A 11 HAS

Language Typology and Language Universals

HSK 20.1

Handbücher zur
Sprach- und Kommunikationswissenschaft

Handbooks of Linguistics
and Communication Science

Manuels de linguistique et
des sciences de communication

Mitbegründet von
Gerold Ungeheuer

Herausgegeben von / Edited by / Edités par
Armin Burkhardt
Hugo Steger
Herbert Ernst Wiegand

Band 20.1

Walter de Gruyter · Berlin · New York
2001

Language Typology and Language Universals

Sprachtypologie und sprachliche Universalien

La typologie des langues et les universaux linguistiques

An International Handbook /
Ein internationales Handbuch / Manuel international

Edited by / Herausgegeben von / Edité par
Martin Haspelmath · Ekkehard König
Wulf Oesterreicher · Wolfgang Raible

Volume 1 / 1. Halbband / Tome 1

Walter de Gruyter · Berlin · New York
2001

⊚ Gedruckt auf säurefreiem Papier, das die
US-ANSI-Norm über Haltbarkeit erfüllt.

Die Deutsche Bibliothek — *CIP-Einheitsaufnahme*

> Language typology and language universals : ein internationales Handbuch / ed. by Martin Haspelmath .... – Berlin ; New York : de Gruyter
> (Handbücher zur Sprach- und Kommunikationswissenschaft ; Bd. 20)
> Vol. 1. – (2001)
> ISBN 3-11-011423-2

© Copyright 2001 by Walter de Gruyter GmbH & Co. KG, D-10785 Berlin
Dieses Werk einschließlich aller seiner Teile ist urheberrechtlich geschützt. Jede Verwertung außerhalb der engen Grenzen des Urheberrechtsgesetzes ist ohne Zustimmung des Verlages unzulässig und strafbar. Das gilt insbesondere für Vervielfältigungen, Übersetzungen, Mikroverfilmungen und die Einspeicherung und Verarbeitung in elektronischen Systemen.
Printed in Germany
Satz: Arthur Collignon GmbH, Berlin
Druck: WB-Druck, Rieden/Allgäu
Buchbinderische Verarbeitung: Lüderitz & Bauer-GmbH, Berlin
Einbandgestaltung und Schutzumschlag: Rudolf Hübler, Berlin

Preface

Subject Matter

The approximately 6,000 languages spoken on this planet differ from one another in many ways. And yet there are limits to this diversity, and within the diversity it is possible to discern certain regular patterns and to formulate certain generalizations. Such regularities within cross-linguistic variation and such limits of the observable variation are the subject matter of language typology and the study of universals.

Language typology and the study of language universals are concerned with the diversity of human languages from different, but complementary points of view. Language typology tries to uncover the patterns of variation and to identify the different language types that exist. The study of language universals tries to find universally valid, basic principles which hold for all languages.

The concept 'language universals' has been defined in a variety of ways. On the one hand, it denotes properties which every human language possesses, which are not subject to variation: automatic language acquisition by children, double articulation, variability through time, social and stylistic differentiation, etc. In principle, all languages are capable of expressing the same content, i. e. there are cognitive and communicative functions that can be fulfilled by all languages. On the other hand, the term 'language universals' has also been used for more specific structural properties that are common to all languages. Since we have only a very limited knowledge of human languages (at most one tenth of all languages have been described and analyzed), such empirical universals can only be formulated as hypotheses, constantly falsifiable by new findings. But even pervasive properties, not universal in the strict sense of the word, but only properties of the vast majority of languages ('universal tendencies') are of great interest. Finally, there is a very narrow, albeit very widespread, concept of universals, which is restricted to such properties of linguistic structure as can be derived from the genotypical properties of the human mind. Such universals are assumed to be innately given.

The goal of language typology is to map out the variation space filled by the languages of the world, to find regular patterns and limits of variation. On the one hand, the number of different techniques employed by languages to solve the problem of expressing certain meanings is not unlimited, but is retricted in most cases to a small number of recurrent strategies. On the other hand, there are connections and correlations between structural properties, such that the choice of an option in one domain severely limits or even uniquely determines the options in other domains. Such correlations are formulated as implicational universals or implicational hierarchies. In this respect language typology is inextricably intertwined with research on language universals and with the empirical discovery of such universals. There is also an interesting interrelation between language typology and the analysis of individual languages. The analysis of a specific language is by necessity based on methodologically and theoretically sound terms and concepts which are provided by language typology. The material for typological comparisons, in turn, is provided by analyses of individual languages.

Goals and Structure of the Handbook

It is the goal of this handbook to provide a comprehensive survey of the history, the theories and the methodology of language typology and the study of language universals, as well as of the current debates and controversies in these fields. The first two chapters of the book are concerned with the theoretical foundations of the study of language universals and of language typology (Chapter I) as well as the connections between these fields and other disciplines (Chapter II). They are followed by two chapters on the history of these fields as well as on different approaches (Chapters II and III). Further foundations for the subsequent chapters are provided by the chapters on current approaches (Chapter V), on functional explanations and methodology (Chapter VI), and on the onomasiological or conceptual basis of language comparison (Chapter VII). From Chapter VIII to Chapter XII the perspective is a semasiological one, i. e. these chapters are concerned with the patterns and limits of cross-linguistic variation. The structure of these chapters is determined by generally accepted distinctions between levels of linguistic analysis, by the usual distinctions between categories, grammatical and phonological devices, structures and constructions. In keeping with the panchronic tradition of language typology, all of these chapters are written both from a synchronic and a diachronic perspective. Chapter XIII is dedicated to a discussion of those parameters of variation which are regarded as central by many typologists, since they play a prominent role in many implicational generalizations. Chapter XIV deals with general questions and principles of areal typology, as well as with the properties of languages in those regions which are characterized by striking areal properties. Diachronic aspects of language typology and the study of universals are the central concern of the concluding chapters XV and XVI. In the final chapter, the general discussion of historical processes in Chapter XV is illustrated by means of some particularly clear examples of typological change taken from different language families.

The authors of the individual sections and chapters are for the most part internationally known experts for the relevant topics from four continents. This handbook is not only intended for the expert in the fields of typology and language universals but also for all those interested in linguistics. It is specifically addressed to all those who specialize in individual languages, for whose analysis it provides basic orientation, placing each language within the space of what is possible and common in the languages of the world.

Vorwort

Gegenstand des Handbuchs

Die etwa 6.000 Sprachen, die auf der Erde gesprochen werden, unterscheiden sich auf vielfältige Weise. Aber es gibt Grenzen der Verschiedenheit, und auch innerhalb der Verschiedenheit lassen sich Muster erkennen und Verallgemeinerungen formulieren. Regularitäten innerhalb der sprachlichen Variation und Grenzen der Variation sind der Gegenstand der sprachlichen Universalienforschung und der Sprachtypologie.

Sprachtypologie und Universalienforschung beschäftigen sich mit der Verschiedenartigkeit der menschlichen Sprachen aus unterschiedlichen, aber komplementären Blickwinkeln. Die Sprachtypologie versucht, die Regelhaftigkeit der Variation hinter der Vielfalt der menschlichen Sprachen zu erkennen. Die Universalienforschung sucht nach allgemeingültigen, allen Sprachen der Welt zugrunde liegenden Prinzipien.

Der Begriff der sprachlichen Universalien ist auf verschiedene Weise verstanden worden. Zum einen bezeichnet er Eigenschaften, die ganz offensichtlich der menschlichen Sprache als solcher eigen sind, die also nicht der Variation unterliegen: der automatische Spracherwerb im Kindesalter, die doppelte Gegliedertheit (,Artikulation'), die historische Veränderlichkeit, die soziale und stilistische Differenziertheit, usw. Im Prinzip können alle Sprachen dasselbe ausdrücken, d. h. es gibt kognitive und kommunikative Funktionen, die von allen Sprachen erfüllt werden. Zum andern ist der Begriff der Universalien aber auch für spezifischere Struktureigenschaften verwendet worden, die, soweit wir sehen, alle Sprachen besitzen, die aber nicht so sein müssten. Da wir nur eine recht beschränkte Kenntnis von den menschlichen Sprachen haben (höchstens ein Zehntel aller Sprachen sind einigermaßen umfassend beschrieben worden), können solche empirischen Universalien immer nur als Hypothesen formuliert werden, die durch neue Einsichten falsifiziert werden könnten. Aber auch allgemeine Eigenschaften, die nicht in diesem Sinne universal sind, sondern nur einer überwältigenden Mehrheit der Sprachen zukommen, sind durchaus von Interesse („universale Tendenzen"). Schließlich gibt es einen recht engen, aber gleichwohl verbreiteten Universalienbegriff, der sich auf solche Eigenschaften der Sprachstruktur beschränkt, die aus den sprachspezifischen genotypischen Eigenschaften des menschlichen Geistes ableitbar sind.

Die Sprachtypologie beschäftigt sich mit den Gemeinsamkeiten und Unterschieden zwischen den Sprachen der Welt, insbesondere mit den Regelmäßigkeiten und Grenzen, die innerhalb der Verschiedenheit beobachtet werden können. Zum einen ist die Anzahl der verschiedenen Techniken, mit denen Sprachen die ihnen gestellten Aufgaben lösen, nicht unbegrenzt, sondern meistens auf eine überschaubare Anzahl von Strategien beschränkt, die sich immer wieder finden. Zum andern gibt es Zusammenhänge und Korrelationen zwischen Struktureigenschaften, so dass die Wahl einer Option in einem Bereich die Optionen in einem anderen Bereich beschränkt. Solche Korrelationen werden als Implikations-Universalien oder Implikations-Hierarchien formuliert. In dieser Hinsicht ist die Typologie nicht von der Universalienforschung zu trennen. Typologie, soweit sie sich nicht nur mit Klassifikation, sondern auch mit Implikationen und Korrelationen beschäftigt, ist immer gleichzeitig auch Universalienforschung im Sinne der empirischen Universalien. Darüber hinaus stehen Sprachtypologie und die einzelsprachliche Analyse in einer interessanten Wechselbeziehung: Die Beschreibung einer Einzelsprache setzt methodisch und theoretisch fundierte Analysebegriffe und Konzepte voraus, die ihr die Sprachtypologie zur Verfügung stellt. Andererseits liefern erst die einzelsprachlichen Analysen der Sprachtypologie das zu vergleichende Material.

Zielsetzung und Konzeption des Handbuchs

Ziel des Handbuches ist es, einen umfassenden Überblick über Geschichte, Theorien, Methodologie und Diskussionsstand der Sprachtypologie und Universalienforschung zu geben. Auf zwei einleitende Kapitel über sprachtheoretische Grundlagen von Universalienforschung und Typologie (Kap. I) und die Verzahnung dieser Gebiete mit anderen Disziplinen (Kap. II) folgen zwei Kapitel über Geschichte und Richtungen (Kap. III und IV). Weitere Grundlagen für die folgenden Teile werden in den Kapiteln über gegenwärtige Ansätze (Kap. V), über funktionale Erklärungsprinzipien und Methodologie (Kap. VI) sowie über die onomasiologische Basis, die übereinzelsprachlichen Bezugspunkte eines Sprachvergleichs (Kap. VII), gelegt. Von Kap. VIII bis Kap. XII ist die Perspektive eine semasiologische. Die Systematik der Gliederung des Handbuchs orientiert sich an den verschiedenen Ebenen der Sprachanalyse, den üblichen Unterscheidungen von Kategorien, grammatischen und phonologischen Mitteln, Strukturen und Konstruktionen. Entsprechend der panchronen Tradition der Sprachtypologie wird in diesen systematischen Kapiteln neben der synchronen auch die diachrone Perspektive stets mit einbezogen. Kap. XIII ist der Diskussion der Parameter der Variation gewidmet, denen man in der typologischen Diskussion eine zentrale Rolle zugeschrieben hat, also Parametern, mit denen eine Fülle von anderen variierenden Eigenschaften korrelieren. Gegenstand von Kap. XIV sind die allgemeinen Fragen und Prinzipien der Arealtypologie sowie die typologischen Eigenschaften der Sprachen solcher Regionen, für die besonders markante areale Gemeinsamkeiten festgestellt worden sind. Diachrone Aspekte von Typologie und Universalienforschung stehen im Mittelpunkt der abschließenden Kapitel XV und XVI. Die allgemeine Diskussion historischer Prozesse von Kap. XV wird im darauf folgenden Kapitel durch Beispiele markanten typologischen Wandels aus einigen Sprachfamilien exemplifiziert.

Die Autorinnen und Autoren der einzelnen Artikel des Handbuchs kommen aus vier Kontinenten. Das Handbuch richtet sich nicht nur an Typologen und Universalienforscher, sondern an alle an Sprachwissenschaft Interessierten, insbesondere an alle Spezialisten für verschiedene Einzelsprachen, denen mit diesem Handbuch für die Analyse der jeweiligen Sprache eine Orientierung im Raum des für die Sprachen der Welt Möglichen gegeben werden soll.

Préface

Le sujet

On parle sur notre planète environ 6.000 langues dont les différences sont considérables. Dans une diversité apparente, on peut cependant discerner des structures et des configurations communes qui permettent de formuler des règles plus générales. Trouver ce qui est régulier dans la diversité linguistique et montrer où sont les limites de la variation, voilà le champ d'investigation de ceux qui s'occupent de la typologie et des universaux linguistiques.

Si la typologie linguistique et la recherche des universaux ont un centre d'intérêt commun dans la diversité des langues humaines, leur point de vue est différent, voire complémentaire. Les représentants de la typologie essaient d'identifier, derrière la diversité apparente des langues humaines, la régularité de certaines variations, tandis que le but des partisans de la recherche universaliste et universalisante est la découverte de principes valant pour toutes les langues du monde.

Il existe cependant plusieurs acceptions de la notion d'universaux linguistiques. Ce terme est utilisé d'une part pour désigner les propriétés qui, de toute évidence, sont essentielles pour le langage humain en tant que tel et qui, par là, ne sont pas susceptibles de varier: la capacité des enfants à apprendre une langue, la double articulation du langage, le changement permanent des langues au cours de leur histoire, la variation du langage selon des paramètres sociaux et stylistiques etc. Aux propriétés de ce type s'ajoute le fait que, puisque tout peut être en principe exprimé dans n'importe quelle langue, il existe des fonctions cognitives et communicatives universelles susceptibles d'être exprimées par toutes les langues. Dans une deuxième acception, le terme « universaux linguistiques » s'applique à des propriétés structurales spécifiques qu'on a trouvées dans toutes les langues connues, bien qu'elles soient, dans une certaine mesure, contingentes. Comme les linguistes sont loin de connaître toutes les langues humaines (des descriptions satisfaisantes n'existent que pour – tout au plus – un dixième), ce type d'universaux empiriques n'admet que la forme d'une hypothèse qui peut s'avérer fausse après de nouvelles découvertes. Si ces propriétés générales ne sont pas des universaux au sens propre du terme, leur base empirique n'étant constituée que par un grand nombre de langues particulières, elles ne sont cependant pas dépourvues d'intérêt dans la mesure où elles reflètent des « tendances universelles ». Finalement, les linguistes emploient le terme d'universaux encore dans une troisième acception, assez étroite, il est vrai, mais tout de même très répandue. Les partisans de ce concept universaliste présupposent que les universaux linguistiques découlent des propriétés qui, parmi les propriétés innées de l'esprit humain, correspondent au génotype.

La typologie linguistique s'occupe d'une part de ce qui est commun à toutes les langues, de l'autre de leur diversité, surtout des régularités et des limites qu'on peut observer dans la diversité apparente. En premier lieu, le nombre des techniques employées pour résoudre les tâches communicatives n'est pas illimité; il existe en général, bien au contraire, un nombre restreint de stratégies qu'on ne cesse de retrouver dans d'autres langues. Ensuite on peut observer des relations, voire des corrélations entre des propriétés structurales, de sorte que le choix d'une possiblité dans un domaine réduit le nombre de celles dans un autre. Dans ce contexte, on parle d'« universaux d'implication » ou de « hiérarchie implicationnelle ». C'est là même un domaine où se recoupent la typologie et la recherche universaliste: c'est que la typologie, dans la mesure où elle dépasse le seul domaine de la classification pour s'occuper d'implications et de corrélations, correspond en quelque sorte à la recherche d'universaux empiriques. Il existe en outre une relation mutuelle très intéressante entre la typologie linguistique et l'analyse d'une langue particulière. S'il est vrai que cette dernière présuppose des concepts basés sur une théorie et une méthode explicites mises à sa disposition par la typologie, c'est en même temps l'analyse des langues particulières qui constitue la base empirique pour le travail de la typologie.

L'objectif et la structure du manuel

Ce manuel présente un panorama de l'histoire, des conceptions, des théories, des méthodes et de l'état présent tant de la typologie linguistique que de la recherche universaliste. Les deux premiers chapitres sont consacrés aux bases théoriques de la typologie et de la recherche universaliste (chapitre I) et aux relations qu'entretiennent ces deux domaines avec d'autres disciplines (chapitre II). Suivent deux chapitres traitant de l'histoire, des tendances et des écoles qui ont jalonné cette recherche (chapitres III et IV). Avec les chapitres V (« Les tendances actuelles »), VI (« Les principes d'explication ») et VII (« Fondements du codage typologique »), s'achève la série des articles de base.

Les chapitres VIII à XII adoptent une perspective sémasiologique. Ils décrivent la variation interlinguistique par le biais des différents niveaux de l'analyse linguistique, les catégories grammaticales et leurs moyens d'expression. Conformément à la tradition panchronique de la typologie linguistique, la perspective diachronique trouve sa place à l'intérieur de ces chapitres dont la conception générale est plutôt systématique et synchronique. Dans le chapitre XIII, parmi les paramètres de la variation, sont mis en relief ceux auxquels on a attribué un rôle central dans la discussion typologique; il s'agit donc de paramètres qui, d'habitude, sont en relation avec bon nombre d'autres propriétés linguistiques. Le chapitre XIV s'occupe de questions générales et de principes de la typologie aréale ainsi que de propriétés typologiques des langues qu'on trouve dans des régions où ont été constatés des traits communs particulièrement saillants. Les chapitres XV et XVI sont axés sur les aspects diachroniques tant de la typologie que de la recherche universaliste. Si, au chapitre XV, sont présentées les évolutions historiques, elles sont illustrées dans le chapitre XVI à l'aide d'exemples provenant de familles de langues où le changement typologique est particulièrement saillant.

Les auteurs des articles de ce manuel sont pour la plupart des spécialistes qui, tout en étant originaires de quatres continents, jouissent d'une renommée internationale. Le manuel ne s'adresse cependant pas aux seuls spécialistes, que ce soit en typologie ou en recherche universaliste, mais à tous ceux qui s'intéressent à la linguistique en général, et notamment à ceux qui se proposent d'analyser une langue particulière. On voudrait leur fournir, avec ce manuel, un instrument de travail qui leur permette non seulement d'analyser cette langue, mais de s'orienter en même temps dans l'espace des possibilités qui se manifeste dans les langues du monde.

Contents/Inhalt/Contenu

Volume 1/1. Halbband/Tome 1

Preface V
Vorwort VII
Préface IX
Common abbreviations/Häufige Abkürzungen/Abréviations fréquentes XIX

I. Foundations: Theoretical foundations of language universals and language typology
Grundlagen: Die sprachtheoretische Fundierung von Universalienforschung und Sprachtypologie
Fondements: les bases théoriques de la typologie linguistique et de la recherche universaliste

1. Wolfgang Raible, Language universals and language typology 1
2. Bernard Comrie, Different views of language typology 25

II. Foundations: Points of contact between language universals/language typology and other disciplines
Grundlagen: Berührungspunkte von Universalienforschung und Sprachtypologie mit anderen Disziplinen
Fondements: les points de contact entre la recherche universaliste, la typologie linguistique et d'autres disciplines

3. Doris Tophinke, Handlungstheorie, Kommunikationstheorie, Lebenswelt 40
4. Kai Buchholz, Sprachphilosophie 62
5. François Rastier, Sciences cognitives et Intelligence Artificielle 75
6. Heiner Böhmer, Künstliche Sprachen und Universalsprachen 85
7. Derek Bickerton, Biological foundations of language 95
8. Wolfgang Raible, Linguistics and Genetics: Systematic parallels . . . 103
9. Jürgen Dittmann, Sprachpathologie 123
10. Franz Dotter, Gebärdensprachforschung 141
11. Wolfgang Schnotz, Textproduktions- und Textverstehensforschung 154
12. Harald Haarmann, Sprachtypologie und Schriftgeschichte 163

III. History and prehistory of universals research
Geschichte und Vorgeschichte der Universalienforschung
Histoire et préhistoire de la recherche universaliste

13. Pierre Swiggers, Alfons Wouters, Philosophie du langage et linguistique dans l'Antiquité classique 181

14.	Jakob Hans Josef Schneider, Sprachtheorien im Mittelalter	192
15	Werner Hüllen, Reflections on language in the Renaissance	210
16.	Lia Formigari, Theories of language in the European Enlightenment	222
17.	N. N., Schulen des Strukturalismus	entfällt

IV. History and approaches of language typology
Geschichte und Richtungen der Sprachtypologie
Histoire et écoles de la typologie linguistique

18.	Werner Hüllen, Characterization and evaluation of languages in the Renaissance and in the Early Modern Period	234
19.	Georg Bossong, Die Anfänge typologischen Denkens im europäischen Rationalismus	249
20.	Martin Haase, Sprachtypologie bei Edward Sapir	264
21.	Heidi Aschenberg, Typologie als Charakterologie	266
22.	Esa Itkonen, The relation of non-Western approaches to linguistic typology	275

V. Current approaches to language typology and universals research
Gegenwärtige Ansätze von Sprachtypologie und Universalienforschung
Les tendences actuelles dans le domaine de la typologie linguistique et de la recherche universaliste

23.	Martin Haase, Sprachtypologie und Universalienforschung bei Joseph H. Greenberg	280
24.	Hubert Haider, Parametrisierung in der Generativen Grammatik	283
25.	Daniel Jacob, Die Hegersche Noematik	293
26.	Yakov G. Testelets, Russian works on linguistic typology in the 1960–1990s	306
27.	Hansjakob Seiler, The Cologne UNITYP project	323
28.	Christiane Pilot-Raichoor, Gilbert Lazard, le RIVALC et la revue *Actances*	344

VI. Explanatory principles, principles of organization, and methods in typology and language universals
Erklärungsprinzipien, Ordnungsprinzipien und Methoden für universalistische und typologische Fragestellungen
Les principes d'explication, les principes structurants et les méthodes appliquées aux questions d'ordre universaliste et typologique

29.	John A. Hawkins, The role of processing principles in explaining language universals	360
30.	Claus D. Pusch, Ikonizität	369

31.	Wolfgang Ullrich Wurzel, Ökonomie	384
32.	Ralph Ludwig, Markiertheit	400
33.	Revere D. Perkins, Sampling procedures and statistical methods	419

VII. Communication-theoretic prerequisites and language-independent *tertia comparationis* as bases of typological coding
Kommunikationstheoretische 'Vorgaben' und außersprachliche *tertia comparationis* als Grundlage sprachtypenbezogener Kodierung
Fondements du codage typologique: les données communicatives et les *tertia comparationis*

34.	Heidi Aschenberg, Sprechsituationen und Kontext	435
35.	Doris Tophinke, Sprachliches Handeln, Kommunikantenrollen, Beziehungsaspekte	444
36.	Raymund Wilhelm, Diskurstraditionen	467
37.	Waldfried Premper, Universals of the linguistic representation of situations ('participation')	477
38.	Hans-Jürgen Sasse, Scales between nouniness and verbiness	495
39.	Anne Reboul, Foundations of reference and predication	509
40.	Jan Rijkhoff, Dimensions of adnominal modification	522
41.	José Luis Iturrioz Leza, Dimensionen der verbalen Modifikation	533
42.	Robert I. Binnick, Temporality and aspectuality	557
43.	Peter Mühlhäusler, Universals and typology of space	568
44.	Wolfgang Klein, Deiktische Orientierung	575
45.	Wolfgang Raible, Linking clauses	590
46.	Jorunn Hetland, Valéria Molnár, Informationsstruktur und Reliefgebung	617
47.	Elisabeth Stark, Textkohäsion und Textkohärenz	634

VIII. Morphological techniques
Morphologische Techniken
Les techniques morphologiques

48.	Georg Bossong, Ausdrucksmöglichkeiten für grammatische Relationen	657
49.	Vladimir A. Plungian, Agglutination and flection	669
50.	Johanna Rubba, Introflection	678
51.	Laurie Bauer, Compounding	695
52.	Gregory Stump, Affix position	708
53.	José Luis Iturrioz Leza, Inkorporation	714

IX. Typology of morphological and morphosyntactic categories
 Typologie morphologischer und morphosyntaktischer Kategorien
 La typologie des catégories morphologiques et morphosyntaxiques

54.	Jan Award, Parts of speech	726
55.	Martin Haase, Lokalkasus und Adpositionen	736
56.	Peter Mühlhäusler, Personal pronouns	741
57.	Ekkehard König, Intensifiers and reflexive pronouns	747
58.	Martin Haase, Local deixis	760
59.	Jouko Lindstedt, Tense and aspect	768
60.	Dietmar Zaefferer, Modale Kategorien	784
61.	Greville G. Corbett, Number	816
62.	Nikolaus P. Himmelmann, Articles	831
63.	Bernd Kortmann, Adverbial conjunctions	842

Volume 2/2. Halbband/Tome 2

X. Syntactic Typology
 Syntaktische Typologie
 Typologie syntaxique

64. Béatrice Primus, Word order typology
65. Gilbert Lazard, Le marquage différentiel de l'objet
66. Leonid Kulikov, Causatives
67. Konstantin I. Kazenin, The passive voice
68. Konstantin I. Kazenin, Verbal reflexives and the middle voice
69. Vladimir P. Nedjalkov, Resultative constructions
70. Ray Freeze, Existential constructions
71. Leon Stassen, Predicative possession
72. Maria Koptjevskaja-Tamm, Adnominal possession
73. Ekkehard König, Internal and external possessors
74. Kaoru Horie, Complement clauses
75. Leon Stassen, Comparative constructions
76. Vera I. Podlesskaja, Conditional constructions
77. Peter Siemund, Interrogative constructions
78. Viktor S. Xrakovskij, Exhortative constructions
79. Laura A. Michaelis, Exclamative constructions
80. Knud Lambrecht, Dislocation
81. Hans Bernhard Drubig, W. Schaffer, Focus constructions
82. Leon Stassen, Noun phrase coordination
83. Bertil Tikkanen, Converbs
84. Andrej A. Kibrik, Reference maintenance in discourse

XI.	Lexical typology
	Lexikalische Typologie
	La typologie lexicale

85. Peter Koch, Lexical typology from a cognitive and linguistic point of view
86. Cecil H. Brown, Lexical typology from an anthropological point of view
87. Cliff Goddard, Universal units in the lexicon
88. Niklas Jonsson, Kin terms in grammar
89. Brenda Laca, Derivation
90. Robert MacLaury, Color terms
91. Ewald Lang, Spatial dimension terms
92. David Gil, Quantifiers
93. Åke Viberg, Verbs of perception

XII.	Phonology-based typology
	Typologie auf phonologischer Basis
	Typologie du domaine phonologique

94. David Restle, Theo Vennemann, Silbenstruktur
95. Thomas Krefeld, Phonologische Prozesse
96. Aditi Lahiri, Metrical patterns
97. Larry M. Hyman, Tone systems
98. D. Robert Ladd, Intonation

XIII.	Salient typological parameters
	Typologisch besonders markante Parameter
	Paramètres typologiques particulièrement saillants

99. Peter Auer, Silben- und akzentzählende Sprachen
100. Walter Bisang, Finite vs. non-finite languages
101. Aleksandr E. Kibrik, Subject-oriented vs. subjectless languages
102. Johannes Helmbrecht, Head-marking vs. dependent-marking languages
103. Mark C. Baker, Configurationality and polysynthesis
104. Katalin É. Kiss, Discourse configurationality

XIV.	Typological Characterization of language families and linguistic areas
	Typologische Charakterisierung von Sprachfamilien und Sprachbünden
	La caractéristique typologique de familles et d'aires linguistiques

105. Östen Dahl, Principles of areal typology
106. Hans Goebl, Arealtypologie und Dialektologie

107.	Martin Haspelmath, The European linguistic area: Standard Average European
108.	Jack Feuillet, Aire linguistique balkanique
109.	Karen Ebert, Südasien als Sprachbund
110.	Christel Stolz, Thomas Stolz, Mesoamerica as a linguistic area
XV.	**Diachronic aspects of language types and linguistic universals: Basic concepts** **Diachronische Aspekte von Sprachtypologie und Universalienforschung: Grundfragen** **Aspects diachroniques de la recherche typologique et universaliste: concepts fondamentaux**
111.	Wulf Oesterreicher, Historizität: Sprachvariation, Sprachverschiedenheit, Sprachwandel
112.	Andreas Blank, Pathways of lexicalization
113.	Claude Hagège, Les processus de grammaticalisation
114.	John Ole Askedal, Conceptions of typological change
115.	Sarah Grey Thomason, Contact-induced typological change
116.	Peter Mühlhäusler, Typology and universals of Pidginization
117.	Peter Cornelius Muysken, Creolization
118.	Hans-Jürgen Sasse, Typological changes in language obsolescence
119.	Helmut Lüdtke, 'Tote' Sprachen
120.	Dieter Wanner, From Latin to the Romance Languages
121.	Jan Terje Faarlund, From Ancient Germanic to modern Germanic languages
122.	Lars Johanson, Vom Alttürkischen zu den modernen Türksprachen
123.	Antonio Loprieno, From Ancient Egyptian to Coptic
124.	Stefan Weninger, Vom Altäthiopischen zu den neuäthiopischen Sprachen
125.	Wolfgang Schulze, Die kaukasischen Sprachen

Common abbreviations
Häufige Abkürzungen
Abréviations fréquentes

	ENGLISH	DEUTSCH	FRANÇAIS
ABL	ablative	Ablativ	ablatif
ABS	absolutive	Absolutiv	absolutif
ACC	accusative	Akkusativ	accusatif
ADJ	adjective	Adjektiv	adjectif
ADV	adverb(ial)	Adverb, adverbial	adverbe, adverbial
AGR	agreement	Kongruenz	accord
AOR	aorist	Aorist	aoriste
ART	article	Artikel	article
ASP	aspect	Aspekt	aspect
AUX	auxiliary	Auxiliar	auxiliaire
CAUS	causative	Kausativ	causatif
COMP	complementizer	Komplementierer	
COND	conditional	Konditional	conditionnel
CONV	converb	Konverb	converbe
DAT	dative	Dativ	datif
DEF	definite	definit	défini
DEM	demonstrative	demonstrativ	démonstratif
DET	determiner	Determinator	déterminant
DO	direct object	direktes Objekt	complément d'objet
DU	dual	Dual	duel
DUR	durative	durativ	duratif
ERG	ergative	Ergativ	ergatif
EXCL	exclusive	exklusiv	exclusif
FOC	focus	Fokus	focalisation
F	feminine	feminin	féminin
FUT	future	Futur	futur
GEN	genitive	Genitiv	génitif
IMP	imperative	Imperativ	impératif
IMPF	imperfect(ive)	imperfektiv, Imperfekt	imparfait, imperfectif
INCL	inclusive	inklusiv	inclusif
INESS	inessive	Inessiv	inessif
INF	infinitive	Infinitiv	infinitif
INTR	intransitive	intransitiv	intransitif
IO	indirect object	indirektes Objekt	complément indirect
LOC	locative	Lokativ	locatif
M	masculine	maskulin	masculin

N	noun	Nomen	nom
NEG	negation, negative	Negation, negativ	négation, négatif
NP	noun phrase	Nominalphrase	syntagme nominal
NOM	nominative	Nominativ	nominatif
OBJ	object	Objekt	objet
OBL	oblique	oblique	oblique
PARF			parfait
PASS	passive	Passiv	passif
PERF	perfect	Perfekt	
PFV	perfective	perfektiv	perfectif
PL	plural	Plural	pluriel
POSS	possessive	possessiv, Possessor	possessif
PP	prepositional phrase	Präpositionalphrase	groupe prépositionnel
PRED	predicate	Prädikat	prédicat
PRES	present	Präsens	présent
PRET	preterite	Präteritum	prétérit
PROG	progressive	Progressiv	progressif
PTCP	participle	Partizip	participe
REFL	reflexive	reflexiv	réfléchi
REL	relative	Relativmarker	relatif
SG	singular	Singular	singulier
SUBJ	subject	Subjekt	sujet
SUJ			sujet
TOP	topic	Topik	topic
TR	transitive	transitiv	transitif
V	verb	Verb	verbe
VP	verb phrase	Verbalphrase	syntagme verbal

I. Foundations: Theoretical foundations of language universals and language typology
Grundlagen: Die sprachtheoretische Fundierung von Universalienforschung und Sprachtypologie
Fondements: les bases théoriques de la typologie linguistique et de la recherche universaliste

1. Language universals and language typology

1. Introduction: a necessary change of perspective
2. Different levels of observation and abstraction
3. Some problems arising for language typology
4. Universals as a solution to problems raised by typology
5. Advantages of the universalist view
6. The shortcomings of traditional views
7. References

"Es ist schon ein großer und nöthiger Beweis der Klugheit oder Einsicht zu wissen, was man vernünftiger Weise fragen sollte. Denn wenn die Frage an sich ungereimt ist und unnöthige Antworten verlangt, so hat sie außer der Beschämung dessen, der sie aufwirft, bisweilen den Nachtheil, den unbehutsamen Anhörer derselben zu ungereimten Antworten zu verleiten und den belachenswerthen Anblick zu geben, daß einer (wie die Alten sagten) den Bock melckt, der andere ein Sieb unterhält." Kant 1781/1903: 52.

1. Introduction: a necessary change of perspective

Before tackling the question of language universals, language types, and the relationship holding between them, let us first clarify the different meanings of the concept 'language'.

1.1. Language as utterance

There is no doubt that the main function of human language is to communicate with others, thus creating societal links. Hence, whenever we are addressed by others or speak ourselves, language means 'utterance'. Utterances may be long and complex like a speech, or short and simple like an interjection or an exclamation, a "yes" or a "no" − the most frequent case being utterances which consist of one, two or more units linguists call 'clauses' or, in logical terms, 'propositions'.

Communication by language is based on social convention. Hence, the utterances we engage in or exchange with others always reflect a socially accepted or 'ratified' activity: somebody has to be *welcomed*; we engage in *smalltalk* with her or him, asking *questions*, giving *answers* or *making jokes*; somebody *asks* us *for the way*, gives us a *recipe*, or engages in *gossip* with us; we *buy* something in a shop, we *flirt* with a member of the opposite sex, *explain* the arcana of a computer program to a friend; somebody may *tell* us *a tale* or try to *recommend* to us the *novel* she or he has just read. Other, more privileged persons *pass judgement* on somebody, make an *injunction* or *pronounce a verdict*. Such outstanding persons may also *read a paper* before a large audience, or *give a sermon* to the parish; they may *teach a course* in economics, or *give a keynote speech* at a conference; some people of very high standing address a whole nation in a *State of the Union address*, or even the entire − then catholic − world ("urbi et orbi") in a lengthy *Encyclical* titled e.g. "fides et ratio."

The italicized terms in the preceding paragraph describe social activities or 'acts' accompanied − or even only made possible − by the use of language ('SPEECH ACTS'). Language thus is a kind of SOCIAL SEMIOTIC (→ art. 3; art. 35, § 4.3; Halliday 1979; cf. for similar approaches Eckert (ed.) 1998; Forgas (ed.) 1985; Giglioli ²1990; Gumperz 1971;

Hickmann (ed.) 1987; Slobin (ed.) 1996; Totman 1985; Varro (ed.) 1994 etc.). Language – in the present case: its manifestation in speech – thus does not come in words or sentences such as "the farmer killed the duckling", "Alfred bat Eugène" or "Alexander vicit Darium"; speech manifestations of language come first and foremost in socially accepted types of utterances. Without such socially acknowledged utterance types or 'communicative genres' human communication would hardly be possible (cf. most convincingly Bakhtin 1979/1986; in an historical perspective: Frank & al. (eds.) 1997; → art. 36).

Now, although all the above examples have in common their being types of utterances, in a certain respect they cannot be seen as being on the same level. The State of the Union address or the papal encyclica are long and highly elaborate written texts (orally performed in the case of the address), whereas the joke, smalltalk, gossip are less elaborate, and oral into the bargain.

In order to take into account this difference, such text types can best be arranged on a scale. With Douglas Biber (1986; 1988) its one end could be termed 'interactive text', the other one 'edited text'. With Peter Koch and Wulf Oesterreicher (1985; 1994) we might say 'conceptually oral' and 'conceptually written' (i.e. highly planned and edited) text.

For a similar distinction Karl Bühler (1934: 48–69) had already introduced a pair of Greek terms used by Wilhelm von Humboldt in the 19th century: language as *enérgeia* vs. language as *érgon*, that is to say language as an activity or a process (involving present partners), as opposed to language as something created and produced, for instance a book. What is increasing from one end of this scale to the other one is, among other things, the amount of planning.

But there is more. Proposing his scheme, Bühler – a psychologist – solves *en passant* and without any fuss a problem that was most intricate if not unsolvable to most post-Saussurean linguists: the clash between the one and the many, the individual and society: speech events in the narrow sense of *parole* are of necessity individual phenomena limited in time and space, as opposed to a *langue* whose socially encompassing character – *la langue est un fait social* – was beyond doubt. The horizontal dimension of the following scheme overcomes this limitation by interpreting the opposition – or better: the scale – between the individual and society as a constitutive characteristic of *parole* itself: the less utterance types are anchored in situations necessitating the presence of communication partners ('situationsgebunden'), the more does the radius of communication grow in space *and time* ('situationsentbunden', 'intersubjektiv'). The progress in the Bühlerian approach is directly visible when we project – as did Bühler himself – Saussurean *parole* and *langue* onto his scheme: they appear now as diametrically opposed.

The corresponding 'Vierfelderschema' proposed by Bühler looks like this:

degree of abstraction	Degree of intersubjectivity and planning	
	low	high
lower	**Sprechereignis** (Saussurean *parole*)	**Sprachwerk** (planned product)
higher	**Sprechakt** (speech act)	**Sprachgebilde** (Saussurean *langue*)

Fig.: 1.1 Karl Bühler's 'Vierfelderschema'

1.2. A first definition

To sum up the first meaning of the concept under discussion: Not only does language take shape in utterances (i.e. texts) which can be attributed to socially conventionalized text types (→ art. 3, § 2.1; art. 6, § 1.3; art. 35, § 4.3; art. 36; art. 44, § 5): at the same time these types can be arranged on a scale between "speech events" (Bühler) like 'smalltalk', and e.g. the 'encyclical' as an instance of a "Sprachwerk", i.e. a highly planned and elaborate type of text existing not only in papal Latin, but moreover in parallel translations into a large number of other languages.

Although such elaborate products tend to come as written texts, there is by no means a necessary link between writing and the Bühlerian "Sprachwerk." The elaborate speech of an American Indian chief would have conformed to this description as well, and hence should be located close to the right hand end of the scale, the "Sprachwerk", too.

1.3. Linguistic variation

Between 1911 and 1940, Jacques Damourette and Édouard Pichon published seven volumes of a French grammar under the heading of *Des mots à la pensée. Essai de grammaire de la langue française*. Apart from the intellectual adventure of an entirely novel linguistic terminology, the present-day reader is overwhelmed by some 35,000 authentic examples showing first and foremost one thing: wellnigh anything goes in this language. Forms and constructions no French grammarian or linguist would ever have admitted as possible and no traditional grammar would have dared to mention even in footnotes were well documented — and can still be found — in the reality of 'language as tokens'. It should not come as a surprise that quite a lot of these specimens, but not all by far, were utterances made in spoken everyday language, let alone the immense scale of further utterance types that were taken into account.

This raises the problem of linguistic variation, of the 'boundaries' of languages, and the relationship holding between 'languages' and 'dialects'. Even if grammars like the one written by Damourette & Pichon reflect linguistic reality, linguistic data need to be filtered through a theory of variation (e.g. Koch & Oesterreicher 1990) according to the dimensions 'space', 'social stratum', 'medium', and, again, 'utterance types' (see above § 1.1) with the different degrees of planning they imply.

Nevertheless, grammars such as the one of Damourette & Pichon draw our attention to the fact that the grammars we all have to rely on are (and of necessity have to be) idealized constructs created by professional linguists. Hence, typologists should complement the information put at our disposal by such grammars with the thorough analysis of text corpora representing a certain variety of utterance types, thus going beyond the traditional (and by no means totally avoidable) analysis of examples found in reference grammars. (→ art. 111).

2. Different levels of observation and abstraction

The introduction started from language as the observable, directly accessible Saussurean *parole*. While doing this, an important modification was introduced, though: 'Language' as *parole* can be seen as manifesting itself on a scale. This picture has to be complemented by the phenomenon of linguistic variation as sketched in § 1.3.

The Bühlerian scale was generated by the projection onto *parole* of a somewhat more abstract perspective — a look from the level of UTTERANCE TYPES or TEXT TYPES. It should be underlined that, even if these types are more abstract than sheer *parole* phenomena, those who use the social semiotic called 'language' always are perfectly aware of the existence of utterance types. During our lifelong linguistic socialization, we get passively — privileged persons sometimes even actively — acquainted with a large number of them.

However, if we climb one further step on the ladder of abstraction, we definitely quit the domain of everyday knowledge, getting into a sphere quite familiar to linguists, if rather alien to average speakers: this is the level of de Saussurean *langue*, i.e. the domain of 'language as a system'. Whilst normal humans may still speak of 'words' and 'sentences', 'questions' and 'answers', linguists deal with entities such as 'word class', 'subject', 'article', 'apposition', 'relative clause', 'determiner', 'head', 'phoneme', 'clefting', SANSKRIT 'bahuvrīhi', ANCIENT GREEK 'sýndesmos', and the like. In a positive way: linguists do "par science, ce que les autres font seulement par coutume" (Claude Lancelot in the Préface of the famous *Grammaire générale et raisonnée* of Port Royal published in 1650).

Linguists get such concepts either — by induction — from direct, methodical observation of 'language as *parole*' (e.g. "distributional analysis"), mediated by 'language as utterance types'; or they draw on a model of grammar they are familiar with, and which may be more or less adequate to this purpose. In cross-linguistic studies, there is some chance that data from at least part of the languages of a sample come from grammars written by others, the authors of the studies thus lacking a thorough knowledge of some of the languages at stake. Here lies a major problem that has to be considered in more detail (see below § 3.3).

However, once we have accepted the intermediate layer of text types ordered on a scale, our traditional concept of *langue* has to be modified in a way which was again already outlined by Bühler in his above-mentioned "Vierfelderschema". Corresponding to the speech event ("Sprechereignis") and the "Sprachwerk" on the *parole* level, he suggests, on the *langue* level, the terms "Sprechakt" (speech act) and "Sprachgebilde".

This is tantamount to saying that there are two possible ways to conceptualize *langue* and 'grammar': one that became familiar in post-Saussurean linguistics: here the system is seen as a global and overall system of rules producing any speech event whatever; and another one which sees the system parallel to the types of utterances it is needed for, that is as an always only 'partial', emergent system producing the socially ratified text types we became used to and want to use in particular cases (cf. Hopper 1998).

An example will show what is meant. A FRENCH judgement — even if it is going on for several pages — always comes in one single sentence. It has the overall structure *The court (...) given that (...) given that (...) given that (...) on behalf of these motifs (...) convicts / condemns / acquits / proves not guilty / fines / dismisses / rejects (...)*. The entire description of the case, the arguments of the parties, the deliberation of the court etc., is linguistically conceived of as a series of adverbials, each one headed by a "given that" (mostly realized as *attendu que* or *considérant que*), and internally constructed according to a highly complex syntax admitting up to ten or more hierarchical levels of hypotactical embedding (cf. Krefeld 1987).

This presupposes, on the *langue*-level, the existence of syntactic means allowing such complex constructions: in FRENCH this means, among other things, conjunctions functioning on the respective levels of embedding, the possibility of expressing all the relevant logical relations on these levels, and of making clear to the reader or hearer that, whenever s/he is quitting a certain level, s/he actually quits it, and on which level s/he arrives next.

This complex subordinating machinery did not exist in FRENCH from the beginning. It was created by way of grammaticalization in centuries of development according to the demands made by specific situations of social communication. (This leaves us with one further example of "discourse — or more precisely: utterance types — shaping grammar".)

As soon as these demands disappear, the corresponding means of expression tend to vanish as well: witness the levelling of the difference between coordination and subordination in the system of LOUISIANA FRENCH, a language that was never used as a written language (cf. Stäbler 1995; 1995a), or witness the simplified techniques allowing for the linking of propositions in emerging CREOLE LANGUAGES (Raible 1994).

On the other hand, we may observe how e.g. CREOLE LANGUAGES which up to date did not have to cope with complex types of written texts and their specific demands, have to develop the adequate means, as often by first borrowing them from the language serving as an acrolect in a given situation, in most cases ENGLISH, FRENCH, or PORTUGUESE (cf. e.g. Ludwig 1996, Kriegel 1996) — a phenomenon that could be observed as well for the early stages of written ROMANCE LANGUAGES in the Middle Ages, where the corresponding acrolect was LATIN (cf. e.g. Raible 1992: 203ff.). Creole writers are even aware of the fact that they have to draw on European tradition and its linguistic patterns when describing for instance a Caribbean landscape (here the problem is not on the level of vocabulary, as one might presume):

"Écrivant en créole, j'ai été confronté à cette difficulté d'exprimer la belleté [beauté in continental French] des mornes [hills] et des ravines, le mystère de certains visages, faute de disposer d'outils pour le faire." (Confiant 1994: 173).

Peter Mühlhäusler's contribution on Universals of Pidginization (→ art. 116), based among other things on the comprehensive survey published in Wurm & al. (1996), starts from a similar assumption, viz. of pidgins that may be less or more complex according to the demands made by users and specific communicative needs in specific situations. A similar view of gradience has been put forward by John H. McWhorter (1998) as regards CREOLE LANGUAGES. The contribution of Hans-Jürgen Sasse on changes that can be observed in language obsolescence admits the same kind of view, with the reduction of complex syntax being even a topic in the relevant discussion (→ art. 118, § 2). We should, hence, not only consider language obsolescence, but also its logical counterpart, the evolution of language systems, their "Ausbau" or "emergence" (Kloss 1978; Hopper 1998).

The Bühlerian concept of *langue*, then, is not an overall system comprising all the possibilities, but a scalar one, running parallel to the demands made by socially ratified utterance types. If we engage in smalltalk, we do not need a syntactic armour going from head to foot. The "pragmatic mode" of Talmy Givón or Eleanor Rosch will do.

All this is visualized in the following scheme that, with its three levels of increasing abstraction, shows at the same time three different meanings of the concept 'language':

degree of abstraction	Degree of intersubjectivity and planning	
	low ↔ high	
lower (token level)	**Sprech-ereignis** (speech event)	↔ **Sprachwerk** (planned product)
intermediate (utterance types₁)	e.g. smalltalk	↔ e.g. FRENCH judgement
higher (*langue* level; types₂)	**Sprechakt** (speech act)	↔ **Sprachgebilde**

Fig.: 1.2 Expanded Bühlerian conception showing three meanings of 'language': as token, as type and as system ('*langue*')

Some will associate the intermediate level with the concept of 'style' — which is tantamount to saying that 'style' is a domain of linguistics, too.

While components of the system may be necessary for all types of utterances (phonology, a large part of the morphological apparatus and simple syntactic devices), components allowing e.g. in ENGLISH the condensation of clauses into nominal syntagms ("on account of"), certain epistemic and a large number of speech act verbs reflecting ever more sophisticated utterance types (e.g. Traugott 1987), or complex syntax, etc., are not.

3. Some problems arising for language typology

We are now acquainted with three meanings of 'language' depending on three levels of abstraction. Language typologists add one further step on this ladder of abstraction. Instead of analyzing one single historical language and its system (perhaps even according to types of utterances it generated, i.e. by the analysis of a corpus), typologists "cross-linguistically" compare the systems of historical languages, or at least parts of them. This may lead to a series of problems.

1. *Language systems reply to demands.* — Once we have accepted that language systems develop parallel to the demands that are made on them (see above § 2): are we then entitled to consider e.g. ENGLISH or FRENCH data as being on a par with the French based CREOLE spoken in Guyana? Are we allowed to simply compare phenomena from such languages? (The question does not imply a judgement of value, it is a matter of 'Ausbau' — although some linguists might be prone to suspect 'political incorrectness'.)

2. *"Pure" systems might be an invention of linguists.* — In the Bühlerian view, *langue* has not only to be seen as a scalar phenomenon (visualized in the horizontal dimension of figures 1.1 and 1.2). At the same time, we should realize that a language system exists only in the "heads" of individual speakers, that these speakers move around and that, above all, more often than not they are bi- or even trilingual, giving rise to phenomena such as language contact, the mixing and interference between languages (→ art. 115), language obsolescence (→ art. 118), Pidgins (→ art. 116), Creoles (→ art. 117), and the like. Then, the question to be asked is: do there exist "pure" language systems? Could it be that such pure systems are nothing but idealized abstractions based on the observations of a particular human species called 'linguists'?

3. *Categories are not cross-linguistically comparable.* — Children acquiring their first language begin with holophrases. Belonging to a zero category, it stands to reason that they cannot by definition be attributed to one of the grammatical categories (although parents may have different ideas on the topic). Then, in a second step, the child makes what is called "two word utterances", thus discovering at the same time the blessings of rule-governed combining. However, the resulting two categories must not be identified with 'nouns' and 'verbs', at the most they might be considered as something like pre-verbs and pre-nouns. Conceptually speaking, they might correspond to the opposition between discrete and continuous entities, e.g. 'objects' and 'persons' as opposed to 'states', 'events', 'properties'. Only after this second step implying two different categories of signs does the rest of the categories used in adult speech emerge little by little. And here, again, things get complicated: The emerging categories are not identical from language to language, with the speakers of some languages using e.g. 'adjectives', 'adverbs', 'articles', 'enunciatives', 'noun class markers', while others do not (→ e.g. art. 38). And even if they were to develop similar categories, e.g. a verb class, it might be rather difficult to compare them.

One further problem is that the number of categories ascribed to a language may differ according to the model of grammar applied for the description (see above § 2).

Let us take the example of infinitives. Non-finite forms are opposed to finite ones. A *finite* form in, say, ANCIENT GREEK is specified according to

(a) three persons,
(b) two numbers and what remains of a dual,
(c) four moods (indicative, subjunctive, optative, and imperative),
(d) three diatheses (active, medium or middle, passive),
(e) five tenses (present, imperfect, aorist, perfect, pluperfect),
(f) finally affirmation and negation.

Greek "infinitives" only lack person, number, and mood. They allow all three diatheses, four of the five tenses, and affirmation/negation. The only difference between non-finite forms termed 'infinitives' and equally non-finite 'participles' is that the participles, which at the same time partake in the nominal system, allow (nominally marked) number.

Now what is called 'non-finite' in a language like ANCIENT GREEK would be rather "finite" in the verbal system of, say JAPANESE. Given such intrinsic differences (as to similar questions cf. Croft 1990: 11−18; → art. 28, § 3), are we then entitled to compare ANCIENT GREEK with JAPANESE, let alone Greek verbs with Japanese ones? What would be the necessary *tertium comparationis* (→ art. 100). And what about MODERN GREEK and other languages of the Balkans whose speakers have totally disposed of their 'infinitives' in the meantime? (→ art. 108). − While some typologists become more and more aware of the problems raised here (cf. e.g. Anward & al. 1997; → art. 54), others consider it to be less important: → e.g. Isaak Š. Kozinskij in art. 26, § 3.1.

4. *The bias of 'traditional' analysis.* − If we start from socially ratified utterance types as being one of the privileged goals of language production, and if language systems force us to break down complex utterances into units called 'propositions' (see above § 1.1), the usual "logically" inspired approach attributing *reference* to elements of the noun class, whereas verbs would *predicate* (→ art. 39), will have its risks, too.

A holistic approach would give reference first and foremost to utterances and propositions representing e.g. an event in its totality (→ art. 37, § 1). A well-known example of this kind of approach was given by the way Paul J. Hopper and Sandra A. Thompson looked at the concept of 'transitivity' (1980; cf. Rastier 1998: 447). The advantage of this kind of view becomes evident when we analyse languages such as FINNISH or GUSIILAY, the latter a language belonging to BAK-group of the NIGER-CONGO family.

While analyzing our Standard Average European languages, we became accustomed to looking for the expression of 'aspect' − that is: of something undoubtedly characterizing an entire situation or a state of affairs − in the verb, i.e. in the predication. FINNISH imparts this task instead to the noun having the function of the direct object: in case the situation to be expressed is thought of as perfective, the object appears as an accusative; if the situation is seen as imperfective, the partitive has to be chosen instead. Hence, an element of a proposition that traditionally has been seen as *referring* is responsible for part of what normally would be conceived of as *predicating*. In GUSIILAY something similar happens with the pronominal element expressing the agent of a proposition: in its reduced form it marks the imperfectivity of the proposition, in its full form perfectivity (Tendeng 2001).

A similar behaviour of pronouns is reported for HAUSA (Kraft & Kirk-Greene 1990). As was shown by Nicholas Evans (1985), in KAYARDILD all non-subject dependents of a verb carry modal case marking (usually in addition to their regular case marking) which carries tense/mood information for the clause. Andrej Kibrik mentions the case of XERENTE where nominative pronouns mark evidentiality, aspect, and intensivness of action (→ art. 84, end of § 6; Kibrik is drawing on Harold Popovich). Rachel Nordlinger mentions as further candidates for such features PITTA, GURNU, BAAGANDJI, YAG DII and IAI (cf. Nordlinger & Sadler 2000).

Interestingly enough, Paul J. Hopper and Sandra A. Thompson, while being 'progressive' in taking into account discourse, go one step behind former achievements in a contribution where they again link the noun/verb distinction to the discourse functions of referring and predicating [1984].

This example is likely to show one more risk implied in looking in a traditional way at phenomena which could be typologically relevant. Not only may verbal systems (and nominal ones) differ from language to language as regards the extension and the intension of their categories (see above § 3.3); there are even verbal systems doing seemingly strange things, and the same thing holds for nominal ones (→ art. 40). Eventually both of them can collaborate in fulfilling certain tasks, for instance in referring on the level of an entire proposition.

In addition to the problems arising from the different scope of language systems depending on the utterance types we take into consideration, there are at least three further ones:

5. *As a process, a language system implies historical depth.* – Since grammaticalization – as a dynamic process creating new devices and categories from older ones – has become ever more important not only in linguistic theory in general, but also in language typology (→ art. 113): are we then entitled to consider as being on a par e.g. the ATHABASKAN language SOUTH SLAVE with ROMANCE LANGUAGES such as SPANISH, FRENCH or PORTUGUESE, i.e. languages endowed with an ample written documentation of language change encompassing the span of about 2,000 years? This is why theorists of grammaticalization, while working with a representative language sample taken from the languages of the world (→ art. 33; as to the factor of historical depth, cf. ibid. § 3.1; art. 38, § 4), tend to draw on European material (thus coming from languages that do not necessarily belong to their corpus into the bargain) as soon as 'typical' grammaticalization processes have to be documented (e.g. Bybee & al. 1994: 68f.).

At the same time, this kind of view introduces history into typology. This aspect is all the more important as a language system of necessity *has* historical depth: It encompasses the solutions of the past as well as those of the present and the future (e.g. "the butcher's shop" vs. "the shop of the butcher"). They belong to different utterance types, they may belong to speakers of different age, and to the different 'stylistic' levels that make up *langue* in the Bühlerian sense.

6. *Criteria for typologizing.* – It has already been mentioned that normal human beings know and currently use text types and their names in everyday communication (see above § 2). They even know – by intuition – the criteria according to which such utterance types tend to be named (Raible 1988).

Now what are the criteria a typologist should rely upon? Are they self evident? Should it be the medium length of words in a language, the number of color terms, the number of lexical items available for time distinctions or for orientation in space? Or should we better classify languages according to the existence of a verb for the concepts TO BE or TO BECOME? Should we copy Dante who, at the beginning of the 14th century, in his *de vulgari eloquentia*, classified the ROMANCE LANGUAGES according to their expressions for YES into *(h)oc, oïl,* and *si(c)* languages, a kind of classifying even accessible to 'normal' human beings – especially as there exist quite a lot of similar cases. Should we rely on one single criterion or should we take into account a whole series of features? In short: where do such criteria for the definition of language types come from that might be self-evident and could be acknowledged by the totality of linguists? Even if categories in two languages were on a par (see above point 3): what would be the parameters to be chosen for comparison?

7. *Typological vs. areal vs. genetic relationship.* – A last problem to be mentioned in this context is the fact that typology has to take into account not only 'History' (witness the 'historical depth' of § 3.5 above, or the socially ratified utterance types as typical outcomes of diachronic processes), but also the factors 'Area' and 'Genetic Relationship' (cf. e.g. Croft 1990: ch. 6; → articles 105; 106; 108; 109): Indeed, an 'eternal' topic in the pertinent discussion is the question whether genetically related languages can be different on the level of typology.

4. Universals as a solution to problems raised by typology

There are two ways to tackle the problems outlined in the preceding section. One could take into account what typologists have done in the past, and, in case they were aware of the problems, how they mastered them.

Another way could be a consideration of the general aspects behind the – seemingly most difficult, if not aporetical – situation described. The insight that possibly could be gained by doing so could show us either a sure way out of a situation that seems to be without issue, or, in the worst case, perhaps even convince us that there is no escape at all. Here the second way will be chosen.

4.1. The basis of understanding and the hierarchy of levels

It is well known that all linguistic data are interpreted data — 'raw', uninterpreted data simply do not exist in the domain of language. Alphabetic written language, for instance, has passed through a writing system that prescribes word boundaries, orthography, and a punctuation that needed understanding and the syntactic analysis of what was to be written.

Unfortunately, the same thing holds for taped live discussions — irrespective of our being active participants or linguistic observers. We have to apprehend and to understand what is being said. This holds all the more for transcribed texts. In order to take just one example: witness the intricate problem of silence in a dialogue. To which one of two or more persons engaged in a dialogue or a polylogue are we to ascribe silence? (The problem is far from being trivial since silence conveys meaning; cf. Meise 1996; Bakhtin 1979/1986: 68f.). Transcribing taped language is a hermeneutic act par excellence.

Now what is the basis of our interpretations? A good example is provided by the way we process visual information. Looking out of a window into a garden and onto a neighboring forest, I think I am perfectly aware of where I am and of what I see. Nevertheless, the sheer quantity of visual information makes it impossible for me to truly see, i.e. to consciously perceive all and in any detail. What I am conscious of is only a quite small part of the overall information. This is why any illusionist or magician whatever has a more than easy job with all of us, although we perfectly know that they cheat us.

What we see is first of all what we expect to see, and perhaps a small amount of truly new information, for instance something that 'is going on' or 'is happening' — in terms of Gestalt psychology this is the known phenomenon of the 'Gestalt' that always appears before a 'Hintergrund' (the figure - ground pattern). All the rest is not seen as tokens, but — at the most — as types. The reduction of enormous amounts of information to 'communicative genres', 'types', 'scripts', 'frames', 'schemes', 'patterns', 'roles', is the secret of human information processing (→ art. 3, § 2.1 as to the implications for social action and our understanding of 'world'; as to the role of 'contextualization' → art. 35, § 4.3).

Apart from proper nouns, the signs we use in language are types, too. This is why we can even handle complex textual information, interpreting and understanding it in the framework of a certain utterance type fixing for instance the truth values that will hold (the relation to 'reality' is thoroughly different in a *novel* or a *tale* as opposed to a *judgement* or a *balance*, thus showing that the utterance type has consequences for the interpretation of its components.)

In a more general way, this can be formulated as one of the central insights of phenomenology as outlined e.g. by Edmund Husserl in 1901. Husserl speaks of the relationship holding between Parts and Wholes (^{4}1928: § 24). In our perception, there is an ascending hierarchy ('Stufenfolge') of *partial wholes* ('Teilganze'), each of them being a whole as concerns the level(s) beneath and only a part with respect to the level(s) above. In this hierarchy (relatively) stable and (relatively) unstable contents always blend into larger partial wholes giving rise to a surplus called 'Einheitsmoment' in the wording of Husserl, or to a 'Gestaltqualität' — this is the term used by Christian v. Ehrenfels, who 'invented' Gestalt theory in a seminal article published in 1890. This unifying element has its base in a relationship of one-sided or mutual foundation ('einseitige', 'wechselseitige Fundierung') between the parts and the newly emerged whole. (A head/modifier-relation can be seen as a relation of 'one-sided foundation', the two parts of an *if-then*-correlation would be an example of the relationship called 'mutual foundation'.)

In a quite abstract way:

"Stücke sind wesentlich mittelbare oder fernere Teile des Ganzen, dessen Stücke sie sind, wenn sie mit anderern Stücken durch verbindende Formen zu Ganzen geeinigt sind, die selbst wieder durch neuartige Formen Ganze höherer Ordnung konstituieren." (Husserl ^{4}1928: 280.)

In the meantime, this view has been amply confirmed by all we know about the neural basis of visual perception. It is clear that the same view can be applied to speech production and perception (cf. e.g. Spinicci 1992; MacKevitt (ed.) 1996; Hubel 1995; Milner & Goodale 1996.). This approach had, indeed, an immense impact on structuralism (cf. e.g. Holenstein 1976: 13–55).

4.2. A phenomenological perspective

The phenomenological perspective is relevant to our problem in a twofold way. (1) In understanding some of the mechanisms in human language processing we may regard as universal (see below § 4.4), and (2) in understanding the mutual roles of typology and universalism in an overall conception.

The second aspect still needs a closer look. The principle holding for visual perception — or for speech perception and production — starts from the assumption that there is a sequence of levels, with some units on a lower level being integrated into one new unit on a higher level, giving rise to the surplus called 'Einheitsmoment' or 'Gestaltqualität'. When we master a language, the more the levels under discussion are inferior, the less are we aware of the processes going on. Only when learning a foreign language — which slows down all the otherwise automated tasks — do we become again aware of such inferior processes of integrating parts into wholes or, in speech production, of taking conceptual wholes to linguistic pieces. It is clear that the relation holding between such parts and wholes can be described as 'parts *having a function* (or a role) in a larger whole'.

Now, whenever we try to theoretically understand a complex matter, we use an approach similar to the one described — with one crucial difference, though: The more we ascend on the scale of theoretical levels, the less are we aware of the existence of such levels. (Some of us might even deny the possibility of their existence.) Witness the problems normal human beings have with the concept of *langue* (see above § 2), or witness the endeavors of the Bourbaki group of mathematicians to create a level encompassing different branches of their discipline.

The advantage is, nevertheless, that once we have found such a level encompassing units of a lower level, we are able to gain what is called 'insight', for instance the insight into certain principles holding for a whole range of phenomena one would otherwise have seen as being different. An example that is well-known among linguists are politeness phenomena. Although their manifestations differ from language to language and from culture to culture, they can be mapped onto universally holding mechanisms of facework (Brown/Levinson [1974] 1987 following Erwing Goffman). And very often they even leave deep traces in grammaticalization and in grammar (see below § 5.2.1).

4.3. Concepts vs. Significations

In the eyes of Aristotle, this search for universals was, incidentally, what made the difference between a true 'science' (*epistēmē*) and a discipline that is only opinion-based (*doxa*): a science, apart from being reasonable, has to have a subject common to mankind and to rely on principles holding for all of us (*Posterior Analytics*, c. 33; 88 b 30ff.). This is why, instead of writing some more *artes grammaticae*, the mediaeval Schoolmen called Modists, starting from the observation of LATIN, eventually created what can be seen as the outlines of a true *grammatica universalis*, largely transcending the original conception of a description of parts of speech by the foundation of a new, additional syntactic component termed 'diasynthetica' (Raible 1987 — see fig. 1.3 on p. 10).

One of their special merits in this field is the clear distinction between the domains of CONCEPTS and SIGNIFICATIONS: concepts, with their specific *modi intelligendi*, originate by a first act of mental imprinting in perception (*prima impositio*), whereas significations with the specific *modi significandi* of the respective word classes only originate in a subsequent *secunda impositio* — a process incidentally called *duplex articulatio*, however in a sense different from the one the term has after André Martinet (cf. e.g. Rosier 1983; Meier-Oeser 1997: 992f.; Wörner 1997: 1055f.; → art. 14, § 4; the only point where we should refrain from getting inspired by the Modists is the idea that the *modi essendi* of a *res* are reflected by the *modi intelligendi* — this is why the doctrine was also termed *grammatica speculativa*).

Thus the Modists established a clear distinction between a realm of concepts supposed to hold for all of us, and the domain of significations, linked to *voces*, i.e. to signs used by the speakers of historical languages.

Another achievement of Modist thinking was a characterization of parts of speech we would nowadays call prototypical. They all have a key function — nouns expressing e.g. the *modus esse*, i.e. the mode of things that exist, verbs the *modus fieri*, i.e. the mode of processes. But given the multifold character of reality and the limited number of parts of speech, many contents are grammatically treated "as if" they belonged to a certain category — like LATIN *nemo* or *nullus* signifying 'no one' while having the linguistic form of something that exists, i.e. the *modus esse*.

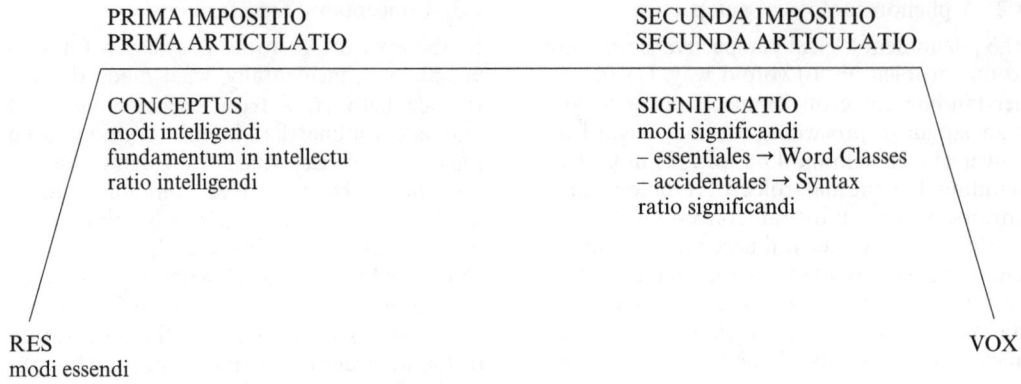

Fig.: 1.3 Sign model of the Modists cf. Raible 1987.

Ideas similar to Modist thinking may be found e.g. in Croft 1991: 101ff.; → art. 54.

The fact that for instance speakers engaged in verbal periphrases (like SPANISH *sigue hablando*, ENGLISH *I will come*, FRENCH *j'ai fini de parler*) — well-known for eventually transforming verbal systems — throughout the world draw on the same concepts, does indeed speak in favour of basic concepts common to all of us: COME, GO, BEGIN, START, CONTINUE, TERMINATE, GET, TAKE, GIVE, MAKE, HEAR, SEE, and the like. (cf. e.g. Raible 1996; Wierzbicka 1996; Casad (ed.). 1996; → articles 85; 86; 87; cf. below § 5.2). Such concepts — apart from 'hear' and 'see' they are accessible as well to deaf or even blind children — make possible the 'bootstrapping' necessary to the acquisition of our first language, be it as speakers or as signers.

Only later in the process of ontogenesis does the evolution of our conceptually and our linguistically based systems become more intertwined (Vygotskij 1962), complicating things a lot. Nevertheless, there is good neurological evidence for the separation of what is popularly called 'thought and language' (see below § 4.5).

Hence, the key for the problems outlined above in § 3 could lie in looking for and, above all, in finding *the conceptual level(s)* beyond the *langue*-level of one or more historical languages. It is, among other things, the crucial question of the *tertium comparationis*.

4.4. Tertia comparationis: What is common to languages?

Given the problems shown in § 3, it goes without saying that any 'reasonable' typologizing — that is taking into account the caveat put forward by Kant, cited in the epigraph to this article, and taking into account the criteria Aristotle formulated for the difference between an 'art' and true 'science' (§ 4.3) — has to start from a *tertium* common to more than one language. In the wording of Wilhelm von Humboldt:

"Die lichtvolle Erkennung der Verschiedenheit erfordert etwas Drittes, nämlich ungeschwächt gleichzeitiges Bewusstseyn der eigenen und fremden Sprachform. Dies aber setzt in seiner Klarheit voraus, dass man zu dem höheren Standpunkt, dem beide untergeordnet sind, gelangt sey, und erwacht auch dunkel erst recht da, wo scheinbar gänzliche Verschiedenheit es auf den ersten Anblick gleich unmöglich macht, das Fremde sich, und sich dem Fremden zu assimiliren." (Humboldt 1829/1963: 156).

Here usually two approaches are distinguished:

(a) The construction of a *tertium* t_a for the languages $L_1^a \ldots L_n^a$, the construction of a *tertium* t_b for the languages $L_1^b \ldots L_n^b$, etc. Then, on the basis of t_a and t_b, the construction of a *tertium* $t_{ab}^{\wedge}$ common to both groups of languages, and so on. This would be the classical way of induction.

In case we confined ourselves to a *tertium* holding only for 'partial' systems of languages $L_1^a \ldots L_n^a$ instead, we would have to make the tacit assumption that we know what the partial systems common to all languages are, that is we would shift the problem, begging the question into the bargain. Partisans of this approach usually refrain from formulating 'universals of language' because, in their opinion, the empirical basis is too small. At any rate there is not the slightest basis for a distinction between e.g. 'absolute' vs. 'statistical' universals (as originally proposed by Greenberg) in this approach (→ e.g. art. 26, § 3.1).

(b) Partisans of the other approach are starting, in an axiomatic way, from what is thought to be common to all languages, i.e. from *essential universals* of 'language'. These are properties no language could lack without losing its status as a language. 'Axiomatic' is used here in the sense it originally had in Ancient Greek mathematics (Szabó 1960): an assumption I start from (Greek *axióō* means '*in my opinion* this is true'), not the eternal truth of the well-known God's Truth discussion in linguistics.

It goes without saying that plausibility is not harmful in this case; this is why we draw on the (phenomenological) insights gained in the discussion of the principles of human perception (see above § 4.1).

(c) It is clear that both ways, the inductive and the deductive one (one of its forms is called 'onomasiological'), may be — and as often are — combined in what Charles Sanders Peirce called 'abduction'. Peirce aimed his theory of abduction ("studying facts and devising a theory to explain them" — Collected Papers 5.145; 171) to be a "logic of discovery". Good examples of this third way are Hansjakob Seiler and Gilbert Lazard (→ articles 27; 28).

As to the second way to find *tertia*: In a famous article of 1960, Charles Hockett outlined a series of principles that could in part be regarded as such essentials in the sense of (b). In 1974, Eugenio Coseriu has formulated five essential universals in a perhaps less known contribution.

	HOCKETT	COSERIU
1	*Semanticity*	*Semanticity*
2	*Interchange-ability*	*Otherness* ('Alterität'): Language is directed to others
3	*Productivity*	*Creativity*
4		*Historicity*: Languages are subject to change
5	*Common Channel*	*Exteriority*: Language materializes, it has to be 'exteriorized'

A sixth essential, having an intermediate position between the first group and the following one, was suggested in 1988 by Wulf Oesterreicher.

	HOCKETT	OESTERREICHER
6	partially implied in: *Discreteness*	'*Discoursivity*': Something we want to 'exteriorize' has to be broken into pieces and to be linearized

To the five essential universals we can add some further ones, this time not principles whose absence would deprive language of its essence. Interestingly enough, human languages share most of them with genetics (→ art. 8, § 4.2).

	LANGUAGE	GENETICS
7	DOUBLE ARTICULATION or DUALITY (also in Hockett)	
8	ARBITRARINESS of signs (also in Hockett)	Holds to a large extent even for Genetics
9	RECURSIVITY (also in Hockett)	see art. 8, § 4.7.
10	As a rule, simple and complex SIGNS REFER TO TYPES	[direct 'reference' instead]

Hockett still adds Displacement, meaning what Karl Bühler termed 'situationsentbundenes Sprechen', i.e. one of the manifest differences between human an animal language (animals do not communicate about past or future, at least not in the way humans do).

Neither Principle 7 (Double Articulation) nor Principle 8 (Arbitrariness of signs) are essential properties of a language on the level of the essentials 1 to 5. As regards Arbitrariness, the example of sign languages shows, at least in a first phase, a considerable amount of iconicity (→ art. 10; as to iconicity in general → art. 30) that tends to dwindle, though, when a sign language develops into a more complex language system (like e.g. American Sign Language [ASL] with its origins in 18th century French Sign Language).

Principles 11 to 16 are — theoretically — based on the considerations made on the subject of Parts and Wholes, implementing the Discoursivity (Discreteness) principle (6).

Their relevance to linguistics will be self-evident. Again, they hold for both linguistics and genetics.

	LANGUAGE & GENETICS
11	TWO DIFFERENT KINDS of signs: 'Signs proper' and 'Signs organizing other signs'
12	DIFFERENT CLASSES as well of 'Signs proper' as of 'Signs organizing signs'
13	Principle of HIERARCHY
14	Principle of COMBINATORIAL RULES used to merge types of Sign Classes (Principle 12) with types of Sign Kinds (Principle 11) into larger, hierarchically higher units, i.e. complex signs (Principle 13)
15	Linking the principles of hierarchy (13) and of combinatorial rules (14): WHOLES ARE ALWAYS MORE THAN THE SUM OF THEIR PARTS ('Einheitsmoment', 'Gestaltqualität')
16	Some of the complex signs created by combinatorial rules (Principle 14) are PRIVILEGED UNITS that are more 'stable' or independent than others

As one can easily see, Principles 6 through 16 can — to a large extent — be interpreted as the more concrete shape Principles 1 to 5 may take by implementation.

Three examples will show different aspects arising from these principles and their combination.

4.4.1. Accentuating Semanticity

The principle of Semanticity (1), together with the principle of Privileged Units (16), makes clear why certain signs — simple and complex ones — have a particular status: they correspond e.g. to perceptually privileged types of *designata*. On a lower level of hierarchy, such privileged signs correspond to types of discrete entities (e.g. objects, persons), taking shape in *word*-signs and in features as often linked to them: perfectivity vs. imperfectivity, telic vs. non-telic, stative vs. non-stative, etc.; on a higher level, they relate to events, situations, i.e. to types of configurations of persons and/or objects, linked for instance in a common activity. Linguistically, they are grouped around the highly unstable and unsaturated category *verb*. On a still higher level, we encounter utterance types (above § 1.1) as instances of relatively stable units.

On the two last-mentioned levels, events and utterance types, terms such as *proposition, sentence, situation, 'Sachverhalt', speech act, face threatening act, scheme, frame, script, actancy, valency, semantic role, ϑ-role*, come into play. Interestingly enough, most of them are units considered as basic by text theory and psychological studies of text production and text processing (→ art. 11, § 2.2).

4.4.2. Accentuating formal aspects

The essential of Discoursivity (or Discreteness of units in the wording of Hockett), together with the essentials of Otherness and Exteriority, relate, among other things, to the principle of the two Kinds of Signs (11): One of the fundamental problems to be solved in speech communication is that all a speaker intends to communicate has to be broken down into smaller signs, and that these discrete units have to be linearized in the act of speaking. This has to be done in a way that allows for hearers (the representatives of Otherness) to reconstruct the intended whole from a series of scattered parts. Since only two neighboring elements can be immediately merged, and since this is certainly not sufficient to construct complex signs by combinatorial rules (witness the phenomenon of discontinuous linguistic entities or the case of the FRENCH judgement, above § 2), there exist two kinds of signs (or sign components): those that directly transport pieces of semantic information, and others whose primary task is putting together, on the different levels of hierarchy, linearized parts that belong together.

Linguistically, this gives rise to the whole apparatus of *syntax, word classes, morphemes, syntagms, clauses, constituency, dependency, congruence, agreement, government, binding, heads, dependents, head-marking, dependent-marking, modifiers, modi significandi accidentales*, and the like.

4.4.3. Other aspects

The principle of Creativity or Productivity (3) is implemented, among other things, by the principles of Reference to Types (10) and Combinatorial Rules (14), such that — together with the rest of the principles 11 to 16 — the outcome will always satisfy principle 15, with the resulting Whole being more than the sum of its Parts.

In another sense, these principles manifest themselves in a compartmentalization of linguistic tasks. The principle of Double Articulation (7) allows us to – theoretically – distinguish Phonology from all the rest. The principles of 'Discoursivity' (6), of Otherness (2), and of Reference to Types (10) lead to socially ratified utterance types as well as to grammatical paradigms.

4.5. Evidence coming from neighboring disciplines

If it were only for these principles – the five essential and the eleven implementational ones – languages could and would be far more different than they actually are. One reason why they are less different than should be expected could be that some of these principles are 'wired' into our brains in a specific manner. This should not come as a surprise: evolution tends to draw on strategies that have proved successful. This is why the 'phenomenological' principle of Hierarchy (13) may be seen as holding for all kinds of perception (cf. Riedl 1989: 220–43; see above § 4.1).

As regards word classes for instance, the opposition between 'verbs' and 'nouns' (→ art. 38) – irrespective of the differences we encounter in the systems of different natural languages – corresponds, indeed, to an opposition between entities our conceptual apparatus is programmed to recognize (see above § 3). The area of our brain named after Carl Wernicke is above all devoted to assigning to and retrieving meaning (concepts) from signs that refer to types of discrete entities. Concepts referring to types of situations and actions are linked, by an associative network, to the area named after Paul Broca (→ art. 9).

When we speak, the task of the Broca area is to break complex ideas (corresponding for instance to what we would call a 'proposition' or even to larger entities) down into smaller units which have to be linearized and grammatically tagged in real time; when we hear, this area does the real time analysis ("parsing") of the grammatically tagged incoming series of signs and the successive synthesis into a coherent structure, to which a complex meaning can be assigned.

As is shown by event-related brain potential (ERP) measures, the two phases can be clearly distinguished by changes in potential (typically 200 and 400 msec after the onset); this holds true also for a third phase necessary in unclear cases where a top-down reanalysis has to be carried out. Each one of these parsing phases, initial bottom up and secondary top down analysis, is subserved by distinct brain systems (cf. Friederici 1997; 1997a; Friederici & al. 1998; Friederici & al. 1999; Hahne & al. 1999; Meyer & al. 2000).

There is cerebral evidence not only as regards the different content types – 'verbs', types of 'nouns' being, e.g., retrieved from different brain areas – but also for the cerebral difference between the concepts and their linguistic implementation, reflecting the Modistic distinction between 'concepts' and 'significations' [above Figure 1.3]; cf. Grabowski & al. 1998; Tranel & al. 1997 and 1997a; Damasio & al. 1993; 1992; Friederici & al. 2000.

In the case of numbers and their cerebral representation, there is evidence suggesting that animals, young infants and adults possess a biologically determined, domain-specific representation of number and of elementary arithmetic operations based on language-independent concepts. This is indirectly confirmed for instance by Susan Schaller (1991): her deaf-mute pupil dubbed Ildefonso who – at age 27 – had not even come into contact with sign language, let alone phonetic or written language, had no problems with elementary arithmetic and with number concepts. As is also well-known, exact arithmetic is, on the other hand, acquired in a language-specific format transferring even poorly to a different language (Dehaene & al. 1998; 1999).

In order not to suggest too close a linkage between the genetic basis and phenomena we regard as typical for our natural languages, a caveat is in order, though: There are speakers whose first language is one of the sign languages deaf people use. In this case, the Broca area does exactly the same job it does in vocal speech: it parses and combines units into larger units in perception, and it analyses and linearizes them in the process of sign production. This is true for native signers, native speakers (of ENGLISH in this case) and speakers of both a sign language (ASL) and ENGLISH (cf., based on functional magnetic imaging: Bavelier & al. 1998; Neville & al. 1998; 1997; cf. also Poizner & al. 1987.).

This means that the basic faculty of combining parts into wholes, and of analyzing wholes into parts, is in principle independent of the quality of the signs at issue: vocal speech, written language, or language consisting of signs made by hand, gesture or facial expression (→ art. 10, where also some differences, mostly due to the modalities of signing, are outlined). Nevertheless, it stands to reason that, in the case of sign languages, the input — before reaching the Broca area — has to be processed in a different way, implicating in this case large parts of the right hemisphere that are less active in vocal or even written language processing.

It should be mentioned that the 'wiring' of concepts and processes into our brain cannot, as a rule, currently be shown by direct physiological evidence, for instance by a detailed view on the functioning of particular neuronal networks. At the moment, most assumptions are based on the indirect evidence given by an increased regional blood flow in activated cerebral areas (positron emission tomography [PET], with low resolution in time) or by changes in the paramagnetic properties of hemoglobin, depending on its oxygenation state (functional magnetic resonance imaging [fMRI], with high temporal and spatial resolution). Other evidence stems from changes in potential or magnetic field due to the firing of neuronal networks in certain brain areas (event-related brain potential [ERP]). Magnetoencephalography (MEG, most expensive) with a temporal resolution in the range of 10^{-3} sec may even register changes brought about by the firing of individual neurons.

The generally indirect evidence we encounter in this domain has its consequences. Whenever a neurophysiologist working on the level of neural tissue is asked for her or his opinion about the basis of cognitive processes, one is likely to hear an agnostic *non liquet* or "we don't know anything for sure", while neuroscientists or neuropsychologists — with their top down view — are much more prone to theorizing on the basis of their observations and findings. A mediation between the two perspectives should always take into account the above-mentioned Principle 15 (in the domain of Life Wholes are always more than the sum of their Parts; cf. above § 4.4; cf. also art. 8, § 4.2 as regards the bridging between 'matter' and 'mind').

5. Advantages of the universalist view

What is the answer given by the universalist approach to the problems raised in § 3? In spite of the evidence coming from adjacent fields of research (aphasiology, neurolinguistics, genetics; see above § 4.5), the considerations outlined in § 4.4 seem to be rather general. Of what use are they, then?

The use lies, first of all, in the possibility of epistemologically classifying approaches to language typology and to language universals, and recognizing what their respective bases are. It permits us, then, to formulate tasks to be fulfilled and problems to be solved, and hence the comparison of the different implementations of an identical task in different languages. This is to say that it provides the necessary *tertium*.

5.1. Enhancing the formal aspects

Noam Chomsky's approach — as instantiated in the Minimalist Hypothesis — starts from a concept of the modularity of Mind, separating the semantico-conceptual module from the formal-syntactic one. His approach emphasizes the aspects outlined above in § 4.4.2. It starts from the assumption of a universal Logical Form already 'wired' into the brains of children. Differences between languages are assumed to result from the fact that the principles presupposed by Universal Grammar are not equally strong in the input coming from different languages. This leads to different linearizations and types of expression once the Logical Form has to be transposed into a real chain of phonological, lexical etc. items (→ art. 24).

In a certain sense, this echoes the discussions on word order in French Enlightenment. Since FRENCH word order with the subject in the first place and the predicate following was conceived of as the universal logical form (inspired by Aristotelian logic), some put forward the idea that e.g. Cicero, before speaking or writing a sentence in the LATIN way, had to have conceived of it in the FRENCH one (→ art. 19, § 3.2.2).

Another approach was proposed by Klaus Heger. It is based on three principles: An ascending scale of ever more complex signs ('Signemränge'), a corresponding dynamic conception of signs not restricted to words, finally a form of representation called 'Aktantenmodelle'. Their canonical form is a two place predicator that attributes a 'relator' to an 'actant'. (In case the relator has more than one place, the number of actants — under the heading of a pro-actant — may be augmented.) Relators can only be continuous concepts, the most important ones being the temporal and the causal relator. It can easily be seen that Heger was not inspired by traditional Aristotelian logic, but by predicate logic or its linguistic homologue, dependency grammar.

The 'noematic' *tertium* created by Heger allows the analysis and the description of entire texts, not only propositions, thus encompassing far more than the Minimalist Hypothesis. Nonetheless, it was only designed as a *tertium* for the comparison of languages, with Heger never claiming a *transitus ab intellectu ad rem* in the sense that all — or even some — of its components had a basis in the psychophysical 'reality' of speech production and reception (→ art. 25). It is evident, though, that the conception is close to universalist positions, and it does not come as a surprise that it is echoed, e.g., in the UNITYP or the RIVALC approaches (→ articles 27; 28).

5.2. Starting the conceptual way

Universalistic approaches may differ in the importance they attribute to the principle of Semanticity. Speakers start from the ideas, the concepts or intentions they want to communicate, and hearers retranslate the chain of sounds and words they perceive into ideas or concepts. Why, then, not start from the conceptual side? Most radical in this sense is William Croft (1991). This gives *function* a most prominent place in typology. One major advantage is that in doing so we may define, as *tertia*, identical tasks languages have to cope with. One of them will serve as a first example.

5.2.1. Tasks on the level of propositions and above

Both the partisans of an inductive way — as represented e.g. by the well-known contribution Joseph H. Greenberg made in 1963 (→ art. 23) — and the followers of axiomatic views have underlined the importance constituent ordering has in propositions. What has been considered above in § 4.4 shows that in doing so, typologists implicitly or explicitly start from the following assumptions:

1. that there is a Privileged Unit (Principle 16) called proposition;
2. that it is essentially made up of units centering around two basic Word Classes (Principle 12), viz. nominals and verbals;
3. that a verb is an unstable, 'unsaturated' unit having *valency*, thus enabling a certain number of nominals to be — conceptually and linguistically — linked to it;
4. that valency may range from 0 to 3, depending on the verbal concept at stake, and that bi-valency is a frequent constellation;
5. that there are Combinatorial Rules (principle 14) allowing for the partial wholes or components — dubbed e.g. X,Y,Z,V — to merge into a higher unit thanks to Signs Organizing Signs (12) that mark the syntactic role they play in the higher unit;
6. that, given the principles of Semanticity and of Signs Referring to Types (Principles 1 and 10), there are conceptual roles corresponding to the syntactic ones, yielding concepts such as *actor, patient, beneficiary*, etc.

This is tantamount to saying that this kind of investigation, while often thought to be purely 'typological' or even 'descriptive', is necessarily based on a whole series of (unavoidable) universalist prerequisites.

Based on the common *tertium* constituted by these assumptions — essentially a *tertium* linked to what linguists call the task of forming propositions — one can, indeed, define types: first of all types according to the linear order the constituents {X,Y,Z,V} have in (certain kinds of) propositions. This alone has led to the formulation of a series of 'implicational' universals put forward by Greenberg and others (→ articles 23; 64). But, above all, thoughts given to this topic and successive observations across a great variety of languages led to types according to the mapping of conceptual roles onto syntactic ones, and to the use that is made to this end of Signs Organizing Signs (Principle 11; morphemes, position).

That this mapping, together with constituent ordering, must be important is shown by the fact that very often speakers of languages have special means permitting them to change both this order and the mapping of conceptual roles onto syntactic ones that is linked to it. The respective devices are called *diatheses*: like 'active', 'passive', 'middle', 'antipassive', 'causative', 'experiencer-diathesis'.

While implementing the same conceptual 'roles', languages may considerably differ in the way they mark and order the constituents of propositions. In this context, typologists most often speak e.g. of 'accusative', 'ergative', and as often 'mixed' languages (→ art. 26, § 3.2; art. 28, § 4; articles 37; 125).

There is an immense body of linguistic data and a great number of studies by now that are devoted to the mapping of conceptual roles onto syntactic ones. The only problem is that, whereas syntactic roles are easy to define given their limited number and definite formal properties, conceptual roles, their number and their definition tend to be subject to discussion among linguists (cf. e.g. Croft 1991: 155ff.). Here the idea of prototypicality proves helpful, as does taking into account the meaning of the respective verb (cf. Koch 1981). The broad activities on this sector manifest themselves in the present handbook: → e.g. art. 2, § 3.1; art. 26, § 2; articles 28; 37; 66−70.

This example demonstrates the importance typologists attribute to a typology based on the *tertium* constituted by the task of forming propositions. Speakers of languages have indeed multifold, often grammaticalized possibilities of ordering the elements in propositions. To these one may add the technique of clefting, allowing, among other things, a freer ordering of elements where the order of actants is relatively fixed.

Another example on the level of propositions are studies on relativization as carried out e.g. by Edward Keenan and Bernard Comrie (1977) or Christian Lehmann (1984). Contrary to the opinion of some scholars, their basis is not only semantic, but also conceptual.

If we ask ourselves why speakers create so many different techniques, the answer is that phenomena such as František Daneš's Functional Sentence Perspective are not ends in themselves, but one of the means allowing for speakers to link a sequence of propositions in a way that serves the interests of hearers and speakers (→ art. 45). 'Pragmatic' and 'textual' issues add to the purely 'syntactic' ones, providing us with the means to linguistically express 'Relevance' (Sperber & Wilson ¹1986/1995). Propositions are, indeed, only partial wholes having themselves a function in higher units that originate by linking and merging propositions into utterance types (see above § 2).

Another universal cognitive prerequisite permanently translated into linguistic forms is a scheme first proposed by James Harris (Harris 1751). Humans use it in order to conceptualize another view on 'actions', viz. 'action' conceived of as a sequence of at most five phases. It starts with a PRE-INITIAL phase followed by the INITIAL one; next are the MIDDLE or PROGRESSIVE phase, i.e. an action just going on, then the TERMINAL phase, that is an action coming to its end, and finally the POST-TERMINAL phase, the concept of an action seen from beyond its end.

Now speakers tend to highlight one of these phases in their propositions, and according to the phase that is being expressed, the verb forms can be attributed to different AKTIONSARTEN. Since they were first described for POLISH by Sigurd Agrell (1908), there exists an enormous amount of terminology in this sector, more often than not even mixing up 'aspect' and 'Aktionsart' (there may be affinities between aspects ['imperfectivity' and 'perfectivity'] and Aktionsarten, but the two categories should be kept distinct; cf. for an overview Iturrioz 1993). All five phases may be expressed either by 'simple' verbs, by prefixes, preverbs etc. − or by verbal periphrases which are themselves common starting points for grammaticalization: with the pre-initial phase giving rise, for instance, to new future forms, whereas the post-terminal one usually ends up in new perfects (cf. for instance Bybee & al. 1994; Lehmann 1995: 29−32.).

In this context, speakers all over the world tend to use the same verbal concepts in order to paraphrase the respective phases (cf. above § 4.3): for instance epistemic or modal concepts (WILL, SHALL, TO HAVE TO), verbs of movement (TO GO) in order to express the pre-initial or the terminal phase (like the FRENCH type *je vais venir, je viens de chanter*; cf. Radden 1996 for an overview over COME and GO); the middle or 'progressive' phase can be expressed by concepts such as TO BE, TO STAND, TO LIE, TO CONTINUE, plus a nominalized verb form such as in SPANISH *está cantando, sigue cantando* or its ENGLISH equivalent *s/he is singing*; for the terminal phase, we find paraphrases such as SPANISH *acaba de cantar*, literally 's/he terminates singing'; the post-terminal phase is usually paraphrased by concepts such as TO HAVE, TO BE FINISHED WITH (cf. the LATIN type *Caesar legiones habebat coactas* 'for Cesar the legions were contracted ones'; we may find as well equivalents of the FRENCH type *j'ai fini de faire qch* that gave rise to perfects and perfectives in French based CREOLES; cf. Michaelis 1993).

An equally well-known case is the concept TO TAKE frequently used as the first element in verb series in order to express the initial phase (often we have to take something before we can do something with it). This occurs even in languages to which verbal series in the strict sense are alien such as to most European ones: cf. the SPANISH type *tomo y me voy* 'I start going' (literally 'I take and go'), a type of expression which is not restricted to SPANISH but can be found in many European languages as was shown in great detail by Coseriu (Coseriu 1966).

A last example of a both conceptual and functional approach, this time based on both pragmatics and concepts, are politeness phenomena. Here, the universal mechanisms are identical: the dignity of the person addressed has to be augmented in the eyes of others ("positive face" in terms of Brown/Levinson 1987), whereas the speaker himself is submissive (e.g. "your humble servant"); at the same time the act of intrusion into the personal sphere of the person addressed has to be mitigated, usually by all kinds of indirectness, e.g. by special moods ("negative face"; → art. 35, § 3.5).

SPANISH and its LATIN AMERICAN varieties are good examples of one of the effects both strategies can have on grammar: *Vuestra Merced* ('Your Grace'), which today has become *Usted*, is the polite form of address, using the indirect third person instead of the second one; in large parts of Latin America the polite address *vos* (originally 2PL) has replaced the too direct form *tú* 2SG, making the paradigm 'irregular' at the same time:

	LATIN AMERICAN SPANISH	EUROPEAN SPANISH
	'I sing' etc.	'I sing' etc.
1SG	*(yo) canto*	*(yo) canto*
2SG	*(vos) cantá(i)s*	*(tú) cantas*
3SG	*(él/Usted) canta*	*(él/Usted) canta*
1PL	*(nosotros) cantamos*	*(nosotros) cantamos*
2PL	*(Ustedes) cantan*	*(vosotros) cantais*
3PL	*(Ustedes) cantan*	*(ellos/Ustedes) cantan*

Another well-known example are JAPANESE honorifics (cf. Prideaux 1970; Lewin 1959: §§ 62; 68; 138f.; 167f.).

5.2.2. Tasks beneath the level of propositions

Let us take another example of a different solution to an identical problem: Speakers of all languages have to apprehend and to linguistically process real world objects — a task giving rise to another privileged unit (above Principle 14), nouns. When cross-linguistically observing the techniques applied to this task, one may formulate a scale of possibilities. It ranges from ABSTRACTION (making nouns out of the content of propositions), over COLLECTION (e.g. 'a flock of birds'), MASS AND MEASURE ('an ounce of gold'), CLASSIFICATION BY VERBS, NOUN CLASSIFICATION, CLASSIFICATION BY ARTICLES, NUMERAL CLASSIFICATION, to NAMEGIVING (cf. Seiler 1986).

Speakers of different languages choose different techniques, but never all of them. Classification of objects by different verbs — mostly in the domain of verbs indicating the position or movement of something — is a highly elaborate technique in an ATHABASKAN language like CHIPEWYAN; GERMAN has a little bit of this 'exotic' technique ('die Kleider *hängen*, die Schuhe *stehen*, die Unterwäsche *liegt* im Schrank', 'der Kamin *sitzt* auf dem Dach', 'die Schraube *sitzt* auf der Mutter' ['the screw is fixed on the nut']), whereas the feature is totally alien to ROMANCE LANGUAGES, which would use the same verb in all the above cases, e.g. the most simple linguistic form of the concept TO BE AT A PLACE. The same holds e.g. for verbs of movement where we may distinguish different types of realization, e.g. 'verb-framed' and 'satellite-framed' techniques: In ENGLISH, there is, e.g., a tendency to use a general verb of movement like *to walk*, adding satellites like *in*, *out*, *across* to it. This results in syntagms like *to walk in* or *out* where a verb-framed language like SPANISH would have specific verbs such as *entrar, salir, subir, bajar* etc. (Talmy 1985; 1991).

Another example has to do with principle 10, Signs Referring to Types. What do speakers of languages do in order to refer to tokens, instead? An answer is given by the dimension of IDENTIFICATION of the UNITYP project (→ art. 27, § 3).

The examples show that formulating a specific task as a *tertium held universally valid* and looking both for the solutions found in a variety of languages and the factors on which the solutions depend is a powerful tool in so-called functional typology. The application of this principle seems to have been particularly successful in Russian typology (→ art. 2, § 3.1; art. 26, §§ 2−4 for convincing examples).

Typically, what functional typology results in is discovering CONTINUA and SCALES.

5.3. The emergence of conceptual continua and linguistic scales

Indeed, once we have formulated an invariant task and observed the cross-linguistic variance historical languages exhibit, we often come to discover CONCEPTUAL CONTINUA and LINGUISTIC SCALES that correspond to them. A well-known example is the hierarchy which is sometimes termed 'Silverstein' or 'Kozinsky hierarchy' (after its discoverers,

Michael Silverstein or Isaak Kozinskij; first ideas in this direction may be found in Hale [1973]), or simply 'animacy hierarchy'. In terms of phenomenology or Gestalt psychology, it reflects the saliency of the 'objects' we are talking of, the most important ones being the speech act persons, then humans in general, animals, plants, discontinuous and concrete entities, mass, abstract entities. Here again concepts are linked to a pragmatic framework.

The effectiveness of such a hierarchy can be shown for instance in differential object marking across a large variety of languages (→ art. 65). In SPANISH, (grammatical) objects are marked either by position alone or with an additional *a* – (*veo a Pedro,* 'I see Pedro' as opposed to *veo el automóbil* 'I see the car'). In SPANISH, the feature deciding in favour of *a* for grammatical objects is being a member of the class of humans, whereas VALLADER, the version of RHETO-ROMANSH spoken in the Lower Engadine, only highlights the speech act persons, or more precisely, the 2nd and the 3rd one (I am not a salient person to myself as a grammatical object). The same animacy scale plays a crucial part in "split ergativity": as was put forward by Isaak Kozinskij, ergative case marking exhibits a universal tendency to implicate nominals of lower animacy (→ art. 26, § 3.2) – which gives especially personal pronouns as typical exponents of humans a particular role in case marking often commented upon (→ e.g. art. 125, § 4.2.2 as regards the case of CAUCASIAN LANGUAGES).

In the case of linguistically processing real world objects (see above § 5.2.2), the principle underlying the scale of enumerated techniques is a continuum between 'predicativity' and 'indicativity'. Predicativity is realized in an optimal way by the technique of abstraction – like *the pan cooks over* → *the cooking over of the pan*; indicativity is optimally realized by proper names which may nonetheless be expressed as well in a predicative way – "Dances with Wolves" for a person or "where they killed each other" as the HUICHOL version of the toponym *Guerra* 'war' – thus linking the ends of the scale into a Möbius-strip. (→ art. 27, § 5.3; for this kind of proper names → also art. 41, § 7.)

If we try to grasp a phenomenon like the linguistic scale(s) suggested for the concept of *transitivity* (see above § 3.4), it is evident that one perceptual continuum is projected onto several linguistic subscales: one being indeed the nature of the grammatical 'subject' and 'object' or, in a more neutral wording, of the actants (animacy hierarchy), another the degree of definiteness of the implied actants, still another tense and/or aspect (perfectivity and/or resultativity make an action more transitive – a fact that may give rise to 'split ergativity' dependent on tense categories: → e.g. art. 125, § 4.4), the thematic or rhematic character of the two nominal constituents, affirmation/negation, etc. (Hopper & Thompson 1980; Tsunoda 1985; 1994; → articles 26; 28, § 7; 125).

This kind of view makes us understand what at first might look exotic – like the case of perfectivity/imperfectivity being expressed by the grammatical object in FINNISH. The imperfectivity-perfectivity opposition being one parameter in the conceptual Whole called 'transitive proposition', its expression can be taken over by an obligatory constituent different from the verb, e.g. the Parts representing the patient or even a form representing the actor (GUSIILAY, where, again, the animacy continuum comes into play, the device being restricted in this form to nominals belonging to classes 1 [humans, SG] and 2 [humans, PL]; see above § 3.4). "The sheer number and typological diversity of languages in which this phenomenon is found argue strongly that it is by no means marginal. Rather the possibility that TAM information is directly contributed to the clause by dependent nominal arguments, must be accounted for within any theory of universal grammar" (Nordlinger & Sadler 2000).

What is crucial for such scales is that they reflect the translation of perceptual or conceptual continua into linguistic forms and features by necessarily introducing cutoffs, turning points and borderlines: the number of signs, of discrete categories and word classes is limited according to the above Principle 10 (types). – More scales brought about by exactly this basic problem may be found in → art. 38, esp. §§ 3 and 4.

Hence, what we observe once we have engaged in this kind of viewing language data are CONCEPTUAL CONTINUA and linguistic SCALES that correspond to them – continua that may manifest themselves in grammatical distinctions, with the speakers of different languages grammatically marking different points in the conceptual continuum, thus giving rise to different *types of linguistic realization.*

A last example shall show the basic process as applied to first language acquisition. If an object falls onto the floor, this is a salient event already to toddlers. Hence, such (prototypical) events are projected onto specific linguistic forms the child has encountered in the speech of peers and adults and which seem to be related to the concept. This is why children use for instance GERMAN perfect forms as resultatives and perfectives: *is runterfanna* ('ist runtergefallen', 'has fallen down and now lies there') as opposed for instance to *is da* ('ist da', 'lies there'). As a consequence, less salient and less resultative events – such as the barking of a dog or the cooking over of a pan on the stove – are attributed to the opposed imperfective, iresulative etc. category.

In this general sense, we might even interpret "Principles and Parameters" as *conceptual* Principles that are projected onto *syntactic, formal* Parameters. (→ art. 28, § 6.5 as to grammatical evolution typically starting from salient or prototypical instances.)

5.4. Some typically 'human' factors

There are universal factors beyond those that are wired into our brains or based on our conceptual apparatus. Their 'typically human' nature becomes most evident when we compare once more the genetic with the linguistic system. Cellular processes are energetically optimized by evolution, thus leaving no conceivable scope for economy (→ art. 8, § 4.9.2). Human communication, characterized among other things by the principles of Otherness and of Exteriority (above § 4.4, Principles 2 and 5), implies two psychophysical systems, that is speakers who may e.g. be more or less explicit in what they produce, giving rise to phenomena like the "Principle of Least Effort" (Zipf 1949). This is why economy (→ art. 31) and markedness (→ art. 32) are most important factors in human languages, leading for instance to permanent language change.

Markedness is a special form of economy since it takes shape in less marked vs. more marked units both on the formal and on the content level: there are less marked vs. more marked linguistic categories as well as semantic units. What is less marked usually conveys less information or, semantically speaking, less intension, having instead a wider range of applicability or extension.

This is one further aspect of well-known categorial scales and conceptual hierarchies like 'subject – direct object – indirect object – genitive construction', and it is related to "implicational universals": "If a category in a hierarchy is accessible to relativization, the categories above will be all the more accessible to it"; in differential object marking: "if a less animate category is differentially marked as an object, the more animate ones will be marked *a fortiori*"; or in ergative marking: "if a more animate category is marked as ergative, the categories of lower animacy will be marked as well".

Economy and markedness are universal phenomena in human language. Unfortunately, both are factors that never lead to stable situations or types: what is economical or optimal on one level leads to an increased effort and to reduced optimality on another one: witness e.g. simple phoneme systems leading to complex phoneme segments; conversely, the price to pay for short segments is a complex phoneme system that leads to increased efforts in pronunciation. Generally speaking, parameters of economy tend to be contrary to each other, often leaving us with a rather blurred overall picture (→ e.g. art. 31, § 6).

Whilst economy serves above all the interests of speakers, and markedness those of speakers and hearers, there is another 'human' factor that has to be taken into account with regard to speech perception, especially as regards parsing. As has been mentioned (see above § 4.4.5), the main task of the Broca area is the real time analysis of the grammatically tagged incoming series of signs (Parts) and the successive synthesis into a coherent structure (Whole). This has consequences for the perceptually optimal position of grammatical tags (→ art. 29).

One of the tasks of 'prepositions' or 'postpositions' is to mark the role a noun phrase (an 'actant') has with respect to the verb. Now, as was shown for the first time by a mathematician, the topologist René Thom, the best place for such linking morphemes is between the elements to be linked. If '*' is the operator and X, Y are the operands, Polish notation in mathematics – with its canonical $*(X, Y)$ form – could by no means be a convenient solution in the linearization of linguistic signs. Instead, a perceptually good solution would be the type $X*Y$, i.e. with the operator *between* the operands. According to Thom (1973), this is why V(S)O ordering more often than not leads to the type V *Prep* N, whereas in (S)OV ordering the type N

Post V is preferred (→ art. 2, § 2.2). (Things might be complicated by taking into account head vs. dependent marking as an additional factor.)

At the same time, this example shows again that what is perceptually optimal on one level may be less so on another one: Since the same principle should apply to actants having the shape of subordinate clauses, we should − in the case of an object clause − have the type $(S)Cl_{obj}*V$ and hence $(S)[sov]_{obj}*V$. As was shown e.g. by Francesco Antinucci (1977), this could lead to a typical pitfall for hearers. As a consequence, we often observe that ordering in dependent clauses differs from ordering in matrix sentences − which prevents misanalysis (cf. Raible 1992).

6. The shortcomings of traditional views

If we take into account the 'traditional' field of Typology and the − often excellent − work that was done in this domain, the above considerations on the topic of Universals as necessary in order to ask the right questions in Typology might appear somewhat gratuitous. But even granted this, a threefold caveat will not be amiss:

1. We do need the universalist view − in particular the level of Principles (see above § 4.4) and of concepts (see above § 4.3) − in order to find or to construct the *tertium comparationis* indispensable in typology. The categories of historical languages are different to such an extent that a simple comparison of seemingly identical categories is bound to be misleading, unless this comparison is supported by functional, conceptual and cognitive criteria (see above e.g. §§ 4.2; 4.3; 5.2; 5.2.1; 5.2.2). This is an answer to the problem raised in § 3.3 (Categories are not cross-linguistically comparable) and it is − at least to a large extent − the secret behind Isaak Kozinskij's opposite claim that categorial differences were of little importance (see above § 3.3).

2. There is an important caveat regarding the 'comparability' of languages: *Langue* in the sense of de Saussure is a construct corresponding to the sociology of Émile Durkheim and his school (that was contemporary to de Saussure). A more realistic view, taking into account, among other things, linguistic variation (§ 1.3), would prefer to conceptualize language systems according to the communicative tasks to be fulfilled, that is language should rather be seen as a scale (see above figures 1.1 and 1.2), or even better as multi-dimensional space. As there is (in parallel to the extension of communicative tasks) a scale of Pidgins merging, e.g., into a scale of Creoles, language systems may be more or less developed or 'sophisticated' (see above § 2, 'Ausbau' as opposed to 'language obsolescence'). While comparing parts of such systems across different languages, we always have to take into account at least the text or utterance type, the area, the social space it is used in. This is all the more important as we have seen that history has to be introduced into typology (see above § 3.5).

3. Another caveat holds for the comparability of languages with respect to 'historical depth' and documentation through history (the issue was raised above in § 3.5; → art. 111). Principle (4), Historicity, makes change a phenomenon inextricably linked with any language at any moment of its existence (see above § 4.4). If in a cross-linguistic approach we concentrate on types e.g. on the basis of the expression of 'possession' or 'marking of objects' (→ art. 65), what we observe may well correspond to the picture we take of an intermediate state on a scale of development. What is important and truly fascinating are not the intermediate states we can observe in a series of languages, giving rise to 'types' of expression for possession or object marking, but the *conceptual continuum* or the *cognitive (mental, semantic) maps* behind such developments − thus meeting the expectations of Leibniz (*Nouveaux essais sur l'entendement humain*):

"On enregistrera avec le temps et mettra en dictionnaires et en grammaires toutes les langues de l'univers, et on les comparera entre elles; ce qui aura des usages très grands tant pour la connaissance des choses [...] que pour la connaissance de notre esprit et de la merveilleuse variété de ses opérations."

7. References

Agrell, Sigurd. 1908. *Aspektveränderung und Aktionsartbildung beim polnischen Zeitworte: Ein Beitrag zum Studium der indogermanischen Präverbia und ihrer Bedeutungsfunktionen.* (Lunds Universitets Årsskrift.) Lund.

Antinucci, Francesco. 1977. *Fondamenti di una teoria tipologica del linguaggio.* (Studi linguistici e semiologici, 7.) Bologna: Mulino.

Anward, Jan & Moravcsik, Edith & Stassen, Leon. 1997. "Parts of Speech: A Challenge for Typology". *Linguistic Typology* 1-2: 167–83.

Bakhtin, Michail M. 1979/1986. *Speech genres and other late essays*. Translated by Vern W. McGee. Ed. by Caryl Emerson. (University of Texas Press Slavic series, 8.) Austin: University of Texas Press. – In Russian: *Estetika slovesnogo tvorčestva*. Moskva: Iskusstvo 1979.

Bavelier, Daphne & Corina, David & Jezzard, Peter & Clark, V. & Karni, A. & Lalwani, A. & A, Rauschecker, J.P. & Braun, A. & Turner, R. & Neville, Helen J. 1998. "Hemispheric specialization for English and ASL: left invariance-right variability". *Neuroreport* 9.7: 1537–42.

Biber, Douglas 1986. "Spoken and written textual dimensions in English: resolving the contradictory findings". *Language* 62: 384–414.

Biber, Douglas. 1988. *Variation across speech and writing*. Cambridge: Cambridge University Press.

Brown, Penelope & Levinson, Stephen C. 1987 (^{1}1974). *Politeness: some universals in language usage*. (Studies in interactional sociolinguistics, 4.) Cambridge: Cambridge University Press.

Bühler, Karl. 1934. *Sprachtheorie. Die Darstellungsfunktion der Sprache*. Jena: Fischer.

Bybee, Joan & Perkins, Revere & Pagliuca, William. 1994. *The Evolution of Grammar. Tense, Aspect, and Modality in the Languages of the World*. Chicago & London: The University of Chicago Press.

Casad, Eugene H. (ed.). 1996. *Cognitive linguistics in the redwoods. The Expansion of a new paradigm in linguistics*. Berlin & New York: de Gruyter.

Confiant, Raphaël. 1994. "Questions pratiques d'écriture créole". In: Ludwig, Ralph (ed.). *Écrire la parole de nuit: la nouvelle littérature antillaise*. (Collection Folio: Essais, 239.) Paris: Gallimard, 171–180.

Coseriu, Eugenio. 1966. "Tomo y me voy. Ein Problem vergleichender europäischer Syntax". *Vox Romanica* 25: 13–55.

Coseriu, Eugenio. 1974. "Les universaux linguistiques (et les autres)". In: Heilmann, Luigi (ed.). *Proceedings of the Eleventh International Congress of Linguists*. Bologna–Florence, Aug. 28–Sept. 2, 1972. Bologna: Il Mulino, 47–73.

Croft, William. 1990. *Typology and universals*. (Cambridge Textbooks in Linguistics.) Cambridge/ GB & New York: Cambridge University Press.

Croft, William. 1991. *Syntactic categories and grammatical relations: the cognitive organization of information*. Chicago: University of Chicago Press. [Rev. Ph.D. thesis of 1986].

Damasio, Antonio R. & Damasio, Hanna C. 1992. "Brain and language". *Scientific American* 267.3: 63–71.

Damasio, Antonio R. & Tranel, Daniel T. 1993. "Nouns and verbs are retrieved with differently distributed neural systems". *Proceedings of the National Academy of Sciences of the U.S.A.* 90.5: 4957–60.

Damasio, Hanna C. & Grabowski, Thomas J. & Tranel, Daniel T. & Hichwa, Richard D. & Damasio, Antonio R. 1996. "A neural basis for lexical retrieval". *Nature* 380.6574: 499–505.

Damourette, Jacques & Pichon, Édouard. 1911–1940. *Des mots à la pensée. Essai de grammaire de la langue française*. 7 vols. Paris: D'Artrey.

Dehaene, Stanislas & Dehaene-Lambertz, G. & Cohen, Laurent. 1998. "Abstract representations of numbers in the animal and human brain". *Trends in Neuroscience* 21.8: 355–61.

Dehaene, Stanislas & Spelke, E. & Pinel, P. & Stanescu, R. & Tsivkin, S. 1999. "Sources of mathematical thinking: behavioral and brain-imaging evidence". *Science* 284.5416: 970–74.

Evans, Nicholas R. D. 1985. *Kayardild: the language of the Bentinck Islanders of North West Queensland*. Canberra: Australian National University Dissertation.

Frank, Barbara & Haye, Thomas & Tophinke, Doris (eds.). 1997. *Gattungen mittelalterlicher Schriftlichkeit*. (ScriptOralia, 99.) Tübingen: Narr.

Grabowski, Thomas J. & Damasio, Hanna C. & Damasio, Antonio R. 1998. "Premotor and prefrontal correlates of category-related lexical retrieval". *Neuroimage* 7.3: 232–43.

Eckert, Penelope. 1998. *Language variation as social practice*. (Language in society.) Oxford: Blackwell.

Ehrenfels, Christian v. 1890. "Über Gestaltqualitäten". *Vierteljahresschrift für wissenschaftliche Philosophie* 14: 249–292.

Forgas, Joseph P. (ed.). 1985. *Language and social situations*. (Springer series in social psychology.) New York: Springer.

Friederici, Angela D. 1997. "Menschliche Sprachverarbeitung und ihre neuronalen Grundlagen". In: Meier, Heinrich & Ploog, Detlev. *Der Mensch und sein Gehirn. Die Folgen der Evolution*. (Veröffentlichungen der Carl Friedrich von Siemens Stiftung, 7.) München: Piper, 137–56.

Friederici, Angela D. 1997a. "Neurophysiological aspects of language processing". *Clinical Neuroscience* 4.2: 64–72.

Friederici, Angela D. & Hahne, Anja & von Cramon, D. Yves. 1998. "First-pass versus second-pass parsing processes in a Wernicke's and a Broca's aphasic: electrophysiological evidence for a double dissociation". *Brain and Language* 62.3: 311–41.

Friederici, Angela D. & von Cramon, D. Yves. & Kotz, Sonja A. 1999. "Language related brain potentials in patients with cortical and subcortical left hemisphere lesions". *Brain* 122.6: 1033–47.

Friederici, Angela D. & Opitz. Bertram & von Cramon D. Yves. 2000. "Segregating Semantic and Syntactic Aspects of Processing in the Human Brain: an fMRI Investigation of Different Word Types". *Cerebral Cortex.* 10.7: 698-705.

Giglioli, Pier Paolo. ²1990. 1972. *Language and social context. Selected readings.* (Penguin language and linguistics.) Harmondsworth: Penguin Books.

Greenberg, Joseph H. 1963. "Some universals of grammar with particular reference to the order of meaningful elements". In: Greenberg, Joseph H. (ed.). *Universals of language.* Cambridge: MIT, 58-90.

Greenberg, Joseph H. 1974. *Language typology. A historical and analytic overview.* (Janua linguarum, series minor, 184.) The Hague & Paris: Mouton.

Günther, Hartmut & Ludwig, Otto (eds.). 1994. *Schrift und Schriftlichkeit. Writing and its use. Ein interdisziplinäres Handbuch internationaler Forschung. An interdisciplinary handbook of international research.* Vol. I. Berlin & New York: de Gruyter.

Gumperz, John J. 1971. *Language in social groups. Essays.* (Language science and national development.) Stanford, Calif.: Stanford University Press.

Hahne, Anja & Friederici, Angela D. 1999. "Electrophysiological evidence for two steps in syntactic analysis. Early automatic and late controlled processes". *Journal of Cognitive Neuroscience* 11.2: 194-205.

Hale, Kenneth. 1973. "A note on subject-object inversion in Navajo". In: Kachru, Braj B. (ed.). *Issues in linguistics. Papers in honor of Henry and Renée Kahane.* Urbana etc.: University of Illinois Press, 300-309.

Halliday, Michael A. K. 1979. *Language as social semiotic. The social interpretation of language and meaning.* London: Arnold.

Harris, James. 1751. *Hermes, or a philosophical inquiry concerning language and universal grammar.* London 1751.

Hickmann, Maya. (ed.). 1987. *Social and functional approaches to language and thought.* Orlando/FLA: Academic Press.

Hockett, Charles F. 1960. "The origin of speech". *Scientific American* 203.3: 88-96.

Holenstein, Elmar. 1976. *Linguistik, Semiotik, Hermeneutik. Plädoyers für eine strukturale Phänomenologie.* Frankfurt/M: Suhrkamp.

Hopper, Paul. 1998. "Emergent grammar". In: Tomasello, Michael (ed.), 155-75.

Hopper, Paul J. & Thompson, Sandra A. 1980. "Transitivity in grammar and discourse". *Language* 56: 251-99.

Hopper, Paul J. & Thompson, Sandra A. 1984. "The discourse basis for lexical categories in Universal Grammar". *Language* 60: 703-52.

Hubel, David H. 1995. *Eye, brain, and vision.* (Scientific American: Library series, 22.) New York: Freeman.

Humboldt, Wilhelm von. 1829/1963. "Über die Verschiedenheiten des menschlichen Sprachbaues". In: Humboldt, Wilhelm von. *Schriften zur Sprachphilosophie.* Ed. Andreas Flitner & Klaus Giel. Darmstadt: Wissenschaftliche Buchgesellschaft, 144-367.

Husserl, Edmund. ⁴1928. *Logische Untersuchungen.* Vol. II/1, Untersuchungen zur Phänomenologie und Theorie der Erkenntnis, Untersuchung III ("Zur Lehre von den Ganzen und Teilen", 225-93.) Reprint 1968. Tübingen: Niemeyer.

Iturrioz Leza, José Luis. 1993. "Bibliografía temática sobre aspecto, modos de acción y clases de predicados". *Función* 13-14: 73-134.

Jakobson, Roman & Halle, Morris. 1971. "The revised version of the list of inherent features". in: Jakobson, Roman. 1971. *Selected Writings. I. Phonological Studies.* The Hague: Mouton, 738-42.

Kant, Immanuel. 1781/1903. *Kritik der reinen Vernunft. Die transcendentale Logik, Einleitung III.* In: *Kants gesammelte Schriften.* Königlich Preußische Akademie der Wissenschaften (ed.) 1903, vol. IV, Berlin: Reimer, 52-54.

Keenan, Edward & Comrie, Bernard. 1977. "Noun phrase accessibility and universal grammar". *Linguistic Inquiry* 8: 63-99.

Kloss, Heinz. ²1978. *Die Entwicklung neuer germanischer Kultursprachen seit 1800.* (Sprache der Gegenwart, 37.) Düsseldorf: Pädagogischer Verlag Schwann.

Koch, Peter. 1981. *Verb — Valenz — Verfügung. Zur Satzsemantik und Valenz französischer Verben am Beispiel der Verfügungs-Verben.* (Reihe Siegen, 32.) Heidelberg: Winter.

Koch, Peter & Oesterreicher, Wulf. 1985. "Sprache der Nähe — Sprache der Distanz. Mündlichkeit und Schriftlichkeit im Spannungsfeld von Sprachtheorie und Sprachgeschichte". *Romanistisches Jahrbuch* 35: 15-43.

Koch, Peter & Oesterreicher, Wulf. 1990. *Gesprochene Sprache in der Romania: Französisch, Italienisch, Spanisch.* (Romanistische Arbeitshefte, 31.) Tübingen: Niemeyer.

Koch, Peter & Oesterreicher, Wulf. 1994. "Schriftlichkeit und Sprache". In: Günther, Hartmut & Ludwig, Otto (eds.), vol. I: 587-604.

Kraft, Charles H. & Kirk-Greene, Anthony H. M. 1990. *Hausa.* (Teach yourself books.) London: Hodder and Stoughton.

Kriegel, Sibylle. 1996. *Diathesen im Mauritius- und Seychellenkreol.* (ScriptOralia, 88.) Tübingen: Narr.

Krefeld, Thomas. 1987. *Das französische Gerichtsurteil in linguistischer Sicht: Zwischen Fach- und Standessprache.* (Studia romanica et linguistica, 17.) Frankfurt: Peter Lang.

Ladefoged, Peter & Maddieson, Ian. 1996. *The sounds of the world's languages*. (Phonological theory.) Oxford: Blackwell.

Lehmann, Christian. 1984. *Der Relativsatz. Typologie seiner Strukturen. Theorie seiner Funktionen. Kompendium seiner Grammatik*. (Language Universals Series, 3.) Tübingen: Narr.

Lehmann, Christian. 1995. *Thoughts on grammaticalization*. Revised and expanded version. München & Newcastle: Lincom Europa.

Lewin, Bruno. ⁴1996 (¹1959). *Abriss der japanischen Grammatik: auf der Grundlage der klassischen Schriftsprache*. Wiesbaden: Harrassowitz.

Ludwig, Ralph. 1996. *Kreolsprachen zwischen Mündlichkeit und Schriftlichkeit. Zur Syntax und Pragmatik atlantischer Kreolsprachen auf französischer Basis*. (ScriptOralia, 86.) Tübingen: Narr.

MacKevitt, Paul. (ed.) 1996. *Integration of natural language and vision processing*. 4 vols. vol. 3: *Theory and grounding representations*. Vol. 4: *Recent advances*. Dordrecht: Kluwer.

McWhorter, John H. 1998. "Identifying the Creole prototype: vindicating a typological class". *Language* 74: 788–818.

Mayberry, R.I. 1993. "First-language acquisition after childhood differs from second-language acquisition: the case of American Sign Language". *Journal of Speech and Hearing Research* 36.6: 125–70.

Meier-Oeser, Stephan. 1997. "Zeichenkonzeptionen in der Philosophie des lateinischen Mittelalters". In: Posner & al., Vol. I, 984–1022.

Meise, Katrin. 1996. *Une forte absence. Schweigen in alltagsweltlicher und literarischer Kommunikation*. (ScriptOralia, 89.) Tübingen: Narr.

Meyer, Martin & Friederici, Angela D. & von Cramon D. Yves. 2000. "Neurocognition of auditory sentence comprehension: event related fMRI reveals sensitivity to syntactic violations and task demands". *Brain Research. Cognitive Brain Research* 9.1: 19–33.

Michaelis, Susanne. 1993. *Temps et aspect en créole Seychellois: valeurs et interférences*. (Kreolische Bibliothek, 11.) Hamburg: Buske.

Milner, A. David & Goodale, Melvyn A. 1996. *The visual brain in action*. (Oxford psychology series, 27.) Oxford: Oxford University Press.

Neville, Helen J. & Bavelier, Daphne & Corina, David & Rauschecker, J. & Karni, A. & Lalwani, A. & Braun, A & Clark, V. & Jezzard Peter & Turner, R. 1998 "Cerebral organization for language in deaf and hearing subjects: biological constraints and effects of experience". *Proceedings of the National Academy of Sciences of the U.S.A.* 95.3: 922–9.

Neville, Helen J. & Coffey, S.A. & Lawson, D.S. & Fischer, A. & Emmorey, K. & Bellugi, Ursula. 1997. "Neural systems mediating American sign language: effects of sensory experience and age of acquisition". *Brain and Language* 57.3: 285–308.

Nordlinger, Rachel & Sadler, Louisa. 2000. "Tense as a nominal category". In: Butt, Miriam & King, Trancy Holloway (eds.) *Proceedings of LFG 2000*. Stanford: CSLI Publications.

Oesterreicher, Wulf. 1988. "Sprechtätigkeit, Einzelsprache, Diskurs und vier Dimensionen der Sprachvarietät". In: Thun, Harald (ed.). *Das sprachtheoretische Denken Eugenio Coserius in der Diskussion*. Vol. I. Tübingen: Narr, 355–86.

Poizner, Howard & Klima, Edward S. & Bellugi, Ursula. 1987. *What the hands reveal about the brain*. (The MIT Press series on issues in the biology of language and cognition.) Cambridge/MA: MIT Press.

Posner, Roland & Robering, Klaus & Sebeok, Thomas A. (eds.). 1997. *Semiotik. Ein Handbuch zu den zeichentheoretischen Grundlagen von Natur und Kultur. Semiotics. A Handbook on the Sign-Theoretic Foundations of Nature and Culture*. (HSK 13.1 & 2.) Berlin: de Gruyter.

Prideaux, Gary Dean. 1970. *The syntax of Japanese honorifics*. (Janua linguarium: series practica, 102.) The Hague: Mouton.

Radden, Günter. 1996. "Motion metaphorized: the case of 'coming' and 'going'". In: Casad, Eugene H. (ed.), 421–58.

Raible, Wolfgang. 1987. "Comment intégrer la syntaxe dans la sémantique? La solution des grammairiens scolastiques", in: Lüdi, Georges & Stricker, Hans & Wüest, Jakob. *Romania ingeniosa. Festschrift für Prof. Dr. Gerold Hilty zum 60. Geburtstag*. Bern: Peter Lang, 497–510.

Raible, Wolfgang. 1988. "? Qué son los géneros? Una respuesta desde el punto de vista semiótico y de la lingüística textual". In: Garrido Gallardo, Miguel A. (ed.). *Teoría de los géneros literarios*. Madrid: Arco/Libros, 303–39.

Raible, Wolfgang. 1992. "The pitfalls of subordination. Subject and object clauses between Latin and Romance". In: Brogyanyi, Bela & Lipp, Reiner (eds.). *Historical Philology. Greek, Latin, and Romance. Papers in honor of Oswald Szemerényi*. Amsterdam & Philadelphia: Benjamins, 299–337.

Raible, Wolfgang. 1994. "Literacy and Language Change". In: Čmejrková, Světla & Daneš, František & Havlová, Eva (eds.). *Writing vs. Speaking. Language, Text, Discourse, Communication*. Proceedings of the Conference held at the Czech Language Institute of the Academy of Sciences of the Czech Republic, Prague, October 14–16, 1992. (Tübinger Beiträge zur Linguistik, 392.) Tübingen: Narr, 111–25.

Raible, Wolfgang. 1996. "Kognition und Sprachwandel". *Akademie-Journal* 1/1996: 38–43.

Rastier, François. 1998. "Prédication, actance et zones anthropiques". In: Forsgren, Mats & Jonasson, Kerstin & Kronning, Hans (eds.). *Prédication, assertion, information. Actes du colloque d'Uppsala en linguistique française, 6−9 juin 1966. (Studia Romanica Upsaliensia, 56.) Uppsala: Acta Universitatis Upsaliensis, 445−61.

Riedl, Rupert. [7]1989. Die Strategie der Genesis. Naturgeschichte der realen Welt. (Serie Piper, 290.) München: Piper.

Rosier, Irène. 1983. La grammaire spéculative des modistes. (Publications de l'Université de Lille III. Linguistique.) Lille: Presses Universitaires.

Schaller, Susan. 1991. A man without words. New York: Simon & Schuster.

Seiler, Hansjakob. 1986. Apprehension. Language, Object, and Order. Part III: The Universal Dimension of Apprehension. (Language Universals Series, 1/III.) Tübingen: Narr.

Slobin, Dan Isaac (ed.). 1996. Social interaction, social context, and language. Essays in honour of Susan Ervin-Tripp. Mahwah/NJ: Erlbaum.

Spinicci, Paolo. 1992. La visione e il linguaggio: considerazioni sull'applicabilità del modello linguistico all'esperienza. Milano: Guerini.

Sperber, Dan & Wilson, Deirdre. 1995 ([1]1986). Relevance: Communication and cognition. Oxford/UK: Blackwell. French as: Sperber, Dan & Wilson, Deirdre. 1989. La pertinence. Paris: Éditions de Minuit.

Stäbler, Cynthia K. 1995. Entwicklung mündlicher romanischer Syntax. Das 'français cadien' in Louisiana. (ScriptOralia, 78.) Tübingen: Narr.

Stäbler, Cynthia K. 1995a. La vie dans le temps et asteur. Ein Korpus von Gesprächen mit Cadiens in Louisiana. (ScriptOralia, 79.) Tübingen: Narr.

Szabó, Árpád. 1960. "Anfänge des Euklidischen Axiomensystems". Archive for the History of Exact Sciences 1: 38−106.

Talmy, Leonard. 1985. "Lexicalization patterns: Semantic structure in lexical forms". In: Shopen, Timothy (ed.). Language typology and syntactic description. vol. 3 Grammatical categories and the lexicon. Cambridge: Cambridge University Press, 36−149.

Talmy, Leonard. 1991. "Paths to realization. A typology of event conflation". In: Proceedings of the Annual Meeting of the Berkeley Linguistic Society. 17: 182−187.

Tendeng, Odile. 2000. Le Gusiilay: un essai de systématisation. Une contribution à l'étude du Ióola Ph. D. thesis Freiburg.

Thom, René. 1973. "Sur la typologie des langues naturelles: essai d'interprétation psycho-linguistique". In: Gross, Maurice & Halle, Morris & Schützenberger, Paul (eds.). The formal analysis of natural languages: proceedings of the 1. International Conference on the Formal Analysis of Natural Languages, Rocquencourt, France, April 27−29, 1970. (Janua linguarum: Series maior, 62.) The Hague: Mouton, 233−48.

Tomasello, Michael (ed.). 1998. The new psychology of language: cognitive and functional approaches to language structure. Mahwah/NJ: Erlbaum.

Totman, Richard. 1985. Social and biological roles of language. The psychology of justification. London: Academic Press.

Tranel, Daniel T. & Damasio, Hanna C. & Damasio Antonio R. 1997. "A neural basis for the retrieval of conceptual knowledge". Neuropsychologia 35.10: 1319−27.

Tranel, Daniel T. & Logan, Christine G. & Frank, Randall J. & Damasio, Antonio R. 1997a. "Explaining category-related effects in the retrieval of conceptual and lexical knowledge for concrete entities: operationalization and analysis of factors". Neuropsychologia 35.10: 1329−39.

Traugott, Elizabeth Closs. 1987. "Literacy and language change: the special case of speech act verbs". Interchange 18, 32−47.

Tsunoda, Tasaku. 1985. "Remarks on transitivity". Journal of Linguistics 21: 385−96.

Tsunoda, Tasaku. 1994. Article "Transitivity". In: Asher, Ronald E. & Simpson, J.M.Y. (eds.). The Encyclopedia of Language and Linguistics. Vol 9: 4670−77.

Varro, Gabrielle (ed.). 1994. Language, the subject, the social link: essays offered to Andrée Tabouret-Keller. (International journal of the sociology of language, 109.) Berlin: Mouton de Gruyter.

Vygotskij, Lev S. 1962. The collected works of L. S. Vygotsky. (Cognition and language.) New York: Plenum Press.

Wierzbicka, Anna. 1996. Semantics: primes and universals. Oxford: Oxford University Press.

Wörner, Markus H. 1997. "Zeichenkonzeptionen in der Grammatik, Rhetorik und Poetik des lateinischen Mittelalters". In: Posner & al., Vol. I, 1046−59.

Wurm, Stephen Adolphe & Mühlhäusler, Peter & Tryon, Darrell T. (eds.). 1996. Atlas of Languages of Intercultural Communication in the Pacific, Asia, and the Americas. (Trends in Linguistics Documentation, 13.) Berlin & New York: de Gruyter. vol. I [maps] and vol. II.1, II.2 [texts].

Zipf, George Kingsley. 1949. Human behavior and the principle of least effort: an introduction to human ecology. Cambridge/MA: Addison-Wesley.

Wolfgang Raible, University of Freiburg i. Br. (Germany)

2. Different views of language typology

1. Preliminary remarks
2. Typological parameters
3. Theoretical concepts
4. Areal typology
5. References

1. Preliminary remarks

Linguistic typology can be defined as the systematic study of crosslinguistic variation. This definition presupposes that there are certain general principles governing variation among languages, and I shall simply make this presupposition. One feature of this definition that might at first sight seem strange is that it makes no mention of the notion 'linguistic type'. Indeed, some approaches to linguistic typology do make crucial use of the notion 'linguistic type', albeit interpreting this notion in different ways, while other approaches make little or no use of the notion, a point to which I shall return below.

Linguistic typology does, however, assume that we have some yardstick against which to assess crosslinguistic variation. Nearly all current work in linguistic typology makes a further assumption, namely that this yardstick or these yardsticks relate to significant factors of linguistic structure. This is not logically necessary, as can be seen by comparing one of the few recent works in linguistic typology that does not make this assumption, namely Vennemann (1984).

Theo Vennemann is concerned most directly with word order typology and in the 1984 article, in contrast to much of his own earlier work, he argues that the notion of ideal linguistic type, such as being consistent in the position of the head of a phrase (consistently head-final or consistently head-initial), is not to be interpreted as a natural correlation of logically independent parameters (the position of the noun in the noun phrase, the position of the adposition in the adposition phrase, etc.), but rather as an essentially arbitrary yardstick against which languages can be measured.

Thus, a language can be assessed for its degree of adherence to consistent head-initiality, or more precisely for the ways in which it adheres to or departs from consistent head-initiality, but this does not assign any inherent greater naturalness to consistent head-initiality than to any other combination of head-initiality and head-finality across constituents. Vennemann draws an analogy to the cardinal vowels of the International Phonetic Association (IPA) (International Phonetic Association 1999).

For instance, the IPA identifies four primary cardinal vowels within the continuum of front unrounded vowels that the human tongue is capable of producing. Positions 1 and 4 are defined in clearly significant anatomical-phonetic terms, as respectively the highest tongue position in which a vowel can be produced without giving rise to friction, and the lowest tongue position that is physically possible. However, positions 2 and 3 are defined so that the distances between 1 and 2, 2 and 3, and 3 and 4 are equal. There is no claim that positions 2 and 3 are significant for the phonetic production of any particular language or for language in general, rather they provide a measure against which particular degrees of front vowel height in particular languages can be calibrated.

While there may well be some aspects of crosslinguistic variation that are appropriately handled in this way, the area that has come to be known as linguistic typology has concerned itself primarily with patterns of crosslinguistic variation that are claimed to provide deeper insight into the nature of language than just a convenient measuring stick.

One aspect of crosslinguistic variation is constituted by the restrictions on this variation, i.e. by logically possible variants that are not in fact found to occur in natural language and are believed, moreover, to be in principle excluded. While it is not always easy to draw a distinction between linguistic typology and language universals, I will in general assume that such restrictions are rather the domain of language universals, which distinguish between what is and what is not possible in human language, and not treat them, other than incidentally, in this article.

It may be useful to mention at this point some general works that provide more detailed overviews of the area of linguistic typology, namely Joseph H. Greenberg (1974), Timothy Shopen (1985), Bernard Comrie (1989), William Croft (1990), and Masayoshi Shibatani and Theodora Bynon (1995). The last mentioned is particularly relevant in that in it a number of prominent typologists set out their own assessment of their approaches to linguistic typology.

A distinction that has played a major role in distinguishing different approaches to linguistic typology is the difference between holistic and partial typologies (Comrie 1991; Lehmann 1978). The extreme instance of a holistic typology would be the possibility of characterizing the whole of the structure of a language by means of one particular feature, from which everything else would be predictable, somewhat like cloning a whole organism from just one cell. This would then constitute, in the strongest sense, a linguistic type.

Although there have perhaps been times in the history of linguistics when linguists have dreamed of something like this, most typologies in fact are more restrictive than this, and are thus in the technical sense partial, although they vary considerably in the extent to which a particular typological parameter is deemed to be determinative for other aspects of a language's structure.

In what follows, I will first examine certain typological parameters, in part to ascertain the extent to which they go — beyond being merely statements of particular differences between languages — in the direction of constituting significant constellations of parameter values that tend to cooccur.

2. Typological parameters

2.1. Morphological typology

The first typological parameter to have been widely used in linguistic typology is morphological structure; Edward Sapir (1921, chapter 6) provides one of the most insightful accounts of this parameter.

Morphological typology actually involves two partially independent parameters. One is whether or not the language in question permits morphemes to be combined to form polymorphemic words or not. Languages which do not allow such combinations are called isolating. While perhaps no language is completely isolating, some languages certainly come very close, for instance VIETNAMESE, where the plural, for instance, even of pronouns, is formed by means of a separate word *chúng*, so that 'I' is *tôi*, 'we' is *chúng tôi*.

Languages that allow morphemes to be combined into words in principle do so in two different ways. The first possibility, termed agglutinating, is for the individual morphemes, each expressing a single element of meaning, to be strung linearly one after the other, as in TURKISH example (1).

(1) TURKISH
adam-lar-dan
man-PL-ABL
'from the men'

Here, the semantic element of plurality has its own morpheme *-lar*, while the semantic element of motion from has its own morpheme *-dan*.

In a fusional language, like RUSSIAN, the exponents of different semantic elements are fused together, so that by comparing nominative singular *stol* 'table' with dative singular *stol-u*, nominative plural *stol-y*, and dative plural *stol-am*, there is no possibility of segmenting the number-case affixes *-u*, *-y*, *-am* into a segment sequence expressing number and a segment sequence expressing case. (Fusional languages are sometimes also called (in)flectional, though this term is potentially confusing, since agglutinating languages also show the contrast between inflectional and derivational morphology, i.e. the other sense of 'inflectional'.)

As Sapir noted, this tripartite typology — isolating, agglutinating, fusional — can be captured by means of two indices. The index of synthesis says whether or not a language allows morphemes to be combined into words and, if so, to what extent; for instance, one could calculate the average morpheme to word ratio across comparable texts in different languages, so that a truly isolating language would have an index of 1; more precise numerical methods are discussed, for instance, in Altmann & Lehfeldt (1973).

For a language whose index of synthesis is higher than 1, the index of fusion defines the extent to which the exponence of combinations of semantic elements is expressed by means of a single indivisible affix; a truly agglutinating language would have an index of fusion of 1.

This approach has the advantage that it is not necessary to give distinct recognition to a fourth type of language as a primitive category, namely polysynthetic languages, characterized (with some variation among different linguists) as languages that combine large numbers of morphemes into a single word, typically so that many clauses consist of just a single polymorphemic word, like SIBERIAN YUPIK ESKIMO example (2).

(2) SIBERIAN YUPIK ESKIMO (Jacobson 1997: 2—3)
Angya -ghlla -ng -yug -tuq.
boat -AUG -ACQ -DES -3SG
'He wants to acquire a large boat.'

Languages like SIBERIAN YUPIK ESKIMO simply have a high index of synthesis. (In this example, the index of fusion is low, although there is one instance of fusion, namely the combination of third person and singular number in *-tuq*.)

The question that now arises, and one that will arise throughout this section, is whether the typology established in this way is significant beyond its initial limited goal of providing a characterization of one aspect of the morphological structure of words in the language in question. As already implied, probably no language is an ideal representative of any of the ideal types (isolating, agglutinating, fusional), since even VIETNAMESE, for instance, has noun compounding. The question is thus rather whether or not there are other, logically independent features that correlate or tend to correlate with the different morphological types. One possibility would, for instance, be serial verbs, as in SRANAN sentence (3).

(3) SRANAN (Sebba 1987)
Lon go teki a buku tyari go gi
run go take the book carry go give
a leriman.
the teacher
'Run and fetch the book and take it to the teacher.'

In a serial verb construction, a single event is encoded by means of a sequence of verbs (which may be interrupted by other material), which are typically morphologically unmarked or minimally marked. The serial verb construction often serves to encode content that would be encoded by means of inflectional morphology in languages that have inflectional morphology. There seems to be a good (though by no means absolute) correlation between absence of inflectional morphology and occurrence of serial verbs (Lefebvre 1998: 356—57), not surprisingly so since in the absence of inflectional morphology some other means must be found of expressing these relations.

2.2. Word order typology

In the revival of language typology studies that followed on the appearance of Greenberg (1966), one of the major topics of research was word order, no doubt in part because this was the focus of Greenberg's own seminal paper. Greenberg's paper succeeded in showing that the distribution of word order, or more accurately constituent order, is far from random across the languages of the world, in particular that certain correlations of word order are frequent while others are rare or even nonexistent.

For instance, languages that have (subject-)object-verb as their basic clause order hardly ever have the order 'relative clause — noun' within the noun phrase; the only well-attested counterexamples are the various forms of CHINESE. Perhaps even more importantly for future work, in the appendix to the 1966 article Greenberg classified the languages of his sample according to four word order parameters, as set out in (4).

(4) order of subject, object, and verb within the clause
order of adposition and noun phrase within the adpositional phrase
order of dependent genitive relative to the head noun
order of adjective relative to the head noun

Some logical combinations were simply absent from Greenberg's corpus. (Later work has, however, often come up with languages illustrating the combinations completely absent from Greenberg's sample.) But even for other combinations, some were extremely rare, while others were much more frequent. In particular, the four combinations given in (5) were found to be particularly common crosslinguistically

(5) VSO, AdNP, NG, NA
SVO, AdNP, NG, NA
SOV, NPAd, GN, AN
SOV, NPAd, GN, NA

Since the four parameters listed in (5) are logically independent of one another, the fact that they cooccur so frequently is likely to be a significant fact about crosslinguistic variation, and much work of the last few decades in linguistic typology has been devoted to ascertaining just what mechanism underlies the correlation.

Early work concentrated on extracting formal properties, the most consistent being that then adopted by Vennemann, as in Vennemann (1972), where he argued that, if one abstracts away from the subject noun phrase, each of the first three types in (5) can be characterized in terms of head position: the first two are consistently head-initial, while the third is consistently head-final. (The fourth type is head-final except for adjective position. Matthew Dryer (1988) argues that the fourth type is actually more widespread crosslinguistically than the third type, suggesting perhaps that adjective order is not to be explained as part of the same constellation of factors as the other parameters.) A useful summary of the development to this stage of the history of word order typology is included in Hawkins (1983).

Some more recent work has tended to go in different directions in seeking an explanation for the correlations of (5).

For instance, John A. Hawkins (1994) argues that the observed correlations are a result of the operation of parsing preferences, with combinations of word orders that are easier to parse being preferred crosslinguistically over those that are not. In addition, the search for reliable parameters going beyond word order that nonetheless correlate with word order continues. For instance, although there are some counterexamples, it seems that there may be a correlation between the occurrence of light verbs, i.e. verbs of minimal semantic content that combine with a nonverbal lexical element to fill what would otherwise be gaps in the verb lexicon, and verb-finality, as in JAPANESE example (6), where *benkyoo* is a noun.

(6) JAPANESE
Gakusei wa benkyoo su-ru.
student TOP study do-PRES
'The student studies.'

2.3. Pro-drop

A typological parameter that played a major role in the generative grammatical literature, more specifically in the approach known as Principles and Parameters (Chomsky 1981; see also section 3.4), is that of pro-drop. According to this parameter, languages would be divided into those that are pro-drop and those that are not.

Characteristic of pro-drop languages, like ITALIAN, is first of all that unstressed pronouns (in the case of ITALIAN: subject pronouns) are normally dropped, so that 'I believe' is normally *credo* rather than *io credo*. This goes hand in hand with the fact that the inflectional morphology of the verb encodes the person-number of the subject, so that *credo* 'I believe' contrasts with *credi* 'you believe', *crediamo* 'we believe', etc. But the claim was that yet further properties correlate with this distinction between pro-drop and non-pro-drop languages. In ITALIAN, for instance, it is in general possible to postpose subjects after the verb, so that alongside (7) one can also say (8).

(7) ITALIAN
Gianni è arrivato.
John be.PRES.3SG arrive.PRETPTCP

(8) *È arrivato Gianni.*
'John has arrived.'

Although there are differences in the functional sentence perspective of (7) and (8), they share the same basic meaning, and do not, for instance, differ as statement versus question. Finally, ITALIAN allows so-called long-distance WH-movement, so that alongside a statement like (9) one can have a WH-question like (10).

(9) ITALIAN
Credi che X partirà.
believe.PRES.2SG that X leave.FUT.3SG
'You believe that X will leave.'

(10) *Chi credi che partirà?*
who believe.PRES.2SG that leave.FUT.3SG
'Who do you believe will leave'?
(lit. '*Who do you believe that will leave?)'

Note that the literal translation of (10) into ENGLISH is impossible.

Since the four properties are logically independent of one another, if they do indeed correlate crosslinguistically this would be a significant empirical discovery, and of course if a principled basis could be found for the correlation so much the better. Unfortunately once one extends the search beyond the few languages originally considered, problems start to arise, suggesting that the correlation may actually not hold crosslinguistically.

For instance, languages like CHINESE and JAPANESE that lack encoding of the person-number of the subject of the verb nonetheless permit, and typically prefer, omission of subject pronouns. Long-distance WH-movement, as in (10), might seem a particularly striking feature, but its problematic status is demonstrated by HUNGARIAN, which is basically parallel to ITALIAN in sentences like (7)−(9), but where some speakers allow and others disallow long-distance WH-movement, as in (11), where the "%" sign indicates variation in speaker judgments.

(11) HUNGARIAN
% *a fiú [aki mondtam, hogy*
the boy who say.PRET.SG1 that
elvette a pénzt]
take.away.PRET.3SG the money
'the boy that I said took away the money'
(lit. '*the boy that I said that took away the money')

This example illustrates that it is dangerous to base typological generalizations on just a handful of languages. In recent work within the Principles and Parameters approach, the pro-drop parameter has indeed virtually disappeared from discussion.

2.4. Head-marking versus dependent-marking

Suppose that we have a construction consisting of a head and a dependent, such as the translation equivalent of *the man's house*, where *house* is head and *the man's* is dependent. There are in principle several ways in which the relation between the two constituent might be marked. There might be no marking, as in HARUAI example (12). Both constituents might be marked, as in TURKISH example (13). Only the head might be marked, as in HUNGARIAN example (14). Or only the dependent might be marked, as in the ENGLISH translation, repeated as (15).

(12) HARUAI
nöbö ram
man house

(13) TURKISH
adam-ın ev-i
man-GEN house-3SG

(14) HUNGARIAN
az ember ház-a
the man house-3SG

(15) *the man's house*

In work that has had a major impact on recent linguistic typology, Johanna Nichols (1986) proposes that the distinction between (14) and (15), in particular, is a significant typological parameter, i.e. whether a language (or a particular construction in a particular language) is head-marking – like HUNGARIAN in (14) – or dependent-marking – like ENGLISH in (15) (→ art. 102). The recognition of the possibility of both head-marking and dependent-marking types is important for general linguistic theory – as Nichols (1986: 116) notes, many traditional and recent models of syntactic structure treat language as being basically dependent-marking and thus require extra machinery in order to accommodate head-marking languages. Our main concern here, however, is possible correlations between the head-marking versus dependent-marking parameter and other features of language. Nichols (1990) goes a considerable way towards providing such correlations, which have been amplified in later work.

First, it turns out that even if a particular language is mixed in terms of its value for head-marking versus dependent-marking, as most languages are once one takes into account the full range of relevant constructions, there are correlations between particular constructions and the likelihood of occurrence of head-marking versus dependent-marking.

For instance, it turns out that even in languages that are overwhelmingly dependent-marking, it is not unusual to find some verb agreement, especially subject-verb agreement, whereby the verb is marked to show the relationship between subject and verb. ENGLISH is an almost exclusively dependent-marking language. Yet verbs in ENGLISH agree, albeit minimally, in person-number with their subject, as in (16)–(17).

(16) *The boy sees the man.*

(17) *The boys see the man.*

Indeed, it is a general property of Indo-European and a number of other languages to be basically dependent-marking but to have subject-verb agreement.

By contrast, the link between a dependent clause and the matrix clause on which it is dependent is crosslinguistically much more likely to be marked on the dependent than on the matrix clause, for instance by means of a subordinating conjunction or a subordinating form of the verb of the dependent clause; in other words, crosslinguistically the type *John left because he was hungry* is more likely to be grammaticalized as an instance of subordination than is *John was hungry, so he left*.

ABKHAZ is an overwhelmingly head-marking language, as seen in the possessive construction of example (18), for instance.

(18) ABKHAZ (Hewitt 1979: 116)
    sarà sə-y^{w}nə̀
    I   1SG-house
    'my house'

However, combinations of matrix and dependent clauses are marked by using special affixes on the dependent verb, such as the nonfinite marker *-lak″* in (19).

(19) ABKHAZ (Hewitt 1979: 39)
    D-an-aa-làk″   *də-šə̀.*
    3SGF-when-come-NONFIN 3SGF-kill
    'When she comes, kill her.'

But correlations involving the head-marking versus dependent-marking parameter can be even more striking than this.

For instance, Nichols (1990) argues that the geographical distribution of languages having gender is strikingly restricted, though with an equally striking exception. In general, languages with gender tend to occur only in areas where most of the other languages have gender (a "gender hotbed"). However, a language that is head-marking may easily have gender whether or not it is located in a gender hotbed.

2.5 Hawkins' semantic typology

In this section, one further example of a typological parameter will be considered to illustrate further the range of possibilities, namely the kind of semantic typology introduced by Hawkins (1986), although examples will be taken from RUSSIAN rather than repeating Hawkins' GERMAN examples.

Hawkins is concerned overall with the extent to which a language's surface syntax directly reflects semantic distinctions, and the discussion here will be restricted to grammatical relations. The question that arises is thus the extent to which the syntactic relations ("grammatical relations") of the language, here especially subjects, are in one-one correspondence with semantic roles. In ENGLISH, there is a rather loose relationship, so that a subject can be an agent as in (20), a patient as in (21), or a natural force as in (22), or a patient of a subordinate verb as in (23).

(20) *Tanya opened the window.*

(21) *The window opened.*

(22) *The wind opened the window.*

(23) *This problem is easy to solve.*

Moreover, in comparing (20) and (21), note that ENGLISH does not need to mark the verb in any overt way to indicate the change in the pairing of syntactic and semantic relations, or equivalently the shift from transitive verb in (20) to intransitive predicate in (21).

In RUSSIAN, by contrast, there is a much closer correlation between syntactic relations and semantic roles, although the correlation is still far from absolute. Moreover, in many instances where the correlation is not maintained, special marking is needed in order to indicate this. The RUSSIAN equivalents to (20)−(23) are given in (24)−(27).

(24) RUSSIAN
    Tanja   otkryla   fortočku.
    Tanya.NOM opened.F   window.ACC

(25) *Fortočka   otkryla-s'.*
    window.NOM opened.F-REFL

(26) *Fortočku   otkrylo   vetrom.*
    window.ACC opened.NT   wind.INS

(27) *Ètu problemu   legko   razrešit'.*
    this problem.ACC easy.NT solve.INF

To understand these examples, it is necessary to note that in the past tense RUSSIAN verbs agree in gender(-number) with their subject, while predicate adjectives also agree in gender(-number) with their subject; *Tanja* is a woman's name, while *fortočka* 'window' (actually, a small window for ventilation) and *problema* 'problem' are feminine. Moreover, in the relevant examples there is correlation between morphological case and syntactic relation, with subjects in the nominative and direct objects in the accusative.

In (25), the patient does indeed show up as subject (the sentence has no agent), but the verb has to be marked with the so-called reflexive suffix to indicate this. While a literal translation of ENGLISH (22) is grammatical in RUSSIAN, the more idiomatic rendering is as in (26), where the patient remains as direct object, the natural force is expressed using the instrumental case, and the verb is impersonal, marking the absence of any agent.

In ENGLISH sentence (23) *this problem* is grammatically subject of the whole sentence (cf. the agreement in *these problems are easy to solve*), while in RUSSIAN sentence (27) *ètu problemu* remains direct object of the infinitive, moved to sentence-initial position by the general RUSSIAN rule preposing topics.

Indeed, even where RUSSIAN and ENGLISH are grammatically alike in having syntactic relation-changing rules like the passive, the rule is typically more restricted in RUSSIAN, e.g. RUSSIAN does not allow nondirect objects to become subjects (cf. ENGLISH *I was given a book*), and has heavier restrictions on the semantic classes of verbs that can be passivized (e.g. no equivalent of *I am loved* using the passive). The usual RUSSIAN functional equivalent of the ENGLISH passive is simply to prepose the direct object, without changing the syntactic relations.

This typology provides a powerful tool for investigating correlations between semantic roles and syntactic relations crosslinguistically. Thus, Franz Müller-Gotama (1994) shows that while languages having a close correlation between semantic roles and syntactic relations are predictably rather alike in this respect, languages that lack such a tight correlation can differ in the ways in which they depart from the correlation; in particular, he shows that ENGLISH and INDONESIAN share the general phenomenon of a low correlation but have rather different ways of abandoning the correlation.

3. Theoretical concepts

3.1. Typology, description, and theory

One way of using typology would be simply as a tool for linguistic description. One would select a particular area of investigation, devise a typology for describing the crosslinguistic variation found in that area, and perhaps extract theoretical generalizations from the result. Of course, the various stages are by no means automatic, in particular one has to come up with an adequate typology of the empirical domain, and even typologically ordered empirical data do not provide automatic access to significant theoretical generalizations. But despite these caveats, this unselfconscious approach to doing typology has in fact produced some of the most significant results in typological work over the past few decades.

The St. Petersburg (formerly Leningrad) typological school (→ art. 26) is a fine illustration of the successes of this method. Since the late 1960s this group has published, under the editorship of Aleksandr A. Xolodovič, Viktor S. Xrakovskij, Vladimir P. Nedjalkov (→ art. 69), and others, a series of classic typological studies investigating such topics as causatives (→ art. 66), passives and voice (→ art. 26, § 2; art. 67) more generally, imperatives (→ art. 78).

I will concentrate here on resultatives, the topic of Nedjalkov (1988), since the fact that this collection is available in an ENGLISH-language edition makes it particularly accessible; for the general framework adopted by the school, reference may be made to Vladimir P. Nedjalkov and Viktor P. Litvinov (1995). The parameters that are relevant for the typology of resultatives are set out primarily in Nedjalkov and Sergej Je. Jaxontov (1988).

In addition to a range of semantic distinctions within the resultative and carefully drawn semantic distinctions between resultatives and neighboring concepts (like the perfect), an important parameter is the diathesis relation between resultative and corresponding nonresultative, i.e. the syntactic relations corresponding to the semantic roles in nonresultative and resultative.

In terms of the symbols S (single argument of an intransitive predicate), A (more agentlike argument of a transitive predicate), and P (more patientlike argument of a transitive predicate), one could describe resultatives as being S-oriented (the subject of the resultative corresponds to the S of the nonresultative), P-oriented (the subject of the resultative corresponds to the P of the nonresultative), or A-oriented (the subject of the resultative corresponds to the A of the nonresultative). (In Nedjalkov (1988) a different terminology is used, respectively subjective, objective, and possessive resultative. There are also some other, crosslinguistically less widespread types.)

These are illustrated by means of ENGLISH examples (28)−(33), where the even-numbered sentences are nonresultative, the odd-numbered ones resultative.

(28) *The water has frozen.*

(29) *The water is frozen.*

(30) *Malcolm has closed the door.*

(31) *The door is closed.*

(32) *I have finished my work.*

(33) *I am finished my work.*

The third type is very marginal in ENGLISH, and not all speakers will accept (33), and indeed languages differ typologically in which of the possibilities they allow, with A-oriented resultatives being distinctly less common than the other two.

Close attention is also paid to the semantic features of verbs, and on this basis a number of implicational universals are formulated and justified against the wide-ranging empirical material.

For instance, verbs expressing a change of state can be divided into those where the resulting state is visually perceivable and those where it is not. Some languages, such as NIVKH (Nedjalkov & Jaxontov 1988: 29) allow resultatives of verbs denoting actions with visually perceivable results, such as 'to tear', 'to break', but not those denoting actions whose resultant states are not visually perceivable, such as 'kiss'.

Some verbs even undergo a slight change of meaning to ensure that they do denote a perceivable resulting state, e.g. (34) means not 'the vodka has been drunk', since if all the vodka had been drunk there would be no perceivable signs that vodka had ever been present in the glass, but rather 'the vodka has been partially drunk', 'the vodka is not quite finished', i.e. there is visual evidence that some, but not all of the vodka has been drunk.

(34) NIVKH
    arak   ra-ɣəta-d'.
    vodka drink-RES-FIN

This thus leads the authors to formulate the implicational universal that if a language has resultatives formed from verbs that denote a resulting state that is not visually perceivable, then it will also have resultative formed from verbs that denote a resulting state that is visually perceivable.

A large number of typological studies devoted to particular empirical domains follow essentially this pattern, albeit often restricting the range of typological parameters that are considered explicitly. One example of this is Comrie (1975) on causative constructions. This article examined only one aspect of morphological causative constructions, namely the syntactic expression of the causee, and came up with a universal tendency. If one assumes syntactic relations to be arranged on a hierarchy, from top to bottom: subject − direct object − indirect object − other, then there is a tendency crosslinguistically for the causee (the one caused to carry out a certain action) to be expressed by the syntactic relation that is highest on this hierarchy and that is not already present in the clause.

This can be illustrated by data from one variety of TURKISH. If the basic verb is intransitive, then the subject slot is filled but the direct object slot is vacant, so the causee will show up as direct object, as in (36) in relation to (35).

(35) TURKISH
    Hasan öl-dü.
    Hasan die-PRET
    'Hasan died.'

(36) *Ali Hasan-ı   öl-dür-dü.*
    Ali Hasan-ACC die-CAUS-PRET
    'Ali killed Hasan.' (lit. 'Ali caused Hasan to die.')

If the basic verb is transitive, as in (37), then the causee shows up as an indirect object, as in (38).

(37) *Müdür mektub-u imzala-dı.*
    director letter-ACC sign-PRET
    'The director signed the letter.'

(38) *Ali mektub-u müdür-e*
    Ali letter-ACC director-DAT
    imzala-t-tı.
    sign-CAUS-PRET
    'Ali got the director to sign the letter.'

If the verb is ditransitive, then the first slot available is "other", and in this (now somewhat archaic) variety of TURKISH the causee shows up with the postposition *tarafından* 'by', as in (40).

(39) *Müdür Hasan-a   mektub-u*
    director Hasan-DAT letter-ACC
    göster-di.
    show-PRET
    'The director showed the letter to Hasan.'

(40) *Ali Hasan-a   mektub-u müdür*
    Ali Hasan-DAT letter-ACC director
    tarafından göster-t-ti.
    by   show-CAUS-PRET
    'Ali got Hasan to show the letter to the director.'

This framework permits a substantial amount of order to be brought into what might otherwise seem to be massive crosslinguistic variation in the expression of the causee. It should be emphasized, however, that even in this early work the universal was claimed only to be a tendency, since counterexamples were known. Thus, instead of (40) TURKISH also permits doubling on the dative, as in (41), though with greater restrictions, for instance the word order is much more fixed in (41) than in (40).

(41) *Ali müdür-e   mektub-u Hasan-a*
    Ali director-DAT letter-ACC Hasan-DAT
    göster-t-ti.
    show-CAUS-PRET

Subsequent work has shown that semantic factors are also relevant to the expression of the causee, so that in JAPANESE, for instance, use of the indirect object marker *ni* rather than the direct object marker *o* in (43) implies that the causee retains greater control over the action.

(42) JAPANESE
Taroo ga   Ziroo o   ik-ase-ta.
Taro NOM Jiro ACC go-CAUS-PRET
'Taro made Jiro go.'

(43) *Taroo ga   Ziroo ni   ik-ase-ta.*
Taro NOM Jiro DAT go-CAUS-PRET
'Taro got Jiro to go.'

For a recent statement of the various factors that are relevant, reference may be made to Jae Jung Song (1996).

What is shared by all the above mentioned work is the use of a descriptive framework against which typologically varied languages are measured, the framework being of course accommodated where necessary to the needs of new empirical material.

3.2. Prototypes

In section 3.1 it was emphasized that the choice of typological framework for the investigation of a particular empirical area is not guaranteed in advance. One significant factor in the progress of typological research in recent years has been the recognition that new tools must be used if typological order is to be drawn out from what appears to be empirical chaos. One example of such an important tool is the notion of prototype.

In classical Aristotelian classification, items are defined in terms of necessary and sufficient conditions. A given item either satisfies these conditions, in which case it is an instance of the concept in question, or it does not, in which case it is not an instance of the concept in question. By contrast, a prototype definition is in terms of a "best instance" of a particular concept, such that other instances will fall closer to or more distant from this best instance, without there being any clear cut-off point between the set of instances satisfying the definition and the set of instances not satisfying the definition.

The classic case of the successful application of the notion of prototype in linguistics is Brent Berlin and Paul Kay's study of color terms across various languages (Berlin & Kay 1969). Previous studies had investigated the boundaries between color terms, and essentially come to the conclusion that there are no universals. For instance, the ENGLISH word *yellow* does not have the same boundaries as its French dictionary equivalent *jaune* (e.g. some things that are *jaune* in French would be *brown* in ENGLISH) or as its GERMAN dictionary equivalent *gelb* (e.g. some things that are *gelb* in GERMAN would be *orange* in ENGLISH). Berlin & Kay, by contrast, examined the focus (i.e. the prototype) of each color term, coming to a number of surprising conclusions.

First, while individuals are often hesitant even in their own usage about identifying boundaries of color terms, and will often shift judgments between experimental sessions, they are generally consistent over identifying the focus of a color term, for instance in answer to the question "what is the best value for color term X", the choice being made from a color chart.

Secondly, there is striking consistency across languages. For instance, the Philippine language HANUNOO at first sight has a color system radically different from that of ENGLISH. Its word *(ma)lagti'* covers ENGLISH 'white' and also other light tints; *(ma)biru* covers 'black' and other dark tints; *(ma)rara'* covers 'red, orange, maroon'; and finally *(ma)latuy* covers both 'yellow' and lighter tints of 'green' and 'brown'. However, the focus for *(ma)lagti'* is the same as for *white*, the focus of *(ma)biru* is the same as for *black*, the focus of *(ma)rara'* is the same as for *red*, and the focus of *(ma)latuy* is the same as for *green*.

Thirdly, on comparing languages that have different numbers of basic color terms – HANUNOO, for instance, has only the four cited – Berlin & Kay found clear evidence for a hierarchy (see section 3.3), as set out in (44).

(44)   white   black
                  red
         green   yellow
                  blue
                  brown

If a language has only two color terms (the minimum found), then they have as their foci 'white' and 'black'. If there is a third term, it has the focus of 'red'. If there is a fourth term, it has the focus of either 'green' or 'yellow', and if there is a fifth term, it has the focus of the other of these. A sixth item has the focus of 'blue', a seventh that of 'brown'. Although subsequent work has uncovered some counterexamples to this hierarchy, it nonetheless stands as an important strong universal tendency (→ art. 90).

But perhaps most important for approaches to typology, it shows that it is important to ask the right typological question, although there is no guarantee in advance as to what the right question will be. Asking questions about the boundaries of color terms does not lead to typological results of any significance. Asking questions about the foci of color terms leads to significant results in lexical typology.

3.3 Hierarchies and continua

As has already been intimated in the discussion of section 3.2, the notion of hierarchy plays an important role in current approaches to linguistic typology, as does that of scale. The only difference between the concepts 'hierarchy' and 'scale' is that the former implies a clear directionality (one end is higher than the other), while the other does not, and the difference between them is not of great significance. Instead of 'scale' many linguists use the term 'continuum', though given the rather specialized sense this term may bring with it from mathematics it is perhaps best avoided.

In section 3.2 the hierarchy of color terms was presented. Another hierarchy that has played an important role in recent typological thinking is the hierarchy of syntactic relations, one form of which was used by Edward Keenan and Comrie (1977) to try to establish order within cross-linguistic variation in accessibility to relative clause formation. By accessibility to relative clause formation is meant the possibility of the notional head of the relative clause occupying a particular function in the relative clause itself. In ENGLISH, for instance, direct objects are accessible to relative clause formation, as in (45), whereas in MALAGASY they are not (see below).

(45) *The student whom the woman saw soon left.*

Note that what is relevant is the role of the notional head in the relative clause (where it is direct object), not in the main clause (where it is subject). In what follows, I will take for granted a number of amendments that have been made to the account in Keenan & Comrie (1977), following by and large that given in Comrie (1989: 155−60).

The hierarchy relevant for relative clauses is as given in (46), with corresponding ENGLISH examples given, in order, in (47)−(50):

(46) Subject
      Direct object
      Nondirect object
      Possessor

(47) *the student who gave the book to the teacher*

(48) *the book that the student gave to the teacher*

(49) *the teacher to whom the student gave the book*

(50) *the teacher whose student bought the book*

Note that the top three positions are arguments of the verb, while the fourth is a constituent of a noun phrase.

The basic intuition underlying accessibility to relative clause formation is that positions higher in the hierarchy are more accessible than those lower down, which in terms of crosslinguistic variation receives the following interpretation. If a given language can relativize on a particular position on the hierarchy, then it must be able to relativize on all higher positions.

In fact, for each position on the hierarchy there is at least one language that can relativize on that position, on all higher positions (to be consistent with the universal), but not on any lower position (to establish empirically the validity of the hierarchy).

For instance, in MALAGASY only subjects are accessible to relative clause formation; in KINYARWANDA, only subjects and direct objects are accessible; in the Fering dialect of NORTH FRISIAN only subjects, direct objects, and nondirect objects are accessible, while in ENGLISH all four positions are accessible.

The accessibility hierarchy as applied to relative clauses has the effect of restricting the range of permitted crosslinguistic variation, and thus operates at the interface of language universals and linguistic typology. For present purposes, what is important is that it provides a principled way of classifying the possibilities of accessibility to relative clause formation.

A particularly rich use of hierarchies is to be found in Greville C. Corbett (1983), where various instances of variation across Slavic languages are handled elegantly by means of the notion of hierarchy. A simple set of examples will suffice to illustrate the kinds of phenomena that are involved.

Many Slavic languages, like many other European languages, have polite plural address forms, e.g. the use of the second person plural form referring to a single addressee. They vary in the number marked on predicative elements that would be expected to agree in number with a subject that is plural in form for politeness but singular in reference. In RUSSIAN, for instance, past tense verbs in such a case are plural, while in CZECH they are singular, as in (51)–(52).

(51) RUSSIAN
  Vy ždali.
  you wait.PL
  'You waited.'

(52) CZECH
  Vy jste čekal.
  you be.2PL wait.3SGM
  'You waited.'

If, however, predicates are arranged on a hierarchy from most verblike to most nounlike, it turns out that in each language plural agreement is found for more verblike predicates, singular agreement for more nounlike predicates, but that the cut-off point varies from language to language. This can be seen even in CZECH sentence (52), where the auxiliary verb is plural even though the (in CZECH) nonfinite lexical verb is singular.

In fact, with respect to the Slavic example just cited one might use the term scale rather than hierarchy, since it is not obvious that the scale from more verblike to more nounlike is directed in the same way as are the hierarchies for color terms and accessibility to relative clause formation. Such scales play an important role in the UNITYP approach to linguistic typology, as described in summary form in Seiler (1995), for instance. Example (53), taken from Seiler (1995: 292), shows the interaction between two scales.

(53)

	haben	besitzen	gehören
Vater	–	–	–
Sohn	+	–	–
Kopf	+	?	–
Haar	+	+	–
Intelligenz	+	+	–
Hose	+	+	+
Haus	+	+	+

The three verbs on the horizontal axis have as translation equivalents respectively 'have', 'possess', and 'belong'. The nouns on the vertical axis are 'father', 'son', 'head', 'hair', 'intelligence', 'pants', 'house'. The plus signs mean that it is possible to combine that verb with that noun, e.g. to produce sentences like (54)–(55) but not (56).

(54) *Das Kind hat Intelligenz.*
  'The child has intelligence.'

(55) *Das Kind besitzt Intelligenz.*
  'The child possesses intelligence.'

(56) **(Die) Intelligenz gehört dem Kind.*
  '(The) intelligence belongs to the child.'

The nouns selected for the vertical axis form a scale of possessa, while the verbs selected for the horizontal axis form a scale of possessing. Their interaction forms a set of implicational universals, such that if a given verb is possible with a particular noun, then it will also be possible with all nouns below that noun – as the items are arranged in (53); if a particular noun is possible with a given verb, then it will also be possible with all verbs to the left of that verb – again, as arranged in (53).

As a final example of recent use of the notion of scales to provide insight into crosslinguistic variation we may cite Haspelmath (1993), which investigates the derivational relations between transitive and intransitive pairs of verbs. In some instance, the transitive verb is derived from the intransitive one, as in ARABIC *darasa* 'he learned' versus *darrasa* 'he taught'. In others, the relation is the inverse, as in RUSSIAN *katat'* 'to roll (TR)' versus *katat'-sja* 'to roll (INTR)'. For a given semantic concept, some languages will go one way, others the other, so that for instance the relation between 'find' and 'be found, turn up' is expressed with a derived intransitive in RUSSIAN (*najti, najti-s'*), but with a derived transitive in TSEZ (*esu-r, esu*).

However, it is possible to arrange verbs according to their meaning into a scale running, for the lexical items investigated by Haspelmath, from 'boil' to 'split', such that verbs nearer the 'boil' end are more likely to have a derived transitive, those nearer the 'split' end a derived intransitive. This can in turn be correlated with the likelihood of particular events happening spontaneously, i.e. it can be given an explanatory basis.

3.4. Principles and Parameters

Although generative grammar and linguistic typology are often seen as incompatible approaches to the study of general properties of language, it would be inappropriate to close this section without mentioning one approach within generative grammar that is very close to work in linguistic typology, namely the Principles and Parameters approach first outlined in Chomsky (1981) and presented in detail, for instance, in Liliane Haegeman (1994).

As in much current generative grammar, the initial impetus behind the Principles and Parameters approach came from considerations of learnability, i.e. the way in which a child rapidly acquires his or her native language.

One way of approaching this problem would be to say that certain properties of language are universal and are, moreover, part of the fixed genetic endowment of the child as a member of the human species.

Other properties show limited crosslinguistic variation, such that it is not implausible to assume that they might be values for a parameter, such that children would be born genetically endowed with knowledge of these parameters and their values, but would have to work out from the data of the language they hear what particular value each parameter has in the particular language to which they are exposed. For this to provide a practical solution to the learnability problem, it is important that the number of parameters be limited.

As an illustration, one can take the headedness parameter, i.e. whether phrases in the language in question are head-initial or head-final, harking back to the discussion of word order typology in section 2.2.

Children would be born knowing that they have to select one or other value for this parameter, but only on exposure to relevant data would they be able to decide what the value is for the language in question. Parameters thus serve to capture both the variation among languages and the restricted nature of this variation, much as linguistic typology does.

Indeed, while there remain many differences between the work of generative grammarians following the Principles and Parameters approach and linguistic typologists, for instance with regard to theory-driven versus data-driven approaches, to the admissibility of abstractness of representations, it is clear that Principles and Parameters on the one hand and linguistic typology on the other have the potential for fruitful interaction. (Whether this is true of Minimalism, a later development within generative grammar, seems less clear.)

4. Areal typology

It has long been noted that languages in contact with one another, even if not genetically related or at least not particularly closely related genetically, often come to share certain features in common. Languages which share a substantial number of features as a result of contact are said to constitute a 'Sprachbund' or linguistic area.

The first such linguistic area to be investigated in detail is the Balkan Sprachbund (→ art. 108), for which Helmut Wilhelm Schaller (1975) presents an overview, although other linguistic areas have also been identified; South Asia (Masica 1976; → art. 109) and Meso-America (Campbell et al. 1986; → art. 110) are among the best known. The Balkan Sprachbund will be used to provide a brief illustration.

The core languages of the Balkan Sprachbund are MODERN GREEK, ALBANIAN, BULGARIAN, MACEDONIAN, and RUMANIAN, with some of the features spreading to other neighboring languages, such as SERBO-CROATIAN, especially its SERBIAN variety. These languages belong to different branches of the Indo-European family: Each of MODERN GREEK and ALBANIAN constitutes a separate branch on its own, BULGARIAN and MACEDONIAN are Slavic, while RUMANIAN is Romance (Italic). Nonetheless, they have certain features in common that are not shared by languages that are more closely related genetically, such as the other Slavic and Romance languages.

For instance, the same form is used for both possessors and indirect objects, so that RUMANIAN has *fete* as genitive-dative of *fată* 'girl', ALBANIAN has genitive-dative *lumi* of *lum* 'river', BULGARIAN uses the preposition *na* to translate both 'of' and 'to', e.g. *na Bălgarija* 'to Bulgaria', and MODERN GREEK uses the reflex of the ANCIENT GREEK genitive in both possessor and indirect functions: *tu anϑrópu* 'of, to the man'. Perhaps even more striking is the Balkan loss of the infinitive, otherwise a characteristic category of most European languages, so that 'give me [something] to drink' comes out literally as 'give me that I drink', as in (57)−(60).

(57) MODERN GREEK
 Δós   mu   na   pjó.
 give.IMP.2SG I.DAT that .drink.PRES.1SG

(58) ALBANIAN
 A-më   të   pi.
 give.IMP.2SG-I.DAT that drink.PRES.1SG

(59) BULGARIAN
 Daj   mi   da   pija.
 give.IMP.2SG I.DAT that drink.PRES.1SG

(60) RUMANIAN
 Dă-mi   să   beau.
 give.IMP.2SG-I.DAT that drink.PRES.1SG

Some linguists have noted areal features that seem to have quite wide geographic ranges. Thus Matthew Dryer (1988) observes that Adjective-Noun order is clearly a minority pattern across most of the world, but achieves majority status across most of northern Eurasia.

One question that arises, and which will be the focus of discussion here, is the precise relationship between such observations and the more general concerns of linguistic typology, since examination of this relationship can also throw light on the nature of such more general concerns.

Perhaps the most crucial difference between an 'areal type' and the notion of 'type' in general typological studies is that the various parameters that go to make up an areal type are preferably independent of one another, not only logically, but also in the sense of not correlating with one another typologically. The reason for this is that the notion of areal type is only significant if the languages comprising the relevant language area share a significant number of non-correlating features.

If a group of languages share a number of correlating features, then this is no more significant areally than if they share a single one of these features, or little more significant if the correlations are not absolute. In the case of the Balkan Sprachbund, the fact that there is no known logical or typological connection between merger of genitive and dative cases on the one hand and loss of the infinitive on the other is a piece of evidence in favor of the supposition that the languages share a number of features that have arisen as the result of contact. More generally, the features that constitute an areal type do not, by definition, constitute a holistic or wide-ranging type in the sense appropriate for general linguistic typology, where one is interested precisely in correlations independent of such historical factors as contact. This difference between areal type and the general notion of linguistic type can be put to good use in historical work, as is demonstrated by Orin Gensler (1993), who investigates whether there are significant typological parallels between Insular Celtic languages on the one hand and Mediterranean Afroasiatic languages on the other. While it had been noted for a long time that there are similarities between Insular Celtic and Mediterranean Afroasiatic languages, before Gensler's work it had not been satisfactorily demonstrated that these similarities were significant. Gensler examines the various features noted in earlier work, comparing each of them with that feature's distribution across the languages of the world.

Some of the features turn out to be very common crosslinguistically, such as relative clauses introduced by an invariable linker (like ENGLISH *that*), and thus the fact that they are shared by Insular Celtic and Mediterranean Afroasiatic languages is not areally significant. On the other hand, other features turn out to be extremely rare crosslinguistically, and thus the fact that a number of them cooccur in both Insular Celtic and Mediterranean Afroasiatic languages is likely to be of areal significance. One such feature is the use of a predicative particle identical to a locative particle, as in Welsh example (61).

(61) WELSH
 Y   mae   ef yn ffermwr.
 PTCL be.PRS.3SG he in farmer
 'He is a farmer.'

Crucial to the conclusion of the project is the determination that the features that are found to be both rare cross-linguistically and common to Insular Celtic and Mediterranean Afroasiatic are not in turn features that cluster together in those languages in which they are found, i.e. Insular Celtic and Mediterranean Afroasiatic languages really are characterized by a significant number of independent rare features.

To summarize this section, the notion of areal type is important for present concerns precisely because of the way in which it differs from the notion of type in general linguistic typology. In the case of areal typology, we are interested in rare combinations of features that are likely to point to historical contact as the only possible basis for the shared similarities. In the case of general linguistic typology, we are interested in finding parallels across languages that are independent of any historical relation between them.

5. References

Altmann, Gabriel & Lehfeldt, Werner. 1973. *Allgemeine Sprachtypologie. Prinzipien und Meßverfahren*. (UTB, 250.) München: Fink.

Berlin, Brent & Kay, Paul. 1969. *Basic color terms: their universality and evolution.* Berkeley: University of California Press.

Bynon, Theodora. 1995.

Campbell, Lyle & Kaufman, Terrence & Smith-Stark, Thomas. 1986. "Meso-America as a linguistic area". *Language* 62: 530–70.

Chomsky, Noam. 1981. *Lectures on government and binding.* (Studies in generative grammar, 9.) Dordrecht: Foris.

Comrie, Bernard. 1975. "Causatives and universal grammar". *Transactions of the Philological Society* 1974: 1–32.

Comrie, Bernard. ²1989. *Language universals and linguistic typology. Syntax and morphology.* Oxford: Blackwell.

Comrie, Bernard. 1991. "Holistic versus partial typologies". In: Bahner, Werner & Schildt, Joachim & Viehweger, Dieter (eds.). *Proceedings of the Fourteenth International Congress of Linguists. Berlin, August 10 – August 15, 1987.* Vol. 1. Berlin: Akademie-Verlag, 139–48.

Corbett, Greville G. 1983. *Hierarchies, targets and controllers: agreement patterns in Slavic.* (Croom Helm Linguistic Series.) London: Croom Helm.

Croft, William. 1990. *Typology and universals.* (Cambridge textbooks in linguistics.) Cambridge: Cambridge University Press.

Dryer, Matthew S. 1988. "Object-verb order and adjective-noun order: dispelling a myth". In: Hawkins, John A. & Holmback, Heather (eds.). *Papers in universal grammar: generative and typological approaches.* (*Lingua* 74.2/3.) Amsterdam: Elsevier, 185–217.

Gensler, Orin. 1993. *A typological evaluation of Celtic/Hamito-Semitic syntactic parallels.* Ph.D. dissertation, University of California, Berkeley.

Greenberg, Joseph H. ²1966. "Some universals of grammar with particular reference to the order of meaningful elements". In: Greenberg, Joseph H. (ed.). *Universals of language. Report of a conference held at Dobbs Ferry/NY, April 13-15, 1961.* Cambridge/MA: MIT Press.

Greenberg, Joseph H. 1974. *Language typology: a historical and analytic overview.* (Janua linguarum, Series minor, 184.) The Hague: Mouton.

Haegeman, Liliane. 1994. *Introduction to Government and Binding theory.* (Blackwell textbooks in linguistics, 1.) Oxford: Blackwell.

Haspelmath, Martin. 1993. "More on the typology of inchoative/causative verb alternations". In: Comrie, Bernard & Polinsky, Maria (eds.). *Causatives and transitivity.* (Studies in Language Companion Series, 23.) Amsterdam & Philadelphia: Benjamins, 87–120.

Hawkins, John A. 1983. *Word order universals.* (Quantitative analyses of linguistic structure, 3.) New York: Academic Press.

Hawkins, John A. 1986. *A comparative typology of English and German: unifying the contrasts.* London: Croom Helm.

Hawkins, John A. 1994. *A performance theory of order and constituency.* (Cambridge studies in linguistics, 73.) Cambridge: Cambridge University Press.

International Phonetic Association. 1999. *Handbook of the International Phonetic Association: A guide to the use of the International Phonetic Alphabet.* Cambridge: Cambridge University Press.

Jacobson, Steven A. 1977. *A grammatical sketch of Siberian Yupik Eskimo, as spoken on St. Lawrence Island, Alaska.* Fairbanks: Alaska Native Language Center.

Keenan, Edward L. & Comrie, Bernard. 1977. "Noun phrase accessibility and universal grammar". *Linguistic Inquiry* 8: 63–99.

Lefebvre, Claire. 1998. *Creole genesis and the acquisition of grammar. The case of Haitian creole.* (Cambridge studies in linguistics, 88.) Cambridge: Cambridge University Press.

Lehmann, Winfred P. 1978. "Conclusion: toward an understanding of the profound unity underlying languages". In: Lehmann, Winfred P. (ed.). *Syntactic typology: studies in the phenomenology of language.* Austin/TX: University of Texas Press, 395–432.

Masica, Colin P. 1976. *Defining a linguistic area: South Asia.* Chicago: University of Chicago Press.

Müller-Gotama, Franz. 1994. *Grammatical relations: a cross-linguistic perspective on their syntax and semantics.* (Empirical approaches to language typology, 11.) Berlin & New York: Mouton de Gruyter.

Nedjalkov, Vladimir P. (ed.) 1988. *Typology of resultative constructions.* (Typological studies in language, 12.) Amsterdam & Philadelphia: Benjamins.

Nedjalkov, Vladimir P. & Jaxontov, Sergej Je. 1988. "The typology of resultative constructions". In: Nedjalkov, Vladimir P. (ed.), 3–62.

Nedjalkov, Vladimir P. & Litvinov, Viktor P. 1995. "The St. Petersburg/Leningrad typology group". In: Shibatani, Masayoshi & Bynon, Theodora (eds.). *Approaches to language typology.* Oxford: Clarendon Press, 215–71.

Nichols, Johanna. 1986. "Head-marking and dependent marking grammar". *Language* 62: 56–119.

Nichols, Johanna. 1990. "Some preconditions and typical traits of the stative-active language type (with reference to Proto-Indo-European)". In: Lehmann, Winfred P. (ed.). *Language Typology 1987: Systematic balance in language. Papers from the Linguistic Typology Symposium, Berkeley, 1-3 december 1987.* (Amsterdam studies in the theory and history of linguistic science, ser. 4, Current issues in linguistic theory, 67.) Amsterdam & Philadelphia: Benjamins.

Sapir, Edward. 1921. *Language: an introduction to the study of speech.* (A Harvest Book.) New York: Harcourt, Brace & World.

Schaller, Helmut Wilhelm. 1975. *Die Balkansprachen: eine Einführung in die Balkanphilologie.* (Sprachwissenschaftliche Studienbücher.) Heidelberg: Winter.

Sebba, Mark. 1987. *The syntax of serial verbs. An investigation into serialisation in Sranan and other languages.* (Creole language library, 2.) Amsterdam & Philadelphia: Benjamins.

Seiler, Hansjakob. 1995. "Cognitive-conceptual structure and linguistic encoding: language universals and typology in the UNITYP framework". In: Shibatani & Bynon (eds.), 273–325.

Shibatani, Masayoshi & Bynon, Theodora (eds.) 1995. *Approaches to language typology.* Oxford: Clarendon Press.

Shopen, Timothy (ed.) 1985. *Language typology and syntactic description.* 3 volumes. Cambridge: Cambridge University Press.

Song, Jae Jung. 1996. *Causatives and causation. A universal-typological perspective.* (Longman linguistic library.) London: Longman.

Vennemann, Theo. 1972. "Analogy in generative grammar, the origin of word order". In: Heilmann, Luigi (ed.). *Proceedings of the Eleventh International Congress of Linguists. Bologna-Florence, Aug. 28. Sept. 2., 1972.* Vol. 2. Bologna: Il Mulino, 79–83.

Vennemann, Theo. 1984. "Typology, universals and change of language". In: Fisiak, Jacek (ed.). *Historical syntax.* (Trends in linguistics, studies and monographs, 23.) Berlin: Mouton, 593–612.

Bernard Comrie, Max Planck Institute for Evolutionary Anthropology, Leipzig (Germany)

II. Foundations: Points of contact between language universals/language typology and other disciplines
Grundlagen: Berührungspunkte von Universalienforschung und Sprachtypologie mit anderen Disziplinen
Fondements: les points de contact entre la recherche universaliste, la typologie linguistique et d'autres disciplines

3. Handlungstheorie, Kommunikationstheorie, Lebenswelt

1. Prämissen
2. Handlungs- und kommunikationstheoretischer Rekurs
3. Universale Aspekte kommunikativen Handelns
4. Zitierte Literatur

1. Prämissen

Die Existenz von Sprache ist stets an soziale Wirklichkeit gebunden. Ihr Entstehen, ihre Weiterentwicklung und Ausdifferenzierung sowie auch ihr Sterben vollziehen sich innerhalb von Kommunikationszusammenhängen und sozialen Beziehungssystemen. Diese sozial-kommunikative Bindung kann als universaler Hintergrund des natürlichen Vorkommens von Sprache angesehen werden. Hier liegt es nahe, dieses Verhältnis von sozial-kommunikativem Geschehen und Sprache in einer universalistischen Perspektive zu thematisieren und die (Inter-)Dependenzen von Sprache und sozialer Wirklichkeit genauer zu bestimmen. Dies bedeutet einerseits, ihre Bedeutung für sozial-kommunikative Prozesse zu diskutieren, und andererseits, nach deren strukturellen Konsequenzen auf den einzelnen Organisationsebenen der Sprache zu fragen. Eine solche Theoretisierung des Zusammenhangs ist die Voraussetzung für die Analyse der kontingenten, also einzelsprachlichen und lebensweltspezifischen Ausprägungen dieses Verhältnisses. Brigitte Schlieben-Lange hat für die Sprachwissenschaft auf die Möglichkeit und Wichtigkeit einer solchen Perspektive hingewiesen:

„Es ist aber auch möglich, eine Universalpragmatik zu entwerfen, die die Bedingungen sinnvollen Sprechens zu untersuchen hätte, ebenso wie die sprachwissenschaftliche Universalienforschung Universalien der Sprache feststellt. [...] Es sei darauf hingewiesen, daß sich die Entscheidung darüber, was nun universell und was einzelgesellschaftlich ist an der menschlichen Rede, äußerst problematisch ist (genauso wie bei den Universalien der Sprache). Als universell darf nur angenommen werden, was zum 'Miteinander-Reden' unerläßlich ist, nur das, ohne das sinnvolle Kommunikation unmöglich wäre" (Schlieben-Lange 1979: 67).

Eine solche sprachwissenschaftliche Universalpragmatik, wie sie Brigitte Schlieben-Lange hier intendiert, ist noch immer Programm. Eine allgemein akzeptierte sprachwissenschaftliche Universalpragmatik gibt es nicht. Es existiert vielmehr eine Reihe von sprachwissenschaftlichen Disziplinen, die sich in unterschiedlicher Weise auf pragmatische Konzepte, hier vor allem auf das Handlungskonzept, beziehen und zusammen den Bereich der sprachwissenschaftlichen Pragmatik bilden. Zum Kern dieser sprachwissenschaftlichen Disziplinen zählen die Soziolinguistik, die Textlinguistik (→ Art. 11) und etwa auch die Gesprächsanalyse (vgl. dazu Schlieben-Lange 1979: 11f.).

1.1. Warum gibt es keine Universalpragmatik?

Das Fehlen einer linguistischen Universalpragmatik hat fachgeschichtliche Gründe. Die Auseinandersetzung mit pragmatischen

Fragestellungen innerhalb der Sprachwissenschaft ist nachhaltig von der Unterscheidung zwischen der 'competence' und der 'performance' bestimmt, die Noam Chomsky (1965) in Anknüpfung an die Unterscheidung von 'langue' und 'parole' de Saussures getroffen hat (vgl. Fiehler 1995). Danach ist der zentrale Gegenstand die Kompetenz im Sinne des grammatischen Systems einer Sprache, und diese kann ohne Rekurs auf den kommunikativ-pragmatischen Zusammenhang von Sprache beschrieben werden (Chomsky 1991: 7). Schon de Saussure argumentiert in Auseinandersetzung mit der zeitgenössischen sprachwissenschaftlichen Forschung:

„Nach unserer Ansicht ist das Studium der äußeren sprachlichen Erscheinungen sehr fruchtbar. Aber es ist falsch, zu behaupten, daß man ohne sie den inneren Organismus einer Sprache nicht kennen könne" (de Saussure 1916/1967: 26).

Im Strukturalismus dokumentiert sich dies in den Techniken der Segmentierung und Klassifikation, die die phonologische, morphologische und syntaktische Struktur einer Sprache ohne Bezugnahme auf die kommunikativ-pragmatischen Verhältnisse ermitteln. In der generativen Grammatik findet diese Annahme ihren deutlichen Ausdruck etwa in der nativistisch begründeten Vorstellung einer „autonomen" Syntax (vgl. Fanselow & Felix 1987: 65ff.; → Art. 24). Kommunikation gilt in der generativen Grammatik nicht als Grundbestimmung von Sprache, sondern ergibt sich aus einer Nutzbarmachung der an sich zweckfreien Sprache:

„[...] language is designed as a system that ist 'beautiful', but in general unusable. It is designed for elegance, not for use, though with features that enable it to be used sufficiently for the purposes of normal life" (Chomsky 1991a: 49).

Die Trennung von Performanz und Kompetenz hat eine spezifische Rangordnung von Fragestellungen innerhalb der Sprachwissenschaft bewirkt. Es ist der Bereich der Kompetenz oder des Sprachsystems, der aus der Sicht vieler Sprachwissenschaftler das Zentrum der Forschungen markiert. Fragen, die die performative Seite der Sprache betreffen, bilden danach eher nachgeordnete Forschungsbereiche. Sie werden als Ergänzungen oder Erweiterungen der sprachsystematischen Analysen betrachtet.

Die sogenannte kommunikativ-pragmatische Wende der Sprachwissenschaft in den 70er Jahren (vgl. Helbig 1990: 13ff.) hat diese Hierarchie nicht wirklich aufheben können. Kritisiert werden kann, daß Untersuchungen, in denen die kommunikativ-pragmatische Perspektive in Ergänzung sprachsystematischer Untersuchungen betrieben werden, letztlich die Trennung von Kompetenz und Performanz nur bestätigen. Pragmatisch sind Untersuchungen danach nur dann, wenn sie die Forschungsperspektive umkehren und die kommunikativ-pragmatischen Verhältnisse zum Ausgangspunkt der Analyse machen (vgl. Ehlich 1986; 1993). Auch die Annahme einer „kommunikativen Kompetenz" (Hymes 1986) läßt die Dichotomie letztlich unangetastet.

1.2. Pragmatische Ansätze

Eine konsequent pragmatische Herangehensweise zeichnet die Textlinguistik in ihrer frühen Etablierungsphase in den 70er Jahren aus. Es wird versucht, Texte in ihrer Struktur konsequent von den kommunikativ-pragmatischen Bedingungen aus zu erschließen. Die Frage nach dem Wesen von Textualität soll nicht als Appendix zu sprachsystematischen Untersuchungen betrieben werden, sondern der Text, die „natürliche Vorkommensweise von Sprache" (Helbig 1990: 167), zur Schlüsselkategorie einer Pragmatik der Sprache werden (vgl. hierzu auch Schlieben-Lange 1979: 110f.; 1988: 1208).

Auch die Funktionale Grammatik beinhaltet eine grundsätzliche Kritik an der Ausklammerung kommunikativ-pragmatischer Fragestellungen aus der grammatischen Analyse. Nach Talmy Givón hat diese zu einer einseitigen Sicht auf die Sprache geführt: „the separation of 'competence' from 'performance' also allowed the detaching of linguistics from language as a socio-cultural phenomenon, expression and instrument" (Givón 1984: 9). Versucht wird nun, die grammatischen Strukturen vor dem Hintergrund kognitiver sowie kommunikativer Funktionen zu erschließen. Mit dieser Ersetzung des formalistischen Konzepts von Grammatik, wie es dem Strukturalismus und dem Generativismus zugrunde liegt, durch ein funktionalistisches wird die Trennung von Kompetenz und Performanz grundsätzlich aufgehoben.

Jochen Rehbein verweist darauf, daß die verzögerte Berücksichtigung der Zusammenhänge von Grammatik und Kommunikation mit einem „Bedürfnis nach Regel-Konstruktion" (Rehbein 1988: 1190) zu tun hat. Dieses verstellt die Sicht auf die funktionale Einbindung von Sprache in Handlungs- bzw. und

Kommunikationszusammenhänge und wird erst allmählich überwunden.

Es sind gerade auch Ansätze innerhalb der Kognitiven Linguistik – generativistische Spielarten hier ausgenommen –, die eine Überwindung der Trennung von Kompetenz und Performanz fordern. So sprechen sich Gert Rickheit und Hans Strohner für eine „Etablierung der Linguistik als Kommunikationswissenschaft" aus, deren Voraussetzung es ist, die Trennung kompetentieller und performativer Bereiche sprachwissenschaftlicher Forschung aufzugeben (vgl. Rickheit & Strohner 1993: 19).

2. Handlungs- und kommunikationstheoretischer Rekurs

In der Frage nach den universalen kommunikativ-pragmatischen Bedingungen von Sprache ist ein Rekurs auf kommunikations- und handlungstheoretische Modelle notwendig, wie sie außerhalb der Sprachwissenschaft entwickelt worden sind.

Diese Modelle menschlichen Handelns und menschlicher Kommunikation, wie sie in der Philosophie, der Anthropologie, der Sozialphilosophie, der Soziologie und der (Sozial-)Psychologie vorliegen, bilden allerdings keinen kohärenten Zusammenhang. Die Ansätze divergieren deutlich und beantworten die Fragen nach den Funktionen, den Bedingungen, den Wirkungen und Bewertungen, den Mitteln und Formen des menschlichen Handelns sehr unterschiedlich (vgl. Lumer 1990).

Hier wirkt sich auch eine jeweils fachspezifische Perspektivierung des Gegenstands aus.

- Philosophischen und auch anthropologischen Konzepten geht es ganz grundsätzlich um die Frage nach dem Wesen des menschlichen Handelns.
- Soziologische Handlungstheorien betrachten demgegenüber vor allem die wirklichkeitskonstitutiven Aspekte des Handelns, die Fähigkeit des Handelns zur Stiftung von Sozialwelt.
- Psychologische Konzepte schließlich konzentrieren sich auf das Individuum und untersuchen das Handeln vor dem Hintergrund psychischer Faktoren.

Dies spiegelt sich deutlich in den wissenschaftlichen Kategorien, die den theoretisch-konzeptionellen Kontext bilden. In soziologischen Theorien sind dies Kategorien wie etwa 'Identität', 'Norm', 'Wert', 'Rolle', 'Status' und 'Routine'. Psychologische Modelle hingegen diskutieren das Handeln im Zusammenhang mit Begriffen wie 'Einstellung', 'bewußte und unbewußte Motive', 'Persönlichkeitsstruktur', 'Emotion' oder 'Stimmung'. In anthropologischen Theorien finden sich Begriffe wie 'Intention', 'Motiv', 'Zweck' oder 'Plan'. Sie decken sich mit denen anderer Handlungstheorien, sind hier jedoch in einem generalisierenden, das Menschsein an sich betreffenden Sinn gemeint.

Handeln spielt eine zentrale Rolle auch in Disziplinen wie der Ökonomie, der Jurisprudenz, der Ethik und der Theologie. Dort steht jedoch nicht die theoretische Reflexion über das menschliche Handeln im Vordergrund, sondern unter Bezug auf das menschliche Handeln geht es um Fragen der Verantwortung, der Schuld und um Sanktionen für deviantes, unerwünschtes oder nicht-tolerables Handeln.

Für die Frage nach den universalen Interdependenzen von Sprache und sozialer Wirklichkeit sind philosophische, vor allem aber soziologische Handlungs- und Kommunikationstheorien relevant. Als besonders instruktiv erweisen sich dabei die Lebenswelt- und Alltagswelt-Theorien der Phänomenologie und Sozialphänomenologie sowie auch die auf phänomenologischen Überlegungen mitbasierenden Ansätze des Symbolischen Interaktionismus und der Ethnomethodologie. In ihnen findet sich einmal die Sprache bereits ganz grundsätzlich berücksichtigt, und sie bieten Anschlußstellen für spezifisch sprachwissenschaftliche Fragestellungen. Entscheidend aber ist, daß diese Theorien Annahmen machen, deren Relevanz sich gerade auch im Zusammenhang linguistisch-kognitivistischer Fragestellungen bestätigt. Dies betrifft etwa die zentrale Rolle von Körperlichkeit und Sensualität für die Wirklichkeitskonstruktion und -repräsentation. Dies eröffnet Möglichkeiten einer integrativen Konzeption, die kognitivistische und pragmatische Fragestellungen der Linguistik zusammenführt.

Im folgenden werden aus der Perspektive der genannten Theorien zentrale Aspekte sozialer Sinnstiftung durch Handlung und Kommunikation vorgestellt. Sie liefern den Hintergrund und die Folie für die daran anschließende, im engeren Sinne sprachwissenschaftliche Diskussion universaler Aspekte des sprachlichen Handlungs- und Kommunikationsgeschehens. Es ergibt sich somit ein problembezogenes Vorgehen. Für eine begriffs- und fachgeschichtliche Darstellung der linguistischen Pragmatik sei auf Brigitte Nerlich und David D. Clarke verwiesen (Nerlich 1995; 1995a; Nerlich & Clarke 1996).

2.1. Soziogenese von Wirklichkeit

Die Sozialphänomenologie ist das Ergebnis der Übertragung phänomenologischer Überlegungen auf die Soziologie. Nach Ilja Srubar hat sich diese dadurch ergeben, daß die Soziologie in den Husserlschen Überlegungen eine Möglichkeit sah, die Frage der Konstitution einer sinnhaften sozialen Realität im Handeln und durch das Handeln zu thematisieren. Diese war in den vorausgegangenen soziologischen Konzeptionen stets offen geblieben, so auch bei Max Weber (Srubar 1991: 170). Sinn bzw. eine sinnhafte Realität mußte als gegeben angenommen werden, um dann das individuelle Handeln als auf diese sinnhafte Realität bezogen zu konzipieren. Das Handeln wurde als sinnorientiert, nicht aber als sinnkonstituierend aufgefaßt. Diese Möglichkeit eröffnet nun die Phänomenologie:

„Konnte man mit Husserl davon ausgehen, daß sich der Weltsinn als die geltende Gegebenheitsweise der Welt in den intentionalen Akten des Bewußtseins konstituiert, dann konnte man auch daran gehen, die Konstitution der sozialen Wirklichkeit als eines sinnhaften Handlungszusammenhangs in den diese Wirklichkeit hervorbringenden Akten – also im sozialen Handeln selbst – zu verorten, [...]" (Srubar 1991: 170).

Die Umsetzung erfolgte im Rahmen der Handlungstheorie von Alfred Schütz, der mithin als der Begründer der Sozialphänomenologie gelten kann. Nach Richard Grathoff besteht das Programm von Schütz in der „Konstitution der Sozialwelt als Welt sinnhaften Handelns aus und in den setzenden und deutenden Akten des alltäglichen Handlungserlebens" (Grathoff 1995: 35). Dieser Ansatz wurde weiterverfolgt vor allem durch Peter L. Berger und Thomas Luckmann (Berger & Luckmann 1966/1980).

Entscheidend für die sozialphänomenologische Konzeption ist die Annahme, daß die Sinnkonstitution nicht im „Erlebnisstrom des handelnden Subjekts" (Srubar 1991: 172) erfolgt, sondern in der Begegnung. Sie erfolgt in der sogenannten „Wir-Beziehung", die als ein sich in der face-to-face-Situation zwangsläufig ergebendes Verhältnis zwischen den Beteiligten angesehen wird. Sie ist der Ort, an dem sozialer Sinn entsteht, ist aber eben selbst – so die Annahme – noch keine soziale oder intersubjektive Konstellation. Diese ergibt sich erst mit der Herausbildung und Verfügbarkeit von sozialen Sinnschemata, die die Wir-Beziehung bzw. die face-to-face-Situation sozial interpretieren (vgl. Schütz & Luckmann 1979: 93). Mit der Herausbildung sozialer Sinnschemata in der Wir-Beziehung wird die Realität „mit einem Sinnkleid überzogen – sie wird zur sinnhaften Welt" (Srubar 1991: 172).

Grundannahme der sozialphänomenologischen Konzeption ist ferner, daß die Sinnschemata nicht das Ergebnis, sondern notwendige Voraussetzung von Subjektivität sind. Die Intersubjektivität wird der Subjektivität vorgeordnet: „Jeder ausgeprägten, konkreten Subjektivität des Handlungserlebens und Sinnverstehens geht 'Intersubjektivität' bereits voraus" (Grathoff 1995: 106). Dies unterscheidet den Ansatz von Schütz deutlich von dem Husserls. Bei Husserl wird eine vom Subjekt ausgehende Kommunikation noch als Voraussetzung von Intersubjektivität gedacht (vgl. dazu Grathoff 1995: 186; Srubar 1991: 175). Die Fundierungsrichtung wird in der soziologischen Adaption der phänomenologischen Konzeption durch Schütz also umgekehrt (Grathoff 1995: 186).

Ein solcher Ansatz, der die Konstitution von Wirklichkeit nicht als subjektive Leistung begreift, führt in der Konsequenz zu einer Theorie der Sozio- oder Autogenese sozialer Wirklichkeit. Hierbei handelt es sich nach Srubar (1991: 70) um einen neuen „Theorietypus", dessen Thema die „Mechanismen" sind, die in der Autogenese sozialer Wirklichkeit wirksam sind.

2.1.1. Wissen und Typik

Eine zentrale Bedeutung innerhalb der sozialphänomenologischen Konzeption besitzt die Kategorie des Wissens, die eine kognitive Dimension der Betrachtung sozialer Wirklichkeit eröffnet. Es geht nicht nur um die Autogenese sozialer Wirklichkeit als Ergebnis von Kommunikation und Handeln, sondern auch um das Wissen von dieser sozialen Wirklichkeit im „Denken" (Schütz & Luckmann 1979: 28f.). Das Wissen ist die Voraussetzung dafür, daß das Individuum sich in seiner Wirklichkeit orientieren und adäquat agieren kann.

„All diese mitgeteilten und unmittelbaren Erfahrungen schließen sich zu einer gewissen Einheit in der Form eines Wissensvorrats zusammen, der mir als Bezugsschema für den jeweiligen Schritt meiner

Weltauslegung dient" (Schütz & Luckmann 1979: 29).

Dieses Wissen über die soziale Wirklichkeit, das vom Individuum im Laufe seines Lebens erworben wird, hat eine spezifische Struktur. Es ist ein Wissen, das die soziale Wirklichkeit in ihren typischen Strukturen erfaßt.

„Wir werden in eine Welt hineingeboren, die von dieser umgangssprachlich vermittelten Typik stets schon vorgeprägt ist. Auch schon in den frühesten Phasen unseres Spracherwerbs nehmen wir etwa Hunde als typische Hunde, Mütter und Freunde als typisch solche wahr. Nicht das konkret-einzigartige Gegenüber, sondern der in Vorerfahrungen gründende Typ bestimmt meist unser Alltagshandeln" (Grathoff 1995: 51).

Schütz hat die wahrnehmungsstrukturierende Rolle der Typik sowie auch ihre soziale Konstituierung und Bearbeitung ausführlich beschrieben (vgl. Schütz & Luckmann 1979: 277ff.). Typik hat danach zentralen Stellenwert im Rahmen einer Theorie wirklichkeitskonstitutiven sozialen Handelns. Es ist die Voraussetzung sowohl für das Wiedererkennen von Phänomenen in der Wirklichkeit als auch für die Wiederholung von Handlung und ermöglicht damit Praxis im Sinne stabiler, in ihren typischen Aspekten repetitiver Handlungs- und Kommunikationsabläufe in den Lebenswelten. Nach Srubar (1991: 173) ist es die Genese von Typik, die den zentralen Gegenstand der Lebenswelttheorie bildet:

„Die pragmatische Genese dieser Typik, ihre pragmatisch bedingte Gliederung in zeitliche, räumliche und soziale Dimensionen, die Entstehung und das Wirken von Relevanz- und Motivationsstrukturen, die dieser Typik zugrunde liegen – dies sind Probleme, die eine Theorie der Lebenswelt zu thematisieren hat" (Srubar 1991: 173).

2.1.2. Habermas und Luhmann

Die Vorstellungen einer Auto- oder Soziogenese von Lebenswelt sind auch außerhalb des sozialphänomenologischen Theorierahmens aufgegriffen worden. Jürgen Habermas (1981) schließt an die phänomenologische Konzeption an, wobei er allerdings als sinnkonstituierend nur das kommunikative, nicht aber das instrumentelle Handeln annimmt (vgl. dazu kritisch Waldenfels 1985: 94 ff.). Ebenso spielt die Leiblichkeit, die in der face-to-face-Begegnung bestimmend ist (vgl. Schütz & Luckmann 1984: 112), bei Habermas keine Rolle.

Auch in die Systemtheorie Niklas Luhmanns fließen phänomenologische Überlegungen ein. Dies gilt vor allem für das Konzept der Autopoiesis, wie Luhmann es in Anknüpfung an Humberto R. Maturana und Francisco F. Varela entwickelt. Gesellschaft wird als soziales System aufgefaßt, das sich durch die Operation der Kommunikation aus sich selbst heraus reproduziert (Luhmann 1995: 29f.). Die Konzeption der Selbst-Reproduktion wird auch auf den Menschen angewandt. Dieser wird als ein psychisches System begriffen, das operativ geschlossen ist, d.h. das nur sich selbst, seine kognitiven Operationen hat, um Wirklichkeit zu erfassen. Entscheidende Annahme Luhmanns ist dabei, daß Kommunikation zwar die Existenz psychischer Systeme voraussetzt, die Kommunikation als konstitutive Operation von sozialen Systemen aber eine eigene, unabhängige Ebene bildet. Dies führt dann zu der in der Formulierung irritierenden Aussage Luhmanns (1995: 37): „Nur die Kommunikation kann kommunizieren".

Dieses Konzept der Kommunikation ersetzt in der Systemtheorie Luhmanns den Intersubjektivitätsbegriff, der für die Konzeption der Autogenese in der Phänomenologie grundlegend ist. Die Vorstellung von Intersubjektivität wird mit dem Verweis auf die Abgeschlossenheit des psychischen Systems grundsätzlich abgelehnt; „das 'Inter' widerspricht dem 'Subjekt'" (Luhmann 1995: 171).

Gleichzeitig mit dem Subjektbegriff verliert auch das Konzept der Handlung an theoretischer Relevanz. Es ergibt sich ein Kommunikationsbegriff, der an das Organon-Modell Karl Bühlers anschließt, aber – eine „handlungstheoretische Begriffsfassung" (Luhmann 1995: 179) vermeidend – die Bühlerschen Termini 'Darstellung', 'Ausdruck' und 'Appell' durch 'Information', 'Mitteilung' und 'Verstehen' ersetzt (Luhmann 1995: 179). Kommunikation wird dann zu einem Ereignis, dem drei Selektionen zugrunde liegen:

„Irgendein Kommunikationsinhalt muß anders sein, als er sein könnte. Irgend jemand muß sich entschließen, dies mitzuteilen, obwohl er es auch unterlassen könnte. Und irgend jemand muß dies Geschehen [...] verstehen, obwohl er sich ebenso gut mit ganz anderen Dingen befassen oder die Differenzen und Selektionen auch übersehen oder nicht erfassen könnte" (Luhmann 1995: 179).

Diese Konzeption macht Sprache zum zentralen Kommunikationsmedium. Anders als das nonverbale Verhalten, das von den Beteiligten wahrgenommen wird und informativ sein kann, nicht aber als Mitteilung gemeint sein muß, liegen mit der Verwendung von Sprache stets sowohl 'Information' und als auch 'Mitteilung' vor. Eine Ausnahme macht hier allenfalls das Selbstgespräch. Diese „Differenz von Information von Mitteilung" in der Sprache kann kaum ignoriert werden (Luhmann 1995: 196).

2.1.3. Konversationsanalyse

Der sozialphänomenologische Ansatz ist auch für die Sprachwissenschaft wichtig geworden. Dies ergibt sich daraus, daß in den sozialphänomenologischen Arbeiten gerade den Konversationsprozessen und damit auch der Sprache die Aufmerksamkeit gilt. Es sind aus dieser Sicht ganz wesentlich die alltäglichen sprachlichen Konversationsprozesse, in denen sich Gesellschaft konstituiert (vgl. auch Srubar 1991: 175). So hat die Sprache „eine Vorzugsstellung im gesamten menschlichen 'Konversationssystem'" und das Gespräch besitzt „wirklichkeitsstiftende Macht" (Berger & Luckmann 1966/1980: 163f.).

In einer ähnlichen Weise widmet sich auch die von Harold Garfinkel entwickelte Ethnomethodologie der alltäglichen Konversation (vgl. Garfinkel 1967). Dies folgt der Grundannahme der Ethnomethodologie, nach der die Gesellschaft im Prozeß des alltäglichen Kommunikationsgeschehens zwischen den Gesellschaftsmitgliedern hervorgebracht wird. Wie in der Sozialphänomenologie wird dieser Prozeß als ein autogenetischer begriffen, und das Forschungsprogramm besteht entsprechend darin, die Mechanismen aufzuzeigen, die die Herstellung sozialer Ordnung und die Sinnkonstitution im interaktiven Geschehen bewirken.

Dieses Interesse an der Konversation und die Nähe zur Sozialphänomenologie sind nicht zufällig. Garfinkel ist in den 50er Jahren Schüler von Talcott Parsons, und sein Konzept der Ethnomethodologie entsteht im Kontext von und in kritischer Auseinandersetzung mit dessen funktionalistischer Konzeption von Gesellschaft (dazu § 2.2). Gleichzeitig besucht er Vorlesungen von Alfred Schütz an der „New School of Social Research" und wird mit dessen sozialphänomenologischem Denken bekannt (vgl. dazu Collins im Vorwort von Hilbert 1992: X).

Die Mechanismen der interaktiven Sinnkonstitution müssen in jeder beliebigen Interaktion auffindbar sein. Dies ist der generelle Anspruch, der sich aus dem ethnomethodologischen Ansatz ergibt. Er führt zu einem radikal empirischen Verfahren, das die Emergenz sozialen Sinns in ganz unterschiedlichen interaktiven Prozessen aufzeigt und dabei auch eine detaillierte Beschreibung der sprachlichen Formen, die dies bewirken, vornimmt.

Diese intensive Auseinandersetzung mit dem sprachlichem Material hat die Ethnomethodologie auch für die im engeren Sinne sprachwissenschaftliche Gesprächsanalyse interessant gemacht. So bildet sie den theoretischen Hintergrund für die konversationsanalytischen Arbeiten von Emanuel A. Schegloff, Harvey Sacks und Gail Jefferson, die in der Umsetzung der ethnomethodologischen Grundannahmen die Mechanismen der Konstitution und Organisation des Gesprächs, also etwa das Eröffnen und Beenden des Gesprächs oder den Sprecherwechsel herausarbeiten (Schegloff & Sacks 1973; Sacks & al. 1974).

2.1.4. Symbolischer Interaktionismus

Auch der Symbolische Interaktionismus basiert auf der Vorstellung von gesellschaftskonstituierender sozialer Handlung. Er bildet eine Nebenströmung der amerikanischen Soziologie, die in Anknüpfung an die Handlungstheorie von George Herbert Mead und in Abgrenzung zur Soziologie von Talcott Parsons entsteht (vgl. Joas 1984a). In den 60er Jahren entwickelt sich ein verstärktes Interesse am Symbolischen Interaktionismus, auch wird er mit phänomenologischen Ansätzen verknüpft. Eine Darstellung der methodologischen Grundlagen des Symbolischen Interaktionismus liefert Herbert Blumer (1973/1995), auf den auch die Bezeichnung zurückgeht.

Anders als bei Talcott Parsons (1937) und ähnlich wie in der (Sozial-)Phänomenologie setzt die Konzeption des sozialen Handelns im Symbolischen Interaktionismus nicht das Individuum voraus. Vielmehr wird das Handeln als eine komplexe soziale Aktivität begriffen, die überhaupt erst die Voraussetzungen für die Genese von Individualität und Intentionalität schafft (vgl. Joas 1984a: 213; Wenzel 1992). Auch die sozialen Normen, sozialen Regeln und sozialen Werte, die eine Gesellschaft bestimmen, werden nicht als Voraussetzung, sondern als Ergebnis der sozialen Interaktion verstanden (Blumer 1973/1995: 37).

Nach dem Symbolischen Interaktionismus orientieren sich die Menschen in ihrer Wirklichkeit auf der Basis der Bedeutungen, die die Phänomene ihrer Wirklichkeit für sie haben. Diese werden in der sozialen Interaktion herausgebildet und bestätigt, aber auch fortlaufend bearbeitet und verändert.

Im Anschluß an Mead unterscheidet der Symbolische Interaktionismus symbolische und nicht-symbolische Interaktionen. Von zentraler Bedeutung sind die symbolischen Interaktionen, bei denen die interaktive Handlung so gewählt wird, daß sie eine bestimmte Bedeutung zum Ausdruck bringt, und die gleichzeitig von interpretativen Prozessen bestimmt sind, in denen die Bedeutung der einzelnen interaktiven Handlung ermittelt wird. Die sprachliche Interaktion ist dem Bereich der symbolischen Interaktion zugeordnet (Mead 1934/1968: 94f.). Nicht-symbolisches Handeln liegt im Falle „reflexartiger Reaktionen" vor (Blumer 1973/1995: 29). Blumer gibt hier das Beispiel eines Boxers, dessen Reaktionen auf die Angriffe seines Gegners keine symbolischen Handlungen sind.

2.1.5. Emergenz sozialer Wirklichkeit und die Rolle des Einzelnen

Entscheidend für alle Konzeptionen, die von der Autogenese sozialer Wirklichkeit ausgehen, ist, daß diese nicht als das Ergebnis individueller Handlung aufgefaßt wird. Soziale Wirklichkeit ergibt sich weder aus den individuellen Handlungen, noch ist die Konstituierung sozialer Wirklichkeit deren Absicht. Ort der Emergenz sozialer Wirklichkeit ist ein soziales Geschehen, das vom Individuum weder vorhersehbar noch völlig kontrollierbar ist. Es ist stets mehr als die Summe der einzelnen individuellen Handlungen, die in sie eingehen. Dieses „Mehr" ist das Ergebnis des Zusammenspiels, der Synchronisierung und Abstimmung individueller Handlungen im sozialen Geschehen.

Die Rede vom „Verlust der Subjektivität" bezieht sich auf diese Annahme einer eigenen, nicht vom Subjekt kontrollierbaren Dynamik der Sozialwelt (Waldenfels 1987: 115ff.; 1990: 72ff.). Allerdings handelt es sich dabei zunächst einmal um einen wissenschaftlichen Befund, der sich auf die Rolle der Konzepte 'Subjekt' und 'Subjektivität' im Rahmen der Beschreibung sozialer Prozesse bezieht. In den Lebenswelten selbst ist die Zurechnung von Handlung auf den Einzelnen natürlich möglich und auch wichtig. Die Konzepte 'Verantwortung' und 'Schuld', wie sie etwa im Rechtsbereich, aber auch im Bereich religiöser Praxis eine zentrale Rolle spielen, basieren auf der Zuschreibung des Handlungsergebnisses an Subjekte.

Nach Bernhard Waldenfels (1980: 177ff.) ist das bestimmende Moment des kommunikativen Geschehens seine „Ko-Produktivität". Im Anschluß an die sprachwissenschaftliche Unterscheidung in syntagmatischen Kontrast und paradigmatische Opposition wird die Kommunikation als ein offener Prozeß gefaßt, der ein paradigmatisch-selektives und ein kombinatorisch-syntagmatisches Moment umfaßt.

Der einzelne Kommunikationsbeitrag ist so zu wählen, daß er an seiner spezifischen Stelle in das kommunikative Geschehen paßt und so in Kombination mit den vorangegangenen Kommunikationsbeiträgen ein kohärenter Text entsteht (zur Übertragung auf die Textlinguistik vgl. Tophinke 1999). Gleichzeitig bleibt stets offen, welche Reaktionen der einzelne Kommunikationsbeitrag auslöst und in welcher Weise die Kommunikation im Anschluß daran fortgesetzt wird. Damit ergibt sich ein Kommunikationszusammenhang, in den subjektive Aktivität zwar eingeht, der aber nicht insgesamt etwas Subjektives ist.

Das Konzept der 'Koproduktion' oder „Ko-Produktivität" ist gerade auch in sprachwissenschaftlicher Hinsicht instruktiv. Es betont nicht nur den Aspekt der Gemeinsamkeit, sondern auch die Produktivität des sprachlich-kommunikativen Geschehens, die einen gemeinsamen Gesprächstext entstehen läßt. Der Ausdruck 'Kooperation', der begrifflich ähnlich verwendet wird (vgl. etwa den Band von Liedtke & Keller 1987), akzentuiert demgegenüber den Aspekt der „Arbeit" (zur Definition von 'Kooperation' vgl. auch Ehlich 1987).

2.2. Zum Movens sozialen Geschehens

Mit der Frage nach der Konstitution von Wirklichkeit im sozialen Handeln eng verbunden ist die Frage nach dem Movens sozialen Handelns. Hier spielen vor allem teleologische und utilitaristische Argumentationen eine Rolle, die sich auf die Kategorien 'Funktion' und 'Zweck' stützen.

Wenn Max Weber formuliert: „Jede denkende Besinnung auf die letzten Elemente sinnvollen menschlichen Handelns ist zunächst gebunden an die Kategorien: 'Zweck' und 'Mittel'", so ist schon seine Theorie einer teleologischen Grundannahme bestimmt (Weber 1904/1991: 24). Parsons übernimmt diese Grundannahme Webers in seiner „struktur-funktionalen Theorie sozialer Systeme" (1964/1981: 486):

3. Handlungstheorie, Kommunikationstheorie, Lebenswelt

„Die Grundeinheit aller sozialen Systeme ist das Individuum als Handelnder, d.h. als eine Einheit, die grundsätzlich dadurch gekennzeichnet ist, daß sie die Erreichung von 'Zielen' anstrebt, [...] Handeln ist in diesem Bezugsrahmen notwendig entlang einem 'normativen', 'teleologischen' oder vielleicht noch besser 'voluntaristischen' 'Koordinaten'- oder Achsensystem strukturiert" (Parsons 1964/1981: 486).

Bei Parsons erfolgt diese funktionalistische Ausrichtung in kritischer Auseinandersetzung mit soziologischen Theorien wie dem Behaviorismus mit seinem „Reiz-Reaktions-Schema", deterministischen Modellen, die menschliches Handeln an die gattungsmäßige Ausstattung des Menschen binden oder es ursächlich-situativ fassen, und idealistisch-historischen Konzepten, die das Handeln als Folge des Wirkens eines überpersonalen Geistes begreifen (vgl. Joas 1996: 219).

Parsons integriert verschiedene Aspekte dieser Richtungen und führt sie in seinem Zweck-Mittel-Schema zusammen (vgl. Joas 1996: 219). Die gattungsmäßige Ausstattung des Menschen und die daraus resultierende Bedürfnislage werden allerdings nur mehr indirekt mit dem sozialen Handeln gekoppelt. Das soziale Handeln bildet nach Parsons einen komplexen systemischen Zusammenhang. Und es sind diese komplexen sozialen Handlungssysteme, in denen Lösungen zur Befriedigung der spezifischen menschlichen Bedürfnisse – und in Erweiterung des Bedürfniskonzepts dann auch kulturspezifische Bedürfnisse – entwickelt werden (Parsons 1964/1981: 487).

Funktionalistische Annahmen spielen auch in der Sozialphänomenologie Thomas Luckmanns eine Rolle. Als „Grundfunktion" sozialen Handelns wird die „Regelung von Lebensproblemen (Arbeit, Geschlecht, Macht)" (Luckmann 1992: 148) angesehen. Sie erfolgt auch bei Luckmann vor dem Hintergrund gattungsspezifischer Handlungsnotwendigkeiten, die dem Überleben dienen:

„[...] in ihrer gattungsspezifischen leiblichen Verfassung müssen Menschen von ihrer Geburt an bis zu ihrem Tode manche genau bestimmten Dinge tun, wenn sie überleben wollen, und andere Dinge, bei denen gewisse Entscheidungsmöglichkeiten offenstehen" (Luckmann 1992: 154).

Die Institutionalisierung problemlösender Handlungen trägt zur „Entlastung" des Individuums bei (Luckmann 1992: 155). Der Einzelne kann bei der Lösung der Probleme, die sich ihm in seinem Leben stellen, auf das institutionalisierte Repertoire an Lösungen zurückgreifen. Gleichzeitig muß ein Handeln, das institutionalisierten Regeln folgt, nicht gerechtfertigt werden (Luckmann 1992: 157).

Für die funktionalistischen und teleologischen Konzeptionen ergeben sich jedoch eine Reihe von Problemen. In der Alltagswelt der Handelnden sind Zielsetzungen oftmals weder angebbar, noch werden sie reflektiert. Dies gilt etwa für ein Handeln, das aus Interesse oder Neugier erfolgt und in der Selbsterfahrung des Handelnden nicht in die Komponenten Zweck und Mittel getrennt ist (Joas 1996: 229). Gleiches gilt für alle Formen routinierten Handelns, dessen Zwecke oder Funktionen nicht mehr reflektiert werden. Wichtig sind Funktionen, Absichten und Ziele allerdings auch in diesen Zusammenhängen als Kategorien der Interpretation erfolgter Handlungen, die es erlauben – etwa im Rechtsbereich – Verantwortung für das Handeln und Schuld zuzuweisen.

Auch im Rahmen wissenschaftlicher Theoriebildung erweist sich eine dichotomische Trennung des Handelns in Zweck und Mittel, Problemlage und Lösung oder Funktion und Erfüllung als schwierig. So lassen sich alle Formen kreativen und innovativen Handelns vor dem Hintergrund von Zielen, Zwecken oder Funktionen nicht sinnvoll bestimmen. Das überraschende und unerwartete Moment, das dieses Handeln auszeichnet, entgeht einer funktionalistischen oder teleologischen Konzeption, denn es kann nicht sinnvoll angenommen werden, daß dieses vor dem Handeln als dessen Zielsetzung oder Bestimmung verfügbar ist. Waldenfels (1990: 90) weist darauf hin, daß die Möglichkeiten der Erklärung für ein kreatives und innovatives Handeln in einem funktionalistischen Rahmen begrenzt sind:

„Denkt man Handeln innerhalb einer teleologischen, einer normativen oder einer faktischen Ordnung, so erscheint es als Weg zum Ziel, als Fall einer praktischen Regel oder als *Wirkung* einer Ursache. Alles Handeln ist im Grunde *reproduktiv*, was die Ordnung selber angeht, *produktiv* ist es nur im Rahmen vorgegebener Ordnungen, indem es den Spielraum variabler Mittel, wechselnder Situationen und nicht vollständig kalkulierbarer Randbedingungen nutzt" (Waldenfels 1990: 90).

Ein weiterer Kritikpunkt betrifft die den funktionalistischen und teleologischen Konzepten inhärente Bestätigung der Geist-Körper-Dichotomie. Diese besteht in der Trennung einer vorgängigen Denkphase, in der die Zwecksetzungen erfolgen, von der Handlungs- bzw. der Ausführungsphase. Nach

Hans Joas liegt hier die Vorstellung vor, „daß zunächst im Erkennen der Welt Orientierungen gefunden werden, die dann im Handeln verfolgt werden", und er führt weiter aus: „Als wäre der natürliche Zustand des Menschen träge Ruhe, beginnt das Handeln nach dieser Denkweise erst, wenn zuvor in der erkannten Welt sinnvolle Zwecke festgelegt wurden und dann – in einem separaten Willensakt – der Entschluß zur Verfolgung eines solchen Ziels gefaßt wurde" (Joas 1996: 231). Mit dieser Vorstellung verbunden ist eine Nachordnung des körperlichen Handlungsvollzugs gegenüber der durch geistige Aktivität bestimmten Phase der Zwecksetzung. Zwar wird die Handlung durchaus als (auch) körperliche begriffen, ihre Einheit und ihr Wesen ergeben sich aber wesentlich daraus, das Mittel zum Zweck bzw. die Erfüllung einer Funktion zu sein.

Joas entwickelt eine alternative Handlungskonzeption, die von der Körperlichkeit als Grundbedingung des Menschen ausgeht. Diese Körperlichkeit eröffnet nach Joas Bewegungsmöglichkeiten, erzeugt Bewegungsgewohnheiten und -fertigkeiten. Intentionalität und Zwecksetzungen sind dieser Körperlichkeit nicht vorgeordnet, sondern ergeben sich in einem reflexiven Prozeß, der sich diesen Bewegungsmöglichkeiten und -fertigkeiten zuwendet und sie dann gezielt einsetzt:

„Die Setzung von Zwecken geschieht [...] nicht in einem geistigen Akt vor der eigentlichen Handlung, sondern ist Resultat einer Reflexion auf die in unserem Handeln *immer schon* wirksamen, vor-reflexiven Strebungen und Gerichtetheiten. In diesem Akt der Reflexion werden solche Strebungen thematisch, die normalerweise ohne unsere bewußte Aufmerksamkeit am Werke sind. Wo aber ist der Ort dieser Strebungen? Ihr Ort ist unser Körper: seine Fertigkeiten, seine Gewohnheiten und Weisen des Bezugs auf die Umwelt stellen den Hintergrund aller bewußten Zwecksetzungen, unserer Intentionalität, dar. Die Intentionalität selbst besteht dann in einer selbstreflexiven Steuerung unseres laufenden Verhaltens" (Joas 1996: 232).

Nimmt man die Körperlichkeit zum Ausgangspunkt, ist damit nicht nur ein anderes Movens für das Handeln gewonnen, sondern vor allem auch eine andere Gegebenheit der Wirklichkeit impliziert. Sie ist ganz wesentlich ein Handlungsraum, der durch vergangenes und gegenwärtiges Handeln sowie auch die Möglichkeiten zukünftigen Handelns bestimmt ist:

„Unsere Wahrnehmung erscheint so strukturiert von unseren Handlungsfähigkeiten und Handlungserfahrungen. Auch wenn wir keine aktuelle Handlungsabsicht verfolgen, ist uns die Welt nicht als äußerliches Gegenüber unserer Innerlichkeit gegeben, sondern im Modus möglicher Handlungen" (Joas 1996: 233).

3. Universale Aspekte kommunikativen Handelns

3.1. Kommunikation und Wirklichkeit

Wie für das Handeln im Allgemeinen, so gilt auch für das sprachlich-kommunikative Handeln im Besonderen, daß es wirklichkeitskonstitutive Leistung erbringt: Es kommt nicht nur in den Lebenswelten vor, sondern hat wesentlich Anteil an ihrer Konstitution. Dies gilt in mehrfacher Hinsicht. Einmal realisieren sich die Lebenswelten mit jedem Kommunikationsereignis. Zum anderen werden in der sprachlichen Kommunikation die sozialen Sinnschemata vermittelt und bestätigt, die in ihnen relevant sind. Vgl. hierzu aus sozialphänomenologischer Sicht Schütz & Luckmann (1984), die der Sprache eine hervorragende Rolle zuschreiben:

„Sprache ist das hauptsächliche Mittel des gesellschaftlichen Aufbaus jeder *menschlichen* Wirklichkeit; sie ist aber auch das Hauptmedium der *Vermittlung* einer bestimmten, also geschichtlichen, gesellschaftlich schon aufgebauten Wirklichkeit" (Schütz & Luckmann 1984: 209).

Der schriftliche und auch der mündliche Text stehen in einem anderen Verhältnis zu den Informationen bzw. Inhalten der Wirklichkeit als das Bild. Utz Maas spricht in einem schrifttheoretischen Zusammenhang von der „wortwörtlichen Fixierung" von Inhalten im schriftlichen Text. Dieser steht eine weniger eindeutige und weniger spezifische Fixierung im Falle bildlicher Mnemotechniken gegenüber. Die bildlich-graphische Darstellung eines Sachverhalts oder Ereigniszusammenhangs kann in ihrer Versprachlichung in eine „*Paraphraseklasse* von Texten" überführt werden, die den Sachverhalt oder Ereigniszusammenhang in seinen wesentlichen Momenten in einer äquivalenten, gleichwohl sprachlich-formal ganz unterschiedlichen Weise fassen (Maas 1992: 12 f.). In der Übertragung auf das kommunikative Geschehen, das sich dieser Medien bedient, bedeutet dies, daß mit der Bildlichkeit stets ein größerer Interpretationsspielraum verbunden ist als mit der Schriftlichkeit bzw. Sprachlichkeit. Damit ist das Medium 'Sprache' dort von Vorteil, wo

3. Handlungstheorie, Kommunikationstheorie, Lebenswelt

es um ein in semantisch-pragmatischer Hinsicht möglichst eindeutiges Verständnis geht.

Helmuth Feilke weist aus einer systemtheoretischen Sicht darauf hin, daß Sprache Themen in einer schematisierten Form bereithält, auf die dann im Kommunikationsgeschehen zurückgegriffen werden kann. Diese Schematismen sind das Ergebnis selektiver Prozesse, die die Komplexität der Sachverhalte und damit die Möglichkeiten ihrer Thematisierung reduzieren. Sie entwickeln oft eine binäre Struktur, die das Thema als Frage von „Bewertungs- und Entscheidungs-Alternativen" faßt. Feilke gibt hier das Beispiel des Themas 'Wiedervereinigung', das binäre Schematismen wie 'Anschluß oder Beitritt', 'Großmachtstreben oder Europäisierung' entwickelt hat (1994: 86).

Die Entwicklung von Schematismen ist begleitet von der Ausbildung spezifischer Formen von Kommunikation und Textualität. So bilden Gesellschaften spezifische Gattungen mündlicher und schriftlicher Textualität aus, die dazu dienen, die Gegenwart zu vermitteln und zu regulieren, aber auch die Vergangenheit zu rekonstruieren sowie die Zukunft zu projektieren. Nach Jörg R. Bergmann und Thomas Luckmann (1997) besitzt jede Gesellschaft einen „kommunikativen Haushalt", der Textgattungen bereithält, die ihre relevanten Kommunikationsprozesse strukturieren und ihr Gelingen absichern:

„The elementary function of communicative genres in social life is to organize, routinize, and render (more or less) obligatory the solutions to recurrent communicative problems [...]. The communicative problems for which such solutions tend to be socially established, are in the main those which have to do with the communicative aspects of those kinds of social interaction which are important for the maintenance of a given social order" (Bergmann & Luckmann 1995: 291).

Textgattungen besitzen dabei einen unterschiedlichen geschichtlichen Skopus. Sie strukturieren entweder die alltägliche und mit alltäglichen Inhalten befaßte Kommunikation, bestätigen damit alltägliches Wissen sowie alltägliche Praktiken und erzeugen auf diese Weise ein „kommunikatives Gedächtnis" (Assmann 1988: 10ff.), oder aber sie „rekonstruieren" die großen Daten der Geschichte und schaffen so ein „kulturelles Gedächtnis" (Assmann 1988: 12ff.).

In beiden Fällen kommen Zuschreibungen von Verbindlichkeitsgraden, von Wahrheits- und Geltungsansprüchen hinzu, die die Erwartung an die von den Textgattungen strukturierten Kommunikationsprozesse sowie die Orientierung an ihnen weitergehend regulieren (vgl. hierzu aus kognitionstheoretischer Sicht Schmidt & Weischenberg 1994: 219).

Schriftliche Gedächtnisarbeit entwickelt andere Textgattungen als die mündliche. Nicht nur ergeben sich mit dem schriftlichen oder mündlichen Medium spezifische äußere Gestaltqualitäten, denen spezifische Produktions- und Rezeptionspraktiken korrespondieren. Vor allem setzt die Entlastung von der Memorierungsarbeit im Falle der Schriftlichkeit kognitive Kapazitäten frei, die in die Arbeit am sprachlichen Text einfließen und zu einer Ausarbeitung der 'konzeptionellen' Seite von Sprache in Richtung auf 'distanzsprachliche' Strukturen führen kann (Koch & Oesterreicher 1994). Dies erhöht nicht nur die Komplexität der schriftlichen Textgattungen, sondern stößt Veränderungen des Sprachsystems an, die das kognitive Potential stärker ausschöpfen (Raible 1992: 191ff.; Raible 1994: 5f.; Raible 1996: 76).

Dennoch verfügen auch mündliche Gesellschaften über Textgattungen, mit denen es gelingt, umfassende Inhalte des kulturellen Gedächtnisses zu tradieren. In der Regel ist dies die Aufgabe einer Gruppe von Spezialisten, die dabei spezifisch mündliche Mnemotechniken wie etwa den Reim, formelhafte Wendungen, eine wiederholende Zurichtung des Inhalts nutzen (vgl. Assmann & Assmann 1983: 269ff.; Raible 1994: 2ff.).

Die Wirklichkeitskonstruktion im kommunikativen Geschehen erstreckt sich auch auf den Kontext. Auch der Kontext wird konstruiert, ist das Ergebnis einer im kommunikativen Geschehen erfolgenden „Kontextualisierung" (Auer 1986). Zwar erfolgt die Kommunikation unter bestimmten situativen Bedingungen, die vor und unabhängig von der sprachlichen Kommunikation bestehen, es sind aber jeweils nur bestimmte Momente der Situation, die in die Interpretation des Kommunikationsgeschehens eingehen und darin Bedeutung gewinnen. Welche dies sind und in welcher Weise sie relevant werden, wird in der sprachlichen Kommunikation bestimmt. Dies geschieht durch „indexikalische Aktivitäten" (Cicourel 1973/1975: 135) auf sprachlicher und nicht-sprachlicher Ebene, die es einmal an ein gemeinsames „hic et nunc" binden und einen „konkreten Horizont" erzeugen (Coenen 1985: 294), die zum anderen aber auch weitere Verweisungskontexte oder „Interpretationsfelder" (Prandi 1994: 21ff.) eröffnen, die den Hintergrund

und den Rahmen für das Verstehen der kommunizierten Sinnzusammenhänge liefern (vgl. Moeschler 1994).

Ähnlich wird in kognitionswissenschaftlichen Zusammenhängen der konstruktive Charakter des Kontextes hervorgehoben. Nach Hans Strohner kommt es im sprachlichen Kommunikationsprozeß zur Aktivierung von Situations-, Partner- und Selbstmodellen. Sie bilden konstitutive Elemente der „kognitiven Pragmatik", durch die die Kognition „Anschluß an das übergeordnete Sozialsystem" erhält (Strohner 1995: 118ff.). Partner- und Selbstmodell enthalten danach Vorstellungen über die eigene Rolle und die eigenen Fähigkeiten, sowie über Rolle und Fähigkeiten des Kommunikationspartners. Situationsmodelle enthalten Wissen über typische Kommunikationssituationen. Ihre Aktivierung reguliert das Kommunikationsgeschehen, indem sie etwa die inhaltliche Entfaltung begrenzt, bestimmte situative Elemente für die Kommunikation relevant macht und andere ausblendet. Erfolgreiche Kommunikation setzt nach Strohner eine gewisse Übereinstimmung der von den Kommunikationspartnern aktivierten kognitiven Modelle voraus (Strohner 1995: 121). Wenn sich die kognitiven Modelle in der Praxis als geeignet erweisen, stabilisiert und bestätigt dies gleichzeitig auch die sozialen Rollen und Beziehungsmuster, die in den Modellen repräsentiert sind.

3.2. Die Soziogenese von Sprache

Sprache ist aber nicht nur ein soziales Phänomen insofern, als sie Anteil hat an der Konstruktion sozialer Wirklichkeit. Die Sprache selbst gewinnt in der Lebenswelt ihre Form (vgl. Taylor 1988: 35–42). Sie ist ein soziogenetisches oder – in Aufnahme der beschriebenen Begrifflichkeit von Srubar (1991) – ein autogenetisches Phänomen. Geht es in einer soziologischen Perspektive vor allem um die wirklichkeitskonstitutiven Leistungen sprachlichen Handelns, so ist es dieser soziogenetische Aspekt, daß Sprache selbst ihre spezifische Form im kommunikativen Geschehen findet, der in sprachwissenschaftlicher Hinsicht im Vordergrund steht.

Die Genese, Weiterentwicklung und Ausdifferenzierung sowie auch der Tod von Sprachen sind das Ergebnis des komplexen sprachlich-interaktiven Geschehens in den Lebenswelten (→ Art. 118). Wie in § 2.1 beschrieben sind sie als soziogenetische Prozesse nicht auf individuelles Handeln zurückführbar, sondern ergeben sich aus der „Ko-Produktivität" des kommunikativen Geschehens. Bei Herbert H. Clark findet sich in diesem Zusammenhang der instruktive Vergleich mit einem Walzertanz:

„Waltzing is the joint action that emerges as Astaire and Rogers do their individual steps in coordination, as a couple. Doing things with language is likewise different from the sum of a speaker speaking and a listener listening. It is the joint action that emerges when speakers and listeners – or writers and readers – perform their individual actions in coordination, as ensembles" (Clark 1996: 3).

Clark weist ferner auf den weithin emergenten Charakter der Strukturen des kommunikativen Geschehens hin. Sie entwickeln sich, erscheinen mit der Kommunikation, ohne daß die Partizipanten dies so hätten vorher bestimmen können: „Much of the structure of conversations is really an emergent orderliness" (Clark 1996: 351). So läßt sich dann für das Ergebnis, die spezifische Struktur des Gesprächstextes, der entstanden ist, nicht mehr angeben, welche Anteile die Partizipanten an seinem Entstehen haben. Die einzelnen sprachlichen Beiträge können zwar den Beteiligten zugeordnet werden, ihre inhaltliche und formale Struktur ist aber als das Ergebnis der Einlassung auf das kommunikative Geschehen anzusehen.

In diesem Geschehen ist nicht nur der sprachliche Beitrag, sondern etwa auch das Schweigen relevant, das als signifikantes Schweigen Einfluß auf den Verlauf des kommunikativen Geschehens nimmt (vgl. Bachtin 1986: 68f., der auf den aktiven Charakter des Schweigens verweist; auch Meise 1996). Bernhard Waldenfels spricht in diesem Zusammenhang von der „'Verflechtung' des eigenen und fremden Verhaltens, die sich zu einer 'Zwischenleiblichkeit'" ausformt. Gleichzeitig weist er das kommunikationstheoretische Modell vom Sender und Empfänger als vereinfachend zurück. Seine Kritik richtet sich gegen die Vorstellung, „daß nämlich Eigenes und Fremdes säuberlich zu trennen sind und daß eine symmetrische Verteilung der eigenen und fremden Beiträge ein Höchstmaß gleichzeitiger Rationalität und Sozialität verkörpert" (Waldenfels 1990: 52f.).

Die Künstlichkeit von Plansprachen, die mit oder auch ohne Anlehnung an natürliche Sprachen zur leichteren Verständigung zwischen Sprechern verschiedener Sprachen konstruiert werden, besteht gerade auch darin, daß sie nicht in diesem Bereich der

„Zwischenleiblichkeit", den das interaktive Geschehen konstituiert, entstehen. Ihre Struktur ist das Ergebnis gezielter und zumeist individueller Planung. Allerdings treten auch diese in einen soziogenetischen Prozeß ein, sobald sie sprachpraktische Bedeutung erlangen und Kommunikationsprozesse in den Lebenswelten tragen. Allerdings haben sich, abgesehen vom ESPERANTO, keine der projektierten Plansprachen durchsetzen können. Sie sind ganz überwiegend individuelle, theoretische Entwürfe geblieben.

In der Perspektive auf die Soziogenese von Sprache ist auch die Annahme eines instrumentellen Charakters zu relativieren. Als soziogenetisches Phänomen verändert sich Sprache notwendig mit den Lebenswelten, ist sie immer in Bearbeitung und niemals fertiges Werkzeug oder Gebrauchs-Objekt. Die Vorstellung, daß je nach Bedarf und situativer Gegebenheit innerhalb definierter Ausdrucksmöglichkeiten ausgewählt wird, ist allenfalls in einem alltagsweltlichen Rahmen richtig, als wissenschaftliches Modell aber vereinfachend. Sprache ist, wie Taylor (1988: 38) hervorhebt, nicht „ein Vorrat fertiger Ausdrücke gleichsam, die man nur abzurufen braucht, um sie in der Rede zu verwenden".

Auch vor dem Hintergrund nativistischer Annahmen, wie sie die Generative Grammatik macht, kann die Relevanz dieser soziogenetischen Dimension der Sprache für die Erklärung sprachlicher Strukturen auf ihren verschiedenen Organisationsebenen nicht geleugnet werden. Schließlich bleibt gerade auch unter der Annahme einer angeborenen Universalgrammatik erklärungsbedürftig, wie es zu der enormen Diversifizierung von Sprachen kommt (vgl. Trabant 1998: 20).

Sowohl für die Ebene der textuellen und diskursiven Organisation von Sprache als auch für die grammatische Ebene liegen Ansätze vor, die die Bindung von Sprachstrukturen an das kommunikativ-pragmatische Geschehen ganz grundsätzlich berücksichtigen und damit in einem weiten Sinne der Vorstellung der Soziogenese von Sprache folgen. Die Anforderungen, Gegebenheiten, Prinzipien oder Strategien, die das sprachliche Kommunikationsgeschehen bestimmen, werden als strukturbildende und strukturgebende Momente verstanden. Dies gilt etwa für die ethnomethodologisch orientierten gesprächsanalytischen Untersuchungen (vgl. § 2.1), sowie für die verschiedenen Ansätze der funktionalen Pragmatik (vgl. etwa Ehlich 1991; die Beiträge in Brünner & Graefen 1994 und in Connolly 1997) und funktionalen Grammatik (vgl. etwa Dik 1989; Halliday 1994; Givón 1984; 1997; die Beiträge in Devriendt & al. 1996), die von der Funktionalität sprachlicher Strukturen für die Kommunikation und auch die Kognition ausgehen. Auch Harald Weinrich (1982; 1993) geht in seinen Grammatiken systematisch von der kommunikativen Situation aus und wählt deshalb die Bezeichnungen 'Textgrammatiken' oder „Dialoggrammatik[en]" (Weinrich 1993: 18). Sprecher und Hörer werden als die „primären Gesprächsrollen der Sprache" begriffen, die gemeinsam eine „kommunikative Dyade", die „Grundeinheit der linguistischen Beschreibung", bilden (Weinrich 1993: 18).

3.2.1. Körperlichkeit

Nach Joas (1996: 233) ist die Wirklichkeit uns „im Modus möglicher Handlungen" gegeben (vgl. § 2.2). Diese handlungstheoretische Annahme trifft sich mit kognitivistischen Konzeptionen innerhalb der Linguistik, die ebenfalls auf die zentrale Bedeutung der leiblich-körperlichen Aspekte der Sprache bzw. der sprachlichen Kommunikation verweisen. So nimmt Mark Johnson ähnlich wie Hans Joas an, daß die Wahrnehmung von Wirklichkeit und auch das Denken bestimmt sind von der körperlichen Erfahrung und der körperbasierten Orientierung und Aktivität in der Wirklichkeit. Johnson spricht hier vom „human embodiment":

„The centrality of human embodiment directly influences what and how things can be meaningful for us, the ways in which these meanings can be developed and articulated, the ways we are able to comprehend and reason about our experience, and the actions we take. Our reality is shaped by the patterns of our bodily movement, the contours of our spatial and temporal orientation, and the forms of our interaction with objects" (Johnson 1987: XIX).

Auch die Prototypentheorie nach George Lakoff geht davon aus, daß die Wirklichkeitswahrnehmung des Menschen entscheidend mitbestimmt wird durch seine Körperlichkeit. Neben dem Prinzip der Gestaltwahrnehmung sowie der Fähigkeit zur bildlichen Vorstellung werden die Bewegungsmöglichkeiten des menschlichen Körpers und das Bewegungsgefühl als strukturierende Momente der Erfahrung und kognitiven Repräsentation von Wirklichkeit angenommen. Als universale Prinzipien der menschlichen Wirklichkeitswahrnehmung erzeugen sie erste, vorkonzeptuelle Strukturen, die die Basis für die sprach- und kulturspezifischen Konzeptbildungen bilden. Ihre Fundierung in der universalen kognitiv-körperlichen Ausstattung des Menschen ist gleichzeitig der Grund dafür, daß sich die sprach- und kulturspezifischen Wirklichkeiten und Konzeptbildungen nicht völlig unterscheiden, sondern in einem gewissen Rahmen vergleichbar sind (Lakoff 1987: 302).

Eine solche Konzeption, die von einer körperbasierten Konzeptualisierung von Wirklichkeit ausgeht, führt zu einem veränderten Begriff von Semantik. Es kann nicht mehr davon ausgegangen werden, daß sich Bedeutung oder Sinn auf der Basis rein geistiger Aktivität ergibt. Vielmehr muß angenommen werden, daß Bewegungserfahrungen, -muster und visuelle Eindrücke in die Bedeutungs- und Sinnkonstitution mit eingehen (Lakoff 1987; Johnson 1987).

Auch im Rahmen der linguistischen Konzeptualisierung speziell sprachlicher Phänomene ist die Berücksichtigung ihrer Fundierung in der körperlich-sensuellen Erfahrung erforderlich. Dies gilt allerdings nur für Phänomene wie etwa den Schrifttext, die Silbe, den Satz, das Wort oder den Laut, die Wahrnehmungsqualitäten besitzen und nicht nur einen theoretischen Status haben. Für den Schrifttext etwa bedeutet dies, auch seine äußere Gestalt und die an seine materiale Realisierung gebundenen Wahrnehmungsqualitäten als bestimmende Momente des lebensweltlich-praktischen Umgangs mit ihm zu berücksichtigen. Der Schrifttext kann nicht nur über seine im engeren Sinne sprachliche Struktur definiert werden. Er ist, wie Kress & al. (1997: 257) hervorheben, ein „multi-modal[es]" Phänomen. Entsprechendes gilt auch für den mündlichen Gesprächstext. Hier sind es ganz anders rhythmisch-intonatorische Eigenschaften, die im dynamischen Zusammenspiel von Sprechgeschwindigkeit, Lautstärke, Tonhöhe seine Wahrnehmungsqualitäten ausmachen.

Die Annahme eines konstruktiven, von der Körperlichkeit des Menschen ausgehenden Charakters der Wirklichkeit hat auch die Konsequenz, daß die sprachliche Grundfunktion der Deixis, wie sie Karl Bühler (1934/1982) systematisch entwickelt hat, weder an einen geometrischen Raumbegriff noch an einen physikalischen Zeitbegriff gekoppelt werden kann. Es ist ein Raum-Zeit-Begriff anzusetzen, der auf der körperlich-sensuellen Erfahrung von Zeit und Raum beruht. Dies macht anthropozentrische und anthropomorphe Konzeptionen des Raum- und Zeitbegriffs für die Sprachwissenschaft relevant, wie sie vor allem in der Phänomenologie entwickelt worden sind (Husserl 1940; Merleau-Ponty 1966: 239ff.; Waldenfels 1999: 200ff.).

Harald Weinrich weist darauf hin, daß das Konzept der Deixis von einem dyadischen, nicht, wie noch bei Bühler selbst, von einem monadischen Raum- und Zeitbegriff ausgehen muß (Weinrich 1988: 82). Auf die Rolle eines dyadisch konstituierten Raumes verweist ebenfalls Charles Taylor in seiner Auseinandersetzung mit Habermas (Taylor 1988: 40f.). Auch hat nach Weinrich das Zeigen seinen Ursprung nicht in einer Zeigegeste, die in der dyadischen Situation sogar redundant oder auch unpassend ist, sondern innerhalb des dyadischen Geschehens in der „Zuwendung und Blickstellung zweier Leiber" (1988: 83). Sie eröffnet einen Raum, der den Orientierungsrahmen für den Verweis darstellt. Präpositionen wie 'zwischen' oder 'gegen' erhalten ihre Bedeutungen vor dem Hintergrund dieses dyadisch konstituierten Raumes:

„Daraus folgt, daß nicht nur die eine oder andere Zeigegeste, sondern das gesamte nonverbale Verhalten in der kommunikativen Dyade, das sich aus der Zuwendung und Blickstellung zweier Leiber ergibt, in der Sprache strukturell präsent ist. Das kann man am besten an den Bedeutungen der Präpositionen zeigen, die diese Strukturen abbilden" (Weinrich 1988: 83).

Die Richtigkeit der Annahme einer anthropozentrischen und anthropomorphen Raumkonzeption zeigt sich in Grammatikalisierungsprozessen. Der Körper bzw. die Körperteile ("body parts") sind es hier, die neben „environmental landmarks" als „source concepts" dienen (Heine 1995: 121; zur Kritik an der Universalität anthropozentrischer und anthropomorpher Konzeptionen vgl. Levinson 1996).

3.2.2. Typik

Beide Dimensionen der Sozialbindung von Sprache, ihre wirklichkeitskonstitutive Leistung sowie ihre Soziogenese, basieren auf Typisierungsprozessen. Es konstituieren sich Inhalte, Objekte, Phänomene mit typischen Strukturen, die dann wiederum typische oder charakteristische Momente der jeweiligen Lebenswelten sind. Gleichzeitig ist auch die Herausbildung von Sprache ein Prozeß, bei dem typische, eben die für die jeweilige Sprache oder die Sprachvarietät charakteristischen Mikro- und Makrostrukturen entstehen. Dies sind Universalien der Sozialbindung von Sprache, und ihre Gültigkeit ist unabhängig davon, welche kognitiven Prozesse und Instanzen als Voraussetzungen und Randbedingungen anzunehmen sind. Sie gelten auch dann, wenn man nativistischen Annahmen folgt.

Sprachliche Typik ist der Hintergrund und die Voraussetzung für das Erkennen von sprachlichen Veränderungen, Abweichungen und Sonderentwicklungen. Nur vor dem Hintergrund typischer, d.h. stabiler, erwartbarer Strukturen werden diese sichtbar. Dies gilt für die gezielte Abweichung, wie sie sowohl im alltäglichen als auch im literarischen Spiel mit Sprache vorkommt, als auch für den versehentlichen, unkontrollierten Versprecher. Ebenfalls setzen die Prozesse des Sprachwandels, die sich als soziogenetische der Kontrolle des Individuums entziehen, typische sprachliche Strukturen voraus. Gleichzeitig erzeugen sie neue, relativ stabile sprachliche Strukturen.

Niklas Luhmann verweist darauf, daß Typik grundsätzlich durch zwei Momente bestimmt ist, die er als „Kondensation" und als „Konfirmierung" (Luhmann 1992: 108) bezeichnet. Die Kondensation entspricht der Auszeichnung oder dem Erkennen bestimmter, für die Typik charakteristischer Strukturen in einem komplexen Zusammenhang; sie ist die „Reduktion auf Identisches, [...] wenn man aus der Fülle des gleichzeitig Aktuellen etwas Bestimmtes zur wiederholten Bezeichnung herauszieht" (Luhmann 1992: 108). Die „Konfirmierung" bezieht sich demgegenüber auf das generalisierende Moment von Typik. Sie muß so unspezifisch sein, daß sie die Anpassung an die Andersartigkeit der jeweiligen Situation erlaubt: „Genau diese Reduktion auf Identisches hat jedoch die andere Seite: daß sie in einer anderen Situation erfolgen und deren Andersheit einarbeiten muß" (Luhmann 1992: 108). Für die Sprache bzw. die Einzelsprachen als typische Phänomene bedeutet dies, daß ihre Strukturen so generell bzw. unspezifisch sein müssen, daß sie in unterschiedlichen kommunikativen Situationen einsetzbar sind. Dies erzeugt eine Spannung zwischen der Einzigartigkeit des konkreten Kommunikationsereignisses und der notwendigen Unspezifik der Sprache. Sprachliche Kommunikation erbringt die Leistung, ein einzigartiges Ereignis mit allgemeinen, d.h. typischen Mitteln zu realisieren.

Spezialisierungen entstehen vor dem Hintergrund dieser Überlegungen als Ergebnisse von Prozessen, die die Spezifik des Kommunikationsereignisses und die Typik bzw. Allgemeinheit der sprachlichen Struktur einander annähern. Folgt man hier der als universal angenommenen Differenz zwischen dem „Inhaltsaspekt" und dem „Beziehungsaspekt" (Watzlawick & al. 1967/1990: 53ff.) oder der ähnlichen Unterscheidung von „Sach- und Sozialdimension" von Kommunikation (Luhmann 1987: 119), so lassen sich hier verschiedene Typen von Spezialisierungen erkennen.

– Fach- oder berufssprachliche Spezialisierungen zielen darauf, die inhaltlich-informative Seite der Kommunikation durch eine spezifische Terminologie zu optimieren; auch entwickeln sie spezifische Text- oder Diskurstypen, die die Kommunikation auf die berufs- und fachspezifisch relevanten Aspekte hin ausrichten (zum Verhältnis von Fachsprachlichkeit und Textualität vgl. Koch 1988).
– Anders dienen Spezialisierungen, wie sie in Form von Familiolekten, Gruppensprachen faßbar sind, vor allem der Stabilisierung des Beziehungsaspekts.

Neben solchen Spezialisierungen sind aber auch Globalisierungsprozesse beobachtbar, in denen eine Sprache ihren Geltungsraum ausdehnt und die Allgemeinheit der Sprache und die Besonderheit des konkreten Kommunikationsgeschehens weiter auseinander treten. Diese Globalsprachen, hier etwa das ENGLISCHE im Bereich der Internet-Kommunikation, ermöglichen einen weltumspannenden inhaltlich-informativen Austausch, der allerdings stets mit Schwierigkeiten auf der Beziehungsebene zu tun hat. Es divergieren die kulturspezifischen Situations- und Partnermodelle (vgl. § 3.1); hier sind Mißverständnisse möglich, die im kommunikativen Geschehen zu bearbeiten sind.

3.2.3. Funktionalität

Ein zentraler Begriff innerhalb der kommunikativ-pragmatisch orientierten Sprachwissenschaft ist die Funktion. Verschiedene funktionale Relationen lassen sich unterscheiden.

Hier besteht zum einen eine funktionale Beziehung zwischen der Kommunikation und der Sprache. Kommunikation kann als die universale Funktion von Sprache angesehen werden (Nuyts 1993: 205). Hieraus ergeben sich spezifische strukturelle Anforderungen an die Sprache, wie sie die funktionalistischen Ansätze im Bereich von Grammatik und Pragmatik zugrunde legen. So kann etwa in der Perspektive kommunikativer Funktionalität angenommen werden, daß die Grammatik so organisiert ist, daß sie die Bedeutungsentnahme erleichtert und so den Verstehensprozeß unterstützt. Dies ist dann gegeben, wenn sowohl strukturelle Einfachheit als auch Informativität vorliegen (vgl. Hopper & Traugott 1993: 64; Comrie 1981/1995: 26).

Aus der Konkurrenz von Einfachheit und Informativität ergeben sich Spannungen, deren Lösung zu Sprachwandel- und Grammatikalisierungsprozessen führen kann. Auch die in einem natürlichkeitstheoretischen Rahmen angenommenen Prinzipien der Ikonizität, Uniformität und Transparenz folgen dieser funktionalen Sicht auf Grammatik (vgl. Mayerthaler 1981; Wurzel 1984; → Art. 30; 31; 32). Die sprachlichen Formen sind natürlicherweise so beschaffen, daß sie die Informationsentnahme optimal unterstützen. Vor dem Hintergrund einer soziogenetischen Auffassung sprachlicher Entwicklungsprozesse ist es auch in diesem Zusammenhang möglich, die sich in der Konkurrenz verschiedener funktionaler Prinzipien einstellende Struktur als emergentes Phänomen zu fassen, das weder intentional, noch kontrolliert entsteht.

Kommunikation ist aber ihrerseits nicht Selbstzweck, sondern steht in einem funktionalen Verhältnis zur sozialen Wirklichkeit. Dies eröffnet eine zweite funktionale Dimension. Kommunikation dient der Konstitution, der Stabilisierung, der Thematisierung und der Reflexion sozialer Wirklichkeit. In dieser funktionalen Dimension eröffnen sich pragmatische Bedeutungsebenen, die über die semantische Informativität im engeren Sinne hinausgehen. Sprache vermittelt nicht nur Informationen, sondern trägt soziale Differenzierungen und transportiert soziale Bedeutungen, die an der Form von Sprache festgemacht sind.

Gruppen- und Regionalsprachen etwa ergeben sich nicht allein vor dem Hintergrund spezifischer informationeller oder inhaltlicher Kommunikationsbedürfnisse und Prozesse, sondern auch aus dem Interesse heraus, Identität durch spezifische sprachliche Formen zum Ausdruck zu bringen. Die Genese der Formen, die in diesem Sinne eine expressive und identitätsstiftende Funktion erfüllen, folgt nicht notwendig den Prinzipien von Einfachheit und Ökonomie; die von William Labov (1972/1980) als Ergebnis einer Untersuchung von 1962 beschriebene „soziale Stratifikation des /r/ in New Yorker Kaufhäusern" ist hierfür ein Beispiel. Sie ist sogar ganz im Gegenteil mit Anstrengung da verbunden, wo es darum geht, neue Formen in einem Bereich zu etablieren, der schon von spezifischen Formen besetzt ist.

Mithin gilt für beide Dimensionen sprachlicher bzw. kommunikativer Funktionalität, worauf Jan Nuyts hinweist, nämlich daß sich Formen der Sprache und der Kommunikation niemals allein aus Funktionen ableiten lassen: „One cannot infer form from function, in language or in any other system" (Nuyts 1995: 299). Eine solche Abhängigkeit der Form von der Funktion besteht nur in den Fällen, in denen genau eine Form funktional ist. Sie liegt nur dort vor, wie Waldenfels in einer Kritik an funktionalistischen Handlungskonzepten feststellt, wo „der Handelnde vor Probleme gestellt ist, die weder einen Formulierungs- noch einen Erwiderungsspielraum zulassen, wo es also eine einzig richtige oder zumindest eine beste Lösung gibt" (Waldenfels 1990: 91f.).

Dieser Fall ist aber gerade im Bereich des Sprachlichen nicht gegeben. Hier gibt es auf allen Ebenen der sprachlichen Organisation nicht nur eine einzige funktionale Lösung. Dies dokumentiert allein die Vielfalt grammatischer, sowie textueller und diskursiver Strukturen, die sich in den Sprachen zeigen.

Was die in einem handlungs- und kommunikationstheoretischen Zusammenhang vor allem interessierende Dimension der wirklichkeitskonstitutiven Funktion von Kommunikation anbetrifft, so wird von einer Reihe von kommunikativen Grundfunktionen ausgegangen, die weitgehend in allen Gesellschaften auftreten.

Dies gilt etwa für die Zeichentheorie von Charles Morris, die in der Frühphase der linguistischen Pragmatik eine zentrale Rolle spielt und die auch den Terminus 'Pragmatik' (1938/1983) einführt (Posner 1997). Morris entwickelt das Modell einer dreidimensionalen Semiotik, bei der die Pragmatik den Teilaspekt der Semiotik bildet, in dem es um das Verhältnis des „Sprachenbenutzers" zum Zeichen geht. In dieser Bestimmung soll sie als Ergänzung zu dem von Alfred Tarski und Rudolf Carnap entwickelten Konzept einer formalen Semantik und Syntax dienen. Es werden vier „Zeichenverwendungen" unterschieden, und zwar die 'informative', 'valuative', 'inzitive' und die 'systemische'. Sie

„stellen die Absichten dar, zu denen ein Individuum Zeichen als Mittelobjekte zur Leitung des eigenen oder fremden Verhaltens herstellt" (Morris 1946/1981: 183).

Auch für die von John L. Austin (1962) und John R. Searle (1969) entwickelte Sprechakttheorie, die ebenfalls großen Einfluß auf die Entwicklung sprachpragmatischer Forschungen genommen hat, ist die Annahme von Grundfunktionen bestimmend. Sie bilden die Basis ihrer Sprechaktklassifikationen. Klassifikationskriterium ist die Illokution des Sprechakts, die angibt, wie der propositionale Gehalt des Sprechakts aufzufassen ist. Searle nimmt fünf zentrale Illokutionen an, die ihn zur Unterscheidung von fünf Typen von Sprechakten veranlassen. Dies sind *Repräsentativa*, die der Sachverhaltsdarstellung dienen, *Direktiva*, die den Hörer zu einer Handlung bewegen wollen, *Kommissiva*, mit denen sich der Sprecher zu etwas verpflichtet, *Expressiva*, die emotionale Zustände zum Ausdruck bringen, sowie *Deklarativa* (Searle 1976).

Diese funktionalistischen Sprechaktklassifikationen haben im Bereich der Textlinguistik und hier vor allem in der Texttypologie zentrale Bedeutung gewonnen. Texte werden als komplexe Sprechakte oder Sprechhandlungen begriffen, die ihre Einheit wesentlich dadurch gewinnen, daß sie eine spezifische Illokution oder Funktion besitzen (Große 1976; Brinker 1992; Rolf 1993; Franke 1987; Motsch 1996; Brandt & Rosengren 1992; Roulet 1998; Kotschi 1996; Heinemann & Viehweger 1991).

In Orientierung an der Sprechaktklassifikation wird von spezifischen textuellen Grundfunktionen ausgegangen, die zur Entwicklung entsprechender Textsorten oder Texttypen führen. Wolfgang Heinemann und Dieter Viehweger etwa nehmen „vier Primärfunktionen des Kommunizierens" (1991: 149) an, die zu einer ersten Differenzierung von Texten in vier Gruppen führen; dies sind das „Sich Ausdrücken", das 'Kontaktieren', das 'Informieren' sowie das 'Steuern'. Ähnlich nimmt auch Eckard Rolf an, daß „wir auch mit Texten nur eine begrenzte Anzahl grundlegender Dinge tun bzw. zu erreichen versuchen. Und es zeigt sich darüber hinaus, daß wir mit den Gebrauchstextsorten im Grunde genommen genau dieselben Zwecke verfolgen wie mit den Sprechakten" (Rolf 1993: 166).

Im Anschluß an das in § 2.2 skizzierte handlungs- und lebenswelttheoretische Modell einer sich im Interaktionsgeschehen herausbildenden Funktionalität ergeben sich wichtige Konsequenzen für die Konzeption sprachlicher, kommunikativer oder textueller Funktionalität. Wird die Genese von Wirklichkeit radikal in das interaktive Geschehen verlegt, so muß auch für die Funktionen und Zwecksetzungen von Sprache angenommen werden, daß sich ihre Genese zusammen mit den spezifischen sprachlichen bzw. textuellen Formen im kommunikativen Geschehen vollzieht. Sie können nicht den Formen vorgeordnet werden. Textfunktionen etwa setzen in einer solchen Perspektive stets schon Kommunikation und die Verfügbarkeit von symbolischen Formen, die diese kommunikativen Prozesse ermöglichen, voraus (Tophinke 1999; in allgemeiner Perspektive auch Feilke 1994: 74ff.).

Auch ist unter der Annahme der Soziogenese von Sprache ein dynamisches und zugleich interaktives Konzept von Funktion notwendig. Dieses muß einerseits den Prozeßcharakter der Herstellung und Veränderung funktionaler Bestimmungen berücksichtigen und zugleich erfassen, daß dieser Prozeß gemeinsam betrieben wird, die Herstellung einer funktionalen Bestimmung eine gemeinsame Leistung ist.

Die Relevanz eines solchen Konzepts wird augenfällig mit Blick auf den Dialog. Dieser ist, sofern es sich um einen echten Dialog handelt, bei dem die Gesprächspartner einen Handlungsspielraum besitzen, in seiner Entwicklung offen. Dies betrifft den Inhalt des Dialogs, aber auch seinen funktionalen Charakter. Die Offenheit ergibt sich daraus, daß das sprachliche Verhalten der Beteiligten an einem Dialog nicht völlig vorhersehbar ist. Es handelt sich um einen Fall von 'Koproduktion'. Der entstehende Text ist ein gemeinsames Produkt, das sich in der wechselseitigen Einlassung auf den anderen sowie in Anknüpfung an dessen Beiträge ergibt und das sich der Kontrolle des Einzelnen entzieht (vgl. § 2.1).

Der Grad der Offenheit ist natürlich je nach Art des dialogischen Geschehens und der Größe des Handlungsspielraums, den die Gesprächsteilnehmer darin haben, verschieden. Sie kann aber nicht völlig verschwinden, ohne daß dies auch den dialogischen Charakter, der Freiheitsgrade notwendig voraussetzt, zerstört. Diese Offenheit des kommunikativen Geschehens, die es auch gestattet, die funktionale Bestimmung des Dialogs zu verändern, kommt in Redewendungen wie „Ein Wort gibt das andere" deutlich zum Ausdruck. Dies gilt auch dann, wenn die Kommunikation durch eine verbindliche Texttypik und eine daran gebundene Funktion vorbestimmt ist. Auch hier ist das Situations- oder Kommunikationsmodell, das die Texttypik relevant und verbindlich macht, von den Beteiligten in der Kommunikation zu bestätigen und anzuerkennen.

Diese Annahmen stehen nicht im Widerspruch zu der alltagspraktischen Vorstellung, daß Sprechen funktional und intentional ist. Für die an der Situation Beteiligten ist es in der Planung und in der Rekonstruktion der kommunikativen Situation wichtig, anzunehmen, daß sie eine spezifische Absicht verfolgen bzw. verfolgt haben. Nach Michele Prandi handelt es sich dabei um ein Alltagsmodell der Kommunikation, das als ein wesentliches Moment der „natürlichen Einstellung" von Kommunikanten eine instrumentalistisch-intentionalistische Perspektive hat:

„For the partners of a communicative event, language is a tool which makes it possible to communicate. Now, we can't at the same time perform an action and cast a problematic eye on the tools we cannot dispense with. It is essential to the nature of an instrument to be seen by its user as something 'at hand' [...] To put it in familiar terms, we could say that natural attitude encapsulates a functional view of language while keeping in the shade its specific structural properties [...]" (Prandi 1994: 18f.).

Die Sprechakttheorie ist wegen ihrer vereinfachenden Sicht in diesem Punkt kritisiert worden (z.B. Wunderlich 1972; Maas & Wunderlich 1972; Clark & Carlson 1990). Die Illokution wird jeweils dem einzelnen Sprechakt bzw. dessen Akteur zugeschrieben und ihr Entstehen damit in eine dem Sprechakt vorausgehende individuelle Planungsphase verlegt. Die Ko-Produktivität des kommunikativen Geschehens, die sich auch auf die Illokution oder Funktion bezieht, kann so nicht erfaßt werden. Dem Kommunikationspartner kommt als Adressat des Sprechaktes zwar eine wichtige Funktion zu, der Sprechakt selbst bleibt aber ein individueller Akt.

„Der wichtigste Punkt dabei ist, daß eine sprachliche Äußerung als interpersonaler Sprechakt, oder – anders formuliert – als ein Handlungszug im Rahmen eines gegebenen Kontextes zu verstehen ist. Mit dieser Auffassung ist gleichzeitig eine Kritik an jener anderen Auffassung verbunden, die das Herstellen faktischer Beziehungen praktisch leugnet: Diese andere Auffassung reduziert den Kommunikationsakt nämlich daraufhin, daß der Sprecher gewisse inhaltliche Intentionen hat, daß er physikalische Signale an den Hörer übermittelt, und daß dieser die Intentionen dann rekonstruiert" (Maas & Wunderlich 1972: 117).

Nach Konrad Ehlich (1993a: 596) hat sich im Zusammenhang dieser Kritik eine terminologische Differenzierung ergeben. Die Sprechhandlung, verstanden als „selbständige Handlungseinheit" (1993a: 596), die sich im interaktiven Geschehen formiert, wird von ihren bestimmenden Momenten, den Sprechakten, unterschieden. Damit ergibt sich eine Begriffsbestimmung für die Sprechhandlung, die sich ähnlich schon bei Bühler (1934/1982: 48ff.) findet.

3.2.4. Form

Die Form des Handelns bzw. der Sprache ist für die wirklichkeitskonstitutive Leistung von Sprache von zentraler Bedeutung. Sprache tritt in den Lebenswelten zunächst einmal als Form in Erscheinung und diese sprachliche Form ist zentraler Anhaltspunkt für die Interpretations- und Verstehensprozesse im kommunikativen Geschehen.

Niklas Luhmann weist aus einer systemtheoretischen Perspektive darauf hin, daß Sprache immer zugleich „Medium" und „Form" ist. Sie ist ein Medium insofern, als sich in ihr Gesellschaft konstituiert; sie ist Form insofern, als sie immer nur als Form erscheint, und die Formungen und Differenzen zwischen den Formungen für die Differenzierung von Informationen und Bedeutungen genutzt werden. Schriftlichkeit und Mündlichkeit sind in dieser Perspektive nicht nur Medium der Sprache, sondern bereits allgemeine Ebenen der Formung:

„Für Sprache kann nach all dem gut verdeutlicht werden, daß sie als Form und als Medium zugleich fungiert. [...] Ins Bewußtsein dringt die Sprache als Formung des Wahrnehmungsmediums ein – zunächst akustisch, seit Erfindung der Schrift auch optisch" (Luhmann 1995: 208).

Sprachliche Formen vermitteln semantische, aber auch pragmatische Bedeutungen. Sie zeigen sozio-kulturelle Zugehörigkeiten und Abgrenzungen an und verorten den Text innerhalb eines lebensweltlichen Bereichs. Diese Annahme ist grundlegend für kulturanalytische Arbeiten, die Handlungs- und Sprachformen als „kulturelle Formen" fassen. Kultur entspricht danach der Fülle an Formen insgesamt, die sich in einer Praxis herstellen und darin bedeutsam sind; sie ist die „Form der Praxis" (Maas 1985: 97). Für die Formen wird ein enger Bezug zu den Lebensverhältnissen angenommen. Sie sind das „Material, in dem das Leben gelebt wird" (Maas 1985: 99), und gleichzeitig von diesen Lebensverhältnissen strukturiert.

Diese kulturelle Signifikanz der Form gilt natürlich ganz grundsätzlich für die Schriftlichkeit und die Mündlichkeit. Allerdings macht Schriftlichkeit, sofern der Schrifttext nicht zerstört wird, die Form dauerhaft verfügbar und eröffnet so besondere Stilisierungs- und Überarbeitungsmöglichkeiten. Carl Bereiter nimmt im Rahmen des Schrifterwerbs eine Stufe des „unified writing" an, auf der diese Stilisierungsmöglichkeiten exploriert werden und der Text als ein „thing to be fashioned" entdeckt wird (Bereiter 1980: 87).

Sprachliche Kommunikation ist natürlich niemals rein sprachlich, sondern allenfalls „dominantly verbal" (Petőfi 1990: 208). Sie ist stets begleitet von mimischen und gestischen „Äußerungen", die als nicht-sprachliche Formen am Kommunikationsgeschehen wesentlichen Anteil haben (Clark 1996: 392). Die Linguistik hat die Verflechtung des mündlichen Textes mit den begleitenden nicht-sprachlichen gestischen oder mimischen „Äußerungen" bislang eher vernachlässigt und sich auf den sprachlichen Text konzentriert. Dabei spielen die nicht-sprachlichen Äußerungen für die Verstehensprozesse auf semantischer und auch pragmatischer Ebene eine wichtige Rolle. Sie können die Bedeutung der sprachlichen Äußerung mit ihrem je spezifischen Repertoire an gestischen und mimischen Ausdrucksformen unterstützen, oder auch eine eigene, gegenläufige Bedeutungsebene eröffnen, wie es etwa beim sogenannten „double bind" (Watzlawick & al. 1967/1990: 195ff.) der Fall ist.

Einen zentralen Stellenwert haben diese Überlegungen in phänomenologischen Zusammenhängen, in denen das Kommunikationsgeschehen insgesamt betrachtet und es nicht auf Sprachlichkeit reduziert wird. Hier wird etwa auch darauf hingewiesen, daß nicht-sprachliches und sprachliches Handeln einander ähnlich sind. Nach Waldenfels (1998: 86ff.) hat das Handeln wie die Sprache eine dialogische Qualität. Auch hat die Form des Handelns wie die der Sprache symbolischen Charakter; Handlungsformen sind wie die Sprachformen „kulturelle Formen".

In universalistischer Perspektive interessieren die natürlichen Begrenzungen, die für die Formdimension von Sprache gelten. In Orientierung an den Theorien über die körperlich-sensuelle Aneignung von Wirklichkeit (vgl. § 3.2.1) ergeben sich diese mit den Wahrnehmungs- und Differenzierungsmöglichkeiten des menschlichen Sinnesapparates. Im Falle der Mündlichkeit sind dies einmal die artikulatorischen Differenzierungsmöglichkeiten, aber auch die auditiven sowie kinästhetisch-propriozeptiven Diskriminierungsmöglichkeiten. Nur was artikulierbar, hörbar und spürbar ist und sich in diesen Dimensionen von anderem unterscheiden läßt, kann für die Sprache relevant werden (vgl. auch Trabant 1998: 185). Im Falle der Schriftlichkeit wirken sich vor allem die visuellen, aber auch die taktilen Diskriminierungsmöglichkeiten aus. Die Schriftzeichen müssen sich vom Trägermaterial abheben und so beschaffen sein, daß sie identifizierbar und unterscheidbar sind.

Die körperlich-sensuelle Ausstattung des Menschen definiert in diesem Sinne einen Spielraum, innerhalb dessen sich Sprache in ihrer Form entwickeln kann. Die Engführung auf spezifische Formen wird dann allerdings nicht mehr allein durch die sich aus dieser Ausstattung ergebende Funktionalität bestimmt. Hier spielen kulturelle Bewertungen und kulturelle Bedeutungen eine Rolle, die an spezifische Formen gekoppelt sind. Auch kann es zu einer kreativen Auslotung des Spielraums kommen. Im Bereich der Schriftlichkeit etwa folgt die Gestaltung der Schriften nicht immer dem Prinzip der Lesbarkeit. Es können sich ganz im Gegenteil sogar beinahe unleserliche Formen entwickeln. So wird etwa die Textura im 14. Jahrhundert in Deutschland mit starken Verzierungen versehen, die die Textlektüre erheblich erschweren (vgl. Bischoff 1986: 179).

Die Rede vom Sprachgebrauch, wie sie sich in pragmatischen Zusammenhängen oft findet, suggeriert, daß die formale Umsetzung einer kommunikativen Absicht und die formale Umsetzung der Information weitgehend unproblematisch ist. Annahme ist die Kontrollierbarkeit der sprachlichen Form im kommunikativen Geschehen, die allenfalls durch psychische Verfaßtheiten, die die Konzentration auf die Sprache behindern oder erschweren, gestört sein kann.

Aus phänomenologischer Sicht ist diese Sicht problematisch. So verweist Herman Parret auf das mit der Kommunikation stets gegebene Risiko des Mißlingens: „communication is always a risky task" (Parret 1994: VII). Maurice Merleau-Ponty führt aus, daß uns zwar Wörter mit einer lexikalischen Bedeutung zur Verfügung stehen, die Intention aber mit ihrer formalen Umsetzung in die Sprache stets eine Veränderung erfährt. Sie wird „selbst erst letztlich fixiert":

„So ist die Sprache denn die paradoxe Leistung, in der wir mit Worten, deren Sinn gegeben ist, und mit verfügbaren Bedeutungen eine Intention zu erfüllen suchen, die grundsätzlich den Sinn der Worte, in die sie sich überträgt, überschreitet und modifiziert und selbst erst letztlich fixiert" (Merleau-Ponty 1966: 443).

Dies führt zu einer „Nicht-Koinzidenz von Gemeintem, Gelebtem und Gesagtem" (Waldenfels 1980: 158), die sich dynamisierend auf die Sprache auswirkt: „Die Nicht-Koinzidenz von Gemeintem, Gelebtem und Gesagtem, die Inadäquation von Ausgedrücktem und Ausdruck hält die Sprache in Bewegung" (Waldenfels 1980: 158).

Diese Dynamisierung wirkt in zweifacher Hinsicht. Die Erfahrung der Nicht-Stimmigkeit führt einmal zu Anschlußäußerungen, die um eine weitere Annäherung an das Gemeinte bemüht sind, hält also das kommunikative Geschehen in Gang. Sie führt darüber hinaus zur Ausbildung neuer sprachlicher, etwa lexikalischer Formen, die eine bessere sprachliche Umsetzung des Gemeinten ermöglichen und diese dauerhaft für die Kommunikation bereithalten.

4. Zitierte Literatur

Assmann, Aleida & Assmann, Jan. 1983. „Schrift und Gedächtnis". In: Assmann, Aleida & Assmann, Jan & Hardmeier, Christof (eds.). *Schrift und Gedächtnis. Beiträge zur Archäologie literarischer Kommunikation.* München: Fink, 265–84.

Assmann, Jan. 1988. „Kollektives Gedächtnis und kulturelle Identität". In: Assmann, Jan & Hölscher, Tonio (eds.). *Kultur und Gedächtnis.* Frankfurt/M.: Suhrkamp, 9–19.

Auer, Peter. 1986. „Kontextualisierung". *Studium Linguistik* 19: 22–48.

Austin, John Langshaw. 1962. *How to do things with words.* Oxford: Clarendon.

Bachtin, Michail M. 1986. „The problem of speech genres". In: Emerson, Caryl (ed.). *Michael Bachtin. Speech genres and other late essays.* Austin: University of Texas Press, 60–102.

Berger, Peter L. & Luckmann, Thomas. [1]1966/1980. *Die gesellschaftliche Konstruktion der Wirklichkeit. Eine Theorie der Wissenssoziologie.* Frankfurt/M.: Fischer.

Bergmann, Jörg R. & Luckmann, Thomas. 1995. „Reconstructive genres of everyday communication". In: Quasthoff, Uta (ed.). *Aspects of oral communication.* Berlin: de Gruyter, 289–304.

Bereiter, Carl. 1980. „Development in writing". In: Gregg, Lee W. & Steinberg, Erwin R. (eds.). *Cognitive processes in writing.* Hillsdale/NJ, 73–93.

Bischoff, Bernhard. 1986. *Paläographie des römischen Altertums und des abendländischen Mittelalters.* Berlin: Erich Schmidt.

Blumer, Herbert. [1]1973/1995. „Der methodologische Standpunkt des Symbolischen Interaktionismus". In: Burkart, Roland & Hömberg, Walter. *Kommunikationstheorien.* Wien: Braunmüller, 23–39.

Brandt, Margareta & Rosengren, Inger. 1992. „Zur Illokutionsstruktur von Texten". *Zeitschrift für Literaturwissenschaft und Linguistik* 86: 9–51.

Brinker, Klaus. 1992. *Linguistische Textanalyse. Eine Einführung in Grundbegriffe und Methoden.* Berlin: Schmidt.

Brünner, Gisela & Graefen, Gabriele (eds.). 1994. *Texte und Diskurse: Methoden und Forschungsergebnisse der funktionalen Pragmatik.* Opladen: Westdeutscher Verlag.

Bühler, Karl. [1]1934/1982. *Sprachtheorie.* Stuttgart: G. Fischer.

Chomsky, Noam. 1965. *Aspects of the theory of syntax.* Cambridge/MA: MIT Press.

Chomsky, Noam. 1991. „Linguistics: personal view". In: Kasher, Asa (ed.). *The Chomskyan turn.* Cambridge/MA & Oxford: Blackwell, 3–25.

Chomsky, Noam. 1991a. „Linguistics and cognitive science: problems and mysteries". In: Kasher, Asa (ed.). *The Chomskyan turn.* Cambridge/MA & Oxford: Blackwell, 26–53.

Cicourel, Aaron, V. [1]1973/1975. *Sprache in der sozialen Interaktion.* München: List.

Clark, Herbert H. & Carlson, Thomas B. 1990. „Speech acts and hearers' beliefs". In: Davis, Steven (ed.). *Pragmatics. A reader.* New York; Oxford: Oxford University Press, 177–98.

Clark, Herbert H. 1996. *Using language.* Cambridge: Cambridge University Press.

Coenen, Herman. 1985. *Diesseits von subjektivem Sinn und kollektivem Zwang. Schütz – Durkheim – Merleau-Ponty. Phänomenologische Soziologie im Feld des zwischenleiblichen Verhaltens.* München: Fink.

Comrie, Bernard. [1]1981/1995. *Language universals and linguistic typology. Syntax and morphology.* Oxford/UK & Cambridge/MA: Blackwell.

Connolly, John H. (ed.). 1997. *Discourse and pragmatics in functional grammar.* Berlin & New York: de Gruyter.

Devriendt, Betty & Goossens, Louis & van der Auwera, Johan (eds.) 1996. *Complex structures: a functionalist perspective.* Berlin & New York: de Gruyter.

Dik, Simon C. 1989. *The theory of functional grammar. Part I: The structure of the clause.* Dordrecht: Reidel.

Ehlich, Konrad. 1991. „Funktional-pragmatische Kommunikationsanalyse – Ziele und Verfahren". In: Flader, Dieter (ed.). *Verbale Interaktion*. Stuttgart: Metzler, 127–43.

Ehlich, Konrad. 1986. „So – Überlegungen zum Verhältnis sprachlicher Formen und sprachlichen Handelns, allgemein und an einem widerspenstigen Beispiel". In: Rosengren, Inger (ed.). *Sprache und Pragmatik*. Bd. 5. Stockholm: Almqvist & Wiksell, 279–98.

Ehlich, Konrad. 1987. „Kooperation und sprachliches Handeln". In: Liedtke, Frank & Keller, Rudi (eds.). *Kommunikation und Kooperation*. Tübingen: Niemeyer, 19–32.

Ehlich, Konrad. 1993. „Pragmatik, Linguistische Pragmatik". In: Glück, Helmut (ed.). *Metzler Lexikon Sprache*. Stuttgart: Metzler, 482–83.

Ehlich, Konrad. 1993a. „Sprechhandlung". In: Glück, Helmut (ed.). *Metzler Lexikon Sprache*. Stuttgart: Metzler, 596.

Fanselow, Gisbert & Felix, Sascha W. 1987. *Sprachtheorie. Bd.1: Grundlagen und Zielsetzungen*. Tübingen: Francke.

Feilke, Helmuth. 1994. *Common sense-Kompetenz. Überlegungen zu einer Theorie 'sympathischen' und 'natürlichen' Meinens und Verstehens*. Frankfurt/M.: Suhrkamp.

Fiehler, Reinhard. 1995. „Weichenstellungen der Sprachwissenschaft und ihre Folgen oder: Zum Verhältnis von Grammatik und Pragmatik". In: Kertész, András (ed.). *Sprache als Kognition – Sprache als Interaktion: Studien zum Grammatik-Pragmatik-Verhältnis*. Franfurt/M.: Lang, 19–58.

Franke, Wilhelm. 1987. „Texttypen – Textsorten – Textexemplare: Ein Ansatz zu ihrer Klassifizierung und Beschreibung". *Zeitschrift für Germanistische Linguistik* 3: 263–81.

Garfinkel, Harold. 1967. *Studies in ethnomethodology*. Englewood Cliffs/NJ: Prentice-Hall.

Givón, Talmy (ed.). 1997. *Grammatical relations: a functionalist perspective*. Amsterdam & Philadelphia: Benjamins.

Givón, Talmy. 1984. *Syntax. A functional-typological approach*. Bd. 1. Amsterdam & Philadelphia: Benjamins.

Grathoff, Richard. 1995. *Milieu und Lebenswelt. Einführung in die phänomenologische Soziologie und die sozialphänomenologische Forschung*. Frankfurt/M.: Suhrkamp.

Große, Ernst Ulrich. 1976. *Text und Kommunikation. Eine linguistische Einführung in die Funktionen der Texte*. Stuttgart: Kohlhammer.

Habermas, Jürgen 1981. *Theorie des kommunikativen Handelns*. 2 Bde. Frankfurt/M.: Suhrkamp.

Halliday, Michael Alexander Kirkwood. 1994. *An introduction to functional grammar*. London: Arnold.

Heine, Bernd. 1995. „Conceptual grammaticalization and prediction". In: Taylor, John R. & MacLaury, Robert E. *Language and the cognitive construal of the world*. Berlin & New York: de Gruyter, 119–35.

Heinemann, Wolfgang. & Viehweger, Dieter. 1991. *Textlinguistik. Eine Einführung*. Tübingen: Niemeyer.

Helbig, Gerhard. 1990. *Entwicklung der Sprachwissenschaft seit 1970*. Opladen: Westdeutscher Verlag.

Hilbert, Richard A. 1992. *The classical roots of ethnomethodology: Durkheim, Weber and Garfinkel*. Chapel Hill; London: University of North Carolina Press.

Hopper, Paul J. & Closs Traugott, Elisabeth. 1993. *Grammaticalization*. Cambridge: Cambridge University Press.

Husserl, Edmund. 1940. „Grundlegende Untersuchungen zum phänomenologischen Ursprung der Räumlichkeit der Natur". In: Farber, Marvin (ed.). *Philosophical essays in memory of Edmund Husserl*. Cambridge/MA: Harvard University Press, 307–25.

Hymes, Dell. 1968. „The ethnography of speaking". In: Fishman, Joshua A. (ed.). *Readings in the sociology of language*. Den Haag: Mouton, 99–138.

Joas, Hans. 1984. „Symbolischer Interaktionismus (Chicago-Schule)". In: Kerber, Harald & Schmieder, Arnold. *Handbuch Soziologie. Zur Theorie und Praxis sozialer Beziehungen*. Reinbek: Rowohlt, 595–98.

Joas, Hans. 1984a. „Handeln, soziales". In: Kerber, Harald & Schmieder, Arnold (eds.). *Handbuch Soziologie. Zur Theorie und Praxis sozialer Beziehungen*. Reinbek: Rowohlt, 210–14.

Joas, Hans. 1996. *Die Kreativität des Handelns*. (Suhrkamp-Taschenbuch Wissenschaft, 1248.) Frankfurt/M: Suhrkamp.

Johnson, Mark. 1987. *The body in the mind. The bodily basis of meaning, imagination, and reason*. Chicago: University of Chicago Press.

Koch, Peter. 1988. „Fachsprache, Liste und Schriftlichkeit in einem Kaufmannsbrief aus dem Duecento". In: Kalverkämper, Hartwig (ed.). *Fachsprachen in der Romania*. Tübingen: Narr, 15–60.

Koch, Peter & Oesterreicher, Wulf. 1994. „Schriftlichkeit und Sprache". In: Günther, Hartmut & Ludwig, Otto (eds.). *Schrift und Schriftlichkeit. Writing and its use*. 1. Halbband. Berlin & New York: de Gruyter, 587–604.

Kotschi, Thomas. 1996. „Zur Interaktion zwischen Textkonstitutionsstruktur und Informationsstruktur in Texten aus mündlicher Kommunikation. Erkundungen am Beispiel des Spanischen". In: Gil, Alberto & Schmitt, Christian (eds.). *Kohäsion, Kohärenz, Modalität in Texten romanischer Sprachen*. Bonn: Romanistischer Verlag, 1–31.

Kress, Gunther & Leite-García, Regina & van Leeuwen, Theo. 1997. „Discourse semiotics". In: van Dijk, Teun A. *Discourse studies. A multidisciplinary approach. Vol. 1: Discourse as structure and process.* London: SAGE, 257–91.

Labov, William. 1980. „Die soziale Stratifikation des /r/ in New Yorker Kaufhäusern". In: Dittmar, Norbert & Rieck, Bert-Olaf (eds.). *William Labov: Sprache im sozialen Kontext.* Königstein/Ts.: Athenäum, 25–48.

Lakoff, George. 1987. *Women, fire, and dangerous things. What categories reveal about the mind.* Chicago: University of Chicago Press.

Levinson, Stephen C. 1996. „Relativity in spatial conception and description". In: Gumperz, John J. & Levinson, Stephen C. (eds.). *Rethinking linguistic relativity.* Cambridge/UK: Cambridge University Press.

Liedtke, Frank & Keller, Rudi (eds.) 1987. *Kommunikation und Kooperation.* Tübingen: Niemeyer.

Luckmann, Thomas. 1997. „Allgemeine Überlegungen zu kommunikativen Gattungen". In: Frank, Barbara & Haye, Thomas & Tophinke, Doris (eds.). *Gattungen mittelalterlicher Schriftlichkeit.* Tübingen: Narr, 11–17.

Luckmann, Thomas. 1992. *Theorie des sozialen Handelns.* Berlin & New York: de Gruyter.

Luhmann, Niklas. 1992. „The form of writing". *Stanford Literature Review* 9.1: 25–42.

Luhmann, Niklas. 1987. *Soziale Systeme.* Frankfurt/M.: Suhrkamp.

Luhmann, Niklas. 1995. *Soziologische Aufklärung 6: Die Soziologie und der Mensch.* Opladen: Westdeutscher Verlag.

Lumer, Christoph. 1990. „Handlungstheorien". In: Sandkühler, Hans Jörg (ed.). *Enzyklopädie zu Philosophie und Wissenschaften.* Band 2. Hamburg: Meiner, 511–14.

Maas, Utz. 1985. „Kulturanalyse und Sprachwissenschaft". In: Ballmer, Thomas T. & Posner, Roland. *Nach-Chomskysche Linguistik. Neuere Arbeiten von Berliner Linguisten.* Berlin: de Gruyter, 91–101.

Maas, Utz. 1992. *Grundzüge der deutschen Orthographie.* Tübingen: Niemeyer.

Maas, Utz & Wunderlich, Dieter. 1972. *Pragmatik und sprachliches Handeln.* Frankfurt/M.: Athenäum.

Mayerthaler, Willi. 1981. *Morphologische Natürlichkeit.* Wiesbaden: Athenaion.

Mead, George Herbert. [1]1934/1968. *Geist, Identität und Gesellschaft.* Frankfurt/M.: Suhrkamp.

Meise, Katrin. 1996. *Une forte absence: Schweigen in alltagsweltlicher und literarischer Kommunikation.* Tübingen: Narr.

Merleau-Ponty, Maurice. 1966. *Phänomenologie der Wahrnehmung.* Berlin & New York: de Gruyter.

Moeschler, Jacques. 1994. „How do we know that what we mean is understood?" In: Parret, Herman (ed.). *Pretending to communicate.* Berlin & New York: de Gruyter, 33–47.

Morris, Charles William. [1]1946/1981. *Zeichen, Sprache und Verhalten.* Frankfurt/M. etc.: Ullstein.

Morris, Charles William. [1]1938/1983. *Foundations of the theory of signs.* Chicago: University of Chicago Press.

Motsch, Wolfgang. 1996. „Ebenen der Textstruktur. Begründung eines Forschungsprogramms". In: Motsch, Wolfgang (ed.). *Ebenen der Textstruktur. Sprachliche und kommunikative Prinzipien.* Tübingen: Niemeyer, 3–33.

Nerlich, Brigitte & Clarke, David D. 1996. *Language, action and context: the early history of pragmatics in Europe and America 1780–1930.* Amsterdam & Philadelphia: Benjamins.

Nerlich, Brigitte. 1995. „The 1930s: at the birth of a pragmatic conception of language". *Historiographia linguistica* 22/3: 311–34.

Nerlich, Brigitte. 1995a. „Language and action: German approaches to pragmatics". In: Jankowsky, Kurt R. (ed.). *History of linguistics 1993. Papers from the sixth international conference on the history of the language sciences.* Amsterdam & Philadelphia: Benjamins, 299–312.

Nuyts, Jan. 1993. „On determining the functions of language". *Semiotica* 94: 201–32.

Nuyts, Jan. 1995. „Functionalism vs. formalism". In: Verschueren, Jef & Östman, Jan-Ola & Blommaert, Jan (eds.). *Handbook of pragmatics.* Amsterdam & Philadelphia: Benjamins, 293–300.

Parret, Herman (ed.). 1994. *Pretending to communicate.* Berlin & New York: de Gruyter.

Parsons, Talcott. 1937. *The structure of social action.* New York: McGraw-Hill Co.

Parsons, Talcott. [1]1964/1981. „Systematische Theorie in der Soziologie. Gegenwärtiger Stand und Ausblick". In: Jonas, Friedrich. *Geschichte der Soziologie 2. Von der Jahrhundertwende bis zur Gegenwart.* Opladen: Westdeutscher Verlag, 480–94.

Petőfi, János S. 1990. „Language as a written medium: text". Collinge, Neville E. (ed.). *An encyclopaedia of language.* London: Routledge, 207–43.

Posner, Roland. 1997. „Pragmatics". In: Posner, Roland & Robering, Klaus & Sebeok, Thomas A. (eds.). *Semiotik: ein Handbuch zu den zeichentheoretischen Grundlagen von Natur und Kultur.* Teilband 1. Berlin & New York: de Gruyter, 219–46.

Prandi, Michele. 1994. „Meaning and indexicality in communication". In: Parret, Herman (ed.). *Pretending to communicate.* Berlin & New York: de Gruyter, 17–32.

Raible, Wolfgang. 1992. *Junktion: eine Dimension der Sprache und ihre Realisierungsformen zwischen Aggregation und Integration.* (Sitzungsberichte der Heidelberger Akademie der Wissenschaften, Philosphisch-Historische Klasse. Bericht 1992, 2.) Heidelberg: Winter.

Raible, Wolfgang. 1994. „Orality and literacy". In: Günther, Hartmut & Ludwig, Otto (eds.). *Schrift und Schriftlichkeit. Writing and its use.* 1. Halbband. Berlin & New York: de Gruyter, 1−17.

Raible, Wolfgang. 1996. „Kognitive Grundlagen des Sprachwandels". In: Michaelis, Susanne & Thiele, Petra (eds.). *Grammatikalisierung in der Romania.* Bochum: Brockmeyer, 61−80.

Rehbein, Jochen. 1988. „Ausgewählte Aspekte der Pragmatik". In: Ammon, Ulrich; Dittmar, Norbert & Mattheier, Klaus J. (eds.). *Soziolinguistik.* (Handbücher zur Sprach- und Kommunikationswissenschaft, 3.2) Berlin & New York: de Gruyter, 1181−95.

Rickheit, Gert & Strohner, Hans. (1993). *Grundlagen der kognitiven Sprachverarbeitung.* Tübingen: Francke.

Rolf, Eckard. 1993. *Die Funktionen der Gebrauchstextsorten.* Berlin: de Gruyter.

Roulet, Eddy. 1998. „Speech acts, discourse structure, and pragmatic connectives". In: Kasher, Asa (ed.). *Pragmatics. Critical concepts. Bd. V: Communication, interaction and discourse.* London & New York: Routledge, 430−47.

Sacks, Harvey & Schegloff, Emanuel A. & Jefferson, Gail. 1974. „A simplest systematics for the organization of turn-taking for conversation". *Language* 50: 696−735.

Saussure, Ferdinand de. ¹1916/1967. *Grundfragen der allgemeinen Sprachwissenschaft.* Ed. Bally, Charles & Sechehaye, Albert. Berlin & Leipzig: de Gruyter.

Schegloff, Emanuel A. & Sacks, Harvey. 1973. „Opening up closings". *Semiotica* 8: 289−327.

Schlieben-Lange, Brigitte. 1979. *Linguistische Pragmatik.* Stuttgart: Kohlhammer.

Schlieben-Lange, Brigitte. 1988. „Text". In: Ammon, Ulrich (ed.). *Sociolinguistics: An International Handbook of the Science of Language and Society.* Bd. 2. Berlin & New York: de Gruyter, 1205−15.

Schmidt, Siegfried J. & Weischenberg, Siegfried. 1994. „Mediengattungen, Berichterstattungsmuster, Darstellungsformen". In: Merten, Klaus & Schmidt, Siegfried J. & Weischenberg, Siegfried (eds.). *Die Wirklichkeit der Medien.* Opladen: Westdeutscher Verlag, 212−36.

Schütz, Alfred & Luckmann, Thomas. 1979. *Strukturen der Lebenswelt.* Band 1. Frankfurt/M.: Suhrkamp.

Schütz, Alfred & Luckmann, Thomas. 1984. *Strukturen der Lebenswelt.* Band 2. Frankfurt/M.: Suhrkamp.

Searle, John R. 1969. *Speech acts. An essay in the philosophy of language.* Cambridge: Cambridge University Press.

Searle, John R. 1976. „A classification of illocutionary acts". *Language in Society* 5: 1−23.

Srubar, Ilja. 1991. „Phänomenologische Soziologie als Theorie und Forschung". In: Herzog, Max & Graumann, Carl Friedrich. *Sinn und Erfahrung. Phänomenologische Methoden in den Humanwissenschaften.* Heidelberg: Roland Asanger, 169−82.

Strohner, Hans. 1995. *Kognitive Systeme. Eine Einführung in die Kognitionswissenschaft.* Opladen: Westdeutscher Verlag.

Taylor, Charles. 1988. „Sprache und Gesellschaft". In: Honneth, Axel & Joas, Hans. *Kommunikatives Handeln. Beiträge zu Jürgen Habermas' „Theorie des kommunikativen Handelns".* Frankfurt/M.: Suhrkamp, 35−52.

Tophinke, Doris. 1999. *Handelstexte. Zu Textualität und Typik kaufmännischer Rechnungsbücher im Hanseraum des 14. und 15. Jahrhunderts.* (ScriptOralia, 114.) Tübingen: Narr.

Trabant, Jürgen. 1998. *Artikulationen. Historische Anthropologie der Sprache.* Frankfurt/M.: Suhrkamp.

Waldenfels, Bernhard. 1980. *Der Spielraum des Verhaltens.* (Suhrkamp-Taschenbuch Wissenschaft, 311.) Frankfurt/M.: Suhrkamp.

Waldenfels, Bernhard. 1985. *In den Netzen der Lebenswelt.* (Suhrkamp-Taschenbuch Wissenschaft, 545.) Frankfurt/M.: Suhrkamp.

Waldenfels, Bernhard. 1987. *Ordnung im Zwielicht.* Frankfurt/M.: Suhrkamp.

Waldenfels, Bernhard. 1990. *Der Stachel des Fremden.* (Suhrkamp-Taschenbuch Wissenschaft, 868.) Frankfurt/M.: Suhrkamp.

Waldenfels, Bernhard. 1998. *Grenzen der Normalisierung.* Frankfurt/M.: Suhrkamp.

Waldenfels, Bernhard. 1999. *Sinnesschwellen.* Frankfurt/M.: Suhrkamp.

Watzlawick, Paul & Beavin, Janet H. & Jackson, Don D. ¹1967/1990. *Menschliche Kommunikation. Formen, Störungen, Paradoxien.* Bern: Huber.

Weber, Max. ¹1904/1991. „Die 'Objektivität' sozialwissenschaftlicher und sozialpolitischer Erkenntnis". In: Sukale, Michael (ed.). *Max Weber. Schriften zur Wissenschaftslehre.* Stuttgart: Reclam, 21−101.

Weinrich, Harald. 1982. *Textgrammatik der französischen Sprache.* Stuttgart: Klett.

Weinrich, Harald. 1988. „Über Sprache, Leib und Gedächtnis". In: Gumbrecht, Hans Ulrich & Pfeiffer, Karl Ludwig (eds.). *Materialität der Kommunikation.* Frankfurt/M.: Suhrkamp, 80−93.

Weinrich, Harald. 1993. *Textgrammatik der deutschen Sprache.* Mannheim: Dudenverlag.

Wenzel, Harald. 1992. „Der interaktionistische Ansatz". In: Dascal, Marcelo & al. (eds.). *Sprachphilo-*

sophie. Halbband 1. Berlin & New York: de Gruyter, 732−45.

Wunderlich, Dieter. 1972. „Sprechakte". In: Maas, Utz & Wunderlich, Dieter. *Pragmatik und sprachliches Handeln.* Frankfurt/M.: Athenäum, 69−188.

Wurzel, Wolfgang Ulrich. 1984. *Flexionsmorphologie und Natürlichkeit.* Berlin: Akademie-Verlag.

Doris Tophinke, Universität Freiburg i.Br.
(Deutschland)

4. Sprachphilosophie

1. Einleitung
2. Die wissenschaftstheoretische Diskussion des Universalienbegriffs
3. Syntaktische Universalien
4. Semantische Universalien
5. Pragmatische Universalien
6. Zusammenfassung
7. Zitierte Literatur

1. Einleitung

Anknüpfungspunkte zur Sprachphilosophie gibt es im Bereich der linguistischen Universalien- und Sprachtypologieforschung fast ausschließlich in bezug auf den ersten Themenbereich − die Universalienforschung. Das liegt darin begründet, daß sich die Sprachphilosophie in erster Linie für sprachliche Phänomene interessiert, die (zumindest dem ersten Anschein nach) für alle Sprachen gelten und damit unabhängig von bestimmten Einzelsprachen sind. Um diese Selbstbeschränkung der Sprachphilosophie zu verstehen, muß man wissen, daß Sprachphilosophie fast immer als Hilfsmittel für die Beantwortung anderer Fragen aufgefaßt wurde. Es handelt sich dabei beispielsweise um die Fragen nach dem richtigen Denken, der korrekten Erkenntnis oder dem rationalen Argumentieren.

Besonders aufschlußreich für die linguistische Universalienforschung ist in diesem Zusammenhang das in der Philosophie vielfältig diskutierte Verhältnis zwischen Logik und natürlicher Sprache. Innerhalb der neueren philosophischen Strömungen wurde dieses Thema in der hermeneutischen, phänomenologischen, dialogischen, konstruktiven und analytischen Philosophie aufgegriffen. Es wurden dabei sowohl logikaffirmative als auch logikkritische Programme vertreten. Auf der einen Seite wurde behauptet, alle zentralen Funktionen der Sprache ließen sich in logischen Notationen ausdrücken und dadurch klar darstellen. Auf der anderen Seite machte man auf die konkreten Verwendungszusammenhänge von Sprache − Sprachspiele, Lebensweisen, Geschichten und Kulturformen − aufmerksam und trat einer logischen Fundierung der Sprachbetrachtung mit Skepsis entgegen. Diese divergierenden Standpunkte werden in diesem Artikel, getrennt nach den sprachlichen Dimensionen Syntax, Semantik und Pragmatik, dargestellt.

Zuvor sei jedoch ein zweiter Zusammenhang zwischen Sprachphilosophie und Universalienforschung ins Auge gefaßt: die **Wissenschaftstheorie der Linguistik**. Dieser Aspekt eignet sich gleichzeitig zur Einführung in die Universalienproblematik, da im Zentrum der wissenschaftstheoretischen Auseinandersetzung mit dieser Problematik die Frage nach der angemessenen und präzisen terminologischen Verwendung des Ausdrucks 'linguistische Universalie' selber steht.

2. Die wissenschaftstheoretische Diskussion des Universalienbegriffs

Auch wenn die linguistische Universalienforschung historische Vorläufer und Inspirationsquellen besitzt (vgl. Martinet 1967: 125), so kann doch das von Joseph Greenberg, James Jenkins und Charles Osgood verfaßte *Memorandum concerning language universals* (Greenberg & Jenkins & Osgood 1963) zu Recht als Gründungsurkunde dieses sprachwissenschaftlichen Forschungszweiges gelten (→ Art. 23). Der programmatische Text, der die systematische Diskussionsgrundlage für die wegweisende Universalienkonferenz bildete, die im April 1961 in Dobbs Ferry stattfand, präsentiert die Grundidee der Universalienforschung zunächst auf intuitive Weise:

„Underlying the endless and fascinating idiosyncrasies of the world's languages there are uniformities of universal scope. [...] Language universals are by their very nature summary statements about characteristics or tendencies shared by all human speakers" (Greenberg & Jenkins & Osgood 1963: 255).

Diese allgemeine Darstellung wird im Verlauf des Memorandums nicht nur insofern differenziert und konkretisiert, als explizit auf verschiedene Anwendungsgebiete der Universalienforschung − z. B. Phonologie, Syntax, Semantik und diachrone Sprachbetrachtung − aufmerksam gemacht wird, sondern auch dadurch, daß eine Typologie von sechs verschiedenen Sorten linguistischer Universalien vorgeschlagen wird:

a. allgemeine Universalien (unrestricted universals)
b. implikative Universalien (universal implications)
c. Äquivalenzuniversalien (restricted equivalence)
d. statistische Universalien (statistical universals)
e. statistische Eigenschaftskorrelationen (statistical correlations)
f. universelle Häufigkeitsverteilungen (universal frequency distributions).

Dabei betreffen die ersten drei Universalienarten solche Eigenschaften, die alle Einzelsprachen ausnahmslos besitzen, wohingegen die letzten drei Arten Aussagen darstellen, mit denen lediglich behauptet wird, daß eine hohe statistische Wahrscheinlichkeit besteht, daß eine Einzelsprache eine bestimmte Eigenschaft besitzt. Dieser Unterschied ist allerdings nicht mit demjenigen zwischen analytischen und empirischen Eigenschaften natürlicher Sprachen zu verwechseln. Vielmehr weisen Greenberg, Jenkins und Osgood ausdrücklich darauf hin, daß sie Eigenschaften, die aus rein definitorischen Gründen auf alle Sprachen zutreffen, aus der Universalienforschung ausschließen wollen. Die ursprüngliche Forschungsidee war also stark empirisch ausgerichtet, was unter anderem auch dadurch deutlich wird, daß ein unproblematischer Übergang von allgemeingültigen zu statistischen Universalien gemacht werden kann, wenn in bezug auf eine als universell angenommene Eigenschaft ein Ausnahmefall gefunden wird. Im einzelnen lassen sich die angeführten Universaliensorten folgendermaßen charakterisieren: Allgemeine Universalien besitzen die logische Form $\bigwedge_{x \, Sprache}. x \, \varepsilon \, \Phi$. Mit solchen Universalien wird behauptet, daß *alle* Einzelsprachen eine bestimmte Eigenschaft Φ besitzen (z. B. diejenige, Vokale zu beinhalten). Demgegenüber ist die logische Form implikativer Universalien $\bigwedge_{x \, Sprache}. x \, \varepsilon \, \Phi \to x \, \varepsilon \, \Psi$.; mit dieser Universalienform ist also die schwächere Behauptung verbunden, daß nur für diejenigen Sprachen, die eine bestimmte Eigenschaft Φ besitzen (z. B. diejenige, den Dualis aufzuweisen), gilt, daß sie auch eine bestimmte andere Eigenschaft Ψ besitzen (z. B. diejenige, den Plural aufzuweisen). Äquivalenzuniversalien schließlich besitzen die Form $\bigwedge_{x \, Sprache}. x \, \varepsilon \, \Phi \leftrightarrow x \, \varepsilon \, \Psi$. Implikative Universalien und Äquivalenzuniversalien eignen sich damit als Darstellungsmittel sprachtypologischer Überlegungen. Statistische Universalien besagen in Analogie zu allgemeinen, daß die meisten Einzelsprachen eine bestimmte Eigenschaft besitzen, und statistische Eigenschaftskorrelationen besagen in Analogie zu implikativen Universalien, daß für die meisten derjenigen Sprachen, die eine bestimmte Eigenschaft Φ besitzen, gilt, daß sie auch eine bestimmte andere Eigenschaft Ψ besitzen. Universelle Häufigkeitsverteilungen bestehen schließlich darin, daß behauptet wird, die Ausprägung bestimmter sprachlicher Parameter (z. B. der Anteil semantisch redundanter Ausdrücke am Gesamtumfang der Ausdrücke einer Sprache) sei in allen Sprachen ähnlich stark. Diese Universalienkonzepte wurden mehrfach zum Gegenstand von Kritik, Verbesserungs- und Ergänzungsvorschlägen gemacht.

So stellte beispielsweise André Martinet die gesamte Grundidee der Universalienforschung in Frage (Martinet 1967). Er rückte die Universalienforschung methodisch in die Nähe der logisch orientierten Sprachwissenschaft (generative und Transformationsgrammatik), obwohl er ihre empirische Stoßrichtung klar erkannte. Martinet war nämlich der Auffassung, daß allein schon das Forschungsziel, universelle Eigenschaften der Einzelsprachen entdecken zu wollen, die Gefahr in sich berge, bestehende Unterschiede gar nicht als solche zu erkennen. Man müsse demgegenüber die definitorische Eigenheit aller natürlichen Sprachen, zweifach (d. h. phonematisch und monematisch) artikuliertes verbales Verständigungswerkzeug zu sein, in der Sprachwissenschaft stets im Auge behalten. Am Beispiel einer Einzeluntersuchung Greenbergs über syntaktische Universalien machte Martinet in diesem Sinne deutlich, daß ein angemessenes Verständnis sprachlicher Strukturen nicht möglich ist, wenn man von der Funktion absieht, die diese Strukturen im Zusammenhang der menschlichen Verständigung besitzen.

Im Gegensatz zu Martinets grundsätzlich kritischer Position steht Eugenio Coseriu der Universalienforschung positiv gegenüber.

Seine ausführliche Stellungnahme zur Problematik linguistischer Universalien (Coseriu 1974) ist dementsprechend eher als Differenzierungsvorschlag denn als Kritik zu verstehen. Neben Coserius Warnung, daß Universalien der Sprache nicht mit universellen Eigenschaften sprachwissenschaftlicher Methoden oder mit universellen Eigenschaften der Struktur der Wirklichkeit verwechselt werden dürfen, sind hier insbesondere drei von Coseriu unterschiedene Universalienarten zu erwähnen:

a. mögliche Universalien (universaux possibles)
b. notwendige Universalien (universaux essentiels)
c. empirische Universalien (universaux empiriques).

Mögliche Universalien sind sprachtheoretische Beschreibungskategorien, die insofern universell sind, als sie unabhängig von bestimmten Einzelsprachen definiert werden. Da solche Kategorien – z. B. Verb, Präfix oder Aufforderungsfunktion – nicht in (allen) bestehenden Sprachen realisiert sein müssen, werden sie als 'möglich' qualifiziert. Notwendige und empirische Universalien sind dagegen in allen Einzelsprachen zu finden. Dabei sind notwendige Universalien solche Eigenschaften der Einzelsprachen, die bereits im Begriff der Sprache enthalten und deshalb notwendig in allen Sprachen anzutreffen sind. Sie entsprechen den im *Memorandum* explizit ausgeschlossenen definitorischen Eigenschaften. Die empirischen Universalien von Coseriu entsprechen Greenbergs, Jenkins' und Osgoods allgemeinen Universalien. Coseriu macht deutlich, daß diese Universalien stets hypothetisch sind, da ihr universeller Charakter auf Induktion beruht, während sich die zwingende Universalität der notwendigen Universalien der Deduktion verdankt. Sein wichtigster wissenschaftstheoretischer Beitrag zur Universalienforschung besteht schließlich darin, daß er den Sinn der Suche nach notwendigen und empirischen Universalien klar hervorhebt:

„[...] tous les universaux essentiels ne sont pas immédiatement évidents et le fait qu'on puisse les déduire n'implique aucunement leur banalité scientifique [...], leurs conséquences, en ce qui concerne la structuration des langues [...], sont souvent encore moins évidentes. [...] Certains universaux empiriques effectivement présents dans toutes les langues pourraient, sans doute, être dus au hasard: c'est une possibilité qu'on ne peut pas exclure d'avance, bien qu'elle soit en réalité infime, étant donné le nombre des langues de l'humanité. Mais les autres devraient alors être motivés [...], ils devraient être déterminés, ou bien par des raisons d'ordre pratique (les langues, étant des 'techniques' historiques, sont gouvernées aussi par l'intelligence pratique), ou bien par la constitution physique et psychique de l'homme et par les conditions de la vie sur la Terre. Du reste, certains universaux statistiques pourraient, eux aussi, être motivés dans ce sens. C'est, précisément, cette possibilité de motivation qui détermine l'intérêt des universaux empiriques, non seulement pour la linguistique, mais pour tous les sciences de l'Homme" (Coseriu 1974: 51–53).

Coseriu erweitert das ursprüngliche Universalienkonzept also um die von Martinet eingeklagte funktionale oder sogar anthropologische Fundierung.

In einer umfangreichen wissenschaftstheoretischen Stellungnahme zur Universalienforschung versuchte Hans-Heinrich Lieb, verschiedene Universalienkonzepte mit Hilfe formaler Darstellungsmittel zu präzisieren und diese Konzepte dann auf ihre Adäquatheit hin zu überprüfen (Lieb 1975). Korrektheit und Fruchtbarkeit von Liebs Beitrag können an dieser Stelle nicht ausführlich beurteilt werden; es muß hier genügen, einen interessanten Punkt in Liebs Darstellung herauszugreifen. Lieb betrachtet nicht verschiedene Universalienarten, sondern unterschiedliche Möglichkeiten, Universalienforschung zu betreiben. Er stellt einen naiven, einen semantischen und einen pragmatischen Ansatz vor. Bei der Beurteilung dieser Ansätze spielt die terminologische Verwendung des Ausdrucks 'Sprache' innerhalb einer Sprachtheorie in Liebs Argumentation eine zentrale Rolle. Durch diese Akzentsetzung wird ein Problem sichtbar gemacht, das mit Universalienarten wie Coserius notwendigen Universalien verbunden ist: Es ist nicht gleichgültig, ob sich die terminologische Verwendung des Ausdrucks 'Sprache' in der sprachwissenschaftlichen Theoriebildung als angemessene Beschreibung eines vorgängigen (alltäglichen) Sprachgebrauchs oder als Normierungsvorschlag zukünftiger Sprachverwendung zu näher zu spezifizierenden Zwecken versteht.

Im Rahmen des *Kölner Universalienprojekts* (→ Art. 27) wurde schließlich der im *Memorandum* noch unberücksichtigte Aspekt der verschiedenen Funktionen von Sprache zur methodischen Grundlage der Universalienforschung gemacht (vgl. Seiler 1978). Dabei wurden sprachliche Universalien als diejenigen Prim-Operationen aufgefaßt, die für das menschliche Sprechen konstitutiv sind (vgl. Boom 1978: 72). Die Entdeckung und Darstellung solcher Prim-Operationen beruht sowohl auf introspektiven wie auf empirischen Verfahren.

Insgesamt ergibt die wissenschaftstheoretische Diskussion um den linguistischen Universalienbegriff, daß unterschiedliche Auffassungen darüber bestehen, in welchem Maße das praktische Fundament des menschlichen Sprechverhaltens einerseits und dasjenige der sprachwissenschaftlichen Theoriebildung andererseits bei der Universalienforschung Berücksichtigung finden müssen. In den folgenden Abschnitten wird sich zeigen, daß diese Frage auch die sprachphilosophischen Auseinandersetzungen um das Verhältnis von Logik und natürlicher Sprache beherrscht.

3. Syntaktische Universalien

Die Syntax beschäftigt sich damit, welche möglichen Zusammensetzungen von Zeichen zu größeren Zeichenverbindungen korrekte Zeichenketten darstellen. Dabei wird von der Bedeutung und Funktion der Zeichen abgesehen. Ausgangspunkt moderner sprachphilosophischer Gedanken zum Problem syntaktischer Universalien ist das Verhältnis von formallogischer Syntax und Syntax der natürlichen Sprachen. Um diesen Gedanken systematisch nachzugehen, bietet es sich nach traditioneller Auffassung an, bei der Syntax der Prädikatenlogik erster Stufe zu beginnen. Die vollständige Spezifizierung dieser Syntax besteht in der Aufzählung der Grundzeichen der prädikatenlogischen Sprache und in der anschließenden Angabe der Kombinationsregeln für die Grundzeichen. Grundzeichen der Sprache der Prädikatenlogik erster Stufe sind: die Junktoren ($\neg$, $\wedge$, $\vee$, $\rightarrow$, $\leftrightarrow$), die Quantoren ($\bigvee_x$, $\bigwedge_x$), die Grundnominatoren (a, b, c, ...), die Gegenstandsvariablen (x, y, z, ...), die Grundprädikatoren (Φ, Ψ, Ξ, ...) und die Kopula (ε). Die syntaktischen Kombinationsregeln geben an, wie Zeichen der verschiedenen syntaktischen Kategorien zusammengesetzt werden können, so daß syntaktisch wohlgeformte Ausdrücke (sogenannte Formeln) entstehen. Formeln der Prädikatenlogik erster Stufe sind zum Beispiel '$a\ \varepsilon\ \Phi$', '$a\ \varepsilon\ \Phi \rightarrow a, b\ \varepsilon\ \Psi$' und '$\bigvee_x . x\ \varepsilon\ \Xi$.'. Diese Form der logischen Syntax besitzt einerseits Ähnlichkeiten mit der Syntax (oder Grammatik) der natürlichen Sprache, zeigt andererseits aber auch grundsätzliche Unterschiede von dieser. Zu den Ähnlichkeiten: Der prädikatenlogische Ausdruck '$a\ \varepsilon\ \Phi$' und die natürlichsprachlichen Sätze 'Peter ist nett' und 'Susanne ist Kettenraucherin' besitzen beispielsweise dieselbe syntaktische Form. Dasselbe gilt für '$a\ \varepsilon\ \Phi \wedge b\ \varepsilon\ \Psi$' und 'Susanne ist Kettenraucherin und Martin hat Schnupfen'. Zentrale Unterschiede zwischen der Syntax der Prädikatenlogik erster Stufe und der Syntax der natürlichen Sprache bestehen darin, daß

a. die Syntax der Prädikatenlogik erster Stufe insofern nicht so restriktiv ist wie diejenige der natürlichen Sprache, als sie bestimmte Kombinationen nicht ausschließt, die aus semantischen Gründen in der natürlichen Sprache nicht vorkommen
b. einige syntaktische Kategorien der Prädikatenlogik eine andere syntaktische Struktur besitzen als die funktional äquivalenten syntaktischen Kategorien der natürlichen Sprache
c. die angemessene syntaktische Charakterisierung natürlicher Sprachen ein größeres Inventar an syntaktischen Kategorien erfordert als es in der Prädikatenlogik zur Verfügung gestellt wird.

Dazu einige Beispiele:

a. Die Syntax der Prädikatenlogik erster Stufe bietet keine Möglichkeit, den Satz 'Susanne ist Kettenraucherin' als wohlgeformt und 'die Donau ist Kettenraucherin' als nicht-wohlgeformt auszuweisen.
b. Der Satz 'Alle Laubfrösche sind grün' erhält in der Prädikatenlogik die syntaktische Form '$\bigwedge_x x\ \varepsilon\ \Phi \rightarrow x\ \varepsilon\ \Psi$.'. Rein syntaktisch liegen hier zwei völlig unterschiedliche Zeichenketten vor.
c. Ausdrücke wie 'die', 'hinein', 'irgendein' und 'sehr' lassen sich keiner der angeführten syntaktischen Kategorien zuordnen.

Ausgehend von dieser Problemlage wird im folgenden dargestellt, welche Vorschläge es gibt, die genannten Beschränkungen durch Erweiterungen der logischen Syntax zu beheben. Im Gegenzug dazu wird anschließend auch auf grundsätzliche Kritik an syntaktischen Universalien hingewiesen.

Auf die erste der angeführten Beschränkungen hat bereits Ludwig Wittgenstein aufmerksam gemacht. In seinem 1913 entstandenen Manuskript *Notes on Logic* erscheint diese Einsicht in Form der konkreten Forderung: „Every right theory of judgment must make it impossible for me to judge that 'this table penholders the book'" (Wittgenstein 1957: 234). Im Rahmen seiner später im *Tractatus Logico-Philosophicus* entworfenen Bildtheorie der Satzbedeutung wird klar, daß diese syntaktische Forderung eng an die Semantik geknüpft ist. Die Zusammensetzungsmöglichkeiten der Namen zu sinnvollen Sätzen macht Wittgenstein dort nämlich davon abhängig, in welcher Weise die einfachen Gegenstände (die Bedeutungen der Namen) zu Sachverhalten kombinierbar sind. Diese Kombinationsmöglichkeiten der Gegenstände werden wiederum durch die Form beziehungsweise die internen Eigenschaften der Gegenstände festgelegt, so daß dann, wenn alle Gegenstände gegeben sind, auch alle möglichen Sachverhalte gegeben sind (vgl. Wittgenstein 1922: 2.0124). Wegen der grundsätzlichen Schwierigkeiten von Wittgensteins frühem Atomismus, einfache Gegenstände anzugeben, wurde das dargestellte Programm − auch von Wittgenstein selbst − nicht weiterverfolgt. Stattdessen hat man versucht, das Problem der Aussonderung von Sätzen wie 'die Donau ist Kettenraucherin' mit Hilfe von **Bedeutungspostulaten** beziehungsweise **Prädikatorenregeln** zu lösen. Für das genannte Beispiel könnte das etwa durch die Regeln '$x \; \varepsilon \; Kettenraucherin \Rightarrow x \; \varepsilon \; Mensch \wedge x \; \varepsilon \; weiblich$' und '$x \; \varepsilon \; Fluß \Rightarrow x \; \varepsilon' \; Mensch$' geschehen. Auch in dieser neuen Variante ist man jedoch von der syntaktischen Ebene zur semantischen übergegangen.

Dem Problem der syntaktischen Verschiedenheit zwischen bedeutungsgleichen Sätzen der natürlichen Sprachen und der Prädikatenlogik hat sich Noam Chomsky zu nähern versucht: Er betrachtete die syntaktische Struktur eines natürlichsprachlichen Satzes als seine **Oberflächen-** und die syntaktische Struktur des entsprechenden logik- oder universalsprachlichen Satzes als **Tiefenstruktur**. Die Überführung von Tiefen- in Oberflächenstruktur sollte durch Transformationsregeln bewerkstelligt werden. Auch dieses Problem ist allerdings nicht auf syntaktischem Wege zu lösen, sondern erfordert die Einbeziehung der semantischen Dimension (vgl. Schneider 1975: 66−72). Beim späten Wittgenstein, auf den die Rede von Oberflächen- und Tiefengrammatik ursprünglich zurückgeht, wird die Tiefenstruktur sogar mit der pragmatischen Ebene identifiziert. Das wesentliche hinter der „Gleichförmigkeit der Erscheinungen" der sprachlichen Ausdrücke ist für Wittgenstein nämlich die *Verwendung der Ausdrücke* (Wittgenstein 1953: §§ 11, 664; vgl. dazu auch Wittgenstein 1922: 4.002).

Dem dritten Problem − der Forderung nach einem reichhaltigeren Inventar an syntaktischen Kategorien − versuchte man in der Warschauer Schule durch die **Kategorialgrammatik** und in der Erlanger Schule durch die Syntax der **Orthosprache** zu begegnen. Die Kategorialgrammatik geht auf Arbeiten von Stanisław Leśniewski und Kazimierz Ajdukiewicz zurück (Leśniewski 1929; Ajdukiewicz 1935). Sie stieß später unter anderem bei Richard Montague, David Lewis und Max Cresswell auf große Resonanz (vgl. z. B. Cresswell 1973). Die Grundidee der Kategorialgrammatik besteht darin, durch bestimmte Kombinationen der syntaktischen Kategorien n (= Name) und s (= Satz) weitere syntaktische Kategorien zu erzeugen. Die Regel dazu lautet: 'Wenn A und B syntaktische Kategorien sind, dann sind auch $(A\backslash B)$ und (A/B) syntaktische Kategorien'. Einstellige Prädikatoren besitzen in dieser Grammatik beispielsweise die syntaktische Kategorie $n\backslash s$. Ein Ausdruck α dieser Kategorie ist syntaktisch dadurch ausgezeichnet, daß dann, wenn links von ihm ein Name β steht, der gesamte Ausdruck $\alpha\beta$ ein Satz ist. Die meisten einstelligen Satzoperatoren (z. B. der Negator) gehören zur Kategorie s/s. Sie ergeben in Verbindung mit einem rechts von ihnen stehenden Satz wieder einen Satz. In dem Satz 'Peter trägt die blaue Hose' können die syntaktischen Kategorien zum Beispiel folgendermaßen angegeben werden:

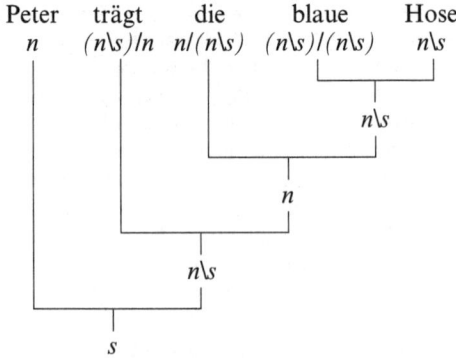

Abb. 4.1: Syntaktische Kategorien am Beispiel 'Peter trägt die blaue Hose'

Ähnlich wie die Kategorialgrammatik besitzt auch die von Paul Lorenzen und Oswald Schwemmer vorgeschlagene Orthosyntax mehr syntaktische Kategorien als die Prädikatenlogik erster Stufe. Sie versteht sich jedoch nicht als Werkzeug zur angemessenen Beschreibung der Syntax natürlicher Sprachen, sondern als rationale Grammatik. Das heißt, die Kategorien der Orthosyntax sind als Normierungsvorschläge aufzufassen. Sie erlauben es, exemplarische Fälle verständlichen Redens zu entwerfen, und sollen dadurch mittelbar der vernünftigen Verständigung dienen. Die Orthosyntax begreift sich

4. Sprachphilosophie

also nur insofern als universal, als sie – auf der Grundlage einer gemeinsamen Handlungspraxis – unabhängig von den Eigenarten einer Einzelsprache einführbar sein soll (vgl. Lorenzen & Schwemmer 1973: 38; Lorenzen 1980: 78). Die die prädikatenlogische Syntax überschreitenden orthosyntaktischen Kategorien sind zusätzliche Prädikatorenkategorien, zum Beispiel Ding- und Geschehnisprädikatoren (Q und P), zusätzliche Partikeln, zum Beispiel Tat- und Geschehniskopula (π und κ), sowie Kasusmorpheme und Präpositionsorthogramme.

Wie schon an verschiedenen Stellen deutlich wurde, besteht der wesentliche Kritikpunkt an universalistischen Behauptungen im Rahmen der Syntax darin, die Möglichkeit einer reinen Syntax überhaupt in Frage zu stellen. Schon an den syntaktischen Kategorien der Prädikatenlogik zeigt sich, daß diese gar nicht unabhängig von der Semantik zu verstehen sind. Beim Aufbau der Kategorialgrammatik standen semantische Überlegungen sogar im Vordergrund. Josef Schächter hat in diesem Zusammenhang sehr treffend zwischen der Grammatik des Materials und der Grammatik der Bedeutung unterschieden. Inspiriert von Wittgensteins Analogie zwischen Sprache und Schachspiel illustrierte er diesen Unterschied folgendermaßen:

„Die Grammatik des Materials ist etwa einem Buche über das Schachspiel zu vergleichen, das aber nicht wie die üblichen Lehrbücher des Schachspiels abgefaßt ist, sondern das sich mehr von der äußeren Seite mit dem Schachspiel beschäftigt, d. h. es beschäftigt sich hauptsächlich mit dem Aussehen der Figuren und deren Einteilung danach, allerdings kommen hier und da auch Hinweise über Züge und Stellungen vor. Der Grammatik der Bedeutung aber entspricht ein Lehrbuch des Schachspiels, in dem hauptsächlich von Zügen und Stellungen die Rede ist und das Material nur insofern berücksichtigt wird, als es für diese von Belang ist" (Schächter 1935: 20).

Bloße Grammatik des Materials findet sich also dort, wo sprachliche Unterschiede nur die Laut- oder Schriftgestalt betreffen und keine Bedeutungsunterschiede anzeigen. Für die logische Grammatik ist die Grammatik des Materials daher laut Schächter völlig uninteressant. Viel zu selten ist dabei allerdings bemerkt worden, daß die angebliche semantische Fundierung der Oberflächensyntax gar nicht ohne weiteres gegeben ist. Die Kategorien logischer Syntax reichen nämlich oft nicht aus, um – zusammen mit dem Inhalt der Lexeme eines Satzes – die jeweilige Bedeutung zu errechnen. Dies hat Hans Julius Schneider am Phänomen der **syntaktischen Metapher** und am nicht abgeschlossenen Charakter der Orthosprache deutlich gezeigt (vgl. Schneider 1992; 1993). Eine syntaktische Metapher liegt dann vor, wenn identische syntaktische Strukturen unterschiedliche semantische Funktionen besitzen, wie zum Beispiel die Sätze 'Im Wartezimmer sitzt der angebliche Lord' und 'Im Wartezimmer sitzt der schottische Lord' veranschaulichen. Ein anderes plastisches Beispiel sind die vielfältigen semantischen Funktionen des Genitivs in Phrasen wie 'das Haus des Bäckers', 'der Tod des Bäckers', 'die Hand des Bäckers', 'der Traum des Bäckers', 'die Vergangenheit des Bäckers' und 'die Krankheit des Bäckers'. Die Bedeutung dieser sprachphilosophischen Einsicht erklärt Schneider unter Hinweis auf Wittgenstein:

„Als kompetente Sprecher wissen wir, daß sein Haus dem Bäcker auf eine andere Weise zugehört als sein Tod: Er besitzt sein Haus oder wohnt dort zur Miete, aber seinen Tod besitzt er weder, noch hat er ihn gemietet. Worauf es nach Wittgenstein beim Verständnis unserer Sprachfähigkeit ankommt, ist, daß wir in der Lage sind, die grammatische Struktur, die wir zum Ausdruck des *einen* Verhältnisses benutzen, in einem aktiven Schritt auf *andere* Verhältnisse, auf neuartige Anwendungsfälle, zu übertragen, zu projizieren. Nicht das, worüber gesprochen wird, spiegelt (quasi 'von Natur aus') seine eigene Struktur in der Struktur der Sprache, sondern *wir* übertragen die bekannte grammatische Form (man könnte sagen: 'mißbräuchlich') von einem Praxisfeld auf ein anderes. Als Sprecher werden wir im Regelfall damit (erstaunlicherweise) verstanden, und als Hörer verstehen wir beide Gebrauchsweisen ohne Nachfrage" (Schneider 1996: 22).

4. Semantische Universalien

Die Semantik beschäftigt sich mit der Bedeutung von Zeichen. Bei der philosophischen Untersuchung des Verhältnisses von Logik und natürlicher Sprache stehen im Bereich der Semantik zwei Bedürfnisse im Vordergrund: dasjenige nach Methoden des vernünftigen Argumentierens (vgl. z. B. Næss 1971) und dasjenige nach Methoden des Aufbaus präziser Wissenschaftssprachen (vgl. z. B. Kamlah & Lorenzen 1973). In beiden Fällen ist der Wunsch grundlegend, wahre von falschen Aussagen nachprüfbar voneinander unterscheiden zu können. Ausgehend von der syntaktischen Struktur des einstelligen Elementarsatzes ($a \ \varepsilon \ \Phi$) lassen sich in diesem Zusammenhang drei zentrale semantische Funktionen auszeichnen: das Benennen von Gegenständen durch Nominatoren (Referenz), das Klassifizieren von Gegenständen durch das Zu- und Absprechen von Prädikatoren (Prädikation) und das Überprüfen der Angemessenheit der mit den Elementarsätzen gemachten Aussagen (Wahrheit). Wegen der universellen Ansprüche, die sowohl mit dem rationalen Argumentieren als auch mit der sprachlichen Fixierung wissenschaftlicher Erkenntnisse verknüpft sind, wird in der Sprachphilosophie oft davon ausgegangen, daß die drei genannten semantischen Funktionen unabhängig von bestimmten Einzelsprachen seien. Was damit genau beansprucht wird und wie sich diese Ansprüche rechtfertigen lassen, soll in diesem Abschnitt dargestellt werden. Zuvor sei jedoch wenigstens darauf hingewiesen, daß auch in der Semantik – ähnlich wie im Bereich der Syntax – verschiedene Erweiterungen des Inventars an Bedeutungskategorien vorgeschlagen wurden. In diesen Zusammenhang gehören unter anderem Edmund Husserls Überlegungen zu einer **reinen Grammatik**, die eine „Formenlehre der Bedeutungen" zur Aufgabe hat, sowie die in Analogie zur Kategorialgrammatik konzipierte Semantik der **Typentheorie** (vgl. Husserl 1900/01, II/1: 294–342; Gardies 1975; Raible 1980; Nef 1991: 43–64; Gamut 1991: 75–91).

Die semantische Funktion der **Referenz**, des Benennens von Gegenständen, geschieht mit Hilfe von Nominatoren. Nominatoren lassen sich in verschiedene Sorten einteilen. Diese Sorten sind der Demonstrator (z. B. 'dies', 'das da'), die deiktische Kennzeichnung (z. B. 'diese Flöte', 'dieser Baum'), die bestimmte Kennzeichnung (z. B. 'die Flöte von Pan', 'die älteste Japanerin'), der Eigenname (z. B. 'Pan', 'Paris') und die Indikatoren (z. B. 'du', 'jetzt'). Als Standardfall eines Gegenstandes faßt man in diesem Zusammenhang in der Regel raum-zeitliche Partikularia (z. B. Einzeldinge oder -ereignisse) auf (vgl. Strawson 1974: vii). Dieser Ausgangspunkt führt häufig zu einem grob verallgemeinernden ontologischen Postulat, das die Existenz eines vorgegebenen Reiches von Individuen behauptet. In neueren Theorien wird dieser postulierte Individuenvorrat häufig als Diskursuniversum bezeichnet. Daß die semantische Funktion von Nominatoren eine differenziertere Betrachtung erfordert, wird jedoch rasch deutlich, wenn man Beispiele wie 'Schizophrenie', 'Mickey Maus', 'Madame Bovary', 'das britische Königshaus', 'die Feuerwehr', 'die Gotik', 'die Unesco' und 'die Zahl π' näher ins Auge faßt. Aus diesem Grund wurde auch der Vorschlag gemacht, die Funktion der Nominatoren nicht unter Rückgriff auf Gegenstände zu erklären, sondern umgekehrt die Rede von Gegenständen auf die Funktion von Nominatoren (und Prädikatoren) zurückzuführen:

„Wir verstehen unter 'Gegenstand' *alles* 'dasjenige', dem ein Prädikator zugesprochen werden kann oder worauf man durch Eigennamen oder deiktische Handlungen (Kennzeichnungen) hinzeigen kann in einer für den Gesprächspartner verständlichen Weise. [...] Wir haben keinerlei Anlaß, uns auf Beschränkungen einzulassen, die zusätzlich fordern, jedem Gegenstand müsse, damit er überhaupt ein Gegenstand ist, von vornherein, in einer Ontologie 'a priori', der Prädikator 'sinnlich greifbar' oder sonst irgend ein Prädikator zugesprochen werden" (Kamlah & Lorenzen 1973: 42).

Von anderer Seite werden logisch-genetische Rekonstruktionen angeboten, mit denen die Rede von Individuen verständlich gemacht werden soll (vgl. z. B. Quine 1960; Lorenz 1981).

Ähnliche Probleme gibt es im Zusammenhang mit der **Prädikation**. Hier bestehen Berührungspunkte zwischen der linguistischen Universalienforschung und dem traditionellen philosophischen Universalienproblem. Bei diesem Problem geht es um die Frage, ob die Bedeutung von Prädikatoren reale (oder mentale) Gegenstände – z. B. Ideen im Sinne des Neuplatonismus oder Mengen – sind oder nicht (vgl. Bocheński 1956; Stegmüller 1956/57; Landesman (ed.) 1971; Kamlah & Lorenzen 1973: 172–179). Eine Alternative zu realistischen und mentalistischen Positionen im Universalienstreit bietet die Auffassung, wonach es neben der Funktion von Prädikatoren, Gegenstände von anderen Gegenständen zu unterscheiden, keine zusätzlichen Bedeutungen gibt. Der Versuch einer logisch-genetischen Rekonstruktion dieser prädikativen Unterscheidungsfähigkeit, ausgehend von elementaren Lehr- und Lernsituationen, verankert den Gebrauch von Prädikatoren nicht in den Strukturen der Welt oder des Denkens, sondern im menschlichen Handeln (vgl. Lorenz 1996).

Ähnlich wie Engpässe der Syntax auf die Semantik verweisen, führen also semantische Probleme, die mit Referenz und Prädikation (→ Art. 39) verbunden sind, zur Pragmatik. Neben diesen allgemeinen kritischen Überlegungen, die durch die Aufhebung des Unterschieds zwischen logischem Subjekt und Prädikat im logischen Atomismus ergänzt werden (vgl. Ramsey 1925), gibt es aber auch Einwände gegen die semantische Universalität des Nominator-Prädikator-Schemas, die sich anderer Argumente bedienen. Diese Angriffe orientieren sich an besonderen Satzsorten und an den Eigenschaften wenig beachteter Einzelsprachen: Sätze, die ersichtlich keine Nominator-Prädikator-Struktur aufweisen, sind natürlich Einwortsätze wie zum Beispiel 'Hallo!', 'Hilfe!', 'Feuer!', 'Fort!', 'Nicht!' (vgl. Wittgenstein 1953: § 27). Auf weitere Abweichungen von der Nominator-Prädikator-Form hat Martinet hingewiesen:

„Soit encore [...] la croyance mainte fois exprimée que tout énoncé de toute langue se compose d'un sujet et d'un prédicat. Sans aller très loin, il suffit d'écouter parler le français pour constater qu'à tout instant, on s'y passe de sujet ou, si l'on veut, le sujet s'y confond avec le prédicat: *voici le panier, il y a des fruits chez l'épicier* (prononcé normalement /ja de .../), *défense de fumer, le temps d'aller prendre les billets*; sans parler, bien entendu, des énoncés à l'impératif. Un aprioriste évoquera l'étymologie, analysera *voici* en *vois (i)ci*, trouvera un sujet dans le *il* d'*il y a*, postulera *il y a* devant *défense de fumer* et, par exemple, *il me faut* devant *le temps d'aller*, bref, retrouvera toutes les roueries et tous les faux-fuyants de l'analyse logique traditionelle" (Martinet 1967: 127).

Der aus der Logik stammende Anspruch, daß die Nominator-Prädikator-Form in deskriptivem Sinne als universale Satzstruktur aufzufassen sei, wurde auch unter Hinweis auf außereuropäische Sprachen in Zweifel gezogen. Prominentester Vertreter dieser Untersuchungsstrategie ist Benjamin Lee Whorf. Dieser ist ganz allgemein der Meinung, daß wichtige Grundannahmen der Logik und der Theorie der Wissenschaftssprache auf kontingenten Eigenschaften der europäischen Sprachen beruhen. Derartige Grundannahmen als universal anzusehen, sei genauso verfehlt, als wollte ein Botaniker aus der ausschließlichen Erforschung von Nutzpflanzen und Treibhausrosen allgemeine Aussagen über die Pflanzenwelt ableiten. Das konkrete Studium des Semitischen, Chinesischen und Tibetanischen, der afrikanischen Sprachen und der amerikanischen Eingeborenensprachen würde hier eine große Menge an Fehlurteilen ans Licht bringen (vgl. Whorf 1956: 214 f.). In bezug auf die Nominator-Prädikator-Struktur hat Whorf insbesondere am Beispiel der Indianersprache Nootka, die überhaupt keine Sätze dieser Art kennen soll, zu zeigen versucht, daß es sich bei dieser Struktur nicht um eine universale handelt. So sei zum Beispiel der Nootka-Satz 'tl'imshya'isita'itlma', der soviel bedeutet wie 'er lädt Leute zu einem Festessen' (oder 'gekochtes Essende holen tut er'), nicht in Nominator und Prädikator aufzubrechen. Um den Unterschied zwischen dem Nootka-Satz und seiner Übersetzung verständlich zu machen, vergleicht Whorf die semantische Komposition von Nootka-Sätzen mit chemischen Verbindungen, die Nominator-Prädikator-Struktur dagegen mit rein mechanischen Mischungen. Er warnt davor, allein aus der Übersetzung auf die Struktur der fremden Sprache schließen zu wollen:

„Our Indian languages show that with a suitable grammar we may have intelligent sentences that cannot be broken into subjects and predicates. Any attempted breakup is a breakup of some English translation or paraphrase of the sentence, not of the Indian sentence itself. We might as well try to decompose a certain synthetic resin into Celluloid and whiting because the resin can be imitated with Celluloid and whiting" (Whorf 1956: 242).

Beim Vergleich des chinesischen Satzes 'Yutang chouyan' mit dem englischen Satz 'Yutang smokes' kommt auch Tsu-Lin Mei zu dem Ergebnis, daß die Nominator-Prädikator-Struktur des Satzes keine universelle Gültigkeit beanspruchen kann (Mei 1961).

In enger Verzahnung mit den dargestellten Funktionen der Referenz und der Prädikation steht natürlich das Problem der **Wahrheit**. Die Erörterung dieses Problems im Rahmen einer Beziehung zwischen Sprache und Welt (also als ein semantisches Problem) führt in der Regel zu folgender Wahrheitsbestimmung: 'Ein Satz ist wahr, wenn der von ihm dargestellte Sachverhalt tatsächlich existiert'. Der Satz 'Peter trägt die blaue Hose' ist nach dieser Auffassung also genau dann wahr, wenn Peter die blaue Hose trägt. Im Sinne des frühen Wittgenstein läßt sich dieses Wahrheitskonzept auch dadurch umschreiben, daß man den Satz als ein mögliches „Bild der Welt" versteht, das man an die Welt halten kann um zu entscheiden, ob es ihr entspricht oder nicht (vgl. Wittgenstein 1922: 4.01). Die Frage, wodurch der Satz dabei zum Bild wird, was sein „Gesetz der Projektion" ist, war für Wittgenstein von größter Bedeutung. Sie verlor leider in der nachfolgenden Tradition des logischen Empirismus von Carnap über Tarski bis zu Montague immer mehr an Beachtung, tritt aber in der analytischen Philosophie unter dem Stichwort 'Wahrheitsbedingungen' als Gegenstand der Diskussion auf. Einen besonders ausführlichen und scharfsinnigen Beitrag zu dieser Diskussion lieferten Gordon Baker und Peter Hacker (Baker & Hacker 1984: 121−242). Im Bereich der Wissenschaftssprachen lassen sich materiale Wahrheitsbedingungen oft durch die technische Beherrschung wissenschaftlicher Verfahren (z. B. des Messens) und durch terminologische Normierungen genauer festlegen als im Alltag. Dies gilt auch für bestimmte andere Lebensbereiche wie das Handwerk und die Jurisprudenz. In den meisten Lebenssituationen, in denen Sprache verwendet wird, ist jedoch nicht genau geregelt, welche Verteidigungspflichten mit dem Äußern eines Elementarsatzes verbunden sind. Hier ist man auf die Vielfalt der alltäglichen Gebrauchsweisen der Sprache verwiesen (vgl. Janich 1996). In der Spätphilosophie Wittgensteins erscheint diese Einsicht, die die Antwort auf die erwähnte Frage nach den Projektionsregeln zwischen Satz und Welt darstellt, als Verwiesenheit an die Mannigfaltigkeit der Sprachspiele (vgl. Hintikka 1976). In ähnlicher Weise wurde das Wahrheitsproblem auch in der phänomenologisch-existentialistischen Tradition von der rein wissenschaftlichen Dimension abgelöst und in grundlegendere anthropologische Zusammenhänge (z. B. die personalistische Einstellung zur Welt oder die Grundstruktur des Daseins als Sorge) eingebettet (vgl. Tugendhat 1967; Buchholz 2000, 179−182). Pirmin Stekeler-Weithofer hat den gemeinsamen Boden der verschiedenen kritischen Stellungnahmen zu den formalistischen und objektivistischen Wahrheitsauffassungen in der Sprachphilosophie besonders deutlich offengelegt:

„Wie verwandt trotz der verschiedenen Sprachen zumindest die Zielsetzung der Analysen des Existenzialismus, des Pragmatismus und dann der logisch-pragmatischen Sprachanalyse sind, zeigt sich gerade an ihrem gemeinsamen 'humanistischen', von Gegnern daher als anthropozentrisch kritisierten Grundsatz, 'den Barwert der Wahrheit […] in Erfahrungsmünze umzurechnen'. Es ist dies nur eine andere Formulierung des phänomenologisch-hermeneutischen Anspruchs, unser Reden, besonders über 'objektive' Dinge und Wahrheiten, streng auf unsere existentielle Grundsituation als Menschen zu beziehen, auf ihren 'Sitz im Leben'" (Stekeler-Weithofer 1996: 1012).

Aus kultur- beziehungsweise sprachrelativistischer Sicht befaßte sich Kwasi Wiredu mit der Wahrheitsproblematik. Am Beispiel der afrikanischen Sprache Akan, die keine Ausdrücke für 'wahr' und 'Tatsache' kennt, sondern nur die Form 'te saa' ('ist so'), zeigt er, daß weder bestimmte Wahrheitstheorien noch das Wahrheitsproblem als solches universalen Charakter besitzen (Wiredu 1996).

5. Pragmatische Universalien

Das Untersuchungsfeld der Pragmatik ist die Sprache, wie sie uns in ihrem tatsächlichen Gebrauch entgegentritt. Die Pragmatik interessiert sich für den gesamten funktionalen Zusammenhang, in den konkrete sprachliche Äußerungen (→ Art. 34) eingebunden sind. Dieses Forschungsziel hat John Langshaw Austin, einer der prominentesten Pragmatiker, klar auf den Punkt gebracht: „The total speech-act in the total speech situation is the *only actual* phenomenon which, in the last resort, we are engaged in elucidating" (Austin 1962: 147). Ein derartiger Anspruch scheint von vornherein jedem Universalitätsgedanken zuwiderzulaufen. Dennoch war gerade Austin, trotz seiner ausgeprägten Sensibilität für feinste Nuancen der Sprachverwendung, einer der ersten, die allgemeine Einsichten in die pragmatische Dimension der Sprache zutage fördern wollten. Austin betonte, daß es neben der von der Logik in den Vordergrund gestellten repräsentativen Funktion der Sprache (lokutionäre Rolle) auch das Verfolgen von Zwecken (illokutionäre Rolle) und das Hervorbringen von Reaktionen (perlokutionäre Rolle) mittels Sprache gebe (→ Art. 35).

Ausgehend von Austins Arbeiten schlug John Roger Searle später eine Typologie von fünf verschiedenen Arten **illokutionärer Akte** vor. Searle beanspruchte, mit dieser Typologie ein vollständiges Klassifikationsschema vorgelegt und dadurch die Ansicht einiger Sprachtheoretiker widerlegt zu haben, daß der Sprachgebrauch in unzählige Formen zerfalle (vgl. Searle 1975: 369). Die fünf Typen sind im einzelnen:

a. darstellende Äußerungen (z. B. 'Oslo ist die Hauptstadt von Norwegen.')
b. direktive Äußerungen (z. B. 'Fahren Sie mich bitte zum Hauptbahnhof!')
c. kommissive Äußerungen (z. B. 'Ich bringe Dir den Schlüssel morgen vorbei.')
d. expressive Äußerungen (z. B. 'Es tut mir sehr leid, daß ich mich verspätet habe.')
e. deklarative Äußerungen (z. B. 'Ich taufe dieses Schiff auf den Namen 'Queen Mary'!').

Diese illokutionären Akttypen können als eine bestimmte Sorte pragmatischer Univer-

4. Sprachphilosophie

salien angesehen werden. Eine zweite Sorte solcher Universalien sind die von Herbert Paul Grice vorgeschlagenen **Konversationsmaximen**. Im Unterschied zu Searles Klassifikation sind diese Maximen allerdings nicht als adäquate Beschreibungen des Sprachverhaltens gedacht, sondern als universelle Normen, die beherzigt werden müssen, wenn man beim Sprechen das Ziel der rationalen Verständigung verfolgt. Einige Beispiele für Konversationsmaximen sind die Regeln 'Gib alle wichtigen Informationen!', 'Sage nichts, was Du für falsch hältst!', 'Rede verständlich!', 'Vermeide Unklarheit und Mehrdeutigkeit!' (vgl. Grice 1975). Eine Verbindung zwischen Searles und Grices Überlegungen leistet Jürgen Habermas' **Universalpragmatik**. Die Grundidee dieses Ansatzes ist die Beschreibung von „allgemeinen Voraussetzungen kommunikativen Handelns" (Habermas 1976: 174). Dabei wird das Ziel kommunikativen Handelns als die Herbeiführung von Einverständnis zwischen den Kommunikationsteilnehmern verstanden und die Voraussetzungen für dieses Ziel als im vorhinein gemeinsam anerkannte Geltungsansprüche bestimmt. Diese universalen Geltungsansprüche seien − in Anlehnung an Grice − die gegenseitige Verpflichtung auf Wahrheit, Richtigkeit, Wahrhaftigkeit und Verständlichkeit. Den ersten drei Arten von Geltungsansprüchen korrespondierten dabei − in Anlehnung an Searle − die Sprechhandlungsfunktionen Darstellung, Mitteilung und Ausdruck. Weiterführende Überlegungen zum theoretischen Status der von Searle und Grice angebotenen Universalien und zur gegenseitigen Ergänzung von syntaktischen und pragmatischen Universalien finden sich bei Siegfried Kanngießer (vgl. Kanngießer 1976).

Darüber hinaus wurden auch in bezug auf die von Searle und Grice vorgeschlagenen Universalienarten Einwände von Seiten der anthropologischen Sprach- und Kommunikationsforschung vorgebracht. Michelle Z. Rosaldo untersuchte beispielsweise, ob Searles Typologie auch auf die Sprache der auf den Philippinen beheimateten Ilongoten angewandt werden kann. Sie fand heraus, daß die von der westlichen Kultur sehr verschiedene soziale und institutionelle Organisation der Ilongoten *alle* illokutionären Akttypen Searles problematisch erscheinen läßt (Rosaldo 1982: 212−222). Die Kategorie der darstellenden Äußerungen etwa sei insgesamt mit großer Vorsicht zu genießen: Der Inhalt einer Äußerung werde bei den Ilongoten nämlich im allgemeinen nicht deshalb akzeptiert, weil er mit den Gegebenheiten in der Welt übereinstimme, sondern weil der Sprecher es durch rhetorisches Geschick verstehe, sich als Person in ein gutes Licht zu rücken. Ähnliche Probleme gebe es mit direktiven und deklarativen Äußerungen. Kommissive und expressive Äußerungen fehlten wegen eines radikal anderen Personenverständnisses bei den Ilongoten sogar nahezu völlig:

„To Westerners, taught to think of social life as constituted by so many individuated cells, prosocial impulses and drives may seem a necessary prerequisite to social bonds, and so the notion of a world where no one 'promises', 'apologizes', 'congratulates', 'establishes commitments', or 'gives thanks', may seem either untenable or anomic. Certainly, when in the field, I was consistently distressed to find that Ilongots did not appear to share in my responses to such things as disappointment or success, and that they lacked expressive forms with which to signal feelings of appreciation, obligation, salutation, and regret, like our 'I'm sorry' or 'good morning'. Repeatedly, I was outraged to find that friends who had arranged to meet and work with me did not appear at the decided time − especially as they would then speak not of commitments broken, or of excuses and regrets, but of devices (such as gifts) that might assuage the generally unexpected and disturbing anger in my heart. To them, it mattered that I was annoyed (a dangerous and explosive state), but not that someone else, in carelessness, had hurt and angered me by failing to fulfill commitments I had understood as tantamount to promises" (Rosaldo 1982: 217 f.).

Während diese Kritikpunkte die Gesamtidee von Searle massiv ins Wanken bringen können, lassen sich die gegen Grice vorgebrachten anthropologischen Einwände (vgl. Balagangadhara & Pinxten 1989) nicht in vollem Umfang aufrechterhalten. Die Beschreibung von Situationen, in denen Chinesen, Inder oder Navahos aufgrund ihrer kulturellen Traditionen unkooperativ handeln, kann nämlich deshalb nicht als Einwand akzeptiert werden, da Grice niemals behauptet hat, daß sich Kommunikationspartner faktisch immer kooperativ verhalten. Er plädiert vielmehr dafür, daß Kommunikationspartner dies tun *sollten*. An dieser Stelle weisen Balagangadhara und Pinxten dann allerdings zu Recht darauf hin, daß die große Bedeutung, die dem rationalen Argumentieren als Norm in der westlichen Kultur beigemessen wird, nicht kulturell neutral ist. Sie beruhe vielmehr auf einer kulturell bedingten entpersonalisierten Auffassung der Gesprächspartner in einem Argumentationsprozeß. Diese Auffassung hänge wiederum sehr eng damit zusammen, daß das Leben in den abendländischen Gesellschaften stark von den Institutionen der Rechtsprechung und der Wissenschaft geprägt sei.

Den vorgestellten pragmatischen Universalienkonzepten, die in den Traditionen der analytischen Philosophie und der Transzendentalpragmatik entwickelt wurden, stehen Überlegungen gegenüber, die aus der phänomenologisch-existentialistischen Philosophie, dem Dialogismus, dem Konstruktivismus und der Sprachspielpragmatik erwachsen sind. In allen diesen Traditionen werden Erwägungen zu pragmatischen Universalien in der *condition humaine* (→ Art. 3) verankert. Wie die *condition humaine* näher zu bestimmen ist beziehungsweise welche ihrer Facetten als grundlegend angesehen werden, ist dabei jedoch keineswegs einheitlich.

Als Vertreter der phänomenologisch-existentialistischen Richtung sind in erster Linie Georg Misch, Karl Jaspers, Wilhelm Schapp, Martin Heidegger und Hans Lipps zu nennen. Misch und Lipps gehen im Vergleich zu Austin genau umgekehrt vor. Sie sehen die praktischen Zusammenhänge, in denen Sprache verwendet wird, nicht als ein über die Logik hinausgehendes Forschungsfeld, sondern als eigens zu thematisierende Vorbedingung für den Aufbau der Logik. In diesem Sinne sprechen sie von einer „hermeneutischen Logik" und einer „Logik auf lebensphilosophischem Boden". Die jeweils einmaligen und einzigartigen Situationen, in denen sich der Mensch wiederfindet und aus denen heraus er Entscheidungen trifft, sowie das **Leben als Ganzes** bilden dabei die Grundlage für jedes bedeutungshaltige Reden (vgl. Lipps 1938: 20−30; Misch 1994: 567−570). In Anknüpfung an diese Tradition hat Schapp später den Lebenshintergrund, ohne den sprachliche Ausdrücke bloße Hülsen bleiben, mit den verschiedenen, ineinandergreifenden **Geschichten** identifiziert, in die wir Zeit unseres Lebens verstrickt sind. Zu dem theoretischen Problem, Wörtern und Sätzen Bedeutungen zuzuweisen, vertritt Schapp dementsprechend eine klare Position: „Ohne Beziehung zu den Geschichten tappen wir [...] vollständig im Dunkeln" (Schapp 1959: 296). Die existentiellen Angelpunkte, von denen her schließlich Heidegger und Jaspers den Sinn von Sprache verständlich machen wollen, sind die **Sorge** und das **Umgreifende** (vgl. Heidegger 1927: § 34; Jaspers 1947: 403−405).

Im Gegensatz zur phänomenologisch-existentialistischen Tradition, in der der jeweils Einzelne mit seinen individuellen Lebensvollzügen zur Grundlage der Sprachphilosophie gemacht wird, steht im Dialogismus das Verhältnis zwischen Sprecher und Angesprochenem im Vordergrund. Insbesondere in den Schriften Martin Bubers und Ferdinand Ebners bildet dieses Verhältnis den Ausgangspunkt für weitreichende Überlegungen zur Rolle der Sprache im menschlichen Leben (vgl. Ebner 1921; Buber 1954). In Bubers Unterscheidung der Grundworte 'Ich-Du' und 'Ich-Es', die die zwei möglichen Haltungen des Menschen zur Welt angeben sollen, wird besonders deutlich greifbar, was das Dialogische an der Philosophie des Dialogs ist: Das Grundwort 'Ich-Es' (oder 'Ich-Er' beziehungsweise 'Ich-Sie') steht für eine Haltung, bei der ein Ich über unpersönlich aufgefaßte Gegenstände spricht. Mit dem Grundwort 'Ich-Du' soll dagegen zum Ausdruck kommen, daß beim Sprechen jemand angeredet wird, dem sich ein Ich mit der ganzen Tiefe und dem unausschöpflichen Geheimnis der **persönlichen Begegnung** widmet. Nur diese zweite Form des Sprechens soll dabei als Dialog oder Gespräch im eigentlichen Sinne verstanden werden.

Im Konstruktivismus wird wiederum eine andere Dimension zur pragmatischen Basis des Sprechens gemacht: das **Handeln**. Es wird dort davon ausgegangen, daß der Mensch durch sein Handeln und auf der Grundlage seiner natürlichen Bedürftigkeit und Ausstattung unterschiedliche Kulturformen und Fertigkeiten ausbilde, die sich einerseits zu kulturellen Traditionen verfestigen und andererseits durch individuelle Aneignung und Umgestaltung verändern könnten. Dies gelte auch für das sprachliche Handeln, das als Form des vermittelten Handelns (vgl. Kambartel 1976) auf nichtsprachliches Handeln angewiesen bleibe und ständig Gefahr laufe, in leeres Gerede abzugleiten (vgl. Lorenzen & Schwemmer 1973: 17−20). Dementsprechend wird die Beschreibung und Normierung universaler Sprachformen in der konstruktiven Philosophie von der Entdeckung und Erfindung universaler nichtsprachlicher Handlungsschemata abhängig gemacht. Dies wird an Lorenzens Versuch, universale logische Strukturen in der natürlichen Sprache durch den Rückgriff auf nichtsprachliche Handlungsformen (z. B. Würfeln und Tauchen) sichtbar zu machen, besonders deutlich (vgl. Lorenzen 1968).

4. Sprachphilosophie

Auch in der Tradition der Sprachspielpragmatik wird auf die enge Verwobenheit sprachlicher und nichtsprachlicher Handlungsanteile hingewiesen (vgl. Wittgenstein 1953: §§ 7, 23). In einer Weiterführung von Wittgensteins Gedanken weist beispielsweise Jakob Meløe darauf hin, daß die Übersetzung von einer Sprache in die andere nur auf der Basis gemeinsamer nichtsprachlicher Tätigkeitsformen möglich ist (Meløe 1986: 115−118). **Sprachspiele** im Sinne Wittgensteins sind Formen der Sprachverwendung, die in ihrer elementaren Gestalt auf Abrichtung und natürlichen Fähigkeiten beruhen (Wittgenstein 1953: §§ 7, 25) und sich im Zusammenhang der vielfältigen menschlichen Lebensformen zu immer feineren und komplizierteren Spielen aufbauen lassen. Sie besitzen insofern universalen Charakter, als sie von Wittgenstein als die jeweils nicht weiter zu hinterfragenden Fundamente der Sprachverwendung aufgefaßt werden (Wittgenstein 1953: §§ 654−656). Diese Fundamente im einzelnen sichtbar und interpersonell verfügbar zu machen, kann als das Grundanliegen der Sprachphilosophie Wittgensteins angesehen werden. Die Mittel dafür sind Sprachspiele in einem zweiten Sinne − unterschiedliche Beschreibungsweisen realer oder fiktiver Sprachverwendungsformen. Die systematische Ausarbeitung dieser Beschreibungsweisen zu einer universalen Methode der Sprachbetrachtung befindet sich jedoch noch in den Anfängen (vgl. Buchholz 1998; 1998/99).

6. Zusammenfassung

Die linguistische Universalienforschung findet ihr sprachphilosophisches Spiegelbild in den Auseinandersetzungen um das Verhältnis von Logik und natürlicher Sprache. Diese Auseinandersetzungen sind in ihrer vollen Tragweite nur auf dem Hintergrund allgemeiner philosophischer Fragestellungen zu verstehen. Sie bewegen sich zwischen zwei entgegengesetzten Polen. Auf der einen Seite steht die Auffassung, daß logische Strukturen die wesentlichen Aspekte des menschlichen Lebens und Erkennens abstecken. Auf der anderen Seite wird gefordert, logische Strukturen in ihren praktischen Bezügen zu erörtern und die vielfältigen Möglichkeiten, die das menschliche Leben eröffnet, nicht vorschnell theoretischer Verengung preiszugeben. Für die Sprachbetrachtung bedeutet dies, daß einerseits die offensichtliche Eigenschaft der Verbalsprache, ein einheitliches und klar strukturiertes Medium zu sein, in den Vordergrund gerückt wird und daß andererseits die eleganten und vielfältigen Anpassungsmöglichkeiten dieses Mediums an die Besonderheiten seiner jeweiligen Verwendungssituation betont werden. In diesem Spannungsfeld einen Ausgleich unter Berücksichtigung der verschiedenen Teileinsichten in das Funktionieren der Sprache zu schaffen, stellt eine große und wichtige Herausforderung an die zukünftige Sprachphilosophie dar (vgl. Schnelle 1976). Für alle Debatten um Universalitätsansprüche in diesem Zusammenhang wäre eine eingehende Beschäftigung mit den empirischen Befunden der linguistischen Universalienforschung sicher sehr hilfreich.

7. Zitierte Literatur

Ajdukiewicz, Kazimierz. 1935. „Die syntaktische Konnexität". *Studia Philosophica* 1: 1−27.

Austin, John Langshaw. 1962. *How to Do Things with Words* (The William James Lectures, 1955.) Cambridge/MA: Harvard University Press.

Baker, Gordon Park & Hacker, Peter Michael Stephan. 1984. *Language, Sense and Nonsense.* Oxford: Blackwell.

Balagangadhara, S. N. & Pinxten, Rik. 1989. „Comparative anthropology and rhetorics in cultures. Reflecions on argumentation theories and forms of life". In: Maier, Robert (ed.). *Norms in Argumentation* (Studies of Argumentation in Pragmatics and Discourse Analysis, 8.) Dordrecht: Foris, 195−211.

Bocheński, Innocentius M. 1956. „The problem of universals". In: Bocheński, Innocentius M. & Church, Alonzo & Goodman, Nelson. *The Problem of Universals.* Notre Dame/IN: University of Notre Dame Press, 35−54.

Boom, Holger van den. 1978. „Eine Explikation des linguistischen Universalienbegriffes". In: Seiler, Hansjakob (ed.). *Language Universals* (Tübinger Beiträge zur Linguistik, 111.) Tübingen: Narr, 59−78.

Buber, Martin. 1954. *Die Schriften über das dialogische Prinzip.* Heidelberg: Schneider.

Buchholz, Kai. 1998. *Sprachspiel und Semantik.* München: Fink.

Buchholz, Kai. 1998/99. „La conception Wittgensteinienne de la philosophie". *Philosophia Scientiae* 3: 171−184.

Buchholz, Kai. 2000. „Nachwort. Vom Schrecken des Todes und des Lebens". In: Shakespeare, William. *Hamlet.* München: Goldmann, 169−224.

Coseriu, Eugenio. 1974. „Les universaux linguistiques (et les autres)". In: Heilmann, Luigi (ed.). *Proceedings of the XIth International Congress of Linguistics.* Vol. 1. Bologna: Il Mulino, 47–73.

Cresswell, Max J. 1973. *Logics and Languages.* London: Methuen.

Ebner, Ferdinand. 1921. *Das Wort und die geistigen Realitäten.* Regensburg: Pustet.

Gamut, L. T. F. 1991. *Logic, Language, and Meaning.* Vol. 2. Chicago & London: University of Chicago Press.

Gardies, Jean-Louis. 1975. *Esquisse d'une grammaire pure.* Paris: Vrin.

Greenberg, Joseph H. & Jenkins, James J. & Osgood, Charles E. 1963. „Memorandum concerning language universals". In: Greenberg, Joseph H. (ed.). *Universals of Language.* Cambridge/MA: M.I.T. Press, 255–264.

Grice, Herbert Paul. 1975. „Logic and conversation". In: Davidson, Donald & Harman, Gilbert (eds.). *The Logic of Grammar.* Encino/Calif.: Dickenson, 64–75.

Habermas, Jürgen. 1976. „Was heißt Universalpragmatik?" In: Apel, Karl-Otto (ed.). *Sprachpragmatik und Philosophie.* Frankfurt a. M.: Suhrkamp, 174–272.

Heidegger, Martin. 1927. *Sein und Zeit* (Jahrbuch für Philosophie und phänomenologische Forschung, 8.) Halle: Niemeyer.

Hintikka, Jaakko. 1976. „Language-games". *Acta Philosophica Fennica* 28: 105–125.

Husserl, Edmund. 1900/01. *Logische Untersuchungen.* 2 Bde. Halle: Niemeyer.

Janich, Peter. 1996. *Was ist Wahrheit?* München: Beck.

Jaspers, Karl. 1947. *Von der Wahrheit.* München: Piper.

Kambartel, Friedrich. 1976. „Symbolic acts". In: Ryle, Gilbert (ed.). *Contemporary Aspects of Philosophy.* Stocksfield & London: Oriel Press, 70–85.

Kamlah, Wilhelm & Lorenzen, Paul. 1973. *Logische Propädeutik* (BI-Hochschultaschenbücher, 227.) Mannheim: Bibliographisches Institut [1967].

Kanngießer, Siegfried. 1976. „Sprachliche Universalien und diachrone Prozesse". In: Apel, Karl-Otto (ed.). *Sprachpragmatik und Philosophie.* Frankfurt a. M.: Suhrkamp, 273–393.

Landesman, Charles (ed.). 1971. *The Problem of Universals.* New York & London: Basic Books.

Leśniewski, Stanisław. 1929. „Grundzüge eines neuen Systems der Grundlagen der Mathematik". *Fundamenta Mathematicae* 14: 1–81.

Lieb, Hans-Heinrich. 1975. „Universals of language: Quandaries and prospects". *Foundations of Language* 12: 471–511.

Lipps, Hans. 1938. *Untersuchungen zu einer hermeneutischen Logik.* Frankfurt a. M.: Klostermann.

Lorenz, Kuno. 1981. „Semiotic stages in the genesis of individuals". *Fundamenta Scientiae* 2: 45–53.

Lorenz, Kuno. 1996. „Artikulation und Prädikation". In: Dascal, Marcelo & Gerhardus, Dietfried & Lorenz, Kuno & Meggle, Georg (eds.). *Sprachphilosophie* (Handbücher zur Sprach- und Kommunikationswissenschaft, 7.) Vol. 2. Berlin & New York: de Gruyter, 1098–1122.

Lorenzen, Paul. 1968. „Logische Strukturen in der Sprache". In: Ders. *Methodisches Denken.* Frankfurt a. M.: Suhrkamp, 60–69.

Lorenzen, Paul. 1980. „Rationale Grammatik". In: Gethmann, Carl Friedrich (ed.). *Theorie des wissenschaftlichen Argumentierens.* Frankfurt a. M.: Suhrkamp, 73–94.

Lorenzen, Paul & Schwemmer, Oswald. 1973. *Konstruktive Logik, Ethik und Wissenschaftstheorie* (BI-Hochschultaschenbücher, 700.) Mannheim: Bibliographisches Institut.

Martinet, André. 1967. „Réflexions sur les universaux du langage". *Folia Linguistica* 1: 125–134.

Mei, Tsu-Lin. 1961. „Subject and predicate, a grammatical preliminary". *The Philosophical Review* 70: 153–175.

Meløe, Jakob. 1986. „Über Sprachspiele und Übersetzungen". In: Böhler, Dietrich & Nordenstam, Tore & Skirbekk, Gunnar (eds.). *Die pragmatische Wende* (Suhrkamp-Taschenbuch Wissenschaft, 631.) Frankfurt a. M.: Suhrkamp, 113–130.

Misch, Georg. 1994. *Der Aufbau der Logik auf dem Boden der Philosophie des Lebens.* Freiburg & München: Alber.

Næss, Arne. 1971. *En del elementære logiske emner.* Oslo: Universitetsforlaget.

Nef, Frédéric. 1991. *Logique, langage et réalité.* Paris: Editions Universitaires.

Quine, Willard Van Orman. 1960. *Word and Object.* Cambridge/MA: M.I.T. Press.

Raible, Wolfgang. 1980. „Edmund Husserl, die Universalienforschung und die Regularität des Irregulären". In: Brettschneider, Gunter & Lehmann, Christian (eds.). *Wege zur Universalienforschung* (Tübinger Beiträge zur Linguistik, 145.) Tübingen: Narr, 42–50.

Ramsey, Frank Plumpton. 1925. „Universals". *Mind* 34: 401–417.

Rosaldo, Michelle Z. 1982. „The things we do with words: Ilongot speech acts and speech act theory in philosophy". *Language in Society* 11: 203–237.

Schächter, Josef. 1935. *Prolegomena zu einer kritischen Grammatik* (Schriften zur wissenschaftlichen Weltauffassung, 10.) Wien: Springer.

Schapp, Wilhelm. 1959. *Philosophie der Geschichten.* Leer: Rautenberg.

Schneider, Hans Julius. 1975. *Pragmatik als Basis von Semantik und Syntax.* Frankfurt a. M.: Suhrkamp.

Schneider, Hans Julius. 1992. „Kann und soll die Sprachphilosophie methodisch vorgehen?" In: Janich, Peter (ed.). *Entwicklungen der methodischen Philosophie* (Suhrkamp-Taschenbuch Wissenschaft, 979.) Frankfurt a. M.: Suhrkamp, 17–33.

Schneider, Hans Julius. 1993. „ 'Syntaktische Metaphern' und ihre begrenzende Rolle für eine systematische Bedeutungstheorie". *Deutsche Zeitschrift für Philosophie* 41: 477–486.

Schneider, Hans Julius. 1996. „Wittgensteins Begriff der Grammatik und das Phänomen der Metapher". In: Schneider, Hans Julius (ed.). *Metapher, Kognition, Künstliche Intelligenz.* München: Fink, 13–31.

Schnelle, Helmut. 1976. „Zum Begriff der sprachanalytischen Rekonstruktion von Sprachausschnitten". In: Wunderlich, Dieter (ed.). *Wissenschaftstheorie der Linguistik* (Athenäum Taschenbücher, 1204.) Kronberg: Athenäum, 217–232.

Searle, John Roger. 1975. „A taxonomy of illocutionary acts". In: Gunderson, Keith (ed.). *Language, Mind, and Knowledge* (Minnesota Studies in the Philosophy of Science, 7.) Minneapolis: University of Minnesota Press, 344–369.

Seiler, Hansjakob. 1978. „The Cologne project on language universals". In: Seiler, Hansjakob (ed.). *Language Universals* (Tübinger Beiträge zur Linguistik, 111.) Tübingen: Narr, 11–25.

Stegmüller, Wolfgang. 1956/57. „Das Universalienproblem einst und jetzt". *Archiv für Philosophie* 6/7: 192–225/45–81.

Stekeler-Weithofer, Pirmin. 1996. „Der Streit um Wahrheitstheorien". In: Dascal, Marcelo & Gerhardus, Dietfried & Lorenz, Kuno & Meggle, Georg (eds.). *Sprachphilosophie* (Handbücher zur Sprach- und Kommunikationswissenschaft, 7.) Vol. 2. Berlin, New York: de Gruyter, 989–1012.

Strawson, Peter Frederick. 1974. *Subject and Predicate in Logic and Grammar* (University Paperbacks, 538.) London: Methuen.

Tugendhat, Ernst. 1967. *Der Wahrheitsbegriff bei Husserl und Heidegger.* Berlin: de Gruyter.

Whorf, Benjamin Lee. 1956. *Language, Thought, and Reality.* Cambridge/MA: M.I.T. Press.

Wiredu, Kwasi. 1996. „The concept of truth in the Akan language". In: Ders. *Cultural Universals and Particulars.* Bloomington/IND: Indiana Univ. Press, 105–112.

Wittgenstein, Ludwig. 1922. *Tractatus Logico-Philosophicus.* London: Routledge & Kegan Paul.

Wittgenstein, Ludwig. 1953. *Philosophische Untersuchungen.* Oxford: Blackwell.

Wittgenstein, Ludwig. 1957. „Notes on logic". *The Journal of Philosophy* 54: 230–245.

Kai Buchholz, Institut Mathildenhöhe, Darmstadt (Deutschland)

5. Sciences cognitives et Intelligence Artificielle

1. Périodisation
2. Les postulats de la recherche cognitive
3. Les deux principaux paradigmes
4. Incidences sur la linguistique
5. La sémantique cognitive
6. Perspectives
7. Références

Dans la tradition philosophique occidentale, le langage a toujours été considéré comme un moyen de connaissance. La linguistique cognitive renoue avec cette tradition, qui préexistait à la formation de la linguistique comme discipline académique et scientifique au début du dix-neuvième siècle. Mais elle le fait évidemment dans des conditions nouvelles.

1. Périodisation

Dans l'histoire de la linguistique cognitive, qui s'étend sur la seconde moitié de ce siècle, on peut distinguer deux phases principales.

La première, de 1955 à 1975 environ, a été préparée par la cybernétique, dans laquelle la linguistique ne jouait qu'un rôle discret. Au début des années cinquante, la théorie de l'information commence à influencer des théories linguistiques; d'autre part se développent les premiers traitements automatiques du langage (traduction, analyse et synthèse de la parole). Par ailleurs, dès 1955, Noam Chomsky utilise la théorie des langages formels pour construire sa grammaire générative. Or, la théorie de langages formels établit une stricte parenté entre la théorie des grammaires et la théorie des automates. A la constitution théorique de la linguistique par la théorie des langages formels pourrait ainsi s'ajouter une validation expérimentale: par son implantation informatique, une grammaire doit pouvoir engendrer automatiquement toutes les phrases correctes d'une langue.

La psycholinguistique, constituée au début des années soixante sous l'impulsion de George A. Miller, se donne corrélativement pour tâche de valider les conceptions chomskyennes. Les liens ainsi établis entre linguistique formelle, psychologie cognitive et informatique concrétisent le paradigme dit *symbolique* du cognitivisme classique: la pensée est conçue comme une suite réglée d'opérations sur des symboles, à l'image des algorithmes informatiques.

Le langage de la pensée, repris par Jerry Fodor à une tradition philosophique millénaire, joue pour le cerveau le même rôle que le langage-machine pour l'ordinateur (cf. *The Language of Thought,* 1975). Il structure les représentations mentales en propositions logiques que les langues auraient pour tâche d'exprimer. La linguistique n'a plus alors de rapport privilégié avec les sciences sociales: selon Chomsky, elle doit se réduire à la psychologie, puis «rentrer dans la biologie»; et la grammaire universelle est considérée comme une composante (hypothétique) du patrimoine génétique. Ce programme explicitement réductionniste dérive de la thèse de l'unité de la science, formulée par le Cercle de Vienne à la fin des années vingt.

Ces objectifs et thèmes de recherche, caractérisés par le primat de la syntaxe et de l'approche formelle de la cognition, sont contestés ou abandonnés depuis le milieu des années soixante-dix par des auteurs issus de la sémantique générative (George Lakoff, Charles Fillmore, Ronald Langacker notamment). Il en résulte un déplacement d'intérêt de la syntaxe vers la sémantique, lexicale notamment; et une mise en cause du format logique des représentations.

Les grammaires cognitives apparues au milieu des années quatre-vingts conçoivent les opérations linguistiques comme des parcours au sein d'un espace abstrait, et témoignent d'un néo-localisme généralisé (George Lakoff, Leonard Talmy, Ronald Langacker). Au paradigme du calcul, elles opposent celui de la perception. Elles retrouvent cependant des thèmes de la philosophie transcendantale, comme celui du schématisme: les schèmes (ou *frames*) sont des formes de l'imagination qui rendent compte de la compréhension du langage comme constitution de scènes mentales. Un renouveau des thèmes phénoménologiques permet aussi d'insister sur le rôle de l'expérience corporelle dans le parcours de l'espace sémantique (Terry Winograd, Mark Johnson).

2. Les postulats de la recherche cognitive

Quitte à nous restreindre ici aux disciplines «centrales» de la recherche cognitive, cherchons les raisons qui ont conduit à leur regroupement. Il repose sur trois postulats d'ordre philosophique.

1) Le dualisme traditionnel entre l'esprit et le cerveau doit être restreint, peut-être jusqu'à disparaître. Le cognitivisme orthodoxe maintient cependant certaines formes de dualisme, qui permettent précisément le fonctionnalisme, au sens que Hilary Putnam a donné à ce mot: comme la computation, en tant que processus formel, est indépendante de son instanciation matérielle dans l'implémentation, les cerveaux et les ordinateurs peuvent fonctionner de manière analogue voire identique.

2) L'homme peut simuler artificiellement les processus mentaux. Ce second postulat, dont les mots mêmes d'*intelligence artificielle* résument les ambiguïtés, a pu être interprété de diverses façons. L'interprétation minimaliste se limite à simuler les «sorties», sans se préoccuper de reproduire les opérations dont elle procède. Dans le domaine du dialogue homme-machine, cela a pu conduire à des systèmes écholaliques dont l'archétype demeure l'*Eliza* de Weizenbaum. Avec plus d'ambition, on peut estimer que pour produire des «sorties» comparables, il est nécessaire de simuler les opérations mentales dont elles résultent. Enfin, l'interprétation maximaliste peut se formuler ainsi: pour simuler aussi fidèlement que possible le fonctionnement cérébral, il faut traiter l'information par des réseaux de neurones formels. C'est là le principe des modèles connexionnistes. De la simulation de «sorties», comme les paroles, on en vient même à concevoir la simulation des tissus cérébraux eux-mêmes.

Comme on le voit, la notion de simulation peut être comprise de trois manières principales, correspondant à trois degrés croissants de fidélité : au premier degré, la coopération entre la linguistique et l'informatique peut suffire; au deuxième, la collaboration avec la psychologie devient nécessaire; au troisième, il faut recourir aux neurosciences.

3) Un troisième postulat, gnoséologique celui-ci, définit la connaissance comme un ensemble de représentations symboliques du réel. Si l'on convient que penser consiste à

opérer sur des représentations et que le raisonnement se réduit à un calcul, une machine opérant sur des symboles serait capable de raisonner sur des connaissances. Cela soutient la comparaison entre cerveau et ordinateur considérés comme deux systèmes matériels de calcul sur des représentations symboliques.

Ce troisième postulat sous-tend le projet de simulation, qui apparaît dans la version maximaliste du cognitivisme, tant en Intelligence Artificielle (IA) qu'en psychologie cognitive: on connaîtra véritablement le fonctionnement du cerveau quand on aura pu le simuler par des machines traitant des symboles. Dans le domaine de la linguistique, cela entraîne que l'on connaîtra véritablement les facultés langagières humaines et les langues quand on sera parvenu à produire et énumérer automatiquement toutes les phrases grammaticales de toutes les langues attestées (voire possibles).

Cependant, il est clair que la simulation informatique ne valide rien : si un concept est techniquement opérationnel, il ne devient pas pour autant opératoire dans la théorie. Enfin, on ne doit pas assimiler sens et connaissance sans s'interroger sur leur rapport : convenons qu'il n'est ni simple, ni immédiat, et que la recherche cognitive s'est jusqu'à présent organisée autour d'une gnoséologie spontanée restée largement implicite.

3. Les deux principaux paradigmes

Les trois postulats que nous venons de préciser sont fondamentaux, dans la mesure où ils sont partagés par les deux principaux paradigmes rivaux, le cognitivisme dit *classique* (ou *orthodoxe*) et le connexionnisme. On peut les associer à deux types de philosophies (philosophie analytique et phénoménologie), deux ontologies implicites (pensée du discret et pensée du continu), voire deux poétiques (métaphore de l'ordinateur et métaphore du cerveau).

3.1. Cognitivisme orthodoxe

Selon le paradigme cognitiviste classique: (i) Le monde est composé de choses et d'états de choses. (ii) Les connaissances sont des représentations symboliques de ces choses et de ces états de choses. (iii) L'IA, la linguistique et la psychologie ont notamment pour tâche de construire des représentations symboliques des connaissances elles-mêmes, de manière à pouvoir opérer sur ces représentations.

La division du travail entre les disciplines centrales est alors celle-ci : (i) La psychologie cognitive traite avec prédilection du raisonnement, des inférences sur les connaissances, de leur stockage, de leur réquisition ; (ii) l'IA s'attache au problème de la *représentation des connaissances*; (iii) la linguistique lui propose des modèles pour le faire.

Ce premier paradigme met en œuvre une conception traductionniste du sens : le sens d'un symbole est sa traduction en d'autres symboles, ou plus précisément ce qu'il a de commun avec sa traduction. Pour ce qui concerne spécifiquement la linguistique, ce dispositif théorique entraîne deux conséquences majeures : (i) le sens linguistique est en dernière analyse dénotatif : les symboles linguistiques désignent des objets du monde ; (ii) la tâche de la linguistique consiste à représenter les symboles des langues naturelles par les symboles des langages formels, dans un processus de représentation conçu comme une traduction symbolique.

3.2. Connexionnisme

Le paradigme *connexionniste*, développé notamment en IA, est issu d'un courant de la cybernétique qui entendait simuler informatiquement l'activité cérébrale au moyen de réseaux de neurones formels. Pour autant que l'on puisse le caractériser généralement, le paradigme connexionniste s'organise autour de la cognition entendue comme formation, apprentissage et réquisition de connaissances. Mieux, *cognitif* vaut pour toute interaction complexe d'un organisme avec son milieu, et non plus seulement pour l'activité mentale dite supérieure, censée culminer chez l'homme avec le langage, voire les langages. La notion même de connaissance est alors étendue : (i) Les connaissances ne sont pas définies comme des représentations. On rompt avec la théorie du reflet. (ii) Elles ne sont pas nécessairement conscientes ou accessibles. Le cerveau ne se résume pas au cortex, ni le système nerveux au cerveau. (iii) Elles ne sont pas nécessairement conceptuelles, au sens rationaliste du terme. (iv) Elles ne sont pas non plus nécessairement symboliques, au sens logique du terme.

Alors que le cognitivisme orthodoxe traite avec prédilection du raisonnement et d'opérations réglées sur des symboles, le connexionnisme s'attache particulièrement au problème de la perception (biologique ou artificielle), et accorde une importance particulière au contexte — au sens spatial, temporel, voire intentionnel. En effet, toute perception d'un phénomène dépend étroitement de son environnement ; elle dépend aussi de facteurs temporels. Les systèmes connexionnistes donnent d'ailleurs leurs meilleurs résultats dans la perception automatique du langage, notamment pour la reconnaissance de formes incomplètes ou bruitées. Et dans ce paradigme néo-associationniste, les opérations linguistiques sont conçues à l'image des activités perceptives. Au niveau symbolique privilégié par le cognitivisme classique, il oppose un niveau subsymbolique (Paul Smolensky) formé par les constituants des symboles. Il a un rôle de médiation entre le symbolique et le physique d'une part, le symbolique et le biologique d'autre part.

La logique perd alors de sa précellence : on ne programme plus une machine, on la «conditionne»; on n'écrit pas de règles, on spécifie des liaisons entre des «neurones formels»; on n'obtient pas de résultats (ou du moins des suites de symboles interprétées comme des résultats), on repère des activations temporaires ou stables de certaines parties d'un réseau.

3.3. Les métaphores centrales

Corrélativement, les deux paradigmes s'appuient sur des ontologies contrastées. Le cognitivisme hérite de l'ontologie atomiste du positivisme logique, alors que l'ontologie spontanée du connexionnisme n'est pas logiciste, mais «physiciste» : l'objet n'est pas une entité discrète et dotée d'une identité à elle-même, mais une singularité sur un espace continu, et dont les saisies peuvent varier indéfiniment.

Enfin, les deux paradigmes se sont développés autour de deux métaphores contrastées. Pour le cognitivisme orthodoxe, le pôle métaphorique est constitué par l'ordinateur. Ainsi, en psychologie cognitive, les sujets sont supposés *traiter de l'information* en temps réel, en série ou en parallèle ; *compiler* du texte, puis l'exécuter ; *stocker des informations* dans différentes mémoires (mémoires tampon, registres, etc.) ; le tout à l'aide d'un *superviseur* allouant des ressources à des processeurs spécialisés. A la modularité des systèmes informatiques, Fodor fait en outre correspondre une modularité de l'esprit, en affirmant que «les seuls modèles de processus cognitifs qui semblent même lointainement possibles représentent ces processus comme computationnels» (1975 : 27). De telles conceptions ont été fort répandues dans le milieu des recherches cognitives, et ont retenti naturellement sur la conception du langage. Cependant, le fait que l'intelligence humaine ait pu déléguer certaines de ses tâches à des ordinateurs ne justifie aucune analogie concernant leur fonctionnement, et encore moins leur structure.

À cette réduction computationnelle répond chez les connexionnistes la métaphore neuronale. David E. Rumelhart, Geoffrey E. Hinton et James L. McClelland l'affirment nettement : «Nous voulons remplacer la 'métaphore de l'ordinateur' comme modèle de l'esprit par la 'métaphore du cerveau' comme modèle de l'esprit» (McClelland et Rumelhart 1986 : 75). De fait, le vocabulaire des connexionnistes fourmille d'emprunts à la neurophysiologie : *inhibition, activation, neurones formels*, etc.

3.4. La connivence secrète des paradigmes

Ainsi, le contraste entre les deux paradigmes semble parfaitement accusé. Dans la préface de la nouvelle édition de leur célèbre *Perceptrons* (1969), Marvin Minsky et Seymour Papert proposent cette liste d'oppositions (1988 : viii) :

symbolic	*connectionnist*
logical	*analogical*
serial	*parallel*
discrete	*continuous*
localized	*distributed*
hierarchical	*heterarchical*
left-brained	*right-brained*

Cependant, la métaphore cognitiviste entre esprit et ordinateur et la métaphore connexionniste entre ordinateur et cerveau se laissent lire ensemble, pour peu que l'on convienne que la matière pense et que la dualité entre esprit et cerveau doit se réduire jusqu'à disparaître.

En outre, si elles s'opposent sur la nature des opérations mentales, les deux problématiques concordent pour mettre en œuvre une conception mentaliste du langage, qui explique les faits linguistiques par les états mentaux ou cérébraux qu'ils reflèteraient. Secondairement, elles partagent l'objectif d'une simulation informatique des processus mentaux. D'où sans doute la connivence secrète des deux paradigmes, avec cette différence que le cognitivisme veut penser le cerveau à l'image de l'ordinateur, et le connexionnisme l'ordinateur à l'image du cerveau.

4. Incidences sur la linguistique

La linguistique cognitive a eu et conserve un impact considérable sur l'ensemble de la discipline, sous le rapport des relations avec les disciplines voisines, la définition même de l'objet et des objectifs, la conceptualisation, et enfin les applications techniques. Au plan épistémologique, la linguistique reste la principale science sociale qui soit partie prenante du regroupement des sciences cognitives (angl. *Cognitive Science*). D'où des relations nouvelles avec l'IA, et renouvelées avec les neurosciences.

4.1. Une linguistique cognitive

La linguistique générale, constamment développée depuis le XIXème siècle, prend pour objet trois grandes diversités : la diversité synchronique des langues (on en compte encore cinq mille au bas mot), leur diversité diachronique (dans leurs permanences et changements historiques), leur diversité interne (dialectes, sociolectes, etc.).

La linguistique générale, discipline descriptive et non prédictive, s'est vue contestée par les grammaires *universelles* qui entendent engendrer jusqu'aux langues possibles. Elles marquent une rupture, qui touche la méthodologie (par l'utilisation de diverses logiques comme *organon*), la nature des théories (qui visent la formalisation), enfin le statut de la linguistique comme science : de science sociale, elle pourrait devenir une branche des mathématiques (selon Richard Montague), ou des sciences de la vie (selon Noam Chomsky). Cependant, les grammaires cognitives non formelles qui se développent depuis quinze ans ne sont pas moins universalistes : elles s'attachent à décrire les opérations mentales élémentaires qui seraient à l'œuvre dans toutes les langues.

Au delà de la constitution d'une linguistique cognitive, les théories cognitives ont influencé l'ensemble des secteurs de la linguistique, et des concepts produits par la linguistique cognitive connaissent une diffusion remarquable dans l'ensemble de la discipline : par exemple, le concept de typicalité est à présent d'un usage courant en lexicologie.

4.2. Les applications

Enfin, de nouveaux domaines de la linguistique appliquée se rattachent aux recherches cognitives par leur insertion dans le champ de l'IA. C'est le cas du dialogue Homme-Machine (à présent Personne-Système), de la synthèse et de l'analyse automatiques de la parole, de la génération et de la compréhension automatiques de textes, de la représentation des connaissances. Que l'on se propose ou non la simulation des processus mentaux, ces recherches ont fait la preuve d'intérêt heuristique. Cependant, il conviendrait de distinguer avec soin l'*informatique linguistique* (branche de l'informatique qui utilise des connaissances issues de la linguistique pour réaliser des produits d'ingéniérie), et la *linguistique informatique,* qui emploie des moyens informatiques pour stocker et exploiter ses données.

Rappelons cependant que les traitements automatiques du langage ne concernent jusqu'à présent qu'un petit nombre des langues vivantes, 1% environ, d'ailleurs apparentées pour la plupart. Dans ce domaine restreint qualitativement, mais étendu géographiquement, il reste que la maîtrise sociale du langage est en voie de connaître un tournant comparable en importance à celui de l'écriture ou de l'imprimerie.

5. La sémantique cognitive

5.1. Les principaux modèles

La problématique du cognitivisme orthodoxe était dominée par la syntaxe et la théorie des grammaires. Les contestations sont d'abord venues de praticiens de l'IA spécialisés dans les traitements automatiques du langage. La théorie des dépendances conceptuelles de Roger Schank (présentée en 1973—1975) prétendait faire l'analyse automatique de textes en se passant de l'analyse syntaxique, et transcrivait tout simplement les mots en primitives conceptuelles. La centralité et l'autonomie de la syntaxe, tout comme le caractère logique de la sémantique se trouvaient de fait déniées. Yorick Wilks portait le débat sur le plan théorique en récusant les prétentions de la sémantique logique à détenir la question du sens linguistique.

En psychologie cognitive, depuis les premiers travaux de Roger Quillian sur la mémoire sémantique représentée par des chemins d'activation sur un réseau (1966), se développaient par ailleurs des modèles du «lexique mental» inspirés par la tradition associationniste, comme la théorie de l'activation propagée de Allan Collins et Elizabeth Loftus. Ils ne devaient rien dans leur principe à la sémantique formelle, quelles qu'aient été par la suite les discussions sur le statut logique de ces réseaux.

En outre, les travaux de Eleanor Rosch et de ses collaborateurs sur la typicalité, publiés à partir de 1972, mettaient indirectement en cause la théorie lexicale des conditions nécessaires et suffisantes développée par Charles Morris et Rudolf Carnap (théorie des postulats de signification), et s'appuyaient sur des expériences indiscutées à l'époque. Les travaux de Rosch concluaient à une appartenance floue des «concepts» à leurs catégories, ce dont les sémantiques logiques, intensionnelles ou extensionnelles, ne pouvaient rendre compte. Conscients du danger, Fodor et ses collaborateurs ont tenté de justifier par des arguments expérimentaux le modèle de Carnap, mais sans grand succès. En effet, le lexique a toujours été une des pierres d'achoppement des sémantiques formelles, et le mouvement progressif de réhabilitation du lexique depuis vingt ans a d'ailleurs coïncidé avec les difficultés croissantes du cognitivisme orthodoxe.

Plus généralement, les échecs subis par le modèle computationnel de l'esprit propre au cognitivisme orthodoxe ont conduit progressivement la linguistique et la psychologie cognitives à s'éloigner des modèles formels, et à mettre notamment en doute le format propositionnel des états mentaux.

Ces causes externes n'ont évidemment agi que sous l'effet de causes internes, et le cognitivisme classique a échoué en sémantique sous l'effet d'une contradiction: à supposer que le sémantique s'identifie au mental, le prétendu caractère formel des états et processus mentaux ne peut s'autoriser de la sémantique formelle contemporaine, qui se caractérise par un antipsychologisme, et, mieux, par un antimentalisme de principe.

On avait cependant assisté, dans la décennie 1975–1985, à une mentalisation de la sémantique formelle, sous le couvert de la théorie computationnelle de l'esprit: chez Fodor, par exemple, le processus de connaissance culminait dans la manipulation formelle des symboles du «langage de la pensée» (cf. 1975). Et l'ouvrage illustre de Philip N. Johnson-Laird, *Mental Models* (1983), tentait comme l'indique son titre de concilier la psychologie et la théorie des modèles, au juste prix d'un appauvrissement réciproque.

5.2. La place de la sémantique

En 1986, Ronald Langacker pouvait encore écrire, sans trop exagérer, à propos de la théorie linguistique contemporaine: «Les points d'accord général comprennent ceux-ci: (a) le langage est un système fermé sur lui-même (*self-contained*), susceptible d'une caractérisation algorithmique, et dont l'autonomie est suffisante pour qu'il puisse être étudié isolément, indépendamment de préoccupations cognitives plus larges; (b) la grammaire (la syntaxe en particulier) est un aspect indépendant de la structure linguistique, distinct à la fois du lexique et de la sémantique; et (c) son sens est justiciable de l'analyse linguistique, et il est correctement décrit par une sorte de logique formelle fondée sur des conditions de vérité» (1986: 1).

A cela il opposait: «Les structures grammaticales ne constituent pas un système formel autonome ou un niveau de représentation: elles sont bien au contraire symboliques par nature, et permettent la structuration et la symbolisation conventionnelle du contenu conceptuel. Le lexique, la morphologie et la syntaxe forment un continuum d'unités symboliques, qu'on ne peut diviser qu'arbitrairement en composants séparés» (1986: 2). Ainsi la contestation de la tripartition de Morris et Carnap permettait de redéfinir l'économie de la linguistique, et notamment la place de la sémantique en son sein. Si les constatations de Langacker sont globalement admises par les chercheurs qui se réclament de la linguistique cognitive (sauf ceux qui sont les plus proches du cognitivisme orthodoxe de Chomsky et Fodor), ils ne sont aucunement unifiés, et il faut distinguer les auteurs qui ont entrepris de psychologiser une sémantique issue de la sémantique formelle (Jackendoff par exemple) et ceux qui, comme Langacker, tentent de rompre avec la philosophie analytique.

Les débats qui se développent depuis une quinzaine d'années sont dominés par la sémantique et ils développent d'ailleurs des arguments naguère formulés par la sémantique générative. De fait, les grammaires cognitives, comme celle de Langacker, sont à base sémantique, et décrivent les relations syntaxiques comme des opérations mentales de type perceptif (balayage ou *scanning*, etc.).

5.3. Langage et pensée

La linguistique cognitive part du postulat que «le langage est une partie intégrante de la cognition humaine» (Langacker 1987: 11), ou le considère comme «un produit de processus cognitifs» (Harris 1990: 7). Autant dire qu'elle se place sous la dépendance ou dans le champ d'une «science cognitive» qui voudrait déposséder la philosophie du problème de la faculté de connaître, ou du moins rivaliser avec elle. Cette subordination épistémologique de la linguistique redouble la subordination de son objet.

Le postulat cognitif rappelle fort celui des grammairiens philosophes du XVIIIème, qui plaçaient la grammaire sous la dépendance de la logique, en convenant que les règles de la grammaire reflètent les opérations de l'esprit humain. Autant dire que la linguistique cognitive prolonge à sa manière le courant des grammaires philosophiques (→ art. 19, § 3.2.2).

Pour la linguistique cognitive, la psychologie, si logicisée soit-elle, l'emporte sur la logique, et les phénomènes linguistiques sont rapportés à des processus mentaux qui sont censés les expliquer. Cette valeur étiologique conférée aux processus mentaux suppose deux thèses, tout à fait traditionnelles en Occident depuis Platon, et qui ont toujours empêché la constitution d'une linguistique autonome : (i) le langage est un produit de la pensée ; (ii) le langage est un instrument de la pensée. A ces deux titres, il est considéré comme le produit et le moyen d'un processus de connaissance. Une approche fonctionnelle s'impose alors : «Si le langage est un des outils conceptuels de l'homme, il ne doit être non pas étudié de façon autonome, mais considéré par rapport à sa fonction cognitive : interpréter, ordonner, fixer et exprimer l'expérience humaine» (Geeraerts 1991 : 27).

Si personne parmi les cognitivistes ne conteste l'autonomie peut-être relative de la pensée, tous dénient celle du langage. C'est à cette dénégation que la sémantique se doit d'occuper dans la linguistique cognitive un rôle central : en effet, le sens est identifié — comme il l'a toujours été jusqu'à Saussure — à des représentations. En outre, les représentations sont généralement réduites à des concepts. On conclut alors, avec Jackendoff, que «la structure sémantique est la structure conceptuelle» (1983 : 85) ; ou encore avec Langacker : «le sens est identifié avec la conceptualisation» (1986 : 3). Si l'on récuse les théories logiques du concept — comme l'ont fait peu ou prou toutes les sémantiques cognitives en s'affirmant comme telles — deux voies s'ouvrent alors.

Soit l'on construit, dans le cadre de la linguistique, une théorie des idées et l'on crée une nouvelle idéologie : c'est la voie proposée notamment par Langacker : «La sémantique linguistique doit alors entreprendre l'analyse structurale et la description explicite des entités abstraites comme les pensées et les concepts» (1986, ibid.), c'est-à-dire que l'on poursuit l'entreprise non-critique (au sens kantien) des grammairiens philosophes des Lumières. Soit l'on s'en remet à la psychologie, comme plusieurs le recommandent, depuis Steinthal. Certains, comme Jackendoff, identifient tout simplement la sémantique et la psychologie cognitive : «Etudier la sémantique du langage naturel, c'est étudier la psychologie cognitive» (1983 : 3).

Si la linguistique n'est pas autonome, la sémantique ne l'est pas non plus. Qu'on en juge : «Ni la forme ni le sens des expressions ne peuvent être adéquatement décrits sans référence aux connaissances encyclopédiques des locuteurs, à leur capacité de transposer des concepts de domaines concrets vers des domaines abstraits, et à leur usage de représentations superpositionnelles et de schèmes à satisfaction de contraintes pour intégrer des sources multiples d'information» (Harris, 1990 : 7).

Si la non-autonomie du langage, et celle du niveau sémantique particulièrement, sont proclamées, la linguistique devient-elle une science de l'esprit ? Langacker dit partager avec Lakoff «la vision (devenant rapidement réalité) d'une linguistique non objectiviste qui reflète la pleine richesse de notre vie mentale» (1988 : 385). Langacker entend par là que son objet n'est pas limité au langage — et il ne prétend pas reconnaître le caractère herméneutique que la linguistique partage avec les autres sciences sociales.

Par le postulat de non-autonomie, les cognitivistes renoncent en fait à délimiter l'objet de la linguistique, pour se conformer à des objectifs, comme celui de refléter «la pleine richesse de notre vie mentale», programme qui pourrait être celui d'une phénoménologie, et qui fut celui d'une idéologie — au sens non péjoratif du terme — à la Destutt de Tracy.

Une ambiguïté demeure : la linguistique et particulièrement la sémantique n'est pas simplement rapatriée dans la philosophie qui a éternellement détenu la question du sens, elle est reversée dans la psychologie cognitive, dont la caution scientifique laisse d'ailleurs à désirer. Ainsi, bien que les sémanticiens cognitivistes reprochent pour la plupart à Chomsky «d'établir l'autonomie du langage au dépens de la sémantique» (Vandeloise 1991 : 74), certains comme Jackendoff entendent réaliser son programme : absorber la linguistique dans la psychologie (cf. Chomsky,

1984). En cela, l'ouverture cognitive, conforme à «la croyance populaire qui voit dans le langage un appendice de nos facultés cognitives générales» (Vandeloise, ibid.), cache en fait un réductionnisme banal, la réduction étant bien entendu présentée comme un enrichissement.

Si le langage n'est pas considéré comme autonome, cela tient ici à la perspective étiologique adoptée par la linguistique cognitive: en recherchant les causes des faits linguistiques, on place leur explication ailleurs, en l'occurrence dans la sphère psychologique, et l'on néglige que les sciences sociales ne peuvent accéder qu'à des conditions, non à des causes, et n'exhiber que des régularités, plutôt que des règles au sens technique.

5.4. Les difficultés du mentalisme

Le mentalisme en linguistique a un long et glorieux passé. On peut en distinguer à présent deux formes principales. (i) Le mentalisme logique a présidé depuis le milieu du XIIIème siècle jusqu'à nos jours au programme des grammaires universelles; et (ii) depuis le milieu du XIXème (si l'on se réfère à Steinthal) au programme psychologiste dont les grammaires cognitives sont la formulation la plus récente. Ainsi, Geeraerts souligne à bon droit la parenté entre une certaine sémantique historique fin de siècle et la sémantique cognitive: chez des auteurs comme Max Hecht ou Jacques van Ginneken, on trouve clairement formulées l'idée que les lois sémantiques sont de nature psychologique et que de ce fait la sémantique «tombe dans la psychologie». Mis à part le fait que la notion de loi est absente de la linguistique cognitive, et qu'elle rejette de fait la perspective diachronique, on comprend alors pourquoi «la linguistique cognitive peut reprendre le programme des préstructuralistes» (Vandeloise 1991: 90).

Les théories mentalistes de la signification linguistique, et notamment celles qui se réclament d'une psychologie, nous paraissent cependant se heurter aux difficultés suivantes.

La première tient à l'universalisme des théories mentalistes. Le cognitivisme orthodoxe prétendait l'avoir hérité du rationalisme classique. Les formes nouvelles du cognitivisme, dont relève la sémantique cognitive, ne s'en réclament plus, mais demeurent universalistes, dans la mesure où elles réitèrent des gestes caractéristiques de la philosophie transcendantale.

L'unité de l'esprit humain n'étant généralement pas mise en doute, et les significations étant rapportées à des représentations ou des opérations mentales, personne ne formule l'hypothèse qu'il existe autant de sémantiques que de langues, soit cinq mille au bas mot. Or, c'est le problème de la diversité des langues qui fait le départ entre la philosophie de la signification et la sémantique linguistique. La sémantique cognitive relève alors, pour l'essentiel, de la tradition philosophique – ce qui au demeurant ne lui enlève rien. La recherche des primitives conceptuelles, universaux et archétypes cognitifs se situe par exemple à l'évidence dans cette tradition.

La seconde difficulté tient au fait que les états et processus mentaux sont évidemment mal connus, et que leur valeur explicative en souffre. Leur unité doit être mise en doute, et ils ne sont d'ailleurs peut-être pas connaissables par une discipline scientifique unifiée. D'une part, les faits psychophysiologiques se caractérisent par des degrés de complexité fort divers et rien à l'heure actuelle ne permet de saisir l'unité de ce que l'on résume sous le terme obscur mais commode de *pensée*. En outre, un abîme sépare les faits psychophysiologiques et les phénomènes vécus. Bien des difficultés de la psychologie cognitive tiennent sans doute à ce qu'elle a élu domicile dans cet abîme, et qu'elle traite des phénomènes comme des objets, par des méthodes qui miment celles des sciences de la vie. Quand la sémantique cognitive considère les significations comme des représentations, elle s'expose aux mêmes difficultés, et se voit alors contrainte d'objectiver un espace phénoménologique où elle déploie les significations.

Une troisième difficulté apparaît dans la mise en rapport du mental et du linguistique. Deux voies s'ouvrent ici. La voie représentationnaliste met en rapport des unités linguistiques et des éléments de pensée, les propriétés des unités linguistiques étant expliquées par celles des éléments de pensée qu'ils représente. Se posent alors des problèmes classiques de la correspondance mot / concept et de l'effabilité. Ainsi Ray Jackendoff regrette que «le langage n'assigne pas systématiquement un mot par concept» (1987: 324) alors que Walter Kintsch se félicitait d'une correspondance presque exacte. Et là où Jerrold J. Katz posait que toute proposition mentale peut être exprimée par une phrase dans toute langue naturelle, Dan Sperber et Deirdre Wilson estiment qu'en général les pensées et les phrases ne se correspondent pas terme à terme (1989 : 287 ; ces auteurs croient que concepts et pensées sont discrets et dénombrables).

Ces faux problèmes demeurent par le maintien d'une séparation entre le linguistique et le conceptuel, caractéristique du dualisme, et telle que les significations sont rapportées à une sphère non linguistique. La sémantique y gagne certes une valeur explicative — fondée sur le postulat que le représenté jouit d'une supériorité sur le représentant, mais à la condition d'être déliée des langues.

Une autre voie permet de mettre en relation le langage et la pensée d'une manière moins naïve, ou du moins sans recourir nécessairement à la notion de représentation. Elle rapporte les faits linguistiques à des opérations de la pensée, et nous la dirons pour cela *opérationnaliste*. Elle a donné lieu à deux courants de recherche distincts. Le premier, inspiré par Terry Winograd, s'est développé en IA dans la décennie 1972−1982, puis tomba vite dans l'oubli ; il a pris le nom de *sémantique procédurale* (cf. Miller et Johnson-Laird, 1976 ; Johnson-Laird, 1983). Le slogan *meanings are procedures* permettait de définir le sens d'un symbole comme l'ensemble des procédures qui lui sont associées, à l'image de certains symboles dans les programmes informatiques. Rapportée à la pensée, la sémantique procédurale supposait bien entendu une conception computationnelle de l'esprit. Elle eut cependant l'intérêt de ne pas limiter la signification à la référence, et de conférer à l'inférence une place primordiale. Le second courant, dominé par des linguistes (Langacker, Lakoff, Talmy, notamment) et développé dans la décennie suivante, prend explicitement ses distances à l'égard du paradigme dit symbolique, et rapporte la signification à des opérations dans des espaces mentaux.

Le courant représentationnaliste et le courant opérationnaliste ne sont pas dualistes de la même façon et ne mettent pas en rapport par la même méthodologie les deux niveaux qu'ils distinguent. Le premier part d'une préconception logique du niveau mental, pour en rapporter les unités aux unités linguistiques. La description vise alors à rédimer l'imperfection des langues en les rationalisant — avec un insuccès constant, puisque les langages logiques qui structurent le niveau mental ont été conçus pour se passer des langues, en évitant par là leurs défauts prétendus. Le second courant entend plutôt, à l'inverse, partir de la description linguistique pour décrire l'espace mental, en considérant le langage comme une «fenêtre» sur la cognition. Ce souci empirique lui confère une capacité descriptive certainement meilleure, bien que la séparation entre son objet (les langues) et son objectif (décrire la cognition) affaiblisse évidemment sa prétention scientifique, au profit d'une philosophie spontanée dépourvue de dimension réflexive.

6. Perspectives

Cependant, la sociologie actuelle de la recherche linguistique la rend plus docile à la demande sociale. Alors que la linguistique historique et comparée s'était développée dans les universités, les recherches actuelles sont aussi menées dans des laboratoires de recherche à financement public et dans des entreprises privées. La diversification et la division de la collectivité des linguistes pourrait présager un éclatement de la discipline. La linguistique générale, et son objet les langues, irait rejoindre la philologie dans quelque glorieux conservatoire des sciences sociales. La linguistique universelle, développée en informatique linguistique, avait pour projet de rejoindre l'IA et la psychologie cognitive parmi les sciences et techniques de la cognition et de la communication.

Malgré tout, le programme théorique de l'IA a perdu beaucoup de son crédit avec le recul du cognitivisme orthodoxe. Par ailleurs l'informatique linguistique a été bouleversée par l'essor récent de la linguistique de corpus liée aux applications sur Internet : on assiste ainsi à l'apparition d'une nouvelle philologie électronique, dont la *Text Encoding Initiative,* qui vise à uniformiser les codages d'échange des documents, présente le développement le plus connu.

Il reste que si la scission de fait entre la linguistique universelle (qui traite du langage), et la linguistique générale (qui prend pour objet les langues) venait à se consommer, y compris dans le domaine académique, la seconde, exclue de fait du champ des sciences cognitives, trouvera sa place dans une sémiotique générale des cultures. Elle pourrait articuler les sciences sociales et les sciences cognitives en faisant la part des facteurs culturels dans la cognition. C'est là une question d'avenir, autant pour les sciences sociales que pour les sciences cognitives elles-mêmes.

De fait, les divers courants de pensée qui se sont développés ces dix dernières années, comme l'énaction, la vie artificielle, le constructivisme, la phénoménologie naturalisée, l'herméneutique matérielle, sont d'autant plus intéressants qu'ils ne se présentent pas comme des théories globales et conservent des liens privilégiés avec des secteurs disciplinaires : l'énaction avec la biologie, la vie artificielle avec l'informatique, le constructivisme avec la psychologie, la phénoménologie naturalisée avec la philosophie, l'herméneutique matérielle avec les sciences du langage.

Aussi, les recherches cognitives entrent sans doute dans une nouvelle phase d'interdisciplinarité, non plus fusionnelle, mais fédérative. Le fonctionnalisme computationnel a unifié les disciplines cognitives par une communauté de postulats : uniformité du symbolique, ubiquité du format propositionnel, théorie calculatoire des processus. Corrélativement, elles utilisaient délibérément les mêmes concepts et les mêmes moyens de représentation : réseaux sémantiques, modules séquentiels, etc. Cette forme d'unité est une application tardive et sans doute ultime du programme de la Science unifiée que proposait jadis le positivisme logique.

Par contraste, les affinités entre les problématiques alternatives qui se développent à présent dans les diverses disciplines ne suffisent pas à décréter une levée de fait des frontières entre elles. Si la perspective de l'herméneutique matérielle permet de renouveler la sémiotique, restée fort tributaire du positivisme logique, cela permettra d'approfondir les distinctions entre les langues, les langages et les autres systèmes de signes, en caractérisant mieux leurs régimes herméneutiques. On pourra alors mieux spécifier la médiation sémiotique entre le «physique» et le «représentationnel». Enfin, en posant le problème de la phylogenèse des cultures, relier les sciences de la culture aux formes d'intelligibilité issues des sciences de la vie.

7. Références

Bobrow, Daniel G. & Collins, Allan (ed.). 1975. *Representation and Understanding: Studies in Cognitive Science.* (Language, thought, and culture.) New York: Academic Press.

Brugman, Claudia & Lakoff, George. 1988. «Cognitive Topology and Lexical Networks». In: Small, Steven L. & al. *Lexical Ambiguity Resolution. Perspectives from Psycholinguistics, Neuropsychology, and Artificial Intelligence.* San Mateo/CA: Kaufman.

Chomsky, Noam. 1988. *Language and Problems of Knowledge.* (Current studies in linguistics series, 16.) Cambridge/MA: MIT Press.

Collins, Allan M. & Loftus, Elizabeth F. 1975. «A Spreading-Activation Theory of Semantic Processing.» *Psychological Review* 82.6: 407−428.

Dreyfus, Hubert L. 1984. *Intelligence Artificielle. Mythes et limites.* Paris: Flammarion [tr. de *What Computers Can't Do.* Seconde édition revue et augmentée. New York. 1979: Harper & Row].

Dubois, Danièle (ed.). 1991. *Sémantique et cognition. Catégories, prototypes, typicalité.* (Sciences du langage.) Paris: CNRS.

Fauconnier, Gilles. 1984a. *Espaces mentaux. Aspects de la construction du sens dans les langues naturelles.* (Propositions.) Paris: Éditions de Minuit.

Fauconnier, Gilles. 1984b. «Y a-t-il un niveau linguistique de représentation logique?» *Communications* 40: 211−228.

Fillmore, Charles. 1982. «Frame semantics». In: *Linguistics in the Morning Calm.* Séoul: Hanshin, 111−137.

Fodor, Jerry A. 1975. *The Language of Thought.* (The language & thought series.) Cambridge/MA: Harvard University Press.

Fodor, Jerry A. 1983. *The Modularity of Mind.* Cambridge/MA: MIT Press [tr. fr. Paris: Éditions de Minuit. 1986].

Fodor, Jerry A. 1987. *Psychosemantics.* (Explorations in cognitive science, 2.) Cambridge/MA: MIT Press.

Gardner, Howard. 1985. *The Mind's New Science: A History of the Cognitive Revolution.* New York: Basic Books.

Geeraerts, Dirk. 1991. «Grammaire cognitive et sémantique lexicale». *Communications* 53: 17−50.

Harris, Catherine. 1990. «Connectionism and Cognitive Linguistics». *Connection Science* 1-2: 7−33.

Jackendoff, Ray. 1983. *Semantics and Cognition.* Cambridge/MA: MIT Press.

Jackendoff, Ray. 1987. *Consciousness and the Computational Mind.* Cambridge/MA: MIT Press.

Johnson, Mark. 1992. «Philosophical implications of cognitive semantics». *Cognitive Linguistics* 3-4: 345−366.

Johnson-Laird, Philip N. 1983. *Mental Models: Towards a cognitive science of language, inference, and consciousness.* Cambridge/MA: Cambridge University Press.

Johnson-Laird, Philip N. 1988. «La représentation mentale de la signification». *RISS* 115: 53−69.

Kintsch, Walter. 1974. *The Representation of Meaning in Memory.* Hillsdale/NJ: Erlbaum.

Lakoff, George. 1987. *Women, Fire, and Dangerous Things: What Categories Reveal About the Mind.* Chicago/ILL.: Univ. of Chicago Press.

Langacker, Ronald. 1986. «An Introduction to Cognitive Grammar». *Cognitive Science* X.1: 1−40.

Langacker, Ronald. 1987. *Foundations of Cognitive Grammar: Theoretical Prerequisites* (vol. 1). Stanford/CA: Stanford University Press.

Langacker, Ronald. 1988. Compte rendu de Lakoff 1987. *Language* 64.2: 383−395.

Langacker, Ronald. 1991a. *Foundations of Cognitive Grammar: Descriptive Applications* (vol. II). Stanford/CA: Stanford University Press.

Langacker, Ronald. 1991b. «Noms et verbes». *Communications* 53: 103−154.

McClelland, John & Rumelhart, David N. (eds.). 1986. *Parallel Distributed Processing.* 2 vols. Cambridge/MA: MIT Press.

Miller, George A. & Johnson-Laird, Philip N. 1976. *Language and Perception.* Cambridge/MA: Cambridge University Press.

Minsky, Marvin. 1975. «A Framework for Representing Knowledge». In: Winston, Paul (ed.). *The Psychology of Computer Vision.* New York: McGraw-Hill, 99−128.

Minsky, Marvin & Papert, Seymour. 1969. *Perceptrons.* Cambridge/MA: MIT Press [nouvelle édition revue. 1988].

Putnam, Hilary. 1988. *Representation and Reality.* Cambridge/MA: MIT Press.

Pylyshyn, Zenon W. 1984. *Computation and Cognition. Toward a foundation in cognitive science.* Cambridge/MA: MIT Press.

Quillian, Roger. 1968. «Semantic Memory». In: Minsky, Marvin (ed.). *Semantic Information Processing.* Cambridge/MA: MIT Press, 227−270.

Rastier, François. 1991. *Sémantique et recherches cognitives.* Paris: PUF.

Sabah, Gérard. 1989. *L'Intelligence Artificielle et le langage.* 2 vols. Paris.

Schank, Roger C. & Abelson, Robert P. 1977. *Scripts, Plans, Goals and Understanding. An inquiry into human knowledge structures.* Hillsdale/NJ: Erlbaum.

Smolensky, Paul. 1988. «The Proper Treatment of Connectionnism». *Behavioral and Brain Sciences* 11.1: 1−74.

Sowa, John F. 1984. *Conceptual Structures. Information processing in mind and machine.* (The Systems Programming Series.) Reading/MA: Addison-Wesley.

Sperber, Dan & Wilson, Deirdre. 1989. *La pertinence.* Paris: Éditions de Minuit [trad. fr. de *Relevance.* Londres: Blackwell].

Talmy, Leonard. 1988. «Force Dynamics in Language and Cognition». *Cognitive Science* 12: 49−100.

Vandeloise, Claude. 1986. *L'espace en français. Sémantique des prépositions spatiales.* (Travaux linguistiques.) Paris: Seuil.

Vandeloise, Claude. 1991. «Autonomie du langage et cognition». *Communications* 53: 69−102.

Weizenbaum, Joseph. 1981. *Puissance de l'ordinateur et raison de l'homme.* (Série L'Homme face à l'ordinateur.) Boulogne-sur-Seine: Éditions d'Informatique.

Wilks, Yorick. 1976. «Philosophy of language». In: Charniak, Eugene & Wilks, Yorick (eds.). *Computational Semantics.* Amsterdam & New York: North-Holland, 205−234.

Winograd, Terry A. & Flores, Fernando. 1986. *Understanding Computers and Cognition.* Norwood/NJ: Ablex.

Winograd, Terry A. 1972. *Understanding Natural Langage.* New York: Academic Press.

Winograd Terry A. 1976. «Towards a procedural Understanding of Semantics». *Revue internationale de philosophie* 30.117/118: 261−303.

Winograd, Terry A. 1983. *Language as a Cognitive Process.* Reading/MA: Addison-Wesley.

François Rastier, Paris, INaLF−CNRS (France)

6. Künstliche Sprachen und Universalsprachen

1. Begriffsklärungen
2. Geschichtlicher Abriß
3. Beispiele für einzelne Universalsprachen
4. Charakteristika von Universalsprachen
5. Leistungen und Grenzen
6. Zitierte Literatur

1. Begriffsklärungen

Künstliche Sprachen sind ein Produkt menschlicher Spracherfindungstätigkeit. In einer „Typologie der sprachlichen Erfindungsfunktion" steckt Alessandro Bausani (1970: 11−39) ein weitgespanntes Anwendungsfeld dieser Tätigkeit ab, das von Tabuwörtern in Stammeskulturen bis zu poetischer Sprache reicht. Einige Produkte der Spracherfindungsfunktion gehen auch Universalienforschung und Typologie an. So behandelt der vorliegende Band Gebärdensprache (→ Art. 10) sowie Pidgins und Kreolsprachen (→ Art. 116, 117). Der vorliegende Artikel beschäftigt sich mit den künstlich entworfenen Weltsprachen. In der Literatur werden sie mit einer ganzen Reihe von Termini bezeichnet (vgl. Blanke 1985: 51−61): **Plansprachen, Welthilfssprachen** (engl. **auxiliary languages**), **Universalsprachen, Verkehrssprachen** u. a. In der vorliegenden Darstellung wurde der Terminus „Universalsprache(n)" gewählt, da er die am weitesten reichende historische Tiefendimension aufweist (Blanke 1985: 55).

2. Geschichtlicher Abriss

Die Idee der Universalsprache ist eingebettet in einen größeren Gedanken-Komplex. Hier verbindet sich die Suche nach der ersten, ursprünglichen Sprache aller Menschen mit der Bemühung, ein Instrument vollkommener Erkenntnis und ein sprachliches Zeichensystem für die zukünftige Kommunikation der gesamten Menschheit zu finden (Eco 1997: 84f.). Diese enge Verknüpfung ergab sich vor dem biblischen Horizont des Mythos der Sprachverwirrung infolge des „Turmbaus zu Babel" (Genesis 11) [Eco 1997: 24−32]. Die weltweite und perfektionierte Verständigung mittels einer Universalsprache soll den allgemeinen Frieden zwischen Völkern und Glaubensgruppen (wieder)herstellen. Die Suche nach dem Sprachursprung, die maßgeblich von Arno Borst (1957−63) dargestellt wurde, verband sich allerdings nur zeitweise mit dem universalsprachlichen Anliegen und ist weitgehend als eigenständiges Thema zu sehen.

Erste Universalsprachen wurden in Europa im 17. Jahrhundert entworfen. Diese Projekte nährten sich aus einer Tradition, die von Mittelalter und Renaissance her kam und einerseits die skizzierte ideelle Seite (Turmbau-Mythos), andererseits mögliche Techniken der Realisierung einer Universalsprache umfasst. Verfahren der Kombinatorik von Buchstaben wurden zuerst von der spanisch-jüdischen Mystik des 13. Jahrhunderts (Kabbala) (Scholem 1980) und dem katalanischen Philosophen Raimundus Lullus (1232/5−1316) ausgebildet. Die Vertreter der ekstatischen Kabbala beschäftigten sich im Zusammenhang mit ihrem Ziel mystischer Gottversenkung mit den Techniken reiner Buchstaben-Umstellung, der Zuordnung von Zahlen zu Buchstaben, dem Akrostichon (vgl. Eco 1997: 40f.; Eco 1992: 47−58; Benedikt 1985: 380−384). Lullus repräsentierte in seiner *Ars magna* metaphysisch-religiöse Gehalte durch Buchstaben, die auf komplexe geometrische Figuren projiziert wurden (Eco 1997: 65−81).

Kabbala und Lullismus bilden den Fundus, auf dem die gesamte weitere Universalsprachen-Tradition in Europa direkt oder indirekt aufbaute (Eco 1997: 127−142). Die Renaissance-Philosophie führte die Buchstabenkombinatorik fort. Darüber hinaus führte die sie kennzeichnende enge Verbindung von Naturwissenschaft, Astrologie und Naturmystik (Gerl 1989: 57f.) zur Beschäftigung mit Bildern als Mitteln einer Universalsprache. Hier stammen die wichtigsten Beiträge von Giordano Bruno (1548−1600) (vgl. Yates 1982, Sturlese 1991) und Athanasius Kircher (1602−1680), der Hieroglyphen- (*Oedipus Aegytiacus*, 1652−54) und chinesische Schrift (*China illustrata*, 1667) untersuchte (vgl. Reilly 1974: 53−59 u. 126f.). Eine andere Linie reicht von der magischen Figur *Monas Hierglyphica* (1564) des Alchimisten John Dee (French 1972) zu den Manifesten der Rosenkreuzer (1614/15) (Yates 1975; Eco 1997: 199 u. 188−191). Schließlich bildeten Techniken der Geheimsprachen eine wichtige Inspirationsquelle (vgl. Strasser 1988: 19−27). Die Geheimschriftentradition nutzend entwarfen Athanasius Kircher und andere Gelehrte Ziffern-Systeme mit universalsprachlichem Anspruch, sogenannte Polygraphien (Eco 1997: 206−216; Strasser 1988: 155−195).

Zu den von Mittelalter und Renaissance ererbten Elementen kamen im 17. Jahrhundert entscheidende Grundgedanken. Francis Bacon wies auf die Ungenauigkeit des gewöhnlichen Sprachgebrauchs hin, die zu Missverständnissen und reinen Terminologiekonflikten führen könne (Eco 1997: 219). René Descartes formulierte in einem Brief an Marin Mersenne vom 20. November 1629 (Adam & Tannery 1956: 76−82) die Prinzipien der Vereinfachung der Grammatik und der philosophischen Konstruktion des Wortschatzes, die er beide deutlich trennte.

Nach diesen Vorbereitungen aus verschiedenen Richtungen wurden seit den vierziger Jahren des 17. Jahrhunderts mehrere konkrete Vorschläge zu Universalsprachen gemacht, überwiegend in England: die *Common Writing* (1647) von Francis Lodwick (Salmon 1972), die *Ars signorum* (1661) von George Dalgarno und der *Essay towards a Real Character* (1668) von John Wilkins. Wilkins wurde in seiner Grammatik von philosophischen Grammatiken des Spätmittelalters und der Renaissance beeinflusst (Salmon 1992: 212–215).

Gottfried Wilhelm Leibniz beschäftigte sich mit dem Entwurf einer Universalsprache (vgl. Couturat 1901: 64–79) im Rahmen seines umfassenderen philosophischen Vorhabens einer „Characteristica universalis" (Eco 1997: 277), wandte sich in letzter Konsequenz aber von dem Projekt ab, u. a. weil er nicht an eine eindeutig nachvollziehbare und evident feststehende Einteilung der Welt glaubte (Gerhardt 1978: 503–509), wie sie die Konstruktion des Wortschatzes philosophischer Sprachen erfordert. Dieselbe Relativierung wurde in der *Encyclopédie* der französischen Aufklärer (Encyclopédie 1966) und den Überlegungen der sogenannten „Idéologues" erkennbar (Eco 1997: 294–298) und bewirkte schließlich, dass sich philosophische Projekte nur noch schwer durchsetzen konnten, selbst wenn man bis ins 20. Jahrhundert hinein bemerkenswerte Entwürfe verzeichnen kann (vgl. Eco 1997: 299–321; Bausani 1970: 135–137).

Welthandel und friedensbedrohende Nationalismen führten Ende des 19. Jahrhunderts dazu, dass die Universalsprachenidee wieder auflebte. Allerdings stand nun nicht mehr die Verbesserung der Erkenntnis, sondern die Ermöglichung weltweiter Kommunikation im Vordergrund. Die neuen Universalsprachen griffen vor allem im Bereich des Wortschatzes, z. T. auch in der Grammatik auf die gegebenen natürlichen Sprachen zurück. Es entstanden viele, oft als 'Welthilfssprachen' bezeichnete künstliche Sprachen (vgl. Bausani 1970: 111–135): *Volapük* (Johann Martin Schleyer, 1879); *Esperanto* (Ludvik Lejzer Zamenhof, 1887); *Mundolingue* (Lott, 1889); *Latino sine flexione* (Peano, 1903); *Ido* (Beaufront, 1907); *Occidental* (Edgar von Wahl 1922); *Novial* (Otto Jespersen, 1928) u. v. a. Aleksandr Duličenko (1989: 51) hat ca. 900 Projekte zu einer Universal- oder Plansprache gezählt. Die meisten dieser Projekte sind jedoch nicht über die Anfänge hinausgekommen. Die einzige Universalsprache, die heute ihrer Anhängerschaft und äußeren Entwicklung nach als bedeutend gelten kann, ist das Esperanto (vgl. Forster 1982: 41; Strasser 1988: 259; Blanke 1985: Tabelle 2). Die Entstehung von Welthilfssprachen wurde bald von einer sprachwissenschaftlichen Diskussion begleitet: Befürworter (Schuchardt 1904, de Courtenay 1907) und Gegner (Brugmann & Leskien 1907) standen einander gegenüber. In den dreißiger Jahren bildete sich dann die Disziplin der „Interlinguistik" aus (vgl. Schubert 1989b).

3. Beispiele für einzelne Universalsprachen

Im folgenden sollen wichtige Universalsprachen aus dem 17. Jahrhundert und der Zeit um 1900 kurz dargestellt werden.

Die Sprachen von Wilkins (*Essay towards a Real Character*) und Dalgarno (*Ars Signorum*) zeichnen sich durch folgende Hauptzüge aus:

– Der Wortschatz wird nach philosophischen Prinzipien konstruiert, d. h., die Konstruktion stützt sich ab auf eine hierarchische Gliederung der Welt nach aristotelischem Vorbild. Jeder Gattung (z. B. Tier, Metall, Gefühl) entspricht eine Silbe aus „Konsonant + Vokal", weniger abstrakten, in der Hierarchie weniger hoch liegenden Arten (z. B. Hund, Eisen, Wut) entsprechen einzelne Laute. So wird das Wort *Debi* 'Blitz' bei Wilkins wie folgt konstruiert:

De = 'Gattung „Element"'
b = 'erster Unterschied'
i = 'vierte Art'

das heißt:
Deb = 'erstes Element' = 'Feuer'
+ *i* = 'vierte Art des Feuers'

das heißt:
debi = 'vierte Art des Feuers' = 'Blitz'
(vgl. Eco 1997: 250 f.; Blanke 1985: 128)

Entsprechend ist *deba* die dritte Art des Feuers (*deb* + *a*) – in Wilkins' Hierarchie ist das der Komet – und so weiter. Bei Wilkins, der von der in Abschnitt 9.2 erwähnten Bildertechnik beeinflusst ist, repräsentieren neben Lauten auch Striche Gattungen und Arten. Den besten Eindruck von der bildlichen Seite der Universalsprachen des 17. Jahrhunderts geben die Photographien bei Strasser (1988) und die Reproduktionen bei Subbiondo (1992).

Die solchermaßen systematisch konstruierten Lexeme sollen die Vollkommenheit der Sprache gewährleisten, da sie dem Wesen der Dinge entsprechen (Wilkins' *Real Character*) (Clauss 1992: 54).

– die Grammatik reduziert alle Vollwortarten auf das Nomen (Dalgarno 1661: 62; Frank 1992: 265). Verben werden durch „Kopula + adjektivales Nomen oder Präsenspar-

tizip eines Nomens" repräsentiert (Dalgarno 1661: 64 f.; Frank 1992: 266–268). Wilkins fasst alle Funktionswörter in einer Wortart „Partikel" zusammen (Blanke 1985: 128).
− die Grammatik kennt keine unterschiedlichen Flexionsklassen, also Konjugationstypen und Deklinationstypen (Dalgarno 1661: 66; Frank 1992: 269)
− syntaktische Relationen werden bei Dalgarno durch Präpositionen angezeigt (1661: 76 f.).
− die Tempora sind eher differenziert, bei Wilkins ergibt sich ein kompliziertes Tempus-Modus-Aspekt-System aus 30, z. T. nicht anwendbaren Konstellationen (Frank 1992: 270–273).
− Wortstellung ist: Subjekt + Kopula + prädikatives Nomen + Objekt (Dalgarno 1661: 72 f.; Frank 1992: 266)

Lodwicks Sprache (vgl. Salmon 1972; Eco 1997: 267–275) unterscheidet sich stark von dem Wilkins-Dalgarno-Typ. Auch er hat im Bereich der Lexeme nur eine Wortklasse. Für ihn ist dies aber das Verb und nicht das Nomen. Viele Nomina wie 'Trinker', 'Trunkenbold', 'Getränk' lassen sich direkt aus Verben ableiten. Das bezeichnete Ereignis, im Beispiel also 'trinken', ist das konstitutive Element von Sätzen. Lodwick geht dabei soweit, Derivationsbeziehungen umzudrehen, wenn Konkreta involviert sind: *hand* wird auf *to handle*, *land* auf *to land* zurückgeführt. Mit der Verbzentrierung kommt er modernen linguistischen Auffassungen nahe (Dependenzgrammatik, moderne Funktionale Grammatik). Ein weiterer bedeutender Unterschied zu Wilkins und Dalgarno liegt darin, dass sich seine Sprache auf reine Graphie reduziert, ohne dass er eine Lautkomponente hätte. Um ein zentrales Zeichen als Lexemrepräsentanten in der Mitte gruppieren sich Indices für grammatische Parameter (Tempora, Modi, Steigerungsstufe usw.).

Nach der Darstellung der englischen Systeme des 17. Jahrhunderts sollen die erwähnten Welthilfssprachen näher erklärt werden. Das Esperanto (vgl. Dahlenburg & Liebig 1981; Blanke 1985: 226–295) entnimmt seine Wörter verschiedenen europäischen Sprachen. Beispiele: Altgriechisch (*kaj* = 'und'), Latein (*jam* = 'schon'), Französisch (*tre* = 'sehr'), Spanisch (*en* = 'in'), Englisch (*jes* = 'ja'), Russisch (*kolbaso* = 'Wurst'), Deutsch (*tago* = 'Tag'). Die Wörter gehören den bekannten Wortklassen an. Die Wortklassenzuordnung wird durch Endungen geregelt: *-o* (Substantiv), *-i* (Infinitiv eines Verbs); *-a* = Adjektiv; *-e* = Adverb. Präpositionen, Konjunktionen und unregelmäßige Adverbien haben keine Endung. Der Übergang von der einen in die andere Wortart ist besonders einfach: *manki* 'fehlen' ↔ *manko* 'Mangel'; *nordo* 'Norden' ↔ *norda* 'nördlich'. Es gibt eine Vielzahl von Derivations-Affixen, die oft eindeutiger auf bestimmte Inhalte festgelegt sind als in natürlichen Sprachen, wie kontrastive Tabellen (Blanke 1972) zeigen. Zwei Beispiele:

(1) (a) Esperanto
    (Dahlenburg & Liebig 1981: 218)
    mal- 'Gegenteil'
    varma 'warm' − *malvarma* 'kalt'
   (b) Esperanto
    (Dahlenburg & Liebig 1981: 221)
    -ujo 'Behälter'
    mono 'Geld' −
    monujo 'Geldbeutel'

Der kategoriale Apparat der Grammatik ist dem Durchschnitt europäischer Sprachen angepasst mit Tendenz auf möglichste Vereinfachung. Er umfasst:

− die üblichen sechs Personen der Konjugation
− drei Zeitstufen ohne Vor- und Nachzeitigkeit: Vergangenheit, Gegenwart, Zukunft
− Imperativ und Konjunktiv
− Konditional
− vier syntaktische Grundrelationen: Subjekt (Nominativ), direktes Objekt (Akkusativ), indirektes Objekt (Dativ), Nominalattribut (Genitiv)

Morphologisch werden diese Kategorien ebenfalls mit dem Ziel größtmöglicher Einfachheit markiert, vor allem fehlen Allomorphe und Flexionsklassen. Im folgenden eine Übersicht (Zirkumflexe über Konsonanten markieren im Esperanto Zischlaute):

− Personen: einsilbige Pronomina
  mi = 'ich'; *vi* = 'du', 'ihr', 'Sie';
  li = 'er', *ŝi* = 'sie', *ĝi* = 'es'
  ni = 'wir', *ili* = 'sie' (Plural)

− Infinitiv: *-i* (z. B. *stari* = 'stehen')
− Vergangenheit: *-is* (z. B. *staris* = 'stand')
− Gegenwart: *-as* (z. B. *staras* = 'steht')
− Zukunft: *-os* (z. B. *staros* 'wird stehen')

− Singular beim Nomen: *-o*,
− Plural beim Nomen: *-oj*
− Singular beim Adjektiv: *-a*;
− Plural beim Adjektiv: *-aj*

– Subjekt: –;
– dir. Objekt: Suffix *-n*;
– indirektes Objekt: Präposition *al*;
– Nominalattribut: Präposition *de*

Andere syntaktisch-semantische Relationen zwischen Verb und Substantiven werden durch Präpositionen gekennzeichnet: *kun* = 'mit'; *por* = 'für'; *per* = 'durch'; *en* = 'in'; *el* = 'aus'; *pri* = 'über', 'betreffs' u. a.

Grundwortstellung ist SVO, das Adverb steht gewöhnlich vor dem Verb. Zwischen einem Substantiv und einem auf dieses bezogenen Adjektiv herrscht Numerus-Kongruenz.

Beispielsätze:

(2) (a) Esperanto
(Dahlenburg & Liebig 1981: 31)
Li televid-as.
3.SG.M fernseh-PRES
'Er sieht fern.'
(b) Esperanto
(Dahlenburg & Liebig 1981: 31)
La fenestr-o-j de la dom-o est-as modern-a-j.
ART Fenster-N-PL PRP-Gen ART Haus-N COP-PRS modern-ADJ-PL
'Die Fenster des Hauses sind modern.'
(c) Esperanto
(Dahlenburg & Liebig 1981: 31)
Ina jam bon-e kompren-as la situaci-o-n
Ina schon gut-ADV versteh-PRES ART Situation-N-OBJ
'Ina versteht die Situation schon gut.'
(d) Esperanto
(Dahlenburg & Liebig 1981: 38):
Ŝi send-is al ŝi poŝtkarto-n.
3.SG.F schick-PRET PRP-Dat 3.SG.F Postkarte-OBJ
'Sie hat ihr eine Postkarte geschickt'

Im Esperanto-Dialekt Ido (vglo. Blanke 1985: 183–201) werden eine Reihe von Regelungen verändert und dem Anspruch nach verbessert (Forster 1982: 122f.): Plural *-i* statt *-oj*; das *-n* des direkten Objekts ist fakultativ, Aufgabe der Zirkumflexe bei der Orthographie, Verfeinerung der Wortbildung (vgl. Blanke 1985: 193).

Volapük (vgl. Bausani 1970: 113f.; Blanke 1985: 204–218) entnimmt den Großteil seiner Vokabeln aus dem Englischen, verfälscht sie dabei aber, weil sie lautlich vereinfacht werden: *nol* (< *knowledge*). Die assoziative Anknüpfung an den europäischen Wortschatz ist also großenteils nicht gegeben. Volapük hat einen reicheren Bestand an grammatischen Kategorien als Esperanto und Ido. Bei den Tempora gibt es Vorzeitigkeit und Unterscheidung zwischen Imperfekt und Perfekt. Das Passiv ist synthetisch und verzeichnet spiegelgetreu alle Kategorien des Aktivs. Die syntaktischen Grund-Relationen zwischen Substantiven und Verb werden mittels Kasus ausgedrückt. Präfigierung spielt eine außerordentlich wichtige Rolle, sowohl bei der Tempusmarkierung in der Konjugation als auch bei der Wortbildung.

4. Charakteristika von Universalsprachen

Die geschilderten Beispiele erlauben nun, einige Charakteristika von Universalsprachen zu bestimmen. Sieht man von den Eigenschaften ab, die die Soziolinguistik angehen – wie etwa die Bildung einer Sprachgemeinschaft *ex post* oder die Zusammensetzung einer solchen Sprachgemeinschaft (Stocker 1996) –, sind folgende Aspekte hervorzuheben:

(A) Die Systeme von Wilkins, Dalgarno und Lodwick haben einen anderen Status als diejenigen von Zamenhof (Esperanto) oder Schleyer (Volapük). Alle sind im wesentlichen das Werk einzelner Menschen. Aber die englischen Universalsprachen des 17. Jahrhunderts sind vollkommene Erfindungen und enthalten keine Bestandteile aus gegebenen natürlichen Sprachen. Lautstruktur, Lexik und Grammatik werden auf allgemeine Prinzipien über die Beschaffenheit der Sprache und das Wesen der Dinge abgestellt. Dagegen nehmen die Welthilfssprachen sehr viele Elemente aus gegebenen empirischen Sprachen auf. Dieser Unterschied wird in der Literatur gewöhnlich durch die von Couturat & Léau (1907) propagierte Unterscheidung zwischen **apriorischen** und **aposteriorischen** Sprachen gefasst (Blanke 1985: 100f.). Trotz der grundsätzlichen Verschiedenheit bezüglich der Art ihrer Entstehung haben apriorische und aposteriorische Sprachen viele Eigenschaften gemeinsam.

(B) Die Struktur von Universalsprachen zeigt typische Merkmale auf den verschiedenen Sprachebenen:
– phonetisch: Man möchte ein Lautsystem schaffen, das möglichst jedem Volk entgegenkommt. So geht Wilkins von allgemeinen Überlegungen zur Lauterzeugung aus (vgl.

Subbiondo 1992: 206), ebenso Dalgarno (Cram 1992: 196). Für das phonologische Denken im Zusammenhang mit Welthilfssprachen ist eine Äußerung Lev Trubetzkoys charakteristisch: „Eine künstliche Sprache mit dem Anspruch auf wirklich internationale Geltung muß ein solches Lautsystem besitzen, das für kein Volk in der Welt unüberwindbare Schwierigkeiten bieten würde" (Trubetzkoy 1939: 198). Bei den Vokalen werden die Eckpunkte des Vokaldreiecks eines dreistufigen ([i], [e], [a], [o], [u]) oder zweistufigen ([i], [a], [u]) Vokalsystems als günstiger Phonembestand angesetzt. Für die Konsonanten schwanken die Vorschläge stärker, der minimale Bestand, den Trubetzkoy fordert, umfasst: [p], [t], [k], [s], [m], [n], [l], [j] und [w] (vgl. Trubetzkoy 1939: 206).

Apriorische Sprachen unterscheiden sich von aposteriorischen dadurch, dass dort oft auch mit optischen Zeichen gearbeitet wird (Wilkins, Lodwick). Welthilfssprachen dagegen werden durchweg mit lateinischen Buchstaben geschrieben, da von allen Alphabeten das lateinische das am weitesten verbreitete ist (Blanke 1985: 88).

− lexikalisch: Der Wortschatz beruht bei apriorischen Sprachen auf einer sachlichen Analyse der Welt. Eine vergleichbare Erkenntnisbemühung fehlt bei den aposteriorischen Sprachen. Dennoch ist die rationale Gliederung auch hier nicht abwesend. Sie drückt sich aus in der größeren Klarheit der Verteilung unterschiedlicher Ausdrucksfunktionen an die Derivationsaffixe im Vergleich zur Polyfunktionalität bei natürlichen Sprachen. Ein Beispiel wäre die Vielzahl der Bezeichnungen für Orte im Deutschen (*Küche*, *Bücherei*, *Reisfeld* u. a.) im Gegensatz zum einfachen *-ejo*-Suffix des Esperanto (vgl. Blanke 1981: 79). Der Wortschatz der rein apriorischen Sprachen wird nach Regeln systematisch konstruiert. Der lexikalische Bestand aposteriorischer Sprachen zeichnet sich dagegen durch Internationalität aus, da er oft mehreren Sprachen entnommen ist.

− grammatisch: Es soll eine einfache und regelmäßige Grammatik geschaffen werden. Dies bedeutet, dass Flexionsklassen, Allomorphie oder suppletive Paradigmen vermieden werden. Hier erkennt man Tendenzen, die die Natürlichkeitstheorie (Mayerthaler & Fiedl 1993: 610−612) in nicht-künstlichen Sprachen unterschiedlichen Typs herausgearbeitet hat und die auf bestimmten abstrakteren Erklärungsprinzipien der Universalienforschung und Typologie beruhen (→ Art. 29−32). In Universalsprachen beobachtet man sowohl Tendenzen einer universalen morphologischen Natürlichkeit (Mayerthaler 1981), bei der prototypische Kategorien wie der Singular morphologisch weniger aufwendig realisiert werden als fernerliegende (Esperanto: Substantiv im Singular auf *-o*, im Plural auf *-o* + *-j*) als auch Tendenzen einer systembezogenen morphologischen Natürlichkeit (Wurzel 1984), bei der es um größtmögliche Geschlossenheit und Einheitlichkeit eines gegebenen Sprachsystems geht (Esperanto: Tempora werden einheitlich repräsentiert nach dem Prinzip „Vokal + *-s*").

Apriorische Systeme neigen dazu, den Wortklassenbestand zu reduzieren. Ob Funktionswörter oder Affixe die grammatischen Funktionen markieren, ist ein Entscheidungsspielraum, der von verschiedenen Sprachen unterschiedlich ausgefüllt wird. So werden in den Konjugationsparadigmen des Esperanto die Personen durch freie grammatikalische Morpheme repräsentiert, während das Volapük die Personen mittels Suffixen anzeigt. Der Kategorienbestand, der hinter den grammatischen Wortformen steht, kann entweder reich verzweigt sein und stärker differenzieren oder sich auf das Elementare und Nötige beschränken. So haben Wilkins und das Volapük ein kompliziertes Tempussystem mit Aspekten und Zeitfolge, Lodwick und das Esperanto dagegen beschränken sich auf die drei Zeitstufen „Vergangenheit", „Gegenwart" und „Zukunft".

− die Klarheit in Wortschatz und Grammatik soll vor allem durch das Prinzip erzeugt werden, dass eine Ausdruckseinheit einer Inhaltseinheit entspricht und umgekehrt (Maxwell 1989: 108 f.). Polysemie und Polyfunktionalität werden unterbunden.

− bei der Grundwortstellung entscheiden sich Universalsprachen überwiegend für den Linearisierungstyp SVO. Aus der Sicht linguistischer Theorien, die ein Optimierungsprogramm bei der natürlichsprachlichen Wortstellung annehmen (Condillac 1947: 518−539 u. 83−86; Bartsch & Vennemann 1972: 136; Hawkins 1994: 77), stellt SVO eher eine Kompromisslösung (Dik 1989: 333) zwischen den der Optimierung dienenden Extremen VSO und SOV (Greenberg 1966) dar. Die empirische Sprachtypologie kann dies durch die Beobachtung ergänzen, dass der SVO-Typ in den Sprachen mit den größten Sprecherzahlen die Grundwortstellung ist: europäische Sprachen, Chinesisch, Bantusprachen, viele Sudan-Sprachen Westafrikas

und austronesische Sprachen (vgl. Ineichen 1979: 137 f.).
(C) Die Vereinfachung bei der Grammatik, die Klarheit bei der Wortbildung und die Bekanntheit oder Konstruierbarkeit der Grundwörter sollen dazu beitragen, dass Universalsprachen für alle leichter erlernbar sind (Blanke 1985: 83−87).
(D) Die Universalsprachen erstreben eine optimale, d. h. möglichst einfache und durchsichtige Struktur. Ein Sprachwandel größeren Umfangs würde diese gefährden. Hinzu kommt, dass sie durch die sie begründenden Schriften (z. B. Schleyer 1880, Zamenhof 1887) gleich von Anfang an in festen Grenzen definiert vorliegen und die Gründer häufig darauf achteten, dass ihr ursprünglicher Entwurf unangetastet blieb (vgl. Forster 1982: 41−57). Ein gewisser Wandel zeigt sich im Fall des Esperanto dennoch. Er betrifft zwar im wesentlichen den Wortschatz und Wortbildungsmechanismen, aber nicht nur (vgl. Piron 1989). Der Wandel kann sich unkontrolliert vollziehen oder kontrolliert, beim Esperanto-Weltbund z. B. durch Diskussion im „Lingva Komitato" (Sprachkomitee) und der „Akademio" (Forster 1982: 162−164).

5. Leistungen und Grenzen

Universalsprachen beinhalten gegenüber natürlichen Sprachen bestimmte Leistungen. Von dem, was Universalsprachen gegenüber natürlichen Sprachen leisten, ist aus der Sicht von Universalienforschung und Typologie Folgendes von Interesse:

− Universalsprachen stellen eine Ergänzung zur Universalienforschung dar. „Man sieht darin u. a. ein sprachwissenschaftliches Phänomen, ein (...) Experiment, das es mit wissenschaftlichen Methoden zu erforschen gilt." (Blanke 1981: 3). Dies gilt auch für apriorische Sprachen (Frank 1992: 264; Cram 1992: 191). Eine Sprache, die durchgängig, in allen ihren Bestandteilen, bewusst geschaffen wird, ist von Anfang an von einem Reflexionsprozess über Gestaltungsprinzipien bestimmt. Ihr Schöpfer muss mindestens alle essenziellen Universalien realisieren, die eine Sprache als solche ausmachen (Coseriu 1988: 237 f.). Sie sollte weiterhin möglichst empirische Universalien, also sehr weit verbreitete Lösungen der Repräsentation von Inhalten durch Lautketten, befolgen (Coseriu 1988: 236 u. 238). Die Interlinguistik hat dies in Listen von Forderungen zusammengefasst, die

eine Universalsprache prinzipiell zu erfüllen hat (Sapir 1925: 134 f., Maxwell 1989).

Es eröffnen sich auch ganz konkrete Anknüpfungspunkte zwischen Teildiskussionen innerhalb der Typologie und Universalienforschung und den vorgeschlagenen Universalsprachen. So könnte man eine Parallele sehen zwischen den Welteinteilungen von Wilkins und Dalgarno und der Forschung nach semantischen Primitiven, die Anna Wierzbicka (1996) unternimmt. Doch Wilkins und Dalgarno ordnen ihre Ausdruckseinheiten, also Buchstaben oder Laute, Gattungen und Arten zu, d. h. komplexen Bündeln von Merkmalen, während ein semantisches Primitiv ein einfaches Merkmal ist. Ausserdem haben sie den Anspruch, sich an den Dingen selbst auszurichten, während Wierzbicka empirische Daten verschiedener Herkunft, aber überwiegend sprachlicher Art, zu Grunde legt: Paraphrasierung, grammatische Verhältnisse, Befunde des Spracherwerbs, Kritik von Wörterbuchdefinitionen u. a. Ein weiterer konkreter Bezug eröffnet sich im grammatischen Feld. Wilkins und Dalgarno schlagen eine Reduktion aller Wortarten auf die eine Klasse des Nomens vor, Lodwick dagegen sieht das Verb als grundlegende Wortklasse. Diesen Reduktionsdiskussionen entspricht die moderne typologische Problematik der Nomen-Verb-Distinktion (Broschart 1991).

− Die Wortbildung in Universalsprachen ist deutlich besser organisiert als die in natürlichen Sprachen. Ferdinand de Saussure und in neuerer Zeit vor allem Hans-Martin Gauger sehen Durchsichtigkeit als das Wesen von Derivation und Komposition an (Gauger 1971; de Saussure 1972: 180−184). Die Durchsichtigkeit wird allerdings dadurch behindert, dass Wortbildungsprogramme natürlicher Sprachen verschiedene Bedeutungen realisieren können, also polyfunktional sind (Gauger 1971: 173). Gauger erwähnt demgegenüber die Möglichkeit idealer Systeme mit Monofunktionalität und daher vollkommen durchsichtiger Wortbildung, was in den Universalsprachen angestrebt wird.

Gegenüber den genannten Leistungen weisen Universalsprachen andererseits Aspekte auf, die man als Grenzen auffassen kann.
− Zunächst ergeben sich Grenzen der Praktikabilität. Diese betreffen in erster Linie die philosophischen Universalsprachen. So kritisiert Eco die mangelnde Konsequenz bei den Welteinteilungen, die Unmöglichkeit einer konsequenten enzyklopädischen Erfassung aller Phänomene und die Schwierigkeit

für Sprecher und Hörer, sich die entstandenen Lexeme zu merken (Eco 1997: 239−242 u. 255−265).
− Da bei der Gestaltung von Universalsprachen rationale Gesichtspunkte vorherrschen, kann man fragen, ob Universalsprachen alle sprachlichen Funktionen wie z. B. Ausdruck, Appell, Darstellung (Bühler 1934: 24−33) oder phatisch, metasprachlich, poetisch (Jakobson 1960) abdecken können. Universalsprachen scheinen im Wesentlichen die Darstellungsfunktion zu erfüllen. Wenn dies für apriorische Universalsprachen, bei denen ein Erkenntnisideal im Vordergrund steht, gilt, kann man Vergleichbares nicht von den aposteriorischen Sprachen behaupten. Diese haben sich aus den Quellsprachen Mittel verschafft, um die drei Bühlerschen Funktionen zu erfüllen. Die Erfahrung von Esperanto-Sprechern zeigt ausserdem, dass die metasprachliche Funktion in Universalsprachen besonders intensiv realisiert wird (Ertl & Lo Jacomo 1994: 97). Heftig umstritten war die poetische Funktion (Blanke 1985: 81−83). Heute gibt es viele Übersetzungen von Weltliteratur in Esperanto (Blanke 1996: 210).
− Universalsprachen legen sich unvermeidlich auf einen Sprachtyp fest. So ist Esperanto agglutinierend, mit starker Tendenz auf Suffigierung. Die Elemente der Präfigierung, die etwa in den polynesischen Sprachen eine wichtige Rolle spielen, sind relativ schwach. Anteile des isolierenden und flektierenden Sprachtyps sind ausgeschlossen. Obwohl die Präfigierung im Volapük wesentlich stärker ist, handelt es sich auch hier um eine agglutinierende Sprache.
− Damit verbunden ist ein gewisser Eurozentrismus im Wortschatz der meisten aposteriorischen Universalsprachen (Eco 1997: 334 f.), die sich vorwiegend an Englisch, den romanischen Sprachen, Latein und Griechisch orientieren. Auch der Aristotelismus der Welteinteilung bei Wilkins und Dalgarno impliziert einen europäischen Charakter der resultierenden Lexeme. Besonders Wilhelm von Humboldt (1836: 433 f.) und Benjamin Lee Whorf (1956: 212−214) vertraten die These, Sprachen bildeten Begriffswelten aus, die als Weltbilder aufzufassen seien. Sprachen mit unterschiedlichen Wortklassen und grammatischen Kategorien wie etwa das von Whorf so genannte „Standard Average European" im Gegensatz zu den nordamerikanischen Indianersprachen würden unterschiedliche Auffassungen von Zeit, Raum, Handlungsinitiierung und anderen grundsätzlichen Aspekten transportieren. Die eurozentrischen Universalsprachen, so lautet nun der Vorwurf, nivellierten tendenziell diese Unterschiede und exportierten europäische Denkungsart (Ertl & Lo Jacomo 1994: 91 u. 97 f.). Dagegen wird darauf hingewiesen, dass sich diese Beschränkung durch die Vermittlungs-Rolle von Welthilfssprachen bei der internationalen Kommunikation allmählich im Zuge der Praxis aufheben lässt (Ertl & Lo Jacomo 1994: 98).
− Universalsprachen sind wesentlich starrer gegenüber Prozessen des Sprachwandels als natürliche Sprachen. So stellt Eco fest, dass das System von Wilkins bestimmte Schwierigkeiten für die Bildung von Neologismen bietet (1997: 257). Wenn dies auch in den aposteriorischen Sprachen kein Problem darstellt, so scheint doch deren grammatische Struktur oder Lautstruktur nicht veränderbar zu sein. Doch schon Ferdinand de Saussure wies darauf hin, dass selbst künstlich geschaffene Weltsprachen nach großer Verbreitung und längerer Benutzung sich zwangsläufig ändern (1972: 111). In der Tat stellt Claude Piron (1989) mehrere Phänomene des Wandels im Esperanto fest: Ersatz von Präpositionalphrasen durch Adverbien auf *-e* (z. B. *aprile* statt *en aprilo*); Verbalisierung aller möglichen Morpheme (z. B. *blu* 'blau' > *blui* 'einen Eindruck von „Blau" machen'); einige neue Funktionswörter u. a. Generell kann man fragen, ob und in welchen Bereichen Resistenz gegen Sprachwandel ein Nachteil ist und in welchen ein Vorteil.
− Das Ziel der leichten Erlernbarkeit und die eineindeutige Zuordnung von Inhalt- und Ausdrucksseite der sprachlichen Zeichen führt dazu, dass das Vokabular reduziert wird (Wilkins 1668: 453 f.). Dass dies gleichzeitig eine Verarmung und De-Poetisierung des reichen metaphorischen Vorrats natürlicher Sprachen bedeutet, ist der hauptsächliche Angriffspunkt der utopie-kritischen Auseinandersetzung mit Universalsprachen (Orwell 1949: Appendix; Kimminich 1995: 163).
− Es wurde auf die Bezüge zwischen Natürlichkeitstheorie und Universalsprachen hingewiesen. Gegenpositionen zur morphologischen Natürlichkeit sehen die Allomorphien produzierenden Kurzformen und die Suppletivformen in natürlich gewachsenen Sprachen eher als kommunikativ günstig und erwünscht an (Werner 1988). Ähnliches gilt für den bei vielen Universalsprachen beobachtbaren Verzicht auf Kongruenz auf Grund ihrer Redundanz. Ob ein solcher Verzicht nützlich ist, erscheint aus informationstheoreti-

scher (Lyons 1968: 87–89) und syntaktischer Sicht (Raible 1993: 15–22) zweifelhaft.

Dass die sprachwissenschaftliche Diskussion um die Natürlichkeit sich auf Universalsprachen ausweiten lässt, ist nur ein Beispiel dafür, wie Universalienforschung und Typologie für die Gestaltung von Universalsprachen fruchtbare Information an die Hand geben können (vgl. Jespersen 1930: 148).

6. Zitierte Literatur

Adam, Charles & Tannery, Paul. 1956. *Œuvres de Descartes. Band 1: Correspondance I.* Paris: Cerf.

Bartsch, Renate & Vennemann, Theo. 1972. *Semantic structures: a study in the relation between semantics and syntax.* Frankfurt a. M.: Athenäum.

Bausani, Alessandro. 1970. *Geheim- und Universalsprachen: Entwicklung und Typologie.* Stuttgart: Kohlhammer.

Benedikt, Heinrich E. 1985. *Die Kabbala als jüdisch-christlicher Einweihungsweg. Band 1: Farbe, Zahl, Ton und Wort.* Freiburg i. Br.: Bauer.

Blanke, Detlev. 1981. *Plansprache und Nationalsprache. Einige Probleme der Wortbildung des Esperanto und des Deutschen in konfrontativer Darstellung.* Berlin: Akademie-Verlag.

Blanke, Detlev. 1985. *Internationale Plansprachen. Eine Einführung.* Berlin: Akademie-Verlag.

Blanke, Detlev. 1996. „Übersetzen in eine Plansprache – für Europa?". In: Salevsky, Heidemarie (ed.). *Dolmetscher- und Übersetzerausbildung gestern, heute und morgen.* Frankfurt a. M.: Lang, 207–214.

Borst, Arno. 1957–63. *Der Turmbau von Babel. Geschichte der Meinungen über Ursprung und Vielfalt der Sprachen und Völker.* 4 Bde. Stuttgart: Anton Hiersemann.

Broschart, Jürgen. 1991. „Noun, verb and PARTICIPATION". In: Seiler, Hansjakob & Premper, Waldfried (eds.), *Partizipation. Das sprachliche Erfassen von Sachverhalten.* Tübingen: Narr, 65–137.

Brugmann, Karl & Leskien, August. 1907. *Zur Kritik der künstlichen Weltsprachen.* Straßburg: Verlag von Karl J. Trübner.

Bühler, Karl. 1934. *Sprachtheorie.* Jena: Gustav Fischer.

Clauss, Sidonie. 1992. „John Wilkins' Essay towards a Real Character: Its place in the seventeenth century episteme". In: Subbiondo 1992, 45–68.

Condillac, Etienne Bonnot de. 1947. *Œuvres philosophiques* (ed. Georges Le Roy). Bd. 1. Paris: Presses Universitaires de France.

Coseriu, Eugenio. 1988. „Die sprachlichen und die anderen Universalien". In: Jörn Albrecht & Thun, Harald & Lüdtke, Jens (eds.), *Energeia und Ergon. Sprachliche Variation – Sprachgeschichte – Sprachtypologie.* Bd. I. Tübingen: Narr, 233–262.

Courtenay, Baudouin de. 1907. „Zur Kritik der künstlichen Weltsprachen". In: Haupenthal 1976, 59–110.

Couturat, Louis. 1901. *La logique de Leibniz d'après des documents inédits.* Paris: Presses Universitaires de France.

Couturat, Louis & Léau, Léopold. 1907. *Les nouvelles langues internationales.* Paris: Hachette.

Cram, David. 1992. „Language Universals and 17th Century Universal Language Schemes". In: Subbiondo 1992, 191–203.

Dahlenburg, Till & Liebig, Peter. 1981. *Taschenlehrbuch Esperanto.* Leipzig: VEB.

Dalgarno, George. 1661. *Ars signorum.* Facsimile-Nachdruck (English Linguistics 1500–1800, 116). Menston: Solar Press.

Dik, Simon C. 1989. *The Theory of Functional Grammar. Part I: The Study of the Clause.* Dordrecht: Foris.

Duličenko, Aleksandr D. 1989. „Ethnic Language and Planned Language: On the Particulars of the Structural-Genetic and the Functional Aspect". In: Schubert 1989a, 47–61.

Eco, Umberto. 1992. *Das Foucaultsche Pendel.* München: Deutscher Taschenbuchverlag (Titel der ital. Originalausgabe: *Il pendolo di Foucault.* Rom, 1988).

Eco, Umberto. 1997. *Die Suche nach der vollkommenen Sprache.* München: Deutscher Taschenbuchverlag. (Titel der ital. Orignalausgabe: *La ricerca della lingua perfetta.* Rom & Bari 1993.)

Encyclopédie ou dictionnaire raisonné des sciences, des arts et des métiers. Nouvelle impression en facsimilé de la première édition de 1751–1780. Stuttgart-Bad Cannstatt: Frommann Holzbog.

Ertl, István & Jacomo, François Lo. 1994. „Umberto Eco, l'espéranto et le plurilinguisme de l'avenir". In: *Language Problems and Language Planning* 18.2: 87–112.

Forster, Peter G. 1982. *The Esperanto Movement.* Den Haag & Paris & New York: Mouton.

Frank, Thomas. 1992. „Wilkins' Grammar: The verb phrase". In: Subbiondo 1992, 263–275.

French, Peter J. 1972. *John Dee. The World of an Elizabethan Magus.* London: Routledge and Kegan Paul.

Gauger, Hans-Martin. 1971. *Durchsichtige Wörter.* Heidelberg: Winter.

Gerhardt, Carl Immanuel (ed.). 1978. *Die philosophischen Schriften von Gottfried Wilhelm Leibniz. Band V: Leibniz und Locke.* Hildesheim: Olms.

Gerl, Hanna-Barbara. 1989. *Einführung in die Philosophie der Renaissance.* Darmstadt: Wissenschaftliche Buchgesellschaft.

Greenberg, Joseph H. 1966. „Some Universals of Language with Particular Reference to the Order of Elements". In: ders. (ed.) *Language Universals.* Den Haag: Mouton, 73–113.

Haupenthal, Reinhard (ed.). 1976. *Plansprachen. Beiträge zur Interlinguistik.* Darmstadt: Wissenschaftliche Buchgesellschaft.

Humboldt, Wilhelm von. 1830–1835. „Ueber die Verschiedenheit des menschlichen Sprachbaues und ihren Einfluss auf die geistige Entwicklung des Menschengeschlechts". In: Flitner, Andreas & Giel, Klaus (eds.). 1963. *Wilhelm von Humboldt: Schriften zur Sprachphilosophie.* Darmstadt: Wissenschaftliche Buchgesellschaft, 368–756.

Ineichen, Gustav. 1979. *Allgemeine Sprachtypologie.* Darmstadt: Wissenschaftliche Buchgesellschaft.

Jakobson, Roman. 1960. „Linguistics and Poetics". In: Thomas A. Sebeok (ed.). *Style in Language.* Cambridge/MA: Technology Press of Massachusetts: 350–377.

Jespersen, Otto. 1930. „Interlinguistik – eine neue Wissenschaft". In: Haupenthal 1976, 148–162.

Kimminich, Eva. 1993. „Vom Gottesgeschenk zum Herrschaftsinstrument. Beobachtungen zu utopischen und Universalsprachen des 17. Jahrhunderts". In: *Zeitschrift für französische Sprache und Literatur* 103.2: 153–164.

Lyons, John. 1968. *Introduction to Theoretical Linguistics.* Cambridge: Cambridge University Press.

Mayerthaler, Willi. 1981. *Morphologische Natürlichkeit.* Wiesbaden: Akademische Verlagsgesellschaft Athenaion.

Mayerthaler, Willi & Fiedl, Günther. „Natürlichkeitstheoretische Syntax/Syntactic Naturalness". In: Jacobs, Joachim & Arnim von Stechow & Wolfgang Sternefeld & Theo Vennemann. 1993. *Syntax. Ein internationales Handbuch zeitgenössischer Forschung* (HSK 9). Berlin & New York: de Gruyter, 610–635.

Orwell, George. 1949. *Nineteen Eighty-Four.* London: Martin Secker & Warburg.

Piron, Claude. 1989. „A few notes on the evolution of Esperanto". In: Schubert 1989a, 129–142.

Raible, Wolfgang. (1993), *Sprachliche Texte – Genetische Texte. Sprachwissenschaft und molekulare Genetik* (Sitzungsberichte der Heidelberger Akademie der Wissenschaften 1993/1), Heidelberg: Winter.

Salmon, Vivian. 1972. *The works of Francis Lodwick.* London: Longman.

Salmon, Vivian. 1992. „ 'Philosophical Grammar' in John Wilkins' *Essay*". In: Subbiondo 1992, 207–236.

Sapir, Edward. 1925. „Memorandum zum Problem einer internationalen Hilfssprache". In: Haupenthal 1976, 133–147.

Saussure, Ferdinand de. 1972. *Cours de linguistique générale* (Tullio de Mauro ed.).

Schleyer, Johann Martin. 1880. *Volapük. Die Weltsprache.* Sigmaringen. Nachdruck: Hildesheim: Olms. 1982.

Scholem, Gershom. 1980. *Die jüdische Mystik.* Frankfurt a. M.: Suhrkamp.

Schubert, Klaus. 1989a. (ed.). *Interlinguistics: Aspects of the Science of Planned Languages.* Berlin & New York: Mouton & de Gruyter.

Schubert, Klaus. 1989b. „Interlinguistics – its aims, its achievements, and its place in language science." In: Schubert 1989a, 7–44.

Schuchardt, Hugo. 1904. „Bericht über die auf Schaffung einer Universalsprache gerichtete Bewegung". In: Haupenthal 1976, 46–58.

Stocker, Frank. 1996. *Wer spricht Esperanto? Kiu parolas Esperanto?* Unterschleissheim: Lincom Europa.

Strasser, Gerhard F. 1988. *Lingua Universalis. Kryptologie und Theorie der Universalsprachen im 16. und 17. Jahrhundert* (Wölffenbütteler Forschungen 38). Wiesbaden: Harassowitz.

Sturlese, Rita. 1991. *Giordano Bruno: De umbris idearum.* Florenz: Olschki.

Subbiondo, Joseph L. 1992 (ed.) *John Wilkins and 17th-Century British Linguistics.* Amsterdam & Philadelphia: John Benjamins.

Tesnière, Lucien. 1959. *Éléments de syntaxe structurale.* Paris: Klincksieck.

Trubetzkoy, Nikolai S. 1939. „Wie soll das Lautsystem einer künstlichen internationalen Hilfssprache beschaffen sein?". In: Haupenthal 1976, 198–216.

Werner, Otmar. 1988 „Natürlichkeit und Nutzen morphologischer Irregularität". In: Boretzky, Norbert (ed.). *Beiträge zum 3. Essener Kolloquium über Sprachwandel und seine bestimmenden Faktoren.* Bochum: Brockmeyer, 289–316.

Whorf, Benjamin Lee. 1956. *Language, Thought and Reality.* Cambridge/MA: MIT Press.

Wierzbicka, Anna. 1996. *Primes and Universals.* Oxford: Oxford University Press.

Wilkins, John. 1668. *An Essay towards a Real Character and a Philosophical Language.* Facsimile-Nachdruck 1968 (English Linguistics 1500–1800, 119). Menston: Solar Press.

Wurzel, Wolfgang & Wurzel, Ullrich. 1984. *Flexionsmorphologie und Natürlichkeit.* Berlin: Akademie-Verlag.

Yates, Frances A. 1975. *Aufklärung im Zeichen des Rosenkreuzes.* Stuttgart: Klett. (Engl. Originalausgabe: *The Rosicrucian Enlightenment.* London 1972.)

Yates, Frances A. 1982. *Lull and Bruno. Collected Essays I.* London: Routledge and Kegan Paul.

Zamenhof, Ludvik Lejzer. 1887. *Doctor Esperanto: Lingvo Internacia.* Warschau.

Heiner Böhmer, Universität Mainz (Deutschland)

7. Biological foundations of language

1. Introduction
2. Linguistic studies
3. Animal 'language' experiments
4. Language deprivation
5. Aphasic and dysphasic syndromes
6. Brain-imaging procedures
7. Evolutionary studies
8. Conclusions
9. References

1. Introduction

More than thirty years have elapsed since the publication of Lenneberg's classic work on the biological foundations of language (Lenneberg 1967). The major issue then was the extent to which language constitutes an innate and genetically-based faculty as opposed to a learned skill. No one could claim that this issue has been entirely resolved, although no-one, then or now, would dispute that to acquire a full human language involves both some degree of biological predisposition and some degree of learning. The dispute has, all along, been one of "how much?" rather than one of "whether or not". However, during the intervening years the balance has clearly swung in favor of a richer and more complex innate component, even though evidence for the precise genetic mechanisms involved remains tantalizingly vague.

Evidence that bears on the issue comes from a variety of fields: from areas within linguistics, in particular the search for language universals and the study of language acquisition; from attempts to teach language to chimpanzees; from the windows on the language faculty afforded by various types of deprivation and by various dysphasic and aphasic syndromes; from direct studies of the brain's role in language; and, most recently, by a recrudescence of interest in language evolution. As yet, none of these fields has provided a thread that would link all the available evidence into a single coherent whole, so that the only way to proceed is to briefly review each field in turn. However, as suggested in the final section, evolutionary studies seem to offer the highest probability of acting as a unifying force in future research.

2. Linguistic studies

2.1. The search for a universal grammar

When Lenneberg (1967) first appeared, the idea that it would be possible to uncover significant universals of language was little more than a pious hope based on the purely theoretical considerations spelled out in Chomsky (1965). The earliest generative grammars were still closely bound to individual languages, and consisted of large numbers of language-specific rules. In the years that followed, these were progressively reduced to a small handful of abstract principles – the Theta Criterion, the Case Filter, and the Empty Category Principle (Chomsky 1981: 36, 49, 250), among others – which applied across all languages and without exceptions. The last of these is particularly impressive; empty categories (such as the subject and object of talk in *He doesn't have anyone to talk to*) have no representation accessible to the senses and therefore it is hard to see how any rules or principles involving them could be learned.

Clearly, however, the presence of universals – even unlearnable universals – cannot in and of itself prove the existence of an innate language-specific mechanism. Universals might in principle derive from the pragmatic nature of the world or the way the brain analyzes that world. The situation has not been helped by a paradoxical unwillingness, on the part of most nativist linguists, to explore the biological, neurological or evolutionary implications of their findings.

2.2. Acquisition and the connectionist challenge

Support for nativism came also from the study of language acquisition. This was seen as requiring a "poverty of the stimulus" argument. Since the generativity of the language faculty was potentially infinite, and could embrace the production of completely novel sentences, no amount of inductive learning, and no finite corpus (such as the actual linguistic input received by the child) could account for the post-acquisitional status of the child's grammar. Moreover, in the course of acquiring language, most if not all children will produce sentence-types different in kind from any they receive as input. It was therefore widely concluded that the child must possess some kind of innate, language-specific "acquisition device". One factor indicating the probability of such a device is the earliness of the date by which complex syntactic structures are mastered. Experimental work by Crain (1991) has shown that such structures can be reliably produced by children as young as age three.

In the late 1980s, however, a strong challenge to innateness emerged from the study of articifial intelligence. Known as CONNECTIONISM (sometimes referred to as "neural networks" or "parallel distributed processing"), this approach (McLelland & Rummelhart 1986) claimed that a network of simple interconnected processing units, comparable to a network of neurons in the brain, could draw regularities from input data and even learn exceptions to those regularities. The example originally chosen was the acquisition of English regular and irregular past tense forms, although the approach was soon extended to the acquisition of similar morphological subsystems in other languages. Results continue to be controversial (cf. Pinker & Prince 1988, Marcus 1995) despite improvements in the connectionist model (e. g. McWhinney & Leinbach 1991).

However, the strongest argument against connectionism comes from the areas to be discussed in § 4.1−4.2. If, as appears to be the case, children can acquire types of complex linguistic structure that are not represented in the input they receive, this cannot in principle be accounted for by any kind of connectionist model. So far, connectionists have not even attempted to deal with this issue. Indeed, a persistent obstacle to uncovering the biological infrastructure of language has been the confinement of arguments within narrow disciplinary limits. Proposals that may seem convincing on evidence from a single field often fail dismally when confronted by evidence from several fields.

3. Animal 'language' experiments

From the 1960s on, a number of comparative psychologists have attempted to teach language-like systems to several different species (for a critical review of the literature, see Wallman 1992). Given that the mere absence of humanlike vocal organs could form a major barrier to language acquisition in these species, such systems generally employed manual gesture or symbolic objects that could be physically manipulated. Chimpanzees were the commonest subjects, but projects involving gorillas, orangutans, dolphins, sea-lions and even an African grey parrot have reported similar results. Initial optimism about the linguistic capacities of other species faded following an influential study (Terrace et al. 1979) which showed that apes had not acquired syntax and suggested that their use of symbols involved mere association rather than true reference.

Work by Savage-Rumbaugh (1985) and her associates dealt principally with the latter issue, and showed fairly convincingly that, given suitable experimental procedures, referential properties could be acquired (albeit not without difficulty) by chimpanzees. However, work purporting to show that bonobos (pigmy chimpanzees) could also acquire some degree of syntax (Greenfield & Savage-Rumbaugh 1991) is much less conclusive. Although one subject, Kanzi, could apparently understand instructions of the degree of complexity shown by "Go to the refrigerator and get the orange", Kanzi's productive capacities were hardly more impressive than those of his chimpanzee predecessors. Pending some new breakthrough, one can say with some confidence that no other species can acquire even rudimentary forms of natural language syntax.

One cannot immediately conclude from this that syntax forms an innate human capacity. In principle, one could claim that general cognitive advances since the pongid-hominid split have made it possible for humans to acquire syntax. However, the full significance of the animal "language" experiments cannot be appreciated until they are compared with results from language deprivation studies (→ § 4 below).

4. Language deprivation

Although many linguists have been slow to avail themselves of such opportunities, much light can be shed on the biological status of language by considering cases in which children have, for one reason or another, been deprived of the well-formed input normally received from parents and other caregivers. Such cases fall into the three classes discussed below.

4.1. Creoles

The period of European colonial expansion (1500−1900) saw the setting-up of a number of plantation communities in which speakers of diverse languages were brought together (as slaves or indentured laborers) in areas remote from their homelands for labor-intensive agriculture (mainly sugar-growing). Lacking a common language, these workers developed PIDGINS — rudimentary systems of verbal communication lacking most characteristic language structures, for examples see Bickerton (1995: 162–3). However, such systems were quickly replaced by CREOLES — full natural languages which strikingly resemble one another in their typology, and each of which contains at least some features that are not found in the ancestral languages of their original speakers.

While the precise circumstances that surround the creation of creoles remain controversial, historical research by Roberts (1998) confirms that, as proposed in Bickerton (1984), these languages are created in one generation, by children, on the basis of radically degenerate input. If confirmed, these results tend to support the existence of a robust, innate language faculty that can produce an output much richer and more complex than the input it receives.

4.2. Sign language

Further support for such a faculty comes from the acquisition of SIGN LANGUAGE (→ art. 10). During the last few decades, sign language has been shown to possess all the characteristic properties of spoken language, save one: it is not normally transmitted from parents to children. In at least ninety per cent of cases, deaf children are born to hearing parents. Parents attempt to communicate with these children by what is known as "HOME SIGN" — ad hoc gestures bearing little relation to the units of developed sign languages. More than two decades ago, it was demonstrated that deaf children exposed to home sign developed novel signs and assembled them into sequences more complex than any they received (Goldin-Meadow 1979).

More recently, studies in Nicaragua (Kegl & Iwata 1989) have shown similar developments on a community scale. Prior to the Sandinista regime there were no schools or other institutions for the deaf, who normally remained isolated from one another. Subsequently, in the face of fruitless attempts to teach speech, the first wave of children in the new schools developed a language of their own (*Lenguaje de Signos Nicaraguense*) which quickly gave way to a more complex system (*Idioma de Signos Nicaraguense*) as a second wave of younger children acquired it.

These studies have not had the impact they deserve. Sign languages, though generally accepted nowadays as 'real' languages, still do not carry quite the same prestige as spoken languages. Moreover, modality differences make them difficult to compare with spoken languages from the viewpoint of language universals. However, the fact that the development of sign languages bears so strong a resemblance to the development of creole languages forms powerful evidence in support of the contention that the human brain contains an innate faculty, not for the acquisition of language, but rather for its creation.

4.3. Individual deprivation

However, several cases in which isolated individuals were deprived of linguistic input until adolescence or later show that, if there is such an innate faculty, that faculty requires at least some (so far undetermined) minimum of input if a full natural language is to develop. "Genie", a Californian child kept in silence and isolation by her demented father, was mute when she finally escaped at age thirteen (Curtiss 1977). After years of intensive training she was able to produce only "immature, pidgin-like sentences" (Pinker 1994: 291). "Chelsea", another Californian born deaf and wrongly diagnosed as retarded, did not receive appropriate treatment until age thirty-one (Curtiss 1989). She was then fitted with a hearing aid and given intensive therapy, but again, although she had no problem in acquiring vocabulary, she too failed to acquire any kind of natural language syntax.

Cases such as these strongly suggest the existence of a limited 'window' for the acquisition of syntax, one that would close irrevocably somewhere around the onset of puberty. Such windows of opportunity are widely found, in a variety of species, for behaviors with a well-established biological basis.

5. Aphasic and dysphasic syndromes

Traditionally, in both medicine and biology, much has been learned from the analysis of abnormal conditions, whether these result from accidental trauma or genetic defect. For those concerned with the biology of language, such areas constitute an obvious place to look, and the wide availability of subjects for many of these conditions makes them particularly tempting. However, the interpretation of results is often highly problematic.

5.1. Aphasia

5.1.1. Traumatic Aphasia

In aphasia studies there are two major caveats that are not always fully appreciated. The first involves the relationship between neurological damage and language deficiency. If damage in region X is accompanied by a defect in linguistic capacity Y, a natural conclusion (or at least one that was natural before techniques of brain-imaging became widely known) is to assume that X is where Y is executed. Logically, this is not necessarily the case. X might be an area through which signals must pass (en route from W to Z) in order for Y to be produced. The second caveat is still more general. Suppose you had to find out how a television set worked. Suppose your only resources were a warehouse full of television sets and a hammer. All you could do would be to hit the sets with the hammer in different places and see what difference each blow made to the way they worked. It is somewhat doubtful whether you would ever be able to discover either the basic principles of television or how a set actually worked.

A further though unrelated problem in interpreting aphasia studies lies in the fact that most descriptions are written by medical professionals with limited knowledge of linguistics, while most linguists have limited knowledge of the brain. Due to these and other difficulties, it is hardly unfair to say that a century's research has added disproportionately little to the pioneering work of Broca and Wernicke. We know that damage to Broca's area often (but not always, and only to varying degrees) results in AGRAMMATISM, a condition in which utterances lack syntactic structure and function words are absent or only sporadically present (→ Art. 9). Until fairly recently it was widely believed that Broca's area was the seat of grammatical competence and that trauma to it destroyed that competence, while Wernicke's aphasia left syntax intact but led to semantic deficits. However, in some cases damage to one of these two "language areas" will produce systems characteristic of damage to the other (for a general overview of the situation see Caplan 1992). Moreover, we now know from both brain imaging procedures (see § 6 below) and lesion studies that several other areas besides Broca's are involved in the processing of sentences. For instance, lesions affecting the basal ganglia (Lieberman et al. 1992) and the cerebellum (Leiner et al. 1991) have been shown to produce agrammatism.

Some recent studies such as Cornell et al. (1993) have shown that even subjects whose utterances are radically ungrammatical can often (but again, not always!) judge whether sentences are ungrammatical or not. Indeed, this is far from the only issue that is plagued by unpredictable variation. It is clear from studies such as Ojeman (1991) that the precise localization even of language functions (such as the representation of words) that do seem to be at least partially localized will differ from one individual to another. Furthermore, since no two strokes affect exactly the same areas of the brain, it is almost impossible to make any significant generalization about aphasia that cannot be contradicted from empirical studies.

5.1.2. Progressive Aphasia

While most studies have concentrated on aphasias that result from some kind of trauma, some recent studies have begun to explore aphasias that may result from conditions such as Alzheimer's or Parkinson's disease, which develop gradually over a period of time. One of these is a condition described as PRIMARY PROGRESSIVE APHASIA (Mesulam 1982) which may be nonfluent (incorporating phonological distortions) or fluent, involving severe anomia but sparing other aspects of language and cognition. However, as with the traumatic aphasias, there is immense interindividual variation. One case studied by Tyler et al. (1997) involved serious deficits in syntactic processing as well as in semantic combination, while individual word meanings, and cognition in general, remained intact. Although such cases, where impairment cuts across the normal syntax-semantics distinction, may be hard to interpret in terms of current models of language processing, they provide further evidence of an at least partial independence of language and cognition.

5.2. Dysphasia

During the last decade in particular, it has begun to seem possible that we will learn more about the way language is instantiated in the brain (and even perhaps its genetic infrastructure) from dysfunctions of the developing brain than from traumas of the mature brain. Some of the dysphasic conditions surveyed below couple mental retardation with severe language deficits; others, interestingly enough, do not.

5.2.1. Specific Language Impairment

Specific Language Impairment (SLI) is a condition that mainly affects grammatical morphology. Subjects either omit or misplace grammatical morphemes, although other aspects of language, as well as cognitive functions, may remain unaffected, and IQs generally fall within the normal range. The study of a large family half of whose members exhibit SLI suggests that the condition is controlled by a single dominant gene (Gopnik & Crago 1991). However, the precise status of the condition remains controversial, with allegations that SLI is accompanied by subtle cognitive deficits (Vargha-Khadem et al. 1995). Studies of SLI in languages other than English that have richer morphology (e.g. Italian) show less severe effects, leading to claims that, while clearly genetic in origin, it may result from a perceptual rather than a purely linguistic deficiency (Leonard 1998; → art. 8, § 8). SLI is better known to most linguists than other conditions that affect language, and ongoing research should help to clarify the picture.

5.2.2. Williams' Syndrome

Williams' Syndrome (WS), a condition studied by Ursula Bellugi and her colleagues (Bellugi et al. 1994) involves subjects with IQs in the 40s or 50s, who when they reach adulthood are still incapable of living alone. Despite this, they produce syntactically flawless complex sentences (even though the content of these may be pragmatically bizarre) and have rich vocabularies. The condition is accompanied in over 90% of cases by a microdeletion involving an elastin gene on chromosome 7 that leads to a stenosis of the aorta (Ewart et al. 1994). There are also interesting neurological consequences; in a comparison between WS and Down's Syndrome (DS) subjects, Jernigan and Bellugi (1990) found that while cerebral volume was reduced below that of normal controls, neocerebellar volume, though sharply reduced in DS cases, was at least equal to that of normals in WS cases. This finding constitutes an interesting link with recent research on the functions of the neocerebellum.

5.2.3. Angelman's and Down's Syndromes

In contrast, Angelman's Syndrome (AS), a condition only identified in the 1960s, and not systematically studied until two decades later, causes both mental retardation and serious language problems (Clayton-Smith 1993; Buntinx et al. 1955). In some cases, subjects have no speech at all; in a large majority of cases, subjects can produce utterances of no more than two or three words, and in all cases they are incapable of maintaining a normal conversation. A similar conjunction of cognitive and linguistic deficits is found in the much more thoroughly studied condition known as Down's Syndrome (DS). According to Rondal (1995: 9) "the spontaneous combinatorial language of DS individuals remains largely telegraphic ... It is characterized by a reduced use of function words ... The lack of appropriate feature marking on pronouns and anaphors may render the referring expressions opaque to the nonfamiliar interlocutor."

However, the genetic origins of these conditions remain puzzling. Although language deficits in AS and DS seem to closely resemble one another, their sources are quite diverse: AS involves a deletion or distomy on chromosome 15, DS involves a trisomy on chromosome 21. Yet a deletion on chromosome 15 is also responsible for Praeger-Willi Syndrome, a condition which (as far as language is concerned) gives rise to only minor articulatory problems. Comparison of the sites involved and the behavioral consequences of deletions therein should afford us further insights into the genetic basis of language.

5.2.4. Autism

One of the commonest, best-known and most widely-studied condition affecting language is autism. Autism involves severe language impairment: in the worst case, complete or virtually complete absence of most or all linguistic functions. However, as with DS, there is a considerable range of individual variation, such that the author of one study reported "each child generated a profile of linguistic abilities and disabilities which were special to him" (Churchill 1978: 21). The disabilities, however, seem to preclude, in virtually all cases, anything more than the stringing together of two- or three-word utterances.

However, it is far from clear that autism (despite the opinion of some researchers) is

primarily linguistic in origin. When faced with tasks such as the execution of simple commands (e.g. "Put the spoon in the cup", many autistic children perform far worse than Kanzi or other trained apes. In autism, language problems would appear to be consequences of far more general cognitive problems, such as an inability to form generalizations that are well within the reach of normal individuals in other primate species. Eventually, studies of autism may help to tease apart the neurological infrastructures of language and cognition, but we are still a long way from reaching this goal.

6. Brain-imaging procedures

During recent years, the development of various brain-imaging techniques, in particular POSITRON EMISSION TOMOGRAPHY (PET) and MAGNETIC RESONANCE IMAGING (MRI) have opened up the possibility, unknown to earlier generations, of studying the human brain while it is actually performing particular linguistic functions. These procedures are not quite the transparent windows on neural activity that popular accounts might suggest. One problem is that any linguistic task inevitably activates processes involving attention, memory and other nonlinguistic functions; these must be subtracted if the precise areas that handle language are to be delimited.

Indeed, at least some researchers have concluded that "functional imaging studies of language have shown little more than what Carl Wernicke knew" (Nadeau & Crosson 1997: 455). Most, however, would agree that the classic Broca-Wernicke model of language functions must now be abandoned for a much more complex picture. One of the most striking findings has been the involvement of the neocerebellum in language tasks (Leiner et al. 1991). Indeed, a growing body of evidence implicates a variety of subcortical sites, in addition to cortical sites extending well beyond the traditional language areas and, in some cases, changing or reducing the functions assigned to these (Raichle et al. 1994, Binder et al. 1997).

The general picture that emerges from these studies is one in which storage of lexical items is quite sharply localized (Hart & Gordon 1992) while syntactic and phonological processing are much more diffused, and involve the co-operation of a variety of areas both inside and outside the cortex.

7. Evolutionary studies

If language indeed has a specific biological infrastructure, then that infrastructure developed through regular processes of biological evolution. Those processes should in principle be recoverable, despite the absence of direct fossil evidence frequently cited to justify indifference or agnosticism towards language evolution.

Unfortunately, until quite recently, few linguists even among those who believed that language formed part of human biology expressed interest in attempting to determine how language could have evolved. In consequence, the field came to be dominated by non-linguists, who showed little awareness of the fact that any adequate theory must explain not merely the developments that produced language, but also why language has the properties that it does have, rather than some other set of properties.

Much recent work in the field seeks to derive language from social intelligence, a trend sparked by Humphrey (1976) and perhaps most fully developed in the work of Dunbar (1996). However, dozens of studies of both wild and captive populations have shown that other primates possess a high degree of social skill, and negotiate complex social situations in a way that seems, to at least one observer, hardly 'inferior to that of human beings' (de Waal 1982: 51). If this is the case, it is hard to see how a selective pressure towards language can have arisen in the sphere of social relations. Moreover, social intelligence theories have failed to provide any account of why language has the features it does, rather than other features.

The proposal that language evolved in at least two discrets stages, with a structureless protolanguage preceding true language (Bickerton 1990) seems now to be quite widely accepted. It avoids the problems raised by direct derivation from prior animal call systems (see Burling 1993 for discussion) while maintaining continuity between primates and humans. Since other primates can produce protolinguistic utterances (see § 3), no biological changes would have been needed; our ancestors simply had to do voluntarily what other primates can do under instruction, although precisely what precipitated the behavioral change remains unclear.

This proposal implies that the evolution of syntactic structure was the crucial development in the emergence of language as we now know it. But did syntax emerge gradually or abruptly? While general evolutionary principles might seem to predict the former (a position defended by Pinker & Bloom 1990, Newmeyer 1991), a variety of considerations combine to make this implausible (Bickerton 1995, 1998; for an alternative version of "catastrophic" evolution, see Berwick 1997). The possibility that syntax resulted from the co-option of some prior adaptation deserves thorough research. If syntax was indeed created in this way, it would help to explain why its biological foundations have proven so evasive. At the same time, syntax would appear both less anomalous and less novel than some accounts have suggested.

8. Conclusions

While the precise extent to which language is pre-determined by biological factors remains unclear, the evidence surveyed above argues strongly for a broader rather than a narrower innate basis. For instance, comparison of the range of deprivation cases surveyed above with the results of animal "language" experiments renders less plausible claims that syntactic capacity might be a function of increased cognitive capacity. Both Genie and Chelsea tested with intelligence levels were well within the normal range; in addition, Chelsea had not undergone any traumatic experience that might be blamed for her inability to acquire syntax. If cognitivist claims were correct, both subjects should have acquired syntax. In fact, both acquired only what apes can be taught – the stringing together of meaningful symbols based solely on semantic and pragmatic considerations. Similar restrictions also seem to apply in many dysphasic syndromes, although failure to take into account the protolanguage/language distinction makes many clinical reports hard to assess. But again, the selective sparing of syntax in Williams' Syndrome cases further supports a sharp disjunction of language and cognition.

The variety of the fields relevant to the biology of language has proved a handicap that can only be overcome by setting the problem squarely within a single framework, one capable of integrating all of the problem's varied aspects. Despite its long history of often baseless speculation, the field of language evolution seems at present among the likeliest to provide such a framework. Evolution is central because, if language is indeed a biological adaptation, it must have evolved somehow, and speculation can now be constrained by extensive findings in the various fields surveyed above.

Unless some dramatic new source of information is discovered, the picture of the language faculty that is emerging will probably show the following set of features. The faculty will be seen as essentially disjoint. One component involves the capacity to acquire a vocabulary and use it for communicative purposes. At least the potentiality for this appears to be shared by a variety of species, and it may thus be assumed to have a biological basis that is not entirely human-specific (although no-one can doubt that the capacity has undergone enormous extension within the hominid line). Another component involves the capacity to process and produce a wide variety of speech sounds. This capacity has not been discussed in the present account, since few would dispute its innate character; for instance, recent experiments have shown that neonates can reliably distinguish speech sounds. A third capacity, clearly limited to humans at least in its present form, involves the assembly of words (or signs) into complex structures. While this capacity may result from a preadaptation, its refinement has surely taken place within the last few hundred thousand years, if not more recently still.

Such an overall evolutionary model can now be tested against findings in the fields of theoretical linguistics, neurology and aphasiology, among others. Such testing should yield some of the most exciting developments in twentyfirst-century studies of human cognition.

9. References

Bellugi, Ursula & Wang, Paul & Jernigan, Terry L. 1994. "Williams' Syndrome: An unusual neuropsychological Profile". In: Broman, Sarah H. & Grafman, Jordan (eds.) *Developmental Behavioral neuroscience.* Hillsdale NJ: Erlbaum, 201–232.

Berwick, Robert C. 1997. "Syntax facit saltum: Computation and the genotype phenotype of language." *Journal of Neurolinguistics* 10: 231–249.

Bickerton, Derek. 1984. "The language bioprogram hypothesis". *Behavioral and Brain Sciences* 7.1: 173–221.

Bickerton, Derek. 1990. *Language and Species.* Chicago: Univ. of Chicago Press.

Bickerton, Derek. 1995. *Language and human behavior.* Seattle: Univ. of Washington Press.

Bickerton, Derek. 1998. "The case for a catastrophic emergence of syntax". In: Hurford, James R. & Studdert-Kennedy, Michael & Knight, Chris (eds.). *Approaches to the evolution of language: Social and cognitive bases.* Cambridge: Cambridge Univ. Press.

Binder, Jeffrey R. & Frost, Julie A. & Hammeke, Thomas A. & Cox, Robert W. & Rao, Stephen M. & Prieto, Thomas. 1997. "Human brain language areas identified by magnetic resonance imaging". *Journal of Neuroscience* 17. 1: 353−362.

Buntinx, Inge L. & Kennekam, Raoul & Brouwer, Obele F. & Stronk, Hans & Beuten, Joke & Mangelschots, Kathelijne & Fryns, J. P. 1995. "Clinical profile of Angelman syndrome at different ages". *American Journal of Medical Genetics* 56.2: 176−183.

Burling, Robbins. 1993. "Primate calls, human language and nonverbal communication". *Current Anthropology* 34: 25−53.

Caplan, David. 1992. *Language: Structure, processing, and disorders.* Cambridge MA: MIT Press.

Chomsky, Noam. 1965. *Aspects of the theory of syntax.* Cambridge MA: MIT Press.

Chomsky, Noam. 1981. *Lectures on government and binding.* Dordrecht: Foris Publ.

Churchill, Don W. 1978. *Language of autistic children.* New York: Halsted Press.

Clayton-Smith, Jill. 1993. "Clinical research on Angelman syndrome in the United Kingdom: Observation of 82 affected individuals". *American Journal of Medical Genetics* 46: 12−15.

Cornell, Thomas L. & Fromkin, Victoria A. & Mauner, Gail. 1993. "A linguistic approach to Broca's aphasia: A paradox resolved". *Current Directions in Psychological Science* 2.2: 47−52.

Crain, Stephen. 1991. "Language acquisition and the absence of experience". *Behavioral and Brain Sciences* 14: 597−650.

Curtiss, Susan. 1977. *Genie: A psycholinguistic study of a modern-day "wild child".* London: Academic Press.

Curtiss, Susan. 1988. "Abnormal language acquisition and the modularity of language". In: Newmeyer, Frederick J. (ed.). *Linguistics: The Cambridge Survey* (Vol. 3). Cambridge: Cambridge Univ. Press. 90−116.

De Waal, Frans. 1982. *Chimpanzee politics: power and sex among apes.* New York: Harper & Rov.

Dunbar, Robin. 1996. *Grooming, gossip and the evolution of language.* London: Faber and Faber.

Ewart, A. K. & Jin, W. & Atkinson, D. & Morris, C. A. & Keating, M. T. 1994. "Supravalvular aortic stenosis associated with a deletion disrupting the elastin gene". *Journal of Clinical Investigations* 93.3: 1071−1077.

Goldin-Meadow, Susan. 1979. "Structure in a manual communication system developed without a conventional model". In: Whitaker, Haiganoosh & Whitaker, Harry A. (eds.). *Studies in neurolinguistics* (Vol. 4). New York: Academic Press, 125−209.

Gopnik, Myrna & Crago, Michael. 1991. "Familial aggregation of a developmental language disorder". *Cognition* 39.1: 1−50.

Greenfield, Pamela & Savage-Rumbaugh, Sue. 1991. "Imitation, gramatical development, and the invention of proto-grammar by an ape". In: Krasnegor, Norman A. & Rumbaugh, Duane M. & Studdert-Kennedy, Michael & Scheifelbusch, D. (eds.). *Biological and behavioral determinants of language development.* Hillsdale NJ: Erlbaum, 235−258.

Hart, John & Gordon, Barry. 1992. "Neural subsystems for object knowledge". *Nature* 359: 60−64.

Humphrey, Nicholas K. 1976. "The social function of the intellect". In: Bateson, Peter P. G. & Hinde, Robert A. (eds.). *Growing points in ethology.* Cambridge: Cambridge Univ. Press, 303−318.

Jernigan, Terry L. & Bellugi, Ursula. 1990. "Anomalous brain morphology on magnetic resonance images in Williams' syndrome and Down's syndrome". *Archives of Neurology* 47: 529−533.

Kegl, Judy & Iwata, Gayla A. 1989. "Lenguaje de signos Nicaragüense: A pidgin sheds light on the 'creole'? ASL". *Proceedings of the Fourth Annual Meeting of the Pacific Linguistics Society.* Eugene OR.

Leiner, Henrietta C. & Leiner, Alan L. & Dow, Robert S. 1991. "The human cerebro-cerebellar: its computing, cognitive and language skills". *Behavioral Brain Research* 44: 113−128.

Lenneberg, Eric H. 1967. *Biological foundations of language.* New York: Wiley.

Leonard, Lawrence B. 1998. *Children with specific language impairment.* Cambridge MA: MIT Press.

Lieberman, Philip & Friedman, J. & Feldman, L. S. 1990. "Syntactic deficits in Parkinson's disease". *Journal of Nervous and Mental Disease* 178: 360−365.

Marcus, Gary. 1995. "The acquisition of the past tense in children and multilayered connectionist networks". *Cognition* 56.3: 271−279.

McLelland, James L. & Rummelhart, David E. 1986. *Parallel distributed processing: Explorations in the microstructure of cognition.* Cambridge MA: MIT Press.

McWhinney, Brian & Leinbach, John. 1991. "Implementations are not conceptualizations: Revising the verb learning model". *Cognition* 40: 121−157.

Mesulam, M.-Marsel 1982. "Slowly progressive aphasia without generalised dementia". *Annals of Neurology* 11.6: 592−598.

Nadeau, Stephen E. & Crosson, Bruce. 1997. "Subcortical aphasia: Response to reviews". *Brain and Language* 58: 436–459.

Newmeyer, Frederick J. (ed.). 1991. *Linguistics: the Cambridge Survey.* Vol. 4,4. Cambridge: Cambridge University Press.

Ojeman, George A. 1991. "Cortical organization of language". *Journal of Neuroscience* 11: 2281–2287.

Pinker, Steven. 1994. *The language instinct.* New York: Morrow.

Pinker, Steven & Bloom, Paul. 1990. "Natural selection and natural language". *Behavioral and Brain Sciences* 13: 707–784.

Pinker, Steven & Prince, Alan. 1988. "On language and connectionism: Analysis of a parallel distributed processing model of language acquisition". *Cognition* 28: 73–193.

Raichle, Marcus E. & Fiez, J. A. & Videen, T. O. & McLeod, A. M. & Pardo, J. V. & Fox, P. T. & Petersen, S. E. 1994. "Practice-related changes in human brain functional anatomy during non-motor learning". *Cerebral Cortex* 4.1: 8–26.

Roberts, Sarah J. 1998. "The role of diffusion in the genesis of Hawaiian Creole". *Language* 74: 1–39.

Rondal, Jean A. 1995. *Exceptional Language development in Down syndrome.* Cambridge: Cambridge Univ. Press.

Savage-Rumbaugh, Sue. 1985. *Ape language: From conditioned response to symbol.* New York: Columbia Univ. Press.

Terrace, Herbert S. & Petitto, Laura A. & Sanders, Robert J. & Bever, Thomas G. 1979. "Can an ape create a sentence?" *Science* 206: 891–902.

Tyler, Lorraine K. & Moss, Helen E. & Patterson, Karalyn & Hodges, John. 1997. "The gradual deterioration of syntax and semantics in a patient with progressive aphasia." *Brain and Language* 56.3: 426–476.

Vargha-Khadem, Faraneh & Watkins, Kate & Alcock, Katie & Fletcher, Paul & Passingham, Richard. 1995. "Praxic and nonverbal cognitive deficits in a large family with a genetically transmitted speech and language disorder." *Proceedings of the National Academy of the Sciences USA*, 92.3, 930–933.

Wallman, Joel. 1992. *Aping language.* Cambridge: Cambridge Univ. Press.

Derek Bickerton, University of Hawaii (USA)

8. Linguistics and Genetics: Systematic parallels

1. Basics
2. Language as a Metaphor in Molecular Biology
3. Linguistic Vocabulary in Microbiology
4. Structural Similarities
5. Program or Encyclopedia?
6. The Awareness of Biologists
7. A Relation between DNA and Language Types?
8. Language Genes?
9. References

"Life depends on the interaction of tens of thousands of genes and their protein products, orchestrated by the regulatory logic of each genome. If we are to comprehend this logic, we must hope that it can be dissected into a series of interlinked modules or networks, each of which can be studied in relative isolation. But even then the complexity of a single module can be daunting. As our knowledge increases, diagrams of gene regulatory networks look increasingly like explosions in a spaghetti factory. We need fresh methods to explore the behaviour of such networks." (Dearden & Akam 2000: 131.)

1. Basics

In order to understand the following comparison, some facts have to be recalled first.

Any cell – irrespective of its being part of a complex organism or its functioning as a one-cell organism – contains the so-called "genetic information" necessary for the reproduction and formation of the whole organism. This information is part of the genome embodied in the double helix of desoxyribonucleic acid (DNA). The double helix or "duplex" has two intertwined strands of DNA. Each one is a long polymer of subunits called *nucleotides* with the four bases adenin, thymin, guanin, and cytosin, abbreviated as A, T, G, and C. The nucleotide T always pairs with A, C with G.

Functionally, nucleotides come as triplets, that is to say that three of them form a codon. Most of them code for one of the 20-odd (21 in the case of man) amino acids, with four of the 64 possible combinations of three nucleotides having the additional function of a start or a stop codon.

The genome – for instance the human one – contains hundreds of thousands of genes or functional subunits of the DNA-strands. Most of them are responsible for the production of specific chains of amino acids, the so-called polypeptides (proteins) which fold into very specific forms fulfilling crucial functions in living cells.

When a gene coded in a DNA-sequence is transformed into a protein, in a first step an enzyme called RNA-polymerase (RNA = ribonucleic acid) makes a replica of the strand of nucleotides forming the gene at stake. This primary replica consisting of RNA is usually subject to further modification: in eukaryotes certain stretches of RNA (termed "introns") are removed, leaving the remaining "exons" (a Greek term which means 'going out') to be fused and finally transported out of the nucleus. Besides that, the ends of the RNA strand are modified, and sometimes specific nucleotides are substituted for others.

Once the RNA molecule has been worked over, it is used by the cell to produce polypeptides. To that end, the RNA molecule – then referred to as "messenger RNA" (mRNA) – is transported to one of the ribosomes in the cytoplasm, i.e. to another enzyme or macromolecule. Using the information contained in the sequence of codons represented by the strand of mRNA, a ribosome produces the corresponding chain of amino acids which folds up into a very specifically shaped protein.

This basic knowledge should be complemented by a contextual knowledge condensed into the following five points (Raible 1993, largely based on Monod 1970):

1. Our cells have two kinds of basic substances: in the domain of the double helix, the substances are the NUCLEOTIDES embodying genetic information. For the rest of the cell, the basic substances are AMINO ACIDS which are chained into large macromolecules doing the "work" that has to be done in the cell.
2. As regards the interior organization of cells, these two classes of macromolecules belong to two separated domains, with the nucleus harboring the DNA. However, the nucleus is only a feature of EUKARYOTIC cells, the components all multicellular organisms consist of. The cells called PROKARYOTES, for instance bacteria such as the omnipresent *Escherichia coli*, do not have such a compartmented nucleus. In this case, the genome lies in the cytoplasm.
3. Chemically, the macromolecules in both domains are formed by two different classes of bonds. (1) When their respective units are put together in order to build larger structures, this is achieved by COVALENT BONDS. A covalent bond is a relatively stable, strictly speaking chemical unit where two or more atoms share common electrons. Covalent bonds create chemical *configurations*. (2) The overwhelming number of bonds which give the molecules their specific shape or conformation are of NON-COVALENT nature: weak interactions, hydrophobic interactions, hydrogen bonds. They result in *conformational* interactions (as opposed to configurations). The advantage of conformations is that neither their formation nor their dissolution needs much energy. At the same time, the respective processes are very fast.
4. Most of the cytoplasm consists of water. Amino acids are partly hydrophilic, partly hydrophobic. Now when, according to the instructions contained in the chain of mRNA, chains of amino acids are formed by the ribosomes, the whole compound folds up into a three-dimensional macromolecule according to the degree of hydrophilia or hydrophobia of its components. As often even so-called scaffolding proteins (chaperons) are used in order to guarantee a specific three-dimensional (steric) structure.

   The special kind of folding, mostly stabilized by hydrogen bonds and sometimes also by specific covalent bonds making up for the overall shape of the macro-molecule, is the basis of an infinity of specific three-dimensional structures in the domain of complex proteins.
5. The resulting steric form is crucial for the functioning of processes in cells: a very large part of such processes is based on the "recognition" – this is a frequently used metaphor – of molecules by each other: Molecule surfaces are fitting like a positive into a negative, protruding forms fit into caved, convex into concave forms, and so on. Here a further common metaphor is the metaphor of the key and the lock.

Above all, the low-energy non-covalent bonds (see above § 1.3) and the "recognition" of molecules by fitting forms are responsible for the fact that cells in our bodies are able to perform processes of synthesis and catalysis with an incredible speed consuming the least possible amount of energy. All these processes are energetically optimized by evolution, leaving thus little room for further economy.

2. Language as a metaphor in molecular biology

Since its beginnings in the middle of the 19th century, molecular biology has been associated with the metaphor of language, especially language in its form of an alphabetic script (Raible 1993: 8–10).

This use of written language as a metaphor has a long history. It starts with the early atomists Leucippus and Democritus (v B.C.). Their basic idea was that the whole complex, manifold, beautiful, fragrant and colored world surrounding us is nothing but appearance, whereas in reality all was thought to consist of atoms and the void between them. According to what is told us in Aristotle's *Metaphysics* about the doctrine of these two pre-socratic philosophers, their visible model for the invisible structure of matter was alphabetic script. The variety of the visible world would be due to the fact that the atoms are differently shaped – just as an A differs in shape from an N; that their order may be different – as the sequence AN is different from NA; finally their relative position in space may differ: a rotation of 90 degrees makes an N out of a Z (Aristotle, *Metaphysics* A4, 985b15ff.).

The central idea behind this conception is the reduction of immense varieties onto a restricted set of elements (here the 20-odd letters of the Greek alphabet making up for a possibly infinite variety of written texts).

In 1869, Friedrich Miescher discovered the existence of nucleic acid in the center of living cells. In 1893, just before his death, he put forward the idea that the relation holding between the letters of our alphabet and the enormous number of words their combination results in could explain the relationship between the information contained in the nuclei of our cells and the variety of life forms ("daß aller Reichtum und alle Mannigfaltigkeit erblicher Übertragungen ebenso gut darin ihren Ausdruck finden können, als die Worte und Begriffe aller Sprachen in den 24 bis 30 Buchstaben des Alphabets").

It was not until 1943 that the same idea was put forward again, this time by the Austrian physicist Erwin Schrödinger, in a series of conferences given in Dublin under the heading "What is life?" He suggested a genetic alphabet similar to the Morse code. Mutations would be due to mistakes in the process of reading and copying the code. However, it took another decade before the chemical nature of Schödinger's alphabet was understood. At first, Oswald Avery proved in 1944 that the nucleic acids – and not the proteins – contained the genetic information necessary to unfold the functions of a pneumonic bacterium. When reading Avery's contribution, Erwin Chargaff even added the idea of a "grammar of biology" (Blumenberg 1981, ch. 22).

Both Miescher and Schrödinger were confirmed in 1953 by the discovery of Francis Crick and James Watson who showed that the long strands of DNA (Schrödinger's punched Morse tapes) have the structure of a double helix, and by the series of momentous discoveries that followed this breakthrough. The metaphor of language in the form of alphabetic script has been omnipresent in molecular biology since 1953.

3. Some of the linguistic vocabulary used in the texts of microbiology

In the U.S., the National Center for Biotechnology Information (NCBI) is running a large data base called Medline. Until 1997, this base had a subset in molecular genetics comprising some 700,000 full-text documents starting from about 1966. In 1998, this subset was merged with the general biological data base, the resulting whole containing now some nine million full-text documents. Since this data base permits searching for any expression, it is easy to demonstrate the presence of the language and the script metaphor in the whole range of texts in molecular biology.

Right from the beginning in 1953, the four nucleotide bases abbreviated by A, T, G, and C were called the "letters of the genetic alphabet". RNA-polymerase is *reading* (found in ca. 44,500 documents as of 2000; the numbers always cover a period of ten years) DNA-sequences with their *reading-frame/s* (27,700 docs.). This process is called *transcription* (81,000 docs. in 1997; 148,100 in 2000 and a total of 212,300 for the family *transcr** in 2000), and this happens thanks to *transcription factors* (92,300 docs. in 2000), a topic needing further comment in a later section (see below § 4.3). Associated with transcription is an immediate process of *proof-reading* or *proof reading* (700 docs. as of 2000).

The result is called a *copy* (20,000 docs. in 2000) subject to further *editing* (2,100) or *copy editing* (52). The resulting string of mRNA will be *translated* (20,000 docs. in 1997, 75,400 for translat* in 2000) into a polypeptide. This is made possible because the triplets of nucleotides *encode* or are *coding for* amino acids (130,000 docs. for code*/coding in 1997, 253,000 in 2000). The whole process is called *gene expression* (245,400 docs. as of 2000).

The use of the metaphor does not end here, though. The genome of lots of species is being *deciphered* actually (830 docs. for decipher* as of 2000). The result is stored in large *data bases* modelling the sequences of nucleotides as sequences of the letters A, T, G, and C. The same is true for protein data bases symbolizing one amino acid by one letter (the sequence *mgqtgkk...* for instance stands for *methionin-glycin-glutamin-threonin-glycin-lysin-lysin...*). This is tantamount to saying that sequences of nucleotides or amino acids corresponding to triplets of nucleotides "materialize" – in a somewhat hybrid way – in data bases as sequences of letters. As a consequence, there are 7,100 documents containing *data base(s)* in 2000.

When the molecular section of Medline was still separated from the rest of biology, there were already 27,000 documents containing (gene-) *library, libraries*; there are 47,000 in 2000 (with 9,400 instances of *gene library/ies*, 6,950 of *genomic library/ies*). Recurrent sequences of nucleotide "letters" as well as recurrent sequences of amino acids in proteins are called *motif, motifs* (12,000 documents in 1997, 29,900 in 2000). Recently a new metaphor is being used more and more: the genome is like an *encyclop(a)edia* (54 docs. in 1997, 225 as of 2000). *Dictionary* is still relatively rare in genetic contexts, though the number of instances is increasing rapidly (913 docs. by 2000). Parts of this encyclopedia may be *formatted* in a different way, like *bold* or *italic text* (see §4.8).

Large data bases of necessity use classification criteria. In 1999, Medline used about 19,000 hierarchically ordered description terms or "main headings" – even there the linguistic metaphor is most evident: *reading frame* (classifying 9,073 docs. as of 1999), *transcription* (68,440), *transcription factor* (79,704), *gene expression* (138,773), library/libraries: *gene library; genomic library* (4,715).

Written language and processes related to writing make up for most of the metaphors. Apart from the concept of *translation* which is ambigous in this respect, vocal language is used relatively seldom in this context, the most conspicuous case being the family *silenc** with 4,300 occurrences as of 2000: esp. *gene silencing* (500); a relatively new topic is *posttranscriptional gene silencing* (33), a phenomenon whose basic mechanisms remain to be fully understood. (Here the usual metaphor is 'knocking out' a gene (9,700 cases of *knockout*, 1,300 of *knock out* as of 2000).

A last metaphor that should be noted is *genomic imprinting* (3,200 docs. by 2000): it serves to characterize regions in the genome that are marked by methylation: imprinted regions are observed to be more methylated and less *transcriptionally* active.

4. Structural similarities as the deeper reason behind the language metaphor

Under the above heading 'basics' (see above § 1), the present author succeeded in avoiding language as a metaphor (apart from the terms "to code for" and "information", though), showing thus that it should – at least in principle – be possible to describe some of the fundamental processes in molecular biology *without* borrowing from language and alphabetic script.

4.1. Linearity as a fundamental problem

Nevertheless, language is not only a metaphor biologists "live by" (without being very aware of the fact that they are using it, though: see below § 6). There is a deeper relationship between the way the "grammar of biology" and the grammar of natural languages are working.

In both cases, information is coded into a linear sequence of basic elements, nucleotides in one, phonemes or letters in the other case. Since this coded sequence of elements is of necessity linear, both systems have to cope with the same fundamental problem: how can a one-dimensional medium transmit the information required for the construction of three- (or even more-) dimensional entities?

The complexity of the information to be transmitted becomes evident when we imagine that all of us originated from one single egg-cell whose genome was replicated billions of times by successive divisions of cells, so-called *mitoses*. Nevertheless, the result was not an amorphous heap of identical cells, i.e. something similar to yeast. Instead, what took shape in the embryonic evolution process was a well-structured three-dimensional body. Since this is a process, the outcome of the reading of linear code-sequences was even four-dimensional.

This is tantamount to saying that the code contained in any cell of our emerging body had to be read very selectively such that, by differentiation of cells occurring in the right place and at the right time, a highly complicated organism with highly specialized compounds of cells took shape. The entire information necessary to carry out this process came from our genome (and the specific composition of the egg plasma of the fertilized oozyte, see below § 4.3).

The same kind of process takes place in human speech. What we want to utter are complex ideas and representations − like the present article. Those ideas are broken down into sections encompassing a series of subsections made out of paragraphs, the paragraphs themselves consisting of linked sentences and propositions. Sentences are again broken down into entities called clauses, phrases, words, and the still linear sequence of words consists of letters. This will be the input for readers whose task is to reconstruct, out of a linear sequence of phonemes or letters, the complex representation the speaker or writer started from.

Although the first part of this process − the breaking down of the complex representation into successive hierarchical layers of pieces resulting eventually in a linearized sequence of basic elements − does not have its counterpart in genetics, the subsequent reconstruction by the reader (or hearer) does indeed. In order to achieve this, genetic processes rely on principles strikingly similar to those holding in language.

Whereas the result of this process of reconstruction tends to be rather volatile and elusive in language (readers or hearers may come up with a reconstruction that is somewhat far from the ideas of the speaker or writer), in the genetic counterpart the result of the cellular reading processes is mostly material, visible and palpable: it is a living body. Genetic reading processes tend to be highly reliable thanks, among other things, to a considerable amount of redundancy in genetic information.

4.2. The basic principles in both systems

In both systems, the principles allowing the reconstruction of multi-dimensional wholes from linear sequences of basic elements are identical:

− double articulation,
− different classes of 'signs',
− hierarchy,
− combinatorial rules on the different levels of hierarchy, and
− linking the principles of hierarchy and combinatorial rules: wholes are always more than the sum of their parts.

Double articulation means that in language we make words out of sounds (in alphabetic script: out of letters) which, by themselves, are − in principle − meaningless. Only groups of sounds are meaningful, just as only triplets of nucleotides "signify" (in the wording of molecular biology: code for) an amino acid. On the level of the double articulation which comprises hierarchy and functional classes, in genetics amino acids are combined into multiform and multifold proteins showing the specific steric and other properties needed for the functioning of specific cells, with cells themselves combining into functional units called for instance organs, such as the liver or an eye. They are again parts in a larger whole − with the respective whole always exceeding the sum of its smaller components.

In the domain of Life this principle, clearly put forward in the seminal thesis of Émile Boutroux (^{1}1875, ^{2}1991), bridges at the same time the seemingly antinomical Cartesian gap between Mind and Matter by introducing the idea of a continuum.

4.3. The discovery of regulating proteins in genetics

Originally, microbiologists thought that there was a clear distinction between the world of nucleotides and the world of proteins. The idea of this distinction was even enhanced by the fact that in eukaryotic cells − as opposed to prokaryotic ones (see above § 1.2) − the nucleus with its genome is separated from the rest of cytoplasm (see above § 1.1). Since the genome contains genes − i.e. "meaningful" subunits of the long strands of DNA − it was thought that all these genes were responsible for the proteins functioning in the cytoplasm, and giving the cell its specific characteristics. Very soon it became clear, though, that proteins, too, play a most important part when a gene is read, transcribed into a strand of mRNA and translated into a protein.

Firstly, all those enzymes making up the "machinery" of transcribing, proof-reading, editing, and finally translating, are — or mainly consist of — proteins, too. It should not come as a surprise that an egg-cell does not have to start from scratch (or *ab ovo* ...), but is already equipped with the necessary proteins (like RNA-polymerase, ribosomes, other specific proteins). But it should also be clear that such proteins are themselves products of specific genes lined up in the genome.

Secondly, the machinery reading and transcribing genes has to "know" which genes are to be transcribed — the human genome is supposed to contain more than 40,000 of them. It is beyond any doubt that the specific properties of specific cells and compounds of cells are the result of the expression of very specific genes — the right genes in the right place and at the right time. But from the observation of relatively simple organisms like *Escherichia coli*, a prokaryote, it became clear that in order to be transcribed, genes have to be marked beforehand by proteins that occupy nearby stretches of DNA, recognizing a specific sequence of nucleotides on the DNA, so-called *binding sites*. These proteins, themselves products of other genes, are called *activators* or *repressors*, according to the effect they have on the transcription of the gene at stake.

The discovery of such regulatory systems was so novel that it was immediately honored by a Nobel prize (given to Jacques Monod and François Jacob). Eventually it led to the discovery of lots of so-called *transcription factors*.

Activators and repressors do not only act locally. As we know from eukaryotic gene studies, there are classes of activators and repressors that can also act at the distance of some 1,000 base pairs "upstream" or "downstream" of the respective genes. The corresponding binding sites on the DNA are called *enhancers* and *silencers* because the proteins binding to them can multiply the effect of classical activators resp. repressors. With one of their ends enhancer or silencer proteins occupy their binding-site on the DNA, with the other one they attach themselves to so-called *co-activators* or adapter molecules which themselves are linked, by so-called *basal factors*, to the RNA-polymerase. (It will become clear later why enhancer or repressor proteins can bridge the distance of several 1,000 base pairs on the DNA: see below § 4.8).

In the complex of coactivators there is still another protein called *TATA binding-protein*. It "recognizes" another functional binding-site upstream of the coding sequence of the gene and, by doing this, brings the RNA-polymerase in a position that allows for it to be near to or exactly on the start codon signalling the coding region of the gene which is going to be read or transcribed. A protein occupying on the DNA the binding site of a silencer prevents the expression of one or more genes.

The most simple forms of transcriptional control were found in prokaryotes (see above § 1.2) where often binding sites for activators and repressors overlap, thus creating an "on/off" switch regulating gene expression by answering to regulatory stimuli. In addition, the genes of prokaryotic cells tend to be "switched on" by default. The presence of an operator then switches off the gene; the exchange of a subunit of RNA-polymerase, the so-called *sigma-factor*, enables RNA-polymerase to switch to a different subset of genes, for instance under the influence of a heat shock.

Apart from marking a certain gene by binding for instance to a specific binding site on the (flexible) DNA, the task of activators is binding at the same time to a specific protein engaged in the process of reading DNA-sequences, giving it — by allosteric modification — the shape it needs in order to fulfill its specific function, for instance the function of an RNA-polymerase. As often such transcription factors have a third binding site for *co-factors* (which e.g. may be *hormones* coming from adjacent cells). This makes regulation processes in eukaryotes much more complicated and hence much more selective.

As was recalled at the beginning, in these processes nearly everything is brought about by the fact that molecules have or get the appropriate shape in order to fit into certain parts of other molecules (see above § 1.5).

4.4. As have signs in language, DNA and proteins have two different functions

For the genetic code, i.e. the DNA-sequences, this means that they have at least two different functions:

— one of them, represented by the coding sequence of genes, is coding for proteins.

− The other − totally different one − represented by binding-sites, is to passively make possible a functional marking by other proteins whose task is to activate (or to block) the process of reading specific genes.

At the same time this implies that there must be two totally different kinds of genes and, as a consequence, of proteins translated from these genes:

− proteins that give the cell its specific shape and its typical metabolic functions,
− and proteins whose task is to regulate the reading of other genes.

What corresponds to the combinatorial rules, i.e. to the "grammar of biology", are different classes of such regulatory proteins on different levels of hierarchy corresponding to different classes of binding-sites. Such binding-sites are characterized by specific sequences of nucleotides, the above-mentioned "motifs" discovered on the DNA (see above § 3; below §§ 4.6; 6.1).

4.5. The two categories of signs in language

Linguists know that the same kind of regulatory processes are necessary for the functioning of language. If we take the − relatively simple − example of units we call propositions, we know that they consist of different classes of signs, for instance 'verbs' and 'nouns'. A verb like 'to give' has three positions open for signs belonging to the class of nouns: somebody who is giving, something that is given, and one instance receiving what is being given. In English, one of those places may be coded as a subject place, one as an object place, one as the place of an indirect object.

The respective signs fit into these positions because of a specific "regulatory" information, for instance case markers (or position markers). There might be other signs such as 'adjectives', and there might be such "regulatory mechanisms" as case agreement which could link the good adjective to the appropriate noun, welding the two of them into a higher unit. In this way one can translate all the regulatory information which is present in a chain of linguistic signs into specific positive forms fitting into specific negative forms of other signs.

If we take as an example the first line of the tale Horace is telling us about the town mouse and the country mouse, we have a linear sequence

> "[olim] rusticus urbanum murem mus paupere fertur accepisse cavo"
> (It is said that [once upon a time] the land mouse received the town mouse in its poor hole.)

which, translated into a two-dimensional scheme with appropriate forms, could be represented as shown in Fig. 8.1.

As soon as we cut off the regulatory information (in language, position in a sequence of signs may play an important part in this context), we won't be able to integrate the parts into a whole any more:

> accipe- cavu- ferr- mure- mure- paupere- rusticu- urbanu-.

In language, there are lots of signals beneath and above the sentence level fulfilling such "regulatory functions": a conjunction putting into a relationship two propositions, an 'if' corresponding to a following 'then', an 'either' with its subsequent 'or'; a 'firstly' makes us wait for the 'secondly', etc. As in the case of the tale told by Horace, a text might start with 'once upon a time' (*olim* in Latin), signalling to the hearer or reader that, with respect to truth functions, what follows has to be understood in a way which is very different from the kind of understanding appropriate for a text starting with "The monthly meeting of the board of IBM took place on Thursday ... at ...". This is, among

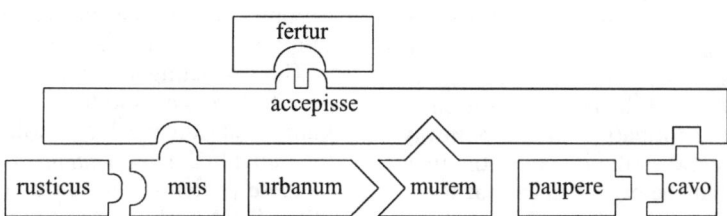

Fig.: 8.1 This kind of representation translates instructions given by grammar into complementary forms.

other things, why most written texts have at their beginning the name of a textual genre: it automatically favors certain readings while ruling out or blocking other ones.

4.6. Hierarchy: morphogenesis and highest ranking genes

A considerable difference between linguistic texts and genetic ones lies in the fact that we are free to invent new textual genres with their respective rules, whereas "nature" always starts from the same genre we could term, for instance, "morphogenesis".

All the forms of life go back to organisms consisting of one cell. All of them developed out of such a single cell by successive differentiation brought about by mutations and by adaptation to the world inside and outside the respective newly emerged species.

This means that, the more we go back in phylogenesis, i.e. to the origins of life, the more we will find similar or even identical solutions. Since in their embryogenesis all living beings repeat the ways and the detours their species has taken during the process of evolution, similar regulatory tasks will be fulfilled by similar means.

Now one of the first of these tasks is the orientation of an emerging body according to an anterior-posterior axis, and this means: the compartmentalization or segmentation of the originating body. A worm, a frog, a mouse, a human being start from one single egg-cell which successively divides into two, four, eight, sixteen, and so on cells, forming, in a first phase, something like a tennis ball. (Instead of tennis ball, biologists have a technical term, *blastula,* for this state.) Then a phase called *gastrulation* follows in which the ball takes the shape the tennis ball would have if we pressed our thumb into it, giving thus the former blastula an *ectoderm*, a *mesoderm*, and an *entoderm*, as well as an anterior-posterior axis. This identical topological task has to be fulfilled in all four cases mentioned before.

Biologists have learned for a long time that in vertebrates the ectoderm will develop into the skin and the nerve system, that muscles, bones, blood originate in the mesoderm, and that one of the results of the entoderm will be the formation of the pathway food is taking between the intake to the final excretion of what the organism cannot use.

Around 1983, a momentous discovery was made by microbiologists: the discovery of a series of highest-ranking genes. In the nucleotide sequences of those genes, a shared motif was found, termed the *homeobox* (geneticists tend to draw boxes around a specific linear sequence of letters which, in their data bases, correspond to nucleotides; in French the expression is clearer: *homéoséquence*). The corresponding class of genes is called *homeobox genes* or – abbreviated – *hox genes*.

Now these hox genes belong to a class of genes whose task is a kind of regulation which brings about a gross compartmentalization of the originating body (called "parasegments" in the case of the fruit fly). Whereas the suppression or, in the language of geneticists, the "knocking-out" of hierarchically inferior genes normally has few, if any consequences for the phenotype, i.e. the developed body, blocking or suppressing hox genes has major, often lethal consequences.

The bizarre outcomes of compartmentalization defects are illustrated by the names given to some of the hox genes of the fruit fly *Drosophila melanogaster*, one of the favourite research objects in genetics: *nanos* (Greek for 'dwarf'), *hunchback, bithorax* (a phenotype which, as a consequence, has also two pairs of wings instead of one), *trithorax, krüppel* (cripple), *hedgehog, antennapedia* (a fly that has legs instead of antennae), *sine oculis* (Latin for 'without eyes'), *fushi tarazu* (Japanese for 'one (segment) is lacking', a lethal mutation) *Polycomb* (a fly that shows sex combs not only on the first, but also on the other pairs of legs). (The names reflect the international character of research in genetics and/or the education of the researchers.)

What defines the class of hox genes on the level of DNA is the above mentioned shared motif of 180 nucleotides. The chain of amino acids which corresponds to this homeobox in the translated protein folds into four main so-called alpha-helices. The third of these helices, the "recognition helix", fits into a specific segment of the DNA, and several amino acids on one face of this helix contact the respective nucleotide bases on the DNA, thus forming one of the above-mentioned transcription factors (see above § 4.3).

The contacting amino acids vary from hox gene to hox gene and hence determine which binding-site on the DNA will be chosen by the individual *homeodomain protein*. The task of these proteins is to mark certain sections of the DNA and either to trigger or to totally prevent the reading of genes specific for a certain segment of the body (see below § 4.8).

4.7. Linear iconicity of selector genes and cellular memory

It came as a big surprise when geneticists – working on a subset of hox genes involved in the patterning of the anterior-posterior axis of the fruit fly – found that the ordering of these so-called *selector genes* on the DNA-sequence corresponds to the ordering of the parasegments – whose emergence and development is triggered – on the anterior-posterior axis of the body. What was even more exciting is the fact that the genes coding for these homeodomain proteins are – in the same order – in the genome not only of *Drosophila melanogaster*, but also of worms (*Caenorhabditis elegans*), frogs (*Xenopus laevis*), mice, and men. (This was matter for some more Nobel prizes.) No less surprising was the fact that the DNA-sequences – and, above all, the protein-sequences resulting from the DNA – were largely identical in the same range of creatures.

This means that the basic signalling system which turned out to be successful in early stages of evolution, resulting in the anterior-posterior orientation and the segmentation of the emerging body, was conserved and is still functioning in the compartmentalization even in species belonging to a much later stage of development. Hence, the selector genes of, say, the fruit-fly have their homologues in humans.

The genes belonging to this class are called *selector genes* because their function is to select and to trigger other, hierarchically lower genes, making possible differentiation in the formation of regions in the emerging body. It is therefore crucial that these genes are activated where they are wanted and switched off where they are not wanted. In this context, at least two equally important tasks have to be fulfilled.

1. Since the regulatory proteins translated from selector genes define regions in an early embryonic state of the originating body, and since these regions are more and more differentiated by successive division of cells, the organism has to ensure that the key regulators retain their transcriptional state throughout cell proliferation. There is good evidence that general cellular mechanisms exist that "freeze" important regulators in their transcriptional state, yielding the cell a kind of "memory" (Paro & Hogness 1991) of its identity within the whole. (The consequences of a loss of identity can be seen in cancer cells.)

   Although in principle any cell of our body contains all the information needed to reconstruct the whole body, this cellular memory with its enhancing or its blocking activity explains why it is so difficult to clone a body from any cell whatever, and this is why geneticists (and physicians) are so interested in the still undifferentiated, so-called stem-cells of embryos (cf., e.g., Thomson & al. 1998).

2. In addition, the successful gene regulatory system established by selector genes has been adopted to other patterning processes, e.g. in the compartmentalization of the limbs. This means that there may be a certain kind of recursivity in regulatory processes.

   Generally speaking, it is evident that a successful genetic program may be used again and again in other parts of the body – witness polarity genes like *Sonic hedgehog* (first discovered in Drosophila; see above § 4.6) effective both in the polarization of our limbs and our brain, the program providing us with five fingers and five toes, or the program giving our fingers and our toes rounded tips (cf. e.g. Shubin & al. 1997).

Hence, what seems to emerge is a regulatory mechanism activating, according to different segments of the emerging body, ever more specific genetic subprograms while blocking at the same time other ones; and on the other hand a mechanism that makes possible the use of one and the same program in different parts of the body. In case the same program is used in another part of the emerging body, the necessary differences may be brought about, among other things, by the process of mRNA-editing (see above §§ 1 & 3) which corresponds to the context sensitive processing of linguistic signs.

4.8. Where language and script could still learn from genetics

Up to now, the fact has been stressed that the strands of DNA are linear. This is true as long as we speak for instance of reading and copying a strand of DNA into a strand of mRNA by RNA-polymerase. In this case what happens is a transcription nucleotide by nucleotide (or "letter by letter").

Nevertheless, it is undeniable that, apart from its functional one-dimensionality, even the strands of DNA, i.e. the double-helix, have steric properties. Whereas the genes, that is the parts of DNA coding for proteins, contain a linear message, other parts, for instance the binding-sites upstream of the coding sequence of the gene, are "recognized" by regulating proteins on behalf of their steric properties.

Apart from the double-sided character of DNA, with some stretches encoding proteins, others functioning as a binding-site for regulatory proteins which corresponds to a similar bi-partition in linguistic signs (see above §§ 1.5 & 4.4) – on closer examination it looks like a necessity that the genetic code should exploit its three-dimensional qualities.

The human genome consists of nearly three billions of genetic letters, i.e. base-pairs in the double-helix of DNA. If this duplex were a string only, any one of our cells should contain a thread of about 200 cm and a diameter of 2 nanometers. It should be clear that this thread does not exist in a linear form, though. Instead, there are proteins serving as architectural elements: The double helix winds roughly twice around a complex of *histones* forming a *nucleosome*. (A nucleosome even contains equal masses of DNA and histone proteins.) The resulting series of nucleosomes is a second-order thread much thicker, much more compact and, naturally, considerably shorter than the first-order one. This second-order thread takes again the shape of a helix, making a third-order thread out of it which possibly forms another helix resulting in a fourth-order thread. In this coiled state the DNA is called *chromatin,* and strands of chromatin are called *chromosomes*. Thus, the chromosomes visible at mitosis correspond to a highly folded and twisted, densely packed form of DNA.

The different degrees of compacted DNA first explain why enhancer or silencer proteins, although binding on the DNA at a distance of several 1,000 base pairs, can shortcut the long way to the gene to be expressed or repressed: in its chromatin state, there is a high probability for distant regions to get into each other's vicinity (see above § 4.3).

At the same time, the compact state of the DNA is important for the general understanding of regulation processes described above (see §§ 4.6 & 4.7) because the DNA of genes – which has to be transcribed into strands of mRNA – is not very well accessible in the compact and coiled state of chromatin. In order to be accessible, parts of the chromatin structure have to be unwound.

The genetic system profits from these different states of DNA. It proves advantageous to tag parts of the DNA already in its compact chromatin state as "readable" or "not readable". This makes the access to the strands of DNA which are relevant for specific cells or cell groups very economic. At the same time, it facilitates the phenomenon called "cellular memory" by making inheritable the transcriptional status of the cell in the process of division (see above § 4.7).

This is exactly what can be observed for instance in *Drosophila melanogaster* (e.g. Cavalli & Paro 1998). Here at least two different sets of regulatory genes belonging to the *trithorax* and to the *Polycomb* group participate in this high order tagging of chromatin. The Polycomb group of genes – as an example – is responsible for HERITABLE SILENCING throughout development (cf. e.g. Paro & al. 1998; Pirrotta 1998; 1997; Shao & al. 1999). This means the maintenance of the repressed ("not readable") state of selector and other homeotic genes.

Indeed, it was found that the Polycomb group proteins are compacting repressed genes in the form of a second or third-order thread of DNA. A different subset of regulatory proteins, the trithorax group, seem to be able to KEEP ACTIVE regions of DNA in an open, "readable" form, thereby helping to maintain a "memory" for the activated key regulators in a region of the body.

In short, this adds another hierarchic level to the regulatory system of development: while we have already seen that proteins can bind to regions of DNA in order to activate or to repress the transcription of a gene, this class of regulators can "freeze" the transcriptional state of genes at a structural basis. They presuppose a molecular machinery operating not on the level of linearized DNA strands, but on the higher level of chromatin, i.e. a 'chromatin' or 'nucleosome remodeling machine'. Biologists have termed it 'chromatin accessibility complex', abbreviated as CHRAC (e.g. Varga-Weisz & al. 1997; Varga-Weisz & Becker 1998).

For geneticists this is at the same time tantamount to saying that there is a considerable difference between the processes observed *in vitro*, and the *in vivo* processes taking place in living cells. This is why those working on chromatin remodeling try to artificially create an *in vivo* environment in their *in vitro* experiments. At the same time, signalling on the chromatin level would explain the phenomenon of linear iconicity observed on the level of high ranking selector genes (see above § 4.7): There would be no advantage if all kinds of genes were scattered in a random way along the DNA. Instead, it should prove advantageous if groups of subordinate genes were relatively close to the regulating higher ranking genes.

In this context, it is not without interest to have a look at the evolution of writing. Whereas spoken language of necessity is one-dimensional, written language comes in two dimensions. In the history of alphabetic script, we can observe an increasing tendency to exploit what is made possible by the existence of a second dimension. Western alphabetic script starts as *scriptio continua*, that is to say as a single thread of letters without spaces. This translates the continuous stream of speech into a continuous thread of letters.

But there is evolution in alphabetic script. In the first centuries A.D. we observe the first attempts at punctuation. Starting from the 8th century, spaces between words are generalized, making words *visible*. Both achievements enormously facilitate the process of reading. A true revolution takes place in the epoch of scholasticism. By 1200, scholastic manuscripts exhibit all the achievements we are inclined to attribute to the invention of printing in the 15th century. Writers use different colors and different fonts. They make alineas, they generalize punctuation. Chapters get titles which are enhanced and which reappear in a table of contents, at the beginning or at the end of the text. Alphabetically ordered registers are invented. On the top of the pages we have running column titles; on the margins we find summaries of the steps of argumentation in tiny script.

The result of this new kind of layout is a quick and easy access to information. Readers are able to get an idea of the structure of even very long texts instead of deciphering long and monotonous strands of letters (a process obligatorily linked with reading out loud). A reader opening a book showing this kind of layout knows at every moment where he or she is in his or her reading process which, since 1200, has become more and more silent (Raible 1991; 1994).

In comparing this evolution in alphabetic script with the genetic information system, we see that to a certain extent the layout of texts follows principles already realized in the densely packed and coiled "genetic texts". As may be expected (see above §3), geneticists themselves draw once again on the comparison with written text: "The idea of a combinatorial 'code' of histone modifications has been proposed to complement the information stored in DNA sequences, in much the same way that highlighting written words in bold or italics complements the information that they carry" (Paro 2000: 579). Others speak of "the language of histone modifications" or of a "histone code" (Strahl & Allis 2000).

At the same time it is evident that, in this respect, the possibilities of written texts are limited since written texts are two-dimensional whereas chromatin has three dimensions. Nevertheless, it could be that there is still some surprise left in the further evolution and the layout of written texts. (Up to now, hypertext only implements techniques known since 1200, making them much more efficient, though.)

4.9. What is similar and what is different in both systems?

In spite of all structural similarities mentioned (for the basic principles: see above § 4.2), there are some major differences between the linguistic and the genetic system, too.

1. *Sender and receiver in genetics?* The point that has been made up to now is a striking and systematic similarity due to the fact that both the linguistic and the genetic system have to cope with the same basic problem: to construct polydimensionality out of a linearized code. One should not overstress this similarity, though, by asking for instance for the sender or the receiver in genetics. There is nothing that corresponds to the two autonomous psychophysical systems acting as speaker and hearer in human communication.

2. *A different role of economy.* Above it was said that cellular processes are energetically optimized by evolution (see above § 1, *in fine*). Since human language comes from a sender and goes to a hearer, human communication always implies human beings, i.e. two psycho-physical systems. Hence, economy is a major factor in human communication and one of the inevitable activators of language change. In genetics, the potential for economically induced change in an already economically

optimized system — lacking the liabilities of psycho-physical systems — is minimal. This means that change in genetic systems is brought about by different factors.

At the same time this means that authors are mistaken when explicitly denying the status of a language to DNA by arguing that the law of Zipf — based on economy: frequent signs tend to be shortened — does not apply to genetics (e.g. Tsonis & al. 1997).

3. *Synonymy and homophony vs. polysemy.* Both the genetic system and the systems of natural languages have double articulation. On the second level, the genetic system makes use of the 20-odd amino acids where the natural languages use their word-signs. There is a decisive difference between the two systems on this level, though: In the genetic system, there exist $4^3 = 64$ possible triplets of the four "letters" A, T, G, and C to which correspond only 20-odd amino acids. This means that there is "synonymy" in the genetic system, whereas true synonymy is extremely rare in natural languages. What is normal instead is polysemy and even homonymy: The number of necessary signs is so high that, as a means of economy, signs tend to have more than one meaning (in the case of homonymy the meanings are even totally different). Witness such examples as English *lies* or *fly*. Natural languages heavily rely upon the syntactic and/or semantic context for disambiguation.

4. *Volatile vs. palpable sense.* As was already mentioned above (see above § 4.1), the result of gene transcription and expression is something material and palpable as in the case of our bodies, whereas the result of the reading process for instance in the case of a novel rests something highly immaterial and volatile, subject to interpretation by different readers. This depends, however, on the text genre: reading a patent specification should lead to something rather concrete. On the other hand genetically inherited properties (like behaviour) may be "volatile" as well.

5. *Selective vs. linear reading* (see above § 4.1). In the domain of genetics, the same "text" exists up to billions of times in one and the same body, and it is read very selectively in any cell. Whilst the regulating elements in texts of natural language facilitate the reconstruction of a sense out of linearly scattered elements, needing a mostly linear reading of the text, regulatory proteins are designed to make possible a specific and selective reading of selected genes in one cell — such that, nevertheless, the aggregation of individual cells forms an ordered and functioning whole which is far more than the sum of its parts (see above § 4.2). Nevertheless, printed texts increasingly enable (depending on the genre, though) selective reading techniques, too (see above § 4.8).

6. *Creativity vs. replication.* The primary aim of genetics is high fidelity replication. Texts in natural languages may express whatever comes into our minds — facts as well as fiction, description of what is as well as description of what will never come into existence, and so on. Nevertheless, evolution shows us that there is another kind of potential creativity in the genetic code: it allows for mutations due largely to flaws in the reading process. The fate of such mutations may be determined in terms of trial, success, and error.

5. The genome as a program or as an encyclopedia

If the genome is seen as a text and the body of a eukaryote as what corresponds to its "sense", we might ask ourselves what the nature or genre of DNA is as a text.

In describing genetic processes, the word 'program' was already used (e.g. above § 4.7.2). This is one possibility. Computer programs are texts, too (Raible 1999: 19ff.); they consist of command lines, mostly so-called conditioned instructions ("if X and not Y or R, then (do) F"). The activation of RNA-polymerase on a certain gene follows exactly this pattern: "IF activator *a* AND activator *b* AND NOT repressor *c* AND ... AND ... THEN READ gene *f*". "If anything, the language of the genes is much more like a programming language whose constraints we do not know (or whose programs we do not know)" (Berwick 1996: 295).

The regulatory signals in the above example of Horace (see above § 4.5) might be interpreted in the same way, i.e. as instructions in a program — this is congruent with the interpretation of grammatical informations as instructions given to the reader or hearer (e.g. Weinrich 1993: 17 etc.).

Whilst the metaphor of a program may apply to both the "grammar of biology" and the grammar of human language, another type of text, a non-algorithmic one this time, might be used and *is* used as well: the metaphor of an encyclopedia (see above § 3, *in fine*). Indeed, the encyclopedia shares with the program the feature that linear reading is not necessary: thanks to the fact that hierarchy is a characteristic of programming languages, too, the procedures of a computer program may be written in any order whatever. It is necessary however to link (for instance by the instruction GOSUB) those procedures to instructions on a higher level.

This is tantamount to saying that, if we choose the metaphor of an encyclopedia, the genome is a very specific encyclopedia: one that comprises articles (genes) giving instructions as to what other articles (genes) are to be read, at what time this should happen, and under which specific conditions. Like procedures in a program that are not linked any more to instructions on a higher level, in such an encyclopedia there might be articles no one will read any longer since they are not linked any more to reading instructions coming from a hierarchically higher level. This is why deciphering all the genes of a genome can only be a first step in a still very lengthy investigation: in any event one has to determine whether there is at least one superordinate gene triggering the reading process of this specific gene. If this is not the case, the gene is like an unused procedure in a program: apart form making the program text longer, it does no harm at all; at the best, it reflects an anterior state in the process of building such a program.

6. Are biologists aware of the structural similarities?

The vast majority of scientists doing research in microbiology are familiar with the metaphors outlined above in sections 2 & 3, and they use them whenever they speak of the basic processes sketched in section 1. Seldom are they aware, though, of the basic problem posed by the linearity of DNA-code as opposed to the three or even four dimensions of the resulting phenotype (see above § 4.1), one of the rare exceptions being e.g. Walter Gehring (1985: 137).

Nevertheless, some biologists tackle the problems of DNA-coding with linguistic means. They divide in two groups, one of them being more speculative, the other one aiming at practical and directly viable results.

6.1. Detecting regularities in DNA by linguistic methods

If we take the example of deciphering the human genome, one of the most prominent aims of microbiology is detecting coding sequences (genes) and binding sites in the interminable strands of DNA: at the most 5% (others speak of 10%) of it are thought to represent genes, the rest has different functions. In this case, the idea to write e.g. an algorithm for the detection of protein coding sequences in the DNA suggests itself. "The usefulness of a grammar for the representation of biological knowledge is now amply acknowledged" (Bentolila 1996: 336) – the number of laboratories working on this topic seems to be rather small, though.

Let us take the following five rewriting rules where s stands for a non-terminal symbol, A, C, G, T for the nucleotides, and ε for an empty string (Searls 1997: 334f. – The symbol s can be replaced by the symbols to the right of the arrow):

$$s \to GsC \quad s \to CsG \quad s \to AsT$$
$$s \to TsA \quad s \to \varepsilon$$

The repeated application of these rules leads to strings like:

$$s \Rightarrow AsT \Rightarrow AAsTT \Rightarrow AACsGTT \Rightarrow$$
$$AACTsAGTT \Rightarrow AACTCsGAGTT,$$

and by application of the empty element rule, eventually the string *AACTCGAGTT*.

Let us assume that after an intermediate string of, say, 30 nucleotides the motif *AACTCGAGTT* recurs, and let us further assume that this entire string with the repeated motif is transcribed into a string of RNA. In all probability it will then take the shape of a loop or a leaf: the two repeated sequences – being dyad symmetric thanks to the underlying rewriting rules – match perfectly in the reverse order (the final T of the first one binding with the first A of the second one, and so on) and hence will form the stalk, the intermediate 30 nucleotides making the contours of the leaf.

Such dyad symmetric repeated motifs are real and extremely important: they make up for the typical cloverleaf-structure of a kind of RNA – termed transfer RNA or tRNA – specialized in "recognizing" amino acids and transporting them to the ribosomes where they are chained to polypeptides according to the information given by a string of mRNA (see above § 1). The same kind or other types of symmetrical motifs often characterize binding sites for proteins on the DNA.

Since one can make overt by such methods "hidden" regularities, lots of approaches aim at finding such properties − e.g. motifs in the DNA, "parsing" of genes (yielding for instance exons and introns; e.g. Dong & Searls 1994; Jiménez Montaño 1994; Ratner & Amikishiev 1996; Asai & al. 1998); the recognition of regulatory regions (e.g. Rosenblueth & al. 1996), even the entire regulation process of a gene (Bentolila 1996; Collado-Vides 1996 & 1996a; Pérez Rueda & Collado-Vides 2000; van Helden & al. 2000).

So-called hidden Markov models (HMMs), algorithms shaped according to the models of context-free grammar, turned out to be powerful tools for the detection of so-called *homologs:* viz. chains of amino-acids sharing common function and evolutionary ancestry without being entirely identical since the function of divergent proteins may be conserved through evolution even though sequence elements are free to change in some areas. The concept of HMMs, based on the similarity of protein families (or of the underlying DNA) is used to statistically describe the so-called consensus sequence of a protein family and to detect new members belonging to the same family.

Nevertheless, HMMs operate, by definition, on the probability of *linear* transitions between elements (nucleotides, amino acids, letters, sounds, words). This makes them very useful on a purely local basis, e.g. in the recognition of words from sound patterns in speech recognition programs. A HMM based on sound patterns cannot detect relations holding between words, though, to say nothing of relations between non adjacent words. In the same way, it is beyond the scope of a HMM detecting consensus sequences of proteins to tell us anything about why there will be, in the folded state of the respective polypeptide chain, a hydrogen bond between, say, amino acids$_{14}$ and $_{53}$, or why the zinc-atom in amino acid$_{55}$ will create a covalent bond with elements of e.g. amino acids$_{32}$, $_{111}$, $_{145}$ and $_{199}$ (for these kinds of bonds, see above § 1.3).

This is why context-sensitive grammars are more adequate in genetics proper. Admitting, among other things, recursivity, they are being applied not only in DNA research; they prove helpful in the analysis of protein sequences, too. All of them operate on DNA or polypeptides represented as strings of letters (see above § 3). The better known results (frequent DNA or protein motifs, binding sites, genes with their location, their reading frames and sequence structure, DNA or protein consensus sequences, etc.) are integrated into the "dictionary" of such algorithms, the more do they become powerful. A good example are Simone Bentolila (1996) or, generally speaking, analyses making use of large data bases, e.g. a data base of protein consensus sequences (e.g. the Protein families database *Pfam*, containing 2,290 families as of June 2000) or data bases of regulatory sequences (e.g. Pérez Rueda & Collado-Vides 2000 for *E. coli*; van Helden & al. 2000 for yeast).

All these approaches indirectly show that the genetic system *has* the properties of a true language with its "grammar" or grammatical regularities − the type of rewriting rules leading to dyad symmetry in the above example was even used by Noam Chomsky in 1957 in order to show that such strings cannot be generated by linear processing and that, instead, hierarchy (genes that function on specific levels), categories (in genetics: 'activator'/'promoter', 'enhancer', 'silencer'/'repressor', 'operator', 'inductor', 'binding site', etc.) and transformation rules are necessary.

Nevertheless, one basic problem persists: these algorithms are essentially bottom-up models holding for cells (e.g. *Escherichia Coli*), at the most for cell assemblies (yeast) or cell compounds. The complementary top-down component necessary to understand the processes of embryogenesis − with its hierarchical levels and corresponding categories − still remains in the dark, or, at the best, in twilight. Now that the human genome has been successfully 'deciphered', the true complexity of the 'grammar of biology' will become visible.

6.2. General aspects of a "grammar of biology"

Macroscopic views on the matter tend to remain somewhat more general and more speculative.

When Lucien Tesnière developed his concept of a dependency grammar, one of the central metaphors he used − valency − came from chemistry. Signs belonging to the class of verbs have up to three free valencies for signs belonging to the class of nouns. According to the kind of valency they may play different parts – subject, direct object, and so on. The scheme in figure 8.1 (see above § 4.5) re-translated this into appropriate forms.

As linguists discovered the usefulness of chemically inspired concepts for their proper domain, chemists discovered language as a metaphor – not only in the domain of genetics (see above § 2), but in chemistry in general. Witness for instance the approaches made by Pierre Laszlo (1993; cf. 1995; 1986) or by Claude Kordon (1993) in biochemistry. In this kind of consideration the division of compounds into *conformations* and *configurations* (see above § 1.3) may play an important part. Conformations are, for instance, interpreted as one of the two articulations in chemical language, configurations as the other one.

Such approaches suggest e.g. a "molecular grammar" consisting of the rules that govern the assembling of molecular units into messengers and their higher-order structures such as hormones, DNA-binding proteins or transcription complexes (Ratner 1993; Ji 1997: 21); the authors are able to discover in the genetic system nearly all the features attributed to human language by Charles Hockett 1960; cf. e.g. Ji 1997: 21, 23–8).

While being speculative, the authors of such contributions at least tackle a problem normally not mentioned by the first group of authors. If at the most 5 to 10% of the DNA contained in a genome is represented by genes, what is the function of the rest? Answers must take into consideration the difference between *in vivo* and *in vitro* analysis of the genome, i.e. the above mentioned fact that the normal state of the genome is chromatin, not a first-order thread of DNA. Lots of the regulatory proteins produced by selector genes of the homeobox class bind to the DNA in its chromatin state, "freezing it" and hence either keeping the genes contained in long sections of DNA open for further reading in this part of the body, or preventing them from being expressed (see above § 4.8).

Answers could be given taking into account the topology of chromatin and the physical properties the DNA needs both for bending in a certain way (e.g. around histones, see above § 4.8) and for bringing classes of genes and classes of binding sites into a good position in the second, third and perhaps even fourth-order thread the DNA represents in its chromatin state. This conforms to the fact that – in terms of base pairs on the first-order thread of DNA – enhancers or silencers often are at a very great distance from the gene or group of genes whose expression they activate or repress (see above § 4.3). Research done in the domain of 'chromatin remodeling machines' (see above § 4.8) or the so-called 'matrix- or scaffold-associating regions' of chromatin (dubbed MARs and SARs) gives hints in this direction: the architecture of chromatin in its different states is turning out to be crucial for transcription processes (e.g. Maric & al. 1998, Girard & al. 1998.).

In this context, partisans of a theory of cell language make far-reaching hypotheses, assuming for instance that 90 to 95% of DNA could incorporate "spatiotemporal genes", with their function being "the control of the folding patterns (or conformational states) of DNA and the topology of chromosomes" (Ji 1997: 32). The non-coding parts of DNA in eukaryotic genomes are thought to encode "a language which programs organismal growth and development" (Bodnar & al. 1997).

7. A mediated link between kinds of DNA and types of human languages

Strictly speaking, sections 7 and 8 do not belong to the topic of this article in its narrow sense. Nevertheless, they have been added because the issue they deal with is not only *related* to both the present volume and the present article, but of some more general interest for linguistics into the bargain.

Starting from about 1965, Luigi Luca Cavalli-Sforza published a lot of biometric studies which were increasingly based on DNA-analysis. They rely upon the fact that there is always variation in the genome of the same species. A basic example: since we have synonymy in the genetic code (see above § 4.9.3), the same amino-acid may be encoded by two or more different triplets of nucleotides. On a higher level, genes may have *alleles* at chromosomal loci which often lead to more or less visible differences in the phenotype (e.g. diseases). Another method assesses the variation among *microsatellites* which – in eukaryotes – occur either as repeated codons in genes or as highly repetitive non-coding sequences of 10 to 50 groups consisting e.g. of the nucleotides AC or ACCC which are scattered over the genome (Moxon & Wills 1999).

Most of the eukaryotic cells have their "power plants", the *mitochondria*. They are organelles in the cytoplasm and must once have been independent cells since they have their own genome, the mitochondrial DNA (mtDNA). There exist "dialects" in mtDNA, and since we always inherit it from our mothers, studying mtDNA in large samples which, then, are statistically processed, leads to further hypotheses as to the diachrony of genetic variety.

Now since differences in the phenotype often – albeit never of necessity – correspond to differences in language, one can try to map genetic variety (mtDNA, alleles, microsatellites) onto linguistic variety. In nearly every case this leads to macroscopic results, suggesting for instance that Amerinds must have come in three immigration waves from Asia across the Bering Strait – then a land passage – into America. There is for instance a T-allele (a T instead of a C) at a certain locus on the (male) Y-chromosome that occurs only in the Western Hemisphere, i.e. the Americas. Some 90% of South America's indigenous people and 50% of those in North America share that genetic marker due to a common ancestor (Underhill & al. 1996).

On a less macroscopic level, the mtDNA method has no good selectivity because of a simple social fact. Roman Jakobson stated that there are three kinds of communication: through language, through goods and services – and, an insight based on Claude Lévi-Strauss, through women. Given both the normal, peaceful exchange of women and the frequent abduction (witness the rape of the Sabine women as one of the innumerable cases), mtDNA analysis cannot but lead to coarse-grained results. Specializing on alleles, e.g. on the (male) Y chromosome, and on microsatellites, instead, shows more precise results suggesting for instance that men were far more sedentary throughout history.

Linking – in an indirect way – the interpretation of variation in the human genome with linguistic diversity suggests that the common ancestors of mankind should have lived in Africa about 200,000 years ago, that spreading of the human species must have started from there about 150,000 years ago, and that West Asia was first settled around 100,000 years ago; that Oceania was occupied first from Africa, more or less at the same time as East Asia, and that from East Asia both Europe and America were settled.

Prehistoric human colonization in the Pacific seems to have happened in two phases, the second one in an express-train like manner starting only 6,000 years ago (Gray & Jordan 2000, based on the comparison of 5,185 lexical items in 77 languages projected onto the results of mtDNA analysis; Cann 2000).

As to Europe (which genetically speaking is relatively homogeneous), the observable gradients in the analysis of DNA variance suggest the spread of agriculture from the Middle East in the period 10,000–6,000, a migration to the north (Uralic languages), and a migration from the region below the Urals and above the Caucasus to most of Europe (Indo-European languages). At the same time it becomes clear, that, in the meantime, e.g. Lapps and Finns genetically became rather europeanized (Jin & al. 1999; Cavalli-Sforza 1997: 7719f., Cavalli-Sforza & al. 1994; 1993).

It should be clear, however, that there are elements of uncertainty. One of them is the dependence of the molecular clock on assumptions such as the calibration date and mutation rate. Another is the reliance on the particular genetic subsystem under study instead of an overall picture mediated by a plurality of features. A third factor are recent fossil data that could also be interpreted as speaking in favour of a multiregional evolution and subsequent interbreeding of humans (Thorne & al. 1999).

At any rate, this method of genetic analysis proves helpful for glottochronology, above all in cases much under discussion (African, Amerindian languages) where e.g. analyses given by Joseph H. Greenberg on the basis of a certain kind of frequent vocabulary are confirmed by the analysis of genetic closeness resp. distance (Ruhlen 1994). Nevertheless, this method – especially by extending the assessment of genetic distance or closeness to larger regions of human DNA – could lead to different and possibly more blurred results according to the number and the kind of alleles examined.

8. Are there direct links between the genome and human language capacity?

It stands to reason that our language capacity is genetically determined. Disagreement only concerns the extent of this determination. Some think there is a bioprogram leading from poor care-giver input to perfectly structured and constructed human languages as in the case of CREOLES evolving from PIDGIN input (→ art. 7); others think that the amount and quality of care-giver input is far more important, the evolution of our language capacity being an experience-expectant process (Greenough & al. 1987 established the useful distinction between 'experience-expectant' and 'experience-dependent' brain plasticity).

In 1991, Myrna Gopnik and Martha B. Crago described a condition currently termed 'specific language impairment' (SLI): As could be shown by a series of experiments, certain members of an ENGLISH speaking family apparently were not able to use nouns and verbs in vocal speech with the appropriate grammatical endings. Typical phenomena were the omission of the -*s* of the third person singular of verbs, of the plural -*s* of nouns, and of the -*ed* of past forms. The understanding of syntax on the sentence level did not seem to be impaired, though (Gopnik & Crago 1991).

Although the condition was known for some decades, this contribution became notorious thanks to Steven Pinker: "The K family, three generations of SLI sufferers, whose members say things like *Carol is cry in the church* and cannot deduce the plural of *wug*, is currently one of the most dramatic demonstrations that defects in grammatical abilities might be inherited" (1994: 323).

Since the condition of SLI would point to the existence and innateness of a putative grammatical subsystem in the brain, the issue became extremely controversial, setting off about 500 contributions on the topic between 1991 and 1999.

What remained more or less uncontroversial is a link to (autosomal, since both sexes are concerned) heredity. However, in the meantime four points became evident: (1) SLI is not a rare condition. It is said to concern between 3 and 6% of otherwise unimpaired children. (2) It is linked to the production and the reception of *vocal* speech (most salient is slow and bad articulation), not to the conceptual side of language production or understanding. (3) The condition is accompanied by a general delay in language acquisition manifesting itself, among other things, in poor vocabulary. (4) The overwhelming number of the studies were carried out (and continue to be carried out) with ENGLISH speaking children and controls.

However, the rare studies made with SLI affected children speaking different languages, e.g. FRENCH, HEBREW, GERMAN, ITALIAN, SPANISH, MODERN GREEK, FINNISH, JAPANESE, do not as a rule exhibit an identical pattern of grammatical symptoms. Italian children with SLI closely resemble the controls in their production of noun plural inflections (bambin*o*/bambin*i*; donn*a*/donn*e*), third person copula forms (sono − sei − è, ero − eri − er*a*), first person singular and plural verb inflections (amo − amia*mo*), and third person singular verb inflection (amo − ami − a*ma*). What was produced with much lower percentage were the (unstressed) articles and clitics (*il*/i, *la*/le, *lo*/gli, the *l'* in *l'*abbiamo sentito) and third person plural verb inflections (mando − mandi − manda − mandiamo − mandate − *mandano*) with their three syllables and the unstressed -*no* ending. (Le Normand & al. 1993; Bortolini & al. 1997; Leonard & Bortolini 2000; Leonard 1998: part II, ch. 4 gives a detailed overview over the phenomena observed in a series of languages.)

Given the different nature of symptoms in different languages, a definition of SLI by purely linguistic criteria seems to be impossible. SLI affected children speaking FRENCH and ITALIAN not only showed symptoms different from ENGLISH. Starting in the early as 1970's, studies carried out by Paula Tallal and her colleagues gave hints as to additional factors in the possible etiology: the nature, the duration and the context of phonemes and grammatical morphemes − and auditory stimuli in general − proved to be a most important factor. Furthermore, by repetition tasks it became evident that children with SLI had a diminished capacity of the phonological working memory (e.g. Montgomery 1995; ITALIAN children perform e.g. much better with disyllabic third person plural forms such as *fanno* or *stanno* than with the trisyllabic type *vedono*). Psychophysical tests employing simple tones and noises and imaging techniques with a high temporal and spatial resolution (especially magneto-encephalography) show that persons with SLI have severe auditory perceptual deficits for brief − but not long − tones in particular sound contexts. Similar phenomena can be observed with poor readers, thus linking to a certain extent SLI with dyslexia (cf. Wright & al. 1997; Montgomery & Leonard 1998; Nagarajan & al. 1999).

The basis is a phenomenon well-known in audiology, so-called masking: the term refers to a natural limitation in the human ability to detect any particular sound that is presented simultaneously − or within a small fraction of a second − with other masking sounds. In normal individuals this masking of particular speech sounds by preceding or following sounds is not sufficient to impair speech processing − in SLI children it is. They require hundreds of milliseconds between acoustic events to discriminate between them, while children of the same age and intelligence level only need tens of milliseconds. Since auditory feedback is defective, speech production and articulation of such children is worse than with normals.

This etiology explains most of the differences between the phenomena observed in various languages. In a language like HEBREW where inflection is to a large extent brought about by changing vowels − i.e. not consonants − between the three consonants of the verbal root, morphology is much less likely to be impaired by such a limitation in the capacity of decoding auditory input. In ITALIAN, the unstressed article *il* is always followed by a consonant (i*l* ri*go*re, i*l* m*er*cato), before vowels it appears in a reduced form (*l'*amico).

A specific training program for auditory discrimination (incidentally a computer game) is said to advance such children within four weeks in a way that normally would have taken two years, suggesting thus that SLI is rather not related to higher cognitive or even grammatical functions as was supposed by the 'grammar gene' hypothesis (Tallal & al. 1996).

In the meantime, biologists try to localize the genetic basis the condition undoubtedly has. In the family investigated by Gopnik & Crago (1991), there seems to be an anomaly on chromosome 7 (Fisher & al. 1998). Bioinformatic analyses should permit to further circumscribe the relevant sector and to − perhaps − detect a specific gene (Lai & al. 2000). Nevertheless, the responsibility of one single gene for 'grammar' is highly improbable. This holds all the more as the effects of the anomaly under discussion are rather unspecific: they concern auditory discrimination, velocity of speech processing, and a speech production that is always accompanied by articulation difficulties (affected members of the family are said to suffer from a severe orofacial dyspraxia making their speech more or less incomprehensible to normal listeners). One could even add, in many cases, dyslexia.

Thanks to Steven Pinker (1994: 64f.), George Pullum's unmasking of "The great Eskimo vocabulary hoax" became widely known among linguists and a large reading public. Unfortunately, it might well be that for a rather long period the putative 'language gene' or 'grammar gene' responsible for SLI could play a role similar to the ESKIMO vocabulary hoax in linguistic textbooks.

What remains is the general claim of a genetically determined disposition to learn languages. In an indirect way, the existence of a corresponding genetic apparatus is shown by children suffering from Williams syndrome. Here the cause of the syndrome is known: one copy of the aforementioned chromosome 7 lacks a tiny section which may contain up to 15 genes, some of them already identified. The brain of such children is smaller, their mean IQ score is 60. Nevertheless, their language capacity seems to be nearly unimpaired on the level of sentences and sentence chaining (the overall coherence of the texts they produce being quite peculiar, though). This gives them a remarkable linguistic ability. Some of them display also a strong musical talent (Lehnhoff & al. 1997).

Human language is a complex system. It is built on principles whose effectiveness has been confirmed by genesis and morphogenesis (see above § 4.2), adding to them an apparatus for speech production and reception. Given the complexity of the genetic system whose "linguistic" aspects have been outlined above, it is unlikely that one single gene should be responsible for language capacity or even for one of its major components. As is shown by SLI, the impairment or disruption of any of a number of these components can impair language development, which, as it stands, is not as autonomous as is sometimes presumed. At the same time, the example makes clear that it may be dangerous to jump to conclusions on the basis of data coming from one single language.

9. References

Asai, K. & Itou, K. & Ueno, Y. & Yada, T. 1998. "Recognition of human genes by stochastic parsing". *Pacific Symposium on Biocomputing*: 228−39.

Bentolila, Simone 1996. "A grammar describing 'biological binding operators' to model gene regulation". *Biochimie* 78.5: 335−50.

Berwick, Robert C. 1996. "The language of the genes". In: Collado-Vides, Julio & al. (eds.), 281−96.

Blumenberg, Hans. 1981. *Die Lesbarkeit der Welt*. Frankfurt a. M.: Suhrkamp.

Bodnar, J.W. & Killian, J. & Nagle, M. & Ramchandani, S. 1997. "Deciphering the language of the genome". *Journal of Theoretical Biology* 189.2: 183–93.

Bortolini, Umberta & Caselli, M.C. & Leonard, Laurence B. 1997. "Grammatical deficits in Italian-speaking children with specific language impairment". *Journal of Speech, Language, and Hearing Research* 40.4: 809–20.

Boutroux, Émile. ²1991 ¹1875. *De la contingence des Lois de la Nature*. (Collection Dito.) Paris: Presses Universitaires de France.

Cann, Rebecca L. 2000. "Talking trees tell tales". *Nature* 405.6790: 1008–09.

Cavalli, G. & Paro, Renato. 1998. "The Drosophila Fab-7 chromosomal element conveys epigenetic inheritance during mitosis and meiosis". *Cell* 93.4: 505–18.

Cavalli-Sforza, Luigi Luca & Piazza, Alberto 1993. "Human genomic diversity in Europe: a summary of recent research and prospects for the future". *European Journal of Human Genetics* 1.1: 3–18.

Cavalli-Sforza, Luigi Luca & Menozzi, Paolo & Piazza, Alberto. 1994. *The history and geography of human genes*. Princeton, NJ: Princeton University Press.

Cavalli-Sforza, Luigi Luca. 1997. "Genes, peoples, and languages". *Proceedings of the National Academy of Sciences of the U.S.A.* 22;94.15: 7719–24.

Collado-Vides, Julio 1996. "Towards a unified grammatical model of sigma 70 and sigma 54 bacterial promoters". *Biochimie* 78.5: 351–63.

Collado-Vides, Julio 1996a. "Integrative representations of the regulation of gene expression". In: Collado-Vides, Julio & al., 179–203.

Collado-Vides, Julio & Magasanik, Boris & Smith, Temple F. (eds.). 1996. *Integrative approaches to molecular biology*. Cambridge/MA: MIT Press.

Dearden, Peter & Akam, Michael. 2000. "Segmentation *in silico*". *Nature* 406.6792: 131–32. [The authors are highlighting the importance that should be attributed to the contribution of von Dassow & al. 2000.]

Dong, Shan & Searls, David B. 1994. "Gene structure prediction by linguistic methods". *Genomics* 23.3: 540–51.

Fisher, Simon E. & Vargha-Khadem, Faraneh & Watkins, Kate E. & Monaco, Anthony P. & Pembrey, Marcus E. 1998. "Localisation of a gene implicated in a severe speech and language disorder". *Nature Genetics* 18.2: 168–70.

Gehring, Walter. 1985. "The molecular basis of development". *Scientific American* 253.4: 136–46.

Girard, Franck & Bello, Bruno & Laemmli, Ulrich K. & Gehring, Walter J. 1998. "In vivo analysis of scaffold-associated regions in Drosophila: a synthetic high-affinity SAR binding protein suppresses position effect variegation". *EMBO Journal* 17.7: 2079–85.

Gopnik, Myrna & Crago, Martha B. 1991. "Familial aggregation of a developmental language disorder". *Cognition* 39.1: 1–50.

Gray, Russell. D. & Jordan, Fiona M. 2000. "Language trees support the express-train sequence of Austronesian expansion". *Nature* 405.6790: 1052–55.

Greenough, William T. & Black, J.E. & Wallace, C.S. 1987. "Experience and brain development". *Child Development* 58.3: 539–59.

Hockett, Charles F. 1960. "The origin of speech". *Scientific American* 203.3: 88–96.

Ji, Sungchul 1997. "Isomorphism between cell and human languages: molecular biological, bioinformatic and linguistic implications". *Biosystems* 44.1: 17–39.

Jiménez Montaño, Miguel Angel 1994. "On the syntactic structure and redundancy distribution of the genetic code". *Biosystems* 31: 11–23.

Jin, L. & Underhill, Peter A. & Doctor, V. & Davis, R.W. & Shen, P. & Cavalli-Sforza, Luigi Luca & Oefner, P.J. 1999. "Distribution of haplotypes from a chromosome 21 region distinguishes multiple prehistoric human migrations". *Proceedings of the National Academy of Sciences of the U.S.A.* 96.7: 3796–800.

Kordon, Claude. 1993. *The language of the cell* (translated from *Langage des cellules*). (McGraw-Hill horizons of science series.) New York: McGraw-Hill.

Lai, Cecilia S.L. & Fisher, Simon E. & Hurst, Jane A. & Levy, Elaine R. & Hodgson, Shirley & Fox, Margaret & Jeremiah, Stephen & Povey, Susan & Jamison, D. Curtis & Green, Eric D. & Vargha-Khadem, Faraneh & Monaco, Anthony P. 2000. "The SPCH1 Region on Human 7q31: Genomic Characterization of the Critical Interval and Localization of Translocations Associated with Speech and Language Disorder". *American Journal of Human Genetics* 67: 357–68.

Laszlo, Pierre. 1986. *Molecular correlates of biological concepts*. (Comprehensive biochemistry, 34A, Section 6, A History of biochemistry.) Amsterdam: Elsevier.

Laszlo, Pierre. 1993. *La parole des choses ou le langage de la biologie*. (Collection savoir: Sciences.) Paris: Hermann.

Laszlo, Pierre. 1995. *Organic reactions. Simplicity and logic*. Chichester: Wiley.

Le Normand, M.T. & Leonard, Laurence B. & McGregor, K.K. 1993. "A cross-linguistic study of article use by children with specific language impairment". *European Journal of Disorders of Communication* 28.2: 153–63.

Lehnhoff, Howard M. & Wang, Paul P. & Greenberg, Frank & Bellugi, Ursula. 1997. "Williams syndrome and the brain". *Scientific American* 277.6: 68–73.

Leonard, Laurence B. ²2000. *Children with specific language impairment.* (Language, speech and communication.) Cambridge/MA & London: MIT Press.

Leonard, Laurence B. & Bortolini, Umberta. 2000. "Grammatical morphology and the role of weak syllables in the speech of Italian-speaking children with specific language impairment". *Journal of Speech, Language, and Hearing Research* 41.6: 1363–74.

Maric, Chrystelle & Hyrien, Olivier. 1998. "Remodeling of chromatin loops does not account for specification of replication origins during Xenopus development". *Chromosoma* 107.3: 155–65.

Monod, Jacques. 1970. *Le hasard et la nécessité. Essai sur la philosophie naturelle de la biologie moderne.* Paris: Éditions du Seuil.

Montgomery, James W. 1995. "Sentence comprehension in children with specific language impairment: the role of phonological working memory". *Journal of Speech and Hearing Research* 38.1: 187–99.

Montgomery, James W. & Leonard, Laurence B. 1998. "Real-time inflectional processing by children with specific language impairment: effects of phonetic substance". *Journal of Speech and Hearing Research* 41.6: 1432–43.

Moxon, Richard E. & Wills, Christopher. 1999. "DNA Microsatellites: Agents of Evolution?" *Scientific American* 280.1: 72–77.

Nagarajan, Srikantan & Mahncke, Henry & Salz, Talya & Tallal, Paula & Roberts, Timothy & Merzenich, Michael M. 1999. "Cortical auditory signal processing in poor readers". *Proceedings of the National Academy of Sciences of the U.S.A.* 96: 6483–88.

Palacios, O.A. & Stephens, Christopher R. & Waelbroeck, Henri. 1998. "Emergence of algorithmic language in genetic systems". *Biosystems* 47.3: 129–47.

Paro, Renato. 2000. "Formatting genetic text". *Nature* 406.6796: 579–80.

Paro, Renato & Hogness, D.S. 1991. "The Polycomb protein shares a homologous domain with a heterochromatin-associated protein of Drosophila". *Proceedings of the National Academy of Sciences of the U.S.A.* 88: 263–67.

Paro, Renato & Strutt, H. & Cavalli, G. 1998. "Heritable chromatin states induced by the Polycomb and trithorax group genes". *Novartis Foundation Symposium* 214: 51–61; discussion 61-6: 104–13.

Pérez Rueda, Ernesto & Collado-Vides, Julio. 2000. "The repertoire of DNA-binding transcriptional regulators in Escherichia coli K-12". *Nucleic Acids Research* 28.8 :1838–47.

Pinker, Steven. 1994. *The language instinct. How the mind creates language.* New York: William Morrow & Company.

Pirrotta, Vincenzo. 1997. "Chromatin-silencing mechanisms in Drosophila maintain patterns of gene expression". *Trends in Genetics* 13.8: 314–18.

Pirrotta, Vincenzo 1998. "Polycombing the genome: PcG, trxG, and chromatin silencing". *Cell* 93.3: 333–36.

Popov, O. & Segal, D.M. & Trifonov, E.N. 1996. "Linguistic complexity of protein sequences as compared to texts of human languages". *Biosystems* 38: 65–74.

Raible, Wolfgang. 1991. *Die Semiotik der Textgestalt. Erscheinungsformen und Folgen eines kulturellen Evolutionsprozesses.* (Abhandlungen der Heidelberger Akademie der Wissenschaften, phil.-hist. Klasse, 1991.1.) Heidelberg: Winter.

Raible, Wolfgang. 1993. *Sprachliche Texte – Genetische Texte. Sprachwissenschaft und molekulare Genetik.* (Sitzungsberichte der Heidelberger Akademie der Wissenschaften, phil.-hist. Klasse, 1993.1.) Heidelberg: Winter.

Raible, Wolfgang. 1994. "Orality and Literacy". In: Günther, Hartmut & Ludwig, Otto (eds.). *Schrift und Schriftlichkeit. Writing and Its Use. An Interdisciplinary Handbook of International Research.* Berlin & New York: De Gruyter. 1–17.

Raible, Wolfgang. 1999. *Kognitive Aspekte des Schreibens.* (Schriften der Philosophisch-historischen Klasse der Heidelberger Akademie der Wissenschaften, 14.) Heidelberg: C. Winter.

Ratner, V.A. 1993. "Comparative hierarchic structure of the genetic language" (in Russian). *Genetika* 29: 720–39.

Ratner, V.A. 1993. "The genetic language: grammar, semantics, evolution" (in Russian). *Genetika* 29: 709–19.

Ratner, V.A. & Amikishiev, V.G. 1996. "Analysis of motifs of functional MDG2 sites in assuring its possible molecular functions" (in Russian). *Genetika* 32.7: 902–13.

Rosenblueth, David A. & Thieffry, Denis & Huerta Moreno, Araceli & Salgado Osorio, Heladia & Collado-Vides, Julio 1996. "Syntactic recognition of regulatory regions in Escherichia coli". *Computer Applications in the Biosciences* 12.5: 415–22.

Ruhlen, Merritt. 1994. *On the origin of languages. Studies in linguistic taxonomy.* Stanford, Calif.: Stanford University Press.

Shao, Zhaohui & Raible, Florian & Mollaaghababa, Ramin & Guyon, Jeffrey R. & Wu, Chaoting & Bender, Welcome & Kingston, Robert E. 1999. "Stabilization of chromatin structure by PRC1, a Polycomb complex". *Cell* 98.1: 37–46.

Shubin, Neil & Tabin, Clifford J. & Carroll, Sean. 1997. "Fossils, genes and the evolution of animal limbs". *Nature* 388.6643: 639–48.

Strahl, Brian D. & Allis, C. David. 2000. "The language of covalent histone modifications". *Nature* 403.6765: 41–45.

Tallal, Paula. 1976. "Rapid auditory processing in normal and disordered language development". *Journal of Speech and Hearing Research* 37: 561–71.

Tallal, Paula & Miller, Steve L. & Bedi, Gail & Byma, Gary & Wang, Xiaoqin & Nagarajan, Srikantan S. & Schreiner, Christoph & Jenkins, William M. & Merzenich, Michael M. 1996. "Language comprehension in language-learning impaired children improved with acoustically modified speech". *Science* 271: 81–84.

Thomson, James A. & Itskovitz-Eldor, Joseph & Shapiro, Sander S. & Waknitz, Michelle A. & Swiergiel, Jennifer J. & Marshall, Vivienne S. & Jones, Jeffrey M. 1998. "Embryonic stem cell lines derived from human blastocysts". *Science* 282.5391: 1145–47.

Thorne, Alan & Grün, Rainer & Mortimer, Graham & Spooner, Nigel A. & Simpson, John J. & McCulloch, Malcolm & Taylor, Lois & Curnoe, Darren 1999. "Australia's oldest human remains: age of the Lake Mungo 3 skeleton". *Journal of Human Evolution* 36.6: 591–612.

Tsonis, Anastasios A. & Elsner, J.B. & Tsonis, Panagiotis A. 1997. "Is DNA a language?" *Journal of Theoretical Biology* 184: 25–29.

Searls, David B. 1997. "Linguistic approaches to biological sequences". *Computer Applications in the Biosciences* 13: 333–44.

Underhill, Peter A. & Jin, L. & Zemans, R. & Oefner, P.J. & Cavalli-Sforza, Luigi Luca. 1996. "A pre-Columbian Y chromosome-specific transition and its implications for human evolutionary history". *Proceedings of the National Academy of Sciences of the U.S.A.* 93.1: 196–200.

van Helden, Jacques & Rios, A.F. & Collado-Vides Julio. 2000. "Discovering regulatory elements in non-coding sequences by analysis of spaced dyads". *Nucleic Acids Research* 28.8: 1808–18.

von Dassow, George & Meir, Eli & Munro, Edwin M. & Odell, Garrett M. 2000. "The segment polarity network is a robust developmental module". *Nature* 406.6792: 188–92.

Varga-Weisz Patrick D. & Wilm, Matthias & Bonte, Edgar & Dumas, Katia & Mann, Matthias & Becker, Peter B. 1997. "Chromatin-remodelling factor CHRAC contains the ATPases ISWI and topoisomerase II". *Nature* 388.6642: 598–602. (With an erratum published in *Nature* 389.6654: 1003.)

Varga-Weisz, Patrick D. & Becker, Peter B. 1998. "Chromatin-remodeling factors: machines that regulate?" *Current Opinion in Cell Biology* 10.3: 346–53.

Weinrich, Harald. 1993. *Textgrammatik der deutschen Sprache*. Mannheim etc.: Dudenverlag.

Wright, Beverly A. & Lombardino, Linda J. & King, Wayne M. & Puranik, Cynthia S. & Leonard, Christiana M. & Merzenich, Michael M. 1997. "Deficits in auditory temporal and spectral resolution in language-impaired children". *Nature* 387.6629: 176–78.

Wolfgang Raible, University of Freiburg i.Br., (Germany)

9. Sprachpathologie

1. Aphasien aus kontrastiv-linguistischer Sicht
2. Aphasien bei Mehrsprachigen
3. Zitierte Literatur

1. Aphasien aus kontrastiv-linguistischer Sicht

1.1. Die Fragestellung

Da die Erforschung der Aphasien nach dem Zweiten Weltkrieg vornehmlich von angelsächsischen Arbeitsgruppen vorangetrieben wurde (Bates & Wulfeck 1989: 111), dominierte eine englischzentrierte Sichtweise. Sie führte in Bezug auf Beeinträchtigungen der grammatischen Verarbeitung zu Hypothesen, die auf andere Sprachen nicht übertragbar sind: Das Engl. unterscheidet sich wegen der strikten Regelung der Wortstellung und der Verarmung der Flexionsparadigmen typologisch von den meisten anderen Sprachen, die unter neurolinguistischen Gesichtspunkten betrachtet wurden (Bates et al. 1988: 331). Die Erforschung der einzelsprachlichen und universalen Merkmale der Aphasien, die, nach sporadischen Beobachtungen in den 40er und 50er Jahren, seit Mitte der 80er Jahre des letzten Jahrhunderts intensiv vorangetrieben wird, hat deshalb in erster Linie Auffälligkeiten in Morphologie und Syntax zum Gegenstand (Bates & Wulfeck 1989: 112; Obler 1996). Diesem Thema ist § 1.3. gewidmet. Vorangestellt werden eine Definition von 'Aphasie' und eine Beschreibung gängiger Aphasie-Typologien, soweit dies zum Verständnis des Folgenden notwendig erscheint.

1.2. 'Aphasie' – Definition und Typologien

Aphasien sind **erworbene**, nicht auf eine gestörte Sprachentwicklung zurückgehende Beeinträchtigungen der Sprachverarbeitung, betreffen also **sprachbezogene** Verarbeitungsprozesse, während andere kognitive Funktionen vergleichsweise verschont sind, und zwar als Folge eines **Hirnschadens**, wobei unterschiedliche Ätiologien (vaskulär: z. B. Schlaganfall; nicht-vaskulär: z. B. Tumor, Schädel-Hirn-Trauma) in Frage kommen (Wallesch & Kertesz 1993: 98; Huber et al. 1997: 135f.). Die Hirnschädigung ist lokal begrenzt, '**umschrieben**', mithin sind Aphasien von Sprachstörungen als Folge diffuser degenerativer Hirnerkrankungen (z. B. bei Morbus Alzheimer) oder als Folge nicht-fokaler Hirnschädigungen, z. B. bei Multi-Infarkt-Demenz (Bayles 1993), zu unterscheiden. (Vgl. aber das hiervon abweichende Konzept der „primary progressive aphasia" bei Mesulam 1982; → Art. 7.) Weiterhin sind Aphasien **zentrale** Sprachstörungen, die alle expressiven und rezeptiven sprachlichen Modalitäten betreffen (Huber et al. 1997: 80). Somit sind sie von den Dysarthrien als Störungen der Sprechmotorik (Huber 1997) und der Sprechapraxie, einer zentralen Störung der 'Programmierung' der Sprechmotorik (Rosenbek 1993), zu unterscheiden.

Die aphasischen Symptome können als Beeinträchtigungen auf den verschiedenen Ebenen der Sprachverarbeitung beschrieben werden. Auf der phonetisch-artikulatorischen Ebene kommt es zu 'Lautentstellungen', z. B. dem Verfehlen des Artikulationsortes eines Lautes (Ziegler 1991). Auf der segmental-phonologischen Ebene treten 'phonematische Paraphasien' auf (Dittmann 1991: 44ff.), die als Auslassungen, Hinzufügungen, Ersetzungen oder Vertauschungen von Phonemen beschrieben werden und zur Produktion von Neologismen führen können. Auf der lexikalisch-phonologischen Ebene kommt es zu Wortfindungsstörungen (Dittmann 1991: 79ff.), aber auch zu formbezogenen Ersetzungen ('formale Paraphasien'; z. B. Zielwort *Schnecke*, geäußert *Schelle*; Blanken 1990). Störungen auf der lexikalisch-semantischen Ebene (Gurd & Marshall 1993; Badecker & Caramazza 1993) führen zu semantischen Paraphasien (vgl. Zielwort *Zaun*, geäußert *Garten*). Semantische Paraphasien betreffen Elemente der offenen Klasse, d. h. Inhaltswörter. Störungen der Verarbeitung von Elementen der geschlossenen Klasse (freie grammatische Morpheme, 'Funktionswörter', **FW**) werden im Kontext der Störungen auf der morphologisch-syntaktischen Ebene untersucht (De Bleser & Bayer 1993; Friederici & Saddy 1993). Hier werden Auslassungen und fehlerhafte Ersetzungen von FWn ebenso beobachtet wie Auslassungen und fehlerhafte Ersetzungen von gebundenen grammatischen Morphemen. Dominieren fehlerhafte Ersetzungen in Verbindung mit komplexen, aber ungrammatischen syntaktischen Konstruktionen, spricht man von 'Paragrammatismus' (Ehinger et al. 1990: 70). Als typische syntaktische Abweichungen werden Satzverschränkungen und Satzteilverdopplungen wie in *Bei der Arbeit einfach hörte es einfach auf langsam auf* angesehen (Huber & Schlenck 1988). Dominieren die Vereinfachung von Flexionsformen (z. B. durch INF-Gebrauch beim V) und Auslassung von FWn in Verbindung mit vereinfachten syntaktischen Konstruktionen, spricht man von 'Agrammatismus' (Tesak 1990). Eine beispielhafte Äußerung für schweren Agrammatismus ('Telegrammstil') auf die Frage, wie es mit der Krankheit angefangen habe: *Ein, zwei, drei, vier Tage ... eh ... Flugzeug ... Sonne scheint und so ... vier Tage und zwei Tage ... bewusstlos und umfallen* [...] (Huber et al. 1997: 113; vgl. § 1.3.).

Im dt. Sprachraum unterscheidet man vier aphasische 'Standardsyndrome' (Huber et al. 1997: 107ff.): (i) Globale Aphasie mit dem Leitsymptom Sprachautomatismen (formstarre, nicht intentionsgerecht eingesetzte Wendungen oder Silbenkombinationen; Blanken et al. 1988), außerdem mit stark eingeschränktem Sprechfluss und schwer bis sehr schwer gestörter Kommunikation. (ii) Wernicke-Aphasie mit den Leitsymptomen Paragrammatismus und Paraphasien, außerdem mit unauffälligem oder überschießendem Sprechfluss ('Logorrhoe') und mittelgradig bis schwer gestörter Kommunikation. (iii) Broca-Aphasie mit dem Leitsymptom Agrammatismus, eingeschränktem Sprechfluss und mittelgradig bis schwer gestörter Kommunikation. (iv) Amnestische Aphasie mit dem Leitsymptom Wortfindungsstörungen, außerdem mit unauffälligem Sprechfluss, aber mit Suchverhalten und Satzabbrüchen bei leicht bis mittelgradig gestörter Kommunikation. 'Nicht-Standard-Syndrome' (Huber et al. 1997: 130ff.) sind die Leitungsaphasie mit herausragender Störung des Nachsprechens und die transkortikalen Aphasien mit verschontem Nachsprechen bei Beeinträchtigung von Spontansprache und/oder Sprachverständnis. Im angloamerikanischen Raum begnügt man sich häufig mit einer groben Einteilung der Aphasien in 'flüssige' und 'nicht-flüssige' auf der Grundlage solcher Parameter wie Sprechgeschwindigkeit, Satzlänge und Prosodie (Huber et al. 1997: 132). 'Flüssig' wären demnach Wernicke-, amnestische und Leitungsaphasie, 'nicht-flüssig' Broca-, und Globalaphasie sowie einzelne Fälle von amnestischer Aphasie.

Da bei etwa 90% der Menschen die linke Hemisphäre sprachdominant ist (Lateralisation), kommt es zumeist nach linkshemisphärischen Hirnschäden zu Aphasien (Huber et al. 1997: 81). Tritt bei Rechtshändern nach rechtshemisphärischer Läsion eine Aphasie auf, spricht man von 'gekreuzter Aphasie' (genauer Malin et al. 1994: 57). Die klassische Lokalisationsauffassung (Willmes & Poeck 1993: 1536) weist der Broca-Aphasie eine prärolandische, temporale Läsion zu, der Wernicke-Aphasie eine retrorolandische (temporo-parietale) Läsion, der amnestischen Aphasie eine kleine retrorolandische Läsion unterhalb der Sylvischen Furche und der Globalaphasie eine große perisylvische (d. h. das gesamte Versorgungsgebiet der Arteria cerebri media betreffende) Läsion. Doch skizziert dies lediglich eine Tendenz, denn von einer Eins-zu-eins-Entsprechung zwischen Läsionsort und Syndrom kann man angesichts großer individueller Varianz nicht sprechen, und die Beteiligung subkortikaler Strukturen ist damit noch gar nicht angesprochen (u. a. De Bleser 1988; Willmes & Poeck 1993; Huber et al. 1997: 85; → Art. 7). Immerhin erhärten diese neuropsychologischen Daten die Hypothese einer kritischen Beteiligung perisylvischer Strukturen an sprachbezogenen Prozessen (Wallesch & Kertesz 1993: 132).

1.3. Universale und einzelsprachliche Ausprägungen von Aphasien

Seit man erkannte, dass die am Engl. orientierte Beschreibung der morphologischen Probleme nicht-flüssiger AphasikerInnen als 'Auslassungen' eine unzulässige Vereinfachung darstellt, steht die Erforschung des Agrammatismus im Zentrum der kontrastiven Aphasiologie. Deshalb wird im folgenden, entsprechend der Forschungslage, fast ausschließlich die Sprachproduktion nicht-flüssiger AphasikerInnen betrachtet. Die Berücksichtigung flüssiger Aphasien (u. a. Friederici et al. 1991; MacWhinney et al. 1991b; MacWhinney & Osmán-Sági 1991a; Tzeng et al. 1991; Slobin 1991; Bastiaanse et al. 1996) würde den Rahmen dieses Artikels sprengen, ebenso der Einbezug der wenigen kontrastiven Arbeiten zum Sprachverstehen (u. a. Bates et al. 1987; Friederici et al. 1991; MacWhinney et al. 1991b; Vaid & Pandit 1991; Nicol et al. 1996).

Wegweisend für die kontrastive Aphasiologie war die Argumentation von Yosef Grodzinsky (1984), der zeigte, dass die Auslassung von Flexionsformen zwar im Engl. zu existierenden Formen führt (vgl. *boy-s* (PL) → *boy-Ø* (SG)); dt. *Jungen, Junge*, z. B. im Ital. aber nicht-existierende (wenngleich aussprechbare) Formen entstehen würden, die von den nicht-flüssigen PatientInnen tatsächlich nicht produziert werden (vgl. *rosso*, dt. *rot*, der Stamm *ross-* ist kein Wort). Im Hebräischen bestehen die Wurzeln der Wörter nur aus Konsonanten, so dass aussprechbare Formen erst durch grammatische Interfixe entstehen (vgl. Wurzel *L_M_D*, dt. *lernen*, 3.SG.M.PRES. *lomed*, 3.SG.M.PRET. *lamad*, 3.SG.M.FUT. *yilmad* etc.). Wäre Agrammatismus auf morphologischer Ebene universal durch die Auslassung von Flexionsformen gekennzeichnet, müsste er für das Hebr. zu Mutismus − zum Verstummen − führen. Tatsächlich kommt es aber zu fehlerhaften Ersetzungen.

Das internationale Projekt CLAS I (Cross-Language Aphasia Study, Phase I) verglich die Ausprägungen des Agrammatismus in 14 europäischen und asiatischen Sprachen (Menn & Obler (eds.) 1990; Menn & Obler 1990b; Menn et al. 1995: 84ff.). Aus diesem Projekt, seiner Fortsetzung CLAS II (*Aphasiology*, 10, Nr. 6, 1996) und weiteren Einzelstudien lassen sich folgende **einzelsprachenspezifische** Merkmale des Agrammatismus ableiten: (1) In Sprachen mit Wurzelformen, die existierende Wörter sind (Engl.: INF des V's, Nom.SG. des Ns), können scheinbar (!) Flexionsformen ausgelassen werden (vgl. *boys* → *boy-Ø*). Wenn Sprachen Person- und Numerus-Formen am V haben, gibt es eine Tendenz, wonach das V in einer geläufigen (1. oder 3. Pers. SG.) oder in einer Form, die keine Kongruenz erfordert, gewöhnlich einer infiniten Form, erscheint (schwächer markierte Form); bei PatientInnen, die keinen 'Telegrammstil' zeigen, ist das Repertoire der verwendeten V-Formen stark eingeschränkt

(Slobin 1991: 158 zum Türk.). Beim N ist der Nom. SG. eine präferierte Ersatzform. Im Dt. würde die Auslassung der Flexionsform beim V zwar zu einer existierenden Form führen (vgl. *geh-Ø* aus *geh-e, geh-st* etc.), diese ist aber eine stark markierte Form, nämlich eine SG-Form des IMPs, und stark markierte Formen kommen als 'Ersatzformen' nicht in Frage (so auch im Isländ., Hindi und Ital.). Als Default-Form tritt deshalb im Dt. überwiegend der INF (Stamm + *en*) auf, also eine flektierte Form (De Bleser et al. 1996: 177). Da die Hypothese der Ersetzung (gegebenenfalls durch das Ø-Allomorph) die Daten aller Sprachen abdeckt, ist es sinnvoll, sie auch für das Engl. zu postulieren und die Auslassungshypothese aufzugeben (Obler 1996: 533), zumal auch die infinite 'V+*ing*'-Form als Ersatz für flektierte V'en vorkommt (Lorch 1986: 97). Diese Auffassung impliziert die Hypothese, dass in agrammatischer Produktion sehr wohl von morphologischen Mitteln, und zwar auch von Flexionsmorphologie, Gebrauch gemacht wird (De Bleser et al. 1996: 178). Viele nicht-flüssige Aphasiker haben herausragende Schwierigkeiten mit V'en, und zwar beim Satzverstehen (Nicol et al. 1996: 610 f.) und in der Produktion, wo es auch zur Auslassung des finiten V's kommt. Ob dieses Problem auf die Flexionsmorphologie zurückzuführen ist (Lorch 1986: 104 für das Finn.), ist unklar, denn Elizabeth Bates et al. (1991a: 222) fanden eine Beeinträchtigung der V-Verarbeitung auch im verbflexionslosen Chin., allerdings für eine Aufgabe des Handlungsbenennens mit N-V-Komposita (aber Yiu/Worrall 1996: 641). Von großer theoretischer Relevanz ist in diesem Zusammenhang das von Bates et al. (1991b) vertretene „competition model": Flexionsformen (und FW) bei Aphasie sind zwar besonders fehleranfällig, andererseits hängt die Fehlerrate aber von der Frequenz und dem Informationsgehalt (kurz: der „cue validity") der jeweiligen Einheit in einer Sprache ab. In Sprachen mit reicher Flexionsmorphologie (Dt., Ital.) ist die „cue validity" der Flexionsformen hoch, entsprechend sind sie besser erhalten als in Sprachen, in denen ihre „cue validity" niedrig ist (wie im Engl.). Im Engl. wiederum kommt der Wortstellung eine höhere „cue validity" zu. Allerdings kann es nach Bates et al. (1991b: 127) vorkommen, dass sprachliche Einheiten mit hoher „cue validity" schwierig zu verarbeiten sind, also ein großes Maß an „cue cost" aufweisen. Dieser Faktor, der höhere Anfälligkeit verursacht, ist dann gegen die „cue validity" aufzuwiegen. Bei nicht-flüssigen türk. AphasikerInnen, also in einer agglutinierenden Sprache, sind, in Übereinstimmung mit dem „competition model", Flexionsformen vergleichsweise gut erhalten, und zwar bei Nomina besser als bei V'en. Die PatientInnen bedienen sich mithin nicht eines 'Telegrammstils' (Slobin 1991: 152). Im Gegensatz dazu fanden MacWhinney & Osmán-Sági (1991a: 176 f.) bei ungar. nicht-flüssigen AphasikerInnen, also ebenfalls in einer agglutinierenden Sprache, einen erheblichen Anteil an Ersetzungen von Kasusallomorphen durch das Ø-Suffix, das ist die NOMform. Man könnte spekulieren, dass die im Vergleich zum Türk. ungleich größere Komplexität der ungar. Nominalflexion und die Tatsache, dass die ungar. Flexionsparadigmen phonologisch weniger regulär sind als die türk. (MacWhinney & Osmán-Sági 1991a: 168), im Ungar. einen „cue-cost"-Faktor einführen, der den Effekt der „cue-validity" überwiegt, so dass auch hier das „competition model" greifen würde.

(2) In Sprachen, deren V'en Person- und Numerusformen haben (Ital., Dt., Hebr.), kommt es zu Ersetzungen dieser Formen und damit zu Kongruenzverletzungen (Ital. *la bambina *sono* / statt *è; das Mädchen *bin* / statt *ist*); dieser Fehlertyp kann in Sprachen, die keine Person-/Numerus-Kongruenzmarkierung am V haben (Japan.), nicht auftreten.

(3) In Sprachen mit reicher Kasusmarkierung am N (Dt., Isländ., die slav. Sprachen) kommt es zu fehlerhaften Ersetzungen von Kasusformen; in Sprachen ohne Kasusmarkierung am N (die roman. Sprachen) können solche Fehler nicht auftreten. — (4) In Sprachen mit Regelung der Wortfolge (z. B. strikte V-zweit-Beschränkung im Aussage-Hauptsatz; Schwed.) treten Wortfolgefehler auf; Verletzungen syntaktischer Regeln sind auch in Sprachen mit relativ freier Wortfolge möglich (z. B. Hauptverb am Satzende im Finn.). Innerhalb komplexer NPn sind bei Sprachen, die postnominale ADJe haben (Frz.), diese weniger fehleranfällig als pränominale ADJe. Letztere werden auch in Sprachen, die keine postnominalen ADJe kennen (Dt., Schwed., Poln., Engl.), häufig nachgestellt (Ahlsén et al. 1996: 553 ff.). — (5) Die Frequenz der Auslassung von FWn wird durch ART und Pronomina (germ. und roman. Sprachen) mitbestimmt; in artikellosen Sprachen (Russ., Japan.) und Sprachen, in denen der Gebrauch der 'Pronomina' von dem in den indoeuropäischen Sprachen ab-

weicht (Japan.), verschiebt sich zwangsläufig die Auslassungsstatistik. Auch im Finn. als einer agglutinierenden Sprache ohne ART als freies grammatisches Morphem und mit nicht-obligatorischen Personalpronomina ergeben sich aus strukturellen Gründen sowohl in agrammatischen Äußerungen als auch im Telegrammregister von NormalprobandInnen niedrige Auslassungsraten von FWn, zugleich erhöht sich hierdurch die Rate grammatikalisch korrekter Sätze (Tesak & Niemi 1997: 148; Niemi et al. 1990: 104 ff.). Wenn FW regulär weggelassen werden können, wie im Chin., sind pathologische Auslassungen auch nicht zu diagnostizieren, was wiederum den Vergleich mit anderen Sprachen verfälschen kann (Bates et al. 1991b: 142 f.). Hingegen können auch unter diesen strukturellen Bedingungen fehlerhafte Ersetzungen (z. B. von „noun classifiers" bei chin. Broca-AphasikerInnen; Tzeng et al. 1991: 194 ff.) beobachtet werden. Berthold Simons et al. (1988: 43 ff.) berichten von ihrem mandarin-chinesisch sprechenden Patienten TY, er habe, wegen der Ersetzungsfehler bei Nominal-Klassifikatoren, aber auch wegen Verstößen gegen die Konstituentenordnung, trotz des neurologischen Befundes und der nicht-flüssigen Redeweise „eher paragrammatisch" als agrammatisch gewirkt.

Auslassungen des bestimmten ARTs bei nicht-flüssigen AphasikerInnen nehmen nicht mit dem Grad der morphologischen Komplexität des Systems zu, wie man erwarten könnte, vielmehr sind sie im Engl. am häufigsten, gefolgt vom Ital. und Dt. (Bates et al. 1991b: 132). Dieser Befund steht in Einklang mit der „cue validity"-Hypothese des „competition model", ebenso die hohe Auslassungsrate des bestimmten ARTs in obligatorischer Stellung, die MacWhinney & Osmán-Sági (1991a: 180) bei nicht-flüssigen ungar. AphasikerInnen fanden, denn der bestimmte ART im Ungar. hat keine Kasus-, Numerus- und Genusmarkierung und mithin niedrige „cue-validity". Die Fehlerraten bei FWn scheinen sich allerdings nicht nur im Sprachvergleich, sondern auch individuell stark zu unterscheiden (Tesak & Niemi 1997: 149 f.). − (6) Es kommt zu Auslassungen von Inhaltswörtern. Die Auslassung finiter V'en wird gelegentlich mit deren hoher 'syntaktischer Ladung' erklärt, also etwa den Informationen über die strikte Subkategorisierung i. S. von Noam Chomsky (1965: 95). Für Nomina-Auslassungen (Finn., Serbo-Kroat.) könnte das komplexe Kasussystem der betreffenden Sprachen verantwortlich sein, mithin der hohe „cue-cost"-Faktor im Sinne des „competition model"; diese Frage bedarf weiterer Klärung. − (7) Vergleiche zwischen dem sog. Telegrammstil bei Agrammatismus und dem Telegrammregister von NormalprobandInnen im Niederl., Dt., Finn. und Schwed. ergaben, dass diese sich in relevanten Merkmalen unterscheiden (Tesak & Dittmann 1991; Tesak et al. 1995; Ahlsén 1993; Tesak & Niemi 1997). Im Niederl. fand Tesak (1994: 339 ff.) im Gegensatz zum Dt. zwar eine Übereinstimmung zwischen Agrammatismus und Telegrammstil hinsichtlich der Auslassungsrate von FWn insgesamt, doch zeigte eine differenzierte Analyse nach den einzelnen FW-Typen, dass deren Auslassungsraten sich sehr wohl unterscheiden: So fehlen z. B. Determinatoren in niederl. Telegrammen fast vollständig, werden aber im untersuchten Korpus von den agrammatischen Patienten in 43% der obligatorischen Kontexte produziert. Dies spricht gegen die rechnerische Subsumierung der entsprechenden grammatischen Morpheme unter **eine** Klasse 'FW'. − (8) In Sprachen mit extensiver Komposita-Bildung (Chin.) werden Teile von Komposita ausgelassen. Für das Dt., ebenfalls eine kompositafreundliche Sprache, bestätigt sich dies in den Daten von Stark & Dressler (1990: 292, 297) zwar nicht, aber Hittmair-Delazer et al. (1994: 32) fanden bei vier Broca-AphasikerInnen in der Gruppe mehr Auslassungen als bei PatientInnen anderer Syndrome (N=11). Da die Leistungen der einzelnen Broca-PatientInnen von 0 bis 13 Fehler reichten (Fehlersumme im gesamten Korpus: 43), ist angesichts der geringen Gruppengröße eine Generalisierung derzeit nicht möglich.

Welches sind die **universalen** Charakteristika des Agrammatismus? (i) Da Menn & Obler (1990a: 14) das Vorliegen reduzierter syntaktischer Konstruktionen zur Operationalisierung von 'Agrammatismus' verwenden, kann dieses Merkmal nicht als universales Charakteristikum aus den Daten von CLAS I herausgeholt werden. Zu konstatieren ist immerhin, dass man reduzierte Syntax bei nicht-flüssiger Aphasie in allen untersuchten Sprachen vorfindet, und zwar über alle PatientInnen und alle Sprachen hinweg in vergleichbarer Weise (Yiu & Worrall 1996: 640). Die PatientInnen tendieren außerdem zum Gebrauch der jeweiligen kanonischen Wortfolge (Slobin 1991: 161; auch Bates et al. 1988: 344 f. für das Dt.). − (ii) Auslassungen von FWn waren für einige Sprachen ebenfalls Operationalisierungskriterium, kommen aber in allen Sprachen vor, jedoch mit unterschiedlicher Frequenz. Dabei werden sog. leere V'en (das sind Hilfsverben in Vollverbfunktion, die weniger bedeutungshaltig sind als Inhaltsverben) und Hilfsverben am häufigsten ausgelassen, gefolgt von Pronomina und ARTn. − (iii) FW-Ersetzungen kommen in allen Sprachen vor; in Sprachen mit Genus des Pronomens scheinen diese besonders fehleranfällig. − (iv) Wo die Unterscheidung von Ersetzung und Auslassung gebundener grammatischer Morpheme möglich ist, sprechen die Daten dafür, dass sie ersetzt werden. Allerdings ist die Ersetzungsrichtung nicht einheitlich, sondern nur in der Tendenz durch die Markiertheitshypothese − die schwächer markierte Form ersetzt die stärker markierte − zu erkären, da auch die entgegengesetzte Richtung vorkommt und offensichtliche Zufallsproduktionen beobachtet wurden (Paradis 1988: 136). Bezüglich der gebundenen grammatischen Morpheme ist Agrammatismus somit ein universell einheitliches Phänomen: Gebundene grammatische Morpheme werden fehlerhaft ersetzt, nicht ausgelassen. Damit ist die Abgrenzung gegen den sog. Paragrammatismus in diesem Merkmal zwar nivelliert (Bates et al. 1991b: 137; Obler 1996: 524), man muss aber betonen, dass, gegen Bates & Wulfeck (1989: 129), flüssige und nicht-flüssige Aphasiker sehr wohl qualitative und quantitative Unterschiede im Muster der Substitution gebundener grammatischer Morpheme zeigen können (Niemi & Laine 1989: 156 zum Finn. und MacWhinney & Osmán-Sági 1991a zum Ungar.). Zu dieser Frage ist weitere Forschung notwendig. − (v) Komplexe Modal- und Tempusformen des V's werden vermieden, ebenso PASS-Sätze und Modalkonstruktionen. − (vi) Einige optionale FW werden im Übermaß verwendet, darunter satzinitiale Konjunktionen wie *und* und *dann*, im Japan. die satzfinalen Diskurssignal-Partikeln; diese FW haben gemeinsam, dass sie keine syntaktische Verarbeitung erfordern. − (vii) Die PatientInnen weichen u. U. auf Ausrufe oder formelhafte Wendungen aus, um einen Sachverhalt mitzuteilen. − (viii) Die PatientInnen tendieren zur direkten im Gegensatz zur indirekten Redewiedergabe. − (ix) Die PatientInnen verfügen über kommunikative (diskurspragmatische) Fähigkeiten wie Diskurssteuerung und Strukturierung von Erzählungen, wobei durch die morpho-syntaktischen Probleme explizite Kohärenzherstellung allerdings eingeschränkt sein kann.

1.4. Alexie, Agraphie und Schriftsysteme

1.4.1. Die Fragestellung

Auf die erworbenen Störungen der Schriftsprachverarbeitung (Huber 1997), die Alexien (Kay 1993) und Agraphien (Roeltgen & Rapcsak 1993), kann hier nicht allgemein eingegangen werden. Im vorliegenden Zusammenhang interessiert jedoch die unterschiedliche Beeinträchtigung schriftsprachlicher Leistungen von PatientInnen mit Hirnschaden in Abhängigkeit vom jeweiligen Schriftsystem, wobei mehrsprachige PatientInnen zunächst außer Betracht bleiben (→ § 2.3.).

Für diese Forschung bietet sich insbesondere das Japan. an, das zwei unterschiedliche Schriftsysteme kombiniert: **Kanji** (Stalph 1996: 1413 ff.) ist ein vom Chin. abgeleitetes morphemisch-logographisches Schriftsystem ('Morphogramme'), in dem ein graphisches Symbol ein lexikalisches Morphem repräsentiert. **Kana** dagegen sind Silbenzeichen, die zwei isomorph aufgebaute Systeme bilden (Stalph 1996: 1418 ff.): Katakana wird u. a. für nicht aus dem Chin. stammende Fremdwörter und Eigennamen verwendet, Hiragana dient im Wesentlichen der Schreibung von FWn. In der typischen Kanji-Hiragana-**Mischschrift** werden die Morphemgrenzen in vielen Fällen verwischt. Will man die schriftsprachliche Leistung von japan. ProbandInnen in Kanji und Kana vergleichen, ergeben sich Probleme (Paradis et al. 1985: 3 f.): Zwar können prinzipiell alle japan. Nomina in Kana verschriftlicht werden (das Umgekehrte gilt nicht), doch ist mit einem Effekt mangelnder Vertrautheit zu rechnen, wenn ein üblicherweise in Kanji geschriebenes Wort in Kana präsentiert wird und umgekehrt. Weiterhin stellt sich ein unerwünschter Längeneffekt ein, wenn ein Wort in Kanji mit einem, in Kana mit mehreren Zeichen symbolisiert wird; ebenso ein Komplexitätseffekt aufgrund der unterschiedlichen Struktur der Schriftzeichen. Der in der Forschung zumeist angestrebte Vergleich der schriftsprachlichen Leistungen in Kana vs. Kanji hinsichtlich der syllabischen (bzw. phonologischen) und der visuellen (graphemischen) Dimension wird durch diese unerwünschten Effekte als in der Regel unkontrollierte Faktoren kontaminiert.

1.4.2. Neuro- und psycholinguistische Evidenzen zur Frage der differentiellen Verarbeitung von Kanji und Kana

Sasanuma & Fujimura (1971) zeigten, dass japan. PatientInnen mit Aphasie und begleitender Sprechapraxie im Gegensatz zu PatientInnen ohne Sprechapraxie beim Lesen und Schreiben in Kana mehr Fehler machten als in Kanji. Die AutorInnen führen das Problem dieser PatientInnen auf die mit der Sprechapraxie gegebene Beeinträchtigung abstrakter phonologischer Prozesse zurück, die in die Verarbeitung von Kana-Schriftzeichen involviert seien, während bei Kanji-Zeichen zumindest im Fall einer Schädigung der phonologischen Verarbeitung unter Umgehung phonologischer Prozesse ein direkter Zugang zu den lexikalischen Einheiten möglich sei (auch Sasanuma & Fujimura 1972). Für eine differentielle Verarbeitung von Kana und Kanji sprechen auch die Daten zum Vorkommen von Agraphie im Japan.: Am häufigsten findet man gestörte Kanji- bei normaler oder relativ verschonter Kana-Verarbeitung (Roeltgen & Rapcsak 1993: 271). Die auftretenden Fehler werden als „visuell" bzw. „visuell-räumlich" beschrieben, während für den einzigen beschriebenen Fall von Kana-Agraphie das Fehlermuster nach Meinung der Autoren auf ein Problem der Phonem-Graphem-Konversion hinweist (Tanaka et al. 1987). Allerdings kann man aus diesen pathologischen Befunden nicht schließen, dass bei der **normalen** Verarbeitung von Kanji keine phonologisch vermittelte Verarbeitung stattfinde (Sasanuma et al. 1992).

Tatsächlich mehren sich die Studien, die aus Forschungen an NormalprobandInnen den Schluss ziehen, dass auch in die Verarbeitung von Kanji und der ebenfalls morphographischen chin. Schrift (Li 1996: 1404 f.) phonologische Prozesse integriert sind: so Perfetti & Zhang (1991; 1995) zum Chin., Osaka (1989; 1990) und Wydell et al. (1993) für Kanji. Allerdings ist die 'Natürlichkeit' der Testaufgaben (Einzelwortverarbeitung!) anzuzweifeln, und Schlüsse auf die Verarbeitung der normalen japan. Kanji-Kana-Mischschrift sind nicht a priori zulässig. Möglicherweise sind bei den einschlägigen Befunden die schon erwähnten (→ § 1.4.1.) unkontrollierten Frequenz- und Komplexitätseffekte im Spiel (Leong & Tamaoka 1995 für Kanji; Seidenberg 1985 zum Chin.; aber Quian et al. 1994). Zu beachten ist weiterhin, dass bei Aufgaben mit Arbeitsgedächtnisbelastung (so bei Tzeng et al. 1977) phonologische Rekodierung ohnehin zu erwarten ist, mithin phonologische Effekte nicht unreflektiert dem Leseprozess zugeschrieben werden dürfen (Koda 1990; Xu 1991; Hu & Catts 1993). Schließlich ist für vergleichende Untersuchungen relevant, dass Kana-Zeichen möglicherweise nicht unter allen Bedingungen beim Lesen phonologisch rekodiert werden müssen (Besner & Hildebrandt 1987; Hirose 1992: 912 f.; Buchanan & Besner 1993; Leong & Tamaoka 1995). Auch hier ist die Verallgemeinerung von der Einzelwortverarbeitung auf das Lesen im Kontext problematisch, so dass die Frage zur Zeit als ungeklärt betrachtet werden muss.

1.4.3. Die Hypothese der differentiellen Lateralisation von Kanji und Kana

Der unterschiedliche Charakter von Kanji und Kana legt die Hypothese einer differentiellen Lateralisation der Verarbeitung durchaus nahe: eine eher ganzheitliche für Kanji in der rechten und eine eher analytische Verarbeitung für Kana in der linken Hemisphäre. Mit den klinischen Daten ist diese Hypothese aber nicht vereinbar: Nach Shimada & Otsuka (1981), Paradis et al. (1985: 196) und Hasuike et al. (1986) gibt es keinen Hinweis darauf, dass Kanji bei rechts- und Kana bei linkshemisphärischen Läsionen stärker beeinträchtigt wird. Bei PatientInnen sowohl mit Kanji-Agraphie und -Alexie als auch bei solchen mit reiner Kanji-Agraphie finden sich linkshemisphärische Läsionen (Roeltgen & Rapcsak 1993: 271). Auch Daten von PatientInnen mit durchtrenntem Corpus callosum (der direkten Verbindung zwischen den beiden Hemisphären) und mit linkshemisphärischen Läsionen legen nahe, dass beide Schriftsysteme linkshemisphärisch verarbeitet werden (Iwata 1984). Den differentiellen Schädigungen der Schriftsysteme scheinen eher intrahemisphärische, nämlich links-temporale (Kana) und links-parietookzipitale (Kanji) Läsionen zu korrespondieren (Paradis et al. 1985: 177 ff.; Hamasaki et al. 1995), wobei die Verhältnisse für Lesen und Schreiben unterschiedlich sein könnten (Kawahata & Nagata 1988).

Untersuchungen an NormalprobandInnen zur Frage, ob morphographische Schriftzeichen rechtshemisphärisch und Kana-Zeichen linkshemisphärisch verarbeitet werden, haben bislang nicht zu eindeutigen Ergebnissen geführt, doch wird häufiger eine differentielle Lateralisation angenommen (u. a. Sasanuma et al. 1977; Hatta 1977; Tzeng et al. 1979;

Cheng & Yang 1989; Leong et al. 1985; Rastatter et al. 1989). Aus methodischen Gründen und wegen der erwähnten Frequenz- und Längeneffekte (→ § 1.4.1.), beurteilen Paradis et al. (1985: 196) diese Befunde äußerst skeptisch, zumal die klinischen Evidenzen gegen eine differentielle Lateralisation sprechen.

2. Aphasien bei Mehrsprachigen

2.1. Definitionen

Da schätzungsweise die Hälfte der Weltbevölkerung als zwei- oder mehrsprachig bezeichnet werden kann (Manuel-Dupont et al. 1992: 193), ist die Erforschung von Aphasien bei Mehrsprachigen keineswegs ein neurolinguistisches Randgebiet. Sie setzt selbstverständlich die Definition von 'Mehrsprachigkeit' voraus. Das kann mittels solcher Klassifikationssysteme geschehen, wie sie u. a. Palij & Aaronson (1992: 64 ff.) und Obler et al. (1995: 140 f.) vorgelegt haben: Wichtige Kriterien sind das Erwerbsalter (vor allem die Unterscheidung zwischen bilingualem L1-Erwerb, L2-Erwerb des Kindes und L2-Erwerb des Erwachsenen; Klein 1984: 27), die (sozialen und situativen) Kontexte des Erwerbs und die prämorbide Beherrschung bzw. die Frage der Dominanz einer Sprache bei Beginn der Erkrankung.

Die Diagnose selbst kann bei polyglotten AphasikerInnen mittels des „Bilingual Aphasia Test" (Paradis 1989a) erfolgen, der für 106 Sprachenpaare vorliegt (Stand: Okt. 2000). Der für das Dt. entwickelte „Aachener Aphasie Test" (AAT; Huber et al. 1983) ist auch in einer ital. (Luzzatti et al. 1991) und einer niederl. Fassung (Graetz et al. 1992) verfügbar.

2.2. Ausprägungen der Aphasien und der Wiedererlangung sprachlicher Fertigkeiten bei Mehrsprachigen

Möglicherweise gilt für Aphasien bei Mehrsprachigen generell, dass die Defizite in allen Sprachen gleichartig sind (Obler et al. 1995: 133): Wenn ein Patient in einer Sprache eine Broca-Aphasie zeigt, zeigt er sie auch in der/den anderen Sprache(n); zeigt er in einer Sprache eine amnestische Aphasie, zeigt er sie auch in der/den anderen, etc. Zwar wurde die Hypothese aufgestellt, das Syndrom könne in einzelnen Fällen für jede der Sprachen ein anderes sein – 'differentielle Aphasie', doch ist dies umstritten: Zwei der in der Forschungsliteratur diskutierten drei (!) Fälle lassen sich nach Paradis (1993: 279; 1996: 171 f.) dadurch erklären, dass die PatientInnen in ihrer jeweiligen Muttersprache (Engl. bzw. Span.) agrammatische, im Hebr. aber nur scheinbar paragrammatische Symptome zeigten. Wie in § 1.3. gezeigt, sind Substitutionen grammatischer Morpheme im Hebr. strukturell bedingt. Es handelt sich also um Fehlinterpretationen aufgrund der Vernachlässigung einzelsprachlicher Unterschiede in den Ausprägungen von Aphasien.

Die viele Jahrzehnte dominierende Hypothese, im Fall von Aphasie bei Mehrsprachigen seien **alle** Sprachen betroffen (Penfield & Roberts 1959: 187) – 'parallele Aphasie', gilt nicht ausnahmslos. Es ist möglich, dass eine Sprache gar nicht betroffen ist – 'selektive Aphasie' (u. a. Paradis & Goldblum 1989). Wenn ein Patient nach Eintreten der Aphasie in Sprache A ein höheres Leistungsniveau zeigt als in Sprache B, dann liegt dies meistens daran, dass er auch prämorbid Sprache A besser beherrscht hat. Im Einzelfall ist die prämorbide Beherrschung allerdings oft schwer zu kontrollieren (Stark et al. 1994: 86; Juncos-Rabadán 1994: 71). Es kommt aber vor, dass eine Sprache stärker betroffen ist, als die prämorbide Beherrschung erwarten lässt (Obler et al. 1995: 134). Ein methodisches Problem des Vergleichs der Schweregrade von Aphasien in verschiedenen Sprachen ergibt sich aus den einzelsprachlichen Unterschieden in den Ausprägungen von Aphasien (Bates et al. 1991b: 142 ff.; Obler et al. 1995: 134 f.; Nicol et al. 1996: 610). Bei der Diagnose von Aphasien bei Mehrsprachigen sind deshalb die Charakteristika der beteiligten Sprachen im Detail zu berücksichtigen, und es liegt auf der Hand, dass sprachvergleichende aphasiologische Studien eine Voraussetzung der Untersuchung von Aphasien bei Mehrsprachigen darstellen (Paradis 1988: 146 ff.).

Die Wiedererlangung der sprachlichen Fertigkeiten verläuft in den meisten Fällen für beide/alle Sprachen parallel (Paradis 1977: 65), doch kommt auch nicht-parallele Wiedererlangung vor (Paradis 1989b: 117; Obler et al. 1995: 134). Die Zahlenangaben über die Wiedererlangungsmuster divergieren, und man muss sehen, dass sich auf solche Zahlen ohnehin keine verlässliche Statistik gründen lässt, weil eher 'interessante' Fälle publiziert werden, und dies sind ohne Zweifel die mit nicht-parallelem Verlauf (Albert & Obler 1978: 141).

Folgende Klassifikation der Wiedererlangung wurde vornehmlich von Paradis entwickelt (Paradis 1977: 65 ff.; Paradis 1989b: 117; Paradis 1993: 278f.): (1) Parallel: beide/alle Sprachen werden gleichzeitig und im selben Maße wiedererlangt; (2) differentiell: eine Sprache wird besser wiedererlangt als die andere/n; (3) sukzessive: erst nachdem eine Sprache maximal wiedererlangt ist, beginnt die Wiedererlangung der anderen; (4) selektiv: eine Sprache wird gar nicht wiedererlangt; (5.1) antagonistisch: zunächst wird Sprache A wiedererlangt, im Zuge der Wiedererlangung von Sprache B verschlechtert sich die Leistung in A, und B ersetzt schließlich A; (5.2) alternierend antagonistisch: die jeweils wiedererlangte Sprache wechselt in Intervallen von 24 Stunden bis zu 8 Monaten; (6) gemischt: die Sprachen werden systematisch intrasententiell, manchmal intramorphemisch, auf allen linguistischen Ebenen (Phonologie, Morphologie, Syntax und/oder Lexikon) gemischt. – Die verschiedenen Typen der Wiedererlangung schließen sich nicht gegenseitig aus. So kann sich z. B. der Typ mit der Zeit ändern (etwa vom sukzessiven zum antagonistischen), oder zwei Typen können koexistieren (z. B. alternierender Antagonismus zweier Sprachen mit sukzessiver Wiedererlangung einer dritten; Paradis 1993: 279).

Zusätzlich zu den sechs Typen der Wiedererlangung werden noch Fälle sog. paradoxen und sog. zwanghaften Übersetzens beschrieben. Von 'paradoxer Übersetzung' (Paradis et al. 1982) spricht man, wenn PatientInnen aus Sprache A, die sie in der Spontansprache beherrschen, in Sprache B übersetzen können, die ihnen in der Spontansprache oder anderen Produktionsaufgaben nicht zugänglich ist, ohne dass sie das Umgekehrte können. 'Zwanghaftes Übersetzen' (Lebrun 1983: 25; Perecman 1984: 57 f.; Lebrun 1991: 6f.) liegt vor, wenn polyglotte PatientInnen unaufgefordert ihre eigenen oder die Äußerungen anderer übersetzen, wobei zumeist Einzelwörter, in einigen Fällen ganze Phrasen betroffen sind. Es handelt sich um ein transitorisches Phänomen, das auch in der Schriftsprache auftreten kann. Luc P. De Vreese et al. (1988: 253) vermuten einen vorsprachlich-konzeptuellen Ursprung. – Schließlich ist bei polyglotten Aphasikern auch die Unfähigkeit, überhaupt zwischen den Sprachen zu übersetzen, beobachtet worden (Paradis et al. 1982).

Sprachmischung ist bei polyglotten Aphasikern selten (Perecman 1984: 44 f.; Obler et al. 1995: 137; Lebrun 1991: 3) und wird mit Wortfindungsstörungen in der jeweils aktuell gesprochenen Sprache in Verbindung gebracht (Obler et al. 1995). Einen möglicherweise einschlägigen Fall berichtet Anton Leischner (1988). Ebenfalls selten scheinen bei polyglotten AphasikerInnen Interferenzen, die fälschliche Übertragung von Konstruktionen aus einer Sprache in die andere, vorzukommen. Treten sie aber auf, dann in der Regel aus der dominanten in eine weniger gut beherrschte Sprache, so dass der Verdacht naheliegt, dies sei auch prämorbid schon geschehen (Obler et al. 1995: 137).

Sprachmischungen, dem intrasententiellen Code-switching bei bilingualen Normalsprechern vergleichbar, sind von Sprachwahlbeeinträchtigungen („language-choice problem"; Obler et al. 1995: 136) zu unterscheiden, d. h. dem Verlust oder der Einschränkung der Fähigkeit polyglotter PatientInnen, die der Kommunikationssituation angemessene Sprache zu wählen, obwohl sie grundsätzlich verfügbar wäre. Hier handelt es sich um eine mit der Situationseinschätzung zusammenhängende Fertigkeit, deren Beeinträchtigung sich in der Wahl einer für den jeweiligen Gesprächszug unangemessenen Sprache (De Vreese et al. 1988: 246) bzw. in einem unsystematischen, wie es scheint grundlosen Sprachwechsel äußert (Lebrun 1991: 2). Diese Beeinträchtigung ist nicht im engeren Sinne 'aphasisch', und sie wird auch eher im Zusammenhang mit Demenzen gesehen (De Vreese et al. 1988: 246ff.).

Über die Faktoren, die für die Muster nicht-paralleler Wiedererlangung verantwortlich sein sollen, sind viele Hypothesen aufgestellt worden (Paradis 1989b: 125 ff.; Obler et al. 1995: 135): Genannt wurden der Schweregrad der Aphasie (je schwerer, desto eher nicht-parallele Wiedererlangung), die Schädigung eines hypothetischen Mechanismus, mittels dessen zwischen den Sprachen hin und her geschaltet werden könne (dessen Existenz man heute nicht mehr postuliert), affektive und emotionale Faktoren (die den Nachteil haben, kaum operationalisierbar zu sein), die Lerngeschichte jeder Sprache, der prämorbide Grad der Beherrschung und Unterschiede in der Struktur der Sprachen (wofür die Evidenzen nach Paradis (1994: 127) aber schwach sind). Manche ForscherInnen (wie Leischner 1979: 147) geben der Sprache der Umgebung des Patienten (zumeist der Klinik) die größte Chance, als erste oder besser wiedererlangt zu werden; Yvan Lebrun (1995: 14f.) vermutet allerdings, dass dies nur zutrifft, wenn der Patient die betreffende Sprache früh erlernt hat. Die von Ribot 1882 aufgestellte Hypothese, die zuerst erworbene Sprache werde auch zuerst wiedererlangt ('Ribots Regel'), wurde durch abweichende Einzelfälle immer wieder in Frage gestellt (vgl. die Kritik bei Lambert & Fillenbaum 1959: 28), und sie galt definitiv als widerlegt, als sich herausstellte, dass sie nur auf 26 von 56 PatientInnen zutraf, deren Daten Albert & Obler (1978: 95 ff.) reanalysierten. Auch eine Studie von Ramamurthi & Chari (1993) an 88 indischen bilingualen AphasikerInnen ergab keinen Vorteil der Muttersprache. Obler & Mahecha (1991) reanalysierten 156 Fallbeschreibungen polyglotter AphasikerInnen im Hinblick auf das Zutreffen (R) bzw. Nichtzutreffen (−R) von Ribots Regel; es ergibt sich als schwer interpretierbares Ergebnis, dass −R signifikant mit dem Vorliegen einer rechtshemisphärischen Läsion und Linkshändigkeit korreliert.

Die von Albert & Obler (1978) analysierten Daten sprechen eher für die von Pitres im Jahre 1895 aufgestellten Hypothese, die zur Zeit des Ereignisses dominante Sprache habe die Chance, zuerst und besser wiederhergestellt zu werden (Lebrun 1995); allerdings sind auch gegen diese Regel Einzelfallbeschreibungen angeführt worden (Lambert & Fillenbaum 1959: 28). 'Pitres' Regel gilt nach Albert & Obler (1978: 153) vor allem für PatientInnen unter 60 Jahren und mit geringerer Wahrscheinlichkeit für Aphasien vaskulärer Ätiologie als für durch Traumen verursachte.

Paradis (1994: 410) erwägt die Hypothese, die Wiedererlangung von L2 vor L1 stehe „in some cases" (!) in Zusammenhang mit dem Grad an Automatisierung der Sprachbeherrschung ('implizites Wissen') bzw. mit metasprachlichem ('explizitem') Wissen und der differentiellen anatomischen Lokalisation dieser Wissenstypen: L1 ist die 'automatisch' beherrschte Sprache, über die weniger gebildete Menschen kaum metasprachliches Wissen haben. Explizites Wissen über L1 setzt in der Regel eine formale Bildung voraus. Im gesteuerten L2-Erwerb wird ebenfalls explizites Wissen erworben. Denkbar ist deshalb, dass die Wiedererlangung von L2 vor bzw. statt L1 in einigen Fällen darauf zurückzuführen ist, dass metasprachliches Wissen von L2 kompensatorisch aktiviert wird (auch Paradis 1995c: 216). Während die sprachliche Kompetenz im Sinne des impliziten Wissens bei beiden Sprachen beeinträchtigt sein kann, ist das für L2 erworbene explizite Wissen, das nach Paradis in anderen Hirnarealen lokalisiert ist, erhalten: Aphasie betrifft implizites sprachliches Wissen; metasprachliches Wissen wie auch andere Aspekte des episodischen und enzyklopädischen, deklarativen Wissens bleiben verschont (Paradis 1995b: 6). Ein von Obler & Mahecha (1991: 61), allerdings nur als Trend, aufgezeigter Zusammenhang zwischen niedrigerer Bildung und nicht erfolgter Wiedererlangung von L1 (−R) könnte dann, positiv gewendet, auf die Möglichkeit der Nutzung expliziten Wissens von L1 bei der Wiedererlangung der Muttersprache durch PatientInnen mit metasprachlichen Kenntnissen in L1 verweisen, allerdings muss man möglicherweise den Faktor des häufigeren Umgangs mit Sprache bei Gebildeteren, unabhängig vom Stand des metasprachlichen Wissens, berücksichtigen.

Nach Ramamurthi & Chari (1993: 63) gibt es zwar keinen pauschalen Vorteil für die prämorbid am besten beherrschte Sprache, doch fanden sie bei ihren bilingualen AphasikerInnen (N=88) Evidenzen dafür, dass die Sprache, die für gedankliche Routinen, Kopfrechnen und Gebete genutzt wird, also für früh erworbene und überlernte Fähigkeiten, gegen Beeinträchtigungen stärker gefeit ist. Carme Junqué et al. (1995: 202) fanden bei 50 katalanisch-span. bilingualen AphasikerInnen einen Vorteil der prämorbid dominierenden Sprache, konnten aber, da diese bei den meisten PatientInnen auch die Muttersprache war, zwischen diesen beiden Kriterien nicht unterscheiden.

Nicht zuletzt ist ein Einfluss der Schriftsprachbeherrschung denkbar: Die Visualisierung sprachlicher Elemente, die in der Regel eher für Standardvarietäten gegeben ist, könnte die Restitution begünstigen und nicht verschriftlichte Sprachen bzw. Varietäten (man denke an die dt. Dialekte) benachteiligen (Paradis 1977: 81f.). Diese Frage ist aber empirisch nicht geklärt (Paradis 1989b: 126).

Da alle möglichen Fälle von Wiedererlangung belegt sind, verwundert es nicht, dass eine einheitliche 'Regel' für die 'erste' Sprache noch nicht gefunden ist (Paradis 1989b: 134). Zwischen dem Wiedererlangungsmuster und der Lage, Größe oder Ursache der Läsion, dem Typ oder Schweregrad der Aphasie, dem Typ von Bilingualismus, dem Strukturtyp der Sprache, Faktoren des Erwerbs oder des habituellen Gebrauchs finden sich keine Korrelationen (Paradis 1995c: 211).

Paradis (1994: 410) vertritt aber die Auffassung, seine Hypothese der kompensatorischen Nutzung metasprachlichen Wissens (vgl. oben in diesem Abschnitt) könne „einige", und seine erweiterte „activation threshold hypothesis" (dazu Paradis 1989b: 132; 1993: 282f.) komplementär dazu „die meisten Fälle" von nicht-paralleler Wiedererlangung erklären (Paradis 1994: 410). Da sich letztere auf die anatomische Lokalisation mehrerer Sprachen bezieht, wird sie unten (→ § 2.4.1.) dargestellt.

2.3. Beeinträchtigungen der Schriftsprache bei Mehrsprachigen

Beeinträchtigungen der Schriftsprache bei mehrsprachigen PatientInnen sind nur kursorisch beschrieben worden, wobei das Bild vielfältig ist: Von den acht in Paradis (1989b: 124f.) der Forschungsliteratur entnommenen Fällen zeigen fünf differentielle, zwei parallele und einer selektive Wiedererlangung.

Zu bedenken ist der Einfluss unterschiedlicher Schriftsysteme auf Ausprägung und Schweregrad der Schriftsprachbeeinträchtigung. Ein relevanter Faktor ist die unterschiedliche Korrespondenz zwischen Graphemen und Phonemen. Diese ist bei Transkriptionssystemen am größten, während orthographische Systeme die Korrespondenz mehr, wie in der ital. Orthographie, oder graduell weniger realisieren, wie etwa in der Abfolge dt., frz., engl., schließlich morphographische Schrift, letztere ohne Korrespondenz (→ § 1.4.1.). In Abhängigkeit von dieser Eigenschaft der jeweiligen Orthographie kann die schriftsprachliche Leistung eines Patienten in Bezug auf die betreffenden Sprachen variieren: Wenn ein engl.-chin. bilingualer Patient aufgrund einer Frontalhirnläsion in der phonologischen Verarbeitung beeinträchtigt ist, kann dies zu einer stärkeren Störung der Schriftsprachverarbeitung in der Sprache mit Graphem-Phonem-Korrespondenz (Engl.) führen, während im Fall einer temporo-parietalen Läsion bei verschonter phonologischer Verarbeitung die Beeinträchtigung in der Sprache mit morphographischem Schriftsystem (Chin.) stärker sein kann (Paradis 1977: 83).

Auch kann die schriftsprachliche Leistung in Abhängigkeit vom Schriftsystem variieren, in den betreffenden Sprachen aber etwa identisch sein: Ein franz.-dt. bilingualer Patient konnte nach einem Insult in beiden Sprachen nur noch Einzelbuchstaben, stenographische Texte dagegen völlig normal lesen (Paradis 1989b: 125). Peuser & Leischner (1974) berichten von einem dt.-engl. bilingualen Aphasiker, der in beiden Sprachen bessere schriftsprachliche Leistungen in phonetischer Transkription als in der normalen Orthographie zeigte, was auf eine Nutzung der Graphem-Phonem-Korrespondenz hindeutet.

2.4. Mehrsprachigkeit, Aphasie und die Repräsentation von Sprachen im Gehirn

2.4.1. Hypothesen über die intrahemisphärische Repräsentation mehrerer Sprachen im Gehirn

Paradis (1993: 282) diskutiert vier Hypothesen über die Repräsentation zweier Sprachen in der sprachdominanten Hemisphäre des Gehirns: Nach der „extended system hypothesis" sind die Sprachen in ihrer Repräsentation nicht differenziert, sondern das bilinguale System ist gegenüber einem monolingualen erweitert. Die Abwahl z. B. einer syntaktischen Konstruktion in Sprache A statt Sprache B funktioniert nicht anders als die Abwahl einer Konstruktion X statt Y innerhalb einer Sprache. Die „dual system hypothesis" dagegen postuliert zwei getrennte neutrale Systeme für die beiden Sprachen. Nach der „tripartite system hypothesis" sind die Einheiten, die in beiden Sprachen identisch sind, in einem gemeinsamen Substrat repräsentiert, die unterschiedlichen hingegen in sprachspezifischen Substraten. Die „subsystems hypothesis" schließlich geht davon aus, dass jede Sprache als Subsystem eines umfassenden sprachlichen Systems repräsentiert ist, nämlich der modular konzipierten 'Sprachkompetenz' als Gesamtheit sprachlicher Funktionen. Lokalisatorisch bedeutet dies (Paradis 1989b: 131), dass beide Sprachen in den für Sprache relevanten Arealen von unterschiedlichen neuronalen „circuits" verarbeitet werden, die anatomisch „intricately intervowen", gleichwohl differentiell pathologisch zu beeinträchtigen sind (ein nicht ganz einfacher Gedanke). Kern der „subsystems hypothesis" ist die „activation threshold hypothesis": Nach dieser Hypothese haben die 'Spuren' oder 'Engramme', die die Sprachfähigkeit im Substrat repräsentieren, Schwellenwerte, deren Höhe u. a. von der Gebrauchshäufigkeit und dem Zeitpunkt des letzten Gebrauchs abhängt. Bei längerem Nichtgebrauch kann der Schwellenwert so hoch sein, dass eine Spur nur noch für das Verstehen, nicht aber für die Produktion (die mehr 'Energie' erfordert) zur Verfügung steht. Die Abwahl einer passenden Spur wiederum hängt ab von der Aktivation, die sie selbst erfährt, und der Hemmung (der momentanen Erhöhung der Schwellenwerte) konkurrierender Einheiten. Wenn ein bilingualer Sprecher sich für eine Sprache 'entscheidet', wird die nichtgewählte Sprache partiell deaktiviert, d. h. der Schwellenwert wird erhöht.

Nach Paradis kann allein die „subsystems"-Hypothese alle Daten von Aphasien bei Mehrsprachigen erklären: Nicht-parallele Wiedererlangung ist demnach nicht als Resultat der selektiven Zerstörung der Repräsentation einer Sprache im Gehirn, sondern (im Sinne des „inhibitory control"-Modells von Green 1986) als die temporäre oder permanente Störung von aktivierenden und inhibitenden Prozessen zu verstehen. Genauer (Paradis 1993: 283): Aphasie kann bewirken, dass eine Sprache nicht 'disinhibiert' werden kann, d. h., der Aktivationsschwellenwert kann nicht genügend gesenkt werden. Wenn dies permanent geschieht, führt es zu selektiver Wiedererlangung; geschieht es temporär, liegt sukzessive Wiedererlangung vor; betrifft es abwechselnd beide Sprachen, ist antagonistische Wiedererlangung die Folge. Ist der Aktivationsschwellenwert für eine Sprache höher als für die andere, führt dies zu differentieller Wiedererlangung. Ist hingegen die Deaktivierung (Anhebung des Aktivationsschwellenwertes) einer Sprache beeinträchtigt, kommt es zu Sprachenmischung. Auf diese Weise gelangt Paradis zu einer einheitlichen Erklärung der Muster nicht-paralleler Wiedererlangung (→ § 2.2.).

Paradis geht mit seiner „subsystems"- und „activation threshold"-Hypothese davon aus, dass zwei Sprachen im Gehirn lokalisatorisch im selben Substrat repräsentiert sind. (Vgl. auch die Diskussion in Gomez-Tortosa et al. 1995; Hines 1996; Gomez-Tortorsa et al. 1996; Paradis 1996). Entsprechend wendet sich Paradis (1995d) auch gegen die „context-of-acquisition"-Hypothese, die besagt, in unterschiedlichen Kontexten erworbene Sprachen (z. B. Elternhaus vs. Schule) seien neurofunktional stärker getrennt als im selben Kontext erworbene (Lambert & Fillenbaum 1959: 29 f.). Bei bilingualen AphasikerInnen sollten nach Lambert & Fillenbaum also eher differentielle Phänomene erwartbar sein, wenn die Repräsentationen von L1 und L2 stärker getrennt sind, d. h. bei spätem L2-Erwerb. Die Evidenzen dafür sind schwach (Lambert 1969: 101 f.). Paradis (1995b: 2 f.) wendet sich mit dem Argument gegen diese Hypothese, die separate funktionale Organisation zweier Sprachen im Sinne von „koordinierten Sprachsystemen" (Ervin-Tripp & Osgood 1954/1986: 12 f.; Albert & Obler 1978: 227), i. e. ein linguistisches Konstrukt, müsse keineswegs zu einer entsprechenden cerebralen Organisation, i. e. ein neurolinguistisches Konstrukt, führen: Während sich die interne Struktur der Grammatik unterscheiden könne, könne das sie bedienende Substrat identisch sein. Als Beleg führt Paradis Fälle von differentieller Wiedererlangung angesichts des Erwerbs von zwei Sprachen im selben Kontext (Sasanuma & Park 1995) bzw. von paralleler Wiedererlangung angesichts des Erwerbs in unterschiedlichen Kontexten an (Junqué et al. 1995).

Allerdings sprechen die Daten einer vieldiskutierten Studie von Kim et al. (1997) an NormalprobandInnen und mittels des Verfahrens der funktionellen Magnetresonanz-Tomografie eher für eine partiell differentielle Repräsentation der Sprachen bei spätem L2-Erwerb (genauer: bei Jugendlichen). Die Daten dieser Studie sind mit der „context-of-acquisition"-Hypothese und für den späten L2-Erwerb mit der „dual system"-Hypothese kompatibel, während sie die Hypothese eines einheitlichen Substrates von L1 und L2 („subsystem hypothesis") für den späten L2-Erwerb zu widerlegen scheinen. Es wird also, sollten sich die Kim-et al.-Befunde replizieren lassen (vgl. Klein et al. 1995, allerdings für eine Gruppe mit L2-Erwerbsbeginn im Alter von durchschnittlich 7,3 Jahren), darum gehen, einen stringenten Bezug zwischen den Lokalisationsdaten von NormalprobandInnen und den Wiedererlangungsmustern von mehrsprachigen AphasikerInnen unter Berücksichtigung der Erwerbsgeschichte, insbesondere des Erwerbsalters, und des Läsionsortes herzustellen.

2.4.2. Differentielle Lateralisation

Seit Albert & Obler (1978: 238 ff.) in einem Forschungsüberblick über experimentelle und klinische Studien bei Bilingualen eine stärkere Beteiligung der rechten Hemisphäre an der Sprachverarbeitung als bei Monolingualen postulieren, wird dieses Thema kontrovers diskutiert (Springer & Deutsch 1995: 260). Die Studien an NormalprobandInnen sind wegen methodischer Probleme vor allem von Paradis (Paradis 1990: 578 f.; dagegen Berquier & Ashton 1992 und die Erwiderung in Paradis 1992; auch Paradis 1994: 408 f.) heftig kritisiert worden. Dabei wird u. a. die Auswahl der Stimuli (typischerweise Einsilber, Zahlen oder Einzelwörter), die es unzulässig erscheinen läßt, auf die Lateralisation sprachlicher Strukturen generell oder gar des Sprachgebrauchs zu verallgemeinern, und die mangelnde Unterscheidung zwischen der sprachsystematischen (Phonologie, Morphologie, Syntax, Lexikon) und der pragmatischen Ebene (Inferenzen, Situationskontext, Prosodie etc.) kritisiert (Paradis 1994: 408 f.; vgl. auch die Kritik von Paradis 1995d an Wuillemin et al. 1994). Letzterer Punkt ist insofern von entscheidender Bedeutung, als die Hypothese einer stärker rechtshemisphärischen Verarbeitung für pragmatische und nonverbale Aspekte der Kommunikation zutreffen könnte, nicht aber für die grammatische Verarbeitung (Paradis 1995a). Wenngleich Paradis (1994: 409) die Hypothese vertritt, die Sprachen bei Bilingualen würden im selben Maße von der linken Hemisphäre bedient wie bei Monolingualen, so spekuliert er doch, dass Sprecher sich in L2, vor allem bei weniger guter Beherrschung, stärker auf pragmatische Aspekte – Interferenzen aus dem situativen Kontext, Weltwissen, emotionale Prosodie usw. – verlassen könnten, um Defizite ihrer morphosyntaktischen Kompetenz in L2 zu kompensieren. Für diese pragmatischen Fähigkeiten wird aber eine stärker rechtshemisphärische Repräsentation angenommen (auch Paradis 1995b: 6).

Vor allem gibt es nicht die geringste klinische Evidenz für eine stärkere Asymmetrie der Sprachrepräsentation bei Bilingualen als bei Monolingualen (Mendelsohn 1988; Zatorre 1989; Paradis 1990: 580). In ihrer Analyse einer Reihe von aphasiologischen Studien zur Rolle der rechten Hemisphäre bei Bilingualen (u. a. Albert & Obler 1978) zeigt Doreen Solin (1989: 113), dass diesen fundamentale Fehlinterpretationen der Daten zugrundeliegen und schlägt vor, diese Hypothese aufzugeben. Auch Rumjahn Hoosain (1992) berichtet in einem Überblick über experimentelle und klinische Studien zu Chinesisch-Englisch Bilingualen, es fänden sich keine Anhaltspunkte für eine stärkere Beteiligung der rechten Hemisphäre an der Sprachverarbeitung als bei Monolingualen.

Studien zur Inzidenzrate gekreuzter Aphasien (→ § 1.2) bei Mehrsprachigen führten zu der Auffassung, diese sei etwas höher als bei Monolingualen, woraus der Schluss auf eine stärker bilaterale Repräsentation von Sprache bei Mehrsprachigen gezogen wurde. Doch sprechen die nichtsignifikanten Unterschiede, die sich u. a. bei Prithika Chary (1986: 195) fanden, nach Solin (1989: 112 f.) gegen diese Hypothese. Vergleichbare Ergebnisse berichten auch Karanth & Rangamani (1988) und Ramamurthi & Chari (1993), so dass man bei derzeitigem Stand der Forschung davon auszugehen hat, dass es keine statistisch signifikant höhere Inzidenzrate gekreuzter Aphasien bei Bilingualen als bei Monolingualen und mithin keinen Hinweis auf stärker bilaterale Verarbeitung bei ersteren gibt (Paradis 1990: 580).

3. Zitierte Literatur

Ahlsén, Elisabeth. 1993. „On agrammatism and telegram style: An exemplifying discussion of Swedish data". *Nordic Journal of Linguistics* 16: 137–152.

Ahlsén, Elisabeth & Nespoulous, J.-L. & Dordain, M. & Stark, J. & Jarema, G. & Kadzielawa, D. & Obler, L. K. & Fitzpatrick, P. M. 1996. „Noun phrase production by agrammatic patients: a cross-linguistic approach". *Aphasiology* 10: 543–559.

Albert, Martin L. & Obler, Loraine K. 1978. *The Bilingual Brain: Neuropsychological and Neurolinguistic Aspects of Bilingualism*. New York: Acad. Press.

Badecker, William & Caramazza, Alfonso. 1993. „Disorders of lexical morphology in aphasia". In: Blanken, G. & Dittmann, J. & Grimm, H. & Marshall, J. C. & Wallesch, C.-W. (eds.). *Linguistic Disorders and Pathologies*. (HSK, 8). Berlin/New York: de Gruyter, 181–186.

Bastiaanse, Roelien & Edwards, Susan & Kiss, K. 1996. „Fluent aphasia in three languages: aspects of spontaneous speech". *Aphasiology* 10: 561–575.

Bates, Elizabeth & Friederici, Angela D. & Wulfeck, Beverly. 1987. „Grammatical morphology in aphasia: Evidence from three languages". *Cortex* 23: 545–574.

Bates, Elizabeth & Friederici, Angela D. & Wulfeck, Beverly B. & Juarez, Larry A. 1988. „On the preservation of word order in aphasia: Cross-linguistic evidence". *Brain and Language* 33: 323–364.

Bates, Elizabeth & Wulfeck, Beverly. 1989. „Comparative aphasiology: A cross-linguistic approach to language breakdown". *Aphasiology* 3: 111–142.

Bates, Elizabeth & Chen, Sylvia & Tzeng, Ovid & Li, Ping & Opie, Meiti. 1991a. „The noun-verb problem in Chinese aphasia". *Brain and Language* 41: 203–233.

Bates, Elizabeth & Wulfeck, Beverly & MacWhinney, Brian. 1991b. „Cross-linguistic research in aphasia: An overview". *Brain and Language* 41: 123–148.

Bayles, Kathryn A. 1993. „Pathology of language behavior in dementia". In: Blanken, G. & Dittmann, J. & Grimm, H. & Marshall, J. C. & Wallesch, C.-W. (eds.). *Linguistic Disorders and Pathologies.* (HSK, 8.) Berlin/New York: de Gruyter, 388–409.

Berquier, Anne & Ashton, Roderick. 1992. „Language lateralization in bilinguals: more not less is needed: a reply to Paradis (1990)". *Brain and Language* 43: 528–533.

Besner, Derek & Hildebrandt, Nancy. 1987. „Orthographic and phonological codes in the oral reading of Japanese Kana". *Journal of Experimental Psychology: Learning, Memory, and Cognition* 13: 335–343.

Blanken, Gerhard. 1990. „Formal paraphasias: A single case study". *Brain and Language* 38: 534–554.

Blanken, Gerhard & Dittmann, Jürgen & Haas, J.-Christian & Wallesch, Claus-W. 1988. „Producing speech automatisms (recurring utterances): Looking for what is left". *Aphasiology* 2: 545–556.

Buchanan, Lori & Besner, Derek. 1993. „Reading aloud: Evidence for the use of a whole word non-semantic pathway". *Canadian Journal of Experimental Psychology* 47: 133–152.

Chary, Prithika. 1986. „Aphasia in a multilingual society: A preliminary study". In: Jyotsna Vaid (ed.). *Language Processing in Bilinguals.* Hillsdale, NJ: Erlbaum, 183–197.

Cheng, Chao-Ming & Yang, Mu-Jang. 1989. „Lateralization in the visual perception of Chinese characters and words". *Brain and Language* 36: 669–689.

Chomsky, Noam. 1965. *Aspects of the theory of syntax.* Cambridge, MA: MIT Press.

De Bleser, Ria. 1988. „Localisation of aphasia: Science or fiction". In: Denes, G. & Semenza, C. & Bisiacchi, P. (eds.). *Perspectives on Cognitive Neuropsychology.* Hove: Erlbaum, 161–188.

De Bleser, Ria & Bayer, Josef. 1993. „Syntactic disorders in aphasia". In: Blanken, G. & Dittmann, J. & Grimm, H. & Marshall, J. C. & Wallesch, C.-W. (eds.). *Linguistic Disorders and Pathologies.* (HSK, 8.) Berlin/New York: de Gruyter, 160–169.

De Bleser, Ria & Bayer, Josef & Luzzatti, Claudio. 1996. „Linguistic theory and morphosyntactic impairments in German and Italian aphasics". *Journal of Neurolinguistics* 9: 175–185.

De Vreese, Luc P. & Motta, Massimo & Toschi, Andrea. 1988. „Compulsive and paradoxical translation behaviour in a case of presenile dementia of the Alzheimer type". *Journal of Neurolinguistics* 3: 233–259.

Dittmann, Jürgen. 1991. „Phonematische Störungen bei Aphasie". In: Blanken, G. (ed.). *Einführung in die Linguistische Aphasiologie. Theorie und Praxis.* Freiburg/Br.: HochschulVerl., 43–88.

Ehinger, Annette & Lutzenberger, Claudia & Dittmann, Jürgen & Blanken, Gerthard. 1990. „Spontane Sprachproduktion bei Wernicke-Aphasie: eine Pilotstudie". *Neurolinguistik* 4: 69–81.

Ervin-Tripp, Susan & Osgood, Charles E. 1954/1986. „Zweitsprachenerwerb und Bilingualismus". In: Raith, Joachim et al. (eds.). *Grundlagen der Mehrsprachigkeitsforschung.* (ZDL, Beiheft 52.) Stuttgart: Steiner, 12–18.

Friederici, Angela D. & Saddy, Douglas. 1993. „Disorders of word class processing in aphasia". In: Blanken, G. & Dittmann, J. & Grimm, H. & Marshall, J. C. & Wallesch, C.-W. (eds.). *Linguistic Disorders and Pathologies.* (HSK, 8.) Berlin/New York: de Gruyter, 169–181.

Friederici, Angela D. & Weissenborn, Jürgen & Kail, M. 1991. „Pronoun comprehension in aphasia: a comparison of three languages". *Brain and Language* 41: 289–310.

Gomez-Tortosa, Estrella & Martin, Eileen M. & Gaviria, Moises & Charbel, Fady & Ausman, James I. 1995. „Selective deficit of one language in a bilingual patient following surgery in the left perisylvian area". *Brain and Language* 48: 320–325.

Gomez-Tortosa, Estrella & Martin, Eileen M. & Gaviria, Moises & Charbel, Fady & Ausman, James I. 1996. „Selective deficit of one language in a bilingual patient: Replies to Paradis and Hines". *Brain and Language* 54: 174–175.

Graetz, Patty & De Bleser, Ria & Willmes, Klaus. 1992. *Akense Afasie Test.* Lisse: Swets & Zeitlinger.

Green, David W. 1986. „Control, activation and resource: A framework and a model for the control of speech in bilinguals". *Brain and Language* 27: 210–223.

Grodzinsky, Yosef. 1984. „The syntactic characterization of agrammatism". *Cognition* 16: 99–120.

Gurd, Jennifer M. & Marshall, John C. 1993. „Semantic disorders in aphasia". In: Blanken, G. & Dittmann, J. & Grimm, H. & Marshall, J. C. & Wallesch, C.-W. (eds.). *Linguistic Disorders and Pathologies.* (HSK, 8.) Berlin/New York: de Gruyter, 153–160.

Hamasaki, Tomoyuki & Yasojima, K. & Kakita, K. & Masaki, H. & Ishino, S. & Murakami, M. & Yamaki, T. & Ueda, S. 1995. „Alexie-agraphie pour l'écriture kanji après lésion temporale postéro-inférieure gauche". *Revue Neurologique* 151: 16–23.

Hasuike, Reiko & Tzeng, Ovid & Hung, Daisy. 1986. „Script effects and cerebral lateralization: The case of Chinese characters". In: Vaid, Jyotsna (ed.). *Language Processing in Bilinguals.* Hillsdale/NJ: Erlbaum, 275–288.

Hatta, Takeshi. 1977. „Recognition of Japanese kanji in the left and right visual fields". *Neuropsychologia* 15: 685–688.

Hines, Terence M. 1996. „Failure to demonstrate selective deficit in the native language following surgery to the left perisylvian area". *Brain and Language* 54: 168–169.

Hirose, Takehiko. 1992. „Recognition of Japanese Kana words in priming tasks". *Perceptual and Motor Skills* 75: 907–913.

Hittmair-Delazer, Magarete & Andree, Barbara & Semenza, Carlo & De Bleser, Ria & Benke, Thomas. 1994. „Naming by German compounds". *Journal of Neurolinguistics* 8: 27–41.

Hoosain, Rumjahn. 1992. „Differential cerebral lateralization of Chinese-English bilingual functions?" In: Harris, Richard Jackson (ed.). *Cognitive Processing in Bilinguals* (Advances in Psychology, 83.) Amsterdam: North-Holland, 561–571.

Hu, Chieh Fang & Catts, Hugh W. 1993. „Phonological recoding as a universal process? Evidence from beginning readers of Chinese". *Reading and Writing. An Interdisciplinary Journal* 5: 325–337.

Huber, Walter. 1997. „Alexie und Agraphie". In: Hartje, Wolfgang & Poeck, K. (eds.). *Klinische Neuropsychologie.* Stuttgart/New York: Thieme, 169–190.

Huber, Walter & Poeck, Klaus & Weniger, Dorothea & Willmes, Klaus. 1983. *Der Aachener Aphasietest.* Göttingen: Verl. für Psychologie Hogrefe.

Huber, Walter & Schlenck, Klaus-Jürgen. 1988. „Satzverschränkungen bei Wernicke-Aphasie". In: Blanken, G. & Dittmann, J. & Wallesch, C.-W. (eds.). *Sprachproduktionsmodelle.* Freiburg/Br.: HochschulVerl., 111–149.

Huber, Walter & Poeck, Klaus & Weniger, Dorothea. 1997. „Aphasie". In: Hartje, Wolfgang & Poeck, K. (eds.). *Klinische Neuropsychologie.* Stuttgart/New York: Thieme, 80–143.

Iwata, Makoto. 1984. „Kanji vs Kana: Neuropsychological correlates of the Japanese writing system". *Trends in Neurosciences* 7: 290–293.

Juncos-Rabadàn, Onémiso. 1994. „The assessment of bilingualism in normal aging with the bilingual aphasia test". *Journal of Neurolinguistics* 8: 67–74.

Junqué, Carme & Vendrell, Pere & Vendrell, Josep M. 1995. „Differential impairments and specific phenomena in 50 Catalan-Spanish bilingual aphasic patients". In: Paradis, Michel (ed.). *Aspects of Bilingual Aphasia.* Oxford: Pergamon, 177–209.

Karanth, Prathibha & Rangamani, G. N. 1988. „Crossed aphasia in multilinguals". *Brain and Language* 34: 169–180.

Kawahata, Nobuya & Nagata, Ken. 1988. „Alexia with agraphia due to the left posterior temporal lobe lesion: Neuropsychological analysis and its pathogenetic mechanisms". *Brain and Language* 33: 296–310.

Kay, Janice. 1993. „Acquired disorders of reading". In: Blanken, G. & Dittmann, J. & Grimm, H. & Marshall, J. C. & Wallesch, C.-W. (eds.). *Linguistic Disorders and Pathologies. An International Handbook.* (HSK, 8.) Berlin/New York: de Gruyter, 251–262.

Kim, Karl H. S. & Relkin, Norman R. & Lee, Kyoung-Min & Hirsch, Joy. 1997. „Distinct cortical areas associated with native and second languages". *Nature* 388: 171–174.

Klein, Denise & Zatorre, Robert J. & Milner, Brenda & Meyer, Ernst & Evans, Alan C. 1995. „The neural substrates of bilingual language processing: evidence from positron emission tomography". In: Paradis, Michel (ed.). *Aspects of Bilingual Aphasia.* Oxford: Pergamon, 23–36.

Klein, Wolfgang. 1984. *Zweitspracherwerb. Eine Einführung.* Königstein/Ts.: Athenäum-Verl.

Koda, Keiko. 1990. „The use of L1 reading strategies in L2 reading". *SSLA* 12: 393–410.

Lambert, Wallace E. 1969. „Psychological studies of the interdependencies of the bilingual's languages". In: Puhvel, Jean (ed.). *Substance and Structure of Language.* Berkeley: Univ. of California Press, 99–125.

Lambert, Wallace E. & Fillenbaum, S. 1959. „A pilot study of aphasia among bilinguals". *Canadian Journal of Psychology* 13: 28–34.

Lebrun, Yvan. 1983. „Cerebral dominance for language: A neurolinguistic approach". *Folia Phoniatrica* 35: 13–39.

Lebrun, Yvan. 1991. „Polyglotte Reaktionen". *Neurolinguistik* 5: 1–9.

Lebrun, Yvan. 1995. „The study of bilingual aphasia: Pitres' legacy". In: Paradis, Michel (ed.). *Aspects of Bilingual Aphasia.* Oxford: Pergamon, 11–21.

Leischner, Anton. 1979. *Aphasien und Sprachentwicklungsstörungen. Klinik und Behandlung.* Stuttgart/New York: Thieme.

Leischner, Anton. 1988. „Die Aphasien der Polyglotten und ihre Beziehungen zur Vergleichenden Aphasieforschung. Beobachtungen an einer tschechisch-deutschen Aphasikerin". *Neurolinguistik* 2: 101–125.

Leong, Che Kan & Wong, Stephen & Wong, Angie & Hiscock, Merrill. 1985. „Differential cerebral involvement in perceiving Chinese characters: Levels of processing approach". *Brain and Language* 26: 131–145.

Leong, Che Kan & Tamaoka, Katsuo. 1995. „Use of phonological information in processing kanji and katakana by skilled and less skilled Japanese readers". *Reading and Writing* 7: 377–393.

Li, Jie. 1996. „Das chinesische Schriftsystem". In: Günther, Hartmut & Ludwig, Otto (eds.). *Schrift und Schriftlichkeit. Writing and Its Use.* (HSK, 10.2.) Berlin/New York: de Gruyter, 1404–1412.

Lorch, Marjorie Perlman. 1986. *A Cross-Linguistic Study of Verb Inflections in Agrammatism.* Boston University Graduate School (Dissertation).

Luzzatti, Claudio & Willmes, Klaus & De Bleser, Ria. 1991. *Aachener Aphasie Test (AAT). Versione Italiana.* Firenze: Organizzazioni specioli.

MacWhinney, Brian & Osmán-Sági, Judit. 1991a. „Inflectional marking in Hungarian aphasics". *Brain and Language* 41: 165–183.

MacWhinney, Brian & Osmán-Sági, Judit & Slobin, Dan I. 1991b. „Sentence comprehension in aphasia in two clear case-marking languages". *Brain and Language* 41: 234–149.

Malin, Jean-Pierre & Widdig, Walter & Duncan, David & Sindern, Eckart. 1994. „Gekreuzte Aphasie oder das Problem der cerebralen Organisation von Sprache. Linguistische Analyse und PET-Studie". In: Ohlendorf, Ingeborg M. et al. (eds.). *Sprache und Gehirn.* Freiburg/Br.: HochschulVerlag, 55–62.

Manuel-Dupont, Sonia & Ardila, Alfredo & Rosseli, Monica & Puente, Antonio E. 1992. „Bilingualism". In: Puente, Antonio E. & McCaffrey, R. J. (eds.). *Handbook of Neuropsychological Assessment: A Biopsychosocial Perspective.* New York: Plenum Press, 193–210.

Mendelsohn, Susan. 1988. „Language lateralization in bilinguals: Facts and fantasy". *Journal of Neurolinguistics* 3: 261–292.

Menn, Lise & Obler, Loraine, K. (eds.). 1990. *Agrammatic Aphasia. A Cross-Language Narrative Sourcebook.* 3 vols. Amsterdam/Philadelphia: Benjamins.

Menn, Lise & Obler, Loraine K. 1990a. „Methodology. Data collection, presentation, and guide to interpretation". In Menn, Lise & Obler, L. K. (eds.). *Agrammatic Aphasia.* Vol. 1. Amsterdam: Benjamins, 13–36.

Menn, Lise & Obler, Loraine K. 1990b. „Crosslanguage data and theories of agrammatism". In: Menn, Lise & Obler, L. K. (eds.). *Agrammatic Aphasia. A Cross-Language Narrative Sourcebook.* Amsterdam: Benjamins, 1369–1389.

Menn, Lise & O'Connor, Michael P. & Obler, Loraine K. & Holland, Audrey. 1995. *Non-Fluent Aphasia in a Multilingual World.* (Studies in Speech Pathology and Clinical Linguistics, 5.) Amsterdam: Benjamins.

Mesulam, M.-Marsel. 1982. „Slowly progressive aphasia without generalised dementia". *Annals of Neurology* 11: 592–598.

Nicol, Janet L. & Jakubowicz, C. & Goldblum, Marie-Claire. 1996. „Sensitivity to grammatical marking in English-speaking and French-speaking non-fluent aphasics". *Aphasiology* 10: 593–622.

Niemi, Jussi & Laine, Matti. 1989. „The English language bias in neurolinguistics: new languages give new perspectives". *Aphasiology* 3: 155–159.

Niemi, Jussi & Laine, Matti & Koivuselkä-Sallinen, P. 1990. „A fluent morphological agrammatic in an inflectional language?" In: Nespoulous, Jean-Luc & Villiard, P. (eds.). *Morphology, Phonology, and Aphasia.* New York: Springer, 95–107.

Obler, Loraine K. 1996. „Early cross-language discussion of agrammatism". *Aphasiology* 10: 533–542.

Obler, Loraine K. & Mahecha, Nancy R. 1991. „First language loss in bilingual and polyglot aphasics". In: Seliger, Herbert W. & Vago, R. M. (eds.). *First Language Attrition.* Cambridge: Cambridge Univ. Press, 53–65.

Obler, Loraine K. & Centeno, Jos & Eng, Nancy. 1995. „Bilingual and polyglot aphasia". In: Menn, Lise & O'Connor, M. & Obler, L. K. Holland, A. (eds). *Non-Fluent Aphasia in a Multilingual World.* With contributions by J. Centeno et al. Amsterdam: Benjamins, 132–143.

Osaka, Noayuki. 1989. „Eye fixation and saccade during kana and kanji text reading: Comparison of English and Japanese text processing". *Bulletin of the Psychonomic Society* 27: 548–550.

Osaka, Naoyuki. 1990. „Spread of visual attention during fixation while reading japanese text". In: Groner, Rudolf & d'Ydewalle, G. & Parham, R. (eds.). *From Eye to Mind. Information Acquisition in Perception, Search, and Reading.* Amsterdam: North-Holland, 167–178.

Palij, Michael & Aaronson, Doris. 1992. „The role of language background in cognitive processing". In: Harris, Richard Jackson (ed.). *Cognitive Processing in Bilinguals.* Amsterdam: North-Holland, 63–87.

Paradis, Michel. 1977. „Bilingualism and aphasia". In: Whitaker, Haiganoosh & Whitaker, H. A. (eds.). *Studies in Neurolinguistics,* Vol. 3. New York: Acad. Press, 65–121.

Paradis, Michel. 1987. „The neurofunctional modularity of cognitive skills: Evidence from Japanese alexia and polyglot aphasia". In: Keller, Eric & Gopnik, M. (eds.). *Motor and Sensory Processes of Language.* Hillsdale/NJ: Erlbaum, 277–289.

Paradis, Michel. 1988. „Recent developments in the study of agrammatism: their import for the assessment of bilingual aphasia". *Journal of Neurolinguistics* 3: 127–160.

Paradis, Michel. 1989a. *Bilingual Aphasia Test (German Version). Stimulus Book.* Hillsdale/NJ: Erlbaum.

Paradis, Michel. 1989b. „Bilingual and polyglot aphasia". In: Boller, François & Grafman, J. (eds.). *Handbook of Neuropsychology,* Vol. 2. Amsterdam: Elsevier, 117–140.

Paradis, Michel. 1990. „Language lateralization in bilinguals: Enough already". *Brain and Language* 39: 576–586.

Paradis, Michel. 1992. „The Loch Ness Monster approach to bilingual language lateralization: a response to Berquier and Ashton (1990)". *Brain and Language* 43: 534—537.

Paradis, Michel. 1993. „Multilingualism and Aphasia". In: Blanken, G. & Dittmann, J. & Grimm, H. & Marshall, J. C. & Wallesch, C.-W. (eds.). *Linguistic Disorders and Pathologies. An International Handbook.* (HSK, 8.) Berlin/New York: de Gruyter, 278—288.

Paradis, Michel. 1994. „Neurolinguistic aspects of implicit and explicit memory: Implications for bilingualism and SLA". In: Ellis, Nick C. (ed.). *Implicit and Explicit Learning of Languages.* London: Acad. Press, 393—419.

Paradis, Michel. 1995a. „Foreword". In: Menn, Lise & O'Connor, M. & Obler, L. K. & Holland, A. *Non-Fluent Aphasia in a Multilingual world. With contributions by Jos Centeno et al.* Amsterdam/Philadelphia: Benjamins, xix—xxi.

Paradis, Michel. 1995b. „Introduction: The need for distinctions". In: Paradis, Michel (ed.). *Aspects of Bilingual Aphasia.* Oxford: Pergamon, 1—9.

Paradis, Michel. 1995c. „Epilogue: Bilingual aphasia 100 years later: consensus and controversies". In: Paradis, Michel (ed.). *Aspects of Bilingual Aphasia.* Oxford: Pergamon, 211—223.

Paradis, Michel. 1995d. „Another sighting of differential language laterality in multilinguals, this time in Loch Tok Pisin: Comments on Wuillemin, Richardson, and Lynch 1994". *Brain and Language* 49: 173—186.

Paradis, Michel. 1996. „Selective deficit in one language is not a demonstration of different anatomical representation: Comment on Gomez-Tortosa et al. (1995)". *Brain and Language* 54: 170—173.

Paradis, Michel & Goldblum, Marie-Claire & Abidi, Raouf. 1982. „Alternate antagonism with paradoxical translation behavior in two bilingual aphasics". *Brain and Language* 15: 55—69.

Paradis, Michel & Hagiwara, Hiroko & Hildebrandt, Nancy. 1985. *Neurolinguistic Aspects of the Japanese Writing System.* Orlando: Acad. Press.

Paradis, Michel & Goldblum, Marie-Claire. 1989. „Selective crossed aphasia in a trilingual aphasic patient followed by reciprocal antagonism". *Brain and Language* 36: 62—75.

Penfield, Wilder & Roberts, Lamar. 1959. *Speech and Brain Mechanisms.* Princeton, NJ: Princeton Univ. Press. (4. print New York 1976).

Perecman, Ellen. 1984. „Spontaneous translation and language mixing in a polyglot aphasic". *Brain and Language* 23: 43—63.

Perfetti, Charles & Zhang, Sulan. 1991. „Phonological processes in reading Chinese characters". *Journal of Experimental Psychology: Learning, Memory and Cognition* 17: 633—643.

Perfetti, Charles & Zhang, Sulan. 1995. „Very early phonological activation in Chinese reading". *Journal of Experimental Psychology: Learning, Memory and Cognition* 21: 24—33.

Peuser, Günter & Leischner, Anton. 1974. „Störungen der phonetischen Schrift bei einem Aphasiker". *Neuropsychologia* 12: 557—560.

Qian, Gaoyin & Reinking, David & Yang, Ronglan. 1994. „The effects of character complexity on recognizing Chinese characters". *Contemporary Educational Psychology* 19: 155—166.

Ramamurthi, B. & Chari, P. 1993. „Aphasia in bilinguals". *Acta Neurochirurgica — Supplementum* 56: 59—66.

Rastatter, Michael P. & Scukanec, Gail & Grilliot, Jeff. 1989. „Hemispheric specialization for processing Chinese characters: Some evidence from lexical decision vocal reaction times". *Perceptual and Motor Skills* 69: 1083—1089.

Roeltgen, David P. & Rapcsak, Steven Z. 1993. „Acquired disorders of writing and spelling". In: Blanken, G. & Dittmann, J. & Grimm, H. & Marshall, J. C. & Wallesch, C.-W. (eds.). *Linguistic Disorders and Pathologies. An International Handbook.* (HSK, 8.) Berlin/New York: de Gruyter, 262—278.

Rosenbek, John C. 1993. „Speech apraxia". In: Blanken, G. & Dittmann, J. & Grimm, H. & Marshall, J. C. & Wallesch, C.-W. (eds.). *Linguistic Disorders and Pathologies. An International Handbook.* (HSK, 8.) Berlin/New York: de Gruyter, 443—452.

Sasanuma, Sumiko & Fujimura, Osamu. 1971. „Selective impairment of phonetic and non-phonetic transcription of words in Japanese aphasic patients. Kana vs. Kanji in visual recognition and writing". *Cortex* 7: 1—18.

Sasanuma, Sumiko & Fujimura, Osamu. 1972. „An analysis of writing errors in Japanese aphasic patients: Kanji vs. Kana words". *Cortex* 8: 265—282.

Sasanuma, Sumiko & Itoh, M. & Mori, K. & Kobayashi, Y. 1977. „Tachistoscopic recognition of kana and kanji words". *Neuropsychologia* 15: 547—553.

Sasanuma, Sumiko & Sakuma, Naoko & Kitano, Kunitaka. 1992. „Reading kanji without semantics: Evidence from a longitudinal study of dementia". *Cognitive Neuropsychology* 9: 465—486.

Sasanuma, Sumiko & Park, Hea Suk. 1995. „Patterns of language deficit in two Korean-Japanese bilingual aphasic patients — A clinical report". In: Paradis, Michel (ed.). *Aspects of Bilingual Aphasia.* Oxford: Pergamon, 111—122.

Seidenberg, Mark S. 1985. „The time course of phonological code activation in two writing systems". *Cognition* 19: 1—30.

Shimada, Mutsuo & Otsuka, Akira. 1981. „Functional hemispheric differences in kanji processing in Japanese". *Japanese Psychological Review* 24: 472—489.

Simons, Berthold & Stachowiak, Franz-Josef & Stadie, Nicole. 1988. „Vergleichende Aphasieforschung. Zum 80. Geburtstag von Anton Leischner". *Neurolinguistik* 2: 41—50.

Slobin, Dan I. 1991. "Aphasia in Turkish: Speech production in Broca's and Wernicke's patients". *Brain and Language* 41: 149−164.

Solin, Doreen. 1989. "The systematic misrepresentation of bilingual-crossed aphasia data and its consequences". *Brain and Language* 36: 92−116.

Springer, Sally P. & Deutsch, Georg. ³1995. *Linkes − rechtes Gehirn*. Heidelberg: Spektrum, Akad. Verl.

Stalph, Jürgen. 1996. "Das japanische Schriftsystem". In: Günther, Hartmut & Ludwig, Otto (eds.). *Schrift und Schriftlichkeit. Writing and Its Use*. (HSK, 10.2.) Berlin/New York: de Gruyter, 1413−1427.

Stark, Jaqueline Ann & Dressler, Wolfgang U. 1990. "Agrammatism in German: Two case studies". In: Menn, Lise & Obler, L. K. (eds.). *Agrammatic Aphasia. A Cross-Language Narrative Sourcebook. Vol. 1*. Amsterdam: Benjamins, 281−441.

Stark, Jacquelin & Stark, K.-Heinz & Pons, Christiane & Hager, Manuela. 1994. "Vienna, une ville molto bella por todos Personen der: Wernicke-Aphasie bei einem polyglotten Wiener Touristenführer". In: Ohlendorf, Ingeborg M. et al. (eds.). *Sprache und Gehirn*. Freiburg/Br.: Hochschul-Verlag, 79−96.

Tanaka, Yasufumi & Yamadori, Atsushi & Murata, Shinji. 1987. "Selective Kana agraphia: A case report". *Cortex* 23: 679−684.

Tesak, Jürgen. 1990. "Agrammatismus. Ergebnisse und Probleme der Forschung". *Neurolinguistik* 4: 1−41.

Tesak, Jürgen. 1994. "Dutch telegraphese". *Linguistics* 32: 325−344.

Tesak, Jürgen & Dittmann, Jürgen. 1991. "Telegraphic style in normals and aphasics". *Linguistics* 29: 1111−1137.

Tesak, Jürgen & Ahlsén, Elisabeth & Göri, Gábor & Koivuselkä-Sallinen, Paivi & Niemi, Jussi & Tonelli, Livia. 1995. "Patterns of ellipsis in telegraphese: A study of six languages". *Folia Linguistica* 29: 297-316.

Tesak, Jürgen & Niemi, Jussi. 1997. "Telegraphese and agrammatism: a cross-linguistic study". *Aphasiology* 11: 146−155.

Tzeng, Ovid J. L. & Hung, Daisy L. & Wang, William S.-Y. 1977. "Speech recording in reading Chinese characters". *Journal of Experimental Psychology: Human Learning and Memory* 3: 621−630.

Tzeng, Ovid J. L. & Hung, Daisy L. & Cotton, Bill & Wang, Willian S.-Y. 1979. "Visual lateralisation effect in reading Chinese characters". *Nature* 382: 499−501.

Tzeng, Ovid J. L. & Chen, Sylvia & Hung, Daisy L. 1991. "The classifier problem in Chinese aphasia". *Brain and Language* 41: 184−202.

Vaid, Jyotsna & Pandit, Rama. 1991. "Sentence interpretation in normal and aphasic Hindi speakers". *Brain and Language* 41: 250−274.

Wallesch, Claus-W. & Kertesz, Andrew. 1993. "Clinical symptoms and syndroms of aphasia". In: Blanken, G. & Dittmann, J. & Grimm, H. & Marshall, J. C. & Wallesch, C.-W. (eds.). *Linguistic Disorders and Pathologies. An International Handbook*. (HSK, 8.) Berlin/New York: de Gruyter, 98−119.

Willmes, Klaus & Poeck, Klaus. 1993. "To what extent can aphasic syndroms be localized?" *Brain* 116: 1527−1540.

Wuillemin, Dianne & Richardson, Barry & Lynch, John. 1994. "Right hemisphere involvement in processing later-learned languages in multilinguals". *Brain and Language* 46: 620−636.

Wydell, Taeko N. & Patterson, Karalyn E. & Humphreys, Glyn W. 1993. "Phonologically mediated access to meaning for kanji: Is a 'rows' still a 'rose' in Japanese kanji?" *Journal of Experimental Psychology: Learning, Memory and Cognition* 19: 491−514.

Xu, Yi. 1991. "Depth of phonological recoding in short-term memory". *Memory and Cognition* 19: 263−273.

Yiu, Edwin M.-L. & Worrall, Linda E. 1996. "Agrammatic production: a cross-linguistic comparison of English and Cantonese". *Aphasiology* 10: 623−647.

Zatorre, Robert J. 1989. "On the representation of multiple languages in the brain: Old problems and new directions". *Brain and Language* 36: 127−147.

Ziegler, Wolfram. 1991. "Sprechapraktische Störungen bei Aphasie". In: Blanken, G. (ed.). *Einführung in die linguistische Aphasiologie. Theorie und Praxis*. Freiburg/Br.: HochschulVerlag, 89−119.

Jürgen Dittmann, Freiburg i.Br.
(Deutschland)

10. Gebärdensprachforschung

1. Zur Sozio- und Psycholinguistik der Gebärdensprachen
2. Zur Geschichte der Gebärdensprachforschung
3. Gebärdensprache und Gestik/Mimik
4. Epistemologische und methodologische Überlegungen
5. Zur Beschreibung der Gebärdensprache
6. Lexikon
7. Diskurs
8. Zum Vergleich zwischen Gebärden- und Lautsprache
9. Zitierte Literatur

1. Zur Sozio- und Psycholinguistik der Gebärdensprachen

Die besondere Situation der Gehörlosen und ihrer optischen Sprachen macht es notwendig, diese kurz zu umreißen.

Gebärdensprachen (in der Folge mit 'GS' abgekürzt) sind dadurch entstanden, daß Gehörlose, denen eine Lautsprache (in der Folge mit 'LS' abgekürzt) akustisch nicht zugänglich war, optische Kommunikationssysteme entwickelten. GS stellen natürliche Sprachen dar, welche an die Bedingungen des optischen Kanals angepaßt sind. Sie sind von anderen optischen Kommunikationssystemen, wie 'Lautsprachbegleitendem Gebärden' (setzt eine LS Morphem für Morphem in optische Zeichen – z.B. 'Signed English' – um), 'Lautsprachunterstützender Gebärde' (kodiert nur wichtige Informationen aus der LS-Produktion; Wisch 1990: 185–90) und Fingeralphabeten (kodieren Buchstaben geschriebener LS) zu unterscheiden.

Bei Ausfall des akustischen verbessert die kompensatorische Nutzung des optischen Kanals die kommunikativen Möglichkeiten Gehörloser und schwer Hörbehinderter entscheidend. Aufgrund der 'Streusiedlung' der Gehörlosen und der Politik der Integration der Gehörlosen in die 'hörende' Gesellschaft bieten sich spezielle bilinguale Konzepte der Gehörlosenbildung an (Holzinger 1995, Dotter & Holzinger 1995b). Die Realität sieht freilich anders aus: Gehörlose waren, weil sie die LS nicht oder nur schlecht beherrschten, seit jeher eine auffällige Behindertengruppe (vgl. die Alltagsmeinung, daß LS 'den Menschen ausmache') – in sozialkommunikativer Hinsicht wurden sie dagegen wegen der Kommunikationsbarrieren kaum wahrgenommen. Die den Gehörlosen gegenüber angewandten Bildungsmethoden sind davon z.T. gekennzeichnet: Nicht wenige auch heute noch gängige Theorien und praktische Ansätze sprechen sich gegen den systematischen Einsatz der GS aus. Manche bezweifeln auch den Sprachstatus von GS bzw. ihre ausreichende Leistungsfähigkeit im Vergleich zu LS. Wir stehen damit vor der einmaligen Situation, daß Wissenschaftler sich mit wissenschaftlichen Argumenten gegen den Gebrauch bzw. die Anerkennung einer Minderheitensprache wenden (Dotter 1991). Obwohl die meisten Argumente von Nicht-Linguisten kamen (Ausnahme: Gipper 1980), zeitigten sie z.T. bis heute bedeutende Auswirkungen auf die Gehörlosenbildung (Wisch 1990: 132–53; Fischer & Lane 1993).Tendenzen in Richtung der Verwendung von GS in der Gehörlosenbildung verstärken sich allerdings zunehmend.

Die in der Vergangenheit z.T. extreme Isolation einzelner Gehörloser bzw. Gehörlosengemeinschaften, sowie die aus mangelnden Kommunikationsmöglichkeiten und Informationen erwachsenden psychosozialen Auswirkungen haben zu einigen schwerwiegenden Folgeproblemen geführt, welche die sprachwissenschaftliche Arbeit an GS beeinflussen:

1. Linguisten finden vor allem lexikalisch sehr variantenreiche, kleinräumig gültige bzw. stark differierende individuelle Systeme vor, was die Erstellung von Standard-Lexika für einzelne GS erschwert.

2. Manche Gehörlose entwickeln nur zu ganz bestimmten Dolmetschern ein Vertrauensverhältnis; manche der in § 1.1. genannten Varianten stellen für Dolmetscher, die nicht Kinder von Gehörlosen sind, tatsächlich ein Problem dar.

3. Mangelnde Leistungsfähigkeit individueller Sprachsysteme und teilweises Fehlen von Fachwortschatz: Vielen Gehörlosen-Gemeinschaften und vor allem einzelnen Gehörlosen standen nicht die Möglichkeiten zur Verfügung, ihre Sprachen weiterzuentwickeln (vgl. Woll 1994; zum sich möglicherweise zur 'Kontaktsprache' unter Gehörlosen entwickelnden „International Sign" Supalla & Webb 1995).

4. GS unterliegen – wie LS-Minderheitensprachen – dem Sprachkontakt mit den um-

gebenden, dominanten LS und einer allfälligen LS-Schriftkultur (Ebbinghaus & Heßmann 1990 und 1994/95, Lucas 1994). Beispiele für den Einfluß von LS bei Neubildungen: Lehnübersetzungen, wie EIERSTOCK aus EI + STOCK (zum Schlagen); bei Eigennamen: Verwendung ablese-identischer oder -ähnlicher Gebärden (DONNER für 'Dotter' oder PIDGEON für 'Pidgin'; Dubuisson & Desrosiers 1994); zum Mundbild siehe 5.2.1 [Glossen für Gebärden erscheinen in Großschreibung; deutsche Glossen beziehen sich auf die Österreichische Gebärdensprache (ÖGS), englische auf die Amerikanische (ASL)].

2. Zur Geschichte der Gebärdensprachforschung

Die in § 1 beschriebene Situation hat sowohl dazu geführt, daß GS lange überhaupt nicht systematisch linguistisch untersucht wurden, als auch dazu, daß die Forschung in verschiedenen Ländern mit großen zeitlichen Unterschieden einsetzte. Sie begann in Holland 1953 (Bernard T.M. Tervoort), in den USA mit William C. Stokoe 1960, in Großbritannien und Schweden in den 70er Jahren, in den meisten übrigen Ländern in den 80er bzw. zu Beginn der 90er Jahre. Nach wie vor bezieht sich die Hauptmasse der Arbeiten auf einige wenige der insgesamt etwa 100 bekannten GS, nämlich ASL, Britische (BSL), Schwedische (SSL) u.a.

Als Bibliografie vgl. Joachim & Prillwitz 1993 (Online-Version siehe Internetadresse der Universität Hamburg in Abschnitt 9); zur Information über einzelne GS Grimes 1984 und Deuchar 1996: 555; zur linguistischen Analyse Boyes Braem 1990, Holzinger 1993 und Valli & Lucas 1995 als Einführungen.

Die erste Phase der GS-Forschung war z.T. daran orientiert, den Sprachstatus dieser optischen Kommunikationssysteme zu belegen. Diese Legitimations-Absicht führte zum Versuch, möglichst viele Kategorien der LS auch in GS nachzuweisen (Stokoe 1960 ging dezidiert anders vor; vgl. Anderson 1992: 274–76). Damit wurden fast zwangsläufig auch weniger angemessene Hypothesen formuliert. Z.B. wurde die Ikonizität der GS heruntergespielt, da eine weitgehende Arbitrarität als Kennzeichen von LS – und damit implizit aller anderer Sprachtypen – angesehen wurde. Die – meist implizit – dahinterliegende Vorstellung, daß eine 'entwickelte' Sprache nur wenig Ikonizität aufweisen dürfe, wurde inzwischen auch innerhalb der LS-Forschung relativiert, welche Ikonizität als ein wichtiges Kodierungsprinzip erkannte (Haiman 1985, Dotter 1995).

Kennzeichen der GS-Forschung bis in die 80er Jahre war eine vorwiegend beschreibungsorientierte Vorgangsweise. Erst danach entstanden viele Arbeiten, welche die vorhandenen Daten – insbesondere in der Phonologie – mittels Übertragung formaler Modelle der generativen Grammatik zu beschreiben versuchen (vgl. Lucas 1990 und unten § 5.2.3.3).

3. Gebärdensprache und Gestik/ Mimik

Die semiotische Nutzung gestisch-mimischer Aktionen ist phylogenetisch alt und spielt auch in LS-Produktionen eine wichtige, oft unterschätzte Rolle. Aufgrund dieses Alters haben manche Autoren sogar den Ursprung der LS aus gestisch-mimischen Systemen postuliert (Hewes 1996, Armstrong & Stokoe & Wilcox 1995, Emmorey & Reilly 1995).

Vom Erscheinungsbild her existieren (aufgrund des gemeinsamen Übertragungskanals) tatsächlich Überschneidungsbereiche zwischen Gestik/Mimik als Kundgabesystem, das entweder allein oder in Verbindung mit LS eingesetzt werden kann (z.B. Deixis, 'adverbielle' Funktionen im weitesten Sinn, Zählen mit den Fingern), und den gestisch-mimischen Teilen der GS-Systeme. Diese Elemente werden aber in GS für ein Sprachsystem (und damit für evolutionär jüngere Zwecke) genutzt (in LS sind sie wahrscheinlich weniger systematisiert bzw. obligatorisch), weisen also gegenüber Gestik/Mimik klare Unterschiede bezüglich Funktion und Kontexten auf.

4. Epistemologische und methodologische Überlegungen

Auf GS können dieselben Analyse- und Beschreibungsmethoden angewendet werden wie auf LS. Aber die im Gegensatz zu LS größere Bedeutung von Ikonizität und Simultaneität (s. unten § 8) verändert die Anwendung (so muß Segmentation teilweise sequentiell und teilweise simultan erfolgen).

Optische Wahrnehmung ist (ohne Berücksichtigung der Zeit) dreidimensional, akustische im Vergleich dazu ein- oder maximal zweidimensional. Es ist daher zu erwarten, daß der im Vergleich zu LS unterschiedliche Übertragungskanal von GS sich in teilweise unterschiedlichen Sprachstrukturen abbildet (Bellugi & Klima 1991, Meier 1992: 173–75).

Da sowohl sprachwissenschaftliche Axiome als auch Analyse- und Beschreibungsmethoden an LS entwickelt wurden, ist es wahrscheinlich, daß Forschungsergebnisse bezüglich Sprachen im optischen Kanal sowohl zu einem gewissen Revisionsbedarf in der Theorie führen, als auch daß die Anwendung bestimmter Methoden zu nicht eindeutigen Ergebnissen führt (beide Phänomene sind ja bei der Bearbeitung 'exotischer' LS immer wieder aufgetreten).

Auf diese Sachlage können Linguisten auf verschiedene Weise reagieren; idealtypisch: Entweder mit der Hypothese, daß die Ergebnisse der LS-Forschung (insbesondere Kategorien und Systemrelationen) einfach auf GS übertragbar seien: Dies tun vor allem Vertreter von Theorien, die eine 'Universalgrammatik' postulieren, welche zusätzlich zum jeweils aktuellen Zeitpunkt als bereits gesichert angesehen wird. Oder man erwartet, daß GS Phänomene aufweisen, die in LS nicht oder graduell unterschiedlich zu finden sind (z.B. ist in GS die Merkmalhaftigkeit von Kongruenzverben bezüglich ihres Objekts die am wenigsten markierte Variante).

Beide Positionen können als epistemologisch hinderliche Filter wirken. Die GS-Forschung ist durch die Anwendung beider konkurrierender Hypothesen gekennzeichnet (dies führt auch zu terminologischen Inkonsistenzen; vgl. Begriffe wie 'Silbe', 'Klassifikator', 'Inkorporation').

5. Zur Beschreibung der Gebärdensprache

5.1. Dauer von Zeichenproduktion und Informationsübertragung

Unter der Annahme einer relativ gleichen Geschwindigkeit der Informationsübertragung in GS und LS ergibt sich aufgrund der langsameren Produktion von Gebärden im Vergleich zu LS-Wörtern, daß während der Dauer von GS-Zeichen wesentlich mehr Information übertragen werden muß, als LS-Wörter normalerweise beinhalten (Bellugi & Fischer 1972). Dies kann nur durch die im optischen gegenüber dem akustischen Kanal größere Menge simultan übermittelbarer Information plausibel gemacht werden.

5.2. Phonetik und Phonologie (Bausteinbereich, 'formational domain')

5.2.1. Zeichenaufbau

Gebärdensprachliche Morpheme lassen sich mittels der sogenannten 'sublexikalischen Elemente' beschreiben, welche zumindest teilweise simultan erscheinen (zur Verwendung der Begriffe 'Phonetik'/'Phonologie' – anstatt der von Stokoe vorgeschlagenen „cherology" – vgl. Liddell & Johnson 1989: 206f. und Wilbur 1990: 96–8). Die relevanten Kategorien finden sich (allerdings nicht vollständig übereinstimmend) in allen umfassenden Beschreibungen von GS nach dem sogenannten 'Parametermodell' (Friedman 1977, Klima & Bellugi 1979, Liddell & Johnson 1989, Wilbur 1987; als Übersicht über die Parameter und deren Werte Prillwitz et al. 1989; zu Unterschieden zwischen einzelnen Systemen Zahwe 1994 und Holzinger 1993: 19–57). Dieses setzt manuelle und nicht-manuelle 'Parameter', d.h. Komponenten von Gebärden, an.

Bei den manuellen Parametern werden unterschieden: Handform (etwa 20–30 distinktive Handformen pro einzelner GS mit ca. 5–10 in allen GS vorhandenen 'Grundformen'), Handstellung bzw. -orientierung, Ausführungsstelle (etwa 15–20 distinktive Ausführungsstellen am Körper, weitere im sogenannten Gebärdenraum in Körpernähe bzw. bei zweihändigen Gebärden auf der 'nicht-dominanten'/'schwachen' Hand) und Bewegung.

Diese Beschreibungsgrößen sind zum Großteil bereits im ursprünglichen, sogenannten 'Aspektmodell' von Stokoe 1960 vorhanden, welches drei simultan realisierte Komponenten („Chereme") ansetzt, nämlich „tab" (Ausführungsstelle), „dez" (Handform) und „sig" (Bewegung). Für einige der genannten Parameter existieren weitere Differenzierungen, z.B. Subparameter der Handform (z.B. Gestrecktheit bzw. Gespreiztheit einzelner Finger), Handstellung (Lage und Richtung der Handfläche) oder Bewegung (z.B. Bewegungsrichtung, Art der Ausführung).

Bei den nicht-manuellen Parametern werden u.a. Gesichtsausdruck/Mimik, Augenausdruck, Blickrichtung, Kopf- und Oberkörperhaltung bzw. -bewegung, sowie Mundgestik und Mundbild unterschieden. MUNDBILD bezeichnet die vollständige oder unvollständige Artikulation eines LS-Worts simultan zu einer Gebärde (in seltenen Fällen auch alleinstehend) ohne Stimmeinsatz, MUNDGESTIK GS-bezogene Produktionen (so wird 'Wetter' mit entsprechendem Mundbild produziert, 'Wind' mit der Mundgestik 'blasen').

5.2.2. Notationssysteme und Verschriftung

Vorauszuschicken ist hier, daß in vielen frühen Arbeiten eine klare Unterscheidung zwischen phonetischer und phonologischer Ebene unterbleibt. Vielfach wird die sogenannte 'Stokoe-Notation' verwendet (Stokoe & Croneberg & Casterline 1965, Brien et al. 1992), ausführlicher sind Prillwitz et al. 1989 („HamNoSys", phonetisch orientiert) und die segment-orientierte (phonologisch orientierte) Notation von Liddell & Johnson 1989 (vgl. auch Miller 1994b; zu weniger bekannten Systemen Holzinger 1993: 58–62). Während diese Systeme die erwähnten Gebärdenkomponenten notieren, kommt „SignWriting" (Sutton 1981) einer Zeichennotation (ikonischen Bilderschrift) nahe.

5.2.3 Phonologische Beschreibungsmodelle

Für die Werte der genannten Parameter können Minimalpaare gefunden werden, welche ihre bedeutungsunterscheidende Funktion nachweisen. War die frühe GS-Forschung (Stokoe) von einem eher simultanen Aufbau gebärdensprachlicher Zeichen ausgegangen, führten die Analysen von Liddell & Johnson 1989 zu einer grundlegend sequenzorientierten Auffassung. Die von diesen Autoren entwickelte Beschreibungsmethode kann als heute weitgehend anerkannte Arbeitsgrundlage für phonologische Modelle gelten.

5.2.3.1. Bewegungs-/Halt-Modell

Liddell & Johnson 1989 schlagen vor, die in Gebärden erkennbaren Halt- und Bewegungsphasen als Segmente zu interpretieren, deren Abfolge die nunmehr primär sequentielle Grundstruktur von Gebärdenzeichen ergibt: Eine Gebärde wird so interpretiert, daß sie normalerweise mit einem Haltsegment beginnt, dem ein Bewegungssegment folgt, welches wieder von einem Haltsegment begrenzt werden kann.

Für die Beschreibung der Haltphase wird das entsprechende Bündel artikulatorischer Merkmale (Handform, -stellung, nicht-manuelle Merkmale) verwendet. Ein Bewegungssegment wird als Übergang von einer Haltphase zur anderen mit entsprechenden Parameterwert-Wechseln definiert, das aber auch spezifische Parameter aufweist. Es werden Morphemstrukturregeln bzw. -beschränkungen verwendet und phonologische Regeln des Zusammenhangs von zugrundeliegender und Oberflächenstruktur formuliert.

Nicht nur, daß mit diesem Modell eine grundsätzliche Ähnlichkeit zwischen LS und GS hergestellt wird, da nun auch in GS sequentiell angeordnete Segmente angesetzt werden: Es liefert auch die Grundlage für die später mehrfach (z.B. Perlmutter 1992) erfolgte Gleichsetzung von Haltphasen mit Konsonanten, bzw. von Bewegungsphasen mit Vokalen der LS, sowie für die Anwendung von Silbenkonzepten auf GS. Liddell 1990 stellt den Ansatz zu einem dezidiert phonologisch orientierten Bewegungs-/Halt-Modell dar, welches zwölf unabhängige Beschreibungsebenen ('tiers' der Autosegmentalen Phonologie) enthält.

5.2.3.2. „Hand-Tier"–Modell

Wendy Sandler (1992) faßt Handform und „location" (Halt ist ein Spezialfall davon) als sequentiell angeordnete, abstrakte „timing slots" auf. Sie führte mehr Hierarchiebeziehungen innerhalb der Ebenen ein und wies der Handform eine spezielle Beschreibungsebene (eben das „hand tier") zu. Sandler leitete auch einen 'prosodic turn' in der GS-Phonologie ein, indem sie annahm, daß Handform und Ausführungsstelle innerhalb von 'Silben' der GS invariant und damit prosodischen Elementen von LS gleichzustellen seien. Dies wird erreicht durch Verlagerung von Bewegung (= Veränderung der Ausführungsstelle) und Handformveränderung auf hierarchisch niedrigere Ebenen, in denen Schwesterknoten zeitliche Abfolgen repräsentieren. Unterschiedliche Parameterwerte solcher Schwesterknoten repräsentieren dann eine Veränderung in der Zeit.

5.2.3.3. Modelle mit Silbenkonzept

Im Lauf der Analyse der GS-Phonologie wurden verschiedene Modelle eingesetzt, die durch einen Transfer von LS-bezogenen Theorien auf GS charakterisiert sind (Ausnahme: Uyechi 1996). Diese Modelle geben unterschiedliche Interpretationen bezüglich der Wortstruktur in GS: Im Fall lautsprachähnlicher (sequentieller) Silben wurde zu Beginn für jede Bewegung-Halt-Kombination bzw. jede Einzelbewegung eine Silbe gezählt, sodaß 'Mehrsilbigkeit' durchaus häufig erschien. Analysen aus der Generativen Grammatik tendieren in letzter Zeit dazu, einfache Lexeme mit unmarkierten Produktionsver-

läufen als strukturell adäquat zu einzelnen (komplexen) Segmenten (= Lauten) der LS anzusehen (Hulst 1993 und 1995). Dazu muß aber eine Silbenstruktur ohne Anlaut angenommen werden. Aus dieser Sicht erscheinen GS typologisch als Sprachen mit vorwiegend monosyllabischen Lexemen.
In der Diskussion waren weiters:

a. Silben ohne Segmente. – Ronnie B. Wilbur (1990: 88–92) anerkennt die von Vertretern segmentaler Modelle festgestellten sequentiellen Phänomene in GS, betrachtet Segmente aber bezüglich der phonologischen Beschreibung als redundant. Sie setzt drei Ebenen an, nämlich Handform, -orientierung und Lokalisierung. Bewegung ist immer dann gegeben, wenn auf mindestens einer dieser Ebenen zwei verschiedene Merkmalsmatrizen verwendet werden müssen.

b. Das „Moren"-Modell (Perlmutter 1992) – Dieses setzt am Bewegungs-/Halt-Modell und am „Hand-Tier"-Modell an und führt zusätzlich Silben ein, die durch Moren als „subsyllabische prosodische" Einheiten strukturiert sind, welche (entsprechend dem Verständnis aus der LS) sowohl die Zeitstruktur von Silben als auch über ihre Anzahl pro Silbe das ‚phonologische Gewicht' der jeweiligen Silbe bestimmen.

c. Simultane Silben – Diane Brentari (1995) schlug – im Verständnis der GS als Simultanität verwendenden Sprachen – vor, die nichtdominante Hand in zweihändigen Gebärden als simultane ‚unbetonte' Silbe anzusehen. Dies findet sich in Brentari 1998 nicht mehr.

Bezüglich weiterer Modellvorschläge und Diskussion vgl. Corina & Sandler 1993, Coulter 1992, Brentari 1998, Uyechi 1996 und Wilbur 1990: 92–105.

5.2.3.4. Uyechi

Lionda Uyechi (1996) setzt gegen den einfachen Transfer von LS-Analyseergebnissen auf GS ein dezidert GS-spezifisches Modell. Um den (im Vergleich zu LS) dynamischeren und stärker simultanen Charakter von GS zu repräsentieren, setzt sie für jeden der drei Hauptparameter Handform, Ausführungsstelle und Orientierung sogenannte „transition units" an, die den Bewegungsablauf in diesen drei Dimensionen beschreiben. Diese ‚Übergangseinheiten' sind in einer sogenannten „cell" (vergleichbar der Silbe in LS) vereint und durch eine „time unit" koordiniert.

Uyechi trägt auch der Tatsache Rechnung, daß manche phonologischen Einheiten der GS morphosyntaktische oder semantische Funktion haben.

5.3. Gebärdensprache und das Bausteinprinzip ('doppelte Gliederung') von Sprache

Auch die Zeichen von GS sind aus kleineren Bausteinen aufgebaut. Allerdings besteht zwischen bedeutungsunterscheidenden und -tragenden Elementen von Zeichen keine so scharfe Trennung wie in LS: In nicht wenigen Fällen funktionieren bausteinartige (also den distinktiven Merkmalen der LS entsprechende) Zeichenkomponenten gleichzeitig bedeutungstragend; z.T. eher lexikalisch (z.B. adverbiell), z.T. eher morphosyntaktisch (z.B. Klassifikatoren). In manchen Bereichen stellt diese Doppelfunktion geradezu den Normalfall dar (Gee 1992, vgl. die „semantic phonology" in Armstrong & Stokoe & Wilcox 1995: 12–15).

5.4. Morphosyntax

Eines der wesentlichen Kennzeichen von GS ist die Verwendung des dreidimensionalen Raums in der Morphosyntax und im Diskurs (zur ASL Winston 1995: 88). Dieser Raum wird verwendet, um Personen und Objekte in einer Art kognitiver Landkarte (1:1- oder 1:n-Abbildung referierter Topographie) zu positionieren, ihre syntaktisch-semantischen Rollen zu kodieren, und um Referenzpunkte (s. § 5.4.1.5) zu setzen (Emmorey & Corina & Bellugi 1995, Keller 1998). Hervorzuheben ist die Rolle der nicht-manuellen Komponente: Der Skopus nicht-manueller Komponenten reicht vom Einzelzeichen über Phrasen bis hin zu ganzen Propositionen; sie übernehmen auch Diskursfunktionen. Die Mimik z.B. erfüllt neben der Kodierung adverbieller Konzepte (bis zu Satzadverbialen wie Bekräftigung, Zweifel) auch grammatische oder pragmatische Funktionen (Markierung von Fragen, Verneinungen, Topikalisierungen, Relativ- und Konditionalsätzen usw.).

5.4.1. Konzept- bzw. Zeichentypen (Wortarten) und Morphologie

5.4.1.1. Objektkonzepte (Nomina)

Dieser Kodierungstyp weist wenig Morphologie auf (kein Genus und Kasus, Numerus eingeschränkt), syntaktische Beziehungen sind vor allem aus der Serialisierung erkennbar.

5.4.1.2. Aktions-/Ereigniskonzepte (Verben)

Zu den Verben vgl. Deuchar 1984, Engberg-Pedersen 1993, Janis 1995, Johnston 1991, Liddell 1980, Padden 1988, Pizzuto 1986. Alle Verben sind modifizierbar bezüglich simultaner manueller oder nicht-manueller Modalkonzepte. Bezüglich ihres morphologischen Verhaltens (beschrieben unter 'Modulation', 'Flexion', tw. auch 'Inkorporation') sind folgende (nicht disjunkte) Gruppen von Verben zu unterscheiden:

1. Einfache Verben ('plain verbs'). – Diese können (aus verschiedenen Gründen, wie: Intransitivität, Subjekt/Objekt in Experiencer-Rolle oder feste Ausführungsstellen am Körper) bezüglich syntaktisch-semantischer Rollen räumlich nicht modifiziert (nicht an verschiedenen Orten oder in verschiedene Richtungen hin ausgeführt) werden. Eine Rollenkodierung ist aber mittels Indexgebärden oder nicht-manueller Kodierungen (Blickrichtung, Körperhaltung) möglich.

2. Lokationsverben ('spatial verbs', 'verbs of motion and location'). – Lokationsverben kodieren primär Bewegungen zwischen verschiedenen Orten bzw. die Position einer Entität an einem bestimmten Ort. Um dies auszudrücken, wird das Verb mit (vorher für Referenten definierten) Raumpunkten als Ausgangs- und/oder Endpunkt bzw. Position übereingestimmt. Die meisten Raumverben können mittels Klassifikatoren bezüglich involvierter Objekte/Personen modifiziert werden (Gegenbeispiele in der ÖGS: BRINGEN, KOMMEN).

3. Kongruenz- (Übereinstimmungs-) Verben ('agreement verbs'). – Bei diesen werden (im Raum lokalisierte) Partizipanten als Anfangs- und/oder Endposition der Verbgebärde ('Kongruenzmorphem') kodiert. Normalerweise wird die Agens- /Subjektrolle zu Beginn und die Patiens-/Objektrolle am Ende dargestellt; bei manchen Verben (z.B. NEHMEN) in umgekehrter Reihenfolge (die Salienzhierarchie ist dabei: Indirektes Objekt > Direktes Objekt > Subjekt). Engberg-Pedersen 1993: 214–21 spricht auch von pragmatischer Kongruenz von Verben mit dem Topic.

Einige Autoren fassen Kongruenz- und Raumverben ohne Klassifikatoren zu einer Verbklasse zusammen (vgl. Engberg-Pedersen 1993: 161). In morphologischer Hinsicht weisen diese beiden Verbtypen große Ähnlichkeiten auf (z.B. räumliche Modifizierung bezüglich Referentenloci, einfache Bewegungsmorpheme).

5.4.1.3. Objektbezogene Merkmalskonzepte (Adjektive)

GS besitzen keine Kopula, daher zeigen die Kodierungen nicht-attributiver Eigenschaftskonzepte statt Adjektiv-Eigenschaften ein ähnliches Verhalten wie (intransitive) Verben.

5.4.1.4. Aktions-, merkmals- und propositionsbezogene Merkmalskonzepte (Adverbiale)

1. Lokal- und Temporaladverbien. – Solche Konzepte werden entweder als manuelle Lexeme (Aarons & Kegl & Neidle 1995) oder durch die Produktion von Verben auf einer Raumposition oder einer sogenannten 'Zeitlinie' (einer Raummetapher) kodiert (Holzinger 1993: 65–68). Eine Hauptzeitlinie verläuft (zumindest für GS in europäisch-westlichen Kulturen) aus Sicht der Gebärdenden von hinten (Vergangenheit) nach vorn (Zukunft). Lexikalische Temporaladverbien beinhalten oft auch eine entsprechende Position oder Bewegungsrichtung auf solchen Zeitlinien als ikonisches Bauelement (GESTERN weist nach hinten, MORGEN nach vorn).

2. Modaladverbien und Aspektkodierungen. – Vor allem durch Bewegungsparameter, z.T. auch nicht-manuell, können sowohl modale als auch viele aspektuale Konzepte (z.B. durativ, iterativ, habitualis, kompletiv, aber auch Intensivierung, augmentativ oder distributiv) an Verben und z.T. an prädikativen Adjektiven kodiert werden (Klima & Bellugi 1979: 243–315; hierher gehören wohl auch die von Jacobowitz & Stokoe 1988 als beschränkte 'Tempuskodierung' bezeichneten Erscheinungen).

5.4.1.5. Partizipantenreferenz und Stellvertreterformen (Pronomina)

1. Anwesende Partizipanten. – Werden solche Partizipanten nicht mit einem vollständig referierenden Lexem (Eigenname oder Nomen) kodiert, so kann dies mittels deiktischer Elemente geschehen: Für Dialogpartner (2. Person) sind dabei Zeigegeste (Index) und Blickrichtung gleichgerichtet, für andere (3. Person) bleibt der Blick des Gebärdenden hauptsächlich auf den Dialogpartner gerichtet, während der Index (meist mit kurzer Blickbegleitung) auf den entsprechenden Referenten (Person, Objekt) zeigt. Possessiva werden ähnlich wie die Personalpronomina, aber mit anderer Handform und -orientierung kodiert.

2. Abwesende Partizipanten. – Diese werden mit einem Lexem eingeführt, dem dann durch einen Index ein Referenzpunkt im Raum ('Lokus') zugewiesen wird. Jede weitere Referenz kann durch die Ausführung einer Gebärde am etablierten Lokus (oder zumindest in dessen Richtung), entsprechender Indizierung und/oder Blickrichtung und Körperorientierung kodiert werden (Ahlgren & Bergman 1994). Während LS-Pronomina wegen der Linearität der LS-Produktion im Verlauf der Äußerung an entsprechenden Stellen immer wieder völlig neu produziert werden müssen, kann in GS zu dem einmal definierten Raumpunkt 'zurückgekehrt' werden ('referential indexing'). Aufgrund der Spezifität dieser Kodierungsform wird diskutiert, ob nun der etablierte Lokus oder der ihn jeweils aktualisierende Index 'das Pronomen darstellen' (Mandel 1977, Wilbur 1979, Liddell 1995). Schließt man jedoch GS-spezifische Zeichentypen nicht aus, so bietet sich auch die Lösung an, daß beide Elemente in Kombination die Kodierung darstellen.

3. Demonstrativa. – Die eben beschriebenen Stellvertreterformen können intensiviert werden und sind dann wahrscheinlich als Demonstrativa zu interpretieren. Zimmer & Patschke 1990 nannten eine von ihnen beschriebene (teilweise simultan mit anderen Lexemen auftretende) Kodierungsform „Determinatoren". Betrachtet man deren Funktionen (Hervorhebung, Betonung, Bezugnahme auf Vorerwähntes), so können sie hier eingeordnet werden.

4. 'Klassifikatoren'. – Es handelt sich hier um Kodierungen, die hauptsächlich mittels Handform und Anordnung der Hände Objektkonzepte innerhalb eines Verbs bzw. simultan zu einem solchen (vorwiegend mit manipulativen, Bewegungs- und Lokationsverben) repräsentieren (Brennan 1990, Johnston 1991, Schick 1990, Supalla 1986). Sie dienen zur Darstellung manipulierter bzw. sich bewegender oder an einer Position befindlicher Objekte bzw. von Instrumenten. Sie werden manchmal als Kongruenzmorpheme bezeichnet, z.T. auch als Proformen (Edmondson 1990: 196) oder klassifikatorische Verbstämme (Engberg-Pedersen 1993). Von der Kodierungsform her sind veränderbare ('deskriptive') und nicht veränderbare ('abstrakte', 'semantische') Klassifikatoren zu unterscheiden. Die veränderbaren kodieren Form, Größe bzw. Handhabung von Objekten mittels Handform („size and shape specifiers" und „handling classifiers") bzw. Umrißwiedergabe durch Bewegungsverlauf („tracing"; diese treten als selbständige Zeichen auf und müssen an Verben durch handformkodierte Klassifikatoren repräsentiert werden).

5.4.1.6. Relationskonzepte (Adpositionen und Konjunktionen)

Diese Konzepte werden relativ selten (und dann oft in GS-Varianten unter LS-Einfluß; Ausnahmen: spezielles kommunikatives Erfordernis und wichtige Konjunktionen wie UND, ABER, ODER) als Lexeme kodiert, sondern sind (z.B. bei Lokalrelationen) in die Bewegung der Verbgebärden integriert oder werden durch ikonische Serialisierung ausgedrückt.

5.4.1.7. Zahlkonzepte (Numeralia)

Über die Handform werden Kodierungen für Zahlbedeutungen (von 2–5) in Lexeme 'eingesetzt' ('inkorporiert'). Die Zahl der ausgestreckten Finger gibt die Grundzahl an, welche durch spezifische Handorientierung und -bewegung eine Stellen- (Zehner, Tausender usw.) oder Kategoriezuordnung (z.B. Ordinalzahl) erhält. Für Zahlen über fünf existieren unterschiedliche Kodierungsstrategien.

5.4.2 Morphologische Prozesse

Ein solcher Prozeß verbindet bestimmte Nomen-Verb-Paare (zumindest in ASL): Während Handform, Ausführungsstelle und Bewegungsrichtung identisch sind, unterscheiden sich Paare wie PRODUCE/PRODUCTION durch die Art der Bewegung, die beim Nomen weniger weit geht und eine höhere Muskelspannung aufweist (Supalla & Newport 1978). Zur 'Inkorporierung' von Zahlen vgl. oben § 5.4.1.7

5.4.3. Lexem oder Morphem?

Aufgrund der Simultaneität ist es methodisch schwierig, zu entscheiden, ob eine bestimmte Bedeutung mittels Formveränderung eines gegebenen Zeichens (also 'morphologisch') oder durch Hinzufügung eines zusätzlichen Zeichens (also 'lexikalisch') kodiert wird. Falls Typmodelle aus der LS-Forschung auf GS angewandt werden, bestehen folgende Möglichkeiten: Wird der 'isolierende' Typ auf GS übertragen, so sind z.B. simultan zu anderen Zeichen produzierte adverbielle Kodierungen eher als 'Individuen', damit als (simultane) Lexeme zu betrachten. Überträgt man den 'polymorphemischen' Typ, so sind gewisse (aber nicht vollständige) Übereinstimmungen zwischen diesen Kodierungen und entsprechenden Verbmorphemklassen in Indianersprachen festzustellen (Engberg-Pedersen 1993).

Ähnliches gilt teilweise auch für die sequentielle Segmentation: Sind rollenkodierende Referenzpunkte im Raum als Flexionsmorpheme von Verben oder – in Analogie zu den Lokalinformation kodierenden Raumpunkten – als Lexeme (Proformen) zu interpretieren? Wie in manchen afrikanischen Sprachen kann ein und dasselbe Zeichen als Lexem und in grammatischer Funktion verwendet werden (z.B. FINISH als Verb und Aspektkodierung). GS sind also Sprachen, die Stufenübergänge zwischen Morphem- und Lexemstatus zeigen, verbunden mit sowohl sequentieller als auch simultaner Lexem-/Morphemkombination.

5.4.4. Syntax

5.4.4.1. Serialisierung

Die Anordnung der Zeichen in GS ist sequentiell mit zusätzlichen simultanen Elementen (Miller 1994a, Neidle & al. 1999). Als vorherrschende sequentielle Grundwortfolgen werden SVO und SOV mit insgesamt relativ starken Variationsmöglichkeiten angegeben (Brennan & Turner 1994, Coerts 1994), soweit diese Kategorien überhaupt verwendet werden (aus Diskursanalysen ergeben sich auch Indizien für eine Topic-Comment-Grundordnung). In Lokativpropositionen ('X liegt auf Y') ist eine Tendenz zur Voranstellung der Lokation feststellbar (Volterra et al. 1984).

5.4.4.2. Satztypkodierung

Für die nicht-manuellen Satztypkodierungen gilt, daß sie während der Dauer des entsprechenden (Teil-)Satzes produziert werden. Hauptsächlich nicht-manuell/mimisch werden Entscheidungsfragen, Subordination und Topikalisierung kodiert. Für Ergänzungsfragen kommt ein initiales und/oder finales Fragewort hinzu (Dubuisson & Miller & Pinsonneault 1994).

Relativsätze besitzen im Normalfall interne Köpfe, die aber durch bestimmte Zusatzkodierungen wie Intensivierung, Umstellung oder Wiederholung hervorgehoben werden können.

Für Temporal- und Konditionalsätze gilt zusätzlich ikonische Anordnung. Topikalisierungen weisen z.T. auch eine längere manuelle Produktionsdauer auf (Liddell 1980). Negation kann nicht-manuell (Kopfschütteln) wie manuell (Negationsgebärden) ausgedrückt werden (Bergman 1995); darüber hinaus können Verben durch Übernahme der ikonischen Bewegung aus Negationsgebärden verneint werden.

5.4.4.2.1. Direkte und indirekte Rede

In beiden Fällen werden die referierte(n) gebärdende(n) Person(en) durch einen bzw. mehrere Referenzpunkte kodiert. Bei direkter Rede werden Äußerungen zu den entsprechenden Referenzpunkten durch Bewegungsrichtung und Körperorientierung in Beziehung gesetzt. Bei indirekter Rede bleibt der Bezug zu den Referenzpunkten durch Indizierung und Bewegungsrichtung aufrecht, während die Körperorientierung (also die 'Rollenübernahme' durch die Gebärdenden) fehlt.

6. Lexikon

Für bestimmte Gebärden (sagen wir genauer: Glossen, so wird auch das methodische Problem der lautsprachorientierten Glossennamen deutlich) können aufgrund der bestehenden Variationsbreite nicht alle Realisierungen, sondern bloß einzelne sogenannte 'Zitatformen' angegeben werden (es geht hier nicht um phonetische Produktionsvariation, sondern um Bedeutungsvarianten; vgl. die Beispiele unten). Dies hat zu einer Vielzahl von Interpretationen geführt, wie z.B., daß GS 'analoge Kodierungen' oder 'descriptive signs' besäßen, bzw. pantomimische oder eben mimisch-gestische Elemente einsetzten (welche nicht mehr zum GS-System zu zählen seien), schließlich, daß im Lexikon ein 'produktiver' (variantenreicher, nur mit Zitatformen repräsentierbarer) und ein 'stabiler' („frozen"; einem LS-Lexikon entsprechender) Teil zu unterscheiden seien (Brennan 1994). Macken & al. 1993 bezeichnen die Zeichen, die zum 'produktiven' Lexikon gehören, als „richly grounding symbols", die auch in LS (aber dort selten) auftreten.

Zu dieser Zeichenklasse gehören jedenfalls bestimmte Objekt- und Aktionskonzepte, für die Form bzw. Bewegung im dreidimensionalen Raum konstitutiv sind. Durch die Möglichkeit ikonischer Kodierung (Wiedergabe einzelner konkreter Aspekte des kodierten Sachverhalts, z.B. von Positionen, Richtungen oder Bewegungsweisen im Raum bzw.

von Objektklassen durch bedeutungstragende Komponenten wie Handform, -orientierung oder Art der Bewegung) können diese sehr stark differenziert werden (vgl. die Diskussion zu den „polymorphemischen Verben" bei Engberg-Pedersen 1993; dies bedeutet auch, daß in GS viele 'morphologische' Veränderungen fakultativ sind). Beispielsweise berücksichtigt eine Gebärde für SCHACHTEL z.T. deren Größe und Form und kann daher sehr unterschiedlich produziert werden. Analog können bei der Ausführung der Gebärde DRÜCKEN simultan das Objekt, welches gedrückt wird, die Richtung des Drückens, unterschiedlicher Körpereinsatz bzw. Schwierigkeitsgrad etc. kodiert werden.

Ähnliche Erscheinungen sind bei variablen Klassifikatoren anzutreffen. So kann ein Klassifikator am Komplex TÜR-ÖFFNEN die Form der Türklinke wiedergeben; zusätzlich können Zweiflügeligkeit durch Zweihändigkeit, die Art der Tür oder die Öffnungsrichtung durch Bewegungsparameter wiedergegeben werden.

Es erscheint schwierig, wenn nicht unmöglich, eine 'verbale' Grundform anzunehmen, von der alle möglichen Varianten durch 'morphologische' Modifikation abgeleitet werden (phänomenbezogen wäre allenfalls ein Grundelement der Bewegung als 'kleinster gemeinsamer Nenner' aller vorstellbaren Varianten anzusehen). Nur für ganz bestimmte Zeichenkombinationen, etwa wenn die Bedeutung 'zweite' in ein 'unkomplettes Morphem' („root") 'Wettbewerbsrang' eingefügt wird, ist eine solche Interpretation plausibel.

Konzepten (oder Konzeptmengen), die durch Glossen wie SCHACHTEL, DRÜCKEN oder ABTROCKNEN wiedergegeben werden, würde nicht ein Lexem, sondern eine offene Klasse möglicher Kodierungen entsprechen, die referenten- und situationsabhängig mit großer Variationsbreite realisiert und daher lexikographisch immer nur beispielhaft mittels einiger Vertreter repräsentiert werden kann. Die Zeichengestaltung erfolgt aber trotzdem nicht wirklich analog, sondern in Abstufungen. Es liegt also eine gewisse Klassifikation/Abstraktion vor, nur sind nicht alle möglichen Formen regelhaft vorhersagbar.

Weitere Zusatzdifferenzierungen von Gebärden (auch für von bestehenden Gebärden abgeleitete Neubildungen) sind (besonders in der ASL) durch Integration von Handformen des Fingeralphabets (als Repräsentanten des Anfangsbuchstabens eines LS-Wortes: z.B. C-Form für COMPUTER; Battison 1978), oder (besonders in europäischen Gebärdensprachen) durch Mundbild/-gestik möglich (Ebbinghaus & Heßmann 1994/95).

7. Diskurs

Neben dem Sammelband Winston 1999 zur ASL kann hier lediglich auf einzelne weitere Arbeiten verwiesen werden: Zur verbalen Interaktion vgl. Mcilvenny & Raudaskoski 1994; zur Sprecherperspektive Engberg-Pedersen 1995, Lillo-Martin 1995 und Poulin & Miller 1995; zur Rolle des Blicks Bahan & Supalla 1995; zur Diskurspartikeln bzw. Textsorten Zeshan 2000: 227–40 bzw. 245–60.

8. Zum Vergleich Gebärdensprache – Lautsprache

8.1. Die gemeinsame Basis

GS und LS teilen die Möglichkeiten und Bedingungen des humanen konzeptuellen Systems inklusive semiotischer und pragmatischer Prinzipien. Sie teilen auch die Prinzipien der internen Organisation (Prototypen, Vagheit, Markiertheitsrelationen, Präferenzregeln usw.) und des Erwerbs (vgl. Teil 3 in Ahlgren & Bergman & Brennan 1994, Vol. 2; Meier & Willerman 1995; Volterra & Erting 1990). GS-Zeichen sind strukturierte Gestalten wie Zeichen der LS und weisen wie diese rhythmische Strukturierungsmöglichkeiten auf.

8.2. Gebärdensprache als Sprachtyp

Im Bausteinbereich ist die Zahl der distinktiven Merkmale mit mindestens 50 bedeutend höher als in LS. Die Bewegung ist z.B. eine wichtige Komponente, die Funktionen vom 'materiellen' Träger der GS-Produktion bis zum Träger von Bedeutung umschließt und daher mit keinem konstitutiven Element von LS vergleichbar ist. Die nicht-manuelle Komponente übernimmt mehr Funktionen als Suprasegmentalia und Ton in LS.

In der Morphosyntax besteht zwar eine große Modulationsfähigkeit von GS-Zeichen, diese kann aber mit LS-typologischen Begriffen ('flektierend' usw.) nicht zureichend beschrieben werden (GS werden sowohl mit isolierenden als auch mit morphologiereichen LS verglichen: Klima & Bellugi 1979, Prillwitz et al. 1985). Vergleiche, wie die von aspektualen Strukturen in GS mit Verbserialisierung in LS (Metlay & Supalla 1995), sind noch bezüglich ihrer Validität zu prüfen.

Ein Kodierungsmittel, das in keinem der in LS verwendeten ein Pendant hat (es ist nur aufgrund der Verwendung des dreidimensionalen Raums verfügbar), sind die Referenzpunkte im Raum. GS weisen also eine im Vergleich zu LS unterschiedliche Gliederung von Kodierungsebenen bzw. -kategorien auf und sind daher als Typ von LS als Typ zu unterscheiden.

8.3. Phänomene, die zumindest eine teilweise Revision der Sprachtheorie nahelegen

8.3.1. Sequentialität und Simultaneität

Im optischen Kanal sind die lineare Zusammensetzung von Zeichen aus Lautelementen, sowie die lineare Ordnung von Zeichen, wie sie für die LS angenommen werden, in dieser Striktheit nicht notwendig und daher auch nicht vorhanden. In GS kann die Kodierung mancher Konzepte, die in der LS mittels der sequentiellen Kombination eines Lexems mit einem Morphem oder zweier Lexeme erfolgen müßte, simultan stattfinden; die Ausnutzung des dreidimensionalen Raums ermöglicht einige charakteristische Kodierungsstrategien z.B. für Partizipanten.

Auch GS wird in der Zeit produziert und ist daher stark sequentiell orientiert (z.B. können Abfolge und Dauer semiotisch genützt werden); pro Sequenz können aber mehr Elemente simultan angeboten werden als in LS. Die simultan-sequentielle Struktur des Zeichenaufbaus in LS und GS ist also verschieden, genauer: in GS besteht eine stärkere Orientierung in Richtung Simultaneität. Dies gilt nicht nur für den Aufbau einfacher Zeichen, sondern für die gesamte Morphosyntax. Als Beispiele seien hier genannt: sequentielle Phänomene sind in der LS Laute und ihre Kombinationen, in der GS der Wechsel von Bewegungsmodi, die Herstellung eines Kontakts zwischen 'Artikulatoren', Wechsel von Handformen; als motorische Produktionseinheit erscheint in der LS die Silbe, in der GS eine noch näher zu beschreibende 'Produktionseinheit'.

Simultane Phänomene sind in der LS die Merkmale von Lauten und die Kombination von Lautsegmenten mit suprasegmentalen Elementen (Teile dieser Erscheinungen sind — wahrscheinlich unangemessenerweise — wie die gesamte Mimik/Gestik als 'parasprachlich' definitorisch aus LS ausgeschlossen), in der GS Komponenten- wie Zeichenkombination (Dotter & Holzinger 1995a).

8.3.2. Arbitrarität und Ikonizität

Ursprünglich wurde die Ansicht vertreten, GS seien nicht ikonischer als LS (Klima & Bellugi 1979: 26−32; Deuchar noch 1996). Phonetischer Symbolismus und Onomatopöie stellen in LS die Ausnahme dar. Ikonizität ist hingegen ein wesentliches Prinzip der Zeichenbildung in der GS: Im Lexikonbereich wird ca. ein Drittel bis die Hälfte des Gesamtvokabulars eines Erwachsenen als relativ ikonisch (inklusive 'transparente' bzw. 'transluzente' Lexeme) eingestuft. Es gibt zwar besonders bei Einzelzeichen und in Komposita De-ikonisierungsprozesse (diachrone Ökonomisierung und reduktive Formen im Diskurs, Frishberg 1975), speziell für Wortneubildungen werden aber oft ikonische Kodierungsstrategien eingesetzt (Morford & Singleton & Goldin-Meadow 1995). Und auch die für das grammatische System der GS wesentlichen räumlich-ikonischen morphosyntaktischen Prozesse verlieren diachron ihre Ikonizität gerade nicht (Holzinger & Dotter 1997). Dies kann mit den vom jeweiligen Übertragungskanal gebotenen Möglichkeiten erklärt werden: Die menschliche Erfahrung und Konzeptualisierung wird durch visuelle Erscheinungen und räumliche Muster dominiert (man vergleiche auch die wesentlich höhere Kapazität optisch und kinästhetisch grundgelegter Metaphern im Vergleich zu der akustisch basierter in beiden Sprachtypen).

Wenn nun ein Kanal benützt wird, in dem visuelle Erscheinungen und räumliche Muster/Gestaltung direkt repräsentiert werden können, wird diese ikonische Repräsentationsart bevorzugt werden, welche in LS nicht möglich ist (Cameracanna et al. 1994). Auch im morphosyntaktischen Bereich besteht dieser Unterschied: Für ikonische Kodierungen müssen LS hauptsächlich auf die Zeit-(Abfolge)-dimension zurückgreifen (z.B. die relative Ordnung von Subjekt und Objekt übereinstimmend mit der Salienz in der Ereigniswelt). Die Ikonizität der GS im Grammatikbereich ist dagegen sowohl räumlich als auch zeitlich grundgelegt. GS bieten damit ikonische Strategien, welche in LS nicht vorhanden sind, können aber die in LS zur Verfügung stehenden Kodierungsstrategien ebenfalls nutzen.

Sowohl für Ikonizität als auch für Simultaneität ist bemerkenswert, daß entsprechende Kodierungsformen relativ spät erworben werden (Macken & Perry & Haas 1993: 39f.).

8.3.3. Folgerungen für die Sprachtheorie

Daß sprachtheoretische Festlegungen (z.B. Hockett 1960), die ja ausschließlich Abstraktionen aus LS-Forschung darstellen, aufgrund der Erkenntnisse der GS-Forschung revisionsbedürftig seien, wurde seit den 70er Jahren festgestellt (Mandel 1977). Die Arbitrarität sprachlicher Zeichen ist sowohl hinsichtlich ihrer Funktionen als auch ihres Ausmaßes zu relativieren und ist jedenfalls keine notwendige Bedingung für Zeichenstatus. Ikonische Kodierungsstrategien sind für Sprachen konstitutiv, müssen allerdings bezüglich Übertragungskanal, Teilbereich des Sprachsystems und Sprachentwicklungsphase differenziert werden. Auch die Sequentialität von Zeichen muß als Charakteristikum von Sprachen aufgegeben werden. Bezüglich LS sollten wir außerdem prüfen, ob wir die Rolle der 'parasprachlichen' non-verbalen Elemente in der Kommunikation adäquat beschreiben.

9. Zitierte Literatur

Aarons, Debra & Kegl, Judy & Neidle, Carol. 1995. „Lexical tense markers in ASL". In: Emmorey & Reilly (eds.), 225–53.

Ahlgren, Inger & Bergman, Brita. 1994. „Reference in narratives". In: Ahlgren & Bergman & Brennan (eds.), Vol. 1: 29–36.

Ahlgren, Inger & Bergman, Brita & Brennan, Mary (eds.). 1994. *Perspectives on sign language structure*. 2 Vols. Durham: Int. Sign Linguistics Assoc.

Anderson, Stephen R. 1992. „Linguistic Expression and its Relation to Modality". In: Coulter, 273–90.

Armstrong, David F. & Stokoe, William C. & Wilcox, Sherman E. 1995. *Gesture and the nature of language*. Cambridge: Cambridge University Press.

Bahan, Benjamin J. & Supalla, Samuel J. 1995. „Line segmentation and narrative structure: A study of eyegaze behavior in ASL". In: Emmorey & Reilly, 171–91.

Battison, Robbin M. 1978. *Lexical Borrowing in ASL: Phonological and morphological restructuring*. Silver Spring, MD: Linstok Press.

Bellugi, Ursula & Fischer, Susan. 1972. „A comparison of sign language and spoken language". *Cognition* 1: 173–200.

Bellugi, Ursula & Klima, Edward. 1991. „Eigenschaften räumlich-visueller Sprachen". In: Prillwitz, Siegmund & Vollhaber, Tomas (eds.). *Gebärdensprache in Forschung und Praxis*. Hamburg: Signum, 135–66.

Bergman, Brita. 1995. „Manual and nonmanual expression of negation in SSL". In: Bos & Schermer, 85–103.

Bos, Heleen & Schermer, Trude (eds.). 1994. *Sign language research*. Hamburg: Signum.

Boyes Braem, Penny. 1990. *Einführung in die Gebärdensprache und ihre Erforschung*. Hamburg: Signum.

Brennan, Mary. 1990. *Word formation in BSL*. Stockholm: Univ. of Stockholm.

Brennan, Mary. 1994. „Pragmatics and productivity". In: Ahlgren & Bergman & Brennan, Vol. 2: 371–90.

Brennan, Mary & Turner, Graham H. (eds.). 1994. *Word order issues in sign language*. Durham: Int. Sign Linguistics Assoc.

Brentari, Diane. 1995. „Sign language phonology: ASL". In: Goldsmith, John A. (ed.). *The Handbook of phonological theory*. Cambridge/MA & Oxford: Blackwell, 615–39.

Brentari, Diane. 1998. *A prosodic model of sign language phonology*. (Language, speech and communication.) Cambridge/MA & London: MIT.

Brien, David et al. 1992. *Dictionary of British Sign Language/English*. London & Boston: Faber

Cameracanna, Emanuela & al. 1994. „How visual spatial-temporal metaphors become visible in sign". In: Ahlgren & Bergman & Brennan, Vol. 1: 55–68.

Corina, David & Sandler, Wendy. 1993. „On the nature of phonological structure in sign language". *Phonology* 10: 165–207.

Coulter, Geoffrey R. (ed.). 1992. *Current issues in ASL Phonology*. San Diego etc.: Academic Press.

Coerts, Jane. 1994. „Constituent order in Sign Language of The Netherlands and the function of orientations". In: Ahlgren & Bergman & Brennan, Vol. 1: 69–88.

Deuchar, Margaret. 1984. *BSL*. London: Routledge & Kegan.

Deuchar, Margaret. 1996. „Spoken language and sign language". In: Lock & Peters, 553–70.

Dotter, Franz. 1991. „Gebärdensprache in der Gehörlosenbildung: Zu den Argumenten und Einstellungen ihrer Gegner". *Das Zeichen* 17: 321–32.

Dotter, Franz. 1995. „Nonarbitrariness and iconicity: coding possibilities". In: Landsberg, Marge E. (ed.). *Syntactic iconicity and freezes*. Berlin & New York: Mouton de Gruyter, 47–55.

Dotter, Franz & Holzinger, Daniel. 1995a. „Typologie und Gebärdensprache: Sequentialität und Simultanität". *Sprachtypologie und Universalienforschung* 48: 311–349.

Dotter, Franz & Holzinger, Daniel. 1995b. „Vorschlag zur Frühförderung gehörloser und schwer hörbehinderter Kinder in Österreich". *Der Sprachheilpädagoge* 27.4: 1−21.

Dubuisson, Colette & Desrosiers, Jules. 1994. „Names in Québec Sign Language and what they tell us about Québec deaf culture". In: Ahlgren & Bergman & Brennan, Vol. 2: 249−59.

Dubuisson, Colette & Miller, Christopher & Pinsonneault, Dominique. 1994. „Question sign position in LSQ (Québec Sign Language)". In: Ahlgren & Bergman & Brennan, Vol. 1: 89−103.

Ebbinghaus, Horst & Heßmann, Jens. 1990. „Deutsche Wörter in der Deutschen Gebärdensprache". *Das Zeichen* 11: 60−71.

Ebbinghaus, Horst & Heßmann, Jens. 1994/95. „Formen und Funktionen von Ablesewörtern in gebärdensprachlichen Äußerungen". *Das Zeichen* 8: 480−87 und 9: 50−61.

Edmondson, William H. 1990. „Segments in Signed Languages: Do they exist and does it matter?" In: E., W. H. & Karlsson, Fred (eds.). *SLR '87: Papers from The Fourth International Symposium on Sign Language Research.* Hamburg: Signum, 66−74.

Emmorey, Karen & Corina, David & Bellugi, Ursula. 1995. „Differential processing of topographic and referential functions of space". In: Emmorey & Reilly, 43−62.

Emmorey, Karen & Reilly Judy S. (eds.). 1995. *Language, Gesture, and space.* Hillsdale & Hove: Lawrence Erlbaum.

Engberg-Pedersen, Elisabeth. 1993. *Space in Danish Sign Language − The semantics and morphosyntax of the use of space in a visual language.* Hamburg: Signum.

Engberg-Pedersen, Elisabeth. 1995. „Point of view expressed through shifters". In: Emmorey & Reilly, 133−54.

Fischer, Renate & Lane, Harlan (eds.). 1993. *Blick zurück.* Hamburg: Signum.

Fischer, Susan D. & Siple, Patricia (eds.). 1990. *Theoretical issues in Sign Language research*, Vol. 1: Linguistics, Chicago & London: Univ. of Chicago Press.

Friedman, Lynn A. 1977. „Formational Properties of ASL". In: Friedman, Lynn A. 1977a, 13−56.

Friedman, Lynn A. 1977a. *On the other hand: new perspectives on American sign language.* (Language, thought, and culture.) New York: Academic Press.

Frishberg, Nancy. 1975. „Arbitrariness and iconicity: Historical change in ASL". *Language* 51: 696−719.

Gee, James P. 1992. „Reflections on the Nature of ASL and the Development of ASL Linguistics: Comments on Corina's Article". In: Coulter, 97−101.

Gipper, Helmut. 1980. „Vorwort". In: Van Uden, A. *Das gehörlose Kind.* Heidelberg: Groos, 11− 18.

Grimes, Barbara F. (ed.). [10]1984. *Ethnologue.* Dallas: Wycliffe Bible Translators.

Haiman, John. 1985. *Natural syntax.* Cambridge etc.: Cambridge University Press.

Hewes, Gordon W. 1996. „A history of the study of language origins and the gestural primacy hypothesis". In: Lock & Peters, 571−95.

Hockett, Charles F. 1960. „The origin of speech". *Scientific American* 203.3: 88−96.

Holzinger, Daniel. 1993. *Forschungsbericht: Linguistische Analyse von Gebärdensprachen.* (Scientia, 35). Innsbruck: Institut für Sprachwissenschaft.

Holzinger, Daniel. 1995. „Gebärden in der Kommunikation mit gehörlosen Kindern". *Hörgeschädigtenpädagogik* 49: 81−100, 163−80.

Holzinger, Daniel & Dotter, Franz. 1997. „Typologie und Gebärdensprache: Ikonizität". *Sprachtypologie und Universalienforschung* 50: 115−42.

Hulst, Harry van der. 1993. „Units in the analysis of sign". *Phonology* 10: 209−41.

Hulst, Harry van der. 1995. „Dependency relations in the phonological representation of signs". In: Bos & Schermer, 11−38.

Jacobowitz, E. Lynn & Stokoe, William C. 1988. „Signs of tense in ASL verbs". *Sign Language Studies* 60: 331−40.

Janis, Wynne D. 1995. „A crosslinguistic perspective on ASL verb agreement". In: Emmorey & Reilly, 195−223.

Joachim, Guido H. G. & Prillwitz, Siegmund. 1993. *International bibliography of sign language.* Hamburg: Signum.

Johnston, Trevor. 1991. „Spatial syntax and spatial semantics in the inflection of signs for the marking of person and location in AUSLAN". *Int. Journal of Sign Linguistics* 2: 29−62.

Keller, Jörg. 1998. *Aspekte der Raumnutzung in der deutschen Gebärdensprache.* Hamburg: Signum.

Klima, Edward S. & Bellugi, Ursula. 1979. *The Signs of Language.* Cambridge, MA: Harvard University Press.

Liddell, Scott K. 1980. *ASL Syntax.* The Hague: Mouton.

Liddell, Scott K. 1990. „Structures for representing handshape and local movement at the phonemic level". In: Fischer & Siple, 37−65.

Liddell, Scott. 1995. „Real, surrogate, and token space: Grammatical consequences in ASL". In: Emmorey & Reilly, 19−41.

Liddell, Scott K. & Johnson, Robert E. 1989. „ASL: The phonological base". *Sign Language Studies* 64: 195−277.

Lillo-Martin, Diane. 1995. „The point of view predicate in ASL". In: Emmorey & Reilly, 155−170.

Lock, Andrew & Peters, Charles R. (eds.). 1996. *Handbook of human symbolic evolution*. Oxford: Clarendon Press.

Lucas, Ceil (ed.). 1990. *Sign Language Research*. Washington: Gallaudet University Press.

Lucas, Ceil. 1994. „Language contact phenomena in deaf communities". In: Ahlgren & Bergman & Brennan, Vol. 2: 261–68.

Macken, Elizabeth & Perry, John & Haas, Cathy. 1993. „Richly grounding symbols in ASL". *Sign Language Studies* 81: 375–94.

Mandel, Mark. 1977. „Iconic devices in ASL". In: Friedman, Lynn A. 1977a, 57–107.

Mcilvenny, Paul & Rautaskoski, Pirkko. 1994. „Sign language and deaf interaction: a preliminary study of sign talk in Northern Finland". In: Ahlgren & Bergman & Brennan, Vol. 2: 269–92.

Meier, Richard P. 1992. „A psycholinguistic perspective on phonological segmentation in sign and speech". In: Coulter (1992), 169–88.

Meier, Richard P. & Willerman, Raquel. 1995. „Prelinguistic gesture in deaf and hearing infants". In: Emmorey & Reilly, 391–409.

Metley, Donald S. & Supalla, Ted. 1995. „Morphosyntactic structure of aspect and number inflections in ASL". In: Emmorey & Reilly, 255–84.

Miller, Christopher. 1994a. „Simultaneous constructions and complex signs in Quebec Sign Language". In: Ahlgren & Bergman & Brennan, Vol. 1: 131–47.

Miller, Christopher. 1994b. „A note on notation". *Signpost* 37: 191–202.

Morford, Jill P. & Singleton, Jenny L. & Goldin-Meadow, Susan. 1995. „The genesis of language: How much time is needed to generate arbitrary symbols in a sign system?". In: Emmorey & Reilly, 313–32.

Neidle, Carol & Kegl, Judy & MacLaughlin, Dawn & Bahan, Benjamin & Lee, Robert G. 1999. *The syntax of American Sign Language: Functional categories and hierarchical structure*. Cambridge, Mass.: MIT Press.

Padden, Carol A. 1988. *Interaction of morphology and syntax in ASL*. New York: Garland.

Perlmutter, David M. 1992. „Sonority and syllable structure in ASL". In: Coulter 1992, 227–61.

Pizzuto, Elena. 1986. „The verb system of Italian Sign Language". In: Tervoort, Bernard T. (ed.). *Signs of Life: Proceedings of the 2nd European Congress on Sign Language Research*. Amsterdam: Univ. of Amsterdam, 17–31.

Poulin, Christine & Miller, Christopher. 1995. „On narrative discourse and point of view in Quebec Sign Language". In: Emmorey & Reilly, 117–31.

Prillwitz, Siegmund et al. 1985. *Skizzen zu einer Grammatik der Deutschen Gebärdensprache*. Hamburg: Forschungsstelle DGS.

Prillwitz, Siegmund et al. 1989. *HamNoSys. Version 2.0. Hamburg Notation System for Sign Languages*. Hamburg: Signum.

Sandler, Wendy. 1992. „Linearization of phonological tiers in ASL". In: Coulter 1992, 103–29.

Schick, Brenda. 1990. „Classifier predicates in ASL". *International Journal of Sign Linguistics* 1: 15–40.

Stokoe, William C. 1960. *Sign Language Structure: An outline of the visual communication system of the American deaf*. Buffalo: Univ. of Buffalo.

Stokoe, William C. & Casterline, Dorothy C. & Croneberg, Carl G. 1965. *A dictionary of ASL on linguistic principles*. Washington: Linstok Press.

Supalla, Ted. 1986. „The classifier system in ASL". In: Craig, Colette (ed.) *Noun classes and categorization*. Amsterdam & Philadelphia, 181–214.

Supalla, Ted & Newport Elissa L. 1978. „How many seats in a chair? The derivation of nouns and verbs in ASL". In: Siple, Patricia (ed.). *Understanding Language through Sign Language Research*. New York: Academic Press, 91–132.

Supalla, Ted & Webb, Rebecca. 1995. „The grammar of International Sign: A new look at pidgin languages". In: Emmorey & Reilly, 333–52.

Sutton, Valerie. 1981. *Sign writing for everyday use*. Boston & Newport Beach: The Sutton Movement Writing Press.

Tervoort, Bernard T.M. 1953. *Structurele analyse van visueel taalgebruik binnen een groep dove kinderen*. 2 Deele. Amsterdam: Noord-Hollandsche Uitgevers.

Uyechi, Linda. 1996. *The geometry of visual phonology*. Stanford: CSLI Publ.

Valli, Clayton & Lucas, Ceil. ²1995. *Linguistics of ASL*. Washington: Gallaudet Univ. Press.

Volterra, Virginia & Erting, Carol J. (eds.) 1990. *From Gesture to language in hearing and deaf children*. Berlin etc.: Springer.

Volterra, Virginia et al. 1984. „Italian Sign Language: The order of elements in the declarative sentence". In: Loncke, Filip & Boyes Braem, Penny & Lebrun, Yvan (eds.). *Recent research on European sign languages*. Lisse: Swets & Zeitlinger, 19–48.

Wilbur, Ronnie B. 1979. *ASL and Sign Systems*. Baltimore: University Park Press.

Wilbur, Ronnie B. 1987. *ASL: Linguistic & applied dimensions*. Boston etc.: College-Hill.

Wilbur, Ronnie B. 1990. „Why syllables? What the notion means for ASL research". In: Fischer & Siple, 81–108.

Winston, Elizabeth A. 1995. „Spatial mapping in comparative discourse frames". In: Emmorey & Reilly, 87–114.

Winston, Elizabeth (ed.). 1999. *Storytelling and conversation: discourse in deaf commuities*. Washington D.C.: Gallaudet University Press.

Wisch, Fritz-Helmut. 1990. *Lautsprache UND Gebärdensprache*. Hamburg: Signum.

Woll, Bencie. 1994. „The influence of television on the deaf community in Great Britain". In: Ahlgren & Bergman & Brennan, Vol. 2: 293—301.

Zahwe, Claudia. 1994. *Zur Struktur der Deutschen Gebärdensprache*. Hausarbeit Universität Köln.

Zeshan, Ulrike. 2000. *Gebärdensprachen des indischen Subkontinents*. München: Lincom.

Zimmer, June & Patschke, Cynthia. 1990. „A class of determiners in ASL". In: Lucas, 201—10.

Wichtige Internet-Adressen

Deaf World Web:
http://dww.deafworldweb.org/

Gallaudet Research Institute:
http://gri.gallaudet.edu/

Universität Hamburg, Zentrum für Deutsche Gebärdensprache:
http://www.sign-lang.uni-hamburg.de/

Liste bekannter Gebärdensprachen
http://www.sil.org/ethnologue/families/Deaf_sign_language.html

Sign Linguistics Resource Index
http://www.vuw.ac.nz/~nzsldict/

Sign Writing Homepage
http://www.SignWriting.org/

Franz Dotter, Universität Klagenfurt,
(Österreich)

11. Textproduktions- und Textverstehensforschung

1. Textproduktion
2. Textverstehen
3. Ausblick
4. Zitierte Literatur

Ein Text ist ein Kommunikationsinstrument, mit dem ein Autor bzw. Textproduzent einem Leser bzw. Textrezipienten eine Mitteilung über einen Sachverhalt macht (Bühler 1934). Dabei versucht der Autor, das Bewußtsein des Lesers mittels sprachlicher Formulierungen so zu steuern, daß der Leser versteht, was der Autor meint. Das Gelingen dieser Kommunikation erfordert, daß der Autor bestimmte pragmatische Kooperationsprinzipien einhält, die zugleich vom Leser implizit als gültig angenommen werden (Clark 1993; Grice 1967). Textkommunikation besteht jeweils aus Textproduktion und aus Textrezeption. Eine systematische Erforschung von kognitiven Prozessen der Textproduktion findet erst seit den 80er Jahren statt, während die Forschung zum Textverstehen etwa ein Jahrzehnt älter ist und insofern bereits zu etwas differenzierteren Modellvorstellungen geführt hat.

1. Textproduktion

1.1. Textproduktion als Problemlösen

Die Erforschung des Schreibens hat sich in den vergangenen zwei Jahrzehnten grundlegend verändert. Stand bis in die 70er Jahre die Analyse von Texten als Produkten des Schreibens mittels rhetorischer Kategorien im Vordergrund, wobei versucht wurde, die Merkmale kommunikationswirksamer Texte zu identifizieren, erfolgte in den 80er Jahren eine kognitive Wende in der Textproduktionsforschung, in der man sich verstärkt den mentalen Prozessen beim Schreiben sowie deren Koordination zuwandte (Eigler 1998; Galbraith & Rijlaarsdam 1999).

Den Beginn dieser kognitiven Wende kennzeichnet ein von John R. Hayes und Linda Flower (1980) entwickeltes Modell der Textproduktion. In diesem Modell wird in Anlehnung an Newell & Simon (1972) der Prozeß des Schreibens als Lösung eines komplexen Problems angesehen. Dieses Problem besteht darin, einen Text über einen bestimmten Sachverhalt für bestimmte Adressaten mit dem Ziel zu verfassen, ihnen Wissen über den Sachverhalt zu vermitteln, ihnen eine bestimmte Sichtweise nahezulegen, sie eine bestimmte Argumentation nachvollziehen zu lassen usw. Der Textproduzent muß dabei nicht nur Wissen über das Thema besitzen, sondern auch auf Wissen über die Adressaten, über Darstellungsmöglichkeiten und Darstellungskonventionen zurückgreifen können.

Die Textproduktion selbst bildet ein durch Rückmeldung geregeltes System von rekursiven Planungs-, sprachlichen Umsetzungs- und Revisionsprozessen, deren Koordination von einer zentralen Exekutive gesteuert wird.

Die Planung beinhaltet das Setzen von Zielen sowie die Erinnerung und Organisation von Wissen. Die sprachliche Umsetzung erfolgt durch Formulierung von Phrasen und Sätzen entsprechend bestimmter Kohärenz- bzw. Kohäsionskriterien, und die Revision besteht im Lesen, Korrigieren und Editieren des geschriebenen Texts.

In dem Modell von Hayes & Flower (1980) erinnert der Textproduzent das in den Text eingehende Wissen ausschließlich aus dem Gedächtnis, was für umfangreiche Texte über komplexe Inhalte nicht realistisch ist. Der Prozeß der Textproduktion erfolgt im allgemeinen vielmehr durch ein Zusammenspiel von internen Informationen, die aus dem Gedächtnis abgerufen werden, und externen Informationen, die in Form von Dokumenten vorliegen (Eigler 1997).

Die bei der Textproduktion stattfindenden Prozesse folgen nicht schrittweise aufeinander, sondern gehen zum Teil ineinander über bzw. finden parallel statt und beeinflussen einander wechselseitig. Beispielsweise sind die Ziele des Schreibens häufig nicht klar vorab definiert und mit einer bestimmten Textsorte assoziiert, sondern können im Prozeß des Schreibens selbst entwickelt, elaboriert und präzisiert werden. Auf diese wechselseitige Beeinflussung der verschiedenen Teilprozesse beim Schreiben hat de Beaugrande (1984) in seinem *parallel-stage-interaction model* hingewiesen.

Die von Hayes und Flower beschriebenen Teilprozesse finden nicht bei jedem Akt des Schreibens statt. Textproduzenten können auch Prozesse überspringen und dadurch suboptimale Texte verfassen, oder sie können zur Entlastung ihrer kognitiven Verarbeitungskapazität relativ mechanischen Schreibgewohnheiten folgen. Frederiksen & al. (1986) betonen deshalb, daß der Prozeß der Textproduktion sowohl ein komplexes Problemlösen als auch ein einfaches Routinehandeln sein kann. Die Autoren haben ein Modell der Textkommunikation entwickelt, welches sich sowohl auf die Textproduktion als auch das Textverstehen bezieht. Beides wird als Prozeß der Vermittlung zwischen konzeptuellen und textuellen Strukturen mittels kognitiver Prozesse angesehen.

Die konzeptuellen Strukturen beinhalten zum einen FRAMES, also globale Bedeutungsstrukturen mit einer spezifischen, z.B. narrativen, deskriptiven oder argumentativen Formbestimmtheit. Zum anderen enthalten sie Propositionen, also lokale Bedeutungsstrukturen, die für bestimmte Sachverhalte spezifische Prädikationen vornehmen.

Die textuellen Strukturen bestehen ihrerseits aus globalen Einheiten – z.B. übergreifenden rhetorischen Strukturen – und aus lokalen Einheiten – Phrasen und Sätzen, die durch Syntax und durch kohäsionsstiftende sprachliche Mittel gekennzeichnet sind (→ Art. 47).

Nach Frederiksen & al. (1986) konstruiert ein Individuum bei der Textproduktion globale Bedeutungseinheiten bzw. Frames, setzt diese in lokale Bedeutungseinheiten bzw. Propositionen um und drückt diese dann sprachlich aus. Dabei werden die aufeinanderfolgenden Einheiten durch globale Topikalisierung und durch lokale kohäsionsstiftende Mittel entsprechend der übergeordneten Framestruktur verknüpft. Die Textproduktion wird hier als ein interaktiver Prozeß angesehen, der prinzipiell auf verschiedenen Ebenen Entscheidungen und konstruktive Aktivitäten erfordert. Diese müssen jedoch nicht notwendig aufgrund eines bewußten Reflexionsprozesses vollzogen werden, sondern können beim routinehaften Schreiben auch weitgehend automatisiert stattfinden.

1.2. Textproduktion als Wissenswiedergabe und als Wissenstransformation

Da der Prozeß der Textproduktion immer den Einschränkungen des Arbeitsgedächtnisses unterworfen ist, besteht ein wesentliches Problem beim Schreiben in der Koordination der verschiedenen Teilprozesse. Nach Carl Bereiter und Marlene Scardamalia (1987) sind deshalb bei der Vermittlung von Fähigkeiten des effektiven Schreibens Koordinationshilfen anzubieten, die dazu beitragen, das komplexe Problem der Textproduktion in handhabbare Teilprobleme zu untergliedern.

Novizen haben bei der Textproduktion häufig deshalb Schwierigkeiten, weil sie dazu tendieren, das Schreiben als einen einheitlichen Prozeß anzusehen, der nicht in unterschiedliche Teilprozesse untergliedert ist. Sie rufen Wissen aus dem Gedächtnis ab, prüfen dieses auf seine thematische Passung und setzen es direkt in sprachliche Formulierungen um bzw. schreiben einfach auf, was ihnen einfällt. Sie verausgaben ihr thematisches Wissen, ohne es weiter zu bearbeiten. Diese Strategie der Textproduktion wird als Wissenswiedergabe (*knowledge telling*) bezeichnet.

Erfahrene Textproduzenten hingegen vollziehen konstruktive Aktivitäten auf verschiedenen Ebenen, nehmen eine elaborierte Planung entsprechend den jeweiligen Kommunikationszielen im Hinblick auf bestimmte

Adressaten vor und revidieren den geschriebenen Text hinsichtlich des Inhalts, der Darstellungsstruktur und der Oberflächenstrukturmerkmale. Diese Strategie der Textproduktion wird als Wissenstransformation (*knowledge transforming*) bezeichnet. Ideen werden hier nicht einfach aus dem Gedächtnis abgerufen, sondern im Hinblick auf die jeweiligen kommunikativen Ziele konstruiert und evaluiert.

Das epistemische Schreiben kann als ein Spezialfall dieser Wissenstransformation angesehen werden: Schreiben ist hier eine Veränderung der äußeren Situation des Textproduzenten, indem dieser eine externe Repräsentation seines eigenen Denkens schafft und damit auf dieses Denken selbst reflexiv Bezug nehmen kann (Kellogg 1994).

Bei der Wissenstransformation ist die Textproduktion nicht nur von inhaltlichem Wissen über den Gegenstand, sondern auch vom Diskurswissen über die linguistischen Regeln zur Behandlung eines Themas abhängig. Dementsprechend wird zwischen einem Problemraum für den Inhalt (*content space*) und einem Problemraum für die rhetorischen Aspekte des Schreibens (*rhetorical space*) unterschieden. Bei der Strategie der Wissenstransformation ist der Schreibende ein planender, vergleichender und prüfender Akteur, der ständig zwischen beiden Problemräumen hin und her wechselt.

Als Ergebnis entsteht nicht nur ein reflektierter Text mit einem hohen Organisationsgrad. Der Textproduzent entdeckt auch selbst neue Seiten am darzustellenden Inhalt und elaboriert oder reorganisiert sein eigenes Wissen. Durch Berücksichtigung von Wissen über Inhalte, über Konventionen, soziale Kognitionen und verschiedene Gewichtung von Teilprozessen kann es zu sehr unterschiedlichen Entwicklungsverläufen bei der Textproduktion kommen (Jechle 1992).

1.3. Schreibenlernen

Nach Bereiter & Scardamalia (1987) gilt es demnach beim Schreibenlernen, von einer Strategie der Wissenswiedergabe zu einer Strategie der Wissenstransformation überzugehen, indem Hilfen zur Koordination der verschiedenen Teilprozesse eines reflektierten Schreibens angeboten werden. Sie sollen den Lernenden angesichts der Komplexität der Aufgabe darin unterstützen, seine begrenzte kognitive Verarbeitungskapazität in Abhängigkeit vom jeweiligen Kontext bei der Verfolgung kommunikativer Ziele adäquat einzusetzen. Diese Unterstützung kann z.B. die Konkretisierung von Zielen betreffen oder in der Empfehlung geeigneter Mittel – einer sog. prozeduralen Erleichterung – bestehen.

Außerdem gilt es, Lernende dafür zu sensibilisieren, wann welche Teilaktivitäten des Schreibprozesses zu vollziehen sind, da die Qualität von Texten weniger vom globalen Ausmaß verschiedener Teilaktivitäten, sondern vor allem vom Zeitpunkt abhängt, zu dem diese Aktivitäten durchgeführt werden (Breetvelt & al. 1994). Da eine reflektierte Textproduktion entsprechend der Strategie der Wissenstransformation in hohem Maße der bewußten Kontrolle unterworfen ist, wurden kognitive Modelle der Textproduktion um metakognitive Komponenten erweitert (Winter 1992).

Neuere Ansätze zur Erforschung der Textproduktion, die seit den 90er Jahren stärker vertreten werden, kritisieren die bisher vorherrschende kognitive Perspektive der Forschung und betonen die soziale Natur des Schreibens bzw. dessen Situiertheit innerhalb bestimmter kultureller Praktiken (Galbraith & Rijlaarsdam 1999). Der Autor eines Texts ist demnach immer in eine soziale und linguistische Gemeinschaft mit bestimmten Interessen und Sichtweisen eingebunden (→ Art. 36). Dementsprechend werden inzwischen sozio-kognitive Modelle des Textproduzierens entwickelt, in denen die Ziele des Schreibens sowie die Planung und Realisierung von Texten hinsichtlich ihrer Übereinstimmung mit den Konventionen bzw. diskursiven Praktiken einer sozialen Gemeinschaft untersucht werden (Flower 1994).

2. Textverstehen

2.1. Kognitive Mechanismen des Textverstehens

Prozesse des Textverstehens basieren auf einer Vielzahl kognitiver Funktionen, zu denen u. a. Wahrnehmung, Lernen, Gedächtnis, Denken und Problemlösen gehören. Dementsprechend wird versucht, Theorien des Textverstehens in allgemeine Theorien der menschlichen Kognition zu integrieren. Schematheoretische Ansätze gehen davon aus, daß das allgemeine Weltwissen eines Individuums in Form hierarchisch organisierter kognitiver Schemata gespeichert ist. Bei diesen Schemata handelt es sich um mentale Datenstrukturen, die bisherige Erfahrungen verallgemeinern und typische Zusammenhänge eines Realitätsbereichs repräsentieren (Anderson & Pearson 1984). Textverstehen basiert diesem Theorieansatz zufolge auf einem Wechselspiel von auf- und absteigenden Schema-Aktivierungen, das durch die vorliegende Textinformation angeregt wird und bei dem sich eine bestimmte Konfiguration aktivierter Schemata herausbildet, die als beste Interpretation des Texts gilt.

Walter Kintsch und Teun A. van Dijk (1978) haben in einem Modell der kognitiven Textverarbeitung zu beschreiben versucht, wie beim Textverstehen Mikro- und Makropropositionen vom Leser zu einem kohärenten Ganzen verknüpft werden. Infolge der begrenzten kognitiven Verarbeitungskapazität erfolgt die Kohärenzbildung in mehreren Zyklen. In jedem Zyklus wird eine bestimmte Anzahl von Propositionen ins Arbeitsgedächtnis eingelesen und anhand bestimmter Kohärenzkriterien zu einem sog. Kohärenzgraphen verknüpft.

Ein Teil des Arbeitsgedächtnisses fungiert als Kurzzeitspeicher, in dem eine bestimmte Anzahl der bisher verarbeiteten Propositionen aufbewahrt und zum nächsten Zyklus mitgetragen wird, um so eine Verknüpfung der neuen Propositionen mit dem bisher Gelesenen zu erleichtern. Je nachdem, ob sich für die neuen Propositionen noch Anknüpfungspunkte im Kurzzeitspeicher befinden oder nicht, oder ob diese ggf. erst inferiert werden müssen, verläuft die Verarbeitung unterschiedlich leicht und flüssig. Bruce K. Britton und S. Gulgoz (1991) fanden, daß die Revision technischer expositorischer Texte mit Hilfe dieses Modells zu weit höheren Lern-Erfolgen führte als eine Revision durch professionelle Autoren.

In ihrem als Produktionssystem konzipierten CAPS/READER-Modell gehen M.A. Just & Patricia Carpenter (1992) davon aus, daß die für die Textverarbeitung relevanten kognitiven Prozeduren in Form von Produktionsregeln für die Informationsaufnahme, die Enkodierung von Wortbildern und Wortbedeutungen, die Bestimmung semantisch-syntaktischer Wortfunktionen und die semantische Verknüpfung von Phrasen gespeichert sind, und daß darüber hinaus durch zielspezifische Produktionsregeln auch unterschiedlichen Verarbeitungs-Strategien Rechnung getragen werden kann.

Die Produktionen kommunizieren miteinander über das Arbeitsgedächtnis. Die Prozesse der Wort-Enkodierung, der Bestimmung semantisch-syntaktischer Wortfunktionen und der Verknüpfung von Phrasen bilden keine starr aufeinanderfolgenden Verarbeitungsstufen, sondern beeinflussen einander ständig wechselseitig, indem 'höhere' Prozesse auf 'niedrigere' Einfluß nehmen und umgekehrt. Die Autoren gelangen mit Hilfe dieses Modells zu relativ guten Vorhersagen über die Bewegung der Augen beim Lesen in Abhängigkeit von den Eigenschaften des Texts sowie den individuellen Zielsetzungen des Lesers.

Konnektionistische Ansätze wenden gegen die Theorie kognitiver Schemata und die Modellierung kognitiver Prozesse mit Hilfe von Produktionssystemen ein, die Regelhaftigkeit kognitiver Prozesse ginge nicht auf die Wirkung von Verarbeitungsregeln zurück, sondern sei lediglich das äußere Erscheinungsbild des Funktionierens sog. neuronaler Netzwerke. Ein solches Netzwerk besteht aus einer großen Zahl einfacher Verarbeitungs-Einheiten − den Netzwerkknoten − die miteinander über gewichtete Verbindungen kommunizieren. Jede dieser Verarbeitungs-Einheiten befindet sich zu einem bestimmten Zeitpunkt in einem bestimmten Aktivationszustand und beeinflußt über exzitatorische und inhibitorische Verbindungen den Aktivationszustand anderer Einheiten. Die kognitive Verarbeitung besteht hier im Prinzip darin, daß sich das Netzwerk durch ein Wechselspiel von aktivierenden und hemmenden Einflüssen zwischen den verschiedenen Netzwerkknoten auf einen bestimmten Aktivationszustand einschwingt, der am besten zur jeweiligen Eingabe paßt.

Ein konnektionistisches Modell zum Verstehen von natürlichsprachlichen Sätzen haben Waltz & Pollack (1985) entwickelt. Ebenfalls auf konnektionistischen Verarbeitungsprinzipien basiert das Konstruktions-Integrations-Modell von Walter Kintsch (1988). Diesem Modell zufolge durchläuft die Verarbeitung der Sätze eines Texts jeweils eine Konstruktions- und eine Integrationsphase. In der Konstruktionsphase werden dem Arbeitsgedächtnis aufgrund assoziativer Aktivationsausbreitung rasch neue Knoten hinzugefügt, welche teils zur Oberflächenstruktur, teils zur Textbasis, teils zum referentiellen Situationsmodell gehören, und mit dem bisherigen Arbeitsgedächtnis-Inhalt kombiniert.

Sobald eine gewisse Zahl von Knoten aktiviert ist, beginnt die Integrationsphase. Grundlage dieser Integration ist ein aus den aktivierten Knoten bestehendes konnektionistisches Netzwerk. In diesem Netzwerk bestehen sowohl zwischen den Knoten der Oberflächenstruktur, den Knoten der Textbasis und den Knoten des Situationsmodells, als auch zwischen den Knoten verschiedener Verarbeitungsebenen exzitatorische und inhibitorische Verbindungen. In der Integrationsphase schwingt sich das Netzwerk auf einen stabilen Aktivationszustand ein, der als Interpretation der vorliegenden Textinformation gilt.

2.2. Mentale Repräsentationen beim Textverstehen

Textverstehen kann als Versuch der Rekonstruktion der vom Autor bei der Textproduktion externalisierten mentalen Repräsentationen verstanden werden. Theorie-Ansätze zum Textverstehen gehen davon aus, daß beim Verstehen eines Texts multiple mentale Repräsentationen konstruiert werden (van Dijk & Kintsch 1983). Dabei lassen sich folgende Repräsentationsebenen unterscheiden, die zugleich als Ebenen der Textverarbeitung angesehen werden können:

− die Ebene der Textoberfläche,
− die Ebene der Textbasis,
− die Ebene des referentiellen mentalen Modells,
− die Kommunikationsebene und
− die Genre-Ebene.

Die *Ebene der Textoberfläche* repräsentiert die gesamte sprachliche Information des Texts, also Formulierungen, syntaktische Konstruktionen usw. Die *Ebene der Textbasis* repräsentiert den semantischen Gehalt in Form von Propositionen. Bei diesen Propositionen handelt es sich um komplexe Symbole, die den Gegenstand des Texts beschreiben. Das *referentielle Modell* ist eine ganzheitliche mentale Repräsentation des im Text dargestellten Sachverhalts (bzw. des darin beschriebenen Referenten), die anhand der Textbasis und des sachbezogenen Weltwissens konstruiert wird. Die *Kommunikationsebene* bezieht sich auf den pragmatischen kommunikativen Kontext, in den der Text eingebettet ist. Hierzu gehört die Identifikation der vom Autor verfolgten Kommunikationsabsicht und die Identifikation des Agenten der Kommunikation. Bei narrativen Texten bleibt der Agent der Kommunikation meist als unsichtbarer Beobachter des Geschehens implizit. Manchmal tritt er jedoch auch − z.B. als Ich-Erzähler − explizit hervor. Die *Genre-Ebene* bezieht sich auf die Textsorte und die entsprechende Textfunktion, z.B. des Erzählens, des Beschreibens, des Erklärens, des Überzeugens, des Unterhaltens usw.

Die Forschung zum Textverstehen konzentrierte sich bisher vor allem auf die Beschaffenheit der Textbasis und des referentiellen Modells. Die Textbasis besteht aus Propositionen, die einer bestimmten Gegebenheit ein bestimmtes Attribut zuschreiben oder durch die zwischen verschiedenen Gegebenheiten bestimmte Relationen spezifiziert werden. Propositionen besitzen eine Prädikat-Argument-Struktur. Zustandsprädikate werden an der Textoberfläche meist durch Adjektive, Prozeß- und Aktionsprädikate durch Verben signalisiert. Die Propositionsargumente werden an der Textoberfläche durch Nominalphrasen ausgedrückt. Die semantischen Rollen dieser Argumente (wie z. B. Agent, Objekt, Rezipient usw.) werden durch Präpositionen, Artikelflexionen usw. signalisiert (Chafe 1994).

Hinsichtlich der Ebene des referentiellen Modells wurden verschiedene Theorien formuliert, die von der gemeinsamen Annahme ausgehen, daß beim Verstehen eines Texts eine ganzheitliche mentale Repräsentation des dargestellten Sachverhalts konstruiert wird. Sanford & Garrod (1981) sprechen hier von Szenarien, van Dijk & Kintsch (1983) von Situationsmodellen, Johnson-Laird (1983) von mentalen Modellen.

Grundsätzlich ermöglicht ein Text die Konstruktion einer Vielzahl von mentalen Modellen, die dem Sinngehalt des Texts gleichermaßen Rechnung tragen. Der Leser konstruiert jedoch normalerweise nur ein Modell von hoher Typikalität. Die mentale Repräsentation der Textoberfläche scheint einem besonders raschen Verfall unterworfen zu sein. Die propositionale Textbasis wird langsamer vergessen, und die geringste Vergessensrate findet sich auf der Ebene des referentiellen Modells (Kintsch & al. 1990; Schmalhofer & Glavanov, 1986).

Die propositionale Textbasis und das referentielle Modell dürften jeweils unterschiedlichen Zwecken dienen. Es ist anzunehmen, daß die Konstruktion der Textbasis einen geringeren Verarbeitungs-Aufwand erfordert, auch für das Speichern vager bzw. schwer verständlicher Aussagen geeignet ist, viel von der Struktur des Texts bewahrt und insofern gut für die Wiedergabe des betreffenden Sinngehalts geeignet ist. Vom referentiellen mentalen Modell hingegen wird angenommen, daß es einen höheren Verarbeitungs-Aufwand erfordert und besonders für jene Prozesse geeignet ist, die man gewöhnlich als Inferenzen bezeichnet. Wiedergaben fallen hingegen weniger genau aus, weil die Struktur der Sprachäußerung hier nicht bewahrt wird und eine Wiedergabe deshalb als freie Beschreibung des betreffenden Modells stattfinden muß.

Einige neuere Untersuchungen haben gezeigt, daß lexikalische und syntaktische Informationen beim Textverstehen auch unmittelbar als Hinweise für die mentale Modellkonstruktion verwendet werden können, womit die Existenz einer eigenen propositionalen Textbasis in Frage gestellt wird (Perfetti & Britt 1995).

2.3. Kohärenzbildung beim Textverstehen

Ein Text unterscheidet sich von einer beliebigen Aneinanderreihung von Sätzen durch seine Kohärenz. Das Verstehen von Texten ist demnach ein Prozeß der mentalen Kohärenzbildung. Dabei kann man zwischen lokaler und globaler Kohärenzbildung unterscheiden. Bei der lokalen Kohärenzbildung werden semantische Zusammenhänge zwischen den unmittelbar aufeinanderfolgenden Sätzen, bei der globalen Kohärenzbildung semantische Zusammenhänge zwischen größeren Textabschnitten mental rekonstruiert. Wenn ein Text wenig kohärent und der Leser wenig motiviert ist oder eine geringe Arbeitsgedächtnisspanne besitzt, so werden die Bemühungen um globale Kohärenzbildung reduziert. Häufig gelingt deshalb Lesern nur die lokale Kohärenzbildung, während die übergeordneten Zusammenhänge nicht ins Blickfeld kommen (Albrecht & O'Brien 1993).

2.3.1. Inferenzen

Ein integraler Bestandteil der Kohärenzbildung beim Textverstehen ist das Ziehen von Inferenzen, da da der Autor eines Texts vieles wegläßt, was vom Leser leicht selbständig ergänzt werden kann (Rickheit & Strohner 1985). Dabei können je nach mentaler Repräsentationsebene unterschiedliche Inferenzmechanismen angenommen werden.

Inferenzen anhand einer propositionalen Repräsentation erfolgen mit Hilfe von Symbolverarbeitungsregeln, die mittels sog. Bedeutungspostulate, von vorhandenen Propositionen ausgehend, neue Propositionen generieren.

Inferenzen anhand eines referentiellen Modells bestehen hingegen in der Manipulation des Modells und dem Ablesen der gesuchten Information (Johnson-Laird 1983). Dabei sind zwar Konstruktions- und Ableseprozesse erforderlich, die regelgeleitet ablaufen. Es werden jedoch keine logischen Schlußregeln benötigt, weshalb hier auch von Pseudo-Inferenzen gesprochen wird.

Hinsichtlich des Umfangs der beim Textverstehen gezogenen Inferenzen existieren unterschiedliche theoretische Positionen. Nach der von McKoon & Ratcliff (1992) vertretenen minimalistischen Hypothese werden die kausalen Antezedenzen von im Text beschriebenen Ereignissen nur inferiert, wenn diese Inferenzen für die lokale Kohärenzbildung erforderlich sind. Graesser & al. (1994) hingegen nehmen in ihrer sog. konstruktionistischen Hypothese an, daß beim Lesen eines Texts drei Arten von Inferenzen vollzogen werden:

(a) Inferenzen, die die Verstehensziele des Lesers betreffen,
(b) Inferenzen, die das Auftreten eines Ereignisses oder einer Aktion erklären, und
(c) Inferenzen, die auf lokaler oder globaler Ebene Kohärenz im referentiellen mentalen Modell herstellen.

Graesser & al. (1997) vertreten die Auffassung, daß diese Hypothesen für jeweils unterschiedliche Bedingungen gültig sind. Demnach trifft die minimalistische Hypothese dann zu, wenn sehr schnell gelesen wird, der Text nicht global kohärent ist und der Leser wenig Hintergrundwissen hat. Die konstruktionistische Hypothese wird dann als gültig angesehen, wenn zum Zweck des Vergnügens oder des Wissens-Erwerbs mit vergleichsweise geringer Geschwindigkeit gelesen wird, wenn der Text global kohärent ist und wenn der Leser hinreichend Hintergrundwissen besitzt.

2.3.2. Textgesteuerte Kohärenzbildung

Angesichts der begrenzten kognitiven Verarbeitungskapazität können sich jeweils nur Teile der Information auf den verschiedenen Repräsentationsebenen im Fokus der Aufmerksamkeit und Konzentration befinden. Der Leser muß deshalb wissen, wovon im Augenblick die Rede ist, um im Falle eines Themenwechsels den Fokus entsprechend verschieben zu können (Chafe 1994; Gernsbacher 1990).

Die hierzu erforderlichen Steuerungssignale werden jeweils durch Topic-Angaben vermittelt. Der Leser identifiziert die Topic-Angabe, vergleicht sie mit dem bisher fokussierten Referenten und behält je nach Übereinstimmung oder Nicht-Übereinstimmung den Fokus bei oder sucht innerhalb der mentalen Repräsentation nach einem neuen Referenten. Dabei wird dem Leser signalisiert, ob ein Topic-Wechsel stattgefunden hat, ob eine kleine oder große Fokus-Verschiebung notwendig ist, wo der neue Topic zu suchen ist und anhand welcher Merkmale dieser identifiziert werden kann. Beispielsweise kann der Topic eines Satzes durch syntaktische Mittel unterschiedlich stark markiert sein (Givón 1983). Dabei signalisiert der Grad der Markiertheit dem Leser die Größe der erforderlichen Fokus-Verschiebung. Eine geringe Markiertheit wird vom Leser als Hinweis darauf interpretiert, daß der bisherige Topic beibehalten wurde. Eine starke Markiertheit wird als Indiz gewertet, daß ein Topic-Wechsel stattgefunden hat (Fletcher 1985).

Die als Anaphora, d.h. zur Bezugnahme auf eine bereits eingeführte Entität verwendeten Worte und Phrasen können als Suchanweisungen nach der betreffenden Entität aufgefaßt werden. Beispielsweise wird durch ein singulares Pronomen signalisiert, daß der Referent zuvor explizit an der Sprachoberfläche genannt wurde, daß er sich noch innerhalb des aktuellen Aufmerksamkeitsfokus befindet und anhand von Geschlecht und Numerus eindeutig identifiziert werden kann. Im Vergleich zu einem Pronomen stellt ein Nomen bzw. eine Nominalphrase einen wesentlich ausführlicheren „Steckbrief" des zu suchenden Referenten bereit. Dabei bieten eine Rekurrenz − also die Wiederholung eines bereits zuvor verwendeten Nomens (z.B. „Hubschrauber") − oder ein entsprechendes Synonym (z.B. „Helikopter") eine reichhaltigere Beschreibung des Referenten als eine lexikalische Generalisierung (z.B. „Fluggerät"). Im Falle der Verwendung eines Synonyms wird der Bezug auf den gemeinten Referenten erst auf der Ebene der propositionalen Repräsentation erkennbar, während dieser Bezug im Falle einer Rekurrenz bereits an der Sprachoberfläche signalisiert wird.

Die verschiedenen Suchparameter müssen jeweils aufeinander abgestimmt sein: Je größer die erforderliche Fokus-Verschiebung bzw. je größer der Suchbereich ist, in dem der Referent zu finden ist, und je mehr der darin enthaltenen Entitäten dem Referenten ähnlich sind, desto reichhaltiger muß die Beschreibung des Referenten sein, um diesen ohne Schwierigkeiten finden zu können. Die Beschreibung des Referenten muß jedoch keineswegs möglichst ausführlich sein. Sie muß lediglich so reichhaltig sein, daß dieser problemlos identifiziert werden kann (vgl. Gernsbacher 1990).

Die mentale Kohärenzbildung wird durch eine thematisch kontinuierliche Darstellung wesentlich unterstützt. Thematische Kontinuität kann dabei sowohl in räumlicher, zeitlicher, kausaler und intentionaler Hinsicht als auch im Hinblick auf die an einem Geschehen teilnehmenden Personen bestehen (Zwaan & al. 1995).

2.3.3. Lesergesteuerte Kohärenzbildung

Textverstehen ist ein intentionaler, zielorientierter Prozeß. Entsprechend ihrer jeweiligen Intentionen setzen Leser unterschiedliche Verarbeitungs-Strategien ein. Diese Verarbeitungs-Strategien sind mentale Programme, die die Abfolge und Gewichtung der einzelnen Verarbeitungs-Prozesse beeinflussen, um den Erwerb, das Einprägen sowie den Abruf und die Anwendung von Wissen zu verbessern (van Dijk & Kintsch 1983).

Mikrostrategien richten sich auf das Verstehen der aufeinanderfolgenden Textaussagen und deren semantische Verknüpfung. Makrostrategien hingegen richten sich auf das Herausarbeiten der Hauptideen eines Texts. Makrostrategien werden − verglichen mit Mikrostrategien − in der individuellen Lerngeschichte relativ spät erworben. Bei einer Behaltensstrategie konzentriert sich die Verarbeitung auf die Bildung einer propositionalen Repräsentation, da eine Wiedergabe des Texts hier relativ genau ausfällt.

Bei einer Verstehens-Strategie steht die Bildung eines mentalen Modells im Vordergrund, da so eine bessere Grundlage für die Beantwortung von Verständnisfragen oder die Anwendung des Gelernten geschaffen wird. Während bei der Verarbeitung von literarischen Texten die mentale Repräsentation der Oberflächenstruktur besser enkodiert wird, liegt bei der Verarbeitung von expositorischen Texten und Zeitungen der Hauptakzent auf der Enkodierung des referentiellen mentalen Modells (Zwaan 1994).

Damit es zu einer flexiblen adaptiven Textverarbeitung kommt, müssen die verfügbaren Verarbeitungs-Strategien situations- und anforderungsgerecht ausgewählt, koordiniert und in ihrer Ausführung überwacht werden. Die metakognitive Verarbeitungs-Regulation geschieht normalerweise weitgehend automatisiert. Nur wenn Verstehensprobleme auftauchen, die mit den automatisierten Prozessen nicht bewältigt werden können, wird sie zum Gegenstand bewußter Reflexion und Kontrolle (vgl. Forrest-Pressley & al. 1985). Mängel in der Verarbeitungs-Regulation können durch inadäquate Verstehensstandards bedingt sein. Selbst relativ routinierte Leser merken oft nicht, daß sie einen Text nicht hinreichend verstehen (Baker 1985).

3. Ausblick

Textproduktion und Textverstehen dienen einer gemeinsamen gesellschaftlichen bzw. kulturellen Funktion: der Zirkulation von Wissen (Eigler 1997). Obgleich beide somit einander ergänzende bzw. aufeinander bezogene Komponenten der Kommunikation mit Hilfe schriftlicher Texte sind, wurden Forschungsarbeiten in beiden Bereichen lange relativ unabhängig voneinander durchgeführt. Die von der etwas jüngeren Forschung zur Textproduktion erhobenen Befunde sind noch weniger reichhaltig und die von ihr entwickelten Modelle etwas weniger elaboriert als die der Forschung zum Textverstehen, wo in annähernd drei Jahrzehnten sowohl eine Fülle empirischer Befunde gesammelt als auch relativ sophistizierte Modelle der kognitiven Verarbeitung von Texten entwickelt wurden (vgl. Schnotz 1994).

Die empirischen Untersuchungen zum Textverstehen wurden zum Teil mit natürlichen und zum Teil mit artifiziellen, speziell für experimentelle Zwecke hergestellten Texten durchgeführt (Graesser & al. 1997). Bei der Verwendung der einen oder der anderen Art des Textmaterials gehen Gewinne hinsichtlich der ökologischen Validität jeweils auf Kosten der experimentellen Kontrolle von Texteigenschaften und umgekehrt. Die Forschung zum Textverstehen sollte versuchen, ihre theoretischen Modelle sowohl durch Befunde aus Untersuchungen in ökologisch validen Settings mit natürlichen Texten als auch durch Befunde aus Experimenten mit artifiziellen, nach kontrollierten Gesichtspunkten konstruierten Texten abzusichern.

Angesichts neuerer Entwicklungen in der Kognitions- und Sprachpsychologie, der Linguistik und der Forschung zur Künstlichen Intelligenz bietet sich sowohl bei der Erforschung der Textproduktion als auch der Erforschung des Textverstehens eine multidisziplinäre Kooperation an. Psychologische Konzepte haben inzwischen Eingang in die Linguistik gefunden, und umgekehrt liefern linguistische Analysen Anregungen für die psychologische Theoriebildung. Die Untersuchung sprachlicher Strukturen und deren Verwendung im Rahmen der Textkommunikation kann als eine spezifische Art des Zugangs zur Struktur und Funktionsweise des menschlichen kognitiven Systems angesehen werden.

4. Zitierte Literatur

Albrecht, J.E. & O'Brien, E.J. 1993. „Updating a mental model: maintaining both local and global coherence". *Journal of Experimental Psychology: Learning, Memory, and Cognition* 19: 1061–1070.

Anderson, R.C. & Pearson, Paul David. 1984. „A schema-theoretic view of basic processes in reading comprehension". In: Pearson, Paul David (ed.). *Handbook of reading research*. New York: Longman, 255–291.

Baker, L. 1985. „Differences in the standards used by college students to evaluate their comprehension of expository prose". *Reading Research Quarterly* 20: 297–313.

Bereiter, Carl & Scardamalia, Marlene. 1987. *The psychology of written composition*. (The psychology of education and instruction.) Hillsdale/NJ: Erlbaum.

Breetvelt, I. & van den Bergh, H. & Rijlaarsdam, G. 1994. „Relations between writing processes and text quality: When and how?" *Cognition & Instruction* 12: 103–123.

Britton, Bruce K. & Gulgoz, S. 1991. „Using Kintsch's computational model to improve instructional text: Effects of repairing inference calls on recall and cognitive structures". *Journal of Educational Psychology* 83: 329–345.

Bühler, Karl. 1934. *Sprachtheorie. Die Darstellungsfunktion der Sprache*. Jena: Fischer.

Chafe, Wallace L. 1994. *Discourse, consciousness, and time. The flow and displacement of conscious experience in reading and writing*. Chicago: University of Chicago Press.

Clark, Herbert H. 1993. *Arenas of language use*. Chicago: University of Chicago Press.

de Beaugrande, Robert Alain. 1984. *Text production. Toward a science of composition*. (Advances in discourse processes, 11.) Norwood: Ablex.

Eigler, Gunther. 1997. „Textproduzieren als konstruktiver Prozeß". In: Weinert, Franz Emanuel (ed.). *Psychologie des Unterrichts und der Schule* (Enzyklopädie der Psychologie, Themenbereich D, Praxisgebiete, Serie 1, Pädagogische Psychologie, Bd. 3), Göttingen: Hogrefe, 365–395.

Eigler, G. 1998. „Zum Stand der Textproduktionsforschung". *Unterrichtswissenschaft* 26: 3–14.

Fletcher, C.R. 1985. "The functional role of markedness in topic identification". *Text* 5: 23–37.

Flower, Linda. 1994. *The construction of negotiated meaning: A social cognitive theory of writing*. Carbondale: Southern Illinois University Press.

Flower, Linda. 1998. *Problem-solving strategies for writing in college and community*. (Community life in literature.) London: Harcourt Brace College Publishers.

Forrest-Pressley, Donna-Lynn & MacKinnon, G. E. & Waller, T. Gary (eds.) 1985. *Metacognition, cognition, and human performance* (Vol. 1). New York: Academic Press.

Frederiksen, Carl H. & Donin-Frederiksen, J. & Bracewell, R.J. 1986. "Discourse analysis of children's text production". In: Matsuhashi, Ann (ed.). *Writing in real time. Modelling production processes*. Norwood: Ablex, 255–290.

Galbraith, D. & Rijlaarsdam, G. 1999. "Effective strategies for the teaching and learning of writing". *Learning and Instruction* 9: 93–108.

Gernsbacher, Morton A. 1990. *Language comprehension as structure building*. Hillsdale/NJ: Erlbaum.

Givón, Talmy (ed.). 1983. *Topic continuity in discourse: A quantitative cross-language study*. (Typological studies in language.) Amsterdam & Philadelphia: Benjamins.

Graesser, A.C. & Millis, K.K. & Zwaan, R.A. 1997. "Discourse comprehension". *Annual Review of Psychology* 48: 163–189.

Graesser, A.C. & Singer, M. & Trabasso, T. 1994. "Constructing inferences during narrative text comprehension". *Psychological Review* 101: 371–395.

Grice, M. P. 1967. *Logic and conversation. The William James Lectures*. Harvard: Harvard University.

Hayes, John R. & Flower, Linda. 1980. "Identifying the organization of writing processes". In: Gregg, Lee W. & Steinberg, Esther R. (eds.). *Cognitive processes in writing*. Hillsdale/NJ: Lawrence Erlbaum, 3–30.

Jechle, Thomas. 1992. *Kommunikatives Schreiben. Prozeß und Entwicklung aus der Sicht kognitiver Schreibforschung*. (ScriptOralia, 41.) Tübingen: Narr.

Johnson-Laird, Philip N. 1983. *Mental models. Towards a cognitive science of language, influence, and consciousness*. Cambridge: Cambridge University Press.

Just, M.A. & Carpenter P.A. 1992. "A capacity theory of comprehension: individual differences in working memory". *Psychological Review* 99: 122–149.

Kellogg, Ronald T. 1994. *The psychology of writing*. New York: Oxford University Press.

Kintsch, Walter & van Dijk, Teun A. 1978. "Toward a model of text comprehension and production". *Psychological Review* 85: 363–394.

Kintsch, Walter. 1988. "The role of knowledge in discourse comprehension: A constructive-integration model". *Psychological Review* 95: 163–182.

Kintsch, Walter & Welsch, D. & Schmalhofer, F. & Zimny, S. 1990. "Sentence memory: A theoretical analysis". *Journal of Memory and Language* 29: 133–159.

McKoon, G. & Ratcliff, R. 1992. "Inference during reading". *Psychological Review* 99: 440–466.

Newell, Allen & Simon, Herbert A. 1972. *Human problem solving*. Englewood Cliffs: Prentice Hall.

Perfetti, C.A. & Britt, M.A. 1995. "Where do propositions come from?" In: Weaver, Charles A. & Mannes, S. & Fletcher, C.R. (eds.). *Discourse comprehension: Essays in honor of Walter Kintsch*. Hillsdale/NJ: Lawrence Erlbaum, 11–34.

Rickheit, Gert & Strohner, Hans (eds.). 1985. *Inferences in text processing*. (Advances in psychology, 29.) Amsterdam: North-Holland.

Sanford, Anthony J. & Garrod, Simon C. 1981. *Understanding written language: Exploration of comprehension beyond the sentence*. Chichester: Wiley.

Schmalhofer, F. & Glavanov, D. 1986. "Three components of understanding a programmer's manual: verbatim, propositional, and situational representations". *Journal of Memory and Language* 25: 279–294.

Schnotz, Wolfgang. 1994. *Aufbau von Wissensstrukturen. Untersuchungen von Kohärenzbildung bei Wissenserwerb mit Texten*. (Fortschritte der psychologischen Forschung, 20.) Weinheim: Beltz.

van Dijk, Teun A. & Kintsch, Walter. 1983. *Strategies of discourse comprehension*. New York: Academic Press.

Waltz, D.L. & Pollack, J.B. 1985. "Massively parallel parsing: A strongly interactive model of natural language interpretation". *Cognitive Science* 9: 51–74.

Winter, Alexander. 1992. *Metakognition beim Textproduzieren*. (ScriptOralia, 40.) Tübingen: Narr.

Zwaan, R.A. 1994. "Effects of genre expectations on text comprehension". *Journal of Experimental Psychology: Learning, Memory, and Cognition* 20: 920–933.

Zwaan, R.A. & Magliano, J.P. & Graesser, A.C. 1995. "Dimensions of situation model construction in narrative comprehension". *Journal of Experimental Psychology: Learning, Memory, and Cognition* 21: 386–397.

*Wolfgang Schnotz,
Universität Koblenz-Landau (Deutschland)*

12. Sprachtypologie und Schriftgeschichte

1. Einleitung
2. Zum Verhältnis von Schrift, Begriffswelt und Sprache im Horizont kultureller Evolution
3. Zur Problematik der Autonomie von Schrift gegenüber der gesprochenen Sprache
4. Zum Verhältnis von Sprachtyp und Schriftart
5. Aspekte einer fortschreitenden Phonetisierung: Motivation und Anwendungstechniken
6. Zum Verhältnis von Silbenstrukturen und Schriftart
7. Zur Problematik der Präzision von Alphabetschriften für die Lautwiedergabe
8. Zitierte Literatur

1. Einleitung

Die Impulse, denen die Originalschriften in der Alten Welt und im vorkolumbischen Amerika ihre Entstehung verdanken, waren andere als die, die in der Forschung zur Schriftgeschichte traditionellerweise genannt werden. Die Motivation, Schrift als Informationstechnologie einzusetzen, bestand nicht primär darin, gesprochene Sprache sichtbar, fixierbar und damit wiederverwendbar zu machen. Diese Motivation ist entwicklungsbezogen sekundär, und sie greift konsequent erst mit der Einführung rein phonographischer Schriftsysteme (Silben-, Segmental- und Alphabetschriften). Insofern sind alle diejenigen Definitionen von Schrift, die sich vorrangig am Verhältnis von Schriftzeichen und sprachlichem Zeichen orientieren, recht eng gefasst.

Vor allem die amerikanische Schriftforschung konzentriert sich auf Schrift in ihrer Bindung an die Lautung von Sprache, auf das, was als „true writing" bezeichnet wird. Ein Buchtitel wie der von DeFrancis (1989) – *Visible Speech* – zeigt seine Verwurzelung in dieser Tradition. Frühstadien der Schriftentwicklung wie die altsumerische Piktographie, das Schlagwortprinzip der Indus-Schrift, die altchinesische Ideographie oder die olmekische Logographie bleiben dabei definitorisch außer Betracht, obwohl es sich hierbei unzweifelhaft um Schrifttechnologien handelt.

Um auch der Entfaltung einer graduellen Annäherung von Schriftzeichen an die Lautung von Sprache in der Schriftevolution Rechnung zu tragen, ist es sinnvoll, Definitionen von Schrift nicht exklusiv mit dem gesprochenen Code einer Sprache zu assoziieren, sondern auch die sprachunabhängige Ideenwelt, die das Kulturmilieu einer Sprachgemeinschaft prägt, mit einzubeziehen (Abbildung 12.1). Ursächlich war die Verschriftung ein Prozess der Visualisierung sprachunabhängiger Begriffe, und nicht sprachlicher Zeichen. Unter Bezugnahme auf eine kulturbezogene Definition von Schrift ist es möglich, den eigentlichen Impulsgeber für die

Schriftprinzipien

Schrifttypen	Schriftvarianten	Fixierung einer Äußerung (Gedankensequenz)	Fixierung eines Begriffs (Einzelbegriffs)	Fixierung der Lautstruktur	
				Lautgruppe	Einzellaut
	(Bilderzählung)	+	–	–	–
Logographie	1. Piktographische Symbole	–	+	–	–
	2. Ideographische Symbole	–	+	–	–
	3. Abstrakt-logographische Symbole	–	+	–	–
Phonographie	4. Segmentalschrift (Zeichen für Lautsegmente)	–	–	+	–
	5. Syllabische Schrift (Silbenschrift)	–	–	+	–
	6. Alphabetische Schrift (Buchstabenschrift)	–	–	–	+

Abbildung 12.1: Varianten logo- und phonographischer Schreibweisen

Entwicklung des Schriftgebrauchs aufzudekken, nämlich das Bedürfnis, Ideensequenzen (d. h. Verkettungen von Einzelbegriffen) zu fixieren. Bei diesen Ideensequenzen konnte es sich um die Koppelung numerischer und denominativer Begriffe (z. B. in den altsumerischen Warenlisten; Walker 1990: 19 ff.), um eine narrative Sequenz magischer Begriffe (z. B. in den altchinesischen beschrifteten Orakelknochen; Keightley 1985: 42 ff.), um die Konfiguration von Autoritätssymbolen (z. B. auf altägyptischen Schminkpaletten; Haarmann 1992: 212 f.) oder um eine komplexe Verquickung verschiedener Symbolebenen handeln (z. B. die Vernetzung von numerischen Begriffen und magisch-religiöser Symbolik in der Maya-Numerologie; Ifrah 1987: 461 ff.).

2. Zum Verhältnis von Schrift, Begriffswelt und Sprache im Horizont kultureller Evolution

Wenn zu Beginn der Geschichte der Informationsverarbeitung das Streben nach einer Technologie entscheidend war, gedankliche Inhalte festzuhalten, wenn sich also das Anfangsstadium der Schriftverwendung weitgehend sprachungebunden entfaltete, dann spielte konsequenterweise die Typik von Sprachen keine nennenswerte Rolle für das Entstehen von Schrift in irgendeinem Kulturkreis. Wohl aber wurden die Ausarbeitung und der Einsatz von Schrift überall und von Anbeginn von den spezifischen Bedingungen des lokalen Kulturmilieus beeinflußt. Die Art und Weise, wie Schriftzeichen in ein System integriert wurden, stand jeweils in Abhängigkeit zum Repertoire der verfügbaren Kultursymbole, nicht von der silbischen oder segmentalen Struktur der lokalen Sprache oder ihrer grammatischen Strukturen (Abbildung 12.2).

Das Anfangsstadium der Schriftanwendung ist eine Phase der Herausforderung des abstrakten Denkvermögens durch die Bedürfnisse einer aufstrebenden Zivilisation, ein ständig wachsendes Maß an Informationen zu akkumulieren und wiederverwendbar zu machen. Die Art und Weise, wie das abstrakte Denken funktioniert und für die Schöpfung einer Originalschrift eingesetzt wird, weist auf eindeutige Kulturabhängigkeit (s. Haarmann 1998 zu Funktionen des kulturabhängigen abstrakten Denkens im Prozess der Schriftschöpfung). Dies ist ein entscheidender Grund dafür, weshalb in den Originalschriften die kulturelle Realität nach spezifisch lokalen Bedingungen ver„zeichnet" wird (Haarmann 1992: 124 ff.). Das Zeichenpotential der ältesten Texte, die zum Zweck der Informationswiederverwendung produziert wurden, war direkt assoziiert mit der Ideenwelt der Menschen, die in einem gegebenen Kulturmilieu interagierten, also auch des „Lesers".

Die Zeichenkonfigurationen in den ältesten sumerischen und altchinesischen Texten weisen keine lineare Aneinanderreihung auf, wie es der Linearität gesprochener sprachlicher Zeichen entsprechen würde. Vielmehr muß die Gedankenlogik des Textinhalts entsprechend seiner inhaltlichen Kohärenz erschlossen werden. Auch hier, bei der Rezeption der alten Texte, ist die Fähigkeit zum

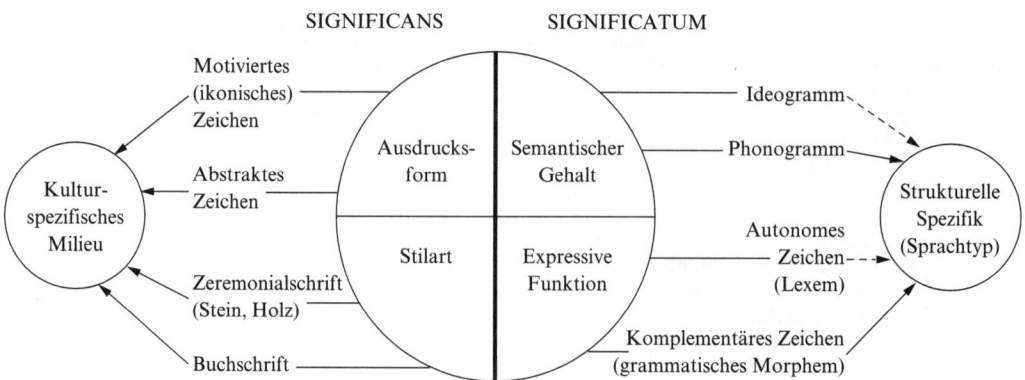

Abbildung 12.2: Die Infrastruktur des graphischen Zeichens (in Anlehnung an Curto 1989:20)

abstrakten Denken entscheidend, denn die eigentliche Dekodierungsleistung besteht darin, logische Gedankenketten trotz des Fehlens direkter Beziehungen zur Linearität sprachlicher Zeichensequenzen zu rekonstruieren. Das Endergebnis dieses Dekodierungsprozesses konnte sprachlich mit erheblichem Spielraum formuliert werden, Sprache war aber nicht die essentielle Basis, weder für die Produktion, noch für die Rezeption solcher Texte.

Was die Visualisierung der kulturellen Begriffswelt betrifft, so war das Aktionsfeld für die menschliche Abstraktionsfähigkeit praktisch unbegrenzt, und die Schöpfer der Originalschriften haben in ihren Heimkulturen mit vielfältigen Alternativlösungen experimentiert. In dieser Hinsicht besonders illustrativ ist das Studium der Determinativ- und Logogrammsysteme, die ein wesentlicher Bestandteil aller Schriftarten des Altertums und der vorkolumbischen Schriften Amerikas sind. Die Festlegung von Schreibkonventionen für Determinative und Logogramme, d. h. die Auswahl figuraler Motive unterschiedlicher Abstraktionsgrade und deren Kombinatorik zur Wiedergabe begrifflicher Inhalte, ist in jeder Regionalkultur spezifisch, unabhängig von dem universalen Charakter vieler Grundbegriffe wie 'Mann', 'Frau', 'Sonne', 'Berg', 'Hand', 'schlafen' oder 'trinken' (Abbildung 12.3).

Die Frage nach dem Verhältnis von Sprachtypologie und Schriftgeschichte kann sich sinnvoll erst auf Perioden in der Evolution von Schriftarten beziehen, als die Assoziation des Schriftbildes mit den Lautstrukturen gesprochener Sprache relevant wurde. Die Strategien einer gezielten Anwendung von Schriftsystemen auf bestimmte Sprachen bringen unweigerlich die Problematik struktureller und sprachtypologischer Spezifika ins Spiel, und dies führt uns in das Dickicht der Experimentiergen mit Schriftzeichenrepertoires und Sprachstrukturen. Unter diesem Gesichtspunkt betrachtet ist die Geschichte der Schrift die Geschichte einer sukzessiven Aufgabe begriffsorientierter Schriftzeichen (d. h. von Logogrammen und Determinativen) zugunsten einer fortschreitenden Phonetisierung.

3. Zur Problematik der Autonomie von Schrift gegenüber der gesprochenen Sprache

Die Funktionen von Schriftsystemen sind prinzipiell autonom, unabhängig davon, bis

Sprache	Ideogramm	Erläuterungen
Sumerisch	▽	Umriß der weiblichen Scham
Ägyptisch	𓁐	sitzende Frau
Mykenisch-Griechisch	𐀀	stehende Frau, mit einem Rock bekleidet
Chinesisch	女 ⟶ 女	

a) Schriftzeichen für ›Frau‹

Sprache	Ideogramm	Erläuterungen
Sumerisch		Umriß eines Penis
Ägyptisch		sitzender Mann
Mykenisch-Griechisch		Torso eines Mannes mit Beinen
Chinesisch	田力	田 ein Reisfeld / 力 ein arbeitender Mann ⟶ 男

b) Schriftzeichen für ›Mann‹

Abbildung 12.3: Die logographische Wiedergabe der Begriffe „Mann" und „Frau" in verschiedenen Originalschriften

zu welchem Grad sie sich den phonetischen und morphologischen Strukturen von Sprachen anpassen. Schriftsysteme operieren nach eigenen Prinzipien, die in partieller, aber nicht vollständiger Wechselbeziehung zu sprachlichen Strukturen stehen. Schriftsysteme, die sich dem Ideal einer Eins-zu-Eins-Entsprechung von Laut und Schrift annähern, sind seltene Ausnahmen (s. u.).

Die Autonomie der Schrift manifestiert sich unter anderem im Variantenreichtum der Organisationsprinzipien, nach denen Schriftsysteme mit Sprachstrukturen korrelieren. Die Anwendung einer syllabischen, segmentalen oder alphabetischen Schreibweise steht nicht in Abhängigkeit zur Struktur einer Sprache oder zu dem von ihr vertretenen Sprachtyp. Der Umstand, dass das Akkadische mit Hilfe eines Syllabars, das Altägyptische mittels einer Segmentalschrift und das Phönizische mit einem Konsonantenalphabet geschrieben wurden, hat kulturhistorische Gründe. Ebensogut könnte man das Akkadische mit ägyptischen Hieroglyphen nach dem Segmentalprinzip oder das Phönizische mit einem Syllabar schreiben. Die letztere Alternative wurde historisch realisiert in den Zeichen der Byblos-Schrift mit syllabischem Wert (Martin 1962).

Die unterschiedlichen Prinzipien, nach denen phonographische Schriften organisiert sind, deuten auf eine verschiedenartige Gewichtung der Kriterien, die für die Wiedergabe von lautlichen Eigenschaften als relevant erachtet werden. Im Fall der Silbenschrift liegt das Hauptaugenmerk auf der silbischen Segmentierung von Lexemen, wobei die Ganzheit des Wortkörpers unberücksichtigt bleibt. Letzteres Kriterium ist aber entscheidend für die Organisation der ägyptischen Hieroglyphenschrift. Deren Zeichen geben die segmentale Struktur von Einzelwörtern wieder, wobei in der Schreibung lediglich die Konsonanten Berücksichtigung finden. Je nach dem, ob ein Wort ein-, zwei- oder dreisilbig ist, unterscheidet die Hieroglyphenschrift zwischen Ein-, Zwei- und Dreikonsonantzeichen (Brunner 1967: 8 ff.). Aus dem Bestand der Einkonsonantzeichen rekrutiert sich der größte Teil des semitischen Alphabets, dessen ältestes Inventar in der proto-sinaitischen Schrift ausgebildet ist und dessen entwicklungsbezogener Prototyp die phönizische Buchstabenschrift ist (Healey 1990).

Traditionell werden bei den Alphabetschriften drei Arten unterschieden: Konsonantenalphabete (z. B. phönizisch, hebräisch, arabisch), vollständige Alphabete (z. B. griechisch, lateinisch, kyrillisch) und silbische Alphabete, d. h. solche Alphabete, deren Konsonanten nach Silbenvokalen variiert werden (z. B. indische Alphabete, amharische Schrift). Es gilt hier eine vierte Art hervorzuheben, die allerdings nur in einem einzigen historischen Schriftsystem realisiert worden ist, und zwar im koreanischen Hangul-System. Das Besondere dieses Schriftsystems liegt darin, dass die individuellen Schriftzeichen jeweils Einzellaute wiedergeben, dass aber die Schreibweise syllabisch orientiert ist. Das heisst, dass die Schriftzeichen jeweils in silbischen Blocks assoziiert werden, dies in Anlehnung an chinesische Schreibkonventionen. Schriftsysteme wie das indische Devanagari oder das amharische sind gleichsam typologische Brückenglieder zwischen rein silbischer und rein alphabetischer Schreibweise.

Wenn das Primat der Autonomie der Schrift gilt, muss es auch möglich sein, Sprachen unabhängig von ihrer strukturellen Spezifik mit verschiedenen Schriften zu schreiben. Die Geschichte der Schriftsprachen und ihrer Literalität bietet zahlreiche Beispiele für Schriftwechsel, auch für die Parallelität verschiedener Schriften in Anwendung auf dieselbe Sprache. Einige seien hier aufgeführt:

ALTÄGYPTISCH
– Segmentalschrift in drei Varianten (Hieroglyphen seit ca. 3100 v. Chr., Hieratisch seit ca. 1500 v. Chr., Demotisch seit dem 7. Jh. v. Chr.);
– Alphabet
(koptisch-christliche Literalität seit dem 3. Jh. n. Chr.).

ALTGRIECHISCH
– Linear B (seit dem 17. Jh. v. Chr.);
– Kyprisch-Syllabisch (seit dem 11. Jh. v. Chr.);
– Alphabet (seit dem 8. Jh. v. Chr.).

MAYA
– präkolumbisches Syllabar mit ideographischer Komponente (seit dem 3. Jh. n. Chr.);
– Lateinschrift spanischer Prägung (seit dem 16. Jh.).

ALTIRISCH
– Ogham (vom 3. bis 5. Jh. n. Chr. in Gebrauch);
– Lateinschrift (seit dem 5. Jh.).

VIETNAMESISCH
– ideographisches Vietnamesisch (Nom); (seit dem 13. Jh.);
– Lateinschrift französischer Prägung (Quoc Ngu); (seit dem 17. Jh.).

SWAHILI
– arabische Schrift (seit dem 17. Jh.);
– Lateinschrift englischer Prägung (seit dem 19. Jh.).

JAPANISCH
– chinesische Schrift (Kanji zur Schreibung von Wortstämmen);
– Hiragana (Syllabar zur Schreibung grammatischer Morpheme);
– Katakana (Syllabar zur Schreibung nichtchinesischer Entlehnungen und Fremdwörter).

Abgesehen von den Originalschriften der Welt, deren Entstehungs- und Entwicklungsbedingungen jeweils mit den Lokalsprachen assoziiert waren, ist die Wahl von Schriftarten für einzelne Sprachen durch kulturhistorische Strömungen und politische Trends bestimmt worden, weniger durch Überlegungen, in wieweit sich ein Schriftsystem für einen bestimmten Sprachtyp eignet. Im Einzugsgebiet dominanter Kulturen entsteht gleichsam ein Sog, der Nachbarkulturen zumeist alternativlos an die zivilisatorischen Institutionen des Zentrums bindet (s. Haarmann 1992: 361 ff. mit einem Abriss der Geschichte sekundärer Schriftadaptionen).

Beispiele dafür bieten die regionalen Adaptionen der chinesischen Schrift an der Peripherie des chinesischen Kulturkreises. Während sich das chinesische System der Ideographie, das für eine Sprache vom isolierenden Typ geschaffen worden war, prinzipiell für das − ebenfalls strukturell isolierende − Vietnamesische eignete, war die chinesische Schrift ein Ballast für agglutinierende Sprachen wie Japanisch oder Koreanisch. Zur Überwindung der Schwierigkeiten, die chinesische Schrift für diese Sprachen mit ihrer vom Chinesischen abweichenden Sprachstruktur zu adaptieren, wurden zusätzlich zum chinesischen Zeichenrepertoire, mit dem Wortstämme geschrieben werden, lokale phonographische Schriften geschaffen: die Syllabare Hiragana und Katakana für das Japanische, die Alphabetschrift Hangul für das Koreanische.

Für das Meroitische in Nubien gab es zu den kulturellen Institutionen der ägyptischen Zivilisation keine Alternative. Im Zuge der Akkulturation wurde auch die ägyptische Schrift übernommen, die in zwei Varianten, in einer hieroglyphischen für zeremoniale Zwecke und in einer kursiven Gebrauchsschrift, adaptiert wurde. Ebenfalls ohne Alternative blieb die Adaption und Weiterentwicklung der olmekischen Schrift in Zentralamerika, die von den Maya, Zapoteken und den Trägern der Kultur von Teotihuacan im Tal von Mexiko adaptiert wurden. Die zapotekische Schrift diente auch zur Schreibung des Toltekischen, Aztekischen und Mixtekischen.

Die Adaption der Lateinschrift zur Schreibung der Sprachen in Westeuropa war kulturhistorisch vorgegeben. Einerseits übernahm das Lateinische lange Zeit sämtliche zivilisatorischen Funktionen in den nachantiken Staatsgründungen, und zwar als Kanzleisprache, Schrift- und Bildungssprache, andererseits war es das Medium der damals führenden Weltanschauung, des Christentums und seiner Amtskirche. In Osteuropa waren die Verhältnisse komplexer. Die Schriftschöpfungen des sogenannten „Slawenapostels" Kyrillos (der für die Schöpfung der Glagolica, nicht der Kyrillschrift, verantwortlich ist) und seines Schülers Kliment von Ohrid (der die Kyrillica geschaffen hat und sie zur Ehrung seines Lehrers nach ihm benannte) modifizierten das Spektrum lokaler und interregionaler Schriften in Osteuropa. Das griechische Alphabet war in den mittelalterlichen Staaten der Slawen wegen des religiösen Schrifttums in dieser Sprache vertraut. Die lokalen Varianten der Kyrillica wurden als nationale Schriften angesehen, entsprechend gepflegt und tradiert.

Bei der Neuverschriftung nichtrussischer Sprachen im zaristischen Russland seit dem 18. Jahrhundert war die Wahl der Schriftart im wesentlichen abhängig von der religiösweltanschaulichen Orientierung. Die kyrillische Schrift wurde für Sprachen verwendet, deren Sprachgemeinschaften zum russisch-orthodoxen Glauben bekehrt worden waren (z. B. Tschuwaschisch, Mordwinisch, Tscheremissisch). Dies galt ebenfalls für das Komi-Syrjänische, das schon seit Ende des 14. Jahrhunderts in einer Lokalschrift, dem Abur-Alphabet, geschrieben worden war. Die Abur-Schrift war von dem russischen Missionar Stephan von Perm für das Syrjänische geschaffen worden. Das ältere religiöse Schrifttum in syrjänischer Sprache, das hauptsächlich im 15. Jahrhundert entstanden war, wurde seit Ende des 18. Jahrhunderts teilweise in die Kyrillica transliteriert und später vollständig durch die kyrillisch geschriebene Literatur ersetzt.

Im Süden Russlands hatte der Islam Geltung, und die neuen Schriftsprachen in jener Region bedienten sich naturgemäß einer islamischen Institution, der arabischen Schrift. Hauptträger für das islamische Gedankengut bei den Muslimen Russlands war das Tatarische, in dem eine reichhaltige religiöse und wissenschaftliche Literatur entstanden ist. Die arabische Schrift fand Anwendung bei größeren Ethnien (z. B. bei Aserbaidschanern, Usbeken und Tadschiken) und bei kleineren Sprachgemeinschaften (z. B. bei Tschetschenen, Kabardinern und Kumyken), und zwar bei den muslimischen Völkern Mittelasiens und im Kaukasus (Baldauf 1993).

Ebenfalls religiös motiviert war die Wahl der hebräischen Schrift zur Schreibung des Karaimischen, einer türkischen Sprache, deren Sprecher Judaisten sind. Dies ist ein Relikt aus der Zeit, als das Turkvolk der Chasaren, deren Reich im 10. Jahrhundert zerstört wurde, den Judaismus als Staatsreligion angenommen hatte. Auch die Juden verwendeten die hebräische Schrift für ihre Alltagssprachen, die aschkenasischen Juden für das Jiddische, die orientalischen Juden für verschiedene Lokalsprachen: Jüdisch-Georgisch, Jüdisch-Tatisch, Bucharisch (Jüdisch-Tadschikisch) u. a. Tatisch wurde in zwei Schriftsystemen geschrieben: in arabischer Schrift (bei den tatischen Muslimen), in hebräischer Schrift bei den „Bergjuden" (russ. *gorskie evrei*).

Die Lateinschrift, die bis zum Ende der zaristischen Ära für nur wenige Sprachen Russlands in Gebrauch war (und zwar Estnisch, Lettisch, Litauisch; ausserdem Deutsch und Französisch als Bildungssprachen), weitete ihren Geltungsbereich in den 1920er Jahren erheblich aus. Entsprechend der Devise Lenins, wonach „die Lateinschrift die Revolution im Osten" bedeute, wurde die Graphie zahlreicher älterer, bis dahin in kyrillisch oder arabisch geschriebener Sprachen latinisiert und neue Sprachen in dieser Schriftart verschriftet (Isaev 1979: 59 ff.). Die spätere Umstellung auf die Kyrillica, die in den 1930er Jahren erfolgte, war ebenso ideologisch motiviert wie die anfängliche Wahl der Lateinschrift. Der von Lenin propagierte kulturelle Pluralismus wurde von Stalin erheblich eingeschränkt, und die kyrillische Schrift wurde zum Garanten für eine zentralistische Kontrolle des kulturellen Lebens aller Sowjetvölker unter Führung des Russischen und des Russentums.

4. Zum Verhältnis von Sprachtyp und Schriftart

In Anbetracht der dominanten Einwirkung kulturhistorischer Strömungen auf die Wahl von Schriften für einzelne Sprachen ist die Frage zum Verhältnis von Sprachtyp und Schriftart nur sinnvoll, wenn man sie auf die Bedingungen von Originalschriften bezieht. Die meisten dieser Schriften sind für die Wiedergabe von agglutinierenden Sprachen geschaffen worden, d. h. für Sprachen mit lexikalischen und grammatischen Morphemen. Diese Verhältnisse treffen auf die elamische und sumerische Schrifttradition in Mesopotamien, auf die Indus-Schrift, auf die altägyptische Schriftkultur und auf die Schriftentwicklung im präkolumbischen Mesoamerika zu. Die Sprachen der frühen Agrargesellschaft in Südosteuropa sind nicht bekannt.

Daher können über das Verhältnis zwischen der alteuropäischen Schrift und den Strukturen jener Sprachen keine Angaben gemacht werden.

Lediglich ein Schriftkulturkreis weicht mit seinen kulturellen und sprachtypologischen Bedingungen deutlich von allen anderen ab, und zwar der chinesische. Hier waren die Entwicklungsbedingungen für eine Annäherung der Schrift an sprachliche Strukturen im wesentlichen andere als in anderen Regionen mit alter Schrifttradition. Das Chinesische ist eine Sprache des isolierenden Typs. Es gibt keinen Unterschied zwischen lexikalischen und grammatischen Morphemen. Da es keine Flexion gibt, existieren auch keine Morpheme der letzteren Kategorie. Im Altchinesischen entsprach ein Lexem einem Morphem, und jedes Wort war einsilbig. Die Bedeutung sprachlicher Äusserungen ist abhängig von den Sequenzen der lexikalischen Morpheme im syntagmatischen Zusammenhang. Diese Strukturtypik wird auch monothetisch genannt.

Unter Einschluss des chinesischen, sprachstrukturellen Sonderfalls der Schriftgeschichte lässt sich zum Verhältnis von Sprachtyp und Schriftart allgemein sagen, dass je nach Sprachtyp der Prozess der Phonetisierung entweder unvollkommen bleibt (wie im Fall der chinesischen Logographie) oder im Gegenteil beschleunigt wird (wie bei der Entwicklung von Syllabaren und Alphabeten). Die Geschichte der Originalschriften veranschaulicht dabei den Sachverhalt, dass die genannte Wechselbeziehung nicht wie ein Systemautomatismus funktioniert, sondern durch die Dynamik kultureller Konventionen variiert wird. Besonders illustrativ für die Veranschaulichung der Wechselbeziehung (in ihrer kulturellen Variabilität) zwischen sprachtypischen Merkmalen und Schriftart ist die Ausbildung des chinesischen (hier im Anschluss) und des altsumerischen (s. u.) Schriftsystems.

Die Anfänge des Schreibens in China sind noch nicht endgültig eruiert. Der Schriftgebrauch der Shang-Periode, der um 1200 v. Chr. einsetzt, und dessen typische Textform die narrativen Sequenzen von Fragen und Antworten in den Orakelinschriften sind, zeigt bereits einen vollständig entwickelten Zeichenschatz (Keightley 1985). Die Entwicklung der Schrift bis zu diesem Stadium ist unbekannt. Die ideographischen und logographischen Symbole der Orakelinschriften deuten auf piktographische Zeichenursprünge hin. Das Prinzip der Logographie eignet sich besonders für das Chinesische, da hier ein Schriftsymbol einem Lexem und einem Morphem entspricht. Zusätzlich repräsentiert dasselbe Schriftzeichen eine Silbe. Allerdings hat es zu keiner Zeit der Schriftentwicklung in China eine Eins-zu-Eins-Korrelation von ideographischen Symbolen und Silbenstrukturen gegeben. Die Zahl der Schriftsymbole ist größer als die der im Chinesischen vorkommenden Silben.

Ein wesentlicher Grund für diese Diskrepanz ist die Existenz von Tonemen, deren System in den regionalen Varianten des Chinesischen sehr verschieden ausdifferenziert ist. In der Standardschriftsprache (Mandarin-Chinesisch) werden vier Toneme unterschieden, im Kantonesischen, zu dem auch das Chinesische von Hong Kong gehört, gibt es neun Toneme. Aufgrund der beschränkten Silbenzahl und des Umstands, dass alle Lexeme einsilbig sind, ist es im Chinesischen zur Bildung zahlreicher Homophone gekommen. Genauer gesagt sind Tausende von chinesischen Lexemen homophon. Dies sind Wörter mit der gleichen Silbenstruktur, deren Bedeutungsunterschiede sich aus ihrer Assoziation mit einem jeweils anderen Stimmton ergeben. In der lateinischen Transliteration chinesischer Wörter wird der Stimmton mit einem diakritischen Zeichen markiert, das ungefähr den linearen Stimmverlauf bildhaft wiedergibt. Da in der ideographischen Schreibweise des Chinesischen der Ideengehalt das entscheidende Kriterium ist, finden homophone Wörter aufgrund ihrer Bedeutungsunterschiede im Schriftbild eine jeweils individualisierende Repräsentanz. Insofern ist es nicht erforderlich, in der chinesischen Schreibweise Stimmtonunterschiede zu kennzeichnen (Abbildung 12.4).

Das logographische Prinzip der chinesischen Schrift zeigt seine Effektivität bei der Differenzierung von homophonen Wörtern mit unterschiedlichem Stimmton, ebenso bei der Individualisierung konkreter Begriffe. Probleme stellen sich bei der Schreibung abstrakter Begriffe, die sich nur schwierig oder gar nicht mit Hilfe ideographischer Zeichen darstellen lassen. Als Hilfsmittel in solchen Fällen wird die Technik des Schreibens nach dem Rebusprinzip angewendet (Coulmas 1996: 81 f.). Ein ideographisches Zeichen zur Wiedergabe eines konkreten Begriffs wird übertragen auf ein Wort mit ähnlicher oder gleicher Lautung, das einen abstrakten Begriff bezeichnet (z. B. das Zeichen 來 zur Schreibung von chines. leg_1 'Weizen', mit dem sekundär auch das homophone leg_2 'kommen' geschrieben wurde). Die Assoziierung des lautlich eindeutigen Zeichens mit seinen unterschiedlichen Bedeutungen ergibt sich allein aus dem Textzusammenhang. Die Schreibung nach dem Rebusprinzip bietet nicht nur eine technische Erleichterung im Hinblick auf die Schreibung abstrakter Begriffe, sie bedingt auch eine ökonomische Reduktion des Zeicheninventars.

Das Primat der Individualisierung konkreter Begriffe in der Schreibung durch ein nach seiner Strichkonfiguration spezifisches Zeichen hat in der Schriftgeschichte Chinas eine Explosion des Zeichenbestandes hervorgerufen. Der Zeichenbestand der Orakelinschrif-

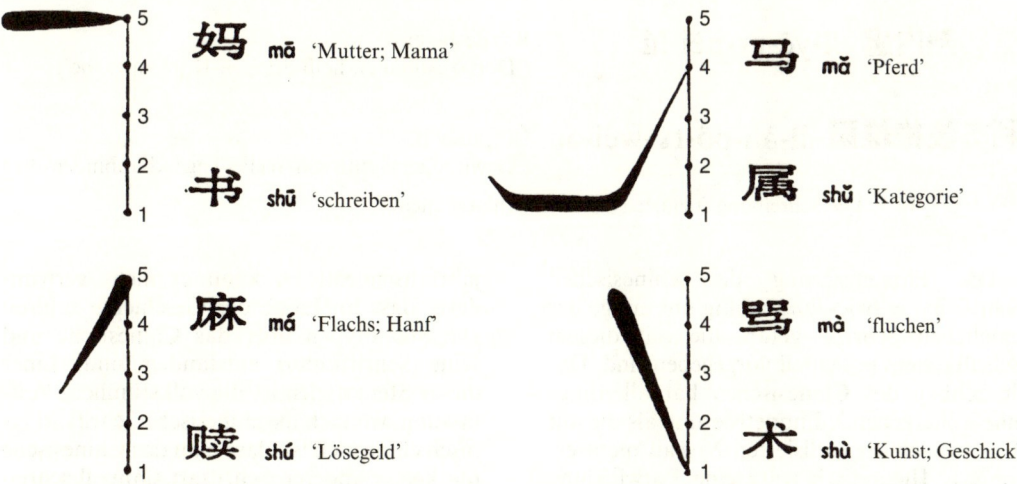

Abbildung 12.4: Stimmtonunterschiede des Chinesischen in Lautung und Schreibung

ten der Shang-Zeit, der im 12. und 11. Jahrhundert v. Chr. in Gebrauch war, belief sich auf rund 2 500 Symbole. Während der Han-Dynastie (202 v. Chr.–220 n. Chr.) stieg die Zahl der Schriftzeichen auf etwa 10 000 an. Im 12. Jahrhundert schließlich hatte sich der Zeichenbestand mehr als verdoppelt und umfaßte ca. 23 000 Einzelzeichen. Die umfangreichsten Wörterbücher führen rund 50 000 Zeichen auf.

Anforderungen an eine Phonetisierung der chinesischen Schrift resultierten ausser aus der Konfrontation mit der abstrakten Begriffswelt auch aus der Namenschreibung. Insbesondere ausländische Namen, deren lautliche Komponenten im Chinesischen bedeutungslos sind, können nicht anders als nach dem phonetischen Prinzip adaptiert werden. Zu diesem Zweck werden die Silben in Namen mit jeweils einem lautähnlichen chinesischen Wort wiedergegeben. Mehrsilbige Namen werden daher als Sequenz lexikalischer Morpheme geschrieben. Die Bedeutung der chinesischen Wörter in ihrer silbischen Repräsentanz ist bei der Schreibung von Namen gänzlich irrelevant. Daher ergibt sich bei der Schreibung ausländischer Namen eine Synchronizität von Silbensequenzen mit Annäherung an das chinesische Lautsystem und von Elementen einer semantischen Nonsense-Verkettung (Abbildung 12.5).

Sprache gleichsam zur Perfektion ausgebaut ist (s. u.). Eine für das Chinesische konzipierte Silbenschrift mit konventionell festgelegten individuellen Zeichen für spezifische Silbenstrukturen hätte den Vorteil, dass die Zahl der Schriftzeichen, die derzeit verwendet werden, drastisch reduziert würde. Andererseits wären Zusatzzeichen zur Unterscheidung homophoner Lexeme und zur Differenzierung der Toneme erforderlich.

Dass die chinesische Schrift potentielle Alternativen einer Anpassung an andere als monothetische Sprachstrukturen bietet, verdeutlicht die Entwicklung dieser Schriftart im japanischen Kulturkreis. Kanji, das System chinesischer Schriftzeichen, dient zur Schreibung von Wortstämmen. Für die spezifischen Bedürfnisse der Schreibung grammatischer Morpheme des Japanischen wurde das Syllabar Hiragana geschaffen, dessen Zeichen sich aus dem Repertoire chinesischer Zeichen rekrutieren. Das Gleiche gilt für das andere japanische Zeichensystem, Katakana, das zur silbischen Transliteration nichtchinesischer Lehnwörter verwendet wird. Insofern werden japanische Texte in drei Schriftsystemen geschrieben, wobei jedes der Systeme spezifische Funktionen erfüllt.

Angesichts des Sachverhalts, dass sich die Schrift als kulturelle Institution in China so tief verwurzelt hat – die Schrifttradition ist

迭更斯 tié-kə̄ŋ-sɯ   Dickens
('wiederholt-ändern-dieses')

柴霍甫斯基 zʰái-xuò-fǔ-sɯ-cī   Tschaikovsky
('Feuerholz-plötzlich-anfangen-dieses-Grundlage')

里約熱內盧 lĭ-yē-ɽɤ̀-nèi-lú   Rio de Janeiro
('Dorf-zustimmen-heiß-drinnen-Kohlenpfanne')

利奧波德維爾 lì-àu-pō-tɤ́-wéi-ə̄ɽ   Léopoldville
('Gewinn-geheimnisvoll-Welle-Tugend-anbinden-du')

Abbildung 12.5: Die Schreibung fremder Namen im Chinesischen

Die Phonetisierung der chinesischen Schrift hat entwicklungsmäßig nur einige der möglichen Schritte getan, die mit diesem Schriftsystem potentiell vorgegeben sind. Der Sprachbau des Chinesischen hat allerdings eine weitergehende Phonetisierung als die auf dem tatsächlich realisierten Niveau nicht erfordert. Theoretisch wäre eine Entwicklung denkbar gewesen, wie sie im Syllabar der Yi-

jahrtausendealt –, kann es nicht verwundern, dass im Laufe der Geschichte zahlreiche Stereotypen über das Chinesische und seine Schriftkultur entstanden sind. Einer dieser Stereotypen ist die volkstümliche Auffassung, wonach die chinesische Schrift so typisch chinesisch ist, dass man das Chinesische mit keiner anderen Schriftart sinnvoll schreiben könne.

Der beste Gegenbeweis ist die Existenz von Pinyin, einem Transliterationssystem zur Wiedergabe des Chinesischen in Lateinschrift. Dieses seit 1958 bestehende System wird einerseits in der wissenschaftlichen Literatur, andererseits als offizielles Transliterationssystem chinesischer Namen von der UNO und ebenso in den Massenmedien verwendet. Toneme werden im Pinyin mit diakritischen Zeichen markiert. Um 1913 wurde auch ein nationalchinesisches Alphabet konzipiert, dessen Zeichen sich teils von chinesischen Ideogrammen ableiten, teils Neuschöpfungen sind, und bei dem die Toneme durch diakritische Sonderzeichen (Punkt, Strich) markiert werden (Jensen 1969: 172f.). Aufgrund der politischen Wechselfälle haben sich diesem Alphabet mit chinesischem Lokalkolorit keine Entfaltungschancen geboten.

Es gibt zahlreiche Beispiele für die Schreibung monothetischer Sprachen mit Hilfe von Alphabetschriften. Die Schrift zur Wiedergabe des Thai ist ein silbisches Alphabet, das im 13. Jahrhundert aus der Khmer-Schrift abgeleitet wurde. Die Khmer-Schrift ihrerseits ist ein Ableger des südindischen Schriftenkreises. Besonders komplex ist das Vokalsystem des Thai, das insgesamt 24 einfache Vokale und Diphthonge unterscheidet.

Ein lebendes Beispiel dafür, dass man eine monothetische Sprache in Lateinschrift schreiben kann, finden wir in der modernen Graphie des Vietnamesischen. Die 22 lateinischen Buchstaben, die adaptiert wurden, reichen bei weitem nicht aus, um alle phonematischen Differenzierungen zu kennzeichnen. Es gibt zahlreiche Zusatzzeichen, ein graphisch ergänztes đ (zur Bezeichnung eines dentalen Verschlußlauts) sowie verschiedene Konsonantenverbindungen wie ng, ph oder gh, die aber Einzellaute bezeichnen. Diakritische Zeichen werden einerseits zur Bezeichnung der Kürze sowie des Öffnungsgrades von Vokalen verwendet (z. B. *â* versus *ă*), andererseits zur Kennzeichnung der Stimmtonkorrelation. Das Vietnamesische kennt sechs Toneme, von denen eines, der Normalton, unbezeichnet bleibt, während die übrigen jeweils mit spezifischen Tonhöhenzeichen markiert werden (Abbildung 12.6).

Der allgemeine Eindruck, den die Graphie des Vietnamesischen auf einen Europäer macht, ist der höchster Komplexität. Dieser Eindruck ist allerdings zu relativieren, wenn man damit die komplizierte Schreibweise des älteren, auf der chinesischen Schrift basierenden Nom-Systems vergleicht. Vom Standpunkt ihrer schrifttechnischen Effektivität aus betrachtet wäre die moderne vietnamesische Schrift ohne weiteres auf das Chinesische übertragbar.

5. Aspekte einer fortschreitenden Phonetisierung: Motivation und Anwendungstechniken

Sprachliche Strukturen und Schriftart stehen in einer lediglich mittelbaren Beziehung zueinander. Dies kann man daran erkennen, dass die Phonetisierung der Schrift zwar durch bestimmte strukturtypische Merkmale der zu schreibenden Sprachen angeregt wird, dass dieser phonetische Anpassungsmechanismus aber keine zwingende Notwendigkeit für das Schreiben ist. Die grammatischen Strukturen bestimmter Sprachen (und zwar solche des agglutinierenden, flektierenden und polysynthetischen Typs) stellen für das Schreiben eine besondere Herausforderung dar.

Formantien der paradigmatischen Morphologie (grammatische Morpheme) und solche der syntagmatischen Morphologie (Ableitungsformantien wie Prä-, In- und Suffixe) mit ihrem anikonischen Charakter entziehen sich einer Repräsentation durch logographische oder ideographische Zeichen in der Schrift. Eine agglutinierende Sprache wie das Sumerische machte besondere Prioritäten in den Schreibkonventionen erforderlich. Die altsumerische Piktographie berücksichtigte im wesentlichen nur Wortstämme. „The Sumerian writing never attempted to render the language phonetically correct, exactly as it was spoken" (Thomsen 1984: 20). Der

fallender Ton	à ằ ầ è ề ì ò ồ ờ ù ừ ỳ
steigender Ton	á ắ ấ é ế í ó ố ớ ú ứ ý
tiefer Ton	ạ ặ ậ ẹ ệ ị ọ ộ ợ ụ ự ỵ
fallend-steigender Ton	ả ẳ ẩ ẻ ể ỉ ỏ ổ ở ủ ử ỷ
unterbrochen-steigender Ton	ã ẵ ẫ ẽ ễ ĩ õ ỗ ỡ ũ ữ ỹ

Abbildung 12.6: Die Markierung der Toneme im Vietnamesischen (ohne Normalton)

Schreibung von Basislexemen wird Priorität eingeräumt, wobei grammatische Morpheme weitgehend unberücksichtigt bleiben. Dieses Schlagwortprinzip (engl. *catch word principle*) ist in der sumerischen Schrifttradition immer aufrecht erhalten worden, auch noch in der Zeit des Wandels zur Keilschrift.

In dem Fall, dass das Schlagwortprinzip zur Schreibkonvention (bzw. zur Konvention der Schriftanwendung) wird, macht sich die Schrift nicht abhängig von den Spezifika der Sprachstruktur. Allerdings entstehen durch die Vernachlässigung grammatischer Morpheme Diskrepanzen zwischen der sprachlichen Realisierung eines Textes und dessen Verschriftung. Diese Diskrepanzen konnten nur dadurch ausgeglichen werden, dass entsprechende Anforderungen an den Benutzer von schlagwortverschrifteten Texten gestellt wurden, nämlich einen Grossteil der grammatischen Beziehungen zwischen den Schlagwörtern sinnvoll zu rekonstruieren. Angesichts der Spannbreite an begrifflichen Assoziationen und grammatischen Beziehungen zwischen den Schlagwörtern waren Missverständnisse und textuelle Fehlinterpretationen beim Lesen nicht ausgeschlossen.

Das Schlagwortprinzip ist in den sumerischen Texten nie aufgegeben worden. Dies ist unter anderem daran zu erkennen, dass in sumerischen Texten überwiegend (und zwar bis maximal 60%) Logogramme und Determinative verwendet wurden. Der Anteil der Syllabogramme schwankt zwischen 36% und 54%. Erst mit der Adaption der sumerischen Schrift für das Akkadische wird das Schlagwortprinzip aufgegeben, und zwar zugunsten einer Dominanz syllabischer Schreibweise. In akkadischen Texten steigt der Anteil der Syllabogramme an der Gesamtzahl der verwendeten Zeichen (bis maximal 400) auf 86% bis 96% an. Gleichzeitig nimmt die Zahl der verwendeten Logogramme drastisch ab (4% bis 7%).

Der Vorteil dieses Phonetisierungsschubs in der Schriftentwicklung liegt auf der Hand: Texte binden sich in ihrer Schriftform mehr an die Lautsequenzen der Sprache, die Gedankengänge sind eindeutiger festgelegt, und damit unterliegen die vom Schreiber intendierten Textinhalte weniger als im Fall des Schlagwortprinzips den Unsicherheiten interpretativer Auslegung auf Seiten des Lesers.

Vergleiche darüber, wie unterschiedlich ein und derselbe Text zu verschiedenen Zeiten aufgezeichnet wurde, kann man anhand sumerischer Lehrtexte anstellen, also von Texten, die wegen ihres zeitlosen belehrenden Inhalts in verschiedenen Perioden immer wieder neu redigiert wurden. Ein solcher Text sind die *Unterweisungen des Šuruppak für seinen Sohn Ziudsudra*, die in einer älteren Version aus der Zeit um 2600 v. Chr. und in einer um 1850 v. Chr. entstandenen jüngeren Version erhalten sind (Abbildung 12.7). Im älteren Text bleibt weitaus mehr vom Inhalt der ergänzenden Interpretation des Lesers überlassen als in der jüngeren Textversion, die die sprachliche Zeichensequenz weitaus präziser verschriftet.

Nach neueren Erkenntnissen war auch die alte Indus-Schrift nach dem Schlagwortprinzip organisiert (Parpola 1986: 408). Die Sprache der Träger der Indus-Kultur war aller Wahrscheinlichkeit nach eine Variante des Dravidischen, also eine agglutinierende Sprache. Geschrieben wurden nur Wurzelwörter, Endungen und Ableitungssuffixe blieben unberücksichtigt. An dieser Schreibweise hielt man bis in die Endphase der Schriftverwendung (d. h. bis ca. 1800 v. Chr.) fest. Wenn die Deutung der kretischen Hieroglyphen auf

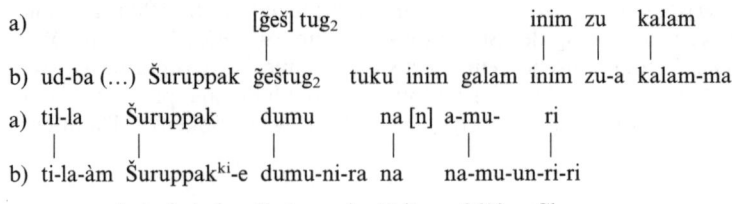

a) Archaischer Text aus der Zeit um 2600 v. Chr.
b) Altbabylonischer Text aus der Zeit um 1850 v. Chr.

Übersetzung:
'(An jenem Tag) gab (Šuruppak), der weise, der, der sich wohl auszudrücken weiß, der in Sumer lebte, Šuruppak gab (seinem) Sohn Unterweisungen.'

Abbildung 12.7: Unterschiedliche Schreibweisen eines sumerischen Lehrtextes (*Unterweisungen des Šuruppak*)

dem Diskos von Phaistos nach Haarmann (1995: 97 ff.) zutrifft, war auch dieses System nach dem Schlagwortprinzip organisiert. Im Hinblick auf die Evolution der Schrift stellt sich die Organisation von Schriftsystemen auf der Basis des Schlagwortprinzips als archaisch dar.

Die Autonomie der Schrift gegenüber der lautlichen Spezifik und dem grammatischen Bau einer Sprache bestätigt sich ebenfalls in kulturellen Zusammenhängen, die außerhalb der mesopotamischen Schrifttradition stehen. Ein illustratives Beispiel für die Wirksamkeit des kulturhistorischen Prinzips ist die Adaption des altägäischen Schriftsystems Linear A für das Mykenisch-Griechische. Die adaptierte Variante wird Linear B genannt (Hooker 1980, Chadwick 1990). Verglichen mit der späteren Alphabetschrift ist die Schreibung des Griechischen mit dem Syllabar Linear B ziemlich umständlich. Die Silbenstrukturen werden nur unvollkommen wiedergegeben, silbenschließende Konsonanten bleiben ebenso wie viele flexivische Elemente unbezeichnet (Abbildung 12.8). Die mangelnde Präzision in der Lautwiedergabe war aber kein Hindernis, Linear B beizubehalten. Jahrhundertelang wurde damit Griechisch geschrieben. Als die Griechen mit Schrift in Kontakt kamen und zu experimentieren begannen, waren ihnen lediglich die kretischen Schriften vertraut. Insofern gab es zu diesen keine realen Alternativen.

Das älteste, erst seit kurzem bekannte Schriftdokument in Linear B ist eine Weihinschrift aus dem heiligen Bezirk von Olympia, die aus dem 17. Jahrhundert v. Chr. stammt (Godart 1995). Aus dem 15. Jahrhundert v. Chr. stammen die Linear B-Inschriften aus den Palastarchiven von Knossos. Auch im Palastbezirk von Khania in Westkreta sind Bruchstücke von Tontäfelchen mit griechischen Inschriften in Linear B gefunden worden. Die längste Schrifttradition in Linear B ist aus den mykenischen Kulturzentren des griechischen Festlandes (Mykenae, Tiryns, Pylos, Theben, Orchomenos, Eleusis) bekannt. Nach 1200 v. Chr. verliert sich die Schrifttradition im „dunklen Zeitalter" des griechischen Festlandes. Auf Kreta sind Nachwirkungen der linearen Schriftsysteme bis in die klassisch-griechische Periode nachweisbar (s. Duhoux 1981, Haarmann 1995: 129 f. zu linearen Inschriftfragmenten aus dem 3. Jahrhundert v. Chr.).

Linear B ist keine Originalschrift, sondern von einem älteren ägäischen Schriftsystem,

Silbenschreibung in Linear B (transliteriert)	Schreibung des Altgriechischen (alphabetisch)
ko-wo	κόρϝος
do-so-mo	δοσμόν
te-o-jo	θεοῖο
da-mo	δάμωι
ka-ko	χαλκῶι
po-ro	πώλω
i-qo	ἵπποι
si-a₂-ro	σίαλονς
a-ne-mo	ἀνέμων
do-e-ro-i	δοέλο-ι
de-so-mo	δεσμοῖς
te-me-no	τέμενος
we-to	ϝέτος
we-te-i	ϝέτει
qi-si-pe-e	ξίφεε
tu-we-a	θύϝεα
pa-we-pi	φάρϝεσφι
e-qe-ta	ἐπέτᾱς
su-qo-ta-o	συβώτᾱο
ra-wa-ke-ta	λᾱϝᾱγέτᾱι
e-qe-ta-e	ἐπέταε
e-qe-ta	ἐπέται
e-re-ta-o	ἐρετάων
e-qe-ta-i	ἐπέτα-ι
i-je-re-u	ἱερεύς
i-je-re-wo	ἱερῆϝος
a-(pi-)po-re-we	ἀμ(φι)φορῆϝε
ka-ke-we	χαλκῆϝες
ka-ke-u-si	χαλκεῦσι

Abbildung 12.8: Beispiele für die Schreibung des Griechischen in Linear B

Linear A, abgeleitet worden. Die Hälfte des Zeichenbestandes ist aus dem Inventar von Linear A übernommen, die übrigen Zeichen sind Neuschöpfungen. Mit Linear A wurde das Minoische geschrieben. Da trotz etlicher Lautäquivalenzen zwischen den Zeichen beider linearer Systeme der silbische Wert vieler Linear A-Zeichen ungeklärt bleibt, können Linear A-Texte noch nicht gelesen werden. Mit grosser Wahrscheinlichkeit jedoch handelt es sich beim Minoischen um eine nicht-indoeuropäische Sprache.

Das Lautsystem und die Silbenstrukturen des Minoischen waren offensichtlich einfacher als die des Mykenisch-Griechischen. Dies wird deutlich bei der Lesung von Linear B-Syllabogrammen und ihrer Assoziation mit griechischen Lexemen. Die Zeichen von Linear B geben die griechische Lautung nur unvollkommen wieder. Vokallängen werden gar nicht bezeichnet. Konsonantenhäufungen finden nur in wenigen Sonderzeichen ihre Entsprechung. Insofern ist es recht umständlich, eine Sprache mit zahlreichen Konsonantenclustern wie das Griechische mit dem Linear B-Syllabar zu schreiben.

6. Zum Verhältnis von Silbenstrukturen und Schriftart

Der Prozess der Phonetisierung von Schriftzeichen war langwierig und endete in den meisten Kulturen der Alten Welt im Entwicklungsstadium von Silben- und Segmentalschriften. Nach neuesten Erkenntnissen kannte auch die Maya-Schrift im präkolumbischen Amerika das Prinzip einer syllabischen Schreibweise (Coe 1992: 231 ff., 280 f.). Verwendet wurden Logogramme und Syllabogramme. Die Entzifferung von Maya-Texten wird außerordentlich durch die Multivalenz (engl. *polyvalence*) vieler Zeichen erschwert. Als Logogramme verwendete Zeichen können auch als Syllabogramme fungieren (und umgekehrt). Außerdem existieren mehrere Zeichen zur Schreibung derselben Silbe.

Die Zusammensetzung der Zeicheninventare in den Lokalschriften zeigt eine erhebliche Variationsbreite. Früher nahm man an, dass das Zeichenrepertoire in einer Silbenschrift relativ begrenzt wäre, und man dachte dabei in erster Linie an die ältesten Syllabare wie das sumerische, akkadische oder das kretische Linear B. Bezieht man allerdings rezente Silbenschriften in die Betrachtung mit ein, so stellt sich heraus, dass es auch Syllabare gibt, die mit einer grossen Zahl von Einzelzeichen operieren.

Ein illustratives Beispiel ist die Silbenschrift der Yi (frühere chinesische Fremdbezeichnung Lolo), einer nicht-chinesischen Ethnie in Südchina. Aus einem Bestand von Tausenden historischer Zeichenvarianten, die seit dem 14. Jahrhundert in Gebrauch waren, wurde die Yi-Schrift im Jahre 1975 standardisiert (Abbildung 12.9). Das moderne Schriftsystem setzt sich aus 819 Einzelzeichen zusammen. Von diesen Zeichen dienen 756 zur Schreibung einheimischer, 63 zur Wiedergabe fremder Silbenstrukturen in Lehnwörtern. DeFrancis (1989: 144) hebt hervor, dass das Syllabar der Yi „deserves special attention as the best example of a 'pure' syllabic system because of its one-to-one correspondence between syllabic sound and syllabic representation". Die Schrift, die hier in vollständiger Abhängigkeit zur komplexen Lautkombinatorik der Yi-Sprache steht, ist auf die Integration einer Vielzahl von Zeichen für Silbenkonstruktionen angewiesen.

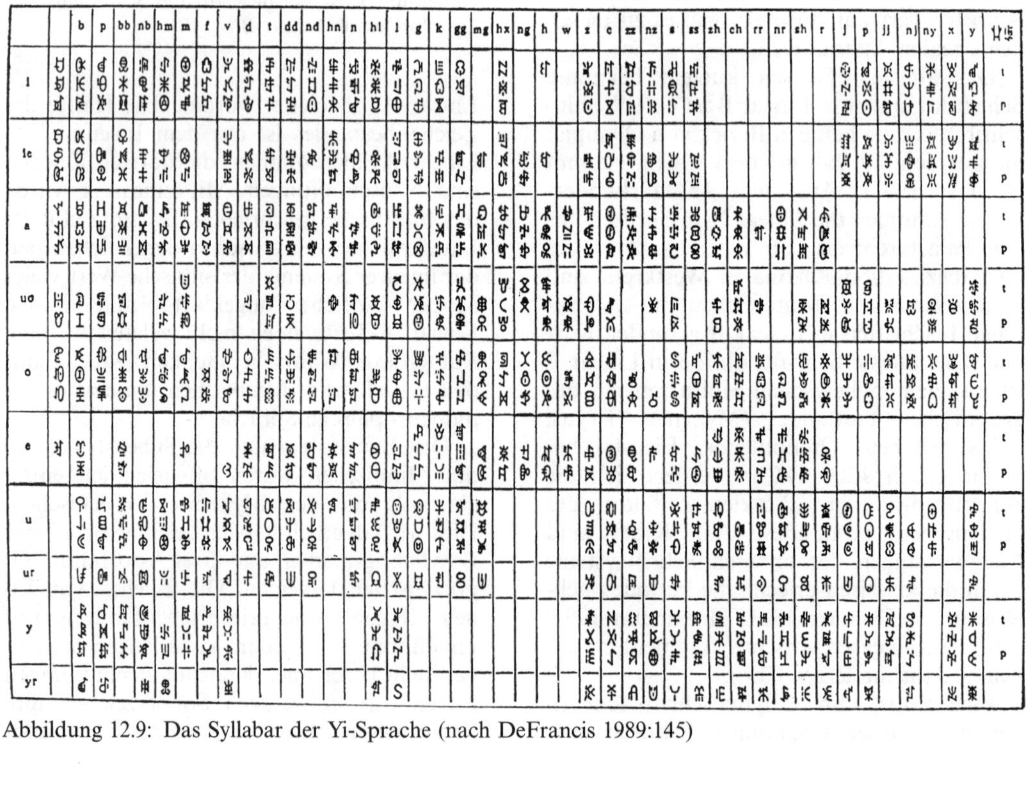

Abbildung 12.9: Das Syllabar der Yi-Sprache (nach DeFrancis 1989:145)

Sprachen, deren Lautkombinatorik in Silbenstrukturen einfacher ist als im Fall der Yi-Sprache oder deren Silben weniger exakt verschriftet werden, kommen mit entsprechend weniger Silbenzeichen aus. Gemessen am Maximalinventar der Yi-Schrift verwenden alle historischen und rezenten Syllabare weniger Zeichen. Das Inventar der akkadischen Keilschrift setzte sich aus maximal 400 Zeichen zusammen, wovon je nach Textgestaltung zwischen 85 % und 95 % Syllabogramme waren. Linear B, mit dem das Mykenisch-Griechische geschrieben wurde, verwendete 73 Silbenzeichen. Das Inventar des Kyprisch-Syllabischen, das zum Schreiben des Eteokyprischen und des arkadischen Griechisch diente, bestand aus 55 Einzelzeichen. Die modernen japanischen Syllabare (Hiragana und Katakana) kommen mit jeweils 48 individuellen Syllabogrammen aus.

7. Zur Problematik der Präzision von Alphabetschriften für die Lautwiedergabe

Alphabetschriften sind ein paradoxes Phänomen. Vom technischen Standpunkt sind Schriften, die nach dem alphabetischen Prinzip organisiert sind, unbestreitbar flexibler in ihrer Anpassung an die Lautstrukturen einer beliebigen Sprache als Silbenschriften. Die optimalen Möglichkeiten einer Phonetisierung, die in Alphabeten angelegt sind, werden aber in der Regel nicht vollständig ausgeschöpft. Dies ist am Tatbestand veralteter Orthographien in vielen Sprachen festzustellen, die aufgrund des Primats der Traditionsbindung der Schriftkultur nicht modernisiert werden (s. u.).

Eine alphabetische Schreibweise bietet eine Präzision in der Wiedergabe linearer Lautsequenzen an, die keine Silbenschrift leisten kann. Wenn die Anpassung der Schrift an die Lautung als Ideal angesehen wird, ist das Alphabet die effektivste Technik, diesem Ideal näher zu kommen. Andererseits wird bei der alphabetischen Schreibweise der assoziative Zusammenhang der Laute in Silben zerrissen (Miller 1994: 108). Das evolutive Entwicklungsstadium der Silbenschrift ist daher mehr als nur eine weniger präzise Vorstufe alphabetischer Schreibweisen, es repräsentiert eine symbiotische Verbindung zwischen Schreibtechnik und intuitivem Wissen über die kompositorische Technik der Silbenbildung auf Seiten des Benutzers. Merkverse und Kinderreime, die in Silbenform memoriert werden, sind aus den meisten Schriftkulturen bekannt. Die ersten Schriftzeichen, die japanische Kinder im Vorschulalter lernen, sind Silbenzeichen des Hiragana-Systems, in dem Kinderbücher geschrieben werden. Auf diese Weise werden japanische Kinder auf ganz natürliche Weise an die Strukturen ihrer Muttersprache gewöhnt.

Ein stärkeres Maß an Anpassung bedingt eine grössere Abhängigkeit vom Sprachbau und gleichzeitig eine Schwächung der Autonomie der Schrift. In Alphabetschriften erreicht das Prinzip der Phonetisierung seine maximale Effizienz. Schrifttypologische Übergangsformen zwischen Syllabaren und Alphabeten sind die sogenannten silbischen Alphabete, bei denen die Schreibung von Konsonanten unterschiedliche vokalische Silbenqualitäten berücksichtigt. Beispiele hierfür bieten die Alphabete des indischen Schriftkreises und das Amharische. Silbische Alphabete stehen in Abhängigkeit zur Lautstruktur der mit ihnen geschriebenen Sprachen. Das Zeicheninventar der amharischen Schrift ist mit 182 Einzelsymbolen recht umfangreich. Der wesentliche Grund liegt in der Komplexität des Vokalsystems, weshalb sich jedes der 26 Konsonantenzeichen in sieben Grundvarianten ausdifferenziert (Abbildung 12.10).

Es ist hier hervorzuheben, dass sich Aussagen zur Flexibilität und Effizienz von Alphabeten auf die Grundtechniken ihrer Adaption beziehen. In dem Maße, wie sich alphabetische Schreibweisen von Lautstrukturen abhängig machen, stellt sich das Problem, wie die Schrift auf sprachhistorische Veränderungen reagiert. Diesbezüglich zeigen sich in der Geschichte vieler Schriften grosse Diskrepanzen, weil die Schrift als kulturelle Institution häufig nicht mit den Lautveränderungen Schritt hält. Das Englische und Französische bieten Beispiele dafür, wie stark graphische Konventionen und Lautentwicklung divergieren können. In beiden Sprachen finden wir mittelalterliche Schreibkonventionen, die im Vergleich zur modernen Lautung wie kulturhistorischer Ballast anmuten. Hier zeigen sich deutlich schrifttechnische Nachteile, wenn nämlich die Normen einer einmalig adaptierten Alphabetschrift nicht entsprechend der sprachlichen Lautentwicklung sukzessive fortgeschrieben werden.

Die Zahl der Einzelzeichen in Alphabetschriften kann je nach Sprache sehr verschieden sein. Das Lautsystem des Maori auf Neuseeland ist einfach. Diese Sprache kommt da-

Lautwert	Konsonant					+ə od. vokallos	+o
	+ä	+u	+i	+a	+e		
h	ሀ	ሁ	ሂ	ሃ	ሄ	ህ	ሆ
l	ለ	ሉ	ሊ	ላ	ሌ	ል	ሎ
ḥ	ሐ	ሑ	ሒ	ሓ	ሔ	ሕ	ሖ
m	መ	ሙ	ሚ	ማ	ሜ	ም	ሞ
š	ሠ	ሡ	ሢ	ሣ	ሤ	ሥ	ሦ
r	ረ	ሩ	ሪ	ራ	ሬ	ር	ሮ
s	ሰ	ሱ	ሲ	ሳ	ሴ	ስ	ሶ
q	ቀ	ቁ	ቂ	ቃ	ቄ	ቅ	ቆ
b	በ	ቡ	ቢ	ባ	ቤ	ብ	ቦ
t	ተ	ቱ	ቲ	ታ	ቴ	ት	ቶ
ḫ	ኀ	ኁ	ኂ	ኃ	ኄ	ኅ	ኆ
n	ነ	ኑ	ኒ	ና	ኔ	ን	ኖ
ʼ	አ	ኡ	ኢ	ኣ	ኤ	እ	ኦ
k	ከ	ኩ	ኪ	ካ	ኬ	ክ	ኮ
w	ወ	ዉ	ዊ	ዋ	ዌ	ው	ዎ
ʻ	ዐ	ዑ	ዒ	ዓ	ዔ	ዕ	ዖ
z	ዘ	ዙ	ዚ	ዛ	ዜ	ዝ	ዞ
j	የ	ዩ	ዪ	ያ	ዬ	ይ	ዮ
d	ደ	ዱ	ዲ	ዳ	ዴ	ድ	ዶ
g	ገ	ጉ	ጊ	ጋ	ጌ	ግ	ጎ
ṭ	ጠ	ጡ	ጢ	ጣ	ጤ	ጥ	ጦ
p̣	ጰ	ጱ	ጲ	ጳ	ጴ	ጵ	ጶ
ṣ	ጸ	ጹ	ጺ	ጻ	ጼ	ጽ	ጾ
ḍ	ፀ	ፁ	ፂ	ፃ	ፄ	ፅ	ፆ
f	ፈ	ፉ	ፊ	ፋ	ፌ	ፍ	ፎ
p	ፐ	ፑ	ፒ	ፓ	ፔ	ፕ	ፖ

Abbildung 12.10: Das silbische Alphabet des Amharischen

her mit lediglich 13 Buchstaben des lateinischen Alphabets aus. Komplex sind die phonetischen Strukturen des seit dem 5. Jahrhundert n. Chr. geschriebenen Armenischen, dessen Alphabet aus 38 Einzelzeichen besteht. Der Konsonantismus dieser Sprache ist sehr differenziert. Zu seinen Besonderheiten gehören zahlreiche Sibilantenqualitäten und Afrikatae.

Von den zahlreichen Alphabetvarianten, die im Laufe der vergangenen dreitausend Jahre entstanden sind, waren etliche sehr erfolgreich. Das phönizische, aramäische, lateinische, kyrillische, arabische Alphabet, die indische Brahmi-Schrift und einige andere Alphabete wurden als Basisschriften für zahlreiche Sprachen adaptiert (Haarmann 1994: 339 ff.). Anhand der qualitativen Differenzierung des Zeichenbestands der Basisschriften kann man ermessen, wie sich die Lautstrukturen der Sprachen voneinander unterscheiden, für die die Basisschriften geschaffen worden sind. Dem lateinischen Alphabet fehlen die zahlreichen Nuancen der in der Kyrillica durch individuelle Zeichen wiedergegebenen qualitativen Unterschiede zwischen Sibilanten, Affrikatae und palatalisierten Lauten.

Aus kulturhistorischen Gründen wird das Portugiesische mit der Lateinschrift geschrieben. In Anbetracht des komplexen Konsonantismus dieser Sprache, der durch lateinische Buchstaben nur recht unvollkommen repräsentiert wird, wäre die Anwendung der kyrillischen Schrift weitaus präziser. Im tschechischen Alphabet wird die in der Lateinschrift fehlende Differenzierung von Vokallängen und von Konsonantenqualitäten durch diakritische Zeichen ausgeglichen.

Die Buchstaben der allermeisten Alphabete sind arbiträr. Eine Ausnahme stellt die koreanische Hangul-Schrift mit ihrer Markierung von Artikulationsmerkmalen dar (Watt 1989: 284). Allein kulturhistorische Gründe sind ausschlaggebend für die Zuordnung der äusseren Form der Buchstaben zu bestimmten Lautwerten. Um aufzuzeigen, wie willkürlich die Konventionen der Korrelation von Schriftzeichen und Laut sind, sei hier auf das Beispiel von s im lateinischen Alphabet hingewiesen. Im Deutschen werden mit ⟨s⟩ sowohl [s] (z. B. in *Wasser*), [z] (z. B. in *Reise*) und [ʃ] (z. B. in *Spalte*) bezeichnet. Im Polnischen ist neben dem einfachen s (für [s]) die Konsonantenverbindung ⟨sz⟩ (für [ʃ] wie in *Warszawa*) in Gebrauch. Die ungarische Graphie kennt ebenfalls diese Differenzierung, allerdings in der umgekehrten Lautzuordnung; ⟨s⟩ steht für [ʃ], während ⟨sz⟩ das stimmlose [s] wiedergibt.

Vorteile und Nachteile verschiedener alphabetischer Schreibweisen für Sprachen mit unterschiedlichen Lautstrukturen kann man anhand der Verschriftungsexperimente der sowjetischen Sprachplanung exemplarisch studieren (Isaev 1979). Der Wechsel von zwei, teilweise drei Alphabeten innerhalb weniger

12. Sprachtypologie und Schriftgeschichte

Jahre beweist einerseits, dass prinzipiell keine Schrift auf irgendeine Sprache festgelegt ist, und es zeigt andererseits, dass bestimmte Schriftarten sich besser als andere für die Lautwiedergabe bestimmter Sprachen eignen. Beispielsweise offenbart sich der Vorteil der kyrillischen Schrift in ihrer Anwendung auf das Aserbaidschanische mit seinem komplexen Konsonantismus. Das Kyrillische bietet individuelle Zeichenformen dort an, wo der lateinische Buchstabenbestand auf diakritische Zusatzzeichen angewiesen ist (Abbildung 12.11).

Die in den 1920er Jahren favorisierte Lateinschrift besitzt ein schmaleres Angebot an Konsonantenzeichen als die Kyrillica. Die meisten Sprachen in der ehemaligen Sowjetunion, d. h. die Sprachen Eurasiens, zeichnen sich durch einen Konsonantismus aus, der erheblich differenzierter ist als das Lautsystem süd- und mitteleuropäischer Sprachen. Die kyrillische Schrift ist insgesamt geeigneter für die Wiedergabe der Lautstrukturen eurasischer Sprachen. Die prinzipiellen Vorteile dieser Schrift gegenüber dem lateinischen Alphabet sind allerdings dahingehend zu relativieren, dass auch die Adaption der Kyrillica für die nichtrussischen Sprachen Russlands in erheblichem Umfang die Verwendung diakritischer Zusatzzeichen erfordert hat. Der Grundbestand an kyrillischen Zeichen ist durch diakritische Variationen um ein Mehrfaches erweitert worden (Abbildung 12.12).

Die meisten Sprachen, die ein Alphabet verwenden, demonstrieren mit ihren Schreibkonventionen verschiedene Grade einer unvollkommenen bzw. inkonsequenten Phonetisierung. Das Ideal, wonach geschrieben wird, wie man spricht, wäre theoretisch mit Hilfe einer alphabetischen Schreibweise zu erreichen. Tatsächlich gibt es keine Schriftsprache der Welt, die eine perfekte (d. h. hundertprozentige) Eins-zu-Eins-Korrelation von Laut und Schriftzeichen entwickelt hätte.

Diejenige Sprache, die dem Ideal einer vollkommenen Korrelation am nächsten kommt, ist das Finnische. Das finnische Lautsystem ist im Hinblick auf qualitative Unterschiede verhältnismäßig einfach, komplex dagegen ist die phonematische Quantitätenkorrelation sowohl im Vokalismus als auch im Konsonantismus. Die qualitativen Lautdifferenzierungen werden sämtlich durch individuelle Buchstaben bezeichnet. Dies sind insgesamt 24. Auf diese trifft eine Eins-zu-Eins-Korrelation zu. Zusätzlich gibt es zwei Zeichen-

Lateinschrift		Kyrillica		Arabische Schrift	
1922–1933	1933–1939 seit 1991	1940–1958	1958–1991	bis 1922	
A a	A a	A a	A a	ا, آ	a
B b	B b	Б б	Б б	ب	b
V v	V v	В в	В в	و	v
K k	Q q	Г г	Г г	ق	g¹
G g	Ƣ ƣ	Ғ ғ	Ғ ғ	غ	ɣ
D d	D d	Д д	Д д	د	d
E e	E e	Э, Е э, е	E e	ا..., ە	e
Ə ə	Ə ə	Ə ə	Ə ə	ە ,ا	ä
Z z	Z z	Ж ж	Ж ж	ژ	ž
Z z	Z z	З з	З з	ز	z
I i	I i	И и	И и	ای, ی	i
Ƚ ƚ	ь ь	Ы ы	Ы ы	ی	ï
J j	J j	Й й	J j	ی	y
Q q	K k	К к	К к	ك	k
Ɔ ɔ	G g	Ҝ ҝ	К к	گ	g²
L l	L l	Л л	Л л	ل	l
M m	M m	М м	М м	م	m
N n	N n	Н н	Н н	ن	n
O o	O o	О о	О о	و, او	o
Ө ө	Ө ө	Ө ө	Ө ө	و, اؤ	ö
P p	P p	П п	П п	پ	p
R r	R r	Р р	Р р	ر	r
S s	S s	С с	С с	س, ث, ص	s
T t	T t	Т т	Т т	ت	t
Y y	U u	У у	У у	و, او	u
U u	Y y	Ү ү	Ү ү	و, اۆ	ü
F f	F f	Ф ф	Ф ф	ف	f
X x	X x	Х х	Х х	خ	x
H h	H h	һ h	һ h	ه	h
Ç ç	C c	Ч ч	Ч ч	چ	č
C c	Ç ç	Ҹ ҹ	Ҹ ҹ	ج	j
Ş ş	Ş ş	Ш ш	Ш ш	ش	š
N̡ n̡	N̡ n̡	—	—	(ك)	ŋ
—	—	Е е	—	—	ye
—	—	Ю ю	—	—	yu
—	—	Я я	—	—	ya

¹ + dunkler Vokal
² + heller Vokal

Abbildung 12.11: Schriftsysteme des Aserbaidschanischen

Basis-zeichen	Sonder-zeichen	Basis-zeichen	Sonder-zeichen	Basis-zeichen	Sonder-zeichen	Basis-zeichen	Sonder-zeichen
А а		И и		П п		Ц ц	
	ä		й		п'		ц
	ă		й		п		цъ
	æ		ки		пп		цэ
	аа		i		пъ		цә
	аь		ï		пI		цI
Б б		Й й			пIу		цц
В в		К к			пIпI		цу
	в'		к'					цIцI
Г г			қ	Р р			ц
	г'		к		р'			дь
	ғ		иж	С с			ць
	ӷ		к̆		ç	Ч ч	
	гъ		қ		сс		ч,
	гь		къ	Т т			ч'
	гв		кь		т'		χ
	гу		кв		ҭ		ӌ
	гI		кI		тт		чъ
	гь		кк		ть		чв
	гьь		кх		тл		чI
	гьв		ку		тэ		чч
	гьу		қь		ҭэ		чIв
	гIв		қь		тш		чIчI
Д д			къв		тI		
	дж		къь		тIу	Ш ш	
			кIв	У у			шъ
	дь		кIь		ȳ		шь
	дә		къу		ў		шв
	дз		кIу		ӱ		шә
	джь		кхъ		ý		шI
	джь		кхъу		ý		шIу
	дзу		кIкI		ý'		
Е е		Л л			уу	Щ щ	
	е'		л'		уь		ъ
	ĕ		љ		У	Ы ы	
	ә		ль		уу		ӹ
	ә'		ль		У̱		ь
	ӓ		лI			Э э	
	'е		льль	Ф ф			ээ
	'ӛ	Н н		Х х		Ю ю	
Ё ё			н̨		х̌	Я я	
	є		н'		х'		яь
Ж ж			н'		хъ		h
	ж,		њ		хь		h'
	ӝ		нг		хi		ħ
	жъ		нъ		хх		ђ
	жь	О о			ху		j
	жв		ö		х̌ә		q
	щә		e		хIв		w
	щъу		ё		хъу		I
З з			оо		хьхь		II
	ҙ		ɵɵ				'
	ӟ		оь				з
			'е				зә

Abbildung 12.12: Varianten der Kyrillica für nichtrussische Schriftsprachen in Russland.

kombinationen mit ⟨n⟩ als erster Komponente (und zwar ⟨ng⟩ und ⟨nk⟩), womit die Laute [ŋ] (z. B. in *kuningas* 'König', gesprochen wie in deutsch *Rang*) und [ŋk] (z. B. in *henki* 'Leben; Odem', gesprochen wie in deutsch *Ranke*) bezeichnet werden. Diese Lautbezeichnungen stehen außerhalb einer vollkommenen Schrift-Laut-Entsprechung. Eine perfekte Entsprechung würde ein Sonderzeichen für n in diesen Zeichenkombinationen erfordern.

Von den Individualzeichen treten drei lediglich in Lehnwörtern auf (⟨f⟩, ⟨g⟩, ⟨z⟩). In finnischen Wörtern kommen ⟨b⟩ und ⟨d⟩ nur im Inlaut (und zwar in obliquen Formen) vor, im Anlaut sind diese stimmhaften Konsonanten auf Lehnwörter beschränkt. Die Quantitätenkorrelation wird konsequent markiert, und zwar die Kürze durch Einfachschreibung, die Länge durch Doppelschreibung:

Kurzer Vokal vs. langer Vokal
rima 'Sprosse' *riimu* 'Reim'

Einfacher Konsonant vs. Doppelkonsonant
mato 'Wurm' *matto* 'Teppich'

Wenn hier über Strategien nachgedacht wird, wie sich Schrift der Lautung anpassen kann, und wenn konkrete Einzelfälle unter dem Gesichtspunkt analysiert werden, in welchem Ausmaß sich ein Schriftsystem dem Ideal einer vollkommenen Lautwiedergabe annähert, sollte man bedenken, daß Idealforderungen, die theoretisch an ein Schriftsystem zu stellen sind, nicht nur die lineare Lautsequenz des Wortkörpers betreffen, sondern ebenfalls satzphonetische Besonderheiten, Eigenheiten der Prosodie und Intonationsmerkmale einschließen. Gemessen an einem solchen Idealniveau ist jedes Alphabet, ebenso das finnische, ein Kompromisssystem und höchst unvollkommen. Andererseits wäre der Umgang mit einer 'perfekten' Schrift sehr umständlich. „A truly complete script, representing all of our phonological knowledge, even if theoretically possible, would be too cumbersomely inefficient and confusing to read" (Miller 1994: 108).

9. Zitierte Literatur

Anati, E. 1989. *Origini dell'arte e della concettualità*. Mailand: Jaca Book.

Baldauf, I. 1993. *Schriftreform und Schriftwechsel bei den muslimischen Russland- und Sowjettürken (1850−1937): Ein Symptom ideengeschichtlicher und kulturpolitischer Entwicklungen*. Budapest: Akadémiai Kiadó.

Brunner, H. ^{2}1967. *Abriss der mittelägyptischen Grammatik*. Graz: Akademische Druck- und Verlagsanstalt.

Chadwick, J. 1990. „Linear B". In: *Reading the past* 1990: 137−195.

Coe, M. 1992. *Breaking the Maya code*. London: Thames and Hudson.

Coulmas, F. 1996. *The Blackwell encyclopedia of writing systems*. Oxford: Blackwell.

Curto, S. 1989. *La scrittura nella storia dell'Uomo*. Mailand: Cisalpino.

DeFrancis, J. 1977. *Colonialism and language policy in Viet Nam*. Den Haag: Mouton.

DeFrancis, J. 1989. *Visible speech. The diverse oneness of writing systems*. Honolulu: University of Hawaii Press.

Dezső, L. & Hajdú, P. (eds.) 1970. *Theoretical problems of typology and the northern Eurasian languages*. Budapest: Akadémiai Kiadó.

Duhoux, Y. 1981. „Les Etéocrétois et l'origine de l'alphabet grec". *l'Antiquité Classique* 50: 287−294.

Godart, L. 1992. *L'invenzione della scrittura. Dal Nilo alla Grecia*. Turin: Einaudi.

Godart, L. 1995. „Un'iscrizione in Lineare B del XVII secolo A.C. ad Olimpia". In: *Rendiconti dell'Accademia nazionale dei Lincei. Classe di Scienze morali, storiche e filologiche*, s. 9, v., 445−447.

Günther, H. & Ludwig, O. (eds.) 1994. *Schrift und Schriftlichkeit. Writing and Its Use*. Berlin/New York: Walter de Gruyter.

Haarmann, H. ^{2}1992. *Universalgeschichte der Schrift*. Frankfurt/New York: Campus.

Haarmann, H. 1994. *Entstehung und Verbreitung von Alphabetschriften*. In: Günther & Ludwig 1994: 329−347.

Haarmann, H. 1995. *Early civilization and literacy in Europe. An inquiry into cultural continuity in the Mediterranean world*. Berlin/New York: Mouton de Gruyter.

Haarmann, H. 1998. „Writing technology and the abstract mind". *Semiotica* 122, 69−97.

Harris, W. V. 1989. *Ancient literacy*. Cambridge, Massachusetts/London: Cambridge University Press.

Healey, J. F. 1990. „The early alphabet". In: *Reading the past* 1990: 197−257.

Heine, B. & Schadeberg, Th. C. & Wolff, E. (eds.) 1981. *Die Sprachen Afrikas*. Hamburg: Helmut Buske.

Hooker, J. T. 1980. *Linear B − An introduction*. Bristol: Bristol Classical Press.

Ifrah, G. ^{2}1987. *Universalgeschichte der Zahlen*. Frankfurt/New York: Campus.

Isaev, M. I. 1979. *Jazykovoe stroitel'stvo v SSSR (processy sozdanija pis'mennostej narodov SSSR)*. Moskau: Nauka.

Jensen, H. ³1969. *Die Schrift in Vergangenheit und Gegenwart*. Berlin: VEB Deutscher Verlag der Wissenschaften.

Keightley, D. N. ²1985. *Sources of Shang history. The oracle-bone inscriptions of Bronze Age China*. Berkeley/Los Angeles/London: University of California Press.

Loprieno, A. 1995. *Ancient Egyptian – A linguistic introduction*. Cambridge/New York: Cambridge University Press.

Martin, M. 1962. „Revision and reclassification of the Proto-Byblian signs". *Orientalia*, NS 31: 250–271; 339–363.

Miller, D. G. 1994. *Ancient scripts and phonological knowledge*. Amsterdam/Philadelphia: John Benjamins.

Parpola, A. 1986. „The Indus script: a challenging puzzle". *World Archaeology* 17: 399–419.

Parpola, A. 1994. *Deciphering the Indus script*. Cambridge: Cambridge University Press.

Reading the past. Ancient writing from cuneiform to the alphabet (introduced by J. T. Hooker). London: British Museum Publications 1990.

Störk, L. 1981. „Ägyptisch". In: Heine et al. 1981: 149–170.

Thomsen, M.-L. 1984. *The Sumerian language. An introduction to its history and grammatical structure*. Kopenhagen: Akademisk forlag.

Walker, C. B. F. 1990. „Cuneiform". In: *Reading the past* 1990: 17–73.

Watt, W. C. 1987. „The Byblos matrix". *Journal of Near Eastern Studies* 46: 1–14.

Watt, W. C. 1989. „Getting writing right". *Semiotica* 75: 279–315.

Harald Haarmann,
Helsinki (Finnland)

III. History and prehistory of universals research
Geschichte und Vorgeschichte der Universalienforschung
Histoire et préhistoire de la recherche universaliste

13. Philosophie du langage et linguistique dans l'Antiquité classique

1. Introduction
2. Le contexte de la réflexion grammaticale
3. L'élaboration d'un modèle grammatical
4. Conclusions
5. Bibliographie

1. Introduction

La linguistique telle qu'elle a pris forme et s'est développée dans l'Antiquité classique est, pour la caractériser en termes généraux, une recherche des structures grammaticales de langues individuelles – en l'occurrence, le grec ou le latin – sans que cet examen s'appuie sur une comparaison typologique de langues et sans qu'il soit basé sur une réflexion méthodologique prenant comme objet le statut des catégories ou la validité des concepts linguistiques mis en œuvre et transposés d'une langue à l'autre. Il n'en reste pas moins que l'Antiquité classique mérite sa place dans un aperçu de l'histoire de la typologie linguistique et de la recherche des universaux linguistiques, étant donné que cette période a vu la création d'un modèle de description linguistique, fondé sur la notion de classes de mots, qui a été constamment utilisé dans l'histoire de la linguistique occidentale et qu'elle a doté d'un remplissage sémantico-ontologique les catégories linguistiques attribuées au grec ou au latin.

Le modèle de description grammaticale qui a été élaboré dans l'Antiquité classique est donc axé autour de la morphologie, et plus particulièrement autour du modèle des parties du discours (classes de mots), auxquelles on assigne des catégories telles que le nombre, le genre, la personne, etc. qui chacune peuvent prendre des valeurs particulières (telles que: singulier/duel/pluriel; masculin/féminin/neutre, etc.). Il s'agit donc d'une description de type WORD-AND-PARADIGM, prenant comme unités de description les mots (et non des morphèmes ou des syntagmes), catégorisés, en fonction de traits formels et sémantiques, dans des séries paradigmatiques. [Pour des aperçus globaux de la réflexion linguistique dans l'Antiquité, cf. Steinthal 1890–1891[2], Robins 1951, Pinborg 1975, Baratin & Desbordes 1981, Hovdhaugen 1982, Swiggers & Wouters 1990, Householder 1995, Taylor 1995].

2. Le contexte de la réflexion grammaticale

La grammaire dans l'Antiquité est une discipline qui s'est dégagée de la rhétorique et de la philosophie. À l'égard de la rhétorique (ou de la poétique), elle a défini un objet d'étude propre; par rapport à la philosophie, elle a emprunté des éléments de la démarche philosophique, tout en ajoutant progressivement des perspectives linguistiques propres. Nous examinerons brièvement les rapports les plus importants entre la grammaire, la rhétorique et la philosophie. [Sur les rapports entre grammaire et rhétorique, voir Belardi 1985 et Swiggers & Wouters 1995; sur les rapports entre grammaire et philosophie, voir Coseriu 1969–1972, Blank 1982, Gambarara 1984, Belardi 1985, Hennigfeld 1994, Ildefonse 1997, Swiggers & Wouters 1998a].

La grammaire a longtemps constitué une discipline unitaire avec la rhétorique. Les deux disciplines se partagent le champ de la λέξις, c.-à-d. l'expression du sens qu'ont les mots (cf. Aristote, *Poétique* VI, 26, 1450b: 12−50). La grammaire, unie à la rhétorique, s'oppose à la dialectique qui prend pour objet les aspects logiques des contenus propositionnels ou des modalités locutoires. Si Aristote, dans sa *Poétique*, intègre l'analyse grammaticale à un examen global de la λέξις (cf. *Poétique* XX−XXII), Denys d'Halicarnasse (2 moitié du 1er s. av. J.-C.) intègre la grammaire à l'étude de la composition du discours, qui est structuré en fonction des principes constitutifs de la beauté et des mérites de l'expression littéraire (cf. Schenkeveld 1983 et Swiggers & Wouters 1995). Denys distingue trois branches: l'étude des formes langagières qui doivent être combinées dans le discours, l'étude des moyens permettant d'obtenir une combinaison harmonieuse, et l'étude des procédés par lesquels on modifie les mots dans le discours en fonction d'un usage particulier. C'est à l'intérieur de sa discussion de la «belle harmonie» du discours que Denys aborde des questions de grammaire et qu'il présente un petit traité sur les éléments (γράμματα) du discours: leur nombre, leur nature, leur classification et leur combinaison en syllabes. C'est par la matière même du discours que l'étude grammaticale est intégrée à l'étude du discours comme combinaison (σύνθεσις); dans l'activité didactique, le champ de la λέξις fonctionne donc comme un domaine unitaire (cf. *De compositione uerborum* 25.134,21−135,12). Cet enracinement de la grammaire dans l'étude unitaire de la λέξις explique pourquoi, dans l'introduction de la *Technê grammatikê* de Denys le Thrace (voir *infra*), on trouve la définition et l'articulation suivantes de la grammaire:

«La grammaire est la connaissance empirique des usages généraux des poètes et prosateurs. Elle a six parties: la première est la lecture experte à haute voix qui respecte la prosodie; la deuxième, c'est l'explication des expressions littéraires dans les œuvres; la troisième, c'est l'établissement de notes sur le vocabulaire rare et sur la thématique; la quatrième, c'est la recherche de l'étymologie; la cinquième, c'est le dégagement de l'analogie; la sixième, c'est l'appréciation de compositions littéraires, ce qui est, de toutes parties, la partie la plus noble de la science.»

Quant aux rapports entre grammaire et philosophie, ceux-ci sont particulièrement importants, étant donné que la philosophie antique a influencé pendant des siècles l'évolution de la discipline grammaticale et a contribué à fixer sa fonction et son métalangage. La linguistique occidentale se nourrit, à la base, de préoccupations philosophiques.

L'intérêt linguistique des philosophes grecs s'est d'abord porté sur les propriétés sémantiques des mots: la synonymie, l'antonymie et la paronymie; il a abouti, dans les *Catégories* d'Aristote, à une théorie sémantique basée sur les relations entre la chose, le nom et le contenu. En fonction des relations existant entre ces trois entités, Aristote définit l'équivocité, l'univocité et la paravocité (cf. *Catégories* I 1, 1a: 1−15). La réflexion philosophique sur les rapports entre chose et nom a donné lieu à une tradition philosophico-linguistique prenant comme objet de réflexion le caractère motivé ou non motivé du signe linguistique, tradition dans laquelle le *Cratyle* de Platon occupe une place cruciale. [Sur le *Cratyle* et son rôle dans l'histoire de la réflexion sur le langage, voir Derbolav 1959]. La réflexion philosophique a également été à l'origine de la lente élaboration d'un modèle descriptif de la structure des langues − structure postulée en l'occurrence pour le grec mais s'avérant d'applicabilité plus large. L'élaboration de ce modèle descriptif s'est nourrie de divers apports philosophiques et la justification de certaines catégories ou sous-catégories linguistiques s'est largement inspirée de vues philosophiques (→ § 3).

3. L'élaboration d'un modèle grammatical

Comme nous l'avons déjà relevé (§ 1), le modèle grammatical élaboré dans l'Antiquité classique est un modèle de type WORD-AND-PARADIGM (cf. Hockett 1954: 210; Robins 1959), axé sur la morphologie conçue comme une description de classes de mots. Ce modèle s'est élaboré à partir d'une division macro-structurelle de la phrase: les «parties du discours» (grec *μέρη τοῦ λόγου*; latin *partes orationis*) correspondent d'abord aux macro-segments de la phrase en tant qu'unités discursives avant d'accéder à un statut foncièrement morphologique, en tant que classes de mots.

L'origine de ce modèle se trouve dans le *Sophiste* de Platon, dialogue dans lequel Platon pose le problème de l'existence de discours faux (cf. Swiggers 1984). Ceux-ci ne peuvent exister que par et dans un acte du langage: celui de l'énonciation. Or, comme le montre l'étranger éléate dans le dialogue en question, l'énonciation, si elle est une suite de mots, est toujours plus qu'un simple assemblage de paroles. Le discours correspond en effet à un principe d'organisation, qui est un principe de *liaison* (συμπλοκή) entre deux entités. Le discours existe par une liaison qu'on établit entre deux unités macro-sémantiques: ce qu'on affirme et ce dont on affirme quelque chose. Les deux 'genres' de signes qui sont utilisés pour exprimer ces deux unités sont appelés *verbe* (ῥῆμα) et *nom* (ὄνομα). Pour qu'on puisse avoir une prédication, le verbe doit être lié à un sujet: cette première liaison (πρώτη συμπλοκή) est la base indispensable du λόγος. C'est par le verbe qu'on indique que quelque chose est, a été ou sera (tel), ou qu'on indique la négation de ces états de choses (au sens de: *states of affairs*). Platon fait une distinction entre deux niveaux: (a) le niveau de la dénomination (l'acte de *dénommer*: grec ὀνομάζειν), niveau auquel on prend les unités *nom* et *verbe* comme unités séparées; (b) le niveau de la prédication ou de l'énonciation prédicative (l'acte d'*énoncer*: grec λέγειν), le niveau auquel un verbe est utilisé avec une valeur «actualisante» de sorte que quelque chose est énoncé à propos d'un certain sujet. Le λόγος correspond donc à un acte de prédication et la possibilité du mensonge réside dans la dualité des niveaux de la dénomination et de la prédication. En effet, toute prédication doit s'appliquer à un objet, mais le locuteur peut combiner n'importe quel ῥῆμα avec n'importe quel ὄνομα, puisque la langue comporte une articulation indépendante de ces deux classes. L'énoncé peut donc correspondre à un fait et être vrai (p. ex. «Platon parle»); mais l'énonciation peut aussi affirmer un fait non réel, voire impossible (p. ex. «La chaise parle»); et dans ce cas-là, on a un discours faux: «Ainsi un assemblage de verbes et de noms, qui, à ton sujet, énonce, en fait, comme autre, ce qui est même, et, comme étant, ce qui n'est point, voilà, ce semble, au juste, l'espèce d'assemblage qui constitue un discours faux.» (*Sophiste* 262 d). Platon a ainsi cerné la structure fondamentale de toute prédication langagière en dégageant les deux unités constitutives de la structure prédicative: le nom et le verbe.

Si Platon a fourni les bases d'une description structurale du langage, Aristote fournira des éléments de caractérisation morphologique nécessaires pour la distinction en classes de mots. Dans le *Peri Hermeneias*, Aristote différencie nettement le nom et le verbe: le nom est défini par lui comme un son vocal possédant une signification conventionnelle, sans référence temporelle, et dont aucune partie ne présente de signification quand elle est prise séparément, alors que le verbe est défini comme ce qui ajoute à sa signification lexicale l'idée du temps: «Je dis qu'il signifie, en plus de sa signification propre, le temps: par exemple, *santé* est un nom, tandis que *se porte bien* est un verbe, car il ajoute à sa propre signification l'existence actuelle de cet état» (*Peri Hermeneias* 16 b). Il faut noter ici que, pour Aristote, le propre du verbe est d'énoncer un prédicat par rapport à une époque temporelle non spécifiée (un «présent» non déterminé); le temps grammatical est une «inclinaison» du verbe, qui permet d'identifier une *forme verbale* comme un 'cas' du verbe: «Une expression comme *ne se porte pas bien* ou *n'est pas malade* n'est pas un verbe: bien qu'elle ajoute à sa signification celle du temps et qu'elle appartienne toujours à un sujet, cette variété ne possède pas de nom. On peut l'appeler seulement un verbe indéfini, puisqu'elle s'applique indifféremment à n'importe quoi, à l'être et au non-être. Même remarque pour *il se porta bien* ou *il se portera bien*; ce n'est pas là un verbe, mais un 'cas' de verbe; il diffère du verbe en ce que le cas marque le temps qui entoure le temps présent» (*Peri Hermeneias* 16 b: 12−19). À cela s'ajoute que, dans l'optique d'Aristote, le verbe (lexical) est analysable en «être + contenu prédicatif» (formellement: une forme conjuguée du verbe «être» + le participe présent du verbe lexical). Cette analyse, qui n'explicite pas le rôle du verbe copule (cf. *Peri Hermeneias* 21 b: 6−9: «ainsi *l'homme se promène* aura pour négation, non pas *le non-homme se promène*, mais *l'homme ne se promène pas*. Il n'y a, en effet, aucune différence entre dire *l'homme se promène* et dire *l'homme est se promenant* »), est à l'origine du procédé couramment appliqué dans la grammaire médiévale et dans les grammaires générales des Temps Modernes, qui consiste à poser une structure «S est P» comme sous-jacente à toute occurrence d'un verbe prédicatif (avec ou sans sujet détaché). Cette analyse, qui transpose une structure logique à diverses structures grammaticales possibles (en surface), est à la base des théories syntaxiques prenant comme objet la constitution des propositions. [Pour l'intérêt historique de l'analyse en «S est P», voir Swiggers 1989a, b. Sur l'importance du *Peri Hermeneias* pour la conception du langage comme reflet expressif de la pensée, voir Arens 1984, Montanari

1984—1988, Hennigfeld 1994: 71—9 et Weidemann 1991].

Dans le chapitre XX de sa *Poétique*, Aristote reconnaît quatre composantes du discours qu'il appelle *nom* (ὄνομα), *verbe* (ῥῆμα), *jonction* (σύνδεσμος) et *membre articulaire* (ἄρθρον). [Cf. Rosén 1990; Swiggers & Wouters, à paraître]. Aristote n'a pas réussi à mettre en place les concepts proprement grammaticaux permettant d'isoler des séries à comportement phrastique moins autonome (clitiques, prépositions, particules) ou permettant de définir les oppositions de comportement entre les classes de mots qui partagent la caractéristique de la non-variabilité. Il n'en reste pas moins qu'il nous fournit une classification sommaire des composantes du discours, un cadre définitionnel (avec des concepts phonétiques, morphologiques et sémantiques tels que φωνή 'voix', σύνθετος 'composé', σημαντικός 'ayant signification'), des indices d'ordre morpho-syntaxique (marquage du temps, statut autonome ou non autonome et position dans la phrase). Comme principal apport linguistique d'Aristote, on retiendra surtout l'élargissement du modèle macro-syntaxique légué par Platon à l'aide de classes ayant une fonction de relateur ou de joncteur. [Sur les conceptions linguistiques ou philosophico-linguistiques d'Aristote, voir Arens 1984, Ax 1992, Rosén 1994].

Le modèle grammatical ainsi constitué subira une transformation importante due à l'apport crucial de la dialectique stoïcienne. [Sur les conceptions linguistiques des Stoïciens, voir Pohlenz 1939, Egli 1967, Lloyd 1971, Hagius 1979, Frede 1987, Baratin 1991, Atherton 1993]. Celle-ci était articulée autour d'une théorie de la signification opérant avec trois unités: l'énoncé, le λεκτόν (contenu notionnel) et les objets. Ces unités n'assument leur statut qu'au niveau de la proposition: celle-ci est la combinaison d'un prédicat (incorporel) et d'un terme sujet (appellatif ou nom propre). Le terme sujet doit présenter une flexion: entre le terme fléchi et l'objet qui possède la qualité ou la caractéristique signifiée par le nom fléchi, il y a une relation de 'survenance', pour laquelle les Stoïciens utilisent le verbe τυγχάνειν. La théorie du λεκτόν (cf. Frede 1994) permet de lier des catégories conceptuelles à des classes morpho-syntaxiques.

Dans leur analyse des structures linguistiques, les Stoïciens distinguent cinq parties du discours: le nom propre (ὄνομα), le nom commun ou appellatif (προσηγορία), le verbe, le σύνδεσμος et l'ἄρθρον. Cette classification prépare la voie au modèle des huit parties du discours (voir *infra*), étant donné que la classe des σύνδεσμοι comportait, à côté des conjonctions, une sous-classe de joncteurs prépositifs, c.-à-d. les prépositions, et étant donné que la classe des ἄρθρα était subdivisée en articles 'limitatifs', c.-à-d. les pronoms personnels, et articles 'non limitatifs', à savoir les articles définis et les pronoms relatifs. Mais le principal apport grammatical des Stoïciens a été celui d'une théorie des accidents (συμβεβηκότα) des classes de mots. L'intérêt accordé par les Stoïciens à ces accidents s'explique par la perspective générale de leur théorie sémantique: celle-ci accordait un sens à chaque partie du discours et ce sens peut être décomposé en valeurs catégorielles, à savoir nombre, genre, cas, diathèse, mode, temps et personne.

Cette réflexion sur les catégories grammaticales a été particulièrement importante dans les processus d'autonomisation de la grammaire: l'examen des faits grammaticaux permettait de montrer que les faits linguistiques ont leur statut propre qui ne coïncide pas toujours avec celui des choses réelles ni avec celui des constructions conceptuelles (d'où p. ex. l'emploi d'un pluriel comme *Athènes* pour un singulier, ou le phénomène de la *constructio ad sensum*).

Les doctrines philosophiques de l'Antiquité grecque ont fourni ainsi à la grammaire une perspective d'analyse, quelques éléments de classification et certains paramètres de définition et d'analyse. Le contact avec les textes littéraires et la nécessité de l'enseignement des langues feront évoluer la grammaire vers une discipline s'intéressant à l'établissement de classes d'unités (à divers niveaux) et à l'identification de traits formels (couplés parfois avec des propriétés sémantiques), traits formels permettant de définir des classes de mots distinctes par leurs comportements. Cette nouvelle étape de la grammaire sera l'œuvre des philologues alexandrins qui, dès le 3e siècle av. J.-C., s'occupaient de l'édition et du commentaire des grands textes littéraires de l'Antiquité grecque. [Sur l'activité philologique et grammaticale des Alexandrins, voir Pfeiffer 1968, Ax 1991 et Schenkeveld 1994]. L'apport des premières générations de philologues nous est connu principalement à travers des remarques (ou scholies) sur des textes, surtout les épopées d'Homère (cf. Erbse 1980). Ces remarques nous permettent de leur attribuer un modèle d'analyse linguistique opérant avec huit classes de mots, à savoir le nom, le verbe, le participe, l'article (y compris le pronom relatif), le pronom, la préposition, l'adverbe et la conjonction. De plus, les grammairiens alexandrins disposaient d'une terminologie pour les cas et, en partie, pour les temps (déjà étudiés par les Stoïciens en tant que formes signifiant des distinctions temporelles externes et internes) et pour les modes verbaux [cf. Matthaios 1997, qui étudie les conceptions des grammairiens alexandrins telles qu'elles apparaissent dans leurs commentaires sur les textes littéraires].

Le premier manuel dans lequel le schéma canonique des huit parties du discours (cf. Robins 1966, 1986 et Lallot 1988) est présenté de façon explicite, est la *Technê grammatikê* de Denys le Thrace, texte dont l'authenticité a été contestée par certains chercheurs (cf. Law & Sluiter eds. 1995), mais dont le noyau peut être daté à notre avis du IIe–Ier siècle avant J.-C. [Pour des traductions et études récentes de ce texte, voir Lallot 1989; Kemp 1986, 1991: 303–316, Swiggers & Wouters 1998b (avec une traduction allemande de Wilfried Kürschner), Seldeslachts & Swiggers & Wouters, à paraître; pour les τέχναι γραμματικαί préservées sur papyrus, voir Wouters 1979 et Swiggers & Wouters 1994]. Les huit parties du discours y sont énumérées et traitées dans l'ordre suivant: ὄνομα 'nom' (à la fois le nom appellatif et le nom propre), ῥῆμα 'verbe', μετοχή 'participe', ἄρθρον 'article' (et aussi pronom relatif), ἀντωνυμία 'pronom', πρόθεσις 'préposition', ἐπίρρημα 'adverbe', σύνδεσμος 'conjonction'. Chacune de ces parties du discours est définie et est analysée en traits formels, le plus souvent morphologiques, mais parfois syntaxiques ou positionnelles (dans le cas de la préposition) et sémantico-syntaxiques (dans le cas de la conjonction). Chacune des parties du discours est aussi exemplifiée par une série de formes appartenant à la partie du discours en question et rangées éventuellement en sous-classes.

Pour illustrer la démarche des grammairiens de l'Antiquité, nous prendrons comme exemple leur description du nom. Cette classe englobe chez eux les éléments à flexion nominale, c'est-à-dire les substantifs (y compris les noms propres) et les adjectifs. Le nom est d'abord décrit d'après les traits formels (et, conjointement, sémantiques) qui le caractérisent. Les traits catégorisants en question sont les suivants:

- *genre* (avec 3 valeurs possibles: masculin/féminin/neutre);
- *espèce* (avec 2 possibilités: primaire ou dérivée, l'espèce dérivée étant généralement subdivisée en: noms patronymiques, noms possessifs, noms comparatifs, noms superlatifs, noms diminutifs, noms tirés de noms [= dénominaux], noms tirés de verbes [= déverbaux]);
- *figure* (avec 3 réalisations possibles: figure simple, ou composée, ou surcomposée)
- *nombre* (avec 3 valeurs possibles: singulier/duel/pluriel);
- *cas* (avec, en grec, 5 possibilités: nominatif (ou «cas direct»), vocatif, génitif, datif et accusatif; et, en latin, 6 possibilités, vu que l'ablatif s'y ajoute encore).

Ce traitement du nom en fonction d'accidents correspondant aux catégories grammaticales qui articulent la structure de la langue (grecque ou latine) permet un aperçu exhaustif des sous-classes de cette partie du discours et, dans la pratique pédagogique, une caractérisation exhaustive de chaque forme nominale qu'on rencontre dans les textes littéraires (ce type d'exercice est appelé *partitio* dans le monde latin, et c'est de là qu'est issue notre notion moderne de *parsing* [*grammar*]).

Il est important d'observer que ce dispositif de présentation est flexible et que la dynamique de la didactique grammaticale et l'évolution de la théorisation ont été responsables de réorganisations, d'ajouts et de suppressions, de précisions, de légères déviations dans (a) le nombre d'accidents assignés à certaines parties du discours (ainsi, les degrés de comparaison sont-ils posés comme un accident du nom, chez certains grammairiens latins), (b) le nombre de valeurs ou réalisations assignées à certaines catégories (comme p. ex. celle du mode, dans le cas du verbe. [Sur cette dynamique, voir Swiggers & Wouters 1994; pour un aperçu des classifications chez les grammairiens latins, voir les notes dans Swiggers 1985; pour une analyse du système des parties du discours chez les grammairiens de l'Antiquité, voir Schoemann 1862].

Le schéma des parties du discours constitue la partie essentielle des manuels (τέχναι) grammaticaux; une description de la syntaxe se fera attendre jusqu'au IIe siècle après J.-C. avec l'œuvre d'Apollonius Dyscole. Celui-ci fournit dans son traité Περὶ συντάξεως (traduction et commentaire dans Householder 1981 et Lallot 1997; voir aussi Sluiter 1990) une analyse du statut syntaxique de l'article (livre I), du pronom (livre II), du verbe (livre III) et de la proposition et de l'adverbe (livre IV), mais il est essentiel de faire remarquer, avec Lallot (1994; 1997 I: 62 ss.), que son analyse ne fait nullement intervenir la notion de *fonction* syntaxique, comme le prétend Bécares Botas (1987: 36 et suiv.). En effet, Apollonius Dyscole ne dispose pas d'un outil conceptuel permettant de dégager des notions telles que 'complément' ou 'attribut'. On chercherait donc en vain une description syntaxique autonome dans les écrits grammaticaux grecs. [Sur l'absence d'une théorie syntaxique chez les grammairiens grecs, voir Donnet 1967; sur la lente élaboration d'une syntaxe à Rome, voir Baratin 1989].

À l'époque où Apollonius s'occupait d'analyse syntaxique, le modèle des parties du discours constituant le noyau des manuels grammaticaux avait déjà été transmis au monde romain (cf. Taylor 1991). Les grammairiens romains ont transformé l'héritage grec, et plus particulièrement alexandrin, en l'appliquant à un objet nouveau: le latin. [Sur le rôle et la position des grammairiens dans le système éducatif et dans la société dans l'Antiquité, voir Kaster 1988, Hovdhaugen 1991]. Chez les grammairiens romains, l'enseignement grammatical couvrait diverses phases, de l'apprentissage des lettres et de la lecture à l'emploi de figures rhétoriques, la place centrale étant occupée par la grammaire au sens strict. Ce *cursus studiorum* correspondait à celui des écoles alexandrines, mais les manuels grammaticaux latins reflètent de façon beaucoup plus fidèle l'intégration de la rhétorique (élémentaire) à l'instruction grammaticale.

Dans le transfert de la grammaire grecque au monde romain, on peut distinguer deux niveaux correspondant à deux phases chronologiques. Le premier niveau est celui du transfert de certaines idées (ou réflexions générales) à propos de la structure et de la nature du langage; le second niveau est celui du transfert, de l'adoption et de l'adaptation de modèles grammaticaux structurés autour du schéma des parties du discours. Le premier niveau est attesté dans les écrits de Varron (= Marcus Terentius Varro, 106-27 av. J.-C.), le premier grammairien romain dont on a conservé de larges extraits. [Sur Varron, voir Dahlmann 1932, Collart 1954, Taylor 1975, 1988]. Son *De lingua Latina* n'a été conservé que fragmentairement. Il comprenait, en 25 livres, une description morphologique et une description syntaxique du latin; cette dernière a été complètement perdue. La description morphologique chez Varron est particulièrement intéressante dans l'optique d'une histoire de la typologie linguistique: elle fournit des notions-clés de validité générale pour la description de structures linguistiques. Au centre de la théorie morphologique de Varron se trouve la notion de *declinatio* que l'auteur explique nettement dans le passage suivant (*De lingua Latina* VIII, 9.21−23):

« Il y a deux espèces de *declinatio*, la *declinatio* volontaire et la *declinatio* naturelle. La *declinatio* volontaire est celle qui est le résultat de la volonté d'un individu, qui se sépare de celle des autres. Ainsi par exemple, quand trois hommes ont acheté à Éphèse chacun un esclave, l'un appellera son esclave d'après le nom du marchand Artémidore et il le baptisera *Artemas*, l'autre appellera son esclave *Ion(a)*, d'après le nom de la région d'*Ionie*, et le troisième l'appellera *Ephesius*, parce qu'il l'a acheté à Éphèse. [...].

22. J'appelle, par contre, *declinatio* naturelle celle qui est basée, non sur la volonté des individus agissant séparément, mais sur un accord général. Une fois que les noms ont été imposés, ils les déclinent en cas de la même façon, et ils diront de la même façon (au génitif), *Artemidori, Ionis, Ephesi*, et ainsi de même dans les autres cas.

23. Parfois les deux espèces se rencontrent ensemble, et de telle façon que dans la *declinatio* volontaire on marque les processus de la nature, et dans la *declinatio* naturelle les effets de la volonté. »

Chez Varron, la *declinatio* est donc le procédé par lequel les mots entrent dans la langue ou assument une forme linguistique: les uns sont des créations individuelles alors que d'autres sont des instances de types lexicaux et leur forme est celle que le système de la langue assigne à toutes les formes ayant le même statut paradigmatique et la même fonction morpho-syntaxique. La *declinatio* naturelle est celle qui est imposée par le système de la langue; elle peut se greffer sur une forme construite par *declinatio* volontaire quand celle-ci prend un cas flexionnel. Varron constitue un jalon important dans l'histoire de la typologie linguistique, étant donné qu'il est un des premiers à expliciter la notion de *rapport*, et plus particulièrement *rapport de proportionnalité*, entre des formes. En effet, dans la langue, les paradigmes sont constitués à partir de rapports structuraux existant entre des séries de formes. Une application grammaticale très intéressante de l'exploitation des rapports structuraux dans la langue, en combinaison avec la notion de *declinatio*, nous est offerte par la réduction en quatre classes de mots à laquelle aboutit Varron. N'adoptant pas les huit parties du discours de la grammaire grecque, Varron reconnaît quatre classes ou espèces de mots (*De lingua Latina* VI, 5.36):

« Les espèces de mots en *declinatio* sont de quatre types: l'un qui signifie par surcroît les temps et n'a pas de cas, comme *leges* (tu liras) et *lege* (lis), qui viennent de *lego* (je lis); l'autre qui a des cas mais qui ne signifie pas de temps, comme *lectio* (lecture) et *lector* (lecteur) de *lego* (je lis); le troisième qui a les deux, à savoir temps et cas, comme *legens* (lisant) et *lecturus* (disposé à lire) de *lego* (je lis); le quatrième qui n'a ni l'un ni l'autre, comme *lecte* (avec choix) et *lectissime* (avec beaucoup de choix) de *lego* (je choisis). »

Les quatre espèces de mots ainsi retenues correspondent à des fonctions différentes dans la langue: les noms remplissent la fonction d'appellation; les verbes, celle d'énonciation; les participes ont le rôle de jonction, selon Varron; et les adverbes ont la fonction d'étayage. Il est intéressant d'observer que, chez Varron, on assiste à une inversion de la démarche des technographes antiques: alors que chez eux les accidents étaient des spécifications ultérieures de catégories qu'on avait posées, Varron établit des catégories de mots en tant que celles-ci épuisent les combinaisons logiques, en partant de la présence ou de l'absence de deux traits, à savoir temps et cas. La contribution originale de Varron réside dans l'emploi de ces traits pour mettre en place une combinatoire fermée qui permet de fixer le nombre minimal des parties du discours. On a ici l'exemple d'un modèle descriptif, appliqué au latin, qui opère avec des marques à valeurs typologiques auxquelles correspondent des valeurs binaires (absence ou présence: −/+).

Le second niveau dans la transposition de la grammaire grecque au monde romain est constitué par l'adoption et la transformation de l'héritage alexandrin appliqué au latin. Cette phase, qu'on peut suivre en détail à partir du 3ᵉ siècle de notre ère consiste en une série de manuels grammaticaux (*artes grammaticae*) [édition Keil 1857−1880; voir aussi Barwick 1922] qui adoptent et systématisent le contenu des τέχναι γραμματικαί de l'Antiquité grecque. Ce qui caractérise en général la grammaticographie latine par rapport à celle du monde grec est l'ajout à la partie phonétique et morphologique d'une section de rhétorique et de stylistique où sont traités les figures rhétoriques et les « vices et vertus » de l'expression langagière (*uitia et uirtutes orationis*). Dans l'optique d'une histoire de la description et de la typologie des langues, c'est la section de morphologie dans les manuels grammaticaux latins qui doit retenir notre attention. Cette partie est structurée autour des classes de mots, les *partes orationis*, correspondant aux μέρη τοῦ λόγου des grammairiens grecs (voir *supra*). Par rapport aux textes grecs, on relève néanmoins deux différences importantes:

(1) alors que la tradition grecque adopte un ordre fixe (nom, verbe, participe, article, pronom, préposition, adverbe, conjonction), les grammairiens latins utilisent un des trois ordres suivants (cf. Swiggers 1995: 166−167):
− nom, pronom, verbe, participe, adverbe, conjonction, préposition, interjection (= ordre **y**);
− nom, pronom, verbe, adverbe, participe, conjonction, préposition, interjection (= ordre **d**, qui est celui des *artes* de Donat);
− nom, verbe, participe, pronom, préposition, adverbe, interjection, conjonction (= ordre **p**, qui est fondamentalement l'ordre des *technai* grecques, la seule différence consistant dans la disparition de l'article et dans le dédoublement de l'adverbe en *aduerbium* et *interiectio*).

(2) le monde latin s'est, très tôt déjà, illustré par la production de manuels d'apprentissage, ce qui s'explique par la diffusion du latin dans les différentes régions de l'Empire et par l'extension d'un réseau d'écoles dans les territoires colonisés. À partir de la fin du 3ᵉ siècle (Marius Plotius Sacerdos), on voit se multiplier les descriptions grammaticales, se dégageant du contexte de l'enseignement rhétorique. À partir de Donat (= Aelius Donatus), l'artigraphie grammaticale s'autonomise grâce à la production de manuels grammaticaux (*artes grammaticae*), qui suscitent leurs propres commentaires (les *artes* de Donat seront commentées par Servius et Pompeius). Plusieurs de ces manuels ne visent que le niveau de l'instruction élémentaire et certains d'entre eux ont été rédigés à l'usage d'un public grécophone apprenant le latin (p. ex. l'*Ars grammatica* de Dosithée et le traité de Macrobe sur les rapports entre les systèmes verbaux du grec et du latin).

Chronologiquement, la série des manuels grammaticaux latins est constituée par les textes contenus dans le schéma 13.1 [nous donnons les noms des auteurs latins dans leur forme latine]:

[Quintus Remmius Palaemon]	*Ars*	[1er s.]?
[Aemilius Asper]	*Ars*	[fin 2e–début 3e s.]?
[Marius Plotius Sacerdos]	*Artium grammaticarum libri tres*	[2e moitié du 3e s.]?
Marius Victorinus	*Ars grammatica*	1re moitié du 4e s.?
[Victorinus]	*Ars*	[1re moitié du 4e s.]?
Donatus	*Ars minor*	v. 340–360
Donatus	*Ars maior*	v. 340–360
Flavius Sosipater Charisius	*Artis grammaticae libri V*	v. 360
Diomedes	*Artis grammaticae libri III*	v. 370–380
Probus	*Instituta artium*	milieu du 4e s.?
Dositheus	*Ars grammatica*	2 moitié du 4 s.
[Augustinus]	*Ars pro fratrum mediocritate breviata*	[fin 4e s.]?
Consentius	*Ars de nomine et verbo*	1re moitié du 5e s.?
Audax	*De Scauri et Palladii libris excerpta per interrogationem et responsionem*	6e s.?
Priscianus Caesariensis	*Institutionium grammaticarum libri XVIII*	v. 526–7

Schéma 13.1: Manuels grammaticaux latins

L'importance de ces textes réside dans l'exploitation d'une structure originalement conçue pour le grec et appliquée maintenant au latin. Cette structure comporte une description progressive des niveaux constitutifs de la langue à partir des lettres jusqu'aux parties du discours et aux procédés rhétoriques et stylistiques. La présence d'un dispositif grec face à un objet pour lequel il n'avait pas été construit, en combinaison avec l'idée que le latin dérive du grec ou serait un dialecte du grec, explique deux tentatives chez les grammairiens latins: celle de reconnaître en latin des séries de formes qui n'existent qu'en grec, comme le mode optatif, et celle de dédoubler certaines formes latines, comme l'ablatif, en deux valeurs, par exemple l'ablatif avec préposition (qui sera le *sextus casus*) et l'ablatif sans préposition (qui sera le *septimus casus*). Ces deux tentatives sont les manifestations d'une même démarche sous-jacente: la mise en corrélation des structures du grec et de leur sens avec les structures du latin.

Chez Priscien, le dernier grammairien latin de l'Antiquité, on trouve un retour aux doctrines grecques et une récupération des descriptions syntaxiques des grammairiens grecs, et tout particulièrement d'Apollonius Dyscole dont il traduit de longs passages. [Sur Priscien et sur l'insertion de son œuvre dans les activités grammaticales à Byzance, voir Robins 1988; 1993: 87–110]. Si, dans ses *Institutiones grammaticae*, Priscien n'innove guère en matière de morphologie – il maintient les huit parties du discours que les autres grammairiens latins avaient reconnues avant lui –, il prépare, en syntaxe, la voie à une analyse qui s'intéresse aux rapports de rection et de dépendance dans la structure phrastique. Toutefois, il n'a pas développé la notion de fonction syntaxique et ne dépasse pas ainsi le niveau de théorisation atteint par Apollonius Dyscole.

4. Conclusions

La grammaire – ou, plus globalement, la réflexion sur le langage dans l'Antiquité – n'a pas de visée typologique explicite: d'une part, elle ne pratique pas la comparaison de structures (si l'on excepte quelques transpositions ou équivalences établies entre les systèmes casuels ou les systèmes temporels du grec et du latin – ces transpositions ne se font pas par référence à un *tertium comparationis*); d'autre part, elle ne témoigne guère d'une conscience de solidarités structurelles caractérisant des types grammaticaux (p. ex. des rapports de solidarité entre l'ordre des constituants et la présence de prépositions et de postpositions). Enfin, si la grammaire sous l'influence d'une philosophie à vocation universaliste – semble postuler des catégories linguistiques universelles, on ne peut pourtant pas dire qu'il y a une recherche *empirique* des universaux ou des tendances générales, ce qui est une condition essentielle de validité typologique.

Il n'en reste pas moins que la grammaire et la philosophie du langage dans l'Antiquité méritent une place dans un aperçu historique de la typologie linguistique: c'est à l'Antiquité classique que remonte l'approche de la morphosyntaxe qui est typique de la linguistique occidentale. Les fondements du 'métalangage' typologique – ou du dispositif typologique — ont été posés par les philosophes et les grammairiens de l'Antiquité. Dans cet héritage, on retiendra en particulier:

(1) le modèle descriptif global, qui dans un mouvement ascendant, passe des éléments graphophonétiques aux syllabes, ensuite aux mots et aux combinaisons de mots. Ce principe d'arrangement réglé et de hiérarchie est formulé par Apollonius Dyscole dans son traité de syntaxe:

« Bien à l'avance déjà, les éléments, mentionnés en premier en tant que matière indivisible, préfigurent cela, car les enchaînements d'éléments ne se font pas au hasard, mais selon les règles de la construction — et c'est de là, pratiquement, qu'ils ont tiré aussi leur nom. Au niveau suivant, la syllabe obéit au même principe, puisque les constructions de syllabes doivent, pour produire le mot, être effectuées selon les règles. Et il est clair que, dans la même logique, les mots, qui sont les parties de la phrase complète bien construite, sont soumis à leur tour à la congruence de la construction. En effet, le contenu de pensée qui est le signifié conjoint à chaque mot est, si l'on peut dire, un 'élément' de la phrase, et, de même que les éléments produisent les syllabes par leurs enchaînements, de même la construction [qui assemble] les contenus de pensée produira, si l'on peut dire, des 'syllabes' par l'enchaînement des mots; ou encore, de la même façon que les syllabes donnent le mot, de même la congruence des contenus de pensée donne la phrase complète » (Περὶ συντάξεως § 2, traduction de Lallot 1997 I: 96);

(2) la concentration du modèle descriptif sur le mot et les accidents qui 'surviennent' à des mots en tant que représentants d'une classe: cette incidence 'lexématique' du modèle constitue à la fois sa force heuristique (le mot est une notion très opérationnelle quand on se place au point de vue de l'usage linguistique et de la conscience des locuteurs) et sa faiblesse théorique (la définition, ou la 'définissabilité' du mot pose de redoutables problèmes de méthode);

(3) le recours à des 'caractéristiques' (formelles, auxquelles on associe des propriétés sémantiques): on assiste là à la postulation de concepts abstraits, et plus particulièrement à l'établissement de *catégories* linguistiques, dont l'usage est une condition de base de toute classification typologique. Toutefois, on doit noter que l'établissement de ces catégories chez les grammairiens grecs et latins a été le résultat d'une analyse presque exclusivement immanente, ne faisant pas intervenir l'idée d'une solidarité (partielle ou totale) de certaines catégories ni celle de contraintes s'exerçant sur les catégories (ou leur réalisation linguistique);

(4) la reconnaissance d'une double hiérarchie: d'abord celle qui explique l'imbrication d'unités plus petites dans des ensembles plus larges (cf. (1), ci-dessus), ensuite celle qui se dégage à l'intérieur du système des parties du discours, où le nom et le verbe se profilent comme les deux classes principales. Leur fonction prééminente se laisse reconnaître à deux propriétés, l'une morphologique et l'autre syntaxique. La première, c'est que le nom et le verbe sont les parties du discours qui ont le plus grand nombre d'accidents (le participe est une classe de mots qui combine leurs accidents); la seconde correspond à une observation fondamentale, qui sous-tend l'analyse logique traditionnelle en sujet et prédicat et qui, d'autre part, fonctionne comme constante (implicite) dans toute analyse en constituants immédiats ultimes, à savoir que la structure minimale d'une phrase est: nom (sujet) + verbe, ou — formulation plus prudente — qu'il suffit d'avoir un nom (sujet) et un verbe (conjugué) pour avoir une phrase minimale. Cette idée qu'on rencontre chez Donat (Keil 1857−1880, vol. IV: 355, 372) est formulée de façon succincte chez l'auteur qui a codifié l'essence de la grammaticographie latine, à savoir Isidore de Séville (6e siècle): « Sed omnes [partes orationis] ad illa dua principalia reuertuntur, id est, ad nomen et uerbum, quae significant personam et actum. Reliquae appendices sunt et ex his originem trahunt » (*Etymologiae* I, chap. XIII. § 1; cf. Swiggers 1985: 286).

5. Références

Arens, Hans. 1984. *Aristotle's Theory of Language and its Tradition. Texts from 500 to 1750. Selection, translation, commentary.* Amsterdam: Benjamins.

Atherton, Catherine. 1993. *The Stoics on Ambiguity.* Cambridge: University Press.

Ax, Wolfram. 1991. « Sprache als Gegenstand der alexandrinischen und pergamenischen Philologie ». In: Schmitter, Peter (ed.). *Sprachtheorien der abendländischen Antike* (Geschichte der Sprachtheorie, vol. 2). Tübingen: Narr, 275−301.

Ax, Wolfram. 1992. « Aristoteles ». In: Dascal, Marcelo & Gerhardus, Dietfried & Lorenz, Kuno & Meggle, Georg (eds.). *Sprachphilosophie. Ein internationales Handbuch zeitgenössischer Forschung.* Berlin − New York: Mouton de Gruyter, 1. Halbb., 244−259.

Baratin, Marc. 1989. *La naissance de la syntaxe à Rome.* Paris: Éd. de Minuit.

Baratin, Marc. 1991. «Aperçu de la linguistique stoïcienne». In: Schmitter, Peter (ed.). *Sprachtheorien der abendländischen Antike* (Geschichte der Sprachtheorie, vol. 2). Tübingen: Narr, 193−216.

Baratin, Marc & Desbordes, Françoise. 1981. *L'analyse linguistique dans l'Antiquité classique* I: *Les théories.* Paris: Klincksieck.

Barwick, Karl. 1922. *Remmius Palaemon und die römische Ars Grammatica.* Leipzig: Dieterich [Réimpression anastatique, Hildesheim: Olms, 1967].

Bécares-Botas, Vicente. 1987. *Apolonio Díscolo. Síntaxis.* Introd., trad. y notas (Bibl. Clásica Gredos, 100). Madrid: Gredos.

Belardi, Walter. 1985. *Filosofia, grammatica e retorica nel pensiero antico.* Roma: Ed. dell' Ateneo.

Blank, David L. 1982. *Ancient Philosophy and Grammar.* Chico: Scholars Press.

Collart, Jean. 1954. *Varron grammairien latin.* Paris: Les Belles Lettres.

Coseriu, Eugenio. 1969−1972. *Die Geschichte der Sprachphilosophie von der Antike bis zur Gegenwart* (2 vols). Tübingen: Narr.

Dahlmann, Hellfried. 1932. *Varro und die hellenistische Sprachphilosophie.* Berlin: Weidmann.

Derbolav, Josef. 1972. *Platons Sprachphilosophie im Kratylos und den späteren Schriften.* Darmstadt: Wissenschaftliche Buchgesellschaft.

Donnet, Daniel. 1967. «La place de la syntaxe dans les traités de grammaire grecque, des origines au XIIe siècle». *L'Antiquité Classique* 36: 22−48.

Egli, Urs. 1967. *Zur stoischen Dialektik.* Bâle: Sandoz.

Erbse, Hartmut. 1980. «Zur normativen Grammatik der Alexandriner». *Glotta* 58: 236−258.

Frede, Michael. 1978. «Principles of Stoic Grammar». In: Rist, John M. (ed.). *The Stoics.* Berkeley & Los Angeles & London: University of California Press, 26−76.

Frede, Michael. 1987. «The Origin of Traditional Grammar». In: Frede, Michael. *Essays in Ancient Philosophy.* Oxford: Clarendon Press, 338−359. [Réimpression de «The Origin of Traditional Grammar». 1977. In: Butts, Richard E. & Hintikka, Jaakko (eds.). *Historical and Philosophical Dimensions of Logic, Methodology, and Philosophy of Science.* Dordrecht: Reidel, 51−79].

Frede, Michael. 1994. «The Stoic notion of a *lekton*». In: Everson, Stephen (ed.). *Language.* Cambridge: University Press, 109−128.

Gambarara, Daniele. 1984. *Alle fonte della filosofia del linguaggio: «lingua» e «nomi» nella cultura greca arcaica.* Roma: Bulzoni.

Hagius, Hugh. 1979. *The Stoic Theory of the Parts of Speech.* [Diss. Columbia University].

Hennigfeld, Jochem. 1994. *Geschichte der Sprachphilosophie. Antike und Mittelalter.* Berlin − New York: de Gruyter.

Hockett, Charles F. 1954. «Two models of grammatical description». *Word* 10: 210−234.

Householder, Fred W. 1981. *The syntax of Apollonius Dyscolus. Translated and with a commentary* (Amsterdam Studies in the Theory and History of Linguistic Science, III: Studies in the History of Linguistics, 23). Amsterdam: Benjamins.

Householder, Fred W. 1995. «Plato and his predecessors», «Aristotle and the Stoics on Language», «Dionysius Thrax, the *Technai* and Sextus Empiricus», «Apollonius Dyscolus and Herodian». In: Koerner, E. F. Konrad & Asher, Robert E. (eds.). *Concise History of the Language Sciences, from the Sumerians to the Cognitivists.* Oxford: Elsevier, 90−93, 93−99, 99−103, 111−115.

Hovdhaugen, Even. 1982. *Foundations of Western linguistics. From the beginning to the end of the first millennium A. D.* Oslo: Universitetsforlaget.

Hovdhaugen, Even. 1991. «The Teaching of Grammar in Antiquity». In: Schmitter, Peter (ed.). *Sprachtheorien der abendländischen Antike* (Geschichte der Sprachtheorie, vol. 2). Tübingen: Narr, 377−391.

Ildefonse, Frédérique. 1997. *La naissance de la grammaire dans l'antiquité grecque* (Histoire des doctrines de l'Antiquité Classique, 20). Paris: Vrin.

Kaster, Robert A. 1988. *Guardians of Language. The Grammarian and Society in Late Antiquity.* Berkeley − Los Angeles − London: University of California Press.

Keil, Henricus. 1857−1880. *Grammatici Latini.* 7 vols., Leipzig: Teubner. [Réimpression anastatique, Hildesheim: Olms, 1961].

Kemp, Alan J. 1986. «The *Technê Grammatikê* of Dionysius Thrax. Translated into English». *Historiographia Linguistica* 13: 343−363. [Réimpression dans Taylor, Daniel J. (1987), *The History of Linguistics in the Classical Period.* Amsterdam − Philadelphia: Benjamins, 169−189].

Kemp, Alan J. 1991. «The Emergence of Autonomous Greek Grammar». In: Schmitter, Peter (ed.). *Sprachtheorien der abendländischen Antike* (Geschichte der Sprachtheorie, vol. 2). Tübingen: Narr, 302−333.

Lallot, Jean. 1988. «Origines et développement de la théorie des parties du discours en Grèce». *Langages* 92: 11−23.

Lallot, Jean. 1989. *La grammaire de Denys le Thrace.* Traduction annotée. Paris: CNRS.

Lallot, Jean. 1994. «Le problème des fonctions syntaxiques chez Apollonius Dyscole». In: De Clercq, Jan & Desmet, Piet (eds.). *Florilegium Historiographiae Linguisticae. Études d'historiographie de la linguistique et de grammaire comparée à la mémoire de Maurice Leroy* (Bibliothèque des Cahiers de l'Institut de Linguistique de Louvain, 75). Louvain-La Neuve: Peeters, 131−141.

Lallot, Jean. 1997. *Apollonius Dyscole. De la construction (Περὶ συντάξεως). Texte grec, accom-*

pagné de notes critiques. Introduction, Traduction, Notes exégétiques, Index (Histoire des doctrines de l'Antiquité Classique, 19). 2 vols., Paris: Vrin.

Law, Vivien & Sluiter, Ineke (eds.). 1995. *Dionysius Thrax and the Technē Grammatikē.* Münster: Nodus.

Lloyd, A. C. 1971. «Grammar and Metaphysics in the Stoa». In: Long, A. A. (ed.). *Problems in Stoicism.* London: Athlone Press, 58−74.

Matthaios, Stephanos. 1997. *Untersuchungen zur Grammatik Aristarchs: Texte und Interpretation zur Wortartenlehre.* 2 vols. [Diss. Göttingen].

Montanari, Elio. 1984−1988. *La sezione linguistica del Peri hermeneias di Aristotele*, vol. I: *Testo*, vol. II: *Commento.* Firenze: Università degli Studi.

Pfeiffer, Rudolf. 1968. *History of Classical Scholarship. From the Beginnings to the End of the Hellenistic Age.* Oxford: Clarendon Press.

Pinborg, Jan. 1975. «Classical Antiquity: Greece». In: Sebeok, Thomas A. (ed.). *Historiography of Linguistics.* The Hague-Paris: Mouton, vol. I, 69−126.

Pohlenz, Max. 1939. «Die Begründung der abendländischen Sprachlehre durch die Stoa». *Nachrichten von der Gesellschaft der Wissenschaften zu Göttingen, Philologisch-historische Klasse* I 3, 6: 151−198. [Réimpression dans: *Kleine Schriften*, I. Hildesheim: Olms, 39−86].

Robins, Robert Henry. 1951. *Ancient and Medieval Grammatical Theory in Europe with particular reference to modern linguistic doctrines.* London: Bell & Sons.

Robins, Robert Henry. 1959. «In Defense of WP». *Transactions of the Philological Society* 58: 116−144.

Robins, Robert Henry. 1966. «The Development of the Word Class System of the European Grammatical Tradition». *Foundations of Language* 2: 3−19.

Robins, Robert Henry. 1986. «The *Technē grammatikē* of Dionysius Thrax in its Historical Perspective: The Evolution of the Traditional European Word Class Systems». In: Swiggers, Pierre & Van Hoecke, Willy (eds.). *Mot et parties du discours/Word and Word Classes/Wort und Wortarten* (La Pensée linguistique, 1). Leuven − Paris: Peeters, 9−37.

Robins, Robert Henry. 1988. «Priscian and the Context of his Age». In: Rosier, Irène (ed.). *L'héritage des grammairiens latins de l'Antiquité aux Lumières. Actes du colloque de Chantilly, 2−4 septembre 1987.* Paris & Louvain: Peeters, 49−55.

Robins, Robert Henry. 1993. *The Byzantine Grammarians. Their Place in History* (Trends in Linguistics. Studies and Monographs, 70). Berlin & New York: Mouton de Gruyter.

Rosén, Haiim B. 1990. «Zu Text und Interpretation der grammatischen Abschnitte in Aristoteles' *Poetik* und zur Umdeutung und Umformung der Redeteileinteilung bis ins orientalische Mittelalter». In: Niederehe, Hans Josef & Koerner, Konrad (eds.). *History and Historiography of Linguistics. Papers from the Fourth International Conference on the History of the Language Sciences (ICHoLS IV) (Trier, 24.−28. August 1987).* Amsterdam & Philadelphia: Benjamins, vol. I, 111−121.

Rosén, Haiim B. 1994. «Aristotle's Thoughts on Language. An Outgrowth of an «Intellectual Climate». In: De Clercq, Jan & Desmet, Piet (eds.). *Florilegium Historiographiae Linguisticae. Études d'historiographie de la linguistique et de grammaire comparée à la mémoire de Maurice Leroy.* Louvain-la-Neuve: Peeters, 87−95.

Schenkeveld, Dirk M. 1983. «Linguistic Theories in the Rhetorical Works of Dionysius of Halicarnassus». *Glotta* 61: 67−95.

Schenkeveld, Dirk M. 1994. «Scholarship and Grammar». In: *La philologie grecque à l'époque hellénistique et romaine* (Entretiens sur l'Antiquité Classique, Tome XL). Vandœuvres − Genève: Fondation Hardt, 263−306.

Schoemann, Georg Friedrich. 1862. *Die Lehre von den Redetheilen nach den Alten.* Berlin: W. Hertz.

Seldeslachts, Herman & Swiggers, Pierre & Wouters, Alfons. (à paraître). *The Technē Grammatikē of Dionysius Thrax. An English Translation with a Historical and Linguistic Commentary.* Leuven: Peeters.

Sluiter, Ineke. 1990. *Ancient Grammar in Context. Contributions to the Study of Ancient Linguistic Thought.* Amsterdam: VU University Press.

Steinthal, Heymann. 1890−1891². *Geschichte der Sprachwissenschaft bei den Griechen und Römern mit besonderer Rücksicht auf die Logik.* Berlin: Dümmler, 2 vols.

Swiggers, Pierre. 1984. «Théorie grammaticale et définition du discours dans le *Sophiste* de Platon». *Les Études Classiques* 52: 15−17.

Swiggers, Pierre. 1985. «Isidore de Séville et la codification de la grammaire latine». *Studi Medievali* 3ᵉ série, XXV: 279−289.

Swiggers, Pierre. 1989a. «Structure propositionnelle et complémentation dans l'histoire de la grammaire». *Lingua e Stile* 24: 391−407.

Swiggers, Pierre. 1989b. «La *Grammaire* de Port-Royal et le 'parallélisme logico-grammatical'». *Orbis* 33: 29−56.

Swiggers, Pierre. 1995. «L'héritage grammatical gréco-latin et la grammaire au Moyen Âge». In: Welkenhuysen, Andries & Braet, Herman & Verbeke, Werner (eds.). *Medieval Antiquity* (Mediaevalia Lovaniensia, Series I / Studia XXIV). Leuven: University Press, 159−195.

Swiggers, Pierre & Wouters, Alfons 1990. «Langues, situations linguistiques et réflexions sur le langage dans l'Antiquité». In: Swiggers, Pierre &

Wouters, Alfons (eds.). *Le langage dans l'Antiquité* (La Pensée linguistique, 3). Leuven–Paris: Peeters, 10–46.

Swiggers, Pierre. 1994. «*Technè* et *Empeiria*: La dynamique de la grammaire grecque dans l'Antiquité à la lumière des papyrus grammaticaux». *Lalies. Actes des sessions de linguistique et de littérature* 15 (Aussois, 29 août–3 sept. 1994): 83–101.

Swiggers, Pierre. 1995. «From Technique to Τέχνη». In: Abbenes, Jelle & Slings, Simon & Sluiter, Ineke (eds.). *Greek Literary Theory after Aristotle. A Collection of Papers in Honour of D.M. Schenkeveld*. Amsterdam: VU University Press, 17–41.

Swiggers, Pierre. 1998a. «Philosophical Aspects of the *Technê Grammatikê* of Dionysius Thrax». In: Lorenzo, Franco & Berrettoni, Pierangelo (eds.). *Grammatica e Ideologia nella storia della linguistica. Proceedings of the Symposium at Acquasparta, 8–10 Ottobre 1993*. Perugia: Istituto di Linguistica dell' Università degli Studi di Perugia.

Swiggers, Pierre. 1998b. *De Tékhnē Grammatikē van Dionysius Thrax. De oudste spraakkunst van het Westen* (Orbis Linguarum, 2). Leuven: Peeters.

Swiggers, Pierre. (à paraître). «Grammatical Theory in Aristotle's *Poetics*, Ch. XX».

Taylor, Daniel J. 1975. *Declinatio: A Study of the Linguistic Theory of Marcus Terentius Varro* (Amsterdam Studies in the Theory and History of Linguistic Science III: Studies in the History of Linguistics, 2). Amsterdam: Benjamins.

Taylor, Daniel J. 1988. «Varro and the Origins of Latin Linguistic Theory». In: Rosier, Irène (ed.). *L'héritage des grammairiens latins de l'Antiquité aux Lumières. Actes du colloque de Chantilly, 2–4 septembre 1987*. Paris & Louvain: Peeters, 37–48.

Taylor, Daniel J. 1991. «Roman Language Science». In: Schmitter, Peter (ed.). *Sprachtheorien der abendländischen Antike* (Geschichte der Sprachtheorie, vol. 2). Tübingen: Narr, 334–352.

Taylor, Daniel J. 1995. «Classical Linguistics: An Overview», «Varro and Early Latin Language Science», «Roman Linguistic Science in the Early Empire». In: Koerner, E. F. Konrad & Asher, Robert E. (eds.). *Concise History of the Language Sciences, from the Sumerians to the Cognitivists*. Oxford: Elsevier, 93–90, 103–107, 107–111.

Weidemann, Hermann. 1991. «Grundzüge der Aristotelischen Sprachtheorie». In: Schmitter, Peter (ed.). *Sprachtheorien der abendländischen Antike* (Geschichte der Sprachtheorie, vol. 2). Tübingen: Narr, 170–192.

Wouters, Alfons. 1979. *The Grammatical Papyri from Graeco-Roman Egypt. Contributions to the Study of the 'Ars grammatica' in Antiquity* (Verh. Kon. Ac. Wet. België, Kl. Lett., Jg. 41, Nr. 92). Brussel: Paleis der Academiën.

Pierre Swiggers – Alfons Wouters,
Université Catholique de Louvain (Belgique)

14. Sprachtheorien im Mittelalter

1. Voraussetzungen mittelalterlicher Sprachtheorien
2. Entwicklungen bis zum 13. Jahrhundert
3. Sprachlogik
4. Die *Grammatica speculativa* der Modisten
5. Zusammenfassung und Ausblick
6. Zitierte Literatur

1. Voraussetzungen mittelalterlicher Sprachtheorien

1.1. Erste historische Bezüge

Die mittelalterlichen Sprachtheorien setzen die antiken Traditionen fort, wie sie bei Platon und Aristoteles ausgebildet sind. Hier sind vor allem für die Antike der platonische Dialog *Kratylos* und *De interpretatione* des Aristoteles zu nennen. Außer *De interpretatione* sind weitere Quellen der mittelalterlichen Sprachtheorien: Aurelius Augustinus' *De doctrina christiana* und *De magistro* und A. M. S. Boethius' Kommentierung der logischen Schriften des Aristoteles. Hinzu kommen die grammatischen Lehrbücher des Donat (Rom 4. Jh.) und Priscian (Konstantinopel, um 500), die kommentiert werden, so das *Commentum in Maiorem Donatum Grammaticum* des Sedulius Scottus aus dem 9. Jh. Die Donat- und Priscian-Kommentare des Remigius von Auxerre († ca. 908) behandeln bereits die wichtigen Themen, wie den Buchstaben, die Silbe und die Redeteile. Mit dem Priscian-Kommentar des Wilhelm von Conches († 1154) beginnt eine selbständige sprachphilosophische Entwicklung im lateinischen Mittelalter. Die *Summa super Priscianum* des Petrus Helias (Mitte des 12. Jh.) gilt als die Autorität. Die beiden Priscian-Kommentare des Jordanus von Sachsen († 1237) und des Robert Kilwardby († 1279) zeigen sehr deutlich den Einfluß der aristotelischen Logik und Ontologie.

1.2. Grammatik und Sprache – Trivium

Das frühe Mittelalter behandelt die Sprache im Rahmen der *artes liberales*. Das Trivium hat sie zum Gegenstand: die *artes sermocinales* (Sprachwissenschaften) im Unterschied zu den *artes reales* (Sachwissenschaften – vgl. Schneider 1992). In erster Linie ist von der Sprache in der Grammatik zu handeln. Autoren wie Cassiodorus (6. Jh.) *Institutiones*, Martianus Capella (5. Jh.) *De nuptiis Philologiae et Mercurii*, Isidor von Sevilla († 636) *Etymologiae*, Hrabanus Maurus († 856) *De institutione*, Alkuin († 804) *Didascalica* sehen es in gleicher Weise (vgl. Schneider 1995: 74 f.): Die Grammatik lehrt die rechte Weise unseres Sprechens, Redens und Schreibens. Sie ist die Grundvoraussetzung jedes weiteren Wirklichkeitserkennens.

Die Gelehrtenwelt des Mittelalters sprach Lateinisch. Das LATEINISCHE ist ihre 'universale' Sprache. Der Unterschied zwischen Bildungs- und Volkssprache wird als Mehrsprachigkeit erfahren. In der Regel beruft man sich auf Aristoteles *De interpretatione* (c. 1, 16 a 5–8): „Und wie nicht alle (Menschen) mit denselben Buchstaben schreiben, so sprechen sie auch nicht alle dieselbe Sprache. Die seelischen Widerfahrnisse (Vorstellungen, Erg. d. Verf.) aber, für welche dieses (Gesprochene und Geschriebene) an erster Stelle ein Zeichen ist, sind bei allen (Menschen) dieselben; und überdies sind auch schon die Dinge, von denen diese (seelischen Widerfahrnisse) Abbildungen sind, (für alle) dieselben." (Übers. H. Weidemann). Sprachunterschiede sind nur Variationen der „äußeren Sprache"; sie sind Oberflächenerscheinungen; während die hinter ihnen stehende „innere (mentale) Sprache" oder „gedachte Sprache" von solchen Varianten nicht betroffen und davon unabhängig ist. Entsprechend kann aus der deskriptiven Grammatik einer bestimmten Sprache, die in den Grammatiken des Priscian und Donat als bereits geleistet vorausgesetzt wird, eine rationale, d.h. 'universale' Grammatik herausgezogen werden.

1.3. Logik und Sprache – Trivium

Man pflegt die sprachtheoretischen Beiträge des Mittelalters gewöhnlich unter dem Titel der Sprachlogik abzuhandeln. Seinen Grund hat es darin, daß sprachtheoretische Überlegungen sehr oft im Anschluß an die Rezeption der aristotelischen Schrift *Perì hermēneías* vollzogen werden, die Teil der logischen Schriften des Aristoteles ist und vom Aussagesatz (*lógos apophantikós*) handelt und vom Nomen und Verbum als seinen Bestandteilen.

In *De interpretatione* (16 a 4) hatte Aristoteles die Sprachzeichen *sýmbola* genannt; d.i. ein Zusammenfall von Ausdruck bzw. Lautgebilde (*tà en tē phōnē*) und Bedeutung (*pathēmata*). Wie sich die Schriftzeichen zum Wort verhalten, so verhalten sich die Wörter zu ihren Bedeutungen: sie sind *sýmbola* der Begriffe (*pathēmata*). Unter Berücksichtigung der aristotelischen Schrift *De sensu et sensato* (437 a 12–15) ergibt sich dieses Bild: Sprache besteht aus Wörtern, wobei jedes Wort ein 'Merkmal' oder 'Zeichen' ist. Undeutlich bleibt allerdings, von was das Wort ein konventionelles Zeichen ist: von den „in der Seele festgemachten Gedanken" (also Begriffen) oder von den Dingen außerhalb der Seele?

Anicius Manlius Severinus Boethius († 524) löst das Problem in seinem Kommentar von *De interpretatione* (vgl. Schneider 1995: 72 ff.): Im Unterschied zum bloßen Laut (*vox*, *sonus*) ist der Sprechakt (*locutio*) ein artikulierter Laut (*articulata vox*); damit dieser ein bezeichnender sei, d.h. signifikativ, muß ihm eine Vorstellung (*imaginatio*) hinzugefügt werden, die ihn mit dem Bild im Geist verbindet. Der „bezeichnende Sprechakt" ist ein „artikulierter Laut, der von sich her bezeichnet". Er besteht aus Nomen und Verbum als seinen Teilen und umfaßt auch die Aussage (*oratio enuntiativa*). Namen gebrauchen wir nicht, um Dinge zu bezeichnen, sondern jene geistigen Gehalte, wie z.B. Begriffe, die in uns von den Dingen entstanden sind. Da nun die gesprochenen Wörter zur Bezeichnung solcher geistigen Gehalte eingesetzt worden sind, hat Aristoteles Recht, wenn er sie „Zeichen der Gedanken" (*animae passionum notae*) nennt. Sprache bezeichnet in erster Linie die Gedanken (*intellectus*, *imagines* oder *similitudines rerum*), und nicht die Dinge selbst. Erst in zweiter Hinsicht bezeichnet sie auch die Dinge; und zwar durch die Gedanken.

Nach Boethius gibt es drei Reden (*orationes*): eine, die mit Buchstaben geschrieben ist; eine andere, die durch die gesprochene Sprache ausgedrückt wird; und schließlich eine, die im Geist verbunden ist (vgl. Kretzmann 1967: 367 f.). Problematisch ist, was Boethius mit diesem Ausdruck meint: Ist die geistige Rede („mental discourse" – Kretzmann) in Anlehnung an Augustinus die nonverbale „innere Sprache"? Eine weitere Schwierigkeit bietet die Unterscheidung zwischen Objektsprache (*prima impositio nominis*) und Metasprache (*secunda impositio nominis*).

Von Bedeutung für die folgende Entwicklung wird die Unterscheidung zwischen der Einsetzung eines Wortes (*impositio*) und seiner Bedeutung (*intentio*); vgl. u. § 3.2.3.

1.4. Sprache und Wissenschaft – der theologische Hintergrund

Sprachtheorien im lateinischen Mittelalter stehen immer auch im Horizont der christlichen Intellektualität, welche diese Epoche charakterisiert. Das betrifft in erster Linie die Frage nach einer angemessenen Rede von Gott. In dem Maße, in dem sich die Theologie seit dem 12. Jh. als Wissenschaft herausbildet, wächst auch das wissenschaftliche Interesse an der Sprache. In gleichem Zuge steigt das Bedürfnis, Grammatik und Logik (Dialektik) wissenschaftlich in der Auslegung der Hl. Schrift einzusetzen. Deutlich ist das schon bei Berengar von Tours († 1088) und ganz klar bei Petrus Abælard († 1142) zu sehen.

In theologischer Erkenntnisabsicht liegt selbstverständlich die angemessene Rede von Gott. Hier sei eine Tradition erwähnt, die mit Johannes Scotus Eriugena († um 877) einsetzt, auf die ich aber nicht näher eingehen kann: die Tradition der negativen Theologie: Da unser ganzes Denken und Sprechen nicht an das Wesen Gottes heranreicht, kann von Gott auch nichts in eigentlichem, sondern nur in übertragenem Sinne und „per metaphoram" ausgesagt werden. Die Sprache in Metaphern und Symbolen ist daher, obgleich uneigentliche Rede von Gott, dennoch die angemessenere (vgl. Schneider 1995: 86 ff.). Die negative Theologie hat Auswirkungen auf das Verständnis von Sprache: Zunächst in Hinsicht auf den vierfachen Schriftsinn; dann aber unter dem Stichwort des „integumentum" oder „involucrum", das im Anschluß an den Kommentar des Bernhard Silvestris (12. Jh.) zu Martianus Capella *De Nuptiis Philologiae et Mercurii* in der Schule von Chartres von Bedeutung wird.

2. Entwicklungen bis zum 13. Jahrhundert

Wie man *De divisione philosophiae* des Dominicus Gundissalinus (ca. 1140) entnehmen kann, besitzt die Grammatik im Rahmen der *septem artes liberales* eine herausragende Stellung. Im frühen Mittelalter wird sie zwar noch nicht in den Rang einer Wissenschaft erhoben; das geschieht erst im 13. und 14. Jh., in der Tradition der *Grammatica speculativa*. Man kann aber bereits im 12. Jh. von einer 'spekulativen Grammatik' sprechen, insofern in dieser Zeit theoretische Überlegungen angestellt werden über eine allgemeine Grammatik, Wortdefinitionen, Redeteile und semantische Probleme: Bedeutung versus Referenz (vgl. Fredborg 1988: 177 ff.).

2.1. Historische Bezüge

Die moderne Historiographie der Grammatik im 12. Jh. kann sich in der Hauptsache auf folgende Quellen stützen, die sich an Priscian anschließen: auf die anonyme *Glosule* der *Institutiones grammaticae* des Priscian, auf den anonymen *Tractatus Glosarum Prisciani* und auf eine Glosse, bekannt unter dem Namen *Promisimus*. Hinzuweisen ist ferner auf die Schulen von Wilhelm von Conches, Ralph von Beauvais und Gilbert von Poitiers; weiter auf die *Summa 'Breve sit'* des Robert von Paris (ed. Kneepkens II 1987) und auf die *Summa in arte grammatica* des Robert Blund (ed. Kneepkens III 1987). Vor allem aber ist die große Grammatik des Petrus Helias zu nennen; das *Doctrinale* des Alexander de Villa Dei und der *Graecismus* des Eberhard von Béthune kommen hinzu (vgl. Kneepkens 1995: 239 ff.).

Selbstverständlich steht an erster Stelle der Text der *Institutiones grammaticae* des Priscian selbst, der im lateinischen Mittelalter zu einem Schlüsseltext geworden ist. Die *Institutiones grammaticae* umfassen 18 Bücher: Das 1. und ein einleitender Teil des 2. Buchs behandeln: *vox*, *littera* und *syllaba*. Nach einleitenden Bemerkungen über *dictio* und *pars orationis* erörtern der größere Teil des 2. Buchs und die Bücher 3 bis 16 die verschiedenen Teile der Rede: *nomen* (2.–7. Buch), *verbum* (8.–10. Buch), *participium* (11. Buch), *pronomen* (12.–13. Buch), *praepositio* (14. Buch), *adverbium* (15. Buch), *interiectio* (15. Buch) und *coniunctio* (16. Buch). In diesen Büchern, *Priscianus maior* genannt (im Mittelalter auch unter dem Titel *Etymologia* geläufig), bietet Priscian eine Definition oder Beschreibung eines jeden Redeteils und listet die entsprechenden akzidentellen Bestimmungen auf. Die beiden letzten Bücher, *Priscianus minor*, im Mittelalter auch *De constructionibus* oder *Diasynthetica* genannt, befassen sich mit der Konstruktion der Pronomen (17. Buch), der Nomen und Verben (18. Buch). Das Werk endet mit einer Diskussion einiger Besonderheiten der GRIECHISCHEN und LATEINISCHEN Syntax. In diesen beiden letzten Büchern besitzt das lateinische Mittelalter die einzige systematische Abhandlung über die LATEINISCHE Syntax.

2.2. Semantik

In bezug auf die Semantik scheint die Frage nach der Identität des *enuntiabile* — z.B. 'Abraham glaubte, daß Christus geboren werden wird'; 'wir glauben, daß Christus geboren ist' (derselbe Aussageinhalt, der durch die Zeitform verschieden wird) — nicht eigentlich ein grammatisches, sondern ein logisches Problem zu sein. Für die Grammatik ist eher von Bedeutung die Frage nach der *unitas nominis*: ob etwa die Bedeutung des Adjektivs 'albus' dieselbe bleibt, auch wenn es in der Geschlechtsform variiert. Von besonderer Bedeutung für die grammatische Theorie ist die Frage nach der Einsetzung eines Wortes, um etwas anzudeuten (*impositio vocis ad significandum*). Hier kommt es auf die Absicht des Sprechers an; also darauf, was der Sprecher hat sagen wollen. Das steht im Gegensatz zur Ansicht des Boethius, der die Bedeutung eines Wortes vom Standpunkt des Hörers aus festlegt (vgl. Rijk II.I 1967: 139—42).

Das Problem der *impositio vocis* wird vornehmlich unter der Frage nach den „*causae inventionis* der Redeteile" behandelt: warum Wörter eine primäre Bedeutung und eine sekundäre semantisch-syntaktische Eigenschaft besitzen. Wörter sollten „nach der spezifischen Natur ihres Ursprungs bewertet werden und nicht nach der Art ihrer Konstruktion". Die *causa inventionis* ist die Frage nach der Daseinsberechtigung eines Wortes: warum es so eingesetzt wurde, wie es eingesetzt wurde. Der Grund ist die Absicht des Sprechers: die Bedeutung, die der Sprecher seinem Ausdruck hat geben wollen.

Abælard behauptet, daß die Bedeutung eines Wortes seiner syntaktischen Funktion vorausgehe. Wilhelm von Conches fordert eine systematische Behandlung der *causa inventionis* für jede Stufe der grammatischen Beschreibung. So bezeichnet beispielsweise das Nomen eine Substanz (ein Was) und eine Qualität (von was, von welcher Art) und Verben eine Tätigkeit oder ein Erleiden. Alle akzidentellen Eigenschaften der Wortklassen — die Arten der Nomen, Kasus, Geschlecht, Person oder Modus — sind auf ihre besondere semantisch-syntaktische *causa inventionis* zurückzuführen.

Mit Petrus Helias unterscheidet Wilhelm von Conches bezüglich der akzidentellen Eigenschaften zwischen sekundären Bedeutungen bzw. Bezeichnungen und reinen formalen Eigentümlichkeiten wie z.B. die Eigentümlichkeit der Konjugation bei Verben. Diese Eigentümlichkeiten lassen sich generalisieren: Sie sind allgemeine Eigentümlichkeiten, die in jeder Sprache vorkommen. In jeder Sprache werden z.B. Verben konjugiert.

Die grammatischen Diskussionen des 12. Jhs. bringen eine Neuerung hinzu: die Unterscheidung zwischen der prinzipiellen Bedeutung eines Wortes (*significatum*) und der Referenz, der Bezugnahme (*nominatum*). So bedeutet nach Wilhelm von Conches z.B. der Ausdruck 'Mensch' eine durch eine allgemeine Qualität bestimmte Substanz (*significatum*); und er nimmt Bezug auf (*nominatum*): (1) Individuen oder (2) die Form ('Mensch ist eine Art') oder (3) referiert auf sich selbst ('Mensch ist ein Nomen'). Der Bezug (*nominatum*, bei Anselm von Canterbury — † 1109 — *appellatum* genannt) ist der Gegenstand, dem ein Name gegeben wurde. Außer bei Interjektionen bezieht man sich in dem Prozeß der Namengebung primär auf die „Zitationsform" (*caput*), d.h. auf den Nominativ Singular bei Nomen oder die erste Person Singular Präsens Indikativ bei Verben. Alle anderen Formen sind von dieser abgeleitet. Nur Nomen und Adjektive haben ein entsprechendes *nominatum*; Verben dagegen nicht. Außerdem hat die Bedeutung (*significatum*) eines Wortes nicht denselben Umfang (Extension) wie sein *nominatum*.

Die Unterscheidung zwischen Bedeutung und Referenz erhält ihre Bedeutsamkeit im Kontext eines Satzes: Sie erlaubt den Logikern zu bestimmen, ob ein Satz wahr ist oder nicht. Das führt im übrigen auch zu einer „realistischen" Tendenz in der Universalienfrage (vgl. Fredborg 1988: 181—86).

2.3. Syntax

Hinsichtlich der Syntax (*congruitas, constructio*) (vgl. Kneepkens 1990: 161), d.i. die Anordnung der Wörter zu einem sinnvollen Satz, widmet man sich in der grammatischen Analyse dem LATEINISCHEN. Eine abstrakte syntaktische Analyse wird noch nicht diskutiert.

Ein erster Zugang ist die Analyse des kleinsten Satzes, bestehend aus Nomen und Verb, Subjekt und Prädikat. Im Anschluß an Aristoteles ist die Funktion des Nomens, Subjekt zu sein, von dem etwas ausgesagt wird; während das Verb anzeigt, was ausgesagt wird. Für das Wortpaar 'Subjekt – Prädikat' verwendet man neue Termini: *suppositum*: das, wovon etwas ausgesagt wird; und *appositum*: das, was ausgesagt wird.

In den grammatischen, die Syntax betreffenden Diskussionen werden vor allem folgende Themen berührt: die Rolle der Pronomen bzw. der Interrogative 'Wer' und 'Was'. Nach Wilhelm von Conches kann ein Pronomen, obgleich es nicht Teil der beiden Hauptredeteile (Nomen, Verb) ist, dieselbe Funktion erfüllen wie Eigennamen, da es wie Eigennamen auch einen unmittelbaren Bezug (Referenz) aufweist (vgl. Rosier & Stefanini 1990: 285ff.).

Ein weiteres Thema ist die Doktrin vom *verbum substantivum*, der Bedeutung und kopulativen Funktion des Verbs 'esse' im Aussagesatz. Seine Bedeutung hat grammatisch zwei Aspekte: zum einen Verb zu sein (*vis verbi*); und zum anderen als Kopula aufzutreten (*vis substantivi*); entsprechend hat es eine kopulative und prädikative Funktion. In diesem Zusammenhang spielt die traditionelle Unterscheidung zwischen der transitiven und intransitiven Konstruktion eines Satzes eine entscheidende Rolle: So ist nach Wilhelm von Champeaux († 1122) der Satz 'Sokrates est albus' grammatisch intransitiv konstruiert; d.h. es gibt keine Transitivität oder keinen Wechsel der Person von 'Sokrates' und 'albus'. Die grammatische Intransitivität der Person wird LATEINISCH durch Maskulin Nominativ Singular, auf '-us' endend angezeigt, wo das grammatische Geschlecht dem realen Geschlecht des Sokrates korrespondiert.

In der Schule des Gilbert von Poitiers verschwindet die Intransitivität. Zum einen unterscheidet man zwischen dem Nomen, das Subjekt des Satzes ist, und dem Nomen, das den Bezug festhält, d.i. die Person, von welcher der Satz spricht. Zum anderen geht man davon aus, daß in einem normal angeordneten Satz – Nomen-Verb-Nomen – das vor dem Verb plazierte Nomen eine Substanz bezeichnet und nach dem Verb plaziert eine Qualität. Entsprechend unterscheidet man zwischen der personalen und substantivischen Konstruktion des Verbs: Verben sind personal konstruiert in Verbindung mit dem Subjekt, aber substantivisch in Verbindung mit einem Nomen oder Adjektiv, das an Prädikatsstelle steht. Diese grammatische Interpretation führt zur Unterscheidung zwischen dem grammatisch-logischen Subjekt eines Satzes (*suppositum appositioni*) und der außersprachlichen Person, von welcher der Satz handelt (vgl. Fredborg 1988: 186–95).

Eine weitere Entwicklung der Grammatiktheorien der LATEINISCHEN Syntax ist die Einführung des Begriffs 'regimen', den Priscian schon entwickelt hatte (vgl. Kneepkens 1978: 108ff.). Zunächst eingeführt als semantische Bestimmung eines Wortes durch ein anderes, wird das *regimen* bei Petrus Helias (1993: 1051.24–26) zu einem Instrument, die Konstruktion bzw. Syntax eines Satzes zu vervollkommnen: So erfordert das Verb den Nominativ zur Vollkommenheit der Syntax bzw. der Satzkonstruktion; z.B. wenn ich sage 'Lego', dann bezeichne ich den Akt des Lesens, der jemandem inhäriert (*inesse*), und so zeige ich an (*significo*), daß der Satz von etwas spricht (*sermonem fieri de aliquo*). Der Nominativ nämlich bezeichnet das, wovon die Rede ist (*de quo fit sermo*); und daher zieht jenes Verb den Nominativ syntaktisch (*in constructionem*) mit sich; denn anders gäbe es keinen syntaktisch vollkommen konstruierten Satz (*aliter non erit perfecta constructio*).

Das 12. Jh. bringt besonders durch den Begriff des *regimen* und durch die grammatischen Konstituentien *suppositum / appositum* weitreichende Neuerungen in die Syntax. Mit Hilfe dieser grammatischen Strukturelemente lassen sich bestimmte semantische Probleme klären. Solche semantischen Probleme gehören zu beiden Disziplinen: zur Grammatik ebenso wie zur Logik. Es kommt daher zu engeren Verschmelzungen beider Disziplinen. Selbstverständlich hat die Grammatik die Aufgabe, die Regeln zu finden, aufgrund derer ein grammatisch wohlgeformter Satz zu bilden ist. So liefert sie die Grundlage für die logisch-semantischen Untersuchungen.

3. Sprachlogik

3.1. Logisch-semantische Analysen im 12. Jahrhundert

Einen ersten bedeutenden Schritt in Richtung einer logisch-semantischen Sprachanalyse vollzieht Anselm von Canterbury (vgl. Jacobi 1995: 84 ff.; Schneider 1995: 98 ff.). Der gewöhnliche Sprachgebrauch (*usus loquendi*) wird anhand logischer Begrifflichkeit einer Kritik unterzogen. In *De grammatico* etwa zeigt Anselm, daß Priscian Unrecht hat, wenn er meint, daß alle Nomen Substanz und Qualität in einem bezeichnen; denn die Sprache selbst unterscheidet zwischen Nomen, die

Substanzen bezeichnen, und solchen, die Qualitäten bezeichnen, wie es die denominativen Nomina tun. Die Unterscheidung zwischen *appellatio* (Benennen; Referenz) und *significatio* (Bedeuten) erlaubt eine logisch-semantische Kritik des Sprachgebrauchs. Es kommt nämlich darauf an, den gemeinten, intendierten Sinn eines Satzes herauszustellen. Sprache und Grammatik geraten unter die Obhut der Logik.

Ganz deutlich wird das bei Petrus Abælard (vgl. Jacobi 1995: 91–96; Schneider 1995: 91 ff.). In seiner *Dialektik* behauptet er (Petrus Abælard 1956: 140 und 135): Um den richtigen Sinn einer Aussage und die Tiefenstruktur der sprachlichen Äußerung mit Hilfe der Dialektik zu ermitteln, solle man sich nicht scheuen, gegen die Regeln der Grammatik zu verstoßen. In seinem Kommentar zu Aristoteles' *Perì hermēneías* unterscheidet er bei Wörtern wie Nomina und Verba, die für sich allein etwas bezeichnen, daß sie einerseits Sachen bedeuten (*significatio de rebus*) und andererseits Verständnisse (*intellectus*) bzw. verstehbare Gehalte (*significatio de intellectibus*); denn die aristotelische *Kategorienschrift* handelt von den einfachen Redeteilen (*de simplicibus sermonibus*) „gemäß ihrer Bezeichnung von Dingen"; *Perì hermēneías* hingegen handelt von ihnen gemäß der Bezeichnung von verstehbaren Gehalten. Die Konstruktion des Verständnisses ist unverzichtbar für den Wirklichkeitsbezug: Sieht man nämlich auf die Ursache der Einführung eines Sprachzeichens (*secundum causam inventionis vocis*), so ist es eingeführt worden, um Verständnisse zu konstituieren. Kategorematische Ausdrücke „bezeichnen Sachen, indem sie verstehbare Gehalte schaffen, die zu den Sachen gehören (Abælard)." (Jacobi 1995: 91). Über Nomina und Verba ist daher zu handeln, insofern aus ihnen eine Aussage gebildet werden kann. Wörter haben dabei einen zweifachen Bedeutungsaspekt: Sie können auf konkrete Dinge verweisen oder aber den Begriff bzw. Dinge als gedachte vergegenwärtigen. Nomina und Verba, die unabhängig von ihrer syntaktischen Funktion in einer Spracheinheit, dem Satz, auf einen Begriffsinhalt oder verstehbaren Gehalt verweisen, werden zu den Bedeutungsträgern der Aussage (*oratio*).

Abælard dringt in der Weise zu einer syntaktisch-semantischen Analyse sprachlicher Einheiten vor. Es kommt darauf an, unter den möglichen Verbindungen verstehbarer Gehalte (Reden) jene Aussagen herauszufinden, die allein die Eigenschaft haben, wahr oder falsch zu sein. Hier kann man eine zweifache Weise des Wirklichkeitsbezuges unterscheiden: gelingende Referenz durch Begriffe oder Begriffskombinationen ('ein laufender Mensch') und Wahrheit von Aussagen ('Sokrates sitzt'). Im ersten Fall spricht Abælard davon, daß Begriffe „erfüllt" bzw. „nicht erfüllt" sind. Im zweiten Fall zergliedert er eine Aussage wie 'Sokrates sitzt' in den verstehbaren, aussagbaren Gehalt und dessen Bejahung bzw. Verneinung: das Behauptungsmoment bzw. die urteilende Stellungnahme des Sprechers. Ergänzt man den unvollständigen Satz 'daß Sokrates sitzt' durch 'Es ist wahr' zu einem vollständigen Satz, so kommt dadurch kein neuer verstehbarer Gehalt hinzu, sondern nur die Behauptung. Wahrheit wird zu einer Funktion von Aussagen.

Abælard macht auf eine Reihe sprachlicher Wendungen aufmerksam ('es ist gut, daß ...'; 'es ereignet sich, daß ...', 'es trifft ein, daß ...'; 'es ist möglich, unmöglich, notwendig, wahr, falsch, daß ...'), die alle einen abhängigen Satz, erfordern. Diese Sprachbeispiele sollen zeigen, daß die aristotelische Strukturbeschreibung von Aussagen – daß nämlich in einer Aussage etwas von etwas ausgesagt wird – nicht korrekt ist. Den abhängigen Satz nennt Abælard *dictum propositionis*: das in der Aussage Gesagte; und dieses bezeichnet kein Subjekt im ontologischen Sinn, keine Sache mit Eigenschaften. Das in der Aussage Gesagte und das, was den aussagbaren Gehalt zu einer vollständigen Aussage macht, verhalten sich nicht wie Subjekt und Prädikat zu einander. Das, was durch den Satz 'Sokrates sitzt' bezeichnet wird, ist der Sachverhalt, 'daß Sokrates sitzt', der im DEUTSCHEN durch einen 'daß-Satz' und im LATEINISCHEN durch die Infinitiv + Akkusativ-Konstruktion (AcI) wiedergegeben wird.

Nach Gilbert von Poitiers, der die traditionelle triadische Struktur von Sprache – Ding, Begriff, Wort bzw. Sprachzeichen – übernimmt, hat man zu unterscheiden zwischen dem, wovon die Rede ist, und dem, was gesagt wird; denn das Nomen ist eingesetzt worden, um das zu bezeichnen, wovon die Rede ist; und das Verb, um das Ausgesagte zu vertreten (Schneider 1995: 97f.). Indem Gilbert in logisch-semantischer Sicht Formbegriffe auf ihre Sinnelemente hin analysiert, Oberbegriffe bildet oder Allgemeinbegriffe spezifiziert, betreibt er Kategorienanalyse. Dabei kommt es zu einer Unterscheidung zwischen „natürlicher Beschreibungssprache" und der „Sprache der Theoriebildung" (Jacobi 1995: 96ff.). Seine semantischen Analysen des *verbum substantivum*, der *unitas nominis*, des *enuntiabile* und der *propositio* scheinen im Zusammenhang mit der *Ars Meliduna* und der terministischen Logiktradition zu stehen (vgl. Rijk 1967 II.I, 292 ff., 306 ff., 319 ff., 357 ff.).

Die logisch-semantischen Sprachanalysen des 12. Jhs. weisen eine gemeinsame Tendenz auf: grammatische Strukturbeschreibungen werden mit logisch-semantischen Analysen verknüpft. Sprachanalysen werden zu einem Thema der Wissenschaft. Allerdings verschwindet die Grammatik als selbständige „Wissenschaft von der Sprache" (*scientia de lingua*) nicht.

So greift Dominicus Gundissalinus die Auffassung des Al-Fārābī (ca. 870−950) auf, wonach die Grammatik sich als „Wissenschaft von der Sprache" auf die „äußere Sprache" (*logos exterior cum voce*) bezieht und so der Logik vergleichbar ist, die sich auf die „innere Sprache" (*logos interior*) bezieht (vgl. Schneider 1995: 99ff.). Insofern die Grammatik jene Sprachregeln untersucht, in denen viele Sprachgemeinschaften übereinstimmen, kann sie allgemein sein. An sich kümmert sie sich jedoch darum nicht, sondern untersucht das, was jeder besonderen Sprache eigentümlich ist. Die Logik hingegen lehrt jene Regeln, wodurch Wahres von Falschem geschieden wird; d.h. sie lehrt allgemeine Regeln, worin alle Menschen in den Reden übereinkommen; denn − in Anlehnung an Aristoteles − die Gedanken, Begriffe von Dingen sind bei allen Menschen dieselben; und auf diese bezieht sich die Logik. Insofern befaßt sich auch die Logik mit der Sprache, da sie die Gedanken untersucht, sofern sie durch Reden bezeichnet werden; d.i. den aussagbaren und verstehbaren Gehalt. Daher gibt die Logik allgemeine Regeln sowohl für den *logos exterior cum voce* als auch für den *logos interior*.

Avicenna (Ibn Sīnā, † 1037) trifft in dem Zusammenhang eine folgenreiche Unterscheidung: Die Logik behandelt die „zweiten Intentionen", die den ersten beigelegt werden; d.h. sie befaßt sich mit den Strukturprinzipien des Verstandes bzw. mit den Gesetzen des Denkens, der inneren Sprache. Mit Avicenna wird so eine Unterscheidung zwischen Objektsprache und Metasprache möglich.

3.2. Logisch-semantische Analysen im 13. und 14. Jahrhundert

Entscheidend für die weiteren sprachlogischen und sprachtheoretischen Überlegungen ist die Frage: ob Wörter bzw. die Sprachzeichen die Gedanken (bzw. Begriffe, Urteile, Sätze) im Geist bezeichnen oder die Dinge außerhalb des Denkens.

Vorherrschend bleibt zunächst die von Boethius festgelegte aristotelische Auffassung von Sprache: Das Wort, als Lautgebilde (*vox*) verstanden, ist ein konventionelles Ausdrucksmittel, wodurch der Sprecher dem Hörer Gedanken von Dingen mitteilt. Es bezieht sich auf den Verstandesbegriff; denn nur so ist es bezeichnend; d.h. nur so hat es Bedeutung. Die Sache (*res*), von der etwas ausgesagt wird, wird im Verstandesbegriff (*conceptus mentis*) repräsentiert; und nur insofern sich das Wort auf diesen, im Verstand bleibenden Begriff einer Sache bezieht, bezeichnet es auch die Sache.

Sprache − so machen etwa Bonaventura († 1274) und Heinrich von Gent († 1293) deutlich − hat einen deklarativen Charakter. Sie ist das lautliche, sinnliche „Gewand" des Verstandesbegriffs, der im Erkennenden oder im Geist verbleibt, wenn es nach außen gesprochen wird. Heinrich − wie auch Albert der Große († 1280) und Thomas von Aquin († 1274/5) − schließt sich der Position des Aristoteles an, wonach das Wort *ad placitum* bezeichnet. Er hält diese Position für angemessener als die Position der Stoiker, nach der Wörter „einen natürlichen Ursprung haben, da der Laut des Wortes eine natürliche Ähnlichkeit mit dem Ding habe." Berücksichtigt man, daß nicht jede Sache, die durch ein Wort, vermittelt über den Verstandesbegriff, bezeichnet wird, „sinnlich" ist, dann muß das Wort einen rationalen Ursprung haben; d.h. es muß ad placitum oder *voluntarie* eingesetzt worden sein. Mit jedem sprachlichen Ausdruck ist daher ein willentliches Moment verknüpft und eine im Verstandesbegriff erfaßte allgemeine Vorstellung. Nur in diesem Sinne ist das Lautgebilde Sprache (vgl. Schneider 1995: 105−09).

3.2.1. Thomas von Aquin

Im Unterschied zum bloßen Laut − so hält Thomas von Aquin in seiner Kommentierung einer berühmten Stelle aus der aristotelischen *Politik* (ad 1253 a 7) fest −, der Gemütsbewegungen wie Trauer, Freude, Zorn und Furcht anzeigt (in der Tradition der *Grammatica speculativa* wird Ähnliches unter dem Redeteil der Interjektion behandelt, vgl. u. § 4.2.3), zeigt die menschliche Sprache Nützliches und Schädliches, Gerechtes und Ungerechtes an. Eine Verständigung darüber stiftet die menschliche Gemeinschaft. Die Sprache ist ihr konstitutives Prinzip. Im übrigen — so bemerkt Thomas in seinem Kommentar zu Aristoteles' *Perì hermēneías* (I, 2. 16 a 3) — ist das der Grund, weshalb diejenigen, die verschiedenen Sprachgemeinschaften angehören, nicht gut miteinander leben können, da sie nicht dieselbe Sprache sprechen. Das ist nicht allein ein Problem der Übersetzung, sondern in dieser Bemerkung liegt auch die Frage nach der Möglichkeit einer allgemeinen Grammatik verborgen, die zwar nicht von der Sprache überhaupt, doch aber von den einzelnen gesprochenen Sprachen abstrahiert.

Thomas entwickelt im Zusammenhang von bezeichnendem Wort, Verstandesbegriff und Sache, was man in der Thomas-Literatur *verbum mentis*-Lehre zu nennen pflegt. Unter dem *verbum mentis* versteht Thomas das Erkannte selbst; d.h. das, was der Verstand von einer Sache erfaßt. Es ist das Medium, in dem der Verstand etwas als etwas — sei es im Begriff, oder sei es im Aussagesatz — begreift und im äußeren Wort darstellt. Ontologisch gesehen ist das *verbum mentis* bzw. das im Begriff Erkannte (*conceptiones*) zwar ein Akzidens, da es in der erkennenden Seele wie in seinem Subjekt ist; aber deutlich schreibt Thomas der Sprache eine eigene Wirklichkeit zu. Sprache ist ein Ausdrucksgeschehen. In ihr drückt der Verstand das aus, was ist, als das, was es ist; oder er zeigt in ihr das Vorliegen oder Bestehen eines Sachverhalts an und so die Wahrheit der Aussage. Das gesprochene und geschriebene Wort ist Ausdruck der erkannten Sache. Es soll das „innere Wort" (*verbum mentis*), das Erkannte, Verständnisse, Gedanken mitteilen, offenbar machen. Sein Wesen besteht darin, Gedachtes zu bezeichnen. Zwar bezeichnen die Sprachzeichen zunächst das Ding oder einen Sachverhalt (*esse rei*); weil aber das von einer Sache Erkannte immer sprachlich vermittelt ist, bezeichnen Wörter vermittels der Konzeptionen Sachen oder Sachverhalte.

Insofern ist nach Thomas der in der spekulativen Grammatik so genannte *modus significandi*, die kategoriale Bedeutung der Wortarten, eng verbunden mit dem *modus intelligendi* (vgl. u. § 4). Die Bezeichnungsweise läßt sich nicht von der Erkenntnisweise trennen. Im Kontext der Erörterung der Frage nach einer angemessenen Rede von Gott präzisiert Thomas den Status der Bezeichnungsweise. In bezug auf den *modus significandi* ist „jeder Name mit Mangel behaftet", da unser Verstand an die Sinneserkenntnis gebunden ist und sie nicht „übersteigen" kann (*Summa contra gentiles* I, c. 30). Da nun — wie Thomas öfters betont — das Erkannte im Erkennenden ist auf die Weise des Erkennenden (*omne quod recipitur in aliquo, recipitur in eo per modum recipientis, Summa theologiae* I, 75, 5c), so ist auch der *modus significandi* abhängig von der Weise des das Erkannte aufnehmenden Verstandes; denn „durch den Namen drücken wir Dinge oder Sachen auf die Weise aus, in der wir sie mit dem Verstand begreifen" (*Summa contra gentiles* I, c. 30). Wenn wir daher *modi significandi* wie Nomen, Verb und Partizip verwenden, dann tun wir das nicht im logischen, sondern im grammatischen Sinne (*In Sent.* I, d. 22, q. 1, a. 1 ad 3): So bezeichnet das Nomen Substanz und Qualität als „etwas Selbständiges" (*ut aliquid subsistens*), von dem etwas ausgesagt wird; aber nicht als eine Substanz „secundum rem". Dieses „Selbständige", das durch den *modus significandi* — hier das Nomen — bezeichnet wird, ist abhängig von der Weise der Verstandeseinsicht, betrifft also nicht das Ding selbst.

Da nun das Sprachzeichen immer bezogen ist auf den Verstandesbegriff (*verbum mentis, intentio intellecta*) und dieser ein im Lichte der Vernunft erleuchteter ist, hat die Sprache den Charakter des Entwurfs. Sie ist eine welterschließende und weltentwerfende Kraft eigenen Rechts (vgl. Schneider 1995: 114−19).

3.2.2. Johannes Duns Scotus

Mit Johannes Duns Scotus († 1308) zeichnet sich eine Entwicklung in der mittelalterlichen Sprachauffassung ab, die von Wilhelm von Ockham († 1349/50) konsequent durchgeführt wird. Schrift, Wort und Begriff bezeichnen Sachen (*res*); sie sind auf je ihre Weise Zeichen der Dinge. Zwar bezeichnet das Wort unmittelbar den Begriff, insofern dieser Zeichen der Sache ist und sie repräsentiert, und durch den Begriff vermittelt die Sache. Im Grunde aber ist das, was durch den sprachlichen Laut (*vox*) bezeichnet wird, die Sache (vgl. Schneider 1996: 395 f.).

Hier sind freilich Differenzierungen einzuführen: Der Begriff von etwas kann nicht im Wort sein; denn dann müßten sich Lateiner und Griechen ohne Schwierigkeit verstehen können. Die Bedeutung kommt zu dem die erkannte Sache bezeichnenden Wort hinzu. Sie gründet in dem aktuellen Erkenntnisvollzug des Verstandes, in dem die Sache als erkannte ein intentionales Sein besitzt. Sprach- und Erkenntnisebene sind von einander zu trennen.

Weiter bezeichnet das Wort die im Begriff repräsentierte Sache nicht als existierende; denn als existierendes wird ein Ding auch nicht erkannt. Was erkannt wird, ist vielmehr seine Wesenheit; und diese verhält sich gegenüber dem Sein indifferent. Diese Differenz von Sein und Wesen oder (wie Duns Scotus sagt) „Washeit" (*quidditas*) – wobei die grundlegende Bestimmtheit 'Seiendes' (*ens*) jene Washeit meint, der ein Sein zukommen kann oder besser gesagt: der das Sein nicht widerstreitet – führt zu einer stringenten Analyse des Aussagesatzes, der die grammatische Form von Subjekt und Prädikat hat, genauer von Subjekt, Kopula und Prädikatsnomen. In dem Satz 'Caesar ist Mensch' – so Duns Scotus in der ersten Fassung seines *Perì hermēneías*-Kommentars – wird das 'ist' nach Art eines Akzidens ausgesagt, wie ein dem Wesen von außen Hinzutretendes. Der Satz ist wahr, unabhängig davon, ob Caesar existiert oder nicht; denn das Prädikatsnomen 'Mensch' hat nicht zum Bedeutungsinhalt die Existenz von Caesar. Folglich ist das 'ist' als Kopula (*tertium adiacens*) aufzufassen; es ist kein – wie Kant sagt – „reales Prädikat". Das Existenzprädikat (*secundum adiacens*) drückt keine Eigenschaft von Dingen aus, es verhält sich zur Wesenheit 'Caesar' nicht wie eine ihr zukommende akzidentelle Bestimmung.

Singuläre Existenzsätze wie 'Sokrates ist bzw. existiert' sind dann so zu verstehen, daß das im Prädikat ausgedrückte Wirklichsein dasselbe ist, was auch der Subjektsbegriff in sich enthält, nämlich das Sein des Subjekts, das „esse Soctratis". Versteht man das Seiende (*ens*) als Nomen, so bezeichnet es ein Subjekt, das eine Wesenheit hat: das „geeignet ist zur aktuellen Existenz".

In diesem Sinne läßt sich das *ens* als Modus entfalten, in dem sich das Subjekt zur aktuellen Existenz verhält. Die Bedeutung des Existenzprädikats 'ist' (*res verbi*) als Wirklichkeit (*actualitas*) drückt einen Modus aus, nämlich die wirkliche Inhärenz (*actualis inhaerentia*) des Prädikats im Subjekt; d.h. die Weise, in der der Verstand etwas von etwas aussagt oder verneint, also den Verstandesvollzug der „Zusammensetzung" (*compositio*) oder „Trennung" (*divisio*). Diese Synthesisleistung des Verstandes vollzieht sich unabhängig von der aktualen Existenz dessen, worauf sich der Satz bezieht. Entsprechend sind die *modi significandi* abhängig zu denken von dem Verstandesvollzug der Synthesis.

3.2.3. Wilhelm von Ockham

Was bei Duns Scotus in gewisser Weise noch zusammengeht, wird bei Wilhelm von Ockham streng auseinandergehalten: Ausdrucksebene, Sprachebene und kognitive Ebene. Nach ihm wird die Zeichenfunktion der Sprache anders und neu gedeutet. Roger Bacon († nach 1292) hatte das zwar schon vorbereitet; aber Ockham zieht die Konsequenzen (vgl. Schneider 1995: 110ff., 129ff.): Verstandesbegriffe und die aus Begriffen (*termini*) zusammengesetzten „Reden" (*orationes*) sind natürliche Zeichen der Dinge; während die Sprachzeichen (die gesprochene und geschriebene Sprache) kraft Übereinkunft bezeichnen, also nicht eigentlich natürlich sind. Dabei handelt die Logik nur von diesen natürlichen, mentalen Zeichen, die nach Augustinus „keiner Sprache angehör(en)"; die Grammatik hingegen von der äußeren Sprache. In dem Kontext ist entscheidend, daß sowohl die geschriebene (*oratio scripta*), die gesprochene (*oratio prolata*) als auch die mentale Sprache (*oratio concepta*) Dinge bezeichnen; also nicht Zeichen der Gedanken in der Seele (*passiones animae*) sind, sondern eben dasselbe bezeichnen, was auch der Verstandesbegriff (*conceptus mentis*) bezeichnet: die Dinge außerhalb des Verstandes (*res extra animam*) – so Ockham in seinem *Perì hermēneías*-Kommentar (lib. 1, prooem. § 2; vgl. auch *Summa logicae* I, c. 1).

Man kann von einer Art Parallelität zwischen mentaler Sprache, welche der Logiker untersucht, und äußerer Sprache reden, welche der Grammatiker untersucht: von den allgemeinen Strukturen des Denkens, der inneren Sprache, zu handeln, kommt dem gleich, von den allgemeinen Strukturen der äußeren Sprache zu handeln (vgl. Panaccio 1995: 185f.). Zwar korrespondieren gesprochene Sprache (*oratio vocalis*) und mentale Sprache; von Bedeutung ist aber die Trennung beider. Dabei ist die gesprochene der mentalen Sprache untergeordnet. In der mentalen Sprache verfügen die Menschen über eine allgemeine sprachliche Struktur, die den besonderen Sprachen, die sie in der Kommunikation verwenden, vorausgeht.

Am Anfang stehen die einfachen Termini, die die äußeren Dinge im Geist repräsentieren; das sind sprachlich und grammatisch gesehen die Wörter (*dictiones*) und logisch-sprachlich gesehen die Begriffe (*conceptus*). Aus ihnen lassen sich Sätze (*propositiones*) bilden. Die semantisch-syntaktische Analyse der Sätze ist abhängig von der Semantik der in ihnen auftretenden Termini. Allein wichtig ist dabei zu unterscheiden, für was die jeweiligen Termini in einem Satz stehen; d.h. entscheidend ist die Zuordnung mentaler Urteilstermini zu ihren Signifikaten (Suppositionstheorie). Die grammatische Struktur der geformten Sätze, also die *congruitas orationis*, aber auch der Wohlklang (*ornatus sermonis*), ist ohne Bedeutung für die mentale Sprache, da sie nur die äußere Sprache betrifft.

Bei der Analyse der Syntax der mentalen Sprache greift Ockham auf eine Auswahl aus den von Donat und Priscian beschriebenen acht Redeteilen zurück: Nomen, Verb, Adverb, Konjunktion und Präposition. Das Partizip, mit dem Verb durch 'seiend' verknüpft, hat dieselbe semantische Funktion; eine eigene Behandlung scheint verzichtbar. Das Pronomen scheint im Vergleich mit dem Nomen auch nicht eigens behandelt werden zu müssen. Zur Interjektion äußert sich Ockham nicht. Bezüglich des Nomens kann man bloße grammatische Kategorien von logisch-semantischen unterscheiden: So gehört das Geschlecht − 'lapis' (maskulin) und 'petra' (feminin) im LATEINISCHEN Synonyme − der grammatischen Oberfläche zu; es hat keine Entsprechung in der mentalen Sprache; ebenso die Figur eines einfachen und eines zusammengesetzten Wortes. Anderes gilt für den Kasus eines Nomens: 'homo est homo' (ein Mensch ist ein Mensch) und 'homo est hominis' (ein Mensch gehört einem Menschen). Beide Sätze haben einen verschiedenen Wahrheitswert, weil die Prädikatsnomina 'homo' (im Nominativ) und 'hominis' (im Genitiv) verschiedene semantische Werte haben. Die mentale Sprache hat also hinsichtlich desselben mentalen Begriffs (*conceptus*) zu unterscheiden; d.h. der grammatischen Struktur entspricht etwas in der logischen Syntax der mentalen Sprache (vgl. Panaccio 1995: 188). Allerdings bleiben in der Sicht Ockhams diese grammatischen Verhältnisse von nur sekundärer Bedeutung für die Analyse der mentalen Sprache.

Bedeutsamer ist die Theorie der Eigentümlichkeiten der Termini (*proprietates terminorum*). Es lassen sich solche Termini, die eine ganz bestimmte und sichere Bedeutung haben, das sind die kategorematischen Termini, von solchen unterscheiden, die für sich genommen keine bestimmte Bedeutung haben, das sind die synkategorematischen Termini, die keinen Bezug aufweisen, d.h. keinen Referenten haben; ihre Bedeutung also nur im Kontext eines Satzes gewinnen; wie z.B. die quantifizierenden Termini: 'omnis', 'nullus', 'totus' und die Präpositionen: 'praeter', 'inquantum' usw. Die kategorematischen Termini sind die ursprünglichen, irreduziblen semantischen Einheiten, aus denen ein Satz gebildet wird, der in der Differenz von 'wahr' und 'falsch' steht. Hier unterscheidet Ockham (*Summa logicae* I, c. 33) zwischen Nomen, die konkrete Einzeldinge bezeichnen, die zu dem Zeitpunkt, wo das Sprachzeichen ausgesprochen wird, anwesend sind: 'Mensch' bezeichnet in dem Fall alle aktuell existierenden Menschen. Und Nomen, die sich auf vergangene, gegenwärtige und zukünftige Dinge erstrecken: 'Mensch' bezeichnet in diesem Fall die einzelnen Menschen zu jeder Zeit. Nur in diesem Fall bleibt die Bedeutung des Ausdrucks 'Mensch' konstant; während sie sich im anderen Fall wandelt. Entscheidend ist dabei, daß die kategorematischen Termini sich ohne Vermittlung durch mentale Entitäten auf extramentale Dinge beziehen; die Logik rein extensional aufgebaut ist.

Diesen beiden Bezeichnungsweisen kann man eine weitere hinzufügen: sie drückt die verschiedenen Modalitäten aus, nach der ein sprachliches oder mentales Zeichen etwas im Geist hervorruft. Diese Bezeichnungsweise behandelt Ockham unter dem Titel der „konnotativen Termini". Die kategorematischen Termini lassen sich also differenzieren in solche Termini, die eine Konnotation aufweisen und solche, die keine aufweisen: die „absoluten Termini" wie 'Mensch' und 'Lebewesen', die man in modernen Sprachtheorien natürliche Arttermini („natural kind terms") zu nennen pflegt (vgl. Panaccio 1995: 190). So bezeichnet der Terminus 'Mensch' alle Menschen unerachtet der Differenzen zwischen ihnen; während der konnotative Terminus 'Vater' zwei Bezeichnungsweisen hat: eine erste, wonach er die konkreten Väter bezeichnet und eine zweite, wonach er sich nicht auf ein konkretes Einzelding bezieht, sondern eine Bedeutung hervorruft, die mit ihm verbunden ist: das Haben von Kindern. Die konnotativen Termini sind bei weitem zahlreicher als die natürlichen Arttermini. Zu ihnen zählt Ockham die bei Aristoteles genannten Paronyme, im Mittelalter *denominativa* genannt, wie z.B. 'gerecht', dem der abstrakte Terminus 'Gerechtigkeit' korrespondiert. Weiter Termini der Relation, wie z.B. 'Vater'. Die Einführung der konnotativen Termini erlaubt eine Erweiterung der logisch-semantischen Satzanalyse über die natürlichen Arttermini hinaus.

Zu dieser Erweiterung gehört auch die Unterscheidung zwischen den *nomina primae impositionis*, denen auf mentaler Sprachebene die *intentiones primae* korrespondieren; und den *nomina secundae impositionis*, denen die *intentiones secundae* entsprechen. Diese Differenz führt dazu, objektsprachliche Termini von metalinguistischen zu unterscheiden. Für den Logiker sind dabei die *intentiones secundae* von Interesse; für den Grammatiker dagegen die *nomina secundae impositionis*, wie z.B. die grammatischen Nomina 'Konjunktion' oder 'Figura'.

Die zweiten Intentionen sind solche, die den ersten beigelegt werden. Porphyrius († ca. 301) hat sie in seiner *Isagoge* in den Prädikabilien, den sog. *quinque voces* aufgezählt: Gattung, Art, Differenz, *proprium* und Akzidens. Für Ockham sind diese Universalien nichts anderes als Sprachzeichen: Der kategorematische Terminus 'Sinnenwesen' z. B. (*animal* = Gattungsbegriff) ist allgemein oder ein Allgemeinbegriff, weil er die vielen individuellen Sinnenwesen bezeichnet. Insofern sind die Termini 'Gattung', 'Art' und 'Unterschied' Namen zweiter Intention und werden metasprachlich verwendet, weil sie in einer letzten semantischen Analyse mentale Zeichen darstellen: 'Der Mensch ist eine Art'. Der Satz ist so zu verstehen, daß das mentale Zeichen 'Mensch' auf eine bestimmte Weise aussagbar ist, nämlich auf die Weise der Art; d.h. als ein Allgemeinbegriff, der sich durch weitere semantische Besonderheiten, wie 'vernunftbegabt' auszeichnen läßt. Ähnlich verfährt Ockham auch mit den aristotelischen Kategorien: 'Substanz', 'Quantität', 'Relation' usw., die eine Klassifikation von mentalen Sprachzeichen darstellen, also zweite Intentionen bezeichnen, und nicht die Dinge selbst klassifizieren.

Dieser Differenzierung zwischen Objekt- und Metasprache dient auch die Suppositionstheorie: Der schon seit dem 12. Jh. bekannte Ausdruck 'suppositio' soll die semantisch-referentielle Funktion eines Terminus in einem Satz klären; also zeigen, für was ein Terminus in einem Satz steht (vgl. Panaccio 1995: 194 ff.). Ockhams Suppositionstheorie erlaubt, die konfuse normale Sprache des Alltags, vor allem von den in ihr auftretenden Mehrdeutigkeiten zu „reinigen". Ockham unterscheidet in seiner *Summa logicae* (I c. 63—77) (1) die „personale Supposition" (*suppositio personalis*): 'ein Mensch läuft': Hier bezeichnet der Terminus 'Mensch' die konkreten individuellen Menschen. (2) Die „materiale Supposition" (*suppositio materialis*): '‹Mensch› ist ein deutsches Wort': Hier bezeichnet das gesprochene, aber auch mentale Sprachzeichen 'Mensch' sich selbst; das konventionelle Sprachzeichen 'Mensch' bezieht sich auf sich selbst als Wort oder als Begriff. (3) Schließlich die „einfache Supposition" (*suppositio simplex*): 'Mensch ist eine Art': Hier bezeichnet das Wort 'Mensch' den Begriff 'Mensch', dem es untergeordnet ist; oder — so kann man auch sagen — der Begriff bezieht sich auf sich selbst.

Die Suppositionstheorie erlaubt also den verschiedenen Sprachgebrauch eines selben Terminus zu klären. Sie ergänzt insofern die Theorie der Metasprache, die durch die Unterscheidung der ersten und zweiten Intentionen bereits begründet ist. Die materiale Supposition gestattet eine Untersuchung der konventionellen Sprache; die einfache Supposition die der mentalen Sprache. In diesem Kontext spielt allerdings die personale Supposition die entscheidende Rolle. Durch sie wird die Verwendung eines Terminus, sei es Subjekt, sei es Prädikat, zur Bezeichnung der individuellen Dinge festgelegt. Insofern ist sie die Basis sowohl der konventionellen als auch der mentalen Sprache.

4. Die *Grammatica speculativa* der Modisten

4.1. Historische Entwicklung

Nach allgemeiner Auffassung der modernen Mediävistik bildet die Tradition der *Grammatica speculativa*, die auch ein neues Genre, die *Summa grammatica* oder Abhandlungen über die *Modi significandi* (Bedeutungsweisen) geschaffen hat, der bedeutendste mittelalterliche Beitrag zur Sprachphilosophie (vgl. Kobusch 1996: 77 f.).

Am Anfang dieser Tradition steht wohl die um 1245 entstandene *Summa grammatica* des Roger Bacon. Aber in vielen Hinsichten ist seine Summa nicht mit den Abhandlungen über die *Modi significandi* der Modisten zu vergleichen. Ein sonst wohl unbekannter Magister der Artistenfakultät im Paris der ersten Hälfte des 13. Jhs., Jordanus, fordert mit Aristoteles (*Anal. Post.*, c. 33; 88 b 30ff.), daß die Grammatik, um Wissenschaft zu sein, einen universalen Gegenstand haben muß: die Sprache. Bei Robert Kilwardby ist die Idee einer *grammatica universalis*, die spätere *grammatica speculativa*, ganz deutlich ausgebildet: Sprache hat ein dreifaches Sein: in der Schrift, im Ausspruch und im Geist. Dabei ist dieses geistige Sein, das Sprache auszeichnet, da bei allen Menschen dasselbe, das Allgemeine und so Gegenstand der Wissenschaft. Insofern die Sprache im Geist auf die Weise des Allgemeinen ist, d.h. durch Abstraktion von den besonderen Sprachen, ist sie dann Erkenntnisgrund der besonderen äußeren Sprachen; insofern sie im Geist durch Affekt und Vorstellung ist, ist sie Prinzip des sinnlichen äußeren Wortes. Nach Kilwardby gibt es daher eine Parallelität zwischen den *modi significandi* und den *modi intelligendi*: die äußere Sprache enthält und repräsentiert dasselbe, was auch die innere Sprache enthält und darstellt (vgl. Sirridge 1995: 123 ff.; Schneider 1995: 112 ff.). Die epistemologische, ontologische und semantische Ordnung korrespondieren einander.

Inaugurator der Modistentradition im engeren Sinn ist Martinus von Dacien († 1304) mit seinem *Tractatus de modis significandi*. (vgl. Roos 1952: 121ff.) Martinus gehört zu einer Schule von dänischen Magistern, die zwischen 1260 und 1290 an der Pariser Artistenfakultät lehrten (vgl. Pinborg 1967: 67). Der bekanntere aus dieser Schule ist jedoch Boethius von Dacien († vor 1284), dessen *Quaestiones* zu Priscianus Maior, *De modis significandi*, um 1270 entstanden sind (vgl. Pinborg 1967: 77). Das umfangreichste Werk der Modistentradition ist die 1280 entstandene, unvollendete *Summa grammaticae* des Johannes Dacus (zweite Hälfte des 13. Jhs.) (vgl. Pinborg 1967: 87). Zu nennen sind noch die kleineren Werke des Simon von Dacien, die *Domus grammatice* und sein Priscian-Kommentar.

Neben der Bedeutung der dänischen Modistenschule dürfte allerdings der bekannteste Modist Thomas von Erfurt (erste Hälfte des 14. Jhs.) sein. Seine berühmte *Grammatica speculativa* wurde lange Zeit für ein Werk des Johannes Duns Scotus gehalten. Erst Martin Grabmann hat es als ein authentisches Werk des Thomas von Erfurt entdeckt. Martin Heidegger schrieb über ihn seine Habilitationsschrift noch unter dem Titel: „Die Kategorien- und Bedeutungslehre des Duns Scotus". Neben Thomas von Erfurt ist der aus Flandern stammende Siger von Courtrai († 1341) zu nennen, der Schüler des Modisten Radulphus Brito war. Schließlich sei noch der Traktat über die *Modi significandi* des Belgiers Michael von Marbais erwähnt (vgl. Pinborg 1967: 90).

Um 1330 setzt bereits die Kritik an der Theorie von den *Modi significandi* ein. An erster Stelle ist zu nennen die nominalistische Kritik des Erfurter Magisters Johannes Aurifaber, die er in seiner *Determinatio de modis significandi* vorträgt (vgl. Pinborg 1967: 193). Bedeutender ist jedoch die wohl von Pierre d'Ailly († 1420) stammende Schrift *Destructiones modorum significandi*. Weitere Kritik wird von anderer Seite vorgetragen: von Adam de Wodeham und Gregor von Rimini († 1358).

Nach 1300 sind keine neuen Entwicklungen in der Tradition der Modisten mehr zu verzeichnen (vgl. Pinborg 1988: 256). Die humanistische Kritik wird etwa durch Lorenzo Valla eingeleitet. Angriffe gegen die modistische *Grammatica speculativa* organisiert Alexander Hegius († 1498) in seiner *Invectiva in modos significandi*. (vgl. Percival 1988: 814). Die spekulative Grammatik wird als ungeeignet erachtet, irgendetwas Bedeutendes zur Klärung und zum Verständnis der Sprache beizutragen (vgl. Ashworth 1992: 153—55).

4.2. Theorien und Hintergründe

4.2.1. Charakter der *Grammatica speculativa*

Die Frage nach der 'Universalität' der Sprache und entsprechend nach einer allgemeinen Grammatik wird in der Tradition der *Grammatica speculativa* thematisiert. Es geht um die Allgemeinheit der Sprache, um die Sprache als solche. Von ihrer Realisierung in den bestimmten gesprochenen Sprachen wird abstrahiert. Insofern ist sie Gegenstand der Theorie. Die Grammatik wird in Anlehnung an den aristotelischen Wissenschaftsbegriff — Einheit des Subjekts, Allgemeinheit und Notwendigkeit der Aussagen über ihren Gegenstand — zu einer Wissenschaft von der Sprache. Die *Grammatica speculativa* versteht sich als Philosophie, als 'reine' Theorie der Sprache. Es geht um jene allgemeine Struktur von Sprache, die jeder besonderen Sprache zugrundeliegt.

Die Modisten wenden sich ihrem Untersuchungsgegenstand, der Sprache, zu im Rahmen der triadischen Struktur, die Aristoteles herausgestellt hat: Wort bzw. Sprachzeichen, Begriff (*conceptus mentis*) und Sache (*res*). Sie greifen dafür auf andere Ausdrücke zurück: *modus significandi*, *modus intelligendi* und *modus essendi* (vgl. Rosier 1995: 137). Die *modi significandi* sind die verschiedenen Weisen des Bezeichnens, durch die ein besonderer Aspekt 'mitbezeichnet' wird: so bezeichnet etwa das Verb, indem es seine eigene Bedeutung hat, die Zeit mit.

Nun hat Aristoteles in *Perì hermēneías* behauptet, daß die Sprachzeichen von Nation zu Nation verschieden; während die Gedanken bei allen Menschen dieselben sind. In der *Grammatica speculativa* kommt es also darauf an nachzuweisen, daß auch die *modi significandi* bei allen Menschen dieselben sind; denn nur so hat sie die Sprache als ihren universalen Gegenstand. Der aristotelischen Vorgabe muß man daher hinzufügen, daß auch die Bedeutung des Sprachzeichens und die durch die *modi significandi* konstituierte besondere Form der Bedeutung universal sind: Mögen also die Laute als Laute nicht dieselben sein bei allen Menschen; so sind sie es doch im Sinne der Ordnungsweise und des Begriffs: der Bedeutung (Jordanus; vgl. Kobusch 1996: 81f.). Insofern kann auch die besondere Form der Bedeutung eines Wortes bei allen invariant sein; und so ist sie von der bloßen Lautgestalt verschieden.

Diese Invarianz des Ausdrucks, d.h. des Wortes, insofern es eine Bedeutung hat (*articulata vox*), und die Invarianz der besonderen Bedeutungsformung durch die *modi significandi* gründet mittelbar in der „Natur der Dinge", dem *modus essendi* und unmittelbar in der Verstehensweise, dem *modus intelligendi*. Die Seinsweisen (*modi essendi*) und Verstehensweisen (*modi intelligendi*) sind bei allen Menschen ähnlich; und so sind sie Grund der Bezeichnungsweisen (*modi significandi*). Insofern ist der *modus significandi* abhängig vom *modus intelligendi*. Die Bezeichnungsweisen sind in der Seele, die sie verursacht. Der *modus intelligendi* ist im Verstand wie das „Erkannte im Erkennenden"; da aber doch nur − wie Martinus von Dacien meint − als ein „Sein in der Seele" (*esse in anima*); d.h. als ein „esse intentionale"; denn jedes Allgemeine ist ein „ens intentionale". Das Allgemeine bzw. das „esse rationale" ist ein „vermindertes Sein" (*esse diminutum*) und vom Verstand verursacht (vgl. Schneider 1995: 121). Insofern stellen die *modi significandi* jene Bedeutungsformen bereit, die der Sprecher einem Wort hat geben wollen. So aber ruhen sie ontologisch auf den *modi intelligendi* und letztlich auf den *modi essendi* auf.

Im Kontext der triadischen Struktur der *modi significandi*, *intelligendi* und *essendi* ist die Sprache als ein bedeutungsbehaftetes Zeichen Ausdruck der Gedanken, Begriffe des Geistes oder des Erkannten; also des *conceptus mentis*. Die Grammatik handelt daher nicht von dem Laut als solchem, der *vox* qua *vox*, die als Phonem Gegenstand der Physik ist. Sie handelt vielmehr von dem Laut, insofern er Bedeutung hat, und von den mit dieser Bedeutung mitbezeichneten besonderen Aspekten. Jedes Wort nämlich hat nicht nur eine bestimmte Bedeutung, sondern auch eine Mitbedeutung, eine in einer bestimmten Kategorie geformte Bedeutung. Z.B. sagt das Wort 'homo' etwas Zusammengesetztes aus: aus dem bezeichnenden Wort (Laut) und der bezeichneten Sache (Bedeutung). Der bedeutungsbehaftete Laut wird in der mittelalterlichen Sprachphilosophie *dictio* genannt. Insofern thematisiert der Grammatiker zwar auch den Laut, aber nur als bedeutenden; d.h. nur insofern er als artikulierter Zeichen der Sache selbst ist. Hier kann man eine zweifache Artikulation unterscheiden: den Laut im Hinblick auf die zu bezeichnende Sache (*impositio vocis*) und im Hinblick auf das Mitzubezeichnende. Gleichwohl wird nicht die Lautstruktur der Sprache thematisiert, sondern die Bedeutung des Sprachzeichens und die durch die *modi significandi* konstituierte besondere Form der Bedeutung. In dem *modus significandi* liegt daher eine bestimmte „Bewandtnis, die es um die Bedeutung hat" (Heidegger 1972: 309 [251]).

Die *Grammatica speculativa* ist eine *scientia sermocinalis*: Wissenschaft von der Sprache. Sie untersucht zwar nicht die verschiedenen besonderen Sprachen und Idiome; davon sieht sie ab. Sie sieht aber nicht von der Sprache überhaupt ab, sondern begreift die Sprache als die allen Einzelsprachen zugrundeliegende. Da jede Sprache eine bestimmte Struktur und Gliederung hat, ist die *Grammatica speculativa* jene Disziplin, die die eine universale, allen besonderen Sprachen zugrundeliegende grammatische Struktur untersucht.

4.2.2. Prinzipien der Grammatica speculativa

Entsprechend dem aristotelischen Wissenschaftsverständnis hat auch der Grammatiker die Aufgabe, seinen Gegenstand – die Sprache – auf die ihn gründenden Prinzipien bzw. Ursachen zurückzuführen. Diese, Sprache konstituierenden Prinzipien sind in der Grammatik die *principia constructionis*, durch die eine sinnvolle Anordnung der Ausdrücke ermöglicht wird. Der Laut, der Buchstabe, die Silbe, der Akzent und das Wort sind die Prinzipien der *Grammatica speculativa* (vgl. Kobusch 1996: 82ff.):

1. Laut: Das erste grundlegende Prinzip ist der Laut. Dabei ist für den Grammatiker nur der grammatische Aspekt des Lautes von Interesse, nicht sein physikalischer. Die Grammatik thematisiert den Laut, insofern er als ein Zeichen der Gedanken des Geistes aufgefaßt werden kann, die man artikulieren und anderen mitteilen will; d.h. sofern der Laut ein in Buchstaben ausdrückbarer artikulierter Laut ist. In dieser Hinsicht hat man den in Buchstaben ausdrückbaren artikulierten Laut wie 'homo' zu unterscheiden von Lauten, die zwar artikuliert sind, aber nicht in Buchstaben ausdrückbare, wie z. B. das Wehklagen der Geschundenen. Umgekehrt gibt es Laute, die zwar in Buchstaben ausgedrückt werden können, die aber inartikulierte Laute sind, z.B. das Quaken der Frösche („quac cra"). Und schließlich gibt es Laute – wie das Muhen der Kühe –, die sowohl inartikuliert als auch buchstabenlos sind. In der Grammatik wird allein der in Buchstaben ausdrückbare und artikulierte Laut thematisiert, insofern er die Grundlage der Buchstaben und Silben, die für sich keine Bedeutung haben, wie auch der bedeutungsbehafteten Wörter und Sätze darstellt.

2. Buchstabe: Der Buchstabe ist das erste und kleinste Element in der Lautanalyse. Er ist das Element der Sprache, das selbst kein Element mehr enthält. Wichtig ist hierbei die Unterscheidung von gesprochenem und geschriebenem Buchstaben. Man kann sich auf das Sprachverständnis des Aristoteles berufen: Das gesprochene Wort verhält sich zu dem Gedanken, den es ausdrückt, wie die Schrift zum Wort; es ist Zeichen der Gedanken wie der geschriebene Buchstabe Zeichen des gesprochenen Worts ist. Der Buchstabe drückt insofern ein Bezeichnungsverhältnis aus. Ihm kommen verschiedene Bestimmungen zu, äußere und innere. Äußere Bestimmungen sind die Zeit (Kürzung oder Dehnung in der Aussprache), die Hauchung (Klangweise), ferner Verdoppelung oder Umstellung eines Vokals oder Konsonanten, der Übergang von einem Vokal in einen Konsonanten; das alles geschieht um des Wohlklangs willen. Daneben hat jeder Buchstabe auch innere Bestimmungen: besonders die „Figur", die ihn sichtbar macht, und die „Bedeutung", die durch die Art der Aussprache ausgedrückt wird.

3. Silbe und Akzent: Die Silbe ist die kleinste Zusammenstellung von Buchstaben. Nach Priscian ist sie die Zusammenstellung von Buchstaben, die einen Akzent trägt, durch einen Luftstoß hervorgebracht wird und für sich noch nichts Bestimmtes bezeichnet, obgleich sie Teil des kleinsten bedeutungsbehafteten Ausdrucks, des Wortes ist. Der Akzent bezeichnet die Betonung oder Klangfarbe der Silbe.

4. Wort: Das Wort (*dictio*) ist die kleinste, inkomplexe Einheit unter den bedeutungsbehafteten Ausdrücken; der Satz hingegen die komplexe Einheit. Bedeutung hat ein artikulierter Laut dann, wenn beim Hörer ein bestimmter Begriff konstituiert wird, den der Sprecher hat mitteilen wollen. „Bezeichnen" heißt daher – so lautet die seit Abælard (vgl. Schneider 1995: 93) geläufige Definition – „einen Begriff zu konstituieren" (*intellectum constituere*). Wille und Vorstellung sind die grundlegenden Elemente dieses Konstitutionsaktes. Jedes Wort hat, unabhängig von seinen in den *modi significandi* modifizierten Bedeutungsformen, also von seiner Mitbedeutung, eine ihm eigene grundlegende Bedeutung. Entsprechend geht diese Grundbedeutung den *modi significandi* voraus. Sie wird zunächst vom Intellekt konstituiert, indem dieser den artikulierten Laut, das Wort, als Zeichen des von der Sache herrührenden Begriffs einsetzt und dann durch die Mitbedeutung, die *modi significandi* modifiziert (zum zugrundeliegenden semantischen Modell → Art. 1, § 4.3).

Die Grammatik unterscheidet – aufgrund der Bezeichnungspaare Substanz und Qualität – verschiedene Wortarten oder Wortklassen: Bezeichnet ein Wort Substanz und Qualität, dann ist es ein Nomen; bezeichnet es ohne Qualität, dann ein Pronomen; bezeichnet es Tätigkeiten oder Erleidungen in Verbindung mit einer Substanz, dann ist es ein Partizip; ohne Substanz ein Verb. Die anderen Wortklassen: Präposition, Adverb, Konjunktion und Interjektion betreffen nicht die Sachen, sondern deren Umstände.

4.2.3. Darstellung der *modi significandi*

Nach Boethius von Dacien ist Gegenstand der Grammatik ausschließlich der *modus significandi*, nicht aber die Verbindung zwischen Sprache und Wirklichkeit. Diese herauszustellen ist eine Aufgabe, die durch den *modus intelligendi* zu erfüllen ist; denn was vor der Sprache liegt (die außersprachliche Wirklichkeit) betrachtet nicht der Grammatiker, sondern der Philosoph. Gegenstand der Grammatik ist allein die Formstruktur der in den *modi significandi* konstituierten Sprache. Die *modi significandi* sind dabei Eigenschaften des Sprachzeichens. Was ihren ontologischen Status angeht, so sind sie nur im bereits bedeutungsbehafteten Ausdruck (*dictio*) wie in ihrem Subjekt. Gegenstand der Grammatik ist daher die Weise, den intendierten Gedanken durch die angemessene Sprache auszudrücken und anderen mitzuteilen. Dabei untersucht sie die allgemeine Struktur der Sprache selbst; d.h. den *modus significandi* hinsichtlich der einzelnen Redeteile (*partes orationis*) (vgl. Schneider 1995: 121 f.). Diese einzelnen *modi significandi* der Redeteile sind nun (vgl. Kobusch 1996: 85 ff.):

1. Nomen: Das Nomen bezeichnet etwas als eine in sich ruhende, permanente Entität, d.i. als Substanz, und als einen bestimmten Begriff, grammatisch gesehen als eine Qualität. Wenn − so hatte schon Thomas von Aquin erklärt (vgl. o. § 3.2.1) − in grammatischem Zusammenhang von Substanz die Rede ist, dann meint man damit nicht die aristotelische Kategorie der Substanz, sondern den Seinsmodus, der sowohl den realen Dingen in der Außenwelt als auch den Gedankendingen zukommt. Nomen können daher Dinge, bloß Gedachtes (z.B. Chimären), Positives ('Glaube'), Negatives ('Unglaube') bzw. Privationen ('Blindheit') bezeichnen. Entscheidend ist, daß das Nomen eine in sich ruhende, selbständige, permanente Entität bezeichnet; und so haben es die antiken Grammatiker wie Donat und Priscian gemeint, wenn sie sagen, daß das Nomen Substanz und Qualität bezeichnet, daß es nach Art einer Substanz und einer Qualität bezeichnet.

Bei den Nomina hat man die verschiedenen *modi significandi* der gemeinsamen Namen, die wie z.B. 'Haus' mehreren Einzeldingen zukommen, von den verschiedenen *modi significandi* der Eigennamen zu unterscheiden. Weiter sind, entsprechend dem Begriffspaar 'Substanz' und 'Qualität', die Gattungs-, Art- und Geschlechtsnamen, die Diminutiva und Kollektiva von den verschiedenen Arten der Adjektive (Thomas von Erfurt listet 24 verschiedene Arten auf) auseinanderzuhalten. Diese *modi significandi* bestimmen den Namen wesentlich; akzidentell werden die Namen aber auch noch durch andere Modi wie Geschlecht, Zahl, Figur (*simplex*, wie 'dives' (reich), *composita*, wie 'praedives' (überreich) und *decomposita*, wie 'inexpugnabilis' (unüberwindlich)), Kasus und Person bestimmt. Dabei gilt die Person nach traditioneller Auffassung als ein Akzidens des Verbums.

2. Pronomen: Auch das Pronomen bezeichnet nach Art einer Substanz; allerdings ohne Qualität; d.h. es zeigt etwas nicht in seiner Bestimmtheit an, sondern gänzlich unbestimmt, d.i. ohne qualitative Bestimmtheit: die „reine Substanz" (*substantiam meram*). Von Bedeutung ist in diesem Zusammenhang, daß das Pronomen auch „als Zeichen gestufter Präsenz" (Kobusch 1996: 87) verstanden werden kann. Nach Auffassung des Martinus von Dacien und Thomas von Erfurt bezeichnen Demonstrativpronomina, zu denen auch die Personalpronomina zu rechnen sind, eine Sache unter der Rücksicht ihrer sinnlichen oder auch geistigen Anwesenheit. Im höchsten Maße präsent ist das Personalpronomen 'ich', da der Sprecher über aktuelle Selbsterkenntnis, d.h. über Selbstgegenwärtigkeit verfügt. Das Personalpronomen 'du' hingegen und andere Demonstrativpronomina verhalten sich indifferent in bezug auf Abwesenheit und Anwesenheit; sie deuten also eine geringere Präsenz an. Die Relativpronomina schließlich bezeichnen eine Sache in ihrer Abwesenheit; d.h. durch sie wird eine erkannte, dann aber vergessene Sache wiedererinnert.

3. Verbum: Das Verbum ist der dritte Modus significandi. Wie schon in Aristoteles' *Perì hermēneías* ausgeführt, läßt sich sein Charakter im Gegensatz zum Nomen bestimmen. Bezeichnet das Nomen nach Art einer Substanz, so das Verbum nach Art des Werdens: „Wie nämlich jedes Nomen die Sache nach Art eines Habitus und in ihrem Verharren bezeichnet, so bezeichnet jedes Verbum die Sache nach Art des Werdens und als im Werden befindliche" (Boethius Dacus 1969: 185). Das eigentlich spezifische Wesen des Verbums liegt nach Boethius von Dacien und Thomas von Erfurt aber darin, daß es den Charakter des „Abständigen oder Trennenden" (*modus distantis*) hat: Insofern nämlich das Verb das Ausgesagte vertritt, bezeichnet es eine von der zugrundeliegenden Sache bzw. Substanz, von der etwas ausgesagt wird, unterschiedene Wesenheit (*essentia distincta*): das, was ausgesagt wird. Dem widerspricht nicht, daß das Verb 'est', das in jedem Verb gleichsam als „Wurzel" (*radix*, Thomas v. Erfurt) eingeschlossen ist, mit Berufung auf Aristoteles' *Perì hermēneías* eine „Zusammensetzung" (*compositio*) bezeichnet; denn der Grund dieser Zusammensetzung liegt in der Inhärenz des Ausgesagten im Subjekt (*inhaerens alteri secundum esse*). Der Modus der Abständigkeit kommt dem Verb wesentlich zu; hingegen der *modus inhaerentis* nur akzidentell. Hinsichtlich der übrigen akzidentellen Bestimmungen des *modus significandi* des Verbs hat man nach der (1) Qualität zu unterscheiden: Indikativ, Imperativ, Optativ, Konjunktiv und Infinitiv; (2) nach der Konjugation: Zeit, Zahl, Modus und Person, durch die das Verb gebeugt wird; (3) nach dem Geschlecht: Aktiv, Passiv und Neutrum; die übrigen vier Bestimmungen sind: Zahl, Figur, Zeit und Person.

4. Partizip: Das Partizip steht in der Mitte zwischen Nomen und Verbum. Mit dem Verbum hat es gemeinsam, daß es nach Art des Werdens bezeichnet; mit dem Nomen, daß es unmittelbar mit der Substanz verbunden ist. Es bezeichnet nicht die Substanz, sondern deren Tätigkeit und Leiden.

5. Adverb: Das Adverb bezeichnet eine nähere Bestimmung des Verbs oder Partizips; entweder (1) nach der Bestimmtheit der bezeichneten Sache oder (2) nach der Bestimmtheit der *modi significandi*:

(1) Hier gibt es vier Arten von Adverbien: Adverbien der Kategorie des Ortes ('wo', 'hier', 'dort' usw.), der Quantität ('viel', 'wenig' usw.), der Qualität ('weise', 'klug', 'schön' usw.) und des Anrufs (*vocandi*) ('Oh Heinrich, lies').

(2) Nach der Bestimmtheit der Zusammensetzung, der Zeit und des Modus unterscheidet man Adverbien, die die Inhärenz des Verbums näher bestimmen: Adverbien des Fragens ('warum'), des Zweifelns ('vielleicht'), der Bejahung oder Verneinung ('auch' oder 'eben nicht'); Zeitadverbien ('jetzt') und Adverbien, die das Verb im Hinblick auf seinen Modus bestimmen: notwendig, kontingent, möglich oder unmöglich, weiter des Wünschens und Ermunterns ('wohlan', 'hoffentlich').

6. Konjunktion: Die Konjunktion verknüpft zwei äußere Glieder eines Satzes (*extrema*): Substantive oder Adjektive oder auch Sätze. Je nachdem, ob die beiden Glieder auf einander hingeordnet sind oder nicht, kann man unterscheiden: die kopulative Konjunktion ('und'), die disjunktive ('oder'), die kausale ('weil') und die schlußfolgernde ('also'). Von Wichtigkeit ist, daß man bei allen synkategorematischen Ausdrücken wie z.B. 'oder ob' (im Sinne von 'vel'), 'ob' (im Sinne von 'si'), 'oder' (im Sinne von 'an') und 'ganz' (im Sinne von 'totus') und 'ganz' (im Sinne von 'omnis') ihre Bedeutung und Funktion, die sie in einem Satz haben, auseinanderhält. Diese Ausdrücke hätten keine Bedeutungsunterschiede, wenn sie nicht verschiedene Funktionen in einem Satz erfüllten. Die Bedeutung der Konjunktion wird durch den synkategorematischen Ausdruck im Ganzen eines Satzes oder einer Rede festgelegt; und wird zurückgeführt auf die Funktion, die der synkategorematische Ausdruck in einem Satz hat. Nach dem Sprachgebrauch des Priscian heißt die grammatische Funktion entweder „Kraft" (*vis*) oder – weniger gebräuchlich – „Funktion" (*officium, potestas*). Für die Grammatiker des 12. Jahrhunderts kann 'Funktion' sowohl die Bedeutung eines Wortes als auch seine syntaktische Eigentümlichkeit heißen, die ihm auf Grund seiner spezifischen Bedeutung zukommt. Bei allen synkategorematischen Termini (Konjunktionen, Präpositionen, quantifizierende Termini) ist ihre Bedeutung jedoch abhängig von der Funktion, die sie in einem Satz haben (siehe o. § 3.2.3).

7. Präposition: Die Präposition bezeichnet eine Sache oder einen Sachverhalt, indem sie eine Kasusform zu einer bestimmten Bedeutung verbindet und auf den im Verb ausgedrückten Akt bezieht. Die Präposition bezeichnet das Verhältnis, in dem eine Kasusform – wie z.B. der Akkusativ – zu dem Akt steht, den das Verb ausdrückt; in diesem Fall das Verhältnis des Zieles; oder das Verhältnis der Kausalität beim Ablativ.

8. Interjektion: Die Interjektion unterscheidet sich von allen anderen *modi significandi* dadurch, daß sie Gefühle repräsentiert; also nicht etwas durch einen Begriff bezeichnet, wie es etwa die Nomen und Verben tun. Sie kann ein Ausdruck der Freude oder des Schmerzes sein, wenn es sich um Gegenwärtiges, und der Furcht, wenn es sich um Zukünftiges handelt. Sie kann aber auch Ausdruck einer Bewunderung sein. So bezeichnet die Interjektion, die aus dem Adverb 'oh' gebildet und mit dem Vokativ 'Heinrich' verbunden ist, nicht eine Sache; sie ist kein *actus signatus*, ein Akt der Bezeichnung, wie Thomas von Erfurt erklärt; sondern durch sie vollzieht sich der Akt selbst: in dem 'oh' liegt ein Aktvollzug (*actus exercitus*), der nicht erst ein Bezeichnungsverhältnis ausdrückt, sondern vollzogen wird. Man kann darin erste Ansätze einer Sprechakttheorie von Sprache erkennen.

4.2.4. Syntax

Nach der Darstellung der *modi significandi* der acht Redeteile, die sich auf die *Etymologia* beziehen, folgt die Darlegung der *modi significandi* hinsichtlich der Syntax, der *constructio* bzw. der *Diasynthetica*. Hier spielt die bereits eingeführte Unterscheidung der transitiven und intransitiven Konstruktion eines Satzes eine große Rolle. Das Kriterium der Unterscheidung ist nach Thomas von Erfurt die Abhängigkeit des in einem Satz an erster Stelle Genannten (*primum constructibile*) von dem an zweiter Stelle Genannten (*secundum constructibile*) und umgekehrt: 'Sokrates läuft' ist intransitiv konstruiert, weil das dort an zweiter Stelle Genannte, also das Prädikat bzw. Verb abhängt von dem an erster Stelle Genannten (*suppositum*), dem Subjekt; oder in 'Sokrates liest gut' ist das Adverb 'gut' abhängig vom Verb. Dagegen ist ein Satz wie 'Ich schlage Sokrates' transitiv konstruiert, weil entweder das an erster Stelle Genannte 'Ich schlage' nicht vom dem an zweiter Stelle Genannten abhängt; oder wie in 'video legentem librum' das 'video' zumindest in obliquo von dem an zweiter Stelle Genannten, dem Partizip 'legentem' abhängt. Die Unterscheidung zwischen transitiver und intransitiver Konstruktion ist allerdings nur metaphorisch gemeint, gleichsam in Anlehnung an einen realen Wechsel oder Übergang.

5. Zusammenfassung und Ausblick

Die Tradition der *Grammatica speculativa* hält an der von Aristoteles und stärker noch von A. M. S. Boethius herausgestellten triadischen Struktur fest: Wort, d.h. Sprache im ganzen (*modus significandi*) – Begriff, d.h. Denken und Gedachtes (*modus intelligendi*) – Sache, Dinge, d.h. Wirklichkeit (*modus essendi*). Zwar gründet der *modus significandi* ontologisch im *modus intelligendi* und letztlich im *modus essendi*; aber die entscheidenden Verhältnisse zwischen Sprache und Denken und zwischen Sprache und Wirklichkeit bzw. Sache (*res*) werden nicht eigentlich geklärt.

Was das Verhältnis zwischen gesprochener und mentaler Sprache angeht, so führt die Einschränkung des Gegenstands der Grammatik als *scientia sermocinalis* auf die allgemeine Formstruktur der Sprache als solcher dazu, die Inhaltsebene von der Ausdrucksebene der Sprache zu trennen. Damit wird die Tendenz gefördert, Sprache als ein Zeichensystem aufzufassen, das als ein solches unabhängig von der wirklichkeitserschließenden Kraft der Sprache zu sein scheint. Dadurch ist auch das andere Verhältnis zwischen Sprache und Wirklichkeit betroffen. Bei Martinus von Dacien hat die Sprache, der *modus significandi*, zwar noch einen Sachbezug; bei Boethius von Dacien aber nicht mehr; denn für Boethius bildet die Sprachebene als Zeichenebene einen selbständigen Seinsbereich. Es wird eine Zeichentheorie (Semiotik) im Unterschied zur Bedeutungstheorie (Semantik) vorbereitet.

Mit Thomas von Erfurt, der die Tradition der *Grammatica speculativa* zum Ende führt, beginnt bereits ihre Auflösung. Thomas behauptet zwar noch, daß die Ausdrucksebene (*modus significandi*), die psychologisch-kognitive Inhaltsebene (*modus intelligendi*) und die ontologische Ebene (*modus essendi*) korrespondieren. Aber unter dem Einfluß des Nominalismus können diese Ebenen auch so verstanden werden, daß sie selbständig gegeneinander sind. So ist es nach Johannes Aurifaber überflüssig, der Sprache eine, im *modus significandi* dargelegte, eigene Form zuzuschreiben; denn die Gliederung der Sachen und der Begriffe als natürlicher Zeichen der Dinge genügt, um auch die Gliederung der Sprache zu erklären. Der artikulierte Laut wird signifikativ und bekommt seine Bedeutung durch den Sprachgebrauch (vgl. Schneider 1995: 122 f.). Hier setzt sich die Ockhamsche Wissenschaftstheorie als Sprachkritik durch.

Trotz dieser, der *Grammatica speculativa* eignenden inneren Problematik lassen sich im ganzen gesehen die sprachphilosophischen und sprachlogischen Überlegungen des Mittelalters auffassen als jene grundlegenden Sprachtheorien, von denen die gegenwärtige Sprachphilosophie lebt; und nicht nur sie: Sprachtypologien, Universalienforschung und die Idee einer allgemeinen Grammatik bleiben virulent. Hinzuweisen ist vor allem auf die Unterscheidung zwischen Bedeutung und Referenz eines sprachlichen Ausdrucks, die eine logisch-semantische Analyse des Sprachgebrauchs erlaubt. Hinzuweisen ist ferner auf die Entdeckung, die Abælard gemacht hat und die gegenüber dem aristotelischen Sprachverständnis einen Fortschritt bedeutet: nämlich die Entdeckung des Sachverhalts, der im Deutschen durch einen 'daß-Satz' wiedergegeben wird und sich dem aristotelischen Kategorien-Schema entzieht. Adam de Wodeham und Gregor von Rimini diskutieren unter dem Titel des *complexe significabile* ausdrücklich die Frage nach dem Signifikat eines ganzen Satzes. Im Anschluß an Gottlob Frege, Bertrand Russell, Willard van Orman Quine und Hilary Putnam werden diese Fragen in der sprachanalytischen Philosophie breit erörtert.

Auch wird man darauf hinweisen dürfen, daß die Überlegungen zur Interjektion erste Ansätze einer Sprechakttheorie bieten. Weiter sind die Traditionen der Sprachlogik zu erwähnen, die in Wilhelm von Ockham einen Höhepunkt erfahren. Die Differenz zwischen Objektsprache und Metasprache, die Idee einer Idealsprache, die für die Wissenschaft im Sinne einer formalisierbaren Sprache von Bedeutung ist, darf man nicht übergehen. In gleichem Zuge ist aber auch die welterschließende Kraft der Sprache zu erwähnen, wie sie in der *verbum-mentis*-Lehre des Thomas von Aquin dargelegt wird und in der Hermeneutik der Gegenwart unverzichtbar ist. Überblickt man die mittelalterlichen Anstrengungen zu einer Theorie der Sprache im ganzen, so darf man mit Fug und Recht behaupten, daß in ihnen ein Spektrum sprachtheoretischer Überlegungen erscheint, von denen moderne Sprachtheorien zehren.

6. Zitierte Literatur

Ashworth, Elisabeth J. 1992. „Traditional Logic". In: Schmitt, Charles B. & Skinner, Quentin (eds.). *The Cambridge History of Renaissance Philosophy*. Cambridge: Cambridge University Press, 143–72.

Boethius Dacus. 1969. *Modi significandi sive Quaestiones super Priscianum Maiorem*. In: Pinborg, Jan & Roos, Heinrich (eds.). *Corpus Philosophorum Danicorum Medii Aevi*, Vol. 4, Kopenhagen: G. E. G. GAD.

Bursill-Hall, Geoffrey L. & Ebbesen, Sten & Koerner, Konrad (eds.). 1990. *De ortu grammaticae. Studies in Medieval Grammar and Linguistic Theory in Memory of Jan Pinborg*. (Amsterdam Studies in the Theory and History of Linguistic Science, 43.) Amsterdam & Philadelphia: Benjamins.

Ebbesen, Sten (ed.). 1995. *Sprachtheorien in Spätantike und Mittelalter*. (Geschichte der Sprachtheorie, 3.) Tübingen: Narr.

Fredborg, Karin Margareta. 1988. „Speculative Grammar". In: Dronke, Peter (ed.). *History of Twelfth-Century Western Philosophy*. Cambridge: Cambridge University Press, 177–95.

Heidegger, Martin. 1972. *Die Kategorien- und Bedeutungslehre des Duns Scotus* (Tübingen 1916). In: *Gesamtausgabe*, Bd. 1: Frühe Schriften, Frankfurt/M.: Klostermann, 189–411.

Jacobi, Klaus. 1995. „Sprache und Wirklichkeit: Theoriebildung über Sprache im frühen 12. Jahrhundert". In: Ebbesen, Sten (ed.), 77–108.

Kneepkens, Corneille Henri Joan Marie. 1978. „Master Guido and His View on Government: On Twelfth-Century Linguistic Thought". *Vivarium* 16.2: 108–41.

Kneepkens, Corneille Henri Joan Marie. 1987. *Het Iudicium Constructionis: Het Leerstuk van de Constructio in de 2de Helft van de 12de Eeuwe. Een Verkennende en Inleidende Studie gevolgd door kritische uitgaven van Robertus van Parijs, ⟨Summa 'Breve sit'⟩ en Robert Blund, ⟨Summa in arte grammatica⟩ en door een werkuitgave van Petrus Hispanus (non-papa), ⟨Summa 'Absoluta cuiuslibet'⟩*. 4 Bde., Nijmegen: Ingenium Publ.

Kneepkens, Corneille Henri Joan Marie. 1990. „Transitivity, Intransitivity and Related Concepts in 12th Century Grammar. An explorative study". In: Bursill-Hall, Geoffrey L. & al., 161–89.

Kneepkens, Corneille Henri Joan Marie. 1995. „The Priscianic Tradition". In: Ebbesen, Sten (ed.), 239–64.

Kobusch, Theo. 1996. „Grammatica speculativa (12.-14. Jahrhundert)". In: Borsche, Tilman (ed.). *Klassiker der Sprachphilosophie. Von Platon bis Noam Chomsky*. München: Beck, 77–93.

Kretzmann, Norman. 1967. „Semantics, History of". In: Edwards, Paul (ed.). *The Encyclopedia of Philosophy*. Bd. 7, New York & London: Macmillan, 358–406.

Kretzmann, Norman & Kenny, Anthony & Pinborg, Jan (eds.). 1988. *The Cambridge History of Later Medieval Philosophy*. Cambridge: Cambridge University Press.

Panaccio, Claude. 1995. „La philosophie du langage de Guillaume d'Occam". In: Ebbesen, Sten (ed.), 184–206.

Petrus Abælard. 1956. *Dialectica*. Ed. Lambert Marie de Rijk. Assen: Van Gorcum.

Petrus Helias. 1993. *Summa super Priscianum*. 2 Vols. Ed. Leo Reilly. Toronto: Pontifical Institute of Medieval Studies.

Percival, W. Keith. 1988. „Changes in the approach to language". In: Kretzmann, Norman & al., 808–17.

Pinborg, Jan. 1967. *Die Entwicklung der Sprachtheorie im Mittelalter*. (Beiträge zur Geschichte der Philosophie und Theologie des Mittelalters, 42/2.) Münster: Aschendorff.

Pinborg, Jan. 1988. „Speculative grammar". In: Kretzmann, Norman & al., 254—69.

Rijk, Lambert Marie de. 1967. *Logica modernorum: A Contribution to the History of Early Terminist Logic*. Bd. I: *On the Twelfth Century Theories of Fallacy* (1962). Bd. II.I: *The Origin and Early Development of the Theory of Supposition*. Bd. II.II: *Texts and Indices*. Assen: Van Gorcum.

Roos, Heinrich. 1952. *Die modi significandi des Martinus de Dacia. Forschungen zur Geschichte der Sprachlogik im Mittelalter*. (Beiträge zur Geschichte der Philosophie und Theologie des Mittelalters, 37/2.) Münster & Kopenhagen: Aschendorff & Arne Frost-Hansen.

Rosier, Irène & Stefanini, Jean. 1990. „Théories médiévales du pronom et du nom général". In: Bursill-Hall, Geoffrey L. & al., 285—303.

Rosier, Irène. 1995. „Res significata et modus significandi: Les implications d'une distinction médiévale". In: Ebbesen, Sten (ed.)., 135—68.

Schneider, Jakob Hans Josef. 1992. „Scientia sermocinalis / realis. Anmerkungen zum Wissenschaftsbegriff im Mittelalter und in der Neuzeit". *Archiv für Begriffsgeschichte* XXXV: 54—92.

Schneider, Jakob Hans Josef. 1995. „Der Begriff der Sprache im Mittelalter, im Humanismus und in der Renaissance". *Archiv für Begriffsgeschichte* XXXVIII: 66—149.

Schneider, Jakob Hans Josef. 1996. „Utrum haec sit vera: Caesar est homo, Caesar est animal, Caesare non existente. Zum Peri-hermeneias-Kommentar des Johannes Duns Scotus". In: Honnefelder, Ludger & Wood, Rega & Dreyer, Mechthild (eds.). *John Duns Scotus. Metaphysics & Ethics*. (Studien und Texte zur Geistesgeschichte des Mittelalters, 53.) Leiden & New York & Köln: Brill, 393—412.

Sirridge, Mary. 1995. „The Science of Language and Linguistic Knowledge: John of Denmark and Robert Kilwardby". In: Ebbesen, Sten (ed.)., 109—34.

Jakob Hans Josef Schneider,
Universität Tübingen (Deutschland)

15. Reflections on language in the Renaissance

1. The era
2. Latin grammaticography
3. The first grammars of vernaculars
4. Grammars of non-European languages
5. The historical perspective
6. References

1. The era

'Renaissance' is the commonly accepted cover-term for a set of intellectual and mental developments, each of which had its own origin and topic, but which occurred concomitantly and, by influencing each other, gave the period a homogeneous character. Its temporal limits are generally given as the middle of the 15th and the end of the 16th centuries, but there are important works which were published in the Renaissance spirit well before these datelines (e. g. Dante's *De vulgari eloquentia*, shortly after 1305) and well after (e. g. Bacon's *Novum organum scientiarum*, 1620). As always, it proves difficult to periodize an intellectual and mental movement.

The spatial boundaries of the Renaissance, however, can be delimited more exactly, mainly on linguistic grounds. It started in northern Italy, notably at the Medici court in Florence, around 1400, and spread to the regions of the Romance, the Germanic and the Slavonic languages. In a dialectical way, it was Latin which delimited the area. As the universal means of communication for all intellectual discourse during the Middle Ages, Latin came under attack (i) because of the rediscovery of classical Latin (and Greek) and the ensuing wave of Humanist studies and (ii) because of the awakening of national vernaculars and their consolidation in analysis and description, without however losing its strongholds in university life and education. Thus, the Renaissance applied to those regions in Europe where Latin was either taught or could be challenged. Some scholars regard this process as the birth of modern Europe (Robins 1990: 107; Eco 1993). It excluded the *Slavia orthodoxa* (as opposed to the *Slavia Romana*), because Old Church Slavonic had there taken the place and the functions of medieval Latin in the west.

Although the many facets of Renaissance culture have a clearly detectable affinity to each other, there are of course some which do not directly pertain to language and linguistics. To them belong the general enjoyment of and curiosity about the world, as opposed to the medieval *vanitas mundi*; the style of urban life in general and court life in particular; the respect for learning outside theology; and the new styles in architecture and the visual arts. But there are other features which had a direct influence on linguistic reflections and practice.

(i) The re-discovery of classical Latin and Greek did not (in the strict sense) originate in but was strongly boosted by the Turkish conquest of Constantinople in 1453, which brought many representatives and many hitherto unknown old texts to the west. This created a new understanding of the historicity of languages and culture, in particular in Italy, where classical Latin and classical (Roman) culture were seen and imitated as the essentials of one's own past. Moreover, it created new ways of analysing and teaching original Latin as distinct from its medieval 'corruptions'.

(ii) Political circumstances with slowly evolving central courts and their accompanying institutions, for example, in Spain, France, England, and the Czech lands, created a certain administrative and commercial need for linguistic uniformity which could only be fulfilled by what can be called upgraded versions of the vernaculars. In Italy, the powerful court in Florence took the place of a central agency. In Germany, the Reformation had a similar unifying effect (at least in the Protestant parts of the country) with its main linguistic project, Luther's translation of the Bible (1534). Thus, the new appreciation of vernaculars (Ribhegge 1998) had its philological, political, commercial, and religious motives. They were supported by the introduction of Johannes Gutenberg's invention, the printing press with movable letters (1452–55, the first 42-line Bible), which allowed books to be deployed much more easily all over Europe than previously and, consequently, demanded a relative linguistic uniformity, mainly in spelling. All this created a new appreciation of people's native languages in general, resulting (a) in their linguistic description, and (b) in their comparison. There also arose a marked interest in the historical development of national languages.

Features (i) and (ii) will be elaborated on subsequently. This will be done by pointing out the contribution of particular authors to the general linguistic development, which will itself be sketched as overlapping identical features of their works. The method means that many eminent names of the intellectual life of an era which was very rich in them cannot be mentioned at all, let alone analysed. For general linguistic information on the era and its authors, see, besides the usual bibliographies, Ahrens 1969, Percival 1975, Brekle 1975, Padley 1976–1988, Michael 1985, Robins 1990, Auroux 1992, Eco 1993, Caravolas 1994, Borst 1995 (in particular vol. III/1 and III/2), Tavoni 1998, Gardt 1999; for particular linguistic information on the authors mentioned, see, besides the usual works of biographical reference, the significant articles in Stammerjohann 1996.

2. Latin grammaticography

2.1 The teaching of Latin in the *trivium* was dominated by a fixed set of textbooks, namely the *Ars minor* by Donatus (4th cent.), the *Doctrinale puerorum* by Alexander of Villadei (b. ca. 1170), and a compilation of Donatus and Priscian (6th cent.) called *Ianua [cum rudibus primam cupientibus artem]* probably from the 13th century. They centred in the traditional eight parts of speech (Matthews 1994: 29–38). (Dionysius Thrax: noun including adjective, verb, participle, article, pronoun, preposition, adverb, and conjunction; Priscian: the same without 'article' and additionally with 'interjection' [Michael 1985: 48; Robins 1990: 38–40; 65–67; Matthews 1994: 38–43; for Dionysius Thrax in general see Robins 1993: 41–86, Priscian in general, see Robins 1993: 87–110]) and the parsing of sentences according to *suppositum* (subject) left of the verb and *appositum* (object) right of the verb, thus presupposing a quasi natural word-order. The relation between verb and nouns to the right (i. e. zero or object) was called *intransitio* or *transitio*. The verbs were broken down into subclasses according to semantic types, such as active, passive, and neuter, and according to the cases they govern to the right. Whoever wanted to change the grammaticography of Latin had to challenge such concepts and their terms.

The first to do so, if only timidly, was Guarino Veronese (1374–1460) with his *Regulae grammaticales* (before 1418). Quite a number of grammars were written under his influence, the first complete one being *Rudimenta grammatices* (1468) by Niccolò Peretto

(1429–1480). Guarini dispensed with concepts such as *suppositum* and *appositum*, using *agent* and *patient* instead, and such as *transitio* and *intransitio*, but left the main traits of the system intact (Percival 1975: 239). This earliest work of the Humanists can be seen both as "developing or breaking from tradition" (Tavoni 1998: 3).

There is much more challenge to tradition in Lorenzo Valla's (1407–1457) *Elegantiarum linguae Latinae libri sex* (ca. 1444). He showed his independence of mind by refuting the hypothesis of Hebrew as the first language of mankind on philological reasons. In his mainly stylistically orientated compendium, he insisted on the usage of the language by the classical writers as the guideline for all grammar, thus taking grammar out of its self-contained existence and making it accountable for language use – in the classical past and even in the writer's own present (Grafton 1997).

The real Humanist innovations came from outside Italy. Johannes Despauterius (ca. 1480–1520) followed Valla in teaching Latin through the old sources. He deduced descriptive rules from them. In 1527–30, Robert Estienne (ca. 1503–1559) published all his works with a complete new set of classical texts replacing the ones used in former centuries. Georgius Haloinus (?1470–?1536), in his *Restauratio linguae Latinae* (1533), took this idea to an extreme in proposing to teach Latin as a vernacular together with the children's mother-tongue without any grammar and only by reading selected classical texts.

The major Humanist innovations appeared between 1540 and the end of the century. They are connected with the names Scaliger, Ramus, and Sanctius.

Julius Caesar Scaliger (1484–1558) published his *De causis linguae Latinae libri tredecim* in 1540. He claimed that grammaticography was a science and not an art and gave it a systematic framework with Aristotelian concepts. The phonetic substance of language is its *causa materialis*, the meaning of words its *causa formalis*. Pronouncing the words is their *causa efficiens*, and the purpose of this their *causa finalis* (Tavoni 1998: 11). He did not speak of *partes orationis* but of *species dictionis*. Contrary to Valla, but also to Erasmus and Linacre (see below), he maintained that grammar did not follow language use (and usage) but underpinned it with philosophical reasoning.

Petrus Ramus (1515–1572), better known as an anti-Aristotelian philosopher than all the other Humanist grammarians, wrote Greek, Latin, and French grammars (*Grammatica*, and *Rudimenta grammaticae Latinae*, both 1559). His main innovation is the definition of the parts of speech strictly according to formal criteria. In the Aristotelian manner, he differentiated between *categoremata* and *syncategoremata*, but contrary to Aristotle he did not use semantic criteria for definition. His most important measure is 'number'. The *categoremata* are *voces numeri* and the *syncategoremata voces sine numero*. The former are again broken down into those *cum genere et casu* and those *cum tempore et persona*. Thus he hoped to gear grammar more to the practical needs of people, i.e. lawyers, teachers, etc., than other grammarians did. Of course, Ramus is also well-known for introducing the largely ineffective principle of dichotomies into grammar as he did in all scientific disciplines.

Franciscus Sanctius Brocensis (1523–1601) was somewhat of a plagiarizer in his *Minerva seu de causis linguae Latinae* (1587), salvaging ideas from Scaliger and Ramus. He claimed that cases are not governed by certain subclasses of verbs, as the more traditional view held, but that cases had their own basic meanings which were the same in every case. His fame, however, rests on his theory of ellipses, in which he again had a forerunner, namely Thomas Linacre (?1460–1524) in his *De emendata structura Latini sermonis* (1524). Both grammarians argued that Latin, in its daily use, deleted units (words, clauses) of sentences in performance because they were implied in the understanding of an utterance anyway. This had its systematic repercussions. Sanctius, for example, did not acknowledge that there were intransitive verbs. He said that in this case a cognate object was being deleted. (It is an argument which reappeared in the grammar of Port Royal (1662) and was claimed by the representatives of early versions of present-day transformational grammar to have prepared their concept of a deep vs. a surface structure of language (Lakoff 1969; → Art. 18).

For Greek grammars and Byzantine linguistics see Percival 1975: 245–47, 259–60 and Robins 1993.

2.2. Humanist grammar writing was a pan-European affair. Italian, (present-day) Belgian, French, Spanish, and English authors have been named. Besides, highly influential grammars with many editions and adaptations appeared in various European countries, for example Antonio de Nebrija's (?1444–1522) *Introductiones Latinae* (1481) in Spain, William Lily's (?1468–?1523) *A Short Introduction of Grammar* and *Brevissima institutio seu ratio grammaticae cognoscendae* (both posthumous 1547) in England, and Philipp Melanchthon's (1497–1560) *Grammatica Latina* (1525/26) in Germany. Other authors were tremendously influential in countries other than their own, like Despauterius in France and Ramus in England. And there were Humanists whose influence was more on the literary than on the grammatical side, like Erasmus of Rotterdam (?1469–1536). All these erudite men were famous for their personal contributions to the new grammaticography, but their works had even more identical properties. This was the four-level approach of *littera, syllaba, dictio*, and *oratio*. With few exceptions (e. g. Despauterius), there was only little discussion of phonetics (*littera, syllaba*) beyond the identification of vowels and consonants, which were named as letters, the centre of grammatical analysis being the definition of word-classes and parts of speech respectively (*dictio*). In them the difference between declinables (*categoremata, significantia*) and indeclinables (*syncategoremata, consignificantia*) was essential. Otherwise the number of word-classes varied from four up to ten in various groupings. The subclass 'noun' embraced substantives and adjectives. In the treatment of verbs, mood, i. e. the manner of speaking, had primacy over tense. The definitions of word-classes oscillated between formal and semantic criteria, most authors mixing them, Ramus using only formal and Melanchthon only semantic ones. How to reconcile a (in present-day terms) structural with a semantic view of grammar can be called the central problem of Humanist grammar (Padley 1976: 30).

The paradigms of grammatical morphology play an important role. Lily, for example, who defined four declinable and four indeclinable parts of speech, listed six cases and seven genders in five declensions, six modes and five tenses in four conjugations, and three concords. He even defined a Latin 'article' (*hic, haec, hoc*).

With few exceptions (e. g. Linacre), only scant attention was paid to syntax (*oratio*). *Suppositum* and *appositum* were replaced by the more logical *subjectum* and *praedicatum*. They were both determined by case, which brings the notion of government into play, and by their position relative to the verb. "As a general rule, however, some of the most basic theoretical terms are left undefined and unexplained, their use simply being taken for granted" (Perceival 1975: 233/34). Although Latin is sometimes compared to the vernaculars (by Despauterius, for example, with French and Dutch, by Lily with English), the idea does not occur to the many authors that languages other than Latin might each have their 'own grammar' and that a special relation might prevail between 'universal' and 'specific' language structures. Latin was *the* language *per definitionem*. Although the concepts used were supposed to be universals, the idea itself and a term expressing it did not enter the minds of Humanist authors. In this respect, linguistic research was still in its pre-scientific phase. It was only Francis Bacon (1561–1626) who distinguished between *literary grammar* and *philosophical grammar*, the former pertaining to national languages, the latter to the "analogy between words and things, or reason" (see Hüllen 1989: 46).

3. The first grammars of vernaculars

3.1. Early grammaticography in Italy took place in the context of the century-long *questione della lingua*, in which scores of linguists discussed which of the various Italian dialects should become the standard language of the country. Tuscan was actually the only natural candidate, because it was the dialect of Dante, Petrarch, and Boccaccio, and because, in the absence of a central power, the Medici court in Florence counted as the most influential one. Leon Battista Alberti (1401–1472), an all-round educated man best known as the architect of the Palazzo Rucellai in Florence, wrote the first vernacular grammar of the country, the *Grammatica della lingua toscana* (finished around 1443, surviving in a 1503 copy, not printed until 1908). His aim was to regularize contemporary Tuscan usage and, thus, to show that it was as rule-governed as classical Latin. His descriptive framework was the concepts and terms of Priscian (Grafton 1997).

Contrary to him and following Giovanni Francesco Fortunio's (ca. 1470–1517) example in his *Regule grammaticali della volgar lingua* (1516), Pietro Bembo (1470–1547), in his

Prose della volgar lingua (published 1525), made the archaic form of Tuscan, as used by the three literate heroes, the guidelines of the new Italian language to be created, which for him was only a written, not a spoken, code (Gensini 1996). For Bembo, modern language usage had to imitate the beauties of their style (Marx 1998). A rhetorical approach to grammar, in the Ciceronian sense, began, one which would prevail for a long time in Italian reflections on language. Both (and many other) grammarians saw the vernacular of their own time as parallel to classical Latin, out of which it developed historically by blending with the 'corrupting' language of invaders, and which they wanted to standardize in the way in which, for example, Cicero had standardized Latin.

As Alberti's grammar was never printed, Antonio de Nebrija's *Grammática de la lengua castellana* (1492) was in fact the first of a vernacular to have public influence (Bahner 1986: 95−100). The political conditions of the work have often been pointed out. The consolidation of the state under Ferdinand and Isabella and the dawn of the Golden Age of the empire demanded the parallel consolidation of a national language. Its standard was not literature, as in the case of Italy, but classical Latin. The supremacy of Castilian was to be ensured by showing that it could be cast in the forms of a traditional Latin grammar, a process by which the vernacular was removed from natural but 'corrupt' everyday usage and made artificial, just as Latin and Greek were artificial to 15th century speakers. Consequently, Nebrija's model grammarians were again Donatus and Priscian and the early Italians, such as Valla and Guarino Veronese. However, Nebrija also had to cope with obvious divergences from Latin, Castilian being a language without declensions. He defined five cases expressed by prepositions, thus identifying Castilian with and at the same time contrasting it to classical Latin. Furthermore, he added the gerund to the traditional eight parts of speech (Tavoni 1998: 32).

For the Portuguese grammars of Fernão de Oliveira (1507−after 1581; publ. 1536) and João de Barros (?1496−1570; publ. 1539/40), see Tavoni 1998: 40−41.

It is significant that the first grammar of French, Jacobus Sylvius' (Jacques Dubois, 1478−1555) *In linguam Gallicam isagωge* (1531) appeared in Latin. The author, a practising doctor, probably relied on the Latin competence of his readers, possibly other doctors or foreign students of the University of Paris, rather than on their knowledge of French. The book contains an elaborate treatment of phonetics and the etymologies of French words, whereas the grammatical part proper consists only of morphology and no syntax. It is likewise significant that the first grammar of French written in the language, Johannes Drosaeus' (Jean Drosée, d. ca. 1550) *Grammaticae quadrilinguis partitiones* (1544) treated French alongside Hebrew, Greek, and Latin, showing that Latin structures were also valid for the other three languages (Padley 1988: 324). Only with Louis Meigret (ca. 1500−ca. 1558) and his *Tretté de la grammare françoeze* (1550) did French grammaticography come into its own. He was interested in the various ways in which the French language appeared in daily use and made the royal court, the law chancelleries, the judicial court, and those educated people who knew the language well the arbiters of correct and elegant usage. For Meigret, they were the ones who had recognized that true French had been "enriched by the profession and experience of Latin and Greek" (Padley 1988: 336). For the first time, a nationalist tone appeared in grammar writing, because the standard of the language was not found in its Latinized character *per se* but in the fact that this character had been adopted by the eminent speakers and institutions of the country (Schmidt 1998).

It mirrors the situation in the region that the early German grammars were written in Latin (in spite of their partly German titles), because the language was not yet in a state to ensure wide readability. Laurentius Albertus (Ostrofrancus, ca. 1540−1583) wrote his *Teutsch Grammatick oder Sprachkunst* (1573) out of love for his native language (as he writes), whose age, richness, and beauty deserved its being treated according to the accepted rules of grammar. He described the older forms of the language as well as its dialects, which gave so many words different meanings. Albertus Ölingerus (fl. 1573), who plagiarized Laurentius Albertus widely in his *Underricht der Hoch Teutschen Sprach: Grammatica seu Institutio verae Germanicae linguae* (1573), meant his grammar to be a tool for teaching German to French speakers. It is amusing that the two authors maintained in Latin that German facilitated the acquisition of foreign languages, and that the famous Humanist Johannes Sturmius

(1507–1589) underlined in his preface the fact that vernaculars should be learnt according to the "rules of the art" (Reifferscheid 1970 [1887]: 301–02, 509–10). For the two authors, these rules were set down by Melanchthon who had faithfully followed Donatus in his grammar (Brekle 1975: 313). Only five years later, Johannes Clajus (1535–1592) made the German dialect of Martin Luther's Bible translation the substance of his work: *Grammatica germanicae linguae, ex Bibliis Lutheri germanicis et aliis eius libris collecta* (1578). At least for the time being, German had come into its own.

The first grammar of the English language, William Bullokar's (ca. 1531–1609) *Bref Grammar for English* (1586), has been called a simple application of Latin norms as they appear in John Colet's (?1467–1519) contribution to Lily's Latin grammar of 1557. But R. H. Robins shows (1994) that this was the only way at that time to give a vernacular its national dignity. It must be proved "a perfect ruled tongue, / conferable to grammar art / as any rules long" (after Robins 1994: 21). The only way for Bullokar to do this was to define in English eight parts of speech and five cases of nouns with the help of prepositions and of word-order relative to the verb, to determine five tenses marked with the auxiliaries *have* and *shall/will*, and to explain articles, missing in Latin, as markers of succeeding nouns. This work was facilitated by the fact that already the Latin examples and paradigms of Lily's grammar had been furnished with English translations (Vorlat 1975: 8). There are cross-references to Latin grammar, but with the replacement of cases by prepositions, the observation of the syntactic function of word-order and the integration of articles into the system William Bullokar also noted deviations from his model language.

The developments in the Czech-speaking region were largely determined by the fact that the intellectual life of the country was fully integrated into the Renaissance and Humanist movements, but that the speakers of the Slavonic languages, nevertheless, had their own interests which differed from those in western Europe. "Rather than foster a rupture between the modern Slavic languages and the older literary language of the Slavs, Slavic grammarians, historians and writers kept alive for centuries the memory of their common origin and patrimony, a memory that was confirmed by the identity of their name (*slověnski*) despite the great diversity of local designations [...]" (Stankiewizc 1984: IX). Since the Counter Reformation with its varying results the individual languages came come into focus as national vernaculars and not only as dialects of an ideal supranational idiom. But even then the awareness of national independence was felt to be under the umbrella of the one Slavonic culture.

Since the 15th century, lively contacts with western developments manifested themselves, for example in lexicography by references to Ambrogius Calepinus (ca. 1435–ca. 1509), Petrus Dasypodius (c. 1490–1559), and Adrianus Junius (Hüllen 1999). Donatus' grammatical terminology had already been introduced in the second half of the 14th century, as can be seen from Claretus de Solentia's (d. 1379) *Vocabulař grammatický*. The Latin grammars of Niccolò Perotto and Philipp Melanchthon were published in special Prague editions (1477 and 1572). That the upgrading of the vernacular profited from the particularly happy reign of a monarch, in this case Charles IV (reigned 1346–78), prefigured the later situation, for example, in Spain with Ferdinand and Isabella (reigned 1479–1516) and in England with Elizabeth I (reigned 1558–1603). That the development of the vernacular depended heavily on a Reformatory assault against the Church, in this case led by Jan Hus (ca. 1370–1415), again prefigured later occurrences, at least in Germany. Around 1410, the Reformer had even published *De orthographia Bohemica*, the pathbreaking book on Czech spelling. Later, the *Kralice Bible* (1579–94) just as the Luther Bible set the linguistic standards in their respective countries for at least two centuries. Contrary to the developments in Germany, however, the Hussite reformation also turned against a second dominant, not indigeneous, language, *viz.* German.

The first Czech grammar, *Grāmatyká Czeská w dwogij stránce* (1533), had Beneš Optat (d. 1559), Petr Gzell (no dates avail.), and Václav Philomates (fl. 16th cent.) as its authors. It is modelled on Donatus. Another grammar, the *Grammatica česká* (MS 1571) written by Jan Blahoslav (1523–1671) and heavily dependent on the former, unfortunately did not see publication until 1857. The author was an archivist of the Czech brethren and, besides elevating the status of the national vernacular, wished to provide preachers with an elaborate work of linguistic reference. The first complete codification of the Czech language, the *Grammaticae bohemicae ad leges naturalis methodi conformatae [...] libri duo* (1603) was written by the Slovak Laurentius Benedicti Nudožerinus (Vavřinec Benedykt Nedožerský, 1555–1615). It followed the principles of Ramus' Latin grammar and used examples from the *Kralice Bible*.

For the development in other West Slavonic languages, see Stankiewicz 1984 and Tavoni 1998: 114–119.

3.2. Just like Humanist grammar writing, vernacular grammar writing was a pan-European affair. Not only were grammars published in the native regions, they also came from other countries and were devoted to 'foreign' languages. In particular, grammars of Italian, the most prestigious of all the vernaculars, appeared in France, in (today) Switzerland and Belgium, and in England. The first comprehensive grammar of French, John Palsgrave's (d. 1554) *Lesclarcissement de la langue francoyse* (1530) (Stein 1998), came from the pen of an English author. The 'indigenous' as well as the 'foreign' grammars were frequently addressed to non-native learners inside and outside their own country. Cristóbal de Villalón (1510–?1562), for example, addressed his *Grammática castellana* (1558), which was published in Antwerp, to the people from Biscay and Navarre, to the French and the Italians, to the Flemish, the English, and the Germans (Tavoni 1998: 40). As only a small section of the native population of any of the countries concerned enjoyed formal education in its own tongue, the need to provide linguistic material to non-native speakers, who either lived together in polyglot regions or crossed language borders in ecclesiastical, martial, or commercial engagements, must have been a powerful incentive for publishing grammars. In 1477, Adam of Rotweil (fl. 1477–1481) published in Venice *Introito e porta*, the first (German-Italian) textbook for foreigners (Hüllen 1999), and by the end of the 16th century the European continent was covered with textbook families which arranged side by side up to eight foreign languages, including Latin as a vernacular.

The grammaticography of vernaculars between the middle of the 15th and the end of the 16th centuries was diversified in the languages covered but still unified in the method of description. In spite of all the personal touches to the grammars and the occasional observation of divergences between Latin and national languages, the old Latin model always loomed in the background. This means that the old system of universals was still adhered to. Subjecting the vernaculars to its rules was the only way of giving them national prestige and a standard. Petrus Ramus and the grammarians who followed him were the most courageous authors in claiming their own method.

The early grammaticography of vernaculars described the status of the languages, in their own time, but did this with the help of a historical comparison. It concerned the old standard of classical Latin, which was supposed to have fallen into corruption and was to be rejuvenated, and it also concerned the newly discovered age of the vernaculars themselves.

4. Grammars of non-European languages

Among the old languages, the Humanist studies were devoted mostly to Latin, with Greek lagging far behind, and among the new ones what could be called the pertinent vernaculars of Europe. This created borderline cases, some of them previous to the 15th century, like Icelandic and Celtic, some contemporary, like Provençal and Catalan, some a little later, like Finnish.

The dominance of the Latin concepts and terms in grammaticography had many causes, among them that they actually fitted, to a certain extent, the vernaculars under description. From historical hindsight, we know that this was so because these languages belonged to the (later so-called) Indo-European group of languages. An exception like Basque, whose first grammar appeared in 1587 (Robins 1990: 117) could not prevail against this.

However, non-European vernaculars were known and treated at that time, too. There are two cases to be considered. The first concerns Hebrew and Arabic, the second other non-European languages.

(i) Hebrew grammaticography (Kukenheim 1951, Bacher 1974, Klijnsmit 1998) lived on in the Jewish tradition of the Provençe and Spain, after 1492 (the expulsion of the Jews) also in other countries (Percival 1986). As one of the three sacred languages and in the context of cabbalistic mysticism (Eco 1993, Kilcher 1998), it also attracted the curiosity of the Humanists. Johannes Reuchlin (1455–1522), for example, wrote *De rudimentis He-*

braica (1506) and *De arte cabalistica* (1517). Nicolas Clenardus (1493/4−1542) published his authoritative *Luąh hadiqduq. Tabula in grammaticen Hebraeam* (1529) (Swiggers 1996). Christian grammarians of Hebrew used Latin grammar as a point of reference for their explanations, and even Jewish grammarians gave Latin paradigms of Hebrew nouns and verbs. This was the case, for example, with Baruch Spinoza (1632−1677) in his *Compendiae grammatices lingvae Hebraeae* (1677), although he did not accept the Latin classification of parts of speech (Gruntfest 1979). "Since the description of Latin determined the grammatical frame-work other languages were described in, Spinoza's terminology doesn't differ very much from the traditional Latin terminology" (Klijnsmit 1986: 10).

Via Hebrew studies in Spain, there was also contact with the rich Arabic grammatical tradition (Versteegh 1977, Versteegh, Koerner and Niederehe 1983; Diem 1983).

(ii) The knowledge of extra-European vernaculars came to Europe in the wake of the great voyages. Although it was for a long time the custom that colonizers and missionaries did not learn the indigenous languages, but kidnapped natives, made them bilingual (often in Europe), and then used them as interpreters (Salmon 1992), so-called missionary linguistics (Hovdhaugen 1996) started to produce descriptive treatments, grammatical and lexical, of South American languages from ca. 1550 on, after Bartholomé de Las Casas (1474−1566) had succeeded in convincing the Spanish missionaries that the Indians of South-America came from Paradise and Babel just as everybody else. However, these treatments often remained secret in the archives of the Church for a long time, and very likely many have not even today been published. Among the authors, the members of the Societas Jesu with their special linguistic training (Caravolas 1994) and also Franciscan monks were outstanding in South America and Asia. The Latin grammars of Manuel Alvares (1526−1582) and Antonio de Nebrija frequently served them as a model of description.

'Missionary linguistics' with reference to North American languages is not much different, except that it is part of the general literature on the voyages between old England and New England and the settlement there (e. g. Koerner 1989). In the case of the Algonkian language, spoken in present-day Carolina, for example, we have the writings of Thomas Harriot (1560−1621) who developed a phonetic script for noting down what he heard, and moreover collected the names of things which he saw (*A Briefe and True Report of the New Found Land of Virginia*, 1588). Sometimes the Algonkian lexemes have no English equivalents, and there is a glimpse of the awareness of linguistic relativity when Thomas Harriot points out that it is 'inconvenient' to list, for example, the Algonkian words for trees (Salmon 1992).

Information about China and the Chinese language reached Europe quite abundantly (Schreyer 1992), but was limited to a description of the nature and the functions of characters.

However, all these linguistic contacts did not break the dominance of Latin in European grammaticography. Reuchlin, for example, adapted the Hebrew partition into nouns, verbs, and particles to the Latin system of word-classes. Even the non-Indo-European Basque was subjected to it (Lafon 1972: 1744−45). We must regard the contact with these exotic languages as an investment in the linguistic future of Europe. Nevertheless, it is noteworthy that this investment started to be amassed during the Renaissance.

5. The historical perspective

5.1. With his *De vulgari eloquentia* (shortly after 1305), Dante Aligheri (1265−1321) is generally credited with having written the first treatise on historical linguistics by turning four observations into a systematic view, namely (i) that all languages are in a constant flux, (ii) that some languages are in closer affinity to one another than others, (iii) that some variants of one language are in closer affinity to one another than others, and (iv) that geographical conditions, like nearness/distance, and temporal conditions, like short/long periods, determine this development. Using such insights and starting from the Biblical story of the one language spoken in Paradise, commonly assumed to be Hebrew, and the dispersion of peoples after the Flood and/or after Babel, he found three language families in the world, as far as he knew it (Germanic in northern Europe, Latin in southern Europe, and Greek in the southeast of Europe and Asia) and fourteen dialects in Italy grouped according to whether they were spoken west of or east of the Apennine mountains.

An early English representative of a similar view is Roger Bacon (1214−1294), who mentioned the various nations in Europe which speak various dialects (Ahrens 1969: 60−61, Kühlwein 1971: 4−10). In his profound discussion of the art of translation he treated dialects as 'languages' on a lower level. Both authors showed remarkable insight into the historical and social development of languages, combining the Greek concept of 'dialect' with the more general concept of 'language'.

For obvious reasons (see above), this historical perspective was focused in an unprecedented way in the Renaissance. This initiated a broad stream of thought in which many people, mostly Humanist grammarians, were involved. Sound changes according to the principle of *permutatio litterarum* between Latin and Greek vs. the contemporary vernaculars were studied systematically, mostly together with the establishment of word etymologies. Structural identities, like word-classes, were identified, and with them also structural divergences, for example, prepositions instead of Latin case markers or analytical constructions with an infinitive and an auxiliary instead of the Latin future tenses. Naturally, the three Romance languages were the primary candidates for this kind of historical and comparative work, which resulted in hypotheses on language history, language contact, and language mixture.

In Italy, it was Bartolomeo Benvoglienti (d. 1486) in his *De analogia huius nominis 'verbum' et quorundam aliorum, et latina lingua graecam antiquiorem non esse* (ca. 1482−85) who founded a philological method of diachronic investigation which was independent of the Bible. The general idea of Italian Renaissance studies, as expressed, for example, by Pietro Bembo, was that Italian grew out of Latin by corruption because of the admixture with the languages of conquerors. Others, like Lorenzo Valla, gave Italian (Tuscan) more independence by stating that Latin 'died' and made the way free for the birth of a new language from various sources. There is also the issue of whether Latin stemmed from (the Aeolian dialect of) Greek or not. One linguist, Giovanni Nanni (Annius, 1432−1502), together with other representatives of the Florence Academy, maintained that Tuscan sprang directly from Etruscan, which sprang from Aramaic, which came from Noah after the Flood. He proved this hypothesis, which freed national Italian from the burden of 'foreign' Latinism, by faked material in his *Commentaria super opera diversorum auctorum de antiquitatibus loquentium* (1498). His combination of linguistic studies with national ambitions proved to be a frequently observed pattern (→ Art. 26).

French Humanists tended to go in the same, rather nationalistic, direction, either by maintaining that Greek, not Latin, was the direct source of French, or that an old version of 'Gallic' was the source of Greek and all the rest. In the *Traicté de la conformité du langage françois avec le grec* (1565), Henri Estienne, for example, placed French on a par with Latin because, for him, both languages originated from Greek. In *[D]e prisca Celtopaedia libri quinque* (1556), Jean Picard (fl. ca. 1556) made the Gauls the original speakers of Greek, out of which came Latin and Italian. Finally, Guillaume Postel (1510−1581) combined the national with the religious tone: he proved by an etymological derivation that 'Gaul' meant 'one who escaped the waters of the Flood', and that, consequently, Noah was a Gaul just like his son Japhet and his grandson Gomer, thus guaranteeing the seniority of French over all known languages of Europe (Tavoni 1998: 53−54). Such genealogies freed French from any dependence on Latin, but also on contemporary Italian.

In Spain, we find as the most common theory, just as in Italy, that the vernacular Castilian developed by way of corruption out of classical or vulgar Latin. There were only differences of opinion on whether the Latinate quality of the present language was stressed as in Nebrija's grammar of Castilian, or whether it was a specific new quality of the spoken language as in the *Diálogo de la lengua* (1535) by Juan de Valdés (fl. 1520−1530). It was Bernardo José Aldrete (1565−1645) who wrote "the closest thing to a historical grammar [of Castilian and Latin] that was produced in Spain at this time" (Tavoni 1998: 58) with *Del Origen, y principio de la lengua castellana o romance que oi se usa en España* (1606).

Apart from these mainstream theories, there was also quite a number of linguists who made out Basque to be the pre-Roman, and thus the originally national, language of Spain. Gregorio López Madera (fl. 1586−

1638), finally, established an autochthonous old-Castilian as Spain's original idiom in his *Discursos de la certidumbre de las reliquias descurbiertas en Granada desde el año 1588 hasta el de 1598* (1601).

For deliberations pertaining to this topic in Portuguese writings, see Tavoni 1998: 58−59.

5.2. Motives for historical and comparative investigations into various languages were quite different in the German-speaking regions (which included today's Flemish and Dutch) from those in the regions of the Romance languages. There was no *questione della lingua* here, at least not before the *Deutsche Sprachgesellschaften* were active in the succeeding century. In the German area, it was the element of foreignness, of the dissimilarity of languages, instead of the Latin similarity, that people had to cope with. The first erudite ambition was therefore to catalogue the languages of this world. This was the motive behind Theodor Bibliander's (Buchmann, ?1504−1565) works (e. g. *De ratione communi omnium linguarum et literarum comentarius*, 1548), although he, the author of a Hebrew grammar and translator of the *Koran*, also intended in them to support Christians against the heathens. He described the mixture of peoples, political and social developments as well as education as the reasons of language change.

This was also the motive behind Konrad Gessner's (1516−1565) *Mithridates: De differentia linguarum, tum veterum, tum quae hodie apud diversas nationes in toto orbe terrarum in usu sunt* (1555), a compilation of twenty-two languages on the basis of The Lord's Prayer. From a more pedagogical point of view, the many polyglot dictionaries and textbooks, both genres serving foreign language learning (Claes 1977, Stankiewicz 1984, Lindemann 1994, Niederehe 1995), again had this motive (Hüllen 1999). Adrianus Junius (1511−1575) wrote his *Nomenclator, omnium rerum propria variis linguis explicata indicans* (1567), i. e. a polyglot, onomasiological and encyclopedic dictionary to prove that Europe, both the Romance and the Germanic areas, was dominated by one homogeneous culture, which could be expressed by many, in this case by six, languages. It was the most popular example of this type of book, which spread like a network over northern Europe. The many cognates which appeared as translations of each other side by side in these nomenclators had their own tendency to create a basis for language comparisons.

For the historical backgrounding of this variety of languages the Bible was used as an explanatory model. Noah's sons Schem, Ham, and Japhet wandered in different directions after the Flood, developing their own dialects and later languages because of the geographical separation of speakers. Although by now distinct as mother-languages, they continued to live on in their later daughter-languages. Thus, after Dante's early example, the idea of language groups again became the subject of discussion. Bibliander, for example, recognized the relationship between Hebrew and Arabic. Hieronymus Megiser (ca. 1453−1618), author of dictionaries and of a collection of plurilingual specimens (The Lord's Prayer again), also wrote *Institutionem linguae turcicae libri quatuor* (1612), i. e. a grammar and a vocabulary of Turkish, recognizing a different linguistic type in this language. There was naturally a general interest in tracing the path of the Japhetic, i. e. one's own, languages. This caused national undertones to appear. The Scythian tradition (Metcalf 1974) was created: Aschkenaz and Gomer inherited their language from their father Japhet; it changed into the Scythian, which covered all of Europe, then into the Phrygian, which was the oldest version of Greek, and then into the Old Italian, Old Celtic, Gothic, and Slavonic languages. The political twist appears when the Celts are declared not to be the ancient Gauls but the forerunners of the Germanic tribes, a view which makes French come from Germanic and not directly from Greek (see above). This is how Adrianus Junius explained the genealogy in *Animadversorum libri* (1556).

Modern linguists see the discovery of the Indo-European language group prefigured in these constructions (Metcalf 1974, Diderichsen 1974, Tavoni 1998: 64−65). There are certainly some features which the achievements of the 16th and the 19th centuries have in common: the assumption of an extinct source language, *lingua matrix*, which lives on in later daughter-languages and can be traced back by etymologies which depend on phonetic similarities and regular changes. The great difference is that, in the earlier century, the belief in the infallible Bible determined what must have happened in history and, moreover, created an evaluative criterion, because the language of Paradise, the mother of all languages, was not only the first but also the most perfect one (→ Art. 18).

Independent from all the theological or historical derivations, the knowledge of the various language groups in Europe was occasionally seen as a positive factor on purely linguistic grounds, which could be instrumentalized for various purposes. Sigismundus Gelenius (Zigmund Hrubý z Jelení, 1497–1554), for example, compiled his *Lexicum symphonum, quo quatuor linguarum Europae familiarum Graecae, scilicet, Latinae, Germanicae ac Slavinicae concordia consonantiaque indicatur* (1537). The author was a Czech Humanist who worked with the publisher Froben in Basle. He listed what would nowadays be called 'cognates', i. e. words whose etymological relationship could be found out by their sound similarity. This was done in order to facilitate language acquisition. His Slavic lexemes, however, represented an artificial language consisting of Czech and Croatian elements. Wherever the parallelism could not be shown in all four languages, he just noted three of them. Gelenius' understanding of etymology was of course time-dependent. He did not, for example, distinguish loan words from others. But his knowledge of European language relations, which for the first time included the Slavonic languages, mostly Czech (Bohemian), and his endeavour to apply them to some practical task, is nevertheless noteworthy (Přívratská 1994).

How close linguistic deliberations, when freed from the major traditions of the Bible, came to nineteenth century findings and even to present-day knowledge of language-groups can be seen from Joseph Justus Scaliger (1540–1609) in his *Diatriba de europaeorum linguis* (1599). He discarded the idea that Hebrew was the Paradisical idiom of mankind and also that Latin descended directly from Greek. He defined eleven language groups, among them four major ones (Latin, Greek, Germanic, and Slavonic) and seven minor ones (Albanian, Tartar, Hungarian, Finnish, Irish, Old British, and Cantabrian (i. e. Basque; see Borst III/1, 1221). His criterion was the word for God with four letters in every idiom (*Deus, Theos, Godt, Boge*). He maintained that these groups were not interrelated, i. e. he saw the differences but not the similarities in his test words. But it is not quite clear whether he really believed in this. At least his work betrays a certain scepticism of the wild ruminations on the migration of peoples after Babel with linguistic repercussions which tended to lead directly to one's own country.

6. References (selected)

Arens, Hans. 1969. *Sprachwissenschaft. Der Gang ihrer Entwicklung von der Antike bis zur Gegenwart.* Second ed. Freiburg and München: Alber.

Auroux, Silvain (ed.). 1992. *Histoire des idées linguistiques. Tome 2: Le développement de la grammaire occidentale.* Liège: Mardaga.

Bacher, Wilhelm. 1974. *Die hebräische Sprachwissenschaft vom 10. bis 16. Jahrhundert.* Amsterdam: Benjamins. Reissue of 1895–1928.

Bahner, Werner. 1986. "Sprachwandel und Etymologie in der spanischen Sprachwissenschaft des Siglo de oro". In: Quilis & Niederehe, 95–116.

Borst, Arno. 1995. *Der Turmbau von Babel.* Vols. I, II/1, II/2, III/1, III/2, IV. Stuttgart: Hiersemann 1957–62. Reissue: München: dtv.

Brekle, Herbert Ernst. 1975. "The seventeenth century". In: Sebeok, 277–382.

Caravolas, Jean-Antoine. 1994. *La didactique des langues. [1] Précis d'histoire I 1450–1700. [2] Anthologie I. À l'ombre de Quintilien.* Montreal: Press de l'Univ. de Montréal/Tübingen: Narr.

Claes, Franz. 1977. *Bibliographisches Verzeichnis der deutschen Vokabulare und Wörterbücher, gedruckt bis 1600.* Hildesheim: Olms.

Diederichsen, Paul. 1977. "The foundation of comparative linguistics: Revolution or continuation?" In: Hymes, 277–306.

Diem, Werner. 1983. "Sekundärliteratur zur einheimischen Arabischen Grammatikschreibung". In: Versteegh, Koerner & Niederehe, 195–250.

Eco, Umberto. 1993. *La ricerca della lingua perfetta nella cultura europea.* [German trans. München: Beck 1994, Engl. trans. Oxford: Blackwell 1996]. Rom & Bari: Laterza.

Gardt, Andreas. 1999. *Geschichte der Sprachwissenschaft in Deutschland.* Berlin: de Gruyter.

Gensini, Stefano. 1996. "Pietro Bembo". In: Stammerjohann, 88–90.

Gruntfort, J. 1979. "Spinoza as a linguist". In: Israel Oriental Studies IX, 105–128.

Guthmüller, B. 1998. *Latein und Nationalsprachen in der Renaissance.* Wiesbaden: Harrassowitz.

Hovdhaugen, Even. 1996. "Missionary grammars – an attempt at defining a field of research". In: Idem, *... and the Word was God. Missionary Linguistics and Missionary Grammar.* Münster: Nodus, 9–22.

Hüllen, Werner. 1989. *'Their Manner of Discourse'. Nachdenken über Sprache im Umkreis der Royal Society.* Tübingen: Narr.

Hüllen, Werner. 1999. *English Dictionaries 800–1700: The Topical Tradition.* Oxford: Clarendon Press.

Hymes, Dell (ed.). 1977. *Studies in the History of Linguistics. Traditions and Paradigms.* Bloomington and London: Indiana Univ. Press.

Kilcher, Andreas. 1998. *Die Sprachtheorie der Kabbala als ästhetisches Paradigma.* Stuttgart/Weimar: Metzler.

Klijnsmit, Anthony J. 1986. *Spinoza and Grammatical Tradition.* Mededelingen vanwege het Spinozahuis, 49. Leiden: Brill.

Klijnsmit, Anthony J. 1998. "Standstill or Innovation?". *Helmontica* 49, 148–49: 39–71.

Koerner, Konrad. 1989. "Towards a history of Amerindian linguistics." In: William Cowan (ed.): Actes du Vingtième Congrès des Algonquinistes. Ottawa: Carleton Univ., 179–192.

Kühlwein, Wolfgang. 1971. *Linguistics in Great Britain. History of Linguistics I.* Tübingen: Niemeyer.

Kukenheim, Louis. 1951. *Contribution a l'histoire de la grammaire grècque, latine et hebräique à l'époque de la Renaissance.* Amsterdam: Noord-Hollandsche Uitg.-Mij.

Lafon, René. 1972. "Basque". In: Thomas A. Sebeok (ed.): Current Trends in Linguistics. Vol. 9 [2]: Linguistics in Western Europe. The Hague and Paris: Marten, 1744–1792.

Lakoff, Robin. 1969. "[Review of] Grammaire générale et raisonner, ou La grammaire du Port-Royal. Ed. by Herbert E. Brekle [...] Stuttgart–Bad Cannstatt 1966." *Language* 45, 343–364.

Lindemann, Margrete. 1994. *Die französischen Wörterbücher von den Anfängen bis 1600. Entstehung und typologische Beschreibung.* Tübingen: Niemeyer.

Matthews, Peter. 1994. "Greek and Latin linguistics". In: Giulio Lepschy (ed.): History of Linguistics. Vol. II: Classical and Medieval Linguistics. London: Longman, 1–133.

Metcalf, George J. 1974. "The Indo-European hypothesis in the sixteenth and seventeenth centuries". In: Hymes, 233–257.

Michael, Ian. 1985. *English Grammatical Categories.* Reissue. Cambridge: Cambridge Univ. Press.

Niederehe, Hans-Josef. 1994. *Bibliografía cronológica de la lingüística, la gramática y la lexicografía del español (Bicres). Desde los comienzos hasta el año 1600.* Amsterdam: Benjamins.

Padley, G. A. 1976–1988. *Grammatical theory in Western Europe 1500–1700.* Vol. 1: *The Latin Tradition*; vol. 2: *Trends in Vernacular Grammar 1*; vol. 3: *Trends in Vernacular Grammar 2.* Cambridge: Cambridge Univ. Pres. 1976, 1985, 1988.

Percival, W. Keith. 1975. "The grammatical tradition and the rise of the vernaculars". In: Sebeok, 231–275.

Perceival, W. Keith. 1986. "The reception of Hebrew in sixteenth-century Europe: The impact of the Cabbala". In: Quilis & Niederehe, 21–38.

Přívratská, Jana. 1994. "Dictionary as a textbook – textbook as a dictionary: Comenius' contribution to Czech lexicography". In: Werner Hüllen (ed.): The World in a List of Words. Tübingen: Niemeyer, 151–158.

Quilis, Antonia & Niederehe, Hans-J. (eds.). 1986. *The History of Linguistics in Spain.* Amsterdam: Benjamins.

Reifferscheidt. 1970. Albert Oelinger [and] Laurentius Albertus. Allgemeine Deutsche Biographie. Bd. 24. Berlin 1887. Reissue: Berlin: Duncker & Humblot, 301–02 [and] 509–10.

Ribhegge, W. 1998. "Latein und die nationalen Sprachen bei Erasmus von Rotterdam, Martin Luther und Thomas More". In: Guthmüller, 151–180.

Robins, Robert H. 1990. *A Short History of Linguistics.* Third edition. London: Longman.

Robins, Robert H. 1993. *The Byzantine grammarians: their place in history.* Berlin: Mouton de Gruyter.

Robins, Robert H. 1994. "William Bullokar's 'Bref Grammar for English': Text and context". In: Günther Blaicher and Brigitte Glaser (eds.): Anglistentag 1993 Eichstätt. Proceedings. Tübingen: Niemeyer, 19–31.

Salmon, Vivian. 1992. "Thomas Harriot (1560–1621) and the English origins of Algonkian linguistics". *Historiographia Linguistica* XIX: 1, 25–56.

Schmitt, C. 1998. "Der Anschub der französischen Volkssprache durch das Latein im Zeitalter von Humanismus und Renaissance". In: Guthmüller, 117–130.

Schreyer, Rüdiger. 1992. *The European Discovery of Chinese (1550–1615) or The Mystery of Chinese Unveiled.* Amsterdam: Stichting Neerlandistick.

Sebeok, Thomas. A. (ed.). 1975. *Current Trends in Linguistics. Vol. 13: Historiography of Linguistics.* The Hague/Paris: Mouton.

Stankiewicz, E. 1984. *Grammars and Dictionaries of the Slavic Languages from the Middle Ages up to 1850. An annotated bibliography.* Berlin: Mouton.

Swiggers, Pierre. 1996. "Nicolas Clenardus". In: Stammerjohann, 195–96.

Stammerjohann, Harro (ed.). 1996. *Lexicon Grammaticorum. Who's Who in the History of World Linguistics.* Tübingen: Niemeyer.

Stein, Gabriele. 1997. *John Palsgrave as Renaissance Linguist.* Oxford: Clarendon Press.

Tavoni, Mirko. 1998. "Renaissance linguistics." In: Giulio Lepschy (ed.): *History of Linguistics. Vol. III: Renaissance and Early Modern Linguistics.* London: Longman, 1–148.

Versteegh, Cornelius H. M. 1977. *Greek Elements in Arabic Linguistic Thinking.* Leiden: Brill.

Versteegh, Cornelius H. M. & Konrad Koerner & Hans-Josef Niederehe. 1983. *The History of Linguistics in the Near East.* Amsterdam: Benjamins.

Vorlat, Emma. 1975. *The Development of English Grammatical Theory 1586−1737.* Leuven: Univ. Press.

Werner Hüllen, Universität Essen (Deutschland)

16. Theories of language in the European Enlightenment

1. Problems and methods
2. Semantic primes and mental language
3. Enunciational epiphanies: the parts of speech
4. Enunciational epiphanies: analytical order and language typology
5. Conclusions
6. References

1. Problems and methods

The problem of universals in eighteenth-century philosophy is in many ways related to the theory of the formation of ideas and the status of concepts, and to the classic and medieval debate on this subject. From this point of view, the canonical discussion of the problem is found in John Locke's *Essay on Human Understanding*. However, the theory of ideas is only one of the fields where the question of language universals, as we intend it today, should be investigated. The presence of observable regularities in all natural languages is a theme common to many different epistemological areas. In the present study, two such areas will be examined. The first is the research on cognitive psychology. When eighteenth-century philosophers discuss language, this usually happens in the context of a theory of cognitive representations. The main purpose of studying the structure and functioning of language is to ascertain the existence of universal mental predispositions. The second epistemological domain is that of grammatical studies. The existence of invariants common to all known languages is the fundamental assumption behind the scientific project of a general grammar, pursued in the course of the eighteenth century along the lines of the Port-Royalist program. This project was not necessarily incompatible with cognitive theories belonging to the empiricist tradition which, in fact, were often integrated in their positions by philosophers who pursued the Port-Royalist program. Studies of cognitive psychology and grammar theories will be discussed, respectively, in the second and third section. This is, of course, an entirely conventional division, since, in reality, the two areas are closely interrelated if not juxtaposed.

Anthropological theories is another area that addresses, albeit indirectly, the problem of universals. Philosophers describe the origin and development of language according to modalities common to all natural languages. They explain the various stages of their formation and transformation on the basis of 'natural' and therefore universally human, psychological mechanisms, treating them as largely predictable historical processes. On this subject, which cannot be dealt with in the present article, a vast literature is extant (see especially Gessinger & Rahden 1989).

We do not find a true linguistic typology before the comparatist program, whose beginnings are usually identified with Friedrich Schlegel's essay *Ueber die Sprache und Weisheit der Indier*. But the observation of variants, and the characterization of languages on the basis of these variants, is also a transversal practice found in different areas of eighteenth-century culture, from grammar theories to the theory of mind, anthropology, or literary theory. We shall deal with this aspect in the fourth section. It is worth anticipating, however, that the debate on the unity/diversity of languages, in this period, is never split between the extreme positions that were to develop over the next two centuries (universality of linguistic structures vs. linguistic relativism, innatism vs. learning). Certainly, the very notion of language universals implies the existence of categories that are prior to the empirical performance of sentences, and this is undoubtedly true for eighteenth-century language philosophers as well. The principles of general grammar, writes Nicolas Beauzée in an often cited passage of his *Grammaire générale*, precede language, are immutable and general, and the purpose of specific grammars is to relate "the arbitrary institutions and the usage of idioms to the general principles of language" (Beauzée 1767: I, X). Yet, it is precisely the conception of *a priori* current in Enlightenment philosophy that serves to mitigate the opposition between the universality of linguistic categories and the specificity of their actualisations in the various languages. Up to Kant's philosophical revolution, the notion of *a priori* does not imply the idea of unconditioned. This is clearly explained, for example, by authors such as Johannes Heinrich Lambert and Johann Gottfried Herder. *A priori* and *a posteriori* are correlated terms, which refer simply to the order in which we know (Lambert 1764: I, §§ 636−637). The *a priori* is a *prius* in regards to the *posterius* only in purely empirical terms; it is its condition, but it is not an unconditioned condition (Herder 1799: I, 22−23, 70) or, in Kantian terms, a transcendental condition. In our case, this means that language universals are certainly *a priori* in the order of causation (given structures of the human mind generate given linguistic structures which in turn are reflected in actual languages) but are *a posteriori* in the order of discovery (from the study of sentences in natural languages we infer the deep structures of language and from these the structure of the mind). They are *a priori* in the sense that they are part of the human onto- and phylogenetic heritage, but they can be identified only inductively, on the basis of a comparison between languages or the analysis of a single language. We will return to this question in the second section of the article, trying to explain the apparent contradiction between the idea of a general grammar as an inventory of necessary principles and the definition of language universals as potentialities that are variously realized, or not realized, in natural languages.

Even in eighteenth-century anthropological research the distinction between nature (*a priori*) and culture (*a posteriori*) does not imply any theoretical incompatibility between the two components of human identity. The problem was to ascertain what sort of animal is the man created by God, or man in the state of nature, and what he has become through a process of acculturation whose beginnings are lost in the mists of time. *A priori* and *a posteriori* are, respectively, structural and acquired elements. In the same way, within the study of language, there is no contradiction between a research aimed at ascertaining characteristics so regular as to be considered universal and the description of the ways in which those characteristics manifest themselves historically in speech. Therefore, the identification of invariants can coexist without contradiction with the investigation of diversities. Linguistic typology, as Dominicy argues (1992: 435), is not incompatible with a general grammar, on the contrary it serves to reinforce the connection between the theory of ideas and the data produced by linguistic observation.

2. Semantic primes and mental language

The notion of the arbitrariness of the sign, that Locke had taken from the previous tradition, giving it a much more radical status and placing it at the centre of his semiotic theory, soon became a commonplace in all discussions on language. At the same time, however, the scientific project of a general grammar was continued and enriched, and this occurred without any great theoretical and terminological breaks with the previous century. The procedures for the analysis of mental contents presented in the *Essay on Human Understanding* merge with the method for analysing ideas and signs introduced by Condillac. The influence of Locke's philosophy does not hinder the development of grammatical studies, to the point that even some theoreticians of the 'rationalist' general grammar, such as Du Marsais, can declare themselves his followers. This apparent paradox − the convergence between a notion of the arbitrariness of language and the search for its universal structures − deserves some explanation.

The notion of the arbitrariness of the sign, which is the core of Locke's semiotic theory, was one of the theoretical offsprings of the seventeenth-century scientific revolution. One of its sources was the critique of the essentialist metaphysics of the scholastic tradition: Hans Aarsleff (1982: 56), for example, has indicated a precedent in Robert Boyle's treatise on *The Origin of Forms and Qualities* (1666). Another source was the rejection of all notions of an original conformity between *signum* and *signatum* upheld by the *Logosmystik* tradition. This double rejection conditions Locke's entire theory of meaning (Formigari 1988: 99−131). In the eighteenth century, the theory of arbitrariness proves functional to the epistemological and political revolution of European Enlightenment. On account of its intimate relationship with knowledge via the formation of ideas, and of its constitutive power in their regard, language can both hinder and promote the procedures of scientific discovery and the development of knowledge, it can both hide and reveal prejudice and fraud, thus preventing or encouraging the emancipation of civil and political society. On the other hand, the omnipresence of the notion of arbitrariness in eighteenth-century philosophical literature can be misleading. In spite of the diffusion and the variety of uses of the notion, there are other aspects of linguistic philosophy that, implicitly or explicitly, limit the arbitrariness of signs. Some of these limitations are social in origin, and therefore contingent and acquired; others, however, are structural, deeply rooted in the human mind, and more in general, in the inclinations of the human psyche. The latter are the ones that are most germane to the present discussion.

To properly address the question of the invariants, we must go to the roots of Locke's notion of arbitrariness. According to Locke, there are no real essences to which the meaning of terms can be referred or, if there are, they are inaccessible to us. The representations on the basis of which we think and argue (ideas) are arbitrarily constituted: "when we quit particulars, the generals that rest are only creatures of our own making; the general nature being nothing but the capacity they are put into, by the understanding, of signifying or representing many particulars. For the signification they have is nothing but a relation that, by the mind of man, is added to them" (Locke 1690: III, iii, 11). This may be more or less true depending on whether we are dealing with natural objects or objects that have no model in nature, but it remains valid in any case. As for natural objects: "the sorting of them under names is the workmanship of the understanding, taking occasion, from the similitudes it observes amongst them, to make abstract general ideas, and set them up in the mind, with names annexed to them, as patterns or forms" (Locke 1690: III, iii, 13). As for objects that do not have a natural model, the intellect "unites and retains certain collections, as so many specific ideas; whilst others, that as often occur in nature, and are as plainly suggested by outward things, pass neglected, without particular names or specifications" (Locke 1690: III/v/3). Having established these premises, the risk was that of reducing language to a pure aggregation of names designating private mental representations. How does Locke's "speaker" avoid this danger?

There are various kinds of limits to the constitutive power of language, as I have noted above. There are conditions imposed by the norms of linguistic usage, clusters of meanings deposited in natural languages to which the speaker is bound. These are contingent and acquired conditions. It is on these conditions that Locke particularly insists, as shown, incidentally, by the examples he adopts. They consist of pragmatic factors, social motivations, which induce speakers to assign names to classes of objects, to select given traits and organize them linguistically. These factors can all be classified under the notion of *habit*, later introduced by David Hume to explain the possibility of linguistic communication. But beyond these contingent limitations, there are also structural conditions that limit arbitrariness.

A first condition is the existence of invariant meanings, that is, meanings that cannot be further analysed. They are expressed by terms that are indefinable but incontrovertible, and are not vulnerable to misunderstanding due to differences between languages. Such are the names of simple ideas, to use again one of Locke's examples. These primary experiences that originate in inner and outer experience are the same for all sane men, and the words that designate them are the only ones that have a non-arbitrary reference. In eighteenth-century cognitive psychology the existence of semantic universals having their origin in sensorial experience is never questioned. Content universals (which we shall call "semantic primes", borrowing the expression from Goddard 1996) are paramount among the factors that make understanding possible. The priority of natural signs over artificial signs — a recurrent theme in the description of the origin and therefore of the nature of language — is an extension of this principle: interjections, physiognomic and pathognomonic expressions, have the immediacy of the names of simple ideas, they immediately express primary experiences such as pain, love, joy, desire, disgust, etc. Gestures, while they may be used to designate more complex things, have the same ostensive power, which preserves them from arbitrariness. Thus, notwithstanding the insistence on the arbitrariness of linguistic signs, the continuity between natural and institutional signs remains, with rare exceptions, a thesis that is taken for granted. Even when it is questioned (as, for example, in Herder's *Abhandlung über den Ursprung der Sprache* [1772]), the properties of things are still considered to be the first signs through which reality communicates with man. They represent already a primary source of information on the world, and guarantee an iconic basis to institutional signs. Thought is the linguistic elaboration of these semantic primes.

Another limitation to the arbitrariness of language is the fact that the elaboration of data, their symbolical transformation, and the manipulation of symbols occur thanks to universal mechanisms. Arbitrariness is limited to the semantics of names, which is founded on classifications of *realia* that are greatly influenced by pragmatic factors, but does not pertain to the procedures through which linguistically expressible thought is generated. In the cognitive psychology of the Enlightenment these procedures are widely accepted as universal and integrated in a theory of faculties.

In commenting on, and in trying to explain, the fact that the *Grammaire* of Port-Royal is so lacking in references to and comparisons with languages other than French, Raffaele Simone observes that these languages are used as 'metalanguages': "the use of this metalinguistic technique implies that aspects that are not superficially evident in a language can only be brought to light through the use of another language where, on the contrary, they are present" (Simone 1996: 101). In other words, the deep structure of language can be inferred from the study of a single language, with other languages occasionally employed as analytical tools. This holds also for eighteenth-century grammars. Language comparisons are not an integral part of theory, since this is considered to be sufficiently supported by the study of a single language and by occasional metalinguistic references. This is why the general grammars of the time have so few references to extra-European languages, in an age that already had abundant documentary evidence at hand and where the peculiarity of alien verbal forms was increasingly drawing the attention of scholars. Beauzée lists sixteen languages on which he supposedly based his general grammar (1767: I, 15), but, in fact, he focuses his analysis on French, using Latin now and then as a metalanguage. Thus, the comparison with alien languages is not constitutive of the theory. The dominant idea is that there is a *potential* universality of grammatical forms, inherent in (mental) language, and that this universality is independent of its actualisation in the various languages.

3. Enunciational epiphanies: the parts of speech

Barrie E. Bartlett (1972: 16) describes very appropriately the relation between language universals and the contingency of natural languages, when he says that the *langue* is nothing but a sub-system of the possibilities inherent in the *langage*, including phonetic possibilities. In other words, within a general grammar, language universals should be seen as the potentialities of language, contingently actualized in natural languages. The purpose of general grammars is to provide a critical exposition of the necessary elements of language, to be used as the basis for the study of all natural languages (as indicated by the subtitle of Beauzée's classic *Grammaire générale* [1767]). This means that it must describe the mechanisms that mediate between the universality of thought forms and the contingency of natural grammars. In Bartlett's terms (1972: 17), we could say that general grammars describe the actualising tools employed by the various natural languages to express the necessary categories and relationships of language.

Thus, the epiphanies of thought in speech take different forms. Sentences never reflect univocally the articulation of thought, if only because the spoken or written sequence is linear, it develops in time, whereas the act of thought is a unity whose parts appear simultaneously. The strategies used in expression and communication never actualize the forms of verbal thought univocally. They embody it in different ways.

But even while complicated by the diversity of natural languages, the homology between logic and language remains undisputed up to the middle of the nineteenth century, and is favoured by a view of logic as the logic of ideas (see Auroux 1993: 180), that is, as a metalanguage of the natural language, as a description of the structures that underlie linguistically expressible thought.

This is the ultimate foundation of general grammar, which is nothing but the critical exposition of the procedures of natural logic

(Beauzée 1767: I, xxxii), reconstructed through its empirical linguistic manifestations. Having natural languages as their starting point, Beauzée and the other *grammairiens-philosophes* can use the inductive method even while affirming the principles of grammar to be *a priori*. In a passage of the preface to the *Grammaire générale* (1767: I, x−xi), Beauzée clearly illustrates this issue. Grammatical science is posterior to natural languages because linguistic usage must exist *before* we reduce it to the system of language.

One of the aspects of Enlightenment language theory that better expresses this logical-grammatical homogeneity is the theory of the parts of speech, "the nucleus of the theoretical structure of Western grammar" (Auroux 1988: 80), a discovery "as solid, stable, and fundamental in the history of humanity as Pythagoras's theorem" (Auroux 1993: 27). All languages must possess grammatical categories, since in all languages specific traits of thoughts must have corresponding traits in the spoken sequence, in agreement with the criterion of grammaticality.

This principle may very well be defined as a language universal. But while all languages have speech parts, not all languages have *all* the parts of speech: in other words, not all languages actualize universals in the same way. This fact must be explained in the context of general grammar; the peculiarities of natural languages must be traced back to common linguistic functions, related to the analytic expression of thought (Beauzée, 1767: I, 234). In view of the fact that not all languages have the article, for example, Beauzée concludes that the article is not essential to speech. What is essential is the *function* of articles, which is actually an adjectival function: it serves to focus the attention of the mind on a given entity, or group of entities, to whom the general name is applied. It is worth stressing this distinction between grammatical categories, which are contingent, and their function, which is universal. Taking Beauzée's argument to the extreme it would be possible to state that in fact no language has articles. Some may express *through* articles the adjectival function that is common to all. No matter how peculiar are the modes in which a given natural language actualizes a universal function of language, no natural language will ever create a new part of speech. What is essential in a natural language is essential in all languages, since the foundation of them all is reason, which manifests itself through the identity of the principles necessary to the analysis and communication of thought (Beauzée 1767: I, 310). The difficulty that arises from the peculiarities of certain languages is overcome by reducing a given part of speech to a more general function, as in the case of the article; or, alternatively, by classifying the essential functions of the parts of speech as virtual or actual, according to the case. Thus, for example, temporality is essential to the verb, but in some languages, such as Chinese, it remains at a virtual stage.

An even more explicit confirmation of the view of language universals as virtual elements variously realized in natural languages can be found in the theory of syntax. The relations instituted between words are the analogue of the relations that exist between the ideas that those words express (Beauzée 1767: I, 3). Consider, for example, the grammatical actualization of the number: what is essential is the (universal) use of singular and plural. The dual, found in some languages, is redundant. Plurality pertains to *two* as much as to *one thousand*, why then not distinguish as many specific pluralities as there are numbers? (Beauzée 1767: II, 86, 87). Consider declension, that is the possibility of varying the inflections of words in order to add an accessory idea to the main one. Various languages actualize in contingent ways the necessary function of expressing accessory ideas: some through the use of prepositions, others through the use of cases, and others through a mixture of both. What is more, cases having the same name in different languages do not necessarily have the same value (Beauzée 1767: II, 161−162).

Such a theory of the parts of speech evidently presupposes a theory of ideas having a strong rationalistic bent. The system of ideas is at one with reason, and language is its epiphenomenon. Anything that diverges from it must be ascribed to usage, to the impact of emotional factors that do not pertain to grammatical science, but at best to the art of rhetoric. We have illustrated an extreme example of this position in Beauzée's *Grammaire*. We shall now use Condillac's Grammar, the first part of his *Cours d'études* (1775), to see how the sensualist approach to the relationship between thought and language modifies, to some extent, and only a limited one, the issue. This approach questions the existence of a fixed system of logical-ontological categories, but does not exclude the fact that common potentialities be actualized in the various natural languages. Condillac's 'psychologism' (if we may anachronistically employ a term that will enter philosophical usage only a century later) is particularly evident in his notion of languages as analytical instruments. This means that languages are tools that allow us to section, distinguish, and order in succession mental contents, which we perceive as unities. They allow us to move from the simultaneity of thought to the linearity of language. The mind's eye is akin to the eye of the body: in their natural state, our thoughts are confused pictures. We are able to distinguish their parts only because we have learned the art of ordering in succession ideas that arise all together in the same moment. This art was born with languages and, like languages, it has been gradually refined (Condillac 1775: 132−133).

The parts of speech are means employed by language to analyze thought. They are not born at once together with language, but develop gradually, as the needs and the knowledge of individuals and communities expand. Condillac had already described this genesis in the *Essai sur l'origine des connoissances humaines* (1746: II/i, 9−10). Therefore, in his Grammar the diversity of the actualizations found in the various languages seems to be less of a problem for him than for Beauzée, who on this subject had adopted a theory that was "too powerful" (Auroux 1988: 88) and therefore more vulnerable to falsification. But the empirical origin and the purely instrumental character ascribed by Condillac to the parts of speech do not imply for him their arbitrariness. On the contrary, their necessity derives precisely from their semiotic nature. Because words are the signs of our ideas, the system inherent in natural language must be based on the system inherent in our knowledge. Thus, languages have different types of words only because our ideas belong to different classes; they have means to connect ideas only because the only way we think is by connecting ideas (Condillac 1775: 27).

The formation of ideas, as the formation of the corresponding morpho-syntactic links, follows general psychological laws that regulate the thoughts of all men. The needs that lead us to analyze thought are common to all, and the means used for this analysis are the same everywhere, more or less sophisticated according to the cultural level of the speakers, but basically subject to the same rules in all languages. Studying grammar means studying the methods used by human beings to analyze thought: the language system is imprinted in each speaker ("le système du langage est dans chaque homme qui parle" [Condillac 1775: 63]).

As we can see, the fact that Condillac applies the genetic method to the theory of the formation of grammatical categories, thus introducing into the general grammar the contingency of historical events and anthropological evolution, does not lead to the denial of the existence of universal mechanisms underlying the parts of speech. Certainly, the nature of universals is different: in sensualist theories they are not conceived of as a set of innate mechanisms but as a set of mental operations that are acquired and refined in the course of philogenetic development. But this is not enough to undermine the homology of language and thought. On this issue, therefore, the distinction between 'rationalist' and 'empiricist' grammars is not at all clearcut. This and other similar distinctions, while undoubtedly useful, must be applied with caution. Philosophical rationalism does not necessarily imply a 'transcendental' notion of grammatical structures, nor, on the other hand, does the use of the genetic method imply their contingency. I will limit myself to two authors, Lambert and Herder, who illustrate this point well. Lambert, usually considered as a representative of the rationalist tradition, albeit an eclectic version of it, tends to acknowledge that the 'metaphysical' impotence of languages, that is, their inability to faithfully reproduce the ontological and logical structure of reality, is in fact functional to their semantic power. Herder, usually celebrated as the precursor of the romantic idea of *Weltbild* and the father of the genetic method, affirmed that the parts of speech are inherent in fundamental metaphysical categories.

In *Neues Organon* (1764), there are various sections where Lambert discusses the parts of speech, questioning to what extent they represent classes of things and relationships between classes and to what extent, instead, they are arbitrary. The existence of parts of speech in all languages is essential, in the sense that in them we find the manifestation of the variations, determinations and relationships of the *realia*. But, in actual natural languages anomaly reigns. This would be clearly evidenced by a comparison with an ideal metalanguage, a comparison which is impossible and which may be substituted by a comparative study of languages (Lambert 1764: III, § 127).

In the absence of this ideal language, then, Lambert bases his analysis largely on German. Here, too, Greek, Latin, and, occasionally, Hebrew are only used as metalanguages. The study of the way in which psychological and pragmatic elements influence the morphosyntactic structure of the various languages serves as a systematic discursive counterpoint to his description of the general grammar. The gap between the actual morpho-syntactic structures (of natural languages) and the ideal structure (of language) is presented by Lambert not only as inevitable but, in the last analysis, as functional to the development and the productivity of natural languages (1764: III, § 277 ff.).

Arbitrariness, which creates this discrepancy between the structure of natural languages and the metaphysical structure of reality, is what gives the speaker freedom of usage and derivation. If we tried to modify the morpho-syntactic structure of our language in order to reduce the arbitrary element in favor of the metaphysical one, we would end up linking words to rigid meanings without eliminating the possibility of errors (Lambert 1764: III, § 279). The impossibility of reforming natural languages is due to their specific structure, subsumed in the notion of *linguistic type*, which we shall deal with in the fourth section of this essay.

As for Herder, in a passage of the *Metakritik* (1799), he describes the origin of the various parts of speech and shows how the fundamental metaphysical categories (being, force, space, time) constitute the texture of all languages.

"Die ersten Begriffe von Sein, Dasein, Fortdauer, Kraft gaben selbständige Worte (*nomina and pronomina substantiva*) mit Vor- und Zusätzen des Ortes und der Zeit, als ihren Bestimmungen (Präpositionen) und Modifikationen (*casus*). Die an ihnen bemerkten Eigenschaften gaben unselbständige Worte (*nomina und pronomina adiectiva*) die Dasselbe oder ein Andres in Geschlechtern, Gattungen, endlich der Art nach bezeichneten; welche Ähnlichkeiten und Unterschiede, als selbständige Begriffe gedacht, neue Bestandwörter mit bestimmenden Artikeln und Endungen wurden. Die in den Dingen bemerkte Kraft schuf sich gleichfalls ihren Ausdruck, *verba*. Die *verba substantiva* Sein, Werden u. f. bezeichnen diese Kraft selbständig; thätige und leidende *Verba* weisen sie auf ihren Gegenstand hin; so ward die Welt der Vernunft, d. i. der Ursachen und Wirkungen bezeichnet. Das Maas der Dinge endlich drücken Zahlwörter, Grade und mancherlei andre Partikeln aus; der Grundbau der Rede in allen Sprachen ist Typus eines zusammenhängenden Acts des wirkenden Verstandes" (1799; II: 306–307).

Certain features of natural languages, so constant as to be considered universal features of language, are organizing principles, which are at work already in pre-linguistic experience. The morphology of natural languages is nothing but the gradual actualization of these forms. These are so deeply introjected in our linguistic conscience that they are perceived as *a priori* forms, which indeed they are in regards to the formation of language.

The case of Herder, like that of Condillac, shows that the method of genetic reconstruction is not at all incompatible with the thesis of the universality of deep structures. All the philosophers of the time rely on a representational theory of the mind, which goes hand in hand with a notion of thought as mental language. Reconstructing the genesis of the formal conditions of representation and studying their presence in natural languages are one and the same process.

This sort of psychologism tends to validate the general laws of language by comparing them to the representational procedures of the mind, to trace the origin of fundamental linguistic categories to pre-verbal cognitive processes. Semiotic analysis is, therefore, an indispensable tool for the production of a "natural history of the soul", and, indeed, the psychological literature of the last decades of the century is an inexhaustible collection of observations on language (Formigari 1994: chap. 4). If we browse through the issues (1783–1793) of the *Magazin zur Erfahrungsseelenkunde*, edited by Carl Philipp Moritz, and follow the column "Sprache in psychologischer Rücksicht", we can readily notice how essays on themes pertaining to "psychological general grammar" (representational motivation of impersonal verbs vs. tendency to personification, the origin of prepositions in modalities of corporeal experience, the use of deixis in relation to spatial and temporal representational activity, use of pronouns and *Selbstgefühl*, etc.) exist side by side with discussions of linguistic pathologies (deaf-and-dumbness, aphasia), i.e., cases where what is severed is precisely the connection between the representational power of the mind and the verbal articulation of the world of representations.

4. Enunciational epiphanies: analytical order and language typology

But let us return to the *grammairiens-philosophes* to discuss another aspect of their theories, which can be subsumed under the headings of language universals and typology. It is the question of analytic order (*ordre analytique*), this mental prototype to which the order of words can be related. Analytic order can be variously actualized in different constructions. Thus, the question of the gap between the universality of language and the specificity of natural languages resurfaces in the debate on natural word order and the use of inversions. Does the organization of the parts of speech in the sentence have to conform to a "natural" hierarchy characteristic of logical categories? does it have to be the image of the succession of ideas? or can it model itself on variable and empirically determined cognitive forms? The issue has important anthropological consequences: is it possible to claim that different people think and feel differently, according to the different word order found in their respective languages? This position lends itself, among other things, to nationalist considerations on the superiority of one's language over that of one's neighbors.

We find echoes of the debate even in the field of literature: what are the limits to stylistic freedom? What are the limits that we must set on the subversive power of 'lower' faculties in fictional works? Significantly, it is in a famous handbook of rhetoric, Lamy's *Rhétorique* (in the 1701 edition), as Ulrich Ricken has noted (1994: 113–114), that the debate is expanded to take into account the problem of the relation of language and thought in general. Speech must analyze a simultaneous whole, a complex mental image (since this is how thought manifests itself in our mind), translating it into successive verbal elements. If a greater liberty in the disposition of verbal elements can achieve this result more effectively, then the natural word order must be considered more like a burden, to which languages like French, which lacks inflections, are subject, but others, such as Latin for example, are not.

I refer the reader to Ricken (1994: chap. 9, 111–133) for a concise outline of the debate, in which the greatest philosophers and men of letters of the time took part, and for a brief note on its antecedents in the *querelle des anciens et des modernes* of the former century. For a more exhaustive discussion, I refer the reader to a previous work by the same author (Ricken 1978: 83–169), which remains to date the most systematic study on this subject.

Let us consider once again the Grammars of Beauzée and Condillac as examples of comparable but significantly different positions. We have seen how the positions of grammarians on the question of verbal categories could hardly be classified in any clear-cut way under the headings of "rationalism" and "empiricism" (→ § 3). On the question of word order, however, the two positions are more clearly differentiated, at least in regards to the consequences that the two schools derive from it.

Beauzée defines analytic order as the order where ideas constituting one and the same thought are arranged in speech in such a way as to reflect the relations that connect the ideas to each other and to the thought as a whole (Beauzée 1767: I, vii). Analytic order, continues Beauzée, is both the result of the analysis of thought and the basis for the analysis of speech in all languages. Sense perception is the natural prototype which generates words in all languages (Beauzée 1767: II, 2). It is the compass that stirs us through the specific usages of natural languages (Beauzée 1767: II, 65, 77). It is the only mechanism that can guarantee the correspondence between mental and verbal language. It is a necessary and universal rule, the immutable touchstone of all possible languages (Beauzée 1767: II, 467–468).

In natural languages this prototype is actualized in two different ways. The analytic order can be faithfully reproduced through direct construction, which corresponds to the actual succession of the ideas. Alternatively, in the case of inverted construction, the analytic order can be suggested through the use of inflections, which morphologically relate the words to one another according to the analytic order. For example, in the Latin sentence *Diuturni silentii finem odiernus dies attulit*, the agreement of the genitive case is what makes it possible to place the adjective *diuturni* before the noun *silentii*, in spite of the fact that in the analytic order the noun comes first. The expression *diuturni silentii* can precede *finem*, even though the latter is the cause of the oblique inflection of *silentii diuturni* and therefore precedes the expression in the analytic order (Beauzée 1767: II, 468–471). But whatever procedures are employed, the analytic order remains the deep structure of mental language and, therefore, the original rule of all languages (Beauzée 1767: II, 465). Beauzée, like Du Marsais — and against the opinion of Charles Batteux, Condillac, Diderot (which shall be later followed by Court de Gébelin) — holds for direct construction as the only one which adequately actualizes the universal prototype of all sentences.

Condillac had already refuted the theory of direct construction in the *Essai sur l'origine des connoissances humaines* (1746: 92−94), and returned to the question in the *Grammaire* (1775: 305−310). Here, he even attacks the use of the term 'inversion', which suggests an order that goes contrary to the natural order, whereas in fact it is simply different from the direct one. Once again, Condillac supports his argument with the consideration that thought, being simultaneous, has no order whatsoever that can be considered natural to it. Thought follows neither the direct nor the inverted order. The mind grasps simultaneously all the ideas it considers, and this is how we would voice them if it were possible to replicate this mental procedure. The two orders (direct and inverse) are both equally 'natural' (Condillac 1775: 306−307).

All languages use inversions; in many cases, in fact, these are necessary and, for this reason, they must become natural ("et si elles sont nécessaires, il faut bien qu'elles deviennent naturelles"; Condillac 1775: 310). The fundamental difference between Beauzée and Condillac's positions turns precisely on this point: the distinction between what *is* natural and, therefore, constitutes a universal model, and that which *becomes* universal because it is expedient to the function of organizing the experience that pertains to language.

The rationalist theory of natural order (the "opinion ancienne", the "doctrine reçue", as Beauzée calls it), had served as the basis for a classification of languages which was to be very successful. Gabriel Girard, in his *Vrais principes de la langue française* (1747), had divided languages into three classes: analogous languages, such as French, Italian, Spanish, which follow prevalently the direct order; transpositional languages, such as Latin and the Slavic languages, which use the inverted order with the help of inflections; and mixed languages, such as Greek. He had also listed a series of internal variants to these classes.

In such a less than rigorous classification even the notion of natural order loses importance. In any case, Girard's classification cannot be considered a true typology. This term does not apply even to purely taxonomic classifications, such as the monumental, four-volume study, *Mithridates*, by J. Ch. Adelung (1732−1806), later continued by Johann Severin Vater (1772−1826), where languages are divided according to lexical criteria in mono- and polysyllabic (see Koerner 1995 for a concise history of the origins of language classification). In any case, even classifications that come closer to the notion of typology or can be considered as forerunners of the future notion of typology (for the controversial case of Adam Smith 1761, see Noordegraf 1977, Coseriu 1983, Plank 1987, Haggblade 1983), never question the fundamental assumption of a homology of thought and language.

The diversity of natural languages is commonly associated in the eighteenth century with the complex of factors that constitute the *genius* of languages. The term *genius* is used to explain the morpho-syntactic variations found in natural languages as different and idiosyncratic ways of realizing the principles of language. It does not necessarily imply that such variations are arbitrary or accidental. On the contrary, as Paolo Ramat observes, the term can be even used in a sense that "excludes the historical dimension" (1995: 30). Very appropriately, Ramat recalls a passage where Girard states that the origin and kinship of languages cannot be determined on the basis of lexical borrowings and etymology, but only on the basis of their genius. This notion is very common. In the *Etymologie* entry written by Turgot for the great *Encyclopédie*, for example, it is raised to the status of a true methodological principle.

If there is a key term for the future developments of linguistic typology, this is the word *genius* used in the above sense. To fully support this claim, it would be necessary to produce a textual survey that is beyond the scope of the present article. I will limit myself to offering, as an example, an author we have already mentioned, Lambert, who identifies the genius of a natural language with the language 'type', that is, with the specific way in which a natural language actualizes the general conditions of language. Incidentally, even in the passage by Herder cited above, the term *Typus* was used in this sense: it indicated a *modus operandi* of the intellect, which manifests itself in the morphology of natural languages.

In *Semiotik*, the third volume of his *Neues Organon* (III §§ 315–328), Lambert explains that (i) the many irregularities found in the variable parts of speech are of accidental nature and are not, therefore, constitutive of the genius or type; (ii) that in no natural language the type is constituted by what is common to all languages. From these two propositions we may infer that (i) the diversity of natural languages is not based on an arbitrary element but on the contrary on intrinsic and necessary traits; and (ii) these traits, notwithstanding their necessary character, cannot be identified with the structures of the *grammaire raisonnée*.

To produce a positive definition of type, Lambert puts together two orders of factors. On the one hand he lists what we may call the impressionistic qualities of natural languages (languages that are more virile, more communicative, more suited to scientific works or to artistic ones), echoing characterizations that were much in fashion in the literary *querelles* on the comparative merits of languages (Lambert 1764: III, § 318). On the other hand, he indicates as constitutive of the type of a given natural language its ability to assimilate foreign words, archaisms and idiomatic expressions, bending them to its physiognomy. This assimilative power pervades all aspects of natural languages, from phonetics to etymology. A similar definition of type will emerge at the beginning of the nineteenth century. Anticipating the celebration of inflectional languages, which will be one of the characteristic traits of the *Romantik*, Lambert (1764: III, § 129) argues that the comprehensiveness of a language is a function of its ability to compose and derive new words from its roots. Only a language that excels in this (such as German among the modern languages) makes it possible to elaborate a *theory* of composition and word derivation capable of identifying the *type* of languages.

5. Conclusions

I have used a handful of texts to exemplify the eighteenth-century debate on notions that can in some way be subsumed in those of language universals and linguistic typology. The field would bear a much more extensive investigation, starting from the vast production of general grammars. The choice of dealing only with Beauzée and Condillac among the *grammairiens-philosophes* is certainly reductive. It would be necessary to extend the analysis at least to the works of Du Marsais and the other encyclopedists (for this, I refer the reader to Auroux 1979) and to James Harris's *Hermes* (see Joly 1972). The appended bibliography contains a few essential indications for future research. In any case, I think it is possible to draw a few conclusions from the quick survey offered in the present article: (i) the homology between linguistic and ideal structures is a central notion in both cognitive and grammatical studies of the eighteenth century; (ii) this notion belongs to various philosophical camps and, with the differences to be expected, is common both to the philosophers who claim allegiance to the rationalist tradition and to those who rely on a program of experimental research and the use of the genetic method; (iii) the belief that there are deep structures prior to speech does not preclude the possibility of using the inductive method, which is, in fact, characteristic of all the general grammars of the century; (iv) these structures are considered to be virtual characteristics of language, destined to be actualized empirically in various ways.

Philosophers and scholars had never perceived the unity/diversity of natural languages as a contradiction. In the past, various cultural factors had favored this more catholic attitude. One of these was the great influence of the biblical myth of the original unity and subsequent dispersion of mankind, whose influence was widely felt in the collective imagination, independently of intentional uses. Another factor was the idea, derived from the tradition of Christian Platonism, that historical experience must reflect the archetypes of nature and reason in a confused fashion, through the distorting mirror of subjectivity and arbitrariness. In the age of Enlightenment, the more philosophers detach themselves from an exemplaristic metaphysics, the more their attention focuses on the modalities of mental representations. These modalities are seen as the natural foundation of languages, that which generates their virtual structures. Yet, the empirical conditions of their actualization are as varied as those modalities and structures are universally human. *(translated by Gabriel Poole)*

6. References

Aarsleff, Hans. 1982. *From Locke to Saussure. Essays on the Study of Language and intellectual History.* Minneapolis: University of Minnesota Press & London: Athlone Press.

Adelung, Johann Christoph. 1806–1817. *Mithridates oder allgemeine Sprachenkunde*, 4 vols. Berlin: Voss.

Auroux, Sylvain. 1973. *L'Encyclopédie. Grammaire et langue au XVIIIe siècle*. Paris: Mame.

Auroux, Sylvain. 1979. *La sémiotique des Encyclopédistes. Essai d'épistémologie historique des sciences du langage*. Paris: Payot.

Auroux, Sylvain. 1986. "Les parties du discours dans la stratégie cognitive de la grammaire générale." *Zeitschrift für Phonetik, Sprachwissenschaft und Kommunikationsforschung* 39.6: 685–694.

Auroux, Sylvain. 1988. "La grammaire générale et les fondements philosophiques des classements des mots". In: Bernard Colombat (ed.). *Les parties du discours* (= *Langages* 92): 79–91.

Auroux, Sylvain. 1993. *La logique des idées*. Montréal & Paris: Bellarmin-Vrin.

Bartlett, Barrie E. 1972. Introduction to: Beauzée 1767. 13–51.

Bartlett, Barrie E. 1980. "Les rapports entre la structure profonde et l'énoncé au XVIIIe siècle". In: Sylvain Auroux & Jean-Claude Chevalier (eds.). *Histoire de la linguistique française* (= *Langue française* 48): 28–43.

Bartlett, Barrie E. 1982. "Lo statuto epistemologico delle classi di parole nella 'Grammaire générale' di Beauzée". In: Dino Buzzetti & Maurizio Ferriani (eds.). *La grammatica del pensiero. Logica, linguaggio e conoscenza nell'età dell'Illuminismo*. Bologna: Il Mulino, 57–75.

Beauzée, Nicolas. 1767. *Grammaire Générale*, ed. by B. E. Bartlett. Stuttgart-Bad Cannstatt: F. Fromman Verlag 1974. 2 vols. (= *Grammatica universalis*, ed. by H. Brekle, 8/1–2).

Chevalier, Jean-Claude. 1968. *Histoire de la syntaxe. Naissance de la notion de complément dans la grammaire française (1530–1750)*. Genève: Librarie Droz.

Condillac, Etienne Bonnot de. 1746. *Essai sur l'origine des connoissances humaines*. In: *Œuvres philosophiques*, ed. by G. Le Roy. Paris: Presses Universitaires de France.

Condillac, Etienne Bonnot de. 1775. *Cours d'étude pour l'instruction du Prince de Parme: Grammaire*, ed. by U. Ricken. Stuttgart-Bad Cannstatt: F. Fromman Verlag 1986 (= *Grammatica universalis*, ed. by H. Brekle, 19).

Coseriu, Eugenio. 1983. "Adam Smith and the Beginnings of Language Typology". *Historiographia Linguistica* 10: 1–12.

Dominicy, Marc. 1992. "Le programme scientifique de la grammaire générale". In: Sylvain Auroux, *Histoire des idées linguistiques* II, Liège: Mardaga, 424–441.

Du Marsais, César Chesneau. 1797. *Œuvres choisies*. I–III, ed. by H. E. Brekle. Stuttgart-Bad Cannstatt: Fromman 1971 (= *Grammatica universalis*, ed. by H. Brekle, 5).

Du Marsais, César Chesneau. 1987. *Les véritables principes de la grammaire*, ed. by F. Douay-Soublin. Paris: Fayard.

Formigari, Lia. 1988. *Language and Experience in 17th-century British Philosophy*. Amsterdam & Philadelphia: Benjamins.

Formigari, Lia. 1994. *La sémiotique empiriste face au kantisme*. Liège: Mardaga.

Gessinger, Joachim & Wolfart von Rahden (eds.). 1989. *Theorien vom Ursprung der Sprache*, 2 vols. Berlin & New York: Walter de Gruyter.

Girard, Gabriel. 1747. *Les vraies principes de la langue française*, ed. by P. Swiggers. Genève & Paris: Slatkine, 1982.

Goddard, Cliff. 1996. "Cross-linguistic Research on Metaphor". *Language and Communication* 16/2: 145–151.

Haggblade, Elisabeth. 1983. "Contributors to the Beginnings of Language Typology". *Historiographia Linguistica* 10: 13–24.

Hassler, Gerda. 1997. "Sprachtheoretische Preisfragen der Berliner Akademie in der 2. Hälfte des 18. Jahrhunderts. Ein Kapitel der Debatte um Universalien und Relativität". *Romanistik in Geschichte und Gegenwart* 3/1: 3–26.

Herder, Johann Gottfried. 1799. *Metakritik zur Kritik der reinen Vernunft. I. Verstand und Erfahrung. II. Vernunft und Sprache* (Bruxelles: Culture et civilisation, 1969 = Aetas kantiana, 91).

Joly, André. 1972. Introduction to: James Harris. *Hermès ou recherches philosophiques sur la grammaire universelle*. Genève: Libr. Droz, 1–144.

Joly, André. 1976. "Le débat sur les parties du discours à l'époque classique". *Zeitschrift für Phonetik, Sprachwissenschaft und Kommunikationsforschung* 29/5–6: 464–467.

Koerner, Konrad. 1995. *Professing Linguistic Historiography*. Amsterdam & Philadelphia: John Benjamins (ch. 8, "Toward a History of Linguistic Typology", pp. 151–170).

Lambert, Johann Heinrich. 1764. *Neues Organon*. In: *Philosophische Schriften*, hrsg. von H.-W. Arndt. Hildesheim: Olms, 1965–1969. I–II.

Locke, John. 1690. *An Essay concerning Human Understanding*. London.

Monreal-Wickert, Irene. 1977. *Die Sprachforschung der Aufklärung im Spiegel der grossen französischen Encyclopädie*. Tübingen: Narr.

Noordegraf, Jan. 1977. "A few Remarks on Adam Smith's Dissertation". *Historiographia linguistica* 4: 59–67.

Pellerey, Roberto. 1993. *La théorie de la construction directe de la phrase. Analyse de la formation d'une idéologie linguistique*. Paris: Larousse.

Picardi, Eva. 1977. "Some problems of Linguistic Classification in Linguistics and Biology". *Historiographia Linguistica* 4: 31–57.

Plank, Frans. 1987. "The Smith-Schlegel Connection in Linguistic Typology: Forgotten fact or fiction?". *Zeitschrift für Phonetik, Sprachwissenschaft und Kommunikationsforschung* 40: 196–214.

Ramat, Paolo. 1995. "Typological Comparison: Towards a Historical Perspective". In: Masayoshi Shibatani & Theodora Bynon, *Approaches to Language Typology*. Oxford: Clarendon Press, 27–47.

Renzi, Lorenzo. 1976. *Histoire et objectifs de la linguistique*. In: *History of Linguistic Thought and Contemporary Linguistics*, ed. by H. Parret. Berlin & New York: W. de Gruyter, 633–657.

Ricken, Ulrich. 1978. *Grammaire et philosophie au siècle des Lumières. Controverses sur l'ordre naturel et la clarté du français*. Villeneuve d'Ascq: Presses Universitaires de Lille.

Ricken, Ulrich. 1994. *Linguistics, Anthropology and Philosophy in the French Enlightenment. Language Theory and Ideology*. London & New York: Routledge.

Robins, Robert Henry. 1973. "The History of Language Classification". *Current Trends in Linguistics*, ed. by Thomas A. Sebeok. The Hague: Mouton. XI. 3–41.

Simone, Raffaele. 1996. "Unicità del linguaggio e varietà delle lingue in Port-Royal". In: Daniele Gambarara & Stefano Gensini & Antonino Pennisi (eds.). *Language Philosophies and the Language Sciences*. Münster: Nodus Publikationen. 85–103.

Smith, Adam. 1761. "Considerations concerning the first formation of languages, and the different genius of original and compounded languages". *The Philological Miscellany* I: 440–479. Reprint in: Adam Smith, *A Dissertation on the Origin of Languages*, Tübingen: Narr, 1970.

Lia Formigari Università di Roma I,
La Sapienza (Italy)

17. Die Schulen des Strukturalismus

Der an dieser Stelle vorgesehene Artikel muß leider entfallen.

IV. History and approaches of language typology
Geschichte und Richtungen der Sprachtypologie
Histoire et écoles de la typologie linguistique

18. Characterization and evaluation of languages in the Renaissance and in the Early Modern Period

1. The era
2. 'Evaluation' in Greek and Roman linguistics
3. National claims in the Renaissance and the Early Modern Period
4. The exceptional case: Comenius
5. Universalism vs. beginnings of relativism
6. References (selected)

1. The era

There is hardly a better example of the difficulties of periodizing European intellectual and mental life than the so-called Early Modern Period. (For the Renaissance: → Art. 15). The name suggests that we should regard it as the preparatory phase for the Modern Period, which, by general consent, is the Enlightenment of the 18th century. But the years between 1600 and 1699 are certainly also to be seen as having their own qualities. Outstanding philosophers like Francis Bacon (1561–1626), René Descartes (Cartesius, 1596–1650), Thomas Hobbes (1588–1679), Baruch (Benedict de) Spinoza (1632–1677), and John Locke (1632–1704) performed and ensured a definite break with scholastic philosophy, and made the reflections and experiences of the individual human being the starting point for all philosophical knowledge. Moreover, outstanding scientists like Johannes Kepler (1571–1630), Galileo Galilei (1564–1642), Isaac Newton (1642–1727), and Robert Boyle (1626–1691) changed people's understanding of the world around them as never before and, additionally, conceived and strengthened the idea of the worldly progress of learning. The works of these men are certainly achievements in their own right, although they are also inalienable conditions for the century to come.

The years between 1600 and 1699 can, on the other hand, also be viewed as an era of consolidation in which the innovations of the Renaissance came into their own, not of course without breeding new conflicts. This pertains, for example, to religious life, in which the existence of the countries of the Reformation north of the Alps was established for good, in spite of (or as a result of) the catastrophe of the Thirty Years' War. It also pertains to the nationalization of grammaticography. In all the countries where grammars of vernaculars first appeared (→ Art. 15), they initiated a large-scale production of more grammars, and also of dictionaries. These grammars started to use language-specific and not Latin categories, as John Wallis (1616–1703) did in his *Grammatica linguae anglicanae* (1653), although written in Latin. This was a significant step, even if the authors were not always successful in doing what they promised to do. Whereas the Humanist interest in classical Latin and Greek was confined to the universities as the centres of learning and led to an early peak of philological activity there, a general eagerness to describe and to learn national languages was manifested in polyglot dialogues and vocabularies. It was encouraged by the new conditions of travel and of commerce, in which the growing new sciences had an important share. Avoiding the term 'Early Modern Period', we could speak of a Humanist and a Scientific phase of the Renaissance with the year 1600 as the watershed.

We would also be justified in doing this because of some general, typically Renaissance, features present in both phases, such as the enjoyment of and curiosity about the world and the belief in its perfectibility, as opposed to the medieval *vanitas mundi*, the style of life and education, the respect for learning outside theology, and new styles of architecture and the visual arts. Although Baroque building and Dutch landscape painting, for example, moved away quite drastically from the earlier artistic modes of expression, they strengthened and deepened the most characteristic Renaissance features, *viz.* interest in the visible reality of this world.

The chronological limits of the Early Modern Period coincide almost exactly with the 17th century. The spatial boundaries are the same as those of the (first phase of the) Renaissance, with a distinctly greater importance accorded to those countries north of the Alps which confessed to the various churches of the Reformation. The countries of origin and the living places of the philosophers and scientists mentioned above testify to this.

Naturally, there were era-specific features, some of which pertain less and others which pertain more to linguistic reflections and practice. To the former belong ideas circling around the problems of 'language and knowledge' and 'language and science'. In fact, all the philosophers mentioned meditated on the role which language plays in cognition and in the accumulation of scientific knowledge, and they influenced thinking about language in the narrow linguistic sense, for example by grammarians, to no small extent. Again, all of the scientists mentioned theorized on how to avoid the speculative elements of language-in-use which would contaminate their arguments, and this means how to create a true and objective scientific style.

Besides the ever-present work of consolidation in grammar writing and dictionary compiling, there are some facets of linguistic work which, although resting on earlier conceptions, give the Early Modern Period its own character.

(i) The general interest in the European vernaculars grew into a broad stream of comparative linguistic activities whose main aim was to establish one's own language as 'better' than other ones. Various criteria were used as yardsticks for these evaluations, eminent among them the so-called Adamic language in the interpretations given to it. They established the rather old notion of a perfect language in a contemporary form.

(ii) The self-assertive characterization of national languages created the beginnings of the idea of a national genius of each language. This prepared for many linguistic concepts in later centuries.

(iii) The philosophical background as incorporated, above all, in Cartesian thinking lent new support to the concept of universals in languages. It influenced both the planning of so-called universal languages and the grammaticography of national languages in various ways. At the same time, a number of deliberations, above all in Lockean philosophy, prepared what in succeeding centuries was to become the highly influential idea of linguistic relativism.

These three features of linguistic reflection will be elaborated on subsequently, limited, however, to publications on German, English, and French. Some reflections on Comenius will be added. Moreover, some preparatory remarks will be made on 'evaluation' in Greek and Roman linguistics as a background to the developments in the Early Modern Period. For general linguistic information on the era and its authors, see, besides the usual bibliographies, Arens 1969, Brekle 1975, Robins 1990, Auroux 1992, Eco 1993, Borst 1995, Matthews 1994, Gardt 1999; for particular linguistic information on the authors mentioned, see, besides the usual works of biographical reference, the relevant articles in Stammerjohann 1996.

2. 'Evaluation' in Greek and Roman linguistics

At all times, human language awareness has not only been descriptive, but also evaluative. Linguists observe and describe, for example, the syntactic and rhetorical structures of a text and the meanings and illocutions they convey, but they also judge these illocutions and meanings as being either true or false and the structures as being either right or wrong, good or bad, beautiful or ugly, etc. The criteria which underlie these judgments were various and they constantly changed during the history of language use and usage. In such praises and verdicts there were alive measures of philosophical correctness (e. g. in name giving), of structural perfection (e. g. in grammar), of stylistic standardization (e. g. in dialects), or of acoustic pleasantness (e. g. in prosody). All of them can be found in Greek and Roman linguistics. Of course, they arise from the various conditions of language use and established usage, which change according to time and circumstance.

The highest criteria of such evaluative decisions are *intelligibility* and *acceptance*. 'Intelligibility' characterizes one's own language in contrast to a foreign one and is a prerequisite for communication. It depends on interlingual comparison. 'Acceptance' characterizes a certain variety (dialect) of a language in contrast to other varieties. It depends on intralingual comparison. The history of evaluation in linguistics shows (see below) that the two kinds of comparison tend to fuse and to become mixed up. This means that an utterance in a foreign language is liable to be regarded as wrong, bad, ugly, etc. because of its unintelligibility.

The fact that the Greeks reflected only on their own language and called all foreigners *barbaroi*, i. e. people who speak unintelligibly, signals clearly that their decision was made only in favour of their own idiom and excluded all foreign ones. This was so in spite of the fact that they must have had plenty of experience of foreign languages, in particular in the Hellenistic period after Alexander (323 BC to battle of Actium 31 BC) and in the Imperial period. The same signal comes from the privileged position of the Attic dialect and the standard position of the Athenian classical authors, contrary to other dialects and also contrary to the spoken variety inside and outside Greece, the *koiné*.

Consequently, grammars as tools for language teaching, for example Dionysius Thrax's (ca. 170−90 BC) *Techné* (Robins 1993, Law & Sluiter 1995), were written only on the standardized variety of Greek, i. e. neither on a foreign language nor on a different dialect. Interestingly enough, quite a number of Greek thinkers came from outside Attica. For example, among the Stoics, Zeno originated from Cyprus and was a Phoenician, and Chrysippus came from Cilicia (today southern Turkey) (Matthews 1994: 50). We can speculate on the possibility that their origins, which forced them to learn Greek as a foreign language, gave these 'barbarians' the heightened awareness for an analysis of Greek by tacit comparison with their own native tongues. But the fact that the Stoic school was active in Athens and nowhere else testifies to the cultural weight of the relevant language and its relevant dialect and the concomitant evaluation by the cultured class.

In Roman linguistics, things are slightly, but not much different. It is true that the Romans accepted Greek as a second language of the Empire, learnt it as a second language and implied it in their linguistic reflections. This was due to their acknowledgement of the superiority of Greek culture and also to the structural similarity of the two languages. But there must have been contacts with almost all the vernaculars spoken around the Mediterranean and in some parts of trans-alpine Europe. They failed to make any impression. Latin and Greek were evaluated as the languages of the Empire and all the foreign idioms fell outside the Latinate culture.

Language evaluation in favour of their own tongues shows in the practical application of linguistics by Greeks and Romans, rather than in theoretical arguments on a meta-level. In the light of these deliberations, however, an early argument about the truth of language, a central point of significance, becomes important. It concerns the names which the gods and goddesses, the heroes and heroines were given by Homer (second half 8th cent. BC) and by Hesiod (ca. 700 BC). The argument is that a name must indicate the essential characteristics of the person, his or her life, tasks, and importance. Names must be telling (to use the modern term). This is even demanded where there are two or several names for one person. They must all be 'true', showing that the truth has various aspects. (Hector's son, for example, was *Skamandros* for his father, after the river of his home town, and *Astyanax*, 'protector of the town', for the public. So there were two truths, a private and a public one.) The true names, in particular of goddesses and gods, guaranteed that the whole report, for example of the Homeric epics, was true, that the reality of the world (*kosmos*) lived in the language (Liebermann 1991). They were the mythological explanation of the semiotic quality and intelligibility of a language and this means they explained communication. Of course, this explanation later changed into the philosophical ideas about language and reality (Schmitter 1991). Plato's (428−349 BC) *Kratylos* shows that this is actually a debate on the nature of the linguistic sign, and as the guarantee of the meaningful sign depends on intelligibility, this argument is in fact the basis of the Greeks' assessment of their own language as the only one that counted.

There is a similar argument in the other parent tradition of European linguistics, the Hebrew one. It lies again in the problem of names, this time of those plants and animals which were nominated by Adam in the presence of God, as the text of the Jahwist (Genesis chap. 2; Schenk 1991) reports. Again, this act of nomination guaranteed intelligibility and communication, because the names conferred upon the things of nature by Adam were supposed to denote their essence. The story of Babel (Genesis, chap. 10) replaced this correspondence between the sign and the referent by 'confusion', i.e. by some restricted form of communication. Unlike the Greek sources, the Biblical report not only marks the pivotal argument for the intelligibility of the linguistic sign in one's own language, commonly assumed to be Hebrew, but also gave an explanation of the existence of a multitude of languages, which cause a new problem for the evaluation process. The Homerian and Hesiodean argument vanished in later Greek and Roman philosophy and linguistics. The story of Paradise and Babel, taken as the infallible word of God, however, was to be influential for many succeeding centuries, the last of these being the seventeenth.

Greek grammaticography was also concerned about the stylistic norm of the language, thus providing the yardsticks for more evaluative judgements. Aristotle's successor Theophrastus (b. ca. 370 BC) defined four 'virtues of speech', namely *correctness, clarity, appropriateness*, and *elegance*. For Diogenes Laertius (b. ca. 370 BC), these 'virtues' were *Greekness* (hellēnismós), i.e. faultlessness in respect of *appropriateness*, i.e. matching of speech and subject matter; of *elegance*, i.e. avoidance of colloquialisms, of *clarity*, and additionally *brevity*. 'Vices' of speech are *barbarisms*, i.e. the use of vocabulary which is contrary to the custom of the Greeks of good repute, and *solecisms*, i.e. speech put together incongruously with reference to meaning (Matthews 1994: 50).

Concern about the standard of Greek vis-à-vis the development of the *koiné* was felt equally by the Romans vis-à-vis the development of Vulgar Latin. Quintilian defined grammar as 'the knowledge of correct speech', and his measures of correctness were very similar to the Greek ones. Speech should be *free of error*, it should be *clear* and *elegant*, which included *appropriateness*. When a single word was wrong, this was a *barbarism*, when more words were wrong, it was a *solecism* (Matthew 1994: 52). Barbarisms and solecisms were rather mechanically classified as *addition, deletion, transposition,* or *substitution.*

The 'virtues' and 'vices' of speech are familiar to all the grammarians and rhetoricians of the medieval centuries. They form the criteria of prescriptive grammar and stylistic education. Many Renaissance authors (e.g. Guarino Veronese (1374–1460), Lorenzo Valla (1407–1457), Henri Estienne (1531–1598), Antonio de Nebrija (ca. 1444–1522), Franciscus Sanctius Brocensis (1523–1601)) wrote grammars as well as books on rhetoric. They explained the stock of yardsticks for evaluative judgments. In particular, correctness, clarity, appropriateness, and elegance will play a major role in the 16th and 17th centuries, when national languages were weighed against one another.

Similar to the situation in ancient Greece and Rome, the unique dominance of Latin in the Middle Ages did not leave an opportunity for the linguistic assessment of other ('foreign') languages. The only qualifications generally made were that Hebrew was supposed to be the oldest language of mankind, the one used by God and Adam in Paradise, which had (somehow) survived Babel, and that, together with Hebrew, Latin and Greek were 'holy' languages, because the Bible was written in or had been translated into them, and because they were used on the sign on the cross.

3. National claims in the Renaissance and the Early Modern Period

3.1. Biblical references

In the Renaissance, there is a qualitative difference between reflections on the history of Romance languages as opposed to reflections on the history of the Germanic ones. All of them served to give the respective languages the status of a national vernacular in its own right. But in the cases of Italian, French, and Spanish, this was done by reference to the Latin tradition, whereas in the cases of German and English this was done by distancing from rather than by referring to it.

Admittedly, even in respect of the former three (Italian, French, and Spanish), there were authors who strove for more linguistic independence. Giovanni Annius (Nanni, 1432–1502) made Etruscan the origin of Italian (Tuscan); Guillaume Postel (1510–1581) declared a hpyothetical old form of Gaulish to be the mother-language of French and Latin alike; and Gregorio López Madera (fl. 1586–1638) did the same with Old Castilian and Spanish. But the majority of linguists in the Romance area acknowledged sensibly the Latin source of their vernaculars and still found a way of securing its present-day (i.e. 16th and 17th centuries') national sovereignty (→ Art. 15). Moreover, there was the obvious affinity of Italian, French, and Spanish to classical Latin, which had been powerfully revived in its contemporary version. Quite a number of grammarians, e.g. Antonio de Nebrija and Petrus Ramus (1515–1572), wrote Latin as well as Spanish and French, grammars.

For the latter two (German and English), however, the Latin tradition was 'foreign', although it was present in an influential way. But the spirit of the time gave the German and English linguists the task of proving that and why their own languages were nevertheless valuable in themselves.

The general framework of their arguments for doing this was the Bible, understood as a reliable report of the history of mankind, in particular of (pre-historic) migrations and their consequences for the development and the deployment of languages. There were three points of reference (contributions in Gessinger & Rahden 1987, Schenk 1991, Eco 1993):

(i) the story of Genesis, chapter 2, where God asks Adam to name the animals of Paradise and later also his wife, Eve. The language in which God and Adam conversed and which was used in the act of nomination was generally taken to be Hebrew, although doubts began to arise whether this was Hebrew as (if only few) people knew it. Moreover, the language of Paradise was taken to be perfect, because the names expressed their referents adequately. What would later be discussed in philosophy as the natural or the conventional basis for semiotic meaningfulness was here resolved by a theological argument. The adequacy of the linguistic sign was guaranteed by its being used by the prelapsarian man, Adam, in the presence of God.
(ii) the story of Genesis, chapters 9 and 10, where Noah, after escaping from the Flood, sends his three sons, Cham, Schem, and Japhet, into the world, where their progeny multiplied and founded a variety of languages. In spite of all its exegetical problems, the Biblical table of peoples and languages which results from this is unique as a panorama of world settlement, world history, and global language development, all regarded for the first time as following the guidance of the one God (Borst 1995: I, 114–133). The table is something like the foundation document of all ethnography and historiography covering the countries and languages round the Mediterranean, the central part of Europe, and what is today called Central Asia. Japhet with his son Gomer and his grandson Aschkenaz stood for the European countries north of the Alps and for Central Asia, i.e. for the non-Semitic peoples and languages.
(iii) the story of Genesis, chapter 11, where God punishes the hybris of humankind in building the Tower of Babel by confusing their languages, and that is by blocking communication. The peoples disperse in various directions, thus creating 72 different languages in all. There has been much controversy on the contradiction between chapters 9–10 and 11. In the former, the scattering of humankind happens after the Flood, in the latter after the rise of Babylonian culture. Taking into consideration the fact that literary historiography as given in the Bible need not be conclusive in any way, we can say that Genesis, chapters 9 and 10, gives reasons for the variety of languages, chapter 11, however, for their mutual unintelligibility. The number 72 must be taken as corresponding to general Biblical number symbolism. In fact, many mythologies contain the story of a crumbling tower, indicating the dangers of a too ambitious erection of stone buildings.

Whereas Genesis, chapter 2, gave a theological reason for the adequacy of the linguistic sign, chapter 11 gives a theological reason for its inadequacy. In the shape of meaningful names, which ensure communication, the former is guaranteed by God and Adam, the prelapsarian human being. The latter is imposed on mankind as a punishment by God in the shape of 'foreignness', i.e. failing communication. Thus, the human use of the linguistic sign is drawn into the disaster of the Fall just as human morality is. This all means that the central problem of semiosis, the possibilities and dangers of signifying, was present in the intellectual world of the Old Testament.

3.2. National hypotheses

The various spokesmen for national languages claimed that their respective vernaculars could be salvaged from the wreck of human history after Babel (Eco 1993 [1994: 105–113]). Either they made Adam one of their first speakers, or they identified these with one of the sons or grandsons of Noah, or they looked for the origin of their languages among the seventy-two of Babel. The important fact is that the idea of a nation as a linguistic unity (which would in later centuries become so important) was underpinned by a theological argument. In one way or the other, every nation claimed to possess God's own language. For Giovanni Annius, Etruscan was a direct daughter-language of Noah's Aramaic. Guillaume Postel claimed the same for the old version of Gaulish. Gregorio López Madera left it open whether Old Castilian stemmed from Noah or from Babel. In both cases it enjoyed the dignity of old age over Latin.

The most daring of such derivations is found in Johannes Goropius Becanus' (1519–1572) *Origines antverpianae sive cimmeriorum becceselana, novem libros complexa* (1569). In long-winded etymologies, which came in for criticism even in his life-time, he showed that the *Cimmerii*, who stemmed from Gomer, Japhet's eldest son and Noah's grandson, were the founders of Antwerp, which made the dialect of this town the most original language of Europe. A slightly different genealogy was drawn up by Abraham Mylius (van der Mijl, fl. 1612) who placed 'Belgian' beside Persian, Greek, and Latin, i. e. beside the three sacred languages, as a *lingua matrix* in *lingua belgica; sive de linguae illius communitate tum cum plerisque aliis, tum presertim cum latina, graeca, persica [...]* (1612).

The Swede Georg Stiernhielm (1598–1672) instrumentalized the Scythian tradition to show that Gothic, identical with Scythian, and its succeeding language Swedish is Europe's most ancient language. Moreover, it was not corrupted in Babel. This conforms with the idea that Sweden, politically highly influential during the Thirty Years' War, was the mythical Atlantis and the source of European culture. Finally, Georg Philipp Harsdörffer (1607–1658) published his *Schutzschrift für die Teutsche Spracharbeit [...]* (1644), where in an often quoted passage (Hüllen 1995: 318) he attributed to German a special faculty for the perfect onomatopoeic imitation of natural sounds, with the assumption that Adam must have used German when he named and characterized the animals in Paradise.

3.3. The German *HaubtSprache*

The national hypothesis entails that one language must by its speakers be regarded as superior to all the others. The main criteria for this judgment are age and purity – age because it places the origin of a language nearest to the perfect language in Paradise, and purity because not having mixed with other languages means that the original qualities were kept intact. All the spokesmen for the Germanic languages claimed that these were superior to the Romance ones, because they remained "unpolluted over many thousand years" (Harsdörffer; see Hüllen 1995: 318), whereas the others, but also English, had become mixed.

Besides these arguments, a permanent multilateral comparison started, in which early stereotypes of language evaluation began to manifest themselves. Harsdörffer, for example, maintained that German had a greater wealth of words than Hebrew, a more perfect system of word-formation than Greek, more precise word-meanings than Latin, more euphony of pronunciation than Spanish, more poetic pleasantness than French, and a more perfect structure than Italian. This not only betrays what European languages were famous for, the comparison also brought some of the classical criteria for judging languages to the fore, such as philosophical correctness, structural perfection, stylistic standard, and phonetic pleasantness (see above).

Justus Georgius Schottelius (1612–1676) is perhaps the most influential promoter of High German in the 17th century with his *Ausführliche Arbeit Von der Teutschen HaubtSprache* (1641) (Brekle 1975: 314–317, Padley 1985). The bulky book combines a discussion of linguistic ideas in the so-called eulogies (*Lobreden*) with a grammar stressing above all the generative principles of word-formation, and a dictionary of German rootwords (*Stammwörter*). He sets out to explain that German is one of the richest languages in words, that it is euphonious, pure, beautiful in style, semantically precise, and, consequently, perfect. It is "according to nature", because, according to Schottelius, all experts are unanimous in their judgment on its excellence, and such unanimity must come from "intelligible nature". The system of word-formation guarantees the age of the language, because, again according to Schottelius, German root-words are to be found in all other European tongues. *Verdoppelung*, i.e. composition and derivation, provides the wealth of words and semantic precision. Schottelius finds the same onomatopoeic meaningfulness as Harsdörffer, but he does not link it with Adam's act of name-giving. Rather, he sees a more general divine element in it, without which the whole language could not be explained (Hüllen 1995).

In the absence of a central academy, the German *Sprachgesellschaften* set themselves the aim of upgrading the native tongue. Germans should become aware of its excellence and should cherish and cultivate it. Harsdörffer and Schottelius, both members of the *Fruchtbringende Gesellschaft* (Fructifying Society), worked for this aim. They used many ideas which in former centuries had resulted in the concept of 'Greekness', even if terms like 'appropriateness' and 'elegance' did not appear (but see below). It is true that their language had a distinctly national ring. Yet it is certainly unjustifiable to see in the favourable treatment of Germanic languages in general and of German in particular the beginnings of a path that would later lead to Nazism (Jones 1966: 214).

3.4. The special history of English

English was a language little known on the Continent during the Renaissance. Only around 1570 did it make its appearance in those polyglot textbooks which show Europe's interest in vernaculars (Hüllen 1999). The English themselves had a very bad opinion of their own language at that time. They called it 'rude', 'gross', 'barbarous', 'base', 'vile', etc. – features which had in common that the language was characterized by them as ineloquent (Jones 1963: 7). This pertained, above all, to vocabulary and style and was to be remedied by coining new words from other languages and by introducing rhetorical tropes and figures. Richard Sherry (fl. 1550) did this, for example, in his *Treatise of Schemes and Tropes* (1550) and Thomas Wilson (ca. 1525–1581) in *The Arte of Rhetoricke* (1560). These and many other books of the same kind brought the old concepts of 'barbarism' and 'solecism' with all their sub-concepts into play. Generally, the superiority of classical Greek and Latin, but also of contemporary French, Italian, and Spanish, was acknowledged. Many authors, like Sir Thomas Elyot (ca. 1490–1546), Robert Recorde (ca. 1510–1558), or Roger Ascham (1515–1568), argued for the improvement of English by the adaptation of Latinized, mostly French, words. This expansion of English by neologizing stimulated a controversy about so-called 'inkhorne termes', still historiographically known as the 'hard-word debate' (Leisi 1998). The issue was that speakers without a Latin background could not understand the new words. Most authors accepted borrowing as the only means of making English eloquent, but rejected borrowing out of vanity. George Putenham (ca. 1520–ca. 1601), for example, developed quite a complex attitude in *The Arte of English Poesie* (1589). He approved of loans only if they filled a gap in the indigenous vocabulary or did the work of several native terms, moreover if they were euphonious to the English ear, and if they were approved of by the court and the higher circles of society.

The general critical attitude towards the English language changed around 1575, when a new positive way of thinking about the vernacular came into being. Above all others, the reason was the general reputation of the Elizabethan poets (Sir Philip Sidney (1554–1586), Edmund Spenser (ca. 1552–1599), Michael Drayton (1563–1631), William Shakespeare (1564–1616), Christopher Marlowe (1564–1593), George Chapman (ca. 1559–1634), and others) and prose writers (St Thomas More (1478–1535), Sir Philip Sidney, Roger Ascham, and others). Whereas in the earlier part of the century the general endeavour had been to improve the native tongue for an unlettered public with the help of foreign tongues, authors were now persuaded by the great poets and playwrights of their time that English itself had enough resources for this.

"But how hardly soeuer you deale with your tongue, how barbarous soeuer you count it, how little soeuer you esteeme it, I durst my selfe undertake (if I were furnished with learnyng otherwyse) to wryte in it as copiously for varietie, as compendiously for breuity, as choycely for woordes, as pithily for sentences, as pleasauntly for figures, and euery way as eloquently, as any writer should do in any vulgar tongue whatsoeuer." (George Pettie, 1548–1589, *The Civile Conversation of M. Steeuen Guazzo* [...], 1581; Jones 1966: 178).

The new belief in the national language was, of course, also a consequence of the national exuberance under Elizabeth I. It no longer considered the abilities of the public but the love of the nation as a whole. Richard Mulcaster (ca. 1530–1611), *The First Part of the Elementarie*, 1582), placed English on a par with Latin. Just as the Romans had brought Latin to excellence and had equalled Greek in their translations, so the English would do with their native tongue – out of love for their country. "I loue Rome, but London better, I fauor Italie, but England more, I honor the Latin, but I worship the English." (see Jones 1966: 193). As George Pettie had already done, Richard Mulcaster enunciated the (seen from present-day linguistics) quite advanced idea that no language is finer *per se* than another one, but that it is made so by its speakers.

It almost goes without saying that this patriotic reflection made use of the language's own history and that the admiration of the Romance languages on the Continent gave way to a more favourable observance of the Germanic ones. In *The Arte of English Poesie* (1589), for example, George Puttenham followed the history of English from the original languages of the 'British', still alive in the Celtic parts of the country, via the Saxon invasion, the Scandinavian ('Danish') influx, the first wave of Latin borrowings, and the final decisive change caused by Norman French after the invasion of 1066, which had made the country for some time culturally trilingual (Saxon, Latin, French) (Bailey 1991: 32–34). In these deliberations, history was valued because of its relevance for the present state of the language, in particular its vocabulary, and its separation into northern and southern dialects. Of them the southern was determined to be the more prestigious one because of the presence of the court, the universities, and the large towns in this area, but, significantly, also because of the absence of 'Danish' elements. So even Scandinavian was detrimental to the purity of the old Saxon language. It was Richard Verstegen (Rowlands, ca. 1565–1620) who combined in *A Restitution of Decayed Intelligence* (1605) such ideas with the Biblical genealogy as we know it from the Continent. In his insistence on the Saxon, i. e. Germanic, roots and character of English, thought of as alien to the heavy influx of Latinate elements in the author's own time, he regarded the native language in the light of the privileges of Germanic in the way in which Goropius Becanus had claimed them (Bailey 1991: 38). According to Verstegen, Tuisco, an immediate descendant of Japhet, was the founder of Old Saxon. Moreover, he (Verstegen) developed the surprising idea that it was the advantage of Babel to make people of one language stay together and found a nation. This is why he favoured genuine Anglo-Saxon monosyllabic words, whereas polysyllables revealed to him the corruption caused by foreign linguistic interventions. He and other linguists used these ideas to prove that English was as excellent a language as any other in Europe. In the course of the 17th century, the so-called antiquarians, like William Camden (1551–1623), Robert Hare (d. 1611) or Meric Casaubon (1599–1671), regarded their country as the most noble of the 'Teutonic nations', even finding words of praise for the "Hunns and Gothians", who had rather been held in disrepute by the Elizabethans. This movement tied in with the religious controversy of the time, in that the Puritans preferred the English translation of the Bible (e. g. William Tyndale's (d. 1536), 1525, ca. 1530, 1531) because it used words of Germanic stock, whereas the Catholics ('Papists') were reproached for their inclination to use hard Latinate vocabulary. There was a heated controversy on this, e. g. in William Turner's (d. 1568) *The huntyng and fyndyng out of the Romish foxe* (1543).

Even in the earlier decades of the 16th century, authors had tried to characterize their English vernacular in its own style as plain, useful, homely, unadorned, etc., although the superiority of the classical languages and the Romance vernaculars was generally accepted. In the later years of the 16th and in the 17th centuries, the excellence of the English language was occasionally attributed to both its qualities, the Saxon origin and the Latin refinement. Raphael Holinshed (d. ca. 1580), the famous author of the *Chronicles* (first volume 1577), maintained that English excelled over all other European languages.

In 1614, Richard Carew (1555–1620) published his essay *The Excellency of the English Tongue* as a chapter in William Camden's famous *Remains Concerning Britain*. It was plagiarized in an anonymous pamphlet *Vindex Anglicus, Or the Perfections of the English Language [...]* (1644), and in 1688 found its way into Guy Miège's (1644–ca. 1718) *The English Grammar* (Bailey 1991: 38–43, Howatt 1984: 54–60). The text praised English under four headings, *viz.* 'facility', 'copiousness', 'significancy', and 'sweetness', and in doing this new ideas were introduced into the discussion.

Facility applied to grammar, in particular to the relative paucity of English morphology. Together with the dominance of monosyllabic words it was said to ensure the easy learnability of English. For the first time, a special property of a vernacular was praised because it made the language easy to learn for foreign speakers. In fact, grammatical 'simplicity' would become a recurrent category in English grammars of the following century. *Copiousness* was found in the fact that English adopted so many words from other languages. Again, this was a new criterion for language evaluation, because it ousted the hitherto almost sacred notion of 'purity'. Miège was an early author for whom 'mixture' and 'unitability' are natural and positive phenomena in languages. *Significance* was understood as semantic precision of words, but also as stylistic versatility and appropriateness. It is the negation of 'barbarism' as well as of 'solecism'. *Sweetness*, finally, pertained to the phonotactic level of English on which it was supposed to excel other European languages:

"The Italian is pleasant but without sinews as a still fleeting water. The French, delicate, but over nice as a woman, scarce daring to open her lippes for fear of marring her countenance. The Spanish majesticall, but fulsome, running too much on the O, and terrible like the divell in a play. The Dutch manlike but withall verie harsh, as one readie at everie word to picke a quarrel." (see Hüllen 1995: 325).

English, however, borrows the positive qualities of these languages for its own 'sweetness'. Such multilateral comparisons, relying on vague psychological impressions from the relation between vowels and consonants in a language, were frequent at the time (see below).

Like the other European languages, English as a national vernacular had come into its own by the end of the 17th century. English linguists employed the same historical derivations as the spokesmen for the continental languages, but with their praise of simplicity and language mixture they also introduced new arguments into the discussion.

3.5. The 'genius of language'

The Early Modern Period also saw the beginnings of an idea which established a close link between a language and its speech community in a way which should not be taken for granted. It is revealed in the newly developing term *genius of language (génie de la langue, Genius (Geist) der Sprache)* which enjoyed a rapidly growing popularity after 1635, and which, *verbatim* or just conceptually, became important in the linguistics of the 18th century and even dominant in that of the nineteenth. For the 17th century, it is only the initial phase of its historical life which can be traced (Haßler 1984).

'Genius of language' was then and has always been a fairly vague concept. Adopting the meaning of Latin *genius* as well as *ingenium*, the term hypothesized that speech communities (peoples) have characters in the same way in which individual human beings are said to have them, and that languages indicate these characters by their phonotactic substance, their vocabulary, etymology, syntactic structure and by other rather vague, predominantly stylistic, qualities. This made the genius-of-language concept a part of the evaluative and competitive national attitude (see above). For individual authors the genius of their own language was always great and admirable, that of other languages, however, at least partly deficient or even totally ridiculous and despicable. Not only in this general attitude but even in the choice of criteria of evaluation do the classical norms of language evaluation, in particular the admixture of intelligibility and acceptance, again come to the fore, without, however, being specifically referred to.

Amable de Bourcey (1606—1671), an expert of Greek and oriental languages, is generally (Christmann 1976, Schlaps 1999) credited with having used the term for the first time in a discourse before the French Academy entitled "Sur le dessin de l'Académie, et sur le different génie des langues" (1635). He attributed *le génie des langues* to such societal qualities as the form of government, modes of conversation, customs, and the temperament of people. Without using the conspicuous term, yet in the same spirit, Estienne Pasquier (1529—1615) had already compared some European vernaculars in *Les recherches de la France* (1621) by stating "que nos langages tant en particulier comme en general accompagnent la disposition de nos esprits." (Christmann 1976: 74).

Dominique Bouhours (1628—1702) is a typical, although hardly original, representative of the genius-of-language concept when he equates the various "talens de peintres" with the different "genies des langues", i. e.

the qualifications of certain men with that of a language. At the same time, he shows an almost ridiculous arbitrariness in criteria selection (far removed from any classical predecessor) when he compares the Romance languages to types of women:

"Ainsi pour ne parler que de leur genies, sans rien decider de leur naissance, il me semble que la langue Espagnol est une orgueilleuse qui les porte haut; qui se pique de grandeur; qui aime le faste, et l'excés en toutes choses. La langue Italienne est une coquette toûjours parée et toûjours fardée, qui ne cherche qu'à plaire, et qui ne se plaist qu'à la bagatelle. La langue Françoise est une prude; mais une prude agreable, qui toute sage et toute modeste qu'elle est, n'a rien de rude ni de farouche. C'est une fille qui a beaucoup de traits de sa mère, je veux dire de la langue Latine [...]" (see Christmann 1976: 72).

The airiness of these arguments is only surpassed by the endlessly repeated anecdote according to which Charles V is said to have claimed that he spoke Spanish to God, Italian to his friends, French to his mistress, and German (by which he must have meant present-day Dutch, if at all) to his soldiers, or to his horses (Gerhardi 1993: 30). It is obvious that such statements are much more significant for the history of national stereotypes than for that of linguistic ideas (Stanzel 1998).

The most telling example of the genius concept in Britain, Guy Miège's treatise on the excellency of the English tongue (1688, see above), is the representative of a different facet of the problem. It places a heavier stress on the properties of the language than on those of the people who speak it. Whereas the previously mentioned authors tended to explain the language with the help of its society, Miège tends to explain the society with the help of its language. He chooses those qualities (facility, significance, copiousness, sweetness) which enable the language to mirror all things of the world and all notions of the human mind for the purpose of human communication. Miège's argument, just like that of Harsdörffer and Schottelius, is thus placed next to that of a perfect language, and it is the pride in possessing it which distinguishes its speakers (Paxman 1991).

Seen against the background of the so-called 'plain style movement', we can detect even here a tacit but historically interesting reservoir of ideas about the English national character. The self-deprecatory characterization of English as plain, humble, simple, coarse, etc. (see above) had always been slightly ambivalent, as the adjectives used to describe it could also be taken as positive moral qualities. The 'plain but honest', 'common but well meaning' stereotype behind them was to some extent in conflict with the idea of ornateness and decoration which underpinned the linguistic innovations of the Renaissance. The language of *Piers Ploughman* and the translated Bible always had a strong position against that of Sidney and Spenser. When the members of the Royal Society (founded in 1660) propagated the plain style as "their manner of discourse" (Hüllen 1989), they had Bacon's epistemological deliberations in mind. According to him, matter was more important than choice words and a text had to be an exact mirror of what people know by experience and by induction, and of nothing else. It was Bacon's struggle against the Ciceronianism of this period and his plea for a direct and honest scientific language which the members of the Royal Society referred to. But by doing this they approached unintentionally, as it were, the 'plain but honest' idea, by which the English language was supposed to indicate the character of the indigenous people. The new scientific style was again characterized by adjectives ('unadorned', 'plain', 'naked', 'masculine', etc.) with distinct moral undertones (Hüllen 1989: 107–112). In his *History of the Royal Society* (1667), Thomas Sprat (1635–1713) declared this to be the true scientific (Baconian) and at the same time the true English style. "There can be little doubt that Sprat intended the connection between national character and language to be apparent." (Paxman 1991: 32), even if he did not mention this explicitly.

From historiographical hindsight, we quickly recognize the shortcomings of the genius-of-language concept. It lies in the pitfalls of establishing societal clichés and stereotypes and in confounding linguistic structures of any level for language use. The famous *clareté*, which would evolve as the outstanding feature of the genius of French in the succeeding century, is not a property of the French language as such but of its use, following the guidance of highly regarded philosophical and stylistic ideas (Schlieben-Lange 1988, Hüllen 1996). This shows most clearly when the genius of language is, for example, identified with the poetic and esthetic principles of French, as Claude Lancelot (ca. 1615–1695) did in his *Nouvelle methode pour apprendre facilement et en peu de temps le langage latine* (2nd ed., 1650) and as we find it in discussions on the translatability of Homer's epics into English (Jones 1966: 240).

4. The exceptional case: Comenius

Linguistic nationalism, not in the modern sense but in that which prevailed in the 16th and 17th centuries, had one of its conceptual origins in theology. The Renaissance linguists and historians found ways to apply the Biblical account of the origin of mankind and the whole relevant context of theology to individual nations, claiming for each of them God's own support. This gave the ensuing competition between nations and their languages the most powerful incentive imaginable, and it is not totally inconceivable that this incentive caused, thanks to a long-term, if subconscious, influence, the heated and frequently biased controversies which linguistic nationalism experienced in the 19th and 20th centuries.

There is at least one author of the 17th century who shows that national rivalry was not the only possible consequence in the given situation: Johannes Amos Comenius (Jan Amos Komenský, 1592–1670). His many linguistic works, both theoretical and applied, i.e. on language and on language teaching, culminated in *De rerum humanarum emendatione consultatio catholica* (discovered as a manuscript as late as 1935, printed 1966), whose fifth part is *Panglottia*. Agreeing in principle with the contemporary ideas on Adamic language and the punishment of Babel, Comenius attributed to every national language in the world the essential task of promoting knowledge in general and the wisdom of God in particular (Přívratská 1996). He saw three ways of doing this: people must learn either all the languages of this world (*pantoglottia*), or some of those which are of regional importance (*polyglottia*), or only one (*monoglottia*), which could only be a universal language. The first and the third possibilities were, of course, impossibilities. Comenius' realistic way out of this situation was to postulate that everybody had to learn their native vernacular well, that those who needed them had to learn one of the so-called *linguae principales* (German, French, the Slavonic languages seen as a group of dialects), and that it was the task of the future to develop a universal language which would unite all humankind and would allow *pansophia*, the all-embracing knowledge of God, to come into being and to spread. The learned languages Greek and Latin were outside this programme, but Latin could, at least for the time being, serve as a universal idiom.

The most noteworthy characteristic of this pedagogical model is the total absence of all national animosity and ensuing competition. It is well known that Comenius loved his mother-tongue. He worked for decades on a Czech dictionary, only to see all his papers destroyed in the great fire of Leszno (1656). He also mentioned the well-known observations on the advantages and drawbacks of individual languages, as authors had described them to prove their evaluative comparisons. But for him all languages were equal as a tool for eternal salvation. He used theology to unite mankind, not to separate its nations.

5. Universalism vs. beginning of relativism

5.1. It was the perhaps strongest incentive of Renaissance and Early Modern linguistics to come to terms with the great number of vernaculars in Europe without giving up such traditional ideas as intelligibility, acceptance, Biblical explanations, and semiotic perfection. This is why the old universalism attached to the all-dominant Latin language gave way to a linguistic awareness of multiple languages which, however, still shared some of the traditional properties. What hitherto had been said with reference to one language (Latin) had now, at least partly, to be said with reference to many.

The new universalism of the 17th century developed in the context of Cartesian thinking. Its peak were the three influential books from the monastery of Port Royal: (i) Claude Lancelot: *Nouvelle méthode pour apprendre [...] la langue latine* (1644), (ii) Antoine Arnould and Claude Lancelot: *Grammaire général et raisonnée [...] de Port-Royal* (1660), and (iii) Antoine Arnauld and P. Nicole: *La logique ou l'art de penser de Port-Royal* (1662). All three books appeared in a number of versions and were translated into the main European languages.

The amount of linguistic studies on Claude Lancelot and Antoine Arnould (1612–1694) is by now unmanageable. It concerns the history of ideas as incorporated in these books, the relative contributions of the authors to their publications, divergences between these, a possible hiatus between the programme and its execution, at least in the grammar, and other topics (Chomsky 1966, Brekle 1975: 333—382; Auroux 1993). Leaving all this and other Cartesian (Port Royal) authors like Bernard Lamy (1640—1715), Géraud de Cordemoy (1620—1684), or Blaise Pascal (1623—1662), and furthermore the discussion on Noam Chomsky's reception of Cartesian linguistics (Lakoff 1969, Salmon 1979 [1969]: 63—86, Aarsleff 1982: 101—119) aside, we can state, above all, that there is an obvious homogeneity between the *grammaire* and Cartesian philosophy. There is the axiomatic dichotomy between spirit (*raison*) and body which repeats itself in the linguistic dichotomy of the structural and the phonetic parts of language. Whereas thinking, i.e. the activity of *raison*, is universal to all humankind, bodies are not. Language is secondary to thinking, a tool to express thoughts necessary only for communication between human beings. Semiotically, i.e. concerning its 'body', language is arbitrary. This entails that all languages are identical in so far as they express thoughts, but that they differ in the signs which they choose in order to do this. The aim of the *grammaire* is to show exactly this. Note the third subtitle: *[... contenant] Les raisons de ce qui est commun à toutes les langues, & des principales differences qui s'y rencontrent.*

Although different in its philosophical presuppositions, Descartes' dichotomy of *res extensae* and *res cogitans* repeated formally the dichotomy of 'body' and 'soul' which St Augustine (354—430) had already made, including that of 'pure thinking' (before the Fall) and 'thinking with the help of signs' (after the Fall) (Haßler 1984: 9—13), and also the dichotomy of 'substance' and 'accidence' in medieval philosophy. Although again different in its philosophical presuppositions, the Port Royal Grammar repeated linguistically a universalism which had, for example, been claimed by the *Modistae* (13th to 14th centuries, Bursill-Hall 1971) on the grounds that the structures of Latin agreed with the structures of thought as Aristotle, for example, had defined them in his categories. The philosophical dichotomy of *res extensae* and *res cogitans* thus had its preceding model in the assumption of the *Modistae* that languages are identical in substance but different in accidence.

There were also Renaissance linguists, i.e. authors much nearer in time to those of Port Royal, who claimed that language had underlying semantic (logical) structures which, in cases of diverging usage, could even be reconstructed. This meant placing the Modistic axiom of the structures of thought and speaking into each sentence. To them belong Julius Caesar Scaliger (1484—1558), who underpinned linguistic performance with the Aristotelian concepts of *causa materialis* and *causa formalis* (*De causis linguae latinae libri tredecim*, 1540); Thomas Linacre (ca. 1460—1524), who treated ellipsis in daily language use as an amendable deficiency of the perfect underlying sentence structure (*De emendata structura Latini sermonis*, 1524), and Franciscus Sanctius Brocensis (1523—1601), who followed Linacre in this argument (*Minerva seu de causis linguae Latinae*, 1587). The parallels between these three authors and some chapters of the Port Royal grammar, for example the famous one on the relative clause, have often been pointed out (e.g. Lakoff 1969, Padley 1985: 233—244, 283—324), just as the parallels between the relevant chapters of this grammar and modern generative theory have been (→ Art. 15).

The three books from Port Royal thus combined new philosophical presuppositions (which made them modern) with old linguistic assumptions (which made them traditional), applying methods of analysis to all languages which had previously been applied only to Latin. In fact, Arnauld and Lancelot almost always use the structures of French, whenever they do not use those of Latin, Greek, or Hebrew. Practically, for example in matters of language teaching, their grammar had the effect of moving French into the model position which Latin had held before.

It almost goes without saying that the undertaking of Port Royal found followers in many countries. Naturally, it became the leading model for the writing of grammars in the France of the 18th century. But its influence was also great in Britain and Germany. Didactically, the theory developed that learning one's own language according to a method which stressed its universal character was the best preparation for learning foreign languages. Archibald Lane's (fl. 1695—1700) *A Rational and Speedy Method of Attaining to the Latin Tongue* (1695) and *A Key to the Art of Letters* (1700) followed exactly this aim. The danger that an author simply declared the structures of his own vernacular to be the universal ones was, of course, great. Mark Lewis (fl. 1670–1678), for example, wrote *Institutio grammaticae puerilis* (1670), according to his own words an introductory grammar to English, Latin, and Greek. In his preface he says:

"The Regularitie of the English-tongue appears from this assertion almost Universally true: Whatever Tongue hath less Grammar than the English, is not intelligible; whatever hath more, is superfluous. [...] Thus we may compute what Grammar any language hath for necessity (as in the English) what for ornament (as in the Latin and Greek). (see Göbels 1999).

5.2. The English counterpart of the Port Royal grammar is John Wilkins' (1614–1672) *Essay Towards a Real Character, And a Philosophical Language* of 1668. It is neither a grammar, nor a treatise on logic, nor a treatise on the method of teaching — and this probably prevented the *Essay* from achieving the general recognition which the *Grammaire générale et raisonnée* enjoyed (and still enjoys). It is a treatise on 'Philosophical Grammar' as the third part of the construction of a system of written (i.e. character) and spoken (i.e. language) signs, which were to be understood by the speakers of all languages in the way in which digits or the signs of the zodiac are: they have the same meaning for everybody and can, thus and if necessary, be pronounced by everybody in their own languages. After the 'Prolegomena' in the first part of the *Essay*, the second explains the semantic aspect of this language and is in fact a comprehensive word-thesaurus (Hüllen 1999), and the fourth develops the universal system in its phonetic and graphic signs. There were several such universal language plans in Britain during the 17th century (Slaughter 1982, Hüllen 1989), that of John Wilkins (Aarsleff 1982: 239–277) being the most elaborate one. Obviously, Arnauld & Lancelot and Wilkins had different points of departure for their treatments: the former set themselves a very traditional task, i.e. the writing of a grammar, but did it in a way which was overtly quite innovative, but nevertheless contained many traditional elements. The latter started an entirely new enterprise (for which he erroneously claimed hieroglyphs and Chinese characters as models), which had the traditional views of the universal qualities of all languages as a prerequisite.

The difference between Arnauld & Lancelot and Wilkins manifests itself equally in the two books:

(i) After discussing sounds and letters in the first part, the second part of the *Grammaire* starts by explaining "[...] trois operations de nostre esprit: concevoir, iuger, raisonner":

"*Concevoir*, n'est autre chose q'vn simple regard de nostre esprit sur les choses, soit d' vne maniere purement intellectuelle; [...]. *Ivger*, c'est affirmer qu'vne chose que nous concevons, est telle, ou n' est pas telle. [...] *Raisonner*, est se servir de deux jugements pour en faire vn troisième. (Brekle 1966: 27–28).

These are the truly Cartesian foundations. The grammar then proceeds to define the word-classes and their 'accidence' on the basis of *concevoir* (nouns with gender and cases marked by prepositions; articles, pronouns, prepositions outside case markings, adverbs; verbs with persons, numbers, tenses, and modes, as infinitives and participles, gerunds, etc.; auxiliaries, conjunctions and interjections). There then follows a short treatment of 'syntax or construction' on the basis of *juger*. The third level of *raisonner* is dismissed as being a combination of the first two. The various chapters deserve their fame because of the brilliance and elegance of the treatment, above all perhaps the explanation of the genitive (chap. VI), of the cases and the various uses of articles (chap. VII), of the relative pronouns (chaps. IX and X), and the classification of prepositions (chap. XI). But the linguistic substance of these chapters, inside their Cartesian embeddings, as it were, coincides with many traditional analyses. "My point here is that this type of analysis, though eminently acceptable to Cartesian philosophy, had been made a thousand times by medievalist and humanist grammarians" (Padley 1985: 302, and *passim* in a similar way).

(ii) The 'philosophical grammar' in John Wilkins' *Essay* (Salmon 1979 [1975]: 97–126, Göbels 1999) rests on a universal ordering of reality, which starts with the most abstract *praedicabilia* and *praedicamenta*, then proceeds to the Aristotelian categories (substance; quantity, quality, action, and relation as accidence) and finally arrives at a universal order according to genera, difference, and species. Wilkins obviously adopted the long tradition of Aristotelian and Scholastic ontology. It is part of the three-level approach which he found in Francis Bacon but which was just as traditional, according to which a *word* is the name of a *notion*, which is the mental representation of a *thing*. Thing and *notion* are universal for all humankind, and it is the task of a universal language to find a direct iconic representation for them. Indeed, the Baconian programme of the Royal Society to increase knowledge and apply it for the good of society was the strongest incentive for the Universal Language plan as Cartesian anthropology was for the *Grammaire*.

Wilkins' grammatical system looks rather radical. Following the old difference between things that exist out of themselves and those that do not (*categoremata* and *syncategoremata*) he distinguished between *integrals* and *particles*, explaining that verbs are not an independent word-class among the integrals because they are adjectives plus copula (the only necessary particle). This argument also occurred in the *Grammaire*. What he explained in detail about integrals (*nouns, adjectives, derived adverbs*) and particles (essential: *copula*; occasional and substitutive: *pronoun* and *interjection*; occasional and connexive: *preposition, conjunction*, and *original adverb*; occasional and declarative: *article, modal, tense-marker*) coincides in many cases with the contents of Renaissance and earlier grammarians. Salmon (1979 [1975]: 97−126) recognizes affiliations to Thomas of Erfurt (fl. 1300), Juan Caramuel (y Lobkowitz, 1606−1682), Thomaso Campanella (1568−1639), Gerard Johannes Vossius (1577−1649), and Julius Caesar Scaliger, and, through them, older grammarians as early as Priscian (fl. 6th cent. AD).

More original than all the rest is Wilkins' concept of so-called *transcendental particles*.

"Those particles are here stiled *Transcendental*, which do circumstantiate words in respect of some Metaphysical notion; either by enlarging the acception of them to some more general signification, then doth belong to the restrained sense of their places: or denoting a relation to some other Predicament or Genus, under which they are not originally placed." (See Göbels 1999).

This pertains to the literal and metaphorical meanings of words, to derivations and compositions (e. g. *act, actor, actress, acting*, etc.), and to semantic relations between words (e. g. *actor, stage, theatre, performance, costume, role*, etc.). Together with the great thesauraus of lexemes, the systematic treatment of these phenomena makes Wilkins a representative of structural semantics *avant la lettre*.

Europe-wide, John Wilkins' reputation has always been that of a planner of a universal language, comparable, for example, with Gottfried Wilhelm Leibniz (1646−1716). In Britain, however, his ideas also became the model for many descriptive grammars of English which intended to make the language visible in its universal aspects. Indeed, the *Grammaire* and the *Essay* together became the most frequently mentioned works of reference in these books. The works of Archibald Lane and Mark Lewis have already been mentioned. The majority of these works appeared in the 18th century (Göbels 1999).

In spite of the various similarities, the two treatises, appearing in 1660 and 1668, seem to have been written independently of each other.

5.3. The strongest argument for linguistic universalism is the independence of thinking from the linguistic sign. Consequently, the strongest argument for relativism is the opposite assumption, i. e. the dependence of the two upon each other. The idea already announced itself in the early grammars of the Romance languages, where the right of the vernaculars, i. e. of language usage, was claimed against the standards of classical Latin. In the 17th century we find a whole series of utterances which spoke of the superiority of language over thought and thus prefigured the relativist position, even if only as a fact worthy of criticism. Indeed, this idea forms part of the philosophical history of that century.

In his doctrine of the four idols, Francis Bacon, who did not elaborate a consistent linguistic theory at all, criticized various 'fallacies' of language use. In particular, the idols of the market-place and the idols of the theatre show that people tend to follow uncontrolled and traditional habits of language use rather than make the language follow their ways of critical thinking. In his deliberations on grammar, Bacon suggested a comparison of languages in their structures which might lead to a truly relativist result:

"[...] there will be obtained in this way signs of no slight value but well worthy of observation (which a man would hardly think perhaps) concerning the dispositions and manners of peoples and nations, drawn from their languages" (see Hüllen 1989: 46).

Even the Cartesian authors acknowledged a certain influence of the language on the ways of thinking, mainly caused by uncritical usage. Words, which denote notions of things, are frequently mistaken as denoting the things themselves. Descartes himself accepted that *imagination* and *passion* estranged language use because they are dependent on certain states of the body. And in the *Grammaire* we find again and again that language use is registered as something contradicting *raison*. Baruch Spinoza stressed the difference between universally valid concepts and the ethnically dependent and era-specific linguistic expressions. In strict contradiction to Descartes, Thomas Hobbes propounded the so-called sensualist position by saying that knowledge (ideas) is first in the senses and then in the mind. It is memorized with the help of language as 'marks' and communicated with the help of language as 'signs'. These are arbitrary (Isermann 1991). It was finally John Locke who prepared the way for relativism more than any other philosopher. Ideas in the human mind are stimulated by the sensual experience of reality, but they are not its direct image. Words are names of ideas and not of reality. As simple ideas are combined by the creative human intellect to form complex ideas, so word meanings refer more often than not to something which does not exist in reality but 'only' in the mind. As the various peoples have their own ways of combining ideas, language is dependent on them. There are no longer any inborn ideas, there is no independence of thought and language, and consequently there are no universal structures of languages which differ 'only' in the substance of their signs. Ideas are now stimulated by experience, but combined by the human mind. Language is dependent on this combination, and the various languages differ accordingly.

It is hardly possible to overestimate the importance of René Descartes on the one hand and John Locke on the other in their impact on the linguistic developments of the succeeding centuries. Next to Wilkins and the *Grammaire*, John Locke became the most frequently quoted author in the grammars of the following century.

6. References

Aarsleff, Hans. 1982. *From Locke to Saussure*. London: Athlone.

Arens, Hans. 1969. *Sprachwissenschaft. Der Gang ihrer Entwicklung von der Antike bis zur Gegenwart.* Second ed. Freiburg and München: Alber.

Auroux, Sylvain (ed.). 1992. *Histoire des idées linguistiques*. Tome 2: Le développement de la grammaire occidentale. Liège: Mardaga.

Auroux, Sylvain. 1993. *La logique des idées*. Montreal and Paris.

Bailey, Richard W. 1991. *Images of English. A Cultural History of the Language*. Ann Arbor: Univ. of Michigan Press.

Borst, Arno. 1995. *Der Turmbau von Babel*. Vols. I, II/1, II/2, III/1, III/2, IV. Stuttgart: Hiersemann 1957–62. Reissue: München: dtv.

Brekle, Herbert Ernst (ed.). 1966. *Grammaire générale et raisonnée ou la grammaire de Port Royal*. Edition critique présentée par [...]. Stuttgart-Bad Cannstatt: Frommann.

Brekle, Herbert Ernst. 1975. *The seventeenth century*. In: Sebeok 1975, 277–382.

Bursill-Hall, G. L. 1971. *Speculative Grammars in the Middle Ages*. The Hague: Mouton.

Chomsky, Noam. 1966. *Cartesian Linguistics: A chapter in the history of rationalist thought*. New York: Harper & Row.

Christmann, Hans Helmut. 1976. "Bemerkungen zum génie de la langage." In: A. Barrera-Vidal, E. Ruhe, and P. Schunck: *Lebendige Romania. Festschrift für Hans-Wilhelm Klein* [...]. Göppingen: Kümmerle, 65–79.

Eco, Umberto. 1993. *La ricerca della lingua perfetta nella cultura europea*. [German trans. München: Beck 1994, Engl. trans. Oxford: Blackwell 1996.] Rom-Bari: Laterza.

Gardt, Andreas. 1999. *Geschichte der Sprachwissenschaft in Deutschland*. Berlin: de Gruyter.

Gerhardi, Gerhard C. 1993. "The 'génie des langues' and the rise of linguistic nationalism." In: H. Kreuzer, K. Riha, and C. W. Thomsen (eds.): *Von Rubens zum Dekonstruktivismus*. [...] Festschrift für Wolfgang Drost. Heidelberg: Winter, 26–40.

Gessinger, Joachim & Wolfert von Rahden (eds.). 1987. *Theorien vom Ursprung der Sprache*. Two vols. Berlin: de Gruyter.

Göbels, Astrid. 1999. *Die Tradition der Universalgrammatik im England des 17. und 18. Jahrhunderts*. Münster: Nodus.

Haßler, Gerda. 1984. *Sprachtheorien der Aufklärung zur Rolle der Sprache im Erkenntnisprozeß*. Berlin: Akad. Verlag.

Howatt, Anthony P. R. 1984. *A History of English Language Teaching*. Oxford: Oxford Univ. Press.

Hüllen, Werner. 1989. *'Their Manner of Discourse'. Nachdenken über Sprache im Umkreis der Royal Society*. Tübingen: Narr.

Hüllen, Werner. 1995. "Good language – bad language. Some case studies on the criteria of linguistic evaluation in three centuries." In: Klaus D. Dutz and Kjell-Åke Forsgren (eds.): *History and Rationality: The Skövde Papers in the History of Linguistics*. Münster: Nodus, 315–334.

Hüllen, Werner. 1996. "Some yardsticks of language evaluation 1600–1800 (English and German)." In: Vivien Law and Werner Hüllen (eds.): *Linguists and Their Diversions. A Festschrift for R. H. Robins* [...]. Münster: Nodus, 275–306.

Hüllen, Werner. 1999. *English Dictionaries 800–1700: The Topical Tradition.* Oxford: Clarendon.

Isermann, Michael. 1991. *Die Sprachtheorie im Werk von Thomas Hobbes.* Münster: Nodus.

Jones, Richard Foster. 1966. *The Triumph of the English Language.* Reprint. Stanford: Univ. Press.

Lakoff, Robin. 1969. [Review of] *Grammaire générale et raisonner, ou La grammaire de Port-Royal.* Ed. by Herbert E. Brekle [...] Stuttgart-Bad Cannstatt 1966. Language, 45, 343–364.

Law, Vivien & Ineke Sluiter (eds.). 1995. *Dionysius Thrax and the 'Techne Grammatike'.* Münster: Nodus.

Leisi, Ernst & Christian Mair. 1998. *Das heutige Englisch. Wesenszüge und Probleme.* Eighth edition. Heidelberg: Winter.

Liebermann, Wolf-Lüder. 1991. *Sprachauffassungen im frühgriechischen Epos und in der griechischen Mythologie.* In: Schmitter 1991a, 26–53.

Matthews, Peter. 1994. "Greek and Latin linguistics." In: Guilio Lepschy (ed.): *History of Linguistics.* Vol. II: *Classical and Medieval Linguistics.* London: Longman, 1–133.

Padley, G. A. 1985. *Grammatical Theory in Western Europe 1500–1700.* [Vol. 2:] Trends in Vernacular Grammar I. Cambridge: Cambridge Univ. Press.

Paxman, David B. 1991. "The genius of English: Eighteenth-century language study and English poetry." In: *Philological Quarterly* 70, 27–46.

Přívratská, Jana. 1996. Panglottia – Comenius' model for language unification. In: Kurt R. Jankowsky (ed.): *Multiple Perspectives on the Historical Dimensions of Language.* Münster: Nodus, 75–80.

Robins, Robert H. 1990. *A Short History of Linguistics.* Third edition. London: Longman.

Salmon, Vivian. 1979. *The Study of Language in Seventeenth Century England.* Amsterdam: Benjamins.

Schenk, Wolfgang. 1991. "Altisraelitische Sprachauffassungen in der Hebräischen Bibel." In: Schmitter, 1991a, 3–26.

Schlaps, Christiane. 1999. Das Konzept eines 'deutschen Sprachgeistes' in der Geschichte der Sprachtheorie. In: Andreas Gardt (ed.): *Nation und Sprache.* Berlin: de Gruyter.

Schlieben-Lange, Brigitte. 1988. "Die Traditionen des Sprechens und die Traditionen der klar-konfusen und klar-distinkten Idee über das Sprechen." In: Jörn Albrecht, Jens Lüdtke, and Harald Thun (eds.). *Energeia und Ergon [...]. Vol. 3: Das sprachtheoretische Denken Eugenio Coserius in der Diskussion* (2). Tübingen: Narr, 451–462.

Schmitter, Peter. 1991. "Vom 'Mythos' zum 'Logos': Erkenntniskritik und Sprachreflexion bei den Vorsokratikern." In: Schmitter, 57–86.

Schmitter, Peter (ed.). 1991a. *Geschichte der Sprachtheorie. Vol. 2: Sprachtheorien der abendländischen Antike.* Tübingen: Narr 1991.

Sebeok, Thomas A. (ed.). 1975. *Current Trends in Linguistics.* Vol. 13: *Historiography of Linguistics.* The Hague/Paris: Mouton.

Slaughter, M. M. 1982. *Universal Languages and Scientific Taxonomy in the Seventeenth Century.* Cambridge: Cambridge Univ. Press.

Stammerjohann, Harro (ed.). 1996. *Lexicon Grammaticorum. Who's Who in the History of World Linguistics.* Tübingen: Niemeyer.

Stanzel, Franz K. (ed.). 1998. *Europäischer Völkerspiegel. Imagologisch-ethnographische Studien zu den Völkertafeln des frühen 18. Jahrhundert.* Heidelberg: Winter.

Werner Hüllen, Universität Essen
(Deutschland)

19. Die Anfänge typologischen Denkens im europäischen Rationalismus

1. Einleitung: Kritik der Geschichte der Sprachtypologie
2. Die Wiederentdeckung rationalistischer Vorläufer der Sprachtypologie
3. Rationalistische Vorläufer der Sprachtypologie im zweiten Universalismus
4. Schlußbemerkung
5. Zitierte Literatur

1. Einleitung: Kritik der Geschichte der Sprachtypologie

Die Anfänge der Sprachtypologie wurden und werden immer noch mit dem Beginn der morphologischen Sprachklassifikation im frühen 19. Jh. gleichgesetzt: Ahnherren und Begründer der Disziplin sind die deutschen Romantiker, also Friedrich Schlegel, August Wilhelm Schlegel und Wilhelm von Humboldt; mit ihnen hebt eine Entwicklungslinie an, die über Fauriel (vgl. Sgoff 1994: 21 ff.), Schleicher, Steinthal und Misteli bis hin zu Georg von der Gabelentz und Nikolaus Finck das ganze 19. Jh. umfaßt und mit Namen wie Sapir, Skalička, Milewski und Uspenskij bis weit in das 20. Jh. hineinreicht (vgl. beispielsweise die klassische Darstellung von Horne 1966 sowie die kritischen Anmerkungen von Coseriu 1976).

Ein rezentes und recht typisches Beispiel ist Whaley 1997; diesem Einführungswerk ist eine „(brief) history of typology" vorangestellt, in der die Wurzeln des typologischen Ansatzes bei den deutschen Romantikern und ihrer Vorstellung vom Sprachorganismus gesucht wird. Diese wird als „difficult to grasp because far removed from the current conception of language" empfunden (Whaley 1997: 19). Dementsprechend führt im Grunde kaum eine Brücke von den traditionellen Ansätzen der Sprachtypologie hin zu dem, was man heute als „Typologie" zu bezeichnen pflegt; im Grunde beginnt die wirklich noch lebendige Tradition dieser Richtung im Rahmen der heutigen amerikanisch geprägten Linguistik nicht mit Sapir, auch nicht mit Bloomfield, sondern mit Greenberg, und hier insbesondere mit seinem Ansatz zu einer Wortstellungstypologie von 1963 (dies ist nicht mehr der Greenberg von 1954, der in der Tat noch ganz in der Tradition des 19. Jh.s steht). Zwar wird die Kontinuität der Forschung als historisches Faktum anerkannt, aber die Prähistorie und die „eigentliche" Historie, das heißt die Geschichte nach diesem oft als „seminal" bezeichneten Beitrag von Greenberg, stehen recht unverbunden nebeneinander; das Interesse an Vorläufern ist bestenfalls museal, in den meisten Fällen schlicht inexistent.

In der heutigen Typologie befaßt man sich kaum mehr mit der klassischen, aus der Frühzeit der deutschen Romantik stammenden Fragestellung einer Einteilung in „geformte" und „formlose", oder in „isolierende / agglutinierende / flektierende / polysynthetische" Sprachen. Nur gelegentlich wird die alte, auf August Wilhelm Schlegel zurückgehende Diskussion über den „analytischen" und den „synthetischen" Sprachbau wieder aufgegriffen und mit neuen Einsichten weitergeführt (Fleischmann 1982, Schwegler 1990).

Insgesamt bewegt sich die typologische Forschung heute auf anderen Bahnen als denen, die ihr von ihren Begründern vorgezeichnet worden sind; der Zusammenhang ist eher in der historischen Kontinuität als in Gemeinsamkeit der Fragestellungen zu suchen. Die Berufung auf die Geschichte der Disziplin bleibt im Äußeren stecken; der Rückgriff auf eine überkommene Begrifflichkeit befruchtet kaum die heutige Diskussion. Dies hat verschiedene Ursachen, von denen ich zwei besonders herausarbeiten möchte: den GEGENSTANDSBEREICH, und das ZIEL der Sprachtypologie.

GEGENSTAND der traditionellen Typologie des 19. Jh.s war der morphologische Bau der Sprachen. Gefragt wurde nach dem Verhältnis von grammatischen und Wurzelelementen, modern gesprochen, von Grammem und Lexem: die Verbindung zwischen beiden konnte mehr oder weniger fest, mehr oder weniger „organisch" sein (Flexion vs. Agglutination), Grammeme konnten ganz fehlen (Isolation) oder zu einem in europäischen Sprachen unbekannten Komplexitätsgrad ausgebaut sein (Polysynthese). Der syntaktische Bau kam nicht ins Blickfeld; Fragen wie die Anordnung der Satzglieder, oder auch der Ausdruck von Subordinationsbeziehungen, wurden nicht behandelt. Man glaubte, in der Beziehung von Wurzel und Affix den Schlüssel für eine allgemeine Charakteristik der Sprache in der Hand zu haben, das, was ihr innerstes Wesen ausmachte.

Dieser Ansatz steht heutigem linguistischem Denken ziemlich fern; auch wenn man aus heutiger Sicht bereit ist, die Fragestellung als solche für beachtenswert zu halten, wird man kaum so weit gehen wollen, sie in das Zentrum der typologischen Klassifikation zu rücken. Dies gilt um so mehr, als sich mittlerweile allenthalben die Einsicht durchgesetzt hat, daß man eine Sprache ohnehin nicht einheitlich klassifizieren kann, daß also immer mehrere Kriterien zusammenwirken müssen, und daß daher Charakterisierungen wie „agglutinierend/flexivisch" usw. immer nur eine Teilwahrheit repräsentieren können.

Ganz allgemein stehen in der heutigen Typologie syntaktische Kriterien im Vordergrund, und wenn man überhaupt eine globale Charakterisierung von Sprachen als Ziel der Typologie ansieht, dann wird man ein Kriterium wie „VO vs. OV" als fundamental annehmen, nicht ein morphologisches; nach heutiger Auffassung wäre es wohl am ehesten ein solches syntaktisches Kriterium, was es erlaubt, aus dem Lindenblatt den Lindenbaum zu erschließen, wie Georg von der Gabelentz dies in dem berühmten Passus formuliert hat, der mit Recht als Tauf-Urkunde der Sprachtypologie gilt:

„welcher Gewinn wäre es auch, wenn wir einer Sprache auf den Kopf zusagen dürften: Du hast das und das Einzelmerkmal, folglich hast du die und die weiteren Eigenschaften und den und den Gesammtcharakter! — wenn wir, wie es kühne Botaniker wohl versucht haben, aus dem Lindenblatte den Lindenbaum construiren könnten. Dürfte man ein ungeborenes Kind taufen, ich würde den Namen *Typologie* wählen." (Gabelentz 1891/1901 [1984]: 481; Hervorhebung vom Autor)

Der andere Punkt wurde bereits kurz angesprochen. Als ZIEL DER TYPOLOGIE wird man heute nicht mehr primär eine Globalcharakterisierung von Sprachen ansehen, die dann letztlich in einer Klassifikation der Sprachen der Welt einmündet. Typologien sind von ihrem Anspruch her nicht mehr holistisch, vielmehr ist man sich darüber klar geworden, daß etwas, was ein beherrschendes Prinzip in einer Sprache ist, keiner anderen Sprache ganz und gar fremd sein kann. Die Unterschiede zwischen den Sprachen beziehen sich immer nur auf partielle Systeme; umfassende Klassifikationen sind nicht nur als utopisch, sondern als geradezu dem Wesen der Sprache widersprechend erkannt, da man heute die Autonomie ihrer modularen Komponenten betont und die Suche nach dem einen entscheidenden Grundprinzip der individuellen Einzelsprache aufgegeben hat.

Fassen wir zusammen. Im Vergleich zu der Entwicklung der „klassischen" Sprachtypologie, von den Schlegels und Humboldt bis Sapir und Skalička, schlägt die typologische Forschung heute in zweierlei Hinsicht andere Wege ein: im Zentrum steht nicht mehr die Morphologie, verstanden als die Beziehung von Lexem und Grammem, sondern die Syntax; und statt eines holistischen, auf die „Gestalt" der Einzelsprache gerichteten Ansatzes wird heute eine Denkweise bevorzugt, die von der Modularität des Sprachbaus ausgeht und Eigenschaften einer Sprache je für sich betrachtet, ehe eventuelle Zusammenhänge im Sinne von Implikationen und Implikations-Hierarchien ermittelt werden.

2. Die Wiederentdeckung rationalistischer Vorläufer der Sprachtypologie

In der aktuellen Literatur zur Sprachtypologie läßt man, wie soeben dargelegt, die Geschichte der Sprachtypologie im frühen 19. Jh. beginnen, mit der Folge, daß heutige Fragestellungen kaum mehr einen Bezug zu früheren Stadien der Fachentwicklung aufweisen. Es ist jedoch international relativ wenig beachtet worden, daß es außer den genannten auch noch andere Wurzeln des sprachtypologischen Denkens gibt, daß dieses weiter in die Vergangenheit zurückreicht als bislang angenommen, und vor allem, daß es in der Vorgeschichte der Disziplin Ansätze gibt, die dem heutigen Denken in mancher Hinsicht näher stehen und mehr Impulse geben könnten als die Typologie des 19. Jh.s.

Die Entdeckung einer Vorgeschichte der Sprachtypologie ist in erster Linie ein Verdienst von Hans Helmut Christmann. Seine Schülerin Irene Monreal-Wickert (Monreal-Wickert 1976, 1977; vgl. Coseriu 1976) hat gezeigt, daß bereits in der Linguistik der europäischen Aufklärung ein Sprachdenken vorliegt, das als typologisch bezeichnet werden kann. Es läßt sich zeigen, daß ein typologischer Ansatz sogar noch erheblich früher erkennbar ist und daß man insbesondere den italienischen Philosophen und Dichter Tommaso Campanelli als Vorläufer dieser Art von Sprachbetrachtung berücksichtigen muß (vgl. Bossong 1990: 210−29; 1992: 10−12). Das typologische Denken ist im Rahmen eines sprachwissenschaftlichen Rationalismus entstanden, der sich in Europa seit Ende des 16. Jh.s allmählich Bahn gebrochen hat, um dann im 17. und 18. Jh. nahezu uneingeschränkt zu herrschen. Die Verwurzelung der Sprachtypologie in dieser geistesgeschichtlichen Strömung aufzuzeigen, ist das primäre Ziel dieses Beitrags. Ebenso soll aber auch darauf reflektiert werden, inwiefern das „Gedankenkapital" jener Epoche für die heutige Reflexion noch relevant sein kann. Die historische Einordnung der eigenen Position kann zu deren heilsamer Relativierung führen, und darin scheint mir letztlich der Sinn jener Disziplin zu liegen, die seit einiger Zeit mit großer Intensität betrieben wird: der Historiographie der Linguistik.

2.1. Standortbestimmung der Sprachtypologie

Ehe auf die Geschichte, oder besser Vorgeschichte, der Sprachtypologie näher eingegangen wird, ist es angebracht, zunächst noch eine kurze Standortbestimmung der Disziplin vorzunehmen: was erlaubt es, einen sprachwissenschaftlichen oder sprachtheoretischen Ansatz als „typologisch" zu bezeichnen? Wie bekannt, und wie eben schon angedeutet, stammt der Name von Georg von der Gabelentz, er wurde im Jahre 1891 vergeben; dennoch scheint niemand Schwierigkeiten damit zu haben, auch schon die Gebrüder Schlegel, Humboldt und andere Gestalten des 19. Jh.s als „Typologen" zu klassifizieren. Mit welcher Berechtigung? Ebenso stellt sich natürlich diese Frage, wenn man Sprachforscher des 17. und 18. Jh.s als Vorläufer des „typologischen" Denkens charakterisiert: wie läßt sich dies begründen?

Es scheint mir sinnvoll, die Typologie als „allgemeine vergleichende Sprachwissenschaft" zu definieren. Dies befindet sich in voller Übereinstimmung mit dem Programm, welches Louis Hjelmslev gegeben hat und das so bekannt ist, daß es sich erübrigt, es *in extenso* zu zitieren; hier nur ein kurzer Ausschnitt:

„Aufgabe [der Sprachtypologie] ist in letzter Instanz, die Frage zu beantworten, welche Sprachstrukturen überhaupt möglich sind, und warum gerade diese Sprachstrukturen möglich sind und nicht andere [...]. Allein durch die Typologie erhebt sich die Linguistik zu ganz allgemeinen Gesichtspunkten und wird zu einer Wissenschaft." (Hjelmslev 1963 [1968]: 113)

In diesem Sinne ist Sprachtypologie also diejenige Wissenschaft, welche die allgemeinen Prinzipien des menschlichen Sprachbaus aus der Erfassung der einzelsprachlichen Verschiedenartigkeit abzuleiten sucht; Erkenntnis über die universale Sprachfähigkeit des Menschen (Saussures *langage*) soll aus der Analyse der Vielfalt der Einzelsprachen (Saussures *langue(s)*) gewonnen werden. Der Weg führt von den Sprachen zur Sprache; die generelle Forschungsstrategie ist induktiv, die Methodik vergleichend. Und dieser Vergleich ist, wie von Hjelmslev klar formuliert, nicht areal, historisch oder genetisch gebunden; er ist vielmehr allumfassend, oder sollte es zumindest dem Anspruch nach sein, auch wenn die Einlösung dieses Anspruchs letztlich utopisch bleibt. Das Programm der Sprachtypologie ist es also, durch den Vergleich möglichst vieler und vielfältiger Einzelsprachen zur Erkenntnis der Bandbreite der „Verschiedenheit des menschlichen Sprachbaues" zu gelangen, um von da aus die sprachlichen Universalien als die zugrundeliegenden Invarianten bestimmen zu können. Mit einem solchen Typologiebegriff ist es selbstverständlich möglich, von „Typologie" avant la lettre zu sprechen, und so hat man ganz fraglos etwa Wilhelm von Humboldt als Typologen charakterisiert, obgleich ja der Terminus, wie soeben gezeigt, erst Generationen später von Georg von der Gabelentz aus der Taufe gehoben worden ist. Und mit derselben Berechtigung lassen sich Sprachtheoretiker der vorangegangenen Jahrhunderte unter diesem Begriff subsumieren, auch wenn der Terminus „Typologie" noch nicht geboren war, und auch wenn keine historische Kontinuität zwischen diesen Vorläufern und dem, was später kam, nachzuweisen ist.

2.2. Universalismen und Partikularismen in der Geschichte der Sprachtheorie

Man kann die Geschichte der Sprachtheorie (verstanden als eine Beschäftigung mit Sprache im Sinne der Sprachwissenschaft oder der Sprachphilosophie) einteilen in Perioden, in denen die Perspektive der Universalien im Vordergrund stand, und solche, in denen es eher um die Einzelsprachen in ihrer unwiederholbaren Spezifizität ging. Im Sinne dieser Einteilung (vgl. Sharadzenidze 1976) habe ich vorgeschlagen, die Geschichte der Sprachtheorie in Westeuropa einzuteilen in Perioden des Universalismus und des Partikularismus, wobei sich in großen Zügen das folgende Bild ergibt (vgl. Bossong 1990).

- Erste Periode des Universalismus: die mittelalterlich-scholastische Sprachtheorie des Modismus und verwandter Strömungen (→ Art. 14);
- erste Periode des Partikularismus: die Beschäftigung mit den vom LATEINISCHEN emanzipierten Nationalsprachen in Humanismus und Renaissance (→ Art. 18);
- zweite Periode des Universalismus: die Sprachtheorie im Zeichen des Rationalismus im ausgehenden 16. sowie im 17. und 18. Jh.;
- zweite Periode des Partikularismus: die Neubewertung der Einzelsprachen seit Mitte des 18. Jh.s sowie die historisch-vergleichende Sprachwissenschaft im 19. Jh.;
- dritte Periode des Universalismus: die Hauptströmungen der Sprachwissenschaft des 20. Jh.s nach Saussure.

Die Autoren und Ansätze, die hier zu besprechen sind, müssen auf dem Hintergrund der rationalistischen Sprachtheorie des 17. und 18. Jh.s gesehen werden. Der vorliegende Beitrag bewegt sich also im Rahmen des zweiten Universalismus; dies muß zunächst noch etwas genauer ausgeführt werden.

Sprachtypologie geht von der Verschiedenheit der Einzelsprachen aus, um die universalen Gesetzmäßigkeiten zu erfassen, welche dieser Verschiedenheit zugrundeliegen; beide Aspekte gehören notwendig zusammen, und so kann sich ein sprachtypologischer Ansatz im Prinzip sowohl in Perioden des Universalismus wie auch in Perioden des Partikularismus entfalten. Bezüglich der oben genannten

Perioden der Sprachtheorie in Westeuropa kann man folgendes feststellen.

Im ersten Universalismus, in der scholastischen Sprachphilosophie, fehlte ein Interesse an einzelsprachlicher Vielfalt. Die Bemühungen der Sprachdenker zielten darauf ab, anhand der Universalsprache LATEIN die logische Struktur von Sprache überhaupt abzulesen. Der Gebrauch des Wortes *grammatica* ist symptomatisch: er bezeichnet sowohl die Grammatik als Beschreibung der Sprachstruktur, als auch die historische Einzelsprache LATEIN als diejenige Sprache, die formal im „Grammatik"-Unterricht erlernt wurde und die als einzige galt, in der es so etwas wie grammatische Regeln überhaupt gibt. Wegen der überwölbenden Universalität dieser *grammatica* tauchte die Frage der sprachlichen Vielfalt und der Vielgestaltigkeit des Sprachbaus gar nicht erst auf, zumindest war sie für die Sprachreflexion unerheblich. In diesem Programm der Konstruktion einer Universalgrammatik anhand der Strukturen einer Einzelsprache fehlt das vergleichende Element völlig; man kann es also noch nicht als „typologisch" im oben definierten Sinn charakterisieren. Es geht um universale logische Strukturen, nicht um sprachliche Verschiedenheit.

Humanistische Ansätze tauchen bereits früh auf; eine wichtige Wegmarke ist die sprachtheoretische Reflexion von Dante Alighieri. Voll zur Entfaltung kommt der Partikularismus dann allerdings erst in der Epoche der Renaissance. Man entdeckte die Eigenwertigkeit der vielgestaltigen Volkssprachen und gleichzeitig damit auch die Eigenwertigkeit des LATEINISCHEN, das fortan nicht mehr als Repräsentant der Universalgrammatik, sondern als historisch ausgeprägte Einzelsprache gesehen wurde. Dementsprechend werden im LATEINISCHEN jetzt nicht mehr die universalen Formen des menschlichen Denkens gesucht, sondern die − nun auch ästhetisch gewerteten − literarischen Hervorbringungen einer als „klassisch" empfundenen Vergangenheit; und mit diesen Hervorbringungen, mit diesen Vorbildern traten die sich emanzipierenden Volkssprachen in Wettstreit.

Wohl gibt es in der Renaissance Sprachvergleich in erheblichem Ausmaß; dieser Vergleich zielt aber nicht auf die Ermittlung allgemeiner Sprachstrukturen, vielmehr auf die ästhetische Wertung von Einzelsprachen. Das 16. Jh. ist eine Zeit von Sprachenwettbewerb: die Vorzüge und Nachteile der einzelnen europäischen, insbesondere romanischen Sprachen werden abgewogen, sie werden untereinander, und insgesamt mit dem LATEINISCHEN und GRIECHISCHEN, verglichen.

Entscheidend sind zwei Elemente: (1) der Vergleich beruht auf ästhetisch-literarischen Kriterien, nicht auf objektiven Strukturbeschreibungen, er kann also methodisch keine Anspruch auf Wissenschaftlichkeit erheben; und (2) der Vergleich steht im Dienste der Wertung, er ist nicht neutral und objektiv, sondern von subjektiven Einschätzungen getragen, oft auch von einem erwachenden Nationalismus. Den für die Renaissance so typischen Sprachvergleichen fehlt die Bezogenheit auf die sprachlichen Universalien, sie können daher nicht als Vorläufer des typologischen Sprachvergleichs gewertet werden.

Es ist bemerkenswert, daß in der Periode des zweiten Partikularismus das wertende Element gleichfalls präsent ist. Die Sprachtypologie des 19. Jh.s ist durchwegs als vergleichende „Sprachwürdigung" angelegt, von allem Anfang an und bis zum Beginn des 20. Jh.s. Für die Gebrüder Schlegel wie für Humboldt war der flexivische Typus der Höhepunkt der Sprachentwicklung, zu der die Agglutination bestenfalls eine unvollkommene Vorstufe darstellte. Hiermit steht es auch in Zusammenhang, daß die Typologie des 19. Jh.s auf die Erfassung der einzelsprachlichen Individualität abzielt; sie ist auf die organische Ganzheit der Einzelsprache ausgerichtet, auch wenn sie diese als Ausprägung allgemeiner Strukturprinzipien sieht. Zweifellos ist sie als vollwertige „Typologie" im Sinne der eingangs von Hjelmslev gegebenen Definition zu verstehen; aber gerade das Element der Wertung, sowie der organisch-holistische Ansatz, rufen beim heutigen Linguisten ein Gefühl der Fremdheit, ja der Befremdung hervor, das bei der Sprachtheorie anderer Epochen fehlt. Im Grunde sind die Ansätze der rationalistischen Sprachtypologie, der sogenannten Vorläufer im 17. und 18. Jh. uns Heutigen näher und vertrauter als einige gerade der zentralen Elemente der Typologie des 19. Jh.s; hier manifestiert sich, daß wir uns seit langem wiederum in einer Periode des Universalismus befinden.

3. Rationalistische Vorläufer der Sprachtypologie im zweiten Universalismus

Wir kommen somit zum zentralen Thema, den Vorläufern der Sprachtypologie im Zeitalter des zweiten Universalismus. Es ist entscheidend, daß diese Epoche nicht einfach ein Wiederaufleben des mittelalterlich-scholastischen Universalismus bedeutet; die Würdigung der Einzelsprachen in ihrer historischen Gewachsenheit, wie sie die Renaissance-Debatte bestimmt hatte, war vorausgegangen, und damit war ein neues Stadium erreicht, das sich nicht in Wiederholung des Alten erschöpfte. So finden wir in dieser Periode erstmals etwas, was im Vollsinne als Typologie gelten kann: systematischer Vergleich von Einzelsprachen mit dem Ziel der Erhellung universaler Strukturen.

3.1. Empirische Grundlage

Wichtig ist dabei, um welche Einzelsprachen es sich handelt: die empirische Grundlage der typologischen Forschung ist von Epoche zu Epoche verschieden. In der hier interessierenden Zeit sind zwei unterschiedliche Faktoren von Bedeutung.

3.1.1. Lateinisch und Romanisch

Zum einen bewirkt die Ablösung des LATEINISCHEN als Universalsprache und die Emanzipation der einzelnen Volkssprachen, ihre Verschriftlichung und grammatische Normierung sowie ihre Erhebung zu Literatur- und schließlich Nationalsprachen, daß die reale Vielfalt der europäischen Sprachlandschaft ins Blickfeld tritt und in der Sprachtheorie reflektiert wird. Das bedeutet den Vergleich der Volkssprachen untereinander; wie wir gesehen haben, war dies in der Epoche der Renaissance sehr beliebt. Allerdings ist eine solche Übung für die Typologie als Ansatz der Sprachwissenschaft nicht sehr ergiebig, da sich diese Sprachen, zumindest innerhalb der romanischen Familie, allzu ähnlich sind. Ungleich bedeutsamer und für die nachfolgende Entwicklung von zentraler Bedeutung ist der Vergleich zwischen den Volkssprachen insgesamt und dem LATEIN: der strukturelle Unterschied zwischen dem LATEINISCHEN und seinen Abkömmlingen sticht sofort ins Auge, er ist tiefgreifend auf allen Ebenen des Sprachsystems. Dieser Gegensatz war ohnehin für alle, die Lesen und Schreiben lernten (was in der Praxis zu allermeist im Lateinunterricht geschah), ein sprachliches Urerlebnis: der morphosyntaktische Typus des LATEINISCHEN, mit dem man seit frühester Kindheit als „künstlich" erlernter Sprache konfrontiert war (vergleiche Dantes Unterscheidung von *lingua naturalis* und *lingua artificialis*), steht in entschiedenem Gegensatz zu dem Typus der jeweiligen Volkssprachen, die mittlerweile auch einen Status als Schriftsprache erlangt hatten. Aus diesem Gegensatz speist sich die sprachtypologische Reflexion in all den Jahrhunderten, in denen die lateinische Bildung noch neben der volkssprachlichen bestand.

3.1.2. Die Entdeckung außereuropäischer Sprachen

Zum anderen bedeuten die überseeischen Entdeckungen, die Erschließung neuer Welten in Amerika und Asien (Afrika spielt keine Rolle), daß der sprachliche Horizont sich in einem Ausmaß weitet, das mit vorangegangenen Epochen inkommensurabel ist. Im Zeitalter der Entdeckungen tritt auch erstmals in der Menschheitsgeschichte die Vielfalt der menschlichen Sprachen ins Blickfeld, zumindest im Umriß.

Eine zentrale Rolle spielten in diesem Prozeß die Jesuiten, daneben auch Missionare aus anderen Orden, die sich mit den einheimischen Sprachen in einem oft erstaunlichen Maße vertraut machten und grammatische Beschreibungen von Idiomen druckten, die bis dahin als primitiv, barbarisch und regellos gegolten hatten. Erstmals gibt es grammatische Beschreibungen der alten Kultursprachen Asiens; die älteste Deskription des JAPANISCHEN ist auf PORTUGIESISCH verfaßt (Rodriguez 1604–1608), die erste Beschreibung des VIETNAMESISCHEN auf LATEINISCH (Borri 1631).

Auf diese Weise wird in Europa unter anderem bekannt, daß es Sprachen gibt, die mit einem sehr geringen morphologischen Apparat auskommen, und daß eine komplexe flexivische Sprachstruktur keine Voraussetzung für hochrangige literarische Hervorbringungen ist. In der Neuen Welt werden hochentwickelte Reiche bekannt, von denen man bis dahin nicht einmal gewußt hatte, daß sie existieren; und in diesen Reichen wurden Sprachen gesprochen, die zahlreichen Völkern als Verständigungsmittel dienten und deren Grammatik, wie man mit erstaunter Bewunderung feststellte, an Komplexität derjenigen der klassischen Sprachen in nichts nachstand (Anchieta 1595, González Holguín 1607, Montoya 1640).

Reales Wissen über außereuropäische, profund von allem Gewohnten abweichende Sprachen ermöglichte erstmals ein Nachdenken über die wahre Verschiedenheit des menschlichen Sprachbaus, eine Überwindung der Beschränkungen, die durch den engen Erfahrungshorizont früherer Epochen bedingt gewesen waren.

Die Kumulation konkreter Kenntnisse führte so zu einem Fortschritt auch der Erkenntnisse, wie er zuvor nicht möglich gewesen war. Wachsendes Wissen, gepaart mit einer Perspektive, die auf die vernunftbegründeten Universalien der Sprache gerichtet war, machte erstmals Sprachtheorien möglich, die man als „typologisch" im eingangs definierten Sinne bezeichnen kann.

3.2. Rationalistische Ansätze

3.2.1. Tommaso Campanellas *Grammaticalia* (1638)

Der erste Autor, den man in diesem Sinne als Typologen betrachten kann, ist Tommaso Campanella (1568–1639). Der berühmte Verfasser der Utopie *La Città del Sole*, der Jahrzehnte als Gefangener der spanischen Inquisition in Neapel verbrachte, Dichter, Aufklärer und Verteidiger von Galilei, hat in seinen Traktat über die „vernunftgemäße Philosophie" (*philosophia rationalis*), der 1638, also ein Jahr nach Descartes' *Discours de la méthode* erschienen ist, eine Abteilung über „Grammaticalia" eingefügt. Hierin definiert er sein Vorgehen ausdrücklich als „philosophisch" und „vernunftgeleitet": Grammatik wie er sie betreibt, ist keine „Kunst", keine bloße Fertigkeit, vielmehr soll sie eine „Wissenschaft" sein. Die begriffliche Unterscheidung von *ars* und *scientia* (als Übersetzung des griechischen *technē* und *epistēmē* entstanden, vgl. auch Verburg 1981) wird hier auf die Sprachbetrachtung angewendet:

Duplex grammatica: alia civilis, alia philosophica. [...] civilis, peritia est, non scientia. [...] philosophica vero ratione constat; et haec scientiam olet.
„Es gibt zwei Arten von Grammatik: eine bürgerliche, und eine philosophische. Die bürgerliche ist eine Fertigkeit, keine Wissenschaft, hingegen beruht die philosophische auf der Vernunft, und daher hat sie etwas von Wissenschaftlichkeit." (Campanella 1638 [1954]:438)

Ein solcher Passus ist eine frühe Vorwegnahme der oben zitierten Hjelmslev'schen Standortbestimmung der Sprachtypologie. Dies wird noch deutlicher, wenn man sich vor Augen führt, daß Campanella konkret Sprachstrukturen vergleicht, und zwar ohne Beschränkung von Raum und Kultur. Er bleibt nicht bei einer vergleichenden Betrachtung von LATEIN und Romanisch stehen, auch nicht, wie vor ihm etwa Sanctius (Sánchez de las Brozas, 1523–1601) oder Gonzalo Correas (1571–1631), bei der Hinzuziehung der semitischen Sprachen ARABISCH und HEBRÄISCH; vielmehr rezipiert er auch die Informationen, die damals über den Bau ostasiatischer Sprachen nach Europa drangen.

Campanella hatte unter anderem Kenntnis von Cristoforo Borri S. J., der sich von 1610 bis 1623 in Saigon aufgehalten hat und in dem Bericht über seine Mission auch auf den Bau der vietnamesischen Sprache eingegangen ist. Das VIETNAMESISCHE ist ein besonders ausgeprägter Vertreter des (von Humboldt später so genannten) „isolierenden" Typus. Es fiel Campanella auf, daß hier all die Kategorien fehlen, die in europäischen Sprachen die Unterscheidung der Wortarten auf den ersten Blick erkennbar machen: Kasusdeklination beim Nomen, temporale und personale Konjugation beim Verbum. Die Erfahrung dieser so ganz anders gearteten Sprachstruktur machte ihm deutlich, daß Vieles von dem, was man bis dahin als essentiell angesehen hatte, in Wahrheit akzidentell ist. Es lohnt sich, die einschlägigen, für die Geschichte der Sprachtypologie höchst bedeutsamen Stellen hier *in extenso* zu zitieren:

in lingua Cocinchinorum et aliarum orientalium non dantur declinationes verborum aptandae personis, neque temporum varietates, neque varietates verborum aptandae temporibus, et ideo omne verbum est instar impersonalis vel infinitivi. Dinstinctio autem fit per adverbia temporalia, ut si dicerem nunc amo, imposterum amo, ante amo, ita quod non dantur concordantiae temporum, nec personarum, neque casuum, sed particulae adverbiales et adnominales totam orationem construunt et distinguunt, mirifica brevitate ac dicendi facilitate.
„Im VIETNAMESISCHEN und anderen orientalischen Sprachen gibt es keine personale Verbkonjugation, keine unterschiedlichen Tempora und keine temporal differenzierten Verbalkategorien; dementsprechend ist jedes Verb gleichsam unpersönlich oder ein Infinitiv. Die Unterscheidung wird mittels temporaler Adverbien getroffen, wie wenn ich sage *jetzt liebe-ich/später liebe-ich/früher liebe-ich*; es gibt keine temporale, personale oder kasuelle Kongruenz, sondern adverbiale und adnominale Partikeln strukturieren und differenzieren die Aussage, mit wunderbarer Kürze und Einfachheit."
non enim ex hoc est verbum, quod habet modos et tempora, sed ex hoc, quod actum fluentem ab essentia. [...] in lingua Chinensium et Cocinchinensium verba non declinantur personis, nec temporibus variantur, sed notulis [...]: ergo accidunt haec verbo, non essentiant verbum.
„Nicht dadurch läßt sich etwas als Verbum definieren, daß es Modi und Tempora hat, sondern dadurch, daß der Essenz ein Akt entspringt. Im CHINESISCHEN und VIETNAMESISCHEN werden die Verben nicht personal und temporal konjugiert, es werden allenfalls Partikeln hinzugefügt. Also

sind Tempus und Person akzidentell, nicht essentiell für das Verbum." (Campanella 1638 [1954]: 600; 528)

Die Erfahrung wirklich fremder Sprachstrukturen erlaubt es, die Konditionierung der Sprachtheorie durch die eigene (oder mit der eigenen eng verwandte) Sprache zu überwinden. Wenn sich zeigt, daß fast alles weglaßbar ist, was einem naiven Sprachverständnis unabdingbar scheint, wird der Blick auf das frei, was wirklich wesentlich ist. Erst wenn man die tatsächliche Verschiedenheit des Sprachbaus erfaßt, kann man zu den Universalien vordringen; nur die Erkenntnis der Vielfalt ermöglicht die Erkenntnis der zugrundeliegenden Einheit.

Genau dies ist die Aufgabe der Sprachtypologie: aus dem uneingeschränkten Vergleich einzelsprachlicher Strukturen zur Erkenntnis der Konstanten vorzudringen. Es scheint mir bemerkenswert, daß Campanella gerade auf Grund der Erfahrung eines „minimalistischen" Sprachsystems zu dieser Einsicht gelangt ist: wie nichts anderes schärft gerade die Beobachtung der Weglaßbarkeit des Akzidentellen den Blick für die zugrundeliegenden Basisstrukturen.

Für die Sprachtypologie des 19. Jh.s war der „isolierende" Typus *formlos*, er wurde abgewertet gegenüber dem angeblich höher entwickelten flexivischen Typus, der als vollendete Ausprägung des Formungsprinzips galt.

Diese Anschauung wird zumindest von einem modernen Typologen auf den Kopf gestellt; für Uspenskij ist gerade der formlose Typ das Eichmaß (auf Russisch *ètalon*), an dem sich alle Sprachstrukturen messen lassen. Die Komplexitäten flexivischer Sprachen sind aus der Einfachheit der formlosen Metasprache abzuleiten, nicht umgekehrt; der isolierende Typus wird zum Maßstab einer auf die Erkenntnis von Universalien gerichteten Sprachtypologie, der formlose Typus bildet die Metasprache für jeden anderen Typus (vgl. insbesondere Uspenskij 1962: 41 [1968: 55]). Die Modernität des Ansatzes von Campanella wird aus solchen Bezügen zur Diskussion des 20. Jh.s schlagend deutlich.

Fassen wir die wesentlichen Punkte zusammen. Campanella ist, nach heutigem Kenntnisstand, der erste, der Informationen über nicht-flexivische Sprachen auswertet und aufgrund eines über das Indogermanische und Semitische hinausgehenden Vergleichs zu neuen Erkenntnissen über Universalien des menschlichen Sprachbaus gelangt. Durch diese Einbeziehung fremder Sprachstrukturen unterscheidet sich Campanella ebenso von früheren rationalistischen Ansätzen, wie etwa demjenigen von Sanctius oder Correas in Spanien, wie von dem späteren Ansatz der Autoren von Port-Royal: die spanischen Linguisten ebenso wie Antoine Arnauld, Claude Lancelot und Pierre Nicole hatten zwar alle eine rational fundierte Universalgrammatik im Sinn; im Sprachvergleich gingen sie jedoch nicht über den aus den klassischen und modernen Sprachen Westeuropas sowie aus dem ARABISCHEN und HEBRÄISCHEN bekannten flexivischen Typus hinaus, sie gelangten daher auch nicht zu einer wirklichen Relativierung der Strukturen, die sie am eigenen Sprachtypus ablesen konnten.

Campanella hingegen wurde mit seinem Ansatz, der Sprachvergleich und universalistische Perspektive gleichermaßen einschließt, zum ersten Vorläufer einer typologischen Sprachforschung im vollen Sinne der eingangs gegebenen Definition (siehe oben § 2.1). Der Sprachvergleich geht über das Vertraute und Bekannte hinaus; er zielt auf die Erhellung der rationalen Grundlagen der menschlichen Sprachfähigkeit. Die Beschäftigung mit Sprache, die „Grammatik", wird erst dadurch von einer bloßen praktischen Fertigkeit zum Rang einer vernunftbegründeten Wissenschaft angehoben.

3.2.2. Gabriel Girards *Vrais principes* (1747)

Campanella hat Grammatik als eine Wissenschaft betrieben, die vom Sprachvergleich ausgeht, um die Konstanten des Sprachbaus mithilfe von Logik und Vernunft zu erhellen; eine sprachliche Typenlehre hat er nicht aufgestellt. Das klassifikatorische Element, also das „Typologisieren" im landläufigen Sinne, kommt erst bei einem anderen, wesentlich späteren Autor ins Spiel, nämlich bei Abbé Gabriel Girard (1677−1748). Hier findet sich erstmals überhaupt eine Klassifikation der Sprachen, die mit einem universalen Anspruch auftritt: nicht mehr nur die vergleichende Charakterisierung der Einzelsprachen ist anvisiert, sondern eine Einteilung, die vom Anspruch her die Gesamtheit der Sprachen erfassen können soll. Eine genaue Betrachtung dieses Ansatzes ist in mehr als einer Hinsicht instruktiv.

Girards empirische Basis für seine Einteilung der Sprachen ist schmal. Bekannt sind ihm, außer den romanischen, in erster Linie die klassischen Sprachen LATEIN und GRIECHISCH; das RUSSISCHE beherrscht er so gut, daß er offiziell als Dolmetscher fungiert hat;

darüber hinaus hat er wohl vom DEUTSCHEN und KIRCHENSLAVISCHEN eine gewisse Vorstellung, während das CHINESISCHE für ihn „comme d'un autre monde" ist (Girard 1747: 31). Dementsprechend ist seine Theorie nur sehr eingeschränkt als typologisch zu bezeichnen; er ist jedoch immerhin derjenige Autor, der die Diskussion des 18. Jh.s über typologische Fragen entscheidend geprägt hat, dessen Anschauungen rasch zum Allgemeingut geworden sind und der letztlich auch auf die Entstehung der „eigentlichen" Sprachtypologie, nämlich der Theorie der Gebrüder Schlegel, beträchtlichen Einfluß hatte. Girard hat die Weichen des typologischen Ansatzes in Richtung Klassifikation gestellt, und bis heute wirkt die problematische Vermengung von Typologie und Klassifikation in der allgemeinen vergleichenden Sprachwissenschaft nach.

Von der soeben genannten engen empirischen Basis ausgehend postuliert Girard drei Klassen von Sprachen, die er unbekümmert als allgemeingültig für die Sprachen der Menschheit postuliert („les Langues se trouvent distinguées en trois classes", 23). Er ist sich sehr wohl der Neuheit seines Ansatzes bewußt: „je suis [...] le premier qui entreprens de la mettre en œuvre dans la méthode grammaticale, & d'en faire valoir le mérite aux yeux du Public" (23). Es lohnt sich, die Definition dieser ersten universalen Sprachklassifikation überhaupt *in extenso* anzuführen:

Les Langues de la premiere classe suivent ordinairement, dans leur construction, l'ordre naturel & la gradation des idées: le sujet agissant y marche le premier, ensuite l'action accompagnée de ses modifications, après cela ce qui en fait l'objet & le terme. Par cette raison je les nomme ANALOGUES, ainsi que le génie qui les caractérise. Elles ont un article, qu'elles joignent aux dénominations qui ne sont pas individuelles, & n'admettent point de cas: telles sont la Françoise, l'Italienne, & l'Espagnole.
Les Langues de la seconde classe ne suivent d'autre ordre, dans la construction de leurs frases, que le feu de l'imagination; faisant précéder tantôt l'objet, tantôt l'action, & tantôt la modification ou la circonstance: ce qui n'est pourtant pas un défaut, & ne produit aucune ambiguïté, à cause des cas & de la variété des terminaisons qu'elles admettent [...]. Ainsi le nom de TRANSPOSITIVES leur convient parfaitement. Elles ne connoissent pas l'usage de l'Article. Le Latin, L'Esclavon, & le Moscovite sont de cette espèce.
Les Langues de la troisième classe tiennent des deux autres; ayant un article comme les Analogues, & des cas comme les Transpositives: telle est la Langue Grecque; il me semble aussi que la Teutonique appartient également à cette classe. On la nommera, si l'on veut, MIXTE, ou, d'un air plus docte, AMPHILOGIQUE: je ne lui fixe point de nom; parce que je n'en dois plus parler, & que je crains de n'en pas trouver un assez heureux pour être adopté. (Girard 1747: 23−25)

Dieser Ansatz ist nur verständlich, wenn man den Hintergrund der zeitgenössischen sprachphilosophischen Diskussion berücksichtigt. Die zentrale sprachtheoretische Frage des 18. Jh.s ist die Wortstellung. Welche Abfolge der Satzglieder ist logisch, welche ist „natürlich"? Ist „natürlich" die an der Logik orientierte Satzgliedstellung des FRANZÖSISCHEN, oder ist es die freie Wortstellung des LATEINISCHEN, wo sich die Gefühle und Empfindungen unmittelbar ausdrücken? Über dieses Problem wurde erbittert gerungen, zentrale philosophische und anthropologische Positionen wurden an dieser Kontroverse festgemacht (vgl. u.a. Rosiello 1967; Ricken 1976; 1978). Was wir oben als „sprachliches Urerlebnis" bezeichnet haben (siehe oben § 3.3.1), nämlich der Kontrast zwischen dem muttersprachlichen FRANZÖSISCH mit seiner rigiden Wortstellung und dem LATEINISCHEN, dessen Freiheit man mühsam erlernen mußte, wurde zum zentralen Motiv der Sprachreflexion. Während die philosophische Position des Rationalismus die strikte Abfolge SVO als grundlegend, unmittelbar von der universalen menschlichen Logik abgeleitet und damit auch als „natürlich" betrachtete, sah man aus sensualistischer Sicht eher die psychologisch-subjektive Wortstellung des LATEINISCHEN als etwas „Natürliches" an, während die strenge Logik des FRANZÖSISCHEN als künstlich und abgeleitet erschien.

Girard steht fest auf dem Boden des Rationalismus. Seine Grammatik ist methodisch angelegt, für Subjektivität ist kein Raum. Dementsprechend ist für ihn der Primat der logischen Wortfolge ein unhinterfragtes Axiom. Er geht davon aus, daß allen Sprachen eine Wortfolge zugrundeliegt, welche die sachliche Abfolge „Handelnder − Handlung − Ziel der Handlung" unmittelbar linear abbildet − also eine Wortfolge mit den Basiskomponenten Subjekt, Verb, Objekt; SVO, die Basisstellung des FRANZÖSISCHEN, wurde nicht als einzelsprachlich bedingt interpretiert, sondern als unmittelbare Widerspiegelung einer universalen, auf der allgemeinen menschlichen Vernunft basierenden Tiefenstruktur. Dies genau ist der Sinn des Terminus 'analogique': die Wortstellung des FRANZÖSISCHEN und seiner romanischen Schwestersprachen ist der universalen logischen

Konstituentenabfolge analog, bildet sie unmittelbar ab.

Demgegenüber weisen Sprachen vom Typus des LATEINISCHEN Abweichungen von diesem Muster auf, welche durch die Subjektivität des Sprechenden – Girard sagt: „le feu de l'imagination" – bedingt sind. Auf dem Weg von der, modern gesprochen, universalen Tiefenstruktur zur konkret-einzelsprachlichen Oberflächenstruktur wird der logische Satzbau umgewandelt; daher der Terminus *transpositiv*. Wie Girard richtig beobachtet, bieten die grammatischen Endungen des LATEINISCHEN genügend Hinweise auf die grammatische Struktur, so daß keine Ambiguitäten aufkommen. Logisch ist SVO, diese Reihenfolge ist universal und liegt auch dem LATEINISCHEN zugrunde; die Kasusendungen wirken als Platzhalter, welche Permutationen, oder Transformationen, dieser Basisordnung ermöglichen. Während die spätere historisch-vergleichende Sprachwissenschaft im Verlust der Endungen die Ursache für das Festwerden der Wortstellung sah, ging man im 18. Jh. von einer als überzeitlich und universal angenommenen logischen Basis aus, von der nur bei Vorhandensein entsprechender Endungen abgewichen werden kann.

Girards Entwurf einer fundamentalen Zweiteilung aller Sprachen ist vom Standpunkt des Rationalismus aus logisch und kohärent. Wenn man die Grundannahme der Existenz einer universalen Wortstellung akzeptiert, ist es logisch, daß es zwei, und genau zwei grundlegende Sprachtypen geben muß: den Typus, der ebendiese universale Wortstellung unmittelbar abbildet, und denjenigen, der sie transponiert. Sein Ansatz ist völlig in die Diskussion seiner Epoche eingebunden, wo er einen festen Platz hat, weil er einen damals „in der Luft liegenden" Gedanken klar formuliert und systematisiert hat.

Dem universalistisch-logischen Ansatz zufolge ist das Interesse der Zeit primär auf die Syntax gerichtet; die morphologische Wortstruktur interessiert nur indirekt, insofern nämlich als flexivische Endungen, wie die des LATEINISCHEN, eine transpositive Syntax überhaupt erst ermöglichen. Mit der Sprachtypologie Girards sind wir Welten von der späteren morphologischen Typologie entfernt, wie sie die Gebrüder Schlegel begründet haben.

Es ist plausibel anzunehmen, daß, wie Monreal-Wickert (1976: 208 ff.) gezeigt hat, Schlegel über Roch Ambroise Sicard und dessen Abhandlung über die Sprache der Taubstummen (1797) Kenntnis von den Theorien Girards hatte und vielleicht auch oberflächlich in der Wahl gewisser Termini von ihm beeinflußt wurde; ebenso klar scheint es mir aber auch, daß die morphologische Typologie des 19. Jh.s nichts mit der syntaktischen Typologie des Aufklärungszeitalters gemeinsam hat: der gedankliche Ansatz, das erkenntnisleitende Interesse sind völlig anders. Beiden gemeinsam ist die klassifikatorische Perspektive: die Sprachen der Welt werden in separate, dem Anspruch nach alles umfassende Klassen eingeteilt. Indessen sind die Grundkonzeptionen unvereinbar: hier das Verhältnis von Morphem und Lexem, die Verbindung von grammatischer und lexikalischer Information im Wort; dort die Beziehung der grundlegenden Satzbaupläne zu syntaktischen Universalien, die auf logische Kategorien zurückgeführt werden.

Der epistemologische Bruch zwischen den beiden Ansätzen ist vollkommen, es führt keine Brücke aus dem 18. in das 19. Jh.; dementsprechend ist es nicht verwunderlich, daß im 19. Jh. jede Erinnerung an Girard und die anderen Autoren des Rationalismus verloren gegangen ist. Sie ist in unserer Zeit wiederbelebt worden, zunächst weniger von seiten der aktuellen linguistischen Diskussion, als vielmehr im Zusammenhang mit dem allgemeinen Aufleben des Interesses an der Geschichte des Faches, an der Historiographie der Linguistik; es ist aber unbestreitbar, daß die Fragestellung eines Abbé Girard der heutigen typologischen Diskussion sehr viel näher steht als die morphologische Typologie des 19. Jh.s. Spätestens seit Greenberg 1963 steht die Wortstellungsfrage im Zentrum der typologischen Forschung, hat sie sich zu einer primär syntaktisch orientierten Disziplin entwickelt.

Anders als die (Pseudo-?)Rezeption der sogenannten „cartesianischen" Linguistik durch Noam Chomsky hat ein breiter Rückgriff auf das Ideenkapital des europäischen Rationalismus im Rahmen der heutigen Sprachtypologie bisher noch nicht stattgefunden; wie vielversprechend er ist, wie viele Anregungen er bringen könnte, davon mögen die hier gebrachten Zitate und Darstellungen eine Vorstellung vermitteln.

Girards Klassifikation ist noch in einer anderen Hinsicht instruktiv; gerade dieser erste solche Klassifikationsversuch überhaupt zeigt mit exemplarischer Deutlichkeit die Aporien, in die ein klassifikatorischer Ansatz in der Sprachtypologie notwendigerweise gerät. Girard geht zunächst von einem logischen, quasi axiomatischen System aus, mithilfe dessen er eine klar binäre Einteilung der Sprachen der Welt erreicht: analog vs. transpositiv, auf der Grundlage der universalen syntaktischen Tiefenstruktur; *tertium non datur*. Girard trübt selbst dieses an sich klare Bild, indem er ein weiteres Kriterium einführt, das mit der rationalistischen Grundlage des ganzen Entwurfs überhaupt nichts zu tun hat: die Anwesenheit bzw. Abwesenheit nominaler Artikel. Der Autor hat sich nicht entschließen können, bei einem einzigen Kriterium zu bleiben und so die strenge Logik des Systems zu bewahren; vielmehr beobachtet er, aufgrund des „sprachlichen Urerlebnisses" des Kontrastes zwischen LATEINISCH und ROMANISCH (siehe oben § 3.1.1), daß in den analogen Sprachen Artikel vorhanden sind, in den transpositiven hingegen nicht. Er fügt dieses Kriterium hinzu, und muß prompt feststellen, daß damit die einfache Binarität des Modells verloren geht: es gibt, laut Erfahrung, auch eine transpositive Sprache mit Artikel, nämlich das GRIECHISCHE. Mit einer breiteren empirischen Basis wäre auch unschwer zu erkennen gewesen, daß auch die vierte logische Möglichkeit im Rahmen einer solchen Kreuzklassifikation realiter existiert: im CHINESISCHEN beispielsweise haben wir feste SVO-Stellung (also analogen Sprachbau), aber nicht die Spur eines Artikelsystems.

In seinem Bedürfnis, dem „génie de la langue" näher zu kommen und Sprachen wie FRANZÖSISCH und LATEINISCH nicht ausschließlich aufgrund ihrer Wortfolge zu charakterisieren, verfängt sich Girard sogleich in den Fallstricken eines jeden Klassifikationsversuches, der mehr als ein Kriterium nutzt; zwei Kriterien können in Widerstreit zueinander stehen, und es entstehen bereits mit dieser minimalen über Eins hinausgehenden Zahl vier logische Möglichkeiten – oder, im Sinne der Girard'schen Klassifikation, Mischtypen, von denen man nicht so genau weiß, welchem Basistypus sie denn nun zuzuordnen sind. Girard bemerkt diese Schwierigkeit; seinen Formulierungen bezüglich des „amphilogischen" Typus merkt man an, daß er über diese Konsequenz seines Ansatzes nicht erfreut war. Gelöst hat er dieses Problem nicht, genauso wenig wie all die späteren Linguisten, welche Typologie mit Klassifikation verwechseln und ihrer Einteilung der Sprachen mehrere Kriterien zugrunde gelegt haben.

Dieses Problem ist in der Tat unlösbar; wenn man sich nicht entschließt, ein einziges Kriterium als fundamental anzunehmen, muß man mit der Existenz von Mischtypen rechnen. Wie gerade auch die Wortstellungstypologie im Gefolge von Greenberg (1963) gezeigt hat, können solche Klassifikationen interessant sein und wichtige Einsichten in das Funktionieren menschlicher Sprache vermitteln; nur darf man sich nie der Illusion hingeben, als sei damit eine naht- und lückenlose Einteilung der Sprachen in strikt separate Klassen möglich.

3.2.3. Nicolas Beauzées *Grammaire générale* (1767)

Viele Autoren haben sich an der Diskussion um die „natürliche" Wortfolge im Laufe des 18. Jh.s beteiligt. Einen typologischen Ansatz *ante litteram* finden wir indessen nur bei einem von ihnen: bei Nicolas Beauzée (1717–1789), Mitarbeiter an Diderots Enzyklopädie, Sprachlehrer an der École Militaire in Paris und Verfasser einer umfänglichen *Grammaire générale*. Die folgende Darstellung stützt sich im wesentlichen auf das letztgenannte Werk, die 1767 erschienenen beiden Bände der *Grammaire générale*, mit dem bezeichnenden Untertitel *Exposition raisonnée des éléments nécessaires du langage pour servir de fondement à l'étude de toutes les langues*.

Es sollen drei Punkte herausgearbeitet werden, die es gerechtfertigt erscheinen lassen, Beauzée als Ahnherren des sprachtypologischen Ansatzes zu betrachten, drei Aspekte, welche die Modernität der rationalistischen Perspektive und ihre Relevanz auch für die aktuelle Diskussion belegen: (1) die Überlegungen zum Verhältnis von Universalem und Partikularem in der Sprache; (2) die empirische Grundlage des multilateralen Sprachvergleichs; (3) und das Postulat einer universalen logisch-analytischen Wortfolge.

In seiner Einleitung entwirft Beauzée das Programm einer Sprachtheorie und Sprachwissenschaft, in welcher das Verhältnis zwischen Universalem und Partikularem ausdrücklich in den Mittelpunkt gestellt wird. Ziel der Sprachtheorie ist die Erkenntnis dessen, was allen Sprachen gemeinsam ist, was notwendig allen Sprachen zugrundeliegt; nur wenn Sprachtheorie auf dieses Ziel gerichtet ist, verdient sie den Namen 'Wissenschaft'. Die alte Unterscheidung von *ars* und *scientia* wird auch von Beauzée wieder aufgenommen und mit neuen Nuancen bereichert: die „allgemeine Grammatik" bezieht sich auf die vernunftgeleitete Spekulation über die unveränderlichen Grundlagen allen Sprechens; einzelsprachliche Grammatiken hingegen sind praktische Hilfsmittel zum Erlernen des realen Sprachgebrauchs, der auch von Willkür und Zufälligkeiten geprägt ist.

Die „grammatische Wissenschaft" liegt den Einzelsprachen voraus, während die „grammatische Kunst" ihnen nachfolgt. Erkenntnis der ewigen und universalen Grundgesetze der Sprache ist nur möglich aufgrund der Beobachtung, insbesondere der Erfassung der realen grammatischen Vielgestaltigkeit der Einzelsprachen: Universalgrammatik bezieht sich zwar auf das, was allen Einzelsprachen vorausliegt, epistemologisch muß sie indes von der einzelsprachlichen Diversität ihren Ausgang nehmen. Mit diesem Paradox sieht sich jede typologisch orientierte Sprachwissenschaft konfrontiert; es ist von Beauzée begrifflich scharf erfaßt und mit unübertrefflicher Klarheit formuliert worden:

La Grammaire générale est une science, parce qu'elle n'a pour objet que la spéculation raisonnée des principes immuables & généraux du Langage. Une Grammaire particulière est un art, parce qu'elle envisage l'application pratique des institutions arbitraires & usuelles d'une langue particulière aux principes généraux du Langage. [...] La science et l'art se doivent des secours mutuels, sans lesquels ils ne nous seroit pas possible d'en acquérir une connoissance solide. En premier lieu, l'art ne peut donner aucune certitude à la pratique, s'il n'est éclairé & dirigé par les lumières de la spéculation [...]. En second lieu, la science ne peut donner aucune consistance à la théorie, si elle n'observe avec soin les usages combinés & les pratiques différentes, pour s'élever par degrés jusqu'à la généralisation des principes. Ces principes, en eux-mêmes, sont déterminés & invariables: mais par rapport à nous, ils sont, comme les objets de toutes nos recherches, environnés de ténèbres, de doutes, d'incertitudes; la voie de l'observation & de l'expérience est la seule qui puisse nous mener à la vérité. (Beauzée 1767: I, x–xiv)

Besser könnte man das Programm der Sprachtypologie auch heute nicht formulieren. Wie in dem eingangs zitierten, für die Sprachtypologie unseres Jh.s zentralen Diktum von Hjelmslev wird auch hier die Linguistik erst dadurch zu einer Wissenschaft im eigentlichen Sinne, daß sie auf die allgemeinen Prinzipien des menschlichen Sprachbaus abzielt; und der Weg zur Erkenntnis solcher Universalien kann nur über eine solide Empirie führen. Mit einem Wort: eine so konzipierte Sprachtypologie läßt sich als „empirische Universalienforschung" definieren.

Bei der Begründung seiner Theorie ist Beauzée um eine möglichst breite empirische Basis bemüht. Laut eigenen Angaben hat er Grammatiken nicht nur der europäischen Hauptsprachen einschließlich DEUTSCH, SCHWEDISCH, LAPPISCH, WALISISCH, IRISCH und BASKISCH, sondern auch semitischer Sprachen, des CHINESISCHEN sowie des „Peruanischen" (QUECHUA) konsultiert (p. xv).

Für seine Zeit und im Vergleich mit praktisch allen anderen Werken dieser Art ist Beauzées Sprachenkenntnis tatsächlich bemerkenswert; er stellt keine These auf, ohne eine solide empirische Untermauerung zumindest zu versuchen. Auch in dieser Hinsicht ist sein Ansatz durchaus als „typologisch" in einem modernen Sinn zu charakterisieren.

Allerdings sollte man die Breite seiner Sprachkenntnisse auch nicht überschätzen: trotz der beeindruckend wirkenden Menge der Sprachen, die er aufzählt, ist der Schwerpunkt seiner Ausführungen auf einem systematischen Vergleich zwischen LATEINISCH und FRANZÖSISCH aufgebaut, also auf demjenigen sprachlichen Kontrast, den wir oben als „sprachliches Urerlebnis" des gebildeten Europäers bezeichnet hatten (siehe oben § 3.1.1).

Immerhin kommen nicht nur die romanischen Sprachen ITALIENISCH und SPANISCH, sondern auch die germanischen Sprachen DEUTSCH, ENGLISCH und SCHWEDISCH (das er selbst aktiv beherrscht hat) so systematisch ins Blickfeld wie bei keinem anderen zeitgenössischen Autor. Auch das Hebräische wird fast immer berücksichtigt, wenn auch an der Tiefe seiner Kenntnisse (bei dieser dritten „klassischen" Sprache des *homo trilinguis*) gewisse Zweifel angebracht sind.

Hinsichtlich der Tiefe der Erkenntnis etwa des Baus ostasiatischer Sprachen bleibt Beauzée allerdings weit hinter den oben charakterisierten Intuitionen von Tommaso Campanella zurück. Bei ihm ist keine Rede von einer universalen Wortartendefinition, bei der wegen des Fehlens bestimmter Eigenschaften in bestimmten Sprachen vom Akzidentellen auf das Essentielle abgezielt würde, er bleibt vielmehr im Vordergründigen, am Bau europäischer Sprachen Abgelesenen stecken. Immerhin bringt Beauzée des öfteren Beobachtungen, die bei keinem früheren Autor zu finden sind und die ein genuines typologisches Interesse des Autors belegen, so etwa, wenn er den nachgestellten Artikel im SCHWEDISCHEN und im BASKISCHEN miteinander in Beziehung setzt (I, 313 f.); oder wenn die Kasussysteme des BASKISCHEN und des „Peruanischen" miteinander verglichen werden (II, 139).

Beauzée nimmt die Beschreibungen der Grammatiken, die ihm vorliegen, nicht als primäre Daten, vielmehr bemüht er sich immer, den Erscheinungen selbst auf den Grund zu gehen. Er ist sich im klaren darüber, daß die gängigen Beschreibungen allzu oft von den Vorgaben der lateinischen Schulgrammatik abhängen und daß man, um zu einer vorurteilsfreien, sachgerechten Einschätzung zu kommen, die jeweilige Struktur aus sich heraus und auf Grund der gegebenen Beispiele erhellen muß.

Ein gutes Beispiel ist die Behandlung der hebräischen Relativpartikel *asher*, die eben nicht, wie in den damals gängigen Grammatiken noch allenthalben nachzulesen, ein Relativpronomen, sondern ein unveränderlicher Subordinator ist, nach dem der obligatorische Gebrauch eines resumptiven Pronomens funktional notwendig und eben gar nicht „pleonastisch" ist (I, 369). Was in unserer Zeit von Lucien Tesnière als „disjonction de l'élément translatif et de l'élément anaphorique" bezeichnet und in den Rahmen einer umfassenderen Typologie der Relativsatzbildung eingebracht worden ist (Tesnière 1959: 570ff.), erscheint hier bei Beauzée zum ersten Mal in seiner Eigenwertigkeit erkannt und korrekt beschrieben. Der typologisch-rationalistische Ansatz führt dazu, daß die Strukturen auch bei einer so wohlbekannten und oft beschriebenen Sprache wie dem Hebräischen hier erstmals adäquat erfaßt werden.

Die „Allgemeine Grammatik" von Beauzée steckt voller zukunftsweisender Theorien und Beobachtungen. So bietet ihr Autor zum ersten Mal etwas, was man als allgemeine Tempus-Theorie im Sinne der heutigen Linguistik bezeichnen könnte, nämlich ein apriorisches Begriffssystem, auf das die Tempussysteme der wichtigsten europäischen Einzelsprachen projiziert werden (I, 422 ff.). Das zugrundeliegende System wird als universell, der davon gemachte Gebrauch, die Auswahl und die Wertigkeit der einzelnen Kategorien hingegen als einzelsprachlich charakterisiert. Damit wird ein hoher sprachtheoretischer Anspruch erhoben und teilweise auch schon eingelöst, wie er dann erst wieder in unserem Jh. zum Tragen kommen wird.

Gilt dies bereits für die Behandlung grammatischer Einzelphänomene wie 'Tempus', 'Kasus', 'Präpositionen' oder 'Relativsatzbildung', so gilt es noch mehr bezüglich des zentralen Problemfeldes, das die Diskussion des 18. Jh.s wie kein anderes beherrscht hat: die Wortstellung (II, 464−533). Im Rahmen dieses Beitrags kann hierauf nur summarisch eingegangen werden.

Beauzée steht fest auf dem Boden des rationalistischen Ansatzes. Allen Sprachen liegt ein „ordre analytique" zugrunde, der als universal postuliert wird, weil er die Gesetze von Vernunft und Logik unmittelbar abbildet. Diese analytische Ordnung ist „natürlich", nicht die rhetorische, emotional geprägte Ordnung der klassischen Autoren. Die „analytische Ordnung" ist, so würden wir heute sagen, ikonisch: sie folgt der Wirklichkeit, für die sie steht − zuerst das handelnde Subjekt, dann die Handlung selbst, und schließlich das Objekt, auf das sich die Handlung bezieht.

Für die rationalistischen Grammatiker-Philosophen des 18. Jh.s hatte die Abfolge S[ubjekt]−V[erb]−O[bjekt] den Status einer selbstevidenten Naturgesetzlichkeit. Keiner hat den grundlegenden Charakter dieser Abfolge so klar betont und herausgearbeitet, keiner so sehr darauf insistiert wie Nicolas Beauzée. SVO ist für ihn der unmittelbare Ausfluß von etwas, was man als „logische Tiefenstruktur" der Sprache, aller menschlicher Sprachen, bezeichnen könnte. Die „isolierende", also ohne morphologische Markierung der Kasusrelation auskommende Struktur des FRANZÖSISCHEN spiegelt diese Tiefenstruktur unmittelbar auch an der Oberfläche; in Sprachen wie dem LATEINISCHEN fungieren die Kasusendungen gleichsam als Platzhalter und ermöglichen es so, von dieser Basisordnung abzuweichen. Diesem Ansatz entsprechend ist für Beauzée die von Girard getroffene Einteilung in analoge und transpositive Sprachen etwas ganz Natürliches und Grundlegendes, etwas, das nicht weiter hinterfragt wird.

Die Problematik, die sich bei Girard dadurch ergeben hatte, daß er zu dem Basiskriterium der Wortfolge noch das Sekundärkriterium der Anwesenheit bzw. Abwesenheit von Artikelsystemen hinzugefügt hatte, wird von Beauzée strikt vermieden: für ihn gibt es nur eine einfache Einteilung in analoge und transpositive Sprachen, je nachdem, ob die analytische Wortfolge eingehalten wird oder nicht. Der klassifikatorische Ansatz ist bei ihm also konsequenter und klarer als bei seinem Vorgänger. Ihm verdankt die syntaktische Sprachtypologie des 18. Jh.s ihre klassische, bis heute gültige Ausprägung. Wir wollen diese Darstellung beschließen mit einem Zitat, in dem diese Typologie und die rationalistische Grundauffassung, die ihr zugrundeliegt, besonders klar zum Ausdruck kommt:

Il est donc évident que, dans toutes les langues, la parole ne transmet la pensée, qu'autant qu'elle peint fidèlement la succession analytique des idées qui en sont l'objet. Dans quelques idiômes, cette succession des idées est représentée par celle des mots qui en sont les signes; dans d'autres, elle est seulement désignée par les inflexions des mots, qui, au moyen de cette marque de relation, peuvent, sans conséquence pour le sens, prendre dans le discours telle autre place que d'autres vûes peuvent leur assigner. Mais à travers ces différences considérables du génie des langues, on reconnoit sensiblement l'impression uniforme de la nature, qui est une, qui est simple, qui est immuable, & qui établit partout une exacte conformité entre la progression des idées & celle des mots qui les représentent. (Beauzée 1767: II, 471)

4. Schlußbemerkung

Das 19. Jh. hat sich von solchen Fragestellungen so völlig abgekehrt, daß selbst die Erinnerung an sie verloren gegangen ist (siehe oben § 3.2.2). Die Typologie im Gefolge des Ansatzes der Gebrüder Schlegel und Wilhelm von Humboldts wurde morphologisch; sie bezog sich auf das Wort und seine interne Beschaffenheit. Dies gilt übrigens nicht erst für die deutschen Romantiker, sondern bereits auch schon für den schottischen Philosophen und Nationalökonomen Adam Smith, dessen *Dissertation on the origin of languages* (1761) mit der Unterscheidung von „compounded" und „uncompounded languages" als Vorläufer der Schlegel-Humboldtschen Sprachtypologie gelten kann; Smith steht am Anfang einer kontinuierlichen Entwicklungslinie, die das gesamte 19. und noch Teile des 20. Jh.s umfaßt. Über alledem sollte jedoch gerade aus heutiger Sicht nicht der Blick auf diejenigen Vorläufer des 17. und 18. Jh.s verstellt werden, bei denen die heutige Linguistik eine Sensibilität für Fragestellungen wiederentdecken kann, die in unserer Zeit im Mittelpunkt des Interesses stehen. Die Tatsache, daß die heutige Typologie zum überwiegenden Teil syntaktisch ausgerichtet ist und gerade die Wortstellungsproblematik in das Zentrum ihrer Überlegungen stellt, sollte den Blick freilegen auf das Gedankenkapital und auf die Argumentationen, die lange Zeit diskreditiert waren und deren Eigenwert man erst heute wieder erkennt. Die Diskussionen um die Wortstellungstypen und die philosophisch-rationalistische Grundlegung der Syntax, wie sie im 18. Jh. geführt wurden, sind heute aktueller als sie im 19. und im frühen 20. Jh. jemals gewesen waren.

5. Zitierte Literatur

Anchieta, P. José de. 1595. *Arte de gramática da lingua mais usada na costa do Brasil.* Coimbra [ed. Julio Platzmann. Leipzig 1874].

Arnauld, Antoine & Lancelot, Claude. 1660. *Grammaire générale et raisonnée contenant les fondemens de l'art de parler expliqués d'une manière claire et naturelle: les raisons de ce qui est commun à toutes les langues, et des principales différences qui s'y rencontrent, et plusieurs remarques nouvelles sur la langue française.* Paris [ed. Michel Foucault. Paris: Paulet 1969].

Arnauld, Antoine & Nicole, Pierre. 1662. *La logique ou l'art de penser: contenant, outre les règles communes, plusieurs observations nouvelles, propres à former le jugement.* Paris [ed. Louis Marin. Paris: Flammarion 1970].

Beauzée, Nicolas. 1767. *Grammaire générale ou exposition raisonnée des éléments nécessaires du langage, pour servir de fondement à l'étude de toutes les langues.* 2 vols. Paris [Faksimile-Ausgabe von Bartlett, Barrie E. Stuttgart: Frommann 1974].

Borri, Cristoforo. 1631. *Relatione della nuova missione del Padre della Compagnia di Giesù al Regno dell Cocincina.* Roma.

Bossong, Georg. 1990. *Sprachwissenschaft und Sprachphilosophie in der Romania. Von den Anfängen bis August Wilhelm Schlegel.* Tübingen: Narr.

Bossong, Georg. 1992. „Reflections on the history of universals. The example of the *partes orationis*." In: Auwera, Johan van der & Kefer, Michel (eds.). *Meaning and Grammar: Cross-linguistic Perspectives.* Berlin: Mouton de Gruyter, 3−16.

Campanella, Tommaso. 1638. *Philosophiae rationalis pars prima, continens Grammaticalium libros tres.* Paris [ed. Firpo, Luigi. Milano: Mondadori 1954].

Chomsky, Noam. 1966. *Cartesian linguistics. A chapter in the history of Rationalist thought.* New York: Harper & Row.

Correas Íñigo, Gonzalo. 1625. *Arte de la lengua española castellana.* Salamanca [ed. Alarcos García, Emilio. Madrid: CSIC 1954].

Coseriu, Eugenio. 1968. „Adam Smith und die Anfänge der Sprachtypologie". In: Brekle, Herbert & Lipka, Leonhard (eds.). *Wortbildung, Syntax und Morphologie. Festschrift zum 60. Geburtstag von Hans Marchand.* The Hague: Mouton, 46−54.

Coseriu, Eugenio. 1976. „Sulla tipologia linguistica di Wilhelm von Humboldt. Contributo alla critica della tradizione linguistica". In: Heilmann, Luigi (ed.). *Wilhelm von Humboldt nella cultura contemporanea.* Bologna: Il Mulino, 133–64.

Finck, Franz Nikolaus. 1901. *Die Klassifikation der Sprachen.* Marburg.

Finck, Franz Nikolaus. 1909. *Die Haupttypen des Sprachbaus.* Leipzig [Nachdruck Darmstadt: Wissenschaftliche Buchgesellschaft 1965].

Fleischman, Suzanne. 1982. *The future in thought and language. Diachronic evidence from Romance.* Cambridge: Cambridge University Press.

Gabelentz, Georg von der. 1891/²1901. *Die Sprachwissenschaft. Ihre Aufgaben, Methoden und bisherigen Ergebnisse.* Leipzig [mit einer Studie von Eugenio Coseriu, neu herausgegeben von Gunter Narr und Uwe Petersen, Darmstadt 1984].

Geckeler, Horst & Schlieben-Lange, Brigitte & Trabant, Jürgen & Weydt, Harald (eds.). 1981. *Logos semantikos. Studia linguistica in honorem Eugenio Coseriu (1921–1981).* 5 vols. Berlin & Madrid: de Gruyter & Gredos.

Girard, Abbé Gabriel. 1747. *Les vrais principes de la langue françoise ou la parole réduite en méthode, conformément aux loix de l'usage: en seize discours.* Paris: Le Breton [édition précédée d'une introduction par Pierre Swiggers, Genève: Droz 1982].

González Holguín, P. Diego. 1607. *Gramática y arte nueva de la lengua general de todo el Perú llamada lengua qquicha o lengua del Inca.* Lima.

Greenberg, Joseph H. 1954. „A quantitative approach to the morphological typology of language". In: Spencer, R. F. (ed.). *Method and perspective in anthropology.* Minneapolis, 192–220 [wieder in: *International Journal of American Linguistics* 26 (1960), 178–94].

Greenberg, Joseph H. 1963. „Some universals of grammar with particular reference to the order of meaningful elements". In: ders. (ed.). *Universals of language.* Cambridge/MA: M.I.T. Press, 58–90.

Hjelmslev, Louis. 1963. *Sproget. En introduktion.* København [zitiert nach der deutschen Ausgabe von Otmar Werner. *Sprache. Eine Einführung.* Darmstadt: Wissenschaftliche Buchgesellschaft 1968].

Horne, Kibbey M. 1966. *Language typology. 19th and 20th century views.* Washington: Georgetown University Press.

Humboldt, Wilhelm von. 1835. *Ueber die Verschiedenheit des menschlichen Sprachbaues und ihren Einfluss auf die geistige Entwicklung des Menschengeschlechts.* Berlin [Nachdruck in: *Schriften zur Sprachphilosophie.* Darmstadt: Wissenschaftliche Buchgesellschaft 1963].

Milewski, Tadeusz. 1969. *Językoznawstwo.* Warszawa: Państwowe Wydawnictwo Naukowe [engl. Version: *Introduction to the study of language.* The Hague & Paris: Mouton 1973].

Monreal-Wickert, Irene. 1976. „Sprachtypologie statt Sprachgeschichte: eine rationalistische Antwort auf den Sensualismus". In: Niederehe, Hans-Josef & Haarmann, Harald (eds.). *In memoriam Friedrich Diez. Akten des Kolloquiums zur Wissenschaftsgeschichte der Romanistik, Trier.* Amsterdam & Philadelphia: Benjamins, 197–220.

Monreal-Wickert, Irene. 1977. *Die Sprachforschung der Aufklärung im Spiegel der großen französischen Enzyklopädie.* Tübingen: Narr.

Montoya, Antonio Ruiz de. 1640. *Arte, bocabulario, tesoro y catecismo de la lengua guaraní.* Madrid [ed. Julio Platzman. Leipzig 1876].

Parret, Herman (ed.). 1976. *History of linguistic thought and contemporary linguistics.* Berlin: de Gruyter.

Ricken, Ulrich. 1976. „Die Kontroverse Du Marsais und Beauzée gegen Batteux, Condillac und Diderot. Ein Kapitel der Auseinandersetzung zwischen Sensualismus und Rationalismus in der Sprachdiskussion der Aufklärung". In: Parret (ed.), 460–87.

Ricken, Ulrich. 1978. *Grammaire et philosophie au Siècle des Lumières. Controverses sur l'ordre naturel et la clarté du français.* Villeneuve d'Ascq: Publications de l'Université de Lille.

Rodriguez, João Tçuzzu S.J. 1604–1608. *Arte da lingoa de Iapam.* 4 vols. Nagasaki [Faksimile-Edition von Doi Tado & Mitsuhashi Ken. Tôkyô; Benseisha 1975; jap. Übersetzung von Doi Tado. Tôkyô: Sanseido 1955].

Rosiello, Luigi. 1967. *Linguistica illuminista.* Bologna: Il Mulino.

Sanctius Brocensis, Franciscus. 1587. *Minerva, seu de causis linguae latinae.* Salamanca [sp. Übersetzung von Fernando Riveras Cárdenas. Madrid: Cátedra 1976].

Sapir, Edward. 1921. *Language.* New York: Harcourt, Brace & Co. [dt. Übersetzung von Conrad P. Homberger. München: Max Hueber 1961].

Schlegel, Friedrich. 1808. *Über die Sprache und Weisheit der Indier.* Heidelberg [ed. E. Behler & al., München 1975].

Schlegel, August Wilhelm. 1818. *Observations sur la langue et littérature provençales.* Paris [ed. Gunter Narr. Tübingen: Narr 1971].

Schleicher, August. 1850. *Die Sprachen Europas in vergleichender Übersicht.* Bonn.

Schwegler, Armin. 1990. *Analyticity and syntheticity. A diachronic perspective with special reference to Romance languages.* (Empirical approaches to language typology, 6.) Berlin: Mouton de Gruyter.

Sgoff, Brigitte. 1994. *Claude Fauriel und die Anfänge der romanischen Sprachwissenschaft.* Diss. München.

Sharadzenidze, T. 1976. „On the two trends in modern linguistics and the two sources of these trends". In: Parret (ed.), 62–84.

Sicard, Roch Ambroise. 1797. *Cours d'instruction d'un sourd-muet de naissance pour servir à l'éduca-*

tion des sourd-muets. Et qui peut être utile à celle de ceux qui entendent et qui parlent. Paris.

Skalička, Vladimír. 1969. *Typologische Studien*. Braunschweig & Wiesbaden: Vieweg.

Smith, Adam. 1761. *A dissertation on the origin of languages or considerations concerning the first formation of languages and the different genius of original and compounded languages*. London [ed. Eugenio Coseriu. Tübingen: Narr 1970].

Steinthal, Heymann. 1850. *Die Klassifikation der Sprachen, dargestellt als die Entwicklung der Sprachidee*. Berlin.

Steinthal, Heymann. 1860. *Charakteristik der hauptsächlichsten Typen des Sprachbaus*. Berlin [rev. von Franz Misteli. Berlin 1893].

Tesnière, Lucien. 1959. *Éléments de syntaxe structurale*. Paris: Klincksieck.

Uspenskij, B[oris] A. 1962. *Principy strukturnoj tipologii*. Moskva: Nauka [englische Version: B. Uspensky, *Principles of structural typology*. The Hague & Paris: Mouton 1968].

Whaley, Lindsay J. 1997. *Introduction to typology. The unity and diversity of language*. Thousand Oaks/CA: Sage Publications.

Verburg, Pieter A. 1981. „*Ars* oder *Scientia*, eine Frage der Sprachbetrachtung im 17. und 18. Jahrhundert". In: Geckeler & al. (eds.). I: 207−14.

Georg Bossong, Universität Zürich,
(Schweiz)

20. Sprachtypologie bei Edward Sapir

1. Edward Sapirs Leben und Werk
2. Sapirs typologisches Raster
3. Sprache und Denken
4. Zitierte Literatur

1. Edward Sapirs Leben und Werk

Edward Sapir (1839−1952) wurde in Lauenburg (Pommern) als Sohn orthodoxer Juden geboren und emigrierte mit seinen Eltern im Alter von fünf Jahren nach Amerika, wo sich die Familie in New York niederließ. Nach einem Studium der germanischen und allgemeinen Sprachwissenschaft an der Columbia Universität wurde er − unter dem Einfluss seines Lehrers Franz Boas − schnell zum herausragendsten Experten der amerikanischen Indianersprachen (Koerner 1984: Teil I). Seine Arbeiten zur allgemeinen Sprachwissenschaft (darunter zur Typologie), später auch zur allgemeinen Kulturwissenschaft und Psychologie gründen sich auf die genaue Kenntnis der Struktur sehr unterschiedlicher Indianersprachen, der INDOGERMANISCHEN und AFRO-ASIATISCHEN (SEMITISCHEN) Sprachen. Neben seinen AMERINDISCHEN Sprachstudien veröffentlicht Sapir im Jahre 1921 ein Grundlagenwerk der allgemeinen Sprachwissenschaft, das Buch *Language. An introduction to the study of speech*, dessen zentrales und längstes sechstes Kapitel sich den Typen sprachlicher Struktur widmet.

2. Sapirs typologisches Raster

Edward Sapirs Typologie ist klassifikatorisch. Es geht ihm darum, die sprachliche Vielfalt zu systematisieren, wobei wie in den typologischen Ansätzen Friedrich und August Wilhelm von Schlegels und Wilhelm von Humboldts die Morphologie im Vordergrund steht („morphologische Typologie").

Sapir ordnet die Sprachen zwar vier relativ allgemeinen Gruppen zu, ansonsten werden sie aber durch eine kombinatorische Merkmalsmatrix klassifiziert, wobei Merkmale nicht nur an- und abwesend (also diskret) sein können, sondern auch graduell (leicht oder hochgradig) abgestuft werden. Schon wenn man von der Möglichkeit der Graduierung absieht, ergeben sich rechnerisch 375 Kombinationsmöglichkeiten (Klassen).

2.1. Morphologische Verfahren

In der Nachfolge der klassischen Typologie unterscheidet Sapir fünf morphologische Verfahren:

a) das *isolierende* Verfahren: es gibt nur Wurzeln; als Mittel der morphosyntaktischen Auszeichnung dient lediglich die Wortstellung,
b) das *agglutinierende* Verfahren: Wörter setzen sich zusammen aus Wurzeln und relativ leicht abtrennbaren Affixen (die möglicherweise auch als gebundene Wurzeln aufgefasst werden können),
c) das *fusionierende* Verfahren: Wurzeln (bzw. Flexionsstämme) werden mit Flexionselementen versehen, die mit jenen semantisch und phonologisch eng verbunden sind (also im Gegensatz zu den Affixen des agglutinierenden Verfahrens nicht leicht abtrennbar sind),

d) das *symbolische* Verfahren: Die Wurzeln an sich werden morphologisch verändert (also nicht mit gesonderten Flexionselementen versehen).

Im Gegensatz zu seinen Vorläufern verwendet Sapir für die letzten beiden Verfahren nicht den Begriff *flexivisch*, da Flexion nicht nur symbolisch (wie im ARABISCHEN) oder fusionierend (wie im GRIECHISCHEN) erfolgen kann, sondern auch agglutinierend (wie im TÜRKISCHEN) und sogar isolierend (wie im TIBETISCHEN).

In Erweiterung der älteren morphologischen Typologie wendet Sapir die Merkmale des morphologischen Verfahrens nicht auf die Sprache als Ganzes an, sondern ordnet sie bestimmten Konzeptbereichen zu: So werden im ENGLISCHEN Tempus und Numerus fusionierend bzw. symbolisch enkodiert, die Derivation erfolgt (abgesehen von Konversion) fusionierend, während syntaktische Relationen in überwiegendem Maße isolierend (also durch die Wortstellung) angezeigt werden. Im SALINA, einer südwest-kalifornischen Indianersprache, sind weniger abstrakte morphosyntaktische Kategorien wie Numerus oder Tempus nicht grammatikalisiert (bzw. noch weniger abstrakt, d. h. lexikalisch-derivativ enkodiert), in allen anderen Konzeptbereichen werden fusionierende Verfahren verwendet. Ähnlich verhält sich das TÜRKISCHE, in dem Numerus ebenfalls stärker derivativ enkodiert ist als z. B. im LATEINISCHEN; allerdings verwendet das TÜRKISCHE agglutinierende Verfahren. Das CHINESISCHE zeichnet sich dadurch aus, dass neben den Lexemen nur abstrakt-relationale Konzepte ausgedrückt werden, und zwar mit isolierenden Verfahren.

2.2. Synthesegrad

Unabhängig vom morphologischen Verfahren klassifiziert Sapir Sprachen nach ihrem Synthesegrad:

− in *analytischen* Sprachen entspricht jedem Konzept ein Wort (CHINESISCH),
− in *synthetischen* Sprachen können die Wörter in (Teil-) Konzepte analysiert werden (LATEINISCH, ARABISCH, FINNISCH),
− in *polysynthetischen* Sprachen ist der Synthesegrad noch höher, d. h. ein Wort ist in zahlreiche (Teil-) Konzepte zerlegbar (als Beispiel führt Sapir eine Reihe von Indianersprachen an: CHINOOK, NOOTKA und YANA).

Die Merkmale *analytisch, synthetisch* und *polysynthetisch* bilden ein Kontinuum, auf dem sich Sprachen diachron entwickeln können.

Kritisch ist anzumerken (auch in Hinblick auf die folgenden Ausführungen), dass Sapir das, was er 'Konzept' nennt (die deutsche Übersetzung spricht von 'Begriff'), nicht genau definiert.

3. Sprache und Denken

Obwohl Sapirs Typologie in der Tradition Humboldts steht, wendet er sich gegen eine evolutionistische Typologieauffassung, nach der die Sprache die „geistige Entwickelung des Menschengeschlechts" spiegelt (Humboldt 1832). Dem Vorwurf Greenbergs (1974: 28−31), Sapirs Typologie suche nach dem „Bauplan" („basic plan", Sapir 1921: 127) oder „Geist" der Sprache („structural 'genius'", Sapir 1921: 127) als Ausdruck der tieferen Einheit, die sich auch in der Kultur bzw. im „Nationalcharakter" der Sprachgemeinschaft manifestiere (Greenberg 1974: 28), widerspricht Sapir (1921: 232): „It is impossible to show that the form of a language has the slightest connection with national temperament." Es ist daher um so unverständlicher, warum die Annahme eines unmittelbaren Zusammenhangs von Sprache und Weltanschauung bzw. Mentalität unter der Bezeichnung „Sapir-Whorf-Hypothese" mit Sapir in Zusammenhang gebracht wird.

In seinen späteren Arbeiten beschäftigt sich Sapir mit einem Gebiet, das er „Kulturpsychologie" nennt. Judith T. Irving rekonstruiert 1994 den Text einer Vorlesungsreihe zu diesem Thema. In einer Vorlesung lehnt Sapir (1994: Kapitel 11) die Annahme einer „primitiven Mentalität" explizit ab, denn die Menschen unterschieden sich nicht in der „Logik", sondern nur in unterschiedlichen Erfahrungen. Somit kann Sapir nicht im eigentlichen Sinne als 'Mentalist' bezeichnet werden, sondern erweist sich als Sprach- und Kulturwissenschaftler, der anthropologische, soziologische und psychologische Fragen in die Linguistik einbezieht (Sapir 1929: 214).

4. Zitierte Literatur

Sapir (1949: 601−617) enthält ein Schriftenverzeichnis. Nachträge dazu finden sich in Koerner (1984: 211−218) zusammen mit einer Bibliographie zur Rezeption insbesondere der Sapir-Whorf-Hypothese (xxii−xxviii).

Greenberg, Joseph H. 1974. *Language Typology. A historcal and analytic overview.* (Janua Linguarum, Series Minor, 184.) Den Haag & Paris: Mouton.

Humboldt, Wilhelm von. 1832. *Ueber die Verschiedenheit des menschlichen Sprachbaues und ihren Einfluss auf die geistige Entwickelung des Menschengeschlechts.* Ursprünglich: *Über die Kawi-Sprache auf der Insel Java, nebst einer Einleitung über die Verschiedenheit des menschlichen Sprachbaues und ihren Einfluss auf die geistige Entwicklung des Menschengeschlechts.* Abhandlungen der Königlichen Akademie der Wissenschaften zu Berlin. Aus dem Jahre 1832, Th. 2−4; wieder in: Humboldt, Wilhelm von 1963. *Werke in fünf Bänden.* Hrsg. von Flitner, Andreas & Giel, Klaus. Bd. 3: *Schriften zur Sprachphilosophie.* Darmstadt: Wissenschaftliche Buchgesellschaft: §8: 368−756.

Koerner, Konrad. 1984. *Edward Sapir. Appraisals of his life and work.* Edited with an introduction by Konrad Koerner. Amsterdam & Philadelphia: Benjamins.

Sapir, Edward. 1921. *Language. An introduction to the study of speech.* New York: Harcourt & Brace. Deutsche Übersetzung: *Die Sprache. Eine Einführung in das Wesen der Sprache.* München: Hueber 1961.

Sapir, Edward. 1929. „The status of linguistics as a science", *Language* 5: 207−214; Wieder in: Sapir 1949: 160−166.

Sapir, Edward. 1949. *Selected Writings of Edward Sapir in Language, Culture and Personality.* Edited by David G[oodman] Mandelbaum. Berkeley & Los Angeles: University of California Press [Second Printing 1951].

Sapir, Edward. 1994. *The Psychology of Culture. A Course of Lectures.* Reconstructed and edited by Judith T. Irvine. Berlin & New York: Mouton de Gruyter.

Martin Haase, Technische Universität Berlin (Deutschland)

21. Typologie als Charakterologie

1. Einleitung
2. Wilhelm von Humboldt
3. *Le génie de la langue*
4. Heyman Steinthal
5. Franz Nikolaus Finck und Ernst Lewy
6. Vilém Mathesius
7. Eugenio Coserius Sprachtypologie
8. Schlußbemerkung
9. Zitierte Literatur

1. Einleitung

Das Konzept der Charakterologie in der Bedeutung einer neu zu begründenden linguistischen Teildisziplin („linguistic characterology") hat Vilém Mathesius auf dem Ersten Internationalen Linguistenkongreß in Den Haag 1928 vorgestellt (cf. id. 1930). Mit diesem Begriff knüpft er an Traditionen der Romantik an, namentlich an Traditionen Wilhelm von Humboldts, zu denen sich auf dem Gebiet der Sprachtypologie insbes. Heyman Steinthal (1850/1856; 1860) und Franz Misteli (1893) als unmittelbare Fortsetzer, des weiteren Georg von der Gabelentz (1891/²1901/1969), Franz Nikolaus Finck (1899; 1910/³1936), Ernst Lewy (1942/²1964) und Eugenio Coseriu (in verschiedenen Publikationen) zählen. Während bei Mathesius das Projekt einzelsprachbezogener Charakteristik kritisch, nämlich aus skeptischer Einschätzung der Möglichkeit einer systematischen Typologie begründet ist, erscheint es bei Humboldt als positives Korollar seiner Sprachtheorie: Das Programm der Sprachcharakteristik hat seine Fundamente in einem Denken, das der Individualität und Organizität von Sprachen Rechnung tragen soll.

2. Wilhelm von Humboldt

Die Perspektivität der von Humboldt skizzierten Sprachcharakteristik erhält ihre Konturen im Kontext eines zunächst anthropologisch, später sprachanthropologisch zentrierten Denkens (cf. Menze 1965), in dem Empirie und Spekulation miteinander verbunden werden. Bereits in den Schriften zu Anthropologie und Geschichte artikuliert sich das Bemühen, gleichsam komplementär zur Kantischen Philosophie die Möglichkeitsbedingungen der Erkenntnis des Individuellen in immer neuen Dichotomien zu fassen. So betrachtet Humboldt es als „eigenthümliche [...] Natur des menschlichen Geistes", „das Allgemeine" zu suchen „und das Einzelne in ein Ganzes zusammenzufassen" (Humboldt 1791/I: 87). Der anthropologisch-erkenntnistheoretischen Akzentuierung des Sachverhalts korrespondiert in anderen Schriften eine ontologisch-platonisierende: das Einzelne repräsentiert das Allgemeine, das Individuum das Ideal (resp. die Idee), die Erscheinung das Wesen (cf. u. a. id. 1797/II: 327; 1821/IV: 54 ff.; cf. auch Borsche 1981: 201 ff.; Steinthal 1860: 22 ff.). Angewendet auf die Sprachthematik resultiert aus diesen Gedanken ein zentrales Forschungsanliegen: die Erschließung der allgemeinen Sprachidee im Ausgang von der Individualität und von der Verschiedenheit der Einzelsprachen (cf. Humboldt 1812/III: 296).

Dem Verständnis einzelsprachlicher Individualität hat Humboldt sich mit einer Konstellation untereinander verbundener, immer wieder neu nuancierter Begriffe anzunähern gesucht, u. a. *innere Form, Bau, Organismus, charakteristische Form, Charakter, Geist, Nation*. Unter den genannten Begriffen hat der Begriff der *inneren Form* als Prinzip aller sprachlichen Individuation unbedingte Priorität (cf. dazu Coseriu 1970: 55; Borsche 1989; Dezsö 1979: 108); Humboldt faßt die *innere Form* zunächst als den „intellectuelle[n] Theil" der Sprache, dann als ein geistiges Prinzip im weiteren Sinne, das im Zusammenwirken mit verschiedenen Intentionalitätsmodi die „spracherzeugende Kraft" formiert und „individuelle Gestaltungen" hervorbringt, „in denen der individuelle Charakter der Nation" zutage tritt (id. 1830/1835/VII: 87). Die innere Form erweist sich als ein einheitsstiftendes Strukturprinzip, das den sprachlichen „Stoff" zu einem phonetisch, morphosyntaktisch und semantisch individuell gegliederten Ganzen ausprägt.

Den Gedanken der „charakteristischen" Ausformung der Einzelsprachen hat Humboldt in mehreren Begriffen zu fassen versucht. Für die Ebene speziell der grammatischen Verfahren wählt er die Begriffe *Bau* bzw. *Organismus* (cf. ib., 87 ff. u. ö.; cf. auch Borsche 1989: 52 ff.), deren Formprinzipien seiner Auffassung zufolge geradezu exemplarisch in „Wortbildung" und „Wortfügung" („Isolierung der Wörter, Flexion und Agglutination", cf. Humboldt 1830/1835/VII: 109) in Erscheinung treten: Diese bezeichnen den „Angelpunkt" des sprachlichen Organismus, nach dem sich dessen Vollkommenheit bemesse (ib.). − Des weiteren verwendet Humboldt den Begriff *charakteristische Form*, um seine Vorstellung der individuellen, alle sprachlichen Ebenen erfassenden Durchgestaltung zum Ausdruck zu bringen (cf. ib., 48), bzw. den Begriff *Charakter*, mit dem er sich dem „Wesen" von Sprache konkreter anzunähern hofft (ib., 165). Der *Charakter* bezeichnet die individuelle Gestaltung von Sprachen „nach Vollendung ihres Baues" (ib., 167), dank der sie ihre Leistungen als literarisch-ästhetisches Ausdrucks- resp. Verständigungsmittel nunmehr voll entfalten können (cf. dazu auch Trabant 1994: 265 f.; Steinthal 1848/1856: 92 ff.; Lehmann 1988: 5). Auch für den Begriff des Geistes wählt Humboldt in diesem Zusammenhang eine konkretere Fassung: Es ist der „Geist eines Volks" (Humboldt 1830/1835/VII: 168), von dem jede Sprache ihre „bestimmte Eigenthümlichkeit" erhält (ib., 171), wie dieser umgekehrt durch die Sprache geprägt wird; Sprache und Volksgeist, Sprache und Nation bedingen und formen sich wechselseitig (cf. ib.). − Auch der Gedanke einer essentiellen Verbindung von Einzelnem und Allgemeinem findet sich in diesem Kontext wieder: Nicht das „einzelne Seyn des Individuums" gilt es zu erforschen, „sondern das allgemeine, das in jedem einzelnen bestimmend hervortritt. Jede erschöpfende Charakterschilderung muss dies Seyn als Endpunkt ihrer Forschung vor Augen haben" (ib., 179).

Humboldts Überlegungen zur Sprachcharakteristik gründen im Gedanken einer notwendigen Vermittlung von Allgemeinem und Individuellem, der Erschließbarkeit der Idee im Ausgang von der Erscheinung. Das Konzept der *inneren Form* als eines einheitsbegründenden sprachlichen Individuationsprinzips sichert ein organologisches Sprachverständnis, das die Entdeckung von *Zusammenhängen* in den Techniken einer Einzelsprache in Aussicht stellt. Humboldts Nachfolger werden im allgemeinen die spekulativen Aspekte seiner Begrifflichkeit beiseite lassen und diese anders orientierten methodologischen und metatheoretischen Konzepten anschließen (cf. infra). − Der Rekurs auf Nation und Geist zur Erklärung sprachlicher Individuation wird allerdings − auch außerhalb der Sprachtypologie − Anlaß zu ideologisch eingefärbten Hypothesen geben, die der Sprachwissenschaft in der Regel nicht zur Ehre gereicht haben (cf. Römer 1985/²1989: 124 ff.).

3. *Le génie de la langue*

Exkurs: Der im frühen 17. Jahrhundert in Frankreich geprägte Begriff *génie de la langue* (cf. Christmann 1977: 91) ist als linguistisches Konzept ebenfalls mit dem Programm charakterisierender Sprachbeschreibung verknüpft. Wichtige Präzisierungen erhält dieser Begriff zunächst im Kontext sensualistischer Erkenntnistheorie, in Condillacs *Essai sur l'origine des connaissances humaines* (1746), wo dieser die wechselseitige Beeinflussung von Sprach- und Volksgeist (*génie de la langue*/*génie des peuples*) abhandelt (id. 1746/1973: 259 ff.; zum Einfluß Condillacs auf Humboldt cf. Christmann 1977: 94).

Der Versuch, über das Konzept des *génie de la langue* Sprachcharakteristik und Sprachklassifikation miteinander zu verbinden, findet sich dann bei Girard, der den je individuellen Geist einer Sprache durch den je individuellen Volksgeschmack erklärt (id. 1747/1982: 22). U. a. nach dem Kriterium der Abbildung der Ideenfolge durch die Wortfolge unterscheidet Girard drei verschiedene Sprachklassen und damit drei verschiedene Formen des *génie de la langue*: 1. *langues analytiques*: Widerspiegelung der Ideenfolge durch die Wortfolge, „ordre naturel"; 2. *langues transpositives*: freie Wortfolge; 3. *langues mixtes*: Charakterzüge aus den beiden ersten Gruppen (cf. ib.: 23 ff.). − Die später am Begriff des *génie de la langue* orientierten Untersuchungen sind in der Regel eindeutig charakterisierend angelegt (cf. z. B. Dauzat 1949/1977), indem sie − bisweilen über den Weg des Sprachvergleichs − das Wesen einer Einzelsprache erfassen sollen.

4. Heyman Steinthal

Humboldts Gedanken zur Sprachcharakteristik werden zunächst von Steinthal fortgeführt, dessen sprachtypologische Position sich maßgeblich in einer ebenso sympathetischen wie kritischen Exegese der Sprachtheorie Humboldts herausbildet (cf. Ringmacher 1996). Der Duktus von Steinthals Kommentaren erinnert an Denkstil und Diktion des Kommentierten selbst: bei beiden eine pathetisch schattierte Metasprache; das Bedürfnis, das einmal Gedachte immer wieder neu zu nuancieren; der Versuch, das eigene Denken durch − keineswegs immer klare − Einbindung philosophischer Konzepte zu konturieren, wobei allerdings Steinthal die Kantisch inspirierte 'dualistische' Anschauungsweise Humboldts durch Orientierung an der Dialektik Hegels zu überwinden bestrebt ist (cf. Steinthal 1860: 23 ff.). Steinthal würdigt an Humboldts „Denkweise" insbesondere die „Richtung auf die *Einzeleigenthümlichkeit*" (id. 1850/1856: 13), vermißt jedoch eine „Classification der Sprachen", die durch dessen „individuelle Forschung" verhindert worden sei (ib.: 57). Diesen 'Widerspruch' Humboldts zu überwinden, d. h. Charakteristik und Klassifikation miteinander in Einklang zu bringen, ist Steinthals erklärtes Ziel. In der Entwicklung seiner Konzepte weicht er verschiedentlich von Humboldt ab, so etwa in der Bestimmung des Begriffs *Organismus*, der nun nicht mehr nur den „Bau" einzelner Sprachen, sondern als „Gesammtorganismus" die Sprachidee selbst bezeichnet (id. 1860: 312). Die Klassifikationskriterien sollten nach Steinthal nicht „ab extra" an die Sprachen herangetragen werden, sondern als „organische" Merkmale den einzelsprachlichen Organismus und ihn als „Glied" des „Gesammtorganismus" charakterisieren, in anderen Worten: seine Position als Repräsentant der Sprachidee angeben (cf. ib.). Die je besondere Gestaltung der Sprachorganismen führt Steinthal in Berufung auf Humboldt auf den „sprachschaffenden Geist" oder das „Volksbewußtsein" zurück (ib.: 316; cf. dazu Knobloch 1988: 184 ff.; Ringmacher 1996: 191 ff.); dieses präge der Sprache die innere Form ein, die Steinthal − enger als Humboldt − als das „eigenthümliche System der grammatischen Kategorien einer Sprache" auslegt (id. 1860: 316).

Die von Steinthal angestrebte Verbindung von Klassifikation und Charakterisierung erfolgt somit über den Begriff des Organismus, der, gleichsam 'homologisiert', als Sprachstruktur und als Sprachidee das Auseinandertreten von Besonderem und Allgemeinem „in nuce" unterbinden soll. Die organologische Theorie soll die Möglichkeit sichern, das einzelne Sprachgebilde über die grammatischen Kategorien als exemplarische Kriterien seiner Organizität nicht nur bis in den kleinsten Winkel, sondern auch in seinem individuellen Wesen zu durchleuchten (zur Neubearbeitung der *Charakteristik* durch Misteli 1893 cf. Ringmacher 1996: 202 ff.).

5. Franz Nikolaus Finck und Ernst Lewy

Finck und sein Schüler Lewy versuchen, in je spezifischer Akzentuierung Humboldtscher Konzepte und unter Einbeziehung psychologischer bzw. kultursoziologischer Erklärungsmuster Klassifikation und Charakterisierung zu vereinen (cf. dazu auch Hartmann 1962: 40 ff.). Während Finck in seiner Schrift

Der deutsche Sprachbau als Ausdruck deutscher Weltanschauung in Orientierung an Burnes Temperamentenlehre Sprachtypus und Volkspsyche als einander entsprechend korreliert (Finck 1899: 12 ff.), distanziert er sich in *Haupttypen des Sprachbaus* ausdrücklich von dem Versuch, die „Eigentümlichkeiten der Sprachen aus der geistigen Eigenart der Völker zu erklären" (id. 1910/³1936: VIII). Den sprachwissenschaftlichen Typbegriff definiert er hier durch das „Gemeinsame" und „Charakteristische" (ib.: 1). Die Schwierigkeit einer Balance zwischen individualisierender Charakterisierung und generalisierender Typisierung nimmt er deutlich wahr (cf. ib.: 2 f.). Seine auf der Grundlage von „Zerlegen" und „Verbinden" durchgeführte morphologische Typologie (cf. ib.: 5) soll nicht nur eine ausreichende Anzahl, sondern auch eine hinsichtlich ihrer „besondere[n], eigenartige[n] Formen" große Spannbreite von Typen bereitstellen, um eine strukturelle Zuordnung aller vorkommenden Sprachen zu ermöglichen (ib.: 3).

Bei Lewy finden sich mehr noch als bei Finck wichtige Überlegungen zur Ausführbarkeit einer charakterisierenden Typologie. Das Bemühen um eine ganzheitliche, die grammatischen Formen als Ausdruck „geistige[r] Kategorien" deutenden Sprachbeschreibung (Lewy 1942/²1964: 14) artikuliert sich in der Wiederaufnahme von Konzepten Humboldts: *Bau* versteht Lewy als „die ordnungsmässige Beziehung der einzelnen Teile eines Ganzen zu einander" (ib.: 13), die Termini „grammatisches System, Bau oder Struktur einer Sprache, Form, auch: innere Form, besagen ungefähr dasselbe" (ib.: 14). Sprachtypen haben nach Lewy lediglich ordnende Funktion, indem sie „einzelne Züge eines grammatischen Systems zusammenfügen [...] oder auf einander beziehen" (ib.: 17). – Für die Erklärung der Verschiedenheit der Sprachen holt Lewy weiter aus als seine Vorgänger, indem er nicht nur die „Verschiedenheit des Geistes", sondern auch die „Verschiedenheit der Wirtschaftsformen" geltend macht (ib.: 18; cf. dazu die Kritik von Spitzer 1944).

Auch in späteren Arbeiten hält Lewy am Programm der charakterisierenden, das „Wesen" von Sprache erfassenden Typologie fest (cf. id. 1951/1961: 10), beurteilt nun jedoch die Möglichkeit einer Parallelisierung von „Geistesart und Sprachgestaltung" eines Volkes zunehmend skeptisch (ib.: 17). Wiederum in Bezugnahme auf Humboldt sucht er ein individualisierendes Sprachverständnis zu sichern, indem er vom Begriff des Typus als eines einheitlichen Strukturbegriffs Abstand nimmt: keine „wirkliche Sprache" sei mit „einigen Formeln" darstellbar, diese „Wahrheit" habe Humboldt „deutlicher gesehen [...] als alle seine Nachfolger"; vielmehr sei anzunehmen, daß jede Sprache verschiedene typologische Züge in sich vereine (ib.: 15).

Eine grundlegende methodologische Schwierigkeit der Sprachcharakteristik liegt nach Lewy darin beschlossen, daß wir über kein Kriterium verfügen, welches uns garantiert, daß wir das „Charakteristische" einer Sprache wirklich erfaßt haben. Lewy denkt diesen Sachverhalt empirisch: solange wir nicht ein „Verzeichnis sämtlicher möglicher Sprachzüge" besäßen, könne der Sprachtypologe immer nur vom begrenzten Radius der eigenen Kenntnisse ausgehen; dies zeige, „wie sehr noch die Charakteristik von der Subjektivität des Charakterisierenden abhängt" (id. 1934/1961: 66). Dieser Gedanke, der auf den ersten Blick an eine konzeptionelle Schwäche des charakterologischen Programms zu rühren scheint, legt dessen hermeneutischen Grundansatz frei.

6. Vilém Mathesius

Mathesius aktualisiert auf der Basis des funktionalistischen Sprachverständnisses der Prager Schule das Programm der Sprachcharakteristik mit neuen Konzepten. Da er eine systematische Typologie auf dem Wissensstand seiner Zeit nicht für durchführbar hält, sollten im Rahmen der einzelsprachbezogenen Charakterologie die Grundlagen für alle weitere typologische Forschung erarbeitet werden (id. 1930: 56). Mathesius' Vorstellungen zufolge bezieht die synchronisch vorgehende Charakterologie ihre Kategorien aus der allgemeinen Sprachwissenschaft; im Unterschied zur deskriptiven Grammatik, die eine vollständige Inventarisierung aller in einer Sprache vorfindlichen formalen und funktionellen Elemente vorzunehmen habe, behandele die Charakterologie allein „the important and fundamental features of a given language at a given point of time [...] and tries to ascertain relations between them" (ib.). Wie allerdings die Ermittlung der 'wichtigen' und 'fundamentalen' Züge im einzelnen vonstatten gehen soll, verschweigt Mathesius. – Den Sprachvergleich betrachtet er als für die Charakterologie äußerst bedeutsames Verfahren (cf. ib.).

Die Tradition der Charakterologie ist Mathesius zufolge durch Humboldt begründet worden, der die charakteristischen Züge einer Sprache mit dem Volksgeist in Verbindung gebracht, darüber hinaus aber auch den Versuch einer systematischen Typologie vorgelegt habe (ib.: 56 f.). − Wie weit Mathesius' eigene Position allerdings von Positionen Humboldts entfernt ist, verdeutlicht schon ein Blick auf die Terminologie: statt *Organismus, innere Form, Sprachgeist* erscheinen bei ihm Begriffe wie *linguistic structure, synchronic interrelations, value, functional point of view* (ib.: 56 f.), die den zuerst genannten zwar nicht gänzlich fremd, jedoch als einem anderen Paradigma verpflichtet gegenüberstehen.

7. Eugenio Coserius Sprachtypologie

Coseriu hat vor dem Hintergrund einer umfassenden Sprachtheorie für die Arbeit in den linguistischen Einzeldisziplinen eine Reihe von Konzepten entworfen, welche die sprachwissenschaftliche Diskussion nachhaltig beeinflußt und stimuliert haben (einen Überblick gibt Albrecht 1988). Die durch ihn begründete „Synthese von idealistischer und strukturalistischer Sprachwissenschaft" (cf. Christmann 1974: 76 ff.) kommt in den Überlegungen zur Sprachtypologie in besonderer Weise zum Tragen: Im Zuge einer intensiven Auseinandersetzung mit der idealistischen Sprachauffassung Humboldts korrigiert Coseriu nicht nur dessen Vereinnahmung für die klassische Typologie (cf. Albrecht 1988: XXVIII); vielmehr erarbeitet er in der Humboldt-Exegese auch die eigene, mit Denkmitteln des Strukturalismus präzisierte Begrifflichkeit (cf. insbes. Coseriu 1972; 1980a/1988; 1983/1988).

In den Schriften Humboldts sieht Coseriu „entwicklungsfähige Ansätze zu verschiedenen Typologien" angelegt, und zwar, erstens, zu „einer 'integralen' Sprachtypologie" (die er selbst vertritt, cf. infra), zweitens, zu einer „Typologie der Sprachgestaltungsarten" und, drittens, zu einer „'partiell-charakterisierenden' Typologie" (Coseriu 1972: 134). Entgegen einer verbreiteten Annahme habe Humboldt eine „ausführliche Klassifikation der Sprachen als solche [...] nicht gegeben" (ib.).

Coseriu entwickelt sein Verständnis des Sprachtypus als einer der Einzelsprache „integrierten", ihr jeweils spezifischen Strukturebene im Ausgang von solchen Textpassagen Humboldts, in denen dieser den Gedanken einzelsprachlicher Individuation durch ganzheitliche Gestaltungsprinzipien begrifflich zu fassen sucht (cf. Coseriu 1980a/1988: 164 ff.; 1980b/1988: 186 ff.); als der eigenen Auffassung in besonderer Weise affin erweist sich dabei Humboldts Konzept der charakteristischen Form (cf. 2.), das Coseriu mit seinem Begriff des Sprachtypus identifiziert (id. 1990: 138). Ein weiterer wichtiger Gewährsmann in diesem Zusammenhang ist von der Gabelentz: mit der Vorstellung, der „Gesammtcharakter" von Sprachen könne mittels „Induction" erschlossen werden, und zwar im Rahmen einer zu diesem Zweck eigens zu begründenden Typologie (cf. von der Gabelentz 1891/²1901/1969: 481), habe dieser ebenfalls den Gedanken „realer" sprachlicher „Gestaltungszusammenhänge" vertreten (Coseriu 1980b/1988: 186).

Die strukturalistische Orientierung wird in der funktionellen Interpretation des Sprachtypus als oberste einzelsprachliche Strukturebene deutlich. Die erste sprachliche Strukturebene, die *Norm*, beinhaltet nach Coseriu die mit einer Sprache tradierten, tatsächlich realisierten Redetechniken; die zweite Ebene, das *System*, enthält die innerhalb einer Sprache möglichen Techniken, d. h. die „funktionellen Oppositionen", in deren Rahmen die Norm sich wandelt; der *Typus* schließlich, als letzte Ebene, gibt jene Möglichkeiten vor, denen entsprechend das System sich verändern kann (cf. id. 1980a/1988: 166). Er umfaßt „die Typen von Funktionen und Verfahren eines Sprachsystems, die funktionellen Prinzipien einer Sprachtechnik, und stellt somit die zwischen den einzelnen Teilen eines Sprachsystems feststellbare funktionelle Kohärenz dar" (ib.). Coseriu legt Wert darauf festzustellen, daß der Typbegriff der „strukturell-funktionellen Typologie im Sinne Humboldts" nicht als „Konstrukt", sondern als „reales Faktum" zu verstehen sei (1980b/1988: 187). Gleichwohl wird man diesem Begriff auch „Abstraktion" und „Idealisierung" unterstellen müssen, denn anders wäre seine Prinzipfunktion nicht zu gewährleisten und, wie Albrecht zu bedenken gibt, z. B. typologische Inkohärenz (mit der nach Coseriu prinzipiell gerechnet werden muß, cf. id. 1980a/1988: 169) nicht darstellbar (Albrecht 1988: XXVIII). − Daß bezüglich der Erklärung von typologischem Wandel durch das Drei-Ebenen-Modell der *regressus ad infinitum* droht, haben nicht nur Coserius Kritiker gesehen (cf. Lehmann

1988: 8f.); Coseriu selbst hat darauf hingewiesen (cf. id. 1971a/1988: 182).

Während in den bisher vorgestellten Theorien die Begründung dafür, welche Eigenschaften einer Sprache als charakteristisch zu gelten haben, bloß *implicite*, aus dem organologischen Sprachverständnis hergeleitet werden konnte, rechtfertigt Coseriu „typologische Relevanz" durch den „funktionellen Status der Merkmale" und durch ihren Zusammenhang: „bloße Kopräsenz" reiche nicht aus (cf. 1980a/1988: 171), vielmehr sei, wie die Definition des Typus verdeutlicht, „funktionelle Kohärenz" der Merkmale erforderlich (cf. supra).

Coseriu hat seine Auffassung von Sprachtypologie an mehreren Sprachen exemplifiziert (cf. id. 1971/1988; 1980b/1988; 1987). Für das Deutsche und das Altgriechische hat er, ausgehend von ganz verschiedenartigen Fakten (von Partikeln, präfigierten Verben und der Nominaldetermination), gezeigt, daß diese durch ein einziges „typologische[s] Gestaltungsprinzip" miteinander verbunden seien, nämlich durch den in allen Fällen „wirksamen Bezug auf Kontexte und auf Situationen" (1980b/1988: 193). – Ein für das Vulgärlatein und für die romanischen Sprachen von ihm ermitteltes typologisches Prinzip weist die 'Ikonizität' bestimmter Ausdrucksfunktionen hinsichtlich bestimmter Bezeichnungsfunktionen nach. So stellt Coseriu fest, daß anders als im Lateinischen im Vulgärlatein und in den romanischen Sprachen „innere", „paradigmatische" Bestimmungen, d. h. materielle Determinationen am Wort selbst, für „innere" (nicht durch den Satz aktualisierte, sondern als „Klassifizierung der Wirklichkeit" durch das Wort mitgebrachte) Funktionen eintreten (wie z. B. im Falle von Genus und Numerus); und daß entsprechend „äußere", „syntagmatische" Bestimmungen, d. h. materielle Determinationen außerhalb des Wortes, „äußere" (erst durch den Satz aktualisierte) Funktionen ausdrücken (z. B. Kasus, Steigerungsstufen; cf. Coseriu 1971/1988: 212; zu diesen nicht leicht verstehbaren Zusammenhängen cf. auch Rohrer 1988; Eckert 1986: 97ff.).

Die integrale Sprachtypologie Coserius kann seinem eigenen Verständnis zufolge nur bedingt mit der Sprachcharakteristik in Zusammenhang gebracht werden, da „nicht jede Charakterisierung von Sprachen an sich schon typologisch" sei (id. 1980a/1988: 161 f.). Die Synthese von Gedanken Humboldts und Konzepten der strukturell-funktionellen Linguistik begründet eine Position, die mit den eingangs skizzierten Theorien in der Forderung übereinstimmt, Typologie habe die individuellen Gestaltungsprinzipien von Sprachen zu erfassen. Während Steinthal, Finck und Lewy die Charakterisierungskonzeption über die Klassifikation einzulösen suchen, ist Coserius Sprachtypologie konsequent einzelsprachbezogen (cf. Lehmann 1988: 20).

8. Schlußbemerkung

Auch außerhalb der Typologie hat es immer wieder Versuche gegeben, das individuell Wesentliche einer Sprache zu erfassen. Die Sprachcharakteristik hat insbesondere in der Romanistik Interesse gefunden, da sie hier in nahezu programmatischer Verbindung mit dem Sprachvergleich (cf. Kuen 1953/1970: 420ff.) für die Ermittlung der individuellen Züge einer romanischen Sprache im Kontrast zu den mit dieser verwandten Sprachen zur Anwendung gelangen konnte (cf. u. a. Christmann 1979; Kuen 1953/1970; Lausberg 1947). In der Diskussion speziell des Französischen standen insbesondere zwei Fragen zur Debatte: die nach seiner *clarté*, einem im Kontext der französischen Klassik in Orientierung an der antiken *perspicuitas* begründeten Sprachideal (cf. Lausberg 1950: 182ff.; Weinrich 1961); und die nach seiner Abstraktheit (cf. Brøndal 1936; dazu Albrecht 1970 und id. 1995). – Die entscheidende Schwäche der Charakterisierungskonzeption ist auch in der Romanistik gesehen worden: „daß sich [...] bestimmte Grundsätze für das, was wichtig, beweisend und für das, was nebensächlich, zufällig ist, nicht geben lassen [...]" (Meyer-Lübke 1901/²1909: 61).

Nicht immer ist eine klare Abgrenzung zwischen der typologischen und der nicht genuin typologischen Sprachcharakteristik möglich: Beide orientieren sich – mehr oder weniger differenziert – an Begriffen und Ideen Humboldts, wie *innere Sprachform* (z. B. Weisgerber 1925/1964), *organisches und unteilbares Ganzes* (Wartburg 1943/²1962: 182), *Bau/Sprachbau* (Lausberg 1947: 108; Wartburg 1943/²1962: 181), *Geist/Sprachgeist* (z. B. Lerch 1933: 1; Vossler 1925; Spitzer 1922: 290ff.; Wandruszka 1959/1967). Hinzukommt noch, daß in diesen und vergleichbaren Studien bisweilen mit Kategorien gearbeitet wird, die aus der Sprachtypologie selbst stammen, wie etwa die von A. W. Schlegel geprägten Begriffe *analytisch/synthe-*

tisch (cf. Schlegel 1818/1971: 16 ff.; cf. z. B. Lerch 1933: 214; Weinrich 1963). Die Orientierung dieser Arbeiten an den oben genannten Konzepten verdeutlicht auf jeden Fall, daß nach einem ganzheitlichen Prinzip gesucht wird, das in verschiedenen Ausprägungen in einer Sprache in Erscheinung tritt.

Wie sollten nun die nicht typologisch orientierten Charakteristiken von den genuin typologischen grundsätzlich unterschieden werden? In Anlehnung an Gedanken Coserius (cf. 7.) könnte zumindest *idealiter* folgende Überlegung richtungweisend sein: Während die einfache Charakteristik im Hinblick auf die darzustellende Eigenschaft mit dem deskriptiven Nachweis der *Kopräsenz* der Fakten sich bescheiden kann, hat die typologische Charakteristik noch einen Schritt weiter zu gehen und deren *funktionale Kohärenz* durch ein Prinzip zu begründen.

„Typologie als Charakterologie" bezeichnet eine Vielfalt von Positionen, die allesamt mehr oder weniger direkt an Humboldt anschließen. Während bei Steinthal, Finck und Lewy das Projekt der Charakteristik durch Beschreibung klassenbildender Prototypen eingelöst werden soll, hat die Charakterologie der Auffassung von Mathesius zufolge – in Ermangelung zunächst aussichtsreicherer Forschungsmethoden – die Grundlagen für die weitere typologische Arbeit bereitzustellen (ebenso Pottier 1968: 310 f.). Das von Skalička konstatierte Fehlen einer „feste[n] theoretische[n] Grundlage" (id. 1958/1979: 318) hatte nicht zuletzt zur Folge, daß das ursprünglich im Idealismus verwurzelte Programm der Sprachcharakteristik mit recht heterogenen Forschungsrichtungen verbunden werden konnte: mit der Völkerpsychologie, mit dem Funktionalismus resp. Strukturalismus und, zumindest ansatzweise, mit der phänomenologisch orientierten Typologie (cf. Hartmann 1962: 40 ff.). Unbeschadet aller theoretischen Divergenzen stimmen diese Positionen darin überein, daß sie „zumindest in ihrer Fragestellung und in ihren Absichten" *holistisch* sind, indem sie Sprachtypen als ganzheitliche Strukturierungsformen von Einzelsprachen verstehen (cf. Coseriu 1990: 135). Vermutlich hat die Charakteristik nicht zuletzt deshalb in so heterogenen sprachwissenschaftlichen Kontexten Fuß fassen können, weil sie, verknüpft mit der Vorstellung einzelsprachlicher Organizität, das Interesse und die Modalität geisteswissenschaftlicher Erkenntnis geradezu exemplarisch repräsentiert: das Interesse an Individualität, die Reduktion individueller Erscheinungsvielfalt auf Prinzipien.

9. Zitierte Literatur

Albrecht, Jörn. 1970. *Le français langue abstraite?* Tübingen: Beitr. zur Linguistik.

Albrecht, Jörn. 1988. „τὰ ὄντα ὡς ἔστω λέγειν: Über die Schwierigkeit, die Dinge zu sagen wie sie sind, und andere davon zu überzeugen". In: Albrecht, Jörn et al. (eds.). Vol. I, XVII–XLV.

Albrecht, Jörn. 1995. „Le français langue abstraite? Neue Antworten auf eine alte Frage aus der Sicht der Prototypensemantik". In: Hoinkes, Ulrich (ed.). *Panorama der Lexikalischen Semantik. Thematische Festschrift aus Anlaß des 60. Geburtstags von Horst Geckeler.* Tübingen: Narr, 23–40.

Albrecht, Jörn & Lüdtke, Jens & Thun, Harald (eds.). 1988. *Energeia und Ergon. Sprachliche Variation – Sprachgeschichte – Sprachtypologie.* 3 vols. Tübingen: Narr.

Borsche, Tilmann. 1981. *Sprachansichten. Der Begriff der menschlichen Rede in der Sprachphilosophie Wilhelm von Humboldts.* Stuttgart: Klett-Cotta.

Borsche, Tilmann. 1989. „Die innere Form der Sprache. Betrachtungen zu einem Mythos der Humboldt-Herme(neu)tik". In: Scharf, Hans-Werner (ed.). *Wilhelm von Humboldts Sprachdenken: Symposium zum 150. Todestag.* Essen: Hobbing, 47–65.

Brøndal, Viggo. 1936. *Le Français Langue Abstraite.* Kopenhagen: E. Munksgaard.

Christmann, Hans-Helmut. 1974. *Idealistische Philologie und moderne Sprachwissenschaft.* München: Fink.

Christmann, Hans Helmut. 1977. „Zu den Begriffen 'Génie de la langue' und 'Analogie' in der Sprachwissenschaft des 16. bis 19. Jahrhunderts". *Beiträge zur Romanischen Philologie* XVI: 91–94.

Christmann, Hans Helmut. 1979. „Wesenszüge der italienischen Sprache in Geschichte und Gegenwart". *Italienische Studien* 2: 119–135.

Condillac, Étienne Bonnot de. 1746/1973. *Essai sur l'origine des connaissances humaines.* Précédé de „L'archéologie du frivole" par Jacques Derrida. Anvers-sur Oise: Galilée.

Coseriu, Eugenio. 1970. „Semantik, innere Form und Tiefenstruktur". *Folia Linguistica* 4: 53–63.

Coseriu, Eugenio. 1971a/1988. „Synchronie, Diachronie und Typologie". In: Albrecht, Jörn et al. (eds.). Vol. I, 173–184.

Coseriu, Eugenio. 1971b/1988. „Der romanische Sprachtypus. Versuch einer neuen Typologisierung der romanischen Sprachen". In: Albrecht, Jörn et al. (eds.). Vol. I, 207–224.

Coseriu, Eugenio. 1972. „Über die Sprachtypologie Wilhelm von Humboldts". In: Hösle, Johannes & Eitel, Wolfgang (eds.). *Beiträge zur vergleichenden Literaturgeschichte. Festschrift für Kurt Wais zum 65. Geburtstag.* Tübingen: Niemeyer, 107–135.

Coseriu, Eugenio. 1980a/1988. „Der Sinn der Sprachtypologie". In: Albrecht, Jörn et al. (eds.). Vol. 1, 161–172.

Coseriu, Eugenio. 1980b/1988. „Partikeln und Sprachtypus. Zur strukturell-funktionellen Fragestellung in der Sprachtypologie". In: Albrecht, Jörn et al. (eds.). Vol. 1, 185–193.

Coseriu, Eugenio. 1983/1988. „Sprachtypologie und Typologie von sprachlichen Verfahren". In: Albrecht, Jörn et al. (eds.). Vol. 1, 195–206.

Coseriu, Eugenio. 1987. „Le latin vulgaire et le type linguistique roman (A propos de la thèse de Humboldt: „Es sanken Formen, aber nicht die Form")". In: Herman, József (ed.). *Latin vulgaire – latin tardif.* Actes du 1er colloque international sur le latin vulgaire et tardif (Pécs, 2–5 septembre 1985). Tübingen: Niemeyer, 53–64.

Coseriu, Eugenio. 1990. „Typologie: ganzheitliche Typologie versus Teiltypologie. Einleitung Plenarsitzung 4". „Überblick über die Ergebnisse der Plenarsitzung 'Typologie: ganzheitliche Typologie versus Teiltypologie'". In: Bahner, Werner & Schildt, Joachim & Viehweger, Dieter (eds.). *Proceedings of the Fourteenth International Congress of Linguists. I. Berlin, August 10–August 15, 1987.* Berlin: Akad.-Verl., 134–138 und 237–242.

Dauzat, Albert. 1947/1977. *Le génie de la langue française.* Paris: Guénégaud.

Dezsö, L. 1979. „On Typological Characterologies". *Acta Linguistica Academiae Scientiarum Hungaricae* 29: 107–128.

Di Cesare, Donatella. 1990. „The Philosophical and Anthropological Place of Wilhelm von Humboldt's Linguistic Typology". In: Mauro, Tullio de & Formigari, Lia (eds.). *Leibniz, Humboldt and the Origins of Comparativism.* Amsterdam/Philadelphia: Benjamins, 157–180.

Eckert, Gabriele. 1986. *Sprachtypus und Geschichte. Untersuchungen zum typologischen Wandel des Französischen.* Tübingen: Narr.

Finck, Franz Nikolaus. 1899. *Der deutsche Sprachbau als Ausdruck deutscher Weltanschauung.* Marburg: Elwert.

Finck, Franz Nikolaus. 1910/³1936. *Die Haupttypen des Sprachbaus.* Leipzig: Teubner.

Gabelentz, Georg von der. 1891/²1901/1969. *Die Sprachwissenschaft. Ihre Aufgaben, Methoden und bisherigen Ergebnisse.* Tübingen.

Geckeler, Horst. 1988. „Die Sprachtypologie von Eugenio Coseriu und Vladimir Skalička". In: Albrecht, Jörn et al. (eds.). Vol. 3, 55–70.

Girard, Abbé Gabriel. 1747/1982. *Les vrais principes de la langue françoise.* Genf: Droz.

Greenberg, Joseph H. 1963/²1966. „Some Universals of Grammar with Particular Reference to the Order of Meaningful Elements". In: Greenberg, Joseph H. (ed.). *Universals of Language. Report of a Conference held at Dobbs Ferry, New York, April 13–15, 1961.* Cambridge. Cambridge, Mass.: MIT Press, 73–113.

Hartmann, Peter. 1956. *Zur Typologie des Indogermanischen.* (Untersuchungen zur Allgemeinen Grammatik, 2.) Heidelberg: Winter.

Hartmann, Peter. 1962. „Zur Erforschung von Sprachtypen: Methoden und Anwendungen". *Innsbrucker Beiträge zur Kulturwissenschaft* Sonderheft 15: 31–55.

Humboldt, Wilhelm von. 1791/1903. „Ueber die Gesetze der Entwicklung der menschlichen Kräfte". In: Leitzmann, Albert (ed.). Vol. 1, 86–96.

Humboldt, Wilhelm von. 1797/1904. „Ueber den Geist der Menschheit". In: Leitzmann, Albert (ed.). Vol. 2, 324–334.

Humboldt, Wilhelm von. 1812/1904. „Ankündigung einer Schrift über die Vaskische Sprache und Nation, nebst Angabe des Gesichtspunctes und Inhalts derselben". In: Leitzmann, Albert (ed.). Vol. 3, 288–299.

Humboldt, Wilhelm von. 1821/1905. „Ueber die Aufgabe des Geschichtsschreibers". In: Leitzmann, Albert (ed.). Vol. 4, 35–56.

Humboldt, Wilhelm von. 1824–26/1906. „Grundzüge des allgemeinen Sprachtypus". In: Leitzmann, Albert (ed.). Vol. 5, 364–473.

Humboldt, Wilhelm von. 1827–1829/1907. „Ueber die Verschiedenheiten des menschlichen Sprachbaues." In: Leitzmann, Albert (ed.), Vol. 6, 111–303.

Humboldt, Wilhelm von. 1830–1835/1907. „Ueber die Verschiedenheit des menschlichen Sprachbaues und ihren Einfluß auf die geistige Entwicklung des Menschengeschlechts". In: Leitzmann, Albert (ed.). Vol. 7, 1–344.

Knobloch, Clemens. 1988. *Geschichte der psychologischen Sprachauffassung in Deutschland von 1850 bis 1920.* Tübingen: Niemeyer.

Kuen, Heinrich. 1953/1970. „Versuch einer vergleichenden Charakteristik der romanischen Schriftsprachen". In: Kuen, Heinrich. *Romanistische Aufsätze.* Nürnberg: Carl, 419–437.

Lausberg, Heinrich. 1947. „Vergleichende Charakteristik der italienischen und der spanischen Schriftsprache". *Romanische Forschungen* 60: 106–122.

Lausberg, Heinrich. 1950. „Zur Stellung Malherbes in der Geschichte der französischen Schriftsprache". *Romanische Forschungen* 62: 172–200.

Lehmann, Christian. 1988. „Zu Eugenio Coserius Sprachtypologie". In: Albrecht, Jörn et al. (eds.). Vol. 3, 3–22.

Leitzmann, Albert (ed.). 1903−1918. *Wilhelm von Humboldt. Gesammelte Schriften.* 15 vols. Berlin: de Gruyter.

Lerch, Eugen. 1933. *Französische Sprache und Wesensart.* Frankfurt a. M.: Diesterweg.

Lewy, Ernst. 1934/1961. „Innere Form, Systematik, Sprachgeographie". In: Lewy, Ernst. *Kleine Schriften.* Berlin: Akad. Vlg., 65−67.

Lewy, Ernst. 1942/²1964. *Der Bau der europäischen Sprachen.* Tübingen: Niemeyer.

Lewy, Ernst. 1951/1961. „Die Lehre von den Sprachtypen". In: Lewy, Ernst. *Kleine Schriften.* Berlin: Akad. Vlg., 9−21.

Mathesius, Vilém. 1930. „On Linguistic Characterology with illustrations from Modern English". In: *Actes du premier Congrès International de Linguistes à La Haye du 10−15 avril 1928*, I. Leiden: Sijthoff, 56−63. (1972. Wendeln: Kraus).

Menze, Clemens. 1965. *Wilhelm von Humboldts Lehre und Bild vom Menschen.* Ratingen: Henn.

Meyer-Lübke, Wilhelm. 1901/²1909. *Einführung in das Studium der Romanischen Sprachwissenschaft.* Heidelberg: Winter.

Misteli, Franz. 1893. *Charakteristik der hauptsächlichsten Typen des Sprachbaues.* Neubearbeitung des Werkes von Prof. H. Steinthal. Berlin: Dümmler.

Pottier, Bernard. 1968. „La typologie". In: Martinet, André (ed.). *Le langage.* Paris: Gallimard, 300−322.

Raible, Wolfgang. 1989. „Romanistik, Sprachtypologie und Universalienforschung. Plädoyer für eine integrale Romanistik". In: Raible, Wolfgang (ed.). *Romanistik, Sprachtypologie und Universalienforschung. Plädoyer für eine integrale Romanistik.* Tübingen: Narr, VII−XXXI.

Ringmacher, Manfred. 1996. *Organismus der Sprachidee. H. Steinthals Weg von Humboldt zu Humboldt.* Paderborn/München: Schöningh.

Rohrer, Christian. 1988. „Zur Untersuchung von nicht-relationellen und relationellen Funktionen. Versuch einer logischen Rekonstruktion". In: Albrecht, Jörn et al. (eds.). Vol. 3, 71−79.

Römer, Ruth. 1985/²1989. *Sprachwissenschaft und Rasssenideologie in Deutschland.* München: Fink.

Schlegel, August Wilhelm. 1818/1971. *Observations sur la langue et la littérature provençales.* 1818: Paris. 1971: Tübingen: Spangenberg.

Skalička, Vladimír. 1958/1979. „Über den gegenwärtigen Stand der Typologie". In: Skalička, Vladimír. *Typologische Studien.* Braunschweig/Wiesbaden: Vieweg, 312−328.

Spitzer, Leo. 1922. *Italienische Umgangssprache.* Bonn u. a.: Schröder.

Spitzer, Leo. 1944. „Sobre un nuevo método de tipología lingüística". *Anales del instituto de lingüística* II (Universidad nacional de Cuyo): 109−127.

Steinthal, Heyman. 1848/1856. „Die Sprachwissenschaft Wilhelm von Humboldts und die Hegelsche Philosophie". In: Steinthal, Heyman. 1856, 1−170.

Steinthal, Heyman. 1850/1856. „Die Classifikation der Sprachen". In: Steinthal, Heyman. 1856, 1−91.

Steinthal, Heyman. 1856. *Gesammelte sprachwissenschaftliche Abhandlungen.* Berlin: Dümmler.

Steinthal, Heyman. 1860. *Charakteristik der hauptsächlichsten Typen des Sprachbaues.* Berlin: Dümmler.

Trabant, Jürgen (ed.). 1994. *Wilhelm von Humboldt. Über die Sprache. Reden vor der Akademie.* Tübingen/Basel: Francke.

Vossler, Karl. 1925. *Geist und Kultur in der Sprache.* Heidelberg: Winter.

Wandruszka, Mario. 1959/1967. *Der Geist der französischen Sprache.* Hamburg: Rowohlt.

Wartburg, Walther von. 1943/²1962. *Einführung in Problematik und Methodik der Sprachwissenschaft.* 1943: Halle. 1971: Tübingen: Niemeyer.

Weinrich, Harald 1961. „Die *clarté* der französischen Sprache und die Klarheit der Franzosen". *Zeitschrift für romanische Philologie* 77: 528−544.

Weinrich, Harald. 1963. „Ist das Französische eine analytische oder synthetische Sprache?". *Lebende Sprachen* 8: 52−55.

Weisgerber, Leo. 1925/1964. „Das Problem der inneren Sprachform und seine Bedeutung für die deutsche Sprache". In: Gipper, Helmut (ed.). *Leo Weisgerber. Zur Grundlegung der ganzheitlichen Sprachauffassung. Aufsätze 1925−1933.* Düsseldorf: Schwann, 36−49.

Heidi Aschenberg, Universität Heidelberg (Deutschland)

22. The relation of non-Western approaches to linguistic typology

1. Background
2. Sanskrit
3. Tamil
4. Classical Arabic
5. Japanese
6. Conclusion
7. Special abbreviations
8. References

1. Background

In the non-Western world there have been long-lasting linguistic traditions of high scientific value in India (= the Sanskrit tradition and, to a somewhat lesser extent, the Tamil tradition) and in the Islamic cultural sphere (= the Classical Arabic tradition). Also the relatively short tradition of indigeneous Japanese linguistics deserves to be mentioned in this context. Of course, some forms of linguistic thinking have existed in other cultures too.

The traditions which are under scrutiny here are characterized by the fact that the oldest extant grammar has had a decisive influence on subsequent linguistic research. Each of these grammars concentrates on one language only, namely Sanskrit, Tamil, or Classical Arabic. In fact, it seems to be a universal truth, also confirmed by the history of Western linguistics, that linguistic theorizing starts, and must start, by concentrating on one single language (which in the West was either Classical Greek or Latin). This explains the lack of the typological aspect in the Sanskrit, Tamil, and Classical Arabic traditions (as well as in the Japanese tradition).

It follows that if one wishes to investigate the non-Western approaches to linguistic typology, one has to make use of an 'indirect' method. An attempt has to be made to evaluate to what extent the various descriptive frameworks have been determined by the typological peculiarities of those languages for the description of which they have been devised and, inversely, to what extent they would lend themselves to the description of typologically dissimilar languages.

2. Sanskrit

Pāṇini's (c. 400 B.C.) grammar *Aṣṭādhyāyī* ('Eight Chapters') constitutes the essence of the Sanskrit tradition. According to the expert opinion, it still qualifies as the best grammar of a single language ever written. In the present context it is not possible to go into the technical details that justify this opinion. A very thorough introduction to Pāṇini is presented in the dozen volumes in which S. D. Joshi and J. A. F. Roodbergen have edited and explicated central passages from Patañjali's (c. 150 B.C.) 'Great Commentary' (see e.g. Joshi & Roodbergen 1975). Book-length introductions are provided by Sharma (1987) and Cardona (1988). Shorter overall accounts are given e.g. by Pinault (1989), Itkonen (1991: 5–87), and Kiparsky (1993).

It is generally agreed that Pāṇini's grammar constitutes a 'device' which takes semantic representations as its input and aims at generating — via a great number of intermediate stages — the 'surface forms' of all and only correct sentences of Classical Sanskrit as its output. The semantic representation centers around the notion of 'action' (*kriyā*), which is divided into three (semantic) subcategories anticipating the (formal) distinctions between the active, personal passive, and impersonal passive endings of the verb. An action involves participants that exemplify one or more of the following semantic roles (*kāraka*): agent, patient, recipient, instrument, location, source. These roles represent a 'shallow' semantic level in the sense that they correspond, roughly, to the case endings of Sanskrit (excluding the genitive). However, the roles of agent and patient require a special treatment: the agent may be expressed by the active endings of the verb (plus the nominative) or by the instrumental (in connection with the passive endings) or by the genitive (in connection with deverbal nouns), whereas the patient may be expressed by the passive endings of the verb (plus the nominative) or by the accusative (in connection with the active endings) or by the dative (in the sense of 'goal') or by the genitive (in connection with deverbal nouns). In addition, all semantic roles may be encoded by derivational affixes as part of the meaning of the word to be derived.

Because the six roles represent a 'shallow' level of semantics, there is no need for an 'intermediate' level corresponding to the grammatical functions 'subject' and 'object'. Sanskrit is a free word-order language, which means that the word order, being dependent on the speaker's communicative intention, is no concern for the grammarian.

The semantic representation containing e. g. the information 'Devadatta is cooking rice' is the starting point for several possible derivations, because — depending on which grammatical rule is chosen first — the derivation may ultimately result in an active sentence or a passive sentence or a nominal sentence (with *paktā/pācakaḥ* = 'cooker', and no copula) (see 1a−c).

(1) (a) Sanskrit
    Devadatta-ḥ odana-m- pac-ati
    D.-NOM   rice-ACC   cook-ACT
    'D. is cooking rice'

  (b) *Devadatte-na odana-ḥ pac-yate*
    D.-INSTR   rice-NOM cook-PASS
    'Rice is being cooked by D.'

  (c) *Devadatta-ḥ odana-sya*
    D.-NOM   rice-GEN
    paktā/pācaka-ḥ
    cooker(NOM)/cooker-NOM
    'D. is a cooker of rice'

The phenomena which could be handled by the notion of syntactic governance are handled here indirectly, namely by means of semantic roles: these are determined by the meaning of the verb plus the choice of one of the three semantico-syntactic categories of the verb (cf. 1a−c). The morphosyntax of verbal complements is in turn determined by rules assigning forms to semantic roles.

The formalism developed by Pāṇini follows the structure of Sanskrit rather closely. Kiparsky's (1993) insistence that Pāṇini's grammar be considered 'generative' in the technical sense of this word seems to indicate, however, that it could have been developed to deal with typologically dissimilar languages to the same extent as current generative grammars can.

3. Tamil

The grammar *Tolkāppiyam* ('Old Book'), which was composed around 100 B.C., describes the earliest stage of Old Tamil (cf. Lehmann 1994); at the same time, it is the oldest extant document of this languae. It consists of three parts which deal with phonology, morphology-syntax-semantics, and poetics, respectively. It is probable that the third part has been composed three or four hundred years later that the first two. The preface of the book expresses indebtedness to a Sanskrit research tradition, but this tradition is definitely non-Pāṇinian in character.

Commentaries on *Tolkāppiyam* that have been written between 1000−1700 are available. According to Chevillard (1996: 23−24), the commentary tradition has in several respects improved upon the theory expounded in *Tolkāppiyam*.

The second part of the grammar has been analyzed by Sastri (1945) and Chevillard (1996). It is centrally concerned with the agreement between nouns and verbs. Nouns are divided into a 'high class' and a 'low class'; the high class has three subcategories: 'masculin' and 'feminin' in singular and 'human' in plural; the low (= 'non-human') class has two subcategories: singular and plural; thus, there are five subcategories in all. The basis for these subcategories is purely semantic. They are systematically expressed by the verbal inflection, and much less systematically by the nominal inflection. Thus, the verb agrees with the semantic subcategory of the subject noun, except that — since the singular form of the noun may stand for the plural — the verb may in such cases be said to express the plural, rather than to agree with a (pre-existent) noun in plural.

The basic difference between nouns and verbs is that they inflect in case and in tense, respectively. Apart from the vocative, there are seven cases (although the 'case' for location is actually expressed by 19 post-positions). Case endings may be either interchanged or deleted without any semantic motivation (for confirmation of this rather surprising fact, see Lehmann 1994: 29, 39, 42). There are seven semantic roles, roughly corresponding to the Pāṇinian *kārakas*, on the one hand, and to the (basic) Tamil case endings, on the other. Verbs are either 'non-independent' (= non-finite) or 'independent' (= finite). The former are either ad-verbal or ad-nominal. The latter are either 'full' verbs (i.e. express the tense explicitly) or 'suggestive' verbs (i.e. contain the tense only implicitly). The finite verb is the only 'complete word' because no other word can constitute a sentence all alone. To be sure, it too 'desires' other words, but these need not be overtly expressed. For instance, the verb form *uṇṭāṉ* may either stand alone or be complemented, depending on the context (see 2a−d).

(2) (a) Tamil
un-ṭ-āṉ vs.
eat-PRET-3.P.M
'He ate' (Lit. 'Ate-he')
uṇ-ṭ-āḷ
eat-PRET-3.P.F
'She ate' (Lit. 'Ate-she')

(b) cāttaṉ uṇ-ṭ-āṉ
S.(M)   eat-PRET-3.P.M
'Sāttan ate'

(c) cōṟṟ-ai uṇ-ṭ-āṉ
rice-ACC eat-PRET-3.P.M
'He ate rice'

(d) cāttaṉ cōṟṟ-ai uṇ-ṭ-āṉ
S.(M)   rice-ACC eat- PRET-3.P.M
'Sāttan ate rice'

In sum, the second part of *Tolkāppiyam* represents a non-abstract analysis of the Old Tamil sentence structure based, essentially, on the noun vs. verb distinction. Old Tamil is a rather strictly verb-final language, subordinate clauses with non-finite verbs being placed before the one finite verb that concludes the sentence. Interestingly, the commentators give several examples that deviate from the verb-final order.

4. Classical Arabic

The Arab linguistic tradition starts with Sībawaihi's (d. 793) grammar *Al-kitāb* ('The Book'), which analyzes Classical Arabic, i. e. the language stage characteristic of the Koran and of ancient Bedouin poetry. The representatives of this tradition have taken its homogeneity and continuity for granted. Recently it has been claimed, however, that Sībawaihi originally provided his theory with 'actionist' or 'operational' underpinnings which were not taken up by his successors. Yet even those who advocate this view admit that Sībawaihi's phonology and morphosyntax "are basically identical to that of the later grammarians" (Bohas & Guillaume & Kouloughli 1990: 48).

The endings of the three cases of Classical Arabic, i. e. nominative, accusative, and genitive, are provided by the three (short) vowels of the language, namely -*u*, -*a*, and -*i*, respectively. Moreover, the distinction between the indicative (of the 'imperfect' tense, equalling the present) and the subjunctive is expressed by the distinction between -*u* and -*a*. It is the central task of the Arab tradition, or at least of its morphosyntactic part, to account for this variation (see 3 a−c).

(3) (a) Classical Arabic
yaktub-u   zayd-un risālat-an
write-IND.IMPF Z.-NOM letter-ACC
'Z. is writing a letter' (Lit. 'Zayd he-is-writing a letter')

(b) ... ḥattā yaktub-a
so-that write-SUBJU
'... so that he should write'
(Lit. '... so that he-should-write')

(c) marra zayd-un bi rajul-in
went Z.-NOM past man-GEN
'Zayd went past a man'

Inspection of examples like these made it natural to think that the verb 'causes' − in a metaphorical sense − the -*u* vs. -*a* distinction in the following nouns, and that the 'particle' (here the preposition *bi*) 'causes' the occurrence of the -*i* ending. In just the same way the 'particle' (i. e. conjunction) *ḥattā* 'causes' the occurrence of the subjunctive marker -*a*. Such observations gave rise to a notion of 'governance' and to a corresponding three-way classification of the word classes: a) nouns are governed and do not govern; b) verbs govern and are governed; c) particles may or may not govern, but are not governed. (A member of a given word class cannot govern another member of the same class.) Expectedly, there are borderline cases which must be related − by means of (theoretical) analogy (*qiyās*) − to the 'clear cases'. For instance, participles are verb-like nouns whereas (indeclinable) pronouns are particle-like nouns; the perfect of the copula is a particle-like verb, whereas the emphatic marker *'inna* is a verb-like particle (cf. Owens 1988, Bohas & Guillaume & Kouloughli 1990). Although the Arabs claimed to have no interest in other languages, the three-way classification of word classes was occasionally asserted to be universal (cf. Versteegh 1995: 26, 40−41).

The notion of governance is only the more natural because in a VSO language like Classical Arabic the 'causes' (= verbs and prepositions) precede their 'effects', as they should. From the VSO order it also follows that transitive verbs are taken to be connected more closely to the nominative (= 'subject') than to the accusative (= 'object'). Thus, the notion of 'verb phrase' would be impossible in this framework. The VSO order is regarded as canonical although 'pragmatically' motivated deviations from it are acknowledged as fully permissible.

This rather simple picture is made more complex by the other basic sentence type, namely the nominal sentence (with no copula in the 'imperfect') (cf. 4a).

(4) (a) Classical Arabic
zayd-un rajul-un
Z.-NOM man-NOM
'Zayd is a man'

First, it is not easy to apply the notion of governance to a sentence like this. Second, a sentence like this exemplifies a 'topic vs. comment' structure which cannot be easily applied to 'verbal sentences' like those given above. However, the force of theoretical analogy ultimately led the Arab grammarians to make both of these moves, i.e. postulating 'invisible governors' for nominal sentences and imposing the 'topic vs. comment' structure on verbal sentences.

There is some 'external evidence' to support the view that it is indeed the formal variation between case endings which constitutes the core of the Arab tradition. Because biblical Hebrew had lost the corresponding endings, the descriptive framework of Arab linguistics could be applied only unsystematically in the first complete grammar of biblical Hebrew, which was written in the 11th century (cf. Kouloughli 1989: 288−289).

5. Japanese

It is very interesting to note that in spite of a cultural tradition of high quality that started already in the second millenium B.C., there has been, apart from phonetics and lexicology, no genuine linguistics in China. The first indigenous grammar of Chinese was written only at the end of the 19th century. Apparently those interested in linguistic matters were absorbed by the intricacies of the Chinese characters. To be sure, such broad distinctions as 'full' vs. 'empty' words and words for actions vs. words for states were known since the 14th century (cf. Casacchia 1989: 446−447).

For a long time, Japan was under the Chinese cultural influence. At the end of the 17th century there arose a nationalist movement that attempted to consolidate the independence of Japanese thinking also in the domain of language. The most important grammarian was Nariakira Fujitani (1738−1779), who developed a descriptive framework for Japanese that is even today accepted as largely adequate (cf. Saeki & Yoichiro 1981). Its core is a four-fold division of word-classes: *na* (= nouns), *yosoi* (= verbs and adjectives), *kazashi* (= demonstrative pronouns, adverbs, conjunctions, interjections), and *ayui* (= postpositions, auxiliaries, suffixes of the verbal or adjectival predicate). Of these terms, the last three mean ornaments for the body, the head, and the feet, respectively. In this way the basic word order is encoded into the names of the word-classes. This apparatus may be illustrated by means of example (5 a); the morpheme boundary in the verb follows Fujitani's analysis:

(5) (a) Japanese
kinoo   niwa   de   otoko ga
yesterday garden LOC man   SUBJ
inu o   nagu-tta
dog OBJ hit-PRET
'Yesterday a man hit a dog in the garden'

Here *kinoo* is a *kazashi*; *niwa, otoko*, and *inu* are *na*; *nagu-* is a *yosoi*; *de, ga, o*, and *-tta* are *ayui*. The class of *ayui* is further divided into 50 subclasses on the basis of distributional criteria. It may be added that the topic marker *wa*, which plays an important role in the Japanese sentence structure, is just one *ayui* among others (see 6a).

(6) (a) kinoo   niwa   de   otoko wa
        yesterday garden LOC man   TOP
        inu o   nagu-tta
        dog OBJ hit-PRET
        'The man hit a dog yesterday in the garden'

6. Conclusion

Tamil and Japanese are SOV languages; Classical Arabic is a VSO language; Sanskrit is a language with a (relatively) free word order. In spite of these differences, all traditions reviewed here share the common feature that the language which they investigate exhibits systemic suffixal (and in the case of Japanese, also postpositional) variation. Grammatical description seems to have originated in the wish to capture the nature of this variation. Classical Arabic is the prototypical instance of a language with word-**internal** (= 'Ablaut'-type) change, and yet − as was noted above − the central question in the corresponding tradition has been how to account for the occurrence of the three case **endings**. The interest in formal variation quite naturally leads to the establishing of distinct word classes. The word-class systems are very explicit in the Arabic and Japanese traditions. In the Tamil tradition, the original fourway classification given in *Tolkāppiyam* was not very coherent, apart from the noun vs. verb division, but it was amended by later commentators. In the Pāṇinian tradition nouns and verbs are named by means of abbreviations standing for the collections of their respective endings, and indeclinable words are considered as nouns by default, their 'endings' being automatically deleted. These systems should be compared with the four-way classification of Marcus Terentius Varro, based on the presence vs. absence of case and/or tense, or with the eight-way classification of Apollonius Dyscolus (cf. Itkonen 1991: 199, 202–203).

On the basis of the available evidence, it seems natural to assume that the lack of a systematic variation between grammatical morphemes might constitute an obstacle to the emergence of linguistic research. With the aid of this assumption, it could conceivably be explained why there never developed a genuine linguistic tradition in China. The speculative character of this type of 'explanation' goes without saying.

7. Special abbreviations

ACT	active
IND	indicative
INSTR	instrumental
P	person
SUBJU	subjunctive

8. References

Bohas, G. & Guillaume, J.-P. & Kouloughli, D. E. 1990. *The Arabic linguistic tradition.* London and New York: Routledge.

Cardona, George. 1988. *Pāṇini: His work and traditions, Vol.* I. Delhi u. a.: Motilal Banarsidass.

Casacchia, Giorgio. 1989. "Les débuts de la tradition linguistique chinoise et l'âge d'or de la linguistique impériale". In: Auroux, Sylvain (ed.). *Histoire des idées linguistiques, tome* 1. Liège-Bruxelles: Mardaga, 431–448.

Chevillard, Jean-Luc. 1996. *Le commentaire de Cēṉāvaraiar sur le Collatikāram du Tolkāppiyam.* Pondicherry: Institut français de Pondichéry.

Itkonen, Esa. 1991. *Universal history of linguistics: India, China, Arabia, Europe.* Amsterdam and Philadelphia: Benjamins.

Joshi, S. D. & Roodbergen, Jouthe Anton Foke. 1975. *Patañjali's vyākaraṇa-mahābhāsya. Kārakāhnika.* Poona: University of Poona.

Kiparsky, Paul. 1993. "Pāṇinian linguistics". In: R. E. Asher (ed.). *The encyclopedia of language and linguistics.* Oxford: Pergamon Press, vol. 1: 6, 2918–23.

Kouloughli, Djamel. 1989. "Le débuts de la grammaire hébraïque". In: Auroux, Sylvain (ed.). *Histoire des idées linguistiques, tome* 1. Liège-Bruxelles: Mardaga, 283–292.

Lehmann, Thomas. 1994. *Grammatik des Alttamil.* Stuttgart: Steiner.

Owens, Jonathan. 1988. *The foundations of grammar: An introduction to medieval Arabic grammatical theory.* Amsterdam: Benjamins.

Pinault, Georges-Jean. 1989. "Le système de Pāṇini". In: Auroux, Sylvain (ed.). *Histoire des idées linguistiques, tome* 1. Liège-Bruxelles: Mardaga, 371–400.

Saeki, Tetsuo & Yoichiro, Yamanai (eds.) 1981. *Kokugogaisetsu.* Osaka.

Sastri, Subrahmanya. 1945. *Tolkāppiyam-collatikāram.* Annamalainagar: Annamalai University.

Sharma, V. Venkatarama. (ed.). 1982. *Taittirīyaprātiśākhya: with the bhāsya padakramasadana of Māhiseya.* New Delhi: Meharchand Lachhmandas.

Versteegh, Kees. 1995. *The explanation of linguistic causes: Az-Zaǧǧaaǧi's theory of grammar.* Amsterdam and Philadelphia: Benjamins.

Esa Itkonen, University of Turku
(Finland)

V. Current approaches to language typology and universals research
Gegenwärtige Ansätze von Sprachtypologie und Universalienforschung
Les tendances actuelles dans le domaine de la typologie linguistique et de la recherche universaliste

23. Sprachtypologie und Universalienforschung bei Joseph H. Greenberg

1. Überblick über das Werk
2. Individuelle und generelle Typologie
3. Typologische Universalienforschung
4. Zitierte Literatur

1. Überblick über das Werk

Joseph Harold Greenbergs (*1915) Weg von einzelsprachlicher Forschung zur Sprachtypologie und zur Universalienforschung lässt sich anhand seiner Publikationen nachvollziehen (Croft & Denning & Kemmer 1990: xix−xxxiii): Seine afrikanistischen Arbeiten (vorrangig in den vierziger und fünfziger Jahren) machen ihn mit typologisch auffälligen Sprachen bekannt und führen ihn zur Frage der Sprachklassifikation; zunächst auf dem Gebiet der afrikanischen Sprachen (Greenberg 1963a); später folgen Arbeiten zur Klassifikation der amerikanischen Sprachen (Greenberg 1987) und zur indo-germanischen Sprachfamilie (Greenberg, in Vorbereitung). Die Frage nach der Sprachgenealogie führt Greenberg zur Sprachtypologie (vgl. den diesbezüglichen Aufsatz in Greenberg 1957: § 3: 35−45; 1974) und schließlich zur Universalienforschung (Greenberg 1963b). Wie noch zu erläutern sein wird, eröffnet Greenbergs typologischer Ansatz auch Einblicke in Prozesse der Sprachveränderung, denn er ist von vornherein diachronisch angelegt (Greenberg 1974: 9f., 57−72). So überrascht es nicht, dass sich Greenberg ebenfalls mit diachronischen Fragestellungen auseinandersetzt (Greenberg 1978; 1979), in neuerer Zeit insbesondere mit Grammatikalisierungsprozessen (Greenberg 1991).

Arbeiten zur Afrikanistik, Sprachklassifikation, Typologie, Universalienforschung und Diachronie charakterisieren sein Gesamtwerk, dessen Höhepunkt wahrscheinlich die Leitung des großen Universalienprojekts in Stanford darstellt, das genaugenommen ein sprachtypologisches Forschungsprojekt ist.

2. Individuelle und generelle Typologie

Joseph Greenberg steht in der Tradition der Typologieforschung humboldtscher Prägung (Humboldt 1832) und ist vom europäischen Strukturalismus beeinflusst. Seine Verbundenheit mit der europäischen Linguistik zeigt sich besonders in seinem historischen Überblick über die Typologie (Greenberg 1974: 35−49). In Auseinandersetzung mit Humboldt (1832) und Sapir (1921) entwickelt er einen eigenen typologischen Ansatz. Die „klassische Typologie" suche − so Greenberg (1974: 28−31) − nach der Individualität einer Sprache; man könnte auch vom „Bauplan" („basic plan", Sapir 1921: 127) einer Sprache sprechen. Der Bauplan ist sozusagen der „Geist" der Sprache („structural 'genius'", Sapir 1921: 127). Dieser sei in der Tradition der klassischen Typologie nur ein Ausdruck der tieferen Einheit, die sich auch in der Kultur bzw. im „Nationalcharakter" der Sprachgemeinschaft manifestiere (Greenberg 1974: 28).

Einem solchen Ansatz der INDIVIDUALISIE-RENDEN oder INDIVIDUELLEN TYPOLOGIE oder

SPRACHCHARAKTERISTIK (→ Art. 21) stellt Greenberg sein eigenes Konzept einer VERALLGEMEINERNDEN oder GENERELLEN TYPOLOGIE gegenüber. Im Mittelpunkt dieses Ansatzes steht die Entdeckung von Verallgemeinerungen über Sprachen (*nicht* Sprache!, „lawlike generalizations in languages", Greenberg 1974: 29). Auf diese Weise sei es möglich, das Konzept der „möglichen menschlichen Sprache" („possible human language", *ib.*) auf der Basis einer empirischen Analyse zu beschränken. Haben Sprachen typischerweise die Eigenschaften ϕ und ψ, so sind folgende Sprachtypen denkbar: (1) Sprachen mit ϕ und ψ (notiert ϕ, ψ), (2) Sprachen, die *nicht* ϕ (notiert als: $\sim\phi$), wohl aber ψ aufweisen, (3) Sprachen mit ϕ, aber ohne ψ (notiert: $\sim\psi$), und (4) Sprachen, die durch $\sim\phi$ und $\sim\psi$ charakterisiert sind. Wenn nun in einer genügend großen Stichprobe Sprachen vom Typ (3), $\phi, \sim\psi$, nicht zu finden sind (zur Repräsentativität einer Stichprobe siehe unten), dann kann geschlossen werden, dass die Eigenschaft ψ die Eigenschaft ϕ als Voraussetzung hat, also ϕ impliziert ψ ($\phi \rightarrow \psi$); ϕ ist also gegenüber ψ merkmalloser und hat die größere Distribution.

Während die individuelle Typologie oder Sprachcharakteristik die Grammatik einer Sprache holistisch behandeln muss, greift die generelle Typologie einzelne Aspekte heraus, die übereinzelsprachlich verglichen werden können. Zwar sucht sie nicht nach dem Geist einer Sprache, geht aber auch über die sprachlichen Phänomene hinaus, da übereinzelsprachliche Verallgemeinerungen durchaus psychologisch (Greenberg 1974: 28) oder funktional (Croft & al. 1990: xv) erklärt werden können. Der vorläufige Charakter der Verallgemeinerungen („Universale" im Sinne Greenbergs) ergibt sich zwingend aus der Tatsache, dass nicht alle Sprachen überblickt werden können. Es können lediglich Typen von Sprachen festgestellt werden.

3. Typologische Universalienforschung

Das von Greenberg geleitete Universalienprojekt an der Universität Stanford (Greenberg & al. 1978) vereinigt Fragestellungen der Universalienforschung mit denen der Typologie. Die Eröffnungstagung in Dobbs Ferry (1961) wird als bahnbrechend für die moderne Linguistik angesehen (Croft & al. 1990: x).

3.1. Greenbergs Universalienbegriff

Greenberg versteht unter sprachlichen Universalien zunächst „Verallgemeinerungen über empirische Beobachtungen" („empirical generalizations", Greenberg 1966: 9). Da die Menge aller Sprachen unüberblickbar ist, haben solche empirische Verallgemeinerungen auch nur einen vorläufigen Charakter. Erhärtet werden sie zwar durch statistische Untersuchungen über eine große, wenn auch nicht repräsentative Sprachenstichprobe (zum Problem der Repräsentativität: Rijkhoff et al. 1993; → Art. 33), dennoch sind sie nicht im eigentlichen Sinne universal.

3.2. Greenbergs Forschungsprogramm

Im Sinne der Universalienforschung ergibt sich jedoch ein Programm: Die ermittelten Universalien müssen an neuen Sprachen überprüft werden und werden dadurch immer allgemeiner (sofern sie nicht falsifiziert werden). Insofern ist Greenbergs Universalienforschung ein Forschungsprogramm: Im ständigen Fortschreiten einer allgemeinen Universalienforschung nähert sich die Wissenschaftlergemeinschaft durch kumulative Evidenz immer mehr dem im eigentlichen Sinne Universalen. In dieser Hinsicht ist Greenbergs Programm „hermeneutisch". Greenberg selbst (1974: 17−20) bezieht sich in seiner Unterscheidung von Klassifikation und Typologie explizit auf Wilhelm Dilthey (1883). Statistiken über große Stichproben können den hermeneutischen Charakter der Universalienforschung relativieren; in neuerer Zeit ist darüber hinaus deutlich geworden (Rijkhoff & al. 1993), dass die Verknüpfung von Klassifikation und Typologie die Möglichkeit bietet, Stichproben von hoher Repräsentativität zusammenzustellen.

3.3. Greenberg-Universalien

Unter Greenberg-Universalien versteht man die oben beschriebenen implikativen Universalien. Die Bezeichnung bezieht sich zunächst auf die von Greenberg und seinen Mitarbeitern besonders im Zuge des Stanforder Projekts aufgestellten Verallgemeinerungen (Greenberg 1963c, Greenberg & al. 1978) als auch auf diejenigen Universalien, die in nachfolgenden Arbeiten ermittelt worden sind.

Inzwischen gibt es eine ständig aktualisierte Datenbank solcher Universalien an der Universität Konstanz (Plank & Filimonova 1999). Unterschieden werden *absolute Universalien*, also solche, gegen die bisher keine

Gegenbeispiele gefunden wurden, und *statistische Universalien*, die zumindest über eine große Zahl von Sprachen Gültigkeit haben. Theoretisch besteht kein grundsätzlicher Unterschied zwischen den beiden Typen von Universalien, denn die sogenannten *absoluten Universalien* werden nicht als definitorisch (oder axiomatisch) angesehen, sondern als potentiell statistisch, d.h. als empirisch überprüfbar (im Sinne des Forschungsprogramms). Somit unterscheiden sie sich von den deduktiven Universalien theoretischer Ansätze (z.B. den Prinzipien in der „Universalgrammatik" generativistischer Prägung).

Die bekanntesten Greenberg-Universalien (aus Greenberg 1963b) beschäftigen sich mit Wortstellungsfragen bzw. dem Zusammenspiel von Wortstellung und Morphologie. Hier sind Beispiele für statistische (fast absolute) Universalien (Greenberg 1963: 78 f. bzw. Plank & Filimonova 1999: Datensatz 3 bzw. 5):

U2 In languages with prepositions the genitive almost always follows the governing noun. [Formel:] Adp NP → N G

U5 If a language has dominant SOV order and the genitive follows the governing noun, then the adjective likewise follows the noun. [Formel:] SOV & N G → N Adj

Als Gegenbeispiel gegen Universale 2 gelten die Sprachen Skandinaviens, auch z.B. DEUTSCH und ENGLISCH haben zumindest eine Genitivkonstruktion, die dem Universal widerspricht; Gegenbeispiele gegen Universale 5 finden sich in Sprachen Mittelamerikas (z.B. HUICHOL; Plank & Filimonova 1999: 5).

Verallgemeinerungen wie die oben angeführten Universalien könnten Anlass geben, Kategorien wie Subjekt, Verb, Objekt, Nomen & Verb, Adjektiv, Genitiv usw. als für alle Sprachen gültig anzusehen. Eine solche Annahme ist jedoch nicht zwingend. Die „Eigenschaft einer Sprache" („property of a language", Greenberg 1974: 55 f.) wird nur zum Zweck der Typologie mit solchen Kategorien der grammatischen Beschreibung verbunden:

„precisely because in the absence of theoretical constraints on the form of the grammar, a wide variety of statements could be made without any great importance being attached as to whether it actually did or could appear in the grammar." (Greenberg 1974: 56)

3.4. Diachronie

Greenbergs Forschungsprogramm umfasst auch einen diachronen Aspekt (Greenberg 1969), den die implikativen Universalien nahelegen: Das Ausbleiben gewisser Kombinationen sprachlicher Eigenschaften muss sich aus Prozessen des Sprachwandels erklären. Das Grammatikalisierungsmodell scheint hier besonders geeignet zu sein, solche Zusammenhänge deutlich zu machen: Für das Greenberg-Universale 2 muss z.B. angenommen werden, dass die Entstehung von Präpositionen in einem Zusammenhang zur Grammatikalisierung von Kasus steht (in diesem Falle besonders des Genitivs).

Praktisch alle Richtungen zeitgenössischer typologischer Forschung sind von Greenbergs Arbeiten beeinflusst worden (vgl. die Wertschätzung in der Joseph Greenberg gewidmeten Festschrift von Croft & al. 1990). Die Fortführung des Forschungsprogramms gehört zu den explizit formulierten Aufgaben der *Association for Linguistic Typology* (ALT). Dabei sei nicht vergessen, dass weitere Arbeiten Joseph H. Greenbergs in Vorbereitung sind bzw. zur Publikation anstehen.

4. Zitierte Literatur

Die von Croft & al. (1990) herausgegebene Festschrift enthält eine Bibliographie der Publikationen Joseph H. Greenbergs (bis 1990).

Croft, William & Denning, Keith & Kemmer, Suzanne (eds.) 1990. *Studies in Typology and Diachrony. For Joseph H. Greenberg.* (Typological studies in language, 20.) Amsterdam & Philadelphia: Benjamins.

Denning, Keith & Kemmer, Suzanne (eds.). 1990. *Selected Writings of Joseph H. Greenberg.* Stanford: Stanford University Press.

Dilthey, Wilhelm. 1883. *Einleitung in die Geisteswissenschaften.* Nachdruck in: *Gesammelte Schriften.* Leipzig & Berlin: Teubner 1922, Bd. I.

Greenberg, Joseph H. 1957. *Essays in Linguistics.* Chicago & London: University of Chicago Press.

Greenberg, Joseph H. 1963a. *The Languages of Africa.* Bloomington: Indiana University Press; Den Haag: Mouton.

Greenberg, Joseph H. 1963b. „Some universals of grammar with particular reference to the order of meaningful elements". In: Greenberg. 1963c: 58–90 (2. Aufl. 1966: 73–113).

Greenberg, Joseph H. (ed.). 1963c. *Universals of Language.* Cambridge/MA: MIT Press (2. Aufl. 1966).

Greenberg, Joseph H. 1966. *Language Universals. With special reference to feature hierarchies.* (Janua Linguarum, Series Minor, 59.) Den Haag & Paris: Mouton.

Greenberg, Joseph H. 1969. „Some methods of dynamic comparison in linguistics". In: Puhvel, Jan (ed.). *Substance and Structure of Language*. Berkeley & Los Angeles: University of California Press, 147–203.

Greenberg, Joseph H. 1974. *Language Typology. A historical and analytic overview*. (Janua Linguarum, Series Minor, 184.) Den Haag & Paris: Mouton.

Greenberg, Joseph H. 1978. „Diachrony, synchrony and language universals". In: Greenberg & al. (eds.) 1978: I, 61–92.

Greenberg, Joseph H. 1979. „Rethinking linguistics diachronically". *Language* 55: 275–90.

Greenberg, Joseph H. 1987. *Language in the Americas*. Stanford: Stanford University Press.

Greenberg, Joseph H. 1990. *Selected Writings*. Cf.: Denning & Kemmer (eds.). 1990.

Greenberg, Joseph H. 1991. „The Last Stages of Grammatical Elements: Contractive and Expansive Desemanticization". In: Traugott, Elisabeth Closs & Heine, Bernd (eds.). *Approaches to grammaticalization*. 2 vols. Amsterdam & Philadelphia Benjamins: I, 300–14.

Greenberg, Joseph H. (in Vorbereitung): *The Eurasiatic Family. Indo-European and its nearest relatives*. Stanford: Stanford University Press.

Greenberg, Joseph H. & Ferguson, Charles A. & Moravcsik, Edith A. (eds.) 1978. *Universals of Human Language*. 4 vols. Stanford: Stanford University Press.

Humboldt, Wilhelm von. 1832. *Ueber die Verschiedenheit des menschlichen Sprachbaues und ihren Einfluss auf die geistige Entwicklung des Menschengeschlechts*. Ursprünglich: *Über die Kawi-Sprache auf der Insel Java, nebst einer Einleitung über die Verschiedenheit des menschlichen Sprachbaues und ihren Einfluss auf die geistige Entwicklung des Menschengeschlechts*. Abhandlungen der Königlichen Akademie der Wissenschaften zu Berlin. Aus dem Jahre 1832, Th. 2–4; wieder in: Humboldt, Wilhelm von 1963. *Werke in fünf Bänden*. Hrsg. von Flitner, Andreas & Giel, Klaus. Bd. 3: *Schriften zur Sprachphilosophie*. Darmstadt: Wissenschaftliche Buchgesellschaft, 368–756.

Plank, Frans & Filimonova, Elena. 1999. *Universals Database. Searchable Archives*. http:www.ling.uni-konstanz.de/proj/sprachbau.htm .

Rijkhoff, Jan & Bakker, Dik & Hengeveld, Kees & Kahrel, Peter. 1993. „A method of language sampling". *Studies in Language* 17: 189–203.

Sapir, Edward. 1921. *Language. An introduction to the study of speech*. New York: Harcourt & Brace.

Martin Haase, Technische Universität Berlin
(Deutschland)

24. Parametrisierung in der Generativen Grammatik

1. Einleitung
2. Parameter in der Grammatiktheorie: Drei Fallbeispiele (Subjazenz, pro-drop, Verb-Zweit)
3. Parametertheorie: Vom GB zum Minimalistischen Programm
4. Universalien, Typologie und Parametertheorie: Wege zum selben Ziel
5. Generative Grammatik als Typologie- und Universalientheorie
6. Zitierte Literatur

1. Einleitung

'So then always that knowledge is worthiest [...] which considereth the simple forms or differences of things, which are few in number, and the degrees and coordinations whereof make all this variety.' (Francis Bacon)

Die Generative Grammatik versteht sich als Forschungsprogramm mit dem Ziel der Modellierung der kognitiven Fähigkeit zum Erwerb und Gebrauch der komplexen Symbolverarbeitungsfertigkeit, über die Grammatik als formale Wissensbasis einer Sprache gesteuert wird. Wie jede empirische Wissenschaft folgt auch die Generative Grammatik der von Francis Bacon aphoristisch skizzierten Vorgangsweise, und wie jede empirische Wissenschaft sucht sie nach den Invarianten der Struktur des Gegenstandbereichs und den Grenzen seines Variationsraumes.

Die Theorie der Invarianten ist für Chomsky (1981: 3 f.) die Theorie der Universalgrammatik („UG"). Die Theorie der UG ist gleichzeitig auch die Theorie des kognitiven Ausgangszustandes (Spracherwerbsdisposition, vgl. Chomsky 1959: 57), der jeden Menschen, in Sonderheit jedes Kind, in die Lage versetzt, rasch und effektiv aus der angebotenen sprachlichen Erfahrung die Wissensinhalte zu extrahieren, die die Grammatik der jeweiligen Sprache determinieren. Da die spezifischen Eigenschaften dieser kognitiven Disposition allen Menschen gemeinsam ist, müßten sie sich als Invarianten in den Produkten dieser Disposition, also in den Grammatiken menschlicher Sprachen, aufspüren lassen. Doch die Grammatik ist nicht direkt beobachtbar, sondern nur die von ihr gesteuerte Produktion und Perzeption sprachlicher Ausdrücke. So ist der wissenschaftliche Zugriff auf die Struktur der kognitiven Disposition über die Analyse der sprachlichen Muster nur indirekt möglich. Er geht zwangsläufig über die Analyse der Grammatiksysteme natürlicher Sprachen.

Die Grammatik selbst wird als ein modulares System betrachtet, d. h. bestehend aus einem Ensemble wechselwirkender Subsysteme mit jeweils eigenständiger Funktionsarchitektur: Die Subsysteme selbst kommunizieren nur über Input-Output-Beziehungen, d. h. es gibt keine direkte Wechselwirkungen zwischen der Regel eines Subsystems und der eines anderen. Diese Systemarchitektur erschwert das Identifizieren von Systeminvarianten in den Produkten des Systems: Einzelne phänomenologisch identifizierte Eigenschaften des Produkts lassen sich schon deswegen nicht einfach als korrespondierende einzelne Eigenschaften des sie konstituierenden Systems deuten, weil sie Resultate eines komplexeren Gesamtsystems sind. Es läßt sich durch bloße Inspektion der Phänomenologie nicht eruieren, welches Modul welchen Anteil an den beobachteten Produkteigenschaften hat.

Dazu kommt, daß die Funktionsmodule begrenzte Variabilität aufzuweisen scheinen. Dies erschwert die Identifikation der Quelle möglicher Invarianten. Gebrochen durch die modulare Wechselwirkung ist das Erscheinungsbild von Systeminvarianten in den Produkten, d. h. den Formen sprachlicher Ausdrücke, fragmentiert und gestreut. Sie enthüllen sich daher oft erst dem systematischen, formal kontrollierten Blick.

Die begrenzte modulare Variabilität wird über das Mittel der Parametrisierung erfaßt: Invariante Prinzipien enthalten justierbare Bestimmungsstücke mit begrenztem Wertebereich. Je nach einzelsprachlich gesteuerter Justierung des Parameterwertes ergibt sich eine andere Instantiierungsform eines invarianten Prinzips in der Grammatik der jeweiligen Sprache. Der Vergleich der einzelsprachlichen Eigenschaften auf der Suche nach Invarianten setzt daher voraus, daß der Platz der jeweiligen Eigenschaften in dem sie bedingenden System der Grammatik eruiert wird. Die Invarianten der Grammatik werden dann erst aufgrund des systematischen Vergleichs der Grammatiken, nicht der Rohdaten, ermittelt. Parametrisierte Invarianten der Grammatiken können mitunter aufgrund der modularen Interaktion so maskiert sein, daß sie sich dem methodisch unbewaffneten Blick überhaupt entziehen. Es gibt aber auch den Fall, daß sich Parametrisierungsinstanzen in leicht erkennbaren Mustervariationen in den Strukturen der Sprachen niederschlagen. Das ist dann eine Quelle der phänomenologischen Typologie. Ein Beispiel dafür sind etwa die Abfolgemuster, die die Greenbergsche Wortstellungstypologie beschreibt (vgl. Haider 1994 b, 1997).

2. Parameter in der Grammatiktheorie: Drei Fallbeispiele (Subjazenz, pro-drop, Verb-Zweit)

Parametrisierung wird im Prinzipien- und Parametermodell (Chomsky 1981) zu einem Hauptgegenstand des theoretischen Interesses. In dieser Generation der Theorieentfaltung erst gelingt es der Generativen Grammatik, ihrem Anspruch zumindest exemplarisch gerecht zu werden und eine Theorie der Invarianten der Grammatik zu entfalten, in der die übereinzelsprachliche Variation nicht als Störfaktor auffällt. Die Variation wird als Resultat der Optionen im Parameterraum gedeutet und im Modell als Regelfall abgeleitet. Beispielgebend dafür war die theoretische Behandlung der Lokalitätsbedingungen (Subjazenzbedingung) für Extraktion aus eingebetteten Sätzen (Rizzi 1982).

Die Motivation der Auswahl der Fallbeispiele liegt in ihrem Problemhintergrund. Subjazenz ist das Beispiel eines − in der neueren Theoriebildung unerwünschten − Regelparameters. Die Erörterung des pro-drop Parameters (Null-Subjekt-Phänomen) und des Verb-Zweit-Phänomens konzentriert sich auf das Problem der Identifikation des Parameters im Grammatiksystem.

2.1. Subjazenz

Italienisch verletzt offenbar eine Generalisierung, die für Englisch und Deutsch zutrifft, nämlich: Extraktion aus eingebetteten Fragesätzen ist unzulässig. Diese Generalisierung war theoretisch als Lokalitätsbedingung rekonstruiert worden (Subjazenzbedingung; Chomsky 1977). Danach darf zwischen zwei Positionen auf dem Ableitungspfad nicht mehr als eine Konstituentengrenze einer bestimmten Kategorie liegen (= **Grenzknoten**). Im Beispiel (1) sind die potentiell relevanten Konstituentengrenzen durch „{" und „[" gekennzeichnet. Letztere ist die Grenze des einfachen Satzes.

(1) (a) *tuo fratello*, [*a cui* {*mi domando* [*che storie* {*abbiano raccontato* – – }]}]
   (b) **dein Bruder*, [*dem* {*ich mich frage*, [*welche Geschichten* {*sie* – – *erzählt haben*}]}]
   (c) **your brother*, [*to whom* {[*I wonder* [*which stories* {*they have told* – – }]}]

Im Englischen und Deutschen ist die mit „{" bezeichnete Grenze die für Subjazenz relevante Konstituentengrenze. Rizzi (1982) erkannte, daß Italienisch nicht als Widerlegung der aufgrund der germanischen Evidenz als invariant behaupteten Lokalitätsbedingung betrachtet werden muß, wenn die Kategorie der Grenzknoten einen einzelsprachlich zu justierenden Parameter bildet. Er wies nach, daß die Subjazenzbedingung für Italienisch empirisch korrekt funktioniert, wenn im Italienischen die in (1) mit eckiger Klammer notierten Grenzen Grenzknoten bilden, nicht aber die mit geschweifter Klammer notierten. In (1 a) liegt zwischen der Ausgangsstelle „– –" des Relativausdrucks und seiner aktuellen Position nur eine Grenze der fraglichen Kategorie, nämlich die Satzgrenze des eingebetteten Satzes. Im Deutschen hingegen ist die relevante Grenze die linke Mittelfeldgrenze, und damit verletzt (1 b) die Bedingung. Analoges gilt für Englisch.

Es hatte sich auch gezeigt, daß ein Nominalausdruck in allen drei Sprachen eine Kategorie mit Grenzknotenwirkung bildet. Daher war zu erwarten, daß Italienisch sich bezüglich Extraktion aus Sätzen, die in Nominalausdrücken eingebettet sind, so verhalten müsse wie Deutsch und Englisch: Zusammen mit dem jeweils anderen Grenzknoten erwirkt die Grenze des Nominalausdrucks stets eine Verletzung der Lokalitätsbedingung:

(2) (a) * … [*a cui* {*temo* (*possibilità* [*che* {*abbiano racconta tutto* – – }])}]
   (b) * … [*dem* {*ich* (*die Möglichkeit* [*daß* {*sie alles erzählt haben*}]) *fürchte*}]
   (c) * … [*to whom* {*I fear* (*the possibility* [*that* {*they told everything* – – }])}]

Was zur Ungrammatikalität in (2) führt, ist im Italienischen die Abfolge der Grenzen „(" und „[", im Deutschen und Englischen die der Grenzen „{" und „(", wobei „(" die Konstituentengrenze des Nominalausdrucks ist. Invariant ist das Grundmuster: Das Überspringen mehr als eines Grenzknotens führt zur Ungrammatikalität. Abstraktion über der Kategorie der Grenzknoten ergibt somit das invariante Lokalitätsprinzip. Die zu instantiierenden Parameterwerte bilden die Kategorienmenge der Grenzknoten.

(3) Subjazenzprinzip: * … XP … [$_G$ … [$_G$ – –] …] …
   Parameterwerte für „[$_G$":
   (a) Italienisch: (, {.
   (b) Deutsch, Englisch: {, [.

Das Subjazenzprinzip läßt sich alternativ implementieren: Es kann entweder als direkte Beschränkung für Verschiebungsoperationen oder als Wohlgeformtheitsprinzip über die resultierenden Repräsentationen (Bedingung für das Bilden von Pfaden) fungieren.

2.2. Pro-drop

Viel Raum in der Parameterdiskussion erhielt die ebenfalls von Rizzi initiierte Diskussion des Nullsubjektphänomens in romanischen Sprachen. Rizzi (1982, 1986) formulierte die Standardhypothese: Danach sind Null-Subjekte pronominale Leerelemente, die phonetisch nicht realisierten Personalpronomina entsprechen. Die Notation für diese Leerelemente ist *pro*. Sprachen mit derartigen Leersubjekten werden als *pro-drop* Sprachen bezeichnet. Mit der *pro-drop*-Eigenschaft sah Rizzi ein Syndrom grammatischer Phänomene des Italienischen verknüpft:

(4) *Pro-drop-Syndrom*
   (a) Referentiell interpretierbare Null-Subjekte
   (b) Absenz von Subjektsexpletiva
   (c) Extraktionsmöglichkeit für Subjekte aus *that*-t-Kontexten (und W-Sätzen)
   (d) Postverbale Subjekte (in VO-Sprachen)

Einer typologischen Prüfung hielt dieses Syndrom nicht Stand. Sowohl van der Auwera (1984) als auch Gilligan (1987) stellten fest, daß einzig die Korrelation von *pro-drop* mit dem Fehlen von Subjektsexpletiva ausnahmslos gilt. Die Eigenschaften (4 c, d) korrelieren nicht in der theoretisch geforderten Weise mit der Eigenschaft (4 a): In Gilligans sprachvergleichender Studie werden u. a. Finnisch, Georgisch und Cochabamba-Quechua als *pro-drop*-Sprachen aufgelistet, die keine Extraktion von Subjekten aus *that-t*-Kontexten tolerieren. Ferner verweist er auf eine Zahl von Sprachen, die trotz *pro-drop* keine Möglichkeit der Subjektsinversion aufweisen (Gilligan 1987: 144–146). Das Phänomen ist auch im generativen Rahmen bekannt (cf. Adams 1987, Grewendorf 1986).

Daneben gibt es aber auch Sprachen mit alternativer, postverbaler Position des Subjekts, aber ohne pro-drop (z. B. Babungo, Duka, Tagalog und Yebamba). Dies zeigt, daß *pro-drop* für Subjektsinversion weder eine notwendige (vgl. Müller & Rohrbacher 1989: 39) noch eine hinreichende Bedingung bilden kann. Da aber auch die Extraktion aus eingeleiteten, eingebetteten Sätzen nicht notwendigerweise mit dem Vorliegen der *pro-drop* Eigenschaft verknüpft ist (vgl. Gilligan 1987: 146), reduziert sich das *pro-drop* Syndrom auf die Null-Subjekt Eigenschaft (4 a, b).

Dieser empirische Befund kommt nicht unerwartet, denn der theoretische Zusammenhang hinter dem Syndrom (4) ist nicht befriedigend expliziert. Das *pro-drop*-Syndrom in der Zusammenstellung (4) besteht in Rizzis (1982, 1986) System aus zwei implikativen Verhältnissen. In seiner Analyse impliziert die Zulässigkeit von Null-Subjekten die Zulässigkeit von postverbalen Subjekten. Dies wiederum impliziert, daß sie extrahiert werden können, ohne gegen die Restriktionen von Extraktionen aus der präverbalen Position zu verstoßen.

Diese Implikationen folgen allerdings nicht zwangsläufig aus dem Prinzipiensystem der Grammatik. Es ist wohl richtig, daß die postverbale Position Extraktionen ermöglicht, die in der präverbalen Position unzulässig wären (vgl. 5 a, b), doch gilt dies nicht generell. Englisch etwa hat ein postverbales Subjekt mit Expletivum an der gewöhnlichen Subjektstelle (5 c), doch das postverbale Subjekt selbst ist nicht extrahierbar (5 d). Die Präsenz des Expletivums kann nicht der Störfaktor sein, denn im Niederländischen ist ein Expletivum in analogen Konstruktionen obligatorisch (5 e):

(5) (a) *Who$_i$ would [to have dinner with e$_i$] please you?
  (b) ?Who would it please you [to have dinner with e$_i$]?
  (c) There has happened something
  (d) *What e$_i$ has there happended e$_i$?
  (e) Wat is *(er) e$_i$ gebeurd?
     Was ist (EXPL) passiert
     (Niederl.)
     [EXPL = Expletivum]

Das Nullsubjekt-Phänomen als Beobachtungskategorie wird von unterschiedlichen grammatischen Verhältnissen gespeist: Nullsubjekte sind Null-Klitika (Beispiel: Italienisch) oder Null-Topiks (Beispiel: Chinesisch). Ferner ist zu unterscheiden, ob in der gegebenen Sprache Nullsubjekte generell zulässig sind oder nur eingeschränkt auf semantisch nicht gehaltvolle Subjekte, d. h. Subjektsexpletiva. Isländisch etwa ist eine Sprache, in der nur die Expletivsubjekte stumm bleiben (7 b), nicht aber referentielle Subjektspronomina (8 b).

(6)   [+REF]]-REF]
  (a) + + pro-drop Beispiel: Italienisch
  (b) − + expletiv-drop Beispiel: Isländisch

(7) (a) *Piove* [It.]
     (Es) regnet.)
  (b) *i gær rigndi* (**Φad*) [Isl.]
     Gestern regnete es.
  (c) *(Φad) rigndi i gær* [Isl.]
     Es   regnete gestern.

Das Expletivsubjekt tritt bei Witterungsverben zwar als Vorfeldexpletiv auf (7 c), nicht aber an der strukturellen Subjektsposition im Mittelfeld. Referentielle Subjekte können im Isländischen nicht unterdrückt werden (vgl. 8 b). Dies würde Klitisierbarkeit erfordern. Isländisch ist aber eine Sprache ohne Pronominalklitisierung.

(8) (a) (*Lei/lui*) *ha comprato il libro*
     (Sie/er) hat gekauft das Buch
  (b) *i gær hefur *(hann) keypt bókina*
     Gestern hat (er) gekauft
     bókina
     Buch-DEF

Der am Italienischen exemplifizierte Fall ist der eines Null-Klitikums: Italienisch ist eine Sprache mit Pronominalklitisierung. Im finiten Satz werden die Klitika an das Finitum klitisiert. *Pro-drop* ist ein Folgephänomen des Zusammentreffens von Subjektsklitikum und Subjektskongruenz am Finitum. Der Klitisierung eines manifesten klitischen Subjekts entspräche eine redundante Spezifikation am Ziel der Klitisierung, dem finiten Verb: Das Subjektsklitikum repräsentiert dieselbe Wertematrix für Person und Numerus wie die Kongruenzmatrix des Finitums (Safir 1985, Haider 1994a). Das kongruierende Klitikum bleibt in Sprachen mit syntaktischer Klitisierung phonetisch stumm. Konsequenterweise sind Nullsubjekte, wenn es sich nicht um semantisch leere Argumente handelt, in *nichtfiniten* Kontexten im Italienischen unzulässig (vgl. Rizzi 1982: 127):

(9)   *A proposito di Mario, ritengo*
     Was Mario angeht, (so) glaube (ich)
  (a) [*poter* [*lui/*pro disporre di*
     können er   verfügen über
     fondi considerevoli]]
     ansehnliche Finanzmittel
  (b) [*che* [*lui*/pro *possa disporre di*
     daß er   kann verfügen über
     fondi considerevoli]]
     ansehnliche Finanzmittel

Verben mit nicht-referentiellen Subjekten (z. B. Witterungsverben) sind in dieser Konstruktion allerdings zulässig. Dies ist Evidenz dafür, daß Italienisch eine Kombination von Bedingungen für Nullsubjekte erfüllt: Zum einen gibt es syntaktische Klitisierung an das Finitum, woraus sich *pro-drop* für referentielle Subjekte ergibt. Zum anderen weist Italienisch auch die am Isländischen exemplizierte Eigenschaft des Wegfalls von Expletivsubjekten auf. Letzteres unterliegt nicht dem Kongruenzerfordernis.

In Topik-prominenten Sprachen (→ Art. 129, 132) ergibt sich das Phänomen der Nullsubjekte in Gestalt von Null-Topiks. Zu beachten sind auch die unterschiedlichen Interpretationsbedingungen für die Null-Argumente:

(10) (a) *Zhangsan shuo [Lisi xihuan – –]*
 [Mand.Chin.]
 Zhangsan sagt, Lisi liebe (ihn/sie/es)
 (b) *Zhangsan shuo [– – xihuan Lisi]*
 Zhangsan sagt, er liebe Lisi

In (10a) ist das Null-Topik ein Objekt. Dieses muß im Unterschied zu einem Null-Subjekt disjunkt interpretiert werden (Huang 1989: 187). Das Null-Subjekt in (10b) hingegen kann disjunkt interpretiert werden, oder auch anaphorisch, mit Bezug auf das Matrixsubjekt. Das Nullsubjekt in Klitik-Sprachen verhält sich bezüglich den Interpretationseigenschaften wie ein Personalpronomen.

Die theoretisch und empirisch adäquate Parametrisierung der *pro-drop*-Eigenschaft ist umstritten (vgl. Jaeggli & Safir eds. 1989, Haider 1994a). Nach Rizzi (1986) ergibt sich der *pro-drop*-Parameter aus einer formalen Eigenschaft der Kongruenzkategorie, die als funktionale Kopfposition in der Phrasenstruktur betrachtet wird:

(11) ... [$_{AGR-P}$ [e] [$_{AGR'}$ [AGR$^\circ$ [... [V-P]]]]]
 ...

Die Leerstelle „[e]" in der Spezifikatorposition der funktionalen Phrase AGR-P (**agreement phrase**) mit dem funktionalen Kopfelement AGR$^\circ$ wird in pro-drop Sprachen über Kongruenzmerkmale des Finitums formal als pronominal identifiziert. Der Parameter ist die Eigenschaft des AGR-Kopfes (vgl. Rizzi 1986: 519), ein Kongruenzverhältnis mit einer pronominalen Leerstelle eingehen zu können. Diese muß überdies referentiell identifiziert werden. Das geschieht über die Werte der Numerus- und Personmerkmale. Sprachen, die nur die erste Bedingung erfüllen, weisen nach Rizzi *pro-drop* nur für nicht-referentielle Subjekte auf. Unerklärt bleibt damit aber, wie es kommt, daß eine Sprache wie Isländisch zwar nicht-referentielle Null-Subjekte aufweist, aber trotz morphologisch explizitem Kongruenzparadigma für Numerus und Person referentielle Null-Subjekte nicht zuläßt. Die oben als Alternative erörterte Deutung über die Verknüpfung mit Pronominalklitisierung erfaßt diese Konstellation: Referentielles *pro-drop* entspricht stummer Klitisierung an eine kongruierende funktionale Kategorie.

2.3. Verb-Zweit

Die Bezeichnung ist potentiell irreführend, da es um die Zweitstellung des Finitums geht. In allen derzeit gesprochenen germanischen Sprachen (einschließlich Jiddisch und Afrikaans, aber mit Ausnahme des Englischen) nimmt das Finitum in nicht-eingeleiteten Sätzen eine spezielle Position ein:

(12) (a) [(XP) [v-fin [.......]]]
 (b) [Spec [Kopf [Komplement]]]
 (c) [$_{FP}$ [Spezifikator] [$_{F'}$ [F$^\circ$ [Komplement]]]]

Die Struktur eines V-2-Satzes (12a) ist eine Instanz der allgemeinen Struktur von Konstituenten mit funktionalem Kopf (12b), oder versehen mit Kategorievariablen in (12c). Ein funktionaler Kopf ist eine Kopfposition im Strukturschema (12c), deren Kategorie über das an der Position verwaltete Merkmal bestimmt ist. Sie kann durch Umsetzung von lexikalischen Köpfen besetzt werden, die das Merkmal der funktionalen Kopfposition morphologisch realisieren: Die Finitposition in (12a) ist die Kopfposition der funktionalen Konstituente, die den Satz überdacht. Das Verb in der funktionalen Kopfposition realisiert die Finitmerkmale und steht in Beziehung zu einer Lücke an seiner Grundposition als Verb. Die Spec-Position (= **specifier**) in (12), in der Feldertermininologie als Vorfeld bezeichnet, ist eine Rangierposition. Sie steht frei für die Umstellung von einzelnen Konstituenten. Die universell dreigliedrige Struktur funktionaler Konstituenten ist der Erklärungshintergrund für einen Aspekt des V-2-Phänomens, nämlich der „Zweit"-Stellung des Finitums: Das Finitum nimmt die Kopfposition ein, somit gibt es nur eine einzige Konstituentenposition davor.

Diese Position steht einer einzigen, relational nicht weiter eingeschränkten Konstituente offen. Das ist die kanonische Struktur des Deklarativsatzes. Ist die erste Position unbesetzt, so ergibt sich ein V-erst Muster, das als Frage- oder Konditionalindikator fungiert. In den germanischen Sprachen mit finaler Verbstellung ist die spezielle Position des Finitums deutlich zu erkennen:

(13) (a) *daß er das einsah*
(b) *Das sah er ein*

In den kontinentalskandinavischen Sprachen bietet einerseits die freie Verfügbarkeit der ersten Position (14b) und andererseits die Stellung der Negation relativ zum Finitum (14a vs. 14c) Referenzpunkte für die Identifikation des V2-Musters.

(14) (a) *at jeg ikke har drukket kaffe* [Dänisch]
    daß ich nicht habe getrunken Kaffee
(b) *Kaffe har jeg ikke drukket*
    Kaffee habe ich nicht getrunken
(c) *Jeg har ikke drukket kaffe*
    Ich habe nicht getrunken Kaffee

Eine systematisch vergleichende Untersuchung der germanischen V2-Grammatik im Rahmen der Generativen Grammatik bietet Vikner (1994). Koopman (1984) analysiert ein analoges Phänomen in den westafrikanischen Kru-Sprachen, in Sonderheit Vata und Gbadi.

Wenn im Schema (12) die Spec-Position systematisch unbesetzt bleibt, ergibt sich, wenn das Finitum die Kopfposition einnimmt, eine V1-Struktur. Diese Struktur ist eine Grundkonfiguration der Satzstruktur keltischer Sprachen. Walisisch zeigt deutlich eine komplementäre Distribution von Finitum und nicht-finitem Verbum, was Sproat (1985) mit folgendem Satzpaar demonstriert:

(15) (a) *Gwelodd Siôn ddraig*
    sah   Siôn Drachen
    Siôn sah einen Drachen
(b) *Gwnaeth Siôn weld ddraig*
    tat   Siôn sehen dragon
    Siôn sah einen Drachen

Unter der Annahme, daß die Position des nicht-finiten Verbs die Grundposition des Verbs ist, ergibt sich die V1-Struktur durch Umstellung des Finitums in die satzinitiale funktionale Kopfposition (vgl. Emonds 1980, Sproat 1985). Walisisch ist folglich eine SVO-Sprache mit Finitumstellung.

Die keltische Erststellung des Finitums und die germanische Erst- bzw. Zweitstellung des Finitums sind Instantiierungsvarianten des generellen Schemas funktionaler Konstituenten (12 a). In den modernen Germanischen Sprachen (zur Diachronie vgl. Battye & Roberts 1995) ist die Realisierung der Spec-Position ein Satzmodusindikator (V2 als Deklarativ-, V1 als Interrogativstruktur). In den keltischen Sprachen wird nur das Muster ohne realisierte Spec-Position instantiiert. Das ergibt die keltische V1 Struktur. Die exakte Feststellung der für die Finitumstellung verantwortlichen Parametrisierung ist kontrovers (vgl. Haider & Prinzhorn 1986; Lightfoot & Hornstein 1994). Der theoretische Aspekt wird im folgenden Abschnitt wieder aufgegriffen.

3. Parametertheorie: Von GB zum Minimalistischen Programm

Was ist ein möglicher Parameter? Die Antwort auf diese Frage wurde im Laufe der Theorieentwicklung zu präzisieren getrachtet. Im GB-Modell (Chomsky 1981) war der Parameterraum kaum eingeschränkt. Es wurden Regelparameter zugelassen (Beispiel: Subjazenz), ebenso wie Relationsparameter (Beispiel: pro-drop) oder Strukturparameter (Beispiel: Konfigurationalitätsparameter; Hale 1993; → Art. 103). Die Vielfalt möglicher Parameter geht zu Lasten einer restriktiven UG-Theorie als Theorie der Invarianten. Je mehr Freiraum der Parametrisierung offen steht, desto geringer ist die durch UG festgelegte Einschränkung des Möglichkeitsspielraumes. Daraus erwächst ein gravierendes Lernbarkeitsproblem: Wie kann eine UG mit großem Parameterspielraum die Treffsicherheit des Kindes beim Erwerb der spezifischen Parameterkonstellation, die die Grammatik der Muttersprache ausmacht, gewährleisten und wie vermag das Kind die korrekten Parameterwerte überhaupt zu identifizieren? Die Brisanz dieser Frage wird deutlich bei Regelparametern. Wenn ein Kind die Parameterwerte für die Subjazenzbedingung sprachspezifisch justieren sollte, müßte es den Beitrag der Subjazenzregel im Konzert der grammatischen Bedingungen isolieren können, um alternative Justierungen vergleichend ausprobieren zu können. Damit stünde es aber vor demselben Problem wie der Forscher: Es müßte durch probeweises Fixieren Rückschlüsse vom Ergebnis auf die Wertwahl für den Parameter ziehen. Daß ein Kind so vorginge, dafür gibt es aber keine Anhaltspunkte. Daher wird versucht, Regelparameter zu eliminieren. Regelparameter wären Parameter des Berechnungssystems der Grammatik. Diese sind in ihrem Ergebnis global, und daher für das Kind nicht anhand lokaler Information identifizierbar. Parameter sollten über Eigenschaften des Inventars, nicht der Regeln, identifizierbar sein. Chomsky (1981: 7) betont mit Verweis auf epistemologische Priorität für den Erwerb, daß dem Kind die Identifizierung von Parameterwerten nur dann gelingen kann, wenn mit dem jeweiligen Wert des Parameters eine spezifische Datenqualität korreliert, die als stabiles Muster erkennbar ist.

Chomsky (1989: 44) fordert, die Parametrisierung auf **binäre** Parametrisierung **funktionaler** Kategorien einzuschränken, mit den Werten (+/− stark]. Der Effekt der Parametrisierung ist, die Abgleichung der Merkmale im Zuge der Derivation zu steuern. Die Merkmale werden stets in einer strukturellen Konstellation abgeglichen, nämlich zwischen einem funktionalen Kopf F und dem Element in seiner Spezifikatorposition (vgl. 12 c). Die Derivation eines komplexen Ausdrucks beginnt mit den lexikalischen Bestandteilen (**numeration**), die dem Lexikon entnommen werden. Diese werden zu Strukturen gefügt (*merge*-Operation). Über diesen Strukturen laufen Verschiebungsoperationen ab. Am Ende der Derivation steht eine Repräsentation (**logische Form**, kurz LF), die die Schnittstelle zur konzeptuellen Struktur bildet. In der Derivation gibt es eine sprachspezifisch zu setzende Abzweigung, an der die morphologische Form abgelesen wird (**spellout**), die phonetisch realisiert wird (**phonetic form**, kurz PF). Denn, so die Annahme, die Sprachen unterscheiden sich in der Setzung der Abzweigung, nicht in der Derivationsprozedur selbst (vgl. 16). Ist die Abzweigung früh in der Derivation, ist der Anteil der Derivationsschritte, der 'unsichtbar' abläuft eben größer. Die Setzung der Abzweigung ist es, die durch die Werte der funktionalen Merkmale bedingt wird: Starke Merkmale müssen vor der Abzweigung abgeglichen werden, schwache Merkmale erst auf der Derivationsstrecke, die zwischen der morphologischen Abzweigestelle und LF liegt.

(16)   Derivation:
       {numeration} ---→ + ---→ LF
                        ↕
                        PF

Als Veranschaulichungsfall möge das V-2 Phänomen dienen: Die Umsetzung des Finitums muß im Minimalistischen Programm durch ein Merkmal mit dem Wert [+stark] ausgelöst werden, das in der funktionalen Kopfposition, die das Finitum in V2-Sprachen einnimmt, geprüft wird. Der dafür erforderliche Derivationsschritt setzt das betroffene Verb in die erforderliche Position um. In V2-Sprachen erfolgt wegen des Stärkemerkmals die Umsetzung **vor** der PF-Abzweigung.

Generell geht das aktuelle Modell der Generativen Grammatik (Chomsky 1995: 'Minimalistisches Programm' kurz MP) von der Annahme einer einzigen, universellen, funktional parametrisierten Derivationsprozedur aus, und infolgedessen auch von einer einzigen, universellen, funktional parametrisierten Satzstruktur (**universal base hypothesis**) als Resultat der Derivation. Diese Strukturen verdanken ihre sprachspezifische Form ausschließlich der einzelsprachlichen Wertematrix der funktionalen Merkmale und der dadurch bewirkten variablen Setzung von **spellout**. Am Beispiel von V2 illustriert, ergibt sich folgendes Bild:

Wenn die für die Ableitung eines Satzes erforderlichen Derivationsschritte allen Grammatiken gemein sind, so impliziert dies, daß auch nicht-V2-Sprachen das Finitum umsetzen, allerdings ohne PF-Effekt. Denn der Derivationsschritt erfolgt nach der PF-Abzweigung. In der Theorieversion von Chomsky (1995) wird die post-PF-Umsetzung modifiziert und auf die Umsetzung von Merkmalen eingeschränkt. Das heißt, es wird nicht das finite Verb selbst stumm umgestellt, sondern dessen Merkmale werden abgetrennt und an den funktionalen Kopf gereicht. Vor der PF-Abzweigung ist die Merkmalsabtrennung wegen der morphologischen Integrität mit dem Träger nicht möglich. Damit erzwingt die PF-wirksame Merkmalsumstellung die Umstellung des Trägers.

Die Parametrisierung über die Setzung der PF-Abzweigung hat ihre Vorläufer bereits in der LF-Konzeption der GB-Theorie, und zwar in der Untersuchung der typologisch zu beobachtenden Variation der Fragesatzstrukturen (→ Art. 100). Es gibt zumindest drei Typen von Fragesatzstrukturen bei Ergänzungsfragen:

(17)   Fragesatzstrukturen (alternativ)
       (a) Frageausdruck in der kanonischen Satzgliedposition
       (b) Genau ein Frageausdruck pro Satz in spezieller initialer Position

(c) Sämtliche Frageausdrücke pro Satz in spezieller initialer Position

Im Chinesischen, ein Beispiel für (17 a), bleibt der Frageausdruck in seiner Satzgliedposition (vgl. 18 a), während im Englischen der Frageausdruck in eine spezielle Position am Satzanfang tritt.

(18) (a) *Tā mǎi*
      'er/sie kaufen-PERF
      le shéme? [Mand. Chinesisch]
      was'
      Was hat er/sie gekauft?
   (b) *What did he buy*

In Fragen mit mehr als einem Frageausdruck repräsentiert Englisch den Fall (17 b). Bulgarisch ist ein Beleg für den Typ (17 c). Die Tatsache, daß im Bulgarischen Klitika (vgl. 20 a) die Abfolge der Frageausdrücke nicht unterbrechen dürfen, wird verständlich, wenn die Frageausdrücke eine Konstituente bilden (Rudin 1988):

(19) (a) *Whom did you tell what?*
   (b) **What whom did you tell?*
   (c) **Whom what did you tell?*

(20) (a) **Koj ti e kakvo*
      wer dir hat was
      kazal? [Bulgarisch]
      gesagt
      Wer hat dir was gesagt
   (b) *Koj kakvo ti e kazal*
      wer was dir hat gesagt

Die Verteilung wird über folgende Merkmalszuschreibung erfaßt: Im Chinesischen sind beide Interrogativmerkmale – das des Frageausdrucks und das des funktionalen Kopfes – schwach. Daher erfolgt vor der Abzweigung zu PF keine Umsetzung, da schwache Merkmale erst nach der Abzweigung geprüft werden. Im Englischen, und in vielen anderen Sprachen, ist das Merkmal des funktionalen Kopfes stark. Es muß daher abgeglichen werden. Die Merkmale der Interrogativausdrücke sind schwach. Es genügt daher, wenn ein einziger Interrogativausdruck umgestellt wird. Im Bulgarischen sind beide Merkmale stark, das Kopfmerkmal und das der Interrogativphrasen. Daher werden alle Interrogativausdrücke in die Position versetzt, in der die starken Merkmale geprüft werden können. Damit sind drei der vier möglichen Verteilungen des Stärkemerkmals abgedeckt: Bulgarisch entspricht (21 a), Englisch (21 b) und Chinesisch (21 c).

(21)   Interr. F-Kopf   Interrogativ-Phrase
   (a) stark   stark
   (b) stark   schwach
   (c) schwach   schwach
   (d) schwach   stark

Der Fall (21 d) ist bei Ergänzungsfragen im Ergebnis nicht vom Fall (21 a) zu unterscheiden: Die starken Merkmale der Interrogativausdrücke erzwingen die Umsetzung. Der Unterschied läßt sich nur in Entscheidungsfragen feststellen: Ein starkes Merkmal erfordert eine morphologische Stütze, beispielsweise durch ein vorangestelltes finites Verb (vgl. Englisch, Deutsch). In der Belegung (21 d) werden alle Frageausdrücke umgestellt, in der Entscheidungsfrage tritt aber keine Umstellung des Finitums oder Einsetzung einer Fragepartikel an der Kopfposition auf.

Die Merkmalsbelegung in (21) erzeugt die distributionellen Unterschiede über die Festlegung, daß starke Merkmale vor der Abzweigung zu PF (vgl. 12) in der Spezifikator-Kopf-Konstellation geprüft werden. Daher sind die Umsetzungen auf der PF-Repräsentation erkennbar. Die schwachen Merkmale bei nicht versetzten Interrogativausdrücken werden auf LF geprüft, ebenfalls in Spezifikator-Kopf-Konstellationen. Es treten dieselben Umstellungen auf, allerdings in verschiedenen Phasen der Derivation und daher auch mit verschiedenem Ergebnis auf der PF-Repräsentation. Auf LF hingegen sind die Fragesatzstrukturen aller erörterten Sprachen gleich: Alle Frageausdrücke stehen in Form von Frageoperatoren an der Spitze der Satzstruktur in Spezifikatorpositionen. Dies wird im Derivationsverlauf nach der PF-Abzweigung durch dieselben Umstellungsoperationen erreicht, die je nach Merkmal auch vor der PF-Abzweigung operieren. Die Annahme der post-PF-Verschiebung ist einerseits durch die semantische Äquivalenz der unterschiedlichen Muster und andererseits durch die Beobachtung motiviert, daß die Effekte grammatischer Beschränkungen, die für prä-LF-Verschiebungen gelten, auch in Sprachen zu beobachten sind, die Interrogativausdrücke nicht versetzen (Huang 1982).

Diese Beispiele illustrieren eine empirisch relevante Konsequenz der Methode: Was immer in einer Sprache für Grammatikverhältnisse auf der PF-Repräsentation auftreten, sie sind auch Bestandteil der Grammatik jeder anderen Sprache. Diese paradox erscheinende Aussage gewinnt an Konsistenz durch die Parametrisierung der PF-Abzweigung:

Wenn ein Derivationsschritt in einer Sprache einen PF-Effekt ergibt, in der anderen aber nicht, dann deswegen, weil er in letzterer Grammatik aufgrund der Stärkeparametrisierung des verantwortlichen Merkmals erst nach der Abzweigung zu PF stattfindet.

Die derzeit aktuelle Modellgeneration der Generativen Grammatik zielt auf eine geschlossene und kumulative Erfassung typologischer Unterschiede ab: Jede Grammatik einer Einzelsprache verfügt über alle Derivationsverfahren und führt diese auch durch. Einzelsprachliche Unterschiede und typologisch relevante Verknüpfungen ergeben sich ausschließlich über Variation im Derivationsablauf. Die einzige Variable ist die durch die Stärkemerkmale gesteuerte Positionierung der Abzweigung zu PF. Sie ist im Ergebnis ein komplexer **Rangierparameter** für die einzelsprachliche Positionierung der PF-Abzweigung im Derivationsablauf.

Im generativen Umfeld gibt es aber auch Konzeptionen, die der traditionellen typologischen Sichtweise näher stehen. Parameter werden als **Partitionierungsparameter** verstanden. Die Grammatiken der einzelnen Sprachen bilden unterschiedliche Instantiierungen des von UG zugelassenen Spielraumes. Die Parameter erzeugen mit ihrer binären Wertbelegung **disjunkte** Teilmengen von Grammatiken. Insgesamt partitionieren die Parameterbelegungen die Menge der Grammatiken im UG-Raum in Teilmengen. Typologische Cluster ergeben sich unter anderem aufgrund von Konsistenzbedingungen: Bestimmte Parametersetzungen engen die Möglichkeiten für Folgeparameter ein. Beispiel: Ist eine Sprache nicht Topik-prominent (= Folge von Parameter Px) und werden Pronomina nicht klitisiert (= Folge von Parameter Py), so gibt es keine referentiell interpretierten Null-Subjekte (Folge von Parameter Pz). Die Belegung des Parameters Pz ist somit durch die Belegung von Parameter Px und Py bereits auf den entsprechenden Wert festgelegt.

Die Partitionierungskonzeption schließt auch die Annahme einer universellen Satzstruktur aus (Ablehnung der **universal base hypothesis**): Die jeweilige Satzstruktur ist eine Funktion von UG-Prinzipien und einzelsprachlichem Inventar. Die Grammatik der Einzelsprache entspricht jener (partiellen) Instantiierung von UG, die für die Verarbeitung des einzelsprachlichen Inventars aktiviert werden muß. Da das morphologische Inventar einzelsprachlich in Kategorie und Umfang variiert, wird nicht angenommen, daß die funktionale Architektur, die der Verwaltung der morphologischen Merkmale dient, universell sei. Es wird vielmehr vorausgesetzt, daß je Sprache jene minimale UG-konforme Konstellation aktiviert ist, die für die strukturelle Verortung genügt. Beispielsweise wird, im Unterschied zum Minimalistischen Programm, für eine kongruenzlose Sprache wie Chinesisch nicht angenommen, daß in ihrer Satzstruktur eine funktionale Kategorie für Subjekt-Verb Kongruenz bereitstünde. Chinesisch weist keine Kongruenz auf, daher wird keine für Kongruenz benötigte funktionale Kategorie aktiviert. Dem ist nicht so im Minimalistischen Programm. Die universale Satzstruktur enthält eine Kongruenzkategorie. Da sie im Chinesischen morphologisch nicht wirksam ist, wird angenommen, daß die Merkmalsbelegung so ist, daß sie ihre Wirksamkeit in der Derivation erst nach der PF-Abzweigung entfaltet und deswegen stumm bleibt.

4. Universalien, Typologie und Parametertheorie: Wege zum selben Ziel

Das Forschungsprogramm der Generativen Grammatik und das der strukturell orientierten Typologie und Universalienforschung streben dasselbe Ziel an. Beide suchen nach den Invarianten der Grammatiksysteme (Universalien) und den Grenzen des Variationsspielraums für einzelsprachliche Unterschiede zwischen den Grammatiken (Typologische Variation). Die unterschiedlichen methodischen Zugangsweisen erschweren mitunter die Kommunikation und nähren das Bedürfnis, nach einem vereinfachenden Entweder-Oder zu verlangen und die jeweils andere Herangehensweise als grundsätzlich verfehlt zu betrachten. Dabei droht aus dem Blickfeld zu geraten, daß beide Herangehensweisen ausreichend begründet sind und in einem Komplementierungsverhältnis stehen, in dem beide Unternehmen aus den Ergebnissen des anderen Nutzen ziehen können, der umso größer wäre, je enger die Kooperation sich gestalten ließe.

Die Typologie und Universalienforschung geht konstruktionsspezifisch (vgl. Ordnungsschema des Abschnitts X dieses Bandes) vor, und damit paradigmatisch-induktiv. Konstruktionen, definiert über ein Leitparadigma, bilden den Klassifikationsrahmen für die Datengrundlage. Die Frage der Identifikation der einander entsprechenden Konstruktionen in den Einzelsprachen und der Vergleichbarkeit wird zum Problem dieser phänomenologischen Methode (tertium comparationis; → Art. 1). Die Vorgehensweise ist durch die Absicht motiviert, eine möglichst extensive Datenbasis zu erfassen: Je größer die Zahl der Sprachen, desto enger muß aber der Fokus der Betrachtung gestaltet werden, um praktikables Vorgehen gewährleisten zu können.

Die Methode der Generativen Grammatik ist prinzipienorientiert und deduktiv. Die Klassifikation der Daten nach Konstruktionen ist kein theoretisches Kriterium, sondern bestenfalls ein heuristisches Moment. **Konstruktionen** sind günstig erstellte Gruppierungen der Daten. Gesucht werden die parametrisierten Invarianten des Grammatiksystems, und nicht die von Konstruktionen. Konstruktionen sind Epiphänomene. Die Invarianten sind, wie die Erfahrung lehrte, nicht konstruktionsspezifisch. **Subjazenz** etwa wirkt in allen Konstruktionen, bei der die Spezifikator-Position der höchsten funktionalen Konstituente durch eine Umstellungsoperation besetzt ist, oder, in repräsentationeller Sichtweise formuliert, Konstruktionen, in denen eine Phrase in der höchsten funktionalen Spezifikator-Position des Satzes mit der Lücke in ihrer Grundposition in Relation gebracht werden muß (vgl. (3) und (22)). Subjazenz fungiert als Lokalitätsbeschränkung für diese Relation. Zu den Konstruktionen, in denen die für Subjazenz relevante Konstellation auftritt, gehören etwa die Relativ- und Fragesatzkonstruktionen mit versetzten Elementen, Komparativkonstruktionen, sowie die Vorfeld-Besetzung in Verb-Zeit-Sprachen.

(22) $[_{XP_i} [\ldots [e]_i \ldots]]$

Jede einzelne Konstruktion repräsentiert ein Bündel an grammatischen Gegebenheiten mit den auf sie einwirkenden Bedingungen und Beschränkungen. Gegenstand der Modellierung aber ist das Wissenssystem, das die Grammatik insgesamt ausmacht. Die Eigenschaften der Konstruktionen zu erklären heißt, ihren Ort im System der Gesamtgrammatik zu bestimmen. Im Unterschied zum extensiven Vorgehen der Typologie ist diese Methode durch eine intensive Herangehensweise an die Grammatik charakterisiert. Ebenfalls bedingt durch die praktischen Arbeitsumstände finden sich dabei Einschränkungen der Anzahl und des Umfangs der bearbeitbaren Grammatiksysteme und deren typologischer Streuung: Für die intensive Erforschung der Grammatik einer Sprache ist sowohl muttersprachliche als auch fachliche Kompetenz unabdingbar, sowie das Korrektiv einer rege interagierenden Expertengemeinde. Diese Umstände sind nicht für jede beliebige Sprache jederzeit gegeben.

Beide Einschränkungen, die enge konstruktionsspezifische Fokussierung der extensiv vorgehenden strukturellen Typologie einerseits und andererseits die zufallsbedingte typologische Streuung der verhältnismäßig wenigen bisher intensiv untersuchten Sprachen, haben es an sich, daß sie mit fortschreitender Forschung schwächer werden. Am Horizont, an dem sich die Linien beider Forschungsstränge treffen sollten, werden sie aufgehoben sein.

5. Generative Grammatik als Typologie- und Universalientheorie

Die Generative Grammatik ist eine Theorie über die Invarianten der Grammatiksysteme und über deren parametrisch konstituierten Variabilitätsraum. Damit ist sie ein Kandidat für eine Theorie der Universalien und der typologischen Variabilität der Grammatiken menschlicher Sprachen. Die Universalien werden in der Theorie der Invarianten erfaßt. Die typologische Auffächerung wird über Parameterkonstellationen modelliert und theoretisch fundiert.

Die Methode, die auf die Ermittlung von Invarianten abzielt, ist zwangsläufig eine Methode, typologische Fragestellungen zu generieren. Denn die typologische Variation ist das Falsifikationsterrain, in dem sich die Theorie der parametrisierten Invarianten bewähren muß. Die Generative Grammatik ist überdies eine Theorie **vernetzter Parameter** im System der Grammatik. Wenn typologische Einzelbefunde modelliert werden, dann immer unter dem Konsistenzerfordernis mit dem Gesamtsystem, und zwar sowohl auf der Ebene der einzelsprachlichen Grammatik als auch auf der Ebene der Theorie der Invarianten.

Praktisch ist es aber derzeit im generativen Rahmen schwierig, die typologische Literatur unmittelbar heranzuziehen. Die Ergebnisse dieser Forschungsrichtung sind meist wegen unterschiedlicher Prämissen mit den theoretischen Fragestellungen der anderen nur bedingt kommensurabel. Umgekehrt ist die für eine aktive Forschergemeinde typische Theoriendynamik der Generativen Grammatik unvereinbar mit der Festlegung einer bestimmten Theorieversion als Referenzrahmen für typologische Forschung. Dies ist aber auch gar nicht erforderlich. Die Forschung innerhalb der Generativen Grammatik hat ein weitläufiges Netz von empirisch abgesicherten Hypothesenpfaden erzeugt, dessen Nutzung ohne Schaden von der jeweiligen Fokussierung der aktuellen Theoriediskussion abgekoppelt werden kann.

6. Zitierte Literatur

Auwera, Johan van der. 1984. „Subject and non-Subject Asymmetries in the Relativization of Embedded NP's". In: de Gest, W. & Putseys, Y. (eds.). *Sentential Complementation.* Dordrecht: Foris, 257–69.

Battye, Adrienne & Roberts, Ian (eds.). 1995. *Clause Structure and Language Change.* Oxford: Oxford Univ. Press.

Chomsky, Noam. 1959. „Review of B. F. Skinner's Verbal Behavior". *Language* 35: 26–57.

Chomsky, Noam. 1981. *Lectures on Government and Binding.* Dordrecht: Foris.

Chomsky, Noam. 1989. Some Notes on Economy of Derivation and Representation. *MIT working Papers in Linguistics* 10: 43–74.

Chomsky, Noam. 1995. *The Minimalist Program.* Cambridge, MA: MIT Press.

Gilligan, Gary. 1987. *A Cross-Linguistic Approach to the pro-Drop Parameter.* Ph-D. Dissertation. USC, Los Angeles.

Haider, Hubert. 1994a. „(Un-)heimliche Subjekte." *Linguistischer Berichte* 153: 372–385.

Haider, Hubert. 1994b. *„Markiertheit" in der generativen Grammatik.* In: J. Jacobs et al. eds. Syntax (Reihe HSK: Handbücher zur Sprach- und Kommunikationswissenschaft) Berlin: de Gruyter, 635–645.

Haider, Hubert. 1997. *„Typological implications of a directionality constraint on projections."* Alexiadou, Artemis & T. Alan Hall. *Studies on Universal Grammar and Typological Variation.* Amsterdam: Benjamins, 17–33.

Haider, Hubert & Martin Prinzhorn (eds.). 1986. *Verb Second Phenomena in Germanic Languages.* Dordrecht: Foris.

Huang, James. 1982. „Move WH in a Language without WH movement." *The Linguistic Review* 1: 369–416.

Huang, James. 1989. „Pro-Drop in Chinese: A Generalized Control Theory." In: Osvaldo Jaeggli & Kenneth J. Safir (eds.). *The Null Subject Parameter.* Dordrecht/Boston/London: Kluwer, 185–214.

Jaeggli, Osvaldo & Savir, Kenneth J. (eds.). 1989. *The Null Subject Parameter.* Dordrecht/Boston/London: Kluwer.

Lightfoot, David & Hornstein, Norbert (eds.). 1994. *Verb Movement.* Cambridge: Cambridge University Press.

Rizzi, Luigi. 1986. „Null objects in Italian and the theory of pro." *Linguistic Inquiry* 17: 501–557.

Rizzi, Luigi. 1982. *Issues in Italian Syntax.* Dordrecht: Foris.

Rudin, Catherine. 1988. „On Multiple Questions and Multiple Wh-Fronting." *Natural Language and Linguistic Theory* 6: 445–501.

Safir, Ken. 1985. *Syntactic Chains.* Cambridge, Mass.: Cambridge University Press.

Williams, E. 1991. „The Argument-Bound Empty Categories." In: Freidin, R. (ed.). *Principles and Parameters in Comparative Grammar.* Cambridge, MA: MIT Press, 77–98.

Hubert Haider, Universität Salzburg (Österreich)

25. Die Hegersche Noematik

1. Hintergründe und Zielsetzungen
2. Das Trapezmodell
3. Noematische Teilsysteme
4. Das Aktantenmodell
5. Weitere Anwendungen des Aktantenmodells
6. Kritik und Würdigung
7. Zitierte Literatur

1. Hintergründe und Zielsetzungen

1.1 Sprachvergleich und Onomasiologie

Ziel der **Noematik** Klaus Hegers ist es, ein **tertium comparationis** zur Verfügung zu stellen für den zwischensprachlichen Vergleich von Strukturen vornehmlich der grammatischen, aber auch anderer sprachlicher Ebenen, bzw. zur außereinzelsprachlich anwendbaren Definition grammatischer Kategorien. Dabei liegen zwei Prinzipien zugrunde: a) die Einzelsprachunabhängigkeit der Kategorien und Strukturen, die den Ausgangspunkt des Vergleichs bilden, ist zu sichern durch eine möglichst weitgehend **deduktive** Herleitung aus einem sorgfältig gewählten Inventar axiomatischer Prämissen;

b) außereinzelsprachliche Kategorien sind auf der begrifflichen Seite der Sprachzeichen zu finden, in den auszudrückenden Inhalten („designanda"), die in jeder Einzelsprache auf spezifische Weise realisiert werden. Der Vergleich verschiedener Sprachsysteme (sei es in typologischer, sei es diachroner Dimension) ist somit grundsätzlich in **onomasiologischer** Perspektive (nach anderer Terminologie in **synthetischer** Perspektive, cf. Lehmann 1989) anzustellen, als die Frage nach den Morphemen, Kategorien und deren Organisation, kurz: nach den Strukturen, die in den verschiedenen Sprachen dem Ausdruck der außereinzelsprachlichen Begriffskategorien dienen. Diese Sichtweise ist kompatibel mit einer funktionalistischen Auffassung von Sprache als problemlösendem Werkzeug, in dem die zu lösenden kommunikativen oder kognitiven Aufgaben über die Sprachen hinweg unterschiedliche Lösungen bzw. Ausdrucksmittel finden. Das Ausgehen von der Funktion/Bedeutung beim typologischen Sprachvergleich ist auch in funktionalistischen Ansätzen zwar nicht immer Praxis, aber häufig geäußerte programmatische Forderung (z.B. Seiler 1986: 13 f; Croft 1990: 11 ff; Wierzbicka 1998: 407f).

1.2. Noematik, Generativismus und funktionale Grammatik

Die Noematik, zusammen mit den darauf aufbauenden Theorieteilen (Aktantenmodell und Signemranghierarchie), ist etwa zeitgleich zur Generativen Grammatik entstanden. Mit dieser teilt sie die weitgehende Zentrierung auf Fragen der Grammatik bei gleichzeitig sehr viel umfassenderem Erklärungsanspruch. Mit ihr teilt sie auch das Bemühen um Definitionsgenauigkeit und Formalisierung, auch wenn die Baumgraphen bzw. die linear formalisierten Ausdrücke des Aktantenmodells (cf. § 4) für etwas ganz anderes stehen als die der Generativen Grammatik, nämlich nicht einzelsprachliche Ausdrucksstrukturen sondern universal-begriffliche Strukturen. In dieser zentralen Rolle der begrifflich-semantischen Ebene für die Darstellung einzelsprachlich-syntaktischer Gegebenheiten liegt der wichtigste Unterschied zum generativen Modell. Evident und explizit ist hingegen die Nähe zu den 'semantischen Dissidenten' der Generativen Grammatik der 60er und 70er Jahre, insbesondere zu der von Charles Fillmore inaugurierten **Kasusgrammatik** (cf. bes. Fillmore 1968; 1971). Mit Fillmore teilt Heger vor allem den Rückgriff auf den verbzentrierten Ansatz von Lucien Tesnière (1959). Allerdings hat sich das Hegersche Modell mit seinem hohen Anspruch an Formalisierung, methodisch-theoretischer Absicherung und Konsistenz und mit seiner theoretischen Reichweite bald von der Kasusgrammatik entfernt. Damit übertrifft das die Noematik in Formalisierungsgrad und Definitionsgenauigkeit auch die sogenannte **Funktionale Grammatik**, selbst da, wo diese sich um Formalisierung bemüht hat (z.B. Dik 1981), obwohl Hegers Theorie gerade mit der Funktionalen Grammatik entscheidende Punkte teilt: auch die Noematik macht die kommunikativen und kognitiven **Leistungen** und Gegebenheiten zum Ausgangspunkt der Darstellung sprachlicher Strukturen und deren Vielfalt in den Einzelsprachen. Hegers **Noematische Teilsysteme** konstituieren sich primär aus den semiotisch-funktionalen, pragmatischen oder kognitiven Kategorien, die auch die funktionalistische Typologie zum Ausgangspunkt nimmt.

1.3. Strukturelle Semantik und Noematik

Die Noematik steht in der Tradition des europäischen Strukturalismus und speziell der Strukturellen Semantik (Hjelmslev, Ullmann, Pottier, Coseriu, Baldinger), die ihrerseits inspiriert war von den von der **nominalistischen** Grundhaltung Humboldts, Saussures, Sapirs und Whorfs, wonach begriffliche Kategorien grundsätzlich festzumachen sind an ihrer sprachlichen Benennung: am sprachlichen Zeichen, bzw. abstrakter, am Beziehungsgeflecht der in einem System vorhandenen Zeichen. Die Unterordnung der Bedeutung unter die konkrete Struktur einer Sprache im Strukturalismus war zudem motiviert durch das Bedürfnis nach einer möglichst objektivierbaren Beschreibungsmethode für die Bedeutung. Eine solche Auffassung schließt aber im Prinzip den semantisch basierten Sprachvergleich aus. Sprachliche Strukturiertheit im Sinne der obengenannten Theorien ist per definitionem die Struktur einer Einzelsprache und nur mit Bezug auf diese gegeben. Um Bedeutungen sprachlicher Zeichen und Kategorien einer Sprache mit denen einer anderen zu vergleichen, bedarf es aus streng strukturalistischer Sicht demnach einer Abbildung der Bedeutungen auf ein System von Begrifflichkeiten, die unabhängig von der Struktur der Einzelsprache gewonnen sind; auch von hier aus ist also die onomasiologische Sichtweise zwingend. Die Noematik ist ein Begriffssystem, das genau diesem Anspruch genügen soll, ohne dabei hinter die methodische Absicherung des semasiologisch-strukturalistischen Bestimmungsverfahrens zurückzufallen.

2. Das Trapezmodell

Das Trapez dient der Klärung verschiedener verschiedener semiotischer Ebenen, die bei der Sprachbeschreibung argumentativ zu berücksichtigen sind. Es geht ursprünglich auf das Dreiecksmodell von Ogden/Richards (1949) zurück. Allerdings wird dieses in mehrfacher Hinsicht uminterpretiert: (1) Es handelt sich nicht, wie bei Ogden/Richards, um eine Modellierung des Zeichengebrauchs, sondern um ein „methodologisches Modell zur Darstellung sprachwissenschaftlicher Fragestellungen" (Heger 1964: 493). (2) Damit einher geht, daß das Modell nicht allein wie bei Ogden/Richards den konkreten Referenzakt repräsentiert, sondern in zwei Abstraktionsschritten auch auf die **Sprache** entweder im Bloomfieldschen Sinne (bei Heger: (Σparole, 1976: 24 ff.) oder im Saussureschen Sinne (**langue**) übertragen wird. Hierzu muß auf der Ausdrucksseite das **Symbol** durch die entsprechende **langue**-Einheit (**Signifikant**) ersetzt werden, auf der Inhaltsseite der **Referent** durch die **Klasse von Referenten**, auf die ein Zeichen auf *langue*-Ebene referiert. Für den von Ogden/Richards als psychischer Prozess verstandenen Referenz-Akt (**reference**) wird die intensional bestimmte 'Bedeutung', also das Saussuresche **Signifikat** eingesetzt. (3) Um das Verhältnis zwischen einzelsprachlicher Semantik und universell bestimmter Begrifflichkeit zu präzisieren, wird die intensional-inhaltliche Ebene in mehrere Aspekte untergliedert: zum einen wird eine Trennung zwischen dem Signifikat als dem vollständigen 'Bedeutungsumfang' eines sprachlichen Zeichens (Heger 1964: 508) in seiner polysemen Vielfalt und dem **Semem** als der jeweils isolierbaren Teilbedeutung vorgenommen. Zum anderen wird eine Ebene angesetzt, auf der Bedeutung als Konjunktion von elementaren Bedeutungs**komponenten** erscheint. Dies ergibt sich einerseits aus der strukturalistischen Strategie der Zergliederung sprachlicher Zeichen in distinktive Einheiten, hier den **Semen** nach Bernard Pottier (1964 u.ö.), andererseits aus dem Bedarf an einem Inventar elementarer Ausgangseinheiten zur Darstellung je einzelsprachlicher Kombinatorik beim Ausdruck universell bestimmter Inhalte, d.h. dem Bedarf an einer Rückführung der Bedeutung auf ein Inventar **semantischer Primitiva**, den **Noemen**. An ein und derselben Systemstelle situieren sich somit, je nach Gewinnungsmethode und Fragerichtung (semasiologisch von der Einzelsprache her oder universell-deduktiv mit onomasiologischer Zielsetzung) die Seme oder die Noeme, beidesmal verstanden als elementare Bedeutungskomponenten.

Hieraus ergibt sich das folgende Schema (Heger 1976: 51; zur weiteren Situierung cf. Raible 1983).

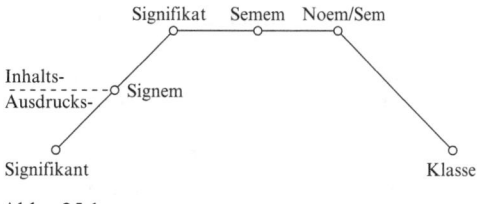

Abb.: 25.1

3. Noematische Teilsysteme

3.1. Konstituierung und Theorie

Die Noematik besteht somit in der Aufstellung von einzelsprachunabhängigen Begriffssystemen, konstituiert aus einem kontrollierten Satz semantischer (besser: begrifflicher) Primitiva. Es ist evident, daß eine völlige Außereinzelsprachlichkeit solcher Systeme nicht zu gewährleisten ist (Heger 1967: 532 ff.; 1976: 4 f.; 1983: § 2.2.2); zum einen wegen der grundsätzlichen Nicht-Hintergehbarkeit der jeweiligen Metasprache bei jeder wissenschaftlichen Erkenntnistätigkeit; zum anderen auch aus ganz praktisch-arbeitsökonomischen Gründen: das Begriffssystem, auf das unterschiedliche Sprachen abgebildet werden sollen, sollte ja nicht komplexer oder wesentlich feinkörniger sein, als die Kategorien der jeweils zu vergleichenden Sprachen; schon gar nicht soll es sich in der Unendlichkeit aller denkbaren begrifflichen Unterscheidungen und Kreuzklassifikationen verlieren. In der Praxis sind die Noeme daher zumindest heuristisch aus den in den zu vergleichenden Einzelsprachen vorfindbaren semantischen Unterscheidungen und Oppositionen gewonnen (z.B. Heger 1967: 54ff. u.ö.). Der notwendige Grad an Außereinzelsprachlichkeit soll dadurch gesichert werden, daß die verschiedenen semasiologisch in mehreren Sprachen als relevant für einen bestimmten Funktionsbereich ermittelten Oppositionen miteinander kreuzklassifiziert werden, so daß jede potentiell relevante Kategorie auch tatsächlich in dem noematischen System vorgesehen ist.

In Teilbereichen lassen sich auch Eingangskategorien bestimmen, deren außereinzelsprachlicher Status per se relativ plausibel ist, etwa bei anthropologischen Universalien wie den Verwandtschaftsbeziehungen oder bei gewissen logischen Kategorien. Dies gilt nicht zuletzt auch für die Bereiche, die den Kommunikationsvorgang und seine Modalitäten selbst betreffen (z.B. Personaldeixis, Modalität, Illokutionstypen, referenzielle Definitheit, Aktantenschema). Als noematisch gelten können somit auch solche Kategorien, die in einer apriorischen Reflexion über den begrifflichen Zusammenhang bestimmt werden können.

Auf die so gewonnenen Schemata potentieller Oppositionen lassen sich die jeweils (semasiologisch) eruierten einzelsprachlichen semantisch-paradigmatischen Oppositionssysteme abbilden („onomasiologische Abbildung", 1983: § 1.4).

Noematische Systeme sind also theoretisch zwar außereinzelsprachlicher Natur; tatsächlich sind sie aber mit Blick auf die zu beschreibenden Strukturen der zu vergleichenden Sprachen konstruiert. Es versteht sich, daß die Forderung nach beliebiger Kreuzklassifizierbarkeit noematischer Strukturen auch ein prinzipiell unendliches System von Positionen generiert. Konkret aufgestellte noematische Systeme sind also per definitionem immer nur **Teilsysteme**. Hiermit setzt sich die Theorie von jeglichem Versuch zur Erstellung umfassender Ontologien oder Kategoriensysteme im Sinne des Porphyrischen Baumes ab (die Noematik ist entstanden in direkter Auseinandersetzung mit dem Entwurf einer exhaustiven Begriffspyramide zu lexikographischen Zwecken durch Hallig/ Wartburg 1963). Dieser nicht-ontologische Status der NT bedeutet auch, daß Noeme dem Anspruch nach zwar **außereinzelsprachliche**, keineswegs aber **außersprachliche** Kategorien sind (Heger 1967: 531 ff.). Die ursprüngliche Auffassung, es bei den noematischen Kategorien mit „mentalen Einheiten" (1967: 531 ff.) zu tun zu haben, wurde schnell wieder fallengelassen: NT sind rein theoretische, beschreibungsmethodisch motivierte Konstrukte ohne ontologischen oder psychologischen Status (1967: 533).

Mit dieser Konzeption von Noemen als Hilfskonstrukten für den Sprachvergleich hat die Noematik einen grundsätzlich anderen Status als die meisten anderen Ansätze, in denen übereinzelsprachliche, komponentielle Begriffsinventare zur Grundlage des Sprachvergleichs gemacht werden, wie etwa in der Theorie semantischer Universalien und Primitiva Ana Wierzbickas (1998 u.ö.): zwar fordert auch Wierzbicka semantische Primitiva und eine daraus zu entwickelnde „universally based metalanguage" als *tertium comparationis* für den typologischen Sprachvergleich (pp. 16, 22 ff., 407 f.) und für die universelle Definition grammatischer Strukturen. Allerdings sucht sie die Primitiva nicht in einem rein methodischen, abstrahierenden Definitionsverfahren, sondern sie unterstellt ihnen gleichzeitig eine reale Existenz als Entitäten der Objektsprachen, als von allen Sprachen geteilter „core" (22) semantischer Grundeinheiten, die in allen Sprachen durch atomare sprachliche Entitäten realisiert, bzw. in einer noch stärkeren Annahme, dem menschlichen Geist angeboren sein sollen (16 ff.).

Mit den Konzepten von **lexical decomposition** der 60er u. 70er Jahre, namentlich denen der Generativen Semantik (Überblick in Dowty 1979: 35 ff.) teilt die Noematik die Intention und das Interesse an der semantischen Explizierung grammatischer Strukturen und den Rückgriff auf komplexe Prädikationshierarchien. Der Unterschied liegt auch hier, neben der wesentlich subtileren Reflexion und Ausgestaltung des noematischen Ansatzes, in der übereinzelsprachlichen Zielsetzung und dem daraus resultierenden deduktiven Zugang. Gleiches gilt für die **conceptual semantics** von Ray Jackendoff (1990 u.ö.). Auch hier liegt der Unterschied im Grad der Detaillierung und theoretischen Fundierung der einzelnen Kategorien, sowie in dem grundsätzlich anderen Verständnis von der Natur der semantischen Grundeinheiten, für deren Ermittlung Jackendoff teilweise **semasiologische** Verfahren vorschlägt (cf. unten 4.4). Es wäre aber lohnend, in einer Gegenüberstellung der beiden Theorien die intuitiven Übereinstimmungen zu analysieren, die sich aus den parallelen Interessen (Beschreibung von Verbsemantik und Syntax) und aus aus der letztlich ähnlichen Heuristik ergeben.

Als generalisierende Systeme semantisch-oppositiver Positionen, auf die die Bedeutungsumfänge der jeweiligen einzelsprachlichen Kategorien abgebildet werden können, sind die NT schließlich auch vergleichbar mit den in der heutigen funktionalistischen Sprachtypologie beliebten **semantic** oder **cognitive maps**: hier wie dort geht es darum zu klären, wo die Einzelsprachen jeweils begriffliche Unterscheidungen und wo sie Neutralisierungen vornehmen, wobei die NT allerdings eher den oppositiven Aspekt zwischen den einzelnen Systemstellen zeigen sollen, während die **semantic maps** eher die Bedeutungs**nähe** der benachbarten Positionen hervorheben. Vor allem aber gilt für die **semantic maps**, daß sie das **Ergebnis** einer empirischen Untersuchung oder zumindest einer induktiven Sichtung über die Sprachen hinweg darstellen, während die NT sich zumindest theoretisch als **Ausgangspunkt** für die typologisch-empirische Untersuchung verstehen. Der Unterschied zwischen Noemen und den Kategorien der **semantic maps** entspricht damit dem von Seiler (1986: 13) aufgestellten Unterschied von **universals** und **invariants**.

3.2. Sprechakt-Spezifizierungen als Beispiel für ein Noematisches Teilsystem

Als einfaches Beispiel des Aufbaus von NT soll hier das System der **Sprechaktspezifizierungen** (≈ Illokutionstypen) dienen, das in Zusammenhang mit dem Aktantenmodell (cf. § 4) in Heger (1976: 275ff) und Heger/Mudersbach (1984: 96ff.) entwickelt wird (zu komplexeren und auch originelleren NT cf. unten § 5). Getreu den Prinzipien der Noematik werden die illokutiven Kategorien ausschließlich aus einer Reflexion über den Kommunikationsvorgang und dessen Instanzen, und aus der Kreuzklassifikation der so gesetzten Prämissen definiert. Prämissen des Systems sind:

a) Die Kategorie der **Assertion**, definiert als die Äußerung einer kommunikativen Intention, die darin besteht, daß der Sprecher für das Zutreffen der geäußerten Proposition die **kommunikative Regreßpflicht** übernimmt und sie damit auch zur Disposition für Zustimmung oder Widerspruch stellt.

b) Die Möglichkeit, in einem Sprechakt die Assertion zu unterlassen, in Erwartung einer späteren Nachlieferung.

c) Die Frage, ob die Nachlieferung der Assertion von dem Sprecher, von dem Hörer oder einer dritten Person erwartet wird.

d) Die Alternative zwischen einer sprachlichen Nachlieferung und einer nichtsprachlichen, letztere in Form der „Herbeiführung des dem propositionalen Gehalt extensional entsprechenden Zustandes oder Vorganges in dem in Frage stehenden Denotata-Bereich" (Heger 1976: 280; cf. das Kriterium der „Anpassungsrichtung Welt-Worte" bei Searle 1977).

e) Die Möglichkeit zur Negation der Aufforderung zur Nachlieferung der Assertion, frei kombinierbar mit der Möglichkeit zur Negation der Proposition.

Die Alternativen c und d ergeben sich nur bei der positiven Wahl der in b beschriebenen Möglichkeit. Ihre Kreuzklassifikation ergibt das folgende Schema (Heger 1976: 281; Heger/Mudersbach 1984: 96):

Assertion nachzuliefern von: in Form:	Sprecher OE	Hörer ŌE	ŌĒ
sprachlich:	vom Sprecher zu beantwortende rhetorische Frage INRH	Frage INT	unbeantwortbare rhetorische Frage INOP
nichtsprachlich:	Versprechen, Zusage, Drohung, etc. PROM	Bitte, Befehl, Verbot, etc. IMP	Wunsch OPT

Abb.: 25.2

Weiter lassen sich auf jede der so gewonnenen Kategorien die in e beschriebenen Alternativen anwenden, was zur Vervierfachung der Möglichkeiten führt. Im Fall der Illokution IMP führt das z.B. zu den 4 Subkategorien:

IMP + P: Befehl etc.
IMP + $\bar{P}$: Verbot
$\overline{IMP}$ + P: (Indifferenz)
$\overline{IMP}$ + $\bar{P}$: Erlaubnis

Weitere Differenzierungsmöglichkeiten ergeben sich, entsprechend der klassischen

Sprechakttheorie, aus dem spezifischen Verhältnis, das zwischen dem Sprecher und der die Assertion nachliefernden Instanz besteht. Bei Betrachtung von über den Einzelsatz hinausgehenden sprachlichen Ereignissen/Ereignistypen bedarf es zudem einer Darstellungsmöglichkeit für die entsprechenden Reaktionen (Antwort auf eine Frage, Ausführung eines Befehls, Erfüllung eines Versprechens ...), die im Aktantenmodell auch zur Verfügung gestellt wird.

4. Das Aktantenmodell

4.1. Allgemeines

Das Aktantenmodell (cf. besonders Heger 1976; Heger/Mudersbach 1984) ist ein Noematisches Teilsystem, das ursprünglich der universellen Definition von sprachlichen Zeichen einer bestimmten Komplexitätsebene (Ränge ≥ 4 der Signemranghierarchie, cf. 5.3) diente. Es beschreibt die Applikation von 1- u. 2-stelligen Prädikaten entweder auf terminale Referenzterme oder auf Argumente in Form rekursiv eingesetzter komplexerer Ausdrücke. Durch die rekursive Offenheit dessen, was an der Argumentstelle ('Aktant') des prädikativen Ausdrucks stehen kann, und durch die völlige Losgelöstheit der noematischen Struktur von bestimmten einzelsprachlich-syntagmatischen Operationen (wie z.B. der attributiven oder prädikativen Setzung von Adjektiven oder Verben zu Substantiven) wird die noematische Prädikat-Argument-Struktur zur generellen Form der syntagmatischen Verknüpfung begrifflich-atomarer Einheiten: in der Abbildung auf einzelsprachliche Strukturen betrifft sie gleichermaßen den internen Aufbau bestimmter Lexembedeutungen wie die Darstellung der Bedeutung komplexer sprachlicher Ausdrücke, die sich aus der syntagmatischen Verknüpfung von Lexemen ergeben, von der Wortkomposition bis hin zu komplexen Satzgefügen und noch weiter: So werden etwa die Satzjunktion, temporale, lokale, aspektuelle, modale Spezifikationen von Vorgängen, illokutive Kategorien, ja selbst die Ausweisung von Denotatabereichen zur Definition von intertextuellen Bezügen in Form von Prädikatenkonstanten dargestellt, die rekursiv auf komplexe Prädikationsstrukturen angewandt werden. Damit wird das Aktantenmodell zum zentralen Element des gesamten noematischen Theorieansatzes, weit über die Darstellung der Verb-Nomen-Beziehung hinaus.

Der Formalismus zur Konstituierung von Ausdrücken des Aktantenmodells hat in Heger/Mudersbach (1984) eine endgültige Festlegung in Form eines systematischen, konsistenten Regelwerks gefunden. Von einem 'axiomatischen' System soll nicht gesprochen werden, da es sich bei dem Formalismus, trotz aller Anklänge an prädikatenlogische Formalismen, zwar um ein Inventar zur systematischen („deduktiven") Generierung beliebig komplexer Ausdrücke handelt, der jedoch allein als Bezugssystem für die **Beschreibung** natürlichsprachlicher Ausdrücke dient, keinesfalls als Kalkül zur deduktiven Überführung von Aussagen in andere Aussagen, sei es auf primärsprachlicher, sei es auf metasprachlicher Ebene (cf. Heger 1976: Fn 116).

Zur Terminologie: das **Aktantenmodell** ist eine allgemeine Theorie über den Aufbau komplexer Bedeutungen sprachlicher Einheiten verschiedener Ebenen in Form einer Prädikationshierarchie, sowie der dazugehörige Notationsformalismus. Dieser Formalismus generiert eine offene Menge möglicher Strukturen (dargestellt zumeist in Form gerichteter hierarchischer Graphen), die, terminologisch nicht ganz konsequent, ebenfalls als **Aktantenmodelle** bezeichnet werden. Zur Problematik des Terminus 'Aktant' cf. 4.3.

Eine ursprünglich eingeführte lineare Notation solcher Modelle in Klammerform (Heger 1976) ist in Heger/Mudersbach (1984) aufgegeben.

4.2. Die wichtigsten Aufbauprinzipien

Zentrales Aufbauelement ist die Prädikation, bestehend aus einem **Prädikator**-Symbol mit Anschlußstellen für eine ein- oder zweistellige Prädikaten-Konstante (**Relator**) sowie für die entsprechende Anzahl von Argumenten (**Aktanten**), die im einfachsten Fall mit einem Referenzterm (**Referenzindikator**) besetzt sind:

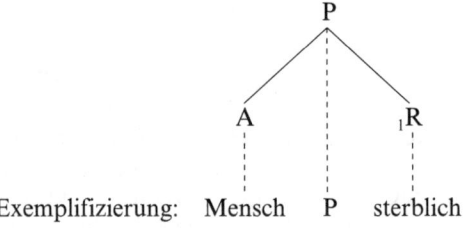

Abb. 25.3: Heger 1976: 115

2-stellige Prädikate sind zur Sicherung der richtigen Zuordnung der Argumente noch einmal intern aufgegliedert in die Angabe ei-

25. Die Hegersche Noematik

ner Relationsdimension und die genaue Spezifikation der vorliegenden Argumentfunktionen:

wandtschaft', mit den jeweils dafür relevanten Argumentfunktionen. Auch die Einführung von 1-stelligen Prädikatenkonstanten

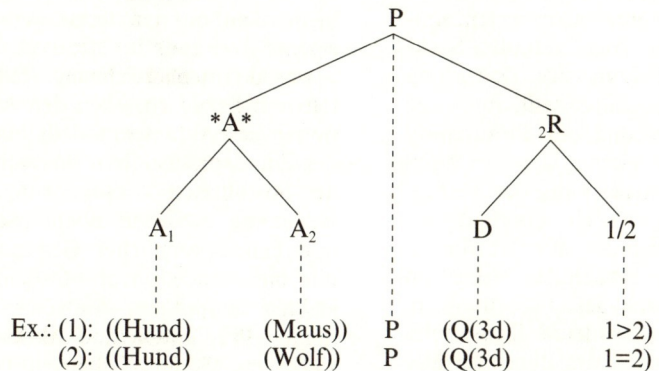

In natürlicher Sprache entsprechen diesen Exemplifizierungen die Formulierungen (1) „Hunde sind größer als Mäuse" und (2) „Hunde sind ebenso groß wie Wölfe"

Abb. 25.4: Heger 1976: 117

Obwohl das Inventar der 2-stelligen Relationenkonstanten im Prinzip offen ist, rangieren sowohl Relationsdimension als auch die zugehörigen Argumentfunktionen über ein eng umgrenztes Inventar an tatsächlich eingeführten Konstanten, deren noematischer Status durch kognitive, logische oder anthropologische Axiome etabliert ist: so etwa die logischen Relationsdimensionen 'Element-Klasse', 'Pars-Totum', 'Quantität', 'Syllogismus', 'Junktion', aber auch Dimensionen wie 'Raum', 'Zeit', 'Denotation/Referenz', 'Ver-

unterliegt im Prinzip der Forderung nach gesichertem noematischen Status. Was einzelsprachlich als drei- oder mehrstellige Relation erscheinen mag (etwa die Bedeutung dreistelliger Verben wie dt. *geben*), ist abzubilden auf komplexe Aktantenmodelle mit rekursiver Schachtelung zweistelliger Relatoren (in der folgenden Darstellung sind diese zweistelligen Relatoren in verkürzter Darstellung in den beiden *Funktor*-Symbolen 'C' 'versteckt', die jeweils zwei Prädikationen in eine − binäre − 'Kausalrelation' bringen):

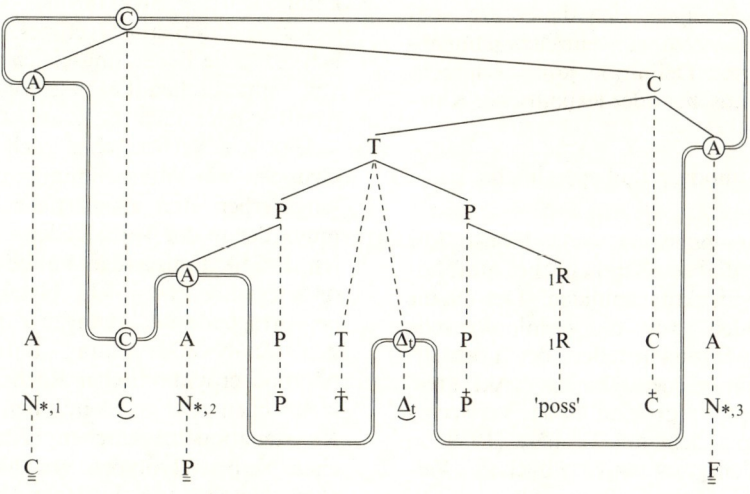

Abb. 25.5: Heger 1984: 72

Dieses Modell ist so zu lesen: „der Referent N_2 beginnt zum Zeitpunkt Δ_t verfügbar ('poss') zu sein. Diese Tatsache hat Folgen für N_3. Dies ist seinerseits die Folge des Handelns/des Zustandes von N_1", wobei es sich hierbei noch nicht um einen assertierten, sondern nur um einen ins Auge gefaßten Sachverhalt handelt. Die ingressive Bedeutung „verfügbar *werden*" ist dargestellt durch die Abfolge $\bar{P}-\overset{+}{P}$ (Doppelung der Prädikation „verfügbar" erst in negierter, dann in affirmierter Form). Die Auswirkung der Verfügbarkeit auf N_3 ist dargestellt durch dessen Stellung im Nachbereich der untergeordneten Kausalrelation C. Die ursächliche Rolle von N1 ist dargestellt durch dessen Stellung im Vorbereich der übergeordneten Kausalrelation C (für eine explizite Darstellung der hier extrem verkürzt dargestellten Kausalrelationen, in der genaugenommen nicht Aktanten, sondern nur Prädiationen in Relation gesetzt werden, cf. Heger/Mudersbach 1984: 51).

Die Doppellinie projiziert den gemeinsamen Bedeutungsumfang einzelsprachlicher Verballexeme „des Gebens" (wie dt. *geben, liefern, beliefern, verkaufen, leihen, schenken* ...) auf das Modell. Die spezifischen Bedeutungen dieser Verben ergeben sich durch die Einbettung dieses Grundmodells in weitere Prädikationen (die graphisch am oberen C anzuschließen wären), etwa zu den weiteren Folgen des dargestellten Vorgangs für die Handlungsbeteiligten (cf. Heger 1976: 162).

Wie diese Projektion einzelsprachlicher Bedeutungsumfänge auf das Aktantemodell zeigt, koinzidiert die Bedeutung einzelsprachlicher Morpheme keineswegs mit den elementaren Komponenten des Aktantenmodells. Gerade deshalb eignet sich dieses als Noematisches Teilsystem zur einzelsprachunabhängig basierten Definition je einzelsprachlicher grammatischer oder lexikalischer Kategorien (cf. 4.3).

4.3. Aktantenmodelle und sprachliche Aktanz

Die Aktantenmodelle lassen sich also nur indirekt auf die einzelsprachliche morphosyntaktische Struktur abbilden. Der Name 'Aktantenmodell' bzw. die terminologische Option, die Argumentstellen der noematischen Prädikationshierarchie als 'Aktanten' zu bezeichnen, birgt eine hohe Verwechslungsgefahr mit dem seit Tesnière (1959) in der Dependenzgrammatik üblichen Verständnis von 'Aktant' als morphosyntaktische Satzteilkategorie in den Einzelsprachen.

Hier wäre die in der Typologie gängigere terminologische Lösung (**Partizipant** = semant./noemat. Argument; **Aktant** = dessen morphosyntakt. Realisierung; cf. z.B. Lazard 1998: 12) vorzuziehen. Allerdings ist das Problem nicht nur ein termiologisches: Hegers eigener Terminus für die syntaktische Kategorie, **Aktantenbezeichnung**, stellt eine unmittelbaren Bezug zwischen den Argumentpositionen des Aktantenmodells und der Syntax der Einzelsprachen her, was sich schlecht mit der postulierten Voraussetzungslosigkeit der Beziehung zwischen noematischem System und einzelsprachlicher Grammatik verträgt und insbesondere auch mit dem oben dargestellten ubiquitären Auftreten der Komponenten **Prädikation** und **Aktant** (Argumentstelle) im Modell. Erklärbar ist die Inkonsequenz wohl dadurch, daß die Argument-Positionen des Aktantenmodells dann, wenn sie mit Referenztermen besetzt sind, auch tatsächlich in der einzelsprachlichen Realisierung nominalen Verbergänzungen entsprechen. So stellen die Aktanten-Anschlußstellen des Modells in Abb. 5, wie die doppelte Linie zeigt, auch gleichzeitig die valenziellen Anschlußstellen für Nominalausdrücke an das durch die Linie repräsentierte Verb des „Gebens" dar. Hier erweist sich die Nützlichkeit des Aktantenmodells für die Darstellung des Phänomens der Valenz: die syntaktischen Anschlußstellen eines bestimmten Verbs (oder auch von Lexemen anderer Wortarten) erscheinen nicht einfach als Leerstellen einer ansonsten opaken Verbbedeutung, sie erscheinen vielmehr motiviert und auch inhaltlich definiert durch die interne semantisch-komponentielle Struktur des verbal ausgedrückten Prädikationsgefüges. Es ist möglich, partielle Bedeutungsgleichheit innerhalb von semantischen Lexemgruppen (etwa die parallele oder auch die konverse semantische Valenz von Verben, aber auch spezifischere Gruppen wie Wahrnehmungsverben, Handlungsverben etc.) als partielle Übereinstimmung der in der Verbalbedeutung abgedeckten Prädikationsgefüge zu beschreiben. In onomasiologischer Sicht bietet das Modell hervorragende Bedingungen zur vergleichenden Analyse/Darstellung unterschiedlicher oberflächensyntaktischer Realisierungen von identischen oder teilidentischen begrifflichen Konstellationen: zwischen bedeutungsähnlichen Verben/Verbtypen verschiedener Sprachen, zwischen verschiedenen Verben/Verbtypen einer Sprache, zwischen verschiedenen diathetischen Formen eines Verbs/Verbtyps etc. (zur Valenz cf. bes. Heger 1985a: § 2.6.2).

Definiert ist damit auch die Unterscheidung zwischen **Ergänzungen** und **Angaben** (**actants** vs. **circonstants**) im Sinne der Dependenzgrammatik: Ergänzungen sind Nominalausdrücke, die solche Argumente des Aktantenmodells bezeichnen, deren Prädikation im Bedeutungsumfang des Verbs enthalten ist. Hingegen sind Angaben Ausdrücke, die neben einem Argument auch die entsprechende 2-stellige Prädikation erst an den verbal ausgedrückten Prädikationskomplex anschließen, indem sie diesen an einer ihrer Argumentstellen einbetten (zu Problemen und Differenzierungen dieser Definition cf. u. a. Heger 1991: 43 f.; 1996).

4.4. Semantische Kasus-Rollen ('Aktantenfunktionen')

Eine der wichtigsten Anwendungen des Modells ist die Definition von semantischen Kasusrollen ('Aktantenfunktionen', cf. bes. Heger 1976: 111 ff., 133 ff., 260 ff.). Hier läßt sich die Noematik eimal mehr von den eher induktiven Verfahrensweisen anderer Ansätze abgrenzen: anders als z.B. in der Kasusgrammatik der 70er Jahre in der Folge Fillmores, deren induktive Zugangsweise sich in immer wieder neuen, einander z.T. widersprechenden Vorschlägen zeigte (cf. hierzu Koch 1983), anders auch als in vielen methodisch strengeren, jedoch erklärtermaßen einzelsprachlich-induktiv vorgehenden Ansätzen wie die von Koch (1981) oder Jackendoff (1990, bes. 25 ff., 46 f., 126 ff.) gewinnt Heger seine Aktantenfunktionen wieder aus einer möglichst geringen Zahl von begrifflichen Grundpostulaten und deren Kombinatorik, wobei das daraus resultierende Inventar den Inventaren der eher empirisch begründeten Ansätze durchaus ähnelt (cf. Heger 1976: 111ff). Das Modell aus Abb. 5 zeigt die drei wichtigsten Aktantenfunktionen: die **Prädikativfunktion** (≈ OBJECT/FACTITIVE bei Fillmore 1968 oder Patiens in vielen Inventaren) ist definiert als diejenige Argumentstelle, die durch das nicht weiter spezifizierte Basisprädikat eröffnet wird, das in der rekursiven Prädikationshierarchie zuunterst steht. Die **Kausalfunktion** (≈ AGENT) ist definiert als Rolle desjenigen Aktanten, der im Vorbereich einer Kausalrelation erscheint, in die die Basisprädikation eingebettet ist (d.h. ein Aktant, der in unspezifizierter Weise an der Ursache des dargestellten Prozesses/Zustandes beteiligt ist, cf. die obige Paraphrase zu Abb.

5). Die **Finalfunktion** (≈ DATIVE bei Fillmore, in anderen Inventaren auch EXPERIENCER/ GOAL/BENEFACTIVE) ist die Rolle desjenigen Aktanten, der im Nachbereich einer Kausalrelation erscheint (d.h. ein Aktant, der in unspezifizierter Weise an der Wirkung des dargestellten Prozesses beteiligt ist; cf. ähnlich Wierzbicka 1988: 426 f. zur Bed. des Dativs). Eine weitere Differenzierung dieser Grund-Trias ergibt sich aus der Unterscheidung nach der bewußten oder unbewußten Beteiligung des Aktanten („unbewußt" + „kausal" > **Instrumentalfunktion**, „unbewußt" + „final" > **Telosfunktion**).

Aktantenfunktionen sind somit nicht allein aufgrund von Prädikatenkonstanten (hier überall die Kausalität) definiert, sondern insbesondere aufgrund der hierarchischen Gegebenheiten des zugrundeliegenden Aktantenmodells. Dies, zusammen mit den in 4.2 nur angedeuteten Präzisierungen der Kausalrelation ermöglicht es, die 'top three' (Givón 1984: 87) gängiger semantischer Rolleninventare (AGENS, PATIENS, DATIV) unter Rückgriff auf nur eine einzige Prädikatenkonstante und in sehr abstrakter Weise zu re-definieren, ohne sich dabei die Probleme einzuhandeln, die die Kasusgrammatik mit der Rückführung des Agens auf die Kausalrelation hatte (cf. Koch 1983), und auch ohne Konzessionen bei der Rigorosität der Definition, etwa in Form eines prototypischen Verständnisses von semantischen Aktantenrollen (wie z.B. Dowty 1991).

Anwendung finden die drei Grundkategorien etwa bei der rein semantischen universellen Definition von übereinzelsprachlichen valenziellen Realisierungsmustern oder Partizipationssystemen wie **Ergativität, Aktivität, Akkusativität** (Heger 1985b) bzw. den darauf operierenden **Diathesen** (z.B. Heger 1985a).

5. Weitere Anwendungen des Aktantenmodells

Das Prinzip, aus möglichst wenig Prämissen möglichst viele Kategorien zur Beschreibung sprachlicher Phänomene abzuleiten, zeigt sich in zahlreichen weiteren Definitionen, die ebenfalls auf dem Aktantenmodell aufbauen, wovon hier nur einige Beispiele gegeben werden können:

5.1. Wortarten

Die Bestimmung von bestimmten einzelsprachlichen oder übereinzelsprachlichen Lexemgruppen aufgrund der von diesen Lexemen abgedeckten Modellkomponenten (wie z.B. bei der Definition von semantischen Valenztypen, cf. 4.3) eignet sich selbstverständlich auch für weitergehende Typisierungen. In Heger (1985) wird eine matrizielle Auflistung wichtiger Komponenten des Aktantenmodells als Basis für die universell gültige Definition von Wortarten gegeben. Eine Wortart ist definiert durch die Modellkomponenten, die im Bedeutungsumfang der Wörter dieser Klasse enthalten sein müssen oder nicht enthalten sein dürfen. So ist das (finite) Verb des Dt. dadurch definiert, daß es einen einen Prädikator, einen Relator (bestimmten hierarchischen Rangs), eine temporale Spezifizierung und einen Anschluß für illokutive Spezifizierung beinhaltet, nicht aber einen Referenzindikator. Das Pro-Verb unterscheidet sich hiervon nur durch die Absenz eines Relators; Substantive beinhalten einen Referenzindikator, einen Prädikator und einen Relator (d.h, ein inhaltliches Prädikat), nicht hingegen eine temporale Spezifizierung, und keine illokutive Spezifizierbarkeit. Pronomina unterscheiden sich hiervon nur durch die Absenz eines Relators und eines Prädikators, etc.

Wortarten sind somit definiert als Konstellationen, die in je einzelsprachgrammatischen Kategorien realisiert sein können. Das Definitionsverfahren als solches ist auf jede Sprache übertragbar, wobei sich unterschiedliche Abdeckungen der Matrix ergeben.

5.2. Modalität

Durch die einfache Einführung einer einstelligen Prädikatenkonstante „Notwendigkeit" ('nec') in das Aktantenmodell gewinnt Heger (1977, 1979) aus der Kombination mit bereits vorgesehenen Modellkomponenten (Anschlüsse für Negation, Quantifikation und zeitliche Situierung an jeder Prädikationsstelle, Assertion,) nicht nur die vier klassischen Modalkategorien der 'Wahrheitstafel' („Notwendigkeit", „Möglichkeit", „Kontingenz", „Unmöglichkeit"), sondern durch Addition der Frage der Übernahme der Kommunikativen Regreßpflicht („Wissen"/ „Nicht-Wissen"/Ø sowie durch die Gegenüberstellung von Modalität und Faktualität der Proposition ein System von 28 (!) modalen Kategorien, für die sich auch einzelsprachliche Realisierungen finden lassen (so läßt sich u.a. die semantische Opposition von span *ser* vs. *estar* auf Positionen dieses Schemas abbilden); durch Einbeziehung der Quantifizierung sind diese sogar noch einmal nach Wahrscheinlichkeitsgraden differenzierbar. Der eigentliche Wert des Aktantenmodells für die Modaltheorie besteht aber in der Anschließbarkeit von Aktantenpositionen in **Kausal-** und **Finalfunktion** (cf. 4.4) an die Modalwerte: hierdurch lassen sich Möglichkeit und Notwendigkeit danach spezifizieren, wer der Garant und wer der Betroffene dieser Modalitäten ist. Je nach Besetzung dieser Aktantenpositionen lassen sich so verschieden begründete Formen der Notwendigkeit/Möglichkeit (alethisch – physikalisch – epistemisch – deontisch – verschiedene Begründungen der Deontik) darstellen; je nach hierarchischer Organisation der aktantiellen Anschlüsse lassen sich verschiedene Relativierungen der Notwendigkeit/Möglichkeit darstellen, z.B. verschiedene Begründungsebenen von „normsetzender Tätigkeit", von „Schuld", verschiedene Gültigkeitsebenen der Formulierung von „Gesetzen" (von der sozialen Gesetzgebung bis zur Formulierung wissenschaftlicher Sätze), aber auch verschiedene Formen der Infragestellung von gesetzhaften Aussagen bzw. von deren Gesetzlichkeit).

5.3. Signemranghierarchie, Textlinguistik

Ein wichtiges Ziel der Noematik und insbesondere des Aktantenmodells war die universell gültige Definition sprachlicher Zeichentypen verschiedener Komplexität. Die Zeichentypen, die in der in Heger (1976) und Heger/Mudersbach (1984) entwickelten **Signemranghierarchie** in einem *bottom-up*-Verfahren ('aszendent') definiert werden, sind teils als Präsisierung, teils als Ersetzung von z.T. notorisch schlecht definierbaren oder auch vorwissenschaftlichen Begriffen wie **free form**, **Wort**, **Proposition**, **Satz**, **Text** zu verstehen, wieder mit dem Ziel der außereinzelsprachlichen Gültigkeit und Anwendbarkeit. Dementsprechend können die bis dato 11 definierten Ränge zunehmender Zeichenkomplexität in **Lexikalische Ränge** (Monem, Autoseme Minimaleinheit, Flexionsform), **Propositionale Ränge** (Kompositionsform, einfache u. spezifizierte Satzbegriffsform), **Satzränge** (sprechaktspezifizierte, assertierte Satzbegriffsform), **Präsuppositionsgefüge und Texträngen** (spezifiziertes, text-assertiertes und spezifiziert/text-assertiertes Präsuppositionsgefüge) gruppiert werden (Heger 1990/91). Von Interesse für grammatische und typologische Fragen sind vor allem die unteren Ränge, bis hinauf zur Ebene der Präsuppositionsgefüge, auf der die möglichen Kohärenzbeziehungen zwischen Sätzen dargestellt werden können. Aus den

Komponenten des Aktantenmodells können 4 Arten solcher Beziehungen abgeleitet werden: Die **assertorische** Präsupposition definiert Relationen zwischen den Assertionswerten zweier Sätze, wie sie durch solche einzelsprachlichen Junktoren wie dt. *aber, zwar, jedoch, sondern, auch,* ausgedrückt werden. Die aktantielle Präsupposition beschreibt klassische Anaphora von Individuentermen, die **Sprecher**-Präsupposition beschreibt Kohärenzen, die sich aus den beteiligten Sprecher- und Hörer-Identitäten ergeben. Die letzte Form der Satz-Satz-Beziehung liegt bereits jenseits typologischer Interessen, ebenso wie die Notationsmöglichkeiten und Fragestellungen, die durch die Definition der höheren Ränge auf der Basis der Kombinatorik des Aktantenmodells eröffnet werden. Nur angedeutet seien hier Extensionen der Theorie in den Bereich der Textlinguistik und der Literaturwissenschaft, wo es um die formale Darstellung von Fragen geht wie komplexe Textgliederungen (z.B. Rahmenhandlung und Episoden), um metatextuelle Verhältnisse und Handlungen (Betitelung durch den Autor oder durch andere, Auftreten des Autors in seinen Texten ...) oder um intertextuelle Bezüge (Text u. Parodie, Text u. Rezension, Text u. Fortsetzungstext, Text-Œuvre eines Autors, Diskursuniversen wie sie innerhalb wissenschaftlicher Schulen oder literarischer Traditionen vorliegen) etc., all dies dargestellt mit den Mitteln des Aktantenmodells unter äußerst sparsamer Hinzufügung vereinzelter weiterer Prädikatenkonstanten (zur genaueren Darstellung cf. Raible 1972, Gülich/Raible 1977 sowie die Beispielsanalyse eines literarischen Textes in Heger 1989).

6. Kritik und Würdigung

Theorieimmanent bleibt, neben der in 4.3 schon geäußerten Detailkritik, als Monendum festzuhalten, daß der außereinzelsprachliche Charakter der Ausgangskategorien (Noeme) in vielen Fällen rein axiomatisch festgelegt ist; eine wirkliche Operationalisierung zur Gewährleistung der Außereinzelsprachlichkeit existiert, über das Verfahren der Kreuzklassifikation hinaus, nicht.

Eine übermäßige Vereinheitlichung könnte man in der Subsumierung pragmatischer, semiotischer und kommunikativer Funktionen unter dem Dach der 'Begriffe' und damit letztlich der sprachlichen **Bedeutung** sehen. So erklärt Heger (1976: 45 f.) explizit alle 3 Funktionsebenen des Bühlerschen Organonmodells zu „Bedeutung". Zwar ist unbestreitbar, daß auch nicht-propositionale Strukturen wie **Thema/Rhema**-Verteilung oder Illokutionstypen den Status von „Auszudrückendem" nicht weniger verdienen als solche propositionalsemantischen Kategorien wie Kausalität oder Verwandtschaftsbeziehungen; dennoch wird durch diese Vereinheitlichung die Beschreibung systematischer Beziehungen zwischen verschiedenen Funktionsebenen (etwa von Affinitäten zwischen bestimmten semantischen Aktantenrollen und Topikalität) erschwert. Auch systematische Erwägungen zum Wechsel der funktionalen Ebene im Rahmen von Grammatikalisierungsprozessen und die daran anschließende Frage, was überhaupt Grammatizität ausmacht, Fragen, aus denen die funktionalistische Typologie wichtige Anregungen bezogen hat, bleiben dabei außerhalb des Blicks. Insgesamt führen die für die Typologie so wichtigen Kategorien und Prozesse der Diskurspragmatik (Thema-Rhema-Gliederung/Topikalisierung u.ä.) in der Noematik ein Schattendasein: die notationelle Möglichkeit zur Indizierung von Komponenten des Aktantenmodells mit Rhematizitätswerten sind in Heger/Mudersbach (1984) ohne Kommentar weggefallen.

Nahezu unerreicht dürfte der hohe Grad an Konsistenz des Modells sein. Mit der Abbildung von sprachlichen Phänomenen der unterschiedlichsten Art auf ein kleines Inventar formaler Darstellungselemente mit einem äußerst geringen Einsatz an Primitiva, Axiomen oder Konstanten wird das Aktantenmodell dem Prinzip der größtmöglichen 'overall simplicity' in einzigartiger Weise gerecht. Man kann allerdings in dem hohen Formalisierungsgrad der Theorie auch eine 'cartesianische' (Chomsky), d.h. die Sprache auf bestimmte Aspekte verkürzende Auffassung sehen, bzw. die Projektion einer Genauigkeit, die im Phänomen Sprache überhaupt nicht gegeben ist. Insbesondere die Empfindlichkeiten des Strukturalismus bezüglich der Definitionsgenauigkeit und Operationalisierung der herangezogenen Kategorien scheinen heute überholt durch die Anerkenntnis ungenauer, prototypikalischer oder oszillierender Kategorien und fließender Grenzen in den natürlichen Sprachen. Zwar ist die Noematik vor dem Vorwurf der unangemessenen Projektion von Genauigkeit, wie überhaupt vor dem häufig an den Strukturalismus gerichteten Vorwurf der Hypostasierung ihrer Beschreibungskategorien im Prinzip gefeit, da sie sich ja nicht als semantische Beschreibung, sondern als rein theoretisches Konstrukt, eben als *tertium comparationis* im Sprachvergleich versteht. Insofern wäre auch zu fragen, ob die indirekt auf die Noematik beziehbare Kritik von Wierzbicka (1996: 9 ff. u.ö) und Goddard (1998: 66 ff.) an zu abstrakten Kategorien in semantischen Metasprachen tatsächlich auf **Metasprachen** anwendbar ist, soweit diese sich als reine methodische Hilfsmittel ohne jeden sprachlichen Status verstehen.

Dennoch liegt hier wohl das wichtigste Versäumnis der Theorie: die oft recht scholastisch, teilweise auch mechanistisch anmutenden Versuche, die einmal aufgestellten noematischen Kategorien auch tatsächlich in den semantischen Kategorien der Einzelsprachen wiederzufinden, haben Heger wiederholt den Vorwurf eingetragen, die Strukturen der Einzelsprachen in ein Prokrustesbett zwängen zu wollen (z.B. Koch 1983). Insgesamt gibt es in der Noematik eine starke Bevorzugung apriorischer Aussagen gegenüber der Offenheit für empirische Entdeckungen. Symptomatisch ist hier die fast völlige Ausblendung der Frage nach der **Grammatikalisierung**, dem diachronen Gegenstück zur Typologie. Ebenfalls fast völlig absent ist bei Heger die Einbeziehung sprachlicher Prototypikalität (mit Ausnahme einiger Aussagen zur universellen Definition von Wortarten bei Heger 1985: 164ff), die sich in der Funktionalen Typologie zu einem der wichtigsten Konzepte bei der Definition übereinzelsprachlicher grammatischer Kategorien und universeller Tendenzen entwickelt hat, zumeist in Form der sogenannten **implicational hierarchies**. Der Grund dafür ist, daß die Noematik (ähnlich wie im Ansatz von H. Seiler, cf. z.B. Seiler 1986: 13 f.) das Universelle per definitionem in den zu lösenden Aufgaben situiert und auf der Seite der Lösungsmöglichkeiten, d. h. der Ausdrucksstrukturen a priori nur die einzelsprachliche Vielfalt erwartet. Symptomatisch hierfür ist die Definition der Kategorie Subjekt in Heger (1982): völlig entgengesetzt zu prototypisch-universalistischen Subjektdefinitionen (wie z.B. Keenan 1976) gibt Heger hier eine klassifikatorisch-exklusive Definition (Subjekt als der einzige Aktant, mit dem das Verb kongruiert), wobei die Reduktion des Subjektbegriffs auf ein einziges, rein formales Kriterium nicht als Mangel, sondern gerade als Vorteil angesehen wird, und wobei in Kauf genommen wird, daß die Definition nur auf eine sehr reduzierte Zahl von Sprachen anwendbar ist. Vergeben wird dadurch allerdings ein zentrales, wenn nicht das zentrale Anliegen der Sprachtypologie, nämlich in der arbiträren einzelsprachlichen Vielfalt die großen Linien, Tendenzen und Optionen, die distributiven Restriktionen und die statistischen Kookkurrenzen unterschiedlicher Kategorien zu konstatieren und vor allem funktional zu erklären: interessanter als eine „wasserdichte" Subjektdefinition für die SAE-Sprachen ist ja die Feststellung, daß das Kriterium der Verbkongruenz über die Sprachen hinweg zwar nicht notwendigweise, aber mit großer Signifikanz kookkuriert mit den anderen von Keenan invozierten Kriterien wie anaphorischer Akzessibilität, Thematizität etc., sowie die Schlüsse, die hieraus über das Funktionieren von Sprache zu ziehen sind.

Insofern ist der in 3.1 gezogene Vergleich zwischen den **semantic maps** der Funktionalen Typologie und den Noematischen Teilsystemen noch etwas zu nuancieren: obwohl die NT ja, anders als die **semantic maps**, nicht Ergebnis sondern theoretisch den Ausgangspunkt einer typologischen Untersuchung darstellen sollen, sieht auch die Noematik ihr Ziel letztlich mehr in der Erstellung als in der Anwendung der NT, weil sie mehr an der Klärung der theoretischen Voraussetzungen für den Sprachvergleich als an dessen tatsächlicher Durchführung interessiert ist. An diesem Punkt ist also ein Desiderat, gleichzeitig aber auch ein noch ungenutztes Potential der Noematik zu sehen: gerade die Noematischen Systeme eignen sich mit ihrer Definitionsstrenge hervorragend als Ausgangspunkt für die Feststellung übereinzelsprachlicher empirischer Tendenzen zu Kategorienkookkurrenz (wie etwa bei der prototypischen Transitivität oder beim prototypischen **subject assignment**) und damit auch für die Definition von induktivempirisch zu verstehenden, prototypischübereinzelsprachlichen Kategorien wie Subjekt, Transitivität etc.

Auch wenn bei der Noematik der letzte Schritt der empirischen Anwendung noch großteils aussteht, ist der Aufstellung Noematischer Teilsysteme ein wissenschaftlicher Erkenntniszuwachs natürlich nicht abzusprechen; er liegt nicht zuletzt in dem hohen heuristischen Wert des kombinatorischen Verfahrens: positive Kehrseite des scholastischen und oft so unrealistisch anmutenden kreuzklassifizierenden Prinzips ist, daß es immer wieder Kategorien 'generiert', die der direkten Intuition nicht zugänglich sind, die aber beim Versuch der Anwendung auf die Einzelsprachen oft überraschende Beschreibungsperspektiven eröffnen. Insbesondere in den Theorien zur Modalität und zu den textuellen Bezügen dürften noch ungehobenen Schätze schlummern, deren Hebung auch heute noch äußerst gewinnbringend wäre.

Schließlich entbindet uns die Anerkennung der fuzziness primärsprachlicher Kategorien nicht von der Verpflichtung zu möglichst genauen Beschreibungskategorien, auf deren Basis gerade die Ungenauigkeit zum Thema gemacht werden kann. Angesichts der Leichtfertigkeit, mit der in Typologie und Kognitiver Linguistik bisweilen intuitive Konzepte oder induktive Befunde zu theoretischen Konstrukten erhoben werden, kann die gedankliche Selbstkontrolle, mit der Heger zahlreiche überkommene grammatische und andere Kategorien einer Dekonstruktion und einer anschließenden Rationalen Rekonstruktion unterworfen hat, bis heute ein Vorbild sein.

7. Zitierte Literatur

Croft, William. 1990. *Typology and Universals*. Cambridge: CUP.

Dik, Simon C. ³1981. *Functional Grammar*. Dordrecht: Foris.

Dowty, David. 1979. *Word Meaning and Montague Grammar*. Dordrecht etc.: Reidel.

Dowty, David. 1991. „Thematic Proto-Roles and Argument Selection". *Language* 67: 565–619.

Fillmore, Charles. 1968. „The Case for Case". In: Bach, Emmon & Harms, Robert T. (eds.). *Universals in Linguistic Theory*. New York: Holt, Rinehart and Winston, 1–88.

Fillmore, Charles. 1971. „Some Problems for Case Grammar". In: O'Brien, Richard (ed.). *Report on the 22nd Annual Round Table Meeting on Linguistics and Language Studies*. Georgetown: Univ. Press, 35–56.

Givón, Talmy. 1984. *Syntax. A Functional-Typological Introduction*. Vol. 1, Amsterdam/Philadelphia: Benjamins.

Goddard, Cliff. 1998. *Semantic Analysis*. Oxford: Oxford University Press.

Gülich, Elisabeth & Raible, Wolfgang. 1977. *Linguistische Textmodelle*. München: Fink.

Hallig, Rolf & Wartburg, Walther v. ²1963. *Begriffsystem als Grundlage für die Lexikographie*. Berlin: Akademie-Verlag.

Heger, Klaus. 1963. *Die Bezeichnung temporal-deiktischer Begriffskategorien im französischen und spanischen Konjugationssystem*. Tübingen: Niemeyer.

Heger, Klaus. 1966. „Valenz, Diathese, Kasus". In: *Zeitschrift für Romanische Philologie* 82: 138–170.

Heger, Klaus. 1967. „Temporale Deixis und Vorgangsquantität ('Aspekt' und 'Aktionsart')". *Zeitschrift für Romanische Philologie* 83: 512–582.

Heger, Klaus. 1976. *Monem, Wort, Satz und Text*. Tübingen: Niemeyer.

Heger, Klaus. 1977. „Modalität und Modus". *Zeitschrift für Romanische Philologie* 93: 1–16.

Heger, Klaus. 1979. „Modalität und Modus II", *Zeitschrift für Romanische Philologie* 95: 382–397.

Heger, Klaus. 1982. „Nominativ – Subjekt – Thema". In: Heinz, Sieglinde & Wandruszka, Ulrich (eds.). *Fakten und Theorien. Beiträge zur romanischen und allgemeinen Sprachwissenschaft, Festschrift für Helmut Stimm zum 65. Geburtstag*. Tübingen: Narr, 87–93.

Heger, Klaus. 1983. „Zum Verhältnis von Semantik und Noematik". In: Stimm/Raible (eds.). 40–44.

Heger, Klaus. 1985a. *Flexionsformen, Vokabeln und Wortarten*. (Abhandl. d. Heidelb. Akad. d. Wiss., Phil.-hist. Klasse, 1985/1). Heidelberg: Winter.

Heger, Klaus. 1985b. „Akkusativische, ergativische und aktivische Bezeichnung von Aktantenfunktionen". In: Plank, Frans (ed.). *Relational Typology*. Berlin/New York: De Gruyter, 109–129.

Heger, Klaus. 1989. „Text Coherence in a Dialogical Presuppositional Group: Chapter XXXI of Unamuno's 'Niebla'". In: Heydrich, Wolfgang et al. (eds.). *Connexity and Coherence – Analysis of Text and Discourse*. Berlin/New York: De Gruyter, 41–99.

Heger, Klaus. 1990/91. „Noeme als Tertia Comparationis im Sprachvergleich". *Romanistisches Jahrbuch* 49/50: 6–30.

Heger, Klaus. 1991. „Vom Stemma zum Aktantenmodell". In: Koch, Peter & Krefeld, Thomas (eds.). *Connexiones Romanicae*. Tübingen: Niemeyer, 41–49.

Heger, Klaus. 1996. „Zum Problem der Gegenüberstellung von 'actants' und 'circonstants'". In: Gréciano, Gertrud & Schumacher, Helmut (eds.). *Lucien Tesnière – Syntaxe structurale et opérations mentales*. Tübingen: Niemeyer, 203-209.

Heger, Klaus & Mudersbach, Klaus. 1984. *Aktantenmodelle. Aufgabenstellung und Aufbauregeln*. (Abhandl. d. Heidelb. Akad. d. Wiss., Phil.-hist. Klasse, 1984/4) Heidelberg: Winter.

Jackendoff, Ray. 1990. *Semantic Structures*. CambridgeMa/London: MIT Press.

Keenan, Edward. 1976. „Towards a Universal Definition of 'Subject'". In: Li, Charles (ed.). *Subject and Topic*. New York etc.: Academic Press, 303–333.

Koch, Peter. 1981. *Verb – Valenz – Verfügung. Zur Satzsemantik und Valenz französischer Verben am Beispiel der Verfügungs-Verben*. Heidelberg: Winter.

Koch, Peter. 1983. „Kasus zwischen Prokrustesbett und Hexerei". In: *Zeitschrift für französische Sprache und Literatur* 93: 225–257.

Lazard, Gilbert. 1989. „Définition des actants dans les langues européennes". In: Feuillet, Jack (ed.). *Actance et valence dans les langues de l'Europe*. Berlin/New York: Mouton de Gruyter, 11–146.

Lehmann, Christian. 1989. „Language Description and General Comparative Grammar", In: Graustein, Gottfried & Leitner, Gerhard (eds.). *Reference Grammars and Modern Linguistic Theory*. Tübingen: Niemeyer, 133–162.

Ogden, Charles K. & Richards, Ivor A. 1949. *The Meaning of Meaning*. New York/London: Routledge/Kegan Paul.

Pottier, Bernard. 1964. „Vers une sémantique moderne". *Travaux de Linguistique et de Littérature* 2.1: 107–137.

Raible, Wolfgang. 1972. *Satz und Text – Untersuchungen zu vier romanischen Sprachen*. Tübingen: Niemeyer.

Raible, Wolfgang. 1983. „Zur Einleitung". In: Stimm/Raible (eds.), 1–24.

Searle, John R. 1977. „A classificaton of illocutionary acts". In: Rogers, A. & Wall, B. & Murphy, J.P. (eds.). *Proceedings of the Texas Conference on Performatives, Presuppositions and Implicatures, Arlington: Center for Applied Linguistics*, 27–45.

Seiler, Hansjakob. 1986. *Apprehension: Language, Object, and Order*. Vol. III. Tübingen: Narr.

Stimm, Wolfgang & Raible, Wolfgang (eds.). 1983. *Zur Semantik des Französischen, Beiträge zum Regensburger Romanistentag 1981*. Wiesbaden: Steiner.

Tesnière, Lucien. ¹1959. *Eléments de syntaxe structurale*. Paris: Klincksieck.

Wierzbicka, Ana. 1988. *The Semantics of Grammar*. Amsterdam: Benjamins.

Wierzbicka, Ana. 1996. *Semantics: Primes and Universals*. Oxford: OUP.

Daniel Jacob, Ludwig-Maximilians-Universität München (Deutschland)

26. Russian works on linguistic typology in the 1960–1990s

1. Morphological typology
2. St.-Petersburg school of grammatical typology: diathesis and voice
3. Isaak S. Kozinsky's works on typology and universals
4. Aleksandr E. Kibrik and functionalism in typology
5. Other trends in research
6. References

The extensive body of literature on linguistic typology produced in Russia during the last decades cannot be adequately presented in a short survey. We focus here on a few research fields and authors in which and by whom we believe the most impressive results have been obtained. They are: morphological typology (§ 1), the works of St.-Petersburg, or Leningrad school of grammatical typology on diathesis and voice (§ 2), Isaak Š. Kozinsky's works on typology and universals (§ 3), and works by Aleksandr E. Kibrik (§ 4). In § 5, we list a few other topics and authors' names that may be of interest for the reader. Publications in the Russian language will be our main concern here; some works published originally or translated into English will be given only a brief mention.

1. Morphological typology

It is customarily acknowledged that the first typological classifications of the world's languages, or, more exactly, different versions of one and the same classification, were successively suggested as early as in the beginning of the 19th century by several German scholars. The base for the classification was the structure of the word, or more precisely, the type of morpheme arrangement in languages. This aspect of morphological typology is sometimes called 'morphemics' (*morfemika* in Russian). After the work of Friedrich von Schlegel (1808), August Wilhelm von Schlegel (1818), Wilhelm von Humboldt (1836), August Schleicher (1859), Friedrich Müller (1876), and some others, it has become a widespread view that, apart from genetic classification, languages can be divided into at least three typological classes: FLECTIVE, AGGLUTINATIVE, and AMORPHOUS, or ISOLATING. Two more labels, ANALYTICAL and SYNTHETICAL, were also used, although less uniformly.

In spite of many attempts, of which those by Edward Sapir (1921 → art. 20) and Joseph H. Greenberg (1960; → art. 23) are probably the best known, to replace this three-valued classification with a set of more flexible multi-valued parameters, the traditional labels have stood the test of time, and their very persistence, after almost 200 years of thoroughgoing criticism, has become itself a fact that needs explanation. Most Russian typologists have always believed that the morphological classes are basically adequate and need only revision and clarification. In his seminal paper of (1965), Sergej E. Jaxontov emphasized that "the traditional and most widespread morphological classification of languages, i.e. their division into flective, agglutinative and amorphous, still holds its scientific value" (1965: 93).

1.1. Analyzing the types: Two groups of features

Summarizing the traditional views on morphological types, Isaak Š. Kozinsky, in his posthumously published note (Kozinskij 1995) outlined two groups of distinctive features. The first group included:

(1) if there is no assimilation on morpheme boundaries, or if such assimilation is motivated by phonological factors only, it is a characteristic of AGGLUTINATION (*aggljutinacija*); if the boundary cohesion effects cannot be predicted from phonology, the language displays FUSION, which is a characteristic of the FLECTIVE type (*flektivnost'*); → art. 49;

(2) phonologically unmotivated changes within roots ([+flective], [−agglutinative]);

(3) phonologically and/or semantically unmotivated difference of grammatical markers for different classes of stems; in other words: many inflectional classes with no or little semantic and/or phonetic background ([+flective], [−agglutinative]);

(4) markers that denote only one single grammatical meaning are [+agglutinative]; syncretistic markers that denote e.g. case, number and gender simultaneously, or person and tense simultaneously, are ([+flective]).

The second group of features concerns the role of synthetic wordforms. Synthetic wordforms, i.e. combinations of roots and grammatical markers within a single word, can be used for:

(5) cross-categorial derivation, e.g. formation of nouns from verbs etc.;

(6) intra-categorial derivation (nouns from nouns etc.);

(7) nominal inflection not related to government (number, definiteness, semantic cases like vocative etc.);

(8) inflection of agreement targets;

(9) inflection and derivation of verbs and other predicate words not related to agreement (aspect, tense, voice, etc.);

(10) inflection of nominals motivated by government (syntactic cases).

If a language exhibits (10), it is called SYNTHETICAL (*sintetičeskij*), if it lacks (10), it is called ANALYTICAL (*analitičeskij*), irrespective of what values the other features take, cf. LATIN vs. SPANISH, RUSSIAN vs. BULGARIAN etc. If a language also lacks (7)−(8), it is usually called ISOLATING (*izolirujuščij*). An isolating language that employs functional words more extensively than morphological markers and in which there is no clearcut distinction between functional and notional words, is called AMORPHOUS.

Kozinsky did not comment on his explication of the traditional notions, or, more exactly, of their current use based partly on linguists' intuition, but he was obviously of the opinion that such an unbalanced classification based on non-elementary, or apparently random, distinctive features needed revision. In particular, it is important for the morphological typology to inquire into the correlation of the features listed in (1)−(4), and if they do really correlate within available samples of languages, to find an explanation for this.

1.2. Sergej E. Jaxontov on isolation and agglutination

Jaxontov, in his (1965) paper, divided morphemes into NOTIONAL MORPHEMES, or ROOTS, and FUNCTIONAL (*služebnye*, lit: 'service') MORPHEMES based on distributional criteria. He assumed further that any functional morpheme is dependent on, or linked to, some root. Functional morphemes that cannot be separated from their roots by any other root are called AFFIXES, those that can be so separated are called PARTICLES. Words that can be linked simultaneously to more than one root also belong to the latter class and are called CONJUNCTIONS.

Affixes can be characterized as FLECTIVE or AGGLUTINATIVE. Flective affixes can denote two, three, or more grammatical categories simultaneously, e.g. Russ. *-a* in *rek-a* 'river' denotes singular and nominative; *-u* in *nes-u* 'I am carrying' denotes the 1st person, singular, and present. An agglutinative affix denotes a value of one single grammatical category. Cf. the declension of the word denoting 'house' in RUSSIAN (*dom*) and in TURKISH (*ev*):

	singular		plural	
	RUSS.	TURK.	RUSS.	TURK.
NOM	*dom*	*ev*	*dom-á*	*ev-ler*
GEN	*dóm-a*	*ev-in*	*dom-óv*	*ev-ler-in*
DAT	*dóm-u*	*ev-e*	*dom-ám*	*ev-ler-e*

Tab.: 26.1 Flective vs. agglutinative affixes

Probably the most important observation made by Jaxontov is that the agglutinative affix is consistently opposed to the lack of any affix, whereby the lack of an affix conveys a meaning that is in some sense 'basic': e.g. in TATAR, a TURKIC language of the Volga area, the plural nominal suffix *-lar* (*at-lar* 'horses') is opposed to zero singular (*at* 'horse').

Among the number forms, the zero form denotes singular; in the case paradigm, it is the marker of nominative; among the person markers, of the 3rd person; among the voice markers, of the active voice; present tense (e.g. in KOREAN or HUNGARIAN), positive degree in adjectives etc. There are no zero forms opposed to agglutinative affixes that mean, for instance, the dative case, or the past tense (→ art. 32 on Markedness).

With flective affixes, on the contrary, such cases are normal, e.g. in RUSSIAN *ryb-Ø* 'fishes (gen. pl.)', *nes-Ø* 'carried' (past tense). The meaning of a form without the agglutinative affix may be very broad and indefinite, cf. subject and object functions of the zero 'nominative' in TURKIC languages (→ art. 122), or forms without the plural marker *-men* in CHINESE that are underspecified with respect to singular and plural; the same holds true for the plural markers in TURKIC languages. On the contrary, the meaning of zero flective affixes cannot be predicted in a similar way. Jaxontov, however, did not try to explain this strongly attested correlation between the lack of phonologically expressed affix and the 'basic' and unmarked meaning in agglutinative systems.

Flective languages are those in which flective affixes prevail, and an agglutinative language is such where agglutinative affixes are typical. Jaxontov noted that "a language in which particles prevail over affixes is called ANALYTICAL, if the language is European, or AMORPHOUS, if it is spoken in Asia, Africa, or Australia" (p. 97).

Agglutinative and analytical (amorphous) languages have one thing in common: in them, a word has a basic form. In those languages a word is an observable object, whereas in flective languages it is an abstract: in real speech, only wordforms can be observed. Genuine zero affixes can only be postulated for languages in which words obligatorily consist of stems and endings, i.e. in flective languages — like zero subject can be postulated only for languages that have the subject vs. predicate opposition for most clauses.

Meanings of grammatical categories may be notional or syntactic: the latter denote syntactic relations and include those 1) of cases, 2) of dependent verbal forms like infinitives, participles, converbs, and 3) the target agreement categories like gender in adjectives, number in verbs etc. (Jaxontov 1975: 107).

Flective and agglutinative languages are non-isolating, since in them syntactic relations are expressed by affixes and partly by function words (particles), and not only by particles and word order, as it is the case with isolating languages. Therefore, in some cases the class to which a language belongs will be determined solely by where word boundaries are traced. For example, if case particles and auxiliaries in the TIBETAN language are separate words, the language is isolating; if they are affixes, the language must be labelled agglutinative.

Later, in his paper of (1977), Jaxontov pointed out that for some languages his criterion of particles vs. affixes, i.e. the separability from the root, yielded an undesirable result. These are languages in which the word order consistently places notional dependents on the one side of the head, and affixes and particles on the other side of it. Instances of this type are TURKIC and DRAVIDIAN languages that employ suffixes only and place all notional dependents to the left of their heads.

For TURKISH, it can be assumed that syntactic markers are not attached to the head of a phrase, but to the whole phrase: *büyük ev* '[a] big house'; *[büyük ev]-in* 'of a big house', *[büyük ev]-e* 'in a big house', *[büyük ev]-deki* 'one who is inside a big house' etc.

According to the standard test to distinguish between an affix and a particle, these markers are affixes, because all notional modifiers (i.e. those containing a root) invariably precede the head noun and cannot be inserted between it and its particles. On the other hand, it is usually assumed that particles, and not affixes, are normally employed with phrases.

A counterpart to TURKISH is probably THAI in which prepositions cannot be separated from the following nouns by any notional material; however, there are postposed function morphemes in THAI too, e.g. directionals. Jaxontov called the languages of this type that defy classification in terms of 'isolating' vs. 'agglutinative' LANGUAGES WITH INSEPARABLE PARTICLES.

There is a continuum with two extremities, one of which are languages with inseparable particles, and another are isolating languages. In between are languages like JAPANESE or EVENKI (TUNGUS-MANCHU family) in which but very few notional words can be inserted between a word and its particle. In JAPANESE, it is, e.g., *dake* 'only': *Nihon-dake-de* [Japan-only-LOC] 'only in Japan', in EVENKI: *knige-rikte-l* [book-only-PL], 'only books'.

In TIBETO-BURMAN languages, some modifiers such as adjectives, numerals and demonstratives, can be inserted between a noun and its grammatical markers, e.g. in TIBETAN: *mi sangpo-nam-la* [person good-PL-DAT] 'to good people', *mi nyi:-la* [person two-DAT] 'to the two people'. In BURMESE, some postverbal markers traditionally called suffixes like *koun* 'completely', *pjan* 'more' and some others can be regarded as separate words inserted between a verb and markers of its syntactic function (Jaxontov 1977: 35).

Agglutinative languages in which, like in flective languages, functional morphemes are unambiguously affixes, stand apart from this continuum. To this group belong languages with a less fixed word order like GEORGIAN or FINNISH, or with elaborate agreement in which affixes are attached to every word in a phrase like SWAHILI.

In his (1991) paper, Jaxontov invoked a well-known distinction between FREE and BOUND MORPHEMES. Morphemes that can be used as a separate utterance are free, those that cannot are bound. Most functional morphemes and roots in flective languages are bound (under the assumption of zero affixes). In non-flective languages, there are bound roots too: e.g. in CHINESE many nouns denoting material objects must obligatorily include the suffix *-zi*; nominal roots without *-zi* may be used as parts of compounds and idioms but not as a separate utterance. However, in non-flective languages, it is normal that roots are free.

Here we can but briefly mention a monograph on morphological typology (Kasevič & Jaxontov [eds.] 1982) in which data from 26 languages of Asia and Africa were thoroughly investigated within a framework of a quantitative study much more advanced in comparison to the pioneer work by Greenberg (1960). In his summarizing article in the volume, Jaxontov (1982) concludes that according to quantitative measuring ISOLATING and AGGLUTINATIVE languages form two homogeneous classes, but FLECTIVE languages are much less consistent. "In general, quantitative data rather confirm than refute the traditional classification" (Jaxontov 1982: 323).

1.3. Vladimir M. Alpatov and Nina V. Solnceva: Isolation and fusion parameters

In his book on the structure of grammatical units in JAPANESE (1979), and in his (1985) paper specially addressing the issue of morphological classification, Vladimir M. Alpatov claimed that the main difference between flective and agglutinative types lies in the kind of the 'grammatical word' mostly employed in a given language.

In flective languages, WORDFORMS$_1$, or flective words, are widely attested. Those are words containing affixes that are attached with fusion, i.e. have variants not predictable phonologically, e.g. in JAPANESE the past markers *-ta* and *-da* are chosen by different verb stems, or the root allomorphs *yon-* and *yom-* 'read' are distributed with respect to affixal morphemes that follow them. With these affixes, the morpheme boundary is often ambiguous. Alpatov calls such cohesive affixes FLEXIONS (*fleksii*).

In agglutinative languages, however, flective words are much less frequent than WORDFORMS$_2$ that consist of a stem and a string of grammatical non-cohesive markers, i.e. those that do not undergo phonologically unmotivated variation. Alpatov calls such markers FORMANTS. Formants can be separated from the stem by other function morphemes but not by notional words. A typical instance of formants are the so-called JAPANESE *ganio* markers — a class of markers that follow the nominal stem and express case meanings (*ganio* is the traditional term for this class of markers composed from their three representatives: *-ga* nominative, *-ni* dative, and *-o* accusative). Formants, but not flexions, can have a non-fixed order: both *-dake-ni* 'only-to' and *-ni-dake* are permissible and identical in meaning.

Some researchers of JAPANESE consider formants to be affixes, others claim that they are separate function words; it is worth noting that many of the former are native speakers of RUSSIAN, and many of the latter are ENGLISH speakers. Instead, Alpatov claims that "in the system of language, there are no 'wordforms', but units belonging to two different classes which we will call 'wordforms$_1$' and 'wordforms$_2$'. Notional wordforms$_1$ contain stems and flexions, notional wordforms$_2$ contain stems, flexions and formants" (Alpatov 1979: 18). Alpatov summarizes his classification as follows (ibid.: 15):

	Flexions	Formants	Function words
Are there non-phonological changes on morpheme boundaries?	yes	no	no
Is the insertion of lexical units possible?	no	no	yes

Tab.: 26.2 Morphological classification according to Vladimir M. Alpatov

Alpatov listed 8 logically possible combinations of these features in a language and pointed out that some language types are unattested, e.g. languages that employ only flexions, only function words, or no grammatical morphemes at all, although there are languages that have typically only formants like the TURKIC languages, flexions and formants, like JAPANESE, or all the three classes like FRENCH or HUNGARIAN. Alpatov emphasized that the feature of fusion is more significant than others traditionally correlated with the flective and agglutinative types, because it directly indicates the type of morphological structure of the word.

It seems, however, that at least one of the types excluded by Alpatov really exists: in his discussion of the language of classical Chinese poetry, Jaxontov (1975) showed that this version of OLD CHINESE lacked any functional morphemes whatsoever; following Boris A. Uspenskij (Uspenskij 1965: 114, 116), Jaxontov called this type "completely amorphous".

Nina V. Solnceva's investigation on isolating languages (1985) is based on data from CHINESE, THAI, VIETNAMESE, KHMER and some lesser-known languages of Southeast Asia like LAHA, PUPEO (both belong to the KADAI family) and CHRU (Austronesian) that were studied within the Soviet-Vietnamese linguistic project of the 1970–80s, of which Solnceva was one of the leaders. Solnceva claimed that the languages of Southeast Asia are not at all 'amorphous': this label originated from the impression that OLD CHINESE (WENYAN), the formal language of China until the beginning of the 20th century, had made upon European linguists. MODERN CHINESE idioms and other languages of Southeast Asia do possess inflectional affixes, although the latter do not express syntactic relations.

What really distinguishes isolating from non-isolating languages is not the lack of morphology, but its special, viz. non-syntactic, character (Solncev 1995). Since no syntactic relations are expressed within a word, they are expressed outside it via word order and function words.

Some of inflectional affixes like CHINESE progressive verbal marker *-zhe*, or iterative *-go* cannot be separated from the stem by other words and therefore behave exactly as normal agglutinative affixes. Of more interest are, however, other inflectional affixes in languages of this type that can be separated from the stem by other words and phrases; Solnceva's central claim is that they are also agglutinative markers. For example, a marker of the perfective aspect can be separated from its verb by a direct object phrase:

CHAM language:
ai nan ca   lo   mu ni
he   plough this piece of ground
ploh co
PRF ?
'He ploughed this piece of ground'

SHOKCHANG dialect of KHMER:
co' rin Ibo:t comriEn no:h hoj
sing this song   PRF
'(he) sang this song'

LAHA language:
zĕn kon to'w mum
I close door PRF
'I closed the door'

In CHINESE, some adverbials also must occupy the position between the two parts of a complex verb stem, cf. *nian-shu* 'to learn, to study', lit.: 'learn-book':

CHINESE
nian-le san-nian de shu
learn-PRF three-year ATTR book
'He studied for three years'

*nian-shu-le san-nian
learn-book-PRF three-year

Solnceva emphasized that the ability of some parts of a word to be employed separately is not correlated to isolation and may be found in a language of any type. In naming this phenomenon she coined a cumbersome term "a word's common-or-separate existence" (*slitno-razdel'noe suščestvovanie slova*). A particular instance of the "common-or-separate existence" is incorporation. Solnceva also mentioned some well-known cases of affixes displaced from their stems like *the king of England's palace* – contrary to the traditional view, she regarded such cases not as morphological marking of constituents longer than a word, but as morphological marking of stems by separated affixes.

In light of this broader view on agglutination, Solnceva presented the following version of morphological classification based on two parameters: the LOCUS of marking the syntactic relations (within or outside a word) and what she called "TECHNIQUE (*texnika*) of morpheme linking" – fusion or agglutination understood as lack of fusion (p. 157):

"Technique"	Syntactic relations expressed within vs. outside the word	
	Non-isolating	Isolating
Fusion	INDO-EUROPEAN	TIBETAN
Agglutination	TURKIC	CHINESE, VIETNAMESE, KHMER etc.

Tab. 26.3: Morphological classification according to Nina V. Solnceva

Solnceva pointed out that the traditional notions of flexion vs. agglutination were based on two independent parameters. The first one was the 'technique', the second one subsumed the inherent characteristics of morphemes. CHINESE and other languages of Southeast Asia are agglutinative according to both, because the inherent characteristic, viz. the lack of syncretistic affixes, suggests the agglutinative type, as well as the 'technique'. The question whether there is any correlation between the two parameters remains open: in agglutinative languages, syncretistic affixes are also found, e.g. in JAPANESE *-gata* means 'high degree of politeness' and 'plural', whereas *-tachi* means 'plural' and 'neutral politeness' simultaneously.

The feature of 'technique' is by no means elementary. Solnceva involves several features of fusion suggested by Aleksandr A. Reformatskij (1965: 73) such as:

(1) stems do not occur without affixes;
(2) stems undergo changes;
(3) affixes have non-standard variants.

Since for instance BAHASA INDONESIA, unlike CHINESE, takes ambiguous values of (2)–(3), Solnceva characterized it as 'fusio-agglutinative', a sort of mixed-type language. She discussed also the problem addressed earlier by Jaxontov – the fact that many marked forms in isolating languages can be replaced by unmarked forms, cf. in CHINESE *ta zuotian lai* 'he came yesterday' and *ta mingtian lai* 'he will come tomorrow' where none of the temporal or aspectual markers are employed. She sees an explanation for this fact in that non-syntactic categories tend to be facultative (p. 206) – which seems to be untrue for languages of other types, however.

Later Jaxontov (1991) argued against Alpatov and Solnceva's view on agglutination pointing out that fusion is no easily distinguishable feature to base a classification on.

"If we try to distinguish between flective and agglutinative affixes according to the degree of their cohesion with their stems, we are faced to a large number of intermediate or unclear cases. There is a much more definite borderline between monosemic and syncretistic affixes" (Jaxontov 1991: 98).

Jaxontov pointed out that, for instance in the agglutinative TURKISH language the affix of the present tense *-iyor* undergoes no change after stems containing front vowels, contrary to the general rule of synharmonism: *gel-iyor* 'he comes' etc. In another TURKIC language, BASHKIR, the choice of the three allomorphs of the plural marker in nouns: *-lar*, *-dar* and *-tar*, although phonetically motivated, is not purely phonological, because other affixes beginning in *l-* in the same position do not change.

To sum up, the researchers agree in that the classes of the traditional morphological typology can be reduced to two distinct parameters: analytical vs. synthetical (syntactic relations are vs. are not expressed within the word) and agglutination vs. flexion. However, it has been a matter of debate as to which feature of agglutination is of fundamental value — the 'technique' of morpheme arrangement and the degree of cohesion (Alpatov, Solnceva), or the monosemic (nonsyncretistic) character of affixes (Jaxontov). In flective languages, the word normally consists of a stem and an affix (or affixes), whereby some affixes may have null forms — much like in syntax where a sentence may obligatorily consist of a subject phrase and a predicate phrase. In languages belonging to other types, the word, if the values of grammatical categories are semantically unmarked, normally coincides with the stem. This latter fact seems to be a serious empirical generalization that still waits for a theoretical explanation.

2. St.-Petersburg school of grammatical typology: diathesis and voice

The Leningrad — or nowadays St.-Petersburg — school of grammatical typology arose in the 1960s around the group of scholars researching structural typology in the Leningrad department of the Institute of Linguistics of the Academy of Sciences, USSR; now it is called the "group for typological studies of languages in the St.-Petersburg Institute of Linguistic Investigations" (*gruppa tipologičeskogo izučenija jazykov; Sankt-Peterburgskij Institut lingvističeskix issledovanij*). The group was founded and led by Aleksandr A. Xolodovič (1906–1977), a specialist in JAPANESE and one of the most outstanding Russian grammarians of his generation (as to his merits see Ogloblin & Xrakovskij 1990). The group included Viktor S. Xrakovskij, Vladimir P. Nedjalkov, Natalia A. Kozinceva, Elena E. Kordi, Leonid A. Birjulin, Inga B. Dolinina among others; many participants in the group's project belonged to the Leningrad State University and the Leningrad Institute for Oriental studies; there were also some participants from Moscow and other cities. (An outline of the history, methods, and results of the group's work may be found in Xrakovskij & Ogloblin 1991; Kozinceva 1991).

Since the late 1960s, the St.-Petersburg school of grammatical typology has issued a series of publications, including many individual and collective monographs that contain fundamental results in many aspects of typology, mostly of verbal categories:

- causative (Xolodovič [ed.] 1969; → art. 66);
- voice and diathesis (Xrakovskij [ed.] 1978; 1981; → art. 67–69);
- resultative (Nedjalkov [ed.] 1983) cf. especially the English version of the same book, revised and enlarged (Nedjalkov [ed.] 1988);
- constructions with sentential arguments (Xrakovskij [ed.] 1983; 1985);
- iterative (Xrakovskij [ed.] 1989) (later translated into English (Xrakovskij [ed.] 1997));
- imperative (Xrakovskij [ed.] 1992; Xrakovskij & Volodin 1980; → art. 79);
- conditional (Xrakovskij [ed.] 1998; → art. 76);
- inceptive (Nedjalkov 1987);
- reciprocal (Nedjalkov 1991 → art. 69).

Below we address probably the best known achievement of the St.-Petersburg school — its typology of diathesis and voice, and specially of passives (Xolodovič [ed.] 1974). Xolodovič and his collaborators believed that all the categories listed above belong to a universal set of grammatical meanings that show only very restricted differences across languages.

The main theoretical influences on the St.-Petersburg theory of voice and related categories were first of all the works by Lucien Tesnière (1959), and later by Charles Fillmore (1968), and an outstanding achievement in typology of verbal categories by Akaki Šanidze, the author of the fundamental description of the Georgian grammar (Šanidze 1953), to whom the book (Xolodovič [ed.] 1969) was dedicated. Published many times in GEORGIAN, Šanidze's book has never been translated into any other language, and its outstanding linguistic message, especially concerning the problem of valence-changing derivations, has unfortunately gone mostly unnoticed outside Georgia. Outlines of the group's view on diathesis and voice were first presented in Xolodovič (1970) and Mel'čuk & Xolodovič (1970), and a more elaborate version of the theory is contained in Xrakovskij (1974).

The basic notion suggested by the school for the verbal categories is that of DIATHESIS (Russ. *diateza*). It can be seen that one and the same verbal lexeme can have different subcategorization frames, or in the Russian tradition – GOVERNMENT PATTERNS (*modeli upravlenija*), i.e. different correspondences from the participants of the verb to morphosyntactic marking (cases, prepositions, agreement and word order); cf. different government patterns for a finite verb (e.g. *goes*) and its non-finite form (e.g. *going*), or for active and passive counterparts such as *builds* and *is built*. Different correspondences found between the participants of a predicate lexeme and grammatical relations like subject, direct object etc. for different wordforms of the lexeme are called DIATHESES. A diathesis that is denoted in a verb with regular morphological marking is called VOICE.

Therefore the category of voice is a formal device to mark a change of government patterns with one and the same verbal lexeme. Consider the difference in government patterns in active and passive wordforms: *The boy has written a letter* and *A letter is written by the boy*.

X (Agent)	Y (Patient)
the boy subject	a letter object

X (Agent)	Y (Patient)
by the boy *by*-phrase	a letter subject

The correlation between the two government patterns is regular: many other pairs of clauses differ exactly like those two. Since the difference is regularly marked in the verb morphology of ENGLISH, the category of voice, by definition, is present in the language. Among all diatheses, one can be distinguished as the UNMARKED (*isxodnaja*). In the unmarked diathesis,

(1) all participants of the predicate are expressed by syntactic arguments;
(2) any participant corresponds to a separate referent;
(3) the thematic roles hierarchy (Agent > Patient > Benefactive) corresponds to the hierarchy of grammatical relations (Subject > Direct object > Indirect object).

All the other diatheses except the unmarked one are called DERIVED (*proizvodnye*). The voice that corresponds to the unmarked diathesis is called ACTIVE. A derived diathesis in which the participant corresponding to the subject in the unmarked diathesis is not expressed by the subject, is called PASSIVE diathesis, and the corresponding voice is called PASSIVE VOICE.

According to the given definition, constructions without agentive phrases (*The work was finished*), as well as constructions without any subject, are passive: RUSSIAN active *My s nimi dogovor-ilis'* [we.NOM with them make-treaty-PAST] 'We made a treaty with them' vs. passive *S nimi dogovor-en-o* [with them make-treaty-PAST.PASS-3SG.NEUT] '(A treaty) was made with them'; in the latter sentence, there is no subject, and the verbal predicate *dogovor-en-o* 'treaty-was-made' shows the passive form and the default agreement (3 sg. neutr.).

The definition also does not specify how the passive construction treats the participant that is the direct object in its active counterpart. This participant may be the subject in the passive construction, or remain the direct object, or be left unexpressed. The difference between the diatheses may be expressed not only by voice forms, but also by function words or by word order, cf. OLD CHINESE *ren sha hu* 'The man kills the tiger' and *hu sha yu ren* 'The tiger is killed by the man'. In the passive construction the position of subject before the verb predicate *sha* 'kill' is occupied by the Patient *hu* 'tiger', whereas the Agent *ren* 'man' is expressed by the function word *yu* 'by'.

There are also pairs of diatheses not distinguished formally at all, e.g. infinitive clauses in FRENCH that can be used both in active and passive diatheses: *J'ai vu manger des chiens* 'I saw the dogs eating' or 'I saw the dogs being eaten', cf. also *The river abounds in fish* vs. *Fish abound in the river*.

In (Xrakovskij 1990), a calculus for the markedness of diatheses was suggested. There are languages in which the expression of an Agent in passive is impossible or restricted in use. In POLISH passive, the Patient may be the direct object in accusative, but in this construction the subject cannot be expressed and remains unspecified, e.g.: *Skradziono mu zegarek* [steal.3SG.NEUT he.DAT watch.ACC] 'His watch was stolen'. This type of passive, although not widespread, directly contradicts "Burzio's generalization" in the *Government and Binding* theory requiring that a verb may case-mark an accusative object only if it has a subject (Burzio 1986).

In ENGLISH, both direct and indirect objects may be promoted to subject in passive: *He gave me a book* vs. *A book was given to me; A book was given by him to me* vs. *I was given a book by him*.

In languages with dummy, or expletive, subject lexemes, the position of subject in the passive constructions may be occupied by such a lexeme, cf. in GERMAN *Alle Kinder tanzen* 'All children are dancing' vs. *Es wird von allen Kindern getanzt* (the same). Xrakovskij also listed some characteristic additional meanings that may be conveyed by passive constructions like resultative (*The money is stolen*), or potential (JAPANESE *kare ni ko:hi ga nom-enaj* [he DAT coffee SUBJ drink-NEG.-MOD.PASS] 'He cannot drink coffee'), etc. Passive can be combined, however, with a very restricted set of such meanings.

The methodological framework of the St.-Petersburg typological school is predominantly empirical and descriptive: their interest is mainly in finding general grammatical notions and features that may be equally employed in all languages and cover various data in a descriptively adequate way. A calculus of types on the basis of initial notions enables the researcher to find all relevant characteristics of a given category in a language under investigation. Explanatory goals may be included, but are not central.

3. Isaak Š. Kozinsky's works on typology and universals

Isaak Š. Kozinskij (1947−1992), or Isaac Kozinsky, as he spelled his name in his works published in English, addressed the typological issues most widely discussed in the 1970−1980s: ergativity, voice, word order and order of affixes, grammaticalization, grammatical relations − for a survey of his works see Testelec (1995). His outstanding contribution to linguistic typology, partly unpublished until now and mostly unnoticed by colleagues during his short lifetime, now is gradually gaining the attention it deserves.

3.1. Empirical universals: Problems of method

In his dissertation on grammatical universals (1979), Kozinsky offered several fundamental ideas that concern the methodological foundations of this research field. First, he explicitly formulated one of the principles on which the Greenbergian 'paradigm' in linguistic typology had been based: "Basic categories and notions of general linguistics elaborated mainly on the data of INDO-EUROPEAN languages ('phoneme', 'word', 'part of speech' [...], are adequate enough for description of many other languages of the world" (Kozinskij 1979: 10); universal definitions of grammatical notions "agree very well with the practice of denoting some phenomena in different languages with the same terms based on intuition [...]. Therefore non-critical use of the data from grammatical descriptions [...] can be regarded as a permissible, and, in practice, most often the only possible method" (ibid.: 31f.).

This is the fundamental assumption of any research work based on a large sample of languages − so large that a researcher has to rely mostly on data which s/he is not able to verify. This assumption proved right in the light of the subsequent discoveries in the field of grammatical typology based on large samples of languages − suffice it to mention Matthew Dryer's (1988) classification of languages into 'left-branching' and 'right-branching' types, an empirically found correlation later explained by John Hawkins (1990), or 'head-marking' and 'dependent-marking' classes of languages discovered by Johanna Nichols (1986; → articles 2, § 2.4; 29; 102).

Kozinsky made an invaluable contribution to the method of statistical verification of empirical universals. He showed that the distinction suggested by Joseph H. Greenberg between 'statistical' and 'absolute' universals is completely illusory: in fact, all empirical universals of the type first explored by Greenberg are statistical. "The claim that if some proposition is true for all languages in a representative sample, it is expected to be true with high probability for all existing languages, seems to be generally accepted in linguistics. However, nothing is easier than to demonstrate that the claim is wrong" (Kozinskij 1979: 15).

Let us take a sample consisting of 100 languages. If there is no language in the sample that lacks some characteristic X, the probability that no language outside the sample lacks the same characteristic either is very small. Indeed, if we assume that the general set of languages consists of 5,000 elements (our conclusions will not change if we assume any other number between 1,000 and 50,000), the probability that X is true for all languages, is 100/5000 = .02. Therefore the reliability of the hypothesis in question is only 2%! To obtain a 90% reliability, we have to include 90% of the world's languages in our sample — which is obviously an unfeasible task.

The only reasonable way to interpret the data is to suggest a statistical claim. In the given case it may sound as follows: with the probability 95%, there are no more than 3% of exceptions in the general set; or, if we take a higher probability of 99%, there are no more than 4,5% of languages in the general set that lack the characteristic X. Therefore, the only kind of empirical generalizations available to a researcher, who is not able to look up the data in all languages of the world or at least in their majority, are statistical universals, that is of the form: 'for the majority of languages, e.g. for 90% of them, X is true'.

Kozinsky employed standard statistical methods to test the reliability of correlational universals, i.e. of propositions that two features X and Y are non-accidentally related. As was shown by Greenberg, such correlations (implications and equivalences) are "the most numerous and instructive" (Kozinskij 1979: 17).

Kozinsky's solution of the problem of exceptions to linguistic universals (Kozinskij 1979; 1985) was one of his most important achievements. The reliability of a universal depends on several factors of which the number of exceptions is by no means decisive. The more exceptions are found, the easier is to find the INTERVENING FACTOR, i.e. a feature F which can, although not obligatorily, occur in languages that run counter to the universal U.

"Therefore, the following recommendation should not seem paradoxical: given that exceptions are found for a universal U, its formulation and the definitions of relevant features are to be suggested in such a way that the number of exceptions be maximal (certainly, if its statistical reliability is kept within an accepted limit). Afterwards it is enough to check the statistical reliability of another correlation 'U or F'. If the latter correlation proves to be reliable, F is the intervening factor in case" (Kozinsky 1979: 34).

Kozinsky used the following example in order to show how this method works. In languages that have both subject and object agreement in the verb, affixes that mark agreement with subject or object may precede the verbal stem (s-V, o-V) or follow it (V-s, V-o). In order to check whether the two features: s-V and o-V are interrelated, Kozinsky compiled a sample of 120 languages, all of which have bivalent cross-reference agreement. In the sample, 68 languages have at least one form of the o-V type, and 79 languages have at least one s-V form. Under the assumption that the two features are independent (the null hypothesis), the most probable number of languages that have both o-V and s-V, is $(68 \times 79)/120 \approx 45$. In his sample Kozinsky found 57 languages that share o-V and s-V, that is 12 more than the expected number. Is this difference enough to reject the null hypothesis ('the features are not related') and to accept the correlation hypothesis? A statistical χ^2 test shows that a positive correlation between both really exists with a 90% probability. Other tests show that the dependence is bidirectional, i.e. equivalent, and may be presented in form of two symmetric universal implications:

Universal 87: (o-V → s-V):
If a bipersonal paradigm contains prefixes which agree with the object (o-V), it contains also (the same or other) prefixes that agree with the subject (s-V).
Exceptions: TUNICA, DARGWA, TABASSARAN, BURUSHASKI, AYUANA, USARUFA, GADSUP, AWA, KATE, UMANAKAINA, TONKAWA, BATS.

Universal 88: (s-V → o-V):
If a bipersonal paradigm contains prefixes which agree with the subject (s-V), it contains also (the same or other) prefixes which agree with the object (o-V).
Exceptions: KAYUWAWA, OTOMI, TZOTZIL, IJIL, NANDI, SUK, LUO, BUGINESE, BARE'E, NENEMA, NIGUMAK, AKKADIAN, ARABIC, HEBREW, SAMARITAN, GE'EZ, BERBER, TSIMSHIAN, PARENGI, SORA, RUANG.

In spite of many exceptions, both universals are statistically reliable. Large numbers of exceptions help to find the intervening factors that show a remarkable symmetry: all exceptions for U_{87}, except TONKAWA, are verb-final, and 17 of 22 exceptions for U_{87} are verb-initial languages. Therefore two more universals may be suggested, both conforming the statistical tests for reliability:

Universal 89:
If a bipersonal paradigm contains forms s-V-o but no forms o-V-s, the language is verb-initial.

Exceptions: AKKADIAN, LUO, SORA, PARENGI, RUANG.
Universal 90:
If a bipersonal paradigm contains forms o-V-s but no forms s-V-o, the language is verb-final.
Exception: TONKAWA.

Exceptions to a statistically reliable universal thus can suggest new valuable universals – in fact, they often must be welcomed by the researcher.

Kozinsky also suggested simple and effective methods to verify universals in order to exclude external factors like areal or genetic affinity of languages that may result in a biased and thus not representative sample.

"If at least one of the features is not found outside a small geographic area, it is useful to define a somewhat broader area in which the initial area would be included [...] After that, a new sample of languages is to be chosen from this broader area only, so that all or at least the majority of languages with the 'suspicious' characteristics in question be included in it. For this new sample, statistical tests must be applied. If the correlation proves statistically reliable, it may be accepted as a universal in spite of its areal distribution" (Kozinskij 1979: 39).

This method helps to brush away correlations of little interest like the dependence of a scanty phonological system and the dual number (in Oceania) and to maintain valuable correlations, like that between morphosyllabism and phonological tones (in Southeast Asia).

This very simple method, not known to most typologists until now, has become of special interest after Matthew Dryer proved the existence of "large linguistic areas" (Dryer 1989; → art. 105) which provide additional problems for the verification of universals. Kozinsky's method, although quite reliable, seems a lot more simple and elegant than other, sometimes very sophisticated, methods of linguistic sampling, partly borrowed from sociology or biology, that have been suggested later (Dryer 1989; Perkins 1989; Rijkhoff & al. 1993; → art. 33 on Statistical Methods).

3.2. Split ergativity

In the 1970s, it was discovered that not all the logically possible combinations of ergative and accusative characteristics are present in world's languages. Independently of Michael Silverstein (1976), whose work was not available to Kozinskij until his candidate thesis was defended (it had been written in 1974), Kozinsky suggested a more full and exact version of what was later called ANIMACY HIERARCHY of split ergativity. A portion of his dissertation concerning this group of universals was published later (Kozinskij 1980).

As it is thereafter known, for ergative case marking there is a universal tendency to involve nominals of lower animacy; if animate nouns have an ergative marking, inanimates have one too; if personal pronouns have an ergative marking, nouns have one too etc., whereas accusative case marking is more typical for nominals of higher animacy.

"For the opposition of accusative vs. nominative case marking, 3rd person pronouns behave like 1st and 2nd person pronouns but not like nouns. For this opposition [...] a following sequence can be suggested: 1st, 2nd and 3rd person pronouns; human proper nouns; human nouns; nouns denoting animals; other nouns. For the opposition of ergative vs. nominative case marking, a clear distinction is found only between 1st and 2nd person pronouns, on the one hand, and all the rest of nouns, on the other hand, whereby 3rd person pronouns belong to the latter" (Kozinskij 1979: 148).

Note that, unlike Silverstein, Kozinsky pointed out that the hierarchy for ergative case marking is not the same as that for the accusative marking.

3.3. Universals of constituent order

Based on his sample of 200 languages, Kozinsky discovered many universals concerning word order, order of agreement between affixes and root, and dependencies thereof, such as his Universal 46: "If a bipersonal paradigm contains constructions s-o-V and o-V-s, it contains also the construction s-V-o" (Kozinskij 1979: 158). He emphasized specially that the order of affixes and the order of arguments and verb are by no means the same. Kozinsky mentioned, for instance, Hans-Jürgen Pinnow's (1966) hypothesis that the PROTO-MUNDA word order was SVO (in modern MUNDA languages it is SOV) only because the order of affixes is s-V-o; likewise Winfried P. Lehmann assumed that compound nouns of the V+O order suggest SVO order, and compounds of the O+V type in INDO-EUROPEAN languages (*bene-facere* in LATIN and the like) suggest that the PROTO-INDO-EUROPEAN language had the SOV order (Lehmann 1975). Assumptions like these that word order and order of affixes are normally the same are based solely on a priori grounds and can be easily proved false by empirical tests.

It turns out, indeed, that the s-V-o order is extremely rare in the SVO languages, and incorporated objects of the O+V order are as frequent in SVO languages as they are in the SOVs; incorporation of the V+O type is found only in verb-initial languages. Kozinsky's Universal 96 claims that if an incorporated direct object precedes the verb root, the subject precedes the verb predicate; a symmetric Universal 97 exists as well: if an incorporated direct object follows the verb root, the subject follows the verb predicate.

Kozinsky found also that the six Greenbergian orders of S, O and V are distributed in his sample in the following way: 50% SOV, 30% SVO, 15% VSO, 5% VOS; OSV and OVS were not represented at all. He hypothesized that in the basic order no more than one of the following three principles can be violated:

(1) subject precedes direct object (proposed by Greenberg);
(2) verb predicate and direct object are adjacent — ten years later, the same principle was independently suggested in Russell Tomlin's book where it was called 'Verb-Object Bonding' (Tomlin 1986);
(3) subject and direct object are adjacent.

The order of the principles determines the distribution of the language types and their percentage in the sample: in the most widespread order none of the principles is violated; in the second, only the third principle — the least important one — is violated, etc. Several years later, the distribution of the types found by Kozinsky was independently confirmed by Hawkins (1983) and Dryer (1988) who compiled, or had access to, much larger samples (→ art. 64).

4. Aleksandr E. Kibrik and functionalism in typology

Although in Russian linguistic works terms like 'functionalism' and 'function' are often encountered, many authors employ them in a rather vague sense, and these terms are rarely explanatory within an elaborated framework competitive to formal theories. This is partly due to the empirical and descriptive trend still dominating in Russian linguistics; explanatory theoretical projects raised little, if any, enthusiasm or even were unnoticed until the late 1980s — for instance, Generative Grammar has been viewed for decades as merely a new method of language description.

Aleksandr E. Kibrik was one of the first Russian linguists who realized that the further development of empirical studies and typology had little prospect without a convincing explanatory theoretical framework. His interest regarding linguistic typology originated from his extensive studies of many unwritten languages of the former Soviet Union in more than 30 linguistic field trips of Moscow State University led by him since 1967.

Apart from the typological stimulus, Kibrik's functionalism originated from his disappointment in the formally oriented and purely descriptive and empirical "Meaning — Text" framework proposed by Igor' A. Mel'čuk and Aleksandr K. Žolkovskij (Mel'čuk 1974), that had been dominant in Russia until approximately the mid-1980s. The author presented his views in a series of papers (Kibrik 1979a; 1979–1981; 1980a; 1980b; 1983; 1984; 1985; 1989; 1990). Revised versions of these papers were collected in (Kibrik 1992). He has published some of his works in English (Kibrik 1979b; 1985a; 1985b/1986; 1997).

Kibrik pointed out that linguistic theories differ in what they believe is the main group of factors determining the structure of language: either the circumstances of language acquisition or the circumstances of language use by humans. The former is typical for formal theorists, and the latter for functionalists whose program Kibrik believes to be far more prolific. Language tends to have a structure optimized with respect to the circumstances of its use.

In Kibrik's view, language is a simple mechanism that enables humans to correlate certain meanings with certain forms; the real difficulty lies in discovering this correlation. Language acquisition is quick and successful exactly because language is simple; complex and cumbersome descriptions are therefore always inadequate (the Simplicity Postulate). Semantic and cognitive structures determine the structure of grammar and constitute the explanatory base of linguistic typology. Descriptive typology (How-typology, in Kibrik's terms) such as that of the St.-Petersburg school, has to be accompanied, if not succeeded, by explanatory studies (Why-typology).

Kibrik invokes a group of principles most of which, as he himself points out, have been in some or other form suggested in works of the functionalist trend before, inter alia:

- Economy Principle: Achieve your purpose with the least possible effort (cf. Peškovskij 1956: 125; → art. 31 on Economy);
- Priority Principle: Of several possibilities, chose the most important (cf. Bergel'son & Kibrik 1981);
- Dynamic Stereotype Principle: Mind and use the links between objects that frequently go together (cf. Haiman 1985: 71f.).
- A more general Iconicity Metaprinciple common to all sign systems: the coded experience is easier to store, change and share if the code is maximally isomorphic to the experience (Givón 1985; → art. 30 on Iconicity).

In particular, the linearization process tends to be iconic: "what is juxtaposed in thought, remains juxtaposed on the linear axis, if other factors do not intervene"; moreover, "what is first actualized in the mind of the speaker, is linearly first" (Kibrik 1992: 35).

This accounts for the continuity of word order, as well as for the most widespread order of inflectional affixes in a verb: ROOT + ASPECT + TENSE + MOOD (cf. Bybee 1985, and earlier, independently of Bybee, Kibrik 1980a). The latter order reflects the hierarchy of how verbal meanings are embedded into one another. For instance, indicative mood denotes roughly 'X is true' where the variable X stands for a meaning that includes temporal and aspectual specifications: 'it is true that in a given moment of time, some action is or is not completed'. Present tense may denote 'X happens in the moment of speech' where X stands for some action that includes an aspectual meaning, e.g. an action may be completed or not etc. The order of conjuncts reflects priority hierarchies, cf. Cooper & Ross 1975, Laufer 1987: *husband and wife, teachers and pupils, ladies and gentlemen, sooner or later*, and the like.

Another example of how Kibrik applies those general principles to typology is his explanation of the distribution of basic coding strategies of semantic roles with different classes of verbal predicates (Kibrik 1992: 186−91). The four main instances (Agent with intransitive verbs; Patient with intransitive verbs; Agent with transitive verbs; Patient with transitive verbs) show 15 logically possible systems of alignment, of which, however, only two are widely attested within the available sample of languages: the NOMINATIVE-ACCUSATIVE system that treats the Agent and the intransitive Patient alike and differently from the transitive Patient, and the ERGATIVE-ABSOLUTIVE system that treats the Patient and the intransitive Agent alike and differently from the transitive Agent. Much less attested are the ACTIVE (Agent and Patient are treated differently throughout), the CONTRASTIVE (intransitive argument vs. transitive Agent vs. transitive Patient), and the NEUTRAL (no distinctions at all) systems (→ art. 101).

Most of the alignment possibilities are not at all attested, e.g.: Agent with intransitives plus Patient with transitives vs. Agent with transitives vs. Patient with intransitives, or: Agent and Patient with transitives alike vs. Agent with intransitives vs. Patient with intransitives, and the like. Kibrik explained this bias in favour of the two systems involving the three explanatory principles that follow:

- Semantic Motivation Principle: what is semantically identical must be coded identically, what is semantically different must be coded differently;
- Economy Principle: semantic differences that can be inferred otherwise must be neutralized. This concerns specially the paradigmatic oppositions that are context bound;
- Distinction Principle: to distinguish those semantic differences that cannot be easily recovered from the context: this concerns syntagmatic oppositions like Agent vs. Patient with transitives and also context free paradigmatic oppositions like temporal or spatial characteristics.

It can be seen now that ergative, accusative, and active systems of alignment are the most optimal with respect to the three principles. Accusative and ergative systems are semantically motivated, economic (they do not distinguish Agents and Patients with intransitives, where roles are unambiguous anyway), and distinctive where necessary (with transitives). The conflict between the Economy Principle and the Semantic Motivation Principle is resolved in favour of the former. The active system, on the other hand, is semantically motivated, distinctive, but not entirely economical (the same conflict is resolved in favour of the Semantic Motivation Principle).

All the other logically possible systems are, however, much less optimal, because they violate more than one Principle of the three listed above. In this way, their non-existence or extreme rarity can be accounted for. Of special importance is Kibrik's recently published typology of clause structure that fully represents his method (Kibrik 1997); since it is available in English, we leave it outside this survey.

Under Kibrik's influence, functionalism has become a widespread methodology in Russian typology in last years, e.g. in dissertations (Kibrik A. A. 1988; Kazenin 1997; Tatevosov 1997; Kalinina 1998; Ljutikova 1998).

5. Other trends in research

The following research fields and works (but not only these) also deserve mention:

(1) typology of aspect (Čertkova [ed.] 1997; 1998);

(2) typology of parts of speech systems; in this field, two collections of papers may be mentioned: (Žirmunskij & Sunik [eds.] 1965; Alpatov [ed.] 1990);

(3) 'contentive' typology, a typological theory suggested by Georgij A. Klimov (1983). The discovery of the active type was Klimov's achievement (Klimov 1977); his version of Ivan I. Meščaninov's (1975) stadial typology that assumes unidirectional historical development of types (active > ergative > accusative) has been, however, a target of criticism;

(4) Typology of polypredicative constructions, especially works by Vera I. Podlesskaja (1993), and the Novosibirsk school of syntactic typology are to be mentioned. The latter includes a group of researchers led by Maja I. Čeremisina residing in Novosibirsk and other cities of Siberia. This school produced more than 15 collections of papers and monographs containing remarkably interesting presentations of the syntax of polypredicative constructions in TURKIC, MONGOLIAN and TUNGUS-MANCHU languages of Siberia, as well as in some of the so-called PALEOSIBERIAN languages within a common framework elaborated by Čeremisina: (Čeremisina, Maja I.(ed.) 1980a; 1980b; 1980c; 1981a; 1981b; 1982; 1985; 1986; 1987; 1989; 1990a; 1990b; Čeremisina & Skribnik [ed.] 1988).

6. References

Alpatov, Vladimir M. 1979. *Struktura grammatičeskix edinic v sovremennom japonskom jazyke*. (= The structure of grammatical units in the modern Japanese language).Moskva: Nauka.

Alpatov, Vladimir M. 1985. "Ob utočnenii ponjatij 'flektivnyj jazyk' i 'aggljutinativnyj jazyk'" (= On clarification of the notions 'flective language' and 'agglutinative language'). In: Solncev & Vardul' (eds.), 92−101.

Alpatov, Vladimir M. (ed.) 1990. *Časti reči. Teorija i tipologija* (= Parts of speech: Theory and typology). Moskva: Nauka.

Bergel'son, Mira B. & Kibrik Aleksandr E. 1981. "Pragmatičeskij 'Princip prioriteta' i ego otraženie v grammatike jazyka" (= The pragmatic Priority Principle and its reflection in the grammar of language). *Izvestija AN SSR. Serija literatury i jazyka*, 4: 343−355.

Burzio, Luigi. 1986. *Italian Syntax: A government-binding approach*. (Studies in natural language and linguistic theory, 1.) Dordrecht: Reidel.

Bybee, Joan. 1985. "Diagrammatic iconicity in stem inflection relations". In: Haiman, John (ed.). *Iconicity in syntax*. Amsterdam: Benjamins, 11−47.

Čeremisina, Maja I. (ed.) 1980a. *Analitičeskie sredstva svjazi v polipredikativnyx konstrukcijax* (= Analytical linking devices in polypredicative constructions). Novosibirsk: [publisher not specified].

Čeremisina, Maja I. (ed.) 1980b. *Podčinenie v polipredikativnyx konstrukcijax* (= Subordination in polypredicative constructions). Novosibirsk: Nauka.

Čeremisina, Maja I. (ed.) 1980c. *Polipredikativnye konstrukcii i ix morfologičeskaja baza* (= Polypredicative constructions and their morphological basis). Novosibirsk: Nauka.

Čeremisina, Maja I. (ed.) 1981a. *Padeži i ix ekvivalenty v stroe složnogo predloženija v jazykax narodov Sibiri* (= Cases and their equivalents in the structure of complex sentences in the languages of the peoples of Siberia). Novosibirsk: [publisher not specified].

Čeremisina, Maja I. (ed.) 1981b. *Sintaksis altajskix i evropejskix jazykov* (= Syntax of Altaic and European languages). Novosibirsk: Nauka.

Čeremisina, Maja I. (ed.) 1982. *Strukturnye i funkcional'nye tipy složnyx predloženij* (= Structural and functional types of complex sentences). Novosibirsk: [publisher not specified].

Čeremisina, Maja I. (ed.) 1985. *Polipredikativnye konstrukcii v jazykax raznyx sistem* (= Polypredicative constructions in languages of different types). Novosibirsk: [publisher not specified].

Čeremisina, Maja I. (ed.) 1986. *Strukturnye tipy sintetičeskix polipredikativnyx konstrukcij v jazykax raznyx sistem* (= Structural types of synthetic polypredicative constructions in languages of different systems). Novosibirsk: Sibirskoe otdelenie AN SSSR.

Čeremisina, Maja I. (ed.) 1987. *Pokazateli svjazi v složnom predloženii* (= Markers of linking in complex sentences). Novosibirsk: [publisher not specified].

Čeremisina, Maja I. (ed.) 1989. *Predloženie v jazykax Sibiri* (= Sentence in the languages of Siberia). Novosibirsk: [publisher not specified].

Čeremisina, Maja I. (ed.) 1990a. *Morfologija glagola i struktura predloženija* (= Morphology of verb and sentence structure). Novosibirsk: [publisher not specified].

Čeremisina, Maja I. (ed.) 1990b. *Sistemnost' na raznyx urovnjax jazyka* (= Systemity on different levels of language). Novosibirsk: Sibirskoe otdelenie AN SSSR.

Čeremisina, Maja I. & Elena K. Skribnik (eds.) 1988. *Komponenty predloženija* (= Components of the sentence). Novosibirsk: [publisher not specified].

Čertkova, Marina Ju. (ed.) 1997. *Trudy aspektologičeskogo seminara filologičeskogo fakul'teta MGU* (= Works of the aspectological seminar at the filological faculty of the Moscow State University). T. 1. Moskva: Izdatel'stvo MGU.

Čertkova, Marina Ju. (ed.) 1998. *Tipologija vida: problemy, poiski, rešenija* (= Typology of aspect: problems, search, solutions). Moskva: Jazyki russkoj kul'tury.

Cooper William E. & Ross, John Robert. 1975. "Word order". In: Grossman, Robin E. (ed.). *Papers from the Parasession on Functionalism*. Chicago: Chicago Linguistic Society.

Dryer, Matthew S. 1988. "Object-verb order and adjective-noun order: dispelling a myth". *Lingua* 74: 185–217.

Dryer, Matthew S. 1989. "Large linguistic areas and language sampling". *Studies in language* 13: 257–92.

Fillmore, Charles J. 1968. "The case for case". In: Bach, Emmon & Harms Robert T. (eds.), *Universals in lingistic theory*. New York: Holt, Rinehart & Winston, 1–88.

Givón, Talmy. 1985. "Iconicity, isomorphism and non-arbitrary coding in syntax". In: Haiman, John (ed.), *Iconicity in syntax*. Amsterdam: Benjamins, 187–219.

Greenberg, Joseph H. 1960. "A quantitative approach to the morphological typology of language". *International Journal of American Linguistics* 26, 178–94.

Haiman, Larry M. 1983. "Form and substance in language universals". In: Butterworth, Brian & al. *Explanation for language universals*. (Linguistics, 21,1.) Berlin: Mouton Publ.

Hawkins, John A. 1983. *Word order universals*. (Quantitative analyses of linguistic structure.) New York: Academic Press.

Hawkins, John A. 1990. "A parsing theory of word order universals". *Linguistic inquiry* 21: 223–261.

Humboldt, Wilhelm von. 1836. *Ueber die Verschiedenheit des menschlichen Sprachbaues und ihren Einfluss auf die geistigen Entwickelung des Menschengeschlechts*. Berlin: Dümmler.

Jaxontov, Sergej Je. 1965. "O morfologičeskoj klassifikacii jazykov" (= On morphological classification of languages). In: Serebrennikov & Sunik (eds.), 93–99.

Jaxontov, Sergej Je. 1975. "Grammatičeskie kategorii amorfnogo jazyka" (= Grammatical categories in an amorphous language). In: Jarceva Viktorija N. & Agnija V. Desnickaja & Fedot P. Filin & Vladimir Z. Panfilov (eds.). *Tipologija grammatičeskix kategorij. Meščaninovskie čtenija*. Moskva: Nauka, 105–19.

Jaxontov, Sergej Je. 1977. "Nekotorye priznaki izolirujuščego tipa jazykov" (= Some features of the isolating type of languages). In: Xrakovskij Viktor S. (ed.). *Problemy lingvističeskoj tipologii i struktury jazyka*. Leningrad: Nauka, 29–36.

Jaxontov, Sergej Je. 1982. "Sravnenie i klassifikacija jazykov po dannym kvantitativnogo analiza" (= Comparison and classification of languages on the base of quantitative analysis). In: Kasevič & Jaxontov (eds.)., 305–323.

Jaxontov, Sergej Je. 1991. "Tipologija morfemy" (= Typology of morpheme). In: Vardul' Igor' F. (ed.). *Morfema i problemy tipologii*. Moskva: Nauka, 86–107.

Kalinina, Elena Ju. 1998. *Nefinitnye skazuemye v nezavisimom predloženii* (= Nonfinite predicates in finite clauses). Dissertacija na soiskanie učenoj stepeni kandidata filologičeskix nauk. Moskva: MGU.

Kasevič Vadim B. & Jaxontov S. Je. (eds.). *Kvantitativnaja tipologija jazykov Azii i Afriki* (= Quantitative typology of languages of Asia and Africa). Leningrad: Izdatel'stvo Leningradskogo universiteta. 1982.

Kazenin, Konstantin I. 1997. *Sintaksičeskie ograničenija i puti ix objasnenija* (= Syntactic constraints and ways of their explanation). Dissertacija na soiskanie učenoj stepeni kandidata filologičeskix nauk. Moskva: MGU.

Kibrik, Aleksandr E. 1979a. "Podležaščee i problema universal'noj modeli jazyka" (= Subject and the problem of the universal model of language). *Izvestija AN SSSR. Serija literatury i jazyka*, 4: 309–17.

Kibrik, Aleksandr E. 1979b. "Canonical ergativity and Daghestan languages". In: Plank, Frans (ed.). *Ergativity: towards a theory of grammatical relations*. London: Academic Press, 61–77.

Kibrik, Aleksandr E. 1979–1981. "Materialy k tipologii ergativnosti" (= Materials for the typology of ergativity). *Institut russkogo jazyka AN SSSR. Problemnaja gruppa po eksperimental'noj i priklad-*

noj lingvistike. Predvaritel'nye publikacii, 127–30; 140–41.

Kibrik, Aleksandr E. 1980a. "Sootnošenie formy i značenija v grammatičeskom opisanii" (= Relation of form and meaning in a grammatical description). *Institut russkogo jazyka AN SSSR. Problemnaja gruppa po eksperimental'noj i prikladnoj lingvistike. Predvaritel'nye publikacii*, 132: 3–10.

Kibrik, Aleksandr E. 1980b. "Predikatno-argumentnye otnošenija v semantičeski ergativnyx jazykax (= Predicate-argument relations in semantically ergative languages). *Izvestija AN SSSR. Serija literatury i jazyka* 4: 324–35.

Kibrik, Aleksandr E. 1983. "Lingvističeskie postulaty" (= Linguistic postulates). *Mexanizmy vyvoda i obrabotki znanij v sistemax ponimanija jazyka. Trudy po iskusstvennomu intellektu.* (Učenye zapiski Tartuskogo universiteta, 621), 24–39.

Kibrik, Aleksandr E. 1984. "Ot taksonomičeskoj tipologii k tipologii dinamičeskoj" (= From taxonomic to dynamic typology). In: *Vsesojuznaja konferencija po teoretičeskim voprosam jazykoznanija. (Tipy jazykovyx obščnostej i metody ix izučenija).* Moskva: [publisher not specified].

Kibrik, Aleksandr E. 1985a. "Tipologija i zadači opisatel'noj lingvistiki" (= Typology and the tasks of descriptive linguistics). In: Solncev & Vardul' (eds.), 74–80.

Kibrik, Aleksandr E. 1985b/1986. "The meaning-form correspondence in grammatical description". In: Lehmann, Winfred P. (ed.). *Language typology 1985. Papers from the Linguistic Typology Symposium, Moscow, 9–13 december 1985.* (Amsterdam studies in the theory and history of linguistic science, 4, 47.) Amsterdam & Philadelphia: Benjamins.

Kibrik, Aleksandr E. 1985c. "Toward a typology of ergativity". In: Nichols, Johanna & Woodbury, Anthony (eds.). *Grammar inside and outside the clause. Some approaches to theory from the field.* Cambridge: Cambridge University Press, 268–323.

Kibrik, Aleksandr E. 1989. "Tipologija: taksonomičeskaja ili objasnitel'naja, statičeskaja ili dinamičeskaja?" (= Typology: taxonomic or explanatory, static or dynamic?) *Voprosy jazykoznanija* 1: 5–15.

Kibrik, Aleksandr E. 1990. "Jazyk" (= Language). In: Jarceva, Viktorija N. (ed.). *Lingvističeskij enciklopedičeskij slovar'.* Moskva: Sovetskaja enciklopedija, 604–06.

Kibrik, Aleksandr E. 1992. *Očerki po obščim i prikladnym voprosam jazykoznanija (universal'noe, tipovoe i specifičeskoe v jazyke)* (= Essays in general and applied linguistics: universal, typical and specific aspects of language). Moskva: Izdatel'stvo Moskovskogo Universiteta.

Kibrik, Aleksandr E. 1997. "Beyond subject and object: Toward a comprehensive relational typology". *Linguistic Typology* 1: 279–346.

Kibrik, Andrej A. 1988. *Tipologija sredstv oformlenija anaforičeskix svjazej* (= Typology of marking of anaphoric dependencies). Dissertacija na soiskanie učenoj stepeni kandidata filologičeskix nauk. Moskva: Institut jazykoznanija AN SSSR.

Klimov, Georgij A. 1977. *Tipologija jazykov aktivnogo stroja* (= Typology of languages of the active type). Moskva: Nauka.

Klimov, Georgij A. 1983. *Principy kontensivnoj tipologii* (= Principles of contentive typology). Moskva: Nauka.

Kozinceva, Natalia A. 1991. "Rezul'taty raboty gruppy za 30 let" (= Results of the group's work for 30 years). *Voprosy jazykoznanija* 4: 108–11.

Kozinskij, Isaak Š. 1979. *Nekotorye grammatičeskie universalii v podsistemax vyraženija subjektno-objektnyx otnošenij* (= Some grammatical universals in the subsystems of expression of subject and object relations). Dissertacija na soiskanie učenoj stepeni kandidata filologičeskix nauk. Moskva: MGU.

Kozinskij, Isaak Š. 1980. "Nekotorye universal'nye osobennosti sistem sklonenija ličnyx mestoimenij" (= Some universal characteristics of declension systems of personal pronouns). In: Vardul', Igor' F. (ed.). *Teorija i tipologija mestoimenij.* Moskva: Nauka, 50–62.

Kozinskij, Isaak Š. 1985. *K voprosu ob isključenijax iz lingvističeskix universalij* (= On the problem of exceptions to language universals). In: Solncev & Vardul' (eds.)., 133–43.

Kozinskij, Isaak Š. 1995. "Parametry morfologičeskoj klassifikacii" (= Parameters of the morphological classification). *Voprosy jazykoznanija* 1: 144–45.

Laufer, Natalia I. 1987. "Linearizacija komponent sočinitel'noj konstrukcii" (= Linearization of the components of the coordinate construction). In: Kibrik, Aleksandr E. & Narin'jani, Aleksandr S. (eds.). *Modelirovanie jazykovoj dejatel'nosti v intellektual'nyx sistemax.* Moskva: Nauka, 167–76.

Lehmann Winfried P. 1975. "A discussion of compound and word order". In: Li, Charles N. (ed.). *Word order and word order change.* Austin: University of Texas Press.

Ljutikova, Ekaterina A. 1998. *Intensifikatory i tipologija refleksiva* (= Intensifiers and typology of reflexive). Dissertacija na soiskanie učenoj stepeni kandidata filologičeskix nauk. Moskva: MGU.

Mel'čuk, Igor' A. 1974. *Opyt teorii lingvističeskix modelej 'Smysl ↔ Text'* (= An essay in the theory of linguistic models 'Meaning ↔ text'). Moskva: Nauka.

Mel'čuk, Igor' A. & Xolodovič, Aleksandr A. 1970. "K teorii grammatičeskogo zaloga" (= Toward a theory of grammatical voice). *Narody Azii i Afriki* 4: 111–24.

Meščaninov, Ivan I. 1975. *Problemy razvitija jazyka.* (= Problems of language development). Leningrad: Nauka. 1975.

Müller, Friedrich. 1876. *Grundriss der Sprachwissenschaft.* Wien: Hölder.

Nedjalkov, Vladimir P. (ed.). 1983. *Tipologija rezul'tativnyx konstrukcij* (= Typology of resultative constructions). Leningrad: Nauka.

Nedjalkov, Vladimir P. 1987. "Načinatel'nost' i sredstva ee vyraženija v jazykax raznyx tipov" (= Inceptives and means of their expression in languages belonging to different types). In: Bondarko, Aleksandr V. (ed.). *Teorija funkcional'noj grammatiki. Vvedenie. Aspektual'nost'. Vremennaja lokalizovannost'. Taksis.* (= Theory of functional grammar. Introduction. Aspectuality. Temporal localization. Taxis). Leningrad: Nauka: 180—195.

Nedjalkov, Vladimir P. (ed.). 1988. *Typology of resultative constructions.* (Typological studies in language, 12.) Amsterdam & Philadelphia: Benjamins.

Nedjalkov, Vladimir P. 1991. "Tipologija vzaimnyx konstrukcij" (= Typology of reciprocal constructions). In: Bondarko, Aleksandr V. (ed.), *Teorija funkcional'noj grammatiki. Personal'nost'. Zalogovost'.* (= Theory of functional grammar. Person. Voice). St-Petersburg: Nauka: 276—312.

Nichols, Johanna. 1986. "Head-marking and dependent marking grammar". *Language* 62: 56—119.

Ogloblin, Aleksandr K. & Xrakovskij, Viktor S. 1990. "A. A. Xolodovič: tvorčestvo i naučnaja škola" (= A. A. Xolodovič: his activity and scientific school). In: Xrakovskij, Viktor S. (ed.). *Tipologija i grammatika* (= Typology and grammar. In memorian for A. A. Xolodovič). Moskva: Nauka.

Perkins, Revere D. 1989. "Statistical Techniques for Determining Language Sample Size". *Studies in Language* 13: 293—315.

Peškovskij, Aleksej M. 1956 (¹1914). *Russkij sintaksis v naučnom osveščenii* (= Russian syntax from the scientific view). Moskva: Ministerstvo Prosveščenija RSFSR.

Pinnow, Hans-Jürgen. 1966. "The verb in Munda languages". In: Zide, Norman H. (ed.). *Studies in comparative Austroasiatic linguistics.* (Indo-Iranian monographs, 5.) The Hague etc.: Mouton.

Podlesskaja, Vera I. 1993. *Složnoe predloženie v sovremennom japonskom jazyke. Materialy k tipologii polipredikativnosti* (= Complex sentence in Modern Japanese. Materials for typology of polypredicative constructions. Moskva: Institut vostokovedenija.

Reformatskij, Aleksandr A. 1965. "Aggljutinacija i fuzija kak dve tendencii grammatičeskogo stroenija slova" (= Agglutination and fusion as two tendencies in the grammatical structure of the word). In: Serebrennikov & Sunik (eds.), 64—92.

Rijkhoff, Jan & Bakker, Dik & Hengeveld, Kees & Kahrel, Peter. 1993. "A method of language sampling". *Studies in language.* 17: 169—203.

Sapir, Edward. 1921. *Language. An introduction to the study of speech.* (A Harvest book.) New York: Harcourt, Brace & World.

Schlegel, August Wilhelm von. 1818. *Observations sur la langue et la littérature provençales.* Paris.

Schlegel, Friedrich von. 1808. *Über die Sprache und Weisheit der Inder. Ein Beitrag zur Begründung der Alterthumskunde.* Heidelberg: Mohr und Zimmer.

Schleicher, August. 1859. *Zur Morphologie der Sprache.* (Mémoires de l'académie des sciences de St. Petersbourg. Série VII, tome 1, n° 7.) St. Petersburg.

Serebrennikov, Boris A. & Sunik, Orest P. (eds). 1965. *Morfologičeskaja tipologija i problema klassifikacii jazykov* (= Morphological typology and the problem of the classification of languages). Moskva & Leningrad: Nauka.

Silverstein, Michael. 1976. "Hierarchy of features and ergativity". In: Dixon, Robert M. W. (ed.). *Grammatical categories in Australian languages.* (Linguistic series, 22.) Canberra: Australian Institute of Aboriginal Studies, 112—71.

Solncev, Vadim M. 1995. *Vvedenie v teoriju izolirujuščix jazykov v svjazi s obščimi osobennostjami čelovečeskogo jazyka* (= Introduction to the theory of isolating language related to general properties of the human language). Moskva: Izdatel'skaja firma 'Vostočnaja literatura RAN'.

Solncev, Vadim M. & Vardul', Igor' F. (eds.). 1985. *Lingvističeskaja tipologija* (= Linguistic typology). Moskva: Nauka.

Solnceva, Nina V. 1985. *Problemy tipologii izolirujuščix jazykov* (= Problems of typology of the isolating languages). Moskva: Nauka.

Šanidze, Ak'ak'ı. 1953. *Kartuli gramat'ik'is sapudzvlebi* (= Foundations of Georgian grammar). I. Morpologia. Tbilisi: Tbilisis saxelmc'ipo universit'et'is gamomcemloba.

Tatevosov, Sergej G. 1997. *Tipologičeskie problemy kvantifikacii v estestvennom jazyke* (= Typological problems of quantification in natural language). Dissertacija na soiskanie učenoj stepeni kandidat filologičeskix nauk. Moskva: MGU.

Tesnière, Lucien. 1959. *Éléments de syntaxe structurale.* Paris: Libraire C. Klincksieck.

Testelec, Jakov G. 1995. "I. Š. Kozinskij i lingvističeskaja tipologija 1970-x — 1990-x godov" (= I. Š. Kozinsky and linguistic typology of the 1970s — 1990s). *Voprosy jazykoznanija* 1, 126—40.

Tomlin, Russell. 1986. *Basic word order: functional principles.* (Croom Helm linguistic series.) London: Croom Helm.

Uspenskij, Boris A. 1965. *Strukturnaja tipologija jazykov.* Moskva: Nauka.

Xolodovič, Aleksandr A. (ed.). 1969. *Tipologija kauzativnyx konstrukcij. Morfologičeskij kauzativ* (= Typology of causative constructions. Morphological causative). Leningrad: Nauka.

Xolodovič, Aleksandr A. 1970. "Zalog. Opredelenie. Isčislenie" (= The voice: definition and calculus). In: *Kategorija zaloga. Materialy konferencii.* Leningrad: [publisher not specified].

Xolodovič, Aleksandr A. (ed.). 1974. *Tipologija passivnyx konstrukcij. Diatezy i zalogi* (= Typology of passive constructions. Diatheses and voices). Leningrad: Nauka.

Xrakovskij, Viktor S. 1974. "Passivnye konstrukcii" (= Passive constructions). In: Xolodovič (ed.), 5–45.

Xrakovskij, Viktor S. (ed.). 1978. *Problemy teorii grammatičeskogo zaloga* (= Problems of theory of grammatical voice).Leningrad: Nauka.

Xrakovskij, Viktor S. (ed.). 1981. *Zalogovye konstrukcii v raznostrukturnyx jazykax* (= Voice constructions in languages of different structure). Leningrad: Nauka.

Xrakovskij, Viktor S. (ed.). 1983. *Kategorii glagola i struktura predloženija* (= Verbal categories and the structure of the clause). Leningrad: Nauka.

Xrakovskij, Viktor S. (ed.). 1985. *Tipologija konstrukcij s predikatnymi aktantami* (= Typology of constructions with clause arguments). Leningrad: Nauka.

Xrakovskij, Viktor S. (ed.). 1989. *Tipologija iterativnyx konstrukcij* (= Typology of iterative constructions). St.-Petersburg: Nauka.

Xrakovskij, Viktor S. 1990. "Markirovka diatez: opyt isčislenija" (= Marking the diatheses: a tentative calculus). In: *Vsesojuznaja konferencija po lingvističeskoj tipologii. Tezisy dokladov.* Moskva: Institut jazykoznanija AN SSSR.

Xrakovskij, Viktor S. (ed.). 1992. *Tipologija imperativnyx konstrukcij* (= Typology of imperative constructions). St.-Petersburg: Nauka.

Xrakovskij, Viktor S. (ed.). 1997. *Typology of iterative constructions.* (LINCOM studies in theoretical linguistics, 4.) Munich: LINCOM Europa.

Xrakovskij, Viktor S. (ed.). 1998. *Tipologija uslovnyx konstrukcij* (= Typology of conditional constructions). St.-Petersburg: Nauka.

Xrakovskij, Viktor S. & Ogloblin, Aleksandr K. 1991. Gruppa tipologičeskogo izučenija jazykov LO Instituta jazykoznanija AN SSSR: teoretičeskaja programma, issledovatel'skie principy, rabočie priemy (= Group for typological study of languages in the Leningrad department of the Institute of linguistics, Academy of Sciences of the USSR; theoretical program, research principles, working methods). *Voprosy jazykoznanija*, 4, 96–108.

Xrakovskij, Viktor S. & Volodin, Aleksandr P. 1980. *Semantika i tipologija imperativa. Russkij imperativ* (= Semantics and typology of imperative. Imperative in Russian). Leningrad: Nauka.

Žirmunskij, Viktor M. & Sunik, Orest P. (eds.). 1965. *Voprosy teorii častej reči na materiale jazykov različnyx tipov* (= Issues in the theory of parts of speech on the data of languages belonging to different types). Leningrad. Nauka.

*Yakov G. Testelets,Institute of Linguistics,
Russian Academy of Sciences, Moskau
(Russia)*

27. The Cologne UNITYP project

1. Introduction
2. Brief characterization
3. An illustrative example: The universal dimension of identification
4. Other dimensions examined
5. Some basic thoughts
6. References

1. Introduction

UNITYP is the name of a research group and stands for "Language Universals Research and Language Typology." The complete descriptive title in German is: "Sprachliche Universalienforschung und Typologie unter besonderer Berücksichtigung funktionaler Aspekte". The group's headquarters was the Institute of Linguistics at the University of Cologne, Germany. It began in 1972 as an individual project, developed into a "Unit" ("Forschergruppe") by 1978, and ended as an official group in 1992. UNITYP ideas live on and are reflected in the work of former associates and members of the group, but also of scholars who got to know the project by its publications only. Further developments of the theory and of its application are being worked out by this writer. Work was and still is funded by different institutions. Most of our work has been or still is being published in the following series:

1. *akup* (= Arbeiten des Kölner Universalienprojekts), edited by H. Seiler, 1973–1992. Numbers 16–89. Köln: Institut für Sprachwissenschaft.
2. *LW* I–III, edited by H. Seiler, 1973–1975: *Linguistic Workshop* I (= *Structura*,

vol. 4), II (= *Structura*, vol. 8), III (= *Structura*, vol. 9), Munich: Wilhelm Fink Verlag.
3. *Language Universals*, edited by H. Seiler, 1978. Papers from the conference held at Gummersbach/Cologne, Germany, 3—8 october 1976 (= *Tübinger Beiträge zur Linguistik*, vol. 111). Tübingen: Gunter Narr Verlag.
4. *LUS*, edited by H. Seiler, 1982, ff: *Language Universals Series*. Tübingen: Gunter Narr Verlag. Eight volumens published so far, vol. I in three parts.

In addition, there exists a great number of unpublished papers and manuscripts. A bibliographical guide to UNITYP publications appeared in *LUS* 5 (1985) 62—7, which is a complete list from the beginning to 1983 (inclusive). A listing of all the *akup* titles is on the back pages of every number.

Two rather detailed reports on the work of UNITYP are available to this date: one in ENGLISH (Seiler 1995: 273—325) with the dimension of possession serving as an *exemplum*, the other in GERMAN (Seiler 1993: 163—86), exemplified by the dimension of oppositeness. The present overview featuring the dimension of identification purports to concentrate on the more recent developments of the project. For an appraisal of this author's personal contribution to language universals research see Christian Lehmann (1985: 225—41).

2. Brief characterization

At the beginning of our work is the insight that a number of structural phenomena in a given language, although differing both in form and in meaning, can be grouped together under a common functional denominator. An example would be ANCIENT GREEK as presented in § 3.4.2 with its array ranging from relative clauses over genitive constructions and quantifiers to demonstratives. Their common function is the representation of identification. The next step is ordering according to similarities and differences: adjective- and genitive constructions are closer to one another, have more properties in common, than have both with demonstratives. The result is a continuum, i. e. a continuous progression from relative clauses to demonstratives, or from demonstratives to relative clauses. The next step is one of interpretation: Considering the end points of the continuum we say that representing identification can be achieved either by content, i. e. by 'predicativity', or by reference, i. e. by 'indicativity'. 'Predicativity' means that the envisaged function is represented by way of predicating or defining: Relative clauses or even full clauses. 'Indicativity' means that the envisaged function is represented by way of pointing or indexically: demonstratives. The intermediate structures (participles, genitives, etc.) as well as the end points exhibit copresence of both functional principles, i. e. 'predicativity' and 'indicativity', but at different ratios: They are negatively correlated in the sense that, as we move from one step to another, an increase of 'indicativity' correlates with a decrease of 'predicativity', and vice versa. There is a middle range on the continuum, were the two principles are about equal in force.

Continua are hierarchies, and hierarchies are, in turn, chained implicational generalizations. We are in this respect deeply indebted to the pioneering work of Joseph H. Greenberg (1963). A difference lies in the fact that, on account of the two complementary or negatively correlated principles, our continua can be read in two directions: from 'indicativity' to 'predicativity' or vice versa. As a further distinction we can, corresponding to an intuitively chosen functional domain — e.g. identification — set up cross-linguistic continua, called dimensions, with a gradience of different 'techniques'. What distinguishes UNITYP most clearly from other universalistic and typological approaches is the teleonomic view on language as a goal-directed activity. Its purpose is the representation of cognitive-conceptual content.

The activity of ordering structures along the lines of continua in language after language leads to uncovering a limited set of functional principles, as 'indicativity' and 'predicativity', plus a limited set of parameters instantiating the distinctions between the different functional dimensions. Universality may thus be described first of all in the form of "doing", i. e. of operational principles and parameters. Linguistic structure results from gradient construction. The same is true for cognitive-conceptual content. There is no difference in principle between operations and parameters on the linguistic level and those pertaining to the level of cognitive-conceptual content. An integrated search on both these levels produces a *tertium comparationis* that is a prerequisite for language typology.

Universalism and typology should thus be distinguished, but not separated from one another. Dimensional continua are the preferred pathways for grammaticalization and for language change.

3. An illustrative example: The universal dimension of identification

This summarizes the results of an inquiry based on earlier attempts but recently developed further (Seiler 2000).

3.1. Delimitation of the database

We chose our database so as to cover an array of phenomena that are traditionally assigned to the two categories of 'determination' vs. 'modification'. As to their delimitation, we encounter in the literature a bewildering variety of opinions. In the older versions of Generative Grammar, DET comprised demonstratives and articles. For various linguists (Trubetzkoy 1939, Moravcsik 1969, Krámsky 1972) determination comprises demonstratives, articles, adjectives, genitives, and relative clauses. Greenberg (1963) extends the notion to include object-verb relations. Vennemann (1974) even goes as far as to include all endocentric constructions. Each one of these proponents may very well have his implicitly or explicitly formulated reasons for his choice. But then their statements concerning universality will differ accordingly.

A principled and explicit choice of the database is therefore of primary importance. Our own choice is determined by notional considerations (see § 3.2). We shall maintain the terms 'determination' and 'modification' when reporting on the work of others and on our earlier work, but we shall use the term 'identification' in their stead for our present-day choice of data.

3.2. The notion of Identification, pretheoretically

1. An entity or object ("Gegenstand") is involved. The notion of object may be assumed to be known – see my book on *Language, Object, and Order* (Seiler 1986).
2. Identification involves the interaction of two partners, tentatively designated as 'operand' and 'operator'. No a priori decision is made as to which one of the partners has which role.
3. Identification is brought about in three phases:
   A. By content, i. e. by perspectivating on properties of the object. This serves primarily the formation of concepts.
   B. By reference, i. e. by perspectivating on the referent of the object. This serves primarily the actualization of the concept.
   C. Between A and B we have the domain of the object itself. Anything that is appertaining to it or constitutes it is in perspective.

This pretheoretical insight is notional, i. e. it pertains to a level outside any particular language, but not outside language itself. It is the level of the *exprimendum* – that which is to be expressed by means of language, of any language. It will be our task to replace this intuition by a more explicit systematization.

3.3. The universal dimension of identification: A tentative reconstruction

Figure 27.1 on p. 326 represents processuality on a cognitive-conceptual, and by that virtue universal, level. Processuality continues on a level intermediate between the universal and the language-specific. Operational content of the level of universality translates on the intermediate level into a sequence of techniques tentatively set up as follows.

This schema is to be understood as an idealization. The status of the techniques is ianus-like: On the one hand they constitute the successive steps or positions replaced by the arrows in the universal scheme. On the other hand they pertain to linguistic encoding and thus to variation. Variation occurs in two senses:

(a) among the techniques themselves: In certain languages some techniques are not represented by any grammatical means, e.g. Relativization. In other languages some techniques merge, e.g. Appurtenance and Possession. The relative order of techniques may change accordingly.
(b) Variation within a technique: Each technique may exhibit an array of variants instantiated by the structures of the particular language, e.g. Possessivity by adjectives, genitives, pronouns. The two negatively correlated curves visualize the gradual increase vs. decrease of the two operational principles of 'Indicativity' vs. 'Predicativity', as one moves along the sequence of techniques in either of

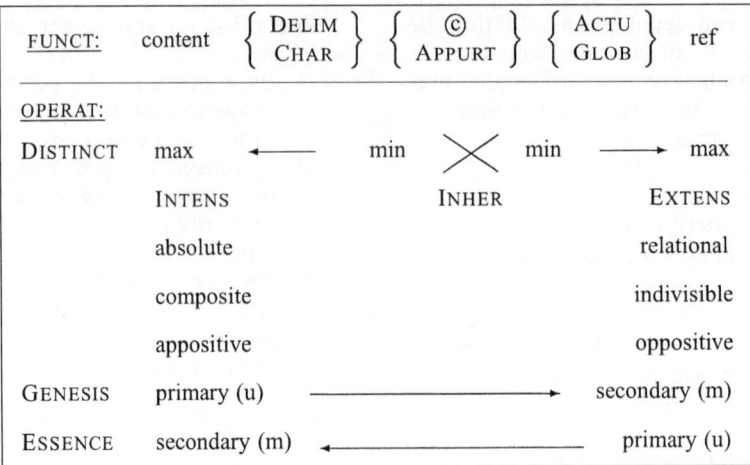

[Abbreviations: FUNCTions, OPERations, DISTINCTions, DELimitation, CHARacterization, © = Kernel Concept, APPURTenance, ACTUalization, GLOBalizaton, ref/erence); INTensionality, INHERence, EXTensionality]

Figure 27.1 Schematic representation of functions and operations involved

PRED – REL – NOM – LOC – QUAL – APPURT – POSS – PRON – QUANT – DEICT

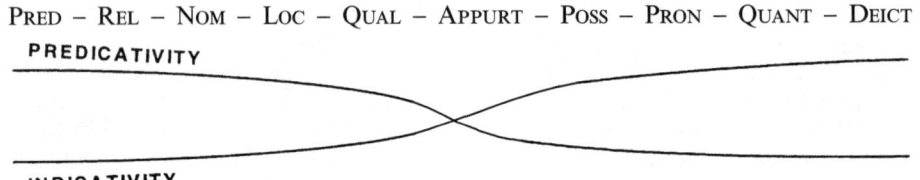

[Abbreviations: PREDication, RELativization, NOMinalization, LOCalization, QUALification, APPURTenance, POSSessivity, PRONominalization, QUANTification, DEICTics]

Schema 27.2: The sequence of techniques

the two directions. Inversion of their respective ratios takes place in a medial range, approximately at the position of APPURTenance.

The dimensional view connects the language-specific facts and universality in a succession of three levels: 1. the universal level, 2. the intermediate level of the different techniques, and 3. the level of the linguistic data. Levels 1. and 3. are taken in an absolute sense, level 2. in an idealized, relative sense. The succession from 1. to 3. is certainly not generative in the sense that it will generate concrete language structures. But it is dynamic ex post to the extent that it will enable us to trace back the pathways from actual language data to their universal sources.

3.3.1. The universal schema

Figure 27.1 is in need of further explication. Above the solid line we have the function or *repraesentandum* of Identification in its three major domains: "by content", "by reference", and as 'Kernel Concept' ©. The curved brackets include on the above line the results, and on the line below that which produces the result. Thus: Delimitation by Characterization, Actualization by Globalization, and the Kernel Concept by Appurtenance.

Below the solid line the operations fulfilling the above mentioned functions are represented in a flow-chart-like manner. There are three major routines: 1. making distinctions, 2. pursuing the perspective of genesis, 3. pursuing the perspective of the essence of identification.

Ad 1. Operations must have a starting point (Seiler 1986: 154; Broschart 1996). In our case the appropriate starting point seems to lie in the middle range, i. e. the Kernel Concept. Here the distinctions are inherent, neutralized. From there the distinction goes in two opposite directions, step by step, indicated by the arrows, until a maximum is reached. The maxima are labeled INTENSIONALITY VS. EXTENSIONALITY respectively. The two are complementary: Intensionality is defined by the set of properties constituting a class, e.g. the "class of squirrels". Extensionality is defined by the class of individuals that can be referred to, e.g. "one actual squirrel visible for the hearer". In the immediate neighbourhood of the Kernel Concept ("squirrel") the distinction is minimal. There are two different minima: minimal intension, and minimal extension. This is the point of inversion, symbolized by the cross.

Since intensionality and extensionality are complementary, one cannot be thought of without the other. This in turn, operationallywise, means that when moving in one direction, e.g. toward maximal intensionality, one has to keep in mind that inevitably the move in the opposite direction, i. e. toward extensionality, must be carried out (Broschart, p.c.). Intensionality and extensionality are the cover terms for a number of parameters. Each parameter comprises two opposite poles. Each parameter implies the next below: absolute/relational → composite/indivisible → appositive/oppositive.

(a) Absolute/relational: Maximal content identification is brought about by predications of properties that are, in principle, independent of one another. Our term here is *"absolute"*. One might think of a guessing game where the object to be identified is narrowed down by a number of predications: "I see something that you don't see and that is brown ... has four feet ... a bushy tail ... etc." Maximal reference identification is brought about by the relation of cohesion between a referencer and the thing referenced. Our term here is *"relational"*. Demonstratives (local deictics) open up a slot to be filled by gestural pointing: "this squirrel — pointing".
(b) Composite/indivisible: Maximal content identification is brought about by an aggregate of predications, and the object to be identified thus appears as *composite*. Maximal reference identification, since it is relational, cannot be composite, must be *indivisible*. The object appears as an 'individuum'.
(c) Appositive/oppositive: With maximal content identification the predicates constituting the object are lined up in *apposition*. With maximal reference identification a pointed out individual virtually stands in *opposition* to other imaginable objects of the same class.

Ad 2. The routine labeled GENESIS. Let us assume that our first move was toward content identification. We are now tuned to the genetic perspective, which says that an object must first be established — by predicative defining — before it can be referenced. Thus, content identification is primary and unmarked (u), while reference identification is secondary and marked (m).

Ad 3. The routine labeled ESSENCE. Let us, on the other hand, assume that our first move was toward reference identification. Now we are tuned to the perspective of what is the essence of identification, which says that reference is in fact the essence of identification.

The relation between genesis and essence corresponds to an old insight as formulated by Aristotle (*Physics* VIII 261a, 13−14), that in the process of growth the genetically posterior is prior according to its essence, its nature.

3.3.2. About the status of this reconstruction

It is called a reconstruction because it tries to explicate what has been intuitively posited in the first place (see § 3.2); and intuitively posited it must be, or else we would not have been able to assemble the relevant data and to delimitate their domain. On the basis of this reconstruction we can now be more explicit about the delimitation: Identification implies the copresence — at varying and negatively correlated ratios — of the two operational principles: 'indicativity' (by reference) vs. 'predicativity' (by content) plus the principle of 'inherence' (in the Kernel Concept"). One might, e.g., wonder why personal pronouns 'I', 'thou' are not included in the dimension. The answer is that 'I' and 'thou', albeit instantiating the 'indicative', referential principle, do not show any reflexes of the 'predicative', contensive principle: The only content of 'I' is self-referential, i. e. 'the person saying *I*'.

The reconstruction integrates a succession of several levels: The cognitive-conceptual level of the function, i. e. the *exprimendum* plus the operations of distinction, genesis, and essence, for which universality may be claimed. It stands outside any individual language ("aussereinzelsprachlich"), but not outside language altogether.

The intermediate level of the techniques, which includes a maximum of cross-linguistic possibilities and may thus be termed "übereinzelsprachlich" (above the individual language). Finally the level of the individual languages with their intra-language continua.

There is no immediate connection between the language-specific fact and universality:

Phenomena of individual languages can never be universal at the same time. However, they do partake in universality precisely by virtue of the succession of levels. – The ways of linguistic inquiry are not unidirectional, as if, e.g., going from cognitive-conceptual to intermediate techniques to language-specific. There is rather a constant shift from "bottom-up" to "top-down", from 'concrete' to 'abstract', and vice versa. Thus, the ingredients of the universal level: domains, distinctions, operational principles, parameters, are not "invented". They are gained from factual observations plus rational reflection and ordering on the basis of these observations. The hypothesis (above § 2.) that there is no difference in principle between operational principles and parameters on any of these levels remains to be tested, and the test will consist in pointing out its usefulness (see § 3.4.4).

3.4. About the evidence

The principal methodological tool of our research is the continuum (more on this notion § 5.3). There are cross-linguistic continua and intra-language continua. In both cases the task consists in substantiating the claim that we are in fact presented with a continuum. Our earlier dimensional research has produced a number of cross-linguistic continua (more on these see § 4). In this section we shall concentrate on pointing out intra-language continua, because here observational adequacy can most readily be tested. A further task will consist in pointing out the operational parameters motivating the dynamic obtaining in these continua.

3.4.1. Modern Standard German

In several publications (Seiler 1978, 1985, with references to descriptive work by others) I posited the following graphical representation for the continuum of nominal determination (now called identification) in GERMAN:

The graph iconically represents normal word order of determinants with regard to a head noun (HN). Some determinants precede HN (predetermination), some others follow it (post-determination). Each position pre and post is filled by a determiner class. The interest was concentrated on the predeterminer classes: material adjectives, color adjectives, evaluating adjectives, affective adjectives, numerals, anaphoric participles, definite article and possessive pronouns (same slot), demonstratives, all quantifier, emphasis. A somewhat artificial example that encompasses all these was

(1) alle diese meine erwähnten zehn schönen roten hölzernen Kugeln des Spiels, die ich dir jetzt gebe

Continuity becomes visible when applicability of determiners to a particular head noun is being tested:

(R_1) (i) The range of head nouns for which a determiner D is potentially applicable increases with the positional distance of that determiner from the head noun.

Thus, in our example (1) D_1 = hölzern 'wooden' applies to a smaller number of Ns, viz. to those characterized by the feature [+ solid object], whereas D_2 = rot 'red' applies to more possible Ns, viz. to those with the features [+ solid object] or [− solid object]. Again, there are more nominal notions which are potentially schön 'beautiful' than there are notions potentially rot 'red'. The countable notions (zehn 'ten') outnumber those being potentially 'red'; the 'aforementioned' ones (erwähnten) outnumber the 'countable'; the things which are potentially 'mine' (meine) outnumber the 'aforementioned' ones; things deictically pointed out and being close to the speaker (diese) outnumber things potentially 'mine', and alle 'all' seems to be all-inclusive and to outnumber everything else. (R_1) (i) thus captures a

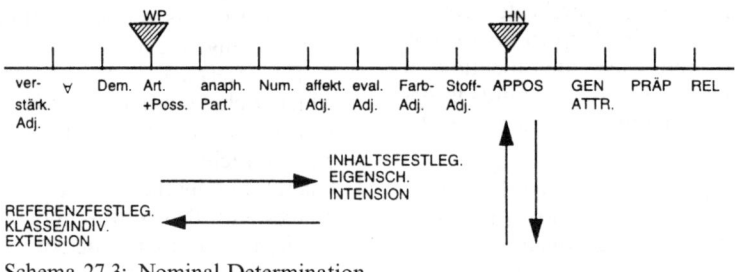

Schema 27.3: Nominal Determination

continuum, where distance iconically portrays a measure of applicability of a D with regard to N. Applicability may involve different degrees of compatibility or of potential *inherence* of D in N.

A corollary of (R_1) (i) says that if a determiner Dj, has wider application than a determiner Di, its force or potential for singling out from the totality of objects the one(s) that the speaker wants to refer to is increased. Hence we formulate the following concomitant regularity:

(R_1) (ii) The potential of a determiner D for singling out the object denoted by N increases proportionally with the positional distance of D from N.

Thus, if I say *zehn schöne Kugeln* 'ten pretty balls', there may be several tens fulfilling the same condition, whereas if I say *diese zehn schönen Kugeln*, 'these ten pretty balls', the choice is narrowed down to those in proximity of the speaker.

(R_1) (ii) again captures a continuum where distance is again iconically portrayed by word order, but with a functional correlate which has to do with the identification of reference: one of the basic options of identification altogether.

The converse of distance is closeness, and normal word order manifests regularity (R_2), the converse of (R_1):

(R_2) Determiners indicate properties more or less inherent in the concept expressed by the HN. The degree of naturalness of such an inherence relation of a D_i vs. a D_j increases proportionally with the closeness of the D with regard to the HN.

The material adjective *hölzern* 'wooden', closest in line to the N *Kugeln*, can be said to be more inherent to such a solid body than would be the color adjective *rot* 'red'. An empirical correlate of this can be seen in the following tetrachoric table:

(2) (i) *hölzerne Kugeln* − *Holzkugeln*
    (ii) *rote Kugeln* − **Rotkugeln*

It is important to see that variation − in our case variation of word order − lends additional support to the analysis.

(3) (i) *die drei heiligen Könige*
    'the three holy kings'

which represents the normal, unmarked word order and refers to any 'holy kings', who happen to be 'three' in number, but for whom "three-ness" is not essential. In contrasting

(3) (ii) *die heiligen drei Könige*
    'the three wise men from the East'

the determining numeral and the N are almost like members of a compound. In fact we find numerous compounds showing *Drei-König(s)* − as a first member. The numeral 'three' is presented as an integrated component of the notion of the 'Magi', and, accordingly, has its position right next to the N.

Affective adjectives can be homonymous with evaluating ones, e.g. *arm* 'poor'. Yet, they are a distinct class, and in normal word order they precede the evaluating ones:

(4) (i) *armer reicher Mann!*
    'poor rich man!'

This is not a contradiction, precisely because there are in fact two different positional classes. In contrast with *reich*, *arm* is affective and endearing, being outside the domain of material wealth, which latter pertains to evaluation. If we invert the order:

(4) (ii) *reicher armer Mann!*

reich is the adjective removed from the domain of material wealth (evaluation), assuming some such affective connotation as "rich in spiritual values". The principles of (R_1) and (R_2) are thus confirmed: Increasing the distance between a determiner and N means moving toward referential identification, which, in turn, is linked to the speech act (affection). Diminishing the distance means moving toward inherence and toward identification of content.

In sum, the discussion of examples (1) to (4) shows 1. that this kind of a continuum is the locus of 'doing', i. e. that it embodies what speakers do when they want to represent distinctions of content; 2. that such doing consists in intellectual motion, and that the motion can be effectuated in two opposite directions: toward reference or toward inherence and further on toward content; 3. that such motion is in successive steps, and that each step or position embodies both principles, although in different proportions: reference vs. inherence/content. Thus, one and the same element − e.g. *arm* or *reich* − can be used either more referentially or more inherently (content-oriented) according to its position with regard to N. Increasing the amount of inherence/content vs. increasing the amount of reference are two converse operations.

What are the domains of these operations? There are two boundaries that partition the continuum. One is represented by the transition from predeterminers via the head noun to the postdeterminers (about the latter see below). The other is represented by the transition from 'modifiers' to 'determiners' in the traditional sense. This its the turning point (WP of schema 27.3). I have shown (opp. citt.) that at this point several things change: 1. the elements to the "left" do not license positional variation – neither among themselves (e.g. *meine diese ..., *diese alle ...) nor with respect to the preceding elements to the "right" (e.g. *zehn die ..., *schöne diese ..., etc.) 2. They do not license relativization. Relativization is possible with

(5) (i) *hölzerne Kugeln* vs. *Kugeln, die hölzern sind*
    (ii) *schöne Kugeln* vs. *Kugeln, die schön sind*

Next in order is an area of transition:

(6) (i) *zehn Kugeln* vs. (?) *Kugeln, die zehn sind*
    (ii) *meine Kugeln* vs. (?) *Kugeln, die meine sind*

and an area of "no trespassing":

(7) (i) *die Kugeln* vs. * *Kugeln, die die sind*
    (ii) *diese Kugeln* vs. * *Kugeln, die diese sind*
    (iii) *alle Kugeln* vs. * *Kugeln, die alle sind*

This means that 'modifiers' in the traditional sense can be transformed into a predicate (predicativity), while 'determiners' in the traditional sense cannot (indicativity). The existence of a transitional zone is an instance of "local squishyness" which corresponds to the overall continuum as formulated in (R_1) and (R_2). Variation is an observable, an indication of the existence of operations along a dimensional ordering, and of a corresponding function. Other observables include implication and squishyness. It is interesting to note that implications may go in two directions as indicated by (R_1) and (R_2). Thus, considering (R_1) we might say: To the extent that reference is determined by the definite article *der*, it can be determined by a demonstrative *dieser*, while the reverse is not true. In comparison with the definite article the demonstrative effectuates a further narrowing down of reference by singling out the objects in the speaker's proximity. On the other hand, considering (R_2) we might say: By virtue of its opposition to the indefinite *ein*, the definite article introduces some such component as "presupposed to be identifiable by the hearer", not present in the demonstrative. In this perspective the definite article substantially determines the content of the noun.

Now, what about the postdeterminers? In my earlier publications (Seiler 1978, 1985), from which the schema (27.3) in the above is taken, I included them into the serialization scheme, overrunning, as it were, from the head noun to the right. In GERMAN these are: Appositions, genitive constructions, prepositional attributes, and relative clauses. It is certainly true that these embody identification ('determination') of content to variable degrees. But this kind of variation is not reflected by regularities of serialization as with the predeterminers. One cannot expect the entire range of linguistic expressions of identification to be assembled in one continuum of one particular language. That is why the evidence for our above reconstruction must be based on language comparison (see §§ 3.4.2 and 3.4.3).

To sum up this discussion we note the following:

1. The overall domain formerly called 'determination' exhibits a threefold partition into (a) the "centre" with greater or lesser inherence, (b) the "left" with greater of lesser reference identification, and (c) the post determiners with regularities other than serialization and presumably representing identification of content.
2. These subdomains are the *locus* of certain operations effectuating a respective increase vs. decrease of the corresponding functions.
3. The operations are motivated by certain parameters: (a) distance vs. closeness, which apparently have to do with the degree of *cohesion* between determinant and head noun; (b) *extension*, i. e. referentiality of the denoted object vs. *intension*, i. e. properties inherent in the denoted object.

3.4.2. Ancient Greek

The data are partly from my own collections, partly from the *Ausführliche Grammatik des Griechischen* by Kühner & Gerth (1955) presenting ample materials and useful frequency indications. At this point, I can only summarize the results of this enquiry. As for terminology, I closely follow the traditional use as adopted in Kühner & Gerth. ANCIENT GREEK differs from MODERN GERMAN in that a wider range of relevant data can be ordered in continuous fashion, specifically including predicative ones, such as relative clauses and participials. As a hypothesis we propose to include the following relevant phenomena in the following order:

Relative clauses and further attributive constructions → Participial-, prepositional-, adjective-, genitive constructions → → Constructions with possessive pronouns, with pronominal adjectives, with quantifiers → → Articles and demonstratives.

Schema 27.4: Continuum of phenomena in ANCIENT GREEK

The inclusion of precisely these phenomena is *prima facie* warranted by the fact that one and the same gender-differentiated element ho, hē, tó corresponding to GERMAN *der, die, das* appears within the limits of (27.4) in the following functions: (a) as a demonstrative, (b) as an article, (c) as a relative pronoun. The statement is somewhat simplified but true in its essence. It is paralleled by exactly the same functional tripartition of the corresponding GERMAN *der, die, das,* viz. (a) as a demonstrative, (b) as an article, and (c) as a relative pronoun.

Our task consisted in justifying the order of (27.4), and, specifically, in showing that it is the order of a continuum. Such a continuum, to be sure, would hold for ANCIENT GREEK and could not be claimed to have universal status. The task, then, consisted in extracting, just as we did in the above summary for GERMAN, those "ingredients" that could be used, along with similar "ingredients" in other languages, for the reconstruction of the true invariant.

Continuous ordering in (27.4) becomes apparent when observing the syntacto-semantic relations between the three structural categories of S(ubstantive), ART(icle), and different kinds of attributes (variable x) – and specifically their relative word order. The grammarians posit two basic types: Type A, called attributive order, and type B, called predicative order. Type A comes in three variants; the examples are construed; a structural formula is added in parenthesis:

(8) A_1: ho anḕr ho agathós
       'the good man'
       the man the good (ART S ART X)

The first article belongs to the nominal syntagm in its entirety, the second article links the substantive and the attribute in the way of a joint or link; hence the term of "Gelenkartikel". This is the "Gelenkstellung".

(9) A_2: anḕr ho agathós
       'the good man'
       man the good (S ART X)

Here, the nominal syntagm lacks an article, is indefinite; the sole article again is in "Gelenkstellung".

(10) A_3: ho agathòs anḗr
       'the good man'
       the good man (ART X S)

Here, the sole article along with the substantive forms a kind of a bracket around the attribute. All three variants share the property of tying together the substantive and the attribute into a closely-knit unit that stands in *opposition* to other such units: "the good man contrasting with the bad man". It is also stated that the strength of the link is greatest with A_1, less so with A_2, and still less with A_3. Type B comes in two varieties:

(11) B_1: ho anḕr agathós
       'the good man'
       the man good (ART S X)

(12) B_2: agathòs ho anḗr
       '(he is) good, the man'
       good the man (X ART S)

Both B_1 and B_2 license paraphrases with a predicate: "the man who is good", "as far as, if, because he is good".

Now the evidence for continuous ordering:

1. If we visualize (27.4) as a linear sequence, then the data show us that frequency of type B increases steadily from "left" to "right".

2. The cline of cohesion as pointed out for the subtypes of A: $A_1 > A_2 > A_3$ is distributed evenly over the positions from "left" to "right": To the left of the genitives we find numerous instances of marked cohesion (attraction of case in the relatives, subtypes A_1 and A_2 elsewhere), to the "right" we find the sole A_3, which vanishes altogether at the position of the demonstratives.

3. If we assume that the constructions to the "left" by reason of their essentially predicative nature are predominantly content identifying, and those to the "right" by reason of their deictic character predomi-

nantly reference identifying, then we come to realize that the frequency distributions of types A and B respectively run in an opposite direction: Strong cohesion counterbalances predominant predicativity so as to provide the possibility of expressing identification of both content and reference. The same holds for 'predicative' B dominating in the area of deixis.

There is also evidence for a partition of the overall continuum into three subdomains. It is brought about by two kinds of converse relationship. One, situated between the positions of adjectives and genitives of substantives, has to do with the relation of *part and whole* within type B: Within the adjective constructions the substantive appears as a divisible whole and the adjective represents a subset or a partial aspect of the substantive. Within the genitive constructions, the relationship is reversed: The genitive appears as the divisible whole, and the substantive represents a subset or a partial aspect.

The other turning point, located between personal and possessive pronouns exhibits complementary behavior: the former always being coded according to B, the latter always according to A.

To sum up this rapid survey of ANCIENT GREEK we note the following: 1. The range of data considered as relevant for Identification exhibits a common formal denominator: *ho, hē, tó.* 2. It is ordered in a continuum. 3. The continuum is partitioned into three subdomains: one central, the other two lateral. 4. The dynamic within the overall continuum is motivated by the following parameters: (a) cohesion ("Gelenkartikel"), (b) part/whole, (c) opposition (A) vs. apposition (B).

3.4.3. Other languages

Three more languages have been looked into in greater detail: TOLAI (Eastern Austronesian) on the basis of Ulrike Mosel's syntax (Mosel 1984); SAMOAN (Austronesian — Polynesian) on the basis of U. Mosel and Even Hovdhaugen's Reference Grammar (Mosel & Hovdhaugen 1992); and CAHUILLA (Northern Uto-Aztecan) on the basis of the author's Grammar, Texts and Dictionary (Seiler 1977, 1970, 1979). The languages differ widely among themselves and from the ones studied thus far.

Continua can be detected for all of them, but their range differs. TOLAI shows a rather fixed sequential order of both pre- and postdeterminers (Mosel 1984: 19). The parameter of *cohesion* is effective throughout: A "connective particle" appears between determiners and the nucleus (head noun) in a middle range before and after the latter. Cohesion between demonstrative, article and N is assured by the relational character of the respective elements. Cohesion between N and possessor phrases is assured by other special elements: possessive markers and classifiers.

In SAMOAN, only one restricted subdomain of Identification shows continuous ordering. These are postnuclear verbs and verbal constructions denoting properties. Examples:

(13)   *pupuni   mafiafia   samasama*
       curtain (spec.pl.) thick   yellow
       'the thick yellow curtains'

The ordering obeys the principle of *inherence*: Of two successive modifying verbs the one that designates a property more strongly inherent in the Kernel concept is ordered closer to the head noun. The other verb ordered more at a distance accordingly contributes more to the reference than to the content of the Kernel Concept.

The parameter "*oppositive* vs. *appositive*" manifests itself, with special preference for the appositive, content identifying pole. The following constructions show an appositive relationship with regard to the nucleus: 'Article + demonstrative', 'relative clause', and 'article + numeral' — all postnuclear, and all coded as NPs more or less closely related to the central nucleus of the overall noun phrase.

CAHUILLA differs substantially from the languages considered thus far (→ articles 41; 53): The basic syntactic relations take place not between words but within words. Subject, direct object and indirect object are coded as obligatory verbal prefixes. Lexical representatives of these relations appear in loose appositive association. All syntactic categories appear in predicative, sentence-generating function: Verbs, nouns, adjectives, quantifiers, personal and local-deictic pronouns. The sentence in CAHUILLA receives its content by successively elaborating predicates. As a consequence, we do not find any attributive relation between words. There are relative participles but no relative clauses. There is no NP. Nevertheless we find the same operational ingredients as before: There is a *continuum* of descriptivity within the majority of lexical nouns. In this way, identification of content manifests itself in different degrees of transparency. It appears as if it were *inherent* in the Kernel concept. Ubiquitous predication contributes to the process of identification. Identification of reference is brought about by an intricate system of local-deictic relational pronouns that are widely distributed over the sentences in the texts and that at the same time assure *cohesion*. They may also stress *oppositiveness*, thereby counterbalancing the overall *appositive* tenor.

3.4.4. Explanatory potential

UNITYP has never considered language universals research as an end in itself. Its findings must be fruitful in view of further insights with regard to both an individual language and language in general (*la langue*). How this is to be understood can be briefly demonstrated within the domain of our foregoing *exemplum* and with special reference to the initial schema (27.1).

1. Intellectual movement from two complementary minima toward the respective opposite maxima is reflected by the widespread preference for mirror image ordering of determiner categories with regard to the head noun, as observed by Greenberg (1963: 68).

2. Assuming that such movement is in successive steps of equal distance from the middle we may predict a tendency for syncretism and/or parallelism of the respective equidistant categories, since, in the end, they contribute to the same overall function. We have seen how demonstrative and relative pronouns, both occupying maximal distance from the head noun, exhibit partially identical representation in GERMAN (§ 3.4.1) and GREEK (§ 3.4.2).

Another example would be adjectives of appurtenance and genitives of appurtenance, both being close to APPURT(enance) but on different sides. Consider

(14) (i) *the Jakobsonian features*
(ii) *Jakobson's features*

(i) refers to features "à la Jakobson", identified by content: someone else besides Jakobson may have proposed them. (ii) denotes features identified referentially and attributed to Jakobson and only to him. In a famous article, Jacob Wackernagel (1908: 125f.) showed that in Indo-European the adnominal genitive was of very limited use and that relations of appurtenance of both varieties (i) and (ii) were preferentially represented by adjectives.

A third example would be the definite vs. indefinite article in a language like GERMAN. Both have in common their generic vs. specific (vs. intermediate) uses, but otherwise they differ substantially: The indefinite conveys the idea of divisibility (compositeness) of the N, and it is an introducer (of content). The definite is a linker and conveys a global view of the N (referentially). Consider the table with the examples (15).

Like and unlike properties of the definite vs. the indefinite article can be visualized as follows:

(15) generic

 ↑ 1 Ein Mensch ist kein Computer 1' der Mensch ist kein Computer
   2 ein Mann der Tat   2' der Mann des Tages
   3 Ein Mann steht draußen   3' Der Mann soll hereinkommen

 ↓   divisible (composite), introducing   linking, global
specific

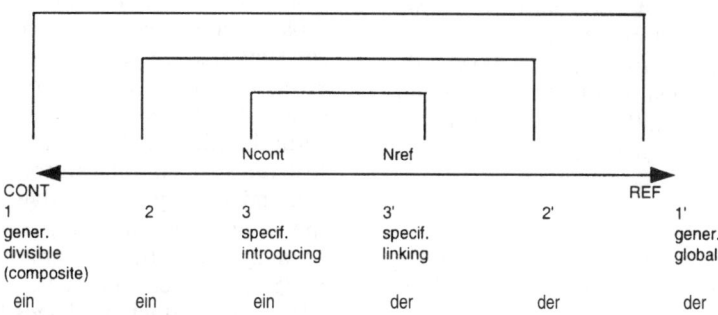

Schema 27.5: Definite and indefinite article

A very similar schematic representation for the FRENCH articles *un* and *le* has already been proposed by Gustave Guillaume (see Wilmet 1972: 37, Valin, ed., 1971: 45f.).

3. Middle range = turning point. We have seen that in different languages the middle range is structurally delimited from the two extreme ranges. We have also seen that the middle range is the *locus* of constructions having to do with appurtenance or partial inherence in the Kernel Concept. Since it is also the *locus* of inversion of the dominance relationship between content and reference identification, we predict that this be reflected in different languages fulfilling the two conditions just mentioned. In GERMAN these are constructions of measuring: *ein Liter Milch*, of counting: *ein Klumpen Gold*, of collectivizing: *eine Herde Kühe*; but also compounds: *ein Goldklumpen, eine Kuhherde*. A comparison between the two syntagms of *ein Liter Milch* and *frische Milch* shows that in the latter the adjective is the satellite and the substantive is the nucleus – both syntactically and semantically (Seiler 1960: 13). But in *ein Liter Milch, ein Liter* is syntactically the nucleus and semantically the satellite, whereas *Milch* is syntactically the satellite but semantically the nucleus (Löbel 1986: 95f.). Such phenomena of inversion have a bearing on the widely discussed question of headness (Corbett & al. [eds.] 1993). Our dimensional schema (27.1) predicts that neither maximal reference identifiers nor maximal content identifiers are fulfledged heads.

4. Linking function. It emanates from the deictics (demonstratives, definite article), because these are relational: The definite article opens a slot for anaphoric reference to discourse-pragmatic facts. Our dimensional schema predicts that this linking function be not confined to deictics but that it may manifest itself with decreasing force in the direction toward content identification, e.g. with quantifiers: For Teop (Bougainville, Papua New Guinea) Mosel and Spriggs (1996) report that "adjectival attributes are not tightly bound to the nominal head." "When a noun is combined with both an adjective and a numeral, the numeral is repeated" – as a linker – "with the adjective":

(16) *a   bua inu   a   bua voon*
      ART.I.SG two house ART.I.SG two new
      "The two houses are new" or "the two new houses"
      [ART.I. = article of gender I.]

5. Characterization emanates from constructions which, in principle, have sentence status. However, it is not confined to these. Our schema with its two gradient and negatively correlated copresent principles predicts that such copresence may extend as far as to the demonstratives. Thus

(17) *dieser Lafontaine*

is not only referential but at the same time asserts content – either negative or positive. Possessive pronouns may oscillate between a referentially oriented or a content oriented representation. Consider

(18) (i) *in diesem unsereN Land*
         (adjective inflexion, content oriented)
     (ii) (as *in diesem schönen Land*)
     (iii) *in diesem unsereM Land*
         (pronominal inflexion, referential)
         (after Plank 1992: 453f.)

The copresence of strong vs. weak adjective inflexion in GERMANIC belongs into this context.

These and many more phenomena can be better understood by postulating both for the speaker/hearer and for the linguistic analyst a processual thinking that follows the lines as visualized in our schemas (27.1) and (27.2).

4. Other dimensions examined

The dimensions to be briefly presented and discussed below were proposed and elaborated at different times within a time-span of over 25 years. They may represent different stages of our way toward understanding universality, the difference being either in theoretical explicitness or in factual support or in both. However, the general direction of our research has remained constant.

4.1. Apprehension

This is thus far the most extensive and the most detailed presentation of a dimension. It explains how language grasps and represents concepts that correspond to objects (things) or items. It is an attempt to give an explicit, systematic and comprehensive picture of the natural order of a vast array of linguistic structures which differ in form and in meaning, and yet appear as variant options corresponding to the invariant theme: the object or thing. It is in three volumes: Volumes LUS 1/I (Seiler & Lehmann [eds.] 1982) and LUS 1/II (Seiler & Stachowiak [eds.] 1982) contain contributions by all the members of the UNI-

TYP group. They survey the entire range and the order of the relevant phenomena, and represent the various techniques (subcontinua) as they appear in a sizeable number of individual languages. LUS I/III (Seiler 1986) is a synthesis and a justification of the continuous dimensional order of the different techniques of Apprehension ranging from Abstraction to Namegiving and thereby manifesting the dynamic passage from dominant predicativity (Abstraction) to dominant indicativity (Namegiving).

The overall dimension divides into three major areas, one central, two peripheral: 1. Relational techniques: Abstraction, Collection, Mass and Measure. 2. Classificatory techniques: Classification by Verbs, Classification by Articles, Numeral Classification. 3. indexical techniques: Agreement in Gender and Number, Namegiving. As with the dimension of Identification, I have shown for Apprehension (Seiler 1986: 154 f.) that the medial range (classificatory techniques) marks a turning where indicativity and predicativity are about equal in force, thereby neutralizing each other. It is also the area of a markedness reversal, from which progressive differentiation, i. e. markedness proceeds toward the outward positions. In this sense, Abstraction at the one end, and Namegiving at the other would be the most marked, i. e. the most complex techniques, although marking is produced by different means.

The motivation for dynamicity is pointed out for each technique by a limited number of "dynamic traits" — a concept that is now, i. e. in our recent work, more systematized and renamed as 'parameters' (see § 5.4).

4.2. Nomination

The dimension was originally referred to as "Die Prinzipien der deskriptiven und der etikettierenden Benennung" (Seiler 1975: 2—57). The naming of objects, properties, processes, etc., is a problem to be solved by every language. For solving the problem there is a whole array of options, both within one and the same language and crosslinguistically. The dimension spans between maximally descriptive (i. e. predicative), and maximally labeling (i. e. indicative). One of the options ('Techniques') in this dimension is derivation. Consider the following continuum in GERMAN:

(19)   *Lehrer — Tänzer — Schneider — Arzt*
       Lehrer: einer, der lehrt 'someone who teaches';
       Tänzer: einer, der tanzt 'someone who dances' — but not everyone who dances is a dancer;
       Schneider: ≠ *einer, der schneidet* 'someone who cuts';
       Arzt: = ?

There is a — usually diachronic — drift along the continuum from more descriptive to less descriptive to labeling. And there is also a drift in the opposite direction, which manifests itself by "doing etymology" — by no means confined to professionals: "What is the *etymon* ("true meaning") of 'Arzt'?" The layman usually concentrates his etymological curiosity precisely on the most labeling words (place and person names). The aim is to detect descriptivity behind labels.

4.3. Possession

It was clearly stated that linguistic possession presupposes conceptual possession (Seiler 1983: 3). The latter has been intuitively defined (op.cit.: 4 f.) as a relationship of appurtenance between a substance and another substance. Substance A, called the *possessor*, is prototypically [+ animate], more specifically [+ human], and still more specifically [+ EGO] or close to the speaker. Substance B, called the *possessum*, is either [+ animate] or [− animate]. It prototypically includes reference to the relationship as a whole and to the *possessor* in particular.

Semantically, the domain of possession has been defined as bio-cultural. It is the relationship between a human being and his kinsmen, his body parts, his material belongings, his cultural and intellectual products. In a more extended view, it is the relationship between parts and whole of an organism.

Syntactically speaking, possession is a relation between nominal and nominal, which is not mediated by a verb. Predication, specifically a verb of possession, does contribute to the expression of possession — but only to the extent that such a predication or such a verb refers to the particular mode of possessive relationship and to nothing else. It is an instance of (metalinguistic) reference from code to code.

The structures representing possession both within a particular language and in cross-linguistic comparison have been arranged in an overall continuum, called a dimension. It is a continuum of increasing explicitness of the possessive relationship. There are two functional principles pervading the dimension: inherent possession vs. established possession. Inherent possession ('indicativity') means that the possessive relationship is inherently given in one of the terms involved, viz. the *possessum*: The *possessum* contains reference to the *possessor*. Semantically, this kind of representation implies more intimate possession: Prototypically, of "self" to his kinsmen, his body parts, etc. To the extent that such a possession is represented as being less inherently given, less intimate, it is established by explicit means, which are, in principle, means of predication ('predicativity'). The two functional principles are thus converse. They complement each other in the sense that they are copresent in all structures representing possession.

The dynamics pervading the dimension have been formulated (op.cit.: 80 ff.) as two converse "pulls" or strategies constantly at work and counterbalancing each other: 1. The "pull" from inherent possessive relationship ('egocentricity') toward establishing a possessive relation. 2. The inverse "pull" going from established to inherent relationship and to "self-orientation". A zone of transition from predominantly adnominal to predominantly adverbal relations was found (op.cit.: 55 ff.) to be represented by markings of genitive, location, existence, and directionality. Typological and diachronic correlates of this dynamic were pointed out (op. cit: 82 ff.)

4.4. Localization

A collective volume (Müller-Bardey & Drossard [eds.] 1993) contains studies by several former UNITYP members. In two comprehensive articles (Seiler 1997, 1999) I examined in more detail the continua of localization in some individual languages: ANCIENT GREEK, and, based on the work of Drossard (1993), Finno-Ugric and Eastern Caucasian languages. It was found that the dimension of localization spans from inherent and less complex toward established and more complex localization. The latter includes a deictic centre along with the object to be localized ('figure'), a localizer, and an object of reference ('ground'), whereas the former can do without the deictic centre. In grammatical terms we have a progression from inessive to adessive, to hyperessive, to allative (to uphill/downhill). The relations to the "left" are preferentially represented by nominal clauses, those to the "right" by verbal clauses.

As with all the other dimensions, there is a cutoff point or rather a transition area somewhere in between; its exact localization varies from language to language. Two converse dynamic strategies were found: *Centralization*, which reinforces the bond between the verb and the locality − *decentralization*, which weakens the bond. The dimensions of localization and of participation share a common denominator which resides in the dynamic leading to the emergence of the respective categories: They have the same origin − the nominal clause; the same centre − the verb; and the same converse strategies: toward the centre − toward the periphery. Yet, localization and participation are two distinct domains, where the latter surpasses the former in scope. The more complex relations are construed on the basis of the simple ones. Observations on the order of development of locative pre- or postpositions in children (Johnston & Slobin 1979) lend further support to this view.

4.5. Participation

This is the most complex dimension (→ articles 27; 37). Research began wirth an overview of the entire domain, presented as a series of lectures first (Seiler 1984) and in published form later (Seiler 1988). A voluminous publication with contributions by UNITYP members and associates followed (Seiler & Premper [eds.] 1991). There are good summaries of the individual contributions by Gilbert Lazard (1994: 92 f.) and Bernard Comrie (1994: 22 f.). What is meant by the term of participation is the representation of a "Sachverhalt" (state of affairs) by the means of language. The latter are essentially predicates. Nominalizations, type *the destruction of Carthago by the Romans*, are excluded because their primary function is not the representation of a "Sachverhalt" but rather, derivatively, the representation of a "Sachverhalt" as a thing. The central terms of participation are *participatum* (something participants take part in) and *participant* (the one who or something which participates in a participatum).

Work on this dimension, as with all the others, started from the assumption that in conceptual processing a "Sachverhalt" is neither monolithic nor an immediately given as such but that it is rather progressively construed, going from the less complex to the gradually more complex. The task, then, is to reconstruct this process on the basis of the linguistic data. A second assumption, then, states that there is no difference in principle between processuality on the conceptual level and processuality on the linguistic level. We have a starting point of maximal indicativity represented by holophrastic expressions, nominal clauses and be-clauses; an area of transition represented by phenomena of transitivity; and at the other end maximal predicativity represented by complex *participata* (causative constructions and the like). To the "left" of transitivity we observe an increasing exfoliation of the *participatum* (noun/verb distinction, verb classes); to the "right" an increasing exfoliation of participants (case marking, serial verb constructions). We thus have a directionality of increasing complexity. All the steps, called 'techniques', communicate between a conceptually determined function and potentially a variety of options on the side of linguistic expression (Broschart 1991: 30). The separation of the techniques from one another and also their continuous ordering is an idealization.

We have significant language-specific evidence that adjacent techniques have more properties in common than more distant techniques. We also have evidence that in certain languages a particular technique is missing (e.g. case marking, verb serialization, etc.), or that techniques merge. But such statements are only thinkable on the background of the aforementioned idealization. The dimension of participation connects with the dimension of junction as described by Wolfgang Raible (1992) (see also the appreciation in Seiler 1995: 12 f.). Junction is understood as the linking between two representations of two states of affairs ("Sachverhalte").

4.6. The dimension of oppositeness

The work is by Seiler (1993 and 1995). The following techniques can be distinguished (linguistic reflexes in parentheses): 1. Symmetrical (kin terms); 2. Complementary (non-graded antonyms, also called "complenyms"); Graded (graded antonyms); 4. Situated (local-temporal opposites); 5. Dissociated (temporal or factual contrast, contrastive stress); 6. Negated (constituent negation, sentence negation). The dimensional ordering leads us from concrete relations (Symmetrical, Complementary) to increasingly abstract ones (Dissociated, Negated). It also leads us from inherent oppositions to increasingly established oppositions with the gradual emergence of an opposition operator (negation). Six parameters could be identified that are operational in the distinction between the techniques. Some of these are used for the definition of techniques in other dimensions as well.

4.7. The dimension of numeration

Work by Seiler (1990 and 1992). The idea that numeration would represent a universal linguistic dimension may derive some plausibility from the fact that the underlying cognitive-conceptual operation, viz. the act of counting, is of a dimensional nature. Our reconstruction shows three techniques as defined by the specification of three parameters. The parameters are: 1. A *frame*. One does not count in the abstract vacuum. The most natural and suggestive frame is the human body with its major functions such as locomotion, use of hands, etc. 2. Such a frame implies some *entities* fulfilling the functions, as the limbs, the hands, specifically the fingers of a hand. 3. To the extent that they are considered as being alike with regard to a particular function, it becomes necessary to distinguish them. This is done by spatio-temporal ordering, i.e. by *serialization*. The conceptual content of numeration can thus be explicated by an ordered sequence of three parameters leading toward its construction. The interplay of these three parameters leads to positing three techniques of numeration:

1. *Atoms:* represented by the low numerals that are usually accompanied by pointing gestures ('indicativity').
2. *Bases:* marks of hierarchical packaging ('iconicity'), e.g. 'hand' = package of five, 'person' = package of twenty (digits).
3. *Calculus:* linguistically implemented by syntactic rules and by rules of interpretation ('predicativity'). It has been shown (op.cit. 203 ff.) how the dimension represents a primary locus of language change and of typological differentiation within the respective domains.

5. Some basic thoughts

5.1. Aims

Why should we engage in language universals research and language typology? What do we want to explain? It is a fact that, although languages do indeed differ significantly and considerably, no one would deny that they have something in common; how else could they be labeled "language"? There is obviously unity among them. Neither diversity *per se* nor unity *per se* is what we want to explain. There is no reason for considering either one of them as primary, and the other as derived. What we do want to explain is "equivalence in difference" (Jakobson 1959/1971: 262), which manifests itself, among other ways, in the translatability from one language to another, the learnability of any language, language change — which all presuppose that speakers intuitively find their way from diversity to unity.

Generally then, our basic goal is to explain the way in which language-specific facts are connected with a unitarian concept of language — 'die Sprache', 'le langage'. Considering such a statement one might come to think that the most efficient way to reach our goal would be to posit an algorithm leading from unity to diversity and/or from diversity to unity. While the idea of explaining the facts of language by ways of an algorithm is cherished by many linguists, it is nevertheless true that to this day it has remained an ideal that has never been reached. In our case the ways leading to an understanding of how universality is connected with individual languages are marked by too many intermediate shifts between observation and systematization. An algorithm is therefore out of the question.

As stated above (§ 2.), our approach takes the *teleonomic* character of language as a goal-directed activity into account. In a first approximation it can be said that the goal has two facets: (1) achieving cognition, and (2) representing cognition — both by means of a semiotic system. Language is thus our primary means of thinking and of achieving cognitive insight, and it is at the same time the means for representing such insight. The foremost notions are those of *operationality* and *processuality*, as against the conception of language being a "formal" or "abstract object", a thing. This echoes, of course, the famous Humboldtian dictum of language not as product (*érgon*), but rather as an activity (*enérgeia*) (W. von Humboldt 1972: 148). It means for us that the spoken or written word is considered as the output, the end product, the result (Benveniste 1952/1966: 117) of mental operations, which we will have to reconstruct on the basis of the data in an abductive way.

5.2. Universality

Language universals research in mainstream linguistics is still committed to the maxim as pronounced by Bloomfield (1933: 20): "The only useful generalizations about language are inductive generalizations", and as followed up by this statement of Hockett's (1963: 1): "This admonition is clearly important, in the sense that we do not want to invent language universals, but to discover them". It was Eugenio Coseriu (1974: 47—73) who showed us, among other related things, how to distinguish between generalizations and (essential) universals. It is the approach as outlined in the foregoing that purports to show that neither do we want to invent universals nor can we reach universality by purely inductive generalizations. What is needed, instead, is an abductive procedure combining factual observation and ordering (in the form of continua), and rational reflexion.

The classical Greenbergian 'universals' in their form as implicational statements (Greenberg 1963: 58 ff.) preserve their full validity as generalizations, in spite of the numerous counter-examples that have been reported since then. But both generalizations and counter-examples need to be integrated into a comprehensive frame that is essentially determined by the purposive function as fulfilled by the relevant phenomena. It is a frame within which interesting hypotheses can be formulated and tested, as, e.g., what will happen to the technique of abstraction in a language showing numeral classification (dimension of apprehension).

It will hopefully have become clear that what is universal in language are not certain properties, no matter whether isolated or implicationally related, and always incurring the risk of being disproved as universals by counter-examples. Universality, instead, is essentially processual. It is the principles ('indicativity', 'predicativity', 'iconicity', 'inherence') and parameters (e.g. relational/absolute, control/non-control, time-stable/temporary, etc.). It is the *repraesentandum* in the first place, i. e. that which is to be represented by the means of language; that which is (tacitly) presupposed by all our language activities, e.g. translation, explanation, including "doing linguistics"; that which is in need of explication by way of reconstruction as exemplified above in § 3. Whether we want to call it cognitive-conceptual or otherwise is less important than the view that, albeit being outside any particular language ("aussereinzelsprachlich"), it is nevertheless an integrated part of universality in language.

5.3. Continua

We find continua on different hierarchical levels:

1. a continuum pertaining to a particular morpho-syntactic domain in a particular language, as, e.g., the continuum of different classes of adjectives, numerals, pronouns, demonstratives in GERMAN.
2. a continuum of different techniques in different languages under the common denominator of a particular function, as, e.g. apprehension or participation.
3. a continuum on the cognitive-conceptual level, as reconstructed in § 3.

While a scale, a "yardstick", is a purely static instrument for measuring, a continuum in our sense embodies dynamics, i. e. intellectual movement in two converse directions. Invariably we found that there are two opposites: 'indicativity' vs. 'predicativity', and a transitory area with a turning point characterized as 'inherent' or 'iconic' or both. Naturally, a continuum implies a sequence of steps or positions. The two opposite principles, 'indicativity' vs. 'predicativity', are copresent in each of the steps, although at different ratios: maximal 'indicativity' correlates with minimal 'predicativity' and minimal 'indicativity' with maximal 'predicativity'. The ordering of the positions within the continuum is determined by the principle of topological neighbourhood: Linguistic structures from adjacent positions share more properties than structures from distant positions.

One possible visualization of continua, especially dimensional ones, as used in our earlier publications, is by two grading asymptotic curves, which are open-ended on both sides: that is, there are no absolute maxima or minima (see 27.2). This leaves open the possibility that the ends meet with a markedness reversal, i. e. in the figure of a Möbius strip — a possibility for which there is empirical evidence in a number of well-defined cases (Seiler 1986: 137 ff.). Another possible visualization has been used in this publication (27.1); its implications are the same except for the different intermediate techniques, which are left unspecified, their specification being reserved for an intermediate level between the cognitive-conceptual and the language-specific.

Dimensions open up new vistas in the sense that they allow us to show how language phenomena that were hitherto considered to be unrelated can nevertheless be brought together under the denominator of a common function, example: kinship terms, antonyms, and negation under the dimension of oppositeness. For a mathematical interpretation of the "Seilerian" continuum see René Thom (1994: 163−65).

5.4. Principles and parameters

The processual principles that we have recognized so far are: indicativity (deictic, global representation); predicativity (defining representation); inherence and/or iconicity (inherent representation and/or by way of relational similarity). Indicativity and predicativity are understood as two opposite poles of a continuum with a number of intermediate positions or steps. Inherence and/or iconicity mark the position on the continuum where the two gradients viz. indicativity vs. predicativity intersect and are about equal in force. These two never totally exclude each other. They are copresent everywhere, albeit with negatively correlated ratios.

The notion of parameters is relatively new in the development of the UNITYP framework. It was first introduced under the name of "operational traits" in our treatment of the dimension of Apprehension (Seiler 1986), then formulated in a survey of the dimension of Participation (Seiler 1994: 35 f.) and more explicitly in our treatment of the dimension of Opposites (Seiler 1993: 166 f.). The idea is that they are bi-polar, that they form a limited set, and that they determine or define the positions on the continuum of the dimension. Our tentative reconstruction of the dimension of identification (above § 3.3) exhibits a hierarchy of parameters with one superordinated: intensional/extensional, and the subordinated ones related to one another by implication: absolute/relational → composite/indivisible → apposite/opposite. All of these determine just the endpoints of the dimension. For the definition of the intermediate gradient steps, viz. the techniques, the introduction of further parameters will be necessary. Further inquiries related to the parameters will be necessary in order to know what they are and how they are related to one another within the limited set that, in principle, has universal status.

5.5. Dimensions and techniques

The dimension is the highest ranking continuum. It manifests itself on three levels (see § 3.3.1): (a) on the cognitive-conceptual level of the *exprimendum* plus the operations of distinction, genesis, and essence, for which universality may be claimed; (b) on the cross-linguistic level of the techniques, which is intermediate in the sense that it receives its structuration from the cognitive conceptual level and makes available the procedures from which the particular languages choose their individual dimensional make-up; (c) the level of the individual languages with their intra-language continua.

The relationship between the techniques on the dimension is disjunction (in the non-strict sense):

(20)   A v B v C v ... Z
        Where v means "and/or"

This means that the technique represents a position on the continuum of the universal dimension. The total array of techniques within a dimension represents an idealized maximal model of options available for the representation of the common functional denominator. The schema (27.2) visualizes the array of techniques on the dimension of identification. Each technique is defined by the particular configuration of parameters. The relationship between parameters constituting a technique is that of intersection:

(21)   a . b . c ... . Z

A technique, in turn, is understood as comprising an array of variant options that may, again, be ordered in continuous fashion. Thus, e.g. the technique called REL(ativization) (27.2) comprises various options ordered in continuous transition from maximally restrictive to maximally non-restrictive relatives.

Dimension is the term for the overall continuum on the cognitive-conceptual level of the *exprimendum* [(a)]. But it "acts on" the levels "below" – the cross-linguistic level of the techniques [(b)], and the level of the individual languages [(c)] – so that their respective continua are dimensional as well.

5.6. Categories

If in the course of our work we have stressed the importance of processuality and operationality as against categoriality, this surely does not mean that we want to "do away" with categories. It does mean, however, that the nature of linguistic categories must be understood in the framework of continua, instead of reducing continuity to categoriality.

The dimensional view in its abstract representation (27.1) implies that there are a number of steps or positions, called techniques, that make up the dimension. They contrast with each other on the dimension, and at the same time communicate between a conceptually determined function and its linguistic representation. Linguistic categories, in turn, are prototypical instantiations of techniques. As they are grounded in the continuity of dimensions, it becomes understandable why their content may fluctuate from one language to another. Gilbert Lazard (1998) very aptly speaks of the "caractère approximatif de ces "catégories interlangues".

5.7. Sampling

Language universal research must face the problem of sampling (→ art. 33). The standards as set by traditional methods demand that as many languages as possible of widely differing structure, provenience, and descent should be considered. Our own approach is different: It centers around the continuum as a theoretical concept and at the same time as a methodological tool. It is relatively easy, even for the student, to set up an intralanguage continuum corresponding to a particular function – an ease which is also reflected by the relatively high number of monographs (89) as produced by UNITYP members and associates. But the continuum approach necessitates a thorough familiarity with the languages(s) considered, and, specifically, a comprehensive view on a greater number of different phenomena that, at first sight, seem to be unrelated. It is neither possible nor necessary to do this on a great number of languages. If the continuum/dimension is set up in accordance with the facts of language(s), then this teaches us about the overarching function, about the dynamic principles and parameters.

5.8. Language universals research and language typology

There is very little consensus about their interrelation. This appears to be a logical consequence of the lack of agreement with regard to their respective essence, tasks, and methods. As for language universals research we have said what there was to say within the scope of this contribution. Regarding language typology, we have some very substantial and illuminating theoretical work at our disposal. In the first place we should mention Eugenio Coseriu's extensive and intensive thinking, as featured, e.g., in (Coseriu 1972) and in (Coseriu 1980). Ch. Lehmann's thought-provoking discussion of Coseriu's typology (Lehmann 1988) also clarifies several issues. Strangely, much of present-day typologizing is going on as if these insights had never been made accessible.

Regarding the interrelation between universalistics and typology, three major views can be distinguished:

1. Language typology and language universals research are diametrically opposed to one another: The latter seeks to uncover what is common to the class of all human languages; the former looks for those traits that are specific for a group of languages or even for one individual language. This seems to be E. Coseriu's view (1978: 94). A different variant of this view is shown in Robert Austerlitz (1974) who, speaking of the "frustrations of linguistic typology" pointedly states (p. 2): "The deeper we go, the less we typologize; the more we typologize, the less we are likely to descend to significantly deep levels."
2. Language typology and language universals research are not distinct (Greenberg 1974), or at least there is no clearcut distinction between them (Comrie 1985: 237). This is the prevailing view in much of present-day typologizing, especially when inspired by work in the U.S.
3. Language typology and language universals research are complementary activities in the sense that one is unthinkable without the other, but that you cannot do both at the same time. This is the view UNITYP and related work tends to favorize — see, e.g., Fernando Leal (1992: 164f.). I have advocated it in several instalments: In a study on the interrelation between language universals research, language typology, and the writing of individual grammars (Seiler 1979: 363), I presented a schema with two axes: One, horizontal, for language universals research presenting a hierarchy extending from the predominantly operational (dimensions, principles and parameters) via the techniques to the predominantly material (observable facts of the individual languages). The other, perpendicular, axis for language typology cutting the horizontal at the level of the techniques and equally extending in a hierarchy from "fundamental type" to 'technique' to 'synthesis' (these notions obviously being borrowed from Sapir (1921: 82f, 120f.). The fundamental positions on both axes (dimensions, "fundamental type") are connected in equidistance with the position for *functions*, which is the origin for both kinds of hierarchy.

In a contribution to a plenary session on "integral vs. partial typology" (Seiler 1989: 156f.) I showed how languages "choose" from the options, i. e. the techniques constituting one dimension. But, clearly, typological relations may cut across several dimensions thereby determining the actual choices in one individual language. The determining factor here are the "preferred connections" of structural traits (Skalička 1974: 17f.). To illustrate it with an example: in the above (§ 3.4.3) it was said regarding CAHUILLA that this language lacks attributive relations between words, that there is no NP. As a consequence, the different degrees in the identification of content manifest themselves within the noun, i. e. its different degrees of descriptivity. This, in turn is intrinsically connected with the fact that all syntactic categories appear in predicative, sentence-generating function. There is solidarity between these typological traits and the particular way CAHUILLA represents content identification within the respective dimension.

5.9. Diachrony

In several publications I showed that the continuum on all hierarchical levels is the most natural frame for describing and explaining the emergence of innovations (Seiler 1983: 83f.; 1986: 161f.; 1990: 9f.; 1995: 314f.). I am not going to repeat this here. With reference to Identification I have given evidence for positing a turning point in the continuum, which would be located at the position of the definite article in languages like GERMAN (see § 3.4.1). I said that this is the point, where several things change. From the history of GREEK, GERMANIC, and ROMANCE LANGUAGES we know that of all determiners the article is one of the most unstable categories, subject to constant renewal. The definite article notoriously derives from a demonstrative pronoun — which means a shift from more referential to less referential and more contensive. The indefinite article notoriously derives from the numeral for "one" —

which means a shift in the opposite direction on the continuum. These as well as many other comparable facts lend strongest support for the view that the continuum − on all levels − embodies what speakers "do".

Acknowledgements

My first thanks go to the former members, associates, and student helpers of the UNITYP group, whom I have been fortunate to work with during twenty years. It is furthermore my pleasant duty to express − in the name of the entire group − our feelings of deep gratitude to the *Deutsche Forschungsgemeinschaft* for its unfailingly generous support during the active years of UNITYP. − As I now live and work in Switzerland, I have been most fortunate to obtain the support − both moral and financial − of the *Erziehungsdepartement des Kantons Aargau* in Aarau with subsidies for a small research station. My heartfelt thanks go to the Head of the Cultural Section, Dr. André-F. Moosbrugger, without whose judicious and efficient support this new phase of UNITYP would not have been possible.

7. References

Austerlitz, Robert. 1974. "The frustrations of linguistic typology: Limitations or stimulants?" *Acta Universitatis Carolinae. Philologica. Linguistica Generalia* I: 1−6.

Benveniste, Emile. 1952/1966. "La classification des langues". In: *Problèmes de linguistique générale* I. Paris: Gallimard, 117ff.

Bloomfield, Leonard. 1933. *Language*. New York: Holt, Rinehart & Winston.

Broschart, Jürgen. 1991. "On the sequence of the techniques on the dimension of PARTICIPATION." In: Seiler, Hansjakob & Premper, Waldfried (eds.). *Partizipation. Das sprachliche Erfassen von Sachverhalten*. (LUS, 6.) Tübingen: Narr, 29−64.

Broschart, Jürgen. 1996. "On turning language into vision. Towards a geometry of interaction." In: Maaß & Olivier (eds.). *Vision and Language*. Heidelberg, 20−38.

Comrie, Bernard. 1985. "On language typology". In: Seiler, Hansjakob & Brettschneider, Gunter (eds.). 228ff.

Comrie, Bernard. 1994. Review of Seiler, Hansjakob & Premper, Waldfried (eds.). *Partizipation. Kratylos* 39: 22−26.

Corbett, Greville G. & Fraser, Norman M. & Mc Glashan, Scott (eds.). 1993. *Heads in Grammatical Theory*. Cambridge/MA: Cambridge University Press.

Coseriu, Eugenio. 1972. "Über die Sprachtypologie Wilhelm von Humboldts. Ein Beitrag zur Kritik der sprachwissenschaftlichen Überlieferung". In: Hösle, Johannes & Eitel, Wolfgang (eds.). *Beiträge zur vergleichenden Literaturgeschichte. Festschrift für Kurt Wais*. Tübingen: Niemeyer, 107−35.

Coseriu, Eugenio. 1974. "Les universaux linguistiques (et les autres)". In: Heilmann, Luigi (ed.). *Proceedings of the Eleventh International Congress of Linguists*, vol. I. Bologna: Il Mulino, 47−73.

Coseriu, Eugenio. 1976. "Stellungnahme zu den '12 Fragen'". In: Seiler, Hansjakob (ed.). *Materials for the DFG International Conference on Language Universals at Gummersbach 1976*. Köln: Institut für Sprachwissenschaft der Universität, 93−98.

Coseriu, Eugenio. 1980. "Der Sinn der Sprachtypologie". *Travaux du Cercle Linguistique de Copenhague* 20: 157−70.

Drossard, Werner, 1993. "Lokale Relationen: Vom Einfachen (Topologischen) zum Komplexen (Dimensionalen) − Sprachliche Reflexe einer psycholinguistischen Erkenntnis". In: Müller-Bardey, Thomas & Drossard, Werner (eds.). *Aspekte der Lokalisation. Beiträge zur Arbeitsgruppe 'Lokalisation' bei der Tagung der Deutschen Gesellschaft für Sprachwissenschaft in Bremen, 1992*. Bochum: Brockmeyer, 44−86.

Greenberg, Joseph H. 1963/1966. "Some universals of grammar with particular reference to the order of meaningful elements". In: Greenberg, Joseph H. (ed.). *Universals of Language*. Cambridge/MA: MIT Press, 58−90.

Greenberg, Joseph H. 1963/1966. (ed.). *Universals of Language*. Cambridge/MA: MIT Press.

Greenberg, Joseph H. 1974. *Language Typology. A Historical and Analytic Overview*. (Janua Linguarum, series minor, 184.) The Hague: Mouton.

Hockett, Charles F. 1963. "The problem of universals in language". In: Greenberg, Joseph H. (ed.), 1−22.

Humboldt, Wilhelm von. 1972. *Schriften zur Sprachphilosophie*. (Werke in fünf Bänden.) In: Flitner Andreas & Giel, K. Bd. III. Darmstadt: Wiss. Buchgesellschaft.

Jakobson, Roman. 1959/1972. "On linguistic aspects of translation". In: *Selected Writings*, vol. II. The Hague: Mouton, 260−66.

Johnston, Judith R. & Dan Isaac Slobin. 1979. "The development of locative expressions in English, Italian, Serbo-Croatian and Turkish." *Journal of Child Language* 6.3: 529−45.

Krámský, Jiri. 1972. *The Article and the Concept of Definiteness in Language*. (Janua Linguarum, series minor, 125.) The Hague: Mouton.

Kühner, Raphael & Gerth, Bernhard. 1955. *Ausführliche Grammatik der griechischen Sprache*, Satzlehre 1. u. 2. Teil. Hannover: Hahn.

Lazard, Gilbert. 1994. Compte rendu de Seiler, H. & Premper, W. (éds.). *Partizipation*. BSL 89.2: 92−100.

Lazard, Gilbert. 1998. "Grandeur et misère de la typologie". In: *Proceedings of the 16th International Congress of Linguists*. Oxford. Pergamon.

Leal, Fernando. 1992. "Der zweite Grundsatz der operationalen Linguistik". *Zeitschrift für Phonetik, Sprachwissenschaft u. Kommunikationsforschung* 45.2: 164−77.

Lehmann, Christian. 1985. "Hansjakob Seilers Universalienforschung". *Zeitschrift für Sprachwissenschaft* 4.2: 225−41.

Lehmann, Christian. 1988. "Zu Eugenio Coserius Sprachtypologie". In: Albrecht, Jörn, et al. (eds.). *Energeia und Ergon. Sprachliche Variation − Sprachgeschichte − Sprachtypologie. Studia in honorem Eugenio Coseriu*. Bd. III. Tübingen: Narr, 3−22.

Löbel, Elisabeth. 1986. *Apposition und Komposition in der Quantifizierung*. (Linguistische Arbeiten, 116.) Tübingen: Niemeyer.

Moravcsik, Edith. 1969. "Determination". *WPLU* (Stanford) 1: 65−98.

Mosel, Ulrike. 1984. *Tolai Syntax and its Historical Development*. (Pacific linguistics: B, 92.) Canberra: Dep. of Linguistics, Research School of Pacific Studies, The AustralianNational Univ.

Mosel, Ulrike & Hovdhaugen, Even. 1992. *Samoan Reference Grammar*. (Instituttet for Sammenlignende Kulturforskning: Ser. B, 85.) London: Scandinavian Univ. Press.

Mosel, Ulrike & Spriggs, Ruth. 1999. "The interaction of gender, number and possession in Teop (Bougainville, Papua New Guinea)". In: Unterbeck, Barbara &Rissonen, Matti (eds.) *Gender in Grammar and Cognition*. (Trends in Linguistics. Studies and Monographs). Berlin/New York: Mouton de Gruyter.

Müller-Bardey, Thomas & Drossard, Werner (eds.). 1993. *Aspekte der Lokalisation. Beiträge zur Arbeitsgruppe 'Lokalisation' bei der Tagung der Deutschen Gesellschaft für Sprachwissenschaft in Bremen, 1992*. (Bochum-Essener Beiträge zur Sprachwandelforschung, 19.) Bochum: Brockmeyer.

Plank, Frans. 1992. "Possessives and the distinction between determiners and modifiers (with special reference to German)". *Linguistics* 28. 453−468.

Raible, Wolfgang. 1992. *Junktion. Eine Dimension der Sprache und ihre Realisierungformen zwischen Aggregation und Integration*. (Sitzungsberichte der Heidelberger Akademie der Wissenschaften. Philosophisch-historische Klasse, 2.) Heidelberg: Winter.

Sapir, Edward. 1921. *Language. An Introduction to the study of speech*. New York: Harcourt, Brace & World.

Seiler, Hansjakob. 1960. *Relativsatz, Attribut und Apposition*. Wiesbaden: Harrassowitz.

Seiler, Hansjakob. 1970. *Cahuilla Texts with an Introduction*. (Indiana University Publications: Language science monographs, 6). Bloomington: Indiana Univ.

Seiler, Hansjakob. 1975. "Die Prinzipien der deskriptiven und der etikettierenden Benennung". In: Seiler, Hansjakob (ed.). *Structura* 9 (Linguistic Workshop, III.) München, 2−57.

Seiler, Hansjakob. 1977. *Cahuilla Grammar*. Banning/CA: Malki Museum Press.

Seiler, Hansjakob. 1978. "Determination: A functional dimension for interlanguage comparison". In: Seiler, H. (ed.), 301−28.

Seiler, Hansjakob. 1979. "Language universals research, language typology, and individual grammar". *Acta Linguistica Academiae Scientiarum Hungaricae*, Tomus 29.3-4: 353−67.

Seiler, Hansjakob & Hioki, Kojiro. 1979. *Cahuilla Dictionary*. Banning/CA: Malki Museum Press.

Seiler, Hansjakob. 1983. *Possession as an Operational Dimension of Language* (LUS, 2). Tübingen: Narr.

Seiler, Hansjakob. 1984. *Partizipation*. Vorlesungsskript. Institut für Sprachwissenschaft, Universität Köln.

Seiler, Hansjakob. 1985. "Kategorien als fokale Instanzen von Kontinua: gezeigt am Beispiel der nominalen Determination". In: Schlerath, Bernfried & Ritter, Veronica (eds.). *Grammatische Kategorien. Funktion und Geschichte*. Wiesbaden: Reichert, 435−48.

Seiler, Hansjakob. 1986. *Apprehension. Language, Object, and Order. Part III: The Universal Dimension of Apprehension* (LUS, 1/III.) Tübingen: Narr.

Seiler, Hansjakob. 1988. *The Dimension of Participation*. Translated and edited by Fernando Leal (Función, 7.) Guadalajara/México: Universidad de Guadalajara.

Seiler, Hansjakob. 1989. "Language typology in the UNITYP model". In: Bahner, Werner & al. (eds.). *Proceedings of the Fourteenth International Congress of Linguists*. Berlin: Akademie-Verlag, 155−67.

Seiler, Hansjakob. 1990. "A dimensional view on numeral systems". In: Croft, William & al. (eds.). *Studies in Typology and Diachrony. For Joseph H. Greenberg*. (Typological Studies in Language, 20.) Amsterdam & Philadelphia: Benjamins, 188−208.

Seiler, Hansjakob. 1992. "La représentation iconique dans la numération". *Académie des Inscriptions et Belles-Lettres. Comptes Rendus*. Paris, 419−25.

Seiler, Hansjakob. 1993. "Der UNITYP-Ansatz zur Univeralienforschung und Typologie". STUF

[Sprachtypologie u. Universalienforschung] 46.3: 163−86.

Seiler, Hansjakob. 1995. "Cognitive-conceptual structure and linguistic encoding: Language universals and typology in the UNITYP framework". In: Shibatani, Masayoshi & Bynon, Theodora (eds.). *Approaches to Language Typology*. Oxford: Clarendon Pr., 273−325.

Seiler, Hansjakob. 1995a. "Junktion. Zu Wolfgang Raibles gleichnamigem Buch". *Vox Romanica* 54: 12−22.

Seiler, Hansjakob. 1995b. "Du linguistique au cognitif: Par la dimension des opposés". In: Lüdi, Georges & Zuber, Cl.−A. (éds.) *Linguistique et Modèles Cognitifs*. Contributions à l'école d'été de la Société Suisse de Linguistique, Sion 1993. *Acta Romanica Basiliensia* 3: 33−51.

Seiler, Hansjakob. 1997. "Localisation et prédication". In: Fuchs, Cathérine & Robert, St. (éds.). *Diversité des langues et représentations cognitives*. Actes de la Table Ronde Internationale à l'École Normale Supérieure de Paris. Paris, 106−16.

Seiler, Hansjakob. 1999. "Lokalization and predication. Ancient Greek and various other laguages." In: Fuchs, Catherine & Robert, Stéphane (eds.). *Language Diversity and Cognitive Representations*. (Human Cognitive Processing, Vol. 3.) Amsterdam/Philadelphia: John Benjamins, 107−121.

Seiler, Hansjakob. 2000. *Language Universals Research: A Synthesis*. Tübingen: Narr.

Seiler, Hansjakob (ed.). 1978. *Language Universals*. Papers from the Conference held at Gummersbach/Cologne 1976. Tübingen: Narr.

Seiler, Hansjakob & Lehmann Christian, (eds.). *Apprehension. Das sprachliche Erfassen von Gegenständen*. Teil I: Bereich und Ordnung der Phänomene. (LUS, 1/I.) Tübingen: Narr.

Seiler, Hansjakob & Stachowiak, Franz-Josef (eds.). 1982. *Apprehension. Das sprachliche Erfassen von Gegenständen*. Teil II: Die Techniken und ihr Zusammenhang in Einzelsprachen. (LUS, 1/II.) Tübingen: Narr.

Seiler, Hansjakob & Brettschneider, Gunter (eds.). 1985. *Language Invariants and Mental Operations*. International Interdisciplinary Conference at Gummersbach/Cologne 1983. (LUS, 5). Tübingen: Narr.

Seiler, Hansjakob & Premper, Waldfried (eds.). 1991. *Partizipation. Das sprachliche Erfassen von* Sachverhalten (LUS, 6.) Tübingen: Narr.

Skalička, Vladimír. 1974. "Konstrukt-orientierte Typologie". In: *Linguistica Generalia* 1. Studies in linguistic typology. Prague, 17−23.

Thom, René. 1994. "Reflections on Hansjakob Seiler's continuum". In: Fuchs, Cathérine & Victorri, B. (eds.). *Continuity in Linguistics*. Amsterdam & Philadelphia, 155−66.

Trubetzkoy, Nikolaj S. 1939. "Le rapport entre le déterminé, le déterminant et le défini". In: *Mélanges de linguistique offerts à Charles Bally*. Genève: Georg, 75−82.

Valin, Roch (ed.). 1971. *Leçons de linguistique de Gustave Guillaume 1948−1949*. Série A. Structure sémiologique et structure psychique de la langue française I. Québec: Presses de l'Univ. Laval.

Vennemann, Theo. 1974. "Theoretical word order studies: Results and problems". *Papiere zur Linguistik* 7: 5−25.

Wackernagel, Jacob. 1908. "Genitiv und Adjektiv". In: *Mélanges de linguistique offerts à Ferdinand de Saussure*. Paris: Champion, 125−52.

Wilmet, Marc. 1972. *Gustave Guillaume et son école linguistique*. (Langues et culture, 12.) Paris: Nathan.

Hansjakob Seiler,
University of Cologne (Germany) /
Lenzburg (Switzerland)

28. Gilbert Lazard, le RIVALC et la revue *Actances*

1. Présentation et historique
2. Les fondements de la typologie comparative de Gilbert Lazard
3. Les difficultés de la typologie comparative
4. La méthode de la typologie actancielle
5. Les études des cahiers d'*Actances*
6. Bilan, résultats et généralisations
7. Références

1. Présentation et historique

Lorsque Gilbert Lazard prit, en 1984, l'initiative du projet RIVALC «Recherche interlinguistique sur les variations d'actance et leur corrélats», il créait vraisemblablement la première unité de 'Recherche Coopérative sur Programme' du Centre National de la Recherche Scientifique exclusivement consacrée à la 'typologie' − bien que le terme n'apparaisse pas dans le libellé du projet. Il s'agissait alors de mettre en synergie, d'une part, les travaux qu'il avait entrepris depuis plusieurs années dans son séminaire à l'École Pratique des Hautes Études et, d'autre part, ceux de Catherine Paris, directeur de recherche au CNRS, qui animait un groupe «Prédicat-Actants» ayant fait l'objet de deux colloques (mai 1977, mai 1978) et d'une publication (Paris (éd.) 1979).

1.1. Le groupe de typologie et ses objectifs

Le programme prit pour objet d'«étudier, dans des langues de types aussi divers que possible, les variations d'actance, c'est-à-dire les changements dans les relations grammaticales qui lient le prédicat verbal et les termes nominaux principaux (les actants), et de déterminer les facteurs pertinents corrélatifs de ces variations, l'objectif final étant d'atteindre, si possible, des invariants présumés universels» (*Actances* 1, 1985: 7). L'actance fut au centre des recherches typologiques du groupe jusqu'en 1995, date à laquelle une nouvelle formation dut être créée. La responsabilité en fut confiée à Zlatka Guentchéva, directeur de recherche au CNRS, qui définit un nouveau programme sur les «Relations intercatégorielles: les variations aspecto-temporelles et les structures diathétiques (Rivaldi)» ayant pour objectif d'étudier «l'interaction entre les catégories de l'aspect et du temps, la détermination et la quantification des termes nominaux du prédicat et l'organisation diathétique d'un énoncé» (*Actances* 9, 1998: 4). Au fil du temps et au gré des thèmes, le groupe s'est élargi et renouvelé: il réunit régulièrement une vingtaine de personnes (enseignants, chercheurs, doctorants), mais depuis sa création, ce sont près de cinquante spécialistes, participants réguliers ou collègues français ou étrangers invités, qui ont enrichi ces recherches de leur compétence sur une ou plusieurs langue(s).

1.2. *Actances* et publications connexes

Ce sont essentiellement les travaux présentés lors des réunions mensuelles que les cahiers *Actances* regroupent. Comme la présentation du premier numéro d'*Actances* (1985) le précise, il s'agit de «documents de travail» et non à proprement parler d'une revue: les cahiers d'*Actances*, tirés à environ deux cents exemplaires, sont de périodicité variable; à ce jour, neuf numéros on été produits: 1985 (n° 1), 1986 (n° 2), 1987 (n° 3), 1989 (n° 4), 1991 (n° 5 et 6), 1993 (n° 7), 1994 (n° 8) et 1998 (n° 9). Deux revues ont par ailleurs consacré un de leurs numéros aux activités de ce groupe de typologie: *Modèles linguistiques* (1992−1993: XIV) et *Studi italiani di linguistica teorica e applicata* (1997: 2). L'ouvrage de G. Lazard *L'actance* (1994) contient également de nombreuses données issues des travaux du groupe. Les orientations, les principes et les résultats de ces travaux sont explicités dans la présentation de chacun des numéros d'*Actances* ainsi que dans divers articles (notamment 1992; 1995; 1997; 1998; 1998a, b, c) de G. Lazard qui en font la synthèse.

2. Les fondements de la typologie comparative de Gilbert Lazard

Les recherches typologiques ont connu un essor important au cours des quinze dernières années et les approches se sont diversifiées, différant tant sur la nature précise des généralisations qu'elles visent que sur les moyens employés pour y parvenir. Ce sont les particularités de l'approche typologique développée au sein du groupe Rivalc qu'on cherchera ici à mettre en évidence.

L'un des points singuliers concerne précisément le type d'invariants recherchés: bien qu'ils soient strictement construits à partir des seules données linguistiques directement observables, à savoir les variations formelles des énoncés, les invariants proposés ne concernent ni les traits formels observables (tels que ordre, marquage) «ni des instruments grammaticaux, ni des catégories, mais des ensembles de relations qui s'imposent aux instruments et catégories des langues particulières et qui commandent les variations observées». Ils se présentent comme «des cadres qui délimitent le champ des variations possibles» (Lazard 1998a: 6).

Le caractère abstrait et complexe des invariants visés par le programme Rivalc découle d'hypothèses et de choix méthodologiques précis, mais ce n'est que dans les écrits de ces dernières années que G. Lazard, jetant un regard rétrospectif sur les résultats des travaux accumulés au cours des ans et retournant aux sources de la linguistique européenne, a cherché à formuler les fondements d'une démarche qui s'était construite de façon plus intuitive que théorique. En m'appuyant sur de larges extraits des publications de G. Lazard, ainsi que sur son intervention «Grandeur et misère de la typologie» au XVIème congrès des linguistes (Paris, juillet 1997), je propose une lecture composée et orientée − et sans doute déformée − des principes et des questionnements qui ont conduit à l'élaboration d'une méthodologie adaptée au projet de typologie comparative.

Afin d'écarter les malentendus que pourraient susciter certains choix qui peuvent sembler excessivement réducteurs, il est bon de souligner que G. Lazard assume pleinement la complexité et la variabilité des langues, tant dans l'usage que dans le temps: «Le fonctionnement d'une langue comporte une infinité de variations d'un acte de parole à l'autre, d'un locuteur à l'autre et d'un instant à l'autre. Tout cela va de soi» dit-il, mais si «la langue n'existe que par les actes de parole […] eux-mêmes ne sont possibles qu'en vertu du système de la langue» (Lazard 1998b).

Bien que le système ait une «relative malléabilité» en raison de la relation dialectique entre langue et parole, il peut constituer, au prix d'une certaine abstraction, l'objet privilégié d'étude d'une «*science des langues*» à laquelle G. Lazard aspire: «Considérer la langue comme un système synchronique, c'est justement neutraliser les variations de diverses sortes pour ne considérer que ce qui lui permet de fonctionner comme instrument de communication. C'est réduire un ensemble complexe et mouvant de phénomènes à un objet abstrait qui se prête en principe à un traitement rigoureux».

Cette démarche s'inscrit explicitement dans la perspective du «structuralisme fonctionnaliste européen […] dont l'inspiration est puisée dans les intuitions saussuriennes» et qui «vise à serrer au plus près les réalités des systèmes linguistiques» (Lazard 1999: 114). Cette conception restrictive peut sembler surprenante à une époque où la linguistique s'est largement ouverte sur d'autres disciplines, mais elle s'inscrit dans une exigence méthodologique plus générale: c'est du renforcement méthodologique de chaque domaine (élaboration de concepts et d'outils d'analyse appropriés à chaque aspect des langues: historique, pragmatique, etc.) que dépend la fiabilité des résultats obtenus et, par conséquent, leur utilité pour l'interdisciplinarité. Prenant pour objet le système de la langue, G. Lazard retrouve naturellement chez ses prédécesseurs (Meillet, Saussure, Hjelmslev, Benveniste sont les plus cités) les principes et les méthodes qui ont fait de la linguistique de la première moitié du vingtième siècle, via le structuralisme, un modèle pour les 'sciences' humaines: dualité du signe linguistique et stricte distinction de la forme (le signifiant) et du contenu sémantique (la substance du signifié).

Mais c'est tout particulièrement dans la phonologie, modèle réduit à quelques dizaines d'unités, où se sont le mieux élaborés les concepts et les principes utiles à l'analyse de tout «système» linguistique, que G. Lazard puise son inspiration: outre la méthode de découverte par commutation, il retient le principe de pertinence qui «impose au linguiste de ne tenir pour pertinentes sur le plan du signifié que les distinctions qui correspondent à des différences sur celui du signifiant, et réciproquement (Lazard 1998c: 73). C'est clairement sur la définition du phonème que s'appuie G. Lazard lorsqu'il écrit qu'«une unité linguistique se définit non par son contenu, mais par opposition aux autres unités. Elle occupe dans l'espace sémantique toute la place que n'occupe pas ses voisines: elle peut être décrite approximativement en termes de substance, mais elle n'a de définition précise que différentielle» (Lazard 1992: 427).

C'est également en référence à la nature catégorielle et discriminante du phonème dans le continuum sonore qu'il faut interpréter la définition de la «catégorie» grammaticale: une catégorie a «des limites bien définies qui la séparent des catégories voisines: si le sens à exprimer se situe dans ces limites, il est exprimé par la forme, morphème ou construction, qui est le signifiant de cette catégorie. S'il l'est par une autre forme, il est hors des limites en question et relève d'une autre catégorie» (Lazard 1998b).

Ce privilège accordé à la forme ne conduit pas à négliger le sens puisqu'il convient de rejeter comme «stérile» une linguistique qui, ignorant la substance sémantique, prétendrait «analyser les données du discours sans tenir compte du sens» (Lazard 1997: 206−07).

Néanmoins, la part de l'hypothèse structuraliste à laquelle G. Lazard adhère, celle qui invite à concevoir les langues comme des systèmes structurés par des réseaux complexes de relations entre des unités − même si ce n'est bien évidemment qu'un des multiples aspects des langues − a des conséquences dramatiques pour la typologie comparative, car, de ce point de vue, *toutes les langues sont différentes*. C'est évident dans le domaine des sons où le système phonologique conditionne l'identification des sons; c'est bien connu dans le domaine lexical et tout aussi vrai du domaine grammatical, pour lequel G. Lazard rappelle entre autres «combien le maniement des aspects, des prépositions ou des articles est difficile à maîtriser dans une langue étrangère» (Lazard 1992: 428).

L'application méthodique des principes de la linguistique structurale conduit inévitablement à reconnaître que dans tous les domaines et à tous les niveaux les langues catégorisent différemment leurs unités, même si G. Lazard prend clairement ses distances avec l'hypothèse dite de Sapir-Whorf (Lazard 1992: 428).

Il n'en reste pas moins que dans le domaine grammatical «cette situation pose un problème évident aux études typologiques, qui se fondent nécessairement sur la comparaison des langues. Sur quelle base comparer des entités présumées radicalement différentes?» (1992: 428). Ce fait a particulièrement retenu l'attention de G. Lazard qui propose dans «Y a-t-il des catégories interlangagières?» (1992) une réponse globale qui semble très suggestive (voir ci-dessous § 6), mais il est vraisemblable que cette réponse s'est nourrie, entre autres, du travail typologique accompli dans le groupe Rivalc; il est donc intéressant de voir quelle est la solution initiale qu'il a apportée à cette difficulté pour pouvoir néanmoins mener à bien la quête des invariants. C'est sur cette problématique, développée ci-dessous (§ 3), que repose la méthode élaborée pour la typologie actancielle.

3. Les difficultés de la typologie comparative

Partir d'une affirmation des différences pour chercher des invariants est pour le moins une démarche inhabituelle ... Si elle est cohérente avec l'idée qu'une langue est un système, elle se heurte toutefois à de sérieuses difficultés, et notamment à l'écueil terminologique. En effet, la typologie repose nécessairement sur la comparaison des langues, mais la terminologie linguistique, contrairement à celle des sciences, n'est pas unifiée. Elle s'expose à une double approximation, liée à la variabilité des langues et à la pluralité des théories: les linguistes «opèrent avec des appareils conceptuels et des terminologies différentes, et, s'il leur arrive d'user des mêmes termes, ils ne leur donnent pas la même signification» (Lazard 1999: 112−13). Dans ces conditions, les termes utilisés 'nom' 'verbe' 'adjectif' 'sujet' 'temps' 'passif' etc. dans la comparaison typologique ne peuvent représenter que des «notions confuses» (Lazard 1999: 113) et la validité des résultats obtenus ne peut que s'en trouver affectée. La mise en garde n'est pas nouvelle comme le rappelle G. Lazard en citant les propos d'Antoine Meillet qui dénonçait déjà l'«élasticité» des termes en linguistique générale (Lazard 1998b).

G. Lazard se trouve dès lors confronté à un «problème redoutable» (Lazard 1997: 207): comment établir les bases de la comparaison? Si toutes les langues sont différentes, si leur forme est différente et les catégories linguistiques les analysant différentes, où trouver l'élément commun permettant leur comparaison? Il faut bien se résoudre à admettre que «ce que toutes les langues ont en commun, c'est la capacité d'exprimer les *mêmes contenus de sens*. La comparaison exige donc que l'on s'appuie sur le sens» (Lazard 1998a: 11). Ce qui ne va pas sans difficulté pour G. Lazard qui adhère, méthodologiquement du moins, au point de vue saussurien selon lequel «l'univers des sens est un espace amorphe ou qui, en tout cas, semble tel, tant qu'il n'est pas structuré par l'expression langagière. [...] Tel est donc le dilemme: d'un côté des données formelles nettes et bien structurées, mais infiniment variées, de l'autre un contenu sans structure propre, qui se prête à tous les découpages arbitraires. Les premières sont en principe incomparables, le second irrémédiablement flou» (Lazard 1998a: 11−12).

L'idéal serait de disposer d'un *tertium comparationis* indépendant de toute langue. G. Lazard évoque la tentative de Klaus Heger (→ art. 36), mais il ne s'y réfère pas, et s'il fonde quelque espoir sur les recherches cognitives qui peut-être «parviendront à établir l'existence [...] de certaines catégories de la pensée, indépendantes des catégories de chaque langue», on ne peut qu'admettre avec lui que «nous n'en sommes pas là» (Lazard 1998b). Inobservable pensée, «misère» du typologue tout autant que de la typologie ...

G. Lazard est amené à reconnaître que «nous sommes donc contraints à des compromis et à des hypothèses, en nous efforçant d'en réduire la part au minimum et de nous appuyer le plus possible sur les données observables, c'est-à-dire sur les réalisations linguistiques» (Lazard 1997: 208). C'est donc une démarche *inductive*, jugée moins aléatoire, qui sera retenue pour développer la typologie actancielle.

4. La méthode de la typologie actancielle

Au départ, la typologie actancielle repose sur une schématisation fort simple à base de quatre sigles *X*, *Y*, *Z* et *V*, incarnant la solution initiale, pratique et contingente, mise au point par G. Lazard pour répondre à l'épineux problème de la comparaison entre langues.

4.1. La typologie des structures d'actance

L'objectif de départ, exposé dès 1978 dans les «Eléments d'une typologie des structures d'actance: structure ergative, accusative et autres» est de fournir les bases d'une classification des structures d'actance par confrontation des constructions biactancielles et uniactancielles et pour cela «il est commode de représenter ces relations grammaticales par un système de sigles» (1978: 55). La solution empirique mise au point est apparue suffisamment efficace pour que G. Lazard la propose au groupe Rivalc comme un «système de sigles» conventionnel «pour représenter des constructions parfois compliquées» (*Actances* 1 : 10).

Ce n'est cependant que bien plus tard qu'il a cherché à faire de ces sigles un véritable outil de comparaison typologique répondant aux exigences que ses réflexions sur les difficultés de la typologie comparative l'avaient amené à formuler.

Deux aspects essentiels sont retenus: (i) ce que les langues ont en commun c'est un contenu de sens; la comparaison exige donc qu'on s'appuie sur le sens; (ii) les seules données observables sont les énoncés produits; on ne peut donc s'appuyer que sur les données morphosyntaxiques. Ce qui l'amène à formuler l'hypothèse de la construction biactancielle majeure: «Cette hypothèse, c'est que, dans toutes les langues, la construction des phrases d'action, c'est-à-dire de celles qui expriment une action exercée par un agent bien individué sur un patient qui en est affecté réellement constitue la *construction biactancielle majeure* et qu'elle est, dans de nombreuses langues, utilisée aussi pour exprimer des procès qui ne sont pas des actions» (Lazard 1997: 208).

Si cette hypothèse est admise, elle permet de répondre à la première exigence puisqu'«elle suffit à fournir l'ancrage sémantique nécessaire à l'étude des relations actancielles dans des langues aussi diverses qu'on voudra, car, à partir de ce point il est possible de mener cette étude sans autre considération sémantique et de se tenir fermement sur le terrain solide des faits morphosyntaxiques» (Lazard 1997: 209). Il en découle une nouvelle définition des sigles arbitraires:

- X est l'actant représentant l'agent dans les phrases d'action et tout actant traité de même dans des phrases autres que les phrases d'action, mais construites sur le même modèle;
- Y est l'actant représentant le patient dans les phrases d'action et tout actant traité de même dans des phrases autres que les phrases d'action, mais construites sur le même modèle.
- Z est l'actant présent dans la construction uniactancielle majeure.

Ces définitions répondent à la seconde exigence retenue: la stricte distinction du signifiant et du signifié: «Il doit d'abord être entendu que nous employons ici le terme d'*actant* pour désigner les termes de la construction, non les êtres ou les choses qu'ils désignent. Les actants sont des unités appartenant au plan morphosyntaxique: ce sont soit des termes nominaux, soit des indices actanciels intégrés ou associés à la forme verbale [...]. Ils représentent les 'participants' qui, eux, appartiennent au plan conceptuel ou sémantique: ce sont les participants, non les actants qui peuvent être agents ou patients ou expérients, etc.» (Lazard 1997: 209).

Cette redéfinition des sigles a l'atout de clarifier leur rôle: ce sont des outils spécialisés, répondant aux exigences de la typologie comparative plutôt qu'à celles de la description des langues particulières.

Le principe de définition des structures d'actance n'a pas changé. Il a été exposé en détail dans *L'actance* (1994: 24 ss.) et synthétisé dans Lazard 1999: 122−26. Il se résume ainsi: «La comparaison de la construction biactancielle majeure et de la construction uniactancielle fournit immédiatement la définition d'une structure d'actance. Résultant de la comparaison des deux constructions majeures, cette structure peut être légitimement considérée comme la *structure d'actance dominante* de la langue en question [...]. Par définition, si X est traité comme Z, la structure est accusative [$X = Z$]; si Y est traité comme Z la structure est ergative [$Y = Z$]» (Lazard 1997: 210). Trois autres structures de base, moins fréquentes, existent: un traitement identique ($X = Z$ et $Y = Z$ ou $X = Y = Z$) donne une structure neutre; un traitement partiellement identique ($X \approx Z$ et $Y \approx Z$), une structure mixte; un traitement différent ($X \neq Z$ et $Y \neq Z$), une structure disjointe.

A ces cinq types de langue, il faut ajouter le type 'actif' que G. Lazard préfère nommer 'dual' dans lequel la présence de deux constructions uniactancielles également importantes — dans l'une Z est traité comme X, dans l'autre comme Y ($X = Z^x$ et $Y = Z^y$) — ne permet pas de dégager une structure dominante.

Cette schématisation ne donne, bien sûr, en vertu du petit nombre de critères retenus, qu'une information très partielle sur la structure des langues et G. Lazard est bien conscient de ce fait: «La construction des phrases simples reste une donnée d'importance typologique première. Mais il n'en faut pas moins prendre en compte les facteurs seconds avec toute l'attention nécessaire et dans toute leur diversité éventuelle» (Lazard 1994: 61), les facteurs seconds étant ceux qui sont habituellement appelés 'syntaxiques', distinguant par exemple l'ergativité syntaxique de l'ergativité dite morphologique. Il appelle également l'attention sur un autre type de critère, plus rarement pris en compte: «l'extension, au sein de la langue, de la construction des phrases d'action» (*ibid.*) — les langues étendent en effet inégalement cette construction à des situations qui ne correspondent pas à une action véritable.

La schématisation proposée n'a pas pour but d'apporter toutes les informations typologiques souhaitables, mais de donner un point de départ fiable à la comparaison entre langues. Et de ce point de vue elle possède deux propriétés intéressantes: elle a désormais une *base sémantique* claire, mais surtout, bien qu'étant établie à partir des données morphosyntaxiques des langues, elle reste totalement indépendante de ces données puisque le seul critère retenu est un *rapport* formel interne à chaque langue entre construction biactancielle et uniactancielle. Elle est en particulier indépendante des fonctions ou relations grammaticales telles que 'sujet', 'objet', etc. qui n'ont pas de définition stable. Selon les définitions proposées, X (*vs* Y) est, dans n'importe quelle langue, l'expression morphologique de l'agent (*vs* du patient) dans une phrase représentant une situation d'action typique. Cette définition n'implique aucune contrainte ni sur la forme de l'expression — l'encodage grammatical de 'l'actant' X ou Y — ni sur celle du sens.

Ce point est crucial pour le fonctionnement de la méthode — et souvent mal compris. Les sigles X et Y désignent, sur le plan notionnel, les deux 'participants' d'une action, l'un provoquant, l'autre subissant les effets de l'action désignée par le verbe, mais cela ne présume pas de l'existence dans la langue d'une quelconque catégorie de l'agent (ou du patient): si la notion d'agent (ou de patient) peut n'avoir aucune pertinence grammaticale dans une langue, il n'en reste pas moins que le participant agissant (ou subissant) aura une certaine représentation dans la phrase. Cette redéfinition strictement 'typologique' des sigles n'étant apparue que très tardivement, on trouve dans les travaux d'*Actances* un usage moins rigoureux de X, Y, Z et parfois variable d'un auteur à l'autre.

Si cette schématisation est en soi peu informative et si son usage trahit quelques flottements, elle s'est néanmoins révélée fort utile dans la recherche des invariants puisqu'elle fournit les points de repère stables et identifiables dans chaque langue à partir desquels seront observées et comparées les variations liées à l'actance, soit à l'intérieur d'une langue, soit entre plusieurs langues.

4.2. Les variations actancielles

La notion de variation d'actance est le complément essentiel de la méthode de typologie actancielle. Elle est exposée en détail dans *L'actance* (1994: 170−220) et c'est sur elle que repose le véritable travail d'exploration typologique: «L'étude de ces variations et des conditions auxquelles elles répondent est des plus féconde pour le chercheur de linguistique générale car elle permet souvent d'entrevoir, par-delà la diversité des langues, des régularités qui apparemment sont le propre du langage en général» (Lazard 1994: 170). Une variation d'actance «embrasse tout changement, minime ou considérable, dans la construction actancielle, c'est-à-dire dans les relations formelles entre X, Y et V ou entre Z et V» (*Actances* 1:10).

Cette notion très générale permet d'appréhender d'un même point de vue des phénomènes habituellement traités séparément: des variations *massives* comme celles de diathèse tout aussi bien que des variations *minimes*, comme la substitution à l'article *du* dans 'je mange *du* pain', d'une préposition *de* dans 'je ne mange pas *de* pain', qui n'en est pas moins «très significative [puisque] des variations analogues sont conditionnées dans diverses langues, par la forme négative du verbe» (Lazard 1994: 170). Quelquefois apparemment libres ('j'habite à Paris' et 'j'habite Paris'), les variations sont le plus souvent significatives, qu'elles soient *obligatoires* (remplacement de *du pain* par *de pain* en contexte négatif) ou relèvent d'un *choix* du locuteur, qui par exemple, en français, emploiera un passif dans une certaine intention communicative.

Le mode d'observation des variations est énoncé de la façon suivante: «On se propose donc, une fois choisie telle variation actancielle dans telle langue particulière, de déterminer précisément avec quel effet de sens ou quelle différence de visée elle est en *corrélation*. Autrement dit, on s'efforce, dans chaque cas particulier, de saisir, par le moyen de la commutation, quelle est la distinction ou quelles sont les distinctions sémantiques ou pragmatiques pertinentes. Le principe de pertinence est au cœur de la méthode» (*Actances* 1:17).

Les principes de base de l'analyse des variations sont donc fort simples puisqu'il s'agit de la transposition dans le domaine des unités significatives, porteuses de sens, de ceux qui ont été appliqués avec succès aux phonèmes.

Les difficultés de l'analyse dans le domaine du sens tiennent, d'une part à la complexité de l'objet d'étude: la forme étudiée, la construction liant un verbe et des actants, est elle-même un complexe de signes, chacun analysable dans de multiples réseaux de relations grammaticales et sémantiques, d'autre part à la superposition dans tout énoncé de *trois plans d'organisation*, conception également issue du fonctionnalisme européen (Daneš 1964): «1) le plan du contenu sémantique, où l'on peut avoir avantage à distinguer une partie 'notionnelle', qui embrasse les notions convoyées par le verbe et les actants, et une partie 'référentielle' (notions de défini, indéfini, etc.); 2) le plan des relations grammaticales formelles établies entre le prédicat verbal et les actants, appelé plan de l' 'actance' ou des 'relations actancielles'; 3) celui de l'articulation thème-rhème, dite traditionnellement 'perspective fonctionnelle de la phrase' et que nous appelerons plus commodément 'visée communicative' ou simplement 'visée'.» (*Actances* 1:8).

La relative autonomie de ces trois plans, dont l'expression se confond en une unique forme, à savoir la construction observée, est à la source de relations complexes entre forme de la variation, facteurs et fonctions de la variation que G. Lazard appelle le *principe de non-isomorphisme entre les formes et les corrélats*: «En perspective interlinguistique, il n'y a pas de correspondance simple entre les formes des variations d'actance et leurs corrélats, c'est-à-dire les fonctions qu'elles remplissent, en ce sens qu'un même type de variation peut, dans des langues différentes, remplir des fonctions différentes et que, inversement, un même facteur peut déterminer, dans des langues différentes, des variations différentes» (1994: 172). Le marquage différentiel de l'objet (→ art. 65) illustre bien ce principe.

Le champ des variations observables est donc très ouvert et les analyses auxquelles elles se prêtent également variées. Dans la pratique, on pourra ainsi choisir d'examiner la forme d'une variation soit dans sa globalité, en comparant par exemple les diverses constructions d'une langue, soit en ne portant l'attention que sur une portion du signifiant global, telle ou telle variation à l'intérieur d'une construction. Quel que soit le point de départ, on cherche à établir l'ensemble des co-variations décelables et à identifier les domaines de grammaticalisation qui leur sont associés. Il est apparu que les corrélats des variations relevaient le plus souvent des points suivants: (a) nature du procès et rôles des participants, (b) catégorisation des actants, (c) catégories verbales, (d) visée communicative, (e) facteurs syntaxiques (1994: 172). Néanmoins, dans le détail, les points critiques déterminants pour chaque langue et les interactions entre différents facteurs sont extrêmement variables. C'est à ce niveau de détail, apportant des informations précises et précieuses sur le maillage grammatico-sémantique de chaque langue, que se sont attachés les travaux menés dans le cadre du programme.

Comme on le voit, la typologie comparative ainsi conçue repose sur une analyse précise, fine et justifiée de chaque langue. Elle requiert en outre une grande transparence dans la présentation des données, illustrées de nombreux exemples, afin que les caractéristiques, aussi singulières soient-elles, propres au système de chaque langue, deviennent accessibles aux spécialistes d'autres langues. Le but du projet est de faire surgir de la confrontation des langues, et en particulier de leurs différences, la reconnaissance des similitudes. Les principes méthodologiques exposés ci-dessus sont ceux que respectent les participants, même s'ils ne partagent pas nécessairement tous les fondements théoriques de G. Lazard.

5. Les études des cahiers d'*Actances*

Les neuf cahiers d'*Actances* publiés rassemblent près de quatre-vingts articles portant sur une cinquantaine de langues. Ils constituent donc un apport de documentation assez important et précis sur les structures actancielles dans de nombreuses langues, dont beaucoup sont peu connues.

Bien que l'échantillon soit modeste au regard des quelques milliers de langues parlées dans le monde, les langues représentées sont assez diverses et géographiquement dispersées sur les cinq continents. Cette diversité, limitée par les compétences des participants, n'est certes ni statistiquement, ni typologiquement représentative, mais permet néanmoins de formuler certaines hypothèses sur les tendances invariantes. Les études sont généralement centrées sur une langue, quelquefois deux ou plusieurs, à l'exception des articles et présentations de G. Lazard qui situent les résultats des travaux dans une perspective typologique globale. Il est bien évidemment impossible de faire un compte rendu exhaustif et détaillé de ces travaux qui se distinguent souvent par la richesse des variations fines mises an jour dans chaque langue. Je me contenterai donc de donner un aperçu global du contenu des cahiers d'*Actances*.

5.1. Les thèmes abordés

L'étude des variations étant en soi pratiquement illimitée, quelques thèmes ont été retenus pour éviter la dispersion des travaux. Les quatre premiers thèmes furent: le *marquage différentiel de l'objet*, l'incorporation ou plus généralement la tendance à la *coalescence* du verbe et de l'objet ou d'un autre actant, les *diathèses* et la *classification des verbes*.

5.1.1. La gamme des langues

Ces thèmes, essentiellement incitatifs, se sont souvent trouvés intégrés dans des études plus globales portant sur «les relations actancielles en ...», sous des titres divers et avec parfois l'accent mis sur un point particulier; on trouve de telles études, dans *Actances* 1, pour le BERBÈRE par G. Galand, pour le BAFIA (langue bantu) par G. Guarisma, pour le HAYU (langue tibéto-birmane) par B. Michailovsky, pour l'AVAR (langue du Caucase, → art. 125) par C. Paris, pour le FINNOIS et le VOGOUL par J. Perrot; dans *Actances* 2 pour le TUNUMIISUT (langue inuit du Groenland) par P. Mennecier, pour l'OSTIAK (langue ob-ougrienne, ainsi que le VACH dans *Actances* 4) par J. Perrot, pour le BADAGA (langue dravidienne) par C. Pilot-Raichoor; dans *Actances* 3, pour le BIRMAN (D. Bernot) et pour des langues amérindiennes: le GUARANÍ (M. Dessaint), le QUECHUA (P. Kirtchuk) et l'AÑUN (M.-F.

Patte); dans *Actances* 7 pour le DOGON par A. Plungian et pour le LIMBU (B. Michailovsky), langue tibéto-birmane de type dual.

5.1.2. Marquage différentiel de l'objet et coalescence

Les deux premiers thèmes sont proches et l'on observe un continuum de l'objet autonome à l'objet non marqué, qui tend à être coalescent avec le verbe, jusqu'à l'incorporation qui en est une forme extrême. Le marquage différentiel de l'objet a fait l'objet de nombreuses études dans *Actances* 6 et 7 (BAFIA, ZARMA, JUDÉO-ARABE, HÉBREU, ÉLAMITE, BULGARE, MORDVE ERZA, TAMOUL, BADAGA, MANDARIN), mais étant traité ailleurs dans ce volume (→ art. 65), je ne retiendrai que les travaux sur la *coalescence*.

Les études présentées dans *Actances* 1 sur le CHINOIS (A. Cartier), le BANDA-LINDA, OUBANGIEN (F. Cloarec-Heiss), le DREHU, langue mélanésienne (C. Moyse-Faurie) et le PASHTO, langue indo-iranienne (D. Septfonds) soulignent la diversité des critères d'identification: à la proximité entre objet et verbe s'ajoutent des critères accentuels (BANDA-LINDA, PASHTO) essentiellement syntaxiques (CHINOIS) distributionnels (paradigme fermé *vs* ouvert: BANDA-LINDA, DREHU), morphologiques (forme indéterminée *vs* personnelle du verbe: DREHU), etc. La coalescence est en rapport avec des facteurs sémantiques (en CHINOIS: humain, inanimé, lieu en corrélation inverse avec la définitude: générique, indéfini, défini), grammaticaux (aspect en PASHTO) et de visée communicative (objet et verbe appartiennent tous deux à une même unité d'information).

Le DREHU permet d'attirer l'attention sur deux types de coalescence bien distincts: dans un cas, on observe la perte d'individuation de l'objet, la détransitivation de l'ensemble verbe-objet coalescent et la tendance à la lexicalisation (avec possibilité d'apparition d'une nouvelle place d'objet); ces faits sont ceux que l'on attribue habituellement à la coalescence et sont comparables à ce qui se passe en CHINOIS, BANDA-LINDA et PASHTO.

Dans l'autre cas, on observe la coalescence entre un pronom ou un nom propre et le verbe: l'objet est alors bien défini et la transitivité de l'ensemble n'est pas altérée. Ce type de coalescence rejoint une tout autre problématique, celle des pronoms clitiques (*cf.* PASHTO *Actances* 8) et des conjugaisons à pronom objet incorporé (HONGROIS, G. Kassai, *Actances* 2).

5.1.3. Diathèses

Les variations de *diathèse*s, prises au sens large, ont été étudiées, dans *Actances* 2 et 3 pour la plupart, dans les langues qui ont des procédés réguliers de diathèse (passif, antipassif ou autres): OSTIAK (J. Perrot), BASQUE (par G. Rebuschi, et aussi en relation avec l'aspect par J. Boulle) et BERBÈRE (L. Galand); dans *Actances* 4, pour les fonctions des formes réflexives: en BULGARE par Z. Guentchéva et en ESPAGNOL, ITALIEN et FRANÇAIS par S. Fisher.

L'examen des variations de diathèses conduisit G. Lazard (*Actances* 2: 7−57) à dégager, pour le passif et l'antipassif, des fonctions diverses qui se laissent ranger sous trois rubriques:

(1) fonctions syntaxiques: d'une part suppression, respectivement de l'agent ou de l'objet de la construction de base, accusative ou ergative, et d'autre part utilisation de l'autre terme (objet en construction accusative, agent en construction ergative) comme 'pivot' d'une phrase complexe;

(2) fonctions de visée ou pragmatiques: le passif sert à la thématisation de l'objet et/ou à la rhématisation de l'agent; l'antipassif est, dans les langues étudiées (BASQUE, ESQUIMAU), en corrélation avec un objet rhématique, mais ce n'est peut-être pas toujours le cas (*cf.* Lazard 1994: 211);

(3) fonctions sémantiques: le passif est en corrélation avec une certaine rétrogradation de l'agent sur l'échelle d'individuation, il tend à estomper l'agentivité de l'agent; l'antipassif est plus nettement en corrélation avec certaines propriétés du procès (action involontaire, inachevée, imperfective, irréelle, etc.) qu'avec celles de l'objet (qui tend à être ou paraître peu individué).

Cet ensemble de fonctions caractéristiques des diathèses a suscité une série d'études dans des langues qui n'ont pas de procédures généralisées de diathèse et pour lesquelles on s'est demandé, comme le formule clairement le titre de C. Paris: «Comment sont remplies en TCHERKESSE les fonctions dévolues dans d'autres langues aux variations de diathèse» (*Actances* 3), de même en BIRMAN (D. Bernot) et dans *Actances* 2 en THAI (R. Gsell) et en BADAGA (C. Pilot-Raichoor). Dans *Actances* 4, F. Malbran-Labat étudie ainsi les moyens d'expression des fonctions du passif en AKKADIEN.

5.1.4. classification des verbes

La *classification des verbes* est abordée dans divers articles traitant des relations actancielles (*Actances* 1: en BANDA-LINDA, en BAFIA, en PASHTO; en FUTUNIEN par C. Moyse-Faurie, *Actances* 6), mais elle a aussi fait l'objet d'études globales − *Actances* 4: en XÂRÂCÙÙ (C. Moyse-Faurie), TUNUMIISUT (P. Mennecier), HÉBREU (P. Kirtchuk) − et d'autres sur des points plus particuliers: verbes réversibles (dans les langues accusatives, en BERBÈRE, L. Galand, *Actances* 3), *verbum dicendi* (en BIRMAN, D. Bernot *Actances* 4) et verbes 'anti-personnels' (verbes de syntaxe ergative mais sans 'objet', en PASHTO). En prenant en compte la valence verbale, les constructions et les corrélats sémantiques, la comparaison a conduit à ébaucher un cadre provisoire comportant quatre repères sur l'axe de transitivité:

(A) Qualité, état, changement d'état, etc.: verbes uniactanciels.

(B) Activité du corps ou de l'esprit dirigée ou non vers un objet: verbes uni- et bi-actanciels, sans changement d'orientation dans les langues accusatives (type 'manger [quelque chose]', HÉBREU 'aimer, haïr, craindre …'), verbes 'réversibles' (avec changement d'orientation) dans les langues ergatives, ex. TUNUMIISUT 'boire, écouter, chasser …', XÂRÂCÙÙ 'manger, pêcher, être taquin/taquiner …'. S'inscrivent aussi dans cet ensemble les verbes, en BULGARE (Z. Guentchéva, *Actances* 4), de forme réflexive et de sens moyen: 'regarder alentour, craindre, se réjouir …'. En revanche, en INDONÉSIEN (A. Cartier, *Actances* 4), l'ajout d'un actant s'accompagne toujours d'une modification morphosyntaxique incluant le jeu des préfixes/suffixes (N_1 *ber-teriak* 'N_1 pleurer' *vs* N_1 *me-neriak-i* Y 'N_1 pleurer Y', de même 'aimer, jalouser …').

(C) Processus spontanés ou provoqués: verbes uni-, bi-actanciels, 'réversibles' dans les langues accusatives (en BERBÈRE 'ouvrir, remplir …'), verbes avec ou sans agent dans les langues ergatives (en TUNUMIISUT 'ouvrir, verser, fondre …', en XÂRÂCÙÙ: 'raser, brûler …') et en BULGARE les verbes de forme réflexive et de sens médio-passif 's'ouvrir, se perdre, durcir …'.

(D) Action prégnante: verbes biactanciels, nombreux dans toutes les langues.

Cette grille, très grossière et incomplète, permet d'esquisser une classification générale qui semble se confirmer tendanciellement à travers les langues étudiées et aussi de spécifier les procédures de recatégorisation propres à chaque langue.

5.1.5. Sujet

Par la suite d'autres thèmes sont apparus, la question du *sujet* (*Actances* 8), dans des langues où les propriétés subjectales sont moins congruentes que dans des langues comme le FRANÇAIS ou l'ANGLAIS. Les travaux sur le sujet ont confirmé l'hétérogéneité des caractéristiques subjectales propres à chaque langue. Dans certaines langues, il s'identifie aisément: en BAFIA (G. Guarisma), le sujet est indispensable à la prédication et régit, à travers un système d'isophorie/allophorie, les propriétés de coréférence; en MOORE, langue d'Afrique occidentale (R. Kabore), le sujet s'identifie par sa place (devant le verbe), il peut être absent s'il s'agit d'un non-animé, mais on remarque surtout que, le procès n'étant pas orienté, n'importe quel terme de l'énoncé peut remplir la fonction de sujet.

Dans d'autres langues, les propriétés subjectales sont très diverses. C'est le cas de l'IRLANDAIS et du HINDI-OURDOU où la situation est singulièrement complexe pour des langues indo-européennes. En IRLANDAIS (P.-Y. Lambert) la caractérisation du sujet varie, entre autres, selon le type de conjugaison (analytique ou synthétique), la personne, le temps ou les conditions d'emploi (énoncé autonome *vs* réponse elliptique); en HINDI-OURDOU (A. Montaut), le sujet ne s'identifie clairement que dans quelques cas (actant unique d'un verbe intransitif et agent d'un verbe transitif inaccompli), dans les autres cas les propriétés subjectales se répartissent sur plusieurs termes. Les variations sont liées non seulement à l'aspect (nominatif à l'imperfectif *vs* ergatif au perfectif), mais aussi à des propriétés discursives ou sémantiques (entre autres: animé et sujet au génitif, verbe d'expérience et sujet au datif).

Dans d'autres langues enfin, la notion de sujet n'est guère pertinente: pour le JAPONAIS (J.-F. Causeret), les critères habituels (actant obligatoire, accord, place) ne sont pas opératoires, seuls peuvent être retenus quelques phénomènes comme celui d'orientation et de permanence référentielle en rapport avec la présence de *wa* ou de *ga* ...; en BADAGA (C. Pilot-Raichoor), les propriétés du sujet (nécessité morphologique, syntaxique ou référencielle) peuvent s'instancier dans un seul élément (indice personnel) ou se répartir sur plusieurs éléments et interviennent peu dans la syntaxe.

5.1.6. Personne

Le second thème d'*Actances* 8, celui des variations en *personne* est représenté par des langues qui ont plusieurs séries de pronoms ou d'indices personnels, témoignant d'une forte grammaticalisation du phénomène. La distinction attendue entre les deux personnes de l'interlocution (première et deuxième) et la troisième est fréquente: CAXINAUA (langue amérindienne du groupe pano, E. Camargo), TUNUMIISUT (P. Mennecier), PASHTO (D. Septfonds). Toutefois, le TCHOUKTCHE (langue paléo-sibérienne, F. Jacquesson) singularise morphologiquement et syntaxiquement la première personne et requiert un préfixe verbal 'inverseur' lorsqu'elle représente un patient, tandis que le FUTUNIEN (langue polynésienne, C. Moyse-Faurie) différencie clairement la troisième personne – mais seulement au singulier – seule apte à représenter une non-personne: omission possible et fontionnement ergatif du pronom antéposé de $3^{\text{ème}}$ sg. alors qu'aux autres personnes la structure est neutre ($X = Y = Z$). En CAXINAUA également, seule la troisième personne du singulier est omissible.

Les différences de traitement actanciel se manifestent tantôt à l'intérieur de la hiérarchie de personne: TCHOUKTCHE ($1^{\text{ère}}$), FUTUNIEN ($3^{\text{ème}}$ sg.), TUNUMIISUT ($3^{\text{ème}}$ personne agent marquée), tantôt entre pronoms et noms: CAXINAUA (marquage des pronoms en fonction d'actant unique ou d'agent (Z/X *vs* Y), tandis que les noms ne le sont que sous certaines conditions (notamment X marqué *vs* Z/Y non marqué).

La différence de traitement entre noms et pronoms a également été étudiée en FINNOIS et en VOGOUL (J. Perrot, *Actances* 1). Des variations apparaissent également en relation avec le temps-aspect-mode du verbe (PASHTO, FUTUNIEN) et le statut subordonné de la proposition (TUNUMIISUT, TCHOUKTCHE, FUTUNIEN), parfois lié à l'isophorie/allophorie (pour la $3^{\text{ème}}$ personne en TUNUMIISUT).

En PASHTO, qui dispose de trois séries de pronoms/indices personnels, la $1^{\text{ère}}$ personne de la série des préfixes directionnels peut avoir pour fonction de manifester la présence du locuteur dans l'énoncé (empathie, antimédiatif, dédoublement...). Enfin tous les auteurs soulignent les relations évidentes, mais complexes et diverses, entre les pronoms/indices actanciels et les pronoms/indices de possession des syntagmes nominaux.

5.1.7. Catégories verbales

Le dernier cahier d'*Actances* (n° 9) ouvre un nouveau champ d'études centré sur les *catégories verbales*, en gros: temps, aspects et modes, et leur interaction avec l'actance.

Les premières études soulignent la complexité du fonctionnement verbal qui ne se laisse précisément pas réduire à une simple distinction en temps, mode ou aspect. Les études portent sur l'ARMÉNIEN OCCIDENTAL (A. Donabédian), notamment sur l'opposition entre aoriste, parfait et médiatif; sur l'interaction entre aspect et modalité en GREC MODERNE (S. Vassilaki); sur le SUD-DRAVIDIEN (C. Pilot-Raichoor): interprétation aspectuelle des trois 'temps' de base incluant le négatif sans marque; sur deux langues amérindiennes, l'ARAWAK de Guyane (M.-F. Patte) qui manifeste une opposition de trois morphèmes (*-ha* virtuel, visée prospective, *-bo* actuel, visée interne ou 'inspective' et *-ka* réel, visée rétrospective) et le MAYA YUCATÈQUE (V. Vapnarsky) où c'est l'opposition entre formes rétrospectives et prospectives qui est analysée.

La restructuration d'un système verbal et de ses catégories est abordée en GRÉCO de Calabre (M. Katsoyannou), où l'affaiblissement des oppositions aspectuelles et la disparition de la catégorie du mode ont entraîné un renouvellement plus analytique du système, et en HINDI-OURDOU (A. Montaut) où la restructuration, également plus analytique, a eu des conséquences importantes sur l'actance (actant dissocié servant de localisateur à la prédication: ergatif à l'accompli, datif avec les verbes d'expérience et à la modalité déontique, etc.). Deux autres études traitent plus spécifiquement des relations entre temps, aspect et actants: en JAPONAIS (J.-F. Causeret et P. Le Nestour), interaction entre lexique, aspect et transitivité, et en DREHU et XÂRÂCÙÙ (C. Moyse-Faurie), langues qui se signalent par l'existence d'un 'transitionnel' marquant le passage d'une situation à une autre.

Ce rapide survol des questions abordées dans les cahiers d'*Actances* ne peut se substituer à la lecture des articles illustrant ces faits et développant bien des points qui n'ont pu être retenus.

6. Bilan, résultats et généralisations

Au-delà de la diversité et de la richesse des contributions individuelles, il est possible, après plusieurs années de fonctionnement, de faire une évaluation de la démarche adoptée et de relever les résultats les plus marquants qui s'en dégagent.

6.1. La méthode de recherche

La méthode de recherche proposée par G. Lazard, fondée sur l'étude des variations et leurs corrélats, s'est révélée à l'usage très productive. Elle fonctionne efficacement de façon bidirectionnelle: on peut, à partir d'une variation formelle quelconque, étudier tous les corrélats sémantiques et pragmatiques associés et en retour chercher, à partir de ce même ensemble de corrélats, dans d'autres langues, les variations formelles correspondantes (*cf.* ci-dessus l'étude des diathèses § 5.1.3). Elle permet également d'explorer l'espace grammatical dans son aspect multidimensionnel: le signifiant d'une variation actancielle s'inscrit souvent dans plusieurs réseaux grammaticaux délimitant son signifié global que la méthode permet aisément d'identifier. Exemplaire est à ce titre l'étude de F. Malbran-Labat sur le morphème *-ir* en ÉLAMITE (*Actances* 7) où l'on voit que ce morphème, qui intervient en tant que marque actancielle de non-ergatif (marquage différentiel de l'objet) se définit également comme animé (par opposition à *-me*), singulier (par oppositon à *-p*) et comme délocutif (par opposition à *-k* et à *-t*). Informations qui sont précieuses puisqu'elles établissent des connexions vers d'autres champs grammaticaux: nominaux, verbaux, etc., signalant un réseau de relations singulier pour chaque langue.

6.2. La typologie des structures actancielles

La typologie des structures actancielles, qui était le point de départ de ces recherches, a fait apparaître, en se développant, la nécessité d'un élargissement et de certains affinements.

D'une part, la schématisation *X,Y,Z* est insuffisante pour identifier les actants des diverses constructions d'une langue (études évoquées au § 5.1.1. et descriptions des actants en TCHERKESSE, ESQUIMAU et BADAGA, *Actances* 5). Il serait souhaitable de disposer de deux systèmes de schématisation, l'un adapté à la description des structures actancielles des langues, l'autre réservé à la comparaison interlangue.

D'autre part, bien que la caractérisation typologique des langues soit clairement justifiée (rapport entre *X*, *Y* et *Z*, *cf.* § 4.1), les désignations, ergative et accusative, adoptées peuvent conduire à une distorsion des relations effectivement manifestées par les langues: ainsi, le TCHERKESSE est, techniquement ($Y = Z$) une langue 'ergative', mais l'analyse approfondie des relations internes à la langue fait apparaître que, sémantiquement, la langue ne privilégie pas une relation ergative (ni la catégorisation d'un agent), mais une relation possessive, présentant des liens évidents avec la structuration du domaine nominal.

Il semblerait préférable, au minimum, d'adopter, comme pour les autres structures, 'mixte', 'neutre', etc., un étiquetage sans connotations sémantiques, mais probablement aussi de raffiner la schématisation qui s'est révélée − en particulier dans les langues présentant une pluralité de constructions (par exemple en HINDI, A. Montaut, *Actances* 8) − insuffisante pour rendre compte des rapports internes existant entre les diverses constructions: fait qui est pourtant d'une incidence notable dans la caractérisation typologique des langues. C'est manifestement dans ce domaine que le poids des hypothèses s'est le plus fait sentir.

6.3. Résultats

En ce qui concerne les résultats − la présentation des travaux (cf. § 5), aussi incomplète et allusive soit-elle, ayant montré combien sont diverses, dans leur forme, leur extension ou leurs fonctions, les variations qui ont pu être observées en relation avec tel ou tel thème − la comparaison entre langues permet néanmoins de dégager certaines régularités au niveau des corrélations qui ont été relevées, montrant qu'elles fonctionnent toujours dans le même sens.

6.3.1. Modèles de constructions biactancielles

Ainsi, les travaux sur le marquage différentiel de l'objet et la coalescence font apparaître qu'un ensemble de facteurs (définitude, humanitude, etc. concernant l'individuation de l'objet, plénitude et perfectivité du verbe, thématicité de l'objet, etc., (→ art. 65)) conduisent, dans toutes les langues où de telles variations existent, à une certaine 'polarisation' de l'objet, tandis que les propriétés inverses sont en corrélation avec une réduction de sa saillance et avec une tendance, soit à le faire entrer en coalescence avec le verbe, soit à le traiter comme un terme oblique, secondaire. On est ainsi amené à poser l'existence de deux modèles de construction biactancielle: l'une tripolaire [$X - Y - V$], l'autre bipolaire [$X - YV$ ou $X - V(-Y)$] qui se rapproche du modèle uniactanciel [$Z - V$].

6.3.2. Échelle de diathèses

D'autre part, l'étude des diathèses, notamment sur le passif et l'antipassif, avait permis de dégager trois types de fonctions: (a) syntaxiques, (b) de visée communicative et (c) sémantiques, représentant des choix possibles mais non nécessaires, de l'un comme de l'autre.

Dans leur morphologie et leurs fonctions syntaxiques, passif et antipassif sont symétriques (X et Y s'échangent et l'agent − périphérisé ou supprimé au passif − dans l'un subit le même sort que l'objet dans l'autre), mais leurs fonctions sémantiques ne le sont pas: le passif vise à estomper l'agentivité de l'agent tandis que l'antipassif tend à réduire l'effectivité de l'action. Cette dissymétrie trouve sa source dans la relation de chacun des participants à l'action: elle émane de l'agent et aboutit au patient $X \rightarrow V \rightarrow Y$; au passif c'est la relation de l'agent à l'action qui est estompée $(X) \ldots V \rightarrow Y$, tandis qu'à l'antipassif c'est celle de l'action au patient $X \rightarrow V \ldots (Y)$. Cette dissymétrie explique la coexistence dans certaines langues des deux diathèses. Passif et antipassif se situent ainsi également dans une position intermédiaire entre l'actif (de structure accusative ou ergative) et la construction uniactancielle.

	Passif	
	$Y - V(-X)$	
Actif		Uniactanciel
$X - Y - V$		$Z - V$
	$X - V(-Y)$	
	Antipassif	

Cette échelle est assez semblable à celle résultant des études sur l'objet, ce qui n'est pas surprenant puisque les corrélats sont approximativement les mêmes (individuation de l'un ou l'autre actant, effectivité du procès).

L'étude des fonctions sémantiques aboutit ainsi à un intéressant rapprochement des trois premiers thèmes de recherche rappelés ci-dessus (5.1.2. et 5.1.3 ←). Il apparaît en effet que les corrélations de l'antipassif ont des affinités frappantes avec celles des constructions où l'objet est non marqué ou tend à la coalescence avec le verbe. Dans les deux cas l'objet n'est pas le terme majeur de la proposition, il est mis en retrait, traité comme une sorte de qualificatif du prédicat. On peut ainsi considérer les constructions biactancielles bipolaires évoquées ci-dessus comme l'équivalent fonctionnel de l'antipassif dans les langues accusatives. De même que certaines langues ergatives ont à la fois un antipassif et un passif, certaines langues accusatives ont à la fois un passif et l'équivalent d'un antipassif.

6.3.3. Classes de verbes

Les études sur les classes de verbes ont également permis d'établir une échelle de corrélations entre les propriétés morphosyntaxiques des verbes et leurs corrélats sémantiques, suggérant l'esquisse d'une classification allant des verbes uniactanciels représentant une qualité, un état ou changement d'état, etc., aux verbes biactanciels représentant une action prégnante, avec diverses positions intermédiaires.

6.3.4. Transitivité

Les résultats de ces diverses études ont été intégrés dans une théorie de la «transitivité généralisée» (Lazard 1998c). Parti d'une conception scalaire, G. Lazard regroupe initialement «deux échelles de transitivité» (*Actances* 2: 59−68), l'une lexicale, issue de la classification des verbes (différences de construction de différents verbes), l'autre grammaticale, issue des études sur les diathèses (changements de construction avec un même verbe), représentées sous forme d'un continuum où l'on peut distinguer des degrés. La transitivité n'est «pas conçue comme une donnée, mais comme un construit, [...] fort complexe que l'on n'atteint qu'au terme d'une longue série d'analyses» (*Actances* 2: 60) sur le jeu complexe de corrélations entre des formes morphosyntaxiques et des facteurs sémantiques et pragmatiques. Elle prend en définitive (Lazard 1998c) la forme d'un cadre général, formé d'un axe orienté muni de deux repères, la construction biactancielle majeure d'un côté, la construction uniactancielle de l'autre, entre lesquelles il convient de situer les constructions intermédiaires.

Ce cadre, toujours provisoire, pourrait être affiné, étendu (constructions hypertransitives ?), comprendre plusieurs lignes (toutes les constructions ne s'échelonnent pas nécessairement sur la même ligne), etc. Le résultat obtenu n'est pas fondamentalement différent de ceux de tous les travaux menés dans le prolongement de la conception multifactorielle de la transitivité de Hopper et Thompson (1980), mais il s'en distingue par le mode de construction, reposant non pas sur des distinctions conceptuelles établies *a priori*, mais sur les catégorisations effectivement manifestées par les langues qu'il faut situer dans ce cadre.

6.4. Construction d'échelles

L'un des résultats les plus patents de l'étude des variations d'actance est qu'elle conduit, de façon presque immédiate, à construire des échelles, soit fines et spécifiques à telle variation particulière signalant les points critiques correspondant aux catégorisations effectuées dans telle langue ou groupe de langues, soit, par généralisation à partir de la comparaison entre langues, des échelles globales permettant de fixer un *cadre*, tendanciellement *invariant*, indiquant l'ordre dans lequel se distribuent les corrélations.

Ce sont ces cadres généraux qui constituent un apport direct aux recherches typologiques, s'inscrivant dans ce qu'on peut appeler des hiérarchies implicationnelles conditionnelles: «Ils n'impliquent pas la nécessité d'une variation donnée, mais, semble-t-il, imposent, si cette variation existe, un certain type de relation entre sa forme morphosyntaxique et son ou ses corrélat(s). [...] ils se formulent ainsi: si, dans une langue donnée, il y a une variation d'actance en corrélation avec tel facteur sémantique (ou pragmatique), la correspondance entre les deux oppositions ou les deux hiérarchies, l'une morphosyntaxique, l'autre sémantique (ou pragmatique), aura lieu dans un certain sens et non dans l'autre» (Lazard 1994: 222).

Construits à partir de données très concrètes et relativement indépendantes des concepts grammaticaux (les variations formelles observées dans chaque langue), les invariants tendanciels qui s'en dégagent sont abstraits puisqu'ils n'expriment que des relations entre des relations: un certain parallélisme entre des séquences de relations formelles et des séquences de relations sémantiques ou pragmatiques.

6.5. Catégorisations

L'autre apport important de l'étude des variations actancielles concerne les *catégorisations* et fournit des informations précieuses sur la dynamique des langues et les sources de la diversité. On observe en effet que si les variations sont en grande majorité presque toujours en corrélation avec les mêmes grands types de facteurs évoqués au § 4.2. (nature du procès et rôles des participants, catégories des actants, du verbe, etc.), la diversité résultante semble être due en grande partie:

(a) au choix des éléments porteurs de la variation (actant, verbe ou l'ensemble des deux),
(b) aux catégorisations et sous-catégorisations propres à chaque langue concernant les deux grands domaines nominaux et verbaux (le nombre et les relations entre les points critiques révélés par les variations diffèrent de façon importante de langue à langue (*cf.* les études sur la personne, § 5.1.6),
(c) aux hiérarchisations entre les différents facteurs corrélatifs d'une variation (le marquage différentiel de l'objet est généralement dépendant de l'individuation des actants, mais dans certaines langues la priorité est accordée à la définitude, dans d'autres à l'humanitude ou à la visée communicative, etc.).

Un autre facteur important de la diversité est l'extension accordée à telle catégorie dans telle langue. Un exemple frappant à ce propos est donné en THAI par R. Gsell, *Actances* 2:77, où la catégorie d'animé tend à s'étendre à tout ce qui bouge, êtres vivants, mais aussi animés technologiques: voitures, moteurs jusqu'à 'l'argent' qui vient d'être inclus dans cette catégorie! Un autre exemple, plus connu, d'extension est celui des constructions transitives dans les langues européennes qui s'appliquent à toutes sortes de relations entre deux actants.

Deux points sont à souligner. D'une part, les faits grammaticaux, comme les faits lexicaux pour lesquels cela est bien établi, sont susceptibles d'extension polysémique de proche en proche, ce qui confirme qu'une étiquette catégorielle quelconque (nom, animé, présent) n'a de sens véritable qu'à l'intérieur d'une langue où elle se définit exclusivement par ses limites, les termes ou emplois qu'elle inclut et ceux qu'elle exclut.

D'autre part, une catégorisation semble s'établir initialement sur une propriété saillante d'un ensemble d'unités (animé, agent, thème). Puis l'inclusion dans cette catégorie d'unités qui *a priori* ont peu d'affinités avec cette propriété conduit à altérer leurs propriétés fondamentales et à forcer une représentation allant dans le sens de la propriété saillante de la catégorie.

La combinaison de ces deux caractéristiques donne à l'organisation forme / sens des langues une grande souplesse. Selon que la langue maintiendra dans tel ou tel domaine une valeur saillante forte ou tendra à sa dilution, on aura des singularités de traitement plus ou moins marquées (dans beaucoup de langues l'actant représentant l'agent doit être un animé, mais le TCHOUKTCHE offre un cas de catégorisation plus marquée (non-patient) de la première personne, *cf.* § 5.1.6); ou on peut rencontrer, à l'inverse, des extensions plus ou moins importantes, visibles par exemple par comparaison entre langues d'un même groupe (*cf.* par exemple, C. Moyse-Faurie, *Actances* 8:183, la distribution des pronoms antéposés dans six langues polynésiennes allant d'un emploi restreint aux seuls verbes transitifs dérivés en TOKELAU jusqu'à un emploi généralisé à tout type de verbes en TONGIEN), visibles aussi dans la dispersion des valeurs dans une même langue (Z. Guentchéva, *Actances* 4, emplois des formes réflexives en BULGARE) qui peut, comme l'exprime S. Fisher à propos de *se* en ESPAGNOL, conduire à un «singulier 'retour' des formes» («les formes moyennes qui, en ESPAGNOL, ont pris la place du passif périphrastique, deviennent à l'usage des formes actives. Bien loin d'engendrer le passif — comme en GREC — ici le moyen produit l'actif», *Actances* 4:91). Un phénomène de même ordre est décrit en MANDARIN (X. Dan, *Actances* 6, le verbe *gei* 'donner' produit causatif, marque d'agent, mais aussi en interaction avec les propriétés lexicales du verbe, marque d'objet, et avec ses propriétés d'orientation, marque de voix neutre).

Ces derniers exemples témoignent d'une exploitation différentielle (positive ou au contraire par signalement d'un élément absent) des potentialités significatives d'une unité et d'un déplacement de la propriété saillante sur telle ou telle valeur dans telles conditions d'emploi.

Aux faits d'extension répondent aussi, bien sûr, des faits de réduction (par désuétude: le duel dans beaucoup de langues, ou par l'extension d'une catégorie mitoyenne: emplois du passé composé réduisant le passé simple en FRANÇAIS). Non seulement les catégories sont différentes de langue à langue, mais de plus, elles sont loin d'être immuables.

Les travaux d'*Actances* mettent bien en évidence la relation dialectique entre le sens et la forme: l'un modèle l'autre, et réciproquement. On pourrait s'attendre, dans ces conditions, à une infinie diversité, ce qui n'est pas le cas. La pérennité de certaines notions grammaticales 'nom', 'verbe', 'agent', 'temps', tout comme la cyclicité de certains phénomènes: thème > sujet > thème > ..., parfait > prétérit > ..., structure accusative > ergative > ..., semblent indiquer qu'il existe dans la dynamique des langues certains principes régulateurs de la variabilité. Les suggestions faites par G. Lazard à propos des catégories interlangagières pourraient ouvrir des voies de recherche intéressantes.

6.6. Relation entre variations et invariants

C'est pour tenter de répondre aux complexes relations entre variations et invariants que G. Lazard a fait les propositions suivantes: «il existerait non pas, à proprement parler, des 'catégories' interlangagières, mais des notions invariantes autour desquelles les catégories des langues particulières, en quelque sorte, se cristalliseraient préférentiellement. Cette conception [...] signifie, si nous nous représentons l'ensemble des notions possibles comme situées dans un espace multidimensionnel: (1) que certaines portions de cet espace sémantique sont telles que toutes les langues peut-être, beaucoup de langues en tout cas, y construisent des instruments grammaticaux [... par exemple] domaine du temps et de l'aspect [...]. (2) que dans ces portions d'espace que sont les *domaines de grammaticalisation*', certaines régions sont privilégiées: ce sont les *'zones focales'*. Les notions qui y sont situées sont plus fréquemment grammaticalisées que d'autres du même domaine. Beaucoup de langues ont donc des formes dont l'aire (ou mieux le volume) de signification contient l'une ou l'autre de ces zones focales, mais cette aire (ou ce volume) a une extension et une forme variables selon les langues, c'est-à-dire comprend, outre la notion privilégiée, telles ou telles notions voisines» (Lazard 1992: 431−32).

Ce sont ces domaines de grammaticalisation et de zones focales qui fournissent les *invariants*, dans lesquels chaque langue découpe ses propres catégories grammaticales, «mais il est fréquent que les catégories recouvrent ou englobent l'une ou l'autre des zones focales» (*ibid.*). Dans cette perspective de nouvelles questions surgissent, notamment sur le caractère nécessaire ou préférentiel des domaines de grammaticalisation et sur la «force d'attraction», vraisemblablement variable, des zones focales.

Décrire les catégorisations des langues, les situer dans l'espace grammatical et confronter les résultats aux invariants supposés, telles semblent être les principales tâches assignées au linguiste typologue adhérant au projet de G. Lazard.

Les recherches typologiques issues du projet Rivalc de G. Lazard se caractérisent en définitive par leur démarche: de la variation et de la forme à l'invariance et au sens, et par leur caractère évolutif: parties d'une schématisation un peu rigide des structures d'actance, enrichies d'outils conceptuels plus complexes: variations et corrélats, échelles (discrétisation d'un continuum), représentations topologiques (informelles dans la 'topographie' de l'espace sémantique suggérée par G. Lazard (1992: 432), mais explicites dans l'approche de Z. Guentchéva (1990) pour le domaine aspecto-temporel), et zones focales (dérivées de la notion de prototype), tant dans leurs thèmes que dans leur méthode ou leurs objectifs.

La contribution de ces recherches à la typologie reste certes bien modeste au regard de la diversité et de la complexité des langues, mais participe − et aux côtés de maintes autres approches − à une meilleure compréhension des faits de langue.

7. Références

Daneš, František. 1964. «A three-level approach to syntax». *Travaux linguistiques de Prague* 1: 225-240.

Actances 1985-1998 (cahiers du groupe Rivalc/Rivaldi, GDR 749, CNRS), Paris.

Guentchéva, Zlatka. 1990. *Temps et aspect: l'exemple du bulgare contemporain.* (Sciences du langage.) Paris. Éd. du CNRS

Hopper, Paul & Thompson, Sandra. 1980. «Transitivity in grammar and discourse». *Language* 56.2: 251−99.

Lazard, Gilbert. 1978. «Eléments d'une typologie des structures d'actance: structures ergatives, accusatives et autres». *Bulletin de la Société de Linguistique de Paris* 73.1: 49−84.

Lazard, Gilbert. 1992. «Y a-t-il des catégories interlangagières ?». In: Anschütz, Susanne (éd.). *Texte, Sätze, Wörter und Moneme.* Heidelberg, 427−34.

Lazard, Gilbert. 1994. *L'actance.* (Linguistique nouvelle.) Paris. Presses Univ. de France.

Lazard, Gilbert. 1995. «Typological research on actancy». In: Shibatani, Masayoshi & Bynon, Theodora (éds.). *Approaches to Language Typology.* Oxford, 167−213.

Lazard, Gilbert. 1997. «La typologie actancielle». *Studi italiani di linguistica teorica e applicata* 26.2: 205−26.

Lazard, Gilbert. 1998. *Actancy.* (Empirical approaches to language typology, 19.) Berlin. Mouton de Gruyter.

Lazard, Gilbert. 1998a. «L'approche typologique». *La Linguistique* 34.1: 3–17.

Lazard, Gilbert. 1998b. «Grandeur et misère de la typologie». In: *Proceedings of the 16th International Congress of Linguists.* Oxford. Pergamon. Paper 0005.

Lazard, Gilbert. 1998c. «De la transitivité restreinte à la transitivité généralisée». In: Rousseau, André. *La transitivité.* Villeneuve d'Ascq: Presses Universitaires du Septentrion.

Lazard, Gilbert. 1999. «Pour une terminologie rigoureuse: quelques principes et propositions». *Mémoires de la Société de Linguistique de Paris* (Nouvelle série, tome VI). Paris.

Modèles linguistiques 1992-1993, n° 14.2: Relations actancielles.

Paris, Catherine (éd.). 1979. *Relations prédicats-actant(s).* Paris: Selaf.

Studi italiani di linguistica teorica e applicata 1997: 2: «La typologie actancielle».

Christiane Pilot-Raichoor,
LACITO–CNRS, Paris (France)

VI. Explanatory principles, principles of organization, and methods in typology and language universals
Erklärungsprinzipien, Ordnungsprinzipien und Methoden für universalistische und typologische Fragestellungen
Les principes d'explication, les principes structurants et les méthodes appliquées aux questions d'ordre universaliste et typologique

29. The role of processing principles in explaining language universals

1. Correspondences between performance and grammars
2. A hypothesis
3. Some evidence for the hypothesis
4. Competing motivations in performance and grammars
5. Conclusions
6. References

1. Correspondences between performance and grammars

When one compares performance variation within a language and grammatical variation across languages one discovers clear correspondences. The preferred word orders in languages that permit choices are generally those that are productively grammaticalized in languages with fixed orders, dispreferred options are not productively grammaticalized. For example, performance ordering alternations in numerous structures and languages have been argued in Hawkins (1994) to be sensitive to the efficiency and speed with which constituent structure can be recognized. This same efficiency and speed is guaranteed by the grammaticalized word orders of Greenberg's (1963) cross-category correlations, and the relative quantities of preferred to dispreferred orders in languages with performance variation are closely correlated with the quantities of preferred grammars. One much-discussed structural type that is hard to process is a center embedding (see e.g. Frazier 1985). There is a decreasing tolerance for center embeddings of increasing size in performance, in those languages that permit them at all, and in grammatical conventions across languages (Hawkins 1994: 297−308, 315−321). The Keenan-Comrie (1977) Accessibility Hierarchy (AH) is supported both by processing ease and frequency data from performance, and by grammatical data in the form of cut-off points for relativization, and so on (Hawkins 1999).

These kinds of correspondences have been amply documented in morphology as well. The markedness hierarchies of Greenberg (1966) and Croft (1990) (e.g. Sing > Plur > Dual > Trial/Paucal) define (declining) frequency rankings in performance and also grammaticalization rankings. If a language has a separate morphological category for some position low on each of these hierarchies, then it has a separate morphological category for each higher position, and the number of alternative morphological forms that are available to partition references to a given category will be greater (or equal) in higher positions compared to each lower position (Hawkins 1998a). This frequency-grammaticalization correlation has been further developed in Bybee (1985) and its implications for current theories of morphological processing are explored in Bybee (1995).

The precision and extent of this correlation is clearly no accident. Yet it is only relatively recently that sufficient data have been collected from both performance and grammars for us to be able to see the potential generality of the phenomenon. And establishing that there is a correlation is only the first step in explaining why it might be so and how it comes about. In this short paper I shall focus on the correlation itself, since its existence is not fully appreciated in much current linguistics, and I shall illustrate certain processing preferences in syntax and the grammatical universals that correlate with them.

When one pursues this approach to grammatical variation, a number of welcome consequences follow. First, the conventions of grammars turn out to be highly sensitive to processing factors, and better descriptive predictions can be made on this basis than by (ultimately stipulated) grammatical axioms alone. Processing preferences lead to statistical and non-statistical universals, to implicational hierarchies, and to variation in structures for which independently motivated preferences are in competition. Grammatical data can also contribute to psycholinguistic theorizing, since grammars in this view are simply conventionalized processing preferences.

2. A hypothesis

Let us formulate the following working hypothesis:

(1) *Performance-Grammar Correspondence Hypothesis* (PGCH)
Grammars have conventionalized syntactic structures in proportion to their degree of processing preference (as evidenced by frequency of use, acceptability judgements or processing experiments).

From (1) we can derive a number of predictions, including those of (2):

(2) *Predictions of the PGCH*
 (a) If structure A is highly preferred over an alternative A', then A will be productively grammaticalized, A' will not be; if A and A' are more equally preferred, then both A and A' will be productive in grammars.
 (b) If there is a preference ranking A>B>C>D in performance, then there will be a corresponding hierarchy of grammatical conventions (with cut-off points and declining frequencies of languages).
 (c) If two preferences P and P' are in (partial) opposition, then there will be grammatical variation, with both P and P' being conventionalized, each in proportion to the degree of motivation for that preference in a given language type.

In order to test these predictions we need performance variation data from various languages involving structures for which some processing theory can motivate preferences in use. These data can take different forms, as summarized in (1). We then need cross-linguistic grammatical data with respect to these same structures in languages that have fixed the options. To fix an option is understood here to mean that a convention of grammar exists that will generate structure A and not generate a potential competitor A' that exists as an alternative in certain languages and that could be semantically equivalent to A.

If the proposed correlation between performance and grammars is valid, then we will be on our way to a processing theory of grammatical variation. Two theoretical components will still be required. The performance preferences will need to be embedded within an overall psycholinguistic and ultimately neurological model that can explain the processing motivation itself. And we will also need a diachronic theory of change and linguistic evolution explaining how patterns of preference for A over A' at time T can become fixed conventions at T+1, selecting structure A and avoiding A' altogether (see Kirby 1994, 1999).

The first step in this research program is to argue for the correlation itself. What general processing motivations are there for structural preferences in performance? And to what extent do they penetrate into the grammar and explain linguistic universals? Some brief illustrations follow.

3. Some evidence for the hypothesis

One major cause of complexity involves the size of the syntactic domain in which a given grammatical relation or dependency operates. How great is the distance separating interdependent items and how much material needs to be processed simultaneously with the processing of the dependency? In Hawkins (1990, 1994, 1998, 1999) I have argued that there is a correlation between performance and grammar with regard to domain sizes. In those languages and structures in which domain sizes can vary in performance, we see a clear preference for the smallest possible domains. In those languages and structures in which domain sizes have been grammatically fixed, we see the same preference in the conventions. This preference is formulated in (3):

(3) *Minimize Domains:* Given two or more categories A, B, ... related by a rule R of combination and/or dependency, the human processor prefers to minimize the distance between them within the smallest surface structure domain sufficient for the processing of R.

3.1. Domain minimization in constituent recognition domains

The immediate constituents (ICs) of a phrase can typically be recognized on the basis of less than all the words dominated by that phrase. Some orderings reduce the number of words needed to recognize all ICs, compared with other orderings, making IC recognition faster. Compare (4 a) and (4 b):

A CRD is defined in (5).

(5) *Constituent Recognition Domain* (CRD): The CRD for a phrasal mother node M consists of all non-terminal and terminal nodes dominated by M on the path from the terminal node that constructs the first IC on the left to the terminal node that constructs the last IC on the right.

The theory of Early Immediate Constituents (EIC) (Hawkins 1990, 1994, 1998b) predicts that the greater the preference for structure A over A' (measured in terms of higher IC-to-word ratios, i.e. smaller CRDs), the more (or equally) frequent/easy to process/etc. the A structure will be in performance, compared with any B/B' pair with less degree of preference. And preferred structures will be those that occur in general (in the unmarked case) in performance.

For a language like English this amounts to a quantitative preference for shorter PPs before longer ones overall, and the degree of this preference is predicted to be directly pro-

(4) (a)
The gamekeeper $_{\mathrm{VP}}$[looked $_{\mathrm{PP1}}$ [through his binoculars] $_{\mathrm{PP2}}$[into the blue but slightly overcast sky]]
    1   2   3   4   5

(b)
The gamekeeper $_{\mathrm{VP}}$[looked $_{\mathrm{PP2}}$[into the blue but slightly overcast sky] $_{\mathrm{PP1}}$[through his binoculars]]
    1   2   3   4   5   6   7   8   9

The three items, V, PP_1 and PP_2 (where the higher subscript refers to a phrase with greater or equal length in words) can be recognized on the basis of five words in (4 a), compared with nine in (4 b), assuming that head categories such as P immediately project to mother nodes such as PP and render them predictable on-line. Following the procedure of Hawkins (1994: ch. 3), the greater efficiency of (4 a) is captured by dividing the number of ICs by the number of words required to recognize those ICs within the VP Constituent Recognition Domain (CRD) and expressing the result as a percentage. The higher the percentage, the more efficient the ordering is, since the same constituency information can be derived from less input.

(4) (a) VP CRD: IC-to-word ratio
        of 3/5 = 60%   (structure A)
    (b) VP CRD: IC-to-word ratio
        of 3/9 = 33%   (structure A')

portional to the length difference between the two PPs. Performance data from English texts bear this out (Hawkins 1994: 129). Structures like (4 a) and (4 b) were examined in which two PPs were freely permutable with truth-conditional equivalence. Only 11% of them were ordered long before short with 67% short before long and 22% of equal length. The short before long orders plus the equal length PPs (in which either ordering is as efficient as it can possibly be) collectively account for 89% of the data. Moreover, within the 11% of long before short PPs (with lower IC-to-word ratios), a full two thirds involved only a one-word difference in length and there was a gradual reduction in long before short orderings the bigger the length difference. This is shown in (6), in which the top row gives the figures for short before long, PP_1 before PP_2, and the second row long before short, PP_2 before PP_1.

(6) n = 126 $PP_2 > PP_1$ by 1 word
    $[PP_1\ PP_2]$ 69% (27)
    $[PP_2\ PP_1]$ 31% (12)
    by 2−3 words   by 4   by 5+
    86% (30)   91% (10)   100% (41)
    14% (5)   9% (1)   0% (0)

35 structures had PPs of equal length. Similar data from many other languages are presented in Hawkins (1994: ch. 4).

3.2. The Greenbergian word order correlations

For grammars, EIC predicts that conventionalized orders will be those with the smallest CRDs, in general; and as CRD sizes increase, orders will be conventionalized in progressively fewer languages and in progressively fewer structures (in proportion to the degree of EIC's dispreference). This accounts for the cross-category ordering correlations in Greenberg's (1963) universals, two of which are presented in (7) and (8) (see Hawkins 1994: 257, 259 and Dryer 1992):

(7) (a) $_{VP}[V\ _{PP}[P\ NP]] = 161\ (41.4\%)$
        IC-to-word: 2/2 = 100%
    (b) $[[NP\ P]_{PP}\ V]_{VP} = 204\ (52.4\%)$
        IC-to-word: 2/2 = 100%
    (c) $_{VP}[V\ [NP\ P]_{PP}] = 18\ (4.6\%)$
        IC-to-word: 2/4 = 50%
    (d) $[_{PP}[P\ NP]\ V]_{VP} = 6\ (1.5\%)$
        IC-to-word: 2/4 = 50%
        Assume: V = 1 word; P = 1; NP = 2
        EIC-preferred (7a)+(7b) = 365/389 (93%)

(8) (a) $_{PP}[P\ _{NP}[N\ PossP]] = 134\ (39.9\%)$
    (b) $[[PossP\ N]_{NP}\ P]_{PP} = 177\ (52.7\%)$
    (c) $_{PP}[P\ [PossP\ N]_{NP}] = 14\ (4.2\%)$
    (d) $[_{NP}[N\ PossP]\ P]_{PP} = 11\ (3.3\%)$
        EIC-preferred (8a) + (8b) = 311/336 (93%)

The adjacency of V and P, and of P and N, guarantees the smallest possible domain for recognition of the two ICs in question (V and PP within VP, P and NP within PP): two words are sufficient, hence 100% IC-to-word ratios. In the non-adjacent domains of the (c) and (d) orders, ratios are significantly lower and exemplifying languages are significantly less. The preferred (a) and (b) structures collectively account for 93% of all languages.

A related illustration can be given from multiple branching NPs consisting of a head noun (N), a single-word adjective (Adj), and a relative clause (S′), as in the English sentence (9):

(9) $_{NP}[\text{bright students }_{S'}[\text{that Mary will teach}]]$

This structure can be represented as (9′) in which C stands for any constructing category for a relative clause, e. g. a relative pronoun, subordinate clause complementizer, or participial marking on the verb indicating subordinate status, as in Dravidian languages (C. Lehmann 1984: 50−52, Hawkins 1994: 387−393):

(9′) $_{NP}[\text{Adj N }_{S'}[C\ S]]$

There are now 12 logically possible orderings of Adj, N and S′ (ordered [C S] or [S C]). Just four of these have 100% IC-to-word ratios for the NP CRD (all with adjacent Adj, N and C), and these four account for the vast majority of languages:

		Structure	IC-to-word ratio	Attested languages
(10)	(a)	[N Adj [C S]]	3/3 = 100%	Extensive: Romance, Arabic, Ewe
	(b)	[Adj N [C S]]	3/3 = 100%	Extensive: Germanic, Greek, Finnish
	(c)	[[S C] N Adj]	3/3 = 100%	Extensive: Basque, Burmese
	(d)	[[S C] Adj N]	3/3 = 100%	Extensive: Telugu, Turkish, Lahu

A small minority of languages are distributed among the remaining eight orders in direct proportion to their IC-to-word ratios (Hawkins 1990, 1994: 272).

3.3. A center embedding hierarchy in prepositional languages

When non-optimal domains are grammatically permitted, they appear to be hierarchically organized, with grammaticality cutting off at implicationally sanctioned points only. Hawkins (1994: 315−319) presents evidence for the following implicational universal:

(11)   If a language is prepositional, then if the relative clause precedes the head noun (RelN) then a possessive phrase precedes the noun (PosspN), if the possessive precedes then a single-word adjective precedes (AdjN), and if a single-word adjective precedes

then a demonstrative determiner precedes (DemN).

This universal defines a hierarchy of permitted modifiers of the noun that can intervene as center-embedded constituents between the preposition (which constructs PP) and the noun (which constructs NP), as shown in (12):

(12) (a) Prep: [NDem, NAdj, NPossp, NRel]   e. g. Arabic, Thai
    (b) Prep: DemN   [NAdj, NPossp, NRel]   e. g. Masai, Spanish
    (c) Prep: DemN, AdjN   [NPossp, NRel]   e. g. Greek, Maya
    (d) Prep: DemN, AdjN, PosspN   [NRel]   e. g. Maung
    (e) Prep: DemN, AdjN, PosspN, RelN   e. g. Amharic

In the language sample of Hawkins (1983) there are 61 prepositional languages on which the predictions of (11) can be tested. Types (12a) and (12b) are of almost equal frequency, but there is a progressive decline in language numbers from (12c) down to (12e). This is shown in (13) which gives the IC-to-word ratios for all the relevant structures (on the assumption that Dem = 1 word, Adj = 1, Possp = 2, RelS' = 4, and that N or Dem constructs NP while P constructs PP):

(13)
Structure	IC-to-word ratio	no. preposed	ratio postposed	no. postposed
1. $_{PP}[P\ _{NP}[Dem\ N]]$	2/2 = 100%	29 (48%)	2/2 = 100%	32 (52%)
2. $_{PP}[P\ _{NP}[Adj\ N]]$	2/3 = 67%	17 (28%)	2/2 = 100%	44 (72%)
3. $_{PP}[P\ _{NP}[Possp\ N]]$	2/4 = 50%	8 (13%)	2/2 = 100%	53 (87%)
4. $_{PP}[P\ _{NP}[RelS'\ N]]$	2/6 = 33%	1 (2%)	2/2 = 100%	60 (98%)

Both Dem-initial and N-initial NPs are equally efficient in this theory, since both Dem and N can construct NP. But as non-constructing categories of increasing aggregate length (Adj < PossP < RelS') intervene, the distance between P and N increases, and as it does so the number of attested languages declines, and the proportion of postposed to preposed modifiers of N increases. Once again, grammatical structures are avoided across languages in proportion to the degree of EIC's dispreference.

3.4. The Accessibility Hierarchy

Keenan & Comrie (1977) formulate an Accessibility Hierarchy (SU > DO > IO > OBL > GEN) for relativization and certain other regularities across languages. Their main claim is that relativization becomes more difficult the lower one goes down the hierarchy. The precise predictions are formulated as a set of hierarchy constraints, defined in terms of relative clause "strategies". Two strategies are considered different if they differ either in terms of head/relative clause ordering, or in terms of "case-coding". A strategy is [+ Case] if it contains a nominal element in the relative clause that unequivocally indicates which NP position is being relativized on (typically a copy pronoun as in Hebrew, or a case-distinctive relative pronoun as in Russian). [− Case] relatives contain no such element (e. g. *the man that I know* in English) and the position relativized on is empty (or "a gap").

I have argued in Hawkins (1994, 1999) that the following (slightly modified AH) ranking involves increasingly complex domains for relativization, measured in terms of the set of nodes and structural relations that need to be computed in order to match the relative clause head with the co-indexed pronoun or gap in the relative clause:

(14)   SU > DO > IO/OBL > GEN

Hence, relativizations on these positions involve increasingly large relativization domains. Some performance support for this comes from a repetition experiment conducted by Keenan & S. Hawkins (1987) on English speakers, children and adults. Their prediction was that repetition accuracy would correlate with positions on the AH. The data, shown in (15), bear this out (GEN-SU stands for relativization on a genitive within a subject; GEN-DO for relativization on a genitive within a direct object).

(15)   Repetition accuracies for relativization
           SU   DO   IO   OBL   GEN-SU   GEN-DO
Adults   64%   62.5%   57%   52%   31%   36%
Children   63%   51%   50%   35%   21%   18%

The relative ranking SU > DO has been corroborated by a number of further studies in the psycholinguistic literature. For example, Pickering & Shillcock (1992) found significant reaction time differences between the two positions in English in a self-paced reading experiment. Textual frequencies for relativizations on these positions also decline down (14) (Keenan 1975).

As relative clauses with gaps grow in size, there is more structure to process simultaneously with gap identification and filling. This theoretical consideration coupled with performance data such as (15) leads to prediction (16) for grammars:

(16)   If a relative clause gap is grammatical in position P on AH, then gaps will be grammatical in all higher positions on AH.

tion relativized on as easy as it can possibly be.

(18)   ha-isha   [she-Yon natan la
        'the woman that John gave to-her
        et   ha-sefer] (Hebrew)
        DO the book', i.e.
        'the woman that John gave the book to'

Hence we predict (19):

(19)   If a copy pronoun is grammatical in position P on AH, then copy pronouns will be grammatical in all lower positions that can be relativized at all.

27 of Keenan & Comrie's languages have copy pronouns (as a subinstance of [+ Case]). Prediction (19) holds exceptionlessly:

(20)   Pronoun-retaining Languages in Keenan & Comrie's Data
        GEN only: e.g. Japanese, Javanese, Malay, Turkish
        GEN & IO/OBL only: e.g. Toba Batak, Hausa, Welsh
        GEN & IO/OBL & DO only: e.g. Chinese (Pekingese), Kera, Slovenian
        GEN & IO/OBL & DO & SU: Urhobo

This prediction turns out to be exceptionlessly supported. Keenan & Comrie's [- Case] relative clauses are all gap strategies, and all the languages in their sample with [- Case] (40 in all) limit the gap strategy to all and only the following implicationally permitted relativization possibilities:

(17)   [- Case] Languages in Keenan & Comrie's Data
        SU only: e.g. Arabic (Classical), Toba Batak, Malagasy, Minang-Kabau
        SU & DO only: e.g. Chinese (Pekingese), Fulani, Hebrew, Malay
        SU & DO & IO/OBL only: e.g. Basque, Korean, Tamil
        SU & DO & IO/OBL & GEN: Japanese

Conversely, the complexity ranking of (14) leads us to predict that any strategy that eases the processing difficulty of filler-gap identification in larger domains should be increasingly grammaticalized down the AH. A copy pronoun in lieu of a gap, as in Hebrew (18), makes identification of the posi-

These grammatical data reveal two opposite implicational patterns: gaps go from low to high, copy pronouns from high to low. In Hawkins (1999: 259) I have quantified the distribution of gaps to copy pronouns in 24 languages (like Hebrew) that have both: the distribution of gaps to pronouns declines down (14) by 100% to 65% to 25% to 4%, while that of pronouns to gaps increases (0% to 35% to 75% to 96%). The complexity ranking of (14), supported by performance data, coupled with the greater explicitness of the copy pronoun in signalling the position relativized on can explain the variation across grammars.

4. Competing motivations in performance and grammars

Domain minimization is just one of a number of processing preferences that structure the data of performance and, derivatively, the conventions of grammars that have evolved in response to performance data. Variation in the conventions may reflect the fact that a given preference can be optimally satisfied in more than one way (recall the Greenbergian correlations of (7) and (8) and the multiple-branching data of (10)). Or it may point to some (partial) competition between preferences in structures of a given type, with some languages following preference P and others an opposing principle P'. There is a rich tradition of research into competing motivations in typology (Greenberg 1963, Croft 1990), and many of the examples discussed in that context can be explained in terms of competing processing principles here.

4.1. Competing motivations in relative clauses

Consider the variation in relative clause positioning across languages. There is a well-known asymmetry summarized in (21) (Dryer 1992; Hawkins 1983, 1988 1999; C. Lehmann 1984):

(21)

	VO	OV	
NRel	yes	yes	yes = productive
RelN	no	yes	no = unattested or unproductive

VO languages are almost exceptionlessly NRel, while OV languages have either NRel (Lakhota) or RelN (Japanese), distributed 59% to 41% in Dryer's (1992) sample. Domain minimization (in the form of EIC, Hawkins 1990, 1994) predicts that a VO language will prefer NRel within its direct object, thereby positioning N adjacent to V and reducing the constituent recognition domain for VP. OV languages should prefer RelN by this same criterion. But efficient phrase structure recognition is not the only processing consideration here, as we have just seen in discussion of the AH. A (nominal head) filler must also be matched with the position relativized on in the relative clause, and whether this is a gap or a co-indexed pronoun there is a strong advantage to processing the filler first. A gap preceding its filler may not be noticed (Fodor 1983), may lead to structural misidentification and garden paths (Antinucci et al 1979), and will result in an on-line processing delay and much retrospective structure assignment when the filler is encountered. This is why WH-question words are invariably fronted to the left of their gaps (Greenberg 1963, Petronio & Lillo-Martin 1997). Copy pronouns, like other anaphors, are also preferred to the right of their (antecedent-)fillers, since they depend strongly on this latter for their interpretation, just like gaps do. Ordering fillers first permits processing of the filler at the filler, immediate activation of a domain within which the gap or copy pronoun can be identified, and these latter can then be processed on-line without delay by reference to the filler.

The variation data of (21) can be explained in terms of the interaction between Fillers First (FF) and EIC. Both preferences are satisfied in VO languages, which are almost exceptionlessly VO & NRel. But FF is opposed to EIC in OV languages: NRel satisfies FF but results in long VP domains (which then require rules such as Extraposition from NP to reintroduce the adjacency between V and N); RelN satisfies EIC but not FF. Variation results, and a number of other apparent idiosyncracies also fall out of this account. For example, RelN is characteristic of the "rigid" verb-final type, like Japanese. In our terms, these are languages that will have more containing phrases that are head-final, thereby providing a stronger preference for noun-finality in the NP as well. The syntactic form and content of prenominal relatives is also much more restricted than that of their postnominal counterparts. C. Lehmann (1984: 168−173) points out that prenominal relatives are more strongly nominalized, with more participial and non-finite verb forms (as in Dravidian), with more deletion of arguments, and more obligatory removal of model, tense and aspect markers. All of this makes them shorter, and reduces the amount of simultaneous processing. Grammatical restrictions such as these are to be expected in structures that do not satisfy FF and that are associated with an on-line processing delay and possible structural misidentifications.

The choice of the gap versus the copy pronoun strategy is also motivated by different processing advantages. Why are gaps preferred in the higher AH positions and why do the more explicit copy pronouns not extend all the way up? Gaps clearly have certain advantages. In particular, they involve economy of expression (Haiman 1983, 1985) and require less form processing. There are numerous structures in all languages that attest to the advantages of brevity in environments that permit recoverability of the relevant information (control structures, co-ordinate deletions, etc.), and this motivates the gap strategy in the higher, simpler hierarchy positions. There are also other devices that can help to identify the gap in a higher position, such as subject agreement, which is extremely common with subjects and whose occurrence beyond subjects is implicationally structured in accordance with the AH (Moravcsik 1978, Nichols 1986, Primus 1999). For these reasons the advantages of the gap can outweigh its disadvantages at the top of the AH, but as complexity increases, the need for clear identification of the head in the relative gradually predominates. We have a competing motivation, therefore, between (reduced) form processing and explicit dependency marking, with structural complexity increasingly requiring the latter.

4.2. Adjacency and explicit dependency marking

More explicit dependency marking is also found in larger domains other than relativization domains. The non-adjacency of otherwise adjacent interdependent items is highly correlated with explicit formal marking, in both performance and grammars. Restrictive relatives that are non-adjacent to the head in Quirk's (1957) corpus of spoken British English almost all have an explicit WH-relative pronoun or THAT (n=141):

(22) *Restrictive relative clauses with intervening material*
WH = 62% (87) THAT = 34% (48)
ZERO = 4% (6)

The corresponding figures for adjacent restrictive relatives are (n=982): WH=45% (437); THAT=33% (323); ZERO=23% (222). Finite clause complements also prefer an explicit complementizer THAT when separated from a governing verb within a lengthened "complementation domain". Rohdenburg (1996) gives the following figures for sentential complements of the verb *tell* in a written English corpus:

(23) *Finite clause complements with intervening material*
THAT = 100% (35) zero = 0%

The corresponding figures for non-intervening material are (n=171): THAT=54% (92); ZERO=46% (79).

Across languages we see grammatical rules actually conventionalizing this preference for explicit signalling of a dependency in non-adjacent domains, while either formal marking or zero may occur in adjacent domains. Consider the following agreement universal involving case copying (from Moravcsik 1995: 471).

(24) If agreement thru case copying applies to NP constituents that are adjacent, it applies to those that are non-adjacent.

For example, both adjacent and non-adjacent case copying are found in Kalkatunga (a word-marking language according to Blake 1987):

(25) Kalkatunga
 (a) *thuku-yu yaun-tu yanyi*
 'dog-ERG big-ERG white-man
 itya-mi
 bite-FUT'
 (b) *thuku-yu yanyi itya-mi*
 'dog-ERG white-man bite-FUT
 yaun-tu
 big-ERG'

Case copying in non-adjacent domains only is found in Warlpiri (a phrase-marking language):

(26) Warlpiri
 (a) *tyarntu wiri-ngki+tyu yarlki-rnu*
 'dog big-ERG+me bite-PAST'
 (b) *tyarntu-ngku+tyu yarlku-rnu*
 'dog-ERG+me bite-PAST
 wiri-ngki
 big-ERG'

Similarly in highly inflected languages like Latin, separation of Adj and N is made possible by rich morphological agreement on Adj (Vincent 1987), while languages with no discontinuity may or may not have agreement. This alternation between zero and explicit marking of dependency relations is another case of competing motivations. Economy of form arises only in small processing domains in which syntactic (and semantic) properties can be transferred to the dependent category by reference to the independent one. Property transfers across large (and non-adjacent) processing domains are dispreferred, plausibly because these domains are already complex and involve much simultaneous processing. These domains prefer explicit formal marking, which makes the dependent category more self-sufficient and processable independently of the category upon which it depends. Explicit formal marking is required in large domains in both performance and grammar, therefore, and the variation across grammars with respect to formal marking or zero is found in small domains only and is a conventionalization of one or the other option available to a language with both structures.

5. Conclusions

I conclude that there is a profound correlation between performance and grammars. If structure A is highly preferred over A' in performance, then A is regularly grammaticalized, whereas A' is not: the preferred constituent recognition domains in the Greenbergian cross-category correlations (see (7), (8) and also (10)) are minimal ones and minimal domains are also preferred in performance data such as (6). When A and A' are equally preferred, then both are productively grammaticalized: both VO and OV languages, e.g. (7a) and (7b), are productive and both have optimal, minimal domains. If there is a frequency or preference ranking A>B>C>D in performance for structures of a common type, then there will be a corresponding hierarchy of grammatical conventions, with cut-off points and declining language frequencies: the center embedding hierarchy of (13) and the Accessibility Hierarchy of (14) exemplify this. Further grammatical variation may result from competition between two principles P and Q: EIC and Fillers First (21); or explicit dependency marking versus economy (22)−(26).

In all of these areas, performance preferences (elicited through experiments, acceptability judgements or frequencies of use) reflect the extent to which some processing principle is satisfied in a given structure (within a language that disposes of alternatives), and the relative strengths of (partially) opposed principles. These performance preferences provide the input data for conventionalization in language evolution and the motivation for change in response to independently motivated changes such as a shift in basic verb position. It is because grammars have conventionalized processing preferences that processing can explain cross-linguistic variation, just as it explains performance variation. There is a complex interplay of preferences at work in any one structure, however. Difficulty with respect to one preference (Fillers First) can mean advantages with respect to another (EIC). Difficulty is also a matter of degree, not an absolute prohibition. In minority language types like Malagasy (VOS) a universally dispreferred subject-final order can be argued to have competing advantages: a verb with rich valency coding occurs initially in the parse string (Keenan 1978), and this coupled with the universally preferred Verb-Object Bonding (Tomlin 1986) results in the dispreferred subject-final order. More complex structures will require more such advantages in order to be preserved through time.

Grammatical conventions, I submit, are "frozen" processing preferences. There are many such preferences and it will require collaborative work between psycholinguists and grammarians in order to define them precisely and work out how they interact to predict the variation of performance and grammar.

6. References

Antinucci, Francesco, Duranti, Alessandro & Gebert, L. 1979. "Relative clause structure, relative clause perception, and the change from SOV to SVO". *Cognition* 7: 145−176.

Blake, Barry. 1987. *Australian aboriginal grammar.* London: Croom Helm.

Bybee, Joan L. 1985. *Morphology.* Amsterdam: Benjamins.

Bybee, Joan L. 1995. "Diachronic and typological properties of morphology and their implications for representation." In: Feldman, Laurie Beth (ed.). *Morphological aspects of language processing.* Hillsdale, New Jersey: Erlbaum, 225−246.

Croft, William. 1990. *Typology and universals.* Cambridge: Cambridge Univ. Press.

Dryer, Matthew S. 1992. "The Greenbergian word order correlations." *Language* 68: 81−138.

Fodor, Janet D. 1983. "Phrase structure parsing and the island constraints". *Linguistics and Philosophy* 6: 163−223.

Frazier, Lyn. 1985. "Syntactic complexity". In: Dowty, David, Karttunen, Lauri & Zwicky, Arnold (eds.). *Natural language parsing: Psychological, computational, and theoretical perspectives.* Cambridge: Cambridge Univ. Press, 129−189.

Greenberg, Joseph H. 1963. "Some universals of grammar with particular reference to the order of meaningful elements". In: Greenberg, Joseph H. (ed.). *Universals of language.* Cambridge/MA: M.I.T. Press, 73−113.

Greenberg, Joseph H. 1966. *Language universals, with special reference to feature hierarchies.* The Hague: Mouton.

Haiman, John. 1983. "Iconic and economic motivation". *Language* 59: 781–819.

Haiman, John. 1985. *Natural syntax.* Cambridge: Cambridge Univ. Press.

Hawkins, John A. 1983. *Word order universals.* New York: Acad. Press.

Hawkins, John A. 1988. "On explaining some left-right asymmetries in syntactic and morphological universals." In: Hammond, Michael, Moravcsik, Edith A. & Wirth, Jessica R. (eds.). *Studies in syntactic typology.* Amsterdam: Benjamins, 321–357.

Hawkins, John A. 1990. "A parsing theory of word order universals." *Linguistic Inquiry* 21: 223–261.

Hawkins, John A. 1994. *A performance theory of order and constituency.* Cambridge: Cambridge Univ. Press.

Hawkins, John A. 1998a. "A typological approach to germanic morphology". In: Askedal, John Ole (ed.). *Historische germanische und deutsche Syntax.* Frankfurt a. M.: Lang, 49–68.

Hawkins, John A. 1998b. "Some issues in a performance theory of word order". In: Siewierska, Anna (ed.). *Constituent order in the languages of Europe.* Berlin: Mouton de Gruyter, 729–781.

Hawkins, John A. 1999. "Processing complexity and filler-gap dependencies across grammars." *Language* 75: 244–285.

Keenan, Edward L. 1975. "Variation in universal grammar". In: Fasold, Ralph W. & Shuy, Roger (eds.). *Analyzing variation in language.* Washington D.C. Georgetown: Univ. Press.

Keenan, Edward L. 1978. "The syntax of subject-final languages". In: Lehmann, Winfred P. (ed.). *Syntactic typology: Studies in the phenomenology of language.* Austin: Univ. of Texas Press, 267–327.

Keenan, Edward L. & Comrie, Bernard. 1977. "Noun phrase accessibility and universal grammar". *Linguistic Inquiry* 8: 63–99.

Keenan, Edward L. & Hawkins, Sarah. 1987. "The psychological validity of the accessibility hierarchy". In: Keenan, Edward L. (ed.). *Universal grammar: 15 essays.* London: Croom Helm, 60–85.

Kirby, Simon. 1994. "Adaptive explanations for language universals: a model of Hawkins' performance theory." *Sprachtypologie und Universalienforschung* 47: 186–210.

Kirby, Simon. 1999. *Function, selection and innateness: The emergence of language universals.* Oxford: Oxford U.P.

Lehmann, Christian. 1984. *Der Relativsatz.* Tübingen: Narr.

Moravcsik, Edith A. 1978. "Agreement". In: Greenberg, Joseph H., Ferguson, Charles A. & Moravcsik, Edith A. (eds.). *Universals of human language.* Vol. 4. Stanford: Univ. Press.

Moravcsik, Edith A. 1995. "Summing up suffixaufnahme". In: Plank, Frans (ed.). *Double case: Agreement by suffixaufnahme.* Oxford: Oxford U. P., 451–484.

Nichols, Johanna. 1986. "Head-marking and dependent-marking grammar". *Language* 62: 56–119.

Petronio, Karen & Lillo-Martin, Diane. 1997. "WH-movement and the position of spec-CP: evidence from American Sign Language". *Language* 73: 18–57.

Pickering, Martin & Shillcock, Richard. 1992. "Processing subject extractions". In: Goodluck, Helen & Rochemont, Michael (eds.). *Island constraints: Theory, acquisition and processing.* Dordrecht: Kluwer Acad. Publ., 295–320.

Primus, Beatrice. 1999. *Cases and thematic roles: Ergative, accusative, active.* Tübingen: Niemeyer.

Quirk, Randolph. 1957. "Relative clauses in educated spoken English". *English Studies* 38: 97–109.

Rohdenburg, Günther. 1996. "Cognitive complexity and increased grammatical explicitness in English." *Cognitive Linguistics* 7: 149–182.

Tomlin, Russell, S. 1986. *Basic word order: Functional principles.* London: Croom Helm.

Vincent, Nigel B. 1987. "Latin". In: Harris, Martin B. & Vincent, Nigel (eds.). *The romance languages.* Oxford: Oxford U.P., 26–78.

*John A. Hawkins, Los Angeles,
University of Southern California (USA)*

30. Ikonizität

1. Typologie, Universalienforschung und außersprachliche Motivierung
2. Typen von Ikonizität: Begriffsbestimmung
3. Bildhafte Ikonizität
4. Strukturell-diagrammatische Ikonizität
5. Ikonische Motivierung zwischen Grammatik, Kognition und Pragmatik
6. Ikonizität und Sprachwandel
7. Zitierte Literatur

1. Typologie, Universalienforschung und außersprachliche Motivierung

Sprachtypologie und Universalienforschung verfolgen Ziele, die zunächst in unterschiedliche Richtungen zu weisen scheinen: die *holistisch ausgerichtete Typologie* strebt eine Klassifizierung der Sprachen nach strukturell unterschiedenen Sprachtypen an, während die *selektiv-partielle Richtung* der typologischen Forschung aus der Charakterisierung und dem Vergleich einzelner grammatischer Erscheinungen und Konstruktionen übereinzelsprachliche Tendenzen abzuleiten versucht, die jedoch im Falle von Merkmalsbündelungen (*clustering*) wiederum der Typisierung und Klassifizierung der betroffenen Sprache(n) dienen können.

Während also die Typologie die Unterschiede zwischen Sprachen und die Individualität der Einzelsprache(n) betont, richtet sich das Interesse der Universalienforschung auf jene Eigenschaften von Sprachen, die sich aus allgemeingültigen Charakteristika des Sprechens ableiten lassen und daher idealiter allen Sprachen gemeinsam sind oder zumindest durch Vorkommen in einem großen Sprachen-Sample probabilistisch als universale Tendenz formuliert werden können.

Die Divergenz zwischen Typologie und Universalienforschung ist *de facto* jedoch nicht sehr groß, wenn man bedenkt, daß die typologische Forschung − zumindest in ihrer 'klassisch'-holistischen Ausrichtung − durch die Untersuchung differentieller Eigenschaften gerade die Gesamtheit der Sprachen zu erfassen versucht, während die Universalienforschung bei der Suche nach sprachlichen Invarianten zugleich das Maß zulässiger Variabilität auslotet, das in natürlichen Sprachen innerhalb bestimmter grammatischer Domänen bei angenommener übereinzelsprachlicher Ähnlichkeit auftreten kann. Die Frage nach übereinzelsprachlicher Invarianz ist typologischen Untersuchungen also inhärent und Typologie damit stets auch eine Methode der Universalienforschung (Shibatani & Bynon 1995: 19; → Art. 1).

Die typologische Forschung hat sich der übereinzelsprachlichen Invarianz auf unterschiedliche Weisen angenähert. In Joseph H. Greenbergs grundlegenden Arbeiten beispielsweise werden die übereinzelsprachlich als gültig angenommenen Regularitäten und Restriktionen, die in Form von Implikationshierarchien formuliert werden, aus den beobachtbaren sprachlichen Fakten abgeleitet und auf diese zurückprojiziert. Bei dieser Vorgehensweise verbleibt die typologische Betrachtung innerhalb des sprachlichen Systems, dessen abstrakte Strukturen und Kategorien die Grundlage der Erklärung von Invarianz darstellen (Croft 1990: 246 ff.), sofern ein solcher explikatorischer Anspruch überhaupt erhoben wird.

Von daher scheint es gerechtfertigt, eine methodische Parallele zwischen derartigem typologischem Vorgehen und dezidiert formalistischen Betrachtungsweisen wie etwa der Generativen Grammatik zu ziehen (Shibatani & Bynon 1995: 17). Vertreter der Generativen Grammatik chomskyscher Prägung tendier(t)en dazu, die einzelsprachliche Parametrisierung der Universalen Grammatik durch Rekurs auf grammatische − meist syntaktische − Prinzipien zu erklären, wie dies die Hypothese von der kognitiven Autonomie der Sprache fordert (→ Art. 24).

Beiden Herangehensweisen − der Implikationstypologie in der Tradition Greenbergs und der generativistischen Universalienforschung − ist gemeinsam, daß übereinzelsprachliche Invarianz mittels abstrakt-linguistischer Kategorien modelliert und unter weitgehender Abstraktion von semantischen oder pragmatischen Erwägungen untersucht wird (dagegen jedoch Newmeyer 1992).

Diesen formal orientierten typologischen Ansätzen werden für gewöhnlich − und zweifelsohne vereinfachend − die funktional ausgerichteten Schulen gegenübergestellt (Shibatani & Bynon 1995: 16−19; Croft 1990: 155 ff.; 1995). Wie insbesondere Frederick J. Newmeyer (1998) in einem kritischen Vergleich zeigt, handelt es sich um Strömungen der modernen Linguistik, deren Antagonismus weit über den Bereich von Typologie und Universalienforschung hinausreicht. Die funktional-typologischen Ansätze haben sich, aufbauend u.a. auf den Arbeiten Givóns (1979; 1984), einen Objektbereich erschlossen, der inzwischen deutlich über traditionell-typologische Fragestellungen hinausgeht, und konnten sich zu einem eigenständigen grammatiktheoretischen Ansatz entwickeln.

„Functionalism seeks to explain language structure in terms of language function" (Croft 1990: 155). Ausgehend von der Annahme, daß die zentrale Funktion von Sprache der Ausdruck von Erfahrungen und Gedanken ist (Shibatani & Bynon 1995: 17), Erfahrungen aber auf die Gegebenheiten der Wirklichkeit und Gedanken auf die mentalen Konzepte des Sprechers verweisen, bezieht die funktional-typologische Betrachtung das Außersprachliche explizit in die Untersuchung übereinzelsprachlicher Invarianz mit ein. Dadurch werden semantisch-kognitive und pragmatisch-situative Faktoren als Erklärung für übereinzelsprachliche Tendenzen und Universalien verfügbar.

Mit der Berücksichtigung kognitiver und pragmatischer Aspekte möchte sich der funktional-typologische Ansatz eine Dimension des Erklärens erschließen, die über jene des strukturalistisch orientierten Sprachvergleichs (Implikationsuniversalien und -hierarchien, Markiertheitsprinzipien usw.; Croft 1990: 127) hinausgeht. Dabei gilt es jedoch stets zu bedenken, daß im Grunde zwei unterschiedliche Ebenen des Nicht-Sprachlichen betrachtet werden, nämlich die Wirklichkeit, also die Referenzebene der Sprache, und ihre Konzeptualisierung durch die Sprecher. Beide Ebenen werden nicht immer sauber getrennt und sind möglicherweise im Einzelfall auch nicht trennbar, wie sich im hier darzustellenden Fall sprachlicher Ikonizität zeigen dürfte.

Der funktional-typologische Ansatz hat sich mit unterschiedlichen Arten außersprachlicher Motivierung (*external motivations*) von übereinzelsprachlich ähnlichen grammatischen Strukturen befaßt. Neben dem Prinzip sprachlicher Ökonomie (Croft 1995: 128f.; → Art. 31), das mit Markiertheitsgraden interagiert (Croft 1990: 64–94; → Art. 32), kognitiv fundierter Prototypikalität und diskursiven Motivationsfaktoren wie Informationsstruktur und Textrelief (→ Art. 46) oder der *type*- und *token*-Häufigkeit, die auch schon in der einschlägigen Forschung vor der funktionalen Typologie eine wichtige Rolle spielte (Croft 1990: 84ff. und 186ff.), gilt die Ikonizität als die wichtigste und vielleicht am besten untersuchte Art externer Motivierung sprachlich-grammatischer Strukturen.

2. Typen von Ikonizität: Begriffsbestimmung

Ikonizität in der hier intendierten Bedeutung kann im weitesten Sinne beschrieben werden als Ähnlichkeit zwischen sprachlichen Zeichen bzw. Zeichenfolgen und außersprachlichen Referenten und Strukturen, die durch diese Zeichen abgebildet werden: „the principle that the structure of language should, as closely as possible, reflect the structure of experience, that is, the structure of what is being expressed by language" (Croft 1995: 129).

Die Ikonizitätshypothese geht aus von einer Similaritätsbeziehung zwischen sprachlichen Zeichen einerseits und Konzepten andererseits, also zwischen sprachlichen und kognitiven Strukturen (Haiman 1992: 191 u.ö.). Die kognitive Basis von Ikonizität (Haiman 1983: 800) eröffnet eine übereinzelsprachliche Perspektive, die Ikonizität als typologischen Beschreibungs- und Erklärungsparameter interessant macht. Der angenommene tendenziell universale Charakter von Ikonizitätsbeziehungen wird dabei jedoch für die einzelnen Typen und Erscheinungsformen von Ikonizität unterschiedlich bewertet.

Die Frage nach dem Abbildcharakter des sprachlichen Zeichens läßt sich bis in die Sprachphilosophie der griechischen Antike zurückverfolgen (Swiggers 1993; Simone 1995) und manifestiert sich in der Axiomatik moderner Zeichenmodelle: Während das strukturalistische Zeichenmodell de Saussures von (zumindest weitreichender) Arbitrarität in der Zuordnung von Zeichen und Konzept ausgeht (Engler 1962; 1995), unterscheidet Peirce (1960 [1932]) in seiner Semiotik zwischen *Indices*, *Ikonen* und *Symbolen*, die unterschiedliche Similaritätsgrade zu den Konzepten aufweisen (vgl. Jakobson 1971: 346f.; Ransdell 1986).

Der Index verweist auf einen materiell oder diskursiv vorhandenen Referenten, von dessen Präsenz er abhängt („An Index is a sign which refers to the Object that it denotes by virtue of being really affected by that Object." (Peirce 1960: 143 [2.247]); vgl. Posner 1980: 1: „Indexikalische Motivierung tritt auf, wo das Auftreten einer Bezeichnung durch kausale oder andere raumzeitliche Beziehungen mit dem von ihr Bezeichneten verbunden ist"), ohne daß allerdings formalstrukturelle Ähnlichkeit notwendig wäre.

Das Symbol beruht auf einer konventionalisierten Zeichen-Konzept-Zuordnung, die sprach- und kulturspezifisch und damit arbiträr erfolgt.

Das Ikon schließlich ist der Zeichentyp, der eine wahrnehmbare Beziehung zum Signatum i.S. von gemeinsamen Merkmalen aufweist. Auf der Ebene der Ikone unterscheidet Peirce zwischen bildhafter („imagic iconicity" [Fischer & Nänny 1999: XXI]), diagrammatischer und metaphorischer Ikonizität. Zwischen diesen Spielarten von Ikonizität besteht ein qualitativer, die Komplexität tangierender Unterschied:

„[icons] which partake of simple qualities [...] are *images*; those which represent the relations, mainly dyadic, [...] of the parts of one thing by analogous relations in their own parts, are *diagrams*; those which represent [...] by representing a parallelism in something else, are *metaphors*." (Peirce 1960: 157 [2.277])

Da sich Diagramme und Metaphern hinsichtlich der Relationen zwischen Zeichen und Konzept(en) gleichen, ordnen Fischer & Nänny (1999) die Metaphern als Instanzen komplex-semantischer Ikonizität der diagrammatischen Ikonizität unter. Metaphorische Ikonizität, die nach Dressler (1995: 21) den am wenigsten 'ikonischen' Ikonizitätstyp darstellt, soll hier nicht näher betrachtet werden.

Die zweite – und für die Sprachtypologie wichtigere – Erscheinungsform, die strukturell-diagrammatische Ikonizität, gliedert sich wiederum in zwei Subtypen, die John Haiman (1980 u.ö.) als 'Ikonizität durch Isomorphie' (*isomorphism*) und 'Ikonizität durch Motivierung' (*motivation*) bezeichnet. Diese Begriffe sind zu recht als unscharf und mißlich kritisiert worden (Croft 1990: 164f.); vor allem Haimans Verwendung von 'motivation' verstellt den Blick dafür, daß Ikonizität nur eine Dimension von externer Motivierung sprachlicher Strukturen ist, und suggeriert – ungerechtfertigterweise –, daß Isomorphie nicht extern motiviert sei. Allerdings hat sich bislang keine terminologische Alternative durchsetzen können.

Aus dem Gesagten ergibt sich folgendes Gesamtbild der Typen von Ikonizität (nach Fischer & Nänny 1999: XXII):

Signifikant	cocorico/[kokori'ko]
↕	↕
Signifikat	'vom Hahn hervorgebrachter Laut'

Abb.: 30.2 Onomatopöien als Beispiel für lautliche Ikonizität

Bildhafte Ikonizität vollzieht sich also auf der Ebene des isolierten sprachlichen Zeichens. Diese Art von Ikonizität gilt als in den heutigen Sprachen weitgehend unproduktiv und linguistisch wenig interessant, da das isolierte Zeichen als Einzeleintrag des Lexikons die deutlichste Tendenz zu Konventionalisierung und Opakisierung aufweist. Bildhafte Ikone stehen vor diesem Hintergrund da als „a few exceptions listed as curiosities" (Bolinger & Sears, zit.n. Fischer & Nänny 1999: XIX).

Auch sprachliche Systeme wie Gebärdensprachen weisen wider die intuitive Erwartung keinen signifikant hohen Anteil an bildhaften Ikonen auf (→ Art. 10, § 8.3.2; vgl. auch Newmeyer 1992: 758). Im Rahmen der unten in § 6 besprochenen Grammatikalisierung sorgt auch in Gebärdensprachen die diachronische Entwicklung für eine Veränderung der Rolle von Ikonizität.

Doch nicht nur die geringe Frequenz (*type*-Zahl) läßt bildhafte Ikone für die Frage nach sprachlicher Universalität uninteressant erscheinen; Lehrbuchbeispiele wie die onomatopoetischen Tierlaute zeigen bereits bei eng verwandten Sprachen deutliche Diver-

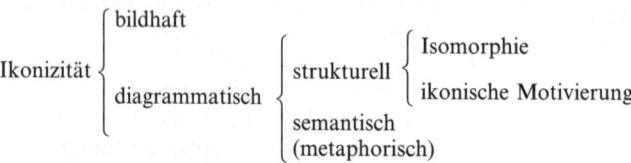

Abb.: 30.1 Typen von Ikonizität

3. Bildhafte Ikonizität

Bildhafte Ikonizität gilt als 'einfache' Art physischer Ähnlichkeitsbeziehung zwischen Zeichen – „usually a morphologically unstructured one" (Fischer & Nänny 1999: XXII) – und Konzept insofern, als beide direkt – im nachfolgenden Modell vertikal – miteinander verbunden sind. Der Signifikant übernimmt seine (lautliche, visuelle, plastische) Form unmittelbar vom Signifikatum. Das anschaulichste Beispiel aus dem Bereich sprachlicher Zeichen sind Onomatopöien.

genzen und scheinen – wie im weiteren Sinne bildhafte Ikone überhaupt – derselben konventionalisierten Form-Inhalt-Relation unterworfen zu sein wie Peirces Symbole. Bildhafte Ikonizität ist daher in der sprachwissenschaftlichen Forschung auf nur peripheres Interesse gestoßen. Allerdings heben Beiträge aus der Erstsprachenerwerbsforschung die große Bedeutung bildhafter Ikone in frühen Phasen des kindlichen Spracherwerbs hervor. Bekannt ist auch die häufige Gebrauchsausweitung dieser Ikone in der Kindersprache durch Konversion. Einzeluntersuchungen zeigen, daß bei Kindern eine übereinzelsprachliche Tendenz feststellbar ist, bestimmte Laute rekurrent mit bestimmten Merkmalen von Signifikaten zu assoziieren (Plank 1979: 129 ff.; Fónagy 1999).

Unter der Annahme, daß sich in der Ontogenese die Phylogenese wiederholt, wäre die bildhafte Ikonizität im Prozeß der Sprachwerdung daher nicht unwichtig. Für die Untersuchung übereinzelsprachlicher Invarianz außerhalb von Fragestellungen, die Formengenese und Etymologie tangieren, scheint diese Spielart von Ikonizität aber wenig ergiebig zu sein.

4. Strukturell-diagrammatische Ikonizität

Wie im o.a. Zitat von Charles Sanders Peirce bereits angesprochen, bezieht sich diagrammatische Ikonizität nicht auf Similaritätsrelationen zwischen Form und Inhalt / Konzept des isolierten Zeichens, sondern auf Ähnlichkeiten, die in Abfolgerelationen komplexer Zeichen und der dadurch ausgedrückten komplexen, da relationalen Konzeptualisierung bestehen: „It is the *perceived* relation in meaning between two concepts that leads to the use of the same form or word or the same shape or structure" (Fischer & Nänny 1999: XXIII; Hervorh. im Orig.). Bei ikonischer Motivierung (im Sinne Haimans) manifestiert sich Ähnlichkeit — wie nachstehend modelliert — auf horizontaler, also syntagmatischer Ebene, während auf vertikaler bzw. paradigmatischer Ebene Similarität nicht notwendig bzw. — nach Kleiber 1993: 106 f. — sogar ausgeschlossen ist. An dem seit Roman Jakobson (1971: 350) in der einschlägigen Literatur oft angeführten Caesar-Zitat läßt sich dies wie folgt veranschaulichen (nach Fischer & Nänny 1999: XXII):

Signifikant	veni	→	vidi	→	vici
	↑		↑		↑
≠					
	↓		↓		↓
Signifikat	'Ereignis'	→	'Ereignis'	→	'Ereignis'

Abb.: 30.3 Ikonizität auf der syntagmatischen Ebene

Die Motiviertheit einer ikonischen Beziehung ergibt sich hier nicht aus den sprachlichen Formen und deren Denotaten, die einheitlich Ereignischarakter haben, sondern aus der Abfolge („Textposition" [Ludwig 1996: 55]) der Zeichen und der (hier: zeitlichen) Abfolge der denotierten Ereignisse.

Diagrammatische Ikonizität ist daher — anders als bildhafte Ikonizität — lexikonunabhängig (daher „résolument grammatical" [Kleiber 1993: 106]) und bezieht sich, wie das Beispiel andeutet, bevorzugt auf die Struktur syntaktischer Konstruktionen (Haiman 1980; 1985a), findet sich jedoch auch in der morphologischen Struktur (Mayerthaler 1980; Bybee 1985; Bybee & al. 1994; Ludwig 1996).

4.1. Ikonizität durch Isomorphie (*isomorphism*)

Mit dem Terminus 'Isomorphie' bezeichnet Haiman die eineindeutige Beziehung von Form und Inhalt, „a one-to-one correspondence between the signans and the signatum" (Haiman 1980: 515). Ikonizität durch Isomorphie zielt auf die Vermeidung von Homonymie („one signans, more than one signata" [Haiman 1980: 516]) und Synonymie („one signatum, more than one signans" [ebd.]) ab.

Isomorphie findet sich bei allen sprachlichen Zeichen; auch die weitgehend arbiträre Form-Inhalt-Zuordnung symbolischer Lexikoneinträge weist eine Tendenz zur Isomorphie auf. Sie trägt zum Gelingen jedweder Kommunikation bei, indem sie Ambiguitäten vermeidet. Dennoch weisen isomorphe Lexeme keine ikonische Qualität auf bzw. ist diese Ikonizität linguistisch nicht von Interesse (Kleiber 1993: 107).

Interessant und relevant ist Ikonizität als 'Isomorphie' unter Bezug auf grammatische Elemente und Konstruktionen, denen *a priori* keine eigene oder zumindest keine einheitliche Semantik zuerkannt werden kann. Demgegenüber postuliert die Ikonizitätshypothese, daß formale Gemeinsamkeiten auch bei solchen sprachlichen Elementen darauf verweisen, daß Gemeinsamkeiten auf der Bedeutungs- und Funktionsebene gegeben sind: „l'unicité de la forme est à travers tous les emplois l'indicateur iconique sur le plan sémantique d'une autre unicité, celle du sens" (Kleiber 1993: 108; vgl. auch Haiman 1985a: 30: „Recurrent identity of form must reflect similarity of meaning"; Fertig 1998: 1074: „sameness of meaning is diagrammed by sameness of form, difference of meaning by difference of form").

Es ist wichtig zu betonen, daß es sich bei der hier in Frage stehenden Bedeutung um konstruktionelle Bedeutung handelt, daß also auch bei Isomorphien die syntagmatischen Beziehungen ausschlaggebend sind. Konstruktionelle Bedeutung ist aber ein Phänomen, das sich nur auf Diskursebene erschließt und von daher auf externe Motivierung verweist. Das Prinzip ikonischer Isomorphie sei an einigen Beispielen illustriert.

Die Funktion der syntaktischen Basiskonstituente 'Subjekt' wird semantisch als äußerst heterogen angesehen. Zwar gilt ein agentives Subjekt als prototypisch, doch können die lexikalische Semantik der prädikativen Ausdrücke und die Diathesen der Subjektkonstituente auch andere Kasusrollen zuweisen, und auch weitere semantische Züge, die das Subjekt typischerweise charakterisieren, wie etwa Definitheit, Topikalität u.dgl., decken nicht alle Fälle ab (Kleiber 1993: 116). Für das Subjekt scheint also keine eineindeutige Form-Inhalt-Beziehung zu bestehen.

Georges Kleiber (1993) argumentiert dagegen (unter Bezugnahme auf Robert W. Langackers Konzeption der Kognitiven Grammatik), daß gerade das Subjekt ein Beispiel für ikonische Isomorphie darstellt, da seine verbreiteten formal-syntaktischen Charakteristika (Bezugspunkt der Verbalkongruenz, Antezedens und Bezugspunkt reflexiver Pronominalisierung usw.) bei aller inhaltlichen Verschiedenheit der lexikalischen Einheiten, die die Subjektrolle einnehmen, auf eine semantische Gemeinsamkeit verweisen: „elles [die subjektspezifischen formalen Charakteristika; A.d.V.] se révèlent iconiques en ce qu'elles traduisent directement la saillance qui constitue le contenu conceptuel du sujet." (Kleiber 1993: 119).

Relativsatz- und Spaltsatzbildung scheinen sich auf den ersten Blick auf ganz unterschiedlichen syntaktisch-funktionalen Ebenen zu bewegen. Während die Relativsatzbildung eine Subordinationstechnik darstellt, die der Verknüpfung von Äußerungen dient, ist die Spaltsatzbildung eine Segmentierungstechnik, durch die eine Äußerung nach vorrangig pragmatischen Kriterien – in erster Linie nach dem Prinzip der sprechersubjektiven Relevanzzuweisung – gegliedert wird. Schachter (1973) zeigte aber, daß zwischen Relativ- und Spaltsätzen formale Gemeinsamkeiten bestehen. So verhalten sich die Konstruktionen im HAUSA (Tschadisch: Afro-Asiatisch) hinsichtlich der Ersetzung des Perfektivitätsmarkers *sun* des unmarkierten Satzes durch den Marker *suka* gleich (Schachter 1973: 23 f.):

(1) HAUSA
   (a) *sun* gaya wa yaron
       'they told the child'
   (b) yaron da *suka* gaya masa / wa
       'the child that they told'
   (c) yaron ne *suka* gaya masa / wa
       'it's the child that they told'

Die Beobachtung Schachters wurde durch Belege aus zahlreichen weiteren Sprachen erhärtet; im ostnepalesischen BELHARISCH (Kirantisprachen: Tibeto-Karenisch: Sino-Tibetanisch) dient derselbe Nominalisierungsmarker *-(k)ha(k)* ebenso zur Bildung von (zirkumnominalen) Relativsätzen wie auch zur Fokussierung, der prominenten Funktion des Spaltsatzes (Bickel 1995).

Auch in einem Großteil der indoeuropäischen Sprachen werden formale Gemeinsamkeiten von Relativ- und Spaltsätzen deutlich. Unter der Prämisse ikonischer Isomorphie deutet dies auf eine beiden Konstruktionen gemeinsame Funktion hin, die Schachter als „semantic process of foregrounding one part of a sentence at the expense of the rest" (Schachter 1973: 19) beschreibt. Das Textrelief und seine Struktur werden jedoch durch den Sprecher geschaffen, der eine komplexe Sachverhaltsdarstellung konzeptualisiert und so die isomorphe Beziehung kognitiv begründet: „grammatical structure reflects conceptual structure." (Croft 1990: 170)

Gleiches gilt für Haimans wohl am häufigsten zitiertes Beispiel für Ikonizität als 'Isomorphie'. Haiman (1980; 1985a: 26 ff.) untersucht, ausgehend von englischen Kontrastpaaren wie (2), die übereinzelsprachlich nachweisbare formale Ähnlichkeit zwischen Protasen in Konditionalgefügen und indirekten Entscheidungsfragen.

(2) ENGLISCH
   (a) I don't know if it is true.
   (b) If it is true, I'll eat my hat.

Er findet für diese Ähnlichkeit eine funktionale Erklärung darin, daß beide Äußerungstypen als Topikalisierungsstrategien eingesetzt werden können, was er als diskurssemantische Äquivalenz deutet, die sich im Gebrauch identischer Marker ikonisch manifestiert (Haiman 1985a: 38).

Isomorphie als externe Motivierung sprachlicher Strukturen wirft zwei an dieser Stelle nicht unwesentliche Fragen auf.

Zum einen wird von einigen Autoren bezweifelt, daß Isomorphie überhaupt als Erscheinungsform von Ikonizität – zumindest im Sinne von Peirce – aufzufassen ist (Newmeyer 1992: 760). Ruft man sich die oben zitierte Definition der diagrammatischen Ikone in Erinnerung – „those which represent the relations, mainly dyadic, [...] of the parts of one thing by analogous relations in their own parts" –, so wird deutlich, daß Isomorphie zumindest keine direkte Similaritätsrelation zwischen sprachlichem Zeichen und Konzept bzw. Realität ausdrückt. Dressler (1995: 35) sieht Isomorphie und die ihr zugrundeliegenden Prinzipien (Synonymien- und Homonymienvermeidung; Gewährleistung von Eineindeutigkeitsrelationen zwischen Form und Funktion) nur als häufige Korrelate, nicht aber als mit Ikonizität identisch an.

Die zweite Frage betrifft den universellen Status von Isomorphie. Haiman erachtet die Invarianz von Form und Bedeutung / Funktion als ein – vielleicht das einzige – Ikonizitätsuniversale (Haiman 1980: 515; Fischer & Nänny 1999: XXIV). In der Tat lassen sich unzählige Erscheinungen des Sprachwandels – zumindest *post festum* – als durch Isomorphie (vor allem: Homonymienvermeidung) begründet erklären. Zugleich sind Homonymie- und daraus resultierende Ambiguitätserscheinungen im synchronischen Schnitt aber keine Seltenheit. Newmeyer (1992: 760 f.) argumentiert, daß eine einfache Äußerung wie *John likes Mary more than Sue* strukturell hochgradig ambig sei und gegen das Isomorphieprinzip verstoße, das aufgrunddessen empirisch nicht haltbar sei. Haiman (1980: 519 ff.) räumt ein, daß systematisch-konstruktionelle Homonymien auftreten können, und geht in solchen Fällen davon aus, „that other tendencies exist [...] which override the requirement of isomorphic correspondence" (Haiman 1980: 528).

Diese Interferenzen können als Konflikt zwischen übereinzelsprachlichen und einzelsprachlich-innersystemischen Tendenzen erklärt werden oder als übereinzelsprachlich-diskursive „competing motivations" im Sinne von Du Bois (1985; vgl. auch Croft 1990: 192–97), z.B. externe Motivation durch das sprachliche Ökonomieprinzip (Haiman 1983).

4.2. Ikonische Motivierung (*motivation*)

Kleiber (1993: 107) weist darauf hin, daß der ikonische Wert von Isomorphie auch deshalb schwer faßbar und kontrovers ist, weil sich dieser Aspekt diagrammatischer Ikonizität bei der Untersuchung sprachlicher Erscheinungen kaum vom zweiten Typ ikonischer Diagramme trennen läßt, der die strukturelle Ikonizität *par excellence* darstellt (ähnlich Croft 1990: 171). Dieser „second type of iconicity [...] is that in which a grammatical structure, like an onomatopoeic word, reflects its meaning directly." (Haiman 1980: 516). Dies nennt Haiman „iconicity of motivation" (ebd.).

Während sich das ikonische Potential der Isomorphie grammatischer Zeichen und Konstruktionen nur durch den distributionellen Vergleich offenbart, ergibt sich das ikonische Potential diagrammatisch-ikonischer Motivierung (hier immer verstanden im Sinne Haimans) als sehr viel unmittelbarere Ähnlichkeitsbeziehung zwischen Form und Konzept. Es ist also nicht überraschend, daß in der engeren Ikonizitätsdiskussion diese Ebene diagrammatischer Ikonizität den breitesten Raum einnimmt und auch benachbarte Theorien, in denen die Ikonizitätshypothese eine Rolle spielt (so etwa die Natürlichkeitstheorie; → Art. 32), vor allem diese Art von Ikonizität betrachten. Auf die Mißlichkeit des (leider fest eingeführten) Haimanschen Terminus wurde bereits hingewiesen. Möglicherweise wäre ein in Anlehnung an Fischer (1999: 352) zu prägender Begriff der diagrammatischen Ikonizität als 'strukturelle Transparenz' geeigneter; Croft (1990: 174) gebraucht den Terminus 'strukturelle Isomorphie'.

Ungeachtet der terminologischen Vorbehalte ist die Bedeutsamkeit und explikative Reichweite der diagrammatischen Ikonizität i.S. von 'Motivierung' beachtlich. Neben dem Lehrbuchbeispiel der Abbildung zeitlicher Abfolge, das durch das oben wiedergegebene Caesar-Beispiel illustriert wurde, gibt es eine Vielzahl von konzeptuellen Relationen, zu deren sprachlicher Abbildung die Linearisierung sprachlicher Zeichen und deren Variierbarkeit ausgenutzt wird. Mit Blick auf markiertheitstheoretische Überlegungen (Ludwig 1996: 39 ff.; → Art. 32) formuliert Haiman (1980: 528) als grundlegendes Prinzip solcher linearisierungsbasierter Ikonizität: „categories that are marked morphologically and syntactically are also marked semantically."

Die Syntax als Ausdrucks- und Beschreibungsebene der Relationen zwischen sprachlichen Zeichen gilt als bevorzugtes Erscheinungsfeld diagrammatisch-ikonischer Motivierung. So vertritt Haiman die Ansicht, daß sich sprachliche Ikonizität in erster Linie syntaktisch und auf der Ebene syntaktischer Relationen durch Positionalität manifestiert. Er geht sogar soweit anzunehmen, daß Sprachen mit elaborierter Morphologie tendenziell weniger ikonisch – also opaker – sind als morphologiearme Sprachen (Haiman 1980: 70; dagegen Ludwig 1996: 55 f.; vgl. auch Dotter 1988). Die typologische Untersuchung diagrammatisch-ikonischer Motivierung ist daher vor allem eine Typologie grammatisch-syntaktischer Konstruktionen unter Rückführung auf parallele kognitive Strukturen (Croft 1990: 172 f.). Form-Konzept-Parallelismen lassen sich dabei für unterschiedliche konzeptuelle Aspekte und Kategorien feststellen, von denen einige kurz vorgestellt werden sollen.

4.2.1. Sequentielle Ikonizität

Die typologische Untersuchung grammatischer Konstruktionen unter ikonizitätstheoretischem Blickwinkel bezieht sich sowohl auf Abfolgerelationen innerhalb der Äußerung, also Ikonizität in der Satzstellung, als auch auf Abfolgerelationen zwischen Äußerungen oder innerhalb komplexer Äußerungsgefüge, d.h. Ikonizität in der Satzverkettung. Caesars oben erwähntes *veni vidi vici* reflektiert die außersprachliche temporale Abfolge dreier Ereignisse durch die sprachliche Anordnung der sie bezeichnenden Verballexeme.

Der universale Status dieser syntaktischen Ikonizitätsrelation zwischen sprachlicher Linearisierung und außersprachlich-temporaler Sequentialität steht außer Frage (vgl. Greenbergs Ansicht: „the order of elements in language parallels that in physical experience or the order of knowledge" [Greenberg 1963, zit. n. Newmeyer 1992: 763]; Jakobson 1965; Haiman 1985a: 75 f.). Allerdings ist die Enkodierung rein temporaler Struktur − also nach der „vorher/nachher"-Relation − nur eine mögliche, und zwar die einfachste, sequentielle Ikonizitätsrelation.

Experimentelle Evidenz und vor allem Beobachtungen aus dem Erstsprachenerwerb (Raible 1992: 131 f.) zeigen, daß auf der „vorher/nachher"-Relation weitere Junktionsrelationen aufbauen, die vom Sprecher/Hörer ebenfalls mit den Abfolgerelationen des sprachlichen Ausdrucks in eine Similaritätsbeziehung gebracht werden können. So entwickelt sich durch ein − ebenfalls übereinzelsprachlich gültiges, kognitiv angelegtes − Prinzip des *post hoc, ergo propter hoc* aus der temporalen Abfolge eine Ursache-Folge-Relation. Neben − bzw. ontogenetisch nach (Raible 1992: 132) − der Konsekutivität kann sich die Finalitätsrelation entwickeln. Diese semantischen Relationen können durch einfache Abfolgerelationen ohne formale Markierung ausgedrückt bzw. − umgekehrt betrachtet − aus der Äußerung durch diagrammatische Ikonizität herausgelesen werden.

Der unmarkiert-implizite Ausdruck ist natürlich in den meisten Sprachen nicht die einzige Möglichkeit der Versprachlichung der genannten semantischen Relationen. Er bildet vielmehr den aggregativen Pol auf der Skala der Satzverkettungstechniken (Raible 1992: 27 ff. → Art. 45, § 3). Auch integrative, elaboriertere Enkodierungsstrategien, die die Abhängigkeit zwischen den zu verknüpfenden Sachverhaltsdarstellungen morphologisch oder morphosyntaktisch markieren, können gewissen ikonischen Restriktionen in der diskursiven Positionierung unterliegen. Bei den Partizipial- und Gerundialkonstruktionen der romanischen Sprachen zeigt Raible (1992: 86), daß „die [...] Relation der Folge [...] aus Gründen der Ikonizität eher nach Nachstellung, die kausale Relation eher nach Voranstellung des Gerundiums oder des Partizips [verlangt]." Hier finden sich allerdings einzelsprachliche Einschränkungen. Haiman (1980; 1985a) zeigt, daß auch die recht komplexe Struktur eines Konditionalgefüges aggregativ ausgedrückt werden kann. So ist (3a) wohl eher als Bedingungssatz in der Bedeutung von (3b) denn als reine Temporalsequenz zu interpretieren (Haiman 1985a: 45):

(3) ENGLISCH
 (a) Smile, and the world smiles with you
 (b) If you smile, the world smiles with you

Erst zum Ausdruck adversativer Konditionalität („even if"), so Haiman, ist die Markierung durch den Junktor (in Haimans Terminologie: durch das Diakritikon) *if* notwendig.

Im Übergangsbereich zwischen inter- und intrapropositionellen Abfolgerelationen finden sich Verbserialisierungen. Auch hier scheint diagrammatische Ikonizität zu gelten, wie das Beispiel (4) von Tai (1985; zit. n. Newmeyer 1992: 759; kritisch hierzu Paris & Peyraube 1993) aus dem CHINESISCHEN zeigt:

(4) CHINESISCH
 (a) Zhāngān [dào túshūguǎn] [ná shū]
  Zhangan [reach library] [take book]
  'John went to the library to get the book'
 (b) Zhāngān [ná shū] [dào túshūguǎn]
  'John took the book to the library'

Es scheint also eine universelle Tendenz zu geben, daß die Konstituentenabfolge in Äußerungen, in denen semantische Relationen wie temporale Sequentialität, Konsekutivität, Finalität oder Kausalität bestehen, durch diagrammatisch-ikonische Motivierung gesteuert wird oder zumindest mitbestimmt werden kann.

4.2.2. Ikonische Distanzmarkierung

Neben ikonisch motivierter Sequentialität ist das Verhältnis von syntagmatisch-syntaktischer vs. konzeptueller Distanz ein Bereich, der als bevorzugter Gegenstand ikonizitätsorientierter Untersuchungen gilt (Haiman 1985a: 102 ff.; Croft 1990: 174 ff.). Haiman (1992: 191 u.ö.) schlägt für diese Art von Ikonizität den Terminus 'Alienation' vor. Die Grundidee dabei ist, daß Zeichen, die in der sprachlichen Realisierung eng zusammen stehen, auch kognitiv affine Konzepte abbilden, während Zeichen, die in der Linearisierung durch andere sprachliche Elemente getrennt werden, auch konzeptuell weiter voneinander entfernt sind: „grammatical distance reflects conceptual distance." (Croft 1995: 130). Es handelt sich hierbei um eine Neuformulierung des Gesetzes von Otto Behaghel (1932), wonach „das geistig eng Zusammengehörige auch eng zusammengestellt wird" (zit. n. Newmeyer 1992: 761).

Haiman (1992 u.ö.) führt Evidenz u.a. aus den Bereichen der Kausativierung und der syntaktischen Beiordnung an. So wird der semantische Unterschied einer Kausativkonstruktion wie *cause to die* zu einem denselben Vorgang bezeichnenden prototypisch transitiven Verb (nach Hopper & Thompson 1980) wie *kill* durch einen größeren Abstand des Agens, i.e. Kausators, zum semantisch zentralen Verballexem gekennzeichnet (Haiman 1992: 191):

(5) ENGLISCH
   (a) I killed the chicken
   (b) I caused the chicken to die

Koordinierte Syntagmen wie im folgenden Beispiel (nach Haiman 1985a: 117)

(6) ENGLISCH
   sweet and sad songs

weisen eine charakteristische Ambiguität auf, die auf konzeptuelle Nähe vs. Distanz verweist: in der einen Lesart beziehen sich die beiden Attribute *sweet* und *sad* auf identische, in einer anderen Lesart auf distinkte Referenten (*sweet songs and sad songs*). Iko-nische Motivierung läßt in der ersten Lesart die Elision des koordinierenden Junktors zu (*sweet sad songs*), nicht jedoch in der zweiten Lesart. Dies wird deutlich, wenn die koordinierten Elemente semantisch widersprüchlich – wie in (7) – oder gar inkompatibel sind (Haiman ebd.).

(7) ENGLISCH
   (a) good and bad news
   (b) ? good bad news

Eine weitere semantische Unterscheidung, die oft durch distanzikonische Mittel gekennzeichnet wird, betrifft alienable vs. inalienable Possession (Haiman 1985a: 130 ff.; Croft 1990: 175 ff., 1995: 131 f.). Zahlreiche Sprachen 'entfernen' alienablen Besitz in der sprachlichen Linearisierung vom Possessor. Im ITALIENISCHEN etwa werden nahe Verwandte als dem – hier im übertragenen Sinne zu verstehenden – Possessor inalienabel erachtet, während Nicht- oder entfernter Verwandte als alienabel konzeptualisiert und in der Äußerungskette durch einen Artikel vom Bezugsreferenten getrennt werden (vgl. auch die Beiträge in Chappell & McGregor 1996):

(8) ITALIENISCH
   (a) Giovanni parla con suo padre.
   (b) Giovanni parla con il suo superiore.

Im KPELLE (Mande: Niger-Kordofanisch) gibt es für nominal bzw. pronominal ausgedrückte Possessoren unterschiedliche Enkodierungsstrategien; sie gehorchen allerdings durchgängig dem Prinzip ikonisch motivierter Distanzmarkierung, da Alienabilität stets mit größerem Linearisierungsabstand zwischen Possessor und Besitztum korreliert (Haiman 1985a: 132; Croft 1995: 131):

(9) KPELLE
   (a) ŋá pérɛi
       'mein Haus'
       (alienable Possession mit pronominalem Possessor: Possessor und Besitztum durch Wortgrenze getrennt)
   (b) ḿ-pôlu
       'mein Rücken'
       (inalienable Possession mit pronominalem Possessor: Possessor und Besitztum durch Morphemgrenze getrennt)
   (c) 'kâlɔŋ ŋɔ pérɛi
       'das Haus des Häuptlings'
       (alienable Possession mit nominalem Possessor: Possessor und Besitztum durch zusätzliches freies Morphem getrennt)

(d) 'kâlɔŋ pôlu
'der Rücken des Häuptlings'
(inalienable Possession mit nominalem Possessor: Possessor und Besitztum durch Wortgrenze getrennt)

Ein anderer Fall der ikonischen Markierung von konzeptueller Distanz, der in Zusammenhang mit Beispielen wie (5) gesehen werden kann, betrifft die Grade von Transitivität. Haimans Ausgangspunkt ist: „the conceptual distance between a verb and its object complement is going to covary with the transitivity of the verb." (Haiman 1985a: 136). Er illustriert dies unter Bezugnahme auf Ergebnisse von Dwight D. Bolinger anhand des spanischen Verbs *contestar* und seinem kontrastierten Gebrauch wie in:

(10) SPANISCH
(a) contestar la pregunta
(b) contestar a la pregunta

Demnach besagt (10a), daß eine Frage vollständig beantwortet wird („*succeed* in answering a question" [Bolinger 1956, zit. n. Haiman 1985a: 137; Hervorh. im Orig.]), während bei (10b) eine unvollständige oder unbefriedigende Antwort gegeben wird („*attempt* to answer the question, but not succeed" [ebd.]). Die Kasusmarkierung stünde hier also in ikonischer Relation zur pragmatischen Bewertung eines Sachverhalts.

Ebenfalls auf das Verhältnis von pragmatischer Bewertung einer Äußerungssituation und ihrem sprachlichen Ausdruck bezieht sich eine Art von diagrammatisch-ikonischer Distanzmarkierung, deren universaler Status durch eine besonders breite Basis an empirischer Evidenz gesichert ist, nämlich die Enkodierung von Respekt und Höflichkeit (Brown & Levinson 1996). Haiman führt zur Untermauerung des ikonischen Prinzips „The more polite the register, the longer the message" (Haiman 1985a: 151) das Beispiel des JAVANESISCHEN (West-Malayo-Polynesisch: Austronesisch) an, wo sich Äußerungen – bei gleicher Konstituentenzahl – je nach Höflichkeitsgrad in der Länge der Konstituenten unterscheiden. In vielen anderen Sprachen finden sich Hinweise auf die Gültigkeit des genannten ikonischen Prinzips, in dem z.B. zur höflichen Anrede zwecks indirekten Ausdrucks markierte Modi mit formal merkmalhaltigeren Formen gewählt oder der Angeredete pluralisch angesprochen wird (Malsch 1986), was wiederum in der Regel in der Verwendung aufwendiger oder längerer Ausdrucksmittel resultiert.

Die bereits erwähnte ikonisch motivierte Differenzierung der Kodierung von alienabler vs. inalienabler Possession, aber auch die pragmatisch basierte Ikonizität von Kasusmarkierungen stellen morphosyntaktische Kontraste dar, die zeigen, daß – anders als Haiman stellenweise insinuiert – diagrammatisch-ikonische Motivierung auch außerhalb der Syntax (verstanden als Linearisierung von prinzipiell freien sprachlichen Zeichen) auftritt.

So zeigt Bybee (1985), daß in der Anordnung von Flexionsmorphemen, die Valenz, Diathese, Aspekt, Tempus, Modus und Personen- oder Numeruskongruenz anzeigen, und dem Verbalstamm eine Ikonizitätsbeziehung besteht: abhängig von der 'Relevanz' der zu kennzeichnenden Kategorien für das Verb, d.h. in Relation zum „extent to which their meanings *directly affect the lexical content of the verb stem*" (Bybee 1985: 11), erscheinen diese nahe beim Verbstamm oder werden von diesem durch andere Flexionsmorpheme getrennt oder aber als freie Morpheme realisiert. Bybee kommt dabei zu folgender Abfolgehierarchie, wobei die verbale 'Relevanz' der Kategorien (vgl. auch Bybee & al. 1994: 22) von links nach rechts abnimmt:

Valenz < Diathese < Aspekt < Tempus < Modus < div. Kongruenzbeziehungen

Valenz wird demzufolge aufgrund großer Bedeutung für die Verbsemantik oft direkt am Verbalstamm lexikalisch oder affixal-derivational gekennzeichnet, während sich Modus nicht auf das Verballexem, sondern die Äußerung insgesamt bezieht und daher konzeptuell vom Verbalereignis entfernter ist; dementsprechend erfolgt die Modusmarkierung weiter vom Verbstamm entfernt, häufig durch nicht-affixale Marker wie Modalpartikeln (eine kritische Würdigung dieser Thesen Bybees liefert Croft 1990: 177 ff.).

Wie die hier nur in Auswahl dargestellten Beispiele zeigen, handelt es sich beim diagrammatischen Ausdruck von Distanz um eine Erscheinung von Ikonizität, die auf verschiedenen sprachlichen Hierarchieebenen und in unterschiedlichsten kommunikativen Domänen auftritt und neben der sequentiellen Ikonizität als empirisch gut gesicherte universale Tendenz gilt. Dabei darf jedoch nicht übersehen werden, daß das Ausgangsdiktum „grammatical distance reflects conceptual distance" ebenso klare Bemessungsparameter für konzeptuelle Distanz verlangen würde, wie diese auf der grammatischen

Seite durch unterschiedliche Fusionsgrade gegeben sind, die durch Kommutationsproben und andere distributionelle Tests nachgeprüft werden können.

Haiman (1985a: 106f.) schlägt vier Parameter der konzeptuellen Nähe vor, nämlich (1) semantische oder physische Gemeinsamkeiten („Two ideas [...] share semantic features, properties, or parts" [ebd.]), (2) gegenseitige Beeinflussung („affect each other" [ebd.]), (3) Nicht-Trennbarkeit („are factually inseparable" [ebd.]) und (4) perzeptive Einheit, „whether factually inseparable or not" (ebd.).

Es ist offenkundig, daß die Operationalisierbarkeit dieser Parameter, abgesehen von intuitiver Bewertung, problematisch ist, da über die kognitive Struktur und Organisation von Konzepten nur wenige gesicherte Erkenntnisse vorliegen. Auch zeigen die zitierten Beispiele, daß die angenommene Ikonizität der sprachlichen Enkodierung häufig — wie etwa im Falle von Respekt und Höflichkeit — weniger auf die Konzeptualisierung des Sachverhalts und der involvierten Referenten verweist als vielmehr auf die pragmatische Interpretation des Sachverhalts und der Referenten.

4.2.3. Weitere Beispiele diagrammatisch-ikonischer Motivierung

Eine Art von Ikonizität, die u.a. von Newmeyer (1992) als eigene Erscheinungsform von ikonischer Motivierung betrachtet wird, jedoch auch als Untergruppe der ikonischen Distanzmarkierung aufgefaßt werden kann (so Haiman 1983), betrifft den Grad konzeptueller Autonomie sprachlicher Ausdrücke. Angewandt auf die Junktionssyntax bedeutet dies: „the grammatical separateness of a clause corresponds to the conceptual independence of the proposition expressed by that clause" (Haiman 1983: 799).

Givón (1985) entwickelt dieses Prinzip zu einer Skala der semantischen Bindung eines subordinierten Verbs an das regierende Verb u.a. anhand der Parameter 'Kasuszuweisung beim Subjekt/Agens', 'Tempus-, Modus- und Aspektmarkierung am untergeordneten Verb' und 'Einfügen oder Fehlen eines Junktormorphems'.

Die folgenden Beispielsätze ordnen sich entlang dieser Skala an, und zwar vom höchsten semantischen Bindungsgrad in (11a) zum niedrigsten in (11e). Dazu verhalten sich, so Givón, die unterschiedlichen Finitheitsgrade des subordinierten Verbs ikonisch: je semantisch autonomer das Verb, desto finiter (Givón 1985: 202).

(11) ENGLISCH
 (a) He made John fall
 (b) He told him to leave
 (c) He wanted him to leave
 (d) He wished that he would leave
 (e) He knew that John left

Haiman (1985b) befaßt sich mit der ikonischen Markierung konzeptueller Symmetrie als 'Koordination'. Wie anhand von Beispiel (3) illustriert, werden (aggregativ oder integrativ) koordinierte Sachverhaltsdarstellungen gemäß dem Prinzip der Tempusikonizität zumindest als aufeinanderfolgend interpretiert, wenn nicht gar eine Verknüpfung durch Konsekutivität oder Kausalität supponiert wird. Haiman (1985b: 72, 1992: 193) geht davon aus, daß zwischen koordinierten sentientiellen Konstituenten offenkundig eine universale Asymmetrie besteht, die eine ikonische Abbildung von Symmetrie auf Satzebene — etwa durch syntaktische Parallelismen — erschwert. Hingegen scheint Symmetrie durch Koordination unterhalb der Satzebene die naheliegende Interpretation zu sein, wie der Kontrast zwischen (12) und der Reziprokkonstruktion in (13) zeigt:

(12) ENGLISCH
 Max hit Harry, and Harry hit Max.
(13) Max and Harry hit each other.

Während (12) eine asymmetrische Lesart (temporale Abfolge) und eine symmetrische Lesart (simultaner Ablauf) erlaubt, hat die intrasententielle Koordination in (13) — freilich morphosyntaktisch gestützt durch das Reziprokpronomen — in erster Linie eine symmetrisch-simultane Lesart. Simultaneität auf sentientieller Ebene kann durch Mittel syntaktischer Koordination abgebildet werden, indem zwei Sachverhaltsdarstellungen ineinander verflochten werden, wie in (14) (Haiman 1985b: 75):

(14) ENGLISCH
 Max and Hortense cleaned out the fridge and started cooking dinner, respectively.

Dennoch zeigt auch dieses Beispiel, daß die Zweidimensionalität der sprachlichen Enkodierung einer ikonischen Abbildung von Symmetrien wie etwa der Simultaneität von Sachverhaltsdarstellungen entgegensteht: auch (14) kommt nicht ohne eine zusätzliche Markierung (Haiman: ein Diakritikon), das Adverb *respectively*, aus.

Eine weitere Spielart von Ikonizität, die in engem Zusammenhang mit der natürlichkeitstheoretischen Annahme zu sehen ist, daß markierte Formen mit markierten Inhalten und Bedeutungen korrespondieren (→ Art. 32), betrifft den Aktivierungsgrad (*predictability*; Givón 1995b) von Diskursreferenten. Haiman (1992 u.ö.) leitet daraus eine diagrammatisch-ikonische 'Motivierung des Unerwartbaren' ab. Er veranschaulicht dies am Kontrast zwischen prototypisch reflexiven Verben wie 'shave' und Verben, deren Objekt typischerweise nicht mit dem Subjekt identisch ist, wie 'kick': im Falle einer nicht-erwartbaren Reflexivität muß ein entsprechendes Pronomen stehen, das bei erwartbarer Reflexivität optional ist:

(15) ENGLISCH
 (a) He shaved (himself)
 (b) He kicked himself

„What is marked by more complex form", so Haimans – weitreichende – Folgerung, „is never a more complex concept, but a more *surprising* one, given the context." (Haiman 1992: 194).

Hopper & Thompson (1985) entwickeln anhand der grammatisch-lexikalischen Kategorien 'Verb' und 'Nomen' eine diagrammatische Kategorialitätsikonizität mit dem Grundprinzip: „The more a form refers to a discrete discourse entity or reports a discrete discourse event, the more distinct will be its linguistic form" (Hopper & Thompson 1985: 151). Die Autoren stellen die als Universale postulierte Existenz der beiden lexikalischen Basiskategorien nicht in Frage, gehen aber von einer Skalarität zwischen Verbalität und Nominalität aus, die sich ikonisch in der Aufwendigkeit der Form und der Bandbreite kompatibler Morpheme manifestiert (→ Art. 38). Das Nomen *bear* weist in (16a) signifikant weniger prototypische Nominalitätszüge auf als in (16b) (Referenz auf eine sichtbare Entität der außersprachlichen Wirklichkeit, *time-stability* u. dgl.) und unterliegt daher deutlichen Restriktionen, was die Kookkurrenz z.B. mit determinierenden Morphemen oder Attributen angeht (Hopper & Thompson 1995: 156):

(16) ENGLISCH
 (a) We went bear-trapping in the woods
 (b) We looked up and saw an old bear lumbering toward our picnic table

Aus ihren zahlreichen Beispielsprachen und Belegen schließen Hopper und Thompson (1995: 158): „Categoriality, i.e. the property of being a prototypical instance of the grammatical category noun or verbs, is thus imposed on linguistic forms by discourse." Die Autoren sehen also die kategoriale Differenzierung bzw. Skalarität und die damit verbundene ikonische Enkodierung als ausschließlich diskursiv motiviert, wobei die Salienz des betreffenden Elements im Textganzen und seine Position im Textrelief – also die Zuordnung zum diskursiven Vorder- oder Hintergrund – das entscheidende Kriterium ist. Semantische 'Universalien' wie 'Dinghaftigkeit' bei Nomina und 'Ereignishaftigkeit' bei Verben werden von Hopper und Thompson als sekundäre, vom diskursiv-pragmatischen Status abgeleitete Generalisierungen gewertet.

5. Ikonische Motivierung zwischen Grammatik, Kognition und Pragmatik

Die Ikonizitätshypothese war eingangs den funktionalen Ansätzen zugeordnet worden, weil sie sprachliche Formen aufgrund externer Motivierungen zu erklären versucht und dabei von einer zentralen Zweckbestimmung der Sprache, „to communicate experience and thought" (Shibatani & Bynon 1995: 17), ausgeht.

Dies ist die Basis für die „kognitive Wende" auch in der Beschäftigung mit Ikonizität insofern, als nicht mehr von einer Similaritätsbeziehung zwischen außersprachlichem Referenten bzw. Sachverhalt und seiner sprachlichen Enkodierung ausgegangen wird, wie dies zuvor vor allem bei bildhaften Ikonen wie Onomatopöien angenommen wurde; vielmehr steht heute innerhalb der ikonizitätsbasierten Ansätze die Relation zwischen Sprachzeichen und Konzepten im Vordergrund. Freilich sind die Fragen der Genese, Struktur, Organisation und zerebralen Lokalisierung der Konzepte alles andere als erschöpfend geklärt.

Geht man davon aus, daß mentale Repräsentationen mit Prototypen arbeiten, die mit den außersprachlichen Referenten in einer Ähnlichkeitsrelation stehen, so wäre ein Ikonizitätsverhältnis, verstanden als Form-Konzept-Similarität, eine zweifach gebrochene und entsprechend schwache Ähnlichkeitsbeziehung. Allerdings haben die Beispiele und

Anwendungen, die bezüglich der diversen Ikonizitätsarten angeführt wurden, deutlich gemacht, daß sich Ikonizität *de facto* häufig nicht oder nicht allein auf die konzeptuelle Ebene, also die mentalen Vorgänge im Sprecher/Hörer, bezieht, sondern sowohl auf das sprachliche System als solches als auch auf die situative Einbettung des Kommunikationsakts, bei dem ikonisch enkodiert wird, verweisen kann.

Die pragmatische Dimension von Ikonizität, wie sie z.B. beim distanzikonisch motivierten höflichen oder respektvollen Ausdruck festgestellt wurde, stellt kein eigentliches Problem dar. Wie Sperber & Wilson (1986) überzeugend zeigen, ist der pragmatisch-situative Kontext nichts außersprachlich Gegebenes, sondern ein im Kommunikationsgeschehen entstehendes, 'ausgehandeltes' Produkt von Perzeptionsvorgängen und kognitiv basierten Komplementärstrategien (*enrichment*).

Problematischer sind dagegen solche angenommenen Ikonizitätsbeziehungen, die auf sprachinterner Basis formuliert werden. So bauen die Parameter, die Givón (1985) für die Bildung der o.a. Bindungshierarchie von Komplementsatzverben anführt, teilweise auf rein innersprachliche Kategorien auf und sind von kognitiven Konzepten unabhängig; Givón sieht dies auch selbst, wenn er einräumt, daß für diese Parameter – die Kasuszuweisung beim Subjekt/Agens und die TMA-Markierung des subordinierten Verbs – Folgendes gilt: „[they] derive their iconic power from *system-internal structural properties*, rather than from immediately obvious *general cognitive principles*" (Givón 1995: 201; Hervorh. im Orig.).

Die Applizierbarkeit des Ikonizitätsbegriffs als definitorisch sprachexterner Motivierung auf solche innersystemischen Erscheinungen erscheint fraglich, wenngleich außer Zweifel steht, daß die innersprachlich-strukturellen Verhältnisse sich häufig auf diskursive oder pragmatische Techniken und Strategien zurückführen lassen, die einen Grammatikalisierungsprozeß durchlaufen haben. Möglicherweise wäre zur Verdeutlichung eine Unterteilung der Ikonizitätshypothese analog zu der in der Natürlichkeitsforschung gemachten Differenzierung zwischen 'übereinzelsprachlicher' vs. 'einzelsprachlichsystembedingter Natürlichkeit' von Nutzen (Wurzel 1987).

Auch unter der Voraussetzung, daß es nicht-sprachextern motivierbare Ikonizität nicht geben kann, da auch innersystemische Verhältnisse – mehr oder minder eindeutig – auf diskursiv-funktionale Ursprünge und Quellen zurückgeführt werden können, zeigt sich anhand des o.a. Beispiels von Givón eine Tendenz zur Ausweitung des Ikonizitätsbegriffs, die nicht in Abrede gestellt werden kann und die explanative Mächtigkeit der Konzeption nicht unbedingt fördert. Newmeyer (1998: 115) kritisiert zu Recht: „there is a tendency to label virtually any functional motivation for a linguistic structure as an 'iconic' one", wodurch 'funktional motiviert' und 'ikonisch' quasi synonymisch würden.

Die Affinitäten zwischen den zentralen sprachextern-funktionalen Motivierungstypen – Markiertheit, Ökonomie, Prototypikalität, Diskurs- und Informationsstruktur und eben Ikonizität – sind evident, wie sich aus den zahlreichen Querverweisen ergibt, die hier im Zusammenhang mit Ikonizitätstypen angebracht wurden, und wie sich auch daran ablesen läßt, daß in der einschlägigen Literatur häufig mehrere Motivierungen verbunden und gemeinsam behandelt werden (z.B. Haiman 1983).

6. Ikonizität und Sprachwandel

Ikonische Motivierung spielt, darauf wurde bereits hingewiesen, im Erstsprachenerwerb eine große Rolle (Slobin 1985), und auch in der Proto-Grammatik von Pidgins und der basilektalen Grammatik von Kreolsprachen, die signifikante Entwicklungsparallelitäten zur sprachlichen Onto- und – vermutlich – zur Phylogenese aufweisen, finden sich vor allem Regularitäten, deren „common denominator […] is that they are extremely iconic" (Givón 1995a: 406; vgl. auch Ludwig 1996). Während aber die Bedeutung von Ikonizität und Ikonisierung in sprachlichen Früh- und Kreationsphasen außer Frage steht, wird der Status von Ikonizität im Sprachwandel unterschiedlich bewertet. Nach der traditionellen, aus der Indogermanistik herkommenden Sichtweise zerstört der Lautwandel die externe Motivierung sprachlicher Zeichen, während analogische 'Verstöße' gegen Lautwandelregularitäten diese Motivierung – und damit auch Ikonizität – wiederherstellen (Haiman 1994: 1633). Damit hängt ein bisweilen in der Literatur vertretenes „Bild des durch De-Ikonisierung gekennzeichneten evolutionären Fortschritts" (Plank 1979: 126) zusammen, nach dem das qualitative Spezifikum menschlicher Kommunikation in seiner Symbolhaftigkeit gesehen wird.

Diese Sichtweise ist erwartungsgemäß nicht ohne Kritik geblieben. Plank (1979: 127) schließt eine tendenziell evolutionäre De-Ikonisierung nicht aus, sieht diese aber vor allem auf die − in heutigen Sprachen bereits als unproduktiv qualifizierte − bildhafte Ikonizität beschränkt. Anders hinsichtlich der diagrammatischen Ikonizität, wo er eine Tendenz zur Ausweitung sieht, die „häufig in Zusammenhang mit systematisierenden, vereinfachenden Entwicklungen jeder Art gebracht [wird]" (Plank 1979: 128).

Die Frage nach dem Zusammenhang von Ikonizität und sprachlichem Wandel stellt sich vor allem in funktional orientierten Sprachwandeltheorien, so etwa bei der Untersuchung von Lexikalisierungs- und Grammatikalisierungsprozessen (Giacalone Ramat 1995). Eine Grammatikalisierung sprachlicher Elemente geht typischerweise aus von Diskursstrategien und den zugrundeliegenden kognitiven Faktoren und führt über die syntaktische Ebene schließlich in den Bereich der Morphologie.

Ausgangspunkt einer solchen Entwicklung sind metonymische oder metaphorische Gebrauchskontexte (Heine & al. 1991; Hopper & Traugott 1993), deren ikonizitätstheoretischer Status aufgrund der erwähnten geringen Ausarbeitung des Typus der metaphorischen Ikonizität hier nicht diskutiert werden kann. Fischer (1999: 352 f.) zeigt jedoch, daß zumindest einige der bei Lehmann (1995 [[1]1982]) zusammengestellten Teilprozesse und Begleiterscheinungen von Grammatikalisierungen Instanzen von − meist isomorpher − Ikonizität sind. So ist etwa die Existenz unterschiedlicher Ausdrucksformen für Futurizität, wie sie − grammatikalisierungstheoretisch als Beispiel der 'Gleichzeitigkeit des Ungleichzeitigen' zu erklären − in vielen Sprachen zu konstatieren sind, insofern isomorph-ikonisch, als diese Ausdrucksmittel je spezifische semantische Nuancen und Gebrauchsrestriktionen zeigen, die auf ihre Ausgangsbedeutung verweisen (Fischer 1999: 353).

Auch formale Erneuerung (*renewal*) wie die 'analogische' Regularisierung von Partizipialformen z.B. im Englischen (Fischer 1999: 352) oder der Ersatz synthetischer durch analytische, auf Periphrasen basierende Verbalformen lassen sich als ikonisch interpretieren: „Renewal cannot be explained by the process of grammaticalisation itself, but is due to a constant pressure for a more iconic (more transparent) isomorphic structure" (Fischer ebd.). Die für die späteren Stadien des Grammatikalisierungsverlaufs charakteristischen Teilprozesse wie etwa der Abbau der lautlichen Substanz grammatikalisierter Elemente werden kontrovers teilweise anti-ikonisch (gemäß der o.a. traditionellen Sicht), teilweise jedoch ebenfalls als Ausdruck von Ikonizität *qua* 'Isomorphie' (Givón 1995b: 49 f.) angesehen.

Die „Möglichkeit der Fluktuation der relativen Symbolizitätsanteile und Ikonizitätsanteile" (Plank 1979: 129) steht in den aktuellen Ikonizitätsansätzen außer Frage (vgl. Fischer 1999: 346); dasselbe gilt für − je nach sprachlicher Betrachtungsebene − unterschiedliche Grade externer Motiviertheit (Giacalone Ramat 1995). Auch wenn das Verhältnis von Ikonizität und Sprachwandel − zumal im Lichte funktional ausgerichteter Sprachwandeltheorien − nicht erschöpfend geklärt ist und, wie Giacalone Ramat (1995: 134 f.) hervorhebt, weitergehender Forschung bedarf, so ist der optimistischen Einschätzung dieser Autorin, daß sich innerhalb der typologischen Untersuchung sprachlicher Varianz und Invarianz die Ikonizitätshypothese und die Grammatikalisierungstheorie zusammenführen lassen (Giacalone Ramat 1995: 135), wohl zuzustimmen.

7. Zitierte Literatur

Bickel, Balthasar. 1995. „Relatives à antécédent interne, nominalisation et focalisation : Entre syntaxe et morphologie en bélharien". *Bulletin de la Société Linguistique de Paris* 90: 391−427.

Brown, Penelope & Levinson, Stephen C. 1996. *Politeness: some universals in language usage.* (Studies in Interactional Sociolinguistics, 4.) Cambridge: Cambridge University Press.

Bybee, Joan. 1985. „Diagrammatic iconicity in stem-inflection relations", in: Haiman (ed.), 11−47.

Bybee, Joan & Perkins, Revere & Pagliuca, William. 1994. *The Evolution of Grammar. Tense, Aspect, and Modality in the Languages of the World.* Chicago & London: University of Chicago Press.

Chappell, Hilary & Mc Gregor, William (eds.). 1996. *The Grammar of Inalienability. A Typological Perspective on Body Part Terms and the Part-Whole Relation.* (Empirical Approaches to Language Typology, 14.) Berlin & New York: Mouton de Gruyter.

Croft, William. 1990. *Typology and universals.* Cambridge etc.: Cambridge University Press.

Croft, William. 1995. „Modern Syntactic Typology", in: Shibatani & Bynon (eds.), 85−144.

Dotter, Franz. 1988. *Nichtarbitrarität und Ikonizität in der Syntax.* (Beiträge zur Sprachwissenschaft, 4.) Hamburg: Buske.

Dressler, Wolfgang U. 1995. „Interactions between Iconicity and Other Semiotic Parameters in Language", in: Simone (ed.), 21−37.

Du Bois, John W. 1985. „Competing motivations", in: Haiman (ed.), 343−65.

Engler, Rudolf. 1962. „Théorie et critique d'un principe saussurien: l'arbitraire du signe". *Cahiers Ferdinand de Saussure* 19: 5−66.

Engler, Rudolf. 1995. „Iconicity and/or Arbitrariness", in: Simone (ed.), 39−45.

Fertig, David. 1998. „Suppletion, natural morphology, and diagrammaticity". *Linguistics* 36: 1065−91.

Fischer, Olga. 1999. „On the Role Played by Iconicity in Grammaticalisation Processes", in: Nänny & Fischer (eds.), 345−74.

Fischer, Olga & Nänny, Max. 1999. „Introduction: Iconicity as a Creative Force in Language Use"; in: Nänny & Fischer (eds.), xv−xxxvi.

Fónagy, Ivan. 1993. „Physei / Thesei. L'aspect évolutif d'un débat millénaire". *Faits de langues* 1: 29−45.

Fónagy, Ivan. 1999. „Why Iconicity?" in: Nänny & Fischer (eds.), 3−36.

Gauger, Hans-Martin. 1993. „Tipología y conciencia lingüística: marca, naturalidad, iconicidad, transparencia, prototipicalidad"; in: Hilty, Gerold (ed.). *Actes du XXe Congrès International de Linguistique et Philologie Romanes, Zurich 1992.* Tome III, Section IV − Typologie des langues romanes. Tübingen & Basel: Francke, 113−24.

Giacalone Ramat, Anna. 1995. „Iconicity in Grammaticalization Processes", in: Simone (ed.). 119−39.

Givón, Talmy. 1979. *On understanding grammar.* New York: Academic Press.

Givón, Talmy. 1984−90. *Syntax. A functional-typological introduction.* Amsterdam & Philadelphia: Benjamins.

Givón, Talmy. 1985. „Iconicity, isomorphism and non-arbitrary coding in syntax", in: Haiman (ed.), 187−219.

Givón, Talmy. 1995a. *Functionalism and Grammar.* Amsterdam & Philadelphia: Benjamins.

Givón, Talmy. 1995b. „Isomorphism in the Grammatical Code. Cognitive and Biological Considerations", in: Simone (ed.), 47−76.

Haiman, John. 1980. „The iconicity of grammar: Isomorphism and motivation". *Language* 56: 515−40.

Haiman, John. 1983. „Iconic and economic motivation". *Language* 59: 781−819.

Haimann, John. 1985a. *Natwal Syntax.* Cambridge: Cambridge University Press.

Haiman, John. 1985b. „Symmetry", in: Haiman (ed.), 73−95.

Haiman, John. 1992. „Iconicity", in: Bright, William (ed.). *International Encyclopedia of Linguistics.* Volume 2. New York & Oxford: Oxford University Press, 191−95.

Haiman, John. 1994. „Iconicity and Syntactic Change", in: Asher, Ronald E. (ed.). *The encyclopedia of language and linguistics.* Oxford etc.: Pergamon Press, 1633−37.

Haiman, John. 1999. „Action, Speech, and Grammar. The Sublimation Trajectory", in: Nänny & Fischer (eds.), 37−57.

Haiman, John (ed.). 1985. *Iconicity in Syntax. Proceedings of a Symposium on Iconicity in Syntax, Stanford, June 24−6, 1983.* (Typological Studies in Language, 6.) Amsterdam & Philadelphia: Benjamins.

Heine, Bernd & Claudi, Ulrike & Hünnemeyer, Friederike. 1991. *Grammaticalization. A Conceptual Framework.* Chicago & London: University of Chicago Press.

Hopper, Paul & Thompson, Sandra. 1980. „Transitivity in Grammar and Discourse". *Language* 56: 251−99.

Hopper, Paul & Thompson, Sandra. 1985. „The iconicity of the universal categories 'noun' and 'verbs'", in: Haiman (ed.), 151−83.

Hopper, Paul & Traugott, Elizabeth Closs. 1993. *Grammaticalization.* Cambridge: Cambridge University Press.

Jakobson, Roman. 1971 [1965]. „Quest for the essence of language", in: ders., *Selected Writings.* II: Word and Language. Den Haag & Paris: Mouton, 345−59.

Kleiber, Georges. 1993. „Iconicité d'isomorphisme et grammaire cognitive". *Faits de langues* 1: 105−21.

Lehmann, Christian. 1995 (¹1982). *Thoughts on Grammaticalization.* (Lincom Studies in Theoretical Linguistics, 1.) München & Newcastle: Lincom Europa.

Ludwig, Ralph. 1996. *Kreolsprachen zwischen Mündlichkeit und Schriftlichkeit.* (ScriptOralia, 86.) Tübingen: Narr.

Malsch, Derry L. 1987. „The grammaticalization of social relationship: The origin of number to encode deference", in: Giacalone Ramat, Anna & Carruba, Onofrio & Bernini, Giuliano (eds.). *Papers from the 7th International Conference on Historical Linguistics.* (Amsterdam Studies in the Theory and History of Linguistic Science, 48.) Amsterdam & Philadelphia: Benjamins, 406−18.

Mayerthaler, Willi. 1980. „Ikonismus in der Morphologie". *Zeitschrift für Semiotik* 2: 19−37.

Nänny, Max & Fischer, Olga (eds.). 1999. *Form miming meaning. Iconicity in language and literature.* Amsterdam & Philadelphia: Benjamins.

Newmeyer, Frederick J. 1992. „Iconicity and Generative Grammar". *Language* 68: 756−96.

Newmeyer, Frederick J. 1998. *Language Form and Language Function.* Cambridge/MA & London: MIT Press.

Paris, Marie-Claude & Peyraube, Alain. 1993. „L'iconicité : un nouveau dogme de la syntaxe chinoise?". *Faits de langues* 1: 69−78.

Posner, Roland. 1980. „Ikonismus in den natürlichen Sprachen". *Zeitschrift für Semiotik* 2: 1−6.

Peirce, Charles S. 1960. *Collected Papers.* Volume II. Elements of Logic. Edited by Charles Hartshorne and Paul Weiss. Cambridge/MA: Belknap Press of Harvard University Press.

Plank, Frans. 1979. „Ikonisierung und De-Ikonisierung als Prinzipien des Sprachwandels". *Sprachwissenschaft* 4: 121−58.

Raible, Wolfgang. 1992. *Junktion. Eine Dimension der Sprache und ihre Realisierungsformen zwischen Aggregation und Integration.* (Sitzungsberichte der Heidelberger Akademie der Wissenschaften, 1992 (2).) Heidelberg: Winter.

Ransdell, Joseph. 1986. „On Peirce's Conception of the Iconic Sign", in: Bouissac, Paul & Herzfeld, Michael & Posner, Roland (eds.). *Iconicity. Essays on the Nature of Culture. Festschrift for Thomas A. Sebeok.* Tübingen: Stauffenburg, 51−74.

Schachter, Paul. 1973. „Focus and relativization". *Language* 49: 19−46.

Shibatani, Masayoshi & Bynon, Theodora. 1995. „Approaches to Language Typology: A Conspectus", in: dies. (eds.), 1−25.

Shibatani, Masayoshi & Bynon, Theodora (eds.). 1995. *Approaches to Language Typology.* Oxford: Clarendon Press.

Simone, Raffaele. 1995. „Foreword: Under the Sign of Cratylus", in: Simone (ed.). vii−xi.

Simone, Raffaele (ed.). 1995. *Iconicity in Language.* (Current Issues in Linguistic Theory, 110.) Amsterdam & Philadelphia: Benjamins.

Slobin, Dan I. 1985. „The child as a linguistic iconmaker", in: Haiman (ed.), 221−48.

Sperber, Dan & Wilson, Deirdre. 1986. *Relevance. Communication and Cognition.* Oxford: Blackwell.

Swiggers, Pierre. 1993. „Iconicité : un coup d'œil historiographique et méthodologique". *Faits de langues* 1: 21−28.

Tai, James H.-Y. 1985. „Temporal sequence and Chinese word order"; in: Haiman (ed.). 49−72.

Wurzel, Wolfgang U. 1987. „System-Dependent Morphological Naturalness in Inflection", in: Dressler, Wolfgang U. (ed.). *Leitmotifs in Natural Morphology.* Amsterdam & Philadelphia: Benjamins, 59−96.

Claus D. Pusch,
Universität Freiburg i.Br., (Deutschland)

31. Ökonomie

1. Was ist Ökonomie in der Sprache?
2. Zur Geschichte des Konzepts
3. Typen von Sprachökonomie
4. Paradigmatische Ökonomie: Ökonomie der Inventare
5. Syntagmatische Ökonomie: Ökonomie der Formen
6. Ökonomie, Markiertheit, Lokalität
7. Zitierte Literatur

1. Was ist Ökonomie in der Sprache?

Wie viele andere linguistische Termini ist der der Ökonomie oder, genauer gesagt, der SPRACHÖKONOMIE, keinesfalls klar und eindeutig. Die verschiedenen in der Literatur zu findenden Begriffe von Sprachökonomie unterscheiden sich teilweise beträchtlich sowohl hinsichtlich ihrer jeweiligen theoretischen Einordnung als auch hinsichtlich der jeweils von ihnen abgedeckten Erscheinungen in der Sprache. Nichtsdestoweniger ist es natürlich im hier gegebenen Zusammenhang notwendig, zunächst einmal wenigstens tentativ zu bestimmen, was unter Sprachökonomie überhaupt zu verstehen ist. Sprachökonomie ist (nach Bußmann 1990: 711)

„Ursache bzw. Anlaß für die Tendenz, mit einem Minimum an sprachlichem Aufwand ein Maximum an sprachlicher Effektivität zu erzielen. Dieses Ziel läßt sich durch verschiedene Maßnahmen anstreben, z. B. Vereinfachung durch Kürzung […], Verwendung von Abkürzungen, Systematisierung und Vereinheitlichung von Flexionsformen oder analogischer Ausgleich zwischen verwandten Formen …"

Diese Bestimmung von Sprachökonomie ist in mehrfacher Hinsicht gut als Ausgangspunkt für die detailliertere Explikation geeignet. Sie ist nicht auf eine spezifische Theorie bezogen, sie engt den Begriff der Ökonomie nicht entweder auf synchrone oder aber auf diachrone Verhältnisse ein, und sie berücksichtigt, daß sich Ökonomie in der Sprache nicht nur in der Vermeidung von quantitativem, sondern auch in der Vermeidung von qualitativem Aufwand äußern kann. (So kann etwa eine Systematisierung von Flexionsformen durchaus auch zu quantitativ aufwendigeren Formen führen, vgl. *er molk > er melkte*).

2. Zur Geschichte des Konzepts

Die Ursprünge des Konzepts der Sprachökonomie liegen in der Lautwandelforschung der zweiten Hälfte des 19. Jahrhunderts. Verschiedene Sprachwissenschaftler, die sich nicht mit der traditionellen philologischen Registrierung von Lautveränderungen begnügten, sondern nach Erklärungen dafür suchten, stellten fest, daß solche Veränderungen (zumindest häufig) offensichtlich zu einer Vereinfachung der Artikulation führen. So konstatierte z. B. William D. Whitney (1868: 28), daß die Haupttendenz des Wandels darin besteht „to make things easy to our organs of speech, to economize time and effort in the work of expressions", und Georg Curtius (1858: 23) formulierte: „Bequemlichkeit ist und bleibt der hauptanlass des lautwandels unter allen umständen". Doch solche Überlegungen fanden in der zeitgenössischen Sprachwissenschaft wenig Akzeptanz und wurden weitgehend als unwissenschaftlich zurückgewiesen.

Etwa fünf Jahrzehnte später nahm Otto Jespersen den Gedanken der Ökonomie des Wandels wieder auf. Jespersen ist davon überzeugt, daß zumindest ein Großteil der Lautveränderungen im Sinne einer generellen „ease theory" durch die das gesamte Handeln des Menschen steuernde „economy of effort" zu erklären ist:

„In thus taking up the cudgels for the ease theory I am not afraid of hearing the objection that I ascribe too great power to human laziness, indolence, inertia, shirking, easygoingness, sloth, sluggishness, lack of energy, or whatever other beautiful synonyms have been invented for 'economy of effort' or 'following the line of least resistance'. The fact remains that there is such a 'tendency' in all human beings ...." (1922: 263).

Zugleich sieht er, daß nicht nur phonologischer, sondern auch morphologischer Wandel entsprechend dieser Tendenz funktioniert:

„... and by taking it into account in explaining changes of sound we are doing nothing else than applying here the same principle that attributes many simplifications of form to 'analogy': we see the same psychological force at work in the two different domains of phonetics and morphology" (a.a.O.).

Auch der Terminus Sprachökonomie („economy of speech") wurde offensichtlich von Jespersen geprägt (1924: 264). Er wendet ihn, terminologisch abgehoben von „economy of effort", ausschließlich auf synchrone Verhältnisse an. „Economy of speech" ist die einzelsprachlich grammatikalisierte Vermeidung von redundanten grammatischen Mitteln, so beispielsweise die Nicht-Symbolisierung des Plurals bei ungarischen Substantiven, wenn sie mit einem Numerale verbunden sind, wie sie auch in deutschen Konstruktionen des Typs *fünf Mann* vorliegt. Was sich für andere Linguisten als 'unlogisch' darstellt, betrachtet Jespersen als „an instance of wise economy" in der Sprachstruktur (208). Wichtig ist für ihn auch die Tatsache, daß die einzelnen Sprachen auf recht unterschiedliche Weise von der Ökonomie Gebrauch machen (264).

Ein erstes systematisch ausgearbeitetes Konzept der Sprachökonomie legt dann Martinet in den fünfziger und sechziger Jahren vor (z. T. unter Bezug auf Frei (1929) und Zipf (1949)). Er geht davon aus, daß die Entwicklung der Sprache bestimmt ist durch „die ständige Antinomie zwischen den Kommunikationsbedürfnissen des Menschen und seiner Tendenz, seine geistige und körperliche Tätigkeit auf ein Minimum zu beschränken" (1963: 164).

Doch das Streben nach dem geringsten Kraftaufwand kann verschieden realisiert werden. Wenn die Sprecher beispielsweise einen neuen Gegenstand benennen müssen, dann können sie entweder eine neue, kurze sprachliche Einheit dafür prägen oder aber den Gegenstand durch die Kombination vorhandener Einheiten beschreiben. Im ersten Fall ergibt sich eine Ersparnis hinsichtlich der Länge der Äußerung, d. h. eine syntagmatische Ersparnis, im zweiten Fall eine Ersparnis hinsichtlich der Belastung des Gedächtnisses, d. h. eine paradigmatische Ersparnis. Beides gleichzeitig ist jedoch nicht zu haben. Spricht man häufig von dem betreffenden Gegenstand, so ist es ökonomischer, eine neue kurze Bezeichnung zu wählen, auch wenn damit das Gedächtnis belastet wird; spricht man dagegen seltener von ihm, so ist es ökonomischer, das Gedächtnis nicht zusätzlich zu belasten, auch wenn damit die entsprechenden Äußerungen länger werden (165). Aufgrund dessen ist zu erwarten, daß häufige Wörter durchschnittlich kürzer sind als seltene, was die Statistik auch erweist (173). Martinet faßt die Sprachökonomie dann in folgender Weise:

„Was man die Ökonomie einer Sprache nennen kann, ist dieses ständige Streben nach dem Gleichgewicht zwischen widerstreitenden Bedürfnissen, denen Genüge getan werden muß: Kommunikationsbedürfnisse auf der einen, Gedächtnisträgheit und Trägheit des Artikulierens – diese beiden in ständigem Konflikt – auf der anderen Seite [...]" (165 f.).

Dabei bezieht sich das Streben nach Kraftersparnis sowohl auf die Vermeidung von quantitativem als auch von qualitativem Aufwand, also etwa von artikulatorisch komplexen Lauten und Lautfolgen, wodurch dann u. a. auch entsprechende phonologische Veränderungen bedingt sind (im Detail dazu 1981: passim). In diesen Zusammenhang gehört auch, daß das Verfahren, „stets dieselbe Form für den selben Begriff zu gebrauchen", als ökonomisch charakterisiert wird (1968: 171).

Für Martinet bestimmt die Sprachökonomie jedoch nicht nur das Funktionieren und die Veränderung der einzelnen Sprachen. Sie ist darüber hinaus zugleich von grundsätzlicher Bedeutung für die Struktur der menschlichen Sprache überhaupt. Das zeigt sich auf beiden „Gliederungsebenen" der Sprache: Die menschliche Sprache ist dadurch charakterisiert, daß sie auf der inhaltlichen Ebene mit einem Inventar von nur einigen tausend „Monemen" (Martinets Terminus für Morpheme) und auf der lautlichen Ebene mit einem Inventar von nur „zwanzig, dreißig Phonemen" auskommt. Beide Gliederungsebenen sind damit jeweils in paradigmatischer Hinsicht streng ökonomisch organisiert und entsprechend gut handhabbar.

Aus der Eingeschränktheit der Inventare resultiert aber, daß sowohl die Moneme als auch die Phoneme jeweils zu komplexeren Einheiten kombinierbar sein müssen, so daß unendlich viele sprachliche Äußerungen gebildet und die lautliche Identität sämtlicher vorhandener Moneme gesichert werden kann. Damit ist für Martinet die spezifische Struktur der menschlichen Sprache und speziell die Existenz der Syntax, die die Moneme zu umfassenderen Zeichen zusammenfaßt, eine unmittelbare Folge der Tendenz zur Ökonomie (1968: 18 ff.).

Seit Ende der siebziger Jahre findet die Problematik der Sprachökonomie wieder stärker das Interesse von funktional orientierten Sprachwissenschaftlern wie Otmar Werner und Elke Ronneberger-Sibold. Sie wird speziell unter dem Gesichtspunkt der unterschiedlichen morphologischen und morphosyntaktischen Symbolisierungstechniken wie Fusion, Agglutination, Isolierung und Suppletion diskutiert, wobei die Vor- und Nachteile der einzelnen Techniken bezogen auf jeweils spezifische Anforderungen der sprachlichen Kommunikation herausgearbeitet werden. In diesem Sinne sieht Ronneberger-Sibold den gesamten Kommunikationsvorgang „als das Zusammenspiel verschiedener psychischer und physischer Tätigkeiten mit verschiedenen, teilweise übereinstimmenden, teilweise einander widerstrebenden Anforderungen an die Sprachstruktur" (1980: 33 f.). Sprachökonomie ist damit

„das Streben nach einem Sprachsystem, das eine unter den gegebenen Umständen optimale Verteilung der Belastungen auf die verschiedenen Performanzbedürfnisse herbeiführt" (236).

Dieses Streben stellt zugleich das Motiv der Sprecher für die Herbeiführung entsprechender Sprachveränderungen dar. Der Ökonomiebegriff ist hier also wie bei Martinet auf das Gesamtsystem bezogen, nicht auf einzelne grammatische Erscheinungen.

Dieser Linie folgt auch Otmar Werner, für den der Sprachwandel „ein gleichmäßig-stetes Bemühen" ist, im System „bei wechselnden kommunikativen Bedürfnissen immer wieder die ökonomische Balance herzustellen" (1984: 186). Diese Balance besteht im wesentlichen darin, daß häufig aneinander „gekoppelt" auftretende Informationen in der Morphologie durch möglichst kurze Formen, also komprimiert, symbolisiert werden, während seltener aneinander „gekoppelt" auftretende Informationen durch längere Formen, also expandiert, symbolisiert werden. Daraus zieht Werner die recht weitgehende Schlußfolgerung: „[...] so entscheidet allein die Gebrauchsfrequenz über die morphologischen Regelungen" (1989: 41). Das hat natürlich wesentliche Konsequenzen für den morphologischen Wandel: „The aim of morphological change is a good mixture – not a uniform language type" (1987: 591).

Damit ist sowohl die Struktur der einzelnen morphologischen Formen als auch die

Struktur des morphologischen Systems durch die auf die Gebrauchsfrequenz zurückgeführte Sprachökonomie determiniert.

Eine entscheidende Rolle spielt die Sprachökonomie in John Haimans Theorie einer 'natürlichen Syntax': Für Haiman sind „the tendencies to maximize iconicity and to maximize economy [...] two of the most important competing motivations for linguistic forms in general" (1985: 18), wobei der Gegenpol der Ökonomie, die Ikonizität, den Isomorphismus von Form und Funktion sowie die Motiviertheit und Transparenz der sprachlichen Zeichen einschließt. Das Verhältnis von Ökonomie und Ikonizität stellt sich dabei jedoch nicht einheitlich dar. Die paradigmatische Ökonomie, d. h. die Tendenz zur Ökonomisierung des Zeicheninventars, ist „more than compatible with iconicity", weil in einem wirklich ökonomischen System immer auch Isomorphismus in dem Sinne herrscht, daß nicht zwei (oder mehr) distinkte Formen die gleiche kommunikative Funktion haben. Hingegen steht die syntagmatische Ökonomie, von Haiman gefaßt als die Tendenz zur Ökonomisierung der Länge oder Komplexität von Äußerungen, im direkten Widerspruch zur Ikonizität, da sie Motiviertheit und Transparenz der sprachlichen Zeichen einschränkt, während Motiviertheit und Transparenz die Ökonomie einschränken (158 f.). Hieraus resultieren widersprüchliche Sprachveränderungen: „An essential attribute of human language, according to this view, is that it is always changing in response to competing pressures [...]" (260).

Alle Linguisten, die sich mit der Ökonomie-Problematik befaßt haben, betrachten diese nicht als bloßes wissenschaftliches Konstrukt zur Beschreibung der Sprache, sondern als eine objektiv gegebene Erscheinung, nämlich als eine Tendenz der Sprecher, mit ihrer Sprache 'sparsam' umzugehen, die deren Struktur entscheidend prägt. Will die Linguistik ein realistisches Bild von der Sprache geben, so muß sie dann natürlich diese Tendenz und ihre Konsequenzen, wie im einzelnen auch immer, in möglichst angemessener Weise widerspiegeln.

3. Typen von Sprachökonomie

Die Sprachökonomie ist ihrem Wesen nach ein umfassendes Phänomen. Will man solche Phänomene in ihrem Umfang und ihrer Strukturierung wissenschaftlich erfassen, so muß man ihre unterschiedlichen Erscheinungsformen ermitteln und sie systematisch zueinander in Bezug setzen, d. h. sie klassifizieren. Dafür ist zunächst zu klären, unter welchen Gesichtspunkten eine solche Klassifizierung überhaupt erfolgen, d. h. auf welchen Unterscheidungen sie beruhen soll.

3.1. Paradigmatische vs. syntagmatische Ökonomie

Wohl allgemein akzeptiert ist heute Martinets grundlegende Distinktion zwischen PARADIGMATISCHER und SYNTAGMATISCHER ÖKONOMIE. Die paradigmatische Ökonomie wird im allgemeinen als Ökonomie der Inventare der Sprache, die syntagmatische Ökonomie als die Ökonomie der sprachlichen Formen (oder auch des Aufwands) gefaßt. Diese beiden Typen von Sprachökonomie sind in sehr unterschiedlicher Weise motiviert (man vgl. nochmals „Gedächtnisträgheit" vs. „Trägheit des Artikulierens" bei Martinet 1963: 165 f.), weshalb sie sich auch in weiten Bereichen widersprüchlich zueinander verhalten.

Es ist faktisch seinem ursprünglichen Zweck als ein Mittel zur Erklärung von phonologischem Wandel geschuldet, daß das Ökonomiekonzept im allgemeinen sowohl auf quantitative als auch auf qualitative Aspekte der sprachlichen Struktur bezogen wird: Um das von Whitney (1868: 28) so formulierte 'Ziel' zu erreichen: „to make things easy to our organs of speech", können phonologische Segmente beispielsweise nicht nur getilgt, sondern auch durch einfachere Segmente ersetzt werden. Eine Ökonomisierung kann also sowohl die quantitative Komplexität, d. h. die Länge, als auch die qualitative Komplexität sprachlicher Einheiten reduzieren. Während die Länge von sprachlichen Einheiten faktisch unmittelbar gemessen werden kann (in Silben/Segmenten, Morphemen oder Wörtern), ist die qualitative Komplexität sprachlicher Formen keineswegs in ebenso unstrittiger Weise zu fassen. Die entscheidende Frage dabei ist, welche Struktureigenschaften grammatischer Einheiten überhaupt als 'komplex', also unökonomisch/wenig ökonomisch, gewertet werden sollen. Hier gibt es recht unterschiedliche Positionen.

3.2. Quantitative vs. qualitative Ökonomie

Wie eben gezeigt praktiziert Haiman einen relativ engen Komplexitäts- bzw. Ökonomiebegriff, indem er der syntagmatischen Ökonomie die Ikonizität als eine konträre und damit unökonomische Erscheinung gegenüberstellt. Bei einer solchen Betrachtungsweise bedeutet zunehmende Ikonizität auch immer zunehmende Komplexität. Doch das ist keine notwendige Konsequenz. So wird etwa in der Geschichte des SCHWEDISCHEN die fusionierende Substantivflexion in eine (weitgehend) agglutinierende Flexion umgewandelt, vgl. dazu z. B. die Veränderung der Flexion des Wortes *hund* 'Hund': N.Sg. *hund*, G.Sg. *hund-s*; N.Pl. *hund-ar*, G.Pl. *hund-a* > N.Sg. *hund*, G.Sg. *hund-s*; N.Pl. *hund-ar*, G.Pl. *hund-**ar**-s*. Im G.Pl. wird also die Form mit dem einheitlichen Kasus-Numerus-Marker *-a* durch eine Form mit dem Numerusmarker *-ar* und dem Kasusmarker *-s* ersetzt. Die neue Flexionsform ist ikonischer (transparenter) als die alte, denn den beiden Kategorien Plural und Genitiv ist nach dem Wandel jeweils ein eigenes Morphem zugeordnet. Die Form ist zugleich auch quantitativ komplexer als die alte, da ein Flexionsmorphem durch zwei ersetzt wurde.

Für Haiman sind Fälle solcherart typische Belege für die „inverse correlation" von syntagmatischer Ökonomie und Ikonizität: Durch die Zunahme von Ikonizität wird notwendigerweise die syntagmatische Ökonomie einer Form reduziert. Doch bei genauerer Betrachtung zeigt sich, daß dabei zwar die quantitative, nicht aber die qualitative Ökonomie reduziert wird. Beim Übergang des G.Pl. *hund-a* > *hund-ar-s* wird vielmehr quantitative Ökonomie der Kürze durch qualitative Ökonomie der Zuordnung ersetzt. Die Eins-zu-eins-Zuordnung von Kategorien und Morphemen ist durchaus ein ökonomisches Verfahren, was auch ihrer Bewertung durch Martinet, Werner, Ronneberger-Sibold u. a. entspricht, die der Ikonizität/Transparenz eine wichtige Rolle im Rahmen der Ökonomie des Systems zuweisen (am ausführlichsten dazu Ronneberger-Sibold 1980: 152f.; 172; 177ff.). Die von Haiman konstatierten Zusammenhänge belegen damit nicht, daß Ikonizität/Transparenz eine 'anti-ökonomische' Erscheinung ist; sie sprechen vielmehr dafür, daß man klar zwischen QUANTITATIVER und QUALITATIVER ÖKONOMIE differenzieren muß, die sich (ähnlich wie paradigmatische und syntagmatische Ökonomie) widersprüchlich zueinander verhalten können.

3.3. Ökonomie in verschiedenen Bereichen der Grammatik

Schließlich ist zu berücksichtigen, daß die Sprachökonomie in den unterschiedlichen Komponenten der Grammatik auftritt. Das ist nicht zuletzt deshalb von Bedeutung, weil sie sich im allgemeinen in den einzelnen grammatischen Bereichen in jeweils spezifischer Weise auswirkt. Entsprechend soll also zwischen ÖKONOMIE IN DER PHONOLOGIE, IN DER MORPHOLOGIE, IN DER SYNTAX UND IM LEXIKON unterschieden werden.

Damit sind zwar nicht alle, aber doch die wohl wichtigsten Gesichtspunkte genannt, unter denen Ökonomiephänomene klassifiziert werden können. Im folgenden soll auf der Grundlage der drei vorgenommenen Distinktionen eine klassifizierende Einordnung der hauptsächlichsten Erscheinungsformen der Sprachökonomie versucht werden.

4. Paradigmatische Ökonomie: Ökonomie der Inventare

Die natürlichen Sprachen verfügen auf all ihren Strukturebenen über Inventare von Einheiten und/oder Kategorien. Solche Inventare sind das Phonemsystem, das Morphem- und das Lexeminventar und das System der morphosyntaktischen Kategorien. Die Inventare sind bekanntlich nicht arbiträr, sondern unterliegen bestimmten Einschränkungen. Diese Einschränkungen sind zum einen durch strikt universelle Vorgaben (wie etwa die Artikulationsmöglichkeiten des Menschen) bedingt, zum andern sind sie aber auch durch das (unbewußte) Streben der Sprecher und damit der Sprachen nach ökonomischen Inventaren motiviert. Die Ökonomie der Inventare wird im allgemeinen als rein quantitative Ökonomie gesehen, aber auch sie hat eine qualitative Seite.

4.1. Quantitativer Aspekt: Begrenzte, relativ eingeschränkte Inventare

Sämtliche Inventare der natürlichen Sprachen sind dadurch charakterisiert, daß sie jeweils nur relativ wenige Elemente umfassen, „a small number of category labels" (Haiman 1985: 16).

Obwohl die Menschen faktisch Hunderte unterschiedlicher Lautsegmente produzieren können, nutzen die natürlichen Sprachen jeweils nur eine relativ kleine Anzahl von distinktiven Lautkategorien, d. h. von Phonemen. Die meisten Sprachen, ca. 70% von ihnen, weisen zwischen 20 und 37 Phonemen auf, so auch das DEUTSCHE mit 34 Phonemen (15 Vokale, 19 Konsonanten). Die Extremfälle bilden u. W. einerseits die Papua-Sprache ROTOKAS, die mit nur 11 Phonemen (5

Vokalen, 6 Konsonanten) auskommt, und andrerseits das !Xũ, eine Khoisan-Sprache, die über 117 Phoneme (24 Vokale, 95 Konsonanten) verfügt. Die Vokalsysteme variieren zwischen drei Vokalen im ADYGHEISCHEN, im ALEUTISCHEN und im marokkanischen ARABISCH und 24 Vokalen (einschließlich der Längen- und Nasalitäts-Distinktionen) im !Xũ.

Die Ausstattung der Konsonantensysteme liegt zwischen sechs Konsonanten im ROTOKAS und dem 'exotischen' Fall von 95 Konsonanten im !Xũ (nach Lass 1984: 134 ff.; Maddieson 1984: 107 ff. und Ladefoged & Maddieson 1996). Die im Verhältnis zu den Artikulationsmöglichkeiten gesehen doch in jedem Fall wenigen Phoneme einer jeden Sprache reichen – partiell ergänzt durch suprasegmentale Mittel – aus, um die Identität und Distinktivität der bedeutungstragenden Einheiten, der Zeichen, in der Sprache zu gewährleisten. Im übrigen sind offenbar keine durch quantitative Ökonomie bedingten Veränderungstendenzen zu beobachten, sehr große Phoneminventare wie das des !Xũ zu reduzieren oder sehr kleine Inventare wie das des ROTOKAS zu erweitern (Maddieson a.a.O.). Für den Abbau und das Hinzukommen von Phonemen sind offenbar immer qualitative Verhältnisse verantwortlich (vgl. 4.2).

Wesentlich größer als die Zahl der Phoneme, aber doch ebenfalls stark begrenzt, ist auch die Anzahl der kleinsten Zeichen der natürlichen Sprache, der Morpheme. Man kann in den modernen Kultursprachen mit jeweils einigen tausend Morphemen rechnen; bei streng synchroner Betrachtung ergeben sich für das DEUTSCHE etwa 5.000 (nach Schnelle/Kranzhoff 1965: 76). Diese niedrige Anzahl ist besonders erstaunlich, wenn man sie mit der Zahl der Lexeme der Sprache vergleicht. Der neueste „Duden" (1996) enthält immerhin mehr als 115.000 Stichwörter, was damit etwa der Menge der Einwortlexeme des modernen DEUTSCHEN entspricht. Auf der Grundlage dieses eingeschränkten Morpheminventars können dann sämtliche kommunikativ relevanten Objekte, Prozesse, Tätigkeiten, Eigenschaften, Relationen usw. durch Lexeme benannt werden. Auch das sich damit ergebende Lexeminventar unterliegt Kriterien der 'Sparsamkeit': Es ist einfach unökonomisch, mehrere unterschiedliche Zeichen mit der gleichen kommunikativen Funktion zu verwenden, wohingegen es durchaus ökonomisch ist, mit einem relativ kleinen Satz von Zeichen möglichst viele unterschiedliche Bedeutungen wiederzugeben.

Hieraus erklärt sich die oft konstatierte Asymmetrie zwischen der häufigen Homonymie und der sehr raren Synonymie in den natürlichen Sprachen (Haiman 1985: 22). Wenn sich im Lexikon (aus welchen Gründen auch immer) doch echte Synonymie ergibt, wird in der Regel ein Glied des jeweiligen Paares abgebaut; vgl. den Abbau der alten Monatsnamen *Hornung* und *Heumonat* zugunsten von *Februar* und *Juni*.

Das Lexeminventar ist (wie gesagt) insgesamt gesehen zwar recht groß, aber natürlich immer endlich. Es ist ein extrem ökonomisches Verfahren, daß aus diesem endlichen Inventar eine unendliche Menge von Äußerungen gebildet werden kann.

Die einzelnen Sprachen machen bekanntlich in sehr unterschiedlicher Weise von morphosyntaktischen Kategorien Gebrauch, was beispielsweise die Kasussysteme gut belegen. Die Zahl der Kasuskategorien kann zwar von Sprache zu Sprache beträchtlich variieren, übersteigt aber kaum ein bestimmtes Maß: Man denke etwa an das UNGARISCHE mit über zwanzig Kasus als eine Sprache mit einem relativ umfangreichen Kasussystem. Auch hier liegt also wieder „a small number of category labels" vor. Dabei ist charakteristisch, daß im Prinzip alle 'syntaktischen' Kasus wie 'Akkusativ', 'Dativ' und 'Genitiv' Generalisierungen in dem Sinne darstellen, daß sie jeweils mehrere, oft sehr unterschiedliche Funktionen zusammenfassen, vgl. etwa den lateinischen Genitiv, der u. a. den *Genitivus subjectivus, objectivus, partitivus, possessivus, qualitatis* einschließt. Auf diese Weise kann das Kasuskategorieninventar entsprechend klein gehalten werden.

Ein instruktives Beispiel für die sparsame Nutzung von Kategorien bieten die Verfahren der Kategorisierung des Subjekts (S) im intransitiven Satz sowie des Agens (A) und des Patiens (P) im transitiven Satz durch die unterschiedlichen Sprachen (Comrie 1981: 117 ff.). Logisch gesehen gibt es fünf verschiedene Möglichkeiten der kategoriellen Gruppierung dieser drei Kasusrollen, nämlich:

(i)   S vs. A vs. P,
(ii) S/A vs. P,
(iii) S/P vs. A,
(iv) A/P vs. S und
(v)   S/A/P ohne Distinktion.

Wenn man berücksichtigt, daß Typ (v) zwar häufig auftritt, aber Kasusklassifizierungen, um die es hier geht, hier keine Rolle spielen (A und P werden im Satz dann meist durch andere Mittel differenziert), bleiben vier Möglichkeiten der kategoriellen Gruppierung, die auch alle belegt sind, aber mit sehr unterschiedlicher Häufigkeit vorkommen: Der dysfunktionale Typ (iv) mit fehlender Differenzierung von A und P im gleichen Satz tritt offenbar nur in bestimmten Nominalphrasen in einigen iranischen Sprachen auf, die sich gegenwärtig in einem Wandelprozeß befinden.

Doch auch die Typen (i) bis (iii), die diese Differenzierung vornehmen, sind nicht gleichmäßig verbreitet. Es gibt nämlich allem Anschein nach nur eine einzige Sprache, das südaustralische WANGGUMARA, die strikt nach Typ (i) S vs. A vs. P funktioniert, während es jeweils sehr viele Sprachen gibt, die den Typ (ii), das akkusativische Kasussystem mit S/A = Nominativ und P = Akkusativ, und den Typ (iii), das ergativische Kasussystem mit S/P = Absolutiv und A = Ergativ aufweisen.

Unter den Typen, die die Differenzierung von A und P im Satz garantieren, präferieren die Sprachen ganz eindeutig diejenigen, die in diesem Bereich mit zwei Kategorien auskommen. Hierzu paßt auch, daß nicht (mehr) funktionale Kategorien oft abgebaut werden, so u. a. der Instrumental im Althochdeutschen.

Auch die Anzahl der in einem Flexionssystem vorkommenden unterschiedlichen Paradigmen (und damit Flexionsklassen) einer Wortart unterliegt ganz offensichtlich starken Beschränkungen. So ergäbe sich z. B., wenn in der lateinischen Substantivdeklination jeder Kasus-Numerus-Marker mit jedem anderen innerhalb eines Paradigmas kombinierbar wäre, die enorme Anzahl von 27.648 unterschiedlichen Substantivparadigmen. Tatsächlich gibt es gemäß der traditionellen Einteilung aber bekanntlich nur fünf.

Ausgehend von entsprechenden Fakten aus vielen Sprachen hat Andrew Carstairs eine These der Paradigmen-Ökonomie formuliert. Sie basiert auf dem Begriff des „Makroparadigmas". Ein Makroparadigma umfaßt diejenigen Lexeme, die entweder strikt gleich flektieren, oder deren Flexionsunterschiede sich aus unabhängigen Eigenschaften ergeben (wie etwa im Fall der lateinischen *o*- Deklination, wo die Unterschiede zwischen *dominus* und *bellum* auf dem Genus beruhen). Das Paradigmen-Ökonomieprinzip besagt, daß die Anzahl der Makroparadigmen in einem Flexionssystem so groß ist wie die der miteinander konkurrierenden Marker in der Position des Paradigmas, in der die meisten unterschiedlichen Marker vorkommen. Beim deutschen Substantiv beispielsweise ist diese Position der N.Pl., wo vier (segmentale) Marker, nämlich -*e*/Ø (Verteilung phonologisch bedingt), -*er*, -*(e)n* und -*s*, konkurrieren. Entsprechend gibt es in der komplexen deutschen Substantivflexion nur vier Makroparadigmen mit ihren Varianten und nicht mehr (für Details vgl. Carstairs 1987: 42 ff.).

Es sei dahingestellt, ob sich diese (etwas minimalistische) Hypothese so halten läßt; auf alle Fälle ist aber die Anzahl der unterschiedlichen Paradigmen in allen Systemen verglichen mit den vorstellbaren Möglichkeiten sehr niedrig. Dazu tragen verschiedene Typen von Veränderungen wie u. a. die Herausbildung von einheitlich flektierenden 'Mischparadigmen' aus zwei Ausgangsparadigmen (vgl. die Vereinheitlichung der alten femininen *n*- und *ō*-Stämme zur gemischten Flexion des Typs Singular *Zunge* − Plural *Zungen* im 18. Jahrhundert) und der vollständige Übertritt der Wörter einer Flexionsklasse in eine andere bei (vgl. den Übertritt aller starken Verben zu den schwachen im AFRIKAANS).

Aus der quantitativen Ökonomie der Inventare resultieren grundlegende universelle Struktureigenschaften der natürlichen Sprache, die diese von allen anderen Zeichensystemen unterscheiden. Die kleinsten segmentalen Einheiten der Sprache, die Phoneme, können aufgrund ihrer kleinen Anzahl und ihrer geringen formalen Substanz nicht selbst als Zeichenform fungieren; sie müssen kombiniert werden, um Zeichenformen zu erhalten. Hieraus ergibt sich die phonologische Gliederung der sprachlichen Zeichen, d. h. die phonologische Struktur.

Im allgemeinen reicht das begrenzte Inventar der Minimalzeichen, also der Morpheme, nicht aus, um alle benennenswerten Objekte, Prozesse, Tätigkeiten usw. zu bezeichnen. Morpheme werden deshalb zu mehrmorphemigen Lexemen zusammengefaßt, die damit dann eine morphologische Struktur aufweisen. Da es auch nur ein begrenztes (wiewohl umfangreiches) Inventar an Lexemen, aber eine unendliche Menge sprachlich zu erfassender Situationen, Ereignisse usw. gibt, müssen Repräsentanten der Lexeme zu Sätzen verknüpft werden, damit die Sprache in der Kommunikation funktionieren kann; entsprechend hat die natürliche Sprache eine syntaktische Struktur. Die spezifische Ausprägung der natürlichen Sprache mit ihren unterschiedlichen Strukturebenen resultiert also faktisch daraus, daß die Sprache auf der Grundlage von eingeschränkten Inventaren beliebig viele Sätze bildet, daß sie „von endlichen Mitteln einen unendlichen Gebrauch machen" muß (Humboldt 1836: CXXII).

4.2. Qualitativer Aspekt: Einfachheit der Elemente und Systematik der Inventare

Die sprachlichen Inventare der unterschiedlichen Ebenen sind nicht nur in quantitativer, sondern auch in qualitativer Hinsicht ökonomisch aufgebaut. Von den Sprachen werden zum einen weniger komplexe gegenüber komplexeren Elementen in den Inventaren und zum anderen systematischere gegenüber weniger systematischen Inventaren bevorzugt.

In der Phonologie sind artikulatorisch einfache (und dabei auditiv möglichst gut unterscheidbare) Vokale und Konsonanten in den Sprachen der Welt wesentlich stärker verbreitet als artikulatorisch komplexere. So hat man bisher eben kein Vokalsystem ohne ein (kurzes oder langes, vorderes oder hinteres) /a/ gefunden, weil dieses der artikulatorisch einfachste, der prototypische Vokal ist. Ähnliches gilt für die beiden anderen 'Eckvokale' des Vokalraums /i/ und /u/; das vordere, nicht-runde /i/ fehlt fast nie im Phonemsystem, das hintere, runde /u/ recht selten (so in bestimmten Indianersprachen wie NAVAHO). Ihre jeweils komplexeren Gegenstücke, das vordere, runde /y/ und das hintere, nicht-runde /ɯ/, kommen dagegen weit seltener vor.

Sämtliche Sprachen weisen bekanntlich orale Vokale auf, aber nur ein Teil von ihnen nasale Vokale, die eine Artikulationsgeste mehr erfordern. Die artikulatorisch einfacheren stimmlosen Verschlußlaute treten häufiger auf als die stimmhaften; Sprachen wie ISLÄNDISCH und HAWAIIANISCH haben überhaupt nur stimmlose Verschlußlaute, viele andere haben mehr stimmlose als stimmhafte. Obstruenten mit einer zusätzlichen sekundären Artikulation wie labialisierte und palatalisierte Verschlußlaute sind viel weniger verbreitet als solche ohne diese usw. usf.

Wie nicht anders zu erwarten, spiegelt sich die Bevorzugung von weniger komplexen Vokalen und Konsonanten gegenüber komplexeren auch im Sprachwandel. So kommen z. B. häufig kontextfreie Entrundungen der vorderen runden Vokale /y/ und /œ/ zu /i/ und /e/ vor, so in der Geschichte des ENGLISCHEN und des JIDDISCHEN, vgl. aengl. *brycge* 'Brücke' > nengl. *bridge*, nicht aber kontextfreie Rundungen von /i/ und /e/ zu /y/ und /œ/. Ebenso werden durch Sprachwandel oft stimmhafte Verschlußlaute kontextfrei zu stimmlosen wie auf dem Weg vom ALT- zum NEUISLÄNDISCHEN, vgl. *gabba* 'verulken' /gab:a/ > /ġaḅ:a/, *blanda* 'mischen' /blanda/ > /bl̥anda/ usw., aber nicht umgekehrt.

Der systematische Aufbau von phonologischen Inventaren zeigt sich besonders deutlich in den Vokalsystemen der unterschiedlichen Sprachen. So überwiegen ganz offensichtlich solche Systeme, in denen die einzelnen Reihen der nicht-niedrigen Vokale, manchmal auch sämtliche Vokale, jeweils durch die gleiche Anzahl in der Höhe paralleler Vokale, vertreten sind, die also die phonologischen Oppositionen ökonomisch nutzen; vgl. z. B. ALEUTISCH mit dem vorderen Vokal /i/, dem hinteren Vokal /u/ und dem niedrigen Vokal /a/, CAYAPA mit den vorderen Vokalen /i ɛ/ und den hinteren Vokalen /u ɔ/, ITALIENISCH mit der vorderen Reihe /i e ɛ/, der hinteren Reihe /u o ɔ/ und dem niedrigen Vokal /a/ und die oralen Vokale des FRANZÖSISCHEN mit der vorderen, nicht-runden Reihe /i e ɛ/, der vorderen, runden Reihe /y ø œ/ und der hinteren (runden) Reihe /u o ɔ/ und den beiden niedrigen Vokalen /a ɑ/.

In vielen Inventaren gibt es weiterhin einen strikten Parallelismus zwischen kurzen und langen Vokalen wie beispielsweise im HAWAIIANISCHEN, vgl. /i ɛ − u ɔ − a/ und /i: ɛ: − u: ɔ: − a:/ und in der norddeutsch geprägten deutschen Standardsprache mit /i e − y ø − u o − a/ und /i: e: − y: ø: − u: o: − a:/ (ohne /ɛ:/) usw.

Nicht zufälligerweise kommen weniger symmetrisch strukturierte und damit weniger ökonomische Vokalinventare wesentlich seltener vor. Einen raren Extremfall stellt der Vokalismus des CHACOBO, einer südamerikanischen Sprache, mit den Vokalen /i − ɨ − ɔ − a/ dar (Lass 1984: 139 ff.). Im Vergleich dieses Viervokalsystems mit dem des CAYAPA (Ecuador) zeigt sich, wie stark sich Segmentinventare hinsichtlich ihrer Systematik unterscheiden können: Das Vokalsystem des CAYAPA wird durch die beiden proportionalen und privativen Oppositionen 'vorn vs. hinten' (/i ɛ/ vs. /u ɑ/) und 'hoch vs. niedrig' (/i u/ vs. /ɛ ɑ/) strukturiert. Dagegen ist das System des CHACOBO durch die beiden isolierten und graduellen Oppositionen 'hoch vs.

mittel vs. niedrig' (/ɨ vs. ɔ vs. ɑ/) und 'vorn vs. zentral vs. hinten' (/i vs. ɨ ɑ vs. ɔ/) gegliedert.

Führt man diese Verhältnisse auf binäre phonologische Merkmale zurück, so ergibt sich, daß das CAYAPA von zwei Merkmalen (etwa [hinten] und [niedrig]), das CHACOBO hingegen von vier Merkmalen (etwa [vorn], [hinten] und [hoch], [niedrig]) distinktiven Gebrauch macht. Die qualitative Ökonomie von Segmentsystemen hat damit auf der Merkmalsebene ein quantitatives Korrelat.

Ein Wandel, der zu einem systematischeren Inventar führt, ist der Abbau des Phonems /ɛ:/ wie in *Bär* in der erwähnten Variante des DEUTSCHEN, wodurch ein symmetrisches System mit sieben (qualitativ verschiedenen) Vokalen entsteht, die jeweils sowohl kurz als auch lang vorkommen. Im melanesischen LIFOU, das über das Verschlußsystem /p t k — d g/ verfügte, wurde ein in Entlehnungen aus dem ENGLISCHEN und FRANZÖSISCHEN vorkommendes /b/ als solches akzeptiert, woraus sich das systematische Inventar /p t k — b d g/ ergab, wohingegen andere, nicht in das System passende Segmente durch bereits vorhandene ersetzt werden (Martinet 1981: 93 f.).

Auch im Lexikon ist die Tendenz zu möglichst wenig komplexen Einheiten zu beobachten. Nicht den einzigen, aber einen sehr wesentlichen Aspekt bildet dabei das Verhältnis der unterschiedlichen Eigenschaften der Lexeme, d. h. ihrer semantischen, phonologischen, syntaktischen und morphologischen Eigenschaften, zueinander (zu einem weiteren Aspekt vgl. unten § 5.1).

Die Eigenschaften der verschiedenen Ebenen können prinzipiell unabhängig voneinander sein, sie können aber auch implikativ voneinander ableitbar sein. Ableitbare Eigenschaften müssen nicht explizit im Lexikon spezifiziert sein. Daher sind Lexeme mit partiell ableitbaren Eigenschaften für die Sprecher (unter sonst gleichen Bedingungen) ökonomischer als solche ohne ableitbare Eigenschaften. Entsprechend sind die Lexikoneinheiten in allen Sprachen hinsichtlich ihrer Eigenschaften in starkem Maße implikativ strukturiert. So ist typisch, daß bestimmte semantische Eigenschaften bestimmte syntaktische Eigenschaften der Lexeme implizieren. Beispielsweise sind in Sprachen mit einem maskulinen und einem femininen Genus in der Regel Bezeichnungen für männliche höhere Lebewesen Maskulina und solche für höhere weibliche Lebewesen Feminina. Das wird durch bestimmte Sprachveränderungen,

auch im DEUTSCHEN, bestätigt. Man vgl. die mit dem Morphem *-el* gebildeten Diminutiva zu Vornamen, die vom Neutrum zum Femininum bzw. zum Maskulinum übergegangen sind: älter *das Gretel, das Hänsel* > *die Gretel, der Hänsel*.

Solche Implikationen können auch wesentlich spezifischer sein. So gilt im DEUTSCHEN u. a., daß hochprozentige alkoholische Getränke immer Maskulina sind; vgl. *der Schnaps, der Korn, der Kirsch* usw. Dieser Implikation schließen sich auch entlehnte Wörter wie *Whisky* und *Rum* aus dem ENGLISCHEN sowie *Wodka* aus dem Russischen an, das dort feminin ist.

Die syntaktische Transitivität/Intransitivität von Verben ergibt sich weitgehend aus der Verbsemantik usw. Auch phonologische Eigenschaften können syntaktische implizieren, z. B. sind im Lateinischen Substantive, die auf *-um* enden, generell Neutra.

Morphologische Eigenschaften der Lexeme, d. h. ihre Zugehörigkeit zu Flexions- und Derivationsklassen, sind häufig durch deren semantische, phonologische und/oder syntaktische Eigenschaften bestimmt. In allen Sprachen mit Flexionsklassen basiert die Klassenzugehörigkeit der einzelnen Lexeme zumindest partiell auf solchen Eigenschaften: Im SWAHILI gehören die Bezeichnungen von Werkzeugen und Instrumenten, also Lexeme mit einer bestimmten semantischen Eigenschaft, in die 3. Substantivklasse, deren Singular mit dem Präfix *ki-* und deren Plural mit dem Präfix *vi-* gebildet wird, vgl. *kisu* 'Messer' — Plural *visu*. Im Lateinischen flektieren die Substantive mit der phonologischen Eigenschaft 'Endung auf *-a*' nach der 1. Deklination, vgl. *femina* 'Frau' — G.Sg. *feminae*. Im ENGLISCHEN bilden die Lexeme der syntaktischen Klasse der Modalverben eine spezielle Flexionsklasse, die u. a. durch das Nicht-Auftreten des Flexivs *-s* in der 3.Ps.Sg. Präs.Ind. gekennzeichnet ist, vgl. *he can* (vs. *he goes*).

Die deutsche Substantivflexion ist ein instruktives Beispiel dafür, daß die Zugehörigkeit zur Flexionsklasse auch durch Kombinationen von unterschiedlichen Eigenschaften determiniert sein kann. Man vgl. die Lexeme mit den Eigenschaften 'maskulin', 'unbelebt' und 'Endung auf Konsonant', die einen speziellen Typ der 'gemischten' Flexion bilden: *Staat* — G.Sg. *des Staates*, D./A.Sg. *dem/den Staat*, Plural *die Staaten* (Wurzel, in Vorb.).

Daß solche Relationen zwischen den unterschiedlichen Eigenschaften von Lexemen existieren, zeigt sich auch in der Sprachveränderung: Das englische Verb *need* ist ursprünglich ausschließlich ein Vollverb mit der Bedeutung 'benötigen' und flektiert entsprechend, vgl. *he needs*. In bestimmten Kontexten entwickelt es später die modale Bedeutung 'brauchen, müssen' und fungiert auch syntaktisch als Modalverb (*I need not come*). Da die syntaktische Eigenschaft 'Modalverb' die morphologischen Eigenschaften determiniert, tritt das modale *need* entsprechend in die Flexionsklasse der Modalverben über und bildet die 3.Ps.Sg.Präs.Ind. ohne das Flexiv *-s*, vgl. *he need not come*. Eine spezielle Angabe der Flexion des modalen *need* im Lexikon wird dadurch eingespart.

Wie 'sparsam' die Sprecher ihre Lexikon-Repräsentationen gestalten, zeigt sich in Fällen, wo sich aufgrund der unabhängig gegebenen Eigenschaften eines Lexems die Flexionsklassen-Zugehörigkeit nicht strikt implizierbar ist, sondern im Prinzip verschiedene Klassen möglich sind. In solchen Fällen bewerten die Sprecher im allgemeinen eine der konkurrierenden Klassen als normaler und präferieren sie, nämlich diejenige, die die meisten Lexeme mit den entsprechenden Eigenschaften enthält. Sie etablieren damit eine tendentielle Implikation zwischen den gegebenen Eigenschaften und der Klassenzugehörigkeit (vgl. Wurzel 1984: 116ff.). Bei den deutschen Verben ist das beispielsweise die schwache Klasse. Hier ist die Klassenzugehörigkeit nicht strikt, aber doch tendentiell impliziert. Das zeigt sich deutlich im Sprachwandel. So treten im modernen DEUTSCHEN starke Verben zur schwachen Klasse über, aber nicht umgekehrt, vgl. *gären – gor > gären – gärte* und *saugen – sog > saugen – saugte*, und entlehnte Verben wie *filmen, streiken* und *joggen* flektieren grundsätzlich schwach.

Solche Verhältnisse lassen sich am angemessensten dahingehend interpretieren, daß immer nur die nicht-präferierte Klassenzugehörigkeit von Lexemen speziell erworben und im Lexikon durch ein spezielles Klassenmerkmal fixiert wird. Geschieht das nicht, ergibt sich 'automatisch' die präferierte Klassenzugehörigkeit. Im DEUTSCHEN hat ein Verb im Lexikon ein Flexionsklassen-Merkmal, wenn es wie *geben* stark flektiert, nicht aber wenn es wie *leben* 'ganz normal' schwach flektiert. Der Übertritt von der starken zur schwachen Konjugation wie bei *gären* und *saugen* bedeutet den Abbau des speziellen Klassenmerkmals; die Lexikon-Repräsentation des betreffenden Lexems wird vereinfacht, wird ökonomischer.

In Sprachen mit unterschiedlichen Flexionsklassen sind auch die Flexionsparadigmen und mit ihnen die gesamten Flexionssysteme, zumindest in sehr starkem Maße, implikativ aufgebaut: Wenn innerhalb eines Paradigmas in einer gegebenen Position eine bestimmte Form erscheint, dann impliziert diese das Auftreten einer bestimmten anderen Form in einer anderen Position (bzw. anderen Positionen). Beim deutschen Substantiv genügt partiell schon die Form des N.Sg. mit ihren nicht-morphologischen Eigenschaften, um daraus alle übrigen Formen des Paradigmas abzuleiten. So erhält ein auf *-e* endendes Femininum generell im G./D./A.Sg. keinen Marker und im gesamten Plural den Marker *-n*, vgl. *die Katze, der/der/die Katze, die/der/den/die Katzen*. Der typische Fall ist jedoch, daß weiterhin die Form des N.Pl. bekannt sein muß, damit man für jedes (reguläre) deutsche Substantiv stufenweise sämtliche Flexionsformen ableiten kann. Vgl. z. B. das Paradigma *Wolf*:

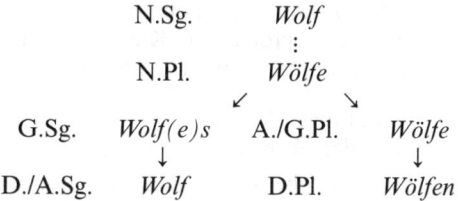

Abb. 31.1: Die implikative Struktur der Substantiv-Paradigmen des DEUTSCHEN

Einsilbige Maskulina auf Konsonant können unterschiedliche Plurale haben (vgl. *Hund – Hunde, Mann – Männer, Park – Parks, Mensch – Menschen*), weshalb hier die Pluralform *Wölfe* angegeben werden muß, doch von dieser führen dann (gegeben die lexikalischen Eigenschaften) eindeutige Wege zu allen übrigen Singular- und Pluralformen.

Um also die Flexion eines deutschen Substantivs zu beherrschen, braucht der Sprecher entweder nur die lexikalische Grundform (den N.Sg.) mit ihren syntaktischen, semantischen und phonologischen Eigenschaften, oder die Grundform und eine weitere Form zu kennen. Hier zeigt sich eine stark kostensparende Strukturierung der Substantivparadigmen innerhalb des Flexionssystems. Einzelne Ausnahmen, die sich diesem Aufbau entziehen, werden in der Regel durch Wandel angeglichen. Man vgl. das Neutrum *Herz* mit seiner traditionellen Flexion N./A.Sg. *Herz*, G.Sg. *Herzens*, D.Sg. *Herzen*; Pl. *Herzen*. Aufgrund seiner Eigenschaften und seiner Pluralform sollte es im Singular jedoch wie *Ohr* flektieren, also mit dem G.Sg. *Herzes* und dem D.Sg. *Herz*. Genau diese Formen setzen sich heute in immer stärkerem Maße durch.

Diese implikative Struktur der deutschen Substantive ist beileibe kein Einzelfall, auch die Flexionsparadigmen anderer Sprachen sind ähnlich ökonomisch aufgebaut (Wurzel, in Vorb.).

5. Syntagmatische Ökonomie: Ökonomie der Formen

Die Ökonomie der Formen favorisiert kurze (quantitativ wenig komplexe) und einfache (qualitativ wenig komplexe) sprachliche Formen im syntagmatischen Zusammenhang. Syntagmatische sprachliche Formen haben eine phonologische, eine morphologische und eine syntaktische Struktur, deren Aufbauprinzipien sich bekanntlich stark unterscheiden. Deshalb muß auch komponentenbezogen spezifiziert werden, was Kürze und Einfachheit von Formen jeweils bedeutet.

5.1. Quantitativer Aspekt: Kürze der Formen

Daß zwischen phonologischer, morphologischer und syntaktischer Kürze sprachlicher Formen zu unterscheiden ist, zeigen die folgenden einfachen Beispiele: Das Substantiv *Abenteuer* mit vier Silben ist phonologisch gesehen zweifelsohne ein quantitativ recht aufwendiges Wort, morphologisch gesehen bildet es aber das quantitative Minimum eines Wortes, denn es besteht aus einem einzigen Morphem. Dagegen ist die Form *liebt* nur einsilbig, enthält aber zwei Morpheme. Die Form *er liebt sie* bildet syntaktisch die Abfolge der Konstituenten NP, V und NP und damit einen vollständigen Satz, phonologisch hat sie aber nur drei Silben, morphologisch nur vier Morpheme. Dagegen ist die Form *Fußballweltmeisterschaftsvorrundenspiel* wohl phonologisch und morphologisch quantitativ sehr aufwendig (zehn Silben, zehn Morpheme), syntaktisch bildet sie als ein Substantiv lediglich eine einzige minimale Konstituente.

Die phonologische Länge von Wörtern bemißt sich in der Anzahl der Silben bzw. der Anzahl und Quantität (lang, kurz, reduziert) der Segmente, die die formale Substanz einer sprachlichen Form ausmachen. Es ist leicht zu sehen, daß die Sprachen insgesamt gesehen phonologisch kürzere, d. h. artikulatorisch weniger aufwendige Wörter gegenüber längeren Wörtern präferieren, wobei es zwischen den Sprachen typologisch bedingte Unterschiede der Wortlänge gibt.

Das DEUTSCHE gehört ähnlich wie das ENGLISCHE zu den Sprachen, in denen nach der Type-Frequenz relativ kurze Wörter dominieren. Zwar kommen gerade hier vielsilbige Komposita wie *Fußballweltmeisterschaftsvorrundenspiel* und Mehrfach-Derivationen wie *Unmißverständlichkeit* vor, doch die typische Wortlänge beträgt zwei bis drei Silben. Das ergibt sich daraus, daß (von wenigen Ausnahmen wie *Holunder* und *Abenteuer* abgesehen) die deutschen Basismorpheme nur ein- oder zweisilbig sind, vgl. *Hund, Katz-e, Gabel, Iltis; schön, offen; leb-en, arbeit-en*. Auch die Grundformen der meisten Lexeme haben damit nur ein oder zwei Silben.

Bei flektierenden Lexemen kann meist nur eine weitere Silbe dazukommen, vgl. *Hunde, Gabeln, Iltisse, schöner, offnere, lebt, arbeitet*, in bestimmten Fällen auch zwei, vgl. *schönere* und *arbeiteten*. Das Streben der Sprecher nach kürzeren Wörtern kommt deutlich beim phonologischen Wandel zum Ausdruck, wo Reduktionen (die typischerweise, jedoch nicht immer, zu kürzeren Wörtern führen) gegenüber Verstärkungen der formalen Substanz eindeutig überwiegen. So haben in allen modernen indoeuropäischen Sprachen die Wörter in der Regel eine geringere formale Substanz als ihre Pendants im (rekonstruierten) Indoeuropäischen. Besonders deutlich wird das im Germanischen mit seinem Anfangsakzent; vgl. das Beispiel S. 395.

In Sprachen wie dem DEUTSCHEN oder dem ENGLISCHEN gibt es nicht nur weit mehr kürzere Wörter als längere, die kürzeren kommen zugleich auch in Texten häufiger vor als die längeren; d. h. sie haben eine höhere Token-Frequenz (Einsilbler machen im DEUTSCHEN nahezu 50% der in Texten auftretenden Wörter aus). Dieser Zusammenhang zwischen Wortlänge und Token-Frequenz ist nicht sprachspezifisch, sondern gilt für alle Sprachen, unabhängig von ihrer spezifischen Struktur. So sind zwar z. B. im TÜRKISCHEN fünf-, sechs- und partiell sogar siebensilbige Verbformen wie *dolurmayabilirdim* 'ich hätte es unterbleiben lassen können, (das/etwas) auszufüllen' ganz regulär bildbar und haben

Indoeuropäisch	Germanisch I	Germanisch II	Althochdeutsch	Mittelhoch-deutsch	Neuhoch-deutsch
*sāgi̯eti	*sōkijit	*sōkīt (got. sōkeit)	suochit	suochet	sucht
4 Silben	3 Silben	2 Silben, Langvokal in der 2. Silbe	2 Silben, Kurzvokal in der 2. Silbe	2 Silben, reduzierter Vokal [schwa] in der 2. Silbe	1 Silbe

Abb. 31.2: Reduktion von Wortsubstanz in der Sprachgeschichte

somit eine relativ hohe Type-Frequenz, aber solche Formen sind in den Texten sehr rar.

Wichtig ist, daß eine sehr hohe Token-Frequenz von Wörtern tendenziell auf ihre formale Substanz zurück wirkt. Zum einen sind hoch token-frequente Wörter oft speziellen phonologischen Reduktionsprozessen unterworfen; vgl. z. B. die Vokalkürzung in mhd. *hāst, hāt* > nhd. *hast, hat*, die sonst nicht eintritt: mhd. *stēst, stēt* − nhd. *stehst, steht*. Zum anderen werden ganz bewußt Kurzwörter unterschiedlicher Typen gebildet: *Kornbranntwein* > *Korn*, *Diskothek* > *Disko*, *Omnibus* > *Bus*, *Kriminalpolizei* > *Kripo*, *Flugzeugabwehrkanone* > *Flak*, *Untergrundbahn* > *U-Bahn* [u:ba:n] und *Lastkraftwagen* > *LKW* [εlka:ve:].

Die sich im Sprachwandel durchsetzende Präferenz der Sprecher für phonologisch kurze Wörter im syntagmatischen Zusammenhang wirkt auf das Lexikon zurück (vgl. oben § 4.2): Lexeme mit quantitativ komplexer formaler Struktur werden verkürzt, wie es beispielsweise die Entwicklung vom Althochdeutschen zum Neuhochdeutschen zeigt, vgl. *ampulla* > *Ampel*, *ampahti* > *Amt*, *ernust* > *Ernst*, *gileisi* > *Gleis*, *markat* > *Markt* und *wintbrawe* > *Wimper*, und die neuen Kurzwörter können die älteren Langformen völlig, d. h. lexikalisch, ersetzen wie in den Fällen *Kinematograph* > *Kino* und *stereophon(isch)* > *stereo*. Hier bedeutet also die syntagmatische Ökonomie zugleich auch paradigmatische Ökonomie.

Die morphologische Länge eines Wortes ergibt sich aus der Anzahl seiner Morpheme. Da das Wort das kleinste selbständige Zeichen darstellt, sind aus weniger Morphemen bestehende Wörter (unter sonst gleichen Bedingungen) leichter zu bilden und vor allem leichter zu perzipieren als aus mehr Morphemen bestehende Wörter. Es ist also ökonomisch, die zu vermittelnde Information in einer Weise zu verteilen, daß vielmorphemige Wörter vermieden werden.

Die Anzahl der in den einzelnen Sprachen pro Wort zugelassenen Derivations- und Flexionsmorpheme ist unterschiedlich. So enthält z. B. die morphologisch längste Verbform im DEUTSCHEN nicht mehr als vier Derivations- und Flexionsmorpheme, vgl. (*sie*) *ver-an-stalt-et-en*, im TÜRKISCHEN im Extremfall immerhin sechs, vgl. nochmals *dol-dur-ma-yabil-ir-di-m* (sich- füllen + KAUS + NEG + IMPOSS + AOR + PRÄT + 1.PS/SG). Sie ist aber nie beliebig groß, sondern bleibt immer relativ eng eingegrenzt. Daß sich die Komposita in bestimmten Sprachen wie DEUTSCH oder CHINESISCH grundsätzlich anders verhalten − z. B. ist im DEUTSCHEN jedes Kompositum prinzipiell erweiterbar, vgl. *Fuß-ball-welt-meister-schaft-s-qualifikation-s-spiel-teil-nehm-er* usw. − ergibt sich daraus, daß die Komposita im Übergangsbereich von Morphologie und Syntax angesiedelt sind und somit auch bestimmte Eigenschaften syntaktischer Konstruktionen haben: Sie enthalten mehr als einen Stamm und sie werden häufig ad hoc vom Sprecher gebildet und dann wieder vergessen, ganz wie syntaktische Phrasen (Bauer 1988: 102 ff.). Komposita sind demgemäß keine typischen Wörter. Entsprechend gibt es, so wie es keinen längsten Satz gibt, auch kein längstes Kompositum. Einen in dieser Hinsicht den Komposita vergleichbaren Status haben die 'Satzwörter' der inkorporierenden Sprachen (→ Art. 53).

Die einzelnen Sprachen nutzen unterschiedliche Techniken, um die Wörter morphologisch kurz zu halten, also um Morpheme einzusparen. Das wichtigste ist die Fusion, die den gesamten fusionierenden (flektierenden) Sprachtyp charakterisiert und die am stärksten ausgeprägt in den älteren indoeuropäischen Sprachen auftritt. Während in agglutinierenden Sprachen wie dem TÜRKI-

SCHEN (im Prinzip) jede Kategorie durch ein eigenes Morphem ausgedrückt wird, vgl. nochmals das obige Beispiel, symbolisiert z. B. das Morphem -ī in einer lateinischen Verbform wie amā-v-ī 'ich habe geliebt' die Kategorien 1.Person, Singular, Indikativ, Aktiv und neben dem Marker -v- auch noch einmal das Perfekt (vgl. Präs. am-ō, Prät. am-ā-ba-m usw.).

Eine weitere, vor allem von agglutinierenden Sprachen praktizierte Möglichkeit besteht darin, redundante Kategoriensymbolisierungen zu vermeiden, so beispielsweise im UNGARISCHEN Pluralmorpheme bei mit einem Zahlwort verbundenen Substantiven wie in öt hajó 'fünf Schiffe' (vgl. oben § 2) oder Plural- und Kasusmorpheme bei attributiven Adjektiven wie in nagy hajó-k-nak 'den großen Schiffen'.

Schließlich werden häufig die jeweils semantisch unmarkierten Kategorien innerhalb von Kategoriengefügen (anders als die markierten) nicht explizit ausgedrückt. So erscheint z. B. in vielen Sprachen in der Verbflexion zwar ein Präterital-Morphem, aber kein Präsens-Morphem, vgl. etwa dtsch. (du) lieb-st — (du) lieb-t-est, lat. amā-s — amā-bā-s und finn. (sinä) rakasta-t — (sinä) rakasta-i-t.

Tilgungen von Morphemen können in Komposita dann vorkommen, wenn sie nicht zu Verständnisproblemen führen vgl. dtsch. Apfel[baum]plantage, Fern[melde]amt und Laub[holz]säge. Fusionen von Morphemen im Sprachwandel resultieren hingegen normalerweise aus dem Streben der Sprecher nach artikulatorisch wenig aufwendigen Wörtern. Sie sind also phonologisch bedingt, werden aber im allgemeinen von der Morphologie akzeptiert (d. h. nicht rückgängig gemacht); man vgl. dazu die Fusion des Stammbildungselements und des Flexivs in der 1.Ps.Sg. Präs.Ind.Akt der lateinischen ā-Konjugation am-ā-ō > am-ō neben am-ā-s, am-ā-mus usw.

Die syntaktische Länge bezieht sich auf die Anzahl der Wörter pro Phrase bis hin zum Satz. Kürzere Phrasen sind bekanntlich einfacher bildbar und perzipierbar als längere Phrasen. Daher ist es entscheidend, daß es syntaktische Verfahren gibt, die eine ökonomische Gestaltung der Phrasen gestatten, ohne daß Information verlorengeht. Eines dieser Verfahren ist das der Pronominalisierung/Pro-Adverbialisierung. Vorerwähnte Nominal- und Adverbialphrasen können ungeachtet ihrer Länge durch Einzelwörter ersetzt werden, so etwa jenes höhere Wesen, das wir verehren durch das Personalpronomen es und in diesem wunderbaren südlichen Land, das ihn immer wieder zum Verweilen einlud durch das Adverb dort.

Personalpronomen der 3.Person und Pro-Adverbien gibt es in allen Sprachen. Das gilt ebenfalls für das vielgestaltige Phänomen der Ellipse. Mittels der Koordinations-Ellipse können unterschiedliche Phrasen reduziert werden; vgl. alte [Frauen] und junge Frauen; alte Männer und [alte] Frauen; sie hat rote Schuhe gekauft und er [hat] braune [Schuhe] [gekauft]; er trinkt Bier und sie [trinkt] Wein. In Frage-Antwort-Konstellationen kann in der Antwort alles das eingespart werden, was in der Frage benannt ist: Wer hat den Wein ausgetrunken? — Kerstin [hat den Wein ausgetrunken].

Situative Ellipsen sind dadurch gekennzeichnet, daß alles weggelassen werden kann, was durch den Kontext bekannt ist: [gib mir] den Hammer (vgl. Schwabe 1994). Die erwähnten Typen von Ellipsen sind jeweils fakultativ. Es gibt jedoch auch grammatikalisierte Ellipsen, so die des (unbetonten) Personalpronomens beim Imperativ in vielen (aber nicht allen) Sprachen; vgl. schreib/schreibt den Brief.

5.2. Qualitativer Aspekt:
 Einfachheit der Formen

Auch die Ökonomie der syntagmatischen Formen hinsichtlich der qualitativen Einfachheit ist jeweils bezogen auf Phonologie, Morphologie und Syntax zu betrachten.

Qualitative Einfachheit der Formen in der Phonologie bedeutet die Vermeidung von Segmentkombinationen, die für den Sprecher artikulatorische Belastungen mit sich bringen. Beispielsweise dominieren in allen Sprachen, in denen Nasal-Verschlußlaut-Verbindungen überhaupt vorkommen, bei weitem die ohne Wechsel der Artikulationsstelle zu bildenden, homorganen Verbindungen der Typen /mp/, /nt/ und /ŋk/, so auch im DEUTSCHEN, vgl. Lump, bunt und Bank.

Nicht-homorgane Verbindungen kommen dagegen nur eingeschränkt oder gar nicht vor, im DEUTSCHEN innerhalb des Morphems regulär nur noch /mt/ wie in Samt und Zimt (< Sammet, Zimmet); /mk/ tritt nur im Einzelfall Imker auf. Mit zwischen den Konsonanten liegender Morphemgrenze gibt es neben /nt/ wie in sinnt und /mt/ wie in kommt zusätzlich auch /ŋt/ wie in singt. Die Kombinationen der Typen /np/, /ŋp/ und /nk/ sind ausgeschlossen (was natürlich nicht für die Fugen von Komposita wie Bahn-karte gilt).

Nicht-homorgane Nasal-Verschlußlaut-Verbindungen werden in der Regel durch Assimilation des Nasals an den Verschlußlaut beseitigt; vgl. einerseits Wörter mit verdunkelter Komposition wie mhd. *ane-boʒ* > *an-boʒ* > nhd. *Amboß* und mhd. *wint-brawe* > nhd. *Wimper* und andrerseits Fremdwörter wie *konkret* und *konkurrieren* mit /n/ > /ŋ/ vor /k/.

Insgesamt gesehen tragen die Sprachen der Ökonomie der qualitativen Einfachheit jedoch nur eingeschränkt Rechnung. So besteht die optimale phonologische Wortstruktur aus einer wechselnden Abfolge von Konsonanten und Vokalen mit folgenden Silbengrenzen /cv&cv& [...]/.

Wenn man nun berücksichtigt, daß jede Sprache ein hinreichend großes Inventar von formal distinktiven Zeichen benötigt, dann hätte eine strikte Realisierung des CV-Musters zur Folge, daß die Wörter relativ lang sein müßten, was der Ökonomie der Kürze der Formen (vgl. oben § 5.1) widerspricht. Eine in jeder Hinsicht maximal ökonomische einzelsprachliche Phonologie kann es deshalb nicht geben. Die einzelnen Sprachen verhalten sich hier unterschiedlich. Beispielsweise sind im Neuhochdeutschen (wie gezeigt) die Wörter durchschnittlich kürzer als im Althochdeutschen, zeigen aber zugleich wesentlich komplexere Konsonantenverbindungen in der Coda; vgl. nochmals *markat* /cvc&cvc/ > *Markt* /cvcccc/ und *ernust* /vc&cvcc/ > *Ernst* /vcccc/.

Ein aus mehreren Morphemen bestehendes Wort hat eine qualitativ einfache morphologische Struktur, wenn das Wort nach den Prinzipien der Transparenz und Ikonizität aufgebaut ist (vgl. oben § 3). Dabei können verschiedene Aspekte unterschieden werden. Morphosemantische Transparenz eines Wortes liegt dann vor, wenn seine Morpheme klar voneinander abgegrenzt sind und wenn sich seine Gesamtbedeutung kompositionell aus den Bedeutungen dieser Morpheme ergibt. Dem folgt der größere Teil der Wörter aller Sprachen; vgl. nochmals *Fuß-ball-welt-meister-schaft-s-vor-rund-e-n-spiel* und *dol-dur-ma-yabil-ir-di-m*. Doch es kommen auch Abweichungen davon vor, wie beispielsweise die stark umgangssprachlichen Varianten von Wörtern wie *geb-en* und *(den) Weg-e-n*, nämlich [geːm] und [veːŋ], zeigen. Hier erscheinen jeweils zwei bzw. gar drei Morpheme quasi ineinandergeschoben; Morphemgrenzen sind nicht auszumachen (sie liegen faktisch jeweils im Nasal).

Solche durch Assimilation entstandenen nicht-transparenten Flexionsformen werden im allgemeinen durch Wandel wieder transparent gemacht. Im MITTELHOCHDEUTSCHEN hatten sich bei bestimmten Verben, deren Stamm auf *-t* ausging, Präterital-Formen herausgebildet, in denen der Tempusmarker *-t* mit dem Stammauslaut verschmolzen war: *aht-en* — Präteritum *(er) ahte*, *trahten* — Präteritum *(er) trahte*. Diese Präterital-Formen wurden im Verlauf der Sprachgeschichte wieder durch transparente Formen ersetzt, vgl. nhd. *(er) acht-et-e*, *(er) tracht-et-e*.

Nicht (mehr) transparente Wortbildungen erhalten bisweilen durch Volksetymologie eine transparente Struktur; vgl. fnhd. *sint-flut* mit 'verdunkeltem' ersten Glied > *sünd-flut* und engl. *hamburger* > *ham-burger* mit Neubildungen wie *cheese-burger* und *fish-burger*. Von Funktions-Form-Ikonismus können wir dann sprechen, wenn jede grammatische und/oder Wortbildungskategorie im Wort durch ein eigenes Morphem symbolisiert ist, was der Strukturbildung der agglutinierenden Sprachen entspricht (im türkischen Beispiel (oben § 5.1) stehen alle Morpheme außer dem letzten jeweils für genau eine Kategorie).

Obwohl aus naheliegenden Gründen eine agglutinierende Struktur zu längeren Wörtern als die fusionierende führt, werden im Sprachwandel manchmal durchaus fusionierende in agglutinierende Formen verändert, wie das oben (in § 3) erwähnte schwedische Beispiel zeigt; vgl. nochmals N.Sg. *hund*, G.Sg. *hund-s*; N.Pl. *hund-ar*, G.Pl. *hund-a* usw. > N.Sg. *hund*, G.Sg. *hund-s*; N.Pl. *hund-a*, G.Pl. *hund-ar-s* usw. Hier setzt sich die Ökonomie des Ikonismus gegen die der morphologischen (und phonologischen) Kürze durch.

Serialisierungs-Ikonismus schließlich bedeutet, daß die Abfolge der Morpheme im Wort dessen kompositionelle semantische Struktur widerspiegelt. So stehen normalerweise Derivationsmorpheme näher beim Stamm als Flexionsmorpheme, gehen ihnen in Suffixsprachen also voraus; vgl. dtsch. *Brau-er-ei-en*, *Alt-er-tüm-er*, *Hinder-niss-e*. Nur sehr vereinzelt kommen Abweichungen davon vor wie *(die) Ei-er-chen* und *Kind-er-chen*. Dabei handelt es sich um echte Ausnahmen, der Bildungstyp ist unproduktiv; vgl. *(die) Häus-chen*, *Männ-chen* (*Häus-er-chen, *Männ-er-chen).

Auch syntaktische Konstruktionen, d. h. Phrasen und Sätze, können qualitativ einfacher oder komplexer sein. Im allgemeinen sind die einfacheren Konstruktionen in ihrer Verteilung auf die Sprachen der Welt und in den Sprachen der Welt weit häufiger. So kann z. B. die Basisreihenfolge von Subjekt und Objekt entweder so geregelt sein, daß das Subjekt dem Objekt vorangeht, also eine der Reihenfolgen SOV, SVO oder VSO auftritt, oder es kann das Objekt dem Subjekt vorangehen, also eine der Reihenfolgen VOS oder OSV (OVS gibt es u. W. nicht) auftreten.

Es zeigt sich, daß in mehr als 99% der Sprachen das Subjekt vor dem Objekt steht und nur ganz vereinzelt wie im MADEGASSISCHEN mit VOS und im HIXKARYANA mit OSV das Objekt vor dem Subjekt erscheint. Diese ungleiche Verteilung ist dadurch bedingt, daß das Agens in Agens-Aktion-Patiens-Konstellationen eine herausragende Rolle einnimmt und das semantische Agens und das syntaktische Subjekt typischerweise übereinstimmen (Comrie 1981: 19 f.). Wir haben es bei 'S vor O' also mit einer ikonischen Subjekt-Objekt-Serialisierung zu tun, die für die Sprecher und speziell die Hörer einfacher ist und deshalb präferiert wird.

6. Ökonomie, Markiertheit, Lokalität

Wenn in linguistischen Diskussionen auch die Konzepte der Sprachökonomie und der MARKIERTHEIT (→ Art. 32) bisweilen als nahezu unversöhnlich gegenübergestellt werden, so ist doch unschwer zu sehen, daß sie sich eng berühren. 'Ökonomie' charakterisiert das Bestreben der Sprecher, „mit einem Minimum an sprachlichem Aufwand ein Maximum an sprachlicher Effektivität zu erzielen" (Bußmann 1990: 711). Demgegenüber bezieht sich 'Markiertheit' direkt auf bestimmte Struktureigenschaften der natürlichen Sprache. Menschen verhalten sich mehr oder weniger ökonomisch, sprachliche Strukturen sind schwächer oder stärker markiert.

Doch auch die Markiertheit sprachlicher Strukturen kann nur ausgehend vom Menschen als Sprecher begründet werden: Sprachliche Strukturen sind umso stärker markiert, je mehr sie die menschliche Sprachkapazität belasten (Wurzel 1998). Die grammatische Seite des „Minimums an sprachlichem Aufwand" (die kommunikativ-pragmatische ist hier irrelevant) besteht in der Vermeidung von markierten/stärker markierten sprachlichen Einheiten. Hier stellt sich dann die Frage, ob Ökonomie und Markiertheit hinsichtlich des involvierten sprachlichen Faktenbereichs die gleiche Domäne haben. Ist also eine grammatische Erscheinung, gleich welcher Art, die für den Sprecher ökonomisch ist, zugleich auch immer als unmarkiert/wenig markiert zu charakterisieren?

Als faktische Evidenzen für die Belastung der menschlichen Sprachkapazität und damit für die Unterscheidung von (stärker) markierten und schwächer markierten/unmarkierten grammatischen Erscheinungen (mGE vs. uGE) werden ziemlich übereinstimmend Zusammenhänge aus verschiedenen linguistischen Bereichen wie die folgenden angesehen:

– aus dem Aufbau einzelsprachlicher Systeme: das Vorhandensein von mGE in einer Sprache setzt das Vorhandensein der ihnen entsprechenden uGE voraus;
– aus dem Spracherwerb: uGE werden vor den ihnen entsprechenden mGE erworben;
– aus der Aphasie: mGE gehen (unter sonst gleichen Bedingungen) vor den ihnen entsprechenden uGE verloren;
– aus dem Sprachwandel: beim grammatisch (d. h. nicht sozial) initiierten Wandel werden mGE durch die ihnen entsprechenden uGE ersetzt.

Diese Charakteristika beziehen sich durchweg auf einzelne grammatische Einheiten (Formen) aller Ebenen, vom Segment über die Segmentverbindung, die Silbe, das phonologische Wort, das Morphem, die (morphologische) Wortform und die syntaktische Konstituente bis hin zum Satz. Man vgl. dazu etwa das Verhältnis zwischen den unmarkierten nicht-runden vorderen Vokalen ('*i*-Typ') und den markierten runden vorderen Vokalen ('*ü*-Typ'), das sich jeweils in den genannten Faktenbereichen spiegelt.

Die Charakteristika sind dagegen nicht sinnvollerweise auf ganze Inventare bzw. Systeme von grammatischen Einheiten anwendbar. Das gilt – entgegen dem ersten Anschein – auch für den Sprachwandel: Beim Wandel wird ja nicht z. B. ein Vokalsystem mit runden vorderen Vokalen durch ein solches ohne diese ersetzt, sondern die Vokale des '*ü*-Typs' werden in ihren konkreten Instanzen von den Sprechern vermieden und durch solche des '*i*-Typs' ersetzt, wodurch sie (vermittelt durch die 'unsichtbare Hand'; Keller 1990: 83 ff.) dann aus dem System verschwinden. Veränderungen in der Syntagmatik wirken so in die Paradigmatik zurück. Der Begriff der Markiertheit, will man ihn nicht verwässern, sollte demnach auf die jeweils einzelnen grammatischen Einheiten beschränkt bleiben.

Damit kommt das Bewertungsprädikat der Markiertheit eben beispielsweise einem Phonem oder einer Flexionsform zu, während man bezogen auf das Phoneminventar oder das Flexionssystem einer Sprache davon abgesetzt von der qualitativen bzw. quantitativen Komplexität sprechen sollte.

Abschließend ist noch kurz auf die Frage einzugehen, was die Sprecher eigentlich 'im Auge haben', wenn sie danach trachten, sich sprachökonomisch zu verhalten. Streben sie in ihrem Sprachverhalten wirklich, wie teilweise angenommen (vgl. oben § 2), ein 'ausgewogenes' und in diesem Sinne ökonomisches Gesamtsystem an?

Die Antwort ergibt sich aus dem Verlauf von Sprachwandelprozessen: Grammatisch initiierter Wandel dient der Vermeidung von Markiertheit und damit der Sprachökonomie (Wurzel 1994: 28 ff.). Doch bekanntlich führt der Abbau von Markiertheit hinsichtlich eines Parameters typischerweise (wenn auch nicht immer) zum Aufbau von Markiertheit hinsichtlich eines anderen, so daß der 'ökonomische Gewinn' faktisch gleich null ist. Man vgl. z. B. nochmals die Herbeiführung von phonologischer Kürze in Fällen wie ahd. *ernust, markat* > nhd. *Ernst, Markt*, die mit der Entstehung von komplexen Konsonantenverbindungen bezahlt wird (oben § 5.2; dort auch weitere Beispiele).

Solche Veränderungen, für die man in allen Sprachen viele Beispiele finden kann, sind völlig unerklärbar, wenn man annimmt, daß die Sprecher beim jeweiligen Wandel faktisch das gesamte System 'im Auge haben', eine ohnehin etwas abenteuerliche Vorstellung. Es bleibt also nur die Schlußfolgerung, daß die Sprecher, die ja die Sprachveränderungen unbewußt herbeiführen, nicht in der Lage sind, wie ein Schachspieler die Konsequenzen eines Wandels im System zu berücksichtigen. Sie streben einfach nach der Vermeidung von Markiertheit hinsichtlich eines bestimmten Parameters, also etwa dem der phonologischen Kürze. Das führt zu einer LOKALEN VERBESSERUNG der grammatischen Struktur, die eben nicht notwendigerweise auch eine globale Verbesserung der grammatischen Struktur darstellt.

Aufgrund der Widersprüchlichkeit der Markiertheitsparameter und der Art und Weise, wie sich Wandel vollzieht, kann es keine allseitige Optimierung des Systems zugleich, aber auch kein gezieltes Bestreben zur Schaffung eines ausgewogenen Systems geben. Da in einem Sprachsystem immer Markiertheit vorhanden ist, die dem ökonomischen Zugriff der Sprecher auf die sprachlichen Mittel im Wege ist, gibt es auch immer die Tendenz zum Markiertheitsabbau. Die grammatische Struktur einer natürlichen Sprache verändert sich auch ohne äußere Einflüsse zu jeder Zeit.

7. Zitierte Literatur

Bauer, Laurie. 1988. *Introducing Linguistic Morphology*. Edinburgh: Edinburgh University Press.

Bußmann, Hadumod. [2]1990. *Lexikon der Sprachwissenschaft*. Stuttgart: Kröner.

Carstairs, Andrew. 1987. *Allomorphy in Inflection*. (Croom Helm linguistics series.) London: Croom Helm.

Comrie, Bernard. 1981. *Language Universals and Linguistic Typology. Syntax and Morphology*. Chicago: University of Chicago Press.

Curtius, Georg. 1858. *Grundzüge der griechischen Etymologie*. Band 1. Leipzig: Teubner.

DUDEN. [21]1996. *Rechtschreibung der deutschen Sprache*. (Duden, 1.) Mannheim: Dudenverlag.

Frei, Henri. 1929. *La grammaire des fautes*. Paris: Geuthner.

Haiman, John. 1985. *Natural Syntax. Iconicity and Erosion*. (Cambridge Studies in Linguistics, 44.) Cambridge: Cambridge University Press.

Humboldt, Wilhelm von. 1836. *Über die Verschiedenheit des menschlichen Sprachbaues und ihren Einfluß auf die geistige Entwicklung des Menschengeschlechts*. Berlin: Dümmler.

Jespersen, Otto. 1922. *Language. Its nature, development and origin*. London: Allen & Unwin.

Jespersen, Otto. 1924. *The Philosophy of Grammar*. London: Allen & Unwin.

Keller, Rudi. 1990. *Sprachwandel: Von der unsichtbaren Hand in der Sprache*. (UTB, 1567.) Tübingen: Francke.

Ladefoged, Peter & Maddieson, Ian. 1996. *The sounds of the world's languages*. (Phonological theory.) Oxford: Blackwell.

Lass, Roger. 1984. *Phonology. An introduction to basic concepts*. (Cambridge Textbooks in Linguistics.) Cambridge: Cambridge University Press.

Maddieson, Ian. 1984. *Patterns of sounds*. (Cambridge studies in speech science and communication.) Cambridge: Cambridge University Press.

Martinet, André. 1963. *Grundzüge der Allgemeinen Sprachwissenschaft*. (Urban-Bücher, 69.) Stuttgart: Kohlhammer.

Martinet, André. 1968. *Synchronische Sprachwissenschaft. Studien und Forschungen*. (Sammlung Akademie-Verlag, 2.) Berlin: Akademie-Verlag.

Martinet, André. 1981. *Sprachökonomie und Lautwandel. Eine Abhandlung über die diachronische Phonologie.* Stuttgart: Klett-Cotta.

Ronneberger-Sibold, Elke. 1980. *Sprachverwendung — Sprachsystem. Ökonomie und Wandel.* (Linguistische Arbeiten, 87.) Tübingen: Niemeyer.

Schnelle, Helmut & Kranzhoff, Jörn A. 1965. „Zur Beschreibung und Bearbeitung der Struktur deutscher Wörter". *Beiträge zur Sprachkunde und Informationsverarbeitung* 6: 65–87.

Schwabe, Kerstin. 1994. *Syntax und Semantik situativer Ellipsen.* (Studien zur deutschen Grammatik, 48.) Tübingen: Narr.

Werner, Otmar. 1984. „Morphologische Entwicklungen in den germanischen Sprachen", In: Untermann, Jürgen & Brogyanyi, Bela (eds.), *Das Germanische und die Rekonstruktion der indogermanischen Grundsprache. Akten des Freiburger Kolloquiums der Indogerm. Gesellschaft, 26.–27. Februar 1981.* (Amsterdam studies in the theory and history of linguistic science, Series IV, Current issues in linguistic theory, 22.) Amsterdam & Philadelphia: Benjamins, 181–226.

Werner, Otmar. 1987. „The aim of morphological change is a good mixture — not a uniform language type". In: Anna G. Ramat, Onofrio Carruba & Giuliano Bernini (eds.), *Papers from the 7th International Conference on Historical Linguistics* (Amsterdam studies in the theory and history of linguistic science, Series IV, Current issues in linguistic theory, 48). Amsterdam & Philadelphia: Benjamins, 591–606.

Werner, Otmar. 1989. „Sprachökonomie und Natürlichkeit im Bereich der Morphologie". *Zeitschrift für Phonetik, Sprachwissenschaft und Kommunikationsforschung* 42: 34–47.

Whitney, William D. (^{2}1867), *Language and the Study of Language. 12 lectures on the principles of linguistic science.* London: Trübner.

Wurzel, Wolfgang U. 1984. *Flexionsmorphologie und Natürlichkeit. Ein Beitrag zur morphologischen Theoriebildung.* (Studia Grammatica, XXI.) Berlin: Akademie-Verlag.

Wurzel, Wolfgang U. 1994. *Grammatisch initiierter Wandel.* Unter Mitarbeit von Andreas Bittner und Dagmar Bittner. (Projekt: Sprachdynamik. Auf dem Weg zu einer Typologie sprachlichen Wandels, I.) Bochum: Brockmeyer.

Wurzel, Wolfgang U. 1998. „On markedness". *Theoretical Linguistics* 24: 53–71.

Wurzel, Wolfgang U. (in Vorb.), „Inflectional system and markedness". To appear in: Aditi, Lahiri (ed.), *Markedness and Language Change.*

Zipf, George K. 1949. *Human Behavior and the Principle of Least Effort. An introduction to human ecology.* Cambridge/MA: Addison-Wesley.

Wolfgang Ullrich Wurzel,
Zentrum für Allgemeine Sprachwissenschaft
Berlin (Deutschland)

32. Markiertheit

1. Einleitung
2. Die Entwicklung der Konzeption
3. Dimensionen der Definition
4. Anwendungsbereiche
5. Theoretische Vermittlungen des Markiertheitsbegriffes
6. Zitierte Literatur

1. Einleitung: 'markiert — unmarkiert', 'merkmalhaltig — merkmallos'

Wie Roman Jakobson (1974) — gewiß einer der „pilgrim fathers" der Markiertheitsforschung (Wurzel 1998: 70) — vermerkt, herrscht im Deutschen um den Begriff der 'Merkmalhaltigkeit' oder auch 'Merkmalhaftigkeit' terminologische Unsicherheit. Oftmals wird er 'Markiertheit' gleichgesetzt; dieselbe Feststellung gilt *mutatis mutandis* für 'Merkmallosigkeit' und 'Unmarkiertheit'.

Jakobson zufolge ist diese Begriffskonfusion durch die Übersetzung der deutschen Begriffe ins ENGLISCHE ('marked' vs. 'unmarked') und deren anschließende anglisierende Rückübersetzung ('markiert' vs. 'unmarkiert') entstanden, bei der der Unterschied zwischen 'Merkmal' ('mark') und 'Eigenschaft' (eigentlich 'feature') verwischt wird. Diese mithin eher zufällig entstandene Synonymie wird heute in der germanophonen Lingusitik gelegentlich zur Differenzierung verschiedener Aspekte von 'Markiertheit' gebraucht (z. B. Mayerthaler 1981, Wurzel 1998, s. u.). Entsprechend schlägt Wolfgang U. Wurzel vor, auch im ENGLISCHEN zwischen 'markedness' und 'featuredness' zu trennen (1998: 61).

Während der Markiertheitsbegriff in verschiedenen Strömungen der germanophonen und anglo-amerikanischen Sprachwissenschaft zwar umstritten, aber fest etabliert ist, nimmt die Rezeption der Markiertheitsdebatte in Frankreich einen geringeren Stellenwert ein. Wohl wird 'markedness' innerhalb der generativen Grammatik mit 'marquage' übersetzt (s. die französische Version Chomsky & Halle 1968); anders als für die Adjektive 'marqué' vs. 'non-marqué' scheint aber die Akzeptanz für den substantivischen Terminus geringer. In anderen Disziplinen der romanischen Linguistik − etwa in der Hispanistik oder der Italianistik − finden sich hingegen differenzierte Anwendungen (im SPANISCHEN 'marcadez', s. z. B. Prado 1982, Gauger 1993; im ITALIENISCHEN 'marcatezza', s. etwa Renzi 1988, Dardano 1994).

2. Die Entwicklung der Konzeption

2.1. Nikolaj S. Trubetzkoy und Roman Jakobson

Die Begründung der Opposition 'merkmalhaft' vs. 'merkmallos', so legt Jakobson in den Dialogen mit Krystyna Pomorska dar, hängt mit Trubetzkoys und Jakobsons Überlegungen zum Binarismus und zur Korrelation zusammen. Während Jakobson den Terminus der Merkmalhaftigkeit schon in den 20er Jahren im literarischen und anthropologischen Zusammenhang gebraucht hatte, so spielt für dessen Übertragung auf den Bereich der Phonologie eine Überlegung eine erhebliche Rolle, die Trubetzkoy in einem Brief an Jakobson, datiert vom 31. Juli 1930, anstellt (zur Markiertheitstheorie von Jakobson, Trubetzkoy und ihren Nachfolgern s. z. B. Andersen 1989; Battistella 1990; Battistella 1996: bes. 19−72). Trubetzkoy legt dar, daß die binäre Opposition

„im Sprachbewußtsein eine besondere Form annimmt: Man stellt die Anwesenheit eines bestimmten Merkmals seinem Fehlen (beziehungsweise das Maximum eines Merkmals seinem Minimum) gegenüber."
(russisches Original in Jakobson 1975: 162; Übers. nach Jakobson & Pomorska 1982: 85).

Denselben, binaristisch gefaßten Gedanken findet man in der in Trubetzkoys *Grundzügen der Phonologie* formulierten Definition der privativen Opposition wieder. Für diesen Oppositionstyp gilt: „ein Glied ist merkmaltragend, das andere merkmallos, z. B. 'stimmhaft' vs. 'stimmlos' (s. Trubetzkoy 1958: 60 ff.). Mit verschiedenen Formulierungen hat Jakobson unterstrichen, daß damit keine 'Gleichberechtigung' der Oppositionsglieder geschaffen wird. Das merkmallose Glied kann konkret des Fehlen der fraglichen Eigenschaft A, ebenso aber die Absenz einer Angabe über die Existenz von A bedeuten:

„As was pointed out in these papers, one of two mutually opposite grammatical categories is 'marked' while the other is 'unmarked'. The general meaning of a marked category states the presence of a certain (whether positive or negative) property A; the general meaning of the corresponding unmarked category states nothing about the presence of A, and is used chiefly, but not exclusively, to indicate the absence of A. The unmarked term is always the negative of the marked term, but on the level of general meaning the opposition of the two contradictories may be interpreted as 'statement of A' vs. 'no statement of A', whereas on the level of 'narrowed', nuclear meanings, we encounter the opposition 'statement of A' vs. 'statement of non-A' ". (Jakobson 1957: 47; ähnlich bereits 1932: 12).

Damit ergibt sich also eine Art Steigerung der 'Merkmallosigkeit' vom ersten zum zweiten Verständnis des negativen Oppositionsgliedes und ein Übergang zu Trubetzkoys gradueller Opposition (Trubetzkoy 1958: 60 ff.), die bis zur genannten Form der Neutralisierung der Opposition im negativen Glied reichen kann. Wenn Jakobson und Trubetzkoy mithin in ihr Konzept des Binarismus den Gedanken der hierarchischen Abstufung der Oppositionsglieder aufnehmen und Jakobson zudem feststellt, daß „die Bestimmung des merkmalhaften und des merkmallosen Terms vor allem von der Zusammensetzung des Bündels distinktiver Eigenschaften als ganzem abhängt" (Jakobson & Pomorska 1982: 86), so wird deutlich, daß der Binarismus eigentlich das Prinzip seiner Überwindung in sich birgt. Konsequenterweise formuliert Wurzel (1998: 66), wohlgemerkt innerhalb eines ausdrücklich auf die Prager Schule gestützten Ansatzes:

„The properties relevant for markedness evaluation are frequently not found in binary realization (G_j has the property P_k or not, but exist in gradual realization [...]. Therefore markedness itself also must be understood to be basically gradual, the common distinction 'marked versus unmarked' is not sufficient. Thus, relative markedness evaluations of the type 'G_1 is more/less marked than G_2 regarding a markedness parameter M_i, arise."

Jakobson wendet die Begriffe 'merkmalhaltig' vs. 'merkmallos' in drei auch für die heutige Bestimmung zentralen Bereichen an: Anthropologie, Phonologie und Morphosyntax.

Bereits in den zwanziger Jahren hat Jakobson darauf hingewiesen, daß es in jeder

Gesellschaft Erscheinungen gibt, die von ihren Mitgliedern als 'normal' und mithin als unauffälliger Regelfall interpretiert werden, während sich andere Phänomene als auffällige, daher aussagekräftige Ausnahmen präsentieren.

Je nach Gesellschaftstyp kann dasselbe Phänomen − Jakobson nennt die Nacktheit − diametral entgegengesetzt bewertet werden (Jakobson 1974: 279; Jakobson & Pomorska 1982: 85). Während ein „Troglodyt [...] sozusagen definitionsgemäß nackt ist", muß sich ein Europäer „erst entkleiden, um nackt zu sein" (1982: 85). Die Merkmalhaftigkeit des Nacktseins in der europäischen Gesellschaft geht etwa aus der Rezeptionsgeschichte von Édouard Manets „Déjeuner sur l'herbe" hervor; die erste Ausstellung dieses Bildes − im Vordergrund zwei Männer in zeitgenössischer französischer Kleidung und eine nackte Frau − hatte im Jahre 1863 sogleich einen Sturm der Entrüstung ausgelöst.

Festzuhalten bleibt, daß hier eine allgemeinere, kultursemiotische Anwendung des Begriffspaars intendiert ist, und zwar auf der Ebene spezifischer gesellschaftlicher Systeme. Im übrigen macht dieses Beispiel Schule; so zitiert Willi Mayerthaler den Nacktbadestrand als Beispiel für Markiertheitsumkehrung in besonderen Kontexten (1981: 55).

Andere theoretische Perspektiven ergeben sich durch Anwendungen in der Phonologie, beispielsweise die Erörterung der Opposition 'kompakt' vs. 'diffus', wofür Jakobson 1944 noch die Termini 'farbig' vs. 'farblos' gebraucht. In einer frühen ontogenetischen Stufe erlernt das Kind den Kontrast 'p' + 'a', mithin die Folge eines diffusen Konsonanten und kompakten Vokals; erst später werden kompakte Konsonanten (/k/) und diffuse Vokale (/u/, /i/) erworben.

Die Opposition 'kompakt' vs. 'diffus' (wie zweitens 'dunkel' vs. 'hell') ist in allen Sprachen der Welt realisiert (Jakobson & Halle 1956: 89), hat also universalen Stellenwert. Innerhalb der Vokale ist 'kompakt' das merkmallose Glied, das − mit Edmund Husserls Begriff − den Erwerb der merkmalhaften, also diffusen Vokale „fundiert" (Husserl 1913); im Konsonantismus ist das Verhältnis umgekehrt. Das merkmallose Glied wird also in der Ontogenese früher erworben und im Aphasiefall später verloren. Interessanterweise bezeichnet Jakobson (1982) zudem die Ausprägung von Merkmallosigkeit als 'Optimalisierung':

„Dieser Unterschied [der unterschiedliche Markiertheitswert von 'kompakt' und 'diffus' in Vokalismus und Konsonantismus] erklärt sich leicht aus der Tatsache, daß die optimalen Vokale kompakt, die optimalen Konsonanten dagegen diffus sind". (in Jakobson & Pomorska 1982: 86).

Im Bereich der Grammatik hat Jakobson die fragliche Opposition etwa bereits in seiner Studie „Zur Struktur des russischen Verbs" (1932) angewendet; hier werden verschiedene grammatische Kategorien markiertheitstheoretisch hierarchisiert, etwa

marked unmarked
perfective imperfective (1932: 3)
passive active (1932: 4)
plural singular (1932: 6)

Insgesamt ist Jakobsons Behandlung der Opposition 'merkmalhaft' vs. 'merkmallos' gewiß nicht völlig kohärent:

„Despite attempts in his retrospective work to present markedness in a unified way, Jakobson's treatment of markedness is neither fully worked out nor wholly consistent, but instead is often speculative, fragmented, and overly broad". (Battistella 1996: 34)

Gleichwohl finden sich in seinen Schriften Leitlinien, die bis heute richtungsweisend sind:

− Die Unterscheidung der Anwendung auf der Ebene eines einzelnen gesellschaftlichen bzw. sprachlichen Systems von der Ebene der Universalien.
− Die Anwendung in verschiedenen Bereichen über Phonologie und Grammatik bis hin zu dem, was man aus heutiger Sicht als gesellschaftliche Pragmatik bezeichnen könnte (etwa im Zusammenhang mit dem Bekleidungsbeispiel).
− Die Heranziehung kognitiver Parameter (Ontogenese und Aphasie).

2.2. Entwicklungen in der Folge von Jakobson und Trubetzkoy

Die Überlegungen zum Markiertheitsbegriff von Jakobson und Trubetzkoy haben ein starkes Echo gefunden. Am Ausgangspunkt der meisten Markiertheitstheorien in dieser Tradition steht, so Edith Moravcsik und Jessica Wirth, eine Korrelation zwischen drei Größen. Demnach gilt im Bereich der menschlichen Perzeption, daß ein Objekt umso leichter wahrgenommen wird,

− je vertrauter, je häufiger es ist;
− je einfacher seine Struktur ist (syntagmatisch);

– je größer die Anzahl seiner Varianten ist (paradigmatisch).

Diese Feststellung trifft auch in der Sprache zu. Moravcsik & Wirth zeigen dies an derselben Stelle am Beispiel des Numerus:

„[...] the singular tends to be simpler in form, more common in usage, and more elaborated in terms of subtypes".
(Moravcsik & Wirth 1986: 2)

Das häufigere, einfacher strukturierte und variantenreichere Glied der Opposition ist also der merkmallose Teil:

„The one of the two entities that is consistently more widely distributed and/or simpler and/or more richly elaborated is called *unmarked*; its complement is the marked member of the opposition".
(Moravcsik & Wirth 1986: 3)

Zu den wichtigsten Erben der Prager Markiertheitsdiskussion zählt Joseph H. Greenberg. In seinen *Language Universals* (1966) werden in diesem Zusammenhang zwei Aspekte diskutiert und problematisiert. Zum einen wird deutlich zwischen einzelsprachlicher und übereinzelsprachlicher Markiertheitsebene geschieden. Zum anderen wird dann das Frequenzkriterium auf beide Ebenen bezogen und vor allem sein Status auf der einzelsprachlichen Ebene hinterfragt. Ein lexikalischer Term oder eine grammatische Kategorie kann demnach übereinzelsprachlich häufig und merkmallos sein, in einer Einzelsprache aber nicht denselben Markiertheitswert besitzen.

Wesentlich ist die Implikationsrelation: einzelsprachlich wird die merkmallose Kategorie von der merkmalhaltigen vorausgesetzt, was zu einer hohen Frequenz führen kann, aber nicht unbedingt muß (Greenberg 1966: 60; 70; vgl. unten zum Begriff 'typologische Markierung' § 3.1.; zum Kriterium der Frequenz s. außerdem Fenk-Oczlon 1991).

Zu den jüngeren, sehr fruchtbaren Ansätzen im Gefolge der Prager Schule gehört die universale und einzelsprachliche Natürlichkeitstheorie (s. u. §§ 2.4., 2.5.) sowie die funktionale Anwendung vor allem von Talmy Givón (s. u. § 2.6.).

2.3. Wandlungen des Begriffs in der formalen Linguistik (Chomsky)

Noam Chomsky greift den Markiertheitsbegriff zunächst im Zusammenhang mit der generativen Phonologie auf (vgl. Battistella 1996: 73 ff.), in seinem 1977 gemeinsam mit Howard Lasnik verfaßten Beitrag über „Filters and Control" werden dann Systeme, die Teil der „core grammar" sind, als „the unmarked case" verstanden.

In den *Lectures on Government and Binding* (Chomsky 1981) wird die Universalgrammatik als eine Menge interagierender Module verstanden, während die „core language acquisition" als Prozeß der Fixierung universaler Prinzipien gesehen wird. Unmarkiertheit erscheint in diesem Zusammenhang als Serie primärer Hypothesen, die dem Sprachlerner zur Verfügung stehen und die er immer dann auswählt, wenn ihm keine gegenteilige Evidenz (beispielsweise durch Korrektur der Rede des Kindes) zur Verfügung steht. Dieser Sicht folgt auch Chomskys Aufsatz über „Markedness and Core Grammar" (1981a).

Battistella (1996: 85) faßt die Entwicklung der späteren generativistischen Markiertheitsdiskussion zusammen:

„For many generative grammarians working in the 1980s Principles and Parameters framework, markedness ends up referring to three related things: (1) a distinction between unmarked and marked periphery; (2) a preference structure imputed to the parameters and parameter values of core grammar; and (3) a preference structure among the rules of the periphery".

Als neuester Aspekt der aus der generativen Markiertheitsdiskussion hervorgegangenen Entwicklungen erscheint die Optimalitätstheorie (s. dazu u. § 5.2.).

2.4. Die universale Natürlichkeitstheorie

Die morphologische Natürlichkeitstheorie nach Mayerthaler (1981; 1987) geht von dem Gedanken aus, daß einerseits universalpragmatische Eigenschaften der Kommunikationssituation und andererseits biologisch-neuropsychologische Prädispositionen des Sprechers bestimmte morphologische Kategorien als elementar, andere als nachgeordnet erscheinen lassen; dieses hierarchische Gefälle wird im Idealfall von Einzelsprachen bei der Enkodierung dieser Kategorien abgebildet.

Eine solche Gradierung herrscht beispielsweise zwischen der Basiskategorie 'Positiv' und den jeweils höher gestaffelten Kategorien 'Komparativ' und 'Superlativ'. Der Positiv wird von allen Sprachen enkodiert und ontogenetisch früh erworben; demnach wäre er die natürlichste und semantisch 'unmarkierteste' der drei Kategorien. Die entgegengesetzten Eigenschaften gelten für den Superlativ; der Komparativ stellt einen Mittelwert dar.

Bei dieser Bestimmung des semantischen Markiertheitsgrades (i. e. auf der „sem-Ebene") orientiert sich Mayerthaler an den Eigenschaften des prototypischen Sprechers, die er in meist binären Oppositionen angibt; der prototypische Sprecher ist belebt, nicht unbelebt, er befindet sich in einer realen, nicht aber einer anderen als der realen Welt, etc. (1981: 13 ff.; 1987: 39 ff.). Je deutlicher eine Kategorie diese Eigenschaften spiegelt, desto weniger komplex, desto perzeptiv zugänglicher und damit desto unmarkierter ist sie. Somit gilt für Markiertheitsrelationen wie das Verhältnis vom Positiv zum Komparativ:

„sem < (A,B) is interpreted as 'A is cognitively less complex than B' " (1987: 41).

Eine Einzelsprache ist nun umso natürlicher, je getreuer, je „konstruktionell ikonischer" sie diese Markiertheitsasymmetrie „enkodiert" oder *symbolisiert* („sym-Ebene") (Zu verschiedenen Anwendungen des Ikonizitätsbegriffs s. Simone 1995). D. h., das unmarkierte Glied der Opposition muß sprachlich entsprechend merkmallos, also phonologisch unaufwendig wiedergegeben werden. So ist lat. *longus* kürzer als *longior*, und dieser Komparativ ist wieder kürzer als der Superlativ *longissimus*. Bei den lateinischen Steigerungsformen koinzidieren folglich sem- und sym-Werte, diese Formen sind konstruktionell ikonisch. Somit ergibt sich der Markiertheitswert insgesamt („m-Wert") aus der Relation von sem- und sym-Wert; im Lateinischen ist der Komparativ bezogen auf den m-Wert markierter als der Positiv und der Superlativ markierter als der Komparativ (s. Mayerthaler 1981: 40 ff.; 1987: 48 ff.).

In der Terminologie Mayerthalers wird also die ursprünglich durch übersetzerisches Mißgeschick entstandene Begriffsdoppelung 'Markiertheit' neben 'Merkmalhaftigkeit' zur Trennung zwischen semantischer und ausdrucksseitiger Ebene ausgenutzt. 'Markiertheit' wird hier demnach letztlich als Begriff für die Relation zwischen Inhalts- und Ausdrucksseite verstanden.

In diesem Sinne werden zwei weitere (eng zusammenhängende) Bedingungen für maximale Unmarkiertheit eingeführt: 'Uniformität' und 'Transparenz'. Beide beziehen sich auf die Eins-zu-Eins-Entsprechung von Form und Funktion. Ein uniformes Paradigma ist eineindeutig organisiert und allomorphiefrei (1981: 34). Ein mehrsilbiges Wort ist dann konstruktionell durchsichtig, wenn es präfigierend oder suffigierend gebildet ist (Mayerthaler 1981: 36; 103 ff.).

Markiertheitsverhältnisse haben in dieser Sichtweise sprachgeschichtliche Folgen: im diachronen Konfliktfall setzt sich in der Regel die unmarkierte gegenüber der markierten Form durch.

2.5. Die einzelsprachliche Natürlichkeitstheorie

Anders als Mayerthaler geht es Wurzel (1984; 1987) um Natürlichkeitsgesetze im morphologischen, insbesondere flektivischen System einer Einzelsprache. Einzelsprachliche morphologische Natürlichkeit bemißt sich an zwei Parametern: 'Systemangemessenheit' („system-congruity") und 'Flexionsklassenstabilität'.

Jedes Sprachsystem zeichnet sich durch bestimmte systemdefinierende Züge aus, also Züge, von denen es ausschließlich (uniforme Systeme wie das Türkische; → Art. 122) oder dominant (nicht-uniforme Systeme wie das Deutsche) bestimmt wird.

Gegenüber diesen definierenden Zügen weisen die Teile, hier genauer die Flexionsklassen des Gesamtsystems, eine mehr oder weniger große Angemessenheit auf; je systemangemessener, desto unmarkierter sind sie. Sprachwandel erfolgt in Richtung auf diese morphologisch unmarkierten, systemangemessenen Flexionsklassen; weniger systemangemessene Verfahren werden abgebaut.

Beispielsweise dominiert im Neuhochdeutschen die Basisformflexion (Sg. *Frau*, Pl. *Frau-en*). Daher gibt es heute im Deutschen eine Tendenz, Stammflexion zugunsten von Basisformflexion abzubauen. So wird *Radi-us, Radi-en* ersetzt durch *Radius, Radiuss- e*; dasselbe gilt für die Pluralformen *Kont-en, Glob-en*, an deren Stelle *Konto-s* und *Globuss-e* treten (Wurzel 1987: 66; → Art. 31).

Wesentlich ist nun, daß bei einem Konflikt des universalen Natürlichkeitsprinzips der Ikonizität mit dem einzelsprachlichen Prinzip der Systemangemessenheit letzteres die Oberhand gewinnt. Im Althochdeutschen gibt es z. B. die mit dem Singular homonyme Pluralform *wort*. Diese Nullpluralbildung ist nichtikonisch, da der universalsemantisch größeren Markiertheit des Plurals eine äußerungsseitig aufwendigere Enkodierung als im Singular entsprechen müßte. Die Nullpluralbildung ist im Althochdeutschen aber systemkongruent; daher gibt sie die Zielklasse im

Sprachwandel ab: Sg. *herza*, Pl. *herzun* wird zu Sg. *herza*, Pl. *herza* (Wurzel 1987: 70).

Kinder bilden gleichfalls Formen, die sich dem dominanten Prinzip des Paradigmas anschließen, obwohl sie damit auf eine Variante verzichten, die aus universaler Sicht ikonischer ist. Im folgenden Beispiel bildet Cédric (4;0) die 2. Pers. Pl. Präs. Ind. bzw. Imperativ mit der 'unikonischen', weil den regelmäßigen Stamm variierenden, aber im Präsensparadigma dominanten *vien*-Form:

(1)   *Allez,* viennez *manger* (statt 'venez').

Das zweite Prinzip einzelsprachlicher morphologischer Natürlichkeit, die Stabilität (einer Flexionsklasse), hängt vom Vorhandensein dominanter oder ausschließlich gültiger paradigmatischer Strukturbedingungen ab. Eine solche Strukturbedingung hat implikativen Charakter, z. B. Wurzel (1987: 77):

„If a German noun is masculine and forms its plural with /e/, then it has /s/ in the G. Sg., cf. *(der) Hund* 'dog' — N. Pl. *Hund-e*: G. Sg. *Hund-(e)-s*, etc."

Wörter mit denselben außermorphologischen, also semantisch-phonologischen Eigenschaften können nun zu verschiedenen, dann komplementären Flexionsklassen gehören, z. B. dt. Sg. *Kino*, Pl. *Kinos* vs. Sg. *Fresko*, Pl. *Fresken*. Stabile und damit unmarkierte Flexionsklassen werden dann durch Wörter mit bestimmten außermorphologischen Eigenschaften konstituiert, die nur einer oder jedenfalls einer dominanten paradigmatischen Strukturbedingung gehorchen.

Wieder hat einzelsprachliche Natürlichkeit Priorität im Sprachwandel sowie Vorrang gegenüber Forderungen universaler Natürlichkeit: eine unstabile Flexionsklasse mit ikonischer Markierung entwickelt sich in Richtung auf eine stabile Klasse, selbst wenn sich diese durch weniger ikonische Markierung auszeichnet.

Während in Wurzels früheren Arbeiten (1984; 1987) der Begriff der Markiertheit trotz der zugrundeliegenden Annahme, wonach Natürlichkeit mit Unmarkiertheit gleichzusetzen ist, keine zentrale Rolle einnimmt, stellt er ihn in jüngeren Beiträgen in den Mittelpunkt (1989; 1991; 1994; 1998). Angeknüpft wird einerseits an die Auffassung, daß sich Sprachwandel in Richtung auf morphologische Unmarkiertheit hin vollzieht, sei es im Bereich der Wortklassen (1989: 228; 233 f.) oder des Wandels von der Subtraktion (markiert) über die Modifikation (mittlerer Markiertheitswert) bis hin zur Addition (unmarkiert) (Wurzel 1998: 58 ff.).

Andererseits rekurriert Wurzel auf allgemeine Prinzipien von Markiertheit: 'Markiertheit' bedeutet (a) größere Komplexität und ist (b) ein relativer Begriff, d. h. nur im Verhältnis zu einem weniger markierten Oppositionsglied sinnvoll. 'Markiertheit' bezieht sich weiterhin (c) auf einzelne Elemente eines Gesamtphänomens statt von vornherein auf dieses Phänomen *in toto* und ist (d) gradueller, skalarer Natur (1989: 229; 1998: 65 f.).

1998 reiht Wurzel weiterhin explizit seine früheren Arbeiten wie auch die natürlichkeitstheoretischen Beiträge von Willi Mayerthaler und Wolfgang U. Dressler in die Tradition der Jakobsonschen Markiertheitstheorie ein (1998: 55). Der zentrale Gedanke von Wurzel 1998 liegt in einer Trennung von Ebenen innerhalb der Markiertheitsdiskussion (ein Konzept, das in breiterer Form von Ludwig 1995, 1996 verfolgt wird). Folgende Niveaus werden geschieden:

(a) die Evidenzebene
(b) die theoretische Ebene
(c) die Ebene der Exemplifizierung der Markiertheitstheorie durch Nachbardisziplinen.

Auf der Evidenzebene führt Wurzel einerseits Bereiche an, die eher als Anwendungsbereiche der Markiertheitstheorie erscheinen (z. B. Sprachwandel), und andere, die (auch) als Evidenzparameter gelten können (wie Aphasie und „slips of the tongue").

2.6. Neuere Verwendungen in der funktionalen Linguistik

Bei Talmy Givón (1990; 1991) konvergieren verschiedene Argumente der Markiertheitsdiskussion; er unterscheidet drei Hauptkriterien für Markiertheit:

(a) Structural complexity: The marked structure tends to be more complex — or larger — than the corresponding unmarked one.
(b) Frequency distribution: the marked category (figure) tends to be less frequent, thus cognitively more salient, than the corresponding unmarked one (ground).
(c) Cognitive complexity: The marked category tends to be cognitively more complex — in terms of *attention, mental effort* or *processing time* — than the unmarked one. (1991: 337)

Sowohl für Kriterium (b) als auch für (c) wird demnach allgemeine psycho-neurologische Evidenz herangezogen; derart ergibt sich auch eine Nähe zum Prototypen-Konzept (Givón 1991: 337 f.; s. u.). Givón wendet den Markiertheitsbegriff dann auf verschiedenen funktionalen Ebenen an:

1. Auf der Ebene der grammatisch-morphologischen Kategorien. Demnach ergeben sich Hierarchien wie z. B. („A < B" : 'A ist unmarkiert bzw. merkmalloser im Vergleich zum markierten bzw. markierteren Glied B') (1990: 948 ff.; 1991: 338 ff.; zu derartigen Markiertheitshierarchien s. weiter Croft 1990: bes. 92 f.): *perfective < imperfective*
2. Auf der Ebene der Satz- bzw. Sprechakttypen: *active < passive; declarative < manipulative*
3. Auf der Ebene der Diskurstypen: *oral-informal < written-formal*.

Derart werden wesentliche, auch pragmatische Anwendungsbereiche der Markiertheitsdiskussion gewiesen (zur Verbindung der Markiertheitskategorien mit der Mündlichkeits-Schriftlichkeitsvarianz s. Ludwig 1986; 1996; s. u.).

3. Hinweise zu einer mehrdimensionalen Definition und zur Dimensionsspezifik einzelner Evidenzparameter

3.1. Die vertikale Definitionsachse

Alle dargelegten Theorien trennen deutlich zwischen einem konzeptionellen und einem formellen Bereich. Für den konzeptionellen Bereich — der, wie sich gezeigt hat, in mehrere Ebenen aufzugliedern ist — wird hier nunmehr von 'kategorieller Markiertheit', für die Enkodierungsseite von 'formeller Markiertheit' gesprochen (analog zu Comrie 1986).

'Kategorielle Markiertheit' umfaßt gleichermaßen eher grammatische wie auch eher lexikalisch-semantische Bedeutungseinheiten; damit wird im Bereich der lexikalischen Semantik der Erkenntnis Rechnung getragen, daß Lexien, abgesehen von Eigennamen, keine einzelnen Exemplare, sondern Bedeutungstypen enkodieren (s. u. zum Zusammenhang von Markiertheit und Prototypik).

Eine Differenzierung zwischen lexikalischer und grammatischer kategorieller Markiertheit wird dann sinnfällig, wenn der Markiertheitsbegriff in Zusammenhang mit der Grammatikalisierungstheorie gebracht werden soll, da sich Grammatikalisierungsprozesse als lexikalisch-kategorielle Demarkierung zugunsten der grammatisch-kategoriellen Seite erfassen läßt (vgl. die kritische Sicht von Lehmann 1989 und dazu Ludwig 1996: 44−6). Zudem läßt sich sinnvollerweise unter 'kategorieller Markiertheit' auch phonologische Markiertheit fassen, die gleichwohl nicht im Skopus dieses Beitrags steht (speziell zur phonologischen Markiertheit s. z. B. Dressler 1989; Liberman 1996).

Die Indizierung des Terminus 'Markiertheit' nach verschiedenen Ebenen hebt im übrigen die Schwierigkeiten einer Trennung von 'Unmarkiertheit' vs. 'Markiertheit' und 'Merkmallosigkeit' vs. 'Merkmalhaltigkeit' auf (d. h. ohne weitere Indizierung werden die Termini synonym).

1. *Unmarkiertheit bzw. Markiertheit$_{KU}$*
   Ebene der universalen Kategorien (KU). Sie entspricht beispielsweise Mayerthalers Opposition markierter bzw. unmarkierter Kategorien (KU) oder Chomskys Überlegungen zu Teilen bzw. präferierten Prinzipien der „core grammar". 'Universal unmarkiert' im strengen Sinne bedeutet, daß eine Kategorie in allen Sprachen der Welt enkodiert ist. Da dieser Status empirisch nicht zu belegen ist, muß er psycholinguistisch-neurologisch wie universalpragmatisch begründet sein.
2. *Unmarkiertheit bzw. Markiertheit$_{KT}$*
   Ebene der typologischen Kategorien (KT). Da nur unmarkierte Kategorien wirklich universal sein können, schafft die Präsenz „außereinzelsprachlich" markierter bzw. markierterer Kategorien typologische Markiertheit (zum Begriff der 'Außereinzelsprachlichkeit', der als Oberbegriff für universale und typologische Markiertheit gelten kann, s. Heger 1976; 1981; → Art. 25). Für entscheidend wird meist die Implikativität der Markiertheitskonstellation erachtet. Entsprechend definieren Forner & al. typologische Markiertheit (1992: 78 f.):

„For any pair of minimally different linguistic structures or characteristics A and B, A is typologically marked relative to B (and B is typologically unmarked relative to A) if and only if every language that has A also has B but not every language that has B also has A. In other words, the presence in any given language of a marked term of a markedness relation implies the presence in that language of the corresponding unmarked term, while the presence of the unmarked term does not imply the presence of the marked term".

Derselbe implikationelle Gedanke wird von William Croft verfolgt (1990, bes. 67−70; 96−98).

3. *Unmarkiertheit bzw. Markiertheit$_{KE}$*
Ebene der einzelsprachlichen Kategorien (KE).
Die außereinzelsprachliche Markiertheit von Kategorien kann sich, aber muß sich nicht im einzelsprachlichen System abbilden; einzelsprachliche Markiertheit wird durch Faktoren wie 'Systemangemessenheit' und 'Flexionsklassenstabilität' bestimmt (s. o. § 2.5.).

4. *Unmarkiertheit bzw. Markiertheit$_{FE}$*
Ebene der einzelsprachlichen Formen (FE). Die materielle Seite der einzelsprachlichen Enkodierung kann, aber muß nicht, ikonisch sein. Daß übereinzelsprachlich unmarkierte Kategorien zur äußerungsseitigen Null-Repräsentation tendieren, ist oft betont worden (so Croft 1990: 71 f.).

3.2. Evidenzparameter

Im Anschluß an die hier dargestellte Markiertheitsdiskussion bzw. weitere Beschreibungen ergibt sich eine Liste von Kriterien und Evidenzbereichen für Markiertheit (MH) bzw. Unmarkiertheit (UM); vgl. weiter die Listen von Croft 1990: 71 f.; Faingold 1995: 151 ff.; Battistella 1996: 70 f.

Entscheidend ist der Gedanke, daß sich die Kriterien jeweils auf unterschiedliche Markiertheitsebenen oder auf Relationen zwischen Markiertheitsebenen beziehen.

Die nachfolgende Liste stellt eine Auswahl dar. Ausgeklammert wurde z. B. der Grad der paradigmatischen Variabilität oder Subspezifikation als Indiz für Merkmallosigkeit, da die genauen Grenzen eines Paradigmas oft schwer bestimmbar sind. Ebenso wurden keine spezifisch diachronen Kriterien in die Liste aufgenommen, da sie mit weitergehenden sprachtheoretischen Prämissen verbunden sind.

Weiter enthält die Kriterienliste keine Hierarchisierung von notwendigen und hinreichenden Bedingungen, um einen Gesamt-Markiertheitswert auf der jeweiligen Ebene zu ermitteln (wie etwa von Mayerthaler intendiert, s. o. § 2.4.). Dennoch sind nicht alle Kriterien gleichrangig. Einige der genannten Punkte haben zweifelsfrei den Status essentieller Definitionskriterien, etwa (A), (B), (E).

Andere haben eher den Status eines empirischen Evidenzbereichs − z. B. der Parameter 'Frequenz' (G).

Die Kriterien werden für UM formuliert, so daß für MH dann die Umkehrung gilt; in jedem Falle sind diese Parameter oppositiver und gradueller Art:

(A) *Semantisch-kategoriell hohe Extensionalität und geringe Intensionalität* eines (inhaltlichen) Begriffs X (UM$_{KU/KT/KE}$)

Dieses Kriterium läßt sich unabhängig auf universaler, typologischer und einzelsprachlicher Ebene verwenden: die hohe Extensionalität der Bedeutung eines einzelsprachlichen Ausdrucks muß nicht unbedingt eine Entsprechung auf universaler Ebene haben.

(B) *Tendenz oder Affinität zur Neutralisation* des von einem einzelsprachlichen Ausdruck E enkodierten semantisch-kategoriellen Begriffs X

Kinder lernen das merkmallose Glied einer Markiertheitsopposition oder einer Markiertheitshierarchie vor dem merkmalhaltigen Glied. Gleichwohl gebrauchen sie es zunächst nicht als unmarkiertes Oppositionsglied im engeren Sinne, sondern als neutralisierten Term für den Ausdruck des gesamten in der Opposition involvierten Kategorienspektrums. Wenn dann ontogenetisch das merkmalhaltige Glied hinzutritt, bleiben simultan zwei Optionen zurück:

(1) die Intension des merkmallosen Glieds wird erhöht; derart wird es zum merkmallosen Oppositionsglied;
(2) im Bedarfsfall kann das merkmallose Glied im Sinne des früheren ontogenetischen Stadiums, d. h. als gesteigert merkmalloser, nämlich neutralisierter Term eingesetzt werden.

Damit zeigt sich ein Zusammenhang zwischen zwei Stufen der Merkmallosigkeit des unmarkierten Glieds; genau dieser Zusammenhang zwischen Merkmallosigkeit und Neutralisation hat öfters zu definitorischen Schwierigkeiten geführt (s. Battistella 1996: 60 f.).

Dieses Kriterium läßt sich mithin nur auf im System einer Einzelsprache verankerte außereinzelsprachliche Kategorien anwenden: UM$_{KU-FE/KT-FE}$

(C) *Kognitiv einfache 'Prozessierung'* (UM$_{KU-E/KT-E/KE-FE}$)

Kognitiv einfacher prozessierbar erscheinen häufig universal oder typologisch primäre Kategorien, die dann natürlich einzelsprachlich verankert sein müssen. Andererseits sind viele Kategorien und Ausdrücke, die in der jeweiligen Einzelsprache zentrale Funktion haben und somit früh erworben werden, einfach prozessierbar, ohne deshalb − wie Wurzel gezeigt hat − universal merkmallos zu sein. Zu diesem Parameter zählt auch die mitunter genannte 'salience' (z. B. Mufwene 1991).

(D) *Ontogenetisch früher Erwerb* (UM$_{KU-E/KT-E/KE-FE}$)

Hierin spiegelt sich wiederum häufig universale UM. Andererseits werden − ähnlich wie im Fall von (C) − insbesondere im morphologischen Bereich auch einzelsprachenspezifische Kategorien bzw. Ausdrücke früh erworben, wenn sie zentral und häufig in dieser Einzelsprache sind, ohne zwingend universal merkmallos zu sein.

(E) *Kommunikativ-pragmatische Priorität* (UM$_{KU/KT}$)

Dazu zählen Überlegungen des Typs, daß sich der prototypische Sprecher zunächst an der realen Welt und am *nunc* etc. orientiert (s. z. B. Mikame 1996).

(F) *Ikonizität bzw. Transparenz*

Merkmallos ist eine eineindeutige Form-Funktions-Beziehung vor allem dann, wenn eine merkmallose Kategorie mit nur einer Form bezeichnet wird − s. die Erklärung zu (B). Die Gleichsetzung von 'Transparenz' und „Eineindeutigkeit in der Form-Funktions-Beziehung" wird von Seuren & Wekker (1986) kritisiert. Außerdem kann man einen Widerspruch zwischen den Kriterien (F) und (A) sehen. Eine gewisse semantische Polyfunktionalität ist aber mit dem Prinzip der Ikonizität verträglich:

− wenn nämlich eine Spezifizierung der wenig intensiven Grundbedeutung auf Diskurs- und nicht auf Systemebene erfolgt;
− wenn eine auf Systemebene angelegte erweiterte Zweitbedeutung aus der Grundbedeutung abgeleitet werden kann.

Dieses Kriterium betrifft die Enkodierungsrelation UM$_{KU-KE-FE}$ bzw., in einem schwächeren Sinne, UM$_{KT-KE-FE}$.

(G) *Frequenz* (UM$_{KU-E/KT-FE/KE-FE}$)

Dieser Parameter hat außereinzelsprachliche und einzelsprachliche Relevanz:

− Er gibt einen Hinweis auf UM$_{KU}$, wenn eine Kategorie von den meisten Sprachen der Welt enkodiert ist.

− Er deutet auf UM$_{KE-FE}$ hin, wenn bestimmte Formen im Gebrauch einer Einzelsprache häufiger sind als andere Formen derselben Sprache.

(H) *Systemangemessenheit und Flexionsklassenstabilität* (UM$_{KE-FE}$)

3.3. Die horizontale Definitionsachse

Vergleicht man nun die Begriffe, die die Standardversion der Natürlichkeitstheorie entwickelt hat, mit einer differenzierten Liste von Sprachfunktionen, so zeigt sich, daß sie nahezu alle auf die Seite der referentiellen Semantik oder Syntax gehören. Prinzipien wie 'Transparenz', die man ja charakteristischerweise auch Wissenschaftssprachen zugrunde legt, dienen der Optimierung bei der Übermittlung von Inhalten, nicht aber (anderen) pragmatischen Zielen.

Im Gegensatz zu dieser Beschränkung erscheint es angemessen, allen sprachlichen − auch pragmatischen − Funktionen Markiertheitshierarchien zuzuweisen. Einzelne Hinweise zu einer solchen Systematisierung finden sich durchaus, etwa zum textuellen Bereich von Dressler (1992) oder zum pragmatischen Bereich von Renzi (1988: bes. 116), Dardano (1994 bes. 399), Givón (s. o.), Waugh & Lafford (1994: 2382). Dennoch muß derzeit diese Ausweitung noch als Desideratum in der Markiertheitsdiskussion gelten und erfordert mithin weitere Untersuchungen.

Als Ausgangspunkt können die drei grundlegenden Sprachfunktionen dienen, die Karl Bühler (1934) in seinem Organon-Modell definiert und Jakobson (1960) in ein erweitertes Modell überführt hat: die *darstellende* bzw. *referentielle* Funktion, zweitens die *expressive* und drittens die *appellative* bzw. *conative* Funktion.

In Kapitälchen sind Subparameter oder Subfunktionen wiedergegeben, die ihrerseits in Markiertheitshierarchien ausdifferenziert sind; bei den formellen Hierarchien bedeutet „A < B": 'A ist unmarkiert bzw. weniger markiert im Verhältnis zu B'.

Auf der linken Seite des Schemas befinden sich die semantisch-syntaktischen Kategorien und Prinzipien, die im wesentlichen Bühlers darstellende Funktion bzw. die referentielle Funktion (Jakobson) erfüllen; dieser Markiertheitstyp soll im Hinblick auf eine referentiell orientierte Syntax 'semantaktisch' genannt werden. Die semantaktische Markiertheit wird exemplarisch mit konkreten Markiertheitshierarchien ausdifferenziert.

Im Mittelbereich der Skala stehen die 'textuellen', rechts die 'pragmatischen' Kategorien und Markiertheitshierarchien.

Es scheint angemessen, im Anschluß an Halliday für den pragmatischen Bereich global die *interpersonelle* Funktion anzunehmen und diese in verschiedene Subfunktionen aufzugliedern (zu Halliday vgl. z. B. den Überblick von Samaniego 1993):

Zunächst die *illokutive* Funktion: gemeint sind die unterschiedlichen in der Kommunikation ständig vollzogenen Sprechakte, wie Aufforderung, Frage, etc.

Dann die *valorative* Funktion (bzw. Bühlers oder Jakobsons expressive Funktion): der Sprechende äußert nicht nur Propositionen, sondern er bewertet sie zudem. Bewertungen und verwendete Bewertungskategorien haben immer eine soziale Implikation, also eine wesentliche Bedeutung für die Beziehung zu Interaktionspartner und sozialer Gruppe.

Schließlich die Funktion des *sozialen Kontaktes:* Jeder kommunikative Akt etabliert oder kontrolliert einen sozialen Kontakt. Diese Funktion kann in mindestens zwei Subfunktionen ausdifferenziert werden. Der Sprecher kann einerseits, etwa durch den Gebrauch bestimmter Anredeformen, seine soziale Nähe oder Distanz zum Interaktionspartner ausdrücken; dies nenne ich die *Funktion der sozialen Distanz*. Der Sprecher kann andererseits seine Relation zur Sprechsituation und zum sozialen Umfeld durch die Wahl bestimmter Sprachregister wie Sozio- und Dialekte anzeigen; damit macht er von der *lektalen Funktion* Gebrauch.

Im Zwischenbereich von referentieller und interpersoneller Funktion wird also die textuelle Funktion lokalisiert; jeder Text umfaßt Strukturen, die – je nach Orientierung der Botschaft – mehr den pragmatischen oder mehr den semantischen Zielen dienen können. Dazu zählen Thema-Rhema, Fokussierungs-Funktion und Metasprache.

Ein derartiger, auf die Pragmatik ausgeweiteter markiertheitstheoretischer Ansatz

Semantaktische Kategorien	Textbezogene Kategorien	Pragmatische Kategorien
dominante Funktion		
darstellende (Bühler) bzw. referentielle Funktion (Jakobson)	textuelle Funktion (Halliday)	interpersonelle Funktion (Halliday) (einschließlich Bühlers expressiver und appellativer Funktion)
Universell		
IKONIZITÄT TRANSPARENZ		ILLOKUTIVE MARKIERUNG Deklarativ < Appell
3. Pers. Neutrum < 3. Pers. Humanum	Thema < Rhema (topic < comment)	VALORATIVE MARKIERUNG positiv < negativ
Singular < Plural	– Fokus < + Fokus	MARKIERUNG SOZIALER DISTANZ soziale Nähe < soziale Distanz
Aspekt < Tempus	– Metakommunikation < + Metakommunikation	LEKTALE MARKIERUNG Lekt mittlerer sozialer Gruppen < Lekt von Mikrogruppen/Supranormen
einfaches Präsens < einfache Vergangenheit, etc.	syntaktische Aggregation < Integration	
Aktiv < Reflexiv < Passiv		
Agens < Patiens, etc.		
Syntax < Morphologie		
Einzelsprachlich		
SYSTEMANGEMESSENHEIT FLEXIONSKLASSENSTABILITÄT		

Abb. 32.1 Übersicht über die MARKIERTHEITS-EBENEN (leicht variiertes Schema von Ludwig 1995)
Das Schema wird in § 4.3 anhand der Beispiele (2)–(14) erläutert.

trägt zudem der etablierten varietätenlinguistischen Rede der diatopisch oder diastratisch als hoch, niedrig u. ä. markierten Register Rechnung (s. etwa Scholz 1997).

4. Anwendungsbereiche

Weitere Anwendungsgebiete des Markiertheitsinstrumentariums als die unter § 4. genannten existieren. Im Zusammenhang mit der Entwicklung der Konzeption wurde bereits auf die diachrone Sprachwissenschaft (These: „Sprachwandel tendiert zur Unmarkiertheit") und den natürlichen Erstspracherwerb (These: „Unmarkierte Kategorien sind ontogenetisch primär") eingegangen. Der Bereich der Sprachkontaktforschung (unten § 4.3.) wird ausführlicher behandelt, da hier verschiedene Gesichtspunkte und Anwendungszonen des Markiertheitsbegriffs zusammentreffen.

4.1. Die Forschung zu Mündlichkeit und Schriftlichkeit

Zu den wesentlichen Ergebnissen der Mündlichkeit-Schriftlichkeits-Forschung zählt, daß inzwischen deutlich zwischen Medium (phonisch-graphischer Aspekt) und Konzeption (die individuell-psychologischen und gesellschaftlichen Funktionen typischer Schriftlichkeit sowie die damit in Zusammenhang stehenden textinternen Merkmale) geschieden wird (s. Koch & Oesterreicher 1994, Raible 1994, Ludwig 1996). Sowohl in medialer wie konzeptioneller Hinsicht erscheint, wie inzwischen auch von Givón dargelegt (s. o.), Mündlichkeit als der merkmallose Pol.

Dies zeigt sich deutlicher, wenn die oben dargelegten Markiertheitskriterien angelegt werden; demnach gilt für Mündlichkeit:

(i) Sie ist onto- und phylogenetisch primär
  (*D: Ontogenetisch früher Erwerb*).
(ii) Sie stellt kognitiv geringere Anforderungen
  (*C: Kognitiv einfache Prozessierung*).
(iii) Mündlichkeit deckt in jeder Gesellschaft die Vielzahl der elementaren, primären Nähebereiche ab, die die öffentlichen Distanzbereiche erst − im Sinne Husserls − fundieren
  (*A: Semantisch-kategorielle Extensionalität; E: Pragmatisch-kommunikative Priorität; G: Frequenz bezogen auf* UM_{KU-E}).
(iv) Sie füllt quantitativ den größeren Kommunikationsraum aus
  (*G: Frequenz bezogen auf* UM_{KE-FE}).
(v) Mündlichkeit kann in jeder Gesellschaft, die über Schriftgebrauch nicht verfügt, sämtliche Kommunikationsbereiche abdecken
  (*B: Tendenz oder Affinität zur Neutralisation*).

Auch die Trennung zwischen universaler und einzelsprachlicher Markiertheit kommt hier zum Tragen. Mündliche Sprachregister sind in vielfacher Hinsicht von der Tendenz zur Markiertheitsreduktion geprägt; dabei können aber Konflikte zwischen einzelsprachlicher und universaler Unmarkiertheit auftreten. Entsprechend kann in einer Einzelsprache − im Sinne von Wurzels Prinzip der Systemangemessenheit − ein (mithin unmarkiertes$_{KE-FE}$) Prinzip verallgemeinert werden, das aus universaler Perseptive markiert ist.

Im gesprochenen SPANISCH insbesondere von Lateinamerika wird beispielsweise zunehmend das synthetische 'Preterito indefinido' (*canté*: merkmallos$_{KE-FE}$, merkmalhaltig$_{KU}$) zuungunsten des analytischen 'Preterito perfecto' (*he cantado*: merkmalhaltig$_{KE-FE}$, merkmallos$_{KU}$) verallgemeinert.

Die Auffassung, daß Mündlichkeit im Verhältnis zur Schriftlichkeit unmarkiert ist, muß in einem Bereich eingeschränkt werden: sie bezieht sich vorrangig auf den Bereich der semantaktischen und textuellen Markierung. Im Falle einzelner pragmatischer Parameter ist Mündlichkeit offen für besondere Markierung, so im Fall der lektalen Markierung.

4.2. Anwendungsbereich Kreolistik

Die Kreolsprachen sind in vieler Hinsicht von den Parametern konzeptioneller, universaler Mündlichkeit geprägt; Konsequenz ist, daß ihre Systeme dominant merkmallos sind, wobei hier Prinzipien der universalen Unmarkiertheit mit einzelsprachlicher Merkmallosigkeit übereinstimmen (Ludwig 1996). Evidenz für diese allgemeine Hypothese liefern verschiedene Ansätze, selbst wenn diese im einzelnen nicht unkritisch übernommen werden dürfen; dazu zählt Bickertons Hypothese des „Bioprogramms" (Bickerton 1981; → Art. 7) oder auch die Hinweise zur besonderen Transparenz und Unmarkiertheit der Kreolsprachen (Muysken 1981; Mufwene 1991).

4.3. Anwendungsbereich Sprachkontaktforschung

Im Bereich der Sprachkontaktforschung ergeben sich verschiedene Anwendungsfelder. Dazu zählt die Forschung zum Erwerb einer zweiten Sprache (L_2), innerhalb derer ein Markiertheitsvergleich der Systeme von L_1 und L_2 (mithin Markiertheit$_{KE-FE}$ zusammen mit dem Vergleich mit universalen Markiertheitsparametern und der Frage von deren Abbildung im System von L_1 oder L_2 Lernprognosen erlaubt. Dieser Ansatz kommt in der „markedness differential hypothesis" zum Ausdruck (Schmid 1995: 270):

„The areas of difficulty that a language learner will have can be predicted on the basis of a systematic comparison of the grammars of the native language, the target language and the markedness relations stated in universal grammar, such that:

(a) Those areas of the target language which differ from the native language and are more marked than the native language will be difficult.
(b) The relative degree of difficulty of the areas of the target language which are more marked than those of the native language will correspond to the relative degree of markedness.
(c) Those areas of the target language which are different from the native language, but are not more marked than those of the native language will not be difficult."

Die „markedness differential hypothesis" läßt sich durchaus auf pragmatische Bereiche ausdehnen — vgl. dazu u. Beispiel (14).

Die Markiertheitstheorie wird weiter in der Forschung zum Kontakt historischer Einzelsprachen herangezogen. Eine Bilanz dieser Anwendungsmöglichkeiten wird von Thomason & Kaufman 1988 gezogen. Thomason & Kaufman stützen sich vorrangig auf das universal-typologische Kriterium „more widespread = less marked" und den ontogenetischen Evidenzparameter „first learned = less marked" (1988: 26 f.).

Die Hauptfrage ist, ob Sprachkontaktsituationen Markiertheit oder Unmarkiertheit generieren. In der älteren Debatte verzeichnen die Autoren beide Positionen (1988: 27—34):

(a) Sprachkontakt führt zur Ausbildung markierter Strukturen (Bailey, Traugott)
(b) Sprachkontakt führt zu einer Reduktion von Markiertheit (Givón, in gewisser Weise Bickerton).

Gemäß Thomason & Kaufman sind beide Tendenzen möglich, wobei kontradiktorische Markiertheitsentwicklungen in derselben Kontaktsituation auftreten können.

Im Folgenden werden beide Tendenzen wie auch die Möglichkeit einer gegenläufigen Markiertheitstendenz auf semantaktischer und pragmatischer Ebene gezeigt.

4.3.1. Semantaktische Markierung

4.3.1.1. Senkung von Merkmalhaltigkeit durch Sprachkontakt (→ Art. 115)

Dieser Typ ist zweifelsohne häufig. Hierher gehören die Überlegungen, daß große typologische Distanz zwischen Sprachen bei Lernprozessen, mündlichen Situationen u. ä. Tendenzen meist der universalen Unmarkiertheit in der entstehenden Kontaktsprache bzw. in der unvollständig erlernten Zielsprache verstärkt.

All diesen Phänomentypen liegt primär die Darstellungsfunktion der Sprache zugrunde: es geht darum, Sachverhalte zu kommunizieren und dafür den adäquaten Ausdruck zu finden: der Aufwand für die kognitive Prozessierung wird einerseits so gering wie möglich gehalten, wobei andererseits die Sicherung der differenzierten Sachverhaltsdarstellung der Reduktion des Prozessierungsaufwandes Schranken auferlegt. Dabei werden die Tendenzen universaler Unmarkiertheit vor allem dann stark ausgeprägt, wenn zwei mündliche Sprachen bzw. eine mündliche Sprache und ein mündliches Register einer Schriftsprache aufeinandertreffen, wenn also die eventuell existierenden Schriftnormen der Kontaktsprachen nicht relevant werden. Dazu einige Beispiele.

Beispiel: Demarkierung von Genusoppositionen im SPANISCHEN von QUECHUA- bzw. MAPUCHE-Sprechern:

Typisch für das lateinamerikanische SPANISCH sind Tendenzen zur Steigerung der formellen und kategoriellen Unmarkiertheit in manchen Bereichen der Endungsmorphologie und der Genusopposition bei aktantieller Markierung (Pronomina). Charakteristisch ist, daß hier die QUECHUA- bzw. MAPUCHE-Interferenz, wo keine Genus-Unterscheidung grammatikalisiert ist, eine in den mündlichen Registern der Zielsprache angelegte Tendenz verstärkt, und zwar oft über den Grad hinaus, in dem ein einsprachiger Substandardsprecher (der Zielsprache) dies realisieren würde. Im folgenden Beispiel ist das enklitische Genusmerkmal neutralisiert (es spricht eine ältere Frau; die darunterstehende kastilische Version ersetzt den grammatischen Kommentar):

(2) *ehtábamo chicoh yo ehtaba máh*
     estábamos chicos yo estaba más
     chiquitit^e y mi hermano máh
     chiquitita y mi hermano más
     grandecit^e
     grandecito

'Wir waren klein ich war kleiner und mein Bruder größer'. (CHILESPANISCH, Korpus R.L.)

Verstärkt wird hier:

- die universale Merkmallosigkeitstendenz zum Abbau des Femininum-Merkmals (KU+FE) (kritisch hierzu Rabofski 1990).
- die einzelsprachliche Tendenz zum Abbau von bestimmter Typen von Postdetermination im gesprochenen CHILENISCHEN (KE+FE).

Dies wird durch MAPUCHE-Interferenz gestützt, und zwar die im MAPUDUNGU nicht vorhandene Genusopposition sowie auch die nicht vorhandene Phonemopposition /o/:/u/.

Beispiel: Senkung der Merkmalhaltigkeit im Bereich der aktantiellen Markierung.

Bekannt ist, daß im amerikanischen SPANISCH beim Objektpronomen tendenziell die Form *lo* generalisiert wird; verloren geht also sowohl die Opposition [humaner Patiens] bzw. *lo* vs. *le* sowie die Genus-Unterscheidung, also *lo* vs. *la*. Bei primären QUECHUA-Sprechern fällt diese Tendenz wieder besonders stark aus (es fehlt die Konkordanz bei einem nahestehenden Referenten):

(3) *Las cosas que tenemos en Calca*
Las cosas que tenemos en Calca
los hemos hecho nosotros los
las hemos hecho nosotros los
calqueños.
calqueños
'Was wir in Calca haben, das haben wir, die Leute aus Calca, gemacht.'
(ANDINES SPANISCH, Peru; Klee 1990: 42)

Hier koinzidieren Substrateinfluß (die nicht vorhandene Genusopposition im QUECHUA), sowie die Tendenz zu einzelsprachlicher und universaler Markiertheit. Häufig kommt auf diesem Wege gleichzeitig lektale Markierung zustande, wenn nämlich – wie in dieser Situation – Nicht-QUECHUA-Sprecher diese Neutralisierung übernehmen, um sich als Mitglieder der andinen Lebenswelt auszuweisen.

Ein anderes Phänomen von Reduktion aktantieller Markierung nach universalen Tendenzen ist die Vereinfachung des Ausdrucks merkmalhaltiger Aktanten bzw. adverbialer Angaben. Dazu machen sich Sprecher des GUADELOUPEKREOLISCHEN kreolische Verfahren zunutze, etwa indem sie eine adverbiale Struktur agentiv reinterpretieren:

(4) *Mardi lui a donné un an* qu'il est de retour.
(GUADELOUPEFRANZÖSISCH, Korpus R.L.; in: Ludwig 1996a: 64)

Dies entspricht genau kreolisch

(5) *Mawdi ba-i   on lanné i*
Dienstag geben-3SG ein Jahr 3SG
viré.
zurückkehren-PFV

während es standardfranzösisch heißen müßte: '*Mardi, cela a fait un an* qu'il est de retour' oder *Il y a eu un an mardi* qu'il est de retour'.

Beispiel: Stärkung der universalen Merkmallosigkeit bei der prädikativen Deixis (Aspekt < Tempus).

Universal ist Aspekt merkmalloser als Tempus; typisch ist die Verstärkung der Kategorie 'Aspekt' durch Sprecher einer mündlichen Sprache mit Aspektdominanz.

Im folgenden Beispiel wird der Reflexiv zur Verstärkung des inchoativ-perfektiven Aspekts eingesetzt. Die aspektuelle Verwendung des Reflexivs läßt sich als metaphorischer Prozeß, und zwar als metaphorische Übertragung der verstärkten personalen auf die aspektuelle Deixis verstehen. Für die vom MAPUCHE beeinflußte Sprecherin typisch ist wieder die konsequente Weiterführung dieser Tendenz über die auch im informellen CHILENISCHEN übliche Grenze hinaus:

(6) *No quería que viniera porque se*
No quería que viniera porque
empezó a llorar.
empezó a llorar
'Er wollte nicht, daß ich käme, weil er dann anfing zu weinen' (CHILESPANISCH, Korpus Ludwig)

4.3.1.2. Entlehnung einzelsprachlich markierter Strukturen aus Schriftsprachen zur Ausweitung merkmalhaltiger Register der Empfängersprache

Insbesondere in Verschriftlichungsprozessen kann Sprachkontakt auch zur Erhöhung semantaktischer Markiertheit genutzt werden. Mündliche Sprachen wie das Kreol tendieren, wenn sie in neuer Weise als 'high variety' verwendet werden, zur Entlehnung etwa von merkmalhaltigen lexikalischen Ausdrücken und morphosyntaktischen Verfahren aus der zur Verfügung stehenden Schriftsprache.

Im folgenden Beispiel sind alle kursiv oder in Kapitälchen gesetzten Wörter Entlehnungen aus dem FRANZÖSISCHEN (Kapitälchen zeigen zunächst den Wechsel zur französischen Standard-Orthographie an):

(7) dé moman konférans an-nou pa'a fèt asi *mod piblisitèr ki* ka *konsisté a énoncé* on sèrten nonb dè vérité ORDINAIRE DU STYLE nou ké gangné fo nou gangné nou ké chanjé LA SITUATION fè nou konfyans èvè nou biten-la ké maché byen nou ké ni on gran politik kiltirèl nou ké ni on gran *politik ékonomik* nou ké ni on gran *politik agrikol* èksétéra rakonté onlo bèl pawol ki pa ni pon sans pon CONTENU épi apré lèwvwè sc population-la rantré akaz a-y [...]
(GUADELOUPEKREOL, Korpus R.L.; in: Ludwig 1996)
'Unsere Konferenzveranstaltungen sind nicht nach dem Reklame-Verfahren gemacht, das darin besteht, eine gewisse Anzahl von allgemeinen Wahrheiten zu verkünden, des Typs 'wir werden gewinnen, wir müssen gewinnen, wir werden die Lage verändern, schenkt uns euer Vertrauen, mit uns werden die Sachen gut funktionieren, wir werden eine große Kulturpolitik haben, wir werden eine große Wirtschaftspolitik haben, wir werden eine große Landwirtschaftspolitik haben', u.s.w., eine Menge schöner Worte, die keinen Sinn haben, keinen Inhalt, und danach, wenn die Versammlung nach Hause zurückkehrt [...]'

Ein anderes Beispiel für die Übernahme markierter Muster zur Erweiterung merkmalhaltiger Register der Zielsprache ist die Ausbildung eines Artikelsystems im MAPUDUNGU (Salas 1992: 40f.).

4.3.2. Textuelle Markierung

Beispiel: Demarkierung der Positionsregeln zum Zwecke der Fokussierung.

Verstärkte Fokussierungen sind ein typisch mündliches Verfahren, das seine Funktionen im Grenzbereich von Expressivität (valorative Markierung) und Verbesserung der Textkohärenz mit dem Ziel der Verdeutlichung des Botschaftsinhalts hat. Quechuasprecher, die ohnehin nicht an der SVO-Grundstellung des SPANISCHEN ausgerichtet sind, verstärken mithin die im SPANISCHEN durchaus angelegte positionale Freiheit zu Fokussierungszwecken, freilich über das sonst zulässige Maß hinaus:

(8) *Julio es.*
(statt *es Julio*)
'Es ist Julio.' (ANDINES SPANISCH, Peru; Benavente 1988: 242)

Beispiel: Entlehnung merkmalhaltiger, integrativer Junktoren zur Herstellung von Textgliederung, argumentativen Schemata u. ä.

Das Kreol ist (auch) im morphosyntaktischen Bereich eine stark aggregative Sprache (zu den Begriffe 'Aggregativität' und 'Integrativität' im Bereich von Lexik, Morphsyntax und Pragmatik s. Ludwig 1996; zu deren Definition spezieller im Bereich der grammatischen Junktion Raible 1992). Da im Kreol viele merkmalhaltige, integrative Junktoren fehlen, greifen bilinguale Sprecher oft auf das FRANZÖSISCHE zurück, sodaß bestimmte Junktoren in ein schriftlicher geprägtes Kreol eingegangen sind, wie *kè, paskè* und *don*:

(9) *mé nou ké di kè fo ni pwogram-la é fo ni on ékip pou apliké pwogram-la paskè si ou pa ni on ékip ki kapab* D'APPLIQUER *program-lasa program-la ké rèsté si papyé i pé ké apliké donk fo i ni a chak domèn déterminé dézom ki konpétan.*
(GUADELOUPEKREOL, Korpus R.L.; in: Ludwig 1996)
'aber wir werden sagen, daß es das Programm geben muß und das es eine Mannschaft geben muß, um das Programm anzuwenden, da, wenn du keine Mannschaft hast, die fähig ist, dieses Programm anzuwenden, das Programm auf dem Papier bleiben wird, es wird nicht angewendet werden, daher ist es nötig, daß es in jedem spezifischen Bereich kompetente Menschen gibt.'

Beispiel: Entlehnung merkmalloser Mittel zur Textgliederung.

Wenn in einer mündlichen Zielsprache keine durch eine besonders offizielle Aussageintention oder schriftliche Textsorte implizierte integrative Textstruktur vorgegeben ist, kommt es auch zur Entlehnung typisch mündlich-unmarkierter, polyfunktionaler Gliederungspartikel, in diesem Fall aus dem SPANISCHEN in das QUECHUA:

(10) *I wakmanta, wak kiti Dios kamachirqan:*

– *Bueno qan llaqta runata nimunki: Llaqta runakuna mikhunkichik huq kutillata p'unchaw sapa p'unchaw-nispa no?*.
('Cierta vez, Dios ordenó al Akakllo: – Bueno, vas a decirle a la gente del pueblo que sólo debe comer una vez al día; así día tras día.')
'Einst befahl Gott dem Akakllo: Gut, geh den Leuten vom Dorf sagen, sie sollen nur einmal am Tag essen; und so Tag für Tag.' (Peruanisches QUECHUA; in: Chirinos & Maque 1996: 349; 188).

Beispiel: Unvollständige Beherrschung von Kohärenzmustern; Kohärenzschwächen.

Für den muttersprachlichen Sprecher des stark aggregativen Kreols (im folgenden Beispiel ein Journalist) wird auch bei fortgeschrittenem Bilinguismus die Verwendung integrativer Junktionstechniken öfters zum Problem:

(11) Une de ces *manifestations dont on aurait aimé assister* un peu plus souvent; une de ces émissions promotionnelles et originales qui ne font qu'enrichir notre patrimoine culturel.
(GUADELOUPEFRANZÖSISCH, France-Antilles, 30.07.94, 8; in: Ludwig 1996a: 65)

Der angemessene Ausdruck im Standardfranzösischen wäre: *auxquelles on aimerait assister un peu plus souvent*.

4.3.3. Pragmatische Markierung

Stellvertretend werden zwei Bereiche angeführt.

4.3.3.1. Valorative Markierung

Häufige valorative Markierungen sind universal typisch für mündliche Register bzw. insgesamt mündlich geprägte Sprachen. Damit ist der Kernbereich dessen gemeint, was üblicherweise als 'Expressivität' oder 'Affektivität' bezeichnet wird. Charakteristisch ist, daß eine Sprache wie das QUECHUA solche – in seinem eigenen System wichtige – valorativ-expressiven Ausdrücke aus dem gesprochenen SPANISCH übernimmt:

(12) *Chaysi huk p'unchay Inka warminta nisqa: – Carajo! Chay wintun mana llank'aqta dejawanchu, huk kanchamanmi wisq'amusaq hasta Qosqo ruway tukunaykama.*
'Así, un día, el Inka había dicho a su mujer: – ¡Carajo! Este viento no me deja trabajar, voy a encerrarlo en una cancha hasta que termine de hacer el Cusco.'
'So, eines Tages hatte der Inka zu seiner Frau gesagt: Carajo! Dieser Wind läßt mich nicht arbeiten, ich werde ihn auf einem Platz einschließen bis ich fertig werde, Cuzco zu errichten.'
(Peruanisches QUECHUA; in: Valderrama Fernandez & Escalante Gutierrez 1982: 19)

4.3.3.2. Lektale Markierung

Lektale Markierungen weisen einen Sprecher als Mitglied einer bestimmten Gruppe aus.

Beispiel: Sprachmischung bzw. Codeswitching als Symbol 'höherer' Gesellschaftszugehörigkeit.

Will ein Guadelouper in einem insgesamt kreolischen Diskurs einer Aussage besonderes Gewicht verleihen und sich sozial aufwerten, wird er sich bemühen, an dieser Stelle französische Elemente einfließen zu lassen, selbst wenn er dieser Sprache kaum mächtig ist: L, eine alte Dame, ist nie zur Schule gegangen und spricht eigentlich nur Kreol. Gleichwohl hat sie im Laufe der Zeit einige französische Wendungen aufgenommen:

(13) ébyen mwen an ka touvé an tan anmwen té MIEUX ki tan aprézan
SC AUSSI BIEN QUE QUAND ou vwè ou té jwenn on granmoun.
an lari fò ou té di bonjou manzè entèl
'Eh bien moi, je pense que c'était mieux de mon temps qu'à présent. Par exemple, quand on rencontrait un adulte dans la rue, il fallait dire «Bonjour Mademoiselle Une telle»'.
(Korpus Ludwig/Telchid & Bruneau-Ludwig 2001)

Zunächst verwendet L das französische Adverb *mieux* statt kreolisch *méyè* oder *pimyé*. Anschließend streut sie französisch *aussi bien que* ein, was weder syntaktisch noch semantisch in den Kontext paßt, bevor sie den folgenden Satz mit *quand* statt kreolisch *lè* einleitet. (Zur Anwendung des Markiertheitskonzepts auf Codeswitching s. Myers-Scotton 1993 u. kritisch dazu Meeuwis & Blommaert 1994).

Beispiel: Inkohärenz lektaler Markierung durch Interferenz einer mündlichen Sprache.

Das GUADELOUPEKREOLISCHE ist wenig nach lektalen Ebenen, nach Stilniveaus untergliedert. Will nun ein kreolophoner, fortgeschritten bilingualer Journalist ein besonders 'hohes' FRANZÖSISCH zur Schau stellen, kann ihn die mangelnde Gewohnheit differenzierter lektaler Markierung in Stilkonflikte bringen. Im folgenden Beispiel kontrastieren das familiär markierte *pour ces gamins* und das gesucht literarfranzösisch markierte *s'adonnent au sein d'* ... unbeabsichtigt stark.

(14) *Des espaces de jeux ont été créés pour ces gamins. C'est ainsi qu'ils s'adonnent au sein d'ateliers spécifiques à la peinture, au dessin, au moulage à l'aide de plâtre.*
(GUADELOUPEFRANZÖSISCH, France-Antilles, 28.07.94, 7; in: Ludwig 1996a: 66)

5. Theoretische Vermittlungen des Markiertheitsbegriffes

5.1. Markiertheit und Prototypikalität

Seit einiger Zeit wird in sprachwissenschaftlichen Beschreibungen ein Konzept aufgegriffen, das in den siebziger Jahren insbesondere von Eleanor Rosch entwickelt worden ist: die 'Prototypikalität'. 'Merkmallosigkeit' und 'Prototypikalität' sind in vieler Hinsicht eng benachbart, ja in einigen Definitionen wird 'Prototypikalität' zu einer speziellen Verwendung von 'Merkmallosigkeit' (Dressler 1990: 85 f., Battistella 1990: 41–44).

Ausgehend von Wittgensteins Konzept der 'Familienähnlichkeit' erscheint der Prototyp als der merkmallose, typischste Vertreter einer Klasse oder Kategorie; im Vergleich zum Prototyp können andere Glieder der Kategorie als peripherer, weniger typisch, m. E. als merkmalhaltiger bestimmt werden. Folgende Charakteristika des traditionellen prototypischen Ansatzes lassen sich nennen (s. Welke 1988: 195 f.; Croft 1990: 125; Kleiber 1990; Taylor 1995; Wierzbicka 1996):

- Eine Kategorie hat einen prototypischen Vertreter, der mit den anderen Gliedern die meisten Merkmale gemein hat.
- Ob ein Element einer Kategorie zugerechnet wird, hängt vom Grad der in Merkmalen faßbaren Familienähnlichkeit mit dem Prototyp ab.
- Zwei Elemente können zur selben Klasse gehören, obwohl sie nur gemeinsame Merkmale mit dem Prototyp, nicht aber untereinander aufweisen.
- Die Peripherie einer Kategorie ist häufig schwer genau zu determinieren.
- Die Merkmale können nach ihrer Wichtigkeit gestaffelt werden.

Croft (1990) sieht die Voraussetzung der Verbindung von Unmarkiertheit und Prototypikalität in der Kombinatorik eines unmarkierten Merkmalbündels (1990: 124 f.; logischerweise können einzelne Merkmale bzw. unmarkierte Wesenszüge keinen Prototypen stellen). Wie im Fall des (Un-)Markiertheitsbegriffs kann die Prototypikalität einer Kategorie ein universales oder außereinzelsprachliches Phänomen sein. So stützt sich der prototypische Ansatz wesentlich auf Arbeiten der kognitiven Psychologie; ein oft genanntes Kriterium für die Bestimmung des Prototyps ist die Frequenz. Eine explizite Trennung zwischen semantischer und grammatischer Prototypikalität wird beispielsweise von Suzanne Kemmer vorgenommen. Semantische Prototypikalität kann Einzelgesellschaften oder – wie die Analyse der Farbbegriffe von Brent Berlin und Paul Kay zeigt – die universale Ebene betreffen; grammatische Prototypikalität ist, so eine von Kemmers Thesen, universaler Natur (Kemmer 1992: 147 f.). Grammatische Protoypikalität wird definiert:

We can define a grammatical prototype as a type of conceived situation (which I will refer to as a 'situation type' following Talmy 1972) that overwhelmingly tends, across languages, to be associated with a particular morphosyntactic form. Grammatical prototypes represent the situation types that are most often kept formally distinct from one another across languages. This tendency toward formal distinctness is a consequence of the privileged cognitive status of these categories. (1992: 148)

Innerhalb der grammatischen Protoypen trennt Kemmer zwischen markierten und unmarkierten Prototypen. Transitivität und Intransitivität wären unmarkierte Prototypen, Reflexivität wäre hingegen ein markierter Prototyp.

5.2. Markiertheit und Optimalitätstheorie

Die Optimalitätstheorie, die seit Beginn der 90er Jahre namentlich von Alan Price und Paul Smolensky entwickelt wurde, nimmt ihren Ausgangspunkt in der zentralen generativistischen Theorie, wonach eine begrenzte Anzahl sprachlicher Universalien Teil des genetischen Erbguts des Menschen sind (s.

den Überblick von Archangeli 1997, weiterhin im WWW „Rutgers Optimality Archive"). Diese Universalien gehen in Beschränkungen („constraints") ein, die hierarchisiert sind; je höher die hierarchische Stufe der jeweiligen Beschränkung, desto weiter verbreitet, mithin desto unmarkierter ist sie.

Zwischen einzelnen Regeln der Hierarchie können Konflikte auftreten; der „evaluator" selektiert dann für einen bestimmten Input die optimale sprachliche Lösung. Alle Regeln sind daher verletzbar; präferiert wird aber die Erfüllung der hierarchisch höher eingestuften Regel. In diesem Sinne bedeutet 'Unmarkiertheit' minimale Verletzbarkeit von Regeln (Archangeli 1997: 25).

Mit der Optimalitätstheorie wird der Markiertheitsbegriff also − wieder − zu einem zentralen Instrument der Sprachwissenschaft.

6. Zitierte Literatur

Archangeli, Diana. 1997. „Optimality theory: An introduction to linguistics in the 1990s". In: Archangeli, Diana & Langendoen, Terence. *Optimality theory. An overview.* (Explaining linguistics.) Malden/MA: Blackwell, 1−32.

Andersen, Henning. 1989. „Markedness Theory: The First 150 Years". In: Tomić 1989: 11−46.

Asher, Ronald E. & Simpson, J.M.Y. (eds.). 1994. *The Encyclopedia of Language and Linguistics.* Vol. 5. Oxford & New York: Pergamon Press.

Battistella, Edwin L. 1990. *Markedness. The Evaluative Superstructure of Language.* (SUNY series in linguistics.) Albany/NY: State University of New York Press.

Battistella, Edwin L. 1996. *The Logic of Markedness.* New York: Oxford University Press.

Benavente, Sonia. 1988. „Algunos rasgos sintácticos del castellano en alumnos universitarios puñenos". In: López, Luis Enrique (ed.). *Pesquisas en lingüística andina.* Lima: Consejo Nacional de Ciencia y Tecnología Universidad Nacional del Altiplano, 237−51.

Bickerton, Derek. 1981. *Roots of Language.* Ann Arbor: Karoma.

Boretzky, Norbert & Enninger, Werner & Jeßing, Benedikt & Stolz, Thomas (eds.). 1991. *Sprachwandel und seine Prinzipien. Beiträge zum 8. Bochum-Essener Kolloquium über Sprachwandel und seine Prinzipien.* Bochum: Brockmeyer.

Bühler, Karl. 1934/1965. *Sprachtheorie. Die Darstellungsfunktion der Sprache.* Stuttgart: Fischer.

Chirinos Rivera, Andrés & Maque Capira, Alejo. 1996. *Eros andino. Alejo Khunku willawanchik.* (Biblioteca de la tradición oral andina, 16.) Edición bilingüe, Cusco: Centro de Estudios Regionales Andinos „Bartolomé de Las Casas".

Chomsky, Noam. 1981. *Lectures on Government and Binding.* (Studies in generative grammar, 9.) Dordrecht: Foris.

Chomsky Noam. 1981a. „Markedness and Core Grammar". In: Belletti, Adriana & Brandi, L. & Rizzi, Luigi (eds.). *Theory of Markedness in Generative Grammar. Proceedings of the 1979 GLOW Conference.* Pisa: Scuola Normale Superiore di Pisa, 123−46.

Chomsky, Noam & Halle, Morris. 1968. *Principes de phonologie générative.* Paris: Seuil.

Chomsky, Noam & Lasnik, Howard. 1977. „Filters and Control". *Linguistic Inquiry* 8: 425−504.

Comrie, Bernard. 1986. „Markedness, Grammar, People, and the World". In: Eckman & Moravcsik & Wirth 1986, 85−106.

Croft, William. 1990. *Typology and Universals.* (Cambridge textbooks in linguistics.) Cambridge: Cambridge University Press.

Dardano, Maurizio. 1994. „Profilo dell'italiano contemporaneo". In: Serianni, Luca & Trifone, Pietro (eds.). *Storia della lingua italiana. Volume secondo: Scritto e parlato.* Torino: Einaudi, 343−430.

Davis, Garry W. & Iverson, Gregory K. (eds.). 1992. *Explanation in Historical Linguistics.* (Amsterdam studies in the theory and history of linguistic Science, Series 4, current issues in linguistic theory, 84.) Amsterdam & Philadelphia: Benjamins.

Dressler, Wolfgang U. (ed.). 1987. *Leitmotifs in Natural Morphology.* (Studies in language: Companion series, 10.) Amsterdam & Philadelphia: Benjamins.

Dressler, Wolfgang U. 1989. „Markedness and Naturalness in Phonology: The Case of Natural Phonology". In: Tomić 1989: 111−20.

Dressler, Wolfgang U. 1990. „The Cognitive Perspective of 'Naturalist' Linguistic Models". *Cognitive Linguistics* 1: 75−98.

Dressler, Wolfgang U. 1992. „Marked and Unmarked Text Strategies within Semiotically Based Natural Textlinguistics". In: Hwang, Shin Ja J. & Merrifield, William R. (eds.). *Language in Context: Essays for Robert E. Longacre.* (Summer Institute of linguistics and The University of Texas at Arlington publications in linguistics, 107.) Dallas: Summer Institute of Linguistics, 5−18.

Eckman, Fred R. & Moravcsik, Edith A. & Wirth, Jessica (eds.). 1986. *Markedness. Proceedings of the 12th Annual Linguistics Symposium of the Univ. of Wisconsin-Milwaukee, held March 11-12, 1983.* New York: Plenum.

Faingold, Eduardo D. 1995. „The Emergence of the Article System in Language Acquisition, Creolization, and History: A Universal Hierarchy of Natural Morphological Markedness". In: Pishwa & Marold 1995: 135−61.

Fenk-Oczlon, Gertraud. 1991. "Frequenz und Kognition – Frequenz und Markiertheit". *Folia Linguistica* 25: 361–94.

Forner, Monika & Gundel, Jeanette K. & Houlihan, Kathleen & Sanders, Gerald. 1992. "On the Historical Development of Marked Forms". In: Davis & Iverson 1992, 77–93.

Gauger, Hans-Martin. 1993. "Tipología y conciencia lingüística: marca, naturalidad, iconicidad, transparencia, prototipicalidad". In: Hilty, Gerold (ed.). *Actes du XXe Congrès International de Linguistique et Philologie Romanes.* vol. III. Tübingen: Francke, 113–24.

Givón, Talmy. 1990. *Syntax. A Functional-Typological Introduction.* Vol. II. Amsterdam & Philadelphia: Benjamins.

Givón, Talmy. 1991. "Markedness in Grammar: Distributional, Communicative and Cognitive Correlates of Syntactic Structure". *Studies in Language* 15: 335–70.

Greenberg, Joseph H. 1966. *Language Universals. With special reference to feature hierarchies.* (Janua Linguarum, Series Minor, 59.) The Hague & Paris: Mouton.

Günther, Hartmut & Ludwig, Otto (eds.). 1994. *Schrift und Schriftlichkeit. Ein interdisziplinäres Handbuch internationaler Forschung.* (Handbücher der Sprach- und Kommunikationswissenschaft, 10.1.) Berlin & New York: de Gruyter.

Heger, Klaus. 1976. *Monem, Wort, Satz und Text.* (Konzepte der Sprach- und Literaturwissenschaft, 8.) Tübingen: Niemeyer.

Heger, Klaus. 1981. "Außersprachlichkeit – Außereinzelsprachlichkeit – Übereinzelsprachlichkeit". In: Weydt, Harald & al. (eds.). *Logos Semantikos. Studia linguistica in honorem Eugenio Coseriu.* Vol. II: *Sprachtheorie und Sprachphilosophie.* Berlin: de Gruyter, 67–76.

Husserl, Edmund. ²1913/1980. *Logische Untersuchungen II/1: Untersuchungen zur Phänomenologie und Theorie der Erkenntnis.* Unveränderter Nachdruck. Tübingen: Niemeyer.

Jakobson, Roman. 1932/1984. "Structure of the Russian Verb". In: Jakobson, Roman 1984, 1–14.

Jakobson, Roman. 1944/⁴1978. *Kindersprache, Aphasie und allgemeine Lautgesetze.* (Edition Suhrkamp, 330.) Frankfurt/Main: Suhrkamp.

Jakobson, Roman. 1957/1984. "Shifters, Verbal Categories, and the Russian Verb". In: Jakobson, Roman. 1984, 41–58.

Jakobson, Roman. 1960. "Linguistics and Poetics". In: Sebeok, Thomas A. (ed.). *Style in Language.* Cambridge/MA: MIT, 350–77.

Jakobson, Roman. 1974/²1979. "Zur Notwendigkeit einer sachlichen und terminologischen Unterscheidung". In: Jakobson 1979, 279 f.

Jakobson, Roman (ed.). 1975. *N.S. Trubetzkoy's Letters and Notes.* (Janua linguarum, series maior, 47.) The Hague & Paris: Mouton.

Jakobson, Roman. ²1979. *Aufsätze zur Linguistik und Poetik.* Ed. Wolfgang Raible. (Ullstein-Buch, 35005.) Frankfurt a.M.: Ullstein.

Jakobson, Roman. 1984. *Russian and Slavic Grammar. Studies 1931–1981.* (Ianua linguarum: Series maior, 106.) Berlin: Mouton de Gruyter.

Jakobson, Roman & Halle, Morris. 1956/1979. "Phonologie und Phonetik". Zit. nach Jakobson 1979, 54–106.

Jakobson, Roman & Pomorska, Krystyna. 1982. *Poesie und Grammatik. Dialoge.* (Suhrkamp-Taschenbuch Wissenschaft, 386.) Frankfurt/Main: Suhrkamp.

Kemmer, Suzanne. 1992. "Grammatical Prototypes and Competing Motivations in a Theory of Linguistic Change". In: Davis & Iverson 1992: 145–66.

Klee, Carol A. 1990. "Spanish-Quechua Language Contact". *Word* 41: 35–46.

Kleiber, Georges. 1990. *La sémantique du prototype. Catégories et sens lexical.* (Linguistique nouvelle.) Paris: Presses Universitaires de France.

Koch, Peter & Oesterreicher, Wulf. 1994. "Schriftlichkeit und Sprache". In: Günther & Ludwig 1994: 587–604.

Lehmann, Christian. 1989. "Markedness and Grammaticalization". In: Tomić 1989: 175–90.

Liberman, Anatoly. 1996. "Phonological Markedness and a Plea for Useful Linguistics". Andrews, Edna & Tobin, Yishai (eds.). *Toward a Calculus of Meaning. Studies in Markedness, Distinctive Features and Deixis.* (Studies in functional and structural linguistics, 43.) Amsterdam & Philadelphia: Benjamins, 55–69.

Ludwig, Ralph. 1995. "Lingüística funcional, la teoría de la marcadez y el español de América: el caso del habla chilena". *Boletín de filología* [Universidad de Chile] 35: 275–316.

Ludwig, Ralph. 1996. *Kreolsprachen zwischen Mündlichkeit und Schriftlichkeit. Zur Syntax und Pragmatik atlantischer Kreolsprachen auf französischer Basis.* (ScriptOralia, 86.) Tübingen: Narr.

Ludwig, Ralph. 1996a. "Langues en contact: Évolutions du créole guadeloupéen". In: Yacou, Alain (ed.). *Créoles de la Caraïbe. Actes du colloque universitaire en hommage à Guy Hazaël-Massieux, Pointe-à-Pitre, le 27 mars 1995.* Paris: Karthala, 57–70.

Ludwig, Ralph & Telchid, Sylviane & Bruneau-Ludwig, Florence. 2001. *Corpus créole. Textes oraux dominicais, guadeloupéeens, guyanais, haïtiens, mauriciens et seychellois: enregistrements, transcriptions et traductions.* En collaboration avec Stefan Pfänder et Didier de Robillard, Paris, à paraître [Études Créoles, Volume spécial].

Mayerthaler, Willi. 1981. *Morphologische Natürlichkeit.* (Linguistische Forschungen, 28.) Wiesbaden: Athenaion.

Mayerthaler, Willi. 1987. „System-Independent Morphological Naturalness". In: Dressler 1987: 25–58.

Meeuwis, Michael & Blommaert, Jan. 1994. „Review Article: The 'Markedness Model' and the Absence of Society: Remarks on Codeswitching". *Multilingua* 13: 387–423.

Mikame, Hirofumi. 1996. „Markierte Perspektive, perspektivische Annäherung des Sprechers an das Objekt und direkte Wahrnehmung. Zur Signalisierung der psychisch-kognitiven Nähe des Sprechers zum Objekt." *Sprachwissenschaft* 21: 367–413.

Moravcsik, Edith A. & Wirth, Jessica. 1986. „Markedness – An Overview". In: Eckman & Moravcsik & Wirth 1986: 1–11.

Mufwene, Salikoko. 1991. „Pidgins, Creoles, Typology, and Markedness". In: Byrne, Francis & Huebner, Tom (eds.). *Development and Structures of Creole Languages. Essais in honor of Derek Bickerton.* (Creole language library, 9.) Amsterdam & Philadelphia: Benjamins, 123–43.

Muysken, Pieter. 1981. „Creole Tense – Mood – Aspect Systems: The Unmarked Case?". In: Muysken, Pieter (ed.). *Generative Studies on Creole Languages.* (Studies in generative grammar, 6.). Dordrecht: Foris, 181–99.

Myers-Scotton, Carol. 1993. *Social Motivations for Codeswitching. Evidence from Africa.* (Oxford Studies in language contact.) Oxford: Clarendon Press.

Pishwa, Hanna & Maroldt, Karl (eds.). 1995. *The Development of Morphological Systematicity. A Cross-linguistic Perspective.* (Tübinger Beiträge zur Linguistik, 399.) Tübingen: Narr.

Prado, Marcial. 1982. „El género en español y la teoría de la marcadez". *Hispania* 65: 258–66.

Rabofski, Birgit. 1990. *Motion und Markiertheit. Synchrone und sprachhistorische Evidenz aus dem Gotischen, Althochdeutschen und Altenglischen für eine Widerlegung der Theorien zur Markiertheit.* Frankfurt/Main etc.: Lang.

Raible, Wolfgang. 1992. *Junktion. Eine Dimension der Sprache und ihre Realisierungsformen zwischen Aggregation und Integration.* (Sitzungsberichte der Heidelberger Akademie der Wissenschaften, Phil.-hist. Klasse, Jg. 1992.2.) Heidelberg: Winter.

Raible, Wolfgang. 1994. „Orality and Literacy". In: Günther & Ludwig (eds.) 1994: 1–17.

Renzi, Lorenzo (ed.). 1988. *Grande grammatica italiana di consultazione.* (Linguistica e critica letteraria.) Bologna: Il Mulino.

Rutgers Optimality Archive: http://ruccs.rutgers.edu/roa.html

Salas, Adalberto. 1992. *El mapuche o araucano. Fonología, gramática y antología de cuentos.* (Colecciones MAPFRE, 1492.5, Colección lenguas y literaturas indígenas, 3.) Madrid: MAPFRE.

Samaniego Aldazábal, José Luis. 1993. „Usos, funciones y significados, según Halliday". In: Matus Olivier, Alfredo & al. (eds.). *Lingüística hoy. Algunas tendencias.* Santiago de Chile: Ediciones Universidad Católica de Chile, 61–74.

Schmid, Stephan. 1995. „Morphological Naturalness in Spanish-Italian Interlanguages". In: Pishwa & Maroldt 1995: 263–91.

Scholz, Arno. 1997. „Das Varietätenspektrum des Italienischen im Wandel". In: Mattheier, Klaus J. & Radtke, E. (eds.). *Standardisierung und Destandardisierung europäischer Nationalsprachen.* (Variolingua, 1.) Frankfurt/Main etc.: Lang, 61–86.

Smith, N.V. 1981. „Consistency, Markedness and Language Change: On the Notion 'Consistent Language'". *JL* 17: 39–54.

Seuren, Pieter A.M. & Wekker, Herman. 1986. „Semantic Transparency as a Factor in Creole Genesis". In: Muysken, Pieter & Smith, M. (eds.). *Substrata versus Universals in Creole Genesis. Papers from the Amsterdam Creole Workshop, April 1985.* (Creole language library, 1.) Amsterdam & Philadelphia: Benjamins, 57–71.

Simone, Raffaele (ed.). 1995. *Iconicity in Language. Papers presented at a conference held Oct. 1992, Rome, Italy.* (Amsterdam studies in the theory of linguistic science, Series 4; current issues in linguistic theory, 110.) Amsterdam & Philadelphia: Benjamins.

Taylor, John R. 1995. *Linguistic Categorization: Prototypes in Linguistic Theory.* 2. Ausg., Oxford: Clarendon.

Thomason, Sarah Grey & Kaufman, Terrence. 1988. *Language Contact, Creolization, and Genetic Linguistics.* Berkeley etc.: University of California Press.

Tomić, Olga M. (ed.). 1989. *Markedness in Synchrony and Diachrony.* (Trends in linguistics, studies and monographs, 39.) Berlin etc.: de Gruyter.

Tomić, Olga M. 1989a. „Introduction". In: Tomić 1989: 1–10.

Trubetzkoy, Nikolaj S. 1958/⁶1977. *Grundzüge der Phonologie.* Göttingen: Vandenhoeck & Ruprecht.

Valderrama Fernandez, Ricardo & Escalante Gutierrez, Carmen (eds.). ²1982. *Gregorio Condori Mamani. Autobiografia.* (Biblioteca de la tradicion oral andina, 2 (2.1).) Cusco: Centro de Estudios Rurales Andinos.

Waugh, Linda R. & Lafford, B.A. 1994. „Markedness". In: Asher & Simpson (eds.), 2378–83.

Welke, Klaus M. 1988. *Einführung in die Valenz- und Kasustheorie.* Leipzig: Bibliographisches Institut.

Wierzbicka, Anna. 1996. *Semantics: Primes and Universals.* Oxford: Oxford University Press.

Wurzel, Wolfgang U. 1984. *Flexionsmorphologie und Natürlichkeit. Ein Beitrag zur morphologischen Theoriebildung.* (Studia grammatica, 21.) Berlin: Akademie-Verlag.

Wurzel, Wolfgang U. 1987. „System-Dependent Morphological Naturalness in Inflection". In: Dressler 1987: 59−96.

Wurzel, Wolfgang U. 1989. „Inflectional Class Markedness". In: Tomić 1989: 227−47.

Wurzel, Wolfgang U. 1991. „Morphologisierung − Komplexität − Natürlichkeit. Ein Beitrag zur Begriffsklärung". In: Boretzky & al., 129−53.

Wurzel, Wolfgang U. 1994. „Natural Morphology". In: Asher & Simpson (eds.), 2590−98.

Wurzel, Wolfgang U. 1998. „On Markedness". *Theoretical Linguistics* 24: 53−71.

Ralph Ludwig, Universität Halle-Wittenberg (Deutschland)

33. Sampling procedures and statistical methods

1. Introduction
2. Statistical inference
3. Sampling
4. Statistical models
5. Possibilities and problems of statistical methods
6. Examples of statistical methods in typological research
7. Conclusion
8. References

1. Introduction

Motivation: There is a fundamental difference of opinion among statisticians as to the conceptual foundations of statistics. One school holds that probabilities are a measure of belief, ranging between 0 and 1, that an event will occur based on evidence and prior beliefs about the likelihood of the event. A second view is that probabilities are frequency measures with odds between 0 and 1 of events happening over the long term. A third view holds that probability is an abstract concept that we can use to accept or reject a hypothesis based on data according to whether those data result in a number above or below a pre-selected significance level between 0 and 1. Each group has substantial criticisms of the other two (Howson & Urbach 1993: 51−74, Glymour & al. 1987: 15−40).

Statistics is complex to use as a research tool, with many opportunities for mistakes that result in invalid, if not foolish, outcomes. So why use a method that has no agreed-upon conceptual basis, is difficult to apply and prone to error? The answer is that despite these shortcomings, STATISTICAL METHODS provide the only known means for validly and reliably summarizing large amounts of data, such as are commonly treated in typological research. Typological linguists will find a substantial number of resources in the domain of statistics to assist them in supporting linguistic hypotheses based on evidence from existing languages.

Joseph H. Greenberg (1963; → art. 23) introduced the use of language samples for drawing inferences about language in general. He made substantial progress without resorting to the use of more formal statistical methods. Bell (1978) provides a useful introduction to sampling for the linguist. Naroll (1973, b, c) furnishes a substantial treatment of various considerations relating to sampling in cultural anthropology, treating concerns that considerably overlap those in linguistics. For linguists the textbook by Woods & al. (1986) is excellent in its coverage of basic inferential statistics and also deals extensively with issues of sampling. Most of the general background statements made in this article may be confirmed there. Blalock (1972) provides an excellent introduction to statistical methods for testing social science hypotheses and Blalock (1964) addresses the theory and practice of causal inferences in nonexperimental research. Cochran (1977) is one of many sophisticated treatments of sampling that emphasize statistical approaches.

Statistical methods quantify the degree to which an assertion in the form of a statistical prediction is corroborated by empirical data. Statistical methods prove invaluable when studying multiple variables and many languages at once. Legitimate typological research does not require using statistical methods (for example, Comrie 1981) but in order to extend results beyond the directly investigated cases, statistical methods are usually necessary. In order to use statistics appropriately, however, the proposed prediction and empirical data must share several characteristics. An appreciation of the role of statistics in typological research requires the introduction of various statistical concepts, some that are obvious but also some that are quite subtle.

CASES are the items investigated, normally languages in typological research. VARIABLES (or attributes) are the characteristics of the cases being evaluated by applying a measuring procedure (a measure) to the attribute. Two of the most common measures are arithmetic MEANS (averages) and STANDARD DEVIATIONS. A frequent goal is to characterize a set of values by a single number; three different measures are frequently used to calculate this number. The mean is the familiar arithmetic average. The mean is sometimes misleading due to values that are OUTLIERS, a few cases whose values are very far from the mean. E.g., means of personal income are subject to the undue influence of the very high incomes of a few people. The MEDIAN is the number at which fifty percent of all values fall below and fifty percent above. The MODE of a distribution is the value that is most frequently found. The mean is most often used by statisticians but the median and mode at times are also useful.

Another measure provides an indication of the dispersion of values. There are others available but statisticians have settled on the STANDARD DEVIATION as the value of choice. Roughly two-thirds of all values in a sample of values that vary fall within one standard deviation of the mean. Roughly 95% of all values fall within two standard deviations about the mean and 99% fall within three standard deviations of the mean. Explanations are more typically aimed at variation, and seek to address questions such as: why does variation in a variable exist? Variation in what other variable(s) might be used to explain the variation seen in a variable?

DESCRIPTIVE statistics provide a method for summarizing large distributions of data.

2. Statistical inference

INFERENTIAL STATISTICS are used to infer what the situation is in the universe of interest based on a portion of that universe, a SAMPLE.

2.1. Types of variables

Three types of variables are normally distinguished in introductory texts. All variables are presumed to have one and only one value for a case, whether the case is defined to be a language, a morpheme, or something else. NOMINAL or CATEGORICAL variables classify cases by terms that define their equivalence or non-equivalence, but no quantitative relationships or ordering among them is suggested or presumed. Basic word order (SOV, SVO, etc.) is a good example of this type of variable. None of the word orders is quantitatively different from the others. Variables that can only take two values such as 'present' and 'absent' are a limiting case of this type of variable. Nominal variables are often represented graphically by HISTOGRAMS or PIE CHARTS (Figure 33.1 is from data in Tomlin 1986: 22, where −V stands for SOV and OSV basic word orders, −V− stands for SVO and OVS, and V− stands for VSO and VOS).

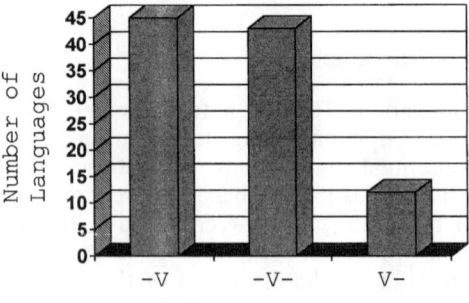

Fig. 33.1: Verb position according to data from Tomlin 1986.

ORDINAL or RANK variables permit a principled ranking of cases based on some property. The value of the variable is normally given a non-negative integer value that indicates the relative ranking of that case with respect to other cases.

Data from Justeson & Stephens (1984: 534 Figure 1) is shown in Figure 33.2 in a cross-TABLE for vowels and consonants in their sample languages.

		Number of Consonants	
Number		≤18	>18
of	≤9	14	11
vowels	>9	13	12

Fig. 33.2: Vowels vs consonants in the sample of Justeson & Stephens 1984.

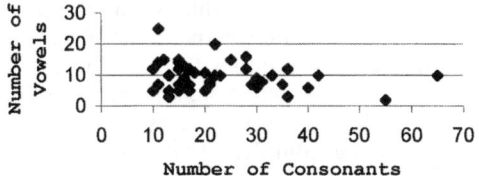

Fig. 33.3: Number of vowels vs number of consonants plotted according to data from Justeson & Stephens 1984.

INTERVAL variables, on the other hand, correspond to measurements of equal-sized units. Data from Justeson & Stephens (1984: 534) are shown in a SCATTERPLOT in Figure 33.3.

In any given study, the appropriate statistical approach depends in part on the measurement levels of the variables under investigation. Variables may also be combined to form scales by a variety of means, adding more complexity to the analysis. Data are recorded for each variable for each case (normally a language but perhaps something else in a language, such as a form type, as in Bybee & al. (1994)). Data will be one of the three types categorical, ordinal, or interval. The distribution of these data provides the distribution to be explained.

2.2. Probability

PROBABILITY here is taken to be the odds (or proportion of times) that a particular event or result obtains. If the method by which the sample was selected matches the method for generating a known distribution, the distribution function may be used to calculate (or look up on a table) the odds that a particular result was obtained. Otherwise, and also instead of calculation, a number of simulations of the empirical data (with the additional stipulation that it was randomly distributed) may be run. After several (perhaps a thousand) simulations have been performed, the odds that the data were generated by chance may be determined, either graphically or by means of counting.

2.3. Expectations

Plausibly similar methods of generating the data using random elements are then attempted with the goal of matching the observed data as closely as possible.

The data distribution of empirical data may take one of several shapes. However, a similar process must plausibly have generated the empirical data to make reasonable the comparison of a random distribution with the empirical data.

2.3.1. Normal distribution

The most important distribution in statistics is the normal (or Gaussian) distribution. Its probabilities comprise the familiar bell-shaped symmetrical curve, with a small number of cases at each end (tail), rising smoothly to a large number of cases in the middle (the mean). A normal curve is completely described by its mean and standard deviation.

2.3.2. Chi-squared distribution

The χ^2 distribution is not symmetrical, but rather varies depending on the number of different values taken by the variables under investigation. Chi-squared distributions are used for testing hypotheses about deviations, for example, the deviation between expected and observed values.

Woods & al. (1986: 144−50) note several requirements of Chi-squared tests that are often ignored and violated by researchers, including expected frequencies of at least five in each cell and independence of observations, and discuss the misleading results obtained if Chi-squared tests are applied to proportions.

2.3.3. Binomial distribution

The Binomial distribution results from discrete trials that can only have two possible outcomes. A histogram of the number of times one of the values occurs in several trials produces the basis for a binomial distribution. Flipping eight coins several times and counting the number of heads that result from each throw of the coins is a common example. Tables that include the frequency of each result and the number of trials give the probability of any result occurring by chance alone.

2.3.4. Multinomial distribution

A Multinomial distribution is an extension of the binomial involving more than two possible outcomes.

2.3.5. Poisson distributions

Poisson distributions result from a count of occurrences of events over space or time. Results are also determined from tables that include probabilities for the likelihood of any positive number of events occurring in the space or time interval by chance given the mean number of times that event occurs over all time or space intervals. For instance, we might ask what is the expected frequency of a particular grammatical construction in a set of sentences by an author when the mean number of times the author uses that grammatical construction in all similar-sized sets of sentences is known.

The benefit of these and other distributions is that they provide a method to quantitatively compare expected values with empirical (observed) values, thereby giving the analyst a clearer idea of the extent of non-randomness of variable values supporting an explanation.

The initial goal of statistical analyses is to establish, by means of a TEST OF SIGNIFICANCE, that empirical results probably did not result from some random process, i. e. by chance. The statistical significance measure varies from 0 to 1 and gives the probability that a data distribution may have been produced by a random process. In the social sciences, practice has suggested that a maximum of .05 (1 chance in 20) is a reasonable level for deciding that a result was unlikely to have been produced by a random process. (This inference will be incorrect about 1 time in 20.) If the researcher is proposing that there is no substantial relationship between two variables, the probability of .05 should be increased to .20 or .30, so that there is less chance that the researcher is correct (Blalock 1972: 162).

2.4. Confidence Intervals

One of the characteristics of estimates based on statistics is that they are not knowable exactly. Knowing the relevant type of distribution makes it possible to confidently predict, however, that, given the sample values, the population's values fall in some interval (the CONFIDENCE INTERVAL) some percentage of the time. The more cases in the sample, the closer will the estimates be to the population values. Increasing the number of cases in the sample narrows the interval of the estimate of the population's values from the sample, but no number of cases less than the number in the total population produces a point or exact estimate.

2.5. Group Significance

If more than a single statistical significance is calculated for a set of data, the significance of the set of results may bring any particular result into doubt. If more than a single test is performed there is an increased probability that the results were obtained strictly by chance. To correct for this, GROUP SIGNIFICANCE tests evaluate whether a set of results would occur by random factors alone. For instance, if one hundred significance tests are performed in the course of a research project, one could be confident that about five of them were statistically significant at the .05 level by chance alone. Distinguishing the significant from the merely statistically significant results is aided by increasing the sample size, but that reduces the statistical significance problem but does not eliminate it.

2.6. Power of a test

Different statistical approaches provide varying degrees of POWER, or capability, to differentiate random from non-random distributions of data. For instance, changing the measurement level for interval level data to ordinal or nominal level data as done in Figure 33.2 (Figure 33.3 shows the interval data that serve as the basis for Figure 33.2.) reduces the power of the test. The generally desired approach is to use the statistical approach with the most power.

2.7. Percentages

Woods & al. (1986: 150 f.) note some pitfalls of reducing observed raw frequencies to PERCENTAGES (a common manner of presentation of results in typological studies). Significant results may be masked by this practice and insignificant results may appear to be spuriously significant.

3. Sampling

Practical motivations for sampling languages include time and other resource constraints. There is not time nor money nor qualified workers to study all of the world's languages directly. In addition, many languages are on the verge of becoming extinct, with no real hope of their being described before they disappear. A selection (or sample) is the only possible alternative. Moreover, because many languages that once were spoken no longer exist, and in the future other languages will also develop, there is no hope that all of the languages of the world could ever be investigated so that a complete database could be developed from which to derive typological principles.

Theoretical reasons for not even attempting complete coverage of all languages also exist. Deming (1950: 247—61) proposes a distinction between SYNTHETIC and ANALYTIC samples. Synthetic samples are employed to obtain some summary characterization of the data. An example might be estimating the number of students expected to register for an upcoming course so that appropriate numbers of textbooks might be ordered. In that case any number of cases up to and including the entire population only improves that estimate.

Analytic samples, on the other hand, are used to draw theoretical inferences. The population characteristics are not the primary interest. Rather, the focus is on theoretical constructs and their relationships. In this case great care is needed to provide only reasonable representation of types and avoid including too many instances of any particular type. If there are too many sample cases then there may be statistical evidence for relationships that do not warrant an explanation.

3.1. Domains

Three sets of (language) objects may be distinguished: (1) the UNIVERSE or scope of applicability of the proposed assertion; (2) the FRAME or set of cases considered in the sampling design; and (3) the SAMPLE or set of cases actually selected (Bell 1978: 126). For instance, the universe might be the set of all languages; the frame, those languages that have been described in published grammars; and the sample, a random selection from the languages in the frame. Transitions between these domains require careful motivation.

3.1.1. Universe

The issue of what the universe is to which inferences are to be drawn is far from straightforward. Bell (1978: 126) states without comment that for research on language universals, the universe of interest is all possible human languages. This seems intuitively correct. However, if each language in the universe is characterized as the set of values for all attributes considered in the study, should the number of cases to be included be proportional to the number of languages in the universe that have a particular set of values for those attributes? The number of languages having the same collection of values (for the same attributes) depends on factors such as area and genetic relatedness, as well as more substantive variables, as noted by Bell (1978: 141—2).

Perkins (1989) proposes that the universe of interest in typological research is language types. Inferences are about LANGUAGE, the general faculty of which individual languages are instances. In this interpretation, a subset of attributes that might be considered is used to establish types and relationships between the types, and the variables of interest to the study are considered after controlling for areal and genetic relationships. Matthew S. Dryer (1989) and Johanna Nichols (1992), perhaps following suggestions by Bell (1978: 142 ff.), argue for a universe of LANGUAGE GROUPS at some time depth, even though time depth is extremely fuzzy and unreliable (see Campbell 1997: 341 ff.).

3.1.2. Frame

Establishing a legitimate frame for the selected universe is open to a variety of reasonable approaches. If the universe to which inferences are to be drawn is comprised of all languages that have ever and will ever exist, the a priori possibility of making this argument easily is not evident. That is, we have no information concerning most of the languages that existed in the past, and none concerning languages that do not yet exist. The reasonable assumption must be made that such languages resemble languages for which records and evidence now exist. Various lists of language names are available that provide fairly complete coverage of the universe of existing languages, with some including selected languages that are no longer spoken. The frame may simply be lists of non-uniformly defined cases. Any list, for instance that of Voegelin (1977), is uneven in its groupings; some of the genetic relationships between the languages listed are well established whereas other groups are from the same general geographic area but have unstudied genetic relationships. No list of well-described languages is extensive enough to be used for an exhaustive frame, but comprehensive lists provide acceptable substitutes.

3.1.3. Sample

The procedure by which a number of objects are selected from the frame produces a smaller set of objects, the sample. These are the objects studied in detail and from which inferences are drawn to the population.

There are a number of procedures used to select a sample of languages from a frame.

They include CONVENIENCE, EXPERT CHOICE, QUOTA, and PROBABILITY SAMPLES. Convenience samples are comprised of cases that are easily available to the researcher. Expert choice samples, sometimes called purposive or judgment samples, reflect a researcher's judgment as to which cases are representative of the intended population. Quota samples match the population on specified selection criteria but otherwise leave the sampler to choose cases by whatever method he desires. Probability samples include a random selection procedure and include simple random, stratified, and cluster sampling, in all of which each sampled case has a definite probability of being selected. Stratified probability samples divide the frame into strata based on some variable and are used to increase diversity over simple random samples and improve the chances of independence of cases.

The most critical distinction for statistical inference is between samples that use some RANDOM SELECTION ELEMENT (probability samples) and those that do not (convenience, expert choice, and quota samples). Naroll (1973: 889) suggests that, since sampling will deviate from the statistically ideal methods, a random element be used to meet the requirement for a probability sample and control for sampling effects via methodological variables that are included in the analysis. Inferences to Language may be made only if the sampling frame includes as broad a range of types of cases as possible and the sampling procedure includes a means for selecting cases that reasonably reflect that range. This requirement may be relaxed for pilot studies and non-statistical studies. However, as soon as STATISTICAL INFERENCES to Language are desirable, sampling must match the assumptions of the statistical method. Blalock (1972: 509−10) notes that using a representative sample is not sufficient to evaluate errors involved. All tests for sampling bias presuppose that results were obtained using a probability sample (Naroll 1973: 911 ff.).

The most frequently-used sampling unit is language. The frame should be constructed so that each language has a known probability of being included in a sample. Lists of languages may provide a sampling frame that is principled, though not exhaustive. Available lists of languages include Voegelin (1966), Voegelin (1978), Ruhlen (1987), Decsy (1985), and Grimes (1996).

To summarize, the universe must be relevant to the theory to be tested; the frame must exemplify the universe of interest; and the sample must be selected in a manner that reflects the frame from which it is selected.

Increasing the sample size decreases the interval around an estimate of the population value, provided the sampled items are independent of each other, at least as much as one would expect by chance. If the sampled items are not independent, then increasing the sample size will spuriously narrow the confidence interval or increase the statistical significance of the result.

3.2. Random Error

Increasing the number of cases in a sample tends to reduce the size of the interval for the estimate; a sample of two randomly-selected values has a very wide interval within which the population's value might be expected to fall. For instance, of two languages chosen at random from all the world's languages, one might have a three-vowel system and the other a nine-vowel system. An estimate of how many vowels on average would be expected in the languages of the population would be six, ((3 + 9)/2 sampled cases). One problem would be the size of the interval that must be used to qualify this estimate, here the best that one can say is that the population mean is, with 95% certainty, between .1 and 11.9. A sample of several hundred values has a much narrower interval, for instance 6 +/− .1 for the expected population mean with 95% confidence. Even here the estimate is qualified with a confidence level which may be interpreted to mean if many samples of this same size were taken, 95% of them would have means that fall within this interval. Increasing the sample size reduces the random error in estimates but does not eliminate it completely.

3.3. Systematic Error (bias)

Though increasing the sample size reduces random error, it does not reduce SYSTEMATIC ERROR. In fact, systematic error may spuriously increase (i. e. decrease its probability) the significance of a result. Naroll 1973a identifies a number of possible sources of systematic error in cross-cultural studies, many of which apply to linguistic typological studies as well. For instance, the variable 'Date-of-Grammar', which records when a particular grammatical description was published, might result in the appearance of spurious results if it is systematically related to other substantive relationships. As the name suggests, systematic error refers to differences in results depending on some measure other than the substantive variables of interest.

Differences between expected and observed values are evaluated using statistical analysis. The differences may be well within what one might expect to occur solely by chance, or highly unlikely to have occurred by chance alone.

Random error results from differences in specific samples due to 'the luck of the draw'. Systematic error, however, may result from variables relating to the selection procedure that systematically skew the data distribution and may spuriously create the appearance or disappearance of structure in the data.

Raoul Naroll suggests that the appropriate control for systematic error is not to ignore it or deal with it in an unsystematic fashion, but to measure the sources of it as variables to be included in the analysis. The effects of bias may be substantial but if they do not account for the associations between substantive variables under investigation they are not viable counter-explanations.

3.4. Galton's Problem

In the late 19th century the first cross-cultural result based on a sample of cultures was presented at the Royal Anthropological Institute. Galton, one of the attendees, objected that it was difficult to evaluate the significance of the results since it was unclear how many independent cases were involved. The problem suggested by Galton has come to be known as GALTON'S PROBLEM (Naroll 1973b: 974). If cases are not independent, the results observed could be the due to borrowing or common history. The situation is completely parallel to that in typological linguistic samples, where languages that are genetically related or are spoken in the same geographical area or in areas in close proximity, tend to have common attributes.

Several means of dealing with Galton's Problem have been proposed and used in cultural anthropology. A linearization of culture groups found in Loftin & Hill (1974: 23−61) provides a means for identifying culture groups that are best considered neighbors. These culture groups may then be used as measures of language neighbors and the borrowing of substantive variable values may be evaluated statistically, as is done in Perkins (1992: 174−76).

3.5. Relationship between languages

Languages may be associated with one another in several ways, most obviously by genetic or areal relationship.

3.5.1. Genetic

Genetic relationships may be measured as to depth, or via an index such as the diversity index of Rijkhoff & al. (1993). Time depth estimates are used as a basis for an assumption of independence by Bell, Dryer, and Nichols, but the research has not been done yet to establish that independence. Other evidence seems to support the assertion that genetic groups are not independent (Perkins 1989).

3.5.2. Areal

Area might be measured by variables such as Hemisphere, Continent, Subcontinent, Region, etc. Dryer (1989) and Perkins (1989) propose and test the size of these effects on a variety of variables. Hemispheric effects appear to be the strongest in the data considered there. Perkins (1992: 172−79) proposes a method to handle the similarity of variable values between neighbors.

3.6. Motivation for Stratification

The usual motivation for stratified probability samples is to reduce the interval estimates for each stratum. However, for cross-cultural and typological samples the motivation is that it tends to maximize independence from diffusion of traits or values for particular variables (Naroll 1973: 898).

3.7. Number of cases

Perkins (1989) evaluates a number of linguistic variables available in the literature and concludes that between about 40 and 140 languages are appropriate (i. e., will show reasonable statistical independence) for the variables evaluated using various grouping levels, from continent to hemisphere. Basic word order and noun phrase order suggested samples of 39 to 54 languages as appropriate. For samples involving phonological variables, a higher number of languages were determined to be appropriate.

The appropriate number of sample cases cannot be known before the data are collected. Only by measuring both the substantive variables and the degree of association of the variables suspected of being sources of non-independence of cases can the appropriate number of independent cases be calculated using the methods described in Perkins (1989). Perkins (1992) used a sample of 49 languages which, following data collection, was reduced to 35 languages in a final set of tests due to lack of independence of cases (1992: 174−79). Bybee & al. (1994) used a sample of 76 languages which, following determination that a significant association of variables with continent area existed, was reduced, for the purpose of statistical testing, to 49 languages to insure independence of cases (1994: 123).

The general strategy being proposed is to use a few more cases than one judges to be independent and then use the method described in Perkins (1989) to reduce the sample size in final tests of the hypothesis. In determining the appropriate number of cases in a sample, the initial estimate may be based on other similar variables and the findings of other researchers.

STEP-WISE SAMPLING (Simon 1997: 405) involves selecting a few cases via a random selection method to determine if the effect of interest is statistically significant with that number of cases. If it is not, then more cases may be sampled and the larger sample tested for statistically significant results. This process may be repeated as desired until it is clear whether data support the hypothesis or not. This strategy is related to the usual need of researchers to balance the cost and effort of selecting a sample against the benefit of the results from that sample. Of course, the requirement of independence of cases remains.

3.8. Selection of cases

Given an estimate of the number of cases to be included in a sample, the problem of selecting which languages to be included in a sample remains.

The first criterion to be met by any process is that it includes a random element. Stratification (grouping) of the sampled frame is usually appropriate to maximize diversity and increase the likelihood that independence of cases is maximized. Within strata, the individual sample cases may be chosen randomly, using a table of random numbers or a computer program that generates random numbers.

3.9. Sampling Requirements

Three important characteristics of samples are: the representativeness of the sample, whether a random process is used in selecting the sample, and whether the sample units are independent.

Leonard (1967: 594−96) provides guidance on choosing samples of representative cases to test inductive generalizations that also apply to choosing samples in typological linguistics.

3.9.1. Aims of research

Depending on the goal of the research, particular samples may be more or less representative. The objective is to have the universe, frame, and sample all provide chances for each case to be selected.

For a study of action nominals, only languages that have action nominals might be relevant (Koptjevskaja-Tamm 1993). For a more general study of phenomena all human languages display, a more inclusive sample would be considered representative.

3.9.2. Reflects population

The sample selected should vary in ways that the population is known to vary. This requirement has been interpreted in several instances of typological research as varying according to language group size (Tomlin 1986, and many others). It is not clear that this is a sound basis for determining cases to be included in a sample, especially when the issue of independence of cases is ignored. Choosing a number of languages based on the proportion of languages of that (genetic) type is basically ad hoc. The number of speakers, number of dialects, or some other proportion could as reasonably be proposed.

A sounder basis is to use a sampling plan that maximizes the diversity of the sample in order to reflect the diversity of the population. Maximizing diversity and representing it adequately are the objectives of the sampling procedures of Perkins (1992) and Bybee & al. (1994). Rijkhoff & al. (1993) propose a method for determining the number of languages to be selected from each genetic group based on a diversity index, which is in turn based on the number of genetically-related sub-groups recognized for each group. This is a substantial improvement over earlier methods.

However, a further consideration is whether sub-population comparisons are to be made or whether all inferences are to the population. If sub-population comparisons are made − as in Nichols (1992) − each sub-population must be adequately sampled to obtain reliable estimates. This may not be possible without violating the principle of independence of cases. Wider comparisons may require fewer cases from each language group.

3.10. Random selection of individual cases

Leonard (1967) agrees that individual sample cases should be selected using a random selection procedure. Unless this requirement is met there is no warrant for using statistical methods. All statistical methods require that empirical data be compared to randomly-generated values and that the empirical data match the randomly-generated values with regard to several critical assumptions, especially that of random selection. Thus, in order to use statistical techniques the sampling method MUST include a random selection procedure — though see Simons (1997: 170−71) for a contrary view. Naroll cites a number of sampling theorists in support of this constraint (Naroll 1973: 890−91).

Researchers in cultural anthropology have attempted to use samples that were not chosen using a random selection procedure and have later been convinced that their samples included unsuspected biases (Naroll 1973: 891−93). There seems to be every reason to assume this will also apply to samples of languages. However, most samples used in linguistic typological research have not been chosen using a random selection procedure, nor are explanations or justifications given, even when statistical results are reported. A table of random numbers or a computer program can provide random numbers and many introductory statistics books explain in detail how to use such tables.

3.11. Proportion of total population

If the sample size is less than about 90% of the population size, the results obtained do not depend on the population size. A sample of 100 from a population of 10,000 provides the same accuracy as a sample of 100 from a population of 1,000,000.

3.12. Independence of cases

Sampled cases must be INDEPENDENT of each other at least to an extent one might expect to occur by chance. Independence means that the values of a variable are not predictable with greater than chance odds given the values of some other variable measurable in the sample.

Woods & al. (1986: 149) note that in applied linguistics the issue of independence of cases is too often ignored. Bell (1978: 142 ff.) proposes that several hundred languages be included in order to insure that cases of RARE TYPES be included and the precision of result be increased. Although these suggestions ignore the requirement of independence of cases, most typological studies have nevertheless followed this reasoning, ignoring the issue of independence of cases.

Sampling requires careful counterbalancing of the requirements for larger numbers of cases to meet the requirements of many tests being run and the requirement for smaller numbers of cases to justify independence of cases.

4. Statistical models

Statistics, in principle, does not produce unequivocal results. Instead there are specifiable odds that the inferred results fall within a range.

A STATISTICAL MODEL is an abstract quantitative representation of a set of measures on variables that captures the investigator's hypothesis about how the variables of interest are related. Inherent in this model are several assumptions, such as the generating procedure for the measures. Empirical data are matched against the model and evaluated for the extent to which the model captures them. If there is not a significant difference between the hypothesized relations, the model, and the pattern of empirical data, the model is said to be corroborated.

Note that the hypothesized model is not thereby proven to be correct. Many other models of similar structure might be evaluated with results that may be better than those actually obtained. Computer programs such as TETRAD (Glymour & al. 1987) permit the evaluation of many possible model configurations and heuristically determine the best-fitting model.

4.1. Univariate models

Univariate models involve a single variable and hypotheses about its value. For instance Tomlin (1986) tests hypotheses about the frequency of occurrence of basic word orders (see Figure 33.1 above). The variable (basic word order) could take on one of several values, but there were no other variables measured to 'explain' the distribution.

4.2. Multivariate analysis

Multivariate analysis involves more than one variable, some of which are the 'causes' (independent variables) and others the effects or results (dependent variables). Other relationships are possible and will be described further below.

4.3. Statistical models and causality

Statistical analysis permits distinguishing several different relationships between variables. Although statistical models are not necessarily best causally interpreted, many, if not most, research efforts have as their goal establishing CAUSAL MODELS. Although it is a topic deserving consideration by any researcher desiring to use statistics, causality is not established by statistics.

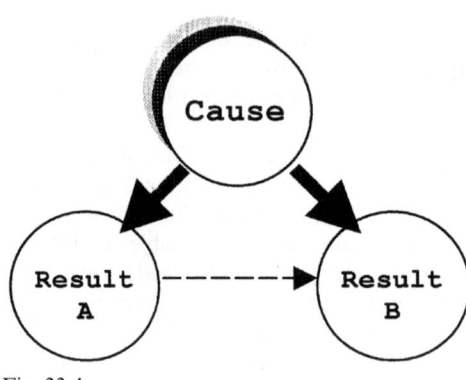

Fig. 33.4

4.3.1. Multiple effects

A single causal factor may have multiple effects (cf. Figure 33.4). For instance, smoking may give a person bad breath and result in lung cancer.

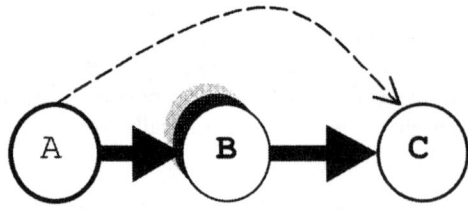

Fig. 33.5

The effects may show evidence of being associated when their common cause is not taken into consideration. When the common cause is taken into account the relationship between the effects is reduced to insignificance. So, for example, there will be some association between bad breath and lung cancer but when their common cause is taken into account, the association will not be accounted for.

4.3.2. Sequences of effects

Another possibility is a sequence of influences between factors, as shown in Figure 33.5, which illustrates an intervening variable between variables A and C. The intervening variable is related to both A and C. It appears there is a relationship between A and C but when B is taken into account the relationship between A and C is revealed to be entirely due to the intervening variable B.

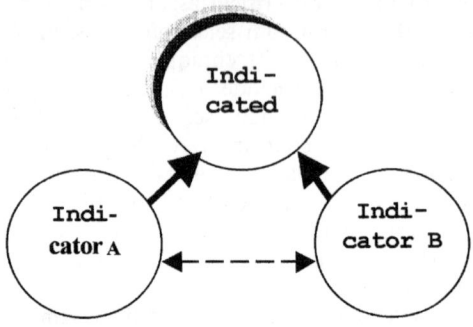

Fig. 33.6

4.3.3. Indicator variables

Another possibility is represented in Figure 33.6. Two variables, Indicator A and Indicator B, are indicators of the Indicated variable, which may itself not be directly measurable because it is purely theoretical. Socio-economic status is an example of this type of variable. There are measures of the variable such as income, education, etc. but the variable itself is not directly measurable.

All of the examples represented by Figure 33.4 through Figure 33.6 are given in their simplest form, but the various structures they represent may be combined into more complex associations between variables.

4.3.4. Implications for a research strategy

Given the flexibility and extendibility of statistical models of the forms represented here, the possible confounding factors of areal effects, genetic relationships, and unevenness or shortcomings in data quality, all of which are of concern in linguistic typological research, can be directly addressed.

4.4. Data Quality Controls

Naroll 1973a provides a strategy for dealing with factors that may systematically affect the model.

The essential point is that including quality control variables in the model may reduce the likelihood of spurious relationships between the substantive variables under investigation. Control factors are characteristics of the data-collection process that may affect the accuracy of data coding (Naroll 1973a: 932). Bias or systematic error may be of different types depending on the stage of their introduction.

Values for quality control variables have three sources: the informant, the grammar writer, and the cross-linguistic researcher. Quality control variables that have been suggested as having a deleterious effect in cultural studies include resource author's occupation, time spent in the field, overall period of work, field experience, the number of language consultants employed, and several others (Naroll 1973a: 935–38).

The strategy Naroll recommends is to treat potential control variables as one would treat any other variables, including them in the analysis with the objective of showing that they have no significant effect. Three levels of sources of data quality problems may be identified, (1) fieldwork-methods level, (2) fieldwork-publication level, and (3) typological-researcher level. In order to evaluate issues of data quality, complete citations for sources of values are required.

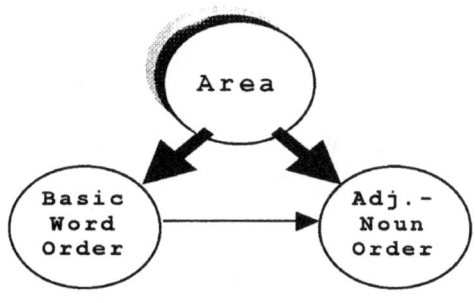

Fig. 33.7

4.5. Example of a Statistical Model

Figure 33.7 represents a model of the relationship of two linguistic variables and Area, a confounding variable that may be the reason for the apparent relationship between the two linguistic variables. Basic Word Order is causally related to Adjective-Noun order. Both of these variables are highly related to Area, however that is coded – perhaps, by a number of different means. Area is causally prior to either of the linguistic variables, hence the direction of the arrows. The relationship between Basic Word Order and Adjective-Noun Order is less pronounced than the relation of either variable with Area. There is a relationship between the two linguistic variables even after Area is taken into account. The model may be supported or rejected by considering empirical data.

4.5.1. Model Testing

Statistical models may be tested using a number of different methods, including Multiple Regression, Log-Linear, and Resampling (among others).

Regression methods were originally developed to handle ratio and interval data, but may be extended to include categorical variables via Logistic regression. Draper & Smith (1981) is the classic treatment of the subject.

Log-linear analysis was designed for dealing with categorical/ordinal variables and provides means for testing a variety of sophisticated models, including a variety of interaction models. Bishop & al. (1975) is the classic treatment of this approach. Regardless of the method, there exist procedures for assessing goodness of fit of the proposed model.

Glymour & al. (1987) provide means for evaluating many models and selecting the one that fits the empirical data best given plausible assumptions about the direction of causality between variables.

Figure 33.8 represents a general model of the research strategy being proposed. Areal and genetic relationships are measured and their influence on the substantive linguistic values and relationships evaluated. Undue influence may be controlled via the analysis or by reducing the number of sample cases.

For multivariate cases it should be noted that because of the mathematics involved, spurious relationships between the substantive variables could only result from the areal or genetic variable being associated with both of the substantive variables.

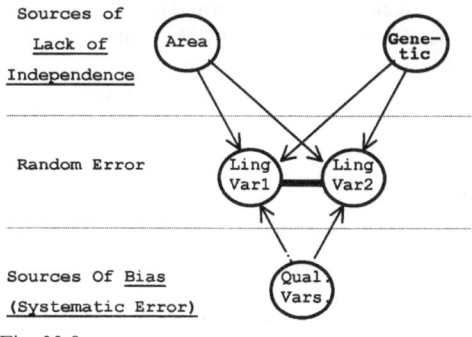

Fig. 33.8

Similarly, with quality control variables, their influence on the substantive linguistic values and relationships may be evaluated along with substantive variables.

5. Possibilities and problems of statistical methods

Statistics provides a substantial tool for analyzing the data commonly treated in typological research, but the use of statistics still presents several potential pitfalls. This section highlights some of the outstanding possibilities and unresolved problems.

5.1. Possibilities

MULTIVARIATE ANALYSIS – statistical testing of the relationship among many variables – provides a means for testing proposals about the interrelationships of several variables. Some of the variables may be methodological variables, such as language area or training of the grammar writer, that are tested for their effects on the relationships between the linguistic variables. Strategies also are provided for testing group significance probabilities when several associations are tested. These strategies comprise the method proposed by Naroll (1973a) and applied in Perkins (1992).

Methods not yet employed in any published typological studies hold promise for producing even more viable results. These include LOG-LINEAR ANALYSIS, RESAMPLING, EXACT METHODS, and CAUSAL ANALYSIS.

Log-linear analysis has been developed to formulate and test models involving many qualitative variables. Modeling several variables, including methodological variables, is relatively straightforward. The method has been extended to deal with ordinal variables. Agresti (1996) provides an introduction to nominal statistics, including log-linear analysis, Bakeman & Robinson (1994) a practitioner's approach to log-linear analysis, and Bishop & al. (1975) much more extensive coverage of log-linear theory and analysis as well as related topics.

Resampling (Simon 1997) or the Bootstrap (Efron & Tibshirani 1993) provide ways to evaluate models and empirical data distributions by simulating many selections of sample data from empirical data. Elements of the methodology have been used for several years (MONTE CARLO SIMULATIONS AND BOOTSTRAPPING, for example), but Simon (1997) has integrated these into a general approach. Many of the assumptions of traditional statistical approaches are not needed with this approach; for instance, small numbers of cases may reasonably be handled and the data may be of any form. The approach is very close to the concrete operations one would use to model the data and provides a clear means for non-statisticians to apply the benefits of statistical reasoning to relevant problems.

Causal modeling is subject to considerable controversy. Glymour & al. (1987) provide an approach to determining causal structures among many variables using artificial intelligence and statistical modeling via a computer program. More mathematically esoteric methods are developing but have yet to be applied to linguistic typological data to deal with the multidimensionality of data. Methods include factor analysis, multidimensional scaling, principal component analysis, and others.

As personal computer hardware becomes faster and software more sophisticated and easy to use, typological studies should benefit from more powerful analyses if researchers put forth effort to explore and learn the techniques. With regard to available data and collaboration on typological research, the World-Wide Web holds significant promise.

5.2. Problems

The requirement of independence of cases conflicts with the requirement that there be enough cases for sufficient POWER to test hypotheses without small numbers or multiple relationships presenting too much of a problem. The number of cases required to make reasonable inferences about a model may be more than can be obtained with independent cases. However, the relationships typically dealt with in typological linguistics are sufficiently robust so that relatively small numbers of cases are sufficient to corroborate them. The power of statistical tests is dependent on the number of cases and, when an effect is small and/or there are several variables involved, is often insufficient to provide conclusive results.

Group significance problems will continue to be a challenge. Since developing samples is expensive in terms of time and money, it is unlikely that a particular sample will only be used to run a single test. For this and other reasons, adequate methods for reconciling practice with the requirement that trials (associations) be independent of each other remains an issue which needs to be addressed.

As the number of variables under consideration increases, a combinatorial explosion of possibilities of alternate models occurs very rapidly. Glymour & al. (1987: 7) note that there are 4^{15} of alternate models possible when as few as 6 variables are considered. Normal practice is to propose a single model and determine if it is unlikely to have occurred by chance alone. This suggests two problems: (1) with six variables there are more than 4^{12} models that one would expect to occur by chance alone; and (2) how does one distinguish the proposed model from those expected to occur by the random distribution of values? Glymour & al. (1987) argue that their heuristic search guided by artificial intelligence and statistical modeling principles, is capable of ranking possible models with respect to empirical data. Further, Naroll (1973a) provides a strategy for ruling out many of the alternative models.

The quality of data available to serve as a basis for typological studies is also an important issue. Nichols (1992: 262 f.) notes the need for more basic grammars, standardized genetic classifications, areal groupings, and information for critical languages such as Tasmanian. The methods proposed by Naroll (1973a) for dealing with quality issues (discussed briefly above) provide a means for addressing most of these difficulties, at least in principle.

The chief obstacle to the profitable use of statistics by typologists is an intellectual one. Typologists have invested considerable time and effort in developing the field but little time in thinking about issues from a statistical perspective, which would require another large investment of time and effort. Resampling techniques provide considerable resources to typologists and are based on intuitively plausible notions that do not require a heavy mathematical investment. Intuitive notions, however, are not sufficient but rather must be used as a basis for analysis by computer to simulate several hundred or thousand similar random processes against which to evaluate empirical results.

6. Examples of statistical methods in typological research

Many samples of languages have been used for typological research. Bell (1978) reviews some of the earlier research involving samples. More recent samples are included here with the goal of providing some examples of different approaches, but not to provide exhaustive coverage of the use of sampling and statistics in typological research.

Joseph H. Greenberg (1963) drew a convenience sample of thirty languages familiar to him and for which adequate grammars were available. His goals were to (1) discover universally-valid statements, mainly about the order of syntactic and morphological elements, and (2) less reliably, adduce conclusions about relative frequencies of language characteristics (1963: 75). The predominance of Indo-European languages and the lack of a random element in the selection process makes the sample quite suspect by current standards, but the statements included have been a fertile starting point for more recent investigations (e.g., Dryer 1992).

John Hawkins (1983) extended Greenberg's (1963) sampling method and drew implicational syntactic relations from the languages used that, because of their universality, do not require the use of statistics.

Graham Mallinson and Barry Blake (1981) constructed samples of 100 languages spread across genetic and typological groupings to investigate the relationship of basic sentence word order to case-marking (1981: 132) and a sample of 150 languages to investigate basic sentence word order with the position of relational expression and their heads (1981: 274). They make no mention of independence of cases or random elements in their sampling procedure and note using languages with unusual relative structures (1981: 274) and for convenience (1981: 275). They do not go beyond using counts and proportions (1981: 148) to make inferences based on their sample. Even counts and proportions are subject to distortion due to sampling inadequacies, however. The Preface (1981:vi) suggests that their treatment is fairly exhaustive of the relevant data so sampling may be beside the point, although issues of independence of cases still apply.

John S. Justeson and Laurence D. Stephens (1984) apply rigorous statistical methods to data from a stratified 50-language sample (1984: 533 ff.) from a frame of data compiled in Ruhlen (1975) to test phonological claims from the literature (1984: 536). They identify the number of cases from linguistic groups for the languages in their sample (1984: 544) but make no argument for representativeness or independence of cases.

Russell S. Tomlin (1986) selected a sample of 402 languages from a frame of 1063 languages consisting of references from his colleagues and the research libraries of the Universities of Michigan and Oregon (1986: 30) to test hypotheses about the relative frequencies of basic sentence word order. The universe of interest for him is the set of all natural human languages. He calculated a measure of fit to determine if potential samples' genetic and areal counts of languages matched those of Voegelin (1977) and settled on a sample that does not differ significantly from that standard (1986: 32) to determine the frequencies of interest to him. Those frequencies are claimed to be representative of the universe of natural languages. Nothing is said about independence of cases or the use of random elements.

Ian Maddieson (1984) constructed a quota sample of 317 languages that is representative of the phonological inventories of the world's extant languages to test a variety of phonological hypotheses from the literature. One central goal was to insure that no duplicate cases of languages were included (1984: 158). Some statistics were calculated (e.g. 1984: 50) even though no random selection process was used nor attention paid to the issue of independence of cases.

Perkins (1992) uses a frame of 1,213 culture/languages, provided by Kenny (1974) using Murdock (1967) and Voegelin (1966), stratified by culture area and language group, and a specified random procedure to produce a sample of forty-nine cases with the maximum attainable cultural and linguistic separation. Bibliographic requirements were applied to languages after they were sampled and researched. If insufficient materials were found, another case was drawn. Since the frame was based on Murdock (1967) there was an improved probability that the language is well described, since the cultures he included are well described. A variety of statistics was used to make inferences concerning the relationship of cultural complexity and morphologized deictics. The associations were evaluated relative to hemispheric differences, similarity between neighbors, and several data quality variables.

Bybee (1985) used a slightly adjusted set of languages from Perkins (1992) to obtain clear results concerning form and meaning in verbal morphology that do not require statistical tests.

Mattew S. Dryer has selected a sample (used in several publications, for example, 1989, 1992) and made statistical inferences about the order of sentence elements based on his own definitions of statistical significance (1989: 270). Those definitions involve what loosely resemble binomial distributions but incorrectly assume the independence of cases between his areas, and involve an adaptation of a binomial test that ignores the requirements of that test, including the requirement that only two possible outcomes exist (1989: Table 26). He uses Chi-squared tests comparing proportions since raw numbers of cases do not work to support his case cleanly (1989: 86−87).

Johanna Nichols (1992) uses a judgment sample of 174 well-described languages that is claimed to be a total sample of the world's language families (1992: 37) but is also representative of the areal groups accepted by experts (1992: 27 ff. but see Campbell 1997: 341 ff.). She selected languages from within families based on the quality of available descriptions, and gives source citations for all codings. Her purpose is to develop hypotheses about within- and between-group syntactic and morphological diversity and stability, rather than to test universal hypotheses about language. She employs Dryer's questionable methodology of declaring universality when a majority of groups in all of her areas evidence the same value for an attribute (1992: 41). She acknowledges that fewer languages may be sufficient to substantiate her claims (1992: 36) and that some of her languages are non-independent (1992: 40), but then calculates significance probabilities using her total sample (1992: 110 ff.). As a result, the significance figures she obtains are not entirely valid.

Joan L. Bybee & al. (1994) use Voegelin (1978) for a frame from which is drawn a probability sample of 76 languages to determine pathways of formal reduction and semantic change in the development over time of grammatical markers associated with verbs. The sample is selected via a specified procedure that aims at diversity of representation, without including too many cases of language isolates or Creoles. One chapter makes extensive use of statistical inference, as does an earlier publication based on the same sample, Bybee & al. (1991).

Twenty six randomly-selected languages from this sample comprise the basis for the sample used by Soteria Svorou (1993: 47), which traces without the use of statistics the semantic and morphological development of spatial morphemes.

Twenty six languages, most from this sample, were also used by Nancy L. Woodworth (1991) to test a hypothesis about sound symbolism in pairs of deictic terms.

7. Conclusion

The use of both sophisticated statistics and sampling methods are still in their early stages in linguistic typology. Recent methods such as resampling and log-linear analysis provide promise of successful approaches to dealing with some of the difficult challenges linguists face in sampling and statistical inference. Sampling and statistics provide a means of formulating and testing theories involving large numbers of cases of language types.

With regard to sampling, attention to the use of random selection procedures, representativeness, and independence of cases are all highly recommended. With regard to statistical analysis, strict adherence to the requirements for applying each statistical test, and to the influence of areal, genetic, and data quality variables all require attention.

8. References

Agresti, Alan. 1996. *An Introduction to Categorical Data Analysis*. (Wiley series in probability and mathematical statistics.) New York: Wiley.

Bakeman, Roger & Byron, F. Robinson. 1994. *Understanding Log-Linear Analysis with ILOG. An Interactive Approach*. Hillsdale/NJ: Erlbaum.

Bell, Allen. 1978. "Language Samples". In: Greenberg, Joseph H. (ed.). *Universals of Human Language*: Volume 1, *Method & Theory*. Stanford/CA: Stanford Univ. Pr., 123−56.

Bishop, Yvonne M. M. & Fienberg, Stephen E. & Holland, Paul W. 1975. *Discrete multivariate analysis: theory and practice*. Cambridge/MA: MIT.

Blalock, Hubert M. Jr. [2]1972. *Social Statistics*. (MacGraw-Hill series in sociology.) New York: MacGraw-Hill.

Blalock, Hubert M. Jr. 1964. *Causal Inferences in Nonexperimental Research*. Chapel Hill: Univ. of North Carolina Pr.

Bybee, Joan L. 1985. *Morphology: a study of the relation between meaning and form*. (Typological studies in language, 9.) Amsterdam & Philadelphia: Benjamins.

Bybee, Joan & Pagliuca, William & Perkins, Revere. 1991. "Back to the Future". In: Traugott, Elizabeth & Heine, Bernd (eds.). *Approaches to grammaticalization*. 2 vols. (Typological studies in language, 19.) Amsterdam & Philadelphia: Benjamins, vol. 2: 17−58.

Bybee, Joan & Perkins, Revere & Pagliuca, William. 1994. *The evolution of grammar: Tense, aspect and modality in the languages of the world*. Chicago: Univ. of Chicago Press.

Carneiro, Robert L. 1973. "Scale Analysis, Evolutionary Sequences, and the Rating of Cultures". In: Naroll, Raoul & Cohen, Ronald (eds.). *A handbook of method in cultural anthropology*. New York: Columbia Univ. Pr., 834−71.

Campbell, Lyle. 1997. "Amerind personal pronouns: A second opinion." *Language* 73.2: 339−51.

Cochran, William. [3]1977. *Sampling Techniques*. (A Wiley publication in applied statistics.) New York: Wiley.

Comrie, Bernard. 1981. *Language Universals and Linguistic Typology. Syntax and Morphology*. Oxford: Blackwell.

Decsy, Gyula. 1985. *Statistical Report on the Languages of the World as of 1985*. (Bibliotheca nostratica, 6.) Bloomington/IND: Eurolingua.

Deming, William Edwards. 1950. *Some Theory of Sampling*. New York: Dover.

Draper, Norman R. & Smith, Harry. [2]1981. *Applied Regression Analysis* (Wiley series in probability and mathematical statistics.) New York: Wiley.

Dryer, Matthew S. 1989. "Large linguistic areas and language sampling". *Studies in Language* 13.2: 257−92.

Dryer, Matthew S. 1992. "The Greenbergian word order correlations". *Language* 68.1: 81−138.

Efron, Bradley & Tibsharani, Robert J. 1993. *An Introduction to the Bootstrap*. (Monographs on statistics and applied probability, 57.) New York: Chapman & Hall.

Glymour, Clark & Scheines, Richard & Spirtes, Peter & Kelly, Kevin. 1987. *Discovering Causal Structure: artificial intelligence, philosophy of science, and statistical modeling*. Orlando: Academic Press.

Greenberg, Joseph. 1963. "Some universals of grammar with particular reference to the order of meaningful elements." In: Greenberg, Joseph (ed.). *Universals of language*. Cambridge/MA: MIT.

Grimes, Barbara F. [13]1996. *Ethnologue: Language Family Index*. Dallas/TEX: Summer Institute of Linguistics.

Hawkins, John A. 1983. *Word Order Universals*. New York: Academic Press.

Howson, Colin & Urbach, Peter. [2]1993. *Scientific Reasoning: The Bayesian Approach*. Chicago: Open Court.

Justeson, John S. & Stephens, Laurence D. 1984. "On the relationship between the numbers of vowels and consonants in phonological systems", *Linguistics* 22: 531–45.

Kenny, James A. 1974. *A Numerical Taxonomy of Ethnic Units Using Murdock's 1967 World Sample.* PhD Diss. Ann Arbor.

Koptjevskaja-Tamm, Maria. 1993. *Nominalizations.* (Theoretical linguistics series.) London: Routledge.

Leonard, Henry S. 1967. *Principles of Reasoning.* New York.

Loftin, Colin & Hill, Robert H. 1974. "A Comparison of Alignment Procedures for Tests of Galton's Problem". In: Schaefer, James M., (General ed.). *Studies in Cultural Diffusion: Galton's Problem.* (Cross-cultural research series.) New Haven/CONN: Human Relations Area Files, 23–61.

Maddieson, Ian. 1984. *Patterns of sounds.* (Cambridge studies in speech science and communication.) Cambridge: Cambridge Univ. Pr.

Mallinson, Graham & Blake, Barry. 1981. *Language Typology: Cross-linguistic Studies in Syntax.* (North-Holland linguistic series, 46.) Amsterdam: North-Holland.

Naroll, Raoul. 1973. "Cross-cultural sampling". In: Naroll, Raoul & al. (eds.), 889–926.

Naroll, Raoul. 1973a. "Data Quality Control in Cross-Cultural Surveys". In: Naroll, Raoul & al. (eds.), 927–45.

Naroll, Raoul. 1973b. "Galton's Problem". In: Naroll, Raoul & al. (eds.), 974–89.

Naroll, Raoul & Cohen, Ronald (eds.) 1973. *A handbook of method in cultural anthropology.* New York: Columbia Univ. Pr.

Nichols, Johanna. 1992. *Linguistic Diversity in Space and Time.* Chicago: Univ. of Chicago Pr.

Perkins, Revere D. 1989. "Statistical Techniques for Determining Language Sample Size". *Studies in Language* 13: 293–315.

Perkins, Revere D. 1992. *Deixis, Grammar, and Culture.* (Typological studies in language, 24.) Amsterdam & Philadelphia: Benjamins.

Rijkhoff, Jan & Bakker, Dik & Hengveld, Kees & Kahrel, Peter. 1993. "A method of language sampling". *Studies in Language* 17: 169–203.

Ruhlen, Merritt. 1975. *A Guide to the Languages of the World.* Language Universals Project. Stanford/CA: Stanford Univ. Pr.

Ruhlen, Merritt. 1987. *A Guide to the World's Languages.* Volume 1: *Classification.* Stanford/CA: Stanford Univ. Pr.

Simon, Julian Lincoln. ²1997. *Resampling: The New Statistics.* Arlington.

Svorou, Soteria. 1993. *The Grammar of Space.* (Typological studies in language, 25.) Amsterdam & Philadelphia: Benjamins.

Tomlin, Russell S. 1986. *Basic Constituent Orders: Functional Principles.* (Croom Helm linguistics series.) London: Croom Helm.

Voegelin, Charles F. & Voegelin, Florence M. 1978. *Classification and Index of the World's Languages.* (Foundations of linguistics series.) New York: Elsevier.

Voegelin, Charles F. & Voegelin, Florence M. 1966. "Index to Languages of the World". *Anthropological Linguistics* 7.

Woods, Anthony & Fletcher, Paul & Hughes, Arthur. 1986. *Statistics in Language Studies.* (Cambridge textbooks in linguistics.) Cambridge: Cambridge University Press.

Woodworth, Nancy L. "Sound symbolism in proximal and distal forms". *Linguistics* 29: 273–99.

Revere D. Perkins, Springville New York (USA)

VII. Communication-theoretic prerequisites and language-independent *tertia comparationis* as bases of typological coding
Kommunikationstheoretische 'Vorgaben' und außersprachliche *tertia comparationis* als Grundlage sprachtypenbezogener Kodierung
Fondements du codage typologique: les données communicatives et les *tertia comparationis*

34. Sprechsituationen und Kontext

1. Die crux relationaler Begriffe
2. Generelle Ansätze
3. Positionen in der Semantik
4. Positionen in der Pragmatik
5. Interaktionale Ansätze in der Soziolinguistik
6. Mündlichkeit und Schriftlichkeit
7. Kontext in der Textlinguistik
8. Konvergenzpunkte
9. Zitierte Literatur

1. Die crux relationaler Begriffe

„'Kontext' kann, grob gesagt, die ganze *Welt relativ zu einem Äußerungsereignis* sein" (Pinkal 1985: 36). Angesichts dieser Feststellung nimmt es nicht wunder, daß dem Begriff des KONTEXTES keine über die Grenzen eines partikularen linguistischen Paradigmas hinausreichende und im Rahmen der Sprachwissenschaft allgemein akzeptierte Bedeutung eignet. Definition und Funktion dieses grundsätzlich relationalen Begriffs sind nicht nur abhängig von der Beschaffenheit des jeweiligen „Äußerungsereignisses", sondern vielmehr auch in hohem Maße festgelegt durch die sprachwissenschaftliche Theorie und Praxis, in denen er Verwendung findet (cf. Duranti & Goodwin 1992: 2).

Dasselbe gilt auch für den Begriff der SPRECHSITUATION resp. SITUATION, der bisweilen im Sinne einer konkreten Ausprägung (neben anderen Ausprägungen) dem Begriff des Kontextes untergeordnet (z. B. van Dijk 1977: 191 ff.; Slama-Cazacu 1961: 148; Lyons 1981: 206; Germain 1973: 21 ff.), bisweilen diesem auch nebengeordnet wird. In dieser Konstellation bedeutet 'Situation' in der Regel 'außersprachliche Wirklichkeit' und 'Kontext' komplementär dazu die 'sprachliche Umgebung' eines Zeichens oder einer Äußerung (z. B. François 1969: 65); im englischen Strukturalismus wurde für die Benennung des sprachlichen Kontextes auch der Begriff CO-TEXT geprägt (z. B. Catford 1967: 31; Lyons 1981: 206; Brown & Yule 1984: 46 ff.).

Wir werden zunächst von solchen Konzeptionen ausgehen, die eine generelle typologische Klassifikation der sprachwissenschaftlich relevanten Kontexte entwickeln (§ 2), um dann in den §§ 3–7 in exemplarischer Form die spezifischen Ausdifferenzierungen der Begriffe 'Sprechsituation' und 'Kontext' vor dem Hintergrund ausgewählter linguistischer Einzeldisziplinen und Positionen vorzustellen. Dabei wird sich zeigen, daß drei zentrale Größen die Diskussion bestimmen: die *Sprechsituation*, der *sprachliche Kontext* (Rede- bzw. Diskurskontext) und das *Wissen* (→ Art. 3, §§ 2; 3).

2. Generelle Ansätze

2.1. Karl Bühlers Feldlehre

In Orientierung an Konzepten der Gestaltpsychologie, denen zufolge alles Partikulare als eingebettet in „wechselnde Ganzheiten" wahrgenommen werde (Bühler 1934/²1965:

155), hat Karl Bühler mit der Lehre von den UMFELDERN eine Theorie vorgelegt, die das Verstehen von Sprachzeichen durch Identifikation der diesen eignenden Kontexte zu erklären beansprucht (cf. ib.: 149).

Bühler teilt bekanntlich die Sprachzeichen in zwei Klassen ein und ordnet diese wiederum zwei Feldern zu, die Zeigwörter dem Zeigfeld und die Nennwörter dem Symbolfeld (ib.: 153). Während der Situationsbegriff dem Zeigfeld korrespondiert, unterscheidet er für die Nennwörter drei Typen von Umfeldern (cf. ib.: 149): Das SYMPRAKTISCHE Umfeld bezeichnet den Bezugsrahmen konventionell geregelter menschlicher Praxis und ermöglicht das Verständnis „empraktischer Nennungen" (wie z. B. „einen schwarzen" im Café, cf. ib.: 155 ff.); das SYMPHYSISCHE Umfeld macht Bühler für die „kontextfreien Namen" geltend, die nicht in einen sprachlichen Zusammenhang eingebettet, sondern auf Etiketten, Schildern und Wegweisern erscheinen (ib.: 159 ff.); das SYNSEMANTISCHE Umfeld schließlich ist der komplexeste Begriff, auf der Ebene der konkreten SPRECHHANDLUNG umfaßt es sämtliche an der Bedeutungskonstitution beteiligten Zeichenvorgänge, also auch Intonation, Mimik und Gestik (ib.: 165 f.).

Auf der Ebene des SPRACHWERKS definiert Bühler dieses Umfeld zunächst denkpsychologisch durch den Begriff der „Stoffhilfen", dank denen eine mit den Wörtern jeweils assoziierte „Sphäre" aktualisiert und eine inhaltliche Zuordnung zu einem bestimmten Seinsbereich vollzogen werde (ib.: 170 ff.).

Als zweites neben den Stoffhilfen wichtiges „Kontextmittel" nennt er die 'connotatio'; damit bezeichnet er den Sachverhalt, daß Wortklassen je bestimmte „Leerstellen" eröffnen, die wiederum nur mit Wörtern bestimmter Wortklassen-Zugehörigkeit besetzt werden können (ib.: 172 f.); hier deutet sich, ohne daß allerdings das Verb ins Zentrum gerückt würde, eine valenztheoretische Sicht *ante litteram* an, die auf die im vierten Axiom der *Sprachtheorie* entwickelte Lehre vom syntaktischen Feld der Zeichen (cf. ib.: 69 ff.) verweist.

Bühlers maßgeblich am Leitfaden des gestaltpsychologischen Feldbegriffs entwickelte Kontexttheorie ist in den komplexen und keineswegs immer klaren Theorieduktus der *Sprachtheorie* mehrfach eingebunden (cf. Aschenberg 1999: Kap. II.1); sie erscheint maßgeblich durch die im Organonmodell fundierte OBJEKTIVE Sprachauffassung perspektiviert (Bühler 1934/²1965: 1): die Umfelder werden nicht als subjektive Apperzeptionsmodi, sondern als objektive 'Umgebungen' der Zeichen konzipiert.

2.2. Eugenio Coserius Umfeld-Lehre

In terminologischer Anlehnung an Bühler hat Eugenio Coseriu (1955/56) das Programm einer Linguistik des Sprechens skizziert, das, thesenhaft zusammengefaßt, folgende Grundüberlegungen zur Theorie der Kontexte enthält:

− Die Umfelder (span. *entornos*) betrachtet Coseriu als *condicio sine qua non* allen Sprechens, da sie nicht allein an der Determination der Referenz der Zeichen (ihrer BEZEICHNUNG), sondern auch an der Konstitution des mit ihnen vermeinten SINNS wesentlich beteiligt seien (cf. ib.: 45; zum Begriff des Sinnes id. 1980/³1994: 64 ff.).

− Obwohl die Umfelder das gesamte Spektrum ihrer Funktionen erst auf der Ebene des konkreten Sprechens entfalten (cf. id. 1955/56: 52), seien sie auch für die Ebene der Einzelsprache, etwa für Personalpronomina und Deiktika bedeutsam, d. h. für solche Ausdrucksmittel, denen aufgrund ihrer Bedeutungsstruktur der Verweis auf eine Bezugsgröße bereits inhärent ist (ib.: 51 f.).

− Gesprochene und geschriebene Sprache seien aufgrund unterschiedlicher Kommunikationsbedingungen (z. B. unmittelbarer Situationsbezug in der ersteren, kompensatorischer verbaler Situationsaufbau in der letzteren) auf unterschiedliche Umfelder verwiesen (cf. ib.).

− Mit der Thematisierung der Umfelder hingen nicht zuletzt auch die Differenzen zwischen den literarischen Gattungen zusammen; während z. B. in der Lyrik weitgehend auf eine Verbalisierung der situationellen Umfelder verzichtet werde, müßten diese in der Epik zumindest in dem Umfang zur Sprache kommen, wie dies für das Verständnis des Textinhalts erforderlich sei (ib.: 52 f.).

Die Lehre von den Umfeldern hat Coseriu in der *Textlinguistik* (1980/³1994) präzisiert. Die unzulängliche Unterscheidung lediglich von sprachlichem und außersprachlichem Umfeld, von „contexte" und „situation" im Sinne Ballys (id. 1932/⁴1965: 43 f.), wie sie sich in älteren Theorien finde (Coseriu 1980/

³1994: 124 ff.), wird durch eine komplexe Klassifikation ersetzt. Diese erfaßt die Umfelder in Form eines strukturierten Begriffsgefüges (ib.: 127), dessen grundlegende Typbegriffe (SITUATION, REGION, KONTEXT, REDEUNIVERSUM) durch weitere Ausdifferenzierung zunehmend präzisiert werden. Die Typbegriffe indizieren bereits, daß die Umfelder völlig unterschiedliche Textdimensionen determinieren.

Situation versteht Coseriu als „die Umstände und Beziehungen in Raum und Zeit, welche durch das Sprechen selbst entstehen" (ib.: 126).

Der Begriff der *Region* und seine verschiedenen Ausprägungen erfassen den Raum, in dem Sprachzeichen bekannt sind, und die Verbreitung lebensweltlicher Kenntnis der bezeichneten Gegenstände, schließlich das soziale und kulturelle Umfeld (ib.: 121).

Der *Kontext* betrifft sowohl sprachliche als auch außersprachliche Zusammenhänge: als EINZELSPRACHLICHER KONTEXT die „Sprache selbst, in der gesprochen wird" (ib.: 128); als REDEKONTEXT die einem Textsegment mittelbar oder unmittelbar vorausgehenden oder folgenden Textpartien; als AUSSERREDEKONTEXT „alle nicht-sprachlichen Umstände" (ib.) wie das materielle, im Sinne Bühlers „symphysische" Umfeld (zur Synopse der Klassifikationen von Bühler und Coseriu cf. Schlieben-Lange 1983: 23), die Konstellationen der Sprechsituation, die verschiedenen Dimensionen des Sprecherwissens.

Das *Redeuniversum*, ein von Urban in Anlehnung an die scholastische *suppositio*-Lehre und an Traditionen der Logik (de Morgan) entwickelter Begriff (Urban 1939/³1961: 197 ff.), versteht Coseriu als ein textuelles Bezugssystem, das die Textaussage als dem Bereich der Mythologie, der Fiktion, der Wissenschaft zugehörig erkennen lasse und so die Modalität des Textsinns begründe (cf. dazu Aschenberg 1999: Kap. II.2).

2.3. Die konstruktivistische Option Georges Kleibers

Im Gegenzug zu den traditionellen „statischen" Kontexttheorien, welche die verschiedenen Kontexttypen 'objektivistisch' als verschiedengeartete Zeichenumgebungen („environnements") mit bedeutungsdeterminierender Funktion akzentuierten, optiert Kleiber (1994) für eine *dynamische, kognitionstheoretisch fundierte, konstruktivistische* und *hierarchisierende* Konzeption. Kleiber unterscheidet drei grundlegende Kontexttypen, den CONTEXTE LINGUISTIQUE, die SITUATION EXTRA-LINGUISTIQUE und die CONNAISSANCES GÉNÉRALES PRÉSUMÉES PARTAGÉES (ib.: 14 u. ö.). Bei diesen Kontexten handele es sich nicht um „quelque chose d'extérieur", sondern um ausschließlich 'interne', d. h. im Gedächtnis repräsentierte, dynamisch aufeinander bezogene kognitive Bezugsgrößen (cf. ib.: 19).

Die *konstruktivistische* Option äußert sich in der gegenüber den traditionellen Theorien behaupteten Umkehrung der Determinations-Relation. Nicht der Kontext lege den Sinn einer Äußerung fest, vielmehr gebe diese vor, welches kontextuelle Modell zu wählen sei (ib.: 18). Die diversen Kontexte seien *hierarchisch* aufeinander bezogen; sofern ein sprachlicher Kontext gegeben sei, habe dieser Vorrang vor dem situationellen Zusammenhang, da der erstere dem Gedächtnis leichter verfügbar sei als der letztere.

Die von Kleiber monierte konzeptuelle Vagheit der traditionellen Kontexttheorien (cf. ib.: 11) kann dem kognitionstheoretischen Modell mindestens genauso angelastet werden. Wie der Autor selbst konstatiert, sind wir noch weit entfernt von gesicherten Erkenntnissen bezüglich der Organisation unseres semantischen Wissens und unseres Weltwissens:

„quelle est la structuration pertinente? Sous forme de prototype? [...] sous forme de *frame* (cadre), de réseau sémantique, etc.? Le débat reste ouvert" (ib.: 19).

3. Positionen in der Semantik

Die Erkenntnis, daß Kontexte für Fragestellungen der SEMANTIK eine zentrale Rolle spielen, ist keineswegs neu. So identifiziert 1910 Karl Otto Erdmann bereits 'Milieu', 'äußere Umstände' (Situation), 'Zusammenhang der Rede' (sprachlicher Kontext), 'Kenntnis des allgemeinsten Gedankenkreises' (Sprecherwissen) (cf. id. 1966: 43) als grundlegende Umfelder für die Determination der Wortbedeutung. Und Stephen Ullmann (1951/²1957: 65) betrachtet die Kontexttheorie gar als den wichtigsten Faktor in der Herausbildung der Semantik des 20. Jahrhunderts.

Während Wortfeldtheorie und strukturelle Semantik Kontexte lediglich auf der Ebene der *langue*, im Sinne von einzelsprachlich organisierten Relationen berücksichtigen, sind all jene Theorien, die in mehr oder weniger direkter Anknüpfung an die Arbeiten des Ethnologen Bronislaw Malinowski sich auf ein pragmatisches Sprachverständnis gründen, auch mit den außersprachlichen, situationellen Kontexten befaßt. Malinowski, dessen sprachwissenschaftliche Konzepte sich unmittelbar aus der Ablehnung des Mentalismus und aus der Beobachtung kommunikativer Prozesse in authochtonen Kulturen herschreiben, vertritt die Auffassung, Sprache sei prioritär als gesprochene Sprache (cf. 1923/[10]1960: 307 ff.) und als „a mode of behavior in practical matters" (ib.: 312) zu untersuchen. Den Kontextbegriff akzentuiert Malinowski auf zweierlei Weise:

1. als „linguistic context", der für gesprochene und geschriebene Sprache in gleicher Weise relevant sei;
2. als „context of situation", der vor allem für die Analyse mündlicher Äußerungen zu berücksichtigen sei (ib.: 307).

John R. Firth zeichnet den CONTEXT OF SITUATION als zentrales Konzept der Semantik aus (id. 1957: 27), versteht dieses jedoch als ein bloßes Konstrukt (id. 1968: 154; cf. dazu auch Robins 1971); dessen inhaltliche Präzisierung hat nie die Gestalt einer ausgereiften Theorie erreicht. Trotz der pragmatischen Orientierung seines Sprachverständnisses geht es ihm in erster Linie um das Systemhafte und Funktionelle am Sprech-Ereignis (cf. id. 1968: 157). Firth faßt den Situationskontext als ein komplexes Strukturgefüge, das folgende Konstituenten aufweist:

1. Personen und ihre Eigenschaften;
2. Gegenstände und Handlungen;
3. Wirkungen der sprachlichen Handlungen (cf. ib.: 177).

Des weiteren sollten Angaben zu den ökonomischen und sozialen Strukturen der jeweiligen Gesellschaft, dem aktualisierten Diskurstyp, dem Kommunikationsmedium und den Typen der Illokution erfolgen (cf. ib.: 178). Der Situationskontext, auf dem die sprachlichen Kontexte – angefangen vom phonetischen bis zum syntaktischen – aufgestuft sind (cf. id. 1957: 33), bildet „the social level" der Analyse und zugleich das Fundament in der Hierarchie der semantischen Beschreibungstechniken (ib.: 1983; cf. dazu auch Lyons 1966; zur Weiterentwicklung dieser Ansätze in der britischen Registerlinguistik cf. Halliday & Hasan 1989; Steiner 1983; Lux 1981; zur semantischen Kontexttheorie cf. Lyons 1977, 2: 570 ff.; id. 1981).

4. Positionen in der Pragmatik

Mit der Auffassung, Sprechen sei wesentlich eine Form menschlichen Handelns, rückt in der PRAGMATIK, wenn auch nur sporadisch in theoretisch expliziter Form, der situationelle Kontext in den Blick (cf. Braunroth et al. 1975: 84).

Während bei den Vertretern der philosophischen Pragmatik über das Kriterium der Angemessenheit als Bedingung des Gelingens von Sprechhandlungen (Austin 1962: 8; 12 ff.; Searle 1969: 18 f.; Duranti & Goodwin 1992: 16 ff.) Situation zumindest als abstrakte Bezugsgröße gedacht wird, finden sich in der linguistischen Pragmatik verschiedentlich Versuche, diese genauer zu bestimmen.

Die Konzeption des „pragmatischen Kontextes" ist nach Dieter Wunderlich immer auf die „idealisierte Sprechsituation" hin entworfen" (id. 1970: 175), für die er folgende Faktoren vorsieht: „Sprecher"; „Angesprochener"; „Zeit der Äußerung"; „Ort und Wahrnehmungsraum des Sprechers"; „Äußerung"; „kognitiver Inhalt der Äußerung"; „Voraussetzungen des Sprechers" (Wissen etc.); „Intention des Sprechers"; „Interrelation von Sprecher und Angesprochenem" (ib.: 178).

Dieser vornehmlich aus der Sprecherperspektive entworfene Situationsbegriff umfaßt nicht nur die grundlegenden Instanzen des Kommunikationsprozesses, sondern auch die in anderen Theorien als eigenständige Typen geführten kognitiven und sprachlichen Kontexte. Das für mündliche Äußerungen entworfene Modell lasse sich mit geringfügigen Änderungen, so der Autor, auch auf Kommunikation im Modus der Schriftlichkeit übertragen (cf. ib.).

Teun A. van Dijk entwickelt den Kontextbegriff im Sinne eines globalen Konstrukts, das auf den Ebenen von *type* und *token* für die Angemessenheit von Äußerungen und von Diskursen aufzukommen hat (id. 1977: 193 ff.). Als erste theoretisch relevante Qualität des Situationskontextes konstatiert er dessen DYNAMISCHEN Charakter: „[...] situations do not remain identical in time, but change. Hence, a context is a COURSE OF EVENTS" (ib.: 192). Unsere jeweils aktuelle Welt betrachtet van Dijk als ein Element aus der Menge *möglicher Welten*. Der aus der Modallogik stammende Begriff der *möglichen Welten* bezeichnet ein zu Explikationszwecken hypothetisch angenommenes Konstrukt, im Hinblick auf welches der aktuelle Kontext jeweils eine Spezifizierung darstellt (ib.: 192;

cf. auch id. 1980: 68 ff.; zur Verbindung von pragmatischer und kognitionstheoretischer Kontexttheorie cf. id. 1977a).

Obwohl der Kontext in den exemplarisch vorgestellten Theorien in der Regel als ein Konstrukt angesehen wird, das auf idealisierte Situationen zu beziehen sei, erweisen sich die komponentiellen Definitionen darin als unbefriedigend, da sie zwar die wichtigsten Situationsfaktoren verzeichnen, jedoch prinzipiell erweiterbar sind (cf. dazu auch Enkvist 1980: 90). Die entscheidende Schwäche des Kontextbegriffs sieht Levinson in dessen prognostischer Insuffizienz:

„Although [...] we may be able to reduce the vagueness by providing lists of relevant contextual features, we do not seem to have available any theory that will predict the relevance of all such features, and this is perhaps an embarrassment to a definition that seems to rely on the notion of context" (id. 1983: 23).

5. Interaktionale Ansätze in der Soziolinguistik

Mit der Untersuchung sozial bedingter Sprachvariation erhält auch in der SOZIOLINGUISTIK der situationelle Kontext Priorität. Zunächst mehrfach als vernachlässigte Kategorie angemahnt (Cazden 1972; Goffman 1964/1972), bezeichnet er hier ein wiederum nach verschiedenen Forschungsrichtungen je spezifisch definiertes Gefüge von Parametern, das jedoch anders als in der Pragmatik auf „empirisch erhobene Sprachdaten" angewendet wird (Kallmeyer & Schütze 1976: 4; cf. Lavandera 1988: 7; Schütze 1987).

Während im Rahmen des durch Labov begründeten „quantitativen Paradigmas" eine auf statistischer Auswertung basierende, gleichsam statische Korrelierung von sprachlichen und situationellen, insbes. sozio-ökonomischen Parametern vorgenommen wird (Lavandera 1988: 2 f.; Labov 1970/72), liegt den verschiedenen Ausrichtungen innerhalb der INTERAKTIONALEN SOZIOLINGUISTIK (Dittmar 1997: 87 ff.; → Art. 3) ein durch Dynamizität bestimmtes Situationskonzept zugrunde, demzufolge sprachliche Äußerungen und situationelle Konstellationen wechselseitig aufeinander einwirken und die Partner aktiv an der Interpretation und Konstruktion der Situation beteiligt sind (cf. auch Bayer 1977: 133 ff.). Als für den interaktionalen Ansatz allgemein grundlegende, freilich im einzelnen je besonders gewichtete und definierte Dimensionen des Kontextverständnisses nennen Alessandro Duranti und Charles Goodwin:

1. „setting" im Sinne eines „social and spational framework", d. h. eines im Gesprächsverlauf durch Intervention der Partner sich beständig ändernden Bezugsrahmens, dessen diskursive und soziale Konstellationen sich insbesondere in den deiktischen und sozialdeiktischen Ausdrücken artikulieren (id. 1992: 6 f.);
2. „behavioral environment", die Art und Weise wie die Partner durch nicht-verbale Ausdrucksmittel den Gesprächsverlauf beeinflussen (ib.: 7);
3. „language as context", Modalitäten der Bezugnahme auf Kontexte und Bildung neuer Kontexte für später folgende Gesprächsschritte (ib.: 7 f.);
4. „genres" nicht nur im Sinne von traditionellen Diskursmustern, sondern als durch das Sprechen selbst erzeugte Organisationsformen von Kontexten (ib.: 8); und
5. „extrasituational context" verstanden als „background knowledge" (ib.: 8 f.).

Zu den diesem Ansatz verpflichteten Forschungsrichtungen zählen insbes. die von Harvey Sacks, Emanuel A. Schegloff und Gail Jefferson praktizierte FORMALE KONVERSATIONSANALYSE; ausgehend von Alltagsgesprächen werden Regeln für die Strukturierung verbaler Interaktionen (Sprecherwechsel, Korrekturen etc.) auf der Grundlage der diese begleitenden Formen sozialen Handelns erfaßt (cf. Dittmar 1997: 89 ff.; Kallmeyer & Schütze 1976: 5; Bergmann 1981: 14 ff.); des weiteren die an Alfred Schütz, Aaron V. Cicourel und Harold Garfinkel anknüpfende INTERPRETATIV KOGNITIVE KONVERSATIONSANALYSE, derzufolge 'Situation' als im wesentlichen durch die Handlungen und Wahrnehmungen der Interaktionspartner produziert verstanden wird.

Innerhalb dieses Ansatzes werden insbes. die Interpretationsleistungen der Kommunikationspartner rekonstruiert sowie die als reflexive Bezugnahme auf das Gespräch und auf dessen soziale Konstellationen sich artikulierenden indexikalischen Ausdrucksmittel untersucht. (cf. Kallmeyer & Schütze 1976: 5).

Als letzte Richtung sei insbes. die mit den Arbeiten von John J. Gumperz verbundene ETHNOGRAPHISCHE KONVERSATIONSANALYSE erwähnt, die verbale Interaktion als Aktualisierung von in einer Gesellschaft geltenden

Normen, Regeln und Wissensbeständen definiert und der Frage nachgeht, wie sprachliches und soziales Wissen menschliches Handeln beeinflussen (cf. Gumperz 1992: 41; Dittmar: 1997: 97 f.). Den Begriff KONTEXTUALISIERUNG benutzt Gumperz, um die sprachlichen wie nicht-sprachlichen Bezugnahmen auf solche Kontexte zu bezeichnen, die, durch gesellschaftliche Konventionen und Traditionen fundiert, z. B. als Präsuppositionen, Erwartungen, kognitive Schemata etc. das Verstehen einer Äußerung lenken (→ Art. 1, § 1; Art. 6, § 1.3; Art. 36).

Kontextualisierung erfolgt z. B. durch *code switching* und in der Form von insbes. prosodischen und parasprachlichen Markierungen (contextualization cues). Als bloße Markierungen verfügen diese Ausdrucksformen nicht über eine referentielle, sondern lediglich über eine steuernde Funktion, indem sie die Inferenzziehung im Verstehensprozeß erleichtern (Gumperz 1993: 231 ff.), oder anders gesagt: CONTEXTUALIZATION CUES werden vom Sprecher eingesetzt, „to enact a context for the interpretation of a particular utterance" (Auer 1992: 25).

Die Orientierung an handlungstheoretischen und kognitionstheoretischen Konzepten hat somit in der jüngeren Forschung zu einer dynamischen Auffassung des Verhältnisses von Sprechen und Kontext geführt:

„[...] context and talk are now argued to stand in a mutually reflexive relationship to each other, with talk, and the interpretative work it generates, shaping context as much as context shapes talk" (Duranti & Goodwin 1992: 31).

6. Mündlichkeit und Schriftlichkeit

In den Forschungen zu SCHRIFTLICHKEIT UND MÜNDLICHKEIT ist die Theorie der Kontexte mit den unterschiedlichen MEDIALEN und KONZEPTIONELLEN Bedingungen (cf. Koch & Oesterreicher 1985: 17 ff.) geschriebener und gesprochener Sprache verknüpft.

Wichtige Überlegungen zu diesem Thema finden sich bereits bei Wegener 1885/1991, der auf der Grundlage eines psychologischen Sprachverständnisses (cf. ib.: 1 f.) die Kontexte aus der Perspektive des Subjekts als „Situation der Anschauung", als „Situation der Erinnerung" und als „Cultursituation" akzentuiert (cf. ib.: 21 ff.). Der expositionelle Aufbau einer Äußerung bzw. eines Textes hängt nach Wegener ab von der Kommunikationssituation und der Konstellation ihrer Faktoren. In dem Maße, in welchem die Kommunizierenden nicht in einer für sie transparenten „Situation der Anschauung" und durch die dieser eignenden Verständigungsmöglichkeiten (Mimik, Gestik, Einschätzung des Gesprächspartners) verbunden sind, obliegt es dem geschriebenen Text, all jene situationellen Faktoren, über die er im Unterschied zur mündlichen Kommunikation nicht verfügt, verbal zu substituieren (cf. ib.: 19 ff.); essentielle Unterschiede zwischen den literarischen Gattungen resultieren aus der unterschiedlichen Verbalisierung der situationellen Kontexte (cf. ib.: 27 f.; cf. zu diesen Fragestellungen u. a. Chafe 1982; Tannen 1982; Rader 1892; Aschenberg 1999).

In den Forschungen zu Mündlichkeit und Schriftlichkeit sind, unter Einbeziehung varietätenlinguistischer Fragestellungen, verschiedene, je nach Untersuchungsrichtung spezifizierte Definitionen von Situation und Redekontext vorgelegt worden. Der im Rahmen der Freiburger Forschungen zur gesprochenen Sprache erarbeitete Kriterienkatalog enthält primär solche Kategorien, die vor allem den sozialen Komponenten von Situationen Rechnung tragen sollen, wie etwa 'Teilnehmerzahl', 'Inszeniertheit von Situationen', 'Öffentlichkeitsgrad', 'Situationsvertrautheit', 'Situationsdistanz' (Schank & Schoenthal 1976: 29 ff.).

An den Situationsbegriff der Freiburger knüpft Hans Siegfried Scherer an, ergänzt die „soziale Dimension" des „situativen Raumes" (1984: 45) jedoch durch die „physische Dimension" (das den physischen Gegebenheiten korrespondierende Raum-Zeitbewußtsein; ib.: 51 ff.) und durch die „informatorische Dimension" (die situationell ausgelösten neurophysiologischen und kognitiven Prozesse der Informationsverarbeitung; ib.: 58 ff.).

Peter Koch und Wulf Oesterreicher (1990: 10 f.) gehen von vier Kontexttypen aus:

1. dem „situative[n] Kontext";
2. dem „Wissenskontext";
3. dem „sprachlich-kommunikative[n] Kontext (auch 'Ko-Text')";
4. den „parasprachlich-" und „nicht-sprachlich-kommunikative[n]" Kontexten.

Während im „Nähesprechen" alle Kontexte zum Einsatz gelangen können, ergibt sich beim „Distanzsprechen" aufgrund der „Situations-" und „Handlungsentbindung" eher ein „Kontextmangel", der gegebenenfalls verbal kompensiert werden muß (ib.: 11).

NÄHE und DISTANZ bezeichnen die Extreme eines Kontinuums, die, im ersten Fall dem Medium des Phonischen, im zweiten dem des Graphischen affin, durch je spezifische Kommunikationsbedingungen und diesen komplementär entsprechende Versprachlichungsstrategien definiert sind (cf. ib.: 12; zum Schweigen in mündlicher Kommunikation und in literarischen Texten cf. Saville-Troike 1985; Meise 1996).

7. Kontext in der Textlinguistik

Die Herausbildung zweier grundlegender Orientierungen in der TEXTLINGUISTIK hat eine analoge Diversifikation in der Konzeption der textuellen Kontexte zur Folge.

Im Rahmen der Erweiterung der Satzgrammatik zur Textgrammatik gilt das Hauptinteresse den einzelsprachlich determinierten TRANSPHRASTISCHEN Relationen (cf. z. B. Trabant 1981: 3; Coseriu 1980/³1994: 16 ff.); der diesem Textverständnis korrespondierende Kontextbegriff bildet die kontextuelle Relationalität als KOHÄRENZ ab, d. h. als semantischen und morphosyntaktischen Zusammenhang von Sätzen, der durch verschiedene Formen der Rekurrenz und Substitution (z. B. Brinker 1985/³1992: 14 ff., 27 ff.; Raible 1979: 65) konstituiert wird; neben den Begriff der Kohärenz tritt bisweilen der der KOHÄSION zur Bezeichnung speziell der morphosyntaktischen Beziehungen an der Textoberfläche (Dressler & de Beaugrande 1981: 50ff.); in diesem Fall erfaßt „Kohärenz" die durch die Tiefenstruktur des Textes aktivierten semantischen Relationen, die Wolfgang U. Dressler und Robert Alain de Beaugrande kognitionspsychologisch, d. h. als durch „Sinnkontinuität innerhalb des Wissens" fundiert interpretieren (cf. ib.: 88; cf. Vater 1992: 32 ff.).

Mit der zweiten Ausrichtung innerhalb der Textlinguistik etabliert sich im Zuge der Wende von einer systemlinguistisch orientierten zu einer verwendungszentrierten Sprachwissenschaft ein wesentlich komplexerer Textbegriff, der auch kommunikativen, pragmatischen und textsortenspezifischen Komponenten Rechnung tragen soll (cf. dazu Gülich & Raible 1977: 21 ff.). Anders als im Fall der Transphrastik, sieht man von den kognitionstheoretischen Deutungsansätzen ab, betreffen die kontextuellen Relationen nun nicht mehr nur sprach- bzw. textinterne, sondern auch oder wesentlich textexterne Zusammenhänge, die je nach Theorie verstärkt an den Textproduzenten oder an den Textrezipienten rückgebunden werden. János S. Petoufi (1981: 2 ff.) schlägt vor, die textuellen Kontexte durch drei Theoriekomplexe zu erfassen:

1. durch die kotextuelle Theorie;
2. durch den Komplex der „Glaubens"- und „Wissenssysteme";
3. durch die „kontextuelle Theorie", welche die Projektion der unter 1. und 2. genannten abstrakten Kontexte in die konkrete Kommunikationssituation darstellt.

Max Scherners wesentlich aus der Perspektive des Textverstehens konzipiertes Modell (id. 1984: 7) beruht auf vier „fundierenden" Begriffen, SPRACHBESITZ (individuelle Sprachkenntnisse, ib.: 63), SITUATION („Wahrnehmungsfeld der Kommunikationsteilnehmer", ib.: 67), KONTEXT (innertextuelle Relation von Textteil und Textganzem, ib.: 68) und HORIZONT („Wissensbestände", „Wertvorstellungen", ib.: 61 f.), ein Bereich, dessen Untersuchung der Wahrnehmungs- und Gedächtnispsychologie sowie der Artificial Intelligence-Forschung obliege.

Die in den textlinguistischen Theorien sich verschiedentlich abzeichnende Hinwendung zu einer kognitionstheoretischen Fundierung der Kontexte ist in anderen Arbeiten noch dezidierter vorgenommen worden, die, sei es unter dem Aspekt des Textverstehens (z. B. van Dijk & Kintsch 1983), der Textproduktion (z. B. Antos & Krings 1989) oder im Rahmen eines interaktiven Modells (Tannen 1993), von vornherein einem kognitionstheoretischen Ansatz folgen.

8. Konvergenzpunkte

'Sprechsituation' und 'Kontext' bezeichnen je nach Forschungsinteresse spezifisch konzipierte und komponentiell ausdifferenzierte Bezugsgrößen, denen sowohl für Analysen auf der Ebene des Sprachsystems wie auch der Sprachverwendung Rechnung getragen werden muß. Die Schwierigkeiten einer theoretisch fundierten und empirisch tragfähigen Konzeptualisierung dieser Begriffe beruht zum einen auf ihrer komplementären Dynamizität im konkreten Kommunikationsereignis, zum anderen auf der mit diesem verknüpften indefiniten Menge faktischer Kontexte.

Empirischer Komplexität kann konzeptuell nur durch idealisierende Reduktion begegnet werden. In den verschiedenen Klassifikationsversuchen treten, z. T. in unterschiedlicher Benennung, immer wieder drei KONTEXTTYPEN auf, die auch aufgrund ihrer ONTISCHEN DIFFERENZ als elementar, d. h. als zugleich konstitutiv und aufeinander nicht rückführbar angesehen werden können: die *Sprechsituation*, der *sprachliche Kontext* (Rede- bzw. Diskurskontext) und das *Wissen* (→ Art. 6).

Die vorgeschlagenen Ausdifferenzierungen dieser Begriffe erscheinen in theoretischer Hinsicht insofern als unbefriedigend, als sie prinzipiell beliebig erweiterbar sind; in praktischer Hinsicht hingegen fungieren sie als heuristische Parameter, deren Eignung sich freilich erst mittels der durch sie erschlossenen Daten und Sinneszuweisungen im Hinblick auf Zielsetzungen der konkreten (sprachwissenschaftlichen) Analyse zu erweisen hat.

9. Zitierte Literatur

Aschenberg, Heidi. 1999. *Kontexte in Texten.* Umfeldtheorie und literarischer Situationsaufbau. Tübingen: Niemeyer.

Auer, Peter. 1992. „Introduction: John Gumperz' Approach to Contextualization". In: Auer, Peter & Di Luzio, Aldo (eds.), 1–37.

Auer, Peter & Di Luzio, Aldo (eds.). 1992. *The Contextualization of Language.* (Pragmatics and beyond, N.S., 22 (1022).) Amsterdam & Philadelphia: Benjamins.

Bally, Charles. 1932/⁴1965. *Linguistique générale et linguistique française.* Bern: Francke.

Austin, John L. 1962. *How to Do Things with Words. The William James lectures delivered at Harvard Univ. in 1955.*. Cambridge/MA: Harvard University Press.

Bayer, Klaus. 1977. *Sprechen und Situation. Aspekte einer Theorie der sprachlichen Interaktion.* (Reihe germanistischer Linguistik, 6.) Tübingen: Niemeyer.

Beaugrande, Robert-Alain & Dressler, Wolfgang. 1981. *Einführung in die Textlinguistik.* (Konzepte der Sprach- und Literaturwissenschaft, 28.) Tübingen: Niemeyer.

Bergmann, Jörg R. 1981. „Ethnomethodologische Konversationsanalyse". In: Schröder, Peter & Steger, Hugo (eds.). *Dialogforschung.* (Jahrbuch des Instituts für Deutsche Sprache, 1980.) Düsseldorf: Schwann, 9–52.

Braunroth, Manfred et al. 1975. *Ansätze und Aufgaben der linguistischen Pragmatik.* (Fischer-Athenäum-Taschenbücher, 2091.) Frankfurt am Main: Athenäum-Fischer.

Brinker, Klaus 1985/³1992. *Linguistische Textanalyse. Eine Einführung in Grundbegriffe und Methoden.* (Grundlagen der Germanistik, 29.) Berlin: E. Schmidt.

Brown, Gillian & Yule, George Udny. 1983. *Discourse Analysis.* (Cambridge textbooks in linguistics.) Cambridge: Cambridge University Press.

Bühler, Karl. 1934/²1965. *Sprachtheorie. Die Darstellungsfunktion der Sprache.* Jena: Fischer.

Catford, John C. 1965. *A Linguistic Theory of Translation. An essay in applied linguistics.* (Language and language learning, 8.) London: Oxford University Press.

Chafe, Wallace L. 1982. „Integration and Involvement in Speaking, Writing and Oral Literature". In: Tannen, Deborah (ed.), 35–53.

Coseriu, Eugenio. 1955/56. „Determinación y entorno. Dos problemas de una lingüística del hablar". *Romanistisches Jahrbuch* VII: 29–54.

Coseriu, Eugenio & Albrecht, Jörn. 1980/³1994. *Textlinguistik. Eine Einführung.* (UTB, 1808.) Tübingen: Francke.

Dijk, Teun A. van. 1977. *Text and Context. Explorations in the semantics and pragmatics of discourse.* (Longman linguistics library, 21.) London: Longman.

Dijk, Teun A. van. 1977a. „Context and Speech Act Comprehension". *Journal of Pragmatics* 1: 211–32.

Dijk, Teun A. van & Kintsch, Walter. 1983. *Strategies of Discourse Comprehension.* New York: Academic Press.

Dittmar, Norbert. 1997. *Grundlagen der Soziolinguistik. Ein Arbeitsbuch mit Aufgaben.* (Konzepte der Sprach- und Literaturwissenschaft, 57.) Tübingen: Niemeyer.

Duranti, Alessandro & Goodwin, Charles (eds.). 1992. *Rethinking context. Language as an interactive phenomenon.* (Studies in the social and cultural foundations of language.) Cambridge: Cambridge University Press.

Duranti, Alessandro & Goodwin, Charles. 1992. „Rethinking context: an introduction". In: Duranti, Alessandro & Goodwin, Charles (eds.), 1–42.

Enkvist, Nils Erik. 1980. „Categories of Situational Context from the perspective of stylistics". *Language Teaching and Linguistics Abstracts* XIII: 75–94.

Erdmann, Karl Otto. 1966. *Die Bedeutung des Wortes. Aufsätze aus dem Grenzgebiet der Sprachpsychologie und Logik.* Darmstadt: Wissenschaftliche Buchgesellschaft.

Firth, John R. 1957. *Papers in Linguistics 1934–1951.* London: Oxford University Press.

Firth, John R. 1964. *The Tongues of Men and Speech.* (Language and language learning, 2.) London: Oxford University Press.

François, Frédéric. 1969. „Contexte et situation". In: Martinet, André & Walter, Henriette (eds.). *La Linguistique. Guide alphabétique.* (Collection guides alphabétiques, méditations.) Paris, Denoel. 64–72.

Germain, Claude. 1973. *La notion de situation en linguistique.* Ottawa/Canada: Ed. de l'Université d'Ottawa.

Giglioli, Pier P. (ed.). 1964/²1972. *Language and Social Context. Selected readings.* (Penguin modern sociology readings.) Harmondsworth/Middlesex: Penguin Books.

Goffman, Erving. 1964/²1972. „The Neglected Situation". In: Giglioli, Pier P. (ed.). *Language and Social Context. Selected readings.* (Penguin modern sociology readings.) Harmondsworth/Middlesex: Penguin Books, 61–66.

Gülich, Elisabeth & Raible, Wolfgang. 1977. *Linguistische Textmodelle. Grundlagen und Möglichkeiten.* (UTB, 130.) München: Fink.

Gumperz, John J. 1992. „Contextuality and understanding". In: Duranti, Alessandro & Goodwin, Charles (eds.), 229–52.

Gumperz, John J. 1992a. „Contextualization Revisited". In Auer, Peter & Di Luzio, Aldo (eds.), 39–53.

Halliday, Michael A. K. & Hasan, Ruqaiya. 1985/²1989. *Language, Context and Text: Aspects of Language in a Social-Semiotic Perspective.* (Language education.) Oxford: Oxford University Press.

Haslett, Beth. 1987. *Communication: Strategic Action in Context.* (Commucication.) Hillsdale/NJ: Erlbaum.

Kallmeyer, Werner. 1974. „Situation". *Linguistik und Didaktik* 18: 161–64.

Kallmeyer, Werner & Schütze, Fritz. 1976. „Konversationsanalyse". In.: Wunderlich, Dieter (ed.). *Wissenschaftstheorie der Linguistik.* (Athenäum-Taschenbücher, 2104.) Kronberg: Athenäum-Verlag, 1–28.

Kleiber, Georges. 1994. „Contexte, interprétation et mémoire: approche standard vs approche cognitive". *Langue française* 103: 9–22.

Koch, Peter & Oesterreicher, Wulf. 1985. „Sprache der Nähe – Sprache der Distanz". *Romanistisches Jahrbuch* 35: 15–43.

Koch, Peter & Oesterreicher, Wulf. 1990. *Gesprochene Sprache in der Romania: Französisch, Italienisch, Spanisch.* (Romanistische Arbeitshefte, 31.) Tübingen: Niemeyer.

Labov, William. 1970/1972. „The Study of Language in its Social Context". In: Giglioli, Pier P. (ed.), 283–307.

Langendoen, Donald T. 1968. *The London School of Linguistics. A Study on the Linguistic Theories of B. Malinowski and J. R. Firth.* (M.I.T. Press Research monograph, 46.) Cambridge/Mass.: M.I.T. Press.

Lavandera, Beatriz R. 1988. „The study of language in its socio-cultural context". In: Newmeyer, Frederick J. (ed.). *Linguistics: The Cambridge Survey. Vol. IV: Language: The Socio-cultural Context.* Cambridge: Cambridge University Press, 1–13.

Levinson, Stephen C. 1983. *Pragmatics.* (Cambridge textbooks in linguistics.) Cambridge: Cambridge University Press.

Lux, Friedemann. 1981. *Text, Situation, Textsorte. Dargestellt am Beispiel der britischen Registerlinguistik, mit einem Ausblick auf eine adäquate Textsortentheorie.* (Tübinger Beiträge zur Linguistik, 172.) Tübingen: Narr.

Lyons, John. 1966. „Firth's Theory of Meaning". In: Bazell, Charles & Firth, John R. (eds.): *In Memory of John R. Firth.* (Longmans' linguistics library.) London: Longmans, 288–302.

Lyons, John. 1977. *Semantics.* 2 Bde. Cambridge & al.: Cambridge University Press.

Lyons, John. 1981. *Language, Meaning and Context.* (Fontana paperbacks, 5923.) London: Fontana.

Malinowski, Bronislaw. 1923/¹⁰1960. „The Problem of Meaning in Primitive Languages". In: Ogden, Charles K. & Richards, Ivor A. *The Meaning of Meaning.* (International library of psychology, philosophy and scientific method.) London: Routledge & Kegan Paul, 296–336.

Malinowski, Bronislaw. 1935/1978. *Coral Gardens and Their Magic. A Study of the Methods of Tilling the Soil and of Agricultural Rites in the Trobriand Islands.* New York: Dover Publications.

Meise, Katrin. 1996. *Une forte absence. Schweigen in alltagsweltlicher und literarischer Kommunikation.* (ScriptOralia, 89.) Tübingen: Narr.

Mounin, Georges. 1966. „La notion de situation en linguistique". *Les Temps Modernes,* 24: 1065–94.

Palmer, Frank R. (ed.). 1968. *Selected papers of J. R. Firth: 1952–1959.* (Longmans' linguistics library, [7].) London: Longmans.

Petőfi, János Sándor 1981. „Kommunikationstheorie, Theorie der Textinterpretation, Aspekte einer Repräsentationssprache". In: Dorfmüller-Karpusa, Käthi & Petőfi, János Sandor (eds.): *Text, Kontext, Interpretation. Einige Aspekte der texttheoretischen Forschung.* (Papiere zur Textlinguistik, 35.) Hamburg: Buske, 1–28.

Pinkal, Manfred. 1985. „Kontextabhängigkeit, Vagheit, Mehrdeutigkeit". In: Schwarze, Christoph & Wunderlich, Dieter (eds.). *Handbuch der Lexikologie.* Königstein/Ts.: Athenaeum, 27–63.

Rader, Margaret. 1982. „Context in written Language: The Case of Imaginative Fiction". In: Tannen, Deborah (ed.), 185–98.

Raible, Wolfgang, 1979. „Zum Textbegriff und zur Textlinguistik". In: J.S. Petöfi (ed.): *Text vs. Sentence. Basic Questions of Text Linguistics. First Part.* Hamburg: Buske, 63–73.

Robins, Robert H. 1971. „Malinowski, Firth and the 'Context of Situation'". In: Ardener, Edwin (ed.): *Social Anthropology and Language*. (ASA monographs, 10.) London: Tavistock, 33−46.

Saville-Troike, Muriel. 1985. „The place of silence in an integrated theory of communication". In: Tannen, Deborah & Saville-Troike, Muriel (eds.). *Perspectives of Silence*. Norwood: Ablex.

Schank, Gerd & Schoenthal, Gisela. 1976. *Gesprochene Sprache. Eine Einführung in Forschungsansätze und Analysemethoden*. (Germanistische Arbeitshefte, 18.) Tübingen: Niemeyer.

Schütze, Fritz. 1987. „Situation". In: Ammon, Ulrich & al. (eds.). *Sociolinguistics/Soziolinguistik* (= Handbücher zur Sprach- und Kommunikationswissenschaft, 3.1.), 157−64.

Scherer, Hans Siegfried. 1984. *Sprechen im situativen Kontext. Theorie und Praxis der Analyse des spontanen Sprachgebrauchs*. (Romanica et comparatistica, 3.) Tübingen: Stauffenberg.

Scherner, Max. 1984. *Sprache als Text. Ansätze zu einer sprachwissenschaftlich begründeten Theorie des Textverstehens. Forschungsgeschichte, Problemstellung, Beschreibung*. (Reihe germanistische Linguistik, 48.) Tübingen: Niemeyer.

Schlieben-Lange, Brigitte. 1983. *Traditionen des Sprechens. Elemente einer pragmatischen Sprachgeschichtsschreibung*. Stuttgart etc.: Kohlhammer.

Searle, John R. 1969. *Speech Acts. An Essay in the Philosophy of Language*. Cambridge: Cambridge University Press.

Slama-Cazacu, Tatjana. 1961. *Langage et contexte. Le problème du langage dans la conception de l'expression et de l'interprétation par des organisations contextuelles*. (Ianua linguarum: Series major, 6.) s'Gravenhague: Mouton.

Steiner, Erich 1983. *Die Entwicklung des britischen Kontextualismus*. (Sammlung Groos, 16.) Heidelberg: Groos.

Stierle, Karlheinz. 1974. „Zur Begriffsgeschichte von 'Kontext'". *Archiv für Begriffsgeschichte* XVIII: 144−49.

Tannen, Deborah (ed.). 1982. *Spoken and written Language. Exploring Orality and Literacy*. (Advances in discourse processes, 9.) Norwood/NJ: Ablex.

Tannen, Deborah. 1982. „The Oral/Literate Continuum in Discourse". In: id. (ed.), 1−16.

Tannen, Deborah. 1993. *Framing in Discourse*. New York: Oxford University Press.

Trabant, Jürgen. 1981. „Wissenschaftsgeschichtliche Bemerkungen zur Textlinguistik". In: Kotschi, Thomas (ed.): *Beiträge zur Linguistik des Französischen*. Tübingen: Narr, 1−20.

Ullmann, Stephen. 1951/²1957. *The Principles of Semantics*. (Glasgow University publications, 84 (84,2,57).) Glasgow: Jackson.

Urban, Wilbur Marshall. 1939³1961. *Language and Reality. The Philosophy of Language and the Principles of Symbolism*. Londo: Allen & Unwin.

Vater, Heinz. 1992. *Einführung in die Textlinguistik*. (UTB für Wissenschaft, Uni-Taschenbücher, 1660, Linguistik, Literaturwissenschaft.) München: Fink.

Wegener, Philipp. 1885/1991. *Untersuchungen über die Grundfragen des Sprachlebens*. Neu herausgegeben von Konrad Koerner. (Amsterdam studies in the theory and history of linguistic science, Series 2, classics in psycholinguistics, 5.) Amsterdam & Philadelphia: Benjamins.

Heidi Aschenberg, Universität Heidelberg (Deutschland)

35. Sprachliches Handeln, Kommunikantenrollen, Beziehungsaspekte

1. Handeln und Sprache
2. Beispiele für die beiden Ansatz-Typen
3. Kommunikantenrollen
4. Dimensionen sprachlicher Koproduktivität
5. Soziale Rollen, Identität, Selbstbild
6. Zitierte Literatur

1. Handeln und Sprache

Die linguistische Pragmatik ist bestimmt von Modellen, die sich auf Konzepte der Handlung oder des Handelns beziehen. Es ist Teil des sprachwissenschaftlichen 'common sense', sprachlich-kommunikative Äußerungen als sprachliches Handeln aufzufassen. Diese „action tradition" innerhalb der Linguistik, wie sie Herbert H. Clark (1992: XII) nennt, hat verschiedene Wurzeln und es lassen sich zwei Richtungen unterscheiden.

− Eine erste steht in der Tradition der philosophischen Ansätze, die davon ausgehen, daß sprachlich-kommunikatives Handeln der Kontrolle von Subjekten unterliegt, die stets absichtsvoll und rational miteinander kommunizieren.
− Eine zweite entstammt dem Zusammenhang soziologischer und sozialphänomenologischer Ansätze, die sprachlich-kommunikatives Handeln ausgehend von gemeinsamen Aktivitäten und Sinnbil-

dungsprozessen fassen. Sprachlich-kommunikatives Handeln basiert danach auf einer Koordination und Koproduktion der Kommunikanten, die Subjektivität nicht voraussetzt, sondern in deren Rahmen sich Subjektivität überhaupt erst entfaltet. Gleichzeitig wird die Kontrollierbarkeit der einzelnen Sprachhandlung relativiert, und es werden Konzepte von Kreativität und Spontaneität wichtig, die dem Vorkommen nicht intendierter, nicht kontrollierter Handlungsergebnisse Rechnung tragen (→ Art. 3).

1.1. Subjektivistische Ansätze

Wesentlichen Anteil an einer handlungstheoretischen Fundierung linguistisch-pragmatischer Forschung haben eine Reihe von Konzeptionen, die im Rahmen der analytischen Philosophie, und hier im Umfeld der sogenannten 'ordinary language philosophy' entstanden sind. Dies sind einmal die Vorstellungen vom SPRACHSPIEL als einer regelgeleiteten, kulturabhängigen sprachlichen Aktivität, wie sie Ludwig Wittgenstein in kritischer Auseinandersetzung mit seinen frühen Arbeiten in Cambridge entwickelt (Wittgenstein 1953). Dies sind zum anderen die sprechakttheoretischen Konzeptionen von John Austin (1998/1962) und John Searle (1997/1969) sowie die sprecherbezogene Bedeutungstheorie und die Theorie der Konversationsmaximen des Philosophen Herbert Paul Grice (1957; 1993/1975).

Diesen Konzeptionen gemeinsam ist die Vorstellung, daß sprachliche Äußerungen als Aktivitäten zu beschreiben sind, deren Bedeutung mit Blick auf den spezifischen Kontext der Aktivitäten und den spezifischen Gebrauch, der darin von ihnen gemacht wird, zu bestimmen sind. Dieses Verständnis sprachlicher Äußerungen spricht etwa deutlich aus dem Titel *How to do things with words*, den Austin für seine Harvard-Vorlesung von 1955 wählt (veröffentlicht unter demselben Titel 1962).

Eine weitere philosophische Richtung, die für die linguistische Pragmatik wichtig wird, ist der amerikanische Pragmatismus, zu dessen Initiatoren Charles Sanders Peirce und William James zählen und der in der zweiten Generation von John Dewey weitergeführt wird. Der amerikanische Pragmatismus nimmt indirekt in zweifacher Hinsicht Einfluß auf die linguistische Pragmatik. Einmal wird die Zeichentheorie von Peirce zur Grundlage der Semiotik von Charles Morris, der in dieser Arbeit den Terminus PRAGMATIK einführt. Er bezeichnet den Forschungsbereich innerhalb der Semiotik, der sich mit der Erforschung der Beziehungen zwischen Zeichen und Interpretanten beschäftigt: „At the same time 'pragmatics' as a specifically semiotical term must receive its own formulation. By 'pragmatics' is designated the science of the relation of signs to their interpreters" (Morris 1938: 30).

Zum anderen verweisen William James und John Dewey in ihren Arbeiten auf die Relevanz der Handlung für das Verstehen und unterstützen so eine Sprachauffassung, nach der wir etwas mit Sprache tun (Dewey 1958; James 1931). Nach Buekens (1995: 428) kann Austin aus dieser Sicht als Vertreter einer britischen Variante des Pragmatismus angesehen werden.

1.2. Interaktionistische Ansätze

Neben diesen philosophischen Konzeptionen sind für die linguistische Pragmatik aber auch Modelle wichtig geworden, die in der Tradition soziologischer Handlungstheorien stehen. Zentrale Bedeutung hat hier die Konversationsanalyse erlangt, die Harvey Sacks, Emanuel Schegloff und Gail Jefferson begründet haben. Sie überträgt ethnomethodologische Vorstellungen, wie sie Harold Garfinkel entwickelt hat, auf die sprachliche Konversation (Sacks & al. 1974; Garfinkel 1967; Heritage 1995). Die Ethnomethodologie wiederum ist in besonderem Maße beeinflußt von der Sozialphänomenologie, wie sie Alfred Schütz unter Zusammenführung soziologischer und phänomenologischer Konzeptionen entwickelt hat (Schütz & Luckmann 1979; 1984).

In großer Nähe dazu wird auch der symbolische Interaktionismus für die Linguistik wichtig. Er basiert auf der soziologischen Handlungstheorie von George Herbert Mead und nimmt ebenfalls (sozial-)phänomenologische Überlegungen auf (Blumer 1995; Mead 1968/1934). In der Weiterentwicklung zur Wissenssoziologie nimmt die Sozialphänomenologie überdies auch direkt Einfluß auf die linguistische Pragmatik (Berger & Luckmann 1980/1966; Luckmann 1992) (→ Art. 3).

1.3. Das Nebeneinander der beiden Ansätze

Die soziologischen Handlungskonzeptionen werden bis heute in philosophischen Zusammenhängen kaum zur Kenntnis genommen. So wird etwa auch die von Mead entwickelte Handlungstheorie, obgleich sie sich ganz wesentlich auf die sprachliche Interaktion bezieht und sein Werk den sogenannten 'linguistic turn' in der Soziologie bewirkt hat, weder von Austin oder Searle noch von Grice rezipiert (Wenzel 1992: 733).

Dies liegt nicht zuletzt in den theoretischen Divergenzen begründet, die zwischen den erwähnten soziologischen und philosophischen Ansätzen bestehen. Es stehen sich Konzeptionen gegenüber, die (sprachliches) Handeln einmal – dies betrifft die analytische Philosophie – vom Subjekt aus konzipieren, und zum anderen – dies gilt für die skizzierten soziologischen und (sozial-)phänomenologischen Ansätze – wesentlich vom interaktiven Geschehen ausgehen.

Nicht zuletzt auch aufgrund der Heterogenität der handlungstheoretischen Konzeptionen hat sich eine einheitliche theoretische Fundierung der linguistischen Pragmatik bislang nicht ergeben (vgl. Schlieben-Lange 1979). Es liegen vielmehr verschiedene Ansätze vor, die sich in unterschiedlicher Weise auf die genannten philosophischen oder soziologischen Handlungskonzepte beziehen. Dabei fließen auch soziolinguistische und linguistisch-anthropologische Konzepte in die linguistische Pragmatik ein und werden mit den Handlungskonzepten verbunden. Aufgegriffen werden hier etwa methodische und theoretische Konzepte, wie sie den soziolinguistischen Arbeiten von William Labov (1972) oder auch der „Ethnographie des Sprechens" von Dell Hymes (1979/1962) zugrunde liegen.

Sowohl die philosophischen als auch die soziologischen Ansätze führen in einer konsequenten Umsetzung zu einer linguistischen Pragmatik, die das sprachlich-kommunikative Handeln in das Zentrum rückt und es zum Ausgangspunkt für morphologische, syntaktische, phonologische und semantische Untersuchungen macht. Ehlich (1987: 280 f.) weist darauf hin, daß dies eine „Revision von analytischen Grundannahmen" bedeutet, nach denen das Sprachsystem das Zentrum und den Ausgangspunkt linguistischer Analyse bildet. Diese Revision ist jedoch in der linguistischen Pragmatik nicht wirklich erfolgt. Die pragmatische Analyse wird noch immer wesentlich als Ergänzung und Erweiterung sprachsystematischer Analysen begriffen und betrieben.

1.4. Begriffliche Vielfalt

Entsprechend der vielfältigen theoretischen Ansätze ist auch die Terminologie innerhalb der linguistischen Pragmatik uneinheitlich.

Termini wie *Sprechhandlung, Sprachhandlung, Äußerungshandlung, Sprechakt, sprachliche Aktivität* sind definiert innerhalb der einzelnen Untersuchung. Sie können so verschiedene Bedeutungen haben. Im Falle von Sprechhandlung etwa kann es sich einmal um die Übersetzung des in der Sprechakttheorie verankerten *speech act* handeln, der Terminus kann aber auch eine spezifische Bedeutung haben. Dies ist etwa in der Sprechakttheorie von Wunderlich (1976) der Fall, die 'Sprechakte' und 'Sprechhandlungen' systematisch unterscheidet.

Auch der Terminus linguistische Pragmatik selbst wird unterschiedlich verwendet. Oft bezeichnet er in einem weiten Sinne den Bereich linguistischer Forschungen, der sich nicht mit der Grammatik beschäftigt. Neben einer solchen Bestimmung *e negativo* liegen aber auch Ansätze vor, die auf eine theoretische Fundierung und eine systematische Verortung pragmatischer Fragestellungen innerhalb der Linguistik zielen. Die Bezeichnung 'linguistische Pragmatik' hat darin jeweils eine spezifische Bedeutung.

Letzteres gilt etwa für die Sprechakttheorie von Dieter Wunderlich. Die Pragmatik bildet hier einen Teilbereich der Sprechakttheorie. Ausgehend von seiner Konzeption der Sprechakttheorie, die er als eine „Erweiterung der Theorie der Bedeutung in natürlichen Sprachen" (Wunderlich 1976: 119) versteht, die zu einer Klärung der Bedeutung nicht-deklarativer Sätze beitragen soll, umfaßt die Pragmatik den Teilbereich, der sich mit Bedeutungen in Abhängigkeit vom Kontext beschäftigt. In der Semantik, die innerhalb der Sprechakttheorie betrieben wird, wird demgegenüber vom Kontext abstrahiert. So lassen sich nach Wunderlich die Sprechakte des Fragens und Aufforderns semantisch beschreiben (1976: 119), während die Sprechakte des Warnens und des Ratschlags pragmatisch erfaßt werden müssen, weil sie immer kontextuell verankert sind (1976: 175 ff.).

Auch der funktionalen Pragmatik liegt ein spezifischer Pragmatik-Begriff zugrunde. Als pragmatisch werden allein solche Untersuchungen begriffen, die das sprachliche Handeln als Teil des gesellschaftlichen Handelns begreifen und es in Abgrenzung zur strukturalistischen Analyse systematisch vor dem Hintergrund seiner gesellschaftlichen Zwecksetzungen analysieren (Rehbein 1977; Brünner & Graefen 1994; Ehlich 1991). Eine solche Perspektive schließt etwa zeichentheoretische Modellierungen der linguistischen Pragmatik aus, weil sie diese auf eine „Wissenschaft vom Zeichen" reduzieren (Rehbein 1992).

2. Beispiele für die beiden Ansatz-Typen

Die Konzeption der Konversations-Implikaturen von Herbert Paul Grice soll in § 2.1 als einflußreiches und prominentes Beispiel für den auf das handelnde Subjekt zentrierten Typ von Handlungsmodellen dargestellt werden. Als ein instruktives Beispiel für die Modellierung von Kommunikation als das Ergebnis gemeinsamer Aktivitäten und Sinnbildungsprozesse wird anschließend in § 2.2 das phänomenologische Kommunikationsmodell von Bernhard Waldenfels (1980; 1987) in einigen für die linguistische Pragmatik relevanten Aspekten skizziert.

2.1. Kommunikation als prinzipiengeleitete rationale Aktivität

Die Konzeption der Konversations-Implikaturen, die Grice (1957; 1993) entwickelt hat, hat in der Linguistik zentrale Bedeutung erlangt. Sie findet in fast allen Einführungen in die Linguistik bzw. in die linguistische Pragmatik Erwähnung. Aus einer analytisch-philosophischen Perspektive geht es um die Prinzipien, die dem Erfassen von Bedeutung in der Kommunikation sowie dem Zustandekommen von Kommunikation zugrunde liegen.

Nach Grice (1957; 1993) umfaßt die kommunikative Handlung verschiedene Arten von Bedeutungen. Dies sind einmal die 'konventionale Bedeutung' (Grice 1993: 247), die der wörtlichen Bedeutung des Gesagten entspricht, sowie auch die Präsuppositionen dieser wörtlichen Bedeutungen, die nach Grice stets konventional impliziert sind. Impliziert werden darüber hinaus vom Sprecher auch konversationelle Bedeutungen der sprachlichen Handlungen, die sich – anders als die Präsuppositionen – nicht aus dem Gesagten ergeben. Sie können dem Gesagten sogar widersprechen (Kemmerling 1991).

Erschlossen werden diese konversationalen Implikaturen des Sprechers vor dem Hintergrund verschiedener Konversationsmaximen, deren Gültigkeit in der Kommunikation unterstellt wird. Dieses Erschließen der konversationalen Implikaturen kann als besondere Form pragmatischer Inferenz gefaßt werden (Levinson 1994: 100 ff.). In den Konversationsmaximen, die Grice ansetzt, drückt sich insgesamt ein allgemeines 'Kooperationsprinzip' aus, das Grice im Sinne eines Postulats in allen Fällen sprachlicher Kommunikation für gegeben annimmt:

„Mache deinen Gesprächsbeitrag jeweils so, wie es dem akzeptierten Zweck oder der akzeptierten Richtung des Gesprächs, an dem du teilnimmst, gerade verlangt wird. Dies könnte man mit dem Etikett Kooperationsprinzip versehen" (Grice 1993: 248).

Dieses Kooperationspostulat wird durch vier Konversationsmaximen entfaltet, die im Gegensatz zum allgemeinen Kooperationspostulat keine universelle Gültigkeit haben. In Orientierung an Kantschen Kategorien unterscheidet er die Maximen der QUANTITÄT, der QUALITÄT, der RELATION und der MODALITÄT.

Die Maxime der QUANTITÄT betrifft die Informativität. Die Äußerung soll so informativ sein, wie es für die Kommunikationszwecke notwendig ist, nicht mehr und nicht weniger (Grice 1993: 249). Die Maxime der QUALITÄT verlangt, daß die Äußerung wahr sein soll (Grice 1993: 249). Die Konversationsmaxime der RELATION fordert die Relevanz der Äußerung in der Kommunikation (Grice 1993: 249 f.). Die Maxime der MODALITÄT schließlich bezieht sich auf die Äußerungsform, die so gewählt sein soll, daß ihr die Bedeutung klar zu entnehmen ist (Grice 1993: 250).

Die Konversationsmaximen können im Gegensatz zum allgemeinen Kooperationsprinzip „storniert" werden (Grice 1993: 264). Dies ist etwa bei der Ironie gegeben; auch sind Äußerungen keineswegs immer wahr oder informativ. Nach Grice wird in solchen Fällen das Aussetzen einer Konversationsmaxime durch den Sprecher angezeigt. Dies kann in Form einer expliziten Formulierung geschehen oder aber durch die ungewöhnliche Verwendung eines Ausdrucks, der normalerweise auf eine konversationale Implikatur schließen läßt (Grice 1993: 264).

Das Gricesche Modell steht in der Tradition der analytischen Philosophie, und es verfolgt dabei eine besondere Perspektive. Die Analyse der Kommunikation zielt auf die Verstehensprozesse des Individuums; sie ist im Kern intentionalistisch (Verschueren 1999: 46 ff.; Rolf 1994: 35 ff.). Damit unterscheidet sie sich deutlich von den Theorien einer gemeinsam, interaktiv und koproduktiv bewerkstelligten Kommunikation. Auch dürfen die Konversationsmaximen, die er für das kommunikative Handeln ansetzt, nicht mit den pragmatischen Regeln identifiziert werden, wie sie im Anschluß an Wittgenstein etwa in der Sprechakttheorie von Searle diskutiert werden (Meggle 1997: 313 f.). Diese pragmatischen Regeln sind objektive Regeln, die unabhängig von den jeweils subjektiven Intentionen der Kommunikanten gelten (hierzu etwa Searle (1997/1969: 96 ff.). Für Grice sind in seiner intentionalistischen Perspektive aber gerade die subjektiven Absichten, Einstellungen und Erwartungen Ansatz- und Ausgangspunkt der Analyse.

Die Konzeption der Konversationsmaximen und Implikaturen, wie Grice sie entwickelt hat, zielt nicht zuvörderst auf eine Kommunikationstheorie. Vielmehr geht es um eine Semantik auf „intentionalistischer Basis" (Meggle 1997: 317), die von der analytisch-philosophischen Annahme ausgeht, daß sich die Bedeutung von Ausdrücken nur unter Rekurs auf ihren Gebrauch in der Kommunikation bestimmen läßt. Die Beschäftigung mit der Kommunikation im Rahmen einer Semantik ergibt sich als Konsequenz aus dieser Annahme.

2.1.1. Weiterentwicklungen

In Auseinandersetzung mit dem Griceschen Modell entstehen in den 60er und 70er Jahren weitere Ansätze, die in der Regel ebenfalls aus analytisch-philosophischer Sicht die von Grice behandelten Fragestellungen aufgreifen (für einen Überblick vgl. Liedtke 1995: 30 ff.).

In diesen Zusammenhang gehört etwa die „Lehre von den Unglücksfällen", in der John L. Austin (1998/1962), ausgehend von den Fällen des Mißlingens, die notwendigen Bedingungen für ein erfolgreiches sprachliches Handeln expliziert. Hintergrund ist seine Theorie der Sprechakte, nach der Äußerungen performativ sind, also illokutionäre Rollen haben; sie drohen, warnen, versprechen oder bitten. Ein Gelingen der sprachlichen Handlung bzw. der performativen Äußerung setzt dann einmal voraus, daß diese zustande kommt, die Äußerung also performativ ist und die Illokution ausgedrückt wird. Zum anderen muß nach Austin die performative Äußerung ehrlich vollzogen werden. Der Sprecher muß es ehrlich meinen, und er muß auch die Konsequenzen übernehmen, also etwa ein angekündigtes Versprechen erfüllen (Austin 1998: 35 ff.).

In den 70er Jahren unternehmen Gordon & Lakoff (1975) den Versuch, das Konzept der Konversationspostulate in eine generative Semantik zu integrieren. Ferner werden in Auseinandersetzung mit der Griceschen Konzeption verschiedene Modifizierungen und Neuerungen vorgeschlagen. Kasher (1976) etwa schlägt ein Rationalitätsprinzip vor, nach dem der Gesprächsbeitrag so gewählt wird, daß das intendierte Ziel möglichst effektiv und mit geringem Aufwand umgesetzt wird. Auf der Annahme einer praktischen Rationalität basiert auch das „Prinzip der Höflichkeit", das Penelope Brown und Stephen S. Levinson (1996/[1]1978) diskutieren. Danach verhalten Kommunikanten sich höflich, weil sie dann davon ausgehen können, daß die anderen dies auch tun. Dies verringert die Gefahr einer Irritation des Selbstbilds in der Kommunikation.

Aus jüngerer Zeit stammt das Konzept der Relevanz von Deirdre Wilson und Dan Sperber, das an die Stelle verschiedener Maximen ein zentrales Prinzip, die Relevanz, setzt (Sperber & Wilson 1995; Wilson & Sperber 1998). Danach erwartet ein Hörer, daß eine Äußerung so relevant ist, daß es sich lohnt, sie zu verarbeiten, und daß der Sender sich vor dem Hintergrund seiner Möglichkeiten und Ziele um maximale Relevanz bemüht hat (Sperber & Wilson 1995: 270 f.).

Anders als Grice, der die Rationalität und Kooperativität sprachlichen Handelns einfach postuliert, argumentieren Sperber & Wilson (1995) und Wilson & Sperber (1998) kognitivistisch. Das Prinzip der Relevanz wird auf ein universales, kognitives Bestreben zurückgeführt:

„The criterion proposed in *Relevance* is based on a fundamental assumption about human cognition: that human cognition is relevance-orientated; we pay attention to information that seems relevant to us" (Wilson & Sperber 1998: 8).

Die Relevanz einer Information steht dabei im Zusammenhang mit den „contextual effects", die ihre Verarbeitung begleiten (Sperber & Wilson 1995: 108). Diese ergeben sich dann, wenn sich neue Information in den informationellen Kontext alter Informationen einpassen läßt. Im besten Fall kann das Individuum die neue Information erfolgreich mit der alten Information verbinden. Möglich ist aber auch, daß sich inferentiell kein Zusammenhang zwischen alter und neuer Information herstellen läßt. Die Relevanz einer Information ist nach Sperber & Wilson (1995: 265 f.) um so bedeutender, je größer der Kontextualisierungseffekt ist und je leichter er sich einstellt.

Angenommen werden zwei Prinzipien der Relevanz, die sich einmal auf die KOGNITION und einmal auf die KOMMUNIKATION beziehen.

— Auf die Kognition bezieht sich das kognitive Prinzip der Relevanz, nach dem die menschliche Kognition stets nach einer Maximierung der Relevanz strebt: „Cognitive principle of relevance. Human cognition tends to be geared to the maximization of relevance" (Wilson & Sperber 1998: 9).
— Für die Kommunikation kann maximale Relevanz nicht immer erwartet werden. Nicht immer besitzt der Sprecher für den Hörer relevante Informationen, nicht immer möchte er sie preisgeben, auch können „umständliche Formulierungen" vorliegen. Das kommunikative Prinzip der Relevanz fassen Wilson & Sperber aus diesen Gründen nicht als Prinzip maximaler, sondern nur als Prinzip optimaler Relevanz: „Communicative principle of relevance. Every act of overt communication communicates a presumption of its own optimal relevance" (Wilson & Sperber 1998: 11).

2.1.2. Kritik

Zentrale Prämisse des Griceschen Modells und der meisten der Nachfolgemodelle ist, daß der kommunikative Umgang mit Sprache stets rational und kontrolliert erfolgt (Kemmerling 1991: 234). Hier setzt die Kritik an. Danach handelt es sich um eine Idealisierung, die den tatsächlichen Verhältnissen nur zum Teil gerecht wird. So bleibt etwa das kreative Handeln ausgeklammert, das zufällige, nicht intendierte Resultate hat (Joas 1996). Auch die Erklärung von routinierten oder spontanen Handlungen, deren Kontrolle aus verschiedenen Gründen nicht vollständig erfolgt, wird vor dem Hintergrund der Prämisse schwierig (→ Art. 3).

Ferner verweisen phänomenologische Studien darauf, daß Gedachtes oder Intendiertes und dessen Äußerung in der sprachlichen Kommunikation nicht identisch sind. Das Gedachte verändert sich mit der sprachlichen Artikulation (Merleau-Ponty 1966). Diese Problematik kann eine intentionalistische Modellierung der Kommunikation nach Grice nicht erfassen.

Kritik an dem Griceschen Modell läßt sich auch aus einer ethnographischen Perspektive üben. Aaron Cicourel kritisiert, daß die in der Griceschen Konzeption vorgenommene Trennung zwischen der wörtlichen Bedeutung, die eine situationsunabhängige, stabile 'Kernbedeutung' darstellt, und den verschiedenen, im jeweiligen situativen Zusammenhang implizierten weiteren Bedeutungsaspekten, unzulässig ist. Seiner Ansicht nach wird dabei nicht gesehen, daß die Verarbeitung sprachlicher Informationen immer einen spezifischen kulturellen und alltagspraktischen Rahmen hat, der das Verstehen im Kern beeinflußt. Gefordert wird deshalb eine ethnographisch orientierte soziolinguistische Basis für die Semantik (Cicourel 1991: 37).

Ähnlich beklagt auch Elinor Ochs-Keenan die fehlende ethnographische Basis und den fehlenden ethnologischen Vergleich. Nach ihrer Ansicht sind die Verhältnisse, wie sie sich für die Konversation in den westlichen Gesellschaften feststellen lassen, nicht auf nicht-westliche Gesellschaften übertragbar. Ferner wirken immer sozial-situative Faktoren auf die Konversation ein. Universalität kann mithin für das Gricesche Konversationspostulat und die Konversationsmaximen nicht behauptet werden. Gleichwohl bietet nach Ochs-Keenan (1976: 79) die Gricesche Konzeption integratives Potential. Sie erlaubt es, ethnographische Einzelstudien in einen größeren, vergleichenden Zusammenhang zu stellen.

Auch Susan Ervin-Tripp sieht ein Problem darin, daß dem Griceschen Modell indoeuropäische Sprachen zugrunde liegen. Wie die Grammatiktheorie in der Beschäftigung mit nicht-indoeuropäischen Sprachen und ihren spezifischen Strukturen zu Veränderungen gezwungen ist, so muß ihrer Ansicht nach auch die Pragmatik die konversationellen Verhältnisse in den nicht-indoeuropäischen Sprachen einarbeiten. Sprachen erfüllen in den verschiedenen gesellschaftlichen Bereichen verschiedene Funktionen, und je nach Funktion variiert auch die Bewertung von Wahrheit, Relevanz und Informativität. So läßt sich etwa sehr schnell zeigen, daß die Qualitätsmaxime häufig nicht gilt:

„In each society there is utility communication that remains truth-based, and communication is marked when it is not truthful; but in other types of circumstances veridical report can be subordinated to alternative values such as entertainment, secrecy, or face" (Ervin-Tripp 1987: 48).

In diesem Zusammenhang verweist Ervin-Tripp auf die von Heath (1983) vorgenommene vergleichende Studie über das Erzählen in den ethnisch unterschiedlichen amerikanischen Städten Trackton und Roadville. Während es in Trackton um ein schlagfertiges, unterhaltsames Erzählen geht und die Wahrheit nachrangig behandelt wird, ist sie in Roadville ein wichtiges Moment.

Ervin-Tripp (1987: 51) nimmt weiter an, daß die Vorstellung absichtsvollen, kontrollierten Sprachhandelns durch eine verbreitete Methodik forciert wird. So werden die Vorstellungen über die sprachliche Interaktion oft auf der Basis der Introspektion und nicht auf der Basis systematischer Beobachtungen entwickelt. In der introspektiven Auseinandersetzung mit dem erlebten sprachlich-kommunikativen Geschehen und in seiner Rekonstruktion rücken Zielsetzung und Kontrolle ebenso in den Vordergrund, wie dies etwa in der narrativen Rekonstruktion von erlebten Ereignissen der Fall ist. Ähnlich verweist auch Prandi (1994) darauf, daß die Vorstellung absichtsvollen, gezielten Sprachhandelns einem Alltagsmodell der Kommunikation entspricht. Sie entspricht der 'natürlichen Einstellung' der Kommunikanten, ist in wissenschaftlicher Hinsicht aber nicht adäquat.

2.2. Kommunikation als interaktive Sinnbildung

Eine von der Konzeption der Konversationsmaximen sich deutlich unterscheidende Modellierung von Kommunikation unternimmt Waldenfels (1980; 1987). Aus einer phänomenologisch-philosophischen Perspektive wird Kommunikation nicht von einem Individuum aus konzipiert, sondern als ein interaktiver Prozeß beschrieben, der auf einer „gemeinsame[n] Produktivität der Kommunikation" (1980: 174) basiert.

Waldenfels (1980: 177) nimmt die in der strukturalistischen Linguistik getroffene Unterscheidung von syntagmatischem Kontrast und paradigmatischer Opposition auf und überträgt diese auf die Ebene der Kommunikation bzw. des Dialogs. Angenommen wird, daß die einzelnen Dialog- oder Kommunikationsbeiträge einen syntagmatischen Zusammenhang bilden. Gleichzeitig steht jede einzelne Äußerung in einem paradigmatischen Verhältnis zu den Äußerungen, die an der entsprechenden Stelle im Kommunikationsgeschehen ebenfalls hätten geäußert werden können, nicht aber selegiert wurden.

Ein kohärenter dialogischer Zusammenhang ergibt sich in dieser Perspektive dann, wenn die Selektion der Äußerungen so erfolgt, daß sich in der Kombination mit den vorhergehenden Äußerungen ein kohärenter Zusammenhang ergibt. Dies ist der Fall, wo die einzelne Äußerung nur im 'Kontext' der vorangegangenen verständlich ist und sich ihre Bedeutung daraus ergibt, daß sie Antwort oder Reaktion auf eine vorangegangene Äußerung ist. Dieses Mitführen vorangegangener Äußerungen als sinnstiftendes Moment bezeichnet Waldenfels (1980: 177) als 'Kontextbildung' bzw. 'Kontextfortbildung'.

Der so erzeugte Zusammenhang zwischen einzelnen Äußerungen kann mehr oder weniger eng sein. Grenzfälle von Kommunikation ergeben sich, wo entweder das kombinatorische oder das selektive Moment fehlen. Eine Kombination, die keinen Selektionsspielraum hat, entspricht in einer psychologischen Perspektive einem „zwanghaften" Verhalten (Waldenfels 1980: 178). Aber auch der Theaterdialog, der den Schauspieler auf den Rollentext festgelegt, ist weitgehend bestimmt durch das Fehlen von Selektionsmöglichkeiten. Der spiegelverkehrte Fall liegt vor, wo zwar Selektionsmöglichkeiten gegeben sind und auch eine Selektion erfolgt, das Moment der Kombination aber fehlt. Hier machen die Äußerungen einander nicht zum 'Kontext', und es ergibt sich kein Zusammenhang (Waldenfels 1980: 178).

Eine fehlende oder mangelnde Kontextfortbildung bestimmt das Ende eines Dialogs. Sie liegt aber auch innerhalb des dialogischen Geschehens vor, und zwar an den Grenzen von Strukturierungseinheiten wie der Episode oder der Diskurseinheit (s. § 4.1). Der Zusammenhang, den die Kontextfortbildung erzeugt, ist an diesen Stellen notwendig schwächer als innerhalb der Strukturierungseinheiten.

Ein dialogisches Geschehen ist nach diesem Modell in seiner Entwicklung stets mehr oder weniger offen. Der einzelne Kommunikant kann seinen Beitrag zwar absichtsvoll und zielgerichtet planen, auch Reaktionen provozieren, angesichts des Selektionsspielraums, den jeder Kommunikant hat, bleibt die Reaktion auf seine Äußerung aber für ihn unvorhersehbar. Auch ist immer ein Abbruch des dialogischen Geschehens durch den Kommunikationspartner möglich.

Offenheit ist mithin eine allgemeine Eigenschaft 'normaler' Kommunikation, und sie ist auch in den institutionalisierten und formellen Formen des Gesprächs gegeben. Das Verhalten muß hier zwar die spezialisierten Zielsetzungen und Vorgaben berücksichtigen, es bleibt aber auch hier stets ein Spielraum.

Waldenfels (1980: 178 f.) spricht von „pragmatische[n] Regeln, [...] die bestimmte Möglichkeiten der Kontextfortbildung ausschließen, ohne eine bestimmte vorzuschreiben" (Waldenfels 1980: 178 f.).

Die 'Kontextbildung' ist nach Waldenfels das Wesen der Kommunikation. Diese Annahme ist verbunden mit einer Kritik an Kommunikationsmodellen, die davon ausgehen, daß das Kommunikationsgeschehen auf der Basis eines sich wiederholenden Wechsels von Sprecher- und Hörerrolle beschrieben werden kann. Der Sprecher übernimmt nicht einfach die Rolle des vorherigen Sprechers, sondern er kommt dem anderen entgegen, indem er an dessen Äußerung anschließt, diese zum 'Kontext' der eigenen macht. Es liegt in diesem Sinne nicht nur abwechselnde Produktion vor, sondern 'Koproduktion' (1980: 180).

3. Kommunikantenrollen

Im Prozeß des sprachlich-interaktiven Geschehens übernehmen die Beteiligten verschiedene Rollen oder Funktionen. Sie werden als Kommunikanten-, Gesprächs-, Partizipanten- oder auch Teilnehmerrollen bezeichnet. Ihre Verteilung verändert sich im Geschehen ständig. Es handelt sich in diesem Sinne um okkasionelle funktionale Differenzierungen, die an den Verlauf des konkreten Kommunikationsgeschehens gebunden sind. Anders als die sozialen Rollen transportieren sie keine sozialen Sinn- oder Ordnungsstrukturen (s. § 5).

Bühler (1982/1934), der das Konzept des 'Rollenträgers' einführt, unterscheidet zwischen dem Sprecher und dem Hörer als den „zwei natürlichen Rollenträger[n] der aktuellen Sprechhandlung" (1982: 381) und einem dritten „hinzugedachten" Rollenträger (1982: 381); dies sind *er*, *sie* oder *es* als dritte Person.

In Anknüpfung an Bühler nimmt Weinrich die 'Gesprächsrollen' des Sprechers und Hörers an und macht die 'kommunikative Dyade', die Sprecher und Hörer bilden, zum Ausgangspunkt der grammatischen Beschreibung. Personen und auch Sachen im Kontext der Dyade weist er eine 'Referenzrolle' zu:

„Der Sprecher und der Hörer sind die primären Gesprächsrollen der Sprache. Ihre Rollenbedeutungen werden mit den gleichnamigen semantischen Merkmalen 'SPRECHER' und 'HÖRER' angegeben. Alles was sonst noch zur Gesprächssituation gehört, es mag sich dabei um Personen oder um Sachen handeln, fassen wir in einer großen Restkategorie zusammen, die wir Referenzrolle ('3. Person') nennen" (Weinrich 1993: 87).

Die Rollen des Sprechers, Hörers und die Rolle der Person oder der Sache, über die gesprochen wird, bilden die drei Rollen, die in unterschiedlicher Weise in den Sprachen auch grammatikalisiert sind. In einer erweiterten Perspektive, die das sprachlich-interaktive Geschehen insgesamt und auch die Personen im engeren und weiteren Umfeld der Kommunikation in den Blick nimmt, lassen sich weitere Rollen diskutieren.

Eine solche Perspektive findet sich etwa bei Goffman (1969/[1]1959). Ausgehend davon, daß das interaktive Geschehen dem Geschehen auf dem Theater gleicht, wir uns in der Interaktion ähnlich dem Schauspieler darstellen oder aber zum Publikum gehören, unterscheidet er verschiedene Teilnehmerrollen. Die drei zentralen Rollen sind der 'Darsteller', der 'Zuschauer' und der „Außenseiter" (Goffman 1969: 132). Weiter werden eine Reihe von 'Sonderrollen' unterschieden, so etwa der 'Denunziant' (1969: 133), der den Darsteller an die Zuschauer verrät, der 'Claqueur' (1969: 134), der auf der Seite des Darsteller steht und ihm immer Beifall gibt, oder der 'Beobachter' (1969: 134), der das Geschehen genau registriert. Alle diese Rollen, die in Orientierung an dem Theatergeschehen beschrieben werden, finden sich — so Goffman (1969) — auch in der Alltagsinteraktion.

Im Rahmen einer allgemeinen Charakterisierung des kommunikativen Kontextes nimmt auch Verschueren verschiedene Kommunikantenrollen an. In einer funktionalen Perspektive unterscheidet er zunächst den 'utterer' und den 'interpreter' (Verschueren 1999: 82). Sie bilden eine „subcategory of what could be called a presence, i. e. the totality of persons who are 'present' at or in the vicinity of a speech event" (1999: 82). Je nachdem, ob die Interpretanten mehr oder weniger in das Kommunikationsgeschehen involviert sind, können sie 'addressees' oder nur 'side participants' sein (Verschueren 1999: 83). Möglich ist auch, daß Personen Interpretanten sind, ohne aber Adressaten oder 'side participants' zu sein. Verschueren (1999: 83) bezeichnet diese als „non-participants" und rechnet diesen den 'bystander', der kaum oder nur am Rande interpretierend tätig ist, den 'overhearer', den 'listenerin' und den 'eavesdropper' zu (Verschueren 1999: 83). Alle diese Personen markieren nach Verschueren relevante Rollen im Kommunikationsgeschehen. Sie sind „ingredients of the communicative context" (1999: 77 ff.).

Diese Bestimmung der Kommunikantenrollen erfolgt aus der Perspektive eines externen Beobachters, der – ähnlich wie bei Goffman (1969) – auf die 'Bühne' des Kommunikationsgeschehens blickt. So kann er etwa auch noch einen Lauscher hinter der Tür erfassen. Diese Beobachterperspektive ist deutlich eine andere als die der Teilnehmer am Kommunikationsgeschehen selbst, denen etwa ein Lauscher hinter der Tür verborgen bleibt.

Eine solche Teilnehmerperspektive liegt dem Ansatz von Herbert H. Clark und Thomas B. Carlson (1992: 217 ff.) zugrunde, die ansonsten eine mit Verschueren (1999) weitgehend identische Typologie der Kommunikanten- bzw. Hörerrollen vorschlagen. Hier werden die Hörer nicht zunächst als Interpretanten verstanden, die sich durch ihre Wahrnehmungs- und Deutungsaktivitäten dem Kommunikationsgeschehen zuordnen. Die Hörerrollen werden vielmehr vom Sprecher aus definiert, der sie in seinem Äußerungsverhalten in systematisch unterschiedlicher Weise berücksichtigt und damit entscheidet, wer an der Kommunikation teil hat (Clark & Carlson 1992: 219).

Dieser Relevanz der Sprecherrolle trägt ein Kommunikationsbegriff Rechnung, wie ihn Niklas Luhmann (1995) aus einer systemtheoretischen Perspektive entwickelt. Danach ist die bloße Wahrnehmung von Informationen, und zwar auch solcher Informationen, die aus der Beobachtung von Kommunikation resultieren, nicht schon Kommunikation. Diese liegt erst dann vor, wenn jemand sich in der Absicht der Mitteilung von Informationen auf einen Adressaten in seinem Wahrnehmungsraum bezieht, dieser dessen Absicht der Mitteilung von Information erfaßt und daraufhin ein Verstehen oder ein Mißverstehen stattfindet. Luhmann spricht in einer systemtheoretischen Abstraktion von einer für Kommunikation vorauszusetzenden Unterscheidung von 'Information', 'Mitteilung' und 'Verstehen' (Luhmann 1987: 212 ff.; 1995: 115). Mithin ist weder eine sprachliche Äußerung kommunikativ, die zwar wahrgenommen und gedeutet werden kann, die aber nicht mit einer Mitteilungsabsicht verbunden ist, noch ist jemand an Kommunikation beteiligt, der zwar die Mitteilungsabsicht wahrnimmt, nicht aber als Adressat der Mitteilung gesehen wird. Auch liegt keine Kommunikation vor, wenn zwar Informationen mitgeteilt werden, diese aber keinen Hörer erreichen.

Ähnlich machen auch Sperber & Wilson (1995) das Vorliegen bzw. das Signalisieren einer Mitteilungsabsicht, die 'ostension', zur Voraussetzung von Kommunikation. Sie muß von dem Adressaten inferentiell erschlossen werden:

„Ostensive-inferential communication consists in making manifest to an audience one's intention to make manifest a basic layer of information. It can therefore be described in terms of an informative and a communicative intention" (Sperber & Wilson 1995: 54).

Vor dem Hintergrund eines solchen Kommunikationsbegriffs konstituieren allein die aufeinander bezogenen Äußerungs- und Wahrnehmungsaktivitäten von Sprecher und Adressat Kommunikation. Personen wie der Lauscher hinter der Tür oder auch der unfreiwillige Zuhörer am Rande der Szene, die mithören, nicht aber Adressaten sind, gehören in das Umfeld der Kommunikation. Zwar beziehen sie sich selbst in ihren Wahrnehmungsaktivitäten auf das Kommunikationsgeschehen, sie können aber, solange sie sich auf die rezeptiv-kognitive Aktivität beschränken, keinen Einfluß auf das Kommunikationsgeschehen nehmen.

Möglich ist allerdings, daß sie in der Kommunikation Bedeutung haben oder erlangen. Dies ist für einen Mithörer außerhalb des Wahrnehmungsraums des Sprechers einmal dann der Fall, wenn der Sprecher um dessen Anwesenheit weiß oder aber glaubt, daß ein Mithörer anwesend ist. Der Mithörer ist hier thematisch, er gehört zu den relevanten situativen Momenten des Kommunikationsgeschehens. Versuche, den Mithörer durch ein leises Sprechen auszuschalten oder aber ihn indirekt als Mithörer anzusprechen, sind mögliche Formen der Reaktion auf die Anwesenheit; Clark & Schaefer (1992: 262 ff.) beschreiben dies in ihrer Diskussion des 'overhearers'. Relevant für das Kommunikationsgeschehen werden Mithörer zum anderen dann, wenn sie sich selbst mit einer sprachlichen Äußerung in das Kommunikationsgeschehen einschalten.

Schließlich können Zuschauer, Zuhörer, Mithörer oder Lauscher noch in einer anderen Weise in der Kommunikation relevant werden. So kann der Mithörer inhaltlich relevant werden, wo die Kommunikanten dessen Anwesenheit sprachlich thematisieren. Hier erhält er dann die Referenzrolle einer dritten Person.

Diese Verständnis von Kommunikation unterscheidet sich deutlich von dem weiten Kommunikationsbegriff, den Watzlawick & al. (1990) aus einer psychologischen Perspektive ansetzen. Sie machen zwar ebenfalls die Mitteilung für die Kommunikation relevant, nehmen aber an, daß das menschliche Verhalten immer „Mitteilungscharakter" hat (Watzlawick & al. 1990: 51). Dies kann weder vermieden noch verneint werden. Gleichzeitig wird davon ausgegangen, daß jedes Verhalten Einfluß auf andere nimmt, weil diese sich dem Mitteilungscharakter nicht entziehen können. Das wahrgenommene Verhalten wird interpretiert, und damit wird gleichzeitig auch schon kommuniziert. So gilt für Watzlawick & al. (1990: 53): „Man kann nicht nicht kommunizieren".

Gegen eine solche Ausweitung des Kommunikationsbegriffs und für die Abgrenzung eines kommunikativen Geschehens im engeren Sinne sprechen auch die interaktiven Aktivitäten der Kommunikanten, die selbst eine Begrenzung der Kommunikation nach außen vornehmen. So verlangen die Aktivitäten des Sprechers notwendig eine Rückmeldung von den Adressaten bzw. Hörern. Sie sind die Voraussetzung dafür, daß der Sprecher sich weiter äußert (s. u. § 4.2.2 'grounding').

Helmut Henne (1979: 124) unterscheidet drei Hörertypen, die sich in der Art der rückmeldenden Aktivitäten unterscheiden: Neben dem aktiven Hörer, der aufmerksam ist und dies rückmeldet, nimmt er den 'passiven Hörer' an, der nicht zuhört und dessen fehlende Rückmeldung zum Ende der Konversation führt, sowie den 'simulierenden' Hörer, der nur scheinbar aufmerksam ist. Ein Lauscher sowie auch ein zufälliger Mithörer oder Interpretant sind auch aus dieser Perspektive nur dann relevant, wenn rückmeldende Aktivitäten stattfinden, die der Sprecher erkennen kann.

Auch gibt es 'Gebote' der Höflichkeit, die das Verhalten der Personenrollen im Umfeld und ihr Verhältnis zum Kommunikationsgeschehen regulieren und damit ebenfalls Grenzziehungen intendieren. So ist etwa das Mithören oder Belauschen von Gesprächen verpönt. Auch gilt es, eine Unterhaltung so zu führen, daß niemand unfreiwillig zum Mithörer wird. Die Einhaltung dieser Höflichkeitsgebote ist allerdings nicht immer möglich. Es gibt Konfliktbereiche, wie etwa Zugabteile oder Restaurants, wo die räumliche Nähe Personen im Umfeld zu Mithörern wider Willen macht.

Die Abgrenzung der Kommunikation nach außen ist also nicht nur aus einer kommunikationstheoretischen Perspektive sinnvoll anzunehmen, sondern sie erfolgt auch in der Praxis selbst. Es ist systematisch zu unterscheiden zwischen

— den Personenrollen, die allein von einem Beobachter als in einer sozialen Szene anwesend erfaßt werden,
— ihrer Relevanz im Kommunikationsgeschehen, etwa in der Rolle der dritten Person, und
— den Kommunikantenrollen, die das Kommunikationsgeschehen initiieren und aufrechterhalten.

4. Dimensionen sprachlicher Koproduktivität

Sprachlich-kommunikatives Handeln läßt sich niemals auf den Austausch semantischer Informationen reduzieren. Es konstituiert vielmehr stets auch ein soziales Ereignis, das Hintergrund und Bezugsrahmen für die Verstehensprozesse ist. Die Initiierung und das Aufrechterhalten des sozialen Ereignisses sowie auch dessen Bestimmung sind im sprachlich-interaktiven Geschehen von den Kommunikanten zu leisten. Dies umfaßt

— gemeinsame strukturierende und verständnissichernde Aktivitäten,
— die Definition des Gesprächs und seine räumliche und soziale Verortung,
— die Bestimmung seiner Funktionalität und
— die Klärung des Verhältnisses der Kommunikanten im Rahmen des sozialen Geschehens.

Ein Erfolg dieser gemeinsamen Aktivitäten ist keineswegs sicher. Die Kommunikanten unterscheiden sich ihren Persönlichkeiten sowie in ihren Motivations-, Interessen- und Kenntnislagen. Auch können kulturelle Unterschiede vorliegen, die sich auf das Gesprächsverhalten auswirken und die eventuell zu Mißverständnissen führen. So müssen sich die Kommunikanten oft mit einem Kommunikationsgeschehen arrangieren, das für sie unbefriedigend bleibt. Auch besteht, wo Interessenlagen divergieren, immer das „Risiko auf Ablehnung" (Luhmann 1995: 119).

Das Vorliegen solcher Divergenzen muß dennoch nicht notwendig als Hindernis für das kommunikative Geschehen begriffen werden. Es erhöht den kommunikativen Aufwand, weil Verstehensprobleme bearbeitet werden müssen, es verhindert aber nicht das Zustandekommen von Kommunikation. Möglicherweise macht gerade auch die Begegnung mit Andersheit Kommunikation interessant und wichtig. Sie läßt neue Informationen erwarten und bietet die Chance neuer Erfahrungen. Argumente für eine solche Annahme ergeben sich etwa im Anschluß an Überlegungen von Merleau-Ponty (1966: 411 ff.) über die Rolle und die Bedeutung der sozialen Welt und des Anderen: „... so auch ist die Spannung meiner Existenz auf einen Anderen hin ein unbestreitbar am Horizont meines Lebens Wirkliches" (1996: 411 f.).

4.1. Interaktive Strukturierungen des Gesprächs

Die sprachliche Interaktion ist eine Geschehen, in dem nicht nur der einzelne Kommunikant mit der Planung und Realisierung einer Äußerung strukturierende und produktive Leistungen erbringt. Auch gemeinsam erzeugen die Kommunikanten Strukturierungen des Kommunikationsgeschehens.

Eine zentrale Strukturierungseinheit ist der TURN, der in der ethnomethodologischen Konversationsanalyse untersucht worden ist (Sacks & al. 1974; Schegloff 1996; vgl. auch Heritage 1995). Eine deutsche Übersetzung dieses Terminus ist schwierig, so daß er zumeist unübersetzt in das Deutsche übernommen wird, seltener auch behelfsweise durch 'Redebeitrag' oder 'Gesprächsschritt' wiedergegeben wird.

Die konversationsanalytischen Arbeiten zeigen, daß das „turn-taking", der Sprecherwechsel, strengen interaktiven Regelungen unterliegt. Dies gilt gerade auch in informellen Alltagsgesprächen. Innerhalb solcher Alltagsgespräche ergeben sich „transition-relevance-places" (Sacks & al. 1974: 703), an denen sich Optionen des Sprecherwechsels eröffnen. An diesen Stellen erfolgt entweder eine Zuweisung der Sprecherrolle durch den jeweils aktuellen Sprecher an einen Beteiligten, oder aber die Beteiligten weisen sich selbst den nächsten 'turn' zu, d. h. sie signalisieren ihrerseits Interesse an der Übernahme des 'turn'. Ob es zu einem Sprecherwechsel kommt, hängt von der Akzeptanz oder Ablehnung der Zuweisungen ab.

Die Organisation des Sprecherwechsels ist in diesem Sinne ein „interactionally managed system" und 'lokal' organisiert (Sacks & al. 1974: 725). Es wirkt zwar über die gesamte sprachliche Konversation hinweg strukturierend und regulierend, organisiert das Geschehen aber immer nur an den „transition relevance-places". Sacks & al. (1974: 725) sprechen deshalb auch von einem „local management system".

Die Organisation des Sprecherwechsels ist in institutionalisierten Gesprächen weitergehend geregelt. Sacks & al. (1974: 729) nennen hier u. a. Zeremonien, Debatten, Seminare, therapeutische Gespräche und Interviews. In den Gesprächen, die einen solchen institutionellen Rahmen haben, kommen soziale Zielsetzungen und auch soziale Rollen ins Spiel und diese nehmen Einfluß auf die Organisation des Sprecherwechsels. Im Falle der Diskussion etwa werden dem Moderator besondere Rederechte zugestanden. Ihm sind häufige Redebeiträge erlaubt und ihm allein obliegt die Zuweisung des Rederechts. Auch werden Kriterien wie die Chronologie der Zeichen, mit denen die Beteiligten ihr Interesse an der Übernahme des 'turns' anzeigen, für die 'turn'-Zuweisung relevant.

Unterschieden werden kann zwischen einer mehr oder weniger starken Formalität der institutionalisierten Gespräche (Heritage 1995: 407 ff.). Weniger formelle Gespräche finden sich etwa im medizinischen und psychiatrischen Bereich oder auch in der Geschäftswelt. Hier sind die Spielräume für die inhaltliche und formale Gestaltung des Gesprächs groß, damit eine flexible Anpassung an die Bedürfnis- und Interessenlagen möglich ist. Einen formelleren Charakter besitzen institutionelle Gespräche, die im öffentlichen Raum stattfinden und Zuschauer oder Zuhörer haben, wie etwa die Konversation im Gerichtssaal. Die Freiheiten der Beteiligten sind hier stärker eingeschränkt.

Die Behandlung dieser institutionalisierten Gespräche ist in einem konversationsanalytischen Rahmen allerdings schwierig. Dies gilt insbesondere für die Fälle formeller Konversation, die über eine längere Phase des Gesprächs hinweg entfaltet werden. Diese können ausgehend von der ethnomethodologischen Grundannahme lokal organisierter interaktiver Aktivitäten nicht mehr beschrieben werden (Heritage 1995: 409).

Neben dem 'turn' wird deshalb auch die DISCOURSE UNIT als wichtige Strukturierungseinheit der sprachlichen Interaktion diskutiert. Nach Hausendorf & Quasthoff (1995: 221) bildet diese den strukturellen Rahmen etwa für die Erzählung eines Witzes in der Konversation, für ein Argument, das in einer Diskussion vorgebracht wird, für eine Einladung, die ausgesprochen wird, oder eine

Wegbeschreibung, die in einem Gespräch erfolgt. Ihre Grenzen werden im sprachlichen Kommunikationsgeschehen durch 'Diskursmarker' angezeigt. Ihre interne Struktur folgt spezifischen Mustern. Auch ist in der Regel einer der Kommunikanten für die 'discourse unit' 'verantwortlich' (vgl. Hausendorf & Quasthoff 1995: 221). Als Einheit, die in diesem Sinne eine längere Phase des sprachlich-kommunikativen Geschehens in ihrer Struktur vorzeichnet, ist die Diskurseinheit nicht mit dem lokal organisierten 'turn' kongruent (Hausendorf & Quasthoff 1995: 222). Eine Diskurseinheit kann durchaus mehrere 'turns' umfassen.

Als eine weitere interaktiv konstituierte Strukturierungseinheit wird die EPISODE diskutiert. Anders als die Diskurseinheit, deren Einheit wesentlich auf einem Muster basiert, ist die Episode über das Thema definiert. Nach Linell & Korolija (1997) besteht in einer Konversation stets eine Spannung zwischen dem Beibehalten und dem Wechsel des Themas. Einerseits erleichtert Thema-Kontinuität das Verstehen, andererseits ist die Konversation bestrebt, sich neuen Themen zuzuwenden und mithin das Thema zu wechseln. Die Episode entspricht in diesem Zusammenhang genau der Phase, in der die Beteiligten an einem Thema festhalten (Linell & Korolija 1997: 197). Sie ist als Einheit innerhalb des sprachlichen Interaktionsgeschehens dadurch definiert, daß sie von etwas Bestimmtem handelt.

4.2. Verständnissicherung

Helmuth Feilke (1994) weist darauf hin, daß es in der Kommunikation nicht um das 'Meinen', sondern stets nur um das 'Verstehen' geht. Das Meinen ist eine kognitive Aktivität, die für Kommunikationspartner unsichtbar abläuft, und solange Gemeintes im kognitiven Vorstellungsraum bleibt, kann es für die Kommunikationspartner und mithin für das Kommunikationsgeschehen keine Rolle spielen. Erst in dem Moment, wo der Kommunikant Gemeintes sprachlich oder auch nichtsprachlich zu verstehen gibt, wird dieses in der Kommunikation relevant und kann Verstehens- und Sinnbildungsprozesse initiieren und orientieren.

Anhaltspunkt und Basis für die Verstehensprozesse bilden die spezifischen sprachlichen und auch nicht-sprachlichen Formen, in denen etwas Gemeintes in der Konversation erscheint. Diese sprachlichen Formen sind als konventionelle Zeichen oder Symbole mit spezifischen Bedeutungen gekoppelt, und sie können so die Verstehensprozesse der Kommunikanten orientieren. Relevant für das Kommunikationsgeschehen ist mithin, „was gesagt wird, nicht primär, was gemeint ist" (Feilke 1994: 75).

Dies setzt voraus, daß die Kommunikanten mit den sprachlichen Formen und den sozialen Bedeutungen, die sie transportieren, vertraut sind. Auch benötigen sie eine gemeinsame Wissensbasis. Hörmann (1980: 26) etwa betont, daß der „Hörer immer schon wissen muß, was sinnvoll ist". Schmidt (1994: 147) setzt ähnlich voraus, daß die Kommunikanten eine „Übereinstimmung in ihren Lebensformen" aufweisen. Die Chance der Verständigung wird darüber hinaus durch eine Reihe von partnerbezogenen Aktivitäten und Strategien erhöht, die im Zuge des Kommunikationsprozesses wirksam sind. Hierzu zählen ein informativer Zuschnitt der Äußerung, aber auch Reparatur- und Reformulierungsaktivitäten.

4.2.1. Reziprozität der Perspektiven

Ein viel diskutiertes Konzept im Zusammenhang eines vorauszusetzenden, geteilten Wissens- und Lebenshorizontes ist die „Reziprozität der Perspektiven". Damit ist einmal die Tatsache beschrieben, daß der Hörer beim Sprecherwechsel zum Sprecher wird und der Sprecher im gleichen Zug zum Hörer. In der Vorstellung von Schütz, der das Konzept zuerst ausgearbeitet hat, sowie auch in der Ethnomethodologie (Cicourel 1975: 31 ff.) ist darüber hinaus die Austauschbarkeit der Standpunkte und die wechselseitige Annahme dieser Austauschbarkeit gemeint. Die Kommunikanten gehen davon aus, daß der andere in ihrer Position als Sprecher oder Hörer die Gesprächssituation ähnlich erlebt.

„Der allgemeine Grundsatz lautet ja: der andere erfährt, versteht die Welt ungefähr – *ceteribus paribus* – so, wie ich sie erfahren, verstehen würde, wenn ich mich in seiner Lage befände. Der andere versteht also auch das, was ich tue, ungefähr so, wie ich mich verstehen würde, wenn ich an seiner Stelle wäre" (Schütz & Luckmann 1984: 119).

Bei Schütz & Luckmann hat das Konzept der „Reziprozität der Perspektiven" im Zusammenhang gesellschaftlichen Handelns zentralen Stellenwert. Es handelt sich um die „wichtigste der auf die Gesellschaftlichkeit der Lebenswelt bezogenen Annahmen" (Schütz & Luckmann 1984: 95). Neben einer „Reziprozität der Perspektiven" wird auch eine „Reziprozität der Motive" angenommen. Danach unterstellen Kommunikanten, daß ihre (Sprach-)Handlungen, wo sie sich ähneln, auf ähnlichen Motiven beruhen (Schütz & Luckmann 1984: 119).

Diese Unterstellung der 'Reziprozität' leitet das (sprachliche) Handeln. Sie macht Wirkungen beim Hörer kalkulierbar, gleichzeitig schafft sie Sicherheit im kommunikativen Geschehen, weil wechselseitig angenommen werden kann, daß sowohl das eigene Handeln verstehbar ist, als auch das Handeln des Kommunikationspartners richtig verstanden wird.

Eine kritische Bewertung des Konzepts findet sich bei Waldenfels (1990: 52 ff.; 1998: 114). Diese richtet sich gegen die der „Reziprozität der Perspektiven" zugrunde liegende Vorstellung, daß als Voraussetzung für sprachliche Kommunikation ein hinreichendes Maß an Gleichheit oder Symmetrie zwischen den Kommunikanten zu erzeugen ist. Nach seiner Ansicht bilden Gleichheit und Symmetrie nicht die Voraussetzungen für Kommunikation. Es sind vielmehr gerade Andersheit und Asymmetrie, die „Frage und Antwort", also ein kommunikatives Geschehen in Gang setzen und in Gang halten:

„Doch eines gerät dabei aus dem Blick: die Asymmetrie eines Antwortens, das aus dem Anhören kommt, das dem fremden Anspruch entspricht, aber nicht mit ihm konvergiert. Frage und Antwort gehen jedem Konsens voraus" (Waldenfels 1998: 114).

Eine Reziprozität der Perspektiven ergibt sich nach Waldenfels (1998) erst durch den Bezug auf gemeinsame soziale Ordnungs- und Sinnstrukturen. Diese werden durch die sozialen Rollen, in denen die Kommunikanten einander immer schon begegnen, in die sprachliche Interaktion hineingetragen (s. § 5).

4.2.2. 'Grounding'

Die erfolgreiche Verständigung in der sprachlichen Kommunikation setzt geteiltes Wissen, einen „common ground" (Clark 1992: 4) voraus. Dieses Wissen muß im sprachlichen Geschehen aktiviert und in Anpassung an die spezifischen Inhalte in der Kommunikation erweitert und aktualisiert werden. Dies geschieht dadurch, daß die Äußerungsinhalte als Teil des geteilten Wissens betrachtet und diesem hinzugefügt werden. Clark & Brennan (1991) bezeichnen diese Aktivitäten der Kommunikanten als 'grounding'.

Entscheidend ist dabei, daß die Kommunikanten das Gefühl gewinnen, daß das Gesagte soweit verstanden worden ist, wie es für die Zwecke der aktuellen Kommunikation notwendig ist. Dies ist das „grounding criterion" (Clark & Brennan 1991: 129), von dem die Kommunikanten ihre verständnissichernden Aktivitäten abhängig machen. Erst wenn es erfüllt ist, wird das Kommunikationsgeschehen inhaltlich weitergeführt. Anzeichen dafür sind sprachliche und nicht-sprachliche Signale, mit denen die Hörer dem Sprecher das Verstehen zurückmelden. Eine große Rolle spielen hier Interjektionen wie etwa „Oh Gott", „ah ja" oder „mh" sowie auch das Anzeigen der Aufmerksamkeit durch Blickkontakt.

Die Techniken des 'grounding' sind abhängig von der Zielsetzung und dem Medium der sprachlichen Interaktion (Clark & Brennan 1991: 148). Sie sind im Medium der Schriftlichkeit grundsätzlich anderer Art als im mündlichen face-to-face-Dialog. Nach Clark & Brennan (1991: 148) sind die Kommunikanten bemüht, die 'grounding'-Aktivitäten auf ein Minimum zu reduzieren.

Besonders deutlich zeigen sich die 'grounding'-Aktivitäten in Gesprächen, an denen Personen mit Sprachschwierigkeiten teilnehmen. In einer Analyse von Gesprächen zwischen Aphasikern und Nichtaphasikern konnten etwa Anderson & al. (1997) feststellen, daß letztere weitreichende 'grounding'-Aktivitäten unternehmen. Dieses Verhalten ist nach Anderson & al. (1997) allerdings kritisch zu bewerten da, wo es dem sprachlichen Verhalten gegenüber Kindern in frühen Phasen des Spracherwerbs ähnelt.

4.2.3. 'Recipient design'

Als ein allgemeines Prinzip interaktiver Aktivitäten nehmen Sacks & al. (1974: 727) den partnerbezogenen Zuschnitt der Äußerungen an, das 'recipient design':

„By 'recipient design' we refer to a multitude of respects in which the talk by a party in a conversation is constructed or designed in ways which display an orientation and sensitivity to the particular other(s) who are the co-participants" (Sacks & al. 1974: 727).

In einer ähnlichen Bedeutung sprechen Clark (1992: 201 ff.), Clark & Schaefer (1992: 248 ff.) vom 'audience design', wobei es hier eng verbunden ist mit der Annahme des 'common ground' als Gesprächsvoraussetzung. Die Sprecher gestalten die Äußerungen auf der Basis ihrer Annahmen und ihres Wissens über die Annahmen und das Wissen ihres Publikums.

Das Publikum einer Äußerung umfaßt dabei alle Personen, von denen der Sprecher glaubt, daß sie zuhören (Clark & Schaefer 1992: 248). Dies sind neben dem Sprecher selbst, der als „monitor" (Clark & Schaefer 1992: 250) seine Äußerungen kontrolliert, die Partizipanten, an die die Äußerung gerichtet ist. Dies sind entweder direkt angesprochene Adressaten oder aber auch Mithörer. Annahme ist, daß der Zuschnitt der Äußerungen systematisch davon abhängt, welche der Hörerrollen angesprochen ist.

Nach Clark & Schaefer (1992: 249 ff.) ergibt sich dies daraus, daß die Sprecher sich für die Hörer in Abhängigkeit von deren Rolle verantwortlich fühlen. Es sind in erster Linie die Partizipanten, und darunter die Adressaten, um deren Verstehen die Sprecher bemüht sind und für die sie ihre Äußerung zuschneiden. So gilt das „grounding criterion" (Clark & Brennan 1991: 129) in der Regel nur in Bezug auf den Adressaten. Ob Mithörer verstanden haben, ist für den Sprecher im Normalfall unwichtig, die Weiterführung des Gesprächs erfolgt auch ohne ihre Rückmeldung.

Viele formale Eigenschaften der Äußerung ergeben sich aus einem partnerbezogenen Zuschnitt. So kommt es etwa dem Hörer entgegen, wenn der Sprecher eine Sprache oder eine Sprachvarietät wählt, die der Adressat gut beherrscht. Weiter dienen Reformulierungs- und Wiederholungsaktivitäten dazu, das Gemeinte in einer für die Adressaten besser verständlichen Weise zu fassen, wenn diese Verständnisschwierigkeiten signalisieren. Auch markieren Satzakzente und Satztopologie relevante Teile einer Äußerung und unterstützen so das Verstehen. Sie lassen sich als Konsequenzen eines „information management" (Tomlin u. a. 1998) fassen, das den Informationsfluß mit Blick auf den Hörer gestaltet. Das „focus-management" etwa, das Tomlin u. a. (1998: 93) annehmen, verfolgt die Strategie, den Hörer auf neue, auch unerwartete Information hinzuweisen.

„As we have seen, speakers try to make some information more prominent or salient to their listeners. Depending on which language they are using, they have a number of devices at their disposal in order to achieve this goal of focusing information" (Tomlin u. a. 1998: 100).

4.2.4. Korrekturen

In engem Zusammenhang mit den Aktivitäten des 'grounding' und des 'recipient design' stehen korrigierende, optimierende und reparierende Aktivitäten. Sie bearbeiten Äußerungen, die Verständnisprobleme bereiten. Die Ursachen können aus verschiedenen Gründen auf der Seite des Hörers liegen. Er kann etwa unaufmerksam oder unkonzentriert sein, oder aber es kann ihm ein entsprechender Wissenshorizont fehlen. Möglich ist aber auch, daß die Äußerung in ihrer sprachlichen Form ein Verstehen erschwert und sie nicht geeignet ist, das Gemeinte zu transportieren. Dies ergibt sich ganz allgemein daraus, daß ein interaktives Geschehen zwar in der Regel absichtsvoll und zielgerichtet betrieben wird, aber niemals vollständig kontrollierbar ist (s. o. § 2.2). Die idiomatische Wendung „Ein Wort gibt das andere" bringt dies zum Ausdruck. Hier ergeben sich etwa Notwendigkeiten, Äußerungen zurückzunehmen oder zu entschärfen. Zum anderen ist auch die individuelle Äußerung nicht vollständig kontrollierbar. Das Gesagte bringt das Gemeinte oft nur unzureichend zum Ausdruck, oder aber es ist mißverständlich. Hier sind ebenfalls nachträgliche Bearbeitungen notwendig.

Wie die Konversationsanalyse herausgearbeitet hat, ist die Organisation von Reparaturen zentrales Moment in der mündlichen Kommunikation (Schegloff & al. 1977). In einem textlinguistischen Rahmen stellen Gülich & Kotschi (1996) für die mündliche Interaktion drei Typen von Aktivitäten fest, die insgesamt das „Textherstellungsverfahren" bestimmen. Neben der „Versprachlichung" und der Redebewertung/-kommentierung" sind dies auch Aktivitäten der „Bearbeitung". Als „Paraphrasen", „Korrekturen", „Exemplifizierungen" oder „Generalisierungen" (Gülich & Kotschi 1996: 74) zielen sie auf eine nachträgliche Verbesserung oder Ergänzung von Äußerungen, um das Gemeinte präziser zum Ausdruck zu bringen. Diese Bearbeitungen sind auf der Oberfläche des Gesprächstextes sichtbar, für das Französische etwa an 'Indikatoren' wie *c'est-à-dire, donc, en d'autres termes* (Gülich & Kotschi 1996: 74). Daß sie gleichzeitig auch zu den typischen und frequenten Merkmalen konzeptioneller Mündlichkeit gehören, wie sie Koch & Oesterreicher (1990) bestimmt haben, verweist auf die Relevanz korrigierender und optimierender Aktivitäten in der Konversation.

4.3. Kontextualisierung

Das Konzept der Kontextualisierung geht zurück auf John J. Gumperz, der es in den 50er und 60er Jahren im Rahmen ethnographisch-linguistischer Studien entwickelt hat (vgl.

dazu Gumperz 1992: 39; → Art. 34, § 5). Angenommen wird, daß mit den interaktiven Aktivitäten immer auch Kontexte erzeugt werden, die als Interpretationsrahmen für die einzelnen Äußerungen dienen. Nach Auer (1992: 4) umfaßt die Kontextualisierung alle sprachlichen und nicht-sprachlichen Aktivitäten im Interaktionsgeschehen, „which make relevant, maintain, revise, cancel ... any aspect of context which, in turn, is responsible for the interpretation of an utterance in its particular locus of occurrence" (Auer 1992: 4).

In der Annahme, daß es die Kommunikanten selbst sind, die das Gespräch kontextualisieren, ergibt sich ein Kontextbegriff, der sich von statischen und deterministischen Kontextbegriffen unterscheidet. Zwar besitzen die Kommunikanten (soziale) Eigenschaften – sie haben etwa einen bestimmten Beruf, sind Mann oder Frau, haben eine bestimmte Ausbildung –, ob und welche dieser Momente aber zu Bestimmungsmomenten des Kontextes werden, hängt von dem Kommunikationsgeschehen ab. Sie haben nicht zwangsläufig Einfluß auf seinen Verlauf. Feilke (1994: 366) weist darauf hin, daß Kommunikationssituationen in aller Regel mehrere Kontexte zugewiesen werden können, sie „mehrfach kontextualisierbar" sind. Auch kann sich die Relevanz der sozialen Eigenschaften im Laufe des Gesprächs verändern. Nach Auer (1986: 23) handelt es sich um ein „(Ethno-)Konstrukt", das geeignet ist, „in einer zwar revidierbaren, aber für alle praktischen Zwecke ausreichenden Weise die Situation zu definieren".

In einer kognitivistischen Perspektive kann die Kontextualisierung als Fall pragmatischer Inferenz begriffen werden, die die für die individuellen Sinnbildungsprozesse notwendigen Verstehenshorizonte aufbaut bzw. aktiviert und mitführt. Gumperz (1994/1982: 3) selbst spricht von einer „conversational inference". Während das Konzept der Kontextualisierung jedoch immer beide Dimensionen, die interaktiv-konstruktive und die kognitive, im Blick hat, bezieht sich das Inferenzkonzept stärker auf die kognitive Verarbeitung des Individuums.

Gumperz unternimmt eine Spezifizierung des Konzepts der Kontextualisierung. Danach bezieht es sich vor allem auf die Aktivierung des Wissens über „activity types", wie sie nach Gumperz (1992: 44) etwa „interview, job interview, discussion, conference, committee meeting" darstellen. Diese „activity types" werden im Anschluß an Alfred Schütz als Typisierungen von Interaktionen („typifications", 1992: 45) begriffen, die Kulturen und Sprachgemeinschaften im Laufe ihrer Kommunikationsgeschichte vornehmen. Sie werden von den Individuen im Rahmen ihrer Interaktionserfahrungen angeeignet (Gumperz 1992: 45; → Art. 36).

Den Kontextualisierungsprozessen sind notwendig soziogenetische Prozesse vor- und nebengeordnet, die Kontexte etwa im Sinne solcher „activity types" oder Interaktionstypen überhaupt erst erzeugen und zum Bestandteil des Kommunikationswissens machen. Hier wiederum ist im Anschluß an Koch & Oesterreicher davon auszugehen, daß es universelle, „anthropologisch begründbare" (1994: 588) Eigenschaften von Kommunikationssituation sind, die in die Genese solcher „activity types" oder Interaktionstypen eingehen. Koch & Oesterreicher diskutieren in diesem Zusammenhang die „raumzeitliche Nähe oder Distanz der Kommunikationspartner", „Öffentlichkeit", „Vertrautheit der Kommunikationspartner", „Emotionalität", „Situations- und Handlungseinbindung" sowie das „Verhältnis des Referenzbezugs zur Sprecher-origo" (Koch & Oesterreicher 1994: 588).

Feilke zeigt auf, daß die Kontextualisierung die notwendige, orientierende und verständnissichernde Verbindung erzeugt zwischen dem Wissen, das die Kommunikanten etwa über solche 'activity types' in die Interaktion mitbringen, und der Erfahrung der konkreten Kommunikationssituation. Das Wissen von den Phänomenen der Welt ist als ein Wissen über die typischen Strukturen dieser Phänomene zu abstrakt, um damit eine vollständige Bestimmung der Kommunikationssituation zu erzielen: „Das aktuelle Haus, z. B., und auch das aktuell in einer Gesprächssituation Geschehende sind je individuell in besonderer Weise determiniert und können insofern nicht Gegenstand meines Wissens sein" (Feilke 1994: 219). Hier setzen die kontextualisierenden Aktivitäten ein. Sie machen das abstrakte Wissen für die Interpretation der aktuellen Situation nutzbar, indem sie es in spezifischer Weise auf die Wahrnehmung der Situation beziehen und so konkretisieren.

4.3.1. Kontextmarker

Die Aktivitäten der Kontextualisierung basieren auf spezifischen Eigenschaften der sprachlichen Formen, die als 'contextualization cues' oder Kontextmarker fungieren:

„I argue that conversational interpretation is cued by empirically detectable signs, contextualization cues, and that the recognition of what these signs are, how they relate to grammatical signs, how they draw on socio-cultural knowledge and how they affect understanding, is essential for creating and sustaining conversational involvement and therefore to communication as such" (Gumperz 1992: 42).

Verschiedene Eigenschaften der sprachlichen und der nicht-sprachlichen Aktivitäten können in einer Interaktion als 'contexualization cues' fungieren. Im Bereich des Sprachlichen sind dies etwa die Lexik, die textuelle Struktur, der Stil, die spezifische Varietät, aber auch intonatorische und prosodische Eigenschaften sowie Stimmqualitäten (vgl. dazu Auer 1986; Selting 1995; Hausendorf & Quasthoff 1995; Couper-Kuhlen & Auer 1991). Auch die Lexik wirkt kontextualisierend. Blommaert & Verschueren (1998: 33 f.) zeigen im Rahmen einer Studie zur öffentlichen Debatte von Immigration, Rassismus und Nationalismus in Belgien u. a. auch die Kontextualisierungseffekte auf, die spezifische Lexeme im öffentlichen Diskurs haben.

Besonders deutlich wird der Kontextualisierungseffekt von sprachlichen Formen auch beim Kodewechsel (Ervin-Tripp 1996: 26 ff.). Ein Wechsel der Sprache führt notwendig auch zu einer Veränderung des Kontexts. Dies ist in besonderer Weise in diglossischen Zusammenhängen der Fall, in denen die Sprachen deutlich getrennten Bereichen gesellschaftlicher Kommunikation zugeordnet sind. Hier verändert der Wechsel der Sprache innerhalb eines Gesprächs den Kontext. Aber auch innerhalb einer Sprache tragen die diaphasischen, diastratischen und diatopischen Varietäten zu einer jeweils spezifischen Kontextualisierung bei. Dies läßt sich in Gesprächen strategisch einsetzen. Regionale Varietäten etwa besitzen das Potential, einen Kontext der Nähe, Vertrautheit und Sicherheit zu erzeugen, und werden in dieser Eigenschaft etwa in öffentlichen Reden oder auch in der Werbung eingesetzt. Ervin-Tripp (1996: 28 ff.) zeigt auf, daß schon Kinder die Kontextualisierung von Sprache erfassen können und selbst zur Kontextualisierung beitragen.

Ein solches konstruktivistisches Konzept des Kontexts berührt die Frage nach der Existenz und Relevanz einer von aller Interaktion unabhängigen Realität. So plädiert etwa Verschueren (1999: 109) für die Annahme eines realen Kontexts, der sich neben dem interaktiv konstruierten Kontext auf die sprachliche Interaktion auswirkt. Als Beispiel führt er das laute Geräusch an, das als Phänomen des realen Kontexts die sprachliche Interaktion stört. Es existieren danach verschiedene Typen von Kontexten: ein von aller Interaktion unabhängiger realer Kontext und ein von den Kommunikanten interaktiv erzeugter Kontext. Als einen dritten Typ ließe sich dann noch der individuelle Kontext ergänzen, den die Kommunikanten unabhängig voneinander und in Abhängigkeit von individuellen Relevanzsetzungen und Interessenlagen bilden.

Gegen die Notwendigkeit, einen realen Kontext zusätzlich anzusetzen, spricht allerdings, daß das Geräusch zwar real existiert, es aber nicht das Geräusch „an sich" ist, das für die sprachliche Interaktion relevant wird, ebensowenig wie dessen individuelle Wahrnehmung. Vielmehr ist es die Art und Weise seiner Bewältigung und Thematisierung in der sprachlichen Interaktion, die maßgeblich ist. Die Geräusche wirken in diesem Sinne zwar auf die Interaktion ein, es ist aber die Interaktion, die bestimmt, welche Bedeutung sie darin erlangen, wie sie bewertet und aus dem Geräusch resultierende Verständigungsprobleme bearbeitet werden.

4.3.2. Indexikalität

Eng verbunden mit der Kontextualisierung ist die Indexikalität. Als Konzept, das aus der formalen Logik stammt, zielt die Indexikalität auf die Abhängigkeit bestimmter sprachlicher Ausdrücke von der jeweiligen Äußerungssituation (Richter 1988). Indexikalische Ausdrücke sind hier zunächst Deiktika wie Personal- und Demonstrativpronomina sowie Orts- und Zeitadverbien (hier, jetzt, morgen, dort).

Bühler (1982/1934) hat die Indexikalität in seiner Sprachtheorie systematisch behandelt und der Linguistik erschlossen. Angenommen werden ein ZEIG- und ein SYMBOLFELD, die Bezugsfelder für die Interpretation der sprachlichen Ausdrücke bilden und so eine präzise Interpretation der indexikalischen Ausdrücke ermöglichen:

„Das Zeigfeld der Sprache im direkten Sprechverkehr ist das hier-jetzt-ich-System der subjektiven Orientierung; Sender und Empfänger leben wachend stets in dieser Orientierung und verstehen aus ihr die Gesten und Leithilfen der *demonstratio ad oculos*. [...] Das sprachliche Symbolfeld im zusammengesetzten Sprachwerk stellt eine zweite Klasse von Konstruktions- und Verständigungshilfen bereit, die man unter den Namen Kontext zusammenfassen kann; Situation und Kontext sind also ganz grob gesagt die zwei Quellen, aus denen in jedem Fall die präzise Interpretation sprachlicher Äußerungen gespeist wird" (Bühler 1982/1934: 149).

Beide Felder werden durch indexikalische und symbolische Aktivitäten von den Kommunikanten aufgebaut. Im Falle des Zeigfeldes sind es vor allem die indexikalischen Ausdrücke bzw. – wie Bühler sie nennt – die sogenannten „Zeigwörter" (Bühler 1982/1934: 107 f.), die seinen Aufbau bewirken. In ihrer von der jeweiligen Kommunikationssituation abhängigen Referenz erzeugen sie ein situatives Wahrnehmungs- und Bezugsfeld, in dem die Referenten der Zeigwörter zentrale Bezugspunkte bilden. Die „Grundzeigwörter" sind *hier, jetzt, ich*, die die „Sprecher-origo" markieren (Bühler 1982/1934: 102 ff.).

Als Teil des Zeigfeldes versteht Bühler (1982/1934: 124) auch den sprachlichen Text, dessen Teil die aktuelle Äußerung ist. Hier ist es ein anaphorischer Gebrauch von indexikalischen Ausdrücken bzw. Zeigwörtern, der das textliche Zeigfeld erzeugt. Das Symbolfeld, der (gedachte) Kontext, wird demgegenüber wesentlich aufgebaut durch symbolische Ausdrücke, die sogenannten „Nennwörter" (1982/1934: 149).

Prandi (1994: 23) zeigt allerdings auf, daß nicht nur die einfachen Zeigwörter, sondern auch komplexe bzw. „gesättigte" Ausdrücke wie Nominalphrasen (*the dog*) oder Sätze (*the dog is running*) stets indexikalische Funktion besitzen. Es ist die Referenz von 'the dog' zu verstehen und etwa auch, warum diese Behauptung gemacht wird. Äußerungen – eben auch solche, die Nennwörter enthalten – sind mithin stets indexikalisch.

Nach Prandi (1994: 25) werden nicht alle Informationen eines Textes oder Diskurses erfaßt, sondern sie werden nach Relevanzkriterien selegiert. Die Interpretationsfelder entstehen in diesem Sinne nicht als Ergebnis einer passiven Rezeption. Sie haben vielmehr konstruktiven Charakter: „The field is no more to be considered as the object of a sort of passive reception; it becomes, at a variable extent, the object of an active construction under the personal responsibility of the interpreter" (Prandi 1994: 25).

Einen zentralen Stellenwert hat das Konzept der Indexikalität in der Ethnomethodologie und weist hier starke Ähnlichkeit mit dem Konzept der Kontextualisierung auf. Angenommen wird, daß Sprache als soziales Medium in jeder konkreten Interaktion immer auch soziale Bedeutungshorizonte mitführt bzw. diese „anzeigt". Gleichzeitig ist jede individuelle Erfahrung sozial vorstrukturiert durch die Ausdrucksmöglichkeiten, die die Sprache als soziales Medium bereithält. Indexikalität wird in diesem Rahmen verstanden als die Aktualisierung der sozialen Bedeutungshorizonte in der konkreten sozialen Interaktion durch sprachliche Ausdrücke. Ein Verstehen in der sozialen Interaktion setzt das Erfassen der indexikalischen Aktivitäten und damit der sozialen Bedeutungshorizonte voraus (Cicourel 1975).

Nicht nur sprachliche Äußerungen haben indexikalischen Wert. Nach Cicourel sind für den Ethnomethodologen neben den sprachlichen Äußerungen auch alle nicht-sprachlichen Handlungen als „indexikalische Entfaltungen der alltäglichen Welt" (Cicourel 1975: 114) aufzufassen. Sprachliches und nicht-sprachliches Handeln unterscheiden sich dabei in ihrem indexikalischen Potential nicht (Cicourel 1975: 135).

Gumperz schlägt eine begriffliche Trennung von Indexikalität und Kontextualisierung vor. Danach handelt es sich bei den 'contextualization cues' zwar um 'indexical signs' (Gumperz 1992: 50), sie machen aber anderes für die Interaktion relevant. Kontextualisierungsmarker aktivieren in erster Linie spezifische Interaktionsmuster, während die indexikalischen Ausdrücke vor allem Inhalte verfügbar machen. Kontextualisierung führt zur Aktivierung eines Interpretationsrahmens für die Interaktion, sie erzeugt nicht auch schon die Interaktionsinhalte (vgl. Gumperz 1992: 45).

4.3.3. Situationsmodelle

Den sprachlich-interaktiven Aktivitäten der Kontextualisierung korrespondieren kognitive Aktivitäten der Beteiligten. Was den unmittelbaren situativen Kontext einer face-to-face-Kommunikation anbetrifft, so lassen sich diese fassen als Aufbau und Aktivierung eines kognitiven Modells, das die relevanten Eigenschaften des situativen Kontextes repräsentiert.

Solche kognitiven Modellbildungs- und Modellaktivierungsprozesse, die die Beteiligung an einer Konversation begleiten, sind bislang allerdings weitgehend unabhängig von den interaktiven Prinzipien und Techniken der Konversation untersucht worden. Dickinson & Givón (1997) halten dies für problematisch und weisen darauf hin, daß gerade die Annahme eines dynamischen situativen Kontexts eine kognitivistische Perspektive notwendig macht. Denn der dynamische situative Kontext ist für die Kommunikanten allein in Form von kognitiven Modellen des Kontexts gegeben, die sie aufbauen und mitführen. Sie nehmen die interaktiv als relevant markierten situativen Eigenschaften auf und führen sie in einer kohärenten Gesamtstruktur, dem Modell, zusammen. Es sind dann diese kognitiven Modelle des situativen Kontexts, die die Wahrnehmung und das Verhalten im Kommunikationsgeschehen bestimmen:

„Much like other kinds of information available to the organism, the current speech situation must be selectively extracted from the 'external' situation, and converted into a mental representation. It is only this on-going mental model of the speech situation that is relevant to the process of face-to-face communication. Fundamentally, then, the dichotomy between 'situational' and 'cognitive' is false" (Dickinson & Givón 1997: 93).

Dickinson & Givón (1997: 94 ff.) verorten das Situationsmodell im Arbeitsgedächtnis, wo es Hintergrund und Bezugsrahmen für die Verstehensprozesse ist.

Die Annahme kognitiver Modelle, die relevante Aspekte der Kommunikationssituation repräsentieren, spielt eine zentrale Rolle in kognitionswissenschaftlichen Forschungen (Strohner 1995). Neben dem Partner- und Selbstmodell bildet das Situationsmodell hier eine wichtige Komponente der 'kognitiven Pragmatik', die es dem Kommunikanten erlaubt, über den semantischen Sinn hinaus weitere pragmatische Sinndimensionen zu erschließen (Strohner 1995: 118 ff.).

Angenommen wird, daß wir als Teil unseres Wissens über Modelle typischer Kommunikationssituationen verfügen, vor deren Hintergrund wir die jeweils aktuelle Kommunikation interpretieren. Sie sind das Ergebnis der Repräsentation typischer Kommunikationserfahrungen. Solche Modelle enthalten Informationen über Ablauf, Organisation, funktionale Bestimmungen sowie inhaltliche Ausrichtungen der typischen Kommunikationssituationen. Vor allem aber verorten sie das Gespräch innerhalb der sozialen Sinn- und Ordnungsstrukturen und weisen den Kommunikanten soziale Rollen zu (→ Art. 36). Nach Strohner (1995: 119) stellt dies eine Verbindung zwischen der individuellen Kognition und dem Sozialsystem her.

Veränderungen gesellschaftlicher Kommunikationsprozesse im privaten und auch im öffentlichen Bereich, Spezialisierungen oder auch Globalisierungen führen notwendig zu einer Veränderung des Repertoires an relevanten Situations- bzw. Kommunikationsmodellen. Modelle verlieren ihre Bedeutung, andere werden ausdifferenziert und umgebaut, oder es kommen neue hinzu.

Die Situationsmodelle reduzieren die Offenheit des interaktiven Geschehens, indem sie das Gespräch in seinen relevanten Eigenschaften vorzeichnen. Dies bietet Orientierung für die individuellen Sprachplanungs- und Verstehensprozesse. Voraussetzung ist allerdings, daß die kognitiven Modelle, mit denen die Kommunikanten das aktuelle Kommunikationsgeschehen interpretieren, in wesentlichen Aspekten übereinstimmen (Strohner 1995: 119). Vor allem aber müssen ähnliche kognitive Modelle als Bestandteile des Wissens verfügbar sein. Dies entspricht Annahmen, wie sie auch den Vorstellungen einer vorauszusetzenden 'Reziprozität der Perspektiven' sowie eines vorauszusetzenden gemeinsamen Wissens zugrunde liegen.

5. Soziale Rollen, Identität, Selbstbild

Das Kommunikationsgeschehen ist in besonderem Maße beeinflußt von der sozialen Rolle und dem sozialen Status, der den Beteiligten in der sprachlichen Interaktion zugewiesen wird. Deterministische Modelle allerdings, die davon ausgehen, daß die Rolle und der Status sich unmittelbar auf das sprachliche Kommunikationsgeschehen auswirken, übersehen, daß Rolle und Status in der sprachlichen Kommunikation überhaupt erst signalisiert, thematisiert und somit relevant gemacht werden müssen. Eine soziale Rolle, um die die Kommunikanten nicht wissen oder die in der konkreten Situation nicht relevant wird, nimmt auch keinen Einfluß auf das Kommunikationsgeschehen.

Auch besitzen Kommunikanten verschiedene soziale Rollen, die im konkreten sprachlich-interaktiven Geschehen nicht alle gleichzeitig relevant sind. Die Kommunikanten müssen mithin in der Interaktion anzeigen, in welcher Rolle sie sich sehen und wie sie von den anderen gesehen werden wollen.

Dies setzt das Wissen um soziale Rollen und das Erfassen der sozialen Rolle im konkreten Kommunikationsgeschehen voraus. Dies geschieht auf der Basis sprachlicher und auch nicht-sprachliche Symbole, die die Kommunikanten verwenden, um die relevante soziale Rolle und die Erwartung ihrer Berücksichtigung in der sozialen Interaktion zu signalisieren. Sie lassen sich als Rollenmarker fassen. Ein wichtiges Symbol ist der Sprachstil; aber auch die Kleidung, die Körperhaltung oder das Interaktionsverhalten geben Hinweise auf die soziale Rolle. Die Deutung der sozialen Rolle auf der Basis solcher Symbole geht natürlich oft fehl und muß dann im Zuge des kommunikativen Geschehens korrigiert werden.

Diese Inszenierung in der Interaktion ist nicht zu verhindern oder auszublenden. Wir kommunizieren immer im sozialen Raum und stehen zu den Kommunikationspartnern immer in einem bestimmten sozialen Verhältnis, kommunizieren in einer spezifischen sozialen Rolle.

„Der Andere begegnet mir immer schon als Dritter. Er bewegt sich in einem sozialen Medium, sofern er sich als Bruder, Frau, Nachbar, Kollege, Mitbürger, Altersgenosse, Europäer und schließlich als Mitmensch äußert, und für mich selbst gilt dasselbe. Wer sich nur als er selbst äußern würde, wäre wie jemand, der in einer Privatsprache mit anderen spräche" (Waldenfels 1997: 116 f.).

Nach Waldenfels ergibt sich eine Austauschbarkeit der Perspektiven, wie sie in der Sozialphänomenologie für die Interaktion angenommen wird, erst wirklich vor dem Hintergrund der sozialen Rollen. Sie bringen Ordnungs- und Sinnstrukturen einer geteilten sozialen Wirklichkeit in die Interaktion ein und überbrücken so die Fremdheit und Andersheit des Gegenübers (Waldenfels 1997: 116 f.).

Diese Inszenierung sozialer Rollen erfüllt aber nicht nur soziale Effekte in dem Sinne, daß das Signalisieren und die Zuweisung von Rollen im konkreten Kommunikationsgeschehen soziale Ordnungs-, Machtverhältnisse und Sinnstrukturen bestätigt und tradiert. Neben dieser sozialkonstitutiven Funktion hat sprachlich-interaktives Handeln auch psychische bzw. psychosoziale Effekte. Im sprachlichen Interaktionsgeschehen erfolgen die Ausbildung, Bestätigung und Stabilisierung der Identität, kommt es aber ebenso auch zu Irritationen und Infragestellungen des Selbstbilds.

Wie in phänomenologischen Zusammenhängen hervorgehoben wird, ist die Genese von Identität wesentlich auf den Anderen und das Andere angewiesen. In einem sehr konkreten Sinne gilt dies etwa für die Geburt. Wir werden von Anderen geboren und diese geben uns unseren Namen (Meyer-Drawe 1990). Auch wird die Rolle des Anderen besonders augenfällig, wenn man sich vergegenwärtigt, daß wir uns selbst in der Interaktion nicht vollständig sehen können. Insbesondere bleibt uns unser Gesicht in der Interaktion immer verborgen. Wir sind hier angewiesen auf die anderen, die uns unser Gesicht geben: „... ich begegne mir im Blick der Anderen" (Waldenfels 1997: 31).

In einer stärker linguistischen Perspektive ist diese psychosoziale Dimension der sprachlichen Interaktion in der Erzählforschung aufgezeigt worden. Wenn Personen erzählen, schildern sie nicht nur Ereignisse, sondern sie präsentieren und erleben sich auch als eine Person mit bestimmten Eigenschaften und finden dieses Selbstbild in der Reaktion der Zuhörer mehr oder weniger bestätigt. Goffmann (1969; 1974) vergleicht das Geschehen in der face-to-face-Interaktion mit dem Theaterspielen. Ähnlich dem Schauspieler inszenieren wir uns in der Interaktion.

Das Individuum ist danach in der face-to-face-Interaktion doppelt präsent, einmal in einer Rolle und gleichzeitig als Darsteller der Rolle bzw. als Selbst. Beides, die Rolle und das Selbst, sind eng miteinander verbunden, sie sind aber niemals identisch. Die Rolle ist immer an die konkrete Inszenierung bzw. an ein konkretes interaktives Handeln gebunden. Das Selbst ergibt sich zwar aus erfolgreichen Inszenierungen und ist in diesem Sinne von den Konstellationen der Rolleninszenierungen abhängig, es existiert als Selbstbild aber (relativ) unabhängig von den konkreten Inszenierungen. Es ist genau das, was in der szenischen Rolle zum Ausdruck gebracht wird (Goffman 1969: 230 ff.).

Miller & al. beschreiben in einer empirischen Studie an amerikanischen Kindern aus verschiedenen kulturellen Milieus, daß die narrativen Praktiken der Selbstdarstellung im Erzählen in der Auseinandersetzung mit den Bezugspersonen erworben werden. Allerdings variieren die narrativen Praktiken kulturspezifisch, und die Autoren vermuten, daß dies auch mit einem kulturell variierenden Verständnis des 'Selbst' zu tun hat (Miller & al. 1990: 305 f.).

Erzählen birgt immer auch die Möglichkeit negativer Erfahrung. Ein positiver Effekt des Erzählens ist dabei von dem Erzähler allein nicht zu bewirken. Er hängt nicht zuletzt auch von situativ variierenden und vom Erzähler nicht zu kontrollierenden Faktoren ab, wie etwa dem Interesse der Kommunikationspartner und ihrem Entgegenkommen.

Auch spielt der Grad der individuellen Verfügbarkeit über narrative Praktiken eine Rolle.

Die Möglichkeit negativer Erfahrungen, und hier der Störungen des Selbstbildes, steht nach Brown & Levinson (1996) in engem Zusammenhang mit der Konstituierung eines „Prinzips der Höflichkeit". Sie gehen davon aus, daß „Höflichkeit" genau dazu dient, kritische und unangenehme Erfahrungen für die Kommunikationsteilnehmer zu vermeiden. Sie legen dabei eine Alltagsrationalität zugrunde, nach der sich die Kommunikanten an das Prinzip halten, weil sie dann einigermaßen sicher sein können, daß dies auch die anderen Kommunikanten tun. Dies bedeutet allerdings keineswegs, daß sie dem Prinzip der Höflichkeit immer folgen. Wo sie dies nicht tun, müssen sie allerdings damit rechnen, daß man auch ihnen „unhöflich" begegnet. Brown & Levinson (1996) verstehen das Höflichkeitsprinzip als universal, heben allerdings hervor, daß es in den Kulturen und Sprachgemeinschaften in jeweils spezifischer Form erscheint.

Goffman hat die identitätsbildenden und -stabilisierenden interaktiven Techniken unter dem Stichwort 'Imagepflege' („facework") untersucht (Goffman 1978: 10 ff.). Imagepflege wird dabei als eine von den inhaltlichen Dimension weitgehend unabhängige Aktivität gefaßt, in der es um die Präsentation und Bestätigung von Selbstbildern geht. Nach Goffman lassen sich verschiedene Techniken der Imagepflege unterscheiden, die alle darauf zielen, in der Interaktion das eigene 'face' und das der anderen zu wahren. Goffman (1978) unterscheidet protektive Techniken, die dem Schutz des 'face' der anderen dienen, und defensive Techniken, die auf die Wahrung des eigenen 'face' zielen. Beide Richtungen der Imagepflege in der Interaktion müssen in gleichem Maße Berücksichtigung finden.

Watzlawick & al. (1990: 68) weisen darauf hin, daß es grundsätzlich zwei Arten von Beziehungen in der Kommunikation gibt, die symmetrische und die komplementäre. Im ersten Fall liegt ein „Streben nach Gleichheit und Verminderung von Unterschieden" vor, im letzten Fall ergänzen die Kommunikanten einander in ihrer Ungleichheit. Der eine nimmt eine „inferiore, sekundäre" Position ein, der andere die „superiore, primäre". Hintergrund dieser Vorstellungen ist die psychologische Annahme eines sich stets ausgleichenden Beziehungssystems. Der Charakter der Kommunikation ist nach Watzlawick & al. (1990: 69 f.) eng an die Definition der sozialen Rollen und sozialen Situationen gebunden. So sind Arzt-Patienten-Gespräche stets komplementär; andere Gespräche sind in ihrer Bestimmung zunächst offen. Hier muß dann der Charakter im Zuge des Gesprächs interaktiv bestimmt werden. In Beziehungen erfolgt zuweilen die Festlegung auf eine der beiden Formen der Kommunikation.

5.1. Geschlechtsrollen

Seit den frühen 70er Jahren ist die Frage nach einem unterschiedlichen Gesprächsverhalten von Frauen und Männern Gegenstand gesprächsanalytischer Forschungen. Nach West & al. (1998) liegt der Wert der frühen Untersuchungen vor allem darin, daß sie die Aufmerksamkeit der Forschung erstmals auf die Sprache von Frauen gerichtet haben. Die in den frühen Arbeiten häufig vertretene Annahme aber, daß Frauen als Konsequenz einer geschlechtsspezifischen Organisation des Alltagslebens in den westlichen Zivilisationsgesellschaften eine eigene Sprache sprechen, vereinfacht die sprachlichen Verhältnisse stark.

In der Folge hat es zahlreiche Untersuchungen gegeben, die vergleichend das Gesprächsverhalten von Männern und Frauen untersucht haben (vgl. die Literaturhinweise in Redeker & Maes 1996). Die Ergebnisse divergieren allerdings, und dies spricht dafür, daß neben dem Geschlecht bzw. der Geschlechtsrolle, wie sie im relevanten Kontext der jeweiligen Interaktion definiert ist, eine Reihe weiterer Faktoren im Spiel sind, die zudem situativ variieren. West & al. (1998: 137) weisen darauf hin, daß die Forschung die sprachlichen Verhältnisse außerhalb der westlichen Welt vernachlässigt hat. Möglich ist, daß hier andere Zusammenhänge zwischen dem Sprachverhalten in der Interaktion und den Geschlechtsrollen bestehen. Auch ist die westliche Welt kein homogener Raum; auch hier gibt es — das zeigen ja die divergierenden Befunde — ganz unterschiedliche Verhältnisse. Eine Generalisierung der Befunde ist kaum möglich.

Die Schwierigkeiten zeigen sich etwa, wenn man allein die Annahmen über ein geschlechtsrollenspezifisches Unterbrechen in Gesprächen untersucht. Nach Tannen (1990) zeichnen sich Frauen in Gesprächen untereinander durch ein emotional engagiertes, kooperatives Gesprächsverhalten aus. Die Gesprächsbeiträge sind — vereinfacht gesprochen — relativ kurz und Unterbrechungen sind eher selten. Redeker & Maes (1996) allerdings stellen in einer kritischen Prüfung dieser These für eine Gruppe von akademisch geschulten Personen in leitenden beruflichen Positionen fest, daß Frauen und Männer gleich häufig unterbrechen. Jedoch konnten sie bestätigen, daß Unterbrechungen in reinen Frauengruppen insgesamt seltener vorkommen als in reinen Männergruppen. Nach den Autorinnen ist mithin davon auszugehen, daß sich Frauen in der Kommunikation mit Männern deren Gesprächsverhalten anpassen.

Hier zeigt sich exemplarisch, daß Frauen in ihrem Gesprächsverhalten keineswegs festgelegt sind. Es verbietet sich ein deterministisches Modell. Vielmehr scheinen Frauen, wo dies im Rahmen der Alltags- und Berufswelten notwendig wird oder hilfreich ist, ihr Interaktionsverhalten strategisch zu verändern. Dabei bleiben 'klassische' Verhaltensweisen durchaus verfügbar und relevant. Es handelt sich in diesem Sinne um eine 'pragmatische' Erweiterung des Verhaltensrepertoires. Sie korrespondiert mit Ansprüchen auf soziale Rollen, die Männern vorbehalten waren, aber auch mit Veränderungen der traditionellen Frauenrolle.

6. Zitierte Literatur

Anderson, Anne H. & Robertson, Alastair & Kilborn, Kerry. 1997. „Dialogue despite difficulties: a study of communication between aphasic and unimpaired speakers". In: Givón, Talmy (ed.), 1−39.

Auer, Peter. 1986. „Kontextualisierung". *Studium Linguistik* 19: 22−48.

Auer, Peter. 1992. „Introduction. John Gumperz' approach to contextualization". In: Auer, Peter & di Luzio, Aldo (eds.), 1−37.

Austin, John Langshaw. 1998 (^{1}1962). *Zur Theorie der Sprechakte (How to do things with words)*. Stuttgart: Reclam.

Berger, Peter L. & Luckmann, Thomas. 1980 (^{1}1966). *Die gesellschaftliche Konstruktion der Wirklichkeit. Eine Theorie der Wissenssoziologie.* Frankfurt/M: Fischer.

Blommaert, Jan & Verschueren, Jef. 1998. *Debating diversity: analysing the discourse of tolerance*. London: Routledge.

Blumer, Herbert. 1995 (^{1}1973). „Der methodologische Standpunkt des Symbolischen Interaktionismus". In: Burkart, Roland & Hömberg, Walter (eds.). *Kommunikationstheorien*. Wien, 23−39.

Brown, Penelope & Levinson, Stephen C. 1996 (^{1}1878). *Politeness: some universals in language usage*. Cambridge: Cambridge University Press.

Brünner, Gisela & Graefen, Gabriele. 1992. „Zur Konzeption der funktionalen Pragmatik". In: Brünner, Gisela & Graefen, Gabriele (eds.). *Texte und Diskurse. Methoden und Forschungsergebnisse der funktionalen Pragmatik*. Opladen: Westdeutscher Verlag, 7−21.

Buekens, Filip. 1995. „Pragmatism". In: Verschueren, Jef & Östman, Jan-Ola & Blommaert, Jan (eds.). *Handbook of pragmatics*. Amsterdam, Philadelphia: Benjamins, 424−29.

Bühler, Karl. 1982 (^{1}1934). *Sprachtheorie*. Stuttgart & New York: Fischer.

Cicourel, Aaron V. 1991. „Semantics, pragmatics, and situated meaning". In: Verschueren, Jef (ed.). *Pragmatics at issue. Selected papers of the International pragmatics conference. Antwerpen 1987.* Volume 1. Amsterdam & Philadelphia: Benjamins, 37−66.

Cicourel, Aaron, V. 1975. *Sprache in der sozialen Interaktion*. München: List.

Clark, Herbert H. (ed.). 1992. *Arenas of language use*. Chicago: University of Chicago Press.

Clark, Herbert H. & Brennan, Susan E. 1991. „Grounding in communication". In: Lauren B. & Levine, John M. & Teasley, Stephanie D. (eds.). *Perspectives in socially shared cognition*. Resnick, Washington/DC: American Psychological Association, 127−49.

Clark, Herbert H. & Carlson, Thomas B. 1992. „Hearers and speech acts". In: Clark, Herbert H. (ed.), 205−47.

Clark, Herbert H. & Schaefer, Edward F. 1992. „Dealing with overhearers". In: Clark, Herbert H. (ed.), 248−74.

Couper-Kuhlen, Elisabeth & Auer, Peter. 1991. „On the contextualization function of speech rhythm in conversation: Question-answer sequences". In: Verschueren, Jef (ed.). *Levels of linguistic adaptation. Selelected papers of the 1987 International Pragmatics Conference*. Vol. II. Amsterdam & Philadelphia: Benjamins, 1−18.

Dewey, John. 1958. *Experience and nature*. New York: Dover.

Dickinson, Connie & Givón, Talmy. 1997. „Memory and conversation: Toward an experimental paradigm". In: Givón, Talmy (ed.), 91−132.

Ehlich, Konrad. 1987. „So − Überlegungen zum Verhältnis sprachlicher Formen und sprachlichen Handelns, allgemein und an einem widerspenstigen Beispiel". In: Rosengren, Inger (ed.). *Sprache und Pragmatik. Lunder Symposium 1986.* Stockholm: Almqvist & Wiksell, 279−98.

Ehlich, Konrad. 1991. „Funktional-pragmatische Kommunikationsanalyse − Ziele und Verfahren". In: Flader, Dieter (ed.). *Verbale Interaktion*. Stuttgart, 127−43.

Ervin-Tripp, Susan. 1987. „Cross-cultural and developmental sources of pragmatic generalizations".

In: Verschueren, Jef & Bertuccelli-Papi, Marcella (eds.). *The pragmatic perspective. Selected papers from the 1985 International Pragmatics Conference.* Amsterdam & Philadelphia: Benjamins, 47–60.

Ervin-Tripp, Susan. 1996. „Context in language". In: Slobin, Dan Isaac & al. (eds.), 21–36.

Feilke, Helmuth. 1994. *Common sense-Kompetenz. Überlegungen zu einer Theorie 'sympathischen' und 'natürlichen' Meinens und Verstehens.* Frankfurt/M: Suhrkamp.

Garfinkel, Harold. 1967. *Studies in ethnomethodology.* Englewood Cliffs/NJ: Prentice-Hall.

Goffman, Erving. 1978. *Interaktionsrituale. Über Verhalten in direkter Kommunikation.* Frankfurt/M.: Suhrkamp.

Goffman, Erving. 1969 (^{1}1959). *Wir alle spielen Theater. Die Selbstdarstellung im Alltag.* München: Piper.

Goffman, Erving. 1974. *Frame analysis. An essay on the organization of experience.* New York: Harper & Row.

Gordon, D. & Lakoff, George. 1975. „Conversational postulates". In: Cole, Peter & Morgan, Jerry L. (eds.). *Speech acts.* (Syntax and semantics, 3.) New York: Academic Press, 83–106.

Grice, Herbert Paul. 1957. „Meaning". *The Philosophical Review* 66: 377–88.

Grice, Herbert Paul. 1993 (^{1}1975). „Logik und Konversation". In: Meggle, Georg (ed.). *Handlung, Kommunikation, Bedeutung.* Frankfurt/M.: Suhrkamp, 243–65.

Gülich, Elisabeth & Kotschi, Thomas. 1996. „Textherstellungsverfahren in mündlicher Kommunikation". In: Motsch, Wolfgang (ed.). *Ebenen der Textstruktur. Sprachliche und kommunikative Prinzipien.* Tübingen: Niemeyer, 37–80.

Gumperz, John J. 1992. „Contextualization revisited". In: Auer, Peter & Di Luzio, Aldo (eds.). *The contextualization of language.* Amsterdam & Philadelphia: Benjamins, 39–53.

Gumperz, John J. 1994 (^{1}1982). *Discourse strategies.* Cambridge: Cambridge University Press.

Hausendorf, Heiko & Quasthoff, Uta M. 1995. „Discourse and oral contextualizations: vocal cues". In: Quasthoff, Uta M. (ed.), 220–55.

Heath, Shirley Brice. 1985. *Ways with words: language, life, and work in communities and classrooms.* Cambridge (UK): Cambridge University Press.

Henne, Helmut. 1979. „Die Rolle des Hörers im Gespräch". In: Rosengren, Inger (ed.). *Sprache und Pragmatik. Lunder Symposium 1978.* Lund: CWK Gleerup, 122–34.

Heritage, John. 1995. „Conversation analysis: Methodological aspects". In: Quasthoff Uta M. (ed.), 391–418.

Hörmann, Hans. 1980. „Der Vorgang des Verstehens". In: Kühlwein, Wolfgang & Raasch, Albert (eds.). *Sprache und Verstehen.* Bd. 1. Tübingen: Niemeyer, 17–29.

Hymes, Dell. 1979 (^{1}1962). „Die Ethnographie des Sprechens". In: Hymes, Dell. *Soziolinguistik. Zur Ethnographie der Kommunikation.* Frankfurt/M: Suhrkamp, 29–97.

James, William. 1931. *Pragmatism: a new name for some old ways of thinking. Popular lectures on philosophy.* New York: Longmans, Green, and Co.

Joas, Hans. 1996. *Die Kreativität des Handelns.* Frankfurt/M.: Suhrkamp.

Kasher, Asa. 1976. „Conversational maxims and rationality". In: Kasher, Asa (ed.). *Language in focus: Foundations, methods and systems: essays in memory of Yehoshua Bar-Hillel.* Dordrecht: Reidel, 197–216.

Kemmerling, Andreas. 1991. „Implikatur". In: Stechow, Arnim von & al. (eds.). *Semantik: ein internationales Handbuch der zeitgenössischen Forschung.* Berlin & New York: de Gruyter, 319–33.

Koch, Peter & Oesterreicher, Wulf. 1990. *Gesprochene Sprache in der Romania: Französisch, Italienisch, Spanisch.* Tübingen: Niemeyer.

Koch, Peter &. Oesterreicher, Wulf. 1994. „Schriftlichkeit und Sprache". In: Günther, Hartmut & Ludwig, Otto (eds.). *Schrift und Schriftlichkeit. Writing and its use.* 1. Halbband. Berlin & New York: de Gruyter, 587–604.

Labov, William. 1972. *Sociolinguistic patterns.* Philadelphia: University of Pennsylvania Press.

Levinson, Stephen C. 1994 (^{1}1983). *Pragmatik.* Tübingen: Niemeyer.

Liedtke, Frank. 1995. „Das Gesagte und das Nicht-Gesagte. Zur Definition von Implikaturen". In: Liedtke, Frank (ed.). *Implikaturen: grammatische und pragmatische Analysen.* Tübingen: Niemeyer, 19–46.

Linell, Per & Korolija, Natascha. 1997. „Coherence in multi-party conversation". In: Givón, Talmy (ed.), 167–205.

Luckmann, Thomas. 1992. *Theorie des sozialen Handelns.* Berlin & New York: de Gruyter.

Luhmann, Niklas. 1987. *Soziale Systeme.* Frankfurt/M.: Suhrkamp.

Luhmann, Niklas. 1995. Soziologische Aufklärung 6: Die Soziologie und der Mensch. Opladen: Westdeutscher Verlag.

Mead, George Herbert. 1968 (^{1}1934). *Geist, Identität und Gesellschaft aus der Sicht des Sozialbehaviorismus* (Suhrkamp-Taschenbuch Wissenschaft, 28). Frankfurt/M.: Suhrkamp.

Meggle, Georg. 1997. *Grundbegriffe der Kommunikation.* Berlin & New York: de Gruyter.

Merleau-Ponty, Maurice. 1966. *Phänomenologie der Wahrnehmung.* Berlin & New York: de Gruyter.

Meyer-Drawe, Käte. 1990. *Illusionen von Autonomie: diesseits von Ohnmacht und Allmacht des Ich.* München: Kirchheim.

Miller, Peggy L. & Potts, Randolph & Fung, Heidi & Hoogstra, Lisa & Mintz, Judy. 1990. „Narrative practices and the social construction of self in childhood". *American Ethnologist*, 17 (2), 292–311.

Morris, Charles William. 1938. „Foundations of the theory of signs". In: Neurath, Otto & Carnap, Rudolf (eds.). *Foundations of the unity of science. Toward an international encyclopedia of unified science. Vol. 1, No. 2*. Chicago: University of Chicago Press, 1–59.

Ochs-Keenan, Elinor. 1976. „On the universality of conversational implicature". *Language in society* 5: 67–80.

Peirce, Charles Sanders. 1968. *Schriften. Band 1: Zur Entstehung des Pragmatismus*. Apel, Karl-Otto (ed.). Frankfurt/M.: Suhrkamp.

Peirce, Charles Sanders. 1970. *Schriften. Band 2: Vom Pragmatismus zum Pragmatizismus*. Apel, Karl Otto (ed.). Frankfurt/M: Suhrkamp.

Prandi, Michele. 1994. „Meaning and indexicality in communication". In: Parret, Herman (ed.). *Pretending to communicate*. Berlin & New York: de Gruyter, 17–32.

Redeker, Gisela & Maes, Anny. 1996. „Gender differences in interruptions". In: Slobin, Dan Isaac & al., 597–612.

Rehbein, Jochen. 1977. *Komplexes Handeln: Elemente zur Handlungstheorie der Sprache*. Stuttgart: Metzler.

Rehbein, Jochen. 1992. „Theorien, sprachwissenschaftlich betrachtet". In: Brünner, Gisela & Graefen, Gabriele (eds.). *Texte und Diskurse. Methoden und Forschungsergebnisse der funktionalen Pragmatik*. Opladen: Westdeutscher Verlag, 25–67.

Richter, Heide. 1988. *Indexikalität. Ihre Behandlung in Philosophie und Sprachwissenschaft*. Tübingen: Niemeyer.

Rolf, Eckard. 1994. *Sagen und Meinen: Paul Grices Theorie der Konversations-Implikaturen*. Opladen: Westdeutscher Verlag.

Sacks, Harvey & Schegloff, Emanuel A. & Jefferson, Gail. 1974. „A simplest systematics for the organization of turn-taking for conversation". *Language* 50: 696–735.

Schegloff, Emanuel A. 1996. „Turn organization: on intersection of grammar and interaction". In: Ochs, Elinor & Schegloff, Emanuel A. & Thompson, Sandra A. (eds.). *Interaction and grammar*. Cambridge (UK): Cambridge University Press, 52–133.

Schegloff, Emanuel A. & Jefferson, Gail & Sacks, Harvey. 1977. „The preference of self-correction in the organization of conversational interaction". *Language* 51: 361–82.

Schlieben-Lange, Brigitte. 1979. *Linguistische Pragmatik*. Stuttgart: Kohlhammer.

Schmidt, Siegfried J. 1994. *Kognitive Autonomie und soziale Orientierung. Konstruktivistische Bemerkungen zum Zusammenhang von Kommunikation, Medien und Kultur*. Frankfurt/M: Suhrkamp.

Schütz, Alfred & Thomas Luckmann. 1979. *Strukturen der Lebenswelt*. Band 1. Frankfurt/M.: Suhrkamp.

Schütz, Alfred & Thomas Luckmann. 1984. *Strukturen der Lebenswelt*. Band 2. Frankfurt/M.: Suhrkamp.

Searle, John R. 1997 (^{1}1969). *Sprechakte. Ein sprachphilosophischer Essay*. Frankfurt/M: Suhrkamp.

Selting, Margret. 1995. *Prosodie im Gespräch. Aspekte einer interaktionalen Phonologie der Konversation*. Tübingen: Niemeyer.

Sperber, Dan & Wilson, Deirdre. 1995 (^{1}1986). *Relevance: Communication and cognition*. Oxford/ UK: Blackwell.

Strohner, Hans. 1995. *Kognitive Systeme. Eine Einführung in die Kognitionswissenschaft*. Opladen: Westdeutscher Verlag.

Tannen, Deborah. 1990. *You just don't understand: Women and men in conversation*. New York: Morrow.

Tomlin, Russell S. & Forrest, Linda & Ming Pu, Ming & Kim, Myung Hee. 1998. „Discourse semantics". In: Van Dijk, Teun A. (ed.). *Discourse as structure and process*. London: Sage, 63–111.

Verschueren, Jef. 1999. *Understanding pragmatics*. London & New York: Arnold.

Waldenfels, Bernhard. 1980. *Der Spielraum des Verhaltens*. Frankfurt/M.: Suhrkamp.

Waldenfels, Bernhard. 1987. *Ordnung im Zwielicht*. Frankfurt/M.: Suhrkamp.

Waldenfels, Bernhard. 1990. *Der Stachel des Fremden*. Frankfurt/M.: Suhrkamp.

Waldenfels, Bernhard. 1997. *Topographie des Fremden*. Frankfurt/M.: Suhrkamp.

Waldenfels, Bernhard. 1998. *Grenzen der Normalisierung*. Frankfurt/M.: Suhrkamp.

Watzlawick, Paul & Beavin, Janet H. & Jackson, Don D. 1990. *Menschliche Kommunikation. Formen, Störungen, Paradoxien*. Bern: Huber.

Weinrich, Harald. 1993. *Textgrammatik der deutschen Sprache*. Mannheim: Dudenverlag.

Wenzel, Harald. 1992. „Der interaktionistische Ansatz". In: Dascal, Marcelo & al. (eds.). *Sprachphilosophie*. Halbband 1. Berlin & New York: de Gruyter, 732–45.

West, Candace & Lazar, Michelle M. & Kramarae, Cheris. 1998. „Gender in discorse". In: Van Dijk, Teun A. (ed.). *Discourse as social interaction*. London: Sage, 119–43.

Wilson, Deirdre & Sperber, Dan. 1998. „Pragmatics and time". In: Carston, Robyn & Uchida, Seiji (eds.). *Relevance theory. Applications and impli-*

cations. Amsterdam & Philadelphia: Benjamins, 1–22.

Wittgenstein, Ludwig. 1953. *Philosophical investigations / Philosophische Untersuchungen*. Oxford: Blackwell.

Wunderlich, Dieter. 1976. *Studien zur Sprechakttheorie*. Frankfurt/M.: Suhrkamp.

*Doris Tophinke, Universität Freiburg i. Br.
(Deutschland)*

36. Diskurstraditionen

1. Traditionalität
2. Komplexitätsgrade von Diskurstraditionen
3. Diskurstraditionen und Universalität
4. Diskurstraditionen und Sprachgeschichte
5. Zitierte Literatur

1. Traditionalität

1.1. Funktion und Tradition

Jeder Text oder Diskurs, ob geschrieben oder gesprochen, steht in Traditionen, er ist präzisen Normen unterworfen. Kommunikation ist auf die Einhaltung von (meist implizit bleibenden) Konventionen angewiesen. Bei den NORMEN der Kommunikation handelt es sich zumeist um informell erworbene, habitualisierte Regelkomplexe, die einem ständigen Wandel unterworfen sind. Die Durchbrechung oder Mißachtung der kommunikativen Normen — jenseits einer gewissen Variationsbreite, die die Voraussetzung der individuellen Realisation wie auch des historischen Wandels darstellt — führt zu Verständigungsschwierigkeiten und im Extremfall zum Mißlingen des Kommunikationsaktes.

Der einzelne Äußerungsakt läßt sich solchermaßen immer nur in dem Spannungsverhältnis zwischen Tradition und Funktion bestimmen: Die Tradition ermöglicht überhaupt erst die Verständigung; die Funktion betrifft die jeweilige Aussageabsicht. Gegenüber der oftmals vorherrschenden funktionalistischen Ausrichtung, wie sie etwa für weite Teile der Soziolinguistik charakteristisch ist, soll hier die Traditionsgebundenheit, die *Traditionalität* der menschlichen Rede betont werden.

1.2. Diskurstradition und Einzelsprache

Es ist notwendig, zwischen zwei Arten von Traditionen, und somit von Normen, zu unterscheiden, durch die eine sprachliche Äußerung geprägt wird: zwischen den Einzelsprachen und den Diskurstraditionen.

Der einzelsprachliche Charakter eines jeden Textes oder Diskurses leuchtet unmittelbar ein: Jede sprachliche Äußerung — von dem Gruß *Buon giorno!* bis zu einem literarischen Meisterwerk wie Petrarcas *Canzoniere* — muß sich notwendigerweise einer historisch gewachsenen Einzelsprache (hier des Italienischen) bedienen. Sicher kann sich ein Text/Diskurs auch mehrerer Einzelsprachen zugleich bedienen, und er kann auch einzelsprachliche Regeln durchbrechen: In beiden Fällen wird die prinzipielle Gültigkeit der einzelsprachlichen Norm allerdings nicht außer Kraft gesetzt, da solche Normabweichungen überhaupt nur vor dem Hintergrund des eigentlich zu Erwartenden (der Norm) als 'Abweichungen' identifiziert werden können.

Ebenso unausweichlich ist jedoch die zweite Art der traditionellen Prägung der menschlichen Rede: Jeder Text/Diskurs steht in einer bestimmten Diskurstradition, er befolgt die Regeln einer bestimmten Textgattung. So wie der Sprecher für seinen Äußerungsakt eine bestimmte Einzelsprache oder ein einzelsprachliches Register auswählt — anstelle des standarditalienischen *Buon giorno!* kann er auch das regionale *Buon dì!* oder, je nach Situation, das französische *Bonjour!* verwenden —, so muß er sich auch für eine bestimmte Diskurstradition — den Gruß, die Gedichtsammlung oder irgendeine andere der traditionellen Formen — entscheiden. So wie es keine sprachliche Äußerung 'außerhalb' einer historischen Einzelsprache geben kann — unser Sprechen ist notwendig Italienisch, Französisch usw. —, so kann es auch kein Sprechen 'außerhalb' einer bereits etablierten Diskurstradition geben: Unser Sprechen bedient sich notwendig der Form des Grußes, der Gedichtsammlung, des Telephongesprächs, des Briefes usw.

Jede Rede ist einzelsprachlich, und sie ist gattungshaft, diskurstraditionell geprägt. Die Kommunikationsformen des Alltags, wie etwa der Gruß, sind dabei prinzipiell nicht weniger regelgeleitet als etwa die literarischen Formen wie die Gedichtsammlung: Auch die 'Gattungen' der Alltagskommunikation sind einer historischen Beschreibung zugänglich (→ Art. 1, § 1.1, 4.1; Art. 3, § 3.1; Bergmann & Luckmann 1995; zur Geschichte der Höflichkeit und insbesondere zu der historischen Situierung bestimmter Grußtypen vgl. etwa Radtke 1994a.)

1.3. Die drei Ebenen des Sprachlichen

In etwas systematischerer Form lassen sich die hier referierten Überlegungen wie folgt präzisieren. Mit Eugenio Coseriu (1994: 46−63) können wir drei Ebenen des Sprachlichen unterscheiden: die UNIVERSELLE Ebene des Sprechens, die HISTORISCHE Ebene und die AKTUELLE Ebene des jeweiligen individuellen Textes. Wie Peter Koch und Wulf Oesterreicher deutlich gemacht haben, müssen wir auf der historischen Ebene jedoch zwei Dimensionen auseinanderhalten: die Einzelsprachen und die Diskurstraditionen (vgl. etwa Koch 1997: 43−49; Oesterreicher 1997: 19−21). Dies bedeutet, daß jeder individuelle sprachliche Äußerungsakt (jeder 'Text') durch universale Sprechregeln, sowie durch die historischen Regeln (Normen) der jeweils gewählten Sprache und der jeweils gewählten Diskurstradition bestimmt wird: Der individuelle Text oder Diskurs steht somit immer in den zwei prinzipiell zu unterscheidenden Traditionen der Einzelsprache und der Diskurstradition.

Die folgenden Ausführungen gliedern sich in drei Teile. Nach einer knappen Charakterisierung der Diskurstraditionen und ihrer unterschiedlichen Komplexitätsgrade (s. u. § 2), möchte ich das Verhältnis der Diskurstraditionen zur Universalität näher beleuchten (s. u. § 3); sodann wird uns das Verhältnis der Diskurstraditionen zu den Einzelsprachen und dabei insbesondere die Wechselwirkung zwischen der Geschichte der Diskurstraditionen und der Sprachgeschichte beschäftigen (s. u. § 4). Die Diskurstraditionen erweisen sich dabei als ein zentraler Gegenstand sowohl der systematischen als auch der historischen Sprachwissenschaft.

2. Komplexitätsgrade von Diskurstraditionen

Bei den Diskurstraditionen lassen sich im wesentlichen drei Komplexitätsgrade unterscheiden: die Diskursuniversen, die Text- oder Diskursgattungen und die Formeln. Es ist zu betonen, daß es sich hierbei jeweils um historisch wandelbare Regelkomplexe oder Normen handelt, die von typologisierenden Konstrukten unterschieden werden müssen.

2.1. Diskursuniversen

Die Diskursuniversen bilden gleichsam Klassen von Text- oder Diskursgattungen. Für die Gegenwart lassen sich (zumindest) die Bereiche der 'Literatur', des 'Alltags', der 'Wissenschaft' und der 'Religion' unterscheiden (zu den 'Sinnwelten' oder 'Kommunikationsbereichen' vgl. auch Steger 1998). Ein besonderes Interesse kommt hierbei der Ausgliederung der unterschiedlichen Diskursuniversen zu (vgl. Schlieben-Lange 1983: 146 f.).

Ein reiches Anschauungsmaterial liefert uns die relativ gut erforschte Geschichte des literarischen Diskursuniversums: So läßt sich detailliert nachvollziehen, wie die Merkmale von 'Literatur' (Fiktionalität, Handlungsentbindung usw.) erst im Laufe eines jahrhundertelangen Entwicklungsprozesses herausgebildet wurden (vgl. Gumbrecht 1988). Folglich erscheint es als angemessen, „die immer wieder gescheiterten Bemühungen um eine 'Literaturdefinition' zu ersetzen durch eine Rekonstruktion jenes Ausdifferenzierungsprozesses von Kommunikationssituationen, aus dem − auch − die 'Literatur' hervorging" (Gumbrecht 1980: 410). Als historische Größen sind die Diskursuniversen − wie alle Diskurstraditionen − nicht ableitbar oder definierbar; vielmehr können sie allein in ihrer historischen Entwicklung nachvollzogen und beschrieben werden.

2.2. Text- oder Diskursgattungen

Bei den Gattungen handelt es sich um Diskurstraditionen eines mittleren Komplexitätsgrades. Dies bedeutet unter anderem, daß Gattungen meist einem bestimmten Diskursuniversum zugeordnet werden können, dem sie gemeinsam mit anderen Gattungen angehören: So sind der Roman oder das Sonett charakteristisch für das literarische Diskursuniversum, das Telephongespräch oder der Privatbrief gehören dem Alltag an usw.

In der literaturwissenschaftlichen Gattungslehre wie auch in der Textlinguistik hat sich die Ansicht herausgebildet, daß deutlich zwischen zwei Texttypenbegriffen unterschieden werden muß: Texttypen können zum einen als klassifikatorische Konstrukte, zum anderen als historisch beschreibbare, im Bewußtsein der Sprecher/Schreiber verankerte

Normen aufgefaßt werden (vgl. Todorov ²1976; Isenberg 1983). Im ersten Fall möchte ich von 'Textsorten', im zweiten Fall von 'Gattungen' sprechen. Hervorzuheben ist dabei, daß sowohl der klassifikatorische Textsortenbegriff als auch der historische Gattungsbegriff gleichermaßen auf den literarischen wie den nicht-literarischen Bereich angewendet werden können: In Hinsicht auf ihre Gattungshaftigkeit besteht kein prinzipieller Unterschied zwischen literarischen und nicht-literarischen Textformen. Im Gegenteil erlaubt es allein ein umfassender Texttypenbegriff, die möglichen Unterschiede in der Ausbildung und Überlieferung literarischer, wissenschaftlicher, alltäglicher usw. Gattungstraditionen zu erkennen (vgl. Wilhelm 1996: 8−11).

Als Normen der Textproduktion und Textrezeption sind die Gattungen im Bewußtsein der Sprecher verankert. Sie sind in erster Linie als 'Gattungsvorstellungen' zu beschreiben. Die Gattungsforschung hat vornehmlich die Aufgabe, diese Normenvorstellungen zu rekonstruieren, da nur sie einen realistischen Zugang zu den Kommunikationsabläufen der Vergangenheit wie auch der Gegenwart erlauben (vgl. Janik 1985).

Einen unmittelbaren Einblick in das jeweils epochenspezifische Gattungsbewußtsein eröffnen uns solche metakommunikativen Äußerungen wie die *Gattungsnamen* und die expliziten *Intentionserklärungen*. Insbesondere muß jedoch auch versucht werden, die mit den jeweiligen Gattungskonzepten verbundenen textuellen Formen möglichst präzise zu beschreiben. Die Gattungsbestimmung hat somit in erster Linie hermeneutisch vorzugehen: Sie muß zunächst danach fragen, welche präzisen Kommunikationssituationen und welche erkennbaren textuellen Muster in einer Epoche mit einem bestimmten Gattungskonzept (Gattungsnamen) verbunden sind. Zugleich müssen wir jedoch immer auch mit mehr oder weniger deutlich ausgeprägten Diskrepanzen zwischen den expliziten Kategorisierungen durch Gattungsbezeichnungen und den impliziten Normvorstellungen der Sprecher/Schreiber rechnen (zur Bedeutung der historischen Gattungsnamen für die Rekonstruktion des jeweiligen Gattungsbewußtseins vgl. u. a. Raible 1996; Wilhelm 1996: 22−25; Frank 1997; Schlieben-Lange 1997; Selig 1997). Dabei können die einzelnen Gattungen durchaus in sehr unterschiedlichen Dimensionen charakterisiert sein.

Unter den Dimensionen, in denen Gattungen 'definiert' sind, sind vor allem der texterne, sowie die beiden textinternen Bereiche der Ausdrucks- und der Inhaltsseite zu nennen. Als Beispiele für die rekurrenten Muster in der ausdrucksseitigen Strukturierung sind etwa die Textgliederungsverfahren und die jeweilige Makrostruktur von Bedeutung, im inhaltsseitigen Bereich sind insbesondere die gattungstypischen Erzählmuster und Argumentationsformen von Interesse (vgl. Wilhelm 1996: 25−28).

Die immer wieder aufgestellte Forderung nach einer „verbindlichen Gattungssystematik" erscheinen unter diesem Gesichtspunkt als im Ansatz verfehlt (Raible 1996: 72): Als Diskurstraditionen sind die Textgattungen durch „Dynamik, beständige[n] Wandel und beständiges Hinaustreten über das Gegebene" charakterisiert; primäre Aufgabe der Gattungsforschung kann somit nur die „Erfassung und Beschreibung dieses kulturellen Wandels" sein (Raible 1996: 72). Regelrechte 'Gattungssysteme' lassen sich dagegen bestenfalls für engumgrenzte kommunikative Teilbereiche und für präzise synchronische Schnitte erstellen.

2.3. Formeln

Als Formeln können wir diejenigen textgliedernden Versatzstücke bezeichnen, die eine übereinzelsprachliche Verbreitung besitzen. So läßt sich der traditionelle Märchenanfang *Es war einmal* in sehr vielen Sprachtraditionen nachweisen, etwa FRANZÖSISCH *Il était une fois,* ITALIENISCH *C' era una volta,* SPANISCH *Érase una vez* usw. (Coseriu ³1994: 188 f.). Die Formel *Es war einmal* kann als ein traditionelles Verfahren der Textgliederung gelten, das unabhängig von der jeweiligen Sprachgemeinschaft verwendet wird.

Einen ähnlichen Status besitzen die typischerweise zur Erzähleröffnung verwendete Narratio-Formel *Wisset* (oder *Voi dovete sapere* u. ä.; vgl. Koch 1988a: 40; Wilhelm 1996: 227 f.), die Formel ITALIENISCH *avvenne che,* FRANZÖSISCH *il advint que,* KATALANISCH. *esdevenc-se que* usw., die in der Erzählung einen neuen Handlungsschritt einleitet (vgl. Wilhelm 1997: 415) oder die Überleitungsformel des Typs *ora lasciamo stare/ritorniamo a,* die parallele Handlungen miteinander verknüpft (vgl. Schlieben-Lange 1987: 775; Wilhelm 1996: 133−36).

Es fällt auf, daß diese Formeln mehr oder weniger deutlich an einzelne Gattungstraditionen gebunden sind. So ist die Formel *Es war einmal* ein typisches Merkmal des Märchens. Die Formel *avvenne che* findet sich dagegen in erster Linie in der mittelalterlichen Novellistik und in der Historiographie (vgl. Stein 1997: 200−202), die Überleitungsformel *ora lasciamo stare* ist charakteristisch für die Epik und wiederum für die Historiographie. Die Narratio-Formel des Typs *Wisset* ist dagegen seit der Antike in Urkunden und Briefen belegt, sie tritt jedoch auch in der Novellistik auf.

Die textgliedernden Formeln können solchermaßen gattungsspezifisch sein, wie die Märcheneröffnung; sie können jedoch auch in mehreren, z. T. recht unterschiedlichen Gattungen auftreten. Gleichwohl scheinen die Formeln immer an eine oder mehrere Gattungen gebunden zu sein: Sie zählen zu den regelhaften Gestaltungsmitteln im Innern präziser Traditionslinien. Das jeweils verwendete Formelinventar bildet somit zweifellos eines der wesentlichen Bestimmungsmerkmale einer Gattung.

Als Diskurstraditionen eines niedrigeren Komplexitätsgrades, gleichsam als traditionelle Bausteine für Texte oder Diskurse, können weiterhin bestimmte Sprechakte oder Sprechakttypen gelten (→ Art. 3, § 3.2.3; Art. 35, § 1.4).

3. Diskurstraditionen und Universalität

Als habitualisierte, einem stetigen Wandel unterworfene Regelkomplexe bilden Diskurstraditionen historisch-kontingente und somit keineswegs universale Größen. Gleichwohl kann uns die Beschäftigung mit den Diskurstraditionen in mehrerer Hinsicht zu der Frage der sprachlichen Universalität führen. Ganz grundlegend ist hier bereits das 'Generizitätspostulat', das die Prägung jeglicher sprachlichen Äußerung durch präzise diskurstraditionelle Normen hervorhebt (s. u. § 3.1).

Hieran anschließend stellt sich jedoch die Frage, inwieweit im historischen Wandel der Diskurstraditionen ebenfalls rekurrente Gesetzmäßigkeiten am Werk sind, die eine universale Gültigkeit beanspruchen können (s. u. § 3.2). Schließlich soll hier noch das Verhältnis zwischen den Diskurstraditionen und den universalen Diskurstypen erörtert werden (s. u. § 3.3).

3.1. Generizitätspostulat

Das Generizitätspostulat besagt, daß kein Text oder Diskurs 'außerhalb' einer etablierten Diskurstradition produziert und rezipiert werden kann. Die „Generizität" kann in der Tat, wie Stempel (1975: 175) betont, „als Bedingung interaktioneller Verständigung" gelten; oder, anders ausgedrückt: „Es gibt keine Rede, die nicht generisch ist" (*ibid.*).

Die Annahme einer unabdingbaren Generizität der menschlichen Rede läßt sich unmittelbar aus der grundlegenden *Historizität* des Sprechens ableiten. Textuelle Formen wie das Telephongespräch oder der Brief, das Sonett oder der Roman können immer nur als Exemplare einer historischen Reihe hervorgebracht und verstanden werden: Sprachliche Kommunikation beruht notwendig auf Konventionen. Folglich könnte ein Text oder Diskurs „nur um den Preis der Unverständlichkeit absolut, d. h. von allem Erwartbaren isoliert sein", wie Jauß (1972: 109) zu Recht betont.

Die diskurstraditionelle Praxis steht immer „im Spannungsfeld von Konvention und Innovation" (Koch 1997: 61). Und dies bedeutet nicht zuletzt, daß auch bei der Herausbildung 'neuer' Diskurstraditionen „in den neuen Traditionen [...] gewisse Konstitutiva der zurückliegenden Traditionen eine Zeitlang erhalten [bleiben], auch wenn sie im Hinblick auf den kommunikativen Zweck eigentlich dysfunktional sind" (Koch 1997: 64). Die Generizität erscheint solchermaßen als ein charakteristischer Ausdruck für die *Traditionalität* jeglichen kommunikativen Handelns.

Wie bereits angedeutet (s. o. § 2.2), sind Diskurstraditionen − wie etwa die Gattungen der Novelle oder des Zeitungsberichts − nicht nur ausdrucksseitig (etwa durch die Verwendung eines bestimmten Formelinventars), sondern oftmals auch inhaltsseitig (etwa durch eine mehr oder weniger deutlich vorgegebene Erzählstruktur) geprägt: Die Diskurstradition gibt somit oftmals bereits eine bestimmte Darstellungsweise, eine 'Form' für die Bewältigung der Erfahrungswelt vor (zu den traditionellen Aufbauprinzipien der Zeitungsnachricht vgl. etwa Koch 1997: 64f.). So stellt sich hier jedoch die Frage, inwieweit eine solche weitreichende traditionelle Festlegung überhaupt die Realisation individueller Aussageabsichten erlaubt und inwieweit − allgemeiner gefragt − die Generizität Raum läßt für einen Gattungswandel und insgesamt für einen historischen Wandel der Diskurstraditionen. Die Diskussion des Generizitätspostulats führt uns somit unmittelbar zu der Frage nach den charakteristischen 'Mechanismen' des Gattungswandels.

3.2. Gattungswandel

Das Generizitätspostulat widerspricht ebensowenig der Annahme eines stetigen Gattungswandels, wie die weitestgehende Erfüllung einzelsprachlicher Konventionen einen Sprachwandel verhindert. Offensichtlich lassen die diskurstraditionellen wie die einzelsprachlichen Normen dem Sprecher gleichwohl immer einen hinreichend großen Variationsspielraum, der zur Ausgangsbasis oftmals weitreichender Innovationen werden kann. (Wegweisend sind hier Saussures Überlegungen zu der „identité diachronique", die als eine „série d'identités synchroniques dans la parole" aufgefaßt werden kann; vgl. Saussure 1972: 250). Oesterreicher (1997: 30 f.) spricht in diesem Zusammenhang von je unterschiedlichen „Freiheitsgraden", die eine mehr oder weniger deutlich ausgeprägte „Diskursvarianz" erlauben (zur Dynamik von Diskurstraditionen vgl. insbesondere auch Koch 1997: 59–70).

In spezifischerer Weise läßt sich der Gattungswandel anhand der unterschiedlichen Typen von GATTUNGSINTERFERENZEN illustrieren. Hierbei wird insbesondere deutlich, daß die Entstehung neuer Gattungen niemals eine *creatio ex nihilo* darstellt, sondern vielmehr als eine neuartige Kombination bereits vorliegender traditioneller Textbausteine zu gelten hat.

Ich möchte hier vier Grundtypen von Gattungsinterferenz unterscheiden. Zur Illustration beziehe ich mich dabei auf die Analyse eines umfangreichen Textkorpus von italienischen Flugschriften aus der ersten Hälfte des 16. Jahrhunderts (zum folgenden vgl. insbesondere Wilhelm 1996: 297 f.).

– Eine GATTUNGSÜBERSCHNEIDUNG liegt dann vor, wenn ein Text zwei von den Sprechern/Schreibern selbst unterschiedenen Gattungen angehört. Eine solche Gattungsüberschneidung kann insbesondere dann auftreten, wenn Gattungsunterscheidungen auf verschiedenen Ebenen vorgenommen werden. Wie wir gesehen haben, können Gattungen eher ausdrucksseitig oder eher inhaltsseitig charakterisiert sein. So kann etwa, in dem untersuchten Korpus, derselbe Text einmal der Gattung *avviso* (der Brieflugschrift) und einmal der Gattung *entrata* (dem Bericht von dem feierlichen Einzug eines Herrschers) zugerechnet werden; daneben gibt es allerdings zahlreiche *avvisi*, die andere Themenbereiche behandeln (etwa kriegerische Handlungen oder Entdeckungen in der Neuen Welt), und es gibt zahlreiche *entrate,* die andere textuelle Formen (wie etwa die *historia*, das Gedicht in der Oktavenstrophe) bevorzugen. In den Texten, die zugleich eine *entrata* und einen *avviso* darstellen, kann man jedoch sagen, daß sich eine inhaltsseitig und eine ausdrucksseitig charakterisierte Gattungstradition 'überschneiden'.

– Von GATTUNGSMISCHUNG möchte ich dagegen dann sprechen, wenn Interferenzen zwischen solchen Gattungen auftreten, die sich grundsätzlich gegenseitig ausschließen, da die für sie charakteristischen Unterscheidungsmerkmale auf derselben Ebene liegen. So bedient sich die *frottola-barzelletta* einer durch die Wiederholung des Refrains ausgezeichneten metrischen Struktur, die *historia* dagegen einer Reihe von Strophen in *ottava rima*. Diese beiden metrischen Formen – die Balladenform und die Dichtung in der Oktavenstrophe – schließen sich gegenseitig aus. Allerdings ist die *historia* nicht allein durch ein metrisches Schema, sondern darüber hinaus durch eine große Anzahl sprachlicher Organisationselemente wie vor allem bestimmte Gliederungssignale charakterisiert. Die für die *historia* gattungstypischen Gliederungssignale – etwa die Verwendung einer genauen Datumsangabe als Signal der Erzähleröffnung – können nun jedoch auch in die Exemplare anderer Gattungen Eingang finden. Sie nehmen hier geradezu einen Zitatcharakter an, insofern das Element der einen Gattung in einem an eine andere Gattungstradition anknüpfenden Text 'zitiert' wird. Textkonstituierende Verfahren aus unterschiedlichen Gattungstraditionen können solchermaßen in einem Text 'vermischt' auftreten.

– Eine GATTUNGSKONVERGENZ liegt schließlich dann vor, wenn mehrere deutlich unterschiedene Gattungen eine analoge Entwicklung nehmen. So läßt sich etwa zeigen, daß in der ersten Hälfte des 16. Jahrhunderts die *historia,* die *frottola-barzelletta* und weitere Formen der Versflugschrift sich in weitgehend analoger Weise von einer mündlich aufgeführten über eine semi-oral verbreitete zu einer literarischen, nicht mehr aktualitätsbezogenen Kommunikationsform entwickeln. Inwieweit eine solche Konvergenz im pragmatischen ('textexternen') Bereich auch eine

Annäherung der jeweiligen textuellen Organisationsform nach sich zieht, mußte in dem analysierten Fall allerdings offenbleiben.
- Die der Gattungskonvergenz gegenläufige Entwicklung, die GATTUNGSDIFFERENZIERUNG, läßt sich anhand zahlreicher Fälle illustrieren. Von Bedeutung ist hier etwa die allmähliche Unterscheidung eines okkasionellen und eines periodischen Journalismus, wie sie sich bereits in einer Serie von *avvisi* aus dem Jahre 1546 andeutet. Aus einer einzigen Gattung, der Briefflugschrift, entwickeln sich hier mehrere verschiedene Gattungen, bis hin zur *gazzetta* und zum Briefroman.

Die unterschiedenen Formen der Gattungsüberschneidung, der Gattungsmischung, der Gattungskonvergenz und der Gattungsdifferenzierung erlauben bereits eine erste Typisierung gattungsgeschichtlicher Prozesse. Es wird somit möglich, im Innern der auf den ersten Blick oftmals zufällig erscheinenden textuellen Organisationsformen präzise historische Entwicklungsstränge nachzuzeichnen. Anhand differenzierter empirischer Arbeiten müßte allerdings ermittelt werden, welche weiteren Typen der Gattungsinterferenz auftreten können und inwieweit diese tatsächlich 'universale' Verfahren des Gattungswandels darstellen. Obwohl es sich bei den Diskurstraditionen zweifellos um „Größen der historischen Ebene" handelt, läßt sich vermuten, daß „die Relationen und Prozesse, die ihre Dynamik ausmachen [...], universaler Natur [sind]" (Koch 1997: 71).

3.3. Universale Diskurstypen?

Eine der (vermeintlichen) „Aporien" (vgl. Schnur-Wellpott 1983) der herkömmlichen Gattungsforschung ist darauf zurückzuführen, daß immer wieder versucht wurde, die historisch beschreibbaren Gattungstraditionen auf universale oder als universal gesetzte Diskurstypen zurückzuführen (vgl. Kuon 1988: 238 Anm. 2). So möchte auch Peter Koch (1987: 125) die Diskurstraditionen als „historische Konkretionen [...] universaler Diskurstypen" bestimmen, wobei sich jeweils zwischen *essentiellen* und *kontingenten* Diskursregeln unterscheiden ließe. Dies bedeutet beispielsweise für den Brief, daß „jede Brieftradition als unabdingbaren Kern die [...] Konstitutiva des Kommunikationstyps Brief" enthalten muß (Koch 1987: 142).

Wenn wir die Historizität der Diskurstraditionen ernstnehmen, dann läßt sich eine solche Betrachtungsweise allerdings nicht aufrechterhalten. Die Geschichte einer Gattung, etwa auch die Geschichte einer der zahlreichen Brieftraditionen, ist prinzipiell offen. Gerade die Geschichte des *avviso*, der Briefflugschrift, zeigt, wie eine bestimmte historische Gattung, die zunächst durchaus einen Briefcharakter besitzt, nach und nach sämtliche 'Briefmerkmale' ablegen kann (vgl. Wilhelm 1996: 205−73).

Eine Gattung kann sich durchaus aus einem universalen Diskurstyp, dem sie zu einem bestimmten Zeitpunkt angehört, 'heraus' und in einen anderen Diskurstyp 'hinein' entwickeln. Eine Unterscheidung zwischen 'essentiellen' und 'kontingenten' Gattungsmerkmalen ist somit nicht möglich: Alle Eigenschaften einer Diskurstradition sind als historisch wandelbar und somit als kontingent anzusehen.

Das Verhältnis zwischen den universalen Diskurstypen und den historisch wandelbaren Diskurstraditionen läßt sich jedoch noch auf eine ganz andere Weise betrachten. Nehmen wir als Beispiel den Diskurstyp des 'Erzählens'. Dem Erzählen darf sicher − neben anderen Formen der Sachverhaltskonstitution wie dem 'Beschreiben' und dem 'Argumentieren' − ein universaler Status zugesprochen werden: Das Erzählen ist geradezu als eine anthropologische Konstante zu betrachten (Gumbrecht 1980: 407).

Wenn jedoch, wie es den Anschein hat, in allen Gesellschaften in irgendeiner Form vergangenes Geschehen und Erleben mit sprachlichen Mitteln abgebildet wird, so stellen sich die jeweiligen Erzählanlässe und die diesen entsprechenden textuellen Formen in sehr vielfältiger Weise dar. Eine historische Erzählforschung − eine 'Geschichte des Erzählens' − muß somit der Frage nachgehen, in welchen spezifischen Diskurstraditionen in den jeweiligen Epochen erzählt wird, d. h. in welchen beschreibbaren Gattungen sich der universale Diskurstyp des Erzählens niederschlägt (vgl. Wilhelm 1995: 50 f.).

Dabei müssen wir uns allerdings bewußt sein, daß eine solche Betrachtungsweise keineswegs zu einer überzeitlich gültigen 'Gattungsdefinition' führen kann: Selbst wenn wir feststellen, daß in einer bestimmten historischen und sozialen Situation die Novelle ein bevorzugtes Instrument des schriftlichen und des mündlichen Erzählens ist (vgl. Wehle [2]1984), so können wir hieraus nicht folgern, daß die Novelle notwendig ('essentiell') eine erzählende Gattung bildet. Wir können keineswegs ausschließen, daß sich die Novelle – oder eine bestimmte Novellenform – im Laufe ihrer Geschichte von dem erzählerischen Muster entfernt.

Die Diskurstraditionen, selbst wenn sie zu einem bestimmten Zeitpunkt als historische Konkretionen eines universalen Diskurstyps erscheinen, sind keineswegs 'essentiell' auf einen solchen universalen Typ festgelegt. Die universalen Diskurstypen scheinen somit immer nur – in einer synchronischen Perspektive – zur Klassifikation von Diskurstraditionen dienen zu können; sie dürfen uns jedoch nicht dazu verleiten, die Diskurstraditionen in einer überzeitlich gültigen Form 'definieren' zu wollen.

4. Diskurstraditionen und Sprachgeschichte

Als historische Größen sind Diskurstraditionen „an kulturelle Gruppen gebunden", die als Träger ('Benutzer') dieser Diskurstraditionen fungieren; dabei ist jedoch zu beachten, daß die Trägergruppen der Diskurstraditionen „sich allenfalls zufällig mit Sprachgemeinschaften decken" (Koch 1988: 343): Diskurstraditionen sind „prinzipiell unabhängig von Einzelsprachen" (*ibid.*). So ist die Geschichte des Romans, aber auch die Geschichte des Telephongesprächs oder des Gerichtsurteils prinzipiell unabhängig von der Geschichte des Französischen, des Deutschen usw.

Gleichwohl läßt sich die Ansicht vertreten, daß den Diskurstraditionen eine herausragende Rolle in der Sprachgeschichte zukommt, daß die Sprachgeschichtsschreibung ganz wesentliche Impulse von einer Geschichte der Textgattungen erhalten könnte (vgl. etwa Schank 1984; Radtke 1994; Wilhelm 1996; Steger 1998; Aschenberg [im Druck]; Weidenbusch [im Druck]). Diese Auffassung soll hier unter drei verschiedenen Gesichtspunkten näher betrachtet werden.

Zunächst möchte ich zeigen, daß es – trotz der prinzipiellen Unabhängigkeit der Diskurstraditionen von den Einzelsprachen – oftmals zu Traditionen der einzelsprachlichen Gestaltung von Diskurstraditionen kommt (s. u. § 4.1). Sodann werde ich mich der Frage zuwenden, welche Rolle den Diskurstraditionen in einer soziolinguistisch orientierten Sprachgeschichtsschreibung zufallen könnte (s. u. § 4.2). Schließlich soll die Bedeutung der Diskurstraditionen bei der sprachhistorischen Bewertung medialer Umbrüche diskutiert werden (s. u. § 4.3). Diese Überlegungen sind insgesamt von der Überzeugung getragen, daß gerade in einer historischen Perspektive das Ineinandergreifen diskurstraditioneller und einzelsprachlicher Faktoren deutlich gemacht werden kann.

4.1. Einzelsprachliche Charakterisierung von Diskurstraditionen

Eine charakteristische Verschränkung diskurstraditioneller und einzelsprachlicher Fakten läßt sich anhand der traditionellen italienischen Versdichtung illustrieren. So besteht grundsätzlich kein Zweifel daran, daß die Opposition 'Vers *versus* Prosa' eine rein diskurstraditionelle Erscheinung betrifft: Die metrischen Formen, die die Versdichtung auszeichnen (Sonett, Oktavenstrophe usw.) sind als (vor allem ausdrucksseitig charakterisierte) Textgattungen zu betrachten. Einzelsprachliche Unterschiede spielen dabei zunächst keine Rolle. So kann man etwa zeigen, daß die Sprache der italienischen Versdichtung des 20. Jahrhunderts mit der Sprache der zeitgenössischen Prosaliteratur grundsätzlich identisch ist.

Es ist jedoch ein unstrittiges sprachhistorisches Faktum, daß in der traditionellen ITALIENISCHEN Versdichtung bis hin zu Carducci eine in grammatischer (*avea, partia* gegenüber *aveva, partiva* usw.) und lexikalischer Hinsicht (*augello, alma* gegenüber *uccello, anima* usw.) ausgezeichnete Sprachform verwendet wird, so daß man die italienische Dichtungssprache bis zum Ende des 19. Jahrhunderts geradezu als eine eigene diaphasische Varietät des Italienischen betrachten kann (vgl. Coseriu 1988: 282). Hier ist es jedoch wesentlich klarzustellen, daß diese einzelsprachliche Differenzierung von Dichtungs- und Prosasprache keineswegs notwendig aus der (diskurstraditionellen) Bestimmung von Vers und Prosa hervorgeht. So kann man etwa zeigen, daß in der zeitgenössischen französischen Literatur zwar auch eine gattungsmäßige Unterscheidung von Vers und Prosa, jedoch keine einzelsprachlich charakterisierte Dichtungssprache existiert. Bei der italienischen Dichtungssprache handelt es sich um eine epochal begrenzte, nur historisch zu erklärende, kontingente Erscheinung. Die Ausbildung einer eigenen dichtungssprachlichen Varietät kann als ein Beispiel für die Traditionen der einzelsprachlichen Gestaltung von Diskurstraditionen gelten. Sie resultiert aus der Traditionalität jeglicher Kommunikation. Sie ist jedoch keineswegs aus der funktionalen und textuellen Bestimmung der Versdichtung ableitbar (vgl. Wilhelm 1996: 347).

Die an bestimmte Diskurstraditionen gebundenen einzelsprachlichen Muster bezeichnen ein zentrales Aufgabengebiet der Sprachgeschichtsschreibung. Es liegt jedoch auf der Hand, daß solche traditionellen Festlegungen nur dann präzise beschrieben werden können, wenn es gelingt, die diskurstraditionellen und die einzelsprachlichen Fakten in der Analyse deutlich zu trennen

4.2. Historische Soziolinguistik

Die Soziolinguistik ist im wesentlichen darum bemüht, sprachliche Variation mit Hilfe sozialer Parameter einsichtig zu machen. Auch die historische Soziolinguistik oder die soziolinguistisch ausgerichtete Sprachgeschichtsschreibung versucht solchermaßen, zwischen eher 'volkstümlichen' und eher 'gelehrten' Formen zu unterscheiden (vgl. etwa zum Italienischen D'Achille 1994). Wenn wir jedoch bedenken, daß die menschliche Rede nicht nur jeweils funktionalen Gesichtspunkten gehorcht, sondern in erheblichem Maße auch traditionell geprägt ist, dann müssen wir uns hier vor allzu einfachen Zuweisungen hüten. Insbesondere die oftmals im Innern präziser Gattungstraditionen perpetuierten einzelsprachlichen Konventionen müßten wahrscheinlich stärker berücksichtigt werden, als dies bislang geschehen ist. Nicht selten kann nämlich ein und dieselbe sprachliche Form eine völlig unterschiedliche soziolinguistische Einordnung erfordern, wenn sie in jeweils unterschiedlichen Gattungstraditionen verwendet wird.

Auch hier möchte ich mich auf zwei Beispiele aus dem Bereich der italienischen Flugschriften des 16. Jahrhunderts beschränken. So sind — in der Verbmorphologie — die regionalen Formen des Typs *semo* und *havemo* in der Mitte des *Cinquecento* grundsätzlich als 'volkstümlicher' einzustufen als die von den Grammatiken vorgeschriebenen florentinischen Formen *siamo* und *abbiamo*. Die Form *havemo* charakterisiert somit erwartungsgemäß eine volkstümliche Briefflugschrift der späten dreißiger Jahre. Eine völlig andere Bewertung erfordert dieselbe sprachliche Form jedoch in einer zeitgenössischen Versflugschrift. Hier erscheint *semo* als eine dichtungssprachliche Parallelform, wie sie in der gelehrten poetischen Tradition seit Petrarca präsent ist und wie sie von den Grammatikern selbst als dichterische Sonderform verzeichnet wird (vgl. Wilhelm 1996: 389−95). Dieselbe sprachliche Form kann hier einmal als Indikator für ein volkstümliches Italienisch, einmal als Element einer hochstehenden dichtungssprachlichen Varietät gewertet werden.

Eine ähnliche Überlegung läßt sich — im syntaktischen Bereich — anhand der Verwendung des *accusativus cum infinitivo* nach den Verben des Sagens anstellen. Dieser latinisierenden Konstruktion wird gemeinhin ein 'gelehrter' Charakter zugeschrieben. In den Briefflugschriften stellt diese Form, die hier fast immer mit dem Verb *essere* im Infinitiv verwendet wird, jedoch ein überaus verbreitetes, aus der Tradition der Kanzleisprache übernommenes, 'volkstümliches' Muster dar. In den Versflugschriften dagegen, ob diese nun eine eher volkstümliche oder eine eher gelehrte Ausrichtung haben, fehlt diese Form fast vollständig. Wiederum läßt sich eine präzise sprachliche Form (ein vermeintlicher Latinismus) nicht in der Opposition 'volkstümlich *vs.* gelehrt', sondern allein im Rückgriff auf die traditionelle Sprachform bestimmter Gattungen hinreichend 'erklären' (vgl. Wilhelm 1996: 486−90).

Die Diskurstradition erscheint somit als eine geradezu notwendige Größe, die es dem Sprachhistoriker erlaubt, die in den Texten auftretenden sprachlichen Formen in befriedigender Weise einzuordnen.

4.3. Mediale Umbrüche

Mit Peter Koch (1988: 343) können wir davon ausgehen, daß die Sprecher/Schreiber früherer Epochen „sich meist in erster Linie als Praktiker einer Diskurstradition [...] und erst in zweiter Linie als Vertreter einer bestimmten Sprache oder Sprachvarietät verstanden und letztere denn auch nach den Maßstäben diskurstraditioneller Effizienz auswählten." Zu präzisieren wäre dabei allenfalls, daß die Wahl einer bestimmten Sprache oder Varietät nicht allein funktionalen Gesichtspunkten folgt, sondern oftmals bereits traditionell vorgegeben ist (s. o. §§ 4.1/ 4.2). Ohne Zweifel folgt hieraus jedoch, daß eine sozialgeschichtlich orientierte Sprachgeschichtsschreibung den Diskurstraditionen einen zentralen Platz einräumen muß: Die Diskurstradition erweist sich geradezu als das geeignete Bindeglied, das es uns erlaubt, den sprachlichen Wandel in realistischer Weise auf den (im weitesten Sinne) sozialen Wandel zu beziehen. Der „Einfluß externer Faktoren auf den Sprachwandel" kann, wie Gerd Schank (1984: 762) betont, gerade „am Wandel einzelner Textsorten [= Gattungen im hier definierten Sinn] konkreter erforscht werden." In den Worten von Peter Koch (1997: 57 f.): „Das eigentliche Bindeglied zwischen der externen und der internen Sprachgeschichte stellen [...] die Diskurstraditionen dar."

Dieser Ansatz läßt sich etwa anhand der großen medialen Umbrüche wie der erstmaligen Verschriftlichung der romanischen Volkssprachen seit dem 10., 11., 12. Jahrhundert oder der durch den Buchdruck ausgelösten medientechnischen Revolution illustrieren. Insbesondere die Verschriftlichung vormals nur mündlich verwendeter Sprachformen kann überhaupt nur anhand einzelner Diskurstraditionen sinnvoll nachvollzogen werden. So hat Peter Koch (1990: 122) darauf aufmerksam gemacht, daß die *Listen* „eine der typischen 'Breschen' sind, durch die romanische Volkssprachen im Mittelalter früh in das Medium Schrift vordringen". Dieser Umstand erklärt sich nicht zuletzt durch die „relative kommunikative Nähe" und gleichzeitig die „obligatorische Verwendung der Schrift", welche die Kommunikationsform der Liste auszeichnet (Koch 1990: 155). Es wird deutlich, daß gerade eine Orientierung an den Diskurstraditionen − wie hier an den „listenhaltigen Diskurstraditionen" (Koch 1990: 147) − eine Annäherung an das zeitgenössische Bewußtsein der Sprecher/Schreiber ermöglicht und uns somit den Schlüssel für eine nachvollziehbare 'Erklärung' der oftmals sehr unterschiedlich motivierten Verschriftlichung volkssprachlicher Varietäten an die Hand gibt (vgl. auch Koch 1993). Von großer Bedeutung ist hier auch die Frage der Verschriftlichung von Diskurstraditionen. Das Eintreten in den Bereich der schriftlichen Kommunikation zieht hier oftmals einen tiefgreifenden Wandel der textuellen Organisationsformen nach sich, wie sich etwa anhand der Heldenepik oder in Medizin und Pharmazie zeigen läßt (vgl. Oesterreicher 1993: 277−79; Buck 1998).

Eine verstärkte Berücksichtigung der Diskurstraditionen drängt sich jedoch auch dann auf, wenn wir versuchen, die sehr weitreichenden sprachhistorischen Konsequenzen jener zweiten großen „révolution de la communication" (Eisenstein 1991: 60) zu ermessen, die die Verbreitung des Buchdrucks mit sich brachte (vgl. auch Grosse & Wellmann [eds.] 1996). So läßt sich etwa anhand des Italienischen zeigen, daß der Zusammenhang zwischen der Ausbreitung des Buchdrucks und der Kodifizierung und Durchsetzung einer einheitlichen Standardsprache nicht einsichtig gemacht werden kann, solange man nicht die Umbrüche im Bereich der Diskurstraditionen und insbesondere die Ausgliederung eines eigenständigen literarischen Diskursuniversums reflektiert.

Zu Beginn des 16. Jahrhunderts sind die Bereiche des literarischen und des nicht-literarischen Schreibens noch nicht so deutlich getrennt wie in späteren Jahrhunderten. Im Gefolge des neuen typographischen Kommunikationsmittels entwickelt sich erst ganz allmählich eine eindeutige Abgrenzung der Diskursuniversen des 'Alltags', der 'Literatur', der 'Wissenschaft' usw. Dieses diskurstraditionelle Faktum − die Herausbildung eines eigenständigen literarischen Diskursuniversums − stellt nun jedoch, zumindest für Italien, die unabdingbare Voraussetzung für eine eindeutig 'literarisch' motivierte Sprachnormierung dar, die sich ganz gezielt an den großen Modellautoren des *Trecento* orientiert.

Die Ausbreitung des Buchdrucks, die Kodifizierung der Volkssprache und die Herausbildung eines 'autonomen' literarischen Diskursuniversums − die Bereiche „nascita del libro, nascita del volgare, nascita del sistema letterario" in den Worten von Amedeo Quondam (1983: 588) − bilden hier eine untrennbare Einheit. Dabei stellt jedoch gerade die diskurstraditionelle Neuerung das unverzichtbare Bindeglied zwischen dem medien- und sozialgeschichtlichen Geschehen und der sprachhistorischen Entwicklung dar.

5. Zitierte Literatur

Aschenberg, Heidi. (im Druck). „Schwerpunkte der historischen Textsortenlinguistik: Aufgabenbereiche". In: Ernst & al. (eds.).

Bergmann, Jörg R. & Luckmann, Thomas. 1995. „Reconstructive genres of everyday communication". In: Quasthoff, Uta (ed.). *Aspects of oral communication*. Berlin: de Gruyter, 289−304.

Besch, Werner & Reichmann, Oskar & Sonderegger, Stefan (eds.). 1984/1985/²1998−. *Sprachgeschichte. Ein Handbuch zur Geschichte der deutschen Sprache und ihrer Erforschung*. (Handbücher zur Sprach- und Kommunikationswissenschaft, 2,1 & 2,2.) Berlin & New York: de Gruyter.

Buck, Susanne. 1998. *Zwischen Texttradition und Methode. Gattungsentwicklung volkssprachlicher Medizin und Naturkunde in der französischen Renaissance*. Dissertation Freiburg.

Coseriu, Eugenio. 1988. *Einführung in die Allgemeine Sprachwissenschaft.* (Uni-Taschenbücher, 1372.) Tübingen: Francke

Coseriu, Eugenio. ³1994. *Textlinguistik. Eine Einführung.* ed. v. Jörn Albrecht. (Uni-Taschenbücher, 1808.) Tübingen: Narr.

D'Achille, Paolo. 1994. „L'italiano dei semicolti". In: Luca Serianni & Pietro Trifone (eds.). *Storia della lingua italiana.* Torino: Einaudi, 2: 41–79.

Eisenstein, Elizabeth L. 1979. *The printing press as an agent of change: communications and cultural transformations in Early-Modern Europe.* 2 vols. Cambridge: University Press. –

Eisenstein, Elizabeth. 1991. *La révolution de l'imprimé à l'aube de l'Europe moderne.* Paris: La Découverte. (Franz. übers.)

Ernst, Gerhard & Gleßgen, Martin-Dietrich & Schmitt, Christian & Schweickard, Wolfgang (eds.) (im Druck). *Romanische Sprachgeschichte.* (Handbücher zur Sprach- und Kommunikationswissenschaft.) Berlin & New York: de Gruyter.

Frank, Barbara. 1997. „'Innensicht' und 'Außensicht'. Zur Analyse mittelalterlicher volkssprachlicher Gattungsbezeichnungen". In: Frank & al. (eds.), 117–36.

Frank, Barbara & Haye, Thomas & Tophinke, Doris (eds.) 1997. *Gattungen mittelalterlicher Schriftlichkeit.* (ScriptOralia, 99.) Tübingen: Narr.

Grosse, Rudolf & Wellmann, Hans (eds.). 1996. *Textarten im Sprachwandel nach der Erfindung des Buchdrucks.* (Sprache – Literatur und Geschichte, 13.) Heidelberg: Winter.

Gumbrecht, Hans Ulrich. 1988. „Beginn von 'Literatur' Abschied vom Körper?". In: Smolka-Koerdt, Gisela & Spangenberg, Peter M. & Tilmann-Bartylla, Dagmar (eds.). *Der Ursprung von Literatur. Medien, Rollen, Kommunikationssituationen zwischen 1450 und 1650.* (Materialität der Zeichen.) München: Fink, 15–50.

Isenberg, Horst. 1983. „Grundfragen der Texttypologie". In: Daneš, František & Viehweger, Dieter (eds.). *Ebenen der Textstruktur.* (Linguistische Studien, A 112.) Berlin: Akademie d. Wiss. d. DDR, 303–42.

Janik, Dieter. 1985. „Die heuristische Funktion und der Erklärungswert der Gattungsvorstellung für die Literaturgeschichte". In: Janik, Dieter: *Literatursemiotik als Methode. Die Kommunikationsstruktur des Erzählwerks und fünf weitere Studien.* Darmstadt: Wiss. Buchges., 89–104.

Jauß, Hans-Robert. 1972. „Theorie der Gattungen und Literatur des Mittelalters". In: Jauß, Hans-Robert & al. (eds.), 1: 107–38.

Jauß, Hans-Robert & Köhler, Erich (eds.). 1968ff. *Grundriß der Romanischen Literaturen des Mittelalters.* Heidelberg: Winter.

Koch, Peter. 1987. *Distanz im Dictamen. Zur Schriftlichkeit und Pragmatik mittelalterlicher Brief- und Redemodelle in Italien.* Unveröff. Habilitationsschrift Freiburg.

Koch, Peter. 1988. „Externe Sprachgeschichte I/ Storia della lingua I". In: Holtus, Günter & Metzeltin, Michael & Schmitt, Christian (eds.). *Lexikon der Romanistischen Linguistik.* Tübingen: Niemeyer, 4: 343–60.

Koch, Peter. 1988a. „Fachsprache, Liste und Schriftlichkeit in einem Kaufmannsbrief aus dem Duecento". In: Hartwig Kalverkämper (ed.). *Fachsprachen in der Romania.* (Forum für Fachsprachen-Forschung, 8.) Tübingen, 15–60.

Koch, Peter. 1990. „Vom Frater Semeno zum Bojaren Neacşu. Listen als Domänen früh verschrifteter Volkssprache in der Romania". In: Raible, Wolfgang (ed.). *Erscheinungsformen kultureller Prozesse. Jahrbuch 1988 des Sonderforschungsbereichs 'Übergänge und Spannungsfelder zwischen Mündlichkeit und Schriftlichkeit'.* (ScriptOralia, 13.) Tübingen: Narr, 121–65.

Koch, Peter. 1993. „Pour une typologie conceptionnelle et médiale des plus anciens documents/ monuments des langues romanes". In: Selig, Maria & Frank, Barbara & Hartmann, Jörg (eds.). *Le passage à l'écrit des langues romanes.* (ScriptOralia, 46.) Tübingen: Narr, 39–81.

Koch, Peter. 1997. „Diskurstraditionen: zu ihrem sprachtheoretischen Status und ihrer Dynamik". In: Frank & al. (eds.), 43–79.

Kuon, Peter. 1988. „Möglichkeiten und Grenzen einer strukturellen Gattungswissenschaft". In: Albrecht, Jörn & Lüdtke, Jens & Thun, Harald (eds.). *Energeia und Ergon. Sprachliche Variation, Sprachgeschichte, Sprachtypologie. Studia in honorem Eugenio Coseriu.* (Tübinger Beiträge zur Linguistik, 300.) Tübingen: Narr, 3: 237–52.

Oesterreicher, Wulf. 1993. „Verschriftung und Verschriftlichung im Kontext medialer und konzeptioneller Schriftlichkeit". In: Schaefer, Ursula (ed.). *Schriftlichkeit im frühen Mittelalter.* (ScriptOralia, 53.) Tübingen: Narr, 267–92.

Oesterreicher, Wulf. 1997. „Zur Fundierung von Diskurstraditionen". In: Frank & al. (eds.), 19–41.

Quondam, Amedeo. 1983. „La letteratura in tipografia". In: Asor Rosa, Alberto (ed.). *Letteratura italiana.* Torino: Einaudi, 2: 555–686.

Radtke, Edgar. 1994. „'Alltag' in der italienischen Sprachgeschichtsschreibung". In: Sabban, Annette & Schmitt, Christian (eds.). *Sprachlicher Alltag. Linguistik – Rhetorik – Literaturwissenschaft. Festschrift für Wolf-Dieter Stempel. 7. Juli 1994.* Tübingen: Niemeyer, 419–33.

Radtke, Edgar. 1994a. *Gesprochenes Französisch und Sprachgeschichte. Zur Rekonstruktion der Gesprächskonstitution in Dialogen französischer Sprachlehrbücher des 17. Jahrhunderts unter besonderer Berücksichtigung der italienischen Adaptationen.* (Beihefte zur Zeitschrift für romanische Philologie, 255.) Tübingen: Niemeyer.

Raible, Wolfgang. 1996. „Wie soll man Texte typisieren?". In: Michaelis, Susanne & Tophinke, Doris (eds.). *Texte − Konstitution, Verarbeitung, Typik.* (Edition Linguistik, 13.) Unterschleissheim/München: Lincom Europa, 59−72.

Saussure, Ferdinand de. 1972. *Cours de linguistique générale.* Publ. par Charles Bally et Albert Sechehaye. Avec la coll. de Albert Riedlinger. Édition critique préparée par Tullio de Mauro. (Payothèque.) Paris: Payot.

Schank, Gerd. 1984. „Ansätze zu einer Theorie des Sprachwandels auf der Grundlage von Textsorten". In: Besch, Werner & al. (eds.). 1: 761−68.

Schlieben-Lange, Brigitte. 1983. *Traditionen des Sprechens. Elemente einer pragmatischen Sprachgeschichtsschreibung.* Stuttgart: Kohlhammer.

Schlieben-Lange, Brigitte. 1987. „Sprechhandlungen und ihre Bezeichnungen in der volkssprachlichen Historiographie des romanischen Mittelalters". In: Jauß, Hans-Robert & al. (eds.), 3: 755−6.

Schlieben-Lange, Brigitte. 1997. „Das Gattungssystem der altokzitanischen Lyrik: Die Kategorisierungen der Dichter und der Poetologen". In: Frank & al. (eds.), 81−99.

Schnur-Wellpott, Margit. 1983. *Aporien der Gattungstheorie aus semiotischer Sicht.* Tübingen: Narr.

Selig, Maria. 1997. „Das Buch im Mittelalter − Überlegungen zu Kommunikationstypik und Medialität". In: Frank & al. (eds.), 137−60.

Steger, Hugo. ²1998. „Sprachgeschichte als Geschichte der Textsorten, Kommunikationsbereiche und Semantiktypen". In: Besch, Werner & al. (eds.). 1: 186−204.

Stein, Peter. 1997. *Untersuchungen zur Verbalsyntax der Liviusübersetzungen in die romanischen Sprachen. Ein Versuch zur Anwendung quantitativer Methoden in der historisch-vergleichenden Syntax.* (Beihefte zur Zeitschrift für romanische Philologie, 287.) Tübingen: Niemeyer.

Stempel, Wolf-Dieter. ²1975. „Gibt es Textsorten?". In: Gülich, Elisabeth & Raible, Wolfgang (eds.). *Textsorten. Differenzierungskriterien aus linguistischer Sicht.* (Athenäum-Skripten Linguistik, 5.) Wiesbaden: Akademische Verlagsgesellschaft Athenaion, 175−79.

Todorov, Tzvetan. ²1976. „Les genres littéraires". In: Todorov, Tzvetan. *Introduction à la littérature fantastique.* (Collection points, 73.) Paris: Éditions du Seuil, 7−27.

Wehle, Winfried. ²1984. *Novellenerzählen. Französische Renaissancenovellistik als Diskurs.* München: Fink.

Weidenbusch, Waltraud. (im Druck). „Schwerpunkte der historischen Textsortenlinguistik: Exemplarische Fallstudien". In: Ernst & al. (eds.).

Wilhelm, Raymund. 1995. „Mündliche Unterhaltungserzählungen im Due-Trecento. Zur historischen Pragmatik mündlichen Erzählens zwischen Alltag und Literatur". *Romanistisches Jahrbuch* 46: 47−73.

Wilhelm, Raymund. 1996. *Italienische Flugschriften des Cinquecento (1500−1550). Gattungsgeschichte und Sprachgeschichte.* (Zeitschrift für romanische Philologie, Beihefte, 279.) Tübingen: Niemeyer.

Wilhelm, Raymund. 1997. „[Rez.] Sabine Philipp-Sattel: 'Parlar bellament en vulgar'. Die Anfänge der katalanischen Schriftkultur im Mittelalter. Tübingen 1996". *Romanistisches Jahrbuch* 48: 410−16.

Raymund Wilhelm, Universität Heidelberg (Deutschland)

37. Universals of the linguistic representation of situations ('participation')

1. Introduction
2. Situations and linguistic representations
3. Types of situations (or predicates)
4. Case roles
5. Actancy (valence, argument structure)
6. Actancy variation (valence alternation)
7. Transitivity
8. Conclusion
9. References

1. Introduction

One of the standard answers given to the question of what the primary functions of language are, is cognition and communication (see, e.g., Givón 1995: xv; Halliday 1970: 143). We know and communicate things about the world. But the things we talk about are not only "things", but people, or locations, or relationships between things, i. e. states of affairs, in GERMAN SACHVERHALTE, which is literally a nominalization of an expression meaning "how things behave or relate". Cf. Ludwig Wittgenstein (1921: § 2.01): "Der Sachverhalt ist eine Verbindung von Gegenständen (Sachen, Dingen)", or as Peter Abælard stated: Sentences do not refer to things but *quidam rerum modus habendi se* (cited from Prechtl & Burkard 1996, s.v.

Sachverhalt; cf. Smith 1992). Moreover, we are typically not only interested in static relationships between things or in relating properties, classifications, possessions or the like, but we also wish to know and communicate what is going on in the world, what people or animate objects do, and to whom or to what they are doing it and with what effects.

There is a tendency among linguists and philosophers of language and mind, to accentuate the relevance of EVENTS in human thinking or their conceptual correlate, propositions, on the one hand, and SENTENCES as the typical form of their linguistic representation, on the other. Sometimes they are even considered to be primary (vis à vis concrete objects/concepts and words); cf. the following selection of statements: "Sentences, not words, are the essence of speech, [...]" (Whorf 1942/56: 258); "Der Satz ist die primäre Bedeutungseinheit; alle Vorstellungen sind von propositionaler Struktur" (Rohs 1979: 17); "Alles intentionale Bewußtsein überhaupt ist propositional" (Tugendhat 1979: 20); "The coding of propositional-semantic information remains a constant requirement in communication, regardless of what other communicative functions are to be satisfied" (Givón 1984: 136); "Propositions are taken to be the principle values of all the various currencies of information" (Crimmins 1994: 3377).

One reason for speaking of "propositions" is that the focus of interest is not so much on the structure of what happens out there in the "real" world but on the way the human mind processes its perceptions. The processing which results in linguistic representations can in part be conceived of as a process of selection, "typification" and "perspectivization" (Fillmore 1968; Seiler 1988: 116, 134). The terminology makes it clear that we are dealing with a conceptual level. In linguistic frameworks which do not distinguish between a conceptual and a semantic level and/or in frameworks where both are ultimately the same, the term proposition can also be used as a linguistic term in a narrower sense: proposition then becomes the semantic content, the meaning of a sentence.

In frameworks which differentiate between a semantic and a cognitive-conceptual level, propositions are to be considered conceptual entities: assuming fundamental structuralistic principles (→ art. 17), two sentences (types, not tokens) not only have different meanings within a language but can never have the same meaning interlinguistically, because the meaning of the elements is ultimately defined by the structure of the given language as a whole, which is different.

Furthermore, the semantic structure of a complex sign (for instance, a sentence) differs according to the differences in syntactic structure across languages (cf. Immler 1991; Sasse 1991: 93). From a conceptual perspective, however, expressions within a language and across languages can be compared: sentences can express the same proposition and, in this sense, have the same meaning. Thus, the conceptual level is often considered the locus of tertia comparationis and therefore a point of departure for language comparison and universals research.

Having pointed out the difference between events, propositions as their cognitive representations, and the corresponding linguistic expressions, it must be stated that, as comprehensive, more neutral terms for "event" ("Ereignis"; cf. Frawley 1992: 183; Stassen 1997: 13), "state of affairs", "Sachverhalt", "process" (e.g. Rupp 1965: 181; Mugler 1988: 15; Lazard 1994: 68 et passim), "Szene" ("scene"; Schulze 1998), or "SITUATION" (Comrie 1976: 41; Lehmann 1991: 188; 1994; Maienborn 1996) are often used (but note the special role of this term in situation semantics [Barwise 1991]). For an overview of the relationships in the notional field of event, proposition, fact, state of affairs etc. see, e.g., Ehrich 1991.

2. Situations and linguistic representations

We have to define in more detail what we mean by "situation" and consider what linguistic representations we find in language. In both tasks we must be aware that we have to distinguish not only what a possible situation or a possible linguistic representation is, but also, that there are more vs. less typical instances of both. This does not necessarily need to be seen as a disadvantage or lack of a neat definition, as long as we can observe some correlations between typical situations and typical linguistic representations.

2.1. Situations

As indicated in § 1, in typical situations, something is happening and one or more entities are involved. Thus a situation is something which is internally relational, implying at least two entities (in a wider sense). There are situations which are more typical than those showing the property just described. More typical are situations with some additional features: When something happens, there seems to be some "dynamicity" involved. As dynamicity is a gradable concept, we can imagine more typical situations, depending on the level of dynamicity. This can be correlated with what happens with the objects involved: some objects change (either their position or their, typically physical, state). Furthermore, there are situations in which some object(s) (typically human), change the position and/or the, typically physical, state of other objects; that is, we have to consider the number of entities involved in the situation. But there are also situations which are less typical than those mentioned, those which have no dynamicity at all, i. e., which are simply static. Even in this domain, there seems to be a gradience of typicality, which depends on how abstract one or both of the relata are. To be more specific, if the situation concerns the mere existence of something, this is a kind of atypical situation. The same holds true for assigning properties to things or classifying things. This leads more and more into the domain of metalinguistic statements, where we are probably least inclined to classify them as referring to typical situations.

In conclusion, we can propose a minimal internal relation, i. e. a relation between two entities, as a common conceptual denominator for a situation, regardless of how typical it may be (where one entity is especially prone to a varying degree of abstractness). In Klaus Heger's system (→ art. 25), where situations are conceptually ("noematically") represented by so-called actant models ("Aktantenmodelle"), this situation (!) is formally reflected by the duality of "actant" vs. "relator" as the minimal requirement for the representation of a situation. The relation as such is provided by the "predicator" (Prädikator), which again is just the result of the act of predicating or predication.

The occurrence of the term predication refers us back to a more linguistic perspective. But predication is also a logical term. Of course, in the history of the respective disciplines, the logical and the linguistic concepts of predication have been intricately interwoven with each other, but this cannot be discussed here in detail. At any rate, in predicate logics (→ art. 39), propositions are made up of argument(s) and a predicate (or a predicate and its argument(s), the order depending on convention). Both are combined in an act of predication (thereby assuming their function, being in a predicative relationship). The product is also often called a predication. In other words, the term predication is used in two ways: it is the act which results in a proposition, or it is a synonym for proposition (cf. Waßner 1992: 329, 141).

2.2. Linguistic expressions

Consider some well-known examples from well-known scholars:

(1) (a) *The farmer killed the duckling.*
    (Sapir 1921: 82)
 (b) *The ducks ate the old bread.*
    (Plank 1995: 1184)
 (c) *John buttered the toast in the bathroom with a knife at midnight.*
    (Davidson 1967: 107, cited, inter alia, by Maienborn 1996: 41)
 (d) *Poor John ran away.*
    (Leonard Bloomfield 1933/35: 161)
 (e) *ésti díkaios ánthropos.*
    'Man is just.'
    (Aristotle, *De interpretatione* 19b27)
 (f) *Flying planes can be dangerous.*
    (Chomsky 1965: 21)

For the sake of convenience, the sentences are already ordered here according to their degree of typicality. The situation expressed by the first expression (1a) is dynamic and contains two animate entities, one of which causes a (dramatic) change in the other. Situation (1b) is similar, but the active entity is not human (yet still animate), while the affected entity is inanimate. Situation (1c) is similar, except that (the active entity is again human and) the affected entity is not (yet) eliminated, so is less affected. Example (1d) relates an event that is dynamic, but there is only one entity. Sentence (1e) is static, telling us that a (permanent) property applies to an entity (person).

The last example (1f) is different in many respects. First, one entity is not only static, but also abstract (possibility). Second, the other entity seems to be a bit abstract as well. Possibility is somehow predicated of a situation, namely, "flying planes". So we would have a complex situation: a situation with another situation as a component part. But is flying planes really a situation? Somehow, it seems to be cut off, for there is no concrete event specified (a flying plane at a given time and in a given space). In one reading, there even seems to be a missing participant, namely someone flying planes, a role which must normally be involved in such a flight-situation — and which is normally expressed: if we try to reformulate the situation into what we have presented as a good structure for representing situations (a sentence), we get into trouble. First, we must insert an indefinite pronoun, which results in *Someone flies planes*. We can accept that as a given situation. However, this is different from what is meant in the context of the original expression. As an equivalent to (1f) (in one reading), we must say:

(2)   If someone flies planes, this can be dangerous.

On the other hand, it seems that not all aspects of a situation need to be expressed. In (1c), for instance, local and temporal circumstances of the situation (situation-situating elements, as it were) are specified. This is not the case in the other examples. And even in the Davidsonian case, there is no unique, definite space and time mentioned. Observations of this kind lead us to the following questions: Can situations be represented by expression types other than canonical sentences? What elements can a situation contain and which of them must be linguistically expressed?

2.3. Participation, predication, and the sentence

In the linguistic representation of a situation, there seem to be more central and more peripheral elements. The centrality of an element depends on the (cognitive representation of the) situation and its linguistic representation in detail, which again depends on the restrictions of the lexemes and grammar of a given language. In a sentence, it is typically the verb which represents the central part of the situation, because, to a great extent, it controls the occurrence of other elements, based on its inherent relationality. Therefore, establishing a noun-verb distinction is a fundamental step in participation (see Broschart 1991a). On a structural level, we speak of ACTANT(S) (or ARGUMENT(S)) vs. predicate; within a cognitive perspective, we distinguish PARTICIPANT and — accordingly — PARTICIPATUM. As indicated, the decision as to what is central depends largely on the perspective of the speaker, whose task or freedom is

(i)   to decide on what s/he may leave out when expressing the situation (which can be considered predominantly a matter of valence, see Broschart 1991a; Mosel 1991), or

(ii)   to decide on what perspective or orientation s/he gives to the expression of the situation (point of view, attention flow, according to the pragmatics of the linguistic context or situation the expression is embedded in; for an overview and further references see DeLancey 1985; Ono 1991; Serzisko 1991; Wunderlich 1993; cf. § 6.2 below); the relevant functional domain or sub-dimension of participation is known as orientation or valence change, with voice as the main strategy. But one should remember that first of all, the speaker has

(iii) the choice of selecting a predicate, which means that s/he makes a predecision about what s/he can possibly do or change linguistically with respect to aspects (i) and (ii).

The question as to how the choice of the predicate delimits valence or strategies of valence change is, to be precise, also a typological question, i. e. is answered differently by different languages, according to the interrelated organization of their lexicon and grammar, of, for instance, the givenness of inherent verb classes or fixed valence patterns. Furthermore, the central status of the predicate does not necessarily mean that it is the 'first' element in a cognitive or pragmatic respect, i. e. speech planning, cf. Knobloch 1994: 107f. Here the notion of subject as "grammaticalized topic" (cf. Givón 1984: 137ff.) and "predication base" comes into play (cf. Sasse 1995).

Thus, in principle, what is central and what is peripheral, is a matter of conceptualization and linguistic expression on lexical and morphosyntactic grounds. This is also a reason for the dispute about the distinction between actants and circumstantials, objects and adverbials, arguments and satellites, obligatory and optional elements.

The distinction is "there": local or temporal specifications, as in (1c), can be seen as peripheral, because they merely "locate" (to a certain extent) in space and time what is going on. What typically matters in the first place is what is going on, and what makes up the basic representation of the situation. Linguistically, this is reflected in that the "additional" specifications are omissible without rendering the sentence ungrammatical, and in that these same elements are encoded using special "material" like adpositions (*in, with, at*), as opposed to the more basic, unmarked expressions for "subject" and "object", for who does something to whom or what.

But clear-cut definitions always pose problems here; this is why Klaus Heger, from the point of view of a *tertium comparationis*, for instance, only speaks of actants, maintaining that the distinction is based not on a binary opposition, but on an arbitrarily divisible continuum ("einem beliebig unterteilbaren Kontinuum", 1991: 44). What plays the role of an instrument in a situation, for example, may typically be conceived of as a peripheral element (*open a door (with a knife)*), but, on the other hand, it can even be "incorporated" in the most central element, the verbal predicate, as in *to stab* (G. 'erdolchen', Heger, ibid.), cf. also *to knife*.

Considering this flexibility, a situation or proposition can be enhanced in principle by an infinite number of specifications, though of differing pertinence. But a detailed exploration of this domain does not seem to be necessary for the definition of a linguistic concept of a situation, which is characterized by a selective, reductionistic trait (see above § 1). The existence of a certain core is maintained as sufficient for speaking of a proposition, the core typically consisting of participatum and participant(s).

These two components are related to two fundamental linguistic acts called *reference* and *predication* by Searle (1969) or "Nomination" and "Prädikation" by Knobloch (1994). And again, there is an asymmetry between participatum and participant in the sense that the former, with its typical exponent, the verb, is the central element of the sentence: "A situation consists of a center, which may be called PARTICIPATUM, [...]" (Lehmann 1991: 189). "... the central information conveyed in an utterance normally relates to the state of affairs rather than an individual; that is why we expect the state of affairs expression to be obligatory, [...]" (Sasse 1991: 82). "Le verbe est le centre et le nœud de la phrase, [...]" (Lazard 1994: 18, based on Lucien Tesnière 1959).

There is considerable flexibility as to what component of the situation is expressed by what syntactic component. Therefore, although there are prototypical correlations between what we regard as participant and what we regard as participatum, we can linguistically treat participata as participants. Ramsey (1925/90: 12) demonstrates this by contrasting *Socrates is wise* with *Wisdom is a characteristic of Socrates*, saying that in both expressions, the same proposition is involved, but the perspective or the style differs.

The way we want to express a proposition may differ according to what aspect of it is important to us (or to other speech act participants), for instance. This holds true even if there are preferred situation representation strategies in a given language. From a logical or conceptual point of view, propositions need not even be structurally represented as sentences. This again represents a continuum, a continuum of nominalization (Lehmann 1982; Koptjevskaja-Tamm 1993; cf. Noonan 1985; → art. 45): expressions can be more or less sentence-like. That-clauses, for instance, are minimally nominalized.

Another significant category is infinitive constructions, "followed" by constructions in which original verbs behave more or less like nouns, taking no subjects or objects but attributes as representations of participants. They also represent propositions in a wider sense. The same can even be maintained for nominal structures with a participant expression as head and a participatum expression as modifier. See the following examples:

(3) *barking of a dog* vs. *a barking dog*
(Sasse 1991: 75, after Gabelentz 1901: 310)

(4) *I expect* ⎫
     I predict ⎬ *that you will* ⎫
                                   ⎬ *occupy the city*
     I order ⎫   ⎭
     I forbid ⎬ *you to* ⎭

(5) (a) *Da die Erde rund ist, sind die Antipoden nicht sichtbar.*
    (b) *Die runde Gestalt der Erde bewirkt die Unsichtbarkeit der Antipoden.*
    (Heger 1976: 154)

(6) (a) *That Elliot entered the room annoyed Floyd.*
    (b) *Elliot's entering the room annoyed Floyd.*
    (c) *For Elliot to enter the room would annoy Floyd.*
    (Noonan 1985: 42)

Zeno Vendler (1972: 68) explains, concerning (4): "... here the same proposition, your occupying the city, is claimed to be expected in thought and is being predicted, ordered, and forbidden in words" (proviso: 'you' refers to the same person). Cf. William Foley & Robert D. Van Valin in their article on "information packaging in the clause" (1985), in which, with respect to a sentence and its passive voice paraphrase, they remark: "These two sentences contain the same basic information, namely the hitting of the ball by the boy, [...]" (p.282). The structures that occur as subjects in (6) are described by Noonan (1985: 42) as "syntactic configurations that are notionally predications, i. e. consist of a predicate and a string of arguments".

Concerning (5), Heger (1976: 154) takes both sentences as linguistic exemplifications of the same actant model, i. e. the same logical, noematic structure. Thus situations or propositions (or: predications in a wider sense) are basically seen as mental objects, thoughts and unitary ideas ("Gesamtvorstellungen" – Gabelentz 1901: 225, 310; Wundt 1900: 240 ff. [this reference by Thümmel 1993: 281]). Following Georg von der Gabelentz, they stand at the beginning and at the end of the communication act. The speaker analyzes it and the hearer seeks to reconstruct it. What lies in-between, the linguistic expression, is variable, may be given as predication (in a narrow sense) or as attribution, but is completely the same regarding the content ("inhaltlich völlig gleich").

In view of this content or conceptual invariant, there is a typological or universal aspect in which it may be useful to consider non-sentence-like expressions as representations of propositions. Extending the "distance" between propositional content and linguistic structure enables the typologist to describe the (basic) structure of a sentence in some languages as, e.g., possessive (action-noun-like) as opposed to rective (verb-like), while the strategy making these structures function as sentences is an additional feature such as a TAM marker.

The distinction between logical-conceptual predication (predication in a wider sense) and predication (in a narrow sense) as "sentence-constituting operation" (Sasse 1991: 80) leads to a typological relativization of the correlatedness of the notion "sentence" with subject-predicate structure (see Sasse 1991), i. e., to the consideration of a bigger set of variants to a common invariant.

On the other hand, we may distinguish between participation in a wider sense, considering all representations of situations in detail, including different types of nominalization, and participation in a narrower sense, with declarative, assertive sentences as its primary research objects, disregarding to a certain extent matters of propositional modalities (→ articles 42; 59; 60).

3. Types of situations (or predicates)

Situations, in terms of their linguistic representation, have been divided into different classes. As can be expected from what was mentioned in § 2.3, this classification has been accomplished predominantly from the perspective of the predicates. When this is done, the problem arises as to how narrow vs. how wide the classification should be or could be. In one extreme, there can be as many classes as there are predicates in a given language (this has at least the disadvantage of being language-specific), for "every verbal lexeme embodies a type of situation" (Lehmann 1991: 189, similarly Givón 1984: 86).

A common, but in itself very simple classification is that of quantitative valence (for an overview of fundamental aspects of valence see, e.g., Helbig 1992; Mosel 1991): predicates can differ as to the number of arguments they (can or must) take; this leads to the traditional labels of INTRANSITIVE, TRANSITIVE and DITRANSITIVE predicates. This can be supplemented, according to the language, by morphosyntactic aspects of case marking (GOVERNMENT in the traditional sense). More information is involved and, accordingly, results in more classes, when qualitative aspects of valence are considered by establishing semantic case-frames (Fillmore 1968). Predicates that fit into such frames share common role structures which can be taken as evidence for the existence of certain types of situations.

Another principle of analysis is the semantic decomposition of verbs. This can be done from a more pragmatic perspective (e.g. Koch 1981; cf. Raible 1992: 123, 138 ff.) or, more commonly, by the identification of atomic predicates like BE, NOT or CAUSE (cf. Foley & Van Valin 1984; Jackendoff 1990) or, even more commonly, by analyzing the internal time structure ("inherent aspectual properties", Comrie 1976) of situations/predicates (which is, by combination of features of different types, only gradually distinct from the aforementioned approach) leading to the distinction of aspectual types (→ art. 42).

The most prominent parameter used in this respect is that of dynamicity, resulting in the two classes of *static* (*stative*) vs. *dynamic* predicates (*punctual* vs. *durative* is sometimes given as the first distinction, as in Comrie 1976: 41 ff.). One finds as second in a hierarchy of relevant factors punctual vs. durative (Lyons 1977, ch. 12.4 and 15.6), *telic* vs. *atelic* (Lehmann 1991; 1994) or controlledness (Dik (1978: 34), who introduces +/− *telic* in 1993: 375 at a third level of subclassification). Further instances of a third level distinction are *static* vs. *dynamic* (Comrie 1976) and Lehmann (1991; 1994).

The latter author's typology is special in two respects. First, the parameters he uses are confined to aspectual characters, treating the concept of control separately (cf. François 1989, esp. p. 230), relating to the properties of participants in a given situation (1991: ch. 3.6.2.). Second, dynamicity is conceived of as a gradual concept. Sharp distinctions are made only between telic and atelic situations, which again are subdivided according to whether they are punctual or whether the situation is bounded on just one side, giving ingressive (or "inchoative", "events that unfold", Frawley 1992: 183) and terminative (or "resultative", "events that come to an end", l.c.: 184) situations.

To summarize, two to three parameters are commonly established (selected from dynamicity, punctuality, telicity, and control) resulting in four (e.g. Chafe 1970, ch. 11; Dik 1978; Vendler 1957), five (Lyons 1977), six (Dik 1993) or seven (François 1989: 237 f., Lehmann 1994) types of predicates. (For further classifications which are empirically based on the encoding of participants, and with semantic implications concerning, for instance, the affectedness of the object, see below §§ 6 and 7). Fig. 37.1 shows Lehmann's table concerning "time stability and types of situations" (1994: 3298; presentation modified).

Notwithstanding the fact that a number of inherent participant properties need to be considered, such as +/− animate or +/− propositional (see the overview in Lehmann 1991: § 5, esp. p. 205), which can, along with the number of participants, feed a further subclassification of predicates, as in Lehmann 1991: § 4, the roles played by the participants involved in situations, or rather, dependent on these situations, need to be accounted for.

4. Case roles

As indicated in § 2.3, predicates, as situation cores, determine to a great extent the role of their participants, a fact which can also be used as a means of predicate classification (cf. § 3). To achieve this, Fillmore (1968) has, inter alia, established a set of roles, elaborated by himself and others, partly on differing principles. A very comprehensive "checklist" of roles that are met in the literature is given by Barry J. Blake (1994: 68−71; for further references, see ibid. and, e.g., Palmer 1994). The list comprises the following roles (also called semantic roles, semantic relations, deep cases, thematic roles or θ-roles): AGENT, PATIENT (or OBJECT, OBJECTIVE, THEME, GOAL), INSTRUMENT, EXPERIENCER, LOCATION, SOURCE, PATH, DESTINATION, RECIPIENT, PURPOSE, BENEFICIARY, MANNER, EXTENT, POSSESSOR. (The list reflects the order chosen by Blake, except that he begins with the patient; the last role is not exemplified as a complement to a verb, but as a modifier of a noun.)

In the sense that participation has, as its onomasiological or "deductive" point of departure, to do with the notional level of situations, it should indeed be a possible aim of research to establish a universal set of such roles. But no such commonly accepted set exists as of yet. This comes perhaps as no surprise, considering the diverging definitional principles, ranging between philosophical, language-universalistic, general linguistic, typological or single language grammar-writing perspectives.

static	atelic	atemporal	class membership
			property
↕		durative	state
			process
	telic	terminative	
		ingressive	event
dynamic		punctual	

Fig. 37.1: Time stability and types of situations (after Lehmann 1994)

Frank R. Palmer (1994: 5) summarizes the difficulties as follows:

"There are three problems with such notional roles. First, like all such notional features, they cannot be defined in any precise way, with the result that it is not always possible to apply them unambiguously. Secondly, it is always possible to suggest more distinctions, so that there is, in principle, no limit to the number of possible roles. Thirdly, they are often partly based on the grammatical distinctions noted in languages, as is obvious in Fillmore's list, and so are not truly notional."

In a way, the situation is comparable to what was explained above, concerning the question of establishing situation types: the types looked for should be conceptually significant yet at the same time linguistically relevant, that is, they should reflect linguistic distinctions, but not be so specific that they are useful for representing "only" properties of a single language, without setting a basis for comparison.

In other words, the problem is how abstract the roles should be. Just as every predicate embodies a type of situation (see the citation of Lehmann at the beginning of § 3), every predicate also generates its own role(s) ("... in principle, there are as many case roles as there are verbs", Givón 1984: 127; see also Koch 1981). As Blake (1994: 71) illustrates, "the verb *hit* implies a hitter and a hitee, the verb *scrape* implies a scraper and a scrapee, and so on."

Thus, to arrive at a limited number of entities, one has to generalize; this by itself leads to more and more abstract concepts, which are broader and at the same time, as regards their intension, more empty. And since this is a linguistic enterprise, the operations of abstraction are methodologically oriented towards linguistic, i. e. morphosyntactic, i. e. ultimately formal distinctions. Thus, a drift takes place which shifts the character of the roles from meaning to function, from semantics to syntax, from content to form.

How does the theory of semantic roles cope with these implications? One possible consequence is demonstrated by von Stechow (1991), who takes the existence of roles such as THEME, AGENT, INSTRUMENT, etc. for granted, but rejects any semantic significance of the role names: for him, they are merely labels whose literal meaning cannot be taken seriously.

Another reaction to the problem of role meanings and the delimitation of role functions is Comrie's conception of semantic roles as a continuum with no sharp distinctions: "... it is not so much a set of discrete semantic relations, but rather a continuum, the labels representing different points along this continuum" (1981: 53).

A further proposal has been made by David Dowty (1991; cf. also the elaboration in Primus 1995) who in fact offers a componential analysis of roles, giving the possibility of a hierarchy of roles by subsuming some roles under others as subcategories, thereby avoiding the necessity of defining wholly separate categories. Specifically, agent and patient are assigned the character of "proto-roles", which are defined by clusters of features.

The fewer features are positively specified for an argument in a given situation, the less prototypical it is as an agent or patient. At the same time, it represents another role. For instance, a prototypical agent is characterized as, among other things, causative, volitional and sentient. In case it is sentient but not volitional and not causative, it represents not a prototypical agent, but a role commonly called experiencer. On the other hand, if it is causative but not volitional and not sentient, it takes on a role known as instrument.

The concept of prototypicality is also applied in other approaches. What they have in common is the special relevance of only (or mainly) two roles or relations and that these relations are not defined absolutely, but rather as resulting from the relation to the predicate and its other argument(s) when present. The difference lies in the conceptual status of these two relations as semantic and/or (morpho-)syntactic. Foley & Van Valin (1984; cf. also the concept of "hyperroles" in Kibrik 1997) postulate two relations called "actor" and "undergoer" which are described as "generalized semantic relations between a predicate and its arguments" (p. 29).

Thus, though generalized, they are still considered semantic, as "macroroles which subsume particular groups of Fillmorean case roles or Gruberian thematic relations" (p. 30). By what criteria is this subsumption achieved? Foley & Van Valin (1984: 27): "... actor and undergoer are the two arguments in a transitive predication, either one of which may be the single argument of an intransitive verb". This statement has, on the one hand, semantic implications insofar as transitivity can be understood as a semantic concept, but, on the other hand, directs attention to the syntactic structure of the clause.

Similarly, Palmer (1994) distinguishes between NOTIONAL ROLES and GRAMMATICAL ROLES. Notional roles represent the bigger set of specific semantic-conceptual roles as signifiés. Two of these roles, namely agent and patient, can be taken as the prototypical instantiations of two grammatical roles, labeled AGENT and PATIENT respectively (abbreviated A and P). These roles are now called "grammatical", which indicates their morphosyntactic localization: they are grammaticalized notional roles. This, of course, makes them less semantic. This syntactic definition has a further consequence: the single argument of an "intransitive" clause is assigned a different grammatical role: S (for "single argument", p. 10).

To conclude: The question of identifying a limited number of semantic roles leads, on conceptual as well as on formal grounds, to a reduction of the number of roles by generalization: on the one hand, prototypical situations seem to be "transitive", moving from an agent/source/cause to a patient/goal/effect (cf. Halliday 1985: 101 ff. or the "vector representation" of DeLancey 1985: 47 f.). In correlation with this, prototypical sentences contain two arguments. The relevance of these somewhat simplifying assumptions will be further substantiated in the course of the following sections by, in discussing both aspects: the formal one of the encoding of actants in a predication, as well as the semantics of the relationship between the exponency of actants and their (semantic-conceptual) roles and the notion of transitivity.

5. Actancy
   (valence, argument structure)

5.1. Role assignment (grammatical roles)

Under the assumption that in participation, languages express participants with differing roles, the question arises as to what specific means of overt coding of these roles languages use; this area of linguistic phenomena is also known as relational typology (cf. Plank (ed.) 1985; Primus 1995). Apart from word order and cross-referencing ("indirect marking", Graham Mallinson & Blake (1981: 41 f.), or "indexation", Croft 1990: 30), case marking can, with certain restrictions to be discussed shortly, be seen as the basic device for "role assignment" (cf. Broschart 1991: 45 ff.).

However, language does not do this in a direct way, i.e. by establishing one-to-one correspondences between a morphological case or an adposition (both are formal types of case markers capable of signaling case) and a "deep case", i.e. semantic role (Blake 1994: 132). This is reflected in the distinction, with no sharp boundary, between "grammatical" cases with abstract meanings and "concrete" cases which signal semantic roles more directly (see, e.g., Lazard 1994/98: 4 f.).

Given that typical clauses exhibit one or two actants (this term normally referring to the syntactic realization of participant[s]; cf. Palmer 1994: 3, 8), the system of case assignment can be seen as organized according to the principles of economy and efficiency (→ art. 31); the kind of semantic roles involved in a given situation is predominantly inherent in the predicate. Thus, the task of case marking is mainly carried out in order to establish syntagmatic contrasts (cf., e.g., Heger 1985: 109).

Two consequences of these functional "duties" are that, (i) in a clause with two arguments, only one of them needs a marker, whereas the other can be left unmarked, and (ii) a case marker in a clause with one argument need not be paradigmatically distinguished from the markers occurring in clauses with two arguments, and therefore need not be marked either.

The topic of this section, ACTANCY, covers a great deal of what is often called valence, one difference being that valence focuses on properties of predicates, whereas actancy deals with the systematic organization of morphosyntactic machinery in its contribution to the representation of situations (→ art. 28); Comrie (1993) puts this under the heading of "argument structure". As regards the perspective of valence, arguments can be necessary and/or can trigger, if an argument is present, the exponence of a certain case.

A very comprehensive and consistent treatment of actancy is presented by Lazard (1994/98). His declared method is to proceed strictly from expression to content, starting from empirical facts about formal means (see p. xii, 35), in combination with taking into consideration the different logical possibilities which exist (see also Bossong, e.g. 1985). As a consequence, the three types of argument, referred to as A, P and S at the end of § 4 above, are simply called X, Y and Z by

Lazard. A comparison of transitive (two argument) and intransitive (one argument) clauses, and the observation of their markings, leads to the postulation of five systems of case marking (which may or may not characterize a language as a whole). These systems are called "structures d'actance" by Lazard. He gives the following list (1994/98: 33; cf. Comrie 1978: 392):

accusative: $X = Z$ (and $Y \neq Z$)
ergative: $Y = Z$ (and $X \neq Z$)
neutral: $X = Z$ and $Y = Z$
mixed: $X \sim Z$ and $Y \sim Z$
disjunct: $X \neq Z$ and $Y \neq Z$

The first two situations are typologically the most prominent. The third (NEUTRAL) means that there is in fact no case marking at all. The forth (MIXED) reflects the situation that, in one respect, for instance indexation (or, in Lazard's words, "indices actanciels"), the system is accusative, whereas in another respect, for instance, the distribution of case markers (Lazard: "relateurs"), the structures behave ergatively. The fifth case represents the special case that in certain constructions, Z is marked differently both from X and from Y or, put differently, that X and Y both receive markings that differ from Z (TRIPARTITE marking). The "mixed" type must not be confused with the so-called "ACTIVE" type (Klimov 1972/1974), which Lazard (1994/98: 43 f.) adds to the list separately and which he prefers to name "dual structure" (1994/98: 43). The relevant formula reads:

$Z^x = X$ and $Z^y = Y$

"(where Z^x and Z^y represent the active and the inactive single actant, respectively)" p. 43). Although it is easy to state that, in a sentence with one argument (Z), the mark is identical with the mark of one of the arguments (X or Y) in a two-argument predication, the methodological abstraction from meaning poses the problem of how to recognize whether it is the X or the Y with which identity holds. Thus, a minimal semantic condition is required: the recognition of sameness vs. difference in meaning (specifically: of role) in pairs of uniactant and biactant constructions, which is applied intra-linguistically and cross-linguistically (see Lazard 1994/98, esp. p. 26, 35).

Accordingly, the question of the semantic interpretation of the structures is approached by Lazard only after their formal identification. In the "semantic" approaches mentioned in § 4, the point of departure was the assumption that typical two-place predicates have agents and patients. Lazard's argument is, however, that this must not be stated a priori. To bring the semantic assumption in line with the structural facts, one has to either weaken the semantic concept of agent and patient (allowing more arguments to be agent-like or patient-like) or ultimately arrive at defining Agent and Patient as grammatical relations (Palmer's "grammatical roles", as could be seen in § 4). In this respect, Palmer's and Lazard's approaches converge. Palmer's "problem" and that of others in describing the linguistic mechanisms of actancy is in a way with how to eliminate semantics; Lazard's "problem" is with how to put semantics in again.

There are many situations in which it is not possible to assign roles in terms of "agency" or "patiency", for instance, in many situations involving perception. Following Lazard, the proper argument is to observe empirically that, indeed, agents and patients are typically encoded by a certain construction in a language, and that many languages use the same constructions for other situations as well: situations with less clearly distributed semantic roles (1994/98: 40). "To sum up, it is clear that sentences expressing an action, with an agent and a patient — let us call them, for brevity's sake, "action sentences" — are widely used as the syntactic model for the construction of sentences expressing different kinds of other processes" (1994: 41). Avery Andrews (1985: 68) describes things along similar lines, speaking of "grammatical functions" (where PTV means 'primary transitive verbs'):

"Languages always seem to have a standard way or small set of ways in which they normally express the Agent and Patient of a PTV. If an NP is serving as argument of a two-argument verb, and receiving the morphological and syntactic treatment normally accorded to an Agent of a PTV, we shall say that it has the grammatical function A; if it is an argument of a verb with two or more arguments receiving the treatment normally accorded to the Patient of a PTV, we shall say that it has the grammatical function O. [...] An NP in an intransitive sentence that is receiving the treatment normally accorded to the single argument of a one-argument predicate will be said to have S function".

Note the expression "receiving the treatment normally accorded to ...", which corresponds to Lazard's "used as model": this leaves open the question of to what extent an A is an agent or a P is a patient; it rather implies the weak assumption that there might be some semantic relevance or even iconicity, but that it does not necessarily have to be so; there could be a discrepancy between semantics (agentive) and grammar (non-agentive). At the least, the description is neutral.

One can conclude then that there is a tendency to use a small number of marking patterns for a larger number of functions, which is made possible, as proposed at the beginning of the section, by the inherent semantics of the predicates. Whether one adheres to a stronger connection between case marking and semantics or not, one can classify languages typologically according to the degree to which different semantic types of situations are, in terms of their morphosyntactic coding, "absorbed" by the "black hole" of a predominant structural pattern. Lazard uses the notion "assimilation" to capture this tendency (1994: 41, 45, 66 et passim), Blake speaks of "conflation" (1994: 122, 137); Kibrik of "mixedness" (1997: 318 et passim); Werner Drossard has studied a different aspect of this phenomenon, subsuming it under the concept of the "leveling out" of case marking ("Kasus-Nivellierung", see Drossard 1991). Because leveling out has something to do with the continuum of central/grammatical vs. peripheral/semantic, we will return briefly to the topic in the next section.

The nominative-accusative case marking system will occasionally be called SA/P, the ergative-absolutive system SP/A (following Blake 1994: 119 ff.).

5.2. Syntactic functions (grammatical relations)

There is a level of categories which has not been mentioned yet, although it is quite central to traditional occidental grammar and to modern frameworks such as Relational Grammar. First and foremost, it includes the notions of subject and object. They have been called, in the tradition of generative grammar, "syntactic functions" — in contradistinction to "syntactic categories" like noun and verb — or "grammatical relations" (Comrie 1981: 59 ff.). Since they have been established in the course of the description of specific languages, viz. ANCIENT GREEK and LATIN, the application and usefulness of these terms in the description of typologically different languages, of languages with strongly differing types of actancy (clause structure), have come to be a problem (cf. Li (ed.) 1976; Plank (ed.) 1985).

To cope with this problem, strategies similar to the one mentioned in §4 have been used; in particular: componential analysis and statements about the relevance of features for the task of cross-linguistic comparison, resulting, for instance, in varying degrees of reduction of features, for example, the disqualification of semantic criteria. In a grammar based on ENGLISH, the subject can simply be defined by a specific position in the phrase structure. At the other extreme, Edward L. Keenan (1976) has identified multiple features (or "factors") of a different nature, which can be used as a checklist for "subjecthood".

While this is certainly a useful basis, critical voices express the caveat that it would also be too simplistic, to consider the "best" subject that which manifests just the highest number of features. Thus Ruqaiya Hasan & Peter H. Fries (1995: XXV) maintain that language comparison should be neither too formal nor too "notional", but "recognize the dialectics of function and form" (ibid.; cf. Himmelmann 1986; Croft 1990: 13−17). The Functional Grammar of Halliday (1985) can be seen as one manifestation of this dialectic principle, which is referred to in the joint publication of Hasan and Fries.

Halliday (1985: 32−37) refers back to the 19th century analysis of subject by Gabelentz into three component concepts: psychological, grammatical, and logical subject. The point is that all three aspects − in modern terms: pragmatic, syntactic, and semantic (role), respectively − may coincide in basic clause structures found in "average standard European", but are logically and linguistically independent in terms of cross-linguistic comparison and intra-linguistic variation of syntactic structure.

Definitional approaches to subject can vary with regard to their relying on one of the three aspects mentioned. Pragmatically based approaches focus on the functions of information packaging in the context of discourse, defining "subject" as what a sentence "is about", the "topic" or "theme". Andrews informs us that his concept of subject "might be described as 'semantically based'" (1985: 151). His definition is based on the categories A, P (or "O"), and S described in §§ 4 and 5.1: "Most often, one finds one grammatical relation associated with A and S, and another with O. The former sort of grammatical relation we will call 'subject', the latter 'object'." Note that he characterizes his approach as semantic despite his calling subject and object "grammatical relations" (apparently following Comrie 1981) and A, O, S "grammatical functions".

A similar solution is presented by Palmer (1994: 14f.) but based solely on syntactic relationships (cf. Blake 1994: 2): Just as A, P, and S have been introduced, defined as "grammatical roles" (as opposed to semantic roles) and orthographically marked by using initial capitals, Subject and Object are introduced as "grammatical relations", where SUBJECT is defined as comprising S and A in an actancy system where S = A, leaving then OBJECT for P (cf. Andrews). In an ergative system, the constellation S = P is called ABSOLUTIVE, the grammatical role A being assigned the grammatical relation ERGATIVE.

But there are other, less "terminological" conceptions, focusing on subject as a special typological category with a certain cluster of functions correlated with specific properties. There must be a specific coding device which "cumulatively" (Kibrik 1997) signals a semantic role (typically, i. e. in basic sentences: agent/actor) and the (pragmatic) topic (cf. Sasse 1995). If role and pragmatic function are coded separately, no special syntactic relation like "subject" exists. The coding device itself, as described by Kibrik (1997), corresponds to the definitions of Andrews/Palmer, differing in two respects:

(i) It is derived from a strictly semantic basis insofar as A, O, S as well as A/S and O/S are correlated with hyperroles, resulting from metonymic extensions which originate in the primary roles agent/cause and patient/effect (cf. Lazard's paradigmatic action sentences).
(ii) Not only A/S but also O/S is termed "subject" on a syntactic level.

In contradistinction to these, the most general functional conception of subject is maintained by Givón (1984: 135ff.). Being a pragmatic case role coding the (primary) topic of a sentence, the subject is a universal category. Typological variation rests more on syntactic regularities than on case marking (Givón 1995: 252), so in ergative languages A is considered to be the subject in spite of being marked and coded differently from S (which is the subject in a uniactant clause; Givón 1984: 140).

Considering the whole set of actants figuring in a sentence, the subject is but one in a set of syntactic relations. The two sets can be correlated using the conception of center (core) vs. periphery, sometimes conceived of as a continuum. Central participants are more dependent on the predicate in two respects: formally, in terms of their presence and marking, and semantically, in the semantic role they realize.

While central arguments are thus semantically determined by the predicate, correlating with the fact that a given case or the grammatical role/function itself bears less inherent semantics (see at the end of § 5.1, concerning the assimilation aspect of A and P), peripheral participants are to a greater extent expected to display one-to-one correspondences between "grammatical relation and semantic role" (Blake 1994: 64); "peripheral grammatical relations tend to be semantically homogeneous" (p. 49). A related conception emerges out of the demand that a greater number of semantic roles must, depending on the verb, be assigned to a small number of grammatical roles (the problem of linking). This is not performed arbitrarily, but there is a universal tendency which has been formulated as an access hierarchy (for different variants and discussion see Fillmore 1968; Comrie & Keenan 1979; Dik 1978; François & Broschart 1994). Here is Givón's version ("topic hierarchy" − 1984: 139):

agt > dat[ive]/ben[efactive] > pat > loc[ative] > instr[ument]/assoc[iative] > mann[er]

(Associative can be taken as a synonym of comitative.) The hierarchy is read in the sense that "if the simple clause has an agent argument, it will be the subject". It is a hierarchy because it implies that it is always the leftmost instance which is the primary candidate for being the subject of the clause. In this sense, agent as the prototypical subject comes into play, and by this the relevance of a specific semantic role in connection with, e.g., the subject.

6. Actancy variation (valence alternation)

6.1. Introduction; individuation hierarchy

Languages which tend to represent argument structure on a more semantic basis ("role-related" languages) will, accordingly, display a larger inventory of case marking patterns and variations. But apart from this, there are other motivations, in any language, for variation. Syntactically, there may be a need for re-assigning a certain role to a certain grammatical relation to make it able to undergo certain syntactical operations which are restricted to that relation — for instance the subject in the domain of relative clause formation or coreference effects in clause linkage (→ articles 45; 74).

Pragmatically, speakers use strategies to present situations from differing perspectives, or to express connotations of politeness or distance. Semantically, formal variations can be reflections of low control of an Agent, low degree of dynamicity of the situation, low degree of its completeness, or a low degree of affectedness of the Patient. The properties may depend on the nature of the situation as well as on the inherent properties of the participants.

There is a universal tendency such that the less "salient" or animated or individuated a participant is, the less likely is it to be coded as subject. This generalization has been discussed by R. M. W. Dixon, Michael Silverstein and others under such terms as animacy hierarchy, agency hierarchy, or empathy hierarchy (see, e.g., Ono 1991: 328 et pass. for more terms and references). Lazard (1994: 185 ff., esp. 202) proposes the "supercatégorie d'individuation" as the general factor at work (referring to Hopper & Thompson 1980: 279). The instances on the hierarchy are (with minor variations of position and impact/effectivity depending on the language):

SAP 1 < SAP 2 < SAP 3 < PN < human < animate < inanimate < mass

(cf. Lehmann 1991: 205). (SAP = speech act participant, PN = proper noun.) The variations of argument structure manifest themselves, in general terms, in: change of valence in the sense of a change of the participants to be expressed obligatorily; change of case marking and related means; change of the assignment of semantic roles to grammatical roles and relations. Techniques or strategies related to these aspects are: verb classes / valence, whereby specific participant exponencies are lexically determined; valence, whereby actants can be omitted; differential marking (mostly concerning the object; → art. 65), which can also mean changes in indexation, voice (→ art. 67), and split marking (→ art. 26, § 3.2).

Before commenting on voice and split marking, one preparatory remark should be made: there is not only a hierarchy of roles and other actant properties, but also a continuum of formal centrality vs. periphery of the actants in relation to the predicate which has to be taken into consideration (cf. Lazard 1994: 68 ff.). It manifests itself in the probability of occurrence in the languages of the world, in obligatoriness of presence in sentences, determination of a specific case by verbal government, and the formal exponence of the case marker (and its semantic specificity). Thus, a most central actant tends to be obligatorily present and unmarked (and grammaticalized). A peripheral argument tends to be optional and marked, possibly morphologically complex (and with "concrete" semantics). In other words, it is a manifestation of the gradience of indicativity.

The case hierarchy tends to be structured as follows (Blake 1994: 89, 157):

(7) NOM ACC/ERG GEN DAT LOC ABL/INST
     OTHERS

The notion of centrality is correlated with the phenomenon of role assimilation described at the end of § 5.1 and is also operational in case marking variation, along with the agency hierarchy.

6.2. Voice

In terms of its functional load, voice (diathesis) represents one of the main syntactic devices for "information-packaging" (Foley & Van Valin 1985). It is a means of valence changing, i.e., rearranging the correlations between roles and grammatical relations (or cases), so it may be called a "role-remapping" device. It can be more or less compelling (in the sense of the factors mentioned in § 6.1) in a given language to remove the central actant from its position (demotion), either leaving it unexpressed or coding it in a peripheral case. Typically, another participant then assumes the central position (is promoted).

In contrast to other strategies of case marking changes, voice alternation originates in a special inflectional marker on the verb. Parallel strategies exist in nominative (SA/P) languages and ergative (SP/A) languages: PASSIVE and ANTIPASSIVE. In accusative languages, it is the A that is demoted, in ergative languages it is P. A common function is to encode situations with lower "transitivity" (see below § 7). This means, for instance, that in an accusative language, the Patient is encoded as subject when it happens to be higher on the individuation scale than the Agent. In an ergative system, antipassive coding can signal that an action is less completed or that the Patient is less completely affected than in the active version.

But there are also asymmetries: for peripheral arguments to be promoted to subject in SA/P systems, they first have to be promoted to object. In an SP/A system, however, any peripheral argument, not just the one encoded as ergative in the basic construction, is directly promoted to the most central position, the absolutive (Blake 1994: 89 f.). This way, one of the effects of voice distinctions is that the most central argument becomes accessible to even more semantic roles (cf. Drossard 1991: 448 f.; for details concerning this section and for supplementary voice distinctions, → articles 41; 67).

6.3. Split marking

Split marking refers to the fact that language often displays neither a thoroughly ergative nor a thoroughly accusative case marking but, dependent on conditions which vary from language to language but show cross-linguistic regularities, "sometimes" (or in some grammatical domains, which is distinguished as "mixed" marking, see § 5.1) use ergative, "sometimes" accusative markings. The regularities can be described or explained in terms of prototypical situations and the agentivity scale:

The prototypical situation describes an action in which an agent does something which affects another entity. The prototypical A is an agent, high on the agentivity scale; the prototypical P a patient, low on that scale. Deviations from this basic pattern can result in a switch from one case marking pattern to another, for instance, from ergative-absolutive (or SP/A) to nominative-accusative (or SA/P) marking. At least the following factors play a role:

(i) the semantic class of the predicate (e.g. action verb vs. experiencer verb),
(ii) tense-aspect-mood (e.g imperfective vs. perfective; → art. 59),
(iii) person (e.g. 1/2 vs. 3),
(iv) subordination.

In each case, the first term of the opposition correlates with accusative (SA/P) marking. Factor (iii) is, of course, associated with the scale of individuation and as such with features of the participants, the others with more general "dynamicity"-properties of the situation as it is represented; together, all three can be put in the context of the aforementioned comprehensive prototype of a situation, which has also been discussed in the framework of a generalized notion of transitivity.

7. Transitivity

According to a standard definition, transitivity refers to verbs: transitive verbs are those which are two-place; the second argument is in the accusative (i. e. represents the direct object), and the whole construction can be passivized. Verbs which do not comply with these formal properties are by definition intransitive. While the terms are still used, for the sake of convenience, to distinguish the corresponding predicate types, the term transitivity has come to be used more and more in a much broader sense which is based on the common notional tradition of the term, namely, that in a typical proposition, the effects of an action "pass over" from an actor to a goal (cf. Lyons 1968: 350). So it is the whole situation, including the roles of the participants, that makes up transitivity (cf. Halliday 1970: 144 ff.). In such a framework, transitivity is

(i) a semantic-conceptual notion, which
(ii) can be attributed not (only) to verbs, but to sentences, which
(iii) is not a binary, but a gradual concept and
(iv) the value of which in a given case results from specifications in a set of linguistic factors which can be seen as determining transitivity or as reflexes of it.

This concept has been elaborated in an especially significant way by Paul J. Hopper and Sandra A. Thompson (1980). The components of transitivity they identify include, inter alia, the parameter of punctual vs. non-punctual predicates, the agency of Agents and the individuation of Patients (p. 252). Positive or more positive specifications imply higher transitivity. What has been largely unspecified is the relative weight of the individual factors in determining the degree of high vs. low transitivity (for some discussion see Seiler 1988: 20 ff., 151 ff.).

Tasaku Tsunoda (1994) has presented a scale of instances with decreasing transitivity, founded on a selection of relevant binary distinctions comprising semantic (linguistic expression of two participants, impingement, change) as well as morphosyntactic aspects (case [marking] frame, possibility of corresponding passive or antipassive constructions, or related reflexive, or reciprocal constructions): point of departure is the (prototypically transitive) case with completely positive specifications (*Brutus killed Caesar*); the scale then shows eleven instances with increasingly lower transitivity characterized by increasingly more "minus" specifications, arriving at an all minus instance exemplified by *It is cold today.*

Lazard (1994: 167f., 220, 231ff., 247ff.) establishes a transitivity scale starting from the traditional dichotomy between transitive (two-place) vs. intransitive (one-place) predicates. He "inserts" intermediate categories which comprise structures which "marginalize" ("marginaliser") one of the two arguments of a "two-place" predication, thereby making it less transitive, but also not quite intransitive (in the sense of displaying only one actant).

Such downgradings can be observed, first, as valence-based: It is not an obligation but a tendency or "general possibility" (and therefore, an invariant or universal) that languages do not construct all clauses by using the model of action clauses. Even if there is much assimilation, some minor classes of predicates are established showing special codings. And there are certain correlations between this formal appearance, intra- as well as cross-linguistically, as is the case with "verbs of cognition" (→ art. 93).

Second, similar constructions can be the result either of voice strategies, rendering one argument optional or peripheral, or of coalescence / incorporation (→ art. 53), disindividuating an argument by making it part of the predicate. Thus semantic-conceptual transitivity based on parameters of individuation of the actants, completeness of the situation, and the perspective with which the situation is seen and communicated by the speaker (cf. Lazard 1994: 218, 250) decreases when the linguistic distance of the participants/actants to the participatum/predicate is reduced, but it decreases as well when the distance is enlarged.

8. Conclusion

The preceding sections have shown relationships among differing types of situations, and demonstrated that linguistic structures can be related to situations in different, non-arbitrary ways. Transitivity alternations tend to result in the representation of different situations, yet, in contrast, one and the same situation can be expressed differently by means of valence changing devices, yielding a varying transitivity "value". This only shows us that the distinction between a situation vs. its "information packaging", the distinction between the propositional content and other communicative aspects of utterances, between content and intent in context, is an analytical device which must not conceal the fact that both stand in reality, i. e. in linguistic structure, in complex interrelationships.

As the position of this contribution in its context indicates, the domain of participation as the representation of situations is linguistically instantiated by a full scale, or net, of linguistic devices as subsystems (techniques, subdimensions, in the terminology of Seiler & Premper 1991; → art. 27), which in turn serve to represent situations not just as such, but as a function of communicative purposes. This means that, in trying to give a full account of the functional load and the systematic interplay of the linguistic devices, not just the representational part of the language functions has to be considered, but also the textual and the situational context (→ articles 34; 35; 44; 45; 46; 47). After having been more and more involved in "predicative" linguistic machinery, we are now more indicative, indexical, and pragmatic (→ art. 27 for a special understanding of the polar opposition between predicative and indicative phenomena). This refers back to the context of this article and reinforces the general assumption that language can be seen as a problem-solving device, an instrument, but a fundamental one, for the tasks human beings may wish to fulfill. Talking about situations is one of them.

9. References

Abraham, Werner. 1988. *Terminologie zur neueren Linguistik*. 2., völlig neu bearb. u. erw. Aufl. (Germanistische Arbeitshefte, Ergänzungsreihe 1.) Tübingen: Niemeyer.

Andrews, Avery. 1985. "The major functions of the noun phrase". In: Shopen (ed.) 1985: Vol. I: 62–154.

Asher, Ronald E. & Simpson, J.M.Y. (eds.). 1994. *The Encyclopedia of Language and Linguistics*. 9 Vols. Oxford: Pergamon Press.

Barwise, John. 1991. "Situationen und kleine Welten". In: Stechow & Wunderlich (eds.) 1991: 80−9.

Bechert, Johannes & Bernini, Guliano & Buridant, Claude (eds.). 1990. *Toward a typology of European languages*. (Empirical Approaches to Language Typology, 8.) Berlin: Mouton de Gruyter.

Blake, Barry J. 1994. *Case*. Cambridge: Cambridge University Press.

Bloomfield, Leonard. 1933/1935. *Language*. New York / London: Henry Holt and Company.

Bolinger, Dwight. 1977. *Meaning and form*. (English Language Series, 11.) London: Longman.

Bossong, Georg. 1985. "Markierung von Aktantenfunktionen im Guaraní. Zur Frage der differentiellen Objektmarkierung in nicht-akkusativischen Sprachen". In: Plank (ed.) 1985: 1−29.

Broschart, Jürgen. 1991. "Noun, verb, and PARTICIPATION (A typology of the noun/verb-distinction)". In: Seiler & Premper (eds.) 1991: 65−137.

Broschart, Jürgen. 1991a. "On the sequence of the techniques on the dimension of PARTICIPATION". In: Seiler & Premper (eds.) 1991: 29−61.

Chafe, Wallace L. 1970. *Meaning and the structure of language*. Chicago: The University of Chicago Press.

Chomsky, Noam. 1965. *Aspects of the theory of syntax*. Cambridge/MA: The M.I.T. Press.

Comrie, Bernard. 1976. *Aspect: An introduction to the study of verbal aspect and related problems*. Cambridge: Cambridge University Press.

Comrie, Bernard. 1978. "Ergativity". In: Lehmann, W. (ed.) 1978: 329−94.

Comrie, Bernard. 1993. "Argument structure". In: Jacobs & al. (eds.) 1993: 905−14.

Comrie, Bernard & Keenan, Edward L. 1979. "Noun phrase accessibility revisited." *Langage* 55: 649−664.

Comrie, Bernard. 1981. *Language universals and linguistic typology. Syntax and morphology*. Oxford: Basil Blackwell.

Cooreman, Ann M. & Fox, B. & Givón, Talmy. 1984. "The discourse definition of ergativity". *Studies in Language* 8: 1−34.

Crimmins, M. 1994. Article "Proposition". In: Asher & Simpson (eds.). Vol 6: 3377−80.

Croft, William. 1990. *Typology and Universals*. Cambridge: Cambridge University Press.

Davidson, Donald. 1967/1980. "The logical form of action sentences". In: Rescher (ed.) 1967: 81−120. Reprinted as "essay 6" in Davidson 1980. *Essays in actions and events*. Oxford: Clarendon; cited thereafter.

DeLancey, Scott. 1985. "On active typology and the nature of agentivity". In: Plank (ed.) 1985: 47−60.

Dik, Simon C. 1978. *Functional grammar*. (North-Holland Linguistic Series, 37.) Amsterdam: North-Holland.

Dik, Simon C. 1991. "Functional grammar". In: Stechow & Wunderlich (eds.) 1991: 368−94.

Dowty, David. 1991. "Thematic proto-roles and argument selection". *Language* 67,3: 547−619.

Drossard, Werner. 1991. "KASUSMARKIERUNG: Zur Zentralität und Peripherizität von Partizipanten". In: Seiler & Premper (eds.) 1991: 446−81.

Drossard, Werner. 1991a. "Verbklassen". In: Seiler & Premper (eds.) 1991: 150−82.

Ehrich, Veronika. 1991. "Nominalisierungen". In: Stechow & Wunderlich (eds.) 1991: 441−58.

Fillmore, Charles J. 1968. "The Case for Case". In: Bach, Emmon & Harms, R. T. (eds.). 1968. *Universals in Linguistic Theory*. New York: Holt, Rinehart & Winston, 1−88.

Foley, William & Van Valin, Robert D. 1984. *Functional syntax and universal grammar*. (Cambridge Studies in Linguistics, 38.) Cambridge: Cambridge University Press.

Foley, William A. & Van Valin, Robert D. 1985. "Information packaging in the clause". Shopen (ed.) 1985: Vol. I: 282−364.

François, Jacques & Broschart, Jürgen. 1994. "La mise en ordre des relations actantielles: Les conditions d'accès des rôles sémantiques aux fonctions de sujet et d'objet". *Langages* 113: 7−44.

François, Jacques. 1989. *Changement, causation, action. Trois catégories sémantiques fondamentales du lexique verbal français et allemand*. Genève: Droz.

Frawley, William. 1992. *Linguistic semantics*. Hillsdale/NJ: Lawrence Erlbaum.

Gabelentz, Georg von der. 1901. *Die Sprachwissenschaft. Ihre Aufgaben, Methoden und bisherigen Ergebnisse*. Leipzig: Tauchnitz (2., vermehrte und verb. Aufl.). 2. Neuauflage 1970, Tübingen: Narr.

Givón, Talmy. 1984. *Syntax: A functional-typological introduction*. Vol. I. Amsterdam & Philadelphia: Benjamins.

Givón, Talmy. 1995. *Functionalism and grammar*. Amsterdam: Benjamins.

Halliday, Michael Alexander Kirkwood. 1970. "Language structure and language function". In: Lyons (ed.) 1970: 140−65.

Halliday, M. A. K. 1985. *An Introduction to Functional Grammar*. London: Edward Arnold.

Hasan, Ruqaiya & Fries, Peter H. (eds.). 1995. *On subject and theme: A discourse functional perspective*. Amsterdam & Philadelphia: Benjamins.

Hasan, Ruqaiya & Fries, Peter H. 1995. "Reflections on subject and theme: An introduction". In: Hasan & Fries (eds.) 1995: xiii-xlv.

Heger, Klaus. 1976. *Monem, Wort, Satz und Text*. (Konzepte der Sprach- und Literaturwissenschaft, 8.) Tübingen: Niemeyer. 2., erw. Aufl.

Heger, Klaus. 1985. "Akkusativische, ergativische und aktivische Bezeichnung von Aktantenfunktionen". In: Plank, Frans (ed.), 109−129.

Heger, Klaus. 1991. "Vom Stemma zum Aktantenmodell". In: Koch, Peter & Krefeld, Thomas (eds.). 1991. *Connexiones Romanicae. Dependenz und Valenz in romanischen Sprachen.* (Linguistische Arbeiten, 268.) Tübingen: Niemeyer, 41−9.

Helbig, Gerhard. 1992. *Probleme der Valenz- und Kasustheorie.* (Konzepte der Sprach- und Literaturwissenschaft, 51.) Tübingen: Niemeyer.

Himmelmann, Nikolaus. 1986. *Morphosyntactic Predication: A functional-operational appproach.* Arbeiten des Kölner Universalien-Projekts (akup) Nr. 62.

Hopper, Paul & Thompson, Sandra A. 1980. "Transitivity in Grammar and Discourse". *Language* 56: 251−99.

Immler, Manfred. 1991. "Is semantics universal, or isn't it?". In: Zaefferer (ed.) 1991: 37−59.

Jackendoff, Ray. 1990. *Semantic structures.* Cambridge, MA: The MIT Press.

Jacobs, Joachim & Stechow, Arnim von & Sternefeld, Wolfgang & Vennemann, Theo (eds.). 1993/1995. *Syntax. Ein internationales Handbuch zeitgenössischer Forschung. An International Handbook of Contemporary Research.* (Handbücher zur Sprach- und Kommunikationswissenschaft, 9,1 (1993) & 9,2 (1995)) Berlin & New York: de Gruyter.

Keenan, Edward L. 1976. "Toward a universal definition of subject'". Li (ed.) 1976: 303−33.

Kibrik, Aleksandr E. 1997. "Beyond subject and object: Toward a comprehensive relational typology". *LT* 1−3: 279−346.

Klimov, Georgij A. 1972/1974. "K xarakteristike jazykov aktivnogo stroja". *Voprosy jazykoznanija* 4: 3−13; engl. transl. "On the character of languages of active typology". *Linguistics* 131: 11−26.

Knobloch, Clemens. 1994. *Sprache und Sprachtätigkeit. Sprachpsychologische Konzepte.* (Konzepte der Sprach- und Literaturwissenschaft, 52.) Tübingen: Niemeyer.

Koch, Peter. 1981. *Verb − Valenz − Verfügung. Zur Satzsemantik und Valenz französischer Verben am Beispiel der Verfügungsverben.* Heidelberg: Winter.

Koptjevskaja-Tamm, Maria. 1993. *Nominalizations.* London & New York: Routledge.

Lazard, Gilbert. 1978. "Eléments d'une typologie des structures d'actances: structures ergatives, accusatives et autres". *Bulletin de la société linguistique de Paris* 73/1: 49−84.

Lazard, Gilbert. 1984. "Actance variations and categories of the object". In: Plank (ed.) 1985: 269−92.

Lazard, Gilbert. 1985. "Anti-impersonal verbs, transitivity-continuum and the notion of transitivity". In: Seiler & Brettschneider (eds.) 1985: 115−23.

Lazard, Gilbert 1994/98. *L'Actance.* (Linguistique Nouvelle.) Paris: Presses Universitaires de France. English Translation by David Wolton & Keith Gregor 1998. *Actancy.* (Empirical approaches to Language Typology, 19.) Berlin: Mouton de Gruyter.

Lehmann, Christian. 1982. "Nominalisierung: Typisierung von Propositionen". In: Seiler & Lehmann (eds.) 1982: 66−83.

Lehmann, Christian. 1991. "Predicate classes and participation". In: Seiler & Premper (eds.) 1991: 183−239.

Lehmann, Christian. 1994. Article "Predicates: Aspectual types". In: Asher & Simpson (eds.). Vol. 6: 3297−302.

Lehmann, Winfred P. (ed.). 1978. *Syntactic typology: Studies in the phenomenology of language.* Austin: University of Texas Press.

Li, Charles N. (ed.). 1976. *Subject and topic.* New York: Academic Press.

Lyons, John. 1968. *Introduction to theoretical linguistics.* Cambridge: Cambridge University Press.

Lyons, John (ed.). 1970. *New horizons in linguistics.* (Pelican books.) Harmondsworth: Penguin Books.

Lyons, John. 1977. *Semantics.* Cambridge: Cambridge University Press. (2 vols.).

Maienborn, Claudia. 1996. *Situation und Lokation. Die Bedeutung lokaler Adjunkte von Verbalprojektionen.* (Studien zur deutschen Grammatik, 53.) Tübingen: Stauffenburg.

Mallinson, Graham & Blake, Barry J. 1981. *Language Typology. Cross-Linguistic Studies in Syntax.* (North-Holland Linguistics Series, 46.) Amsterdam: North-Holland.

Maslov, Yuriy S. 1985. "An outline of contrastive aspectology". In: Maslov, Yuriy S. (ed.) 1985. *Contrastive studies in verbal aspect in Russian, English, French and German.* Translated and annotated by James Forsyth in collaboration with Josephine Forsyth. (Studies in Descriptive Linguistics, 14.) Heidelberg: Julius Groos, 1−44.

Mosel, Ulrike. 1991. "Towards a Typology of VALENCY". In: Seiler & Premper (eds.) 1991: 240−51.

Mugler, Alfred. 1988. *Tempus und Aspekt als Zeitbeziehungen.* (Studien zur Theoretischen Linguistik, 9.) München: Wilhelm Fink.

Myhill, John. 1992. *Typological discourse analysis: Quantitative approaches to the study of linguistic function.* Cambridge, MA: Blackwell.

Noonan, Michael. 1985. "Complementation". In: Shopen (ed.) 1985. Vol. II: 42−140.

Ono, Yoshiko. 1991. "The Function of the Japanese Passive". In: Seiler & Premper (eds.) 1991: 309−80.

Palmer, Frank R. 1994. *Grammatical roles and relations*. (Cambridge Textbooks in Linguistics) Cambridge: Cambridge University Press.

Plank, Frans (ed.). 1985. *Relational typology*. (Trends in Linguistics. Studies and monographs, 28.) Berlin: Mouton de Gruyter.

Plank, Frans. 1995. "Ergativity". In: Jacobs & al. (eds.) 1995: 1184−99.

Prechtl, Peter & Burkard, Franz-Peter (eds.). 1996. *Metzler Lexikon Philosophie. Begriffe und Definitionen*. Stuttgart: J.B. Metzler.

Primus, Beatrice. 1995. "Relational typology". In: Jacobs & al. (eds.) 1995: 1076−109.

Raible, Wolfgang. 1992. *Junktion. Eine Dimension der Sprache und ihre Realisierungsformen zwischen Aggregation und Integration*. Heidelberg: Carl Winter.

Ramsey, Frank Plumpton. 1925/90. "Universals". *Mind* 34: 401−17. Reprinted 1990 in: *Philosophical Papers*. Ed. by D. H. Mellor. Cambridge: Cambridge University Press, 8−30.

Rescher, Nicholas (ed.). 1967. *The logic of decision and action*. Pittsburgh: The University of Pittsburgh Press.

Ritter, Joachim & Gründer, Karlfried (eds.). 1971ff. *Historisches Wörterbuch der Philosophie*. Darmstadt: Wissenschaftliche Buchgesellschaft.

Rohs, Peter. 1979. "Transzendentalphilosophie oder sprachanalytische Bedeutungstheorie?". *Philosophisches Jahrbuch* 86: 16−41.

Rupp, Heinz. 1965. "Zum deutschen Verbalsystem". *Neuphilologische Mitteilungen* 66: 179−99.

Sapir, Edward. 1921. *Language: An introduction to the study of speech*. New York: Harcourt, Brace & Company.

Sasse, Hans-Jürgen. 1991. "Predication and sentence constitution in universal perspective". In: Zaefferer (ed.) 1991: 75−95.

Sasse, Hans-Jürgen. 1995. "Prominence typology". Jacobs & al. (eds.) 1995: 1065−75.

Schulze, Wolfgang. 1998. *Person, Klasse, Kongruenz − Fragmente einer Kategorialtypologie des einfachen Satzes in den ostkaukasischen Sprachen. Band 1: (in zwei Teilen): Die Grundlagen*. München/Newcastle: LINCOM Europa.

Searle, John Robert. 1969. *Speech acts: An essay in the philosophy of language*. Cambridge.

Seiler, Hansjakob & Brettschneider, Gunter (eds.). 1985. *Language invariants and mental operations*. (Language Universals Series, 5.) Tübingen: Narr.

Seiler, Hansjakob & Lehmann, Christian (eds.). 1982. *Apprehension. Das sprachliche Erfassen von Gegenständen. Teil I: Bereich und Ordnung der Phänomene*. (Language Universals Series (LUS), 1/I.) Tübingen: Narr.

Seiler, Hansjakob & Premper, Waldfried (eds.). 1991. *Partizipation. Das sprachliche Erfassen von Sachverhalten*. (Language Universals Series (LUS), 6.) Tübingen: Narr.

Seiler, Hansjakob. 1988. *The dimension of* PARTICIPATION. (= *Función*, 7.) Universidad de Guadalajara.

Serzisko, Fritz. 1991. "ORIENTIERUNG". In: Seiler & Premper (eds.) 1991: 273−308.

Shopen, Timothy (ed.). 1985. *Language Typology and Syntactic Description*. Vol. I: *Clause structure*. Vol. II: *Complex constructions*. Vol III. *Grammatical categories and the lexicon*. Cambridge: Cambridge University Press.

Smith, B. 1992. "Sachverhalt". In: Ritter & Gründer (eds.). Vol. 8: 1102−4.

Stassen, Leon. 1997. *Intransitive predication*. (Oxford Studies in Typology and Linguistic Theory.) Oxford: Clarendon Press.

Stechow, Arnim von. 1991. "Syntax und Semantik". In: Stechow & Wunderlich (eds.) 1991: 90−148.

Stechow, Arnim von & Wunderlich, Dieter (eds.). 1991. *Semantik / Semantics. Ein internationales Handbuch der zeitgenössischen Forschung. An International Handbook of Contemporary Research*. (Handbücher zur Sprach- und Kommunikationswissenschaft, 6) Berlin & New York: de Gruyter

Tesnière, Lucien. 1959. *Eléments de syntaxe structurale*. Paris: Klincksieck.

Thümmel, Wolf. 1993. "Der amerikanische Strukturalismus". In: Jacobs & al. (eds.) 1993: 280−97.

Tsunoda, Tasaku. 1985. "Remarks on transitivity". *Journal of Linguistics* 21: 385−96.

Tsunoda, Tasaku. 1994. Article "Transitivity". In: Asher & Simpson (eds.). Vol 9: 4670−77.

Tugendhat, Ernst. 1979. *Selbstbewußtsein und Selbstbestimmung. Sprachanalytische Interpretationen*. (stw, 221.) Frankfurt/M.: Suhrkamp.

Vater, Heinz. 1978. *Probleme der Verbvalenz*. (KLAGE 1.) Trier: L.A.U.T.

Vendler, Zeno. 1957. "Verbs and times". *The Philosophical Review* 66: 143−60.

Vendler, Zeno. 1972. *Res cogitans: An essay in rational psychology*. Ithaca. Cornell University Press.

Waßner, Ulrich Hermann. 1992. *'Proposition' als Grundbegriff der Linguistik oder Linguistische Apophantik*. Münster & Hamburg: Lit.

Whorf, Benjamin Lee. 1942. "Language, mind and reality". *The Theosophist* 63. Reprinted in Whorf, Benjamin Lee. 1956. *Language, thought, and reality. Selected writings of Benjamin Lee Whorf*, ed. by John B. Carroll. Cambridge/MA, 246−70.

Wittgenstein, Ludwig. (1921) 1960. *Tractatus logico-philosophicus*. Schriften Bd. 1. Frankfurt/M.: Suhrkamp.

Wunderlich, Dieter. 1993. "Diathesen (Valency changing)". In: Jacobs & al. (eds.) 1993: 730−47.

Wundt, Wilhelm. 1900. *Völkerpsychologie. Eine Untersuchung der Entwicklungsgesetze von Sprache, Mythus und Sitte. Erster Band: Die Sprache*. Leipzig: Wilhelm Engelmann.

Zaefferer, Dietmar (ed.). 1991. *Semantic universals and universal semantics*. Berlin: de Gruyter.

*Waldfried Premper,
University of Tübingen (Germany)*

38. Scales between nouniness and verbiness

1. The Non-Discreteness Hypothesis of parts of speech
2. Language-specific 'Category Squishes'
3. Crosslinguistic continua
4. Other possible types of continua
5. Proposals for explanations, problems and suggestions for future research
6. References

1. The Non-Discreteness Hypothesis of parts of speech

The hypothesis that word classes (parts of speech) differ by degree has long been discussed in the linguistic literature. In earlier works, considerations to this effect were usually made in relation to the observation that the traditional definition of word classes depends on a mixture of morphological, semantic, and syntactic criteria, which do not necessarily coincide in particular instances (cf. Lyons 1977: 423). Rather, what one finds is that the various distinguishing features heavily cumulate in certain cases, often referred to as the 'bona fide' nouns, adjectives, etc., but less so in others, which are considered border-line cases.

The result is that the well-known structuralist postulate that word classes must be characterized by "maximum homogeneity within the class" (cf. Gleason 1965: 130) is not always easy to attain when proceeding from a small set of categories such as the classical one. This is often compensated by the introduction of additional criteria. But the more criteria one introduces, the more classes and/or subclasses will be established, and the fuzzier the boundaries between the traditional larger "holistic" categories become (cf. Crystal 1967: 29—30).

Moreover, a major problem is often posed by hybrid categories (such as infinitives, gerunds, and participles), which combine features otherwise ranked very highly for their diacritic force (e.g. tense + case inflection, nominal inflection + verbal syntax, etc.) and cannot therefore be unambiguously assigned to a single category (cf. Jespersen 1924: 87 and many authors thereafter).

Such considerations have repeatedly led scholars to look upon word classes as prototypes. This idea sneaks in occasionally in early basically discreteness-oriented accounts of parts of speech such as Jespersen's, for instance when he says that the prime function of nouns and adjectives is to denote things and qualities respectively, but "we cannot, of course, expect to find any sharp or rigid line of demarcation separating the two classes" (1924: 81). Prototypicality is explicitly referred to several times in the contributions to the famous Lingua "Word Classes" volume (*Lingua* 17 (1967)), e.g. by David Crystal on ENGLISH (1967: 46; 'centrality of membership') and by Robert Henry Robins on YUROK (1967: 213; 'nuclear members' vs. 'marginal members').

It was not before the early seventies, however, that non-discrete theoretical conceptions such as hierarchies, continua, scales, squishes, fuzzy boundaries, gray areas, cardinal points, and prototypes began to enjoy wide acceptance as descriptive and explanatory tools in linguistics.

To our knowledge, John Robert Ross (1972, 1973) was the first to introduce the notion of 'category squish', elaborating on ideas advanced by George Lakoff (in Lakoff 1970), though the scalar analysis of categorial gradience phenomena (then called 'serial relationship') was predated by works of Randolph Quirk (1965) and Crystal (1967), and its invention is usually attributed to Dwight Bolinger (cf. Anderson 1974 for a brief reference to the earliest sources).

Ross argues that a number of syntactic phenomena speak in favor of the postulation of quasi-continua, instead of fixed, discrete inventories of "syntactic categories" in ENGLISH. For example, gradual differences in the applicability of a cluster of syntactic rules renders the traditional distinction between verbs, adjectives, and nouns in ENGLISH "squishy", with the intervention of at least the following intermediate stages:

(1)   Verb > Present participle > Perfect participle > Passive participle > Adjective > Preposition (?) > "adjectival noun" (e.g., fun, snap) > Noun

The three underlined categories verb, adjective, and noun are something like cardinal points within the hierarchy of (1). Adjectives are "between" verbs and nouns with respect to the applicability of certain syntactic processes. A number of these are shown to apply "mostly" to verbs, "less" to adjectives, and "least" to nouns. For example, "raising" applies more to verbs than to adjectives, as can be seen by comparing (2a) with (2b):

(2) a. We knew / showed / proved / believed / etc. Oliver to like walnuts.
    b. *I am afraid / ready / willing / etc. (of) Oliver to eat walnuts.

Raising is even less applicable for nouns than for the other categories. There are in fact only very few ENGLISH nouns that can undergo raising, such as *likelihood* and, marginally, *tendency* (Ross 1972: 322).

The intermediate stages constitute areas of transition between the cardinal points and are connected by "subsquishes" within the general squish. For example, there is a subsquish between adjectives and prepositions (*proud > opposite > near > like > in*) with respect to the three syntactic rules of "preposition deletion", "PP postponing", and "pied piping" (for details cf. Ross 1972: 319).

A general characteristic of all the nine features examined in Ross (1972) is that "all manifest the same 'funnel direction': nouns are more inert, syntactically, than adjectives and adjectives than verbs" (Ross 1972: 325; hence "Endstation Hauptwort").

The analysis of squishes follows a technique resembling the Guttman scalogram analysis (Guttman 1944), where members of a population are ordered along a continuum of minimal feature differences. In the ideal case, members may be ordered adjacent to each other by the difference of just one feature value. Supposing you have seven items (marked with integers from 1 to 7) and six features A, B, C, D, E, F, an idealized Guttman scale would look like this:

Table 38.1: Idealized Guttman scale

	A	B	C	D	E	F
1	+	+	+	+	+	+
2	+	+	+	+	+	−
3	+	+	+	+	−	−
4	+	+	+	−	−	−
5	+	+	−	−	−	−
6	+	−	−	−	−	−
7	−	−	−	−	−	−

We will demonstrate this technique in section 2 below by giving three examples of category squishes that have been proposed in the literature for three quite divergent languages: ENGLISH, MURRINH-PATHA (non-PAMA-NYUNGAN, Northern Australia), and CAYUGA (Northern IROQUOIAN, Canada). Further category squishes described in the literature include the contributions to the second chapter of Charles-James Bailey and Roger W. Shuy (1973), Lloyd B. Anderson (1974) (all of them on ENGLISH), Ulrike Mosel (1991, on SAMOAN) and Johanna Mattissen (1995, on JAPANESE); cf. also the earlier analyses of 'serial relationship' for ENGLISH in Quirk (1965) and (Crystal (1967).

For more general observations on squishy categories and language-specific prototype concepts of word classes see Plank (1984), Taylor (1995), and sections 3 and 4 below.

2. Language-specific 'Category Squishes'

2.1. The nouniness squish in English

For the various entities that may occupy argument positions in ENGLISH, Ross (1973) proposes a squish between embedded constituent sentences with finite verb forms and (simplex) nouns, called the "nouniness squish":

(3)   that > for to > Q > AccIng > PossIng > Action Nominal > Derived Nominal > Noun

The eight positions in (3) are abbreviations for the following types of complements:

(4) a. that = *that*−clauses (*that Max gave the letters to Frieda*)
    b. for to = *for* NP *to* V X (*for Max to have given the letters to Frieda*)
    c. Q = embedded questions (*how willingly Max gave the letters to Frieda*)

d. AccIng = [NP, +Acc] V+ing X (*Max giving the letters to Frieda*)
e. PossIng = NP's V+ing X (*Max's giving the letters to Frieda*)
f. Action Nominal (*Max's / the giving of the letters to Frieda*)
g. Derived Nominal (*Max's / the gift of the letters to Frieda*)
h. Noun (*letter*)

The degree of nouniness increases from left to right (or from (4a) to (4h)). *That*-clauses are lowest in nouniness, ordinary non-derived nouns are highest. Whilst applying to some point in the hierarchy, each rule also applies to all points lower than that.

Between strict ungrammaticality and full applicability there is usually a gray area where the application of the rule is not fully ungrammatical or may be grammatical in a few instances. Six degrees of grammaticality are distinguished between "splendid ungrammaticality" and "flawless grammaticality" (cf. table 38.2 below): **, *, ?*, ??, ?, OK.

Incidentally, a weak point in Ross's argumentation is the fact that the criteria for the gradation of semi-grammaticality (i. e. the difference between ?*, ?? and ?) are not explicitly stated.

It is not possible to reproduce the entire evidence for the squish here. To illustrate how it works we will confine ourselves to the following features – a selection of Ross's "noun-based phenomena" (1973: 186):

(a) The Island-Internal Sentential NP Constraint (well-formedness of surface structure islands of the form X [S]NP Y);
(b) NP Shift (acceptability of a complement's placement at the end of the sentence);
(c) NP's as Determiner (e.g. *Ed's [that he refused the offer] angered me*, etc.);
(d) Demonstrative as Determiner;
(e) *no / some / little / much* etc. as Determiners;
(f) *the / prior / occasional / frequent* etc. as Determiners;
(g) Plural Agreement with conjoined NPs;
(h) Possessivizability by -'s;
(i) *careful / reluctant / clever* etc. as Determiners;
(j) *other / mere* as Determiners;
(k) *good / bad* as Determiners;
(l) Pied Piping and the Sentential Subject Constraint ("Pied Piping" is Ross's term for syntactic phenomena in which rules which one might expect to affect a smaller constituent either can or must affect a larger one. E.g. in *How proud of you is Mr. Greenjeans?* the entire phrase *proud of you* is moved together with the wh-word.

The Sentential Subject Constraint runs as follows: if a part of a subject is chopped out of it by any rule, the grammaticality of the result will vary directly with the nouniness of the subject. Thus, OK *Of which cars do they figure that the hoods were damaged by the bomb?*, but *To which hoodlums do they think that having to send money was resented by the drivers?*, and ?**Of which kinds of facts do they think that Ted's collecting was amateurish?*)

In tabular form, the (partial) nouniness squish based on the above features looks like this.

There are several ill-behaved points on the scale. For example, columns (i) and (k) are ill-behaved in that there is no fuzziness vertically (i. e. no entity is between grammaticality and ungrammaticality).

Table 38.2: Partial "Nouniness" Squish in ENGLISH

	(a)	(b)	(c)	(d)	(e)	(f)	(g)	(h)	(i)	(j)	(k)	(l)
that S	*	*	*	*	*	*	*	**	*	*	*	*
for to	?*	*	*	*	*	*	*	*	*	*	*	*
Q	?	?*	*	*	*	*	*	*	*	*	*	*
AccIng	?	|??|†		OK ?	??	?*	?*	*	*	*	*	*
PossIng	OK	|?|	OK	OK ?	??	?*	|??|	?*	*	*	*	*
Act.Nom.	OK	OK	OK	OK	OK	OK	?	??	|OK|	??	|*|	?*
Der.Nom.	OK	OK	OK	OK	OK	OK	OK	OK	OK	|?|	OK	?
N	OK	OK	OK	OK	OK	OK	OK	OK	OK	OK	OK	OK

† Horizontally ill-behaved cells are enclosed in parallel vertical lines

2.2 Vouns and nerbs in Murrinh-Patha

Our next example is based on Michael Walsh (1996). In the Northern Australian language MURRINH-PATHA it is possible to set up a class of nouns and a class of verbs and to define these classes in terms of morphological co-occurrence. However, MURRINH-PATHA evidences word-types which do not readily fit into either of these major word-class categories. As in the ENGLISH squish proposed by Ross (1972), "adjectives" can be conceived of as an "intermediate" word type in that they pattern in some ways like nouns and in other ways like verbs. Moreover, there are two more intermediate categories, called "nerbs" and "vouns", which are between plain adjectives and verbs. Nerbs are to be thought of as more nouny and vouns as more verby. In terms of ontological membership, both of them basically denote qualities. Walsh's examples of nerbs cover meanings such as

The version given below is based on the following morphosyntactic criteria:

(a) compatibility with the "propriety suffix" -*ma* 'associated with X';
(b) case inflection;
(c) compatibility with nominal classifiers;
(d) cross-referencing object pronoun;
(e) body-part incorporation;
(f) number indicator;
(g) adverb incorporation;
(h) cross-referencing benefactive pronoun;
(i) tense-aspect-mood suffix;
(j) compatibility with the "primary auxiliary" (signaling subject, class membership, and some basic information about tense, aspect, and mood);
(k) other cross-referencing pronouns.

For reasons of space we will use +, −, and ± signs instead of the original YES, NO, and SOME.

Table 38.3: Adjective-Nerb-Voun Squish in MURRINH-PATHA

	(a)	(b)	(c)	(d)	(e)	(f)	(g)	(h)	(i)	(j)	(k)
Noun	+	+	+	±	±	±	−	−	−	−	−
Adj	+	+	+	+	+	+	−	−	−	−	−
Nerb	±	+	+	+	+	+	+	−	−	−	−
Voun	−	−	−	+	+	+	+	+	+	+†	−
Verb	−	−	−	+	+	+	+	+	+	+	+

† 3rd Singular Subject only.

'quick', 'robber', 'deaf', 'hunter', 'greedy', 'buried', 'sticky', while vouns include 'cramped', 'cruel', and 'crooked'.

For example, *mutmutthe* 'deaf' is a nerb: it patterns with nouns with respect to all the defining co-occurrence features of ordinary nouns but has several additional affixal possibilities akin to those of verbs. It may incorporate a body-part noun (*mutmut-Ø-ye* deaf-3sgØ-ear 'ear-deaf') and it may take a pronominal affix (*mutmut-ngi-ye* 'I'm deaf / inattentive to sound').

The squish is presented here in a strongly simplified version. Many of the original features are omitted since some of Walsh's intermediate categories (nominal classifiers, pronouns, impersonal verbs) are not taken into account; for more details the reader is referred to the original publication. Note that the original table looks much more "ill-behaved" than the simplified one presented here.

It emerges that vouns are very similar to verbs but differ from these by not taking cross-referencing pronominal affixes other than object and benefactive. Furthermore, they allow only 3rd person singular subject 'primary' auxiliaries. Nerbs pattern more like nouns, but are similar to verbs in that they may incorporate adverbs.

2.3. The morphological category squish in CAYUGA

The final example is a very simple morphological category squish in the Northern Iroquoian language CAYUGA adopted from Sasse (forthcoming).

The CAYUGA squish is based on the fact that there is − roughly speaking − no complementary morphology separating the different lexical categories of the language (this is less evident in some of the other Northern Iroquoian languages, though it stands to reason that it is the original historical situation). Instead, lexical categories differ in the 'gaps' they systematically have in relation to the maximum paradigm.

The squish could be extended (and made more complicated) by the addition of certain features that apply only to categories on the lower end of the continuum (i. e. two funnel directions could be assumed), but the partial squish presented below may suffice for the present purpose.

The lexical categories distinguished are the following:

(a) dynamic verbs such as -k- 'eat', -ya'k- 'cut', etc.;
(b) 'transitive' personal static verbs such as -yęti- 'know';
(c) 'intransitive' personal static verbs such as -kowanę- 'be big';
(d) impersonal static verbs such as -na'no- 'be cool'; to this class also belong conventionalized expressions denoting objects specified according to position, condition, etc.; these are called "extended reference forms" (ERF's) and are morphological compounds consisting of a nominal root + static verb form (e.g. ka'ahthraní:yǫ:t 'basket hanging', kanǫhsaté:kęh 'house burnt', etc.);
(e) some of the more fossilized types of ERF's, e.g. those specifying quantification (tekanǫhsá:ke: 'two houses');
(f) minimal reference forms (MRF's) of nominal roots such as kanǫ́hsa' 'house';
(g) 'uninflectives', i. e. simplex forms such as só:wa:s 'dog'.

The inflectional potential in which these categories differ is exemplified by the following categories:

(a) capability of taking 3rd person neuter pronominal prefixes;
(b) capability of taking prepronominal prefixes;
(c) capability of forming tense inflection;
(d) capability of taking non-neuter subject prefixes;
(e) capability of taking human subject + human object prefixes;
(f) capability of forming aspect stems other than the stative.

Below we present the squish in tabular form.

3. Crosslinguistic continua

3.1. Statistical approaches

Heribert Walter's monograph is one of the earliest attempts to exploit the category-squish concept for cross-linguistic comparison (Walter 1981). His study exemplifies a statistically oriented functional-typological approach which enjoyed a certain popularity in the seventies and eighties.

Walter's work rests on the theory of continua developed in the framework of Seiler's UNITYP model, where two funnel directions ("gradients") are usually assumed instead of one (cf. Seiler 1985). The scalar approach is carried out on different levels of analysis. From the language-specific point of view, scales are postulated which have nouns and verbs as prototypical cornerstones, connected by the two gradients of increasing nouniness / decreasing verbiness and decreasing nouniness / increasing verbiness.

According to this view, the intermediate categories such as the various types of participles in ENGLISH and other European languages not only differ in their increase in nominality as Ross suggests, but also gradually lose their verbal characteristics as one moves along toward the right-hand end of the continuum.

The turning point where the two gradients meet may be set up as a typological parameter, i. e. languages may differ in whether they

Table 38.4: Morphological Category Squish in CAYUGA

	(a)	(b)	(c)	(d)	(e)	(f)
dyn. verbs	+	+	+	+	+	+
'trans.' pers. stat. verbs	+	+	+	+	+	−
'intrans.' pers. stat. verbs	+	+	+	+	−	−
impers. stat. verbs and ERF's	+	+	+	−	−	−
some types of ERF's	+	+	−	−	−	−
MRF's	+	−	−	−	−	−
Uninflectives	−	−	−	−	−	−

statistically favor the left-hand or the right-hand side of the turning point (e.g. by having more noun-like or more verb-like categories).

From the general universal-typological perspective of the noun/verb distinction, Walter develops a theory of gradual partial indistinction of nouns and verbs across languages. While he assumes that there is no language that does not differentiate between nouns and verbs at all, nouns and verbs are never totally distinct either; rather, the differentiation is a matter of degree and thus typologically variable.

The typological variation may be calculated on the basis of phenomena such as the formal overlap between nominal and verbal morphology, the frequency of categorially ambivalent stems, etc., yielding individual "indistinction indexes" (I) and "distinction indexes" (D) for each language. Total indistinction is $D = 0/I = 1$, maximal distinction $D = 1/I = 0$. This is exemplified for the three languages GREENLANDIC, HUNGARIAN, and TURKISH. For the first parameter (overlap between nominal and verbal morphology) TURKISH scores $D = 0.73/I = 0.27$, HUNGARIAN $D = 0.62/I = 0.38$, GREENLANDIC $D = 0.3/I = 0.7$.

Although such a statistical approach would seem appealing at first sight since it appears to provide hard and testable criteria, its reliance on atomistic formal coincidences is hardly satisfactory. Partial formal coincidence is not in itself indicative; it is the total sum of formal properties that defines a given word class. The fact that four out of six personal endings of the past tense of the objective conjugation in HUNGARIAN are identical with the possessive affixes on nouns (Walter 1981: 58) is hardly any more significant than the fact that the 3rd person plural ending -*en* of German verbs formally coincides with one of the nominal plural suffixes (*sing-en* : *Lamp-en*).

What is important is the different paradigms in which these forms are located; the forms are thus homophonous, but paradigmatically (and thus semantically) distinct. In terms of the overall paradigm, HUNGARIAN has a splendid noun/verb distinction — nouns and verbs are entirely discrete in their overall morphological pattern. There is a substantial difference between this and the phenomenon observed for CAYUGA in 2.3, where the various categories largely all share the same morphology, but with different degrees of completeness.

3.2. Functionally based prototype approaches

The scalar approach is taken from quite a different angle in two influential studies by Paul Hopper and Sandra Thompson, which appeared in 1984 and 1985. The authors proceed from a functional discourse perspective, assuming that nouns and verbs can universally be taken as lexicalizations of the two fundamental discourse operations of (a) naming a discourse-manipulable participant (→ nouns), and (b) reporting an event (→ verbs). The first is akin to the notion of "discourse referent" (as developed over the years by Lauri Karttunen, cf. Behrens & Sasse forthcoming), while the second is related to what is now widely called the 'episodic' use of verbs in that it pertains to dynamic situations in a narrative chain usually conveyed in the affirmative 'factual' modality.

It is assumed that "the grammars of languages tend to label the categories N and V with morpho-syntactic markers which are iconically characteristic of these categories to the degree that a given instance of N or V approaches its prototypical function" (Hopper & Thompson 1984: 703). This means that the closer a form is to signalizing its prime function, the more category-specific morpho-syntactic indicators it will have.

In other words, the goodness of categorial membership is proportional to the form's indicating the discourse functions postulated as prototypes. For example, nouns are 'best members' when occurring with markers of definiteness, case markers indicating central grammatical relations, number distinctions, etc. because it is assumed that these grammatical markers are associated with their prototypical functions.

The more a noun deviates from the prototypical contexts for which it is said to be designed, the poorer it will be with respect to these markers. The morphosyntactic versatility of nouns is often severely impoverished in peripheral grammatical relations, in the predicate position, and in the scope of negation and other non-factual modalities.

The same is said of verbs, which unfold their entire range of tense, aspect, etc. categories only in episodic contexts, while gradually losing their verbal characteristics in other contexts to the extent that these contexts deviate from the prototype.

The ontological aspect related to this view is that forms denoting first-order entities in the sense of John Lyons (1977: 442) are the best candidates for prototypical nouns and forms denoting dynamic processes the best candidates for prototypical verbs.

Hopper and Thompson conclude by suggesting that "linguistic forms are in principle to be considered as lacking categoriality completely unless nounhood or verbhood is forced on them by their discourse functions" (Hopper & Thompson 1984: 747). This enforcement is said to be scalar: it results in continua which "in principle begin with acategoriality, and which end with fully implemented nounhood or fully implemented verbhood" (ibid.).

There have been a number of studies written in a similar spirit, though with slightly different interpretations of the 'scalar' effects in each case (Givón 1984: 51 ff., Broschart 1987, 1991, Thompson 1988, Pustet 1989, Bhat 1994, etc.). All of them tend to leave two fundamental problems open.

First, the formal behavior of a category in a specific language — a product of the language's individual history — cannot be immediately correlated with "universal functions". The question that follows from this is where the functional force that allegedly shapes grammars into what they are is to be located. A simple statement to the effect that grammar "somehow emerges" out of communication or "fulfills functional needs" would not appear to provide a satisfying answer. For example, it is hard to see in what sense linguistic forms "lack categoriality" — as if there were something like primordial language made up of acategorial forms and then comes discourse and moulds them into good and bad exemplars of nouns and verbs depending on the position in the utterance.

Second, it is not immediately convincing that the functional prototypes underlying the explanations are the correct ones or the only possible ones. For example, languages possess all kinds of grammatical machinery to signalize indefinite, generic, predicative, and non-referential uses of nouns, so that the definite, topical, discourse-referent-indicating noun appears to be only one of several modes of appearance nouns typically take on. It is an empirical fact that nouns (taken as 'lexemes') are on principle neutral with respect to referentiality and predicativity, receiving these values on the level of the actual utterance, so that there is no a priori reason to assume that discourse-referentiality is their prime function.

Playing the devil's advocate, one could say that both formal semanticists and markedness theoreticians would probably be equally happy with the assumption that the predicate noun is the prototypical noun, in that in their view nouns basically denote 'intensional' concepts and are conceived of as predicates, and in that their referential function is often specifically marked. For more on "explanations" cf. section 5 below.

3.3. Nouniness and verbiness in view of the adjective problem

Proceeding from the classical studies by Robert W. M. Dixon (1977), Anna Wierzbicka (1986), and others, many authors have found adjectives a particularly weak category within and across languages. It has long been commonplace that many languages do not have adjectives in any sense familiar from European languages, but use noun or verb forms to express the concepts we usually express by our adjectives.

In the given context, it is interesting to note that most of the squishes proposed so far appear to have adjective-related categories somewhere in the middle: Ross (1972) with adjectives and Ross (1973) with participles as intermediate cardinal points; Walsh (1996) with adjectives, nerbs, and vouns (all of them denoting several subtypes of qualities, including human propensities, dimensions, colors, etc.) as transitional categories, etc.

It is therefore not surprising that much recent work on the fuzzy character of major word classes has centered around adjectives (Givón 1984, Thompson 1988, Pustet 1989, Bhat 1994, Wetzer 1992, 1995, 1996).

Before we proceed, it is necessary to clarify what the different authors understand by 'adjectives' or 'adjectivals'. Most of the typologists working on adjectives explicitly state that they proceed from a semantic type usually called 'property concepts' (or, more vaguely, 'adjectival meanings'). This includes Dixon's seven types of dimension, color, age, value, physical property, speed, and human propensity, of which age, dimension, and value are usually said to be the prototypical ones.

The authors are usually less concerned with the question of whether or not a category of 'adjectives' can be established by hard formal (morphosyntactic) criteria in a given language (a notable exception is Bhat 1994, but Wetzer 1996 explicitly rejects the possibility of clear definitional criteria for "adjective-hood"). Thus, most recent comparative work on 'adjectives' in actual fact pertains to the question of how the above-mentioned semantic types are expressed across languages.

Wetzer's (1992, 1995, 1996) studies are confined to the expression of "protoypical property concepts" (i. e. age, dimension, value) in the predicate position, which he calls 'predicate adjectivals'. On the basis of a sample of 115 languages and against the background of the continuum hypothesis, he shows that 'predicate adjectivals' tend to fall into two major categories, viz. 'verby' and 'nouny' adjectivals. This is not equivalent to saying that some adjectivals are expressed by verbs and others by nouns, an interpretation that Wetzer explicitly rejects as a basis for classification. Rather, it means that predicate adjectivals can be distinguished as to whether they tend toward the nominal or the verbal end of the continuum with respect to certain morphosyntactic criteria.

Wetzer comes up with a classification of languages into four types. Most of them are either "nouny" or "verby languages", in which all prototypical adjectivals are either nouny or verby. In addition, there are also languages which cannot readily be classified in terms of this dichotomy. There are "mixed languages" which have both nouny and verby adjectivals. These can be divided into two subtypes, viz. "split-adjective languages" (where a split is found so that adjectivals are distributed across different lexical categories), and "switch-adjective languages" (where adjectivals are "categorially ambivalent", i. e. may be both verby and nouny). The fourth group comprises languages in which no clear morphosyntactic distinction can be made between nominal and intransitive verbal predicates, with the result that adjectivals cannot be assigned to one or the other.

Finally, Wetzer finds a somewhat puzzling correlation between the nouny/verby split and what he calls "tensedness": nouny encoding of predicate adjectivals tends to go together with tense-marking on verbs, while verby encoding of predicate adjectivals tends to go together with lack of tense-marking on verbs.

Wetzer's approach has been criticized by Bhat (1994) for not taking attributed adjectives into account. This is in fact surprising since traditional lore has it that the proposi-tional act of attribution/modification is the main functional *raison d'être* of adjectives (cf., inter alia, Croft 1991, Sasse 1993). According to Thompson (1988), adjectives are prototypically characterized by their multiple function as referential, attributive, and predicative elements. Bolinger (1967) makes the interesting point that attributive and predicative adjectives are not the same because the latter have a certain time spread whilst the former do not. In any event, the role of adjectives or adjective-like categories in category squishes cannot be properly understood by restricting the investigation to predicative adjectives.

In the present context it is interesting to speculate on the nature of the "squishy" effects that have been observed between nouns and adjectives on the one hand, and between verbs and adjectives on the other. Several authors have pointed to the fact that the notorious linguistic problems of categorization of lexical elements as 'adjectives' or 'nouns' is due to the fact that from a notional perspective, it is very difficult to distinguish between 'properties' and 'objects' (Miller 1985, Behrens 1995). Leila Behrens has pointed out that in ENGLISH, and even more so in HUNGARIAN, there is a great deal of syntactic overlapping between nouns and adjectives, especially due to the fact that both of them share the ability to occur in the prenominal attributive position. Moreover, dictionaries of both languages favor a double categorization (noun + adjective) in particular semantic fields, e.g. age, nationality, human propensities, and materials (Behrens 1995: 21–26).

One may add: similar problems arise with respect to the distinction between 'properties' and 'situations'. Properties may be conceived of as situations and the more they are subject to change the more they may pattern with other change-of-state situations.

This will probably suffice to explain the language-specific differences in subcategorization referred to in the first paragraph of this section. "Property" concepts are most versatile with respect to conventional imagery and perspective; both the boundary between 'objects' and 'properties', and the boundary between 'properties' and 'situations' are fuzzy. It does not come as a surprise, then, that lexical elements denoting 'property' concepts are cross-linguistically rather evenly distributed across lexical categories, that they share morphosyntactic features once with nouns, once with verbs, that their tendency to behave "nounily" or "verbily" is associated with the semantic fields in which they are allocated, and that languages may even have such things as kinship verbs (Evans 1999), human propensity verbs (Sasse forthcoming), and the like.

Several typological parameters emerge out of these findings, which may be established complementarily to Wetzer's. For example, it may be worth investigating HOW nouny or verby adjectives are in a particular language. Leila Behrens (1995) has drawn attention to the importance of investigating the noun/adjective problem in the context of lexical-categorial ambiguity. In an interesting study, Moskovitch (1977) found out that in HUNGARIAN, the most frequent type of lexical-categorial ambiguity is the noun/adjective ambiguity, whereas in ENGLISH this comes second after the noun/verb ambiguity.

Differences like these may well constitute a typological parameter. In general, the correlation between semantic fields such as 'materials', 'human propensities', etc., and the lexicogrammatical categories with which the corresponding expressions are associated is a matter of language-specific lexicalization patterns which may be subject to typological research. In this sense the continuum concept could prove a useful tool of investigation with respect to gradual differences in the semantic fields covered by the various categories and their ambiguity potential.

4. Other possible types of continua

There is still another sense in which the notions of 'nouniness' and 'verbiness' may be and have been interpreted: as a typological feature of languages referring to the basic morphological structure of their content words. In earlier accounts of non-Indoeuropean languages one often encounters statements to the effect that a certain language "has only nouns" (e.g. Finck 1910 and Winkler 1921 for TURKISH, Hammerich 1936 and Mey 1970 for GREENLANDIC, Scheerer 1924 and Capell 1964 for TAGALOG) or "has only verbs" (Lafitau 1724 for IROQUOIAN).

While such an interpretation is certainly inadequate in its strong form, it is true that the phenomena these authors have in mind, namely that verbs in some languages look more like Indoeuropean nouns and vice versa, are fundamental typological traits worthy of investigation. They are the result of certain diachronic processes which may in fact lead to the leveling of the distinctive features that we perceive as characteristic of the nominal or verbal make-up of content words.

In a number of cases where languages are attested over a long period of time it is possible to ascertain the mechanisms by which systems of major lexical categories are radically restructured, and the observations made in this context throw some light on the historical origin of these phenomena (cf. Sasse 1993 on EASTERN ARAMAIC, Claudi & Mendel 1991 on EGYPTIAN and MANDE).

For example, it was found that languages do not seldom replace finite verb forms with participles or with verbal nouns in the course of their historical development. As a result, they may pass a stage where the former participles or verbal abstracts, now the only morphological forms of "verbs", do not very much differ from the inherited nouns both in their distributional potential and as far as gender, number, case, etc. distinctions are concerned.

Unfortunately, phenomena of gradual reduction and gradual building-up of major lexical categories through time have not so far been given sufficient attention in modern linguistics and detailed studies are therefore rare, even though these historical events may play a key-role in the understanding of the possible systems of lexical categories in language. They show that the same basic semantics (e.g. an 'action'), may be perceived in a variety of ways (as an 'object', a 'property', or a 'situation'), and that the possible options of doing so may considerably change over time, resulting in marked differences in conventional imagery.

A different, though related type of parameter, also leading to the postulation of a typological continuum across languages with respect to differences in lexicalization patterns, may be sought in the number of primitive (basic, non-derived) members in each category. It is commonly upheld that nouns and verbs are always open classes (e.g. Robins 1967: 211). This is certainly not the case, at least not as far as their inventories of primitive members are concerned. The inexhaustible number of simplex noun and verb stems found in certain Romance and Germanic languages is probably an atypical phenomenon, chiefly brought about by the enormous amount of borrowing characteristic of the evolution of the European national languages during the past two millennia.

By contrast, some IROQUOIAN languages have a fairly small number of basic nominal roots, which is not enlarged by borrowing; most lexical enrichment in the nominal domain being achieved by "word sentences" of the type "it flies habitually" (= 'aeroplane') or "one sits on it" (= 'chair').

Languages in two geographical areas have become famous for their small inventories of basic verbs: Papua-New Guinea (cf. Foley 1986: 110ff.) and Northern Australia (cf. Schultze-Berndt forthcoming). In the Papuan language KALAM, there are less than 100 verb stems and of these only about 25 are commonly used. Complex verbal semantics is usually conveyed by the serialization of several of these verbs, in that the complex situation is broken down into its constituent sub-situations and each one expressed by a separate verb (e.g. "go-wood-hit-hold-come-put" = 'fetch firewood'). Some of these verbs may also function as "light verbs" combined with common nouns to yield more specific meanings ("eye-perceive" = 'see', "ear-perceive" = 'hear', "thought-perceive" = 'think', etc.).

The "light verb" strategy is even more prominent in some forty languages of Northern Australia, which form a clear linguistic area with respect to this phenomenon. An extreme dearth of inflected verbs is reported for most of these languages, ranging from several hundred to six. An average case is JAMINJUNG, which has around 30, most of them having fairly general meanings such as 'have', 'fall', 'go', 'take', 'hit', 'throw', etc. More specific verbal meanings are expressed by the combination of these verbs with preverbal elements called 'coverbs'. These come from a variety of sources (nouns, adverbials, ideophones, etc., including borrowed items) and form a distinct category of their own.

The impact of cases like these for our understanding of the typology of lexical categorization has not been investigated exhaustively. In particular, much more research must be carried out on questions of semantic compositionality, conventionalization, and productivity (cf. Pawley 1986). The basic question is: what is 'a verb' in these languages? One of the members of the closed class of tense-aspect-mood-person-inflecting lexical units? Or the entire multi-word string associated with a complex semantic unit (a 'unitary concept')?

Incidentally, there is evidence that systems of this kind occasionally represent intermediate stages between a phase of reduction (toward a smaller inventory of verb stems, eventually ending up as a closed set of "light verbs") and the creation of a new morphologically rich verb system (by means of the grammaticalization of component parts of the multi-word string into affix positions, as in several of the Papuan languages).

5. Proposals for explanations, problems and suggestions for future research

In the previous sections, we have already foreshadowed several of the explanations usually offered in the literature for the various types of continua found in the domain of the major word classes. The explanations vary with the explanatory goals and with the perspective in which the squishy phenomena are investigated (language-specific or typological, grammar-oriented or discourse-oriented, etc.).

The following list of proposals is perhaps representative:

(1) There is a gradation of grammatical (morphological, syntactic) versatility from nouns as the most inert category through dynamic verbs as the most versatile one.
(2) There is a gradation of inherent relationality from lexical items denoting objects through lexical items denoting dynamic situations involving active participants. This is manifested in the argument-taking properties of different lexical categories and subcategories.
(3) There is a gradation of time-stability between lexical items denoting more time-stable entities (encoded as nouns) and less time-stable situations (encoded as verbs).
(4) Nouns and verbs encode prototypical discourse functions. There are several types of deviations from these prototypes, which manifest themselves in grammar, motivated by non-prototypical positions in the utterance.
(5) Nouns and verbs encode prototypical clusterings of semantic types and grammatical functions, motivated by the innate cognitive make-up of the human being. These result in natural 'markedness' phenomena. There are several types of deviation from these prototypes, including underdifferentiation, due to language-specific conditions.

(6) The degree of the differentiation of major lexical categories is a matter of a language's refinement or 'optimality': from more "primitive" languages to more "elaborate" ones.
(7) The distinction between the ontological categories 'objects', 'properties', and 'situations', which are assumed to constitute the semantic types underlying the formal word class distinctions, is in itself fuzzy in the sense that it allows for different perspectives producing Janus-faced entities (something that may be construed in different ways, e.g. either as an 'object', or as a 'property'). This explains both the fuzzy boundaries between language-specific formal categories and the different types of categorization across languages.
(8) The gradient character of linguistic categories is an effect of complex mapping relationships between grammar and different dimensions of meaning ('semantic maps').

None of these proposals have gained great acceptance as the sole explanation for the facts. One may speculate that the reason for this resides in the possibility that there are several converging factors rather than only one.

No. 1 is a purely form-oriented statement, usually given by authors concerned with language-specific squishes (e.g. Ross). It is not to be regarded as an "explanation" in the proper sense, unless it is coupled with some idea about the "reason" for the degrees of formal versatility observed.

If one does not want to resort to the idea that the reason might simply be found in the properties of some "innate universal grammar", no. 1 has to be coupled with at least one of the other concepts. The most popular one is no. 3 (time-stability), originally propagated by Givón (1979: 320f. and subsequent publications) and since echoed by most of the authors cited in the preceding sections. However, critical voices have not been lacking. The time-stability concept has been reproached by Hopper & Thompson with being too hard to apply in practice: "Many V's denote highly stable situations, e.g. 'to tower'; however ... N's may denote temporary situations ('fire', 'fist') or entities which may not be perceived directly (abstractions such as 'justice')" (Hopper & Thompson 1984: 705–6).

It has also been pointed out by Thompson (1988) and Wetzer (1996, esp. 292ff.) that prototypical adjectivals denote fairly stable concepts, so that their intermediate position would not be justified on the assumption of a time-stability criterion. But if operationalizability is the issue here, no. 4, which is essentially Hopper & Thompson's criterion, does not do any better (cf. the critique in section 3 above).

Explanation no. 2 sounds plausible, but is contradicted by the actual linguistic evidence: an action nominal may be a formal noun and yet be linked to a considerable number of arguments, whereas an intransitive verb may have only one argument and yet look very "verby". We may probably disregard the glottogonic approach of no. 6, occasionally proposed in earlier literature, but also as recently as in Wald (1971).

This leaves us with those proposals which aim at correlations between semantic and grammatical properties of linguistic entities: the 'prototypical clustering' concept of no. 5, which is essentially manifested in Croft's (1991) approach (cf. also Broschart 1991 for a related 'markedness' concept), the "Janus-face" concept alluded to in sections 3 and 4 (no. 7), which – at least in part – can be traced back to Jespersen (1924), and the 'multidimensional mapping' concept, originally due to Anderson (1974).

The problem with the 'prototypical clustering' concept is that it runs into trouble with languages that do not conform to the European pattern since this is modeled on the classical correlations of objects = referential entities = nouns, properties = attributive entities = adjectives, situations = predicative entities = verbs, correlations whose 'prototypicality' is questionable even for well-known European languages and which have simply been generalized from the works of the Alexandrian grammarians (cf. Sasse 1993a). All of the scalar concepts proposed so far proceed from these three cardinal points. In other words, the universal EXISTENCE of nouns, verbs, and to a lesser extent, adjectives as grammatical categories has never been called into question, it is only their degree of differentiation and discreteness that is the subject of investigation in continuum approaches to word classes.

Two questions thus remain open. First, it is doubtful whether the entire phenomenology of major word classes within and across languages can be adequately treated in terms of continua. We have already seen that squishes may be "ill-behaved" at certain points. In MURRINH-PATHA, the intermediate categories, which were left out for expository purposes in section 2.2, display a considerable number of ill-behaved points. In CAYUGA there is one category which stands totally outside the squish presented in 2.3 (or constitutes part of a different squish, as it were), viz. static verbs denoting animates (kinship verbs, etc.). This means that partial squishes often look quite convincing, but as soon as the entire range of possible criteria is taken into account they tend to become messy.

Second, what to do with languages with an entirely different 'system architecture' such as some of the Polynesian languages (Broschart 1997), some of the Philippine languages (Himmelmann 1991), and some of the polysynthetic languages of North America (see references in Sasse 1993), where a great deal of mismatching between the components usually assumed to form prototypical clusters is found? Note that the CAYUGA squish presented in 2.3 is not in actual fact a scale between nouns and verbs but between the language-specific categories of 'uninflectives' and "tense-aspect-mood-person-inflected lexical entities".

One could of course maintain that the former are the prototypical nouns and the latter the prototypical verbs. It is doubtful, however, whether such an interpretation really pinpoints the typological character of this language (cf. Sasse 1993a). What is immediately striking here is that there is an astonishing amount of mismatches between the larger ontological categories (objects, properties, situations) and the formal categories.

Moreover, morphology and syntax do not match either, which has led Iroquoianists to distinguish between syntactic nouns, morphological nouns, etc. There is no harm in doing this, but it must be clear that it is tantamount to admitting that such a language does not conform to the theory of universal prototypes. The discussion of the noun/verb distinction has predominantly centered around the question of word classes being more or less distinct; the possibility of 'otherness' is seldom taken into account.

Proposal no. 7 has the advantage of providing a rational basis for the treatment of both continuous and non-continuous phenomena, of both ambiguities and differences in formal marking, and of both languages with similar and languages with different 'system architectures'. However, there is one additional proviso: it is necessary to develop a complete decomposition of the various semantic and grammatical dimensions relevant in the respective domains, factorizing them into different independent parameters and allowing for different types of mapping and different types of 'lexicalization patterns' in the sense of Talmy (1985). This is in fact what proposal no. 8 (Anderson's solution) suggests. For further details on what such a multidimensioal approach could look like, the reader is referred to Sasse (1993a), Behrens (1995), and Behrens & Sasse (forthcoming).

At least three separate components of analysis should be distinguished and mapped onto each other:

(1) the semantic organization of vocabulary on different hierarchical levels, from the most basic ontological categories (such as 'objects', 'qualities', situations") to the finer semantic fields (such as 'food', 'materials', 'human propensities', etc.);
(2) the lexicogrammatical 'domains' in which grammaticalization has been commonly observed, i. e. important distinctions which are relevant for the constitution of grammatical categories since they are frequently conventionalized, be it by morphological marking, syntactic rules, or systematic ambiguity (cf. Talmy 1985);
(3) the lexical and grammatical categories established language-specifically on formal grounds. A specific mapping relationship between these components constitutes what we might call a 'lexicogrammatical type' (reflecting a certain lexicalization-cum-grammaticalization pattern).

If one looks upon language from this perspective, fuzziness comes as no surprise: it is the complex relationship between these different strands, including the fact that a limited number of conventionalized grammatical categories is available to express a multitude of semantic concepts, that is the ultimate source of the phenomena that we perceive as gradient both within and across languages.

Other factors may join in, such as the competition of different patterns of analogy, the coexistence of archaic and innovative material, etc.

The idea of decomposition is not absent from traditional approaches to word classes, and more recently John Lyons, William Croft, Ronald Langacker, and others have explicitly proposed parameters for decomposition. Nevertheless, the idea of the universal validity of at least 'prototypical' holistic categories is not at the same time abandoned. However, it has largely been overlooked that this rests on a bias rooted in the linguistic tradition, which leads linguists to take for granted that there must be prototypical form-meaning correlations which serve as cornerstones even if everything in between is squishy. Whether or not "nouniness" and "verbiness" in the sense usually understood are really universal cognitive entities has yet to be shown. As also noted in the recent pogrammatic sketch by Anward, Moravcsik & Stassen (1997), this remains one of the most fundamental open questions in word class research.

6. References

Anderson, Lloyd B. 1974. "Distinct Sources of Fuzzy Data: Ways of Integrating Relatively Discrete and Gradient Aspects of Language, and Explaining Grammar on the Basis of Semantic Fields". In: Shuy, Roger W. & Bailey, Charles-James N. (eds.). *Towards Tomorrow's Linguistics*. Washington, D.C., 50–64.

Anward, Jan & Moravcsik, Edith & Stassen, Leon. 1997. "Parts of Speech: A Challenge for Typology". *Linguistic Typology* 1-2: 167–83.

Bailey, Charles-James N. & Shuy, Roger W. (eds.). 1973. *New Ways of Analyzing Variation in English*. Washington, D.C.: Georgetown University Press.

Behrens, Leila. 1995. "Categorizing Between Lexicon and Grammar". *Lexicology* 1: 1–112.

Behrens, Leila & Sasse, Hans-Jürgen. 1999. *Qualities, Objects, Sorts, and Other Treasures: GOLD-digging in English and Arabic*. Arbeitspapier Nr. 35 (NF). Köln: Institut für Sprachwissenschaft.

Bhat, Durbhe Narayana Shankara. 1994. *The Adjectival Category. Criteria for Differentiation and Identification*. (Studies in Language Companion Series, 24.) Amsterdam & Philadelphia: Benjamins.

Bolinger, Dwight. 1967. "Adjectives in English: Attribution and Predication". *Lingua* 18: 1–34.

Broschart, Jürgen. 1987. *Noun, Verb, and PARTICIPATION*. (akup, 67.) Köln: Institut für Sprachwissenschaft.

Broschart, Jürgen. 1991. "Noun, Verb, and Participation (A Typology of the Noun/Verb-Distinction)". In: Seiler, Hansjakob & Premper, Waldfried (eds.). *Partizipation. Das sprachliche Erfassen von Sachverhalten*. Tübingen, 65–137.

Broschart, Jürgen. 1997. "Why Tongan Does it Differently: Categorial Distinctions in a Language without Nouns and Verbs". *Linguistic Typology* 1-2: 123–65.

Capell, Arthur. 1964. "Verbal Syntax in Philippine Languages". *Philippine Journal of Science* 93: 231–49.

Claudi, Ulrike & Mendel, Daniela. 1991. "Noun/Verb Distinction in Egyptian-Coptic and Mande: A Grammaticalization Perspective". In: Mendel, Daniela & Claudi, Ulrike (eds.). *Ägypten im afro-orientalischen Kotext. Gedenkschrift Peter Behrens* (Afrikanistische Arbeitspapiere, Sondernummer 1991.) Köln, 31–53.

Croft, William. 1991. *Syntactic Categories and Grammatical Relations. The cognitive organization of information*. Chicago: University of Chicago Press.

Crystal, David. 1967. "English". *Lingua* 17: 24–56.

Dixon, Robert M.W. 1977. "Where Have All the Adjectives Gone?" *Studies in Language* 1: 19–80. [Reprinted as Dixon, Robert M.W. 1982. *Where Have All the Adjectives Gone?*. Berlin].

Evans, Nicholas. 1999. "Kinship Verbs". To appear in Comrie, Bernard & Vogel, Petra (eds.). *Anthology of Word Classes*. Berlin: Mouton-de Gruyter.

Finck, Franz Nikolaus. 1910. *Die Haupttypen des Sprachbaus*. (Aus Natur und Geisteswelt, 268.) Leipzig & Berlin: Teubner.

Foley, William A. 1986. *The Papuan Languages of New Guinea*. (Cambridge language surveys.) Cambridge: Cambridge University Press.

Givón, Talmy (Tom). 1979. *On Understanding Grammar*. (Perspectives in neurolinguistics and psycholinguistics.) New York: Academic Press.

Givón, Talmy (Tom). 1984. *Syntax. A Functional-Typological Introduction*, vol. 1. Amsterdam & Philadelphia: Benjamins.

Gleason, Henry A. 1965. *Linguistics and English Grammar*. New York: Holt, Rinehart and Winston.

Guttman, Louis. 1944. "A Basis for Scaling Qualitative Data". *American Sociological Review* 9: 139–50.

Hammerich, L. L. 1936. *Personalendungen und Verbalsystem im Eskimoischen*. (Det Kgl. Danske Videnskabernes Selskab, Historisk-filologiske Meddelelser, 23.2.) Copenhagen.

Himmelmann, Nikolaus. 1991. *The Philippine Challenge to Universal Grammar*. Arbeitspapiere des Instituts für Sprachwissenschaft der Universität zu Köln, NF 15.

Hopper, Paul J. & Thompson, Sandra A. 1984. "The Discourse Basis for Lexical Categories in Universal Grammar". *Language* 60: 703–52.

Hopper, Paul J. & Thompson, Sandra A. 1985. "The Iconicity of the Universal Categories 'Noun' and 'Verb'". In Haiman, John (ed.). *Iconicity in Syntax*. (Typological studies in language, 6.) Amsterdam & Philadelphia: Benjamins, 151–86.

Jespersen, Otto. 1924. *The Philosophy of Grammar*. London: George Allen & Unwin.

Karttunen, Lauri. 1976. "Discourse Referents". In: McMawley, James D. (ed.). *Notes from the Linguis-*

tic Underground. (Syntax and Semantics, 7.) New York: Academic Press, 363−85.

Lafitau, Joseph-François. 1724. *Mœurs des sauvages ameriquains, comparées aux mœurs des premiers temps.* Paris.

Lakoff, George. 1970. *Irregularity in Syntax.* (Transatlantic series in linguistics.) New York: Holt, Rinehart & Winston.

Langacker, Ronald W. 1987. "Nouns and Verbs". *Language* 63: 53−94.

Lyons, John. 1977. *Semantics.* Volume 2. Cambridge: Cambridge University Press.

Mattissen, Johanna. 1995. *Das Nomen im Japanischen. Abgrenzung und Subklassifizierung.* Theorie des Lexikons: Arbeiten des Sonderforschungsbereichs 282, Nr. 65. Düsseldorf: Heinrich Heine Universität.

Mey, J. 1970. "Possessive and Transitive in Eskimo". *Journal of Linguistics* 6: 57−80.

Miller, Jim E. 1985. *Semantics and Sytax: Parallels and Connections.* (Cambridge studies in linguistics, 41.) Cambridge: Cambridge University Press.

Mosel, Ulrike. 1991. "The Continuum of Verbal and Nominal Clauses in Samoan". In: Seiler, Hansjakob & Premper, Waldfried (eds.). *Partizipation. Das sprachliche Erfassen von Sachverhalten.* (Language universals series, 6.) Tübingen: Narr, 138−49.

Moskovitch, W.A. 1977. "Polysemy in Natural and Artificial (Palnned [sic!]) Languages". In: *Statistical Methods in Linguistics* 1: 5−28.

Pawley, Andrew. 1986. "Lexicalization". In: Tannen, Deborah & Alatis, James E. (eds.). *Languages and linguistics. The Interdependence of Theory, Data, and Application.* (Georgetown Round Table in Languages and Linguistics 1985.) Washington, D.C.: Georgetown University Press, 98−120.

Plank, Frans. 1984. "24 grundsätzliche Bemerkungen zur Wortarten-Frage". *Leuvense Bijdragen* 73: 489−520.

Pustet, Regina. 1989. *Die Morphosyntax des 'Adjektivs' im Sprachvergleich.* (Continuum, 7.) Frankfurt am Main: Lang.

Quirk, Randolph. 1965. "Descriptive Statement and Serial Relationship". *Language* 41: 205−17.

Robins, R. H. 1967. "Yurok". *Lingua* 17: 210−29.

Ross, John Robert. 1972. "The Category Squish: Endstation Hauptwort". *Chicago Linguistic Society* 8: 316−28.

Ross, John Robert. 1973. "Nouniness". In: Fujimura, Osamu (ed.). *Three Dimensions of Linguistic Theory.* Tokyo: TEC, 137−257.

Sasse, Hans-Jürgen. 1993. "Syntactic Categories and Subcategories". In: Jacobs, Joachim & von Stechow, Arnim & Sternefeld, Wolfgang & Vennemann, Theo (eds.). *Syntax. An International Handbook of Contemporary Research.* Berlin: de Gruyter, 646−86.

Sasse, Hans-Jürgen. 1993a. "Das Nomen − eine universale Kategorie?" *Sprachtypologie und Universalienforschung* 46: 187−221.

Sasse, Hans-Jürgen. Forthcoming. *Cayuga.* (Languages of the World/Materials, 182.) München: LINCOM Europa.

Scheerer, Otto. 1924. "On the Essential Difference Between the Verbs of the European and the Philippine Languages". *Philippine Journal of Education* 7: 1−10.

Schultze-Berndt, Eva. Forthcoming. *Simple and Complex Verbs in Jaminjung. An investigation of event categorization by generic verbs in an Australian language.* Diss. University of Nijmegen.

Seiler, Hansjakob. 1985. "Linguistic Continua, Their Properties, and Their Interpretation". In: Seiler, Hansjakob & Brettschneider, Gunter (eds.). *Language Universals and Mental Operations.* International Interdisciplinary Conference held at Gummersbach/Cologne, Germany. (Language Universals Series, 5.) Tübingen, 14−24.

Talmy, Leonard. 1985. "Lexicalization Patterns". In: Shopen, Timothy (ed.). *Language Typology and Syntactic Description III: Grammatical categories and the lexicon.* Cambridge: Cambridge University Press, 57−149.

Taylor, John R. ²1995. *Linguistic Categorization. Prototypes in Linguistic Theory.* Oxford: Clarendon Press.

Thompson, Sandra A. 1988. "A Discourse Approach to the Cross-linguistic Category 'Adjective'" In: Hawkins, John A. (ed.), *Explaining Language Universals.* Oxford: Blackwell, 167−85.

Wald, Lucia. 1971. "On the Formation of the Opposition Between Noun and Verb". *Linguistics* 67: 83−90.

Walsh, Michael. 1996. "Vouns & Nerbs: A Category Squish in Murrinh-Patha (Northern Australia)". In: McGregor, William (ed.), *Studies in Kimberley Languages in Honour of Howard Coate.* München: LINCOM Europa, 227−52.

Walter, Heribert. 1981. *Studien zur Nomen-Verb-Distinktion aus typologischer Sicht.* (Structura, 13.) München: Fink.

Wetzer, Harrie. 1992. "'Nouny' and 'Verby' Adjectivals: A Typology of Predicative Adjectival Constructions". In: Kefer, Michel, van der Auwera, Johan (eds.). *Meaning and Grammar: Cross-linguistic Perspectives.* (Empirical Approaches to Language Typology, 10.) Berlin: Mouton de Gruyter, 223−62.

Wetzer, Harrie [Henricus M.]. 1995. *Nouniness and Verbiness: A Typological Study of Adjectival Predication.* [Ph.D. dissertation: Nijmegen, Katholieke Universiteit.]

Wetzer, Harrie. 1996. *The Typology of Adjectival Predication.* (Empirical approaches to language typology, 17.) Berlin: Mouton de Gruyter.

Wierzbicka, Anna. 1986. "What's in a Noun? (Or: How do nouns differ from adjectives?)". *Studies in Language* 10.2: 353–89.

Winkler, Heinrich. 1921. *Die altaische Völker- und Sprachenwelt*. (Osteuropa-Institut in Breslau, Quellen und Studien, 6. Abt., Heft 1.) Leipzig & Berlin: Teubner.

Hans-Jürgen Sasse, University of Cologne (Germany)

39. Foundations of reference and predication

1. Introduction
2. Reference and predication as propositional acts
3. A brief history of 'reference' and 'predication'
4. The apparent parallelism between logic and grammar
5. Parallelism debunked
6. Propositions and reference
7. An ontological basis for the distinction between reference and predication
8. Events
9. Reference and predication in possible worlds logic
10. Conclusion
11. References

1. Introduction

Reference and predication can be seen as species of speech acts which, at the logico-linguistic level, yield **referring expressions** and **predicates**. We will deal here mainly, but not only, with referring expressions and predicates.

We will begin by a sketch of the **speech acts** view of reference and predication as given in Searle (1969). We will then give an overview of the history of the distinction, with two main landmarks, Aristotle and Frege. We will afterwards discuss the apparent parallelism between logic and grammar and show that it is only surface deep. This comes, among other things, from the fact that all NPs do not refer and we will turn back to reference and to the conditions of its success. This will lead us to the distinction between **sentence** and **proposition**.

We will then turn to yet another foundation for the distinction, i.e. ontology and the distinction between **particulars** and **universals**. The distinction between referring expressions and predicates can nevertheless still be attacked through apparent counter-examples to Buridan's law. We will show that these counter-examples are only valid at the linguistic level, but not at the relevant level of logic.

We will then treat **events**, their relation to particulars and, hence, to reference and will deal with the paradox of the imperfective. Finally, we will expose Kripke's notion of **rigid designators** and discuss the application of the reference/predication distinction in possible worlds logic.

2. Reference and predication as propositional acts

2.1. The reference act

Searle (1969) has argued that reference and predication are two varieties of **propositional acts**, that is, acts which, conjointly, produce propositions. We will begin, as Searle himself does, by the reference act. Searle is only concerned with what he calls **unique definite reference** (i.e. proper names and definite descriptions), of which a standard example could be:

(1)   *Pussy* is on *the mat*.

In (1), we have two uniquely referring expressions, **Pussy** and **the mat**, one a proper name and the other a definite description.

Searle, however, is careful to set aside some uses of proper names or definite descriptions, such as those in (2 b) and (3 b):

(2) (a) *Socrates* was a philosopher.
    (b) *"Socrates"* has eight letters.
(3) (a) Sam kicked *the bucket*. It fell down with a crash.
    (b) Sam kicked *the bucket*. The funeral will take place next saturday.

(2 b) is a case of *mention* — as indicated by the inverted comas — (where *Socrates* does not refer), as opposed to (2 a) which is a case of *use* (where *Socrates* refers). *Kicked the*

bucket in (3 b) is an **idiom** (where *the bucket* does not refer) as opposed to a standard use in (3 a) (where *the bucket* refers).

Searle gives a whole range of conditions for the accomplishment of a propositional act of reference. Here, given that the reference act consists in an utterance, by a speaker S, speaking to an adressee A, and using an expression R denoting an object X, we will primarily be concerned with what Searle calls the *semantic rules*:

(1) R only occurs in the context of a sentence whose utterance can constitute the accomplishment of an illocutionary act.
(2) R is only used if there exists an object X such that, either R contains an identifying description of X or S can complete R by such a description of X, and such that, through the use of R, S has the intention of isolating or identifying X for A.
(3) Uttering R is tantamount to identify or to extract X for A.

Expression R is what is called below a **referring expression**.

2.2. The predication act

Let us now turn to the predication act. Just as the referring act produces at the logico-linguistic level a referring expression, the predication act produces at the logico-linguistic level a **predicate**. Searle begins by a three parts distinction between (a) a **predicate** (or **predicative expression**), (b) a property and (c) the use of a predicate to attribute a property. Just as he gives rules for the act of reference, Searle gives rules for the act of predication. Again, we will only be concerned here with the semantic rules:

(1) P (the predicate) is only used in the context of a sentence, T, whose utterance can constitute the accomplishment of an illocutionary act.
(2) P is only uttered in T if the utterance of T implies an actual reference to X.
(3) P is only uttered if X belongs to a category or a type such that it is logically possible that P is true or false of X.
(4) The utterance of P is tantamount to questioning the truth or falsity of P about X.

We will not be widely concerned here with illocutionary acts as such (but see § 6.1.) and we will mainly note that reference entails uttering a referring expression under some conditions and that predication entails uttering a predicate under some conditions. The distinction between referring expression and predicate has a long and venerable history, as we will now see.

3. A brief history of reference and predication

We turn to an history of the logico-linguistic distinction between referring expression and predicate, with two main characters in the history of logic, e. g. **Aristotle** and **Frege**.

3.1. Aristotle

Aristotle has come down in the history of philosophy as the founder of logic (see his *Organon*; in Aristotle 1984). Intriguingly enough, he was not concerned with what is usually called **propositional calculus** (which deals with the combination of propositions and connectives to produce other well-formed propositions), but rather with what might be called (in a rather anachronistic way) **predicate calculus**. That is, Aristotle was mainly interested in the internal structure of simple propositions in as much as it plays a role in syllogistic reasoning. In other words, Aristotle was interested in what is common between examples (4) and (5):

(4) All men are mortal
     Socrates is a man
     So Socrates is mortal.

(5) All horses bite
     Eclipse is a horse
     So Eclipse bites.

Obviously, these examples have the same form, i.e. "All Fs are G, a is F, so a is G". The problem here is to know how to combine elements (the letters in the form above) to yield correct sentences which can then be used in syllogisms.

The notion which Aristotle introduced was the notion of a **predicable**, or, in other words, of what can be predicated of something. Aristotle established a list of the kinds of things which can be predicated:

(a) a definition of the essence of the thing,
(b) a distinctive property of the thing,
(c) the genus of the thing,
(d) a differentiating property of the thing,
(e) an accidental property of the thing.

They are respectively illustrated by the examples under (6):

(6) (a) Man *is a rational animal.*
    (b) Man *is a laughing animal.*
    (c) Man *is an animal.*
    (d) Man *is rational.*
    (e) Man *is white.*

3.2. Frege

Frege was the greatest innovator in logic since Aristotle and was indeed the founder of modern logic. He introduced the notion of predicate (see Frege 1980a), defining it as a function which would take one or more argument (see § 4.2.). On his view, a predicate is any expression which, in conjunction with a singular term (a referring expression), yields a sentence. In other words, though for Aristotle, sentences such as "Socrates is mortal" are to be represented as **a is M**, for Frege, they must be represented as **Ms** where **M** is a predicative function which takes as an argument a singular term, in this instance **s**, to yield the proposition **Ms (Mortal(Socrates))**. Frege thus founded the **predicate calculus**, which deals with the internal structure of propositions.

4. The apparent parallelism between logic and grammar

4.1. Reference and predication in logic and grammar

The first thing to point out, as far as the parallelism between logic and grammar is concerned, is that whereas **reference** is a logical notion, **predication** is both a logical and a grammatical notion. At first glance, this might throw doubt on the parallelism between grammar and logic. However, there are distinctions which seem closely similar: the first one, between **subject** and **predicate**, belongs to grammar in the traditional sense, while the second one, between **topic** and **comment**, belongs to linguistics and is based on the difference between what it is that we talk about and what it is that we say about it. There is yet another distinction in linguistics, and more precisely in syntax, which seems to mirror the reference/predication distinction: it is the distinction between **NPs (Noun Phrases)** and **VPs (Verb Phrases)**, where it may seem, at first glance, that NPs correspond to referring expressions, while VPs correspond to predicates.

If we come back to Aristotle, it might seem that the parallelism is strong. Let us examine example (7):

(7) (a) All men are mortal.
    (b) Socrates is a man.
    (c) Thus, Socrates is mortal.

In each of sentences (7 a–c), there is a referring expression, subject, topic or NP (*men, Socrates, Socrates*) and a predicate, comment or VP (*are mortal, is a man, is mortal*). Thus, it does seem that the grammatical distinction between subject and predicate, the linguistic distinction between topic and comment and the syntactic distinction between NP and VP closely mirror the logical distinction between referring expression and predicate.

4.2. Binary and n-ary predicates in logic and grammar

On the whole, the sentences which we have examined until now have had a fairly simple structure, of type [x is G] where x is a referring expression and *is G* is the predicate. It should be noted however that the verb *to be* can have several meanings, as can be seen in examples below:

(8) (a) Socrates is human.
    (b) This bracelet is gold.
    (c) Hesperus is Phosphorus.

The first **is**, in (8 a), is the **copula**: it is the link between the referring expression and the adjective which is applied to it and it can either be seen as a part of the predicate or as a dummy linguistic element which can be omitted in the logical representation of (8 a) (as in Frege's analysis, where (8 a) is represented not as **s is M** but as **Ms**). The second **is** *is* the **is of constitution**: that is, it says what kind of material an object (or a type of object) is made of (what it is which constitutes it). The third **is** is the **is of identity**: it says that two referring expressions refer to the same object (see below, § 9.1. and § 9.2.). What is of interest right now is mainly the first **is**, the copula.

Indeed, the sentences which we have met with until now, such as those in (7), are quite simple and all have the same linguistic structure (NP-copula-NP/adjective), which strongly mirrors the referring expression/predicate distinction of logic. There are however sentences with much more complicated structure as far as the distinction referring expression/predicate is concerned. The predicates in (7 a–c) all allow only one referring expression: in other words, they are **unary predicates**, i.e. predicates with a single argument place. There are, however, also predicates which allow more than one argument place, as the examples in (9) show:

(9) (a) The cat ate the mouse.
    (b) John gave Mary the book.

The predicate in (9 a) is a **binary predicate**, i.e. a predicate with two argument places (respectively *the cat* and *the mouse*) and the predicate in (9 b) is a **trinary predicate**, i.e. a predicate with three argument places (respectively *John, Mary* and *the book*). In principle, predicates can have any number of argument places, though the number of argument places that predicates actually have is probably limited.

It should be noted that the number of argument places of a predicate does not alter the apparent parallelism between grammar and logic. If the logical distinction actually is between referring expressions and predicates, the grammatical/syntactic distinction is between NPs and VPs. Just as predicates in logic can be unary, binary or n-ary, verbs can have a subject NP and any number of complement NPs or PPs. It should be noted that this has been taken into account in various types of syntax, such as, for instance, **Government and Binding (Generative Grammar)** where it appears as the question of **thematic roles** (or **θ-roles**) (see Higginbotham 1985) and in **Case Grammar** (see Fillmore 1987), where it has a central place.

Thus, the difficulty for the parallelism between logic and grammar does not come from the number of argument places of the predicate.

5. Parallelism debunked

5.1. Apparent parallelism

As was pointed out before, as long as referring expressions are considered as equivalent to NPs, there is no problem with the parallelism between logic and grammar. But in order for the parallelism to stand, NPs must refer. Is that always the case? Let us have a look at one type of NPs, indefinite descriptions. Indefinite descriptions can appear in any position, but, notably, in subject or complement position or inside the predicate with a copula (the verb *to be*). Let us cast our minds back to (4), *Socrates is a man*. *A man* in (4) is an indefinite description, which appears inside the predicate (as would an adjective, *human*, for instance) and is used as an attribute of *Socrates*. As an indefinite description, it is an NP and thus apparently a referring expression, yet it is obvious that it does not refer.

Let us now have a look at an indefinite description in a subject position:

(10)   **A cat** was sitting under the table.

In (10), the indefinite description **a cat** is in subject position. The question is, does it refer? This brings us to another question: what is it to refer? Or, more specifically, how should we define **reference**? Before we answer that question, we should outline Russell's analysis of indefinite descriptions (see Russell 1994). According to Russell, indefinite descriptions, such as **a cat**, do not refer to any specific individual: what they do is saying that there exists an (indefinite) individual which belongs to the *N* category, i.e. for **a cat, there exists an (indefinite) individual which is a cat**. Thus the proper analysis of (10) would not be 11 a), but (11 b):

(11) (a) was sitting under the table (a cat).
    (b) $\exists x$ (cat(x) & sitting under the table(x))
    (There exists x such that x is a cat and x is sitting under the table)

In other words, indefinite descriptions do not refer, they just assert the existence of an individual of a given kind, without specifying which particular individual.

5.2. NPs do not always refer

Apart from indefinite descriptions, do all NPs refer? The first thing to note is that if, in order to refer, referring expressions must designate specific individuals in the world, then any referring expression which refers to a fictional or mythical individual (for instance, *Sherlock Holmes* or *unicorns*) does not refer. This, however, does not mean that all referring expressions which are not indefinite descriptions and which do not designate fictional or mythical individuals do refer (but see below, § 9.4.).

Let us examine definite descriptions (e.g. *the cat*). In his famous Theory of descriptions, **Russell** (1994) did not only deal with indefinite descriptions. He also turned his attention to definite descriptions and proposed an existential analysis of them, just as he had done for indefinite descriptions. He, however, did not think that definite and indefinite descriptions are entirely equivalent from a semantic point of view. Though indefinite descriptions have a simple existential analysis, according to which the proposition would be true if there exists at least one object which satisfies both the description and the predicate applied to it, definite descriptions have a mixed existential reading, according to which the proposition would be true if there is one object, and only one, which satisfies both the description and the predicate applied to it. Thus *The cat was sitting under a table* would be interpreted as *There is one and only one x, such as x is a cat and x is sitting under the table*. Hence, on Russell's view, a definite description is not a referring expression anymore than an indefinite description is.

This thesis has been challenged in part by Donnellan (1966) who proposes a distinction between **attributive** and **referential** uses, with a specific application to definite definitions. Donnellan's pet example is (12):

(12)   Smith's murderer is mad.

Donnellan points out that the expression *Smith's murderer* can be interpreted in two widely different ways: a) as *Smith's murderer whoever he is*, that is the speaker does not know (or believe that he knows) who Smith's murderer is; b) as *Smith's murderer standing there in the dock*, that is the speaker knows (or believes that he knows) who Smith's murderer is. The first use corresponds to Russell's analysis of definite description, that is, it asserts the existence of a single individual who both is Smith's murderer and is mad: this use of definite descriptions was called by Donnellan the **attributive use** and it certainly is not referring. By contrast, the second use is referring and was named by Donnellan the **referential use**.

Thus, there does seem to be quite a number of NPs which, indeed, do not refer: indefinite descriptions, which never do, and all the attributive uses of definite descriptions. What about other kinds of NPs, such as pronouns or proper names? We will come back to proper names later on, when we discuss the notion of **rigid designator** below (see § 9.3.). Let us just say for now that proper names generally refer. Pronouns are usually supposed to refer as well as do demonstrative descriptions (**this/that cat**), though it has been argued (see Reboul 1994, Bezuidenhout 1997) that the referential/attributive distinction can be applied to personal pronouns (indexicals included) as well as to definite descriptions. I will not discuss this here: let us just say that the matter can only be approached through a pragmatic view of attributive and referential uses, an issue about which Donnellan has been rather cautious.

Still, the main thing is that some NPs do not refer and that the one-to-one correspondance between NPs and referring expressions flounders. If this is the case then there is no true parallelism between logic and grammar and this leads us to the distinction between **sentence** and **proposition** and to the definition of **reference**.

6. Propositions and reference

6.1. Logic vs. grammar: proposition vs. sentence

The distinction between **sentence** and **proposition** has a one-to-one correspondance with the distinction between **grammar** and **logic**. Or, in other words, **propositions** are to logic as sentences are to grammar. A sentence can be defined from a syntactico-linguistic point of view as a complete and grammatical sequence of words, both completeness and grammaticality being determined through the putative sentence compliance with linguistic rules. Just as sentences are well-formed sequences according to grammar, propositions are well-formed formulae according to logic. This could be thought as restauring parallelism. But as we shall see, it does not.

Let us come back to example (12):

(12)   Smith's murderer is mad.

As pointed out above, the sentence in (12) can receive two different interpretations depending on whether the definite description *Smith's murderer* is used attributively or referentially. These two different interpretations correspond to two different propositions, the attributive interpretation to (13a) and the referential one to (13b):

(13)   (a) There is one and only one x, which is such that x is Smith's murderer and X is mad.
        (b) Is mad (Smith's murderer).

Thus, we have here a single sentence, but two propositions corresponding to two possible interpretations of the sentence in question. This is the first indication that there is some problem with the putative parallelism between logic and grammar.

There is more however: just as a single sentence can correspond to two (or more) different propositions, two sentences can correspond to one and the same proposition as shown by the examples below:

(14) (a) The cat ate the mouse.
     (b) The mouse was eaten by the cat.

These two examples correspond to the same proposition:

(15)   There is a single x, there is a single y, such that cat (x) and mouse (y) and ate (x, y).

This is where the parallelism between grammar and logic falls through. Sentences do not have a one-to-one correspondance with propositions: they tend to be ambiguous, either, as we have just seen, at the pragmatic level, or at the syntactico-semantic level. This means that the same sentence can be interpreted in a range of was, depending on the number of syntactic, semantic or pragmatic ambiguities which it can give raise to.

There is more however to the notion of proposition. Let us have a look on examples (16):

(16) (a) How beautiful this building is!
     (b) Is this building beautiful?
     (c) I wish that this building were beautiful.
     (d) I believe that this building is beautiful.

In all examples under (16), the same proposition (*this building is beautiful*) is expressed in either a non-embedded ((16a) and (16b)) or an embedded position ((16c) and (16d)), but different attitudes are expressed relative to it: astonishment in (16a), ignorance in (16b), desire in (16c) and belief in (16d). Thus another way of characterizing propositions (which is entirely compatible with the definition in terms of well-formedness indicated above) is that the proposition is the thing which is common to all the examples under (16), no matter what attitudes are taken by the speakers relative to that proposition.

The same thing can be said about illocutionary force. Searle (1969) distinguished two parts in any utterance, the **illocutionary force indicator** and the **propositional content indicator**, which correspond respectively in example (17) below, to the preface (**I order that** ...) and to the complement sentence (**John leaves**):

(17) (a) I order that John leaves.

But, basically, the same propositional content, that is, the same proposition, can be accompanied by all types of illocutionary forces, which can be indicated explicitly or implicitly:

(17) (b) I promise that John will leave.
     (c) John will leave and that is a menace.

Thus propositions not only can be the object of different attitudes (called, for that reason, **propositional attitudes**), they can also be the object of different illocutionary forces.

Yet another way of characterizing the proposition is to say that it can be evaluated as to its truth value: that is a proposition is by definition something which is true or false. This, it should be noted, does not entail that the speaker or the adressee is actually able to evaluate the truth-value of the proposition.

We thus seem to arrive at a four-fold definition of **proposition:**

(i)   A proposition is a well-formed formula, subject to the laws of logic.
(ii) A proposition can be evaluated as to its truth or falsity.
(iii) A proposition can be the common element in sentences expressing different attitudes.
(iv) A proposition can be accompanied by different illocutionary forces and can be the common element in the utterances expressing them.

6.2. A definition of **reference**

Let us now come back to reference and non-reference: as seen above, referring expressions and non-referring expressions do not make identical contributions to the propositions in which they occur. This was shown in the analysis of example (12), which corresponds to two different propositions, depending on whether the definite description is taken to be used attributively or referentially. According to the **direct reference theory** (see Recanati 1993), what enters the proposition, when the NPs in the sentence are referring, are not so much referring expressions but the referents themselves, that is the object in the world to which the referring expressions in the sentence refer. What enters the proposition in the case of non-referring NPs is a variable bound by a quantifier (in the case of definite and indefinite descriptions, usually, the existential quantifier, ∃), and a predicate,

which is something quite different. This allows us to give a definition of reference:
An NP is referring if and only if its contribution to the proposition expressed by the utterance where it occurs is an individual.

NPs which always refer are generally considered to be proper names, demonstratives and pronouns, while NPs which never refer are indefinite descriptions. Some NPs, such as definite descriptions, may refer or not refer depending on the use the speaker is making of them.

7. An ontological basis for the distinction between reference and predication

7.1. Particulars versus universals

Given what has just been said regarding the contribution of referring and non-referring NPs to propositions, it should be clear that NPs which refer contribute reference to propositions, while NPs which do not contribute bound variables and predicates. This difference between reference and predication can be seen from the point of view of the attribution of truth value. For instance, the evaluation of the truth-value of the proposition expressed in (12) may be very different depending on whether (12) is taken to express proposition (13 a) or proposition (13 b): if it is taken to express proposition (13 a), then it is true if and only if there exists a single individual who both is Smith's murderer and is mad; if it is taken to express proposition (13 b), it is true if only if the specific individual who is taken to be Smith's murderer, Jones for instance, is mad.

Truth-evaluation has to do with what is taken to be the structure of the world, and the difference between referent and predicate has often been seen as closely corresponding to the old philosophical and ontological distinction between particulars (specific objects in the world) and universals (properties) (see, for instance, Strawson 1992). Thus the reference part of a proposition would be constituted by particulars, while the predicate part of a proposition would correspond to universals. This, however, supposes that the ontology accepts universals, something about which, to say the least, some philosophers have been rather reluctant. This would mean that over and above red things in the world, there would also be an object which is redness.

There is however an alternative view according to which the truth value of the proposition would be evaluated by ensuring that the particular designated by the referring expression has the property described by the predicate. On this view, there would only be red objects, belonging to the set of all red objects in the world and there would be no need of an additional entity of redness. Thus, truth-evaluation would proceed through ensuring that the particular belongs to the extension of the property, that is, that it belongs to the set of all things which have the property in question. In (13 b), this would mean that the particular designated by *Smith's murderer* belongs to the extension of the property *being mad*. In (13 a), where there is no authentic referring expression, the attribution of the truth-value would depend on ensuring that the intersection between the set of things which have the property of *being Smith's murderer* and the set of things which have the property of *being mad* is not the nulset.

Thus there is an ontological foundation for the difference between reference and predication. This ontological foundation, as well as the direct reference view, has some consequences on the relation between reference and predication.

7.2. Buridan's law

The philosopher Buridan proposed a law according to which the reference of an expression must be specifiable in a way which does not involve first determining whether the proposition in which the expression occurs is true (see Geach 1980). In other words, the referring expression should determine its referent (the particular to which it refers) independently of the predicate and of the fact that the predicate does or does not apply to the particular, i.e. without ensuring first that the proposition is true. The basis for this law is obvious: truth-evaluation of propositions in which authentically referring expressions occur depends on whether the particulars designated by the referring expressions in question belong or not to the extension of the predicates which are applied to them in the proposition. Thus, accepting that the identity of the particular should be determined **via** its appartenance to the extension of the predicate would amount both to evaluating the truth-value of the proposition before identifying the particular, which seems to be impossible and to a weakening of the difference between reference and predication or between particulars and universals.

Hence, on the face of it, it seems that Buridan's law should be enforced. Yet, there does seem to be quite a few counter-examples to it, some of them having to do with the identification of the particular being refered to, while others have to do with the identification of the type of the particular. Let us look at the examples below:

(18) (a) The boss fired the worker because *he* was a convinced communist.
(b) The teacher has punished John because *he* is short-tempered.
(c) The teacher has punished John because *he* was ill-mannered.

(19) (a) Have a look at *John's sonata*. It is lying on the piano.
(b) Have you heard *John's sonata*? It's atonic.
(c) I listened *to John's sonata* yesterday. It lasted half an hour.

In the examples under (18), the problem is with the assignment of the third person pronoun. In (18a), not only can the pronoun not determine its referent independently, it is not clear whether it refers to the boss or to the worker if one does not take into account both the predicate (*was a convinced communist*) and the context: the pronoun will be interpreted as referring to the boss if the fact described occurs in Pre-Gorbatchev USSR, while it will be interpreted as referring to the worker if the fact described occurs in the USA. In (18b), the pronoun could refer to John's teacher, rather than to John, if the predicate (*is short-tempered*) is taken into account as an explanation of the teacher's behaviour, while in (18c) the pronoun probably refers to John if the predicate (*was ill-mannered*) is taken into account. In other words, the third person pronoun, though it can and very often is solved without taking account of the predicate, may also in a fair number of cases be resolved only through the predicate which is applied to it.

The examples under (19) are slightly different in that there is no doubt what the referent is in all of them: it is John's sonata. Unfortunately, the expression *John's sonata* is ambiguous in that it can designate either the **material object** (the musical partition), as in (19a), the **cognitive object**, as in (19b), or the **event** which is the execution of the partition as in (19c). What discriminates between these interpretations is, in each case, the predicate: only a material object can be lying on the piano, while only a cognitive object can be atonic, and only an execution can be an event and have a duration.

Thus, it seems that Buridan's law meets with a number of counter-examples and the distinction between reference and predication appears to be rather harder to sustain than it looked on first glance.

7.3. Buridan's law and the sentence/proposition distinction

Let us come back to the sentence/proposition distinction. According to Buridan's law, the reference of an expression must be specifiable in some way that does not involve first determining whether the proposition in which the expression occurs is true. The question is: is Buridan's law truly put in jeopardy by examples like those in (18) or in (19)? A first answer to that question, which will have to be improved afterwards, is that all these examples are examples of sentences and not of propositions and that Buridan's law applies at the level of proposition and not at the level of sentence. This, it should be noted, is tantamount to saying that Buridan's law is a law of logic and not a law of grammar or linguistics.

So far, thus, our answer to the challenge apparently raised against Buridan's law by examples such as (18) and (19) is to say that Buridan's law must be complied with, but at the level of logic. There is, indeed, some doubts as to whether it could be obeyed at the level of grammar. I will rapidly develop this argument. It has to do, it should be noted, with the well-known notion of the underdetermination of language. We already have met with examples of linguistic underdetermination: examples of definite descriptions which can be interpreted as either attributive of referential are quite good examples of what is meant by linguistic underdetermination. Indeed, it can be said that linguistic underdetermination occurs whenever a given sentence can receive several different interpretations, i.e. whenever it is ambiguous. It should be noted that, though the sentences in (19) contain an ambiguous NP, *John's sonata*, these sentences themselves are not ambiguous: this comes from the fact that the predicates grammatically select one meaning of the ambiguous NP rather than another as was explained before. It does it through what has come to be known as the

restriction selections of a verb. For instance, the restriction selections of the verb **to eat** impose that the **agent** of the action (i.e. the subject of the active verb) should be an animate being and that the **patient** (i.e. the complement of the active verb) should be an edible substance. In the same way the restriction selections of the predicate in the sentences under (19) respectively select the meaning *John's sonata as a material object, John's sonata as a cognitive object* and *John's sonata as an event*.

The picture is rather different for the examples under (18) and the linguistic underdetermination is more important there (just as it is for example (12)), as the predicate, though it helps attributing the right referent to the pronoun, can only do so with the assistance of contextual or encyclopaedic knowledge. I will not go here in the details of the model one could propose of how this is done. I shall only remark that the linguistic underdetermination of referring expressions (among other linguistic expressions) could only constitute a counter-example to Buridan's law if it contaminated the proposition. But there is no reason to think that this is the case (the interpretations of (18) can be given through quite straightforward propositions, with no ambiguity in them) and thus Buridan's law, as long as it is considered, as it should be, as a logical law and as long as one keeps in mind the distinction between sentence and proposition, stands as it is. So does the distinction between reference and predication at the logical level.

8. Events

We have already met with the notion of event when we discussed John's sonata in § 7.3. As we shall see, it has quite an important role to play in the referring expressions/predicate distinction.

8.1. Davidson and the logical form of action sentences

Quite a lot of our examples have been of the type **NP copula NP/adjective**. However, in natural language, a good number of sentences are **action sentences**, sentences which describe actions or events such as John's taking a walk in the parc, Shem's kicking of Shawn, John's gift to Mary, or the fall of Constantinople. Davidson interested himself in the problem of what logical form one should attribute to such sentences (see Davidson 1980). His approach consisted in pointing out that, just as NPs are divided between referring expressions and non-referring expressions (notably indefinite descriptions), the description of actions and events in discourse can be divided between non-referring descriptions (action sentences) and referring descriptions (for instance defnite descriptions referring to events).

Thus, according to him, action sentences such as (20) should be interpreted as (21) indicates, that is as asserting the existence of an event which is such and such:

(20)   John came.

(21) $\exists x \,((\text{came (John)}) \, x)$
(There is an x which is such that it is a coming by John).

Thus, Davidson introduces a new type of entity in the ontology: **events**. The question as far as the distinction between reference and predication is concerned is whether the introduction of events in the ontology affects or weakens in any way the distinction.

As a matter of fact, there is no reason to suppose it does. What the propositional form of action sentences such as (20) says is just that there exists an individual which belongs to the extension of the predicate *being a coming by John*. It certainly modifies the relation between reference and predication in as much as, before Davidson, the logical form of a sentence such as (20) would simply have been taken to be (22):

(22)   Came (John)

It should be noted, however, that (22) can be found embedded in (21) and that, indeed, what (21) says is both that John (a particular) belongs to the extension of the universal *came* and that there is an (indefinite) particular which is such that it belongs to a subset of the set of *comings*, the subset of *comings by John*. This entails that (22) must be true if (21) is. Thus, Davidson's extension of the ontology to include events does not menace the reference/predication distinction in logic anymore than do linguistic supposed counter-examples to Buridan's law.

8.2. Vendler's ontology of events

Before Davidson's reflexions on events, Vendler (1957) had made a classification of event types (which are dumped together by Davidson), organising them in an ontology. That ontology can be said to depend on the fact that the event is or is not leading to a change of state and on whether its duration is or is not limited to the moment when the change occurs. Let us look at the examples under (23):

(23) (a) John ran.
(b) John built a house
(c) John won the 100 meters race.

In (23a), what happens is identical all along the duration of the event described: at all instants during the event which is John running, John ran. The event does not imply a change of state in John or in anything else. This type of event is called by Vendler an **activity**. In (23b), by contrast, what happens is not identical all along the duration of the event described. This event, the building of a house by John, is made of a great number of different sub-events and it does imply a change of state, namely the existence of a house where there was no house before. The apparition of this change of state at a given moment in a durative event is called by Vendler a **culmination** and events that culminate are called **accomplishments**. In (23c), we have a third kind of events which has the peculiarity of implying a change of state (after the event, John is the winner of the hundred meters race, which he was not before), though it has no duration: it only describes the culmination of the event. These events are called **achievements**.

The three-fold vendlerian distinction between activities, achievements and accomplishments has been used by a lot of people working on time and events. It has led to a definition, by Asher (1997) of an **event** (reduced here to achievements and accomplishments) as that which implies a change of states in an object or a situation, and of a **state** as what obtains in an object or a situation between events. As we shall see in the next section events are very important for the referring expressions/predicates distinction, and not only on the basis of their contribution to the proposition (see § 8.1.).

8.3. Evolving reference

The role that events play in the referring expressions/predicates distinction can best be seen from the point of view of **evolving reference**. Evolving reference can be easily described from example (24):

(24)   John has caught the fat and lively chicken which lives in his back yard. He has killed **it**, he has prepared **it** for the oven, he has cut **it** into four pieces and he has roasted **it** with thyme for an hour.

In (24), the thing which is refered to **via** the third person pronoun in the last clause (i.e. *he has roasted it with thyme for an hour*) does certainly not share all the properties of the thing which was refered to in the first sentence through the (referring) definite description *the fat and lively chicken which lives in his back yard*. In fact, it certainly does not share with it the properties of being fat, lively and of living in John's back yard, and, though it may still be called *a chicken*, it certainly does not belong to the same category as the specimens of poultry which are called by that name when they are alive.

Quite generally, the problem of evolving reference is the problem raised by reference to an object through a description in a sentence or a sequence of sentences describing one or more events which have changed the state of the object to such an extent that it does not satisfy the description anymore, though it still refered to as if it did. It is especially central to third person pronoun interpretation as it is generally considered that third person pronouns are interpreted through substitution of their antecedent NP. It is thought that, given that third person pronouns and their antecedents generally are coreferential, the object they refer to has the same properties, no matter when it is refered to. Here, however, though there is no ambiguity about which NP the antecedent of the third person pronoun is, the substitution can certainly not be said to preserve truth value, because the properties of the object have not been preserved. Evolving reference thus raises two problems: how are third person pronouns actually interpreted and how is the identity of the object preserved throughout the changes which it is submitted to? We will only answer the first one: this means pointing out that third person pronouns, when they are not in the scope of a quantifier, are probably interpreted much more directly than has generally been thought.

8.4. The paradox of the imperfective

Apart from evolving reference, action verbs do play an important role in the proposition expressed. As seen above (see § 8.1.), they describe events which can be integrated in the proposition under an existential quantifier.

This is generally true of all verbs, though at some tenses the generalization may fail.

Let us look at examples (25):

(25) (a) Mary pushed the cart.
(b) Mary was pushing the cart.
(c) Mary built a house.
(d) Mary was building a house.

Whereas in (25 a) and (25 b), despite the change of tense from the simple past to the past progressive, the event is supposed to have occured, in (25 c) and (25 d), the change from the simple past to the past progressive strongly implies that the event described may not have been completed.

It should be clear that, in Vendler's terms, *to push a cart* describes an activity while *to build a house* describes an accomplishment. In some verbs of accomplishment, such as *to build a house, to draw a circle, to make a dress*, etc. the passage from the simple past to the past progressive implies that the event was not completed. This has a few disturbing consequences: for instance what was Mary doing while she was building a house if she did not build a house? And what is it that she was building if there is no house which she built?

The answers to such questions are not and cannot be simple. What seems clear is that there is an asymmetry between simple past and past progressive in examples such as (25 c) and (25 d) in as much as (25 c) implies (25 d), while (25 d) does not imply (25 c). This means that (25 c) could be given an analysis in terms of Davidson's proposal regarding action sentences, while (25 d) could not.

The peculiarity of such sentences can be seen when it is observed that the logical asymmetry between (25 c) and (25 d) does not occur between (25 a) and (25 b): (25 a) implies (25 b) and (25 b) implies (25 a). In other words, they are logically equivalent and they can both receive the same Davidsonian analysis.

So how should sentences like (25 d) be analysed? The most simple answer to that is that they can be analysed in the standard referring expressions/predicate way, as:

(26) (a) was building a house (Mary).

On the other hand, sentences such as (25 c) could be analysed in the standard way as (26 b) and in a Davidsonian way as (26 c):

(26) (b) $\exists x$ (house (x) & built(Mary, x))
(c) $\exists x, \exists y$ (house (y) & (built(Mary, y) x).

None of interpretations (26 b) and (26 c) are available for (25 d). Thus the problem raised by some sentences at the past progressive is that of the proposition which they express and which differ from that which they express at the simple past.

9. Reference and predication in possible world logic

What we have been concerned with until now is reference and predication and the propositions which they conjointly produce when evaluated relative to the real or actual world, i.e. the world which we inhabit. How propositions produced through reference and predication should be evaluated relative to other worlds, the so-called **possible worlds**, is the subject of this section. It should be remembered that Kripke developped possible worlds logic, building on propositions by Barcan Marcus (see Marcus 1993). One of his aims was to account for identity statements and it is toward those sentences which we will now turn, beginning with a quick sketch of the problems they raise and outlining Frege's solution, before turning to Kripke's solution. We will then speak about the notion of rigid designator and outline a possible worlds solution to the problem of expressions referring to fictional objects.

9.1. Identity statements and triviality: Frege's view

The stepping point for Kripke was a question which had exercised Frege's ingenuity at the turn of the century: essentially it was the question of the triviality or nontriviality of identity statements. Let us take an identity statement such as (27):

(27)   Hesperus is Phosphorus.

The question which bothered Frege (see Frege 1980b) was whether or not a statement such as (27) could be informative. Given that it is generally considered that expressions which have the same extension (i.e. which refer to the same thing) are substituable **salva veritate**, an identity statement such as (27) can be considered equivalent to (28) or (29):

(28)   Hesperus is Hesperus.

(29)   Phosphorus is Phosphorus.

Given that *Phosphorus* and *Hesperus* both designate the same individual, i.e. Venus, and given the substituability **salva veritate** of referring expressions which have the same extension, (27) should be equivalent to both (28) and (29) which are tautologies. Tautologies are propositions which are both necessarily true and obviously necessarily true, hence uninformative or trivial. (28) and (29) are clearly non-informative, but what about (27)?

The solution proposed by Frege was to say that proper names such as *Hesperus* and *Phosphorus* do not only have a **denotation** (their extension or reference): they also have a **sense** (respectively *the Evening Star* and *the Morning Star*). This allows him to distinguish between (27) on the one hand, (28) and (29) on the other hand. Though (28) and (29), being of form [a = a], are truly tautologies (the referential expressions on either side of the **is** are identical), (27), being of form [a = b] is not (the referential expressions on either side of the **is** are not identical).

Thus the sense/denotation distinction allowed Frege to solve the problem of the non-triviality of (some) identity statement.

9.2. Identity statements and triviality:
     Kripke's view

Kripke (see Kripke 1981) was essentially troubled by the same question as Frege was. However he rejected Frege's solution, denying that, as far as proper names are concerned, they had a sense. According to him a proper name only has a denotation or reference, it does not have a sense. Thus Kripke found himself faced with the problem of the possible triviality of identity statements, even when the names used on either side of **is** are not identical: given that they refer to the same thing and that their only semantic contribution is their referent, all identity statements seem to be necessarily tautologous, i.e. trivial.

One solution might have been to deny that identity statements are necessarily true: if they are only contingently true, then they are not tautologous. In his modal logic, Kripke used the notion of **possible worlds**: he hypothesizes that, apart from the actual world in which we live, we create possible worlds each time we make a supposition, describe the way things should be rather than the way things are, etc. All these possible worlds (to which there is no limit apart from the fact that they must be possible, i.e. contradictory propositions cannot both be true in the same possible world) together with the actual world (which is obviously possible) make the set of possible worlds. Given this set, Kripke defines **possibility** for a proposition as the fact that the proposition is true at at least one possible world or at a set of possible worlds. He defines **necessity** for a proposition as the fact that the proposition is true at all possible worlds.

Thus, the problem for the triviality or non-triviality of identity statements reduces itself to the question of whether identity statements, when true, are true at all possible worlds or only at some possible worlds. As Kripke points out, it is hard to see how a statement about the identity of Hesperus and Phosphorus could be true at some possible worlds and false at other possible worlds: it may not have a truth value at possible worlds where Venus does not exist, but at all worlds where Venus does exist, Hesperus is Phosphorus. The only possibility for Hesperus not to be Phosphorus would be if the rules of English were changed in such a way that either Hesperus or Phosphorus does not refer to Venus anymore. But this would hardly be relevant for the problem of identity statements.

Thus, according to Kripke, not only do proper names only have reference, identity statements, when true, are necessarily true. It seems to leave Kripke in something of a quandary because, given those two hypotheses, it seems that he has no other option than to say that identity statements are trivial.

Kripke, however, rejects this thesis. He distinguishes between necessity and contingency on the one hand and **a priori** and **a posteriori** knowledge on the other hand. Though identity statements when true are necessarily true, nevertheless some necessarily true propositions are not knowable **a priori**: they can only be known **a posteriori** and this is the case for identity statements which are both necessarily true and knowable **a posteriori**. Given that **a posteriori** knowledge is not trivial, identity statements are not trivial either, though they are necessarily true.

9.3. Rigid designators and possible worlds

As we have seen above (see § 9.2.), Kripke rejects the reference/denotation distinction for proper names. He does not think that proper names have anything like a sense and, according to him, their only semantic weight is their reference. What is more, as is shown by the fact that identity statements involving proper names are necessarily true at all possible worlds where their referents exist, proper names refer to the same individual in all the possible worlds where this individual exists. As Kripke pointed out, a big difference between descriptions and proper names is that though proper names refer to the same individual at all possible worlds, descriptions do not: the properties which they attribute to their referents may not be true of that referent in another possible world. Let us look for instance at the examples below:

(30) (a) Helmut Kohl could have lost the last elections.
(b) The present chancellor of Germany could have lost the elections.

Both (30a) and (30b) happen to be true in the real world and the proper name *Helmut Kohl* and the description *the present chancellor of Germany* happen to be coreferential in this world, but in any possible world in which it is true that Helmut Kohl lost the last elections, the description *the present chancellor of Germany* would not refer to him.

Thus, there is a specificity to proper names: they are always referential and their reference is both the same in all possible worlds and given once and for all. This explains why Kripke calls them **rigid designators**: they are **designators** because they are referential and they are **rigid** because they refer to the same thing at all possible worlds.

Kripke indicates how the link between a given proper name and its referent is created: there is a baptism and it is that baptism (which, of course, does not have to be religious or official, though it does have to be minimally public) which is the cause of the very strong and, indeed, indestructible, link between the proper name and its referent. This account of how the relation between proper names and their referents is established explains why Kripke's theory is known as the **causal theory of reference**.

Thus, according to Kripke's theory, which is generally well received, proper names contribute their referents to the propositions expressed by the sentences where they occur.

9.4. Expressions referring to fictional individuals: the possible worlds solution

To close this investigation on reference and predication, we will now turn to the vexing subject of reference to fictional characters: strictly speaking and in this, our real world, names supposedly referring to fictional character all refer to the same thing, that is, nothing. This, though hardly controversial, is nevertheless a rather disagreable conclusion, given that we have strong intuitions to the contrary, i.e. strong intuitions that when we refer to Sherlock Holmes, we are not at all referring to the same thing as when we refer to Hercule Poirot.

Searle (1969) proposed a solution to that problem of which I will only say that, for him, reference to fictional characters is possible because, though these characters do not exist in reality, they do exist in the fiction. This solution was thoroughly refined when Lewis tackled the problem (see Lewis 1983) in terms of possible worlds. Lewis pointed out that though Sherlock Homes and Hercule Poirot do not exist at our real world, they did exist in (different) possible worlds. He made the hypothesis that the titles of the books or stories in which fictional characters occur are a means of selection of the relevant set of possible worlds. For instance, in (31), the expression *In The Aventures of Sherlock Holmes* is a way of selecting only the worlds where the set of propositions expressed in the sentences of which *The Adventures of Sherlock Holmes* is constituted are true:

(31) In *The Adventures of Sherlock Holmes*, Sherlock Holmes is a bachelor.

Incidentally the proposition expressed in (31) is true at the possible worlds concerned.

Thus, there is a solution in terms of possible worlds to the problem of the reference of names denoting fictional characters.

10. Conclusion

I have been trying here to give a short overview of all the problems raised by the notions of reference and predication, as well as by indicating their antiquity. Perhaps a list of a few main points in the exposition above should be given at this stage:

(i) Reference and predication are propositional acts which jointly yield propositions and which separately yield respectively referring expressions and predicates.
(ii) Despite the apparent parallelism between logic and grammar, they are in fact quite different and sentences should not be confused with propositions, anymore than NPs should be confused with referring expressions.
(iii) The representation of events raises spe-

cific problems for the referring expression/predicate distinction though these problems can be solved.
(iv) Reference and predication work in the same way in possible worlds logic, though possible worlds logic has the advantage of allowing for the notion of **rigid designator**, which appears to be a good description of proper names.
(v) It also offers a solution to the problem of reference to fictional characters.

11. References

Aristotle/Barnes, Jonathan. ed. 1984. *The Complete Works of Aristotle*. The Revised Oxford Translation. Princeton: Princeton Univ. Press.

Asher, Nicholas. 1997. "Evénements, faits, propositions et anaphore évolutive". In: *Verbum* XIX/1−2, 137−176.

Bezuidenhout, Anne. 1997. Pragmatics, Semantic Underdetermination and the Referential/Attributive Distinction. In: *Mind* 106/423, 275−409.

Davidson, Donald. 1980. *Essays on Actions and Events*. Oxford: Clarendon Press.

Donnellan, Donald. 1966. Reference and Definite Descriptions. In: *The Philosophical Review* 75, 281−304.

Fillmore, Charles/Dirven, René/Radden, Günter. eds. 1987. *Fillmore's Case Grammar. A Reader*. Heidelberg: Groos.

Frege, Gottlob. 1980a. *Foundations of Arithmetics*. Oxord: Blackwell.

Frege, Gottlob. 1980b. *Philosophical Writings*. Oxford: Blackwell.

Geach, Peter. 1980. *Reference and Generality. An Examination in Some Medieval and Modern Theories*. Ithaca/London: Cornell. Univ. Press.

Higginbotham, James. 1985. On Semantics. In: *Linguistic Inquiry* 16/4, 574−593.

Kripke, Saul. 1980. *Naming and Necessity*. Oxford: Blackwell.

Lewis, David. 1983. Truth in Fiction. In: *Philosophical Papers*, Volume I. New York/Oxford: Oxford Univ. Press, 261−280.

Marcus, Ruth Barcan. 1993. *Modalities. Philosophical Essays*. New York/Oxford: Oxford Univ. Press.

Recanati. 1993. *Direct reference: from language to thought*, Oxford: Basil Blackwell.

Reboul, Anne. 1994. L'anaphore pronominale: le problème de l'attribution des référents. In: Moeschler, Jacques et al.: *Langage et pertinence*, Nancy: Presses Univ. de Nancy, 105−173.

Russell, Bertrand/Urquhart, Alan/Lewis, Allan. Eds. 1994. *The Collected papers of Bertrand Russell*. Foundations of Logic 1903−1905, Volume IV. London: Allen & Unwin.

Searle, John. 1969. *Speech Acts. An Essay in the Philosophy of Language*. Cambridge: Cambridge Univ. Press.

Strawson, Peter. 1992. *Analysis and Metaphysics. An Introduction to Philosophy*. Oxford: Oxford Univ. Press.

Vendler, Zeno. 1957. "Verbs and Times". In: *Philosophical Review* 56, 143−160.

Anne Reboul,
ISC-CNRS (France)

40. Dimensions of adnominal modification

1. Nouns and noun phrases
2. Adnominal modifiers
3. Syntax of adnominal modifiers
4. References

1. Nouns and noun phrases

Some of the most typical modifiers of the noun are the article (**the/a** book), the demonstrative pronoun (**this/that** book), the question word (**whose/which** book), the possessive pronoun (**my/her** book), the numeral (**five** books), the quantifier (**all/some/many** books), the adjective (**old/new** books), the noun phrase (with or without case marker, adposition or other kind of relator; e. g. *the book on the table* [location], *the flowers for mother* [beneficiary] *the child's book* [possessor], *the roof of the house* [part/whole]), and the relative clause (*the book that you gave me this morning*). These and other modifiers will be discussed in § 2, which contains a cross-linguistic overview of the various categories of adnominal modification. § 3 is concerned with the order of adnominal modifiers in the noun phrase.

Before we deal with various categories of noun modifiers, however, we shall devote some attention to the modified constituent, i. e. (head) noun, and to the internal structure of the noun phrase, insofar as this relates to matters of adnominal modification.

1.1. Nouns

This section is mostly concerned with the relationship between adnominal modification on the one hand and nominal subcategories and the occurrence of nouns as a separate word class on the other.

1.1.1. Nouns as a cross-linguistic category

Although it is usually assumed that each language has nouns, there are languages in which the existence of nouns as a distinct word class is at least doubtful. Consider, for example, these remarks about Samoan (Mosel/Hovdhaugen 1992: 77; see Hengeveld 1992 on parts-of-speech systems in general): "Many, perhaps the majority of, roots can be found in the function of verb phrase and NP nuclei and are, accordingly, classified as nouns and as verbs. [...] in Samoan the categorization of full words is not given a priori in the lexicon." For instance: *teine* 'girl', 'be a girl'; *tusi* 'book, letter', 'write'; *salu* 'broom', 'sweep'; *ma'i* 'patient, sickness', 'be sick'. It is basically the presence of non-lexical elements that indicates what particular function such predicates fulfil. If the predicate serves as the head of the clause, it will typically combine with tense-aspect-mood particles; if it serves as the head of the term it will appear with an article, a preposition, etc.

Thus, languages differ in the degree to which nouns can be distinguished from other word classes, but to what extent such differences systematically correlate with morphosyntactic properties of adnominal modifiers is still largely unexplored territory (but cf. Hengeveld et al. 1997).

1.1.2. Nominal subcategories and adnominal modification

Nouns are sometimes subdivided according to the kind of entity they denote. Thus, first order nouns are nouns that are used in relation with first order or spatial entities (*car, knife*), second order nouns are used for temporal entities (*meeting, game*), and higher order nouns denote entities beyond the spatio-temporal dimension (*thought, linguistics*). In addition there are, of course, proper names such as Max or Johanna, but apart from non-restrictive forms of modification (as in e. g. *Max, who had only recently bought a new house, ...*) these nouns are normally severely limited with respect to the various forms of (restrictive) adnominal modification; hence they will be ignored here. Apart from the fact that each noun imposes its own selection restriction on the various (sub)types of modifiers (cf. *a red dress* vs. **a dead dress*; i. e. the feature ± animate plays a role here), the possibility to occur with certain modifiers is often restricted by the kind of entity that is denoted by the noun. For example, strictly speaking only spatial entities can have a certain weight or colour (*big$_A$ car*), whereas only temporal entities can have a certain duration or speed (*brief$_A$ meeting, fast$_A$ game*). Yet it is possible to use first order (spatial) adjectives in combination with higher order nouns, as in *big$_A$ disappointment* (and vice versa, as in *fast$_A$ car*). Such combinations are by no means unusual, but unless they are stored as set phrases or idiomatic expressions they normally require some degree of extra cognitive processing on the part of the addressee to arrive at a meaningful interpretation. For example, when combined with a second order noun such as *speech*, the second order adjective *recent* specifies a property of a temporal entity (the "speech event"). But in *recent book* the same adjective modifies a first order noun, so that the resulting expression stands in need of a special interpretation. In this particular combination, the hearer is forced to conceive the book as a temporal rather than a spatial entity, i. e. *recent* specifies the time of publication. Usually, however, it is rather the other way around in that speakers often use first order adjectives in combination with higher order nouns, as in *big event, fat chance, high hopes, low temperature, flat refusal, open mind* (cf. Lakoff/Johnson 1980; Levinson 1992). This is commonly attributed to the way our cognitive system works: it is assumed that we understand complex, higher order entities in terms of simple spatial notions and categories (cf. "Localist hypothesis"; Lyons 1977: 718).

Finally, although it is generally true that there are certain restrictions as to possible noun-modifier combinations, it is also important to realize that probably all languages can, by metaphorical extrapolation, introduce new, seemingly incompatible modifier-noun combinations (in fact this is especially exploited in more creative forms of language use, such as poetry). It is also worth emphasizing that there is no one-to-one relation between linguistic attribution and ontological attribution: i. e. what can be meaningfully said (predicated) about things denoted by nouns is only partially determined by properties of entities in the extra-linguistic world (cf. Sommer 1965 on the difference between linguistic and ontological predicability).

Another way to characterize nouns is in terms of qualifications such as **singular object noun** (e.g. *dog*; since the bare noun *dog* denotes a singular object), **mass nouns** (*gold, oil*), **collective noun** (*family, team*). This kind of categorization also relates to adnominal modification in that, for example, in many languages mass nouns require a different set of quantifiers (*much water*) than singular object nouns and collective nouns (*many books, many families*). Although this categorization is essentially designed to account for spatial entities it appears that nouns for non-spatial entities can be characterized in terms of the same subcategories; thus 'love' is a mass noun, as in *much love*, and *meeting* is a singular object noun, as in *two meetings* (cf. Lehmann 1990; Dik 1985).

It is important, however, to realize that nouns may have different properties in different languages, even when they are used for the same thing in the external world. For example, in English plural marking is normally obligatory, both with and without a numeral: *a/the horse, (the) two horses*; but **(the) two horse*. In Oromo, on the other hand, plural marking is optional without a numeral and must be absent when the noun is modified by a numeral (Stroomer 1987, 76): *farda* 'horse/horses', *fardoollee* 'horses', *farda lama* [horse two] 'two horses'. Nouns of the Oromo type could be called set nouns, because they seem to designate a certain property of a set of entities (by definition, a set can contain any number of entities, including 'one'). Nouns in Thai and many other SE Asian languages are not marked for number under any circumstances and adnominal numerals appear with a so-called sortal (or: numeral) classifier, as in *rôm sǎam khan* [umbrella three CLF: LONG_HANDLED_OBJECT] 'three umbrellas'. It is assumed that the appearance of a sortal classifier is due to the fact that, contrary to e.g. English, the noun does not include in its lexical meaning the notion of spatial discreteness, boundedness or shape (cf. Hundius/Kölver 1983: 166). In other words, nouns like Thai *rôm* 'umbrella' (which occur with a sortal classifier and which therefore might be called **sort nouns**) are deemed to denote a non-bounded property in the spatial dimension, and since only spatially bounded entities can be counted directly special measures, i.e. classifiers, are needed before such nouns can be modified by a numeral (note that classifiers are also called "individualizers"; cf. Lyons 1977: 462). The employment of sortal classifiers in a language does, however, not necessarily imply that nouns denote a non-bounded property, since it is well known that (erstwhile) classifiers may come to be used for other purposes, such as marking specificity, topicality or definiteness (Adams 1989; Hopper 1986; Bisang 1999 fc.). Furthermore sortal classifiers must be distinguished from *mensural classifiers*, which we also find in Thai: *náamtaan sǎam thûaj* [sugar three cup] 'three cups of sugar' (Hundius/Kölver 1983: 168). Mensural classifiers are different from sortal classifiers in that they occur with mass nouns and always indicate some kind of measure (size, volume, weight).

Some languages (such as Yucatec Maya) are deemed not to differentiate between sortal and mensural classifiers, which may indicate that these languages also do not distinguish between **sort nouns** and **mass nouns**. One could call such nouns **general nouns**, and the classifiers that are used with these nouns: **general classifiers**. Compare (Lucy 1992: 74):

a/one-CLF banana [Yucatec Maya]
'un-wáal há'as   'one/a 2-dimensional banana (the leaf)'
'un-p'éel hà'as 'one/a 3-dimensional banana (the fruit)'
'un-kúul há'as   'one/a planted banana (the tree)'
'un-kúuch há'as 'one/a load banana (the bunch)'
'um-p'íit há'as 'a-little-bit/some banana'

1.2. Noun phrases

In the first section we saw that not every language has a distinct category of nouns and that different languages may use a different kind of noun (e.g. general noun, sort noun, set noun, singular object noun) for the same thing in the external world. In this section we will see that even if a language has nouns, this does not necessarily imply that the language also has noun **phrases** (NPs).

1.2.1. Integral and non-integral noun phrases

In many, perhaps most of the world's languages the adnominal modifier is an integral part of the noun phrase (NP) proper, in which case we speak of an **integral** NP (also called configurational, tight, hierarchical or non-fractured NP). In quite a few languages, however, some or all adnominal modifiers can or must be in an appositional relation with the phrase that contains the head noun (in such cases we speak of appositional modification or flat, loose, scrambled or fractured NPs). That is to say: in these languages the modifier is strictly speaking not a constituent of the NP, but constitutes a referring phrase by itself. In a number of languages (notably those spoken on the Australian continent) appositional modification of the noun seems to be the rule rather than the exception. For instance, Blake (1983: 145) argues that in Kalkatungu "there are in fact no noun phrases, but [...] where an argument is represented by more than one word we have nominals in parallel or in apposition. [...] Each word is a constituent of the clause [...]". Compare:

(1) (a) **Cipa-yi ṭuku-yu yaun-tu**
       this-ERG   dog-ERG big-ERG
       yani   icayi
       white-man bite
    (b) **Cipayi ṭukuyu** yani icayi **yauntu**
    (c) **ṭukuyu cipayi** icayi yani **yauntu**
    (d) **Yauntu cipayi ṭukuyu** icayi yani
    (e) **Cipayi** icayi yani **ṭukuyu yauntu**
    (f) **Yani** icayi **cipayi yauntu ṭukuyu**
       'This big dog bit/bites the white man'

There are also languages in which only certain modifiers are apposed or where appositional modification is the result of restrictions on the internal structure or complexity of the NP. For instance, noun phrases in Yimas "may consist of only two constituents, a modifier and a head, in that order. If more than two modifiers are present for a given noun, one must take an agreement suffix and occur in the scrambled pattern. [...] The scrambled structures have very different properties from the tight noun phrases. They are not single noun phrases at all, but rather two noun phrases in apposition, one consisting of a noun, the other a modifier, nominalized by the agreement suffix" (Foley 1991: 4).

In other languages only certain modifiers are regularly apposed, notably the numeral classifier phrase (Lehmann 1982: 255; see e.g. Comrie (1981: 269) on Nivkh, Lee (1989: 118) on Korean, Wheatley (1987: 851) on Burmese).

It may also be the case that fully integrated modifiers of the noun in one language must be regarded as (non-apposed) constituents at the level of the sentence in another language. This appears to hold, for instance, for the Hixkaryana equivalent of English attributive numerals, which according to Derbyshire (1979: 103) are basically adverbs.

1.2.2. The head of the phrase

Although it has recently been proposed that the determiner is the head of the term (giving rise to the so-called Determiner Phrase or DP analysis; Abney 1987), it is traditionally the noun that is considered to form the nucleus of the NP (Corbett/Fraser eds. 1993). It should, however, be recognized that there are some cases where morpho-syntactic evidence seems to suggest that it is the modifier rather than the noun which serves as the head of the phrase. Consider for instance this example from Finnish, in which the numeral (in the nominative) imposes partitive case on the noun: *kolme poika-a puhu-u Ranska-a* [three: NOM boy-PRTV:SG speak:PRS-3SG French] 'Three boys speak French' (see also e.g. Corbett 1991 on Russian numerals and Rischel 1995 on adjectives in Minor Mlabri; for a general discussion of 'dependency reversal' see Malchukov 2000c).

2. Adnominal modifiers

Adnominal modifiers can be divided into four major categories: qualitative modifiers, quantitative modifiers, locative modifiers, and referential modifiers. Apart from the last category, each of these modifier categories can be expressed by means of lexical elements (involving content words such as verbs, nouns, adjectives) and in the form of grammatical elements (involving articles, determiners, quantifiers and members from other non-lexical word classes). Note, however, that what is expressed by adnominal modification in one language can be realized by phonological or morphological means (e.g. tonal differences, inflection, affixation, derivation, compounding) in another language. For example, in Ossetic definiteness was indicated by shifting stress to the second syllable (Abaev 1964: 12) and in Nivkh adjectives are often incorporated into the head noun (Comrie 1981: 251). Below I will mostly deal with syntactical, i.e. free analytic expressions of adnominal modification.

2.1. Qualitative modifiers

Qualitative modifiers are modifiers which relate to the intrinsic, more or less characteristic properties ("qualities") of the referent and if a language has a class of adjectives, they are typically used to express such qualitative notions like age, value, colour, and size (Dixon 1982). Not every language has a distinct class of adjectives, however, or they may only have a small handful of them. Such languages often use abstract nouns or verbs to specify qualitative properties. In the first case the head noun is modified by a NP, as in this example from Hausa (Schachter 1985: 15): *mutum mai alheri* [person PROPR kindness] 'a kind person', lit. 'a person with kindness'. In the second case the head noun is modified by a qualifying or descriptive (rather than a restrictive) relative clause or participial construction, as in this example from Galela (van Baarda 1908: 35 f.): *awi dòhu i lalamo* [his foot 3:SG be__big] 'his big foot'. When in Galela the word 'big' (i. e. the verb 'to be big') is used attributively, the first syllable must be repeated, which yields the participial form. Additionally a personal pronoun must appear (here: i = 3SG 'it') which is coreferential with the matrix NP *awi dòhu* 'his foot'.

Tamil is a language with only a very small handful of basic, underived adjectives, which comprises such high-frequency items as *nalla* 'good', *periya* 'big', *cinna* 'small', *putu* 'new', *pazaya* 'old' and a few basic colour terms; e. g. *nalla manusan* [good man] 'a good man' (Asher 1982: 62; 187).

Finally there are language with adjectives that either occur as bound forms or as predicates in that they normally require a copula. Sarcee, for example, appears to have only bound adjectival modifiers: *tłi-yáná* [dog-old] 'old dog'. In his description of Sarcee, Cook (1984: 67 f.) adds that such complex forms "are different morphologically and semantically from nouns with a relative clause. The former is like a compound and the latter a phrase, comparable to the English nominal compound 'bláckbird' and phrase 'bláck bírd' " (on this phenomenon see also e. g. Li/Thompson (1989: 119) in Mandarin Chinese). In Ika nearly all adjectives must appear with the lexeme *kawa* which Frank (1990: 32) glosses as 'seem': *paka awʌn? kawa* [cow big seem] 'big cow'.

There is evidence that there are also **grammatical** (i. e. non-lexical) modifiers of the noun that relate to qualitative properties of the referent of the NP. Earlier we saw that there are languages (like Oromo) that employ set nouns, i. e. nouns which do not require a sortal classifier or a plural marker when reference is made to a plural entity; i. e. the noun can be in a direct construction with a cardinal numeral, in which case the so-called plural marker (if available at all) is normally obligatorily absent. It can be argued that the 'plural marker' on a set noun is actually not a number marker but a nominal (more accurately: collective) aspect marker (Rijkhoff 1990; Rijkhoff 1992: 87). The most important difference between a number marker (as we know it from e. g. Dutch and English: obligatory, both with and without a numeral modifier) and a nominal aspect marker (optional without a numeral modifier and in most languages obligatorily absent with a numeral) is that the number marker indicates that we are dealing with a referent that involves multiple singular objects (book+Pl = books) or multiple collectives (family+Pl = families), whereas the so-called plural marker (i. e. nominal aspect marker) on a set noun indicates that the referent is a non-singleton set (cf. Oromo *saree* 'dog/dogs' vs. *sareellee* 'dogs'). In fact, animate nouns in Oromo can also take the singulative suffixes *-(i)ca* (masculine), and *-(i)ttii* (feminine), as in *nama* 'man/men' vs. *namica* 'a/the man' (Stroomer 1987: 83), so that there are actually two ways to specify what kind of set is referred to: a singleton set (noun + singulative suffix) or a non-singleton / collective set (noun + so-called plural suffix).

The reason why these suffixes are better treated as nominal aspect markers than number markers has to with the fact that they do not so much serve to indicate number but rather specify what kind of entity is involved: a singleton set (containing one member) or a non-singleton set (i. e. a collective; note incidentally that in many languages the collective marker has developed into a 'proper' plural marker — see e. g. Comrie 1981: 167). In other words, just as verbal aspect marking is concerned with representations in the temporal dimension (perfective, ingressive, etc.), so nominal aspect marking relates to the way a nominal property is represented in the spatial dimension (i. e. as a collective or as a singular object).

2.2. Quantitative modifiers

Following Brown (1985) we may divide quantitative adnominal modifiers into: [1] absolute non-proportional (*five boys*), [2] relative non-proportional (*many/some/few girls*), [3] absolute proportional (*three of the five boys*), [4] relative proportional (*many/some/few of the girls*), [5] universal (*all students*). Ordinal numerals (*the second child*) indicate the position of a referent in a sequence. Although lower ordinals are often suppletive forms (as in English *first*, *second*), ordinals are commonly derived from cardinal numbers. In some languages, however, the forms are identical (e.g. Babungo; Schaub 1985: 240). Adnominal negators can been regarded as instances of zero quantification (as in *I have* **no** *money*; see e.g. Kahrel/Van de Berg 1994).

Probably all language communities have ways to indicate the cardinal number of a referent, but it is not quite certain that they all have developed adnominal cardinal modifiers for this purpose (Greenberg 1978b: 257; Hurford 1987). For example, in many languages cardinality is indicated by gestures (touching certain body-parts), which do not require verbalization.

As in the case of qualitative modifiers, we can find both grammatical and lexical expressions of adnominal modifiers that relate to quantitative properties of the referent. Restricting ourselves to cardinal numerals we find, for example, that in many Amerindian and Austronesian languages cardinality is expressed by verbs (or at least by lexemes that can only be used predicatively). In the following example from Boumaa Fijian the numeral is the main predicate of a special kind of relative clause (Dixon 1988: 144): *e tolu a gone* [3SG.S be_three ART child(ren)] 'three children' lit. '(the) children who are three'.

In other languages, such as those that belong to the large Bantu family, we find that at least some numerals have properties that are normally associated with nouns, e.g. they belong to a particular gender (traditionally called **noun class** in Bantu linguistics). In this example from Babungo the numeral 'two' agrees in gender with 'hundred', which belongs to noun class 3/4; class 4 is the plural of class 3 (Schaub 1987: 176; 187; C = class): *və̀-ŋgá yì-wáa yì-bɔ̀ɔ* [C2-antelope C4-hundred C4-two] 'two hundred antelopes'.

When cardinal numerals do not display verbal or nominal properties, as in Dutch (*drie boek-en* [three book-PL] 'three books), they are regarded as grammatical (i.e. nonlexical) modifiers of the noun. It was already mentioned that in many languages the numeral is not in a direct construction with the head noun, but must first combine with a so-called sortal classifier and that the (postnominal) numeral+classifier is often said to be in an appositional relationship with the noun. Such is the case, for instance, in Burmese: θwà lè hcàun [tooth four peg] 'four teeth' (Wheatley 1987: 851).

2.3. Locative modifiers

Locative adnominal modifiers have in common that they relate to locative properties, and hence to the identifiability of the referent. As in the case of qualitative and quantitative adnominal modifiers, we can distinguish between grammatical and lexical instances of locative adnominal modification. Grammatical modifiers that belong to this category are of course attributive demonstrative pronouns, which specify the location of a referent relative to a certain reference point, the so-called deictic center, which often coincides with the speaker's position. Demonstratives may also encode information about such diverse phenomena as visibility, shape, height (relative to speaker), and geographical and/or environmental features (Lyons 1977: ch. 15; Levinson 1983: ch. 2; Anderson/Keenan 1985: 259—308). There are languages, however, in which demonstratives are never used attributively (see e.g. Derbyshire (1979: 131) on Hixkaryana) and in other languages they seem to be appositional rather than fully integrated adnominal modifiers (see e.g. Donaldson (1980: 138; 229 ff.) on Ngiyambaa). In some languages demonstratives are formally identical with adverbs so that the same word is used to express 'this', 'here' and 'now' (Anderson/Keenan 1985: 278). Since spatial references often serve as the basis for metaphorical extension into other domains, they may eventually become definite articles or personal pronouns (Greenberg 1978a; Greenberg 1985). In quite a few languages the adnominal demonstrative co-occurs with the definite article (e.g. Hungarian and Abkhaz; cf. Moravcsik 1969: 76; Moravcsik 1997; Manzelli 1990) or a sortal classifier (e.g. Mandarin Chinese, Hmong Miao).

There are several lexical constructions that serve as locative modifiers, such as the possessor phrase, the (restrictive) relative clause, and of course the equivalent of English noun phrases such as *[the book] on the table*. Locative modifiers indicate that the entity referred to by the matrix NP has a place in the spatial, temporal or cognitive dimension. 'Location' is closely connected with 'identification': only entities whose location is known can be identified (hence lexical manifestations of locative modifiers such as genitives and relative clauses mostly occur in definite NPs). To give an example, even though *the house* in the sentences below has not been mentioned before, it can still be identified because in each case the adnominal modifier refers (or contains a reference) to a topical or otherwise identifiable entity: the Van Gogh Museum, the speaker's father, the addressee ('you'): "I bought the house **next to the Van Gogh Museum / my father's** house / the house **that you wanted to buy last year**". By establishing a existential relationship between the referent of the matrix NP (the house) and the identifiable entity referred to in the locative modifier the addressee can — by inference — also identify the referent of the matrix NP. If one knows or accepts that there is a Van Gogh Museum (i. e. that it has a location), then one can also infer the existence (location) of the house, viz. next to the Van Gogh Museum. Thus locative adnominal modifiers such as *(next to) the Van Gogh Museum* enable the addressee to *anchor* or *ground* the referent of the matrix NP (here: *the house*) in conversational space (Prince 1981: 236; Fox/Thompson 1990: 30). The localizing function of prepositional modifiers such as 'next to the van Gogh Museum' is rather obvious, but possessor phrases and relative clauses essentially serve the same purpose.

The relationship between possession and location has been investigated in studies by e. g. Clark (1970: 1978) and Lyons (1967). For example, Clark (1970: 3) has argued that, cognitively, possessed items are located 'at' the possessor and it also has been shown that in many languages markers of possessorship derive from locative elements (see e. g. Claudi/Heine 1986: 316). Possessive constructions have been the subject of several typological studies (Chappell/McGregor eds. 1996; Heine 1997; Manzelli 1990; Plank 1991; Seiler 1983; Ultan 1978). Adnominal possessive pronouns may be free elements (as in English *my book*) or bound forms (as in Gude *laa-kii* [cow-3SG] 'his cow'), but in quite a few languages they may also appear together (for emphasis), as in this example from Hungarian: *az én kabát-om* [the 1SG coat-1SG] 'my coat'. Cross-referencing of the possessor also occurs with nominal possessives, as in this example from Nasioi (Rausch 1912: 119): *nánin bakana danko* [man 3SG spear] 'the man's spear. With proper names and nouns designating kinship relations, however, the pronominal element is not used in Nasioi: *Máteasi bauran* [Mateasi daughter] 'Mateasi's daughter' (note that Nasioi does not mark the possessive relationship by a case marker or adposition). Some languages have a special set of possessive pronouns, but often there is no formal difference between personal and possessor pronouns (Ultan 1978: 36; cf. also Siewierska 1998). Across languages various morpho-syntactic means are used to distinguish between alienably and non-alienably possessed entities (inalienably possessed entities typically include bodyparts and kinship relations). If bound and free forms are used to mark this difference, the bound form is normally used to express inalienable possession (Ultan 1978: 36). In certain Oceanic and Amerindian languages alienable possessive constructions are characterized by the appearance of a so-called possessive or relational classifier (Lichtenberk 1983; Croft 1990: 26–39; Seiler 1983: 35–39), as in these Mokilese examples (Harrison 1988: 66): *nimoai pil* [CLF:DRINK.1SG water] 'my water (for drinking)' and *oai pil* [GENERAL.1SG water) 'my water (for washing)'.

Ultan (1978) also found the following morphosyntactic correlations between nominal and pronominal forms of adnominal possessive modification (G = possessive modifier):

1. "GN constituent order in a nominally possessed construction implies the same order in a pronominal (non-affixal) construction";
2. Personal possessive prefixes always imply a GN order, but not the converse; for personal possessive suffixes there is no such rule".

The localizing/identifying function of restrictive relative clauses is mentioned in e. g. Lehmann's monograph on relative clauses (see also Keenan/Comrie 1977; Lehmann 1986; Givón 1990: 645 f.; Foley 1986: 201); witness:

"Mit einem Relativsatz kann man leicht einen bestimmten Gegenstand durch Spezifikation der Situation, an der er teilhat, identifizieren. So erklärt es sich, daß die typische Relativkonstruktion von einem Definitum begleitet ist [...]" ["With a relative clause one can easily identify a certain object by specifying the situation in which it is involved. This explains that the typical relative clause construction co-occurs with a determiner [...]"] (Lehmann 1984: 402).

Unlike other adnominal modifiers, relative clauses are not only attested before or after the noun, but they may also contain the head noun as an integral constituent of the construction itself; this is so-called head-internal relative clause. The following example is from Imbabura Quechua (Cole 1982, 50 f.):

Marya jari-paj ruwana-ta rura-shka-ka Agatu-pi-mi kawsa-n [María man-for poncho-ACC make-NLZR-TOP Agato-in-VAL live-3] 'The man for whom María made a poncho lives in Agato'. Some languages employ the so-called adjoined relative clause, whose status as an adnominal modifier is not quite clear either for two reasons. Firstly, it precedes or follows the clause rather than the head noun and, secondly, it can often (also) be interpreted as an adverbial clause. This example from Walbiri illustrates (Hale 1976: 78−79): *ŋatjulu-ḷu ṇa yankiri pantu-ṇu, kutja-lpa ŋapa ŋa-ṇu* [1-ERG AUX emu spear-PAST Comp-AUX water drink-PAST] 'I speared the emu which was/while it was drinking water'. Finally there is the so-called corelative construction, which is strictly speaking not an adnominal modifier either. This construction is generally characterized by the fact that it contains a distinctive element, the corelative marker, which is referred to anaphorically by an element in the main clause, as shown in this example from Hindi (from Keenan 1985: 164; on corelatives see also Schwartz 1971; Downing 1978, 399 f.; Lehmann 1984: 122 f.; Givón 1990: 651): *Jis a:dmi ka kutta bema:r hai, us a:dmi ko mai ne dekha* [COREL.M men GEN dog sick is, that man DO I ERG saw] 'I saw the man whose dog is sick' (lit. 'Which man's dog was sick, that man I saw').

2.4. Referential modifiers

The last class of adnominal modifiers is formed by elements that relate to referential properties of a referent, i. e. articles indicating (in)definiteness, specificness, or genericness. They are used, for example, to indicate whether or not a referent is considered to be identifiable by the hearer (± definite reference), whether the speaker refers to a particular token (specific reference), or whether he refers to all tokens or any arbitrary token (generic reference). Definiteness and indefiniteness can be indicated in several ways (for some general overviews of the way (in)definiteness is expressed cross-linguistically, see e. g. Moravcsik 1969; Krámský 1972; Dryer 1989). A language may use special modifiers such as articles to express the notions of definiteness and indefiniteness, but in many languages the definite article is formally identical with the distal demonstrative modifier (Greenberg 1978a; Greenberg 1985). Indefinite articles most commonly derive from the numeral 'one' (Givón 1981).

Although it is true that in many languages the set of (in)definite articles is also used for specific and generic reference (as in English: ***The lion*** *is a dangerous animal* [generic]), there are also languages, such as Samoan, in which articles only mark the ± specific distinction (Mosel/Hovdhaugen 1992: 149; cf. also Greenberg 1978a and Greenberg 1981 on Stage II articles).

Since the equivalents of English modifiers like *other* and *same* also relate to referential (rather than locative, quantitative, or qualitative) properties of the referent of the noun phrase, they can be regarded as a special subclass of referential adnominal modifiers.

3. Syntax of adnominal modifiers

The sequencing of adnominal modifiers relative to each other and the noun has been investigated in a number of studies. With respect to the relative order of demonstrative + numeral + adjective + noun, Greenberg (1966: 86−87) formulated a number of universals, such as (on Universal 20 see cf. Hawkins (1983: 119−120); see also Aristar 1991; Dryer 1992):

Universal 18. When the descriptive adjective precedes the noun, the demonstrative and the numeral, with overwhelmingly more than chance frequency, do likewise.

Universal 19. When the general rule is that the descriptive adjective follows, there may be a minority of adjectives which usually precede, but when the general rule is that descriptive adjectives precede, there are no exceptions.

Universal 20. When any or all of the items (demonstrative, numeral, and descriptive adjective) precede the noun, they are always found in that order. If they follow, the order is either the same or its exact opposite.

With respect to the three adnominal modifier categories demonstrative − (non-lexical) numeral − adjective it appears that they generally adhere to one of the following patterns when they are fully integrated constituents of the NP (Rijkhoff 1990):

dem num A N   dem A N num   num A N dem
dem num N A   dem N A num   num N A dem
A N num dem
N A num dem

Although the pattern [dem A N num] did not occur in Hawkins' sample, there is evidence that the combination [A N] and [N num] is attested in Efik, Zande and other languages of the eastern Benue-Congo and Adamawa-Ubangi groups (Greenberg 1989: 113; Rijkhoff 1992: 271). Note that each of the eight patterns above is an instance of a more general pattern [dem num A N A num dem], in which [i] the locative modifier (dem) is always the first or last in the sequence, [ii] the qualitative modifier (A) is always adjacent to the noun, and [iii] the quantitative modifier (num) never appears between A and N. In other words, it appears that fully integrated modifiers in the simple noun phrase are ordered according to their semantic relevance or scope (cf. also Bybee (1985) with respect to the ordering of aspect, tense, and mood morphemes relative to the verb root). Adjectives specify qualitative properties, which have to do with more or less typical characteristics of the kind of entity defined by the noun and which are not connected with quantity or location. Cardinal numerals (quantitative modifiers) have scope over the noun and the adjectives in that they specify the number of entities involved, with all their qualitative properties. Finally, the demonstrative indicates the spatial position of the referent and since this involves the referent with all its qualitative and quantitative properties we may say that the demonstrative (the locative modifier) has the noun and both its qualitative and quantitative modifiers in its scope (Bartsch/Vennemann 1972; Seiler 1985).

Other ordering patterns than those given above all seem to involve appositional or phrasal modifiers, which appear to be sensitive to different sets of ordering principles than non-appositional and non-phrasal adnominal modifiers (Rijkhoff 1990; Rijkhoff 1992). Yet another reason why adnominal modifiers may deviate from the eight patterns specified above, is that a modifier may have a particular pragmatic function (such as contrastive or counter-assertive focus). In such cases the modifier will often appear in a special position (usually at the beginning or the end of the clause or the NP; cf. Siewierska 1984; Schaub 1985).

Little is known about the position of embedded modifiers (such as genitives and relative clauses) vis-à-vis other adnominal modifiers, but preliminary research indicates that, if they appear in postnominal position, such modifiers tend to occur follow all other postnominal modifiers (Rijkhoff 1997).

4. References

Abaev, V. I. 1964. *A grammatical sketch of Ossetic.* International Journal of American Linguistics: 30–4. Bloomington: Indiana University.

Abney, Steven P. 1987. *The English noun phrase in its sentential aspect.* Ph.D. dissertation, MIT, Cambridge, Mass.

Adams, Karen Lee. 1989. *Systems of numeral classification in the Mon-Khmer, Nicobarese, and Aslian subfamilies of Austroasiatic.* Pacific Linguistics B-101. Canberra: Australian National University.

Anderson, Stephen R. & Edward L. Keenan. 1985. "Deixis". In: Shopen (ed.), Vol. III, 259–308.

Aristar, Anthony Rodrigues. 1991. "On diachronic sources and synchronic pattern: an investigation into the origin of linguistic universals". *Language* 67–1: 1–33.

Asher, R. E. 1982. *Tamil* (Lingua Descriptive Studies 7). Amsterdam: North-Holland.

Baarda, M. J. van. 1908. *Leiddraad bij het bestuderen van 't Galela'sch dialekt, op het eiland Halmaheira* [Manual for the study of the Galela dialect, on the island of Halmahera]. The Hague: Nijhoff.

Bartsch, Renate & Theo Vennemann. 1972. *Semantic structures: a study in the relation between semantics and syntax.* Frankfurt am Main: Athenäum.

Bisang, Walter. 1999. "Classifiers in East and Southeast Asian languages: counting and beyond", in Gvozdanović (ed.), 113–185.

Blake, Barry J. 1983. "Structure and word order in Kalkatungu: the anatomy of a flat language". *Australian Journal of Linguistics* 3–2: 143–175.

Brown, D. Richard. 1985. "Term operators". In: Machtelt A. Bolkestein et al. (eds.), *Predicates and terms in Functional Grammar*, 127–145. Dordrecht: Foris.

Bybee, Joan L. 1985. *Morphology: a study of the relation between meaning and form* (Typological Studies in Language 9). Amsterdam: Benjamins.

Chappell, Hilary & William McGregor (eds.). 1996. *The grammar of inalienability: a typological perspective on body part terms and the part-whole relation.* Berlin: Mouton de Gruyter.

Clark, Eve V. 1970. "Locationals: a study of the relation between 'existential', 'locative', and 'possessive' constructions". *Working Papers in Language Universals* 3 (Stanford University), L1–L36 + xiii.

Clark, Eve V. 1978. "Locationals: existential, locative, and possessive constructions". In: Greenberg et al. (eds.), Vol. 4, 85–126.

Claudi, Ulrike & Bernd Heine. 1986. "On the metaphorical basis of grammar". *Studies in Language* 10–2: 297–335.

Cole, Peter. 1982. *Imbabura Quechua* (Lingua Descriptive Studies 5). Amsterdam: North-Holland.

Comrie, Bernard. 1981. *The languages of the Soviet Union*. Cambridge: Cambridge University Press.

Cook, Eung-Do. 1984. *A Sarcee grammar*. Vancouver: University of British Columbia Press.

Corbett, Greville G. 1991. "The head of the noun phrase: evidence from Russian numeral expressions". *EuroTyp Working Paper 7 of Theme Group 7 (Noun Phrase Structure) of the Eurotyp Programme in Language Typology*. Fachgruppe Sprachwissenschaft, Universität Konstanz.

Corbett, G. & N. M. Fraser (eds.). 1993. *Heads in grammatical theory*. Cambridge: Cambridge University Press.

Croft, William. 1990. *Typology and universals*. Cambridge: Cambridge University Press.

Derbyshire, Desmond C. 1979. *Hixkaryana*. (Lingua Descriptive Studies 1). Amsterdam: North-Holland.

Dik, Simon C. 1985. "Formal and semantic adjustment of derived constructions". In: Machtelt A. Bolkestein et al. (eds.). *Predicates and terms in Functional Grammar*, 1–28. Dordrecht & Providence RI: Foris.

Dixon, Robert M. W. 1982. *Where have all the adjectives gone? and other essays in semantics and syntax*. Berlin: Mouton de Gruyter.

Dixon, Robert M. W. 1988. *A grammar of Boumaa Fijian*. Chicago: University of Chicago Press.

Donaldson, T. 1980. *Ngiyambaa: the language of the Wangaaybuwan of New South Wales*. Cambridge: Cambridge University Press.

Downing, Bruce T. 1978. "Some universals of relative clause structure". In: Greenberg et al. (eds.), Vol. 4, 375–418.

Dryer, Matthew S. 1989. "Article-noun order". In: Wiltshire et al. (eds.), *CLS 25: Papers from the 25th annual regional meeting of the Chicago Linguistic Society. Part one: The general session*: 83–97. Chicago: Chicago Linguistic Society.

Dryer, Matthew S. 1992. "The Greenbergian word order correlations". *Language* 68–1: 81–138.

Foley, William A. 1986. *The Papuan languages of New Guinea*. Cambridge: Cambridge University Press.

Foley, William A. 1991. *The Yimas language of New Guinea*. Stanford: Stanford University Press.

Fox, Barbara A. & Sandra A. Thompson. 1990. "A discourse explanation of the grammar of relative clauses in English conversation". *Language* 66–2: 297–316.

Frank, Paul. 1990. *Ika syntax* (Studies in the languages of Columbia 1). Dalles: Summer Institute of Linguistics.

Givón, Talmy. 1981. "On the development of the numeral 'one' as an indefinite marker". *Folia Linguistica Historica* 2–1: 35–55.

Givón, Talmy. 1990. *Syntax: a functional-typological introduction. Volume II*. Amsterdam: Benjamins.

Goral, Donald R. 1978. "Numeral classifier systems: a Southeast Asian cross-linguistic analysis". *Linguistics of the Tibeto-Burman area* 4–1: 1–72.

Greenberg, Joseph H. 1966. "Some universals of grammar with particular reference to the order of meaningful elements". In: Joseph H. Greenberg (ed.), *Universals of language*. (2nd edition), 73–113. Cambridge: MIT.

Greenberg, Joseph H. 1978a. "How does a language acquire gender markers?". In: Greenberg et al. (eds.), Vol. 3, 48–82.

Greenberg, Joseph H. 1978b. "Generalizations about numeral systems". In: Greenberg et al. (eds.), Vol. 3, 250–295.

Greenberg, Joseph H. 1981. "Nilo-Saharan moveable -k as a Stage III article (with a Penutian typological parallel)". *Journal of African Languages and Linguistics* 3: 105–112.

Greenberg, Joseph H. 1985. "Some iconic relationships among place, time, and discourse deixis". In: John Haiman (ed.), *Iconicity in syntax* (Typological Studies in Language 9), 271–287. Amsterdam: Benjamins.

Greenberg, Joseph H. 1989. "The internal and external syntax of numerical expressions: explaining language specific rules". *Belgien Journal of Linguistics* 4: 105–118.

Greenberg, Joseph H. (ed.). 1966. *Universals of language* (2nd edition). Cambridge: MIT Press.

Greenberg, Joseph H. & Charles A. Ferguson & Edith A. Moravcsik (eds.). 1978. *Universals of human languages. Vol. 1: Method – Theory. Vol. 2: Phonology. Vol. 3: Word structure. Vol. 4: Syntax*. Stanford: Stanford University Press.

Gvozdanović, Jadranka (ed.). 1999. *Numeral types and changes worldwide* (Trends in Linguistics: Studies and Monographs 118). Berlin: Mouton de Gruyter.

Hale, Kenneth L. 1976. "The adjoined relative clause in Australia". In: Dixon (ed.), *Grammatical categories in Australian languages* (Linguistic series No. 22), 78–105. Canberra: Australian Institute of Aboriginal Studies.

Harrison, Sheldon P. 1988. "A plausible history for Micronesian possessive classifiers". *Oceanic Linguistics* 27–1/2: 63–78.

Hawkins, John A. 1983. *Word order universals. Quantitative analyses of linguistic structure*. New York: Academic Press.

Heine, Bernd. 1997. *Possession: cognitive sources, forces, and grammaticalization*. Cambridge: Cambridge University Press.

Hengeveld, Kees. 1992. *Non-verbal predication: theory, typology, diachrony*. Berlin: Mouton de Gruyter.

Hengeveld, Kees & Jan Rijkhoff & Anna Siewierska. Fc. "Parts-of-speech systems as a basic typological parameter". Paper read at the Second International Conference of the Association for Linguistic Typology (ALT), Eugene (Oregon), 10—14 September 1997.

Hurford, James R. 1987. *Language and number: the emergence of a cognitive system.* Oxford: Basil Blackwell.

Hopper, Paul J. 1986. "Some discourse functions of classifiers in Malay". In: Colette Craig (ed.), *Noun classes and categorization* (Typological Studies in Language 7), 309—325. Amsterdam: Benjamins.

Hundius, Harald & Ulrike Kölver. 1983. "Syntax and semantics of numeral classifiers in Thai". *Studies in Language* 7—2: 164—214.

Jones, Robert B. 1970. "Classifier constructions in southeast Asia". *Journal of the American Oriental Society* 90: 1—12.

Kahrel, Peter & René van den Berg (eds.). 1994. *Typological studies in negation.* (Typological Studies in Language 29). Amsterdam: Benjamins.

Keenan, Edward L. 1985. "Relative clauses". In: Shopen (ed.), Vol. II, 141—170.

Keenan, Edward L. & Bernard Comrie. 1977. "Noun phrase accessibility and Universal Grammar". *Linguistic Inquiry* 8—1: 63—99.

Krámský, Jiri. 1972. *The article and the concept of definiteness in language* (Janua Linguarum, Series Minor 125). The Hague: Mouton.

Lakoff, George & Mark Johnson. 1980. *Metaphors we live by.* Chicago: University of Chicago Press.

Lee, Hansol H. B. 1989. *Korean grammar.* Oxford: Oxford University Press.

Lehmann, Christian. 1984. *Der Relativsatz: Typologie seiner Strukturen, Theorie seiner Funktionen, Kompendium seiner Grammatik.* Tübingen: Narr.

Lehmann, Christian. 1986. "On the typology of relative clauses". *Linguistics* 24: 663—680.

Lehmann, Christian. 1990. "Towards lexical typology". In: William Croft et al. (eds.), *Studies in typology and diachrony: Papers presented to Joseph H. Greenberg on his 75th birthday* (Typological Studies in Language 20), 161—185. Amsterdam: Benjamins.

Levinson, Stephen C. 1983. *Pragmatics.* Cambridge: Cambridge University Press.

Levinson, Stephen C. 1992. "Primer for the field investigation of spatial description and conception". *Pragmatics* 2—1: 5—47.

Li, Charles N. & Sandra A. Thompson. 1989 [1981]. *Mandarin Chinese — A functional reference grammar.* Berkeley: University of California Press.

Lichtenberk, Frantisek. 1983. "Relational classifiers". *Lingua* 60: 147—176.

Lucy, John A. 1992. *Grammatical categories and cognition: a case study of the linguistic relativity hypothesis* (Studies in the Social and Cultural foundations of Language 13). Cambridge: Cambridge University Press.

Lyons, John. 1967. "A note on possessive, existential and locative sentences". *Foundations of Language* 3: 390—396.

Lyons, John. 1977. *Semantics* (2 vols). Cambridge: Cambridge University Press.

Malchukov, Andrej L. 2000. *Dependency reversal in noun-attribute constructions: towards a typology* (LINCOM Studies in Language Typology 03). München: Lincom Europa.

Manzelli, Gianguido. 1990. "Possessive adnominal modifiers". In: Johannes Bechert et al. (eds.), *Toward a typology of European languages,* 63—111. Berlin: Mouton de Gruyter.

Moravcsik, Edith A. 1969. "Determination". *Working Papers on Language Universals* 1 (Stanford University), 64—130.

Moravcsik, Edith. 1997. "Parts and wholes in the Hungarian noun phrase — a typological study". In Bohumil Palek (ed.), *Proceedings of LP'96. Typology: prototypes, item orderings and universals.* Prague: Charles University Press, 307—324.

Moser, Ulrike & Even Hovdhaugen. 1992. *Samoan reference grammar.* Oslo: Universitetsforlaget AS.

Plank, Frans. 1991. "On determiners: 1. Ellipsis and inflections, 2. Co-occurrence of possessives". *EuroTyp Working Paper 11 of Theme Group 7 (Noun Phrase Structure) of the Eurotyp Programme in Language Typology.* Fachgruppe Sprachwissenschaft, Universität Konstanz.

Prince, Ellen F. 1981. "Toward a taxonomy of Given-New information". In: Peter Cole (ed.), *Radical pragmatics,* 223—255. New York: Academic Press.

Rausch, P. J. 1912. "Die Sprache von Südost-Bougainville, Deutsche Salomonsinseln". *Anthropos* 7: 105—134, 585—616, 694—994.

Rijkhoff, Jan. 1990. "Explaining word order in the noun phrase". *Linguistics* 28: 5—42.

Rijkhoff, Jan. 1991. "Nominal aspect". *Journal of Semantics* 8—4: 291—309.

Rijkhoff, Jan. 1992. *The noun phrase: a typological study of its form and structure.* Ph.D. diss. University of Amsterdam (revised version to be published by Oxford UP).

Rijkhoff, Jan. 1997. "Word order in the noun phrase of the languages of Europe". In Anna Siewierska (ed.), *Constituent order in the languages of Europe,* ch. 11. Berlin: Mouton de Gruyter.

Rischel, Jørgen. 1995. *Minor Mlabri: a hunter-gatherer language of Northern Indochina.* University of Copenhagen: Museum Tusculanum Press.

Schachter, Paul. 1985. "Parts-of-speech systems". In: Shopen (ed.), Vol. I, 3—61.

Schaub, Willi. 1985. *Babungo*. London: Croom Helm.

Schwartz, Arthur. 1971. "General aspects of relative clause formation". *Working Papers on language Universals* 6 (Stanford University), 139–171.

Seiler, Hansjakob, 1985. "Kategorien als fokale Instanzen von Kontinua, gezeigt am Beispiel der Nominalen Determination". In: B. Schlerath & V. Ritter (eds.), *Grammatische Kategorien: Funktion und Geschichte*, 435–448. Wiesbaden: Dr. Ludwig Reichert.

Seiler, Hansjakob. 1983. *Possession as an operational dimension of language*. Tübingen: Narr.

Shopen, Timothy (ed.). 1985. *Language typology and syntactic description. Volume I: Clause structure. Volume II: Complex constructions. Volume III: Grammatical categories and the lexicon.* Cambridge: Cambridge University Press.

Siewierska, Anna. 1984. "Phrasal discontinuity in Polish". *Australian Journal of Linguistics* 4–1: 57–71.

Siewierska, Anna. 1998. "On nominal and verbal person marking". *Linguistic Typology* 2–1: 1–55.

Sommers, F. 1965. "Predicability". In M. Black (ed.), *Philosophy in America*, 262–281. London: Allen and Unwin.

Stroomer, Harry J. 1987. *A comparative study of three southern Oromo dialects in Kenya (phonology, morphology and vocabulary)* (Cushitic Language Studies 6). Hamburg: Buske.

Ultan, Russell. 1978. "Toward a typology of substantival possession". In: Greenberg et al. (eds.), Vol. 4, 11–50.

Wheatley, Julian K. 1987. "Burmese". In Bernard Comrie (ed.), *The world's major languages*, 834–854. London: Croom Helm.

*Jan Rijkhoff, Dept. of Linguistics,
University of Aarhus (Denmark)*

41. Dimensionen der verbalen Modifikation

1. Zielsetzung
2. Überblick über die Morphologie des Verbs
3. Morphologische Explizitheit
4. Maximale Komplexität
5. Relevanz
6. Satzbereiche und Relevanzgrade als Prinzipien der Morphemstellung
7. Morphemstellung neben anderen Indikatoren der Relevanz
8. -ti als Zeichen der Bereichsabgrenzung bzw. Bereichserweiterung
9. Abbau durch Konversion
10. Kontextbedingte Weglaßbarkeit
11. Affinitäten zwischen Dimensionen
12. Asymmetrie zwischen Prä- und Suffigierung
13. Änderung des morphologischen Status
14. Kindergerichtete Elternsprache
15. Ontogenese
16. Grammatikalisierung und Polyfunktionalität
17. Spezielle Abkürzungen
18. Zitierte Literatur

1. Zielsetzung

Verben können viele Arten von grammatischer Information tragen: 'Valenz', 'Diathese', 'Tempus', 'Aspekt', 'Modus', 'Person', 'Numerus', 'Aktionsart', 'lokale Deixis' etc. Viel ist über den möglichen Zusammenhang zwischen diesen Dimensionen der verbalen Modifikation und zu ihrem kognitiven Hintergrund gesagt worden. Für die einen gibt es z. B. eine mehr oder minder kanonische Reihenfolge der Signale für Modus – Tempus – Aspekt, für andere gilt Aspekt – Modus – Tempus.

Im Rahmen dieses Beitrags kann nun nicht versucht werden, jede einzelne Dimension – und noch weniger jede einzelne für das Verb relevante Kategorie – zu behandeln. Ziel ist es vielmehr, ausgehend von einer Sprache, die eine sehr ausgebaute, explizite Verbalmorphologie aufweist – es geht um die utoaztekische Sprache HUICHOL – allgemeine Überlegungen über die relative Relevanz der verbalen Dimensionen, die Organisation der verschiedenen daran beteiligten Kategorien und die Affinitäten zwischen ihnen anzustellen. Der expansive Charakter des HUICHOL kann entscheidend dazu beitragen, die innere Komplexität der einzelnen Kategorien und Dimensionen wie 'Tempus', 'Aspekt', 'Modalität', 'Lokalisation' und 'Partizipation' besser zu erkennen, und andererseits die vielfältigen Beziehungen zwischen ihnen transparenter zu machen.

Besonders aufschlußreich sind dabei: die Abgrenzung von Bereichen im Vor- und Nachfeld des Verbs (s. u. §§ 6–8); die sukzessive Reduzierung der ausgedrückten Dimensionen mit zunehmender Nominalität der Verbalformen (s. u. § 9); schließlich die Art und Weise, wie Eltern die Explizitheit reduzieren, wenn sie zu Kleinkindern sprechen, sowie der sukzessive Aufbau des Ausdrucks dieser Dimensionen in der Ontogenese (s. u. §§ 14; 15).

2. Überblick über die Morphologie des Verbs

Um das Verständnis zu erleichtern, biete ich in den folgenden Tabellen eine Übersicht über die wichtigsten formalen und semantischen Aspekte der Affixe: Positionen, Funktionen, Kategorien. Tabelle 41.1 zeigt dabei die 18 Positionen, die maximal vor dem Verb-Kern besetzt sein können, und ihre Exponenten; Tabelle 41.2 zeigt das Analoge für die 14 Positionen hinter dem Verballexem.

Die Exponenten der Partizipation (→ Art. 27, § 4.5; Art. 37) verteilen sich über den ganzen Bereich, alle anderen Dimensionen umspannend: Die personalen Formen des SUBJEKTS erscheinen in 17: *ne* '1SG', *pe* '2SG', *te* '1PL', *xe* '2PL', *me* '3PL'. Die Exponenten des OBJEKTS verteilen sich auf mehrere Positionen, der Hierarchie der Kategorie 'Person' folgend: '1/2SG' sowie '1PL' in 12, '2/3PL' in 9. Die Form der 3. Person in 5 hat deiktischen Wert und erscheint nur in Abwesenheit einer expliziten NP: sie verweist auf ein einzelnes Lebewesen und ist in Bezug auf Unbeleb-

tes numerusindifferent (I). In 3 erscheinen die reflexiven Formen des Objekts: *ne* '1SG', '*a* '2SG', *ta* '1PL', *yu* '3SG/PL, 2PL'.

Die Affixe von 18 drücken eine Graduierung des Prädikats bzw. der Assertivität aus: '*a* 'viel, positiv', *tsi-* 'wenig, negativ', *ya-* 'so [deiktisch]'. *Ka*-$_{16}$ ist 'hesitativ', *ka*-$_{13}$ 'Negation', *xika-* 'konditional' (wenn, ob), *ke-* 'Imperativ'.

Die Hauptexponenten der Modalität erscheinen in den Positionen 15, 14, 10: man kann vereinfacht sagen, daß *pi-* das Zeichen der Nähe in der Kommunikation ist, geeignet für augenfällige, einsichtige, offenkundige, auf den unmittelbaren Kontext bezogene Sachverhalte; es ist der Ausdruck der Assertivität schlechthin (AS). *Mi-* ist dagegen das Zeichen der Distanz zwischen dem Sachverhalt und dem Kommunikationsakt, geeignet für alte, überlieferte, berichtete Sachverhalte, für die der Sprecher selber sich nicht verbürgt; es ist im Hinblick auf Assertivität das neutrale Modalmorphem und wird daher oft einfach mit 'MOD' glossiert. Kombinationen mit *ka*-$_{14}$ und *ni*-$_{10}$ drücken verschiedene vom Sprecher verliehene Wichtigkeitsgrade der Information aus und stellen eine formale (FOR) Haltung von Autorität her oder garantieren, daß der Sprecher für die Richtigkeit der Angaben einsteht. Es ist kein diskontinuierliches Morphem, denn jedes Element kann für sich

Tabelle 41.1: Maximal mögliche Präfixe der finiten Verbalformen

18	17	16	15	14	13	12	11	10	9	8	7	6	5	4	3	2	1	0
'a tsi ya	ne pe te xe me	ka	pɨ mɨ	ka	ka	ne ma ta	ti	ni	xe wa	tsi	'u	ha	'i	na nu	ne 'a ta	ti ta ku	RED	SUPPL
			xɨka			⇄						he			wa yu	ka ye		
				ke									heu					
DIST	INTS BEKR	SUBJ	HES MOD	AS FOR KOND	NEG IMP	O	SKAL GENR SORT BEKR EFR KM	FOR EVID INV IR	O	MT	HGR	FIG IP CIS EXP DURCH GLOB	O	QUER CIS TRSL VORN	REFL	AUF AB QUER LIM UPL EP	VPL	DER
KAT	G M	GRF	M			GRF	G GEN M	M	GRF		L M	L M	L M	GRF L	L	L AA P/I	AA	FLEX
DIM	G S	P I	S	J		P I	BB P/I S J	S	P I		L S	L POS	L S	P I	L	BB P	BB	BB
	Klit			Flexiv														
																	Derivativ	

Die Präfixe drücken Begriffe aus, die unter die Dimensionen **G**(raduierung), **M**(odalität), **I**(ndividuation), **P**(artizipation), **L**(okalisation) und Begriffsbildung (**BB**) fallen.

genommen einen unabhängigen Beitrag zur Aussage leisten und unterliegt spezifischen Kookkurrenzbeschränkungen.

Die Exponenten der drei modalen Positionen bilden einen komplexen Ausdruck des formalen Stils; so gekennzeichnete verbale Formen dienen im Diskurs besonders der Mitteilung von festen Glaubenssätzen und überlieferten Lehren (s. Gómez 1999), die in der Regel als zeitlich unbegrenzt (atemporal) angesehen werden. Gerade aus dieser Funktion ergeben sich die Kookkurrenzbeschränkungen mit Tempusmorphemen.

Aber auch die Affixe von 11 und 7/6 haben modale Bedeutungen. Ti_{11} drückt in Verbindung mit tsi_{18} Intensität des vom Prädikat bezeichneten Prozesses (G), GENERALISIERUNG im Hinblick auf das PATIENS (P), UNPERSÖNLICHKEIT (P), aber auch eine Verstärkung der Assertion wie BEKRÄFTIGUNG oder EMPHASE, oder eine Entscheidungsfrage (M) aus. Zuletzt dient es als Zeichen eines Schemas der Textorganisation, indem es die Wiederholung von Exponenten der Modalität in den Hauptprädikaten desselben Satzgefüges (Periode) vermeidet (KONSTANZ DER MODALITÄT).

Tsi_8 hat eine morphotaktische Funktion (MT): in Abwesenheit anderer Elemente muß es die homophonen reflexiven und nicht-reflexiven Objektaffixe identifizieren.

Die Elemente der Positionen 7 bis 4 bilden ein formal und semantisch komplexes System, in dem sehr viele Lokalisationsschemata, aber auch 'Modalität' bezeichnet werden: *u* 'sichtbar', 'etwas, was im Erfahrungsbereich des Sprechers stattgefunden hat', *ha* 'aus eigener Erfahrung', *he* 'hat außerhalb des Erfahrungsbereichs des Sprechers stattgefunden', 'vom Hörensagen'.

Die Elemente von 2 zeichnen sich durch den größten Grad an Polyfunktionalität aus: sie drücken vielfältige lokale Schemata, aber auch daraus abgeleitete Begriffe wie 'Terminativ', 'Pluralität der Handlung' usw. aus, die unter den Begriff 'Aktionsart' fallen.

Auch bei den Grammemen, die dem Verb suffigiert werden können (Tabelle 41.2), verhalten sich P(artizipation) und S(ituierung) hinsichtlich der Nähe zum Nukleus weitgehend komplementär. Modalität kommt am äußeren Rand vor; neu ist hier, daß die Exponenten der letzten Position eine emotionale Komponente beinhalten. Partizipation umfaßt hier Techniken zur Änderung der thematischen Struktur (Erweiterung oder Verminderung der Valenz) wie TR(ansitivierung), KAUS(ativierung), PROM(otion) sowie zur (Änderung der) PERSP(ektivierung) durch verschiedene Orientierungstechniken. (Zur Dimension JUNKTION (J) s. Raible 1992; → Art. 45.)

Für weitere Informationen zur morphologischen Struktur des HUICHOL sei auf einige frühere Arbeiten verwiesen (Iturrioz & Gómez 1988; Iturrioz 1989; 1992; 1999).

3. Morphologische Explizitheit

Wenn wir Beispiel (1) betrachten, stellen wir fest, daß im HUICHOL viele Operationen, die in anderen Sprachen implizit bleiben bzw. aus dem Kontext erschließbar sind, explizit ausgedrückt werden können bzw. müssen, wobei anscheinend ein beträchtliches Maß an Redundanz in Kauf genommen wird: Wir finden dreimal Signale für formale Rede (FOR), dreimal für pluralisches Subjekt (PL.S). Um denselben Sachverhalt im DEUTSCHEN auszu-

Tabelle 41.2: Maximal mögliche Suffixe der finiten Verbalformen

	1	2	3	4	5	6	7	8	9	10	11	12	13	14
	tia ya ta ma	tsi	tia (tɨi)	ya	rie	xɨa	xime rɨme ne/tɨwe we/wawe mɨkɨ/ku	tɨ	xɨ nɨ kai	tsie kɨ	tɨ	ni	tɨ	kaku
DIST	TR FACT KOM	MT	KAUS TR	PROM PAS	PROM PAS	DISTR	INM PGR KAP DESID IMPL FUT	ERW	PERF IMPF	TEMP FUT	ERW KAUSAL	FOR	ERW	leider halt
KAT	THS		THS	THS	THS	AA	AA	T/A	NEX		M		M	
DIM	P		P	P	P	BB	BB	S	J		J		S	

drücken, reichen 5 Morpheme aus, die auf drei autonome Wörter verteilt sind: *wir woll-en lern-en*; im SPANISCHEN sind es vier Morpheme und zwei Wörter: *quere-mos aprende-r*.

(1) Te$_{17}$- ka$_{14}$- te$_{11}$- ni$_{10}$- ta$_3$-
    1PL.S FOR   GEN:PL.S FOR   REFL.1PL
    P   eM   P/I/eM   eM   P/I
    ti$_2$- '**iki** -tɨa$_1$ -ku$_7$ -ni$_{12}$.
    VPL   zeig   KAUS DES:PL.S FOR
    AA/I   P   dM/I/T   eM
    'Wir wollen lernen – queremos aprender'

Beispiel (1) zeigt Morpheme, die dem Verb-Lexem vorangehen und nachfolgen. Die Indexziffern an den Morphemen geben die absolute Position der jeweiligen Klassen vor dem Verb (bei den Präfixen) oder nach dem Verb (bei den Suffixen) an. An den freibleibenden Positionen könnten – unter bestimmten Kookkurrenzbeschränkungen – andere Elemente eingesetzt werden.

In der zweiten Zeile steht der grammatische Kommentar: FOR = 'formal' (generelle Assertion), GENR = 'Generalisator', PL.S = 'pluralisches Subjekt', VPL = 'verbale Pluralität', DES = 'desiderativ', KAUS = 'kausativ'.

Die Buchstaben der dritten Zeile sind Kurzbezeichnungen für die funktionalen Domänen, denen die einzelnen Kategorien zugewiesen werden: P steht für 'Partizipation', I für 'Individuation', M für 'Modalität', A für 'Aspekt', AA für 'Aktionsart', d für 'deontisch' und e für 'epistemisch'.

Sprachen unterscheiden sich voneinander in Bezug auf die Explizitheit in doppelter Weise, einmal durch die Anzahl der Dimensionen, die am Prädikat markiert werden, und zweitens durch den Grad der Entfaltung jeder Dimension in verschiedene Techniken und Kategorien, gemessen an der Anzahl der Exponenten, die für jede Dimension in derselben Äußerung eingesetzt werden können bzw. müssen (→ Art. 1, § 3.3; → Art. 45, Tabelle 45.7).

Jede Operation, die die Argumentstruktur oder eine Valenzmodifikation anzeigt, hinterläßt eine eigene Spur:

– -*tɨa*$_1$ zeigt eine Erweiterung der Valenz um eine neue Rolle, *ta*$_3$- gibt die Person und die grammatische Funktion des neuen Arguments an, während *te*$_{11}$- einer Operation der Generalisierung im Hinblick auf das Patiens (das als direktes Objekt in der nicht markierten Diathese oder als zweites direktes Objekt im Hintergrund in Fall einer Promotion bzw. im Passiv erscheint)

als Exponent dient und außerdem die Pluralität des Subjekts anzeigt.
– 'Modalität' erhält in Beispiel (1) mehrere Exponenten, nämlich *ka*$_{14}$-, *te*$_{11}$-, *ni*$_{10}$-, -*ku*$_7$, -*ni*$_{12}$, die mit Ausnahme des externen Arguments *te*$_{17}$- 'wir' das ganze Wort umklammern.
– Auf die Pluralität des Subjekts wird an drei Stellen verwiesen: *te*$_{16}$-, *te*$_{11}$-, -*ku*$_7$.

Von Redundanz kann jedoch streng genommen nicht die Rede sein, denn jeder Exponent bringt eigene Information, ist im Hinblick auf Kookkurrenzbeschränkungen von den anderen relativ unabhängig, erscheint an einer anderen Stelle und geht mit Exponenten anderer Dimensionen spezifische Beziehungen ein: Polyfunktionalität, kumulative Exponenz, usw. 'Modalität' kann auch durch nur zwei Elemente, nämlich *ni*$_{10}$-/-*ni*$_{12}$ bzw. allein durch das Suffix -*ni*$_{12}$ ausgedrückt werden; was sich dabei ändert, ist das Gewicht, das dem jeweiligen Sachverhalt im Zusammenhang des Textes gegeben wird.

Hinter dem Suffix -*tɨa*$_1$ steckt in Beispiel (1) eine Operation der Erweiterung der Valenz von *'iki* 'kopieren, nachahmen' um einen neuen obligatorischen Mitspieler: das Resultat dieser Operation, die üblicherweise TRANSITIVIERUNG genannt wird, ist ein zweistelliges, transitives Prädikat mit der Bedeutung 'unterrichten, unterweisen, jemandem etwas beibringen'; verbunden mit dem gebundenen reflexiven Pronomen heißt es 'lernen'.

Im DEUTSCHEN und SPANISCHEN gibt es keine offene Markierung der Transitivität, die transitiven Verben *lernen* und *aprender* brauchen nicht einmal eine explizite NP mit der Funktion des direkten Objekts, wie man es für ein transitives Verb erwarten würde; in diesem syntaktischen Aspekt stimmt HUICHOL mit den zwei anderen Sprachen überein, aber nur teilweise, denn im HUICHOL wird die Nichtbesetzung der Leerstelle nicht lediglich durch die Abwesenheit eines gebundenen Pronomens bzw. einer expliziten NP angegeben, sondern explizit durch ein Morphem, welches eine Operation der Generalisierung anzeigt: damit wird zu verstehen gegeben, daß die Handlung des Lernens auf keinen bestimmten Gegenstand bezogen wird, weil es sich um einen generischen Sachverhalt handelt; zugleich wird durch die Kongruenz dieser generische Sachverhalt als Charakterisierung des Subjekts hingestellt.

Die Nominalphrase SPAN. *La Guerra* 'Der Krieg', so heißt der Name eines kleinen Ortes am Rand des HUICHOL-Gebiets, wurde ins

HUICHOL durch eine sehr deskriptive verbale Bezeichnung übersetzt:

(2) Mi- r- a- yu- ta- **kwi** -ti -xi.
     MOD IMPS FIG REFL LIM töt ERW PERF
     'Wo man sich tötete.'

4. Maximale Komplexität

Die morphologische Komplexität zeigt sich nicht nur in der Anzahl der Elemente, die in einer Kette aneinander gereiht werden müssen bzw. können, sondern auch in der Polysemie der einzelnen Exponenten und in der Komplexität der Regeln, die die innere Organisation der Paradigmen und die Kombination von so vielen Exponenten bestimmen.

Im Folgenden wird die Aufmerksamkeit hauptsächlich auf die lineare Komplexität gerichtet. Die relative Anordnung der nebeneinander vorkommenden Elemente und die Kookkurrenzbeschränkungen bestimmen ein System von Positionen und Positionsklassen. Zwischen Positionen und Paradigmen besteht keine ein-eindeutige Entsprechung, denn Elemente desselben Paradigmas können an verschiedenen Positionen und Elemente verschiedener Paradigmen in derselben Position erscheinen (Iturrioz 1999). Somit ist es nicht möglich, ein Wort mit Vertretern aller Paradigmen zu bilden. Eine Verbalform kann immerhin eine maximale Komplexität von beinahe dreißig Morphemen aufweisen, Klitika nicht eingeschlossen.

Das folgende Wort besteht aus 29 Morphemen, das inkorporierte Nomen *tsiikiri* 'Hund:PL:PL' als unanalysiertes Ganzes mitgerechnet, weil es sich hier nicht um einen rein syntaktischen Prozeß handelt (zur Inkorporation → Art. 53).

(3) Tsi_{18} $-me_{17}-$ ka_{16} $-mi_{15}-$ ka_{14}
     ITS   3PL.S   HES   MOD   NEG
     M   P/PT   M   M   M

     $-ka_{13}-$ $te_{11}-$ $(ni_{10}-)$ xe_9- tsi_8-
     FOR   GENR:PL.S FOR   2PL   MT
     M   M   M/P   M   M

     ha_6- nu_4- yu_3- ti_2- **$tsiikiri$** $-ye_2$
     FIG   TRSL   REFL   AUF   Hunde   in
     M   M   P   L/A   L

     $-ku_1-$ KU_0 $-ya_1$ $-tsi_2$ $-tii_3$
     RED   kämpf:SUPPL   DER   MT   KAUS
     L   I   P   P

     $-rie_5$ xia_6 $-xime_7$ $-kai_9$ $(-tsie_{10}$
     APPL   DISTR   NEX   IMPF   TEMP
     P   AA/I   AA   A/T   J

     $/-ki_{10})$ ti_{13} $-kaku_{14}$.
     KAUSAL   ERW   schade
     J   MT   M

'Gerade als sie sich anschickten, euch hinaufzuschicken, damit ihr unterwegs ihre Hunde kämpfen laßt.'

Das Wort enthält nur ein verbales Lexem und ein inkorporiertes Nomen, alle anderen Elemente sind Grammeme, die zum Teil den lexikalischen Begriff bereichern, zum Teil Operationen anzeigen, die Beziehungen zu anderen Sachverhalten im Text und zum Redekontext herstellen. Am rechten Rand des prädikativen Worts erscheint das nexuale Morphem -*kaku*, welches der Vermittlung des Abschnittabgrenzers -*ti* bedarf, wenn es an ein volles (nicht reduziertes) Wort mit modalen und/oder temporalen Morphemen angehängt wird (s. u. § 8).

5. Relevanz

Die Relevanz einiger Kategorien bzw. der jeweiligen Dimensionen für das Verb ist bisher vor allem durch Vergleich zwischen Sprachen erforscht worden (Foley & van Valin 1984; Drossard 1991; Broschart 1987; 1988), und durch den Vergleich diachronischer Prozesse (Bybee 1985; Bybee & Pagliuca 1985; Bybee & al. 1994). Auch im vorliegenden Kontext wird besonderer Wert auf die Morphemstellung gelegt, d. h. auf die relative Nähe zum Stamm, auf die diachronischen und funktionsbedingten Änderungen der Morphemstellung, aber es werden außerdem andere Indikatoren berücksichtigt wie die kontextbedingte Weglaßbarkeit und der schrittweise Abbau der Dimensionen im Rahmen eines komplexen Nominalisierungsprozesses. Die Kategorien, die bei zunehmender Nominalisierung übrigbleiben, sind mit Verbalität weniger inhärent verbunden (s. u. § 9).

Man sollte aber auch die Affinität zwischen Dimensionen – d. h. ihre gegenseitige Relevanz – untersuchen. Für den typologischen Vergleich ist die Verteilung der Dimensionen auf die lexikalischen Hauptkategorien 'Nomen' und 'Verb' ein wichtiger Parameter, die Art ihrer Assoziierung innerhalb einer Wortklasse bzw. übergreifend ein wichtiger Affinitätsindex.

So erweist sich 'Lokalisation' im HUICHOL als eine für das Verb zentrale Dimension, die in vielfältiger Weise den Verbalbegriff bereichert und sich auch als Quelle von partizipativen und individuativen Schemata herausstellt. Im BASKISCHEN spielt sie dagegen eine zentrale Rolle in der Nominalflexion, aber auch hier geht sie sehr enge Beziehungen zu

'Individuation' und 'Partizipation' ein (Iturrioz 1985).

Auf die enge Beziehung zwischen den Begriffen 'Raum' und 'Gegenstand' vom psychogenetischen Standpunkt aus hat Piaget in mehreren Arbeiten hingewiesen (z. B. Piaget 1978; Piaget & Inhelder 1980).

Einige Exponenten sind polyfunktional, und ihre Funktionen organisieren sich in Hierarchien, die Beziehungen zwischen Dimensionen erkennen lassen. Auch die Untersuchung des Erwerbs dieser Kategorien durch Kinder bringt weitere interessante Ergebnisse.

Viele — auf den ersten Blick sehr heterogene — Phänomene wie (Änderung der) Morphemstellung, Wortunterbrechung, Abbau durch Nominalisierung (s. u. § 7; → Art. 38; Art. 45) usw. könnten eine einheitliche Erklärung erhalten, wenn man Morpheme nicht als statische und isolierte Entitäten betrachtet, sondern aus der Perspektive von Prozessen, die ein dynamisches System von Beziehungen zwischen Dimensionen und zum Prädikat bilden.

6. Satzbereiche und Relevanzgrade als Prinzipien der Morphemstellung

Verschiedene Autoren haben nach den Faktoren gefragt, die die relative Reihenfolge der Affixe bestimmen. Die Verteilung der Positionen auf verschiedene Kategorien von Morphemen folgt gewissen allgemeinen Prinzipien, die etwas mit den Beziehungen der Dimensionen zum Prädikat, aber auch zwischen den Dimensionen und den jeweiligen Kategorien, zu tun haben. William A. Foley und Robert D. van Valin (1984: 208 ff.) führen Belege für eine Reihenfolge A-M-T an, was sie darauf zurückführen, daß diese Kategorien als Operatoren über verschiedenen Satzbereichen fungieren, d. h. sich durch das auszeichnen, was van Valin ein „increasingly wider scope", nennt (1984: 41):

giert vor 'Tempus'. Werner Drossard (1991) untermauert diese Reihenfolge mit Beobachtungen zur Kasusmarkierung. Joan L. Bybee (1985) vergleicht eine größere Anzahl von Kategorien in einer größeren Anzahl von Sprachen anhand von zwei miteinander korrelierenden Hauptkriterien (morphonologische Fusion der Affixe mit dem Stamm und die unmittelbare semantische Relevanz der Affixe für den Stamm) und kommt zu folgendem Schluß:

„[the result] can be used to arrange inflectional categories on a scale from which various predictions can be made. For instance, the categories of VALENCE, VOICE, ASPECT, TENSE, MOOD and AGREEMENT are ranked for *relevance to verbs* in that order. From this ranking we can predict the frequency with which categories have lexical, derivational or inflectional expression in the languages of the world, the ordering of affixes, as well as the extent to which the stem and affix have a morphophonemic effect upon one another" (1985: 4−5).

Der Relevanzgrad bestimmt eine hierarchische Ordnung der Kategorien, welche sich in der relativen Nähe der Morpheme zum Stamm widerspiegelt. Dahinter steckt das allgemeine, kognitiv relevante Prinzip des konstruktionellen Ikonismus (Mayerthaler 1981; → Art. 30), d. h. der diagrammatischen Organisation der Ausdrucks- und der Inhaltsebene, der Kovariation von zwei Kontinua (Seiler 1988; 1995).

Da die Häufigkeit der morphonologischen Änderungen und die Relevanz kontinuierliche Attribute sind, bestimmen sie eine skalare und nicht eine dichotomische Einteilung in derivative und flexive Kategorien. Spätere Arbeiten wie etwa Bybee & Pagliuca (1985) sowie Bybee & al. (1994) stützen diesen Ansatz durch den Vergleich von Grammatikalisierungsprozessen.

Es fällt auf, daß die von Bybee vorgeschlagene Reihenfolge mit der von Foley & van Valin nicht übereinstimmt: A-T-M gegen A-

A(spekt)	*M*(odalität)	*T*(empus)
Satz-Nukleus	Core	Satzperipherie
(Prädikat)	(Prädikat + fundamentale Partizipanten: Actor − Undergoer)	(Prädikat + Core + Umstandsangaben)

Schema 41.3: Verhältnis von Aspekt, Modus, Tempus nach Foley & van Valin.

'Aspekt' (im weiteren Sinne des Wortes) liegt demnach dem Partizipatum (zum Begriff → Art. 37) am nächsten, und 'Modalität' rangiert vor 'Tempus'. Werner Drossard (1991)

M-T. Man muß sich fragen, ob diese Divergenz, die sich sicherlich zum Teil aus der Verwendung unterschiedlicher Sprachdaten ergibt, durch Einbeziehung von neuem Material zugunsten der einen oder der anderen Meinung gelöst werden kann, oder ob man nicht annehmen müßte, daß die Erklärung der Reihefolge die Einbeziehung zusätzlicher Faktoren und feinerer Differenzierungen erfordert. Die Morpheme ordnen sich nicht nach globalen Dimensionen, aber auch nicht nach abstrakten Kategorien. Zur selben Funktion können verschiedene Kategorien gehören, die ihrerseits eine variable Anzahl von Distinktionen und semantischen Merkmalen aufweisen, sie können unterschiedlich organisiert und grammatikalisiert sein und dementsprechend auch verschiedene Positionen einnehmen.

Beispiel (3) zeigt, daß Dimensionen und Kategorien wie 'Modalität', 'Tempus', 'Lokalisation' mehrere kookkurrierende Exponenten erhalten, die in verschiedenen, nicht benachbarten Positionen vorkommen und sich, wie unten dargelegt wird, semantisch voneinander unterscheiden und enge Beziehungen mit den umgebenden Morphemen eingehen. Die morphologische Struktur des HUICHOL impliziert mehrere Organisationsebenen.

Die Applikation des Relevanzprinzips unterliegt nach Bybee einigen Beschränkungen:

(a) wenn zwei Morpheme sich in einem Portemanteau-Ausdruck vereinigen,
(b) wenn zwei Morpheme getrennt auf beiden Seiten des Stamms erscheinen,
(c) wenn zwei Morpheme in derselben Position einander ausschließen.

Bezüglich (c) wird in Iturrioz (1999) argumentiert, daß der Rückgriff auf die Position als eine von der Funktion unabhängige Kookkurrenzbeschränkung einer Notlösung – gleichsam einem Deus ex machina – gleichkommt. Wenn in (b) zwei Morpheme getrennt auf beiden Seiten des Stamms vorkommen, kann man zumindest nach den bestimmenden Faktoren dieser Verteilung fragen und u. U. ein Verhältnis zwischen den relativen Entfernungen vom Stamm herstellen. Wenn im Fall (a) die Vereinigung eines Morphems mit dem Stamm in einer morphophonemischen Einheit einen hohen Relevanzgrad dieses Morphems für den Stamm zeigt, könnte dann auch die Vereinigung zweier Morpheme in einem Portemanteau-Ausdruck als Zeichen der gegenseitigen Relevanz bewertet werden? Muß das, was für die Beziehung der einzelnen Morpheme zum Prädikat gilt, auch für die Beziehung der Morpheme untereinander gelten? Ein Morphem kann für andere Morpheme semantisch mehr oder weniger relevant sein, was sich in der Bildung von Morphemblöcken und zuletzt in der Fusion widerspiegeln kann. Diese Phänomene könnten in einer umfassenden Analyse der Prinzipien, die die Ordnung der Affixe bestimmen, eine zufriedenstellende Erklärung finden.

Die Fusion von Affixen verrät nicht ohne weiteres Affinität zwischen Dimensionen oder Kategorien, z. B. zwischen 'Modalität' und 'Lokalisation' in den folgenden Regeln der Verbmorphologie des HUICHOL:

(1)	mi_{15}-/pi_{15}- + ha_6- → ma-/pa-
(2)	ti_{11}- + ha_6- → ra-
(3)	ni_{10}- + $he_{7/6}$- → ne-
(4)	ha_6- + $'i_5$- → he-
(5)	ka_{13}- + $heu_{7/4}$- → kau-/ka-heu-
(6)	te_{11}- + ha_6- → ta-/te-ha-
(7)	te_{11}- + $he_{7/6}$- → te-/te-he- usw.

Schema 41.4: Morphonologische Prozesse (Kontraktion) zwischen Affixen.

In der flexiven Zone der Morphologie kann Fusion die Folge des hohen Grammatikalisierungsgrades sowie der semantischen und phonologischen Markiertheitsverhältnisse der aufeinander treffenden Morpheme sein. Die modalen Affixe *mi*- und *pi*-, die den neutralen Vokal *i* tragen, fusionieren mit allen Affixen der Positionen 7 bis 4, die mit den peripheren glottalen Konsonanten anfangen.

Während die ersten vier Regeln obligatorisch angewandt werden, sind die drei letzten fakultativ, was u. a. auf den markierten Charakter der Vokale bzw. der kumulativen Exponenz für grammatische Distinktionen zurückzuführen ist: /a/ gegenüber /i/ und te_{11}- 'GENR ... + PL.S' gegenüber ti_{11}- 'GENR ... + SG.S/IMPS'. Ti_{11}- wird zu *r*- vor den lokalen Affixen *ha*-, *he*-, *heu*- (*ra*-, *re*-, *reu*-), bleibt jedoch unverändert vor *'u*, dessen Konsonant /'/ ein Merkmal mehr als /h/ hat (+ okklusiv). Die genannten Fusionen sind mechanische, von funktionalen Faktoren unabhängige Prozesse, die ohne Rücksicht auf die Polyfunktionalität der beteiligten Affixe stattfinden.

In agglutinativen Zonen sind formale Änderungen dagegen funktionsabhängige Prozesse. Viele agglutinative Morpheme sind nämlich polyfunktional, wobei mit dem Wechsel der Funktion oft Änderungen in der Form, in der Position und in den kombinatorischen Eigenschaften einhergehen. Das Morphem

-*tia₃* 'KAUS' wird vor -*rie₄* in -*tii* verwandelt, womit -*rie* in seiner primären Funktion 'PROMOVIERUNG DES BENEFAKTIVS' auftritt, denn sonst müßte es als 'PASSIV' verstanden werden: -*tia-rie* kann nur als 'KAUS + PASSIV' verstanden werden – vgl. etwa u. Beispiel (7). Sowohl -*rie* als auch -*ya* werden als Zeichen des Passivs verwendet, aber -*tia-ya* ist eine unmögliche Kombination.

Soll neben PROMOTION auch PASSIV mitbezeichnet werden, dann kommt aus demselben Grund -*tia-ya-rie* nicht in Frage. In diesem Fall übernimmt -*rie* nachträglich diese Funktion und überläßt dem Morphem -*ya* die Funktion der Promotion und seine Position: -*tii-ya-rie* 'KAUS + PROM + PAS'. Zu den Funktionen von -*ya* gehört VALENZERWEITERUNG, aber im Unterschied zu -*tia* kann es nur Transitivierung, nicht Kausativierung bewirken, und außer in dieser Dreierkombination kann es im Unterschied zu -*rie* nicht den BENEFAKTIV in die Funktion des OBJEKTS promovieren.

Die Polyfunktionalität vieler agglutinativer Affixe und die hierarchische Ordnung der Funktionen nach der begrifflichen Distanz zum Stamm (Transitivierung ⇒ Kausativierung ⇒ Promotion ⇒ Perspektivierung) bestimmen die Regeln dieser Art von Zusammenarbeit: nachdem -*rie* 'PROM' die formale und semantische Änderung von -*tia* 'KAUS' in -*tii* 'KAUS:PROM' auslöst, kann es die allgemeine Funktion der Valenzerhöhung dem Morphem -*ya* abtreten und die Funktion 'PASSIV' übernehmen:

-*tia*	-*rie*	-*ya* ⇒	-*tii*	-*ya*	-*rie*
KAUS	PROM	TR	KAUS:PROM	VALENZ	PAS
TR	PAS	PAS			

Schema 41.5: Funktionsverschiebung im Bereich der Partizipation.

Die globalen Exponenten der Nominalisierung (-ME) und der Skala der attributiven Strukturen (-TR) rücken mit zunehmender Grammatikalisierung näher an den Stamm, bis sie eine untrennbare Einheit bilden. Sie ändern ihre paradigmatischen und kombinatorischen Eigenschaften parallel zu den globalen Änderungen, die schrittweise von Nebensätzen zu nominalen oder adjektivischen Lexemen führen (s. u. §9, sowie Iturrioz 1989, 1990).

Die Morpheme bilden nicht ein gleichmäßiges Kontinuum, in dem die Zugehörigkeit zu einer Kategorie oder Dimension, die begriffliche Relevanz für den Stamm und die relative Nähe zum Stamm alleinbestimmend sind. In den präfixalen Positionen 12, 9 und 5 erscheinen verschiedene Objektmorpheme. Die Verteilung wird von ihrem höheren bzw. niedrigeren Rang auf der Skala der Kategorie 'Person' (s. u. § 7.3) bestimmt. Die Zonen der Dimensionen sind nicht scharf abgegrenzt; es gibt Überschneidungen zwischen den Dimensionen, zum Beispiel zwischen 'Lokalisation' und 'Partizipation', zwischen 'Modalität' und 'Partizipation', zwischen 'Tempus' und 'Modalität'.

Es gibt außerdem Diskontinuitäten unterschiedlicher Art, in denen sich verschiedene Formen von Solidarität und Affinitäten zwischen Funktionen verschiedener Dimensionen manifestieren. Bestimmte morphosyntaktische Prozesse liefern Evidenz für die Existenz von Abschnitten in der Morphologie des Verbs und für die gegenseitige Relevanz der sich darin zusammenschließenden Kategorien. Morpheme bilden Blöcke, d. h. Abschnitte mit innerer Kohärenz und relativer Unabhängigkeit vom Nukleus. Damit hängt es zusammen, daß an bestimmten Stellen autonome Wörter bzw. Gruppen von Wörtern den Verbalkomplex unterbrechen bzw. in ihn inkorporiert werden können. Weitere Evidenz bietet die Trennung bestimmter Morphemkombinationen, die ungebildete Leute machen, wenn sie schreiben. Über die Grenzen dieser Abschnitte hinweg können Morpheme auch kooperative Gruppen bilden, indem sie sich für die Erfüllung einer komplexen Funktion verbünden.

Die zu Beginn dieses Abschnitts genannten Autoren stützen sich auf partielle Daten und sehen A, T und M weitgehend als monolithische Kategorien an. Die auf der Basis einzelner Beobachtungen in wenigen Einzelsprachen festgestellten Tendenzen könnten durch die Analyse komplexerer Morphemketten ins rechte Licht gesetzt werden. Es erweist sich als nötig,

– A, T und M als komplexe Dimensionen oder funktionale Domänen aufzufassen;
– Sprachen mit größerer morphologischer Komplexität zu untersuchen, um so
– die Anzahl der betrachteten funktionalen Domänen zu erweitern;
– innerhalb jeder Domäne alle Techniken und Kategorien zu betrachten;
– die Polyfunktionalität vieler Exponenten zu untersuchen, weil in Verbindung mit

den verschiedenen Funktionen Position, Distribution und Kombination sich ändern können;
- nach allgemeinen Prinzipien zu suchen, die hinter den spezifischen Regeln und Skalen stehen, um haltbare Hypothesen über die kognitiven Grundlagen des Systems aufstellen zu können;
- die vielfältigen Beziehungen zu untersuchen, die zwischen den Prinzipien bestehen können, um, wie im letzten Abschnitt (s. u. § 11) dargelegt wird, Affinitäten zwischen Dimensionen zu finden.

6.1. Zwei Arten der Relevanz

Joan L. Bybees Begriff der Relevanz entspricht ziemlich genau dem UNITYP-Begriff der Prädikativität. Während aber Bybee und die meisten Linguisten Kontinua als unidirektional auffassen, werden sie nach UNITYP von zwei gegenläufigen, komplementären Prinzipien gesteuert (→ Art. 27, § 3.3.1). Die Positionen spiegeln diagrammatisch einerseits die relative begriffliche Nähe zum Nukleus des Prädikats bzw. umgekehrt die graduelle Hinwendung zur Redesituation und zur Textpragmatik (Subjekt, Relation Subjekt-Prädikat und 'Modalität') wider.

Neben BEGRIFFLICHER RELEVANZ sollte man auch von PRAGMATISCHER RELEVANZ sprechen. Entgegen der traditionellen Auffassung, nach der es in der Morphologie einen flexiven und einen derivativen Teil gibt (mit einer Übergangszone dazwischen), läßt sich das sprachliche Material so interpretieren, daß zwei komplementäre Kontinua in entgegengesetzten Richtungen verlaufen. Inkorporation und Wortunterbrechung zeigen zum einen, daß syntaktische Phänomene noch in der Nähe des Verbalstamms stattfinden können. Die Tatsache andererseits, daß Subjektaffixe streng genommen nicht von einer syntaktischen Konstituente regiert werden, zeigt, daß sie sich noch als eine Erweiterung der semantischen Struktur des Prädikats darstellen lassen.

Links vom Subjekt erscheinen nur noch einige reduzierte Adverbien (wie '*a-* 'positiv', *tsi-* 'negativ'), die zum Teil noch Intensität der Handlung, aber auch schon modale Komponenten beinhalten: Bekräftigung, Schwächung der Assertivität, subjektive Bewertung des Sachverhalts usw.

(4) (a) *'a- me- mi- pa- pa.*
positiv- 3PL.S- AS- RED- groß
'Sie sind groß'

(b) *tsi -me -mi -pe -pe.*
negativ 3PL.S AS RED groß
'Sie sind klein'.

Diese vom Stamm so entfernten Präfixe bestimmen sowohl den Vokalismus der Wurzel (Vokalharmonie) als auch den positiven oder negativen Wert auf der vom Verb neutral bezeichneten Dimension.

6.2. Dimensionen als komplexe funktionale Domänen

Die Morpheme können einer Anzahl von Dimensionen oder funktionalen Domänen zugewiesen werden. (Sie sind in den Beispielen (1) und (3) jeweils als dritte Zeile notiert.) Innerhalb einer Dimension werden verschiedene Techniken und Kategorien identifiziert, die spezifische Subfunktionen erfüllen. 'Partizipation' umfaßt etwa Operationen wie Erweiterung oder Reduktion der Valenz, Verteilung der thematischen Rollen, Orientierung (Perspektivierung) usw. (→ Art. 37). 'Modalität' deckt ein relativ breites Spektrum von deontischen, epistemischen, kommunikativen und emotionalen Modalitäten mit verschiedenen Eigenschaften ab (→ Art. 60). Dies verhindert einen absoluten Kontrast und zwingt zu feineren Distinktionen. Dimensionen, Techniken und Kategorien sind für das Prädikat mehr oder weniger relevant, was sich u. a. in der Stellung der jeweiligen Exponenten, aber auch in anderen Phänomenen manifestieren kann.

Eine Dimension umfaßt mehrere komplementäre Funktionen, und ihre Exponenz besteht daher oft aus einer Reihe von Exponenten, die nicht immer in derselben Position, ja nicht einmal in benachbarten Positionen vorkommen, so daß eine genaue Beschreibung über globale Urteile hinausgehen muß, um die komplexen Beziehungen zu anderen Dimensionen erfassen zu können.

Während deontische, sprecherbezogene Modalitäten suffixale Positionen vor den Tempusmorphemen besetzen, stehen die Ausdrucksmittel der epistemischen Modalitäten in den extremen, peripheren Positionen hinter den suffixalen Tempusmorphemen. Ka_{16}-, mi_{15}-, ka_{14}-, ka_{13}-, te_{11}-, ni_{10}- und -ni_{12} gehören alle zur Domäne der Modalität.

Jede Dimension ordnet ihre Exponenten entsprechend einer Kombination von allgemeinen und spezifischen, den Funktionen ihrer Kategorien und dem Grad der Grammatikalisierung ihrer Exponenten inhärierenden Prinzipien. Die Frage entsteht nun, nach welchen Kriterien die Exponenten verschiedener Dimensionen angereiht werden, wenn sie in einer Kette miteinander kombiniert werden müssen. Der Grammatikalisierungsgrad der einzelnen Instanzen innerhalb der jeweiligen Dimension muß als bestimmender Faktor betrachtet werden. Dabei muß man berücksichtigen, daß ein polyfunktionaler Exponent je nach Dimension verschiedene Grammatikalisierungsgrade aufweisen kann. So kann $(ti/r)/te_{11}$- als Generalisator neben modalen Affixen vorkommen, was in seiner Funktion als Zeichen einer Entscheidungsfrage nicht der Fall ist. Umgekehrt kann es als GENR nicht mit dem Argument OBJEKT kookkurrieren, wenn es die thematische Rolle PATIENS realisiert. Dasselbe Präfix te_{11}-, umgeben von Positionen der Modalität, drückt in Beispiel (1) zweierlei aus: erstens Pluralität des Subjekts, zweitens generischen Sachverhalt und damit verbunden generisches Patiens.

Diese Operation der Generalisierung impliziert eine Aufhebung der Transitivität: die Rolle des Patiens kann nicht durch eine unabhängige NP erfüllt werden. Diese Operation wird im DEUTSCHEN und SPANISCHEN nicht offen markiert, sondern lediglich durch die Abwesenheit einer NP implizit angezeigt bzw. durch den generischen Charakter des Diskurses nahegelegt. Im Fall eines polyfunktionalen Exponenten ändern sich die Wahlmöglichkeiten auf der Horizontalen mit der Wahl einer spezifischen Funktion für diesen Exponenten auf der Vertikalen:

	$(ti/r)/te_{11}$-		ti_2
1)	SKAL	G/I	LOK
2)	GENR	P/I	AA
3)	SORT	P/I	POS
4)	BEKR	M/I	P/I
5)	EFR	M/I	
6)	KM	M/J/I	
7)	IMPS	J/I	

Schema 41.6: Funktionsverschiebung und Änderung der Kombinatorik.

In allen Instanzen drückt $(ti/r)/te$ zugleich den Numerus des Subjekts aus (*ti/r*- steht für 'SG', *te*- für 'PL'), aber der Bezug auf das Subjekt ist nicht die notwendige Bedingung, sondern eine begleitende Funktion. Dies ändert sich in der letzten Instanz, wo es einen unpersönlichen Sachverhalt bezeichnet, d. h. einen Sachverhalt, der sich auf keinen Referenten des Diskursuniversums bezieht. Die Numerusdistinktion wird dabei aufgehoben und die Position 17, wo in den anderen Fällen Person und Numerus des Subjekts angegeben wird, bleibt leer.

Die Wahl der Dimension ist ein entscheidender Faktor für die Kombination mit anderen Morphemen. Die Kookkurrenzbeschränkungen werden entsprechend der Reihenfolge der Dimensionen nach außen verschoben; $(ti/r)/te$- ist in der Funktion P/I mit allen anderen Morphemen kompatibel, mit einem Objektmorphem (Positionen 7−5−3) allerdings nur unter der Voraussetzung, daß dieses sich nicht auf das Patiens bezieht, sondern auf den promovierten Benefaktiv; in den Funktionen M/I schließt es alle Modalaffixe und in der letzten Funktion das Subjektaffix aus.

Soweit diese Hierarchie eine Verlagerung nach außen impliziert, bestätigt sie die für die Horizontale aufgestellte Hierarchie und bringt Evidenz für eine allgemeine Relevanzhierarchie der Dimensionen. Obwohl jeder Exponent eine spezifische Hierarchie beinhaltet, bleibt die Reihenfolge gleich. Die Position des Exponenten bestimmt außerdem die Ebene der Dimensionen, die seinen Funktionen entsprechen.

6.3. Relevanz-Skala

Die Skala von ti_3- in Schema 41.6 beginnt mit einer sehr relevanten Dimension (Lokalisation) und endet mit Individuation, die im Fall von $(ti/r)/te_{11}$- schon seit der ersten Instanz beteiligt ist. Wenn man daraus folgern kann, daß das Auftreten von Individuation in der Nähe des Stamms genauso markiert ist wie das Auftreten von subjektbezogenen Begriffen in Position 11, dann ist es möglich, eine allgemeine Skala der Relevanz für die verschiedenen Dimensionen aufzustellen. Die Dimensionen, die sich auf die sprachliche Erfassung des Partizipatums beziehen, sind relevanter als diejenigen, die sich auf die pragmatische Umsetzung der thematischen Rollen in Argumentstrukturen beziehen. Auch wenn Exponenten der Individuation in stammnahen Positionen auftreten, können sie sich nicht auf grammatische Relationen wie Subjekt beziehen, sondern nur auf thematische Rollen, vor allem auf das Patiens; sie können sogar primär Pluralität, Dispersion usw. der Handlung ausdrücken. Die Verteilung der mit P(artizipation) verbundenen Morpheme auf die prä- und suffixalen Positionen ist funktional. Die suffixalen Morpheme zeigen Operationen an, die die Rollenstruktur modifizieren, während die präfixalen Morpheme sich auf die darauf aufbauende Argumentstruktur beziehen. Die suffixalen beziehen sich auf den Sachverhalt selbst, die präfixalen auf die Partizipanten. Unter den präfixalen Morphemen besetzen diejenigen, die sich auf thematische Rollen beziehen, stammnahe Positionen, während mit zunehmender Distanz auf die höheren Instanzen der Zugänglichkeitsskala Bezug genommen wird: Objekt und Subjekt. Das externe Argument erscheint in einer äußerst peripheren Position.

7. Morphemstellung neben anderen Indikatoren der Relevanz

Modalität erweist sich insgesamt als die peripherste Dimension. Ihre Exponenten erscheinen wie eine Klammer in den Randpositionen auf beiden Seiten des Verbs. Die nicht markierten Präfixe der Modalität *pi-* und *mi-* gehören in phonologischer Hinsicht zu den ärmsten Affixen, sie bestehen aus einem Konsonanten und dem neutralen Vokal *i*. Im Text, in realen Redesituationen bzw. unter bestimmten kontextuellen Bedingungen (z. B. vor *ma-* '2SG.O') sind modale Morpheme weitgehend weglaßbar:

(5) 'ikɨ'i   ta-   'iyari (pi) ti- u-
    D₁   1PL.POS   Seele AS   GENR EXP
    naki   -ri   -xi.
    erfüll   INGR   PERF
    'Dies erfüllt unseren Geist.'

(6) Tsepa   xewi- ti.   (*pi) ma-
    Vielleicht jmd   SUBJ   AS   2SG.O
    tsi- 'u-   ta-   hiawi -xi.
    MT   HGR   LIM   red   PERF
    'Vielleicht sprach dich jemand an.'

Auch infolge zahlreicher morphonologischer Prozesse können die Exponenten der Modalität verschwinden bzw. verkürzt werden, besonders in Verbindung mit den 'lokalen' Exponenten der Position 7: *pi-ha-mie* 'AS CIS geh:SG' → *pamie*. Aufschlüsse gibt auch die Entwicklung in der Ontogenese (s. u. § 15).

Schließlich ist im Zusammenhang mit der Relevanz zu erwähnen, daß Modalmorpheme in der ersten Stufe der Nominalisierung verschwinden, während Tempus erst in der zweiten Stufe abgebaut wird und Personalaffixe in den darauffolgenden Stufen noch fakultativ bleiben (weitere Einzelheiten in Iturrioz 1990; vgl. Art. → 45, § 3.2.5 und Tabelle 45.1).

7.1. Das externe Argument

Auf das Subjekt verweisen mehrere Exponenten in verschiedenen Positionen, darunter die Präfixe von 17 und 11, die Suffixe *-miki/-ku* 'DESIDERATIV' (7 in Beispiel (1)), *-we/-wawe* 'KAPAZITÄT' usw., aber sie sind weder äquivalent noch redundant, denn sie bezeichnen außer der grammatischen Funktion verschiedene andere spezifische Kategorien. Auf das Subjekt nimmt primär das Morphem te_{17}- in (1) Bezug, dann aber auch te_{11}-; während jedoch te_{17}- '1PL.S' die Person bezeichnet, gibt te_{11}- lediglich den Numerus des Subjekts an; nach Bybee ist die Kategorie 'Numerus' relevanter als 'Person', was sich in der Position widerspiegelt.

Das Morphem ku_7- drückt primär eine subjektbezogene Modalität aus, welche seine Position bestimmt, und nicht die sekundäre Funktion SUBJEKT. Die Kongruenz mit dem Subjekt unterstreicht, daß es sich um eine subjektbezogene Modalität handelt. Das Morphem $(ti/r)/te_{11}$- (ti/r sind, wie erwähnt, morphonologische Varianten für 'SG.S', *te-* steht für 'PL.S') bezieht sich sowohl auf das Subjekt als auch auf das Objekt, aber seine primäre Funktion besteht darin, eine Operation der Generalisierung (s. o. §§ 3; 6.2) im Hinblick auf das patientive Objekt zu bezeichnen. Dies erklärt seine Position unter den Objektaffixen (näheres u. § 7.3). Diese Operation ist in den meisten Fällen die notwendige Bedingung seines Erscheinens. Nur in einem sehr markierten Fall bezeichnet es primär das Subjekt, nämlich wenn es als Zeichen der Impersonalität eines Sachverhalts dient:

(7) Xe-   'ixatsitia -rie -ti xika r-
    2PL.S lehr   PAS NPR wenn IMPS
    a-   niu   -wa -ni.
    CISL reden HAB FOR
    'Wenn man hierher zu sprechen kommt, damit ihr belehrt werdet.'

Der Relevanzgrad einer Kategorie kann auch vom Sprachtyp abhängen, wie ein Vergleich der Kategorie 'Subjekt' in flexiven und in polysynthetischen, verbzentrierten Sprachen zeigt. DEUTSCH *-en* und SPANISCH *-mos* haben dieselbe Funktion wie HUICHOL te_{17}-: sie drücken die Kategorie 'Person' und die grammatische Relation 'Subjekt' aus. Der auffälligste Unterschied besteht in der Position zum Nukleus; während nämlich *-en* und *-mos* suffigiert werden, wird te_{17}- präfigiert. Von einer funktionalen Betrachtungsweise aus erweist sich jedoch die Tatsache als wichtiger, daß in allen drei Sprachen die Personalaffixe des Subjekts die letzte bzw. vorletzte, jedenfalls eine vom Verbstamm sehr weit entfernte Stelle besetzen: SPANISCH *aprende-mos, aprend-ía-mos* (PRÄT), *aprende-r-e-mos* (FUT), *aprende-r-ía-mos* (POT), DEUTSCH *lern-en, lern-te-n*. Von der Position her, die vom Nukleus weiter entfernt ist als die meisten und prototypischen Positionen der Modalität, erweist sich das Subjekt als eine sehr periphere Kategorie. Beim Schreiben ist die Tendenz groß, die Subjektmarker vom Rest des Wortes zu trennen: *Te katenitati'ikitiakuni* 'wir wollen lernen' (s. o. Beispiel [1]).

Die partielle phonologische Identität dieser Präfixe mit den autonomen Personalpronomina ist kein hinreichender Grund für die Trennung, denn die nicht homophonen Affixe werden nicht weniger häufig getrennt geschrieben. Als Mitteilungszentrum des Satzes und Drehpunkt von pragmatisch gesteuerten syntaktischen Operationen verweist das Subjekt mehr als irgend eine andere grammatische Funktion auf satzübergreifende, textkonstituierende Zusammenhänge: das Subjekt tendiert mehr als jede andere grammatische Relation dazu, die Referenz auf eine kleine Anzahl von Gegenständen im Text konstant zu halten und sie dadurch als Figuren des Textes zu konstituieren. Für die Bedeutung des Prädikats ist es jedoch nicht ganz irrelevant. Im Unterschied zu anderen Sprachen kann das Subjekt nämlich nicht als ein rein syntaktisches, von der Semantik des Prädikats unabhängiges Kongruenzphänomen behandelt werden; erstens ist es nicht völlig desemantisiert, denn alle Elemente des Subjekt-Paradigmas haben das Merkmal [+ belebt]. Unabhängig von der syntaktischen Konstituente *'üri*, die den unbelebten Gegenstand 'Pfeil' bezeichnet, praktisch im Widerspruch zu ihr, verweist *me-* im folgenden Beispiel selbständig auf die Belebtheit des Arguments:

(8) *'üri mana me- p- a- ti- hu*
     Pfeil da   3PL.S AS CIS auf geh:PL.S
     -kai.
     IMPF
     'Die Pfeile stiegen herauf.'

'üri bezeichnet hier metonymisch eine Gruppe von pfeiltragenden, d. h. bewaffneten Männern (Soldaten). Dies kommt jedoch erst durch die Anwesenheit von *me-* zum Ausdruck; hätte nämlich *'üri* von sich aus als Symbol der Männlichkeit das Merkmal [+ belebt], dann müßte es hier ein Pluralsuffix bekommen, denn die Pluralmarkierung ist bei belebten Nomina obligatorisch, wenn das Prädikat für das Subjekt als pluralisch markiert ist: *'üri-ma* (mehr Information hierzu → Art. 100 im Band zur Morphologie in dieser Reihe).

Entgegen der geläufigen Tendenz, in der Verbalmorphologie einen derivativen und einen flexiven Teil abzugrenzen, ist es angemessener, von zwei gegenläufigen Gradienten auszugehen, nämlich dem der 'Prädikativität' (ein Begriff, der sich weitgehend mit dem der Relevanz in Bybee (1985) deckt) und dem der 'Pragmatizität'. Obwohl die Prädikativität mit der Nähe zum Nukleus graduell zunimmt, kann man nicht übersehen, daß etwa die Elemente der Position 2 Funktionen haben, die den flexiven Funktionen wie 'Kongruenz' nahekommen.

Im folgenden Beispiel ist die Präsenz der Reduplikation bzw. von *ti-* als Zeichen der Pluralität des Arguments obligatorisch (näheres dazu u. § 7.3):

(9) *Mi- xime- ti me- ni- yu-*
     sterb IMM SIM:IS 3PL.S FOR REFL
     xa- xata -ni ... Ne- mi- ne-
     RED RED FOR 1SG MOD 1SG.REFL
     xata -kai -ti ti, ne- papa-
     RED IMPF ERW ADV 1SG.POS Elter
     ma pita me- -mi yu- ti- xata-
     PL KONTR 3PL.S MOD REFL PL RED
     ke -kai.
     BEN IMPF
     'Sie gingen kurz vor dem Tod zur Beichte. Obwohl ich zur Beichte ging ... Meine Eltern hätten zuerst zur Beichte gehen sollen.'

7.2. Funktionale Bereiche

Die Dimensionen werden nicht en bloc nacheinander angeordnet, sie überschneiden und verzahnen sich, indem ihre Exponenten sich in der Reihenfolge vielfältig abwechseln. Die Anordnung der Morpheme erfolgt also nicht nach Dimensionen, obwohl sie wichtige Anhaltspunkte für die globale Relevanz einer Dimension liefern kann.

Die Morphemstellung zeigt außerdem nicht einen rein graduellen Ablauf. Gruppen von Morphemen, die zu verschiedenen Dimensionen gehören können, bilden hintereinander gelegene, in sich geschlossene funktionale Bereiche, d. h. Abschnitte oder kohäsive Segmente mit relativer Autonomie innerhalb des Wortes.

Zwischen den präfixalen Blöcken existieren Schnittstellen, an denen zwei Operationen stattfinden können: Inkorporation und Wortunterbrechung. Das Subjekt bildet mit den Elementen der umliegenden Stellen einen Bereich, der sich u. a. dadurch auszeichnet, daß dort das modale freie Morphem -*xika* inkorporiert werden kann:

(10) *Pai ri   n- e-   yi-   ni -ke*
     so schon FOR INV geschen FUT LIM
    ne-   xika -ti- 'ena -kai -ti -ni.
    1SG.S wenn GENR hör IMPF ERW FOR
    'Unmittelbar bevor dies geschah, hörte ich vielleicht (diese Sachen).'

Bevor die Konjunktion *xika* inkorporiert wird, verdrängt sie die modalen Präfixe *ka- ni-* aus den Positionen, die sie selber bei der Inkorporation besetzt:

(10) (a) *Pai ri neyinike.*
    (b) *Xika ne(*ka)ti(*ni)'enakaitini.*

Die Kookkurrenzbeschränkungen bilden die Vorstufe der Einbeziehung von *xika* in das Paradigma der modalen Präfixe. Konjunktionen sind keine prominente Kategorie des HUICHOL. Modale Präfixe können nicht von den Subjektpräfixen getrennt werden; sie können nur en bloc vom Rest des Wortes getrennt werden, indem das Wort an dieser Schnittstelle durch andere Konstituenten des Satzes unterbrochen wird, darunter durch das direkte Objekt:

(11) *'Ena pe-   xika tsi kuta 'a-*
    dort 2SG.S KOND denn halt 2SG.POS
    'ürí   'u- ti- xiri   -wa -ni.
    Pfeil HGR PL.P darbring HAB FOR
    'Wenn du denn halt daran gewöhnt bist, deine Pfeile dort darzubringen.'

Zu diesem Bereich gehört auch die Negation, deren Exponent bei der Wiederaufnahme des Wortes wiederholt werden kann:

(12) *pe-   mi- ka- tsi kuta mipai*
    2SG.S MOD NEG denn halt so
    ka- 'ane -ni.
    NEG sein FUT
    'Du wirst denn halt nicht so sein.'

Zu diesem Block gehört noch das Morphem (*ti*/*r*)/*te-* in allen seinen Funktionen: Generalisierung, Intensivierung usw.:

(13) *Tsi- me- pi- ka- te- 'ipá*
    ITS 3PL.S AS NEG INTS Surilho
    (hepai) 'u -'ia -tika.
    wie   HGR riech PL.S
    'Sie riechen sehr wie ein Surilho.'

Der Bereich besteht also aus allen Elementen, die in irgendeiner Weise auf den Sprecher, auf das Subjekt sowie auf die Relation Subjekt-Prädikat Bezug nehmen. Der Block bestimmt eine Schnittstelle, an der das Wort durch ein anderes Wort, durch eine ganze Konstituente bzw. durch mehrere Konstituenten unterbrochen werden kann: *'ipá hepai* 'wie ein Surilho'. Die Tatsache, daß die Adposition *hepai* 'wie' hier elidiert werden kann, aber nicht außerhalb des Wortes, deutet darauf hin, daß sich ihr grammatischer Status geändert hat. Wenn man dieses Wort mit (3) vergleicht, wird man leicht feststellen, daß dort die Unterbrechung an einer ganz anderen Stelle stattfindet, nämlich links von der Position 2 der primär lokalen Präfixe, an einer dem Stamm viel näheren Stelle, was vermuten läßt, daß dort die Unterbrechung einer echten wortbildenden Inkorporation viel näher kommt.

Unterbrechung und Inkorporation kommen im folgenden Beispiel nebeneinander vor, wo das Wort *haka* 'Hunger' als freie Konstituente den Instrumental *-ki* annehmen müßte:

(14) (a) *Wai   te-   p- eu- ta-   ku-*
       Fleisch 1PL.S AS LOK 1PL.REFL DISP
    mexiima haka-   xite   -kie xia.
    sofort   Hunger schneid BEN DIST
   (b) *Wai mexiima hakaki*
      tepeutakuxitekiexia.
      'Wir schnitten uns sofort aus Hunger an verschiedenen Stellen Fleischstücke.'

7.3. Die grammatische Funktion OBJEKT

Die grammatische Funktion ist ein bestimmender Faktor der Position von Pronominalaffixen. Die Subjektaffixe erscheinen links von den Objektaffixen; während die Affixe des Subjekts eine der letzten präfixalen Positionen (Pos. 17) einnehmen und das Subjekt sich so als das externe Argument des Satzes bestätigt, erscheinen die Objektaffixe in mehreren internen Positionen. Die Verteilung der Pronominalaffixe auf diese Positionen wird nicht von der grammatischen Funktion und auch nicht von der semantischen Relevanz für den Stamm bestimmt, sondern von inhärenten Prinzipien der Kategorie, die ihre Instanzen hierarchisch ordnen.

Die meisten Objektpronomina sind erstens hinsichtlich der Position nicht konstant, sondern beweglich; zweitens erscheinen die reflexiven Pronomina in einer dem Nukleus viel näheren Position, obwohl sie sich auf dieselbe Rolle wie die Objektaffixe beziehen.

Die Position der Objektaffixe wird auch von der Hierarchie der Personen und von anderen Faktoren wie demorphologischen Kontext, den thematischen Rollen hinter den Argumenten (Patiens, Benefaktiv ...) usw. bestimmt. Die Affixe der ersten (*ne-* 'mich', *ta-* 'uns') sowie der zweiten Person (*me/ma-* 'dich', *xe-* 'euch') werden in die Position unmittelbar vor oder nach dem GENR (Pos. 11, s. Beispiel (18)) gebracht, die zweite Person Plural *xe-* kann außerdem dem Modalmarker *ni-* (Pos. 10) nachgestellt werden, während die dritte Person Plural (*wa-*) obligatorisch in dieser Position erscheint (Pos. 9, s. Beispiel (3)). Die dritte Person Singular rückt weiter nach rechts in Position 5 und wird so den ersten Exponenten von Lokalisation nachgestellt:

(15) Te- pi- te-   war he- ti-
     1PL.S AS GENR:PL.S 3PL.O INV VPL
     'iki -tia -ni.
     zeig TR   FUT
     'Wir wollen sie unterrichten'

(16) (a) 'aixi ne-   pi- ti- xe-   'u-
         gut 1SG.S AS INTS 2PL.O HGR
         hayewa -kai.
         lass   IMPF
         'Ich hatte euch in einer guten Lage gelassen.'

    (b) 'aixi ne-pi-xe-ti-u-haye-wa-kai.
        'Idem.'

Bestimmte Objektaffixe werden dem GENR vorgestellt. Man muß dabei beachten, daß GENR einen doppelten Bezug hat, nämlich einmal auf das Subjekt (SG:PL), dann aber auch auf das Objekt (Generalisierung, s. o. §§ 3; 6.2); seine Position liegt so erwartungsgemäß zwischen denen des Subjekts und des Objekts.

Die weitere Verlagerung der reflexiven Pronomina nach rechts verrät einen engeren Kohäsionsgrad mit dem Prädikat. Dafür kann zusätzliche Evidenz angeführt werden. Unter anderem können das reflexive *ta-* (Beispiel (1)) und alle übrigen Elemente seines Paradigmas durch den allgemeinen Ausdruck der Reflexivität *yu-* ersetzt werden. Die Kategorie 'Person' wird dabei aufgehoben. Wenn die Rolle des Patiens generalisiert wird, kann *yu-* trotzdem das Prädikat mit Information über ein mögliches Argument bereichern: *yukwaiya* 'Belebtes essen'. Reflexivität ist allein bei belebten Argumenten möglich:

(17) pe-   ka- ti- yu-   kwá'a.
     2SG.S NEG EFR REFL [+ BEL]   ess
     'Frißt du nicht Lebewesen?'

Die genaue Identifizierung der Position muß in jedem Fall garantiert sein. In (1) wird *ta-* als Reflexivum identifiziert und damit auf die 3. Position links von V gewiesen, weil es dem GENR *te-* nachgestellt ist, und weil das morphotaktische Element *tsi-* fehlt. In (18) identifiziert dagegen die Stellung vor GENR *ta-* als nicht-reflexives Objekt:

(18) Me$_{17}$- pi$_{15}$- ta$_{12}$- te$_{11}$- he$_6$- ti$_2$-
     3PL.S AS 1PL.O GENR INV VPL
     'iki -tia$_1$ -ni$_{12}$
     zeig TR   FUT
     'Sie wollen uns (etwas) beibringen.'

Um die Position der gebundenen Pronominalpräfixe und damit ihrer grammatischen Funktionen genau zu kennzeichnen, wird manchmal ein Grenzsignal gesetzt, wenn sie nicht anders identifiziert werden können. In Abwesenheit des GENR verweist das morphotaktische Morphem *tsi-* auf eine Grenze zwischen Morphembereichen, womit Position und Funktion von *ta-* und *ti-* genau identifiziert werden; *ta-* kann auf diese Weise auch nicht mit dem aus einer Kontraktion resultierenden Morphem *ta-* < *te-ha-* verwechselt werden, weil die Position des lokalen Morphems *ha-* auf die von *tsi-* folgen müßte (s. o. Schema 41.4) Schema 41.7 zeigt die Verhältnisse bei den Objektaffixen:

(19) 'Utiarika me- pi- ta-   tsi- ti-
     Schrift   3PL AS 1PL.O MT   VPL
     'iki -tia -ni
     zeig TR   FUT
     'Sie werden uns das Lesen beibringen.'

		TI$_{11}$		NI$_{10}$	HE$_{7-6}$-	NA$_4$-	TI$_2$-
1SG	ne-		ne-				R
2SG	ma-		ma-				E
1PL	ta-		ta-				F
2PL	xe-		xe-	xe-			L
3PL				wa-			
3SG					i-		

Schema 41.7: Verteilung der Objektaffixe.

Die Affixe rücken nach rechts, wenn andere
— etwa modale — Elemente dieses Bereichs
wie *ni-* dies möglich machen. Das Zeichen *'i*
'3SG.O' ist weniger grammatikalisiert als alle
anderen; es kongruiert nicht mit einem Argument, denn es erscheint gerade dann, wenn
das Argument nicht da ist; und es kann
alleinstehend vom Rest des Wortes durch
Einschub autonomer Konstituenten getrennt
werden, was mit *wa-* nicht möglich ist; *'i-* gehört zu einem anderen Morphembereich, der
auch Reflexiva und Lokalisationsaffixe umfaßt, und ist in diesem Beispiel sein einziger
Vertreter:

(20) *'i   yeme mie -ne -ti ke ti*
      3SG.O fast töt PRG SIM:IS BIS CLIT
      netiuyuri
      geschieht
      'Irgend etwas geschieht, was ihn beinahe tötet.'

Der Wechsel der Position ist also ein Zeichen
der Abkehr von den Argumenten und der
Hinwendung zum Nukleus. Die reflexiven
Pronomina werden nur durch die Positionen
der nicht ganz unabhängigen Reduplikation
und des Paradigmas {*ti-, ta-, ku-, ka-, ye-*}
angezeigt, das primär Raumbegriffe (*ti-wiya*
'auf-fliegen, nach oben fliegen'), aber auch
Aktionsarten (*ti-xeiya* 'intensiv sehen, prüfen', *ta-xeiya* 'auf-finden') bezeichnet. In (1)
drückt *ti-* Pluralität der Handlung (Dispersion) aus, während es in (3) auf die Tiefe (vertikale Dimension) des Flusses hinweist: die
großen Flüsse dienen als Orientierungsachse,
alternativ zur Schwerkraft, s. Iturrioz & al.
(1988); *ta-* bezeichnet in (2) und (6) die limitative Aktionsart. Insgesamt gesehen sind
solche Bildungen weitgehend derivativ.

HUICHOL *-ta* ist auch Zeichen von '1PL.O',
aber in der Funktion des direkten Objekts: im
vorliegenden Fall gehört es zum Paradigma
der reflexiven Objektpronomina, die in der
dritten Position links vom Verb erscheinen
und formal nur teilweise mit denen der nichtreflexiven Pronomina identisch sind. *-ta* kann
durch das allgemeine Zeichen der Reflexivität
-yu ersetzt werden, womit keine Person-Numerus-Kongruenz mehr angezeigt und Reflexivität eher als eine inhärente Eigenschaft
des Prädikats dargestellt wird: *te-ka-te-ni-yu-ti-'iki-tia-ku-ni* 'wir wollen lernen' (s. o. Beispiel (1)).

Die reflexiven Pronomina haben in vielen
Sprachen einen mehr oder weniger stark derivativen Charakter (→ Art. 57), sie können
u. a. verschiedene Aktionsarten ausdrücken
wie z. B. 'inchoativ': SPAN. *ir* 'gehen' — *irse*
'ausgehen'; terminativ: *beber agua* 'Wasser
trinken' — *beberse el agua* 'das Wasser austrinken'; sie können aber auch eine verminderte Agentivität bezeichnen: *rompió su pantalón* 'er zerriß seine Hose' — *se rompió el
pantalón* 'er zerriß sich die Hose', usw.

In einigen dialektalen Varianten des SPANISCHEN besteht die Tendenz, das Reflexivum
näher an das Verb zu bringen, was die Tatsache widerspiegelt, daß das Reflexivum im
Sinne von Bybee (1985, Bybee & al. 1994)
eine größere Relevanz besitzt als die nicht
reflexiven Pronomina, d. h. daß es mit dem
Verb eine engere, kohärente Einheit bildet: *se
melte rasgó* → *melte se rasgó* 'es zerriß sich
mir/dir'.

Die Umstellung betrifft nicht nur die Klitika der ersten und zweiten Person, sondern
auch das Zeichen des Plurals in der dritten
Person im Imperativ, wo im Unterschied zu
den anderen Modi die Pronomina immer
nachgestellt werden: *siénte-se-n* (das als vulgär empfunden wird). Auch im DEUTSCHEN
tendiert das Reflexivum dazu, näher beim
Verb zu erscheinen als alle anderen Klitika:
er ergab sich ihnen, er hat sich's anders überlegt.

7.4. Suffixale Exponenten der Partizipation

Die ersten suffixalen Positionen bezeichnen
Modifikationen der Rollenstruktur (Erweiterung der Valenz: TRANSITIVIERUNG, KAUSATIVIERUNG, PROMOTION) sowie Änderungen der
Orientierung des Sachverhalts auf verschiedene zentrale Argumente oder PERSPEKTIVIERUNG (Serzisko 1984: inverse Flexion, Diathese), und zwar in dieser Reihenfolge. Transitivierung und Kausativierung teilen den Exponenten *-tia*, aber die Sprecher des HUICHOL
verwenden einen raffinierten Trick, um den
Unterschied zu markieren. Die größere begriffliche Distanz des Kausativums zum Verb
wird fakultativ durch das morphotaktische
Affix *tsi* angezeigt: V-*tsi-tia*. Wenn *tsi* nicht
eingesetzt werden kann, handelt es sich um
eine transitive Konstruktion mit einem engeren Kohäsionsgrad. *-rie* kann Promovierung
und Passiv bezeichnen, aber wenn beide Operationen realisiert werden, steht *-rie* immer
für das Passiv und in einer dem Stamm ferneren Position. Die Reihenfolge, in der die
verschiedenen Techniken von Partizipation
angegeben werden, entspricht auch hier der
Reihenfolge der Funktionen polyfunktionaler
Exponenten (s. o. Schema 41.5).

Jürgen Broschart (1988) macht den interessanten Vorschlag, daß die Techniken der Partizipation eine Skala bilden, die sich von den maximal impliziten wie N-V-Distinktion zu den maximal expliziten wie Kausativierung erstreckt. Die Position auf der Skala müßte sich u. a. in der Morphemstellung reflektieren. Der Vergleich von Transitivierung und Kausativierung brachte eine Bestätigung für diesen Vorschlag, aber die Tatsache, daß die Morpheme der Orientierung rechts von diesen Techniken erscheinen, scheint dagegen zu sprechen. Eine genauere Analyse dieser Ansätze würde über den Rahmen dieses Beitrags hinausgehen.

7.5. Lokalisation und daraus abgeleitete Begriffe

Der dritte funktionale Bereich umfaßt u. a. die Dimension L ('Lokalisation'), die sich von der Position her als eine für das Verb sehr relevante Funktion — relevanter sogar als Partizipation — erweist, wenn man nur die präfixalen Positionen betrachtet. Es handelt sich um drei Klassen von Morphemen, deren primäre Bedeutung 'Lokalisation' ist: *ti-* 'nach oben, rauf', *ka-* 'nach unten', *ta-* 'auf gleicher Höhe; quer', *ku-* 'rund um, hin und her', *ye-* 'drin'.

Die semantische Struktur dieser Grammeme ist, ohne den begrifflichen Bereich der Lokalisation zu verlassen, sehr komplex, da sie — in Abhängigkeit von der Orientierungsachse im allgemeinen Raum (Schwerkraft, Fluß) und von der inneren räumlichen Konfiguration der Gegenstände — sehr verschiedene Lokalisationsschemata ausdrücken (Iturrioz/Gómez 1988). Hinzu kommt, daß aus diesen ursprünglich lokalen Bedeutungen sich im Laufe der Zeit andere Bedeutungen entwickelt haben, die zu anderen begrifflichen Domänen wie 'Aktionsarten' und 'Individuation' gehören.

Zwischen 'Lokalisation' und 'Aktionsarten' gibt es einen gleitenden Übergang: Begriffe wie 'Distribution', 'Dispersion' können sich auf verschiedene Orte der Handlung oder ihre Anwendung auf verschiedene Objekte beziehen. Die Funktion der Lokalisation wird durch drei Klassen von Exponenten ausgedrückt, die in den Positionen 7−4 (*ha-, he-, heu-, 'u, nu-, na-, wa-*) und 2 (*ti-, ta-, ku-, ka-, ye-*) erscheinen.

Die Anordnung hat mit dem Grad der Prädikativität zu tun. Die Affixe von 2 geben zahlreiche, sehr spezifische räumliche Schemata an, die sich auf den Sachverhalt (Handlung, Zustand usw.) selbst beziehen ('nach oben', 'nach unten', 'nach außen', 'hin und zurück', 'an verschiedenen Stellen' usw.). Die Affixe von 4 drücken noch sehr konkrete Begriffe wie 'an der Spitze', 'hinten' 'quer', 'durch' aus, die sich auf die interne räumliche Struktur von Gegenständen beziehen.

Die Affixe von 7 und 6 sind stark grammatikalisiert und beinhalten sehr abstrakte Begriffe wie 'Figur auf einem Grund', deiktische Begriffe wie 'her', aber auch schon sprecherbezogene Modalitäten wie 'erfahren, erlebt', 'vom Hörensagen' usw.

Die drei Klassen stellen also horizontal und nach außen eine Grammatikalitätsskala dar. Einige Elemente von 2 können noch mit unabhängigen Lexemen identifiziert werden: *ka-* mit der Bedeutung 'nach unten, feststehend' erinnert an *ka* 'sitzen', *ye-* 'drinnen' an das Verb *ye* 'stecken, hineintun', *ku-* 'rund herum' an *ku* 'Schlange', *ti-* nach oben an *ti* 'stehen'.

Ursprünglich waren es also Zusammensetzungen. Daß diese Affixe heute noch eine ziemlich lose Verbindung mit dem Verb eingehen, zeigt Beispiel (3), wo die Wortunterbrechung durch das Nomen *tsükiri* nach dem lokalen Morphem *ti-* 'auf' es möglich macht, daß das Wort mit einem neuen Morphem desselben Paradigmas (*ye-* 'drinnen, auf dem Weg') wiederaufgenommen wird. *Yepiya* 'aufmachen' setzt sich aus *ye-* 'nach außen' und *piya* '(Deckel, Tür ...) wegnehmen' zusammen. Dieser einheitliche Begriff kann mit *ye-* eine erneute semantische Verbindung eingehen: *yeyepiya* '(aufmachen und) hinauslassen'.

Diese Exponenten von Lokalisation sind aber auch eine wichtige Quelle für Aktionsarten (limitativ, distributiv usw.), für Begriffe der Possession oder 'Individuation' und zuletzt für deiktische Begriffe, die stärkere Grammatikalisierungsgrade aufweisen; so kann *ye-* auch den deiktischen Begriff 'weg vom Sprecher' ausdrücken:

(21) *Te- pi -ye- hu.*
1PL.S AS weg geh: PL
'Wir gehen.'

Die verschiedenen Bedeutungen dieser Exponenten können nun auch in der Form einer Grammatikalisierungsskala geordnet werden. Diese vertikale Entwicklung, die anscheinend keine graduelle Entfernung vom Nukleus impliziert, schränkt jedoch die Kombinationsmöglichkeiten dieser Affixe so ein, daß die Entfernung von dem pragmatischen Pol auch diesmal reduziert wird. Mit anderen Worten:

Es findet eine Kontraktion der Verbalmorphologie statt, und die dann entstehenden Ketten sind denen flexiver Sprachen ähnlicher. Wenn *ye-* eine deiktische Bedeutung hat, kann es nicht auf andere lokale Exponenten folgen, die eine weniger grammatikalisierte Bedeutung ausdrücken. Exponenten der Positionen 7−4 zwingen die Elemente der Position 2 dazu, eine weniger grammatikalisierte Bedeutung anzunehmen.

8. *-ti* als Zeichen der Bereichsabgrenzung bzw. Bereichserweiterung

Dieses Morphem hat die Funktion, im suffixalen Teil des Prädikats Grenzen zwischen Morphemgruppen und damit innere Kohäsion und eine gewisse Autonomie dieser Gruppen anzuzeigen, obwohl es hier Unterbrechungen und Inkorporation nicht geben kann. *-ti* markiert den Schluß eines funktionalen Bereichs und zugleich die Hinzufügung eines zusätzlichen Elements desselben. Es kann mit dieser Funktion in einer Reihe von Konfigurationen erscheinen, die in Schmema 41.8 dargestellt sind.

NSatz	NPräd	AA	T/A	MOD	NEX
RedPr-*ti*	V-*ti*-yei	-*ti*-re	-*ti*-kai -ne -xi	-*ti*-ni	-*ti*-kaku

Schema 41.8: Funktionen von *ti* 'ERW'.

ti kann mehrmals im selben Wort erscheinen:

(22) *Ni- kie -pa -ti -kai -ti -ni*
    FOR Haus LOK ERW IMPF ERW FOR
    -ti -kaku
    ERW KONZ
    'Es war das Hausgelände.'

Das erste *-ti* ermöglicht, daß ein temporales Morphem an ein nominales Prädikat angefügt wird, d. h. daß ein gegenständlicher Begriff (*kiepa* 'Hausgelände') temporalisiert wird. Die prototypischen Nomina bezeichnen kompakte, semantisch gesättigte Strukturen. Wenn das Nomen nicht zur prototypischen Instanz dieser Kategorie gehört und infolgedessen nicht einen materiellen, raumzeitlich permanenten Gegenstand bezeichnet, dann bedarf es nicht des Morphems *-ti*. *Taikaiyari* 'Abend' kann auch 'den Abend zubringen' und *tsipuriki* 'Masern haben' bedeuten:

(23) *Mana ni- u- taikai -yarie -ni*
    dort FOR HGR Abend KOMP FOR
    'Dort verbrachte er/sie den Abend.'

(24) *Ne- niwé ni- tsipuriki -kai -ti*
    POS.1SG Kind FOR Masern IMPF ERW
    -ni
    FOR
    'Mein Kind hatte Masern.'

Das zweite *-ti* von (22) ist identisch mit dem von (24); es ermöglicht, daß ein temporalisierter Sachverhalt mit dem Zeichen des formalen Registers ka_{13}-, ni_{10}- und $-ni_{12}$ versehen wird.

Das dritte *-ti* von (22) macht die Anfügung des nexualen Morphems *-kaku* an eine für die Kategorien 'Tempus' und 'Modalität' schon gesättigte Struktur möglich; wenn diese Kategorien wegfallen, kann das gebundene Morphem *-kaku* ohne weiteres angehängt werden; es kann aber auch als Klitikum ohne *-ti* in einer nicht reduzierten Struktur verwendet werden:

(25) (a) *'uxa'a pe- 'ekwa -ne -kaku*
        morgen 2SG.S wasch PRG SIM:VS
        ne- mi- ha- tua -ne -ni
        1SG.S MOD Wasser bring PRG FUT

   (b) *'uxa'a pe-mi-'ekwa-ne-ni-ti-kaku*
       'Während du morgen wäschst,
       ne nemihatuaneni
       werde ich gießen.'

Der einzige Unterschied zwischen beiden liegt darin, daß im zweiten Satz das Futur offen markiert ist. Eine Kombination von beiden ist auch möglich:

(26) *ka- ka- ti- ni- u- yiwe kaku*
    NEG FOR GENR FOR EXP könn SIM:VS
    tikaku.
    KONZ
    'Obwohl dies angeblich nicht passieren sollte.'

In einer dem Stamm näheren Position ermöglicht *-ti* das Anfügen bestimmter Aktionsarten:

(27) *Mi- ti- waika -ti -ne -ni*
    MOD IMPS spiel ERW PGR:SG FUT
    -tsie pi- ka -ti -hari ti -re.
    als AS NEG IMPS trink ERW OBL
    'Während man spielt, soll man nicht trinken.'

(28) *'Ayumieme mi- ti- ku- 'ixatsi*
    deshalb MOD IMPS DISP rat
    -ti -re, mi- ti- 'ena -ti -re.
    ERW OBL MOD IMPS hör ERW OBL
    'Deswegen muß man raten, deshalb muß man gehorchen.'

Dieses -ti setzt voraus, daß es sich um einen unpersönlichen, abstrakten Sachverhalt handelt, der im Prinzip Information hinsichtlich des Täters und des inneren Verlaufs und ähnliche Merkmale ausschließt. Die Bedeutung der Aktionsartaffixe ändert sich entsprechend der neuen semantischen Konstellation: Während -re normalerweise das Futur eines ingressiven Prädikats bildet, bezeichnet es hier eine deontische (agensbezogene) Modalität; während -ne anderweitig die lokale Dispersion einer Handlung bezeichnet (vgl. SPAN. *anda vendiendo*), ist hier das Ablaufen in einem abstrakten Schema zu verstehen. Auch die Zusammensetzung wird durch -ti angezeigt, wenn das erste Glied ein Verbalstamm ist, nicht jedoch, wenn es einer anderen Kategorie wie 'Nomen' gehört. Ein Lexem der lexikalischen Klasse 'Verb', das somit im Hinblick auf Prädikativität bereits abgeschlossen ist, wird durch ein anderes Verb ergänzt, das dadurch zu einem Auxiliar wird:

(29)   *'aixɨ ne- pi -r- e- ti- 'ena*
       gut 1SG AS GENR INV VPL versteh
      -tɨ- yeika.
       ERW geh
      'Ich verstehe gut.'
      [SPAN. *voy entendiendo bien*.]

Diese Art von Zusammensetzung entsteht aus der Reduktion einer Nebenprädikation, deren Exponent -ti Gleichzeitigkeit und identisches Subjekt anzeigt. Ein selbständiger Satz, der eine abgeschlossene Proposition beinhaltet, wird durch einen anderen unvollständigen Satz ergänzt, der auf diese Weise zu einer Nebenprädikation wird:

(30)   *Ne- r- e- ti- 'ena -ti ne-*
       1SG GENR INV VPL versteh SIM:IS 1SG
      pi- yeika -kai.
       AS geh IMPF
      'Beim Gehen hörte ich zu.' (Wörtl. 'zuhörend ging ich')

(31)   *Me- yu- huta tɨ me- pi- tsɨɨki*
       3PL BEL zwei NS 3PL AS Hund:PL
      -ri -ti -kai.
       PL ERW IMPF
      'Es waren zwei Hunde.' (Wörtl. 'sie hundeten zweiend')

9. Abbau durch Konversion

Unter den synchronischen Prozessen soll hier die Nominalisierung hervorgehoben werden. In diesem Prozeß der Umkategorisierung eines Verbs in ein Nomen werden die Dimensionen der verbalen Morphologie stufenweise abgebaut, und zwar entsprechend der relativen Relevanz dieser Dimensionen und der jeweiligen Kategorien für den Verbalbegriff: je relevanter sie sind, desto länger bleiben sie erhalten.

Die Tatsache, daß 'Modalität', 'Aspekt' und 'Tempus' in der ersten Stufe der Nominalisierung zusammengehen, zeigt eine relative Affinität zwischen diesen Kategorien, aber der Abbau der Kategorien wird vom Grammatikalisierungsgrad mitbestimmt; während nämlich alle Affixe der Modalität mit einem Mal wegfallen, einschließlich der modalen Bedeutungen der primär lokalen Affixe der Positionen 7−4, sind zunächst nur die deiktischen Tempusaffixe betroffen. Die agglutinativen Affixe der ersten Nominalisierungsstufe beinhalten noch einen temporalen Bezug auf den Hauptsatz. Von den Morphemen, die Pluralität des Subjekts ausdrücken, fällt in der Nominalisierung zunächst me_{17}- weg, während te_{11}-, das in einer stammnäheren Position erscheint, in der drittletzten Instanz erst fakultativ bleibt.

In Iturrioz (1990) wird ein komplexer Nominalisierungsprozeß beschrieben, der sich in einer Abfolge von zumindest acht Schritten vollzieht. Der ganze Prozeß führt von vollständigen Satzstrukturen zu Eigennamen. Jeder Schritt involviert einen Abbau von morphologischen und syntaktischen Entfaltungsmöglichkeiten der vorangehenden Struktur.

Beim ersten Schritt verschwinden alle modalen und temporalen Morpheme von Hauptsätzen. Aus der finiten Struktur (25b) resultiert so (25a), wo das modale Morphem *mi-* und das temporale Morphem *-ni* nicht mehr erscheinen können.

Eine Dimension braucht nicht mit einem Mal zu verschwinden, ihre Kategorien können nacheinander abgebaut werden. Während 'Modalität', die pragmatische Kategorie par excellence, in dieser Stufe spurlos verschwindet, schließen diese Strukturen Temporalität nicht ganz aus, denn die subordinativen Konnektoren der Klasse -*ti*, -*kaku* usw. drücken meistens gerade temporale Relationen mit dem Hauptsatz aus. Diese den Klitika nahen Exponenten der Kategorie 'Tempus', die in finiten Strukturen eine Bereichserweiterung verlangen würden, werden nicht ausgeschlossen. Auch Aktionsarten, die interne Zeitschemata wie 'Verlauf' (-*ne* 'PGR') usw. beinhalten, können in diesen Strukturen erhalten bleiben.

In einem zweiten Schritt entstehen attributive Strukturen ohne Temporalität, deren Exponenten lediglich angeben, ob die Nebenprädikation sich auf das Subjekt (-*ti*) oder auf eine andere Rolle bezieht (-*me*). Die Subjektaffixe werden hier fakultativ, während die stärker prädikativen Objektaffixe obligatorisch bleiben, wie in Beispiel (25a).

Der folgende Überblick zeigt die acht Schritte der Reduktion beim Übergang vom Verb zum Nomen. Nominalisierung baut die Morphologie des Prädikats in folgenden Schritten ab:

```
M → T/A → AA → LOK → SUBJ → OBJ
  → PART → REFL → GENR
              BEL    UNBEST
```

Schema 41.9: Schritte der Reduktion von Exponenten verbaler Dimensionen bei der Nominalisierung.

Die Dimension der Partizipation wird zuletzt abgebaut. Die zwei letzten Kategorien werden in den letzten, stärker nominalen Instanzen als BEL(ebtes Objekt) und UNBEST(immte Referenz) uminterpretiert. Während *yu*- auf eine inhärente Eigenschaft des Patiens des transitiven Nomens verweist, hat (*ti/r*)/*te*- nur noch mit der pragmatischen Funktion der Referenz zu tun, die für das Nomen weniger semantische Relevanz besitzt als die Morpheme der Possession:

(32) (a) *Ti-   yu- mie -ka -me*
         GENR BEL töt   NOMR
    'Mörder.'

(b) *Ne- ti-   teriwa -me*
    1SG GENR schreib NOMR
    'Mein Buch.' (Autor)

(c) *Ti-   ne-   teriwa -me*
    UNBEST 1SG.POS schreib NOMR
    'Mein Buch.' (Leser)

Jede Operation bestimmt eine spezifische Skala, die mit den aus anderen Operationen resultierenden Skalen nicht im Detail übereinzustimmen braucht. Wird etwa Morphemstellung mit Nominalisierung verglichen, stellt man interessante Abweichungen fest.

Die Position ist nicht allein bestimmend. Exponenten derselben Dimension verschwinden zusammen, auch wenn sie verschiedene Positionen besetzen, z. B. Modalmorpheme. Obwohl Subjektaffixe links von den Modalmorphemen erscheinen, bleiben sie obligatorisch, nachdem diese verschwinden. Obwohl Objektaffixe teilweise links von GENR erscheinen können, werden sie zuerst abgebaut. Die Hierarchie der funktionalen Domänen ist mitbestimmend. Während Objektaffixe sich auch auf eine weniger zentrale (promovierte) Rolle wie Benefaktiv beziehen können, muß sich GENR immer auf das Patiens beziehen.

Polyfunktionale Morpheme verschwinden nicht auf einmal, sondern entsprechend der Hierarchie ihrer Funktionen, unabhängig von der Position. In der ersten Stufe verliert (*ti/r*)-/*te*- seine modalen Funktionen, während es als Zeichen der Generalisierung bis zur vorletzten Instanz erhalten bleibt, länger als die Objektaffixe, durch die es nicht mehr ersetzt werden kann, zumal es als Zeichen der Indetermination uminterpretiert vor den Possessivpronomina erscheint: *netiteriwame* 'Buch = was ich geschrieben habe' − *tineteriwame* 'Buch, das ich besitze'. Das Reflexivum *yu*- bleibt ebenfalls bis zur vorletzten Instanz erhalten, allerdings nur mit der Bedeutung 'belebtes (vornehmlich menschliches) Patiens' in der agentiven Interpretation des Nomens: *ti-yu-miekame* 'derjenige, der Menschen tötet'. Die lokalen Funktionen der Affixe der zweiten Position verschwinden zuletzt.

10. Kontextbedingte Weglaßbarkeit

Im Redefluß sind verkürzte Formen üblich, denen Präfixe der Modalität fehlen: '*u-yeika-kai* statt *m-u-yeika-kai*; diese Formen unterscheiden sich dadurch von den Formen der ersten Nominalisierungsstufe wie '*u-yeika-ti*, daß jene noch deiktische Temporalaffixe haben müssen, während in diesen die Satzkonnektoren nur relative Zeit ausdrücken können. 'Modalität' erweist sich insgesamt als die Dimension, die am häufigsten ausgelassen wird.

11. Affinitäten zwischen Dimensionen

Die Affinitäten zwischen den Dimensionen manifestieren sich in einer Reihe von komplexen Beziehungen, die u. a. topologische und prozessuale, diachronische und synchronische, kombinatorische und paradigmatische Aspekte umfassen. Im Hinblick auf Morphemstellung muß man hier zweierlei berücksichtigen, einmal die Opposition 'präfigiert/suffigiert', zum anderen die relative Entfernung vom Stamm.

In der Regel folgt eine Dimension nicht als Ganzes auf eine andere, sondern sie werden miteinander verzahnt, indem die jeweiligen Kategorien einander abwechseln. Die Affinität zwischen Kategorien zweier Dimensionen kann sich darin manifestieren, daß sie sich in einen funktionalen Bereich zusammenschließen bzw. erst durch die Vermittlung eines Erweiterers sich verbinden lassen. Was besagt aber die Tatsache, daß 'Tempus' allein durch Suffixe, 'Modalität' dagegen vorwiegend durch Präfixe ausgedrückt wird?

Die komplexe Exponenz des formalen Registers erscheint jedoch wie eine Klammer auf beiden Seiten des Worts; *ka-ni-V-ni* drückt eine diskursive Kategorie aus, nämlich die Relevanz eines Sachverhalts innerhalb eines Textes oder eines Textabschnitts.

Die Relevanz einer Dimension zeigt sich auch in der Spannbreite ihrer Exponenz, in der Vielfalt der spezifischen Funktionen, die sie beinhaltet, und in der Anzahl der Verbindungen mit anderen Dimensionen, die sie herstellt (Affinitäten). Die Affinität kann sich durch Kookkurrenzbeschränkungen oder durch Bildung kooperativer Gruppen, durch Grammatikalisierung, durch systematische Assoziierung und andere Prozesse manifestieren. So deckt 'Partizipation' praktisch den ganzen präfixalen Bereich und einen guten Teil der suffixalen Positionen ab; andererseits stellt sie Beziehungen zu verschiedenen anderen Funktionen her: zu Wortbildung durch Inkorporation des Objekts und anderer Konstituenten, durch Generalisierung, Intensivierung usw.; zu Topikalisierung durch das Subjekt, zu Perspektivierung durch das Passiv usw., zu Individuation und Modalität durch die Polysemie von *(ti/r)/te-* usw.

Aus der Funktion der Generalisierung leiten sich andere pragmatische Funktionen wie Intensivierung, Bekräftigung, Fragestellung ab. 'Lokalisation' ist dagegen die Quelle anderer derivativer Begriffe (Aktionsarten, einschließlich Pluralität der Handlung), die den Verbalbegriff bereichern. 'Partizipation' zeichnet sich durch den höchsten Grad an pragmatischer Relevanz aus, während sie an begrifflicher Relevanz von 'Lokalisation' übertroffen wird. 'Individuation' ist mit 'Partizipation' systematisch assoziiert (kumulative Exponenz); bestimmte Aktionsarten wie PGR, DES, KAP verbinden sich auch mit der Individuierung der jeweiligen Argumente.

11.1. Ko-Operationen

In Iturrioz & Gómez (1988) werden eine Reihe von Phänomenen beschrieben, wo verschiedene Morpheme sich in einer Operation zusammenschließen, in der sie komplementäre Funktionen erfüllen. Diese Kooperationen können innerhalb einer Dimension (z. B. 'Lokalisation') geschehen oder aber mehrere Dimensionen einschließen. Wird da ein Morphem gewechselt oder auf eine andere Funktion festgelegt, so ändern sich kaleidoskopartig die Funktionen der anderen Morpheme in der kooperativen Gruppe. Der stammnahe Bereichsabgrenzer -*ti* impliziert die Anwesenheit von *(ti/r)/te-* in der Bedeutung UNPERSÖNLICH (Beispiele (27) und (28)). Wird eine andere Instanz des Bereichsabgrenzers gewählt, so wird *(ti/r)/te-* automatisch als GENR usw. interpretiert. Das Perfektivum wird in der Regel von mehreren Morphemen der Positionen 7 und 2 begleitet. Die individuative pluralische Form *te-* des Morphems *(ti/r)/te$_{11}$-* impliziert — gleich in welcher Funktion — die Anwesenheit des Subjektsmorphems *me$_{17}$-*. Diese Kooperationen bilden die Kehrseite der Kookkurrenzbeschränkungen.

11.2. Kookkurrenzbeschränkungen

Sie betreffen in der Regel nicht ganze Dimensionen, sondern einzelne Kategorien bzw. einzelne Instanzen derselben. Jedes Tempusmorphem erfährt hinsichtlich der Kookkurrenz mit dem Modalmorphem -*ni* eine andere Behandlung. Das imperfektive -*kai* bedarf der Zwischenschaltung des Bereichsabgrenzers -*ti*, Beispiel (33):

(33) *Ti$_{11}$- ni$_{10}$- ku$_2$- hiawe -kai$_9$ -ti$_{10}$*
     GENR FOR rund- RED IMPF ERW
     -ni$_{11}$.
     FOR
     'Man unterhielt sich miteinander.'

Das Zeichen des perfektiven Präteritums -*xi* schließt jeden Ausdruck von 'formaler Modalität' aus, aber PERFEKTIV kann auf andere Weise ausgedrückt bzw. erschlossen werden, nämlich aus den Morphemen -*u* 'HGR' und -*ta* 'LIM', die in der Regel das Perfektivum kooperativ begleiten:

(34) (a) *Nunutsi pi- ti- u- ta- kwini*
        Kind AS GENR HGR LIM erkrank
        -xi.
        PERF

    (b) **Nunutsi ka-ti-ni-u-ta-kwini-xi -ni*
        'Das Kind erkrankte.'

    (c) *Nunutsi ka- ti- ni- u- ta-*
        Kind FOR INTS FOR HGR LIM
        kwine (* ni).
        erkrank
        'Idem.'

Nur wenn das nichtformelle Perfektivum ohne -*xi* gebildet wird, muß das Zeichen -*ni* 'FOR' suffigiert werden:

(35) (a) '*Irawe hakaxie -ti p- u-*
 Wolf hunger SIM:IS AS HGR
 nua.
 geh:CIS:PF

 (b) '*Irawe hakaxie -ti ka- ni-*
 Wolf hunger SIM:IS FOR FOR
 nua   -ni.
 geh:CIS:PF FOR
 'Der Wolf kam hungrig (hungernd).'

Dies zeigt, daß die Beschränkungen sich nicht blind auf die inhaltlichen Kategorien selbst beziehen, sondern auf bestimmte Ausdruckstypen. Dabei sorgen die verbleibenden Elemente einer kooperativen Gruppe ('*u-ta-* und die suppletive Form *nua*) dafür, daß die Gesamtbedeutung erhalten bleibt. Die Beschränkungen gelten nicht für das Präsens:

(36) *ka- ti- ni- u- ta- kwi- kwine*
 FOR INTS FOR EXP LIM RED erkrank
 -ni
 FOR
 'Er erkältet sich oft.'

12. Asymmetrie zwischen Prä- und Suffigierung

Die suffixalen Markierungen der Pluralität des Subjekts, die im Bereich der Aktionsarten (-*ne/tiwe* 'PGR', -*we/wawe* 'KAP') liegen, sind unabhängig von inhärenten Merkmalen des Arguments und so den Beschränkungen der präfixalen Morpheme nicht ausgesetzt; folgendes Beispiel veranschaulicht diese Tatsache:

(37) *Tupiriya ti- xuawe kwiniya*
 Pflanze SORT exist Krankheit
 ti- wa- wewie -rie -wawe -ti.
 SORT 3PL mach APPL KAP:PL.S SIM:IS
 'Es gibt verschiedene Pflanzenarten, die ihnen Leiden verschiedenen Typs verursachen können'.

In beiden Verbalformen erscheint das Subjektmorphem -*me* nicht, weil es nur für belebte individuelle Argumente eingesetzt werden kann; aus demselben Grund erscheint die singularische Form *ti-* des Morphems (*ti/r*)/ *te-*, das hier in der Funktion des Sortalis auftritt: hier ist nicht von individuellen Pflanzen die Rede, sondern von mehreren Arten/Typen/Sorten (sortale Pluralität); im Gegensatz dazu steht der Ausdruck der Pluralität in Verbindung mit der Aktionsart -*wawe* 'KAP' nichts im Wege; der entsprechende Singular heißt -*we*. -*kai* 'IMPF' und sogar -*xi* 'PERF' können unter bestimmten Bedingungen weiteres mit den präfixalen Morphemen der Modalität kookkurrieren:

(38) (a) *me- ka- te- n- a- ka- wima*
 3PL FOR GENR FOR FIG unter hüll
 -kai.
 IMPF
 'Sie übten das Einhüllen.'

 (b) *me- ka- te- n- a- ye-*
 3PL FOR GENR FOR FIG innen
 nuiwa -xi.
 geboren PERF
 'Sie kamen da drinnen zur Welt.'

Diese Asymmetrie findet eine Parallele in der kontextbedingten Reduktion der verbalen Wörter und in der Reduktion der kindergerichteten Elternsprache.

13. Änderung des morphologischen Status

Die Kookkurrenz kann auch dadurch ermöglicht werden, daß ein Exponent durch einen anderen ersetzt wird, der zu einem anderen funktionalen Abschnitt gehört. Das modale Suffix -ni_{12} hat mit dem homophonen Futurmorphem -ni_9 insofern noch etwas zu tun, als es mit ihm nicht kookkurrieren kann, nicht einmal durch die Vermittlung des Bereichsgrenzmarkers *ti*. FUTUR ist, mit anderen Worten, mit dem Ausdruck der formalen Redeweise unvereinbar.

Soll trotzdem FUTUR ausgedrückt werden, dann muß das Tempusmorphem -*ni* durch den weniger grammatikalisierten Exponenten der nächstverwandten Kategorie 'Desiderativ' bzw. IMMINENZ mit dem Status einer Aktionsart ersetzt werden: -*miki/-ku* 'DESID/ IMM'. Dieses Suffix drückt in allen anderen Fällen eine deontische, d. h. sprecherbezogene Modalität aus, nämlich einen Wunsch bzw. das Bevorstehen eines Vorgangs.

(39) (a) *Nunutsi pi -ti- ta- kwine.*
 Kind AS INTS LIM erkrank
 'Das Kind wird erkranken.'

 (b) *Nunutsi ka- ti- ni- ta- kwini*
 Kind FOR INTS FOR LIM erkrank
 -miki.
 FUT
 'Idem.'

(40) (a) *ne- p- i- ta- wewie -ni.*
 1SG AS 3SG LIM mach FUT

(b) ne- ka- ni- i- ta- wewi -mi̱ki̱.
1SG FOR FOR 3SG LIM mach FUT
'Ich werde es machen.'

Das Suffix -*miki*/-*ku* kann als eine alternative Weise der Tempusmarkierung aufgefaßt werden, denn es drückt nicht nur den Wunsch oder die Absicht eines Lebewesens aus, sondern auch affine Ideen wie Imminenz eines Vorgangs, Voraussicht/Möglichkeit des Eintretens.

(41) *Pi- ka- wiye -miki.*
AS runter- regn IMM
'Es sieht nach Regen aus.' (wörtl. 'Es will regnen.')

Die Elemente der Klasse 7, die vorwiegend als Ausdrucksmittel von Aktionsarten und deontischen Modalitäten dienen, sind im Unterschied zu den echten Aspekt- und Tempusmorphemen (-*kai* 'IMPF', -*xi* 'PERF', -*ni* 'FUT') mit den propositionalen Modalitäten ohne weiteres kompatibel.

14. Kindergerichtete Elternsprache

Wenn die Eltern mit kleinen Kindern sprechen, reduzieren sie in abgestufter Weise die morphologische Komplexität der Wörter. Dabei fällt es besonders auf, daß diese Reduktion allein den präfixalen Teil trifft, während die Suffixe regelrecht intakt bleiben. So kann *ka-ni-nunutsi-ti-ni* 'FOR-FOR-Kind-ERW-FOR' 'es ist ein Kind') entweder zu *ni-nunutsi-ti-ni* oder *nunutsi-ti-ni* verkürzt werden, aber nicht zu *ka-ni-nunutsi*.

Die Präfixe werden nicht immer alle ausgelassen, die Reduktion wird vielmehr in abgestufter Weise vorgenommen: *ke-ne-u-ka-tsiki* 'IMP IMP EXP unter kämm' → *katsiki* → *tsiki* 'kämm ihn/sie/es'.

Dies scheint auf allgemeine Prinzipien und Operationen der Sprachverarbeitung zurückzugehen, die unabhängig sind von sprachspezifischen grammatischen Regeln. Greenberg stellte eine Asymmetrie in der Verteilung von Präfixen und Suffixen in den Sprachen der Welt fest. Hawkins & Cutler (1988: 306) schlagen folgende psycholinguistische Erklärung für diese allgemeine Bevorzugung der Suffigierung in der mentalen Verarbeitung der grammatischen Information vor: a) die Information von Affixen und Wurzeln wird getrennt verarbeitet, b) die lexikalische Verarbeitung geht der grammatischen voraus, c) die Wurzel besetzt tendenziell die erste Position. Suffixe sind im Sinne der Natürlichkeitstheorie 'natürlicher' als Präfixe in SOV-Sprachen.

Bybee & al. (1994: 19−29) argumentieren, daß die Erleichterung der Verarbeitung allein die Bevorzugung der Suffigierung nicht erklären kann, daß zusätzliche Faktoren wie die Quelle der grammatikalisierten Elemente und die Relevanz der Kategorien mit eine Rolle spielen. Aber Präfixe mit einem relativ hohen Relevanzgrad wie (*ti*/*r*)/*te*- (Generalisierung), welches die Verbvalenz verändert, Aktionsartexponenten wie *ta*/*ti*- (LIMITATIV) und die lokalen Affixe werden oft ausgelassen. Innerhalb des präfixalen Teils scheint jedoch morphologische Reduktion nicht auf extragrammatischen Operationen zu basieren, sondern auf spezifischen morphologischen Regeln der Sprache. Es gilt die allgemeine Implikation: Relevante, stammnahe Morpheme werden nicht ausgelassen, wenn die flexiven Morpheme nicht auch ausgelassen werden, aber nicht umgekehrt. Dies bedeutet, daß weniger relevante Morpheme viel häufiger ausfallen.

15. Ontogenese

Erst im Alter von 23 Monaten beginnen Kinder, komplexe verbale Wörter zu verwenden, wobei suffigierte Wörter bei weitem vorherrschen. Die ersten Morpheme, die verbale Wurzeln begleiten, sind Tempusmorpheme: '*iki chana-si* [*tsana-xi*] 'dies ging kaputt', *utiani* 'werde schreiben', *che-ni* [*pinetsitseni*] 'es wird mich stechen', *nanai-yu* [*tepinanaiyu*] 'wir gehen es kaufen'.

Am häufigsten sind Imperativformen wie *we-ti* (SPAN. *aquí parado*, 'bleib stehen', *tsita-ti* 'bleib sitzen'. Die ersten Präfixe sind Elemente der Position 2 in weitgehend lexikalisierten Verbindungen, die Kinder wahrscheinlich unanalysiert lernen: *ta-pi, ye-pi* 'aufmachen'.

Kinder scheinen also zunächst Suffixe zu lernen. Das früheste Suffix könnte das Zeichen des Imperativs -*ti* sein. Darauf folgen temporale Suffixe, allen voran -*ni* 'FUT', die eng verbunden mit Modalität sind. 'Modalität' und 'Tempus' zeichnen sich durch den größten Grad an kommunikativer Relevanz aus.

Die Modalaffixe werden nicht als Teil der Verbalmorphologie gelernt, sondern zunächst (bis zum Alter von zweieinhalb Jahren) in autonomen Kombinationen oder Syntagmen adverbialer Art: *kani* 'nein', *kena* 'gib her', *kami* 'sieh mal'; sie werden nachträglich in die Verbalmorphologie integriert. Das Zeichen 'i '3SG.O' wird zunächst als autonomes Adverb/Pronomen verwendet: 'i 'nimm', 'i yepi: 'dies aufmachen'. Die sehr prädikativen Morpheme der ersten echt segmentalen Position 2 werden dagegen zunächst als untrennbare Bestandteile des Verbs produziert und hinterher als selbständige Bedeutungsträger erkannt: ka-wiwi 'runterwerfen', ta-wewi 'PERF machen', ye-pi 'aufmachen'.

16. Grammatikalisierung und Polyfunktionalität

Bei polyfunktionalen Exponenten organisieren sich die Funktionen in Hierarchien, die im wesentlichen Grammatikalisierungsskalen entsprechen. Die relative Position in diesen Hierarchien verrät Affinität zwischen den Dimensionen. Je näher am Prädikat die Position des Exponenten liegt, desto relevanter (prädikativer) sind die ersten Funktionen der Skala; mit zunehmender Entfernung vom Stamm wächst auch der pragmatische Charakter der Hierarchie. Die Funktionshierarchie von (ti/r)/te- zeichnet sich durch ein Gleichgewicht zwischen beiden allgemeinen Prinzipien aus, was damit zusammenhängt, daß dieser Exponent in der Übergangs- oder Katastrophenzone liegt.

17. Spezielle Abkürzungen

1, 2, 3	1., 2., 3. Person
A	Aspekt
AA	Aktionsart
ADV	adverbial
AS	Assertiv
BEKR	Bekräftigung
CISL	Cislativ
D	Demonstrativ
DER	Derivativ
DESID	Desiderativ
DIM	Dimensionen
DIST	Distinktionen (innerhalb der Kategorien)
DISTR	Distributiv
dM	deontische Modalität
EFR	Entscheidungsfrage
ELAT	Elativ
eM	epistemische Modalität
EMPH	Emphase
EP	etablierte Possession
ERW	Bereichserweiterer
EXP	Experienz, aus eigener Erfahrung, selbsterfahren
FAKT	Faktitiv
FIG	Figur
FOR	formale Redeweise
FUT	Futur
G	Graduierung
GEN	Generalisierung
GENR	Generalisator
HGR	Hintergrund
I	Individuation
IMP	Imperativ
IMPF	Imperfektiv
IMPS	Impersonal
INGR	Ingressiv
IMM	Imminential
INTS	Intensität
INV	unsichtbar, nicht im Erfahrungsbereich des Sprechers
IR	indirekte Rede
IS	identisches Subjekt
J	Junktion
KAP	Kapazität
KAT	Kategorien
KAUS	Kausativ
KAUSAL	Kausal (Satzkonnektor)
KLIT	Klitikum
KOM	Komitativ
KOMP	Kompositum
KOND	Konditional
KONTR	Kontrast
KONZ	Konzessiv
L	Lokalisation
LIM	Limitativ
M	Modalität
mM	emotionale Modalität
MOD	Morphem der Modalität
MT	morphotaktisch
N	Nomen
NEG	Negation
NEX	Nexus, Satzkonnektoren
NOMR	Nominalisator
NPr	Nebenprädikation
NS	Nebensatz
O	Objekt
P	Partizipation
PAS	Passiv
PAT	Patiens
PERF	Perfektiv
PERSP	Perspektivierung
PGR	Progressiv
PL	Plural
PL.O	pluralisches Objekt
PL.S	pluralisches Subjekt
PROM	Promotion
RED	Reduplikation
RedPr	reduziertes Prädikat (ohne modale und temporale Morpheme)
REFL	Reflexiv

S	Situierung (Tempus, Aspekt, Modalität)
SG.O	pluralisches Objekt
SG.S	singularisches Subjekt
SIM	simultan
SKAL	skalare Begriffe
SORT	Sortalis
SUBJ	Subjekt
SUPPL	Suppletivismus
T	Tempus
TEMP	Temporal (Satzkonnektor)
TERM	Terminativ
THS	thematische Struktur
TR	Transitiv
TRSL	Translativ
UNBST	unbestimmt
V	Verb
VPL	verbale Pluralität

18. Zitierte Literatur

Broschart, Jürgen. 1987. *Noun, Verb and* PARTICIPATION. akup [Arbeiten des Kölner Universalien-Projekts], 67.

Broschart, Jürgen. 1988. *On the sequence of the techniques on the dimension of* PARTIZIPATION. akup [Arbeiten des Kölner Universalien-Projekts], 76.

Bybee, Joan L. 1985. *Morphology: A study of the relation between meaning and form.* Amsterdam & Philadelphia: Benjamins.

Bybee, Joan L. & Pagliuca, William. 1985. „Crosslinguistic comparison and the development of grammatical meaning". In: Fisiak, Jaček (ed.). *Historical Semantics. Historical Word Formation.* (Trends in Linguistics Studies and Monographs, 29.). Berlin: de Gruyter, 59–84.

Bybee, Joan L. & Perkins, Revere & Pagliuca, William. 1994. *The evolution of Grammar. Tense, Aspect, and Modality in the Languages of the World.* Chicago & London: The University of Chicago Press.

Drossard, Werner. 1986. „Kasusmarkierung und die Zentralität von Partizipanten". akup [Arbeiten des Kölner Universalien-Projekts] 63: 1–28.

Drossard, Werner. 1991. „Situierung (Aspektualität, Modalität, Temporalität) und Partizipation mit besonderer Berücksichtigung der Kasusmarkierung". akup [Arbeiten des Kölner Universalien-Projekts], 83: 1–24.

Foley, William A. & van Valin, Robert D. 1984. *Functional Syntax and Universal Grammar.* (Cambridge Studies in Linguistics, 38). London & New York: Cambridge University Press.

Gómez, Paula. 1999. „La función retórica y la categoría de modo: el asertor de registro formal en huichol". *Actas del Primer Congreso Internacional de Retórica en México: El Horizonte Interdisciplinario de la Retórica.* México: Universidad Autónoma de México.

Hawkins, John A. & Cutler, Anne. 1988. „Psycholinguistic factors in morphological asymmetry". In: Hawkins, John A. (ed.). *Explaining Language Universals.* Oxford: Basil Blackwell, 280–317.

Iturrioz, José Luis. 1989. „De la gramática particular del huichol a la tipología: Una contribución a la morfología operacional". *Función* II/2–3: 239–381.

Iturrioz, José Luis. 1990. *Variation und Invarianz bei der formalen und semantischen Beschreibung von grammatischen Morphemen.* akup [Arbeiten des Kölner Universalienprojekts], 80.

Iturrioz, José Luis. 1992. „Zur morphologischen Kodierung der Partizipationstechniken im Huichol". *Zeitschrift für Phonetik, Sprachwissenschaft und Kommunikationsforschung* (ZPSK) 45/2: 122–36.

Iturrioz, José Luis. 1999. „La lengua wixarika: balance de la investigación lingüística". *Actas del Encuentro Amigos de las lenguas utoaztecas*, celebrado en Hermosillo, Sonora, del 19 al 20 de junio de 1997.

Iturrioz, José Luis. & Gómez, Paula. 1988. *Entwurf einer operationalen Morphologie.* akup [Arbeiten des Kölner Universalienprojekts], 69.

Iturrioz, José Luis & Gómez, Paula & Ramírez, Xitkame. 1988. „La dimensión de localización en huichol: Serie funcional y jerarquías de paradigmas". *Función* 8: 111–66.

Mayerthaler, Willi. 1981. *Morphologische Natürlichkeit.* (Linguistische Forschungen, 28.) Wiesbaden: Athenaion.

Piaget, Jean. [7]1978. *La formation du symbole chez l'enfant: imitation, jeu et rêve, image et représentation.* (Actualités pédagogiques et psychologiques.) Paris: Delachaux et Niestlé.

Piaget, Jean & Inhelder, Bärbel. [9]1980. *La psychologie de l'enfant.* (Que sais-je?, 369.) Paris: Presses Universitaires de France.

Raible, Wolfgang. 1992. *Junktion. Eine Dimension der Sprache und ihre Realisierungsformen zwischen Aggregation und Integration.* Heidelberg: Winter.

Seiler, Hansjakob. 1988. *The Dimension of Participation.* Translated and edited by Fernando Leal (= *Función*, 7.) Guadalajara/México: Universidad de Guadalajara.

Seiler, Hansjakob. 1995. „Cognitive-conceptual structure and linguistic encoding: Language universals and typology in the UNITYP framework". In: Shibatani, Masayoshi & Bynon, Theodora (eds.). *Approaches to Language Typology.* Oxford: Clarendon Press, 273–325.

Serzisko, Fritz. 1984. „Orientierung". akup [Arbeiten des Kölner Universalienprojekts], 57: 1–65.

José Luis Iturrioz Leza,
Universidad de Guadalajara (México)

42. Temporality and aspectuality

1. The expression of temporality and aspectuality
2. Tense
3. Aspect and Aktionsart
4. References

1. The expression of temporality and aspectuality

1.1. Temporality and aspectuality in the verb

The principal linguistic expression of temporality is **tense**, the "grammaticalized expression of location in time" (Comrie 1985: 9). Such localization is ultimately relative to a deictic centre or locus, usually the **speech act time (time of utterance)**. Hence tense is a **deictic (indexical)** category (→ Art. 44).

There are three kinds of tenses: (1) **absolute (deictic, primary)** tenses (→ § 2.1.), which locate situations in the past, present, and future times, as in *sang, sings, will sing*; (2) **relative (anaphoric, secondary)** tenses (→ § 2.2.), which locate situations relative to time intervals within those three times, as in *had sung, would sing*; and (3) **metrical** tenses, which indicate degrees of **remoteness** from the deictic centre, e. g., "immediate past" versus "remote past" (→ § 2.3.).

The linguistic expression of aspectuality, which concerns the "different ways of viewing the internal temporal constituency of a situation" (Comrie 1976: 3), has been termed **aspect** or **Aktionsart** ('kind of action'). Goedsche (1940), Garey (1957), Bache (1982), and Smith (1983) argue that what others (e. g., Bybee 1992: 145; Verkuyl 1993: 11) see as a single category in fact encompasses two distinct categorizations (→ § 3.1.): (1) aspect **(grammatical aspect, viewpoint aspect)** (→ § 3.2.), which concerns how situations are viewed at a certain point, as a completed whole or as on-going etc., for example in the Russian opposition of **perfective** *oni pročitali* 'they read, had read' and **imperfective** *oni čitali* 'they read, were reading'; and (2) Aktionsart **(actionality, lexical, aspect situation aspect)** (→ § 3.4.), which involves characterization of situations in terms of the different ways in which they occur, e. g., **semelfactive** (*wag*) versus **iterative** (*waggle*), or **activity** (*read a book for an hour*) versus **accomplishment** (*read a book in an hour*).

Tense is far from universal and fewer languages may have tense than have aspect (Lyons 1977: 678 f., 705; Comrie 1985: 50 ff.). Claims of the tenselessness of particular languages are difficult to evaluate, however, due to the difficulty of distinguishing relative tense from aspect (Lyons 1977: 689; Dahl 1985: 25), for example in creoles and the older Semitic languages (Binnick 1991: 434 ff., 444 ff.; DeCaen 1996).

In tense and aspect, there is only a weak correlation between meaning (semantic category) and form (grammatical category): e. g., the Russian (grammatical) present perfective is a (semantic) future tense; the present perfect (grammatical) tense of Latin serves also as a (semantic) past tense. Under various pragmatic conditions, there may be a shift of the deictic centre **(orientation time, evaluation time)**, so that the use of a tense marker in text or discourse only indirectly reflects its semantic characterization, as in the case of the **historical (narrative) present and future**, e. g., *Napoleon arrives at Saint Helena, where he will die in 1821* (Waugh 1975: 449 f., 466 f.; Comrie 1976: 73; Wolfson 1979; Schiffrin 1981; Chvany 1985: 261 f.), and **epistolary tenses** taking the viewpoint of the reader, as in Latin *eram* 'I was' meaning 'I am'.

For such scholars as Comrie (1976: 9), Lyons (1977: 704), Johnson (1981: 148), and Waugh (1987: 1), grammatical tenses implicitly mark aspect, so that the ancient Greek **aorist** is past in (semantic) tense and perfective in aspect. The absolute grammatical tenses (→ § 2.1.) mark perfective or imperfective aspect, while the relative grammatical tenses (→ § 2.2.) mark **perfect** or **prospective** aspect (→ § 3.2.); in English the simple past and future tenses are polysemously perfective and imperfective.

While the grammatical categories of tense and aspect are usually realized morphologically in the verb (→ Art. 41) (e. g., *sings, sang*), or by use of auxiliary words in syntactic relation to it (e. g., *will sing*), this is not invariably the case, as in Mam (Comrie 1985: 31), which marks tense with a sentence-initial particle. The semantic categories of tense and aspect pertain not to the verb, but to the sentence (Waugh 1975: 456; Lyons 1977: 678; Comrie 1985: 12), if not to the text or discourse (Hopper 1982: 16; Wallace 1982: 207 f.; Kamp & Rohrer 1983: 250).

Tense and aspect interact (→ § 2.4., 3.3) with one another and with Aktionsart, but as well with **mood**, especially **evidentiality** and **inferentiality**; and aspect also with voice.

1.2. Temporality and aspectuality outside the verb

Temporal relationships are expressed by more types of words than the verb. Like phrases headed by verbs, expressions headed by nouns, adverbs, adjectives, and prepositions may be temporally deictic (*this morning, now, present-day, just at present*) or anaphoric (*that afternoon, immediately, contemporary, at that time*) (cf. Anderson & Keenan 1985: 297−301). They may be located in one of the three time spheres (e. g., *ancient Rome, contemporary design, the Buddha to come*). Because living Pompeii, unlike London, is presupposed to exist only in the past, *Pompeii was a bustling city* has an **indefinite** (→ § 2.1.) reading, whereas *London was a bustling city* is only **definite**, referring to a specific point in time. Derivatives of verbs (*her being ill, the aim of the hunters, the discovery of the wreck*) inherit actional and aspectual properties (Bartsch 1986).

Temporal non-verbs interact with tense, aspect and Aktionsart in the verb. Adjectives denoting temporary, "accidental" properties may occur with the progressive (*the children are being difficult*), but ones for essential, permanent properties may not (**the children are being short*). Anaphoric tenses may take their antecedent in an adverbial (Partee 1973, 1984; Hinrichs 1986; Lo Cascio 1986) or even a noun, as in Vet and Molendijk's (1986: 150) French example (1), in which, they argue, the antecedent of the imperfect tenses in *était* and *donnait* is the grand-vizier.

(1)   *Le grand-vizier mourut à l'âge de 88 ans. C'était un homme très sage qui donnait toute satisfaction.*
'The grand-vizier died at the age of 88. He was a very wise man who gave much satisfaction'.

The temporality of noun phrases is just now being explored at conferences and in theses.

2. Tense

2.1. Deictic tense

Deictic or absolute tenses are those in which the **situation time** (the time interval over which the state of event represented by the clause occurs) is related directly to the time of the speech act. Viewed as semantically and/or morpho-syntactically simplex, they are termed **simple** tenses (e. g., the simple past tense or **preterite**). The three possible orderings of situation times relative to the deictic centre − anteriority, overlap (or coincidence), and posteriority − define respectively the semantic **past, present,** and **future** tenses. Joos (1964: 159), inter alia, proposes that the modal character of the grammatical future tense (as in Germanic languages) excludes it as a tense, but Comrie (1985: 43−8), Dahl (1985: 103−8), and Declerck (1991: 10 f.) argue to the contrary.

The deictic tenses are characteristic of finite verb forms in both the indicative and other moods. In dependent clauses with a non-present tense matrix verb, inherently deictic tenses generally function as relative tenses, but under certain conditions remain deictic (→ § 2.2.).

Deictic tenses are also called primary tenses, because they denote **time spheres (axes of orientation, domains, time levels,** or **perspectives)** in relation to which relative or secondary tenses such as the **pluperfect** (*had sung*) and **conditional** (*would sing*) are defined (Lyons 1977: 689). For those who consider tense to map objective time, each deictic tense defines its own domain (Johnson 1981: 151), but for those who take linguistic time to be subjective any number of domains may be possible (Bull 1963: 22); thus Bull (31) places *sings, sang, will have sung,* and *would have sung* respectively on the Present Point, Retrospective Point, Anticipated Point, and Retrospective Anticipated Point axes of orientation.

The time spheres are often defined in non-temporal terms. James (1982: 375) observes that the past tense is used in many languages to mark the hypothetical, the connection between the two sometimes being seen as that they are both "distant from present reality", so that the temporality of tenses is considered by some (e. g., Janssen 1996: 247) as a purely contextual effect. The present and past are seen by Coseriu (1976: 94), Mufwene (1984: 201), and Thieroff (1994: 4) as indicative respectively of the actual (**realis**) and the inactual (**irrealis**). Waugh (1975: 452) writes of the "restrictedness" of the past tense from the domain of the speech situation and Thieroff (4 f.) refers to the categorization of "remote" (past tense) and "non-remote" (present) as "distance". In such theories, the future tense is considered to belong to the sphere of the present (cf. Waugh 1975: 474).

The deictic tenses are called definite because they refer to specific times; as Partee (1973: 602) observes, *I didn't turn the stove off* does not mean 'I have never turned the stove off'. Dry (1983: 21) and Thelin (1990: 60 ff.) relate definiteness to the occurrence of situations on the main narrative line (→ § 3.1.).

2.2. Relative tense

Those tenses in which the situation time is related only indirectly to speech act time, but immediately to a contextually-given **reference time (reference point)** are known as relative or secondary tenses (Lyons 1977: 689). For those scholars who believe tense markers to combine tense with aspect (→ § 1) there are no inherently relative tenses; for Reichenbach (1947: 290), who defines all tenses in terms of the reference point, all tenses are inherently relative. Comrie (1981: 30) rejects such use of reference times for the definition of deictic tenses. Relative tenses are also called **compound** tenses because they are morphosyntactically and/or semantically complex. McCawley (1971: 111) and Partee (1973: 609) observe that relative tenses refer back to times denoted by previous temporal expressions in the text or discourse and suggest a treatment of relative tenses similar to that of pronouns, i.e., as bound variables, from which relative tenses are also called anaphoric tenses (cf. Lo Cascio 1986: 198).

There are three ways of viewing relative tenses, reflected in the names used for particular grammatical tenses, though Bull (1963: 13), in saying that "*anterior, past,* and *perfected* all describe the same order relation to the axis", in effect denies any difference between the three. (The terminology used by scholars is not always consistent, however, with their definitions of the tenses, and traditional names, such as **perfect** for the present perfect, are also commonly used.)

(1) The relative tenses designate secondary times within one of the domains denoted by the primary, deictic tenses, but anterior or posterior to the central point in those domains (Jespersen 1924: 257; Bull 1963: 14; Kamp & Rohrer 1983: 254−7). That is, in **anterior** tenses (anterior past, *had sung*; anterior present, *has sung*; anterior future, *will have sung*), situation times precede their respective reference times. In **posterior** tenses (posterior past, *would sing*; posterior present, 'is about to sing'; posterior future, 'will be about to sing'), situation times follow their reference times. In this type of theory there can be no relatively coincident tenses distinct from the central tenses of the domains themselves; consequently, as Bull (26) notes, there can be no principled account within the theory of tenses such as the **imperfect** tense of the Classical and Romance languages, and Bull accepts an aspectual analysis for the imperfect.

(2) Grammatical relative tenses represent semantic deictic tenses combined with aspect (→ § 3.2). The perfect tenses, in some languages formed with a perfect participle (*been, eaten, sung*), represent perfective aspect along with past (past perfect, *had sung*), present (present perfect, *has sung*), or future (future perfect, *will have sung*) tense. The prospective tenses similarly combine prospective aspect with past (past prospective, *would sing*), present (present prospective, *is (about) to sing*), or future (future prospective, *will be (about) to sing*) tense. The prospective tenses are rarely if ever fully grammaticalized (Dahl 1985: 111 f.). Relatively coincident tenses such as the Romance imperfect represent imperfective aspect (Vogel 1997: 126).

(3) Relative tenses represent deictic tenses in relation to other deictic tenses. (In McCawley 1971: 91, and Hornstein 1981: 120, the relation in question is syntactic subordination; in what McCoard (1978) calls the "embedded past" theory of the perfect, the present perfect derives from a past tense embedded under a present tense.) Thus *had sung* is the past-in-the-past, *has sung* the past-in-the-present, and *will have sung* the past-in-the-future. Similarly, *would sing* is the future-in-the-past, *is (about) to sing* the future-in-the-present, and *will be (about) to sing* the future-in-the-future. Coincident (relatively present) tenses are ignored by many contemporary theorists, though Lo Cascio (1982: 42) writes of the imperfect, which is considered in traditional grammar a present-in-the-past, as a past coincident tense.

Jespersen (1924: 271) says the past and future perfects are ambiguously anterior tenses (*Caesar had thrown a bridge across the Rhine but it had been swept away by the winter floods*) or "permansive", i.e. of perfective aspect (*Caesar had thrown a bridge across the Rhine in the previous season*); these are contextual variants, however. Compositional analyses of morpho-syntactically compound tenses (e.g., Olsen (1994: 18)), in which each element of the form, whether verb or participle, is assigned its own meaning, are controversial; compositionality of the present perfect is especially debated (→ § 3.2.).

Some tenses require more than one reference point. (1) The **conditional perfect** (*would have sung*) is a past-in-the-future-in-the-past (Comrie 1981: 27; Declerck 1991: 391). (2) Colloquial French (Waugh 1987: 21 ff.) and German (Thieroff 1994: 12 f.) have **supercompound (surcomposé)** tenses requiring two reference points (e. g., French *J'ai eu épousé cette femme* 'I had married that woman', i. e., at a time anteceding some point previous to some time in the past), and French dialects have **hypersupercompound** tenses (Waugh 1987: 23) which may require three. (3) The past anterior tense of Romance languages, formed with an auxiliary in the simple past (e. g., French *quand Marie eut terminé son travail, elle rentra* 'when Marie had finished her work, she went home'), which is distinct from the pluperfect, formed with an auxiliary in the imperfect (*Marie avait terminé son travail* 'Marie had finished her work'), differs from it in marking precedence not to a contextually-given reference time, but to an implicit point of reference succeeding it (Vet & Molendijk 1986: 153 f.).

While relative tenses are characteristic of finite verb forms, many languages are said to exhibit relative tense in non-finite verbs (Comrie 1985: 16), but, as noted in → § 1, this is difficult to distinguish from aspect. Inherently anaphoric tenses typically occur in dependent, subordinate clauses, but may occur in independent clauses in **free indirect discourse**, where they are understood to refer back to a previous tense in the discourse (e. g., *had eaten* is dependent on *explained* in *John explained that he wasn't hungry. He had eaten earlier.*) (Rohrer 1986: 93).

Insofar as they do not refer to a specific time, relative tenses are known as indefinite, in contrast to the definite deictic tenses (→ § 2.1). The perfect tenses, for example, simply state that a situation occurred at some time previous to the reference time (*Sue had often visited Rome, Tom had learned to crochet*).

In certain types of dependent clauses, e. g., in **indirect discourse** (*they said/thought/wrote that* [sentence]) (→ Art. 45), deictic tenses may exhibit relative values. The facts are extremely complicated and the appropriate analysis much debated. There are three types of theory. (1) The tense of an embedded, subordinate clause adjusts itself to the tense of the embedding, matrix clause in accord with rules of **Sequence of Tense (Consecutio Temporum)**. Thus in French (Rohrer 1986: 82) the present under a past becomes the imperfect (preterite in English); the simple past, present perfect, and pluperfect become the pluperfect (the imperfect however remains the imperfect); the future and conditional become the conditional; and the future and conditional perfects become the conditional perfect. Syntactic tense adjustment or sequence of tense rules are argued for by Comrie (1985, 1986), Ogihara (1995b), and others; and there have been various proposals (e. g., McCawley 1971) involving the syntactic transformation of underlying tenses.

(2) Embedded verbs generally bear relative tense, as in Reichenbach 1947 (Hornstein 1981). With a past-tense matrix (*They said ...*), a past tense in the subordinate clause (*that Sam was there*) is a relative present and the pluperfect (*that Sam had been there*) a relative past. With a future matrix (*They will say ...*), the past and present are relative past and present respectively (*that the 20th century was strange, that the 21st century is fun*) (Rohrer 1986: 83; Vogel 1997: 35). In *They said that Sam was there*, *was* is past because its reference point, at which the situation obtains, is anterior to speech act time. Deictic uses require special explanation (Lakoff 1970, Costa 1972). The reference of tenses is determined by some kind of anchoring conditions or rules for anaphoric reference, as in Smith 1981, Lo Cascio 1986, Enç 1987.

(3) In "deictic centre" or "absolute reference" theories (see Declerck 1991: 4; Vogel 1997: 17, 22), embedded tenses bear absolute values and the embedded past marks precedence to the deictic centre; deictic uses require no explanation. Comrie (1985: 111 ff., 1986: 278−83) argues against this type of approach.

2.3. Metrical tense

Metrical tenses mark degrees of temporal remoteness from the deictic centre (Chung & Timberlake 1985: 207 f.; Comrie 1985: 83; Dahl 1985: 120 f.), though Comrie cites (85 f.) cases of relative time reference in metrical tense, i. e., involving distance from another, reference time, e. g., in Sotho. The demarcations between metrical tenses is often relative and vague (e. g., "immediate" or "proximate" past vs. "remote" past, i. e., "recently" vs. "long ago") but may be chronological and precise, e. g., "today" (**hodiernal**) versus "before today" (**antehodiernal**) or "yesterday" (**hesternal**) versus "before yesterday" (**ante-

hesternal) (Dahl 1985: 125 f.). A large number of distinctions may be made, up to the seven of Kiksht (Comrie 1985: 100), which distinguishes the pasts "just now", "earlier today (but not just now)", "yesterday or preceding couple of days", "last week", "from a week to a year ago", "from one to ten years ago", and "remote past".

While metrical tense occurs in both the past and the future, the number of distinctions tends to be greater in the past (Chung & Timberlake 1985: 209; Comrie 1985: 87), though symmetrical systems exist, e. g. in Bamileke-Dschang. The choice of an appropriate metrical tense is pragmatic, dependent on a number of contextual factors (degree of personal involvement, spatial distance, social separateness, etc.), and languages differ as to the weighting they assign to subjective and objective factors in judgements of temporal distance (Dahl 1985: 123 ff.).

The present perfect often serves as a recent, and the pluperfect as a distant, past tense (Comrie 1976: 60; 1985: 68, 84; Dahl 1985: 126 f., 136); the *Grammaire Générale* of 1660 describes the French present perfect (*passé composé*) as hodiernal, the simple past as ante-hodiernal (Comrie 1985: 85, 93), and similar usages occur in numerous present-day Romance dialects (Dahl 1985: 125; Vogel 1997: 10 f.).

2.4. Interaction of tense with other categories

There is a correlation of present tense with imperfective aspect and past tense with perfective (Comrie 1976: 66, 71 f.; Lyons 1977: 688; Dahl 1985: 79, 83, 94 f.; Bybee 1992: 145). The past allows a wider range of aspects than the present (the ancient Greek aorist indicative, the English *used to* habitual, and the past perfective of Romance, have no present-tense equivalents) (Comrie 1976: 71); the perfective in the non-past tends to be a future tense, as in Russian (Comrie 1976: 66). Comrie (1976: 80) sees Koranic Arabic as combining aspect and relative tense in its "imperfective" and "perfective" forms; in this and other tenseless languages the imperfective is interpreted out of context as present, perfective as past (Comrie 1976: 82 f.).

In subordinate structures the distinction of past, present perfect, and past perfect is often neutralized, as in *John denied having seen her before, John said he had never seen her before, = John said, "I never saw/have never seen/had never seen her before"* (McCawley 1971: 100).

The past tense is sometimes evidential (i. e., personally experienced or vouched for), as opposed to the inferential present perfect (Binnick 1991: 377, 391). It also readily takes on a range of modal values, such as contrary-to-factness, dubitativeness, possibility, irreality, conditionality, etc. (James 1982). The conditional tense may be reportative, as in French *le roi serait à Paris* 'it appears the king is in Paris' (James 1982: 386); cf. the conditional perfect in *That would have been late Tuesday night?* (Binnick 1991: 392). Ultan (1978) exhibits a range of modal meanings of the future tense: probability, potentiality, inferentiality, suppositionality (*that will be Tom coming in now*), etc.

3. Aspect and Aktionsart

3.1. Definitions of aspect and Aktionsart

The terms "aspect" and "Aktionsart" ("actionality") have received no universally accepted definitions. The names "grammatical aspect" (Dahl 1985, Brinton 1988, Olsen 1994) for aspect and "lexical aspect" (Olsen 1994) for Aktionsart reflect the view that aspect is grammatical, while Aktionsart is lexical. Verkuyl (1972) has pointed out, however, that Aktionsart also concerns phrases and even clauses, and Bybee (1985: 145 f.) that there is a continuum of inflectional and derivational expression of the aspects. The distinction of aspect and Aktionsart is sometimes couched in terms of the supposed objectivity of Aktionsart and subjectivity of aspect (thus Forsyth 1970: 356). Bache (1982: 64 ff.) argues to the contrary that Aktionsart needs not to apply to the real world and that aspect choice is not always free.

Aktionsart is understood in different ways in general linguistics and in certain language-specific disciplines (e. g., Slavic linguistics). In the former, "Aktionsart" refers to an implicit classification of situational expressions (Lyons' (1977: 706) "aspectual character"; Smith's (1986: 100) "situation aspect"; Olsen's (1994: 9) "lexical aspect"), i. e., as **atelic states** (*be happy, vegetate*) and actions (*read, run*), lacking inherent terminations, and **telic** accomplishments (*read a book*) and **achievements** (*spot an error*), which have them (Vendler 1957/67, Dowty 1979); hence the distinction of aspect and Aktionsart in general linguistics is sometimes couched in terms of actual, as opposed to ideal or inherent, phasic structure (i. e., the developmental stages) of situations (Olsen 1994: 9).

In Slavic and other language areas, Aktionsart is taken to concern morphologically marked **procedural** categories (Forsyth 1970: 19f.) such as **inceptive** (Latin *calesco* 'grow warm', Russian *zaplakat'* 'burst into tears'), iterative (*sparkle*), semelfactive (Russian *stuknut'* 'to knock once'), etc. **Aspectualizers** (aspectual auxiliary verbs) such as *begin, continue, keep, resume, stop* are taken (as in Woisetschlaeger 1976, Freed 1979) to form periphrastic Aktionsarten.

The earlier name *Aktionsart* for aspect reflects definitions couched in terms of phasic structure, i.e., "the way in which the action of the verb proceeds" (Karl Brugmann, in Porter 1989: 29); the name *aspect* reflects definitions based on point of view, e.g., "the point of view from which the process is considered, namely either as an on-going action or as an event" (Walter Porzig in Fanning 1990: 32): hence Smith's (1983, 1986) "viewpoint aspect". On the history of definitions of aspect and Aktionsart, see Porter 1989: 26–47; Fanning 1990: 8–50; Binnick 1991: 135–169, 207–214.

The "phasic" or "development" school defines perfective aspect as completed action and imperfective as incomplete; such notions are akin to Aktionsart (which likewise concerns the structures of situations), and are criticized as such by Comrie (1976: 16ff.), Brinton (1988: 3), and Klein (1995: 672). Nonetheless, some scholars recognize "aspects" which resemble Aktionsarten, thus Brinton's (1988: 53) **ingressive** ('begin to [verb]') and **egressive** ('stop [verb]-ing') subcategories of an aspectual category of "phase", and a **continuative** ('continue to [verb]') subcategory of the imperfective.

The "viewpoint school" defines aspect in terms of (non-)totality, (non-)inclusion of (initial and terminal) boundaries, interior versus exterior view, cursive (linear) versus punctual, etc., the central opposition being between the presentation of an internally-structured situation occurring over a time interval (in the imperfective), and that of a situation as an unanalyzable atom occurring at a point in time (the perfective). Klein (1995: 674f., 677) is critical of the vague, metaphorical "viewpoint"; and to "non-totality", "interior view", and the like, opposes Russian examples in the imperfective which nonetheless describe complete situations, including terminal boundaries, e.g., *Včera ja spal do obeda* 'Yesterday I slept till lunchtime'. Notions such as "totality", "bounded", and "cursive" come close to concepts of "culminative", "totalizing", and such Aktionsarten (Dahl 1981: 81).

Contrary to the claim that aspect, unlike tense, is not time-relational (Comrie 1976: 5; Bybee 1992: 145), some theorists (Ducrot 1979: 17; Johnson 1981: 153; Chung & Timberlake 1985: 213; Klein 1995: 688; Boogaart 1996: 223, 227) define aspect precisely as involving the temporal relationship of the situation to a contextually-defined **event frame** or reference time. In the perfective, the situation time in question coincides with the frame; in the imperfective, the frame is within the situation time; in the perfect and prospective, the frame follows and precedes the situation time respectively.

Scholars of what is termed the discourse-pragmatic school see the (perfective and imperfective) aspects as discourse-conditioned and primarily indicative respectively of the **foreground** (i.e. the main narrative line or principal statements) and **background** (the subsidiary, supportive material) of discourse (Hopper 1979: 213–5, 1982: 5; Wallace 1982: 208f.; Thelin 1990: 61) (→ Art. 61). Foreground in narration is characterized by temporal movement, in which there is a sequence of reference points represented by **propulsive** perfective tenses (Forsyth 1970: 9f.; Kamp 1979: 403; Kamp & Rohrer 1983: 253ff.; Thelin 1990: 63); thus *John sat down. He took a pill* (the two accomplishments are perfective) represents a narrative sequence, while *John sat down. He was taking a pill*, with the **ruptive** imperfective *was taking*, is not. (Kamp & Rohrer (1983: 256) point out the possibility of subsidiary narrative lines in relative tenses such as the pluperfect: *He had taken two aspirins. He had swallowed his stomach medicine. He had put drops in his nose.*) Background is characterized by a lack of narrative movement, even a timelessness (Thelin 1990: 60ff.).

Movement of the reference point is associated with those combinations of aspect and Aktionsart in which the boundaries of narrated events are distinct and there is no overlap between them (Ducrot 1979: 11f.; Hopper 1982: 6; Timberlake 1982: 313; Thelin 1990: 63; Dowty (1986) emphasizes the role of the situational types in narrative movement, since atelics lack inherent boundaries. More generally, movement involves changes in state, and even the stative imperfective (*was*) can drive narrative movement where a change of state is inferable (Dry 1981, 1983;

Dowty 1986; Thelin 1990: 64 f.), as in Dry's (1981: 238) example *This time she was pushed out of the frightening fifth dimension with a sudden immediate jerk. There she was, herself again, standing with Calvin beside her.*

Thelin (1990: 62) relates backgrounding and what he calls the **thematic** function, which he further relates to what Dry (1983: 32−5) calls anaphoric reference. Thus (3 d) below, unlike the equivalent (2 c), does not move narrative time and is merely a "comment".

(2) (a) John gave Mary an apple
 (b) and she sat down to take a bite.
 (c) She took the bite deliberately, savoring the taste.

(3) (a) John gave Mary an apple.
 (b) She sat down
 (c) and took a bite.
 (d) She took it deliberately, savoring the taste.

The distinction of **theme** and **rheme** (cf. Ducrot 1979: 2) is roughly that of **topic** and **comment** on the discourse level, and is related to, though not identical with, that of **old and new information** (→ Art. 46). The ultimate purpose of the use of tense, aspect and Aktionsart in backgrounding and foregrounding is to maintain cohesion of the discourse (→ Art. 47), just as (according to Reichenbach (1947)) the reference point serves to maintain cohesion of clauses within the sentence.

Vet & Molendijk (1986: 158) offer synonymous French examples (4, 5) in which nonetheless different aspects appear. They see aspect choice as dependent on Aktionsart and "the predicative structure of the sentence", i.e., in (4) the sentence in the imperfect "predicates something of the moment referred to by the adverbial", while in (5), "it is the time adverbial which predicates something of the event itself." Thus aspect choice is partially dependent on the sorts of discourse phenomena discussed by Thelin.

(4) *Il y a cent ans naissait Franz Kafka.*
 'A hundred years ago (there) was born [imperfect, i.e. imperfective] Franz Kafka.'

(5) *Franz Kafka naquit il y a cent ans.*
 'Franz Kafka was born [simple past, i.e. perfective] a hundred years ago.'

One further discourse factor affecting aspect and tense choice alike is the choice of a **point of view (temporal perspective)** (→ Art. 44),

either **external focalization (event focus,** the point of view of the narrator) or **internal** focalization (**participant focus**, the point of view of the subject) (Kamp & Rohrer 1983: 263 ff.; Fleischman 1991: 28; Thelin 1994: 66 ff.). *Elle vit* [simple past, i. e., perfective] *la lune* 'she saw the moon' is an objective statement, *elle voyait* [imperfect, i. e., imperfective] *la lune maintenant* 'she saw the moon now' represents an experience of the subject. The distinction of viewpoints may provide the underpinnings of the evidential use of the preterite and the inferential use of the present perfect (→ § 2.4, 3.3). Point of view is related to the distinction of **de re** and **de dicto** readings, utilized in Abusch's (1988) solution (Ogihara 1995a, b; Vogel 1997: 33 ff.) to the problem of **double-access** sentences with a deictic though embedded present-tense verb (e. g., *John heard that Mary is pregnant*) (Enç 1987). De dicto readings are attributed to the subject, and de re readings to the narrator; the relatively present embedded tense in *Aristotle believed that the earth was round* reflects the viewpoint of Aristotle, the embedded absolute present tense in *Aristotle knew that the earth is round* that of the speaker.

3.2. Aspect

Perfective and imperfective are universally accepted as aspects; the progressive is widely considered to be a variety of the imperfective (Comrie 1976: 25; Dahl 1985: 92f.; Olsen 1994: 207), as is the habitual (which Brinton (1988: 53) considers an aspect). It is widely assumed that there is one opposition of perfective and imperfective. However, Olsen (1994) concludes that the two are independent of each other, principally because (1) while the imperfective is the unmarked member of the opposition in Slavic (Comrie 1976: 112), it is (arguably) the marked one in ancient Greek (Lyons 1968: 314ff.; Friedrich 1974: 13, 19 ff.); and (2) the two aspects may co-occur (Olsen 1994: 126 f., 130, citing Dahl 1985: 154−181), e. g., in the Bulgarian imperfective aorist (Comrie 1976: 23, 31 f.). Markedness (→ Art. 32) of aspects is, however, contentious (Bybee 1985: 147; Dahl 1985: 19, 69−73; Porter 1989: 39 ff.; Fanning 1990: 54 ff.; Binnick 1991: 149−69). Chung & Timberlake (1985: 239 ff.) contrast "closure" languages such as Russian, in which "the event must be closed at the proposition level; and … the predicate must be telic", and in which the perfective is the marked aspect, with "dynamicity" languages like English, in which "the event must include the frame ... and the event must be a process", and in which the progressive is marked.

Some scholars (Johnson 1981: 154; Dahl 1985: 139; Brinton 1988: 53) admit a perfect aspect, but others consider the perfect the result of interaction of the perfective with tense or another aspect (Olsen 1994: 161, 169 f.; Vogel 1997: 126 f.). In English and Portuguese the perfect and progressive may co-occur (as in *I have been working*), and in Bulgarian the perfect and imperfective (Comrie 1976: 62).

Unlike the other grammatical perfect tenses, the English present perfect does not admit definite past adverbials (*Jane had seen him at noon;* **Jane has seen him at noon*); for reason of this and other peculiarities, the present perfect is often considered (e. g., by Richards (1982: 101) and Michaelis (1994: 113)), to be a non-compositional form unlike the other perfect tenses. For Comrie (1976: 12) it is semantically a past tense, and McCawley (1971: 101 ff.) and Michaelis (1994: 111) analyze it as a past tense within the scope of a present tense.

Its meaning(s), its sundry uses, and the relationship between them are complicated issues arousing much debate (McCoard 1978; Dahl 1985, chapter 5; Fenn 1987; Brinton 1988: 10−15; Binnick 1991: 64 f., 264−81). The present perfect (or perfect aspect in general) is often taken, however, to refer in some way to a state resultant from (relatively) past action (Comrie 1976: 12; Chung & Timberlake 1985: 240; Dahl 1985: 133; Fenn 1987: 209; Thelin 1990: 72; Boogaart 1996: 227; Vogel 1997: 131).

The present perfect in Latin, colloquial French, some dialects of German and Italian, and other languages, also serves as a preterite. This has occasioned some controversy; many see such grammatical tenses as ambiguous (e. g., Vet & Molendijk 1986: 136; Vogel 1997, 10), while Waugh (1987: 2) claims the French tense has one general meaning and Lo Cascio (1986: 202) places the Italian one solely amongst the deictic tenses.

Some scholars (e. g., Johnson (1981: 154)) define the perfect aspect as denoting a relationship of precedence between the terminal bounds of situations and their event frames. Such a definition opens the possibility of a prospective aspect defined as succession of the initial bound after its frame, and some scholars recognize such an aspect (e. g., Comrie 1976: 64 f.; Klein 1992: 537).

3.3. Interaction of aspect with other categories

Aspect interacts with the situation classification, especially in discourse. For unclear reasons, stative expressions are incompatible with the English progressive save under special conditions: **Sue is living and breathing* but *Sue is living in Cairo* (Brinton 1988: 38 ff.). The progressive also does not readily occur with punctual situations; progressive achievements (*he is spotting errors in the copy*) and accomplishments have iterative, serial readings (Comrie 1976: 42; Brinton 1988: 41), and accomplishments (*John was winning the race when he collapsed*) conative ones as well. Similarly, statives in the perfective make reference to the inception and/or termination of states (Ancient Greek *ebasíleuse déka éte* 'he reigned [aorist] for ten years') (Comrie 1976: 50).

Bauer (1970) argues that the various uses of the present perfect result from its interaction with the various Aktionsarten; thus with telic expressions it is **resultative** (*He has found it*), with atelic it is **experiential** (*He has lived in different parts of the world*), or, with certain adverbials, **continuative** (*He has lived in London since 1950*); in the progressive such continuative perfects may be telic (*I have been removing the stones in my garden*) as well.

Aspect interacts as well with procedural Aktionsarten. The procedural prefixes of Slavic typically mark perfective aspect. Aspectualizers combine with imperfective forms, not perfective, even in the case of verbs like *finish* and *stop* (*he stopped running,* **he stopped having run*). Punctual situations require the perfective (Bache 1982: 70); in *When I arrived, Massimo was leaving,* the phrase *was leaving* can only mean 'was about to leave, was going to leave' (Vogel 1997: 68 f.).

The perfect often has inferential (quotative, reportative) uses (Comrie 1976: 108 ff.; Dahl 1985: 159, 152 f.; Binnick 1991: 387 f.), as opposed to the directly evidential past tense. Dahl (153) cites Swedish *Vittnet har lämnet lokalen klockan två,* 'The witness (says that he) has left the premises at two o'clock'.

Aspect interacts also with voice. In some languages the perfect occurs only in the passive, e. g., the Russian construction with predicative past passive participle (*kon'jak vypit* 'the brandy (has been) drunk') has no active counterpart (Comrie 1976: 84; Dahl 1985: 135).

3.4. Aktionsart

Regarding the classification of situational expressions (Brinton 1988: 23−35; Binnick 1991: 179−97), the taxonomy of Vendler (1957/67) has generally been accepted, sometimes with minor modifications such as a category for "series" (Freed 1979: 51 ff.; Brinton 1988: 54 f.), which are state-like but allow *keep* [verb]-*ing: they kept being ill, *they kept understanding French.* The categories in the taxonomy are definable by the features of telicity (having an inherent terminal bound), punctuality (occurrence at an instant), dynamicity (exhibiting change over time), and possibly iterativity (i. e., repetition) (Garey 1957: 106 f.; Chung & Timberlake 1985: 214−22; Brinton 1988: 53−57).

Many schemes of procedural Aktionsarten have been proposed (Schwall 1991, Quesada 1994), but no widely accepted theory exists. The question of the relationship of the specific procedural categories to the situational types, if any, is an open one; Bache (1982: 70) seems to suggest the procedural categories represent language-specific realizations of the broader notional (situational) categories, while Binnick (1991: 148) considers the two categorizations independent.

4. References

Abusch, Dorit. 1988. "Sequence of tense, intensionality, and scope." In: *Proceedings of the 7th West Coast Conference on Formal Linguistics.* Stanford: Calif. Assoc., 1−14.

Anderson, Stephen R. & Keenan, Edward L. 1985. "Deixis." In: Shopen, Timothy (ed.). *Language Typology and Syntactic Description,* volume 3, *Grammatical Categories and the Lexicon.* Cambridge: Cambridge Univ. Press, 259−308.

Bache, Carl. 1982. "Aspect and Aktionsart: towards a semantic distinction." *Journal of Linguistics* 18: 57−72.

Bartsch, Renate. 1986. "On Aspectual Properties of Dutch and German Nominalizations." In: Lo Cascio, Vincenzo & Vet, Co (eds.). *Temporal Structure in Sentence and Discourse.* Dordrecht: Foris Publ., 7−39.

Bauer, Gero. 1970. "The English 'perfect' reconsidered." *Journal of Linguistics* 6: 189−98.

Binnick, Robert I. 1991. *Time and the Verb: A Guide to Tense and Aspect.* New York: Oxford Univ. Press.

Boogaart, Ronny. 1996. "Tense and temporal ordering in English and Dutch indirect speech". In: Janssen, Theo A. J. M. & van der Wurff, Wim (eds.). *Reported Speech: Forms and Functions of the Verb.* Amsterdam & Philadelphia: Benjamins, 213−235.

Brinton, Laurel J. 1988. *The Development of English Aspectual Systems: Aspectualizers and post-verbal particles.* Cambridge: Cambridge Univ. Press.

Bull, William E. 1963. *Time, Tense, and the Verb.* Berkeley: Univ. of Calif. Press.

Bybee, Joan L. 1985. *Morphology: A study of the Relation between Meaning and Form.* Amsterdam & Philadelphia: Benjamins.

Bybee, Joan L. 1992. "Tense, Aspect, and Mood". In: Bright, William (ed.). *International Encyclopedia of Linguistics*, volume 2. New York/Oxford: Oxford Univ. Press, 144−5.

Chung, Sandra & Timberlake, Alan. 1985. "Tense, Aspect and Mood." In: Shopen, Timothy (ed.). *Language Typology and Syntactic Description,* volume 3, *Grammatical Categories and the Lexicon.* Cambridge: Cambridge Univ. Press, 202−58.

Chvany, Catherine V. 1985. "Backgrounded Perfectives and Plot Line Imperfectives: Toward a Theory of Grounding in Text." In: Flier, Michael S. & Timberlake, Alan (eds.). *The Scope of Slavic Aspect.* Columbus, Ohio: Slavica Publ., 247−73.

Comrie, Bernard. 1976. *Aspect.* Cambridge: Cambridge Univ. Press.

Comrie, Bernard. 1981. "On Reichenbach's Approach to Tense." *Papers from the 17th Regional Meeting, Chicago Linguistic Society.* Chicago: Univ. of Chicago, Department of Linguistics, 24−30.

Comrie, Bernard. 1985. *Tense.* Cambridge: Cambridge Univ. Press.

Comrie, Bernard. 1986. "Tense in Indirect Speech." *Folia Linguistica* 20: 265−96.

Coseriu, Eugenio. 1976. *Das romanische Verbalsystem.* Tübingen: Narr.

Costa, Rachel. 1972. "Sequence of Tenses in That-Clauses." *Papers from the 8th Regional Meeting, Chicago Linguistic Society.* Chicago: Univ. of Chicago, Department of Linguistics, 41−51.

Dahl, Östen. 1981. "On the Definition of the Telic-Atelic (Bounded-Nonbounded) Distinction." In: Tedeschi, Philip J. & Zaenen, Annie (eds.). *Tense and Aspect.* (Syntax and Semantics, 14.) New York: Acad. Press, 79−90.

Dahl, Östen. 1985. *Tense and Aspect Systems.* Oxford: Blackwell.

DeCaen, Vincent. 1996. "Ewald and Driver on Biblical Hebrew 'Aspect': Anteriority and the Orientalist Framework." *Zeitschrift für Althebraistik* 9: 129−51.

Declerck, Renaat. 1991. *Tense in English: Its structure and use in discourse.* London and New York: Routledge.

Dowty, David R. 1979. *Word Meaning and Montague Grammar.* Dordrecht: Reidel.

Dowty, David R. 1986. "The Effects of Aspectual Class on the Temporal Structure of Discourse: Semantics or Pragmatics?" *Linguistics and Philosophy* 9: 37–61.

Dry, Helen. 1981. "Sentence Aspect and the Movement of Narrative Time." *Text* 1: 233–40.

Dry, Helen. 1983. "The Movement of Narrative Time." *Journal of Literary Semantics* 12: 19–53.

Ducrot, Oswald. 1979. "L'imparfait en français." *Linguistische Berichte* 60: 1–23.

Enç, Mürvet. 1987. "Anchoring Conditions for Tense." *Linguistic Inquiry* 18: 633–57.

Fanning, Buist M. 1990. *Verbal Aspect in New Testament Greek.* Oxford: Clarendon Press.

Fenn, Peter. 1987. *A Semantic and Pragmatic Examination of the English Perfect.* Tübingen: Narr.

Fleischman, Suzanne. 1991. "Verb tense and point of view in narrative." In: Fleischman, Suzanne & Waugh, Linda R. (eds.). *Discourse-Pragmatics and the Verb: Evidence from Romance.* London/New York: Routledge, 26–54.

Forsyth, John. 1970. *A Grammar of Aspect: Usage and Meaning in the Russian Verb.* Cambridge: Univ. Press.

Freed, Alice. 1979. *The Semantics of English Aspectual Complementation.* Dordrecht: Reidel.

Friedrich, Paul. 1974. "On Aspect Theory and Homeric Aspect." *International Journal of American Linguistics*, Memoir 28: 1–44.

Garey, Howard B. 1957. "Verbal Aspect in French." *Language* 33: 91–110.

Goedsche, C. R. 1940. "Aspect versus Aktionsart." *Journal of English and Germanic Philology* 39: 189–97.

Hinrichs, Erhard. 1986. "Temporal Anaphora in Discourses of English." *Linguistics and Philosophy* 9: 63–82.

Hopper, Paul J. 1979. "Aspect and Foregrounding in Discourse." In: Givón, Talmy (ed.). *Discourse and Syntax.* (Syntax and Semantics, 12) New York: Acad. Press, 213–41.

Hopper, Paul J. 1982. "Aspect between Discourse and Grammar: an Introductory Essay for the Volume." In: Hopper, Paul J. (ed.). *Tense-Aspect: Between Semantics and Pragmatics.* Amsterdam/Philadelphia: Benjamins, 3–18.

Hornstein, Norbert. 1981. "The Study of Meaning in Natural Language: Three Approaches to Tense." In: Hornstein, Norbert H. & Lightfoot, David (eds.). *Explanation in Linguistics.* London: Longman, 116–51.

Jakobson, Roman. 1971. "Shifters, Verbal Categories, and the Russian Verb." In: Jakobson, Roman. *Selected Writings*, volume 2, *Word and Language.* The Hague: Mouton, 130–47.

James, Deborah. 1982. "Past Tense and the Hypothetical: A Cross Linguistic Study." *Studies in Language* 6: 375–403.

Janssen, Theo A. J. M. 1996. "Tense in reported speech and its frame of reference". In: Janssen, Theo A. J. M. & van der Wurff, Wim (eds.). *Reported Speech: Forms and Functions of the Verb.* Amsterdam/Philadelphia: Benjamins, 227–259.

Jespersen, Otto. 1924. *The Philosophy of Grammar.* London: Allen & Unwin.

Johnson, Marion R. 1981. "A Unified Temporal Theory of Tense and Aspect." In: Tedeschi, Philip J. & Zaenen, Annie (eds.). *Tense and Aspect.* (Syntax and Semantics, 14) New York: Acad. Press, 145–75.

Joos, Martin. 1964. *The English Verb: Form and Meanings.* Madison: Univ. of Wisconsin Press.

Kamp, Hans. 1979. "Events, Instants, and Temporal Reference." In: Bäuerle, R. & Egli, Urs & von Stechow, Arnim (eds.). *Semantics from Different Points of View.* Berlin: Springer, 376–417.

Kamp, Hans & Rohrer, Christian. 1983. "Tense in Texts." In: Bäuerle, Rainier & Schwarze, Christoph & von Stechow, Arnim (eds.). *Meaning, Use, and Interpretation of Language.* Berlin: Gruyter, 150–69.

Klein, Wolfgang. 1992. "The Present Perfect Puzzle." *Language* 68: 525–52.

Klein, Wolfgang. 1995. "A Time-Relational Analysis of Russian Aspect." *Language* 71: 669–95.

Lakoff, Robin T. 1970. "Tense and Its Relations to Participants." *Language* 46: 838–49.

Lo Cascio, Vincenzo. 1982. "Temporal Deixis and Anaphor in Sentence and Text: Finding a Reference Time." *Journal of Italian Linguistics.* 7(1): 31–70.

Lo Cascio, Vincenzo. 1986. "Temporal Deixis and Anaphor in Sentence and Text: Finding a Reference Time." In: Lo Cascio, Vincenzo & Vet, Co (eds.). *Temporal Structure in Sentence and Discourse.* Dordrecht: Foris Publ., 191–228.

Lyons, John. 1968. *Introduction to Theoretical Linguistics.* Cambridge: Univ. Press.

Lyons, John. 1977. *Semantics.* Cambridge: Cambridge Univ.

McCawley, James D. 1971. "Tense and Time Reference in English." In: Fillmore, Charles & Langendoen, D. T. (eds.). *Studies in Linguistic Semantics.* New York: Holt, Rinehart & Winston, 97–113.

McCoard, Robert W. 1978. *The English Perfect: Tense-Choice and Pragmatic Inferences.* Amsterdam: North Holland Publ.

Michaelis, Laura A. 1994. "The ambiguity of the English present perfect." *Journal of Linguistics* 30: 111–57.

Mufwene, Salikoko S. 1984. "Observations on Time Reference in Jamaican and Guyanese Creoles." *English World-Wide* 4: 199–229.

Ogihara, Toshiyuki. 1995a. "'Double-Access' Sentences and References to States." *Natural Language Semantics* 3: 177–210.

Ogihara, Toshiyuki. 1995b. "The Semantics of Tense in Embedded Clauses." *Linguistic Inquiry* 26: 663–79.

Olsen, Mari Jean Broman. 1994. "A Semantic and Pragmatic Model of Lexical and Grammatical Aspect." Ph.D. dissertation, Northwestern University.

Partee, Barbara Hall. 1973. "Some Structural Analogies between Tenses and Pronouns in English." *The Journal of Philosophy* 70: 601–9.

Partee, Barbara Hall. 1984. "Nominal and Temporal Anaphora." *Linguistics and Philosophy* 7: 243–86.

Porter, Stanley E. 1989. *Verbal Aspect in the Greek of the New Testament, with Reference to Tense and Mood.* New York: Lang.

Quesada, J. Diego. 1994. *Periphrastische Aktionsart im Spanischen: Das Verhalten einer Kategorie der Übergangszone.* Frankfurt a. M.: Lang.

Reichenbach, Hans. 1947. *Elements of Symbolic Logic.* New York: Macmillan.

Richards, Barry. 1982. "Tense, Aspect, and Time Adverbials, Part I." *Linguistics and Philosophy* 5: 59–107.

Rohrer, Christian. 1986. "Indirect Discourse and 'Consecutio Temporum'." In: Lo Cascio, Vincenzo & Vet, Co (eds.). *Temporal Structure in Sentence and Discourse.* Dordrecht: Foris Publ. 79–98.

Schiffrin, Deborah. 1981. "Tense Variations in Narration." *Language* 57: 45–62.

Schwall, Ulrike. 1991. *Aspektualität: eine semantisch-funktionelle Kategorie.* Tübingen: Narr.

Smith, Carlota S. 1981. "Semantic and Syntactic Constraints on Temporal Interpretation." In: Tedeschi, Philip J. & Zaenen, Annie (eds.). *Tense and Aspect.* (Syntax and Semantics, 14) New York: Acad. Press, 213–37.

Smith, Carlota. 1983. "A Theory of Aspectual Choice." *Language* 59: 479–501.

Smith, Carlota. 1986. "A Speaker-Based Approach to Aspect." *Linguistics and Philosophy* 9: 97–115.

Thelin, Nils B. 1990. "Verbal aspect in discourse: on the state of the art." In: Thelin, Nils B. (ed.). *Verbal Aspect in Discourse: Contributions to the Semantics of Time and Temporal Perspective in Slavic and Non-Slavic Languages.* Amsterdam & Philadelphia: Benjamins, 3–88.

Thieroff, Rolf. 1994. "Inherent Verb Categories and Categorizations in European Languages." In: Thieroff, Rolf & Ballweg, Joachim (eds.). *Tense Systems in European Languages.* Tübingen: Niemeyer, 3–45.

Timberlake, Alan. 1982. "Invariance and the Syntax of Russian Aspect." In: Hopper, Paul J. (ed.). *Tense-Aspect: Between Semantics and Pragmatics.* Amsterdam & Philadelphia: Benjamin, 305–31.

Ultan, Russell. 1978. "The Nature of Future Tenses." In: Greenberg, Joseph H. (ed.). *Universals of Human Language*, volume 3, *Word Structure.* Stanford: Univ. Press, 83–123.

Vendler, Zeno. 1957. "Verbs and Times". *Philosophical Review* 66: 143–60. Revised 1967. In: Vendler, Zeno. *Linguistics in Philosophy.* Ithaca, New York, 97–121.

Verkuyl, Henk J. 1972. *On the Compositional Nature of the Aspects.* Dordrecht: Reidel.

Verkuyl, Henk J. 1993. *A Theory of Aspectuality: The Interaction between Temporal and Atemporal Structure.* Cambridge: Cambridge Univ. Press.

Vet, Co & Molendijk, Arie. 1986. "The Discourse Functions of the Past Tenses in French." In: Lo Cascio, Vincenzo & Vet, Co (eds.). *Temporal Structure in Sentence and Discourse.* Dordrecht: Foris Publ., 133–60.

Vogel, Roos. 1997. *Aspects of Tense.* (Holland Institute of Generative Linguistics Dissertations, 25) Amsterdam: Holland Institute of Generative Linguistics.

Wallace, Stephen. 1982. "Figure and Ground: The Interrelationships of Linguistic Categories." In: Hopper, Paul J. (ed.). *Tense-Aspect: Between Semantics and Pragmatics.* Amsterdam & Philadelphia: Benjamins, 201–23.

Waugh, Linda R. 1975. "A Semantic Analysis of the French Tense System." *Orbis* 24: 436–85.

Waugh, Linda R. 1987. "Marking Time with the Passé Composé: Toward a Theory of the Perfect." *Linguisticae Investigationes* 11: 1–47.

Woisetschlaeger, Erich F. 1976. *A Semantic Theory of the English Auxiliary System.* Bloomington/IND: Indiana Univ. Linguistics Club.

Wolfson, Nessa. 1979. "Conversational Historical Present Alternation." *Language* 55: 168–82.

Robert I. Binnick,
University of Toronto (Canada)

43. Universals and typology of space

1. Introduction
2. The research problem and definitions
3. Deictic vs. non-deictic localization in space
4. Some formal properties of deictic, absolute and intrinsic systems
5. Cognitive consequences
6. Universals and Typology
7. Conclusions
8. References

1. Introduction

As observed by Annette Herskovits (1986: 1) "the domain of space provides a particularly clear view of most of the fundamental issues pertinent to language and cognition". This statement can be interpreted to mean either that spatial expressions are a particularly straightforward illustration of more general properties of human languages, or else that spatial expressions demonstrate more clearly than other areas of language the insufficiency of widespread metalinguistic assumptions such as that language can be studied as a self-contained independent phenomenon.

As pointed out by Gunter Senft (1997: 1), linguistic theories of space have tended to be based on the concepts found in familiar Indo-European languages and universal status has been claimed for them. It is ironic that this view was accepted also by the otherwise fiercely anti-universalist linguist Benjamin Lee Whorf (1954: 158 f.; cf. Malotki 1979). After discussing a number of perceived major differences in the semantics of time in HOPI and Standard Average European languages, Whorf continues

"But what about our concept of 'space', which was also included in our first question? There is no such striking difference between Hopi and SAE about space as about time, and probably the apprehension of space is given in substantially the same form by experience irrespective of language. The experiments of the Gestalt psychologists with visual perception appear to establish this as a fact. But the concept of space will vary somewhat with language, because, as an intellectual tool, it is so closely linked with the concomitant employment of other intellectual tools, of the order of 'time' and 'matter', which are linguistically conditioned. We see things with our eyes in the same space forms as the Hopi, but our idea of space has also the property of acting as a surrogate of non-spatial relationships like time, intensity, tendency, and as a void to be filled with imagined formless items, one of which may even be called 'space'. Space as sensed by the Hopi would not be connected mentally with such surrogates, but would be comparatively 'pure', unmixed with extraneous notions."

The universalist view of spatial concepts continues to dominate linguistics and cognitive science (e.g. Lyons 1977; Talmy 1983), but has been shown to be insufficient by a number of researchers (mainly from the Cognitive Anthropology Research Group of the Max Planck Institute at Nijmegen) working on languages of the Australian and Pacific region.

2. The research problem and definitions

First and foremost it needs to be kept in mind that spatial cognition is distinct from language about space, that therefore not all spatial meanings can be expressed linguistically and that those linguistic expressions one can identify in individual languages cannot be taken for iconic representations of cognitive ability. Attempts directed to project cognitive categories directly onto linguistic ones thus would seem to be misguided.

As regards language about space, fundamental to all understanding of the linguistic encoding of spatial expressions is that locations and directions can be understood only "in relation to some frame of reference taken – however provisorily – as absolute" (Herskovits 1986: 164).

Current research distinguishes between three such frames or perspectives: an *intrinsic*, a *deictic* and an *absolute* one.

- The intrinsic perspective is illustrated by the ENGLISH utterance 'the pedestrian walked in front of the car'. It is assumed that cars have front and rear ends which remain constant wherever the car is located or moved. What is front and what is back is part of the conventionalised lexical information of individual languages. In ENGLISH for moving objects front is in the usual direction of travel, but for static objects there are often only weak conventions (e.g. it is not clear what constitutes the front of a church) and for numerous objects (e.g. eggs, drums) there are no conventions.
- The deictic perspective is speaker centred and relative. The meaning of the utterance 'I saw a pedestrian to the left of the car' depends on my own (on a speaker's) location.

– Finally, an absolute perspective locates entities and events with respect to absolute reference points as in 'Italy is located south of Switzerland.' All three perspectives can be applied both to positions or place and movement through space.

When speaking about location the terminological distinctions between *figure* (or theme) and *ground* is used: In the example 'the cat sat on the mat' the entity to be situated, the cat, is the figure and the entity it relates to, on which the figure is situated, the mat, is the ground.

3. Deictic vs. non-deictic localization in space

The received view about language and space has been until quite recently the deictic one, i. e. that space is seen in egocentric terms as projection from the speaker. Spatial coordinates are projected from the ego in two horizontal (front/back and left/right) and one vertical (up/down) axes. These axes reflect human bodily experience: The reference plane for front and back runs asymmetrically across the centre of the body, the reference plane for left and right runs symmetrically down the centre of the body whilst the up/down plane runs along the base of the feet. Deictic conceptualization is based on the unmarked case of speakers standing upright and facing forward.

Location in space thus depends on the orientation of participants in speech events. What is left to the speakers is right to the interlocutors facing them and vice versa.

The notions of back and front again are governed by the speaker's perspective. There are differences, however, between languages (such as Western Europe Languages) where objects viewed are assumed to face the speaker (hence 'in front of the house' means closer to the speaker than 'behind the house') and other languages (such as TOK PISIN and other languages of Papua New Guinea) where objects are felt to be in alignment with the speaker: 'In front of the house' thus means further away from the speaker than the back of the house.

According to Clifford Hill (1982) Indo-European languages favour the facing perspective in the static mode and the dynamic perspective for the dynamic (movement) mode. Note, however, that this claim has not been subjected to a large scale empirical investigation and note the ambiguity of constructions simultaneously involving a static and a dynamic object as in 'please stop the taxi in front of/behind this parked car'.

Location and orientation in space can be studied *from two perspectives* as pointed out by Charles Fillmore (1982: 35), "first, in terms of the manner in which the socio-spatio-temporal anchoring of a communication act motivates the form [...] and second, in terms of the grammatical and lexical systems in the languages which serve to signal or reflect such anchoring."

The discussion thus far has focussed on the first perspective. As regards the linguistic means employed in signalling location, the following are found:

(a) local and directional prepositions and postpositions (e.g. 'in', 'at' or '-ward' in expressions such as 'heavenward')
(b) adverbs of place ('here', 'there')
(c) demonstratives ('this', 'that')
(d) deictic verbs ('to stand', 'to come', 'to bring')
(e) presentatives (e.g. FRENCH 'voilà')
(f) case markers (e.g. LATIN ablative *dŏmō* 'from home') and others.

Languages differ in their choice of favoured devices or combinations of devices. While there appears to be a trade relationship of the type that languages with few prepositions tend to have other devices, there are considerable differences in the total number of linguistic devices employed in different languages, with Pidgins and Creoles (→ articles 116; 117) at the lower end of the spectrum and a number of ESKIMO languages at the other end (see Senft 1997: 8).

As it is the case with other deictic phenomena (e.g. pronouns), it is not possible to analyse spatial deixis as a determinate closed system. Senft (1997: 10ff.) argues that attempts to identify basic meanings of spatial expressions ignore the importance of contextual and other knowledge and the creative dynamic potential of human languages. The meaning of the same preposition, for instance, can vary vastly.

Consider the following:

'the key is in the door'
'I am a Professor in the University of Oxford'
'the beer is in the mug'
'the patient is in bed'
'the moon is in the sky'
'the foot is in the door'
'the foot is in the slipper'
'the fault in the wiring'

and so on.

A number of universals of spatial terms have been proposed on the assumption that the egocentric system is universal (for a summary see Foley 1997 and Senft 1997). Their validity is undermined by the recent discovery that the egocentric anthropocentric system is not universal and that a number of languages in Australia, Oceania and Latin America operate with radically different absolute systems.

John Haviland (1979: 72 ff.) showed that GUUGU YIMIDHIRR (Northern Queensland) has a four term spatial system whose meanings "correspond roughly to English compass points", or more precisely quadrants from a horizontal plane "rotated slightly clockwise from the corresponding European compass points so that the median of the north quadrant is actually orientated slightly northeast". (Foley 1997: 217). They are:

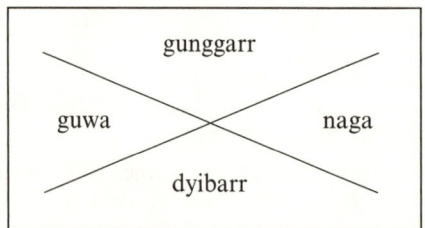

Figure 43.1: Absolute orientation system of GUUGU YIMIDHIRR

These categories are absolutely fixed and not subject to the speaker's orientation. Thus instead of 'give me the cup on your left' one has to say 'give me the northern cup' or in giving directions instead of 'first go right then left' one has to say 'first go west then north'. In order to operate in this language one has to know both one's present position and where north, south, west and east are. As tests by members of the Max Planck Institute demonstrate (Meermann 1994) GUUGU YIMIDHIRR speakers can do this even under difficult conditions, e.g. when in locations distant from home or when travelling by bus at night.

Absolute systems consisting of an axis contrasting seaward with landward and another axis derived from the parts of the sun or prevailing winds are found in a number of Pacific Island languages, e.g. LONGGU (Hill 1997) of the Solomon Islands. Whilst GUUGU YIMIDHIRR speakers do not have an egocentric system at all, LONGGU speakers supplement their absolute system with an egocentric one.

Tenejapa Tzeltal (a Mayan language) described by Penelope Brown and Stephen Levinson 1993 uses a mix of an absolute and intrinsic system. The dominant orientation is the uphill/south, downhill/north one, mirroring the mountainous terrain in which TZELTAL speakers live. There land falls from high-lying south to low-lying north. A secondary transverse axis with the poles unnamed is also used. It is an absolute system for all spatial locations.

Detailed analyses (summarized by Senft 1997: 17 ff.) have established that the TZELTAL uphill/downhill distinction applies both to the horizontal and to the vertical dimensions as well as to proximity. TZELTAL in addition to the absolute system also uses intrinsic description for spatial reference. Neighbouring Mayan languages such as TZOLTZIL (De León 1994) add a deictic system for motion events.

Willem J.M. Levelt (1996: 80; 101) makes reference to MOPAN (spoken in Belize), which exclusively employs an intrinsic system, but provides no further information on this language.

4. Some formal properties of deictic, absolute and intrinsic systems

The choice of spatial perspective has a number of formal consequences, discussed in some detail by Levelt (1996) in particular with regard to converseness and transitivity.

4.1. Converseness

Perspective systems that involve either deictic or absolute axes with polar opposites (left/right or uphill/downhill): If object A is to the left of B, then B is to the right of A. This is not the case with intrinsic systems: If locomotive A is in front of locomotive B it does not follow that B is behind A: They could be travelling in opposite directions and be headed for a collision.

4.2. Transitivity

Transitivity means that if A is to the right of B and B is to the right of C then A is to the right of C. Transitivity again holds for deictic and absolute systems. However, with intrinsic systems, consider:

L $\boxed{X}$ R   R $\boxed{Y}$ L   R $\boxed{Z}$ L

Figure 43.2: Relative orientation

when R and L stand for 'intrinsic right' and 'left' respectively: Z is to the right of X. X also is to the right of Y but Z is to the left of Y.

5. Cognitive consequences

Whilst it is acknowledged that spatial cognition and spatial language are not directly related, there is a growing body of experimental evidence suggesting that habitual spatial perceptions and non verbal actions are influenced by a speaker's linguistic resources.

This can be illustrated with gesturing. William A. Foley (1997: 221) summarizes Haviland's analysis of GUUGU YIMIDHIRR story telling: The same story told by a narrator at different times and facing different directions was accompanied by gestures preserving absolute orientation. Levinson (1996: 113ff.) discusses a range of experiments aimed at determining to what extent subject's responses to memory tasks will reveal their frame of reference.

The basic design is that a subject S sees situation A, an arrow pointing to the right or objectively to the north on a table. After a delay the subject is rotated 180° to face another table, situation B, on which two arrows are located, one pointing to their right, one pointing to their left.

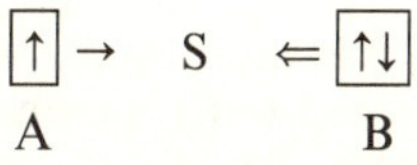

$$\boxed{\uparrow} \rightarrow \quad S \quad \Leftarrow \boxed{\uparrow\downarrow}$$
$$\quad A \qquad\qquad\qquad B$$

Figure 43.3: Experimental design revealing a subject's frame of spatial reference

They are then asked to identify the arrow pointing in the same direction as on the first table. If they select the arrow on the left this suggests an absolute system whilst the selection of the right arrow suggests a relative system determined by their body coordinates. In a number of experiments based on this design DUTCH subjects overwhelmingly behave like relative coders whilst TZELTAL subjects were overwhelmingly absolute coders. What counts for same and what counts for different thus appears to be a function of the subject's linguistic background. These experiments like those carried out with other languages would seem to lend strong support to the linguistic relativity hypothesis: linguistic categories impact on habitual thought.

6. Universals and Typology

Most earlier attempts to formalize universals of spatial expressions (e.g. Talmy 1983) were based on the assumption that the egocentric system of Indo-European languages could claim universal status. This is no longer tenable and a total revision of earlier hypotheses is indicated. This means that researchers have been compelled to carry out a great deal of pretheoretical data based research on non-Indo-European languages. Research on the acquisition of spatial expressions (summarized by Foley 1997: 227ff.) confirms that children do not naturally acquire a particular orientational system but that the categories of their care-givers' language shapes both their expressive devices and the way in which they conceptualize space. Melissa Bowerman (1991: 19) comparing ENGLISH and KOREAN children's acquisition of spatial expressions found that "there was little evidence that they had strong prelinguistic biases for organizing space in a particular way."

Opinions vary as to whether it will be possible to establish universals at all. Roger M. Keesing (1997) seems to suggest that there might be a universal egocentric system. He opines that the majority of 'exotic' languages have orientational systems very much like those of Western European languages either exclusively or in combination with some other system. Like others working on Melanesian languages he distinguishes exoteric from esoteric languages: The former are freely available as languages of wider communication whilst the latter are jealously guarded as insider languages. Their esotericity in some instances manifests itself as deliberately created complexity which renders them difficult to learn and use for outsiders. Implicit in Keesing's argument is that the complexities of some non-egocentric systems of spatial reference may be deliberately introduced complications. Under this interpretation the natural system would be egocentric with the absolute and intrinsic one being abnatural.

Senft's (1997: 23) interpretation is different: He argues that the study of decontextualized spatial terms may be unrevealing and that "the problem should be tackled from the 'meaning and context' side, in an effort to reach the basic meaning and thus reversing the order of research strategies". Foley (1997: 229) similarly concludes that "how we talk about space is not solely, nor perhaps even primarily, the result of our innate biological endowment, but also our history of engaging with our spatial environment and sedimented in our linguistic practices."

Typological work could begin by setting up (at this point of necessity pretheoretical) categories of spatial environment and linguistic practice. Parameters to be considered would include:

(i) To what extent are languages bound to topological space. Some Australian Aboriginal languages can be used only in certain locations, whilst others can be readily transported.
(ii) In some languages (such as SAMU discussed by Shaw & Shaw 1974) it is difficult to make an utterance without indicating locational reference. But in others use of such reference is much less evident.
(iii) The degree to which language use can be disconnected from cultural knowledge, i. e. the degree of their exotericity or esotericity.
(iv) The physical nature of the speaker's environment: Orientation in the desert requires strategies different from orientation at sea or in a forest. Clemens L. Voorhoeve (1997), for instance, relates NIMBORAN speakers' spatial system to their living at the bottom of a valley.
(v) The impact of transport and communication technology: Heeschen (1982: 82) for instance suggests that space is of much more importance in illiterate than in literate communication.

Whilst the requirement for speakers efficiently to orient themselves in their environment must be met somehow, purely functional explanations of spatial terms are rendered problematic by the fact that languages whose speakers live in very similar environments can have quite dissimilar systems and, moreover, that spatial terms can change at a rate that does not match environmental changes.

Typologies of the formal properties of spatial terms would seem to require considerably more and more secure information than is available at present. A complicating factor is that non-verbal signs (pointing and so on) typically accompany and supplement verbal ones. Moreover, as Herskovits (1986: 11 ff.) points out, it cannot be assumed that the production and interpretation of spatial terms are mirror images of each other. Keeping such difficulties in mind, some elements of a formal typology can be identified:

(i) Levinson (1996: 143) suggested the developmental priority of intrinsic systems over relative ones. It follows that the use of a relative system implies the presence of an intrinsic system but not vice versa. Absolute systems do not appear to require an intrinsic system (Levinson 1996: 148).
(ii) Languages can differ in their use of grammatical or lexical devices for spatial expressions. There is a strong tendency for spatial expressions to be lexicalized in most languages.
(iii) As regards the lexical categories used for spatial reference, a distinction can be made between languages employing prepositions and postpositions and others using verbs or adjectives.

Compare:
TZELTAL:

waxal ta ch'uj te' te k'ib
upright LOC plank wood the water jar
'The water jar is standing *on* the plank'.

Or TOK PISIN:

pisin plai raunim diwal
bird fly surround tree
'The bird flew *around* the tree'.

TZELTAL has more than 250 positional adjectives but only one unspecific locative particle. TOK PISIN again has only two locative prepositions.

(iv) An important distinction, particularly when reference to motion events is made, is that between languages that allocate information between the main verb and supporting 'satellites' (e.g. ENGLISH 'walk into', 'go to', 'run up to') and other languages that are verb-framed, i. e. where the core information is expressed by the verb alone (e.g. equivalents of 'to enter' 'to ascend' and so on). English, having Germanic and Romance roots, employs both types, whereas DUTCH, for instance, clearly favours verb + satellite ("de man *rende* het huis *uit*" — 'the man ran out of the house'). French favours verb framed instructions ("l'homme *sortit de* la maison [en courant]" — 'the man left the house [running]' — cf. Talmy 1985).

(v) Languages differ in the number of spatial axes they distinguish. The three way distinction ('up', 'down', 'across') seems favoured (see Levinson 1996: 111).

There are many other potential typological parameters but the literature available makes it difficult to identify those that lend themselves to cross-linguistic comparisons. An interesting supplement to such studies is the search for developmental aspects of spatial expressions of the type carried out by Bernd Heine & al. (1991) or Soteria Svorou (1994), which examines the grammaticalization path (from body part to abstract spatial notion) in a number of languages.

7. Conclusions

As observed by Levinson (1996: 134), "the analysis of spatial terms in familiar European languages remains deeply confused, and those in other languages almost entirely unexplored". Whilst systems other than the putative canonical egocentric system have been numerous, dramatic changes in the linguistic ecology of places such as Australia or Melanesia have led to the erosion of Non-Western modes of thinking. Literacy, a western school system and the intrusion of world languages may yet make the egocentric system universal though its universality will be contingent on history and not reflect nature.

Linguists in the past have treated spatial terms as a system which can be studied independent of context and use. This approach has come under attack from both anthropologically oriented linguists such as Senft (1997) and cognitive scientists such as Herskovits (1986). The latter points out that logical semantics cannot satisfactorily account for speakers uses of spatial expressions. Both approaches conclude that different types of knowledge (world knowledge, pragmatic knowledge, contextual knowledge) interact with biological factors in ways that make any appeal to rules of grammar unworkable.

Whilst the researchers at the Max Planck Institute and others have carried out a great deal of descriptive work, it would be rash to conclude that linguists now have at their disposal sufficient observationally adequate data to proceed to explanations. Their job is not made easier by the fact that spatial orientation interacts in poorly understood ways with temporal and social orientation. Non-egocentric systems of the type discussed here have provided strong counter evidence against earlier typological work and universalist interpretations. This has necessitated the reformulation of research questions and renewed observation of the use of spatial expressions. The next task, that of isolating the parameters needed for classification and typological work is far from completed and such terminology as is employed by current researchers remains deficient as a basis for comparative and typological studies. The development of standard procedures for testing spatial cognition (Senft 1994) as yet is not matched by agreed structural typological parameters and an agreed meta-language.

For some time theoretical linguists have hoped that there might be privileged one to one mappings between parts of language and biologically based mental representation systems. Such evidence as is at hand now suggests that the relationship between spatial knowledge and talk about spatial knowledge is far from straightforward.

Most research to date has focussed on adult systems. Insofar as these systems are the end point of language development, closer attention to the development of spatial languages in children (Bowerman 1996), adult L_2 learners (e.g. Perdue & Schenning 1996) or during pidginization and creolization is likely to provide explanatory parameters in this domain.

8. References

Bierwisch, Manfred. 1996. "How much space gets into language". In: Bloom & al. (eds.), 31–76.

Bloom, Paul & Peterson, Mary A. & Nadel, Lynn & Garrett, Merril F. (eds.) 1996. *Language and Space*. Cambridge, Mass: MIT Press.

Bowerman, Melissa. 1991. "The origins of children's spatial semantic categories: Cognitive vs. linguistic determinants". Paper presented at the "Rethinking Linguistic Relativity" Symposium, MS Nijmegen.

Brown, Penelope & Levinson, Stephen C. 1993. "'Uphill' and 'downhill' in Tzeltal". *Journal of Linguistic Anthropology* 1: 46–74.

De León, Lourdes. 1994. "Explorations in the acquisition of geocentric location by Tzoltzil children". *Linguistics* 32: 857–84.

Dixon, Robert W. M. & Blake, Barry J. (eds.) 1979. *Handbook of Australian Languages*. Amsterdam & Philadelphia: Benjamins.

Fillmore, Charles J. 1982. "Towards a descriptive framework for spatial deixis". In: Jarvella & Klein (eds.), 31–59.

Foley, William A. 1997. *Anthropological Linguistics: An Introduction*. (Language in society, 24.) Oxford: Blackwell.

Haviland, John. 1979. "Guugu Yimidhirr". In: Dixon & Blake (eds.), 27–180.

Heeschen, Volker. 1982. "Some Systems of Spatial Deixis in Papuan Languages". In: Weissenborn & Klein (eds.), 81–109.

Heine, Bernd & Claudi, Ulrike & Hünnemeyer, Friederike. 1991. *Grammaticalization. A conceptual framework*. Chicago & London: The University of Chicago Press.

Herskovits, Annette. 1986. *Languages and Spatial Cognition. An interdisciplinary study of the prepositions in English*. (Studies in natural language processing.) Cambridge: Cambridge Univ. Press.

Hill, Clifford. 1982. "Up/down, front/back, left/right: A contrastive study of Hausa and English". In: Weissenborn & Klein (eds.), 13–43.

Hill, Deborah. 1997. "Finding your way in Longgu: Geographical Reference in a Solomon Language". In: Senft (ed.), 101–26.

Jarvella, Robert J. & Klein, Wolfgang (eds.) 1982. *Speech, Place, and Action. Studies in deixis and related topics*. Chichester: Wiley.

Keesing, Roger M. 1997. "Constructing Space in Kwaio (Solomon Islands)". In: Senft, Gunter (ed.), 127–43.

Levelt, Willem J.M. 1996. "Perspective taking and Ellipsis in Spatial Descriptions". In: Bloom & al. (eds.), 77–108.

Levinson, Stephen C. 1996. "Frames of Reference and Molyneux's Question". In: Bloom & al. (eds.), 109–69.

Lyons, John. 1977. *Semantics*. Cambridge: CUP.

Malotki, Ekkehart. 1979. *Hopi-Raum. Eine sprachwissenschaftliche Analyse der Raumvorstellungen in der Hopi-Sprache*. (Tübinger Beiträge zur Linguistik, 81.) Tübingen: Narr.

Meermann, Horst. 1994. "Gib mir bitte die nördliche Tasse". *MPG Spiegel* 16.4: 4–6.

Perdue, Clive & Schenning, Saskia. 1996. "The expression of spatial relations in a second language: two longitudinal studies". *Zeitschrift für Literaturwissenschaft und Linguistik (LiLi)* 104: 6–34.

Pick, Herbert L. & Acredolo, Linda P. (eds.) 1983. *Spatial Orientation: Theory, Research and Application*. New York: Plenum.

Senft, Gunter. 1994. "Sprache, Kognition and Konzepte des Raumes in verschiedenen Kulturen". *Linguistische Berichte* 154: 413–29.

Senft, Gunter (ed.). 1997. *Referring to Space: studies in Austronesian and Papuan languages*. (Oxford studies in anthropological linguistics, 11.) Oxford: Clarendon Press.

Senft, Gunter. 1997. "Introduction". In: Senft (ed.), 1–38.

Shaw, Daniel R. & Karen A. 1974. "Location – A linguistic and cultural focus in Samo". *Kivung*, 158–72.

Svorou, Soteria. 1994. *The Grammar of Space*. (Typological studies in language, 25.) Amsterdam & Philadelphia: Benjamins.

Talmy, Leonard. 1983. "How language structures space". In: Pick & Acredolo (eds.), 225–320.

Talmy, Leonard. 1985. "Lexicalization patterns: Semantic structure in lexical forms". In: Shopen, Timothy (ed.). *Language typology and syntactic description*. vol. 3 *Grammatical categories and the lexicon*. Cambridge: Cambridge University Press, 36–149.

Voorhoeve, Clemens L. 1997. "Conceptualizations of Space in Nimboram: Some supplementary remarks". In: Senft (ed.), 281–87.

Weissenborn, Jürgen & Klein, Wolfgang (eds.) 1982. *Here and there: Cross-linguistic studies on Deixis and Demonstration*. (Pragmatics and beyond, III, 2/3.) Amsterdam & Philadelphia: Benjamins.

Whorf, Benjamin Lee. 1954. *Language, Thought and Reality*. Cambridge/MA: MIT Press.

Peter Mühlhäusler, University of Adelaide (Australia)

44. Deiktische Orientierung

1. Einleitung
2. Arten deiktischer Ausdrücke
3. Zum Forschungshintergrund
4. Kanonische Verwendung und Verschiebung
5. Objektdeixis
6. Ortsdeixis
7. Zeitdeixis
8. Schlußbemerkung
9. Zitierte Literatur

1. Einleitung

Die sprachliche Verständigung beruht auf dem steten Zusammenwirken von Ausdrucksinformation und Kontextinformation. Mit Ausdrucksinformation ist all das gemeint, was sich aus der konventionalisierten Bedeutung elementarer Ausdrücke („Morpheme") einerseits, aus den gleichfalls konventionalisierten Regeln ihrer Zusammenfügung (Flexion, Wortbildung und Syntax) anderseits ergibt. Die Kontextinformation speist sich aus allen anderen Wissensquellen, über die Sprecher und Hörer in der jeweiligen Redesituation verfügen.

Dies ist zum einen das, was im unmittelbaren *sprachlichen* Kontext zum Ausdruck gebracht wird; es ist zweitens das, was man über seine Sinnesorgane der jeweiligen Situation entnehmen kann; und es ist schließlich das *Weltwissen* der Beteiligten, also ihre mehr oder minder gesicherten Annahmen darüber, wie die Welt beschaffen ist und wie die Menschen handeln oder handeln sollten. Das *Kontextwissen* schwankt von Person zu Person, und es verändert sich fortwährend, nicht zuletzt eben durch die fortlaufende Rede selbst.

In allen natürlichen Sprachen finden sich nun zahlreiche Ausdrücke, die in besonderer Weise auf den Einbezug kontextueller Information hin ausgelegt sind; ihre konventionalisierte Bedeutung sieht gleichsam eine Leerstelle vor, die in bestimmter Weise aus dem Kontext zu ergänzen ist. In dem Satz *Hier sitze ich* bezieht sich der Ausdruck *ich,* so wie er nun einmal im Deutschen konventionalisiert ist, auf den, der gerade spricht; wer der jeweilige Sprecher ist, muß dem Situationswissen entnommen werden; ebenso bezieht sich das Wort *hier* nach seiner reinen Ausdrucksbedeutung auf einen Ort um den jeweiligen Sprecher herum, wobei die genauen Grenzen dieses Ortes recht unbestimmt sind. Die Präsensmarkierung des Verbs *sitzen* drückt aus, daß das Geschehen, dessen Wahrheit behauptet wird, sich auf die Sprechzeit bezieht, oder genauer gesagt auf eine Zeitspanne, welche die Sprechzeit einschließt; was genau diese Zeit ist, geht aus dem Ausdruck selbst nicht hervor; es muß gleichfalls anderen Wissensquellen entnommen werden.

Ausdrücke mit einer strukturell vorgegebenen Leerstelle, die aus dem Situationswissen zu füllen ist, nennt man *deiktisch.* Im ersten Fall bezieht sich die strukturell vorgesehene Leerstelle auf eine Person, im zweiten auf einen Ort, und im dritten auf eine Zeitspanne. Dementsprechend spricht man gewöhnlich von *personaler, lokaler* und *temporaler* Deixis. Ob es auch andere Formen der Deixis gibt, ist umstritten; manche Autoren (etwa Levinson 1983) nehmen an, daß auch die soziale Beziehung zwischen Sprecher und Angesprochenem, wie es sich etwa in den Anredeformen niederschlägt, als deiktisch zu analysieren ist; ein anderer Fall sind Wörter wie *so,* wenn sie nur in Verbindung mit einer Geste zu deuten sind, etwa in *Der Hase war so [Geste] groß.* Eine reichere Typologie schlagen z. B. Rauh 1983 und Herbermann 1988 vor.

Deiktische Ausdrücke sind nicht die einzigen, die strukturell kontextabhängig sind; in dem Satz *Zuvor saß er dahinter* müssen Person, Zeit und Ort dem sprachlichen statt dem situativen Kontext entnommen werden; in diesem Fall spricht man von *Anaphorik.* Deixis und Anaphorik sind nicht immer leicht zu trennen; dies hat viele Autoren dazu veranlaßt, das Wort „Deixis" für alle möglichen Formen der Kontextabhängigkeit zu verwenden (siehe unten § 3).

Ein klares Bild von Form und Funktion deiktischer Ausdrücke zu vermitteln, ist nicht leicht (die beste zusammenfassende Darstellung, allerdings aus einer bestimmten theoretischen Perspektive, bietet Sennholz 1985). Dies hat sechs teils miteinander zusammenhängende Gründe.

(i) Es gibt sehr unterschiedliche deiktische Ausdrücke – Adverbien, Verben, Pronomina –, deren Ausdrucksbedeutung sich in ganz unterschiedlicher Weise aus deiktischen und nicht-deiktischen Komponenten zusammensetzt (siehe unten § 2).

(ii) In den rund hundert Jahren, in denen die Deixis ernsthaft untersucht wird, haben sich drei Forschungsstränge ausgebildet, die bei mancherlei Überschneidungen eine ganz unterschiedliche Perspektive auf das Phänomen einnehmen und so zu einem sehr heterogenen Bild geführt haben (siehe unten § 3).

(iii) Das Phänomen selbst ist nicht einheitlich; schon erwähnt wurde die Verflechtung mit anderen Formen der Kontextabhängigkeit; ebenso wichtig ist, daß es in allen Sprachen möglich ist, vom tatsächlichen Hier-und-Jetzt der Redesituation zu „verschobenen" Redesituationen überzugehen, die dann als Ankerpunkt für die deiktischen Ausdrücke wirken (siehe unten § 4).

(iv) Bei den drei Grundformen, nämlich personaler, lokaler und temporaler Deixis, sind die zugrundeliegenden Referenzbereiche unterschiedlich strukturiert. Während Raum und Zeit durch Beziehungen wie „vor-hinter", „über-unter", „rechts-links" bzw. „vorher-nachher" geordnet sind, gilt dies nicht in vergleichbarer Weise für Personen; dies spiegelt sich in der Ausbildung der einzelnen deiktischen Teilsysteme wieder (siehe unten §§ 5–7).

(v) Es gibt zwar viele Arbeiten zur Deixis, darunter auch solche zu entlegenen Sprachen (vgl. etwa Weissenborn & Klein 1982, Morel & Danon-Boileau 1992); aber nur selten wird an umfangreichem Material untersucht, wie deiktische Ausdrücke tatsächlich in konkreten Redesituationen verwendet werden (eine der seltenen Ausnahmen ist Hanks 1990 zum YUKATEKISCHEN).

(vi) Schließlich ist die Terminologie sehr uneinheitlich. Das Wort „deiktisch" findet sich schon bei Apollonios Dyskolos; dort bezeichnet es Artikel/Demonstrativa und Pronomina in demonstrativer Verwendung (z. B. perì syntáxeōs p.57; p.99 Bkk. etc.; vgl. zur Frühgeschichte des Begriffs Lenz 1997: 7–33). Wörter wie *ich, jetzt, hier* werden von vielen Autoren als „indexikalisch" bezeichnet; Bertrand Russell redet von „egocentric particulars", Reichenbach von „token-reflexive words"; wieder andere Autoren verwenden, wie bemerkt, deiktisch als Oberbegriff für verschiedene Formen der Kontextabhängigkeit (vgl. die Diskussion in Richter 1988).

2. Arten deiktischer Ausdrücke

Deixis findet sich in der Lexik wie in der Grammatik, dabei kommt der Lexik allerdings viel größeres Gewicht zu. So bildet die Ortsdeixis in allen Sprachen oft sehr komplexe lexikalische Subsysteme aus; sie ist aber nur selten grammatikalisiert; hingegen ist die Referenz auf Sprecher und Angesprochenen in sehr vielen Sprachen morphologisch am Verb markiert. Ebenso ist das Tempus in vielen Sprachen deiktisch-relational, d. h. es verweist auf eine Zeitspanne relativ zur kontextuell gegebenen Sprechzeit. Solchen Kategorien gehört traditionell die Liebe der Grammatiker, und sie sind daher auch ausführlich studiert. Viel reichere deiktische Ausdrucksmöglichkeiten finden sich hingegen im lexikalischen Repertoire aller Sprachen. Dies sind:

(a) Adverbien: sie sind auf Orts- und Zeitdeixis beschränkt, dort allerdings in allen Sprachen reich ausgebaut; deutsche Beispiele sind etwa *hier, da, dort, links (von)* für die Ortsdeixis; *jetzt, morgen, vorhin* (im Gegensatz zu anaphorischem *vorher*) für die Zeitdeixis; nicht selten kann ein deiktischer Ausdruck sowohl örtlich wie zeitlich verwendet werden, z. B. *da*.

(b) Pronomina: alle Sprachen haben Pronomina für Sprecher und Angesprochenen; die Pronomina der dritten Person sind vorrangig anaphorisch, können aber oft auch – dann in der Regel mit Zeigegeste – in der Situation gebraucht werden.

(c) Verben: der bekannteste Fall sind hier Bewegungsverben wie *kommen-gehen, bringen-holen;* so drückt *kommen* nach verbreiteter Ansicht eine Bewegung zum deiktischen Zentrum hin aus, *gehen* eine Bewegung vom deiktischen Zentrum weg; allerdings sind die Bedingungen im einzelnen sehr verwickelt (vgl. neuerdings Wilkins & Hill 1995).

(d) Partikel: im DEUTSCHEN werden *hin* und *her* oft als deiktische Partikel angesehen; allerdings gilt dies nur für einige ihrer Verwendungen; andere Sprachen hingegen besitzen oft ein reiches Repertoire vor allem lokaler deiktischer Partikel; dabei ist, wie stets bei Partikeln, die Grenze zu Affixen sehr fließend (→ Art. 58).

(e) Definite Artikel und Demonstrativa: Demonstrativa sind nach der hier vertretenen Auffassung entweder unmittelbar oder doch verschoben deiktisch; ob man auch den definiten Artikel, der sich meist von einem Demonstrativum ableitet, gleichfalls als deiktisch ansehen soll, ist strittig.

Nomina, Adjektive und Quantoren werden gewöhnlich nicht als deiktisch angesehen. Es gibt allerdings klare Ausnahmen, wie z. B. *hiesig, dortig, gegenwärtig* im Deutschen. Und ebenso mag man sich fragen, ob ein Nomen wie *Vergangenheit* nicht gleichfalls deiktisch ist. In der Literatur werden allerdings fast nur das Tempus als grammatikalisierter Ausdruck der Temporaldeixis und Lexeme aus den Wortklassen (a)−(e) behandelt.

3. Zum Forschungshintergrund

Drei Entwicklungslinien bestimmen das heutige Bild der Deixis, eine philologisch-sprachwissenschaftliche, eine psychologische und eine philosophisch-logische. In diesem Abschnitt wird nicht versucht, diese Linien im einzelnen nachzuzeichnen, sondern ihren besonderen Beitrag zur Deixisforschung deutlich zu machen (Ausführlicheres findet sich in Lenz 1997: 7−76).

In der philologisch-sprachwissenschaftlichen Tradition liegt dieser Beitrag zum einen in der mehr oder minder akribischen Untersuchung einzelner Ausdrücke und Teilsysteme in verschiedenen Sprachen − freilich selten in konkreten Redesituationen; zum andern liegt er in dem Gedanken, daß Deiktika etwas mit „Zeigen" zu tun haben. Das Wort selbst kommt von idg. **deik-*, das griech. *deiknymi* 'zeigen' zugrundeliegt, aber auch lat. *dicere* und dt. *zeigen* und *Zeichen.* In den idg. Sprachen sind Deiktika formal eng mit Demonstrativa wie *dieser, jener* verwandt (Brugmann 1904); ähnliches gilt für viele andere Sprachen. Dies ist auch nicht verwunderlich: eine Zeigegeste kann nur aufgrund situativer Information gedeutet werden. So werden denn in der linguistischen Tradition deiktische Ausdrücke und Demonstrativa häufig gemeinsam behandelt, wenn nicht einfach gleichgesetzt (vgl. beispielsweise die Aufsätze in Weissenborn & Klein 1982, Morel & Danon-Boileau 1992 sowie die kritische Diskussion in Himmelmann 1997). Nun sind allerdings viele typische Deiktika wie *ich, jetzt, hier, links* oder gar das Tempus in keiner Weise auf Zeigegesten angewiesen. Um die Gleichsetzung von Deixis und Demonstration zu retten, muß man daher den Begriff 'zeigen' in einem kraß metaphorischen Sinn verwenden, in dem er eigentlich jeden Erklärungswert verliert (das Präteritum „zeigt" in die Vergangenheit).

Der wichtigste Beitrag der Sprachpsychologie liegt in der Vorstellung, daß Deiktika es in besonderer Weise erlauben, die Welt von einem bestimmten Bezugspunkt aus darzustellen. Sie reflektieren daher, nicht anders als beispielsweise bei der Wahrnehmung, eine gewisse subjektive Perspektive (vgl. hierzu Graumann 1992). Der Bezugspunkt ist im Regelfall durch das sprechende Ich gegeben, genau wie er in der Wahrnehmung durch das wahrnehmende Ich gegeben ist. Mit dem Ich sind gewöhnlich bestimmte Attribute verbunden; dies ist die *Rolle* des Ich (etwa als Sprecher), die *Zeit,* zu der es spricht (bzw. eine sonstige Handlung vollführt, beispielsweise sich etwas vorstellt), und schließlich seine *Orientierung im Raum;* zu dieser Orientierung im Raum zählt zunächst einmal die Position des Körpers, aber auch eine gewisse Struktur des Raumes, die sich aus dieser Position aufgrund der Asymmetrien des Körpers ergibt. Deiktische Ausdrücke sind relativ zu diesen Attributen zu deuten.

Nun ist dem menschlichen Geist gegeben, sich diese Attribute anders vorzustellen als sie in der tatsächlichen Redesituation sind: er kann sich eine andere Rolle vorstellen, eine andere Zeit, einen anderen Ort und, damit verbunden, eine andere Orientierung im Raum. Deiktische Ausdrücke spielen diese Verschiebungen in bestimmten Grenzen nach. Man muß daher, wenn man ihre Funktion verstehen will, den KANONISCHEN FALL ebenso wie die verschiedenen VERSCHIEBUNGEN betrachten.

Dieser Gedanke wurde am klarsten von Karl Bühler (1934) in seiner „Zweifelderlehre" ausgearbeitet (Eschbach 1988: 229−99). Bühler teilt die sprachlichen Zeichen in Zeigwörter und Nennwörter; beide verweisen in ein „Feld" − das Zeigfeld und das Symbolfeld. Das Zeigfeld besitzt, einem kartesischen Koordinatensystem vergleichbar, einen Nullpunkt; diese ORIGO ist im kanonischen Fall (der „deixis ad oculos et aures") durch das Ich-Hier-Jetzt bestimmt. Sie kann verschoben werden; so mag man sich im Geiste in eine andere Situation versetzen („Deixis am Phantasma"); weiterhin sieht Bühler eine Verschiebung vor, die Verweise in einem Text möglich macht; Bühler spricht hier von „Anaphorik" bzw. von „anamnestischem Verweis". Später ist der Ausdruck „Textdeixis" in Gebrauch gekommen, der freilich sehr uneinheitlich benutzt wird (Ehlich 1979; Harweg 1990: 177−212).

Bühler knüpft in seinen Überlegungen zwar an Sprachwissenschaftler wie Wegener und Brugmann an; der Terminus „Zeigwort" belegt es. Aber seine Denkweise ist letztlich eine ganz andere; im Mittelpunkt steht die Überlegung „Wie erfahre ich die Welt, wie stelle ich mir die Welt vor, wie beschreibe ich die Welt *von meiner Warte aus*, sei dies nun die augenblicklich gegebene oder eine irgendwie vorgestellte?".

Dieser Gedanke ist sicher mit der Idee des „Zeigens" nicht unvereinbar, bringt aber ein ganz anderes Moment ins Spiel: die Deixis ist ein Sonderfall der Perspektivierung. Er ist in der Folge von vielen Linguisten, mehr aber noch von Sprachpsychologen aufgegriffen worden. Folgenreich war insbesondere die von George A. Miller und Philip N. Johnson-Laird 1976 entwickelte Gegenüberstellung von „deiktischer" und „intrinsischer" Orientierung; erstere ist durch das Ich-Hier-Jetzt gegeben, letztere durch inhärente Eigenschaften eines anderen Bezugsobjektes. So hat ein Auto eine linke und eine rechte Seite, ein Oben und ein Unten, ein Hinten und ein Vorne. Daher kann jemand, der einen Verkehrsunfall beschreibt, die Geschehnisse relativ zu seiner eigenen Position („deiktisch") oder relativ zur Position und den Attributen eines als Bezugsobjekt gewählten Autos („intrinsisch") beschreiben (siehe unten § 6.3); er muß nur klarmachen, welches Bezugssystem gewählt ist (Miller & Johnson-Laird 1976: 396 ff., Levelt 1989: 44−58, Herrmann & Grabowski 1994: 107−52).

Die philosophisch-logische Linie, vertreten durch Zeichentheoretiker wie Charles Sanders Peirce oder Charles Morris und durch Logiker wie Bertrand Russell, Yehoshua Bar-Hillel, Richard Montague, David Lewis oder David B. Kaplan, hat zwei wesentliche Beiträge zum Verständnis der Deixis geliefert.

Der erste bezieht sich auf ihren besonderen Status als Zeichen. So unterscheidet Peirce, der Begründer der modernen Semiotik, zwischen ikonischen, indexikalischen und symbolischen Zeichen, wobei die indexikalischen im wesentlichen deiktischen und anaphorischen Elementen entsprechen (vgl. Nöth 1985: 1−58). Die meisten semiotischen Arbeiten zur Deixis befassen sich mit Grundsatzfragen der Zeichenhaftigkeit; allerdings gibt es eine Fülle neuerer semiotisch orientierter Untersuchungen zur Rolle der Deixis in literarischen Texten (vgl. etwa Green 1995).

Der zweite Beitrag dieses Traditionsstranges bezieht sich auf das Grundproblem der formalen Semantik, nämlich die Frage, unter welchen Umständen ein Satz bestimmter Form wahr ist. Für einen Satz mit einer deiktischen Komponente läßt sich diese Frage unmittelbar gar nicht beantworten; es ist klar, daß bei einer bestimmten Beschaffenheit der Welt der Satz *Ich sitze jetzt hier* wahr, aber auch falsch sein kann, je nachdem, wer redet, wo er redet und wann er redet. Solche Sätze lassen sich daher nicht so ohne weiteres in die klassischen formalen Sprachen, etwa die traditionelle Prädikatenlogik, übersetzen. Sie lassen sich aber sehr wohl mit den Mitteln der modernen formalen Semantik behandeln. Dazu sieht man eine Reihe von „kontextuellen Indices" vor, und die Deutung eines Satzes ist von der Belegung dieser Indices aus dem Kontext abhängig. So läßt sich im Prinzip jede Form der strukturellen Kontextabhängigkeit, darunter auch die deiktische, behandeln (eine sehr klare Darstellung gibt Zimmermann 1991).

4. Kanonische Verwendung und Verschiebung

Die eben skizzierten Entwicklungslinien haben, bei allen Gemeinsamkeiten, im Ergebnis zu einem uneinheitlichen Bild der Deixis geführt. Um eine gewisse Ordnung in dieses Bild zu bringen, ist es sinnvoll, von einem „kanonischen Fall" der Deixis auszugehen, von dem nach bestimmten Prinzipien abgewichen werden kann (dieser Gedanke findet sich, in Anknüpfung an Bühler, sehr schön in Sitta 1991 entfaltet).

Der kanonische Fall ist die Verwendung in der mündlichen Interaktion zu einer bestimmten Zeit an einem bestimmten Ort, bei der neben dem Sprecher zumindest ein Angesprochener beteiligt ist. Diesen Fall als den kanonischen anzusehen, liegt deshalb nahe, weil er in allen Kulturen und in allen natürlichen Sprachen Ausgangspunkt der Kommunikation ist.

Ein Ausdruck ist also im kanonischen Sinne deiktisch, wenn er strukturell auf den Einbezug von Information aus der Redesituation ausgelegt ist. Dafür gibt es zumindest zwei Möglichkeiten. Zum einen kann die referentielle Bedeutung des deiktischen Ausdrucks von einem Bezugspunkt abhängig sein, der in der Redesituation für Sprecher und Hörer identifizierbar ist. Dies ist etwa der Fall bei dem Wort *ich,* zu dessen Verständnis der jeweilige Sprecher zu identifizieren ist, oder bei der einen deiktischen Tempusform, zu deren Deutung die Sprechzeit identifiziert werden muß; ein „Zeigen" ist hierfür nicht nötig, oft nicht einmal möglich.

Zum andern kann er von einer zusätzlichen Geste abhängig sein. Das ist der Fall bei Wörtern wie *dieser, der da, so* in der situativen Verwendung. Beide Möglichkeiten schließen einander nicht aus; so kann es beispielsweise in einer Redesituation einen oder mehrere Angesprochene geben; im ersten Fall ist eine begleitende Geste überflüssig, wenn auf eine bestimmte Person referiert werden soll, im andern hingegen notwendig.

Von diesem kanonischen Fall sind vielfältige, aber nicht beliebige Abweichungen möglich. So kann an die Stelle der situativen Information auch eine andere Form des Kontextwissens treten, beispielsweise etwas, das Sprecher und Hörer noch im Gedächtnis steht, weil es eben passiert ist („Das da war mein früherer Lateinlehrer"), oder weil es gerade gesagt worden ist. Solche Verschiebungen sind in der Lexik und der Grammatik einzelner Sprachen in unterschiedlichster Weise ausgebaut. So ist die anaphorische Verwendung zumeist reich entfaltet; im Deutschen können beispielsweise alle mit Geste verwendbaren Deiktika auch anaphorisch gebraucht werden. Anders ist es bei nicht-gestischen Deiktika wie beispielsweise den Tempus- oder Zeitadverbien. Sie lassen zwar auch bestimmte Verschiebungen zu, allerdings nur sehr begrenzt den anaphorischen Gebrauch (siehe unten § 7.2).

Am Rande sei vermerkt, daß manche Autoren Ausdrücke wie *weiter unten, wie oben bemerkt, darauf kann hier nicht eingegangen werden* als „Textdeixis" von der anaphorischen Verwendung unterscheiden, vgl. etwa Harweg 1990: 177−207.

Der Ersatz der situativen Information durch die im sprachlichen Kontext eingeführte ist aber nicht der einzig mögliche. Wir wollen dies am Beispiel der drei zeitdeiktischen Adverbien *heute, gestern, morgen* illustrieren. Wie alle Lexeme sind sie Bündel aus kategorialen und semantischen Informationen. Kategoriale Informationen sind jene, die festlegen, in welche weitere morphologische und syntaktische Prozesse das Lexem eingehen kann; deiktische Lexeme können vielen Kategorien angehören (siehe oben § 2).

Wesentlich für sie ist nun, daß ihr semantischer Gehalt, anders als bei nicht-deiktischen Lexemen, eine Leerstelle einschließt, die in vorgegebener Weise aus dem Kontext gefüllt werden muß. Aber ihre Ausdrucksdeutung besteht natürlich nicht nur aus dieser Leerstelle, sondern sie umfaßt weitere lexikalische Informationen, die sie zu anderen, vergleichbaren deiktischen Ausdrücken in Kontrast setzen. Die drei Adverbien *heute, gestern, morgen* beziehen sich jeweils auf eine Zeitspanne, und zwar relativ zur Sprechzeit. Sie unterscheiden sich in der Art dieses Bezugs. Das Lexem *heute* referiert im Kontext auf den Tag, der die Sprechzeit einschließt; *gestern* referiert auf den Tag, der dem Tag, der die Sprechzeit einschließt, unmittelbar vorausgeht; *morgen* referiert auf den Tag, der dem Tag, der die Sprechzeit einschließt, unmittelbar folgt.

Dies beschreibt die „kanonische Bedeutung" dieser drei Ausdrücke. Sie umfaßt also zwei Komponenten, eine deiktische (im folgenden kurz „D-Teil" genannt) und eine lexikalische („L-Teil"). Der D-Teil ist bei *heute, gestern, morgen* gleichermaßen „bezogen auf die Sprechzeit"; im L-Teil enthalten die drei Wörter hingegen kontrastierende lexikalische Informationen.

Wie sich D-Teil und L-Teil ausgestalten, hängt wesentlich von der Struktur des jeweiligen Referenzbereichs ab (siehe unten §§ 5−7). Beide Teile erlauben Verschiebungen oder „Umdeutungen". So kann anstatt der realen Sprechzeit eine andere Zeitspanne als Ankerpunkt gewählt werden, z. B. eine Zeit, zu der jemand anderes in der Vergangenheit gesprochen hat, wie in *Er sagte: Kommst du morgen mit?*, oder eine Zeit, an die man sich lebhaft erinnert, wie in der sogenannten „erlebten Rede", die sich in vielen literarischen Texten findet. Bei dieser Verschiebung geht es immer noch um eine bestimmte Zeit − es ist nur eben nicht die wirkliche Sprechzeit. Es ist aber auch möglich, über viele denkbare Sprechzeiten zu verallgemeinern, wie in dem Sprichwort *Was du heute kannst besorgen, das verschiebe nicht auf morgen*. Eine typische Verschiebung der lexikalischen Komponente besteht darin, die Beschränkung auf die Dauer eines Tages aufzuheben, wie in *Heute gibt es kaum noch Stiefelspanner* oder *Die Lösung der Energiekrise ist keine Aufgabe von morgen, sondern von heute*.

Diese Möglichkeiten der Verschiebung gibt es, freilich in unterschiedlicher Form, bei allen deiktischen Ausdrücken (im übrigen auch bei den grammatikalisierten). Wenn man daher die Funktion deiktischer Ausdrücke verstehen will, sind zwei Aufgaben zu lösen: man muß beschreiben, was die deiktische Komponente und die lexikalische Komponente im kanonischen Fall sind, und man muß beschreiben, in welcher Weise sich diese Komponenten verschieben lassen. Dies soll im folgenden exemplarisch für die drei Formen der Deixis veranschaulicht werden.

Wie oben in Abschnitt 1 bemerkt, werden herkömmlich drei Hauptformen der Deixis unterschieden – Personendeixis, Zeitdeixis, Ortsdeixis. Sie entsprechen zum einen den drei Koordinaten der Bühlerschen Origo Ich-Jetzt-Hier, zum andern drei Arten von Referenten, auf die sich die deiktischen Ausdrücke beziehen können – Personen, Zeitspannen, Orte. Beides steht aber oft nicht im Einklang. Man kann sich ja auch deiktisch auf Objekte – z. B. auf *diese* Tasse da – beziehen. Es erscheint daher sinnvoller, nach den möglichen Referenten drei Arten deiktischer Ausdrücke zu unterscheiden.

Dies sind erstens solche, die sich auf Personen oder Objekte beziehen; zu den entsprechenden Deiktika zählen Pronomina wie *ich, du, mein, dein,* die normalerweise keine Zeigegeste verlangen, wie auch Demonstrativa wie *dieser, der da.* Für diese Form der Deixis sage ich hier OBJEKTDEIXIS.

Eine zweite Gruppe bezieht sich auf Orte; im kanonischen Fall sind dies Teilräume des gewöhnlichen dreidimensionalen Anschauungsraums; es kann aber auch beispielsweise der auf zwei Dimensionen reduzierte Raum einer Karte sein; Beispiele für diese ORTSDEIXIS sind *hier, dort, links, drüben.*

Die dritte Gruppe bezieht sich auf Zeitspannen; Beispiele für die ZEITDEIXIS sind zum einen Adverbien wie *jetzt, gestern, vorhin,* zum andern das deiktisch-relationale Tempus. Diese drei Gruppen werden nun etwas eingehender besprochen.

5. Objektdeixis

5.1. Kanonischer Fall

In der kanonischen Redesituation gibt es zumindest zwei Beteiligte, die durch ihre Rolle in der gerade ablaufenden Kommunikation identifiziert sind; das sind der jeweilige Sprecher und der jeweilige Hörer. Für beide sehen alle natürlichen Sprachen deiktische Lexeme vor. Dies sind die vertrauten Personaldeiktika, die als Pronomina oder als grammatikalisierte Markierungen am Verb auftreten können. Sie können durch einen zusätzlichen L-Teil angereichert sein; so bezieht sich *ich* auf den jeweiligen Sprecher, *wir* bezieht sich auf eine Gruppe, zu der der jeweilige Sprecher zählt, *mein* drückt die Relation „dem jeweiligen Sprecher zugehörig" aus, usw.

Nun gibt es in einer normalen Redesituation nur einen Sprecher, der daher durch seine Rolle eindeutig identifiziert ist. Hingegen kann es sehr wohl mehrere Hörer geben, zwischen denen das Wort *du* allein nicht diskriminiert; falls auf einen bestimmten Hörer Bezug genommen werden soll, müssen daher weitere Informationen hinzutreten, entweder sprachliche („du mit der Glatze") oder eben durch eine Zeigegeste.

In einer Redesituation mögen auch andere Personen anwesend sein; ob man diesen eine spezifische kommunikative Rolle „unbeteiligt" vorsieht oder nicht – sie sind jedenfalls nicht über diese Rolle allein identifizierbar; dazu bedarf es einer Zeigegeste.

Ebendies gilt auch für alle Objekte, die in der Situation gegeben sind. Die drei Objektdeiktika *ich – du – dieser* repräsentieren daher unterschiedliche Grade, zu denen ein in der Situation gegebener Referent durch eine bestimmte situative Information, seine Rolle in der Redesituation, identifizierbar ist. Statt von 'Personendeixis' wäre es daher geschickter, von 'Rollendeixis' zu reden. Die meisten Sprachen haben je nach sozialem Verhältnis zwischen Sprecher und Angesprochenem mehr als einen Ausdruck für die Rollendeiktika; dies gilt insbesondere für die Rolle des Angesprochenen, manchmal aber auch für die Rolle des Sprechers („ich Unwürdiger"). Im heutigen Deutsch ist diese SOZIALDEIXIS auf die Wahl zwischen *du* und *Sie,* vielleicht noch auf das etwas altmodische *Ihr* beschränkt; in andern Sprachen ist sie oft sehr elaboriert (Braun 1988).

Bei den nicht-rollenbezogenen Objektdeiktika kann es bis zu vier kontrastierende deiktische Wörter geben (vgl. Anderson und Keenan 1985). Da die Identifikation ja durch die Zeigegeste geleistet wird, würde im Grunde ein Term genügen; dies ist auch oft der Fall, etwa im russ. *etot.* Üblicher sind zwei oder drei, allerdings in unterschiedlicher Ausgestaltung. Im Deutschen etwa hat man *dieser* und (betontes) *der,* beide ergänzbar durch *da.* Zwischen diesen beiden einen lexikalischen Kontrast auszumitteln, ist sehr schwer, wenn nicht unmöglich. Wo ein solcher Kontrast vorliegt, bezieht er sich nach allgemeiner Ansicht entweder auf die Entfernung von dem, der die Zeigegeste vollführt, oder auf die Verknüpfung mit einer Rolle. Als typisches Beispiel für den ersten Fall gilt das englische *this-that-*System (wohlgemerkt in der situativen Verwendung); *that* wird gewählt, wenn das Objekt in der Situation vorhanden, aber weiter entfernt ist.

Als typischer Fall für ein dreigliedriges System werden gewöhnlich lat. *hic-iste-ille* angeführt; mit *hic* wird auf ein Objekt verwiesen, das der Sphäre des Sprechers zugehört, mit *iste* auf ein Objekt, das der Sphäre des Angesprochenen zugehört, mit *ille* endlich auf ein Objekt, das situativ gegeben ist, aber weder in die Sprecher- noch in die Hörersphäre fällt; dieses Objekt kann auch der Sprecher, der Angesprochene bzw. eine dritte Person sein. Ob dies wirklich so zutrifft, ist aber durchaus nicht klar; soweit man es der geschriebenen Sprache entnehmen kann, hat sich das Lateinische im Gebrauch dieser Terme im Laufe der Zeit stark entwickelt (Brugmann 1904); was aber ihre tatsächliche Verwendung in der konkreten Redesituation angeht, so haben wir dafür ohnehin nur das Zeugnis literarischer Dialoge, nicht eben die beste Quelle. Leider ist dies auch nicht sehr viel anders für heute gesprochene Sprachen; so gibt es viele Studien zum spanischen System, das mit *este-ese-aquel* gleichfalls drei Terme für die Objektdeixis aufweist (vgl. etwa Hottenroth 1982); aber sie konzentrieren sich durchweg auf die geschriebene Sprache. Begründete Aussagen über die tatsächliche situative Verwendung in Verbindung mit Zeigegesten sind daher fast unmöglich.

5.2. Verschiebungen

Das bisher Gesagte bezieht sich auf den kanonischen Fall. Welche Verschiebungen gibt es nun? Eine erste besteht darin, die reale Situation durch eine vorgestellte zu ersetzen, beispielsweise durch ein Verb des Sagens oder Denkens: *Semprini sagte: „Ich komme gleich"*. Zweitens können Sprech- und Hörsituation getrennt sein, wie bei göttlichen Geboten (*Du sollst nicht töten!*) oder bei Gebrauchsanweisungen (*Ziehen Sie das rote Kabel durch die linke Öffnung!*). Hier ist nicht ein in der Sprechsituation anwesender Hörer, sondern der jeweilige Adressat gemeint. Drittens ist es möglich, statt über die reale Situation über eine Menge möglicher Situationen zu quantifizieren; dies führt zum „generischen" Ich oder Du: *„Du brauchst nur diesen Knopf zu drücken, und schon fliegt alles in die Luft"*.

Bei einer zweiten Gruppe von Verschiebungen wird der situative Kontext durch einen sprachlich geschaffenen ersetzt; dies führt auf die anaphorische (und, weniger ausgeprägt, die kataphorische) Verwendung. Die Rollendeiktika können hier, soweit Sprecher und Hörer (bzw. Schreiber und Leser) in dieser Rolle identifizierbar sind, unverändert beibehalten werden. Schwieriger ist die anaphorische Verwendung nicht-rollenbezogener Deiktika. An die Stelle der in der Situation vorhandenen treten hier die im Text erwähnten Objekte (oder Personen). Auf diese kann nicht gezeigt werden, außer man verwendet das Wort 'zeigen' in einem völlig vagen Sinne.

Die Funktion der deiktischen Ausdrücke im Text hängt nun davon ab, wie viele mögliche Referenten es gibt und ob diese in eine gewisse Ordnung, eine „Salienzhierarchie" gebracht werden können. Eine solche Hierarchie ergibt sich im einfachsten Fall aus der Reihenfolge der Erwähnung; je kürzer sie zurückliegt, desto salienter ist der betreffende Referent; diese Rangfolge kann durch andere Faktoren, z. B. den grammatischen Status oder den Grad der Fokussierung, überlagert werden. Im Deutschen verweisen *dieser* und *der* auf den salientesten unter den möglichen Referenten, *jener* (soweit es denn noch verwendet wird) auf einen weniger salienten. Das häufigste Element *er, sie, es* läßt sich nur verwenden, wenn nur ein einziger damit bezeichenbarer Referent vorkommt oder als relevant betrachtet wird. Anders gesagt, *dieser* und *der* verweisen auf einen aus einer Menge von Referenten, die gleichfalls durch *dieser* oder *der* bezeichnet werden könnten; *er* drückt keinen solchen Kontrast aus.

Damit sind die wichtigsten Möglichkeiten der Verschiebung genannt; zumindest erwähnt sei noch, daß gelegentlich auch das Weltwissen an die Stelle der situativen oder der textuellen Information treten kann, etwa wenn man sagt *„Wie geht es ihm denn heute?"* und klar ist, daß ein bestimmter Kranker gemeint ist.

5.3. Generelles zur Objektdeixis

Bevor wir nun zur Ortsdeixis kommen, ist es hilfreich, sich noch einmal zusammenfassend einige Punkte der Objektdeixis vor Augen zu führen. Es geht stets darum, ein bestimmtes Objekt (oder auch eine Person) aus einer Menge von Objekten herauszusondern. Im kanonischen Fall sind diese im Anschauungsraum vorhanden und wahrnehmbar, sie können durch ihre jeweilige Rolle in der Situation als Sprecher oder Hörer identifizierbar sein („Rollendeixis"); oder aber sie bedürfen einer zusätzlichen Zeigegeste.

An die Stelle des realen Anschauungsraums kann auch ein anderer Raum treten, der die möglichen Referenten enthält — ein Gedächtnis- oder Vorstellungsraum, in den man natürlich in der Redesituation nicht mehr wirklich „zeigen" kann (in den Kopf kann man nicht zeigen). Ein solcher Raum bewahrt unter Umständen dieselbe Struktur wie der Anschauungsraum; es kann aber auch sein, daß er wesentlich schwächer strukturiert ist: die möglichen Referenten sind beispielsweise vielleicht nur durch die Reihenfolge geordnet, in der sie eingeführt worden sind oder anschließend eingeführt werden (siehe unten § 6.3). Ebendies wird beim anaphorischen Verweis ausgenutzt. Damit ist bereits angedeutet, wie Objekt- und Ortsdeixis zusammenhängen.

6. Ortsdeixis

6.1. Hauptparameter

Der entscheidende Unterschied zwischen Objektdeixis und Ortsdeixis liegt darin, daß mit ersterer auf mehr oder minder klar umrissene Objekte (oder Personen) verwiesen wird, mit letzterer auf Orte, d. h. auf Teilräume eines irgendwie strukturierten Raumes.

Dies hat zwei Konsequenzen. Erstens sind, anders bei Objekten oder Personen, die Grenzen eines Referenten im allgemeinen nicht klar; der Ausdruck *hier* beispielsweise kann sich auf alle möglichen Teilräume beziehen, die (vereinfacht gesagt) die Position des jeweiligen Sprechers enthalten: man denke an *hier auf meinem Hocker* gegenüber *hier in Europa*; anders als bei der Objektdeixis ist die Raumdeixis durch ein Abgrenzungsproblem gekennzeichnet.

Zweitens stehen die Teilräume in bestimmten strukturellen Beziehungen zueinander; der Referenzbereich ist, anders als bei Objekten, in sich vielfältig strukturiert. Die genaue Natur dieser Beziehungen hängt von der Art des Raumes ab. Im kanonischen Fall ist dies der gewöhnliche Anschauungsraum; die Ortsdeixis funktioniert aber auch in Räumen mit stärkerer oder schwächerer Struktur (siehe unten § 6.3). Die Folge ist, daß die Ortsdeixis oft sehr viel komplexere Teilsysteme ausbildet als die Objektdeixis, weil die einzelnen deiktischen Ausdrücke ganz unterschiedliche Eigenschaften des jeweiligen Raums in ihren L-Teil aufnehmen können. So gibt es seit der Pionierarbeit von Henri Frei (1944) eine Fülle detaillierter Studien zur Ortsdeixis in verschiedenen Sprachen und Kulturen. In ihrer sorgfältigen Untersuchung der Ortsdeixis in etwa 150 Sprachen nennt Catriona Hyslop (1993: 19) die folgenden acht „deiktischen Parameter", die in den lexikalischen Gehalt von Deiktika eingehen:

1. Entfernung
   (a) nah/fern in Bezug auf
   – den Sprecher
   – den Hörer
   – Sprecher und Hörer
   – andere an der Sprechhandlung Beteiligte
   (b) gleich weit von Sprecher und Hörer
   (c) dem Sprecher am nächsten/fernsten
2. Sichtbarkeit
   – für Sprecher (und Hörer) sichtbar/ nicht sichtbar
3. Höhe
   – höher/tiefer/gleichhoch, bezogen auf den Sprecher
4. außerhalb/innerhalb
5. auf dieser Seite/auf der entgegengesetzten Seite
6. vor dem Sprecher oder dem Sprecher gegenüber
7. hinter dem Sprecher/dem Hörer
8. Umgebungsparameter
   – im Landesinnern/seewärts
   – bergwärts/talwärts
   – flußaufwärts/flußabwärts
   – die Küste aufwärts/abwärts

Unter diesen acht Parametern ist der erste in seinen verschiedenen Ausprägungen bei weitem der wichtigste. Aber auch Sichtbarkeit und relative Höhe sind oft genutzt; die andern finden sich, naturgemäß, wie man sagen möchte, nur in bestimmten Gegenden. Da manche dieser Merkmale sich bündeln, ergeben sich bisweilen sehr komplexe Subsysteme, die gut ein Dutzend Elemente umfassen können. Am häufigsten sind allerdings auch hier Systeme mit zwei oder drei Termen. Reiche Differenzierungen finden sich durchweg im L-Teil, d. h. in all jenen Merkmalen, die in einer bestimmten Sprache aus dem einen oder andern Grunde lexikalisiert sind, und nicht so sehr im D-Teil. Wenn man die Natur der deiktischen Orientierung verstehen will, scheint es auch hier sinnvoll, zunächst einmal den kanonischen Fall und davon ausgehend die verschiedenen möglichen Verschiebungen zu betrachten.

6.2. Deixis im Anschauungsraum

Der kanonische Fall ist der „gewöhnliche Anschauungsraum", in dem die Menschen miteinander reden, handeln und sich orientieren. So selbstverständlich uns dieses Konzept erscheint, so schwierig ist seine genaue Bestimmung. Fünf Momente scheinen mir konstitutiv:

1. ELEMENTE: Sie bestehen aus einzelnen Orten, die man als Mengen von Raumpunkten auffassen kann.
2. DIMENSIONALE STRUKTUR: Die Orte sind in drei Dimensionen geordnet: Vertikale, Horizontale und Transversale („hinten-vorn").
3. TOPOLOGISCHE STRUKTUR: Die Orte können ganz oder völlig ineinander enthalten sein.
4. REGIO: Jeder Ort hat (mindestens) einen „Nahbereich" oder, wie hier gesagt wird, eine „Regio", um sich. Wie diese Regio nun genau definiert ist, ist offen: es ist gleichsam der Einflußbereich dieses Ortes.
5. ORIGO: Der Raum hat einen ausgezeichneten Ort, der durch die Position und Körperorientierung einer als Bezugspunkt gewählten Person gegeben ist. Die Dimensionen sind in der Regel auf diese Origo bezogen.

Ich nehme nicht an, dass der Anschauungsraum eine metrische Struktur hat. Seine Eigenschaften erlauben es also nur zu sagen, ob ein Ort in die Regio eines andern Ortes (beispielsweise der Position des Sprechers) fällt oder nicht (also „fern") ist, nicht aber, wie weit er davon entfernt ist. Eine Metrik zählt zu den verschiedenen zusätzlichen Strukturen, die dem Anschauungsraum aufgeprägt werden können. Dazu zählen auch geographische Eigenschaften, wie etwa der Unterschied zwischen Berg und Tal, Land und Meer.

Ortsdeiktika verweisen auf Orte, indem sie sich die Raumstruktur zunutze machen. Am einfachsten ist dies bei zweigliedrigen Systemen wie den englischen Adverbien *here* und *there*. Sie verweisen im kanonischen Fall auf einen Ort, der die Origo einschließt (*here*) oder ausschließt (*there*). Die Origo selbst ist durch die Position des Sprechers gegeben. Die Grenzen dieses Ortes sind lexikalisch nicht festgelegt. Für *hier* kann man sich jedoch auf die Regio stützen, d. h. hier bezeichnet die Regio des Sprechers, die von Fall zu Fall sehr unterschiedlich ausfallen kann; darüber, falls es nicht ausdrücklich gesagt wird, kann nur das Weltwissen Auskunft geben. Für *there* ist dies nicht möglich. So gibt es denn auch in einer Redesituation zwar nur ein „here", aber viele „there's". Um ein bestimmtes „there" auszusondern, sind zusätzliche Informationen erforderlich, beispielsweise eine Zeigegeste (die allerdings die Grenzen immer noch offen läßt).

Nun kann allerdings eine Zeigegeste auch sinnvoll mit *here* verbunden werden, etwa wenn man auf einen Punkt an jemandes Schulter deutet oder ihn berührt und sagt: *Die Kugel traf ihn hier* (Klein 1978). Dies legt eine etwas andere Analyse der Ausdrucksbedeutung von *hier* nahe: es referiert auf einen Teilraum der Regio des Sprechers, der durch eine Zeigegeste festgelegt wird; fehlt diese, so wird die Regio als Ganze gewählt. Hingegen bezeichnet *there* einen Ort außerhalb der Regio, der durch eine Zeigegeste festgelegt wird; die Grenzen bleiben offen.

Schwieriger gestaltet sich das Bild bei dreistufigen Systemen; sie können sehr unterschiedlicher Art sein. Das französische System mit *ici : là : là-bas* wird traditionell als ein dreistufiges Distanzsystem gedeutet: *ici* bezeichnet die Regio des Sprechers, die beiden andern Terme jeweils Orte außerhalb dieser Regio; *là-bas* drückt einen größeren Abstand zur Sprecher-Regio aus. Dies ist aber nur in Grenzen mit dem tatsächlichen Gebrauch in Einklang zu bringen (vgl. etwa Smith 1992).

Das deutsche *hier-da-dort-System* läßt sich sicherlich nicht über Distanzunterschiede beschreiben; *da* kann sowohl für *hier* wie für *dort* eintreten (dabei gibt es deutliche dialektale Beschränkungen), allerdings nicht in allen Fällen. In der bislang subtilsten Analyse vertritt Ehrich (1992) die Auffassung, daß *hier* in seiner Ausdrucksbedeutung auf Nähe und *dort* auf Ferne zur Sprecherposition festgelegt sind. Das Lexem *da* ist in dieser Hinsicht nicht markiert; seine bevorzugte Lesart ergibt sich aus einer konversationellen Implikatur, je nachdem, ob es zu *hier* oder zu *dort* in einen polaren Kontrast gesetzt wird.

Manche Sprachen haben mehrere Systeme. Das bekannteste Beispiel ist Spanisch mit dem dreistufigen System *ahí : aquí : allí* und dem zweistufigen *acá : allá*. Ersteres wird zumeist als Rollensystem gedeutet (beim Sprecher, beim Angesprochenen, bei einer dritten Person), letzteres als ein Distanzsystem „nah" und „fern", wobei, wenn ansonsten nichts angegeben wird, die Position des Sprechers der Bezugspunkt ist; im Gegensatz zu den drei ersten Termen sind *acá* und *allá* steigerungsfähig; dies spricht für eine Distanzanalyse. Allerdings wird dieses schöne Bild zumindest durch dialektale und stilistische Präferenzen verwischt; auch ist bislang nicht untersucht worden, welche Rolle Zeigegesten beim Gebrauch dieser fünf Formen spielen (eine eingehende Analyse findet sich in Hottenroth 1982). Angesichts der eminenten Schwierigkeit, über das deiktische System recht gut erforschter Sprachen etwas Gesichertes zu sagen, kann man eine gewisse Skepsis, was entlegenere Sprachen angeht, nicht verhehlen.

Ortsdeiktika wie die bisher genannten sind rein topologisch; sie nutzen nicht die drei Dimensionen des Anschauungsraumes. Was unterscheidet diese drei Dimensionen voneinander? Im normalen Fall sind alle drei Dimensionen durch die Origo und die damit verbundene normale Körperorientierung festgelegt. Maßgeblich für die Transversale ist die Blickrichtung: *vorn* sind all jene Orte, die in Blickrichtung liegen, *hinten* jene, die in entgegengesetzter Richtung liegen. Die Vertikale mit den Polen *oben* und *unten* ist durch die kanonische Kopf-Fuß-Orientierung gegeben, die Horizontale durch die Körperseiten-Asymmetrie: *links* ist, wo bei den meisten das Herz ist, *rechts* ist die entgegengesetzte Seite. Die deiktische Orientierung im Anschauungsraum ergibt sich aus den Körperasymmetrien einer Person, und dies ist im kanonischen Fall der Sprecher.

Nicht alle Sprachen nutzen diese Möglichkeit für die Ortsdeixis; insbesondere die *rechts-links*-Unterscheidung fehlt oft, möglicherweise weil die Körperasymmetrie in dieser Dimension nicht so ausgeprägt ist wie die beiden anderen (einen umfassenden Überblick über die verschiedenen Systeme der Raumreferenz geben Pederson & al. 1998). Für die Vertikale kann man, anders als bei der Transversalen und der Horizontalen, auch eine abstrakte Eigenschaft wie die Schwerkraft als definierendes Kriterium nehmen. In der kanonischen Position (stehend, geradeausblickend) steht diese Definition allerdings mit der deiktischen im Einklang, so daß sich für den Gebrauch von *oben* und *unten* kein Unterschied ergibt.

Dimensionale Deiktika sondern relativ umfassende Teilräume aus, nämlich all das, was beispielsweise links von der Origo liegt; da sich dieser Teilraum aus den Körperasymmetrien allein ergibt, sind Zeigegesten nicht erforderlich.

6.3. Verschiebungen

Das bisher Gesagte betraf die kanonische Redesituation. Zahlreiche Verschiebungen sind möglich, von denen hier nur die wichtigsten betrachtet werden.

Zum ersten kann eine andere Person, beispielsweise der Angesprochene, als Origo gewählt werden. Dies ist häufig, ohne daß es besonders markiert würde, in Aufforderungen der Fall („*Bitte mal nach links drehen!*"). Ebenso kann die Position des Sprechers oder einer anderen Person zu einer anderen Zeit und unter anderen Umständen gewählt werden; dies ist die berühmte Bühlersche „Deixis am Phantasma". Dann verändern sich *links* und *rechts, vorn* und *hinten*, nicht aber *oben* und *unten*, solange die Bezugsperson auch im Phantasma als stehend gedacht ist. An der Verwendung der deiktischen Ausdrücke selbst ändert sich dadurch zunächst nichts. Dies ist anders, wenn real oder in der Vorstellung eine andere Position eingenommen wird (etwa im Bett liegend); dann nimmt der Sprecher in der Regel sein „links und rechts" mit; die beiden übrigen Dimensionen geraten in Konfusionen, die von Fall zu Fall unterschiedlich aufgelöst werden (sowohl die Deckenlampe wie das Kopfende können „oben" sein).

Bei einer zweiten Gruppe von Verschiebungen wird nicht eine spezifische, sondern eine typische Position als Bezugspunkt genommen. So hat ein Auto eine „rechte" und eine „linke" Seite, und zwar relativ zur typischen Position des Fahrers. Viele „intrinsische" Eigenschaften von Objekten haben hier ihren Ursprung; dabei wird jedoch eigentümlicherweise oft eine mentale Rotation um 180 Grad vollzogen: die Vorderseite eines Schrankes ist spiegelbildlich zum „vorn" des normalen Betrachters. (Vgl. die Unterscheidung von „facing" und „aligning" in Hill 1982.)

Bei all diesen Verschiebungen bleibt die Struktur des Raumes selbst unangetastet; es ändert sich lediglich der Bezugspunkt. Es ist aber auch möglich, ihn um eine oder zwei Dimensionen zu reduzieren und damit den üblichen Anschauungsraum zu verlassen. Dies ist beispielsweise bei deiktischer Referenz auf Orte in Landkarten der Fall. Dabei werden die deiktischen Definitionen von *links* und *rechts* sowie von *oben* und *unten* beibehalten (oben ist beim Kopf, unten ist bei den Füßen), und zwar relativ zur Position und Blickrichtung des Betrachters; die Dimension vorn-hinten wird aufgegeben. Reduziert man den Raum um eine weitere Dimension, so bleibt als Ordnungsbeziehung zwischen den verschiedenen Orten nur noch die Reihenfolge, in der sie in die fortlaufende Rede eingeführt werden, d. h. der anaphorische Gebrauch von Ortsdeiktika. Diese Möglichkeit ist recht beschränkt (Ehlich 1979; 1983).

Dimensionale Deiktika sind weithin ausgeschlossen; die einzige Ausnahme ist die sich auf die Materialität des Texts beziehende Redeweise „oben", „unten". Hingegen können topologische Deiktika wie *hier, da, dort* sehr wohl gebraucht werden, oft zur Referenz auf denselben in der Rede eingeführten Ort: *Am Tag darauf kamen wir nach Pontecorvo. Hier/dort/da gibt es ein Spaghettimuseum.*

Die Unterschiede sind nicht leicht zu fassen. Falls, wie in diesem Beispiel, keine Wahl zwischen verschiedenen alternativen Orten zu treffen ist, kann man die ursprüngliche Differenzierung am ehesten dadurch retten, indem man „Regio" als eine Art subjektiver Nähe deutet. Falls hingegen mehrere Orte in den „Gedächtnisraum" eingeführt sind, gibt es wiederum eine Salienzabstufung zwischen ihnen, die im einfachsten Fall durch die Reihenfolge bestimmt ist: was früher eingeführt wurde, gilt als „weiter entfernt". Dabei hat, wie Ehrich (1992: 42−63) gezeigt hat, *da* seinem unmarkierten Charakter entsprechend ein besonders reiches Spektrum von Anwendungen.

6.4. „Dynamische" Ortsdeixis

Alle bisher erörterten Ortsdeiktika sind „statisch" oder „positional", d. h. sie verweisen auf einen Ort oder einen Typ von Orten relativ zur deiktischen Origo. In den meisten Sprachen gibt es jedoch auch „dynamische" Ortsdeiktika. Die wichtigsten darunter sind Adverbien wie *hierhin, dorthin, dahin, hierher, (von) dorther, daher* sowie Bewegungsverben wie *kommen* und *gehen.* Über erstere wird gewöhnlich gesagt, daß sie einen „Weg" oder eine „Richtung" angeben (direktionale Adverbien). Dies ist aber nicht sehr einleuchtend. Wenn sich z. B. *dort* auf Rom bezieht, so führen sehr viele Wege *dorthin,* und man kann aus vielen Richtungen *dorthin* fahren. Um eine Richtung festzulegen, müßte sehr viel mehr angegeben werden.

Was diese Adverbien ausdrücken, ist zweierlei: sie verweisen deiktisch auf einen Ort, und sie geben zudem an, daß es sich bei diesem Ort um einen ZIELORT oder um einen AUSGANGSORT handelt. Diese letztere Information gehört zum L-Teil der Ausdrucksbedeutung; er ist selbst nicht deiktisch.

Ebendiese Unterscheidung zwischen Zielort und Ausgangsort liegt auch der Bedeutung deiktischer Bewegungsverben zugrunde. In dem Satz *Eva verließ das Zimmer* wird gesagt, daß Eva zuerst an einem bestimmten Ort war und dann nicht an diesem Ort war, d. h. die Semantik von *verlassen* spezifiziert die Position von Eva im Ausgangszustand als „am Ort x" und im Zielzustand als „nicht am Ort x"; was x ist, wird durch das direkte Objekt *das Zimmer* angegeben. In anderen Fällen wird es aber nicht angegeben; dann muß es aus dem Kontext ergänzt werden.

Bei manchen Verben gilt nun regelhaft der deiktische Bezugspunkt als Zielort oder auch als Ausgangsort. Am einfachsten ist dies bei den Imperativen *komm!* und *geh!* zu sehen. Im ersten Fall ist das deiktische Zentrum Zielort; über den Ausgangsort ist nichts weiter gesagt, ebensowenig etwas über eine „Richtung". Bei *geh!* hingegen ist das deiktische Zentrum Ausgangsort, und über den Zielort ist nichts weiter ausgeführt, außer daß er eben nicht das deiktische Zentrum ist. Im einfachsten Fall ist dieses deiktische Zentrum durch Position und Körperorientierung des Sprechers gegeben. Es kann aber natürlich verschoben werden.

In dieser Hinsicht unterscheiden sich die deiktischen Bewegungsverben einzelner Sprachen erheblich. So wird beispielsweise im Deutschen das deiktische Zentrum gewöhnlich beibehalten, wenn der Sprecher wechselt *Kommst Du heute abend? − Ja, ich komme.* In andern Sprachen, wie etwa Ungarisch, gilt für die Antwort das deiktische Zentrum des bisher Angesprochenen und nunmehrigen Sprechers, und er sagt sinngemäß *Ja, ich gehe.* In jedem Falle jedoch liegt die deiktische Komponente dieser Verben nicht in der „Richtung" oder dem „Weg", sondern darin, ob ein bestimmter Ort als deiktisches Zentrum verstanden werden soll.

7. Zeitdeixis

Objektdeiktika verweisen auf relativ konkrete Entitäten − Objekte oder Personen (siehe oben § 5); ihr Referenzbereich ist nicht oder nur schwach strukturiert (beispielsweise durch Verwandtschaftsbeziehungen wie Mutter-von, Bruder-von usw.). Ortsdeiktika (siehe oben § 6) verweisen auf eher abstrakte Entitäten, deren Grenzen nicht sehr klar sind: Teilräume eines irgendwie strukturierten Raums; ihr Referenzbereich ist sehr stark strukturiert, durch die drei Dimensionen, durch topologische Beziehungen, und im Einzelfall auch durch zusätzliche Eigenschaften wie Berge, Flüsse, Meere; dies spiegelt sich im L-Teil der Ortsdeiktika wider.

Zeitdeiktika verweisen auf noch abstraktere Entitäten – auf Zeitspannen oder Intervalle. Wie bei Orten sind ihre Grenzen unbestimmt. Ihr Referenzbereich ist in klarer Weise strukturiert. Zeitspannen können ganz oder teilweise ineinander enthalten sein (topologische Struktur), und sie können aufeinander folgen (Ordnungsstruktur). Alle Sprachen haben reiche lexikalische Möglichkeiten, deiktisch auf Zeitspannen zu verweisen; das wichtigste Mittel sind Adverbiale (siehe unten § 7.3). Sehr viele Sprachen haben den deiktischen Ausdruck der Zeit grammatikalisiert; in allen indoeuropäschen Sprachen ist er an die Finitheit gebunden und daher in finiten Sätzen obligatorisch.

7.1. Grammatikalisierte Zeitdeixis im kanonischen Fall

Seit alters wird angenommen, daß man drei Zeiten unterscheiden kann, die sich durch ihr Verhältnis zum wahrnehmenden oder auch zum sprechenden Subjekt unterscheiden: Vergangenheit, Gegenwart und Zukunft. Diese Vorstellung liefert seit fast zweieinhalb Jahrtausenden die Folie für die übliche Analyse der „Zeitformen" des Verbs, wie sie sich immer noch in der Terminologie niederschlägt: die Ausdrücke 'Tempora', 'Gegenwart', 'Vergangenheit', 'Zukunft', 'past', 'present', 'future', um nur einige zu nennen, können sich sowohl auf Zeiten wie auf Formen des Verbs beziehen. Nach dieser Analyse ist das Tempus eine deiktisch-relationale Kategorie des Verbs. Es gibt eine deiktische Origo, (hier t_0 genannt), und die Tempusform markiert, daß eine bestimmte Zeit (nämlich die Zeit des Ereignisses, um das es geht) in einer bestimmten temporalen Relation zu t_0 steht. Sie kann vor t_0 liegen (Vergangenheit), nach t_0 (Zukunft) oder sich mit t_0 überlappen, im Grenzfall gleichzeitig zu t_0 sein (Gegenwart).

Diese klassische deiktisch-relationale Analyse stößt auf viele Probleme (vgl. die ausgezeichnete Darstellung in Fabricius-Hansen 1991), von denen drei hier diskutiert werden sollen. Das erste rührt daher, daß es in vielen Sprachen mehr als drei Tempora gibt. Dafür sind mehrere Lösungen denkbar:

(a) Die zeitlichen Relationen werden verfeinert, indem man relative Entfernungen hinzunimmt, etwa lange vor t_0, kurz vor t_0, lange nach t_0, kurz nach t_0, usw. Eine solche Verfeinerung der Zeitrelation liegt etwa der verbreiteten Analyse von französisch *il va venir* vs. *il viendra* oder *he is going to come* vs. *he will come* als „unmittelbare" vs. „fernere" Zukunft zugrunde. Nach dieser Vorstellung sind die Zeitformen nach wie vor rein temporal-deiktisch definiert; nur sind die Relationen feiner.

(b) Man beläßt es bei den drei einfachen Relationen, nimmt aber zusätzliche Zeitspannen über das deiktische Zentrum hinaus an, relativ zu denen diese Relationen beschrieben werden. Dieser Gedanke wird heute meist Hans Reichenbach (1947) zugeschrieben; er findet sich aber durchgehend schon in der älteren Literatur, beispielsweise bei Hermann Paul (1886).

(c) Man ergänzt die zeitlichen Relationen durch andere Kategorien, die gleichfalls „zeitlich" sind, aber nicht im deiktisch-relationalen Sinne. Dies ist die Vorstellung, die gemeinhin dem Begriff des „Aspekts" zugrundegelegt wird. Zwei Aspektformen eines Verbs unterscheiden sich nicht dadurch, daß sie eine unterschiedliche zeitliche Relation zur Sprechzeit ausdrücken, sondern dadurch, daß sie – beispielsweise – das Ereignis als abgeschlossen oder als im Verlauf befindlich darstellen.

Alle drei Möglichkeiten finden sich in den Sprachen der Welt vielfältig belegt, oft in Verbindung miteinander (Bybee, Perkins & Pagliuca 1994). Sie wahren grundsätzlich den deiktisch-relationalen Charakter des Tempus.

Das zweite Problem ist ganz anderer Art. Man kann es sich anhand einer einfachen Satzfolge wie *Man fand ihn in der Badewanne. Er war tot.* vor Augen führen. Nach der üblichen deiktisch-relationalen Analyse besagt das Präteritum, daß das jeweilige Ereignis vor der Sprechzeit liegt. Dies mag beim ersten Satz stimmen, sicher aber nicht beim zweiten: dort ist das Ereignis sein Totsein, und dies liegt sicher nicht vor der Sprechzeit, sondern es enthält die Sprechzeit. Was vor der Sprechzeit liegt, ist ein SUBINTERVALL des im Satz beschriebenen Sachverhalts, nämlich jene Zeitspanne, über die in der betreffenden Redesituation etwas behauptet wird; dafür sage ich Assertionszeit oder TOPIKZEIT. Das Tempus markiert die relative Lage dieser Topikzeit zur deiktischen Origo. Die Topikzeit ihrerseits kann in unterschiedlichen zeitlichen Relationen zur „Ereigniszeit" stehen. Im obigen Beispiel ist sie in der Ereigniszeit enthalten; sie kann auch davor oder danach sein oder umgekehrt ihrerseits die Ereigniszeit enthalten. Dies führt zu unterschiedlichen zeitlichen Perspektiven auf das Ereignis, also zu dem, was man traditionell „Aspekte" nennt. Der Aspekt ist also gleichfalls eine zeitliche Relation, freilich keine deiktische: es ist die Relation zwischen der Zeit, für die etwas behauptet wird, und der Zeit, zu der das im Satz beschriebene Geschehen besteht (vgl. hierzu Klein 1994).

Das dritte Problem liegt darin, daß der Bezugspunkt in vielen Fällen nicht die Sprechzeit ist. Ein einfaches Beispiel sind Sätze wie *Ich dachte, daß er schläft.* Hier ist die Zeit, über die etwas behauptet wird, die „Zeit des Denkens", diese liegt in der Vergangenheit; sein Schlafen wird nun relativ zu dieser Zeit in der Vergangenheit beschrieben, nicht relativ zur Sprechzeit. Die erste Tempusform *dachte* ist also deiktisch, die zweite *schläft* hingegen nicht. Man kann diese Verwendung, nach dem allgemein hier beschrittenen Weg, als eine von vielen möglichen Verschiebungen des kanonischen Gebrauchs ansehen.

7.2. Verschiebungen der grammatikalisierten Zeitdeixis

Anders als bei der Objekt- und der Ortsdeixis ist der Referenzbereich bei der Zeitdeixis immer ein „Vorstellungsraum": er besteht aus den in einer gegebenen Redesituation relevanten Zeitspannen, über die man etwas sagen möchte und die relativ zur realen Sprechzeit eingeordnet werden.

Eine erste Möglichkeit zur Verschiebung besteht nun darin, ausgehend von der Sprechzeit ein weiteres Intervall einzuführen, das nunmehr als Bezugszeit gilt. Das einfachste Beispiel dafür ist die direkte Rede, wie in *Er sagte: „Ich komme gleich".* Diese Möglichkeit findet sich, soweit man weiß, in allen Sprachen. Vielfach kann man zu diesem Zweck auch Verben des Sagens und Denkens ohne direkte Rede verwenden, wie in *Ich dachte, daß er schläft* oder *Warum hast du mir damals nicht gesagt, daß du krank bist?* Diese Möglichkeit ist stärker beschränkt. In beiden Fällen findet sich das „verschobene Tempus" in einem untergeordneten Satz, während das Tempus im übergeordneten Satz auf die reale Sprechzeit bezogen, also im kanonischen Sinne deiktisch ist. Davon kann gleichfalls abgewichen werden. Drei bekannte und oft diskutierte nicht-kanonische Verwendungen dieser Art sind das historische Präsens, das „praesens tabulare" sowie das Tempus in nicht-faktischen Texten.

Beim historischen Präsens wird ein vergangenes Geschehen im Präsens berichtet: *Kaum komme ich gestern morgen ins Büro, da steht mein Chef in der Tür und sagt, ...* Im Prinzip gibt es, wie schon Bühler (1934) für die Deixis am Phantasma allgemein bemerkt hat, zwei Möglichkeiten, dies zu analysieren. Entweder man nimmt an, daß die Origo in die Vergangenheit verschoben ist, d. h. es ist nicht die reale Sprechzeit, die als Ankerpunkt gilt, sondern eine Zeit in der Vergangenheit; oder man nimmt an, daß sich die Geschehnisse gleichsam jetzt abspielen.

Die erste Analyse scheint zunächst ökonomischer, weil dann nur eine Zeit, eben die Sprechzeit, verschoben werden muß, während bei der zweiten alle Ereignisse ins Jetzt wandern. Allerdings denkt sich der Redende beim historischen Präsens nicht, daß er in der Vergangenheit *spricht,* während die zu berichtenden Geschehnisse so oder so nur in der „Vorstellungswelt" bestehen; auch die Erinnerung ist eine gegenwärtige Vorstellung; deshalb ist die zweite Möglichkeit, oft durch die Metapher „lebhafte Vergegenwärtigung" gekennzeichnet, vorzuziehen. Sie wahrt den deiktischen Charakter des Tempus und betrifft nur die subjektive Repräsention der Zeitspannen und der Ereignisse, die diese Zeitspannen einnehmen.

Beim Praesens tabulare werden einfach Fakten aus der Vergangenheit im Präsens berichtet: *Im Jahre 303 v. Chr. schlägt er die Perser bei Issos.* Hier erscheint der Gedanke, die möglichen Referenten würden in die Gegenwart verschoben, wenig einleuchtend. Diese Verwendung läßt sich jedoch einfach erklären, wenn man annimmt, daß die Topikzeit sehr lang ist: es wird sozusagen eine grundsätzliche Behauptung gemacht, und die Topikzeit schließt lange vergangene Geschehnisse (303 v. Chr.) ebenso wie die Sprechzeit ein. Auch bei dieser Analyse behält das Tempus seinen deiktisch-relationalen Charakter bei.

In beiden Fällen geht es um reale Ereignisse in realer Zeit. Aber in vielen Sätzen bezieht sie sich auf *nur* vorgestellte Ereignisse. Sie lassen sich natürlich überhaupt nicht auf die reale Sprechzeit beziehen. Dies gilt für die vergleichsweise gut erforschte fiktive Literatur (vgl. etwa Green 1995); es gilt aber auch für Filmnacherzählungen, wie in *In der nächsten Szene steigt er aus einem Flugzeug;* und es gilt nicht zuletzt für normative Texte (*Eine Zensur findet nicht statt*). Den letzteren Gebrauch kann man als deiktisch ansehen, wenn man annimmt, daß die Topikzeit nicht nur eine Zeit sein kann, über die etwas behauptet wird, sondern auch eine Zeit, für die — bei deontischen Texten — eine bestimmte Norm gilt. In den beiden anderen Fällen wird der Gebrauch von bestimmten narrativen Konventionen bestimmt; so findet sich bei literarischen Texten das Präsens ebenso wie das Präteritum. Hier ist die Verschiebung vom kanonischen Fall so weit getrieben, daß es kaum noch sinnvoll erscheint, von „deiktisch-relational" zu reden; doch ist dies letztlich eine Frage der Terminologie.

7.3. Deiktische Zeitadverbien

Seit mehr als zweitausend Jahren gilt die Liebe der Grammatiker der deiktischen Kategorie des Tempus. Dies ist angesichts seines quasi-obligatorischen Charakters in vielen Sprachen verständlich. Man muß die Zeit angeben, über die man redet, und dies tut man am besten relativ zu einer Zeit, die in der normalen Redesituation gegeben ist, also der Sprechzeit. Allerdings ist die deiktisch-relationale Leistung des Tempus selbst bei etwas reicheren Systemen sehr unbestimmt, wenn man es mit dem Potential deiktischer Adverbien vergleicht. Sie sind in allen bekannten Sprachen gut ausgebildet, allerdings nicht so differenziert wie das System der Ortsdeixis. Dies hat seinen Grund in der viel einfacheren Struktur des Referenzbereichs. Im nichtverschobenen Fall weisen Ortsdeiktika in ihrem L-Teil drei Arten von Informationen auf: sie können die Art der Relation zur Origo angeben („vor, nach, enthalten in" usw.); sie können diese Relation je nach der Entfernung von der Origo verfeinern; so liegen *vorhin, früher, kürzlich, jüngst, vor langem* alle vor der Origo), und sie können in mehr oder minder bestimmter Form die Grenzen der Zeitspanne angeben, auf die verwiesen wird. Wir haben dies oben (siehe oben § 4) am Beispiel von *gestern, heute, morgen* veranschaulicht; dort wurden auch schon die wesentlichen Verschiebungen genannt.

8. Schlußbemerkung

Zwischen den einzelnen Ausprägungen der Deixis bestehen große Ähnlichkeiten, aber auch charakteristische Unterschiede. Die referentielle Bedeutung von Deiktika ist relativ; sie ist relativ zu Informationen, die im kanonischen Fall in der Redesituation gegeben sein müssen; davon sind in bestimmter Weise Verschiebungen möglich. Die Unterschiede rühren im wesentlichen aus den unterschiedlichen Referenten und der Art, wie der jeweilige Referenzbereich strukturiert ist. Das damit gegebene Bedeutungspotential wird von den einzelnen Sprachen unterschiedlich genutzt; diese Unterschiede liegen sowohl darin, welche Ausdrucksbedeutung Lexeme und grammatische Konstruktionen im kanonischen Fall haben, wie darin, welche Verschiebungen möglich sind.

Unsere Vorstellungen darüber, wie dies tatsächlich in den einzelnen Sprachen funktioniert, sind freilich noch sehr wenig gesichert; zwar gibt es zahlreiche Studien zur Deixis; nur wenige aber haben systematisch zu klären versucht, wie sprachliche und nicht-sprachliche Information, beispielsweise Zeigegesten, in tatsächlichen Redesituationen zusammengebracht werden.

9. Zitierte Literatur

Anderson, Stephen & Keenan, Edward. 1985. „Deixis". In: Shopen, Tim (ed.). *Language Typology and Syntactic Description.* Vol. III, 259–308.

Apollonius Dyscolus. 1981. *The syntax of Apollonius Dyscolus.* Translated, and with commentary by Fred W. Householder. (Amsterdam studies in the theory and history of linguistic science, Ser. 3, 23.) Amsterdam & Philadelphia: Benjamins.

Braun, Friederike. 1988. *Terms of Address. Principles of patterns and usage in various languages and cultures.* Berlin: Mouton.

Brugmann, Karl. 1904. *Die Demonstrativpronomina der indogermanischen Sprachen.* Leipzig: Teubner.

Bühler, Karl. 1934. *Sprachtheorie. Die Darstellungsfunktion der Sprache.* Jena: Fischer.

Bybee, Joan & Perkins, Revere & Pagliuca, William. 1994. *The evolution of grammar. Tense, aspect, mood in the languages of the world.* Chicago: Chicago University Press.

Eschbach, Achim (ed.). 1988. *Karl Bühler's Theory of Language.* Amsterdam & Philadelphia: Benjamins.

Ehlich, Konrad. 1979. *Verwendungen der Deixis beim sprachlichen Handeln. Linguistisch-philologische Untersuchungen zum hebräischen deiktischen System.* Frankfurt/M.: Lang.

Ehlich, Konrad. 1983. „Deixis und Anapher". In: Rauh (ed.), 79–97.

Ehrich, Veronika. 1992. *Hier und Jetzt. Studien zur lokalen und temporalen Deixis im Deutschen.* Tübingen: Niemeyer.

Fabricius-Hansen, Cathrine. 1991. „Tempus". In: von Stechow & Wunderlich (eds.), 441–58.

Fillmore, Charles. 1971. *Santa Cruz Lectures on Deixis.* Bloomington: Indiana University Linguistic Club (unveränderter Neudruck Stanford/CA: CSLI 1997).

Frei, Henri. 1944. „Systèmes de déictiques". *Acta Linguistica* 4: 111−29.

Graumann, Carl-Friedrich. 1992. „Speaking and understanding from viewpoints". In: Semin, Gün & Fiedler, Klaus (eds.). *Language, Interaction and Social Cognition*. London: Sage. 237−55.

Green, Keith (ed.). 1995. *New Essays in Deixis*. Amsterdam & Atlanta: Rodopi.

Hanks, William F. 1990. *Referential Practice. Language and lived space among the Maya*. Chicago: The University of Chicago Press.

Harweg, Roland. 1990. *Studien zur Deixis*. Bochum: Brockmeyer.

Herbermann, Clemens-Peter. 1988. „Entwurf einer Systematik der Deixisarten". In: id., *Modus referentiae*. Heidelberg: Winter. 47−93.

Herrmann, Theo & Grabowski, Jürgen. 1994. *Sprechen. Psychologie der Sprachproduktion*. Heidelberg: Spektrum.

Hill, Clifford. 1982. „Up/down, front/back, left/right. A contrastive study of Hausa and English". In: Weissenborn & Klein (eds.), 13−42.

Himmelmann, Nikolaus. 1997. *Deiktikon, Artikel, Nominalphrase*. Tübingen: Niemeyer.

Hottenroth, Priska-Monika. 1982. „The System of Local Deixis in Spanish". In: Weissenborn & Klein (eds.), 133−53.

Hyslop, Catriona. 1993. *Towards a Typology of Spatial Deixis*. Ph.D. Thesis. National University of Australia.

Jarvella, Robert, & Klein, Wolfgang (eds.). 1982. *Speech, Place, and Action*. Chichester: Wiley.

Klein, Wolfgang. 1978. „Wo ist hier?" *Linguistische Berichte* 58: 18−40.

Klein, Wolfgang. 1994. *Time in language*. London: Routledge.

Lenz, Friedrich. 1997. *Diskursdeixis im Englischen*. Tübingen: Niemeyer.

Levelt, Willem. 1989. *Language Production*. Cambridge/MA: MIT Press.

Levinson, Stephen. 1983. *Pragmatics*. Cambridge: Cambridge University Press.

Miller, George A. & Johnson-Laird, Philip N. 1976. *Language and Perception*. Cambridge/MA: Harvard University Press.

Morel, Mary-Annick & Danon-Boileau, Laurent (eds.). 1992. *La déixis*. Paris: Presses Universitaires de France.

Nöth, Winfried. 1985. *Handbuch der Semiotik*. Stuttgart: Metzler.

Paul, Hermann. 1886. *Prinzipien der Sprachgeschichte*. Jena: Niemeyer.

Pederson, Eric & al. 1998. „Semantic typology and spatial conceptualisation". *Language* 74: 557− 589.

Rauh, Gisa. 1983. „Aspects of Deixis". In: Rauh (ed.), 9−60.

Rauh, Gisa (ed.). 1983. *Essays on Deixis*. Tübingen: Narr.

Reichenbach, Hans. 1947. *Elements of Symbolic Logic*. Berkeley: Univ. of California Press.

Richter, Heide. 1988. *Indexikalität. Ihre Behandlung in Philosophie und Sprachwissenschaft*. Tübingen: Niemeyer.

Sennholz, Klaus. 1985. *Grundzüge der Deixis*. Bochum: Brockmeyer.

Sitta, Georg. 1991. *Deixis am Phantasma*. Bochum: Brockmeyer.

Smith, John Charles. 1992. „Traits, marques et sous-spécification: applications à la déixis". In: Morel & Danon-Boileau (eds.), 257−64.

Stechow, Arnim von & Wunderlich, Dieter (eds.). 1991. *Semantik. Ein internationales Handbuch der zeitgenössischen Forschung*. Berlin: de Gruyter.

Weissenborn, Jürgen & Klein, Wolfgang (eds.). 1982. *Here and there. Crosslinguistic Studies on Deixis and Demonstration*. Amsterdam & Philadelphia: Benjamins.

Wilkins, David & Hill, Debbie. 1995. „When 'go' means 'come'". *Cognitive Linguistics* 6: 209−259.

Zimmermann, Thomas. 1991. „Kontextabhängigkeit". In: von Stechow & Wunderlich (eds.), 156−229.

Wolfgang Klein,
Max-Planck-Institut für Psycholinguistik,
Nijmegen (Niederlande)

45. Linking clauses

1. What is clause linking about?
2. Maintaining reference
3. Hierarchy: downgrading clauses
4. The expression of relations
5. Communicative dynamism
6. Diachronic aspects
7. Overall view and concluding remarks
8. References

1. What is clause linking about?

Human communication is primarily based on utterances, texts, turns in dialogue, not on propositions, sentences or clauses. This makes linking smaller parts — like clauses — into higher units a basic activity of speakers and hearers. In order to show the resulting complexity of human information processing, a first example will be appropriate.

(1) (Cable News Network [CNN], 11.2.1999)
 With Clinton's acquittal on perjury and obstruction-of-justice charges virtually assured, and even a formal censure of the president seeming unlikely, the biggest remaining question is whether either article will get a majority vote.

What will a non-US reader dependent on her/his knowledge of ENGLISH understand in, say, 2019?

- that there is a main clause: *the biggest remaining question is*;
- that there is, depending on this main clause, a following indirect question: *whether either article will get a majority vote*;
- that, preceding the main clause, there are two nonfinite clauses, headed by the preposition 'with' and coordinated by the conjunction 'and': *With Clinton's acquittal on perjury and obstruction-of-justice charges virtually assured, and even a formal censure of the president seeming unlikely*;
- that both of them can be interpreted as nominalized clauses which, in a more explicit form, could read like this: "Clinton is certain to be acquitted on the charges of perjury and obstruction-of-justice" and "even a formal censure of the president seems unlikely";
- that these hybrids between clause and nominal may be functionally interpreted as adverbials;
- that some RELATION holds between these two adverbials and the main clause, but that the nature of this relation is open to interpretation: *while, whereas, since* could be candidates, leading, e.g., to "*Whilst Clinton's acquittal on perjury and obstruction-of-justice charges is virtually assured, and even a formal censure of the president seems unlikely ...*", thus making the relation that holds more explicit;
- that the ordering of the adverbials, the main clause and the dependent clause is not fortuitous — on the contrary: it conveys a certain COMMUNICATIVE DYNAMISM, starting from something that seems to be given (the two adverbial syntagms), and enhancing the main clause — where "the biggest remaining question" underlines the importance of the concluding indirect question *whether either article will get a majority vote*.

Analysing this complex sentence, we already found and exemplified three of the most important techniques speakers use when linking clauses into larger wholes:

1. The technique of creating SYNTACTIC HIERARCHY, thus giving clauses a different status (in the above example: main clause, dependent clause, hybrid between clause and nominal syntagm);
2. the technique of GROUNDING, serving the aims of a certain COMMUNICATIVE DYNAMISM; this technique may overlap with the first one;
3. the technique of ESTABLISHING SPECIFIC RELATIONS like 'condition', 'concessivity', 'causality' etc. among the parts or between the parts and a larger whole.

A fourth linking technique depends largely on our historical and encyclopaedic knowledge: In order to fully understand example (1), we should know that William Jefferson Clinton, member of the Democratic party, was president of the United States in 1999; that there was an investigation against him directed by an independent counsel (Kenneth Starr); that the 445-page Starr report, made public on September 11th 1998, contained 11 grounds for impeachment; that on December 9th 1998 the House of Representatives Judiciary Committee reduced these grounds to four articles of impeachment against the president; that, as a result, the president was impeached on December 19th 1998, with another two articles of impeachment voted down beforehand; that on January 7th 1999 the impeachment trial was opened in the Senate; that in 1999 the Senate had 55 Republican and 45 Democratic members and that a two-thirds majority was needed to convict on either article; that the public was resolutely on the president's side throughout the whole affair, with polls showing "steady disdain for the partisan bickering over Mr Clinton's sexual misdeeds"; and that since − in strictly juridical terms − the charge of perjury (depending on the definition of 'sexual intercourse') was not tenable, there was no conviction to be expected, the only open question being whether either article would obtain more than 50 votes.

In addition to this historical or situational knowledge, readers should be familiar with legal text genres and their vocabulary. One has to know that 'article' can have a very special meaning: as a distinct proposition in a series of such, as in a constitution or an 'impeachment' − the latter term belonging, like its synonym 'arraignment' and other terms in the same context ('charge', 'perjury', 'acquittal', 'trial', 'misdemeanor', 'abeyance'), to the juridical terms inherited from OLD FRENCH (in this case *empescher, empeschement,* in MODERN FRENCH *empêcher* 'to prevent'). The same context gives for instance a very special meaning to 'count', too: that of 'a separate charge in an indictment'.

This leaves us with two more techniques or factors in the domain of clause linking:

4. MAINTENANCE OF REFERENCE: nouns or nominal elements that occur in different parts of the text, but have the same or a similar referent: 'Clinton' ← 'president'; without our historical and legal knowledge we perhaps would never have understood that *either article* in example (1) refers to *perjury charge* as article$_1$ and *obstruction-of-justice charge* as article$_2$;
5. the importance of the legal knowledge, legal thinking, and the whole legal context for the understanding of example (1) suggests an important role for TEXTUAL GENRES, too.

With all this supplementary information, the following example will be understood without any problems. This time the news item was formulated, one day later, by the British Broadcasting Corporation (BBC). It is the answer to the question raised in example (1).

(2) (BBC 12.2.1999)
Bill Clinton has been cleared of all charges in his impeachment trial, leaving him free to carry on as the American president.
In an historic vote, prosecutors failed to secure either of the two counts brought against him in the Senate trial, and could not even muster a simple majority on the first vote. A two-thirds majority was needed to convict on either charge.
On the article of perjury, senators voted 45 guilty, 55 not guilty, with 10 Republicans voting for acquittal. On obstruction of justice, members were split down the middle, voting 50 guilty, 50 not guilty. Five Republicans crossed the aisle to join their Democrat colleagues.

Example (2) clearly shows the REFERENCE MAINTENANCE technique:

(a) Bill Clinton ← him ← (the American President) ← him;
(b) all charges ← either of the two counts ← either charge ← article of perjury ← on [the article of] obstruction of justice;
(c) prosecutors ← Ø;
(d) senators ← 10 Republicans ← members ← five Republicans ← their Democrat colleagues, etc.

Specimens (b) with *on obstruction of justice* instead of *on [the article of] obstruction of justice* and (c) with zero anaphora demonstrate how, in certain contexts, anaphora functions even under elliptical conditions. Specimen (d) is a good example of splitting a whole that functions as a referential frame into different parts referring to the aforementioned totality.

At the same time, example (2) shows the COMMUNICATIVE DYNAMISM typical of newspaper genres: first the most important news, then the evaluation, with the details (paragraph 3) following at the end.

The following sections will treat: the technique of maintaining reference in subsequent propositions, together with the role of textual genres and specific knowledge (§ 2); the techniques relying on syntactic hierarchy (§ 3), the expression of relations (§ 4), communicative dynamism (§ 5), followed by the diachronic aspects, especially grammaticalization (§ 6), and concluding remarks (§ 7).

2. Maintaining reference

The techniques of reference maintenance or reference tracking are extensively treated in article 84 by Andrej A. Kibrik, to whom Bernard Comrie (1999) can be added. This is why only some additions are appropriate.

2.1. Nominal substitution

As has already been said, the maintenance of reference by anaphora crucially depends on encyclopaedic knowledge and at the same time on a certain familiarity with the corresponding textual genres. In the above example (2), we had to be acquainted with a legal usage where some lines of text can be referred to as 'article' or 'count'.

In the following example John Locke resumes five sentences by *This is matter of fact ...*:

(3) (John Locke, *An Essay Concerning Human Understanding* IV, x, § 19).
"$_1$For example, my right hand writes whilst my left hand is still. $_2$What causes rest in one hand and motion in the other? $_3$Nothing but my will, a thought of my mind; $_4$my thought only changing, the right hand rests, $_5$and the left hand moves. $_6$This is matter of fact which cannot be denied".

Jens Lüdtke (1984) aptly called such nouns 'interpretators' since, while resuming an entire passage of a text, they interpret it at the same time: as a kind of speech act like in *promise, obligation, injunction, defense, statement, assertion, question, guarantee*; as a part in an argumentative whole: *premise, conclusion, argument, hypothesis, fact, necessity, possibility*; as a component of a (legal or other) text: *paragraph, count, article, impeachment, arraignment, dogma*; as something translating a rather emotional attitude: *certitude, doubt, hope, desire, wish*.

Such interpretators are to a very large extent products of discourse traditions or textual genres created by literacy. This is shown, among other things, by the fact that a considerable number of English speech act verbs — i. e. verbs corresponding to the aforementioned speech act types — appear for the first time in Early Modern English: *to acknowledge, to advocate, to assert, to concede, to remind, to apologize, to question, to request;* or even later: *to remark, to retort, to state, to accept, to guarantee, to volunteer* (Traugott 1987).

Some of these discourse traditions may appeal as well to our scientific or technical knowledge, as in example (4), where the entire sentence$_2$ describing a complex event is resumed by *this high frequency*:

(4) SPANISH (Patent specification, cited from Raible 1972: 195)
"$_1$Mediante el regulador se limita la corriente en el motor de manera que el vehículo eventualmente no podría arrancar. $_2$Como aquí la corriente a través del motor se encuentra en las proximidades del valor máximo permisible se desconecta y vuelve a conectar el tiristor en una secuencia muy rápida, bajo circunstancias, varias cientos de veces por segundo. $_3$*Esta elevada frecuencia* se aprovecha para conectar, en la posición determinada mencionada del aparato de mando, el contacto punteador".

In a language like GERMAN, to a large extent also in ENGLISH, these interpretators may be used as *nominal* heads cataphorically referring to a subsequent complement *clause*:

(5) "*Der Gedanke, daß* sie ihn besuchen könnte, versetzte ihn in helles Entzücken".

A speaker of SPANISH has the same possibility, with one significant difference, though: the element linking the complement clause to the interpretator serving as head is *de que*: *de* joins a following noun to the preceding one as in *la velocidad de translación* 'the velocity of movement', and *que, si* or *cómo* links a subordinate clause to the matrix sentence. Thus, whereas *de* is due to the nominal character of the head noun, the conjunctions *que, si, cómo* mark the verbal character of the following clause:

(6) SPANISH (*El País*, 8.11.1989)
"La razón por la que este tipo de lucha tiende a prevalecer en nuestra sociedad se debe *al hecho de que una nueva forma de poder político se ha desarrollado* de manera continua desde el siglo XVI.
'... is due to *the fact that* there emerged a new form of political power ...'

Speakers of languages like FRENCH are rather restrictive in this respect. They prefer to introduce an additional verbal element in order to attenuate the communicative 'scandal' of a clause depending on a noun: this is the type *la question de savoir si* instead of the type *the question whether*.

2.2. Inferential processes

Reference tracking by nominal substitution needs an inferential backing based on our encyclopaedic knowledge (→ art. 47, § 5). Usually, such processes are triggered and stimulated by the presence of deictic elements (e.g., "*this* high frequency", "*esta* elevada frecuencia" in example [4].) Often definite articles will do:

(7) (a) Il y avait une bicyclette dans le jardin. *Les rayons* étaient faussés.
    There was a bike in the garden. *The spokes* were broken.
   (b) Nous nous approchâmes d'une maison. *La cheminée* fumait. (Charolles 1999)
    We approached a house. *The chimney* was smoking.

The inferential process is more demanding in cases like the following ones:

(8) Il y avait une bicyclette dans le jardin. *Le moyeu* (or: *le rayon*) était faussé.
    There was a bike in the garden. *The hub* (or: *the spoke*) was broken.

There does not seem to be a major problem in decoding whenever the part in the following sentence is an integrated part of the whole evoked in the first one: as are spokes in the case of a bicycle or the chimney with respect to a house (there are houses with only one chimney). But since a bike has two hubs and 64 to 72 spokes, it takes us a little bit more time to guess what could be meant in cases like (8).

Suffice it to mention in the present context that Roland Harweg (^{1}1964, ^{2}1979: 178−260) gives an invaluable "phenomenology of pronominal linking" listing and classifying more or less all the possibilities existing in this domain. The cases under discussion would fall under the heading "Text-Kontiguitäts-Substitution" (Harweg ^{2}1979: 192−99); another case in point is the theory of supposition as developed by the medieval schoolmen: → art. 14, § 3.2.3 devoted especially to William of Ockham (1285−1349); Peter of Spain (1219−1277) should also be mentioned in this context (e.g., Petrus Hispanus 1577).

2.3. Substitution by zero

A special case of substitution is zero anaphora or 'anaphorical ellipsis' (De Beaugrande & Dressler 1981: 72). A case was already mentioned in example (2) at the end of § 1. This technique is well-known in Indoeuropean languages. Essentially, it is based on two preconditions: (a) The verbs of the language have to be specified as to the grammatical person of the subject ('concord'). (b) As a rule, the participant functioning as the grammatical subject is identical with the subject of the preceding sentence (same subject or ss-constraint).

CLASSICAL GREEK and CLASSICAL LATIN are cases in point. Whenever the ss-constraint is applicable, no subject has to be expressed in a subsequent clause. Languages using this technique tend to develop a special morpheme signaling a different subject (DS-condition) in the subsequent clause. In CLASSICAL GREEK this is the function of the particle *de*, in late LATIN it is *autem*, *vero*, sometimes also *sed* at the beginning of the next clause. As in the case of GREEK *de*, grammatical tradition has it that the meaning of these signals is 'but'. However, one had better leave them untranslated. − For examples see Selig 1992: 138 ff.; Raible 1992: 71−75.

2.4. Diathesis, clefting, extraposition

Reference tracking is one of the reasons why the order of clausal elements can be important. A referent that remains identical in the subsequent clause is like a link − or a pivot (Foley & Van Valin 1984) between clauses − and a pivotal element is always best placed between the parts to be linked. In the case of entire clauses this confers a privileged position on the head of a clause (or, as can be seen in some techniques of clause linking, to the end of the preceding one).

It is well known that order plays a different part in different languages. In some languages, speakers are relatively free, in others the possibilities of changing a "ratified" order are rather restricted. Nevertheless, no language can do without basic ordering principles: hearers have to know beforehand what most probably will come next. This means that there can be a conflict between the expected ordering principle and the one a speaker intends to choose.

The answer to this conflict are institutionalized strategies allowing speakers to "legally" violate basic ordering principles: linguists call them clefting, *genus verbi*, *vox*, diathesis (→ art. 67−69), extraposition, etc., on the main clause level where they allow speakers to bring to the fore those elements that seem relevant to them.

A good example are such Creole languages whose speakers have not developed a technique of diathesis yet. A case in point is GUADELOUPE CREOLE.

(9) (a) GUADELOUPE CREOLE (Ludwig 1990: 34f.)
  Ijénie ka bat Ijenn.
  Eugenie IPFV strike Eugene
  "Eugenie slaps Eugene."
 (b) *bat Ijénie ka bat Ijenn.*
  strike Eugenie IPFV strike Eugene
  "Eugenie truly strikes Eugene."
 (c) *sé bat Ijénie ka bat Ijenn.*
  it.is strike Eugenie IPFV strike Eugene
  "idem."
 (d) *sé Ijénie ki ka bat Ijenn.*
  it.is Eugenie who IPFV strike Eugene
  "It is Eugenie who slaps Eugene."
 (e) *sé Ijénie i ka bat Ijenn.*
  it.is Eugenie she IPFV strike Eugene
  "idem."
 (f) *sé Ijenn Ijénie ka bat.*
  it.is Eugene Eugenie IPFV strike
  "It is Eugene whom Eugenie strikes."

As in many CREOLES, the speaker is free to focus not only on the Agent or the Patient, s/he may even highlight the action by fronting the verb.

Nonetheless, as was shown by Sibylle Kriegel (1996) for SEYCHELLES and MAURITIUS CREOLE, speakers of such languages tend to grammaticalize a new passive form, above all under the pressure of beginning literacy. In other languages, the technique of clefting may even lead to an 'upgrading' of finite verbs by a phenomenon called 'enunciative' (Pusch 1999; 2001; see below § 6).

2.5. Substitution by dummies

Very often, inferential processes (see above § 2.2) also hold for substitution by the dummies we use for nouns, i. e. most often pronouns: here the problem lies in the scope of pronominal anaphora or cataphora. In the following example, the index letters added to the nominals and noun groups (and to the corresponding verbs in case the noun groups are grammatical subjects) show to some extent how reference maintenance functions in a large body of languages.

(10) SPANISH (Sociedad Chilena de Ciencias del Mar, Boletín mayo 2000)
"$_1$Las Jornadas de Ciencias del Mar$_i$ constituyen$_i$ una importante tribuna para el rápido intercambio del conocimiento científico y tecnológico generado en el país. $_2$Los numerosos Simposios, Conferencias y Mesas Redondas, que han tenido lugar durante estas$_i$, han ofrecido un foro para la discusión de los problemas y temas contingentes en Ciencias del Mar$_j$. $_3$Las Jornadas$_i$ han contribuido$_i$ además a difundir el quehacer [the knowhow] en Ciencias del Mar$_j$ entre los estudiantes Universitarios$_k$ de áreas afines a las Ciencias del Mar$_j$, privilegiandolas$_j$ con una masiva asistencia. $_4$*Por lo tanto*, las jornadas$_i$ han ofrecido$_i$ a varias generaciones de jóvenes estudiantes$_k$, un testimonio de cómo se genera el conocimiento en Ciencias del Mar$_j$, contribuyendo *por este medio$_l$* a formar y educar. $_5$Desde 1994 la Corporación ha implementado un sistema de becas para jóvenes investigadores$_{ki}$ con la finalidad de ayudarles$_{ki}$ con los costos de asistencia a este evento$_i$."

As can be easily recognized, the nominal syntagms *Jornadas de Ciencias del Mar* and *Ciencias del Mar* ('oceanography') make up the backbone of this short passage. But in spite of this system of reference tracking, it remains unclear what we should regard as the scope of *por lo tanto* 'therefore' at the beginning of sentence$_4$. Does it refer to sentence$_3$, or to sentences$_{1-3}$? An answer to this question would need a very close and repeated reading, thus showing that linking processes might be more sloppy above the sentence level.

Instead, it is perfectly clear that the scope of the cataphorically used interpretator *testimonio* in sentence$_4$ is the complement clause *se genera el conocimiento en Ciencias del Mar*: both are syntactically linked by *de cómo*, verbally: 'evidence *of how* knowledge in oceanography is generated'. The same thing holds for the following "contribuyendo *por este medio* a formar y educar" − 'thus contributing to education'.

The example of *por lo tanto* 'therefore' shows at the same time that there exists another kind of interpretators: They can as well refer to entire text passages, and they interpret these passages, too − but in quite another way: they establish one of the more or less SPECIFIC RELATIONS — first mentioned in §1, point 3 and henceforward represented with small capitals — that hold between the following sentence and its antecedent(s). In the case of *por lo tanto* the antecedent is seen as a CAUSE, the clause introduced by *por lo tanto* as a CONSEQUENCE.

3. Hierarchy: downgrading clauses

There are more relations of this kind expressed in text (10): At the end of sentence₄ we find the relation of MANNER: '*contributing in this manner* to education' (*contribuyendo por este medio a formar y educar*). Sentence₅ reads: "Since 1994, the Corporation has implemented a system of grants for young scientists *in order to* (*con la finalidad de*) help them reduce the expenses necessary for attending this event". Here the relation of FINALITY is expressed by *con la finalidad de*, i. e. 'with the aim of', consisting of PREP. + ART. + NOUN + PREP., a prepositional group. In example (1) we already encountered *with a formal censure of the president seeming unlikely*, a syntagm that was qualified as a "hybrid between clause and nominal", the special relation holding in this case being open to interpretation.

All these examples show at least two things:

(a) relations like FINALITY, CAUSALITY, CONSEQUENCE, CONDITION, MANNER play an important part in clause linking.
(b) At the same time, there are many possibilities expressing them on different levels of syntactic hierarchy.

The first aspect will be partly treated in § 4, the second one will receive a closer look in the following subsection.

3.1. Aggregation vs. integration

Let us take the example of CAUSALITY as a relation frequently expressed in texts. The most simple way would be the sheer juxtaposition of two clauses as in examples (11a/b):

(11) (a) Joan is ill. She remains at home.

Or with an appropriate exchange of the pronoun and its nominal antecedent:

(b) Joan remains at home. She is ill.

This shows that CAUSALITY, on this level, is a matter of inference, too, and that even the order of the clauses has no importance. Order matters in the next examples where 'this is why', resuming the previous clause, gives it a causal meaning:

(12) (a) Joan is ill. *This is why* she remains at home.
(b) Joan bleibt zu Hause. Sie ist *nämlich* krank.
(c) Joan reste chez elle. *Car* elle est malade.
(d) Joan est malade. *C'est pourquoi* elle reste chez elle.

According to a classical conception of grammar, examples (11a/b) and (12a/d) are specimens of coordination. Example (13b) would be seen as 'subordinating' instead, with order again losing its importance:

(13) (a) *Since* Joan is ill, she remains at home.
(b) Joan remains at home *because* she is ill.

Examples (14a/b) would be said to exhibit subordination, too. Whereas in examples (13a/b) the verb was still finite, now it has become nonfinite, though:

(14) (a) *Being ill*, Joan remains at home.
(b) *With* her daughter Rachel *being ill*, Joan remains at home.

The first version is with same subject (SS), the second one with different subject (DS). Its nonfiniteness makes *being ill* depend on the finite verb of another clause, thus establishing a clear syntactic relation. The character of the relation remains open to interpretation, though, like in the above examples (11a/b). The relations that are usually expressed by such gerunds, infinitives and the like are CAUSALITY, SIMULTANEITY, MANNER, CONDITION and CONCESSIVITY. FINALITY and CONSECUTIVITY seem to be excluded at least in GERMANIC and ROMANCE languages (Stump 1985: 41 ff.; Raible 1992: 79−87; König 1995).

In examples (14a/b), with the nonfinite verb forms, we have reached a certain point on a scale between verbiness and nouniness (→ art. 38; contributions in Vogel 2000), where *being ill* still has verbal characteristics (e.g., *being ill* as opposed to *having been ill*). How should we classify the following example, then?

(15) *On account of* her illness, Joan remained at home.

In this case, the relation that is expressed is again very clear: CAUSALITY. Nevertheless, it would make no sense to speak of 'subordination'. This is why, instead of using 'coordination' and 'subordination', one should prefer more neutral candidates — as are for instance *aggregation* and *integration* (Raible 1992; Bickel 1991: 58 ff. uses integration in a similar context). They are to be seen as the extreme points of a scale admitting a great number of intermediate techniques.

In order to show the remaining, still more integrative possibilities: instead of prepositional noun groups one could use simple prepositions like in (16):

(16) *Wegen ihrer Krankheit blieb Joan heute zu Hause.*

If a language has a rich case marking system, the odds are that one of the case markers will be sufficient to express, e.g., CAUSALITY: In LATIN this is *ablativus causae*, in CLASSICAL GREEK *dativus causae*, in FINNISH an adessive in an INSTRUMENTAL sense:

(17) LATIN (Plautus, *Amphitruo* verse 1118)
mihi   horror
P.PRON.1P.SG.DAT   horror-SG.NOM
membra   misero
limb-PL.ACC   poor-SG.DAT
percipit   dictis
strike-3SG.PERF words-PL.ABL
tuis.
your-2PL.POSS.ABL
"On account of your words, horror struck the limbs of the poor of me."

(18) CLASSICAL GREEK
Xérxēs   tēn
Xerxes-SG.NOM ART.DET.SG.AKK
thálassan orgē̂
sea-SG.ACC wrath-SG.DAT
emastígōsen.
to.whip-3P.SG.AOR.ACT
"Anger made Xerxes whip the sea."

(19) FINNISH
halon   puita
split-1SG.PRES wood-PL.PARTIT
kirvee-llä.
hatchet-SG.ADESS
"I am splitting wood with a/the hatchet."

In the CLASSICAL GREEK example, we could as well use *hyp'orgēs*, i. e. a preposition ('out of wrath'), thus showing the well-known relationship between case marking and nominal affixes (prepositions, postpositions).

3.2. Junction: a universal dimension of language as a conceptual frame for linking techniques

The scale of techniques extending between aggregation and integration is a good *tertium comparationis* for the comparison of languages (→ art. 1, §§ 5.2; 5.3; art. 27, § 4; § 5).

Since all languages have clauses, and since all languages have to fulfill the task of linking individual propositions into larger wholes, the two extreme solutions cannot but exist in all languages: at one end of the scale, at the pole of aggregation, there are two clauses without explicit linking. What remains at the other end of the scale, the pole of integration, is one totally integrated single clause to which, in turn, another one may be added, thus giving the scale the shape of a Moebius strip.

In all languages, such scales represent at the same time a continuum between verbiness and nouniness (it should be clear, though, that 'nouns' and 'verbs' have different implementations, too: → art. 38; art. 54; art. 1, § 3, point 3). This means that somewhere on the scale there has to be a turning point where the respective techniques lose all their verbal properties, being fully integrated into the realm of nouns instead.

In the case of lots of European languages, the first purely nominal technique are prepositional groups like ENGLISH *on account of, on behalf of, with respect to, in spite of*; SPANISH *con finalidad de, (con) respecto a, al respecto de, a causa de, debido a, gracias a, merced a, por causa de*; FRENCH *à cause de, par suite de, pour cause de, en vertu de*; ITALIAN *a causa di, grazie a, a forza di, in virtù di*; GERMAN *infolge von, aufgrund von, in Bezug auf*, etc.

In most cases, such prepositional groups occur for the first time in juridical texts. This is due to the fact that jurists like precision (the underlying idea is ruling out ambiguities) and that prepositional groups offer the most precise possibility of expressing certain relations. As a result, they are relatively rare in other textual genres. Above all, they tend not to occur in the genres of spoken language, thus showing once more the relation holding between the linking techniques and the *Ausbau* of a language system by scripturality. Given the universality of the scale between aggregation and integration, the difference between languages lies in the fact that speakers of different languages may implement different linking techniques. Some of them will be presented in subsections 3.2.1 to 3.2.8.

3.2.1. Intonation

Even before they understand language, babies and toddlers understand intonation contours. And before children discover segmental means of clause linking, they use intonation to this end:

(20) GERMAN (Florian, age 2;4)
Hat der Folian geweint. Hat die Mama liebhabt.
"Has Florian cried. Did mom caress."

(21) *Jetzt zieh ich aus die Schuhe. Jetzt geh ich nicht mehr Garten.*
"Now I take off the shoes. Now I don't go garden any more."

Alongside a clear syntactic parallelism, the child uses a characteristic intonation to link these clauses.

When analyzing the techniques of clause linkage in SEYCHELLES CREOLE, Susanne Michaelis — inspired by Marianne Mithun (1988) — discovered two techniques based essentially on intonation: 'comma intonation' and 'integrative intonation' (Michaelis 1994: 41–50). Comma intonation signals that the information to be given has not come to its end, but that the following information unit should be seen as a conceptually distinct aspect of the whole.

(22) SEYCHELLES CREOLE (Michaelis 1994: 41, 48)
*Mon konpran pyos * anmaser*
1P.SG can hoe C-INT picker
*koko * netway propriyete*
coconut C-INT clean propriety
son met la.
POSS master there
"I am an expert in farming, (I worked as) picker of coconuts, (I) kept clean the propriety of one's master."

By contrast, integrative intonation — i.e. with no intonation break — describes subparts of what is conceived of as a single event (Mithun 1988: 335):

(23) SEYCHELLES CREOLE (Michaelis 1994: 46 f.)
La nou a tire la nou
there 1P.PL MOD quarry there 1P.PL
a vini nou a anmennen
MOD come 1P.PL MOD bring
zet anba langar.
throw down hangar
"Then we quarried (guano), we came and got (it) in order to store (it) in the hangar."

Since integrative intonation makes the pieces of information subparts of a whole, it is not surprising that these parts follow in chronological order.

The basic strategy underlying such phenomena has been aptly described by Brigitte K. Halford (1996): intonation contours reflect units of cognitive planning. This is why even highly complex syntax can be well understood, provided the speaker uses an appropriate intonation, and this is why, a priori, intonation is also a good means to link clauses — whether it is the principal strategy or only an additional one, supporting for instance one of the following techniques.

3.2.1. The technique of clause chaining

Sentences as privileged units refer to situations, events, processes, states. But normally an individual clause is not sufficient to express what we intend to convey to others. This means that the complex representation we want to utter has to be decomposed into a whole series of such clauses. This, again, amounts to saying that, in order to express a coherent whole, speakers have to tag the resulting clauses such that hearers have a fair chance of reconstructing the intended whole. With a metaphor coined by G. Pilhofer (1933) in his grammar of KÂTE (New Guinea) and taken over by Balthasar Bickel (1991), speakers have to lay out tracks (*Fährtenlegen*) that can be discovered by hearers.

In an earlier section, a technique has already been mentioned where the tracks laid out were personal (substitution by nouns, pronouns, zero anaphora, *Personalfährte* in the wording of Pilhofer; see above §§ 2.1; 2.3). There was no difference in the degree of finiteness between the verbs of the respective subsequent clauses, though.

Especially speakers of languages with the basic order SOV have developed a different technique called clause chaining. At the end of a clause the speaker signals to the hearer whether the actual clause is to be seen as downgraded, and whether the subsequent clause will be same subject or different subject. In the words of Thomas Müller-Bardey (1988) who gave a good overview over switch reference in general: "Scheinbar integrierte Sachverhalte werden in Folgen sukzessiver Komponenten-Prädikationen zerlegt, wobei das Subjekt jeweils als Scharnier dient".

HOPI, a UTO-AZTECAN language, has a rather sophisticated system of clause chaining. It functions in the following way (Stahlschmidt 1983; for this phenomenon in North American Indian languages cf. Jacobsen 1983): if the hearer is supposed to expect a different participant as subject of the following clause, the verb closing the first clause ends with the suffix *-q*. As a result, the hearer will have to switch to a different subject (hence the term 'switch reference' first used by William H. Jacobsen [1967]). In case the speaker intends to use the same subject in the following clause, s/he cannot but specify the SPECIFIC RELATION that should hold between the actual and the intended following proposition.

Simplifying things somewhat: given a SS-condition, the first question a HOPI speaker has to decide is whether the relationship should be interpreted as TEMPORAL or not. If this is not the case, the relation will be CONDITIONAL, signaled by the suffix -e'. If the relationship is to be interpreted as TEMPORAL, one possibility is SIMULTANEITY ("concursive relation"), marked by the suffix -kyang. If a simple ANTERIOR/POSTERIOR relation is intended, the suffix -t will do. When TEMPORALITY has to be interpreted as CAUSALITY instead, this is marked by the suffix -qe.

What happens at the end of the first clause can be repeated at the end of the next one (hence 'clause chaining') — until the sequence is closed by an "absolute" form. This is why Pilhofer (1933) qualified the preceding verb forms as *Satzinnenformen* or *Durchgangsformen* as opposed to the absolute *Satzendformen* or *Wechselformen*. — In his grammar of FORE, another New Guinea language, Graham Scott (1978) quotes the example of a woman who was asked to tell in short what had happened to her that day. She did it in one single grammatical sentence that contained about 40 predications, only the last one ("I came down here") ending with an absolute declarative form (Müller-Bardey 1988: 185—88).

Some examples will demonstrate how clause chaining functions in HOPI.

(24) HOPI (Stahlschmidt 1983: 599)
Noq yaw Tötölö-t
and QUOT Grasshopper
nöm-'at   nova-law-q pam
wife-his-SG.NOM eat-DS   he
yaw nöma-y   'awintaq yaw
QUOT wife-his-SG.OBJ tell-DS   QUOT
Isaw pasa-yamuy   aqle
Coyote field-their-PL.OBJ near
maknum-kyango   put'aw
hunt-SS.SIMULT.REL 3P.SG.ALLAT
pitu.
arrive-ABS.FORM
"And while Grasshopper's wife prepared the meal, he told her that, when Coyote was hunting on the fields close to them, he had approached them."

A somewhat simpler example shows temporal sequentiality:

(25) HOPI (Stahlschmidt 1983: 521)
Qavongvaq   yaw   su'ich
The-next-morning QUOT   very-soon
talavai Peeni   taha-hoya-i
morning Peeni-NOM uncle-little-POSS
'a-mum
with-3P.SG.-SOZ
moro-yuwsi-na-t
donkey-SG.NOM-garment-SG.NOM-CAUS-SEQ.REL.SS
nitkya-ta-t
food.for.the.journey-SG.NOM-SEQ.REL.SS
tuuwalo-to.
keep.guard-ABS.PROJECTIVE
"The next day very soon in the morning, Peeni with his little uncle saddled the donkey, got their provisions and started in order to keep guard (on the field)."

While examples like the one alluded to in the grammar of FORE might amaze us as exotic, it is perhaps appropriate to point out that a text in LATIN or CLASSICAL GREEK could contain the same 40 clauses, this time for instance linked all by zero anaphora (although, admittedly, without downgrading). Similar things could even be done with converbs (§ 3.2.5) in European and Eurasian languages, to say nothing of 'stylistic' techniques like *style indirect libre* (§ 3.2.8) or the FRENCH style judgement mentioned in → art. 1 § 2. For similar phenomena in TURKIC languages → art. 122.

3.2.3. The technique of adverbial conjunctions

In this technique of linking, one of the clauses — mostly headed by a conjunction — is downgraded ('subordinate clause') and functions as an optional adverbial modifier of the main clause. The first examples were (13a/b). The technique is very common in most of the European languages. It is extensively described by Bernd Kortmann (→ art. 63). As a result, some additions will be sufficient in the present article.

Kortmann, too, underlines the fact that the *Ausbau* of this technique should be seen as stimulated by literacy. Already at the beginning of the last century, Eduard Schwyzer (1914) drew on literacy as a decisive factor explaining the affinity existing in many respects between European languages. A good example is the *Consolidated version of the treaty on European Union* of 1997 (the 'Treaty of Maastricht'). § 40 (3) reads as follows:

(26) (a) GERMAN: Die Entscheidung gilt als angenommen, *es sei denn*, der Rat beschließt mit qualifizierter Mehrheit, sie zurückzustellen.
 (b) ENGLISH: The decision shall be deemed to be taken *unless* the Council, acting by a qualified majority, decides to hold it in abeyance.
 (c) FRENCH: La décision est réputée approuvée, *à moins que* le Conseil, statuant à la majorité qualifiée, *ne décide* de la tenir en suspens.
 (d) ITALIAN: La decisione si intende adottata *a meno che* il Consiglio, deliberando a maggioranza qualificata, *decida* di tenerla in sospeso.
 (e) SPANISH: La decisión se considerará adoptada *salvo que* el Consejo *decida*, por mayoría cualificada, mantenerla en suspenso.
 (f) PORTUGUESE: A decisão considera-se tomada, *excepto se* o Conselho, deliberando por maioria qualificada, *decidir* suspendê-la.
 (g) FINNISH: Päätös katsotaan tehdyksi, *jollei* neuvosto määräenemmistöllä *päätä* sen lepäämään jättämisestä.
 (h) MODERN GREEK: I apófasi logízete óti échi liftí *ektós an* to Simbúlio, me idikí pliopsifía, apofasísi na paramíni to étema ekkremés.

With the exception of GERMAN, where the normal solution *es sei denn, daß* is slightly different, the languages cited here use the same kind of excluding conjunction heading an integrated clause with a verb we usually would qualify as finite. This holds even for FINNISH where another construction would have been possible. (In the present case, the conjunction *jollei* has two components, the conjunction proper and the negation verb *ei* marked for 3P.SG whereas the negated verb *päättä* is nonfinite.) The tendency favoring the use of adverbial junction corresponds to the overall picture conveyed by the EU treaty.

We get the same 'European' picture with respect to the additional condition expressed as *acting by a qualified majority* in the ENGLISH version: the ENGLISH, FRENCH, ITALIAN, PORTUGUESE versions use one of the 'converbal' forms discussed below in § 3.2.5, whereas GERMAN, SPANISH, FINNISH and MODERN GREEK prefer one of the still more integrative techniques: a prepositional group (the type *mit qualifizierter Mehrheit*) or case-marking: *määrä-enemmistö-llä* [number-majority-ADESS] in the FINNISH example (for this technique see § 3.2.7).

That literacy plays a part in the evolution of such techniques is confirmed by cases in which a European language, e.g., FRENCH, is reduced to the role of a purely spoken language as for instance in the case of LOUISIANA FRENCH (Stäbler 1995; 1995a). Related phenomena may also be linked to language obsolescence (→ art. 118). Other cases in point are CREOLE languages which lost most of the integrating techniques of the European donor language (Raible 1994), leaving speakers with the task of reinventing new ones (Ludwig 1996).

A good example of re-invention is PAPIAMENTO, a Creole language spoken in the Caribbean (Aruba, Bonaire, Curaçao): speakers can downgrade verbs by means of a new conjunctive ('suphuntivo', a verb form without particles; Maurer 1988: 243 ff., 341 f.) and by the gerundial forms (Maurer 1988: 67 f.) discussed in § 3.2.5.

3.2.4. Clauses as participants

Clauses headed by an adverbial conjunction are integrated into a main clause to such an extent that they clearly take on the function of (peripheral) participants. This could not be said, for instance, in the case of clause chaining (§ 3.2.2). The technique of adverbial conjunctions does not generate, in principle, a major problem for the hearer since the conjunction heading the clause functions as a syntactic hinge, indicating into the bargain the SPECIFIC RELATION holding between the adverbial and the main clause.

Since one of the most important topics of human communication is communication itself, there exist a lot of verbs expressing, by their semantic content, communicative or related activities: above all *verba dicendi, sentiendi et sciendi*, encompassing all the speech act verbs. As the participant function they assume is usually the function of an object, or even a subject, this leaves the speakers of this language with the problem how to tag in an adequate way such embedded prepositions. Since the participants functioning as subjects and objects belong to the very core of a predication (§ 7.1), this is something rather unusual. One answer may be special conjunctions for complement clauses, a topic treated to some extent elsewhere (→ art. 74).

In the present context, it should only be mentioned that speakers of ROMANCE languages, like those of their LATIN mother, tend to use — as an additional tag signaling clausal integration — a mood called 'conjunctive' or 'subjunctive'. This is not only the case with speech act complements. The ROMANCE examples (26c to 26f) show that this may hold even for adverbial clauses. Since the information given by the default mood 'indicative' is 'communicative responsibility of the speaker', the subjunctive of necessity conveys a reduction of this responsibility: the hearer can always contradict a statement made in indicative mood, never one in the conjunctive or subjunctive (or in whatever modally downgraded verb form).

This leaves speakers of such languages with a problem generated by a certain kind of matrix verbs in the main clause: viz. verbs expressing, by their meaning, that the speaker can and does assume communicative responsibility. These are above all the *verba dicendi, sentiendi et sciendi* ("I confirm, assert, say ...", the verbs of perception and of knowing "I see, have seen, know ..."). The solution are 'regular exceptions' to the subordinating mood, i. e. the choice of indicative instead.

In this context, CLASSICAL GREEK and LATIN are interesting cases because they use a somewhat different technique to this end: it is called *accusativus cum participio* and *accusativus cum infinitivo*. This means that the speakers of these languages developed a technique allowing them to treat the embedded clause as an accusative — by giving its subject and, if this is possible, also its verb (finite verb downgraded as participle) a case marker.

In the following example (drawn from Longus, *Daphnis and Chloe*, book III, § 15) the main clause reads "Lycaenium seeing Daphnis ... coveted him luring him by gifts". The 'trick' attenuating the 'scandal' of a clause serving as a core participant of the main clause lies in the fact that "Daphnis" has *two* functions in this complex sentence: he is object to 'seeing' and at the same time subject of the embedded clause that explains what the woman saw: that every day he drove his goats by to the fields and back. Similar to its subject, the action of 'driving by' as a participle has the accusative marker that downgrades the whole clause.

(27)   CLASSICAL GREEK:
haútē hē Lykaínion
this DET.SG.FEM Lykainion-SG.NOM.FEM
horôsa
see-PRT.AOR.ACT.NOM.FEM
tòn Dáphnin
DET.SG.MASC Daphnis-ACC
kat'hekástēn hēméran
every day
pareláunonta
drive.by-PRT.PRES.ACT.SG.ACC.MASC
tàs aîgas
the goats-PL.ACC.FEM
hēôthen eis nomēn
in the morning onto pasture
nýktōr ek nomēs
on nights from pasture
epethýmēsen   erastēn
covet-3P.AOR.ACT lover-SG.ACC.MASC
ktēsasthai   dōrois
possess-INF.AOR.MED gifts-PL.DAT
deleásasa.
lure-PRT.AOR.ACT.SG.NOM.FEM
"This Lykainion, observing Daphnis as every day early in the morning he drove his goats by to the fields and home again at the first twilight, had a great mind to beguile the youth by gifts to become her lover."

The embedding procedure is repeated at the end: "she coveted to possess [infinitive] (him) as a lover".

The speakers of ENGLISH are developing a quite similar technique with *for* + ACC + *to* + INF. Christian Mair gives, among other things, a dense description of all types of ENGLISH infinitival constructions (Mair 1990).

Tagging embedded clauses by case marking, i. e., treating them as nouns, not only avoids the problems generated by the fact that a mood is used in order to integrate clauses (Raible 1983; 1992a). It is above all characteristic of techniques that will be described in the following subsection.

The 'scandal' of a clause functioning as core-participant of another clause may be attenuated by other means, e.g., by the interpretators that were already mentioned above in §§ 2.1; 2.4: one of their function was interpreting a clause as a speech act. This is in turn why they can be used — as subjects or objects of the main predication — in a *cataphorical* way in order to introduce a subsequent clause they interpret beforehand: this is the aforementioned type *the idea that*, SPANISH *la idea de que* — see above examples (5), (6) or sentence 4 of example (10).

3.2.5. The technique making use of converbs – gerunds, infinitives, participles, etc.

The more a verb loses its finite properties (in European languages 'finiteness' usually means marked for person, mood, number, tense, aspect, diathesis ...), the more it becomes nonfinite. This means that there exists, according to the number of verbal characteristics lost or left, a scale between finiteness and nonfiniteness, not a clear-cut distinction (see below § 7.2). The resulting forms on the finiteness/infiniteness scale are called 'infinitives', 'gerunds', 'participles'.

Many linguists call these forms 'converbs', thus indicating that they are (a) less finite, i. e. dependent verb forms with (b) an adverbial function (Haspelmath 1995: 26; Nedjalkov 1995: 97 ff.; Nedjalkov 1998 with a somewhat different definition).

In many languages, especially European and Eurasian ones (Bisang 1998: 730 ff.; for Turkic languages: Johanson 1995 and → art. 122), converbs are an important technique of integration, typically mixing verbal and nominal properties.

A case in point is FINNISH. Apart from participles, speakers of FINNISH can use four infinitives. Grammarians call them infinitives I to IV. All of them lack modal information. The most 'verbal' one is infinitive I: Apart from the fact that it can function as an object (without case suffix), it only takes one case, translative:

(28) FINNISH (Raible 1992: 94–103)
isä toi
Father-SG.NOM bring-3SG.PAST
mansikoita
strawberry-PL.PARTIT
syödä-kse-mme.
eat-INF$_I$-TRANSL-1PL.POSS
"The father was bringing strawberries for us to eat".

Personal information is expressed by 'nominal' means, i. e. a possessive suffix.

Infinitive II admits only two cases, inessive and instructive, the latter being one of the marginal cases. The subject of the embedded representation appears as a genitive.

(29) FINNISH
meidän
we-PL.GEN
kirjoitta-e-ssa-mme hän
write-INF$_{II}$-1PL.INESS-1PL.POSS he-3P.SG
luki sanomalehteä.
read-3SG.PAST newspaper-SG.PARTIT

"While we were writing, he was reading a/the newspaper".

Like infinitive II, infinitive III always has case marking, taking still more cases, though. The most frequent ones are inessive, elative, illative, adessive, and abessive.

(30) FINNISH
Vain etukäteen vuokran
only beforehand rent-SG.ACC
maksa-ma-lla voi
pay-INF$_{III}$-ADESS can-3IMPERS.PRES
vuokrata huoneen.
rent-INF$_I$ room-SG.ACC
"Only by paying cash beforehand may one rent the room."

(31) *poika lipsahti*
boy-SG.NOM slip-3P.PAST
baariin kenenkään
snackbar-SG.ILLAT anybody-SG.GEN
huomaa-ma-tta.
remark-INF$_{III}$-ABESS
"Without being remarked by anybody, the boy slipped into the snackbar."

Infinitive IV is a verbal lexeme with nominal properties. It is open to all case suffixes.

(32) *hallituksen kukistu-minen*
government-SG.GEN fall-INF$_{IV}$-NOM
olisi kohtalokasta.
be-3P.COND momentous-SG.PARTIT
"The falling of the government would be momentous."

The last example clearly shows the principle behind a great number of nonfinite constructions. The subject of the embedded proposition appears as a genitive that determines the infinitival form: the type "the government falls" is transformed into "the falling of the government".

Inasmuch as participles are open to all case markers, they have, like infinitive IV, the strongest nominal features. At the same time, they have more verbal characteristics than the latter in that they are marked for tense and diathesis. In line with their verbal and nominal properties, participles may be used in verbal and nominal contexts: as adjectives determining nouns like relative clauses, or as verbal kernels of embedded clauses:

(33) FINNISH
hän on Jumalaa
he-3P.SG be-3P.SG.PRES God-SG.PARTIT
pelkäävä mies.
fear-PART.PRES.ACT.-SG.NOM man-SG.NOM
"He is a godfearing man."

(34) *pojan   syö-ty-ä*
      boy-SG.GEN eat-PART.PERF.PASS-PARTIT
      lähdimme.
      leave-1PL.PAST
      "We left after the boy had eaten."

Those familiar with CLASSICAL LATIN will feel that example (34) could have something in common with LATIN *ablativus absolutus* (cf. Müller-Lancé 1994, especially with respect to its evolution). Its domain of application is much more restricted, though: example (34) could not easily be translated into LATIN by an *ablativus absolutus*.

As regards tense, it tends to disappear relatively soon in infinitivization, but sometimes it may be expressed by nominal means instead. A case in point is SPANISH, where the preposition *tras* 'after' is totally sufficient in order to express a relationship of ANTERIOR to POSTERIOR, even though in this case an infinitive perfect would be available:

(35) SPANISH (*El País*, 11.9.2000)
      "Las investigaciones comenzaron a principio de año, *tras detectarse* un fuerte aumento en el número de las ciudadanas de Europa del Este que exercían la prostitución en la Casa del Campo."
      ... after discover-INF.PRES.REFL ...
      "Investigations started at the beginning of the year *when/after* a considerable augmentation of the number of citizens from Eastern Europe who practised prostitution in the Casa del Campo *was found*."

Generally speaking, one can say that the more a technique is 'nouny', the more are nominal means used in order to express relations holding between clauses. This is the case with the SPANISH preposition *tras* as well as with FINNISH case markers on infinitives: in example (28) translative case was used for the relation of FINALITY; adessive can be used for INSTRUMENTAL relations, inessive for SIMULTANEITY, etc.

This is tantamount to saying that on the one hand in many European languages the relation expressed by a gerund, infinitive, participle depends on the context, certain relations being practically excluded (see above § 3.1). On the other hand, we may state that in languages endowed with a rich case marking system a large set of 'adverbial' relations can be explicitly conveyed by converbs – thanks to their nouniness which admits case marking. As a result, in FINNISH even FINALITY can be expressed converbally (above example [28]).

Another interesting feature is that verbal downgrading implies a total loss of modal information (indicative or assertive mood), thus showing that downgrading by a special mood (conjunctive or subjunctive) is to be seen as a quite particular, if not exotic, linking technique (see above § 3.2.4 and below § 3.2.8).

Table 45.1 summarizes what has been said with respect to FINNISH.

3.2.6. The technique of verb serialization

By definition, the opposition between verbs and converbs presupposes an opposition between finite and nonfinite (given the scale between aggregation and integration, one should better say: less finite) verb forms. This makes sense above all in many European languages where finite verbs are obligatorily marked as to person, number, tense, mood, aspect, diathesis, assertion. Depending on how many of these features are lost, a lot of

Table 45.1: FINNISH infinitival linking techniques between verbiness and nouniness.

		expression of:			
		mood	person	tense, diathesis	cases
more verbal	1. participle used as verb	no	poss. suff.	yes	some
↑	2. infinitive I	no	poss. suff.	no	two
	3. infinitive II	no	poss. suff.	no	two
	4. infinitive III	no	no	no	many
↓	5. infinitive IV	no	no	no	all
less verbal	6. participle used as noun	no	no	partly	all

Desententialization starts with the loss of modal information and a continuous increase in nominal properties, above all in case marking. This allows speakers to 'nominally' express a large set of adverbial relations. Information as to the grammatical person may still be given in the more verbal techniques, though by nominal means. Tense tends to disappear soon, too. – For similar observations in HUICHOL (with an even larger number of intermediate steps due to a richer verbal system) → art. 41 § 9 and table 41.9.

ever more 'nouny' intermediate forms may come into existence.

If, however, the speakers of a language do not have to obligatorily mark verbs for all these features, there will be little room left for converbs and the like. This is the case with languages like CHINESE and VIETNAMESE where the finite/nonfinite distinction does not make any sense. In a language like JAPANESE, the distinction is based exclusively on the feature of ± past (Bisang 1998: 736−40). This is why such languages make use of a different linking technique. It is called 'verb series', where, formally speaking, the two (or more) verbs following one another are on a par.

As a specialist in the matter, Walter Bisang (1998: 732) gives the following definition:

"Verb serialization, as I understand it, is defined as the unmarked juxtaposition of two or more verbs or verb phrases (with or without subject and/or object), each of which would also be able to form a sentence on its own (Bisang 1992: 9). This definition is syntactic and can be morphological with regard to the markedness of the juxtaposition and with regard to the ability of a word to form a sentence on its own.
There are two different subtypes of verb serialization. If there is no grammaticalized verb in a sequence of verbs, we have 'verb serialization in a broad sense', which is in contrast to verb serialization influenced by grammaticalization which is monopredicative and which I call 'verb serialization in a narrow sense' ".

The following example will show, among other things, how this technique functions in CHINESE. There are four verbal elements following one another: 'to kneel', 'to go down', 'to come', and 'to beg'. 'To come' typically confers a deictic meaning on a verb or verbal syntagm it follows. This is like GERMAN 'her-fahren' vs. 'hin-fahren', or, vertically, 'hinauf-steigen' vs. 'herauf-steigen'. Except in lexicalised oppositions such as *bring* vs. *take* or *come* vs. *go*, this component is not translated into ENGLISH.

The component 'go down' expresses the movement of the person kneeling down. Since − according to the lack of a distinction between finite and nonfinite verb forms − it is not clear whether the fourth verbal element, 'to beg' should be integrated or not into the group made up by the three preceding verbs, there exist four different interpretations of the sentence.

(36) MANDARIN CHINESE (Li & Thompson 1973: 98 cited from Bisang 1998: 764)
Nǐ guì-xià-lái   qiú Zhāngsān.
you kneel-go.down-come beg Zhangsan

As FINALITY: "You knelt down in order to beg Zhansan."
As CONSECUTIVE action: "You knelt down and then begged Zhangsan."
As SIMULTANEOUS action: "You knelt down begging Zhangsan."
As alternating action: "You knelt down and begged Zangsan."

The first scholar who recognized the crucial role verb serialization (the current term has been invented much later, though) plays in CHINESE was Wilhelm von Humboldt (1827). In a well-known letter addressed to the French physician Jean Pierre Abel-Rémusat, he underlined the fact that, among other things, all the functions assumed by prepositions in European languages, are taken over by verbs in CHINESE. The *grande thèse* of Claude Hagège (1975) and, somewhat later, the masterly thesis of Walter Bisang (1992), had a similar importance.

Even if, in a strict sense, verb serialization should be limited to languages like MANDARIN CHINESE where no difference between finite and nonfinite verb forms is made, similar phenomena can be observed in languages where speakers distinguish different degrees of finiteness. This means that the more finite forms may have additional verbal features with respect to the less finite ones, or that the less finite ones exhibit additional features themselves − like the nominal markers observed in FINNISH. Bisang refers to such cases as 'asymmetric'. Grammaticalization can occur in all cases, though.

Some examples will be added. The conceptual domain chosen is in most cases 'to take': in order to do something with an object, very often one has to take it first. (The only CHINESE preposition in the original sense of the term, *bǎ*, an object marker, is derived from the verb 'to take'.) − The Far East examples are taken from Bisang (1992: 30 ff.).

(37) (a) THAI: he − take − book − read
"He is reading a book."
(b) KHMER: he − take − garment − directional verb − put − sun
"He puts the garments into the sun."
(c) VIETNAMESE: secretary − take − hand − put − directional verb − pocket
"The secretary put his hand into the pocket."
(d) KHMER: pupil − go − house − take − book − come − school − give − teacher
"The pupil went home and brought the book to the teacher in the school."

The following examples demonstrate how the second member of a verb-verb compound can be downgraded in languages where concord between subject and verb is obligatory.

(38) KILIVILA (Senft 1986: 152)
E   ka-me-si   o kwadewa
and 1P.EXCL-come-PL   to beach
e   ka-bia-si   ma-waga-si
and 1PL.EXCL-push-PL POSS.1PL-boat-PL
i-la   o kwadeva.
3P.UNMARKED-go to beach
"And we run ashore and push our boats onto the beach."

Here the verb in *the boats go* does not have its plural form, but the neutral 3rd person marker and no plural marking at the end (the fully-fledged finite form would be *i-la-si* instead of *i-la*).

Another downgrading feature may be the loss of a person marker on the non-first members of a verbal compound. This can be observed, e.g., in Creole languages like PRÍNCIPE CREOLE where 'full' verbs are specified by a personal affix when the subject remains identical (reference tracking by substitution, see above § 2.1). – Bold face marks the high tone.

(39) PRÍNCIPE CREOLE (Günther 1973: 122)
eli myè se wè   ze awa
then woman his go-PFV get water
tâ   wè kaschi feze ròmòsu
take go house make meal
"Then his wife went for water (and) brought (it) to the house (in order to) prepare the meal."

In the following example the verb *da*, in addition to the loss of the person marker *e* 's/he', has its low tone, not the high one it would have as a verb in its own right. In this case, loss of the high tone might signal a further step in grammaticalization with *da* functioning as a preposition enlarging the valency of the verbal concept.

(40) PRÍNCIPE CREOLE (Günther 1973: 122)
òra   ki   òmi   sé   schiga
hour when husband POSS   arrive-PFV
kaschi e   pwe   ròmòsu
house s/he-3P.SG put-PFV   meal
da 'li
give him
"When her husband came home, she served the meal for him."

Another means frequently used in ROMANCE CREOLES in order to reduce finiteness is imperfectivity as opposed to perfectivity: imperfectivity is usually felt as less finite (see Hopper & Thompson 1980; for examples see Raible 1992: 61–71; Michaelis 1994; Ludwig 1996; see below § 7.2).

Verb serialization can be seen as a construction kit for the expression of complex content. As is shown in examples (37d) or (39), the concept 'to bring' can be decomposed into the simpler conceptual building blocks 'to take', 'to transport' and 'to give' something to somebody. An additional directional component might complete the picture.

In its purest form, verb serialization is typical of Far Eastern languages (see, e.g., Bisang 1998: 734). The underlying principle – i.e. the combination of two or more verbal elements in order to form a more complex content, whether monopredicative (Bisang) or not – can probably be found in all languages, though. This makes verb serialization – in a broad sense – an ideal starting point for grammaticalization and lexicalization. The wider the scale between finite and non-finite verb forms, the higher the number of intermediate products. One of the typical final outcomes is even identical in, e.g., CREOLE LANGUAGES and in CHINESE: new nominal affixes, for instance prepositions.

Another possible outcome is diathesis. An example familiar to speakers of FRENCH, ENGLISH or SPANISH are steps towards a diathesis highlighting the Beneficiary. What is necessary is a verb like GERMAN 'kriegen', 'bekommen', ENGLISH 'to get', or a perception verb like 'to see' or 'to hear'. They have all in common that the first participant is not conceived of as an Agent, but rather as a Beneficiary or someone concerned by an action.

(41) ENGLISH (BBC News 14.7.1999)
As prices for personal computers plummet, Apple *could see* its revenues *diminish*, even as its sells more computers, analysts say.

(42) FRENCH (*Le Monde* 7.3.1994, p. 9)
Majit Jalil Ali Al Mendelavi, vingt-six ans, un médecin irakien, kurde et chiite, qui *s'est vu refuser* l'admission sur le territoire français, (...) devait être renvoyé, samedi 5 mars, en direction d'Amman.

In the European languages cited above, there is again a link to the *Ausbau* of languages, i.e., to literacy with its different textual genres: "The frequency of *se voir* in sentences expressing the passive or topicalizing the experiencer, as well as the fact that *se voir* is commonly used — odd though this may appear from a 'logical' viewpoint — in the administrative and scientific styles when the referent of the patient is an abstract notion, are two important arguments for grammaticalization" (Hagège 1993: 229). Nonetheless, this type of experiencer diathesis may be found in New Guinea languages as well (Foley & Van Valin 1984: 149 ff.).

All in all, it should be clear that not any verb whatever can be integrated into such verbal compounds: there are semantic primes highly likely to be part of such tandem constructs, whereas others will never appear in this kind of context (Raible 1996; Wierzbicka 1998). This is, again, a clear hint to a cognitive basis of such phenomena.

3.2.7. Prepositional groups and nominal affixes

As was shown, for instance, by Adolf Noreen (see below § 4), the number of SPECIFIC RELATIONS humans may want to express when speaking is considerable. One only has to think of the possibilities we have in the domain of temporal or local relations: *before, behind, in front of, beneath, above, below, under, over, right, left*, etc. (→ art. 43; art. 44). All of these local relations may be combined with movement, thus making them dynamic (for instance *thither, hither*). This movement may again be combined with a deictic component, i. e. additionally taking into account the point of view of the speaker or the hearer, etc.

In many European languages, an answer to this challenge are prepositions, prepositional groups, a rich case system, or a combination of both of them. Beyond doubt, the most dynamic of these techniques of integration are prepositional groups. In principle, this technique is productive. As a rule, to a first preposition an element is added that has the function of the semantic core. This again is followed by another preposition, usually one that belongs to the most unmarked prepositions (like *de/di, à/a* in the ROMANCE LANGUAGES, *von* in GERMAN, or *of, to* in ENGLISH).

As regards the semantic core, more often than not it is the precise expression of the intended relation: EXCEPTION, ADDITION, interest as the GOAL of an action (*in addition to, with the exception of, on behalf of, à l'intention de, au détriment de*, to the detriment of, to the disadvantage of, *à condition de, en vertu de*, by virtue of, etc.). If the speakers of a language have converbs at their disposal (see above § 3.2.5), they may be used as well: e.g., FRENCH *compte tenu de* 'on account of'.

Speakers of languages which use the technique of converbs may combine the prepositional technique with converbs in still another way: the increasing nouniness of such constructions can be enhanced by case marking or by nominal affixes having a similar function, while expressing at the same time SPECIFIC RELATIONS. Good examples are the gerundial forms of, e.g., SPANISH, ITALIAN or even LATIN *ablativus absolutus*: ENGLISH *when doing this, while looking at ..., despite having been seen, with Mary now singing*; SPANISH *aún levantándose tardísimo*; ITALIAN *dopo cenato*, LATIN *quies provinciae* quamvis remoto consulari *mansit* 'in spite of the withdrawal of' ...), etc.

In the above example (10), we became first acquainted with a very special kind of interpretator: a pronominal dummy — referring to an entire sentence or even a series of sentences — linked to a preposition, the two of them giving the antecedent passage a special meaning, for instance CAUSE. In this case it was SPANISH *por lo tanto* 'therefore', an equivalent of *por eso*.

This means that a technique which, by its form (PREP + PRON) is highly integrative, can develop into a linking element functioning on a rather aggregative level. In § 6 below it will become manifest that this is also one of the important sources for grammaticalization.

3.2.8. Downgrading by tense and mood

Balthasar Bickel, while discussing the possibilities speakers have when they want to lay out tracks for the hearer, mentions different kinds of *Fährten*: the personal tracks which have received much attention above, local tracks, tracks using topicalisation as described, e.g., in § 2.4. He also briefly mentions temporal or tense tracks (Bickel 1991: 149 ff.).

Since related topics are treated elsewhere (→ art. 42; art. 59), a short look from a European perspective will be sufficient. — Roman Jakobson outlined a general frame for this kind of consideration (Jakobson 1957/1971). There are different relevant types of linkage on the temporal level: the type 'narrated Event in relation to another narrated Event' (symbolized as E^n/E^n) corresponds to a tense like FRENCH *passé simple*: a series of clauses with *passé simple* refers to a series of successive events (temporal iconicity; → art. 30, § 4). Jakobson called this type 'taxis':

(43) FRENCH (Racine, *Phèdre*)
Je le vis, je rougis, je pâlis à sa vue.

A second relevant type is labelled $E^n/E^{ns}/E^s$. It describes a verbal category, called 'evidential', "which takes into account three events — a narrated event, a speech event, a narrated speech event (E^{ns}), namely the alleged source of information about the narrated event. The speaker reports an event on the basis of someone else's report (quotative, i. e. hearsay evidence), of a dream (relative evidence), of a guess (presumptive evidence) or of his own previous experience (memory evidence)." (Jakobson 1957/1971: 135).

There are many languages which have integrated this possibility into their grammar, for instance as a 'quotative' — see above examples (24, 25). A typical example are newspapers in most ROMANCE languages where conditional mood in main clauses makes clear that the author is not willing to assume any communicative responsibility whatever. Another interesting case among European languages is the free indirect speech, in FRENCH *style indirect libre*. Direct speech is transposed into a form where most of its characteristics are conserved — with the exceptions of tense and personal deixis (→ art. 47, § 2.2). If the language under discussion has in its system an option between perfective and imperfective tenses, the imperfective version will be chosen. (Downgrading by imperfective forms has already been mentioned in § 3.2.6 and will be integrated into a more general framework in § 7.2). An example will illustrate this:

(44) FRENCH (Flaubert, *Madame Bovary*, ch. VII)
[...] Ah! il était parti, le seul charme de sa vie, le seul espoir possible d'une félicité! Comment n'avait-elle pas saisi ce bonheur-là, quand il se présentait! Pourquoi ne pas l'avoir retenu à deux mains, à deux genoux, quand il voulait s'enfuir? Et elle se maudit de n'avoir pas aimé Léon; elle eut soif de ses lèvres.

In this passage, *style indirect libre* has come to an end when we read "Et elle *se maudit* ..." with its two occurrences of *passé simple* (as a 'perfective' verb form absolutely excluded from *style indirect libre*), one of them a metacommunicative verb into the bargain ("she cursed herself ...").

Speakers of GERMAN may use a mood, 'Konjunktiv 1' (to be distinguished from 'Konjunktiv 2') as a quotative.

(45) GERMAN
"Ich bin erst gestern angekommen, will Ihnen aber nicht zur Last fallen und reise deshalb schon morgen wieder ab"
will be transformend into the quotative version
"Er *sei* erst gestern angekommen, *wolle* mir aber nicht zur Last fallen und *reise* deshalb schon morgen wieder ab."

Quotative makes clear that the speaker has no communicative responsibility. It should be added, though, that Konjunktiv 1 is a highly literary form. Most speakers of GERMAN cannot actively use the adequate verb forms, taking the forms of 'Konjunktiv 2' or analytical paraphrases instead.

Another case of downgrading by mood could already be observed in the ROMANCE examples (26d to 26f) and it was commented upon above in § 3.2.4.

4. The expression of relations

When speaking of clause linking, one cannot avoid speaking of the SPECIFIC RELATIONS holding between propositions — see, e.g., above §§ 1; 2.5; 3; 3.1; 3.2; 3.2.3 to 3.2.7.

How should such relations be conceived of? Is there an unlimited number of them? Are they universal or restricted to specific languages? If they are universal, are they innate? Or do we have to acquire them?

In order to answer the questions raised here, different approaches are possible. The first one is strictly empirical: we could choose a certain group of languages and observe the relations expressed, e.g., by adverbials. This survey was made by Bernd Kortmann (1997) in a EUROTYP project (→ art. 63). He found a body of relations he termed 'CCC' (CAUSALITY, CONDITION, CONCESSIVITY), and three other groups termed TIME, PLACE, and MODAL. Others speak of logical relations instead of CCC. The existence of such relations in a large sample of languages speaks in favor of universal categories of human thinking.

Kortmann has combined a second approach with the first one: diachrony. Are there certain directions in semantic change? The answer was in the affirmative, with Kortmann even proposing a 'cognitive map' or 'semantic space' explaining the observed changes (→ art. 63, fig. 63.1; 63.2).

In the present article a third approach will be added: the development of the CCC relations in ontogenesis. — The most basic cognitive operation carried out in the domain of CCC relations is putting into relation two events: one event has something to do with another. This is expressed by CIRCUMSTANCE or CONDITIONALITY, and this is why children, observing the speech of their parents, very often start with seemingly tautological utterances:

(46) GERMAN (Florian, age 2;5)
Wenn der Hansi aussteigt, steigt der Hansi aus.
Wenn das selber abgeht, geht es ab.
Wenn ich das Knäckebrot aufgessen hab, hab ich das Knäckebrot aufgessen.

These utterances are not intended as tautological, though, nor as truisms. They only express the delight the child has at beginning to understand how such constructions are used by her/his peers or carers.

Children tend to use one of the conjunctions, in GERMAN preferably *wenn* or similar forms, as a general conjunction applicable to all contexts. The first relation distinguished after CONDITIONALITY is TEMPORALITY:

(47) GERMAN (Florian age 2;10)
Wenn ich geschläfen hab, hab ich ein Kuchen gekriegt.
"When I had slept, I got a cake."
(48) GERMAN (Julian age 3;1)
Wenn Weihnachten war, da hab ich die Kerzen ausgepfeifen.
"When there was Christmas, I 'whistled out' the candles."

Having discovered TEMPORALITY, children are prepared for CAUSALITY: temporal relationships can be interpreted causally, but temporality does not imply CAUSALITY. The child may use GERMAN *wenn* in this sense before starting to use *weil*.

FINALITY is more complicated; (a) it is the relation of CAUSALITY seen from another perspective, (b) intention has to be added.

(49) GERMAN (Julian age 3;1)
Ich hab das Fenster mal bissle sauber gemacht, wenn die Leute rausgucken können.
"I've wiped the window a little bit 'when' the folks can look out." (The child cleaned a steamed window in a railway carriage.)
(50) GERMAN (Florian age 3;4)
Ich hab da was drangebunden. Wenns besser hält.
Verbally: "I wrapped something around it, 'when' it keeps better tight" (The child wrapped the cable of a toy telephone around the doorknob of the toilet.) At this age, this child already distinguishes between *wenn, als* and *weil*.
(51) GERMAN (Julian age 3;4)
[The child tells his father a pseudo dream. The father asks:] *Warum hast du denn die Flaschen in dem Koffer gehabt?* [Answer:] *Weil ich trinken kann.*
"Why on earth did you have the bottles in the bag? — Because [used in a FINAL sense] I can drink."

Similar observations have been reported for instance by Michèle Kail and Jürgen Weissenborn (1991).

It is not without interest that this cognitive evolution reflects more or less the steps a speaker of HOPI had to apply in clause chaining: with the ss-condition holding the first question to be asked is whether the relation is TEMPORAL or not: if it is not temporal, it has to be CONDITIONAL. In the case of TEMPORALITY, s/he has to choose between a SIMULTANEOUS relationship, ANTERIOR/POSTERIOR or CAUSALITY (see above § 3.2.2).

It should be added, though, that the expression of two simultaneous actions remains a true challenge to children (Berman & Slobin 1994: 393–455). As was shown by Emilia Ferreiro (1971), this is due to the lack of cognitive prerequisites that come into existence at the earliest by age seven or eight.

All this is good evidence in favor of a cognitive space — as shown in Table 45.2 — with appropriate building blocks and the corresponding steps in ontogenesis.

On the one hand, table 45.2 explains also why CONCESSIVITY as the most complex relation is acquired last by children. On the other hand it is a good background for the unidirectional semantic change Kortmann observed in 50 European languages. A CONDITIONAL can become TEMPORAL, but not vice versa. The same thing holds for TEMPORAL items evolving into CAUSAL ones, etc. The above examples of children cannot be alleged

Table 45.2: Overview over the 'logical' relations.

	\multicolumn{6}{c}{relation to be expressed}					
	CONDITIONAL	TEMPORAL	CAUSAL	CONSECUTIVE	FINAL	CONCESSIVE
implication	yes	yes	yes	yes	yes	yes
anterior/posterior	±	yes	yes	yes	yes	yes
causation	±	±	yes	yes	yes	yes
effect	±	±	±	yes	yes	yes
intended effect	±	±	±	±	yes	±
unexpected effect	±	±	±	±	±	yes

The table is simplified because it does not take into account the hypothetical possiblilties treated to some extent in Seiler 1993. All combinations possible in this domain are analyzed in Heger & Mudersbach 1984: 62.ff. Cf. also Dancygier 1998.

as counterevidence: the child does not use the linguistic forms as peers do.

A last remark should be made on the number and the systematic ordering of relations. It is relatively simple to put the CCC relations into a certain order because there exists a clear internal relationship. As for the rest, we have the choice between lots of approaches (some of them are synthesized in Raible 1992: 146–53).

One of them deserves a special mention as probably the most fine-tuned attempt in this domain: the theory of *states* by Adolf Noreen (1923). Noreen distinguished between five exterior and four interior states with numerous subdivisions, yielding a total of about 60. Since he gave them LATIN names, we find the names of all the grammatical cases we know from reference grammars of the most remote and exquisite languages, and we possibly find as well all the semantic relations we can think of. Often the distinctions he made prove extremely helpful (for instance the *status classificationis* in cases like *la ville de Paris, this linguist of Noreen*; cf. Raible 1982.)

This shows, among other things, once more the close relationship that holds between 'semantic' relations and grammatical cases.

5. Communicative dynamism

Right from the beginning of this article it was pointed out that clause linking is not an end in itself. Among the aims it serves are grounding and communicative dynamism (§ 1, point 2). Syntactical hierarchy (*ibid.*, point 1), establishing semantic relations (*ibid.*, point 3) and reference tracking (*ibid.*, point 4) all contribute to this basic task.

One of the grounding techniques is clefting (see above § 2.4). Others are diathesis (→ art. 67–69) and syntactic hierarchy, that is the whole scale of techniques selectively described in § 3. Even different types of reference tracking (§ 2) are implied in this task, for instance in the form of the five types of thematic progression described by František Daneš (→ art. 46; art. 47, § 2.3).

This means that communicative dynamism is first and foremost a matter of texts, not of individual sentences or clauses – see above example (2) with its communicative dynamism typical of newspaper genres, example (3), (10) or the GREEK example (27) with its fine tuned exploitation of syntactic hierarchy.

One of the most competent authors on this topic was Étienne Bonnot de Condillac (1715–1780), one of the intellectuals of the French Enlightenment. He was for many years tutor to the Infant of Parma. Between 1769 and 1773, he published the material he had used in this capacity under the title *Cours d'études*. It contains, among other things, a *Logic*, a *Grammar* extensively commented upon in an earlier article by Lia Formigari (→ art. 16), and an *Art of writing*.

Condillac's fundamental idea is that the basis of texts are conceptual building blocks and that, in order to be well understood and to be effective, they have to be put into an appropriate order and to be linked in an adequate way. He called this *la liaison des idées*. In order to demonstrate this to his pupil, he used contemporary authors as good and as bad examples, often generating special effects by modifying the original text. A short passage from a famous funeral address by Bossuet illustrates the procedure:

(52) FRENCH (Condillac, *L'art d'écrire*, book iv)
"O nuit désastreuse! O nuit effroyable, où retentit tout à coup, comme un éclat de tonnerre, cette étonnante nouvelle: Madame se meurt, Madame est morte!"

A cet endroit de l'oraison funèbre de *Madame*, tout le monde répandit des larmes: mais je me trompe fort, que l'on n'en aurait pas répandu, si Bossuet avait dit:
"O nuit désastreuse! O nuit effroyable, où cette étonnante nouvelle: Madame se meurt, Madame est morte, retentit tout à coup comme un éclat de tonnerre."

Bossuet, the author of the good version, used even the interpretator (see above §§ 2.1; 2.4) *cette étonnante nouvelle* in a cataphoric function for the effect he intends: first comes the substituting element yielding the adequate frame of interpretation, then the direct quote that fills this frame. The same technique is used in the above example (1).

The example needs no further comment — apart from the fact that it shows how wrong the members of a certain grammatical tradition (→ art. 19) were when claiming that French *clarté* was due to SV(O) ordering: in the present case, the effect is, above all, based on inversion. This is tantamount to saying — and Condillac says this explicitly — that the order of elements in a sentence is governed by the larger whole it is a part of.

More extensive examples from Condillac cannot be cited here: in manifold ways, this author demonstrates — by slight modifications — the crucial importance of clause linking. Even if every sentence in a series may be perfectly correct in itself, the result can turn out to be a hardly intelligible text: "les phrases ne tiennent plus les unes aux autres". With Condillac, coherence implies all the techniques of grounding by downgrading clauses available in FRENCH.

6. Diachronic aspects

The dimension of junction with its techniques extending between the poles of aggregation and integration is an ideal field for semantic change and for grammaticalization. As regards semantic change, a possible — partial — frame is shown above in Table 45.2 and, above all, in the contribution of Bernd Kortmann (→ art. 63).

A good starting point for grammaticalization are the converbal techniques (§ 3.2.5). This is due to the fact that, *by virtue of their form*, they signify integration whereas, in principle, the specific relation holding between the converbal form and the main verb it depends on remains open to interpretation. However, in case the semantic content given to the converb is identical with one of the specific semantic relations, this form can be grammaticalized, very often yielding a new adnominal element (e.g., a preposition). Table 45.3 illustrates this with some ROMANCE examples.

The type of examples integrated in table 45.3 can easily be found in the respective versions of the above mentioned EU treaty (see above § 3.2.3), alongside with their English equivalents (*during, concerning, pending, barring, notwithstanding, given, granted*).

Table 45.4 shows that the same development can be observed in FINNISH, this time with the help of nonfinite verb forms and the case markers they admit in this language: again, the EU treaty is full of such 'new' prepositions that are constructed, in this language, with a case depending on the meaning of the underlying verb (usually genitive, partitive, illative, elative). In many cases, the other languages of the EU treaty have to fall back on less integrative techniques in order to express the same relations.

Table 45.3: Grammaticalization of converbs in some ROMANCE languages.

relation expressed	FRENCH	ITALIAN	SPANISH	RUMANIAN
MEANS	*moyennant*	*mediante*	*mediante*	
EXCLUSION	*hormis, excepté*	*eccetto*	*excepto, exceptuando*	*exceptînd pe*
DURATION	*durant, pendant*	*durante*	*durante*	
CAUSE	*compte tenu de, vu, attendu*	*tenuto conto di, considerato*	*habida cuenta de, dado, debido a*	*avînd in vedere, considerînd*
CONCESSION	*nonobstant*	*nonostante*	*no obstante*	
RESPECT	*concernant, touchant, suivant*		*concerniente a, siguiendo*	

Table 45.4: Grammaticalization of converbs in FINNISH.

'preposition'	meaning	form	of the verb
huoli-ma-tta	in spite of	INF$_{III}$-ABESS	*huolia* 'to care about'
loukkaa-ma-tta	regardless of	INF$_{III}$-ABESS	*loukata* 'to hurt'
riippu-ma-tta	regardless	INF$_{III}$-ABESS	*riippua* 'depend on'
rajoitta-ma-tta	without prejudice to	INF$_{III}$-ABESS	*rajoittaa* 'to limit'
lähti-e-n	starting from	INF$_{II}$-INSTRUCT	*lähteä* 'depart from'
kulu-e-ssa	during	INF$_{II}$-INESS	*kulua* 'to go by'
sattu-e-ssa	in case	INF$_{II}$-INESS	*sattua* 'to happen'
vaati-e-ssa	in case	INF$_{II}$-INESS	*vaatia* 'to require'
menn-e-ssä	until	INF$_{II}$-INESS	*mennä* 'to go'
kulu-ttu-a	after	PRT.PERF.PASS-PARTIT	*kuluttaa* 'spend time'
tarvitta-e-ssa	where necessary	PASS.INF$_{II}$-INESS	*tarvita* 'to need'

At the end of § 3.2.7, it was already mentioned that the combination NOMINAL AFFIX + DUMMY, with the nominal affix expressing a SPECIFIC RELATION, is an important source for grammaticalization. It leads first to co-ordinating conjunctions: LATIN *própter éa* 'therefore' → *proptérea*.

Propterea normally refers to something antecedent, that is it is used as an anaphoric. The next step in the evolution is cataphoric use: *propterea quod*. When it is used without a dummy interpretator, *quod* has a causal meaning. Since CLASSICAL LATIN, the analytic scheme 'dummy interpretator + prep + *quod*' has become highly productive: *inde quod, ob id quod, ideo quod, idcirco quod, interim quod, postea quod, cum eo quod*, etc. The element *eo, ea* may also be replaced by a more cataphoric element, *hoc*: *hoc ipso quod*, or, with a real nominal interpretator, *hac ratione quod* 'for this reason', etc.

The number of synthetic LATIN conjunctions transferred to ROMANCE is quite small. The bulk of Romance subordinating conjunctions has been newly formed according to the two analytic LATIN moulds PREP + DUMMY + QUOD (LATIN *per hoc quod*) and PREP + QUOD (LATIN *propter quod*). The details — as well as the link to literacy — can be seen in Stempel 1964: 390 ff. or in Raible 1992: 160−70.

It stands to reason that verbal series, too, are ideal starting points for grammaticalization, particularly in languages where a large scale of possibilities between finiteness and nonfiniteness exists. Examples were already mentioned in § 3.2.6.

Another interesting chapter are complementizers. Here a current evolution starts from the introducing matrix verb 'to say'. Karen H. Ebert (1991; for examples in SEYCHELLES CREOLE see Michaelis 1994) has given good examples with all the intermediate steps. Another current evolution starts — once more — from interpretators. This is how LATIN *quo modo* became a complementizer in some ROMANCE languages, cf. especially ITALIAN *como*. A third current starting point are cataphoric dummies (pronouns) introducing direct quote ("I tell you that:", leading to forms like GERMAN *dass/daß*) or *that*.

All the developments mentioned as yet have to do with the downgrading of clauses. As was shown by Claus D. Pusch (1999; 2001), the speakers of GASCON, one of the ROMANCE languages, have developed an 'upgrading' feature from a pivot (see above § 2.4); it is called 'enunciative' and brings GASCON on a par with QUECHUA and a couple of African languages like KIKUYU (Heine & Reh 1983).

In such cases, cleft sentences no longer serve as tags for the reordering of constituents. Although they do not lose entirely their focalizing effect which, in these contexts, is associated with the highlighting of relevant parts of the utterance, they develop into markers of predication focus, a weaker type of focus that often parallels the unmarked theme/rheme order. Enunciatives are the morphologic remains of cleft constructions in such unmarked declarative sentences.

In general, one could say that it should not come as a surprise that, above all, the analytical techniques of junction serve as a starting point for grammaticalization.

7. Overall view and concluding remarks

The preceding sections have shown that clause linking is a fairly complex task: it implies reference tracking in subsequent clauses (§ 2), the expression of SPECIFIC RELATIONS (some of them were treated in § 4), and the exploitation of syntactic hierarchy by a series of techniques extending on a scale between aggregation and integration (§ 3).

The relevant techniques, apart from the most aggregative and integrative ones, are highly language specific, thus making up for the typological aspect of clause linking. In article 63, Kortmann has formulated some characteristics holding for European languages ('euroversals') in one of these techniques, adverbial conjunctions. They show a connection between other features (basic word order, existence of prepositions) and adverbial conjunctions. Basic word order (SOV) was mentioned also with respect to the technique of clause chaining (above § 3.2.2) and clefting (above § 2.4). Authors like Toshio Ohori (1994) show diachronic processes bringing about a change in the dominant type of clause linking, in his case for JAPANESE.

When successfully applied, linking clauses with the help of the appropriate techniques should lead to a well structured, intelligible and effective text − this is why literacy and the related *Ausbau* of languages came into play (cf., e.g., above §§ 2.1; 3.2; 3.2.3; 3.2.6; 3.2.7; 6).

In order to get an overall view, the threads will now be tied in a somewhat different way.

7.1. A layered or encapsulated model of the verb

The following table 45.5 synthesizes some authoritative views expressed with respect to the internal structure of verbal groups and clauses.

If a token of any layer of figure 45.5 − nuclear, core, or peripheral − is joined to any other token of its same type, Foley & Van Valin (1984: 188) speak of 'juncture'. Practically, this concerns above all what Bisang has called a 'monopredicative' verb series (see above § 3.2.6), that is nuclear juncture. The authors call 'nexus' "the nature of the syntactic linkage between two clauses" (1984: 238), proposing three types of nexus characterized by the combination of the features ± embedded and ± dependent: coordination (− embedded, − dependent), subordination (+ embedded, + dependent) and cosubordination (− embedded, + dependent). This is represented in Table 45.6 *Nexus and juncture possibilities* (1984: 263) on the next page.

Up to a point, table 45.6 should be seen as another way of representing the scale between aggregation and integration proposed above in § 3. This holds all the more as the field may be translated into a scalar *syntactic bondedness hierarchy* (1984: 267). At the same time, the centers of interest overlap only partially since Foley & Van Valin are not interested in the SPECIFIC RELATIONS that can be expressed by nexus and juncture, thus putting aside such phenomena as interpretators and grammatical cases expressing SPECIFIC RELATIONS, e.g., CAUSALITY.

'Conjunction' is even more aggregative than the above example illustrating pure aggregation (11a/b) since it combines two totally non-coalescent clauses with 'and', viz.

---

periphery
Kenneth Lee & Evelyn Pike 1984: *margin*; Simon C. Dik 1978: *satellites*
− domain of the peripheral arguments of the verb; for Foley & Van Valin 1984: Beneficiary and all the rest, plus: spatio-temporal setting, i. e., temporal and local adverbials.

  core
  Pike & Pike 1984; Dik 1978: *nucleus*
  − contains the arguments or participants of the core; for Foley & Van Valin 1984: only Agent and Patient; for others: Agent, Patient, Beneficiary.
  − core is the domain where diathesis is effective; cf. Givón 1994.

    nucleus   *participants*
    Foley & Van Valin 1984: "innermost layer"; Hansjakob Seiler 1988: "Par-   (e.g., Seiler 1988)
    tizipatum"; Peter Koch 1981: "konstitutive Sachverhaltsbedingungen" and
    "Art der Sachverhaltsdarstellung".
    − Foley & Van Valin 1984 locate here categories like 'aspect'. This is somewhat problematic because aspect may be realized as a core category (aspect marking on the participants: → art. 1 § 3, point 4).

Figure 45.5: Encapsulated or layered model of the verb resp. clause.
On the basis of William A. Foley & Robert D. Van Valin (1984: 78), the figure shows the conceptual and terminological differences existing between these authors and some other authoritative models of the internal structure of verbs or clauses.

Table 45.6: Nexus and juncture possibilities according to Foley & Van Valin 1984: 263.

Nexus: Juncture	Coordinate	Subordinate	cosubordinate
Peripheral	*Conjunction*	*Adverbial clause* (see § 3.2.3)	*Switch reference* (see § 3.2.2)
	parataxis (see § 3.1, ex. [11a/b])	*That-clause* (see § 3.2.4)	CONJ *'and'* with zero anaphora (see ex. [2]; § 2.3)
Core	*Parataxis* (see § 3.1, ex. [11a/b])	*Core embedding* (see § 3.2.5)	*Verb serialization* (see § 3.2.6, broad sense, ex. [38−42])
	acc. c. inf. (see § 3.2.4, ex. [27])	*Clause embedding* (see § 3.2.4, as subject)	
Nuclear	*Verb serialization* (see § 3.2.6, *stricto sensu*)		*Verb serialization* (see § 3.2.6, *stricto sensu*)

the case of 'maximal disjunctness' in the wording of Christian Lehmann (below § 7.3, point 5).

Maintaining reference (§ 2) concerns on the one hand only the participants, i. e. the core and the periphery in figure 45.5. On the other hand it may concern the whole clause with its nucleus whenever dummies or interpretators − or dummy verbs (*verba vicaria*) like *to do, tun, faire* − are used to this end, with or without one of the SPECIFIC RELATIONS being added (above § 2): they represent entire sentences and even text passages, thus additionally demonstrating that not only nouns, but also clauses, propositions, sentences, and texts refer to something (→ art. 1, § 3, point 4). These are the most interesting cases and, above all, often starting points for grammaticalization (see § 3.2.7).

Maintaining reference also has to do with the order of participants on the main clause level, thus implying techniques allowing to 'reshuffle' participants like diathesis and clefting, the latter actually foregrounding rather than downgrading a clause (above § 2.4).

The more a technique becomes integrative, the more it will interact with the core and the nucleus. In this context, the relations expressed might play a part, too: Hansjakob Seiler has put forward the idea that, by their nature, the SPECIFIC RELATIONS expressed in the dimension extending between the most aggregative and the most integrative techniques are themselves more or less aggregative or integrative. He proposes the following scale, starting with the most integrative ones: TIME, PLACE, MEANS, FINALITY, CAUSE / CONSEQUENCE, CAUSALITY / CONCESSIVITY, INCLUSION / EXCLUSION, CONJUNCTION / DISJUNCTION, CONDITION / COUNTERFACTUALITY (Seiler 1995: 21). All of them seem to be conceived of as peripheral, though.

Things are simpler as regards the downgrading techniques such relations are used with. The periphery, and, in part, the core, have important roles in clause chaining (§ 3.2.2), in the technique of adverbial subordination with conjunctions (§ 3.2.3), and in the technique of converbs (§ 3.2.5). With complement clauses, the core is strongly involved, too − witness the cases of *accusativus cum participio* or *accusativus cum infinitivo* (§ 3.2.4). The same thing holds for diathesis (§ 2.4). According to its definition, the 'core' may be implicated also in the techniques using prepositional groups and nominal affixes (§ 3.2.7). Changes brought about by the grammaticalization of converbal processes (§§ 3.2.5; 6) may even concern the nucleus by the creation of new nominal affixes (e.g., prepositions) enlarging verbal valency.

The technique of verb serialization has, above all, to do with nuclear processes. On the one hand, verb serialization in its narrow sense is a conceptual construction set for "the innermost layer" of verbs, i. e., for the domain called "participatum" by Seiler (1988) and "konstitutive Sachverhaltsbedingung" by Peter Koch (1981): witness the examples cited as illustrations to this end in § 3.2.6. Among other things, the valency of the verb may be increased as a result.

On the other hand, verbal series in the larger sense, e.g., with verbs serving as auxiliaries, are a standard way of analytically expressing tense, aspect, *Aktionsart*, diathesis, etc., thus remodeling entire verbal systems (cf. Raible 1996).

7.2. The complexity of the finite/nonfinite distinction

In 1980, a seminal contribution was published by Paul Hopper and Sandra A. Thompson. Its topic was the concept of transitivity. It inspired Talmy Givón to establish a link between semantic conciseness and grammatical finiteness. The basic idea is that a completed action is more finite than a non-terminated one, that punctual events are more finite than durative ones, that real events are more finite than irreal ones, etc.

In a systematic way this can be represented as in table 45.7. This table suggests that we should distinguish four kinds of finiteness/non-finiteness.

1. in the sense of 'perfectivity' as opposed to 'imperfectivity', 'realis' as opposed to 'irrealis' (downgrading by mood, above § 3.2.8), 'perfective' as opposed to 'imperfective' (downgrading by aspect, above § 3.2.6);
2. in the sense of a loss of finiteness brought about by the loss of distinctions within a category: some ROMANCE languages still have a conjunctive with four tenses, whereas, e.g., FRENCH has lost all tense distinctions in this mood. This reduces the amount of grammatical information conveyed by such forms;
3. in the sense of a less specified system: cp. the CHINESE verbal systems with the ENGLISH one (above § 3.2.6);
4. depending on the last type: presence or absence of domains that are particularly rich in distinctions (e.g., a tense-based system as opposed to an aspect-based one).

7.3. Related conceptions

Sandra A. Thompson has not only contributed, although in an indirect way, to the finiteness discussion. She wrote also, this time together with John Haiman, an important contribution on "'Subordination' in Universal Grammar" (1984). This was followed by an equally important contribution from Christian Lehmann (1988).

Basically, both contributions describe scalar models, too. Haiman & Thompson list seven components:

1. Identity between the two clauses of subject, tense, or mood.
2. Reduction of one of the clauses.
3. Grammatically signaled incorporation of the two clauses.
4. Intonation linking between the two clauses.
5. One clause is within the scope of the other.
6. Absence of tense iconicity between the two clauses.
7. Identity between the two clauses of speech act perspective.

Items 1 to 3 can be found in a more precise and analytic formulation in Foley & Van Valin (1984). Items like 5 or 7 are characteris-

Table 45.7: The different meanings and implementations of finiteness.

	finiteness ranking		content of categories	
	of tense, aspect, modality	of major verb categories	*more finite*	*less finite*
most finite	TENSE		terminated, in sequence	non-terminated, anterior
	MODALITY	INDICATIVE SUBJUNCTIVE PARTICIPIAL INFINITIVE	realis	irrealis
	ASPECT		punctual	durative
	NEGATION		affirmative	negative
least finite		NOMINAL		

The two-dimensional field of finiteness proposed by Talmy Givón manifests the relativity, or, put positively, the different aspects of the 'finiteness' concept. – The two scales (a vertical and a horizontal one) bring different aspects to the fore: on the vertical one, which is in itself twofold, *tense aspect modality* concerns the semantic and grammatical features of the nucleus, partially also of the core. The column with the major verbal categories is dedicated to the categorial and morphological implementation of this kind of finiteness or non-finiteness. There is a correlation between decreasing finiteness and a decreasing number of distinctions a category allows: a tense system has many different tenses, an aspect system has only two of them (perfective/imperfective). The horizontal scale attributes higher or lower finiteness to the categorial *content* transported by tense, mood etc.

tic of the well-known pragmatic and text linguistic approach of Haiman & Thompson, thus being rather alien to the considerations of Foley & Van Valin. Most of these aspects are taken into account in §§ 2, 3 and 4.

Lehmann proposes six scales that are combined into three groups:

Autonomy vs. Integration
1. hierarchical downgrading (parataxis vs. embedding)
2. main clause syntactic level of the subordinate clause (sentence vs. word)

Expansion vs. Reduction
3. desententialization of the subordinate clause (sententiality vs. nominality)
4. grammaticalization (independent predicate vs. grammatical operator)

Isolation vs. Linkage
5. interlacing of the two clauses (complete disjunctness vs. maximal identity)
6. explicitness of the linking (syndesis vs. asyndesis)

Lehmann's approach is the most analytic one and thus an excellent guideline for concrete crosslinguistic analysis. Basically, it is a three-dimensional space, the three dimensions being the headings of the three pairs of parameters he introduces. The subparameters and their instantiations as pairs of opposite notions have been taken into account in the above sections 1 to 6, too.

8. References

Bickel, Balthasar. 1991. *Typologische Grundlagen der Satzverkettung. Ein Beitrag zur Allgemeinen Grammatik der Satzverbindung und des Fährtenlegens.* Zürich: ASAS-Verlag.

Bickel, Balthasar. 1998. Review of Haspelmath & König (eds.). 1995. *Linguistic Typology* 2: 381–397.

Berman, Ruth A. & Slobin, Dan Isaac. 1994. *Relating events in narrative: a crosslinguistic developmental study.* Hillsdale/NJ: Erlbaum.

Bisang, Walter. 1992. *Das Verb im Chinesischen, Hmong, Vietnamesischen, Thai und Khmer. (Vergleichende Grammatik im Rahmen der Verbserialisierung, der Grammatikalisierung und der Attraktorpositionen).* Tübingen: Narr.

Bisang, Walter. 1998. "Adverbiality. The view from the Far East". In: van der Auwera (ed.), 641–812.

Charolles, Michel. 1999. "Associative anaphora and its interpretation". *Journal of Pragmatics* 31.3: 311–26.

Comrie, Bernard. 1999. *Coreference in Grammar and Discourse.* Oxford: Blackwell.

Condillac, Etienne Bonnot de. 1775. *Cours d'étude pour l'instruction du Prince de Parme: L'art d'écrire.*

Dancygier, Barbara. 1998. *Conditionals and predication. Time, knowledge and causation in conditional constructions.* Cambridge: Cambridge University Press.

De Beaugrande, Robert-Alain & Dressler, Wolfgang Ulrich. 1981. *Einführung in die Textlinguistik.* (Konzepte der Sprach- und Literaturwissenschaft, 28.) Tübingen: Niemeyer.

Dik, Simon C. 1978. *Functional Grammar.* (North Holland linguistic series, 37.) Amsterdam: North-Holland.

Ebert, Karen H. 1991. "Vom verbum dicendi zur Konjunktion. Ein Kapitel universaler Grammatikentwicklung". In: Bisang, Walter & Rinderknecht, Peter (eds.). *Von Europa bis Ozeanien – von der Antonymie zum Relativsatz: Gedenkschrift für Meinrad Scheller.* Zürich: Seminar für Allgemeine Sprachwissenschaft, 77–95.

Ferreiro, Emilia. 1971. *Les relations temporelles dans le langage de l'enfant.* Genève: Droz.

Foley, William A. & Van Valin, Robert D. 1984. *Functional syntax and universal grammar.* Cambridge: Cambridge University Press.

Givón, Talmy. 1990. *Syntax: a functional-typological introduction.* Vol. II. Amsterdam & Philadelphia: Benjamins.

Givón, Talmy. 1994. *Voice and inversion.* (Typological studies in language, 28.) Amsterdam & Philadelphia: Benjamins.

Günther, Wilfried. 1973. *Das portugiesische Kreolisch der Ilha do Príncipe.* (Marburger Studien zur Afrika- und Asienkunde, Serie A, 2.) Marburg a. d. Lahn: Selbstverlag.

Hagège, Claude. 1975. *Le problème linguistique des prépositions et la solution chinoise. (Avec un essai de typologie à travers plusieurs groupes de langues).* (Collection linguistique publiée par la Société de Linguistique de Paris, LXXI.) Louvain: Peeters.

Hagège, Claude. 1993. *The language builder: an essay on the human signature in linguistic morphogenesis.* (Amsterdam studies in the theory and history of linguistic science: Series, 4, Current issues in linguistic theory, 94.) Amsterdam & Philadelphia: Benjamins.

Haiman, John & Thompson, Sandra A. 1984. "'Subordination' in Universal Grammar". In: *Subordination. Proceedings of the Tenth Annual Meeting of the Berkeley Linguistic Society.* Berkeley/CA: Berkeley Linguistic Society, 510–23.

Haiman, John & Thompson, Sandra A. 1988 (eds.). *Clause combining in grammar and discourse.* (Typological studies in language, 18.) Amsterdam & Philadelphia: Benjamins.

Halford, Brigitte K. 1996. *Talk units. The structure of spoken Canadian English.* (ScriptOralia, 87.) Tübingen: Narr.

Harweg, Roland. ¹1964 ²1979. *Pronomina und Textkonstitution.* (Beihefte zu Poetica, 2.) München: Fink.

Haspelmath, Martin. 1995. "The converb as a cross-linguistically valid category". Haspelmath & König (eds.), 1−55.

Haspelmath, Martin & König, Ekkehard (eds.). 1995. *Converbs in cross-linguistic perspective: Structure and meaning of adverbial verb forms − adverbial participles, gerunds.* (Empirical Approaches to Language Typology, 13.) Berlin & New York: Mouton de Gruyter.

Heger, Klaus & Mudersbach, Klaus. 1984. *Aktantenmodelle: Aufgabenstellung und Aufbauregeln.* (Abhandlungen der Heidelberger Akademie der Wissenschaften. Phil.-hist. Klasse; Jg. 1984, Abh. 4.) Birkenau/Heidelberg: Bitsch.

Heine, Bernd & Reh, Mechthild. 1983. "Diachronic observations on completive focus marking in some African languages". *Sprache und Geschichte in Afrika* 5: 7−44.

Hopper, Paul J. & Thompson, Sandra A. 1980. "Transitivity in grammar and discourse". *Language* 56: 251−99.

Humboldt, Wilhelm von. 1827. *Lettre à M. Abel-Rémusat, sur la nature des formes grammaticales en général, et sur le Génie de la langue Chinoise en particulier.* Paris.

Jacobsen, Jr., William H. 1967. "Switch reference in Hokan-Cohahuiltecan". In: Hymes, Dell & Bittle, William E. (eds.). *Studies in southwestern ethnolinguistics: meaning and history in the languages of the American Southwest.* (Studies in general anthropology, 3.) The Hague: Mouton, 238−68.

Jacobsen, Jr., William H. 1983. "Typological and genetic notes on switch-reference systems in North American Indian languages". In: Haiman, John & Munro, Pamela (eds.). *Switch-reference and universal grammar. Proceedings of a Symposium on Switch Reference and Universal Grammar. Winnipeg, May 1981.* (Typological studies in language, 2.) Amsterdam & Philadelphia: Benjamins, 151−83.

Jakobson, Roman. 1957/1971. "Shifters, verbal categories, and the Russian verb". In: id. *Selected Writings II. Word and language.* The Hague: Mouton, 130−47.

Johanson, Lars. 1995. "On Turkic converb clauses". In: Haspelmath & König (eds.), 313−47.

Kail, Michèle & Weissenborn, Jürgen. 1991. "Conjunction: Developmental issues". In: Piérraut-LeBonniec, Gilberte & Dolitsky, Marlène (eds.). *Language bases ... discourse bases: some aspects of contemporary French-language psycholinguistics research.* (Pragmatics and beyond; N.S., 17.) Amsterdam & Philadelphia: Benjamins, 125−142.

Kibrik, Andrej A. 1988. *Tipologija sredstv oformlenija anaforičeskix svajzej* [A typology of anaphoric means]. Ph.D. dissertation. Institut jazykoznanija AN SSSR. Moskau.

Kibrik, Andrej A. 1991. "Maintenance of reference in sentence and discourse". In: Lehmann, Winfred P. & Jakusz Hewitt, Helen-Jo (eds.). *Language typology 1988. Typological models in reconstruction.* Amsterdam & Philadelphia: Benjamins, 57−84 [Summary of Kibrik 1988].

Koch, Peter. 1981. *Verb, Valenz, Verfügung. Zur Satzsemantik und Valenz franz. Verben am Beispiel der Verfügungs-Verben.* (Reihe Siegen, 32.) Heidelberg: Winter.

König, Ekkehard. 1995. "The meaning of converb constructions". In: Haspelmath & König (eds.), 57−95.

Kortmann, Bernd. 1997. *Adverbial Subordination. A typology and history of adverbial subordinators based on european languages.* (Empirical Approaches to Language Typology, 18.) Berlin & New York: Mouton de Gruyter.

Kriegel, Sibylle. 1996. *Diathesen im Mauritius- und Seychellenkreol.* (ScriptOralia, 88.) Tübingen: Narr.

Lehmann, Christian. 1988. "Towards a typology of clause linkage". In: Haiman & Thompson, 181−225.

Li, Charles N. & Thompson, Sandra A. 1973. "Serial verb constructions in Mandarin Chinese: Subordination or co-ordination?". *Chicago Linguistic Society* 9: 96−103.

Ludwig, Ralph. 1990. "Abrégé de grammaire du créole guadeloupéen". Ludwig, Ralph & Montbrand, Danièle & Poullet, Hector & Telchid, Sylviane. *Dictionnaire créole français (Guadeloupe).* Paris: Servedit/Éditions Jasor, 17−38.

Ludwig, Ralph. 1996. *Kreolsprachen zwischen Mündlichkeit und Schriftlichkeit. Zur Syntax und Pragmatik atlantischer Kreolsprachen auf französischer Basis.* (ScriptOralia, 86.) Tübingen: Narr.

Lüdtke, Jens. 1984. *Sprache und Interpretation: Semantik und Syntax reflexiver Strukturen im Französischen.* (Tübinger Beiträge zur Linguistik, 237.) Tübingen: Narr.

Maurer, Philippe. 1988. *Les modifications temporelles et modales du verbe dans le papiamento de Curaçao (Antilles Néerlandaises): avec une anthologie et un vocabulaire papiamento-français.* (Kreolische Bibliothek, 9.) Hamburg: Buske.

Mair, Christian. 1990. *Infinitival complement clauses in English: a study of syntax in discourse.* (Studies in English language.) Cambridge: Cambridge University Press.

Michaelis, Susanne. 1994. *Komplexe Syntax im Seychellen-Kreol. Verknüpfung von Sachverhaltsdarstellungen zwischen Mündlichkeit und Schriftlichkeit.* (ScriptOralia, 49.) Tübingen: Narr.

Mithun, Marianne. 1988. "The grammaticalization of coordination". In: Haiman & Thompson (eds.), 331–59.

Müller-Bardey, Thomas. 1988. *Typologie der Subjektverkettung ("Switch reference")*. (Arbeiten des Kölner Universalienprojekts, 70.) Köln: Institut für Sprachwissenschaft.

Müller-Lancé, Johannes. 1994. *Absolute Konstruktionen vom Altlatein bis zum Neufranzösischen: ein Epochenvergleich unter Berücksichtigung von Mündlichkeit und Schriftlichkeit.* (ScriptOralia, 64.) Tübingen: Narr.

Nedjalkov, Igor' V. 1998. "Converbs in the languages of Europe". In: van der Auwera 1998, 421–55.

Nedjalkov, Vladimir P. 1995. "Some typological parameters of converbs". In: Haspelmath & König (eds.), 97–136.

Noreen, Adolf. 1923. *Einführung in die wissenschaftliche Betrachtung der Sprache: Beiträge zur Methode und Terminologie der Grammatik.* Transl. by Hans W. Pollak. Halle a.d.S.: Niemeyer.

Ohori, Toshio. 1994. "Diachrony of clause linkage: TE and BA in Old through Middle Japanese". In: Pagliuca, William (ed.). *Perspectives of grammaticalization.* Amsterdam & Philadelphia: Benjamins, 135–149.

Petrus Hispanus. 1577. *Petri Hispani Summulae logicales: cum Versorii Parisiensis ... expositione / parvorum item Logicalium eidem Petro Hispano adscriptum opus, nuper in partes ac capita distinctum.* Venetiis: Fr. Sansovinus.

Pike, Kenneth Lee & Pike, Evelyn. 1982. *Grammatical Analysis.* Arlington/TX: Summer Institute of Linguistics.

Pilhofer, G. 1933. repr. 1969. *Grammatik der Käte-Sprache in Neuguinea.* (Zeitschrift für Eingeborenen-Sprachen: Beihefte, 14.) Berlin: Reimer; Nendeln, Liechtenstein: Kraus Reprints.

Pusch, Claus D. 1999. "Reanalyse von Spaltsatzkonstruktionen und grammatikalisierte Prädikationsexplizierung. Zur Entwicklung des Enunziativs *que* im Gaskognischen". In: Lang, Jürgen & Neumann-Holzschuh, Ingrid (eds.). *Reanalyse und Grammatikalisierung in den romanischen Sprachen.* (Linguistische Arbeiten, 410.) Tübingen: Niemeyer, 147–59.

Pusch, Claus Dieter. 2001. *Morphosyntax, Informationsstruktur und Pragmatik. Ein universalistischer Blick auf präverbale Marker im gaskognischen Okzitanisch und in anderen Sprachen.* Tübingen: Narr.

Raible, Wolfgang. 1972. *Satz und Text: Untersuchungen zu vier romanischen Sprachen.* (Beihefte zur Zeitschrift für romanische Philologie, 132.) Tübingen: Niemeyer.

Raible, Wolfgang. 1982. "'Regelmässige Ausnahmen' im Bereich der romanischen Nominaldetermination". In: Heinz, Sieglinde & Wandruszka, Ulrich (eds.). *Fakten und Theorien. Beiträge zur romanischen und allgemeinen Sprachwissenschaft. Festschrift für Helmut Stimm zum 65. Geburtstag.* (Tübinger Beiträge zur Linguistik, 191.) Tübingen: Narr, 231-239.

Raible, Wolfgang. 1983. "Knowing and Believing – and Syntax". In: Parret, Herman (ed.). *On believing. Epistemological and semiotic approaches. De la croyance. Approches épistémologiques et sémiotiques.* Berlin & New York: de Gruyter, 275–91.

Raible, Wolfgang. 1992. *Junktion. Eine Dimension der Sprache und ihre Realisierungsformen zwischen Aggregation und Integration.* (Sitzungsberichte der Heidelberger Akademie der Wissenschaften, phil.-hist. Klasse, Jg. 1992, 2.) Heidelberg: Winter.

Raible, Wolfgang. 1992a. "The pitfalls of subordination: Subject and object clauses between Latin and Romance". In: Brogyányi, Béla & Lipp, Reiner (eds.). *Historical Philology: Greek, Latin, and Romance. Papers in honor of Oswald Szemerényi II.* (Current Issues in Linguistic Theory, 87.) Amsterdam & Philadelphia: Benjamins, 299–337.

Raible, Wolfgang. 1994. "Literacy and Language Change". In: Čmejrková, Svetla & Daneš, František & Havlová, Eva (eds.). *Writing vs Speaking. Language, Text, Discourse, Communication. Proceedings of the Conference held at the Czech Language Institute of the Academy of Sciences of the Czech Republic, Prague, October 14–16, 1992.* (Tübinger Beiträge zur Linguistik, 392.) Tübingen: Narr, 111–25.

Raible, Wolfgang. 1996. "Kognition und Sprachwandel". *Akademie-Journal* 1/96, 38–43.

Schwyzer, Eduard. 1914. "Genealogische und kulturelle Sprachverwandtschaft". In: *Universität Zürich. Festgabe zur Einweihung der Neubauten 18. April 1914.* Zürich. Teil V: Philosophische Fakultät I, 133–46.

Scott, Graham. 1978. *The Fore language of Papua New Guinea.* Canberra, A.C.T.: School of pacific studies.

Seiler, Hansjakob. 1988. *The Dimension of participation.* Translated and edited by Fernando Leal. (*Función*, 7.) Guadalajara, México: Universidad de Guadalajara.

Seiler, Hansjakob. 1993. "Satzverbindung im Konditionalgefüge (besonders im Altgriechischen)". *Cahiers Ferdinand de Saussure* 47: 143–58.

Seiler, Hansjakob. 1995. "Review of Raible 1992". *Vox Romanica* 54: 12–21.

Selig, Maria. 1992. *Die Entwicklung der Nominaldeterminanten im Spätlatein: romanischer Sprachwandel und lateinische Schriftlichkeit.* (ScriptOralia, 26.) Tübingen: Narr.

Senft, Gunter. 1986. *Kilivila: the language of the Trobriand Islanders.* (Mouton grammar library, 3.) Berlin: Mouton de Gruyter.

Shopen, Timothy (ed.). 1985. *Language typology and syntactic description.* Vol. 2: *Complex constructions.* Cambridge: Cambridge University Press.

Stäbler, Cynthia K. 1995. *Entwicklung mündlicher romanischer Syntax: das ‹français cadien› in Louisiana.* (ScriptOralia, 78.) Tübingen: Narr.

Stäbler, Cynthia K. 1995a. *La vie dans le temps asteur. Ein Korpus von Gesprächen mit Cadiens in Louisiana.* (ScriptOralia, 79.) Tübingen: Narr.

Stump, Gregory T. 1985. *The semantic variability of absolute constructions.* (Synthese language library, 25.) Dordrecht: Reidel.

Stahlschmidt, Andrea. 1983. *Das Verbalsystem des Hopi. Eine semantische Strukturanalyse der Hopi-Grammatik unter besonderer Berücksichtigung von B. L. Whorfs Thesen zur Zeitauffassung der Hopi-Indianer.* (SAIS Arbeitsberichte aus dem Seminar für Allgemeine und Indogermanische Sprachwissenschaft, 7.) Kiel: Universität Kiel.

Stempel, Wolf-Dieter. 1964. *Untersuchungen zur Satzverknüpfung im Altfranzösischen.* (Archiv für das Studium der neueren Sprachen und Literaturen: Beihefte, 1.) Braunschweig: Westermann.

Thompson, Sandra A. & Longacre, Robert E. 1985. "Adverbial clauses". In: Shopen, Timothy (ed.), 171–234.

Traugott, Elizabeth C. 1987. "Literacy and language change. The special case of speech act verbs". *Interchange* 18: 32–47.

van der Auwera, Johan (ed.). 1998. *Adverbial constructions in the languages of Europe.* Berlin: Mouton de Gruyter.

Van Valin, Robert D. & LaPolla, Randy J. 1997. *Syntax: Structure, meaning, and function.* Cambridge: Cambridge University Press.

Vogel, Petra Maria (ed.). 2000. *Approaches to the typology of word classes.* (Empirical approaches to language typology, 23.) Berlin: Mouton de Gruyter.

Wierzbicka, Anna. 1998. "Anchoring linguistic typology in universal semantic primes". *Linguistic Typology* 2: 141–94.

Wolfgang Raible, University of Freiburg i. Br.
(Germany)

46. Informationsstruktur und Reliefgebung

1. Einleitung
2. Grundlegende Termini und Begriffe
3. Zur Verankerung der Informationsstruktur in der modernen Sprachtheorie
4. Grundprinzipien der Informationsstrukturierung
5. Formale Mittel der Topik- und Fokusmarkierung
6. Informationsstruktur aus typologischer Perspektive: zur Frage der Diskurskonfigurationalität
7. Weitere typologisch relevante Zusammenhänge
8. Reliefgebung in Texten
9. Zitierte Literatur

1. Einleitung

Die Analyse der Sprache läßt sich nicht auf die Beschreibung und Erklärung von formalen Gesetzmäßigkeiten einschränken. Sprachliche Äußerungen sind mehrschichtig: ihre Strukturierung setzt außer der Berücksichtigung von Formcharakteristiken die Beachtung von inhaltlichen Faktoren voraus. Da die Sprache nicht nur der Darstellung von Gedanken dient, sondern gleichzeitig das wichtigste Instrument zur Vermittlung von Information zwischen Kommunikationspartnern bildet, ist auf der inhaltlichen Ebene auch die Bezugnahme auf den kommunikativen Bereich unerläßlich. Die Vermittlung von Information beinhaltet nämlich, daß ein Sender im Laufe mündlicher oder schriftlicher Kommunikation den Wissensvorrat eines Empfängers in relevanter Weise ergänzt. In diesem Prozeß sind zwei grundlegende kommunikative Aspekte involviert: teils geht es darum, daß der Sprecher oder Schreiber das Wissen des Hörers bzw. Lesers richtig einschätzt und als Ausgangspunkt seiner Mitteilung wählt, teils darum, daß er das Relevante deutlich hervortreten läßt. Auf diese Weise wird den beiden Anforderungen Rechnung getragen, deren Erfüllung eine wesentliche Voraussetzung für das Funktionieren der Kommunikation bildet: der Herstellung von *Kohärenz* im Diskurs und der Sicherung der *Informativität* der Äußerung.

Mit verschiedenen sprachlichen und außersprachlichen Mitteln wird die Information vom Sender so gewichtet, daß bestimmte Teile ins Blickfeld gerückt werden, während andere zurücktreten. Durch diese Gewichtung nach Vordergrund und Hintergrund wird ein Informationsrelief aufgebaut. Die Strukturierung von Information und die dadurch entstehende Reliefwirkung werden in der einschlägigen Literatur in Zusammenhang mit zwei sprachlichen Einheiten erörtert: Satz und Text. Bei der Diskussion der Informationsgewichtung auf der Satzebene wird vor allem der Begriff *Informationsstruktur* verwendet, während in der Textlinguistik der *Reliefbegriff*, der aus der Gestalttheorie stammt, eine zentrale Rolle spielt.

Bezüglich der Frage, in welchem Bereich des Sprachsystems die Strukturierung von Information verankert ist, gehen die Meinungen in der Forschung auseinander: in früheren Untersuchungen wurde die größte Aufmerksamkeit den kognitiven und kommunikativen Aspekten der Problematik gewidmet; in der modernen Linguistik dagegen wird die Informationsstruktur vorwiegend als Teil der grammatischen Repräsentation betrachtet. Von Anfang an stand allerdings in beiden Richtungen die Identifizierung der unterschiedlichen sprachlichen Mittel, die zur Kodierung der informationsstrukturellen Gliederung dienen, im Zentrum des Interesses. Darüber hinaus wurden in zahlreichen Arbeiten Vorschläge zur Explizierung der der Informationsstrukturierung zugrunde liegenden Prinzipien gemacht, welche die Anwendung einzelner morphosyntaktischer, topologischer und prosodischer Mittel steuern. Bereits in den sprachvergleichenden Arbeiten der Prager Schule wurde auf die große sprachspezifische Variation in der formalen Gestaltung der Informationsstruktur hingewiesen. Erst neuere typologische Untersuchungen haben aber durch extensive Datenerhebung die Gewinnung typologisch relevanter Aufschlüsse ermöglicht.

Im folgenden wollen wir in Abschnitt 2 zunächst die wichtigsten Termini und Begriffe einführen, die in der Literatur zur Informationsstruktur Verwendung finden. Nach der Präsentation verschiedener theoretischer Analysemöglichkeiten des Phänomens in Abschnitt 3 wird in Abschnitt 4 auf bestimmte Faktoren und Prinzipien eingegangen, die die Strukturierung von Information beeinflussen. In Abschnitt 5 werden die wichtigsten formalen Mittel diskutiert, die in unterschiedlichen Sprachen zur Markierung informationsstrukturell ausgezeichneter Kategorien vorliegen. In den Abschnitten 6 und 7 fassen wir die neuesten im Hinblick auf die Informationsgliederung erzielten Ergebnisse der Typologieforschung zusammen. Abschnitt 8 wird schließlich der Diskussion von Informationsstruktur und Reliefgebung aus textlinguistischer Perspektive gewidmet.

2. Grundlegende Termini und Begriffe

Die Strukturierung von Information in Sätzen ist einer Ebene zuzuordnen, die von der syntaktischen Subjekt-Prädikat-Struktur relativ unabhängig ist. Diese Erkenntnis geht auf den französischen Sprachwissenschaftler Henri Weil (1844) zurück, der auf die Notwendigkeit einer Unterscheidung zwischen der durch kognitive und kommunikative Prinzipien motivierten Serialisierung und der syntaktischen Struktur hingewiesen hat. Daß eine solche Unterscheidung erforderlich ist, läßt sich anhand folgender Beispiele nachweisen:

(1)   *Bill read this book last week.*

(2)   *This book Bill read last week.*

Die Sätze (1) und (2) sind sowohl im Hinblick auf ihren propositionalen Gehalt als auch bezüglich der ihnen zugrunde liegenden syntaktischen Hierarchie identisch. Beispielsweise realisiert *Bill* in beiden Sätzen die syntaktische Funktion Subjekt, während *this book* als Objekt auftritt. Die Umstellung der Konstituenten in Satz (2) im Verhältnis zu Satz (1) führt aber zu einem Unterschied in der jeweils vermittelten Information, indem in (1) über *Bill*, in (2) über *this book* etwas ausgesagt wird.

Für die informationsstrukturelle Funktion von *Bill* bzw. *this book* in den oben angeführten Beispielsätzen werden in der linguistischen Literatur je nach theoretischem Ansatz verschiedene Bezeichnungen verwendet, u. a. *psychologisches Subjekt, Topik, Thema* und *Satzgegenstand*. Durch diese Termini wird − in bestimmter, noch zu diskutierender Weise − auf den Bereich der Äußerung hingewiesen, der den Ausgangspunkt der Mitteilung bildet. Der komplementäre Teil, der Mitteilungskern − in (1) *read this book last week*, in (2) *Bill read last week* − wird *psychologisches Prädikat, Kommentar, Rhema, Satzaussage* oder *Fokus* genannt. Allen Untersuchungen zur Informationsstruktur ist gemeinsam, daß in ihnen eine derartige Spaltung des Satzes in zwei Bereiche vorgenommen wird. Auf diese Bereiche wird durch Begriffspaare wie z. B. *psychologisches Subjekt* vs. *psychologisches Prädikat, Topik* vs. *Kommentar* und *Thema* vs. *Rhema* Bezug genommen.

Die Termini *psychologisches Subjekt* und *psychologisches Prädikat* wurden bereits im vorigen Jahrhundert von Paul (1880) und

v. d. Gabelentz (1891) vorgeschlagen. Ammann (1928), der über den psychologischen Aspekt hinaus den sozialen Charakter des „Sprechaktes" betonte, führte zur Bezeichnung der beiden — auch kontextuell relevanten — Einheiten der Äußerung die Termini *Thema* und *Rhema* ein. Eine systematische und differenzierte Beschreibung der Informationsstruktur liegt jedoch erst seit der Ausarbeitung der Lehre von der Funktionalen Satzperspektive durch die Prager Schule vor (Mathesius 1929, Daneš 1964). In der Theorie der Prager Schule spielte das kontextuell bestimmbare Kriterium *bekannt* vs. *neu* eine zentrale Rolle, vgl. Daneš (1964: 228): „The framework for the dynamism of the utterance represents 'the functional perspective' in a strict sense [...] In this way, an utterance may usually be divided into two portions: the **theme** (or **topic**), conveying the known (given) elements, and the **rheme** (or **comment**), conveying the unknown (not given) elements of an utterance."

Halliday (1967) argumentiert überzeugend dafür, daß das Bekanntheitskriterium allein nicht ausreicht, um alle Aspekte der Informationsstrukturierung zu erfassen. Er unterscheidet u. a. zwischen der Ebene der *thematization* und der Ebene der *information structure*, und betrachtet diese als unabhängige Ebenen der textuellen Organisation, die unterschiedliche Funktionen erfüllen und sich auch verschiedener Formmittel bedienen. Im Unterschied zu Daneš und anderen Prager Linguisten schränkt Halliday das Begriffspaar *theme* — *rheme* auf die *thematization* (die kontextunabhängige Gliederung) ein, betrachtet das Thema als „point of departure for the clause as a message" (1967: 212) und bindet es an die erste Position des Satzes. Seiner Analyse zufolge wären in den Beispielen (1) und (2) die Konstituenten *Bill* und *this book* aufgrund der Erststellung im Satz — unabhängig von ihrem Status als bekannt bzw. nicht bekannt — als Ausgangspunkt der Aussage, d. h. als Thema, anzusehen. Hallidays Bezeichnungen *Thema* — *Rhema* stimmen allerdings weder mit der von Daneš vorgeschlagenen noch mit der in der jüngsten Literatur dominierenden Terminologie überein — nicht nur weil er den Terminus *Thema* von dem Bekanntheitskriterium trennt, sondern auch deshalb, weil er die Bezeichnung *Topik* nicht verwendet.

In Hallidays Modell ist die Ebene der *information structure* — im Gegensatz zur Thema-Rhema-Ebene — auch vom Kontext abhängig. Halliday betont jedoch die Freiheit des Sprechers hinsichtlich der Entscheidung, auf welche Weise ein bestimmter Inhalt vermittelt wird. Nicht die Bekanntheit oder Neuheit des mitgeteilten Inhalts selbst, sondern die Art seiner „Verpackung" sei ausschlaggebend. Halliday weist in diesem Zusammenhang — vor allem in bezug auf englische Daten — auf die entscheidende Rolle der Intonation hin. Abhängig von den Akzentverhältnissen im Satz lassen sich bestimmte Segmente der Äußerung als „information focus" festlegen. In unserem Beispielsatz (1) *Bill read this book last week* können demnach unterschiedliche Konstituenten den Hauptakzent tragen und als Informationsfokus (unten mit Fettdruck markiert) fungieren. Vgl. (3)—(6):

(3) **BILL** *read this book last week.*

(4) *Bill* **READ** *this book last week.*

(5) *Bill read* **THIS BOOK** *last week.*

(6) *Bill read this book* **LAST WEEK.**

Die Sätze (3)—(6) unterscheiden sich bezüglich ihrer kontextuellen Einbettungsmöglichkeiten. Während beispielsweise Satz (3) als Antwort auf die Frage *Who read this book last week?* angemessen ist, kann (5) in einem Kontext, wo nach dem Objekt gefragt wird — wie *What did Bill read last week?* — als angemessene Antwort dienen. In neueren syntaktisch und semantisch orientierten Theorien zur Informationsstruktur wird zur Bezeichnung der hervorgehobenen Konstituente der Terminus *Fokus* bevorzugt; gleichzeitig wird das von den Prager Linguisten eher in funktionalem Sinne verwendete Begriffspaar *Thema* — *Rhema* vermieden. Als Gegenpol zum Fokus werden Termini wie *Präsupposition, offene Proposition, Topik* oder *Hintergrund* eingeführt, die allerdings mit teilweise unterschiedlichem begrifflichem Inhalt verbunden werden.

Die Ansicht, daß für eine vollständige Beschreibung und Erklärung der Gesetzmäßigkeiten der Informationsstruktur eine einzige Ebene nicht ausreicht, wird neuerdings von den meisten Sprachwissenschaftlern vertreten. Zu denjenigen, die für zwei Ebenen in der informationsstrukturellen Gliederung argumentieren, gehören Chomsky (1971), Dahl (1974), Kiefer (1977), Jacobs (1984), Drubig (1991/92) und Lambrecht (1994). Im Gegensatz zu diesen schlägt Molnár (1991) eine Schichtung in drei Ebenen vor (nach Topik — Kommentar, Thema — Rhema und

Hintergrund − Fokus), um dadurch auf die drei von Bühler (1934: 24) angesetzten „Relationsfundamente" der kommunikativen Situation (Gegenstände bzw. Sachverhalte, Empfänger, Sender) Bezug zu nehmen.

In der Literatur finden sich auch andere − theoretisch unterschiedlich orientierte − Vorschläge zur Differenzierung der informationsstrukturellen Funktionen. Im Rahmen der Theorie der Prager Schule hat Firbas (1971) das Konzept der Kommunikativen Dynamik entwickelt, wonach die Elemente im Satz − abhängig von ihrem Beitrag zur Vorantreibung der Kommunikation − hierarchisch geordnet sind. Im Gegensatz zu den früheren Dichotomie-Thesen handelt es sich bei Firbas um einen graduellen Übergang vom Thema, das den niedrigsten Grad an kommunikativer Dynamik trägt, zum Rhema, das den Mitteilungskern enthält.

In einer bedeutenden neueren Arbeit setzt sich Vallduví (1992) − ganz anders als Firbas − mit dem traditionellen Dichotomie-Gedanken auseinander und konstruiert ein 'trinomisches' hierarchisches Modell der Informationsstruktur. Nach der primären Aufspaltung des Satzes in *Focus* und *Ground* (Hintergrund) teilt er in einem zweiten Schritt den Ground in *Link* und *Tail* auf, wobei das *Link* mit dem Satzgegenstand vergleichbar ist und der *Tail* den Rest des *Grounds* umfaßt. In Anlehnung an Halliday betrachtet Vallduví die Strukturierung von Information als ein „packaging phenomenon", das strategische Instruktionen zum Aufbau bzw. zur Modifizierung des Wissensvorrats des Empfängers bereitstellt.

3. Zur Verankerung der Informationsstruktur in der modernen Sprachtheorie

In der Sprachwissenschaft der letzten zwei Jahrzehnte wird die Informationsstruktur vorrangig im Hinblick auf die Topik-Kommentar-Gliederung und die Fokus-Hintergrund-Gliederung untersucht. Während auf der Topik-Kommentar-Ebene der Topikbegriff zentral ist und der Kommentar einfach den restlichen Teil des Satzes umfaßt, ist auf der Fokus-Hintergrund-Ebene der Fokus die relevante Definitionsgröße, und der Hintergrund bildet den Rest. Dieses Verhältnis erklärt vermutlich, warum in der Literatur nicht selten die markierten Begriffe *Topik* und *Fokus* als Gegenpole behandelt werden.

Das Topik-Kommentar-Verhältnis wird in der Regel mit Bezug auf die „aboutness relation" festgelegt (Reinhart 1982, Molnár 1991). In vielen Arbeiten wird aber gleichzeitig die kontextuelle Bindung des Topikbegriffs im Sinne von Bekanntheit oder Vorerwähntheit betont (Gundel 1988, Büring 1997). Diese Bezugnahme auf zwei unabhängige Definitionskriterien hat zu erheblichen Schwierigkeiten in der Topikdiskussion geführt.

Was die Fokussierung anbelangt, so wird diese in der Literatur − vor allem in der generativen Grammatik − als syntaktisches Phänomen betrachtet. Der Vorschlag, ein syntaktisches Fokusmerkmal F einzuführen, das mit beliebigen Knoten der Oberflächenstruktur assoziiert werden kann, stammt von Jackendoff (1972). Durch ein solches Merkmal lasse sich eine Verbindung zwischen der Phonologie − wo der Fokus als Akzent ausbuchstabiert wird − und der interpretativen Komponente herstellen. Ein syntaktisches Fokusmerkmal spielt auch in neueren Fokustheorien eine entscheidende Rolle (Selkirk 1984, Horvath 1986, Rochemont 1986, Rosengren 1991, Uhmann 1991, Hetland 1992, Winkler 1997).

Für die syntaktische Relevanz des Fokus werden in der Literatur vor allem drei Argumente angeführt. Erstens wird auf die Gesetzmäßigkeiten der sogenannten Fokusprojektion hingewiesen, nach denen die syntaktische Position des Satzakzents über den Umfang des Fokusbereiches im Satz entscheidet, vgl. (7) und (8):

(7)   Peter hat DEN JUNGEN *geschlagen.*

(8)   DEN JUNGEN *hat Peter geschlagen.*

Die Fokusprojektion wird normalerweise mit Hilfe von Frage-Antwort-Paaren ermittelt. Der Beispielsatz in (7) kann nicht nur als angemessene Antwort auf die Frage *Wen hat Peter geschlagen?* dienen, er kann auch die Fragen *Was hat Peter getan?* und *Was ist passiert?* beantworten. In (7) liegt also − durch die mögliche Erweiterung der Fokusdomäne über die akzentuierte Konstituente hinaus − Fokusprojektion vor, in (8) dagegen ist die Fokusprojektion blockiert wegen der Erststellung der akzentuierten − und folglich fokussierten − Konstituente. Zum letztgenannten Satz kann man sich nur eine Frage vorstellen wie *Wen hat Peter geschlagen?* Das Phänomen der Fokusprojektion wird ausführlich von Höhle (1982) diskutiert.

Als zweites Argument für den Einfluß syntaktischer Prinzipien auf die Informationsstruktur dient die in bestimmten Sprachen vorliegende strukturelle Fokusposition. So wird z. B. für Sprachen wie Baskisch (Rijk 1978) und Ungarisch (É. Kiss 1981) die obligatorische Versetzung der Fokuskonstituente in eine spezifische syntaktische Fokusposition angenommen. In einigen Arbeiten der generativen Syntaxtheorie wird aber auch für Sprachen, in denen eine oberflächenstrukturelle Position für den Fokus fehlt, eine unsichtbare − auf der Ebene der Logischen Form erfolgende − Fokusbewegung postuliert (Brody 1990, É. Kiss 1991).

Über die Fokusprojektion und die Annahme von festgelegten Fokuspositionen hinaus wird in der Literatur als drittes Argument angeführt, daß beide Typen von Fokusbewegung (auf S-Struktur oder LF) strikten Lokalitätsbeschränkungen („island constraints") unterliegen (Drubig 1994). In Sprachen mit overter Fokusposition läßt sich die Wirkung von Inselbeschränkungen leicht nachweisen: Horvath (vgl. 1986: 101) hat z. B. für das Ungarische überzeugend gezeigt, daß die Bewegung der fokussierten Konstituente aus einer Nominalphrase − einen zusätzlichen Grenzknoten überschreitend − nicht zulässig ist:

(9) * *Kati* [F A FÖLDRENGÉSTŐL]$_i$
 Kati the earthquake-from
 hallotta [NP a hírt, [CP *hogy*
 heard the news-AKK that
 Attila félt t$_i$]]
 Attila feared
 'Kati hat die Nachricht gehört, daß Attila vor dem ERDBEBEN Angst hatte.'

In Sprachen, in denen der Fokus in situ markiert wird, läßt sich die Geltung der Lokalitätsrestriktionen nur indirekt belegen. Der Nachweis, daß hier die gleichen syntaktischen Beschränkungen wirksam sind, setzt aber das Vorhandensein von fokussensitiven Partikeln voraus (*only, even,* Negationspartikeln etc.), wie in Beispiel (10), vgl. Drubig (1994: 37):

(10) *He didn't interrogate*
 [the man who invited the ex-convict
 with the [RED] shirt], but
 1. **the BLUE shirt*
 2. **with the BLUE shirt*
 3. **the ex-convict with the BLUE shirt*
 4. *the man who invited the ex-convict with the BLUE shirt*

Drubig argumentiert dafür, daß in einer replaziven Konstruktion wie (10) die Negation nicht direkt mit dem Fokus *RED* assoziiert werden kann, sondern nur mit der von äußeren Klammern umgebenen Nominalphrase *the man who invited the ex-convict with the RED shirt.* Dies wird als Indiz dafür interpretiert, daß syntaktische Inselrestriktionen auch in Sprachen wie dem Englischen gelten.

Da im Englischen keine feste syntaktische Position für die Markierung des Fokus zur Verfügung steht, muß der Fokus hier mit Hilfe von anderen formalen Mitteln zum Ausdruck gebracht werden. Im Englischen − wie in den meisten europäischen Sprachen − ist die Akzentuierung das wichtigste Fokussierungsmittel. Laut Selkirk (1995: 555) wird jede durch einen Pitch-Akzent ausgezeichnete Konstituente mit einem Fokusmerkmal versehen: „An accented word is F-marked". Für die Fokusprojektion gelten in ihrem Modell folgende Regeln:

„a. F-marking of the **head** of a phrase licenses the F-marking of the phrase.
 b. F-marking of an **internal argument** of a head licenses the F-marking of the head."

Für die von Selkirk vorgeschlagenen Regeln ist die Argumentstruktur von entscheidender Bedeutung. Problematisch ist aber, daß ihr argumentstruktureller Ansatz auf die Konstituentenabfolge keine Rücksicht nimmt und außerdem nicht der Fokussierung in solchen Sprachen Rechnung tragen kann, in denen die Fokusmarkierung nicht primär durch prosodische Mittel ausgedrückt wird. Weiterhin kann mit Hilfe von Selkirks Projektionsregeln die Subjektprominenz in thetischen Sätzen nicht erklärt werden (Sasse 1987, 1996).

Eine ganz andere theoretische Orientierung liegt den Arbeiten von Jacobs (1982, 1983, 1984) zugrunde, in denen die Fokussierung als semantisches Phänomen behandelt wird und formale Methoden zur Beschreibung von Fokus-Hintergrund-Strukturen entwickelt werden. In Jacobs' „relationaler Fokustheorie" wird jede Fokuskonstituente als Fokus eines fokussierenden Elements betrachtet, und jede Fokuskonstituente ist an ein solches Element gebunden. Als Fokusbinder fungieren Lexeme wie Gradpartikeln (z. B. *nur, sogar*), die Negationspartikel *nicht* und Einstellungsverben. In Fällen, wo kein offen fokussierendes Element vorhanden ist, kommt die Funktion der Fokusbindung dem Illokutionsoperator zu. Vgl. (11) und (12):

(11) *Peter besucht nur Gerdas* SCHWESTER.

(12) *Peter besucht Gerdas* SCHWESTER.

Diese Sätze haben laut Jacobs parallele semantische Strukturen (vgl. Jacobs 1984: 30 ff., ASS steht für Assertion):

(13) NUR (λX^{NP} [Peter besucht X's Schwester], Gerda)

(14) ASS (λX^{NP} [Peter besucht X's Schwester], Gerda)

Der Erklärungsansatz von Jacobs könnte zwar eine einheitliche Erfassung sämtlicher Fokussierungsphänomene ermöglichen, die Annahme einer Parallelität zwischen (13) und (14) ist aber nicht unproblematisch. Man muß nämlich davon ausgehen, daß auch in Sätzen mit Gradpartikeln (vgl. (13)) Illokutionsoperatoren vorliegen. In solchen Fällen bleibt offen, welcher Operator als Fokusbinder fungiert.

Die inhaltliche Leistung der Fokussierung besteht nach Jacobs (1988: 91 f.) in der Herstellung eines Alternativenbezugs, eine Idee, die er von Rooth (1985) übernimmt und die auf Jackendoff (1972: 242 ff.) zurückgeht. Jackendoff verwendet allerdings nicht die Bezeichnung „alternative", sondern spricht von „a coherent class of possible contrasts with the focus". Rooth konzentriert sich auf das Phänomen „association with focus", das man in Sätzen mit fokussensitiven Operatoren wie *only* und *even* beobachten kann. Für die Interpretation von Fokus wird in Rooths Ansatz — im Gegensatz zu den oben erwähnten syntaktischen Fokustheorien — keine Bewegung angenommen: der Fokus wird in situ interpretiert. Die in diesem Zusammenhang relevante syntaktische Konfiguration ist das Bestehen eines C-Kommando-Verhältnisses zwischen Fokuspartikel und Fokus.

Für die semantische Interpretation setzt Rooth zwei Ebenen an: die erste expliziert den propositionalen Inhalt, ohne auf das F-Merkmal Rücksicht zu nehmen; auf der zweiten Ebene wird ein „p-set" (vgl. Jackendoffs (1972) „presuppositional set") ausbuchstabiert, das die durch Fokussierung hervorgerufenen Alternativen erfaßt. Diese Alternativen machen ihrerseits die Quantifikationsdomäne für fokussensitive Operatoren aus.

Die von Rooth entworfene Zwei-Ebenen-Semantik wird von Büring (1997) weiter ausgebaut, indem Büring die propositionale Ebene und die Ebene des „p-sets" — von ihm „Fokuswert" genannt — durch eine dritte Ebene, den „Topikwert", ergänzt. Der Topikwert enthält relevante Alternativen zu intonatorisch markierten Topiks. Durch ihren Alternativenbezug weisen markierte Topiks in Bürings Modell offenbar Eigenschaften auf, die auch für Foki charakteristisch sind. Büring argumentiert allerdings mit Nachdruck dafür, daß diese Topiks nicht mit Fokussierung in Beziehung zu setzen sind und schließt sie — als Teil des Hintergrunds — aus dem Fokusbereich aus.

Es hat sich in semantisch orientierten Modellen als schwierig erwiesen, eine saubere Trennung der semantischen und pragmatischen Aspekte der Fokusinterpretation durchzuführen. Das Problem der Grenzziehung zwischen Semantik und Pragmatik ist in der Fokusdiskussion keineswegs neu, schon bei Sgall/Hajičová/Benešová (1973) wurde es explizit angesprochen. Im Rahmen der generativen Semantik haben Sgall et al. ein einheitliches „initiales" semantisch-pragmatisches Niveau als relevante Ebene für die Topik-Fokus-Artikulation befürwortet. Diese Auffassung wurde vor allem dadurch begründet, daß in bestimmten Fällen informationsstrukturelle Gegebenheiten die wahrheitsfunktionale Interpretation des Satzes beeinflussen.

Auch Lambrecht (1994) behandelt formale und kommunikative Aspekte der Sprache innerhalb eines einzigen übergreifenden Systems. Im Gegensatz zu den oben erwähnten Vertretern der generativen Semantik sieht er aber für die Informationsstruktur eine eigene Komponente innerhalb der Satzgrammatik vor, wobei er die Interaktion dieser Komponente mit anderen Submodulen des Systems stark betont.

Rein pragmatisch verankert ist die von Dik (1978) im Rahmen der „Functional Grammar" ausgearbeitete Theorie der Informationsstruktur, die sich in ihrer funktionalen Orientiertheit weitgehend auf die Prager Linguistik stützt. In Diks Ansatz werden drei Funktionsebenen auseinandergehalten, die syntaktische, die semantische und die den beiden anderen übergeordnete pragmatische Ebene, wobei auf der pragmatischen Ebene die zum Kern der Prädikation („predication proper") gehörigen Kategorien *Topik* und *Fokus* von den prädikationsexternen Kategorien *Thema* und *Tail* unterschieden werden.

Auch Vallduví (1992) entwickelt ein pragmatisches Modell der Informationsstrukturierung, das zwar seinen Ausgangspunkt im Prinzipien- und Parametermodell der generativen Grammatik hat (Chomsky 1981), das aber die Informationsstruktur einer eigenständigen sprachlichen Ebene („Informatics") zuordnet und diese den anderen interpretativen Ebenen gleichstellt. Valldují argumentiert nicht nur für den modularen Aufbau des Sprachsystems, sondern auch für eine strikte Abhebung der informationsstrukturellen Komponente von der LF-Komponente, die für die logisch-semantischen Aspekte der Interpretation zuständig ist.

4. Grundprinzipien der Informationsstrukturierung

Bei der Erforschung der Informationsstruktur spielt die Identifikation relevanter Kategorien und die Analyse ihrer Reihenfolge in der Äußerung eine wesentliche Rolle. In typologisch und universalgrammatisch orientierten Arbeiten wird diese Problematik vorwiegend mit Bezug auf die interne Abfolge von *Topik* und *Fokus* bzw. *given* und *new* diskutiert. Einige der Regularitäten, die die Strukturierung von Information steuern, gehen höchstwahrscheinlich auf Prinzipien zurück, deren Wirkung in allen menschlichen Sprachen nachvollziehbar ist. Diese universalen Prinzipien haben ihren Ursprung in unterschiedlichen Bereichen: in der Kognition, in der jeweiligen kommunikativen Situation sowie in strukturellen Gesetzmäßigkeiten. Dabei ist allerdings nicht auszuschließen, daß im Laufe der Sprachentwicklung kognitive und diskursfunktionale Strategien einen gewissen Einfluß auf die Festlegung grammatischer Strukturen ausgeübt haben.

Die kognitiv und pragmatisch motivierten Prinzipien haben zu der häufig vertretenen Annahme geführt, daß die Abfolge *Topik vor Fokus* universale Geltung hat. Diese Regularität wurde in der Prager Schule als Thema-Rhema-Abfolge behandelt (vgl. vor allem Firbas 1971 zur kommunikativen Dynamik); bei Kuno tritt sie als *Information Flow Principle* auf (Kuno 1978: 54, nach Kim 1988), bei Gundel (1988: 229) als *Given Before New Principle*: „State what is given before what is new in relation to it."

Mit diesem Prinzip eng verwandt ist das von Tomlin (1986: 37) vorgeschlagene *Theme First Principle*: „[…] information that is more 'thematic' tends to precede information that is less 'thematic' ". In Tomlins psycholinguistisch verankertem Ansatz hat der thematische Teil der Äußerung, der ihm zufolge dem Satzgegenstand entspricht, vor allem die Funktion, einen Rahmen für den nachfolgenden Diskurs zu schaffen, indem er die Aufmerksamkeit des Hörers in einer bestimmten Richtung lenkt.

Ein weiteres Prinzip, das für die Plausibilität der Reihenfolge Topik vor Fokus spricht, wird von Herring (1990: 164) als *Discourse Iconicity Principle* eingeführt: „Information ideally is placed as close as possible to the part of the discourse to which it relates; i. e. sentences start with what has already been talked about, and end with what is to be talked about next."

Im Widerspruch zu diesen Prinzipien steht allerdings das *First Things First Principle*, das die Universalität der Topik-Fokus-Abfolge in Abrede stellt: „Provide the most important information first." (Gundel 1988: 229, vgl. auch Mithuns *Newsworthiness Principle* 1987: 304 ff., außerdem Behaghel 1932: 254 ff. und Givón 1983: 20). Nach diesem Prinzip steht der fokussierte Teil des Satzes vor dem nichtfokussierten Rest. In solchen Fällen handelt es sich in der Regel um emphatische, kontrastive Fokustypen am Satzanfang. Diejenigen Linguisten, die von einer obligatorischen Topik-Fokus-Dichotomie im Satz ausgehen, sind bei der Anfangsstellung des Fokus zur Annahme eines Topiks im postfokalen Bereich gezwungen. Fraglich ist jedoch, ob ein solcher Vorschlag, der in der einschlägigen Literatur nicht selten gemacht wird (Creider/Creider 1983, Gundel 1988, Herring 1990), berechtigt ist. Die Beantwortung dieser Frage ist weitgehend von der jeweiligen Topikdefinition abhängig.

In der Forschung wurde auch die Frage diskutiert, ob über die oben genannten funktional begründeten Prinzipien hinaus andere Faktoren für die Strukturierung von Information relevant sein könnten. Als wichtige strukturelle Gesetzmäßigkeit mit sprachübergreifender Geltung wurde in diesem Zusammenhang bereits von Behaghel (1923—32) das „Gesetz der wachsenden Glieder" formuliert, das auf eine Erkenntnis des französischen Grammatikers Beauzée (1767) zurückgeht. Diesem Prinzip wird auch in späteren linguistischen Arbeiten große Bedeutung zugeschrieben: zum Beispiel wird es bei Jespersen (1949) unter der Bezeichnung „principle of relative weight" erörtert, während es bei Hawkins (1991/92) — mit einem ganz anderen theoretischen Ausgangspunkt — als „principle of syntactic weight" behandelt wird. In seinem performanzorientierten Ansatz argumentiert Hawkins gegen den entscheidenden Einfluß funktionaler Prinzipien auf die Wortstellung; statt dessen nimmt er an, daß für eine optimale Perzeption das syntaktische Gewicht ausschlaggebend ist: „I believe that words occur in the orders they do so that speakers can enable hearers to recognize syntactic groupings and their immediate constituents [...] as rapidly and efficiently as possible" (Hawkins 1991/92: 197).

Aus typologischer Perspektive wird in Herring (1990) die Relevanz struktureller Prinzipien für die Informationsstruktur erörtert. Anhand typologischer Daten versucht sie nachzuweisen, daß die Wirkung sämtlicher funktionalen Prinzipien von der Basisgliedfolge der jeweiligen Sprache überspielt wird. Diese Gesetzmäßigkeit faßt sie im *Word Order Type Principle* zusammen: „Information structure is determined relative to a language's basic word order, as a rhetorical marking strategy. Verb-subject languages tend to order focus (comment) before topic, in contrast with languages of either the SVO or the SOV type." (Herring 1990: 164). Laut Herring ist das *Word Order Type Principle* das einzige Prinzip, das eine zuverlässige Prognose für die relative Stellung von Topik und Fokus geben kann.

5. Formale Mittel der Topik- und Fokusmarkierung

Die universalen Gesetzmäßigkeiten stellen – in ihrer Interaktion mit sprachspezifisch variierenden, aber grammatisch festgelegten Strukturen – einen gewissen Spielraum zur Verfügung für die formale Realisierung der informationsstrukturellen Kategorien *Topik* und *Fokus*. Die Ausdrucksmöglichkeiten dieser Kategorien sind syntaktischer, morphologischer oder phonologischer Natur. Sie sind in unterschiedlichem Maße markiert, abhängig von den strukturellen Besonderheiten der jeweiligen Sprache (darunter Basisgliedfolge, Konfigurationalität, Verb-Zweit-Charakter usw.). Zum Beispiel ist ein Objekt in der prototypischen Topikposition – d. h. in satzinitialer Stellung – in verschiedenen Sprachen mit unterschiedlichem Markiertheitseffekt verbunden, vgl. den englischen Satz (15) und seine deutsche Entsprechung in (16):

(15) *The pláy, John saw yésterday.*
(Chafe 1976: 49)

(16) (*Wann hat Hans das Schauspiel gesehen?*)
Das Schauspiel hat Hans géstern gesehen.

Während das Topik *the play* in (15) nicht unakzentuiert bleiben darf und oft kontrastiv interpretiert wird (vgl. Chafes „Topics, English Style"), ist die Topikalisierung von *das Schauspiel* im deutschen Satz (16) auch ohne Akzent möglich. Die Wortstellung ist in diesem Fall zwar nicht neutral, das Topik kann aber phonologisch unmarkiert bleiben.

Zur Kennzeichnung des Topiks dienen in den Sprachen der Welt verschiedene intonatorische und strukturelle Mittel, die satzintern oder satzextern eingesetzt werden. Unter den satzinternen Topikmarkierungen werden in der Forschung – über die oben exemplifizierten Topikalisierungstransformationen hinaus – vor allem Topikmorpheme erwähnt (u. a. im Japanischen, Koreanischen und Quechua). Weiterhin wird die Passivkonstruktion als eines der wichtigsten Topikalisierungsmittel betrachtet, die eine Umstellung der Satzglieder und die Beförderung einer nicht-agentivischen Konstituente zum Subjekt beinhaltet. Dadurch wird die unmarkierte Korrelation zwischen dem Subjekt – in der Regel im Nominativ – und dem Topik ermöglicht (Givón 1979, Eroms 1986). Vgl. die Aktantenumpolung bei Passivierung in den deutschen Sätzen (17) und (18):

(17) *Hans   schlägt Peter.*
      Subj. = Agens Akk.obj. = Patiens
      TOPIK

(18) *Peter   wird von Hans*
      Subj. = Patiens präp. Angabe = Agens
      geschlagen.
      TOPIK

Während durch Passivierung pragmatisch unmarkierte Topiks ermöglicht werden, dienen in vielen Sprachen intonatorische Mittel zur Bildung von markierten Topiktypen. Innerhalb des Satzrahmens kann durch einen Akzent auf der Topikkonstituente – zusätzlich zum Fokusakzent – die Topik-Kommentar-Gliederung verdeutlicht werden:

(19) (a) *What happened to your car?*
     (b) *My CAR broke DOWN.*
     (Sasse 1996: 12)

Die prosodische Realisierung des Topikakzents weist allerdings große Variation auf. Dabei sind relevante Unterschiede nicht nur zwischen den Sprachen zu beachten, sondern es stehen auch innerhalb der Einzelsprachen mehrere intonatorische Muster zur Verfügung, die mit unterschiedlichen Interpretationen einhergehen. Große Aufmerksamkeit wird in der jüngsten Forschung – vor allem mit Bezug auf das Deutsche – einem besonderen Akzentmuster gewidmet, das durch die Kombination von einem steigenden bzw. fallend-steigenden Akzent auf dem Topik („Wurzelakzent", mit √ markiert) und einem fallenden Akzent auf dem Fokus gekennzeichnet ist:

(20) (a) *Kann man denn alle Romane von Grass empfehlen?*
(b) *Na ja, √ALle kann man sicher 'NICHT empfehlen (, aber sein ERSter ist zweifellos ein MEISterwerk).* (Jacobs 1997: 92)

Diese intonatorische Kennzeichnung der Topikkonstituente ist nicht nur mit einer Kontrastimplikatur verbunden, sondern sie bewirkt in Sätzen mit bestimmten Quantoren und Operatoren sogar Skopusinversion, d. h. für den Fall (20 b) eine Lesart mit weitem Negationsskopus („es ist nicht der Fall, daß alle Grass-Romane empfehlenswert sind"). Dieses Phänomen wird in einschlägigen Arbeiten in Anlehnung an Jacobs (1982) unter der Bezeichnung „I-Topikalisierung" diskutiert (vgl. hierzu auch Höhle 1991, Büring 1995, Jacobs 1997, Molnár/Rosengren 1997, Hetland 1999). Mit Bezug auf andere Sprachen als das Deutsche wird für vergleichbare Topiks der Terminus „contrastive topic" verwendet (Szabolcsi 1981. É. Kiss 1987, Lambrecht 1994, Molnár 1998).

Zusätzlich zu den satzintern markierten Topikstrukturen werden in der Literatur zwei Haupttypen von satzexternen Topikrealisierungen untersucht, *hanging topic* (*Freies Thema*) und *left dislocation* (*Linksversetzung*), eine Differenzierung, die auf Cinques (1977) Vorschlag bezüglich des Französischen und Italienischen zurückgeht. Vgl.:

(21) *Mary, John saw her yesterday.* HT
(Prince 1985: 67)

(22) *Mary, she saw John yesterday.* LD

Da aber die Kriterien, die der Kategorisierung zugrunde liegen, in den verschiedenen Ansätzen variieren, ist die Abgrenzung der beiden Typen voneinander nicht unproblematisch (vgl. Cinque 1977, Altmann 1981, Cardinaletti 1987). Unabhängig von ihrer Kategorisierung können satzexterne Topikmarkierungen wie Freies Thema und Linksversetzung optional auch mit lexikalisierten Einleitungsfloskeln auftreten (z. B. *as for, concerning, regarding, was ... betrifft*):

(23) *As for Matilda, she can't stand Felix.*
(Reinhart 1982: 9)

In allen satzexternen Topikkonstruktionen bildet die außerhalb des Satzrahmens stehende Konstituente eine eigenständige Akzentdomäne, wobei die Topikinterpretation vom jeweils verwendeten Akzentmuster abhängig ist. Diese markierten Topiktypen dienen vornehmlich als Signale von Topik-Shift bzw. Topik-Kontrast. Im Vergleich zu den strukturell und intonatorisch unmarkierten Topiks unterliegen sie erheblich strengeren Diskursrestriktionen.

Wie für das Topik, gibt es auch für den Fokus ein breites Spektrum von strukturellen Realisierungsalternativen, die sich bezüglich ihres Markiertheitsgrads unterscheiden. Während in der überwiegenden Mehrzahl der europäischen Sprachen die Fokussierung mit Hilfe von prosodischen Mitteln erfolgt, dienen in anderen Sprachen Fokusmorpheme (vgl. Japanisch, Kikuyu, Somali, Quechua) oder bestimmte syntaktische Positionen bzw. Konstruktionen (vgl. Aghem, Akan, Baskisch, Hausa, Ungarisch und Yoruba) zur Fokusmarkierung.

Beim sogenannten „Intonation Focus" (Taglicht 1984) kann der Fokusakzent – unabhängig von anderen Faktoren – einer beliebigen Konstituente im Satz zugewiesen werden:

(24) *He was* HERE.

(25) HE *was here.*

(26) *He* WAS *here.* (Taglicht 1984: 3)

Ein Hauptakzent auf dem finiten Verb (vgl. (26)) kann dabei eine besondere Fokusinterpretation auslösen, den sogenannten Polaritätsfokus bzw. Verum-Fokus (Gussenhoven 1984, Höhle 1988, Drubig 1994), wodurch das Wahrsein eines aus dem Kontext bekannten Sachverhalts hervorgehoben wird.

In anderen Fällen von Fokussierung interagiert jedoch die Prosodie mit bestimmten syntaktischen Strukturen, wobei vor allem den Satzrändern eine entscheidende Rolle zukommt. Der linke Satzrand wird vornehmlich bei besonders markierten, emphatischen Fokussierungen ausgenutzt:

(27) *His name I never found out.*
(Taglicht 1984: 3)

(28) *Nothing could I find anywhere.*
(Jackendoff 1972: 365)

Der Fokussierung in satzinitaler Stellung liegen in den Sätzen (27) und (28) unterschiedliche syntaktische Strukturen zugrunde – in

(27) handelt es sich um Topikalisierung in syntaktischem Sinne, während in (28) „Negative Constituent Preposing" vorliegt. In beiden Beispielen setzt sich offenbar des *First Things First Principle* durch (vgl. Abschnitt 4).

Die Position an der rechten Peripherie des Satzes steht ebenfalls häufig im Dienste der Fokussierung, wie beim sogenannten „Heavy NP Shift" und bei bestimmten anderen Vorkommnissen der Extraposition im Englischen (vgl. Ross 1968 zum „Complex NP Shift", außerdem Rochemont 1978, Rochemont/Culicover 1990). Bei Heavy NP Shift handelt es sich in der Regel um die Rechtsversetzung einer umfangreichen und informationsstrukturell wichtigen Konstituente, die laut Rochemont/Culicover (1990: 24) im Englischen eine obligatorische Fokusinterpretation auslöst:

(29) *John purchased for his wife* A BRAND NEW FUR COAT.

Die notwendige Fokusinterpretation der rechtsversetzten Konstituente in (29) wird von Rochemont/Culicover damit begründet, daß der Satz nur als Antwort auf eine Frage wie (30) — und nicht als Antwort auf (31) — angemessen ist:

(30) *What did John purchase for his wife?*

(31) *For whom did John purchase a brand new fur coat?*

Rochemont/Culicovers Schlußfolgerung bezüglich der obligatorischen Fokusinterpretation der rechtsbewegten NP, die auf der Grundlage von englischen Daten gezogen wird, kann nicht ohne weiteres auf andere Sprachen übertragen werden. Dies läßt sich u. a. anhand von „right detachment" von nichtfokussiertem Material im Katalanischen nachweisen (Vallduví 1992: 131):

(32) *[$_{IP}$El Pau$_1$ [$_{IP}$ [$_{IP=F}$ no l$_2$ 'ha MORT t$_2$ t$_1$] el jutge$_2$]].*
'Paul didn't KILL the judge.'

Es gibt aber auch Sprachen, in denen bestimmte Rechtsversetzungstypen bezüglich ihrer informationsstrukturellen Funktion heterogen sind. Das ist der Fall bei den sogenannten Ausklammerungskonstruktionen, die allerdings auf Sprachen mit einer prädikativen Satzklammer wie Deutsch und Niederländisch beschränkt sind. Vgl. die deutschen Sätze (33) und (34), zitiert nach Haftka (1981: 762):

(33) *In derselben Sekunde schlug der Angsttraum um <u>in den schönsten Traum seines Lebens</u>.*

(34) *(Egon wird diesen Werkstoff nicht wieder verwenden.)*
Er hat schlechte Erfahrungen gemacht <u>mit diesem Material</u>.

Während es sich in (33) zweifellos um die Bewegung einer informationsstrukturell wichtigen Konstituente über die rechte Satzklammer handelt (bei Haftka „Rhema"), zeigt (34) deutlich, daß die Funktion der Ausklammerung im Deutschen nicht auf Rhematisierung bzw. Fokussierung einzuschränken ist. In diesem Zusammenhang ist jedoch wichtig zu beachten, daß für die Ausklammerung u. a. auch Präpositionalphrasen — also nicht nur, wie bei der englischen Konstruktion Heavy NP Shift, Nominalphrasen — in Frage kommen.

Was das Englische anbelangt, sind über die erwähnten Fälle hinaus auch andere syntaktische Fokussierungsstrategien untersucht worden. Zu diesen zählen nach Rochemont/Culicover (1990: 25) weitere Konstruktionen mit einem strukturellen Fokus an der rechten Peripherie des Satzes — wie *directional/locative adverbial preposing* (35), *preposing around „be"* (36) und *presentational „there" insertion* (37):

(35) *Into the room walked* JOHN.

(36) *Under the table was* A CAT.

(37) *There ran into the room* SEVERAL OVEREXCITED FANS.

Im Gegensatz zu Heavy NP Shift und einigen anderen Typen der Extraposition wird hier laut Rochemont/Culicover notwendigerweise das in situ bleibende Subjekt als Fokus interpretiert.

Zu den in der Forschung eingehend diskutierten Fokuskonstruktionen gehört auch die sogenannte Satzspaltung (*Cleft*). Viele Fokusforscher behaupten kategorisch, daß die Clefts die Fokuskonstruktion par excellence darstellen (vgl. vor allem Rochemont/Culicover 1990: 24):

(38) *It was* A BRAND NEW FUR COAT *that John purchased for his wife.*

Die obligatorische Fokusinterpretation der Cleft-Phrase *a brand new fur coat* in (38) wird von Rochemont/Culicover dadurch begründet, daß (38) nur in einem Kontext wie (39) angemessen ist und unter keinen Umständen als Antwort auf (40) vorkommen kann:

(39) *What did John purchase for his wife?*

(40) *Who purchased a brand new fur coat for his wife?*

Überzeugende Einwände gegen die Analyse der Cleft-Phrase als eines obligatorischen Fokus wurden zuerst von Prince (1978) formuliert, die nachgewiesen hat, daß die Fokuslesart der Cleft-Phrase nicht zwingend ist, sondern daß auch das Cleft-Komplement den Fokus enthalten kann, vgl. hierzu (41) aus Delin (1992: 6):

(41) a. *And does the head know?*
b. *No. Oh, wait a minute.*
It was the head who arrANGED it.

Prince unterscheidet zwischen zwei Cleft-Typen: in einem von diesen („stressed focus *it*-clefts") wird die Cleft-Phrase als Fokus interpretiert, beim zweiten Typ („informative-presupposition *it*-clefts") liegt der Fokus innerhalb des Cleft-Komplements. In der jüngsten Forschung werden Vorschläge zu weiteren Differenzierungen von *it*-Clefts gemacht (Delin 1992).

Ganz andere Aspekte der Fokusmarkierung werden vor allem in semantisch orientierten Ansätzen (Jackendoff 1972, Jacobs 1983, Rooth 1985) im Zusammenhang mit den sogenannten fokussensitiven Partikeln (*only, even* etc.) zur Debatte gestellt. Es wird in der überwiegenden Mehrzahl der Analysen behauptet, daß sich diese Partikeln obligatorisch mit dem Fokus des Satzes assoziieren, wobei die Assoziation mit dem Fokus grundsätzlich als eine semantisch relevante Erscheinung behandelt wird (vgl. Abschnitt 3).

Zuletzt soll auf ein Phänomen hingewiesen werden, das sich zwar nicht ohne weiteres unter die Fokusmarkierungen subsumieren läßt, jedoch in bestimmten Sprachen (z. B. Deutsch, Niederländisch, Russisch, Ungarisch) für die informationsstrukturelle Gewichtung auf der Satzebene große Konsequenzen hat: das Scrambling. Scrambling beinhaltet eine optionale Linksbewegung einer oder mehrerer – in der Regel kontextuell gegebener – Konstituenten aus dem Fokusbereich. Die Funktion des Scrambling besteht vor allem darin, den Fokusbereich im Satzinnern einzuschränken. Darüber hinaus wird von Rosengren (1993) gezeigt, daß das Scrambling im Deutschen auch zur Herstellung von mehreren Fokusdomänen dienen kann.

6. Informationsstruktur aus typologischer Perspektive: zur Frage der Diskurskonfigurationalität

Die Sprachen der Welt lassen sich in zwei große Klassen einteilen, je nachdem, ob die grundlegende Satzstruktur durch kasusstrukturelle oder diskurssemantische Faktoren motiviert ist. Sprachen, in denen die Kasus- und Thetarollenzuweisung die Serialisierung auf der Oberflächenstruktur steuern, sind auf der grammatischen Ebene als mehr oder weniger konfigurationell zu betrachten. In denjenigen Sprachen dagegen, in denen die Gliedstellung von der Aufgabe der strukturellen Zuweisung des (Nominativ-)Kasus entlastet ist, ist vor allem der informationsstrukturelle Status der Konstituenten für die Gliedfolge verantwortlich. Bei letzterem Sprachtyp spricht man von *diskurskonfigurationellen* Sprachen, die ihrerseits interne Unterschiede aufweisen und weiter zu differenzieren sind.

Die Beobachtung, daß die syntaktische Subjekt-Prädikat-Struktur nicht in allen Sprachen die grundlegende Satzstruktur repräsentiert, stammt von dem ungarischen Linguisten Brassai (1860). Ihm zufolge läßt sich in bestimmten Sprachen die Struktur eines Satzes primär mit Bezug auf informationsstrukturelle Konzepte festlegen (bei Brassai „inchoativum – bulk"). Hundert Jahre später finden sich ähnliche Gedanken bei Hockett (1958: 201 ff.) und Li/Thompson (1976) – unter den Bezeichnungen *Topik* und *Kommentar*. Anhand von Evidenz aus dem Burmesischen (einer Sprache aus der Sino-Tibetanischen Sprachfamilie) schlagen Li/Thompson eine typologische Klassifizierung der Sprachen vor, die auf die variierende Dominanz („Prominenz") der Begriffe Subjekt und Topik Bezug nimmt.

Unter Einfluß der Konfigurationalitätsdebatte in der generativen Grammatik (Hale 1982, É. Kiss 1987) wird die Frage der Subjekt- bzw. Topikprominenz aus einer neuen Perspektive aufgegriffen. Nach É. Kiss (1995: 13) besteht der relevante Unterschied zwischen subjekt- und topikprominenten Sprachen darin, daß sie die Prädikation auf unterschiedlichen syntaktischen Ebenen repräsentieren. Während die Prädikation – die „notional predication structure" – in topikprominenten Sprachen auf der S-Struktur repräsentiert ist, ist sie in subjektprominenten Sprachen erst auf der Ebene der LF identifizierbar. Topikprominenz wird von É. Kiss auf der Grundlage von zwei Kriterien definiert, die aber nicht unbedingt miteinander korrelieren. Einerseits gilt eine Sprache als topikprominent, wenn ein vorangestelltes arbiträres Argument die gleiche syntaktische Position einnehmen kann wie das Subjekt. Andererseits werden solche Sprachen als topikprominent definiert, in denen kategorische und thetische Urteile durch unterschiedliche syntaktische Strukturen realisiert werden.

In Anlehnung an Li/Thompsons Bezeichnung *Topikprominenz* wird später die Bezeichnung *Fokusprominenz* geprägt, die sich auf die Eigenschaft bestimmter Sprachen bezieht, den Fokus – in der Regel mit kontrastiver Interpretation – an eine bestimmte Position im Satz zu binden.

In diskurskonfigurationellen Sprachen stehen für Konstituenten mit Topik- bzw. Fokusstatus ausgezeichnete Positionen zur Verfügung. In einigen dieser Sprachen müssen beide informationsstrukturellen Kategorien im Satz formal enkodiert werden, während in anderen Sprachen entweder für das Topik oder für den Fokus feste Positionen vorhanden sind.

Der Sprachtyp mit Topik- *und* Fokuskonfigurationalität umfaßt viele europäische Sprachen, unter diesen Italienisch, Katalanisch, Polnisch, Russisch, Rumänisch, Griechisch, Türkisch, Armenisch und einige kaukasische Sprachen – allerdings mit relevanten sprachspezifischen Besonderheiten (vgl. Sasse 1995: 1073). Zu diesem Sprachtyp gehört auch das Ungarische, wo die Fokuskonstituente in der Regel unmittelbar vor dem finiten Verb steht und wo beim eventuellen Vorhandensein von Topikkonstituenten diese die Positionen vor dem Fokus einnehmen müssen. Eine adäquate und grammatisch korrekte Beantwortung der Frage (42) ist im Ungarischen nur dann möglich, wenn die oben genannten Stellungsrestriktionen beachtet werden:

(42) *Hova utazott   Péter?*
      Wohin ist gefahren Peter
      'Wohin ist Peter gefahren?'

(43) a. [FOKUS *LUNDba*] *utazott.*
           nach Lund (er) ist gefahren
           'Er ist nach Lund gefahren.'
     b. [TOPIK *Péter*] [FOKUS *LUNDba*]
           Peter   nach Lund
        utazott.
        ist gefahren
     c. *[FOKUS *LUNDba*] [TOPIK *Péter*]
           nach Lund   Peter
        utazott.
        ist gefahren

Die in (42) erfragte Konstituente *LUNDba* fungiert in der Antwort (43 a) als Fokus und muß folglich in der präverbalen Position stehen. Wenn in der Antwort auch ein Topik realisiert wird, wie in (43 b), muß dies dem Fokus vorangehen. Die Umkehrung der Reihenfolge von Topik und Fokus resultiert in einem ungrammatischen Satz, vgl. (43 c).

Unter denjenigen diskurskonfigurationellen Sprachen, die nur die Topikalität syntaktisch kennzeichnen, sind in der einschlägigen Literatur u. a. Tschechisch und Slowakisch genannt worden. Als weitere Beispiele für topikkonfigurationelle Sprachen werden asiatische Sprachen wie Japanisch und Mandarin angeführt und Indianersprachen wie Quechua (Sasse 1995). Bezüglich des Japanischen ist allerdings nicht auszuschließen, daß diese Sprache gleichzeitig auch fokuskonfigurationell ist. Eine auf den Fokus beschränkte Konfigurationalität liegt nach Angaben in der Literatur u. a. in den Sprachen Aghem (É. Kiss 1995), Walisisch, Bretonisch und Finnisch vor (Sasse 1995).

7. Weitere typologisch relevante Zusammenhänge

Die wichtigste Aufgabe typologischer Untersuchungen im Bereich der Informationsstrukturierung besteht darin, die diskursfunktionalen Eigenschaften natürlicher Sprachen zu grammatisch-strukturell festlegbaren Sprachtypen in Beziehung zu setzen und dadurch implikative Zusammenhänge aufzudecken. Nicht nur in der Diskussion der Diskurskonfigurationalität, sondern auch in anderen Bereichen der Typologie der Informationsstruktur sind die Begriffe Topik und Fokus und die mit ihnen verbundenen Konstruktionen von zentraler Bedeutung.

Bahnbrechend auf dem Gebiet der Topikforschung sind die Arbeiten von Kuroda (1972) und Sasse (1987, 1996), die sich auf die philosophische Tradition von Brentano (1874) und Marty (1895) stützen. Laut Kuroda gibt es zwei grundlegende Formen menschlicher Urteile, zum einen die thetischen, die sich auf die Situation als ungeteiltes Ganzes beziehen, zum anderen die kategorischen, die in zwei Schritten – Benennung und Prädikation – vollzogen werden. Diese beiden Urteilstypen manifestieren sich in bestimmten Satzstrukturen, eine Beobachtung, die später von Sasse übernommen und weiterentwickelt wird. Sasse ist es dabei gelungen, tiefe theoretische Einsichten im Bereich der Thetizität mit einem weiten typologischen Überblick zu verbinden.

Thetische Sätze weisen – im Gegensatz zu kategorischen – eine monolithische Struktur auf, indem sie eine neue Situation als Einheit präsentieren, vgl. (44) und (45) aus Sasse (1987: 558):

(44) *The CAT is miaowing.* (thetisch)

(45) *The CAT is MIAOWing.* (kategorisch)

Die strukturelle Realisierung dieses Unterschieds untersucht Sasse anhand einer großen Anzahl von Sprachen, wobei er für thetische Sätze von vier verschiedenen Konstruktionstypen ausgeht: (i) Subjektakzentuierung (45), (ii) Verb-Subjekt-Abfolge (46), (iii) Subjekt + Relativsatz (47) und (iv) Inkorporation des Subjekts (48). Vgl. Sasse (1996: 12 ff.), außerdem Lambrecht (1994):

(46) *My CAR broke down.*

(47) *Mi si è rotta la MACCHINA.*
      'My CAR broke down.'

(48) *C'est MAMAN qui me bat.*
      'MUM's hitting me.'

(49) *áddigée-juudi* (Boni)
      father:1sPOSS-die:3smPERF
      'My Father died.'

In seinen typologisch ausgerichteten Untersuchungen geht Sasse der Frage nach, wie sich die vier genannten Konstruktionen auf unterschiedliche Sprachtypen verteilen. Gleichzeitig vermittelt er wertvolle Einblicke in die Gesetzmäßigkeiten der Fokusprojektion in verschiedenen Sprachen.

Was die Fokusforschung aus typologischer Perspektive anbelangt, so gibt es zwar eine Reihe von relevanten einzelsprachlichen Untersuchungen, aber nur in wenigen Arbeiten kommt es zu sprachübergreifenden Generalisierungen. Wichtige Daten und Erkenntnisse zur typologischen Charakterisierung der europäischen Sprachen enthalten die im Rahmen des EUROTYP-Projekts durchgeführten Forschungen (É. Kiss (Hrsg.) 1995), deren große Bedeutung auch darin besteht, daß sie theoretische und methodologische Grundlagen für die Erforschung außereuropäischer Sprachen bereitstellen. Interessante, die Grenzen des europäischen Sprachraums überschreitende Untersuchungen stammen von Kim (1988), der Sprachen wie Japanisch, Hindu-Urdu, Tamilisch, Türkisch und Navajo einbezieht, und implikative Beziehungen zwischen dem Greenbergschen Sprachtyp XXIII (ein Typ innerhalb der sov-Sprachen, vgl. Hawkins 1983) und bestimmten Fokustypen feststellt. Kim gehört auch zu denjenigen Linguisten, die auf die Präferenz für Clefts als Fokussierungsstrategie in vso-Sprachen hinweisen. Zu den verbinitialen Sprachen liegen auch wichtige typologische Studien von Creider/Creider (1983) und Payne (1995) vor, die auf der Grundlage relevanter Einzelsprachen Evidenz dafür liefern, daß in diesen Sprachen vor allem pragmatisch markierte Funktionen, wie z. B. kontextuell neue Topiks (Creider/Creider) und kontrastiver Fokus (Payne), in präverbaler Position – am Satzanfang – realisiert werden.

Einen weiten typologischen Ausblick bietet Herring (1990), die die Strukturierung der Information in verbinitialen Sprachen mit der Informationsstrukturierung in anderen Sprachtypen vergleicht. Dabei unterscheidet sie zwischen unmarkierten und markierten Topik- und Fokustypen („continuous topic" und „presentational focus" vs. „shifted topic" und „contrastive focus") und setzt sich hauptsächlich mit der Frage auseinander, welche Prinzipien für die Serialisierung dieser pragmatischen Einheiten entscheidend sind. Herring stellt eine sehr starke Hypothese auf, die besagt, daß die Basisgliedfolge der jeweiligen Sprachen die relative Abfolge von Topik und Fokus determiniert und daß das „word order type principle" alle anderen Prinzipien zur Festlegung der Informationsstruktur überspielt (vgl. Abschnitt 4). Die Verifizierung oder Falsifizierung dieser These bildet eine wichtige Aufgabe für die zukünftige typologisch orientierte Forschung.

8. Reliefgebung in Texten

Die Bezeichnung *Reliefgebung* („mise en relief", Reliefbildung) tritt unseres Wissens zum ersten Mal bei Brunot (1926) auf, zur Markierung von informationsstrukturell ausgezeichneten Konstituenten innerhalb des Satzes. Mit Bezug auf die Satzebene wird der Terminus auch von Müller-Hauser (1943) benutzt – und außerdem von Dressler (1973), beim letztgenannten unter anderem als Synonym von Hervorhebung im Sinne der Funktionalen Satzperspektive. Dressler untersucht auch die Reliefgebung auf der Textebene, wobei er sich an Weinrichs (1964) Terminologie bezüglich der Gliederung des Textes nach Vordergrund und Hintergrund anschließt.

Während Weinrich – anhand von erzählenden Texten der schönen Literatur – den Begriff der Reliefgebung mit Ausgangspunkt von den beiden im Französischen vorliegenden Tempora Imparfait und Passé simple entwickelt und deren Funktion mit der Rolle der

Verbstellung im Deutschen vergleicht, wird bei Dressler die textuelle Reliefgebung auch in Beziehung zu der Aspektproblematik und zu Modalpartikeln gesetzt. In späteren Arbeiten werden vor allem syntaktische Gewichtungsmittel beachtet, wie Haupt- und Nebensätze, Parenthesen und Präpositionalgruppen. Dabei gehen Linguisten wie Posner (1972) und Hartmann (1984) davon aus, daß die syntaktische Unterscheidung zwischen Haupt- und Nebensatz normalerweise dem kommunikativen Unterschied zwischen Haupt- und Nebeninformation entspricht. Ihnen zufolge gibt der Sprecher durch die Wahl der Nebensatzform zu erkennen, daß es sich nicht um assertierte Information handelt, sondern um eine Voraussetzung zur Einschätzung der eigentlichen Aussage, die ihrerseits in Form eines Hauptsatzes präsentiert wird. Durch die Nebensatzform läßt sich laut Hartmann auch signalisieren, daß der Nebensatzinhalt nicht weiter Gegenstand des Diskurses sein soll.

Ein Begriff, der für die Explikation der Informationsstrukturierung in Texten von großer Bedeutung ist, ist die *Informationseinheit*. Dieses Konzept wurde ursprünglich von Halliday (1967) mit Bezug auf die Satzebene eingeführt und aufgrund phonologischer Kriterien definiert. Auf Texte bezogen — mit einem anderen theoretischen Ausgangspunkt — wird der Terminus *Informationseinheit* von Rossipal (1975) und später auch von Brandt (1990) zur Bezeichnung von diskurspragmatisch definierten Entitäten verwendet. Laut Brandt (1990, 1996) vermittelt jede Informationseinheit eine *Information*, die eine eigene Fokus-Hintergrund-Gliederung und eine relativ selbständige Intonationskontur aufweist. Auf diese Einheit rekurrierend modifiziert Brandt Hartmanns These von der Funktion der Nebensatzform als Gewichtungsmittel und gelangt zu der Schlußfolgerung, daß die angenommene Korrelation zwischen syntaktischer Subordination und Hintergrundinformation nicht ausnahmslos gilt. Brandt argumentiert dafür, daß an der kommunikativen Gewichtung auf der Textebene nur solche subordinierten Nebensätze teilhaben, die selbständige Informationseinheiten ausmachen. Eine zufriedenstellende Definition des Begriffes *Informationseinheit* steht allerdings noch aus.

In den Arbeiten zur textuellen Reliefgebung werden insbesondere narrative Texte untersucht, wobei die Begriffe *Vordergrund* und *Hintergrund* in Abhängigkeit von ihrem Beitrag zur Weiterführung der Ereigniskette definiert werden (Klein/Stutterheim 1992, vgl. auch Hopper 1979). In Klein/Stutterheims Ansatz wird die Unterscheidung nach Vordergrund und Hintergrund nicht auf die kommunikative Wichtigkeit im Sinne der funktionalen Satzperspektive bezogen, sondern sie wird aus der Perspektive der globalen Textstruktur interpretiert: „Eine Äußerung zählt zum Vordergrund eines Textes dann und nur dann, wenn sie Bestandteil des narrativen Skelettes ist. Alle anderen Äußerungen sind dem Hintergrund zuzurechnen" (Klein/Stutterheim 1992: 72). Die zum Skelett des Textes gehörigen Vordergrundäußerungen beantworten laut Klein/Stutterheim (1992: 69) die sogenannte „Quaestio" des Textes: „Was ist (dir) zum Zeitpunkt x am Ort y passiert?" Klein/Stutterheim gehen in ihrer Untersuchung vor allem der Frage nach, wie die globalen Bedingungen, die sich aus der Quaestio ergeben, die Informationsentfaltung auf der lokalen Ebene beeinflussen. Die genauere Explizierung des Verhältnisses zwischen globalen und lokalen Beschränkungen der Informationsgewichtung in Texten bildet eine wichtige Aufgabe für die zukünftige textlinguistische Forschung.

9. Literatur

Altmann, Hans. 1981. *Formen der „Herausstellung" im Deutschen. Rechtsversetzung, Linksversetzung, Freies Thema und verwandte Konstruktionen.* (Linguistische Arbeiten, 106) Tübingen: Niemeyer.

Ammann, Hermann. 1928. *Die menschliche Rede. Sprachphilosophische Untersuchungen. Zweiter Teil.* Lahr: Schauenburg.

Beauzée, Nicolas. 1767. *Grammaire générale, ou exposition raisonnée des éléments nécessaires du langage, pour servir de fondement à l'étude de toutes les langues.* Paris: Barbou.

Behaghel, Otto. 1923–1932. *Deutsche Syntax. Eine geschichtliche Darstellung.* 4 Bände. Heidelberg: Winter.

Brandt, Margareta. 1990. *Weiterführende Nebensätze. Zu ihrer Syntax, Semantik und Pragmatik.* (Lunder germanistische Forschungen, 57) Stockholm: Almqvist & Wiksell International Internat.

Brandt, Margareta. 1996. „Subordination und Parenthese als Mittel der Informationsstrukturierung in Texten". In: Motsch, Wolfgang (ed.). *Ebenen der Textstruktur. Sprachliche und kommunikative Prinzipien.* (Reihe Germanistische Linguistik, 164) Tübingen: Niemeyer, 211–240.

Brassai, Sámuel. 1860. 1863–65. „A magyar mondat". (The Hungarian sentence.) *Magyar Akadémiai Értesítő, A Nyelv- és Széptudományi Osztály Közlönye* 1:279–399; 3: 3–128, 173–409.

Brentano, Franz. 1874. *Psychologie vom empirischen Standpunkte.* Leipzig: Duncker & Humblot.

Brody, Michael. 1990. „Some remarks on the focus field in Hungarian". *UCL Working Papers in Linguistics* 2. 201–225.

Brunot, Ferdinand. 1926. *La pensée et la langue. Méthode, principes et plan d'une théorie nouvelle du langage appliquée au français.* Paris: Masson.

Bühler, Karl. 1934. *Sprachtheorie. Die Darstellungsfunktion der Sprache.* Jena: G. Fischer.

Büring, Daniel. 1997. *The meaning of topic and focus. The 59th street bridge accent.* London & New York: Rontledge.

Cardinaletti, Anna. 1987. „Linksperiphere Phrasen in der deutschen Syntax". *Studium Linguistik* 22: 1–30.

Chafe, Wallace L. 1976. „Givenness, contrastiveness, definiteness, subjects, topics, and point of view". In: Li, Charles N. (ed.), 25–55.

Chomsky, Noam. 1971. „Deep structure, surface structure, and semantic interpretation". In: Steinberg, Danny D. & Jakobovits, Leon A. (ed.). *Semantics. An interdisciplinary reader in philosophy, linguistics and psychology.* Cambridge: Cambridge University Press, 183–216.

Chomsky, Noam. 1981. *Lectures on Government and Binding. The Pisa lectures.* (Studies in Generative Grammar, 9) Dordrecht/Cinnaminson: Foris Publications.

Cinque, Guglielmo. 1977. „The movement nature of left dislocation". *Linguistic Inquiry* 8.2: 397–412.

Creider, Chet A. & Creider, Jane T. 1983. „Topic-comment relations in a verb-initial language". *Journal of African Languages and Linguistics* 5: 1–15.

Dahl, Östen. 1974. „Topic-comment structure revisited". In: Dahl, Östen (ed.). *Topic and comment, contextual boundness and focus.* Hamburg: Buske, 1–24.

Daneš, František. 1964. „A three-level approach to syntax". *Travaux Linguistiques de Prague* 1: 225–240.

Delin, Judy. 1992. *Aspects of cleft constructions in discourse.* Arbeitspapiere des Sonderforschungsbereichs 340, 19. Stuttgart: Wissenschaftliches Zentrum der IBM Deutschland.

Dik, Simon C. 1978. *Functional Grammar.* (Publications in Language Sciences, 7) Dordrecht/Cinnaminson: Foris Publications.

Dressler, Wolfgang. 1973. *Einführung in die Textlinguistik.* (Konzepte der Sprach- und Literaturwissenschaft, 13) Tübingen: Niemeyer.

Drubig, Hans Bernhard. 1991/92. „Zur Frage der grammatischen Repräsentation thetischer und kategorischer Sätze". In: Jacobs, Joachim (ed.), 142–195.

Drubig, Hans Bernhard. 1994. *Island constraints and the syntactic nature of focus and association with focus.* Arbeitspapiere des Sonderforschungsbereichs 340, 51. Heidelberg: Wissenschaftliches Zentrum der IBM Deutschland.

Eroms, Hans-Werner. 1986. *Funktionale Satzperspektive.* (Germanistische Arbeitshefte, 31) Tübingen: Niemeyer.

Firbas, Jan. 1971. „On the concept of communicative dynamism in the theory of functional sentence perspective". *Sborník Prací,* A 19: 135–144.

Gabelentz, Georg von der. 1891. *Die Sprachwissenschaft, ihre Aufgaben, Methoden und bisherigen Ergebnisse.* Leipzig: Tauchnitz.

Givón, Talmy. 1979. *On understanding grammar.* New York/San Francisco/London: Academic Press.

Givón, Talmy. 1983. „Topic continuity in discourse: an introduction". In: Givón, Talmy (ed.). *Topic continuity in discourse: a quantitative cross-language study.* Amsterdam/Philadelphia: Benjamins, 1–41.

Gundel, Jeanette K. 1988. „Universals of topic-comment structure". In: Hammond, Michael & Moravcsik, Edith A. & Wirth, Jessica R. (eds.), 209–239.

Gussenhoven, Carlos. 1984. *On the grammar and semantics of sentence accents.* (Publications in Language Sciences, 16) Dordrecht/Cinnaminson: Foris Publications.

Haftka, Brigitta. 1981. „Reihenfolgebeziehungen im Satz (Topologie)". In: Heidolph, Karl Erich & Flämig, Walter & Motsch, Wolfgang (eds.). *Grundzüge einer deutschen Grammatik.* Berlin: Akademie-Verlag, 702–764.

Hale, Ken. 1982. „Preliminary remarks on configurationality". In: Pustejovsky, James & Sells, Peter (eds.). *Proceedings of NELS* 12. Amherst/MA: GLSA, 86–96.

Halliday, M. A. K. 1967. „Notes on transitivity and theme in English". Part 2. *Journal of Linguistics* 3: 199–244.

Hammond, Michael & Moravcsik, Edith A. & Wirth, Jessica R. (eds.). 1988. *Studies in syntactic typology.* (Typological Studies in Language, 7) Amsterdam/Philadelphia: Benjamins.

Hartmann, Dietrich. 1984. „Reliefgebung: Informationsvordergrund und Informationshintergrund in Texten als Problem von Textlinguistik und Stilistik. Zur Verwendung sprachlicher Mittel zum Ausdruck von Haupt- und Nebeninformation". *Wirkendes Wort* 4: 305–323.

Hawkins, John A. 1983. *Word Order Universals.* New York etc.: Academic Press.

Hawkins, John A. 1991/92. „Syntactic weight versus information structure in word order variation". In: Jacobs, Joachim (ed.), 196–219.

Herring, Susan C. 1990. „Information structure as a consequence of word order type". *Proceedings of the 16th annual meeting of the Berkeley Linguistics Society:* 163–174.

Hetland, Jorunn. 1992. *Satzadverbien im Fokus*. (Studien zur deutschen Grammatik, 43) Tübingen: Narr.

Hetland, Jorunn. 1999. „Die Geheimnisse des Akzenttons fall-rise und die 'J-Topikalisierung' des Deutschen". *Sprache und Pragmatik* 50: 48−87.

Hockett, Charles F. 1958. *A course in modern linguistics*. New York: MacMillan.

Höhle, Tilman N. 1982. „Explikationen für 'normale Betonung' und 'normale Wortstellung'". In: Abraham, Werner (ed.) *Satzglieder im Deutschen. Vorschläge zur syntaktischen, semantischen und pragmatischen Fundierung*. (Studien zur deutschen Grammatik, 15) Tübingen: Narr, 75−153.

Höhle, Tilman N. 1988. „VERUM-Fokus". *Sprache und Pragmatik* 5: 1−7.

Höhle, Tilman N. 1991. „On reconstruction and coordination". In: Haider, Hubert & Netter, Klaus (eds.). *Representation and derivation in the theory of grammar*. (Studies in Natural Language and Linguistic Theory, 22) Dordrecht/Boston/London: Kluwer, 139−197.

Hopper, Paul J. 1979. „Aspect and foregrounding in discourse". In: Givón, Talmy (ed.). *Discourse and syntax*. (Syntax and Semantics, 12) New York/San Francisco/London: Academic Press, 213−241.

Horvath, Julia. 1986. *FOCUS in the theory of grammar and the syntax of Hungarian*. (Studies in Generative Grammar, 24) Dordrecht/Riverton: Foris Publications.

Jackendoff, Ray S. 1972. *Semantic interpretation in generative grammar*. (Studies in Linguistics Series, 2.) Cambridge, MA/London: MIT Press.

Jacobs, Joachim. 1982. *Syntax und Semantik der Negation im Deutschen*. (Studien zur theoretischen Linguistik, 1) München: Fink.

Jacobs, Joachim. 1983. *Fokus und Skalen. Zur Syntax und Semantik der Gradpartikeln im Deutschen*. (Linguistische Arbeiten, 138) Tübingen: Niemeyer.

Jacobs, Joachim. 1984. „Funktionale Satzperspektive und Illokutionssemantik". *Linguistische Berichte* 91: 25−58.

Jacobs, Joachim. 1988. „Fokus-Hintergrund-Gliederung und Grammatik". In: Altmann, Hans (ed.). *Intonationsforschungen*. (Linguistische Arbeiten, 200) Tübingen: Niemeyer, 89−134.

Jacobs, Joachim (ed.) 1991/92. *Informationsstruktur und Grammatik*. (Linguistische Berichte, Sonderheft 4) Opladen: Westdtutscher Verlag.

Jacobs, Joachim. 1997. „I-Topikalisierung". *Linguistische Berichte* 168: 91−133.

Jespersen, Otto. 1949. *A modern English grammar on historical principles*. Part VII: Syntax. Completed and published by Niels Haislund. København: Munksgaard.

Kiefer, Ferenc. 1977. „Functional sentence perspective and presuppositions". *Acta Linguistica Academiae Scientiarum Hungaricae* 27: 83−109.

Kim, Alan Hyun-Oak. 1988. „Preverbal focusing and type XXIII languages". In: Hammond, Michael & Moravcsik, Edith A. & Wirth, Jessica R. (eds.), 145−169.

É. Kiss, Katalin. 1981. „Structural relations in Hungarian, a 'free' word order language". *Linguistic Inquiry* 12: 185−213.

É. Kiss, Katalin. 1987. *Configurationality in Hungarian*. Dordrecht: Reidel.

É. Kiss, Katalin. 1991. „Logical structure in syntactic structure: the case of Hungarian". In: Huang, C.-T. James & May, Robert (eds.). *Logical structure and linguistic structure. Cross-linguistic perspectives*. (Studies in Linguistics and Philosophy, 40) Dordrecht/Boston/London: Kluwer, 111−147.

É. Kiss, Katalin. 1995. „Discourse configurational languages. Introduction". In: É. Kiss, Katalin (ed.), 3−27.

É. Kiss, Katalin. (ed.). 1995. *Discourse configurational languages*. New York/Oxford: Oxford University Press.

Klein, Wolfgang & Stutterheim, Christiane von. 1992. „Textstruktur und referentielle Bewegung". *Zeitschrift für Literaturwissenschaft und Linguistik* 86: 67−92.

Kuno, Susumu. 1978. *Danwa no bunpō*. (The grammar of discourse.) Tokyo: Taishukan.

Kuroda, S.-Y. 1972. „The categorical and the thetic judgment: evidence from Japanese syntax". *Foundations of Language* 9: 153−185.

Lambrecht, Knud. 1994. *Information structure and sentence form. Topic, focus, and the mental representation of discourse referents*. Cambridge: Cambridge University Press.

Li, Charles N. (ed). 1976. *Subject and topic*. New York/San Francisco/London: Academic Press.

Li, Charles N. & Thompson, Sandra A. 1976. „Subject and topic. A new typology of language". In: Li, Charles N. (ed.), 457−489.

Marty, Anton. 1895. „Vom Ausdruck einfacher Urtheile. (Insbesondere pseudokategorische Aussagen und ihre innere Form.)". *Vierteljahrsschrift für wissenschaftliche Philosophie* XIX: 277−334.

Mathesius, Vilém. 1929. „Zur Satzperspektive im modernen Englisch". *Archiv für das Studium der neueren Sprachen und Literaturen* 155: 202−210.

Mithun, Marianne. 1987. „Is basic word order universal"? In: Tomlin, Russell S. (ed.). *Coherence and grounding in discourse*. (Typological Studies in Language, 11) Amsterdam/Philadelphia: Benjamins, 281−328.

Molnár, Valéria. 1991. *Das TOPIK im Deutschen und im Ungarischen*. (Lunder germanistische Forschungen, 58) Stockholm: Almqvist & Wiksell International.

Molnár, Valéria. 1997. „Topic in focus. On the syntax, phonology, semantics and pragmatics of the so-called 'contrastive topic' in Hungarian and German". *Acta Linguistica Hungarica* 45, 1−2: 89−166.

Molnár, Valéria & Rosengren, Inger. 1997. „Zu Jacobs' Explikation der I-Topikalisierung". *Linguistische Berichte* 169: 211–247.

Müller-Hauser, Marie-Louise. 1943. *La mise en relief d'une idée en français moderne.* (Romanica Helvetica, 21) Genève/Erlenbach-Zürich: Droz.

Paul, Hermann. 1880. *Prinzipien der Sprachgeschichte.* Tübingen: Niemeyer.

Payne, Doris L. 1995. „Verb initial languages and information order". In: Downing, Pamela & Noonan, Michael (eds.). *Word order in discourse.* (Typological Studies in Language, 30) Amsterdam/Philadelphia: Benjamins, 449–485.

Posner, Roland. 1972. *Theorie des Kommentierens. Eine Grundlagenstudie zur Semantik und Pragmatik.* (Linguistische Forschungen, 9) Frankfurt/M: Athenäum-Verlag.

Prince, Ellen F. 1978. „A comparison of wh-clefts and *it*-clefts in discourse". *Language* 54.4: 883–906.

Prince, Ellen F. 1985. „Fancy syntax and 'shared knowledge' ". *Journal of Pragmatics* 9: 65–81.

Reinhart, Tanya. 1982. *Pragmatics and linguistics: An analysis of sentence topics.* Bloomington, Ind.: Indiana University Linguistics Club.

Rijk, R. P. G. de. 1978. „Topic fronting, focus positioning and the nature of the verb phrase in Basque". In: Jansen, Frank (ed.). *Studies in fronting.* Lisse: Peter de Ridder Press, 81–112.

Rochemont, Michael S. 1978. *A theory of stylistic rules in English.* Ph. D. diss. University of Massachusetts.

Rochemont, Michael S. 1986. *Focus in generative grammar.* (Studies in Generative Linguistic Analysis, 4) Amsterdam/Philadelphia: Benjamins.

Rochemont, Michael S. & Culicover, Peter W. 1990. *English focus constructions and the theory of grammar.* (Cambridge Studies in Linguistics, 52) Cambridge etc.: Cambridge University Press.

Rooth, Mats E. 1985. *Associaton with focus.* Ph. D. diss. University of Massachusetts.

Rosengren, Inger. 1991. „Zur Fokus-Hintergrund-Gliederung im Deklarativsatz und im w-Interrogativsatz". In: Reis, Marga & Rosengren, Inger (eds.). *Fragesätze und Fragen.* (Linguistische Arbeiten, 257) Tübingen: Niemeyer, 175–200.

Rosengren, Inger. 1993. „Wahlfreiheit mit Konsequenzen – Scrambling, Topikalisierung und FHG im Dienste der Informationsstrukturierung". In: Reis, Marga (ed.). *Wortstellung und Informationsstruktur.* (Linguistische Arbeiten, 306) Tübingen: Niemeyer, 251–312.

Ross, John Robert. 1968. *Constraints on variables in syntax.* Ph. D. diss. MIT. Reproduced by the Indiana University Linguistics Club.

Rossipal, Hans. 1975. „Informationsgrammatik". In: Hovdhaugen, Even (ed.). *Papers from the second Scandinavian conference in linguistics.* Oslo: University of Oslo, Department of Linguistics, 260–281.

Sasse, Hans-Jürgen. 1987. „The thetic/categorical distinction revisited". *Linguistics* 25: 511–580.

Sasse, Hans-Jürgen. 1995. „Prominence typology". In: Jacobs, Joachim & Stechow, Arnim von & Sternefeld, Wolfgang & Vennemann, Theo (eds.). *Syntax. Ein internationales Handbuch zeitgenössischer Forschung.* (Handbücher zur Sprach- und Kommunikationswissenschaft, 9.2) Berlin/New York: de Gruyter, 1065–1075.

Sasse, Hans-Jürgen. 1996. *Theticity.* (Arbeitspapier 27) Institut für Sprachwissenschaft, Universität Köln.

Selkirk, Elisabeth O. 1984. *Phonology and syntax: The relation between sound and structure.* Cambridge, MA/London: MIT Press.

Selkirk, Elisabeth O. 1995. „Sentence prosody: Intonation, stress and phrasing". In: Goldsmith, John A. (ed.). *The handbook of phonological theory.* Cambridge, MA/Oxford: Blackwell, 550–569.

Sgall, Petr & Hajičová, Eva & Benešová, Eva. 1973. *Topic, focus and generative semantics.* (Forschungen Linguistik und Kommunikationswissenschaft, 1) Kronberg: Scriptor-Verlag.

Szabolcsi, Anna. 1981. „Compositionality in focus". *Folia Linguistica* XV, 1–2: 141–161.

Taglicht, Josef. 1984. *Message and emphasis. On focus and scope in English.* (English Language Series, 15) London/New York: Longman.

Tomlin, Russell S. 1986. *Basic word order. Functional principles.* London/Sydney/Wolfeboro: Croom Helm.

Uhmann, Susanne. 1991. *Fokusphonologie. Eine Analyse deutscher Intonationskonturen im Rahmen der nicht-linearen Phonologie.* (Linguistische Arbeiten, 252) Tübingen: Niemeyer.

Vallduví, Enric. 1992. *The informational component.* New York/London: Garland.

Watters, John R. 1979. „Focus in Aghem: A study of its formal correlates and typology". In: Hyman, Larry M. (ed.). *Aghem grammatical structure.* (Southern California Occasional Papers in Linguistics, 7) Los Angeles/California: University of Southern California, 137–197.

Weil, Henri. 1844. *De l'ordre des mots dans les langues anciennes comparées aux langues modernes.* Paris: Franck.

Weinrich, Harald. 1964. *Tempus. Besprochene und erzählte Welt.* (Sprache und Literatur, 16) Stuttgart/Berlin/Köln/Mainz: Kohlhammer.

Winkler, Susanne. 1997. *Focus and secondary predication.* (Studies in Generative Grammar, 43) Berlin/New York: Mouton de Gruyter.

Jorunn Hetland, Universität Trondheim (Norwegen)/
Valéria Molnár, Universität Lund (Schweden)

47. Textkohäsion und Textkohärenz

1. Einleitung und Begriffsbestimmung
2. Textsyntax: Ausdrucksseitige Phänomene des Textzusammenhangs
3. Textsemantik
4. Textpragmatik
5. Kohärenz und Kognition
6. Zitierte Literatur

1. Einleitung und Begriffsbestimmung

Seit den sechziger und insbesondere siebziger Jahren ist der primäre Gegenstand sprachwissenschaftlicher Untersuchungen als 'Text' identifiziert worden (vgl. u. a. Hartmann 1971, Van Dijk 1972). Ähnlich wie der Satzbegriff ist allerdings auch der Textbegriff umstritten, da die vielfältigen Richtungen der **Textlinguistik** keine einheitliche, modellunabhängige Textdefinition hervorgebracht haben (vgl. Petöfi 1979 und 1981, Sowinski 1983: 51−54, Vater 1992: 10−26). Durch seine Etymologie verweist der Terminus **Text** allerdings auf einen möglichen 'gemeinsamen Nenner' der verschiedensten Definitionen: **Text** geht auf lat. *textus* 'Gewebe' (aus *texere* 'weben') zurück, womit 'Komplexität', 'Struktur' und 'Zusammenhang' assoziiert werden. Tatsächlich ist v. a. ein (sprachlich) wie auch immer realisierter **Zusammenhang** von sprachlichen Einheiten mit dem Terminus der **Kohärenz** bzw. der **Kohäsion** als prominentes **Textualitäts**-Kriterium angeführt worden (vgl. Berruto 1979: 497 und § 1.1.). Ausprägungen dieses Zusammenhangs auf verschiedenen Ebenen sprachlicher Strukturierung werden Gegenstand der folgenden Betrachtungen sein, wobei eine außereinzelsprachliche Perspektive die Vergleichbarkeit einzelsprachlicher Textbildungsmittel ermöglichen soll. Dabei wird zugunsten einer gegenstandsbezogenen Darstellung auf theorieabhängige Diskussionen innerhalb einzelner textlinguistischer Modelle weitgehend verzichtet (vgl. den umfangreichen Forschungsüberblick von Charolles et al. 1986).

1.1. Definitionen und Relation der Begriffe zueinander

Während **Kohäsion** aus (lat. *cohaesum*, Partizip Perfekt zu *cohaerere* 'zusammenhängen', 'verbunden sein') als fachsprachlicher Terminus bezeichnet werden kann und (fast) ausschließlich in der Sprachwissenschaft definiert und verwendet wird, besitzt **Kohärenz** (aus lat. *cohaerens, -entis*, Partizip Präsens zu *cohaerere*) eine allgemeinsprachliche Bedeutung, v. a. im Adjektiv *kohärent* ('zusammenpassend', 'zusammenhängend'). Maria-Elisabeth Conte 1988 verweist auf diese Polysemie von **Kohärenz**, wenn sie einen privativen Kohärenzbegriff ('Widerspruchslosigkeit') von einem positiven, textlinguistischen ('Zusammenhang', „Integration von Teilen in ein Ganzes", Conte 1988: 133) unterscheidet (vgl. bereits Gutwinski 1976: 26 ff.). Vor allem in der frühen englischsprachigen Literatur zu Textkonstitutionsfragen wird jedoch nur *cohesion (Kohäsion)* verwendet (vgl. u. a. Halliday 1964, Hasan 1968, Gutwinski 1976). M. A. K. Halliday & Ruqaiya Hasan 1976 etablieren *cohesion* als einzigen Terminus. Wesentlich an ihrem Textbegriff (vgl. Halliday & Hasan 1976: 1 f.) ist die Überwindung der 'Konstituenz-Annahme', die vielen transphrastischen Untersuchungen (vgl. § 2.) anhaftet. Texte bestehen nicht aus Elementen niederer Strukturierungsebenen, Sätzen, oder jedenfalls nicht nur (vgl. Heger ²1976). Sie werden durch Sätze realisiert als genuin semantische Einheiten, die „texture", also Strukturiertheit und Zusammenhang, aufweisen (vgl. auch De Beaugrande 1980: 10 ff.). *Cohesion* ist bei Halliday & Hasan 1976 dann entsprechend „a semantic [concept]; it refers to relations of meaning that exist within the text and that define it as a text. Cohesion occurs when the INTERPRETATION of some element in the discourse is dependent of that of another." (Halliday & Hasan 1976: 4). *Cohesion* als „general text-forming relation" (Halliday & Hasan 1976: 9) in diesem Sinne schlägt sich in oberflächenstrukturell manifesten „cohesive ties" (Halliday & Hasan 1976: 3 f.) zwischen (mindestens zwei) sprachlichen Elementen eines Textes nieder und ist insofern „part of the system of a language" (Halliday & Hasan 1976: 5), also ein einzelsprachliches, im übrigen auch graduelles Phänomen. Halliday & Hasan 1976 reflektieren noch nicht die notwendige Unterscheidung in außereinzelsprachliche Aspekte textueller Konstitution, wie sie im folgenden betrachtet werden sollen, und deren jeweilige einzelsprachliche Realisierung. Sie stehen mit ihrem *cohesion*-Konzept dennoch am Anfang einer intensiven und umfangreichen textlinguistischen Diskussion, die *Kohärenz* und *Kohäsion* als Phänomene der Textebene von rein satzinternen grammatischen Fragestellungen trennt (vgl. Halliday & Hasan 1976: 6ff.).

Etwa zeitgleich zu diesen oberflächenstrukturell orientierten Vorstellungen publiziert Teun A. Van Dijk 1972 und 1977 seine grundlegenden textlinguistischen Arbeiten, die nun wieder ausschließlich von *coherence* (neben dem engeren Begriff der *connection*, vgl. § 3.2.) als „one of the central notions of a semantic analysis of discourse" (Van Dijk 1977: 4) sprechen, welche sie ähnlich wie Halliday & Hasan 1976 als semantische Interdependenz von einzelnen Textelementen auffassen (vgl. z. B. Van Dijk 1977: 93). In ihrer richtungsweisenden *Einführung in die Textlinguistik* führen Robert A. De Beaugrande & Wolfgang Dressler 1981 **Kohäsion** und **Kohärenz** nun als zwei der insgesamt sieben Textualitätskriterien zusammen (vgl. kritisch Vater 1992: 31—73) und differenzieren sie folgendermaßen: „Kohäsion [...] betrifft die Art, wie die Komponenten des OBERFLÄCHENTEXTES [...] miteinander verbunden sind. Die Oberflächenkomponenten *hängen* durch grammatische Formen und Konventionen *voneinander ab*, so daß also Kohäsion auf GRAMMATISCHEN ABHÄNGIGKEITEN beruht" (De Beaugrande & Dressler 1981: 4). „Kohärenz betrifft die Funktionen, durch die die Komponenten der TEXTWELT, d. h. die Konstellationen von KONZEPTEN (Begriffen) und RELATIONEN (Beziehungen), welche dem Oberflächentext zugrundeliegen, für einander *gegenseitig zugänglich* und *relevant* sind." (De Beaugrande & Dressler 1981: 5). Die terminologische Unterscheidung in **Kohäsion** als durch formale, oberflächenstrukturell manifeste Mittel der Grammatik hergestellter Textzusammenhang (s. auch den Begriff der **Textsyntax** bei Dressler 1970a und 1972) und **Kohärenz** als semantisch-pragmatischer Sinnzusammenhang von Texten hat sich in der Folge durchgesetzt und soll auch den vorliegenden Ausführungen zugrundeliegen (vgl. u. a. bereits Dressler 1972, Östman 1978, De Beaugrande 1980, Reinhart 1980, Tannen 1984; eine ähnliche Auffassung mit einer verbreiteten, hier nicht weiter verfolgten terminologischen Trennung in **Text** als von kohäsiven Sätzen gebildete theoretische und **Diskurs** als von kohärenten Äußerungen realisierte praktische Einheit hat Coulthard 1977). Dabei nehmen viele Forscher eine Hyponymie-Relation zwischen beiden Begriffen insofern an, als **Kohärenz** häufig allgemein als textbildender Zusammenhang sprachlicher Äußerungen verstanden wird, dessen formale Ausprägung als Spezialfall der **Kohäsion** gesehen werden kann (vgl. u. a. Marello 1979). Der gemeinsame textdefinitorische Nenner beider Begriffe ist sicherlich 'Kontinuität' bzw. 'Konnektivität', d. h. Verbundenheit der Textelemente untereinander, die auf unterschiedlichen Realisierungsebenen beobachtet werden können (vgl. u. a. Bellert 1970, Van Dijk 1972 und 1977, De Beaugrande 1980, Reinhart 1980, Randquist 1985). Viele textlinguistische Beschreibungsansätze gehen seit Van Dijk 1972 und 1977 außerdem von mindestens zwei Ebenen in der Konstitution von Texten aus, wenn sie prinzipiell interphrastische „linear" oder „sequential" oder „microlevel coherence" und „global" oder „macrocoherence" unterscheiden (vgl. u. a. Isenberg 1976, Van Dijk 1977, De Beaugrande 1980, Randquist 1985, Heinemann & Viehweger 1991). Wichtig ist hier festzuhalten, daß die Unterscheidung einer mikro- und makrostrukturellen Konnektivität von Texten nicht mit der oben getroffenen Differenzierung in formal-grammatische Textbildungsmittel (Kohäsion) und semantisch-pragmatischen Textzusammenhang (Kohärenz) identisch ist, vielmehr alle Ebenen textueller Konnektivität innerhalb von Texten auf der Mikroebene oder eben als Eigenschaft von Texten insgesamt untersuchen will.

1.1.1. Kohärenz als textzentrierter Begriff

Konnektivität oder „Zusammenhang" als textkonstitutives Merkmal von sprachlichen Objekten werfen die Frage nach ihrer Entstehung und Lokalisierbarkeit auf. Frühe, v. a. generativ inspirierte textlinguistische Ansätze wie Van Dijk 1972 schreiben Kohärenz den formalen Status eines definitorischen Kriteriums zu, das kompetenten Sprechern parallel zu 'Grammatikalität' von Sätzen Texte als solche zu identifizieren und produzieren erlaube (vgl. Van Dijk 1972: 3 ff., vgl. dagegen u. a. Brinker 1979): 'Textgrammatiken' wären so als modifizierte Satzgrammatiken vorstellbar, wobei sich in der Folgezeit eine Kontroverse über die Notwendigkeit bzw. Erklärungsadäquatheit solcher 'Textgrammatiken' entsponnen hat (vgl. Van Dijk 1972, Dascal & Margalit 1974, Van Dijk 1977 und die Beiträge in Petöfi 1979 und 1981). Wesentlich im vorliegenden Zusammenhang ist die Bestimmung von **Kohärenz** als inhärenter Eigenschaft von Texten und die damit verbundene Annahme der Existenz von Nicht-Texten, d. h. nicht kohärenter Satzfolgen, wofür Van Dijk 1972 folgendes Beispiel gibt:

(1) (Van Dijk 1972: 40)
We will have guests for lunch. Calderón was a great Spanish writer.

Die Kennzeichnung solcher Satzfolgen als 'ungrammatisch', da nicht kohärent, ist in der Folgezeit zurecht kritisiert worden; je nach Ko- bzw. Kontext, durch die eine mögliche Verbindung zwischen den beiden Propositionen inferierbar wäre (vgl. Abschnitt 5.2.), ist angemessener eher mehr oder weniger große Akzeptabilität oder Plausibilität anzusetzen (vgl. Bierwisch 1965, Dressler 1972: 16 ff., auch Schmidt 1973 und die Abschnitte 1.1.2, 3, 4 und 5). Kohärenz als allgemeine textinterne Relation zwischen Texteinheiten verschiedenster Hierarchieebenen begegnet bei Irene Bellert 1970, Wolfgang Dressler 1970b, Horst Isenberg 1971 und 1976, Egon Werlich 1975, Elisabeth Gülich & Wolfgang Raible 1977, Lita Lundquist 1980, Klaus Brinker 1985 u. a.

Bei De Beaugrande & Dressler 1981 wird nun allerdings 'Sinnkontinuität' als die Grundlage der Kohärenz eines Textes, als Kontinuität des durch die Textbestandteile aktivierten Wissens des Rezipienten beschrieben (vgl. De Beaugrande & Dressler 1981: 88). Kohärenz selbst ist mit (semantischen) Relationen von Konzepten offenbar noch textintern lokalisiert, doch der schon bei Robert A. De Beaugrande 1980 angelegte prozedurale Textproduktions- und -rezeptionsansatz bezieht in zunehmendem Maße das sprechende Subjekt in die Beschreibung von Kohärenzphänomenen mit ein (vgl. insgesamt Lundquist 1985).

1.1.2. Kohärenz als verwenderzentrierter Begriff

1978 beschreibt Nils E. Enkvist verschiedene Ausprägungen von Kohärenz, von „Pseudo-Kohärenz", d. h. der Anwesenheit kohäsiver Verbindungen ohne semantischen Zusammenhang (vgl. Bierwisch 1965), über semantische Kohärenz (konsistente Zusammenhänge zwischen miteinander kompatiblen Sachverhalten, vgl. Reinhart 1980) und pragmatische Kohärenz, die beide der formalgrammatischen Kohäsion nicht bedürfen, bis zur vollen Kohärenz bei gleichzeitiger Kontinuität bzw. Konnektivität auf syntaktischer, semantischer und pragmatischer Ebene (vgl. Enkvist 1978: 112). Interessant hier Enkvists abschließende Bemerkung, daß Kohärenz als konstitutive Texteigenschaft vom Hörer immer vorausgesetzt und ein zur kooperativen Rezeption inhaltlich oder formal schwer zugänglicher Texte notwendiger Verstehenskontext notfalls (re-)konstruiert wird (vgl. Enkvist 1978: 124 f.).

Noch expliziter äußert sich János S. Petöfi, der in seiner „Text-Struktur-Welt-Struktur-Theorie" ein elaboriertes und auf einer eigenen zeichentheoretischen Konzeption basierendes Textproduktions- und Textanalysemodell entworfen hat, in verschiedenen Publikationen zur Frage der Lokalisierung von Kohärenz (vgl. z. B. Petöfi 1973). Weder Kohärenz noch Texthaftigkeit sind danach inhärente Eigenschaften sprachlicher Objekte, sondern Ergebnis kognitiver Operationen. Diese Auffassung steht in enger Verbindung zu einer der grundlegenden theoretischen textlinguistischen Arbeiten zum Text- und Kohärenzbegriff, der programmatischen terminologischen Synthese von Katshuhiko Hatakeyama & János S. Petöfi & Emel Sözer 1985 (im folgenden H/P/S 1985). Hier stehen der Sprachverwender und sein Zugang zu sprachlichen Objekten im Vordergrund (vgl. Raible 1989). H/P/S 1985 unterscheiden im wesentlichen zwischen **Konnexität** und **Kohäsion** als sprachlichen Text(produktions)kategorien und **Kohärenz** als Beschreibungskategorie für die einem Text durch den Rezipienten zugeordnete 'Textwelt' (vgl. H/P/S 1985: 58). **Konnexität** bezieht sich im engeren Sinne auf die ausdrucksseitige Verbundenheit aller selbständigen Texteinheiten (vgl. H/P/S 1985: 61−67) und ist eine notwendige, aber nicht hinreichende Bedingung für **Kohäsion**, die eine Konnexität auf der semantisch-thematischen, der Inhaltsebene eines Textes ist (hier überschneidet sich dieser Kohäsionsbegriff mit dem traditionellen Kohärenzbegriff, vgl. Abschnitt 1.1.1., vgl. H/P/S 1985: 67−70). Kohäsion in diesem Sinne ist nun allerdings weder eine notwendige noch hinreichende Bedingung für **Kohärenz**, da dieser Begriff den Text als Objekt verläßt bzw. als relational im Zusammenhang mit dem rezipierenden Subjekt aufzufassen ist (s. ähnlich auch Bókay 1985 und Lundquist 1985). Kohärenz bei H/P/S 1985 ist eine Eigenschaft der 'Textwelt', d. h. der 'Gesamtbedeutung', die der Rezipient einem Text entnehmen kann und zu der er u. U. unter Rekurs auf auch nicht explizit im Textausdruck enthaltene Informationen gelangt (vgl. H/P/S 1985: 70−74, s. auch § 5.). Kohärenz in diesem Sinne ist nun weder eine notwendige noch hinreichende Voraussetzung für **Interpretierbarkeit** (das wären Abgeschlossenheit und Kontinuität des „Textkorrelats"), d. h. die Identifikation einer der 'Textwelt' entsprechenden außersprachlichen Sachverhaltskonfiguration.

Kohärenz als Interpretationsleistung des Rezipienten sprachlicher Objekte wird v. a. in den neueren kognitiv-prozeduralen textlinguistischen Ansätzen untersucht (vgl. Viehweger 1989 als Überblick und im einzelnen Charolles 1983, 1985, 1989, 1994, Langleben 1981 und 1985, Lundquist 1991, Van de Velde, mit psycholinguistischer Ausrichtung Rickheit 1991), auch im Zusammenhang mit maschineller Sprachverarbeitung und Forschungen zur künstlichen Intelligenz (→ Art. 11). Roger G. Van de Velde schreibt Kohärenz als inhaltlichem Zusammenhang eine Existenz innerhalb des Textes („kotextuelle Kohärenz"), dann aber auch außerhalb des Textes zu als Eigenschaft der Kommunikationssituation, der außersprachlichen Sachverhalte und v. a. als Ergebnis der „rezeptiven Kreativität" (Van de Velde 1981: 18). Michel Charolles geht einen Schritt weiter und faßt Kohärenz prinzipiell nicht mehr als Eigenschaft von Texten auf, sondern als a-priorisches Interpretationsprinzip, als Grundlage menschlicher Verstehfähigkeit überhaupt (vgl. z. B. Charolles 1994: 133 f.).

1.2. Extensionale Bestimmungen von Kohäsion und Kohärenz

Halliday & Hasan 1976 behandeln in ihrer einzelsprachlichen Studie „cohesion"-Phänomene als „reference", also Koreferenz und „cross-reference", „substitution", „ellipsis", „conjunction" und „lexical cohesion" (vgl. § 2.). Ähnliche Aufzählungen finden sich z. B. bei Enkvist 1978, der wie auch andere Forscher darüberhinaus temporale Kontinuität, Informationsstruktur in Satz und Text und syntaktische und phonologische Rekurrenzen berücksichtigt (vgl. u. a. bereits Dressler 1970b, Coseriu ³1994, Charolles 1994, Petöfi ²1994, ähnlich Van Dijk in seinen Arbeiten, erweitert um Fragen der Präsuppositionen, Implikaturen und der Informationsstruktur, vgl. Abschnitt 4.1).

Mit der terminologischen Trennung von **Kohäsion** und **Kohärenz** bei De Beaugrande & Dressler 1981 (vgl. § 1.1.) fallen unter **Kohäsion** alle Arten oberflächenstrukturell manifester Rekurrenzen, Parallelismen, Paraphrasen, neben verdichtenden Textbildungsmitteln wie Proformen und Ellipsen. Berücksichtigt werden hier weiterhin grammatische Erscheinungen im weiteren Sinne, die Relationen zwischen Ereignissen der Textwelt signalisieren sollen: Tempus, Aspekt und Junktion als oberflächenstrukturelle Reflexe der Informationsverteilung in Satz und Text (vgl. De Beaugrande & Dressler 1981: Kap. IV). **Kohärenz** ist dagegen extensional bestimmbar als Eigenschaft semantischer Netzwerke, von Konzepten und deren Relationen untereinander, wobei Textelemente verschiedene Wissensstrukturen aktivieren, die über das explizit im Text Enthaltene hinausgehen (vgl. De Beaugrande & Dressler 1981: Kap. V). **Kohärenz** kann detaillierter als verschiedene intrapropositionale semantische Relationen (z. B. Argument-Prädikat-Strukturen), interpropositionale logische, thematische und konzeptionelle Relationen (z. B. 'Erläuterung', 'Beispiel für' u. ä.) gefaßt werden (s. z. B. Van Dijk 1980, Daneš 1989a). H/P/S 1985 fassen in ihrer dreigliedrigen Terminologie unter **Konnexität** auch Erscheinungen morphosyntaktischer Wohlgeformtheit (Kongruenz u. ä.), Rekurrenzen prosodischer, semantischer, referentieller Art und konnektive Relationen zwischen Propositionen (vgl. § 3.2.). Letztere sind in aller Regel bei anderen Forschern bereits der **Kohärenz** zugeordnet. Gleiches gilt nach H/P/S 1985 für **Kohäsions**mittel, die dort im wesentlichen thematische Kontinuität, stilistische Einheitlichkeit (ein selten erwähnter Punkt, vgl. auch Enkvist 1977, Szabó 1985) umfassen. **Kohärenz** als extratextuelle Kategorie betrifft verschiedene kognitive Operationen (vgl. § 5.).

Im folgenden werden Koreferenzbeziehungen und deren Versprachlichungsmöglichkeiten, Tempus und Ellipsen im Text und Fragen der (textuellen) Informationsstruktur, neben insbesondere lexikalischen Rekurrenzen, expliziten Textgliederungsverfahren, Redewiedergabe u. ä. diskutiert (§ 2.), bevor Rekurrenzen der semantischen Ebene, logische und semantische Relationen zwischen Propositionen, zusammen mit dem Komplex 'Textthema' als Kohärenzträger vorgestellt werden (§ 3.). Fragen der kommunikativ-pragmatischen Textdimension (Präsuppositionen, Implikaturen, Konversationsmaximen, Illokutionsfolgen, Diskursanalyse, § 4.) schließen sich an, vor einem Ausblick auf kognitive Voraussetzungen und Operationen von Texten in konkreter Kommunikation (Inferenzen, Schemata, „scripts" u. ä. § 5.).

Dabei ist zu bedenken, daß 'textueller Zusammenhang' im Grunde immer in zwei Dimensionen manifest wird: paradigmatisch über Rekurrenzen auf den verschiedenen Ebenen sprachlicher Strukturierung und syntagmatisch über eine wie auch immer geartete 'Verknüpfung' von Texteinheiten zu einem komplexen Ganzen (vgl. schon Nye 1912 in Dressler 1977).

2. Textsyntax

Wesentlich bei der folgenden Betrachtung formal-grammatischer Textbildungsmittel (**Kohäsion** oder **Textsyntax**) ist Bohumil Paleks 1968 Einsicht, daß 'hypersyntaktische' oder transphrastische Relationen, also oberflächenstrukturelle Erscheinungen über die Satzgrenze hinaus, im Gegensatz zu satzinternen, immer einen obligatorischen semantischen Hintergrund brauchen, um auftreten und interpretiert werden zu können. Texte werden in den ersten textlinguistischen Arbeiten als 'kohärente Folge von Sätzen' (z. B. bei Isenberg 1971, 1976) aufgefaßt, wobei *kohärent* hier v. a. 'oberflächenstrukturell zusammenhängend' meint. In dieser Zeit entworfene 'Textgrammatiken' sind entsprechend als 'Mehrsatz'- oder 'Satzverknüpfungsgrammatiken' konzipiert (vgl. Heidolph 1966, Isenbergs „Theorie der sequentiellen Textkonstitution", Isenberg 1976: 126 ff.), die Kohäsionsmittel verschiedener Ebenen (vgl. Heinemann & Viehweger 1991: 28 f.) zu beschreiben versuchen.

2.1. (Nominal-)Referenz und Textzusammenhang

Die Erscheinung totaler oder partieller Referenzrekurrenzen im Text, deren Identifikation z. T. auf der Bedeutung der Prädikation und auch auf außersprachlichen Wissensstrukturen beruht (vgl. Bellert 1970, Bosch 1983, 1985, Conte 1986 u. a.), schlägt sich ausdrucksseitig in Artikelselektion und Pronominalisierung, allgemein in der kategoriellen Füllung von referentiell aufeinander bezogenen Nominalphrasen nieder (zu übereinzelsprachlichen und typologischen Auffälligkeiten s. Grimes 1975, Hinds 1978, Givón 1983; zu Genus-/Numeruskongruenz zwischen koreferenten Ausdrücken als Kohäsionsmittel s. Bosch 1983, 1985 und Cornish 1994). Es handelt sich um Beziehungen vollständiger Koreferenz (*ein Mann – der Mann*, bei Harweg 1968 „Text-Identitäts-Substitution" oder bei Isenberg 1971 „explizite Referenz"), teilidentische Referenzbeziehungen (*die Kinder – einige davon*) oder referentielle Beziehungen zwischen Nominalphrasen, deren Referenten in einer Kontiguitätsbeziehung stehen (Rekurrenzen einzelner semantischer Merkmale, „Text-Kontiguitäts-Substitution" bei Harweg 1968 oder „implizite Referenz" bei Isenberg, vgl. § 3.1.). Für die Bildung unterschiedlich komplexer 'referentieller Ketten' im Text (vgl. u. a. Harweg 1968, Zhou 1994) kann angenommen werden, daß bei koreferenten nominalen Ausdrücken in der Regel von intensional präzisen, umfassenden und aufgrund des 'deskriptiven Gehalts' der NP eindeutig referierenden Nominalphrasen (zur erfolgreichen Etablierung eines „Diskursreferenten" siehe in diesem Zusammenhang Conte 1980, 1986) bei der ersten Referenz über weniger spezifische bis zu den auf grammatische Informationen beschränkten Proformen kodiert wird (vgl. u. a. bereits Steinitz 1968), d. h. der Aufwand an lexikalischer und morphosyntaktischer Kodierung ist übereinzelsprachlich umgekehrt proportional zur (situativen oder kontextuellen) 'Gegebenheit', 'Zugänglichkeit' des Referenten (vgl. Givón 1979, 1983). U. a. Lundquist verweist in ihren neueren Arbeiten (z. B. 1990) auf das hier operierende Interpretationsprinzip der 'thematischen Kontinuität'. Aufeinanderfolgende Nominalphrasen, die den jeweiligen Aussagegegenstand, das *topic* einer Proposition, kodieren (häufig als grammatisches Subjekt), werden zunächst immer als koreferent dekodiert (vgl. § 2.3.) bis hin zur obligatorischen anaphorischen Subjekt-Ellipse in manchen Sprachen (z. B. Italienisch, → Art. 84), wenn Koreferenz angezeigt werden soll.

Halliday & Hasan 1976 (Kap. 2) untersuchen mit „reference" diese interpretative und referentielle Bezogenheit sprachlicher Ausdrücke aufeinander. Solche Abhängigkeitsbeziehungen müssen als Kohäsionsmittel intratextuell bestehen („endophoric reference", gegenüber „exophoric", also deiktischer Referenz) und sind gerichtet: Geht der Bezugsausdruck dem abhängigen voran, sprechen Halliday & Hasan 1976 von „anaphora" (zum Anaphern-Begriff s. u. a. Kleiber 1994: Anaphern sind nicht an strikte Koreferenz gebunden, s. auch Conte 1988), im umgekehrten Fall von „cataphora" (der sie aber eine genuin satzgrammatische und für die Textkonstitution untergeordnete Rolle zuschreiben, vgl. Cole 1973: 25 ff., Kesik 1989; zu Einzelheiten referentieller Strukturen im Text → Art. 108). „Substitution" (Halliday & Hasan 1976, Kap. 3) beschreibt dagegen den einzelsprachlich-grammatisch geregelten formalen Ersatz identischen lexikalischen Materials (nominal, verbal oder satzförmig) ohne zwingende Referenzidentität bis hin zur Ellipse (vgl. § 2.2.).

Roland Harweg 1968 entwirft ein komplexes Modell textinterner Substitutionsbeziehungen auf der Basis von totaler oder partieller Koreferenz, deren oberflächenstrukturellen Ausdruck er als textkonstituierende „ununterbrochene syntagmatische Substitution" bezeichnet. Nominalphrasen sind danach unterteilbar in „Substituenda", d. h. Ausdrücke, deren Referenz unabhängig vom Vortext feststellbar ist und die andere nicht ersetzen, d. h. mit ihnen nicht koreferent sein können (z. B. Nominalphrasen mit indefinitem Artikel), und „Substituentia" mit den gegenteiligen Eigenschaften (z. B. Personalpronomina — neben weiteren Unter- und Mischklassen). Der gesamte Ansatz geht von der tatsächlichen sprachlichen Realisierung im Text aus und ist insofern einzelsprachlich (bezogen vornehmlich auf das Deutsche) ausgerichtet. Die Verteilung von Substituenda und Substituentia ist entscheidend u. a. für die Delimitation von Texten. Ebenfalls in einzelsprachlicher und oberflächenstruktureller Ausrichtung analysiert Harald Weinrich 1969 die Funktion des definiten Artikels (im Deutschen, später auch im Französischen, vgl. Kallmeyer et al. 1974, Bd. 2: 266—293) als verweisend auf Vorinformation, also anaphorisch, die des indefiniten Artikels als verweisend auf nachfolgende Information, also kataphorisch (diese Unterscheidung wird beim sogenannten 'Nullartikel', soweit existent, neutralisiert; dazu kritisch Raible 1972, Kallmeyer et al. 1974, Bd. 1: 192 ff.), womit eine frühe genuin textuelle Betrachtung nominaler Determinanten entworfen wird. Textinterne Referenzrekurrenzen steuern also die hier untersuchten einzelsprachlichen Markierungen von Definitheit und Indefinitheit sowie Verfahren der Pronominalisierung (vgl. Palek 1968, Isenberg 1971, sowie die Arbeiten von Kleiber und Heim).

Conte verweist in vielen ihrer Arbeiten zur Anapher als 'Rückbezug' im Text auf die notwendige semiotische Differenzierung in Anaphern, die auf totaler oder partieller Koreferenz beruhen (hier ist die Art des Referenzbezuges für die Versprachlichung der Wiederaufnahme ausschlaggebend, vgl. Dressler 1972: 27 f.), Anaphern, die auf Bedeutungsidentität ohne Koreferenz beruhen ('pronouns of laziness') und solche, die Formidentität ohne Koreferenz voraussetzen:

(2)   (Conte 1988: 137)
   — *Guarda là in fondo! Quello è un rododendro.*
   — *Cosa? Me lo puoi sillabare?*
   '— Das ist ein Rhododendron.
   — Ein was? Kannst du es für mich buchstabieren?'

Insgesamt ist die referentielle Kennzeichnung von Nominalphrasen im Text Ausdruck der außereinzelsprachlichen Kategorien 'Neueinführung' und 'Wiedervorkommen', und in dieser Hinsicht sind Pronomina sinnvoller als 'Konnexionsanweisungen', 'Kontinuitätssignale' denn als eigenständig referierende Substitutionsresultate anzusehen (vgl. Kallmeyer et al. 1974, Bd. 1: 217 ff., 226 ff., Brown & Yule 1983: 200 f., Corblin 1995).

2.2. Tempus und Ellipse

Textualität und temporale Relationen zwischen Sachverhalten sind unmittelbar aufeinander beziehbar. Texte als sprachliche Zeichen für Ereignisse und Sachverhalte sind sowohl in ihrer formalen Manifestation als auch in ihrer semantischen Struktur an die prinzipielle Linearität und Sukzessivität menschlicher Erfahrungen und Handlungen von jeweils einer bestimmten Dauer gebunden. So sind temporale Elemente integrale Komponenten der Textsemantik und Textpragmatik, deren oberflächenstrukturelle Kodierung in einzelsprachlich verschiedenen Tempussystemen als Kohäsionsmittel untersucht werden kann (vgl. Lo Cascio 1982, 1986). Dabei muß die gegebenenfalls grammatisch geforderte *consecutio temporum* von der außersprachlich ontologischen Zeitordnung unterschieden werden.

Weinrich 1964/²1971 beschreibt Tempora über drei voneinander unabhängige Faktoren, die als außereinzelsprachliche Kategorien temporaler, auch aspektueller Textstrukturierung gesehen werden können. Tempora signalisieren die „Sprechhaltung" („Besprechen" vs. „Erzählen"), die „Sprechperspektive" („Rückschau" — „Nullstufe" — „Vorausschau") und die „Reliefgebung" (Vordergrund-Hintergrund-Gliederung, vgl. § 3.3.2.), was einzelsprachlich von verschiedenen sprachlichen Mitteln (Wortstellung, Verbalperiphrasen, Adverbien u. ä.) geleistet werden kann. Vor allem die Sprechperspektive betrifft die Versprachlichung von Sukzessivität und Dauer, d. h. die gegenseitige zeitliche Bezogenheit von Ereignissen aufeinander. Die Reichenbachsche Temporallogik mit Ereigniszeitpunkt, Sprechzeitpunkt und Referenzzeitpunkt (vgl. Reichenbach 1947) bezeichnen Hans Kamp & Christian Rohrer 1983 als eine genuin textuelle; v. a. der Bezugszeitpunkt von vorzeitigen Tempora wie dem Plusquamperfekt wird ja kotextuell etabliert. Seit Barbara Partee 1973 wird die Parallelität bestimmter Tempora mit pronominalen Anaphern aufgrund der auch hier vorliegenden Interpretationsabhängigkeit von vorausgehenden Bezugspunkten diskutiert (vgl. Moeschler 1994); sie ist v. a. von Vincenzo Lo Cascio ausgearbeitet worden zur prinzipiellen Opposition von 'deiktischen' und 'anaphorischen' Tempora und Temporaladverbien, wobei erstere zeitliche Relationen in direktem Bezug auf den Sprechzeitpunkt, letztere in nur indirektem Bezug über Abhängigkeit von deiktischen temporalen Elementen versprachlichen. In vielen indogermanischen Sprachen betrifft diese Opposition v. a. Vergangenheitstempora (vgl. beispielsweise Lo Cascio 1982 zum Italienischen). Die Kombinatorik von Tempora, Adverbien und bestimmten Konjunktionen ist ein einzelsprachliches textgrammatisches Phänomen (vgl. Dorfmüller-Karpusa 1988), das gegebenenfalls sekundäre textpragmatische Werte wie die Signalisierung von Redewiedergabe u. ä. erhalten kann (vgl. Fleischman 1991):

(3) (Fleischman 1991: 31f., aus Flauberts *L'Education sentimentale*)
*Au coin de la rue Montmartre, il [Frédéric] se retourna; il regarda les fenêtres du premier étage; et il rit intérieurement de pitié sur lui-même, en se rappelant avec quel amour **il les avait souvent contemplées! OÙ donc VIVAIT-elle? Comment la rencontrer maintenant?** La solitude SE ROUVRAIT sur son désir plus immense que jamais.*

Das *maintenant* in der fettgedruckten Passage bezieht sich natürlich nicht auf die Jetzt-Zeit des Erzählers, von der aus er rückblickend die Ereignisse um Frédéric berichtet, sondern auf das Jetzt Frédérics, das Jetzt seiner Gedanken.

1991 zeigt Co Vet, daß die Alternanz beispielsweise von romanischem Imperfekt und einfachem Perfekt auf inhaltlich unterschiedliche Funktionen zurückgeführt werden sollte: Ersteres stellt ein *setting* eines Textes her, d. h. alle wesentlichen Umstände und das hauptsächliche Thema (was nicht immer nur 'Hintergrundinformation' darstellt!), während Perfekta jeweils ein „change of setting" anzeigen, die Veränderung eines Einzelaspektes bei andauernder Gültigkeit der anderen Kontinuitätsfaktoren (vgl. Vet 1991: 13−18; zum Aspekt als Textbildungsmittel v. a. in nicht-indogermanischen Sprachen s. bereits Grimes 1975).

Neben der obligatorischen Zeitstruktur von Texten ist das Phänomen der oberflächenstrukturellen Unvollständigkeit Gegenstand transphrastischer (s. auch die generative Diskussion um jeweils satzinterne Phänomene, s. bereits Dressler 1972: 32−35 u. a.) Untersuchungen geworden. Daß 'Lükken' in der Oberfläche Kohäsionsträger zwischen benachbarten Texteinheiten sein können (vgl. Marello 1984) nimmt nach Halliday & Hasan 1976 explizit u. a. Lucien Cherchi an. Halliday & Hasan 1976 definieren **Ellipse** als strukturelle Unvollständigkeit in Sätzen, die kotextuell über Präsuppositionen und Inferenzen (vgl. § 4.1. und 5.) gefüllt werden kann. Ellipse ist bei ihnen ein Sonderfall der „substitution" vorangehenden lexikalischen Materials durch eine „Nullvariable" (Halliday & Hasan 1976: 142), also ein primär anaphorisches Kohäsionsmittel im nominalen, verbalen und Satzbereich, das v. a. in Dialogen eine hohe Frequenz hat:

(4) (Halliday & Hasan 1976: 144)
'And how many hours a day did you do lessons?' said Alice, in a hurry to change the subject.
'Ten hours the first day,' said the Mock Turtle: 'nine the next, and so on.'

Grundsätzlich gilt auch hier wieder das interpretative Prinzip der Kontinuität: Ellipse beispielsweise von Auxiliaren mit Tempus-, Modus-, Diatheseanzeige bewirkt die Annahme einer zum Vorgängerausdruck identischen Markierung. Cherchi 1978 und 1985 wendet sich gegen die Annahme 'unvollständiger' Einheiten im Text, die durch Rekonstruktion vervollständigt werden könnten. Er zeigt, daß elliptische Äußerungen die Informationsstruktur in komplexen Äußerungsfolgen offenlegen durch regelhafte Isolierung von *topic* oder *comment* (vgl. § 2.3.), wodurch die einzelnen Äußerungen eng und ko- bzw. kontextuell adäquat miteinander verzahnt werden.

2.3. 'Funktionale Satzperspektive', Wortstellung und Intonation

Frühe transphrastische Ansätze sehen die Informationsorganisation im Text als Erweiterung der Untersuchungen zur ursprünglich satzgebundenen „Funktionalen Satzperspektive" (→ Art. 46) und diskutieren z. T. deren Niederschlag in Kohäsionsphänomenen der Wortstellung und Intonation, die nun die syntagmatische Dimension des Textes betreffen (vgl. Heidolph 1966). Die Entwicklung des Konzeptes der „kommunikativen Dynamik", d. h. die Analyse von Informationseinheiten nach ihrem Beitrag zur Informationsentfaltung (→ Art. 46), operiert mit genuin textuellen Kategorien der 'Gegebenheit' bzw. 'Neuheit' u. ä., ebenso das Danešsche Konzept von 'Thema' und 'Rhema' (→ Art. 46, sowie Tschida 1995, Stark 1997). 'Funktionale Satzperspektive', d. h. die Abhängigkeit der Kodierung sprachlicher Information von ihrem aussagetheoretischen (**topic-comment** oder 'Satzgegenstand' – 'Satzaussage') und referentiellem Status ('alt' – 'neu' – 'definit' – 'indefinit') ist eine universale Erscheinung auch und gerade der Textebene (vgl. Halliday 1974, Sgall 1974, Van Dijk 1972 und 1977, Givón 1979 und 1983, dagegen allerdings Hajicová & Sgall 1988). Übereinzelsprachlich feststellbare serielle und satzinterne Phänomene wie die Voranstellung 'neuer' *topics* vor ihren *comment*, die Nachstellung 'gegebener' *topics*, die Initialstellung von „engen Foki", das Auftreten von Cleft-Konstruktionen (vgl. Primus 1993) sind bestimmt von außereinzelsprachlichen informationsstrukturellen Kategorien textueller Natur. Die folgerichtige Anordnung topologisch und intonatorisch entsprechend kompatibler Sätze im Text ist ein wichtiges Kohäsionsmittel (vgl. bereits Dressler 1970b: 69 f.). Auch die kategorielle Füllung koreferenter anaphorischer NP, ja die Existenz von Kataphora ist z. T. bedingt durch thematische Kontinuität vs. kontrastierende Fokussierung (z. B. Nullsubjekt vs. Subjekt-Pronomina im Italienischen, Auftreten von Pronomina mit Kontrastakzent, vgl. Werth 1984); Ellipsen sind eng an 'Gegebenheit' des 'Fehlenden' gebunden (vgl. Kuno 1977).

Die intonatorische Markierung einzelner Syntagmen beschreibt u. a. David Brazil 1975 und 1978 direkt über die Anwesenheit oder Neueinführung von Referenten in die Diskurswelt („proclaiming tone", oft Fallkontur, für 'neue', „referring tone", oft Steigkontur, für 'gegebene' Referenten). Suprasegmentale Strukturierungen lassen sich in gesprochenen Texten überhaupt sinnvoll mit der Signalisierung von Einheiten oberhalb der Satzebene in Verbindung bringen (vgl. Brazil 1975 und 1978, Couper-Kuhlen 1983, Gibbon & Richter 1984 und Gibbon 1988 und die Beiträge in Tomlin 1987). 'Kontrast' ist weiterhin eine außereinzelsprachliche, genuin anaphorische Relation zwischen Einheiten mehrerer Äußerungen und fordert eine adäquate Kodierung im Text:

(5) (nach Krötsch & Sabban 1990: 83)
 – *Pourquoi tu achètes toujours des pommes de terre?* DES TOMATES *tu dois acheter et non pas des pommes de terre!*

2.4. Weitere oberflächenstrukturelle Kohäsionsmittel

In den Bereich der Kohäsion gehört weiterhin insbesondere die „lexical cohesion" im engeren Sinne (vgl. Halliday 1964, Halliday & Hasan 1976, Kap. 6), d. h. lexikalische Rekurrenzen von wörtlicher Wiederholung des gleichen Lexems mit oder ohne Koreferenz (vgl. Halliday & Hasan 1976: 82 ff.) oder mehrmaliges Auftreten des gleichen lexikalischen Wortstammes (schon in der Rhetorik als *figura etymologica*). Hierzu gehören aber auch phonologische Rekurrenzen, die v. a. in literarischen Texten als Kohäsionsmittel eingesetzt werden (Metrum, Reim, Assonanz u. ä., vgl. z. B. Van Dijk 1972, Kap. 6.2), z. T. um einen Zusammenhang auf der Bedeutungsebene (Kohärenz) erst herzustellen bzw. zu suggerieren (s. auch die mnemotechnische Funktion beim mündlichen Erzählen, vgl. Gumperz et al. 1984). Wiederholung lexikalischer Einheiten kann über bloße Redundanz hinaus einen emphatischen Effekt hervorrufen und insbesondere in dialogischen Texten neben der Signalisierung thematischer Kontinuität z. B. nach Unterbrechungen sekundäre pragmatische Werte wie Zustimmung, Zurückweisung, Signalisierung von Aufmerksamkeit, *turn*-Organisation usw. (verbunden mit jeweils unterschiedlicher intonatorischer Kennzeichnung) übernehmen (vgl. die Beiträge in Bazzanella 1996).

Probleme der temporalen und referentiellen Diskontinuität bei Wahrung der Gesamtkohärenz liegen weiterhin einzelsprachlich unterschiedlichen grammatischen Ausprägungen der Redewiedergabe in Texten zugrunde (*consecutio temporum*, Moduswechsel, indirekte vs. erlebte Rede u. ä., vgl. Longacre 1970, Dressler 1972: 89 ff., Enkvist 1978 u. a.). An der Textoberfläche manifestieren sich außerdem häufig, z. T. textsortenspezifisch, z. B. vermehrt in wissenschaftlichen Texten (→ Art. 36), metatextuelle, speziell textdeiktische Verweisformen (*siehe oben, wie im letzten Kapitel angemerkt* u. ä.), wobei Lexeme temporaler oder lokaler Semantik metaphorisch 'durch den Text führen' (vgl. v. a. Conte 1980, 1981, 1986).

Viele der genannten kohäsiven Mittel werden herangezogen, um genuin textuelle Einheiten wie z. B. den '**Paragraph**' zu identifizieren, welcher typographisch respektive intonatorisch durch bestimmte Grenzsignale (z. B. signifikant längere Pausen als zwischen Einzeläußerungen), auch morphologisch-lexikalischer Art (vgl. Gülich 1970 zu 'Gliederungssignalen', Wunderli 1979 zur Intonation), delimitiert wird und innerhalb dessen spezifische Koreferenzverhältnisse (auch temporal) feststellbar sind bedingt durch seine angenommene 'thematische Einheit' (vgl. Giora 1983, Brown & Yule 1983, Kap. 3, und die typologisch interessanten Arbeiten von Longacre; gegen die Existenz einer 'Paragraph-Texteinheit' s. Coulthard & Montgomery 1981: 87 ff.).

Als medial schriftliches Textgliederungsmittel soll schließlich die Interpunktion Erwähnung finden, die verschiedene Zusammengehörigkeitssignale enthält und Textverstehen, Verarbeitungszeit usw. beeinflussen kann (vgl. Fayol 1989).

3. Textsemantik

3.1. Bedeutungszusammenhang durch Merkmalrekurrenz

Die außereinzelsprachliche Beziehung von totaler oder partieller Koreferenz im Text und die „Text-Kontiguitäts-Substitution" (Harweg 1968, vgl. § 2.1.) können in Abhängigkeit von einzelsprachlichen Bedeutungsstrukturen einzelner Lexeme auch den lexikalischen Kern, die 'lexikalische Bedeutung' von aufeinanderbezogenen NP betreffen. Die Möglichkeit einer koreferentiellen Interpretation von *the minister* und *the man* in

(6) (Halliday & Hasan 1976: 274 f.)
Didn't everyone make it clear they expected the minister to resign? — They did. But it seems to have made no impression on the man.

ergibt sich hier nicht nur aus dem definiten Determinierer der zweiten NP, sondern auch aus der semantischen Rekurrenz der Merkmale [+menschlich], [+männlich] o. ä. in *the man*, welches insgesamt als intensional enger, extensional umfangreicher, also als Hyperonym zu *the minister* gesehen werden kann. Diese Relation existiert übereinzelsprachlich dort, wo „Klasseme" (vgl. Greimas 1966, Coseriu 1967) lexikalisiert vorliegen und einen Übergangsbereich zwischen echter Pronominalisierung und koreferenten definiten NP („Kennzeichnungen") darstellen (vgl. Halliday & Hasan 1976: 274 ff.). In der Regel besteht eine anaphorische Beziehung des Hyperonyms auf das vorangehende Hyponym (vgl. Steinitz 1968, dazu kritisch Kallmeyer et al. 1974, Bd. 1: 197−201). Allgemein muß beachtet werden, daß Beziehungen der Hyponymie Rekurrenzen von einzelsprachlichen Bedeutungsmerkmalen, aber auch Rekurrenzen außersprachlicher Objekteigenschaften als Ursprung haben können, was wiederum die Frage nach der Rolle enzyklopädischen Wissens (neben lexikalischem) bei Kohärenzbildung aufwirft (vgl. § 5 und z. B. Petöfi 1971, Daneš 1983: 8 f.). „Lexical cohesion" mit Koreferenz beruht weiterhin auf den semantischen einzelsprachlichen Relationen der totalen oder partiellen Synonymie, d. h. der weitgehenden Deckungsgleichheit der Denotation. Ungefähre Bedeutungsäquivalenz von Lexemen, Syntagmen oder ganzen Textteilen liegt neben der Synonymie auch der Erscheinung der 'Paraphrase' zugrunde, die ebenfalls als Kohärenzmittel analysiert werden kann (vgl. z. B. Agricola 1979, Fuchs 1985) und in der lexematisch differenten, meist umfangreicheren Wiedergabe eines bedeutungs- oder sogar referenzidentischen Textelementes (oder auch ganzen Textes) besteht. Herman Parret 1989 verweist auf ihre wichtige Funktion in Dialogen oder Mehr-Personen-Gesprächen, da die Paraphrase jeweils neue Bedeutungsaspekte anbietet, die das Verständnis der ursprünglichen Versprachlichung, v. a. bei polysemen Termen, erleichtern soll.

Rekurrenz semantischer Merkmale in heteronymen oder antonymen Lexemen oder Zugehörigkeit zum gleichen Wortfeld (vgl. Trier 1931) liegt, neben außersprachlichem Weltwissen (vgl. § 5.), der semantischen Bezogenheit einzelner Lexeme im Text aufgrund von Kontiguitätsbeziehungen (zu einzelnen Differenzierungen vgl. Harweg 1968: 192−199), d. h. ohne (totale) Koreferenz, zugrunde:

(7) (Isenberg 1971: 162)
Gestern fand eine Hochzeit statt. Die Braut trug dabei ein langes weißes Kleid.

Textgrammatischer Niederschlag dieser speziellen anaphorischen Beziehung ist u. a. die Unmöglichkeit, den definiten Artikel in *die Braut* durch einen demonstrativen Determinierer zu ersetzen (vgl. u. a. Kleiber 1990).

Diese Phänomene beruhen insgesamt auf der signifikanten Rekurrenz semantischer Merkmale im konkreten Text, die Algirdas J. Greimas 1966 bei mindestens einmaliger Rekurrenz eines Merkmals als **„Isotopie"** identifiziert und untersucht. Lexeme, die jeweils über mindestens ein nicht-triviales gemeinsames Merkmal miteinander verbunden sind, bilden Isotopieebenen, ein Text entsprechend einem Gefüge aus (bei polysemen Termen sich gegebenenfalls überlagernden oder überschneidenden) Isotopieebenen (komplexe Isotopien). François Rastier 1972 erweitert den rein semantischen Isotopiebegriff von Greimas auf die Iterativität aller möglicher sprachlicher Einheiten (phonetisch/phonologisch, lexikalisch, syntaktisch usw.) und etabliert so wieder das grundlegende Prinzip der Rekurrenz als textkonstitutives (vgl. § 1.; zum mittlerweile extrem polysemen Isotopiebegriff s. Rastier 1986; vgl. auch Arrivé 1973, Berrendonner 1976 u. a.). Rastier unterscheidet in Inhalts- und Ausdrucksisotopien, in „rhetorische" (Isotopien auf der gleichen sprachlichen Ebene) und „stilistische" (Isotopien auf unterschiedlichen Ebenen) und entwirft eine Hierarchie der Isotopien nach Frequenz und Anzahl rekurrenter Merkmale in einer Isotopieebene. Interessant ist seine Untersuchung „semiologischer Isotopien", die auf der Rekurrenz von Semen beruhen und 'horizontal' in der Entfaltung einzelner Themen oder 'Lesarten' manifest werden, 'vertikal' dagegen bei der metaphorischen Interpretation zweier verschiedenen semantischen Bereichen angehöriger Lexeme über ein gemeinsames Sem.

Die Rekurrenz semantischer Merkmale als strukturierende Eigenschaft einzelsprachlicher lexematischer Felder untersucht Eugenio Coseriu 1967 mit seinen „lexikalischen Solidaritäten", worunter er systematische, semantische (einzelsprachliche) Interdependenz und Vereinbarkeit von Lexemen (vgl. Agricola ²1972) versteht, die z. B. ihrer häufigen Kookkurrenz im Text zugrundeliegen kann (dazu genauer Stati 1979). Lexeme können inhaltlich durch ihre „Klasse" als unterscheidendes Sem bestimmt werden („Affinität", z. B. dt. *fressen* durch [-menschlich]), aber auch durch das „Archilexem" („Selektion", z. B.: dt. *fahren* durch Fahrzeug vs. *fliegen*) oder durch ein einzelnes anderes Lexem („Implikation", z. B. frz. *aquilin* als eine bestimmte Nasenform, also durch frz. *nez*).

3.2. 'Satzverknüpfungsrelationen'

Ein bisher noch nicht diskutiertes Textbildungsmittel ist die syntagmatische Verbindung von Textelementen zu größeren Einheiten, die zu Beginn der textlinguistischen Forschung v. a. als Satzverknüpfung, Koordination und Subordination, in textgrammatischer Perspektive untersucht wurde (vgl. Dik 1968, Dressler 1970a, Isenberg 1971 und 1976 und Lang 1977). Neben einzelsprachlichen Analysen von Konjunktionen, Adverbien usw. (vgl. z. B. Halliday & Hasan 1976, Kap. 5, Gil 1995 u. a.) kann die bereits früh gestellte Frage nach der Äquivalenz von komplexen Sätzen und asyndetisch gereihten Satzfolgen (s. etwa Dressler 1972: 72 f., Van Dijk 1972, 1977 vs. Dascal & Margalit 1974 und die Beiträge in Petöfi 1979 und 1981) als eine genuin semantische (u. U. auch pragmatische) identifiziert werden. Wenn Halliday & Hasan 1976 die Untersuchung englischer **Konnektive** (Terminus nach Van Dijk als Oberbegriff für sprachliche 'Satzverknüpfungselemente', Funktoren mit in der Regel zwei Argumenten, also Konjunktionen, Adverbien, Partikeln usw.) in „additive", „adversative", „causal", „temporal" und „others" gliedern, legen sie eine semantische Einteilung zugrunde, so daß syntagmatische Beziehungen zwischen Propositionen bzw. deren oberflächenstrukturellem Niederschlag als Teil der textuellen Bedeutungsebene auf bestimmte semantische Kategorien zurückgeführt werden können, die ihrerseits außersprachlich-ontologischen Relationen wie 'Ursache — Folge', 'Äquivalenz' u. ä. entsprechen und als „main ordering conditions for sentences in a text" gesehen wurden (Van Dijk 1972: 87 und Kap. 2.5.).

Die hier relevante außereinzelsprachliche Dimension ist die der **Junktion** (vgl. De Beaugrande & Dressler 1981: 76–81, Raible 1992), d. h. der Ausdruck von Relationen zwischen mindestens zwei Ereignissen und Sachverhalten. Für die Kohärenz von Texten ist dabei die außersprachliche Verbundenheit der Sachverhalte wesentlich (vgl. Van Dijk 1977: 48 ff.). Versprachlicht wird diese Dimension zwischen „Aggregation" und „Integration", wobei erstere auf alleiniger Herstellung bzw. Erschließung der Relation durch den Hörer, letztere auf expliziter sprachlicher Signalisierung der Relation durch den Sprecher beruht (vgl. Raible 1992: 30 f.). De Beaugrande & Dressler 1981 unterscheiden vier grundlegende Ausprägungen der Relationen: **Konjunktion** (d. h. 'beides ist in der Textwelt wahr'), **Disjunktion** (d. h. 'nur eines ist in der Textwelt wahr'), **Kontrajunktion** (d. h. 'Unvereinbarkeit in der Textwelt') und **Subordination** (d. h. 'Abhängigkeit' in kausaler, temporaler usw. Hinsicht; hier sind semantische Relationen gemeint, die Konzepte der Textwelt miteinander in Verbindung setzen, so daß diese als in 'semantischen' oder 'thematischen' Netzen von Konzepten und Prädikaten angeordnet vorstellbar sind − vgl. Dressler 1972: 66 ff., De Beaugrande & Dressler 1981: 5 ff., und die Ebene der „intensionalsemantischen Repräsentation" in der „Textstruktur-Weltstruktur-Theorie" von Petöfi, z. B. in Petöfi 1973 und Gülich & Raible 1977: 175 ff.). Diese logischen, semantischen Kategorien sind in keinem Fall eindeutig mit ihrer Versprachlichung in den Einzelsprachen verbunden (vgl. z. B. Van Dijk 1977: 88 f., 1979, Ducrot et al. 1980: 15 ff., und die Unterscheidung in „kanonische" und natürlichsprachige Konnektive im Rahmen der „Textstruktur-Weltstruktur-Theorie": Fritsche 1982, Biasci 1982). Die Kataloge der außersprachlichen semantischen Relationen finden sich in ähnlicher Weise in zahlreichen Arbeiten zur Junktion und Textkohärenz (z. B. zweistellig als reine Konjunktion, Disjunktion, als temporal kausal, konditional, final, konzessiv oder adversativ bei Raible 1992, vgl. auch Van Dijk 1972, Kap. 2.5, 1977, Kap. 3, als einstellig auch lokal, neben Relationen der Implikation, Äquivalenz bei Daneš 1983, 1989a, auch Van Dijk 1980: 29 f.).

Als 'metasprachlich' führt Claudia Biasci 1982 eine Relation der 'Paraphrase' ein; hier sind dann weiterhin die gesamten metasprachlichen und diskursiven „Gliederungssignale" oder „organisateurs textuels" zu nennen (vgl. Gülich 1970, Roulet et al. ³1991, Drescher 1996, Gülich & Kotschi 1996). Neben den semantischen Relationen zwischen Sachverhalten bestehen auf der textuellen Ebene also kompositionelle, funktionale Relationen zwischen einzelnen Textelementen, die zueinander in Beziehungen der Erläuterung, Illustration, Evaluation, Generalisierung, Spezifizierung usw. stehen können (vgl. Van Dijk 1980: 54 ff., Daneš 1983, 1989a; s. auch die Isenbergschen „Vertextungstypen" von 1971, die interpropositionale Relationen referentieller, semantischer oder funktionaler Art vermischen).

Viele natürlichsprachige Konnektive besitzen außerdem neben ihrem semantischen auch einen pragmatischen Wert, worauf Van Dijk immer wieder hingewiesen hat (s. auch Ducrot et al. 1980, Franck 1980). Sie verknüpfen dann nicht Propositionen, sondern Sprechakte, sind also nicht wahrheitswertgebunden, sondern Träger einer pragmatischen Kohärenz (vgl. Van Dijk 1979). Beispielsweise engl. *but* kann äußerungsinitial zusätzlich Überraschung signalisieren, ohne zwingend eine rein adversative Relation zwischen zwei Sachverhalten auszudrücken (*Let's go to the cinema.* − *But I thought we were invited to diner tonight?*).

3.3. Thematischer Textzusammenhang

Über die Existenz lokaler formaler oder semantischer Relationen zwischen einzelnen Textteilen hinaus ist immer auch die einheitliche thematische Orientierung eines Textes als grundlegend für seine Kohärenz angesehen worden (vgl. u. a. Koch 1972, Gutwinski 1976, Viehweger 1976, Agricola 1979, Brinker 1985, Lötscher 1987, Heinemann & Viehweger 1991: 45 ff., Vater 1992: 93 ff.). Die globale Informationsorganisation im Text kann dabei unter verschiedenen Aspekten betrachtet werden.

3.3.1. Textthema und Makrostrukturen

Die Notwendigkeit einer einheitlichen thematischen Orientierung von Einzelsätzen eines Textes weist bereits Ewald Lang 1973 und 1977 nach, indem er die Unabhängigkeit der Textkohärenz von expliziten Kohäsionsmarkern zeigt, solange eine „gemeinsame Einordnungsinstanz" angenommen werden kann:

(8) (Lang 1973: 302)
Peter lernt Französisch, Susi wäscht ab und Rudi sitzt vorm Fernseher. Die Kinder sind IM MOMENT BESCHÄFTIGT.

Auf der Ebene der „vertikalen" oder der „Makrokohärenz" von Texten (vgl. § 1.) ist also jeweils eine zugrundeliegende thematische Basis anzunehmen („topic of discourse", Van Dijk 1977: 148 f.), die die Ausprägungen der „Mikrokohärenz" beeinflußt (z. B. Kompatibilität und Abfolge einzelner Propositionen). Die Annahme einer solchen propositionalen semantischen Textbasis in Analogie zur generativen „Tiefenstruktur" von Sätzen führt Van Dijk zu seinem Konzept der prädikatenlogisch organisierten „Makrostrukturen" (vgl. z. B. Van Dijk 1972, Kap. 3, 1977, Kap. 7), die im Text selbst nicht unbedingt versprachlicht sein müssen (optional in „Thema-" oder „Makrosätzen", die „Makropropositionen" ausdrücken), aus diesem aber über rekursive „Makroregeln" ('Auslassen', 'Selektieren', 'Generalisieren', 'Integrieren', vgl. Van Dijk 1980: 45 ff.) ableitbar sind. Die Einbeziehung kognitiver Prozesse (v. a. von außertextuellen Wissensstrukturen bei der letzten „Makroregel") bei der Erstellung von Makrostrukturen zeigt, daß diese möglicherweise außerhalb der eigentlichen Textsemantik bzw. in einem dynamischen Interaktionsprozeß von Hörerwissen und sprachlicher Information manifest werden, also im Grunde eine kognitive Größe darstellen (vgl. § 5. und Randquist 1985, Vater 1992: 86 ff., bereits Van Dijk 1973).

3.3.2. Informationsorganisation und thematische Entfaltung

Organisation der thematischen Information im Text kann in einer Zweiteilung von 'Vordergrund' und 'Hintergrund' („Reliefgebung" u. a. bei Brandt 1996) oder 'Bekanntes' vs. 'Neues' beschrieben werden, wobei keine Deckungsgleichheit zwischen diesen Kategorien und v. a. keine Identität zwischen 'Textthema' und 'Thema' eines Satzes als kontextuell gegebener Ausgangspunkt (vgl. Daneš 1964 und § 2.3.) angenommen werden darf. In narrativen Texten trägt die Signalisierung der „(main) event line", des 'Vordergrundes', durch einzelsprachlich unterschiedliche formale Mittel (Tempus, Wortstellung, Subordination u. ä., vgl. Hopper 1979, die Beiträge in Tomlin 1987 und Klein & Von Stutterheim 1992, Brandt 1996) zur Erleichterung der Rezeption bei in Abhängigkeit vom jeweils zugrundeliegenden 'Handlungsschema'. In diesem Zusammenhang sollen die strukturalistisch orientierten 'Erzählgrammatiken' (vgl. z. B. Propp 1928, Todorov 1969, Bremond 1973 – vgl. Gülich & Raible 1977) und die eher kognitiv-rezeptionsorientierten „story grammars" (Rumelhart 1980, Thorndyke 1977, Mandler & Johnson 1977 u. a., vgl. Siklaki 1985) Erwähnung finden, die sich hauptsächlich mit der Struktur des außersprachlichen Erzähltextkorrelats befassen, der Konstituierung einer minimalen Erzähltexteinheit („Funktion" oder „Ereignis") und der Verknüpfung mehrerer Handlungs- oder Ereignisschritte zu einer komplexen Erzählung, wobei Fragen der Versprachlichung in aller Regel eine untergeordnete Rolle spielen (vgl. Gülich & Raible 1977: 308; vgl. insgesamt die informative Übersicht in Gülich & Raible 1977, Kap. 3, und Siklaki in Sözer 1985). Für die Kohärenz von Erzähltexten wesentlich ist dabei entweder die textsortenspezifische Anwesenheit von Elementen wie *setting, plot* usw. oder eine allgemeine, in der Regel kausale Ereigniskette, die bei der Rezeption in Rekurs auf wissensbasierte Inferenzen (vgl. § 5.) rekonstruiert wird (vgl. insgesamt genauer Siklaki 1989).

Das Textthema, das nach Wolfgang Klein & Christiane von Stutterheim 1992 durch eine Textfrage („Quaestio") ermittelt werden kann, legt allgemein z. B. die Art der „thematischen Entfaltung" (Brinker), der „referentiellen Bewegung" (Klein & Von Stutterheim), der „thematischen Progression" (Daneš) fest. Die bekannteste Kategorisierung stellen hier wohl die allerdings in Rekurs auf die satzbezogenen Begriffe 'Thema' und 'Rhema' von František Daneš beschriebenen fünf Typen der „thematischen Progression" dar (einfach linear, d. h. das 'Rhema' des vorangehenden Satzes wird jeweils das 'Thema' des nächsten, mit durchlaufendem Thema, d. h. das 'Thema' der einzelnen Sätze bleibt konstant, mit abgeleiteten Themen, d. h. ein 'Überthema' ergibt jeweils die Einzelthemen, mit 'gespaltenem' Rhema, d. h. ein Rhema teilt sich auf und wird zu einzelnen Themen der nachfolgenden Sätze, und schließlich die Progression mit einem 'thematischen Sprung', vgl. u. a. Daneš 1970, 1974: 118 f., 1989b). Diese Typen stehen mit den textinternen Isotopierelationen, genauer dem Verhältnis von Textthema und einzelnen Satzthemen in Verbindung und sind u. U. auch textsortenspezifisch (→ Art. 37). Sie können nach dem 'thematisierten Element' (vorheriges 'Thema' oder 'Rhema'), nach direkter Übernahme oder Ableitung eines 'Themas' aus dem Kotext und der Entfernung des jeweiligen Bezugselementes klassifiziert werden (vgl. Daneš 1989b: 25 f.; dazu genauer Lötscher 1987, Kap. 4). Mit textsortenspezifischer Relevanz zeigen sich die Brinkerschen (u. a. 1985) „Grundtypen thematischer Entfaltung" (deskriptiv, explikativ, argumentativ, narrativ), die in ihrer pragmatischen Fundierung den sehr viel detaillierteren Van Dijkschen „Superstrukturen" als konventionelle Textsortenschemata (→ Art. 37) sehr nahe kommen.

4. Textpragmatik

Mit der Auffassung von Texten als den primären sprachlichen Äußerungen in jeweils konkreten Kommunikationssituationen verbindet sich der Aspekt ihrer 'pragmatischen Kohärenz', d. h. ihrer Situationsadäquatheit, handlungslogischen Konsistenz usw., womit die Ebene systeminterner Kategorien verlassen wird und übereinzelsprachlich gültige 'Kommunikationsregeln' als mögliche Kohärenzträger (vgl. Kummer 1975, Maas & Wunderlich 1972, Wunderlich 1972) in das Blickfeld rücken. Auch hier ist eine zweifache Herangehensweise möglich, nämlich die Untersuchung lokaler, sequentieller Verbundenheit einzelner Äußerungen und dann deren Zusammenhang mit einer möglichen übergeordneten Textfunktion („Makrosprechakt", vgl. z. B. Van Dijk 1977, Kap. 8 und 9, Van Dijk 1980: 92−95).

4.1. Präsuppositionen, Implikaturen und Relevanz

Daß Kohärenz und Textverstehen wesentlich mit den Größen des Sprechers und Hörers zusammenhängen, beschreibt bereits Bellert 1970, wenn sie die semantisch kohärente Interpretation einer Äußerung als abhängig vom Verständnis ihres Ko-Textes inklusive aller sich daraus ergebenden Folgerungen bzw. Schlüsse („Quasi-Implikationen") beschreibt. Besonders „implikative Terme" transportieren nach Bellert einmal über ihre 'Systembedeutung' 'implizierte Propositionen' mit, die im Folgetext versprachlicht werden oder eine wichtige Voraussetzung für sein Verständnis darstellen können („lexikalische", „semantische **Präsuppositionen**", vgl. Franck 1973, auch Charolles 1994: 129; zum Präsuppositionsbegriff als kontextabhängige Voraussetzung für den angemessenen Gebrauch bzw. die angemessene Interpretation von sprachlichen Ausdrücken s. etwa die Beiträge in Franck & Petöfi 1973). Sodann rufen sie aber auch außersprachliches Wissen auf, das ebenfalls automatisch mit bestimmten versprachlichten Konzepten verbunden ist (vgl. § 5.) und der impliziten Verbundenheit einzelner Propositionen zugrundeliegen kann (vgl. Van Dijk 1972: 97 f., Van Dijk 1980: 32 f.). Van Dijk weist 1972 und 1977 auf die notwendige Berücksichtigung von 'Folgerungsbeziehungen' im weitesten Sinne zwischen einzelnen Propositionen hin, die ihre Anordnung mitbestimmen: Präsupponierte Elemente müssen vor darauf bezugnehmenden Assertionen eingeführt worden sein (vgl. Van Dijk 1977: 106). Natürlichsprachige Präsuppositionen und Implikationen (zur Unterscheidung s. u. a. Franck 1973) einer Proposition sind in der Regel weniger zahlreich als logisch mögliche (Kohärenz ist nicht gleich logische Konsistenz!), da hier die kommunikative **Relevanz** im jeweiligen Kontext eine einschränkende Funktion hat (vgl. Van Dijk 1972: 96−100). Der pragmatische Aspekt von Präsuppositionen im Text als Kohärenzträger ist also deutlich (vgl. auch Brown & Yule 1983, die Präsuppositionen, Implikaturen u. a. als genuin pragmatische Phänomene beschreiben).

Diskurskohärenz kann allgemein als Folge der Anwendung des universalen Relevanzprinzips gesehen werden (vgl. Charolles 1994: 136 f.), das Sperber & Wilson 1986 formulieren als maximales Potential an 'Kontexteffekten' (Interpretationsanstrengung durch den Hörer, vgl. Moeschler et al. 1994: 24 ff.). Bereits Reinhart 1980 weist auf das Zusammenspiel von Kohärenz („cohesion"), Konsistenz und Relevanz hin, wobei letztere als Meta-Prinzip im Falle explizit nicht-kohärenter Texte Implikaturen auslöst, die Texten eine implizite Interpretierbarkeit verleihen (vgl. Reinhart 1980: 164 ff.). Relevanz ist in dieser Auffassung die Beziehung zwischen einer Äußerung und ihrem Ko- bzw. Kontext. Relevanz als Konversationsmaxime („Maxime der Relation" bei Grice 1975) beschreibt das Verhalten eines Individuums und ist ein a-priorisches Kommunikationsprinzip. Hauptsächlich dieses Prinzip bedingt die Existenz kontextabhängiger **konversationeller Implikaturen** (im Unterschied zu den ebenfalls wichtigen konventionellen Implikaturen, die ausschließlich auf der einzelsprachlichen Bedeutung von Lexemen oder grammatischen Konstruktionen beruhen), die z. B. eine kohärente Interpretation des Beispiels (1) möglich machen ('wir feiern immer den Geburtstag dieses uns werten spanischen Schriftstellers'). Insbesondere in Dialogen ist die gegenseitige semantische und pragmatische Relevanz der Gesprächsbeiträge (*turns*) ein übergeordnetes Steuerungsprinzip der Sprachproduktion und -rezeption (vgl. Van Dijk 1980: 249 f.).

4.2. Illokutionshierarchien

Der konsistente sequentielle Charakter von Textteilen hängt auch von einer handlungstheoretisch plausiblen Abfolge von Sprechakten ab, die globale pragmatische Textkohärenz von deren Bezogensein auf einen „Makrosprechakt". Motsch & Viehweger 1981, Motsch 1983, Viehweger 1983, Motsch 1996 u. a. nehmen grundsätzlich neben der grammatischen und thematisch-semantischen eine Illokutionsstruktur von Texten an, der sie eine zentrale Rolle zuschreiben. Textanalyse sehen sie als kommunikative Handlungsanalyse. Texte erweisen sich in dieser Sicht als Handlungsmuster, als „ziel- und ergebnisabhängige Schemata zur Realisierung komplexer Handlungsziele" (Viehweger 1983: 101). Häufig existiert eine hierarchische Relation zwischen einer 'Hauptillokution', einer Haupthandlung, einem 'Oberziel', und diesen untergeordneten 'Teilillokutionen', 'Teilzielen' (vgl. etwa Van Dijk 1977, Kap. 8.4, Motsch & Viehweger 1981, Viehweger 1983 u. a.). Die untergeordneten Sprechakte können essentiellen oder nur akzidentellen Charakter haben; beispielsweise verlangen Bitten häufig motivierende oder rechtfertigende Erklärungen, während die Angabe einer 'Beglaubigungsquelle' bei einer Assertion (vgl. z. B. Van Dijk 1972: 215) optional sein kann. „Stützende" Sprechakte sind entweder direkt mit dem dominierenden Sprechakt verbunden („subsidiär") oder sichern indirekt die Kooperationsbereitschaft des Hörers, z. B. durch Beachtung der Regeln (sprachlicher) Höflichkeit („komplementär", vgl. Brandt & Rosengren 1992: 18 ff.). Die Sequenzierung von Illokutionen hängt nach Motsch 1996 u. a. von übereinzelsprachlich gültigen Prinzipien der Illokutionsstruktur ab; die „Illokutionshierarchie" von über- und untergeordneten Sprechakten hat v. a. einer „globalen Adjazenzforderung" zu genügen insofern, als dem dominierenden Sprechakt die dazu subsidiären jeweils unmittelbar vorangehen oder folgen müssen (vgl. weitere Prinzipien bei Brandt & Rosengren 1992: 23 ff.); es gilt, daß eine Illokution jeweils genau eine andere direkt stützt (vgl. Heinemann & Viehweger 1991: 105 ff., Motsch 1996: 190 f.). Die Abfolge von Sprechhandlungen ist dabei nicht mit der Abfolge von Sätzen gleichzusetzen (vgl. u. a. Motsch 1983: 125 ff., auch schon Isenberg 1976), oft sind die Verhältnisse von oberflächenstrukturellen Indikatoren, propositionaler Struktur und zugrundeliegender Illokution kompliziert (s. Rosengren 1983: 136 ff., Brandt & Rosengren 1992).

Ein pragmatischer Kohärenzindikator und Kohärenzträger ist auch die Identifizierbarkeit einer einheitlichen Intention des Textproduzenten. Lundquist 1989 zeigt, wie die „Modalität" eines Textes, d. h. die indizierte Senderintention und seine Einstellung zum Thema (signalisiert über Marker verschiedenster Art wie Verbmodus u. ä.) beim Rezipienten verschiedene Erwartungen über die Illokutionsstruktur im Zusammenhang mit dem jeweils spezifischen Kontext (z. B. Leitartikel in einer Tageszeitung vs. Werbeannonce) hervorrufen, die allerdings im Prozeß der Rezeption immer revidiert werden können.

4.3. Diskursanalyse

Dialoge oder Mehr-Personen-Gespräche sind der 'Normalfall' (vgl. Coseriu 1974) von komplexer sprachlicher Aktivität, also von Texten im weitesten Sinne, und besitzen neben der bisher beschriebenen oberflächenstrukturellen, semantisch-thematischen und illokutionären eine metakommunikative-interaktionelle Dimension, die ebenfalls ihren 'Zusammenhang', also ihre Kohärenz betrifft. Dialogpartner müssen übereinzelsprachlich bestimmte Regeln des 'Miteinandersprechens' beachten, womit ein nicht nur sprachlicher Aspekt der sozialen Interaktion aufgerufen ist. Seit den siebziger Jahren ist die Forschungsrichtung der 'Diskursanalyse' als sozio-pragmatische, varietätenlinguistische und textlinguistische Disziplin mit derartigen Fragen befaßt (vgl. Grimes 1975, Coulthard 1977, Coulthard & Montgomery 1981, Roulet et al. ³1991; zur Argumentationstheorie s. Moeschler 1989). Im Dialog treffen grundsätzlich (mindestens) zwei Sprecher mit je eigenen Weltkonzepten und Absichten aufeinander, verfolgen aber ein (gemeinsames) Ziel. Die einzelnen Repliken (keine syntaktische, sondern eine interaktioniell-pragmatische Einheit) konstituieren füreinander den jeweiligen Hintergrund und sind aufeinander als 'stimulus' – 'response' bezogen, d. h. sie bestimmen die Art des Folgenden, wobei jederzeit die Möglichkeit zur Eigen- oder Fremdkorrektur besteht. Konventionell-interaktionelle Paare von Repliken („turns") werden als „adjacency pairs" (Frage – Antwort, Bitte – Dank usw., vgl. Schegloff & Sacks 1973) bezeichnet, innerhalb derer bestimmte oberflächenstrukturelle Erscheinungen (z. B. Frage-Antwort-Ellipse, Wortstellung usw.) als semantisch oder pragmatisch durch die Gesamtheit des Replikenpaares bedingt analysiert werden müssen (vgl. Langleben 1983). Die Organisation des „turn-taking" (Sacks et al. 1974) gehorcht im Diskurs fundamentalen interaktionellen Regeln, die allerdings z. T. kulturspezifischer Art sind (vgl. Coulthard 1977: 63 f.), z. B. 'nicht mehr als ein Sprecher gleichzeitig', Auswahl des nächsten Sprechers durch den aktuellen über Intonation, Gestik und Augenkontakt (vgl. Coulthard & Montgomery 1981, Kap. 8) mit oder ohne Festlegung des erwarteten Sprechaktes usw.

Für Kohärenz wesentlich erweist sich auf dieser Ebene v. a. handlungslogische 'Vollständigkeit' (weniger logische Konsistenz; vgl. besonders Roulet et al. ³1991: 15 f.).

5. Kohärenz und Kognition

Bereits Bellert 1970 zeigt, daß die anfangs fast mechanisch im Rahmen von Textgrammatiken analysierte Koreferenz (vgl. § 2.1.) keineswegs eine rein innersprachliche Kategorie ist:

(9) (nach Bellert 1970)
Picasso hat Paris verlassen. Der Maler begab sich in sein Atelier an der Mittelmeerküste. Er hält sich dort auf.

Bellert bemerkt zutreffend, daß die Kenntnis der Tatsache, daß Picasso Maler war, keine notwendige Bedingung für eine koreferentielle Lesart der drei Subjekts-NPn ist, diese allerdings enorm erleichtert, wobei aufgrund der schon mehrfach beschriebenen Interpretationsprinzipien der 'thematischen Kontinuität' und der pragmatischen Relevanzmaxime u. ä. Koreferenz inferiert werden kann.

5.1. Kognitive Grundlagen

Menschliches Wissen ist in bestimmten kognitiven Strukturen organisiert, die als 'Netzwerke' mit Konzepten als in der Regel mehrfach miteinander verbundenen 'Knotenpunkten' vorstellbar sind (vgl. z. B. Figge 1994). Konzepte sind beschreibbar über essentielles „determinierendes Wissen" (z. B. 'Sterblichkeit' als Eigenschaft von Lebewesen), „typisches Wissen" und „zufälliges Wissen" (vgl. De Beaugrande & Dressler 1981: 90 ff.), die zunehmend subjektiv sind. Aktiviert werden Konzepte über bestimmte „trigger" oder Schlüsselwörter, Lexeme, während Konnektive (vgl. § 3.2.) bestimmte Operationen der Kenntnisverarbeitung und Wissensaktivierung einleiten können (vgl. De Beaugrande 1980: 165). Zwischen einzelnen Konzepten müssen jeweils kontextabhängige Prozesse der „Aktivierungsverbreitung" (vgl. De Beaugrande & Dressler 1981: 93 f.) und „(Merkmals-)Vererbung" (vgl. De Beaugrande & Dressler 1981: 96 f.) angenommen werden, so daß in aller Regel in einem Text mehr Informationen verstanden werden als explizit versprachlicht sind (vgl. Rieger 1989). Hier findet sich die kognitive Grundlage der Van Dijkschen „Makrostrukturen" (vgl. § 3.3.), die den Prinzipien der 'ganzheitlichen Gestaltwahrnehmung' entsprechen und auf der Basis der „Makroregeln" u. a. unter Einbeziehung extratextueller, inferierter Bedeutungselemente in zyklischen Verstehensprozessen entstehen (vgl. Van Dijk 1973 und v. a. Kintsch & Van Dijk 1978). Um beispielsweise Koreferenzrelationen, Isotopien oder auch „Text-Kontiguitäts-Substitutionen" (vgl. §§ 2. und 3.) als solche in ihrer textbildenden Funktion erkennen zu können, müssen mindestens zwei Wissensbereiche durch sprachliche Textelemente aktiviert werden, nämlich einzelsprachlich-lexikalisches Wissen und außersprachlich-enzyklopädisches Wissen (vgl. Bellert 1970 und das Beispiel (9), De Beaugrande 1980: 19 f. und 231 ff., Van Dijk 1980: 28 ff., Daneš 1983: 8 f. u. a.). Außerdem spielen oft „Interaktionswissen" (vgl. § 4.) und „Textsortenwissen" eine Rolle (vgl. Heinemann & Viehweger 1991: 68). Kohärenz kann so als 'Sinnkontinuität' des Wissens, das durch den Text aktiviert wird, beschrieben werden (vgl. De Beaugrande & Dressler 1981: 88, Van Dijk 1977: 99 f.). Vor allem außersprachliches Wissen ist in 'globalen Mustern' organisiert (vgl. De Beaugrande & Dressler 1981: 93), die als „**frames**", „**scripts**", „**plans**" und „**Schemata**" bezeichnet werden (vgl. De Beaugrande & Dressler 1981: 95 f.). *Frames* sind relativ statische Wissensstrukturen über stereotype Situationen (mit „konzeptuellem Zentrum", z. B. Bestandteile eines Gottesdienstes, vgl. Minsky 1975, Brown & Yule 1983, Kap. 7), während *scripts* und Schemata Wissen über stereotype Ereignisabläufe darstellen (z. B. Einkaufen). *Plans* sind Handlungsschemata, die Informationen über Erreichen von Zielen enthalten (vgl. Schank & Abelson 1977, De Beaugrande 1980: 163 ff.) und individuell variieren können. Die Existenz von *frames* und *scripts* erklärt die in §§ 2. und 3. erwähnte Erscheinung der „impliziten Referenz", da der *frame* 'Hochzeit' eine Braut als Konzept enthält und 'mitaktiviert', woraus sich die oberflächenstrukturelle Definitheit erklären läßt. Auch die Kenntnis des Handlungsziels eines Protagonisten erlaubt Rückschlüsse auf dessen wahrscheinliches Handeln oder das Verstehen vermeintlich irrelevanter Handlungen als sinnvoll und kohärent (vgl. Samet & Schank 1984, De Beaugrande 1980: 164). *Frames* können auch bestimmte Textsortenschemata repräsentieren und so auf der 'Metaebene' Kodierungsprozesse erleichtern (vgl. Minsky 1975, Lundquist 1989).

5.2. Kohärenz und Inferenzen

Eine kohärente Wahrnehmung ist die Grundvoraussetzung für Menschen, um mit ihrer Umwelt in sinnvolle Interaktion treten zu können. Die Wahrnehmung von Kohärenz in Texten ist eine sehr komplexe (als Kohärenz der beschriebenen Sachverhalte, der Senderintention, der Versprachlichung usw.), die bei 'Relevanzproblemen' oder 'Kohäsionsbrüchen' aufgrund von Widersprüchen zwischen der zunächst dekodierten Textbedeutung oder -funktion und bestehenden Wissensstrukturen über Implikaturen und Inferenzen jederzeit herzustellen versucht wird (vgl. Charolles 1983, 1985, 1989, s. auch Rickheit 1991 und den Kohärenzbegriff von H/P/S 1985, vgl. § 1.). Der Textproduzent kann 'Konnexitätsindikatoren' im Text verteilen in Abhängigkeit von einem bestimmten Kommunikationsziel und seinen Hypothesen über Hörerkenntnisse u. ä.; theoretisch besteht allerdings in dieser Perspektive keine notwendige oder hinreichende Bedingung für eine kohärente Textrezeption, auch keine 'Kohärenzgrenze', unterhalb derer keine kohärente Interpretation von Texten mehr möglich wäre (vgl. v. a. Charolles 1985: 3 ff.). Kohärenz verläßt hier freilich die Ebene der sprachlichen Textmanifestation als Objekt und ist eine Kategorie der Rezeption (u. U. auch der Produktion), des wahrnehmenden Subjekts, weil das in § 4. beschriebene Relevanzprinzip die absichtliche Produktion inkohärenter Texte ausschließt. Wird *Text* als Kommunikationsprozeß aufgefaßt, ist Kohärenz das 'Verhandlungsergebnis' kommunikativer und mentaler Vorgänge auf der Basis von grammatischen und lexikalischen Indikatoren und Wissens- bzw. Gedächtnisstrukturen (vgl. die Beiträge in Heinemann & Viehweger 1991, Gernsbacher & Givón 1995, Kap. 1.2.6, bereits De Beaugrande & Dressler 1981: 37 u. a.).

Konzeptwissen kann aktiviert werden über bestimmte kognitive Operationen, die Teil des „prozeduralen Wissens" sind und u. a. Inferenzprozeduren beinhalten, d. h. Konstruktionen von nicht-explizit im Text versprachlichten, aber ausgehend von dort enthaltenen Elementen erschlossenen Propositionsverbindungen, Propositionsteilen oder Propositionen (vgl. Crothers 1979: 16, Heinemann & Viehweger 1991: 73 f., Rickheit 1991). Obwohl **Inferenzen** bei der Textproduktion in aller Regel eingeplant werden, sind sie nicht vorhersagbar und können zu unterschiedlichen Rezeptionsergebnissen führen (vgl. Crothers 1979: 9, Heinemann & Viehweger 1991: 74, s. auch Weingartner in Conte et al. 1989). Edward J. Crothers 1979 entwickelt eine detaillierte Inferenztypologie (vgl. Crothers 1979: 16 ff.), in der er u. a. 'a-priori-' und 'a-posteriori-Inferenzen' unterscheidet; erstere aktivieren enzyklopädisches Wissen sofort bei Auftreten eines bestimmten „triggers", letztere ergänzen die bisher konstruierte Textwelt in Abhängigkeit von beispielsweise anaphorischen Referenzanweisungen bei nicht explizit eingeführten Textreferenten. Van de Velde beschreibt in seinen Arbeiten Kohärenz als „inhaltlichen Zusammenhang" als Ergebnis der Aktivität des Rezipienten, womit er Inferenzen als führende Kraft der Textinterpretation meint (vgl. z. B. Van de Velde 1989a). Inferenzen können auf der Basis verschiedener Arten von Informationen entstehen (phonematisch-graphemisch, syntaktisch, semantisch-logisch, pragmatisch intratextuell und handlungsbezogen, sozio-pragmatisch extratextuell, vgl. z. B. Van de Velde 1985: 262 ff.) und sind beschreibbar als Problemlösungsstrategien, die miteinander interagieren in analytischen („bottom-up", d. h. Dekodierung syntaktischer, lexikalischer usw. Einheiten, die als Konstituenten einer größeren Einheit verstanden werden), sequentiellen („on-line", d. h. Rekonstruktion linearer Verknüpfungen) und holistischen Prozessen („top-down", d. h. die Konstruktion einer globalen Bedeutung, die Rückschlüsse auf einzelne Bedeutungselemente zuläßt — hier wird die wichtige Kategorie der „gemeinsamen Einordnungsinstanz" oder „Makrostruktur" erkennbar, vgl. § 3.3. und Van de Velde 1981). Inferenzen sind bei Van de Velde unterteilt in syntaktische, lexikonbasierte, semantisch-logische und 'handlungsorientierte', die auf der Basis von Sprechakten, *scripts*, Konversationsmaximen u. ä. operieren (s. z. B. Van de Velde 1989b: 185—211).

Mit dem letzten Punkt wird die ganze Spannweite des Kohärenzbegriffes sichtbar, der anders als der oberflächengebundene der Kohäsion als 'sinnvoller Zusammenhang' eine Kategorie von sprachlichen Objekten, aber eben auch versprachlichten Sachverhalten, Kommunikationssituationen und Verhaltensweisen und letztlich v. a. von kreativen Verstehensprozessen ist (vgl. Van de Velde 1981: 8 f.).

Die Diskussion verschiedener Manifestationsmöglichkeiten von Kohärenz hat gezeigt, daß der explizite oberflächenstrukturelle Ausdruck von Kohärenz (also Kohäsion) textintern und textextern (v. a. durch Thematik und Situationsfaktoren, unter denen die subjektiven Ausprägungen von Sprecher- und Hörerwissen eine ausgezeichnete Rolle einnehmen) bedingt sein kann, was eine unterschiedliche Gewichtung der einzelnen 'Kohärenzebenen' (phonetisch-phonologisch, grammatisch, semantisch, pragmatisch usw.) in unterschiedlichen Textsorten bzw. Diskurstraditionen (→ Art. 36) zu konstatieren erlaubt (vgl. Conte et al. 1989: „Part II: Text-Type Specific Aspects of Connectedness", 223−359). Bereits Harweg ²1979 zeigt die Dominanz verschiedener 'Substitutionstypen' (vgl. § 2.1.) in wissenschaftlichen und literarischen Texten (vgl. auch Gutwinski 1976); die Kategorie der 'Fiktionalität' selbst ist u. a. auch über im Vergleich zu 'Alltags-Texten' gelockerten semantisch-referentiellen Kohärenzanforderungen definiert worden. Prinzipiell ist die pragmatisch bedingte Unterscheidung in primär linear bzw. primär hierarchisch organisierte Texte für Kohärenzausprägungen bzw. unterschiedliche Kohärenzannahmen und Inferenzprozesse auf Hörerseite relevant; je nach Textfunktion und Kommunikationssituation sind eine konsistente gegenseitige Bezogenheit einzelner Äußerungen in chronologischer Reihenfolge (z. B. in Kochrezepten), eine globale thematische Einheitlichkeit oder aber eine hohe Variabilität in stilistischer, semantisch-thematischer, ja pragmatischer Ausrichtung (in spontanen Dialogen) Teil des diskurstraditionellen Wissens und somit textsortenspezifische Kohärenzträger (vgl. Hinds 1978).

Kohärenz ist insgesamt sinnvoll zu beschreiben entweder als Kommunikationsaxiom oder phänomenologisches Konzept. In beiden Fällen weist Kohärenz weit über den engen Bereich der 'Textualitätsdiskussion' hinaus und wirft die berechtigte Frage nach der Zugehörigkeit der Textebene zu (einzelsprachlichen) Systemen mit implizierter Entscheidbarkeit über Systemzugehörigkeit oder Abweichung ('Ungrammatikalität') auf.

6. Zitierte Literatur

Agricola, Erhard. ²1972. *Semantische Relationen im Text und im System.* (Janua linguarum, Series Minor, 113) Den Haag/Paris: Mouton.

Agricola, Erhard. 1979. *Textstruktur, Textanalyse, Informationskern.* Leipzig: VEB Verlag Enzyklopädie.

Arrivé, Michel. 1973. „Pour une théorie des textes poly-isotopiques". *Langages* 30: 53−63.

Bazzanella, Carla (ed.) 1996. *Repetition in Dialogue.* (Beiträge zur Dialogforschung, 11) Tübingen: Niemeyer.

Beaugrande, Robert-Alain de. 1980. *Text, Discourse, and Process. Toward a Multidisciplinary Science of Texts.* (Advances in Discourse Processes, 4) Norwood/New Jersey: Ablex.

Beaugrande, Robert-Alain de & Dressler, Wolfgang Ulrich. 1981. *Einführung in die Textlinguistik.* (Konzepte der Sprach- und Literaturwissenschaft, 28) Tübingen: Niemeyer.

Bellert, Irene. 1970. „On a Condition of the Coherence of Texts". *Semiotica* 2: 335−363.

Berrendonner, Alain. 1976. „De quelques aspects logiques de l'isotopie". *Linguistique et sémiologie* 1: 117−135.

Berruto, Gaetano. 1979. „A Sociolinguistic View on Text-Linguistics". In: Petöfi (ed.) 1979, vol. 2, 495−508.

Biasci, Claudia. 1982. *Konnektive in Sätzen und Texten. Eine sprachübergreifende pragmatisch-semantische Analyse.* (Papiere zur Textlinguistik, 41) Hamburg: Buske.

Bierwisch, Manfred. 1965. „Rezension von Zellig S. Harris. 1963. *Discourse Analysis Reprints.* (= Papers on Formal Linguistics, 2) Den Haag". *Linguistics* 13: 61−73.

Bókay, Antal. 1985. „Text and Coherence in a Psychoanalytic Theory of Jokes". In: Sözer (ed.) 1985, 414−438.

Bosch, Peter. 1983. *Agreement and Anaphora. A Study in the Role of Pronouns in Syntax and Discourse.* London u. a.: Academic Press.

Bosch, Peter. 1985. „Constraints, Coherence, Comprehension. Reflections on Anaphora". In: Sözer (ed.) 1985, 299−320.

Brandt, Margaretha. 1996. „Subordination und Parenthese als Mittel der Informationsstrukturierung in Texten". In: Motsch (ed.) 1996, 211−240.

Brandt, Margaretha & Rosengren, Inger. 1992. „Zur Illokutionsstruktur von Texten". *Zeitschrift für Literaturwissenschaft und Linguistik* 86: 9−51.

Brazil, David. 1975. *Discourse Intonation.* (Discourse Analysis Monographs, 1) Birmingham: English Language Research (University of Birmingham).

Brazil, David. 1978. *Discourse Intonation II.* (Discourse Analysis Monographs, 2) Birmingham: English Language Research (University of Birmingham).

Bremond, Claude. 1973. *Logique du récit.* Paris: Editions du Seuil.

Brinker, Klaus. 1979. „Zur Gegenstandsbestimmung und Aufgabenstellung der Textlinguistik". In: Petöfi (ed.) 1979, vol. 2, 3−12.

Brinker, Klaus. 1985. *Linguistische Textanalyse. Eine Einführung in Grundbegriffe und Methoden.* (Grundlagen der Germanistik, 29) Berlin: Erich Schmidt.

Brown, Gillian & Yule, George. 1983. *Discourse Analysis.* Cambridge: Cambridge University Press.

Canisius, Peter & Herbermann, Clemens-Peter & Tschauder, Gerhard (eds.) 1994. *Text und Grammatik. Festschrift für Roland Harweg zum 60. Geburtstag.* Bochum: Brockmeyer.

Charolles, Michel. 1983. „Coherence as a Principle in the Interpretation of Discourse". *Text* 3.1: 71−99.

Charolles, Michel. 1985. „Text Connexity, Text Coherence and Text Interpretation Processing". In: Sözer (ed.) 1985, 1−15.

Charolles, Michel. 1994. „Cohésion, cohérence et pertinence du discours". *Travaux de linguistique* 29: 125−151.

Charolles, Michel (ed.) 1989. *The Resolution of Discourse. Processing, Coherence or Consistency Dissonances.* (Papiere zur Textlinguistik, 54) Hamburg: Buske.

Charolles, Michel & Peytard, Jean (eds.) 1978. *Enseignement du récit et cohérence du texte. (Langue française,* 38) Paris.

Charolles, Michel & Petöfi, János S. & Sözer, Emel (eds.) 1986. *Research in Text Connexity and Text Coherence. A Survey.* (Papiere zur Textlinguistik, 53.1) Hamburg: Buske.

Cherchi, Lucien. 1978. „L'ellipse comme facteur de cohérence". In: Charolles & Peytard (eds.) 1978, 118−128.

Cherchi, Lucien. 1985. „On the Role of Ellipsis in Discourse Coherence". In: Meyer-Hermann, Reinhard & Rieser, Hannes (eds.) *Ellipsen und fragmentarische Ausdrücke.* (Linguistische Arbeiten, 148) vol. 2. Tübingen: Niemeyer, 224−249.

Cole, Peter. 1973. *Indefiniteness and Anaphoricity: The Analogical Extension of a Semantically Based Constraint.* Ann Arbor: University Microfilms International.

Conte, Maria-Elisabeth. 1980. „Coerenza testuale". *Lingua e stile* 15.1: 135−154.

Conte, Maria-Elisabeth. 1981. „Textdeixis und Anapher". *Kodikas* 3.2: 121−132.

Conte, Maria-Elisabeth. 1986. „Coerenza, interpretazione, reinterpretazione". *Lingua e stile* 21.2/3: 357−372.

Conte, Maria-Elisabeth. 1988. „Italienisch: Textlinguistik". In: Holtus, Günther & Metzeltin, Michael & Schmitt, Christian (eds.). *Lexikon der Romanistischen Linguistik.* Bd. IV: *Italienisch, Korsisch, Sardisch.* Tübingen: Niemeyer, 132−143.

Conte, Maria-Elisabeth (ed.) 1989. *Kontinuität und Diskontinuität in Texten und Sachverhalts-Konfigurationen.* (Papiere zur Textlinguistik, 50) Hamburg: Buske.

Conte, Maria-Elisabeth & Petöfi, János S. & Sözer, Emel (eds.) 1989. *Text and Discourse Connectedness. Proceedings of the Conference on Connexity and Coherence Urbino, July 16−21, 1984.* (Studies in Language Companion Series, 16) Amsterdam/Philadelphia: Benjamins.

Corblin, Francis. 1995. *Les formes de reprise dans le discours. Anaphores et chaînes de référence.* Rennes: Presses universitaires de Rennes.

Cornish, Francis. 1994. „Agreement and Discourse: From Cohesion to Coherence". *French Language Studies* 4: 191−213.

Coseriu, Eugenio. 1967. „Lexikalische Solidaritäten". *Poetica* 1: 293−303.

Coseriu, Eugenio. 1974. *Synchronie, Diachronie und Geschichte.* (Internationale Bibliothek für allgemeine Linguistik, 3) München: Fink.

Coseriu, Eugenio. ³1994. *Textlinguistik. Eine Einführung.* Hrsg. u. bearb. von Jörn Albrecht. (UTB, 1808) Tübingen u. a.: Francke.

Couper-Kuhlen, Elisabeth. 1983. „Intonatorische Kohäsion. Eine makroprosodische Untersuchung". *Zeitschrift für Literaturwissenschaft und Linguistik* 13: 74−100.

Coulthard, Malcolm. 1977. *An Introduction to Discourse Analysis.* London/New York: Longman.

Coulthard, Malcolm & Montgomery, Martin (ed.) 1981. *Studies in Discourse Analysis.* London/New York: Routledge.

Crothers, Edward J. 1979. *Paragraph Structure Inference.* Norwood/New Jersey: Ablex.

Daneš, František. 1964. „A Three-Level Approach to Syntax". *Travaux linguistiques de Prague* 1: 225−240.

Daneš, František. 1970. „Zur linguistischen Analyse der Textstruktur". *Folia linguistica* 4: 72−78.

Daneš, František. 1974. „Functional Sentence Perspective and the Organization of the Text". In: Daneš (ed.) 1974, 106−128.

Daneš, František. 1983. „Welche Ebenen der Textstruktur soll man annehmen?". In: Daneš & Viehweger (eds.) 1983, 1−11.

Daneš, František. 1989a. „Report of Roger van de Velde's Paper 'Man, Verbal Text, Inferencing, and Coherence' ". In: Heydrich et al. (eds.), 228−239.

Daneš, František. 1989b. „'Functional Sentence Perspective' and Text Connectedness". In: Conte et al. (eds.), 23−32.

Daneš, František (ed.) 1974. *Papers on Functional Sentence Perspective.* Den Haag/Paris: Mouton.

Daneš, František & Viehweger, Dieter (eds.) 1976. *Probleme der Textgrammatik.* (studia grammatica, 11) Berlin: Akademie-Verlag.

Daneš, František & Viehweger, Dieter (eds.) 1983. *Ebenen der Textstruktur.* Berlin: Akademie der Wissenschaften der DDR.

Dascal, Marcelo & Margalit, Avishai. 1974. „A New 'Revoluton' in Linguistics? – 'Text-Grammars' vs. 'Sentence Grammars'". *Theoretical Linguistics* 1: 195–208.

Dik, Simon C. 1968. *Coordination. Its Implications for the Theory of General Linguistics.* Amsterdam: North Holland Publishing Company.

Dorfmüller-Karpusa, Käthi. 1988. „Temporal and Aspectual Relations as Text-Constitutive Elements". In: Petöfi (ed.) 1988, 134–169.

Drescher, Martina. 1996. „Textkonstitutive Verfahren und ihr Ort in der Handlungsstruktur des Textes". In: Motsch (ed.) 1996, 81–102.

Dressler, Wolfgang Ulrich. 1970a. „Textsyntax". *Lingua e stile* 5: 191–213.

Dressler, Wolfgang Ulrich. 1970b. „Modelle und Methoden der Textsyntax". *Folia Linguistica* 4: 64–71.

Dressler, Wolfgang Ulrich. 1972. *Einführung in die Textlinguistik.* (Konzepte der Sprach- und Literaturwissenschaft, 13) Tübingen: Niemeyer.

Dressler, Wolfgang Ulrich (ed.) 1977: *Current Trends in Textlinguistics.* (Research in Text Theory, 2) Berlin/New York: De Gruyter.

Dressler, Wolfgang Ulrich (ed.) 1978. *Textlinguistik.* (Wege der Forschung, 427) Darmstadt: Wissenschaftliche Buchgesellschaft.

Ducrot, Oswald et al. (ed.) 1980. *Les mots du discours.* Paris: Minuit.

Enkvist, Nils E. 1977. „Stylistics and Text Linguistics". In: Dressler (ed.) 1977, 174–190.

Enkvist, Nils E. 1978. „Coherence, Pseudo-Coherence, and Non-Coherence". In: Östman (ed.) 1978, 109–128.

Fayol, Michel. 1989. „Une approche psycholinguistique de la ponctuation: étude en production et en compréhension". *Langue française* 81: 21–39.

Figge, Udo L. 1994. „Kognitive Grundlagen textlicher Kohärenz". In: Canisius et al. (eds.) 1994, 1–28.

Fleischman, Suzanne. 1991. „Verb Tense and Point of View in Narrative". In: Fleischman & Waugh (eds.) 1991, 26–55.

Fleischman, Suzanne & Waugh, Linda R. (eds.) 1991. *Discourse Pragmatics and the Verb. The Evidence from Romance.* London/New York: Routledge.

Franck, Dorothea. 1973. „Zur Problematik der Präsuppositionsdiskussion". In: Franck & Petöfi (eds.) 1973, 11–42.

Franck, Dorothea. 1980. *Grammatik und Konversation.* (Monographien der Linguistik und Kommunikationswissenschaft, 46) Königstein: Scriptor.

Franck, Dorothea & Petöfi, János S. (eds.) 1973. *Präsuppositionen in Philosophie und Linguistik.* (Linguistische Forschungen, 7) Frankfurt a. M.: Athenäum.

Fritsche, Johannes (ed.) 1982. *Konnektivausdrücke, Konnektiveinheiten. Grundelemente der semantischen Struktur von Texten I.* (Papiere zur Textlinguistik, 30) Hamburg: Buske.

Fuchs, Cathérine. (ed.) 1985. *Aspects de l'ambiguïté et de la paraphrase dans les langues naturelles.* (Sciences pour la communication, 10). Bern u. a.: Lang.

Gernsbacher, Morton A. & Givón, Talmy (eds.) 1995. *Coherence in Spontaneous Text.* (Typological Studies in Language, 31) Amsterdam/Philadelphia: Benjamins.

Gibbon, Dafydd & Richter, Helmut (eds.) 1984. *Intonation, Accent and Rhythm. Studies in Discourse Phonology.* (Research in Text Theory, 8) Berlin/New York: De Gruyter.

Gibbon, Dafydd. 1988. „Intonation and Discourse". In: Petöfi (ed.) 1988, 3–25.

Gil, Alberto. 1995. *Textadverbiale in den romanischen Sprachen. Eine integrale Studie zu Konnektoren und Modalisatoren im Spanischen, Französischen und Italienischen.* (Bonner romanistische Arbeiten, 53) Frankfurt a. M. u. a.: Lang.

Giora, Rachel. 1983. „Functional Paragraph Perspective". In: Petöfi & Sözer (eds.) 1983, 153–182.

Givón, Talmy (ed.) 1979. *Discourse and Syntax.* (Syntax and Semantics, 12). New York: Academic Press.

Givón, Talmy 1983. „Topic Continuity in Discourse: An Introduction". In: Givón, Talmy (ed.). *Topic Continuity in Discourse: A Quantitative Cross Language Study.* Amsterdam/Philadelphia: Benjamins, 1–41.

Greimas, Algirdas J. 1966. *Sémantique structurale. Recherche de méthode.* Paris: Larousse.

Grice, Herbert P. 1975. „Logic and Conversation". In: Cole, Peter & Morgan, Jerry L. (eds.). *Speech Acts. Syntax and Semantics* 3. New York: Academic Press, 41–58.

Grimes, Joseph Evans 1975. *The Thread of Discourse.* (Janua linguarum, Series minor, 207) Den Haag/Paris: Mouton.

Gülich, Elisabeth. 1970. *Makrosyntax der Gliederungssignale im gesprochenen Französisch.* (Structura, 2) München: Fink.

Gülich, Elisabeth & Raible, Wolfgang 1977. *Linguistische Textmodelle. Grundlagen und Möglichkeiten.* (UTB, 130) München: Fink.

Gülich, Elisabeth & Kotschi, Thomas. 1996. „Textherstellungsverfahren in mündlicher Kommunikation. Ein Beitrag am Beispiel des Französischen". In: Motsch (ed.) 1996, 37–80.

Gumperz, John J. & Kaltman, Hannah & O'Connor, Mary Catherine. 1984. „Cohesion in Spoken and Written Discourse: Ethnic Style and the Transition to Literacy". In: Tannen (ed.) 1984, 3–20.

Gutwinski, Waldemar. 1976. *Cohesion in Literary Texts. A Study of Some Grammatical and Lexical*

Features of English Discourse. Den Haag/Paris: Mouton.

Hajicová, Eva & Sgall, Petr. 1988. „Topic and Focus of a Sentence and the Patterning of a Text". In: Petöfi (ed.) 1988, 70−96.

Halliday, M. A. K. 1964. „The Linguistic Study of Literary Texts". In: *Proceedings of the IXth International Congress of the Linguists:* 303−304.

Halliday, M. A. K. 1974. „The Place of 'Functional Sentence Perspective' in the System of Linguistic Description". In: Daneš (ed.) 1974, 43−53.

Halliday, M. A. K. & Hasan, Ruqaiya. 1976. *Cohesion in English.* (English Language Series, 9) London/New York: Longman.

Hartmann, Peter. 1971. „Texte als linguistisches Objekt". In: Stempel (ed.) 1971, 9−29.

Harweg, Roland. ²1979 [1968]. *Pronomina und Textkonstitution.* (Beihefte zu Poetica, 2) München: Fink.

Hasan, Ruquaiya. 1968. *Grammatical Cohesion in Spoken and Written English Part I.* (Programme in Linguistics and English Teaching, 7) London: Longmans, Green.

Hatakeyama, Katshuhiko & Petöfi, János S. & Sözer, Emel. 1985. „Text, Connexity, Cohesion, Coherence". In: Sözer (ed.) 1985, 36−105.

Heger, Klaus. ²1976. *Monem, Wort, Satz und Text.* (Konzepte der Sprach- und Literaturwissenschaft, 8) Tübingen: Niemeyer.

Heidolph, Klaus E. 1966. „Kontextbeziehungen zwischen Sätzen in einer generativen Grammatik". *Kybernetika* 2: 274−281.

Heim, Irene. 1988. *The Semantics of Definite and Indefinite Noun Phrases.* New York/London: Garland.

Heinemann, Wolfgang & Viehweger, Dieter. 1991. *Textlinguistik. Eine Einführung.* (Reihe Germanistische Linguistik, 115) Tübingen: Niemeyer.

Heydrich, Wolfgang & Neubauer Fritz & Petöfi, János S. & Sözer, Emel. (eds.) 1989. *Connexity and Coherence. Analysis of Text and Discourse.* (Research in Text Theory, 12) Berlin/New York: De Gruyter.

Hinds, John. (ed.) 1978. *Anaphora in Discourse.* (Current Inquiry into Language and Linguistics, 22). Edmonton, Champaign: Linguistic Research.

Hopper, Paul. 1979. „Aspect and Foregrounding in Discourse". In: Givón (ed.) 1979, 213−242.

Isenberg, Horst. 1971. „Überlegungen zur Texttheorie". In: Ihwe, Jens (ed.) *Literaturwissenschaft und Linguistik* I. Frankfurt a. M.: Athenäum, 155−172.

Isenberg, Horst. 1976. „Einige Grundbegriffe für eine linguistische Texttheorie". In: Daneš & Viehweger (eds.) 1976, 47−145.

Kallmeyer, Werner & Klein, Wolfgang & Meyer-Hermann, R. et al. 1974. *Lektürekolleg zur Textlinguistik.* 2 vols. (Athenäum Taschenbücher zur Sprachwissenschaft, 2050) Königstein u. a.: Athenäum.

Kamp, Hans & Rohrer, Christian. 1983. „Tense in Texts". In: Bäuerle, Rainer & Schwarze, Christoph & von Stechow, Arnim (eds.). *Meaning, Use, and Interpretation of Language.* Berlin/New York: De Gruyter, 250−269.

Kesik, Marek. 1989. *La cataphore.* Paris: Presses universitaires de France.

Kintsch, Walter & Van Dijk, Teun A. 1978. „Toward a Model of Text Comprehension and Production". *Psychological Review* 85−5, 363−394.

Kleiber, Georges. 1990. „Sur l'anaphore associative: article défini et adjectif démonstratif". *Rivista di linguistica* 2.1: 155−175.

Kleiber, Georges. 1994. *Anaphores et pronoms.* Louvain-la-Neuve: Duculot.

Klein, Wolfgang & Von Stutterheim, Christiane. 1992. „Textstruktur und referentielle Bewegung". *Zeitschrift für Literaturwissenschaft und Linguistik* 86: 67−82.

Koch, Walter A. 1972. *Strukturelle Textanalyse − Analyse du récit − Discourse Analysis.* (Studia semiotica, 1) Hildesheim/New York: Olms.

Krötsch, Monique & Sabban, Annette. 1990. „'Bleu, je veux' − Remarques sur la focalisation en français". *Zeitschrift für Romanische Philologie* 106: 80−98.

Kummer, Werner. 1975. *Grundlagen der Texttheorie. Zur handlungstheoretischen Begründung einer materialistischen Sprachwissenschaft.* (rororo studium, 51) Reinbek bei Hamburg: Rowohlt.

Kuno, Susumu. 1977. „Generative Discourse Analysis in America". In: Dressler (ed.) 1977, 275−294.

Lakoff, Robin. 1971. „If's, And's and But's about Conjunction". In: Fillmore, Charles J. & Langedoen, D. Terence (eds.) *Studies in Linguistic Semantics.* New York: Holt, Rinehart and Winston, 115−156.

Lang, Ewald. 1973. „Über einige Schwierigkeiten beim Postulieren einer Textgrammatik". In: Kiefer, Ferenc & Ruwet, Nicolas (eds.) *Generative Grammar in Europe.* (Foundations of Language, Supplement Series, 13) Dordrecht: Reidel, 284−314.

Lang, Ewald. 1977. *Semantik der koordinativen Verknüpfung.* (studia grammatica, 14) Berlin: Akademie-Verlag.

Langleben, Maria. 1981. „Latent Coherence, Contextual Meanings, and the Interpretation of Text". *Text* 1.3: 279−313.

Langleben, Maria. 1983. „On the Structure of Dialogue". In: Petöfi & Sözer (eds.) 1983, 220−286.

Langleben, Maria. 1985. „A Long Way to the Full Interpretation". In: Sözer (ed.) 1985, 106−137.

Lo Cascio, Vincenzo. 1982. „Temporal Deixis and Anaphora in Sentence and Text: Finding a Reference Time". *Journal of Italian Linguistics* 7.1: 31−70.

Lo Cascio, Vincenzo & Vet, Co (eds.) 1986. *Temporal Structures in Sentence and Discourse*. (Groningen-Amsterdam Studies in Semantics, 5) Dordrecht u. a.: Foris.

Lötscher, Andreas. 1987. *Text und Thema. Studien zur thematischen Konstituenz von Texten*. (Reihe Germanistische Linguistik, 81) Tübingen: Niemeyer.

Longacre, Robert E. 1970. „Sentence Structure as a Statement Calculus". *Language* 46.4: 783−815.

Longacre, Robert E. 1979. „The Paragraph as a Grammatical Unit". In: Givón (ed.) 1979, 115−134.

Lundquist, Lita. 1980. *La cohérence textuelle: syntaxe, sémantique, pragmatique*. Kopenhagen: Erhvervsøkonomisk Forlag S/I.

Lundquist, Lita. 1985. „Coherence: From Structure to Processes". In: Sözer (ed.) 1985, 151−175.

Lundquist, Lita. 1989. „Modality and Text Constitution". In: Conte et al. (eds.) 1989, 103−118.

Lundquist, Lita. 1990. „Un cas d'ambigüité référentielle. Aspects pragmatiques". In: Kleiber, Georges (ed.). *L'Anaphore et ses domaines*. Paris: Klincksieck, 229−249.

Lundquist, Lita. 1991. „La cohérence textuelle révisée. Une étude pragmatique". *Folia linguistica* 25.1/2: 91−110.

Maas, Utz & Wunderlich, Dieter. 1972. *Pragmatik und sprachliches Handeln. Mit einer Kritik am Funkkolleg „Sprache"*. (Athenaion-Skripten Linguistik, 2) Frankfurt a. M.: Athenaion.

Mandler, Jean M. & Johnson, Nancy S. 1977. „Remembrance of Things Parsed: Story Structure and Recall". *Cognitive Psychology* 9: 11−151.

Marello, Carla. 1979. „Text, Coherence and Lexicon". In: Petöfi (ed.) 1979, vol. 2, 618−633.

Marello, Carla. 1984. „Ellissi". In: Coverì, Lorenzo (ed.). *Linguistica testuale. Atti del XV Congresso Internazionale di studi. Genova*. Rom: Bulzoni, 255−270.

Marello, Carla. 1989. „Ellipsis between Connexity and Coherence." In: Conte et al. (eds.) 1989, 119−135.

Metzing, Dieter (ed.) 1979. *Frame Conceptions and Text Understanding*. (Research in Text Theory, 5) Berlin: De Gruyter.

Minsky, Marvin L. 1975. „A Framework for Representing Knowledge". In: Winston, Patrick Henry (ed.) *The Psychology of Computer Vision*. New York u. a.: McGraw-Hill, 211−277.

Moeschler, Jacques. 1989. *Modélisation du dialogue. Représentation de l'inférence argumentative*. Paris: Hermès.

Moeschler, Jacques. 1994. „Anaphore et déixis temporelles: sémantique et pragmatique de la référence temporelle". In: Moeschler, Jacques & Reboul, Anne & Luscher, Jean-Marc & Jayez, Jacques (eds.). *Langage et pertinence, Référence temporelle, anaphore, connecteurs et métaphore*. Nancy: Presses universitaires de Nancy, 339−354.

Motsch, Wolfgang. 1983. „Satz und Sprachhandlung als Grundbegriffe der Textanalyse". In: Daneš & Viehweger (eds.) 1983, 104−132.

Motsch, Wolfgang. 1996. „Zur Sequenzierung von Illokutionen". In: Motsch (ed.) 1996, 189−210.

Motsch, Wolfgang (ed.) 1996. *Ebenen der Textstruktur. Sprachliche und kommunikative Prinzipien*. (Reihe Germanistische Linguistik, 164) Tübingen: Niemeyer.

Motsch, Wolfgang & Viehweger, Dieter. 1981. „Sprachhandlung, Satz und Text". In: Rosengren (ed.) 1981, 125−153.

Neubauer, Fritz (ed.) 1983. *Coherence in Natural-Language Texts*. (Papiere zur Textlinguistik, 38) Hamburg: Buske.

Nye, Irene. 1977 [1912]. „Satzverbindung, besonders bei Livius". In: Dressler (ed.) 1977, 15−22.

Östman, Jan-Ola (ed.) 1978. *Cohesion and Semantics*. (Publications of the Research Institute of the Akademi Foundation, 41) Åbo.

Palek, Bohumil. 1968. *Cross-Reference. A Study from Hyper-Syntax*. (Acta Universitatis Carolinae. Philologica Monographia, 21) Prag: Univ. Karlova.

Parret, Herman. 1989. „Paraphrase as a Coherence Principle in Conversation". In: Conte et al. (eds.) 1989, 281−290.

Partee, Barbara H. 1973. „Some Structural Analogies between Tenses and Pronouns in English". *The Journal of Philosophy* 70: 601−609.

Petöfi, János S. 1971. *Transformationsgrammatiken und eine kotextuelle Texttheorie. Grundfragen und Konzeptionen*. (Linguistische Forschungen, 3) Frankfurt a. M.: Athenäum.

Petöfi, János S. 1973. „Towards an Empirically Motivated Grammatical Theory of Verbal Texts". In: Petöfi & Rieser (eds.) 1973, 205−275.

Petöfi, János S. ²1994. „Coherence". In: Sebeok, Thomas A. (ed.). *Encyclopedic Dictionary of Semiotics*. (Approaches to Semiotics, 73.1) Berlin/New York: Mouton de Gruyter, 1080−1087.

Petöfi, János S. & Rieser, Hannes (eds.) 1973. *Studies in Text Grammar*. (Foundations of Language, Supplement Series, 19) Dordrecht: Reidel.

Petöfi, János S. (ed.) 1979. *Text vs. Sentence. Basic Questions of Text Linguistics*. 2 vols. (Papiere zur Textlinguistik, 20) Hamburg: Buske.

Petöfi, János S. (ed.) 1981. *Text vs. Sentence Continued*. (Papiere zur Textlinguistik, 29) Hamburg: Buske.

Petöfi, János S. & Sözer, Emel (eds.) 1983. *Micro and Macro Connexity of Texts*. (Papiere zur Textlinguistik, 45) Hamburg: Buske.

Petöfi, János S. (ed.) 1988. *Text and Discourse Constitution. Empirical Aspects, Theoretical Approaches.* (Research in Text Theory, 4) Berlin/New York: De Gruyter.

Primus, Beatrice. 1993. „Word Order and Information Structure: A Performance-Based Account of Topic Positions and Focus Positions." In: Jacobs, Joachim & Von Stechow, Arnim & Sternefeld, Wolfgang & Vennemann, Theo (eds.). *Syntax: Ein internationales Handbuch zeitgenössischer Forschung.* 1. Halbband. Berlin/New York: De Gruyter, 880−896.

Propp, Vladimír. 1972 [1928]. *Morphologie des Märchens.* (Literatur als Kunst, 12) München: Hanser.

Raible, Wolfgang. 1972. *Satz und Text. Untersuchungen zu vier romanischen Sprachen.* (Beihefte zur Zeitschrift für romanische Philologie, 132) Tübingen: Niemeyer.

Raible, Wolfgang. 1989. „Phänomenologische Textwissenschaft. Zum Beitrag von K. Hatakeyama, J. S. Petöfi und E. Sözer (Text, Konnexität, Kohäsion, Kohärenz)". In: Conte (ed.) 1989, 101−110.

Raible, Wolfgang. 1992. *Junktion. Eine Dimension der Sprache und ihre Realisierungsformen zwischen Aggregation und Integration; vorgetragen am 4. Juli 1987.* (Sitzungsberichte der Heidelberger Akademie der Wissenschaften. Philosophisch-historische Klasse. Jahrgang 1992, Bericht 2) Heidelberg: Winter.

Randquist, Madeleine G. 1985. „The Barely Visible Glue. Some Aspects of Textual Connectedness". In: Sözer (ed.) 1985, 189−218.

Rastier, François. 1972. „Systématique des isotopies". In: Greimas, Algirdas J. (ed.). *Essais de sémiotique poétique.* Paris: Larousse, 80−106.

Rastier, François. 1986. „Microsémantique et textualité". In: Charolles et al. (eds.) 1986, 147−166.

Reichenbach, Hans. 1947. *Elements of Symbolic Logic.* New York: Macmillan.

Reinhart, Tanya. 1980. „Conditions for Text Coherence". *Poetics Today* 1.4: 161−180.

Rickheit, Gert (ed.) 1991. *Kohärenzprozesse. Modellierung von Sprachverarbeitung in Texten und Diskursen.* Opladen: Westdeutscher Verlag.

Rieger, Burghard B. 1989. „Relevance of Meaning, Semantic Disposition, and Text Coherence: Modelling Reader Expectations from Natural Language Discourse". In: Conte et al. (eds.) 1989, 153−174.

Rosengren, Inger (ed.) 1981. *Sprache und Pragmatik. Lunder Symposium 1980.* (Lunder germanistische Forschungen, 50) Lund: Gleerup.

Rosengren, Inger. 1983. „Die Realisierung der Illokutionsstruktur auf der Vertextungsebene". In: Daneš & Viehweger (eds.) 1983, 133−151.

Roulet, Eddy & Auchlin, Antoine & Moeschler, Jacques et al. ³1991. *L'articulation du discours en français contemporain.* (Sciences pour la communication, 11) Bern u. a.: Lang.

Rumelhart, David E. 1980. „On Evaluating Story Grammars". *Cognitive Science* 4: 313−316.

Sacks, Harvey & Schegloff, Emanual A. & Jefferson, Gail 1974. „A Simplest Systematics for the Organization of Turn-Taking for Conversation". *Language* 50: 696−735.

Samet, Jerry & Schank, Roger C. 1984. „Coherence and Connectivity". *Linguistics and Philosophy* 7.1: 57−82.

Schank, Roger C. & Abelson, Robert P. 1977. *Scripts, Plans, Goals and Understanding. An Inquiry into Human Knowledge Structures.* Hillsdale/New Jersey: Lawrence Erlbaum.

Schmidt, Siegfried J. 1973. *Texttheorie. Probleme eine Linguistik der sprachlichen Kommunikation.* (UTB, 202) München: Fink.

Schlegloff, Emanual A. & Sacks, Harvey 1973. „Opening up Closings". *Semiotica* 8−4: 289−327.

Sgall, Petr. 1974. „Zur Stellung der Thema-Rhema-Gliederung in der Sprachbeschreibung". In: Daneš (ed.) 1974, 54−74.

Siklaki, István. 1985. „Story Grammars as Models for Text Processing". In: Sözer (ed.) 1985, 219−260.

Siklaki, István. 1989. „Macro-Structure, Knowledge Base, and Coherence". In: Conte et al. (eds.) 1989, 309−324.

Sözer, Emel (ed.) 1985. *Text Connexity, Text Coherence. Aspects, Methods, Results.* (Papiere zur Textlinguistik, 49) Hamburg: Buske.

Sowinski, Bernhard. 1983. *Textlinguistik. Eine Einführung.* (Urban-Taschenbücher, 325). Stuttgart u. a.: Kohlhammer.

Sperber, Dan & Wilson, Deirdre. 1986. *Relevance. Communication and Cognition.* Cambridge/Mass.: Harvard University Press.

Stark, Elisabeth. 1997. *Voranstellungsstrukturen und topic-Markierung im Französischen. Mit einem Ausblick auf das Italienische.* (Romanica Monacensia, 51) Tübingen: Narr.

Stati, Sorin. 1979. „Connessioni lessicali". *Studi italiani di linguistica teorica ed applicata* 8: 103−120.

Steinitz, Renate. 1968. *Nominale Pro-Formen.* (Arbeitsstelle Strukturelle Grammatik, Bericht 2) Berlin: Akademie der Wissenschaften.

Stempel, Wolf-Dieter (ed.) 1971. *Beiträge zur Textlinguistik.* (Internationale Bibliothek für allgemeine Linguistik, 1) München: Fink.

Szabó, Zoltán. 1985. „The Importance of Text Coherence for the Global Stylistic Analysis". In: Sözer (ed.) 1985, 526−545.

Tannen, Deborah (ed.) 1984. *Coherence in Spoken and Written Discourse.* (Advances in Discourse Processes, 12) Norwood/New Jersey: Ablex.

Thorndyke, Perry W. 1977. „Cognitive Structures in Comprehension and Memory of Narrative Discourse". *Cognitive Psychology* 9: 77–110.

Todorov, Tzvetan. 1969. *Grammaire du Décaméron.* (Approaches to Semiotics, 3) Den Haag/Paris: Mouton.

Tomlin, Russel S. (ed.) 1987. *Coherence and Grounding in Discourse. Outcome of a Symposium, Eugene, Oregon, June 1984.* (Typological Studies in Language, 11) Amsterdam/Philadelphia: Benjamins.

Trier, Jost. 1931. *Der deutsche Wortschatz im Sinnbezirk des Verstandes. Die Geschichte eines sprachlichen Feldes.* (Germanische Bibliothek, II. Abteilung, 31) Heidelberg: Winter.

Tschida, Alexander. 1995. *Kontinuität und Progression. Entwurf einer Typologie sprachlicher Information am Beispiel des Französischen.* (pro lingua, 25) Wilhelmsfeld: Eggert.

Van de Velde, Roger G. 1981. *Interpretation, Kohärenz und Inferenz.* (Papiere zur Textlinguistik, 33) Hamburg: Buske.

Van de Velde, Roger G. 1985. „Inferences and Coherence in Text Interpretation." In: Sözer (ed.) 1985, 261–298.

Van de Velde, Roger G. 1989a. „The Role of Inferences in Text Organisation". In: Conte et al. (eds.) 1989, 543–562.

Van de Velde, Roger, G. 1989b. „Man, Verbal Text, Inferencing, and Coherence". In: Heydrich et al. (eds.) 1989, 174–217.

Van Dijk, Teun A. 1972. *Some Aspects of Text Grammars. A Study in Theoretical Linguistics and Poetics.* Den Haag/Paris: Mouton.

Van Dijk, Teun A. 1973. „Text Grammar and Text Logic". In: Petöfi & Rieser (eds.) 1973, 17–78.

Van Dijk, Teun A. 1977. *Text and Context. Explorations in the Semantics and Pragmatics of Discourse.* (Longman Linguistic Library, 21) London/New York: Longman.

Van Dijk, Teun A. 1979. „Pragmatic Connectives". *Journal of Pragmatics* 3: 447–456.

Van Dijk, Teun A. 1980. *Textwissenschaft. Eine interdisziplinäre Einführung.* München: Deutscher Taschenbuch Verlag.

Vater, Heinz. 1992. *Einführung in die Textlinguistik. Struktur, Thema und Referenz in Texten.* (UTB, 1660) München: Fink.

Vet, Co. 1991. „The Temporal Structure of Discourse: Setting, Change, and Perspective". In: Fleischman & Waugh (eds.) 1991, 7–25.

Viehweger, Dieter. 1976. „Semantische Merkmale und Textstruktur". In: Daneš & Viehweger (eds.) 1976, 195–206.

Viehweger, Dieter. 1983. „Sprachhandlungsziele in Aufforderungstexten". In: Daneš & Viehweger (eds.) 1983, 152–192.

Viehweger, Dieter. 1989. „Coherence – Interaction of Moduls". In: Heydrich et al. (eds.) 1989, 256–274.

Weingartner, Paul. 1989. „Connectedness of Texts and Relevant Consequences". In: Conte et al. (eds.) 1989, 563–576.

Weinrich, Harald. ^{2}1971 [1964]. *Tempus. Besprochene und erzählte Welt.* Stuttgart u. a.: Kohlhammer.

Weinrich, Harald. 1969. „Textlinguistik: Zur Syntax des Artikels in der deutschen Sprache". *Jahrbuch für internationale Germanistik* 1: 61–74.

Werlich, Egon. 1975. *Typologie der Texte. Entwurf eines textlinguistischen Modells zur Grundlegung einer Textgrammatik.* (UTB, 450) Heidelberg.

Werth, Paul. 1984. *Focus, Coherence and Emphasis.* London. u. a.: Croom Helm.

Wunderli, Peter. 1979. „Satz, Paragraph, Text – und die Intonation". In: Petöfi (ed.) 1979, vol. 2, 319–341.

Wunderlich, Dieter. (ed.) 1972. *Linguistische Pragmatik.* (Schwerpunkte Linguistik und Kommunikationswissenschaft, 12) Frankfurt a. M.: Athenäum.

Zhou, Hengxiang. 1994. „Koreferenzbeziehung und Textprogression". In: Canisius et al. (eds.) 1994, 29–50.

*Elisabeth Stark,
Ludwig-Maximilians-Universität München
(Deutschland)*

VIII. Morphological techniques
Morphologische Techniken
Les techniques morphologiques

48. Ausdrucksmöglichkeiten für grammatische Relationen

1. Vorbemerkung
2. Die grammatischen Relationen
3. Der Ausdruck der grammatischen Relationen
4. Schlußbemerkung
5. Spezielle Abkürzungen
6. Zitierte Literatur

1. Vorbemerkung

In diesem Beitrag soll eine Axiomatik der Ausdrucksmöglichkeiten für grammatische Relationen versucht werden. Die hier vorgestellten Überlegungen basieren auf einer Reihe von früheren Arbeiten des Autors, auf die in der Bibliographie am Ende des Beitrags verwiesen wird; wegen dieses Bezugs sind die folgenden Ausführungen als die Kurzdarstellung einer Doktrin zu sehen, wo ein Gedankengefüge knapp zusammengefaßt wird, nicht jedoch als eine breit entwickelte Detailexposition. Aus demselben Grund sind auch die bibliographischen Hinweise auf ein Minimum reduziert.

Dieses typologische Modell versteht sich als grundlegend; es ist unmittelbar aus bestimmten universalen, das heißt jeder Einzelsprache vorausliegenden, Gegebenheiten des menschlichen Sprachbaus abgeleitet. Typologische Variationsbreite kann nur vor dem Hintergrund solcher Universalien adäquat erfaßt werden; die Universalien geben die Möglichkeiten vor und grenzen sie ein. Typologie und Universalienforschung sind notwendig aufeinander bezogen.

Die Prämissen, von denen die folgenden Überlegungen zu den Ausdrucksmöglichkeiten für grammatische Relationen ausgehen, beziehen sich auf drei Bereiche: die anthropologisch-kognitiven Grundlagen der menschlichen Sprachfähigkeit; die hierarchische Struktur von Sprache; und die Linearität von Sprache in ihrer materialisierten Form. Der erste Bereich ist maßgebend für die Ausgangsfrage: welche grammatischen Relationen sind überhaupt zu unterscheiden? Die beiden anderen Bereiche determinieren die Antwort auf die sodann zu entwickelnde zentrale Frage dieses Beitrags: wie werden die so festgestellten Relationen sprachlich ausgedrückt?

2. Die grammatischen Relationen

Im ersten genannten Bereich ist für die hier betrachteten Zusammenhänge vor allem ein Faktor wichtig: das Basisprinzip des Satzes, nämlich die Assertivität. Von Aristoteles stammt die Unterscheidung von *lógos sēmantikós* und *lógos apophantikós* (PHerm. 4, 17 a, 1); nur in letzterem gibt es in Wahrheit und Lüge. Erst durch die Assertion wird der Satz zum Satz. Sie ist die Basisoperation der menschlichen Sprache. Linguistisch äußert sich dies in grundlegenden Eigenschaften: die Aufgliederung der Welt in überschaubare Einheiten, in denen eine begrenzte Anzahl von Elementen miteinander in Beziehung gesetzt werden; das heißt, einen Schritt näher an den Sprachstrukturen, die Herausbildung jener Grundstruktur, bei der ein oder mehrere Terme einem zentralen Element zugeordnet wird/werden, welches die assertive Funktion trägt; und daraus abgeleitet die Differenzierung von verbalen und nominalen Elementen, die wohl doch universal ist, wie auch immer sie sich im einzelnen ausprägt. Mit Wittgenstein ist die Welt alles, was der Fall ist; der Satz stellt einen Sachverhalt dar, und er sagt ihn darüber hinaus aus. Eine der grundlegenden Begrenzungen der menschlichen Kognition besteht darin, daß wir nur satzförmige Sachverhalte assertieren können, also Sachverhalte als Verbindungen zwischen einigen wenigen Termen und einem zentralen Assertionsträger. Ob wir damit der wahren

(I) Grammatische Grundrelationen

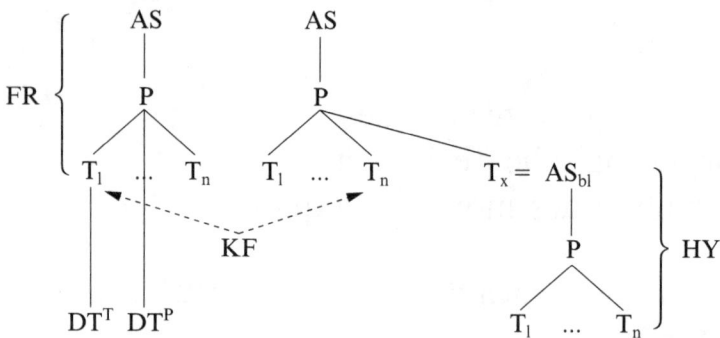

Komplexität der Welt gerecht zu werden vermögen, ist eine Frage, die nur außerhalb der Linguistik gestellt (und ohnehin nicht beantwortet) werden kann.

Der Assertionsträger bindet Terme, setzt sie zueinander und zu sich selbst in Beziehung. Im assertiven Akt wird diese Bindung, diese Beziehung (der reine Sachverhaltsausdruck) in die Dimension der Zeit eingebracht; durch die Einbettung in die Zeitlichkeit wird der Sachverhaltsausdruck zum Satz. Assertion, Term(e) und Prädikat: das ist das Muster, mit dem wir die Welt erfassen und dem wir ebenso unausweichlich verhaftet sind wie der Struktur von Retina und Sehnerv. Jede natürliche menschliche Sprache folgt diesem Muster. Grammatische Relationen bilden so zunächst einmal und auf einer ganz elementaren Ebene dieses grundlegende Muster, diese fundamentale Begrenzung unseres kognitiven Apparats ab. Sie enthalten als Basiskategorien termfähige Ausdrücke einerseits, prädikationsfähige, und das heißt assertierbare, in die Zeitdimension einbindbare, Ausdrücke andererseits.

Der nächste Schritt ist das, was oben als zweiter Bereich genannt wurde: die Hierarchie der Relationen. Grundlegend ist die Beziehung zwischen Term(en) ($T_1 \ldots T_n$) und Prädikat (P) sowie die an dieser Beziehung festgemachte Assertion; hierdurch entsteht der „Satz", das „Urteil": die Behauptung eines Sachverhalts als autonome Äußerung. Ich habe diese Beziehung stets als Fundamentalrelation bezeichnet (FR). Hierarchisch nachgeordnet sind die anderen Grundrelationen, die es in der Sprache gibt: die Satzverknüpfungsrelation, die im wesentlichen auf Termkonstanz, also auf Koreferenz (KF) beruht; die hypotaktische Relation (HY), durch die ein assertierfähiger Komplex in seiner Assertivität blockiert und dadurch einem höheren Assertionsträger untergeordnet wird; die Determinativrelationen (DT), durch welche einem primären Satzelement, sei es Term, sei es Prädikat, eine nähere Bestimmung zugeordnet wird. Diese Relationen können auch kombiniert erscheinen, so etwa wenn die Determination eines Terms aus einem assertionsblockierten Satz besteht, was etwa beim Relativsatz der Fall ist; hierbei werden Koreferenz und Hypotaxe in den Dienst der Determination gestellt. Zusammengefaßt kann man die grundlegenden Hierarchiebeziehungen in der Sprache, welche die grammatischen Relationen bestimmen, darstellen wie in (I).

Die Grundrelationen sind also: die **Fundamentalrelation** als assertierte Relation zwischen Term(en) und Prädikat; die **Hypotaxe** als assertionsblockierte Fundamentalrelation und Einbettung derselben in eine höhere Fundamentalrelation; die **Determination** von Elementen, wobei zwischen Termdetermination und Prädikatdetermination unterschieden werden muß; und die **Koreferenz** als eine die Textkohärenz stiftende semantische Relation zwischen Termen. Diese Relationen liegen der hierarchisch geordneten, und eben dadurch nicht-linearen, Struktur der menschlichen Sprache zugrunde.

3. Der Ausdruck der grammatischen Relationen

3.1. Hierarchie und Linearität

Sprache ist linear; Linearität gehört zu ihren essentiellen Universalien, nicht-linear kann natürliche Sprache nicht gedacht werden, gleich ob sie in ihrer primären Erscheinungsform als Lautsprache oder in einer sekundären Erscheinungsform wie der Schrift erscheint. Ein Zentralproblem menschlicher Sprache besteht genau darin, daß nicht-lineare, hierarchische Strukturen in lineare Ketten überführt werden müssen. Lineare Ketten mit ihrem zeitlichen (oder auch räumlichen) Nacheinander müssen Hierarchiebeziehungen abbilden. Jede Überlegung zu den Ausdrucksmöglichkeiten grammatischer Relationen muß von diesem grundlegenden Paradoxon ihren Ausgang nehmen.

Damit sind wir bei dem dritten der oben genannten Bereiche. Wie gelingt es, Hierarchien linear abzubilden? Diese Frage ist der Angelpunkt einer Axiomatik der morphosyntaktischen Sprachtypologie; aus ihr lassen sich die Basismöglichkeiten zum Ausdruck grammatischer Relationen unmittelbar ableiten. Es sind genau drei solche Möglichkeiten denkbar, die sich durch zwei hierarchisch geordnete binäre Verzweigungen darstellen lassen: der Ausdruck der Relation kann unterbleiben oder erfolgen; und wenn er erfolgt, dann kann entweder die Linearität als solche benutzt werden, oder ein besonderes lineares Element, das auf den Ausdruck der Relation spezialisiert ist.

3.2. Die Ausdrucksmöglichkeiten

3.2.1. Implikation

Zunächst einmal kann der Ausdruck der Relation implizit bleiben; da die Elemente der Lautkette an und für sich bereits bedeutungstragend sind, kann eine Relation unter bestimmten Umständen ohne Schaden unausgedrückt bleiben, nämlich immer dann, wenn sie aus der Bedeutung der Einzelelemente erschlossen werden kann. Ich bezeichne diesen Fall als **Implikation**. Implikation bedeutet einfach den Nicht-Ausdruck einer Relation. Sie kommt vor allem dort systematisch vor, wo die implizite Semantik der beteiligten Elemente so spezifisch ist, daß auf den expliziten Ausdruck der Relation verzichtet werden kann. Im Deutschen etwa sind bestimmte Zeit- und Ortsangaben so eindeutig, daß sie ohne einen Hinweis auf ihre prototypische Funktion (nämlich DT^P) auskommen. In einer Beispielreihe wie

(1) (a) *Oktober ist ungemütlich*
    (b) *Oktober mag ich nicht*
    (c) *Oktober fahre ich weg*

bleiben die Relationen implizit. Natürlich kann mithilfe von *der/ den/ im* die jeweilige Relation expliziert werden. Man kann auch argumentieren, daß die Implikation in (a) und (b) syntaktischer, nicht semantischer Natur ist: da in (a) die Subjektstelle unbesetzt ist, muß *Oktober* Subjekt sein; da sie in (b) besetzt ist, muß *Oktober* Objekt sein; implizit, also indirekt zu erschließen, bleibt die Relation allemal, durch die Stellung der Elemente kommt sie nicht zum Ausdruck. In (c) ist die Relation tatsächlich nur auf Grund der spezifischen Semantik von *Oktober* zu erschließen.

Elemente wie *Oktober* tragen eine spezifische Relation (nämlich DT^P) gleichsam schon in sich, so daß die Implikation hier systematisch und häufig ist. Mir ist indessen kein Fall einer Sprache bekannt, in welcher der Ausdruck der Fundamentalrelation regelmäßig implizit bliebe; hier ist die Notwendigkeit einer klaren Differenzierung der Rollen von $T_1 \ldots T_n$ (Kasusrollen) so evident, daß auf expliziten Ausdruck nicht grundsätzlich verzichtet werden kann. Freilich sind die Fälle wohlbekannt, wo in einem Teil des Paradigmas eine solche Differenzierung unterbleibt, sei es semantisch motiviert (NOM = ACC bei den Neutra in allen indogermanischen Sprachen mit Genus, wegen der semantischen Affinität des Neutrums mit der Objektrolle), sei es auf Grund historisch zufälliger Lautentwicklung (NOM = ACC im deutschen oder altfranzösischen Femininum). Es dürfte jedoch keine Sprache geben, in der zwischen den zentralen Kasusrollen über das ganze Sprachsystem hinweg grundsätzlich nicht explizit differenziert werden kann.

3.2.2. Explikation: Taxemik

Der Implikation tritt die **Explikation** gegenüber: die Relation muß nicht indirekt erschlossen werden, sondern wird explizit zum Ausdruck gebracht. Wegen der Linearität von Sprache kann dies auf zweierlei Weise erfolgen: durch die relative Stellung der in Beziehung tretenden Elemente selbst; oder durch hinzutretende lineare Elemente. Elemente, deren Aufgabe darin besteht, grammatische Relationen zum Ausdruck zu bringen, werden im folgenden „Grammeme" genannt; von den in Bezug tretenden Elementen selbst spreche ich im folgenden zeitweise vereinfachend als von „Lexemen", wobei dies als *pars pro toto* genommen werden soll (es geht im Prinzip nicht um einzelne Lexeme, sondern um syntaktische Konstituenten).

Im erstgenannten Fall wird die relative Position der Lexeme mit Bedeutung aufgeladen, die Linearität wird unmittelbar in den Dienst des Ausdrucks einer hierarchischen Beziehung gestellt. Ich möchte dies hier mit dem Terminus **Taxemik** bezeichnen und definiere: taxemisch ist der Ausdruck einer Relation immer dann, wenn die grammatische Relation zwischen zwei oder mehr Lexemen (Konstituenten) durch deren relative Position zueinander ausgedrückt wird. (Der Begriff „Taxemik" ist analog zu Begriffen wie *Phonemik/Morphemik/Graphemik* zu verstehen: die „Taxis" (*ordo* im Griechischen) wird bedeutungsdifferenzierend verwendet; insofern ist der Terminus genauer als der früher von mir verwendete Begriff der „Position", den ich jetzt an anderer Stelle einsetze (vgl. § 3.2.6).) Implikation und Taxemik unterscheiden sich also dadurch voneinander, daß nur im letzteren Fall die Position bedeutungsdifferenzierend ist; wenn wir eine beliebige hierarchische Relation mit /Ξ/, die lineare Verkettung hingegen mit /∩/ symbolisieren, können wir dies so schreiben:

(II)   Implikation:
       A Ξ B → A ∩ B = B ∩ A
       Explikation/Taxemik:
       A Ξ B → A ∩ B ≠ B ∩ A

An dieser Stelle kann eine Beziehung zu den traditionellen Begriffen der morphologischen Typologie hergestellt werden. Auf einer Idee der Gebrüder Schlegel aufbauend entwickelte Wilhelm von Humboldt (1835 [1963]: 488 ff.) den Begriff des „isolierenden" Sprachtyps, der dann von vor allem im Hinblick auf den Bau des Chinesischen näher ausgeführt worden ist. Im gesamten Verlauf der Entwicklung der Typologie im 19. Jahrhundert ist dann dieser Begriff immer wieder als einer der Eckpunkte einer Skala verwendet worden, die über Agglutination bis hin zur Flexion reicht (Art. 49). Eine vielfach verfeinerte Spätform dieses Grundgedankens finden wir noch bei Nikolaus Finck (1909 [1965]: 12 ff.). Näher an unserer Zeit hat besonders Skalička diesen alten Begriff wieder aufgenommen und originell weiterentwickelt (1979: 339 f.). Das hier vorgeschlagene Modell nimmt die Substanz dieser Diskussion auf, präzisiert sie aber insoweit, als zwischen Implikation und Taxemik differenziert wird; im herkömmlichen Begriff der „Isolation" wird beides miteinander vermengt. Das Chinesische markiert grammatische Relationen nicht implikativ, sondern (vorwiegend) taxemisch. Ob man geneigt ist, eine solche Technik als „isolierend" zu bezeichnen, sei dahingestellt; Elemente, deren Position zueinander bedeutungsdifferenzierend ist, wird man kaum als „isoliert" voneinander bezeichnen wollen. Wie dem auch sei, einfache Beispiele aus wenigen Sprachen sind hinreichend, um an dieser Stelle die taxemische Technik zum Ausdruck der FR zu illustrieren:

(2) (a) *dog bites man* vs. *man bites dog*
    (b) Koyra Chiini (Heath 1999: 11)
        har di o guna woy di
        man DEF IMPF see woman DEF
        vs. *woy di o guna har di*
        „the man sees the woman" vs.
        „the woman sees the man"
    (c) Mandarin
        wŏ rènshi nĭ vs. *nĭ rènshi wŏ*
        ich kennen du
        „ich kenne dich" vs. „du kennst mich"

Taxemik kann sich auch subtiler manifestieren als in der simplen Differenzierung von Subjekt und Objekt. Hierfür zwei Beispiele.

Man kann die Satzgliedstellung des Deutschen so interpretieren, daß die Endstellung des finiten Verb(teil)s als Basisstellung gilt; dementsprechend wäre die Zweitstellung als Ergebnis einer Bewegungstransformation zu interpretieren, die zum Ausdruck der Assertion instrumentalisiert wird

(3) (a) *daß er in kurzer Zeit sein Geld ausgibt/ausgegeben hat*
    (b) *er gibt in kurzer Zeit sein Geld aus*
    (c) *er hat in kurzer Zeit sein Geld ausgegeben*

Während üblicherweise der Ausdruck der Assertion implizit bleibt und von der Finitheit des zentralen Prädikats gleichsam mit übernommen wird, werden im Deutschen taxemische Mittel zum expliziten Ausdruck der Assertion verwendet. Selbst wenn man der These nicht zustimmen mag, daß im Deutschen die Verbendstellung die Basisstellung sei, von der sich die Verbzweitstellung durch Bewegungstransformation ableitet, ist doch die Tatsache unstreitig, daß die Grundrelationen Assertion und Hypotaxe im Deutschen durch eine taxemische Opposition ausgedrückt werden.

Auch im Japanischen wird die Taxemik in den Dienst einer Unterscheidung von Assertion und Hypotaxe gestellt. Relativsätze unterscheiden sich von normalen assertierten Sätzen dadurch, daß sie dem Bezugswort vorausgehen, wodurch das finite Verb, das normalerweise am Satzende steht, unmittelbar vor das entsprechende Nomen zu stehen kommt. Man vergleiche:

(4) (a) *chichi-ga kinō hon-o yonda*
    Vater-NOM gestern Buch-ACC las
    „Vater las gestern ein Buch"
   (b) *chichi-ga kinō yonda*
    hon-*wa ii desu*
    THM   gut ist
    „das Buch, das Vater gestern gelesen hat, ist gut"

Von den drei Relationen, die für die Relativsatzbildung konstitutiv sind, erfolgt die Hypotaxe im Verein mit der Determination durch taxemische Mittel; die Koreferenz bleibt implizit, sie muß — im Unterschied zur indogermanischen Relativsatzbildung mittels von Relativpronomina — aus dem Kontext erschlossen werden: da die durch *yonda* eröffnete Objektstelle frei ist, ist klar, daß das koreferentiell getilgte *hon* hier als *hon-o* zu denken ist. Das Beispiel macht deutlich, daß beim Ausdruck einer mehrfach zusammengesetzten Relation verschiedene Techniken in Kombination eingesetzt können; während im Indogermanischen für die Relativsatzbildung komplexe Grammeme eingesetzt werden, erscheinen im Japanischen die Operationen HY + DT einerseits, KF andererseits durch die Verwendung von Taxemik bzw. Implikation voneinander getrennt.

3.2.3. Explikation: Grammemik

Alles Übrige gehört in den Bereich der **Grammemik**, bei der die grammatischen Relationen durch eigene lineare Elemente ausgedrückt werden. Die Möglichkeiten sind naturgemäß weitaus vielgestaltiger als im Falle der Implikation und der Taxemik; demgemäß ist eine Typologisierung dieses Bereiches nicht von vornherein vorgegeben, vielmehr gibt es eine Reihe von Kriterien, die unabhängig eingesetzt werden können und zu verschiedenen Klassifikationen führen. Es empfiehlt sich daher, das bisher Ausgeführte in (III) kurz zusammenzufassen, ehe auf die verschiedenen Typologien der Grammemik eingegangen wird.

Bei der Subklassifikation der Grammemik sehe ich drei Hauptkriterien, die untereinander kombiniert werden können und müssen (weitere Kriterien sind denkbar). Das einheitliche Haupt-Schema (III) teilt sich also unter dem Punkt *Grammemik* auf in drei Sub-Schemata, die im folgenden getrennt voneinander behandelt werden. Die drei Hauptkriterien lassen sich unter den Stichwörtern Konfiguration, Flexionsgrad und Position darstellen.

3.2.4. Grammemik: Konfiguration

Die **Konfiguration** ist das erste und fundamentalste der drei Kriterien. Hierunter verstehe ich die Verteilung der Grammeme auf die Elemente, deren Relation ausgedrückt werden soll. Eine hierarchisch definierte Relation setzt (mindestens) zwei Konstituenten miteinander in Beziehung. Logischerweise kann ein Grammem im oben definierten Sinn, das heißt ein zusätzliches, für den Ausdruck der Relation spezialisiertes Element, an eine der beiden Konstituenten allein (unilaterale Markierung) oder aber an beide (bilaterale Markierung) angefügt werden; diese Unterscheidung läßt sich zunächst einmal ohne

(III) Die Ausdrucksmöglichkeiten für grammatische Relationen

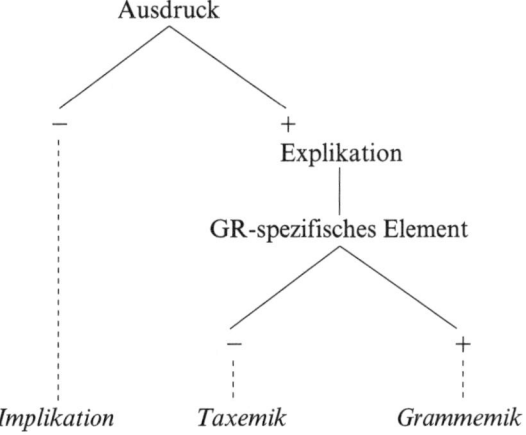

jede Berücksichtigung inhaltlicher Beziehungen, auf einer rein formalen Ebene treffen. Mit Einbeziehung einer inhaltlichen Komponente kann man im Bereich der unilateralen Markierung weiter ausdifferenzieren. In einer hierarchisch definierten Relation gibt es ein dominantes und ein dominiertes Glied; in der angelsächsischen Literatur wird dies als „head" und „dependent" unterschieden (markant etwa bei Nichols 1992: 46 ff.), was man im Deutschen als „Kopf" und „Dependens" wiedergeben kann. Dementsprechend ist es sinnvoll, bei der unilateralen Markierung zwischen **Kopfmarkierung** und **Dependensmarkierung** zu unterscheiden; logischerweise macht eine solche Differenzierung bei der bilateralen Markierung keinen Sinn, da hier sowohl Kopf als auch Dependens Markierungsträger sind. In Analogie und in Fortsetzung zu Schema (III) lassen sich diese Zusammenhänge als binäres Entscheidungsdiagramm darstellen wie in (IV).

Im folgenden gebe ich einige illustrative Belege. Für jeden der drei Markierungstypen werden Beispiele aus dem Bereich der Fundamentalrelation und der adnominalen Determinativrelation gebracht; die formale Parallelität zwischen diesen beiden Relationstypen wird dabei ebenso deutlich wie ihre inhaltliche Unterschiedlichkeit. Man beachte, daß in diesen Beispielen nicht nach den Kriterien Fusionsgrad und Position differenziert wird; diese Kriterien werden in den danach folgenden Abschnitten behandelt. Um Übersichtlichkeit und Vergleichbarkeit zu gewährleisten, wird eine Formel angewandt, die auf Schema (II) aufbaut und die Chiffren /x/ und /y/ für kopf- und dependensmarkierende Grammeme verwendet; /Kx/ bedeutet also „grammemmarkierter Kopf", wobei über den Fusionsgrad von Lexem und Grammem ebensowenig etwas ausgesagt ist wie über die Stellung der Elemente zueinander; /Kx/ kann also sowohl für die konkrete Position /K ∩ x/ (Suffix, Postposition, Endung ...) als auch für die konkrete Position /x ∩ K/ (Präposition, Präfix ...) stehen. Die bilaterale Konfiguration kann sowohl in akkusativischen als auch in ergativischen oder anderen (dualen, aktivischen etc.) Systemen auftreten (vgl. (5c), (7c)). Im Rahmen eines Kasus- oder Konjugationssystems kann eine bestimmte Stelle (z. B. NOM oder 3SG) selbstverständlich nullmarkiert sein; auch Nullmarkierung ist Markierung, wenn sie paradigmatisch entsprechend verankert ist (vgl. (5d)).

Bilaterale Markierung der Fundamentalrelation ist aus indogermanischen Sprachen des älteren Typus, aber auch aus zahllosen anderen Sprachen rund um den Globus wohlvertraut; sie liegt immer dann vor, wenn, traditionell gesprochen, verbale Konjugationsmorpheme mit nominalen Kasusmorphemen „kongruieren":

(5) FR → Kx + Dy
 (a) Deutsch/Lateinisch
  de-r Wind weh-t /
   NOM   3SG /
  Socrate-s curr-it
   NOM   3SG

(IV) Grammemik I: Konfiguration

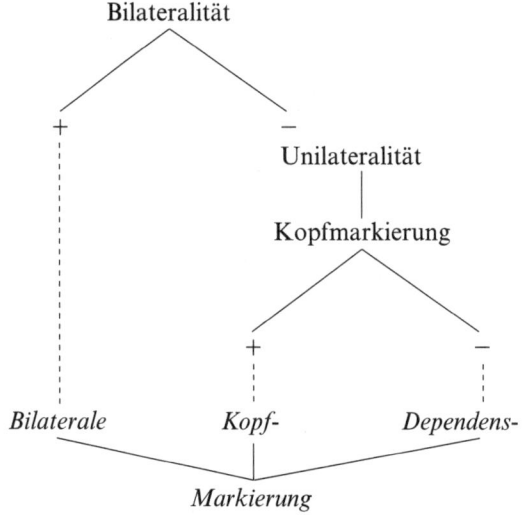

(b) Klassisch-Arabisch
ya-ktub + u ṭ-ṭālib-u
3m-schreib ART-Student-NOM
/katab-a ṭ-ṭālib-u
/schrieb-3m ART-Student-NOM
„der Student schreibt/schrieb"
(c) Georgisch
st'udent'-i c'er-s /
Student-NOM schreib-3SG /
st'udent'-ma da+c'er-a
Student-ERG schrieb-3SG
„der Student schreibt/schrieb"
(d) Quechua
tayta-Ø iskribi-n
Vater-NOM schreib-3SG
„Vater schreibt"

Bilaterale Markierung der adnominalen Determinativrelation ist bei weitem nicht so häufig; klassische sind die Fälle von „pronominaler" Aufnahme des Genitivs beim Possessum:

(6) DT^T → Kx + Dy
(a) Deutsch (Substandard)
de-m Vater sein-Haus
DAT=POSSr POSSm
(b) Türkisch/Quechua
baba-nın ev-i /
Vater-GEN Haus-POSSm /
tayta-pi wasi-n
Vater-GEN Haus-POSSm
„das Haus des Vaters"

Unilaterale Kopfmarkierung der Fundamentalrelation ist in den Sprachen der Welt überaus häufig. Sie liegt immer dann vor, wenn, traditionell gesprochen, zwar ein verbales Konjugationssystem, aber keine nominale Kasusflexion vorliegt. Sehr oft zieht das verbale Prädikat den alleinigen Ausdruck der Fundamentalrelation an sich; wie das Beispiel etwa der romanischen oder semitischen Sprachen zeigt, geht eine typische diachronische Bewegung weg von der bilateralen hin zur unilateralen Kopfmarkierung der FR: die nominale Markierung verschwindet, die verbale bleibt erhalten.

(7) FR → Kx + D
(a) Italienisch/Spanisch
Socrate corr-e / Sócrates corr-e
— 3SG / — 3SG
(b) Hebräisch/Ägyptisch-Arabisch
ha-sṭudenṭ yi-xtov /
ART-Student 3m-schreib /
aṭ-ṭālib b-yi-ktib
ART-Student PRS-3m-schreib
„der Student schreibt"

(c) Guaraní
ha'e o-ñani, o-puka /
er 3ACT-lauf 3ACT-lach /
ha'e i-ro'y, i-rase
er 3INACT-frier 3INACT-wein
„er lief, lachte/er fror, weinte"

Im Unterschied zur Fundamentalrelation ist die Kopfmarkierung in der adnominalen Determinativrelation ausgesprochen selten. Üblicherweise gibt es einen Genitiv (Dependensmarkierung), aber keine spezifische Markierung des Possessums unter Ausschluß des Possessors. Klassische Fälle von Kopfmarkierung bieten das Persische mit seiner Ezâfet-Konstruktion, einige semitische Sprachen mit ihrem sogenannten *status constructus* und auch das Guaraní, wo eine große Anzahl von Nomina in Possessum-Funktion ihre Form von *t-* zu *r-* verändern:

(8) DT^T → Kx + D
(a) Persisch
xâne-ye pedar-e man
Haus-EZF Vater-EZF ich
„das Haus meines Vaters"
(b) Hebräisch
bayit vs.
Haus (status absolutus)
beyt ha-melex
Haus (status constructus) ART-König
„Haus/das Haus des Königs"
(c) Guaraní
ko t-ape vs.
dies Weg (absolut)
yvága r-ape
Himmel Weg (verbunden)
„dieser Weg/der Weg des Himmels"

Die Häufigkeiten sind bei der Dependensmarkierung umgekehrt verteilt: bei der Fundamentalrelation ist sie ausgesprochen selten, während sie bei der adnominalen Determinativrelation eher die Regel als die Ausnahme darstellt. Beispiele für eine ausschließlich nominale Markierung der Fundamentalrelation sind nicht leicht zu finden. Ich gebe ein Beispiel aus dem Japanischen und Koreanischen:

(9) FR → K + Dy
Japanisch/Koreanisch
basu-ga Tôkyô-eki-e ikimasu
bŏsŭ-ga Sŏul-yŏg-ŭro kamnida
Bus-NOM (Name)-Bahnhof-zu geh
„der Bus fährt zum Bahnhof von Tôkyô/Seoul"

Dependensmarkierung der Determinativrelation ist üblich und häufig in den Sprachen der Welt:

(10)   DT^T → K + Dy
(a) *de-s Vater-s Haus/das Haus de-s Vater-s/das Haus von Vater*
(b) Baskisch
   dom   otc-a
   Haus(NOM) Vater-GEN
   „das Haus des Vaters"
(c) Baskisch
   aita-ren etxe-a
   Vater-GEN Haus-ART
   „das Haus des Vaters"

Auch die Genitiv-Konstruktion des Hindi fällt unter diese Kategorie; hier wird die Genitiv-Endung in Form einer Postposition an das POSSr-Nomen angefügt und zugleich an das folgende POSSm in Kasus, Genus und Numerus angeglichen. Trotz dieser Kongruenz bleibt der Kopf als solcher unverändert, so daß eindeutig die Konfiguration K + Dy, nicht die Konfiguration Kx + Dy vorliegt:

(d) Hindi (Kellogg 1893 [1972]: 102)
   rājā   kā   ghar
   König   GENmSG Haus/
   mālī   ke   beṭe
   Gärtner GENmPL Söhne/
   brahman kī   pothī
   Brahmane GENfSG Buch
   „Haus des Königs/Söhne des Gärtners/Buch des Brahmanen"

3.2.5. Grammemik: Flexionsgrad

Neben der Konfiguration muß der **Flexionsgrad** typologisch differenziert werden. Wie die Formulierung schon besagt, handelt es sich hierbei nicht um eine einfache Opposition, sondern um eine graduierte Skala, um ein Kontinuum. Grammeme können in einem Extremfall frei im Satz verschiebbare, autonome Elemente sein; oder sie können, im entgegengesetzten Extremfall, so völlig mit dem dazugehörigen Lexem verschmelzen, daß keine Grenzziehung zwischen beidem möglich ist. Zwischen diesen Polen spannt sich eine Skala von intermediären Lösungen aus, die nach verschiedenen Kriterien aufgegliedert werden kann. Es scheint sinnvoll, an dieser Stelle eine Anbindung des hier vorgestellten Modells an die traditionelle Unterscheidung von Agglutination und Flexion vorzunehmen: so wie wir oben eine Einbindung und gleichzeitig Präzisierung des traditionellen Begriffs der „Isolation" vorgenommen haben, bietet sich auch hier eine genauere Fassung dieser beiden im vorigen — und auch noch in unserem — Jahrhundert so weit verbreiteten Termini an.

Bei der Verwendung dieser Begriffe in der traditionellen typologischen Literatur wurden mehrere Kriterien miteinander vermengt, die getrennt behandelt werden müssen. Darüber hinaus muß selbstverständlich die eurozentrische, idealisierende Betrachtungsweise der traditionellen Typologie vermieden werden, nach der nur der flexivische Typus als „organisch" betrachtet und der agglutinative Typus als „mechanistisch" abgewertet wurde. Von solchen Vorstellungen sind wir heute scheinbar äonenweit entfernt, doch spuken sie gelegentlich immer noch unterschwellig durch die Literatur.

Der Unterschied zwischen agglutinativen und flexivischen Techniken läßt sich auf mindestens vier Kriterien zurückführen; sind alle Kriterien positiv, liegt uneingeschränkt Flexion vor, sind alle negativ, ist die Technik uneingeschränkt agglutinativ. Zwischenlösungen, bei denen die Kriterien unterschiedlich verteilt sind, kommen häufig vor; sie sind als graduierte Abstufungen zwischen der reinen Flexion und der reinen Agglutination zu werten.

Flexion ist idealtypisch gekennzeichnet durch das Vorliegen der folgenden Eigenschaften: Polymorphie, Synkretismus, Funktionskumulierung, Fusion. Agglutination ist idealtypisch gekennzeichnet durch das Fehlen all dieser Eigenschaften. Betrachten wir zunächst das Türkische als prototypischen Vertreter der agglutinativen Technik:

(11) ev   Haus
      evri   Haus-sein
      ev-den   Haus-ABL
      ev-ler-i   Haus-PL-sein
      ev-ler-in-den Haus-PL-sein-ABL
      „Haus/sein Haus/vom Haus/seine Häuser/von seinen Häusern"

Es liegt keine Polymorphie vor: die Relationen werden durch genau eine Form ausgedrückt. Es gibt keinen Synkretismus: jede Form hat genau eine Funktion. Kumulierung findet nicht statt: jede Funktion wird durch eine einzelne separate Form ausgedrückt. Der Fusionsgrad ist gering: zwar sind die Grammeme an das Lexem gebunden (sogar durch Vokalharmonie und gegebenenfalls Konsonantenassimilation mit ihm relativ eng verschmolzen), aber die Bindung ist nicht so fest, daß nicht andere Suffixe dazwischentreten könnten; jedenfalls ändert sich das Lexem nicht unter dem Einfluß des Grammems.

In jeder Hinsicht exakt das Gegenteil finden wir in einer prototypischen Flexionssprache wie dem Latein:

(12) Latein
    (a) GEN.SG.m: *domin-i/reg-is*
    (b) *domin-i*:   GEN.SG.m/NOM.PL.m
    (c) *domin-i*:   NOM+PL+m
    (d) *itineris*:   GEN.SG.n

In beiden Richtungen liegt eine Mehr-zu-Eins-Relation vor, sowohl von der Funktion zum Ausdruck als auch vom Ausdruck zur Funktion (Polymorphie (a) und Synkretismus (b)); in einem Morphem sind mehrere Funktionen unanalysierbar kumuliert (c); und die Verschmelzung geht so weit, daß das Lexem unter dem Einfluß des hinzutretenden Grammems seine Form verändert (d).

Mit Hilfe eines so präzisierten begrifflichen Instrumentariums wird es möglich, die traditionelle Unterscheidung von Agglutination und Flexion genauer anzuwenden; es geht nicht um ein Entweder-Oder, sondern um ein Mehr-oder-Weniger: je nachdem welche der genannten Eigenschaften eine Konstruktion aufweist, tendiert sie eher zu dem einen oder zu dem anderen Pol, kann sie als mehr oder weniger agglutinativ bzw. flexionell klassifiziert werden. Anhand der Entwicklung des Imperfekts vom Lateinischen zum Romanischen soll dies kurz illustriert werden.

Das lateinische Verbalsystem ist insgesamt — entgegen landläufigen Vorstellungen — in höherem Maße von agglutinativen Eigenschaften geprägt als das durch und durch flexivische Nominalsystem. Das *imperfectum* genannte Tempus weist zu drei Vierteln agglutinative Züge auf: als Tempusgrammem (d. h. als Träger des Assertionsbezuges) fungiert durchgehend und ausnahmslos das Morphem *-ba-*, als Personalgrammeme (d. h. als Träger des Aktantenbezuges) fungiert ebenso ausnahmslos die regelmäßige Morphemreihe *-m/-s/-t/-mus/-tis/-nt*. Innerhalb dieses Tempus gibt es also weder Polymorphie noch Synkretismus, und auch die Trennung der Funktionen (Tempus und Person) ist klar vollzogen; nur die Verschmelzung von Lexem und Grammem ist flexivisch. Es ist evident, daß all dies in anderen Tempora des Lateinischen nicht in der gleichen Form gilt, dort dominieren vielmehr die flexivischen Züge (extrem etwa im *perfectum* der unregelmäßigen Verbalklassen). Festzuhalten bleibt, daß das Imperfekt eine Art agglutinative Insel in einem flexivischen Meer bildet — genauer gesagt, hier dominieren die agglutinativen Züge, während ansonsten die flexivischen vorherrschen.

In den romanischen Sprachen gewinnen flexivische Züge auch in diesem Tempus die Oberhand. Vergleichen wir Italienisch und Spanisch. Im konservativen Italienisch hat sich die Funktionstrennung der Grammeme gehalten: in Formen wie *ama-v-ate* und *veni-v-ate* ist *-v-* als Tempusgrammem eindeutig von dem nachfolgenden Personalgrammem getrennt — ein agglutinativer Zug des Lateinischen, der sich erhalten hat. Nur im Bereich der Personalmarkierung ist zunächst eine Zunahme der Flexionalität zu beobachten: durch die mechanisch wirkende Lauterosion sind die Formen *amaba-m* und *amaba-t* im Prinzip zunächst zu *amava* zusammengefallen; hier liegt im Ergebnis ein Synkretismus vor. In Analogie zu der ansonsten dominierenden Endung *-o* für 1SG wurde die Form *amavo* gebildet, die sich von dem *amava* für 3SG eindeutig unterscheidet; das Paradigma wurde also wieder in Richtung Agglutination ausgeglichen, der Zustand des Lateinischen (mit neuen Mitteln) wiederhergestellt. (Bereits in der ältesten Literatur findet man *amavo* neben *amava*, ersteres in Siena und Lucca, letzteres in Florenz; endgültig setzte sich *amavo* erst im 19. Jahrhundert durch, als Manzoni sich in der — für die italienische Nationalsprache maßgeblichen — zweiten Version seiner „Promessi sposi" von 1840 für diese Form entschied; vgl. Rohlfs 1968: II, 286.) Im Unterschied dazu ist das Spanische von allem Anfang an flexivischer: aus *amabatis* wurde *amábais*, aus *veniebatis* wurde *veníais*. Die Präsenz von zwei Grammemen, nämlich *-b-* und *-í-*, zum Ausdruck des Tempus stellt einen Polymorphismus dar; in der Tatsache, daß man bei *-í-* nicht mehr eindeutig zwischen dem Ausdruck der Verbalklasse und der Tempusfunktion unterscheiden kann, kann man eine Kumulierung mehrerer Funktionen in einem Morphem sehen. Darüber hinaus besteht der soeben für das Italienische konstatierte Synkretismus im Bereich der Personalendungen (*amaba* „ich/er liebte") auch im Spanischen, ohne daß es hier zu einem analogischen Ausgleich in Richtung Agglutination gekommen wäre. Das Spanische hat im Imperfekt also drei flexivische Züge neu entwickelt und bis heute bewahrt, die im Lateinischen nicht bestanden hatten. Das hier entwickelte begriffliche Instrumentarium erlaubt eine differenzierte Analyse, die in einigen Punkten den üblichen Vorstellungen vom generell „synthetischen"

Latein und den generell „analytischen" romanischen Sprachen zuwiderläuft.

(V) Grammemik II: Agglutination und Flexion am Beispiel des lateinisch-romanischen Imperfekts

	Lat	Ital I	Ital II	Span
Polymorphie	−	−	−	+
Synkretismus	−	+	−	+
Kumulation	−	−	−	+
Fusion	+	+	+	+
Agglut/Flex	3/1	2/2	3/1	0/4

3.2.6. Grammemik: Position

Gehen wir zum Abschluß auf das dritte der oben genannten Kriterien ein: die **Position**. Grammem und Lexem können in verschiedener Weise zueinander angeordnet sein, wobei die herkömmliche Unterscheidung von Präfix und Suffix zu wenig differenziert ist; weitere Unterscheidungen sind also zu treffen. Es folgt eine summarische Übersicht mit Beispielen aus verschiedenen Sprachen, wobei der jeweilige Verschmelzungsgrad an dieser Stelle unberücksichtigt bleibt; eine Kasusendung wird also gleich wie eine Postposition, ein klitisches Pronomen gleich wie eine Konjugationsform klassifiziert. Manche Klassifikationen sind nicht ohne Willkürlichkeit möglich; so kann man die kasusregierenden Präpositionen des indogermanischen Typus sowohl als Präfixe auffassen, wenn man nur die Präposition als solche im Auge hat; besser − wenn auch ungewohnter − wäre es vielleicht, diese Konstruktionen als Zirkumfixe zu klassifizieren. So müßten viele weitere Details genauer diskutiert werden, was hier aus Raumgründen aber unmöglich ist.

(VI) Grammemik III: die Positionstypen

− **Präfixe**
GRA ∩ LEX (das Grammem geht dem Lexem voraus)
a) einfach
  − nominal: Präpositionen ohne Kasusrektion
  [englisch *in the city*; spanisch *a la vecina*; chinesisch *dào Běijīng* „nach Peking"]
  − verbal: proklitische Personal- oder TAM-Affixe mit fester Position
  [Angolar *n ga eta* „ich IMPF wissen";

Ainu *a-e-kore* „ich-dir-gebe"; Nahuatl *ni-mitz-itta* „ich-dich-sehe"; Ubychisch *a-z-bya-n* „ihn-ich-sehe-PRS"; Persisch *mi-kon-id* „PRS-macht-ihr"]
b) komplex
  − nominal: Präpositionen mit Kasusrektion (auch als Zirkumfix klassifizierbar)
  [Deutsch *in de-r Stadt*, Russisch *v Moskv-e* „in Moskau-PP", Arabisch *bil-madīnat-i* „in.der-Stadt-GEN"]

− **Suffixe**
LEX ∩ GRA (das Grammem folgt dem Lexem)
a) einfach
  − nominal: Postpositionen ohne Kasusrektion, einfache Kasusendungen
  [Japanisch *chichi-no* „Vater-GEN"; Arabisch *al-kitāb-i* „das-Buch-GEN"; Polnisch *polsk-iego lud-u* „polnisch-GEN.SG(Adj) Volk-GEN.SG.m"; Sanskrit *deva-sya* „Gott-GEN.SG.m"]
  − verbal: enklitische Personal- oder TAM-Affixe mit fester Position
  [Lateinisch *venie-ba-tis*; Türkisch *gel-iyor-sunuz* „komm-PRS-ihr"; Ubychisch *a-z-bya-n* „ihn-ich-sehe-PRS"; Persisch *mi-kon-id* „PRS-macht-ihr"; Japanisch *tabe-ta* „essen-PRF"]
b) komplex
  − nominal: Postpositionen mit Kasusrektion, zusammengesetzte (zweistufige) Kasusendungen
  [Deutsch *de-s Frieden-s halber*; Hindi *beṭ-a*/*beṭ-e ko* „Sohn-REC/Sohn-OBL DAT"; Georgisch *deda*/*ded-is-tvis* „Mutter.NOM/Mutter-GEN-für"; Avarisch *wacc*/*wacc-ass*/*wacc-ass-ul* „Bruder.ABS/Bruder-ERG/Bruder-ERG-GEN"; Lesgisch *sew*/*sew-re*/*sew-ren* „Bär.ABS/Bär-ERG/Bär-ERG-GEN"]

− **Zirkumfixe**
GRA ∩ LEX ∩ GRA' (das Grammem besteht aus zwei Bestandteilen, von denen einer dem Lexem vorangeht, der andere ihm folgt)
  − nominal: zirkumfixale Adpositionen
  [Deutsch *um des Friedens willen*; Chinesisch *zài xuéxiào-lǐ* „in Schule-drin"]
  − verbal: zirkumfixale Partizipialformen, zweigliedrige Negationsgrammeme
  [Deutsch *ge-lieb-t*/*ge-lauf-en*; Französisch *Jean ne vient pas*; Amharisch *al-näggärä-m* „NEG-er.hat.gesagt-NEG"; Quechua *manam munani-chu* „nicht ich.will-NEG"]

- **Wechselaffixe**
GRA ∩ LEX ~ LEX ∩ GRA
a) alternierend: das Grammem geht dem Lexem voran oder folgt ihm unter bestimmten Bedingungen (finite vs. infinite Verbalformen, satzphonetischer Kontext)
[Italienisch *me lo dai/dàmmelo* „mir es du.gibst/gib-mir-es!"; Neugriechisch *mu to δínis/δós mu to* „ebenso"; Portugiesisch (Portugal) *quero-te/não te quero* „ich.liebe-dich/nicht dich ich.liebe"]
b) ambivalent: Voran- oder Nachstellung des Grammems stehen in freier Variation
[Deutsch *wegen des Friedens/des Friedens wegen*; Altgriechisch *héneka hygieías* „wegen Gesundheit-GEN"/*lógou héneka* „verbi gratia"]

- **Infixe**
LEX ∩ GRA ∩ LEX'
a) inserierend: das Grammem wird in das Lexem eingefügt, wobei beide ihre Form bewahren
[Tagalog *sulat/s-um-ulat* „schreiben"]
b) mutierend: die Einfügung des Grammems bewirkt eine Veränderung des Lexems; das Grammem manifestiert sich nur durch seine Wirkung]
[Englisch *man/men; mouse/mice; read/read*]

- **Interdigitalisierende Affixe**
„GRA" + „LEX" → Wort
das Grammem hat die Gestalt eines abstrakten Musters, welches der ebenfalls abstrakten Lexemwurzel eine bestimmte konkrete Form aufprägt (Grammemmuster und Wurzel durchdringen sich gegenseitig); die einzelnen Bestandteile des Grammems können präfixal, infixal, zirkumfixal oder suffixal sein, entscheidend ist die Gesamtgestalt des Musters
[Arabisch: Wurzel *ktb* „schreiben" + Muster *XāYiZ* → *kātib* „schreibend"; + *maXYūZ* → *maktūb* „geschrieben"; + *uXYuZ* → *uktub* „schreib"; + *taXXuZū* → *taktubū* „ihr schreibt"; *XāYaZnā* → *kātabnā* „wir korrespondierten"; *iXtaYaZtum* → *iktatabtum* „ihr schriebt euch ein" etc.]

4. Schlußbemerkung

Konfiguration, Flexionsgrad und Position sind voneinander unabhängige Parameter, die getrennt zur Analyse eingesetzt, dann aber miteinander kreuzklassifiziert werden müssen, um eine vollständige typologische Charakterisierung der jeweils zum Ausdruck einer grammatischen Relation verwendeten Technik zu erreichen. Aus dem vorgeschlagenen Modell ebenso wie aus den angeführten Beispielen geht klar hervor, daß die einzelnen Sprachen eine Vielzahl unterschiedlicher Techniken nebeneinander verwenden und daß pauschalierende Klassifizierungen ganzer Sprachsysteme als „isolierend/agglutinierend/flexivisch" endgültig der Vergangenheit angehören. Nur ein differenziertes typologisches Raster erlaubt eine Erfassung der Techniken, welche der Spezifizität und Komplexität der historischen Einzelsprachen gerecht wird.

Und noch ein weiteres sollte aus der Darstellung dieses Modells deutlich geworden sein: universal sind zunächst einmal die grammatischen Relationen selbst; universal und logisch aus den Eigenschaften menschlicher Sprache ableitbar sind aber auch die zu ihrem Ausdruck verwendbaren Techniken: sie können allesamt als Lösungen des Grundproblems der Linearisierung nicht-linearer Strukturen interpretiert werden. Typologisch ausdifferenziert erscheinen die Sprachen durch die spezifische Kombination grammatischer Relationen zu einzelsprachlichen Kategorien, durch die spezifische Auswahl, die sie aus dem universalen Arsenal möglicher Techniken treffen, sowie durch die Gewichtung, die sie den einzelnen Techniken im Rahmen ihres Gesamtsystems zuerkennen. Die Bandbreite der universalen Möglichkeiten determiniert die typologische Vielfalt.

5. Spezielle Abkürzungen

ACT	aktiv
AS	Assertion
DT	Determinativrelation
EZF	Ezafet
FR	Fundamentalrelation
GRA	Grammem
HY	Hypotaxis
IMPF	Imperfektiv
INACT	inaktiv
KF	Koreferenz
LEX	Lexem
P	Prädikat
POSSm	Possessum
POSSr	Possessor
PP	Präpositiv
PRS	Präsens
REC	casus rectus
T	Term
TAM	Tempus-Aspekt-Modus
THM	Thema

6. Zitierte Literatur

Bossong, Georg. 1979a. „Typologie der Hypotaxe". *Folia Linguistica* 13: 33–54.

Bossong, Georg. 1979b. „Prolegomena zu einer syntaktischen Typologie der romanischen Sprachen". In: Höfler, Manfred et al. (eds.), *Festschrift Kurt Baldinger zum 60. Geburtstag*. Tübingen: Niemeyer, I, 54–68.

Bossong, Georg. 1980. „Aktantenfunktionen im romanischen Verbalsystem". *Zeitschrift für romanische Philologie* 96: 1–22.

Bossong, Georg. 1998a. „Éléments d'une typologie actancielle des langues romanes". In: Feuillet, Jack (ed.), *Actance et valence*. (EALT EUROTYP 20–2) Berlin: Mouton, 769–788.

Bossong, Georg. 1998b. „La typologie des langues romanes". In: Holtus, Günter & Metzeltin, Michael & Schmitt, Christian (eds.), *Lexikon der romanistischen Linguistik*, vol. VII. Tübingen: Niemeyer, 1003–1019.

Bossong, Georg. 1998c. „Vers une typologie des indices actanciels. Les clitiques romans dans une perspective comparative". In: Ramat, Paolo & Roma, Elisa (eds.), *Atti del XXX Congresso Internazionale della Società di Linguistica Italiana*. (Pubblicazioni della Società di Linguistica Italiana 39) Roma: Bulzoni, 9–43.

Charachidzé, Georges. 1981. *Grammaire de la langue avar (langue du Caucase Nord-Est)*. Paris: Jean-Favard.

Cohen, Marcel. 1970. *Traité de langue amharique*. Paris: Institut d'ethnologie.

Dumézil, Georges. 1975. *La verbe oubykh. Études descriptives et comparatives (avec la collaboration de Tevfik Esenç)*. Paris: Klincksieck.

Finck, Nikolaus. 1909 [1965]. *Die Haupttypen des Sprachbaus*. (Nachdruck Wissenschaftliche Buchgesellschaft) Darmstadt.

Haspelmath, Martin. 1993. *A grammar of Lezgian*. (Mouton Grammar Library 9) Berlin: Mouton de Gruyter.

Heath, Jeffrey. 1999. *A grammar of Koyra Chiini. The Songhay of Timbuktu*. (Mouton Grammar Library 19) Berlin: Mouton de Gruyter.

Humboldt, Wilhelm von. 1835 [1963]. *Ueber die Verschiedenheit des menschlichen Sprachbaues und ihren Einfluss auf die geistige Entwicklung des Menschengeschlechts*. (Nachdruck in: *Schriften zur Sprachphilosophie*, Wissenschaftliche Buchgesellschaft) Darmstadt: Claassen & Roether.

Kellogg, S. H. 1893 [1972]. *A grammar of the Hindi language*. (Nachdruck Oriental Books Reprint Corporation) New Delhi, Prayaga: Hindi Sahitya Sammelana.

Launey, Michel. 1978. *Introduction à la langue et à la littérature aztéques. 1. Grammaire*. Paris: L'Harmattan.

Lewin, Bruno & Kim, T. Dae. 1976. *Einführung in die koreanische Sprache*. Heilbronn: Gustav Scherer.

Makino, Seiichi & Tsutsui, Michio. 1986 [[18]1994]. *A dictionary of basic Japanese grammar*. Tokyo: Japan Times.

Maurer, Philippe. 1995. *L'angolar. Un créole afroportugais parlé à São Tomé*. Hamburg: Buske.

Nichols, Johanna. 1992. *Linguistic diversity in space and time*. Chicago: University of Chicago Press.

Rohlfs, Gerhard. 1968. *Grammatica storica della lingua italiana e dei suoi dialetti*. Torino: Einaudi.

Schachter, Paul & Otanes, Fe T. 1972. *Tagalog reference grammar*. Berkeley: University of California Press.

Schlegel, August Wilhelm. 1818 [1971]. *Observations sur la Langue et la Littérature Provençales*. (Nachdruck Gunter Narr) Tübingen: Tübinger Beiträge zur Linguistik.

Shibatani, Masayoshi. 1990. *The languages of Japan*. Cambridge: Cambridge University Press.

Skalička, Vladimir. 1979. *Typologische Studien*. (Schriften zur Linguistik 11) Braunschweig, Wiesbaden: Vieweg.

Soto Ruiz, Clodoaldo. 1976. *Gramática quechua. Ayacuchu-Chanca*. Lima: Ministerio de Educación.

Georg Bossong, Universität Zürich (Schweiz)

49. Agglutination and flection

1. Preliminaries
2. Traditional parameters of agglutination
3. Connections between the parameters
4. Agglutination as a manifestation of greater morpheme autonomy
5. The diachronic dimension
6. Special abbreviations
7. References

1. Preliminaries

The terms "agglutination" and "(in)flection", taken in their most general and most established sense, oppose two major techniques of morpheme combination within a word-form, or, to put it slightly differently, two ways of assembling words in natural languages. Since both trace their origins back to (at least) the early 19th century (the term "flection" was proposed by Friedrich von Schlegel in 1808; the term "agglutination" is due to Wilhelm von Humboldt), their actual use is often rather vague; in fact, they cover a variety of heterogenous features, which do not necessarily coexist in all languages. Thus, there is a need for some renewed, more narrow and, perhaps, more precise definitions, made nevertheless against the traditional "holistic" background.

In this overview, we are not in a position to evaluate or even summarize in any detail what has been written about agglutination and flection in a typological perspective. Our proposals rely heavily on some well-known theoretical contributions which include, first of all, Sapir 1921, Greenberg 1960, Skalička 1966, Kasevič & Jaxontov 1982, Dressler 1985 and Dressler et al. 1987; among reference works, Greenberg 1974, Kilani-Schoch 1988 and Croft 1990 may also be recommended.

When speaking about differences in morphological techniques, it seems advisable to isolate at the outset the following three parameters, which can apply, in principle, independently:

(i) the way in which inter-morpheme boundaries are handled within a word-form;
(ii) the extent to which non-phonologically conditioned variation of stems and grammatical markers is attested; and
(iii) the extent to which a symmetry between the semantic and formal organization ("first articulation", to use traditional structuralist terms) of grammatical markers is observed.

The parameter (i) opposes agglutination to **fusion** (the term was coined by Sapir), the parameters (ii) and, especially, (iii), to **flection**. Obviously, the lack of fusion does not necessarily imply the lack of flection (in both senses), and vice versa, although some interrelations do exist. In what follows, we consider these parameters in turn (§ 2), as well as their possible interaction (§3), and then we touch on their more general consequences and diachronic developments (§§ 4 and 5).

2. Traditional parameters of agglutination

2.1. Agglutination as non-fusion

The first parameter treats agglutination as a formal device specifying the shape of word-internal morpheme sequences.

It is generally accepted that words can be thought of as formed by sequences of smaller form-meaning pairs — morphemes. The possibility of linear segmentation does not imply, however, that "one and the same" morpheme remains invariable in all contexts. On the contrary, contextual variation of the shape of morphemes (known as **allomorphic variation**) is pervasive in natural languages.

Not all kinds of allomorphic variation are concerned with the agglutination / fusion distinction, but only those which occur on morpheme boundaries and affect morpheme junctures (a frequently used term for this type of morpheme variation is **sandhi** — more precisely, word-internal sandhi). In other words, the more widespread the fusion, the more likely the linear segmentation of word-forms is to be problematic.

For our purposes, "partial" fusion and "complete" fusion have to be distinguished. **Partial fusion** presupposes that adjacent parts of morphemes undergo certain transformations, but the boundary is still present; by contrast, **complete fusion** makes the boundary disappear and hence surface morpheme segmentation impossible. Below examples of partial (1 a–c) and complete (2 a–b) fusion are given:

(1) (a) Hungarian, forms of non-object 2PL imperative:
ír-jatok 'write'
hoz-zatok 'bring'
mos-satok 'wash' [moššɔtok]
(b) Russian, forms of the verb 'lay':
klad-ú 'I am laying'
lay-PRES:1SG
klas-t' 'to lay'
lay-INF
kla-l 'laid'
lay-PAST(M:SG)
(c) Latin, forms of past participle:
can-ere 'to sing'
sing-INF
can-t-us 'sung'
sing-PTCP:PAST-M:SG:NOM
prem-ere 'to press'
press-INF
pres-s-us 'pressed'
press-PTCP:PAST-M:SG:NOM

(2) (a) Latin
caed-ere 'to hit'
hit-INF
caes-us 'hit'
hit:PTCP:PAST-M:SG:NOM
(b) Russian
mog-ú 'I am able'
can-PRES:1SG
moč' 'to be able'
can:INF

In (1 a), the Hungarian suffix of the 2PL imperative has different allomorphs depending on the last consonant of the verbal stem; in (1 b), it is the Russian root 'lay' which changes its phonological shape depending on the following suffix. Finally, Latin forms such as *pressus* in (1 c) are an example of both root and affix changing in contact with each other. In all three cases, however, despite the sandhi effects conditioned by the phonological shape of adjacent morphemes, the linear segmentation remains unproblematic. By contrast, a natural linear segmentation is impossible in (2 a – b), since one-phoneme markers of Latin past participle and of Russian infinitive are absorbed by the verbal stems, merging in their final part. These markers disappear (as segmental ones), and the only surface trace they leave is the modification of an adjacent morpheme. Another well-known example of complete fusion are French forms such as *du* [dy] 'of the', where the preposition *de* 'of' and the masculine singular definite article *le* have been merged.

Languages where partial (and especially complete) fusion prevails are called **fusional**; accordingly, languages where the non-fusional technique is preferred are called **agglutinative**. Typical examples of fusional languages are classical Indo-European languages (Sanskrit, Ancient Greek, Latin), Slavic languages, many American Indian languages, and others. On the other hand, agglutinative languages (in this and other possible senses of the term) include, first of all, Turkic, most Finno-Ugric, Dravidian, most Austronesian languages, as well as Quechua, many Australian languages, etc. Of course, many intermediate cases are found (which are probably even more frequent than ideal ones). Languages where both fusional and agglutinative features seem to be represented equally well are, for example, Mongolian and Semitic.

2.2. Agglutination as uniformity

The second parameter of agglutination deals with the non-phonological variation of morphemes. Indeed, allomorphic variation may have two principal sources: either shape of the morpheme is different because of different phonological contexts (as demonstrated in § 2.1), or different allomorphs are chosen in different morphological contexts. In this latter case the allomorphic variation does not depend on the phonological environment, but on semantic or grammatical properties of an adjacent morpheme (rather than on its phonological shape).

Two types of non-phonological variation can be distinguished: to wit, stem and affix variation.

Non-phonological stem variation may be called **grammatically conditioned** variation: this is the case where different grammatical markers require different allomorphs of one and the same stem. Cf. the punctual past forms (or "perfect", in the traditional terminology) in Latin (3 a) or the oblique case forms in Hungarian (3 b) and Finnish (3 c):

(3) (a) Latin tense forms of 1SG:

PRES	PERF	
leg-o	lēg-ī	'gather'
can-o	cecin-ī	'sing'
pell-o	pepul-ī	'push'
ter-o	trī-v-ī	'rub'

(b) Hungarian, forms of NOM and ACC (SG):

NOM	ACC	
király	király-ot	'king'
ház	háza-t	'house'
kéz	keze-t	'hand'
madár	madara-t	'bird'

(c) Finnish, forms of NOM and GEN (SG):

NOM	GEN	
pirtti	*pirti-n*	'hut'
lempi	*lemme-n*	'love'
lahti	*lahde-n*	'bay'
leipä	*leivä-n*	'bread'
pako	*pao-n*	'flight'
rae	*rakee-n*	'grain'

In Latin, the past tense is expressed by a special series of personal endings and, often, by one of the past suffixes (-*v*-, -*u*- or -*s*-). These past markers may (but need not) condition some changes of the verbal stem, as shown in (3 a): lengthening of the stem vowel, partial reduplication of the stem, as well as other modifications.

The Hungarian examples in (3 b) demonstrate the difference between the nominative and the oblique stem (a very frequent case in the world's languages); the long vowel of the nominative stem may be shortened in the oblique stem, and an extra-vowel may be added to this before the marker of the accusative (which is -*t* after the vowels and -*Ot* after the consonants). Both changes are not obligatory and concern only a part of word-forms containing a long vowel: thus, the word for 'king' has one and the same stem in all the case forms.

In Finnish, nominative and genitive stems may be opposed by a series of complex alternations of "consonant grades" (note also possible additional alternations of the final vowel). Of special interest is the fact that a given case form need not always trigger one and the same consonant grade (cf. the opposition of forms for 'flight' and 'grain' in (3 c)).

All these variations are not phonologically conditioned — in the sense that we cannot say (at least from a synchronic point of view) that, for example, the vowel lengthening in Latin *lēgī* — or the vowel shortening in Hungarian *kezet* — occurs because of phonological assimilation to a certain adjacent morpheme. These particular phonological alternations can be correctly described only with recourse to grammatical properties of the morphological context. However, it should be borne in mind that historically many cases of non-phonological variation can be traced back to those of phonological variation (as is suggested, in particular, for Hungarian and Finnish declension and at least for some verbal forms in Latin). Gradually, the phonological context may change, and the phonological alternation gets morphologized, i.e. the conditions of its application are reinterpreted in morphological terms. In consequence, there are no hard and fast boundaries between the two types of variation: an intermediate area exists. Nevertheless, extreme cases can be clearly distinguished (cf. also Dressler 1985).

Let us now turn to non-phonological variation of affixes. This type of variation may be called **lexically conditioned** variation. This is the case where different lexical stems require different allomorphs of one and the same affix. The most common type of lexically conditioned variation is known as a difference between various classes of declension or conjugation. Thus, the marker of (non-neuter) nominative plural in Latin is -*ae* for the stems of the traditional 1st declension (like *silv-a* 'forest'), -*ī* for the stems of the 2nd declension (like *anim-us* 'spirit'), -*ēs* for the stems of the 3rd and 5th declensions (like *urb-s* 'city' or *faci-ēs* 'face') and -*ūs* for the stems of the 4th declension (like *lac-us* 'lake'), etc.

There exists another type of affix variation which is not lexically, but grammatically conditioned (more like stem variation considered above). In this case, different markers of one and the same grammeme are chosen in different grammatical contexts (i.e. depending on other grammatical markers in the word-form). Cf. examples (4 a–c):

(4) (a) Mansi, nominal number:
the noun *xāp* 'boat' in its non-possessive and possessive (1PL) forms:

	'boat'	'our boat'
SG	*xāp*	*xāp-uw*
DU	*xāp-iɣ*	*xāp-aɣ-uw*
PL	*xāp-ət*	*xāp-an-uw*

(b) Hungarian, subject person and number and verbal mood:
the verb *jár-* 'walk'

	1SG	2SG
PRES	*jár-ok*	*jár-sz* [ja:rs]
PAST	*jár-t-am*	*jár-t-ál*
COND	*jár-né-k*	*jár-ná-l*

(c) Udmurt, subject person and number and verbal tense:
the verb *min̄-* 'go'

	2SG	3SG
PRES	*min̄-is'ko-d*	*min̄-e*
FUT	*min̄-o-d*	*min̄-o-z*
PERF	*min̄-em*	*min̄-em*

	3PL	1PL
PRES	mïn-o	mïn-is'ko-mï
FUT	mïn-o-zï	mïn-o-m
PERF	mïn-il'l'am	mïn-is'kem-mï

In Mansi (Ob-Ugric branch of the Finno-Ugric family) declension, the markers of dual and plural, as shown in (4a), differ in non-possessive and possessive forms; especially striking is the difference of plural allomorphs (-ət for non-possessive nouns and -an- for possessive ones).

In (4b), the Hungarian endings of 1st and 2nd person singular differ depending on verbal tense and mood; the marker of conditional mood is different, in turn, for 1st and 2nd person. Only the past marker -t- is not subject to variation.

A fragment of Udmurt (Finno-Ugric family) verbal morphology represented in (4c) is even more complicated. The present marker is different for 3rd and non-3rd person (zero vs. -is'ko- resp.); on the other hand, personal endings of 3 SG and PL differ in the present (-e/-o) and the future (-z/-zï). The future marker is invariably -o, while the perfect possesses three different markers for 2–3SG, 1Pl and 3PL; finally, all perfect forms but 1PL have zero personal endings.

By and large, agglutinative morphology is supposed to be bereft of this kind of morpheme variation. In an ideal agglutinative language, stems and affixes are uniform; their choice does not depend on their morphological (as well as phonological, see § 2.1) context. However, in many languages usually considered agglutinative (such as Finno-Ugric) this type of allomorphic variation is recurrent. On the other hand, non-uniformity of stems and affixes is one of the constitutive features of what is traditionally called "flective languages".

2.3. Agglutination as non-cumulation

Inflectional markers may differ depending on how many grammatical meanings (or "grammemes") they convey. Agglutinative patterns here, as well as elsewhere, involve uniformity: each agglutinative morpheme normally expresses only one grammeme. This is the main **semantic** parameter of agglutination.

The opposite trait is usually called **cumulation** (cf. Mel'čuk 1982, among others). A cumulative morpheme, though formally not segmentable into smaller meaningful units, expresses several different grammatical meanings simultaneously. The most common example is the cumulation of number and case grammemes as represented in many declensional systems. Indo-European languages (those which have preserved an old declension) are probably the most familiar case (cf. Russian data in 5a); however, within the Indo-European family, Modern Eastern Armenian displays an "agglutinative" (i.e., non-cumulative) declension, as shown in (5b).

(5) (a) Russian, nominal declension:
the noun *stena* 'wall'

	SG	PL
NOM	sten-á	stén-y
GEN	sten-ý	stén-Ø
DAT	sten-é	stén-am
INSTR	sten-ój	stén-ami

(b) Armenian, nominal declension:
the noun *ban* 'thing'

	SG	PL
NOM	ban-Ø	ban-er-Ø
GEN	ban-i	ban-er-i
INSTR	ban-ov	ban-er-ov
ABL	ban-ich	ban-er-ich

In Russian, not only are declensional markers cumulative — they are also highly homonymous; thus, the forms of GEN:SG and NOM:PL in (5a) are opposed only by their stress patterns. This is typical of many old Indo-European flective systems (and, perhaps, of flective paradigms in general).

Equally well attested is the cumulation of person and number in verbal conjugation, as well as that of tense and aspect. Languages often oppose "durative" (or "imperfective") and "punctual" (or "perfective") past tense markers (cf. Dahl 1985), where aspectual grammemes of durative and punctual are expressed in cumulation with the past tense, as it is the case, for example, in Latin forms like (6a) and (6b). (Note also the grammatically conditioned variation in the markers of 1SG!)

(6) Latin
(a) *scrīb-ēba-m*
write-DUR:PAST-1SG
'I wrote / was writing'
(b) *scrīp-s-ī*
write-PUNCT:PAST-1SG:PUNCT:PAST
'I wrote / have written'

The cumulation of durative and past is often called "imperfect" (following the grammatical tradition of antiquity); interestingly, there is no equally well established term for such a cumulation of punctual and past (perhaps, "aorist" is the most agreed upon).

However frequent this tense-aspect cumulation may be, it is by no means universal, as shown by example (7) from another Indo-European language, Modern Persian:

(7) Persian
   (a) *mi-kon-äm*
       DUR-do:PRES-1SG
       'I do / am doing'
   (b) *mi-kärd-äm*
       DUR-do:PAST-1SG
       'I did / was doing'
   (c) *kärd-äm*
       do:PAST-1SG
       'I did'

Here, aspectual grammemes (*mi-* for durative and zero for punctual, in all verbal forms) are expressed independently of tense (different tense choice corresponding to different stem allomorphs) and of person/number (*-äm* being an invariable marker of 1SG). Thus, aspect and tense in Persian can be said to have an agglutinative (in particular, non-cumulative) expression.

On the opposite side of this scale are languages such as Modern Greek (cf. 8), where at least some verbal word-forms may mark simultaneously not only person, number, tense and aspect, but also voice.

(8) Modern Greek, the verb 'write':

	3SG	3PL
ACTIVE		
PRES:(DUR)	γráf-i	γráf-un
PAST:DUR	é-γraf-e	é-γraf-an
PAST:PUNCT	é-γrap-s-e	é-γrap-s-an
PASSIVE		
PRES:(DUR)	γráf-ete	γráf-onde
PAST:DUR	γraf-ótan	γráf-ondan
PAST:PUNCT	γráf-tik-e	γráf-tik-an

Note that some fragments of paradigm (8) are more "agglutinative" than others; the less agglutinative forms are, obviously, those of present and past durative (imperfective) passive, where all the five grammatical meanings are concentrated in a single non-segmentable suffix. Active past forms, by contrast, are the most agglutinative (thus almost approaching the Persian pattern in 7). Passive past punctual forms lie in between, since they consist of two grammatical markers. One of them (*-tik-*) expresses aspect in cumulation with voice, while tense is expressed in cumulation with subject, person, and number.

The lack of cumulation is often thought of as being the most characteristic parameter of agglutination. In fact, the most striking and easily observable properties of agglutinative languages (such as a considerable length of word-forms and an additive character of most morpheme complexes) are direct consequences of this parameter, because a non-cumulative word-form obviously must be longer than a cumulative word-form with the same grammatical meaning. On the other hand, combinations of (uniform and regular) grammatical markers are more additive than any other combinations of morphemes. All this explains largely why, for many linguists, additiveness is the main property of agglutination; cf. a typical formulation:

"In an agglutinative system, every word contains a root that provides its basic lexical meaning and a string of affixes arranged on either side of the root, each one of which has a meaning of its own, such that the meaning of the whole word is the sum of the meanings of its parts" (Aronoff & Sridhar 1984: 3).

Still, this is not a definition of agglutination, but only a description of one of its very typical consequences.

3. Connections between the parameters

The three parameters of agglutination just discussed (the lack of fusion on morpheme junctures, the lack of non-phonological variation and the absence of cumulation) are, by and large, independent. Languages may have only one or two of them, and any combinations are, in principle, possible. Thus, the Armenian nominal declension has neither fusion nor cumulation, but is characterized by widespread lexically conditioned variation of affixes. The Finnish nominal declension has no (or very little) cumulation, but fusion and grammatically conditioned variation are well represented in Finnish. The Hungarian declension, in turn, has very little cumulation and fusion, but all types of non-phonological variation are well attested, and so on.

On the other hand, some relationships are statistically more recurrent than others. Of special importance is the fact that cumulation implies, as a rule, both phonological (fusion) and non-phonological variation. This is by no means an accident, because, historically, cumulation and non-uniformity are a frequent consequence of fusion, i.e. of phonological assimilation of adjacent morphemes in the speech chain.

4. Agglutination as a manifestation of greater morpheme autonomy

4.1. General remarks

We have considered three traditional parameters specifying what are usually characterized as agglutinative features. Now, the question arises whether these parameters may be accounted for by some other more general property. We have already seen that these parameters are related historically and tend to co-occur in a non-random way.

In search of such a common denominator for all the traditional parameters of agglutination we can direct our attention to the following fact. All manifestations of agglutination can be interpreted as related to one common characteristic, namely, the **greater autonomy** of morphemes in agglutinative languages. In other terms, agglutinative affixes are much closer to roots than non-agglutinative affixes as far as their phonological, morphological, syntactic and grammatical properties are concerned — to the extent that often the boundary between agglutinative affixes and autonomous words is hard to draw. Moreover, another more precise (and probably stronger) claim can be made: the rules specifying how agglutinative morphemes are combined with each other are more syntactic than morphological by their nature and thus are closer to rules specifying how word-forms are combined with each other. In a sense, an ideal agglutinative language is a language without complex word-forms: each morpheme in such a language tends to behave like an autonomous word, and not like a part of a word.

All the traditional parameters described in § 2.1−2.3 are easy to explain assuming this general property. Indeed, both sandhi (and hence complete fusion) and non-phonological variation tend to occur rather word-internally than with respect to autonomous units. (As a rare example of non-phonological variation affecting the choice of an autonomous word within a syntactic construction, the use of the auxiliaries 'be' and 'have' in Romance languages such as French or Italian may be considered.)

However, besides the traditional parameters just discussed, agglutinative languages display many other interesting properties which, in the long run, also follow from the non-autonomous character of agglutinative markers. We shall restrict ourselves to two groups of such properties, which may be included under the headings of syntactic and grammatical autonomy, respectively.

4.2. Manifestations of syntactic autonomy

Syntactic autonomy underlies the agglutinative technique of assembling morphemes and clearly opposes agglutinative and flective/fusional morpheme complexes. A number of particular manifestations of such syntactic autonomy can be distinguished, namely:

− the scope of agglutinative affixes can be extended over several stems, and so one and the same nominal affix can apply, for example, to a coordinated group of nouns (9) or to an analytical word-form (10);

− the linear order of agglutinative affixes within a word-form is more free as compared to flective ones; in particular, agglutinative affixes allow permutations and other variations in their linear order (11−12);

− both agglutinative stems and affixes have a greater freedom as far as their combinability with each other is concerned; the most conspicuous realization of this property are the so-called **transcategorial uses** of agglutinative affixes, when one and the same grammatical marker is allowed to occur on stems of different word classes (nouns, verbs, adjectives, and so on), cf. examples (13)−(15). It is well known that flective languages are not only devoid of transcategorial uses, but even within one and the same word class different grammatical markers of the same category are used (cf. numerous examples of lexically conditioned variation like those mentioned in § 2.2.).

Below, some linguistic data will be listed which exemplify these manifestations of syntactic autonomy.

Constructions of the type (9 a−b) (belonging to the stock examples of typological works) illustrate the possibility of an agglutinative affix to be applicable to a coordinated group.

(9) (a) Turkish
    bayan ve bay-lar
    lady and gentleman-PL
    'ladies and gentlemen'
 (b) Spanish
    clara y precisa-mente
    clear and precise-ADV
    'clearly and precisely'
 (c) Tokharian A (Schmidt 1969: 107)
    kukl-as yuk-as
    cart-OBL:PL horse-OBL:PL
    oṅkälm-ās-yo
    elephant-OBL:PL-INSTR
    'with carts, horses and elephants'

(Note that, in the Tokharian phrase, all the coordinated nouns have a marker of plural oblique stem, but only the last noun bears the marker of the instrumental case.)

Another type of word-like affix is attested in Dogon (Niger-Congo, Mali), where an agentive suffix -nɛ may occur not only on synthetic (10a), but also on analytic word-forms (in (10b), a form of past resultative is given). (ANT = anterior)

(10) Dogon
 (a) dɔnɔ-dɛ
  sell-PRES:HAB(3SG)
  'he sells'
  dɔnɔ-dɛ-nɛ
  sell-PRES:HAB-AGT
  'one who sells, seller'
 (b) dɔn-a be
  sell-ANT be:PAST(3SG)
  'he had sold'
  dɔn-a be-nɛ
  sell-ANT be:PAST-AGT
  'one who had sold, former seller'

If, in English, forms of the type (10b) were possible, they would take the form, for example, *haver sold (for more details, see Plungian 1999); in English, however, derivational morphemes never display such a degree of autonomy. In any case, Dogon is not unique in this respect: for instance, the Basque agentive marker -dun- shows a very similar set of properties.

The possibility of linear permutations of agglutinative affixes within a word-form is illustrated by the data from Eastern Mari and Erzia Mordvinian nominal declension systems (both belong to Finno-Ugric family).

(11) Eastern Mari
 (a) taŋ-βlak-em or taŋ-em-βlak
  friend-PL-1SG
  'my friends'
 (b) čeβer-eš-em or čeβer-em-eš
  beautiful-LOC-1SG
  'in my beautiful ...'

(12) Erzia Mordvinian
 (a) kudo-do-nt'
  house-ABL-DEF:SG
  'from the house'
 (b) kudo-tn'e-d'e
  house-DEF:PL-ABL
  'from the houses'

In Mari, the possessive marker may occur before or after case and number suffixes; the corresponding forms are in free variation. The Erzia example (a fragment of the so-called "definite declension") demonstrates the variability of another kind: this is a variability concerning the linear position of an affix within a paradigm (i.e., depending on the morphological context). Singular case forms, as shown in (12a), require a case marker to precede the cumulative marker of number and definiteness, while in plural forms the order is just the opposite: a case marker follows the marker of the definite plural.

Let us now turn to the phenomenon of transcategorial use of agglutinative affixes. Example (13) illustrates an unusually broad combinability of the diminutive/laudative suffix -ke in Mansi.

(13) Mansi, diminutive marker:
 (a) on nouns:
  sāli 'reindeer'
  sāli-ke 'little (good) reindeer'
 (b) on numerals:
  low 'ten'
  low-ke 'ten good...'
 (c) on verbs:
  toti 'he is carrying (something)'
  toti-ke 'he is carrying (something) with pleasure'

Example (14) gives some Udmurt affixes which may freely occur both on verbal and nominal stems.

(14) Udmurt, grading and negation
 (a) on adjectives (grading):
  vil' 'new'
  vil'-ges '[somewhat] newer'
 (b) on nouns (caritive):
  val 'horse'
  val-tek 'without a horse'
 (c) on verbs:
  malpa-sa 'having thought'
  think-CONV
  malpa-sa-ges 'having thought a little'
  malpa-tek 'not having thought'
  malpa-tek-ges 'having thought not enough'

Besides, many agglutinative languages (from Mansi to Quechua) show a very significant similarity (up to a full identity) between nominal possessive markers, on the one hand, and verbal agreement markers, on the other. For example, in Mansi there is a full coincidence between nominal possessive markers and person/number markers of verbal subjects in the so-called object conjugation (used, roughly, in the case of a definite object). As for person/number markers of the verbal subject in an "objectless" conjugation (when the object is non-definite or is lacking), they differ from possessive markers only in 3rd person; instead, the markers of a 3rd person subject in the objectless conjugation are identical to other nominal markers, namely, to those of nominal number (which are zero for singular, *-iγ* for dual, and *-ǝt* for plural, as shown, in particular, in (4 a)). For a recent overview of this issue, see Siewierska 1998.

It is worth noting that transcategorial uses are most typical of analytic languages (like Polynesian languages), which convey their main grammatical meanings with the help of auxiliaries and not affixes; these auxiliaries usually have a broad combinability and may operate both in nominal and verbal domains. This is another piece of evidence for the set of properties agglutinative affixes share with autonomous words.

Syntactically, autonomous and transcategorial affixes are obviously much more widespread in agglutinative languages than in flective ones; nevertheless, the phenomenon is not restricted exclusively to agglutinative languages. Sporadically, similar examples are found also in flective languages. Spanish coordinated adverbs were already discussed under (9 b); another interesting example concerns the transcategorial use of the Portuguese diminutive/evaluative suffix *-inh-*, cf. (15).

(15) Portuguese diminutive marker
    (a) on nouns:
        livr-o 'book'
        book-M:SG
        livr-inh-o 'small book'
        book-DIM-M:SG
    (b) on adjectivals:
        obrig-ad-o
        oblige-PTCP:PAST-M:SG
        'thank you', lit. '[I am] obliged'
        obrig-ad-inh-o 'thank you, my dear'
        oblige-PTCP:PAST-DIM-M:SG
    (c) on verbs:
        escrev-er 'to write'
        write-INF
        escrev-inh-ar 'to write insipid things'
        write-DIM-INF

4.3. Manifestations of grammatical autonomy

As far as their grammatical autonomy is concerned, agglutinative affixes contrast with flective affixes in a very special way, so that their connection to auxiliaries of analytic languages becomes, once more, quite evident. It is well known that flective languages are characterized by a fairly distinct boundary between inflection and derivation. In flective languages, inflectional markers form equipollent oppositions (cf. Chvany 1993) and are organized into paradigms consisting of a small set of mutually exclusive elements. Derivational markers, on the other hand, are generally non-productive and idiomatic. There are no (or very few) really productive derivational markers; their lack forms a gap separating inflection from derivation in a rather clear manner (the amount of intermediate cases being often negligible).

By contrast, derivational markers found in agglutinative languages are, as a rule, productive; hence they are closer to inflectional markers of flective languages. On the other hand, inflectional markers in agglutinative languages tend to form privative (and not equipollent) oppositions and are less likely to be organized into small commensurable paradigms.

Thus, in agglutinative languages the boundary between "prototypical" (i. e. found in flective languages) inflection and derivation is blurred, since, in many respects, agglutinative derivation approaches inflection, and agglutinative inflection approaches derivation.

So far, the problem of a universal definition of inflection and derivation is still unsolved. It should be noted, however, that the type of grammatical systems found in agglutinative languages is closer to what occurs in analytic and isolating languages; at the same time, the morphological structure of the word (namely, the abundant use of affixes) is more like that of flective languages. Agglutination is intermediate.

Let us take one typical case as a brief illustration of what has just been said. In most agglutinative languages (like Turkic or Finno-Ugric), the plural of nouns is expressed by an affixal marker − similarly to flective Indo-European patterns. However, the semantics of such plural forms is different and is closer to what is encountered in languages where the plural is marked with an auxiliary particle, and not with an affix (as in Korean, Burmese and others). Indeed, forms without a plural marker (whether they have a zero singular marker or no number marking at all, is at issue) do not necessarily denote one object, but may also denote any number of indefinite objects, as well as a set of objects which form a single whole (like 'teeth', 'children', etc.). The same unmarked form is used, as a rule, in numeral constructions, i.e. in those cases where information about the number of objects is already present in the sentence.

Thus, not only number, but also other grammatical categories may be said to be non-obligatory in agglutinative languages (or, at least, to be less obligatory than those of flective languages); they form privative rather than equipollent oppositions and defy their description in terms of inflectional paradigms. This is more typical of analytic grammatical systems where grammatical meanings are conveyed by autonomous markers and are less likely to be obligatory (cf. Bybee & Dahl 1989).

Besides the different nature of grammatical oppositions, inflectional morphemes of agglutinative languages show another property which brings them closer to the derivational domain: they tend to convey derivational meanings almost as frequently as derivational markers themselves do. Grammatical systems of flective languages are organized according to a strong principle that derivational markers apply only to stems, and not to word-forms: stems include only a root and other derivational elements, but not inflectional ones (several counterexamples like the frequently cited German *Kinder-chen* are obviously marginal for flective systems). In agglutinative languages, however, this principle (known also as "inflection outside derivation") seems to be violated more systematically. New words may be derived equally well both from what we would like to call stems and from what we would like to call word-forms. Cf. one characteristic example of agglutinative derivation taken from Basque (in (16), *-tu* is a marker of one of the non-finite verbal forms, usually taken as a citation form).

(16) Basque, denominal verbs (Lafitte 1978: 205)
 (a) *etxe-ra* 'to [a] house; home'
  house-ALL
  etxe-ra-tu 'go home'
 (b) *etxe-ta-ra* 'to houses'
  house-PL-ALL
  etxe-ta-ra-tu 'go to one's own houses'
 (c) *etxe-ko* 'at home'
  house-GEN
  etxe-ko-tu 'get used to'

The Dogon deverbal nouns given in (10) illustrate the same phenomenon: the derivational suffix of agentive nouns occurs after inflectional markers of tense and aspect.

Another manifestation of derivational properties found in agglutinative inflection is the possibility of a double use of one and the same inflectional marker in the word-form (which is clearly at odds with the obligatory status of inflectional markers). Such examples are not uncommon; among them, double plural and case markers are attested most frequently (cf. the interesting material in Plank 1996).

5. The diachronic dimension

All the properties outlined here have an obvious diachronic explanation. Historically, flection arises from agglutination (going through the intermediate stage of fusion), agglutination, in turn, arises from analytic and/or isolating systems. All these are stages of one and the same process, which may be described as a gradual loss of syntactic (and morphological) autonomy of linguistic units; this process is one of the most conspicuous components of grammaticalization (cf. Lehmann 1982/1995; Heine & Reh 1984). Every agglutination seems to be a "yesterday's analytism", i.e. it is morphology which *was* syntax (and in fact did not completely cease to be). Therefore, many genuine morphological notions (such as paradigm, grammatical category, word-form, and so on) pose problems for the description of agglutinative languages; instead, an intermediate "morphosyntactic" terminology seems to cope better when it makes use of notions such as clitics, idiomaticity and productivity, template structure, and so on. Agglutinative languages thus pose serious problems for any attempt to draw a clear boundary between morphology and syntax.

To summarize, the distinction between agglutination and flection appears to be, as we have tried to show, something much more profound than a mere opposition of two different morphological techniques.

6. Special abbreviations

AGT	agentive
ALL	allative
ANT	anterior
DIM	diminutive
PUNCT	punctual

7. References

Aronoff, Mark & Sridhar, S.N. 1984. "Agglutination and composition in Kannada verb morphology". In: Testen, D. et al. (eds.), *Papers from the Parasession on lexical semantics*. Chicago: Chicago Linguistic Society, 3–20.

Bybee, Joan L. & Dahl, Östen. 1989. "The creation of tense and aspect systems in the languages of the world". *Studies in Language* 13: 51–103.

Chvany, Catherine V. 1993. "The evolution of the concept of markedness from the Prague circle to generative grammar". In: Yokoyama, O. T. & Klenin, E. (eds.) 1996. *Selected essays of Catherine V. Chvany*. Columbus (OH): Slavica, 234–241.

Croft, William. 1990. *Typology and universals*. Cambridge: Cambridge University Press.

Dahl, Östen. 1985. *Tense and aspect systems*. Oxford: Blackwell.

Dressler, Wolfgang U. 1985. *Morphonology: the dynamics of derivation*. Ann Arbor: Karoma.

Dressler, Wolfgang U. & Mayerthaler, Willi & Panagl, Oswald & Wurzel, Wolfgang U. 1987. *Leitmotifs in natural morphology*. Amsterdam: Benjamins.

Greenberg, Joseph H. 1960. "A quantitative approach to the morphological typology of language". *International Journal of American Linguistics* 26: 178–194.

Greenberg, Joseph H. 1974. *Language typology: a historical and analytic overview*. The Hague: Mouton.

Heine, Bernd & Reh, Mechthild. 1984. *Grammaticalization and reanalysis in African languages*. Hamburg: Buske.

Kasevič, Vadim B. & Sergej E. Jaxontov. (eds.). 1982. *Kvantitativnaja tipologija jazykov Azii i Afriki* [Quantitative typology of languages of Asia and Africa]. Leningrad: LGU.

Kilani-Schoch, Marianne. 1988. *Introduction à la morphologie naturelle*. Bern: Lang.

Lafitte, Pierre. 1978. *Grammaire basque (navarro-labourdin littéraire)*. Donostia: Elkar.

Lehmann, Christian. 1982/1995. *Thoughts on grammaticalization*. München: LINCOM Europa, 2nd ed..

Mel'čuk, Igor A. 1982. *Towards a language of linguistics: a system of formal notions for theoretical morphology*. München: Fink.

Plank, Frans (ed.). 1996. *Double case*. Amsterdam: Benjamins.

Plungian, Vladimir A. 1999. "Agentive nouns in Dogon: neither derivation nor inflection?" In: Rennison, John (ed.). *Morphologica 1996*. Amsterdam: Holland Academic Graphics, 179–190.

Sapir, Edward. 1921. *Language*. New Work: Harcourt, Brace & World.

Schmidt, Karl Horst. 1969. "Agglutination und Postposition im Tocharischen". *Münchener Studien zur Sprachwissenschaft* 25: 105–112.

Siewierska, Anna. 1998. "On nominal and verbal person marking". *Linguistic Typology* 2: 1–55.

Skalička, Vladimir. 1966. "Ein 'typologisches Konstrukt'". In: V. Skalička. *Typologische Studien*. Braunschweig: Vieweg, 1979, 335–341.

Vladimir A. Plungian
Institute of Linguistics, RAS, Moscow
(Russia)

50. Introflection

1. The term introflection
2. Examples of introflection from the world's languages
3. Theoretical approaches to introflection
4. Conclusion
5. Special Abbreviations
6. References

1. The term introflection

1.1. Definition

Skalička (1979: 54) characterizes **introflection** as a morphological system in which "die Anhäufung der Bedeutungen die Wortwurzel betrifft", that is, one in which word roots are the locus of morphological marking. He contrasts it to his four other language types (isolating, agglutinating, (in)flectional, and polysynthetic) in which word roots retain their integrity, with morphological marking accomplished via suffixation, periphrasis, or compounding. Skalička construes introflection broadly, citing examples from **ablaut** and **umlaut** systems (German alternations such as *Vater: Väter* and *trinken: tranken*; English plurals like *goose: geese*), and notes that, in any particular language, it "nur bis zu einem gewissen Grad zur Geltung kommt" (1979: 54). He finds some degree of introflection in Celtic, Germanic, and Tibetan languages, and cites the more universally accepted examples of Afro-Asiatic languages. His only examples of introflection are small samples from Arabic; he may have been only superficially familiar with the Semitic languages, which display the most extreme forms of introflection.

1.2. Alternate terminology

What Skalička termed **introflection** would be included today in the broad category of **nonconcatenative** or **discontinuous morphology**, particular manifestations of which have spurred recent theoretical innovations, especially as concerns prosodic elements such as the syllable, mora and foot. These include reduplication and what is variously called **shape-invariant** or **templatic** morphology (McCarthy 1982, McCarthy & Prince 1990a, 1990b), the latter being the mapping of root segments onto templates or patterns of fixed CV shape (e. g., CVCCVC or σ σ, where σ = syllable) with morphosyntactic meanings such as plural or perfect. The interdigitating morphology of the Semitic type, known traditionally as **root-and-pattern** (henceforth **R&P**) morphology, continues to be a major focus of interest. In this article, I will focus on theoretical treatments of R&P morphology within the Semitic languages, because these languages are the most extreme examples of introflection, and because they have been the subject of the widest variety of theoretical approaches.

2. Examples of introflection from the world's languages

What follows is a selection of examples of introflection from a wide variety of language families, moving from what might be considered the least to the most radical introflecting techniques.

2.1. Introflection involving individual segments of the root

This would include root/stem-internal modification strategies such as **ablaut, umlaut**, and **consonant mutation**. These are among the longest-known and best-studied phenomena, since they are common in Indo-European languages such as Proto-Indo-European itself as reconstructed, the Germanic and Celtic languages. Examples of plural marking deriving from umlaut (a process of regressive height or roundness assimilation effected by a suffix vowel on a root vowel) such as Modern German *Buch: Bücher, Ofen: Öfen, Rad: Räder* ('book', 'oven', and 'wheel', respectively) and English *foot: feet, mouse: mice* have already been cited. **Ablaut** (also known as **apophony**) also names a change in a vowel of the root, this time of purely morphological motivation within the known history of the language. Examples include past-tense and past-participle formation in Germanic languages such as German and English: German *singen: sangen: gesungen* parallels English *sing: sang: sung*; similarly German *brechen: brachen: gebrochen* and English *break: broke: broken*. As will be noted below, some theorists have proposed that much Semitic R&P morphology is ablaut.

Consonant mutation is a process in which morphologically-marked forms of a word show a change in a consonantal segment (especially the initial segment of the root). Although phenomena labeled as consonant mutation are listed as occurring in widely distinct language families − Athabaskan vs. Bantu, for example − the best-known mutation examples are from the Celtic languages, as shown in (1).

(1)   Gloss   Irish Gaelic   Welsh
    (a) dog   *ku:*   *ki:*
    (b) his dog   *ə xu:*   *i gi:*
    (c) her dog   *ə ku:*   *i xi:*

2.2. Discontinuous markers: circumfixes, suprafixes, transfixes

We should probably include in a discussion of discontinuous morphology morphological markers which, though they do not affect the root, are discontinuous in themselves: **circumfixes**. These are prefix-suffix pairs that consistently convey particular meanings, neither of whose members ever appears alone. These seem particularly common as markers of negation.

(2)   Yucatec Mayan (William Fisher, personal communication)
    (a) *leti*
        'that one'
    (b) **maʔ-** *leti-*   **-ʔi**
        NEG- that one- NEG
        'not that one'
    (c) *ʔinkaat*
        'I want (it)'
    (d) **maʔ-** *inkaat-*   **-ʔi**
        NEG- I want (it)- NEG
        'I don't want (it)'
    (e) *ʃbaaloob*
        'female things'
    (f) **leʔ-** *ʃbaaloob*   **-ʔo**
        DEM- female things- DEM
        'those girls over there'

(3) Lewo (Oceanic) (Robert Early, personal communication)
(a) ne-   ligan -ko
    1.SG.SUBJ- leave- 2SG.OBJ
    'I will leave you'
(b) **na-** ligan -ko   **-ena**
    NOM- leave- 2SG.OBJ -NOM
    'the leaving of you/your being left'

Suprafixes affect the segmental or suprasegmental structure of the root. The vowel changes of languages such as Arabic and Hebrew (see the discussion of R&P morphology in § 2.5) are sometimes classified as suprafixes or 'transfixes' (Kilani-Schoch & Dressler 1985) because they, so to speak, 'spread across' the root, displacing root vowels. Suprafixes signal morphological categories by changing the stress of tone patterns of a root. (4) shows an example from Ancient Greek of stress as a suprasegmental morphological marker.

(4) Ancient Greek (Brugmann 1906: 27f., cited in Becker 1993: 8)
(a) *potós*   'drunk'
    pótos   'a drink'
(b) *dolikhós*   'long'
    dólikhos   '(long) racetrack'
(c) *leukós*   'white'
    leûkos   'whitefish'
(d) *aspʰódelos* 'asphodel (plant)'
    aspʰodelós 'covered with asphodel'

2.3. 'Root-interrupters': subtractive morphology, infixes, reduplication

Root-interrupting morphology imposes discontinuities on a base; **subtractive** morphology truncates the base. The Uto-Aztecan language Tohono O'odham, for example, forms the completive by deleting the final syllable of the base.

(5) Tohono O'odham truncation (data from Hale (1965), cited in Becker (1993: 4))
incompletive completive gloss
huḑuni   *huḑu*   'descend'
ki.ḑiwa   *ki.ḑi*   'shell (corn)'
ta:pana   *ta:pa*   'split'
bidima   *bidi*   'turn around'
dagaṣapa   *dagaṣa*   'give'

Infixes interrupt the base by inserting segmental or syllabic material within the root. A frequently-cited example is the Philippine language Bontok, in which the infix *-um-* changes a noun or adjective base into a copular verb: *fikas* 'strong', *fumikas* 'to be/become strong'; *bato* 'stone', *bumato* 'to be/become stone'; *fusul* 'enemy', *fumusul* 'to be/become an enemy'.

Reduplication is not only very widespread in the world's languages, but also extremely interesting as a theoretical problem. Reduplication is often iconic; for instance, it is used in various languages to mark plural, iterative, distributive, intensive, and similar meanings. The simplest type of reduplication repeats the whole base, as in Bahasa Indonesia *anakanak*, plural of *anak* 'child'. In other cases, only a portion of the base is reduplicated, at either margin of the base. Tagalog forms the irrealis imperfective of verbs by reduplicating the first syllable of the base: *bili* 'buy' becomes *bibili*, *kuha* 'get' becomes *kukuha*; *upo* 'sit' becomes *uupo*. Hausa data exemplify reduplication of base-final material, as well as the fact that the reduplicated portion of the base may have its own prosodic and segmental specifications. The completive of verbs appears to conform to a template *CCe*, with the last consonant in the base filling the C-slots: *cika* 'fill' becomes completive *cikakke*, *jefa* 'throw' becomes *jefaffe*. Durativity or continuous/distributed action is shown in Hausa by prefixing a template CVC onto the base, using the segmental material of the first syllable of the base as follows: *buga* 'beat' becomes *bubbuga* 'keep on beating'; *kikkira* 'call various people' derives from *kira* 'call'. Analysis of reduplication often shows that the shape of the affix is governed not just by phonological constraints of the language, but by specification of a certain syllable shape in the morphology.

2.4. Templatic or shape-invariant morphology

The observation of this last fact — that the shape of reduplicating affixes is often specified in metrical units, and may have its own partial segmental specifications apart from those of the root — led to the development of the notion of **shape-invariant** or **templatic** morphology, according to which the syllabic shape of a morphological marker may be lexicalized; the root then comprises segments in a certain sequence, which are used to fill C and V positions in this syllabic shape. For example, McCarthy & Prince (1994: 12), analyzing data from Shetler (1976), describe reduplicative affixes in Balangao (Austronesian) (see (6)) as consisting of two syllables, the second of which cannot have a coda. This two-syllable affix is filled in with only as much segmental material from the root as is needed. This analysis accounts in a unified way for the common characteristics of affixes derived from very different bases.

(6) Balangao (Austronesian) (McCarthy & Prince 1994: 13)

Base	Reduplicated form Gloss
(a) ka ... ʔuma	ka-**ʔuma**-ʔuma 'always making fields'
(b) ka ... ʔabulot	ka-**ʔabu**-ʔabulot 'believers of everything'
(c) ma ... taynan	ma-**tayna**-taynan 'repeatedly be left behind'
(d) maŋ ... tagtag	ma-**nagta**-tagtag 'running everywhere/repeatedly'

Templatic morphology is thought to be involved not only in affixation, but in the derivation of stems, some basic (lexical), some simultaneously expressing several morpholexical categories. Archangeli (1979: 106–108), for example, discusses a subclass of Yawelmani (Amerindian) verbs whose roots are disyllabic, with a long second vowel and with lexically-specified vowel patterns: *CaCa:(C)-*, *CiCe:(C)-*, *CoCo:(C)-*, and *CuCo:(C)-*, e. g., *p'axa:t'-al* 'might mourn', *hibe:y-al* 'might bring water', *yolo:w-ol* 'might assemble'. By far the most famous example of this phenomenon is the Semitic family of languages, which display the most radical of all introflecting strategies: interdigitation of discontinuous morphemes, discussed in § 2.5. Shape-invariant morphology is a major subject of analysis in Optimality Theory (§ 3.2.4).

2.5. Interdigitation of discontinuous root morphemes with discontinuous 'transfixes': Root and pattern morphology

In R&P morphology, lexemes and grammatical morphemes are either discontinuous or underspecified, and interdigitate or map to one another to form word stems. R&P morphology seems to be attested only in Afro-Asiatic languages (Carstairs-McCarthy, p. c.; Dryer, p. c.); it is most alive in the verbal morphology, with its presence in nominal and other categories varying across Semitic languages. The lexeme may have two, three, or four consonants; these, called consonantal roots, are mapped into templates. In Classical Arabic, stem vowels are also discontinuous morphemes expressing voice; in most other Semitic languages, the stem vowels and the template together signal a morphological category such as preterite, imperative, or agentive noun. Hudson (1974) analyzes the Cushitic language Beja, for example, as having some biliteral (two-consonant) and triliteral (three-consonant) verb roots; these clearly fill positions in templates, as shown in (7).

(7) Beja (Cushitic) (Hudson 1974: 133–135)

	l-w 'burn'	d-b-l 'collect'
(a) 1 SG PRES	anlíiw	adanbíl
(b) 3M SG PRES	inlíiw	danbíl
(c) 1 PL PRES	neelíiw	needbíl
(d) 1 SG PAST iterative	loowán	adaabíl
(e) positive IMP M	liwa	dibil'a
F	liwi	dibil'i
(f) past participle	liwa	dibla

R&P is still robust in the verb system of major Semitic languages. Some examples of stem forms from major Semitic languages are given in (8)-(9).

(8) Preterite stem forms in Classical Arabic (McCarthy 1982) and Modern Hebrew (Bat El 1989)

Binyan Preterite	Arabic (root *k-t-b* 'write')	Hebrew (roots *g-n-v* 'steal'; *g-d-l* 'grow')
I	katab	ganav
II	kattab	nignav
III	kaatab	higdil
IV	ʔaktab	gidel
V	takattab	hitgadel
VI	takaatab	–
VII	ntatab	–
VIII	ktatab	–
IX	ktabab	–
X	staktab	–

(9) Stem forms for Amharic (Yimam 1994: 106–108) and Modern Aramaic (Rubba 1993)

Stem	Amharic *s-b-r* 'break'	Modern Aramaic (Fellihi dialect) *p-l-x* 'work'
infinitive	məsbər	plax-
imperfective	sabr-	palx-(3MSG *paalix*)
perfective	sabbər	plix-
subjunctive	sbər	–
imperative	sibər	ploox
agent noun	sabar	palax-
verbal noun	səbər-	palox-
result/instance noun	sibbir-	pilx-

In Classical Arabic, each stem form can be analyzed into three parts: the lexical root (*k-t-b* 'write', for instance), the vowel melody (in the preterite, *a-a* signals active voice while *u-i* signals passive voice), and the template (CVCVC for Binyan I, CVCCVC for Binyan II, CVVCVC for III, etc.). In Modern Hebrew or Modern Aramaic, on the other hand, verb-root lexemes such as *g-n-v* 'steal' or *p-l-x* 'work' can be extracted, but the stem vowels cannot be analyzed as a morpheme separate from the syllabic shape of the stem; they must be prespecified: Modern Aramaic *CaCaC*- 'agentive noun', for example, contrasts with *CaCoC*- 'verbal noun' in vocalic melody, but no meaning can be connected with the vowels separate from the syllable structure.

The next section reviews theoretical approaches to this highly challenging kind of morphology.

3. Theoretical approaches to introflection

The principal problems that R&P morphology raises for linguistics are (a) what to select as the basic unit of lexical/morphological representation, (b) how to represent the internal structure of words, and (c) how to represent derivational relationships. Clearly, these three issues are intimately related; the crucial decision, however, is (a), since this can dictate the possible options for (b) and (c).

These are problematic issues because R&P systems violate highly-valued ideals of linguistics: that linguistic forms such as morphemes, stems, and words be made up of contiguous segments; that these units combine by simple linear concatenation; and that forms and meanings neatly line up, making word formation a simple matter of transparent combination of the meanings of concatenated forms. If these conditions hold, derivational relationships are also easy to model, since all that are needed are means for describing occurring combinations of forms, whether by descriptive statement in paradigms or item-and-arrangement lists, or by morphological processes in derivations.

These ideals have been incorporated into linguistic theory sometimes quite explicitly. In American structuralism, for example, irregularities such as ablaut ('process morphemes'), 'empty morphs' and 'cranberry morphs' were viewed as significant difficulties; they forced modifications in morphological theory which drove it farther and farther from these ideals (Hockett (1954), Aronoff (1976)). Natural Morphology incorporates the above ideals as universal preferences for morpheme shape and word formation, i. e. as criteria for evaluation for semiotic fitness (Dressler et al. 1987). Golston's (1996) version of Optimality Theory includes CONTIGUITY of a stem as a general constraint.

If we choose to analyze R&P languages as possessing morphemes comprising non-contiguous segments, this is in clear violation of the ideal. In turn, it forces us to modify our models of word formation and derivational relationships so that these accomplish the correct intercalations; it is clear that simple concatenation processes that work for concatenating languages will not do. If on the other hand we choose not to admit discontinuous morphemes, then our models of word formation and derivation must violate the ideals, for instance by positing massive ablaut rules; this option also requires choice of a contiguously-constituted basic form from which others can neatly be derived. It should be noted that these approaches are not mutually exclusive; several accounts of R&P morphology incorporate both isolation of discontinuous morphemes and derivation of some forms from other, already-intercalated forms.

Modern attempts to account for R&P morphology have striven to admit R&P languages into either the typological mainstream (i. e., they are not so different from other languages as they initially appear) or the mainstream of linguistic theory (they may well be typologically strange, but they are accountable using standard theoretical devices); sometimes both. This striving has become more conscious and more explicit in recent decades.

In the summary beginning in the next section, I will describe the choices various linguistic theories have made with respect to (a), (b) and (c) above. I have selected theories based not only on how well-known they have become within linguistics, but also on their relative importance in the current competition among various approaches (for example, generative, functionalist, and cognitivist). Some are also selected for their historical importance, which often means their contribution to later theory.

3.1. The ancients: the Medieval Arab grammarians

The great grammarians of Classical Arabic had a well-developed theory of the language, evolving from the eighth to the fifteenth centuries A.D., many principles of which are shared by modern linguistics (Bohas, Guillaume & Kouloughli 1990; Owens 1988). Most medieval Arabic grammarians combined discontinuous morphemes with a word-based analysis, conceiving of the derivation of word stems as a process mediated by numerous other full forms with the same root. The most basic form of a word, the *maSdar*, (a nominalization), was formed first by combining its vocalized template with a particular root; the result was then available for further modification to produce other forms, "[t]he central idea being that every element in the chain of derivation cumulates the 'grammatical meanings' of those which precede it and adds another one" (Bohas, Guillaume & Kouloughli 1990: 76).

The representation of R&P morphology via paradigms relating numerous forms containing the same lexical root was also proposed, however; and shades of a templatic approach are also found, in that a single verb root, f-ʕ-l 'do', was used to stand in for other roots and hence exemplify all known patterns in all word classes.

Not all the nonlinear elements of the forms − root consonants, vowel melodies, and CV patterns − were viewed as discrete formal units (although they were viewed as contributing distinct meanings to the whole). Strikingly absent in the Arabs' grammatical theories is the isolation of vowel patterns as distinct form/meaning pairings, as in the work of McCarthy (1982).

The reason for the Arabs' preference for word-based morphology seems to be their strong resistance to recognizing roots, vowel melodies, and syllabic shapes of words as discrete *kalima*, the nearest the Arabs come to the notion 'morpheme'. This notion was defined in strictly linear or concatenative terms.

3.2. The generative tradition

3.2.1. Harris

Of major interest in view of later developments is Harris (1941), a classic of American structuralism − "an attempt to state the structure of Hebrew (of 600 B.C.) in terms of a formal method, which asks only what forms exist and in what combinations" (1941: 143). The bulk of the work is devoted to listing the occurring phonemic and morphemic elements plus distribution statements for classes of elements. He gives three types of morphemes: linearly concatenated words and affixes; roots, which consist of consonants only; and "patterns, [which] consist of vowels, vowels plus [length], or vowels plus an affix" (1941: 152). For example, the pattern --*u*- means "active action"; -*a-i-* "object having a particular quality"; *n-a-i-* "middle [voice] action" (Harris 1941: 152; hyphens are consonant positions). Each morpheme type covers "a particular range of meaning: Roots refer to individual phenomena (break, large, stone). Patterns refer to relations of these phenomena (being passive, an object, a quality)" (1941: 152).

Word formation is a generalized description of occurring patterns: minimally, a stem consisting of either a linearly concatenated sequence or a consonantal root intercalated in a pattern. As to nonlinear stem formation, he notes simply that roots and patterns "must occur with each other" (1941: 163) and that roots of 2, 3, or 4 consonants occur "[i]ntercalated in patterns" (1941: 160, morpheme distribution statement number 8). Certain complications of word structure are dealt with under the rubric of morpheme alternations: for example, there are several variants of the active vowel pattern --*u*-, including -*u-u-*, -*a-u-*, and others, which appear in specific phonological or morphological environments. The main alternant is chosen on the basis of its more general distribution and the lack of conditioning factors in its context.

Harris' analysis is symptomatic of the move away from process models in American structuralism (cf. Hockett 1954); but some process language persists, and in some places it seems that an ordered derivation is implied: "The morphophonemic formulas must be considered as operative all the time, even after the morpheme-variant formulas have been applied ... In some cases the order [of application of formulas] is necessary" (1941: 159).

Thus Harris includes both continuous and discontinuous, specified and underspecified morphemes in his model, but does not concern himself with formulating a word formation apparatus that would guarantee the existing intercalations. As to derivational relationships, he appears to limit his interest to morphophonological alternants, and to satisfy himself with simply stating the contexts in which such alternants appear.

3.2.2. Chomsky

Chomsky (1951), while explicitly adopting some elements and assumptions of American structuralism (e.g. Harris' long components and the notion of the morphophoneme), marks the transition to generative treatments of R&P morphology. His analysis is explicitly transformational: "A series of morphological and morphophonemic statements transforming any grammatical sequence of morphemes into a sequence of phonemes" (1951: 4). Chomsky's „major morpheme classes" (1951: 15) comprise discontinuous consonantal roots and vowel patterns as in (10).

(10) (Chomsky 1951: 20–21).
    (a) Roots: $R \rightarrow C^R_1 C^R_2 C^R_3$
                          (:, sometimes, if $C_2 = Y_2$)
    (b) Vocalism: α_1 -- β_2,
                          where $\alpha_1, \beta_2, = V$ or $\emptyset$

R stands for root; C for consonant; the subscript integers give the order. The colon stands for length, and 'Y$_2$' is a semivowel morphophoneme. These are, in effect, morpheme structure rewrite rules similar to phrase structure rules, and not morphemes in themselves. Intercalation of the root and vowel pattern is accomplished by a transformation, morphophonemic statement number 3 (1951: 28): a root and vowel pattern sequence $C_1C_2C_3 + V_1V_2$ is rewritten as $C_1V_1C_2V_2C_3$ (to simplify considerably). Other phenomena having an impact on word structure are handled by other morphophonemic transformations − variations in stem vowel quality or syllable structure, for instance.

This early analysis therefore admits discontinuous morphemes such as consonantal roots as the basic unit of lexical/morphological representation, relying on a transformational derivation to represent the internal structure of words and derivational relationships.

3.2.3. Prosodic Morphology

After being subordinated to phonology and syntax from the late 1950s through the 1960s, morphology re-emerged in the 1970s as a distinct theoretical discipline (Halle 1973, Aronoff 1976). The problems presented by R&P and other kinds of discontinuous morphology led to major innovations in morphological theory, culminating in present-day Optimality Theory.

The major innovation actually began in phonology, with Goldsmith's (1976) Autosegmental Phonology, a system of multilinear phonological representations for tone languages. Tones are analyzed as 'autosegments' represented on a tier parallel to but distinct from that of segments; segments are then mapped or associated to tones by rule. Goldsmith's multidimensional formalism spread well beyond tone studies (see e. g. van der Hulst & Smith 1984; Clements 1985). John McCarthy made similar innovations in morphology (1982), in which he applied the multilinear formalism to Semitic morphology, especially Classical Arabic. McCarthy objected to Harris's (1941) and Chomsky's (1951) treatments of Semitic morphology, claiming that neither was sufficiently restrictive: "The actually attested possibilities of intercalating roots and patterns are much more limited than [Harris's] apparatus allows" (McCarthy 1982: 117); the unconstrained power of transformational rules had already been deemed a major flaw for all generative theories by this time. McCarthy therefore sought a model which would accommodate the independent representation of the analyzable portions of a stem while providing a constrained means of associating them, exactly what Autosegmental Phonology provided. With his Morphemic Tier Hypothesis, McCarthy (1981) posits an analog of the autosegment: the morphemes that make up a word occupy distinct but parallel representational tiers. The representation of a Classical Arabic stem such as *kaatab* 'correspond, perfective active' would look like Figure 50.1. A stem with a derivational affix such as the prefixal /n/ of Binyan VII would be on yet another tier, as shown in Figure 50.2. The segmental tiers were then connected to the CV-tier in word formation by universal and language-specific association conventions, modification rules, and constraints on representations (many imported from autosegmental theory). McCarthy's early model also had more-static properties; e. g., basic/derived relations were encoded in the lexicon as connections between stored words.

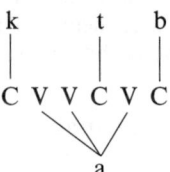

Figure 50.1: Representation of Arabic verb stems in early Prosodic Morphology (McCarthy 1982)

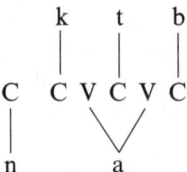

Figure 50.2: PM representation of Arabic verb stem with prefix

McCarthy's account was recognized as a significant gain in economy over previous treatments and it gained instant recognition for its innovation in morphological representation. Although Harris had presaged both phonological and morphological autosegments in his 'long component' idea (1944, 1951), generative theory was at a loss to deal with such phenomena before the innovations of Goldsmith and McCarthy.

McCarthy took the up-to-then most radical step in admitting discontinuous and underspecified elements, having discontinuous root consonants, discontinuous vowel patterns, and underspecified CV templates as morphemes. While modeling word formation as derivation via mapping of discontinuous segmental morphemes to a CV-template and the meeting of other constraints, he also incorporated a lexicon-internal representation of derivational relationships.

The approach McCarthy began evolved into the theory of **Prosodic Morphology (PM)**. McCarthy & Prince (1986, 1990a, 1990b) argued against permitting CV skeleta as morphemes, proposing the Prosodic Morphology Hypothesis: "the templates of reduplicative or templatic morphology are defined in terms of the authentic units of prosody: the mora, the syllable, the foot, and the phonological word" (McCarthy & Prince 1990a: 3). They claimed that prosodic templates provide a more restrictive set of expression units and unify the analysis by using the same units used in phonology. McCarthy & Prince must, however, use certain devices in order to get around the problem that only one of the four stem templates they propose for the Classical Arabic verb system actually "corresponds to a prosodic constituent" (1990a: 35). The devices they use are extraprosodicity (edge elements may be invisible to prosodic constraints) and the notion that the templates are not, in fact, basic, but contain a purely prosodic suffix, to which melodic units (root consonants and vowels) can map. (11) shows what two of the stem morphemes look like under the new analysis. 'σ' represents 'syllable'; 'μ' 'mora'; '+' signifies the morpheme boundary between the suffix and the remainder of the stem.

(11) (a) σ + σ   (b) σ + σ
        | | ∧ |
        μ   μ   μ μ   μ

Thus (11 a) represents a stem comprising two syllables, each with a single mora; the second syllable is a prosodic suffix; both syllables map to morphemic segments. (11 b) shows a stem comprising two syllables, one a base and one a prosodic suffix, but the first syllable contains two morae and the second just one.

The stems are subject to further restrictions, for example **minimality** and **maximality**. Minimality subjects stems to language-particular phonological constraints; maximality sets an upper limit (of two syllables) on prosodic templates. McCarthy & Prince (1990b) develop another interesting notion, **prosodic circumscription**: a morphological process can isolate a prosodic constituent (especially the **minimal word**) from the base and adopt it as its domain of application. McCarthy & Prince (1986, 1990a, 1990b) devote the bulk of their works to defending the Prosodic Morphology Hypothesis, not only for Semitic but also for other languages in which morphological reduplication, hypocoristics, and language games exploit prosodic structure. Word formation is discussed but not in the minute detail applied to the templatic morphemes. Other authors develop complex cyclic mechanisms for word formation (Yip 1987, Farwaneh 1990, Moore 1990).

Word formation in later PM is a process of "template satisfaction" (McCarthy & Prince 1990a: 41), that is, filling out the moras and syllables of the prosodic template with melodic elements by means of conventions, constraints, and rules, some universal and some language-particular. For example, Arabic requires consonantal onsets to all syllables; therefore in the process of filling out a prosodic template with an initial syllable, that syllable will receive a consonant onset. Special rules are still required, however, to handle phenomena that were problematic in the early framework, such as medial geminated root consonants and infixes. McCarthy & Prince (1990a) do not address vowel association in the verb; but a process of "melodic overwriting" (McCarthy & Prince 1990b: 244−246) is posited for derived plurals and diminutives of nouns − the melody (vowel pattern) of the derived category simply replaces the melody of the base, and then standard association conventions may apply.

In the wake of McCarthy & Prince's work, PM has been applied to numerous languages, such as Native American Yawelmani (Archangeli (1991)), Choctaw, Alabama, Tohono O'odham, and Koasati; Japanese; Balangao and Keley-i (Austronesian) (Lombardi & McCarthy (1991)). R&P morphology in other

Semitic languages, such as Hebrew (Bat El 1989, Inkelas 1990) and Modern Aramaic (Hoberman 1991), has also been the subject of study.

The prosodic template has been a persistent bone of contention within PM, with authors variously arguing that they are not needed because the correct syllabification can be gotten via phonological syllabification algorithms (Moore 1990, Bat El 1989); others (Inkelas 1990, Hoberman 1991) insist that prosodic templates are both desirable and necessary. A persistent problem within syllabification theories is the existence of initial complex onsets in some stem templates in languages such as Iraqi Arabic (Broselow 1991) and Modern Aramaic. This is problematic because, given PM's inventory of prosodic units, we cannot distinguish between templates with simple onsets in the initial syllable and templates with initial clusters. This problem is resolved in Optimality Theory (e.g. Golston 1996), which accommodates complex onsets by representing such stems as violating a general syllable-structure-preference constraint 'no complex onset'. Stems that violate this constraint would have an initial cluster, and stems that are not specified as violating this constraint will have simple onsets.

Other problems, such as how to deal with medial gemination, vowel placement, and infixation, are also resolved in Optimality Theory, to which we now turn.

3.2.4. Optimality Theory

The most recent innovation in generative linguistics relevant to R&P morphology is Optimality Theory (OT) (McCarthy & Prince (1994), Prince & Smolensky (1993), Golston (1996)). OT accounts for occurring linguistic forms via their violations of a set of universal principles of markedness, that is to say, features of a phonological (and morphological) representation appear not as, say, mental representations of positive gestures of the vocal tract, but as violations of particular constraints. These constraints apply to both feature makeup and syllable structure and are taken from well-attested cross-linguistic tendencies. The ideal configuration of the vocal tract is rest; articulation of any sound requires moving away from that resting position and expending effort, that is, making 'unnatural' or 'marked' efforts. Therefore the presence of a feature in a representation means the violation of the ideal that would leave the vocal tract at rest. Thus features are represented not in terms of their positive existence, but in terms of the particular constraints they violate. For example, all voiced segments violate the constraint NO VOICE. Voicelessness of sounds brings them closer to the ideal resting state of the vocal tract; hence voicelessness is less marked than voicedness. This is borne out in such broadly attested phenomena as implicational hierarchies in phoneme inventories (where the presence of voiced consonants usually entails the presence of voiceless ones, but not vice-versa) and syllable- or word-final devoicing processes as found in German and other languages. Syllable structure constraints come from a general consensus within the field on what kinds of syllables are preferred, e. g., CV syllables vs. any other type; the sonority hierarchy, etc. (cf. Vennemann 1988).

There are also constraints not directly relevant to the feature makeup of a representation. ALIGNMENT, for example, dictates the "coincidence of edges of morphological and phonological constituents" (McCarthy & Prince 1994: 2); some are theory-specific, such as FAITHFULNESS, which requires "identity of input and output" (McCarthy & Prince 1994: 2). OT output is the target surface form and input is a representation that is optimal with respect to the grammar of the language in question. This grammar consists of a particular ranking of constraints, drawn from a universal set called CON. These constraints are not absolute, but are violable, similar to preference laws (cf. Vennemann 1988); they represent ideals.

Constraints interact and may come into competition (for instance, voicelessness is less marked than voicedness for segments in general, but the competing desirability of a sonorous peak for syllables makes voicing more natural for segments that form syllable peaks, such as vowels, than for segments that occur in syllable margins). A particular language's constraint-ranking resolves competition among constraints that may be equal from a universal perspective. Thus there may be several ways to realize an underlying form, but one is likely to satisfy more constraints according to the ranking within the particular language than another candidate form.

The similarity of this approach to Natural Phonology (Stampe (1980), Donegan (1985)) should be clear. In Natural Phonology, the phonological system of a language develops in a learning child as she discovers which of an inventory of natural processes (which, as a whole, would culminate in a minimally effortful vocal tract gesture) she must suppress in order to attain the adult output. These natural processes are the analog of OT's universal constraints. OT captures the same insight by recognizing that human language uses violations of particular constraints distinctively (i. e. phonemically) (in Natural Phonology terms, the child learns to suppress processes only as far as is necessary to create the phonemic distinctions exploited by her language). "Constraint violations are the distinctive features of ... OT, they represent all phonologically and morphologically relevant contrasts" (Golston 1996: 725).

Golston's (1996) proposed modification of OT, called **direct OT**, simplifies the theory by ridding it of input and output forms and the machinery (a function called GEN) which derives the latter from the former, representing a 'surface' form (at least partially) purely in terms of its violations of markedness constraints ('representation as pure markedness', or RPM). Though not yet fully accepted as the best version of OT, RPM is still representative of the OT approach, and provides an example of OT applied to R&P morphology. Golston supports his revision of OT by presenting thumbnail accountings of several types of traditionally problematic morphology, including discontinuous phenomena such as infixation, circumfixation, templatic reduplicative morphology and templatic non-reduplicative morphology, as found in Semitic. I will give only a bare summary of his analysis here. Golston addresses the problem of the discontinuous consonantal roots by giving them a prosodic shape with underspecified vowels, somewhat like a CV template with the Cs filled in, e. g. [kE.tEb] for Classical Arabic Binyan 1, CV.CVC. The root morphemes are represented as an ordered sequence of consonants, using constraint violations to assure the sequence (the ideal placement for any consonant is initial in a syllable; in order to place a noninitial root consonant such as the /t/ of *k-t-b* in its proper position, it is specified as violating that initial-placement constraint). Vowel melody morphemes are represented as are consonantal roots, using constraint violations to determine which syllable will wind up with a give vowel as nucleus.

A full stem would be characterized by summarizing all of the constraints it violates. In a stem such as *kuttib*, the causative perfective passive of Binyan 2, meaning something like 'was caused to be written', for example, the /k/ receives its phonological feature makeup by violating constraints prohibiting velar and stop tongue gestures; it is placed in initial position by not violating ALIGN, the constraint which calls for syllable-initial placement of consonants. On the other hand, violation of the ALIGN constraint for the first /t/ in the stem places it in the coda of its syllable. *Kuttib* winds up having the segments and syllable structure that it has as a result, broadly speaking, of it violating the fewest constraints of Classical Arabic in the order in which those constraints are ranked for that language. The fact that this stem has two coda consonants, for example, is taken to indicate that Classical Arabic ranks NO CODA at a lower priority than, say, Hawai'ian, which permits no coda consonants whatsoever.

OT is not a total departure from tradition in generative linguistics; it assumes many devices of generative phonological and morphological theory, such as extrametricality, feature-spreading, and licensing. Its ultimate success will hinge on the validity of these assumptions, as well as the defensibility of the various constraints and ranking schemes it proposes.

The status of representations such as [kE.tEb], the vowel melodies, and the tableaus specifying template structure in OT is not clear at this point. Are they meant as distinct items, stored in a lexicon? Or, *pace* Cognitive Grammar (§ 3.3.4), are only full forms stored, with these components *immanent* within them? In OT, "[t]here is no serial derivation" (McCarthy & Prince 1994: 3), and, for each output candidate, "[o]ptimality is computed with respect to all linguistically relevant dimensions, not just one" (McCarthy & Prince 1994: 2), suggesting that the only possibility to incorporate word formation would be via a single-step process in which root morphemes combine with vowel melodies to create output candidates, each of which is then evaluated by the constraint ranking of the grammar, with the least-marked option emerging. This means that contrast between templates (such as infinitive CCaC vs. agentive CaCaC in Modern Aramaic) must be specified by according morpheme status to alternate patterns of constraint violation (CCaC would violate 'no complex onset' while CaCaC would not).

If this is the intended picture, then OT is similar to PM in admitting discontinuous and underspecified morphemes, but it modifies how the template is characterized. Stem template morphemes are specified not as units of prosody such as syllable or foot, but rather as patterns of constraint violation.

3.3. Modern alternatives to the generative tradition

3.3.1. Kuryłowicz

Kuryłowicz (1962, 1973) develops an analysis of R&P morphology within Prague school structuralism, which he characterizes as **apophony** or **ablaut**, i.e., modifications of stem vowels. His main interest is in tracing the rise of the present system, which he claims is the result of the morphologization of vowel alternations which once were phonetically motivated, with syllable structure changes due to syncope. His model is word-based: "every vocalism of the verbal forms ... [and] of the derived classes ... must be traced back ... to the fundamental vocalism *via apophonic transformations*" (1973: 34, italics in original). These modifications are viewed as morphemes, similar to the **process morpheme** notion in American structuralism. Thus he admits no discontinuous morphemes whatever, positing derivation of all forms by modification of a fully-specified word of a basic type.

3.3.2. Natural Morphology

Natural Morphology (NM) is a model which evaluates morphological systems along parameters of 'naturalness' such as transparency and diagrammaticity (Dressler et al. 1987). In early work on Semitic, Dressler (1981) entertains both morpheme-based and word-based analyses, citing **root extraction** (the extraction of triliteral roots from foreign words or native acronyms and use of these in regular nonconcatenative verb formation) as evidence for roots as morphemes in at least educated Semitic speakers. In Kilani-Schoch & Dressler (1985), the root-based analysis is abandoned on two grounds: (1) a discontinuous base is unnatural and hence dispreferred; it would then also require discontinuous transfixes (i.e. the vowel melodies), which Dressler finds "too unnatural for existing at all" (1987: 116); (2) "not all [CV-structures] operate as bases" (1985: 33), that is, it is possible to analyze some as basic and others as derived from these. In their account, basic stems for nouns and verbs are formed in accordance with abstract CV patterns they call morpheme structure constraints or "prelexical morphological rule[s]" (1985: 32). Stems thus derived serve as bases for other operations: ablaut, gemination, reduplication, and affixation. First-order derived words then serve as bases for second-order derivations, e.g., the reciprocal *takaatabuu* 'they corresponded with each other', derives ultimately from *kataba* 'he wrote'. The affinities of this analysis with those of the medieval Arab grammarians and Kuryłowicz should be clear.

Kilani-Schoch & Dressler evaluate Semitic morphology negatively on a number of naturalness parameters. It is low on the diagrammaticity scale: because addition of a derivational meaning is reflected not by addition of a discrete morpheme, but by a change in the vowel/syllable structure of an underlying stem, the constructional iconicity of the resulting morpheme complex is lessened. It rates low on the transparency parameter for the same reason: "the massive use of ablaut in Classical Arabic verb forms jeopardizes the identity of the underlying stems ... and thus diminishes morphotactic transparency" (1985: 39). Semitic also fails by violating Natural Morphology preferences for the size and shape of morphemes: "The optimal size of a grammatical morpheme seems to be ... a [CV] syllable" (Kilani-Schoch and Dressler 1985: 29). Kilani-Schoch and Dressler imply that the rareness of R&P morphology is due to the fact that it "radicalizes" (1985: 36) two cross-linguistic tendencies: (1) the tendency to signal lexical meaning through consonants, and (2) the tendency to signal grammatical meaning through vowels, especially through ablaut and umlaut. Its robustness in Semitic might be attributed to system-dependent morphological naturalness (Wurzel 1987), a kind of inertia in which a particular morphological strategy persists in a language by setting itself as a standard of naturalness within the language, though it may violate universal preferences. Bybee & Newman (1995) challenge the judgment of stem changes as inherently less natural than affixation, however.

3.3.3. Functional Grammar

Functional Grammar (Dik 1981, 1983) is a theory of grammar which focuses heavily on meaning, particularly argument structure and thematic roles. The grammar consists of the **fund**, which comprises **predicate frames** — a crucial construct for representing the meanings of constructions – **terms** (roughly equivalent to lexical items such as words), and a set of rules for deriving nonbasic terms and predicate frames from basic ones. The nonbasic items also reside in the fund. In their basic form, predicate frames are, essentially, underspecified semantic representations of clauses (minus satellite adverbial modifiers) of different types such as transitive, causative, etc. They exist in the lexicon; any particular sentence may be created by inserting terms into them, and adding refinements on the terms such as definite and plural.

An example treatment of R&P morphology within FG is Junger (1987). For Junger, the root is a separate, phonologically discontinuous morpheme; its lexical representation includes the segments of the root in proper order, the morphosyntactic category to which the most basic verb form using the root belongs, specification of the basic binyan for that root (being again the most basic form using that root), and the "number, semantic function of the arguments and selection restrictions on the terms [of argument structure]" (Junger 1987: 52).

The syllabic and vocalic patterns (binyanim) are distinct morphological entities: "[t]he *binyanim* have a semantic, syntactic and morphological value of their own, independent of the semantic and morphological value of the root" (Junger 1987: 63, italics original). They are represented as 'predicate schemes', containing information about the argument structure, morphosyntactic category (= verb), as well as an underspecified root (strangely, the actual phonological shape of the binyan seems to be left out of the representation, although it may be that she is including traditional labels such as 'Paal' and 'Hitpael' in the representations). (12) is a predicate-scheme for the Hifil, a causative binyan:

(12) (Junger 1987: 52)
C.C.C. V B6
(x0) causer (x1) causee [(x2) Go]

'C.C.C' is the schematic lexical root: 'V' specifies that stems of this form are verbs; 'B6' refers to 'binyan 6', in accordance with the traditional numeration of the binyanim; the remainder specifies semantic and syntactic details of argument structure.

A full lexical entry is more complex than just a root morpheme plus a binyan morpheme. The lexical entry is a 'configurational sub-system': "[lexical] entries consist of the basic *binyan* and its predicate scheme ... and of all the *binyanim* derived from the root (and their semantic and syntactic function), as well as of the valency operations for deriving them. This is followed by a list of roots which all share this configurational sub-system, and every root is followed by a list of the *mishqalim* [nominalizations] derived from it" (Junger 1987: 56; italics in original).

Thus Junger wishes to capture a great deal of idiosyncratic detail in her lexicon (i.e., which particular roots occur in which particular binyanim); at the same time, her formalism does allow for capturing crucial generalizations such as the regular meanings associated with particular binyanim, and regular derivational relationships among the binyanim. She uses statistics about usage to discover the particular specifications of the various roots/binyanim. The choice of a basic binyan is made according to usual criteria such as semantic and morphological simplicity, markedness, and "consistency with the rest of the system" (Junger 1987: 70).

To capture productivity in the binyanim, she posits 'predicate formation rules' which change the valency of an input binyan to that of the output binyan (for example, non-causative binyan 1 to causative binyan 5); her claim is that "all syntactic relations as well as morphological and derivational relations between the *binyanim* in the verbal system can be described in terms of valency change (quantitative [= number of arguments] or qualitative [= role of arguments])" (Junger 1987: 62, italics original).

It is notable that Junger makes no attempt to account for the phonological shapes of the occurring verb stems, the very issue which has been the core problem for generative theorists.

3.3.4. Cognitive Grammar

Yet another non-generative framework is Cognitive Grammar (CG) (Langacker 1987, 1991a, 1991b). CG shares with FG the central placement of meaning in describing and explaining linguistic structure; in fact, the preferred strategy in cognitive linguistics in general is to look to meaning to motivate form whenever possible. Cognitive linguistics also adopts principles from cognitive psychology and applies these to language. For instance, categories are often described as organized around a prototype or central member (MacLaury 1991); figure/ground organization features prominently in descriptions of both semantics and syntax (Talmy 1988, Langacker 1987). CG is selected here because, among cognitive-linguistic theories, it has the most detailed morphological and lexical theory, and because at least one lengthy work (Rubba 1993) has been devoted to R&P morphology.

CG's model of the lexicon (in fact, its model for the entirety of a language's grammar) is the **network**. Network models of language have emerged more or less independently in the work of several scholars (Bybee 1985, 1988, Hudson 1984, Lamb 1966, Langacker 1987, 1991a). The network model contrasts with generative models in that it focuses, not on the most economical formal analysis possible, but on cognitively likely representations that a language learner might arrive at, given exposure to data. In fact, the best way to understand CG is to consider it as a model for the gradual development of a grammar in a learner.

The language learner builds a network of mental representations derived from experienced language events. The items in the network are mental representations of phonological forms and of particular conceptual gestalts (complex configurations of concepts which function as the meanings of linguistic expressions). What makes the assemblage a network is connections between these mental representations, both within and across the phonological and conceptual (= semantic) domains. These connections are relationships of three sorts: symbolization, integration, and categorization; these are to be understood as conceptual units in themselves. A symbolic connection is one between a phonological form and its meaning, enabling the basic semiotic function of language. Integration refers to the combination of items to build more-complex items, for instance the integration of morphemes to form a word or words to form a phrase. Categorization means a judgment of partial or full similarity of phonological and/or semantic features between items, whether already stored in the network or newly experienced.

Categorization is of far-reaching importance in CG, as it is the basis for the construction of all relationships among experienced linguistic signs, and is therefore the basic mechanism for constructing and maintaining the network — for learning and using language. To give a highly simplified example, if we, in the course of a conversation, segment out a word with the phonological form /ni/, we can recognize it as an exemplar of the lexical item 'knee': it bears strong phonetic resemblance to the phonological form of this lexical item, and (with support from context) we will likely assume that a meaning is intended which coincides with the body-part concept that is symbolized by that phonological string. We rapidly assign a semantic interpretation to the uttered string, advancing by a small increment our understanding of the discourse. The mental activity involved in this understanding is categorization of the uttered string as the lexical item 'knee'.

It is also crucial that one possible product of a categorization event is a **partial** rather than a full match between the item to be categorized and the standard of comparison. This makes **schemas** possible: for instance, the CV-templates of McCarthy's early work (§ 3.2.3) can be viewed as the product of comparisons of multiple experiences of stems of a certain shape, say CVC.CVC. The actual experiences were of stems with fully specifed consonants and vowels, of course; symbols of underspecified representations such as C and V can be understood as standing for the learner's realization of shared features among the segments of numerous stems.

CG is agnostic as to the ontology of schemas. They may be viewed as either underspecified representations distinct from, though connected to, the items from which they derive, making them similar to morpheme structure rules or lexical redundancy rules in other theories. Alternatively, they may reside entirely in entrenched connections among the items from which they derive, encoding the similarities between them — a situation termed **immanence**. They are often depicted as the former in diagrams used to portray the network, but this is for convenience and is not intended to signal a commitment to one or the other view. The answer to this question is a matter of empirical investigation, presumably through psycholinguistic studies.

In fact, viewing schemas not as distinct representations but as connections among more-fully-specified representations offers a resolution of some of the stickiest problems in morphological theory, such as empty morphs and discontinuous morphemes like the Semitic consonantal root. Linguistic theories have traditionally reified the morpheme as an item that would be stored in a mental lexicon. This allows idealistic criteria such as contiguity and one-to-one correspondence between meaning and form to come into play. The network model offers the option of *not* isolating morphemes, envisioning them rather as relationships of similarity among stored lexical items which may be complex. This makes all morphemes schemas of a kind (after all, when we recognize or utter a morpheme, what we hear or utter is not, ontologically, the morpheme itself, but something we categorize as a physical manifestation of our mental representation). Thus the network model offers us two options: to isolate Semitic roots as discontinuous morphemes, or envision Semitic speakers' knowledge of root morphemes as entrenched judgments of similarity – connections or comparison events – among all the words containing each root. Adopting the former course forces us to face their typological strangeness, and therefore possibly attempt to account for this in some way; the latter course makes Semitic look like every other language in the world, since morphemes in every language can be considered to be connections in the same way.

Figure 50.3 gives a graphic depiction of a portion of a network for Modern Aramaic in highly simplified notation, portraying the basics of the network model: conceptual units (phonological units in plain text, semantic ones in italics) in connected to one other by relationships of symbolization (thicker lines) and similarity/categorization (thinner lines). The data depicted comprise imperative, feminine agentive-noun, and 3rd-person singular feminine future forms based on the roots *d-m-x* 'sleep' and *p-l-x* 'work', shown in (13).

(13)   *d-m-x* 'sleep'   *p-l-x* 'work'
    IMPERATIVE   *dmoox*   *ploox*
    AGENTIVE-N-F   *damaxta*   *palaxta*
    3SG.FEM.FUT   *bdamxat*   *ppalxat*

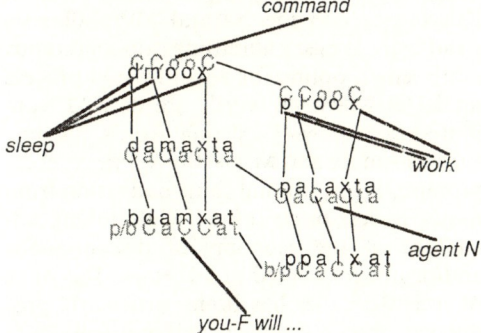

Fig. 50.3: CG Mini-Network

Figs. 50.4 and 50.5 demonstrate how the notion of the morpheme can be derived from the network, not by cutting certain items out and listing them separately, but by focusing in on a particular set of units and relationships while backgrounding others. These figures show the morphemes *d-m-x* 'sleep' and *CCooC* 'command', respectively. As in other theories, the notion 'morpheme' can be defined in CG as a minimal symbolic relationship between a phonological form and a meaning – a relationship not further analyzable into component symbolic relationships. But this can be represented without isolating any morpheme from words it occurs in. Thus we will not be plagued with the need to get them to correctly map to a templatic morpheme in a derivation (a central problem of McCarthy's (1981, 1982) analysis and of Prosodic Morphology in general, e. g., McCarthy & Prince (1990a, b)). At the same time, nothing in CG prevents an OT-type constraint-based explanation for the form of particular stems; in fact, CG explicitly incorporates the notion of simultaneous satisfaction of multiple constraints by all representations in a grammar.

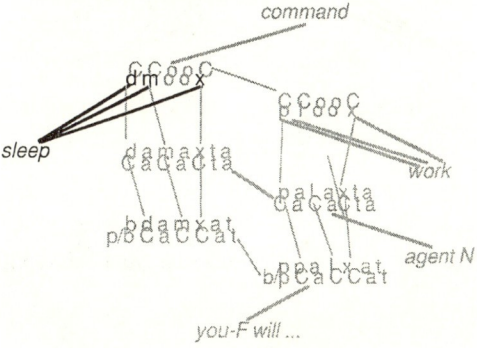

Fig. 50.4: Root morpheme 'isolation'

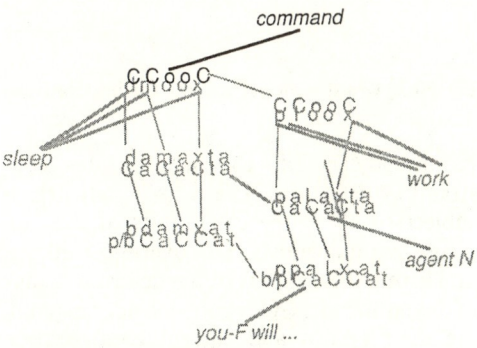

Fig. 50.5: Stem morpheme 'isolation'

CG's analog for inflectional and derivational rules, morpheme-structure rules, and redundancy rules also resides in the network; the **constructional schema** or **schematic symbolic** unit. The internal structure of a datum such as *dmoox* 'sleep!' may be seen also by foregrounding the relevant parts of the network while backgrounding other parts, as shown in Fig. 50.6. A more-general constructional schema that would be available as a template for constructing any imperative on a triliteral root is depicted in Fig. 50.7 (shown, for convenience, in isolation from the network). The unit *C-C-C* 'process' is a schematic version of a root morpheme (**process** is the technical term for **verb** in CG). This represents a Modern Aramaic speaker's knowledge that verbal meanings are in general coded by a sequence of three consonants with varying interspersed material. The schema as a whole is a generalization over the fact that (for regular, triliteral roots), the imperative form comprises the root consonants mapped into the template *CCooC*.

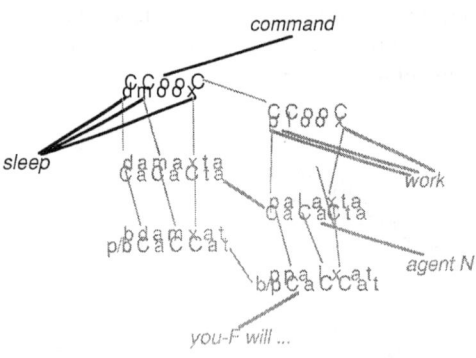

Fig. 50.6: Constructional schema: [[dmoox/*sleep!*]]

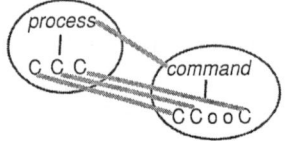

Fig. 50.7: Constructional schema for imperatives

As already noted, CG incorporates constraint satisfaction. The whole network is subject to all of the constraints of the language simultaneously. Discovering, ranking, and listing these is part of the descriptive task of any grammar; CG would consider explaining their genesis and current configuration with reference to cognition as part of the explanatory enterprise of linguistics (contra OT). Constraint satisfaction may be a tool for describing the shapes of morphemes such as the stem templates. For example the Modern Aramaic contrasts

(14) (a) CCaC   infinitive stem
     (b) CaCC   imperfective (non-3 masc. sg.) stem
     (c) CaCaC   agentive noun stem
     (d) CaCoC   verbal noun stem

might be captured by understanding initial 'CC' as 'violate no onset clusters', while no such violation is specified for b, c, or d. Contrasting b vs. c might be accomplished (as already suggested by, among others, Hoberman 1991) by specifying syllable structure in the phonological form of the morpheme, imperative and imperfective requiring one syllable; agentive and verbal noun two syllables.

Thus, with respect to R&P morphology, CG allows us to straddle the positions of isolating discontinuous morphemes vs. taking a totally word-based approach to morphology. Its reliance on analogy as a mechanism for categorizing and building new words is criticized by some; but note that it does make available the existence of rules in the form of schemas extracted from observed similarities among experienced forms. As to such persistent questions as storage of full forms vs. online construction by rule and the inflection-derivation distinction, CG can accommodate a variety of answers more easily than theories that insist on a particular answer.

4. Conclusion

This summary of theoretical approaches to R&P morphology demonstrates that the core issues of how to represent morphemes, word formation, and derivational relationships have indeed preoccupied linguists dealing with this unusual morphology. Intellectual descendants of the Prague school such as Kuryłowicz and the Natural Morphologists steadfastly resist admitting discontinuous morphemes, opting for a word-based process model in which all words are derived from more-basic, already-existing words. Others, such as Junger and McCarthy & Prince, compromise, incorporating some derivation from more- to less-basic forms, while taking advantage of the economy of discontinuous and/or underspecified morphemes. The work of recent decades has been particularly productive theoretically, providing new constructs such as prosodic templates and lexical networks for modeling morphemes.

Formal theories such as PM and OT have tended to background the semantics of the morphemes they study, while FG and CG make this a primary area of concern, studying how introflecting morphemes, similar to their non-introflecting counterparts, code familiar modifications of meaning such as additions to argument structure in transitivization or causativization, or morphosyntactic categories such as aspect or derived nominalization. Overall, recent theoretical work tends towards inclusiveness, portraying introflection as accountable via theories applied to a wide range of morphological marking strategies, rather than as a strategy requiring its own distinct theoretical framework.

5. Special abbreviations

CG	Cognitive Grammar (§ 3.3.4)
CV	consonant vowel
FG	Functional Grammar (§ 3.3.3)
NM	Natural Morphology (§ 3.3.2)
OT	Optimality Theory (§ 3.2.4)
PM	Prosodic Morphology (§ 3.2.3)
R&P	root-and-pattern morphology (§ 2.5)
RPM	representation as pure markedness (§ 3.2.4)

6. References

Archangeli, Diana. 1979. "The Yawelmani dialect of Yokuts". In: Kenstowicz, Michael & Kisseberth, Charles (eds.), *Generative Phonology: Description and theory*. New York: Academic Press.

—. 1991. "Syllabification and prosodic templates in Yawelmani". *Natural Language and Linguistic Theory* 9.2: 231–283.

Aronoff, Mark. 1976. *Word formation in generative grammar*. Cambridge/MA: MIT Press.

Bat El, Outi. 1989. *Phonology and word structure in Modern Hebrew*. Ph.D. dissertation, University of California, Los Angeles.

Becker, Thomas. 1993. "Back-formation, cross-formation, and 'bracketing paradoxes' in paradigmatic morphology". *Yearbook of Morphology* 1–25.

Bohas, G., Guillaume, J.-P., & Kouloughli, D. E. 1990. *The Arabic linguistic tradition*. London: Routledge.

Broselow, Ellen. 1991. "Parametric variation in Arabic dialect phonology". In Broselow, E., M. Eid, and J. McCarthy, (eds.), *Perspectives in Arabic linguistics IV*. Amsterdam and Philadelphia: John Benjamins.

Brugmann, Karl. 1906. *Vergleichende Laut- und Stammbildungs- und Flexionslehre nebst Lehre vom Gebrauch der Wortformen der indogermanischen Sprachen*. 2nd edition. Strasbourg: K. J. Trübner.

Bybee, Joan. 1985. *Morphology: A study of the relation between meaning and form*. Amsterdam: John Benjamins.

—. 1988. "Morphology as lexical organization". In: Hammond, Michael, & Noonan, Michael (eds.). *Theoretical morphology: approaches in modern linguistics*. San Diego: Academic Press.

— & Jean Newman. 1995. "Are stem changes as natural as affixes?" *Linguistics* 33: 633–654.

Chomsky, Noam. 1951. *Morphophonemics of Modern Hebrew*. (Outstanding dissertations in linguistics 12, printed 1979.) New York: Garland.

Clements, George N. 1985. "The geometry of phonological features". *Phonology Yearbook* 2: 223–252.

Dik, Simon. 1981. *Functional Grammar*. 3rd ed. Dordrecht: Foris.

—. 1983. *Advances in Functional Grammar*. Dordrecht: Foris.

Donegan, Patricia J. 1985. *On the natural phonology of vowels*. (Outstanding dissertations in linguistics 13.) New York: Garland.

Dressler, Wolfgang U. 1981. "On word formation in Natural Morphology". *Wiener linguistische Gazette* 26: 3–14.

—, Mayerthaler, Willi, Panagl, Oswald and Wurzel, Wolfgang U. 1987. *Leitmotifs in Natural Morphology*. Amsterdam: John Benjamins.

Farwaneh, Samira. 1990. "Well-formed associations in Arabic: Rule or condition". In: Eid, Mushira and McCarthy, John (eds.). *Perspectives on Arabic Linguistics: Papers from the Second Symposium*. Amsterdam and Philadelphia: John Benjamins.

Goldsmith, John. 1976. *Autosegmental phonology*. New York: Garland.

Golston, Chris. 1996. "Direct Optimality Theory". *Language* 72: 713–748.

Hale, Kenneth. 1965. "Some preliminary observations on Papago morphophonemics". *International Journal of American Linguistics* 31: 295–305.

Halle, Morris. 1973. "Prolegomena to a theory of word formation". *Linguistic Inquiry* 4, 3–16.

Harris, Zellig. 1941. "Linguistic structure of Hebrew". *Journal of the American Oriental Society* 61: 143–167.

—. 1944. "Simultaneous components in phonology". *Language* 20: 181–205.

—. 1945. "Discontinuous morphemes". *Language* 21: 121–127.

—. 1951. *Structural linguistics*. Chicago: University of Chicago Press.

Hobermann, Robert P. 1991. "Formal properties of the conjugations in modern Aramaic". In: Booij, G. and Van Marle, J. (eds.). *Yearbook of Morphology*. Dordrecht: Kluwer, 49–64.

Hockett, Charles. 1954. "Two models of grammatical description". *Word* 10: 210–231.

Hudson, Richard. 1974. "A structural sketch of Beja". *African Language Studies* XV: 111–142.

—. 1984. *Word Grammar.* Oxford: Basil Blackwell.

Inkelas, Sharon. 1990. "Prosodic replacement in Modern Hebrew". In: *Papers from the 26th Regional Meeting of the Chicago Linguistic Society, Vol. 2: The Parasession on the Syllable in Phonetics and Phonology.* Chicago: Chicago Linguistic Society.

Itô, Junko. 1991. "Prosodic minimality in Japanese". In: *Papers from the 26th Regional Meeting of the Chicago Linguistic Society, Vol. 2: Papers from the Parasession on the Syllable in Phonetics and Phonology.* Chicago: Chicago Linguistic Society.

Junger, Judith. 1987. *Predicate formation in the Hebrew verbal system.* Dordrecht: Foris.

Kilani-Schoch, Marianne, & Dressler, Wolfgang U. 1985. "Natural Morphology and Classical vs. Tunisian Arabic". *Studia gramatyczne* 7: 27–47.

Kuryłowicz, Jerzy. 1962. *L'apophonie en sémitique.* 'S-Gravenhage: Mouton & Co.

—. 1973. *Studies in Semitic grammar and metrics.* London: Curzon Press.

Lamb, Sydney M. 1966. *Outline of Stratificational Grammar.* Washington, D.C.: Georgetown U. Press.

Langacker, Ronald W. 1987. *Foundations of Cognitive Grammar, Vol. I: theoretical prerequisites.* Stanford: Stanford University Press.

—. 1991a. *Foundations of Cognitive Grammar, Vol. II: Descriptive application.* Stanford: Stanford University Press.

—. 1991b. *Concept, image, and symbol: the cognitive basis of grammar.* (Cognitive Linguistics Research I). Berlin: Mouton de Gruyter.

Lombardi, Linda, and McCarthy, John. 1991. "Prosodic circumscription in Choctaw morphology". *Phonology* 8: 37–72.

MacLaury, Robert E. 1991. "Prototypes revisited". *Annual Review of Anthropology* 20: 55–74.

Marantz, Alec. 1981. "Re reduplication". *Linguistic Inquiry* 13: 483–545.

McCarthy, John. 1981. "A prosodic theory of nonconcatenative morphology". *Linguistic Inquiry* 12.3: 373–418.

—. 1982. *Formal problems in Semitic phonology and morphology.* Bloomington: Indiana University Linguistics Club.

—, & Prince, Alan. 1990a. "Prosodic Morphology and templatic morphology". In: Eid, Mushira, and McCarthy, John, (eds.). *Perspectives on Arabic Linguistics: Papers from the Second Symposium.* Amsterdam: John Benjamins.

—. 1986/1999. "Prosodic morphology." In: Goldsmith, John (ed.). *Phonological theory: The essential readings.* Oxford: Blackwell, 238–288.

—. 1990b. "Foot and word in Prosodic Morphology: The Arabic broken plurals". *Natural Language and Linguistic Theory* 8: 209–282.

—. 1994. The emergence of the unmarked: Optimality in Prosodic Morphology. Rutgers Optimality Archive. In Merce Gonzalez (ed.), *Proceedings of the North-East Linguistics Society 24.* Amherst, MA: Graduate Linguistic Student Association. 333–379. ROA- 13. Rutgers Optimality Archive, http://ruccs.rutgers.edu/roa.html.

Mester, Armin. 1990. "Patterns of truncation". *Linguistic Inquiry* 21: 478–485.

Moore, John. 1990. "Doubled verbs in Modern Standard Arabic". In: Eid, Mushira, & McCarthy, John, (eds.). *Perspectives on Arabic Linguistics: Papers from the Second Symposium.* Amsterdam: John Benjamins, 55–93.

Owens, Jonathan. 1988. *The foundations of grammar: An introduction to medieval Arabic grammatical theory.* Amsterdam: John Benjamins.

Poser, William. 1990. "Evidence for foot structure in Japanese". *Language* 66: 78–105.

Prince, Alan, and Smolensky, Paul. 1993. *Optimality Theory: Constraint interaction in generative grammar.* Technical Report, Rutgers University, New Brunswick, N. J.

Rubba, Jo. 1993. *Discontinuous morphology in Modern Aramaic.* Ph.D. dissertation, University of California, San Diego. (UMI order #9414747.)

Shetler, Joanne. 1976. *Notes on Balangao grammar.* Huntington Beach, CA: Summer Institute of Linguistics.

Skalička, V. 1979. *Typologische Studien.* Wiesbaden.

Stampe, David. 1980. *A dissertation on Natural Phonology.* New York: Garland.

Talmy, Leonard. 1988. "The relation of grammar to cognition". In: Rudzka-Ostyn, Brygida (ed.). *Topics in Cognitive Linguistics.* Amsterdam: John Benjamins, 165–205.

van der Hulst, Harry & Smith, Norval. 1984. "The framework of nonlinear generative phonology". In: van der Hulst, Harry, (ed.). *Advances in nonlinear phonology.* Dordrecht: Kluwer.

Vennemann, Theo. 1988. *Preference laws for syllable structure and the explanation of sound change.* Berlin: Mouton de Gruyter.

Wurzel, Wolfgang U. 1987. "System-dependent morphological naturalness". In: Dressler et al., 59–96.

Yimam, B. 1994. "Amharic". In: Asher, R. E. (ed.) *Encyclopedia of language and linguistics* 1: 106–108. Oxford: Oxford University Press.

Yip, Moira. 1988. "Edge-in association". *Natural Language and Linguistic Theory* 6.4: 551–578.

Johanna Rubba, California Polytechnic State University, San Louis Obispo (USA)

51. Compounding

1. Defining a compound
2. A language sample
3. Order of elements
4. Types of compound
5. Meanings in tatpuruṣa compounds
6. Tying elements together: morphological effects
7. Tying elements together: phonological effects
8. Delimiting the notion of compound
9. Conclusion
10. References

Despite the fact that compounding is extremely widespread across languages, the category 'compound' is very poorly defined, and the term is frequently found with different referents. In this article I shall therefore begin by providing a definition of a compound, I shall then introduce a sample of thirty-six areally and genetically diverse languages against which possible typological claims will be tested, before going on to consider possible typological influences on compounding in general.

1. Defining a compound

A compound can be defined as a lexical unit made up of two or more elements, each of which can function as a lexeme independent of the other(s) in other contexts. The insistence on functioning as a lexeme is important, because it rules out cases of affixation as being compounds (as for instance the term is used by Boas 1911: 446, when he says "compounds are formed by the use of suffixes"). This should not, however, be read as implying that all relevant inflectional markers are invariably present — many inflectional languages allow the uninflected lexemic base to appear in compounds. The insistence that a compound should form a lexical unit is important since it excludes combinations, for example, of auxiliary and main verb or adverb and verb which are a part of the normal syntactic patterns. However, this definition is not always sufficient to allow the isolation of a particular set of forms for a given language. Other criteria are sometimes appealed to, but these are not always successful. Some of these will be discussed immediately below.

Semantic specialisation is a criterion which is often used, but this is neither necessary nor sufficient. On the one hand, there can be semantic specialisation of structures which are straightforward syntactic combinations (as in English *women's liberation, green light*); on the other, some structures which by other criteria appear to be compounds may nonetheless have compositional semantics (such as English *lady-friend, waiting room*).

Grammatical isolation, in those cases where it can be applied, is more generally helpful. Normally in a compound one of the elements cannot take a full range of inflectional marking, a full range of modifiers, a full range of determiners or auxiliaries (where relevant), and so on. Given an English compound like *nosebleed*, we cannot have *[noses]bleed*, *a [broken nose]bleed*, *a [his nose]bleed*, etc., and given a compound *blackboard* we cannot have *[blacker]board*, *[very black]board*, etc.

Thirdly, in some languages there may be phonological isolation of compounds. In English, some compounds are distinguished from syntactic phrases by stress (contrast *a 'black 'board* and *a 'blackboard*, for instance). In other languages there may be special morphophonemic processes which apply between the elements of compounds, there may be tone sandhi patterns or particular tonal patterns which apply to compounds, there may be some phonological merger between the elements of the compound (Dakota, Hebrew, see section 7), and so on. For instance, in Japanese there is a process known as *rendaku*, whereby the initial segment of the second element in a compound is voiced.

(1) Japanese (Shibatani 1990: 173)
    amadera < *ama tera*
    nun temple
    'nunnery'

In Kpelle, the second element of a compound always takes low tone, independent of the tone it takes in isolation:

(2) Kpelle (Welmers 1973: 280)
    telâŋ-wùlɔ < *telâŋ wúlɔ*
    'peanut oil'

We can now define a compound as a lexical unit made up of two or more elements, each of which can function as a lexeme independent of the other(s) in other contexts, and which shows some phonological and/or grammatical isolation from normal syntactic usage. Even this definition does not always make it clear when compounds are involved, unfortunately. For instance, Frachtenberg

(1922: 319), discussing Coos, says that "Incorporation and compound words are entirely absent". Given that the terminology of 1922 is no longer in general use, this may be difficult to interpret, anyway. But when Frachtenberg (1922: 412) says that "Substantives are often used to qualify other nouns [...] and both nouns retain their nominal character", the confusion for the modern reader increases. While the linguist may be perfectly justified in making such claims, it is not necessarily clear to the consumer of the description what the difference might be between a noun with a substantival qualifier and a compound (see Bauer 1998 for a discussion with reference to English). Similar comments apply to the descriptions of languages as diverse as West Greenlandic and Turkana. So although a certain amount of confusion in the literature means that it is not always clear precisely what is intended in the sources cited, it is hoped that the definition given above presents a focal notion of the way in which the term "compound" will be used here.

2. A language sample

In order to test various hypotheses about typological influences on compounding, a small sample of thirty-six languages was constructed. While a sample of 36 languages is too small to give clear answers on typological matters, it nevertheless allows some conclusions to be drawn and points to areas where further study would be valuable. Although the sample is a sample of convenience in the sense that languages for which descriptions were readily available were used, the languages were carefully chosen to be genetically and areally diverse. Each of the languages is from a different genus (as defined in Dryer 1992), with six languages from each of the large geographical areas used by Dryer (1992), namely 1. Africa, 2. Eurasia (excluding southeast Asia), 3. Southeast Asia and Oceania, 4. Australia-New Guinea, 5. North America and 6. South America. The languages used and the sources of data are indicated below.

1. Africa
    Ewe   (Westermann 1930)
    Hebrew   (Glinert 1989)
    Kanuri   (Lukas 1937)
    Tswana   (Cole 1955)
    Turkana   (Dimmendaal 1983)
    Yoruba   (Bamgbose 1966; Rowlands 1969)

2. Eurasia (excluding southeast Asia)
    Abkhaz   (Hewitt 1979)
    Basque   (Saltarelli 1988)
    Chukchee   (Bogoras 1922)
    Danish   (Allan et al. 1995)
    Finnish   (Karlsson 1983; Sulkala & Karjalainen 1992)
    Tamil   (Asher 1982)

3. Southeast Asia and Oceania
    Cantonese   (Matthews & Yip 1994)
    Cambodian   (Ehrman 1972; Jacob 1968)
    Maori   (Bauer 1993)
    Thai   (Fasold 1969; Hudak 1987)
    Toba-Batak (Nababan 1981; Percival 1981)
    Vietnamese (Thompson 1965)

4. Australia-New Guinea
    Arabana-Wangkangurru (Hercus 1994)
    Kobon   (Davies 1981)
    Mara   (Heath 1981)
    Siroi   (Wells 1979)
    Waskia   (Ross & Paol 1978)
    Yimas   (Foley 1991)

5. North America
    Dakota   (Boas & Swanton 1911)
    Kiowa   (Watkins 1984)
    Takelma   (Sapir 1912)
    Tümpisa Shoshone   (Dayley 1989)
    Tzutujil   (Dayley 1985)
    West Greenlandic   (Fortescue 1984)

6. South America
    Cayuvava   (Key 1967)
    Guarani   (Gregores & Suarez 1967)
    Hixkaryana (Derbyshire 1979)
    Imbabura Quechua   (Cole 1982)
    Paumarí   (Chapman & Derbyshire 1991)
    Pirahã   (Everett 1986)

In terms of the ordering of major constituents, this sample shows the distribution set out in Table 51.1. The sample thus under-represents the number of VSO languages, particularly in comparison with VOS languages, but otherwise gives a reasonably representative picture of the way in which these patterns occur in the languages of the world (Dryer 1989). In Table 51.1, the letters A, E, O, G, N, S represent the six areas listed above.

Table 51.1: Order of major constituents in sampled languages

Word Order	A	E	O	G	N	S	Tot
SOV	1	4	0	4	5	2	16
SVO	3	2	3	1	0	2	11
VSO	2	0	1	0	0	0	3
VOS	0	0	1	0	1	1	3
OVS	0	0	0	0	0	1	1
No data or variable order	0	0	1	1	0	0	2

3. Order of elements

It might be expected that the order of head and modifier nouns in a nominal compound should reflect the order of noun and adjective (including quantifiers, demonstratives, etc. in languages which do not have an identifiable class of adjectives). However, Table 51.2 indicates that this is not necessarily the case. From the data presented here it seems that there is a slight preference for modifier noun + head noun structures, independent of the syntactic order of adjective and noun.

Table 51.2: Order of noun and adjective in relation to modifier and head noun in a noun + noun compound

Word Order	A	E	O	G	N	S	Tot
N-Adj & N-mod	3	0	5	0	2	0	10
N-Adj & mod-N	2	1	0	4	2	2	11
Adj-N & N-mod	0	0	0	0	0	1	1
Adj-N & mod-N	0	4	1	1	2	1	9
insufficient data	1	1	0	1	0	2	5

Interestingly, if the correlation is made with possessor noun and head noun instead of with adjective and noun, there seems to be a slightly better match, despite the fact that there are languages like Arabana-Wangkangurru and Mara which allow the possessor noun to be on either side of the possessed noun, and that in Kiowa a possessor noun can only occur in a compound. The figures are presented in Table 51.3.

Table 51.3: Order of noun and possessor noun in relation to modifier and head noun in a noun + noun compound

Word Order	A	E	O	G	N	S	Tot
N-Poss & N-mod	3	0	4	0	0	1	8
N-Poss & mod-N	1	0	0	0	2	0	3
Poss-N & N-mod	0	0	0	0	1	0	1
Poss-N & mod-N	1	5	1	4	1	2	14
insufficient data	1	1	1	2	2	3	10

However, it is not entirely clear how much weight can be attributed to such figures, given the lack of consistency across languages in the ordering of modifier and head in compounds. Although it might be expected that this would be fixed in any individual language, that is the case only in about half of my sample from any of the areas used. The figures are given in Table 51.4. The figures given in this table show inconsistencies across compounds of all word-classes, but even if only noun compounds are considered, there is considerable inconsistency. The figures for nouns alone are parenthesised in Table 51.4. It must be recalled that many languages are consistent because only one pattern of compound is reported.

Table 51.4: Consistency of ordering of head and modifying elements in compounds (parenthesised figures show just nominal compounds)

Word Order	A	E	O	G	N	S	Tot
Consistent ordering	3	3	4	4	2	2	18
	(3)	(5)	(4)	(6)	(3)	(3)	(24)
Inconsistent ordering	3	3	2	2	3	3	16
	(3)	(1)	(2)	(0)	(3)	(2)	(11)
Unclear or missing	0	0	0	0	1	1	2
					(0)	(1)	(1)

4. Types of compound

The Sanskrit grammarians distinguished four distinct types of compound, one with two sub-types. Each of these will be considered in turn below, with a definition and examples, and a discussion of the cross-linguistic occurrence of the pattern. Although Sanskrit had no verbal compounds and only limited types of adjectival compound, the set of labels is here extended to compounds of these word-classes. It must be borne in mind that descriptions of compounding available in grammars are not necessarily exhaustive, and some patterns may occur which are not reported.

4.1. Tatpuruṣa compounds

Tatpuruṣa compounds are also termed determinative compounds. Following Bloomfield (1933: 235) the term endocentric compound is also current, though it may include rather more than the label tatpuruṣa does. In these compounds there are two elements, one of which acts as modifier to the other. This is the majority pattern for compounds in the languages of the world, and there are very few languages which do not have compounds of this type. As was noted earlier, some of the languages which are reported not to have compounds of this type nonetheless have other constructions which allow sequences of nouns in a modifier-modified relationship. It is not necessarily clear from descriptions whether the difference lies in the lack of phonological or grammatical isolation discussed in section 1. For example, West Greenlandic is reported not to have tatpuruṣa compounds, but does allow constructions such as

(3) West Greenlandic (Fortescue 1984: 117)
     kaataq qisuk
     hammer wood
     'wooden hammer'

which appears to have the same function as things which are called compounds in descriptions of other languages. Similarly, although Turkana is said not to have tatpuruṣa compounds, it does have a "topicalisation strategy" which allows

(4) Turkana (Dimmendaal 1983: 337)
     ɛ-kalèes ɲɪ-dè
     M.SG-ostrich M/N.PL-child
     'ostrich chicks'

instead of the usual

(5) Turkana (Dimmendaal 1983: 337)
     ɲɪ-dè à è-kalèès
     M/N.PL-child of M.SG-ostrich
     'ostrich's chicks'

Languages which are reported as not having tatpuruṣa compounds include the two mentioned above, Hixkaryana, Arabic (Holes 1990: 258–259) and Evenki (Nedjalkov 1997). Dimmendaal (1983: 292) speculates that the lack of compounds in Turkana may correlate with its verb-initial word-order, but languages like Hebrew, Maori or Welsh (Thorne 1993: 340–341) show that there is no necessary link here. Similarly, although it might seem that the lack of compounds in Arabic is due to its introflecting morphology, the fact that some are found in Hebrew (albeit not as frequently as in many other languages) shows that there is no necessary link between the two. Neither is it the case that polysynthetic morphology precludes compounding, since Chukchee and Yimas both have tatpuruṣa compounds. Thus, while it is not obvious whether tatpuruṣa compounding is actually a language universal or not, for those languages which may lack such compounding there does not seem to be any clear correlation with any other feature.

Perhaps surprisingly, most of the languages sampled have compound verbs, except in Africa. A few are described as having compound verbs but not compound nouns. In some cases it is not clear whether the items concerned are best treated as compounds or instances of incorporation (→ Art. 53). In many cases the productivity of verbal compounding is extremely limited, because only a few verbs are allowed in head or in modifying position, because the elements are in the process of becoming grammaticalised, because only nouns from certain semantic fields (e. g. body-parts) can be included in a verbal compound, and so on. Very few of the languages with verbal compounds do not have tatpuruṣa verbal compounds, though Thai is described as having dvandva verbal compounds (see section 4.3.) but no tatpuruṣas, and Pirahã may not have any tatpuruṣa verbal compounds.

In contrast, very few languages are described as having tatpuruṣa adjectival compounds, and the majority of those are from Eurasia (Basque, Danish, Finnish). The types illustrated for Turkana and Tzutujil (the other languages in the sample to show this type) are both extremely limited, in Turkana, for instance, being limited to colour adjectives.

4.2. Karmadhāraya compounds

Karmadhāraya compounds are seen by the Sanskrit grammarians as a sub-type of tatpuruṣa compound. In modern times, two distinct groups of karmadhāraya compounds are usually distinguished. The first is adjective + noun compounds like *blackbird*, the second is noun + noun compounds in which the nouns stand in apposition to each other. Adjective + noun compounds are nowadays seen as being more like regular tatpuruṣa compounds than as a special type. Trivially, adjective + noun compounds are restricted to those languages in which there is a recognisable class of adjectives. In the vast majority of other cases, adjective + noun karmadhāraya compounds exist if there are other tatpuruṣa compounds. The figures are given in Table 51.5.

Table 51.5: Languages which have both tatpuruṣa and adjective + noun karmadhāraya compounds

Word Order	A	E	O	G	N	S	Tot
tatpuruṣa and Adj+N	3	4	4	0	4	3	18
tatpuruṣa but no Adj+N	2	1	0	3	1	0	7
No category of Adj or no tatpuruṣa	1	1	2	3	1	3	11

The second type of karmadhāraya compound is made up of two nouns, each of which independently refers to some aspect of the entity denoted by the compound as a whole. Examples from English include *maidservant, woman doctor* and *fighter-bomber*. Because the entity denoted by the compound can be viewed as having both aspects simultaneously, these compounds are also called appositional (Jespersen 1909–1949, VI: 142). Cross-linguistically, compounds of this type are used especially to mark gender and diminution (e. g. by compounding with the word for 'child'). One of the oddities of this type is that it is not possible to see from the meaning of the compound itself which element is the head; instead, headedness is determined by grammatical features or by parallelism with other structures. Although nothing can necessarily be concluded from the fact that this construction is not discussed in a particular description, karmadhāraya compounds are mentioned in approximately half of the descriptions in my sample, without apparent areal bias (except that they are mentioned for only one South American language, but two others have no tatpuruṣa noun compounds at all, so this is probably not significant).

Karmadhāraya verbal and adjectival compounds are rare, and are difficult to distinguish from dvandvas (see section 4.3.), with which they are often classed or confused. Examples are given below, an adjectival example in (6), a verbal one in (7).

(6) Tswana (Cole 1955: 144)
kgômo ênkgwê-kubidu
ox white.backed-red
'a white-backed red ox'

(7) Siroi (Wells 1979: 55)
bale-far-de
kill-spread-3PL.PRES
'they massacre them'

4.3. Dvandva compounds

Dvandvas, also called copulative compounds (Jespersen, 1909–1949, VI: 142), aggregative compounds (Whitney 1889: 480) or co-ordinative compounds (Bloomfield 1933: 235), have two or more words in a coordinate relationship, such that the entity denoted is the totality of the entities denoted by each of the elements. Dvandvas are rare in English outside a few borrowed place-names (*Alsace-Lorraine, Schleswig-Holstein*) and corporate names (*Fletcher-Challenge, Rank-Hovis-McDougal, Time Warner*), but occur in many other European languages.

(8) Modern Greek (Mackridge 1985: 326)
xart-o-fakela
notepaper-LINK-envelopes
'stationery'

The incidence of dvandva compounds in the languages of the world appears to have strong areal biases, as is indicated in Table 51.6.

Table 51.6: Languages with dvandva compounds

Word Order	A	E	O	G	N	S*	Tot
Dvandva compounds discussed	1	5	5	4	1	1	17
No dvandva compounds discussed	5	1	1	2	5	4	18

* In the description of Pirahã there are some verbal compounds which might be dvandvas but might be tatpuruṣas. This language is omitted from the table.

Interestingly, adjectival dvandvas are discussed only in descriptions of languages from area 2 (Eurasia) which also have nominal dvandvas, and in Cantonese (which is not listed as having nominal dvandvas). Verbal dvandvas are discussed only in descriptions of languages from area 3 (in fact, only in the South-east Asian languages Cambodian, Thai and Vietnamese which also have nominal dvandvas) and in Pirahã, discussed in the note to Table 51.6. These compounds seem to be areally extremely restricted.

A very few languages (Abkhaz, Hebrew, Tamil) may have an overt expression of a word meaning 'and', but this is unusual. In Danish, the element which historically corresponds to 'and' has been phonologically reduced to the point where it is merely a [ə], and homophonous with other link elements:

(9) Danish
saft-e-vand
juice-and-water
'diluted cordial'

Despite an apparently clear distinction between appositional karmadhāraya compounds and dvandvas, the two are frequently (and understandably) confused, for at least three reasons. (a) Both can be glossed by inserting the word 'and' between the two elements: *fighter-bomber* 'fighter and bomber',

Schleswig-Holstein 'Schleswig and Holstein'. (b) While in some languages (e. g. Marathi, see Pandharipande 1997: 518, and Tamil) a distinction is made between the two constructions because noun dvandvas take plural or dual agreement, this difference is not maintained in all languages (or even in all that mark agreement); both singular and plural concord are found under different semantic circumstances in Sanskrit (Gonda 1966: 82). (c) With adjectival and verbal compounds in particular (see section 4.2.), it can be difficult to determine the semantics: is *a bitter-sweet scent* a scent which is defined by being at the intersection of 'bitter' and 'sweet', or one defined by the union of 'bitter' and 'sweet'? It is not even clear how far the question makes sense. Even with nominal compounds there can be doubt: is a *washer-drier* a drier that can also function as a washer (and thus linguistically like *fighter-bomber*) or a machine which is made up of a washer and a drier (and thus like *Schleswig-Holstein*)? And constructions like *merchant-adventurer, queen-mother* and *secretary-treasurer* look in many ways like dvandvas, but unlike prototypical dvandvas provide two labels for a single person, rather than labels for two distinct people (compare *mother-father* discussed immediately below).

In many Indic languages, there is a subset of dvandvas in which the two words compounded are alternatives rather than constituent parts of the entity denoted.

(10) Sanskrit (Whitney 1899: 485)
      jayaparājaya
      victory-defeat
      'victory or defeat'

It is not entirely clear whether this should be treated as a separate type. The distinction between 'and' and 'or' blurs in many cases, since a reference to *mother-father* (as in Kashmiri [Wali & Koul 1997: 284], Malayalam [Asher & Kumari 1997: 399], Marathi [Pandharipande 1997: 518], or Tamil [Asher 1982: 206]) is likely in many cases to refer to one or the other, although it has the potential to refer to both.

Dvandvas may be constructed of examples of the general concept denoted by the semantically specialised compound as a whole. For example,

(11) (a) Vietnamese (Thompson 1965: 128)
          bàn-ghê
          table-chair
          'furniture'

(b) Marathi (Pandharipande 1997: 519)
    tikhat-mīṭh
    pepper-salt
    'spices'

(c) Kannada (Sridhar 1990: 283)
    bassu karu
    bus car
    'vehicles'

In these cases the construction as a whole may be interpreted as an exocentric of some kind (see section 4.4.), though the form is clearly dvandva.

The type illustrated in *the Australian-American relationship* or *the Kennedy-Kruschev meeting* may belong here, in that the two elements are of equivalent status (and in these cases may even be inverted, which is not true of all dvandvas in most languages). However, I prefer to recognise these as a separate type which may be dubbed translative, as in *a Greek-English lexicon*.

4.4. Bahuvrīhi compounds

Bahuvrīhi compounds are also known as possessive compounds, *Dickkopfkomposita*, or exocentric compounds (Bloomfield 1933: 235), although exocentric is a rather more inclusive label. Bahuvrīhi, like the German *Dickkopf*, is an example of the type, in the Sanskrit instance meaning 'having much rice'. In Sanskrit, this label was applied to a compound functioning "as an adjective qualifying some other concept" (Burrow 1955: 215), rather like English *blue-eyed*. In modern usage, however, the term is applied to any compound which is not a hyponym of its own head element. By this definition, English *egghead* (which is not a type of head), *pickpocket* (which is neither a type of pick nor a type of pocket) and *output* (which is neither a type of out nor a type of put) are termed bahuvrīhis or exocentrics, but *blue-eyed* is not.

Approximately half of the languages in my sample across all areas are described as having bahuvrīhis or exocentrics, and there is no apparent correlation with any structural facet of the languages concerned. In Imbabura Quechua there is an interesting construction in which the equivalents of exocentric compounds are created by affix.

(12) Imbabura Quechua (Cole 1982: 94)
      jatun singa-yui
      big nose-POSS
      'one who has a big nose'

The same construction can also be used with a simplex base:

(13) Imbabura Quechua (Cole 1982: 94)
      wasi-yuj
      house-POSS
      'house owner'

This type is much more like the English *blue-eyed*, and would not generally be counted as a bahuvrīhi; it makes the point that other constructions can have the same effect as the bahuvrīhi.

Exocentric verbs and adjectives are certainly possible (witness English *pig out* and *stop-go*), but are rarely discussed in language descriptions. (Parenthetically, we should note for English that *stop-go* as in *stop-go negotiations* may not be an adjective, but may be a complex element functioning as modifier – it has no comparative and cannot be submodified by *very, rather*, it cannot be used as a base from which to derive a noun or adverb, etc.; it is not clear how far this type of analysis is available in other languages.) This type, while not strictly a type of bahuvrīhi, is still of interest, and two examples are presented below. How frequent such types are is difficult to determine, but they appear to be rare.

(14) Finnish (Sulkala & Karjalainen 1992: 361)
      parta-suu
      beard-mouth
      'bearded'

(15) Tzutujil (Dayley 1985: 136)
      b'ojchi7xik < b'o7j chii7
      cotton mouth
      'to woo'

4.5. Avyayībhāva compounds

This class of compounds, recognised by the Sanskrit grammarians, is not generally used by recent scholars. The name means 'conversion to an uninflected', and denotes those adjectival compounds used adverbially (Whitney 1889: 513). The class is listed here only for completeness, and will not be discussed further.

4.6. Synthetic compounds

The isolation of a class of synthetic compounds belongs to much more recent linguistic history than the Sanskrit grammarians, and the class is not particularly well-defined. Synthetic compounds are also called semi-synthetic compounds (Bloomfield 1933: 232), verbal compounds (Roeper & Siegel 1978) and verbal-nexus compounds (Allen 1978: 147). Synthetic compounds have been discussed mainly in the Germanic languages, but the phenomenon is much more widespread (Lieber 1994: 3608).

Synthetic compounds are easier to illustrate than to define. Examples of synthetic compounds from English include *truck-driver, peace-keeping* and *home-made*. This type has been variously defined as being based on word-groups or syntactic constructions (Botha 1984: 2), or as compounds whose head elements are derived from verbs (Lieber 1994: 3607). Some authors restrict the affixes that synthetic compounds may involve (Roeper & Siegel 1978: 199), others do not. Note in any case the apparent inconsistency that while *speech-synthesiser* is classed as a synthetic compound because *synthesiser* is derived from a verb, *speech synthesis* is not, because *synthesis* is not (overtly) derived from *synthesise* (Lieber 1994: 3608). Much of the discussion of these compounds in the literature has centred on the fact that the modifying element in the compound is (usually) interpreted as an argument of the verb from which the head element is derived. A *speech-synthesiser* is a machine which synthesises speech (*speech* being the direct object of *synthesise*). This type of interpretation is much more restricted than is typically the case with other tatpuruṣa compounds (which in this context are frequently referred to as root compounds or primary compounds – rather cavalierly, since roots are not necessarily involved, and it is not clear why synthetic compounds might be thought "secondary").

In my sample no synthetic compounds are described for any of the languages in area 4 (Australia and New Guinea), but this is an accidental gap, since Nash (1986: 37) describes synthetic compounds in Warlpiri as the major productive type of compound in that language. In other areas about half of the languages are described as having something which might be considered to be a synthetic compound. There are at least two hypotheses which might be put forward to explain the ordering of verbal element and nominal argument in a synthetic compound. (a) It might be that the order of verb and argument corresponds to the order of verb and direct object in the syntax. Figures for this hypothesis are given in Table 51.7. (b) It might be that the order of verb and argument corresponds to the order of head and modifier in tatpuruṣa compounds in the same language. Figures for this hypothesis are given in Table 51.8. The totals are not the same in the two tables because information on the ordering of verb and object is missing in one case, some languages do not have ordinary tatpuruṣa compounds with which to make comparisons, etc. Nevertheless, it can be seen that hypothesis (b) is more strongly supported than hypothesis (a), and that the ordering in a synthetic compound relies more on morphological principles than on syntactic ones.

Table 51.7: Correlation of verb and object in a synthetic compound with verb and object in syntax

Word Order	A	E	O	G	N	S	Tot
O-V & CpdN-V	1	1	0	0	1	1	4
O-V & CpdV-N	0	0	0	0	0	0	0
V-O & CpdN-V	2	1	0	0	0	1	4
V-O & CpdV-N	3	0	4	0	1	1	9

Table 51.8: Correlation of verb and object in a synthetic compound with head and modifier in tatpuruṣa compounds

Word Order	A	E	O	G	N	S	Tot
H-M & CpdN-V	1	0	0	0	0	0	1
H-M & CpdV-N	2	0	5	0	1	1	9
M-H & CpdN-V	1	2	0	0	1	1	5
M-H & CpdV-N	0	0	0	0	0	0	0

5. Meanings in tatpuruṣa compounds

One aspect of compounding that is frequently dealt with a great length in discussions of individual languages is the meaning relationships that may hold between the elements (see e. g. Adams 1973; Brekle 1970; De Haas & Trommelen 1993; Hatcher 1960; Lees 1960; Levi 1978; Rohrer 1977; Ryder 1994; Söderbergh 1968; Warren 1978; Žepić 1970). Although it is unfortunately the case that very few descriptions of languages give enough information for it to be obvious what kinds of semantic relationships may be expressed within tatpuruṣa compounds, there is enough information about a few languages (such as English) to suggest that — for at least some languages — there may not be any finite list of relationships. In a detailed survey of just three languages, Bauer (1978: 147) points out that underlying semantic relationships of location appear to be the most common relationships in those languages. The same is true with the sample discussed here. Compounds in which the head is the location of the entity denoted in the modifier (e. g. English *furniture store*) or where the head denotes an entity located at the modifier (e. g. English *bone cancer*) are the types most frequently illustrated or commented on for the languages in my sample across all areas. The next most frequent type to be illustrated is the type where the head is made from the material in the modifier (e. g. English *sandcastle*). Other meanings are illustrated or commented on far more sporadically. While this does not show that other meanings are not also in common use, it does suggest that compounds may be used prototypically to indicate location or source (especially if 'made from', 'made by', 'belonging to' and 'coming from' are all interpreted as sources).

6. Tying elements together: morphological effects

The norm in compounding — possibly because of the morphological isolation of the elements in a compound — is for the elements of a compound to be juxtaposed stems. The compound as a whole may then be inflected for its role in the sentence, if inflection is used in the language concerned. The preference for stem juxtaposition must also be supported by the fact that many languages do not have any inflections which could intervene in a compound. In some descriptions, items which are linked by prepositions are called compounds if they meet some criterion of frequency or lexicalisation. Examples like that in (16) illustrate the general type.

(16)   French
       chemin de fer
       way of iron
       'railway'

Such examples are found in a number of languages, including Hebrew and Toba-Batak, but will not be considered any further here (see further below in section 8).

Where there is not simply juxtaposition of stems, there are two main ways of linking the elements of a compound. The first is by means of some kind of linking element, which thus comes to act as an empty morph. The second is the use of some inflectional form of one of the elements. In some instances it may not be clear which of these is involved, as will be illustrated below.

Linking elements may be purely phonological in the sense that they are there to improve the phonological structure of the resultant word, or they may have morphological origins, in that they may derive from inflectional markings. Cambodian and Yoruba provide examples of the first type. In Cambodian a linking vowel is added, sometimes accompanied by a gemination of the final consonant of the first element.

(17) Cambodian (Ehrman 1972: 51)
    (a) *yian-ə-thaan*
        vehicle-LINK-place
        'garage'
    (b) *riac-cə-kaa*
        royal-LINK-affair
        'government'

The second type is illustrated by Danish, where most of the link elements are derived variously from genitive and plural markers, but occasional ones are borrowed from German.

(18) Danish (Allan *et al.* 1995: 545–546)
    (a) *jul-e-dag*
        Christmas-LINK-day
        'Christmas day' (link is etymologically a genitive)
    (b) *invalid-e-pension*
        invalid-LINK-pension
        'disability pension' (link is etymologically a plural)
    (c) *smør-(r)e-brød*
        butter-LINK-bread
        'open sandwich' (link is etymologically from *og* 'and')

Where nouns are concerned, inflectional elements used in compounds are usually case-markers, though there are instances of other types (e. g. plural markers in Dutch). The most common kind of case marking appears to be that used for possession, whether the possessor or the possessee is the noun marked in the language in question. Contrast, for instance, Finnish which marks the possessor and Takelma which marks the possessee:

(19) Finnish (Sulkala & Karjalainen 1992: 362)
    auto-n-ikkuna
    car-GEN-window
    'car window'

(20) Takelma (Sapir 1912: 242 [226])
    p!iyin sgéʔxabā:
    deer its.hat
    'deerskin hat'

In Hebrew it is difficult to say whether there is juxtaposition of stems or the use of possession-marking, since in construct phrases (used to mark possession) there may be no overt case marking:

(21) Hebrew (Glinert 1989: 38)
    oreH iton
    editor newspaper
    either 'editor of a newspaper' or 'newspaper editor'

There is a wide range of other types of case-marking attested. In Tamil, stems are compounded, but the first element stem is the oblique stem of the noun concerned. In Maidu a marker homophonous with the nominative marker is used on the first (modifying) element of a compound when it would otherwise end in a vowel (the accusative case is unmarked in Maidu):

(22) Maidu (Dixon 1911)
    hi'nī-m-butu
    eye-NOM-fur
    'eye-lash'

In Yimas, the modifying element occurs in the oblique case:

(23) Yimas (Foley 1991: 172)
    num-n numpran
    village-OBL pig
    'domesticated pig'

In Sanskrit, the modifying element of a compound may occur in the accusative, instrumental (abbreviated INST in (24)), dative, locative or ablative case, in keeping with the sense of the compound.

(24) Sanskrit (Whitney 1889: 483)
    (a) *dhana-m-jayá*
        wealth-ACC-winning
        'winning wealth'
    (b) *diví-cara*
        sky.LOC-moving
        'moving in the sky'
    (c) *vāc-ā́-stena*
        incantation-INST-stealing
        'stealing by incantation'

In Finnish, the modifying element of the compound can be in any of the local cases (in (25) ADE means 'adessive' and DERIV means 'derivational marker'):

(25) Finnish (Sulkala & Karjalainen 1992: 362)
    (a) *matka-lla-oloaika*
        journey-ADE-be.DERIV.time
        'the time the journey takes'

(b) *maa-lta-pako*
country-ABL-flee.DERIV
'rural depopulation'

In Hungarian, similar types can be found, but, crucially, only when the head is a verb (FACT means 'factive case'):

(26)   Hungarian (Kiefer 1992: 64—65)
   (a) *tévé-t néz*
      television-ACC watch
      'watch television'
   (b) *új-já-épít*
      new-FACT-build
      'rebuild'

Where verbs are modifiers in compounds, the overwhelming pattern is to use verb stems, but there are languages in which an inflected non-finite verb-form is used, for example Danish, Finnish and Yimas.

(27)   Yimas (Foley 1991: 175)
   ayk-t yaw
   marry-NONFINITE road
   'rules for a proper marriage'

In other languages, though these are a minority, finite verb forms appear in compounds. Consider the following examples of endocentric and exocentric compounds:

(28)   Arabana-Wangkangurru (Hercus 1994: 211)
   yanhi-rnda-tharka-kura
   speak-PRES-stand-PAST.CONTINUOUS
   'they were standing talking'

(29)   Kanuri (Lukas 1937: 15)
   lenəm-aré
   you.go-come!
   'way to and fro'

(30)   Tswana (Cole 1955: 122)
   mo-šwa-oême
   NOUN.CLASS-die-it.standing
   'dead tree, still standing'

Booij (1993) distinguishes between inherent and contextual inflection, where inherent inflections include number for nouns, comparatives, infinitives and participles, and contextual inflection includes markers determined by concord and government from elements elsewhere in the sentence. He suggests (1993: 42) that only inherent inflection can be found within words. The data presented here suggests that this conclusion is not entirely correct. However, in most of the instances in which case is found in a compound, it is either (a) an instance of adnominal marking (usually interpreted as possession-marking from its most common usage) or (b) case which is determined by some other element within the compound (consider the Sanskrit examples in (24) for example). The Arabana-Wangkangurru and Kanuri examples in (28) and (29) are less easily explained in this way, and may be genuine counter-examples. On the whole, Booij's generalisation appears to be true, but it is probably not an absolute universal.

7. Tying elements together: phonological effects

Apart from morphophonemic and morphotonemic changes that are concomitants of the compounding process in languages such as Japanese and Nama, there are languages in which compounding is, or may be, accompanied by a certain amount of phonological merger of the two elements. This may simply be the result of the lexicalisation process, or may be due to constraints (whether weak or strong) on the shape of stems. In either case, the results may be rather more like what, in the morphology of English, are described as blends. Some examples are given below.

(31)   Hebrew (Glinert 1989: 441)
   (a) *rakevel < rakevet kevel*
      train cable
      'cable car'
   (b) *midraHov < midraHa reHov*
      pavement street
      'pedestrian precinct'

(32)   Dakota (Boas & Swanton 1911)
   (a) *ćanze' < ćante ze'*
      heart disturbed
      'be troubled'
   (b) *hãmani < hãyetu mani*
      night walk
      'walk at night'

(33)   West Greenlandic (Fortescue 1984: 116)
   tuttuamia < tuttup amia
   'caribou skin'

(34)   Toba-Batak (Nababan 1981: 91)
   karɛtapi < karɛta api
   carriage fire
   'train'

8. Delimiting the notion of compound

There is a tendency apparent in the literature to call any multi-word lexical item a 'compound'. This includes lexicalised phrases (35), nouns linked by prepositions (36), possessive

+ noun constructions (37), and names derived from syntactic structures (38).

(35) French
comme il faut
as it is.necessary
'proper'

(36) French
pomme de terre
apple of earth
'potato'

(37) (a) *women's liberation*
(b) *cat's paw*

(38) German
Vergißmeinnicht
forget.me.not

While such constructions are certainly listemes (Di Sciullo & Williams 1987), and typically show some degree of loss of semantic compositionality, and while they share with compounds the fact that they are multi-lexeme constructions, there are also differences between these and compounds more closely defined, though we lack a standard terminology to encode the distinction. The terms *composé prépositionnel* 'prepositional compound' (Spence 1969: 5) and compound phrase (Bauer 1978: 47) have been used for the construction in (36), and in German the term *Zusammenrückung* 'consolidation' is used for a number of different constructions including that illustrated in (38) (Fleischer 1975: 61–63). One difference in many of these cases is a lack of the binary structure which typifies compounds. The example in (37 a) lacks any phonological or grammatical isolation (although (37 b) does carry a single stress, and might thus be considered a compound). Part of the reason for the extension of the term 'compound' seems to be a confusion between listeme and word, discussed by Di Sciullo & Williams (1987). If we can accept examples like those in (35)–(38) as listemes of various kinds but not as lexemes, we have a way of restricting the use of the term 'compound'. That is not to deny parallels between compounds narrowly defined and constructions like those in (36) and (37), but simply to suggest that a more careful use of terminology might be helpful in this area.

9. Conclusion

It is not clear to what extent compounding can be regarded as a universal; there are languages which are reported as having no (or extremely few) compounds, but this might be a matter of definition. While the majority of languages that have compounding have endocentric (tatpuruṣa) nominal compounds, there are some which have none of that type, but compounds of other types, for instance exocentrics (Djapu, Morphy 1983: 48, Turkana) or verbal compounds (Paumarí), and the use of verb compounding at the expense of noun compounding is common in western Australian languages (Blake & Dixon 1979: 17). Languages which avoid compounding do not appear to share typological or areal features. The order of modifying and head element in a compound most often seems to reflect the order of possessor and possessed in noun phrases, but the order of modifier and head is frequently variable in compounds. The use of dvandva compounds seems to be an areal feature, but there is no obvious restriction of compound-type according to morphological type or constituent-ordering criteria. However, in languages such as Gumbaynggir, where there is no formal distinction between nouns and adjectives (Eades 1979: 271) there is no grammatical way to demarcate nominal compounds from syntactic structures, and correspondingly no such structures are described. Case-marking languages may mark case internally in a compound, usually either the case which is also used for possession or some other case which is determined by meaning and other elements in the compound. Other inflectional categories appear sporadically in compounds, usually, but not exclusively, inherent inflectional features. Incorporation (→ Art. 53), which is related (and, indeed, may be difficult to distinguish from compounding in some languages), has not been dealt with in this article.

10. References

Adams, Valerie. 1973. *An Introduction to Modern English Word-Formation.* London: Longman.

Allan, Robin & Holmes, Philip & Lundskær-Nielsen, Tom. 1995. *Danish, a comprehensive grammar.* London and New York: Routledge.

Asher, R. E. 1982. *Tamil.* Amsterdam: North Holland.

Asher, R. E. & T. C. Kumari. 1997. *Malayalam.* London and New York: Routledge.

Bamgbose, Ayo. 1966. *A Grammar of Yoruba.* London, etc.: Cambridge University Press.

Bauer, Laurie. 1978. *The Grammar of Nominal Compounding.* Odense: Odense University Press.

Bauer, Laurie. 1998. "When is a sequence of noun + noun a compound in English?" *English Language and Linguistics* 2.

Bauer, Winifred. 1993. *Maori*. London and New York: Routledge.

Blake, Barry J. & Dixon, R. M. W. 1979. "Introduction". In: Dixon, R. M. W. & Blake, Barry J. (eds.). *Handbook of Australian Languages*, Canberra: Australian National University Press, 1−25.

Bloomfield, Leonard. 1933. *Language*. London: George Allen & Unwin.

Boas, Franz. 1911. "Kwakiutl". In: Boas, Franz (ed.). *Handbook of American Indian Languages Part 1*, Washington: Smithsonian Institution, 423−557.

Boas, Franz & Swanton, John R. 1911. "Siouan: Dakota (Teton and Santee Dialects)". In: Boas, Franz (ed.), *Handbook of American Indian Languages Part 1*, Washington: Smithsonian Institution, 875−965.

Bogoras, Waldemar. 1922. "Chukchee". In: Boas, Franz (ed.), *Handbook of American Indian Languages Part 2*. Washington: Bureau of American Ethnology, 631−903.

Booij, Geert. 1993. "Against split morphology". In: Booij, Geert & Marle, Jaap van (eds.), *Yearbook of Morphology 1993*, Dordrecht, etc.: Kluwer, 27−49.

Botha, Rudolf P. 1984. *Morphological Mechanisms*. Oxford, etc.: Pergamon.

Brekle, Herbert E. 1970. *Generative Satzsemantik im System der Englischen Nominalkomposition*. München: Wilhelm Fink.

Burrow, T. 1955. *The Sanskrit Language*. London: Faber and Faber.

Chapman, Shirley & Derbyshire, Desmond C. 1991. "Paumarí". In: Derbyshire, Desmond C. & Pullum, Geoffrey K. (eds.), *Handbook of Amazonian Languages Vol 3*, Berlin, etc.: Mouton de Gruyter, 161−352.

Cole, Desmond T. 1955. *An Introduction to Tswana Grammar*. Cape Town: Longman.

Cole, Peter. 1982. *Imbabura Quechua*. Amsterdam: North Holland.

Davies, John. 1981. *Kobon*. Amsterdam: North Holland.

Dayley, Jon P. 1985. *Tzutujil Grammar*. Berkeley, etc.: University of California Press.

Dayley, Jon P. 1989. *Tümpisa (Panamint) Shoshone Grammar*. Berkeley, etc.: University of California Press.

Derbyshire, Desmond C. 1979. *Hixkaryana*. Amsterdam: North Holland.

Dimmendaal, Gerrit Jan. 1983. *The Turkana Language*. Dordrecht: Foris.

Di Sciullo, Anna-Maria & Edwin Williams. 1987. *On the Definition of Word*. Cambridge, Mass.: MIT Press.

Dixon, Roland B. 1911. "Maidu". In: Boas, Franz (ed.), *Handbook of American Indian Languages Part 1*, Washington: Smithsonian Institution, 679−734.

Dryer, Matthew S. 1989. "Large linguistic areas and language sampling". *Studies in Language* 13.2: 257−292.

Dryer, Matthew S. 1992. "The Greenbergian word order correlations". *Language* 68: 81−138.

Eades, Diana. 1979. "Gumbaynggir". In: Dixon, R. M. W. & Blake, Barry J. (eds.), *Handbook of Australian Languages*, Canberra: Australian National University Press, 244−361.

Ehrman, Madeline E. 1972. *Contemporary Cambodian: Grammatical Sketch*. Washington DC: Dept of State.

Everett, Daniel. 1986. "Pirahã". In: Derbyshire, Desmond C. & Pullum, Geoffrey K. (eds.), *Handbook of Amazonian Languages Vol 1*, Berlin, etc.: Mouton de Gruyter, 200−325.

Fasold, Ralph William August. 1969. *Noun Compounding in Thai*. Abbreviated reprint of 1968 University of Chicago PhD dissertation. Arlington, Va.

Fleischer, Wolfgang. 1975. *Wortbildung der deutschen Gegenwartssprache*. Tübingen: Niemeyer.

Foley, William A. 1991. *The Yimas Language of New Guinea*. Stanford: Stanford University Press.

Fortescue, Michael. 1984. *West Greenlandic*. London, etc.: Croom Helm.

Frachtenberg, Leo J. 1922. "Coos". In: Boas, Franz (ed.), *Handbook of American Indian Languages Part 2*. Washington: Bureau of American Ethnology, 297−429.

Glinert, Lewis. 1989. *The Grammar of Modern Hebrew*. Cambridge, etc.: Cambridge University Press.

Gonda, Jan. 1966. *A Concise Elementary Grammar of the Sanskrit Language*. University, Ala.: University of Alabama Press. Tr. Gordon B. Ford Jr.

Gregores, Emma & Suárez, Jorge A. 1967. *A Description of Colloquial Guarani*. The Hague and Paris: Mouton.

Haas, Wim de & Trommelen, Mieke. 1993. *Morfologisch Handboek van het Nederlands*. 's-Gravenhage: SDU.

Hatcher, Anna Granville. 1960. "An introduction to the analysis of English noun compounds". *Word* 16: 356−373.

Heath, Jeffrey. 1981. *Basic Materials in Mara: Grammar, Texts and Dictionary*. Canberra: Pacific Linguistics Series C, No. 60.

Hercus, Luise A. 1994. *A Grammar of the Arabana-Wangkangurru Language, Lake Eyre Basin, South*

Australia. Canberra: Pacific Linguistics, Series C, No 128.

Hewitt, B. G. 1979. *Abkhaz.* Amsterdam: North Holland.

Holes, Clive. 1990. *Gulf Arabic.* London and New York: Routledge.

Hudak, Thomas John. 1987. "Thai". In: Comrie, Bernard (ed.), *The Major Languages of East and South East Asia,* London: Routledge, 29–47.

Jacob, Judith M. 1968. *Introduction to Cambodian.* London, etc.: Oxford University Press.

Jespersen, Otto. 1909–1949. *A Modern English Grammar on Historical Principles.* 7 vols. London: George Allen & Unwin and Copenhagen: Munksgaard.

Karlsson, Fred. 1983. *Finnish Grammar.* Porvoo, etc.: Werner Söderström.

Key, Harold H. 1967. *Morphology of Cayuvava.* The Hague: Mouton.

Kiefer, Ferenc. 1992. "Compounding in Hungarian", *Rivista di Linguistica* 4/1, 61–78.

Lees, Robert B. 1960. *The Grammar of English Nominalizations.* The Hague: Mouton.

Levi, Judith N. 1978. *The Syntax and Semantics of Complex Nominals.* New York, etc: Academic.

Lieber, R[ochelle]. 1994. "Root compounds and synthetic compounds". In: Asher, R. E. (ed.), *The Encyclopedia of Language and Linguistics,* Vol 7, Oxford, etc.: Pergamon, 3607–3610.

Lukas, Johannes. 1937. *A Study of the Kanuri Language.* Oxford University Press. Reprinted 1967 by International African Institute.

Mackridge, Peter. 1985. *The Modern Greek Language.* Oxford: Oxford University Press.

Matthews, Stephen & Yip, Virginia. 1994. *Cantonese: a comprehensive grammar.* London and New York: Routledge.

Morphy, Frances. 1983. "Djapu, a Yolngu dialect". In: Dixon, R. M. W. & Blake, Barry J. (eds.), *Handbook of Australian Languages, Vol 3,* Canberra: Australian National University Press, 1–188.

Nababan, P. W. J. 1981. *A Grammar of Toba-Batak.* Canberra: Pacific Linguistics Series D No 37.

Nash, David. 1986. *Topics in Warlpiri Grammar.* New York and London: Garland.

Nedjalkov, Igor. 1997. *Evenki.* London and New York: Routledge.

Pandharipande, Rajeshwari V. 1997. *Marathi.* London and New York: Routledge.

Percival, W. K. 1981. *A Grammar of the Urbanised Toba-Batak of Medan.* Canberra: Pacific Linguistics Series B No 76.

Roeper, Thomas & Siegel, Muffy E. A. 1978. "A lexical transformation for verbal compounds", *Linguistic Inquiry* 9.2: 199–260.

Rohrer, Christian. 1977. *Die Wortzusammensetzung im modernen Französisch.* Tübingen: Narr.

Ross, Malcolm with Paol, John Natu. 1978. *A Waskia Grammar Sketch and Vocabulary.* Canberra: Pacific Linguistics Series B No. 56.

Rowlands, E. C. 1969. *Yoruba.* London: Hodder & Stoughton.

Ryder, Mary Ellen. 1994. *Ordered Chaos: The Interpretation of English Noun-Noun Compounds.* Berkeley, etc: University of California Press.

Saltarelli, Mario. 1988. *Basque.* London, etc.: Croom Helm.

Sapir, Edward. 1912. "Takelma". In: Boas, Franz (ed.), *Handbook of American Indian Languages* (1922) 1–296. Reprinted in Golla, Victor (ed), *The Collected Works of Edward Sapir vol VIII,* Berlin and New York: Mouton de Gruyter, 1990: 17–313.

Shibatani, Masayoshi. 1990. *The Languages of Japan.* Cambridge, etc.: Cambridge University Press.

Söderbergh, Ragnhild. 1968. *Svensk Ordbildning.* Norsteds: Svenska Bokförlaget.

Spence, Nicol C. W. 1969. "Composé nominal, locution et syntagme libre". *Linguistique* 2: 5–26.

Sridhar, S. N. 1990. *Kannada.* London and New York: Routledge.

Sulkala, Helena & Karjalainen, Merja. 1992. *Finnish.* London and New York: Routledge.

Thompson, Laurence C. 1965. *A Vietnamese Grammar.* Seattle: University of Washington Press.

Thorne, David A. 1993. *A Comprehensive Welsh Grammar.* Oxford and Cambridge, Mass.: Blackwell.

Wali, Kashi & Koul, Omkar N. 1997. *Kashmiri.* London and New York: Routledge.

Warren, Beatrice 1978. *Semantic Patterns of Noun-Noun Compounds.* Göteborg: Acta Universitatis Gothoburgensis.

Watkins, Laurel J. 1984. *A Grammar of Kiowa.* Lincoln and London: University of Nebraska Press.

Wells, Margaret A. 1979. *Siroi Grammar.* Canberra: Pacific Linguistics Series B No. 51.

Welmers, William E. 1973. *African Language Structures.* Berkeley, etc.: University of California Press.

Westermann, Diedrich. 1930. *A Study of the Ewe Language.* London, etc.: Oxford University Press.

Whitney, William Dwight. 1889. *Sanskrit Grammar.* Cambridge, Mass.: Harvard University Press and London: Oxford University Press. Second edition.

Žepić, Stanko, 1970. *Morphologie und Semantik der deutschen Nominalkomposita.* Zagreb: Philosophische Fakultät der Universität Zagreb.

Laurie Bauer
Victoria University of Wellington
(New Zealand)

52. Affix position

1. Position of affix relative to stem
2. Relative position of affixes
3. Special abbreviations
4. References (selected)

The rubric "affix position" subsumes two related phenomena: (a) the position of an affix relative to the stem with which it joins, and (b) the position of an affix relative to other affixes which accompany it. Both phenomena afford substantive typological generalizations.

1. Position of affix relative to stem

Affixes can be sorted into several types according to the way in which they are positioned relative to a word's stem. The world's languages do not exhibit instances of each type with equal frequency; several explanations have been proposed for this imbalance in the incidence of affix types.

1.1. Types of affixes

In general, affixes can be classified according to the way in which they are positioned relative to any stem with which they join: a prefix precedes its stem (as in Kikuyu *mi-rũũthi* [PL-lion] 'lions'), a suffix follows its stem (as in English *girl-s*), an infix interrupts its stem (as in Oaxaca Chontal *kwepo?* 'lizard', plural *kwe-l-po?*), a circumfix encloses its stem (as in Berber *ta-xd:am-t* 'worker (fem. sg.)', stem *xd:am*), and the segments of an intercalated affix are interspersed among those of its stem (as in Arabic *katab* 'wrote', where the perfective active affix is the vocalism *a...a* and the stem is the consonantal sequence *k...t...b* 'write'). In occasional instances, an affix's position relative to its stem is context-dependent; in Swahili, for example, relative affixes are suffixed in tenseless affirmative verb forms, but are otherwise prefixed (e. g. *wa-na-o-soma* [AGR-TNS-REL-read] 'who are reading', *wa-si-o-soma* [AGR-NEG-REL-read] 'who don't read', but *wa-soma-o* [AGR-read-REL] 'who read').

1.2. Incidence of affix types

Affixes of these different types might be naively expected to appear with equal frequency across the world's languages. In fact, infixes, circumfixes, and intercalated affixes appear only infrequently; because they entail discontinuity in the stem, in the affix, or in both, Greenberg (1966: 92) groups infixes, circumfixes, and intercalated affixes together as discontinuous affixes, and suggests that the presence of discontinuous affixes in a language always implies that of either prefixes or suffixes or both. Prefixes and suffixes appear frequently in languages worldwide; suffixes, however, appear with significantly greater frequency than prefixes (Sapir 1921: 67, Greenberg 1957: 89 ff.). Moreover, affixes encoding certain grammatical properties are particularly likely to appear in suffixal position; case affixes on nouns, for example, are nearly always suffixed (though Hall (1992: 58) cites Biblical Hebrew, Chontal, Cua, Kalispel, Luvale, Sabaic, Sakao, Shuswap, Squamish, Temiar, Zapotec, Zhilha, and Zulu as exceptions), as are mood affixes on verbs (Hawkins & Gilligan 1988: 222 ff.).

Across the world's languages, variations in the incidence of prefixation and suffixation correlate statistically with variations in word order typology. As Greenberg (1966: 92 f.) first noted, languages which favor postpositions and OV word order exhibit an overwhelming and most often exclusive preference for suffixes over prefixes; thus, in Greenberg's thirty-language sample, twelve of the fourteen postpositional languages were exclusively suffixing, as were ten of the twelve OV languages. By contrast, languages which are exclusively prefixing (a small minority cross-linguistically, represented by only a single language in Greenberg's sample) generally exhibit prepositions and VO word order (though Hawkins & Gilligan (1988: 252), citing work by Leon Stassen, note that Mangbetu is an apparent exception). As Hawkins & Cutler (1988: 288) emphasize, neither of these generalizations can be strengthened to a biconditional, since some languages which favor suffixes over prefixes — indeed, a number of exclusively suffixing languages — also favor prepositions and VO ordering.

Suffixation, in other words, is not only the most widespread type of affixation; it is also the least discriminate typologically, appearing freely in both head-initial languages and head-final languages. Prefixation, by contrast, is much more common in head-initial languages than in head-final languages; exclusive prefixation is nearly unique to head-initial languages.

1.3. Explaining the suffixing preference

At least four explanations for the suffixing preference have been considered.

1.3.1. Givón (1979)

The first of these derives from Givón (1979). Givón does not explicitly set out to account for the suffixing preference; he does, however, advance a hypothesis that suggests a particular understanding of this preference. He argues (pp. 275 ff.) that every human language is or has developed from a language of the head-final, SOV type. On the assumption (Givón 1971: 412 f.) that the affix X in a morphological combination X+stem (or stem+X) generally arises, by reanalysis, from the head X of a syntactic combination [X Y] (or [Y X]), Givón's SOV hypothesis entails that suffixes should be pervasive in the world's languages.

Various considerations militate against this explanation. First, Givón's SOV hypothesis rests, in part, on the assumption that the incidence of suffixes in a head-initial language is evidence of a head-final ancestor. But if this is the ONLY sort of evidence favoring the conclusion that some language has a head-final ancestor, then an explanation which attributes the incidence of suffixes in that language to ancestral syntax is circular (as Hall (1992: 94 f.) observes); moreover, the ordering of a language's morphological formatives is not necessarily a direct reflection of the basic word order at some earlier stage in its history, as Comrie (1980), Bybee (1985: 39 ff.), and Haspelmath (1993) have shown. Finally, the proposed explanation implies that on average, suffixes in head-initial languages must be older (being relics of an earlier, head-final stage) than suffixes in head-final languages, and should therefore exhibit a greater degree of grammaticization; but as Bybee et al. (1990: 14 f.) show, this expectation is not confirmed. Indeed, they point to a variety of potential sources for the diachronic development of verbal suffixes within head-initial languages.

1.3.2. Hawkins & Cutler (1988)

An alternative explanation for the suffixing preference is proposed by Hawkins & Cutler (1988) (cf. also Cutler *et al.* (1985) and Hawkins & Gilligan (1988)). Hawkins & Cutler argue that the incidence of prefixation and suffixation is universally constrained by (a) a principle favoring prefixation in head-initial languages and suffixation in head-final languages, and (b) a set of counterprinciples which uniformly favor suffixation in all languages. Adopting the assumption that affixes are always heads in morphological structure, they formulate principle (a) as in (1):

(1) The Head Ordering Principle
The affixal head of a word is ordered on the same side of its subcategorized modifier(s) as P is ordered relative to NP within PP, and as V is ordered relative to a direct object NP. (Hawkins & Cutler 1988: 290)

The Head Ordering Principle, they claim, accounts for the fact that prefixes are more commonly found in head-initial languages than in head-final languages (where the functionally analogous affixes tend to be suffixal). On its own, the Head Ordering Principle wrongly predicts that head-initial languages should favor prefixes over suffixes, which they do not; but Hawkins & Cutler argue that the set (b) of counterprinciples, while simply reinforcing the suffix preference in head-final languages, produces a skewing in favor of suffixation in head-initial languages (so that on average, prefixes and suffixes appear in roughly comparable numbers in such languages).

But what is the nature of these counterprinciples? Hawkins & Cutler argue that they follow from the mechanisms of language processing. Drawing on research in experimental psycholinguistics, they cite a large body of evidence suggesting that in the processes of speech production and comprehension, (i) a word's onset is more salient than its ending, while both are more salient than its middle (cf. Aitchison 1987: 119 ff.); and (ii) stems are, at some stage, processed separately from affixes. In view of these facts, Hawkins & Cutler argue that the suffixing preference can be accounted for simply by assuming that stems are processed before affixes: on this assumption, the ordering of a word's stem before its affix(es) places the stem in the word's most salient position (its onset) and the affix(es) in a position of lesser salience (the word's ending), facilitating the processing of stem before affix; because it fails to facilitate processing in this way, prefixation is to that extent disfavored.

Hawkins & Cutler note two additional factors which may tend to favor suffixation. First, because languages have many fewer affixes than stems, the onsets of prefixed words are phonologically less differentiated than the onsets of suffixed words; moreover, because an affix's content can in some instances be predicted from the syntactic or semantic context (while stems are comparatively unpredictable), the onset of a prefixed word is less informative than that of a suffixed word. In view of these factors, prefixation tends to delay word recognition, and is to that extent disfavored.

1.3.3. Hall (1992)

A somewhat different explanation of the suffixing preference is proposed by Hall (1992). Hall agrees with Hawkins & Cutler's central contention that the suffixation preference follows from principles of language processing, but questions the validity of both the Head Ordering Principle and the assumption that stems are processed before affixes; in addition, he asserts the need for a fuller account of the mechanism by which principles of language processing influence morphological form.

As Hall argues (pp. 49 ff.), the assumption that all affixes are heads (the main premise of the Head Ordering Principle) is not well-motivated. Indeed, most morphological theorists assume either that affixes are never heads (Zwicky 1985, Stump 1995: 247 f.) or that only certain affixes are heads (Williams 1981, Selkirk 1982: 74 ff., Lieber 1992: 77 ff.); the notion that inflectional affixes are heads is particularly difficult to motivate. But if the Head Ordering Principle is dispensed with, then how might one explain the much higher incidence of prefixation in head-initial languages? Hall (pp. 74 ff.) proposes a diachronic explanation: on the assumption that affixes arise historically through the reduction of syntactic heads, head-initial languages should exhibit a higher incidence of prefixation than head-final languages. (Hawkins & Cutler do, however, explicitly question (p. 311) the validity of this diachronic explanation, both on the grounds that affixes do not always derive from syntactic heads and on the grounds that the sorts of words from which affixes derive do not always exhibit the consistency of ordering which the diachronic explanation requires.)

Hall further asserts (p. 160) that existing experimental evidence fails to confirm Hawkins & Cutler's assumption that lexical processing (including stem access) necessarily precedes the processing of syntactic information (including that encoded by a word's inflectional affixes). Still, he agrees that the suffixation preference follows from the fact that prefixes impede processing efficiency (pp. 143 ff.): he shows that by delaying stem access, prefixes delay the point at which a word is recognized; moreover, he argues for a model of lexical access (based on the Cohort Model of Marslen-Wilson & Tyler (1980) and related work) in which prefixed words involve a more complex lexical representation (hence a higher degree of computational complexity in on-line processing) than suffixed words.

Hall employs this model in developing a diachronic account of the linkage between processing efficiency and morphological form (pp. 164 ff.), arguing that at that point in time at which an independent word becomes a candidate for reanalysis as an affix, the likelihood of reanalysis is constrained by its relative cost to the lexical processor: the reanalysis of some word as a prefix is costlier, and therefore less likely to happen, than the reanalysis of some word as suffix.

1.3.4. Bybee et al. (1990)

Bybee et al. (1990) question the validity of such processing explanations for the suffixing preference, arguing that the predominance of suffixes in the world's languages must be attributed to more than one cause. First, they demonstrate that (contrary to what any processing explanation would entail), the suffixation preference is not universally observable. Because of a universal tendency for free person/number markers to be postposed (and thus to develop into suffixes), verb-initial languages often exhibit suffixal agreement; but if person/number suffixes are excluded from consideration, such languages exhibit no clear preference for suffixes over prefixes. Moreover, the high incidence of suffixation in verb-final languages needn't be attributed to a suffixation preference, because it is, in any event, an inevitable manifestation of the more general tendency for such languages to postpose free grammatical markers: in languages of this sort, grammatical markers which become bound naturally emerge as suffixes. Thus, the only type of language that can be convincingly claimed to exhibit a suffixing preference (or a prefixing dispreference) is the verb-medial type, where a verb's preposed grammatical markers are less likely to develop into affixes than its postposed markers.

Bybee et al. entertain (pp. 19 ff.) the possibility that phonological factors favor suffixation over prefixation; two factors, in particular, might seem to afford an explanation of the suffixing preference. The first (originally suggested by Greenberg (1957: 90 f.) is the apparent tendency for assimilation to be anticipatory rather than perseverative – a tendency whose effect should be to rob prefixes of their formal stability, but to leave suffixes comparatively unaffected. Bybee et al. test this hypothesis against evidence from a large sample of languages, and find no grounds for the assumption that assimilation tends to be anticipatory: prefixes are no less stable in form than suffixes.

A second phonological factor which might help account for the suffixing preference is the tendency for the beginnings of words and phrases to be phonologically "stronger" than their ends: thus, prefixes exhibit initial consonants more often than suffixes do, and obstruent-initial prefixes begin with stops and affricates more often than obstruent-initial suffixes do. Nevertheless, Bybee et al. show that this difference in the relative phonological strength of prefixes and suffixes does not correlate with any difference in susceptibility to fusion with the accompanying stem. Thus, they reject the possibility that the suffixation preference has a phonological explanation (a possibility which is, in any event, called into question by the fact that this preference is restricted to verb-medial languages).

Bybee et al. propose an explanation for the worldwide predominance of suffixes which may shed light on the preference for suffixation in verb-medial languages. They observe a strong tendency for free grammatical markers to develop into affixes at clause peripheries; thus, free grammatical markers preposed to the verb in a verb-initial language or postposed to the verb in a verb-final language tend strongly to become affixes. By contrast, they find that in clause-internal positions, the likelihood that a free grammatical marker will develop into an affix on an adjacent verb generally depends on its degree of semantic relevance to that verb – that in accordance with the hierarchy of relevance proposed by Bybee (1985: 13 ff.), markers with higher relevance are more likely to become bound to the adjacent verb. Because verb-final languages are so much more common than verb-initial languages (and because a verb's free grammatical markers are so consistently postposed in a verb-final language), the statistical predominance of suffixes over prefixes in the world's languages must be seen as an effect not only of the suffixing preference in verb-medial languages, but of the strong tendency for clause-peripheral grammatical markers to develop into affixes. Indeed, the latter tendency may help explain the suffixing preference in verb-medial languages: in such languages, an intransitive verb's postposed grammatical markers are more often clause-peripheral than its preposed grammatical markers.

1.4. Properties of infixation

Even more striking than the predominance of suffixes over prefixes is the paucity of infixes in the world's languages. Hawkins & Cutler (1988: 309 f.) suggest that principles of language processing disfavor the incidence of infixation for two reasons. On the assumption that structural discontinuities tend to complicate language processing, infixed words should be relatively hard to process, since their stems – unlike those of prefixed words and suffixed words – lack structural integrity (cf. also Hall 1992: 199, note 2). Moreover, psycholinguistic research has shown that by a variety of criteria, a word's least salient part is its middle; accordingly, situating an affix in a word-internal position may diminish its capacity to convey potentially crucial grammatical information.

Where infixes do exist, their placement is subject to specific kinds of restrictions (Anderson 1992: 206 ff.). The positioning of an infix within a word or stem X is in general insensitive to X's internal morphology; instead, infixes are positioned so as to appear before or after a phonological unit of a particular kind (e.g. after X's first consonant, before X's last syllable, and so on). Typically, the phonological unit beside which an infix is situated is the first or last such unit in X; in some instances, however, this unit is identified by reference to the placement of X's main accent.

2. Relative position of affixes

Two significant generalizations have been proposed concerning the relative ordering of a word's affixes: the first of these pertains to the positioning of inflectional affixes relative to that of derivational affixes; the second concerns the sequencing of a word's inflectional affixes.

2.1. Position of inflection relative to derivation

It is commonly observed that in words which have both inflectional affixes and derivational affixes, the inflectional affixes tend to be positioned peripherally to the derivational affixes (as in *sweetens*, where *-en* is derivational and *-s* is inflectional). This tendency is elevated to the level of theoretical principle by proponents of the Split Morphology Hypothesis, according to which derivational morphology is lexical while (productive) inflectional morphology is extralexical (Anderson 1982, Perlmutter 1988). This hypothesis, however, is disconfirmed by at least two types of evidence.

First, there are instances in which category-changing derivational affixes join with productively inflected stems. Breton presents numerous instances of this kind (Stump 1990): thus, while **socksless* is not a possible privative adjective in English, its Breton counterpart *dileroù* (the result of affixing the denominal adjective-forming prefix *di-* to *leroù* 'socks', which carries the default plural suffix *-où*) is well-formed.

In view of their relative infrequency across languages, examples of this sort might be dismissed as a highly marked phenomenon. But there is a second kind of counterevidence to the Split Morphology Hypothesis which is very widely observable. Very commonly, headed words arising through the addition of a category-preserving derivational affix inflect on their head rather than at their periphery, as in the case of Russian *stučat'sja* 'to knock, hoping to be admitted', in whose inflected forms the derivational suffix *-sja* is external to all inflectional markings (e. g. *stučajutsja* 'they knock hopefully'). To account for such instances, Hoeksema (1984) allows individual inflectional rules to be defined as marking a stem's head rather than its periphery. Stump (1995: 256 ff.), however, questions the assumption that head marking is a stipulated property of individual inflectional rules, since there are instances in which one and the same inflectional affix appears on the head of some headed expressions but at the periphery of others. In Breton, for example, the default plural suffix *-où* marks the head *tok* 'hat' rather than the periphery of the noun *tok-sivi* [hat-strawberries] 'strawberry hull', but marks the periphery rather than the head *ti* 'house' of the noun *tiad* 'houseful': *tokoù-sivi*, but *tiadoù*. Moreover, the assumption that head marking is a stipulated property of individual inflectional rules fails to account for two universally valid generalizations about head marking:

(2) The Coderivative Uniformity Generalization
Where X and Y are headed coderivatives (i. e. arise through the application of the same category-preserving derivational rule), either X and Y both exhibit head marking or neither does (regardless of whether they inflect by means of the same rules).

(3) The Paradigm Uniformity Generalization
Stems that exhibit head marking do so categorically, throughout their paradigm of inflected forms.

Stump shows that generalizations (2) and (3) both follow automatically if one instead assumes that head marking is triggered by a property P which individual rules of category-preserving derivation may, by stipulation, assign to their derivatives; on this assumption, the incidence of head marking can be seen as the effect of a single universal principle sensitive to the presence of this property P (Stump's Head-Application Principle).

Notwithstanding the widespread incidence of head marking, Haspelmath (1993) documents several instances in which an extrafix (i. e. a derivational affix whose position in a word is peripheral to that of any inflectional affix) is resituated with respect to the accompanying inflectional markings. In more archaic forms of Georgian, for example, the indefinite postfix *-me* in *rame* 'anything' follows any case suffixes (e. g. *ra-s-me* [stem-DAT-INDEF]), while in more innovative forms of the language, it precedes them (e.g. *ra-me-s* [stem-INDEF-DAT]); strikingly, diachronic developments of this sort commonly involve an intermediate stage in which the internal inflectional affix is pleonastically doubled by an external counterpart (e. g. *ra-s-me-s* [stem-DAT-INDEF-DAT]). Although it is not unusual for a word's inflectional affixes to be externalized in this way, developments of the opposite sort — a diachronic internalization of inflectional affixes — are unattested. Haspelmath attributes this unidirectionality to the preference principle in (4), whose existence, he suggests, is motivated by both semiotic and psycholinguistic considerations (cf. Bybee (1985: 33), Dressler et al. (1987: 7)).

(4) The Inflection-outside-Derivation Principle
A morphologically complex word is preferred if its inflectional affixes are further away from the root than its derivational affixes.

2.2. Relative position of inflectional affixes

The relative position of a word's derivational affixes is, of course, determined by the function of the affixes themselves (or of the rules introducing them); for instance, the suffix *-er* in *sweetener* follows the suffix *-en* because *-er* derives nouns from verbs while *-en* derives verbs from adjectives. By contrast, the relative position of a word's inflectional affixes is not strictly determined by their function. From one language to the next, affixes which are comparable in their function may differ in their relative positioning (as the imperfect and first-person singular agreement suffixes differ in Latin *amā-ba-m* [love-IMPF-1SG] 'I loved' and Welsh Romany *kamá-v-as* [love-1SG-IMPF] 'I loved'). Indeed, alternative orderings may coexist within a single language; in Mari, for example, the positioning of plural suffixes and possessive suffixes is variable, as in *joltaš-em-βlak* [friend-POSS-PL] ~ *joltaš-βlak-em* [friend-PL-POSS] 'my friends' (Luutonen 1997: 13).

Despite such facts, the world's languages do exhibit certain tendencies in the relative ordering of inflectional affixes. Bybee (1985: 33 ff.) shows that verbal affixes encoding inflectional categories which are highly relevant to a verb's meaning tend to be situated closer to the verb stem than affixes encoding less relevant categories. For instance, because a verb's aspect is more directly relevant to its semantics than its tense, its mood, or its agreement properties are, aspectual affixes are almost never positioned peripherally to affixes expressing tense, mood, or agreement. Thus, in the fifty-language sample on which Bybee's conclusions are based, all eight of the languages in which the exponents of tense and aspect contrasted in their proximity to the verb stem conformed to this generalization; all ten of the languages in which the exponents of mood and aspect contrasted in stem-proximity conformed; and all but one of the thirteen languages in which the exponents of person and aspect contrasted in stem-proximity conformed. Bybee suggests (pp. 38 ff.) that the fact that an affix's stem-proximity tends to correlate positively with its degree of semantic relevance to the stem is a reflection of the fact that stem-affix combinations develop historically from frequently occurring syntactic combinations, and that both the frequency with which two words appear together in syntax and their semantic appropriateness for reanalysis as a single word is a function of their degree of mutual relevance.

3. Special abbreviations

AGR	agreement affix
IMPF	imperfect affix
INDEF	indefinite affix
PL	plural affix
POSS	possessive affix
REL	relative affix
TNS	tense affix

4. References

Aitchison, Jean. 1987. *Words in the mind.* Oxford and New York: Blackwell.

Anderson, Stephen R. 1982. "Where's morphology?" *Linguistic Inquiry* 13: 571–612.

Anderson, Stephen R. 1992. *A-Morphous morphology.* Cambridge: Cambridge University Press.

Bybee, Joan L. 1985. *Morphology: A study in the relation between meaning and form.* Amsterdam: Benjamins.

Bybee, Joan L. & Pagliuca, William & Perkins, Revere D. 1990. "On the asymmetries in the affixation of grammatical material". In: Croft, William & Denning, Keith & Kemmer, Suzanne (eds.). *Studies in typology and diachrony: Papers presented to Joseph H. Greenberg on his 75th birthday.* Amsterdam and Philadelphia: Benjamins, 1–42.

Comrie, Bernard. 1980. "Morphology and word order reconstructions: Problems and prospects". In: Fisiak, Jacek (ed.). *Historical morphology.* The Hague: Mouton, 83–96.

Cutler, Anne & Hawkins, John A. & Gilligan, Gary. 1985. "The suffixing preference: A processing explanation". *Linguistics* 23: 723–758.

Dressler, Wolfgang U. & Mayerthaler, Willi & Panagl, Oswald & Wurzel, Wolfgang U. 1987. *Leitmotifs in natural morphology.* Amsterdam and Philadelphia: Benjamins.

Givón, Talmy. 1971. "Historical syntax and synchronic morphology: An archaeologist's field trip". *Chicago Linguistics Society* 7: 394–415.

Givón, Talmy. 1979. *On understanding grammar.* New York: Academic Press.

Greenberg, Joseph H. 1957. *Essays in linguistics.* Chicago: University of Chicago Press.

Greenberg, Joseph H. 1966. "Some universals of grammar with particular reference to the order of meaningful elements". In: Greenberg, Joseph H. (ed.). *Universals of language.* Cambridge/MA, 73−113.

Hall, Christopher J. 1992. *Morphology and mind.* London and New York: Routledge.

Haspelmath, Martin. 1993. "The diachronic externalization of inflection". *Linguistics* 31: 279−309.

Hawkins, John A. & Cutler, Anne. 1988. "Psycholinguistic factors in morphological asymmetry". In: Hawkins, John A. (ed.). *Explaining language universals.* Oxford: Blackwell, 280−317.

Hawkins, John A. & Gilligan, Gary. 1988. "Prefixing and suffixing universals in relation to basic word order". *Lingua* 74: 219−259.

Hoeksema, Jacob. 1984. *Categorial morphology.* (University of Groningen dissertation.) New York: Garland.

Lieber, Rochelle. 1992. *Deconstructing morphology.* Chicago: University of Chicago Press.

Luutonen, Jorma. 1997. *The variation of morpheme order in Mari declension.* Helsinki: Suomalais-Ugrilainen Seura.

Marslen-Wilson, W. D. & Tyler, L. K. 1980. "The temporal structure of spoken language understanding". *Cognition* 8: 1−71.

Perlmutter, David. 1988. "The split morphology hypothesis: Evidence from Yiddish". In: Hammond, Michael & Noonan, Michael (eds.). *Theoretical morphology: approaches in modern linguistics.* San Diego: Academic Press, 79−100.

Sapir, Edward. 1921. *Language.* New York: Harcourt, Brace & Company.

Selkirk, Elisabeth O. 1982. *The syntax of words.* Cambridge/MA.: MIT Press.

Stump, Gregory T. 1990. "Breton inflection and the split morphology hypothesis". In: Hendrick, Randall (ed.). *The syntax of the modern Celtic languages (Syntax and Semantics, 23).* San Diego: Academic Press, 97−119.

Stump, Gregory T. 1995. "The uniformity of head marking in inflectional morphology". In: Booij, Geert & van Marle, Jaap (eds.). *Yearbook of Morphology 1994.* Dordrecht: Kluwer, 245−296.

Williams, Edwin. 1981. "On the notions 'lexically related' and 'head of a word'". *Linguistic Inquiry* 12: 245−274.

Zwicky, Arnold M. 1985. "Heads". *Journal of Linguistics* 21: 1−29.

Gregory Stump, University of Kentucky (USA)

53. Inkorporation

1. Vorbemerkung
2. Die Verschiedenheit des menschlichen Sprachbaus und der syntaktische Status der Inkorporation
3. Nominalinkorporation als Komposition in der morphologischen Typologie
4. Gegenwärtige grammatiktheoretische und typologische Auseinandersetzung
5. Vier Typen der Inkorporation
6. Inkorporation und Wortunterbrechung
7. Inkorporation als syntaktischer Prozeß
8. Spezielle Abkürzungen
9. Zitierte Literatur

1. Vorbemerkung

Nach Bakers (1988) weitgefaßter Definition ist Inkorporation ein allgemeines grammatisches Phänomen, das als Juxtaposition von zwei funktionalen oder lexikalischen Kategorien charakterisiert werden kann; so kann eine funktionale Kategorie in eine funktionale Kategorie, eine lexikalische in eine funktionale oder eine lexikalische in eine lexikalische inkorporiert werden. Andere Linguisten definieren Inkorporation enger als Komposition eines Wortes (typischerweise Verb oder Präposition) mit einem anderen Wort (typischerweise Nomen, Pronomen oder Adverb). Aber gerade um die Frage, ob es sich um ein morphologisches oder um ein syntaktisches Phänomen handelt, gehen die Meinungen auseinander. Schon die Tatsache, daß diese Frage im Mittelpunkt der Diskussion steht und daß die bisher von beiden Seiten angeführten Argumente keine klare Entscheidung herbeigeführt haben, bestärkt die Ansicht, daß Inkorporation weder in der Syntax noch in der Morphologie eine prototypische Kategorie ist. Ich werde mich im folgenden auf Nominalinkorporation (von nun an NI) beschränken, weil sie die einzige Instanz ist, die vom typologischen Standpunkt bisher umfassend untersucht worden ist. NI ist die Kombination eines Nomens und eines Verbs zu einer komplexen verbalen Form, die einerseits prädikative Funktion hat und andererseits auch die Rolle eines Arguments erfüllt (Gerdts 1998: 99). Sie weist Eigenschaften sowohl einer syntaktischen Konstruktion als auch eines morphologischen Prozesses auf, was eine Verfechterin des morphologischen Ansatzes wie Mithun (1984: 847) zur Charakterisierung der NI als „perhaps the most nearly syntactic of all morphological processes" geführt hat. Der erste Linguist, der auf die syntaktischen Aspekte der Inkorporation sowie auf ihre typologische Relevanz verwies, war Wilhelm von Humboldt, was hier eine besondere Anerkennung finden soll.

2. Die Verschiedenheit des menschlichen Sprachbaus und der syntaktische Status der Inkorporation

Humboldt (1836: Kap. 14) zählt das inkorporierende Verfahren zu den drei fundamentalen Methoden der Organisation von Sprachsystemen neben dem flektierenden (Sanskrit) und dem isolierenden (Chinesisch). Inkorporierende Sprachen behandeln den Satz mit all seinen notwendigen Bestandteilen nicht als eine aus Wörtern konstruierte Einheit, sondern als ein einziges Wort; sie spalten die Einheit des Satzes nicht, sondern tendieren dazu, seine Komponenten in der Einheit des verbalen Wortes als echten Mittelpunkts des Satzes zu binden, indem die Grenzen des Wortes mehr und mehr zu den Grenzen des Satzes hin verschoben werden. Die regierenden und die regierten Elemente werden soweit wie möglich im Verb verbunden wie etwa im folgenden Beispiel aus der „mexikanischen" Sprache (= klassisches Aztekisch oder Nahuatl), die Humboldt für einen prototypischen Repräsentanten des inkorporierenden Sprachbaus hält:

(1)   *ni-   naca-qua*
      1SG.SUBJ Fleisch-ess
      'Ich esse Fleisch.'

Auf den ersten Blick entsteht dadurch ein zusammengesetztes Verb, das genau dem griechischen Wort *kreophagéo* entspricht, bei näherem Hinsehen stellt man dahinter zwei verschiedene Konzeptionen des Satzes fest. Wird nämlich das Substantiv nicht inkorporiert, dann wird es beim Verb durch ein Pronomen vertreten, was einen unabhängigen Beweis dafür liefert, daß das einheitliche strukturelle Schema des Verbs auch die Funktion des Substantivs umfaßt; der Satz erscheint im Prädikatswort abgeschlossen, und das nun appositiv angeschlossene Substantiv bringt eine komplementäre, sekundäre Determination:

(2)   *ni-c-qua   in   naca-tl*
      1SG.SUBJ-3SG.OBJ-ess DET Fleisch-ABS
      'Ich esse (das) Fleisch.'

Falls kein bestimmtes Objekt erwähnt wird, muß beim Verb ein indefinites Pronomen erscheinen, das wenigstens angibt, ob es sich um Personen oder um Gegenstände handelt: *ni-tla-qua* 'ich esse etwas', *ni-te-tla-qua* 'ich gebe jemandem etwas'. Das Subjekt des Satzes wird am Verb ausgedrückt, aber es kann im Unterschied zum Objekt nicht inkorporiert werden. Auch die Erweiterung der Valenz, angezeigt durch das Applikativum *-lia*, erwähnt Humboldt in diesem Zusammenhang:

(3)   *ni-c-chihui-lia*
      1SG.SUBJ-3SG.OBJ-mach-APPL
      in   no-piltzin   ce calli
      DET   1SG.POSS-Sohn   ein Haus
      'Ich mache meinem Sohn ein Haus.'

Humboldt verwendet den Terminus *polysynthetisch* nicht, und seine Darstellung macht deutlich, daß er diesen Begriff nicht von *inkorporierend* unterscheidet. Er stellt einen Zusammenhang her zwischen der Tatsache, daß durch die Angabe von syntaktischen Relationen beim Verb die schematische Struktur des Verbs der schematischen Struktur des ganzen Satzes zu entsprechen tendiert, und der Tatsache, daß die Argumente selbst in das Verb eingegliedert werden, aber er bringt keine Erklärung dafür, warum die Inkorporation, die als definitorisches Merkmal dieses fundamentalen Sprachbautyps angesehen wird, auf das Objekt beschränkt ist. Auf jeden Fall stehen syntaktische Aspekte im Mittelpunkt seiner Überlegungen. Inkorporation hat eine syntaktische Funktion (Satzbildung) und nicht eine morphologische Funktion (Wortbildung). Sein Standpunkt ist weitgehend durch die Sprachwahl bestimmt. Vom Standpunkt des Nahuatl mag seine Beschreibung richtig sein, aber die Frage stellt sich, ob sie auch als allgemeine Theorie einer Überprüfung in anderen Sprachen standhält.

3. Nominalinkorporation als Komposition in der morphologischen Typologie

In der klassischen morphologischen Typologie werden drei kanonische oder ideale Sprachtypen unterschieden, nämlich der isolierende, der agglutinierende und der fusionierende (oder flektierende) Sprachtyp. Diesen drei

Haupttypen wird aber oft ein vierter hinzugefügt, der polysynthetisch oder inkorporierend genannt wird, was nicht bedeutet, daß beide Termini frei füreinander austauschbar sind. Während nämlich mit *polysynthetisch* in der Regel auf die Anzahl der miteinander verknüpften, lexikalischen oder grammatischen Morphemen verwiesen wird, kann *inkorporierend* speziell auf die Möglichkeit referieren, eine Anzahl von lexikalischen Morphemen zu einem komplexen Wort zu kombinieren. Comrie (1981: 45) stützt diese terminologische Differenzierung durch eine Gegenüberstellung der folgenden Beispiele aus dem Tschuktschischen und dem Eskimo:

(4) Tschuktschisch
 tə-meyə-levtə-pəγt-ərkən
 1SG-groß-Kopf-Schmerz-IMPF
 'Ich habe große Kopfschmerzen.'

(5) Eskimo (Sibirisches Yupik)
 angya-ghlla-ng-yug-tuq
 Boot-AUGM-ERWERB-DESID-3SG
 'Er will ein großes Boot erwerben.'

Inkorporation gilt somit als ein weiterdifferenzierendes Merkmal innerhalb des polysynthetischen Typs. Im Unterschied zum Tschuktschischen ist Eskimo zwar auch polysynthetisch, aber nicht inkorporierend, da es in der Regel ein lexikalisches Morphem pro Wort hat; die anderen Morpheme sind grammatischer Art. Hier gilt möglicherweise folgende Implikation: inkorporierend ⇒ polysynthetisch, aber nicht umgekehrt.

Ist Inkorporation ein morphologisches oder ein syntaktisches Verfahren? Kroebers (1909) Definition der Nominalinkorporation als Kombination des Objektsnomens mit dem als Satzprädikat fungierenden Verb in ein einziges Wort hält Sapir (1911: 257) entgegen, daß darin zwei heterogene Bedingungen vermengt werden: eine morphologische (Kombination zu einer komplexen lexikalischen Einheit, Wortbildung) und eine syntaktische, die syntaktische Beziehung, die zwischen den unabhängigen Elementen bestehen muß, welche in das komplexe Wort eingehen. NI muß ein Prozeß entweder der einen oder der anderen Art sein, und nach seiner Meinung handelt es sich um einen Prozeß der Zusammensetzung eines Nominalstamms mit einem Verb, unabhängig von der syntaktischen Funktion des Nomens. Diese Abgrenzung schließt einerseits die pronominale Inkorporation und andererseits auch die Bildung von denominalen Verben mittels derivativer Affixe aus, weil es sich in beiden Fällen um rein grammatische Morpheme handelt.

In der Typologie Skaličkas, wo die Sprachtypen als (prototypische) Konstrukte oder ideale Konstellationen von bevorzugten Zusammenhängen dargestellt werden, gilt Komposition dagegen als distinktives Merkmal des polysynthetischen Typs als solchen. „Seine hervorstechendste Eigenschaft ist das reichliche Vorhandensein von Komposita ... Die wichtigste Besonderheit des polysynthetischen Typs sind die Komposita" (Skalička 1951/1979: 57). Ein Kompositum steht oft dort, wo man in anderen Sprachen eine Ableitung, ein einfaches Wort oder eine syntaktische Kombination von mehreren Wörtern findet, etwa chinesisch *chung^1-kuo^2-hua^4* 'Mitte-Staat-Sprache' für 'Chinesisch' oder dt. *Dampfschiff* gegenüber tsch. *parník* und fr. *bateau à vapeur*.

Auf diese Weise werden die Termini *Inkorporation* und *Komposition* weitgehend gleichgestellt. So sagt Comrie ausdrücklich: „Incorporation refers to the possibility of taking a number of lexical morphemes and combining them together into a single word" (Comrie 1981: 42). Er kann folgerichtig behaupten, daß Inkorporation in beschränktem Maß auch im Englischen möglich ist „as when the lexical morphemes *swim* and *suit* are compounded together to give *swimsuit*." Der Unterschied zwischen Englisch und den eigentlich inkorporierenden Sprachen ist nach seiner Ansicht quantitativer Art und liegt darin, daß in letzteren dieser Prozeß außerordentlich produktiv ist und zur Bildung von sehr langen Wörtern führt (Beispiele (4) und (5); s. auch Biermann (1980: 32)). Mithun (1984: 847) widerlegt mit zwingenden Argumenten die Ansicht, daß Konstruktionen wie *to baby-sit, to mountain-climb, to word-process* als Inkorporation betrachtet werden können; sie sind vielmehr nicht-produktive Rückbildungen aus nominalen Komposita: sie werden meistens nur in semiprädikativen Strukturen gebraucht (*baby-sitting, mountain-climbing, word-processing*) und nicht in finiten Verbformen (*I mountain-climb every Saturday*); in *baby-sit* besteht keine klare thematische Relation zwischen N und V. „The way in which the baby qualifies the sitting is much more typical of the looser semantic relationships generally found between the constituents of nominal compounds." (Mithun 1984: 847) Dies gilt auch für folgende deutsche Konstruktionen, die in der poetischen Sprache produktiv sein können (sie stammen alle aus Paul Celans Gedichten): *schattenverheißend, messerumfunkelt, sonnendurchschwommen, nachtgewiegt, tagenthoben, feigengenährt, sternüberflogen, meerübergossen, schattenentblößt.* Im Deutschen ist Inkorporation allerdings ein produktiver Prozeß: die folgenden Wörter repräsentieren die 6 Typen, die Wurzel (1983) anhand von zwei Parametern (Unterbrechbarkeit und Formenbestand) unterscheidet: *radfahren, kopfrechnen, schutzimpfen, feuerverzinken, notlanden, gewährleisten.* Sie bilden in dieser Reihenfolge ein Kontinuum der Wortigkeit, die links schwer von der Syntax abzugrenzen und rechts sehr lexikalisiert ist.

Man muß Skalička zugutehalten, daß er durch die Unterscheidung von mehreren Kompositionstypen, die verschiedene Funktionen haben, eine nähere Präzisierung des Begriffs *Inkorporation* ermöglicht. Neben den Komposita, die eine Benennungsfunktion erfüllen, gibt es solche, die eine syntaktische Funktion haben und eher zwei Benennungen beinhalten. „Hierher gehören Wörter wie *Münzfernsprecher* oder *sprachbezogen*" (Skalička 1951/1979: 57−8); sie sind leichter durch eine Verbindung von mehreren syntaktischen Konstituenten paraphrasierbar: *auf die Sprache bezogen*. Die Grenzen zwischen diesen beiden Arten von Komposita sind fließend, die Unterschiede haben nicht absoluten, diskret-kategoriellen, sondern prototypischen Charakter. Zu den syntaktischen Komposita gehören die sogenannten Gelegenheits- oder Ad-Hoc-Komposita, die erst in einem spezifischen textuellen Zusammenhang entstehen, indem sie ein schon erwähntes syntaktisches Element als erstes Kompositionsglied wiederaufnehmen:

(6) *Der Minister kündigte die Bereitschaft der Regierung zum Dialog an. Diese Bereitschaftsankündigung / Regierungsbereitschaft / Dialogbereitschaft ...*

Hier liegt ein anaphorischer Gebrauch der Wortbildung vor. Nun scheint in einer Reihe von Sprachen Inkorporation auch mehr eine anaphorische als eine Wortbildungsfunktion zu haben (s. unten). Mit dieser Art von Komposita vergleicht Skalička selbst die prototypische Inkorporation: „Die syntaktischen Komposita sind besonders in einigen Indianersprachen beliebt. Hier verbindet sich das Objekt mit dem Verb zu einem einzigen Wort" (Skalička 1951: 57−8). Mit Inkorporation in diesem engeren Sinne wird die Tendenz bezeichnet, syntaktische Konstituenten (Objekt, Adverbiale usw.) bzw. die lexikalischen Köpfe derselben dem Prädikatswort einzuverleiben; die syntaktischen Beziehungen zwischen unabhängigen Satzkonstituenten werden durch die Zusammenrückung verschiedener Syntagmen zu einem Wort ersetzt, das dadurch zu einem Satzwort wird. Skalička erwähnt noch einen dritten Kompositionstyp, dessen Funktion es ist, „das betreffende Wort in eine bestimmte Klasse einzugliedern, also eine Funktion, die der der Genera in den germanischen Sprachen sowie der der Substantivklassen in den Bantusprachen ähnelt". Mehrere Autoren unterscheiden auch einen klassifikatorischen Inkorporationstyp von der eigentlich syntaktischen (für andere dagegen kompositionellen) Inkorporation. Für die genaue Bestimmung des grammatischen Status und damit auch des typologischen Status der Inkorporation, insbesondere für den Vergleich mit der Komposition wird es sich als nützlich erweisen, mehrere Inkorporationstypen zu unterscheiden, so wie es auch verschiedene Kompositionstypen mit unterschiedlichen formalen und funktionalen Eigenschaften gibt. Die für die gegenwärtige Diskussion noch zentrale Frage, ob Inkorporation ein morphologisch-lexikalisches oder ein syntaktisches bzw. textkonstituierendes Phänomen ist, kann so in einer differenzierteren Form angegangen werden.

4. Gegenwärtige grammatiktheoretische und typologische Auseinandersetzung

Die Sapir-Kroeber-Auseinandersetzung um die morphosyntaktischen Aspekte der Inkorporation wird von gegenwärtigen Typologen anhand neuer Daten aus Sprachen aller Kontinente und im Rahmen gegensätzlicher theoretischer Ansätze weitergeführt. Typologie und Grammatiktheorie sind auf gegenseitigen Einfluß angewiesen. Die formalen und funktionalen Eigenschaften der NI müssen möglichst genau bestimmt werden, damit sie in der typologischen Charakterisierung von Sprachen ohne Mißverständnisse benutzt werden kann, aber auch die neuen Tendenzen in der Grammatiktheorie müssen nach den neuen Erkenntnissen der Typologie beurteilt werden. Schon die Bestimmung der Verbreitung dieses Phänomens unter den Sprachfamilien der Welt bedarf einer möglichst präzisen Definition, aber die Definition sollte nicht unabhängig von den Beobachtungen hinsichtlich der formalen und funktionalen Variation des Phänomens erfolgen. Sapir hielt Inkorporation für eine relevante Eigenschaft vieler Indianersprachen, die zu verschiedenen Sprachfamilien gehören. Ich werde nur einige wenige erwähnen: Irokesisch (Onondaga, Mohawk, Tuscarora, Oneida, Seneca, Cayuga, Huron); Kaddoanisch (Caddo, Wichita, Pawnee, Arikara); Utoaztekisch (Nahuatl, Huichol); Maya (Kanjobal, Aguakatekisch, Mame, Ixil, Chuj, Yukatekisch; Sioux (Lakhota); Tanoanisch (Süd-Tiwa) usw.

Sapir erkennt zugleich, daß die Indianersprachen bemerkenswerte Unterschiede aufweisen sowohl hinsichtlich der relativen Stellung von Nomen und Verb, der impliziten syntaktischen Beziehungen zwischen beiden (Objekt, Instrument, Subjekt usw.), des Koaleszenzgrades sowie auch hinsichtlich der Bedeutung. Manche Sprachen scheinen mit NI-Strukturen generelle, permanente Aktivitäten, andere dagegen partikuläre Ereignisse zu bezeichnen; ersteres hält er für den normalen Fall, wie es sich für Komposita gehört: Nahuatl *ni-c-qua* (spezifische Tätigkeit) vs. *ni-naca-qua* (generelle Tätigkeit). Sapir gibt selber zu, daß dieser wichtige semantische Unterschied im klassischen Nahuatl nicht konstant zu sein scheint, und Merlan (1976) hat nachgewiesen, daß im modernen Dialekt von Huautla NI nicht die wortbildende, sondern eine diskursive Funktion vorherrscht, nämlich die Konstalthaltung der Referenz:

„In terms of discourse, it is possible to show that incorporated nouns serve to maintain coreference with previously introduced lexical nouns. Because lexical properties of nouns are preserved under incorporation, noun incorporation functions as a strong reference-maintaining device intermediate between complete repetition of the coreferential adjunct and complete anaphoric pronominalization ... The use of noun incorporation in Huautla Nahuatl is comparable to means used in other languages to signal coreference at the discourse level." (Merlan 1976: 177−8).

(7) (a) *Na' ni'-neki   ni-tla-powas wan*
        ich 1SG.SUBJ-woll 1SG-GENR-les aber
        aš ni'piya   mošti
        NEG 1SG.SUBJ-hab Buch
        'Ich will lesen, aber ich habe kein Buch.'
    (b) *Na' ni-mic-mošti-maka*
        Ich 1SG.SUBJ-2SG.OBJ-Buch-geb
        'Ich gebe dir ein Buch.'

Neben der anaphorischen hat NI sekundär auch die Funktion, einen generelleren Begriff auszudrücken, oft wird jedoch dieser Begriff erst im Kontext definiert, nicht im Lexikon. Die lexikalisierten, syntaktisch nicht paraphrasierbaren Bedeutungen sind eher selten.

Nicht alle Indianersprachen besitzen diese Technik, soweit man sich auf die vorhandenen grammatischen Beschreibungen verlassen kann, auch wenn es sich um polysynthetische Sprachen handelt. Andererseits wird diese Technik in vielen Sprachen anderer Familien produktiv angewendet, die nicht polysynthetisch sind. Dies hat einige Forscher dazu angeregt, einen nicht-morphologischen Inkorporationstyp anzunehmen, bei dem nicht Wortbildung, sondern eine pragmatische Funktion der Hintergrund-Stellung von Information eine entscheidende Rolle spielt (Sasse (1984), Compes et al. (1994)).

In der aktuellen Diskussion haben sich die Meinungen wieder einmal um die zwei schon dargelegten gegensätzlichen Grundansätze polarisiert, wenn auch bereichert durch neue präzisere Kriterien und formale Mittel. Sogar innerhalb des generativen Lagers und im Rahmen des Government-Binding-Modells haben sich zwei Fronten gebildet. Baker (1988) schlägt eine einheitliche syntaktische Beschreibung vor, während Di Sciullo & Wiliams (1987) und Rosen (1989) u. a. von einem lexikalischen (präsyntaktischen) Prozeß ausgehen, der der Komposition im Englischen ähnelt. Die Funktionalisten andererseits, allen voran Mithun (1984), versuchen die beobachteten Unterschiede auf einer Skala oder Hierarchie von vier prototypischen Strukturen anzuordnen, die sowohl formal als auch funktional voneinander abweichen. Die Frage ist, ob eine einfache D-Struktur oder eine komplexe Skala von Strukturen dem typologischen Vergleich besser dient, den gleitenden diachronischen Übergängen und der Tatsache, daß in derselben Sprache grundverschiedene Inkorporationstypen nebeneinander vorkommen, besser Rechnung tragen kann.

5. Vier Typen der Inkorporation

In diesem Abschnitt folgt eine komprimierte Beschreibung der vier Inkorporationstypen auf der Skala von Mithun (1984).

5.1. Typ I: Lexikalische Komposition

Das Ergebnis dieses Inkorporationstyps sind einheitliche, benennenswerte, institutionalisierte Begriffe. Die Bestandteile und das Resultat können zu jeder lexikalischen Kategorie gehören: N+N ⇒ N; V+V ⇒ V; N+V ⇒ V; N+A ⇒ A. Aber NI wird insofern als ein Spezialfall der Komposition angesehen, als sie die Existenz von „basic lexical composition" impliziert. Das Nomen hat keinen syntaktischen Status mehr, es kann nicht für Kasus, spezifische Referenz oder Numerus markiert werden. Die Valenz des Verbs wird reduziert, N und V verbinden sich zu einem intransitiven Verb, das direkt als N verwendet oder aus dem wieder ein transitives Verb abgeleitet werden kann; in Ergativsprachen bekommt das externe Argument den Kasus Absolutiv.

5.1.1. Typ I.1: Juxtaponierende Komposition

Zu dieser Gruppe rechnet Mithun viele ozeanische relativ analytische Sprachen mit fester Wortstellung wie Mokilesisch, Yapesisch, Tonganisch, Kusaie, Samoanisch usw. Bestimmte Klitika und grammatische Morpheme werden jetzt nicht an das V, sondern an die komplexe Einheit V+N angehängt:

(8) Ponape (mikronesisch)
 (a) *I kanga-la wini-o*
   ich ess-KOMPL Medizin-die
   'Ich nahm all diese Medizin ein.'
 (b) *I keng-winih-la*
   ich ess-Medizin-KOMPL
   'Ich bin mit dem Medizin-Einnehmen fertig.'

(9) Tonganisch (polynesisch)
 (a) *Na'e inu 'a e kavá*
   PRÄT trinken ABS KONN kava
   'e Sione
   ERG John
   'John trank das Kava.'
 (b) *Na'e inu kavá 'a Sione*
   PRÄT trinken Kava ABS John
   'John trank Kava.'

In einigen Maya-Sprachen wie Mam und Kanjobal bleiben N und V getrennte Einheiten, aber syntaktisch sind sie einem intransitiven Verb äquivalent, wie aus den Pronominalaffixen zu ersehen ist. Im Yukatekischen verbindet sich das N mit dem V aber in der Reihenfolge V+N, was nicht den prototypischen Komposita entspricht, aber im Einklang mit der Stellung des Objekts in der syntaktischen Konstruktion steht.

(10) Kanjobal
 (a) *š-ø-a-lo-t-oq in-pan*
   PRÄT-3ABS-2ERG-ess-geh-OPT 1ERG-Brot
   'Du hast mein Brot gegessen.'
 (b) *š-a-lo-w-i pan*
   PRÄT-2ABS-eat-AFF-AFF bread
   'Du hast Brot gegessen.'

(11) Yukatekisch
 (a) *tun pa'as-ik-ø lu'um*
   ASP+A3 scharr-MOD-B3s Erde
   le kaaš-o'
   DEM Huhn-CL
   'Das Huhn kratzt in der Erde.'
 (b) *tun pa'as-lu'um le kaaš-o'*
   ASP+A3 kratz-Erde DEM Huhn-CL
   'Das Huhn kratzt in der Erde.'

Im Lahu (Tibetoburmanisch) werden Kasusmarkierungen getilgt:

(12) (a) *ji̍ thà' dó*
   Alkohol AKK trink
   '(den) Alkohol trinken'
 (b) *ji̍-dò*
   Alkohol-trink
   'Alkohol trinken'

5.1.2. Typ I.2: Morphologische Komposition

Beide Bestandteile können ihre formelle Identität verlieren (Koaleszenz), sie unterliegen den internen phonologischen Prozessen des Wortes. Dies kann sich auch auf ihre semantische Identität auswirken, eine einheitliche, spezialisierte oder nicht komponentielle Bedeutung entsteht. Erwähnt werden hier die australischen Sprachen und Comanche (utoaztekisch).

Der so beschriebene Typ I macht einen sehr heterogenen Eindruck; sogar innerhalb der Mayasprachen verhalten sich die einzelnen Sprachen bezüglich des Koaleszenzgrades sehr unterschiedlich. In vielen Beispielen vor allem des ersten Untertyps verliert das Nomen partiell seinen syntaktischen Status, aber das Resultat könnte noch kein Wort sein. Einige Linguisten wie Gerdts (1998: 91−2) bezeichnen diese Konstruktion als „noun-stripping" und betrachten sie als eine Vorstufe der Inkorporation: N und V bleiben unabhängige Wörter, vor allem vom phonologischen Standpunkt aus; das N kann jedoch nicht vom V getrennt werden und hat keinen Kasusmarker und keine Determinanten bei sich. Bei Typ I.1 befinden wir uns möglicherweise im Bereich der Syntax, und man könnte höchstens formal von nicht-morphologischer Inkorporation, funktional von der Gliederung des Diskurses in größere Informationseinheiten, die als solche fokussierbar sind, deren Bestandteile jedoch in den

Hintergrund treten (Compes et al. 1994). *Weintrinken* bezeichnet sicher einen nennenswerten, institutionalisierten Begriff, aber dies bedeutet nicht, daß in *Wir trinken abends Wein* eine Inkorporation im Sinne einer lexikalischen Komposition vorliegt. Mithun nimmt diese Funktion erst für Typ III an.

5.2. Typ II: Manipulation der thematischen Struktur

Die Manipulation der thematischen Struktur hat Auswirkungen auf den ganzen Satz: ein obliques Argument wird in die Position promoviert, die ein inkorporiertes Nomen leergelassen hat; durch diese Erweiterung der Valenz entsteht ein neues transitives Verb.

(13) Tupinambá (Tupi-Guaraní)
 (a) *s-oβá*
  3SG.POSS-Gesicht
  a-yos-éy
  1SG.SUBJ-3SG.OBJ-wasch
  'Ich wusch sein Gesicht.'
 (b) *a-s-oβá-éy*
  1SG.SUBJ-3SG.OBJ-Gesicht-wasch
  'Ich wusch sein Gesicht.'

(14) Yukatekisch (Maya)
 (a) *k-in-ch'-ø-k*
  INKOMP-1SG.SUBJ-hack-INTR-IMPF
  ché' ichi in-kool
  Baum in 1SG.POSS-Maisfeld
  'Ich beseitigte die Bäume aus meinem Maisfeld.'
 (b) *k-in-ch'ak-ché'-t-ik*
  INKOMP-1SG.SUBJ-hack-Baum-TR-IMPF
  in-kool
  1SG.POSS-Maisfeld
  'Ich beseitigte die Bäume aus meinem Maisfeld.'

Andere Sprachen: Blackfoot (Algonkisch), Oluteco (Maya), Huichol (Utoaztekisch).

An dieser Konstruktion sind Körperteilbezeichnungen und ähnliche Ausdrücke inhärenter Possession oft beteiligt. Mithun definiert II als eine natürliche Extension von I, was die Reihenfolge auf ihrer Skala und die Implikation II ⇒ I auswirkt, aber ihre Analyse ist etwas zweifelhaft. Man muß annehmen, daß ein zunächst durch NI intransitiv gewordenes transitives Verb durch Promotion eines obliquen Arguments wieder transitiv wird, es gibt aber keine unabhängige Evidenz für eine Operation der Promotion. (Für eine genaue Beschreibung der Interaktion der Operationen Inkorporation und Promotion/Applikation im Oluteco siehe Zavala 1999). Das Morphem *-t* wird von Gutiérrez (1997: 105 ff.) als Zeichen der thematischen Transitivität interpretiert, das in allen transitiven NI-Konstruktionen erscheint, aber nicht immer die Anhebung eines obliquen Arguments ermöglicht. Aber in (14) haben wir es wahrscheinlich mit einem dreistelligen alternierenden (nicht orientierten) Verb zu tun (vgl. spanisch: *limpié los árboles de mi milpa* versus *limpié mi milpa de árboles*, wo die diskursive Gliederung der Information die Verteilung der Rollen bestimmt).

Transitive NI-Konstruktionen gehen in einigen Fällen auf dreistellige Prädikate zurück (Maya, Huichol; für Yukatekisch s. Gutiérrez 1997: 103 ff.). In vielen anderen Fällen sollte man eher annehmen, daß die NI einer Inkorporation von Adverbien und anderen freien Angaben gleichkommt, die die thematische Struktur des Verbs nicht modifiziert bzw. keine Transitivität voraussetzt:

Huichol
(15) *Wiki-xi me-pɨ-**tau-kɨxe***
 Vogel-PL 3PL-AS-Sonne-sich.warm.mach
 'Die Vögel machen sich an der Sonne warm.'

(16) *'Iki tɨɨ-ri*
 DEM Kind:PL-PL
 me-pɨ-te-yu-tsinu(-rixi)-ke-we
 3PL-AS-GENR-REFL-Welpe(-PL)-beiß-DISP
 'Diese Kinder beißen wie kleine Hunde.'

5.3. Typ III: Manipulation der Diskursstruktur

Hierbei wird bekannte oder nicht fokussierte Information in den Hintergrund gestellt. Typ III wird gerade im Hinblick auf die Funktion definiert. Aber Mithun betont, daß es sich hier um polysynthetische Sprachen handelt, die unter anderem A und P am Verb markieren und einen vollen Satz bilden, mit fakultativen Argumenten, freier Wortstellung usw. Die Form und der Grammatikalisierungsgrad der NI hängt also von anderen typologischen Charakteristiken der Sprachen ab. Insofern sollte man die Typen aufgrund der formalen Eigenschaften und nicht der Funktion definieren. Bestimmte polysynthetische Sprachen machen mit Strukturen des Typs III, was analytische Sprachen mit Typ I machen: diskursive Gliederung der Information. Formal geschieht diese Reduzierung der Prominenz entweder im syntaktischen Rahmen des Satzes (I) oder im (Satz-) Wort. Von der Form her sind Typ II und Typ III wahrscheinlich identisch; der Unterschied ist funktional begründet: in II wird NI vorwiegend für Wortbildungszwecke und in III für pragmatische Zwecke eingesetzt. Im Hinblick auf die Funktion gehören viele analytische Sprachen von I und die Sprachen von III zusammen. Insgesamt gesehen dürfte Typ I für Wortbildung weniger geeignet sein, während morphologische NI sich leichter auf diese Funktion spezialisieren kann. Die Implikation III ⇒ II ⇒ I soll auch funktional verstanden werden: wenn eine Sprache Typ II/III für diskursive Zwecke verwendet, dann verwendet sie sie auch für Wortbildung. Aber im Nahuatl ist die diskursive Funktion viel produktiver und prominenter als Wortbildung (Merlan 1976). Lexikalisierung tritt natürlich desto stärker ein, je mehr NI für die Funktion der Wortbildung benutzt wird. Mithuns Argumente dafür, daß Sprecher von Typ-III-Sprachen die NI-Konstruktionen als lexikalische, im Gedächtnis gespeicherte Wörter betrachten, halte ich für wenig überzeugend. Im Sinne der Grammatikalisierungsprozesse sollte man annehmen, daß die diskursiv-pragmatische Funktion früher auftritt als die lexikalische und nicht erst in Typ III.

5.4. Typ IV: Klassifikatorische NI

Dieser Typ hat Anlaß zu vielen Kontroversen gegeben; ich möchte ihn im Rahmen der Auseinandersetzung zwischen dem syntaktischen und dem lexikalischen Ansatz behandeln. Er existiert nach Mithun in Sprachen wie Mohawk, Caddo, Wichita, Pawnee, Arikara sowie in einigen australischen Sprachen. Möglicherweise handelt es sich um besondere Fälle eines allgemeineren Inkorporationstyps.

Gunwinggu
(17) *bene-dulg-nang mangaralaljmayn*
beide-Baum-seh Cashewnuß
'Sie sahen einen Cashewnußbaum.'

(18) *bene-red-nang redgenengeni*
beide-Zelt-sehen Zelt-neu
'Beide sahen ein neu eingerichtetes Zelt.'

6. Inkorporation und Wortunterbrechung

Im Hinblick auf die Form unterscheidet sich Huichol von anderen polysynthetischen Sprachen durch einen höheren Polysynthesegrad (Iturrioz 1989), was sich unter anderem darin manifestiert, daß in dieser Sprache (a) nicht nur N-Wurzeln, sondern auch Nomina mit Numerus- und Kasusmorphemen inkorporiert werden (s. 15–16), (b) oblique Argumente werden relativ frei inkorporiert, (c) es können auch komplexe Syntagmen (vor allem modifizierte Nomina) inkorporiert werden, (d) es besteht ein gradueller Übergang zwischen prototypischer Inkorporation mit einer N-Wurzel in unmittelbarer Verbnähe und mit tendenziell lexikalischer Funktion (Wortbildung) einerseits und Wortunterbrechung an verschiedenen Stellen des Verbalkomplexes und in zunehmendem Maße mit diskursiver Funktion. Die meisten Definitionen der Inkorporation beschränken das Phänomen auf die Kombination einer N-Wurzel mit einer V-Wurzel. Im Huichol zeigt schon die Inkorporation des Objekts mehr syntaktische Eigenschaften als viele andere Sprachen, aber die schwache Inkorporation zeigt andererseits auch bestimmte Eigenschaften der lexikalischen Inkorporation. Dies legt eine einheitliche Behandlung beider Phänomene nahe. Aus Platzmangel werde ich hier mit ein paar Beispielen meinen integrativen Ansatz nur andeuten:

(19) Huichol
Tiweweiyame 'iki haika-me
Jäger DEM drei-nSUBJ
p-a-'üri-'i-kai.
AS-FIG-Pfeil-trag-IMPF
'Der Jäger trug diese drei Pfeile.'

Das Demonstrativum und das Numeral bilden nicht eine syntaktische Konstituente; *haikame* hat den Status einer Nebenprädikation, aber es impliziert auf jeden Fall den Bezug auf eine vom Subjekt verschiedene Konstituente („nicht Subjekt") und ist stärker an den Kopf des Nominalsyntagmas gebunden als andere Modifikatoren; in diesem Fall kann es nur das inkorporierte Objekt sein. Es handelt sich um einen klaren Fall „stranded modifier" oder diskontinuierlicher Determination/Modifikation. Am anderen Pol dieses komplexen Prozesses befindet sich die „leichte" Inkorporation des Subjekts und bestimmter Adverbialausdrücke:

(20) Huichol
(a) **Tai tixai**
Feuer etwas
mi-ka-ti-ye-hekia-kai
MOD-NEG-EMPH-in-erschein-IMPF
'Das Feuer war noch keineswegs erschienen.'
(b) *Mi-ka-**tai-tixai**-ti-ye-hekia-kai.*
MOD-NEG-Feuer-etwas-EMPH-in-erschein-IMPF
'Die Feuerentstehung fand noch lange nicht statt.'

Die Eingliederung von *tai* in das komplexe verbale Wort hat den pragmatischen Effekt, die Referentialität zu mindern und eine komplexe diskursive Informationseinheit zu bilden, in der kein Element fokussiert werden darf. Dieses (Satz-) Wort stammt aus einer mytischen Erzählung, in der die Umstände beschrieben werden, unter denen das Feuer erscheinen würde. Diese schwache Inkorporation unterstreicht die Tatsache, daß das Wort *tai* 'Feuer' auf eine noch nicht existierende Entität referiert. An dieser Stelle unmittelbar hinter den Morphemen des Subjekts und der Modalität (Negation eingeschlossen) werden außer dem Subjekt Elemente inkorporiert, die Modalität, eine Verstärkung der Negation usw. ausdrücken (*tixai* 'etwas' + -*ka* 'NEG' = 'absolut nicht'). Es ist keine einfache Unterbrechung, die Verbindung *katixai* kann sich verselbständigen mit der Bedeutung 'nichts'. Unter bestimmten Umständen kann ein Nomen zusammen mit einem Modifikator, d. h. eine komplexe syntaktische Struktur inkorporiert werden:

(21) Huichol
 (a) *Tsɨki waki-ti* **nawi tapɨani-me**
  Hund mager-SUBJ Leder dürr-nSUBJ
  tsi-pɨ-ka-r-ana-ka-kwai-miki.
  OR-AS-NEG-INTS-hinten-↓-ess-DESID
  'Dieser magere Hund macht den Eindruck, ein dürres Leder (herunter-)fressen zu wollen.'
 (b) *tsi-pɨ-ka-r-ana-ka*
  OR-AS-NEG-INTS-hinten-runter
  nawi tapɨani-me *kwai-miki.*
  Leder dürr-nSUBJ ess-DESID
  'macht den Eindruck, ein dürres Leder fressen zu wollen.'
 (c) *tsi-pɨ-ka-r-ana-ka* **nawi**
  OR-AS-NEG-INTS-hinten-runter Leder
  tapɨani *kwai-miki.*
  dürr ess-DESID
  'macht den Eindruck, ein dürres Leder fressen zu wollen.'
 (d) * *nawi tapɨani tsi-pɨ-ka-r-ana-*
   Leder dürr   OR-AS-NEG-INTS-hinten-
  ka-kwai-miki
  runter-ess-DESID
  'macht den Eindruck, ein dürres Leder fressen zu wollen.'

In (b) wird das Wort „geschnitten" an der gewohnten Stelle der NI, unmittelbar vor dem Verbstamm: eine Inkorporation im strengeren Sinne, aber mit der weniger gewohnten Besonderheit, daß es ein komplexes Syntagma ist und daß es das flexive Element *-me* 'auf ein vom Subjekt verschiedenes Argument bezogen' (nSUBJ = Nicht-Subjekt) beibehalten kann, aber nicht muß (c). Außerhalb des Wortes würde das Weglassen dieses Flexionselements zu einem ungrammatischen Satz führen. Satz (c) klingt allerdings natürlicher als (b). Niemand würde hier auf die Idee kommen, in *nawitapɨanikwaiya* ein neues lexikalisches Wort zu sehen.

Der typologische Wert der Inkorporation basiert auf der Existenz einer Skala von Strukturen mit graduellen Unterschieden bezüglich einer Reihe von relevanten Parametern, darunter der Polysynthesegrad. Die Skala müßte entsprechend den hier gemachten Vorschlägen geändert und verfeinert werden. Es könnte aber auch sein, daß es mehrere nicht-reduzierbare NI-Typen gibt, wie es andere Forscher vorgeschlagen haben.

7. Inkorporation als syntaktischer Prozeß

Für Baker (1988) ist Inkorporation ein Prozeß, der von syntaktischen Regeln und Prinzipien gesteuert wird: Uniformity of Theta Assignment, Projection Principle, Head Movement Constraint, Empty Category Principle. NI-Konstruktionen und ihren syntaktischen Paraphrasen wird dieselbe D-Struktur zugewiesen, weil sie die thematische Struktur teilen. Eine Bewegungsoperation juxtaponiert zwei Kategorien der X°-Ebene und hinterläßt eine Spur, die zur Erklärung mehrerer Phänomene herangezogen wird. Seine Definition, das anschließende Beispiel und das Diagramm fassen alle wichtigen Komponenten seines Ansatzes zusammen:

„The verb is morphologically complex: it contains both a basic verb root and a noun root, in addition of a standard collection of agreement, tense and aspect morphemes. The special characteristic of these sentences is that the noun root seems to count as the direct object of the structure, productively receiving a thematic role from the verb root." (Baker 1988: 76)

(22) Onondaga (Woodbury 1975)
 (a) *Pet waʔ-ha-**hwist-ahtu**-ʔt-aʔ.*
  Pat PRÄT-3ms-Geld-verlier-KAUS-ASP
  'Pat verlor Geld.'
 (b) *Pet waʔ-ha-htu-ʔt-aʔ*
  Pat PRÄT-3ms-verlier-KAUS-ASP
  *neʔ o-**hwist**-a.*
  DET PREF-Geld-SUF
  'Pat verlor das Geld.'

Der lexikalische Ansatz geht dagegen vom Prinzip der Unteilbarkeit (Atomizität) des Wortes: Wörter sind gegenüber syntaktischen Operationen opak; diese haben keinen Zugang zu Informationen, die die innere Struktur des Wortes betreffen, und können u. a. die Argumentstruktur des Prädikats nicht ändern; sie müssen deswegen *bartend* als ein von *tend* unabhängiges unergatives Verb betrachten: *John$_j$ bar$_i$tends*. Inkorporation ist ein von lexikalischen Prinzipien und Regeln gesteuerter Prozeß, der u. a. Phrasenstrukturregeln umfaßt: N ⇒ N N, V ⇒ N V.

Syntaktischer Ansatz:

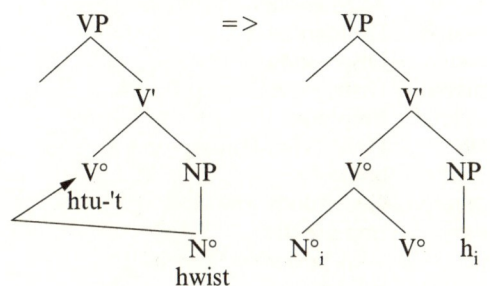

Lexikalischer Ansatz:

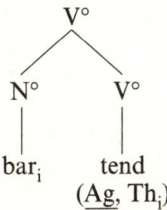

Zugunsten des syntaktischen Ansatzes wird das Phänomen der diskontinuierlichen Dependenzen („stranded modifiers") herangeführt. Das inkorporierte N wird von Elementen spezifiziert oder modifiziert, die außerhalb des V-Syntagmas bleiben:

(23)   Süd-Tiwa (Tanoanisch, Neu-Mexiko)
  (a) *Yede a-seuan-mu-ban.*
       DEM 2SG-Mann-seh-PRÄT
       'Hast du diesen Mann gesehen.'
  (b) [*Yede seuan-ide*] *a-mu-ban*
       DEM Mann-SUF 2SG-seh-PRÄT
       'Hast du diesen Mann gesehen.'

Für Mithun (1984: 106−7) und Rosen (1989) ist dies nicht durch die NI bedingt, denn dasselbe geschieht auch dann, wenn keine NI vorliegt; sie verweisen auf die Existenz in Sprachen wie Mohawk, Onondaga usw. von Konstituenten, die nominale Null-Kerne (N°-Kategorien ohne phonetische Realisierung) modifizieren:

(24) Mohawk (Mithun 1984: 879)
      Kamekwarunyu
      3N.gefleckt.DIST
      wa'-k-[akyatawi'tsher]-u:ni.
      PRÄT-1SG.3N-[Kleid]-machen
      'Ich machte ein geflecktes Kleidungsstück.'

Das sog. „doubling" ist ein Sonderfall mit phonetischer Realisierung des Kopfes:

(25) Mohawk
      *Wa-k-**nuhs**-v:ti:*
      AOR-1s/3N-**Haus**-mach/PF
      [*he:ni:kv o:**nuhs**-eh*].
      DEM PRÄF-**Haus**-SUF
      'Ich habe dieses Haus gemacht.'

In Wirklichkeit erfüllt das inkorporierte Nomen das interne Argument nicht, was übrigens gegen das Thematische Prinzip stoßen würde, denn das Prädikat ist weiterhin transitiv. Das syntaktische Argument kann auch ein anderes N als Kern haben:

(26) Tuscarora
      *Ae-hra-**taskw**-ahk-hwa' ha' **tsi:r**.*
      DUR-3M-Haustier-fang-ASP PART Hund
      'Ich fange gewöhnlich Haustiere.'

Es handelt sich hier um einen von der thematischen Struktur des Verbs unabhängigen Prozeß. Inkorporation erzeugt zwei Typen von Strukturen, je nachdem, ob sie das interne Argument erfüllt oder nicht:

A. N$_i$ + V   B. N + V
    (x, y$_i$)   (x, y)

(A) Die intransitive Inkorporation („compound noun incorporation" in Rosen 1989) entspricht gut dem Schema von Baker und würde mit den notwendigen Vorbehalten die Bezeichnung „syntaktisch" verdienen. Sie zeichnet sich durch folgende Eigenschaften aus:

1. Das Resultat ist ein intransitives Verb; das externe Argument wird in den Ergativsprachen als Absolutiv markiert, weil das inkorporierte Nomen das interne Argument erfüllt;
2. keine Kookkurrenz mit Nullkopfmodifikatoren;
3. keine Duplikation;
4. mehr semantische Transparenz und regelmäßige Paraphrasierbarkeit;
5. volle oder zumindest stärkere Produktivität.

Der lexikalische Ansatz erklärt nicht, warum im Yukatekischen V auf der linken Seite des Kompositums erscheint und daß in anderen Mayasprachen V und N unabhängige Konstituenten bleiben (Gutiérrez 1997: 81). Der syntaktische Ansatz dagegen kann nicht erklären, warum das Agens als Absolutiv markiert wird. Sie wird als charakteristisch für die mikronesischen und polynesischen Sprachen (Tonganisch usw.) betrachtet, aber sie kommt genauso häufig in amerikanischen Sprachen (Huichol, Yukatekisch usw.) vor.

(B) Der zweite Grundtyp der Inkorporation hat die unglückliche Bezeichnung „classifier noun incorporation" bekommen, weil Beispiele wie (22) zu der Ansicht geführt haben, daß das inkorporierte Nomen immer als ein klassifizierender Oberbegriff des syntaktischen Objekts fungiert. In Wirklichkeit sind solche Beispiele nur Sonderfälle eines allgemeineren Schemas:

1. Es handelt sich um prototypische Komposita mit Wortbildungsfunktion, die zwar produktiv sein können, die aber oft eine beschränkte formale und semantische Transparenz zeigen; für sie dürfte der lexikalische Ansatz besser geeignet sein;
2. die thematische Struktur des Verbs und seine Flexions-Morphologie ändern sich nicht, so daß ein transitives Verb transitiv bleibt (Mohawk, Onondaga, Yukatekisch, Huichol usw.);
3. Kookkurenz mit „diskontinuierlichen" Modifikatoren möglich („doubling" eingeschlossen);
4. nicht nur Nomina, auch Elemente anderer lexikalischer Kategorien können so inkorporiert werden, und zwar auch bei intransitiven Verben;
5. bei transitiven Verben kann das syntaktische Objekt zusätzlich inkorporiert werden (intransitive Inkorporation).

Beide Inkorporationtypen kommen oft in denselben Sprachen vor; Eigenschaft 5. impliziert sogar, daß sie auch im selben Wort zusammen auftreten können:

(27) Huichol
'Ayiweka ne-p-u-ti-'**ika-te-hai**-pi.
zum.Glück 1SG-AS-VIS-PL$_P$-Bein-PL-Wasser-wegnehm
'Zum Glück ist meine Beinschwellung zurückgegangen.'

Die Elemente erscheinen immer in dieser Reihenfolge, d. h. die intransitive NI wird zunächst angewendet. Bei der NI des Typs B kommen Lexikalisierungen mit unvorhersagbaren semantischen („Wasser + abnehmen" = „abschwellen") und formellen Veränderungen häufig vor.

8. Spezielle Abkürzungen

↓	nach unten, herab, herunter
1	erste Person
2	zweite Person
3	dritte Person
A	Agens
AKK	Akkusativ
APPL	Applikativum
AS	Assertiv
AUGM	Augmentativ
DESID	Desiderativ
DISP	Disposition
DIST	Distributiv
EMPH	Emphase
FIG	Figur (vom Hintergrund abgehoben)
GENR	Generalisator
IMPF	Imperfektiv
IN	inkorporiertes Nomen
INKOMP	Inkompletiv
INTS	Intensität
KAUS	kausativ
KOMPL	Kompletiv
KONN	Konnektiv
MOD	Modalität
NI	Nominalinkorporation
nSUBJ	nicht-Subjekt
OR	Orientierung (Richtung auf einer Skala)
P	Patiens
PART	Partitiv
PRÄF	Präfix
PRÄT	Präteritum
SUF	Suffix
VIS	visible, sichtbar

9. Zitierte Literatur

Allen, Barbara & Donna B. Gardiner & Donald G. Frantz. 1984. „Noun incorporation in Southern Tiwa". *International Journal of American Linguistics* 50: 292−311.

Baker, Mark C. 1988. *Incorporation: a theory of grammatical function changing*. Chicago: University of Chicago Press.

−. 1993. „Noun incorporation and the nature of linguistic representation". In: William Foley (ed.), *The role of theory in language description*. Berlin: Mouton de Gruyter, 13−44.

Baker, M. C. 1996. *The polysynthesis parameter*. New York: Oxford University Press.

Biermann, Anna. 1980. „Nominalinkorporation". *Arbeiten des Kölner Universalienprojekts 38.* Köln: Universität zu Köln.

Compes, Isabel & Otto Barbara. 1994. *Nicht-morphologische Nominalinkorporation — etwas ganz anderes?* (Arbeitspapiere des Instituts für Sprachwissenschaft, 18.) Köln: Universität zu Köln.

Comrie, Bernard. 1981. *Language universals and linguistic typology.* Oxford: Basil Blackwell.

Di Sciullo, Anna-Maria & Edwin Williams. 1987. *On the definition of word.* Cambridge, Mass.: MIT Press.

Gerdts, Donna B. 1998. „Incorporation". In: Spencer, A. & Zwicky, A. M. (eds.) *The handbook of morphology.* Blackwell Publishers, 84–99.

Gutiérrez Bravo, Rodrigo O. 1997. *La incorporación nominal en maya yucateco.* México, D. F., Escuela Nacional de Antropología e Historia.

Haas, Mary. 1941. „Noun incorporation in the Muskogean Languages". *Language* 17: 311–15.

Hall, Robert A. 1956. „How we noun-incorporate in English". *American Speech* 31: 83–88.

Hill, Archibald A. 1941. „Incorporation as a type of language structure". *Humanistic studies in honor of John Calvin Metcalf.* (University of Virginia Studies I.) Charlottesville: University of Virginia Press, 65–79.

Humboldt, Wilhelm von. 1836. *Über die Verschiedenheit des menschlichen Sprachbaues und ihren Einfluss auf die geistige Entwickelung des Menschengeschlechts.* Berlin: Dümmler.

Iturrioz, José L. 1989. „De la gramática particular del huichol a la tipología: Una contribución a la morfología operacional". *Función* II/2–3: 239–381.

Kroeber, Alfred L. 1909. „Noun incorporation in American Languages". In: Heger, F. (ed.) *Verhandlungen des XVI. Internationalen Amerikanistenkongresses.* Wien/Leipzig: Hartleben, 569–576.

–. 1911. „Incorporation as a linguistic process". *American Anthropologist* 13: 577–584.

Mardirussian, G. 1975. „Noun Incorporation in universal grammar". *Chicago Linguistic Society* 10: 383–389.

Merlan, Francesca. 1976. „Noun incorporation and discourse reference in modern Nahuatl". *International Journal of American Linguistics* 42/3: 177–191.

Mithun, Marianne. 1984. „The evolution of noun incorporation". *Language* 60: 847–893.

–. 1986. „On the nature of noun incorporation". *Language* 62: 32–37.

Preuss, Fritz. 1960/1. „Backformation or noun-incorporation". *Lebende Sprachen* 5: 110–112; 6: 6–7; 7: 37.

Robertson, John S. 1980. *The structure of pronoun incorporation in the Mayan verbal complex.* New York: Garland.

Rosen, Sarah T. 1989. „Two types of noun incorporation: a lexical analysis". *Language* 65/2: 294–317.

Sadock, Jerrold M. 1980. „Noun incorporation in Greenlandic: a case of syntactic word formation". *Language* 56: 300–319.

–. 1985. „Autolexical syntax: a proposal for the treatment of noun incorporation and similar phenomena". *Natural Language and Linguistic Theory* 3: 379–440.

–. 1986. „Some notes on noun incorporation". *Language* 62: 19–31.

Sapir, Edward. 1911. „The problem of noun incorporation in American languages". *American Anthropologist* 13: 250–282.

Sasse, Hans-Jürgen. 1984. „The pragmatics of noun incorporation in Eastern Cushitic languages". In: Plank, Frans (ed.) *Objects: towards a theory of grammatical relations.* London: Academic Press, 243–268.

Skalička, Vladimír. 1968. „Die Inkorporation und ihre Rolle in der Typologie". *Travaux du Cercle Linguistique de Prague* 3: 275–279.

–. 1979 [1951]. „Das Erscheinungsbild der Sprachtypen". In: Skalička, Vladimír. *Typologische Studien.* Braunschweig: Vieweg, 21–58.

Wolfart, H. Christoph. 1971. „Plains Cree Internal Syntax and the Problem of Noun-Incorporation". *Verhandlungen des 38. Internationalen Amerikanistenkongresses.* Stuttgart/München. Bd. III. München, Kommissionsverlag Klaus Renner, 511–518.

Woodbury, Hanni J. 1975. „Onondaga noun incorporation: some notes on the interdependence of syntax and semantics". *International Journal of American Linguistics* 41: 10–20.

Wurzel, Wolfgang U. 1983. „Inkorporierung und ‚Wortigkeit' im Deutschen". In: Tonelli, Livia & Dressler, Wolfgang U. (eds.) *Natural Morphology: Perspectives for the nineties.* Padova: Unipress, 109–126.

Zavala, Roberto. 1999. „External possessor in Oluta Popoluca (Mixean): applicatives and incorporation of relational terms". In: Payne, Doris L. & Barshi, Immanuel (eds.). *External possession.* Amsterdam: Benjamins, 339–72.

José Luis Iturrioz Leza, Universidad de Guadalajara (México)

IX. Typology of morphological and morphosyntactic categories
Typologie morphologischer und morphosyntaktischer Kategorien
La typologie des catégories morphologiques et morphosyntaxiques

54. Parts of speech

1. Semantic classes
2. Semantic class and syntactic function
3. Lexicalization
4. Complex mapping
5. Inflection and government
6. Parts of speech as spread patterns
7. References

The part-of-speech system of a language is a classification of the lexical items of that language with respect to a number of phonological, morphological, syntactic, and semantic properties (Anward, Moravcsik & Stassen 1997). An individual part of speech is, extensionally, a class of lexical items which share a unique set of such properties, or, intensionally, the unique set of properties shared by this class of lexical items.

In order to do typology on part-of-speech systems, it is useful to take part-of-speech systems to be mappings of semantically defined classes of lexical items onto classes delineated by phonological, morphological, and syntactic properties.

1. Semantic classes

To get an idea of the range of conceptual resources made available by natural languages, we may start with the list of lexical items in (1). Wierzbicka (1996), summarizing some 25 years of research, argues that the concepts expressed by the English words and expressions in (1) are both semantic primitives and lexical universals. That is, every language lexicalizes these concepts, and every other concept lexicalized by a natural language can be defined in terms of these concepts.

(1) I, you, someone, something, people, this, the same, other, one, two, many/much, all,
think, say, know, feel, want,
do, happen,
good, bad,
big, small,
when, where, after/before, above/under,
no, because, if/would, can/may,
very,
kind of, have parts,
like

To classify the concepts in (1), we can, for example, use a version of the semantic metalanguage of the Western grammatical tradition — the Aristotelian categories, as they are presented and exemplified in chapter 4 of Aristotle's *Categories* (Ackrill 1963: 5). In modern semantic terminology, these categories are: thing / person, quantity, property, relation, place, time, position, possession, action, and process — a not unreasonable semantic metalanguage. Compare, for example, Jackendoff's more recent set of "ontological categories": thing, event, state, action, place, path, property, and amount (Jackendoff 1990: 22). What needs to be added is chiefly the category of situation, the category expressed by sentences and interjections.

The following variation on the Aristotelian categories, where event subsumes action and process (both mental and physical) and where position and possession have been left out, since they are not instantiated in (1), suffices to classify Wierzbicka's concepts:

(2) *Person/* I, you, someone, some-
    Thing: thing, people
    Event: do, happen, think, say, know, feel, want
    Place: where, above/under, this
    Time: when, after/before
    Relation: because, if/would, can/may
     kind of, have parts
     like
     the same, other
    Property: good, bad, big, small
    Quantity: no
     one, two, many/much/
     very, all

We can begin to chart the diversity of part-of-speech systems by looking at the ways in which the semantic classes in (2) can be mapped onto classes delineated by phonological, morphological, and syntactic properties.

2. Semantic class and syntactic function

To begin with, there is a characteristic mapping of semantic classes onto syntactic functions.

Hopper & Thompson (1984: 708−710) argue that the demands of narrative discourse create two basic uses of words: introducing and deploying participants, and asserting the occurrence of events. Since participants are introduced and deployed in argument positions (subject and object position), and events are asserted to occur in main clause predicate position, these uses sanction two basic prototypical combinations of semantic category and syntactic function:

(3) Person/Thing;   Argument
(4) Event;   Predicate

Croft (1990) equates Hopper & Thompson's two basic uses with the propositional acts of reference and predication, as these are defined by Searle (1969), and then goes on to identify further propositional acts, each one sanctioning a particular combination of semantic category and syntactic function.

A third major propositional act, modification, sanctions the combination in (5), and a minor propositional act of situating an entity in a background dimension sanctions the combinations in (6)−(8).

(5) Property;   Modifier
(6) Place;   Modifier
(7) Time;   Modifier
(8) Quantity;   Modifier

If we also take into account the combination of the semantic category of situation with the syntactic function of independent utterance (root (sentence), in the sense of Emonds 1976), we can summarize the mapping of semantic classes onto syntactic functions by means of the grid in Table 1. The semantic classes are ordered along a rough scale of time-stability (Givón 1984; see also Stassen 1997: 15−16, 578−581 for a recent assessment), from the least stable entities (situation and event) to the most stable entities (person and thing), as well as along an additional scale of spatiotemporal specification (Stassen 1997), which is orthogonal to the time-sta-

Tab. 54.1: Semantic classes and syntactic functions

	root	predicate	predicate modifier	argument modifier	argument
situation	✓				
event		✓			
place			✓	✓	
time			✓	✓	
relation			✓	✓	
property			✓	✓	
quantity				✓	
person/thing					✓

bility scale and extends from place (most specified) through time to relation, where it "meets" the time-stability scale. The syntactic functions are ordered along a scale from root to subject or object (argument) function. Highlighted cells indicate characteristic combinations.

3. Lexicalization

Thus, in a first step, a part-of-speech system can be thought of a distinctive lexicalization of each of the highlighted cells in Table 54.1. That is, a language will provide its users with a unique class of lexemes for each one of these highlighted combinations of semantic class and syntactic function.

The usual names of these lexeme classes are given in (9).

(9)
root, situation	Interjection
predicate, event	Verb
predicate modifier, place	Adverb, Adposition, Conjunction
predicate modifier, time	Adverb, Adposition, Conjunction
predicate modifier, relation	Adverb, Adposition, Conjunction
predicate modifier, property	Adverb
argument modifier, place	Demonstrative
argument modifier, property	Adjective
argument modifier, quantity	Quantifier, Numeral
argument, person/thing	Pronoun, Noun

3.1. Interjections

The combination of the semantic class of situation and the syntactic function of root is lexicalized by interjections.

Interjections normally divide into at least four subclasses (Ameka 1992): expressive interjections ('ouch', 'oh', 'wow', 'aha'), directive interjections ('hush', 'psst', 'hey'), phatic interjections ('mhm', 'yes', 'no', 'huh'), and descriptive interjections ('wham', 'thud', 'bang'), also called ideophones or expressives.

While expressive, directive, and phatic interjections index aspects of the speech event, ideophones signify topical events in an essentially symbolic way. Typical ideophones display phonetic symbolism, often iconic, based on onomatopoeia or phonaestethicism.

3.2. Verbs

The combination of the semantic class of event and the syntactic function of predicate is lexicalized by verbs.

The lexical class of basic verbs will normally lexicalize concepts of motion, posture, process, activity, existence, production, possession, transfer, contact, destruction, and transaction (Dixon 1977, 1980: 280−281, Foley 1986: 113−128, Givón 1980, Tsunoda 1981, and Viberg 1986).

There are Australian languages (Dixon 1976: 615−768, 1980: 280−281) and Papuan languages (Foley 1986: 113−128) which have very small classes of verbs (between 10 and 100). To cover the conceptual range covered by a large class of verbs, some of these languages use combinations of a verb in predicate function and a noun in argument function ('do saliva': spit) or modifier function ('perceive [with] eye': see). Other languages use combinations of a verb in predicate function and one or more verbs in conjunctive predicative function ('go get return give': bring).

There are also languages, for example the Australian language Mangarayi (Merlan 1982), where the class of verbs is split into a small set of inflected verbs and a larger set of non-inflecting verbs which must be governed by an inflected verb.

3.3. Modifier categories

The combinations of the semantic classes of relation, time, place, property, and quantity and the syntactic function of modifier are lexicalized by adpositions, conjunctions and adverbs in predicate modifier (adverbial) function and by demonstratives, adjectives, quantifiers, and numerals in argument modifier (attributive) function.

As pointed out by Schachter (1985), it is not uncommon for classes that lexicalize concepts in modifier function to be small and closed. For example, Yoruba has a small class of adjectives, a common situation in African languages, and may also have exactly one preposition (developed from a verb), Chukchi has only four postpositions, recently developed from nouns, and Archi, a Daghestanian language, has a class of around a dozen basic attributive words, which is fairly heterogeneous, but seems to somehow straddle the property-quantity boundary.

3.4. Pronouns and nouns

The combination of the semantic class of person/thing and the syntactic function of argument is lexicalized by personal pronouns and nouns.

The lexical class of basic **personal pronouns** is defined by the normally obligatory dimensions of person (first, second, and third) and number (at least singular and plural) and the optional dimensions of inclusive/exclusive 1st person plural (which may sometimes have the status of an additional person category; Dixon 1980: 351−356), gender, case, discourse status (e. g. proximal − obviative in Algonquian; Hockett 1966), social status (e. g. speech level in Nahuatl; Hill & Hill 1978), and kinship (e. g. in Lardil; Hale 1966, Dixon 1980: 276).

There are, though, Papuan languages that lack a number distinction in pronouns (Foley 1986: 66−74) and Papuan and Australian languages that lack third person pronouns (Foley 1986: 66−74; Dixon 1980: 356−362). A truly minimal pronominal system has just one first person pronoun and one second person pronoun. Such a system is found in the Papuan language Golin (Foley 1986: 70).

Pronominal concepts may also be expressed by affixes, instead of or beside independent pronouns.

The lexical class of basic **nouns** will typically include items denoting humans, animals, plants, artifacts, inanimate objects, environmental phenomena, and more abstract cultural entities, as well as a number of relational concepts, having to do with kinship, other social relations, name, body parts, plant parts, and parts of inanimate objects and abstract entities (Leisi 1966, Langacker 1987, Silverstein 1987).

Pronouns and nouns can be ordered on an animacy hierarchy (Silverstein 1976):

> I, You > Humans > Animals > Artifacts > Plants > Objects > Abstracts

Cutting across this hierarchy are a number of further distinctions:

> *Individuation*: count items, such as 'head', 'pot', and 'mountain',
> versus mass items, such as 'blood', 'milk', and 'water';

Discourse status: pronouns, such as 'I' and 'you',
versus interrogatives, such as 'who' and 'what',
versus names, such as *Jack* and *Jill*,
versus common nouns, such as 'friend' and 'stone';
Valency: relational nouns, such as 'mother', 'name', 'head' and 'top',
versus non-relational nouns, such as 'woman' and 'pot'.

Relational nouns may be less differentiated than non-relational nouns along the animacy hierarchy: humans, animals, plants and objects always have separate lexicalizations, but distinctions between human body parts, animal body parts, plant parts, and object parts, as well as distinctions between human kin and animal kin, and human status and animal status, may be more or less neutralized. Names may also show less differentiation than common nouns along the animacy hierarchy (Leach 1970: 89−92).

3.5. Variation

As pointed out by Hengeveld (1992, ch. 4), a part-of-speech system, viewed simply as a lexicalization of the highlighted cells in table 1, is subject to two kinds of variation.

First, a language need not use all of the syntactic functions in Table 54.1. A language may lack predicate modifiers, using serial or medial verbs instead. Likewise, a language may lack argument modifiers, and use predicate modifiers (or something equivalent) to express argument modification. Hixkaryana and other Carib languages are examples of languages that approximate this type (Derbyshire 1979), and, incidentally, constitute potential counter-examples to Hengeveld's proposal that absence of argument modifiers entails absence of predicate modifiers. Following Whorf (1945) and Sasse (1988), Hengeveld also proposes that there are languages that lack arguments altogether and express everything through a series of predicates. However, proposed examples of such languages, Wakashan and Iroquoian languages, do not seem to fit the type (Jacobsen 1979, Mithun 2000).

In polysynthetic languages, syntactic functions may, optionally or obligatorily, be realized word-internally, through compounding, incorporation and/or inflection. In particular, argument function may be restricted to pronominal inflection, with independent nouns being used as appositions (Jelinek 1984), and predicate and argument modification may be essentially word-formation processes.

Secondly, a language need not lexicalize all of the highlighted cells in Table 54.1. In particular, all of the modifier categories are cross-linguistically optional. Anward (2000) observes a tendency for languages with adverbs to have adpositions as well, but this needs to be tested against a larger sample. Hengeveld's proposal that languages with adverbs also have adjectives may be better rephrased as a tendency for languages with adpositions also to have adjectives. Even this generalization has counterexamples, though. Ainu is one.

While interjection seems to be a universal part of speech, it is a matter of considerable controversy whether or not both [event; predicate] and [person/thing; argument] need to be distinctively lexicalized. There is no lack of proposed cases of languages where the noun-verb distinction is neutralized. In some languages, such as the Wakashan languages Nootka and Nitinat (Swadesh 1939, Whorf 1945) and the neighbouring Salish languages (Kuipers 1968, Kinkade 1983, Jelinek & Demers 1994), all content words (as opposed to invariable particles) are said to be basically verbal, or predicative, in nature, but also allow an argument use, in which they are interpreted essentially as headless relatives. In other languages, such as Eskimo languages (Hammerich 1951, Johns 1992), all content words are held to be basically nominal, with agentive nouns as the closest equivalent to verbs. In yet other languages, such as various Austronesian languages (Himmelmann 1991, Broschart 1997), it is not even clear which function, predicate or argument, is basic. Indeed, Gil (1994) has argued that in such languages, only [situation; root] is lexicalized.

4. Complex mapping

However, a part-of-speech system is not simply a lexicalization of a subset of the highlighted cells in Table 54.1. The mapping of semantic classes onto formally demarcated classes is far more complex.

First of all, semantic classes may be distinctively lexicalized in non-typical functions as well, which means that semantic classes are often multiply lexicalized. Place, for example, is lexicalized not only by adpositions (*to*), but also by nouns (*direction*) and verbs (*enter*) (Schwarze 1991).

Secondly, lexical items may be used in other functions than the one in which they are lexicalized. A noun such as *iron* may be used not only as argument (*I bought some iron*), but also as predicative (*This metal is iron*), predicate (*Did you iron my shirt?*), and attributive modifier (*I need an iron bar*).

4.1. Lexicalization possibilities

While the semantic class of person/things only seems lexicalizable by nouns, other semantic classes can be lexicalized in several ways.

Event can be lexicalized by action nouns, such as *scandal* and *war*, in argument function.

Place can be lexicalized in argument function, as locational nouns, in predicate function, as verbs of posture, location, and motion, in adverbial function, as adverbs, adpositions and conjunctions, and in attributive function, as demonstratives. Adverbs and adpositions can also be incorporated into verbs as locational/directional affixes and adpositions can be grammaticalized to local case affixes.

The general notions of 'place' and 'path' are typically lexicalized by nouns, while the notions of 'come', 'go' (motion) and 'stand' (posture) are typically lexicalized by verbs.

More specific place and path concepts, such as 'in', 'behind', and 'to' can be lexicalized both by nouns (*interior, rear, way*) and by adverbs and adpositions (*in, behind, to*), as pointed out by Schwarze (1991). Moreover, such concepts can be incorporated into the meanings of motion verbs in certain languages (Talmy 1985).

Certain notions are more likely to be lexicalized by nouns, for example 'left', 'right' and the points of compass. In addition, such notions are not incorporated in the meanings of motion verbs, and they are rarely grammaticalized as case concepts.

Deictic concepts, on the other hand, are typically lexicalized by modifier categories.

Time can be lexicalized in argument function, as temporal nouns, in predicate function, as aspectual verbs and verbs of duration and temporal existence, in adverbial function, as adverbs, adpositions and conjunctions, and in attributive function, as temporal adjectives. Aspectual verbs and temporal adverbs can also be grammaticalized as tense and aspect inflections.

Temporal unit notions, such as 'time', 'day', 'night', 'summer', and 'winter', are typically lexicalized by nouns, while aspectual notions, such as 'start' and 'stop', frequency notions, such as 'repeat' and 'often', duration notions, such as 'take a long while', and notions of temporal existence such as 'occur' and 'take place' (sic!) are typically lexicalized by verbs and adverbs. Temporal relations and points-in-time, deictically anchored or not, are often lexicalized as adpositions (*after*), adverbs (*now*), and adjectives (*early*).

Relation can be lexicalized in argument function, as relational nouns, in predicate function, as stative verbs, in adverbial function, as adpositions, and in attributive function, as relational adjectives. The concepts of 'kind of' and 'part of' are typically lexicalized as nouns. Causal relations are lexicalizable as nouns (*ground, purpose*), verbs (*cause*) and adpositions (*because*), and modal notions have an unusually broad range of alternative lexicalizations (Nuyts 1994): nouns (*risk*), verbs (*can*), adverbs (*perhaps*), and adjective (*possible*). Even the notion of 'like' have several possible lexicalizations. In Swedish, there is the adposition *som* (like), and the adjective *lik* (similar), and in English there is also the verb *resemble*.

Property is also a very versatile category, which can be lexicalized by nouns, verbs, adverbs, and adjectives. There is by now a fairly extensive literature on which subcategories typically go into this category and which lexicalization tendencies these subcategories exhibit. See e.g. Dixon (1977), Schachter (1985), and Wetzer (1996).

Quantity, finally, is another versatile category. Quantity can be lexicalized by nouns (*pair, score*), verbs (*equal, exceed*), quantifiers (*many*) and numerals (*five*).

4.2. Extensions

Lexical items are typically not restricted to just one function, but have a range of syntactic functions. One way to put this is to say that the use of lexical items is typically extended from the function in which they are lexicalized to other syntactic functions as well.

A verb, such as *sing*, which denotes an event in predicate function (10 a), can also be used, with a derivational suffix and nominal inflection, to denote an entity in argument function (10 b) and predicate function (10 c), and, with another derivational suffix and nominal inflection, an event in argument function (10 d).

(10) (a) Leonard Cohen sings.
 (b) The singer must die.
 (c) Leonard Cohen is a singer.
 (d) The singing stopped.

And a noun, such as *stone*, which denotes an entity in argument function (11 a), can also be used to denote an entity in predicate function (11 b), and, with verbal inflection, an event in predicate function (11 c) and, with a derivational suffix and nominal inflection, an event in argument function (11 d).

(11) (a) The stones were heavy.
 (b) This is a stone.
 (c) They stone you when you're playing your guitar.
 (d) The stoning of singers must stop.

Thus, through extension, both verbs, such as *sing*, and nouns, such as *stone*, may fill up the space defined by the syntactic functions of predicate and argument, and the semantic categories of event and person/thing:

Frequent patterns of extension include:

(i) Most parts of speech extend to root (i.e. can be used as single-word utterances).
(ii) Most parts of speech extend to predicate (and/or predicative).
(iii) Nouns and verbs extend to most other functions, although extension of nouns to adverbial may be restricted to locational and/or temporal nouns, and extension of verbs to modifier may be restricted to stative or intransitive verbs.
(iv) Adverbial parts of speech (adverb, adposition) extend to attributive function.
(v) Attributive parts of speech (demonstrative, adjective, quantifier, numeral) extend to adverbial and to argument.
(vi) Ideophones extend to modifier.

4.3. Modes of extension

Kuryłowicz (1936) makes a distinction between syntactic derivation and lexical derivation, arguing that derivational morphology can change either syntactic function (syntactic derivation) or lexical category (lexical derivation). Adverbial derivation, for example *ici-ly* from *icy*, would be an instance of syntactic derivation, while derivation of adnominal adjectives, for example *ic-y* from *ice*, would be an instance of lexical derivation. The distinction works just as well for extensions which involve no derivational morphology – conversions, or "zero-derivations". Thus, conversion of a locational adverb, such as *out*, from adverbial (*We slept out*) to predicative function (*The cat is out*) would be an example of syntactic conversion, while conversion of a locational adverb to predicate function (*He outs with the old equalizer*) would be an example of lexical conversion.

If we unpack Kuryłowicz's distinction, we can see that there are two potential changes associated with derivation and conversion: change of syntactic function and change of semantic category.

In clear-cut cases of syntactic derivation or conversion — what we might call syntactic extension — syntactic function is changed, without change of semantic category. Thus, in the derivation of *icily* from *icy*, syntactic function is changed — from attributive modifier to adverbial — but semantic category — property — is retained. The same holds for predicative conversion of *out*: syntactic function is changed — from adverbial to predicative — but semantic category — place — is retained.

If we look at the two cases of lexical derivation/conversion used as examples, it is plain that the conversion of *out* from locational adverb to verb is more syntactic than semantic, the change of semantic category being somehow a side-effect of the change of syntactic function, while the derivation of *icy* from *ice* is more semantic than syntactic, the change of syntactic function being more of a side-effect in this case. There are also cases of lexical derivation/conversion which involve only a change in semantic category. Property to thing (*beauty → beauty*), thing to property (*man → manhood*), and process to action (*break → break*) are three examples.

The "verbal" conversion of *out* is in fact a special case of syntactic extension, modistic extension (named after the group of medieval grammarians, the modistae, who held that semantic category is predictable from syntactic function), whereby members of a lexical class take on both a new syntactic function and the semantic category that is most typically associated with that function. In the case of *out*, the semantic category involved is of course event. Other examples of the same process would be conversion of "numeral" to "noun" (*Five go down to the sea*) and "noun" to "adjective" (*an orange clockwork*).

The remaining cases of lexical derivation/ extension might be called semantic extension, either semantic extension with a syntactic side-effect, as in the derivation of *icy* from *ice*, whereby members of a lexical class take on a new semantic category and the syntactic function(s) typically associated with that category, or "pure" semantic extension, as in the derivation of *manhood* from *man*, where only a shift in semantic category is involved.

5. Inflection and government

Lexical items are differentiated not only by their characteristic distribution over the cells in Table 1, but also by their patterns of inflection and government in the cells in which they occur.

Hopper & Thompson (1984) argue that the combinations

(3) Person/Thing; Argument
(4) Event; Predicate

are loci for inflectional elaboration. Nominal morphology — inflection for definiteness, number, gender, case, and person agreement — is maximally elaborated in (3), and verbal morphology — inflection for finiteness, tense, mood, aspect, subject agreement, and object agreement — is maximally elaborated in (4).

Croft (1991) argues that inflectional elaboration is a consequence of markedness. Items appear in unmarked form and with maximal paradigmatic elaboration in unmarked contexts (characteristic combinations) and in marked form and with reduced paradigmatic elaboration in marked contexts (non-characteristic combinations). Thus, verbs appear as simple stems with maximal inflectional elaboration in (4), but tend to appear as elaborated stems (participles, nominalizations, etc) with reduced inflection in other, non-characteristic combinations.

The category/function combinations in (3) and (4) are also loci of syntagmatic elaboration, patterns of government. A pattern of government is minimally the core arguments (subject, object, possessor) a given head can take, the cases these arguments appear in, if any, and the positions of these arguments relative to the head. The combinations in (3) and (4) are often associated with distinct patterns of government. In Germanic, for example, verbs in (4) govern subjects, with nominative or dative case, and may also govern direct objects, with accusative case, as well as oblique objects, with dative or genitive case. Nouns in (3) govern only possessors in the genitive case. Subjects and possessors precede their heads, while objects either precede or follow their heads. Syntagmatic elaboration, like paradigmatic elaboration, is maximal in unmarked contexts and likely to be reduced in marked contexts.

In addition to the patterns of inflection and government in (3) and (4), there is a third type of distinctive inflection and government (Stassen 1997, ch. 14): the absence of inflection and government associated with locational adverbs in predicate function and adverbial function.

A strong hypothesis is that there are at most three models for inflection and government operative in a language: the *V model*, with verbal inflection and verbal government (v; v), the *N model*, with nominal inflection and nominal government (n; n), and the *L model*, with no inflection and no government (−; −), anchored in the combinations of (3), (4), and (6), respectively. And these models extend, through a process called take-over by Stassen, horizontally and vertically to other cells in Table 54.1.

Minimally, a language will use L inflection and L and V government, with V inflection, N inflection, and N government as successive elaborations. However, "new" patterns of inflection and government need not be wholly distinct from "older" patterns.

Nominal and verbal inflection may overlap. As Allen (1964), Seiler (1983), and Siewierska (1998), show, possessor agreement is often identical to either subject agreement or object agreement. There are also languages where there is identity between determiner inflection and either finiteness inflection or subject agreement. Nama is a case in point. And there are languages, such as Swedish, where nominal and verbal inflection, although categorically differentiated (nouns inflect for case, number, definiteness, and gender, verbs for voice and finiteness), have roughly the same set of suffixes as exponents (Kvist 1995).

Nominal and verbal government may also overlap. Nouns and verbs may govern the same cases, and their core arguments may be similarly positioned.

Sometimes, such overlaps seem to suggest a fundamental similarity of nouns and verbs. For example, in Eskimo languages, ergative case and genitive case are largely identical. Since possessor agreement and absolutive agreement are identical, as well, and core arguments of both nouns and verbs precede their heads, this has often been interpreted as indicative of a neutralization of the noun − verb distinction in Eskimo (Johns 1992, but cf. also Woodbury 1985).

6. Parts of speech as spread patterns

Since natural languages do not restrict the distribution of their lexical items to one prototypical use per item, the traditional notion of part of speech is best explicated in terms of characteristic **spreads** of lexical items over the cells in Table 54.1. The proposal to interpret parts of speech in this way was first made by Whorf (1945) and Hockett (1958, ch. 26), and has since been elaborated by Hengeveld (1992) and Anward, Moravcsik & Stassen (1997). Extensionally, a part of speech is a class of lexical items which share a pattern of spread. Intensionally, a part of speech is the pattern of spread shared by a class of lexical items.

For example, the English class of concrete nouns, exemplified by *stone*, is partially defined by the spread in (12).

(12)

stone occurs
in unmarked form in [predicative; thing]
    with nominal inflection and government;
in unmarked form in [argument; thing]
    with nominal inflection and government;
in unmarked form in [argument modifier; thing]
    with no inflection and no government.
in unmarked form in [predicate; event],
    with verbal inflection and government;
in marked form in [argument; event]
    with nominal inflection and government;

The distinctive spread patterns of a particular language, its parts of speech, can be identified through an analytic reconstruction of the part-of-speech system of that language, comprising the steps detailed above, and summarized in (13):

(13)   *Analytic Reconstruction of Part-of-speech Systems*

Primary lexicalization
Which of the highlighted category/function combinations in Table 1 are lexicalized?
What are the basic patterns of inflection and government in these combinations?

Secondary lexicalization
Which of the remaining category/function combinations in Table 1 are lexicalized?

Extension
How are lexical items extended from their lexicalization sites to other category/function combinations?

Take-over
How do patterns of inflection and government extend from their basic sites to lexical items in other category/function combinations?

In this interpretation, parts of speech are stable and coherent generalizations over spreads of individual lexical items, centered around one of the highlighted cells in Table 1 ([argument; thing], in the case of *stone*, for example). Such general patterns of spread serve as attractors in language acquisition and language change, and thus work to streamline vocabularies. However, since both competing generalizations and generalizations on different levels of abstraction may be operative in the process, there is no point in reifying such generalizations into entities which are then somehow "realized" by individual spreads.

Likewise, there is no point in taking the parts of speech of a given language to be instantiations of a universal set of parts of speech. Parts of speech are language-specific generalizations over language-specific spreads. And cross-linguistic generalizations are just that, generalizations over language-specific generalizations (see Dryer 1997: 116—119 for a short, but illuminating discussion of these points).

A typological inquiry into part-of-speech systems must start with the best inventory of semantic classes available, and relate them to phonological, morphological, and syntactic properties, as currently conceived, but progress means transcending the initial framework, turning up unexpected regularities, and, possibly, completely revising fundamental assumptions.

7. References

A useful general bibliography of works on the typology of parts of speech, compiled by Frans Plank, can be found in *Linguistic Typology* 1. 185—192 (1997).

Ackrill, J. L. 1963. *Aristotle's Categories and De Interpretatione*. Oxford: Oxford University Press.

Allen, W. Sidney. 1964. "Transitivity and possession". *Language* 40: 337—343.

Ameka, Felix. 1992. "Interjections: the universal yet neglected part of speech". *Journal of Pragmatics* 18: 101—118.

Anward, Jan. 2000. "A dynamic model of part-of-speech differentiation". Vogel & Comrie (eds.), 3—45.

Anward, Jan & Edith Moravcsik & Leon Stassen. 1997. "Parts of speech: a challenge for typology". *Linguistic Typology* 1: 167—183.

Broschart, Jürgen. 1997. "Why Tongan does it differently: categorial distinctions in a language without nouns and verbs". *Linguistic Typology* 1: 123—166.

Croft, William. 1990. "A conceptual framework for grammatical categories." *Journal of Semantics* 7: 245—280.

—. 1991. *Syntactic categories and grammatical relations*. Chicago and London: University of Chicago Press.

Derbyshire, Desmond C. 1979. *Hixkaryana*. Amsterdam: North-Holland.

Dixon, R. M. W. (ed.). 1976. *Grammatical categories in australian languages*. Canberra: Australian Institute of Aboriginal Studies.

Dixon, R. M. W. 1977. "Where have all the adjectives gone?" *Studies in Language* 1: 1—80.

—. 1980. *The languages of Australia*. Cambridge: Cambridge University Press.

Dryer, Matthew. 1997. "Are grammatical relations universal?". In: Joan Bybee, John Haiman, and Sandra A. Thompson (eds.), *Essays on language function and language type*. Amsterdam/Philadelphia: John Benjamins, 115—144.

van Eijk, Jan P. & Hess, Thomas. 1986. "Noun and verb in Salish". *Lingua* 69: 319—331.

Emonds, Joseph E. 1976. *A transformational approach to English syntax*. New York: Academic Press.

Foley, William A. 1986. *The Papuan languages of New Guinea*. Cambridge: Cambridge University Press.

Gil, David. 1994. "The Structure of Riau Indonesian". *Nordic Journal of Linguistics* 17: 179—200.

Givón, Talmy. 1980. "The Binding Hierarchy and the typology of complements". *Studies in Language* 4: 333—377.

—. 1984. *Syntax: A functional-typological introduction*. Amsterdam: John Benjamins.

Hale, Kenneth. 1966. "Kinship reflections in syntax: some australian languages". *Word* 22: 318—324.

Hammerich, Louis L. 1951. "The cases of Eskimo" *International Journal of American Linguistics* 17: 18—22.

Hengeveld, Kees. 1992. *Non-verbal predication*. Berlin/New York: Mouton de Gruyter.

Hill, Jane. H. & Hill, Kenneth C. 1978. "Honorific usage in modern Nahuatl". *Language* 54: 123—154.

Himmelmann, Nikolaus P. 1991. "The Philippine challenge to Universal Grammar". *Arbeitspapier (Neue Folge)* 15. Institut für Sprachwissenschaft, Universität zu Köln.

Hockett, Charles F. 1958. *A course in modern linguistics.* New York: Macmillan.

—. 1966. "What Algonquian is really like". *International Journal of American Linguistics* 32: 59–73.

Hopper, Paul & Thompson, Sandra A. 1984. "The discourse basis for lexical categories in universal grammar". *Language* 60: 703–752.

Jackendoff, Ray S. 1990. *Semantic structures.* Cambridge, Mass: MIT Press.

Jacobsen, William H. 1979. "Noun and verb in Nootkan". In: B. S. Efrat (ed.), *The Victoria Conference on Northwestern Languages,* Heritage Record, No 4, British Columbia Provincial Museum, 83–155.

Jelinek, Eloise. 1984. "Empty categories, case, and configurationality". *Natural Language & Linguistic Theory* 2: 39–76.

Jelinek, Eloise & Richard A. Demers. 1994. "Predicates and pronominal arguments in Straits Salish". *Language* 70: 697–736.

Jespersen, Otto. 1924. *The philosophy of grammar.* London: Allen & Unwin.

Johns, Alana. 1992. "Deriving ergativity". *Linguistic Inquiry* 23: 57–88.

Kinkade, M. Dale. 1983. "Salish evidence against the universality of 'noun' and 'verb'". *Lingua* 60: 25–40.

Koptjevskaja-Tamm, Maria. 1993. *Nominalizations.* London: Routledge.

Kuipers, Aert. H. 1968. "The categories verb – noun and transitive – intransitive in English and Squamish". *Lingua* 21: 610–626.

Kuryłowicz, Jerzy. 1936. "Dérivation lexicale er dérivation syntaxique: contribution à la théorie des parties du discours". *Bulletin de la Société de Linguistique de Paris* 37: 79–92.

Kvist, Ulrika. 1995. "On semantic markedness and Swedish inflectional suffixes". *Papers from the XVth Scandinavian Conference of Linguistics.* Oslo: University of Oslo, 269–276.

Langacker, Ronald W. 1987. "Nouns and verbs". *Language* 63: 53–94.

Leach, Edmund. 1970. *Lévi-Strauss.* London: Fontana Press.

Leisi, E. 1967. *Der Wortinhalt.* Heidelberg: Quelle & Mayer.

Merlan, Francesca. 1982. *Mangarayi.* Amsterdam: North-Holland.

Mithun, Marianne. 2000. "Noun and verb in Iroquoian". In: Vogel & Comrie (eds.), 397–420.

Nuyts, Jan. 1994. *Epistemic Modal Qualifications: On their linguistic and conceptual structure.* Antwerp: Antwerp Papers in Linguistics 81.

Sasse, Hans-Jürgen. 1988. "Der irokesische Sprachtyp". *Zeitschrift für Sprachwissenschaft* 7: 173–213.

Schachter, Paul. 1985. "Parts-of-speech systems". In: Timothy Shopen (ed.), *Language typology and syntactic description.* Vol. 1. Cambridge: Cambridge University Press, 3–61.

Schwarze, Christoph. 1991. "Concept types and parts of speech: the lexicon of space in French". *Journal of Semantics* 8: 333–361.

Searle, J. R. 1969. *Speech Acts.* Cambridge: Cambridge University Press.

Seiler, Hansjakob. 1983. "Possessivity, subject and object". *Studies in Language* 7: 90–116.

Siewierska, Anna. 1998. "On nominal and verbal person marking". *Linguistic Typology* 2: 1–55.

Silverstein, Michael. 1976. "Hierarchy of features and ergativity". In: Dixon (ed.). 1976, 112–171.

—. 1987. "Cognitive Implications of a Referential Hierarchy". In: Maya Hickmann (ed.), *Social and functional approaches to language and thought.* New York: Academic Press, 125–164.

Stassen, Leon. 1997. *Intransitive Predication.* Oxford: Oxford University Press.

Swadesh, Morris. 1939. "Nootka internal syntax". *International Journal of American Linguistics* 9: 77–102.

—. 1955. "Towards greater accuracy in lexicostatistic dating". *International Journal of Amercan Linguistics* 21: 121–137.

Talmy, Leonard. 1985. "Lexicalization patterns: semantic structure in lexical forms". In: Timothy Shopen (ed.), *Language typology and syntactic description.* Vol. 3. Cambridge: Cambridge University Press, 57–149.

Tsunoda, Tasaku. 1981. "Split case-marking patterns in verb types and tense/aspect/mood". *Linguistics* 19: 389–438.

Viberg, Åke. 1986. "The study of cross-linguistic lexicology". In: Östen Dahl (ed.), *Papers from the Ninth Scandinavian Conference of Linguistics.* Stockholm: Stockholm University, 313–327.

Vogel, Petra & Comrie, Bernard (eds.) 2000. *Approaches to the typology of word classes.* Berlin: Mouton de Gruyter.

Wetzer, Harrie. 1996. *The typology of adjectival predication.* Berlin: Mouton de Gruyter.

Whorf, Benjamin Lee. 1945. "Grammatical categories". *Language* 21: 1–11.

Wierzbicka, Anna. 1996. *Semantics: primes and universals.* Oxford: Oxford University Press.

Woodbury, Anthony C. 1985. "Noun phrase, nominal sentence, and clause in Central Alaskan Yupik Eskimo". In: Johanna Nichols & Anthony C. Woodbury (eds.), *Grammar inside and outside the clause.* Cambridge: Cambridge University Press, 66–88.

Jan Award, University of Linköping
(Sweden)

55. Lokalkasus und Adpositionen

1. Allgemeines Schema, Explizitheit
2. Lokalisation zwischen Lokalisatum und Lokale
3. Grammatikalisierung
4. Spezielle Abkürzungen
5. Zitierte Literatur

Die Kategorien *Kasus* und *Adposition* lassen sich nur dann sinnvoll in der grammatischen Beschreibung von Sprachen verwenden, wenn für die Beschreibung dieser Sprachen auch von einer Nomen-Verb-Unterscheidung ausgegangen wird. Beide Kategorien sind in der linguistischen Tradition sehr stark an die Kategorie *Nomen* gebunden, die sich zum Teil sogar durch die Kasusflexion bzw. durch das Hinzutreten von Adpositionen definiert (→ Art. 38).

Die Abgrenzung von Lokalkasus und Adpositionen ist nur einzelsprachlich vorzunehmen. Im folgenden wird — onomasiologisch argumentierend — von Lokalisation im allgemeinen gesprochen, für die Unterscheidung von Lokalkasus und Adpositionen spielt zum einen die Explizitheit der Lokalisation und zum anderen ihr Verhältnis zu Nomen und Verb im Satz eine Rolle.

1. Allgemeines Schema, Explizitheit

Onomasiologisch betrachtet geht es bei der Lokalisation um die Herstellung einer Relation zwischen einem zu lokalisierenden *Lokalisatum (Lokalisandum)* und einem Ort (*Locus* oder *Lokale*). Ein *Lokalisator* kann hinzukommen und die Lokalisation näher bestimmen. Es kann also das folgende einfache Grundschema angenommen werden:

(1) *Lokalisatum (Lokalisator) Lokale*

Über die Abfolge der Ausdrucksmittel kann aus onomasiologischer Sicht keine Aussage gemacht werden (→ Art. 64); die Stellung des *Lokalisators* zwischen *Lokalisatum* und *Lokale* ist jedenfalls ein guter Kandidat für eine präferierte Reihenfolge.

Sprachen können sich nach dem Grad der Explizitheit der Lokalisation unterscheiden, wobei auch ein innersprachliches Kontinuum zu beobachten ist.

1.1. Minimale Lokalisation: Arabisch, Französisch

Im Arabischen können Ortsangaben (z. B. Namen größerer Städte oder — wie im folgenden Beispiel — Inseln) ohne Präposition (Lokalisator), also ohne explizite lokale Markierung verwendet werden, wenn die Lokalisation eindeutig ist, d. h. wenn sie z. B. nach Verben verwendet werden, die eine gezielte Bewegung oder eine örtliche Befindlichkeit ausdrücken. Man kann in diesem Zusammenhang von *inhärenter Lokalisation* sprechen.

(2) Maltesisch (Arabisch)
 U mbagħad mort lura
 und dann geh.PRET.1SG zurück
 Għawdex.
 Gozo
 'Und dann kehrte ich zurück (nach) Gozo.'

Das Französische benötigt — wie für eine romanische Sprache üblich — einen expliziten Lokalisator. Der allgemeinste ist die Präposition *à*, die keine weiteren Auskünfte über die Art der Lokalisation gibt; es ist der Fall einer merkmallosen Lokalisationsmarkierung:

(3) Französisch
 J'habite à Paris.
 'Ich wohne in Paris.'

Wenn Bedarf besteht, die Lokalisation stärker zu explizieren, können andere Präpositionen gewählt werden:

(4) Französisch
 J'habite dans Paris.
 'Ich wohne in(nerhalb) Paris.'

Noch expliziter wird die Lokalisation durch die Verwendung einer Präpositionalgruppe, die die merkmallose Präposition *à* und ein relationales (Lokal-)Nomen ('Inneres') enthält:

(5) Französisch
 J'habite à l'intérieur de Paris.
 'Ich wohne im Innern von Paris.'

Andere relationale Nomina ('Mittelpunkt', 'Herz') können ebenfalls verwendet werden, um die Lokalisation zu explizieren:

(6) Französisch
 J'habite dans le centre/dans le cœur de Paris.
 'Ich wohne im Zentrum/im Herzen von Paris.'

In einigen Fällen, in denen die Lokalisation dem Verb inhärent ist, kann die Präposition ganz fehlen.

(7) Französisch
J'habite Paris.
'Ich wohne in Paris.'

Diese Möglichkeit besteht nur, wenn es sich um ein prototypisches *Lokale* handelt (z. B. die Stadt Paris, vgl. das arabische Beispiel oben) und wenn das Verb, wie in diesem Falle *habiter* ('(be-)wohnen'), eine Lokalrelation anzeigt.

1.2. Explizite Lokalisation

Zur Explizierung der Lokalisation wird ein zu lokalisierender Mitspieler einer Situation oder eine Situation (Lokalisatum), eine Ortsangabe (Lokale) und Angaben über die Art der Lokalisation in Form eines Lokalisators benötigt. Wie oben gezeigt wurde, ist der Lokalisator im Falle minimaler bzw. inhärenter Lokalisation überflüssig. Der Lokalisator kann jedoch auch komplex sein. Besonders in diesem Fall treten noch zusätzliche Elemente auf, die den (komplexen) Lokalisator an das Lokalisatum und das Lokale binden, sogenannte Ligatoren. Ein Beispiel sehen wir in (8).

(8) Französisch
J'habite   à   l'intérieur
'Ich wohne im   Innern
Situation (L-Ligator)   Lokalisator
de   Paris.
von   Paris.'
(P-Ligator) Lokale

Der Lokalisator ist oft ein relationales Nomen (das auf dem Wege der Grammatikalisierung möglicherweise sehr bedeutungsentleert ist und häufig keinen vollwertigen Nominalstatus mehr hat), das mit Hilfe eines Possessiv-Ligators (P-Ligator) an das Lokale gebunden ist. Die Verbindung zwischen dem relationalen Nomen und dem Lokalisatum wird mit einem Lokal-Ligator (L-Ligator) hergestellt, meist eine merkmallose Adposition (wie in Beispiel (8) oben) oder ein allgemeiner Lokalkasus:

(9) Baskisch
etxe-a-ren   ondo-an
Haus-IDV-GEN   Seite-IN
'neben dem Haus'

Das relationale Nomen dieses Beispiels ist allerdings schon weitgehend zu einem Lokalisator mit der Bedeutung 'neben' grammatikalisiert. In den Grammatiken werden solche Lokalisatoren als Adpositionen behandelt (auch wenn sie praktisch nicht ohne die Ligatoren verwendet werden können). Der Grammatikalisierungsprozess ist abgeschlossen, wenn eine reine Adposition entstanden ist:

(10) Baskisch
Ikus-i   arte
seh-PZP   bis
'bis zum (Ge-)Sehen' (= 'auf Wiedersehen')

Die Postposition bedeutet eigentlich 'Zwischenraum'.

Der folgende Grammatikalisierungskanal ist also anzunehmen:

(11) *relationales Nomen > Lokalisator > Adposition*

Da die Klasse der relationalen Nomina prinzipiell offen ist, können mit solchen Lokalisationssyntagmen sehr detaillierte Lokalisierungen vorgenommen werden. Das Tok Pisin verfügt letztlich nur noch über zwei eigentliche Präpositionen (a) *long* 'in, an, bei, entlang usw.' für lokale Relationen und (b) *bilong* 'von' für possessive Relationen. Durch den Einsatz dieser beiden als L- und P-Ligator ist die Bildung von Lokalisationssyntagmen möglich:

(12) Tok Pisin
long   beli   bilong...
lokale Präp. Bauch   Possessivpräp.
L-Ligator   Lokalisator P-Ligator
'im Bauch (= Innern) von'

Es ist im Tok Pisin jedoch auch möglich, die allgemeine Lokalpräposition durch ein Adverb beim Lokalisatum zu spezifizieren (vergleiche auch die deutsche Übersetzung):

(13) Tok Pisin
Mi go insait long   stua.
ich geh innen lokale Präposition Laden
'Ich gehe in den Laden hinein.'

Unter den relationalen Nomina werden in vielen Sprachen vor allem Körperteilbezeichnungen zur Lokalisation verwendet (eine Liste findet sich bei Stolz 1992: 105), wobei oft nicht zu klären ist, ob ein relationales Lexem zunächst eine Körperteilbezeichnung ist oder ein abstraktes relationales Lokalnomen; trotz vereinfachender funktionalistischer Annahmen lässt sich nicht schlüssig nachweisen, ob z. B. baskisch *aurre* eher den Weg von der konkreten Bedeutung 'Gesicht' zum abstrakten relationalen Lokalnomen mit der Bedeutung 'Vorderseite' genommen hat oder ob etymologisch eine umgekehrte Entwicklung anzunehmen ist.

1.3. Ort und Richtung

Die Art der Lokalisation kann auch in Bezug auf den Unterschied *statisch/dynamisch* expliziert werden. Dabei können verschiedene Bewegungsrichtungen unterschieden werden:

(14) Türkisch
  (a) *ev-de*   'im Haus'
                Haus-Lokativ/Inessiv
  (b) *ev-e*   'zum Haus'
                Haus-Dativ (= Allativ)
  (c) *ev-den* 'vom Haus'
                Haus-Ablativ

Stolz (1992: 30) nimmt an, dass diese Dreigliederigkeit zum Prototyp der Lokalisation gehört. Diese Annahme scheint nicht zwingend zu sein, denn es können auch ganz andere Aspekte grammatikalisiert werden. So unterscheidet das Baskische darüber hinaus, ob eine Bewegung terminativ ist (also das Ziel erreicht) oder nur in eine bestimmte Richtung gewendet stattfindet (Destinativ):

(15) Baskisch
  (a) *etxe-an*   'im Haus'
                  (Inessiv)
  (b) *etxe-ra*   'zum Hause'
                  (unspezifischer Direktiv)
  (c) *etxe-runtz* 'in Richtung auf das Haus'
                  (Destinativ)
  (d) *etxe-rain* '(bis) zum Haus'
                  (Terminativ)
  (e) *etxe-tik* 'vom Haus'
                  (Ablativ)

Andere Sprachen unterscheiden die Art der Lokalisation gar nicht explizit. Sie ergibt sich aus dem Kontext:

(16) Tok Pisin
     Mi stap i go long stua.
     'Ich gehe im Laden umher.'
     (lit.: 'Ich bin dabei, in den/dem Laden zu gehen.')

Je nach Zusammenhang sind vielleicht noch andere Übersetzungsmöglichkeiten vorhanden (z. B.: 'am Laden vorbei/entlang').

1.4. Belebtheit

Wenn belebte Wesen (genaugenommen ein mit ihnen assoziierter Ort) als Lokale fungieren, unterscheidet das italienische Präpositionalsyntagma nicht zwischen Wo, Woher und Wohin:

(17) Italienisch
  (a) *Sono da Marco.*
     'Ich bin bei Marco.'
  (b) *Vado da Marco.*
     'Ich gehe zu Marco.'
  (c) *Vengo da Marco.*
     'Ich komme von Marco.'

Hier ist allerdings die Art der Lokalisation durch das gewählte Verb festgelegt, die Lokalisation wird also durch das Lokalisatum (den Sachverhalt selbst) spezifiziert (vgl. § 2).

Die Verwendung spezieller Ausdrucksmittel für einen Bezug auf belebte Wesen findet sich auch in anderen Sprachen. So verfügt das Baskische über eine spezielle Reihe von Postpositionen:

(18) Baskisch
  (a) *Iñaki-ren-gan* 'bei Iñaki'
     Iñaki-GEN-ANIM:IN
  (b) *Iñaki-ren-gana* 'zu Iñaki'
     Iñaki-GEN-ANIM:DIR
  (c) *Iñaki-ren-gan-dik* 'von Iñaki'
     Iñaki-GEN-ANIM-ABL

Das Lokalkasusaffix kann hier nicht direkt an Eigennamen oder Substantive angehängt werden, die belebte Wesen bezeichnen. Stattdessen wird eine Postposition verwendet, die offenbar komplex ist, da sie ihrerseits (zumindest in c) eine Lokalkasusendung enthält. In ähnlicher Weise gibt es im Französischen eine spezielle Präposition für die Lokalisation mit personalem Bezug (etymologisch: 'Haus'):

(19) Französisch
  (a) *chez Marc*
     'bei/zu Marc'
  (b) *de chez Marc*
     'von Marc'

Im Gegensatz zum Italienischen fallen hier allerdings nur Inessiv und Direktiv zusammen, vgl. (a).

Die Sonderbehandlung von belebten Wesen erklärt sich daraus, dass sie untypische Lokale sind.

2. Lokalisation zwischen Lokalisatum und Lokale

Bisher wurde nur der Grad der Explizierung der Lokalisation unterschieden. Daneben muss jedoch ein weiteres Kontinuum angenommen werden: Die Lokalisation kann außer am Lokalisator auch noch am Lokalisatum und am Lokale spezifiziert werden,

d. h. die Nomen-Verb-Unterscheidung vorausgesetzt, kann eine Lokalisation stärker am Verb (als Lokalisatum) oder am Lokal-Nomen verortet sein, oder eben dazwischen stehen. Die stärkere Anbindung ans Lokalisatum wurde schon in Beispiel (13) gezeigt:

(20) Tok Pisin
 Mi [go insait] [long stua].
 ich geh innen lokale Präp. Laden
 Lokaladv. Präpositionalsyntagma
 'Ich gehe in den Laden hinein.'

Die Möglichkeit, das Präpositionalsyntagma unter gewissen pragmatischen Bedingungen voranzustellen oder wegzulassen, stützt die Annahme, dass das Lokaladverb stärker zum Verb gehörig ist.

Im Deutschen wird der Unterschied zwischen lokaler Befindlichkeit und Bewegung am Lokale spezifiziert:

(21) Deutsch
 (a) *Ich radle auf dem Berg.*
 (b) *Ich radle auf den Berg.*

Im Saramakkischen hingegen wird dieser Unterschied beim Lokalisatum spezifiziert:

(22) Saramakkisch (Stolz 1992: 88)
 (a) *A wàka a dì òpòlàni.*
 3SG geh Präp. DF Flugzeug
 'Er ging im Flugzeug umher.'
 (b) *A wàka gò a dì òpòlàni.*
 3SG geh hingeh Präp. DF Flugzeug
 'Er ging zum Flugzeug.'
 (c) *A wàka kò a dì òpòlàni.*
 3SG geh komm Präp. DF Flugzeug
 'Er kam vom Flugzeug.'

Hier werden unterschiedliche Verben in einer seriellen Verbkonstruktion verwendet. Die Richtungsverben sind im übrigen gute Kandidaten für eine Grammatikalisierung: Sie haben fast schon den Status von Lokaladverbien (vgl. deutsch *her* und *hin*) und können möglicherweise sogar zu Präpositionen werden, indem sie mit der allgemeinen Lokalpräposition koaleszieren oder diese ersetzen (siehe § 3.1).

3. Grammatikalisierung

3.1. Entstehung der Affixe

Es ist plausibel, in Lokalkasus das Grammatikalisierungsprodukt von Adpositionen zu sehen: Der Hiat im Inessiv des Baskischen scheint ein Indiz dafür zu sein, dass hier ursprünglich eine stärkere Grenze (Wortgrenze) vorlag:

(23) Baskisch
 etxe-an 'im Haus'

Komplexere Lokalkasus können auch als Adpositionen aufgefasst werden (vgl. dazu auch Plank 1991):

(24) Baskisch
 etxe-ra(d)ino 'bis nach Hause'

Es ist keineswegs zwingend *-(r)adino* zu den Kasussuffixen zu rechnen. Insbesondere aufgrund seiner komplexen Struktur würde es auch zu den Adpositionen gerechnet werden können.

Die Annahme der Entwicklung von Lokalkasus aus Adpositionen beruht auf der Projektion des Explizitheitskontinuums zwischen Adpositionen und Lokalkasus auf die Diachronie:

(25) *Adposition > Lokalkasus > 0*

Den Input für die Adpositionen bilden dementsprechend explizitere Ausdrucksmittel im Bereich der Lokalisation, diese sind: komplexe Adpositionen, Adpositionalgruppen und schließlich für den Fall der nominalen Lokalisation relationale Nomina und für den Fall der verbalen Lokalisation, d. h. der Lokalisation durch ein Verb, (lokale) Verben: Schon Beispiel (22) aus dem Saramakkischen zeigte, wie aus Verben Präpositionen entstehen können. Als Beispiel wird in diesem Zusammenhang jedoch vor allem das Chinesische genannt (Hagège 1975):

(26) Chinesisch (Mandarin, nach Lehmann 1995: 105)
 Nĭ jì gĕi tā sān.
 2SG leih geb 3SG Schirm
 'Du gibst ihm einen Schirm.'

Das Verb 'geben' ist hier bereits zu einer benefaktiv-direktiven Präposition grammatikalisiert.

3.2. Lokale Metaphern

Das Lokalisationsschema wird in manchen Sprachen auch auf Relationen angewandt, die *stricto sensu* nicht in den Bereich der Lokalisation gehören. Das gilt vor allem für die Bereiche 'Instrumental' und 'Komitativ':

(27) Baskisch
lagun-a-rekin
Freund-IDV-KOM
'mit dem Freund'

Die komitative Kasusendung setzt sich offensichtlich aus einer alten Genitivendung (*-(r)e*), dem Adverbialmorphem *-ki* (möglicherweise eine Art Instrumental) und einem Inessiv zusammen. Es handelt sich also um eine zu einem Lokalkasus grammatikalisierte komplexe Postposition. Daneben gibt es im Dialekt der Biskaia auch die Endung *-gaz* für den Instrumental, die sich aus dem in § 1.4. behandelten Belebtheitsmorphem *-ga(n)* und dem Instrumental zusammensetzt. Da der Instrumental in der pronominalen Flexion mit einem sonst auf Lokalkasus beschränktes Formativ *-ta-* gebildet wird (z. B. *nitaz* 'durch mich'), liegt die Annahme nahe, dass es sich ursprünglich um einen Lokalkasus handelt, der lokale Nähe bezeichnet ('Proximativ').

Auch andere abstrakte Relationen werden mit Mitteln der Lokalisation ausgedrückt:

(28) Deutsch
<u>über</u> ein Thema arbeiten/reden ...

Man beachte, dass hier die dynamische Lokalisation Ausgangspunkt der Metapher ist, während in einem explizit statischen Zusammenhang auch die statische Ortszuweisung metaphorisch genutzt wird:

(29) Deutsch
<u>über</u> einem Thema brüten

Zeitangaben werden in vielen Sprachen wie Ortsangaben behandelt: 'zu einer bestimmten Zeit' entspricht dabei 'an einem bestimmten Ort':

(30) Englisch
 (a) *at school*
  'in der Schule'
 (b) *at three (o'clock)*
  'um drei (Uhr)'

Es handelt sich in allen Fällen um metaphorische Verschiebungen der Lokalisation.

4. Spezielle Abkürzungen

ABL	Ablativ
ANIM	animiert
DF	Definit
GEN	Genitiv
IDV	Individualisierer
IN	Inessiv
KOM	Komitativ
PL	Plural
PREP	Präposition
PRET	Präteritum
PZP	Partizip
SG	Singular

5. Zitierte Literatur

Umfangreiche Bibliographien, die hier nicht reproduziert werden sollen, sind in Huppertz (1991) und Stolz (1992) enthalten.

Drossard, Werner & Müller-Bardey, Thomas (eds.). 1993. *Aspekte der Lokalisation*. Bochum: Brockmeyer (= Bochum-Essener Beiträge zur Sprachwandelforschung 19).

Haase, Martin. 1993. „La localisation dans les langues romanes". In: Hilty, Gerold (ed.): *Actes du XXe Congrès de linguistique et philologie romanes*. Tübingen/Basel: Francke: III, 127–136.

Hagège, Claude. 1975. *Le problème linguistique des prépositions et la solution chinoise*. Paris: Société de Linguistique de Paris.

Huppertz, Angelika. 1991. „Bibliography on prepositions." In: Rauh (1991: 9–28).

Lehmann, Christian. 1995. *Thoughts on grammaticalisation*. München: Lincom.

Plank, Frans. 1991. *From case to adposition*. (EUROTYP Working Papers.) Konstanz: University of Konstanz.

Rauh, Gisa (ed.) 1991. *Approaches to prepositions*. Tübingen: Narr (= Tübinger Beiträge zur Linguistik 358).

Stolz, Thomas. 1992. *Lokalkasussysteme. Aspekte einer strukturellen Dynamik*. Wilhelmsfeld: Egert (= Pro Lingua 13).

Martin Haase,
Technische Universität Berlin (Deutschland)

56. Personal pronouns

1. Definitions
2. Pronoun universals
3. Strong and weak pronoun forms
4. Development of pronominal clitics
5. Speech roles of second person pronouns
6. Special roles of first person plural pronouns
7. Pronoun development and implicational universals
8. Pronouns of politeness
9. Formal versus functional typology
10. Conclusions
11. References

1. Definitions

Personal pronouns is the name given to a closed set of words whose perceived principal function has been that they can substitute for nouns and noun phrases. Whilst they are sometimes grouped with other referring expressions (Lyons 1981: 223) their referentiality is neither primary nor constant and the term 'shifters' has been suggested by Jakobson (1957), who emphasized their dependency on situational factors. The substitution function of pronouns suggested by their etymology and a tradition going back to Dionysius Thrax is generally taken to be their primary function, but pronouns "also have a quite different function, which arguably is more basic than that of standing for an antecedent noun or noun phrase. This is their indexical or deictic function" (Lyons 1981: 228).

Personal pronouns designate the roles of persons in a communicative event (speakers, addressees, person(s) spoken about or combinations of these such as speaker plus addressee dyad). Different languages 'carve up' communicative space in different ways, resulting in personal pronoun inventories of various sizes. The main roles are speaker (**1**), hearer/addressee (**2**) and person talked about (**3**). Pronoun forms either stand for these roles individually (e.g. English *I* = **1**) or combinations such as **2** + **2** = (German *ihr*, English *you*, French *vous*) or **1** + **3** (e.g. Tok Pisin *mipela*, the so-called first person plural exclusive). One aspect of universals research has been to formulate constraints on possible combinations of different roles as well as constraints on their combination with other information (such as sex/gender, animacy, number etc).

2. Pronoun universals

The best known but by no means the universal or even 'normal' pronoun system is that consisting of three persons (**1, 2, 3**) and two numbers (singular, plural). Greenberg's universal 42 (1963: 96) reads:

"All languages have pronominal categories involving at least three persons and two numbers."

It should be noted that Greenberg set up this universal as an empirical, falsifiable claim and subsequent research has come up with counter-examples of various types including:

a) The category personal pronoun is not encountered in languages such as Burmese and Japanese.

b) A number of languages make fewer than six distinctions. These include Pidgin languages such as Samoan Plantation Pidgin English and special registers of certain Australian languages (for details see Mühlhäusler & Harré 1990: 256 ff.) but also full languages. Laycock's comprehensive survey (1977) of Papuan languages lists the following counterexamples to universal 42.

(1)   Morwap: 1 vs. not 1
       Amanab: 1 singular vs. not 1
               1 plural
       Awyi, Simog, Daonda and others:
       1, 2, 3, no number distinction

c) The category of number is at best ambiguous (Greenberg 1988), at worst useless when applied to pronouns. Kawi (Old Javanese) has been analysed as having a set of proximates (singular) and distance (roughly equivalent to plural pronouns).

d) It is not clear whether third person is indeed a person category rather than a non-person. Absolute universals cannot be postulated for pronominal gender either but the first two implicational universals postulated by Greenberg (1963: 96) remain valid. The third implicational universal proves more problematic:

Universal 43. If a language has gender distinctions in the noun, it has gender categories in the pronoun.

Universal 44. If a language has gender distinctions in the first person, it always has gender distinctions in the second or third person, or in both.

Universal 45. If there are any gender distinctions in the plural of the pronoun, there are gender distinctions in the singular also.

In the Australian language Ndje'bbana (McKay 1990: 430) we find no gender distinctions in the third person singular (minimal only) but for all three unit augmented forms. If unit augmentation is equated with non-singular (dual or plural for augmented **1 + 2**) then universal 45 needs to be revised.

It must be noted with respect to universal 43 that the number of gender distinctions need not be the same and that complex rules govern the choice of anaphoric pronouns for mixed gender nominal conjuncts: languages such as French, Spanish use **3** plural masculine for mixed masculine/feminine pairs, Icelandic has a separate plural pronoun and Buin, a Papuan language spoken on Bougainville Island (Laycock personal communication 1989), uses the feminine plural pronoun. There is considerable scope for further research in this area.

The assignment of gender to pronouns, according to Laycock (1977: 35), is pragmatically motivated: "I know what sex I am, and I can make a fair guess what sex you are, but it is not always possible to be so sure of a third party." A somewhat complex counter example to universal 44 is the weak pronoun set of Nagala (Laycock 1965: 133) where the difference between second and third person singular is neutralized but the two genders are preserved for the combined **non-1**. This appears to indicate that for this language, gender rather than person is the most important category of the personal pronoun.

Next to gender a range of other information can be packaged with pronouns, including the following (for more comprehensive accounts see Mühlhäusler & Harré 1990: 60 ff.).

kinship	(Adnyamadhanta, South Australia)
interrogativity	(Hiri trade language, Papua New Guinea)
tense	(Iaia, Loyalty Islands)
topic/focus	(Weri, Papua New Guinea)
animacy	many languages
social status, etc.	many languages

Existing descriptions use widely differing labels and it is difficult to formulate any universals at this point. What is evident is that the existing European terminology of number and person is not adequate. Proposals to create a more adequate metalanguage (e. g. Goddard 1997) would not appear to have overcome the problem of a Eurocentric interpretation and the constraints imposed by a syntactic approach.

3. Strong and weak pronoun forms

Pronouns serve a relatively extensive range of grammatical and discursive functions and it is common that different pronoun forms are employed for different purposes. The presence of several sets of forms is found in a large number of unrelated or very distantly related languages, which suggests that universal forces are operative. Whilst it is relatively easy to document such formally different sets, making generalisations as to their function is much more difficult. The particular contrasts include:

a) degree of emphasis: weakening of first and second person pronouns forms for politeness reasons is illustrated by the reduction of stress in the English personal pronouns *I, you* and the existence of special weak forms in language such as French (*je* against *moi*).

b) the degree of cross-referencing: when weaker (often clitic or bound) forms repeat information as to subject, object or other status of pronouns. Consider Kwaio:

(2) Kwaio (Keesing 1988: 146)
tha wane gala nigi naaboni
two men subject arrive yesterday
reference
they two
'Two men arrived yesterday.'

(3) Kwaio
boo ku ngari-a mai naaboni
pig subject bring-it deictic yesterday
reference
I
ta-gala suga-a
future buy it
subject
reference
they two
'It's the pig I bought yesterday they are going to buy.'

The selection of strong or weak pronouns is governed by a range of factors such as topicalization in different languages. Many of these belong to discourse rather than sentence grammar and in the absence of large scale comparative research, universals cannot be postulated. Differential behaviour of weak and strong pronouns has been used for regional typologies, such as Wurm's (1982) treatment of Papuan languages.

4. Development of pronominal clitics

The category a person can manifest itself formally as free pronouns, pronominal clitics, and inflections. Free pronouns can be stressed and stand on their own and in many languages be moved to different syntactic positions. The movement of pronominal clitics is highly restricted in that they are attached to other parts of speech. They do not cohere phonologically with the stem they are attached to, however. Pronominal inflections are bound both syntactically and phonologically.

Available studies (e.g. Dixon 1980 for Australia and Wurm 1982 for Papuan languages, Wanner 1987 for Romance) suggest that clitics and inflections develop out of free pronouns and not vice versa. The number of distinctions in clitics is either the same or less than the corresponding free pronouns but never more.

Sankoff's (1977) longitudinal study of pronominal clitics in Tok Pisin suggests that a number of factors promote their development, including the practice of using pronouns resumptively. Thus *man he come* becomes *man i-kam* in later stages of this language. Indications of he becoming a clitic are that it is no longer used as a free pronoun and that it can be combined with a later free pronoun em as in *em i-kam* 'he arrived'. Her study also suggests that pronominal cliticization begins with the third person singular pronoun followed by second and first singular and subsequently non-singular pronouns.

The functions of pronominal clitics include subject and object referencing or, when clitics become formally identical for all persons, predicate markings. Compare:

(4) Kwaio (Keesing 1988: 72 ff.)
       full pronoun clitic
                     (subject reference)
  1st sg *inau*   ku
  2nd sg *i'oo*   ko
  3rd sg *ngai'a*   ka

(5) Mota (Austronesian)
       full pronoun predicate markers
  1st sg *inau*   /
  2nd sg *iniko*   /
  3rd sg *ineia*   /

5. Speech roles of second person pronouns

Most generalizations about pronoun systems have been made on the basis of ego-centric pronoun systems. Relatively little information is available about alter-centric systems (see Mühlhäusler & Harré 1990: 256 ff.) when the centre of the speech event is the addressee. English baby talk which is inherently child-centred illustrates the latter type (Wales 1996: 56 ff.). Typically, in alter-centred languages there are more forms for the addressee than for the speaker and the unmarked interpretation of inclusive *we* is *you and I* rather than *I and you*. But note that the numerical preponderance of second person forms can also reflect the social requirements of minimizing the threat to the interlocutor's face. An indigenous trade language (Hiri Trade Language Elema) described by Dutton (1983: 91) provides a particularly clear cut example of an altercentred pronoun system. It distinguishes only 4 pronouns:

(6) Elema
    are I, we (inclusive and exclusive)
    eme you (singular, plural, for statements)
    a   you (singular, plural, for questions)
    ere he, she, it, they

In as much as the addressee is not a passive hearer but interacts with the speaker, his/her role is unique.

Thus, arguments against the notion that there can be more than one speaker are paralleled by claims to the effects that there can only be one addressee (McKay 1990). Formal support for this claim comes from Ndje'bbana when the gender in augmented pronouns is governed by a rule of the following type:

If there are two addressees, one of each sex, the female is treated as the augmented person and the augmented feminine form is chosen suggesting one is not dealing with simply mixed gender groups.

6. Special role of 1st person plural pronouns

Because they were perceived to be placeholders for nouns the treatment of pronouns by grammarians has tended to carry over the analytic tools and metalinguistic labels of nominal grammar. This is particularly problematic in the treatment of grammatical categories such as number and gender. Regarding number, Greenberg's universal 42 reflects the conventional arrangement of the type:

(7)   Singular   Plural
    1st   1   1+1, 1+2
    2nd   2   2+2
    3rd   3   3+3

Whilst this grid for arranging pronominal data has been used very widely and whilst it can accommodate the pronouns of a large number of languages, including most Indo European ones, there are two problems:

a) the meaning of the term plural of the so-called first person plural pronoun, as strictly speaking, it does not mean 'more than one speaker' and typically has several meanings (see Mühlhäusler & Harré 1990).

b) data from a range of languages (in particular Philippine and Australian) cannot be felicitously portrayed in this way.

Regarding the first point, Greenberg (1988: 1) notes the ambiguity of first person plurals, in particular their favoured interpretation being dual and suggests a number of additional generalizations including:

a) "The first person inclusive is a favoured category among duals."

b) The existence of a second person dual pronoun implies that of a first person dual pronoun.

c) "When the sole dual pronoun is a first person inclusive, there is almost always a distinction in the plural between a first person inclusive and exclusive."

Whilst these observations can be displayed in an existing traditional model, the resulting system is asymmetric and suggestive of systematic gaps which are in actual fact rarely if ever filled. Conklin (1962) suggested a revised metalanguage to accommodate the data from Ilokano (Philippines):

(8)   Ilokano
    (a) (traditional analysis)

Singular	Dual	Plural
-ko	-ta (incl.)	nayo (incl.)
		-mi (excl.)
-mo		-yo
-na		-da

    (b) (Conklin's analysis)

	[+ restricted]	[− restricted]
[+ speaker, − hearer]	-ko	-mi
[− speaker, + hearer]	-mo	-yo
[+ speaker, + hearer]	-ta	-tayo
[− speaker, − hearer]	-na	-da

This reanalysis was justified by its functional economy and symmetry rather than be appeal to speaker's intuition. The "Ilokano" analysis has subsequently been applied to a range of languages. A revision of Conklin's analysis is given by McGregor (1989: 439 ff.), who suggests the replacement of Conklin's structurally based terminology with one which is sensitive to semantic factors: "What is relevant to the first and second person categories is addition or augmentation: to the speakers or the hearer, may be added one or more others" (1989: 439−40).

The notions of restricted and unrestricted are reserved for the difference between group including the speaker, the former meaning speaker plus one or more members of one non-speaker role (addressee and third person) the latter referring to speaker hearer plus at least one other individual (see McGregor 1989: 445).

7. Pronoun development and implicational universals

Neither children nor pidgin users start off with a fully fledged pronoun system such as is postulated in Greenberg's universal 42 but acquire pronouns in stages: Pronoun mastery presupposes the ability to identify one's self from others in speech roles.

Developmental studies of L1 pronoun acquisition (Charney 1980) confirm that pronoun development proceeds along a small number of pathways. In the absence of developmental evidence for a sufficiently large sample of non-Indo European languages, generalizations have to be tentative.

Combining the insights from child language acquisition with those gained from the longitudinal study of a number of Pidgins, certain implications begin to emerge, including the primacy of the first person singular, the somewhat awkward position of the third person singular, and the importance of paucal and dual over plural.

Pronouns such as English *we* are typically used to refer to speaker plus one (dual) or a few others (paucal) rather than many others (plural). The conventional label 'plural' would seem to hide the fact that the implicational ranking of singular, dual, and paucal for nouns (Greenberg 1963: 94, universal 34: "No language has a dual unless it has a plural") are reversed for personal pronouns. This can be represented in the following developmental hierarchy:

(9) 1st stage:
$\begin{bmatrix} + \text{speaker} \\ - \text{hearer} \end{bmatrix}$ *I*

$\begin{bmatrix} + \text{speaker} \\ + \text{hearer} \end{bmatrix}$ *you and I* (*yumi*)

2nd stage: add
$\begin{bmatrix} - \text{speaker} \\ + \text{hearer} \end{bmatrix}$ *you* (sg.)

3rd stage: add
$\begin{bmatrix} - \text{speaker} \\ + \text{hearer} \end{bmatrix} + \begin{bmatrix} - \text{speaker} \\ + \text{haerer} \end{bmatrix}$ *you* (pl.)

4th stage: add
$\begin{bmatrix} - \text{speaker} \\ - \text{hearer} \end{bmatrix}$ *he, she, it, they*

5th stage: add
$\begin{bmatrix} + \text{speaker} \\ - \text{hearer} \end{bmatrix} + \begin{bmatrix} - \text{speaker} \\ - \text{hearer} \end{bmatrix}$ *we* (excl.)

6th stage: add
$\begin{bmatrix} - \text{speaker} \\ - \text{hearer} \end{bmatrix} + \begin{bmatrix} - \text{speaker} \\ - \text{hearer} \end{bmatrix}$ *they, those things*

This hierarchy also suggests that the indexical and deictic functions of pronouns are developed prior to their referential and anaphoric function, which is most strongly represented by third person pronouns.

8. Pronouns of politeness

Given the key role of pronouns in person deixis or carving up people space, their use for social deixis, i.e. as markers of status and roles is not unexpected. Because of their high token frequency pronouns are ideal markers or reinforcers of social distinction. The work of Brown & Gilman (1970) on address systems is widely acknowledged as the standard account in particular their distinction between *tu* (T) pronouns of solidarity and the *vous* (V) pronoun of respect. Formally, the second person pronoun of respect can be isomorphic with the second person plural (French *vous*) or the third person singular or plural (German *Er, Sie*) or else be formally separate as in Spanish *Usted* (from *vuestra merced* 'your grace') or Dutch *Uw*. Pronouns that signal social distinction or solidarity are found in many of the world's languages though this practice in European languages can be shown to result from diffusion of the Latin and late French and German models (Stone 1985).

More recent studies seem to suggest that the two dimensional model postulated by Brown and Gilman cannot account for the more complex type of social indexicality found in human languages. Brown & Levinson (1987: 15) distinguished three factors determining the level of politeness: relative power, social distance and the ranking of the imposition in performing a face-threatening act. As social deixis is subject to constant monitoring and deliberate changes (as is exemplified in the *you* − *ye* − *thou* debate in British English (Wales 1983)) it is difficult to postulate universals. If number figures in social deixis, singular will denote lesser distance and lesser status than plural. Forms of address for God illustrate the instability of pronouns that combine solidarity and respect. God is addressed as V in French and T in German and by a special pronoun *Gij* in Dutch.

Brown & Levinson's study of politeness phenomena across a wide range of languages suggests a number of trends (statistical universals) in pronoun usage. Greater politeness is signalled by:

a) the omission of 1 and 2 singular pronouns (e.g. in imperatives);
b) the use of indefinite pronouns such as English *one*, French *on*, Tzeltal *maca*;
c) pluralisation of 1 and 2 pronouns. Pluralisation as a distancing device is encountered in a number of languages (Brown & Gilman 1970: 198);
d) the use of third person pronouns for polite address and first person plural inclusive instead of 1st person singular.

The analysis of politeness pronouns has tended to treat these as situation dependent. In actual fact pronouns choice often is situation-creating: a shift to a less polite pronoun, for instance, can create a new situational context.

9. Formal versus functional typology

Pronouns are conventionally characterized as a paradigm of forms and it is further assumed that there "is a considerable tendency for morphophonemic categories to line up or correlate with the semantic ones" (Zwicky 1977: 714). It is further widely held that pronouns agree with the nominals for which they are placeholders in terms of number, case etc. A final widely held assumption is that full pronouns are grammatically equivalent to pronominal verb endings in null-subject or pro-drop languages. None of these assumptions is unproblematic.

As Mühlhäusler & Harré (1990) have shown for a range of languages, there is little empirical support for the view that pronouns are mono-valent in meaning: Wales' (1996) empirical study of English personal pronouns confirms this. She argues that pronoun research should draw on naturally occurring discourses of different types (Wales 1996: 197). Such research would lead to a typology of pronoun functions. In the absence of a sufficient body of data very little can be said about matters such as the role of pronouns in modality, information packaging or social control.

10. Conclusions

The study of pronouns has tended to be driven by the presence of a distinctive class of forms or endings signalling different speech roles. It has further been restricted to either single forms or their use in decontextualized sentences. This, with hindsight, may turn out to be a highly problematic way of proceeding if their social and pragmatic properties are also to be considered. As Wales (1996: xii) argues: "What appears to be a 'syntactic' phenomenon cannot actually be explained satisfactorily syntactically." This, combined with the use of normative rather than empirical data would seem to account for major shortcomings in the areas of universals and typology.

Greenberg's (1963) suggestion that there is an absolute universal of the type that all languages distinguish three persons and two numbers has shown to be in need of revision. A number of implicational universals have turned out to be a better basis for typological research on pronouns, but again progress has been impeded by the lack of comparative data from a range of discourses and insufficient attention to developmental evidence (see also Wiesemann 1986).

11. References

Brown, Penelope & Levinson, Stephen C. 1987. *Politeness — Some Universals in Language Use.* Cambridge: Cambridge University Press.

Brown, R. W. & Gilman, A. 1970. "Pronouns of Power and Solidarity". In: Brown, R. (ed.). *Psycholinguistics.* New York: Free Press, ch. 1.

Charney, Rosallind. 1980. "Speech Roles and the Development of Personal Pronouns". *Journal of Child Language* 7: 509−528.

Conklin, H. C. 1962. "Lexicographical Treatment of Folk Taxonomies". In: Householder & Saporta (eds.), 119−141.

Comrie, Bernard. 1981. *Language Universals and Linguistic Typology.* Oxford: Basil Blackwell.

Dixon, Robert M. W. 1980. *The Languages of Australia.* Cambridge: Cambridge University Press.

Dutton, Thomas E. 1983. "Birds of a Feather: a Pair of rare Pidgins from the Gulf of Papua". In: Woolford & Washabaugh (eds.), 77−105.

Edmonson, Jerold A. & Crawford, Feagin & Mühlhäusler, Peter (eds.). 1990. *Development and Diversity: Linguistic Variations across Time and Space.* Arlington: University of Texas and SIL.

Forchheimer, Paul. 1953. *The category of person in Language.* Berlin: de Gruyter.

Goddard, Cliff. 1997. "Semantic Primes and Grammatical Categories". *Australian Journal of Linguistics* 17.1: 1−42.

Greenberg, Joseph H. 1963. "Some universals of grammar with particular reference to the order of meaningful elements". In: Greenberg (ed.), 73−113.

−. (ed.). 1963. *Universals of Language.* Cambridge, Mass.: MIT Press.

−. 1988. "The first person inclusive dual as an ambiguous category". *Studies in Language* 12.1: 1−18.

Householder, Fred W. & Saporta, Sol (eds.). 1962. *Problems in Lexicography.* Bloomington: Research Centre in Anthropology, Folklore and Linguistics, Indiana University.

Ingram, David. 1978. "Typology and universals of personal pronouns". In: Greenberg (ed.), 213−47.

Jakobson, Roman. 1957. "Shifters, Verbal Categories and the Russian Verb". Harvard University: Department of Russian.

Keesing, Roger. 1988. *Melanesian Pidgin and the Oceanic Substrate.* Stanford: Stanford University Press.

Laycock, Donald C. 1965. *The Ndu Language Family.* (Pacific Linguistics C-T.) Canberra: Australian National University.

−. 1977. "Me and you and the rest". *Irian* 6.3: 33−41.

Luján, Marta 1985. "Binding Properties of Overt Pronouns in null Pronominal Languages". *Chicago Linguistic Society* 21: 424−438.

Lyons, John. 1981. *Language, Meaning and Context.* London: Fontana.

McGregor, William. 1989. "Greenberg on the first person inclusive dual: evidence from some Australian languages". *Studies in Language* 13.437−451.

McKay, Graham R. 1990. "The Addressee: Or is the Second Person Singular?". *Studies in Language* 14.7: 429−432.

Michael, Ian. 1970. *English grammatical categories (and the tradition to 1860).* Cambridge: Cambridge University Press.

Mühlhäusler, Peter & Harré, Rom. 1990. *Pronouns and people*. Oxford: Blackwell.

Mühlhäusler, Peter. 1990. "Towards an implicational analysis of pronoun development". In: Edmondson, Feagin & Mühlhäusler (eds.), 351–370.

Sankoff, Gillian. 1977. "Variability and explanation in languages and culture". In: Saville-Troike (ed.), 59–73.

Saville-Troike, Muriel (ed.) 1977. *Linguistics and anthropology*. Washington: Georgetown University Press.

Stone, G. 1985. "Polish pronominal address in the seventeenth century". *Oxford Slavonic Papers* 18: 55–65.

Wales, Katie. 1983. "Thou and you in Early Modern English: Brown and Gilman reconsidered". *Studia Linguistica* 37: 107–125.

—. 1996. *Personal pronouns in present-day English.* Cambridge: Cambridge University Press.

Wanner, Dieter. 1987. *The development of Romance clitic pronouns.* Berlin: Mouton de Gruyter.

Wiesemann, Ursula (ed.). 1986. *Pronominal systems.* Tübingen: Narr.

Woolford, Ellen & Washabaugh, William (eds.). 1983. *The social context of creolization.* Ann Arbor: Karoma.

Wurm, Stephen A. 1982. *Papuan languages of Oceania.* Tübingen: Narr.

Zwicky, Arnold M. 1977. "Hierarchies of person". *Chicago Linguistic Society* 13: 712–733.

Peter Mühlhäusler,
University of Adelaide (Australia)

57. Intensifiers and reflexive pronouns

1. Terminology
2. Syntactic properties and use types
3. Basic meaning
4. Parameters of variation
5. Intensifiers as sources and targets of language change
6. Intensifiers and reflexive anaphors
7. Special abbreviations
8. References

1. Terminology

Expressions like English x-*self* (*himself, herself, myself, oneself,* etc.), German *selbst, selber,* Latin *ipse,* Italian *stesso,* Russian *sam,* Mandarin *zìjǐ* or Japanese *zisin* and *zibun* exhibit very specific syntactic and semantic properties and play a distinctive role in processes of grammaticalization and semantic change. It therefore seems justified to assign these expressions to a special subclass of function words. The most generally accepted and least misleading categorial labels for such expressions are the terms **intensifier** (cf. Moravcsik 1972; Edmondson & Plank 1978; Baker 1995; Zribi-Hertz 1995, König & Siemund 1999a, etc.) and **emphatic (pronoun)** (cf. Moyne 1971). Other terms, also found in the relevant literature, such as "**emphatic reflexives**" (cf. Cantrall 1973; Kemmer 1995), "**adverbial reflexives**" (cf. Browning 1993), "**appositive reflexives**" or "pronouns of identity" are either highly misleading in their implications and connotations or have not been generally accepted. Whether intensifiers are expressions *sui generis* or can be subsumed under one of the more established minor lexical categories is still an open question. Their interaction with a focus makes them very similar to focus particles like *even, also, only, alone* (cf. König 1991; Ferro 1993). On the other hand, they exhibit the morphological behaviour of adjectives in a wide variety of languages and their role in the marking of reflexive predicates and their nominalizations (e. g. *self-accusation*) have often been seen as a good reason for classifying them as reflexive pronouns or pronouns of identity.

Intensifiers can be found in a wide variety of languages in all parts of the globe and perhaps in all languages. The examples listed above give the misleading impression that there are only one or perhaps two expressions of this class in each language. What we typically find are in fact lexical fields of related, though distinct, expressions, all of which can be assigned to the class of intensifiers. In most languages there seems to be one member of this lexical field which is least restricted in terms of syntactic distribution and semantic selection and may thus be regarded as the core member of this class. This prototypical representative of the class of intensifiers is *selbst* (*selber*) in German, *stesso* in Italian and *zìjǐ* in Mandarin. But in addition to these core members, the following expressions can also be included among the class of intensifiers in these languages (cf. König & Siemund 1996; Hole 1998):

(1) German: *eigen, leibhaftig, persönlich, höchstpersönlich, von selbst, von sich aus, an sich*, etc.
(2) Italian: *in persona, proprio, personalmente, da sè, da solo, di suo*, etc.
(3) Mandarin: *běnrén, běnshen, qīnzi, qīnshǒu, qīnshēn*, etc.

2. Syntactic properties and use types

Syntactically, the most distinctive property of intensifiers can be seen in the fact that they can be adjoined both to NPs and VPs or to projections thereof. The following two examples illustrate this distinction between an **adnominal use** and an **adverbial use**:

(4) *The President himself will attend the ceremony.* (adnominal use)
(5) *The President wrote his speech himself.* (adverbial use)

The assumption that intensifiers can be adjoined to NPs is confirmed by the usual tests (coordination with other NPs, permutation together with the NP, occurrence inside an adpositional phrase, etc.):

(6) (a) *Dr. Watson and even Sherlock Holmes himself think that they have found the murderer.*
(b) German
um [*der Sache selbst*]$_{NP}$ *willen*
'for the sake of the idea itself'

In a wide variety of languages, including English, intensifiers agree with the NPs they are adjoined to with regard to some or all of the features person, number, gender and case and such agreement also shows that intensifiers may either be adjoined to a complex NP or only a constituent thereof:

(7) (a) [[*The work of Picasso*] *itself*]
(b) *The work of* [*Picasso himself*]

The NP to which intensifiers are adjoined can be analyzed as the focus (or better: one focus) of the relevant sentence, as the focus associated with the intensifier, or, in terms of a relational theory of focus (cf. Jacobs 1983), the focus of the intensifier. The most convincing evidence for this analysis is semantic in nature and will be presented in § 3. As far as the syntax is concerned it is the ability of intensifiers to combine with any NP that is used referentially which makes them similar to other focus-sensitive expressions. That intensifiers are stressed rather than the focus they are associated with and that they follow "their" focus is not a completely unique phenomenon but can also be observed in connection with focus-sensitive expressions like *alone* and *too* in English.

In their adverbial use, intensifiers are in construction with a VP or some other projection of the verb. In English the position at the right or left periphery of the VP is a characteristic feature of this use:

(8) (a) *Mary Fisher has earned all that money herself.*
(b) *The President has himself made a deposition.*

In some languages a distinction has to be drawn between two adverbial uses, an exclusive and an inclusive one:

(9) (a) *I have swept this court myself. Nobody helped me.* (exclusive adverbial use)
(b) *I have myself swept this court. I know how difficult that is.* (inclusive adverbial use)

Whereas the contribution of the intensifier in (9 a) and (8 a) can be paraphrased by 'without help' or 'alone', the paraphrase appropriate for (9 b) and (8 b) is something like 'also', 'too'. There is a certain complementarity between the exclusive use and the inclusive use with regard to definiteness, aktionsart and word order, but it does not seem possible to analyze this distinction in meaning simply as a consequence of such syntactic differences. In addition to the existence of minimal pairs like (9), the fact that these two uses interact differently with negation makes the conclusion inescapable that there is a semantic distinction to be drawn. In their inclusive use, intensifiers invariably take wide scope over negation and quantifiers, whereas exclusive intensifiers take narrow scope:

(10) (a) *John did not repair the car himself. Somebody else did it.* (exclusive)
(b) *I did not see much of the show myself. So, don't ask me.* (inclusive)
(c) *I have failed the driving test twice myself.* (inclusive)

Both syntactic and semantic facts suggest that intensifiers also interact with the information structure of a sentence in their adverbial use. As is formally indicated by agreement in languages like English, the focus with which adverbial intensifiers interact is an NP, an agentive subject in the case of the exclusive use and a typically human subject or object in the case of the inclusive use. The interaction of exclusive adverbial intensifiers with the agent role has a formal reflex in languages where intensifiers inflect for case. In those languages exclusive intensifiers are encoded either in the nominative case (e. g. Russian), the ergative case (e. g. Lezgian) or the instrumental case (e. g. Japanese, Hebrew). Examples like (10 a) show that the negation in a sentence with an exclusive intensifier relates to the agentive subject, which can thus be assumed to be the focus ('It was not John who repaired the car'). The interaction with the information structure of a sentence is thus a property of all uses of intensifiers and these expressions also seem to share the property that their focus is invariably a nominal one.

3. Basic meaning

However formidable the problems posed by a formal semantic analysis of intensifiers might be, the basic outlines of their meaning are quite clear. This is true, in particular, of the adnominal use. The most basic fact about the adnominal use and indeed about all uses of intensifiers is that they − or the focusing with which they interact − evoke alternatives to the referent of their focus. This is a property they share with such focus-sensitive expressions as *even, only, too, especially, not...but*, etc. Their second contribution to the meaning of a sentence consists in the fact that they structure the set of referents under consideration (referent of the focus + set of alternatives) in terms of center and periphery (cf. Figure below): The set of alternatives Y is characterized as periphery (entourage) of a center constituted by the referent of the focus X (König 1991: 87 ff.):

(11) (a) *The President himself will come to the final.*
(b) *Even George himself is against the plan.*

In (11 a) the referent of the focus of the adnominal intensifiers is the center by virtue of being high in rank, the relevant periphery being made up by the subordinates or entourage of this powerful person. This aspect of meaning is also apparent in cases where the focus of an intensifier is simply a proper name. If we compare the meaning of (11 b) to that of the corresponding sentence without intensifier it becomes clear that *himself* contributes a characterization of the alternatives under consideration in a situation where the sentence is uttered. The relevant alternatives can only be people somehow related to George taken as center, i. e. colleagues, friends, family, etc.

According to a related, though somewhat different semantic analysis, intensifiers are markers of **discourse prominence** (cf. Baker 1995). Even though this notion is clearly unsuitable as a general cover term for all uses of intensifiers (cf. Kemmer 1995; Siemund 1999), the specific manifestations of discourse prominence distinguished within that theory can also be regarded as different manifestations of a structuring of entities in terms of center and periphery. The conditions for the use of adnominal intensifiers can therefore be spelt out more specifically as follows:

(12) Conditions for the use of adnominal intensifiers:
Adnominal intensifiers relate a center X (= referent of the focus) to a periphery Y of alternative values, such that:

(13) (a) X has a higher rank than Y in a real-world hierarchy.
(b) X is more important than Y in a specific situation
(c) Y is identified relative to X (kinship terms, part-whole, etc.).
(d) X is the subject of consciousness, center of observation, etc. (logophoricity).

The examples in (14) illustrate the four typical contexts distinguished in (13). The Pope is a high-ranking figure, the driver of a car is of central importance in an accident. In (14 c) the food served in a restaurant is identified in relation to the owner and Carl Heine in (14 d) is described from the perspective of a man called Horace:

(14) (a) *The Pope himself is against this view.*
(b) *Most of the passengers suffered light injuries. The driver himself was killed.*
(c) *Lunch hour rush. Marta's tuna sandwiches in heavy demand. Marta herself everywhere and nowhere ...*

(d) *No, Carl Heine was not amiable, but neither was he a bad sort ... He had been that way and then the war had come — the war Horace himself had been to.*

In contrast to focus particles like *only, merely*, on the one hand, and *even, also, too*, on the other, adnominal intensifiers totally lack the implication that the relevant alternative values are either excluded or included as values for the predication of a sentence. Some contexts certainly suggest that alternative values are excluded, as a result of world knowledge that only one person carries out the relevant action:

(15) *The President himself will give the opening speech* (i.e. the President and nobody else).

Other contexts, like (14a), give the very opposite impression.

In addition to the semantic analysis sketched above there is also the view, developed *inter alia* in Edmondson & Plank (1978), in Primus (1992) and Kibrik & Bogdanova (1995) that adnominal intensifiers order the value of their focus and the alternatives evoked on a scale of expectancy, likelihood or remarkability. The referent of the NP to which intensifiers are adjoined is assumed to be characterized as the least likely or least expected and thus most remarkable candidate for the relevant situation among the alternatives under consideration. Intensifiers may thus "correct hearer expectations" (Kibrik & Bogdanova 1995). That analyses along these lines cannot be right is simply shown by the fact that sentences with adnominal intensifiers can be introduced by a clause like *As everyone expected ...* without contradiction.

The semantic analysis of the adverbial use of intensifiers is clearly more complicated than that of the adnominal use and poses some serious problems, none of which has been solved satisfactorily so far. Our semantic intuition as well as the effect of negation provide some evidence for the view that exclusive adverbial intensifiers relate to an Agent subject as focus and take scope over the relevant sentence. Further evidence for this view comes from the fact that such intensifiers agree morphologically with the subject in languages like English. The alternatives evoked in sentences like (9a) and (10a) are alternative agents which could have been asked by the referent of the subject to carry out the relevant task or at least to help carry it out (e.g. *So have me arrested. Or better yet, arrest me yourself*). A negation in such sentences clearly relates to that subject focus, as the paraphrase given above for (10a) shows. In addition to characterizing the agent subject as focus and to excluding alternative agents, exclusive (adverbial) intensifiers also characterize the referent of their focus as the maximally interested party, i.e. as that person who maximally benefits or suffers from the result of the relevant action. It is because of this implication that 'the car' in (10a–b) is construed as John's car and 'this court' in (9) as the one for which the speaker is responsible.

Inclusive adverbial intensifiers are found in three major types of contexts: interaction, reproaches and expressions of empathy (cf. Siemund 1999):

(16) (a) *I can't give you any money. I'm a little short of cash myself.*
(b) *How can you be so generous when you are so poor yourself?*
(c) A: *Children can be very expensive.* — B: *I know. I have three kids myself.*

What intensifiers in their inclusive adverbial use essentially do is characterize the referent of their focus as equally central (hence the paraphrase with 'also, too') with regard to an interaction as an alternative given in the context. As a result of thus rejecting an assumed asymmetry as a basis for some transaction, sentences with inclusive intensifiers eliminate the basis for an interaction, a transfer of goods, the passing on of information and experience, etc.

4. Parameters of variation

4.1. Agreement vs. invariability

The most obvious variant feature in the form of intensifiers across languages is their formal dependence on some other nominal constituent of a sentence: Intensifiers agree with their focus in some languages and they are completely invariable in others. This parameter of variation opposes, for example, Slavic, Romance, the Turkic languages, the Indic languages and English, which exhibit such agreement, to most Germanic languages (e.g. German *selbst/selber*), to Japanese (*zisin*) and Mandarin (*zìjǐ*), where intensifiers are morphologically invariable. The morphosyntactic features which may play a role in this agreement are person, number, gender and case (the so-called φ-features) as is shown by the following examples:

(17) Lezgian (Haspelmath 1993: 187)
Kac-i wič-i laha-na.
cat-ERG self-ERG say-AOR
'The cat itself told me.'

(18) Turkish (person, number, case)
Müdür-ün kendi-si biz-im-le
director-GEN self-3SG we-GEN-with
konuş-acak.
talk-FUT.3SG
'The director himself will talk to us.'

(19) Italian
Il direttore stess-o intervenne
the director self-MASC.SG took.part
alla riunione.
in.the meeting
'The director himself took part in the meeting.'

It is this agreement with a nominal focus which makes intensifiers very similar to adjectives. It is interesting to note in this context that intensifiers do not seem to be subject to the constraint formulated for possible agreement systems by Lehmann (1988: 58): "what can agree in case never agrees in person, and vice versa". Whether intensifiers inflect in a language or not seems to be connected with the general typological affiliation of the language in question, i.e. with whether it is isolating, inflecting or agglutinating, but the tie-up is by no means a perfect one.

4.2. Differentiation between intensifiers and reflexive anaphors

In Slavic languages, Romance languages, in most Germanic languages and in many Bantu languages a clear formal distinction is drawn between intensifiers (e. g. Russian *sam*, Italian *stesso*, German *selbst*) and reflexive anaphors, i.e. referentially used reflexive pronouns (e. g. Russian *sebja*, Italian *si*, German *sich*). The use of the same expression both as intensifier and reflexive anaphor, however, seems to be an equally frequent pattern and perhaps the majority pattern among the world's languages. This pattern is found, for example, in the Finno-Ugric languages, the Turkic languages, the Semitic languages, the Indic languages, in Persian, Mandarin and, of course, in English. In these languages intensifiers and reflexive anaphors are only distinguished distributionally: Reflexive anaphors occur in argument positions other than the (matrix) subject position, whereas intensifiers occur in adjunct positions.

(20) French
(a) *Pierre se deteste.*
'Pierre hates himself.'
(b) *Le président lui-même va nous adresser la parole.*
'The President himself will talk to us.'

(21) Persian (Moyne, 1971)
(a) *hušang xod-aš žāla-rā*
Hushang self-3SG Zhala-ACC
did.
see.PRET.3SG
'Hushang himself saw Zhala.'
(b) *hušang xod-aš-rā did.*
Hushang self-3SG-ACC see.PRET.3SG
'Hushang saw himself.'

(22) Mandarin
(a) *Zhāngsān zìjǐ huì lái.*
Zhangsan self can come
'Zhangsan himself can come.'
(b) *Zhāngsān kànjian zìjǐ.*
Zhangsan look.at self
'Zhangsan is looking at himself.'

Not surprisingly, this typological distinction correlates with a variety of other distinctions between languages. The most striking of these correlations concerns possible further uses of those expressions used as reflexive anaphors, i.e. as markers of co-reference in a local domain. In addition to their referential use, reflexive pronouns are also used as markers of reciprocity, as markers of derived intransitivity, as aspectual markers, etc. in a wide variety of languages. There is no complete agreement as to how many of those extended uses of reflexives are to be distinguished (cf. Geniušienė 1987; Oesterreicher 1992; Kemmer 1993; Cennamo 1993). The following examples from Spanish illustrate the distinctions most frequently made in the literature:

(23) Spanish
(a) *Juan se mató.*
'Juan killed himself.'
(b) *Juan se levantó.*
'Juan got up.'
(c) *La situación se agrava.*
'The situation is deteriorating.'
(d) *Aquí se vive muy bien.*
'One lives here very comfortably.'
(e) *Se venden coches usados.*
'Second-hand cars for sale.'
(f) *Aquí se habla español y catalán.*
'Spanish and Catalan is spoken here.'
(g) *Juan se duerme.*
'Juan is going to sleep.'

These constructions have been arranged in such a way that they form a scale:

> referential (a) > bodily motion (b) > anticausative (c) > facilitative/middle (d) > passive (e) > impersonal (f) > aspectual

This scale could be regarded as encapsulating a series of implicational generalizations of the following kind: If a language uses a reflexive pronoun in a construction at some point of this scale it will also permit this use in all the constructions higher up on this scale. But such strong predictions do not seem to be borne out by the relevant data in all languages. So it seems that what we find here is not an implicational scale, but a grammaticalization scale or cognitive map. Such a scale makes predictions about the possible extensions in the use of reflexive pronouns and about the availability of certain uses in a specific language: If a subset of these constructions is found in a language it will always be a subset of adjacent constructions (cf. Haspelmath 1990; Kemmer 1993). Spanish has all seven constructions, Italian allows the first six and French the first five, etc. The interesting point in the context of the preceding discussion, however, is the fact that the extended uses of reflexive pronouns are only found in those languages which clearly differentiate formally between intensifiers and reflexive anaphors, as in most European languages, many African languages, etc. In other words, the following implicational generalization can be formulated on the basis of our current knowledge (cf. König 1998; König & Siemund 2000a):

(24) **Implicational Generalization**
If a language uses the same expression both as intensifier and as reflexive anaphor, this expression is not used as a marker of derived intransitivity or aspectual marker.

Note that the reciprocal use of reflexive pronouns has not been included into this generalization, since there are languages (e. g. Lezgian) where the same expression is used as an intensifier, as a reflexive marker and as a marker of reciprocity. It seems quite plausible to link the generalization given in (24) to the degree of grammaticalization and the concomitant loss of semantic substance exhibited by the relevant expressions in different types of languages. Due to their semantic substance and their weak degree of grammaticalization, expressions used both as intensifiers and as reflexive anaphors are not also used as essentially grammatical markers.

4.3. Asymmetries: nominal foci vs. pronominal foci

In languages which draw a clear distinction between reflexive pronouns and intensifiers, such as most European languages, intensifiers can be adjoined to both (referential) NPs and pronouns without any restrictions (German *der Direktor selbst* 'the director himself'; *er selbst* 'he himself'), but they cannot occur in argument positions without an accompanying focus. Languages which lack a clear formal distinction between intensifiers and reflexive anaphors may also allow intensifiers in argument positions without accompanying pronouns, i. e. in positions from which they are normally excluded. Such "headless intensifiers" may be excluded from certain grammatical functions (e. g. from subject position) and they may be restricted in their interpretation. In (Standard) English, for example, intensifiers can only be adjoined to subject pronouns (*he himself* vs. **him himself*):

(25) English
 (a) *He himself will give the key-note lecture.*
 (b) *Maggie looked at him. Did he mean herself — herself and the baby?* [Zribi-Hertz 1989: 707]

A similar constraint, or at least preference, has been reported for Cantonese (Matthews & Yip 1994: 85). Quite frequently, however, intensifiers without accompanying pronominal heads can also be found in subject positions of simple sentences:

(26) Turkish (Kornfilt 1997: 304)
 Kendi-si opera-ya git-ti.
 self-3SG opera-DAT go-PRET
 'He himself went to the opera.'

(27) Latin
 Ipse dixit.
 self say.PERF.3SG
 'He himself (i. e. Aristotle) said (it).'

(28) Lezgian (Haspelmath 1993: 187)
 Weleda-n xizan tek pud kasdi-kaj
 Weled-GEN family only three person-SBEL
 ibarat tir: wič, pab Nabisat,
 consisting COP:PRET self, wife N.,
 ruš Cükwer.
 girl C.
 'Weled's family consisted only of three people: W. himself, his wife N. and his daughter C.'

The semantic effect of this use of intensifiers is typically a honorific one. The persons identified by such forms are characterized – sometimes ironically – as being high in rank, as salient in a particular context, or – as in the case of a slightly old-fashioned use of Japanese *zibun* – as adopting a humble attitude towards the hearer (*Zibun-wa Tookyoo kara kimashita* 'I came from Tokyo').

Whenever such "headless intensifiers" are used in complex constructions as markers of co-reference, i.e. in an anaphoric function, the boundary between "headless intensifier" and reflexive anaphor can be very difficult to draw. The relevant structures have been discussed as cases of long-distance binding in a wide variety of languages (Mandarin, Japanese, Korean, Cantonese, Lezgian, English, etc). Here, too, the relevant forms may be restricted to non-subject positions, as is the case in English, but they may also be admissible as subjects, as in Cantonese, Mandarin, Lezgian, etc.

(29) Mandarin
 (a) *Zhāngsān gàosu wǒ zìjǐ méi*
  Zhangsan tell me self have.not
  bèi dàhuì xuǎnshang.
  by conference select
  'Zhangsan told me that he was not selected by the conference.'
 (b) *Zhāngsān rènwei Lǐsì hěn zìjǐ.*
  Zhangsan think Lisi hate self
  'Zhangsan thinks Lisi hates himself/him.'

(30) *Joyce hadn't expected Barry to follow her, for she knew he was a obstinate as herself.*

It is for structures like these that the distinction between **anaphor** and **logophor** plays an important role in the literature. Reflexive anaphors are assumed to be subject to purely syntactic conditions: they are bound in their governing category, i.e. they find their antecedent in a local domain (Chomsky 1981; 1986) or their antecedent is assumed to be a co-argument of the same predicate (Reinhart & Reuland 1993). The notion of logophoricity was first introduced by Hagège (1974) to characterize certain pronouns predominantly found in African languages that refer to the entity in discourse from whose point of view a situation is presented. This term has also been applied to expressions called "headless intensifiers" above. Logophors in that sense are long-distance bound, their antecedent being the closest subject of consciousness (Zribi-Hertz 1989; Koster & Reuland 1991). They exhibit the distributional properties of personal pronouns and have the perspectivizing function just mentioned, they refer to the entity who is the centre of perspective.

The categorization of certain occurrences of intensifiers in argument positions as (perspective) logophors leaves their distinctive function totally unexplained. Given that the distinction between center and periphery of perspective is one manifestation of the structuring intensifiers generally introduced for the focus referent and the alternatives evoked it is not unreasonable to assume that the perspectivizing function of logophors derives from the possible use of these expressions as intensifiers. Moreover, given the restrictions and options in the use of intensifiers with a pronominal focus observed above it is not implausible that logophors that are formally related to both intensifiers and anaphors are simply intensifiers with incorporated or deleted pronominal heads (Baker 1995; König & Siemund 2000a).

4.4. Selectional restrictions

In most European languages the prototypical, central representative of the class of intensifiers (i.e. English X-*self*, French X-*même*, Russian *sam*, Italian *stesso*, German *selbst*, etc.) does not exhibit any sortal restrictions with regard to its focus, other than that the NP (or DP) it is adjoined to should be referential and definite. In these languages, subdivisions of nouns into human and non-human ones, into animate and inanimate ones, etc. do not play any role for the use of these intensifiers. Other members of the lexical field of intensifiers, however, may exhibit such sortal restrictions. In languages such as Japanese, Mandarin, Cantonese, Bengali or Turkish such restrictions seem to be relevant for all intensifiers. In Turkish *kendi* is only used for persons and personifications. In Mandarin *zìjǐ* is primarily used with human nouns and in Japanese *zibun* and *zisin* are only used with human nouns and those denoting higher animals, whereas *zitai* is used with inanimate nouns:

(31) Japanese
 (a) *Taroo-zisin kyouzyu-o sonkeisite iru.*
  Taro-self professor-ACC honours
  'Taro himself honours the professor.'
 (b) *Kono hon-zitai yomunoga muzukasii.*
  this book-self to.read difficult.is
  'This book itself is difficult to read.'

If we look at the whole class of intensifiers in each language, however, we often find analogous sortal restrictions. In Italian, *personalmente* and *in persona* are restricted to human noun phrases and the same applies to German *persönlich*, *leibhaftig*, *in Person*. In Scandinavian languages the invariant post-nominal forms can only be adjoined to a human focus, in contrast to the pre-nominal inflecting form (Norwegian *dronningen selv* 'the Queen herself', but *selve huset* 'the house itself'). Moreover, in some European languages there are also specific adnominal forms for noun phrases denoting a high rank. In German *höchstpersönlich* and the archaic *höchstselbst* are used for this purpose and the Scandinavian languages have superlative forms of the ordinary intensifier for such contexts:

(32) Swedish
Självaste kung-en kunde inte ha
self.SUP king-DEF can.PRET NEG have
det bättre.
that better
'The king himself could not have a better time.'

The pattern of cross-linguistic variation revealed by these facts can roughly be captured by the well-known animacy hierarchy (hierarchy of empathy, individuation, etc.), which has been found to be relevant for a wide variety of variant properties across languages, due to the anthropocentric nature of language:

(33) Animacy Hierarchy
1,2 > 3 [human] > human proper nouns > human common nouns > animate common nouns > inanimate common nouns

Applied to the selectional restrictions relevant for adnominal intensifiers, this hierarchy states that if an adnominal intensifier can combine with a type of noun phrase at a particular point in the hierarchy, it may also combine with all types of noun phrases further to the left. The distinction between human and non-human nouns has already been shown to be relevant for a wide variety of languages. Moreover, this distinction is also relevant for the different uses of intensifiers distinguished above. Exclusive adverbial intensifiers can only select an agentive NP as focus and the inclusive adverbial use seems to be restricted to human experiencers:

(34) (a) *John opened the door himself.* / **The wind opened the door itself.*
(b) *John is very tired himself.* / **The cat is very tired itself.*

The distinction between different participants in a verbal interaction seems to be relevant for certain uses of logophors. In a wide variety of languages logophors (or headless intensifiers) are licensed in contexts without suitable antecedents if they refer to the speaker. Given the special role that the speaker and/or addressee have in a verbal encounter, first person and partly also second person pronouns are acceptable in contexts where third person pronouns are excluded.

(35) Mandarin
Zhè-ge xiăngfă, chúle zìjĭ, zhĭyŏu
this-CL idea besides self only
sān-ge rén zàncheng.
three-CL people agree
'As for this idea, besides myself, only three people agree.'

(36) *On behalf of myself and USAIR, we would like to thank you ...*

There are, however, exceptions to the implicational generalization formulated in (33). Japanese *zitai*, which only combines with nouns denoting objects, is a case in point. Moreover, the restrictions relating to the rank of a person are also not captured in (33). Since such restrictions do not seem to play a role in other patterns of cross-linguistic variation, we probably need a suitably modified weaker version of this hierarchy for intensifiers.

4.5. Lexical differentiations

One of the lexical differentiations typically found in the subclass of intensifiers in European languages is the one between adnominal intensifiers, which invariably follow their focus (e.g. English x-*self*, Italian *stesso*, German *selbst*) and attributive, possessive intensifiers (English *own*, Italian *proprio*, German *eigen*). Such a distinction is found, for example, in the Germanic and Romance languages, but not in the Turkic languages, in the Indic languages, in Caucasian languages, in Mandarin, or in Japanese:

(37) Turkish
(a) *müdür-ün kendi-si*
director-GEN self-POSS.3SG
'the director himself'

(b) *kendi oda-m*
 self   room-1SG.POSS
 'my own room'

Given such interlinguistic equivalences, it should not come as a surprise that sentences with possessive intensifiers typically allow a paraphrase with adnominal intensifiers (*The director's own house* vs. *the house of the director himself*) and that in some languages and dialects reflexive anaphors are derived from possessive intensifiers:

(38) Brabants Dutch (Ad Foolen p.c.)
 (a) *Ik was m'n eigen.*
  I wash my own
  'I wash (myself).'
 (b) *Jan maakt z'n eigen de meeste*
  Jan makes his own the most
  zorgen over z'n eigen.
  sorrows over his own
  'Most of all John is concerned about himself.'

4.6. Patterns of Polysemy

All languages in which intensifiers are clearly attested seem to distinguish at least two uses of these expressions, an adnominal one and an exclusive adverbial one. The syntactic differentiation may not always be as clear as it is in English, German or French. In most Romance languages, for example, we find the intensifiers in their exclusive use adjoined to a pronominal copy of the subject: and thus the distinction between the adnominal use and the adverbial one is less obvious than in other languages:

(39) Italian
 Maria fa lezione lei stess-a
 Maria makes lesson she self-FEM.SG
 ai   suoi bambini.
 to.DEF POSS children
 'Mary teaches her children herself.'

It is only very rarely that specific members of the class of intensifiers seem to be restricted to either the adnominal or the adverbial exclusive use. Japanese is a case in point: *zisin* and *zitai* are only used adnominally, whereas *zibun* is exclusively used as an adverbial intensifier and as reflexive anaphor. An analogous situation can also be found in Lebanese Arabic. Apart from such cases of contextual specialization there seems to be at least one form in most languages which permits both the adnominal and the exclusive adverbial use, even if certain other expressions are restricted to one use only. What does not seem to occur in all languages is the adverbial inclusive use. It seems to be only marginal, at best, in Romance languages other than French. An inclusive intensifier in English is usually translated by an additive focus particle (Italian *anche, nemmeno*; Spanish *tambien*; Portuguese *também*) in these languages:

(40) Italian
 Questo purtroppo   non lo
 this   unfortunately NEG it
 so   nemmeno io.
 know.PRES.1SG neither I
 'Unfortunately, I don't know this myself.'

And in those cases where intensifiers seem to have the requisite additive meaning ("also"), it is not quite clear whether the relevant data are examples of the adnominal or the adverbial use:

(41) Brazilian Portuguese
 Consolei-a, mas eu próprio precisava de consolações.
 'I offered her consolation, but was in need of consolation myself.'

On the basis of these observations we can predict with reasonable certainty that an intensifier in a certain language with an adverbial inclusive use will also have the exclusive use and the adnominal use, but not vice versa. This is expressed by the following (partial) hierarchy:

(42) adnominal/exclusive > inclusive

4.7. Intensifiers as topic markers

One further parameter of variation to be considered here concerns the use of (adnominal) intensifiers as parts of contrastive topics (→ Art. 104). The most distinctive feature of sentences with such topics are two intonation peaks (rise plus fall), whose semantic effect is a double contrast, the evoking of two sets of alternatives. Unfortunately, there is no generally accepted term for such constructions. In addition to the terms "contrastive topic", "intonation topicalization", and "sentence topic", the term "double focusing" has also been used for their identification and characterization.

In those cases where NPs with adnominal intensifiers are used as "contrastive topics", as in the following examples, interesting patterns of variation may be observed across languages (cf. König & Siemund 1999a):

(43) *Myself, I am not in favour of it.*

(44) Cantonese (Matthews & Yip 1994: 85)
Ngóh jihgéi jauh móuh sówaih
I self then not-have objection
bātgwo ngóh lóuhpòh mh jai wo.
but my wife NEG willing PRT
'I don't mind at all myself but my wife is not willing.'

If a language allows such constructions at all it is in such cases that an adnominal intensifier may be separated from its focus, i. e. from the NP it interacts with. In verb-second languages, either the NP or the intensifier may occur in the forefield by itself in addition to exhibiting the usual adjacency, so that we get the following three semantically equivalent options:

(45) German
(a) *Ich /selbst habe \keine Zeit.*
   I self have.PRES.1SG no time
(b) */Selbst habe ich \keine Zeit.*
(c) *Ich habe /selbst \keine Zeit.*
   'Myself, I don't have any time.'

In English intensifiers may exhibit left dislocation in such cases (→ Art. 80), but only in the first and second person, as is shown by a comparison between (43) and the following example:

(46)(a) *Himself, he is not in favor of it.*
   (b) *As for HIM, he is not in favor of it.*

In some languages, such as Romance, intensifiers do not seem to be used as parts of contrastive topics at all:

(47) Italian
La moglie di Piero parla inglese e
the wife of Piero speaks English and
*francese. Piero invece/*stesso non*
French Piero by.contrast/self NEG
parla lingue straniere.
speaks languages foreign
'Piero's wife speaks English and French. Piero himself does not speak any foreign languages.'

5. Intensifiers as sources and targets of language change

Intensifiers play a prominent role in certain pervasive patterns of semantic change, both as targets and as sources of further developments. Those languages in which their etymology is still fairly transparent show that intensifiers typically derive from expressions for body parts ('body', 'soul', 'head', 'eye', 'bone', 'person' (< Latin *persona* 'mask')). The following examples illustrate this historical and synchronic connection (cf. Moravcsik 1972):

(48) Arab. *ʕayn* 'eye'; Arab. *nafs* 'soul'; Amharic *ras-* 'head'; Georgian *tviton, tavi* 'head'; Germ. *leibhaftig* (cf. *Leib* 'body'); Hausa *ni dakaina* 'I with my head'; Hebrew *ʕecem* 'bone'; Hung. *maga* 'seed, body'; Jap. *zi-sin* 'body'; Okinawan Japanese *duna* 'body'; Rumanian *insumi* 'person'; Abkhaz *axə* 'head', etc.

How these concrete meanings developed into the more abstract ones described for intensifiers above is essentially an open question. Some attempts have been made, however, to provide a plausible reconstruction of the basic outlines of these developments (cf. König & Siemund 1999b).

A pervasive historical development which takes its origin from intensifiers is the development of reflexive anaphors, i. e. reflexive pronouns with a purely referential function. As was pointed out above, intensifiers and reflexive anaphors are formally identical in a wide variety of languages, especially non-European languages, so that it is not always clear which use derives from the other. The development of reflexive pronouns in English and in other West Germanic languages as a result of combining personal pronouns and intensifiers (cf. Engl. *her + self > herself*) suggests that intensifiers are the source in this kind of change (cf. Keenan 1996; van Gelderen 1996; König & Siemund 2000b). The derivation of reflexive markers from expressions for body parts in many creole languages points into the same direction. Finally, if reflexive clitics disappear as a result of morphological erosion the renovation of this category typically takes its origin from intensifiers. Clear examples can be found in Brazilian Portuguese and Rheto-Romance (cf. Turley 1997), but also in Scandinavian languages, where the intensifier has to be added to the reflexive pronoun in the case of those verbs denoting remarkable situations of coreference. The two typical patterns of change discussed so far can thus be summarized as follows:

(49) 'body parts' → intensifiers → reflexive anaphors

One of the most interesting problems in the development of reflexive anaphors from intensifiers is the identification of the use of intensifiers (adnominal or adverbial) relevant for such developments. It is quite plausible to assume that it is the adnominal use that led to the development of reflexive anaphors, as in the following example from Old English, where the adjunction of the intensifier *seolf* to a personal pronoun signals coreference unambiguously:

(50)   Old English
        se Hælende sealde hine sylfne for us
        [ÆLet 4 1129]
        'The Savior gave himself for us.'

In those few languages, however, which differentiate lexically between adnominal intensifiers and exclusive adverbial intensifiers, like Japanese (*zisin, zitai* vs. *zibun*), reflexive anaphors are based on the adverbial use.

A further general development taking its origin from intensifiers leads to demonstratives and further to definite articles and personal pronouns:

(51)   intensifiers → demonstrative pronouns → definite articles/personal pronouns

Clear examples of such developments can be found in the Romance languages (cf. Selig 1992), where the Latin intensifier *ipse* developed into a demonstrative pronoun in Catalan (*eix*), Portuguese (*esse*) and Spanish (*ese*). Lat. *ipse*, in turn, is generally assumed to derive from a complex expression containing the demonstrative *is* + intensifier (*ispse* > *ipse*). The additional development of derivatives from *ipse* into definite articles and personal pronouns is illustrated by examples taken from Sardinian (*su, sa; isse, issa*), from dialects of Catalan spoken on the Balearic Islands (*es, sa*) and from the historical development of Greek (Classical Greek *autós* 'self, same' > Modern Greek *aftós* 'that, this; he').

6. Intensifiers and reflexive anaphors

In his typological study of reflexivization, Faltz (1985) distinguishes four basic strategies: First of all verbal reflexives are opposed to NP-reflexives and in a second step the latter are subdivided into "head reflexives" (e.g. Japanese *zibun*), "adjunct reflexives" (e.g. Irish *é féin* 'him-self') and "reflexive pronouns" (e.g. German *sich*). As was shown above, both head reflexives and adjunct reflexives are based on, and probably also derived from, expressions also used as intensifiers. As also briefly noted above, the availability and use of a particular strategy in a language correlates with other grammatical properties of the language in question. Head reflexives and adjunct reflexives are only used referentially, i.e. as reflexive anaphors and perhaps also as reciprocal anaphors. The other possible uses of reflexive markers (anticausatives, middle voice, passives, generic statements, etc.) are only exhibited by pronominal reflexives and verbal reflexives (cf. (23)):

(52)   Russian
        (a) *Èta sobaka kusa-et-sja.*
            this dog   bite-PRES.3SG-REFL
            'This dog bites.'
        (b) *Èta sobaka ukusi-la   (samu) sebja.*
            this dog   bite-PRET.F itself REFL
            'This dog bit itself.'

Pronominal reflexives like German *sich*, Norwegian *sig* or Italian *sè* can generally be combined with intensifiers for emphasis, i.e. to describe remarkable situations of coreference. If the intensifier immediately follows the reflexive pronoun the adnominal use and the exclusive adverbial use of the intensifier are only distinguished in languages in which intensifiers inflect for case, as in the following example from Russian:

(53)   Russian
        (a) *Ivan udari-l   samogo sebja.*
            Ivan beat-PRET self:ACC REFL
            'Ivan beat himself.' (adnominal use)
        (b) *Ivan udari-l   sam   sebja*
            Ivan beat-PRET self:NOM REFL
            'Ivan beat himself.' (exclusive adverbial use)

In languages like German and English, however, the two uses are not formally distinguished. The following German example could be used as an answer to both the question after the victim of some activity (*Who did he ruin?*) and the question after the agent of some activity (*Who ruined him?*) and the English translation exhibits, of course, the same kind of constructional homonymy:

(54)   German
        Er hat sich selbst ruiniert.
        he has REFL self   ruined
        'Has has ruined himself.'

Simple pronominal reflexives and those combined with intensifiers may differ in the binding domain. The observation made *inter alia* by Faltz (1985) and Pica (1984, 1991) for some European languages that complex anaphors find their antecedent in a local domain, whereas long-distance binding only occurs with simple anaphors seems to hold true of many languages (cf. Reinhart & Reuland 1993). The following example from Norwegian is a case in point:

(55) Norwegian (Nynorsk)
(a) *Han$_i$ bad henne$_j$ hjelpe seg$_i$.*
   'He asked her to help him.'
(b) *Han$_i$ bad henne$_j$ hjelpe [seg sjølv]$_j$.*
   'He asked her to help herself.'

There is, however, no perfect correlation between morphological complexity of an anaphor and its domain properties. There are exceptions in both directions. Furthermore, it is not perfectly clear how the correlation or implicational connection is to be formulated. Is it the morphological complexity that matters or is a question of whether the reflexive marker contains an intensifier or not (cf. König & Siemund 2000a)?

If a language has several of the reflexivization strategies distinguished above at its disposal there is an interesting tie-up between the meaning or pragmatics of the sentence and the complexity of the strategy chosen. The correlation in question can roughly be formulated as follows (cf. Haiman 1995; König & Siemund 2000a):

(56) **Correlation between predicate meaning and reflexivization strategies:**
The more complex strategy tends to be used for the more remarkable (i. e. conventionally other-directed) situation; the less complex strategy tends to be used for inherently reflexive verbs and for conventionally non-other directed situations.

As far as the meaning of the sentence and in particular its predicate is concerned, we have to draw a distinction between those predications denoting conventionally other-directed situations (violent actions, emotions, act of communication, etc.), which therefore describe remarkable situation whenever subject and object are co-referent, and those denoting conventionally non-other-directed situations (grooming, defending, preparing, liberating, pride, etc.) and may therefore express perfectly expectable and normal situations of coreference. The distinction between simple vs. complex reflexivization strategy, on the other hand, may take several forms: verbal vs. nominal strategies (e. g. Turkish, Hebrew, Greek), optional vs. obligatory reflexive marker (English verbs of grooming vs. other transitive verbs), simple pronominal reflexives vs. pronouns + intensifiers (Scandinavian), simple intensifiers vs. doubling of intensifiers (Lezgian, Albanian, Japanese, etc.). The following examples from Turkish provide illustration for the preceding remarks. Grooming is typically self-directed. Only very old or very young people are washed, dressed, shaved, etc. Many languages use a verbal strategy of reflexivization or no reflexive marking at all for such unremarkable cases of co-reference. Violent actions, by contrast, especially when they are intended as such, are a clear example of other-directed actions and it is usually the most complex strategy of reflexivization that a language uses for such cases of remarkable co-reference:

(57) Turkish
(a) *yıka-mak*
   'wash something'
(b) *yıka-n-mak*
   'wash oneself'

(58) Turkish
(a) *vur-mak*
   'beat'
(b) *(O) kendi kendi-si-ni vur-du.*
   S/he self self-3SG-ACC beat-PAST:3SG
   'S/he beat him-/herself.'

In the following Russian example the choice of the strategy depends on whether the violent action is intended or not:

(59) Russian
(a) *Ja poreza-l-sja.*
   I cut-PRET-REFL
   'I cut myself (inadvertently).'
(b) *Ja sam sebja poreza-l.*
   I self REFL cut-PRET
   'I cut myself (intentionally).'

7. Special abbreviations

CL	classifier
COP	copula
FEM	feminine
MASC	masculine
PRT	particle
SBEL	subelative case
SUP	superlative degree

8. References

Baker, Carl L. 1995. "Contrast, discourse prominence, and intensification, with special reference to locally free reflexives in British English". *Language* 71: 63–101.

Browning, Marguerite A. 1993. "Adverbial reflexives". *North Eastern Linguistic Society* 23, Vol. I: 83–94.

Burzio, Luigi. 1991. "The morphological basis of anaphora". *Journal of Linguistics* 27: 81–105.

—. 1996. "The role of the antecedent in anaphoric relations". In: Freidin, Robert (ed.), *Current issues in comparative grammar.* Dordrecht: Kluwer, 1–45.

Cantrall, William R. 1973. "Why I would relate own, emphatic reflexives, and intensive pronouns, my own self". *Chicago Linguistic Society* 9: 57–67.

Cennamo, Michela. 1993. *The reanalysis of reflexives: A diachronic perspective.* Naples: Liguori Editore.

Chomsky, Noam. 1981. *Lectures on government and binding.* Dordrecht: Foris.

—. 1986. *Knowledge of language: Its nature, origin and use.* New York: Praeger.

Cole, Peter & Hermon, Gabriella. 1998. "Long distance reflexives in Singapore Malay: An apparent typological anomaly". *Linguistic Typology* 2.1: 57–77.

Edmondson, Jerry A. & Plank, Frans. 1978. "Great expectations: An intensive self analysis". *Linguistics and Philosophy* 2: 373–413.

Everaert, Martin. 1986. *The syntax of reflexivisation.* Dordrecht: Foris.

Faltz, Leonard M. 1985. *Reflexivization: A study in universal syntax.* New York: Garland.

Ferro, Lisa. 1993. "On "self" as a focus marker". *ESCOL '92: Proceedings of the ninth Eastern States Conference on Linguistics.* Ithaca, NY: Cornell University, 68–79.

Frajzyngier, Zygmunt. 1989. "Three kinds of anaphors". In: Haik, Isabelle & Tuller, Laurice (eds.), *Current progress in African linguistics.* Amsterdam: Foris, 194–216.

Geniušienė, Emma. 1987. *The typology of reflexives.* Berlin: Mouton de Gruyter.

Hagège, Claude. 1974: "Les pronoms logophoriques". *Bulletin de la Société de Linguistique de Paris* 69: 287–310.

Haiman, John. 1995. "Grammatical signs of the divided self". In: Abraham, Werner & Givón, T. & Thompson, Sandra A. (eds.). *Discourse grammar and typology.* Amsterdam: John Benjamins, 213–234.

Haspelmath, Martin. 1990. "The grammaticization of passive morphology". *Studies in Language* 14: 25–72.

—. 1993. *A grammar of Lezgian.* Berlin: Mouton de Gruyter.

Hole, Daniel. 1998. "Intensifiers in Mandarin Chinese". *Sprachtypologie und Universalienforschung* 51: 49–68.

Jacobs, Joachim. 1983. *Fokus und Skalen. Zur Syntax und Semantik von Gradpartikeln.* Tübingen: Niemeyer.

Keenan, Edward L. 1996. "Creating anaphors. An historical study of the English reflexive pronouns". UCLA, ms (to appear).

Kemmer, Suzanne. 1993. *The middle voice: A typological and diachronic study.* Amsterdam: John Benjamins.

—. 1995. "Emphatic and reflexive *self*: Expectations, viewpoint and subjectivity". In: Stein, Dieter & Wright, Susan (eds.) *Subjectivity and subjectivization: Linguistic perspectives.* Cambridge: Cambridge University Press, 55–82.

Kibrik, Aleksandr E. & Bogdanova, Ekaterina. 1995. "*Sam kak operator korrekcii ožidanij adresata*". *Voprosy jazykoznanija* 3: 4–47.

König, Ekkehard. 1991. *The meaning of focus particles: A comparative perspective.* London: Routledge.

—. 1998. "Towards a typology of intensifiers". In: Caron, Bernard (ed.) *Proceedings of the XVIth International Congress of Linguists.* Amsterdam: Pergamon (CD-ROM).

— & Siemund, Peter. 1996. "*Selbst*-Reflektionen". In: Harras, Gisela & Bierwisch, Manfred (eds.). *Wenn die Semantik arbeitet.* Tübingen: Niemeyer, 277–302.

— & —. 1997. "On the development of reflexive pronouns in English: A case study in grammaticalisation". In: Böker, Uwe & Sauer, Hans (eds.). *Anglistentag 1996, Dresden, Proceedings.* Trier: Wissenschaftlicher Verlag, 95–108.

— & —. 1999a. "Intensifikatoren und Topikalisierung: Kontrastive Beobachtungen zum Deutschen, Englischen und anderen germanischen Sprachen". In: Wegener, Heide (ed.). *Deutsch kontrastiv.* Tübingen: Stauffenberg, 87–110.

— & —. 1999b. "Intensifiers as targets and sources of semantic change". In: Koch, Peter & Blank, Andreas (eds.). *Historical semantics and cognition.* Berlin: Mouton, 237–58.

— & —. 2000a. "Intensifiers and reflexives: A typological perspective". In: Frajzyngier, Zygmunt (ed.), *Reflexives: Forms and functions*, Amsterdam: Benjamins, 41–74.

— & —. 2000b. "The development of complex reflexives and intensifiers in English." *Diachronica* 17:39–84.

Kornfilt, Jaklin. 1997. *Turkish.* London: Routledge.

Koster, Jan & Reuland, Eric. (eds.) 1991. *Long-distance anaphora.* Cambridge: Cambridge University Press.

Kuno, Susumu. 1987. *Functional syntax: Anaphora, discourse and empathy*. Chicago: Chicago University Press.

Lehmann, Christian. 1988. "On the function of agreement". In: Barlow, Michael & Ferguson, Charles A. (eds.). *Agreement in natural languages: Approaches, theories, descriptions*. Stanford: CSLI, 55–65.

Matthews, Stephen & Yip, Virginia. 1994. *Cantonese: A comprehensive grammar*. London: Routledge.

Moyne, John A. 1971. "Reflexive and emphatic". *Language* 47: 141–163.

Moravcsik, Edith. 1972. "Some cross-linguistic generalizations about intensifier constructions". *Chicago Linguistic Society* 8: 271–277.

Oesterreicher, Wulf. 1992. "SE im Spanischen. Pseudoreflexivität, Diathese und Prototypikalität von semantischen Rollen". *Romanisches Jahrbuch* 43: 237–260.

Pan, Haihua. 1997. *Constraints on reflexivization in Mandarin Chinese*. New York: Garland.

Pica, Pierre. 1984. "Subject, tense and truth: Toward a modular approach to binding". In: Guéron, Jacqueline & Obenauer, Hans-Georg & Pollock, Jean-Yves (eds.). *Grammatical representation*. Dordrecht: Foris, 259–91.

Pica, Pierre. 1991. "On the interaction between antecedent-government and binding: The case of long-distance reflexivization". In: Koster, Jan & Reuland, Eric (eds.). *Long-distance anaphora*. Cambridge: Cambridge University Press, 119–36.

Primus, Beatrice. 1992. "*Selbst* – Variants of a scalar adverb in German". In: Jacobs, Joachim (ed.), *Informationsstruktur und Grammatik*. Opladen: Westdeutscher Verlag, 54–88.

Quirk, Randolph & Greenbaum, Sidney & Leech, Geoffrey & Svartvik, Jan. 1985. *A comprehensive grammar of the English language*. London: Longman.

Reinhart, Tanya & Reuland, Eric. 1991. "Anaphors and logophors: An argument structure perspective". In: Koster, Jan & Reuland, Eric (eds.). *Long-distance anaphora*. Cambridge: Cambridge University Press, 283–321.

Reinhart, Tanya & Reuland, Eric. 1993. "Reflexivity". *Linguistic Inquiry* 12: 657–720.

Selig, Maria. 1992. *Die Entwicklung der Nominaldeterminanten im Spätlatein: Romanischer Sprachwandel und lateinische Schriftlichkeit*. Tübingen: Narr.

Siemund, Peter. 1999. *Intensifiers: A comparison of English and German*. London: Routledge.

Turley, Jeffrey S. 1997 "The renovation of Romance reflexives". *Romance Philology* 51.1: 15–34.

van Gelderen, Elly. 1996. "The emphatic origin of reflexives". *Berkeley Linguistics Society* 22: 106–15.

Zribi-Hertz, Anne. 1989. "Anaphor binding and narrative point of view. English reflexive pronouns in sentence and discourse". *Language* 65: 695–727.

–. 1995. "Emphatic or reflexive? On the endophoric character of French *lui-même* and similar complex pronouns". *Journal of Linguistics* 31: 333–74.

Ekkehard König, Freie Universität Berlin
(Germany)

58. Local deixis

1. Local adverbs and demonstratives
2. Principle of iconicity
3. Diachrony
4. Functional motivation
5. Special abbreviations
6. References
7. Appendix

Deixis can be defined as the anchorage of an utterance in the extralinguistic context (Fillmore 1997: § 1). More specifically, it concerns those "systematic areas of grammar in which the extralinguistic context of the utterance determines the interpretation of linguistic elements: the categories of person, social relations, spatial demonstratives, and temporal reference." (Anderson & Keenan 1985: 307). Here we are concerned with what the authors call "spatial demonstratives", but there is more in this field than demonstratives: local or spatial deixis (sometimes called place deixis, Fillmore 1997: 27) comprises local adverbs, demonstratives, deictic particles, deictic verbs (e. g. movement verbs, such as *to come* or *to go* in English). In what follows I will focus on adverbs and demonstratives, leaving the complex and somewhat intricate problem of deictic verbs to specialised studies (cf. Ricca 1993).

1. Local adverbs and demonstratives

Deictic localisation appears most saliently in so called demonstrative or deictic local adverbs (Diessel 1999). Cf. the English example for a start:

(1) (a) *here*
    (b) *there*

These adverbs und their corresponding demonstratives (a) *this/these* and (b) *that/those* are primarily deictic, i.e. their main function is to refer to a place (a) near to or (b) away from the speaker.

Other adverbs can be used in that way without being necessarily deictic:

(2) English
    up, down, inside, outside, left, right, north, etc.

The reference point of these adverbs can be the speaker or the hearer, in which case they are deictic, i.e. their meaning depends on the extralinguistic context (who the speaker/hearer is, where they stand), but the reference point can also be of a person or an intrinsically oriented object (e.g. *to the left of Peters's car*). Moreover, these adverbs contain other semantic features than that of local distance from participants of the speech act.

I restrict my analyses to those elements that are primarily deictic and differ only with respect to local distance form discourse participants, i.e. those which do not contain other semantic features, even if they are local, too (cf. (2)). That means that I will exclude the feature of visibility as well. It often occurs in the context of distance deixis, but is better treated as a special case, since it is again an additional semantic feature ("additional dimension", Anderson/Keenan 1985: 288).

An interesting case is provided by the presentatives that we find in Russian or French:

(3) Russian
    Vot stol.
    'There is a/the table.'

(4) French
    Voici/Voilà une table.
    'Here/There is a table.'

They have predicate-constituent force, and what is interesting in the present context is that at least the French presentatives can express deictic difference. Etymologically, these are lexicalized syntagms, viz. *vois ici* and *vois là*, meaning 'see here' and 'see there' respectively. Presentatives can be viewed as essentially the same as local adverbs, the main difference being their predicate-constituent function in a language where adverbs do not show that function otherwise (it is thus a language-specific problem or at best a problem of a certain type of language).

Table 1 lists the different levels of deictic distance we encounter in the languages of the world. Whereas the terms 'proximal', 'medial', and 'distal' are frequently used, I have chosen the term 'obvial' for a forth deictic level that can be encountered, although it seems to occur rather infrequently:

Table 1:

Deixis 1	Deixis 2	Deixis 3	Deixis 4
proximal	medial	distal	obvial
here	*(t)here* (with you)	*there, yonder*	*over there*

The first level (proximal) indicates a place near the speaker (or near speaker/hearer, if there is no medial), the second (medial) a place near the hearer (or at least not so near to the speaker), the third level a place away from speaker and hearer (or at least not so near to the speaker), the third level a place away from speaker and hearer. The fourth level a place very far away from speaker and hearer. To imitate the different levels of deictic distance in English, the local adverbs of Scottish English (and of other regional varieties of British English) are used, i.e. *here, there, yonder* (and the demonstratives *this, that, yon,* accordingly), although the translation of medial deixis (especially in the fourfold system) can better be rendered by 'here (with you)'. The first three levels are sometimes referred to as first, second, or third person deixis. This terminology has the disadvantage that there is no proper term for the rare case of a fourth level.

Italian (at least the standard variety based on Tuscan) shows all four levels:

(5) Italian
    (a) 1   2   3   4
        qui qua lì là

Note that the fourfold distinction is an innovation with respect to the threefold Latin (and Romance) system (cf. (5b)). The best translation into English would be:

(b) Italian
1. *qui*
 'here'
2. *qua*
 'here (slightly distant from speaker, or closer to hearer)'
3. *lì*
 'there'
4. *là*
 'over there'

The difference between 1 and 2 or 3 and 4 is rather subtle, and may vary from speaker to speaker, especially when dialects interfere. There seems to be a general preference for the *a*-variant with verbs of movements, e. g. *Vieni qua!* 'come here', although *Vieni qui!* seems to be possible as well. Another fourfold system can be found in Quileute (Anderson & Keenan 1985, cf. appendix). Basque has a threefold system (I add the conventional English translation):

(6) Basque
1	2	3
hemen	*hor*	*han*
here	there	yonder

German has a twofold system, resembling that of standard English:

(7) German
1	3
hier	*dort*
here	there

In all these cases the local adverb is in some way etymologically related to the demonstrative, although it is independent at the synchronic level.

A case that is interesting in this respect is presented by Wolof, a West-African (Niger-Kongo) language: Here the local adverbs are just a special case of the demonstratives with the local (class) prefix *f*-:

(8) Wolof
(a) *fas w-ii fas w-ee*
 horse CL-DCT horse CL-DCT
 'this/that horse'
(b) *f-ii f-ee*
 'here' 'there'
 LOC-DCT LOC-DCT

In Modern French on the other hand, the local adverbs take over the function of marking different levels of deictic distance together with the demonstrative adjective which, when used alone, has lost this differentiation.

(9) French
(a) *ici là*
 'here' 'there'
(b) *cette maison-ci cette maison-là*
 'this house' 'that house'
 ceci cela > ça
 'this' 'that'

In Tamil, we have a basically two-way opposition (proximal distal), which is complemented by a deictically neutral form:

(10) Tamil
(a) *inta anta enta*
 'this' 'that' 'what'
(b) *inge ange enge*
 'here' 'there' 'where'

Again the local adverbs seem to be a special case of the demonstratives.

2. Principle of iconicity

All the above examples involve iconicity (sound symbolism). An approximation of defining the iconicity principle is given here:

Iconicity: A characteristic of the denoted (*denotatum*) correlates with a characteristic of the denoting (*denotans*) and these characteristics manifest some similarity.

This means that deictic distance correlates in some way with certain characteristics of the vowels, and that these characteristics show some similarity with deictic distance. One can easily find counter-examples, though:

(11) Modern Greek
(a) *(e)dó (e)kí*
 'here' 'there'
(b) *aftós ekínos*
 'this' 'that'

The words involved here are all different and of different origin (*ekí* and *ekínos* being related). The iconicity principle is, of course, restricted to phonologically closely related forms (ideally minimal pairs). Typically, the degree of vowel closeness is inversely proportional with deictic distance. German *dies* ('this') and *das* ('that') are good examples just like their English counterparts. English *here* and *there* may be treated as quasi-minimal pairs (correlatives).

Of course, deictics may contain other vowels that fulfill different functions in the deictic element (e. g. agreement). As these vowels do not mark the deictic opposition, they can behave in a 'counter-iconic' way. The Swahili demonstratives consists mainly of agreement vowels:

(12) Swahili
   (a) *h-u-u*   *h-u-o*   *u-le*
       DEM-CL-CL   DEM-CL-DCT   CL-DCT
       'this, that, yon'
   (b) *h-i-i*   *h-i-y-o*   *i-le*
       DEM-CL-CL   DEM-CL-CL-DCT   CL-DCT
       'these, those, yon'

In the case of Latin, the demonstratives do not show different vowels, but are differentiated by consonant clusters:

(13) Latin
    1   2   3
    ipse   *iste*   *ille*
    'this'   'that'   'yon'
    '(with me)'   '(with you)'   '(with him/her)'

Again there is less closeness in the case of ille (most distant), which contains a liquid (approximant) against stop consonants in *ipse* and *iste*. As labial closure can be seen as the prototype of closeness, we have decreasing closeness paired with increasing deictic distance.

In Santa Ana del Valle Zapotec, an American Indian language, deictics differ only suprasegmentally:

(14) Zapotec
   (i) *rèè*   (falling tone)
       'here'
   (ii) *rèé*   (rising tone)
       'there'

The tonal differences reflect the iconicity principle: Rising tone indicates greater distance, falling tone smaller distance. Latin and Zapotec seem to be rather special cases, deictic distance being normally correlated with vowel closeness.

But there still are exceptions. Take Finnish as an example:

(15) Finnish
   (a) *tämä nämä täällä*
      'this' 'these' 'here'
   (b) *tuo nuo tuolla*
      'that' 'those' 'there'

In consideration of the Finnish evidence, the iconicity principle should be formulated in the following way:

The functional opposition of more or less deictic distance corresponds to the formal opposition of more vs. less open vowels or front vs. back vowels in (almost) identical context.

Two parameters are thus taken into consideration: vowel openness and vowel fronting. In her study on deictic iconicity, Woodworth (1991) feels uneasy about the application of more than one parameter at a time. That is why she prefers to treat her data from an acoustic point of view, where she can choose one parameter, namely pitch, i. e. the second formant (for the acoustic motivation, cf. below). Since the two parameters are not complementary, the iconicity principle is rather unproblematic, however. Under certain conditions this (still hypothetical) generalization can be falsified, e. g. if a constellation of **ti* for distant deixis (e. g. distal) and **to* for near deixis (e. g. proximal) can be found. But even if contradictory evidence is eventually found, the iconicity principle remains a valid generalization for a number of languages. Moreover, its functional validity is supported by diachronic evidence.

3. Diachrony

Some of the languages mentioned above show an increase in iconicity or, at least, the loss of counter-iconic forms.

3.1. Italian and French

In traditional Standard Italian (based on Tuscan) we find a threefold demonstrative system (cf. the system of local adverbs under (5)):

(16) Italian
    questo codesto quello
    'this' 'that' 'yon'

This system still prevails in literary style. In spoken Standard Italian the system is usually reduced to two levels:

(17) spoken Standard Italian
   (a) *questo*   *quello*
      'this (one)' 'that (one)'

But this is not the whole story. The system is actually fourfold in the same way as the local adverbs are, since demonstratives are usually reinforced by adding local adverbs in the following way:

(17)
   (b) *questo qui/qua quello lì/là*
      'this here/there' 'that there/yonder'

We see that the medial demonstrative *codesto*, which does not fit into the system, is lost, and an iconically motivated innovation takes place, resulting in a fourfold system again. Moreover, some dialects of central Italy (Umbria, Haase 1999) have a medial adverb *sti* ('there (with you)') which can be combined with *questo*. By analogy they have also created a threefold presentative system:

(18) Italian (Umbrian dialect and other dialects of Central Italy)
(a) *eccolo*
'here it is'
(b) *estolo*
'there (with you) it is'
(c) *ellolo*
'over there (yonder) it is'

As in Latin, there is a complete (and even long) closure in the proximal form (18 a); the distal form (18 c), on the contrary, contains an approximant (in analogy to *lì, là* and *quello*), so there is no closure of the vocal tract; the medial form (18 b) contains a fricative (in analogy to *questo*) together with an obstruent, so it is intermediate.

In modern French only one deictic degree of the Romance demonstratives has survived. A twofold distinction has been reinstalled by using particles grammaticalized from the local adverbs *ici* ('here') et *là* ('there'): *ci* et *là* (cf. (9)).

3.2. Basque

Basque has a threefold demonstrative system (the forms in brackets are the stems in all cases other than the absolutive, which is irregular):

(19) Basque
(a) 1 2 3
 hau (ho/un-) hori (horr-) hura (har)
 this that yon

Parallel to the demonstrative system, there are local adverbs as well (the form in bracket is the stem in all local cases other than the inessive, which is irregular in combination with proximal deixis):

(19) (b) 1 2 3
 hemen (hun-) hor han
 here there yonder

The system of stem-vowel alternation is then as follows:

(19) (c) 1 2 3
 u/o o a

The fact that the vowel /o/ marks less distant deixis is used in the plural paradigm of noun inflexion: Here it replaces /e/ and /a/, which leads to a case syncretism:

(20) (a) *bi-ak / bi-ek*
 2-ABS.PL 2-ERG.PL
 'the two, both (of them)'
(b) *bi-ok*
 2-ABS/ERG.PL
 'the two, both of us/you'

The form *biok* means either something like 'the (closer) two' or 'the two, both here', so one of the two is the speaker or the hearer (it may be both). Welmers (1974: 285) reports a similar phenomenon in Kpelle (Mande, Niger-Kongo).

The deictic /o/ is probably an innovation in Basque, since it is typical of some dialects only (especially Biscayan and Guipuzcoan, from where it got into Standard Basque). It is very popular in terms of address:

(21) Basque (Biscayan and Guipuzcoan dialect)
(a) *lagun maite-ak*
 friends dear-ABS.PL
 '(the) dear friends'
(b) *lagun maite-ok*
 friends dear-ABS/ERG.PL
 'dear friends!'

In contemporary Basque it has spread over the plural conjugation:

(22) (a) *euskaldun-en*
 Basque-GEN.PL
 of the Basques
(b) *euskaldun-on*
 Basque-GEN.PL
 'of us Basques'

Occasionally, it can be found in the singular as well. The following example is taken from a Biscayan text:

(23) Basque (Biscayan)
(a) *larre-an*
 alp-IN.SG
 'on the alp'
(b) *larre-on* (bisc.)
 alp-IN.SG
 'on the alp'

Creoles are an interesting case in this discussion. The following data from Ndjuka, a Surinam Creole, seems to be counter-iconic at first sight. It goes back to the English etymons:

(24) Ndjuka
(a) 1 2
 ya (< here) *de* (< there)
 here there
 3
 anda (< yonder)
 yonder

But, in the modern language, the counter-iconic *de* is usually replaced by a descriptive formation within the language system:

(24) (b) *ape*
    'there': *a* (loc. preposition) + *pe* 'where?' (< *place*)

This intralinguistically created form consists of a local preposition *a* and the grammaticalized word for 'place', meaning 'where' when used alone. It is again a counter-iconic medial form that is replaced.

4. Functional motivation

Since the iconicity principle plays an important role in the languages of the world, it must be motivated in some way: Woodworth (1991) chooses an acoustic approach for merely practical reasons. She does not give a functional motivation. Suter (1991: 225) proposes an interesting explanation from an acoustic point of view again, stating that the deictic sign imitates the acoustic component of the perception of movement: Acoustically, the sound of an insect that flies towards us rises in pitch, as it comes nearer, and falls again, when it flies away. Suter's interesting acoustic motivation, though plausible, is rather speculative, and lies outside the realm of linguistics. In the context of the grammaticalization model, where the speaker's articulatory action plays an important role, a different functional motivation seems to be more promising: If we trace local adverbs and demonstratives back on a chain or channel of grammatization, we do not find lexical items from which they may have developed, as in the case of e.g. adpositions that have developed from lexical items such as 'back(-side)' (> 'behind') in many languages. Note that the words such adpositions have developed from are relational, but not necessarily in relation to the speech-act situation and its participants, as deictics are. This is an important difference between adpositional localisation and the like, better labeled 'Spatial Orientation', and deictic localisation. Local adverbs and demonstratives are the grammaticalization of pointing gestures. Ungrammaticalized pointing takes place in space, but as soon as you want to oppose two pointing directions, they should not be too close to one another. So, when different pointing directions are opposed, a first step of grammaticalization is undertaken (still outside of sound language, but further developed in sign language), by dividing real world space into a limited number of (abstract) pointing sectors. This system has to be transposed into a language based on sound, which is deficient where pointing is concerned. The problem that the community of speakers have to solve is how to remedy this deficiency. The pointing functors (mainly, local adverbs and demonstratives), although related, have to be opposed to one another by means of sound. There is iconicity involved at this stage, since a constellation of relationship and difference that pertains outside spoken language (pointing and different directions) is transposed into a language based on sound. It implies that the sound forms used are related ([quasi-]minimal-pair condition). A straight-forward possibility of opposition is a consonant cluster with vowel alternation. The opposite strategy of vowel maintenance and consonant alternation (as practiced in Latin) is less straight-forward, as consonants can be opposed in multiple ways. Vowel alternation allows for only a restricted set of oppositions. This is not really a problem, as the number of oppositions decreases with increasing grammaticalization. Vocal articulators remedy the problem of indicating spatial distance by different degrees of distance between themselves, i.e. between the tongue (dorsum) and the post-alveolar region of the palate. For more proximal deixis the distance of the articulators is very small, resulting in high/front vowels, for more distal deixis it is greater, resulting in low/back vowels.

Those in favour of an acoustic approach may object that an articulatory approach neglects the fact that the hearer cannot see the pointing gesture of the tongue, since only different vowel sounds can be heard. This is not really an argument against such reasoning, since different sounds are kinesthetically related to the correspondent position of the articulators. That is what makes acoustic correlations as those found by Woodworth (1991) possible. Undoubtedly, acoustic facts, such as those presented by Suter (1991), reinforce the hearer's decoding of the iconic relation.

Finally, a word on iconicity in general seems to be in order: So far, it has become evident that Saussure's arbitrary (or Peirce's symbolic) relation between form and content does not hold for all parts of language. Sapir (1929) and Jakobson (1965) show that some lexical items show iconicity phenomena, although these seem to be exceptions, so that the lexicon can be said to be symbolically organized. But what about grammar? The answer depends on the different grammaticalization channels. Those phenomena that have grammaticalized from lexical words stand in symbolic relation to the content they express (in quite the same way as lexical words). Those grammatical phenomena that have grammaticalized from discourse (such as deictics, topic and focus markers, grammaticalized word order) show a predominantly iconic relationship between form and expression. This implies a new way of dividing grammar into an iconic "syntax" (ritualized discourse) and a symbolic "morphology" (ritualized lexicon).

Acknowledgements

For the Zapotec data, I am obliged to Aaron Broadwell (personal communication). The interpretation in terms of "tonal iconicity" is his idea. The Ndjuka data was provided by George Huttar (personal communication).

5. Special abbreviations

ABS	absolutive
ADV	adverb
ANAPH	anaphora
ART	article
DCT	deictic
DEM	demonstrative
ERG	ergative
FR	French
H	high (tone)
IN	inessive
L	low (tone)
LOC	locative
PL	plural
PR	pronoun
SG	singular

6. References

This article takes up very much of what I have described in Haase (1993) where the same material is discussed.

Anderson, Stephen R. & Keenan, Edward L. 1985. "Deixis", in: Shopen, Timothy (ed.): *Language Typology and Syntactic Description*. Vol. 3. Cambridge etc.: Cambridge University Press.

Diessel, Holger. 1999. *Demonstratives: form, function and grammaticalization*. Amsterdam: Benjamins.

Fillmore, Charles J. 1997. *Lectures on Deixis*. Stanford: Center for the Study of Language and Information.

Haase, Martin. 1993. "Pointing with sounds: Iconicity and deictic localisation". In: Drossard, Werner & Müller-Bardey, Thomas (eds.) *Aspekte der Lokalisation*. Bochum: Brockmeyer (= Bochum-Essener Beiträge zur Sprachwandelforschung 19): 105–119.

Haase, Martin. 1999. *Dialektdynamik in Mittelitalien: Sprachveränderungsprozesse im umbrischen Apenninenraum*. Tübingen: Stauffenberg.

Himmelmann, Nikolaus P. 1992. "Grammaticalization and grammar". *Arbeitspapier* 16 (Neue Folge). Köln: Institut für Sprachwissenschaft.

Jakobson, Roman. 1965. "Quest for the Essence of Language", *Diogenes* 51, again in: id. (1971): *Selected Writings* II. Paris/The Hague: Mouton: 345–359.

Ricca, Davide. 1993. *I verbi deittici di movimento in Europa: una ricerca interlinguistica*. Firenze: La Nuova Italia.

Sapir, Edward. 1929. "A study in phonetic symbolism", *Journal of Experimental Psychology* 12: 225–239, again in: Mandelbaum, David G. (ed.). 1929. Selected Writings. Berkeley: University of California Press, 61–72.

Seiler, Hansjakob. 1990. "Language Universals and Typology in the UNITYP Framework". *Arbeiten des Kölner Universalienprojekts (AKUP)* 82. Cologne: Institut für Sprachwissenschaft.

Suter, Edgar. 1991. "Die Richtigkeit der Laute". In: Bisang, Walter & Rinderknecht, Peter (eds.). 1991. *Von Europa bis Ozeanien – von der Antonymie zum Relativsatz. Gedenkschrift für Meinrad Scheller*. Zürich: Seminar für Allgemeine Sprachwissenschaft, 215–227.

Taylor, Insup. 1976. *Introduction to Psycholinguistics*. New York: Holt, Winston & Rinehart.

Welmers, William E. 1974. *African Language Structure*. Berkeley: University of California Press.

Woodworth, Nancy. 1991. "Sound symbolism in proximal and distal forms", *Linguistics* 29: 273–299.

Martin Haase, Technische Universität Berlin (Germany)

7. Appendix

		proximal	medial	distal	obvial
Akan	DEM	yi		nʊ	
Amharic	DEM	yIh/yIcc(i) M / F		ya/yacc(i) M / F	
	ADV	Izzih		Izziya	
Basque	DEM	hau/hon-	hori/horr-	hura/har-	
	ADV	hemen (hun-)	hor	han	
Bemba	DEM	CL-nó CL-yú (1) (1)	CL-yóò CL-yó (1/2) (2)	CL-lyà (3)	
Cantonese	DEM	ni (H)		go (H)	
Castilian	DEM	este/a/os/as	ese/a/os/as	aquel/aquella...	
	ADV	aquí acá	ahí	allí	allà
Colville	Particle	ixi⁷ proximative			axa⁷ obviative
Dutch	DEM	dit/deze N /M, F, PL		dat/die N /M, F, PL	
	ADV	hier		daar	
Efik	DEM	έmì	órò	ókò	
English	DEM	this/these		that/those	
	ADV	here		there	
Finnish	DEM	tämä/nämä SG PL		tuo/nuo SG PL	
	ADV	täällä		tuolla	
French	Suffix	-ci		-la	
	ADV	ici		la	
Hausa	DEM	nàn		càn	
	ANAPH	nán		cán	
Hungarian	DEM	ez		az	
	Prefix	i-		o-	
Italian (Tuscan)	DEM	questo	codesto	quello	
	ADV	qui	qua	lì	là
Japanese	DEM	kore	sore	are	
	ADV	koko	soko	asoko	
Kirundi	DEM	PR-e	PR-o	PR-a	
Koyukon -Athabaskan	DEM	gonh	eeyet	nəghənh	
	Prefix	do-	no-	aa-	yoo-
Kpelle	DEM	ngi		ti	
Latin	DEM	ipse/hic	iste	ille	
Mandarin	DEM	zhe		na (H > L)	
	ADV	zher		nar	
Maringi	DEM	inye	dunye	anye	
Martuthunira	ADV	nhii/yila		ngunhu/ngula	
Modern Greek	DEM	aft-		ekin-	
	ADV	(e)dho		(e)ki	
Ndjuka	DEM/ADV	ya	de/ape	anda	
Panyjima	ADV	nyiya	panha/pala/	ngunha/ngula	

		proximal	medial	distal	obvial
Portuguese	DEM	este	esse	aquele	
	ADV	aquí cá	aí	alí	(aco)lá
Quileute	DEM	xóʔo	sóʔo	sáʔa	á:çaʔa
Santa Ana del Valle Zapotec	ADV	rèè		rèè	
Sardinian (Sassarese)	DEM	kulthu	kussu	kullu	
Scot. English	DEM	this/these	that/those	yon	
	ADV	here	there	yonder	
Scot. Gaelic	DEM	sinn	seo	siad	
Swahili	DEM	h-CL-CL	h-CL-CL-o ANAPH	CL-le	
Tagalog	DEM	ito	iyan	iyon	
	ADV	dito	diyan	doʔon	
Tamil	Prefix	i-		a-	
	DEM	inta		anta	
	ADV	inge		ange	
Tolomako	DEM/ADV	ka(ho)	tuha	keni	
Turkish	DEM	bu	shu	o	
Wolof	ART	CL-i		CL-a	
	DEM	CL-ii/-ile		CL-eel-ale	
	ADV	fi/fii/file		fa/fee/fale	
Yatye	DEM	na		mɛ	

59. Tense and aspect

1. Introduction
2. Main approaches
3. Tense
4. Aspectuality in the lexicon
5. Grammatical aspect
6. Perfects (anteriors) and resultatives
7. Interaction between tense and aspect
8. Grammaticalization paths
9. Special abbreviations
10. References

1. Introduction

Situation is a general name for anything that a sentence denotes, or an utterance refers to − an event or a state, for instance. Strictly speaking, sentences denote situation types, and utterances refer to situation tokens. (Instead of "situation", the terms "event" or "state-of-affairs" are also used.) **Tense** and **aspect** are grammatical expressions of the temporal properties of situations (→ Art. 42). Tense shows the temporal **location** of the situation, whereas aspect indicates its temporal **shape** or profile. Tense implies the notion of a **reference point** relative to which the situation is located. Aspect is often concerned with the presence or absence of a **bound** or limit that ends or completes the situation in some way or another, though this is not the only way in which the temporal shapes of situations may differ.

Scholarly literature on tense and aspect is vast, and there are but few generally accepted terms. Every study of these matters, including the present one, should therefore be seen as defining its own terms, explicitly or implicitly. Despite these terminological problems there is, however, a growing body of evidence suggesting that languages choose most of their grammaticalized temporal and aspectual categories – tense and aspect **grams** – from a fairly limited set of **cross-linguistic gram types** (Dahl 1985; Bybee, Perkins and Pagliuca 1994), though this is not always obvious when one looks at the mere names of these grams in the written grammars of various languages. In what follows, a convention of writing cross-linguistic gram types with a small initial letter but capitalizing the initial letters of the traditional names of grams in each language will be observed. It will then be possible to say things like "the Latin Perfect is not a perfect, but a perfective past tense".

2. Main approaches

The traditional **structuralist** approach is to describe tense and aspect in each language as a system of forms and their oppositions. Each form is supposed to have a structurally determined, context-independent basic meaning – Roman Jakobson's (1971a/1936) *Gesamtbedeutung* – which is realized through context-dependent "uses", "interpretations" or "special meanings" (Jakobson's *Sonderbedeutungen*; for discussion, see Lindstedt 1985: 17–24).

The grammatical oppositions are commonly thought to have marked and unmarked members (→ Art. 32). Thus, Forsyth's (1970) *Grammar of aspect* is a detailed account of the semantic contrasts between Russian Perfective and Imperfective aspect forms in different contexts, with the basic assumption that only the Perfective positively "means" something, the Imperfective being the semantically unmarked and "empty" member of the opposition, used in positions of neutralization. It is, however, somewhat problematic to use markedness as an explanation when formal marking (the presence of a grammatical morpheme) does not run parallel with the assumed semantic marking (cf. Dahl 1985: 19), or even runs counter to it, as is the case with most Perfective/Imperfective pairs in Russian. Moreover, since an unexpected use of the semantically unmarked member can always be interpreted as neutralization, only the meaning of the marked member can be subject to testable hypotheses in this approach.

In its strictest form, structuralism considers the oppositions and their members to be unique in each language so that there would be nothing that could really be said about, say, the perfective aspect as a cross-linguistic phenomenon; but obviously no interesting typological studies could be made on this basis. In Comrie's influential monograph on aspect, cross-linguistic categories are at the centre of attention, but they are interpreted as semantic entities: grammatical categories of individual languages are expressions for universal semantic categories (Comrie 1976: 9–10). Progressive Aspects of different languages thus grammatically encode the progressive meaning, and Perfects (or at least part of them) encode the cross-linguistic perfect meaning. But Comrie's text is actually written in such a way that nouns such as "progressive" and "perfect" soon begin to look like cross-linguistic grammatical prototypes, not semantic entities as stipulated. Comrie's (1976: 52) claim "The perfect [...] tells us nothing directly about the situation itself, but rather relates some state to a preceding situation" reads as a generalization about certain grammatical categories in different languages, collectively called "the perfect", not as a description of a cross-linguistic semantic feature such as "female" or "adult". Semantic categories do not "tell" or express anything, since they are the things expressed, and, at any rate, the semantics of the perfect is so complex that it would hardly be considered any kind of semantic primitive at all, were it not for the very fact that it is often grammaticalized.

This covert notion of a cross-linguistic grammatical category was operationalized and made explicit by Dahl (1985) and independently by Bybee (1985). Dahl, using typological questionnaires with sentences to be translated in controlled contexts, and Bybee, using reference grammars, convincingly showed that temporal and aspectual meanings which are expressed grammatically in the world's languages cluster around certain prototypical meanings and uses. As they state in their later joint article (Bybee & Dahl 1989: 52): "In fact, our main thesis is that the meanings of grams are cross-linguistically similar, making it possible to postulate a small set of cross-linguistic **gram-types**, identifiable by their semantic foci and associated with typical means of expression" [orig. emphasis]. The claim about "typical means of expression" means that certain meanings are more likely to be expressed inflectionally, others periphrastically.

Bybee, Perkins and Pagliuca's (1994) monograph on the grammaticalization of tense, aspect and modality in the languages of the world is the next step towards the formation of a post-structuralist, **substantialist** approach to tense and aspect:

"Like Dahl 1985, we take the universal categories at the level of future, past, perfective, imperfective (for example) to be the atoms of our theory and refer to them as cross-linguistic gram-types. We neither try to break their semantic foci down into smaller features, nor do we try to group grams into higher categories such as tense, aspect, or mood. The latter represent for us cognitively significant semantic domains, but not structurally significant categories" (Bybee, Perkins and Pagliuca 1994: 3).

Thus, for the structuralist, tense and aspect as grammatically structured wholes are the fundamental categories, whereas for the substantialist approach the really significant categories are grams on the level of "the past tense" or "the imperfective aspect". The substantial approach has certain advantages. First, it implies much stronger hypotheses about what is cross-linguistic. Second, it makes questions like "Is the English Present Perfect really a tense or an aspect?" less important, since defining a gram as a tense or an aspect does not really add anything new to the description of its meaning and use. And third, it liberates the linguist from the obligation of presenting an overall philosophical or cognitive model of situations and temporality every time tense and aspect grams are discussed.

Yet, the traditional structuralist approach retains part of its value; the notion of **opposition** especially cannot be dismissed. The perfective and imperfective aspect, for instance, cannot be conceived of without each other, and obviously a language with only one tense gram would have no tense grams. (Of course one of the tenses can be formally unmarked, and it often is.) This is why it is still useful to discuss tense and aspect as two grammatical domains (see §§ 3−5 below), keeping in mind that there are numerous semantic and functional connections between them (§§ 6−7).

3. Tense

Tense shows the location of the situation in time; in other words, it is the grammatical expression of **temporal reference**. No language is known to encode reference to a fixed calendar time grammatically, so the temporal location is always indicated with respect to a moving **reference point**. In the simplest case, the present moment, the time of the speech act itself, serves as the reference point which provides the distinction between past, present and future situations. According to Reichenbach's (1966/1947: 287−298) useful scheme, a greater number of tenses can be described assuming that the situation (**E**, for "event") is located relative to a secondary reference point (**R**) which can itself be past, present or future with respect to the primary reference point, the point of speech (**S**). Since this S is always involved in temporal reference, directly or indirectly, tense is a deictic category, and this property can be used to distinguish it from aspect (→ Art. 44). However, it is not unusual to find aspect distinctions restricted to certain temporal levels and aspect marking intertwined with tense marking (see § 7 below).

One of the fundamental tenses in the world's languages is the **past tense**, indicating that E precedes S. More often than not, its marking is inflectional, rather than periphrastic (Dahl 1985: 115−117); the **present tense** may be morphologically and distributionally unmarked. In Dahl's (1985) 64-language sample there were, however, more past tense grams restricted to certain grammatical contexts than "simple past tenses" usable for all verbs. The past tense is often marked with the imperfective aspect only, or for stative verbs only, or outside narrative contexts only. There is a universal tendency to regard single, dynamic and bounded events as located prototypically in the past.

In Dahl's (1985: 103−105) sample, there were around 50 languages with a **future tense**, i.e., a grammatical way of referring to future situations (E follows S). Bybee, Perkins and Pagliuca's (1994: 243) 76-language sample contained seventy languages with a gram that had reference to the future as one of its uses, and the total number of grams registered was as high as 156, since most languages had more than one gram with this function. The future seems to be the most common formally marked tense in the languages of the world. This is in an apparent contradiction with the fact that the typologically (or conceptually) basic distinction is often said to be "past vs. non-past", not "future vs. non-future". The reason may be that future time is modally tinged, being by its very nature epistemologically less certain than the present or the past, and this uncertainty often requires formal marking even in languages that do not consistently mark the past. Hausa, for instance, only grammaticalizes aspect, not tense, on the present and past time planes, but it has two grams referring to the future (Brauner & Ashiwaju: 1965: 68−70; Kraft & Kirk-Greene 1973: 81−83).

Futures are more likely to be marked periphrastically than past tenses are, and in this sense they are less grammaticalized as regards their form. Future markers are often excluded from subordinate temporal or conditional clauses. There are languages (such as Finnish) that do not possess a gram that could be labelled a future, and languages whose Futures are so infrequent as to make their identification as a member of this cross-linguistic gram type uncertain (Dahl 1985: 108−109; 2000a: 325−26).

The other side of the modality of the future tense is that those events in future time which are somehow bound to occur are often expressed by the present tense: it is uncommon to find a marked future in sentences like *Tomorrow it is Sunday*. A gram expressing **scheduled future** of this kind is reported in Inuit by Bybee, Perkins & Pagliuca (1994: 250; their term is "expected future"), but it is the only one of its kind in their database. When there are aspect distinctions in the present tense, it is often the imperfective or progressive present (see § 5) which is used for the scheduled future.

The problem of whether the future should be classified as a tense or as a mood is of course not essential to the substantialist approach, but it should be noted that Dahl (1985: 105−107) finds that the temporal factor in most future tenses is more dominant than the modal factors. The modal character of the future does, however, account for the fact that a language may possess several future grams. They often originate as expressions of intention or obligation (Bybee, Perkins & Pagliuca 1994: 254−266), and the distinction between "events that are going to happen because of someone's intention" and "events that are simply predicted to happen" (such as changes in the weather) may be reflected in, say, the choice of the future auxiliary (Dahl 2000a: 309−13).

A language may possess several future and past tenses expressing different **remoteness** degrees, i.e., the temporal distance between E and S (Dahl 1985: 120−128; Comrie 1985: 83−101, 1994: 4561−4562; Bybee, Perkins & Pagliuca 1994: 98−104, 246−247). According to Dahl, the most common remoteness distinction is between 'more than one day away' and 'not more than one day away' (**hodiernal** vs. **pre-hodiernal**), but Bybee et al. find a greater number of less precise distinctions between **immediate** and **remote** tenses. Usually there are only two or three tense grams that enter a remoteness opposition, such distinctions being more common in the past than in the future, and more common in non-narrative past contexts than in narrative past contexts.

All continents provide examples of languages with remoteness distinctions, though the phenomenon is rare in European languages. In Catalan, Occitan and some varieties of Spanish the periphrastic perfect, rather than the simple past tense, is preferred when referring to situations that have occured the same day, even in connected narrative (Dahl 1985: 125; Schwenter 1994; Bybee, Perkins & Pagliuca 1994: 101−102). This is, however, only one expression of the "current relevance" meaning of the perfect (§ 6) rather than a true hodiernal tense.

The distinction between **narrative** and **non-narrative** contexts has already been mentioned as relevant to the use of tense and aspect grams. According to Dahl's (1985: 11) definition, a narrative discourse is "one where the speaker relates a series of real or fictive events in the order they are supposed to have taken place". Weinrich (1964) went so far as to claim that the distinction between narrative and non-narrative forms is more fundamental even in well-known European languages than temporal reference; he claims that the basic function of certain simple past tenses is to be used in narratives, not to refer to the past. His monograph is still a useful corrective against attempts to describe tenses in constructed isolated sentences, but from a typological point of view his thesis is an exaggeration, since certain African languages do possess separate **narrative tenses** (Dahl 1985: 113−114) that do not necessarily occur as the first predicate of the story. Typically they seem to be subordinate verb forms that have been generalized to main clauses after the first, stage-setting past tense form. Hausa uses the same "Relative Aspect" verb forms in relative clauses as in narrative main clauses after the first non-Relative verb form or a narrative-introducing adverbial; a non-Relative Completive (= perfective) Aspect form in a narrative is interpreted as a pluperfect-like flashback, i.e., a past anterior (Brauner & Ashiwaju 1965: 48−49; Kraft & Kirk-Greene 1979: 109, 171−172). (It should be pointed out that narrative tenses are different from the reportative evidentials found in many languages and sometimes erroneously called "narratives"; these will be briefly discussed in § 6 below.)

All tenses that locate E directly with respect to the primary reference point S are called **absolute tenses**; logically they are three — past, present, future — but remoteness and narrativity distinctions may increase their number. **Relative tenses** locate E with respect to a contextually given secondary reference point R (Comrie 1985: 56—64, 1994: 4560). At least in European languages, verb forms with relative time reference are typically nonfinite (not inflected for person). An example of a relative present tense is the Latin Present Participle Active *laudāns* 'praising': it shows that the praising E is contemporaneous with a moment R given by the context, but it does not show anything about the location of E with respect to the point of speech S. The Latin Future Participle Active *laudatūrus* 'about to praise' shows a relative future tense, the Past Participle Passive *laudātus* 'praised' is a relative past tense. Not only participles, but also various adverbial verb forms (gerunds, converbs) typically have relative time reference.

Sometimes relative time reference of this kind is called **taxis** (Jakobson 1971b: 135, 140—142; Bondarko et al. 1987: 234—319). In some languages it can be subsumed within the functions of aspect: imperfective forms may express relative present tense, perfective forms relative past tense.

Forms like the English Pluperfect *had written* can be called **absolute-relative** tenses (traditionally they have also been called "relative tenses", a practice rightly criticized by Comrie 1985: 65, 1994: 4561). The English Pluperfect (Past Perfect) shows (in its non-modal uses) that the situation E is located prior to a contextually given reference point R that precedes the point of speech S. Its counterparts on other temporal planes are the Present Perfect *has written* and the Future Perfect *will have written*; in the grammars of some languages, the future perfect is also known as the Second Future or *futurum exactum*. An example of a different kind of absolute-relative tense is the form *would return* in sentence (1) (Comrie 1994: 4561):

(1)   Mary left at six o'clock; she **would return** an hour later.

Here, Mary's return E is located after the reference point R provided by the first sentence; R is located before the point of speech S. Notice that (1) does not directly tell us what the relative order of E and S is.

If the present perfects of various languages are analysed as absolute-relative tenses, the general scheme of their temporal reference is: "E precedes R, R coincides with S". This is Reichenbach's (1966: 289—290) original analysis, but it has been criticized by Comrie (1985: 78) who seems to find the idea of a distinct R that nevertheless coincides with S meaningless. It is, however, one way of capturing the intuition that *She has written a letter* seems to tell something either about the present or relevant to the present, whereas *She wrote a letter* only relates to a past world. In all tenses, R must be understood to represent 'the time the discourse is about'. But there will be more to say about various kinds of perfects in § 6 below.

4. Aspectuality in the lexicon

In linguistic literature, the terms "tense" and "aspect" are often used asymmetrically. "Tense" only refers to the grammatical expression of temporal reference, not to such lexical expressions as adverbs and adverbial phrases of the type *now* or *in the distant past*. In contrast, it is not unusual to see the term "aspect" to be used about features inherent in the lexical meaning of the verb — about the fact, for instance, that the English *to blink* denotes a punctual event, but *to swim* a more prolonged process. One reason may be that such **lexical aspect, aspectual character** or **inherent aspectual meaning** of the verb always interacts with the grammatical aspect. The interpretation of the Progressive is not the same in *She is swimming* (a process) as in *She is blinking* (a series of punctual events). Another reason is a gap in terminology: if tense is said to express temporal reference grammatically, there is no obvious term for what aspect expresses, the more so as there are various competing theories about the semantic essence of aspect. A wider use of the term **aspectuality**, modelled on "mood : modality", would clarify the situation (→ Art. 42). In Russian linguistic literature, the corresponding term *aspektual'nost'* is already commonplace to express the whole semantic field.

Between the inherent aspectual meaning of verb lexemes and grammatical aspect there is the phenomenon of **derivational aspect**, also called **Aktionsart** or **actionality** (if these two terms are not simply used as a synonym for lexical aspect). Aktionsart was first clearly distinguished from (grammatical) aspect by Sigurd Agrell (1908). Many languages possess various momentary, habitual and other derivative affixes that change the temporal profile of the basic verb in some way or another. The so-called **bounders**, affixal elements or particles that express the completion of an action, such as the English *up* in *to eat up*, are a related phenomenon (Bybee et al. 1994: 87−88). The distinction between derivational and grammatical aspect is one of degree and generality only; obviously bounders can be grammaticalized as markers of the completive/perfective aspect, and habituals can become imperfectives, as has happened in Slavic languages (Maslov 1984: 102−110).

Grammatical aspect may also be morphologically parasitic upon derivational aspect. This is the case with the Slavic Perfective Aspect, which is expressed with Aktionsart prefixes; there is no general Perfective marker applicable to all or most verbs. The Bulgarian Imperfective verb *varjá* 'boil, cook' thus possesses more than twenty prefixal derivatives, which are all of the Perfective Aspect. Some are clearly lexically distinct verbs, others may be considered Aktionsarten of *varjá*, and one or two can be considered its true Perfective counterparts, viz. *svarjá* and the rarer *uvarjá* (Lindstedt 1985: 159−160). Their prefixes are said to be "empty", i.e., adding only an aspectual (general perfective), not an Aktionsart meaning. With other verbs the prefixes *s-* and *u-* still retain their original Aktionsart function.

Outside the Slavic languages, most classifications of the aspectual character (lexical aspect) of verbs are based on Vendler's classic study (1967; originally 1957), Vendler distinguished four different "time schemata" presupposed by verbs. English verbs, or verb + object combinations, that can be used in the Progressive Aspect denote either **activities**, such as 'running', or **accomplishments**, such as 'running a mile', 'drawing a circle'. Activities take adverbials of the type 'for one hour' (*She ran for one hour*), whereas accomplishments typically take adverbials of the 'in one hour' type (*She drew a circle in one minute*). Verbs usually lacking Progressive forms denote either durative **states**, such as 'knowing' or 'loving', or momentary **achievements**, such as 'starting', or 'reaching the summit'. Achievements can, however, be used in the Progressive to show imminence (*The train is leaving*).

Various other classifications of aspectual character have been proposed, but they are usually based on Vendler's system, whose terms remain the best known in the field. It is, however, important to avoid two potential misunderstandings pertaining to them. First, although those beginning with an *a-* seem to denote actions typically performed by agentive beings, there is nothing in Vendler's definitions that would exclude non-agentive situations: 'raining' qualifies as an activity, 'exploding' as an achievement. Some would actually prefer the term **process** instead of "activity", and **punctual event** instead of "achievement". Second − and this may be more seriously misleading − although Vendler's terms seem to refer to different kinds of situation, they only classify linguistic entities, viz. uninflected verb phrases. Consider (2):

(2) (a) *She was running a mile.*
 (b) *She ran a mile in ten minutes.*

It would make sense to say about the situation types denoted by these sentences that (2a) describes an activity, whereas (2b) describes an accomplishment. However, in Vendler's system *run a mile* is an accomplishment irrespective of its tense and aspect; the English Progressive Aspect only modifies its basic meaning, but does not change its class or "time schema". Much confusion arises if these two types of classification are not distinguished.

In one important case this distinction between situation types and uninflected verbs/verb phrases is better supported by post-Vendlerian terminology. This is the distinction between **boundedness** and **telicity** (for a good overview and further bibliography, see Depraetere 1995). Vendler's accomplishments are telic, i.e., they contain a reference to an "inherent or intended endpoint" (Depraetere 1995: 2). Thus, both (2a) and (2b) are telic, the endpoint being the end of a run of one mile. Activities and states are atelic: 'running' (in general), 'raining', 'knowing' and 'loving' are not directed to any endpoint, and even though physical limitations force them to end sooner or later, they are never "completed" in any sense. By contrast, boundedness refers to the actual, not potential achievement of the endpoint: (2b) is bounded, but (2a) is unbounded. In Russian aspectology, telicity is known as *predel'nost'* 'limitedness', a property that unites both Vendler's accomplishments and achievements. In the Western tradition, achievements are not always clearly classified in this respect, but it would seem to be logical to classify them as telic, too: being essentially punctual, they are not only directed to their endpoint, but also contain nothing but the endpoint.

As will be seen in the next section, boundedness is the most central notion grammaticalized as aspect in the world's languages. Aktionsarten and other types of verb derivation, such as transitivizing affixes, often have consequences for telicity, but being closer to lexical semantics, telicity is less apt to be grammaticalized as an inflectional category.

5. Grammatical aspect

The most important aspect distinction in the languages of the world is between the **perfective** and the **imperfective** aspect; Dahl (1985: 70−71) found it in more than half of his 64-language sample. Some languages express the distinction in all verb forms, such as in Russian *stroit'* 'to build (Imperfective)' vs. *postroit'* 'to build (Perfective)': in Russian, no tenses, moods or non-finite forms can neutralize this opposition, with the exception that what is morphologically a Perfective Present is usually interpreted as having future time reference (the Imperfective does possess separate Present and Future tenses). Modern Greek is a language where there are separate perfective ("Aorist") and imperfective forms for the past, present and future. But in many languages this opposition is confined to the past temporal domain, as in Latin and modern Romance languages:

(3) Latin
 Cena-ba-m   *forte,*
 have.dinner-PAST.IMPFV-SG1 by.chance
 cum amic-us **veni-t.**
 when friend-SG.NOM come.PAST.PFV-SG3
 'I happened to be having dinner when a/the friend came.'

In Latin, the perfective past is traditionally called the Perfect, and the imperfective past the Imperfect. "Imperfect" can indeed be used as a cross-linguistic name for imperfective past tenses, but "Perfect" is usually reserved for other uses (see § 6 below).

Sentence (3) also illustrates a minimal narrative context which is cross-linguistically diagnostic for the perfective / imperfective opposition: what *was happening* (imperfective) when an event *happened* (perfective). If a form with the first of these functions excludes stative predicates (Vendler's states), as the English form *was happening* does, it is not a true imperfective, but a **progressive**. Thus, an imperfective is also used as the first predicate in a sentence of the type "I knew what would happen next", but a progressive is not. In Dahl's (1985: 90−95) sample, the progressive was nearly as frequent as the imperfective, and it is not unusual to find both a progressive and an imperfective in the same language, such as Spanish, Portuguese and Italian (for the progressive in European languages, see Bertinetto, Ebert & de Groot 2000). In contrast to the imperfective, the progressive is usually not confined to the past tense, nor is it used with a habitual meaning, and it is clearly more often expressed periphrastically (often with locative expressions) than the imperfective is. When the same language has both an imperfective and progressive aspect, I propose the tentative universal that the progressive is also less grammaticalized in that its use is less compulsory in the appropriate contexts: the imperfective may suffice to express the progressive meaning, but not vice versa.

Most theories about the basic meaning distinction between the perfective and imperfective aspect are based on the concepts of **boundedness** and **totality**. According to Comrie (1976: 3), the perfective "presents the totality of the situation referred to [...] without reference to its temporal constituency: the whole of the situation is presented as a single unanalysable whole" (cf. Bondarko 1990). In a sense, a perfective form like *venit* 'came, arrived' in (3) above can be compared to a count noun in that a complete arrival must contain all of its parts. An imperfective form like *cenabam* 'was eating, was having dinner' is like a mass noun since even a short stretch of having a meal is a perfect instance of this type of activity (Carlson 1981 and forthcoming). Notice that this is not directly related to the duration of the situation, but to its internal homogeneity. A perfective situation, i. e., a situation referred to perfectively, is not necessarily more punctual than an imperfective situation is, but it is similar to a point in being indivisible. Moreover, an imperfective form is often used to describe the state of affairs at a definite moment, such as the present moment, or the moment of the friend's arrival in (3), whereas an perfective accomplishment (such as *She built a house*) necessarily refers to a prolonged interval. It is therefore erroneous to label the imperfective "durative" and the perfective "punctual", as is often done.

It is also said that the perfective refers to a bounded situation, a situation that has reached some kind of limit or endpoint. Since the inclusion of the limit is the most important thing that makes a situation that is referred to perfectively indivisible, obviously this is not in contradiction with the totality definition. Perfective grams of various languages may, however, differ according to the type of bound they express. Lindstedt (1995) has suggested calling the two main types a **temporal bound** and a **material bound**. A material bound presupposes telicity and entails a temporal bound, such as in the following Russian sentence containing a Perfective verb:

(4) On **na-pisá-l**   pis'm-ó.
     he PFV-write-PAST(M) letter-SG.ACC
     'He wrote a/the letter.'

The endpoint of the action has a clear material character: when the letter was finished, the work was done.

Now consider the Russian translation of the following sentence from Dahl's (1985: 74–75) typological questionnaire:

(5) (What did your brother do after dinner yesterday?)
     On **pisá-l**   pís'm-a.
     he (IMPFV)write-PAST(M) letter-PL.ACC
     'He wrote (some) letters.'

Russian must use an Imperfective verb here, because the situation is atelic: the brother spent some time in letter-writing, but he is not reported to have had a definite number of letters to be completed. A Perfective verb (*on* **napisál** *pís'ma*) would force the translation 'He wrote **the** letters'. However, in translating (5) most aspect languages in Dahl's sample make use of the perfective – the Romance languages, for instance, would use their perfective past tenses. This is because their perfective aspect is based on the notion of temporal bound: the brother spent some time in letter-writing and then did something else.

Another type of test sentence for the temporal bound is:

(6) Mary **danced** until midnight.

(7) Mary **danced** for two hours.

Languages that express the temporal bound use the perfective here (notice also the Simple Past instead of the Progressive in English), whereas Russian and other Slavic languages would make use of their imperfectives since dancing is atelic, and no material bound can exist.

In Bulgarian sentences referring to the past, there are two independent aspect oppositions, onne grammaticalizing the material bound (as in Russian), the other the temporal bound (as in Romance languages). In cases like the following the uses of the two perfectives coincide; the verb form used is the so-called Perfective Aorist, a "perfective perfective-past":

(8) Tja **iz-pjá**   pesen-tá za
     she PFV-sing.AOR(SG3) song-DEF.F PREP
     tri minút-i.
     three minute-PL
     'She sang the song in three minutes.'

However, when the bound is only temporal, we have an Imperfective Aorist, an "imperfective perfective-past":

(9) Tja **pja**   pesen-tá
     she (IMPFV)sing.AOR(SG3) song-DEF.F
     tri minút-i
     three minute-PL
     'She sang the song for three minutes.'

Notice in the translations that English only makes use of different temporal prepositions to express the nature of the bound.

Many languages use bounders (see § 5) or other kinds of morphemes – such as auxiliaries with the original meaning 'finish' – to indicate that an action totally affects or consumes the object, or that it involves the whole set of individuals expressed by a plural subject or object, or sometimes that the action has some surprise value (cf. Bybee, Perkins & Pagliuca 1994: 57–61; Dahl 1985: 95, 1994: 243; Bakker & al. 1994: 257–258). This kind of **completive** aspect is best regarded as a relatively weakly grammaticalized expression for the material bound. Completive prefixes are the diachronic source of the Slavic Perfective (cf. § 5), and many neighbouring languages, such as Georgian, Lithuanian, Latvian, German and Hungarian possess systems of verbal prefixes and other bounders with various degrees of grammaticalization. In Finnic (Balto-Finnic) languages such as Finnish, the nominal cases distinguishing a partially-affected object from a totally affected object behave in some contexts like markers of imperfectivity and perfectivity (Heinämäki 1984, 1994). There is thus an area in Central and Eastern Europe where the material bound is often marked, whereas the Western (Romance) system marks the temporal bound, and typically in the past only.

As regards discourse structure, especially narrative discourse, it is possible to say that the perfective or completive aspect denotes an **event**, i.e., a foregrounded situation that moves the plot forward and changes the state-of-affairs in the discourse world, whereas the imperfective aspect denotes a **process** or **state** and therefore describes a background state-of-affairs in that world. The progressive only denotes processes, not states. This threefold classification into events, processes and states necessarily pertains to the situations or situation types themselves, not to linguistic entities à la Vendler (cf. Mourelatos 1981).

A special kind of state is a situation that is habitually repeated, such as:

(10)   *The two children **used to send** me a card at Christmas time.*

Imperfectives, but not progressives, are often employed to express such habitual situations (for the Slavic Imperfective and Perfective in habitual function, see Mønnesland 1984). The English auxiliary *used to* ['ju:stə] is an example of what can be called the **habitual** aspect (Comrie 1976: 26−30; Dahl 1985: 95−102; Bybee, Perkins & Pagliuca 1994: 151−160; cf. also Kučera 1981 for English and Czech). As the English *used to* or the so-called Past Iterative in Lithuanian, the habitual is often restricted to the past. In Bybee, Perkins and Pagliuca's cross-linguistic sample, there were 21 grams expressing habituality without tense restrictions, and 10 grams with the meaning 'past habitual'. There were two cases of specifically present habituals, but both were morphologically unmarked. Imagine that the English Progressive Present (*is reading*) were generalized as a non-habitual present: the English Simple Present (*reads*) would then emerge as such a morphologically unmarked present habitual tense. As shown by Haspelmath (1998), in various languages a new morphologically marked present tense has pushed the old unmarked present into future, habitual or subjunctive uses.

6. Perfects (anteriors) and resultatives

The **perfects** of various languages typically express (1) the relevance of a past situation from the present point of view and (2) detachment from other past facts, i.e., non-narrativity (Comrie 1976: 52−65; Dahl 1985: 129−153; Maslov 1984: 32−47, 1988). The notion of **current relevance** particularly is considered crucial (for its possible explication, see Dahl & Hedin 2000). The English Present Perfect (as in *He has read this book*, or *He's read this one*) is a good example of this cross-linguistic gram type.

In recent literature the perfect is also called **anterior** so as to avoid confusion with the term "perfective (aspect)". It is indeed somewhat misleading that the Perfects of some languages, such as Latin, can be cross-linguistically called perfective past tenses, but not perfects, the crucial difference being the use of the Latin perfect as a main narrative tense. Thus, Bybee, Perkins & Pagliuca's (1994: 54) definition of the anterior is essentially the same as that of the perfect discussed here. Their definition is, however, broader in that it also provides for past anteriors and future anteriors: "an anterior signals that the situation occurs prior to reference time and is relevant to the situation at reference time [...] Anteriors may occur with past or future tense marking". Past perfects (or pluperfects) and future perfects (*futura exacta*) share several properties with present perfects, but they can be described as absolute-relative tenses more easily than the present perfects can (see § 3 above). Notice also that in creole linguistics, "anterior" usually refers to a purely relative past tense (Bakker & al. 1994: 250).

Bybee and Dahl (1989: 67−68) list four typical diachronic sources of the perfect in the languages of the world: (i) copula + past participle of the main verb; (ii) possessive constructions involving a past participle of the main verb (cf. Maslov 1984: 224−248); (iii) main verb + particle meaning 'already'; (iv) constructions involving verbs like 'finish' or 'cast aside'. The two latter sources are by their semantics completive constructions (§ 5), whereas the first two, common in European languages, are originally **resultatives** (Bybee, Perkins & Pagliuca 1994: 53−74). A perfect deriving from a possessive construction may involve a transitive verb meaning 'to have'; if this is the case, it can be called a 'have' perfect, or a *habeo* perfect. As transitive verbs with the meaning 'have' are rare outside European languages, the 'have' perfect is a typically European phenomenon. A copula-based perfect is a 'be' perfect, or a *sum* perfect.

The distinction between resultatives and perfects was established in linguistics only recently, largely owing to the important collective work edited by Nedjalkov (1988/1983). Resultatives "signal that a state exists as a result of a past action" (Bybee, Perkins & Pagliuca 1994: 54). Traditionally the resultative is often subsumed under the category of perfect as a special resultative or "statal" variant of it, or is simply called a "stative". For the criteria for distinguishing resultatives from perfects, the reader is referred to Nedjalkov & Jaxontov (1988), Dahl (1985: 133−135), Bybee & Dahl (1989: 68) and Bybee, Perkins & Pagliuca (1994: 63−69), but the most important single difference should be mentioned here: only resultatives combine with adverbs of unlimited duration, such as 'still' or 'as before'. In English, it is not possible to say *She has still gone (if still is used in its temporal meaning) − in contrast to the resultative construction She is still gone (see also Lindstedt 2000: 366−68).

The perfect is typically a periphrastic gram, being formally close to its resultative (or completive) source. An important exception seems to be the old Indo-European Perfect, as attested in Ancient Greek and Old Indic. A newer inflectional perfect *in statu nascendi* is the active resultative construction in North Russian dialects (Trubinskij 1988: 394; Tommola 2000: 465).

The perfect of current relevance semantically shades into what is usually called the **experiential** (or existential) perfect. In English, these two types are formally differentiated only in rare cases like the following (cf. Comrie 1976: 58−59):

(11)   *Mary **has gone** to Paris.*

(12)   *Mary **has been** to Paris.*

In (11), the fact of Mary's having gone to Paris may be relevant to the present state of affairs in various ways, but typically the sentence at least implicates that she is not present. The experiential perfect of (12) only expresses that the past situation in which Mary went to Paris is less directly part of the present state of affairs, most notably through Mary, who perhaps now knows what Paris is like.

In its narrower definition, an experiential perfect presupposes an animate agent, since it expresses the fact that "certain qualities or knowledge is attributable to the agent due to past experiences" (Bybee, Perkins & Pagliuca 1994: 62). In a broader definition, it only means that "a given situation has held at least once during some time in the past leading up to the present" (Comrie 1976: 58). This notion is further explicated by Dahl & Hedin (2000), who call it "type-focusing event reference" (as opposed to "token-focusing event reference", as in *Mary went to Paris*).

However, experientiality as such is neither a necessary nor a sufficient condition for a gram to be called a perfect. **Experientials proper** are a distinct gram-type, described by Dahl (1985: 139−144); the Japanese *-ta koto ga aru* construction is a well-known example (see also Dahl & Hedin 2000: 388).

Although the experiential meaning may become dominant in the perfect, historically it is usually secondary and derives from the current relevance meaning. The perfect of a particular language may well be compatible with specific past time adverbials. Sentence (13) is ungrammatical in English, to be sure:

(13)   **I **have woken up** at 4 o'clock this morning.*

However, a perfect would be possible − though not the only alternative − in Finnish and Bulgarian, for instance. This is because there is an obvious current relevance reading − I woke up so early that I am now tired. According to Dahl (1985: 137−138), Swedish occupies an intermediate position: a specific time adverbial can combine with the perfect if it is part of the information focus. I assume that the degree of incompatibility of specific time adverbials with the perfect in a particular language shows to what extent it has become a dominantly experiential form.

In some languages the perfect has developed **evidential** functions, or has become a predominantly evidential gram. Evidential, to be distinguished from mood, is, according to Trask (1993 s. v.), "a grammatical category occurring in some languages by which all statements (and sometimes other sentence types) are overtly and obligatorily marked to indicate the source of the speaker's evidence for her/his utterance" (see also Jakobson 1971b: 135; Chafe & Nichols (eds.) 1986; Willett 1988). There are no well-established terms for different types of evidentials. I propose the term **indirective** for the most widespread evidential gram type, which indicates that the speaker has not witnessed the situation he or she is speaking about, but knows of it from hearsay or other kinds of indirect evidence.

Other grammatical and semantic terms in use are **reportative** (also called, somewhat misleadingly, "quotative"), which should be confined to the hearsay case alone, and **inferential**, referring to statements made on the basis of inference, not hearsay. The Scandinavian perfect, for instance, has inferential functions (Haugen 1972; Kinnander 1973; cf. also Weinrich 1964: 84−86 for German), though it has not developed into a real indirective evidential, as have the 'be' perfects of Bulgarian (Lindstedt 1985: 259−276, 2000) and Macedonian (Friedman 1976, 1977; Graves 2000). If a policeman investigates a burglary and sees footprints beneath a window, she or he can say in Swedish:

(14)   Tjuv-en   **ha-r**   **komm-it in**
       thief-DEF.UT have-PRES come-SUP in
       genom det   här fönstr-et
       through DEF.NT here window-DEF.NT
       'The thief must have entered (lit. has entered) the house by this window.'

In Europe, there are two major areas where grammatical evidentiality distinctions are common. One is the Baltic region, comprising the Baltic languages Lithuanian and Latvian and the Finnic languages Estonian and Livonian. The other area can be called the Black Sea area, as it consists of languages around this sea, though it stretches to Central Asia (Haarmann 1970; Dahl 1985: 149−153; Friedman 1986; Johanson 1992: 244−246). The indirectives of this area are generally regarded as having arisen from Turkish influence during the Ottoman reign. However, the tendency to develop indirectives from various sources is typical not only of Turkish, but of the whole Turkic stock, and the area also extends from the Black Sea to regions where such Uralic languages as Komi and Udmurt, farther north, are spoken (Leinonen & Vilkuna 2000).

Most European indirectives are past participles used as finite predicates, or periphrastic forms involving past participles, but not all of them can be shown to have had a perfect as their diachronic source (cf. Ikola 1953 for Estonian and Livonian, and Schmalstieg 1988: 113−121 for Lithuanian).

7. Interaction between tense and aspect

It was pointed out in § 5 above that an imperfective or progressive gram can be used to describe the state of affairs at a single point-in-time:

(15)   Yesterday at two o'clock she **was building** a sauna.

In contrast, bounded situations (events) can be associated with one time point only if they are punctual (achievements):

(16) (a) ?? Yesterday at two o'clock she **built** a sauna.
     (b) Yesterday at two o'clock the sauna **exploded**.

Since the present is also a point-in-time, it is logically impossible to have aspectually bounded forms referring to a single present situation. In various languages perfective presents may be interpreted, for instance, as futures, or present habituals (since a habitual series of bounded situations is in itself a state-like unbounded situation; cf. *Every summer she builds a sauna*). Perhaps the only types of true present perfectives are performatives (*I promise to come*) and commentaries describing sports or other public events in approximate real time.

If a language has a perfective/imperfective opposition, but no past/non-past opposition, perfectives are interpreted as referring to the past, imperfectives to the present, if the context does not indicate any other temporal relation. It is also usual to find the perfective/imperfective opposition confined to the past tense. As pointed out by Dahl (1985: 83), there are actually two typological parameters involved:

(i) whether the perfective aspect is restricted to past time reference;
(ii) whether the use of a distinct past tense marker is restricted to the imperfective aspect.

These two parameters tend to correlate; Dahl assumes that in most cases they both receive either a positive or a negative value. The Slavic languages have a negative value for both parameters, whereas Classical Arabic (as analysed by Comrie 1976: 78−81 and Dahl 1985: 82−83) is positively marked for both: the Arabic Perfective (also called "Perfect") refers to past bounded situations, and the Imperfective (also called "Imperfect") refers to the present without further context, but with contextual indications or appropriate auxiliaries it can also refer to past unbounded situations and to any future situation (bounded or unbounded).

However, as pointed out by Dahl, there are languages which are positively marked for the first of these parameters only. The Classical Greek Aorist is an example of a perfective aspect that is confined to the past tense only, at least in the Indicative Mood; yet both the Aorist (perfective past) and Imperfect (imperfective past) require a past-tense marker (the so-called augment). It is interesting to note that Modern Greek has generalized the aspectual opposition to other temporal domains and is now aligned with the Slavic patterns (Mackridge 1985: 104–116). Dahl (1985: 83) considers it more difficult to find a clear example of a language with the opposite situation, i. e., a language whose perfective aspect is not restricted to past time reference but which only uses a distinct past tense marker with the imperfective. If such languages are indeed rare or non-existent, an implicational universal might be that a morphological past tense marking confined to the imperfective aspect implies a necessary past tense reference for the perfective or, perhaps more succinctly, that if a language has a perfective/imperfective opposition, it always possesses grammatical means of unequivocally referring to the past in both aspects.

When an aspect opposition is confined to the past, it is usual to find **joint marking** for aspect and tense. Both Latin and modern Romance languages have a perfective past tense (such as the Latin Perfect, or the *passé simple* in written French and the *passé composé* in spoken French) and an imperfective past tense (usually called the Imperfect), but no separate markers for tense and aspect can be morphologically segmented.

In **layered marking**, markers of aspect are usually closer to the root than those of tense are if both are bound morphemes (cf. also Bickerton's hypothesis in § 8). To take an example from Modern Greek: in the verb *lípo* 'be absent, missing, lacking' both the augment *é-* and the personal suffixes show the tense; the relative ordering of tense and aspect is relevant to the position of the personal endings and the perfective marker *-s-*:

	imperfective	perfective
non-past sg.1	líp-o	líp-s-o
non-past sg.3	líp-i	líp-s-i
non-past pl.2	líp-ete	líp-s-ete
past sg.1	é-lip-a	é-lip-s-a
past sg.3	é-lip-e	é-lip-s-e
past pl.2	líp-ate	líp-s-ate

In Bulgarian, there is a Russian-like perfective/imperfective opposition in all tenses, but also an additional perfective/imperfective opposition confined to the simple past tense (both in the Confirmative and Indirective evidential series). As illustrated by examples (8) and (9) above, the latter opposition is based on the notion of temporal bound, whereas the "Slavic-style" opposition is based on the material bound. When both aspect oppositions are marked suffixally, the "Slavic-style" opposition, called Perfective/Imperfective, is marked closer to the root than the past-tense aspect opposition, called Aorist/Imperfect. In this example the verb is *pomágam/pomógna* 'to help':

	Imperfective	Perfective
Imperfect sg.1	pomág-a-x	pomóg-n-e-x
Imperfect sg.3	pomág-a-še	pomóg-n-e-še
Aorist sg.1	pomag-á-x	pomóg-n-a-x
Aorist sg.3	pomag-á	pomóg-n-a

The distinction between Aorist and Imperfect is partly marked by the theme vowel (*-a-/-e-*), partly by different personal suffixes, partly by accentual differences. As illustrated in (9), the Imperfective Aorist is used when a situation is bounded temporally, but not materially (Lindstedt 1985: 175–184). Since a material bound always entails a temporal bound, there does not seem to be a place for the Perfective Imperfect. It is, however, used in certain subordinate clauses to denote an unbounded habitual series of events each of which is by itself materially bounded (Lindstedt 1985: 189–198).

The aspectual semantics of a sentence can be described as consisting of different layers. The aspectual character of the predicate lexeme is the innermost layer, whose meaning is modified by grammatically marked aspect, different adverbials, number of the actant NP's and so on (Verkuyl 1972; Lindstedt 1984, 1985: 169–210; Dahl 1994: 245–246). As shown above, the grammatically marked level itself can be layered. Bybee, Perkins & Pagliuca (1994: 21–22) use the term "layering" somewhat differently to refer to the various diachronic sources and age of, say, competing future grams such as the English *will*, *shall*, *is going to* ~ *gonna*; the difference is that this second kind of layering manifests itself paradigmatically, not syntagmatically.

8. Grammaticalization paths

Bybee and Dahl (1989: 54–55) report that between 70 and 80 per cent of the tense and aspect grams found in their typological samples (Bybee 1985; Dahl 1985) belong to the six major gram-types of perfective, imperfective, progressive, future, past and perfect (anterior). Of these, the perfect, the progressive and (to a lesser degree) the future tend to have periphrastic expression, the imperfective, the perfective and the past morphologically bound (inflectional) expression. In the gram-based approach to tense and aspect, the existence of a limited set of cross-linguistic gram-types, as well as the typical meaning-form correlations (such as the propensity of the perfect to be expressed periphrastically), are explained as results of recurrent processes of grammaticalization (→ Art. 113), or universal grammaticalization paths, which repeatedly produce similar results in different languages. It is an open question whether these grammaticalization paths realize a functional teleology of some kind, producing expressions for meanings that are universally needed for human communication, or whether they simply reflect the fact that the normal functioning of human communication and cognition automatically creates changes that tend to be similar everywhere, but do respond to any kind of long-term need or teleology. The latter view is endorsed by Bybee, Perkins and Pagliuca (1994: 297—300); for a compatible theory of language change, see Nyman (1994) and the literature quoted there.

The Evolution of Grammar by Bybee, Perkins and Pagliuca (1994) is a major contribution to the study of the grammaticalization paths of tense, aspect and modality in the languages of the world. They find, for instance, that resultatives and completives (see § 6 above) often develop into anteriors (perfects), which tend to develop further into perfective pasts or simple pasts; an alternative path leads from resultatives to evidentials (pp. 104—105). Progressives, often originating as locative expressions (pp. 128—129), tend to develop into presents or imperfectives (pp. 140—149). Unmarked perfectives can come into existence by becoming opposed to a newly developing imperfective gram; the same applies to the relation between an unmarked present tense and a past gram (pp. 90—91). Futures arise from such modal notions as desire and obligation, but also from movement verbs (either 'going' or 'coming') and (rarely) temporal adverbs (pp. 251—271).

The question of fundamental tense-aspect-mood distinctions and their origins has had an important role in pidgin and creole linguistics (→ Art. 116, Art. 117). The creolist Derek Bickerton (1981) has put forward a Language Bioprogram Hypothesis, according to which true creolization (which to him always means nativization, i.e., the emergence of first-generation native speakers, in certain well-defined sociolinguistic circumstances) always produces the same fundamental grammatical structures, the roots of which lie in the genetically determined human language faculty. He has argued that as regards tense-aspect-mood, the most fundamental markers are those of the anterior (tense), the irrealis (mood) and the non-punctual (aspect), and that they typically occur as preverbal particles or auxiliaries in this order (Bickerton 1981: 58—59, 73—99). His "non-punctual" marker is essentially a progressive/imperfective marker for non-stative verbs; statives are unmarkedly non-punctual.

The Language Bioprogram Hypothesis is not generally accepted by pidgin and creole scholars, but it has had seminal influence on studies of creolization, and this also applies to investigations of tense and aspect systems and their development. The results of recent studies do not generally seem to support the hypothesis that emerging creoles must pass through a stage at which the three grams postulated by Bickerton are employed (see Romaine 1988: 264—274 and the papers in Singler (ed.) 1990). For instance, the configurations of past, anterior (perfect) and perfective markings may differ from creole to creole. Bakker et al. (1994: 258) present a more cautious generalization than Bickerton: all creoles possess at least three markers, one for tense, one for mood and one for aspect, and they are most often placed before the verb in this order.

The main methodological problem is that there may simply not be any creoles that have been created from scratch, without the strong influence of one or more existing languages, as Bickerton's theory would require; therefore, we can not know what a tense and aspect system without a history would be like.

In his paper originally circulated since 1971, Labov (1990) traces the development of tense markers in some creoles, and concludes that they do not appear as a response to some fundamental cognitive and communicative need:

"One might say that a developing grammar serves the need of stylistic variation. But it would be more accurate to say that grammar **is** style. [...] On the whole, grammar is not a tool of logical analysis: grammar is busy with emphasis, focus, down-shifting and up-grading; it is a way of organizing information and taking alternative points of view" (Labov 1990: 45).

Bybee, Perkins and Pagliuca (1994: 299–300) add to this that grammar may also facilitate production through automation. Automated, obligatory grams help the speaker concentrate on the propositional content of the utterance. This kind of argument is functional, but it does not presuppose that grammaticalization has a long-term teleology. When lexical words become tense and aspect markers, the final result of grammaticalization is no more intended by anyone than inflation is a goal of those economic agents whose decisions produce it, jointly and inadvertently. Notice, incidentally, that the claim that grammaticalized (especially inflectional) items facilitate production is indirectly an assertion about what kind of language we are biologically best equipped to process, though it is less specific a claim than Bickerton's bioprogram hypothesis (→ Art. 7, Art. 29).

It is important to note that grammaticalization theories are relevant not only to the question of the origins and diachronic development of tense and aspect grams; they are also a necessary part of their synchronic description or, rather, they make the very distinction between diachrony and synchrony relative rather than absolute (→ Art. 111; cf. Dahl 2000b: 8–18). There are no synchronic steady states to be described. Each gram may have uses that still preserve its earlier meaning; for instance, a future auxiliary that originally meant 'want' may still exhibit this sense in special contexts (as in English *He will have his own way*, with stress on *will*). New and expanding uses of a gram point to its future development, but they are also a synchronic fact.

Grammaticalization processes are synchronically reflected as **grammaticalization clines** (Dahl 2000b: 14–15): the propensity towards the use of a gram decreases monotonically along some dimensions, such as the semantic distance from certain prototypical (focal) contexts, the geographical distance from the centre of innovation, or the age scale from younger to older generations. A multidimensional synchronic cline is a suitable model for describing the gradual change of the Romance perfect (such as the French *passé composé* or the Italian *passato prossimo*) into a general perfective past tense (Squartini & Bertinetto 2000), or the change of the German perfect into an aspect-neutral past tense (Latzel 1974; Thieroff 1992, 1994, 2000). Of course, when a development of this kind has been completed — as is the case with the Russian Past Tense, historically a present perfect — no cline can be observed any longer; but new changes are then already going on elsewhere in the grammar. An adequate description of the tense and aspect system of any language must thus refer not only to the meaning of the individual grams and to the structure of their overall system, but also to the on-going grammaticalization processes as reflected in various kinds of synchronic variation.

9. Special abbreviations

AOR	aorist (= perfective past tense)
IMPF	imperfect (= imperfective past tense)
IMPFV	imperfective
NT	neuter (gender)
PAST	past tense (= preterit)
PREP	preposition
SG1	1st person singular
SG3	3rd person singular
SUP	supine
UT	utrum (gender)

10. References

Agrell, Sigurd. 1908. *Aspektänderung und Aktionsartbildung beim polnischen Zeitworte. Ein Beitrag zum Studium der indogermanischen Präverbia und ihrer Bedeutungsfunktionen*. Lund.

Arends, Jacques & Muysken, Pieter & Smith, Norval (eds.) 1995. *Pidgins and creoles: An introduction*. (Creole Language Library, 15.) Amsterdam & Philadelphia: John Benjamins.

Asher, R. E. & Simpson, J. M. Y. (eds.) 1994. *The encyclopedia of language and linguistics* 1–8. Oxford et al.: Pergamon Press.

Bache, Carl & Basbøll, Hans & Lindberg, Carl-Erik (eds.) 1994. *Tense, aspect and action: Empirical and theoretical contributions to language typology*. Berlin & New York: Mouton de Gruyter.

Bakker, Peter & Post, Marike & van der Voort, Hein. 1995. "TMA particles and auxiliaries." In: Arends et al. (eds.) 1995, 247–258.

Bertinetto, Pier Marco & Ebert, Karen H. & de Groot, Casper. 2000. "The progressive in Europe." In: Dahl (ed.) 2000, 517–558.

Bertinetto, Pier Marco & Bianchi, Valentina & Dahl, Östen & Squartini, Mario (eds.) 1994. *Temporal reference, aspect and actionality, vol. 2: Typological perspectives*. Torino: Rosenber & Sellier.

Bickerton, Derek. 1981. *Roots of language.* Ann Arbor: Karoma.

Bondarko, A[leksandr] V[ladimirovič] 1990. "O značenijax vidov russkogo glagola." *Voprosy jazykoznanija* 1990/4: 5–24.

Bondarko, A[leksandr] V[ladimirovič] et al. 1987. *Teorija funkcional'noj grammatiki: Vvedenie. Aspektual'nost'. Vremennaja lokalizovannost'. Taksis.* Leningrad: Nauka.

Brauner, Siegmund & Ashiwaju, Michael. 1965. *Lehrbuch der Hausa-Sprache.* (Lehrbücher für das Studium der orientalischen und afrikanischen Sprachen, 10.) Leipzig: VEB Verlag Enzyklopädie.

Bybee, Joan L. 1985. *Morphology: A study of the relation between meaning and form.* Amsterdam & Philadelphia: John Benjamins.

Bybee, Joan & Dahl, Östen. 1989. "The creation of tense and aspect systems in the languages of the world." *Studies in Language* 13: 51–103.

Bybee, Joan & Perkins, Revere & Pagliuca, William. 1994. *The evolution of grammar: Tense, aspect, and modality in the languages of the world.* Chicago & London: University of Chicago Press.

Carlson, Lauri. 1981. "Aspect and quantification." In: Tedeschi & Zaenen (eds.) 1981, 31–64.

Carlson, Lauri (forthcoming). *Tense, mood, aspect, diathesis: Their logic and typology.*

Chafe, Wallace & Nichols, Johanna (eds.) 1986. *Evidentiality: The linguistic coding of epistemology.* (Advances in Discourse Processes, 20.) Norwood, New Jersey: Ablex.

Comrie, Bernard. 1976. *Aspect: An introduction to the study of verbal aspect and related problems.* Cambridge: Cambridge University Press.

Comrie, Bernard. 1981. *Language universals and linguistic typology.* Oxford: Basil Blackwell.

Comrie, Bernard. 1985. *Tense.* Cambridge: Cambridge University Press.

Comrie, Bernard. 1994. "Tense." In: Asher & Simpson (eds.) 1994, 4558–4563.

Dahl, Östen. 1985. *Tense and aspect systems.* Oxford & New York: Basil Blackwell.

Dahl, Östen. 1994. "Aspect." In: Asher & Simpson (eds.) 1994, 240–247.

Dahl, Östen. 2000a. "The grammar of future time reference in European languages." In: Dahl (ed.) 2000, 309–328.

Dahl, Östen. 2000b. "The tense-aspect systems of European languages in a typological perspective." In: Dahl (ed.) 2000, 3–25.

Dahl, Östen (ed.) 2000. *Tense and aspect in the languages of Europe.* (Empirical approaches to language typology/EUROTYP 20–6.) Berlin: Mouton de Gruyter.

Dahl, Östen & Hedin, Eva. 2000. "Current relevance and event reference." In: Dahl (ed.) 2000, 385–401.

Depraetere, Ilse. 1995. "On the necessity of distinguishing between (un)boundedness and (a)telicity." *Linguistics and Philosophy* 18: 1–19.

Forsyth, J. 1970. *A grammar of aspect.* Cambridge: Cambridge University Press.

Friedman, Victor A. 1976. "Dialectal synchrony and diachronic syntax: The Macedonian perfect." In: Sanford B. Steever et al. (eds.), *Papers from the parasession on diachronic syntax.* Chicago: Chicago Linguistic Society, 96–104.

Friedman, Victor A. 1977. *The grammatical categories of the Macedonian indicative.* Columbus, Ohio: Slavica.

Friedman, Victor A. 1986. "Evidentiality in the Balkans: Bulgarian, Macedonian, and Albanian." In: Chafe & Nichols (eds.) 1986, 168–187.

Givón, Talmy. 1982. Tense-aspect-modality: The creole prototype and beyond. In: Hopper (ed.) 1982, 115–163.

Graves, Nina. 2000. "Macedonian – a language with three perfects?" In: Dahl (ed.) 2000, 479–494.

de Groot, Casper & Tommola, Hannu (eds.) 1984. *Aspect bound: A voyage into the realm of Germanic, Slavonic and Finno-Ugrian aspectology.* Dordrecht & Cinnaminson: Foris.

Haarmann, Harald. 1970. *Die indirekte Erlebnisform als grammatische Kategorie. Eine eurasische Isoglosse.* (Veröffentlichungen der Societas Uralo-Altaica, 2.) Wiesbaden: Otto Harrassowitz.

Haspelmath, Martin. 1998. "The semantic development of old presents: new futures and subjunctives without grammaticalization." *Diachronica* 15.1: 29–62.

Haugen, Einar. 1972. "The inferential perfect in Scandinavian: a problem for contrastive linguistics." *The Canadian Journal of Linguistics* 17: 132–139.

Heinämäki, Orvokki. 1984. "Aspect in Finnish." In: de Groot & Tommola (eds.) 1984, 153–177.

Heinämäki, Orvokki. 1994. "Aspect as boundedness in Finnish." In: Bache et al. (eds.) 1994, 207–233.

Hopper, Paul J. (ed.) 1982. *Tense-aspect: Between semantics and pragmatics.* (Typological Studies in Language, 1.) Amsterdam & Philadelphia: John Benjamins.

Ikola, Osmo. 1953. *Viron ja liivin modus obliquuksen historiaa.* Helsinki: Suomalaisen Kirjallisuuden Seura. (Suomi 106, 4.) [With a summary in German: "Zur Geschichte des estnischen und livischen Modus obliquus."]

Jakobson, Roman. 1971a [1936]. "Beitrag zur allgemeinen Kasuslehre: Gesamtbedeutungen der Russischen Kasus." In: *Selected writings* II. The Hague & Paris: Mouton, 23–71. [Originally in *Travaux du Cercle linguistique de Prague*, VI.]

Jakobson, Roman. 1971b. "Shifters, verbal categories, and the Russian verb." In: *Selected writings* II. The Hague & Paris: Mouton, 130–147.

Johanson, Lars. 1992. *Strukturelle Faktoren in türkischen Sprachkontakten.* (Sitzungsberichte der Wissenschaftlichen Gesellschaft an der Johann Wolfgang Goethe-Universität Frankfurt am Main XXIX, 5.) Stuttgart: Franz Steiner.

Kinnander, Bengt. 1973. "Perfektum i 'sekundär' användning." *Nysvenska studier* 53: 127–172.

Kraft, G. H. & Kirk-Greene, A. H. M. 1979 [1973]. *Hausa.* Sevenoaks, Kent: Teach Yourself Books.

Kučera, Henry. 1981. "Aspect, markedness, and t_0." In: Tedeschi & Zaenen (eds.) 1981, 177–189.

Labov, William. 1990. "On the adequacy of natural languages: I. The development of tense." [Originally written in 1971.] In: Singler (ed.) 1990, 1–58.

Latzel, Sigbert. 1974. "Zum Gebrauch der deutschen Vergangenheitstempora: Zwei Studien." In: Gelhaus, Hermann & Latzel, Sigbert. *Studien zum Tempusgebrauch im Deutschen.* (Institut für deutsche Sprache, Forschungsberichte, 15.) Mannheim, 169–348.

Leinonen, Marja & Vilkuna, Maria. 2000. "Past tenses in Permian languages." In: Dahl (ed.) 2000, 495–514.

Lindstedt, Jouko. 1984. "Nested aspects." In: de Groot & Tommola (eds.) 1984, 23–38.

Lindstedt, Jouko. 1985. *On the semantics of tense and aspect in Bulgarian.* (Slavica Helsingiensia, 4.) Helsinki.

Lindstedt, Jouko. 1995. "Understanding perfectivity – understanding bounds." In: Bertinetto et al. (eds.) 1995, 95–103.

Lindstedt, Jouko. 2000. "The perfect – aspectual, temporal and evidential." In: Dahl (ed.) 2000, 365–383.

Mackridge, Peter. 1985. *The Modern Greek language.* Oxford: Clarendon Press.

Maslov, Jurij S[ergeevič] 1984. *Očerki po aspektologii.* Leningrad: Izdatel'stvo Leningradskogo universiteta.

Maslov, Jurij S[ergeevič] 1988. "Resultative, perfect, and aspect." In: Nedjalkov (ed.). 1988, 63–85.

Mønnesland, Svein. 1984. "The Slavonic frequentative habitual." In: de Groot & Tommola (eds.) 1984, 53–76.

Mourelatos, Alexander P. D. 1981. "Events, processes and states." In: Tedeschi & Zaenen (eds.) 1981, 191–212.

Nedjalkov, Vladimir P. (ed.) 1988. *Typology of resultative constructions.* (Typological Studies in Language, 12.) Amsterdam & Philadelphia: John Benjamins. [An enlarged translation of *Tipologija rezul'tativnyx konstrukcij (rezul'tativ, stativ, passiv, perfekt)*, Leningrad 1983: Nauka.]

Nedjalkov, Vladimir P. & Sergej Je. Jaxontov. 1988. "The typology of resultative constructions." In: Nedjalkov (ed.) 1988, 3–62.

Nyman, Martti. 1994. "Language change and the 'invisible hand'." *Diachronica* 11: 231–258.

Reichenbach, Hans 1966 [1947]. *Elements of symbolic logic.* New York: The Free Press; London: Collier, Macmillan.

Romaine, Suzanne. 1988. *Pidgin and creole languages.* London & New York: Longman.

Schmalstieg, William R. 1988. *A Lithuanian historical syntax.* Columbus, Ohio: Slavica.

Schwenter, Scott A. 1994. "The grammaticalization of an anterior in progress: Evidence from a peninsular Spanish dialect." *Studies in Language* 18: 71–111.

Singler, John Victor (ed.) 1990. *Pidgin and creole tense-mood-aspect systems.* (Creole Language Library, 6.) Amsterdam & Philadelphia: John Benjamins.

Squartini, Mario & Bertinetto, Pier Marco. 2000. "The simple and compound past in Romance languages." In: Dahl (ed.) 2000, 403–439.

Tedeschi, Philip J. & Zaenen, Annie (eds.) 1981. *Syntax and semantics 14: Tense and aspect.* New York: Academic Press.

Thieroff, Rolf. 1992. *Das finite Verb im Deutschen. Tempus – Modus – Distanz.* (Studien zur deutschen Grammatik, 40.) Tübingen: Narr.

Thieroff, Rolf. 1994. "Das Tempussystem des Deutschen." In: Thieroff & Ballweg (eds.) 1994, 119–134.

Thieroff, Rolf. 2000. "On the areal distribution of tense-aspect categories in Europe." In: Dahl (ed.) 2000, 265–305.

Thieroff, Rolf & Ballweg, Joachim (eds.) 1994. *Tense systems in European languages.* (Linguistische Arbeiten, 308.) Tübingen: Niemeyer.

Tommola, Hannu. 2000. "On the perfect in North Slavic." In: Dahl (ed.) 2000, 441–478.

Trask, R. L. 1993. *A dictionary of grammatical terms in linguistics.* London & New York: Routledge.

Trubinskij, Valentin I. 1988. "Resultative, passive, and perfect in Russian dialects." In: Nedjalkov (ed.) 1988, 389–409.

Vendler, Zeno. 1967. "Verbs and times." In: Z. Vendler: *Linguistic in Philosophy.* Ithaca, New York: Cornell University Press, 97–121. [Revised version of "Verbs and times." *The Philosophical Review* 66 (1957): 143–160.]

Verkuyl, Henk J. 1972. *On the compositional nature of the aspects.* (Foundations of Language, Supplementary Series, 15.) Dordrecht: D. Reidel.

Weinrich, Harald. 1964. *Tempus: Besprochene und erzählte Welt.* Stuttgart: W. Kohlhammer.

Willett, Thomas. 1988. "A cross-linguistic survey of grammaticalization of evidentiality." *Studies in Language* 12: 51–97.

Jouko Lindstedt, University of Helsinki (Finland)

60. Modale Kategorien

1. Zum Begriff der modalen Kategorie
2. Modale Kategorien I: Interne Modalitäten
3. Modale Kategorien II: Illokutionäre Modalitäten
4. Die Interaktion modaler Kategorien mit anderen
5. Zusammenfassung
6. Zitierte Literatur

1. Zum Begriff der modalen Kategorie

1.1. Ist Modalität definierbar?

„In fact, it may be impossible to come up with a succinct characterization of the notional domain of modality and the part of it that is expressed grammatically" (Bybee et al., 1994: 176). Das als Einleitung für den vorliegenden Artikel gewählte Zitat ist symptomatisch sowohl in seiner Form als auch in seinem Inhalt. In seiner Form demonstriert es die Allgegenwärtigkeit von Modalität. Unter seinen 28 Wortformen finden sich fünf Träger modaler Information: Das einleitende Adverbiale *in fact*, das Modalverb *may*, das Modaladjektiv *impossible*, die Indikativform der Kopula (die Konjunktivformen wären *be* und *were*) und die Struktur des Satzes, die diesen als Deklarativsatz ausweist. Vielleicht ist diese Allgegenwärtigkeit mit ein Grund dafür, dass Modalität so schwer begrifflich zu fassen ist. Die im Inhalt des Zitats zum Ausdruck kommende Skepsis bezüglich der Möglichkeit einer präzisen Explikation des Modalitätsbegriffs ist sicher verständlich und weit verbreitet; das gleiche gilt übrigens für den verwandten Modusbegriff: „Of all the widely attested grammatical categories, mood is perhaps the most elusive ..." (Trask 1993: 175). Dennoch soll dieser Artikel mit dem Versuch einer solchen Explikation beginnen. Die hierfür erforderlichen sprachtheoretischen Voraussetzungen sind bescheiden und sollten somit in hohem Maße konsensfähig sein.

Angenommen, Sie sitzen mit Ihrer Begleiterin in einem Café und diese äußert (1):

(1) *Darf hier geraucht werden?*

Wie jeder Fall von normalem Sprachgebrauch schafft auch dieser auf einen Schlag wenigstens zwei Situationen: eine Situation, *in* der gesprochen wird, die jeweilige Sprechsituation (im folgenden auch Metasituation genannt), und eine Situation, *über* die gesprochen wird, die Objektsituation (vgl. Jakobsons (1971: 133) Unterscheidung von *narrated event* und *speech event*). Im Beispielfall überschneiden sich Meta- und Objektsituation weitgehend wegen des 'hier', im Unterschied zur Metasituation ist die Objektsituation freilich keine Sprechsituation, was auch dann gilt, wenn das angesprochene mögliche Rauchverbot auf einen Sprechakt zurückgeht.

Als Kern der Metasituation fungiert im Allgemeinen entweder ein Ereignis, nämlich die jeweils vollzogene sprachliche Handlung oder Illokution selbst, oder einer der Partizipanten dieser Handlung, also der Sprecher oder Adressat. Im Beispielfall ist es ihre Begleiterin, die sich durch die Form ihrer Äußerung als Fragende zu erkennen gibt. Der Kern der Objektsituation kann dagegen von beliebigen Objekten gebildet werden, seien das Dinge (Individuen oder Substanzen), Eventitäten oder aber auch andere Situationen. (Der Kunstbegriff 'Eventität' (englisch *eventity* aus *event or similar entity*) wird hier verwendet, weil das Deutsche ebensowenig wie das Englische einen Oberbegriff für Ereignisse, Aktivitäten und Zustände lexikalisiert hat und weil von den englischen Termini *event* und *eventuality* der eine den Normalgebrauch von *event* unangemessen überdehnt und der andere einen unnötig schwerfälligen Kunstbegriff darstellt.)

Sogar die Annahme von Objektsituationen ohne Kern erweist sich als nötig: Im Beispielfall bezieht sich die Frage ihrer Begleiterin nach dem Bestehen einer Raucherlaubnis auf die Situation selbst, nicht einen darin zu identifizierenden Kern. Während der Kern der Metasituation sich selbst als unter einen bestimmten Begriff fallend präsentiert (Ihre Begleiterin macht durch ihren Diskursbeitrag deutlich, dass sie als nach einem bestimmten Inhalt Fragende aufgefasst werden will), muss dies bei der Objektsituation oder ihrem Kern von außen her geschehen, durch Zuordnung zu einem charakterisierenden Begriff, im Beispiel zum Begriff der Existenz einer örtlichen Raucherlaubnis. Aus diesen drei Bestandteilen: Objektsituation (gegebenenfalls mit Kern), passendem Begriff (Prädikat) und der Zuordnung von ersterem bzw. ihrem Kern zu letzterem (Prädikation) entsteht eine mentale Einheit oder konzeptionelle Struktur, die für alle Sprachen von zentraler Bedeutung ist: eine Proposition. Die von Ihrer Begleiterin im Café zum Ausdruck gebrachte Proposition besteht aus der Cafésituation, dem Begriff der Existenz einer örtlichen Raucherlaubnis und der Zuordnung der Situation zu dem Begriff.

Über den Propositionsbegriff sind Bibliotheken geschrieben worden. Für die gegenwärtigen Zwecke soll es genügen, den mit der hier vorgestellten Propositionskonzeption verbundenen Wahrheitsbegriff zu skizzieren − Propositionen sind traditionell nicht nur Objekte von Einstellungen wie Glauben und Handlungen wie Bestreiten, sondern auch Wahrheitswertträger −, und zwar für die beiden elementaren Fälle (die Wahrheit modalisierter Propositionen baut in operatorspezifischer Weise darauf auf):

Eine elementare thetische − also kernlose − Proposition p mit der Objektsituation c und dem Begriff T ist wahr genau dann, wenn c durch T charakterisiert ist.

Eine elementare kategorische Proposition p mit der Objektsituation c, deren Kern n und dem Begriff T ist wahr genau dann, wenn n in c unter T fällt.

Zum Beispiel ist eine von einer Verwendung von „Nichts geht mehr!" ausgedrückte elementare thetische Proposition wahr genau dann, wenn die Situation, die von dieser Verwendung beschrieben werden soll, durch den Begriff der Abwesenheit von etwas, das noch geht, charakterisiert ist. Dagegen ist eine von einer Verwendung von „Max ist reich." ausgedrückte elementare kategorische Proposition wahr genau dann, wenn Max in der Situation, die von dieser Verwendung beschrieben werden soll, unter den Begriff *reich* fällt.

Unter einer Proposition soll im folgenden eine elementare Proposition oder eine durch bestimmte Operationen modifizierte, z. B. modalisierte, Proposition verstanden werden. Da Sprechsituationen immer Kerne enthalten, entsprechen ihnen immer kategoriale Propositionen, nämlich Gehalte möglicher Sprechhandlungsbeschreibungen. Entsprechend soll im folgenden nicht nur von Meta- und Objekt*situationen*, sondern analog dazu auch von Meta- und Objekt*propositionen* die Rede sein. Wenn also Karl, von der Arbeit nach Hause kommend, zu Eva sagt: „Ich habe Hunger", so lässt sich das beschreiben als Übereinstimmung von Metaproposition und Objektproposition sowohl bezüglich der Situation, nämlich des Heimkommens, als auch bezüglich des Kerns, nämlich Karl, bei gleichzeitiger Differenz der Charakterisierungen: In der Metaproposition will Karl unter den Begriff eines Handelnden fallen, nämlich eines Mannes, der mitteilt, dass er Hunger hat, in der Objektproposition hingegen will er unter den Begriff eines Zustandsträgers fallen, nämlich eines Hungrigen. Wenn alles gutgeht, erweisen sich beide Charakterisierungen als zutreffend: Die Mitteilung ist gelungen und ihr Inhalt ist wahr, Karl hat Hunger und er hat Eva dies mitgeteilt.

Wo ist nun der systematische Ort der modalen Kategorien? Vergleichen wir das oben genannte und hier wiederholte Beispiel (1) mit (2), bei dem ebenfalls Objekt- und Metasituation zum Teil koinzidieren. (1) und (2) haben zwar übereinstimmende Objektpropositionen, die Kerne der Metasituationen und deren Charakterisierungen sind jedoch verschieden.

(1) *Darf hier geraucht werden?*

(2) *Hier darf geraucht werden.*

Die Objektproposition ist in beiden Fällen die, dass in der Objektsituation rauchen als erlaubt gilt. Der propositionale Gehalt der beiden Äußerungen (1) und (2) ist also bei gleichem Situationsbezug gleich. Dennoch unterscheiden sich die Metapropositionen, denn die sprachlichen Mittel, die zum Einsatz kommen, konstituieren bei (1) eine Frage, bei (2) hingegen eine Aussage. Frage und Aussage sind zwei verschiedene Arten von Funktionen, in deren Dienst der gleiche propositionale Gehalt gestellt werden kann; als Defaultinterpretationen der Satzmodi Interrogativ und Deklarativ sind sie zweifelsfrei modale Kategorien. (Dass einige Autoren mit einem engeren Modalitätsbegriff arbeiten, der die Satzmodi und damit die Illokutionstypen ausschließt − z. B. schränken van der Auwera & Plungian (1998) die Modalität auf vier ihrer Ansicht nach in Termini von Notwendigkeit und Möglichkeit definierbare Kategorien ein −, ist wohl eher als Notlösung zu verstehen: Der Vorteil einer leichten Abgrenzbarkeit muss erkauft werden durch den Nachteil einer Entfernung von der terminologischen Tradition.)

Die modalen Kategorien Interrogativ und Deklarativ sollen hier als Ausgangspunkt dienen für eine erste, allgemeine Bestimmung des fraglichen Begriffs:

D 1   Eine *modale Kategorie* ist eine Kategorie der funktionalen Einordnung einer Proposition in den übergeordneten Zusammenhang.

Anders gesagt: Die verschiedenen Antworten auf die Frage, welche Funktion eine Proposition in ihrer Umgebung hat oder welche Rolle sie darin spielt, lassen sich in Kategorien einordnen, und die modalen Kategorien gehören zu dieser Art von Kategorien.

Die Satzmodi, auch Illokutionsmodi genannt, sind also modale Kategorien im Sinne von D 1, denn sie bestimmen die Funktion oder Rolle, die die Objektproposition im übergeordneten Zusammenhang, nämlich der Metasituation, spielen soll. Da sich aus Metasituationen zusammen mit ihren Ereigniskernen immer auch Propositionen bilden lassen, eben die Metapropositionen, ist der hier vorgeschlagene Modalitätsbegriff mit dem von Rescher (1968: 24) verträglich, der definiert: „When such a proposition is itself made subject to some further qualification of such a kind that the entire resulting complex is itself once again a proposition, then this qualification is said to represent a *modality* to which the original proposition is subjected."

Um D 1 als Definition zu verstehen, muss man aber auch umgekehrt annehmen, dass jede Kategorie der funktionalen Einordnung einer Proposition in den übergeordneten Zusammenhang eine modale Kategorie ist. Sind dann aber nicht Schmeichelei und der Versuch, etwas als lächerlich darzustellen, und tausend andere Zwecke auch modale Kategorien? In einem weiteren Sinne (und im Sinne von D 1) ja, aber nicht unbedingt in einem linguistisch interessanten Sinn. Linguistisch interessant sind nicht beliebige modale Kategorien, denn davon gibt es zu viele, anders gesagt, dieser Modalitätsbegriff ist zu feinkörnig, linguistisch interessant sind vielmehr solche modalen Kategorien, die von bestimmten, lokalisierbaren Bestandteilen des Geäußerten ausgedrückt werden.

Ein interessanterer Begriff der modalen Kategorie kann daher nicht mehr universal sein, er muss vielmehr auf Einzelsprachen relativiert werden:

D 2   Eine *einfache modale Kategorie der Sprache L* ist eine mit Hilfe eines elementaren grammatischen oder lexikalischen Mittels von *L* kodierbare modale Kategorie.

Unter einem elementaren grammatischen oder lexikalischen Mittel sei hier ein nicht bedeutungskompositional aufgebautes verstanden, d. h. es kann sich hier um Simplizia, komplexe Wörter oder auch um ganze Konstruktionen, Phraseologismen oder Kombinationen aus lexikalischen und grammatischen Einheiten handeln, sofern ihre Bedeutung sich nicht kompositional aus den Bedeutungen ihrer Bestandteile ergibt. Als eine solche Konstruktion lässt sich z. B. das deutsche Verbzweitsatzmuster mit nicht-interrogativ gefülltem Vorfeld auffassen.

Lexikalische Mittel zur Modalitätskodierung sind vor allem Verben, Noonan (1985) spricht allgemeiner von komplementnehmenden Prädikaten. Noonans 14 Klassen von solchen Prädikaten sind alle modale Kategorien im Sinne von D 1, er selbst nennt freilich nur eine dieser Klassen modal, nämlich die Prädikate der moralischen Verpflichtung und Notwendigkeit. Wegen der Existenz des entsprechenden Verbs ist zum Beispiel 'bitten' eine einfache modale Kategorie des Deutschen, nicht aber 'zum fünfzehnten Mal bitten'. Ist die Modalitätskodierung nur auf grammatische Eigenschaften des Geäußerten zurückzuführen, so spricht man von Modi:

D 3   Ein *Modus der Sprache L* ist eine mit Hilfe eines grammatischen Mittels von *L* kodierbare modale Kategorie.

Die *L*-Modi sind also die modalen Kategorien von *L*, die zugleich grammatische Kategorien von *L* sind. Damit bleiben zwar die kommunikativen Funktionen des Inhalts einer Schmeichelei oder eines Versuch, etwas als lächerlich darzustellen, modale Kategorien, aber erstere ist kein Modus und letztere nicht einmal eine einfache modale Kategorie des Deutschen. Das schließt freilich die Möglichkeit nicht aus, dass es Sprachen gibt, in denen man Dinge sagen kann, deren wörtliche Übersetzungen etwa (3) oder (4) wären:

(3)   *Sie hab-erl-en aber einen schönen Hund.*   (*erl*-Affigierung als Markierung des Blanditiv (Schmeichelmodus))

(4)   *Er verlächerlichsuchte, dass Max einen Hut trug.*

Wir können also mit einer für typologische Zwecke hinreichenden Allgemeinheit festhalten, ohne inhaltliche Restriktionen vorzugeben:

D 4   Eine Kategorie ist eine *einfache modale Kategorie* genau dann, wenn sie eine einfache modale Kategorie wenigstens einer Sprache ist.

D 5   Eine Kategorie ist ein *Modus* genau dann, wenn sie ein Modus wenigstens einer Sprache ist.

1.2. Klassen modaler Kategorien

Betrachtet man die Beispielsätze (1) und (2) oben im Lichte des Gesagten noch einmal, so zeigt sich, dass die gegebenen Definitionen auf sie mehrfach anwendbar sind: Es wird ja nicht nur die Funktion der gesamten Objektproposition in der Metasituation als Gegenstand einer Frage bzw. Aussage kategorisiert, sondern auch die Funktion der erschließbaren untergeordneten Proposition 'dass hier geraucht wird' in der gesamten Objektproposition, und zwar als Gegenstand einer Erlaubnis. Hier geht es nicht um Einbettung einer Objekt- in eine Metasituation, sondern um die Einbettung einer elementaren Objektproposition in eine andere, nicht elementare, die die Zulässigkeit oder deontische Möglichkeit einer Verhaltensform thematisiert. Auch wenn für manchen die Grenzen des hier definierten Begriff der modalen Kategorie zu weit gesteckt sein mögen, dürfte die Zuordnung von Möglichkeit und Notwendigkeit zum prototypischen Kern recht unkontrovers sein: „Modality has to do with necessity and possibility", schreibt z. B. Kratzer (1991), um den Modalitätsbegriff zu umreißen.

'Dürfen' stellt eine einfache modale Kategorie des Deutschen dar, gemäß D 3 liegt sogar ein Modus des Deutschen vor, und zwar genau in dem Maße, in dem der Einsatz modaler Auxiliare als eher grammatisches denn lexikalisches Mittel gewertet wird; zumindest wird man von einem weitgehend grammatikalisierten lexikalischen Mittel sprechen können. 'Dürfen' stellt einen Spezialfall der Möglichkeitskategorie dar: Die in (1) wie in (2) kodierte Proposition ist wahr genau dann, wenn in der mit *hier* bezeichneten Situation die Wahrheit der eingebetteten elementaren Proposition (dass geraucht wird) mit den in dieser Situation gültigen Normen verträglich ist, m. a. W., wenn es in dieser Situation möglich ist, zu rauchen, ohne eine gültige Norm zu verletzen.

Vergleichen wir die metapropositionale Modalisierung durch die Satzmodi Deklarativ und Interrogativ einerseits mit der objektpropositionalen Modalisierung durch das Modalverb *dürfen* andererseits, so fallen verschiedene Unterschiede ins Auge. Zum einen ist die oberste Modalisierung obligatorisch (kein selbständiger Satz ohne Satzmodus), während die propositionsinterne auch entfallen kann. Ein weiterer Unterschied hat zu tun mit der ontologischen Sorte von Ausgangspunkt und Resultat der Modalisierung: Die Einordnung in die Metaproposition bedeutet immer auch Einordnung in eine Handlung (und damit ein Ereignis), denn Kern einer Metaproposition kann ja nur eine Handlung oder ein Partizipant einer solchen sein. Die Einordnung in die nächsthöhere Objektsituation mit Hilfe eines Modalverbs bedeutet hingegen häufig auch Einordnung in einen Zustand, denn Fähigkeiten, Möglichkeiten, Notwendigkeiten etc. sind Dispositionen und somit Zustände, unabhängig davon, ob jeweils eine Aktivität zugrundeliegt (wie in (1) und (2)) oder etwas anderes.

Dieses Kriterium des sortalen Aspekts der Modalisierung hilft schließlich, einen dritten wichtigen Unterschied zu verdeutlichen. Vergleicht man (5) mit (6), so liegt es nahe, (6) aufzufassen als Einordnung der in (5) ausgedrückten Proposition in den Zusammenhang einer übergeordneten Proposition, in dem sie die Funktion des zu Qualifizierenden der Qualifikation *heftig* hätte.

(5) *Hier wird geraucht.*

(6) *Hier wird heftig geraucht.*

Hier liegt aber offenbar eine ganz andere Art von Modalisierung vor, denn hier kann sich die modalisierte Proposition weder in der Situation noch in der ontologischen Sorte des Kerns von ihrer Basis unterscheiden, sondern lediglich im Spezifikationsgrad der Charakterisierung. Daraus folgt, dass diese Art von Modalisierung immer sortenkonstant ist, d. h. sie macht aus Zuständen Zustände, aus Aktivitäten Aktivitäten usw., kurz es handelt sich weder um eine Modalisierung im Sinne einer Illokutionsbildung, noch um eine Dispositionalisierung, sondern um eine modale Ereignis- oder allgemeiner Eventitätsspezifikation. Dass hier gar keine Propositionsmodalisierung vorliegt, geht auch daraus hervor, dass eine die Modifikation in (6) isolierende Paraphrase nicht (7) sondern (8) lautet (vgl. auch die anderen Tests in Bartsch (1972: 26 f.).):

(7) **Es ist heftig, dass hier geraucht wird.*

(8) *Es ist heftig, wie hier geraucht wird.*

Wir werden daher in solchen Fällen von subpropositionaler oder Eventitätsmodalität sprechen. (Nicht zu verwechseln mit Hengevelds (1999) 'event-oriented modalities', die propositionale Modalitäten im hier gebrauchten Sinn darstellen.) Ihre Kategorien sind keine modalen Kategorien im Sinne von D 1 und sollen in diesem Artikel nur am Rand behandelt werden. Als Unterscheidungskriterium kann auch die Negation herangezogen werden: Lässt sich kein Negationsoperator zwischen das zugrundeliegende Prädikat und den Modalisierungsoperator einschieben, so liegt subpropositionale Modalisierung vor:

(9) *Es ist heftig, wie hier nicht geraucht wird.

Der Unterschied zwischen Propositions- und Eventitätsmodifikation spiegelt sich auch im logischen Verhalten wider: Aus der modalisierten Proposition (6) folgt (5), aber nicht umgekehrt. (Die Umkehrung gilt dann, wenn beide Sätze negiert werden.) Bei den Propositionsmodalitäten ist das anders: Weder folgt aus (2) (5), also aus der Raucherlaubnis eine Rauchaktivität, noch umgekehrt, aber bei Hinzunahme einer naheliegenden Zusatzprämisse folgt in der Tat aus (5) (2), nämlich dann, wenn man annimmt, dass sich die Leute hier an die gültigen Normen halten (ein häufiger praktischer Schluss in fremder Umgebung). Wieder anders ist es bei den Illokutionen: Die Existenz oder Nichtexistenz einer Raucherlaubnis und die einer Frage danach oder einer Aussage darüber sind völlig unabhängig voneinander.

Auf der Basis dieser logischen und ontologischen Unterschiede lassen sich drei Klassen von modalen Kategorien im weitesten Sinn bilden:

0. Modale Eventitätsspezifikation: Hier liegt homogene unbedingte logische Abhängigkeit im Sinne einer Verstärkung vor.
1. Propositionskonstitution durch modale Propositionseinbettung: Hier liegen heterogene und oft bedingte logische Abhängigkeiten im Sinne von Abschwächung oder Verstärkung vor.
2. Illokutionskonstitution durch modale Propositionseinbettung: Hier liegt logische Unabhängigkeit vor.

Zwei Gründe sprechen dafür, subpropositionale Modalitäten im Rahmen einer Übersicht über modale Kategorien nicht ganz zu übergehen, obwohl es sich hier um einen deutlich anders strukturierten Phänomenbereich handelt: die terminologische Tradition und das Phänomen der Doppelmodalisierung. Während man den ersteren noch zurückweisen könnte, ist letzterer wohl zwingend genug, um zumindest einige Bemerkungen zu Modaladverbien wie *schnell, schlecht, leicht, sorgfältig, wunschgemäß* zu machen (zur Unterscheidung modaler von anderen Adverbien sowie zur Untergliederung der ersteren vgl. Bartsch 1972). Mit Doppelmodalisierung ist hier das Phänomen gemeint, dass gewisse propositionale Modaloperatoren aus Gründen, die wohl noch nicht recht verstanden sind, nicht oder nur sehr schwer ohne eine subpropositionale Modalisierung verwendbar sind. Beispiele sollen im § 4.4 'Modalität und Diathese' behandelt werden.

Die anderen beiden Modalitätsklassen bilden den Schwerpunkt der vorliegenden Untersuchung und sollen in § 2 und § 3 behandelt werden. Die folgenden Definitionen bauen auf den vorgestellten Befunden auf:

D 6 (a) Eine *externe modale Kategorie* ist eine Kategorie der funktionalen Einordnung einer Proposition in eine unmittelbar übergeordnete Metasituation.

(b) Eine *interne modale Kategorie* ist eine Kategorie der funktionalen Einordnung einer Proposition in eine unmittelbar übergeordnete Objektproposition. Interne modale Kategorien und die Bereiche, in die sie sich gruppieren lassen, sollen daher auch Propositionsmodalitäten heißen.

Bezogen auf die Eingangsbeispiele (1) und (2) sind demnach Interrogativ und Deklarativ externe modale Kategorien (sie tragen zur Bestimmung der Funktion des Geäußerten in einer Sprechsituation bei), Erlaubnis hingegen ist eine interne modale Kategorie (sie legt die Rolle der eingebetteten Proposition 'dass hier geraucht wird' in der gesamten Objektproposition fest).

D 7 Eine *illokutionäre modale Kategorie* ist eine Kategorie der funktionalen Einordnung einer Objektproposition in die Charakterisierung einer unmittelbar übergeordneten Sprechsituation.

Gemäß D 6 und D 7 sind also alle externen modalen Kategorien illokutionär, aber nicht umgekehrt: Da in allen natürlichen Sprachen über Sprechsituationen gesprochen werden kann, können illokutionäre modale Kategorien nicht nur extern, sondern auch intern sein.

Abschließend soll noch auf die Frage eingegangen werden, ob die eingangs behauptete Omnipräsenz modaler Kategorien in dem Sinne wörtlich zu nehmen ist, dass Äußerungen immer eine modale Komponente enthalten müssten. Die Antwort lautet: Im allgemeinen ja, denn jede selbständige Äußerung ist eine Illokution und trägt als solche Information über eine externe modale Kategorie. Eine Ausnahme bilden die Interjektionen, die *per definitionem* keinen propositionalen Gehalt haben.

Anders verhält es sich mit der Frage, ob Propositionen immer eine modale Komponente enthalten müssten. Hier lautet die Antwort ganz klar: nein, denn die Zerlegung von Propositionen in Mutter- und Tochterproposition muss irgendwo ein Ende haben. Die Polaritätskomponente des hier angenommenen Propositionsbegriffs scheint zwar ein modales Element zu enthalten, aber dies gilt nur für den negativen Fall, denn eine negative Proposition ist darstellbar als Einbettung der entsprechenden positiven Proposition unter den elementarsten aller Modaloperatoren, den Matrixsatz-Negationsoperator. Positive Propositionen, also situierte positive Charakterisierungen, brauchen hingegen kein modales Element zu enthalten.

Und mit dieser Überlegung ist der Punkt erreicht, an dem eine Übersicht über die verschiedenen Strukturen von Modaloperatoren angebracht erscheint. Zuvor ist aber noch eine Anmerkung zur hier intendierten Verwendung des Begriffs Modaloperator vonnöten, um möglichen Missverständnissen vorzubeugen. In der Modallogik ist es üblich, zu unterscheiden zwischen Ansätzen, die Modaloperatoren verwenden, und solchen, die mit Modalprädikaten arbeiten. Der Unterschied liegt darin, dass die Leistung der Modaloperatoren wie die der Junktoren und Quantoren und anderer logischer Konstanten bei der Definition der Interpretationsfunktion als logische Wahrheit festgelegt wird, während die Leistung der Modalprädikate durch Bedeutungspostulate als analytische Wahrheit bestimmt wird. Die Verwendung des Terminus *Modaloperator* im vorliegenden Artikel ist eine andere: Sie meint solche Denotate sprachlicher Zeichen, elementarer oder komplexer, die auf Propositionen operieren und aus ihnen modalisierte Propositionen oder Illokutionen mit dem entsprechenden propositionalen Gehalt machen.

1.3. Strukturen von Modaloperatoren

1.3.1. Modalität, Polarität, Dualität

Wenn Negation hier als elementare modale Kategorie aufgefasst wird, so lässt sich dies ganz wörtlich nehmen: Sie bildet nämlich typischerweise zusammen mit anderen elementaren Kategorien komplexe modale Kategorien. So ist die deontische modale Kategorie des Verbots wahlweise auf die elementare Kategorie des Gebots mit innerer Negation oder auf die elementare Kategorie der Erlaubnis mit äußerer Negation zurückzuführen. Aus der Kombination von Negation und einer elementaren deontischen Kategorie entstehen also insgesamt vier deontische Kategorien: erlaubt, geboten, verboten und unterlassbar, die eine sogenannte Dualitätsgruppe bilden (zum Begriff der Dualitätsgruppe vergleiche Löbner 1990), weil man zwei Propositionsoperatoren Duale voneinander nennt, wenn jeweils der eine aus dem anderen definierbar ist mit Hilfe von kombinierter innerer und äußerer Negation: Erlaubt ist, was zu unterlassen nicht geboten ist, und geboten ist, was zu unterlassen nicht erlaubt ist; unterlassbar ist, was zu unterlassen nicht verboten ist, und verboten ist, was zu unterlassen nicht unterlassbar ist.

Im Reich der modalen Kategorien und damit auch der sie kodierenden Modaloperatoren ist also überall dort mit dem Auftreten von Dualitätsgruppen zu rechnen, wo Modaloperatoren frei mit innerer und äußerer Negation kombinierbar sind, was bei internen modalen Kategorien im Sinne von D 6 b. immer der Fall ist. Zur Unterscheidung der vier Kategorien, die eine vollständige Dualitätsgruppe ausmachen, ist es also sinnvoll, hier weiterhin definitorisch festzulegen:

D 8 (a) Eine *implizierende modale Kategorie* ist eine Kategorie der funktionalen Einordnung einer Proposition derart, dass die Mutterproposition die Tochterproposition impliziert.

(b) Eine *implizierte modale Kategorie* ist eine Kategorie der funktionalen Einordnung einer Proposition derart, dass die Mutterproposition von der Tochterproposition impliziert wird.

Beide Kategorien kommen in unbedingten und in bedingten Variationen vor. Als Beispiele mögen die logische Notwendigkeit dienen und ihr deontisches Gegenstück, das Gebot, sowie die logische Möglichkeit und ihr deontisches Gegenstück, die Erlaubnis: 'Notwendigerweise regnet es oder es regnet nicht' impliziert 'Es regnet oder es regnet nicht', 'Hier ist es geboten zu schweigen' impliziert 'Hier wird geschwiegen' unter der Bedingung, dass hier die gültigen Regeln eingehalten werden; 'Es regnet' impliziert 'Möglicherweise regnet es', 'Hier wird geraucht' impliziert 'Hier darf geraucht werden' unter der gleichen Bedingung wie oben.

D 9 (a) Eine *negativ implizierende modale Kategorie* ist eine Kategorie der funktionalen Einordnung einer Proposition derart, dass die Mutterproposition die Negation der Tochterproposition impliziert.

(b) Eine *negativ implizierte modale Kategorie* ist eine Kategorie der funktionalen Einordnung einer Proposition derart, dass die Mutterproposition von der Negation der Tochterproposition impliziert wird.

Auch diese Kategorien kommen in unbedingten und in bedingten Varianten vor. Als Beispiele mögen die logische Unmöglichkeit dienen und ihr deontisches Gegenstück, das Verbot, sowie die logische Nichtnotwendigkeit und ihr deontisches Gegenstück, die Unnötigkeit: 'Es ist unmöglich, dass es regnet und zugleich nicht regnet' impliziert 'Es trifft nicht zu, dass es regnet und zugleich nicht regnet', 'Hier ist es verboten zu rauchen' impliziert 'Hier wird nicht geraucht' unter der Bedingung, dass hier die gültigen Regeln eingehalten werden; 'Es regnet nicht' impliziert 'Es braucht nicht zu regnen', 'Hier wird vor dem Eintreten nicht angeklopft' impliziert 'Hier ist es unnötig, vor dem Eintreten anzuklopfen' unter der gleichen Bedingung wie oben.

Dualitätsgruppen treten auch bei externen modalen Kategorien auf, z. B. wenn Gebot und Verbot durch Satzmodi markiert werden, allerdings sind äußere Negationen bei den häufigsten Satzmodi eher nicht zu erwarten. Dualitätsgruppen können hingegen nicht auftreten bei den subpropositionalen Modalitäten: Wenn geraucht wird, so liegt eine Aktivität und somit eine Eventität vor, die als heftig qualifiziert werden kann; wenn dagegen nicht geraucht wird, ist keine Aktivität mehr vorhanden und somit nichts, was eventitätsmodal qualifiziert werden könnte. (Wer Fälle wie 'Hier wird angestrengt nicht gesprochen' akzeptiert, wird wohl einräumen, dass 'Hier wird angestrengt geschwiegen' eine bessere Formulierung für die gemeinte Aussage ist, und schweigen ist mehr als nur nicht sprechen.)

1.3.2. Argumentstrukturen von Modaloperatoren

Ein wichtiges Kriterium für die Unterscheidung und Einteilung modalisierender Mutterpropositionen ist die Argumentstruktur ihres jeweiligen Hauptprädikators oder Kopfes.

Drei Faktoren sind zu beachten bei einer solchen Differenzierung von Modaloperatoren nach ihrer Valenz: 1. Die Stelligkeit (welche Stellen außer der für die zu modalisierende Proposition gibt es noch?), 2. die grammatische und die semantische Rolle der Tochter- in der Mutterproposition und 3. der Grad der Integration von Tochter- und Mutterproposition sowie, in ikonischer Abhängigkeit davon, der Grad der Integration der entsprechenden Kodierungsmittel (Matrix- und Komplementsatz; vgl. Givón (1990: 516): „The stronger the *semantic bond* is between the two events, the more intimately [sic!] is *the syntactic integration* of the two propositions into a single clause", Hervorhebungen im Original). Noonan (1985) unterscheidet in diesem Zusammenhang sechs Komplementtypen: Parataktische Sätze, indikativische und konjunktivische Hypotaxen, Infinitive, Nominalisierungen und Partizipien. Alle drei oben genannten Faktoren, vor allem die beiden letzteren, sind natürlich der Variation von Sprache zu Sprache unterworfen. Die folgenden Beispiele sind einfachheitshalber dem Deutschen entnommen.

(a) Einstellige Modaloperatoren
Bei einstelligen Modaloperatoren spielt der die Tochterproposition kodierende Konstituentensatz typischerweise die Subjektrolle im Matrixsatz (vgl. (10) und (11)); die zu modalisierende Proposition kann aber auch durch einen Matrixsatz kodiert werden, dem ein Adverbialsatz syntaktisch untergeordnet ist, obwohl dieser die semantisch übergeordnete Mutterproposition kodiert (modale Subordination des Hauptsatzes; vgl. (12) und (13)). In allen vier Fällen liegt hochgradig autonome Kodierung der Teilpropositionen vor. Schwieriger ist die Rolle der Tochterproposition in den Fällen (14)−(16) zu bestimmen, weil hier ein höhrer Integrationsgrad vorliegt: Durch Infinitivphrasen ist die Tochterproposition nur partiell bestimmt, ihre Aktanten müssen aus dem Matrixsatz erschlossen werden, wobei die rekonstruierte Tochterproposition als logisches Subjekt der Mutterproposition fungiert. Die Chomsky-Schule spricht hier von *raising*-Konstruktionen. Man beachte übrigens, dass in (16) der propositionale Möglichkeitsoperator seinerseits subpropositional (durch *leicht*) modalisiert ist.

(10)   *Es ist denkbar, dass Max pfeift.*

(11)   *Es scheint, dass Max pfeift.*

(12) *Max pfeift immer, wenn er guter Laune ist.*
(Dass Max pfeift, ist immer dann der Fall, wenn er guter Laune ist.)

(13) *Max pfeift, weil er guter Laune ist.*
(Dass Max pfeift, ist deswegen der Fall, weil er guter Laune ist.)

(14) *Max scheint zu pfeifen.* (vgl. (11))

(15) *Max dürfte pfeifen.*
(vgl. *Es dürfte, dass Max pfeift vs. Es dürfte der Fall sein, dass Max pfeift.)

(16) *Dieses Problem ist leicht zu lösen.*

(b) Zweistellige Modaloperatoren
Wenn bei zweistelligen Modaloperatoren die Tochterproposition durch einen Subjektsatz kodiert wird, so liegt typischerweise eine evaluative Modalisierung vor; der Integrationsgrad kann dabei unterschiedlich sein (vgl. (17)−(19)). Sonst wird die Tochterproposition eher durch ein Objekt kodiert, sei es ein direktes (vgl. (20)−(22)), sei es ein Genitiv- oder Präpositionalobjekt (23), sei es nominalisiert und inkorporiert in einem Kompositum (24). Weil in (21) bis (23) die Infinitivphrasen als auf das übergeordnete Subjekt bezogen interpretiert (von ihm 'kontrolliert') werden, spricht die Chomsky-Schule hier von *control*-Konstruktionen. Die Integrationsgrade können wieder schwanken.

(17) *Dass Max pfeift, missfällt Eva.*

(18) *Es gefällt Eva, zu pfeifen.*

(19) *Eislaufen begeistert Eva.*
(Wenn sie/jemand eisläuft, so begeistert das Eva.)

(20) *Max will, dass Eva pfeift.*

(21) *Max will pfeifen.* (vgl. Max will, dass Max pfeift.)

(22) *Max kann pfeifen.* (vgl. *Max kann, dass Max pfeift. vs. Max kann das.)

(23) *Max ist fähig zu pfeifen.* (vgl. Max ist dessen/dazu fähig.)

(24) *Max ist kompromissbereit.* (vgl. Max ist dazu bereit, Kompromisse zu machen.)

(c) Dreistellige Modaloperatoren
Auch bei dreistelligen Modaloperatoren ist die Kodierung der Tochterproposition durch einen Subjektsausdruck eher die Ausnahme und kommt typischerweise bei psychologischen Modalitäten vor (25); der Normalfall sind die Rolle des direkten ((26), (27)) oder Präpositionalobjekts ((28), (29)). Die Integrationsgrade können wieder schwanken.

(25) *Dass Max pfeift, nimmt ihm die Angst.*

(26) *Max erzählt Eva, dass Peter gepfiffen hat.*

(27) *Max verspricht Eva zu pfeifen.* (... dass Max pfeift.)

(28) *Max hindert Eva daran zu pfeifen.* (... daran, dass Eva pfeift.)

(29) *Max bereitet Eva aufs Pfeifen vor.* (... darauf, dass Eva pfeift.)

1.4. Kodierungsmittel modaler Kategorien

Die Definitionen D 2 und D 3 haben bereits deutlich gemacht, dass sich Arten modaler Kategorien natürlich nicht nur von der inhaltlichen Seite her unterscheiden lassen, sondern auch gemäß den sprachlichen Mitteln, die jeweils zum Einsatz kommen. Diese sollen im folgenden in einem systematischen Überblick vorgestellt werden. Der ökonomischste, aber zugleich auch am wenigsten transparente Fall ist hier der der fehlenden oder Nullkodierung.

1.4.1. Nullkodierung

Bisweilen bleibt die Präsenz einer übergeordneten Proposition ohne jede explizite Kodierung, dann muss die gemeinte Modalisierung dem Kontext entnommen werden. Ein prominentes Beispiel ist das deutsche Sprichwort in (30), bei dem erst eine Umschreibung wie (31) die Modalisierung sichtbar macht.

(30) *Glück und Glas, wie leicht bricht das.*

(31) *Wie leicht können Glück und Glas brechen.*

Wenn jemand angesichts einer geschlossenen Tür, eines geparkten Autos, eines lesenden Peters (32) bzw. (33) bzw. (34) äußert, dann redet er entweder Unsinn, oder er will seine Aussagen modalisiert verstanden wissen:

(32) *Diese Tür geht nach innen auf.*

(33) *Dieses Auto fährt 250 Stundenkilometer.*

(34) *Peter läuft die 100 Meter in 9,9 Sekunden.*

Die modale Interpretation macht aus Aktivitätsprädikaten Zustandsprädikate vom Typ der Dispositionsprädikate. Freilich hat nicht jedes Aktivitätsprädikat auch eine Dispositionslesart. Bezogen auf ein geparktes Auto ist (35) schlicht falsch und kann nicht im Sinne von (36) uminterpretiert werden:

(35)   *Dieses Auto biegt links ab.*

(36)   *Dieses Auto kann links abbiegen.*

Dies liegt vermutlich daran, dass implizite Dispositionsmodalisierungen nur dann zur Verfügung stehen, wenn damit nicht-triviale Aussagen gemacht werden können. Denken wir uns eine Rennbahn, auf der speziell dafür gebaute Autos im Kreis herumfahren, und zwar immer nur rechtsherum, so dass die Autos entsprechend eingeschränkte Lenkungen haben. In einem solchen Kontext könnte (35) auch erfolgreich als Dispositionsaussage verwendet werden.

Es ist jedenfalls plausibel, anzunehmen, dass implizite Kodierung als Modalisierungsmittel vorkommt. Sie ist zu unterscheiden von Fällen lexikalischer Polysemie, bei denen eine aktuelle und eine modalisierte Lesart koexistieren. Ein Beispiel ist das deutsche Verb *trinken*, das intransitiv verwendet seine Kernbedeutung 'Flüssigkeit zu sich nehmen' nur dann kodiert, wenn es episodisch gelesen wird ('Trinkt Max gerade?'), während es in seiner habituellen Lesart Alkoholkonsum bezeichnet.

1.4.2. Grammatische Kodierung: Modi

Der folgende Abschnitt geht davon aus, dass grammatische Kodierungsmittel in gebundene Gramme (grammatische Morpheme), freie Gramme (Strukturwörter) und Konstruktionen (idiomatisierte Konfigurationen) zerfallen, und behandelt diese, soweit sie modale Information tragen, in der genannten, durch zunehmendes Differenzierungsvermögen gekennzeichneten, Reihenfolge.

(a) Flexionsmorphologische Kodierung: Verbmodi. In ihrem Fragebogen zur Erstellung einheitlich organisierter deskriptiver Grammatiken (Comrie & Smith 1977) rechnen die Autoren mit dem Auftreten der folgenden 14 (und möglicherweise mehr) modalen Kategorien, die als Verbmodi kodiert sein können: Indikativ, Konditional, Imperativ, Optativ, Intentionalis, Debitiv, Potentialis (mit den Subkategorien Abilitativ (± erlernt) und Permissiv), Probabilitiv (Gewissheitsgrad), Evidential, Hortativ, Admonitiv, Narrativ, Konsekutiv und Kontingentiv.

Die Vermutung, dass im allgemeinen nur ein Anfangssegment dieser Folge flexionsmorphologisch kodiert wird, bestätigt sich bei der Durchsicht der nach diesem Schema organisierten Grammatiken. So konstatiert Nedjalkov (1997) für das Evenki die Existenz von sieben Verbmodi: Indikativ, Konditional, Imperativ, Optativ, Debitiv, Probabilitiv, und Admonitiv. Die Affixe für fünf weitere modale Kategorien (Volitiv, Konativ, Petitiv, Andativ, Simulativ) müssen bei finiten Formen mit Modusmarkierern kombiniert werden und werden daher nicht zur Flexionsmorphologie gerechnet.

(i) Synthetische Kodierung der Verbmodi: Wenn ein Konjugationsparadigma einer Sprache eine modale Opposition aufweist, so ist das unmarkierte Glied dieser Opposition immer der Indikativ. Der Indikativ kann im Lichte der obigen Überlegungen kein propositionaler Modaloperator sein, da er mit seiner Hilfe unmodalisierte Propositionen kodiert werden. Er kann aber ein illokutionärer Modaloperator (oder Teil eines solchen) sein, und zwar trägt er dort, wo ihn keine anderen illokutionären Operatoren überschreiben, zur Markierung von Deklarativsätzen und im allgemeinen auch Interrogativsätzen, nicht aber z. B. Imperativsätzen bei.

Der Indikativ kann also auf zweierlei Weise mit anderen Verbmodi in Opposition treten: auf der illokutionären Ebene mit anderen illokutionären Operatoren und auf der propositionalen Ebene mit den propositionalen Modaloperatoren. Im Deutschen zeigt sich das in der Indikativ-Imperativ-Opposition einerseits und in der Indikativ-Konjunktiv-Opposition andererseits. Die Beziehungen können wie folgt verdeutlicht werden:

(37)   *Max pfeift laut.*

(38)   *Max, pfeif laut!* [Wenn Max der Aufforderung nachkommt, gilt (37).]

(39)   *Max pfeife laut.* [Eine Informationsquelle behauptet (37).]

(40)   *Max pfiffe laut.* [Unter anderen Umständen als den gegebenen gilt (37).]

(ii) Analytische (periphrastische) Kodierung der Verbmodi: Je nach Analytizitätsgrad einer Sprache wird modale Information in verbalen Paradigmen entweder rein synthetisch oder rein analytisch (durch Kombination mit Auxiliaren) oder gemischt kodiert. Das Deutsche instantiiert den letzteren Fall: Neben den angeführten synthetischen Modi verfügt es auch noch über die sogenannte *würde*-Periphrase, die mit den Formen des in (40) exemplifizierten, vom Präteritalstamm abgeleiteten Konjunktiv II in Abhängigkeit von zwei Faktoren alterniert: Synkretismus und Stilebene. Eine Formulierung wie (40) wirkt im heutigen Deutsch schon recht gewählt und damit stilistisch markiert, die unmarkierte Alternative dazu ist (41). Bei schwachen Verben fallen im Präteritum Indikativ- und Konjunktivformen zusammen (vgl. (42)), dort muss unabhängig von der Stilebene die Periphrase gewählt werden (vgl. (43)), wenn eine eindeutige Markierung erfolgen soll.

(41) *Max würde laut pfeifen.*

(42) *Max sagte wenig.*

(43) *Max würde wenig sagen.*

(b) Strukturwortkodierung (Modalverben). Die Ähnlichkeit zwischen Auxiliaren als den prototypischen Strukturwörtern im verbalen Bereich und Modalverben ist ebenso bekannt wie die größere Nähe der letzteren zu Vollverben. Es verwundert daher nicht, wenn verschiedene Modalverben verschiedener Sprachen unterschiedliche Grade von Grammatikalisiertheit und damit unterschiedliche Positionen auf der Skala von den klaren Strukturwörtern zu den klaren Inhaltswörtern (die im folgenden Abschnitt behandelt werden) einnehmen. Im Deutschen spiegelt sich die engere Zusammengehörigkeit von Modalverb und seiner Ergänzung gegenüber einem bedeutungsnahen Vollverb und dessen Ergänzung in den auf Modalverben eingeschränkten Merkmalen Abwesenheit der Infinitivpartikel *zu* und Möglichkeit einer Nullanapher:

(44) *Albert konnte nicht folgen. – Albert konnte nicht.*

(45) *Albert vermochte nicht zu folgen. – Albert vermocht's nicht.*

(c) Konstruktionskodierung (Modale Konstruktionen): In Sprachen wie dem Deutschen werden Satzmodi im wesentlichen durch Konstruktionen kodiert. Als eine solche Konstruktion lässt sich etwa das Verbzweitsatzmuster mit nicht-interrogativ gefülltem Vorfeld und deklarativer Intonation auffassen. Weitere konstruktionskodierte Kategorien sind Möglichkeit und Notwendigkeit (durch die sogenannten modalen Infinitive) sowie Konditionalität und Kausalität (durch Verberstkomplementsätze ohne die bzw. mit der Modalpartikel *doch*):

(46) *Der Brief wird sofort geöffnet.*

(47) *Der Brief ist leicht zu öffnen.* (... kann leicht geöffnet werden.)

(48) *Der Brief ist sofort zu öffnen.* (... muss sofort geöffnet werden.)

(49) *Ist der Ruf erst ruiniert, lebt sich's gänzlich ungeniert.* (Wenn der Ruf erst ruiniert ist, ...)

(50) *Für Hans tat sie es gerne, war er doch ihr bester Freund.* (... denn er war ihr bester Freund.)

1.4.3. Lexikalische Kodierung

(a) Wurzelkodierung (monomorphematische Stämme): Für die Struktur des Lexikons einer Sprache ist es wichtig, welche Inhalte auf die nach der grammatischen Kodierung nächstökonomische Weise, nämlich durch lexikalische Wurzeln kodiert werden können. Es ist zu erwarten, dass in allen Sprachen Wurzeln aller Hauptwortarten Modales kodieren können. Im Deutschen sind das Vollverben, Nomina, Adjektive und Adverbien:

(51) *Es stimmt, dass Max schon gekommen ist.*

(52) *Es ist eine Schande, dass Max nicht gekommen ist.*

(53) *Gut, dass Max nicht gekommen ist.*

(54) *Max ist sicher nicht gekommen.*

(b) Kodierung durch komplexe Stämme: (i) Kodierung durch derivierte Stämme und derivationsmorphologische Kodierung: Bei der Kodierung modaler Konzepte durch derivierte Wörter sind die Fälle besonders interessant, bei denen die modale Komponente im Derivationsmittel steckt. Prominente Beispiele sind das patienspotentiale Adjektivierungssuffix *-bar* im Deutschen und seine Entsprechung *-able* im Englischen:

(55) *Das Fahrrad ist noch verwendbar.* (... kann noch verwendet werden.)

(56) *The bike is still usable.* (... can still be used.)

(ii) Kodierung durch nicht-derivative komplexe Stämme: Auch hier ist wieder zu unterscheiden zwischen Stämmen, die erst als ganze eine modale Bedeutung annehmen wie *imstande, außerstande* und solchen, wo der modale Anteil in einer der Komponenten steckt, während die andere die modalisierte Proposition kodiert wie *lebensfähig, kompromissbereit*.

1.4.4. Phrasale Kodierung

Sätze mit verbalen Modaloperatoren, bei denen der Ausdruck der zu modalisierenden Proposition nicht das einzige Komplement bildet, wie z. B. (57), lassen zwei Sichtweisen zu: Entweder das Verb wird als mehrstelliger Modaloperator aufgefasst, der außer dem kritischen Komplement(satz) weitere Ergänzungen braucht (diese Sichtweise wurde in 1.3.2. eingenommen), oder der restliche Matrixsatz wird als syntaktisch komplexer, aber einstelliger Modaloperator gesehen. In diesem Fall kann man von einer phrasalen Kodierung sprechen.

(57) *Eva fragt Maria, ob Max schon gekommen ist.*

2. Modale Kategorien I: Interne Modalitäten

Wie schon erwähnt hängen die Modalitätsdichotomien intern/extern und nicht-illokutionär/illokutionär nur insofern zusammen, als alle nicht-illokutionären Modalitäten interner Natur sind, die illokutionären hingegen teils interner, teils externer. Entsprechend erfolgt die Darstellung der illokutionären Modalitäten zum Teil schon in diesem Abschnitt, zum Teil erst im folgenden. Eine Übersicht über die (partiellen) Korrespondenzen bietet die folgende Tabelle:

2.2. Interne Handlungsmodalitäten
2.2.1. Handlungstendenzmodalitäten
2.2.2. Handlungsdispositionsmodalitäten
2.2.3. Handlungseinflussmodalitäten
2.2.4. Handlungsumstandsmodalitäten
2.2.5. Andativmodalität
2.2.6. Konativmodalität
2.2.7. Simulativmodalität
2.2.8. Deontische Modalitäten

2.3. Interne Einstellungsmodalitäten
2.3.1. Interne Expressive
   a. Interne Exklamative
   b. Interne Optative
2.3.2. Interne telische Modalitäten
   a. Interne volitive Modalitäten
   b. Interne intentionale Modalitäten
2.3.3. Interne epistemische Modalitäten (Informationsquellensdifferenzierung)
   b. Interne Gewissheitsmodalitäten
   c. Interne Verantwortungsmodalitäten
2.3.4. Interne evaluative Modalitäten
2.3.5. Interne Erwartungsmodalitäten (prospektiv)
2.4. Interne Allgemeinmodalitäten
2.4.1. Allgemeine Tendenzmodalitäten
2.4.2. Allgemeine Dispositionsmodalitäten
2.4.3. Allgemeine Einflussmodalitäten
2.4.4. Allgemeine Umstandsmodalitäten
2.4.5. Imminenzmodalitäten
2.4.6. Konditionale Modalitäten
2.4.7. Similativmodalitäten
2.4.8. Alethische (ontische) Modalitäten

3. Modale Kategorien II: Illokutionäre Modalitäten
3.1. Nicht-sententiale Illokutionen
3.1.1. Interjektionen
3.1.2. Phrasale Illokutionen
3.2. Sententiale Illokutionen
3.2.1. Expressive Illokutionen
   a. Exklamative Illokutionen
   b. Optative Illokutionen
   c. Imprekative Illokutionen
3.2.2. Volitive Illokutionen
   a. Volitive Illokutionen mit allgemeinen Zielen
   b. Volitive Illokutionen mit epistemischen Zielen
      i. Erotetische Illokutionen (Volitive mit auto-epistemischen Zielen)
      ii. Assertive Illokutionen (Volitive mit hetero-epistemischen Zielen)
3.2.3. Deklarationen (selbstverifizierende Illokutionen)

2.1. Semimodalitäten

Es gibt Modalitäten (im Sinne von Gruppen von Kategorien), deren Elemente ausnahmslos selbst modaler Natur sind. Dies ist typischerweise überall dort der Fall, wo echte Dualitätsgruppen auftreten, wie bei den vier Begriffen *erlaubt, geboten, verboten, unterlassbar*. Das sind die eigentlichen Modalitäten. Andere Gruppen enthalten hingegen nur zum Teil modale Kategorien. Wir haben in § 1.3.1 Negation als elementare modale Kategorie eingeführt und die Frage postponiert, ob deswegen Polarität eine Modalität ist. Akzeptiert man die Vorstellung, dass Modalisierung bei unmodalisierten Propositionen ihren Anfang nehmen muss, so folgt, dass der andere Wert dieser Kategorie, positive Polarität, keine modale Kategorie ist. Solche Bereiche, deren Kategorien zum Teil modaler Natur sind und somit zum Aufbau modaler Strukturen beitragen, zum Teil aber nicht, wollen wir in Ermangelung eines etablierten Terminus semimodale Kategorienbereiche oder kurz Semimodalitäten nennen.

2.1.1. Polarität

Im Falle der Polarität ist die Bezeichnung Semimodalität besonders angebracht, weil eine ihrer beiden Kategorien, die positive Polarität, amodal ist, während die Negation wegen ihrer zentralen Rolle bei der Konstitution von Dualitätsgruppen und damit im Aufbau modaler Komplexität zumindest modalitätsverdächtig ist. Dass aber auch hier keine prototypische modale Kategorie vorliegt, ergibt sich aus D 1, besteht doch die Funktion der zugrundeliegenden Proposition in der erweiterten einzig darin, den Ausgangspunkt für eine Umkehrung der Wahrheitsbedingungen zu bilden. Ein zweiter Faktor, der die Position der Polarität an der Peripherie der Modalitäten unterstreicht, ist der Umstand, dass ihre Kategorien, also positive Polarität und Negation keine echte Dualitätsgruppe bilden: Der zur Negation duale Operator ist nämlich die Negation selbst. Man nennt sie daher auch selbstdual. Das gleiche gilt für ihr positives Gegenstück. Während also prototypische Modaloperatoren vierelementige Dualitätsgruppen bilden, deren Elemente alle auch Modaloperatoren sind, bilden die Polaritätsoperatoren nur eine zweielementige Dualitätsgruppe, von deren Elementen obendrein eines gar kein Modaloperator ist.

Wie ist die These von der Amodalität der positiven Polarität aber verträglich mit dem spürbaren Modalisierungseffekt, der von expliziten Trägern positiver Polarität ausgeht? 'Es trifft zu, dass Eva fehlt' heißt schließlich etwas anderes als 'Eva fehlt'. Es ist jedoch leicht, diesen Modalisierungseffekt als Implikatur zu erkennen: Wenn der positive Charakter einer Aussage durch einen Matrixsatz explizit gemacht wird, so hat das seinen Grund. Das mag Emphase sein oder Konzession oder anderes, es ist jedenfalls abhängig von der Wahl eines markierten Ausdrucksmittels für positive Polarität und kann deswegen die Annahme, dass positive Polarität an sich keine modale Kategorie ist, nicht erschüttern.

Dafür, dass die negative Polarität mit den zentralen modalen Kategorien aufs engste verknüpft ist, lassen sich nicht nur apriorische, begriffsanalytische Gründe anführen, vielmehr spiegeln auch die Kodierungsmittel der verschiedensten Sprachen diesen engen Zusammenhang häufig wider. So wird das Problem der Bestimmung des Negationsskopus bei Sprachen, die eine Negationspartikel zwischen Modalverb und dependentes Vollverb setzen (eng oder weit), auf verschiedene Weise gelöst. (Für eine Übersicht über die Typologie der Negationsmittel vgl. Payne 1985.) Im Deutschen ist die Defaultinterpretation die mit weitem Skopus (58) und der enge muss durch intonatorische Hervorhebung markiert werden (59) und (60), im Englischen dient eine lexikalische Alternation (de Haan (1997) spricht hier von 'modal suppletion') dem gleichen Zweck: *must* und *need* drücken beide Notwendigkeit aus, aber ersteres hat 'eingebauten' engen Skopus, während die Negation bei letzterem immer nur mit weitem Skopus interpretiert werden kann.

(58) *Das kann nicht sein.*

(59) *Kann sein, kann NICHT sein.*

(60) *Max kann nicht NICHT rauchen.*

(61) *John must not fly to New York tomorrow.*

(62) *John need not fly to New York tomorrow.*

Schließlich drücken Gebärdensprachen, die ohnehin zu höheren Ikonizitätsgraden neigen, die enge Verbindung von Modalität und Negation besonders anschaulich aus, indem sie bei modalen Prädikaten eine besondere, von der Standardnegation verschiedene Negationsform wählen, nämlich die sogenannte Negationsinkorporation (vgl. Deuchar 1984: 89f. et passim).

2.1.2. Realität

Verbmodi werden, in Übereinstimmung mit der Mehrheit der Linguisten, im vorliegenden Text als grammatikalisierte Kodierungsmittel für modale Kategorien aufgefasst (vgl. z. B. Bybee/Fleischman (1995: 2): „As used here, mood refers to a formally grammaticalized category of the verb which has a modal function."). Da nun die Realis-Irrealis-Distinktion sicher zentral für alle Verbmodussysteme ist, könnte man erwarten, dass hier ein zentraler modaler Kategorienbereich vorliegt. Wir haben aber in § 1.4.2.(a)(i) festgestellt, dass der Indikativ als Realisoperator kein Modaloperator sein kann. Es folgt, dass die entsprechende Variationsdimension, die die Kategorien Realis, Irrealis und eventuell noch andere umfasst, eine Semimodalität in unserem Sinn darstellt. Dass dies nicht im Widerspruch zu dem Eindruck einer zentralen Rolle stehen muss, wurde am Beispiel der Polarität deutlich.

Die Nonrealismodalität deckt, ähnlich wie die negative Polarität, einen sehr weiten logischen Raum ab, anders als diese wird sie aber häufig näher spezifiziert. Obwohl diese Kategorie gewissermaßen zwischen positiver und negativer Polarität angesiedelt ist, ist sie von beiden logisch unabhängig: Wer (63) oder (64) äußert, muss damit weder (61) noch (62) implizieren:

(61)　Der Verdacht ist ausgeräumt.

(62)　Der Verdacht ist nicht ausgeräumt.

(63)　Der Verdacht sei ausgeräumt.

(64)　Der Verdacht wäre ausgeräumt.

Die vage Intuition, dass aus (63) in gewisser Weise (61) und aus (64) tendenziell (62) folgt, lässt sich wie folgt präzisieren: (63) ist durch den Konjunktiv als modal subordiniert markiert, d. h. es wird (in der quotativen, nicht in der Optativlesart) präsupponiert, dass die in (61) enthaltende Proposition von einer vom Sprecher verschiedenen Quelle behauptet wird. Der bisweilen naheliegende Schluss auf (61) gilt also nur, wenn diese Quelle recht hat.

Auch (64) ist, zumindest in einer Lesart, als modal subordiniert zu verstehen, hier jedoch unter einer hinreichenden Bedingung, deren Nichtvorliegen zwar nicht behauptet, aber nahegelegt wird, z. B. 'wenn es ein Alibi gäbe'. Um den Schluss von (64) auf (62) zu rechtfertigen, muss also zweierlei hinzukommen: Erstens muss die in der mitgedachten Bedingung enthaltene Proposition tatsächlich falsch sein und zweitens muss diese Bedingung nicht nur hinreichend, sondern auch notwendig sein. Im Beispielfall müssten also zu (64) zwei Prämissen hinzukommen, damit der Schluss von (64) auf (62) gültig ist: Erstens, dass es kein Alibi gibt und zweitens, dass ein Alibi notwendig ist dafür, dass der Verdacht ausgeräumt wird.

Um Struktur in das weite Feld der vom Realis verschiedenen Modi zu bringen, empfiehlt es sich also, die genauen Umstände anzugeben, unter denen ein Schluss auf die vom entsprechenden Realissatz kodierte Proposition oder deren Negation möglich ist (vgl. auch Portner 1999).

2.1.3. Temporalität

Tempus wird einerseits von der Mehrheit der Linguisten nicht als Modalität betrachtet, anderseits widmet John Lyons in seinem Semantikbuch einen ganzen Abschnitt (Lyons 1977: 809−823) dem Thema 'Tense as a modality'. Im Lichte der hier gemachten sprachtheoretischen Annahmen verwundert dies nicht: Tempus ist eine Semimodalität, weil eine der temporalen Kategorien, heiße sie nun Präsens oder Atemporalis, in unmodifizierten elementaren Propositionen zum Tragen kommt und daher keine modale Kategorie ist. Ähnlich wie bei der Polarität handelt es sich hier sicher nicht um eine prototypische Modalität, denn die Leistung der einbettenden Proposition gegenüber der eingebetteten besteht ja nur in der Relativierung von deren Zeitkomponente. Dennoch es gibt mehrere Gründe, sie im Zusammenhang mit den prototypischen Modalitäten zu behandeln. Der eine ist der, dass Temporaloperatoren Dualitätsgruppen bilden (so ist z. B. 'es war immer der Fall' das duale Gegenstück zu 'es war der Fall'), der zweite der, dass zumindest manche Fälle von Notwendigkeit und Möglichkeit eine implizite temporale Komponente enthalten, z. B. 'notwendigerweise immer' (vgl. Thomasons Fußnote 9 in Montague 1974: 259) vs. 'möglicherweise irgendwann', und der dritte, dass viele Sprachen den Unterschied zwischen nachzeitiger Zeitreferenz (Futur) und epistemisch abgeschwächter Modalität (Dubitativ) verwischen (vgl. Bybee et al. 1994: 207 et passim, Enç 1996: 356).

In diesen Zusammenhang gehört auch die Interaktion von Tempus und Modus in Konjugationsparadigmen, z. B. die Neutralisierung der im Indikativ des Deutschen gültigen Präsens-Präteritum-Opposition im Konjunktiv: Die Formen des Konjunktiv I sind offensichtlich vom Präsensstamm abgeleitet und die des Konjunktiv II vom Präteritalstamm (z. B. *tue* von *tut* und *täte* von *tat*). Diesem formalen Unterschied entspricht aber auf der Inhaltsseite kein temporaler, sondern ein modaler Unterschied.

2.2. Interne Handlungsmodalitäten

Wenn eingangs Propositionen als Charakterisierungen von Situationen oder von deren Kernen aufgefasst wurden, so ist dies gut verträglich mit der wohlbegründeten Annahme, dass prototypische Objektsituationskerne menschliche Personen und prototypische charakterisierende Begriffe Handlungsbegriffe sind. Da aber eine systematische Darstellung die prototypischen Phänomene zuerst und die abgeleiteten danach behandeln sollte, werden im folgenden zunächst die verschiedenen Handlungsmodalitäten besprochen, danach die Einstellungsmodalitäten, da Einstellungen Handlungen typischerweise vorausgehen und sie begleiten, und erst dann werden die allgemeinen Modalitäten jenseits von Agenten und deren mentalen Zuständen zur Sprache kommen (obwohl die den allgemeinen zugehörigen logischen Modalitäten natürlich auf einer abstrakten Ebene vielen modalen Kategorien zugrundeliegen).

2.2.1. Handlungstendenzmodalitäten

Handlungstendenzoperatoren kodieren Abschwächungen der zugrundeliegenden Handlungs- oder allgemeiner Verhaltenspropositionen im Sinne einer objektiven Wahrscheinlichkeit. (65) wird nicht schon dann falsch, wenn Anton mal lacht, (66) ist nicht widerlegt, wenn Eva die Einladung dann doch ausschlägt, erst eine überwiegend freundliche Miene Antons oder die Information, dass es für Eva zu dem fraglichen Zeitpunkt eher unwahrscheinlich war, dass sie die Einladung annehmen würde, machen (65) bzw. (66) zu falschen Aussagen, wobei die Grenzen natürlich unscharf bleiben.

(65) *Anton tendiert dazu, finster dreinzublicken.*

(66) *Eva ist geneigt, die Einladung anzunehmen.*

(67) *Eva ist nicht abgeneigt, die Einladung anzunehmen.*

Das deutsche Handlungstendenzverb *geneigt sein zu* tendiert zur Selbstdualität: Zwischen den Sätzen (66) und (67) dürfte wohl nur ein stilistischer Unterschied bestehen. Handlungstendenzoperatoren bewirken immer eine Veränderung der ontologischen Sorte ihrer Argumente: Sie machen aus einer Handlungsproposition (atelisch wie in (65) oder telisch wie in (66) und (67)) eine Zustandsproposition.

2.2.2. Handlungsdispositionsmodalitäten

Die prominenteste Handlungsdispositionsmodalität ist die der Fähigkeit, mit den Kategorien 'fähig' und ihrem negativen Gegenstück 'außerstande'. Die Duale dazu ('innerlich gezwungen' und 'innerlich frei') sind typischerweise nicht lexikalisiert oder gar grammatikalisiert. Manche Sprachen, z. B. das Französische (Beispiele (68) und (69)) und das Mapuche (Smeets 1989: 219) unterscheiden zwischen erlernter und nicht erlernter Fähigkeit:

(68) *Jean ne sait pas chanter.*
    'Hans kann nicht singen (er hat es nicht gelernt)'

(69) *Jean ne peut pas chanter.*
    'Hans kann nicht singen (er ist zu heiser)'

2.2.3. Handlungseinflussmodalitäten

Handlungsdispositionsmodalitäten (innere Faktoren) und Handlungseinflussmodalitäten (äußere Faktoren) werden häufig sprachlich gleich behandelt. Bisweilen kann die Wahl zwischen einer persönlichen und einer unpersönlichen Konstruktion den Unterschied ausdrücken:

(70) *Es drängte Max, das Wort zu ergreifen.* (Disposition)

(71) *Man drängte Max, das Wort zu ergreifen.* (Einfluss)

2.2.4. Handlungsumstandsmodalitäten

Während die eben besprochenen Einflussmodalitäten nur bedingt implizierend sind (der Schluss von (71) darauf, dass Max das Wort ergreift, gilt erst unter der Zusatzprämisse, dass er dem Drängen nachgibt), sind die Handlungsumstandsmodalitäten unbedingt implizierend.

Handlungsumstandsmodalitäten werden typischerweise durch Satzadverbien kodiert, in einigen Sprachen aber auch durch Verben, deren Modalverbstatus bei engeren Moduskonzeptionen natürlich strittig ist. Wieder lassen sich die vertrauten Dualitätsmuster erkennen, bei (72) und (73) offenbar basierend auf einem Paar dualer Adjektive, während bei (74) und (75) ein Paar antonymer, also einfach polar entgegengesetzter Adjektive zugrundeliegt. Die französische (77), englische (78), mittelhochdeutsche (79) und chinesische (80) Entsprechung des deutschen Verbs *wagen* (76) werden zumindest von einigen Grammatikern als Modalverben eingestuft. Das gleiche gilt für die französische Entsprechung zu *geruhen* (81), obwohl hier der Verdacht naheliegt, dass er sich hier um eine subpropositionale Modalität handelt.

(72) *Karl hat feigerweise zugestimmt.*

(73) *Karl hat nicht mutigerweise nicht zugestimmt.*

(74) *Maria ist freiwillig nicht mitgekommen.*

(75) *Maria ist nicht gezwungenermaßen nicht mitgekommen.*

(76) *Eva hat es gewagt/sich getraut/es riskiert zu widersprechen.*

(77) Französisch
    Jean ose venir.
    'Jean wagt es zu kommen.'

(78) Englisch
John dares come.
'John wagt es zu kommen.'

(79) Mittelhochdeutsch
So turre wir wol sprechen.
'So wagen wir es wohl zu sprechen.'

(80) Mandarin
Ta¹ gan³ pi¹ ping² wo.³
3P wagen kritisieren 1P
'Er wagt es, mich zu kritisieren.'

(81) Französisch
Jean daigne venir.
'Jean geruht zu kommen.'

2.2.5. Andativmodalität

Andative Modalitäten kodieren das Aufbrechen der handelnden Person, um die modalisierte Handlung zu tun. Sie werden begleitet von einer allgemeinen konversationellen Implikatur, dass im Normalfall auch die modalisierte Handlung ausgeführt wird. Wie viele andere Sprachen benutzt das Deutsche dazu das gewöhnliche Verb für 'gehen', interessanterweise aber mit einem reinen Infinitiv (vgl. (82)).

(82) *Max ist Maria abholen gegangen.*

Das Evenki bedient sich zum gleichen Zweck eines Suffixes *-na/-ne*, vgl. *d'ev-* 'essen' − *d'ev-ne-* 'essen gehen', *duku-* 'schreiben' − *duku-na-* 'schreiben gehen' (Nedjalkov 1997). Andativoperatoren sind häufig Quellen für Futurmarker, z. B. im Englischen, aber auch im Margi und Cocama (Bybee et al. 1994: 268).

2.2.6. Konativmodalität

Im Gegensatz zu den andativen werden die konativen Modalitäten begleitet von einer allgemeinen konversationellen Implikatur, dass die Durchführung der modalisierten Handlung zumindest zweifelhaft bleibt. Sie kodieren einen Versuch, eine Bemühung der handelnden Person, die modalisierte Handlung zu tun. Wieder benutzt das Deutsche hierzu ein gewöhnliches Vollverb, diesmal mit einem gewöhnlichen *zu*-Infinitivkomplement (vgl. (83)).

(83) *Max hat versucht, Maria abzuholen.*

Das Evenki verwendet zum gleichen Zweck wieder ein Suffix, *-ssal-sse*, vgl. *duku-* 'schreiben' − *duku-ssa-* 'zu schreiben versuchen' (Nedjalkov 1997).

2.2.7. Simulativmodalität

War bei der konativen Modalität die Implikatur, dass die modalisierte Handlung nicht durchgeführt wurde, noch konversationeller und damit leicht zerstreubarer Natur, so ist die gleiche Implikatur bei der Simulativität konventionell und damit fester Bedeutungsbestandteil: Aus (83) folgt analytisch (84) und (85) ist kontradiktorisch:

(83) *Eva tut so, als schliefe sie.*

(84) *Eva schläft nicht.*

(85) *Eva tut so, als schliefe sie, und sie schläft auch tatsächlich.*

Das entsprechende Suffix des Evenki lautet in diesem Fall, *-lakan/-leken*, vgl. *a:sin-* 'einschlafen' − *a:sin-leken-* 'so tun als schliefe man' (Nedjalkov 1997). Am Beispiel des Französischen, wo das Verb *feindre* von manchen Grammatikern zu den Modalverben gerechnet wird, sei schließlich noch die Skopusvariabilität des Simulativoperators bei Kookkurrenz mit anderen Modalen demonstriert:

(86) Französisch
Jean feint de lire.
'Hans tut so, als lese er.'

(87) Französisch
Jean sait feindre de lire.
'Hans kann so tun, als lese er.'

(88) Französisch
Jean feint de savoir lire.
'Hans tut so, als könne er lesen.'

(88) illustriert zugleich, dass zwar Simulativität selbst nur Handlungen zukommen kann, das Simulierte aber nicht unbedingt eine Handlung sein muss, sondern eine beliebige aus Verhalten erschließbare Eigenschaft sein kann.

2.2.8. Deontische Modalitäten

Die Struktur deontischer Modalitäten wird unten (3.2.2.) am Beispiel der volitiven Illokutionen ausführlicher diskutiert werden. Die Beziehung zwischen volitiven und deontischen Kategorien ist übrigens keineswegs in allen Sprachen so transparent wie im Deutschen, wo das Sollen offenbar das heterovolitionale Gegenstück zum Wollen ist. Die deontischen Operatoren des Lateinischen etwa (wie *licet, opus est* etc.) weisen nirgends auf einen solchen Zusammenhang hin.

Eine häufige Grammatikalisierungsquelle von Kodierungsmitteln für deontische Zulässigkeit bilden Ausdrücke für Fähigkeit (vgl. auch van der Auwera & Plungian 1998). Die ASL-Gebärde (ASL steht für American Sign Language) für 'können', nämlich die einfache oder doppelte Präsentation von zwei geballten Fäusten, stammt laut Janzen & Shaffer (2001) aus der entsprechenden parasprachlichen Geste (etwa: 'Schaut mal, wie stark ich bin!'), von der sie erst zum Adjektiv 'stark' lexikalisiert, und schließlich zum Modalauxiliar grammatikalisiert wurde. Dagegen geht die ASL-Gebärde für 'müssen', das hammerähnliche Herabfallen des gekrümmten Zeigefingers der dominanten Hand auf eine unsichtbare Oberfläche, nach der gleichen Quelle auf die parasprachlichen Geste des Auf-etwas-Pochens (Tisch mit Schuldschein oder Brieftasche) zurück, von der sie erst zum Verb 'schulden' der Französischen Gebärdensprache (LSF) lexikalisiert, und schließlich zum Modalauxiliar von LSF und ALS grammatikalisiert wurde.

Wegen des klaren Handlungscharakters der zu modalisierenden Propositionen gehören die deontischen eindeutig zu den Handlungsmodalitäten, die Modalausdrücke selbst stammen allerdings nur zum Teil aus der gleichen Gruppe, zum Teil stammen sie aus dem lexikalischen Bereich der Rechte und Pflichten, zum Teil aber auch aus der Gruppe der Einstellungsmodalitäten, wie z. B. die oben erwähnten volitiven Ausdrücke. Die deontischen Modalitäten lassen sich also häufig nicht nur den Handlungs- sondern zugleich den Einstellungsmodalitäten zuordnen. Deswegen wurden sie als letzte Gruppe der ersteren behandelt, bevor es im folgenden Abschnitt um Einstellungsmodalitäten geht.

2.3. Interne Einstellungsmodalitäten

Wurde die Gruppe der Handlungsmodalitäten dadurch definiert, dass ihre Tochterpropositionen alle Handlungspropositionen und die Modalisierungen dazu alle handlungsspezifischer Natur waren, so gibt es bei den Einstellungsmodalitäten keinerlei Einschränkungen bezüglich der Gehalte der eingebetteten Propositionen mehr, dagegen ist die Charakterisierung der einbettenden Proposition auf mentale Eventitäten beschränkt, die Propositionen zum Gegenstand haben, eben propositionale Einstellungen.

Während interne Einstellungsmodalitäten also sowohl bezüglich der Art der Einstellung als auch bezüglich der Identität des Einstellungsträgers unbeschränkt sind, spezifizieren externe Einstellungsmodalitäten immer die Art der in der jeweils vollzogenen Sprechhandlung ausgedrückten Einstellung des Sprechers. Um den letzteren Fall, der bei Gegenwartsbezug mit einer internen Charakterisierung einer Sprechereinstellung leicht zu verwechseln ist, terminologisch abzuheben, empfiehlt es sich hier, einer Anregung von Ewald Lang (1983) folgend, zu unterscheiden zwischen Einstellungsausdruck und Einstellungsbekundung: Wer mit einer Äußerung von *Ich bin dir dankbar für diese Worte* seinem Adressaten dankt, drückt seine Einstellung aus, wer dagegen mit der Formulierung *Ich danke dir für diese Worte* eine Aussage macht, bekundet seine Dankbarkeit. Nur im ersteren Fall kann eine wörtliche Lüge vorliegen, im letzteren Fall höchstens Verlogenheit.

2.3.1. Interne Expressive

(a) Interne Exklamative: Exklamative drücken eine Einstellung des Erstaunens, des Überraschtseins, des Für-außergewöhnlich-Haltens aus, sie sind kurz gesagt mit allen Einstellungen verträglich, die einen Ausruf (daher kommt ja der Terminus) rechtfertigen. Viele Sprachen haben einen exklamativen Hauptsatzmodus grammatikalisiert (→ Art. 79), in vielen, möglicherweise allen Sprachen gibt es auch eingebettete Exklamative. Zu unterscheiden sind Polaritätsexklamative, die sich typischerweise nicht von eingebetteten Deklarativsätzen unterscheiden ((89), (90)) und die eine satzadverbiale Paraphrase erlauben (91), und Ergänzungsexklamative, die formal oft von Ergänzungsinterrogativen schwer zu unterscheiden sind ((92), (93)), während der semantische Unterschied auf der Hand liegt: Paraphrasen wie (94) sind nur bei Matrixprädikaten möglich, die eine Valenzstelle für exklamative Sätze haben, nicht aber bei solchen, die nur eingebettete Interrogative zulassen wie in (95) (vgl. Zaefferer 1983).

(89) *Eva wundert sich, dass Max ihr geschrieben hat.*

(90) *Es ist erstaunlich, dass Max Eva geschrieben hat.*

(91) *Erstaunlicherweise hat Max Eva geschrieben.*

(92) *Eva wundert sich, wer ihr (nicht) alles geschrieben hat.*

(93) *Es ist erstaunlich, wer Eva (nicht) alles geschrieben hat.*

(94) *Eva wundert sich, dass diejenigen, die ihr geschrieben haben, ihr tatsächlich alle geschrieben haben.*

(95) *Eva fragt sich, dass diejenigen, die ihr geschrieben haben, ihr tatsächlich alle geschrieben haben.

(b) Interne Optative: Optative drücken eine Einstellung des Wünschens, allgemeiner des Für-wünschenswert-Haltens aus, also einer positiven Einstellung (vgl. unten 3.2.1.(b)), und werden häufig nach dem Kriterium der Erfüllbarkeit subkategorisiert, die natürlich bei auf Vergangenes bezogenen Propositionen generell nicht gegeben ist. Dennoch können auch Wunscheinstellungen bezüglich solcher Propositionen als erfüllbar markiert werden, dann nämlich, wenn dem Einstellungsträger der Wahrheitswert der Proposition noch nicht bekannt ist (vgl. (97), erfüllbar, mit (98), unerfüllbar). Nichtverbale Prädikation (99) ist ebenso möglich wie satzadverbiale Kodierung (100). Wünsche mit negativen Inhalten wie (101) werden häufig mit Matrixsatznegation formuliert (102), wohl auf Grund einer mehr oder minder stark idiomatisierten Implikatur, eine Option, die bei entsprechenden Satzadverbialen nicht gegeben ist (103). Der propositionale Gehalt kann bei direktionalem Prädikat auch durch reduzierte Sätze kodiert werden (104).

(96) *Max wünscht sich, dass Eva ihm schreibt.*

(97) *Max wünscht sich, dass Eva ihm geschrieben hat.*

(98) *Max hätte sich gewünscht, dass Eva ihm schreibt.*

(99) *Es ist wünschenswert, dass Eva Max schreibt.*

(100) *Hoffentlich schreibt Eva Max.*

(101) *Hans möchte, dass Max nicht kommt.*

(102) *Hans möchte nicht, dass Max kommt.*

(103) *Hoffentlich kommt Max nicht.*

(104) *Hans wünscht Max zum Teufel.*

2.3.2. Interne telische Modalitäten

(a) Interne volitive Modalitäten: Volitive teilen mit den Optativen die Präferenz des jeweiligen Einstellungsträgers für die Wahrheit des propositionalen Gehalts, im Gegensatz zu diesen spielt die Kategorie der Erfüllbarkeit hier allerdings keine Rolle, da rationales Wollen die Annahme der Erfüllbarkeit in sich schließt. Aus dem gleichen Grund kommen als für die Realisierung der jeweiligen Eventität verantwortliche Agentien nur der Einstellungsträger selbst (vgl. (105)) oder von ihm beeinflussbare Personen (vgl. (106)) in Frage: (107) wirkt nur dann nicht merkwürdig, wenn Hans irgendwie Einfluss auf das Wettergeschehen hat oder zu haben glaubt (weswegen er z. B. einen Regentanz ausführt). (108) hingegen ist Unsinn und (109) nur im übertragenen Sinn zu verstehen: Ziel von Fritz' Wollen ist nicht, dass er Urlaub gemacht hat, sondern dass sein Adressat dies glaubt (vgl. unten 2.3.3. (a), quotative Modalitäten).

(105) *Eva will Urlaub machen.*

(106) *Max will, dass Eva Urlaub macht.*

(107) *Hans will, dass es regnet.*

(108) *Hans will, dass es geregnet hat.*

(109) *Fritz will Urlaub gemacht haben.*

(b) Interne intentionale Modalitäten: Intentionale Modalitäten lassen sich als autovolitive auffassen, also als der Spezialfall der volitiven Modalitäten, bei dem Einstellungsträger und Agens der in der Tochterproposition genannten Eventität immer identisch sind. Bei diesen Modalitäten ist die Tendenz, Matrixsatznegation auf die Tochterproposition zu beziehen, schwächer ausgeprägt als bei den gerade genannten, d. h. (112) wird als Aussage über eine abwesende Einstellung zu einem positiven Gehalt interpretiert, im Gegensatz zu (111), einer Aussage über eine vorhandene Einstellung zu einem negativen propositionalen Gehalt:

(110) *Max beabsichtigt, Eva einen Brief zu schreiben.*

(111) *Max beabsichtigt, nicht lockerzulassen.*

(112) *Max beabsichtigt nicht, lockerzulassen.*

2.3.3. Interne epistemische Modalitäten

Der Terminus epistemisch wird hier in einem weiten Sinne verwendet, der die Differenzierung von Information nach ihrer Quelle (evidentielle Modalität), der subjektiven Sicherheit (Gewissheitsmodalität) und der intersubjektiv vermittelten Gewähr (Verantwortungsmodalität) umfasst. Die genannten drei Variationsdimensionen sind logisch gesehen orthogonal, und obwohl wir in unserer Kultur wohl dazu zu neigen scheinen, direkte Evidenz mit hoher Gewissheit und hoher Gewährleistung zu verbinden, so zeigt doch eine kurze Reflexion, dass oft genug indirekte, nämlich quotative Evidenz zu ebenso hoher oder sogar höherer Gewissheit führt, dann nämlich, wenn der Quelle eine hohe Vertrauenswürdigkeit zugebilligt wird (Welcher Flugschüler würde ein wildes Ausweichmanöver durchführen, wenn ihm der Fluglehrer sagt, dass das Licht, das auf ihn zuzukommen scheint, nur ein Reflex in der Kanzel ist?)

(a) Interne Evidentialitätsmodalitäten (Informationsquellendifferenzierung): Hier ist zunächst zu unterscheiden zwischen direkter Evidenz, also eigener Sinneswahrnehmung, und indirekter Evidenz. Im zweiten Fall ist es noch wichtig, ob der Mangel an eigener Sinneswahrnehmung durch ein nichttriviales Folgerungsverfahren oder durch einen Kommunikationsakt wettgemacht wurde, ob erschlossene Information oder Information aus zweiter Hand vorliegt.

A. Direkte Evidenz
A.1. Visuelle Evidenz (Augenzeuge)

(113) *Ich habe mit eigenen Augen gesehen, dass ein Hund eine Frau gebissen hat.*

(114) Tuyuca
díiga apé-wi
'Er spielte Fußball' (Augenzeugenmodussuffix)

In Sprachen wie dem Deutschen erfordert die evidentielle Modalisierung einen viel höheren Kodierungsaufwand als etwa im Tuyuca (Beispiele (114), (116), nach Barnes 1984), das über eine grammatikalisierte Evidentialitätsmarkierung verfügt.

A.2. Auditive Evidenz (Ohrenzeuge)

(115) *Ich habe mit eigenen Ohren gehört, dass ein Hund laut gebellt hat.*

(116) Tuyuca
díiga apé-ti
'Er spielte Fußball' (Ohrenzeugenmodussuffix)

A.3. Andere Sinnesevidenzen

(117) *Ich habe selbst geschmeckt, dass Zitrone in der Soße war.*

(118) *Ich habe selbst gerochen, dass das Wasser gechlort war.*

(119) *Ich habe selbst gespürt, dass die Erde gebebt hat.*

Die Unmittelbarkeit direkter Evidenz wird häufig betont, um den Schluss auf einen hohen Gewissheits- und Zuverlässigkeitsgrad nahezulegen.

B. Indirekte Evidenz
B.1. Prämissen als Quelle: Inferentielle Evidenz (meist Eigenquelle)

Die Opposition von schwacher und starker Modalität drückt hier den Gegensatz Verträglichkeit mit den Prämissen (120), (121) vs. Folgerung aus den Prämissen (122), (123) aus:

(120) *Auf Grund der Verletzungen ist nicht auszuschließen, dass ein Hund die Frau gebissen hat.*

(121) *Ein Hund kann die Frau gebissen haben.*

(122) *Die Verletzungen lassen keinen anderen Schluss zu, als dass ein Hund die Frau gebissen hat.*

(123) *Ein Hund muss die Frau gebissen haben.*

(124) *Der mutmaßliche Verursacher der Bisswunden ist ein Dackel.*

(125) Tuyuca
 (a) *díiga apé-yi*
 'Er spielte Fußball' (Es gibt konkrete Indizien dafür: spezifischer Inferentialmodus)

 (b) *díiga apé-hi:yi*
 'Er spielte Fußball' (Es ist vernünftig, das anzunehmen: generischer Inferentialmodus)

B.2. Kommunikation als Quelle: Quotative Evidenz (meist Fremdquelle)

(126) *Jemand hat gesagt, dass die Frau ein Hund gebissen hat.*

(127) *Ein Hund soll die Frau gebissen haben.*

(128) *Ein Hund habe die Frau gebissen.*

(129) *Angeblich hat ein Hund die Frau gebissen.*

(130) *Das angebliche Opfer hat sich beschwert.*

(131) *Das mutmaßliche Opfer hat sich beschwert.*

(132) Tuyuca
díiga apé-yigi
'Er spielte Fußball' (Jemand hat mich darüber informiert: Quotativmodus)

(133) *Die Frau will den Hund noch nie gesehen haben.*

Die Beispiele (121), (123), (127) und (128) zeigen, dass das Deutsche im Bereich der indirekten evidentiellen Kategorien und einen höheren Grad an Grammatikalisierung aufweist als bei den direkten, wenn auch höchstens der Konjunktiv I in Beispiel (128) als evidentieller Modus bezeichnet werden kann. Das Tuyuca (Beispiele (125) und (132)) zeigt hingegen eine hohe Systematizität auf einem hohen Grammatikalisierungsniveau. (129) illustriert die Möglichkeit einer satzadverbialen Kodierung der Mutterproposition, die Beispiele (130) und (131) verdeutlichen, dass NP-interne Modalisierungen keineswegs immer die Form eines Relativsatzes annehmen müssen, der Unterschied zwischen den Attributen besteht unter anderem darin, dass nur bei *angeblich*, nicht aber bei *mutmaßlich* der Referent der NP selbst als Informationsquelle in Frage kommt. Schließlich verfügt das Deutsche noch über eine besondere, das autovolitive Modalverb involvierende Konstruktion für den Fall, dass Subjekt und Informationsquelle zusammenfallen (133).

Dass die Unterfälle der indirekten Evidentialität bei hochgradig grammatikalisierten Kodierungsmitteln nicht unterschieden werden, ist zu erwarten. Etwas überraschender ist der Befund, dass viele Sprachen mit dem gleichen Mittel auch eine Art von Exklamativität kodieren, da bei dieser ja häufig sehr direkte Evidenz vorliegt (vgl. Lazard 1999). Eine Erklärungsmöglichkeit liegt in der von Lazard vorgeschlagenen Paraphrase 'apparently', zu deren Lesarten ja sowohl das direkte 'offensichtlich' als auch das indirekte 'scheinbar' zählen. Eine andere geht von einer zugrundeliegenden Indirektheitsfunktion aus und leitet die direkte, aber expressive Verwendung von einen ironisch-untertreibenden Gebrauch ab (vgl. *Der scheint einen guten Gleichgewichtssinn zu haben*, wenn jemand brilliant balanciert). Schließlich wäre auch eine Anwendung des Unglaublichkeitstopos denkbar, der bei den von indirekter Evidentialität ermöglichten Zweifeln an der Glaubwürdigkeit des propositionalen Gehalt den Ausgangspunkt für eine Bedeutungsübertragung bilden könnte (vgl. *Ich traue meinen Augen nicht*).

(b) Interne Gewissheitsmodalitäten: Die Skalierbarkeit von Gewissheit ist Grundlage der subjektiven Wahrscheinlichkeitstheorie, sprachlichen Ausdruck findet der Gewissheitswert in Wettaussagen:

(134) *Ich wette mein letztes Hemd, dass Peter gewonnen hat.*

(135) *Ich gehe lieber keine Wette ein, dass Peter gewonnen hat.*

(136) *Ich wette mein letztes Hemd, dass Peter nicht gewonnen hat.*

Grammatikalisierte Kodierung erfährt von den Gewissheitskategorien am ehesten die Ungewissheit im sogenannten Dubitativ (Beispiel (137) aus dem Imbabura Quechua; Cole 1982) und die emphatische Gewissheit (Beispiel (138) aus der gleichen Sprache). Das letztere Beispiel illustriert zugleich die oben angesprochene Verknüpfung von hoher Gewissheit mit direkter Evidentialität.

(137) Imbabura Quechua (Cole 1982: 164)
Jusi-ka kitu-man chaya-shka-chá
José-TOP Quito-zu ankomm-PERF-DUB
'Vielleicht ist Pedro in Quito angekommen.'

(138) Imbabura Quechua (Cole 1982: 164)
ñuka-ta miku-naya-n-mari
1-ACC ess-DESID-3-EMPH.DIR.EVID
'Ich möchte essen.', 'Es gelüstet mich offenbar heftig zu essen (mein Magen knurrt).'

(c) Interne Verantwortungsmodalitäten: Wenn es im Zusammenhang mit einer Information heißt: *Diese Angaben erfolgen ohne Gewähr*, so will sich der Autor von der Verantwortung für die Folgen freistellen, die sich ergeben könnten, wenn sich die gegebene Information als falsch herausstellt. Verantwortungsbereitschaft ist rationalerweise mit zuverlässigen Evidenzsorten und hoher Gewissheit gekoppelt, logisch aber davon unabhängig. Dennoch lassen sich grammatische Mittel, die einen Verantwortungsgrad indizieren (typischerweise einen reduzierten) kaum von solchen unterscheiden, die Gewissheit oder Evidenz signalisieren.

2.3.4. Interne evaluative Modalitäten

Evaluative Modalitäten gehören schon zu den von Rescher (1968) genannten Kategorien, sie werden typischerweise lexikalisch kodiert wie in den Beispielen (139)−(141). Die von Donaldson (1980: 242) im Ngiyambaa beobachteten Ausdrücke für Lob bzw. Missbilligung scheinen auch nur allenfalls geringfügig grammatikalisiert zu sein.

(139) *Gut, dass du kommst.*

(140) *Schade, dass du gehst.*

(141) *Leider kann ich nicht bleiben.*

GOOD ist übrigens die einzige Gebärde mit adjektivischer Übersetzung, die wohl in BSL (British Sign Language) als auch in ASL (American Sign Language) inkorporierte Negation erlaubt (Deuchar 1984: 118).

2.3.5. Interne Erwartungsmodalitäten (prospektiv)

Auch hier scheint eine grammatische Kodierung eher selten sein, falls es sie überhaupt gibt, insofern dürften die Beispiele (142) und (143) wohl als prototypisch gelten. Negative Erwartungen überlappen sich allerdings mit den exklamativen Modalitäten, bei denen eine weit höhere Grammatikalisierungstendenz zu beobachten ist (vgl. 2.3.1. (a)).

(142) *Die Regierungspartei hat, wie von den meisten erwartet, die Wahlen gewonnen.*

(143) *Gegen alle Erwartungen hat die Regierungspartei die Wahlen gewonnen.*

2.4. Interne Allgemeinmodalitäten

Es spricht alles dafür, dass man sich die Ausdrucksmittel für die internen Allgemeinmodalitäten als Resultate eines Grammatikalisierungs- und damit Abstraktionsprozesses vorzustellen hat, bei dem die Spezifika der entsprechenden Handlungsmodalitäten ausgeblendet wurden, so dass modale Konstruktionen ohne personale Subjekte möglich wurden. Dass das logisch Primäre und Grundlegende sich so als empirisch-evolutionär sekundär und abgeleitet erweist, ist wohl nur auf den ersten Blick paradox: Nach einiger Überlegung erscheint es vielmehr als eine durchaus natürliche Entwicklung, wenn implizit immer schon gültige abstrakte Strukturen erst bei relativ abstraktem Sprachgebrauch auch explizit formulierbar werden.

2.4.1. Allgemeine Tendenzmodalitäten

Die allgemeinen Tendenzmodalitäten verhalten sich wie die Handlungstendenzmodalitäten (vgl. § 2.2.1), d. h. es geht um Abschwächungen der zugrundeliegenden Propositionen im Sinne einer objektiven Wahrscheinlichkeit, im Gegensatz zu den Modalitäten der subjektiven Wahrscheinlichkeit, die oben in § 2.3.3 (b) behandelt wurden. Allgemeine Tendenzmodalitäten werden häufig durch spezielle lexikalische Mittel ausgedrückt (vgl. (147) und (148)).

(147) *Die Einschreibungen zeigen eine rückläufige Tendenz.*

(148) *Die Temperaturen tendieren zu extremen Ausschlägen.*

Auch allgemeine Tendenzoperatoren bewirken eine Vereinheitlichung der ontologischen Sorte ihrer Argumente: Ob der Kern der Tochterproposition ein Zustand, eine Aktivität oder ein Ereignis ist, die Mutterproposition ist immer eine Zustandsproposition. Das deutsche Tendenzverb *tendieren* scheint zur Selbstdualität zu tendieren, was freilich angesichts seiner Vagheit nicht leicht nachweisbar ist.

2.4.2. Allgemeine Dispositionsmodalitäten

Auch dispositionale Modaloperatoren überführen beliebige Propositionen in Zustandspropositionen, im Unterschied zu den Tendenzmodalitäten muss hier aber die Mutterproposition als verdeckte Konditionalisierung der Tochterproposition aufgefasst werden, wobei die (hinreichende) Bedingung freilich unausgedrückt bleibt. Man kann unterscheiden zwischen neutralen (d. h. selbstdualen, Beispiele (149) und (150)), starken (bei Vorliegen der ungenannten Bedingung implizierenden; Beispiele (151)–(153)) und schwachen (bei Vorliegen der ungenannten Bedingung implizierten; Beispiele (154)–(159)) Dispositionsmodalitäten. Wiederum lassen sich auch diese allgemeinen Modalitäten als Generalisierungen der entsprechenden Handlungsmodalitäten auffassen.

(149) *Dieser Wagen neigt zum Übersteuern. (... wenn man damit schnell in die Kurve fährt.)*

(150) *John tends to be optimistic. (... wenn eine schwierige Situation eintritt.)*

(151) *Das Seil muss reißen.*

(152) *Peter ist unbedingt zuverlässig.*

(153) *Dieser Kunststoff brennt unter allen Umständen.*

(154) *Rohöl ist schwer entflammbar.*

(155) *Glas bricht leicht.*

(156) *Das Seil kann reißen.*

(157) *Dieser Kunststoff ist brennbar.*

(158) *Dieser Kunststoff brennt unter Umständen.*

(159) *Der Vorschlag ist konsensfähig.*

In den Fällen (154) und (155) sind die ungenannten Umstände zusätzlich charakterisiert bezüglich des Aufwands, der für die Herbeiführung des jeweiligen Sachverhalts erforderlich ist: Dieser wird im ersten Fall als relativ hoch, im zweiten Fall als relativ niedrig eingestuft (vgl. auch Talmys (1988) Konzept der Kräftedynamik, 'force dynamics').

2.4.3. Allgemeine Einflussmodalitäten

Während bei den Dispositionsmodalitäten Kräftedynamik ein fakultatives Element darstellt, ist sie bei den Einflussmodalitäten essentiell. Sie werden hier der systematischen Vollständigkeit halber erwähnt, obwohl sich reine Beispiele schwer finden lassen. In Formulierungen wie 'Das Dach droht unter Schneelast zusammenzubrechen' ist nicht nur von dem Einfluss und seiner Zielrichtung die Rede, sondern es wird auch eine wertende anthropomorphisierende Metapher eingesetzt.

2.4.4. Allgemeine Umstandsmodalitäten

Die allgemeinen Umstandsmodalitäten, von denen die kausalen und die konzessiven die prominentesten sind, implizieren wie die Handlungsumstandsmodalitäten die zu modalisierende Proposition. Der Modaloperator enthält im Allgemeinen selbst eine Proposition, deren Wahrheit ebenfalls impliziert wird: Aus (160) folgt ebenso wie aus (161), dass (a) ein frischer Wind wehte und (b) alle bester Laune waren, dagegen folgt nur aus (160), dass (a) zur Erklärung von (b) hinreicht, während aus (161) folgt, dass (a) zur Erklärung der Falschheit von (b) hingereicht hätte.

(160) *Weil ein frischer Wind wehte, waren alle bester Laune.*

(161) *Obwohl ein frischer Wind wehte, waren alle bester Laune.*

(162) *Wegen Umbau geschlossen.*

(163) *Trotz Umbau geöffnet.*

Anders bei (162) und (163): Aus beiden folgt, dass (a), das Stattfinden eines Umbaus, für die Erklärung von (b), den Zustand des Geschlossenseins, hinreicht und dass (a) eine Tatsache ist, hingegen folgt nur aus (162) dass (b) auch vorliegt, während (163) das Gegenteil impliziert.

Die Kausativprädikate sind ein Musterbeispiel für hochgradige Integration von Mutter- und Tochterproposition (vgl. § 1.3.2), weil sie die beiden Prädikate verschmelzen: 'fällen' lässt sich ja dekompositional als 'fallen machen' paraphrasieren, wobei das Subjekt des komplexen Verbs als Agens des Machens interpretiert wird (und damit als Agens einer unspezifizierten Ursache) und das direkte Objekt dieses Verbs als Aktant des Fallens und damit der entsprechenden Wirkung (vgl. Payne 1997: 175–186).

2.4.5. Imminenzmodalitäten

Imminenzmodalitäten sind das allgemeine Gegenstück zur Andativmodalität bei Handlungen. Der Übergang kann als Folge einer generalisierenden Grammatikalisierung erfolgen wie bei dem englischen unmittelbaren Futur, das zugleich die Nähe von Tempus und Modalität illustriert:

(164) *Peter is going to fill the bucket.*

(165) *The bucket is going to spill.*

Die folgenden Beispiele stellen sprechaktbasierte allgemeine Imminenzmodalitäten dar, die zugleich eine evaluative Komponente enthalten.

(166) *Der Turm drohte umzufallen.*

(167) *Das Wetter versprach, besser zu werden.*

2.4.6. Konditionale Modalitäten

Was die konditionalen mit den Dispositionsmodalitäten verbindet, ist die Konditionalisierung der Tochterproposition, was sie von diesen unterscheidet ist die explizite Nennung der hinreichenden ((168), (169)) oder notwendigen ((170), (171)) Bedingung.

(168) *Die sachgerechte Lagerung dieser Konserve ist hinreichend dafür, dass sie mindestens zwei Jahre hält.*

(169) *Bei sachgerechter Lagerung hält diese Konserve mindestens zwei Jahre.*

(170) *Nur tagsüber ist ein Sonnenschutz angebracht.*

(171) *Nur wenn es Tag ist, ist ein Sonnenschutz angebracht.*

Wie die Beispiele zeigen, wird konditionale Modalisierung keineswegs nur sentential kodiert. Einen Überblick über Kodierungsformen von Konditionalen vermitteln Comrie (1987) sowie Artikel 76 des vorliegenden Handbuchs. Die meisten Semantiker sind mit Kratzer (1991) der Meinung, dass auch konditionale Modalisierung als Form von Quantifikation interpretiert werden sollte. Diese Quantifikation bleibt allerdings bei generalisierenden *wenn*-Sätzen gewöhnlich implizit, d. h. *wenn* wird dann als *immer wenn* verstanden. Diese Auffassung scheint bei *falls* auf Schwierigkeiten zu stoßen, da hier explizite Quantifikationen wie *immer, manchmal* oder *nie* unmöglich sind. Das Problem löst sich auf, wenn man *falls* im Sinne der Theorie der verallgemeinerten Quantoren als Kennzeichnungsquantor auffasst, also als paraphrasierbar mithilfe einer definiten Singularnominalphrase wie *in dem Fall, dass*. Die quantifizierende Analyse ist auch übertragbar auf die sogenannten 'Unkonditionale' (Zaefferer 1991), die im Gegensatz zu den Konditionalen keine Abhängigkeit, sondern eine Unabhängigkeit ausdrücken:

(172) *Immer wenn er etwas Dummes sagte, wurde Karl getadelt.*

(173) *Egal, was er sagte, Karl wurde getadelt.*

(174) *Immer wenn er etwas sagte, wurde Karl getadelt.*

In (172) wird über eine eingeschränkte Klasse von Äußerungen quantifiziert, nämlich solche mit dummem Inhalt, in (173) und (174) über die uneingeschränkte Klasse aller Äußerungen, d. h. solcher mit beliebigen Inhalten, der Unterschied der Unkonditionalkonstruktion (173) zur parallelen Konditionalkonstruktion (174) besteht nur in der emphatischen Hervorhebung der Unabhängigkeit.

2.4.7. Similativmodalitäten

Similativmodalitäten sind das allgemeine Gegenstück zur handlungsbezogenen Simulativmodalität. Sie können persönlich (175) oder unpersönlich (176) konstruiert werden; sie können außerdem die Falschheit der Tochterproposition im implizieren ((177) in nichtumgangssprachlichem Gebrauch, zumindest laut Duden) oder auch nicht (178):

(175) *Seitdem ist mir, als wäre der Himmel mit einem schwarzen Flor überzogen.*

(176) *Es war, als hätt' der Himmel die Erde still geküsst.*

(177) *Die Tür ist scheinbar verschlossen.*

(178) *Die Tür ist anscheinend verschlossen.*

2.4.8. Alethische (ontische) Modalität

(179) *Gott existiert nicht nur, er muss existieren.*

(180) *Ein Ereignis kann kein Ding sein.*

Wenn in einer theologischen oder philosophischen Debatte Sätze wie (179) oder (180) fallen, dann geht es nicht um einfache Existenz oder Dinghaftigkeit, sondern um deren Position im logischen Raum des Denkbaren: Wer (179) sagt, gibt zu verstehen, dass die Existenz Gottes nicht nur gegeben, sondern gar nicht wegdenkbar ist, wer (180) sagt, erklärt ein Ereignis, das zugleich Ding ist, für undenkbar. Die Philosophen sprechen hier von alethischer Modalität, weil es hier um logische (auf der Bedeutung logischer Operatoren beruhende) oder analytische (auf der Bedeutung nichtlogischer Prädikate beruhende) Wahrheit oder Falschheit geht, um Tautologie oder Kontradiktion, jedenfalls um Verhältnisse, die unabhängig vom Zustand der Welt, Naturgesetzen, Wissens- oder Wollenszuständen oder sozialen Normen sind. Lexikalisiert sind die vier Glieder einer alethischen Dualitätsgruppe im Deutschen zum Beispiel durch die vier Adjektive *denkbar, denknotwendig* (= *undenkbar, dass nicht*), *undenkbar* und *wegdenkbar* (= *nicht undenkbar, dass nicht*). Eine approximative Variante dieser Vierergruppe kann man mit Hilfe entsprechender Adverbien erzeugen: *leicht denkbar, fast denknotwendig* (= *schwer denkbar, dass nicht*) *schwer denkbar* und *leicht wegdenkbar* (= *leicht denkbar, dass nicht*).

Schließlich ist noch anzumerken, dass die gleichen Ausdrücke meist in implizit relativierten Varianten verwendet werden, die von den Höhen philosophischer Debatten in die Niederungen der Alltagskonversation führen. (181) bringt keinen logischen Widerspruch zum Ausdruck, der der Tochterproposition inhärent wäre, sondern einen, der zwischen dieser und einer unterstellten Prämissenmenge (z. B. 'In solchen Kleidern geht man nicht auf solche Parties.' und 'Ich tue nichts, was man nicht tut') besteht.

(181) *Undenkbar, dass ich in diesem Kleid auf die Party gehe.*

Eine andere Deutung würde das *undenkbar* als Hyperbel nehmen: Der Vorgang ist zwar theoretisch denkbar, ihn sich vorzustellen stößt aber praktisch auf so großen Widerstand, dass er eigentlich doch nicht gedacht werden kann.

3. Modale Kategorien II: Illokutionäre Modalitäten

Die Vorstellung, dass ein und dieselbe Objektproposition in verschiedenen Metasituationen zu verschiedenen Zwecken eingesetzt werden kann, hat Wittgenstein (1960: § 22) auf besonders anschauliche Weise formuliert: „"Denken wir uns ein Bild, einen Boxer in bestimmter Kampfstellung darstellend. Dieses Bild kann nun dazu gebraucht werden, um jemand mitzuteilen, wie er stehen, sich halten soll; oder, wie er sich nicht halten soll; oder, wie ein bestimmter Mann dort und dort gestanden hat; oder etc. etc. Man könnte dieses Bild (chemisch gesprochen) ein Satzradikal nennen. Ähnlich dachte sich wohl Frege die 'Annahme'." Diese Zerlegbarkeit der Gesamtillokution in illokutionäre Rolle und propositionalen Gehalt gilt mit einer gleich zu diskutierenden Ausnahme für alle Illokutionstypen und ist unter den damit befassten Wissenschaftlern unkontrovers.

Kontroverser ist die Frage, ob und wenn ja in welche Faktoren die illokutionären Rollen selbst zerlegt werden sollten. Die folgende Darstellung geht davon aus, dass sich sämtliche elementaren illokutionären Rollen in eine Handlungsmodalität (etwas zum Ausdruck bringen) und eine Einstellungsmodalität zerlegen lassen, wobei letztere bei telischen Einstellungen noch einmal danach unterscheidbar sind, ob das 'telos', also das angestrebte Ziel, modalisiert ist, und wenn ja, wie.

3.1. Nicht-sententiale Illokutionen

3.1.1. Interjektionen

Interjektionen sind Ausdrücke, mit deren Hilfe Illokutionen ohne deskriptiven Gehalt vollzogen werden können. Wer „Au!" sagt, signalisiert zwar etwas Ähnliches wie „Das tut weh!", aber nur in letzterem Fall ist „Wo denn?" eine angemessene Reaktion. Da interjektive Illokutionen keinen deskriptiven und somit keinen propositionalen Gehalt haben, bilden sie keine modalen Kategorien im Sinne von D 1.

3.1.2. Phrasale Illokutionen

Searle merkt in einer Fußnote zu 'Speech Acts' (1969: 31) an, dass nicht alle Illokutionen die Form $F(p)$ aufweisen, wobei F für die Illokutionstypindikatoren steht und p für die Propositionskodierung, und dass man für Beispiele wie „Hurrah for Manchester United" oder „Down with Caesar" die Form $F(n)$ annehmen müsse, wobei n ein referierender Ausdruck sei. Dabei scheint er davon auszugehen, dass *Hurrah for* und *Down with* Illokutionstypindikatoren sind und die Beispiele ähnliche Strukturen aufweisen. Beide Annahmen erweisen sich bei genauerer Betrachtung als unrichtig.

(182) *Ein Prosit auf den edlen Spender!*

(183) *Störer raus!*

(184) *Her mit den kleinen Engländerinnen!*

Wer (182) unter entsprechenden Umständen äußert, bringt damit einen Toast auf den Referenten (in seiner Spenderrolle) aus, man kann hier von einer elliptischen performativen Formel ausgehen („Hiermit bringe ich ein Prosit aus"). Für die Interpretation kann man daher die phrasalen Illokutionen des Typs (182) den Deklarationen zuordnen, die unten in § 3.2.3 behandelt werden. Bei (183) und (184) handelt es sich dagegen um verkürzte Wunschsätze, bei denen ein Modalverb wie *sollen* dazuzudenken ist. Bemerkenswert an dem (184) zugrundeliegenden Phraseologismus '*Direktionaladverbial* mit *NP*' ist der Umstand, dass sein Inhalt nicht einfach durch Hinzufügung eines Modalverbs explizierbar ist, vielmehr muss man zu Paraphrasen greifen wie 'Mit *NP* soll es so sein, dass ...'. Dennoch erscheint es wegen der rekonstruierbaren propositionalen Gehalte in allen diesen Fällen angebracht, von modalen Kategorien im hier definierten Sinn zu sprechen und sie für die weitere Interpretation den sententialen und damit propositionsbasierten Illokutionsmodalitäten zuzuordnen, die im folgenden Abschnitt behandelt werden.

3.2. Sententiale Illokutionen

Alle Illokutionstypen mit propositionalem Gehalt drücken eine Einstellung zu diesem Gehalt aus, ihre Gliederung spiegelt daher zum Teil die der internen Einstellungsmodalitäten. Im Gegensatz zu diesen kommt aber immer eine Handlungskomponente dazu, nämlich die des Zum-Ausdruck-Bringens. Bei den expressiven Illokutionen ist damit der Handlungszweck bereits erreicht. Expressive Illokutionen gehören demgemäß zu denjenigen Handlungen, die die märchenhafte Eigenschaft haben, dass ein klares Zum-Ausdruck-Bringen des Wunsches oder der Absicht, etwas zu tun, aus begrifflichen Gründen, also mit analytischer Notwendigkeit, bereits hinreichend ist für eine Erfüllung dieses Wunsches: Niemand kann durch sein Verhalten deutlich machen, dass er etwa seine Freude zum Ausdruck bringen will, ohne zugleich durch das gleiche Verhalten seine Freude zum Ausdruck zu bringen. Andreas

Kemmerling (1999) nennt diesen Handlungstyp 'gricy' und meint, alle elementaren Illokutionen seien dieser Natur.

Mit den übrigen Illokutionen wird ein darüber hinausgehendes, mit Hilfe der ausgedrückten Proposition definiertes Ziel verfolgt. Sie sollen daher hier volitiv genannt werden. Ist das Ziel der volitiven Einstellung nicht, oder jedenfalls nicht notwendigerweise, epistemischer Natur, so liegt eine nichtepistemische Illokution vor, andernfalls eine epistemische. In diesem Fall soll der propositionale Gehalt nicht realisiert, sondern nur angenommen oder gewusst werden. (Eine ausführliche Begründung dafür, wieso eine solche Klassifikation gerade unter typologischen Gesichtspunkten der in Searle (1975) vorgeschlagenen vorzuziehen ist, findet sich in Zaefferer (2001).

3.2.1. Expressive Illokutionen

(a) Exklamative Illokutionen: Gemeinsamer Nenner aller exklamativen Illokutionen (vgl. auch den Artikel 79 dieses Handbuchs und Abschnitt 2.3.1.(a) oben) ist der Ausdruck des Erstaunens über den propositionalen Gehalt, seiner Einschätzung als höchst ungewöhnlich, unerwartet oder auffällig, wobei entweder die Polarität der Proposition Fokus der Einstellung sein kann (Existenz bzw. Nichtexistenz der denotierten Eventität, vgl. (185) und (186)), oder aber der Grad bzw. die Ausprägung der denotierten Charakterisierung ((187), (188); vgl. auch Zaefferer 1983, 1990). In allen Fällen ist eine Fortsetzung durch (189) denkbar. Während (189) die modale Kategorie der Exklamation, bezogen auf einen anaphorisch identifizierten propositionalen Gehalt, lexikalisch und intonatorisch/orthographisch kodiert, zeigen die Beispiele (185) bis (188), wie heterogen die für externe Exklamative zur Verfügung stehenden Konstruktionstypen sind, insbesondere wenn man sie mit den Kodierungstypen der internen Exklamative vergleicht (vgl. 2.3.1.(a)).

(185) *Wirft der mir doch glatt das Glas um!*

(186) *Dass die sich nicht schämt!*

(187) *DAS ist ein Angeber!*

(188) *Wie die herüberschaut!*

(189) *Das ist ja unglaublich!*

Aus Sadock & Zwicky (1985) geht hervor, dass diese Heterogenität sich auch im Sprachvergleich findet, und dass etwa die Verwandtschaft von exklamativen mit interrogativen Strukturen weit verbreitet ist.

(b) Optative Illokutionen: Ist die ausgedrückte Sprechereinstellung zur Objektproposition die des Wünschens oder Ersehnens, so liegt eine optative Illokution vor. Dabei ergibt sich aus dem temporalen Aspekt der Objektsituation eine Trennung zwischen realisierbar und nicht realisierbar: Vorzeitige Propositionen wie in (191) sind nicht realisierbar, andere wie in (190) schon.

(190) *Wenn er nur endlich käme!*

(191) *Wären wir doch nie auf diese dumme Idee verfallen!*

(c) Imprekative Illokutionen: Verwünschungen und Verfluchungen kann man sicher in allen Sprachen der Welt aussprechen und in den meisten gibt es wohl auch idiomatisierte Wendungen dafür. Beispiel (192) macht deutlich, dass Imprekative spezielle Optative sind, nämlich Wünsche zum Schaden des Betroffenen.

(192) *Den Kerl soll der Teufel holen!*

Wie im positiven Fall liegt die Vermutung nahe, dass in vielen Fällen magische Vorstellungen eine Rolle spielen. So verwundert es nicht, dass im Türkischen ein heute nur noch imprekativ verwendetes Suffix auf eine alte Futurmarkierung zurückgeht:

(193) Türkisch (Lewis 1967: 115)
 ev-in yikil-asi
 Haus-2POSS zerstört.werd-FUT
 'Möge dein Haus zerstört werden!'

3.2.2. Volitive Illokutionen

(a) Volitive Illokutionen mit allgemeinen Zielen: Volitive Illokutionen, deren Objekte nicht auf epistemisch erweiterte Propositionen eingeschränkt sind, hier kurz nichtepistemische Illokutionen genannt, umfassen ein weites Spektrum von Untertypen. Zu den Kodierungsmitteln gehören satzmodusbestimmende Verbmodi wie Imperativ, Permissiv, Hortativ und Admonitiv. Die grundlegende Dualitätsgruppenstruktur in diesem Bereich lässt sich am Beispiel der folgenden Kategorien erkennen (schwächere Kategorien wie Nahelegen etc. verhalten sich völlig analog):

1. Gebot   Obligativ
2. Erlaubnis   Permissiv
3. Unterlassungsgebot (Verbot) Prohibitiv
4. Unterlassungserlaubnis   Deobligativ

Entsprechende Beispiele im Deutschen sind die folgenden:

(194) *Gehen Sie hin! / Ich bin dafür, dass Sie hingehen.*

(195) *Gehen Sie ruhig hin! / Ich hab nichts dagegen, dass Sie hingehen.*

(196) *Gehen Sie nicht hin! / Ich bin dafür, dass Sie nicht hingehen.*

(197) *Gehen Sie ruhig nicht hin! / Ich hab nichts dagegen, dass Sie nicht hingehen.*

Wie man sieht, ist der imperative Verbmodus in allen Fällen einsetzbar, die negativen Varianten werden mit *nicht*, die schwachen Kategorien durch die Modalpartikel *ruhig* kompositional erzeugt. Der Vergleich mit den Formulierungen nach dem Schrägstrich zeigt die Variationsbreite des Imperativs: Er kann eine emphatische Volitionalität zum Ausdruck bringen ('Ich verlange nachdrücklich ...'), aber eben auch im Sinne der genannten Formulierungen eingesetzt werden, so dass sogar Vorschläge als vorsichtige Grenzfälle von Volitionalität aufgefasst werden können. Dass (194) und (196) in der ersten Variante auch als Ratschlag bzw. Warnung (als Monitiv) interpretierbar sind, liegt einfach daran, dass Sprechervolitionen ja auch durch Identifikation mit den Interessen des Adressaten motiviert sein können.

(198) *Sie sollen hingehen.*

(199) *Sie können hingehen.*

(200) *Sie sollen nicht hingehen.*

(201) *Sie brauchen nicht hinzugehen.*

Der Vergleich von (194)−(197) mit (198)−(201) demonstriert, dass Modalverbkonstruktionen illokutionär mehrdeutig sein können: Neben ihrer Interpretation als Assertionen, d. h. als Aussagen über unabhängig vom Sprechakt bestehende deontische Verhältnisse gibt es auch eine Interpretation als nichtepistemische volitive Illokutionen, durch deren Vollzug solche Verhältnisse erst geschaffen werden (vgl. Abschnitt 3.2.3.).

Die bisherigen Beispiele haben die grundlegende Dualitätsgruppenstruktur nur für den Fall der adressatenbezogenen Verwendungen gezeigt, allerdings unter Vernachlässigung der Numerusdistinktion. Die gleiche Struktur gilt aber auch für singularische und pluralische sprecherbezogene Verwendungen, also Selbstverpflichtung, Selbsterlaubnis, Selbstverbot und Selbstentpflichtung, sowie für Verwendungen, die sich auf Dritte beziehen.

(202) *Ich will hingehen. / Gehn wir hin!*

(203) *Ich erlaube mir hinzugehen. / Wir erlauben uns hinzugehen.*

(204) *Ich will fernbleiben. / Gehn wir nicht hin!*

(205) *Ich erlaube mir fernzubleiben. / Wir erlauben uns fernzubleiben.*

(206) *Er soll hingehen. / Sie sollen hingehen.*

(207) *Er darf hingehen. / Sie dürfen hingehen.*

(208) *Er darf nicht hingehen. / Sie dürfen nicht hingehen.*

(209) *Er braucht nicht hinzugehen. / Sie brauchen nicht hinzugehen.*

Die zweite Formulierung in (202) illustriert die modale Kategorie des Hortativs (auch Adhortativ oder Exhortativ genannt, vgl. Artikel 78 dieses Handbuchs), für deren Ausdruck viele Sprachen eigene Formen bereitstellen (vgl. Sadock & Zwicky 1985: 177).

(b) Volitive Illokutionen mit epistemischen Zielen: (i) Erotetische Illokutionen oder Fragen werden prototypischerweise durch Interrogativsätze kodiert (→ Art. 77), sie drücken Ich-will-wissen-Einstellungen aus und sind daher in monologischen Situatioinen kaum weniger natürlich als in dialogischen. Sie zielen dabei auf eine bestimmte Art von epistemischer Einstellung, die hier als Spezifikationswissen bezeichnet werden soll und die in natürlichen Sprachen durch diejenigen Verwendungen des Verbs für 'wissen' kodiert wird, die als Komplement einen abhängigen Interrogativsatz oder eine entsprechende Nominalphrase verlangen. Spezifikationswissen ist systematisch verwandt mit Propositionswissen, das in den Verwendungen von 'wissen' mit dass-Sätzen kodiert wird, aber klar unterschieden davon. Über Propositionswissen verfügt, wer von der Wahrheit einer wahren Proposition überzeugt ist, oder, etwas schwächer formuliert, wer eine zutreffende Annahme macht. Über Spezifikationswissen verfügt, wer weiß, welche von einer gegebenen Menge von Propositionen wahr und somit dem Propositionswissen verfügbar sind, und welche nicht. Propositionswissen ist Wissen *von* etwas, Spezifikationswissen ist Wissen *über* etwas.

Polaritätserotetische Illokutionen (Ja-Nein-Fragen) zielen auf eine Spezifikation der Polarität (positiv oder negativ) ihres propositionalen Gehalts, wobei modalisierende Antworten als Teilantworten durchaus hilfreich sein können (vgl. Beispiel (210) unten). Da die zugrundeliegende Proposition aber *per definitionem* bereits polarisiert ist, läuft die Spezifikation auf eine Bestätigung oder Umkehrung der tentativ vorgegebenen Polarität hinaus, was sich bei manchen Sprachen in der Wahl der entsprechenden Antwortpartikel widerspiegelt: Während die englischen Partikeln *yes* und *no* die Polarität der Antwort absolut kodieren, teilen die japanischen Partikeln diese nur vermittelt mit, in Form einer Kongruenz (*hai*) oder Disgruenz (*iie*) mit der Polarität der Frage. Die deutschen Antwortpartikeln *ja*, *nein* und *doch* kodieren primär eine Polaritätsopposition und sekundär (nur bei negativen Fragen) eine Kongruenzopposition (211).

(210) *Hat jemand angerufen?* − *Nein. / Ja. / Wahrscheinlich nicht.*

(211) *Hat niemand angerufen?* − *Nein. / Doch. / Wahrscheinlich nicht.*

Da Polaritätsfragen auf eine Spezifikation der Polarität zielen, ist die vorgegebene Polarität eigentlich irrelevant. Aus Ökonomiegründen könnte man also immer positiv fragen, weshalb eine negativ polare Frage als markiert empfunden wird, was häufig im Sinne einer zusätzlichen Information, nämlich einer mitkodierten Antworterwartung, zu interpretieren ist. (211) ist dementsprechend als negative Tendenzfrage zu werten mit der Erwartung, dass sich die formulierte Hypothese als falsch erweist. Bei Sprachen wie dem Chinesischen, die neben den negativ und positiv polaren Ja/Nein-Fragen auch über eine polaritätsneutrale Ja/Nein-Frageskonstruktion verfügen, ist nur bei ersteren eine Interpretation als Tendenzfrage möglich (vgl. Li & Thompson 1984).

Einen besonderen Fall von koordinativer Verknüpfung von Polaritätsfragen stellen die Alternativfragen dar: Obwohl es sich um eine Konjunktion von Fragen handelt, werden sie mit dem disjunktiven Junktor 'oder' formuliert. *n*-fache Alternativfragen zielen auf die Spezifikation derjenigen Propositionen aus den *n* alternativ vorgegebenen, die zutreffen, wobei konversationell impliziert wird (im Sinne einer Griceschen Implikatur), dass dies für genau eine gilt. Bei Konstituentenfragen geht es um die Spezifikation der interrogativ markierten und somit indefinit gehaltenen Konstituenten (das Koreanische und andere Sprachen verwenden Indefinita als Frageproformen) und zwar im Idealfall um die maximal wahrheitsgemäße Spezifikation, d. h. gewusst werden sollen alle und nur die Entitäten, die die gefragte Eigenschaft aufweisen (212), wobei freilich bei Adverbialfragen häufig auch die Exhaustivität in den Hintergrund rückt (213).

(212) *Wer hat angerufen? / Niemand. / Alle deine Freunde. (Und sonst niemand.)*

(213) *Wo gibt es hier einen Briefkasten? / Dort drüben. / An jeder größeren Kreuzung.*

Wird mehr als eine Konstituente als erfragt markiert, so können diese in verschiedenen koordinierten Teilsätzen stehen (koordinierte Konstituentenfragen, (214)) oder im gleichen Satz (Mehrfachkonstituentenfragen (215)):

(214) *Wer hat angerufen, und wann? / Karl, und zwar um sieben.*

(215) *Wer hat wann angerufen? / Karl um sieben, Eva um acht und Max um neun.*

Der Unterschied liegt darin, dass im zweiten Fall konventionell impliziert wird, dass wenigstens zwei verschiedene Anrufer-Zeitpunkt-Paare vorliegen, was im ersten Fall nicht gilt.

Rhetorische Fragen schließlich implizieren konventionell die Negation der betreffenden Proposition ((216): 'Ich bin's nicht.'), bzw. bei Konstituentenfragen die Negation des existentiellen Abschlusses derselben ((217): 'Niemand'), bisweilen auch mit einer prominenten Ausnahme ((218): 'Von keinem andern als vom Wolferl').

(216) *Bin ich denn dein Dienstmädchen?*

(217) *Wer sitzt schon gerne im Gefängnis?*

(218) *Wessen Bild wird das schon sein auf den Mozartkugeln?*

Echofragen zielen primär nicht auf die Objektsituation, sondern auf die Metasituation: Der Sprecher will wissen, was sein Adressat gesagt hat und paraphrasiert daher das, was er verstanden hat, wobei er das unverstanden Gebliebene durch ein Fragewort ersetzt:

(219) A (im Sturm, schreiend): *Binde mir bitte den ... [unverständlich] zu!*
B (auch schreiend): *Ich soll dir den WAS zubinden?*

Eine beträchtliche Anzahl von Sprachen verfügen über die Kategorie der abhängigen Interrogativsätze (Sadock & Zwicky 1985: 186), die traditionell auch indirekte Fragen genannt werden. Nur ein Teil dieser Sätze trägt aber zur Kodierung von internen Illokutionen im hier explizierten Sinn bei, nämlich genau diejenigen, die als Komplemente von *verba dicendi* auftreten. Bei anderen Matrixprädikaten muss man davon ausgehen, dass auch sie sich auf die Spezifikation der maximal zutreffenden aus einer Reihe von gegebenen Propositionen beziehen. Das Beispiel (220) bestätigt dies, besagt es doch, dass die Spezifikation der Gesamtheit der Wahlkampfteilnehmer bestimmt wird durch die Spezifikation der Gesamtheit der erfolgreichen Geldbeschaffer.

(220) *Wer am Wahlkampf teilnimmt, hängt davon ab, wer genügend Geld für seine Wahlkampagne auftreibt.*

(ii) Assertive Illokutionen (Volitive mit hetero-epistemischen Zielen): Es gibt verschiedene Möglichkeiten, die Faktoren, die in einem assertiven Sprechakt zusammenkommen, zu gewichten. Sprachphilosophen tendieren dazu, den Wahrheitsaspekt ins Zentrum ihrer Definitionen zu rücken, in der hier verfolgten Systematik ist dieser Faktor dem Ziel der Veränderung eines epistemischen Zustands untergeordnet. Assertive Illokutionen drücken Ich-will-dass-du-weißt-Einstellungen aus und sind daher in dialogischen Situationen natürlicher als in monologischen. Sie zielen dabei primär auf Propositionswissen, was aufgrund der gerade gegebenen Explikation dieses Begriffs impliziert, dass der Wahrheitsaspekt nicht zu kurz kommt: Wer mit einer Äußerung von (221) eine prototypische Assertion vollzieht, bringt zum Ausdruck, dass er seinen Adressaten zu der zutreffenden Annahme bewegen will, dass Eva angerufen hat, was voraussetzt, dass er, der Sprecher, diese Annahme teilt. Tut er das nicht, so liegt zwar immer noch eine Assertion vor, aber in einer weniger prototypischen Ausprägung, nämlich eine Lüge. Trifft hingegen die Annahme ohne Wissen des Sprechers nicht zu, so liegt eine prototypische Assertion vor, wenn auch eine mit falschem propositionalem Gehalt.

(221) *Eva hat nicht angerufen.*

Wenn bei den Fragen das Spezifikationswissen und bei den Aussagen das Propositionswissen zentral ist, so heißt das nicht, dass das Spezifikationswissen für die letzteren keine Rolle spielt. Schließlich ist jemand, der eine Ich-will-dass-du-weißt-Einstellung zu einem Propositionswissen zum Ausdruck bringt, gut beraten, dies mit dem Spezifikationswissen abzustimmen, zu dem der Adressat eine Ich-will-wissen-Einstellung hat, sowie überhaupt mit den Annahmen und Hypothesen, die der Adressat hegt.

(222) *Hat Eva angerufen?*

(223) *Wer hat angerufen?*

(224) *Was gibt's Neues?*

(225) *Was ist mit Eva?*

Wer (222) fragt, will Spezifikationswissen haben über die Hypothese, dass Eva angerufen hat, und wer (221) antwortet, will, dass sein Adressat weiß, dass diese Hypothese falsch ist. Wer (223) fragt, will Spezifikationswissen haben über die hypothetische Gesamtheit der Anrufer, und wer (221) antwortet, will, dass sein Adressat weiß, dass Eva nicht dazugehört. Dies ist nur eine partielle Antwort und verlangt eine entsprechende zweigipflige Intonation mit einem ausgeprägten Tief-Hoch-Wechsel von der ersten zur zweiten Silbe und einem umgekehrten Wechsel von der vierten zur fünften Silbe. Wer (224) fragt, will Spezifikationswissen haben über die hypothetische Gesamtheit der Neuigkeiten, und wer (221) antwortet, will, dass sein Adressat weiß, dass Evas fehlender Anruf dazugehört. Wer (225) fragt, will Spezifikationswissen haben über die hypothetische Gesamtheit der relevanten Informationen über Eva, und wer (221) antwortet, will, das sein Adressat weiß, dass ihr fehlender Anruf dazugehört.

Wenn Sprecher die Form ihrer Assertionen auf die von Adressaten gehegten Annahmen und Hypothesen abstimmen, so braucht ihr Wissen darüber nicht nur auf Fragen des anderen zu beruhen, auch selbsterzeugte Erwartungen können diese Rolle spielen. Wer zum Beispiel (226) erzählt, schafft damit einen Hintergrund, vor dem eine Sperrsatzformulierung wie (227) eine effektvollere Fortsetzung darstellt als (221).

(226) *Den ganzen Abend saß ich am Telefon und wartete auf einen Anruf von ihr.*

(227) *Wer nicht anrief, war Eva.*

Soviel zu den externen Assertionen, die mit Hilfe von unterschiedlich strukturierten unabhängigen Deklarativsätzen vollzogen werden. Abhängige Deklarativsätze dienen zur Kodierung von internen Assertionen, allerdings gilt dies wie bei ihren interrogativen Gegenstücken und den internen Fragen nur dann, wenn sie von *verba dicendi* abhängen, ansonsten fungieren sie als Kodierung für propositionale Gehalte beliebiger passender Prädikate oder Relationen.

Abschließend sei noch auf eine interessante Asymmetrie bei der Verwendung der Konstruktion 'Du sollst (nicht) wissen, dass …' hingewiesen. Eine Äußerung von (229) unten kann, einen rationalen Sprecher vorausgesetzt, nur so interpretiert werden, dass jemand anderes als der Sprecher (und natürlich der Adressat) Träger der behaupteten volitiven Einstellung ist, wogegen bei einer Äußerung von (228) eine solche Einschränkung nicht gilt. Nach der hier vertretenen Auffassung von Assertion macht der Sprecher, wenn er sich selbst als Wollenden meint, nur etwas explizit, was im Falle einer bloßen Behauptung von (230) implizit ausgedrückt bliebe, freilich mit einem wichtigen Unterschied in den Wahrheitsbedingungen: Wer (228) in diesem Sinne assertiert, sagt damit erst dann etwas Wahres, wenn er die behauptete Einstellung tatsächlich hat (was u. a. die Wahrheit von (230) impliziert), während die Wahrheit einer Assertion von (230) nur von der Identität des Autobesitzers abhängt.

(228) *Du sollst wissen, dass das Auto nicht mir gehört.*

(229) *Du sollst nicht wissen, dass das Auto nicht mir gehört.*

(230) *Das Auto gehört nicht mir.*

3.2.3. Deklarationen (selbstverifizierende Illokutionen)

Eine Objektsituation kann mit ihrer Metasituation partiell koinzidieren, nämlich dann, wenn in der Sprechsituation über eben diese Situation gesprochen wird. Dann stimmen Objektzeit und Metazeit überein und das gleiche gilt für Objektort und Metaort. Fallen obendrein auch noch charakterisierender Begriff und gegebenenfalls Kern von Objekt- und Metasituation zusammen, so hat man es mit einer selbstverifizierenden Äußerung zu tun. Solche Äußerungen werden in der Sprechakttheorie als Deklarationen bezeichnet, und können mit Sätzen wie (231) oder (232) vollzogen werden:

(231) *Ich bitte Sie, nicht zu rauchen.*

(232) *Es wird gebeten, nicht zu rauchen.*

Beschreibt eine Äußerung von (231) die Metasituation, so charakterisiert deren Kern, der Sprecher, sich darin als einer, der den Adressaten bittet, nicht zu rauchen. Da eine solche Selbstcharakterisierung aber normalerweise auch als Bitte gilt, ist sie meist zutreffend und der Sprecher assertiert etwas Wahres über sich und damit die Situation. Beschreibt eine Äußerung von (232) die Metasituation, so charakterisiert sie diese als eine, in der eine Bitte, nicht zu rauchen, in Kraft ist. Da eine solche Charakterisierung aber nicht nur als Bericht über eine solche Bitte, sondern auch als Ausführung einer solchen interpretiert werden kann, ist sie meist zutreffend und der Sprecher assertiert etwas Wahres über die Situation. Eine Deklaration soll hier also (gegen Searle 1989) als derjenige Spezialfall einer Assertion aufgefasst werden, bei dem die Wahr- oder Falschheit dessen, was gewusst werden soll, abhängt vom Ge- oder Misslingen der Assertion. Gewöhnliche, nicht-deklarierende Assertionen, wie sie oben diskutiert wurden, sind also solche, bei denen die Wahr- oder Falschheit des propositionalen Gehalts unabhängig ist vom Vollzug der Assertion.

Man kann unterscheiden zwischen performativen und resultativen (antizipierenden) Deklarationen. Bei ersteren ist eine Verdeutlichung durch *hiermit* immer möglich (233), bei letzteren wirkt sie eher fehl am Platze (234).

(233) *Ich erlaube Ihnen jetzt (und hiermit), Ihre Sicherheitsgurte zu lösen.*

(234) *Sie können jetzt (?und hiermit) Ihre Sicherheitsgurte lösen.*

(235) [Bei einem Gesellschaftsspiel] *Max, du bist dran.*

Ob (235) als resultative Deklaration zu interpretieren ist, hängt von den jeweiligen Spielregeln ab: Wenn ein Spieler erklären muss, dass er keine Aktionen mehr vornehmen möchte, damit der nächste zum Zug kommen kann, so ist eine solche Interpretation möglich, sonst nicht. (235) exemplifiziert übrigens eine zweite resultative Deklaration: Der Vokativ *Max* ist ja nichts anderes als eine Ernennung von Max zum Adressaten und somit durch 'Max ist mein Adressat (für das Folgende)' paraphrasierbar. Die explizite modale Struktur dessen, was eine Äußerung von (235) ausdrückt, lässt sich daher wie folgt umschreiben: 'Ihr sollt wissen, dass Max mein Adressat ist, und Max soll wissen, dass er dran ist'.

3.3. Modalisierte Illokutionen

Illokutionen sind Handlungstypen mit modalisierten propositionalen Gehalten: Die bloße Darstellung einer Proposition gilt interessanterweise nicht als vollständiger illokutionärer Akt. Die minimal erforderliche illokutionstypdefinierende Modalisierung kann aber noch weiter elaboriert werden. In diesem Fall soll von modalisierten Illokutionen gesprochen werden, obwohl diese Redeweise etwas irreführend ist, da nicht in allen Fällen die Gesamtheit der Faktoren, in die der Illokutionstyp zerlegt werden kann, modalisiert wird. Die Kodierungsmittel für Illokutionstypmodalisierung, lexikalische, phrasale und sententiale Adverbialkonstruktionen, zeichnen sich alle durch einen geringen Grad an Intergriertheit in die Satzstruktur aus. Bezogen auf das Englische sprechen Quirk et al. (1985) deshalb von *disjuncts*, in dem hier gemeinten Fall genauer von *style disjuncts*.

3.3.1. Qualitative Illokutionstypmodifikationen

(236) *Ehrlich gesagt, Ihre Krawatte ist wohl etwas gewagt.*

(237) *Offen gestanden, eine solche Behauptung würde ich nie aufstellen.*

(238) *Im Ernst: Wollen Sie wirklich zurücktreten?*

Wer (236) äußert, macht nicht nur eine Aussage, er qualifiziert diese Assertion zugleich als eine ehrliche, d. h. er bringt nicht nur zum Ausdruck, dass der Adressat wissen soll, dass seine Krawatte gewagt ist, sondern auch, dass er wissen soll, dass dieses Zum-Ausdruck-Bringen ehrlich gemeint ist. Ähnliches gilt für (237): Der Adressat soll auch wissen, dass der Sprecher seine Assertion als offenes Geständnis gewertet wissen will. Schließlich bringt der Fragende in (238) einerseits zum Ausdruck, dass er wissen will, ob sein Adressat wirklich zurücktreten will, andererseits aber auch, dass der andere wissen soll, dass der Sprecher dies im Ernst meint.

3.3.2. Konditionale Illokutionsmodifikationen

Ist die Protasis einer Konditionalkonstruktion ganz aus dem Kernsatz hinausverlagert, folgt ihr also etwa im Deutschen ein Verb-Zweit-Deklarativsatz, so kann sie als Illokutionskonditionalisierung interpretiert werden. Wer z. B. (239) äußert, bringt damit zum Ausdruck, dass sein Adressat wissen soll, dass er, falls er Durst hat, wissen soll, dass im Kühlschrank Bier ist. Ist die Protasis falsch, so ist also keineswegs der ganze Sprechakt nicht vollzogen, es entfällt nur der Wunsch des Sprechers, den Adressaten die Apodosis wissen zu lassen. (Er lässt sie ihn ja trotzdem wissen, aber in diesem Falle ungewollt.)

(239) *Wenn Sie Durst haben, im Kühlschrank ist noch Bier.*

3.3.3. Kausale Illokutionsmodifikatioinen

Jemand, der einen Satz wie (240) äußert, bringt damit nicht nur seinen Willen zum Ausdruck, dass sein Adressat weiß, wo der Whisky ist, der Adressat soll auch wissen, dass dieser Willen seinen Grund hat in der freundlichen Bitte des anderen. Die Struktur kausaler Illokutionsmodifikationen entspricht also völlig der ihrer konditionalen Gegenstücke.

(240) *Weil Sie mich gar so freundlich bitten, hier ist der Whisky.*

3.3.4. Deontische Illokutionsmodifikationen

Deontische Illokutionsmodifikation kann nur kata- oder anaphorisch oder bei Deklarationen auftreten. Die Aussage über die Hartnäckigkeit des Adressaten wird in (241) angekündigt als eine, um die der Sprecher nicht herumkann, die Behauptung, dass der Referent schwierig sei in (242) erfährt eine nachträgliche Qualifikation als zulässig. Deklarierende Äußerungen von (243) und (244) werden im allgemeinen als Bitten interpretiert. Zusätzlich drückt der Sprecher im ersteren Fall aus, dass ihm keine andere Wahl bleibt, als diese Bitte auszusprechen, während er im letzteren Fall betont, dass nichts dem entgegensteht, dass er eine solche Bitte ausspricht. Dies ist sinnvoll vor allem in Kontexten, wo eine Bitte möglicherweise als unangemessen eingestuft werden könnte, allgemeiner in hochgradig formellen Situationen, wo alles verboten ist, was nicht ausdrücklich erlaubt ist.

(241) *Ich muss schon sagen: Sie sind ganz schön hartnäckig.*

(242) *Er ist ein wenig schwierig, kann man sagen.*

(243) *Ich muss Sie bitten, das Rauchverbot zu beachten.*

(244) *Ich darf Sie bitten, hereinzukommen.*

4. Die Interaktion modaler Kategorien mit anderen

4.1. Modalität und Polarität

Über den Status der Polarität als Semimodalität und die Rolle der Negation bei der Konstitution von Dualitätsgruppen wurde bereits ausführlich gehandelt. An dieser Stelle soll noch ein Hinweis auf die Existenz polaritätssensitiver Modaloperatoren nachgetragen werden. Das deutsche Verb *brauchen* in seiner Valenz mit einer *zu*-Infinitivergänzung ist so ein Fall. Mit Akkusativergänzungen drückt es aus, dass etwas nötig ist ((245)–(247)), in der erwähnten Valenz hingegen zusammen mit einem negativen Element Unnötigkeit, wobei der Negator explizit (wie in (249)) oder implizit (wie in (250); *nur* heißt ja 'nicht mehr als') sein kann, aber nicht fehlen darf (vgl. (248)):

(245) *Er braucht Lob.*

(246) *Er braucht es, dass man ihn lobt.*

(247) *Er braucht es, gelobt zu werden.*

(248) **Er braucht gelobt zu werden.*

(249) *Er braucht nicht gelobt zu werden.*

(250) *Er braucht nur gelobt zu werden, schon ist er glücklich.*

4.2. Modalität und Temporalität

Der Status des Tempus als Semimodalität wurde bereits oben unter § 2.1.3 diskutiert, hier sei nur noch ergänzend auf die Rolle hingewiesen, die Tempus bei der Auflösung von modaler Mehrdeutigkeit spielt. Das deutsche Modalverb *müssen* zum Beispiel ist zwar im Prinzip mehrdeutig mit einer deontischen und einer evidentiellen, genauer inferentiellen Lesart, aber die Tempuswahl lässt meistens nur eine Interpretation zu. Da niemand verpflichtet werden kann, etwas getan zu haben, ist (252) nur inferentiell interpretierbar, während für (251) kaum eine andere Deutung als eine deontische in Frage kommt.

(251) *Du musst das Licht anlassen.*

(252) *Du musst das Licht angelassen haben.*

4.3. Modalität und Aspektualität

Bei der Unterscheidung von subpropositionaler und propositionaler Modalität unter 1.2. wurde bereits darauf hingewiesen, an dieser Stelle soll noch einmal daran erinnert werden, dass bei ersterer, die ja auch Eventitätsmodalität genannt wurde, die Aspektualität oder der Eventitätstyp stets unverändert bleibt, während bei letzterer die Aspektualitäten der Charakterisierungen von Mutter- und Tochterproposition logisch unabhängig voneinander sind: Hungrig sein ist ein Zustand, sagen, dass man hungrig ist, ist ein Ereignis; zerbrechen ist ein Ereignis; zerbrechen können oder zerbrechlich sein ein Zustand.

Chung & Timberlake (1985) geben einen typologischen Überblick über die Kategorientrias Tempus, Aspekt und Modus.

4.4. Modalität und Diathese

In § 2 wurde unter der Bezeichnung Doppelmodalisierung ein Phänomen angesprochen, bei dem Werte aus drei logisch unabhängigen Variationsdimensionen, nämlich propositionale Modalität, Diathese und Eventitätsmodalität eine interessante Verbindung eingehen. Dieses Phänomen muss hier, wo es um die Interaktion modaler mit anderen Kategorien geht, aus systematischen Gründen noch einmal angesprochen werden. Mit Doppelmodalisierung wurde der Sachverhalt bezeichnet, dass gewisse propositionale Modaloperatoren aus Gründen, die wohl noch nicht recht verstanden sind, nicht oder nur sehr schwer ohne eine subpropositionale Modalisierung verwendbar sind.

Im Deutschen sind Medium und modaler Infinitiv Konstruktionen, die eine nichtaktivische Diathese zugleich mit einer schwachen Modalisierung (vgl. auch § 2.4.2 Allgemeine Dispositionsmodalitäten) kodieren. Je nach Bezug der dabei im allgemeinen erforderlichen zusätzlichen Eventitätsmodalisierung sind dabei zwei Fälle zu unterscheiden. Innere Eventitätsmodalisierung liegt bei Beispiel (253) vor, wie der Vergleich mit (254) und (255) zeigt.

(253) *Dieses Buch liest sich rasch.* (... ist rasch zu lesen. / ... lässt sich rasch lesen.)

(254) **Es ist rasch möglich, dieses Buch zu lesen.*

(255) *Es ist möglich, dieses Buch rasch zu lesen.*

Anders beim Beispiel (256), wo der Vergleich mit (257) und (258) deutlich macht, dass eine äußere Eventitätsmodalisierung, also eine subpropositionale Qualifikation der Möglichkeit, vorliegt:

(256) *Diese Frage beantwortet sich leicht.* (... ist leicht zu beantworten. / ... lässt sich leicht beantworten.)

(257) Es ist leicht möglich, diese Frage zu beantworten.

(258) *Es ist möglich, diese Frage leicht zu beantworten.

Bei manchen Prädikaten sind beide Skopusmöglichkeiten offen, wie (259)–(261) belegen:

(259) Hierher findet sich's leicht. (... ist leicht zu finden. / ... lässt es sich leicht finden.)

(260) Es ist leicht möglich, hierher zu finden.

(261) Es ist möglich, leicht hierher zu finden.

4.5. Modalität und Numerus

Die für die Paradigmen von Personalpronomina zentralen Kategorien Person und Numerus scheinen wenig geeignet zu sein für eine Interaktion mit modalen Kategorien. Dennoch gibt es auch hier Fälle von Abhängigkeit. So zerfallen die deutschen jussiven, also für die Kodierung von Aufforderungen spezialisierten, Satztypen in die eigentlichen Imperativsätze, die einer Verwendung des Proximalpronomens *du* entsprechen, und die Distaljussive, die von dem verwendeten Distalpronomen *Sie* die Transnumeralität erben: Grammatisch handelt es sich um Pluralformen, semantisch ist aber die Kardinalitätsdistinktion zwischen eins und mehr als eins neutralisiert.

4.6. Modalität und Person

Eine interessante Interaktion von evidentieller Modalität und Person berichtet Lowe (1972) für das Nambiquara: Die drei Kategorien direkte, inferentielle und quotative Evidenz werden jeweils noch einmal unterteilt nach dem jeweils involvierten Subjekt. Je nachdem, ob der Wahrnehmende, der Schlussfolgernde oder der Adressat der fraglichen Mitteilung nur der Sprecher ist, oder der Sprecher zusammen mit dem Adressaten, müssen verschiedene Formen gewählt werden, was natürlich für argumentative Diskurse von Vorteil ist, da sofort erkennbar wird, wo Konsens angenommen wird, und wo nicht.

5. Zusammenfassung

Ausgehend von der Beobachtung, dass prototypische Modalisierungen Einbettungen von Propositionen in übergeordnete Zusammenhänge sind, wurde eine sehr weite Auffassung von Modalität skizziert und in einer Gesamtübersicht dargestellt: Modale Kategorien sind immer Kategorien der Einordnung einer Proposition in etwas Übergeordnetes, sei dies nun eine bloße Charakterisierung wie bei den externen, ausschließlich illokutionären Modalitäten, oder eine volle Mutterproposition, wie dies bei den internen Modalitäten der Fall ist, zu denen die Sprechaktbeschreibungen gehören, aber auch die Modalverbpropositionen, die die verschiedensten Arten von Möglichkeiten und Notwendigkeiten zum Ausdruck bringen.

Bei der Untergliederung hat sich herausgestellt, dass dabei zwei interessante partielle Parallelitäten auftreten, und zwar erstens zwischen den Handlungs- und den allgemeinen Modalitäten und zweitens zwischen den Einstellungs- und den Illokutionsmodalitäten: Die klassischen modallogischen Kategorien wurden den allgemeinen Modalitäten zugeordnet und erwiesen sich in ihrer Struktur weitgehend als Abstraktionen aus Kategorien der Handlungsmodalitäten; die Beobachtung, dass gewisse volitionale und epistemische Einstellungsmodalitäten auch zur Sprechaktbeschreibung verwendet werden, wurde zum Anlass genommen, Illokutionscharakterisierungen und damit Satzmodi aufzufassen als dekomponierbar in eine Handlungskomponente des Zum-Ausdruck-Bringens und in eben solche Einstellungsmodalitäten. Durch diesen Nachweis eines Zusammenhangs zwischen den prototypischen modalen Kategorien der Satzmodi einerseits und den von den Modalverben kodierten Möglichkeiten und Notwendigkeiten andererseits konnte gezeigt werden, dass hinter der oberflächlichen Heterogenität der modalen Kategorien doch eine tiefere Einheit verborgen ist.

Angesichts der Vielfalt an modalen Kategorien, die eine so weite Auffassung des Begriffes mit sich bringt, verwundert es nicht, dass die Kodierungsmittel für diese Kategorien eine noch größere Vielfalt aufweisen, von der Nullkodierung bei Prädikaten mit modalen Interpretationen über die Affixe und die Modalverben bis zu elaborierten Matrixsätzen mit einer Reihe anderer Argumente neben der modalisierten Proposition. Typologische Befunde zu ausgewählten modalen Kategorien wie den Satzmodi oder der Evidentialität oder den partizipanteninternen und -externen sowie den epistemischen Modalitäten liegen ebenso vor (Sadock & Zwicky 1985, Chafe & Nichols 1986, van der Auwera & Plungian 1998) wie Globalübersichten über die zentralen modalen Kategorien (Palmer 1986, Bybee & Fleischman 1995), was fehlt, sind Übersichten über Gesamtheiten von modalen Subsystemen in verschiedenen Sprachen, die zum Beispiel den Eindruck präzisieren oder korrigieren könnten, dass die modalen Subsysteme in einigen Sprachen stärker volitionalitätsorientiert sind, in anderen Sprachen hingegen stärker normenorientiert, und dass das Deutsche den ersteren Typ repräsentiert, das Lateinische den letzteren.

6. Zitierte Literatur

Barnes, J. 1984. „Evidentials in the Tuyuca verb". *Internatonal Journal of American Linguistics* 50: 255–271.

Bartsch, Renate. 1972. *Adverbialsemantik.* Frankfurt am Main: Athenäum.

Bybee, Joan L. & Fleischman, Suzanne (eds.) 1995. *Modality in Grammar and Discourse.* Amsterdam: Benjamins.

Bybee, Joan L. & Perkins, Revere & Pagliuca, William. 1994. *The Evolution of Grammar: Tense, Aspect and Modality in the Languages of the World.* Chicago: University of Chicago Press.

Chafe, Wallace & Nichols, Johanna (eds.) 1986. *Evidentiality: The Linguistic Coding of Epistemology.* Norwood, NJ: Ablex.

Chung, Sandra & Timberlake, Alan. 1985. „Tense, Aspect, and Mood". In: Shopen, Timothy (ed.). *Language Typology and Syntactic Description. Vol. III: Grammatical Categories and the Lexicon.* Cambridge: Cambridge University Press, 202–258.

Cole, Peter. 1982. *Imbabura Quechua.* Amsterdam: North Holland.

Comrie, Bernard, 1987. „Conditionals: A Typology". In: Traugott, Elisabeth C., et al. (eds.) *On Conditionals.* Cambridge: Cambridge University Press, 77–99.

Comrie, Bernard & Smith, Norval. 1977. „Lingua Descriptive Studies: Questionnaire". *Lingua* 42: 1–72.

Deuchar, Margaret. 1984. *British Sign Language.* London: Routledge.

Donaldson, Tamsin. 1980. *Ngiyambaa: the language of the Wangaaybuwan.* Cambridge: Cambridge University Press.

Enç, Mürvet. 1996. „Tense and Modality". In: Lappin, Shalom (ed.). *The Handbook of Contemporary Semantic Theory.* London: Blackwell.

Givón, Talmy. 1990. *Syntax. A functional-typological introduction. Vol. II.* Amsterdam: Benjamins.

Haan, Ferdinand de. 1997. *The interaction of modality and negation. A typological study.* New York: Garland.

Hengeveld, Kees. 2000. „Mood and Modality". In: Booij, Geert & Lehmann, Christian & Mugdan, Joachim (eds.). *Morphology: A Handbook of Inflection and Word Formation.* Berlin: de Gruyter.

Jakobson, Roman. 1971. „Shifters, Verbal Categories, and the Russian Verb". In: Jakobson, Roman. *Selected Writings II: Word and Language.* Den Haag: Mouton.

Janzen, Terry & Shaffer, Barbara. 2001. „Gestures as the Substrate in the process of ASL Grammaticization". In: Cormier, Kearsy, et al. (eds.). *The Effects of Modality on Language and Linguistic Theory.* Austin, TX: Texas Linguistic Forum.

Kemmerling, Andreas. 1999. „Gricy actions". In: Cosenza, Giovanna (ed.). *Paul Grices Heritage.* Turnhout: Brepols.

Kratzer, Angelika. 1991. „Modality". In: Stechow, Arnim von & Wunderlich, Dieter (eds.). *Semantik/Semantics. Ein internationales Handbuch der zeitgenössischen Forschung/An International Handbook of Contemporary Research.* Berlin: de Gruyter.

Lang, Ewald. 1983. „Einstellungsausdrücke und ausgedrückte Einstellungen". In: Ruzicka, Rudolf & Motsch, Wolfgang (Hgg.). *Untersuchungen zur Semantik.* Berlin: Akademieverlag, 305–341.

Lazard, Gilbert. 1999. „Mirativity, evidentiality, mediativity, or other?". *Linguistic Typology* 3: 91–109.

Lewis, G. L. 1967. *Turkish Grammar.* Oxford: Oxford University Press.

Li, Charles N. & Thompson, Sandra A. 1984. „Mandarin". In: Chisholm, William S., jr. (ed.). *Initerrogativity.* Amsterdam: John Benjamins, 47–61.

Löbner, Sebastian. 1990. *Wahr neben falsch: duale Operatoren als die Quantoren natürlicher Sprache.* Tübingen: Niemeyer.

Lowe, I. 1972. „On the relation of the formal and the sememic matrices with illustrations from Nambiquara". *Foundations of Language* 8, 360–390.

Lyons, John. 1977. *Semantics.* 2 vols. Cambridge: Cambridge University Press.

Montague, Richard. 1974. *Formal Philosophy.* New Haven: Yale University Press.

Nedjalkov, Igor. 1997. *Evenki.* London: Routledge.

Noonan, Michael. 1985. „Complementation". In: Shopen, Timothy (ed.). *Language typology and syntactic description. Vol. II: Complex constructions.* Cambridge: Cambridge University Press, 42–140.

Palmer, Frank Robert. 1986. *Mood and Modality.* Cambridge: Cambridge University Press.

Payne, John R. 1985. „Negation". In: Shopen, Timothy (ed.). *Language Typology and Syntactic Description. Vol. I: Clause structure.* Cambridge: Cambridge University Press 1985, 197–242.

Payne, Thomas E. 1997. *Describing morphosyntax. A guide for field linguists.* Cambridge: Cambridge University Press.

Portner, Paul. 1999. „The semantics of mood". In: *Glot International* 4.1: 3−9.

Quirk, Randolph & Greenbaum, Sidney & Leech, Geoffrey & Svartvik, Jan. 1985. *A Comprehensive Grammar of the English Language.* London: Longman.

Rescher, Nicholas. 1968. *Topics in Philosophical Logic.* Dordrecht: Reidel.

Sadock, Jerrold M. & Zwicky, Arnold M. 1985. „Speech Act Distinctions in Syntax". In: Shopen, Timothy (ed.). *Language Typology and Syntactic Description. Vol. I: Clause structure.* Cambridge: Cambridge University Press, 155−196.

Searle, John R. 1969. *Speech acts. An essay in the philosophy of language.* Cambridge: Cambridge University Press.

Searle, John R. 1975. „A Taxonomy of Illocutionary Acts". In: Gunderson, K. (ed.), *Language, Mind, and Knowledge.* Minneapolis: University of Minnesota Press. [Reprinted in: Searle 1979, 1−29, and under the more appropriate title „A Classification of Illocutionary Acts" in: *Language in Society* 5 (1976), 1−23.]

Searle, John R. 1979. *Expression and Meaning.* Cambridge: Cambridge University Press.

Searle, John R. 1989. „How Performatives Work". In: *Linguistics and Philosophy* 12, 535−558.

Smeets, Ineke. 1989. *A Mapuche Grammar.* Doctoral Dissertation, Rijksuniversiteit te Leiden. Leiden.

Talmy, Leonard. 1988. „Force Dynamics in Language and Cognition". *Cognitive Science* 12: 49−100.

Trask, Robert Lawrence. 1993. *A Dictionary of Grammatical Terms in Linguistics.* London: Routledge.

van der Auwera, Johan & Plungian, Vladimir A. 1998. „Modality's semantic map". *Linguistic Typology* 2: 79−124.

Wittgenstein, Ludwig. 1960. *Schriften I: Philosophische Untersuchungen.* Frankfurt am Main: Suhrkamp.

Zaefferer, Dietmar. 1983. „The Semantics of Non-Declaratives: Investigating German Exclamatories". In: Bäuerle, Rainer, et al. (eds.). *Meaning, Use, and Interpretation of Language.* Berlin: de Gruyter, 466−490.

Zaefferer, Dietmar. 1990. „On the Coding of Sentential Modality". In: Bechert, Johannes & Bernini, Giuliano & Buridant, Claude (eds.). *Toward a Typology of European Languages. Proceedings of the Workshop held at Consiglio Nazionale delle Ricerche, Rome, 7−9 January 1988.* Berlin: Mouton de Gruyter, 215−237.

Zaefferer, Dietmar. 1991. „Conditionals and Unconditionals: Cross-linguistic and Logical Aspects". In: Zaefferer, Dietmar (ed.). *Semantic Universals and Universal Semantics.* Berlin: Foris 210−236.

Zaefferer, Dietmar. 2001. „Deconstructing a classical classification: A typological look at Searle's concept of illocution type". *Revue internationale de philosophie.*

Dietmar Zaefferer,
Ludwig-Maximilians-Universität München
(Deutschland)

61. Number

1. Nominal and verbal number
2. Number values
3. Implicational claims (the Number Hierarchy)
4. The nominals involved
5. The expression of number
6. Conclusion
7. Special abbreviations
8. References

1. Nominal and verbal number

What type of category is number? The obvious answer, certainly for speakers of Indo-European languages, is that it is a nominal category, affecting primarily nouns and pronouns. The difference between *head* and *heads*, or the Russian equivalents *golova* and *golovy* is the number of heads involved.

Number may be shown by verbs too in English (and Russian, and many other languages):

(1)   *my friend speaks Russian*

(2)   *my friends speak Russian*

Though number is marked on the verb here as well as on the noun, the essential difference between (1) and (2) is, of course, the number of friends involved. The type of number we are dealing with can be seen particularly clearly in these examples:

(3)   *the sheep drinks from the stream*

(4)   *the sheep drink from the stream*

Though the form of the noun does not change, and the marker of number is on the verb, it still indicates the number of sheep involved. (Example (4) cannot be used in English for the situation in which *one* sheep drinks several times.) In other words, we have nominal number which is expressed on the verb (usually, in English, in addition to being expressed on the noun). Number in English is obligatory (there is no form of a noun which allows us to avoid specifying the number, instead we have to indicate one or more than one), it is relevant to syntax, as the agreement facts show, and it is largely regular (examples like *friend ~ friends*, greatly outnumber those like *sheep ~ sheep* and *criterion ~ criteria*). Thus number is an inflectional category in English: *friend* (singular) and *friends* (plural) are forms of the same lexical item FRIEND.

There are many languages which are broadly comparable to English in this respect. But there are also many languages in which number is fundamentally different: in particular it may be not a nominal category but a verbal one. Moreover, it is often optional, rather than obligatory, and highly irregular, which suggest that it is then a derivational category. For an example we turn to Rapanui (the language of Easter Island, one of the Oceanic languages within Austronesian):

(5) Rapanui (Veronica Du Feu, personal communication)
     ruku
     'dive'

(6) *ruku ruku*
     'go diving'

The form in (6) implies more than one dive, but not necessarily more than one diver. The event is in a sense plural and reduplication is used here to indicate verbal plurality. There are other possibilities for verbal number, the main one being that it may be concerned with the number of participants (thus several eating together may count as different from one eating alone). An important account is that of Durie (1986). Verbal number is found in many linguistic areas: it is particularly widespread in North America (Mithun 1988: 231). It is also found in the South Central Dravidian group of languages of southern India (Steever 1987) and in many languages of Africa (Brooks 1991), the Chadic group being particularly well documented (Newman 1990: 53–87). Verbal number may be restricted to relatively small numbers of verbs, and it rarely shows more than a two-way distinction (one versus several). For typological work it is vital to be clear what type of number is being discussed. Since nominal number shows greater variation, we shall concentrate on that type. The material presented here in summary form is treated more extensively in Corbett (2000).

2. Number values

We now consider the possible values for nominal number. The common ones are singular and plural (as in English and Russian), but there are several more. First, we should note that sometimes number can be 'avoided' as it were, that is there are forms which are outside the number system. An example is the Cushitic language Bayso which at the last count had a few hundred speakers on Gidicho Island in Lake Abaya (southern Ethiopia) and on the western shore of the lake. In Bayso, nouns have a form which represents what we shall call 'general' meaning (the German tradition is to call such forms 'transnumeral'), that is, it is non-committal as to number (Corbett & Hayward 1987). *Lúban* 'lion' denotes a particular type of animal, but the use of this form does not commit the speaker to a number of lions — there could be one or more than that. Other forms are available for indicating reference specifically to one or to more than one lion when required, as we shall see in § 2.4.

(7) Bayso (Dick Hayward, personal communications, Corbett & Hayward 1987)
     lúban   foofe
     lion.GENERAL watched.1.SG
     'I watched lion' (it could be one, or more than that.)

While it is rare to have separate general forms, there are very many languages which can express general meaning, but with a form shared with the singular. This more usual situation, with general identical to singular, can be illustrated from the Cushitic language Arbore. We find pairs like the following:

(8) Arbore (Hayward 1984: 159–183)
     general   *plural*
     kér 'dog(s)'   *ker-ó* 'dogs'
     garlá 'needle(s)' *garlá-n* 'needles'

It is important to stress that, though the morphology may appear comparable to English, the semantics of the forms is quite different: *keró* guarantees more than one dog, while *kér* does not imply only one: it might be one, it might be more than that. (There are other, less frequent number pairings in Arbore.) Systems like this, in which number is not an obligatory category (and so is arguably not inflectional) are common in the world's languages.

From now on we shall assume that number is to be expressed, and consider the possible values of the category.

2.1. The plural

The simplest system, and a common one, has an opposition:

(9)   singular plural

2.2. The dual

The dual refers to two distinct real world entities. If a dual is added to our previous system, we have another common system:

(10)   singular dual plural

Examples can be found all over the world, for instance, in Upper Sorbian, an endangered West Slavonic language. Some of the forms are given in Table 61.1.

It is important to note that the introduction of the dual has an effect on the plural. More generally, a change in system gives the plural a different meaning; if the system is singular-dual-plural, the plural is for three or more real world entities, a point made by Saussure (1971: 161). The dual has long fascinated linguists, a notable early example being Humboldt; see Plank (1989) for discussion and references.

2.3. The trial

Just as the dual is for two, the trial is for referring to three distinct real world entities. Adding it to systems like those just discussed gives the following system of number values:

(11)   singular dual trial plural

Such a system is found in Larike, a Central Moluccan language with 8–10,000 speakers on the western tip of Ambon Island, Central Maluku, Indonesia. Central Moluccan forms part of the Central Malayo-Polynesian subgroup of Austronesian; the data are from Laidig & Laidig (1990). Larike distinguishes singular/dual/trial/plural in its free pronouns (though there are no third person pronouns for non-human referents):

(12)   Larike (Laidig & Laidig 1990)
        Duma hima aridu   naʔa
        house that 1.TRIAL.EXCL own.it
        'We three own that house.'

It also makes these distinctions in its various series of pronominal affixes:

(13)   *Kalu iridu-ta-ʔeu,   au-na-wela*
        if   2.TRIAL-NEG-go   1.SG-IRR-go.home
        'If you three don't want to go, I'm going home.'

It is interesting to note that the dual and trial forms originate from the numerals 'two' and 'three', and that the plural comes historically from 'four'. Such developments are fairly common in Austronesian languages. There are also numerous instances of former trials becoming paucals. This is a potential hazard for the typologist: the term 'trial' is sometimes used according to the form of the inflections (derived historically from the numeral three), even when the forms are currently used for small groups including those greater than three (and so are paucals) and sometimes the term is used according to meaning (for genuine trials). This shows the need for typologists to be careful in the use of terms in this area. The Larike trial is a genuine trial:

"... it should be stated explicitly that Larike trials are true trial forms. In other words, they represent the quantity three, and are not used to refer to the more vague notion of several, as is a paucal or limited plural." (Laidig & Laidig 1990: 92)

Table 61.1: The dual in Upper Sorbian (Stone 1993)

singular	dual	plural
ja 'I'	*mój* 'we two'	*my* 'we'
ty 'you'	*wój* 'you two'	*wy* 'you (all)'
hród 'palace, castle'	*hrodaj* 'two palaces'	*hrody* 'palaces'
dźěłam '(I) work'	*dźěłamoj* '(we two) work'	*dźěłamy* '(we) work'

The Larike trial is 'facultative', a question to which we return in § 3.2 below. Ngan'gityemerri (a Daly language with two dialects, Ngan'gikurunggurr and Ngan'giwumirri, and with 100 speakers, 300 miles SW of Darwin, Australia) has a trial, strictly for three (Nicholas Reid 1990: 118–119 and personal communication) as does Marrithiyel, another Daly family language (Green 1989: 136–139).

These then are languages with genuine trials, appropriate just when referring to three entities. There is a question as to whether there are also languages with quadrals (for reference to four entities). However, having raised the issue of paucals, we shall first continue the analysis of these, and only then return to the question of quadrals.

2.4. The paucal

The paucal is used to refer to a small number of distinct real world entities. It is similar to the English quantifier 'a few' in meaning, particularly in that there is no specific upper bound that can be put on its use. (Its lower bound, like that of the plural, will vary according to the system in which it is embedded.) Let us return to the Cushitic language Bayso. Besides the general number forms, there are also these:

(14) Bayso (Dick Hayward, personal communications, Corbett & Hayward 1987)
lubán-titi foofe
lion-SG watched.1SG
'I watched a lion'

(15) *luban-jaa foofe*
lion-PAUCAL watched.1.SG
'I watched a few lions'

(16) *luban-jool foofe*
lion-PLURAL watched.1.SG
'I watched (a lot of) lions'

Bayso then has a paucal, with singular and plural, giving the following system (in additional to general number):

(17) singular paucal plural

The paucal is used in Bayso for reference to a small number of individuals, from two to about six. Bayso has this system in nouns but not in pronouns: thus the system of number values in a given language can vary according to which part of the grammatical system is examined. This is an essential point for typologists: when we say that a language has a particular number value, we need to be clear about its range of use — whether is it available for most nouns or found just with the personal pronouns, for example.

Systems with just a paucal in addition to singular and plural are rare. It is much more common to find it together with a dual, giving this system:

(18) singular dual paucal plural

Here the meaning of the paucal changes to exclude two. This system is found, for instance in Yimas, a Lower Sepik language with 250 speakers in the Sepik Basin of Papua New Guinea. The paucal is found in the pronoun and in the pronominal affixes on the verb.

"The paucal expresses a set of a few; more than two and usually less than seven, but the exact number varies quite widely according to context. Prototypically, however, it refers to a class of three to five individuals, and is always restricted to humans." (Foley 1991: 216)

The restriction to humans is specific to Yimas, of course.

This system (with dual and paucal) is found widely in Oceanic languages, for instance in Paamese, spoken in Vanuatu. The factors governing the choice of paucal and plural in Paamese have been well described by Crowley (1982: 81): the lower the absolute size of the group, the more likely the paucal is to be used, the larger, the more likely the plural. But for groups in the middle (around six to twelve) then relative number becomes important: if the group is contrasted with some larger group, then the paucal is more likely, if contrasted with a smaller group, this will favour the plural.

2.5. The largest number systems

We now consider whether there are languages with the following system:

(19) singular dual trial quadral plural

Such languages would have a quadral, a set of forms specifically for the quantity four. If such languages exist, they are rare. All the claims come from within the Austronesian family. A well-documented case is Sursurunga (Hutchisson 1986, and personal communications), which has some 4000 speakers in southern New Ireland. The forms labelled quadral are restricted to the personal pronouns, but are found with all of them, the first person (inclusive and exclusive), the second and the third:

Table 61.2: Emphatic pronouns in Sursurunga (Hutchisson 1986 and personal communications)

	singular	dual	"trial"	"quadral"	plural
1 exclusive	iau	giur	gimtul	gimhat	gim
1 inclusive	–	gitar	gittul	githat	git
2	iáu	gaur	gamtul	gamhat	gam
3	-i/on/ái	diar	ditul	dihat	di

Here is an example of a quadral form in use (we retain the traditional label 'quadral' here although we are about to give reasons for replacing it):

(20) Sursurunga (Hutchisson 1986 and personal communications)
gim-hat
1.EXCL-QUADRAL
káwán
maternal.uncle:nephew/niece
'we four who are in an uncle-nephew/niece relationship'

(á is used to indicate schwa (ə); this and other changes from the 1986 paper are based on personal communications from Don Hutchisson.) Besides being used of four, the quadral has two other uses. First, plural pronouns are never used with terms for dyads (kinship pairings like uncle-nephew/niece), and then the quadral is used instead for a minimum of four, and not just for exactly four (Hutchisson 1986: 10). The second additional use is in hortatory discourse; the speaker may use the first person inclusive quadral, suggesting joint action including the speaker, even though more than four persons are involved. These two special uses account for most instances of the quadral. If our terminology is based on meaning, the term 'quadral' is hardly appropriate, when in the majority of its uses the forms are not restricted to denoting foursomes. The forms would be better designated 'paucal'.

Let us consider the rest of the system in more detail (data and judgements from Don Hutchisson, personal communications). The dual is used quite strictly for two people (if there are two it must be used, and if it is used it indicates two). It is also used for the singular when the referent is in a taboo relationship to the speaker. This is a special use which does not alter the fact that its main use is as a regular dual. The trial will be used for three. But, it is also used for small groups, typically around three or four, and for nuclear families of any size. It is therefore not strictly a trial, rather it could be labelled a paucal (an appropriate gloss would be 'a few'). We saw earlier that the trial frequently develops in this way. The quadral, as we have noted, is primarily used in hortatory discourse and with dyad terms; but otherwise it is used with larger groups, of four or more (an appropriate gloss would be 'several'). This too would qualify as a paucal; we therefore have two paucals, a paucal (traditionally trial) and a greater paucal (traditionally quadral).

The following example is particularly helpful for distinguishing the use of the two forms. It is from a letter to Don Hutchisson written in 1976:

(21) Iau lala hol pas gamhat
1.SG greatly think about 2.QUADRAL
kabin ngo iau lu mákái
because that 1.SG HAB see
málálár gamtul mínái i rum
photo 2.TRIAL here in house
'I am thinking about you [QUADRAL] all the time because I often see the picture of you [TRIAL] here in my house.'

The family consists of four members; the quadral is used first (perhaps to stress that all four are included), but then the writer moves to the trial, more normal usage for a small group. The entire family is intended in each case.

The plural, as we would expect, is for numbers of entities larger than what is covered by the quadral; however, there is no strict dividing line (certainly not at the number five). If we use semantic labels, as in the rest of this chapter, we should not call the forms trials and quadrals. Both have functions found with paucals elsewhere. We may therefore represent the system in Sursurunga like this:

(22) singular – dual – paucal – greater paucal – plural

The system is no less interesting since it has a well documented five-valued number category. There are certainly other languages with five number values; we do not have such detailed information as for Sursurunga and there is no certain case of a quadral: it seems that in all cases the highest value in such systems can be used as a paucal. There are several false trails in the literature, that is, suggestions of other Austronesian languages with quadrals, which turn out in fact to have four number values not five. In such cases, the plural may have a form in which the numeral four can be reconstructed.

Besides the split in the paucal, we may also find a split in the plural, with 'greater plurals' of different types. For instance in Syrian Arabic some nouns have a plural *dəbbānāt* 'flies' and an additional form, the greater plural, *dababīn* 'many flies' (Cowell 1964: 369). Greater plurals may imply an excessive number or else all possible instances of the referent. They are as yet poorly researched, except in a few languages.

3. Implicational claims (the Number Hierarchy)

According to Greenberg's universal 34: "No language has a trial number unless it has a dual. No language has a dual unless it has a plural" (Greenberg 1963). This claim appears fully justified. However, it is only a part of the overall typology of systems of number values. Some researchers give a Number Hierarchy, along these lines, suggesting it covers the possible number systems:

(23)   singular > plural > dual > trial

There are two problems with this hierarchy: first, it cannot be modified to include the different systems which have a paucal; and second, the patterns of what we shall call 'facultative' number are problematic.

3.1. Possible systems of number values

The first problem with the Number Hierarchy given above is that it does not account for systems which include a paucal. A modified hierarchy has been proposed:

(24)   singular > plural > dual > paucal/trial

This would account for systems like the following:

(25)   singular plural (Russian)
        singular dual plural (Upper Sorbian)
        singular dual trial plural (Larike)
        singular dual paucal plural (Yimas)

However, it does not allow for systems which include the paucal in a different combination:

(26)   singular paucal plural (Bayso)

We must allow for the paucal to be an option at more than one point, which makes it clear that no straightfoward hierarchy will be adequate. To make progress here we need to draw a distinction between 'determinate' and 'indeterminate' number values. These terms are to differentiate situations where, given the knowledge of real world which the speaker has, we can determine that only one form is appropriate (determinate number) from those where we cannot (indeterminate). Thus, in a language with an obligatory dual, this would be an instance of determinate number, since to refer to two distinct entities only the dual is appropriate. The determinate numbers are basically the numerical ones, (singular, dual, trial, plural). Use of determinate number values is agreed across speakers (different speakers agree that, say, the dual is appropriate for referring to two referents), it remains constant for the same speaker across different occasions, and it does not vary according to the referent (thus elephant-DUAL refers to two elephants just as ant-DUAL refers to two ants).

The indeterminate number values are the paucal, greater paucal and the greater plural. These may vary across speakers (there is no clear dividing line between paucal and plural, for one speaker across occasions), and can vary according to the referent (elephant-PAUCAL may refer to fewer real world entities than ant-PAUCAL). While the determinate numbers can be defined in terms of numerals, the indeterminates correspond to other quantifiers: 'a few', 'many', 'all'.

How then are number systems constrained? First, a language may take any number of the determinate number values, in the order given (i. e. in accord with the old number hierarchy). However, this should be seen as adopting a series of binary choices, and choice after the plural should be seen as removing a part from the range of the plural and hence dividing the plural. This gives the possibilities that are shown in Figure 61.1.

We have chosen to arrange the branches in this figure with the values for larger numbers

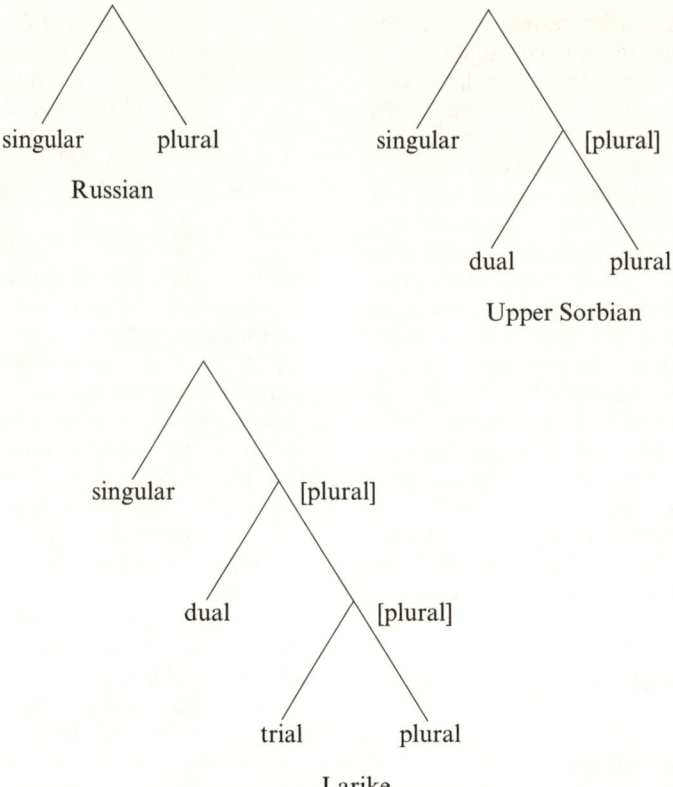

Figure 61.1: Illustration of possible number systems

of entities to the right. '[plural]' indicates what the value would be at that point if no further choices were made; this will be relevant when we consider facultative number. In addition to the determinate number values, languages may further divide up the plural space by taking an indeterminate number value. Most commonly, only one is selected. Some of the possibilities which result are shown in Figure 61.2.

While it is more common for just one indeterminate value to be selected, as in Bayso and in Mokilese (Harrison 1976: 88–89), two is also possible. The Mele-Fila system is based on material from Ross Clark (personal communications); it has a 'constructed system' in the sense discussed in § 5.3 below, cf. Figure 61.3.

Mele-Fila is perhaps the less surprising, in that it takes two indeterminate values of different types. Sursurunga has two paucals. It is tempting to try to add further constraints in order to bring the systems permitted into closer match with those so far recorded. This would be premature since we are still short of data on the larger systems; it is to be hoped that highlighting these examples will encourage others to report on large number systems with indeterminate values included.

Besides making synchronic predictions, typology also makes diachronic predictions in that languages move from one possible system to another. Thus, a language with singular – dual – trial – plural may lose the trial, since the resulting system is allowed by the typology, but it could not lose the dual without first losing the trial. The drift from trial to paucal is easy to understand, since they occur in similar configurations.

We have set out a typology of possible number systems. As we shall see shortly, this same typology imposes further constraints on the number system.

3.2. Facultative number

We have considered how number systems vary according to how many number values they have, that is, how many different numbers of real world entities may be referred to by different means. But they may also differ

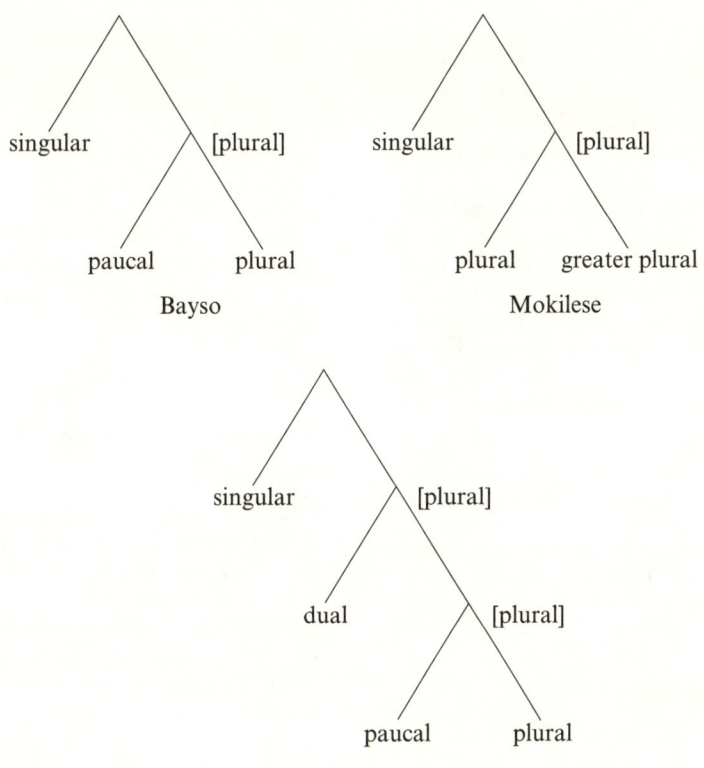

Figure 61.2: Possible number systems including an indeterminate value

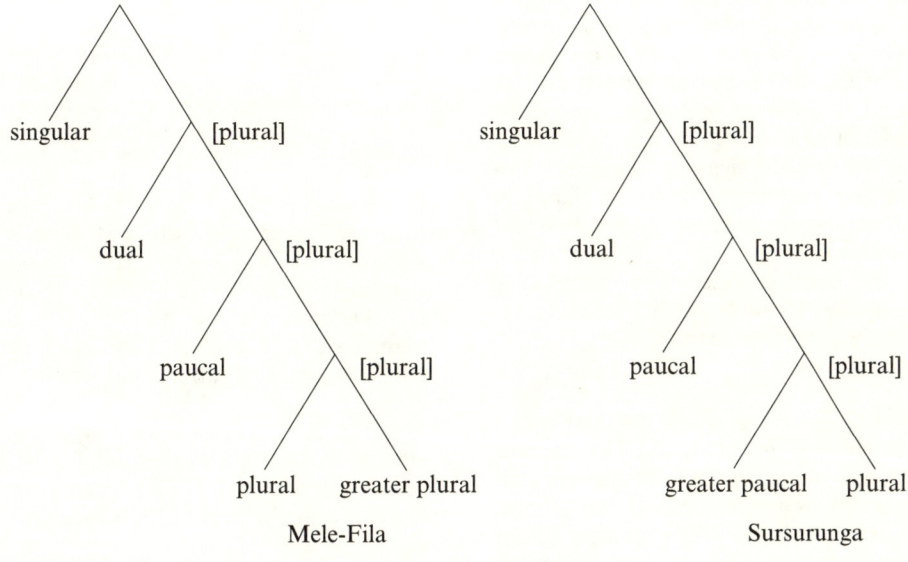

Figure 61.3: Number systems with two indeterminate values

in a more subtle way, according to whether the use of particular values is obligatory or 'facultative' (Greenberg 1966: 28). For instance, in Ngan'gityemerri (as noted in § 2.3) there is singular, dual, trial and plural. The dual must be used to refer to two entities, the plural must be used for four and more. For three entities, the trial is used when the fact of there being three is salient (for example, at the first mention in discourse) but otherwise the plural is used for three. Recall that the trial is strictly for three, and is not a paucal (Reid 1990: 118−119 and personal communication).

Consider now the systems with singular − dual − plural. The use of the dual may be obligatory, as in Sanskrit, or it may be facultative, as in the South Slavonic language Slovene. Here we do not find the same degree of choice as with the Ngan'gityemerri trial, but the important point is that the dual is not obligatory in the way that the plural is in Slovene:

"[...] in non-pronominal noun phrases with, for example, body parts that come in pairs like 'eyes' and 'feet', dual forms tend to be used only when the quantifiers 'two' or 'both' are explicitly stated in the context, and are replaced by the plural when this quantifier is unstated, even if a pair of referents are obviously implicit [...]" (Priestly 1993: 440−441)

Priestly gives the following example:

(27) Slovene (Priestly 1993: 441)
 nóge me   bolijo
 foot.PL 1.SG.ACC hurt.PL
 'my feet hurt'

It is assumed that two feet are referred to, and the dual is not required in this example. Nominals express number obligatorily in Slovene; however, for referring to two entities, the use of the dual is not obligatory. Just as the plural is different in English (no dual) and Sanskrit (with dual), so it is different in Sanskrit (with an obligatory dual) and Slovene (with a facultative dual). A plural in Slovene may be for reference to just two real world entities.

Let us now consider how facultative number relates to the Number Hierarchy, repeated here for convenience:

(28) singular > plural > dual > trial

If we have a system in which the dual is facultative, then in its place the less marked number, the plural, is used. It appears that the hierarchy is making useful predictions, based on markedness. Unfortunately this is only apparent here. Consider again Ngan'gityemerri: it has a trial which is facultative and so we would predict that the less marked dual could be used in its place. But of course this is not the case, the plural is used. This is what is expected if the system is viewed as a set of binary choices (see Figure 61.4).

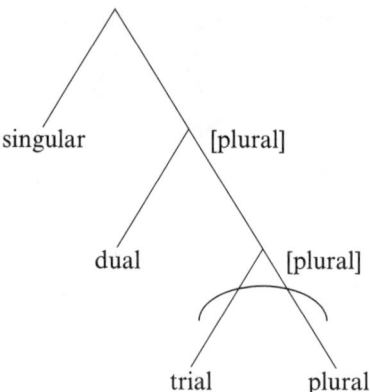

Figure 61.4: The facultative trial of Ngan'gityemerri

The point is that the last choice is facultative. If it is removed, as by the arc in figure 61.4, then Ngan'gityemerri has another possible system, singular − dual − plural, and the plural covers the area otherwise covered by trial and plural.

In Slovene, the situation is as in Figure 61.5:

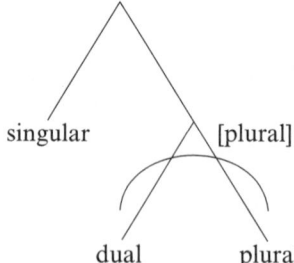

Figure 61.5: The facultative dual of Slovene

If the dual − plural choice is not taken up, then the system reverts to a straightforward singular − plural system. It is tempting to suggest that facultative number can only affect the 'last choice' of number, as in the examples so far. However, there are languages which show the situation is rather more interesting.

Let us consider just Larike, which we considered earlier as an example of a language with a genuine trial. Unlike Ngan'gityemerri, it is not only the trial which is facultative, the dual is as well:

"The Larike plural forms may also be used when referring to quantities of two or three. Thus, in spite of the fact that duals and trials are used to specifically denote twos and threes, plural forms can still be used with the meaning of two or more. In these situations, the choice of whether to use plural versus dual or trial forms depends upon the speaker's desire to specify or focus upon the number of the referent nouns. Although the plural forms are probably most frequently used (even when referring to twos and threes), duals and trials are also quite common, and are often heard in routine conversations as well as in more formal language contexts." (Laidig & Laidig 1990: 93)

We represent this system in Figure 61.6.

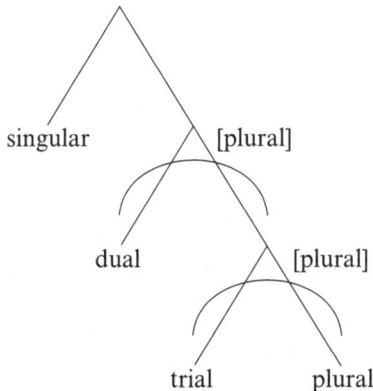

Figure 61.6: The facultative numbers of Larike

We cannot restrict facultative number values to 'the last choice'; rather we must say that if there is facultative number it must involve 'the last choice'. It may involve other numbers, working up from the last choice. Thus it may affect the dual-plural choice in Larike, because it also affects the trial-plural choice. But there could not be, we claim, a language with a facultative dual and an obligatory trial or paucal.

The existence of facultative numbers show how careful the typologist must be: Sanskrit and Slovene both have a dual, but they are rather different duals.

4. The nominals involved

So far we have concentrated on number values. Now we change tack and ask which nominals may be involved in the number system of a language, examining first the basic singular-plural opposition. We might say that we wish to establish the patterns of 'count' or 'countable' nouns in different languages. Unfortunately the terminology here has become rather confused. We shall call 'count' nouns those which are distinguishable for number, rather than those which may be counted. In part we are simplifying by looking at nominals, since, as Allan (1980) has argued, countability is a characteristic of noun phrases and not of nouns. However, as he points out:

"Even though countability is characteristic of NP's, not of nouns, it is nonetheless a fact that nouns do show countability preference — insofar as some nouns more often occur in countable NP's, others in uncountable NP's, and still others seem to occur quite freely in both." (Allan 1980: 566).

Thus, strictly speaking, we are investigating the countability preferences of nominals (we are as interested in pronouns as in nouns). There is considerably more variety in the world's languages than we might have expected. Consider the following Warrgamay example (Queensland, Australia):

(29) Warrgamay (Dixon 1980: 266—268)
yibi-yibi   ŋulmburu-ŋgu
child-REDUP.ABS   woman-ERG
wurrbi-bajun-du buudi-l-gani-y
big-VERY-ERG   take-CONT-UNM
malan-gu
river-ALL
'The very big woman/women is/are taking the children to the creek'

This example indicates that a noun can be marked for number in Warrgamay, as in yibi-yibi 'child', but this is not required; forms like ŋulmburu-ŋgu 'woman' are quite normal; in fact Dixon (1980: 267) says that a noun in this language 'is not normally specified for number' and suggests that this is the typical situation in Australia (1980: 22). Note especially that the verb in (29) does not determine number either (l- and -gani- together indicate continuative and -y- indicates unmarked tense, hence the gloss 'is/are taking', Dixon 1980: 268). To check on the pronouns we turn to Dixon (1981: 39—40) The first and second persons, singular, dual and plural, and the third dual and plural are 'strictly specified for number' and are available only for reference to humans (and occasionally tame dogs). The form filling the third singular slot can range over all persons and all numbers (it can have non-human as well as human reference) but its 'unmarked sense' (1981: 40) is third person singular.

Thus the word for 'woman' is not normally specified for number, while in English it must be. Yet the first and second persons are. Could there be a language in which the word for 'woman' specified number but the first person pronoun did not? It seems not. It was known for some while that the patterns of nominals involved in number distinctions was related to animacy; this observation was taken up and developed by Smith-Stark (1974), who proposed this version of the Animacy Hierarchy:

speaker   >   addressee   >   kin   >   rational   >   human   >   animate   >   inanimate
(1st person   (2nd person
pronouns)   pronouns)

Figure 61.7: The Smith-Stark (Animacy) Hierarchy

Smith-Stark suggested that plurality 'splits' a language if "it is a significant opposition for certain categories but irrelevant for others" (1974: 657). The type of evidence he produced concerned marking of the noun phrase for number (usually by marking on the noun itself) and agreement in number (mainly verbal agreement but with some instances of agreement within the noun phrase). He claims, for instance, that in Georgian if the subject is plural and denotes an animate the verb will be plural, if it denotes an inanimate then the verb will be singular. Thus Georgian nouns are split, and the division is between animates and inanimates.

Various languages make the split at different points. In Kalkatungu, a language of western Queensland with no known remaining full speakers (Barry Blake, personal communication), pronouns (free and bound) and demonstratives distinguish singular, dual and plural (Blake 1979: 31−32, 34−37). There is a dual and a plural marker for nouns; both are "common with kinship nouns", are part of the number system of demonstratives, but are "rarely used" with other nominals (1979: 80−81). And according to Masica (1991: 225−226) in Bengali number is obligatory for pronouns; other plural suffixes are optional.

The hierarchy presented by Smith-Stark is clearly akin to what in other publications has been termed the Animacy Hierarchy or the Topicality Hierarchy. He provides a good deal of data to support his claim, and notes some problematic cases too. Smith-Stark's article (1974) was a major step forward in our understanding of number systems; on the other hand, it is rather confusing in places, and a lot of the relevant data are missing (that remains the case − it has not been followed up as well as it deserved).

It is worth considering the nouns which are off the bottom of the scale, those which do not enter into number oppositions. In English they typically pattern with the singulars, thus *honesty* has the form of a singular and takes singular agreements. This is not the only possible pattern: In Manam (Lichtenberk 1983: 269), mass nouns are treated as plural (unless they refer to a single quantity):

(30)   *daŋ   di-éno*
        water 3.PL-exist
        'there is water (available)'

In various Bantu languages we typically find that some mass nouns are singular and some plural.

The reference to Manam mass nouns being plural unless they refer to a single quantity (when they are singular) recalls English, where mass nouns can also be recategorized as count nouns. There are two motivations. For portions, as in *a coffee and two beers please* and for types, as in *they had two wines at dinner*.

Finally in this section we should note that a goal of the typological investigation of number is to integrate the typology of values (§ 2) with the typology of nominals involved. This is quite a challenge. The point is that Smith-Stark considered only plurals, suggesting that other values, such as the dual, would behave in the same way. If for example, a language has singular, dual and plural, he assumed that the nominals with a dual would be the same as those with a plural. This situation is found, but it is far from being the only possibility. For instance, in Modern Hebrew and in Maltese, there are some nouns with a dual; they are relatively few in comparison with those with a plural, and they are certainly not those at the top of the Smith-Stark Hierarchy. These duals have been analysed as 'minor numbers'; they do not pattern according to the Smith-Stark Hierarchy, but they are counter-examples of a narrowly definable type (Corbett 2000: 95−101). Then there are other apparent number values, which appear to run counter to the hierarchy. For example, associatives, like Central Alaskan Yup'ik *cuna-nku-t* (Chuna-ASSOCIATIVE-PL) 'Chuna and his family/friends'. These apparent exceptions can be shown to involve an additional category and so are outside the scope of the constraints discussed here (Corbett & Mithun 1996). A discussion of these complications is beyond the scope of this chapter.

5. The expression of number

Having discussed the possible number values, and the nominals involved in the number system, we now turn to the question of how number is expressed. There are various means available.

5.1. Number words

Some languages have special 'number words', just for the purpose of indicating number. Thus in Tagalog, virtually any constituent can be pluralized by the word *mga* [maŋa], perhaps best characterized as a clitic (David Gil, personal communication):

(31) *mga   bahay*
      PL   house
      'houses'

(32) *mga   tubig*
      PL   water
      'cups/units of water'

(33) *mga   Marcos*
      PL   Marcos
      'Marcoses'

(34) *mga   ma-puti*
      PL   STAT-white
      'white ones'

Further examples of number words can be found in Dryer (1989). Diachronically, number words are a potential source of number morphology.

5.2. Syntax

In § 1 we saw that nominal number may be marked by agreement. It is worth noting that nominals whose number marking and agreements differ will be more regular with regard to agreement than for nominal marking. Thus English *sheep* is exceptional as far as the Smith-Stark Hierarchy is concerned, if we consider its morphology. In English, animates and most inanimates distinguish number, and so we would expect *sheep* to distinguish number, as *goat* does. If we look at its agreements it is fully regular, however:

(35) *this sheep is grazing*
      (cf. *this goat is grazing*)

(36) *these sheep are grazing*
      (cf. *these goats are grazing*)

5.3. Morphology

Number morphology varies from relative simplicity in some languages to great complexity in others. Even in languages where the main patterns are straightforward, we often find isolated examples of more interesting types.

We start from the notion of 'base' (or 'basic inflectional stem'). The base of a lexical item is the form which cannot be further reduced as far as inflectional categories are concerned. English *play* is the base for the forms *play-s* and *play-ed*. Let us consider a language which has at least two numbers, singular and plural. What are the possible relations between the number forms and the base for a given lexical item (or group of lexical items)? Let us start from a maximally general model, shown in Figure 61.8.

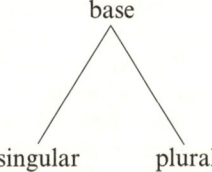

Figure 61.8: Possibilities for number marking

How can the singular and plural forms differ from the base? First they may differ in inflection. Or they can vary from the base through stem formation. These two devices, inflection and stem formation may occur separately or together. The fourth logical possibility is that neither inflection nor stem formation is employed. If this means that the singular form, plural form and basic stem are all identical, then clearly number is simply not marked morphologically for the items in question (as in the case of English *sheep*).

Having considered the possibilities in an abstract way, let us now consider the options in more detail, allowing for different stems:

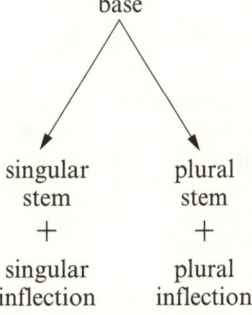

Figure 61.9: Possible stems and inflections

We will now look at examples of number marking, considering in particular whether all the elements identified in the diagram are distinct or not in particular examples. It is important to note that different patterns often coexist within a single language; if an example is given from a particular language this does not mean that the pattern is the norm for that language.

If we start with the relations between the base and the stems, the first logical possibility is that all are distinct. This possibility can be illustrated by the irregular Russian noun, *xozjain* 'landlord'. The base is *xozja(j)-*, the singular stem is *xozja-in-* and the plural stem is *xozja-ev-*. Both stems allow the normal addition of endings. The extreme type of difference is found in cases of suppletion, where there are different stems which are not related by any regular or irregular type of stem formation; their relation is purely semantic. An example is Russian *čelovek* 'person', plural *ljud-i* 'people'. Note that we are indeed dealing with stems here: *čelovek* 'person', takes normal singular inflections, and *ljud-i* 'people' takes plural inflections.

It is unusual for the root and the singular and plural stems all to be distinct, in Russian and more generally. Often we find that the base and the singular stem are identical, as in this diagram:

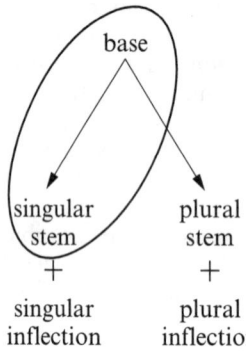

Figure 61.10: Singular stem equals the base

This pattern too can be illustrated from Russian. The noun *krylo* 'wing' has the base *kryl-*, to which the singular endings are added directly (*kryl-o, kryl-a, kryl-u* and so on). The plural stem is *kryl'j-* (the ' marks palatalization of the preceding consonant), as in the nominative plural *kryl'ja*. Why should we say that there is a distinct plural stem here, rather than that the nominative plural ending is palatalization plus *-ja*? The point is that *-a* is a regular nominative plural ending, found on hundreds of nouns which do not have a separate plural stem. The plural endings for the remaining five cases of Russian are also found on other nouns; we would be missing an obvious generalization if we claimed there were special endings right through the plural paradigm while in fact nouns like *krylo* 'wing' differ from other nouns only in having a different stem for the plural.

The next possibility is that the plural stem should be the same as the base:

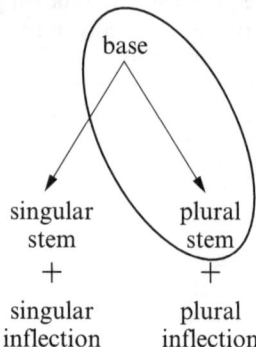

Figure 61.11: Plural stem equals the base

Again the pattern is found in Russian. The noun *bolgarin* 'a Bulgarian' has the base *bolgar-*, and the plural stem is identical, as in forms like the nominative plural *bolgar-y*. The singular stem differs, and is *bolgarin-*. Several nouns denoting nationalities and other social groupings behave in this way.

A final relation of base to stems is that all are identical, diagrammed as follows:

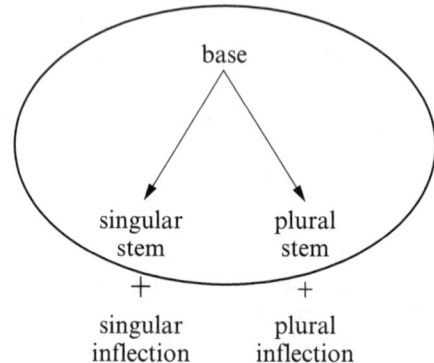

Figure 61.12: Both stems equal the base

This situation is extremely common. Again in Russian we find many nouns like that for 'newspaper', which has the basic stem *gazet-*. The (nominative) singular is *gazet-a* and the (nominative) plural is *gazet-y*. Here, stem formation has no role, and the entire burden of signalling a difference in number is carried by the inflections (endings in this instance).

We move on to look for identities elsewhere in the model. There is a further, initially rather surprising type of identity, shown in the next diagram:

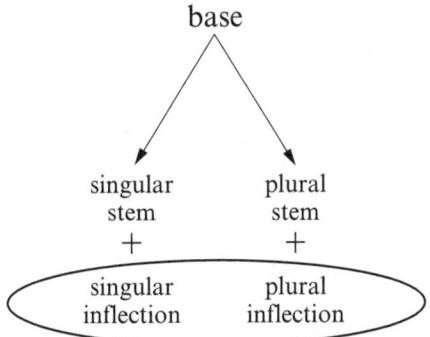

Figure 61.13: Inflections not sensitive to number

This pattern suggests that the inflections used for singular and plural could be identical. This situation regularly occurs in Daghestanian languages for the majority of the large numbers of cases they distinguish (often just the absolutive is an exception). The Akhvakh noun *nido* 'forehead' shows a clear case of identical endings: we take absolutive and ergative endings to illustrate the point:

(37) Akhvakh (Kibrik 1991)
	singular	plural
absolutive	*nido*	*nido-di*
ergative	*nido-la-de*	*nido-di-le-de*

In this example the base is *nido*, and the singular stem is identical to it. The plural stem is *nido-di-*. The absolutive case, in singular and plural, has no ending. In both numbers there is an oblique stem, distinct from the basic singular or plural stem; in the singular it is formed with *-la*, and in the plural with *-le-*. The various oblique case endings are added to this stem; in our example the ergative case is given, and the appropriate ending is *-de*. As with the absolutive, the ending is the same for singular and plural. The point is that information about number is signalled by the differences in the stems: *-di-* indicates plurality for this noun, *-la-* shows singular oblique, and *-le-* plural oblique. Thus, a form like *nido-di-le-de* indicates plurality twice. The endings have no role in the number system, their function is to mark the case of the noun (the case system is extensive). This identity of form of endings in the singular and plural is quite general in Daghestanian languages. It is to be distinguished from occasional syncretisms of form involving small numbers of nouns in languages where the coincidence of form is not systematic.

There is one final pattern of identity, noted earlier, which we should consider again, that in which both stems are identical to the base, and where the stems are identical to the forms with endings (that is, there are no endings). This means that the noun is indeclinable — number is not marked morphologically. There are numerous examples of this situation, both of languages where number is not marked morphologically on particular word classes (English adjectives, for example) or not marked morphologically at all. But it may be found for a subset of a word class within a system where number is usually marked morphologically. Thus in Russian, the majority of nouns distinguish two numbers but some, especially foreign borrowings do not. For example, *taksi* 'taxi' may denote one or more taxis (the ambiguity will often be removed by elements showing agreement in number).

Two special types of number marking deserve a mention. The first is 'inverse' number, where the marker for singularity for some nouns is used to mark plurality for others. This is found, for example in Kiowa (Watkins 1984). The other is 'constructed' numbers. Constructed numbers appear where there is a mismatch between number marking of different elements. Consider the following data from Hopi:

(38) Hopi (Hale 1993: 19)
Pam   wari
that.SG run.PFV.SG/DUAL
'he/she ran'

(39) *Puma   wari*
that.DUAL/PL run.PFV.SG/DUAL
'they (two) ran'

(40) *Puma   yu'tu*
that.DUAL/PL run.PFV.PL
'they (plural) ran'

The pronominal forms on their own make only a two-way distinction, as does the verb. Put together, however, we have a singular-dual-plural system, 'constructed' from the two parts. It must be stressed, however, that this is only a part of the system: animate nouns in Hopi have a straightforward singular-dual-plural system.

This section has attempted to describe the typological space for number marking. But this is just a start: we need to be clear about which forms are the typical ones for given languages, and which occur only sporadically. And then we can investigate the patterns of marking; thus, for instance, we tend to find greater irregularities (and greater use of stem alternations) for the items higher on the the Smith-Stark hierarchy. For pronouns it is common to find suppletion. And yet this patterning is overridden by items such as *geese* and *teeth*, whose distribution in texts between singular and plural is dramatically different from the average (see Tiersma 1982).

6. Conclusion

The category of number remains a challenge for typologists. We need to know more on the relation between nominal and verbal number (§ 1). We now have a fair understanding of the possible number values (sections 2 and 3) and a reasonable idea of the patterns of the types of nominal involved in number systems (§ 4). However, there is a good deal to be done for these two parts of the typology to be integrated. Similarly, while we have a reasonable inventory of the means of number marking (§ 5), we do not know the possible ways in which these means of marking may be distributed over types of nominal. Number, this apparently simple category, is far from being understood.

Acknowledgement

This entry is based on research funded in part by the ESRC (grant R000222419) and the British Academy. This support is gratefully acknowledged.

7. Special abbreviations

ALL	allative
CONT	continuative
HAB	habitual
IRR	irrealis
REDUP	reduplication
STAT	stative
UNM	unmarked

8. References

Allan, Keith. 1980. "Nouns and countability". *Language* 56: 541–567.

Blake, Barry J. 1979. *A Kalkatungu grammar* (Pacific Linguistics, series B, no. 57). Canberra: Department of Linguistics, Research School of Pacific Studies, Australian National University.

Brooks, Bryan. 1991. "Pluractional verbs in African languages". *Afrikanistische Arbeitspapiere* (Cologne) 28: 157–168.

Corbett, Greville G. 2000. *Number.* Cambridge: Cambridge University Press.

Corbett, Greville G. & Hayward, Richard J. 1987. "Gender and number in Bayso". *Lingua* 73: 1–28.

Corbett, Greville G. & Mithun, Marianne 1996. "Associative forms in a typology of number systems: evidence from Yup'ik". *Journal of Linguistics* 32: 1–17.

Cowell, Mark W. 1964. *A reference grammar of Syrian Arabic (based on the dialect of Damascus)* (Arabic series 7). Washington, DC: Georgetown University Press.

Crowley, Terry. 1982. *The Paamese language of Vanuatu* (Pacific Linguistics, series B, no. 87). Canberra: Department of Linguistics, Research School of Pacific Studies, Australian National University.

Dixon, Robert M. W. 1980. *The languages of Australia.* Cambridge: Cambridge University Press.

Dixon, Robert M. W. 1981. "Wargamay". In: Robert M. W. Dixon & Barry J. Blake (eds) *The handbook of Australian languages: II: Wargamay, the Mpakwithi dialect of Anguthimri, Watjarri, Margany and Gunya, Tasmanian,* Amsterdam: Benjamins, 1–144.

Dryer, Matthew. 1989. "Plural words". *Linguistics* 27: 865–95.

Durie, Mark. 1986. "The grammaticization of number as a verbal category". *Berkeley Linguistics Society* 12: 355–70.

Foley, William A. 1991. *The Yimas language of New Guinea.* Stanford: Stanford University Press.

Green, Ian. 1989. Marrithiyel, a language of the Daly River region of Australia's Northern Territory. Unpublished PhD thesis, Australian National University.

Greenberg, Joseph H. 1963. "Some universals of grammar with particular reference to the order of meaningful elements". In: Joseph H. Greenberg (ed.) *Universals of language*, Cambridge, Massachusetts: MIT Press, 73–113.

Greenberg, Joseph H. 1966. *Language universals: with special reference to feature hierarchies.* The Hague: Mouton.

Hale, Kenneth. 1993. "On the human value of local languages". In: André Crochetière, Jean-Claude Boulanger & Conrad Ouellon (eds.) *Proceedings of the XVth International Congress of Linguists, Québec, Université Laval 9–14 August 1992: Endangered Languages: Volume I,* Sainte-Foy: Les Presses de l'Université Laval, 17–31.

Harrison, Sheldon P. (with the assistance of Salich Y. Albert) 1976. *Mokilese Reference Grammar.* Honolulu: University Press of Hawaii.

Hayward, Dick [= R. J. Hayward]. 1984. *The Arbore language: a first investigation: including a vocab-*

ulary. (Cushitic Language Studies 2). Hamburg: Buske.

Hutchisson, Don. 1986. "Sursurunga pronouns and the special uses of quadral number". In: Ursula Wiesemann (ed.) *Pronominal systems* (Continuum 5), Tübingen: Narr. 217–55.

Kibrik, Alexandr E. 1991. "Organising principles for nominal paradigms in Daghestanian languages: comparative and typological observations". In: Frans Plank (ed.) *Paradigms: the economy of inflection* (Empirical Approaches to Language Typology 9), Berlin: Mouton de Gruyter, 255–74.

Laidig, Wyn D. & Laidig, Carol J. 1990. "Larike pronouns: duals and trials in a Central Moluccan language". *Oceanic Linguistics* 29: 87–109.

Lichtenberk, Frantisek. 1983. *A grammar of Manam* (Oceanic Linguistics Special Publication 18). Honolulu: University of Hawaii Press.

Masica, Colin P. 1991. *The Indo-Aryan languages.* Cambridge: Cambridge University Press.

Mithun, Marianne. 1988. "Lexical categories and the evolution of number marking". In: Michael Hammond & Michael Noonan (eds.) *Theoretical morphology: approaches in modern linguistics.* San Diego: Academic Press, 211–34.

Newman, Paul. 1990. *Nominal and verbal plurality in Chadic* (Publications in African Languages and Linguistics 12). Dordrecht: Foris.

Plank, Frans. 1989. "On Humboldt on the dual". In: Roberta Corrigan, Fred Eckman & Michael Noonan (eds.) *Linguistic categorization* (Amsterdam Studies in the Theory and History of Linguistic Science 61). Amsterdam: Benjamins, 293–333.

Priestly, T. M. S. 1993. "Slovene". In: Bernard Comrie & Greville G. Corbett (eds.), *The Slavonic languages.* London: Routledge, 388–451.

Reid, Nicholas J. 1990. *Ngan'gityemerri: A Language of the Daly River region, Northern Territory of Australia.* Unpublished PhD thesis, Australian National University, Canberra.

Saussure, Ferdinand de. 1971. *Cours de linguistique générale* (publié par Charles Bally et Albert Sechehaye avec la collaboration de Albert Riedlinger). Paris: Payot. [Third edition, first edition 1916.]

Smith-Stark, T. Cedric. 1974. "The plurality split". *Chicago Linguistic Society* 10: 657–71.

Steever, Sanford B. 1987. "The roots of the plural action verb in the Dravidian languages". *Journal of the American Oriental Society* 107: 581–604.

Stone, Gerald. 1993. "Sorbian (Upper and Lower)". In: Bernard Comrie & Greville G. Corbett (eds.), *The Slavonic languages.* London: Routledge, 593–685.

Tiersma, Peter M. 1982. "Local and general markedness". *Language* 58: 832–49.

Watkins, Laurel J. 1984. *A grammar of Kiowa.* Lincoln and London: University of Nebraska Press.

Greville G. Corbett, University of Surrey (United Kingdom)

62. Articles

1. Two approaches to the typology of articles
2. Identifying articles
3. Articles derived from demonstratives
4. Articles from other sources
5. Co-occurrence with other determiners
6. Special abbreviations
7. References

1. Two approaches to the typology of articles

The typology of articles has been approached in essentially two ways. The approach adopted by Grasserie (1896) and Krámský (1972) begins with a definition of definiteness and then identifies and classifies various grammatical phenomena which express definiteness in natural languages. The resulting typology is not limited to articles but includes other grammatical phenomena such as word order and verbal agreement. Semantically, such a typology is based on the simple bilateral opposition 'definite' vs. 'indefinite', which is assumed to be universal. Consequently, the typological parameters are exclusively formal. Krámský (1972), for example, subdivides his list of definiteness expressing phenomena according to the following two parameters: the morphological shape of the definiteness markers (independent word, clitic, affix, non-segmental phenomena (order, stress)) and the number of definiteness markers (definite and indefinite, only definite, only indefinite).

The second approach, pioneered by Greenberg (1978), is based on the observation that articles are historically derived from other elements such as demonstratives and numerals. That is, articles are viewed as stages in the adnominal grammaticisation of these elements, the typology of articles then being concerned with identifying different paths of grammaticisation in which articles occur and classifying the different stages of their development on the basis of semantic and formal criteria.

Probably the best-known grammaticisation path for articles is Greenberg's somewhat rudimentary grammaticisation path for articles derived from demonstratives:

(1) DEM → DEF.ART → SPEC.ART → NOUN MARKER

This path may be used briefly to preview some major features of the grammaticisation approach to the typology of articles and to highlight some salient differences with regard to the definiteness-based approach.

Most importantly, from a grammaticisational point of view, definiteness, though undeniably of central importance to the grammar and typology of articles, is only one of a number of meanings that can be conveyed by articles. Thus, for example, specific articles indicate specificity rather than definiteness. Definiteness and specificity are only two salient (and crosslinguistically well attested) stages on the grammaticisation path in (1). Given a sufficiently fine-grained set of criteria, many more stages could be distinguished. Thus, on the one hand, the grammaticisation approach provides a more detailed typological grid for articles and includes a variety of phenomena not considered in the definiteness-based approach (further details in § 3 and 4). On the other hand, the grammaticisation approach excludes some of the phenomena dealt with in the definiteness-based approach, in particular those grammatical structures which appear to be sensitive to definiteness but are not part of a grammaticisation path for articles (such as word order, case markers or verbal agreement).

Furthermore, the grammaticisation approach highlights the problem of distinguishing demonstratives from articles (and various types of articles from each other). In order to establish a grammaticisation path for articles, explicit and operational criteria have to be provided for determining that a given element is no longer a demonstrative but a definite article. This problem is addressed in § 2.

It should be noted that both approaches converge in that they both address the issues of classifying definite and indefinite articles according to their different morphosyntactic shapes (see in particular § 3.2) and according to the paradigmatic relations they enter into (see §§ 4.1 and 5).

The present overview of the typology of articles basically follows the grammaticisation approach as sketched in Greenberg (1978) and further elaborated in Himmelmann (1997) and Laury (1997). It is primarily concerned with articles derived from demonstratives, the most common and widespread type in natural languages.

2. Identifying articles

This section presents some formal (morphosyntactic) and semantic criteria for distinguishing articles from related elements, in particular the elements they are historically derived from, such as demonstratives and numerals (some of these criteria are also relevant to distinguishing different types of articles).

Two essential, though not sufficient formal criteria are as follows. First, articles are grammatical elements which occur only in nominal expressions. Second, their position within such expressions is fixed (i.e. they occur either to the left or to the right of a noun but not alternatively on either side). At first sight, these may seem to be rather trivial criteria. But note that they distinguish articles from, for example, demonstratives in many languages. Demonstratives (more precisely: deictic elements) may appear in at least four different syntactic functions, i.e. as pronouns, as adverbials, as predicates, and as adnominal modifiers. In the first three of these functions they are not in construction with a noun (cf. Fillmore 1982: 47f., Diessel 1999, Himmelmann 1997: 125−130). Furthermore, in many languages (e.g. Swahili, Latin, many Australian languages) demonstratives may occur on either side of a noun when used adnominally (cf. Dryer 1989). Thus, an element which can occur by itself, or one the position of which in nominal expressions is not fixed is, in general, not an article.

A further useful heuristic for identifying articles is obligatoriness in grammatically definable contexts. Such contexts include superlatives (*the greatest singer*), nouns taking complement clauses (*the fact that they lost the game*), and the fact that count nouns cannot be used in core argument positions without a marker for definiteness or specificity.

High textual frequency, often invoked as an argument for claiming that a particular element is an article, is an important but equivocal indicator of articlehood. Unequivocal articles (when not bound formatives) are without doubt high frequency items, found generally at the very top of frequency statistics for a given language sample. Thus, claims that a low frequency item should be regarded as an article are generally met with well justified suspicion. However, the mere fact that a demonstrative or numeral is used more frequently in one language or historical period than in another does not necessarily show that the element in question has become grammaticised as an article. In order for this to be the case it has to be shown that the increase in overall textual frequency correlates with a substantial difference in the semantics and pragmatics of the grammaticising element (cf. Himmelmann 1996: 210–218 and 1997: 28–33, 192–194 for further details on this methodological issue and problems regarding arguments based solely on frequency).

Formal criteria alone are not sufficient for providing a useful and operational definition of articles since there are other kinds of grammatical elements in nominal expressions which share essentially the same formal characteristics (case markers or classifiers, for example). They have to be complemented by semantic criteria. These differ strongly according to the type of article and its historical source. In the remainder of this section only the semantic criteria for distinguishing demonstratives from articles are discussed. The much less well known criteria relevant to other types of articles are briefly mentioned in § 4.

Put simply, articles are distinguished from demonstratives by the fact that they can be used in semantic and pragmatic contexts in which demonstratives cannot be used. The discussion here follows Hawkins (1978, 1991) who, building on the classic work of Christophersen (1939), has presented a very useful systematisation of article use in English which in turn provides a crosslinguistically applicable grid for identifying definite and specific articles semantically.

The first step in establishing such a grid is to identify those contexts in which demonstratives can be used in all languages. Himmelmann (1996) argues that there are four such contexts. The following three of these (illustrated from English Pear Stories, cf. Chafe 1980) are well-known:

(2) **Situational use**
 This guy behind you waits to get back to his seat (referring to a person present in the utterance situation)

(3) **Discourse-deictic use**
 ... and that's the end of **that story** (referring to a preceding stretch of discourse)

(4) **Tracking use** (also called anaphoric use)
 ... and a man comes along with a goat, and **this goat** obviously is interested in the pears

The fourth universal demonstrative use, **recognitional use**, is less widely known. This use is characterised by the fact that the intended referent has to be identified via specific, but presumably shared, knowledge. It can always be (and in fact often is) accompanied by a *you know?* or *remember?*-type of tag question.

(5) **Recognitional use**
 (a) **those dusty kind of hills** that they have out here by Stockton and all
 (b) *hitting one of* **those bounce-back things**, you know, the little thing that had elastic, and it has a ball

Note that in the preceding examples the distal demonstrative *those* occurs in first mentions. Neither the hills nor the bounce-back things have been mentioned before. They are also not visibly part of the actual utterance situation.

Articles derived from demonstratives may or may not be useable in these four contexts. The crucial distinguishing feature, however, is that they are consistently used in some additional contexts in which demonstratives must not be used. For **definite articles** two contexts are of particular importance. One is **larger situation use**, the first mention of entities that are considered to be unique, and hence generally identifiable, in a given speech community. This use is characterised by the fact that the intended referent has to be identified via general knowledge (e. g., *the sun, the Queen, the pub*). The other is **associative-anaphoric use**, i. e. the first mention of an entity that is not unique per se but with respect to a previously mentioned referent, as in:

(6) *The man drove past our house in a car.* ***The exhaust fumes*** *were terrible.*

As stated above, demonstratives cannot be used in these two contexts. In (6) it is impossible to replace *the* in *the exhaust fumes* by either *these* or *those*. Similarly, one cannot say *Her face was burnt by this sun* if *sun* is mentioned for the first time in a given conversation.

Specific articles (which are very common in Niger-Congo and Austronesian languages, among others) may occur in all of the preceding contexts. In addition, however, they may be used in some contexts in which neither demonstratives nor definite articles may occur. A useful diagnostic context in this regard is the introduction of a new participant into the universe of discourse as in the following Tagalog example (so-called **specific-indefinite use**):

(7) Tagalog (Bloomfield 1917: 32/31)
doón   ay   na-kita   nilá
DIST.LOC PM   REAL.STAT-see 3PL.POSS
ang *isá-ng ma-lakí-ng higante*
SPEC one-LK STAT-big-LK giant
'There they saw a great giant ...'

Put more generally, the crucial difference between specific articles on the one hand and demonstratives and definite articles on the other is that in the case of specific article use it is not necessary that the speaker assumes that the intended referent is identifiable for the hearer.

3. Articles derived from demonstratives

There are two basic types of articles derived from demonstratives. One type may be called **phrasal article**. These articles are found at the (left or right) periphery of a nominal expression. In general, they occur only once per nominal expression. The other type may be called **linking article**. These articles are found in between the constituents of a complex nominal expression. They may occur several times in a single nominal expression.

Phrasal articles and linking articles develop from different syntactic constellations. The former derive from a syntagm consisting of DEM-(X)-N or N-(X)-DEM (x representing optional adnominal modifiers such as adjectives, quantifiers, etc.), while the latter derive from a syntagm of the shape N-DEM-X or X-DEM-N. Thus, one major difference between phrasal and linking articles pertains to the fact that linking articles only occur in complex nominal expressions, while phrasal articles occur in both simple and complex nominal expressions.

3.1. Linking articles

Linking articles (which are often also called linkers, ligatures, or connectors) may be indeclinable particles which occur between the major constituents of a nominal expression, as in the following example from Tagalog:

(8) Tagalog (Bloomfield 1917: 24/37)
*apat **na** malalim **na** balón*
four LK deep   LK well
'four deep wells'

Or they may agree with the noun, as in the following Albanian examples:

(9) Albanian (Buchholz & Fiedler 1987: 326)
shok-u   i   mirë
friend-DEF.NOM.SG.M LK.NOM.SG.M good
'the good (male) friend'

(10) Albanian (Buchholz & Fiedler 1987: 326)
shoqja   e   mirë
friend:DEF.NOM.SG.F LK.NOM.SG.F good
'the good (female) friend'

The preceding examples illustrate the use of linking articles with quantifiers and adjectives. Other typical contexts of use include relative clauses and (much more rarely) demonstratives:

(11) Tagalog
*yuung mama **na** bàbaril sa*
iyon-ng mama' na RED1-baríl sa
DIST-LK man   LK RED1-gun LOC
kanyá
kaniyá
3SG.DAT
'that man who was going to shoot at him'

In both Albanian and Tagalog the linking articles are strongly grammaticised. Their use depends exclusively on grammatical factors such as the kind of adnominal modifier. Semantic and pragmatic factors such as definiteness or specificity do not play a role; cf. example (7) above and:

(12) Albanian (Buchholz & Fiedler 1987: 326)
(një) shok   i   mirë
one friend:INDEF.M LK.NOM.SG.M good
'a good (male) friend'

In Albanian, the linking article is also used with genitive modifiers:

(13) Albanian (Buchholz & Fiedler 1987: 356)
roman-i   i   tretë
novel-DEF.NOM.SG.M LK.NOM.SG.M third
i   autor-it
LK.NOM.SG.M author-DEF.GEN.SG.M
'the author's third novel'

In Tagalog the linking article does not form a constituent with either of the two elements it 'links'. In Albanian, however, there is good evidence that it forms a constituent with the modifier, either as a proclitic (in the case of genitive modifiers) or as a prefix (in the case of adjectives). Thus, adjectives, for example, also occur with a linking article in predicative function, as in:

(14) Albanian (Buchholz & Fiedler 1987: 199)
vajz-a   është
girl-DEF.NOM.SG.F be.3SG.PRS
e   bukur
LK.NOM.SG.F pretty
'the girl is pretty'

The development of linking articles roughly follows the bondedness hierarchy proposed by Foley (1980): they occur first with attributes such as relative clauses and adjectives, then with quantifiers, and finally with demonstratives (cf. Himmelmann 1997: 172–183). Gamillscheg (1937) identifies examples such as Latin *porcus ille silvaticus* 'pig that feral' as a possible source construction.

The development of linking articles appears to be totally independent from the development of phrasal articles. In several languages, including Tagalog and Albanian, linking articles freely co-occur with phrasal articles in the same construction.

3.2. Phrasal articles

There are two basic types of phrasal articles. One type, called **NP-article** here, occurs in all types of nominal expressions, including nominal expressions functioning as modifiers within complex nominal expressions (as in *the end of **the** movie*). The definite articles in European languages are prototypical examples of NP-articles.

The other type, called **complement article** (CMA) here, occurs only once per clause-level nominal expression (i.e. a nominal expression which is in construction with a finite verb or one which forms a major constituent in a non-verbal clause). Compare the following examples from the Papuan language Hua:

(15) Hua (Haiman 1977: 58)
fina-roga-**mo** vie
fight-ALL-CMA go.3SG
'He went to the/a fight.'

(16) Hua (Haiman 1977: 58)
fina-roga (*mo) de(-mo)
fight-ALL   man(-CMA)
'a man for fights/a fighting man'

(17) Hua (Haiman 1978: 568)
bura de-ma? (*mo) fu-(mo)
that man-GEN   pig(-CMA)
'that man's pig'

In (15) the nominal expression *finaroga* is the allative complement of the verb 'go' and hence marked by the complement article *mo*. In (16) the same nominal expression functions as a complement of the noun *de* 'man'. In this construction, use of the complement article *mo* is impossible. Similarly in (17), where *bura dema?* 'that man's' functions as a possessive modifier of 'pig'. Further details on the complement article may be found in § 3.2.2.

There is no well-established terminology for many of the phenomena considered in this section, including the distinction between complement articles and NP-articles. Alternative terms for complement articles include 'connective particle' or 'phrase marker'.

3.2.1. NP-articles

The usage conditions for NP-articles vary across languages with regard to many minor details. For the two best known types of NP-articles, the definite and the specific article, the following contexts have been identified as particularly prone to crosslinguistic variation (cf. Greenberg 1978: 64–66 and Krámský 1972: 74–89): a) use with proper names and vocatives; b) use in adpositional phrases (cf. Himmelmann 1998); c) use with other determining elements such as demonstratives and possessors (see § 5). For specific articles there are the following additional grammatical contexts (cf. Greenberg 1978: 66–69): a) the noun functions as the object of a negated verb; b) the noun functions as a nominal predicate; c) the noun appears as part of a compound.

With regard to formal aspects, NP-articles vary along at least two parameters: a) the degree of fusion between article and noun; b) the number of articles in a given system (cf. Krámský 1972: 74–165 and Bechert 1993).

NP-articles typically are phrasal proclitics, occurring on the leftmost periphery of a noun phrase (as in *the three little boys*). Less commonly, they appear as phrasal enclitics as in Balinese *karanjang gede **ne*** 'the big basket (lit. basket big the)'. Very rarely, they are second position clitics, i. e. they appear after the first constituent of a noun phrase. In Bulgarian and Macedonian, for example, the definite article occurs after the noun if the NP consists of just a noun, but if the noun is preceded by one or more modifiers, it occurs immediately after the first modifier:

(18) Bulgarian (Scatton 1984: 164–167, 314 f.)
kníga=**ta**
book:SG.F=DEF.SG.F
'the book'

dvé=**te**   nóvi   knígi
two.F=DEF.PL.F   new:PL   book:PL.F
'the two new books'

Furthermore, NP-articles can be suffixed to the noun, a phenomenon common in North Germanic languages (e. g. Danish *hus* 'house' vs. *hus-et* 'the house') and also found in Rumanian (e. g. *lup* 'wolf(M)' vs. *lup-ul* 'the wolf', *casă* 'a house (F)' vs. *casa* 'the house') and Albanian. Prefixed articles appear to be rare. The definite articles in Berber and Semitic languages possibly belong into this category.

An extremely rare phenomenon is the consistent enclisis of an article to the preceding constituent. This phenomenon is found in North Wakashan (Boas 1911, 1947 and Anderson 1992: 23–37) and the neighbouring Tsimshian languages (Mulder 1994: 30–49). In the following example from Kwakw'ala (North Wakashan) the NP-articles =*i* and =*a* are both glossed as DIST because they convey deictic meanings, a point to which we will return shortly. Here it is only important to register that these articles are phonologically part of the preceding word while grammatically forming a constituent with the following one.

(19) Kwakw'ala (Boas 1911: 554)
lá:'lai: dú:x̌ʷaƛəlax̌a
la:-'la=i   du:qʷ-aƛəla=x̌=a
go-RPRT-DIST   see-accomplish-OBJ-DIST
'nəqá:c'aqi: x̌ʷá:k'una
'nəq-c'aq=i   x̌ʷa:kʷ-n=a
ten-LONG-OBJECT-DIST canoe-??-DIST
məx̌í:s   a:q
məx̌-i:s   la:-q
hollow_thing-beach   go-DIST.VIS.OBJ
'There he discovered ten canoes on the beach.'

Also extremely rare and in need of further investigation are the claims that an NP-article is realised only suprasegmentally, i. e. as a modification of the stress pattern of a noun. Krámský (1972: 186) mentions Ossetic as a language where this phenomenon is found. Another example is the so-called 'definitive accent' in Tongan (Churchward 1953: 25–27). This 'accent', however, appears to be functionally a demonstrative according to the criteria stated in § 2 since, judging from Churchward's examples, it occurs in typically recognitional and anaphoric contexts (Tongan also has a proclitic specific article *e*). Furthermore, the 'definitive accent' formally occupies an otherwise empty slot in the paradigm of enclitic demonstratives (cf. Clark 1974).

As for the number of NP-articles being part of a single system, a variety of phenomena may be distinguished. Typically, there is only one NP-article in a given system which may be either an indeclinable particle (as English *the* or Tagalog *ang*) or it may agree in number, gender and/or case with the noun (as in French, Albanian, Bulgarian, Standard German, etc.). More complex systems arise when NP-articles convey additional information about the referent (**classifying articles**) or speakers' attitude (**emotional** or **honorific articles**). Honorific articles occur primarily with proper nouns (they are widespread Western Austronesian, e. g., Tagalog *si*, Balinese *ni*). Emotional articles are found in certain Polynesian languages where they convey sympathy or belittlement (e. g. Samoan *nāi teine* 'the poor/dear/few girls'; cf. Mosel & Hovdhaugen 1992: 264–267). Krámský (1972: 93–96) reports a fairly elaborate system of classifying articles for Ponca (Siouan).

In a totally different type of system with multiple NP-articles the choice between two (or more) different NP-articles depends on the syntactic construction. For example, in North Germanic languages the definite article for unmodified nouns is a suffix (cf. Braunmüller 1982: 222–242). However, if the noun is preceded by modifiers then a different form of the definite article, i. e. a phrasal proclitic, has to be used (e. g., Danish *mand-en* 'the man' and ***den** gamle mand* 'the old man'). In some of these languages, both forms of the definite article are used together in complex nominal expressions. Thus, Swedish ***den** gamle mann-**en*** 'the old man' includes both a proclitic and a suffixed article.

A third type of system with multiple NP-articles arises when articles encode meanings typically associated with demonstratives such as visibility (VIS vs. INVIS) or distance from a deictic center (PROX, MED, DIST). These articles may be called **deictic articles**. They have been reported for Salish and North Wakashan (according to Boas (1947: 260) the two clitics =i and =a in example (19) above differ with regard to visibility) and several Austronesian languages, for example Tsou (Tung 1964: 218). To date, many aspects of these articles are not very well understood, including the precise nature of the semantic differences between the members of a given paradigm and between these articles and 'true' demonstratives.

Here it will suffice to illustrate the phenomenon from one language. In Lushootseed (Salish) the paradigm of determiners includes the following three elements: *ti* 'the (definite)', *tiʔəʔ* 'this', and *tiʔiɬ* 'that' (glosses from Hilbert & Hess 1977: 5), the latter two obviously being derived in some way from the first one (cf. Montler 1986: 224–236 for a componential analysis of Salish determiners). Although the glosses suggest that *tiʔəʔ* and *tiʔiɬ* are demonstratives, their use appears to be similar to specific articles. That is, in narrative texts they are used not only in typically demonstrative contexts but also in contexts which appear to be interpretable as instances of larger situation, associative-anaphoric or even specific-indefinite use (for the latter cf. also Jelinek & Demers 1994: 731 f.). Thus, the following example contains the first mention of the two protagonists of a traditional story, marked by *tiʔəʔ* (for want of a better gloss here simply glossed as THIS):

(20) Lushootseed (Hilbert & Hess 1977: 14)
tu-huyu-cut-əxʷ **tiʔəʔ**
PAST-make-self-NOW THIS
[sə]saʔliʔ ləgʷ-ləgʷəb
two (humans) RED-youth
'Two youths prepared themselves.'

Some of the multiple NP-article systems reported in the literature turn out, upon closer inspection, to contain demonstratives. Thus, it has been claimed for a variety of German dialects (Heinrichs 1954: 85–103, Hartmann 1982), North Frisian (Ebert 1970) and some Catalan dialects (references and some discussion in Selig 1992: 191) that two definite articles exist in these languages and dialects. One of these so-called definite articles, however, is used only in anaphoric contexts. Hence by the criteria used here, it is not an article but a high-frequency demonstrative (cf. Himmelmann 1997: 54–56, 100).

3.2.2. Complement articles

In addition to the defining feature of complement articles stated at the beginning of this section – i.e. that they occur only once per clause-level nominal expression – these articles also tend to occur after subordinate clauses expressing presupposed information. Thus, in Hua a complement article is commonly found after conditional and temporal adverbial clauses:

(21) Hua (Haiman 1980: 498/30)
zu'-roga-mo bau-ma-mo
house-ALL-CMA be-REL.DES-CMA
kgai'-hi' d-geta havi'
2SG-BEN 1SG.POSS-mind think
havi' hu-da
think do-1SG
'When I am at home I just think about you all the time.'

For a more extensive discussion of complement articles in Papuan languages, representing different stages in their grammaticisation, see Reesink (1994). Complement articles are in all likelihood not restricted to Papuan languages. Elements with similar distribution occur in some American Indian languages (Cayuga, Lakota) and possibly also in Haitian Creole (Lefebvre & Massam 1988).

4. Articles from other sources

This section briefly reviews articles derived from sources other than demonstratives. The review is brief not only because the phenomena to be discussed here are less widespread and less frequently attested in natural languages but also because there are, to date, no indepth studies on which well-supported generalisations could be based.

4.1. Articles derived from 'one'

Indefinite articles derive quite generally from the numeral 'one'. In fact, in many languages the numeral 'one' and the indefinite article are segmentally identical (e.g. French *un/une*, written German *ein/eine*, Turkish *bir*). And even if indefinite article and numeral are not segmentally identical, they generally do not co-occur with each other (*a one book is not well-formed in English; cf. also Moravcsik 1969: 84). An exception is Sinhala where what appears to be an indefinite article freely co-occurs with numerals, including the numeral for 'one'. Examples: *pota-k* 'a book (book.SG-INDEF)', *pot eka-k* 'one book (book. PL one-INDEF)', *pot tuna-k* 'three books (book.PL three-INDEF)', *mee pot tuna* 'those three books'.

When numeral and article are segmentally identical, the major formal criterion invoked in the literature for distinguishing them is that the article is unstressed. This, however, is a rather weak criterion since in most languages numerals do not have to be stressed. Consequently, in some instances it is controversial whether it is actually possible and useful to distinguish between article and numeral (for German, see Bisle-Müller 1991: 100−116, among others). In other instances stronger formal evidence is available for making such a distinction. In Turkish, for example, numeral and article are claimed to occupy different syntactic positions in complex nominal expressions (Lewis 1967: 54). The article intervenes between modifier and noun (*büyük bir tarla* 'a large field') while the numeral precedes the adjective (*bir büyük tarla* 'one large field').

Another kind of formal evidence for indefinite articles is provided by the rather rare phenomenon that an indefinite article derived from the numeral 'one' may be used in plural expressions. In at least one language, Spanish, special plural forms of such an indefinite article exist (cf. *un libro* 'a book' vs. *unos libros* 'some/a few books'). It should be noted, however, that indefinite articles derived from 'one' are typically restricted to the use with singular count nouns, a major difference between definite and indefinite articles. Exceptions to this generalisation include the indefinite articles in Turkish and, possibly, Sinhala. Furthermore, it is occasionally argued that another quantifier (e. g. *some* in English) functions as a plural indefinite article (Chesterman 1991: 44 f.). Fijian and some Polynesian languages are said to have plural indefinite articles derived from sources other than 'one'.

Givón (1981) is the only crosslinguistic study to date that attempts to identify different stages in the grammaticisation of indefinite articles, thereby also providing semantic criteria for distinguishing numerals from articles. One important criterion is the consistent use of the latter in nonspecific-indefinite contexts such as *I am looking for **a book on math**, do you have any?* Another one is the use of the indefinite article with predicate nominals as in *He is **a language professor**.* Furthermore, indefinite articles may occasionally be used in some kinds of generic statements such as *A dodo likes peanuts* (see Chesterman 1991: 32−38 for references and discussion).

As to the formal realisations of indefinite articles, the crosslinguistic variation is much more restricted than in the case of NP-articles. To date, no systems containing multiple indefinite articles have been identified. The major crosslinguistic variation pertains to the position of the indefinite article (before or after the noun) and to its degree of fusion with the noun (indefinite article are clitics in European languages but suffixes in Persian and Sinhala).

It is common to think of definite and indefinite articles as a 'natural pair', i.e. as occurring together in one morphosyntactic paradigm. Crosslinguistically, however, this is the exception rather than the rule (see Moravcsik 1969: 85−89). There are many languages with definite articles lacking indefinite articles (classical Greek, the Celtic languages, Bulgarian, many modern Arabic dialects, etc.). Conversely, there are a few languages with indefinite articles but no definite articles (e. g., Persian, Sinhala). And even if both a definite and an indefinite article are found in a particular language, they do not necessarily exhibit similar morphosyntactic characteristics. In several languages, for example, one article precedes the noun, the other follows it (e. g., Classical Arabic, North Germanic languages).

4.2. Pronominal articles

In many languages, personal pronouns can be used adnominally as in *we students*. This use, however, is generally severely constrained by grammatical and semantic factors and rather infrequent overall. In a few languages, including most of the languages spoken in central Australia (e. g., Mparntwe Arrernte (Wilkins 1989), Yankunytjatjara (Goddard 1985)), third person pronouns are regularly used in anaphoric mentions, e. g.:

(22) Mparntwe Arrernte (Wilkins 1989: 129)
*Artwe **itne** no*
man 3.PL.NOM NEG
ahel-irre-ke artwe
angry-INCH-PAST.COMPL man
mperikerre ikwere
white 3.SG.DAT
'The men didn't become aggressive towards the white man.'

In these languages, then, third person pronouns are used more frequently and in more kinds of contexts than in other languages. This can be interpreted as the beginning of the grammaticisation of an article from a pronoun. Given that third person pronouns are also generally derived from demonstratives, this grammaticisation path for articles is clearly closely related to the one leading directly from demonstratives to articles.

A fully grammaticised pronominal article is found in Nama (Khoisan) where every specific nominal expression is accompanied by a pronominal clitic (in phrase-final position). In the following example both the 1.SG pronoun and the word for 'desert' are followed by such a pronominal clitic, agreeing with the phrasal head in person, number and gender:

(23) Nama
 ti-**ta** ke k!aro-ŋ!hu-**p** ŋ!â
 1.SG-1.SG SUBJ desert-land-3.SG.M LOC
 nî kl?an-mâ.
 FUT.PFV smoke-stay
 'I will pitch in the desert.'

Since there are clitics for all persons and any noun may, in principle, be followed by any clitic (e. g. si-ʔao-**khom** (1.NONSG-man-1.DU.M) 'we two men'), it is sometimes said that in Nama nouns are 'inflected' for person. But note that these elements are clearly clitics (and not affixes) and that their overall distribution corresponds to a strongly grammaticised specific article.

4.3. Possessive articles

There is also evidence that in several languages possessive pronouns can be used well beyond the typical contexts of use for possessive pronouns. This is particularly clear in instances where there is no antecedent for the pronoun, as in the following example from Indonesian:

(24) Indonesian
 karena sungai-**nya** keruh
 because river -3SG.POSS muddy
 '(We couldn't take a bath) because the river was muddy …'

The river referred to here is the river known to everybody in the speech community. It is clear that there is no possessor for the river (i. e. it would be wrong to translate *sungainya* with 'his/her/its river'). Example (24), then, shows a larger situation use of a possessive pronoun, a context highly characteristic of definite and specific articles.

Similar extended uses of possessive pronouns have been reported for several Uralic and Turkic language in which both 3.SG and 2.SG possessive pronouns can be used in this way (cf. Krámský 1972: 173 f., Bechert 1993: 31−36). But in these languages as well as in Indonesian it does not appear to be the case that use of a possessive pronoun is obligatory in all (or a clearly defined subset of) definite or specific contexts. Further research is required to determine their precise usage conditions. A more strongly grammaticised form of the possessive article is found in Amharic (cf. Kapeliuk 1994).

4.4. Further (minor) sources

The sources for articles discussed in the preceding sections certainly do not exhaust all possibilities. In at least four instances it is clear that the source of an article in a given language is not a demonstrative, numeral, or personal or possessive pronoun.

Two instances pertain to the honorific and emotional articles mentioned in § 3.2.1 above. No unequivocal sources for these kinds of articles have been identified so far (for one of the Polynesian emotional-diminutive articles (Samoan *si* and its cognates) it has been suggested that it derives from the word for 'little'). Note that these elements are only considered articles if they are in complementary distribution with other kinds of articles (typically NP-articles). Otherwise, they would be considered simply honorific or diminutive particles without further import to the structure of nominal expressions.

The definite article in Sardinian is derived from the Latin identity pronoun *ipse* 'self' (Selig 1992: 177−185) which was frequently used in anaphoric contexts in late Latin (Selig 1992: 117−120) and also survives as a highly general and frequent marker of anaphoric reference in some Catalan dialects (where it is one of the two so-called definite articles, see § 3.2.1 above).

Finally, in Salish there is a determiner based on the root k^w-which is generally glossed as 'remote, hypothetical, or conjectured' in the grammars of these languages. It is fairly frequent in nominal expressions and occurs in typical anaphoric contexts:

(25) Lushootseed (Hilbert & Hess 1977: 19)
 ɫu-lə-ʔux̌ʷ čəd dxʷʔal **k**ʷi
 WILL-SERIES-go I TOWARD REMOTE
 siʔab ʔab(s)-s-ləx̌-il
 noble HAVE-ABS-light-BECOME
 'I will be going towards the noble man who possesses the daylight.'

This element also appears to be used as a subordinator (complementizer) with modal implications. It is clear that it is in complementary distribution with the deictic determiners mentioned in § 3.2.1 and hence belongs to the paradigm of determiners. It is also reasonably certain that it is not derived from a numeral, deictic, or pronoun. But its origin and precise meaning and function remain to be determined.

5. Co-occurrence with other determiners

One major typological parameter relevant to all articles irrespective of their source is the question of whether or not articles may co-occur with other determining elements such as possessive pronouns and demonstratives. 'True' indefinite articles (as opposed to numerals) generally do not co-occur with any other determiner, for obvious semantic reasons. Specific articles quite generally may co-occur with both possessive pronouns and demonstratives (e. g., Tagalog *ang anák ko* 'my child (SPEC child 1.SG.POSS)'). In many languages, definite articles also freely co-occur with possessive pronouns as in Italian *il mio amico* 'my friend (the my friend)' (cf. Plank 1992). Somewhat less commonly, definite articles may co-occur with demonstratives, for example, in Gulf Arabic (Holes 1990: 175) *haadha l-garaar* 'this decision (PROX DEF-decision)' (similar constructions are found in Hungarian, Welsh and Greek). Co-occurrence phenomena such as the precedings ones have been amply documented in recent work by Plank et al. (Plank 1995) under the label 'overdetermination'. This also includes the co-occurrence of two different forms of an article within the same nominal expression as in the Swedish example **den gamle mann-en** 'the old man' mentioned in § 3.2.1.

Acknowledgements

Many thanks for helpful discussion and data to Kumara Henadeerage (Sinhala), Wayan Pastika (Balinese), Andy Pawley (Polynesian), and Heinz Roberg (Nama). All Tagalog and Indonesian data without source references are from the author's corpora.

6. Special abbreviations

ALL	allative
BEN	benefactive
CMA	complement article
COMPL	completive
DIST	distal demonstrative
INCH	inchoative
INDEF	indefinite
INVIS	invisible
LK	linker (linking article)
MED	medial demonstrative
PM	predicate marker
PROX	proximal demonstrative
REAL	realis
RED	reduplication
REL.DES	relative desinence
RPRT	reportative
SPEC	specific
STAT	stative
VIS	visible

7. References

Anderson, Stephen R. 1992. *A-morphous morphology*. Cambridge: Cambridge University Press.

Bechert, Johannes. 1993. *Definiteness and article systems*. Eurotyp Working Papers I/4.

Bisle-Müller, Hansjörg. 1991. *Artikelwörter im Deutschen*. Tübingen: Niemeyer.

Bloomfield, Leonard. 1917. *Tagalog texts with grammatical analysis*. Urbana: The University of Illinois.

Boas, Franz. 1911. "Kwakiutl". In: Boas, Franz (ed.). *Handbook of American Indian languages*. Washington: Bureau of American Ethnology, I: 425–557.

Boas, Franz. 1947. *Kwakiutl grammar with a glossary of the suffixes*. Philadelphia: The American Philosophical Society.

Braunmüller, Kurt. 1982. *Syntaxtypologische Studien zum Germanischen*. Tübingen: Narr.

Buchholz, Oda & Fiedler, Wilfried. 1987. *Albanische Grammatik*. Leipzig: Verlag Enzyklopädie.

Chafe, Wallace L. (ed.). 1980. *The Pear Stories: Cognitive, cultural, and linguistic aspects of narrative production*. Norwood, N. J.: Ablex.

Chesterman, Andrew. 1991. *On definiteness*. Cambridge: Cambridge University Press.

Christophersen, Paul. 1939. *The articles. A study of their theory and use in English*. Copenhagen: Munksgaard.

Churchward, C. Maxwell. 1953. *Tongan grammar*. London: Oxford University Press.

Clark, Ross. 1974. "On the origin of the Tongan definitive accent". *The Journal of the Polynesian Society* 83: 103–108.

Diessel, Holger. 1999. *Demonstratives: form, function and grammaticalization*. Amsterdam: Benjamins.

Dryer, Matthew. 1989. "Article-Noun Order". *Chicago Linguistic Society* 25: 83–97.

Ebert, Karen H. 1970. *Referenz, Sprechsituation und die bestimmten Artikel in einem nordfriesischen Dialekt.* Bräist/Bredstedt: Nordfriisk Instituut.

Fillmore, Charles J. 1982. "Towards a descriptive framework for spatial deixis". In: Jarvella, Robert J. & Klein, Wolfgang (eds.). *Speech, Place and Action.* Chichester: John Wiley, 31−59.

Foley, William A. 1980. "Towards a universal typology of the noun phrase". *Studies in Languages* 4: 171−200.

Gamillscheg, Ernst. 1937. "Zum romanischen Artikel und Possessivpronomen". In: id. *Ausgewählte Aufsätze von Ernst Gamillscheg.* (Supplementheft XV der Zeitschrift für französische Sprache und Literatur) Jena: Wilhelm Gronau.

Givón, Talmy. 1981. "On the development of the numeral 'one' as an indefinite article". *Folia Linguistica Historica* 2: 35−53.

Goddard, Cliff. 1985. *A grammar of Yankunytjatjara.* Alice Springs: Institute for Aboriginal Development.

Grasserie, Raoul de la. 1896. "De l'article". *Mémoires de la Société de Linguistique de Paris* 9.4: 285−322, 381−394.

Greenberg, Joseph H. 1978. "How does a language acquire gender markers?" In: Greenberg, Joseph H., Ferguson, Charles A. & Moravcsik, Edith (eds.) *Universals of Human Language.* Stanford: Stanford University Press, III: 47−82.

Haiman, John. 1977. "Connective particles in Hua: an essay on the parts of speech". *Oceanic Linguistics* 16: 53−107.

Haiman, John. 1978. "Conditionals are topics!". *Language* 54: 564−589.

Haiman, John. 1980. *Hua: A Papuan language of the Eastern Highlands of New Guinea.* Amsterdam: Benjamins.

Hartmann, Dietrich. 1982. "Deixis and Anaphora in German Dialects: The semantics and pragmatics of two definite articles in dialectal varieties". In: Weissenborn, Jürgen & Klein, Wolfgang (eds.) 1982. *Here and there.* Amsterdam: Benjamins, 187−207.

Hawkins, John A. 1978. *Definiteness and indefiniteness.* London: Croom Helm.

Hawkins, John A. 1991. "On (in)definite articles: implicatures and (un)grammaticality prediction". *Journal of Linguistics* 27: 405−422.

Heinrichs, Heinrich Matthias. 1954. *Studien zum bestimmten Artikel in den germanischen Sprachen.* Giessen: W. Schmitz.

Hilbert, Vi & Hess, Thomas. 1977. "Lushootseed". In: Carlson, Barry F. (ed.). *Northwest Coast Texts.* Chicago: The University of Chicago Press, 4−32.

Himmelmann, Nikolaus P. 1996. "Demonstratives in narrative discourse: a taxonomy of universal uses". In: Fox, Barbara (ed.). *Studies in anaphora.* Amsterdam: Benjamins, 203−252.

Himmelmann, Nikolaus P. 1997. *Deiktikon, Artikel, Nominalphrase: Zur Emergenz syntaktischer Struktur.* Tübingen: Niemeyer.

Himmelmann, Nikolaus P. 1998. "Regularity in irregularity: Article use in adpositional phrases". *Linguistic Typology* 2: 315−353.

Holes, Clive. 1990. *Gulf Arabic.* London: Routledge.

Jelinek, Eloise & Demers, Richard A. 1994. "Predicates and pronominal arguments in Straits Salish". *Language* 70: 697−736.

Kapeliuk, Olga. 1994. *Syntax of the noun in Amharic.* Wiesbaden: Harrassowitz.

Krámský, Jiří. 1972. *The article and the concept of definiteness in language.* The Hague: Mouton.

Laury, Rita. 1997. *Demonstratives in interaction: The emergence of a definite in Finish.* Amsterdam: Benjamins.

Lefebvre, Claire & Massam, Diane. 1988. "Haitian Creole syntax: a aase for *DET* as head". *Journal of Pidgin and Creole Languages* 3: 213−243.

Lewis, G. L. 1967. *Turkish grammar.* Oxford: Clarendon Press.

Montler, Timothy. 1986. *An outline of the morphology and phonology of Saanich, North Straits Salish.* (University of Montana Occasional Papers in Linguistics No. 4) Missoula: University of Montana.

Moravcsik, Edith A. 1969. "Determination". *Working Papers on Language Universals* (Stanford) 1: 64−98.

Mosel, Ulrike & Hovdhaugen, Even. 1992. *Samoan reference grammar.* Oslo: Scandinavian University Press.

Mulder, Jean G. 1994. *Ergativity in Coast Tsimshian (Sm'algyax).* Berkeley: University of California Press.

Plank, Frans. 1992. "Possessives and the distinction between determiners and modifiers (with special reference to German)". *Journal of Linguistics* 28: 453−468.

Plank, Frans (ed.). 1995. *Overdetermination.* Eurotyp Working Paper (Theme 7, No. 24).

Reesink, Ger P. 1994. "Domain-creating constructions in Papuan Languages". In: Reesink, Ger P. (ed.) *Topics in Descriptive Papuan Linguistics.* (Semaian 10) Leiden: Vakgroep Talen en Culturen van Zuidoost-Azië en Oceanië, 98−121.

Scatton, Ernest A. 1984. *A Reference grammar of Modern Bulgarian.* Columbus: Slavica Publishers.

Selig, Maria. 1992. *Die Entwicklung der Nominaldeterminanten im Spätlatein.* Tübingen: Narr.

Tung, T'ung-ho. 1964. *A descriptive study of the Tsou Language.* Taipei: Academia Sinica.

Wilkins, David P. 1989. *Mparntwe Arrernte (Aranda): Studies in the structure and semantics of grammar.* PhD thesis ANU, Canberra.

Nikolaus P. Himmelmann,
Ruhr-Universität Bochum (Germany) and
Australian National University, Canberra
(Australia)

63. Adverbial conjunctions

1. Research background
2. Morphology and syntax
3. Semantics
4. Evolution
5. Universals
6. Special abbreviations
7. References

1. Research background

1.1. The semantic space of adverbial (or: circumstantial, interclausal semantic) relations like Simultaneity, Anteriority, Cause, or Condition is an indispensable part of human cognition (cf. von der Gabelentz 1901^2: 464). Thus most languages (for exceptions cf. § 2.2) have a set of free or bound morphemes which serve, at least in one of their functions, as markers of adverbial relatons holding between two or more propositions. Of these, adverbial conjunctions (henceforth *ACs*), i. e. free morphemes which operate over a subordinate clause serving as an optional adverbial modifier of the main clause (e. g. English *when, while, after, since, because, if*), form if not the largest then certainly the best-known and best-researched subclass. This is due to (a) their status as one of the established (functional, synsemantic) word classes in the (Indo-)European grammar tradition (Lang to appear), and the related fact that (b) the (western and central) European languages, especially those representing Standard Average European (*SAE*), are particularly rich in ACs, both as regards number and semantic diversity. As a matter of fact, the preferred or exclusive use of finite subordinate clauses, which in the case of adverbial clauses are introduced by ACs, are considered as two distinctive traits of Standard Average European (van der Auwera 1998b; → Art. 107). Perhaps the major reason for the richness of SAE languages in ACs (on average 60 per language) is that (a) ACs and adverbial subordination in general involve complex sentences, (b) complex sentences are primarily a phenomenon of planned language use, notably of written language, and (c) the great majority of European languages qualify as *ausbau* languages (Kloss 1967), i. e. fully developed languages with a written form for all communicative purposes. The evolution of rich and diversified inventories of ACs and the borrowing of ACs from more prestigious (especially European) languages, too, can be shown to be linked to a developing literacy (Meillet 1915/16, Raible 1992, Thompson & Longacre 1985; cf. § 4.3).

1.2. As a consequence, it is for the European languages that the form, meaning and history of ACs have been investigated much more thoroughly than for any other (genetic or areal) group of languages. Most of these studies are language-specific though. In general, there exist hardly any cross-linguistic or typological studies of ACs, or of adverbial subordination for that matter (Thompson & Longacre 1985 is an exception). Those few cross-linguistic studies on ACs that do exist are Eurocentric in one way or another. They either look exclusively at ACs in European languages (cf. Kortmann 1997a, 1997b and various contributions to van der Auwera 1998), or make European ACs the starting-point and standard of comparison of cross-linguistic studies (e. g. Traugott 1985 on conditionals or König 1985, 1988 on concessives). European languages will therefore figure prominently in this article, especially when statistical statements will be made. At the same time, there will be three safeguards against a European, or even SAE, bias: (a) care will be taken to point out the major differences between ACs in European and non-European languages; (b) we will avoid making facts from the European languages the basis for generalizations across the languages of the world; (c) linguistic Europe is not reduced to the typical SAE languages, but includes all languages up to Siberia in the Northeast, the Ural mountains in the East and the Caspian Sea, the southern Caucasus, the Black Sea and the Bosporus in the Southeast. Besides covering the well-known Indoeuropean languages in the, linguistically speaking, fairly homogeneous West and Central European core, generalizations across the European languages also cover such typologically diverse languages as Basque, the Celtic languages, Indo-Iranian, Uralic, Altaic, Caucasian and Semitic languages in the geographical periphery of Europe.

2. Morphology and syntax

2.1. The most important distinctive properties of ACs are the following: (a) ACs are non-inflecting free forms, (b) ACs operate over a (typically finite) subordinate clause (thus the alternative term *adverbial subordinators*) which has the status of an optional adjunct (and thus qualifies as an adverbial clause), (c) ACs do not fulfil a syntactic function (e. g. subject, object, adverbial) in the subordinate clause, (d) ACs assume a fixed position at the margin of the subordinate clause.

2.2. By subordinate clause is understood a dependent clause, i. e. a clause which depends for its occurrence on another, the main, clause. Even if it may not be entirely clear (cf. Haiman & Thompson 1984) what exactly constitutes subordination on the clausal level (i. e. hypotaxis), the notion 'subordinate clause' is taken to be universally applicable (→ Art. 45, 74). According to Thompson & Longacre (1985: 171), this also holds for the notion 'adverbial clause': "It appears that all languages have a set of two-clause constructions in which one clause can be said to modify the other in a way similar to the way in which an adverb modifies a proposition". The typological parameter finiteness however, with defining features like tense, mood, aspect, voice marking and subject agreement, cannot claim to possess universal validity. The distinction between languages using preferably or exclusively finite or non-finite subordination patterns is extremely important when considering, for example, the languages of Europe (finiteness being a distinctive trait of SAE; cf. § 1.1). For many other languages it is difficult, if not impossible to operate with these two notions. Isolating languages like Mandarin Chinese, for example, do not have a formal distinction between dependent and independent verb forms in the first place (Bisang 1998: 733; for a general discussion cf. also Lehmann 1988, Koptjevskaja-Tamm 1994, Haspelmath 1995; → Art. 100). There also appear to be languages whose primary or exclusive-linking strategy is not subordination but juxtaposition (e. g. North American languages like Iroquoian; Mithun 1984). In such languages the semantic relation holding between adjacent clauses is not explicitly signalled, but a matter of inference.

2.3. The overwhelming majority of European languages exclusively use clause-initial ACs. But ACs are not restricted to the initial position in the adverbial clause (cf. property (d) in § 2.1). Strictly speaking, this is even true for SAE languages in those cases where the AC is (pre)modified by an adverb (e. g. English *immediately before, soon after*). Another scenario of ACs in non-clause-initial position is the fronting of certain constituents of the adverbial clause. This is possible, for example, for English *though* and *as if* the predicative complement is fronted:

(1) (a) *Rich people though they are, they have no style.*
(b) *Rich though/as they are, they have no style.*

In many languages all or a subset of ACs appear in clause-final position, either exclusively (2 a, b) or as one option (2 c). In the case of Udmurt *ke* 'if' the other option is a clause-medial position between the subject and the verb (3 a), which is also the normal position for various ACs in Ossetic (3 b, c):

(2) (a) Ijo (Niger-Congo; Dryer 1992a: 53)
ǫ   duma tún timi   *sèribi*,
3PL song sing CONT.PAST *while*
arì waìi bó-mi
I turn come-PAST
'While they were singing, I returned'
(b) Ossetic (Indo-Iranian)
mah ahodæn ba-hor-tta-m,
we breakfast pref-eat-PAST-1PL,
tsæugædon-ə bəl-mæ
river-GEN bank-ALL
a-tsæu-ən-ə **razmæ**
prefix-go-INF-GEN *before*
'We had breakfast before we went to the river'
(c) Udmurt (Finno-Ugric)
ki-jad   *biṅgozy śot-i-zy*
hand-INESS:2SG reins give-PAST-3PL
ke, *ton so-je jun kyrmy*
if you it-ACC fast hold-IMP
'If they gave the reins into your hands, hold them firmly'

(3) (a) Udmurt
*ton **ke** myny-sal-yd, ćoryg no*
you *if* go-COND-2SG fish also
luy-sal
be-COND
'If you had gone, there would be fish'
(b) Ossetic
*art **kəm** uə-di,   uəm mah*
fire *where* be-PAST.3SG there we
fe-dta-m   ærmæst sau ævzalə
see-PAST-1PL only   black ruins
'Where the fire had been, we saw only black ruins'

(c) Ossetic
æz televisor-mæ **kuə**
I   TV-ALL   when
kas-tæ-n,   uæd
watch-PAST-1SG then
ærba-tsə-də-stə   mæ nəjjardžə-tæ
prefix-go-PAST-3PL my parents-PL
'When I was watching TV, my parents arrived'

For Mandarin Chinese ACs all three positions can be found. As in the East and Southeast Asian languages in general, the majority of ACs assume either clause-initial position or the position after the topic and/or subject of the clause. A small group of temporal ACs, however, namely ACs derived from a noun meaning 'time' or from relational nouns meaning 'back, front', obligatorily take clause-final position (Bisang 1998: 761 f., 776). Here the grammaticalization path is responsible for the position of the AC (cf. § 4). As the example from Fanti shows (4), there even appear to be languages which employ a clause-initial and a clause-final AC in the same clause:

(4)   Fanti (Niger-Congo)
      se   mi-wi'é   a   mí-kò fi'é
      when 1SG-finish when 1SG-go home
      'When I'm finished, I go home'

The following universal tendencies can be observed with regard to what type of language can be expected to make use of predominantly clause-initial or clause-final ACs (Dryer in Kortmann 1997a: 71). They all confirm the strong correlation between prepositions and clause-initial ACs, on the one hand, and postpositions and clause-final ACs on the other hand.

(5)   If a language is prepositional, it will employ clause-initial ACs.

(6) (a) Clause-final ACs only occur in languages with postpositions.
    (b) If a language primarily employs clause-final ACs, then, if it employs adpositions, those adpositions will be primarily postpositions.

Just like prepositions and postpositions correlate with VO and OV order respectively (→ Art. 64), clause-initial ACs strongly correlate with VO (in Dryer's data 59 of 60 VO languages). The correlation between OV and clause-final ACs is much less pronounced though (38 of 55 OV languages). The same correlations hold for complementizers; subordinating conjunctions in general may therefore be called *verb patterners* (Dryer 1992: 102 f.). Compare § 5 for more correlations between basic word order and properties of ACs and adverbial subordination strategies.

2.4. The properties in § 2.1 help distinguish ACs from other markers of adverbiality and, more generally, from other non-inflecting word classes. Property (a), for example, distinguishes ACs from relative pronouns, which are case-marked, and from the bound markers of specialized (or: conjunctional) converbs (cf. V. Nedjalkov 1995, I. Nedjalkov 1998; → Art. 83) as they can be found in the North Caucasian and Altaic languages (e. g. Lezgian *-waldi, -zamaz*, Chechen *-seh'*, or Karachai-Balkar *-ganlai*: all 'as soon as'). Property (b) distinguishes ACs both from coordinating conjunctions (e. g. English *for*, French *car*, German *denn*, Dutch *want*) and from complementizers (e. g. English *that, whether*). Properties (b), (c) and (d) together distinguish ACs from conjunctional adverbs or "main clause conjunctions" (e. g. English *however, nevertheless*, German *deswegen, deshalb*). The properties in 2.1 also keep ACs distinct from other non-inflecting word classes, notably from prepositions and adverbs, regardless of whether ACs and the latter two are defined in the traditional sense, or as subcategories of the major lexical (head-of-phrase) category P in generative syntax (cf. Emonds 1987).

2.5. ACs are frequently syntactically polyfunctional, i. e. they also (sometimes even primarily) serve other syntactic functions like, using examples from English, preposition (*after, before, since*), adverb (*after, before, since, directly*), interrogative marker (*when*), noun (*while*) or verb (*provided*). Judging on the basis of the European languages, this applies only to a minority of ACs: almost never to phrasal ACs (e. g. English *as soon as, so that, as if*) and only to roughly half of all one-word ACs. In no European language do such "secondary" ACs outnumber "primary" ACs, i. e. lexical items serving exclusively as ACs. This tendency can also be observed in Asian languages (Bisang 1998: 759). The most important other word classes secondary ACs belong to are adpositions, adverbs and interrogative markers, followed by relativizers and complementizers (Kortmann 1997a: 110 f.). These are also the major sources of ACs in the European languages. In cases like *after, when, while* or *directly*, what started life as a member of any of these word classes additionally developed the use as an AC. In fact, serving as an AC can generally be called an overlay function. The reverse direction of change has hardly been documented in the world's languages. In non-European languages, however, other source categories may be much more important. This applies for example to verbs and nouns, which are the most important sources of ACs in serial-verb languages (Bisang 1998: 772–779).

2.6. The great majority of ACs consist of one word. There are only very few languages (e.g. the West Romance languages) where the majority of ACs is phrasal (e.g. French *à moins que*, *à present que*, *aprés que*, *bien que*, *parce que* or Spanish *a menos que*, *antes (de) que*, *dado que*, *hasta que*, *puesto que*, *salvo que*). A fairly small subclass of phrasal ACs is discontinuous, with the discontinuous elements occurring either both in the adverbial clause (like Megrelian *radgan ... -ni* in (7), possibly also in (4) above) or with one element in the adverbial clause and the correlative element in the main clause (e.g. Latin *pro — eo*, English *the — the*, German *je — desto*).

(7) Megrelian (Kartvelian; South Caucasus)
    ma ok'o   tena kobʒire,
    I ought.to it:NOM 1:3:see:OPT
    radgan si taš ragadanki-**ni**
    since/because you so 2:3:say:PRES-SR
    'I ought to see it, since you say so'

Discontinuous ACs need to be distinguished from those instances where ACs are frequently (e.g. English *if — then*) or even typically (but not obligatorily) accompanied by a correlative element in the main clause. In Mandarin Chinese, for example, most ACs occur with correlators (e.g. *zhǐ-yào* 'as long as' — *jiù* 'then', *zhǐ-yǒu* 'only if' — *cái* 'only', *jì-shǐ* 'even if' — *yě* 'too', *suī-rán* 'although' — *dànshi* 'but'; Bisang 1998: 768 f.).

2.7. As pointed out in § 2.5, syntactic polyfunctionality can only be observed for one-word ACs, almost never for phrasal or discontinuous ACs. In fact, the formal complexity of ACs inversely correlates with their syntactic polyfunctionality: The lower the degree of morphological complexity, the higher is the likelihood that the AC additionally belongs to other word classes. Of more than 2,000 ACs in almost 50 European languages, the by far highest proportions of syntactically polyfunctional ACs were found for monosyllabic ACs, immediately followed by polysyllabic, but still monomorphemic ACs (Kortmann 1997a: 110 f.). This inverse correlation does not only hold between formal complexity and syntactic polyfunctionality, but also between formal complexity and semantic polyfunctionality, i.e. polysemy (cf. § 3.2).

3. Semantics

3.1. ACs are commonly classified according to the adverbial relation(s) they express (temporal markers, conditionals, concessives, etc.). The semantic space of adverbial relations can be said to consist of those in (8) to (11). The first three sets represent the three major networks: temporal relations (8), modal relations (9), and CCC relations (10), i.e. causal, conditional and concessive relations as well as relations closely related to these three. Locative and other adverbial relations which cannot be subsumed under any of the three major networks form the set in (11). The exact number of the relations is irrelevant. All languages, however, are claimed to possess morphemes for the marking of at least a subset of these (and possibly additional) adverbial relations (cf. § 5).

(8) TIME
    Simultaneity Overlap   'when'
    Simultaneity Duration   'while'
    Simultaneity
      Co-Extensiveness   'as long as'
    Anteriority   'after'
    Immediate Anteriority   'as soon as'
    Terminus a quo   'since'
    Posteriority   'before'
    Terminus ad quem   'until'
    Contingency   'whenever'
(9) MODAL
    Manner   'as, how'
    Similarity   'as, like'
    Comment/Accord   'as'
    Comparison   'as if'
    Instrument/Means   'by'
    Proportion   'the ... the'
(10) CCC
    Cause/Reason   'because'
    Condition   'if'
    Negative Condition   'unless'
    Concessive Condition   'even if'
    Concession   'although'
    Contrast   'whereas'
    Result   'so that'
    Purpose   'in order that'

Negative Purpose	'lest'
Degree/Extent	'insofar as'
Exception/Restriction	'except/ only that'

(11) OTHER
Place	'where'
Substitution	'instead of'
Preference	'rather than'
Concomitance, Negative Concomitance	'without'
Addition	'in addition to'

3.2. Even if the semantic space of adverbial relations is cut up into such fine distinctions, it is astonishing to see that of more than 2,000 ACs taken from almost 50 European languages the majority (63.5%) is monosemous and that polysemy in most cases is restricted to two meanings (22.5%). No more than 14% of the European ACs can signal three or more adverbial relations as their primary or secondary meanings. As for syntactic polyfunctionality (cf. §§ 2.5 and 2.7), one-word ACs are much more likely to be polysemous (roughly one out of two) than phrasal or discontinuous ACs (roughly one out of four). In fact, a parallel inverse correlation can be observed between the (degree of) formal complexity of ACs and their (degree of) polysemy as was observed for syntactic polyfunctionality: The more formally reduced an AC is, the higher is the proportion (a) of polysemous ACs and (b) of highly polysemous ACs with three or more two meanings (Kortmann 1997a: 123−127).

3.3. From a semiotic point of view, the findings sketched in §§ 2.7 and 3.2 are relevant in various respects. ACs clearly conform to the hypothesis of a balance between form and meaning/function as it is frequently found in functional explanations of form-meaning and form-function asymmetries. This balance, first observed by George K. Zipf (1949) in particular, applies both to the semantic and syntactic polyfunctionality of ACs. In fact, the morphological and semantic analysis of ACs in languages for which reliable frequency statistics are available lends convincing support to Zipf's well-known Economy Principles (→ Art. 31), for example to his Law of Abbreviation (the frequency of use of a word correlates inversely with its formal complexity) or the Principle of Economical Versatility (the frequency of use of a word correlates directly with its number of meanings; cf. Kortmann 1997a: 127−135). Furthermore, the fact that the majority of ACs in the European as well as East and Southeast Asian languages (cf. Bisang 1998: 759) tend to be both monosemous and monofunctional (i. e. 'primary' ACs) is taken to support isomorphism, i. e. the hypothesis that one form tends to have only one meaning and one syntactic function (→ Art. 30).

3.4. In analyzing polysemous ACs across a large number of languages it is possible to identify constraints on polysemy and recurrent polysemy patterns. What is meant by constraints on polysemy is that certain adverbial relations can never or only very rarely be expressed by the same AC (e. g. Condition and Purpose, Posteriority 'before' and Manner/Similarity 'as, like'). For temporal ACs expressing more than one temporal relation the constraint seems to be that the relevant temporal relations must be adjacent on a cognitive map such as Figure 63.1 (cf., for example, (12) and (13)). In almost 50 European languages no polysemous temporal AC was found to violate this "adjacency constraint" (Kortmann 1997a: 186 f.), which is of course also a constraint on possible semantic changes within the temporal domain.

3.5. Searching for recurrent polysemy patterns means searching for adverbial relations that are frequently expressed as primary and/or secondary meanings of polysemous ACs in the languages of the world (e. g. Anteriority/Terminus a quo 'after'/'since' and Cause, Simultaneity Overlap/Co-Extensiveness 'when'/'as long as' and Condition, Simultaneity Duration 'while' and Contrast 'whereas'). That way a lot can be learnt about important paths of semantic change, on the one hand, and about the semantic relatedness of individual adverbial relations, on the other hand. The outcome of these searches can be interpreted on a macrolevel and a microlevel. On a macrolevel only those semantic affinities are taken into account which hold globally between the four networks of CCC, temporal, modal and, as the most important minor network, locative relations. On a microlevel what is considered are the semantic affinities between individual (pairs of) interclausal relations both within and across these four networks. The three most important generalizations on the macrolevel are the following (cf. Figure 63.2): (A) Semantic affinities between interclausal relations belonging to dif-

63. Adverbial conjunctions

		TAQUO 'since'	ANTE 'after'	IMANTE 'as soon as'	SIOVER 'when'	SIDUR 'while'	SICOEX 'as long as'	TAQUEM 'until'	POST 'before'
Grg	mas šem-deg rac	——							
Alb	qëkurse	————————							
Dut	toen		———————						
Goth	þande(i)			—————————————					
Arm	minčev				————————				
Rum	pînă						—————————————		
Mcd	dodeka				—————————————————————				
Blg	dokato					———————————			
Ltn	dum					—————————————————			
Mlt	sakemm						———————		
Grk	óso na							———————	

Grg = Georgian, Alb = Albanian, Dut = Dutch, Goth = Gothic, Arm = Armenian, Rum = Rumanian, Mcd = Macedonian, Blg = Bulgarian, Ltn = Latin, Mlt = Maltese, Grk = Modern Greek

Figure 63.1: Temporal subordinators covering different parts of the network of temporal relations

ferent semantic networks are always unidirectional. For example, temporal relations generally give rise to CCC relations; locative and modal relations feed in to the network of temporal relations and, partly via the latter, to the CCC network. For none of these links does the reverse hold, i. e. neither are CCC subordinators found to develop temporal, locative or modal readings, nor do temporal subordinators come to serve as locative or modal markers. (B) The semantic networks in Figure 63.2 can be classified according to whether they serve exclusively as the source (locative and modal relations) or as the goal (the CCC network) of processes of interpretative enrichment and semantic change; the network of temporal relations serves both as a source domain (for derived CCC meanings) and as a goal (for locative and modal relations). (C) The semantic affinities between these four networks differ in strength: The strongest affinities hold between temporal and CCC relations, whereas the weakest are those between locative and modal relations.

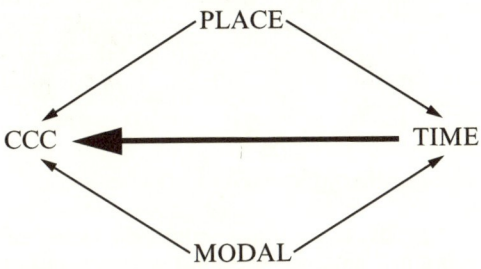

Figure 63.2: The macrostructure of the semantic space of interclausal relations

Some of the most frequently observable polysemy patterns across languages are illustrated in (12) to (20):

(12) Simultaneity Co-Extensiveness 'as long as' — Terminus ad quem 'until'
Latin *quoad*, Italian *fin(tanto)ché, sin(tanto)ché*, Rumanian *cît, pînă (ce, cînd)*; Gothic *þanei, þande(i), und þatei*; Polish *(do)póki*, Russian *poka*, Bulgarian *dokle, do(g)de*, Macedonian *duri*, Serbian/Croatian *dok, dokle*; Albanian *derisa, qjersa*; Classical Greek *mékhri (hoū), éste, héōs*; Lithuanian *iki, lig(i)*, Latvian *kamēr, līdz*; Armenian *minčev (or/zi)*; Hungarian *(a)míg, (a)meddig*; Turkish *kadar*; Lezgian *q'wan*; Maltese *sakemm*

(13) Terminus ad quem 'until' — Posteriority 'before'
Irish *sula*; Rumanian *pînă (ce, cînd)*; Bulgarian *dokle, do(g)de*, Macedonian *duri, pred*, Serbian/Croatian *dok, dokle*; Albanian *derisa, qjersa*; Modern Greek *óso na*; Georgian *vidre(mde/mdis)*; Maltese *qabel ma*; cf. also bound adverbial subordinators: Abkhaz *-aanza*; converbs like Chuvash *-ičćen*, Karachay-Balkar *-gänči*, or Lezgian *-daldi*

(14) Anteriority 'after' — Cause/Reason 'because'
Irish *tar éis (do) (go)*; French *à présent que, maintenant que*, Italian *dopo che*; German *nachdem*, Dutch *nu*; Hungarian *miután*; Macedonian

pošto, Serbian/Croatian *pošto*; Albanian *pasi, mbasi*; Modern Greek *afú, efóso*, Classical Greek *epeí*; Finnish *koska*; Azerbaijani *vara*

(15) Terminus a quo 'since' – Cause/Reason 'because'
Irish *ó*, Scottish Gaelic *ó*; Portuguese *desde que*, French *dès lors que, du moment que*, Italian *dacché, dal momento che*; Danish *siden*, English *since*; Classical Greek *epeí*; Basque *ordutik*

(16) Simultaneity Duration 'while' – Contrast 'whereas'
Welsh *tra*; Catalan *mentre (que)*, Italian *mentre, laddove*, Rumanian *în vreme/timp ce*; Danish *mens/medens*, Icelandic *(á) meðan (að)*, Dutch *terwijl*, English *while, whilst*, German *während, indes(sen)*, Yiddish *beshas ven*; Polish *podczas gdy*, Russian *v to vremja kak*; Lithuanian *tuõ tarpu kai*, Latvian *kamēr*; Albanian *ndërsa*; Armenian *minčder*; Maltese *mentri, waqt li*

(17) Posteriority 'before' – Preference 'rather than'
Irish *sula*, Scottish Gaelic *mus*, Manx *roish (my)*; Spanish *antes (de) que*, Catalan *abans (de) que*, Latin *priusquam*, Italian *prima che*; Dutch *voor(dat), eer(dat)*, English *before*, German *bevor, ehe*; Polish *zanim*; Romani *maŋke*; Finnish *ennen kuin*; Maltese *qabel ma*

(18) Purpose 'in order that' – Cause/Reason 'because'
Spanish *porque*, Catalan *perquè*, Portuguese *porque*, Italian *perché*, Rumanian *pentru că*, Gothic *duþþe (ei)*, Classical Greek *hōs*, Talysh *bəčə gorə (ki)*, Finnish *jotta*, Udmurt *šuysa*, Nenets *je"ämnga*, Turkish *için, diye*, Karachay-Balkar *üçün*, Kalmyk *gihəd*, Lezgian *luhuz/lahana*, Basque *arren*; Ngizim *gàađà* (a Chadic language)

(19) Negative Condition 'unless' – Exception/Restriction 'except/only that'
Spanish *a no ser que, salvo que, excepto que, fuera (de) que*, Catalan *salvant que, llevat que, tret que*, Portuguese *de/a não ser que*, Latin *nisi, praeterquam si, extra quam si*, Italian *tranne che, salvo che, fuorché*, Danish *medmindre, undtagen at*, Icelandic *nema*, Dutch *tenzij*, English *unless, but that*, Gothic *alja*, Polish *chyba że*, Lithuanian *nebeñt*, Modern Greek *ektós óti, ésto ke (an)*, Classical Greek *eàn*, Romani *tini*, Basque *ezean*, Finnish *paitsi siinä tapauksessa*, Hungarian *hacsaknem*

(20) Concession 'although' – Concessive Condition 'even if'
Scottish Gaelic *ged nach*, Spanish *por mucho que*, Catalan *per més que, si bé, malgrat que*, Latin *etsi, quamvis*, Italian *per quanto, ammesso che*, Rumanian *oricît, oricum*, English *though*, German *wenngleich, sosehr*, Gothic *sweþauh ei*, Russian *xot'(i)*, Lithuanian *nórint(s), tegù(l)*, Latvian *lai arí, lai gan*, Albanian *ndonëse, sado/sido (që)*, Chuvash *pulin te*

3.6. In the analysis of adverbial clauses, a distinction is frequently drawn between three levels of linking (Sweetser 1990: 77): a content level (21 a), an epistemic level (21 b) and a metalinguistic or speech act level (21 c). Adverbial clauses as in (21 c), which do not modify the proposition of the main clause but provide the motivation for uttering the main clause, are also known as *speech act adverbial clauses* or *speech act qualifiers* (cf. Thompson/Longacre 1985: 203 f.):

(21) (a) *John came back because he loved her.*
(b) *John loved her, because he came back.*
(c) *What are you doing tonight, because there's a good movie on?*

Many ACs can be used on more than one of these levels, some (like *because*) on all three levels. Only very few of them, however, are used primarily or even exclusively as speech act qualifiers (like the concessive AC *encore que*), or on the speech act and epistemic level but not on the content level (e. g. French *puisque*, Spanish *ya que* Latin *quoniam* Classical Greek *epei*).

4. Evolution

4.1. From a historical point of view, the polysemy patterns in §§ 3.4 and 3.5 reflect frequent paths of semantic change. For example, the most important network-transcending paths of semantic change leading to causal and conditional ACs in the European languages are given in (22):

(22) a. Cause   < Simultaneity Overlap, Anteriority, Terminus a quo; Instrument, Manner, Similarity
     b. Condition < Contingency, Simultaneity Overlap, Simultaneity Co-Extensiveness

What originally was a pragmatic inference and subsequently an additional meaning may over time develop into the only meaning of the AC. In this case the relevant path of semantic evolution can often be reconstructed from the (original) meaning of the morphological material from which the connective is formed. Examples of this are given in (23)–(26).

Evidence from polysemy patterns (cf. Figure 63.2) and from data as in (23) to (26) shows that network-transcending semantic changes undergone by ACs are unidirectional. The CCC network is always a goal domain of semantic change, with Concession as the absolute endpoint (König 1985: 2). Never does this network serve as a starting-point of semantic change in the sense that causal, conditional, contrastive or concessive ACs develop temporal, modal or locative meanings.

The latter two, on the other hand, serve exclusively as source domains. It is to be expected that the predictions concerning semantic change and the constraints on possible directions of semantic change formulated in this section and in §§ 3.4 and 3.5 do not only hold for ACs, but for any kind of adverbial connective.

Another general tendency that can be observed in the semantic development of ACs is the tendency away from polysemy to monosemy and from more polysemous to less polysemous. In Latin and Greek, for example, more than half (53.4%) of the ACs were polysemous, whereas the average proportion in the modern European languages has gone down to about a third (Kortmann 1998b: 215 f.). This tendency is paralleled by a decrease in the syntactic polyfunctionality of ACs over time (cf. §§ 2.5 and 2.7). For the purpose of developing ACs, languages in their earliest stages tend to draw on members of other syntactic categories much more heavily than they do in their latest stages. Later language periods tend to have a larger proportion of ACs exclusively belonging to this syntactic category. These two tendencies together can be viewed as facets of an overall functional differentiation of ACs in the course of the history of a language. On the one hand, ACs become firmly established as

(23) monosemous causal ACs derived from markers of Anteriority:
     Danish   eftersom   after-REL/as, like
     French   puisque   afterwards-COMP
     Italian   poiché   after-COMP
     Spanish   pues que   (etym.: after) COMP

(24) monosemous causal ACs derived from markers of Terminus a quo:
     Albanian   ngase, ngaqë, prejse   from, of-COMP
     Georgian   radgan   INT:INSTR-from
     Irish   ón uair go   from the.hour COMP
     Rumanian   de vreme ce   from time COMP
                 din moment ce   from, out.of moment COMP

(25) monosemous contrastive ACs derived from Simultaneity markers:
     Breton   tra ma   while/time COMP
     Spanish   mientras que   while COMP

(26) monosemous preference markers deriving from adverbs of temporal precedence:
     Albanian   më parë ... sesa   more at.first ... than-how.much
     Danish   snarere end (at)   early:CMPAR than (COMP)
     English   rather than   etymology: < (h)rathe 'quickly, immediately'
     Italian   piuttosto che   more-soon COMP
     Lithuanian greičiau   soon-CMPAR
     Latvian   drīzāk ... nekā   soon-CMPAR ... not-than
     Russian   by skoree ... čem   COND.marker fast-CMPAR ... what:INSTR

an autonomous syntactic category; on the other hand, the inventories of ACs grow and as a consequence there is a neater semantic division of tasks between the members of this inventory.

4.2. In the European languages the most important word classes from which ACs are constructed are adverbs, adpositions (i. e. in most cases prepositions), complementizers, interrogatives and relativizers. These are the word classes which are most frequently found to be incorporated in ACs and which syntactically polyfunctional ACs most frequently belong to (cf. § 2.5). In many other languages, too, these or a subset of these have been found to serve as starting points of grammaticalization paths leading to ACs (on postpositions as the sources of subordinators cf., for example, Genetti 1986 and 1991 for the Tibeto-Burman languages or Harris & Campbell 1995: 291 f. on the Kartvelian language Laz). This is different, for example, for serial verb languages as found in the Far East (cf. Bisang 1998: 734, 770−784). In languages like Mandarin Chinese, Vietnamese, Thai or Khmer the two by far most important source categories of ACs are verbs (including the copula, verbs of volition, and verbs of saying; cf. (27)) and nouns (28−29), both of which play only a marginal role in the formation of ACs in most European languages (with the exception of converb languages, the Celtic languages, and Basque). Among the relevant nouns, 'time' is the most prominent one (28).

As the head noun of relative clauses it developed into a temporal AC meaning 'when, while' in many languages across the world, English *while* itself being a case in point.

Where in European languages temporal and spatial nouns are used in order to form ACs, the former typically develop into temporal ACs and the latter into locative ACs. The languages in the western and the northern periphery of Europe also have temporal ACs which developed from spatial nouns ('length', 'place', 'track, path, way'). Examples are given in (30).

On the evolution of individual semantic classes of ACs, notably causals, conditionals (→ Art. 76), concessive conditionals and concessives, consult König 1985, Traugott 1985, Haspelmath/König 1998, or Kortmann 1997a and 1998b.

4.3. ACs and complex sentences in general are a typical feature of writing (cf. Raible 1992: 165−170, Kortmann 1997a: 46 f.). The evolution of ACs and of large AC inventories goes hand in hand with the development of literary and, ultimately, *ausbau* languages (cf. § 1.1). In this process it may come to the borrowing of ACs by languages with no or a relatively short literary tradition from languages with a long literary tradition. The latter typically are the dominant, most prestigious ones in the relevant area and/or qualify as superstrate languages (e. g. English, Spanish or French in other continents). Cases of borrowing under these conditions have been

(27) follow Chinese: *yóu-yú* [cause/follow/from(C)-PREP(C)] 'owing to, because' (Cause)
arrive Thai: *thy̌ŋ* 'although, even if' (Concession, Concessive Condition)
give Vietnamese: *cho* 'in order to' (Purpose)
Thai: *hâj* 'in order to' (Purpose)
Khmer: *ʔaoy* 'in order to' (Purpose, Result)
seem/be like Chinese: *hǎo-xiàng* 'as if' (Comparison)
Thai: *my̌an-kàb* [V-PREP: with] 'as if' (Comparison)
Khmer: *doːc-cìːə* [V-COP] 'as if' (Comparison)

(28) Simultaneity markers developing from a noun 'time':
Chinese *de shíhou* [ATTR-time], Vietnamese *khi, lúc*, Thai *weelaa*, Khmer *kaːl, pèːl*

(29) moment Thai: *khanàʔ-thîi* [N-REL] 'while' (Simultaneity Duration)
interval/period Thai: *rawàaŋ* 'while' (Simultaneity Duration)
fact/matter Thai: *kaan-thîi-càʔ* [N-COMP-FUT] 'in order to' (Purpose)
way, manner Thai: *yàaŋ-kàb* [N-PREP:with] 'as if' (Comparison)

(30) | Irish | tar eis | over/on track | 'after'
| | fhad is | length and | 'while, as long as'
| Scottish Gaelic | fhad's | length:and | 'as long as'
| Welsh | ar ol | on track | 'after'
| Manx | lurg | track | 'after'
| Icelandic | um leið og | through/to path and/also | 'while, as soon as'
| Finnish | sillävälin kun | D3:ADESS-place when | 'while'
| Basque | bitartean | length-INESS | 'while, as long as'

reported from different parts of the world: for example, the borrowing of ACs from Russian and, in the case of some Balto-Finnic languages, from German and Scandinavian by many non-Indoeuropean languages in the former U.S.S.R. (Comrie 1981: 12 f.); the borrowing of ACs from Spanish by languages in North and Central America (Thompson/Longacre 1985: 204 f.); the borrowing of ACs from English and French by African and Australian languages; the borrowing of ACs from Persian by Turkic and North Caucasian languages (Kortmann 1997a: 366); or the borrowing of ACs from Mandarin Chinese by Vietnamese (Bisang 1998: 784). As these examples show, donor and recipient languages are often typologically very different. Thus it is interesting to observe that borrowed ACs tend to retain the syntactic properties they had in the donor language even if these are foreign to the language type of the recipient language. For example, the clause-initial position of ACs typical of VO languages may well be retained in OV languages, which are typically postpositional and have ACs in clause-final position. Lezgian, a Northeast Caucasian language, is a case in point: Although it is an SOV language with otherwise exclusively clause-final ACs, the ACs borrowed from Persian (an SVO language with clause-initial ACs) occur in clause-initial position. It seems that ACs, like adpositions, are borrowed together with their relative position to the syntactic unit they are operating over (cf. Moravcsik 1978: 122 f., Kortmann 1997a: 366).

5. Universals

5.1. Given the relative scarcity of typological studies on ACs what can at most be identified are tentative candidates for universal tendencies for the non-universal category of ACs (cf. § 1.1). These candidates are based on the set of Euroversals first formulated in Kortmann (1997a), slightly modified in Kortmann (1998a), and tested for the languages of the Far East by Bisang (1998). Three types of universal tendencies will be suggested. The first two are only claimed to apply to languages which have ACs. They are concerned with the form-meaning and form-function relationship of ACs (§ 5.2) and with correlations between the morphosyntax of ACs and language types (§ 5.3). The third type, on the other hand, concerns the universality of markers for individual adverbial relations. The latter tendencies are also meant to hold for languages lacking ACs. All that is claimed in this set of universals is that there is a small number of adverbial relations for which each language will have some adverbial marker (whether free or bound, whether operating over a (finite or nonfinite) subordinate clause or over a main clause). The relevant universals thus have the status of cognitive or conceptual universals (§ 5.4).

5.2. The first two candidates for universal tendencies link up with what was said about the relationship between form and meaning and between form and syntactic function in §§ 2.7, 3.2. and 3.3.

(31) In any language with ACs as the dominant type of adverbial marker, the prevailing type of AC is a one-word item which can be used as AC only (syntactic monofunctionality) and expresses no more than one adverbial relation (semantic monofunctionality, monosemy).

(32) In any language, the majority of polymorphemic one-word ACs and of phrasal (or: multi-word) ACs tend to be monosemous.

5.3. For the European languages it is possible to identify various correlations between morphological properties (e.g. degree of complexity, incorporated material) and syntactic properties (e.g. position in the adverbial clause) of ACs, on the one hand, and the morphosyntactic properties of languages, on the other hand (e.g. basic word order, dominant type of adposition, preferred subordination strategy). For example, it is possible to formulate implicational universals of the kind that in Europe VO languages tend to have morphologically more complex ACs than SOV languages, or that languages not making use of complementizers and/or adpositions in the formation of ACs are SOV (cf. Kortmann 1997a: 286 f.). Despite the considerable heterogeneity of European languages these and related Euroversals cannot claim universal validity, as Bisang has clearly shown for some Asian languages (1998: 762 f.). For instance, SVO languages like Thai or Khmer make no use at all of complementizers in forming ACs. It seems that only one major type of correlations observable in the European languages remains a candidate for universal tendencies, namely correlations between adposition type, i.e. ultimately basic word order, and the position of the AC in the adverbial clause (cf. also (5) and (6) in § 2.3):

(33.1) If a language is predominantly prepositional, it will predominantly use ACs in clause-initial position.

(33.2) If a language predominantly employs clause-final ACs then, if it has any adpositions, it is predominantly postpositional.

(34.1) VO languages tend to employ ACs in clause-initial position.

(34.2) Languages which make use of clause-final ACs tend to be OV.

(33.2) cannot be formulated in a parallel way to (33.1), itself a more modest reformulation of (5), because there are languages which are predominantly postpositional and yet have overwhelmingly clause-initial ACs (e.g. the Uralic languages Finnish, Hungarian, Nenets). The tendencies in (34) cannot be formulated more strongly because there are SVO languages like Mandarin Chinese which also have clause-final ACs.

5.4. Tendencies (35) and (36) make claims concerning the availability of ACs for individual adverbial relations depending on the degree of lexicalization:

(35) One-word ACs: The overwhelming majority of languages which predominantly or exclusively make use of ACs have a one-word AC for the (exclusive or primary) expression of Simultaneity Overlap ('when'), Place ('where'), Similarity ('as'), Condition ('if'), Cause ('because'), Purpose ('in order to'), and Concession ('although').

(36) Any kind of ACs (one-word or phrasal): The overwhelming majority of languages which predominantly or exclusively make use of ACs have some AC for the (exclusive or primary) expression of Simultaneity Duration ('while'), Simultaneity Coextensiveness ('as long as'), Anteriority ('after'), Immediate Anteriority ('as soon as'), Posteriority ('before'), Result ('so that'), Exception ('except that'), Comparison ('as if'), and Proportion ('the ... the').

Especially the adverbial relations in (35) qualify as candidates for conceptual universals. For example, Wierzbicka (1998: 144, 149−152, 178−185) considers five of the seven relations in (35), viz. Simultaneity Overlap, Place, Similarity, Cause, and Condition (explicitly excluding counterfactuals (1998: 182); cf. similarly Bechert 1991: 62 f., 69), and two of the relations in (36), viz. Anteriority and Posteriority, as conceptual primitives and thus as part of her Natural Semantic Metalanguage. For these relations, the argument goes, all languages have some way of lexical marking, i.e. not necessarily ACs. As a further candidate for conceptual universality Wierzbicka (1998: 183 f.) admits Purpose, which in her view may however be cognitively too complex in order to qualify as a primitive. This, it needs to be added, applies even more strongly to Concession, which is perhaps the cognitively most complex member of the semantic space of adverbial relations (cf. König 1988: 157, Kortmann 1997a: 152−157, 208).

6. Special abbreviations

AC	adverbial conjunction
ADESS	adessive case
ALL	allative case
CCC	cause/condition/concession
CMPAR	comparative
CONT	continuous
INT	interrogative
OPT	optative
SAE	Standard Average European
SR	subordinator

7. References

Bechert, Johannes & Bernini, Giuliano & Buridant, Claude (eds.). 1990. *Toward a typology of European languages.* Berlin & New York: Mouton de Gruyter.

Bechert, Johannes. 1991. "The problem of semantic incomparability". In: Zaefferer, Dietmar (ed.). *Semantic universals and universal semantics.* Berlin & New York: Foris, 60–71.

Bisang, Walter. 1998. "Adverbiality: the view from the Far East". In: van der Auwera, Johan (ed.). 641–812.

Blatt, Franz. 1957. "Latin influence on European syntax". *Travaux du Cercle Linguistique de Copenhague* 11: 33–69.

Brugman, Claudia & Macaulay, Monica (eds.). 1984. *Proceedings of the tenth annual meeting of the Berkeley Linguistics Society.* Berkeley: Berkeley Linguistics Society.

Comrie, Bernard. 1981. *The languages of the Soviet Union.* Cambridge: Cambridge University Press.

Dryer, Matthew S. 1992. "The Greenbergian word order correlations". *Language* 68: 81–138.

Emonds, Joseph E. 1987. "Parts of speech in generative grammar". *Linguistic Analysis* 17: 3–42.

Genetti, Carol. 1986. "The development of subordinators from postpositions in Bodic languages". In: Axmaker, Shelley & Jaisser, Annie & Singmaster, Helen (eds.). *Proceedings of the fourteenth annual meeting of the Berkeley Linguistics Society.* Berkeley: Berkeley Linguistics Society, 387–400.

Genetti, Carol. 1991. "From postposition to subordinator in Newari". In: Traugott, Elizabeth Closs & Heine, Bernd (eds.). Vol. II: 227–255.

Haiman, John & Thompson, Sandra A. 1984. "'Subordination' in universal grammar". In: Brugman, Claudia & Macaulay, Monica (eds.). 510–523.

Haiman, John & Thompson, Sandra A. (eds.). 1988. *Clause combining in grammar and discourse.* Amsterdam & Philadelphia: Benjamins.

Haspelmath, Martin. 1995. "The converb (adverbial participle, gerund) as a crosslinguistically valid category". In: Haspelmath, Martin & König, Ekkehard (eds.). 1–55.

Haspelmath, Martin & König, Ekkehard (eds.). 1995. *Converbs in crosslinguistic perspective.* Berlin & New York: Mouton de Gruyter.

Haspelmath, Martin & König, Ekkehard. 1998. "Concessive conditionals in the languages of Europe". In: van der Auwera, Johan (ed.). 563–640.

Hopper, Paul J. & Traugott, Elizabeth Closs. 1993. *Grammaticalization.* Cambridge: Cambridge University Press.

Kloss, Heinz. 1967. "'Abstand languages' and 'ausbau languages'". *Anthropological linguistics* 9: 29–41.

König, Ekkehard. 1985. "Where do concessives come from? On the development of concessive connectives". In: Fisiak, Jacek (ed.). *Historical semantics – historical word-formation.* Berlin: Mouton de Gruyter, 263–282.

König, Ekkehard. 1986. "Conditionals, concessive conditionals and concessives: areas of contrast, overlap, and neutralization". In: Traugott, Elizabeth Closs & ter Meulen, Alice & Snitzer Reilly, Judy & Ferguson, Charles A. (eds.). 229–246.

König, Ekkehard. 1988. "Concessive connectives and concessive sentences: crosslinguistic regularities and pragmatic principles". In: Hawkins, John A. (ed.). *Explaining language universals.* Oxford: Blackwell, 145–166.

Koptjevskaja-Tamm, Maria. 1994. "Finiteness". In: Asher, R. E. (ed.). *The encyclopedia of language and linguistics.* Vol. 3. Oxford: Pergamon Press, 1245–1248.

Kortmann, Bernd. 1997a. *Adverbial subordination. A typology and history of adverbial subordinators based on European languages.* (Empirical Approaches to Language Typology 18). Berlin & New York: Mouton de Gruyter.

Kortmann, Bernd. 1997b. *A cross-linguistic dictionary of adverbial subordinators.* (Linguistic Data on Diskette). Munich: LINCOM EUROPA.

Kortmann, Bernd. 1998a. "Adverbial subordinators in the languages of Europe". In: van der Auwera, Johan (ed.). 457–561.

Kortmann, B. 1998b. "The evolution of adverbial subordinators in Europe". In: Schmid, Monika S. & Austin, Jennifer R. & Stein, Dieter (eds.). *Historical Linguistics 1997. Selected papers from the 13th International Conference on Historical Linguistics, Düsseldorf, 10–17 August 1997.* Amsterdam & Philadelphia: Benjamins, 213–228.

Kortmann, Bernd & König, Ekkehard. 1992. "Categorial reanalysis: the case of deverbal prepositions". *Linguistics* 30: 671–697.

Lang, Ewald. 2001. "Die Wortart 'Konjunktion'". In: Cruse, Alan & Hundsnurscher, Franz & Job, Michael & Lutzeier, Peter Rolf (eds.). *Lexikologie – Lexicology.* Berlin & New York.

Lehmann, Christian. 1988. "Towards a typology of clause-linkage". In: Haiman, John & Thompson, Sandra A. (eds.). 181–225.

Meillet, Antoine. 1915–16. "Le renouvellement des conjonctions". *Annuaire de l'Ecole pratique des Hautes Etudes*: 1–28 [Reprinted in Meillet 1958, 159–174].

Mithun, Marianne. 1984. "How to avoid subordination?" In: Brugman, Claudia & Macaulay, Monica (eds.). 493–509.

Moravcsik, Edith A. 1978. "Language contact". In: Greenberg, Joseph H. (ed.). *Universals of human language*, Vol. I: *Method & theory.* Stanford: Stanford University Press, 93–122.

Nedjalkov, Igor' V. 1998. "Converbs in the languages of Europe". In: van der Auwera, Johan (ed.). 421–456.

Nedjalkov, Vladimir P. 1995. "Some typological parameters of converbs". In: Haspelmath, Martin & König, Ekkehard (eds.). 97–136.

Raible, Wolfgang. 1992. *Junktion. Eine Dimension der Sprache und ihre Realisierungsformen zwischen Aggregation und Integration.* Heidelberg: Winter.

Rudolph, Elisabeth. 1996. *Contrast: adversative and concessive relations and their expressions in English, German, Spanish, Portuguese on sentence and text level.* Berlin & New York: de Gruyter.

Sasse, Hans-Jürgen. 1993. "Syntactic Categories and Subcategories". In: Jacobs, Joachim & von Stechow, Arnim & Sternefeld, Wolfgang & Vennemann, Theo (eds.) *Syntax: an international handbook of contemporary research.* Berlin & New York: de Gruyter, 646–686.

Sweetser, Eve E. 1990. *From etymology to pragmatics. Metaphorical and cultural aspects of semantic structure.* Cambridge: Cambridge University Press.

Thompson, Sandra A. & Longacre, Robert E. 1985. "Adverbial clauses". In: Shopen, Timothy (ed.). *Language typology and syntactic description.* 3 vols. Cambridge: Cambridge University Press, Vol. II: 171–234.

Traugott, Elizabeth Closs. 1985. "Conditional markers". In: Haiman, John (ed.). *Iconicity in syntax.* Amsterdam & Philadelphia: Benjamins, 289–307.

Traugott, Elizabeth Closs & ter Meulen, Alice & Snitzer Reilly, Judy & Ferguson, Charles A. (eds.) 1986. *On conditionals.* Cambridge: Cambridge University Press.

Traugott, Elizabeth Closs & Heine, Bernd. 1991. *Approaches to grammaticalization.* 2 vols. Amsterdam & Philadelphia: Benjamins.

van der Auwera, Johan (ed.) 1998a. *Adverbial constructions in the languages of Europe.* Berlin & New York: Mouton de Gruyter.

van der Auwera, Johan. 1998b. "Introduction". In: van der Auwera, Johan (ed.). 1–23.

von der Gabelentz, Georg 1901². *Die Sprachwissenschaft, ihre Aufgaben, ihre Methoden und bisherigen Ergebnisse.* Leipzig: Weigel.

Wierzbicka, Anna. 1998. "Anchoring linguistic typology in universal semantic primes". *Linguistic Typology* 2: 141–194.

Zipf, George Kingsley. 1949. *Human behavior and the principle of least effort.* Cambridge, Mass.: Addison-Wesley Press.

Bernd Kortmann,
Universität Freiburg (Germany)